THE

MENNONITE ENCYCLOPEDIA

-

THE

Mennonite Encyclopedia

A Comprehensive Reference Work
on the
Anabaptist-Mennonite Movement

VOLUME III

I–N

(For additional I-N articles see Supplement, pp. 1025-1096, Vol. IV.)

Mennonite Publishing House, Scottdale, Pennsylvania
Mennonite Publication Office, Newton, Kansas
Mennonite Brethren Publishing House, Hillsboro, Kansas

1957

EDITORS

Cornelius Krahn, Editor
North Newton, Kansas

Melvin Gingerich, Managing Editor
Goshen, Indiana

Orlando Harms, Associate Editor
Hillsboro, Kansas

PREFACE

The second printing of *The Mennonite Encyclopedia* began in 1969 with Volume I. All available corrections based on information gathered in the editorial offices contributed by the staff and readers of *The Mennonite Encyclopedia* have been made. These corrections are being limited to those that can be made without changing the number of lines in the column.

The editors are also charged with the responsibility of planning for a completely revised edition of *The Mennonite Encyclopedia* when the reprint is exhausted. They solicit suggestions and information for both the reprint of the remaining volumes and the planned revised edition.

February, 1973.   Cornelius Krahn, Editor
                                                    Melvin Gingerich, Managing Editor

KEY TO SYMBOLS AND ABBREVIATIONS

A. Symbols Used for the North American Mennonite Bodies

Church of God in Christ, Mennonite	(CGC)	Krimmer Mennonite Brethren	(KMB)
Conservative (Amish) Mennonite	(CAM)	Mennonite Brethren Church	(MB)
Evangelical Mennonite Brethren	(EMB)	Mennonite Brethren in Christ	(MBC)
Evangelical Mennonite Church	(EMC)	Mennonite Church	(MC)
Evangelical Mennonite Church (Kleine		Old Order Amish Mennonite Church	(OOA)
Gemeinde)	(EMC, KG)	Old Order Mennonite Church	(OOM)
General Conference Mennonite		United Missionary Church	(UMC)
Church	(GCM)		

B. Geographical Abbreviations

States of the United States of America		Countries		Provinces of Canada	
Cal.	California	N.D. North Dakota	Can. Canada	Alta.	Alberta
Col.	Colorado	N.Y. New York	Ger. Germany	B.C.	British Columbia
Ill.	Illinois	Okla. Oklahoma	Neth. Netherlands	Man.	Manitoba
Ind.	Indiana	Ore. Oregon	Par. Paraguay	Ont.	Ontario
Kan.	Kansas	Pa. Pennsylvania	P.R. Puerto Rico	Sask.	Saskatchewan
Minn.	Minnesota	S.D. South Dakota	Sw. Switzerland		
Mo.	Missouri	Va. Virginia		*Other*	
Neb.	Nebraska			Co.	County
				Twp.	Township

C. Bibliographical Symbols

ADB *Allgemeine Deutsche Biographie* 56v. (Leipzig, 1875-1912).

Beck, Geschichts-Bücher Josef Beck, *Die Geschichts-Bücher der Wiedertäufer in Oesterreich-Ungarn* (Vienna, 1883).

Bender, Two Centuries H. S. Bender, *Two Centuries of American Mennonite Literature, A Bibliography of Mennonitica Americana 1727-1928* (Goshen, 1929).

Bibliographie des Martyrologes F. Vander Haeghen, Th. Arnold, and R. Vanden Berghe, *Bibliographie des Martyrologes Protestants Néerlandais. II. Receuils* (The Hague, 1890).

Biogr. Wb. H. Visscher and L. A. van Langeraad, *Biographisch Woordenboek von Protestantsche Godgeleerden in Nederland*, A-L (I, Utrecht), later by J. P. de Bie and J. Loosjes (II, III, IV, V, and installment #29, The Hague) 1903- .

Blaupot t. C., Friesland Steven Blaupot ten Cate, *Geschiedenis der Doopsgezinden in Friesland* (Leeuwarden, 1839).

Blaupot t. C., Groningen . . . *Groningen, Overijssel en Oost-Friesland*, 2v. (Leeuwarden, 1842).

Blaupot t. C., Holland . . . *Holland, Zeeland, Utrecht en Gelderland*, 2v. (Amsterdam, 1847).

BRN S. Cramer and F. Pijper, *Bibliotheca Reformatoria Neerlandica*, 10v. (The Hague, 1903-14).

Catalogus Amst. *Catalogus der werken over de Doopsgezinden en hunne geschiedenis aanwezig in de bibliotheek der Vereenigde Doopsgezinde Gemeente te Amsterdam* (Amst., 1919).

DB *Doopsgezinde Bijdragen* (Amsterdam, 1861-1919).

DJ *Doopsgezind Jaarboekje* vv. 1-48 (Assen, et al., 1901-43, 1949-).

Dirks, Statistik Heinrich Dirks, *Statistik der Mennonitengemeinden in Russland Ende 1905 (Anhang zum Mennonitischen Jahrbuche 1904/05). Gesammelt von Heinrich Dirks, Prediger der Gnadenfelder Gemeinde* (Gnadenfeld, 1906).

Friesen, Brüderschaft P. M. Friesen, *Die Alt-Evangelische Mennonitische Brüderschaft in Russland (1789-1910) im Rahmen der mennonitischen Gesamtgeschichte* (Halbstadt, 1911).

Gbl. *Gemeindeblatt der Mennoniten* vv. 1-85 (Sinsheim, later Karlsruhe, 1870-).

Gem.-Kal. *Mennonitischer Gemeinde-Kalender* (formerly *Christlicher Gemeinde-Kalender*) (various places, chiefly Kaiserslautern, Weierhof, Karlsruhe, 1892-).

Gesch.-Bl. *Mennonitische Geschichtsblätter. Herausgegeben vom Mennonitischen Geschichtsverein* (Frankfurt, later Karlsruhe, 1936-40, 1951-).

Grosheide, Bijdrage Greta Grosheide, *Bijdrage tot de geschiedenis der Anabaptisten in Amsterdam* (Hilversum, 1938).

Grosheide, Verhooren *Verhooren en Vonissen der Wederdoopers, betrokken bij de aanslagen op Amsterdam in 1534 en 1535,* in *Bijdragen en Mededeelingen van het Historisch Genootschap,* Vol. XLI (Amsterdam, 1920).

HRE Herzog-Hauck, *Realencyclopädie für Protestantische Theologie und Kirche,* 24v. (3.ed., Leipzig, 1896-1913).

Inv. Arch. Amst. J. G. de Hoop Scheffer, *Inventaris der Archiefstukken berustende bij de Vereenigde Doopsgezinde Gemeente te Amsterdam,* 2v. (Amsterdam, 1883-84).

Kühler, Geschiedenis I W. J. Kühler, *Geschiedenis der Nederlandsche Doopsgezinden in de Zestiende Eeuw* (Haarlem, 1932).

Kühler, Geschiedenis II,1 *Idem, Geschiedenis van de Doopsgezinden in Nederland II. 1600-1735 Eerste Helft* (Haarlem, 1940).

Kühler, Geschiedenis II,2 *Idem, Geschiedenis van de Doopsgezinden in Nederland: Gemeentelijk Leven 1650-1735* (Haarlem, 1950).

Lietboecxken *Een Lietboecxken, tracterende van den Offer des Heeren,* contained in *Het Offer des Heeren* (see *Offer*).

Loserth, Anabaptismus Johann Loserth, *Der Anabaptismus in Tirol* (Vienna, 1892).

Loserth, Communismus *Idem, Der Communismus der mährischen Wiedertäufer im 16. und 17. Jahrhundert: Beiträge zu ihrer Lehre, Geschichte und Verfassung (Archiv für österreichische Geschichte,* Vol. LXXXI, 1, 1895).

Mart. Mir. D(utch) Tileman Jansz van Braght, *Het Bloedigh Tooneel of Martelaers Spiegel der Doops-gesinde of Weereloose Christenen, Die om 't getuygenis van Jesus haren Salighmaker geleden hebben ende gedood zijn van Christi tijd af tot desen tijd toe. Den Tweeden Druk* (Amsterdam, 1685), Part II.

Mart. Mir. E(nglish) *Idem, The Bloody Theatre or Martyrs' Mirror of the Defenseless Christians Who Baptized Only upon Confession of Faith and Who Suffered and Died for the Testimony of Jesus Their Saviour . . . to the Year A.D. 1660* (Scottdale, Pa., 1951).

ME *Mennonite Encyclopedia* (I, 1955; II, 1956; III, 1957; IV, 1958)

Mellink, Wederdopers A. F. Mellink, *De Wederdopers in de noordelijke Nederlanden 1531-1544* (Groningen, 1954).

Menn. Bl. *Mennonitische Blätter* vv. 1-88 (1854-1941), published variously at Danzig, Hamburg-Altona, and Elbing (W. Prussia).

MHB *Mennonite Historical Bulletin* (Scottdale, Pa.; 1940-   ).

Menn. Life *Mennonite Life* (North Newton, Kan., 1946-).

ML Christian Hege and Christian Neff, *Mennonitisches Lexikon,* 3v., A-R (Frankfurt and Weierhof, I, 1913; II, 1937; III, #31-36, 1938-42; #37-39 at Karlsruhe, 1951-54) *et seq.*

Menno Simons, Opera *Opera Omnia Theologica, of alle de Godtgeleerde wercken van Menno Simons* (Amsterdam, 1681).

Menno Simons, Writings *The Complete Writings of Menno Simons c. 1496-1561. Translated from the Dutch by Leonard Verduin* (Scottdale, 1956).

MQR *Mennonite Quarterly Review* (Goshen, Ind., 1927-).

Müller, Berner Täufer Ernst Müller, *Geschichte der Bernischen Täufer* (Frauenfeld, 1895).

Naamlijst *Naamlijst der tegenwoordig in dienst zijnde predikanten der Mennoniten in de vereenigde Nederlanden* (Amsterdam, 1731, 1743, 1755, 1757, 1766, 1769, 1775, 1780, 1782, 1784, 1786, 1787, 1789, 1791, 1793, 1802, 1804, 1806, 1808, 1810, 1815, 1829).

N.N.B.Wb. P. C. Molhuysen and P. J. Blok, *Nieuw Nederlandsch Biografisch Woordenboek* vv. 1-10 (Leiden, 1911-37).

Offer *Dit Boec wort genoemt: Het Offer des Herren, om het inhout van sommighe opgheofferde kinderen Godts . . .* (n.p., 1562, 1567, 1570, 1578, 1580, Amsterdam, 1590, n.p., 1591, Amsterdam, 1595, Harlingen, 1599). The 1570 edition is cited as reproduced in BRN II, 51-486, including *Een Lietboecxken, tracterende van den Offer des Heeren* (pp. 499-617).

Reimer, Familiennamen Gustav E. Reimer, *Die Familiennamen der westpreussischen Mennoniten* (Weierhof, 1940).

Rembert, Wiedertäufer Karl Rembert, *Die "Wiedertäufer" im Herzogtum Jülich* (Berlin, 1899).

RGG *Die Religion in Geschichte und Gegenwart* (2.ed., 5v., Tübingen, 1927-32).

Schijn-Maatschoen, Geschiedenis I Hermanus Schijn, *Geschiedenis dier Christenen, welke in de Vereenigde Nederlanden onder de Protestanten Mennoniten genaamd worden . . . , Tweede Druk op nieuws uit het Latyn vertaald, en vermeerdert door Gerardus Maatschoen* (Amsterdam, 1743).

Schijn-Maatschoen, Geschiedenis II, which is volume II of the preceding work, entitled *Uitvoeriger Verhandeling van de Geschiedenisse der Mennoniten* (Amsterdam, 1744).

Schijn-Maatschoen, Geschiedenis III, which is volume III of the preceding work, entitled *Aanhangzel Dienende tot den Vervolg of Derde Deel van de Geschiedenis der Mennoniten . . . in het welke noch Negentien Leeraars der Mennoniten . . .* , by Maatschoen alone (Amsterdam, 1745).

TA Baden-Pfalz M. Krebs, *Quellen zur Geschichte der Täufer. IV. Band, Baden und Pfalz* (Gütersloh, 1951).

TA Bayern I Karl Schornbaum, *Quellen zur Geschichte der Wiedertäufer II. Band, Markgraftum Brandenburg (Bayern I. Abteilung)* (Leipzig, 1934).

TA Bayern II *Idem, Quellen zur Geschichte der Täufer, V. Band (Bayern, II. Abteilung)* (Gütersloh, 1951).

TA Hessen G. Franz, *Urkundliche Quellen zur hessischen Reformationsgeschichte. Vierter Band, Wiedertäuferakten 1527-1626* (Marburg, 1951).

TA Württemberg G. Bossert, *Quellen zur Geschichte der Täufer I. Band, Herzogtum Württemberg* (Leipzig, 1930).

TA Zürich L. von Muralt und W. Schmid, *Quellen zur Geschichte der Täufer in der Schweiz. Erster Band Zürich* (Zürich, 1952).

Verheyden, Brugge A. L. E. Verheyden, *Het Brugsche Martyrologium (12 October 1527-7 Augustus 1573)* (Brussels, n.d., [1944]).

Verheyden, Courtrai *Idem, Le Martyrologe Courtraisien et la Martyrologe Bruxellois* (Vilvorde, 1950).

Verheyden, Gent *Idem, Het Gentsche Martyrologium (1530-1595)* (Brugge, 1946).

Wackernagel, Kirchenlied Philipp Wackernagel, *Das deutsche Kirchenlied von der ältesten Zeit bis zu Anfang des XVII. Jahrhunderts,* 5v. (Leipzig, 1864-77).

Wackernagel, Lieder *Idem, Lieder der niederländischen Reformierten aus der Zeit der Verfolgung im 16. Jahrhundert* (Frankfurt, 1867).

Wappler, Thüringen Paul Wappler, *Die Täuferbewegung in Thüringen von 1526-1584* (Jena, 1913).

Wiswedel, Bilder W. Wiswedel, *Bilder und Führergestalten aus dem Täufertum,* 3v. (Kassel, I, 1928; II, 1930; III, 1952).

Wolkan, Geschicht-Buch Rudolf Wolkan, *Geschicht-Buch der Hutterischen Brüder* (Macleod, Alta., and Vienna, 1923).

Wolkan, Lieder *Idem, Die Lieder der Wiedertäufer* (Berlin, 1903).

Zieglschmid, Chronik A. J. F. Zieglschmid, *Die älteste Chronik der Hutterischen Brüder: Ein Sprachdenkmal aus frühneuhochdeutscher Zeit* (Ithaca, 1943).

Zieglschmid, Klein-Geschichtsbuch *Idem, Das Klein-Geschichtsbuch der Hutterischen Brüder* (Philadelphia, 1947).

D. Other Symbols and Abbreviations

A.D.S. Algemene Doopsgezinde Societeit. **MCC** Mennonite Central Committee.

Vereinigung Vereinigung der Deutschen Mennonitengemeinden.

Verband Verband badisch-württembergisch-bayrischer Mennonitengemeinden e. V.

CPS Civilian Public Service. **KfK** Kommission für kirchliche Angelegenheiten (or Kirchenangelegenheiten). **CO** Conscientious objector to military service.

q.v. "quod vide," "which see," is a cross-reference indicating that an article on the subject is to be found in the regular alphabetical order.

* signifies deceased. † indicates that an illustration will be found in the pictorial section at the end of the volume.

AML Amsterdam Mennonite Library

BeCL Bethel College Historical Library. **GCL** Goshen College Mennonite Historical Library.

MAPS AND ILLUSTRATIONS

The maps listed below will be found in the text next to the articles they serve. Illustrations are grouped at the end of each volume. For a complete list of illustrations in Volume III, see pp. 1 f. of pictorial supplement.

Alphabetical List of Maps, Volumes I—IV

Africa, Mennonite Missions
Alberta
Alexandertal Settlement, Samara, Russia
Allen and Putnam Counties, Ohio
Alsace, Upper, France
  Alternative Service Camps (following Civilian Public Service)
Amish, Old Order Communities
Argentina
  Asia, Central (following Siberia)
Austria, 16th Century Anabaptism
Barnaul Settlement, Siberia
Belgium, 16th Century Anabaptism
Bern Canton, Switzerland
Brazil and Adjacent Areas
British Columbia
Bucks and Montgomery Counties, Pa.
California
Canada
Caucasus, Russia
Chaco, Paraguay, Mennonite Colonies
Chicago, Illinois
China, Mennonite Missions
Chortitza Settlement, Russia
Church of God in Christ, Mennonite
Civilian Public Service, Mennonite, U.S.A.
Alternative Service, Mennonite, Canada
Congo, Belgian, Mennonite Missions
Conservative (Amish) Mennonite Church
Cottonwood County, Minnesota
Danzig, Free City of
  Delaware (with Maryland)
East Reserve Settlement, Manitoba
Elkhart and Lagrange Counties, Indiana
Emmental Region, Switzerland
Europe, Anabaptism in 1550
European Mennonitism in 1938
Evangelical Mennonite Brethren and Evangelical Mennonites
Far East, Mennonitism
France
Fraser River Valley, British Columbia
Friesland, Province, Netherlands
Galicia
General Conference Mennonite Church, North America
Germany, West (in two parts)
Groningen, Province, Netherlands
Harvey County, Kansas, and Adjacent Area
Holmes County, Ohio
Hutterites in Canada and U.S.A. (two maps)
Hutterites in Moravia, Slovakia, and Transylvania
Hutterites in Moravia (1530-1622)
Hutterites in Slovakia
Hutterites in Ukraine
  Idaho (with Washington)
Illinois

India, Mennonite Missions and Churches
Indiana
Indonesia
Iowa
Japan
Johnson, Iowa, Washington, and Henry Counties, Iowa
Kansas
Krimmer Mennonite Brethren Church
Lancaster County, Pennsylvania
Luxembourg
Manitoba
Maryland and Delaware
Memrik Settlement, Russia
Mennonite Brethren Church, N.A.
Mennonite Church, North America
Mexico, Mennonite Settlements
Michigan
Mifflin County, Pennsylvania
Missouri
Molotschna Settlement, Russia
  Montana (with Washington)
Nebraska
Netherlands (in two parts)
New York
North Holland, Province, Netherlands
Ohio
Oklahoma
Ontario
  Oregon (with Washington)
Orenburg Settlement, Russia
Palatinate, Germany
Paraguay
Pennsylvania
Rockingham County, Virginia
Russia, European
San Joaquin Valley, California
Saskatchewan
Siberia
Somerset County, Pennsylvania, and Garret County, Maryland
South America
South Dakota, Eastern
Switzerland, 16th Century Anabaptism
Tazewell, Woodford, and McLean Counties, Illinois
Terek Settlement, Russia
Trakt Settlement, Russia
Ukraine, Russia
United States, All Mennonites
Virginia
Volga Region, Russia
Washington, Oregon, Idaho, and Montana
Waterloo County, Ontario
Wayne County, Ohio
West and East Prussia, Germany, and Poland
West Reserve Settlement, Manitoba
Württemberg, Baden, and Bavaria, Ger.
Zagradovka Settlement, Russia

KEY TO SYMBOLS FOR WRITERS IN VOLUME III

Amstutz, Daniel, Biel, Sw.	D.A.	*Driedger, A., Heubuden, Ger.	A.D.
Amstutz, H. Clair, Goshen, Ind.	H.C.A.	Driedger, N. N., Leamington, Ont.	N.N.D.
Amstutz-Tschirren, A. J., Oberbütschel, Sw.	A.-T.	Driver, H. A., Wauseon, Ohio	H.A.Dr.
Andres, Mrs. H. J., Newton, Kan.	J.S.A.	Duerksen, Jacob A., Washington, D.C.	Ja.A.D.
Augsburger, Myron S., Harrisonburg, Va.	M.S.A.	Duerksen, Peter, Neuland, Pa.	P.Du.
Bachman, Leland, Goshen, Ind.	L.A.B.	Dyck, Arnold, Darlaten, Ger.	Ar.D.
*Bachmann, Arnold, Lemberg, Poland	A.Ba.	Dyck, Cornelius J., Chicago, Ill.	C.J.D.
Baker, M. L., Cremona, Alta.	M.L.B.	Dyck, J. A., Niagara-on-the-Lake, Ont.	J.A.D.
Bargen, Bernhard, North Newton, Kan.	B.B.	Dyck, Jakob, Korntal, Ger.	J.Dy.
*Bartsch, Franz, Russia	F.B.	Ebrard, Friedrich August, Zürich, Sw.	F.A.E.
Bean, Dorothy, Chicago, Ill.	D.Be.	Eby, Gladys, Didsbury, Alta.	Gl.E.
Bean, E. W., Lehighton, Pa.	E.W.B.	Ediger, Elmer, North Newton, Kan.	E.Ed.
Bear, Paul E., Scranton, Pa.	P.E.B.	Ediger, Peter J., Fresno, Cal.	P.J.E.
Beck, Carl C., Obihiro, Japan	C.C.B.	Ediger, Walter O., Hutchinson, Kan.	W.O.E.
Becker, Eduard, Darmstadt, Ger.	E.Be.	Eitzen, David D., Rolling Hills, Cal.	D.D.E.
Bender, E. C., Martinsburg, Pa.	E.C.B.	Emmert, Donald R., Monroe, Wash.	D.R.E.
Bender, H. S., Goshen, Ind.	H.S.B.	Enns, J. H., Winnipeg, Man.	J.H.En.
Bender, Mrs. H. S., Goshen, Ind.	E.H.B.	Ens, Gerhard, Gretna, Man.	G.En.
Bender, Mary Eleanor, Goshen, Ind.	M.E.B.	Entz, J. E., Newton, Kan.	J.E.E.
Berg, P. H., Hillsboro, Kan.	P.H.B.	Enz, Jacob J., Chicago, Ill.	J.J.En.
*Bergmann, Cornelius, Jena, Ger.	C.B.	Epp, A. W., Fairview, Okla.	A.W.E.
Bixler, Allen, Dalton, Ohio	A.Bix.	Epp, Arnold, Newton, Kan.	A.Ep.
Bixler, Annie, Dalton, Ohio	A.Bi.	*Epp, David H., Chortitza, Russia	D.H.E.
*Block, Theodor, Oberursel, Ger.	T.B.	Epp, J. H., Hepburn, Sask.	J.H.E.
Bontreger, Eli J., Shipshewana, Ind.	E.J.B.	Erb, Allen H., Lebanon, Ore.	A.H.E.
*Bossert, G., Sr., Stuttgart, Ger.	G.Bo.	Erb, Paul, Scottdale, Pa.	P.E.
*Bossert, G., Jr., Stuttgart, Ger.	G.Bos.	Esh, Glenn, Akron, Pa.	G.Es.
Brackbill, Mrs. Maurice, Harrisonburg, Va.	R.M.B.	Ewert, John L., Meade, Kan.	J.L.E.
Braun, Abraham, Nierstein, Ger.	A.B.	Fast, Henry A., Newton, Kan.	H.A.F.
Brenneman, Virgil J., Iowa City, Iowa	V.J.B.	Fast, J. W., Fairview, Okla.	J.W.Fa.
Brubacher, Ada, Goshen, Ind.	A.Br.	Fellmann, Walter, Mönchzell, Ger.	W.F.
Brubaker, J. Protus, Edwards, Mo.	J.P.Br.	Foth, Johannes, Friedelsheim, Ger.	J.F.
Brunk, Harry A., Harrisonburg, Va.	H.A.B.	Fretz, Clarence Y., Harrisonburg, Va.	C.Y.F.
Bucher, Samuel J., Harman, W.Va.	S.J.B.	*Fretz, J. C., Kitchener, Ont.	J.C.F.
Buller, Vernon H., Huron, S.D.	V.H.B.	Fretz, J. Herbert, Freeman, S.D.	J.H.F.
Burkholder, Harold D., Dallas, Ore.	H.D.B.	Fretz, J. Winfield, N. Newton, Kan.	J.W.F.
Byler, J. N., Akron, Pa.	J.N.B.	Friedmann, Robert, Kalamazoo, Mich.	R.F.
Carper, Mrs. Reuben, Denbigh, Va.	E.W.C.	Friesen, Jacob T., Bluffton, Ohio	J.T.F.
Cattepoel, Dirk, Düsseldorf, Ger.	D.C.	Friesen, J. John, Butterfield, Minn.	J.J.F.
Cernohorsky, Karel, Troppau, Czechoslovakia	K.C.	*Froese, John P., Winnipeg, Man.	J.P.F.
Chester, Edward N., Zephyr, Ont.	E.N.C.	Gaeddert, Gustav R., N. Newton, Kan.	G.R.G.
Claassen, Willard, Newton, Kan.	W.C.	Galle, Christian, Weierhof, Ger.	C.G.
Classen, Mrs. Jonas, West Liberty, Ohio	M.B.C.	Gampp, Harvey, Baden, Ont.	H.Ga.
Coblentz, Simon, Uniontown, Ohio	S.C.	Garber, E. S., Nampa, Idaho	E.S.G.
*Coffman, S. F., Vineland, Ont.	S.F.C.	Garber, Robert E., Nampa, Idaho	R.E.G.
Correll, Ernst, Washington, D.C.	E.H.C.	Gehman, R. H., Newark, N.J.	R.H.G.
Cressman, J. Boyd, Kitchener, Ont.	J.B.C.	Geiser, Samuel, Brügg, Sw.	S.G.
Crous, Ernst, Göttingen, Ger.	E.C.	Gerbrandt, H. J., Altona, Man.	H.J.G.
Decker, David, Olivet, S.D.	D.D.	Gerbrandt, J., Saskatoon, Sask.	J.G.
Dedels, G. W., Sundre, Alta.	G.W.D.	Gerig, Jared F., Fort Wayne, Ind.	J.F.Ge.
*Dedic, P., Graz, Austria	P.De.	Giesbrecht, Gerhard B., Filadelfia, Par.	G.B.G.
DeWind, Henry A., Whitewater, Wis.	DeWind	Gingerich, J. C., Dagmar, Mont.	J.C.G.
Dick, A. A., Mountain Lake, Minn.	A.A.D.	Gingerich, Leroy, Versailles, Mo.	L.G.
Dick, Abram J., Winnipeg, Man.	A.J.Di.	Gingerich, Melvin, Goshen, Ind.	M.G.
Dick, Henry H., Lodi, Cal.	He.H.D.	Gingerich, Simon, Wayland, Iowa	S.Gi.
Dick, I. J., Mountain Lake, Minn.	I.J.D.	Gingrich, Arthur, Markstay, Ont.	A.Gi.
Dick, John R., Omaha, Neb.	J.R.D.	Gingrich, J. E., Johnstown, Pa.	J.E.G.
Diener, Harry A., Hutchinson, Kan.	H.A.D.	Glanzer, Paul J., Saint Lawrence, S.D.	P.J.G.
Diller, Samuel J., Maugansville, Md.	S.J.D.	*Göbel, Gustav, Weierhof, Ger.	G.Go.
Doerksen, J. J., Abbotsford, B.C.	J.J.D.	Goering, Peter W., Lehigh, Kan.	P.W.G.
Dollinger, Robert, Weiden, Ger.	R.Do.	Goerz, H., Vancouver, B.C.	H.G.

Golterman, W. F., Amsterdam, Neth.	W.F.G.	Janzen, H. H., Winnipeg, Man.	H.H.J.
Good, Abram, Wadsworth, Ohio	Ab.G.	Janzen, Samuel, Glenwood Springs, Col.	S.J.
Good, Noah G., Lancaster, Pa.	N.G.	Jeltes, H. F. W., The Hague, Neth.	H.F.W.J.
*Göttner, Erich, Danzig, Ger.	Er.G.	Johnson, Jesse, Galva, Kan.	J.Jo.
Graber, J. D., Elkhart, Ind.	J.D.G.	Jost, Arthur, Reedley, Cal.	A.Jo.
Gramberg, K. P. C. A., Rotterdam, Neth.	K.P.G.	Just, L. R., Fresno, Cal.	L.R.J.
Gratz, Delbert L., Bluffton, Ohio	D.L.G.	Kaap, T. F., Bluffton, Ohio	T.F.K.
Graybill, J. Silas, Doylestown, Pa.	J.S.G.	Kauenhoven, Kurt, Göttingen, Ger.	K.K.
Grout, Arcie, Ferndale, Wash.	A.Gr.	Kauffman, Clyde X., Brutus, Mich.	C.X.K.
Grove, Paul H., Ringwood, Ont.	P.H.Gr.	Kauffman, Floyd, Minot, N.D.	F.E.K.
Grunau, P. C., Enid, Okla.	P.C.G.	Kauffman, J. Howard, Goshen, Ind.	J.H.Ka.
Guengerich, L. Glen, Wellman, Iowa	L.G.G.	Kauffman, Nelson E., Elkhart, Ind.	N.E.K.
Guengerich, Paul T., Parnell, Iowa	P.T.G.	Kauffman, Orie, White Pigeon, Mich.	Or.K.
Haarer, Paul W., Howe, Ind.	P.W.H.	Kauffmann, Ivan J., Hopedale, Ill.	I.K.
*Habegger, Alfred, Lame Deer, Mont.	A.H.	*Kaufman, Ammon, Davidsville, Pa.	A.Ka.
*Hallman, Eli S., Akron, Pa.	E.S.H.	Kaufman, Ed. G., N. Newton, Kan.	E.G.K.
Hallman, H. W., Queensville, Ont.	H.W.Ha.	Kaufman, J. N., E. Peoria, Ill.	J.N.K.
Hamm, H. H., Altona, Man.	H.H.H.	Kaufman, Orlo, Gulfport, Miss.	O.K.
Harder, Bernhard, Hanau, Ger.	B.H.	Kennel, LeRoy E., Lombard, Ill.	L.E.K.
Harder, H. N., Bloomington, Ill.	H.N.H.	Kern, Anton, Graz, Austria	A.Ke.
Harder, J. A., Yarrow, B.C.	J.A.Ha.	King, S. M., Goshen, Ind.	S.M.K.
Harder, Menno S., N. Newton, Kan.	M.S.H.	Kitchin, Jason, Cass City, Mich.	J.Ki.
Harms, Orlando, Hillsboro, Kan.	O.Ha.	*Klaassen, Johann, Heilbronn, Ger.	J.Kl.
Hartzler, H. Harold, Goshen, Ind.	H.H.Har.	*Klassen, C. F., Abbotsford, B.C.	C.F.K.
Hartzler, Levi C., Elkhart, Ind.	L.C.H.	*Kliewer, Fritz, Witmarsum, Brazil	F.K.
Hartzler, Raymond L., Bloomington, Ill.	R.L.H.	Kliewer, Henry A., Tuba City, Ariz.	H.A.K.
*Hege, Christian, Frankfurt, Ger.	Hege	Klockenbrink, F. H., Jr., Amsterdam, Neth.	F.H.K.
*Hege, Otto, Frankfurt, Ger.	O.H.	Koehn, J. A., Livingston, Cal.	J.A.K.
Hein, Gerhard, Sembach, Ger.	G.H.	*Köhler, Walther, Heidelberg, Ger.	W.K.
Hershberger, Mrs. Elmer D., Detroit Lakes, Minn.		Konrad, Gerhard A., Matsqui, B.C.	G.A.K.
	E.D.He.	Kopper, Gerhard, Montau, Ger.	G.K.
Hershberger, Erwin N., Meyersdale, Pa.	E.N.H.	Kopper, George W., Monroe, Wash.	G.W.K.
Hershberger, Guy F., Goshen, Ind.	G.F.H.	Krabill, Russell, Goshen, Ind.	R.Kr.
*Hertzler, Richard, Ludwigshafen, Ger.	R.He.	Krahn, Cornelius, N. Newton, Kan.	C.K.
Hertzler, Silas, Goshen, Ind.	Si.H.	Kraus, C. Norman, Goshen, Ind.	C.N.K.
Hiebert, Clarence, Enid, Okla.	C.H.	Krehbiel, Olin A., Berne, Ind.	O.A.K.
Hiebert, P. C., Hillsboro, Kan.	P.C.H.	Krehbiel, Walter Henry, Reedley, Cal.	W.H.Kr.
Hiebert, P. G., Atmore, Ala.	P.G.H.	Kreider, A. E., Goshen, Ind.	A.E.K.
Hochstetler, John G., Creston, Mont.	J.G.H.	Kreider, Jacob L., Lancaster, Pa.	J.L.K.
Holdeman, Harvey, Bonners Ferry, Idaho	H.Hol.	Kreider, John F., Palmyra, Mo.	J.F.Kr.
Hooley, Orvin H., Burr Oak, Mich.	O.H.H.	*Kroeker, A. J., Mountain Lake, Minn.	A.J.K.
Hoover, N. O., Bloomington, Ill.	N.O.H.	Kuyf, Wilhelmina, Newton, Kan.	W.Ku.
Horn, Delmer J., Niles, Mich.	D.J.H.	Landis, Ira D., Bareville, Pa.	I.D.L.
Horst, Irvin B., Harrisonburg, Va.	I.B.H.	*Lapp, George J., Goshen, Ind.	G.J.L.
Horst, John L., Scottdale, Pa.	J.L.H.	Lapp, John E., Lansdale, Pa.	J.E.L.
Horst, Moses K., Maugansville, Md.	M.K.H.	Lederach, Paul M., Scottdale, Pa.	P.M.L.
Horst, Rufus P., Kansas City, Kan.	R.P.H.	Leendertz, J. M., Hoog Soeren, Neth.	J.M.L.
Horst, S. J., South English, Iowa	S.J.H.	Leendertz, W., Santport, Neth.	W.Le.
Hostetler, D. M., Lowpoint, Ill.	D.M.H.	Lehman, Earl, Goshen, Ind.	E.Le.
Hostetler, Jake H., Mishawaka, Ind.	J.H.H.	Lehman, Sylvan, Lima, Ohio	S.Le.
Hostetler, John A., Scottdale, Pa.	J.A.H.	Leinbach, Oscar, Clark Lake, Mich.	O.L.
Hostetler, S. J., Elkhart, Ind.	S.J.Ho.	Leisy, Mrs. E. E., Dallas, Tex.	E.K.L.
Hostetter, D. Ralph, Harrisonburg, Va.	D.R.H.	Loewen, J. J., Justice, Man.	J.J.L.
Hovens Greve, K., Amsterdam, Neth.	K.Ho.	Lohrenz, G., Winnipeg, Man.	G.L.
*Hübert, Johann, Margokerto, Java	J.H.	Lohrenz, J. H., Hughestown, Hyderabad, India	
Huebert, G. D., Winnipeg, Man.	G.D.H.		J.H.L.
Huffman, J. A., Winona Lake, Ind.	J.A.Hu.		
*Hylkema, C. B., Haarlem, Neth.	C.B.H.	*Loosjes, J., Bussum, Neth.	J.L.
Isaac, Mrs. F. J., Newton, Kan.	A.E.I.	*Loserth, Johann, Graz, Austria	Loserth
Isaak, Mrs. F. F., Winnipeg, Man.	A.J.I.	McBrier, Robert, Nappanee, Ind.	R.McB.
Isaak, Jakob, Fernheim, Par.	J.I.	Martin, J. E., Harrisonburg, Va.	J.E.M.
Jansson, A., Tiege, East Prussia, Ger.	A.J.	Mast, C. Z., Elverson, Pa.	C.Z.M.
Jantzen, G. H., Dallas, Ore.	G.H.J.	Matthijssen, Jan, Pati, Java	J.M.
Janzen, A. E., Hillsboro, Kan.	A.E.J.	Mendel, John S., Chicago, Ill.	J.S.M.
Janzen, Cornelius C., Winnipegosis, Man.	C.C.J.	Metzler, A. J., Scottdale, Pa.	A.J.M.
*Janzen, Heinrich, Waterloo, Ont.	H.J.	Mierau, Hugo J., Danvers, Ill.	H.J.M.
		Miller, Clara, Ithaca, Mich.	C.M.

Miller, Daniel E., Hubbard, Ore.	D.E.M.	*Schertz, H. R., Metamora, Ill.	H.R.S.
Miller, D. Paul, Mankato, Minn.	D.P.M.	Schlegel, L. O., Milford, Neb.	L.O.S.
Miller, Enos, Amboy, Ind.	E.Mi.	Schlegel, Wilfred, London, Ont.	W.Sc.
Miller, Ivan J., Grantsville, Md.	I.J.M.	Schmidt, H. U., Meno, Okla.	H.U.S.
Miller, L. A., Arthur, Ill.	L.A.M.	Schmidt, John F., N. Newton, Kan.	J.F.S.
*Miller, L. C., Manitou Cprings, Col.	L.C.M.	Schmidt, Sam J., Marion, S.D.,	S.J.S.
Miller, Percy J., Lagrange, Ind.	P.J.M.	*Schmitt, Hermann, Deutschhof, Ger.	H.Sc.
Miller, S. J., Grabill, Ind.	S.J.M.	Schowalter, Otto, Hamburg, Ger.	O.S.
Mitchell, Frank R., Meadows, Ill.	F.R.M.	Schowalter, Paul, Weierhof, Ger.	P.S.
*Momber, Wilhelm, Berlin, Ger.	W.M.	Schrag, M. Gordon, Goshen, Ind.	M.G.S.
Mosemann, John H., Goshen, Ind.	J.H.M.	Schrag, Martin H., Goshen, Ind.	M.H.S.
Moyer, S. T., Jagdeeshpore, India	S.T.M.	Schrag, Menno, Newton, Kan.	M.S.
Müller, Daniel, Prehof, Ger.	D.M.	Schrag, Robert, Newton, Kan.	R.Sc.
*Neff, Christian, Weierhof, Ger.	Neff	Schrock, Alta E., Goshen, Ind.	A.E.S.
*Nelson, T. U., Newaygo, Mich.	T.U.N.	Schultz, J. S., Bluffton, Ohio	J.S.Sc.
Neuenschwander, A. J., Wadsworth, Ohio	A.J.N.	Schutter, G. N., Sappemeer, Neth.	G.N.S.
Neufeld, Herman, Vancouver, B.C.	H.Ne.	Shank, Lester C., Harrisonburg, Va.	L.C.S.
Neufeld, I. G., Fresno, Cal.	I.G.N.	Shantz, Sidney S., Hanover, Ont.	S.S.S.
Neufeld, P. T., Inman, Kan.	P.T.N.	Shelly, Maynard, Newton, Kan.	M. Sh.
Nice, Aaron D., Morrison, Ill.	A.D.N.	Shelly, Paul R., Bluffton, Ohio	P.R.S.
Nickel, Elizabeth, Hillsboro, Kan.	E.N.	Shelly, Wilmer S., Hereford, Pa.	W.S.S.
Nickel, J. D., Rosemary, Alta.	J.D.N.	Sherk, J. Harold, Akron, Pa.	J.Ha.S.
Niepoth, Wilhelm, Crefeld, Ger.	W.N.	*Showalter, Timothy, Broadway, Va.	T.S.
*Nijdam, C., Amsterdam, Neth.	C.N.	Shultz, Lawrence W., Milford, Ind.	L.W.Sh.
North, Homer F., Nappanee, Ind.	H.F.N.	Smith, Lena Mae, Newton, Kan.	L.M.S.
Nussbaum, Nathan, New Castle, Pa.	N.N.	Smith, Tilman R., Eureka, Ill.	T.R.S.
Oswald, Walter E., Goshen, Ind.	W.E.O.	Smith, Willard H., Goshen, Ind.	W.H.S.
Oswald, Mrs. Walter E., Goshen, Ind.	N.O.	Smucker, Don. E., Chicago, Ill.	D.E.S.
Pankratz, Peter, West Salem, Ore.	P.Pa.	Smucker, J. N., Goshen, Ind.	J.N.S.
Pannabecker, S. F., Chicago, Ill.	S.F.P.	Snyder, M. S., Salem, Ore.	M.S.S.
*Pauls, H., Elbing, Ger.	H.Pa.	Snyder, W. T., Akron, Pa.	W.T.S.
Pauls, Wilhelm, Didsbury, Alta.	W.P.	*Sommer, Pierre, Grand Charmont, Fr.	P.So.
Peachey, Aaron J., Rittman, Ohio	A.J.P.	Springer, N. P., Goshen, Ind.	N.P.S.
Pellman, Hubert R., Harrisonburg, Va.	H.R.Pe.	Sprunger, Elda, Berne, Ind.	E.Sp.
Penner, Henry D., Medford, Okla.	H.D.P.	Sprunger, Mrs. Ira H., Berne, Ind.	A.H.S.
Penner, Johann Peter, Rosemary, Alta.	J.P.P.	Stahly, Delmar, Akron, Pa.	D.S.
Penner, John I., Kleefeld, Man.	J.I.P.	Stahly, Ralph, Wakarusa, Ind.	R.St.
*Penner, P. W., Hillsboro, Kan.	P.W.P.	Starkey, J. B., New Market, Iowa	J.B.St.
Priddle, H. R., Palmerston, Ont.	H.R.P.	Stauffer, Elam W., Musoma, Tanganyika, Africa	
Quiring, Horst, Korntal, Ger.	H.Q.		E.W.S.
Quiring, Walter, Rosthern, Sask.	W.Q.	*Stauffer, Ezra, Tofield, Alta.	E.S.
Rahn, Ben, Inman, Kan.	B.R.	Steiner, E. G., Berne, Ind.	E.G.St.
Redekop, H. H., Winkler, Man.	H.H.R.	Steiner, James A., Wadsworth. Ohio	J.A.S.
Regehr, J. I., Main Centre, Sask.	J.I.R.	Steingard, Henry, Meade, Kan.	H.St.
*Regehr, Peter, Talma, Russia	P.R.	Stoll, Henry J., Rensselaer, Ind.	H.J.St.
*Regier, D. A., Mountain Lake, Minn.	D.A.R.	Stoltzfus, Abner G., Kinzers, Pa.	A.G.S.
Regier, Walter H., Clinton, Okla.	W.H.R.	Stoltzfus, Grant M., Harrisonburg, Va.	G.M.S.
Reiff, V. E., Elkhart, Ind.	V.E.R.	Stoltzfus, LeRoy S., Bird-in-Hand, Pa.	L.S.S.
Reimer, David P., Giroux, Man.	D.P.R.	Stoneback, George S., Wichita, Kan.	G.S.S.
Reimer, D. J., Morden, Man.	D.J.R.	Storms, Everek R., Kitchener, Ont.	E.R.S.
Reimer, Elmer, Jansen, Neb.	E.R.	Stucky, Gerald, Cachipay, Colombia	G.S.
Reimer, P. J. B., Rosenort, Man.	P.J.B.R.	Stucky, Harley J., N. Newton, Kan.	H.J.S.
Reist, H. F., Premont, Texas	H.F.R.	Stucky, Walter, West Unity, Ohio	W.S.
Rembert, Karl, Crefeld, Ger.	K.R.	Suderman, J. M., Newton, Kan.	J.M.S.
Rempel, Alexander, Göttingen, Ger.	A.R.	Swartzendruber, A. Lloyd, Kalona, Iowa	A.L.S.
Rempel, Hans, Neuland, Par.	H.Re.	Swartzendruber, Harold L., Goshen, Ind.	H.L.S.
Rempel, J. G., Saskatoon, Sask.	J.G.R.	Swartzendruber, Maude, La Junta, Col.	M.Sw.
Reusser, James, Dalton, Ohio	J.Re.	Swope, Wilmer D., Leetonia, Ohio	W.D.S.
Risler, Walter, Crefeld, Ger.	W.Ri.	Taylor, Albert, New Carlisle, Ohio	A.Ta.
*Risser, John D., Hagerstown, Md.	J.D.R.	*Teufel, Eberhard, Stuttgart-Fellbach, Ger.	E.T.
Roth, Paul M., Masontown, Pa.	P.M.R.	Tgahrt, E., West Prussia, Ger.	E.Tg.
Roth, Roy D., Hesston, Kan.	R.D.R.	Thiessen, J. J., Saskatoon, Sask.	J.J.Th.
*Rupp, Jakob, Lemberg, Poland	J.Ru.	Thiessen, John, Newton, Kan.	J.T.
Ruth, Arthur D., Souderton, Pa.	A.D.R.	Thomann, David E., Jersey City, N.J.	D.E.T.
Schaefer, P. J., Gretna, Man.	P.J.S.	*Tilitzky, C. G., Abbotsford, B.C.	C.G.T.
Schantz, Irwin, Loman, Minn.	I.S.	Toews, A. A., N. Clearbrook, B.C.	A.A.T.

Toews, A. R., Windom, Kan.	A.R.T.	Wiebe, Alfred, Seiling, Okla.	A.Wi.
Toews, C. W., Linden, Alta.	C.W.T.	Wiebe, Arthur J., Reedley, Cal.	A.J.W.
Toews, H. P., Winnipeg, Man.	H.P.T.	Wiebe, David V., Hillsboro, Kan.	D.V.W.
Toews, Jacob J., Kitchener, Ont.	J.J.T.	Wiebe, John A., Mountain Lake, Minn.	J.A.W.
Toews, John A., Winnipeg, Man.	Jo.A.T.	Wiebe, Orlando H., Omaha, Neb.	O.H.W.
Toews, J. W., Linden, Alta.	J.W.T.	Wiebe, Willard W., Mountain Lake, Minn.	
Toews, Peter P., Dresden, N.D.	P.T.		W.W.W.
Troyer, David J.,	D.J.T.	Wiens, H. E., Mountain Lake, Minn.	H.E.W.
Troyer, L. E., Meadows, Ill.	L.E.T.	Wiens, Henry P., Lustre, Mont.	H.P.W.
Tschetter, John P., Lewellen, Neb.	J.P.T.	Wiens, J. B., Vancouver, B.C.	J.B.W.
Umble, John S., Goshen, Ind.	J.S.U.	Wiswedel, Wilhelm, Bayreuth, Ger.	W.W.
Ummel, Samuel, Peoria, Ill.	S.U.	Witmer, H. Howard, Manheim, Pa.	H.H.W.
Unger, J. J., Kelowna, B.C.	J.J.U.	Woelke, O., Düsseldorf, Ger.	O.W.
Unruh, Abe J., Montezuma, Kan.	A.U.	Wyse, Ora C., Naubinway, Mich.	O.C.W.
Unruh, Albert, Montezuma, Kan.	A.Un.	*Yntema, J., Haarlem, Neth.	J.Y.
Unruh, J. D., Freeman, S.D.	J.D.U.	Yoder, Edward, Kansas City, Kan.	Ed.Y.
Unruh, N. H., St. Elizabeth, Man.	N.H.U.	Yoder, Gideon G., Hesston, Kan.	G.G.Y.
*Vos, Karel, Middelstum, Neth.	K.V.	Yoder, Glen, Kansas City, Kan.	G.Y.
Wagley, Paul E., Marshall, Mich.	P.E.Wa.	Yoder, J. J., Jr., Belleville, Pa.	J.J.Y.
Wall, P. F., Downey, Cal.	P.F.W.	Yoder, John Miller, Parnell, Iowa	J.M.Y.
Waltner, Erland, N. Newton, Kan.	E.W.	Yoder, Noah, Choteau, Okla.	N.Y.
Warkentin, G. J., Dundurn, Sask.	G.J.W.	Yoder, Paul R., Columbiana, Ohio	P.R.Y.
Warkentin, Peter J., Tofield, Alta.	P. J. Wa.	Yoder, Sam E., Crestview, Tenn.	S.E.Y.
*Warns, J., Wiedenest, Ger.	J.Wa.	Yost, A. L., Moundridge, Kan.	A.L.Y.
Weaver, Norman, Gulliver, Mich.	N.We.	Zehr, B. F., Croghan, N.Y.	B.F.Z.
Weber, L. S., Scottdale, Pa.	L.S.W.	*Zehr, Edmund P., Beatrice, Neb.	E.P.Z.
Wedel, C. C., Montezuma, Kan.	C.C.W.	Zehr, Harold, Rantoul, Ill.	H.Z.
Wenger, A. D., Fentress, Va.	A.D.W.	Zehr, Noah, Middlebury, Ind.	N.Z.
Wenger, Mrs. A. D., Fentress, Va.	L.H.We.	Zijpp, N. van der, Rotterdam, Neth.	vdZ.
Wenger, J. C., Goshen, Ind.	J.C.W.	Zimmerman, E. E., Peoria, Ill.	E.E.Z.
Widmer, Liesel, Bergzabern, Ger.	L.W.	Zook, Ellrose D., Scottdale, Pa.	E.D.Z.

THE

MENNONITE ENCYCLOPEDIA

I

Ibersheim (Yberscheim, Uebersheim), a village in Rheinhessen, Germany, near the Rhine, about eight miles north of Worms, formerly called Ibersheimer Hof. On a map of 1752 it is designated as "Wiedertaufhof."

The time of the coming of the first Anabaptists cannot be ascertained; they stemmed from the region of Bern, Switzerland, and probably came after the Thirty Years' War, likely in the 1650's. The land had been devastated and depopulated by the war. The great electoral estates in and around Ibersheim had been abandoned. The immigrant Mennonites were welcomed as capable farmers to reclaim this land. It was to the advantage of the Ibersheim Mennonites that they received 12-year leases of the crown estates from the elector, giving them a different status from the other Mennonite congregations.

The Ibersheim estate, which was leased as a whole to the Mennonites, was divided among them into 6 parts, later into 12, and finally into 24 still recognizable parts. To it the neighboring villages, Hamm, Eich, Gimbsheim, Alsheim, Osthofen, and Westhofen, owed feudal service. The Mennonites did not exact this service, and the French abolished it during their occupation of the region (1793-1816). In 1816 Ibersheim passed into Hessian control, and in 1822 it became an independent village. Its first mayor was Johannes Forrer (1822-37).

Ibersheim is probably the oldest of the Mennonite churches established after the Thirty Years' War in the Palatinate west of the Rhine. In 1661—three years before the first general Mennonite "Concession"—the inhabitants of Ibersheim had been accepted as subjects of the Palatinate. Upon this Concession all subsequent decisions and measures by the government concerning the Mennonites were based. It states: "That they may for the sake of their faith, for which they are not to be molested, hold no public or private meetings or conventicles attended by others that do not live on the estate, much less attract and mislead others of our subjects." The church chronicle of 1683 makes the first mention of a rental contract.

The charge was soon made that they abused the elector's grace. In May 1671 Inspector and Dean Johannes Jakob Löffler of Osthofen accused them of having baptized a member of the Reformed Church. Investigation revealed that a Jakob Weber, whose grandparents had, however, been Mennonites, had indeed been baptized. The congregation at Ibersheim was fined 100 Talers. They were now secretly but closely watched to note any transgressions against the Concession of 1664. It was observed that 50-100 Mennonites attended their services, whereas the Concession allowed only 20 to meet together. Upon a petition signed by all the Men-

nonites in the Oberamt of Alzey it was decided to modify the wording to permit 20 families instead of 20 persons.

In the contract of lease of 1683, renewed in 1745, 1753, and 1762, ten names occur: Heinrich Neff (Trieb has "Neef"); Konrad Hiestand; Hans Jakob Forrer; Heinrich Gochnauer; Hans Jakob Brubacher; Jakob Dentlinger; Hans Leitweller; Peter Opmann; Heinrich Reif, and Ulrich Hagmann's widow. In 1745 there are 24 lessees listed. On the other hand the list of names required by the Palatine government contains 32 names of renters, and that of 1743 the same number, with a total of 170 persons. Of especial value is the register of 1752, which contains important family names (court records of the Karlsruhe *Generallandesarchiv*). According to a Dutch register there were in Ibersheim in 1732, 56 Mennonite families. (Müller, 212.)

An attempt made by the officer Zachmann of Alzey to have the Mennonites of Ibersheim treated exactly like those in Kriegsheim, Niederflörsheim, Heppenheim, Dackenheim, and Wolfsheim failed. The Ibersheim residents referred to their contract and letter of Concession. The official in charge reported to Zachmann that he was convinced that they were not mere renters, but had their own possessions and domicile. Thus the Mennonites of Ibersheim must have had the right of ownership as early as 1685; this was nowhere else the case in the Palatinate. This official was apparently favorable toward the Mennonites. His letter of 1685 to the elector states, "Everyone must give them the testimonial that they live quietly and peaceably, live in harmony with their neighbors, and have proven themselves more industrious than others, obedient to the government, true and constant in all things."

During the tribulations of the French attack on the Palatinate in 1697 the Ibersheim Mennonites paid the contributions levied by the French. In 1711 they were to be drafted as guards and for military service, but upon their petition a decision was passed on Jan. 27, 1712, confirming their rights to exemption from military service. They repeatedly paid their exemption tax of 12 fl. per head, but were then released from the obligation. In 1742 this tax was again considered and debated over several decades on the ground that only those who leased the land were exempt, and not any later arrivals; furthermore the original number of 20 families had increased to 30. There was also some difficulty in connection with the burial of their dead in the community cemetery, but this was also settled in their favor.

Divine services were at first held in private homes. Later a special room was used for this purpose, described by the Lutheran tutor of the van

1

der Smissen family in Altona, who visited Ibersheim in 1782 with his wards, as follows: "In the lower story of a two-story house is the school, which looked very handsome, clean, and orderly. Above to the right is a little room in which the schoolmaster lives, and to the left the room . . . for the meeting of preachers and elders before the service. Adjoining these rooms is the meeting-hall, which, in addition to the good points in its arrangement, has the defect of being very low. It is evident from the style of the building that the Mennonites built it soon after their arrival here."

The present church was built in 1836. It is the only Mennonite church in South Germany with tower and bell. The church record states, "The new church stands on the site of the old one, but the former church opened on the street, whereas the new one has windows on that side. On the lower floor was the school and a brewery, on the upper the church; but later on the lower floor was used as a church, and the former church became a school and council room. In 1822 the present organ was bought; previously the congregation had not used an organ to accompany its hymns." On Feb. 11, 1866, two new bells were dedicated (*Menn. Bl.*, 1866, 18 ff.). In 1891 the church was incorporated (*Menn. Bl.*, 1891, 24).

The office of preaching was conducted by several preachers chosen from the congregation. The church records name Heinrich Christoph as preacher in 1784, Johann Stauffer in 1787. During the last years before his death in 1822 or 1823 he served alone. He was followed by Daniel Stauffer of Eich, who resigned in 1842. The congregation, following the example of Monsheim and Sembach, now employed a trained minister with an annual salary of 400 fl. A request of an additional sum of 250 fl. from the state was refused (1844). This step was severely reprimanded by the Mennonite church conferences held at Sembach in 1843 and at Monsheim in 1844. The following preachers have served: Bernhard Thiessen 1843-55, Heinrich Neufeld 1856-69, J. Ellenberger II 1869-71, Heinrich van der Smissen 1872-82, Thomas Löwenberg 1883-1917, Emil Händiges 1917-23, Erich Göttner 1923-27, A. Braun 1928-   , Daniel Habegger 1953-   . With the consent of the Ibersheim congregation H. Neufeld in 1856 took over in addition the churches at Eppstein (*q.v.*) and Friesenheim (*q.v.*) (now Ludwigshafen). Since then these three churches have been in charge of one pastor.

In 1803 and 1805 two important conferences were held at Ibersheim, the results of which are known as the Ibersheim Resolutions (*Ibersheimer Beschlüsse*). Both sets of resolutions were signed for Ibersheim by the preachers Jakob Weiss, Heinrich Christoffel, Heinrich Forrer, and Johannes Stauffer, and the deacon Jakob Hiestand.

On May 24, 1874, the new church discipline was adopted (drawn up by H. v. d. Smissen). In 1882 a new parsonage was built.

The Ibersheim church is a member of the Vereinigung, the Conference of South German Mennonites, and the Palatine-Hessian Conference. The latter met at Ibersheim several times.

In 1932 the church had a membership of 120 baptized members; in 1955 the total number, including children, was 185.

Services are held every two weeks in winter, and every three weeks in summer. Communion is observed three times a year, viz., at Easter, Pentecost, and at the harvest festival.   A.B.

A. Trieb, *Ibersheim am Rhein, Geschichte des Ortes seit den frühesten Zeiten mit besonderer Berücksichtigung der Mennonitengemeinde; Menn. Bl.*, 1886, 1891; Müller, *Berner Täufer; ML* II, 397-400.

Ibersheim Resolutions (*Ibersheimer Beschlüsse*) is the name given to the acts of two conferences of South German Mennonites held at Ibersheim June 5, 1803, and June 10, 1805.

The former was called by Valentin Dahlem (*q.v.*) of Mosbach and Peter Weber of Neuwied. A new Ministers' Manual was to be drawn up and issued. In addition resolutions were passed, dealing almost exclusively with church discipline. The age of baptismal candidates was fixed at 14 or 15. A second baptism for persons changing membership from another church was rejected. The bearing of arms and military service were forbidden.

At the second conference the regulation prohibiting members from holding government office was renewed. Preachers were not to be considered in full service until they had had some practice and proved themselves. The council meeting (*Umfrage*) was never to be omitted. A day of prayer and fasting was set for July 28 in all the congregations "on this side of the Rhine and on the Neckar" to avert the distress of military service. Mannhardt therefore calls this meeting at Ibersheim "the sunset glow in the sky of the old Mennonitism in the Rhineland."   NEFF.

W. Mannhardt, *Die Wehrfreiheit der Altpreussischen Mennoniten* (Danzig, 1863) 55; *Menn. Bl.*, 1907, 51 and 60; *ML* II, 400.

Iberville Hutterite Bruderhof, seven miles northeast of Elie, Man., founded in 1919 by eleven families with their preacher Paul Gross, of the Rosedale Bruderhof. Paul Gross died May 10, 1929. Other preachers of the colony were Peter Gross, chosen on March 16, 1924, Paul Gross, chosen on Jan. 15, 1933, and Michael Gross, chosen on Jan. 31, 1937. In 1947 the colony had a population of 143 souls, of whom 57 were baptized members.   D.D.

Ich Sende Euch is the official organ of the Mennonite Collegiate Graduates' Society, the alumni association of the M.C.I. at Gretna, Man., which was organized in 1942, and succeeds the former *Alumni Journal*. First published at Gretna, beginning in August 1942, it was transferred to Winnipeg, Man., July 1, 1944. The present 8-page journal is published five times a year in German. In 1949 the circulation was 800, with Frank Dyck serving as editor. In 1953 it was edited by Paul F. Peters.   G.EN.

Ickelsamer (Ickelsheimer), **Valentin**, an early Protestant-spiritualist opponent of Luther and defender of Carlstadt, studied at the University of Wittenberg. He was the author of the book, *Klag etlicher Brüder* *an alle Christen von der grossen . . . Tyranney, so Endressen Bodensteyn von Karlstadt jetzt von Luther . . . geschieht* (1525), an original and courageous book which sharply attacked Luther and defended Carlstadt (*q.v.*). In consequence of this book he suffered a lengthy imprisonment, during which he asked Luther's pardon, which was granted through the mediation of Justus Menius (*q.v.*). This book is reprinted in *Flugschriften aus der Ref.-Zeit*, No. X (Halle, 1893). Later, as a follower of Schwenckfeld, he became involved in a dispute with Pilgram Marpeck (*q.v.*) in 1542 (*Beiträge*, 278; Loserth, 58, 426). That he was an Anabaptist and a leader of the Peasants' Revolt, as Elector John of Saxony wrote in a letter dated March 27, 1530, and as Jacobs (429) and Wappler (91) also thought, is most unlikely; the elector offers no evidence for the statement. (The letter is found in Einicke, 416 f.) In his book of 1525 Ickelsamer does not mention the Anabaptists; nevertheless it must be admitted that the spirit of the "fanatics" of all kinds, so violently suppressed by Luther, is brought to clear expression in the book. Having studied in Wittenberg he was well aware of the weaknesses in Lutheranism.

NEFF, E.T.

H. Fechner, *Vier seltene Schriften des 16. Jahrhunderts mit einer ungedruckten Abhandlung über Val. Ickelsamer von R. Wiegand;* H. Barge, *Andreas Bodenstein von Karlstadt* II (Leipzig, 1905) 317-24; E. Jacobs, *Die Wiedertäufer am Harz* (Wernigerode, 1899); P. Wappler, *Thüringen; Corpus Schwenckfeldianorum* IV (1914) 68; V (1916) 163, 165; 272 f.; 404; 408 f., 698, 798-806; J. Loserth, *Quellen und Forschungen zur Gesch. der oberdeutschen Taufgesinnten im 16. Jahrh.* (Vienna, 1929); G. Einicke, *Zwanzig Jahre schwarzburgische Ref.-Gesch.* 1521-1541, I; Fr. Thudichum, *Die deutsche Ref.* II (Leipzig, 1909) 281; *Beiträge zur bayr. Kirchengesch.* VII (1902); *ML* II, 400.

Idaho, pop. 524,873, admitted to the union as a state in 1890, has large areas of mountain and arid land, with the population chiefly inhabiting the south. Here, almost on the western border, less than 20 miles from the state capital of Boise, the first Mennonite settlement was begun in February 1899 by David Garber, and the Nampa Mennonite (MC) Church was organized the same year. Two other congregations of this group were later established in Idaho; viz., Filer (1914), some 150 miles southeast, and Indian Cove (1935) near Hammett, some 150 miles south of Nampa. In 1955 these three congregations had a total of 369 members.

The General Conference Mennonites first came to Idaho in 1906, when a settlement was established at Aberdeen, about 200 miles east of Nampa. They organized a congregation in 1907. A second church (Emmanuel), established by division in 1912, three miles south, merged again with the Aberdeen church in 1930. Two other settlements near Aberdeen, the Minidoka mixed settlement (partly GCM, partly Central Conference), and the Dubois settlement (1910-12), both failed. One other G.C.M. settlement, at Caldwell, five miles from Nampa, was founded in 1941; a congregation was organized in 1947. A third church was organized in Filer in 1955. The three G.C.M. congregations in 1955 had a total of 389 members, Aberdeen alone having 327.

A United Missionary church was organized in Filer in 1905. In 1949 it had 69 members. For a short period a Mennonite Brethren church also existed at Aberdeen (founded 1910) and a Central Conference church at Nampa (founded 1907). The Mountain View congregation of the Church of God in Christ, near Bonners Ferry, at the extreme northern point near the Canadian border, was organized in 1936 and had 92 members in 1955.

Thus the total Mennonite membership in Idaho in 1955 was 790, distributed as follows: G.C.M. 389, M.C. 369, C.G.C. 92. The Idaho settlements were all pioneer farming communities, those in the south depending almost exclusively on irrigation, built by settlers of widely varying backgrounds. All are located in or near small towns except those at Nampa, which has over 12,000 inhabitants. The settlements are of mixed background. The Nampa Mennonite (MC) Church operates a city mission in Nampa and a Christian day school called Nampa Mennonite School. The Mennonites (GCM) of Aberdeen built the Salem Deaconess Hospital at American Falls but sold it to the county because of financial difficulties. (*ML* II, 400 f.) H.N.H.

Idsegahuizen, a hamlet in the Dutch province of Friesland, where Leenaert Bouwens baptized six persons in 1557 and four more in 1563. Nothing is known about a congregation here. The newly baptized may have joined the Legemeer (*q.v.*) congregation. vDZ.

Ieper (*Yper,* or *Yperen*), a town in West Flanders, Belgium (1949 pop. 17,154). The town has a rich history. In the Middle Ages it was very prosperous as a result of a flourishing weaving industry; in the 13th century there were more than 80,000 inhabitants. The town has been repeatedly struck by war; in World War I it was nearly completely destroyed. During the raid on Nov. 22, 1914, when the beautiful old Cloth Hall was set on fire, the archives were destroyed. These archives without doubt contained some valuable material about the Anabaptist-Mennonite congregation existing here in the 16th century. Now the information about the Anabaptist movement here is very scarce. There was Anabaptist activity at Ieper as early as about 1538, and there may have been a congregation at this time. Leenaert Bouwens baptized 13 persons here in 1554-56.

There are two important documents, both of 1561, which supplement one another. (*a*) A letter written by the inquisitor Titelman (*q.v.*), at Ieper on Nov. 14, 1561, to the vice-regent Margaret of Parma, informing her that he had destroyed a Mennonite congregation at Ieper, which had been meeting for 10 or 12 months in a woods between Ieper and Meenen (*q.v.*), 80 to 100 persons being present at times. Sometimes they also held meetings in town with an attendance of 38 to 40 persons. A number of heretics had been taken prisoner and the law had taken its course. Most of the Anabaptists, however, had escaped and fled to Armentières or Hondschoote, or were roaming about the country, still seducing the simple people. (This letter is found in P. Besson, *Edicts de Persecutions,* Berne-Neuchatel-Buenos Aires, n.d., 11-14.) (*b*) A hymn, found in the *Lietboecxken van den Offer des Heeren* (No. 23), composed by Anabaptists arrested in 1561 when a meeting was surprised by Titelman and his soldiers. The Dutch martyrbook of 1615 (the *Groot Offerboek*) and later martyrbooks, including van Braght's *Martyrs' Mirror*, which contain this hymn in a prose version, give information which shows that these Mennonites had moved from elsewhere to Ieper to avoid persecution. They were all weavers. A certain Hendrik N. managed to escape, and one woman recanted. The arrested Mennonites, four in number, were strangled and burned at the stake on the market place of Ieper. The trial of the martyr Jacob de Rore (*q.v.*), who was himself active in Ieper, reveals that a certain Lossche Coppen (concerning whom nothing more is known) was active in Ieper, preaching and performing marriages. Titelman's assertion that he had exterminated the Anabaptist congregation of Ieper is not true. Until about 1574 Mennonites were found here, and in 1566 they were said to have held their meetings rather publicly. The following martyrs died at Ieper: Jan Hulle, Maeyken Kocx, Anthonis Schoonvelt, Kalleken Strings, and Laurens van de Walle, all in 1561, Claudine le Vettre in 1568, Dirk Anoot and Willem de Zager in 1569. (*BRN* II, 603-7; A. L. E. Verheyden, "Mennisme in Vlaanderen," ms.)   vDZ.

Igbetti, a town of some 6,000 in Southern Nigeria, West Africa. Still unknown to missionaries in 1919, 25 years later it was the home of the world's largest United Missionary Church (*q.v.*) congregation, with an average Sunday attendance of around 1,000. Its development is largely due to the work of O. L. Traub and G. J. Bolender. Besides the church there is a school with an enrollment of 200, a dispensary, a Bible school, and a normal school.   E.R.S.

IJlst, one of the eleven towns (1947 pop. 1,488, with 154 Mennonites) of the Dutch province of Friesland, the seat of a Mennonite congregation with a rich history dating back to the early days. Richt Heynes, of IJlst, sealed her faith with her martyr's death by drowning at Leeuwarden in 1547. In 1551-57 Leenaert Bouwens baptized 49 persons here. Nothing more is known about this church in the 16th century except that there were two congregations. One of them, apparently of the Waterlander branch, joined the Sociëteit of Friesland (*q.v.*) at its founding in 1695; it had about 35 self-supporting members. This congregation had a church record book listing the baptized members which was begun in 1701. It acquired a new meetinghouse, dedicated on Aug. 12, 1708, by its (lay) preacher Sybren Gosses. The other congregation, always small, was a member of the Groningen Old Flemish Sociëteit in 1710 and probably much earlier. It dates back at least to 1648, when Louwe Mantjes was its preacher, and it was still sending delegates to the Sociëteit in 1815, when the conference was dissolved.

In 1746 at least 15 members of the IJlst Old Flemish congregation were living in Sneek. These members organized an independent congregation under the leadership of Wouter Berends. The Waterlander congregation at IJlst was served by Jelle Sipkes van Teerns 1771-1818. He was an active Patriot (*q.v.*) and a man of importance not only in his home congregation, taking an active political part in the government of Friesland in 1796-98.

In 1819 the two congregations in IJlst merged; they had a total of 102 members. The old Mennonite principle of charitable giving was expressed in the "Ten Kate Foundation," which was established by the brothers Rijkle (1770-1855) and Keimpe (1775-1856) Lammerts ten Kate for the support of the poor.

A new meetinghouse was dedicated on Sept. 27, 1857. A pipe organ was installed in 1881. The membership numbered 135 in 1838, 140 in 1861, 101 in 1900, 84 in 1954. Until 1818 the congregation was served by lay ministers. H. J. Busé, minister at IJlst 1890-1917, wrote a history of the congregation (manuscript). Busé was followed by L. G. Holtz 1918-21, B. H. Rudolphi 1921-30, B. Dufour 1930-35, A. du Croix 1936-39, Miss J. H. van der Slooten 1939-46, H. B. Kossen 1950-56. The pulpit is now (1957) vacant; the pastor of the near-by Sneek congregation has charge of the IJlst congregation. The church has a ladies' circle and a choir.   vDZ.

Inv. Arch. Amst. II, Nos. 2361-63; Blaupot t. C., *Friesland, passim,* see Index; H. J. Busé, *Ter gedachtenis aan het 50-jarig bestaan der nieuwe Doopsgezinde Kerk te IJlst* (Sneek, n.d.-1907); *Naamlijst* 1829, 49 f.; *DJ* 1840, 44; Gorter's *Doopsgezind Lectuur* 1858, 48; *DB* 1861, 145; 1879, 3, 89; 1890, 93-98; 1892, 89-98; 1917, 66-73; *ML* II, 406.

IJmuiden, formerly a village, now a large city with an important harbor and active industry, with population (together with Velsen) of 52,108, with about 425 Mennonites in 1954, located in the Dutch province of North Holland at the mouth of the North Sea Canal, which joins Amsterdam to the sea. The Anabaptists here originally belonged to the adjacent Beverwijk congregation. On Feb. 21, 1909, they organized an independent congregation, acquired a church, and called E. Pekema from Monnikendam as their pastor on July 25, 1909. He served until 1912 and was followed by D. Attema 1912-15, W. Luikinga 1915-d.1928, F. F. Milatz 1929-44, W. Veen 1949-55, and J. P. Jacobszoon 1956- .

The membership of the IJmuiden congregation, numbering 80 when the congregation was founded, was 170 in 1930 and 204 in 1954. During the last years of World War II church life was at a complete standstill; the church was damaged by bombs which destroyed a part of the town, and the population was evacuated. Church services are now (1957) held at IJmuiden and in a rented hall at Westerveld. Church activities include Sunday school for children at IJmuiden and Velsen, ladies' circles at IJmuiden and Santpoort, and a Bible course.   vDZ.

DB 1909, 186; 1910, 191; *De Zondagsbode* XXII (1909-10) Nos. 9, 18, 41; *De Noodbrug,* October 1945; *ML* II, 406.

IJntema, Jan, b. 1894 at Workum, Friesland, d. 1944 at Surhuisterveen, a Dutch Mennonite pastor, who served at Surhuisterveen 1918-22, Oudebildtzijl 1922-26, Dantumawoude 1926-31, Leeuwarden 1931-36, and Haarlem 1936-44; author of *De Doopsgezinden* (Huis ter Heide, 1930, 2d ed. 1930) and *Wij Doopsgezinden* (Amsterdam, 1940, 2d ed. 1941). He also published two articles in the *Doopsgezind Jaarboekje* (1936 and 1937) and a number of sermons. In cooperation with Pastor A. Binnerts (*q.v.*) he founded the A.N.D.P.V. (*q.v.*, Dutch Mennonite Pastors' Association) and served as its secretary-treasurer for many years. vᴅZ.

IJs(s)elstein, a town (1947 pop., 5,311) in the Dutch province of Utrecht, which, together with the village of Benschop (*q.v.*), was governed by the tolerant Ghijsbrecht van Baeck (*q.v.*) in the early 1530's when Anabaptism arose in the Netherlands. The reformer Henric Rol (*q.v.*), who later joined the Anabaptists, was until about 1530 van Baeck's domestic chaplain, and van Baeck's wife, Else van Lostadt (*q.v.*), was herself an Anabaptist. Anabaptist meetings could be held freely at IJselstein. But Anabaptism in this territory soon deteriorated into Münsterism, leaders like Gerrit van Benschop (*q.v.*) preaching revolutionary principles. After 1535 it soon declined, though IJselstein in the following years was still a shelter for Anabaptists persecuted elsewhere. When Else van Lostadt, who had been in prison 1544-48, was set free, all traces of Anabaptism had disappeared in this region. vᴅZ.

Inv. Arch. Amst. I, 28, 33, 39, 55, 104, 230; Kühler, *Geschiedenis* I, 88, 99, 175, 208; Mellink, *Wederdopers*, 231-41.

IJtens, a Dutch Mennonite congregation: see **Ytens**.

Illikhoven (Illekhoven), a village near the Maas River in the Dutch province of Limburg, once belonging partly (north) to the duchy of Gelder, partly (south) to the duchy of Jülich; now belonging partly (north) to the community of Reesteren (1940, 60 inhabitants), partly (south) to the community of Born (1940, 70 inhabitants). A short distance to the west is Vissersweert (*q.v.*), a hamlet on the Maas (1940, 19 houses and 90 inhabitants). About 1545 Menno Simons (*q.v.*) stayed at Illikhoven with Lemke (*q.v.*) and preached at night in a pasture near Vissersweert, and then went by boat to Roermond (*q.v.*). After 1545 Theunis van Hastenrath (*q.v.*) of Illikhoven also preached and baptized here, and about the same time Adam Pastor seems to have visited the congregation. In 1547 a severe persecution struck the small group. Three of its members, Metken (*q.v.*), Jater (*q.v.*), and Lijsken (*q.v.*), were put to death; other Mennonites saved their lives by flight. Yet the congregation was not destroyed; Illikhoven was the center of a Mennonite congregation "on the Maas," which Diderich Verwer represented at Cologne (see **Concept of Cologne**) in 1591. E.C.

Inv. Arch. Amst. I, No. 343; *DB* 1890, 54-61; 1909, 120 f.; W. Bax, *Het Protestantisme in het bisdom Luik en vooral te Maastricht 1505-1557* (The Hague, 1937) *passim;* C. Krahn, *Menno Simons* (Karlsruhe, 1936) 62-64; K. Vos, *Menno Simons* (Leiden, 1914) 83-87, 240-43; E. Crous, "Auf Mennos Spuren am Niederrhein," *Der Mennonit* VIII (1955) 155.

Illingen (Illing), a village (pop. 1,750) in Württemberg, Germany, in which there were Anabaptists in the 16th century. The Hutterite *Geschicht-Buch* (183) states that ten Anabaptists were executed here, but does not give names or dates. Nor is there any other information about the execution of Anabaptists here. The earliest references showing connections with the Hutterites in Moravia are dated 1554 (*TA*, 142). Several families united with them. In

1565 Matthäus Klotz, a carpenter at Stammheim near Calw, born at Illingen, moved to Moravia with his wife and six children and 400 florins in cash (*TA*, 547). Other Anabaptists of Illingen distinguished themselves by steadfastness in suffering and exemplary living.

Illingen was the home of Hans Dauber, who was arrested in 1581 and imprisoned in Hohenurach for his faith. After six years, declaring himself ready to join the state church, he was released. But in 1589 he was again seized "because he could not desist from his perverted manner" (675). He was then taken to Hohenwittlingen (*q.v.*), where he was held prisoner for several decades. After an attempt to convert him in 1608 his tormentors apparently abandoned all hope of his returning to the state church; in a court record they remarked, he "must be commended to God's judgment" (809).

In Illingen Dauber appears to have gained a considerable following (545). Peter Ehrenpreis, in whose possession Menno Simons' *Foundation Book* was found, was one of his followers. Ehrenpreis was the son of the magistrate Wolf Ehrenpreis, whom the pastor bitterly accused before the authorities of failing to take steps against the Anabaptists (562). Peter Ehrenpreis emigrated to Moravia and joined the Hutterites. Upon his return to Illingen he was seized on May 10, 1585, but was dismissed when he promised to join the state church (598 and 616). But in 1596 the pastor Johann Huttenloch in Illingen reported to Wilhelm Holder, abbot of Maulbronn, that although Ehrenpreis had formerly attended the noon services, he now remained away when the sacraments were discussed and hurried out of the church when communion or infant baptism was being observed. On July 5, 1596, he went to Moravia with his family, leaving all his possessions. By his manner of life Ehrenpreis won respect, as is shown in the report of the local pastor: "Like all the Anabaptists Ehrenpreis lives a quiet, honorable, blameless life before the world. With his Anabaptist hymns, which he sings in the vineyards and other places, and through his hypocritical conduct he has won such favor with the majority of the populace, that they would not consent to his being condemned for his Anabaptism. At a public inn recently a councilman, Jörg Augsburger, exclaimed that if a man could be saved here, then this Peter would be saved, and he wished for no other heaven than the one to which Peter would go, and that he was more highly esteemed by a great many than all the Protestant pastors" (687).

It is not at all impossible that this Ehrenpreis was the father of Andreas Ehrenpreis (*q.v.*), an outstanding leader of the Hutterian Brethren (*TA*, 66).

After the emigration of Peter Ehrenpreis there are no more reports about Anabaptist families in Illingen. In 1657 there was a rental record (*Zinsbrief*) concerning Anabaptist property of Illingen leased out by the official management of Anabaptist property. Hᴇɢᴇ.

Wolkan, *Geschicht-Buch; TA Württemberg*, index under "Dauber, Hans"; G. Bossert, "Eine amerikanische Quelle für württembergische Geschichte und Literatur des 16. und 17. Jh.," in supplement to *Staats-Anzeiger für Württemberg*, June 1, 1916; *ML* II, 407.

Illinois, one of the 48 states of the United States, was admitted to the Union as a state in 1818. With an area of 56,400 square miles its greatest length is 385 miles and its extreme breadth 218 miles. It comprises an area larger than Belgium, Switzerland, and Holland combined. One of the most level of the states, its greatest elevation is 1,150 feet above the sea, and its average elevation is 550. The greater part of its area consists of quite level or slightly undulating prairies, though there are hills and bluffs along the rivers and their tributaries and in the northwest and the extreme south. Having rich black soil, Illinois, as a part of the fertile Mississippi Valley, is a prosperous agricultural state. But it is also an important producer of minerals, coal being the most important. It is also one of the most important manufacturing states, with Chicago as the chief industrial city. In 1950 Illinois was fourth state in population, having 8,712,176 inhabitants.

The Mennonites did not come to Illinois in large groups as a colonizing movement but rather as individuals and in small groups. The first ones to settle in the state were of the Amish wing. They came to the central part of Illinois settling in the counties of McLean, Woodford, Tazewell, and Livingston. Peter Maurer, the first of whom there is record, settled in McLean County in 1829, having come from Butler County, Ohio, and two years before that from Alsace. In 1830 two others came, walking, it is said, all the way from Butler County. Others came in the following years, most of the Illinois Amish having arrived by 1850. Many of these immigrants came from Alsace, some coming directly by way of New Orleans and up the Mississippi and Illinois rivers, and others coming by way of New York City, either directly or after a brief sojourn in Pennsylvania or Ohio. Other European areas, besides Alsace-Lorraine, contributed Amish settlers to central Illinois—Hesse, the Palatinate, Bavaria, Baden, and Switzerland. Though usually not the first whites in an area, these first Amish settlers found themselves surrounded by frontier conditions in this part of Illinois when they arrived in the 1830's.

The first church organized among the Amish was that of the Partridge congregation, west of the present Metamora, in Woodford County. This was the first German-speaking church in the state and the second of any denomination to be organized in the county. It continues today as the Metamora congregation located east of the town of that name.

One small group of Amish adhering for a time more to the "old order" in their customs came from Mifflin Co., Pa., and settled in McLean County. Later it became the original church of the Stuckey Amish, or Central Conference of Mennonites, the East White Oak congregation near Danvers.

The first settlements of the Amish and the Mennonites, like those of other Illinois pioneers, were made in the wooded sections along rivers and creeks. This was done for the purpose of having a supply of water and wood and also to avoid the supposedly unhealthful conditions of the undrained prairies. By the 1850's, however, Mennonites, along with others, began to appreciate the value of the prairies and began to make settlements away from the timbered areas.

Though the first Mennonites in Illinois were of the Amish wing, the main line of Mennonites (MC) began to come soon after. In 1833 two families by the name of Kindig came from Virginia by horse-drawn wagons to Tazewell County and started a settlement which became known as the Union congregation near Washington, Ill. There were additional migrants from Virginia and others came from Pennsylvania, Ohio, and Bavaria (Germany). This congregation later merged with Metamora.

About 1840 and later a few Mennonite families came from Bavaria and settled at Scales Mound in Jo Daviess County in northwestern Illinois near Galena. A small congregation was formed but has long since become extinct. The last Mennonite baptismal ceremony was performed about 1878.

In 1843-60 another settlement of Bavarians and other Germans was made near Summerfield, St. Clair County, in the southwestern part of the state. In 1861 this congregation, together with some from Iowa and several in the East, helped organize the General Conference Mennonites.

In the 1830's and 1840's a number of Hessian Mennonites came from Butler County, Ohio, and formed the South Danvers congregation (now known as the Danvers Church) in McLean County. This church was one of the 12 charter congregations which formed the Central Conference of Mennonites in 1908.

Also in the 1840's a small settlement was begun near Freeport in Stephenson County. The first immigrants came from Clarence Center, New York, and others came from Pennsylvania, Ohio, and Canada. Freeport joined the Illinois Conference (MC).

About 1847 several Reformed Mennonite families moved near Sterling in Whiteside County and a few years later organized the only church of this branch in the state. In the 1850's Mennonites from Pennsylvania settled near Sterling and started what became the Science Ridge congregation. In the next decade a few families from Pennsylvania and a few from Sterling settled near Morrison, in the same county, and started the congregation by that name. The membership of this church has remained small. In the 1850's a few families from Ohio and Pennsylvania settled at Gardner in Grundy County. It was here in 1865 that John F. Funk, who lived in Chicago, was ordained to serve as English preacher. This church soon became extinct. In 1858 four families came from Virginia to Cullom in Livingston County and together with others who soon came from Grundy and Woodford County, Illinois, founded the small Cullom congregation. From about 1865 to the time of the Chicago fire in 1871 a small Mennonite congregation, founded by Peter Neff and John F. Funk, existed in Chicago.

Soon after the Civil War some Old Order Amish from Pennsylvania, from Johnson County, Iowa, and from Holmes County, Ohio, came to Moultrie and Douglas counties and, later spreading into Gales County, became the large Old Order Amish community which centers around Arthur.

In 1835 a group of Amish Mennonites from Bavaria, and a few from Butler County, Ohio, settled in the neighborhood of Hennepin, Putnam County. Shortly thereafter most of these moved

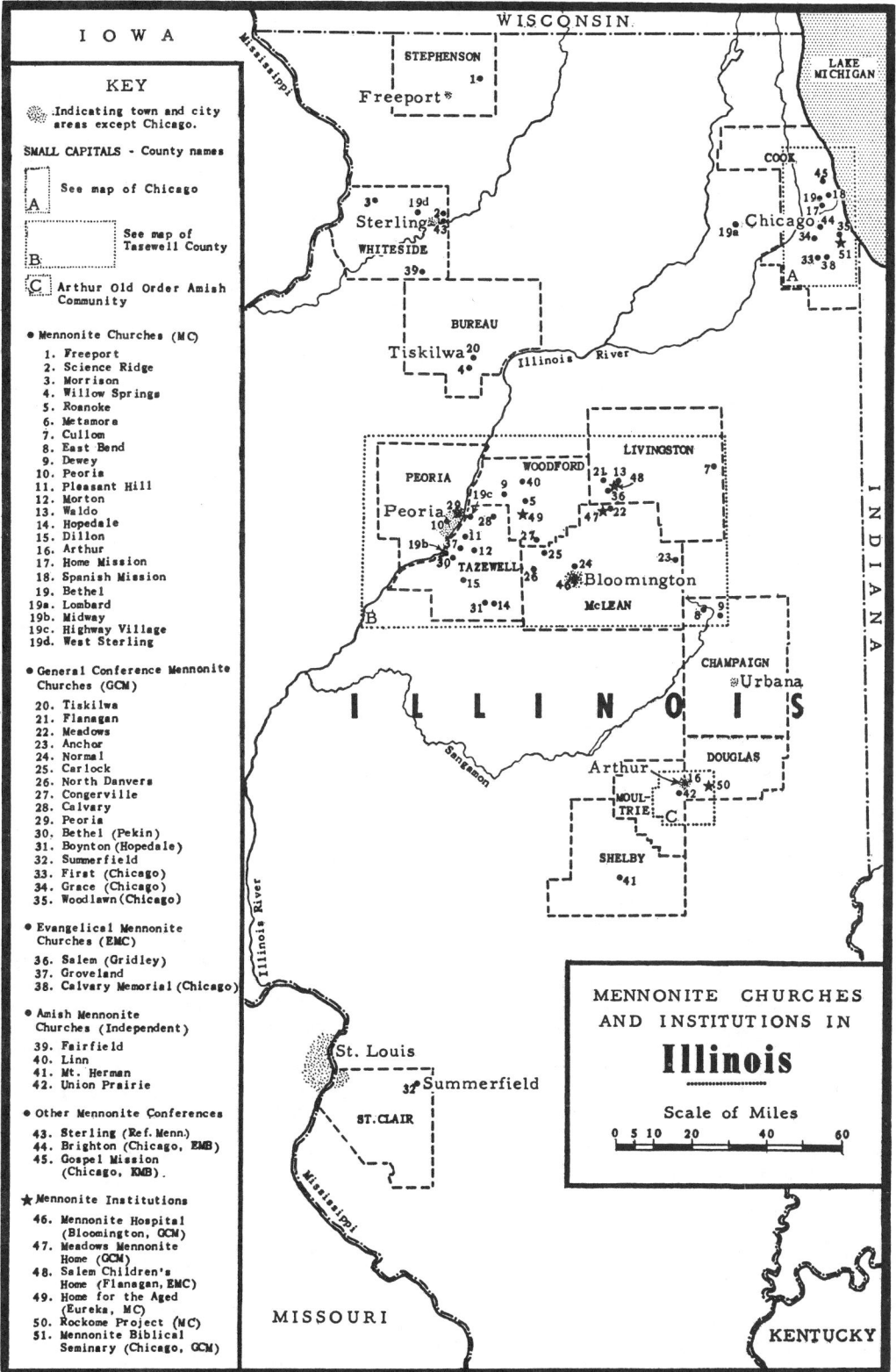

I O W A

WISCONSIN

STEPHENSON
1
Freeport

LAKE MICHIGAN

COOK

45
6
19   18
17
19   44   35
Chicago
34
33   38   51

KEY

Indicating town and city
areas except Chicago.

SMALL CAPITALS - County names

A   See map of Chicago

B   See map of
Tasewell County

C   Arthur Old Order Amish
Community

● Mennonite Churches (MC)

1. Freeport
2. Science Ridge
3. Morrison
4. Willow Springs
5. Roanoke
6. Metamora
7. Cullom
8. East Bend
9. Dewey
10. Peoria
11. Pleasant Hill
12. Morton
13. Waldo
14. Hopedale
15. Dillon
16. Arthur
17. Home Mission
18. Spanish Mission
19. Bethel
19a. Lombard
19b. Midway
19c. Highway Village
19d. West Sterling

● General Conference Mennonite
Churches (GCM)

20. Tiskilwa
21. Flanagan
22. Meadows
23. Anchor
24. Normal
25. Carlock
26. North Danvers
27. Congerville
28. Calvary
29. Peoria
30. Bethel (Pekin)
31. Boynton (Hopedale)
32. Summerfield
33. First (Chicago)
34. Grace (Chicago)
35. Woodlawn (Chicago)

● Evangelical Mennonite
Churches (EMC)

36. Salem (Gridley)
37. Groveland
38. Calvary Memorial (Chicago)

● Amish Mennonite
Churches (Independent)

39. Fairfield
40. Linn
41. Mt. Herman
42. Union Prairie

● Other Mennonite Conferences

43. Sterling (Ref.Menn)
44. Brighton (Chicago, EMB)
45. Gospel Mission
(Chicago, KMB)

★ Mennonite Institutions

46. Mennonite Hospital
(Bloomington, GCM)
47. Meadows Mennonite
Home (GCM)
48. Salem Children's
Home (Flanagan, EMC)
49. Home for the Aged
(Eureka, MC)
50. Rockome Project (MC)
51. Mennonite Biblical
Seminary (Chicago, GCM)

Mississippi

3   19d
Sterling
43

WHITESIDE

39

BUREAU

Tiskilwa 20
4

Illinois   River

PEORIA

WOODFORD

LIVINGSTON

7

9   40

21 13 48
36
47 22

Peoria
29
19c
10   5   49
28
11   27
19b   37   12
25   24
30   23
TAZEWELL   26
15   46   Bloomington

B   31   14   McLEAN   8   9

ILLINOIS

Sangamon

CHAMPAIGN
Urbana

Arthur   DOUGLAS
16
MOUL-   42   50
TRIE
C

SHELBY
41

INDIANA

St. Louis

Summerfield
32
ST.CLAIR

Illinois River

MISSOURI

KENTUCKY

Mississippi

MENNONITE CHURCHES
AND INSTITUTIONS IN

Illinois

Scale of Miles

0 5 10   20   40   60

across the Illinois River into Bureau County, near Tiskilwa, and formed the nucleus of what has become the Willow Springs Church. The Central Conference Mennonite Church in Tiskilwa is an offshoot of this congregation.

Most of the remaining Amish Mennonite congregations in Illinois not already mentioned were outgrowths of settlements mentioned above, with further additions of immigrants from other states in some cases. This includes the Roanoke Church between Eureka and Roanoke, the Goodfield Church near Goodfield, the Pleasant Grove Church near Tremont, the Hopedale Church near Hopedale, the Waldo Church near Flanagan, and the East Bend Church near Fisher. The Goodfield and Pleasant Grove congregations, mentioned above, merged in 1941 and constructed a new church building in Morton. A small Conservative Amish congregation and a larger Mennonite congregation have developed from the Old Order Amish community at Arthur. In 1954 a new congregation was organized at Lombard just west of Chicago.

In 1907 a small independent group of Conservative Amish, mostly from Elkhart Co., Ind., came to Shelbyville in Shelby County. Sometimes called the "sleeping preacher group," they were followers of John D. Kauffman who caused much interest and controversy by his practice of preaching while in trances. An unaffiliated Amish Mennonite congregation, composed largely of withdrawals from the Roanoke and Metamora congregations, exists near Roanoke. Another unaffiliated Amish Mennonite congregation is located near Tampico.

Mennonites of various kinds have also come to Chicago but these groups can perhaps best be discussed in connection with the mission and institutional work of the several branches. There were in 1953 a total of nine congregations and mission stations in Chicago with a combined membership of about 550.

The Mennonite movement into Illinois was largely of the Amish and old-line Mennonite branches. A few decades after the founding of the early settlements, however, splits from these groups began to occur. One of these divisions occurred just after the Civil War when the branch known as the Defenseless Mennonites or "Egly Amish" was formed. Henry Egly, bishop of an Amish church in Geneva Co., Ind., felt that the church was too cold and formalistic and began in the 1860's to emphasize the necessity of a definite experience of regeneration, at the same time, however, insisting on the old customs including dress. He organized his own church in 1866, and the movement spread to other Amish communities. In the Gridley Prairie, or Waldo, congregation in Livingston Co., Ill., Joseph Rediger, one of the ministers, about 1870 led a few members out of the old organization and formed an "Egly" congregation officially called the Salem Defenseless Mennonite Church. The only other congregation of this group in Illinois was organized at Groveland in Tazewell County, with the exception of the work started later in Chicago. In 1953 this group changed its name to Evangelical Mennonite Church.

Another division among the original groups took place when Joseph Stuckey formed the Central Illinois Conference of Mennonites. Stuckey, a bishop in the Yoder Amish Church in McLean County, was more liberal-minded than his fellow bishops and less ready to excommunicate members who did not reach the prevailing Amish standards. Since congregational control was still strong at that time this split from the majority group became apparent only gradually during the 1870's, although Stuckey did not attend the Amish General Conference after 1872. It was not until 1908, however, that a constitution was formally and officially adopted, with nine churches in the Peoria-Bloomington region joining as charter members, besides two in Indiana and one in Nebraska. In 1914 the official name was changed to "The Central Conference of Mennonites." In 1946 this group joined the GCM Church and in 1957 merged with the Middle District.

The Apostolic Christian Church, whose founders included some former Mennonites in Switzerland, and which came to Morton about 1855, gained a number of Amish proselytes in Illinois as elsewhere. For that reason they are sometimes called the "New Amish."

Institutions for the carrying out of aggressive work were slow in appearing among the Mennonites in Illinois as elsewhere. However, the first Mennonite publishing venture of any consequence was carried out in this state, although the group as a whole had nothing to do with its origin. This was the founding of the *Herald of Truth,* and the German edition, *Herold der Wahrheit,* in Chicago, 1864, by John F. Funk, a young Mennonite, who had come to Chicago from Pennsylvania a few years before. In 1867 this enterprise was moved to Elkhart, Ind., where in 1875 it became known as the Mennonite Publishing Company.

Missionary sentiment, which had been developing for some time on the part of individuals, was no doubt stimulated by the evangelistic efforts of John S. Coffman and others in the latter part of the 19th century. The Chicago Home Mission, founded in 1893, was the first such effort of the MC group. Initiative from outside the state as well as from within was responsible for the opening of this work, and control of the institution since 1896 has been shared by the general mission board and the Illinois Mennonites. The Twenty-Sixth Street Mission in Chicago, founded in 1906, was an outgrowth of activity of the Home Mission. This mission was sold to the Central Conference of Mennonites in 1924. A Mennonite (MC) Mexican mission, opened in 1934, and a Negro mission (MC), opened in 1944, are also maintained in Chicago.

In 1919 the Illinois District Mission Board (MC), which had been organized in 1918, opened a mission in Peoria, which was turned over to the Mennonite Board of Missions and Charities in 1921. The Pleasant Hill Rural Mission, between Morton and Peoria, was organized in 1920 and after being under the supervision of the district mission board for some time became a regular congregation. A number of small mission outposts are operated by various congregations.

Another institution in Illinois operated by the M.C. group is the home for the aged at Eureka, opened in 1922. A home for retired church workers, called Rockome, sponsored by the Mennonite Board of Missions and Charities and the Illinois Mennonite Mission Board, is being developed at Arcola, Ill.

Running counter to a trend toward division was the merger of the Amish Mennonites and the Mennonites (MC). Completed in Illinois in 1921, the merger was in the process of development over a long period of time. The various institutional activities mentioned above, supported by both groups, played an important part in bringing about the union. Doctrinally there was no longer anything of consequence to keep them apart.

The Defenseless (Evangelical) Mennonites, besides supporting an active mission program, especially in Africa, opened in 1900 the Salem Orphanage near Flanagan, Ill. Since 1923 the Central Conference of Mennonites and the Defenseless Mennonite (Evangelical) Conferences have shared in its operation. The Defenseless conference also participated in the founding (1919) and maintenance of the Mennonite Hospital at Bloomington, Ill., which was primarily a Central Conference undertaking. Another co-operative activity between the Evangelical (Defenseless) and the Central Conference Mennonites is the maintenance of the Old People's Home (opened in 1923) at Meadows, Ill. The Evangelical (Defenseless) Mennonites operate a mission in Chicago (opened in 1908) and the Evangelical Mennonite Brethren operate one (opened in 1907).

The Central Conference, as noted, carries an important part of the load in operating the Mennonite Hospital at Bloomington, and also shares in the operation of the Salem Orphanage near Flanagan, and the Old People's Home at Meadows. In addition it operates the Mennonite Gospel Mission (founded 1914) in Peoria. The conference also cooperates with other Mennonite groups in supporting the Congo Inland Mission, and, long before the merger with the General Conference Mennonites, it supported Bluffton College at Bluffton, Ohio.

In Chicago, in addition to those activities listed above, mention should be made of the Krimmer Mennonite Brethren mission, opened in 1915. The

General Conference Mennonites have also carried on work there since 1915 with two congregations. A third General Conference church has recently been organized in connection with the Mennonite Biblical Seminary, founded as a graduate theological institution in Chicago in 1944. A total of nine Mennonite congregations with about 550 members are located in Chicago.

As to occupation, most of the Mennonites in Illinois are farmers. In recent decades, however, a larger number have gone into businesses of various kinds and into a number of the professions. Attracted by high wages, some have gone into the factories as laborers. W.H.S.

H. F. Weber, *Centennial History of the Mennonites of Illinois* (Goshen, 1931); ML II, 407-9.

Illinois Mennonite Conference (MC), organized in 1921 by the merger of the earlier Mennonite Conference (MC) of the State of Illinois (formed in 1871) and Amish Mennonite congregations in the state which had been members of the Western District Amish Mennonite Conference. It is the only Mennonite (MC) district conference limited exclusively to one state, including all Mennonite (MC) congregations within and no congregations outside the state. Conference meets annually, usually during the third week in August. There is a ministers' fellowship meeting during the winter months. Regularly ordained or licensed bishops, ministers, and deacons are considered members of conference and transact the business of conference under the leadership of a five-man executive committee. Auxiliary organizations are the Christian Education Cabinet (six members), District Mission Board, State Sewing Circle, and State Mennonite Youth Fellowship. The Christian Education Cabinet sponsors a Christian Workers' Normal—a one-week training course held annually during the Christmas holiday season. A certificate is awarded upon the completion of a three-year course of six units. The District Mission Board publishes *The Missionary Guide* bimonthly. It includes inspirational articles as well as reports of congregational and missionary activities.

The constitution of the Illinois Mennonite Conference does not declare the Dordrecht Confession of 1632 its official confession, but this is the confession commonly used in the congregations. Conference teaches nonresistance to evil, nonconformity to the world, and simplicity in worship, home, and attire, but it does not require a particular costume. It protests against the use of tobacco and alcoholic beverages, forbids members to hold public office requiring the use of the force of the law and administration of the oath, and forbids membership in secret societies and the swearing of oaths. It teaches the ordinances of baptism, communion, footwashing, women's prayer veil, anointing with oil, salutation of the holy kiss, and marriage. A minister may not move from one congregation to another without the consent of both congregations. There is a strong trend toward a trained ministry, although sentiment is still quite strong for the ordination of men from within the conference district. The lot is seldom used in connection with ordinations.

Mennonites began to move to Illinois from eastern

ILLINOIS MENNONITES (1953)

Conference	members	congregations
Illinois Conference (MC)	3,359	18
Central Conference of Mennonites (now Central Dist. Conference, GCM)	2,046	12
Evangelical Mennonite Church (formerly Defenseless Mennonites)	523	4
Evangelical Mennonite Brethren	76	1
Krimmer Mennonite Brethren	?	1
Reformed Mennonite	?	1
Conservative Amish	56	1
Old Order Amish	795	9
Middle District (GCM)	235	3
Amish Mennonite (unaffiliated)	369	3
Total in Illinois	7,459	53

states in 1833. Illinois Mennonite congregations, originally a part of the Indiana conference, received the permission of that conference to form a separate conference in 1871 and met in their own first conference May 24, 1872. There were seven congregations in 1921, with a combined membership of 516. Two of these seven congregations were mission congregations in Chicago. The others were Freeport, Morrison, Sterling, Cullom, and Union (Washington).

Amish Mennonite settlers arrived in Illinois in 1829. Within a decade four congregations had been formed in central Illinois along the Illinois River and its tributaries. Many of the families had come directly from Europe. Others had stopped for a few years in eastern states or Ontario. A few came from older Amish Mennonite settlements in America. In 1921 there were nine Amish Mennonite congregations in Illinois with a combined membership of 1,428, all in the central part of the state. They were at Metamora, Roanoke, Hopedale, Fisher, Flanagan, Tiskilwa, Tremont, Goodfield, and Ohio Station. There is no longer a distinction between Amish Mennonite and Mennonite congregations within the state. Amish Mennonite congregations, particularly, lost heavily to the Egly and Stuckey factions which resulted in the Defenseless Mennonite and Central Conference Mennonite Churches. They lost also to the Apostolic Christians (*q.v.*) and the "Sleeping Preacher" group near Roanoke. One might cite John Alexander Dowie as an example of non-Mennonites who have proselyted members from Mennonite congregations.

Since the merger in 1921 the following seven new congregations have been formed: Arthur, Peoria, Pleasant Hill, Dillon, Bethel (Chicago), Spanish (Chicago), Lombard.

Men such as Henry Albrecht, J. C. Birky, Samuel Gerber, Chancy A. Hartzler, Henry Nice, Daniel Orendorff, Andrew Schrock, J. S. Shoemaker, John Smith, and H. R. Schertz are remembered for their ministry throughout the church, as well as within the conference district. Other more recent leaders have also served in offices on major church-wide boards. At present the conference includes 22 organized congregations and 10 mission outposts, with a total membership of 3,250 in 1955.   N.P.S.

Illinois Mennonite Conference Directory (1947); *Mennonite Yearbook and Directory* (Scottdale, 1905-   ); H. F. Weber, *Centennial Hist. of the Menn. of Illinois, 1829-1929* (Goshen, 1931).

Illinois Mennonite Mission Board (MC) is a subsidiary organization of the Illinois Mennonite Conference. Its purpose is "to work as the missionary and financial auxiliary of the Illinois Mennonite Conference in the following ways: (1) to create and promote missionary interest, and to assist the various congregations in systematizing and extending the work of evangelism. (2) To organize and supervise the missionary work of the Illinois Mennonite Conference not under the direct control of an organized congregation or the Mennonite Board of Missions and Charities. (3) To perform such benevolent or charitable work as may be deemed advisable by the Board, or as the Conference may direct. (4) To acquire and hold title to real estate and other

property, to lease, operate, maintain, and sell or otherwise dispose of the same. (5) For the aforesaid purpose to solicit funds, to receive and hold all donations, bequests, endowments and annuities, etc., as may come under the control of the Board, or as Conference may direct."

The Board is made up of (*a*) one member elected by each local church; (*b*) the superintendent of each extension work (at least two years old) within the Conference; (*c*) two members elected by Conference; (*d*) the Conference member of the Mennonite Board of Missions and Charities.

The Board held its first annual meeting Sept. 13, 1923. The first officers were as follows: pres. S. R. Good; vice-pres. J. A. Heiser; sec. John Roth; treas. S. D. Schertz; and fifth member A. C. Good. The present officers are: pres. Ralph Imhoff; vice-pres. Kenneth G. Good; sec. Ivan J. Kauffmann; treas. Russell Massanari; fifth member or field worker Chris Graber; colporteur John Harnish.

The Pleasant Hill, Arthur, Highway Village, and Dillon churches have been established during the time the Board has been in operation and have been influenced directly or indirectly by the Board. The official organ of the Board is the *Missionary Guide,* published bimonthly beginning with November 1944. Harold Zehr has served as editor for a number of years. The Board also prints a report of its annual meeting. The 1955 budget was $10,450.

The present Board was preceded by the "Illinois District Mission Board," organized July 26, 1917, under the old Illinois Mennonite Conference. The first officers were: pres. S. R. Good; vice-pres. J. J. Summers; sec. A. H. Leaman; treas. J. V. Fortner; fifth member J. D. Conrad. Its first mission project was the Garden Street Mission in Peoria, which was established in May 1919, and turned over to the Mennonite Board of Missions and Charities in 1921. The second project was Pleasant Hill, near Peoria, which was opened as a mission Sunday school on Nov. 21, 1920. After the Amish and Mennonite merger in 1921 and the creation of the new Illinois Mennonite Conference, the Mission Board was given a new name and constitution but continued on the same pattern of organization and work.   I.K.

H. F. Weber, *Centennial History of the Mennonites of Illinois* (Goshen, 1931).

Illinois Old Order Amish Mutual Aid Plan serves the Old Order Amish around Arthur, Ill., and had a total of 820 members in 1953.   H.S.B.

Illkirch, a village in Alsace, in which in compliance with orders issued by Strasbourg, 68 Anabaptists were arrested in 1540, and expelled from the Strasbourg area because they "would not let themselves be converted."

T. W. Röhrich, *Mittheilungen aus der Gesch. der evangelischen Kirche des Elsasses* II (Strasbourg, 1855) 211; Fr. Thudichum, *Die Deutsche Reformation* II (Leipzig, 1909) 622.

Illuminated Manuscripts *among Russian Mennonites.* The art of penmanship and the production of illuminated writings dates back to the Middle Ages. Particularly the initial letters in printing and writing were ornamental, sometimes using many colors.

This was also known as *Kanzleischrift,* practiced in the offices of the royal courts, which was taken over by schools and survived, in some forms, until the 19th century. Among the Mennonites, the Hutterites have practiced this art of penmanship in the writing of their chronicles, but the Pennsylvania-German Mennonites and the Prusso-German Mennonites have also used this art.

H. Görz reports that after the hardship of the pioneer days had been overcome, the elementary schools among the Mennonites of the Ukraine strongly emphasized this art of penmanship (*Frakturen*). Recognition cards were produced by the teacher and the older gifted pupils and distributed among the best pupils of the school. Particularly for Christmas and New Year's Eve they produced the traditional *Weihnachtswunsch* and *Neujahrswunsch,* which carried an appropriate poem pertaining to Christmas or New Year's Eve, which the children presented to their parents on the morning of these holidays, reciting the poetry before they received their presents. The art of penmanship and the production of illuminated manuscripts filled a considerable part of the curriculum of elementary training in Mennonite schools in Russia during the first half of the past century. When, through Cornies' effort, the educational level was raised, this art was discouraged as a waste of time, but it somehow survived and was practiced in some form until the Mennonite communities in Russia disintegrated under the Soviets. Some of the teachers belonging to the "old school," such as J. D. Rempel (now in Germany), hardly ever write a letter which does not have a beautifully illuminated salutation. The practice of producing illuminated wall mottoes can still be found among the Mennonites of South America. Some of the teachers developed into artists in their own right (H. J. Janzen, Joh. H. Janzen, J. P. Klassen, and others). Numerous copies of illuminated manuscripts and Christmas and New Year's greetings have been preserved in Mennonite homes of the prairie states and provinces, and are gradually reaching the Bethel College Historical Library, which is now in possession of a collection of them, some of which were produced in the beginning of the past century.†   C.K.

H. Görz, *Die Molotschnaer Ansiedlung* (Steinbach, 1950) 92.

Illuminated Manuscripts *among the Pennsylvania Mennonites.* The art of fraktur or illuminative writing, as it was practiced by the Pennsylvania Germans in colonial times and down to 1840-50, by which manuscript specimens were written in ornamental capital letters decorated in several colors, is clearly a descendant of the medieval art of manuscript illumination, but came possibly also directly from similar practices in the schools of Middle and South Germany from which the colonial immigrants to Pennsylvania came. It was a form of religious art, almost never applied to secular themes, usually including either Scripture verses or expressions of piety. The block letters were ornamented, and the entire drawing was often ornamented with illuminative borders, overhanging tulips or lotus flowers, birds, angels blowing trumpets, etc. In America it

was chiefly perpetuated by deliberate instruction in German private schools by German schoolmasters, and the coming of the public schools in 1840-50 meant its end.

Among the types of fraktur work to be noted are the illuminated manuscript songbooks of the Ephrata Cloister of the mid-18th century, small plain manuscript songbooks made in Mennonite schools in the early 19th century with illuminated title pages giving the owner's name and the writer's school, illuminated ownership pages to printed songbooks, rewards of merit, copyforms made for pupils in Mennonite schools, bookmarks, baptismal certificates for Lutherans and Reformed, marriage and death registers in Bibles.

The chief geographical area of the practice of fraktur was in central Bucks County; specimens of the art from certain neighboring counties have also been preserved, especially Lehigh. Although Mennonites apparently were among the leaders in the art, they were not the only practitioners. However, the last surviving masters were two Mennonites, Jacob Gross of New Britain, and John H. Detweiler of Perkasie, Bucks Co., noted by Mercer (*Survival,* 432) as still alive at an advanced age in 1897. John D. Souder (1867-1944), a Mennonite of Telford, Bucks Co., revived the art in his late years and is said to have produced nearly 1,000 specimens of fraktur, largely mottoes and anniversary certificates for his friends, though not of the quality of older specimens. Bucks County Mennonite emigrants carried the art of fraktur with them to their settlement near Vineland, Lincoln Co., Ont. (*ca.* 1800), where a number of specimens have been preserved.

One of the noted early fraktur artists was Christopher Dock (*q.v.,* d. 1771), the "pious schoolmaster of the Skippack," who had some 25 of his illuminated texts posted on the walls of his school. Abraham H. Cassel of Harleysville, Pa., whose father was a pupil in Dock's school, had a collection of Dock's illuminated texts, which he gave to the Historical Society of Pennsylvania. The Goshen College Library has a collection of some 30 pieces of fraktur including five small manuscript Mennonite songbooks. Goshen's oldest piece is an illuminated text-copyform made in the Deep Run Mennonite school in Bucks County in 1783.†

In recent times fraktur art has been rediscovered as a part of the rediscovery of Pennsylvania-German folk art, and good specimens have become museum items. The most successful collector was Henry S. Borneman (d. 1953), who published *Pennsylvania German Illuminated Manuscripts, A Classification of Fraktur-Schriften and an Inquiry into their History and Art* (Pennsylvania German Society, Norristown, 1937) with splendid four-color reproductions of 32 specimens. Borneman lists the names of 107 fraktur artists whose work has survived. His *Pennsylvania German Book Plates* (Phila., 1953) has 24 four-color reproductions.†   H.S.B.

H. C. Mercer, *The Survival of the Medieval Art of Illuminative Writing Among Pennsylvania Germans* (reprint from *Proceedings of the American Philosophical Society* XXXVI, 1898, No. 156, 423-32); M. G. Brumbaugh, *The Life and Works of Christopher Dock* (Philadelphia, 1908); J. J. Stoudt, *Consider the Lilies How They Grow* (Pennsylvania German Folklore Society, II,

1937); *idem, Pennsylvania Folk Art* (Allentown, 1948); Frances Lichten, *Folk Art Motifs of Pennsylvania* (N.Y., 1954); *idem*, "Fractur from the Hostetter Collection," *The Dutchman* VI (1954); E. F. Robacker, "Major and Minor in Fraktur," *The Dutchman* VII (1956) 2-7; S. J. Riccardi, "Pennsylvania Dutch Folk Art and Architecture, A Selective Annotated Bibliography," *Bulletin of the New York Public Library* XLVI (1942) 471-83.

Ilp (Den), a village in the Dutch province of North Holland, north of Amsterdam, where there have been Anabaptists from the earliest times. Van Braght (*Mart. Mir*. D 61, E 464) names Seli and Jacob of neighboring Landsmeer as martyrs. In 1673 there was a Waterlander congregation at Landsmeer, to which the Mennonites of Den Ilp belonged. At that time there was also a Frisian congregation at Landsmeer. The congregation contributed liberally to the relief of the Mennonites of Lithuania, Poland, and Prussia in 1727, 1733, and 1736.

During the night of Feb. 4, 1863, both the church and the parsonage were burned down by lightning. With liberal support from other congregations, as far away as Friedrichstadt, Germany, they were able to build a new church and parsonage, which was dedicated on May 7, 1865; an organ was installed in 1901. In 1847 the congregation of Den Ilp and Landsmeer had 116 members; by 1931 the membership had risen to 130. Now (1956) the baptized membership numbers 80. After the death of J. L. de Wagenmaker, who served here as pastor in 1915-51, the pulpit was vacant until 1955, when the pastor of Amsterdam-North assumed charge. vDZ.

Inv. Arch. Amst. I, Nos. 892, 896; II, 2, No. 220; *DB* 1864, 174; 1865, 165 f.; 1902, 144; Blaupot t. C., *Holland* I, 332; II, 204, 232; *ML* II, 409.

Ilpendam, a hamlet in the Dutch province of North Holland, where there was an independent Mennonite congregation in the 17th century belonging to the Waterlander branch. Before 1700 this congregation was united with near-by Den Ilp (*q.v.*). vDZ.

Imbroich (Imbroek), **Thomas von**, an Anabaptist martyr, also known as Thomas Drucker or Thomas of Truden, b. 1533 probably in the village of Imgenbroich, Germany, not far from Aachen, hence his name Imbroich. By trade he was a printer of books, came to Cologne (*q.v.*) in 1554, joined the Anabaptists there, and became an outstanding leader of the Mennonites of the Lower Rhine area. On Dec. 23, 1557, he was arrested and after repeated cross-examination, cruel torture, and vain attempts to convert him was beheaded on March 5, 1558, at the age of 25 years (not May 5, as stated in van Braght's *Martyrs' Mirror*).

In prison Thomas wrote a confession of his faith to make his belief clear to the judges of the Inquisition. A copy of his manuscript was smuggled out to his brethren, and was apparently immediately printed and widely circulated in the next years. The "confession" deals primarily with baptism, and is unusually rich and deep in its exposition of the Scriptures opposing infant baptism. It reveals its author as thoroughly familiar with Menno Simons, under some influence of Melchior Hofmann, and acquainted with the Church Fathers as well as some more recent literature. He was not willing to accept the theological explanations of the Protestant leaders nor of the Catholic scholastic writers, but accepted as truth only the words of the Gospel. His logical clarity made his book an important weapon in the great struggle of the Anabaptists with the state churches.

Felix Reichmann has made a careful study of the printing of the confession in "An Early Edition of Thomas von Imbroich" (*MQR* XVI, 1942, 99-107), in which he holds that the first edition was printed between 1560 and 1600, probably in Alsace, though it might have been in Cologne. The Duke of Jülich published an edict against Anabaptist books, dated March 9, 1560, which Heinrich Bullinger, in a letter of 1562, states was directed specifically against the Imbroich book. Bullinger refers to the great influence of Thomas, which must have been continued through the publication of his confession.

The full title of this first edition of the Imbroich Confession is as follows: *Ein schöne bekanntnus eines frommen und Gottliebenden Christen samt etlichen Sendbrieffen und Christliche Ermanungen auss heiliger Schrift seiner Hausfraven und Brüdern auss der Gefängnus geschrieben. Mit kurtzem und doch wahrhafftigen anzeigungen wie er seinen Glauben durch krafft Gottes (zu Cölln am Reyn) Anno 1558. den 5. Mertz beständig mit seinem blut bezeugt hat allen Christen und Gottesfürchtigen gantz nützlich und tröstlich zu lesen und zu hören. Esaje am 59. Cap*. . . . *n.p., n.d.* (copy in the Landis Valley Museum, Lancaster, Pa.; an early reprint in the Goshen College Library). A Dutch translation was published at Gent in 1579 (copy in Amsterdam Mennonite Library). The *Martyrs' Mirror* of 1660 contains a partial reprint. *Güldene Aepfel in Silbern Schalen* (European editions 1702, 1742; Ephrata, Pa., edition in 1745) contains the confession and the epistles complete. The *Ausbund*, beginning with the 1742 Germantown edition, contains a brief condensation of the confession. This brief form was reprinted as a tract about 1922 by an unknown Amish publisher.

Thomas also wrote seven epistles (*Sendbriefe*), some of which are quite extensive, which were published with his confession. They bear witness to a rare confidence in God and a willingness to die, and contain a wealth of Biblical admonition. Hymn No. 23 in the *Ausbund*, "Would you hear what happened in the year fifty-seven," tells the story of Thomas and his martyrdom in 25 stanzas, but was probably not written by him. It appeared at least as early as between 1563 and 1565 in a Mennonite hymnbook, entitled *Ein schon Gesangbuchlein Geistlicher Lieder*. It appeared first in the *Ausbund* in the 1583 edition. Wolkan (*Lieder,* 99) says it was translated from a Dutch original which he found in the Hamburg *Stadtbibliothek*, and was written by a Dutch Mennonite. It does appear, however, in the first edition of the German book containing Thomas' confession, *ca*. 1560, as *"Ein New Lied."* (Title page reproduced in *ME* I.) NEFF.

Mart. Mir. D I, 402-7 and II, 196-200, E 367-71 and 578-82; Rembert, *Wiedertäufer*, 439 ff.; Wolkan, *Lieder*, 48, 99; W. Scheibler, *Gesch. der evang. Gemeinde Monschau* (Aachen, 1939) 22-24; Müller, *Berner Täufer*, 104; *DB* 1898, 108, article "Imbroich als Gatte und Vater"; Felix Reichmann, "An Early Edition of Thomas von Imbroich," *MQR* XVI (1942) 99-107; *Bibliographie des*

Martyrologes I, 193-203; W. Bax, *Het Protestantisme in het Bisdom Luik* (The Hague, 1937) 303-6; *ML* II, 409.

Imhoff, Catharina Friedli, an Anabaptist martyr, executed for her faith at Bern, Switzerland, Aug. 28, 1537. This martyr is not found in the Dutch edition of van Braght's *Martyrs' Mirror,* but only in the German and English translations. (*Mart. Mir.* E 1129; *ML* II, 409.)

The name Imhof occurs frequently in Switzerland and the Palatinate, and is also found in Illinois.

Immanuel Academy at Reedley, Cal., opened as the Reedley Bible School, Oct. 17, 1927, with two teachers and 31 students. It met until 1932 in a small building on the grounds of the Reedley Mennonite Brethren Church. It was continued until 1937 by the Dinuba Mennonite Brethren Church in the building now known as the Reedley hospital. In 1937-41 the Bible school met in the kitchen of the Dinuba M.B. Church in Dinuba. Then the Reedley M.B. Church reopened its Bible school on its own church grounds and operated it parallel to the Dinuba Bible School 1938-41. In 1941 the schools were combined and named Immanuel Bible School. In 1944 the four-year academy program was started and the name changed to Immanuel Academy. The first four-year class was graduated in 1946. In 1946 the school was moved to the present location in its new building. The academy principals have been J. N. C. Hiebert, August 1943-January 1947; H. R. Wiens, January 1947-July 1950; and Arthur J. Wiebe, July 1950- . The enrollment in recent years has averaged 200. The school is sponsored by the Reedley and Dinuba M.B. churches and the Zion K.M.B. Church in Reedley, which share the cost on a per capita basis. The Fresno M.B. Church also participates on a partial basis.

Immanuel Academy is a first-class accredited high school with a faculty of 12 teachers and five buildings, of which a chapel seating 300 is under construction. The 10-acre campus is located on the banks of the Kings River in Reedley. The annual budget is $55,000, half of which is raised by tuition.
A.J.W.

Immanuel Mennonite Church (GCM), located in Downey, Los Angeles Co., Cal., was organized with 35 charter members as the Mennonite Mission Church, May 12, 1918, at Avenue 19 and Albion Street, Los Angeles. On Nov. 2, 1924, it was organized under its present name, and a church was dedicated at 79th Street and Stanford Avenue, Los Angeles. On July 4, 1953, it moved to the present location at 10335 Paramount Blvd., Downey. The membership in 1955 was 271. It became a member of the Pacific District Conference in 1919. The following ministers have served the congregation since 1924: Albert Claassen, H. B. Dirks, D. D. Eitzen, Albert Jantzen, Wilbert A. Regier, Paul Bauman, H. D. Burkholder, Alfred Regier, and the present pastor, John B. Graber. H.D.B.

Immanuel Mennonite Church (GCM), located at Delft, Cottonwood Co., Minn., a member of the Northern District Conference, was organized on July 28, 1940, with a membership of 85. The group had previously been a part of the Gospel Mennonite Church at Mountain Lake and under its ministry. In 1897 a church was built 1½ miles west of Delft to facilitate the service. In 1906 this structure was moved to Delft, and in 1920 a new church was built. Since its organization in 1940 the group has had its own pastor. The present membership (1955) is 130, with W. M. McDowell as pastor. J.J.F.

Imme Eyckendochter, an Anabaptist martyr "vuytte maeren van Groeningerlandt," was executed with four other women on Jan. 17, 1539, at Delft, Dutch province of South Holland. She was put to death by drowning after she had been put into a sack. Imme was probably an adherent of David Joris. (*Inv. Arch. Amst.* I, No. 749.) vDZ.

Immelhausen, a village in Baden, Germany, 2½ miles south of Sinsheim, has been the seat of a Mennonite congregation for 250 years. The first Mennonites settled there soon after the Thirty Years' War as renters in Immelhausen and on the adjacent estates of Streichenberg, Steinsfurt, Kirchard, and Weiler, having left Switzerland on account of their faith. The authorities welcomed them into the devastated and depopulated country, but did not permit them to hold religious services without special government consent. Apparently the consent to assemble for the "admonition" was sometimes given reluctantly. They probably did not often claim this permission, since the pastors expected them to attend the regular services of the Reformed Church. How unpleasant their meetings were to church circles can be seen in the fact that the church councilors at Heidelberg in 1654 advocated non-toleration of the Mennonites if they refused to be subject to the Reformed Church. Therefore they preferred to assemble quietly, without authorization, in the woods. These secret meetings were discovered in 1654, when a marriage was performed there. The case was inflated to make it appear a public nuisance.

The Mennonites also held services in their homes, for which they had not sought permission. On March 2, 1661, 53 persons were surprised at nine o'clock in the evening in Steinsfurt as they were just beginning a hymn. They were fined 100 guilders, a heavy fine in view of the fact that their total capital amounted to only 6,000 guilders. Max Oberholzer, who had come from the canton of Zürich in 1660, had taken part in this service. His brother, Jakob Oberholzer, the father of 13 children, had come earlier. In a later cross-examination it was learned that he had left the Reformed Church in 1645 on account of the wicked lives of its members, because he was unable to take communion with them with a good conscience. He had united with the Mennonites, since all of them strove to live godly, to avoid vices, and transgressors were separated from them. His mother had previously been a Mennonite. The other participants lived at Rohrbach, Reihen, Ittlingen, Streichenberg, Weiler, Dühren, and Steinsfurt.

The Mennonites declared to the state officials that they would rather leave the country than give up their religious meetings. The authorities, acknowledging the pioneer work of the Mennonites in rebuilding the land, granted them permission to hold their services in an electoral edict on Aug. 4, 1664. The regard their work called forth is revealed in a report of Johann Jakob Lumpert in Hilsbach, Oct. 20, 1666, to the government, stating that the Mennonite families of his district were cultivating the electoral estates at Streichenberg, Immelhausen, Steinsfurt, and Reihen, were still clearing forests and draining marshes, and paid their debts, the poorer ones being aided in the payment of dues by those who had a little more. The electoral estates would have to lie desolate if these families moved away; among the remaining subjects one would hardly find people who could manage such estates.

When in 1671 the Swiss Mennonites had to flee from renewed oppression, leaving their property, they were willingly received in the Kurpfalz. But new congregations arose in the Immelhausen area. According to a register of 1732 there were 160 families in 13 congregations in the Palatinate east of the Rhine. To the Immelhausen church belonged 18 families who lived on adjacent estates; the names listed are Binkele, Frey, Bähr, Brand, Müller, Schaub, Gut, Gerber, Lienhard, Schneider, Huber, Eicher, Moser, Behm, and Oberholzer, whose descendants can in many cases still be found in the South German churches. A descendant of the Oberholzer family, members of which went to Pennsylvania in 1727 to 1732, was J. H. Oberholtzer, who in 1859 was the moving spirit in forming the General Conference Mennonite Church (q.v.). In 1887 the baptized membership numbered 41; there were 15 children. The congregation at this time had no elder, and Christian Schmutz (ordained 1880) was its preacher. There was a meetinghouse in Immelhausen, and meetings were also held at Dühren. In 1891 the Immelhausen estate was still occupied by four Mennonite families. Of these only the Binkele family lived there in 1930. The congregation was severely weakened by emigration to Pennsylvania in the 18th century. In March 1912 it was merged with the newly organized congregation at Sinsheim (q.v.), which the Ittlingen (q.v.) church also joined at the same time.

The issues of the Dutch *Naamlijst* 1766-1802 give some information about Immelhausen, in the issue of 1766 called "Himmelhausen, Durnen en Hönigerhoff," in 1769 "Dieren en Himmelhausen," in 1784 and following years "Diernheim en Himmelhausen." Abraham Zeiset (d. 1787) is named as the elder beginning in 1749. After his departure to the Willenbach congregation in 1783, Johannes Krehbiel was the elder. When Krehbiel moved to Bockshof in 1790, Heinrich Funck became the elder. The following preachers are mentioned in this period: Jacob Mayer 1735-ca. 80, Jacob Plätscher 1761 until after 1802, Jacob Schmutz until about 1780, Michel Bachmann until about 1767, Samuel Bär about 1768-75, Friedrich Müller 1772-ca. 85, Johannes Neff from 1772, and Friedrich Müller from 1786.

At the Immelhäuserhof, near Immelhausen, a conference was held on Oct. 14, 1782, for the purpose of healing the breach between the Amish and the Reist Mennonites. The Swiss delegates were Peter Ramseier, Benedict Wälti, Hans Lehmann, Hans Steiner, and David Baumgartner; from the Palatinate were Christian Hege, Abraham Ellenberger, Johann Stauffer, Michael Stiess, and Johann Möllinger.   HEGE, vDZ.

Müller, *Berner Täufer*, 210 and 213; C. Henry Smith, *The Mennonite Immigration to Pennsylvania in the Eighteenth Century* (Norristown, 1929) 184 and 196; *ML* II, 409 f.

Immersion, a mode of baptism in which the candidate is deeply immersed or completely submerged in water, either in a large baptismal font in the church or in a pool or stream in the open. All Mennonites of modern times who practice immersion follow the latter practice. Immersion may be single, forward (as in Krimmer M.B. practice) or backward (M.B. practice), or trine, forward (Brethren in Christ and Church of the Brethren). The practice of pouring upon the head of a candidate kneeling in a stream, as occasionally practiced in M.C., O.O.A., G.C.M., and some other groups, has no relation to immersion, although it is similar to a practice found in the second-century Christian Church. Immersion came into the M.B.C.-U.M. group through the Brethren in Christ (Swankites) group which merged with it in 1883.

Immersion was the most common practice in the early centuries of church history and on down into the Middle Ages, although the alternate modes of sprinkling and pouring were also used at times. By the time of the Reformation it had been almost entirely displaced in the West, though still practiced in the East.

Immersionists base their practice upon their sincere conviction that the New Testament Greek word for baptize (*baptizo*) means to immerse, upon the circumstantial evidence of certain cases of New Testament baptism (e.g., the Ethiopian eunuch and Jesus), and upon such Scriptures as Matt. 3:16, Acts 8:32, Col. 2:12, and Rom. 6:4. They hold that immersion best symbolizes the new birth experience of death and resurrection with Christ—death to the old life and resurrection to newness of life. The backward posture is based on the idea of burial, while the forward posture with its kneeling and bowing is held to symbolize Christ's suffering and death when He knelt in Gethsemane and bowed His head on the cross, as well as to reflect an attitude of submission by the candidate.

Immersionists are often exclusive in mode, recognizing no other mode as valid and requiring rebaptism of transfers who have not been immersed. This is generally the rule of the M.B. Church in Russia and North and South America, although it was not the case with the M.B. Conference of Ontario before it united with the M.B. General Conference in 1939. This conference had been organized originally (1924?) as an Evangelical M.B. group (Allianz-Gemeinde, q.v.), which practiced immersion but not rebaptism of transfers. No other immersionist Mennonite group, except the K.M.B., requires rebaptism.

All cases known to the writer of the introduction of immersion in Mennonite history, temporary or permanent, are given in the following paragraphs. Conrad Grebel, as an exception to early Anabaptist practice and at the insistence of the candidate, apparently baptized Wolfgang Ulimann by immersion in the Rhine River near Schaffhausen in February 1525. It is not to be understood, however, that Grebel or Ulimann intentionally adopted immersion as a variant form, but rather that Ulimann in his enthusiasm, like Peter who wanted not only his feet but his entire body washed, "did not want only to have a bowl of water poured over him but desired to be pressed under and covered over with water in the Rhine altogether naked" (reported in *Johannes Kessler's Sabbata,* printed in St. Gall, 1902, from the original contemporary manuscript).

Sebastian Franck, who in his *Chronica (q.v.)* of 1531 described a large variety of supposed Anabaptist groups, listing even their minor differences in practice, fails to mention the practice of immersion by any Anabaptist group. The only possible evidence to the contrary is that cited by Friedrich Roth, who quotes (p. 212) Clemens Sender's chronicle, *De Ortu et Progressu,* as saying that some rebaptisms were performed at Augsburg in the Lech River, whereby the men were naked, the women in bathing clothes; the mode of baptism is not stated. The same chronicle reports baptisms in Augsburg as being performed in the homes. It is also known that several of the Augsburg preachers had been baptized by pouring and used this mode in their baptizing.

The assertion that Menno Simons taught immersion is based upon two statements in which Menno refers in passing (not in a direct discussion of the mode of baptism) to baptism as a "dipping in the water" (*induycken in den water*) and as a "baptism in the water" (*doopsel in den water*). Krahn (p. 137) and Horsch ("Did Menno . . .") have shown, however, that Menno elsewhere refers to baptism as "receiving a handful of water" (*handt vol waters*) and as being baptized "with the water" (*met dat water*), and both conclude that Menno had in mind only one form, namely, that of pouring or sprinkling. Bernhardt Rothmann's *Bekenntnisse von beyden Sacramenten* (Münster, 1533) also speaks of baptism in dual terms as "inducking int water" and "int water gedumpelt werden," but says also that baptism means a dipping in (*eyn induckinge*) or sprinkling with water (*waterbesprengung*). Since there is documentary proof that baptism at Münster was performed by "pouring a little water on the head," it is clear that the terminology used by Rothmann was traditional and symbolical, and does not require the actual practice of immersion. The same is true of Menno Simons' terminology. Since immersion was little known in Western Christendom at this time (1530-60), although it was practiced in the Eastern Church, and since there is no evidence of any dispute among the Anabaptists of Western Germany or Holland about the mode, and since it is historically certain that pouring or sprinkling was practiced by the Anabaptists in this area, it is not very likely that Menno conceived practically of baptism as immersion in the modern sense.

Some Dutch Mennonites who were associated with the Collegiants (not an organized church, but a fellowship) were no doubt immersed, since the Collegiants (*q.v.*) twice a year practiced communion and conducted baptismal ceremonies by immersion at their center of Rijnsburg. Immersion was introduced in this group soon after it was established in 1619, probably under Polish Socinian influence (the first Socinian confession of 1574 specified immersion as the mode of baptism), since this was before the introduction of immersion by the English Baptists (1640), who actually took over immersion from the Collegiants.

Under Collegiant influence there was occasional practice of baptism by immersion in the Mennonite congregations at Amsterdam, Leiden, Rotterdam, and Schiedam during the 17th and early 18th centuries. In Surhuisterveen there was a small group of newly immigrated followers of Philipp Mack who practiced immersion. This group emigrated to Pennsylvania about 1720. (See **Brethren Church of the**). They were not Mennonites.

Jan Tammes of Groningen was excommunicated in 1688 from the Old Flemish congregation there because he advocated immersion and freedom for all members to preach as was the case among the Collegiants. Adriaan Houttuyn (*q.v.,* 1700-77), who was a preacher of the Waterlander congregation at Hoorn 1732-77, was an adherent of Collegiant principles including baptism by immersion. He published a booklet in 1752 givng reasons to prefer immersion above sprinkling, also a sermon on immersion in 1770 when he immersed at Rijnsburg.

Under Collegiant influence Arrien Jansen, a deacon in the Leeuwarden (Holland) Mennonite congregation, persuaded a part of the congregation to adopt immersion in 1715. Although in a short time affusion again replaced immersion, the stone immersion font remained in the meetinghouse until 1850. Jansen had promoted the idea since 1674 and caused much dissension. In 1720 he withdrew with his adherents but was readmitted to the congregation in 1725.

The immersion idea was strongly opposed by Bastiaan van Weenighem (1625-97, *q.v.*), an influential elder (ord. 1659) of the Rotterdam Mennonite congregation and a strong leader of the orthodox party with T. J. van Braght. He published two vigorous attacks on immersion in 1666 and 1668, *Nootwendighe verantwoordinge van zeventien redenen* and *Ganze Natuere des Doops.* He was attacked in turn by the Collegiant Joan Arentsz in *Eindelijck Verklaringe der gedoopte Christenen* (1668).

Under the influence of an English Baptist a small part (two preachers and 15 members) of the Hamburg, Germany, congregation adopted immersion and separated from the main body in 1648-50. They were called Dompelaars (*q.v.*), and continued to worship in the Hamburg Mennonite meetinghouse until 1708, when they built a church of their own. With the death in 1748 of their last preacher, Jacob Denner (*q.v.*), they became extinct.

In Crefeld a small Dompelaar movement stirred up the question of immersion *ca.* 1700-30 in the Mennonite Church. Gosen Goyen (*q.v.*), one of the Crefeld Mennonite preachers, was baptized by immersion in the Rhine in 1724. How many members of the Crefeld Mennonites followed Goyen is not known. Jan Crous, who was also a Crefeld Mennonite preacher, opposed Goyen. The small group of pietistic Dompelaars of this area migrated to Pennsylvania in 1719 to become the Church of the Brethren there, who of course practiced immersion.

The Cornelis Ris Confession of 1766 (Hoorn, Holland) says, "We understand under a baptism an immersion or submersion of the entire body in water, or a copious sprinkling of the same (which last mode we in these northern regions almost universally consider more proper, since the benefits [of baptism] are represented thereby)." Since the footnotes of Ris at this point submit a number of reasons against immersion, evidently the recognition of immersion by the Ris Confession as a valid form of baptism was purely theoretical, and immersion was not intended to be practiced by those using the confession; they practiced sprinkling.

Steven Blaupot ten Cate (*Geschiedenis der Doopsgezinden in Friesland*, 1839) asserts that the Ukowallist or Groningen Old Flemish group in Holland (begun in 1630) practiced baptism by immersion, but an earlier detailed description given by Jehring in 1720 (*Gründliche Historie*, 224) of a Ukowallist baptismal service states that the elder "took a dish full of water, . . . knelt down beside the candidates, and baptized each one separately."

The small group of Mennonites in Baden, Germany, who in 1858 followed Michael Hahn (*q.v.*) and are known as the "Hahnische" Mennonites, adopted immersion.

The newly organized Mennonite Brethren group in South Russia, which had its official beginning in the Molotschna settlement on Jan. 6, 1860, adopted immersion in September 1860. Friesen says (*Brüderschaft*, 245): "The Molotschna M.B. congregation came independently to its concept and practice of baptism without personal contact or correspondence with the Baptists, but influenced by their writings." But the M.B. congregation in the Chortitza settlement did not adopt immersion until 1862. A. H. Unruh in his *Geschichte der Mennoniten-Brüdergemeinde* says, "Abr. Unger came into a connection with the Baptist preacher Oncken, and it was under this influence that the question of baptism arose"; in other words, immersion.

A primary source regarding the introduction of immersion into the new movement is the diary of Jakob Becker, now in the Tabor College Library. According to this document Johann Claassen, who had been in St. Petersburg, first brought the idea of immersion to Becker and Bartel and convinced them that the Scripture required immersion. He also gave them a booklet on baptism, "in which I found explained by various doctors and theologians what baptism is. . . . When I with Heinrich Bartel had searched the book through, we were fully convinced that we had not received a Scriptural baptism." A. H. Unruh (p. 67) says that Jakob Reimer was stirred up on the question of baptism by reading the life story of Ann Judson, the Baptist missionary in Burma. Friesen (242) says this was in 1837, and that Reimer's father had learned of immersionists on a journey to Prussia in 1835. Becker, apparently not knowing of Reimer's attitude, says under date of June 9, 1860, "We knew at that time as yet nothing of an immersion," and indicates that Claassen first brought up the question of mode in connection

with the commission of Becker to baptize two women. Becker reports that he then decided to find out what Menno Simons taught on baptism, since the original M.B. declaration of Jan. 6, 1860 (*Ausgangsschrift*), declared "that we in all other points agree with Menno Simons." He was satisfied when he found that Menno taught that the apostolic baptism was nothing else than "in unhindered water" (*im unbeschwerten Wasser*), gathering that this meant immersion in a stream of running water. Becker adds that he discovered further that "several had become acquainted with immersion through books and periodicals, who then also stood for it vigorously." Some additional immersionist literature read, according to Friesen largely introduced through Reimer, was: a tract published by the Free Evangelical Church in St. Gall, Switzerland, in which baptism by immersion was practiced; a tract of Baptist origin; a magazine *Friedensglocke;* and some "old books in which the baptism by immersion" was explained. After studying diligently the Word of God, Menno Simons' works, and other Christian literature, a number were convinced that immersion was the Scriptural baptism. The first application of the new convictions about the mode of baptism occurred on Sept. 23, 1860, in the stream Kuruschan in the Molotschna settlement (half way between Waldheim and Gnadenfeld), when Becker baptized Bartel, Bartel in turn baptized Becker, and Becker then baptized three others in the presence of a "carriage full of brethren and sisters." Other baptisms followed on Oct. 9 and 14. Some prominent leaders of the M.B. movement, such as Heinrich Hübert and Jakob Reimer, were baptized later (May 1861) and only Johann Claassen on June 30, 1862, when most of the members had been baptized. Some of those that were baptized in 1860 were baptized by kneeling in the water and dipping forward three times. At Easter of 1861 it was, however, decided that the mode of baptizing once backwards symbolizes more closely the burial of the Lord Jesus Christ and since that time this mode was the only one used.

About the same time, 1861, under the influence of the Baptist preacher Alf, several Mennonites of the congregation near Adamov, Poland, received baptism by immersion; but they did not unite with the Baptists because they differed on the oath, nonresistance, and footwashing, and because some were immersed forward. The Krimmer Mennonite Brethren (*q.v.*), founded in 1869 in the Crimea, adopted immersion at once as their sole mode of baptism. Elder J. A. Wiebe (*q.v.*), the founder, states in a manuscript, "The Form of Baptism of the K.M.B. Church," after giving Scriptural evidence for baptism while kneeling, "In the small *Martyrs' Mirror* (i.e., Isaac von Dühren's *Geschichte der Märtyrer*, 2nd ed., sold by Gottlieb Schad, Molotschna, 1863) it says clearly on page 8, 'At that time (i.e., in the first century) baptizing was not sprinkling, but the entire person was dipped in and under.' " This supports his initial statement, "We were anxious to have our form of baptism as taught in God's Word and as practiced by the apostolic churches during the persecution times." Wiebe also interpreted certain passages in Menno Simons' works as indicating that Menno taught immersion.

The Allianz-Gemeinde (Evangelical Mennonite Church), founded in the Ukraine in 1905-7, practiced baptism by immersion but without requiring rebaptism of unimmersed transfers; its daughter groups in North and South America have done the same.

In North America immersion was made the exclusive mode of baptism by the River Brethren (Brethren in Christ) Church at its founding in 1770, under Dunkard (Church of the Brethren) influence. The Mennonite Brethren in Christ (now largely United Missionary Church) from the beginning (1875) made the mode of baptism optional, but gradually immersion came into favor; in 1896 it was made the exclusive form. The Missionary Church Association broke off from the Defenseless Mennonites in 1896, partly on the point of making immersion the exclusive mode of baptism.

The E.M.B. Church, which long used pouring only, changed over to immersion about 1925 (by local congregational option, not by conference decision); only one congregation still practices pouring only, and one other permits immersion on request by the candidate. The Evangelical Mennonites (formerly Defenseless Mennonites) originally had only pouring, but now make the mode optional; a growing minority of baptisms are performed by immersion. The Emmanuel independent church at Meade, Kan., has only immersion since 1950. The Apostolic Christian Church, organized in 1832 in Switzerland, adopted immersion as its mode of baptism, requiring its Mennonite fraction (from the Emmental congregation) to be rebaptized. A preacher of this group (Benedict Weyeneth) who visited the Amish Mennonite congregation at Croghan, N.Y., succeeded in detaching a large part of the membership and ministers in 1852 and organizing them as an Apostolic Christian congregation, having led them to believe that immersion was the only true form of baptism.

While the remaining North American Mennonite bodies all recognize immersion as valid baptism and do not require rebaptism of transfers, only with rare exceptions do they allow immersion as an optional mode.

The intensity of feeling by some immersionist Mennonite groups, particularly on requirement of rebaptism of transfers with its attendant implication of invalidation of baptism by pouring or sprinkling, has added at times to the difficulties hindering good inter-Mennonite relations. This was earlier true also of the relations between the Church of the Brethren and Mennonites. On the other hand, the identity of baptismal doctrine and practice between Mennonite Brethren and Baptists has resulted in a greater openness to Baptist influence, both in North America and Russia, and has resulted in some M.B. transfers to the Baptists, both of ministers and members.

Occasionally certain claims for immersion have been made by Baptist and Mennonite historians; e.g., that Menno taught and practiced immersion, that "most Anabaptist congregations gave the baptismal candidates free choice of mode" (implying that immersion was recognized and practiced by the Anabaptists as an alternate mode), and that "there always were immersionists among the Mennonites, at least until 1750 or later." The latter two claims

made by Friesen (*Brüderschaft*, p. 249) were taken over from the French Baptist historian, C. A. Ramseyer (*Histoire des Baptistes*, 1897). But general Anabaptist recognition of immersion or practice of it on an optional basis has not been demonstrated, as is seen above. The general historic practice of Mennonites up to 1860, with few exceptions, was pouring or sprinkling. (See further **Baptism** and **Baptists**, *ME* I.) H.S.B.

In addition to the literature given in the article "*Baptism*," the following should be noted: J. Horsch, "Did Menno Simons Practice Baptism by Immersion?" *MQR* (1927) 54-56; A. H. Unruh, *Die Geschichte der Mennoniten-Brüdergemeinde 1860-1954* (Winnipeg, 1954), particularly "Die Einführung der Tauchtaufe," 67-81; E. Händiges, *Die Lehre der Mennoniten in Geschichte und Gegenwart* (Ludwigshafen, 1921); J. Horsch, *Kurzgefasste Geschichte der Mennoniten-Gemeinden* (Elkhart, 1890). The following writings by Mennonites, all but the first being brief treatises, usually include a treatment of the mode of baptism, and several are polemical anti-immersionist tracts: Heinrich Funck, *Ein Spiegel der Taufe* (Germantown, 1744; English editions 1851 and later); Peter Burkholder, *Eine Verhandlung von der Aeusserlichen Wasser-Taufe* (Harrisonburg, 1816); Johannes Risser, *Glaube und Lehre von der Taufe der Mennoniten in Deutschland* (Berlin, Canada, 1845); J. Holdeman, *Eine Vertheidigung gegen die Verfälscher unserer Schriften, wie auch eine Erklärung und Erläuterung der Absicht der Christlichen Taufe* (Lancaster, 1865); *The Bible Mode of Baptism, By Different Authors* (Published by Abraham Blosser, Dale Enterprise, Va., 1884); Isaak Peters, *Die christliche Wassertaufe, ihr Zweck und ihre Bedeutung* (Elkhart, ca. 1901); L. J. Heatwole, *Baptism Shown to be a Ceremony of Consecration* (Elkhart, 1902); L. H. Shank, *Bible Mode of Baptism* (Elkhart, ca. 1900); E. J. Berkey, *The Bible Mode of Baptism* (Warrenton, 1906); Heinrich Donner, *Unterricht von der heiligen Wassertaufe* (printed at Tiegenhof, 1906, reprint of a first edition of 1792).

Imperial Recesses (*Reichsabschiede*) against the Anabaptists. The legislation of the diet or parliament (Reichstag) of the Holy Roman (German) Empire against the Anabaptists is an important source of information for Anabaptist history. Furthermore, the mandates passed by the diet had considerable influence on the legislation of the subsidiary units of the empire against the Anabaptists, although because of the weakness of the imperial executive authority the mandates were not always executed by the component states. As the supreme legislative body of the Empire the position taken by it, to be sure, had great weight in setting the tone for Europe as a whole in this matter of the Anabaptists, namely, one of harsh persecution intended to effect the complete destruction of the movement. The entire text of all the recesses 1528-66, together with the imperial mandates based upon them, has been published by Gustav Bossert, Sr., in his edition of the Anabaptist documents for Württemberg (*TA Württemberg*, 1929). The contents of the most important recesses is given in the following paragraphs.

The recess of Speyer (*q.v.*) of 1529, Sections 6 and 7, deals with Anabaptism, which is called an ancient heresy: "Each and every Anabaptist and rebaptized person, man or woman of an accountable age, shall be sentenced . . . and brought from life to death by fire, sword, or the like according to the occasion and the person. And the seditious revolutionaries of the notorious blasphemy of rebaptism will . . . by no means be pardoned. But he who confesses his error to recant it, and is willing to accept the punishment and show penitence for it, and would ask for mercy, he may, according to his condition of rank, nature, and youth, be pardoned. But he who disregards these in the opinion that infant baptism is naught, he shall, if he persists therein, be considered an Anabaptist and subject to the above imperial mandate. And none shall be pardoned and be assigned to other places, but shall be bound to stay in his country, which then has to exercise diligent watchfulness that none of these converts backslides. Whoever gives the Anabaptists shelter or help, does not treat them sternly and tolerate them, falls under the ban of the empire." The mandate of Charles V of April 1529, with the same content, then follows.

Section 11 of the imperial recess of Augsburg (q.v.) of Nov. 19, 1530, has the following to say about the Anabaptists: "Some have taught that infant baptism is naught, but that every person when he comes to understanding shall be baptized again; also they do not consider baptism a sacrament. Thereby some have given up all the Christian order and prayers, which are held at baptism, and have made others." Section 10 says: "Regarding the Anabaptists we will retain the decisions and decrees that have been issued, which we want to have renewed here with the counsel and the consent of the electors, princes, and nobility, and decree that children everywhere be baptized . . . ."

The recess of Worms of April 25, 1535, concerns principally the Münster (q.v.) Anabaptists and their "accursed teaching," the tyranny of the tailor who was made their king, the siege of the city and the assistance offered in the siege by the estates to punish the unchristian tyranny. This is the tenor of all the 60 paragraphs. Thus Sections 42 and 43 say that if the temporal authorities do not have sufficient power, the neighboring estates are to assist them, with the exception of those who are in need of help themselves. Paragraph 44, concerning "prevention of future sedition," states that it had been decided in the name of the electors, princes, and other estates for the prevention of these accursed sects and the avoidance of further mischief, because the Anabaptists move from land to land, that neither electors nor princes or other estates shall accept such foreign unknown persons as subjects and citizens in their dominions, without having first ascertained that they are not followers of rebaptism. Section 45 commands that no writings, books, or other material that might promote the accursed sect of Anabaptism shall be printed or offered for sale, but the transgressor shall be severely, quickly punished.

The recess of Speyer of June 10, 1544, Section 74, orders, that since the dangerous and seductive sect of Anabaptists is gaining the upper hand in the Holy Roman Empire Charles has made an agreement with the estates to this effect that whether in the cities or in the country, if one has the duty of denouncing and another the duty of arresting; if the denouncer is negligent, the one who has the duty to arrest shall have the authority to seize the Anabaptists and proceed against them in accord with the decrees. Also the negligent denouncer shall be punished. But all authorities in whose domain such persons are arrested shall diligently strive to have them converted through their scholars and theologians.

The imperial recess of Augsburg of Feb. 14, 1551, states in Sections 87-94 that all Anabaptists of accountable age who do not obey the authorities and swear the required oaths, or are unwilling to recognize any authority shall be executed by fire, sword, or the like. The leaders and preachers of the vice of rebaptism shall by no means be pardoned, but shall be earnestly dealt with, both those who persist in their error and those who fall back into it. But those who confess their error and are willing to recant may, according to rank, nature, youth, and other circumstances, be pardoned.

The imperial recess of Augsburg of Sept. 25, 1555, Section 17, states that all other creeds with the exception of the Catholic and the Augsburg (Lutheran) are not meant in the religious peace, but are wholly excluded. Therewith the general imperial recesses against the Anabaptists close. Concurrently there are, however, the much more numerous mandates (q.v.) and decrees of the individual rulers and imperial cities, issued on the basis of the above recesses or on their own initiative.   LOSERTH.

E. A. Koch and H. C. von Lenckenberg, *Neue und vollständigere Sammlung der Reichsabschiede* (Frankfurt, 1747); *ML* III, 450 f.

In the Service of the King, a 16-page bimonthly official organ of the Bethel Deaconess Home and Hospital Society, Newton, Kan., was begun in January 1942 with ten issues per year, changing in October 1949 to five (now six) issues. The circulation (free) is 2,800. Editors have been Sister Frieda Kauffman 1942-44, Joanna S. Andres 1944-54, Ernst Harder 1955-56, and H. J. Andres 1956- .   H.S.B.

Inanwatan, in the northwest part (called Vogelkop, i.e., Bird's Head) of the island of New Guinea (a Dutch colony). Here the Dutch Mennonite Mission Association opened a mission on Oct. 1, 1950, taking over this area from the Dutch Reformed Church. The Papuas living in this section were partly Christianized in 1915-25. There are now about 60 congregations and mission stations. R. E. H. Marcus, who has been preaching here since October 1950, is now the missionary-pastor, assisted by a large number of native preachers and teachers. From October 1950 to May 1956 P. Messie also served as pastor. In the spring of 1954 Teminabuan (q.v.) became the center of the mission work.   vDZ.

Incarnation of Christ, a doctrine which has been a subject of controversy at various times in church history. Those emphasizing the humanity of Christ at the cost of His deity are probably better known than those emphasizing the divinity more than the humanity. A large wing of the early Anabaptists emphasized the deity of Christ more than the regular Catholic and Protestant churches did, with their historic orthodox creeds. However, this emphasis did not originate with the Anabaptists, but had its roots in early Christendom. The Valentinians at the time of Tertullian emphasized the divinity of Christ and minimized His humanity to the point that they considered Christ born of the Virgin Mary as if He had been passing through her body "as through a pipe," taking none of her human flesh, in order to assure that the Saviour had "other flesh" than that of fallen man so that He would not have part in original sin. Even stronger is the emphasis placed on this by the Gnostic Marcion. Apollinaris and his followers continued this line of thought emphasizing that only thus humanity has a guarantee of salvation. "Our human nature was accepted by Him so that He became a perfect organ of God" (Schoeps, 13). During the Middle Ages this particular emphasis almost completely disappeared with the exception of such groups as the Bogomiles and Cathars. During the Reformation this concern reoccurs particularly among some of the "left-wing" reformers.

In a recent study devoted to this subject, H. J. Schoeps (*Vom himmlischen Fleisch Christi,* 1951) states that Caspar Schwenckfeld was the first of the reformers to emphasize the teaching of the "heavenly flesh" of Christ and that he was directly influenced by the Greek Fathers (26). Schwenckfeld believed in a sinless "glorified humanity" of Christ. "If Christ had the characteristics of a sinful creation, He could not represent us in the presence of God" (28). Schoeps states that Schwenckfeld's concern in this matter was that mankind can be "glorified" or become divine only if Christ was divine. His Christology was closely related to his views regarding the Lord's Supper. "Only through Christ's heavenly body is the spiritual influence from above guaranteed, because only through the glorified humanity of the risen Christ can believers be filled and fed with the Holy Spirit" (36). "Through His spiritualized, raised, and glorified (divine) flesh, Christ, as a second Adam, draws mankind toward Himself into spirituality" (36).

Melchior Hofmann was the originator of this peculiar teaching regarding the incarnation of Christ, as far as the early Anabaptists are concerned. To what extent he was influenced by Schwenckfeld or Sebastian Franck, whom he met in Strasbourg, has not yet been conclusively established. Schwenckfeld says concerning his influence along these lines, "They have both (Hofmann and Franck) taken their errors from our truth, like spiders who suck poison out of a beautiful flower" (*Corpus Schwenckfeldianorum* V, 522 f.). Even though the above influences may have started Hofmann out on his way along these lines, he soon went his own way. It has been definitely established that Hofmann's ideas were taken over by Menno Simons, Dirk Philips, and other representatives of the early Dutch Anabaptists, who added hardly anything new.

This peculiar view regarding the Incarnation was widespread among the early Dutch Anabaptists. That it was also found among the followers of Melchior Hofmann in South Germany as late as 1555 is apparent in the introduction to the "Agreement of the brethren and elders congregated at Strasbourg regarding the question of the source of Christ's flesh," which stated that the ministers and elders had been approached to give an account along these lines by "the followers of Hofmann, as well as the Dutch brethren." This distinction between the two would indicate that some of them were located in South Germany or in the vicinity of Strasbourg

(Brons, 97). At this Anabaptist conference it was emphasized that since the Bible states both that Christ had His flesh from heaven and that He received it from Mary we should "not attempt to know more than can be known," and "that reason should be subordinated to the obedience of Christ."

One of the basic differences between the early Dutch Anabaptist leaders and Schwenckfeld was the claim of the Dutch that Christ was born "in Mary" and not "of Mary," that Mary did not furnish the flesh of the Saviour, but merely His nourishment. Schwenckfeld does not go so far, stating that Christ received the "flesh and tabernacle of His body from Mary, the virgin," and emphasizes that he is not "Hoffmenisch," although he considers the flesh of Christ of "divine origin" (*Corpus Schwenckfeldianorum* VII, 304). Schwenckfeld's views are closely related to his peculiar view of the "deification" of the children of God, in which process he considered it necessary that the flesh of Christ be of divine origin. Hofmann's and Menno's views are closely related to their concept of the Christian church. The church of Christ, which is the body of Christ, can only be transformed into this fitting close relationship to Him if the sole cause of this act is Jesus Christ, her Saviour and head. The church, or the body of Christ, can be without wrinkle and blemish only if Christ was without sin and His human substance was of divine origin. Franck, who shared somewhat the Anabaptist emphasis on the divinity of Christ, did not have their concern regarding the establishment of a visible, pure church and he, therefore, did not agree with them along these lines.

It is here where an apparently speculative thought becomes a basic doctrine of salvation. It was because of this reasoning that the peculiar view regarding the incarnation of Christ became a very important doctrine for Menno and his followers. Although Menno asserts (*Complete Writings,* 430, 439) that he is not particularly teaching and preaching this view, but that he is constantly being lured to defend it, we must conclude that he would not have been so voluminous in writing about this subject and defending it if it had not been basic for him, and that he would not have been attacked by his opponents if he had kept this as a "secret" doctrine. At nearly all public discussions with opponents this matter was on the agenda and discussed in detail. For him and his followers this was an essential part of their doctrine. This is also evidenced by the fact that Adam Pastor was ousted because he stressed the humanity of Christ, and denied His essential deity because he thought God and man (Jesus) could not be of the same essence (Krahn, 67 ff.). In oral and written discussions, this doctrine was a matter of controversy between Menno and a Lasco, Micron, and Faber, as well as at official religious debates at Leeuwarden and Emden. In the writings of Melchior Hofmann, Menno Simons, and Dirk Philips this subject matter is discussed, defended and elaborated on at length. They object seriously to speaking of two "persons" in Christ, the divine and the human, on the grounds that the divine act in the birth of Christ cannot be described in these terms.

At the great Anabaptist conference at Strasbourg in 1555 it was emphasized that since the Bible states both that Christ had His flesh from heaven and that He received it from Mary we should "not attempt to know more than can be known" and "that reason should be subordinated to the obedience of Christ." When pressed by the Reformed for answers along these lines at the Frankenthal Disputation in 1571, the Anabaptists seem to have been intentionally unexplicit. The question posed was: "Concerning Christ. Whether Christ received the nature of His flesh from the substance of the flesh of the Virgin Mary or elsewhere." This question is definitely directed against the teaching of Melchior Hofmann along these lines. Diebold Winter finally said, "We request time to think it over. We are flooded with many words. If there is anything to them we cannot grasp it. We must fear God and cannot yet accept them in such manner."

In an undated edict against the Anabaptists Philip of Hesse stated that "those who hold that Christ did not receive His humanity from the blood of Mary through the work of the Holy Spirit" (*TA Hessen,* 33) were not permitted to live in his realm. This would indicate that there were some followers of Hofmann in South Germany who shared his views on the incarnation. Also Caspar Schwenckfeld stated that "many Anabaptists, particularly in Alsace and the Netherlands," held this view and that he had "debated with many of them, also with M. Hofmann, and proven by Scripture that Christ had really taken His flesh from the Virgin Mary" (Schoeps, 28). This is a quotation from his book *Vom Fleisch Christi* . . . (1561). Already around 1540 he had written a booklet *Vom Fleische Christi* . . . in which he attacked Melchior Hofmann (*Corpus Schwenckfeldianorum* VII, 281 ff.). In his letter to W. Thalhäuser dated Feb. 1, 1539 (*Corpus Schwenckfeldianorum* VI, 483), he states that he has succeeded in convincing some of the followers of Hofmann, including leaders, to accept the true teaching concerning the incarnation of Christ. How widespread Hofmann's views pertaining to this doctrine were in Middle and South Germany has not been studied. That they may have been present as late as 1577 is possible, since the *Formula of Concord* (*q.v.*) starts its condemnation of the Anabaptists under "Intolerable Articles Concerning the Church" with the statement: "That Christ did not receive His body and blood from the Virgin Mary, but brought them with Him from heaven." The body of *Täuferakten,* most of which have been published, must be examined to determine to what extent these views were actually represented among the Middle and South German Anabaptists if at all. There is no evidence of it among any of the numerous Hutterite documents.

The early Anabaptist confessions of faith and writings of the Low Countries emphasize this teaching strongly. The public debates between the Reformed and the Anabaptists of Emden (1578) and Leeuwarden (1596) cover it in great detail. During the 17th century some of the more liberal groups began to give up this doctrine and it thus became one of the first typical Dutch Mennonite characteristics to be dropped. However, the fact that the *Catalogus*

(181-84) lists more than two dozen writings on this subject printed during this century indicates that this was by no means a dead issue in the Dutch brotherhood at this time. When S. F. Rues visited the Dutch Mennonites during the first half of the 18th century, only the conservative groups such as the Old Flemish and the Danzigers were still adhering unitedly to this doctrine (Rues, *Aufrichtige Nachrichten,* 16), while the progressive Mennonites had given up Menno's view and agreed in this matter with the rest of Christendom (p. 97). The Lammerenkrijgh (*q.v.*) and other influences had overshadowed this teaching, and its significance in connection with the attempt to establish a true church "without spot or wrinkle" had been lost sight of. However, such books as the Old Flemish *Onderwyzing des Christelyken Geloofs* . . . by Pieter Boudewyns of 1743, still strongly emphasized this view. This book was reprinted as late as 1825. By 1800 this peculiar view, with a few exceptions, had been forgotten as a "Mennonite doctrine." A complete study of this doctrine and its later development in Holland and other countries (such as Prussia) has not yet been made.   (See also **Formula of Concord, Franckenthal Disputation.)**   C.K.

Menno Simons' Complete Writings (Scottdale, 1956); Dirk Philips, *BRN* X (135-53); Melchior Hofmann, *BRN* V (125-70, 210-14); H. J. Schoeps, *Vom himmlischen Fleisch Christi* (Tübingen, 1951); C. Krahn, *Menno Simons* (Karlsruhe, 1936); I. E. Burkhart, "Menno Simons on the Incarnation," *MQR* IV (1930) 113-39, 178-207; VI (1932) 122-23; W. J. Leendertz, *Melchior Hofmann* (Haarlem, 1883); F. O. zur Linden, *Melchior Hofmann* (Leiden, 1885); A. Hulshof, *Geschiedenis van de Doopsgezinden te Straatsburg* (Amsterdam, 1905); A. Dorner, *Entwicklungsgeschichte der Lehre von der Person Christi* II (Berlin, 1853) 637-43; John Horsch, *Menno Simons* II (Scottdale, 1916); *Corpus Schwenckfeldianorum* V, VI, VII (Leipzig, 1916 ff.); Ch. Hege, *Die Täufer in der Kurpfalz* (Frankfurt, 1908) 124 f.; *TA Baden-Pfalz;* A. Brons, *Ursprung, Entwickelung und Schicksale der* . . . *Mennoniten* (Amsterdam, 1912) 97 ff.; Peter Kawerau, *Melchior Hoffman als religiöser Denker* (Haarlem, 1954); *ML* III, 113-15.

Incorporation: see **Legal Status.**

India Calling is a quarterly publication of 12 to 14 pages, published by the General Conference Mennonite Church missionaries in India, beginning with Aug. 1, 1940. It presents mission and church news of the work in Raipur, Bilaspur, and Sarjuga districts, Madhya Pradesh, India. Editors have been S. T. Moyer, Mrs. F. J. Isaac, Mrs. P. A. Wenger, Edward Burkhalter, and Kenneth Bauman. It is printed in Newton, Kan.   W.K.

India Mennonite Conference (MC) is the name given to the church conference that came into being coextensive with the American Mennonite Mission with headquarters at Dhamtari in the Central Provinces (since 1950 called Madhya Pradesh), India. The American Mennonite Mission began work in the area in 1899, but the India Mennonite Conference was not organized until January 1912. At that time its total membership was 488.

J. S. Hartzler and J. S. Shoemaker visited the India Mission during 1910-11 and with the help of missionaries M. C. Lapp and P. A. Friesen drew up a constitution with rules and discipline for the

India Mennonite Conference. The first session of the Conference convened the first Tuesday of January 1912 in the Bethel Church at Balodgahan. Conference membership consisted of all missionaries (men and women), two lay delegates from each congregation for the first 50 members, and two delegates for every additional 50 members or fraction thereof.

The church ordained four Indian deacons in 1913, and the first Indian minister was ordained on April 30, 1927. In 1953 the figures for ordained nationals in the India church were: deacons 6, ministers 8, and deaconess 1. The constitution of the conference was revised in 1928-29, placing the Conference on a sounder basis organizationally and bringing matters of procedure and discipline up to date. Now conference membership consisted only of ordained persons (lay missionaries and missionary women were no longer members) and the same system of lay representation of two for the first 50 and two for every additional 50 members or fraction thereof was maintained. In 1955 the membership was 1,507.

Another milestone was reached in the Conference on July 1, 1952, when the American Mennonite Mission and the India Mennonite Church were merged under the name "The Mennonite Church in India." The basis of membership remained the same, but the Executive Committee was enlarged to a total of 14 members. The entire work of the church was now organized under four councils of approximately nine members each as follows: (1) evangelistic and pastoral, (2) educational and charitable institutions, (3) medical, and (4) economic aid. Indian pastors are in charge of all the larger congregations and are supported fully by the Indian Church. Missionaries appointed to the area serve co-operatively within the conference framework. Thus the indigenous church is being developed with her roots in the soil of India and with Christ as her head.   J.D.G.

India, Mennonite Missions in. In 1957 there were five distinct Mennonite mission fields in India, all operated by North American Mennonite mission boards. They are given below with statistical information, in order of origin: (1) *Mennonite Church* (MC), state of Madhya Pradesh, language Hindi, area 5,000 sq. mi., field pop. 1,000,000, baptized members 1,500, arrival of first missionaries in India March 24, 1899; (2) *Mennonite Brethren,* state of Andhra Pradesh (Hyderabad), area 5,000 sq. mi.,

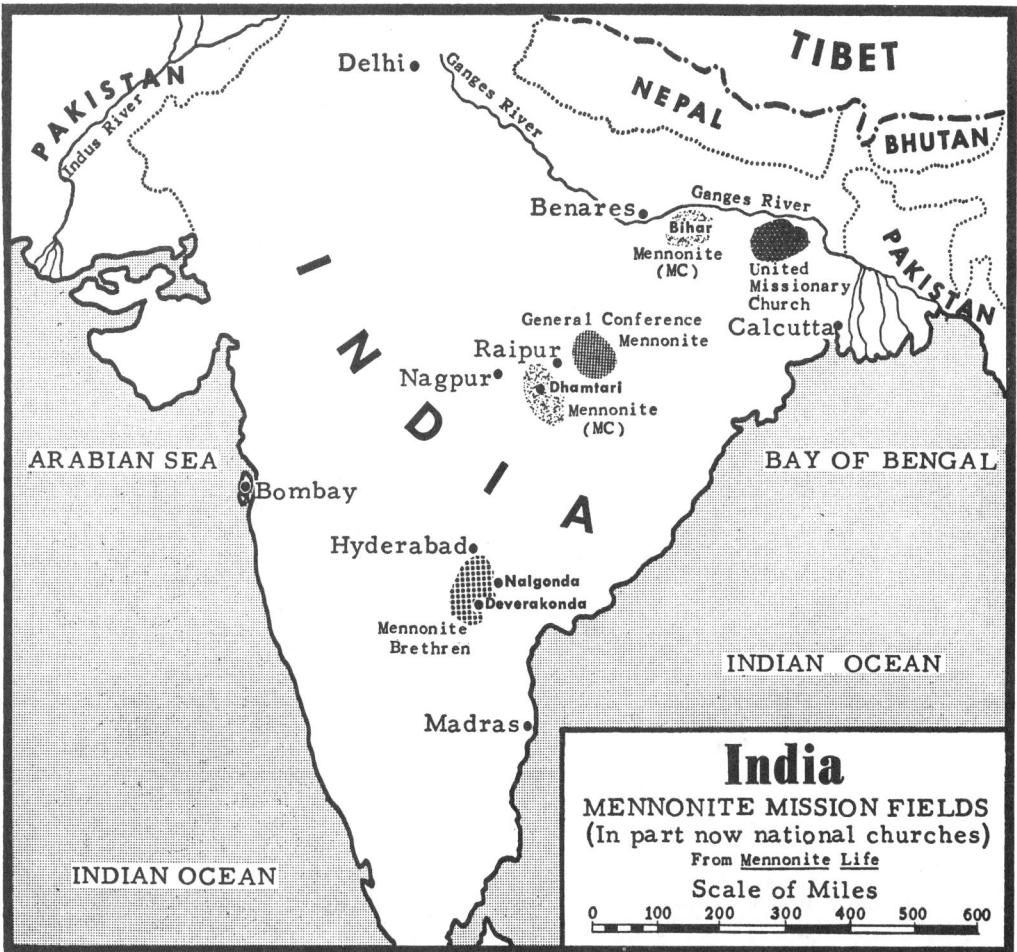

India
MENNONITE MISSION FIELDS
(In part now national churches)
From Mennonite Life
Scale of Miles
0   100   200   300   400   500   600

pop. 2,500,000, members 23,000, language Telegu, arrival of first missionaries Oct. 27, 1899; (3) *General Conference Mennonite Church,* state of Madhya Pradesh, language Hindi, area 4,000 sq. mi. (to which a second contiguous field was recently added), pop. 1,000,000, members 3,600, first missionary arrival Dec. 9, 1900; (4) *United Missionary Church,* state of Bihar, language Bengali, area 1,500 sq. mi., pop. 400,000, first missionary arrival 1925, members 600; a second field was opened in Calcutta in 1956; (5) *Mennonite Church* (MC), second field, state of Bihar, language Hindi, area 4,200 sq. mi., pop. 1,000,000, members 110, established in January 1940. See the map for locations of the fields.

Thus the five Mennonite missions in India today, after almost 60 years of work, have a total of roughly 29,000 members, three fourths of them in the M.B. field. Methods of working have included direct evangelism, educational, medical, and industrial missions, and also leprosy work. The three oldest missions have been major efforts, each with a staff of 30 to 40 missionaries at their height. The M.C. mission in Madhya Pradesh was terminated in 1952, and the direction of the entire work transferred to the indigenous church, although missionaries are still sent to the field in small numbers. The other missions are still operating as American missions, but are working toward indigenization. The G.C.M. mission has taken over an adjoining area from the British Baptists. The M.C., G.C.M., and U.M.C. cooperate with the Union Theological Seminary at Yeotmal, furnishing certain staff members. For a more detailed account of the several American missions in India see the pertinent articles on the entire missions as well as on the major stations and institutions.

The only European Mennonite Mission in India was the work carried on by the Mennonite Brethren in the state of Hyderabad 1890-1914 under the American Baptist Missionary Union. The work, officially supported by the conference, was begun in 1890 by Abraham Friesen, who had been trained at the Baptist Theological Seminary in Hamburg, Germany. It was not an independent work, but rather a portion of the Baptist field and under Baptist general administration. The coming of World War II forced the closing of the work because of difficulties of travel and remission of funds; so the entire field reverted to the Baptists. The missionaries on the field at that time joined the Baptist Church and remained as Baptist workers. In 1910 the membership under their direction had reached 3,000. At its height the Russian M.B. staff in India was seven. The center of their work was Nalgonda. It was to this place that the first American M.B. missionaries came. They located their field adjacent to the Russian M.B. field. The M.B. Church had been visited earlier by representatives of the Russian missionaries and had been giving some financial support to the Russian work.   J.T., H.S.B.

Ed. G. Kaufman, *The Development of the Missionary and Philanthropic Interest Among the Mennonites of North America* (Berne, 1931); A. E. Janzen, *Survey of Mennonite Brethren Missions* (Hillsboro, 1950); G. W. Peters, *The Growth of Mennonite Brethren Foreign Missions* (Hillsboro, 1952); Mrs. H. T. Esau, *First Sixty Years of Mennonite Brethren Missions* (Hillsboro, 1954);

Twenty-Five Years with God in India (GCM, Berne, 1929); R. Ratzlaff, *Fellowship in the Gospel in India, 1900-1950* (GCM, Newton, 1950); S. T. Moyer, *With Christ in the Edge of the Jungles* (GCM, Berne, 1941); G. J. Lapp, *Our Mission in India* (MC, Scottdale, 1921); *Building on the Rock* (MC, Scottdale, 1926); *The Love of Christ Hath Constrained Us* (MC, Scottdale, 1949); E. R. Storms, *What God Hath Wrought, The Story of the Foreign Missionary Effort of the United Missionary Church* (Springfield, 1949); M. C. Lehman, *Our Mission Work in India* (Elkhart, 1939); Mary M. Good, *The Mennonite Church in India* (Elkhart, 1955); C. G. Esch, *Fiftieth Anniversary Souvenir Booklet,* 1906-1956 (Elkhart, 1956).

Indian Cove Mennonite Church (MC), located in a small irrigated farming community in Owyhee County, southern Idaho, near Hammett, a member of the Pacific Coast Conference, was organized in 1935, the first Mennonite settlers, Aaron S. Brubaker and family, having come from Mahoning Co., Ohio, in 1926. Two ministers, A. M. Shenk of Nampa, Ida., and Paul J. Hooley of Limon, Col., were among the 19 charter members. In 1954 the membership was 72, with Paul W. Miller and Amos Shenk as ministers, and Menno S. Snyder as deacon. M.S.S.

Indian Industrial School, Halstead, Kan., was established in 1885 jointly by the Mission Board of the General Conference Mennonite Church and the Halstead Seminary. The school was started with 15 Indian children from Oklahoma, who received regular training in schoolwork and agriculture, housekeeping, and Christian living. In 1887 the school was moved to the Christian Krehbiel farm about one mile southeast from Halstead. During the school year the children received regular instruction and during the summer they helped on the farm, where they lived as a large family. In his report to the Mission Board in 1892-93 Christian Krehbiel stated that he had again received a contract from the government to take 30 pupils for the school year, for each of whom he would receive $125. In 1896 the government discontinued this contract policy of schools for the Indians. Thus after eleven years of operation the Indian Industrial School was closed. Both the Indians and the Mennonite constituency, which was aroused to greater mission efforts, gained by this enterprise. Reports were published in *Christlicher Bundesbote.*   C.K.

H. P. Krehbiel, *The History of the General Conference of the Mennonites of South America* I (1898) 306-9; Ed. G. Kaufman, *The Development of the Missionary and Philanthropic Interest Among the Mennonites of North America* (Berne, 1931) 141-43.

Indian Missions of the General Conference Mennonite Church, from 1880 to 1953. The unifying principle of the General Conference Mennonite Church at its origin was to carry on home and foreign missions. The word "foreign" meant missions among heathen not yet under the influence of the Gospel. Hence when an opening was found in the Indian Territory, now the state of Oklahoma, to carry on mission work among the Arapaho Indians, a school was built for about 25 pupils at Darlington. Mr. and Mrs. S. S. Haury arrived there in May 1880. In a few months other workers arrived, and by August 1881 the school building was completed. On Feb. 19, 1882, this building was destroyed by fire, and four small children lost their lives, among them the infant son Karl of the Haury family.

Despite this terrific loss so early in the mission work, plans were made to build again. A brick building was put up, and when the government buildings at Cantonment, 65 miles northwest of Darlington, could be had free of charge for mission purposes the work expanded. With a government grant of $5,000 for the new building at Darlington, the work at Cantonment was undertaken in the fall of 1882.

Since the Arapaho and Cheyennes lived in close proximity in the Cantonment area, Cheyenne children were also taken into the school. For a number of years both schools had as many children as they could accommodate. The usual number at Darlington was about 50, that at Cantonment about 75. Some Indian children were taken to Kansas as early as 1884, and in 1887 Christian Krehbiel, president of the foreign mission board, at his own expense built an industrial school on his farm about one mile from Halstead. Gradually the schools were closed, when the government ceased giving subsidies to Indian missions.

In the meantime the Indians of both tribes had been allotted land and had settled in groups, and mission stations had been built in the more densely populated areas. Missionaries were placed at these stations to work with the adult Indians as well as with the younger ones. The Indians were largely illiterate in those early days, and only a few could understand English. These helped the missionaries as interpreters.

In 1891 Mr. and Mrs. Rodolphe Petter came from Switzerland to take up the work with the adult Cheyennes at Cantonment. Petter was well prepared to learn the Cheyenne language, knowing French, German, Latin, Greek, Hebrew, and having studied English for a school year at Oberlin College, Ohio, just previously. He reduced the difficult language to writing, compiled a voluminous dictionary, worked out a comprehensive grammar, and translated *Pilgrim's Progress,* and the entire New Testament, as well as large portions of the Old Testament into the Cheyenne language.

At the present time there is one church for the Arapaho Indians at Canton, Okla. Among the Cheyenne Indians there are churches at Longdale, Fonda, Thomas, Clinton, Hammon, and Seiling. The Indian children attend public schools with white neighbor children, and the English language is used almost exclusively in the mission work. Sunday school, daily vacation Bible schools, and young people's retreats are some of the special activities that help to bring Christ to these people.

The General Conference mission work expanded to the Hopi tribe of Arizona in 1893. H. R. Voth, who had spent ten years as a missionary in Oklahoma, was sent to the Hopi and built a mission station at Oraibi. Here also pioneering cost sacrifices. H. R. Voth had lost his first wife through death in Oklahoma while in mission work there, and in Arizona his second wife passed away. Other missionaries came to establish mission work among the Hopi in other villages. The reluctance of the Hopi to accept the Gospel was even more evident here

than in the work among the Arapaho and Cheyenne Indians. However, there are fervent Christians at the various mission stations who work with the missionaries in Sunday schools and other activities such as proclaiming the Gospel over public-address systems in the villages, and women's work. In recent years it was, however, felt that a mission day school was a necessity. Hence a day school building was built with a capacity of about 80 pupils, and a new day for this mission field had come. The attendance has averaged about 52 in the last few years. There are small congregations at Oraibi, Bacabi, and Moencopi, Ariz.

A fourth opening was found among the Northern Cheyennes in southeastern Montana. The Cheyennes in Oklahoma often spoke of their relatives in Montana; so Petter made several trips there to study the possibility of using the Cheyenne translations in mission work there. As a result, in May 1904 G. A. Linscheid began work at Busby, Mont. Mission stations were subsequently built at Lame Deer, Birney, and Ashland, Mont. In this field the Cheyennes did not have the opportunities to learn the English language as early as their southern relatives.

Petter with his second wife, Bertha E. Kinsinger, was transferred to Lame Deer in 1916; and worked there until his death on Jan. 6, 1947.

For fuller details about the mission work among the North Cheyennes see article **Cheyenne Indians.** (*ML* II, 413 f.) A.H.

Indiana. The nineteenth state of the Union, admitted Dec. 11, 1816, having an area of 36,291 square miles and a population of 3,934,224 in 1950, is the location of a number of flourishing Mennonite settlements totaling over 14,000 baptized members. The basic settlements were all established in the quarter century just before the Civil War, 1838-60. There are three: (1) the Swiss (GCM) settlement in Adams County around Berne; (2) the Mennonite (MC) settlement around Goshen in Elkhart County, made by settlers largely from eastern Ohio; and (3) the Amish settlement east of Goshen and west of Nappanee, by settlers from Somerset Co., Pa., and Holmes Co., Ohio. The small community in Allen County north of Fort Wayne was settled by Amish immigrants directly from Alsace and South Germany, some of whom also located in Adams County. Indiana Mennonite history is marked also by five divisions. The Amish divided four times: (1) the Old Order-Progressive (MC) division about 1854-65 in the Elkhart-Lagrange County settlement; (2) the Conservative Amish separation in the same area in 1876; (3) the Central Conference group split in the Clinton Frame congregation in 1892; and (4) the Beachy Amish separation from the Old Order Amish in 1950. The Elkhart County Mennonites suffered three schisms, two major: the Wisler (Old Order) division of 1871-72, and the M.B.C. (Brenneman) division of 1874; and a minor division occurred in 1923-24 when several groups (MC) left to join the Central Conference and the General Conference Church. The following discussion will treat the history by settlements and branches.

Adams County. The first Mennonite settlers in the state were Swiss Mennonites, two Baumgartner

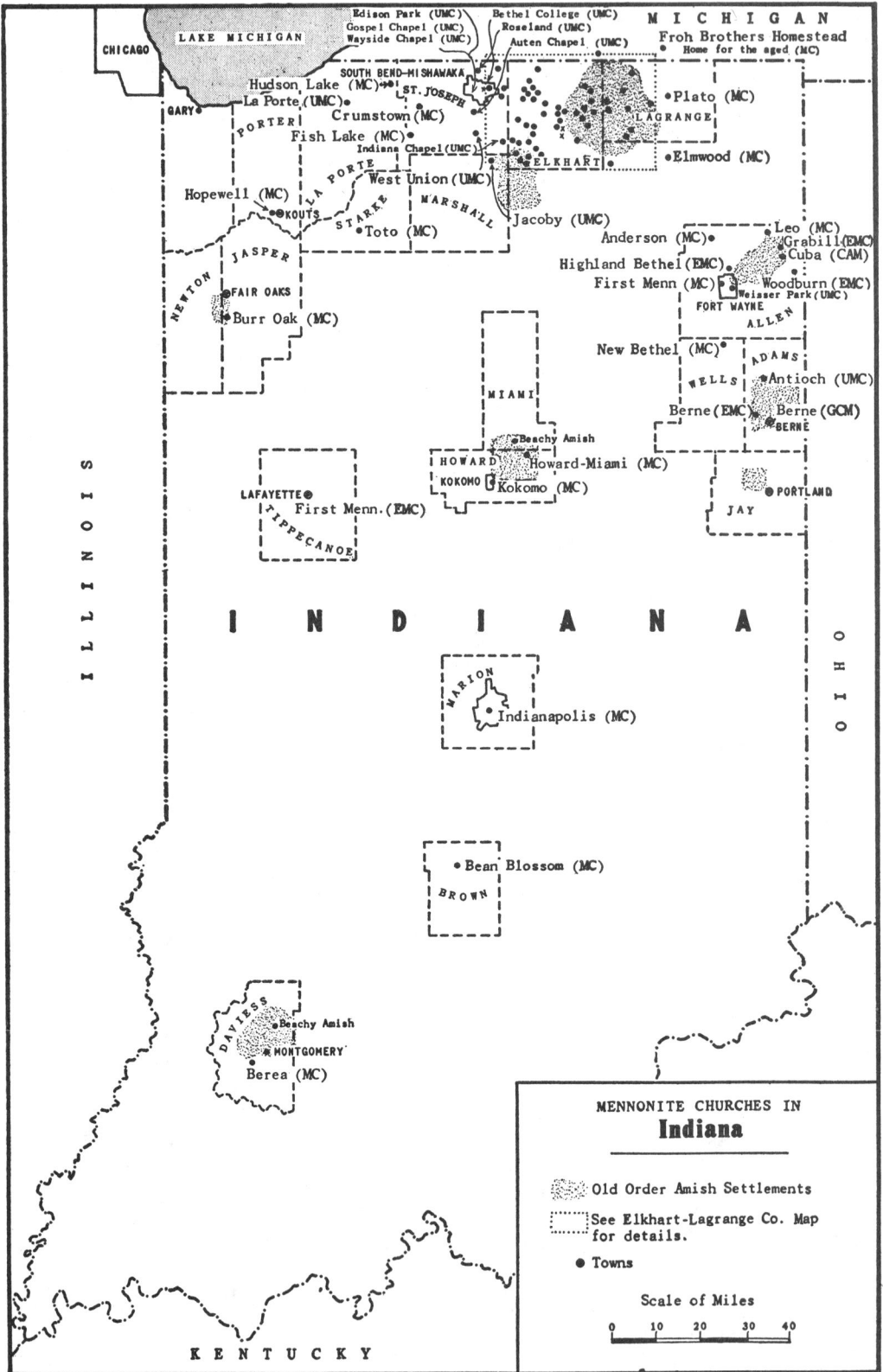

MICHIGAN

LAKE MICHIGAN

CHICAGO

Edison Park (UMC)
Gospel Chapel (UMC)
Wayside Chapel (UMC)

Bethel College (UMC)
Roseland (UMC)
Auten Chapel (UMC)

Froh Brothers Homestead
Home for the aged (MC)

SOUTH BEND-MISHAWAKA

Hudson Lake (MC)
La Porte (UMC)
Crumstown (MC)
ST. JOSEPH

GARY

PORTER

Fish Lake (MC)

Indiana Chapel (UMC)

ELKHART

LAGRANGE

Plato (MC)

Elmwood (MC)

LA PORTE

West Union (UMC)

Hopewell (MC)

KOUTS

MARSHALL

Jacoby (UMC)

Anderson (MC)

Leo (MC)
Grabill (EMC)
Cuba (CAM)

STARKE

Toto (MC)

Highland Bethel (EMC)
First Menn (MC)

Woodburn (EMC)
Weisser Park (UMC)

JASPER

NEWTON

FAIR OAKS

Burr Oak (MC)

FORT WAYNE

ALLEN

New Bethel (MC)

ADAMS

Antioch (UMC)

WELLS

Berne (EMC)

Berne (GCM)

BERNE

MIAMI

Beachy Amish

HOWARD

KOKOMO

Howard-Miami (MC)

Kokomo (MC)

PORTLAND

JAY

LAFAYETTE

First Menn. (EMC)

TIPPECANOE

INDIANA

MARION

Indianapolis (MC)

OHIO

Bean Blossom (MC)

BROWN

DAVIESS

Beachy Amish

MONTGOMERY

Berea (MC)

ILLINOIS

KENTUCKY

MENNONITE CHURCHES IN
Indiana

Old Order Amish Settlements

See Elkhart-Lagrange Co. Map
for details.

● Towns

Scale of Miles

0   10   20   30   40

brothers, Christian and Peter, who migrated from Wayne County, Ohio, to Adams County in 1838, just two years after Adams County was created, and located near Vera Cruz in Wells County, just across the Adams County line. The congregation which developed there was called the Baumgartner Church. In 1839 their aged father, Preacher David Baumgartner, followed his sons to Adams County. Other settlers followed, locating in Lick Township in the western portion of Adams County. In 1845 Christian Baumgartner was chosen by lot and ordained preacher to assist his father. By 1849 there were 16 families in this Baumgartner congregation, among them Augsburger, Baumgartner, Bieri, Bixler, Falb, Gilliom, Habegger, Hirschy, Luginbill, Merillat, Moser, Soldner, Stauffer, Steiner, and Suter. In 1852 a number of Swiss Mennonite families came directly from the Emmenthal in the Canton of Bern and affiliated themselves with the Baumgartner congregation in Adams County. This group brought along two preachers, Ulrich Kipfer and Matthias Strahm. In that same year, 1852, a colony of about eight Swiss Mennonites emigrated from the Swiss Jura mountain region to Adams County and settled near what is now Berne, Ind. Included in the group was a preacher, Peter S. Lehman, who had been chosen by lot and ordained in 1848. This group organized its own congregation instead of uniting with the Baumgartner congregation. In 1853 the aged David Baumgartner ordained Peter S. Lehman, who was selected by lot, to succeed him as elder, who then assumed oversight of both Baumgartner and Berne congregations. By 1858 there had been a three-way division in the Baumgartner congregation: (1) some members withdrew and united with the Evangelical Association; (2) Preacher Matthias Strahm and some members withdrew and joined the "New Mennist" (Apostolic Christian) Church; (3) the remainder of the members continued under the leadership of Ulrich Kipfer as preacher (Christian Baumgartner had asked for release as a preacher). About 1860 the Baumgartner congregation built its first church building. In 1865 Christian Augsburger was chosen by lot and ordained a preacher. In 1869 Preacher Christian Augsburger (1821-1903) and family, and the families of John Stauffer, Peter Steiner, and George Fox withdrew and organized a (MC) congregation. (In 1881 Augsburger attended the Indiana Mennonite Conference—MC—and asked for help in a church difficulty.) His group never prospered, and worshiped in homes and school buildings. The congregation which prospered in Adams County was the congregation at Berne, established in 1852 and served by Elder Peter S. Lehman. Its first meetinghouse was built in 1856-58. Both the Baumgartner and Berne congregations united with the General Conference in 1872. The Berne congregation built a new church in 1879 (enlarged 1886 and 1899), and also in 1911-12. The Baumgartner congregation was merged with the Berne church in 1886. At the same time a portion of the Berne group which had opposed various changes in the life of the church, and who had been having separate services for 15 years, were also reunited with the progressive group in Berne. The outstanding leader in this period was

S. F. Sprunger (q.v.). The Berne congregation has grown greatly, and now has a membership of 1,326. An Amish settlement was also made in Adams County (q.v.), beginning in 1850.

Perhaps the earliest Indiana Mennonite settlement outside Adams County was made at Arcadia in Hamilton County, beginning in 1838, by the Kauffman, Hildebrand, Gascho, and Correll families. No meetinghouse was built until 1881, the membership seems to have remained under 20, and the last member died in 1906.

Elkhart County Amish. The second settlement of Mennonites in northern Indiana was made by four Amish Mennonite families in 1841. They located in Clinton Twp., Elkhart Co. (created as a county in 1830), and Newbury Twp., Lagrange Co. (created as a county in 1832). Preacher Joseph and Elisabeth Miller and their four children, and Deacon Joseph and Barbara Borntreger and five children, came from Somerset Co., Pa., and settled in Clinton Twp., Elkhart Co. Daniel S. and Barbara Miller with their five children, and Christian and Elisabeth Borntreger with two children, also of Somerset Co., Pa., located in Newbury Twp., Lagrange Co. These four families arrived on the Elkhart Prairie in June 1841. In October the same year Emanuel Miller and wife of Ohio arrived in Lagrange County. A little later Preacher Isaac Smucker (Schmucker then) moved into the community, also the following and their families: Jacob Kaufmann, Isaac Miller, and Jonas Hochstetler. The first service of the Amish in Indiana was an Easter service held March 27, 1842, in the home of Preacher Joseph Miller in Clinton Twp., Elkhart Co. There were 14 members in the church at the time of this service. Other Amish settlers from Somerset County who settled in Lagrange County in 1842 were Abraham Herschberger, Joseph Herschberger, Johann Herschberger, Hans Miller, Heinrich Miller, Philip Weirich, Christian Hochstetler, and David Lehman. In the fall of 1842 the following Amish families from Holmes Co., Ohio, arrived in Elkhart County: Johann Miller, Joseph J. Miller, Jonas Miller, David H. Miller, Eli Tschoppen, Velti Yoder, David Schragen, and Deacon Peter Schragen. In 1843 Isaac Smucker was ordained by lot as the first Amish bishop in Indiana. He removed to McLean Co., Ill., in 1850 but returned to Indiana in 1856 and organized the Hawpatch congregation, now known as Maple Grove, Topeka, Ind.

Isaac Smucker was a progressive bishop, mild in discipline, and soon (1845) he was the leader of a less strict faction. But in 1847 a mediation committee resolved the controversy and the schism was healed for a time. In 1852 a preacher Jonas Troyer located in the Clinton district, which about the middle of the century had its separate church organization from that in Lagrange County, and that very year Isaac Smucker ordained him bishop. Bishop Jonas Troyer was also not as strict as some in maintaining the "old order" in the discipline of the church, and soon the Amish were threatened by division both in Elkhart and Lagrange counties. The schism was complete by 1854. Troyer introduced the new custom of holding Amish baptisms in streams, obviously to follow the New Testament precedent: Jesus, for example, was baptized in the Jordan River. In 1863 these progressives, who were destined to merge with the Mennonites (MC) of Indiana, built their first meetinghouse in Indiana, located in Clinton Township and known as Clinton Frame. The more conservative Amish, who tolerated fewer changes, came to be known as Old Order Amish. They also flourished, establishing congregations in Elkhart, Lagrange, Marshall, Newton, Jasper, Howard, Daviess, Adams, Brown, and Allen counties. Today there are approximately 40 congregations of Old Order Amish in Indiana, a remarkable growth from the feeble start of 1841 in Elkhart County. These Old Order Amish wear severely plain dress, wear the beard, use the German in their services, generally shun all modern methods of Christian education such as Sunday schools, evangelistic meetings, build no meetinghouses, drive horse and buggy rather than automobiles, and try to maintain their simple rural culture rather than to conform to what they think of as the "world."

Amish Mennonites. The progressive Amish Mennonites, represented by such early leaders as Isaac Smucker and Jonas Troyer, on the other hand, had no hesitation to allow their congregations to gradually drop the earlier garb of the Amish, shave off their beards, build meetinghouses, introduce the use of English into the services of the church, etc. All these changes were not made in a decade or a generation, but the process of cultural accommodation went on. Progressive Amish Mennonite congregations appeared from 1854 on in various communities of Indiana: in that very year a new congregation was formed in the Amish settlement of Howard-Miami counties, which had been started in 1848; in 1871 this progressive group built their first church building. The Forks Amish Mennonite meetinghouse in Newbury Twp., Lagrange Co., was built in 1864, seven years after the group began to meet separately from the Old Order Amish for their worship services. The Leo Amish Mennonite congregation in Allen County had its beginnings in 1861, its first preacher in 1875, and its first meetinghouse in 1887. The Pretty Prairie Amish Mennonite congregation in Lagrange County had its first settlers in 1864, and its first meetinghouse in 1872, but became extinct. The Hawpatch (Maple Grove now) Amish Mennonite congregation was organized in 1854, and built its first church in 1856. A small settlement of Amish Mennonites was made near Grovertown in Starke County in the 1860's, and a meetinghouse was erected. Bishop Jonas Troyer of Elkhart County lived there for a time. Bishop Isaac Smucker's son, Jonathan P. Smucker, was ordained deacon there in 1873, and preacher the same year. But the congregation died out soon after Smucker removed to Nappanee, Ind., a year or so after his ordination. The West Market Street Amish Mennonite congregation at Nappanee was organized in the 1870's, and in 1875 J. P. Smucker was ordained bishop of the congregation there. The first church building was erected in 1877. A small Amish Mennonite congregation was organized in the Adams County Amish settlement (*q.v.*), which congregation erected a meetinghouse in 1870, but soon became extinct. There were former-

ly Amish settlements in the Peru area and in Clinton County near Edna Mills.

Elkhart County Mennonites. The first Mennonite settlers (not Amish Mennonites) in Elkhart County were John Smith and his son Joseph from Medina Co., Ohio, who settled in Harrison Township, nine miles south and one mile east of Elkhart. Smith bought the farm in 1843 but did not locate on it until the fall of 1845. About the same time Jacob Strohm settled in the same vicinity, having also come from Ohio. In the spring of 1845 the families of Bishop Martin Hoover (1760-1850), his son John Hoover, and Christian Henning removed from Medina Co., Ohio, and also settled in Harrison Township. During the year 1848, 27 more families came to Harrison Township from Wayne, Columbiana, Medina, and Mahoning counties in Ohio, although most of these people were originally from Pennsylvania. Included in the 1848 settlers were Preacher Jacob Wisler (1808-89) from Columbiana Co., Ohio, and Preacher Jacob Christophel (1783-1868), who had left the Rhenish Palatinate in 1818, lived for a time in western Pennsylvania, had been ordained as preacher in Allegheny Co., Pa., in 1827, and had lived for a time in Columbiana Co., Ohio. The first service of the Harrison Township Mennonites, the Yellow Creek congregation, was held in a schoolhouse about a half mile north of the present village of Southwest on Ascension Day, 1848, with 16 people present. Services were held biweekly thereafter. The first log church building was erected in 1849 on the lot now occupied by the Wisler Yellow Creek (frame) meetinghouse. Before his death in 1849 Bishop Hoover had ordained Jacob Wisler as his successor in the bishop oversight of the Mennonites of Elkhart County. For many years Yellow Creek was the Mennonite center in Indiana, and the other churches were merely outposts of the Yellow Creek congregation. All baptisms, ordinations, and communion services were held at Yellow Creek for many years. In 1861 over 600 persons partook of the communion emblems. The (fall) meetings of the Conference were also held in the Yellow Creek meetinghouse.

Within a year or two after the building of the Yellow Creek meetinghouse, there were other small concentrations of Mennonites in outlying districts which occasioned the building of churches or the holding of biweekly services in schoolhouses on the Sundays when no services were held at Yellow Creek. Daniel Moyer (1812-64), who was born in Bucks Co., Pa., but had grown to manhood in Butler Co., Pa., and had lived after his marriage in Ashland Co., Ohio, removed to Elkhart Co., Ind., to a farm west of Jamestown. About 1850 he was ordained as a preacher at Yellow Creek. Soon he and others were worshiping in a log schoolhouse a mile or less north of the present Olive Church. The Olive cemetery was platted in 1855. The new meetinghouse (Olive) on the Baugo was erected in 1862. The Holdeman settlement west of Wakarusa was also started by 1850, and the first log meetinghouse erected in 1851. The settlement of Mennonites in Clinton Township (Clinton Brick) was started as early as 1845, and the first log meetinghouse built in 1854. Mennonites began to locate in

DeKalb County about 1850, but it was not until 1883 that they erected their first Pleasant Valley meetinghouse. This group later became extinct. By 1851 Mennonites had begun to locate in Newbury Twp., Lagrange Co., and in 1874 they erected the Shore meetinghouse. The Emma congregation, a branch of Shore, is also located in Newbury Township. The congregation was organized in 1901 and a church building erected at once. In 1853 Dutch Mennonites from Balk in Friesland migrated to America and settled west of New Paris, Ind. For many years they worshiped in private homes, then in the Neff schoolhouse, and finally in the Christophel and Blosser log meetinghouses. At last, in 1889, the Salem meetinghouse was erected, half of the members being of the Dutch Mennonite settlement. Several Mennonite families located at Rolling Prairie, La Porte County, in the 1850's, but no congregation developed and the settlement died out. About 1853 Mennonites from Ohio and Pennsylvania began to locate in Clay and Owen counties, Indiana, the first known Mennonite settler being Bishop Daniel Funk, then of Logan Co., Ohio, but a Pennsylvanian by birth. The congregation was called Bowers in the course of time, named after Preacher Jacob Bower (Bauer). The first meetinghouse was built in 1861. Three years later the membership was at least 70 with four ministers and two young deacons, but it soon died out. The Gar Creek settlement in Allen County, eleven miles east of Fort Wayne, was started about 1854 but never had its own meetinghouse; a union house of worship was used. About 1865 the Mennonite settlement at Lakeville in St. Joseph County began. Resident ministers who later served there were Peter Y. Lehman, and Michael W. Shank (1833-1905), grandfather of Clarence Shank of the Olive congregation; the meetinghouse was a union building.

One of the most influential leaders in the Mennonite Church (MC), both in Elkhart County and in the church as a whole, was John F. Funk (*q.v.*, 1835-1930), who located in Elkhart in 1867 and founded the Prairie Street Mennonite Church. This congregation built its first meetinghouse in 1871.

It is to be remembered that from the 1840's until 1916 the Mennonites were of two original types: Mennonite and Amish. And from 1854 the progressive Amish Mennonites, in contrast with the Old Order Amish, gradually approached closer to the Mennonites in doctrine and practice, so that in 1917 the two conferences, Indiana-Michigan Mennonite and Indiana-Michigan Amish Mennonite, merged. But even prior to the merger there was in a few cases actually joint conference and bishop care of certain congregations, e.g., the weak Barker Street (*q.v.*) Church. Both Mennonites and Amish Mennonites formed the Middlebury Sunday school (1903) and congregation (1904), but the affiliation was Amish Mennonite through the choice of an Amish Mennonite bishop. (The first Middlebury Amish Mennonite church building was built in 1911.) When Goshen College located in Goshen (from Elkhart) in 1903 a congregation of both Mennonites and Amish Mennonites was formed with a bishop from each of the two groups furnishing joint bishop oversight.

Literary Societies were organized in many of the congregations (MC) of northern Indiana in 1913-28. An over-all organization of the literaries was effected in 1924 and named Northern Indiana Literary Convention; its constitution was adopted in 1927. In 1949 the convention became affiliated with the nation-wide Mennonite Youth Fellowship (MC); consequently a new constitution was written for the convention in that year, reconstituting the convention into a conference-wide MYF organization. This new constitution was adopted in 1950, whereupon the organization took the name Indiana-Michigan Mennonite Youth Fellowship.

Mission Churches (MC). The discovery of a few families of scattered Mennonites in a distant county without church privileges caused the District Mission Board of the merged conferences (organized 1911) to place pastors in such needy fields, and to erect small houses of worship. The Burr Oak congregation near Rensselaer in Jasper County was begun in 1918, and the first church building built in 1925. The Berea congregation in Daviess County was founded in 1920, and a church built in 1925. More recent mission outposts, sponsored either by the district mission board or by congregations, and often created in purely non-Mennonite communities to evangelize the unchurched, are as follows: *Elkhart County:* Belmont, Elkhart, 1929; North Goshen, 1936; East Goshen, 1942; Locust Grove, Elkhart, 1942; Benton, 1944; Sunnyside, Dunlap, 1947; Roselawn, Elkhart, 1949; *St. Joseph County:* Crumstown, 1933; Osceola, 1951; *Lagrange County:* Marion, Howe, 1944; Plato, 1949; *Allen County:* Anderson, *ca.* 1941; *Starke County:* Toto, Knox, 1948; English Lake, 1949; *Kosciusko County:* Syracuse, 1947; *Brown County:* Bean Blossom, 1945; *Wells County:* New Bethel, Ossian, 1949; *Howard County:* Kokomo, 1947; *La Porte County:* Hudson Lake, 1950; Fish Lake, *ca.* 1950; *Noble County:* Kendallville, 1953; *Morgan County:* Mahalasville, 1951; *Daviess County:* Washington, 1953. The total membership of the Mennonite congregations in Indiana (MC) is now (1954) about 6,500, which is more than three fourths of the Indiana-Michigan Mennonite Conference (MC) membership.

General Conference Churches. There are seven congregations of the General Conference Mennonite Church in Indiana. In Elkhart County are Silver Street, a schism from the Clinton Frame congregation (MC) in 1892, and which at present has 153 members, the Eighth Street Church in Goshen, with 304 members, the Warren Street Mennonite Church in Middlebury, having 84 members, and the First Mennonite in Nappanee, with 165 members. In Newton County is a small congregation, Zion at Goodland, with its 58 members, an Alsatian group which has been French-speaking; Topeka in Lagrange County has 235 members. The above five congregations (except Nappanee) are affiliated with the Central Conference (GCM). The Swiss congregation at Berne in Adams County has 1,326 members, and the Nappanee congregation in Elkhart County has 165 members: these two churches are affiliated with the Middle District Conference (GCM). The Berne congregation comprises about 60 per cent of all the G. C. Mennonites in Indiana.

All of these but the Berne and Goodland congregations arose as schisms from M.C. congregations, or were daughters of the schismatic groups.

Evangelical Mennonite Congregations. Formerly known as Defenseless Mennonites, this group arose in Indiana in the years 1864-66 under the leadership of an Amish bishop of Geneva, Adams County, named Henry Egly. Bishop Egly, who experienced a spiritual awakening, led half his congregation into the new group. There are now five congregations of the Evangelical Mennonites in the state: Berne in Adams County (237 members); Fort Wayne (43 members), Grabill (143 members), and Woodburn (179) in Allen County; and Lafayette in Tippecanoe County with 64 members: a total of about 670 in the state. Lafayette is the continuation of a former rural church. The Amish Mennonite settlement at Edna Mills in Clinton County was established by Gingrich, Ehresman, etc., families. The rural Defenseless Church building was erected in 1885 in Tippecanoe County. The old Amish cemetery is located south of Edna Mills, a town about eight miles east of Lafayette.

Old Order Mennonites. The first Mennonite bishop ordained in Indiana, Jacob Wisler of the Yellow Creek congregation in Elkhart County, seceded from the Indiana Mennonite Conference (MC) in 1872, because he could not tolerate the numerous changes in church life, such as the adoption of Sunday schools, four-part singing, evening meetings, the loss of the German language in the church services, and a more favorable attitude toward evangelistic meetings. The "Wisler Mennonites" have not prospered since their founding in 1872. They have had some internal difficulties, and have found it difficult to know what new cultural items to tolerate. In 1907 they divided into two groups, ostensibly over the use of telephones. The more conservative group, which refused to allow the installation of telephones in their homes, also opposed the use of automobiles in later years when they became common. In recent years there has been a degree of unrest in the more conservative group, with a partial shifting of members to the more progressive group, but there are still only two groups in Indiana. The stricter group, whose bishop is William G. Weaver, holds services at three points: County Line Church near Wakarusa; Yellow Creek (frame) Church; and Blosser's Church near Nappanee. Membership in the district totals 102. The more progressive group, whose bishop is William Ramer, holds services every two weeks at Yellow Creek, and every two weeks at Blosser's. (The two groups alternate in the use of their church buildings.) The Ramer group has 150 members. The total Old Order membership is 252.

United Missionary Church (formerly Mennonite Brethren in Christ). Three years after Wisler and his followers withdrew from the Indiana Mennonite Conference (MC) because it was too progressive, Daniel Brenneman seceded in 1874 because it was not progressive enough. He felt that the time had come to launch out in evangelistic work, to emphasize revivals, and the like. He and his followers formed what is now known as the United Missionary Church, the first congregation being Bethel,

eight miles south of Elkhart. This denomination is represented in Indiana by about 27 congregations, all in the northern area of the state, 13 of them with 50 members or less. The membership in Indiana totaled 2,388 in 1953. The congregations and locations are as follows: Antioch, west of Decatur; Auten Chapel, west of South Bend; Bethel, south of Elkhart; Beulah and Zion in Elkhart; Brenneman Memorial and Sunnyfield in Goshen; Osolo, north of Elkhart; Cedar Road, Osceola; Mishawaka; Gospel Center and Edison Park in South Bend; Roseland, north of South Bend; Granger; West Union, south of South Bend; Indiana Chapel, north of Bremen; Bremen; Wakarusa; Oak Grove, west of Wakarusa; Nappanee; Foraker; Lagrange; Garver Lake; Jacoby; South West, west of Goshen; Wayside Chapel; Weisser Park, Fort Wayne.

Conservative Mennonites (formerly Conservative Amish Mennonites). This group was organized as a body intermediate between the Old Order Amish and the Mennonite Church (MC). Although the conference was not organized until 1910, the Conservative Mennonites had been in existence for several decades (since 1880). In 1908 the members in Elkhart County totaled only 35. Today they have over 600 members in five congregations in this county: Griner, Townline, Pleasant Grove, and River View, all in the general area about Middlebury, Ind., and a newly organized (1954) congregation northeast of Nappanee. They also have a congregation of 170 members at Cuba near Grabill in Allen County. The name Amish was dropped in 1955.

Burkholder Amish Mennonites. A more recent body of progressive Amish is that led by Bishop David O. Burkholder of near Nappanee, Ind. There are four congregations of his followers in Indiana: one near Nappanee, and one east of Goshen, both in Elkhart County; one in Miami County; and one in Daviess County. These four congregations have memberships running from 50 to 100 each, a total of about 320. They belong to the Beachy Amish group.

Missionary Church Association. This small body seceded from the Evangelical Mennonite Church (it was then called Defenseless Mennonite) in 1896-98 under the leadership of Joseph E. Ramseyer. It has 15 congregations in Indiana, with 1,739 members, located in Angola, Auburn, Berne (2), Decatur, Fort Wayne (5), Frankfort, Grabill, Mooresville, Woodburn, and Yoder.

Statistical Summary. The following summary will give a picture of the Mennonite membership in Indiana by groups in 1953. (All figures refer to baptized members; unbaptized children are not included.) Mennonite Church (MC), 6,500; General Conference Mennonites, 2,325; Old Order Amish Mennonites, 3,100; Evangelical Mennonites, 670; United Missionary Church, 2,300; Old Order Mennonites, 260; Conservative Mennonites, 770; Burkholder Amish Mennonites, 320; and Missionary Church Association, 1,739. The total of those who still call themselves Mennonites is 13,945.

The Mennonite institutions established in Indiana have been: Mennonite Publishing Co. (*q.v.,* MC) at Elkhart, 1867-1925 (most of its business sold in

1908 to the Mennonite Publishing House at Scottdale, Pa.); Goshen College (MC) at Goshen, 1903-
, previously Elkhart Institute at Elkhart 1894-1903;
Bethel College, South Bend (UMC) 1945- ; Fort
Wayne Bible College (Missionary Church Association) 1904- ; Bethany Christian High School (MC)
at Goshen 1954- .   J.C.W.

J. E. Borntreger, *Eine Geschichte der ersten Ansiedlung der Amischen Mennoniten und die Gründung ihrer
ersten Gemeinde im Staate Indiana, nebst einer kurzen
Erklärung über die Spaltung, die in dieser Gemeinde
geschehen ist* (Elkhart, 1907); *History of Elkhart County,
Indiana* (Chicago, 1881); *Minutes of the Indiana-
Michigan Mennonite Conference 1864-1929;* E. Sprunger,
The First Hundred Years [of the Berne Swiss Com-
munity] (Berne, 1938); *ML* II, 411-13.

Indiana Chapel United Missionary Church, located
four miles southeast of Lakeville, Marshall Co., Ind.,
was organized in 1896. Among the early leaders
were John Rouch and Fred Schutz. In 1953 the
membership was 62, mostly rural, with Wayne
Gerber serving as pastor.   P.E.WA.

Indiana Conference of the United Missionary
Church had its origins in the "Indiana, Michigan,
and Ohio Evangelical United Mennonite Conference." The date of its organization is not clear but
it met in its "sixth annual conference" in Elkhart
Co., Ind., in September 1880. After the Evangelical
United Mennonites became the Mennonite Brethren
in Christ in 1883, the first annual "Conference of
the Mennonite Brethren in Christ of Indiana, Ohio,
Michigan and the West" held its session in Miami
Co., Ohio, in March 1884. After Ohio became a
separate conference in 1942 the Indiana Conference
was confined to one state. The conference meets
annually during the last week of June on its camp-
grounds 7½ miles south of Elkhart. Its committees
are executive, youth, budget, camp meetings, foreign
missions, peace, and reading course examiners. In
1955 its 37 congregations had 2,507 members. The
district superintendent was Kenneth Geiger and the
secretary Gordon Bacon.   M.G.

Indiana-Michigan Amish Mennonite Conference
(1888-1917) was the first of three Amish Mennonite
conferences to be organized after the Amish Mennonite general conference (*Diener-Versammlung*
1862-78, *q.v.*) no longer met and it was the first to
unite with its district Mennonite conference. The
others were the Western A.M. (*q.v.*) (1890-1920)
and the Eastern A.M. (*q.v.*) (1883-1927). The
Indiana-Michigan A.M. Conference held its first
meeting in the Maple Grove Church southwest of
Topeka, Ind., on April 7, 1888. Several of the members of the Amish Mennonite Conference participated in the discussions of the Indiana Mennonite Conference held in October of the same year when
that body passed a resolution favoring a Mennonite
general conference. From the beginning, ministers
of each conference were welcomed in the other and
in the years immediately preceding the merger in
1917 the A.M. Conference was referred to as the
"spring conference" and the Mennonite as the "fall
conference." Before the merger the two conferences
co-operated in organizing a district mission board in
1911. In the year before the merger (1916) the Ind.-

Mich. A.M. Conference reported 11 congregations,
1,539 members, 5 bishops, 13 ministers, and 9 deacons; the Ind.-Mich. Mennonite Conference, 1,728
members (counting the Goshen College joint congregation of 195 members), 24 bishops and deacons,
and 29 ministers. The 11 congregations of the A.M.
conference in 1916 were: Indiana—Forks, Clinton
Frame, Nappanee, Middlebury, Leo, Maple Grove
(Topeka), Howard-Miami, Linn Grove; Michigan—
Fairview, Sunnyside (Comins), Union (Chief).

In the first years after organization Bishop J. P.
Smucker of Nappanee served as moderator or assistant moderator and took an active part in organizational and evangelistic activities. Other leading bishops of the conference were D. D. Miller of
Middlebury; D. J. Johns of Goshen; and Jonathan
Kurtz of Ligonier. These three brethren took a
very active part in promoting the Elkhart Institute (*q.v.*), the first educational effort of the Mennonite Church (MC). D. D. Miller was elected
moderator of the merged conference.   J.S.U.

Indiana-Michigan Mennonite Conference (MC) resulted from the merger of two earlier conferences
in 1916; the Indiana-Michigan Mennonite Conference, and the Indiana-Michigan Amish Mennonite
Conference. The Mennonite (MC) body was at first,
in the 1850's, more or less an extension of the Ohio
Mennonite Conference and was called the Indiana
Conference. It was customary for the Ohio ministers to meet with the Indiana ministers in the fall,
and the Indiana ministers met with the Ohio ministers in the spring. The first such conference of
which minutes have been preserved was held at the
Yellow Creek meetinghouse Oct. 14, 1864. The next
available minutes are of 1867, then 1870. The minutes of 1895 are headed "Indiana-Michigan Conference," although there was no official action to add
the name Michigan to the name of the conference.
The first Indiana-Michigan Amish Mennonite Conference was held at the Maple Grove ("Hawpatch")
A.M. Church near Topeka, Ind., on April 7, 1888.
Thereafter the Amish Mennonite Conference was
the "Spring Conference," and the Mennonite Conference was the "Fall Conference." A close spirit of
fellowship and good will prevailed between the
spring and fall conferences for many years, and there
was considerable attendance at both conferences by
ministers of the other conference. The time finally
came when both conferences appointed a "Committee on Conference Union," which met Feb. 13, 1913.
The work of the committee was well received by
both conferences, and a new *Constitution, Rules, and
Discipline* was prepared, printed, and submitted to
the congregations for ratification. The spring conference of 1916 adopted the new discipline on the
basis of the congregational vote and declared it as
being in effect as of June 8, 1916. The fall conference
of 1916 reported a vote of 1,319 in favor, and 155
opposed, and on that basis also adopted it and declared it to be in effect as of Oct. 12, 1916. Since
1917 the united conference has met annually the first
Wednesday in June.

The Indiana Mennonite (fall) Conference was not
only intimately associated with the Ohio Conference, being for many years a sort of fall meeting of

the same group which met in Ohio in the spring, but it also felt a degree of responsibility for the weak congregations farther west. In 1872, for example, Bishop Daniel Brundage, who for a decade had been a preacher in the Holdeman congregation in Indiana, and who was then living in Missouri, asked permission of the Indiana (and Ohio) Conference in session at the Yellow Creek meetinghouse west of Goshen, Ind., to hold a conference in the fall of each year in Missouri. The request was granted. In fact this was but following the precedent set in 1871 when the Indiana (and Ohio) ministers, also in session at Yellow Creek, granted to "the western brethren" permission to form a "new conference district." The conference was to meet "at a time to be hereafter decided upon in Whiteside County, Illinois." This meeting was held in the Science Ridge meetinghouse near Sterling, Ill., in 1872, the first meeting of the Illinois Mennonite Conference.

The concerns of the Indiana Mennonite Conference related mostly to the year by year problems which the bishops, preachers, and deacons faced, such as whether Mennonites ought to vote in political elections, how best to resist worldliness in attire, whether the Bible calls upon Christians to break social fellowship ("shun") with those who have been excommunicated, how to give pastoral care to weak congregations and scattered members, whether it would not be advisable to have a general conference of all the Mennonites (MC) in the country (1864), how to deal with divorced and remarried people, etc. By the fall of 1868 there was evidently enough autonomy in the Indiana Conference that it felt it necessary to "adopt entire" the resolutions of the Ohio Conference which had been adopted in its spring session of 1868. In 1887, when the Conference was considering the eligibility for membership on the part of a divorced man who was planning to marry a sister in the church, the decisive addresses were made by Bishops John F. Funk of Indiana, and Henry Nice of Illinois. Deacon Joseph Holdeman supported them. The question was posed by Preacher Henry Good of Ohio. (It was decided that the man be received as a member.)

During the first decades of the life of the conference, it was customary for the ordained men to come quietly together with no appointed moderator and no prepared program. The older bishops led in messages of exhortation after the singing of one or more hymns. The entire meeting was conducted in the Pennsylvania German dialect, with the exception of the hymns and Scripture reading, which were in High German. The opening prayer was silent. After the devotional service was over, one or more bishops exhorted the ministers to hold fast to the historic and Biblical principles of the brotherhood. Anyone was then free to make any further remarks or to bring questions before the group for counsel and decision. If the decisions met with too much opposition in the congregations, the ministers did not hesitate to reverse themselves at a later conference. In 1871, for example, the conference urged that (first) cousins should not marry. Because this counsel "caused considerable dissatisfaction," the conference of 1873 decided to leave it to the conscience of the individuals involved "so far as state laws do not prohibit such marriages."

Especially in the 1870's the Indiana Mennonite Conference struggled long and hard with the problems occasioned by the transition from old to new customs relating to new methods of Christian work, the transition from German to English, and the like. Bishop Jacob Wisler (1808-89) of Yellow Creek and his followers seceded from conference in 1871 because it supported the introduction of Sunday schools, and tolerated other changes from the "old order." Thus the Wisler or Old Order Mennonite branch had its beginning. On the other hand, evidently in an effort to prevent another division (although it may have contributed to the Daniel Brenneman secession of 1874), the conference in 1872 decided that calling regular prayer meetings "can not be tolerated."

Gradually the conference began to organize more fully and thus acquire its present form. In the meeting of Oct. 9, 1885, the conference authorized the bishops thereafter to meet on the Thursday afternoon preceding conference to receive in writing all questions to be submitted on the day of conference. Six years later, in 1891, the conference took the new step of choosing a moderator and a secretary as the first item of business for the day. In 1898 it was further decided to "elect a permanent secretary whose duty it shall be to keep a record of the proceedings of conference in a book for that special purpose. He shall serve for a term of three years." In 1904 the spring (Amish Mennonite) conference began to elect a moderator for the next annual meeting of conference, and in 1906 the fall (Mennonite) conference followed suit. Little mention is made of anything like an executive committee in either conference before the merger of 1916. But thereafter the power of the Executive Committee of Conference grew continually until Indiana-Michigan vested more power in its elected Executive Committee of five members than perhaps any other district conference of the Mennonite Church (MC). The man most responsible for this centralization of power was J. K. Bixler (1877-1939), who represented the fall (Mennonite) conference prior to the merger. Other leaders who helped form the modern Mennonite Church of the midwest were Bishop John F. Funk (1835-1930), Bishop David Burkholder (1835-1923), Preacher J. S. Hartzler (1857-1953), Bishop D. A. Yoder (1883-   ), Bishop O. S. Hostetler (1874-   ), and Deacon George L. Bender (1867-1921). On the side of the spring (Amish) conference should be mentioned Bishop Jonathan Kurtz (1848-1940), Bishop D. D. Miller (1864-1955), Bishop D. J. Johns (1850-1942), and Preacher Ira S. Johns (1879-1956). Since the 1940's the conference has tended to be more democratic, and to recognize more fully the rights of bishops and congregations.

At present (1954) the Indiana-Michigan Mennonite Conference includes 66 congregations and mission stations having a total of 8,076 members, served by 31 bishops, 83 ministers, and 34 deacons. In Indiana there are 36 congregations and missions with 6,429 members: 18 in Elkhart County, 6 in Lagrange, 3 in Allen, 2 mission outposts in La

Porte, and one congregation or mission in each of the following counties: Wells, Starke, Porter, Jasper, St. Joseph, Noble, and Daviess. In Michigan there are 30 congregations and missions with 1,563 members; scattered congregations in the following counties: Emmet, Newaygo, Gratiot, Oscoda, Midland, St. Joseph, and Kent; and mission stations in Emmet, Antrim, Manistee, Wayne, Livingston, Lapeer, St. Joseph, Montcalm, Jackson, Huron, Saginaw, and Calhoun counties; as well as 11 mission stations in the Upper Peninsula. There are also three mission points in Kentucky with 34 members, and one in International Falls, Minn., with 52 members.

Within and subject to the conference are also the following semiautonomous organizations: the Indiana-Michigan Mennonite Mission Board (q.v., founded in 1911), operating a chain of rural home mission stations from Kentucky to Northern Michigan; the Christian Workers' Conference, before 1943 called the Sunday School Conference, with its origins going back to 1894; the Women's Missionary and Service Auxiliary (organized in 1917); and the Mennonite Youth Fellowship (founded in 1949, but actually a continuation of the Northern Indiana Literary Convention founded in 1924). The conference also owns and operates Bethany Christian High School at Waterford, south of Goshen, Ind. (founded in 1954). Completely autonomous is the Mennonite Aid Association (founded in 1911), a mutual aid property insurance organization.   J.C.W.

Minutes of the Indiana-Michigan Mennonite Conference 1864-1929 (Scottdale, n.d.), which also contain the minutes of the Ind.-Mich. A.M. Conference, 1888-1916. The conference minutes since 1929 have been published as annual reports in booklet form.

Indiana-Michigan Mennonite Mission Board, an agency of the Indiana-Michigan Mennonite Conference (MC), was organized on Dec. 1, 1911, with the name "Mission Board of the Indiana-Michigan Mennonite Conference." Its first executive committee consisted of N. E. Byers, pres.; B. B. King, vice-pres.; G. L. Bender, treas.; Jacob K. Bixler, sec.; and O. S. Hostetler, fifth member. On Oct. 18, 1913, it was reorganized as the Indiana-Michigan District Mennonite Mission Board. The word "District" was dropped from the name on June 2, 1914. The board was incorporated in Indiana on Aug. 13, 1914, and admitted to do business in Michigan on Dec. 18, 1923. There are at present (1955) 27 mission stations under the board, located in Indiana, Michigan, and Kentucky. It publishes the *Gospel Evangel,* formerly the *Rural Evangel.* During the last fiscal year the board spent $118,293.11.   P.J.M.

Indiantown Mennonite Church (MC), located in northern Lancaster Co., Pa., a member of the Lancaster Mennonite Conference, was the central point for the eastern end of the Hammer Creek-Indiantown District. After worshiping for nine decades in eight private homes, meetinghouses were built in 1819 at both Hammer Creek and Indiantown (the latter in the last Indian reservation in this county). The congregation grew until the middle of the 19th century, when the Reformed Mennonites made a sizable schism. In more recent years there have been additions from Weaverland and from the Old

Order Mennonites, and the congregation is growing. The membership in 1954 was 150. Denver, once a preaching point, is now a thriving outpost of Indiantown. The earlier preachers included Christian Risser, Abraham Brubaker, John R. and Jonas H. Hess, and more recently Noah Hurst, Henry P. Fox, and Isaac Gehman, with Amos S. Horst and Mahlon M. Zimmerman as bishops, and Jacob M. Hurst as deacon.   I.D.L.

Indonesia, formerly the Dutch East Indies, since Dec. 29, 1949, a republic (1950 pop. 80 million), a group of islands in the Malay Archipelago in the Indian and Pacific oceans, of which Java (pop. 49 million and area 50,000 sq. mi.) is the most densely populated tropical country, although Sumatra (pop. 11,000 and area 163,557 sq. mi.) is larger. The Dutch Mennonites, who had previously supported the mission work of other denominations, opened a mission in Java (q.v.) in 1847, which was extended to include Sumatra (q.v.) in 1871 among the Battak (q.v.). This was the first Mennonite mission among non-Christian peoples, which was followed by other missions established in the last quarter of the 19th century by American Mennonite bodies.

Out of this mission work have developed two Mennonite Conferences in eastern Java, the Malay Church with 11 congregations, a membership of 2,410, and a Bible school at Pati, and the Chinese Church with 9 congregations and a membership of ca. 1,500. There is also a small Mennonite church in Sumatra with 101 members in four places.

The Mennonite Central Committee began a relief program in the Pati area in 1949 which was still in operation in 1956. A small relief program was also operated in a region 150 miles south of Medan, Sumatra, in 1948.   H.S.B.

Industrial Home Journal, The, was founded in March 1906 as an 8-page monthly to promote the Industrial School and Hygiene Home for the Friendless (q.v.). The "proprietor and editor" was T. H. Long. The last issue of the Bethel College Historical Library set is dated July 1907.   C.K.

Industrial School and Hygiene Home for Friendless Persons was chartered as a charitable institution by the State of Kansas on Sept. 15, 1890, as a home for orphan children. The pattern of administration was that of a corporation. Although the charter was not granted to the church the members of the corporation and of the Board of Directors were almost exclusively Krimmer Mennonite Brethren, and the institution has always been considered a home mission project of this group, who also assumed the responsibility of providing necessary funds. At the annual conference held on Oct. 19, 1896, at the Gnadenau Church near Hillsboro, Kan., it was announced that the building was ready to begin the work with 20 children, preferably Kansas children. The establishment was motivated and aided by M. E. Gordon, River Brethren of Pennsylvania, who visited the community in 1880 and decided that it would be an excellent location for such an institution. In the beginning a few members of the Board of Directors were River Brethren. Amanda Dohner, a member

MENNONITE CHURCHES IN

Indonesia

- Mennonite congregations
★ Junior High Schools
◊ Medical Clinics

Scale of Miles

0 25 50 75 100   200   300   400

Scale of Miles

0   5   10   20

Scale of Miles

0   10   20

1500 miles to Mennonite Mission in Dutch Mennonite Peninsula, Vogelkop New Guinea.

MOUNT MURIA

Djuana
Pati (Seminary) ★
Kajuapu ◊
Kudus ★
Margoredjo ★
Kedungpendjalin ◊
Taju
Japara ★
Demak
Semarang
Surabaya
Jakarta
Palembang
Singapore
Medan
Natal

JAVA SEA

JAVA

MALAYA

SUMATRA

INDIAN OCEAN

Mennonite Churches in Sumatra (Mandailing Area)
1. Bonan-dolak
2. Penjabungan
3. Kota-nopan
4. Muara-sipongi
5. Pakantan

Mennonite congregations in Java

Javanese Church
1. Pati
2. Djuana
3. Kudus
4. Kajuapu
5. Japara (Djepara)
6. Ngeling
7. Kedungpendjalin
8. Balongkodok
9. Bondo
10. Margokerto
11. Tembelang
12. Bandunghardjo
13. Kelet
14. Margoredjo
15. Tegalombo
16. Banjutowo
17. Puntjil
18. Karangsari
19. Brodjol

Chinese Church
20. Kudus
21. Pati
22. Japara (Djepara)
23. Welahan
24. Petjanga'an
25. Bangsri
26. Taju
27. Blora
28. Demak

of a River Brethren community in Pennsylvania, served as the first matron in the home.

Beginning in 1889 homeless children were brought in from Chicago; 60 to 80 children filled it to capacity. About 1910-15 the orphanage gradually became a home for the aged. Until 1946, when the building was destroyed by fire, it served as a home for the aged under the Krimmer Mennonite Brethren Conference. In 1915 the K.M.B. Conference obtained a new charter and changed the name to Salem Home. After the fire the Salem Home was moved to Hillsboro and housed in a small annex of the Salem Hospital. With completion of the new hospital building now under construction the whole building now utilized by Salem Hospital will become the Salem Home for Aged People (q.v.). M.S.H.

Gemeindeblatt und Waisenheim (Hillsboro, Kan.) 1894 ff.; *Jahrbuch der Krimmer Mennoniten Brüdergemeinde*, 1894 ff.

Industry Among Mennonites *in Russia (and Prussia)*. The industrial enterprises of the Mennonites in general have been presented in the article **Business**, with the exception of Prussia and Russia. Although the Mennonites here were located mostly in rural areas, some significant industries were developed. From the earliest days of the Mennonite settlements in Danzig and Prussia they continually encountered difficulties in finding occupations open to them, since they were not considered citizens. The regulations and edicts issued against them indicate what the occupations were. Among the industries were weaving (*Bortenwirker*) and brewing. In 1749 Danzig had ten Mennonite businessmen, numerous weavers, dyers, brewers, and small craftsmen like shoemakers, tailors, and merchants. The list of Mennonites who left Prussia to go to Russia after 1788 gives a fairly good review of the occupational backgrounds. There were some large estate owners, small-scale farmers, store owners, laborers, and a considerable number of craftsmen, who could possibly be considered the prospective industrialists in Russia. During the 18th and 19th centuries many of the Mennonites of Danzig, Königsberg, and other cities were in business and banking. A. Zimmerman (d. 1919) of Danzig owned a foundry.

In Russia industrial enterprises on a large scale originated among the Mennonites during the second half of the 19th century, particularly as a result of a large-scale farming, which necessitated the production of technical, highly developed agricultural machinery in a country where it was not available. Large-scale wheat raising produced a flourishing milling industry. Among the first industries developed by the Mennonites in Russia was silk production, which, however, disappeared when grain raising overshadowed all other branches of agriculture.

The first large-scale industrialist was P. H. Lepp of Chortitza, who started a foundry in 1860, with A. Koop and C. H. Hildebrand as his apprentices. Chortitza remained the industrial center of the Mennonites. Other places were Alexandrovsk, Halbstadt, and New York. In 1911 the eight largest Mennonite factories producing agricultural machinery and implements accounted for 10 per cent of the total output in South Russia and 6.2 per cent of the output

of all Russia. The following table lists these factories, showing total annual production in terms of rubles and personnel employed.

Firm	Annual Production		Total Employed
Lepp and Wallmann	900,000	rubles	270
A. J. Koop	610,000	"	376
J. G. Niebuhr	450,000	"	350
J. J. Neufeld & Co.	350,000	"	200
J. A. & W. J. Classen	241,000	"	145
Franz and Schröder	209,190	"	153
G. A. Klassen & Neufeld	200,442	"	140
J. Jansen and K. Neufeld	200,000	"	110

(From A. Ehrt, *Das Mennonitentum in Russland*, p. 91 f.)

The Mennonites played a considerable role in the industrial and agricultural development of the country far beyond their immediate communities. The total number of Mennonite-owned larger factories in the Ukraine was 26. Smaller industries were the manufacture of brick, cheese, sausage, soap, starch, furniture, woven goods, and clocks, brewing of vinegar and beer and distilling whisky, print shops ("Raduga," Halbstadt; H. E. Ediger, Berdyansk; H. A. Lenzmann, Tokmak; A. P. Friesen, Davlekanovo, Ufa), and mill construction.

One of the latest industries, which finally surpassed all others, was the milling industry. Over half of all industrial enterprises of the Mennonites in the Ukraine were connected with the milling industry. The foundation for this was the windmill, which had been transplanted from Holland to Prussia and to Russia, having originally been used mostly to regulate the water level of the Low Countries. In the steppes of the Ukraine it was used to grind feed and flour. Some horse-driven mills were also in use. The greater advance came with the introduction of large-scale wheat production, which resulted in the establishment of large motor- and steam-driven mills toward the close of the 19th century. Soon all Mennonite settlements were dotted with large four- to five-story flour mills, in which the wheat was ground into very fine flour to be shipped into all parts of Russia and abroad. By the beginning of World War I Mennonite-owned flour mills could also be found in many railroad centers outside the Mennonite communities. Some of the centers were Chortitza, Alexandrovsk, Halbstadt, Ekaterinoslav, Nikopol, Kharkov, and New York. Some of the largest milling industries were Niebuhr and Co., of Alexandrovsk, J. J. Thiessen of Ekaterinoslav, J. Siemens of Nikopol, and Peter Unger of New York, which had a total annual production of three million rubles. In addition there were many flour businesses, the one owned by Heinrich and Peter Heese, Ekaterinoslav, having an annual turnover of 1.5 million rubles.

In 1908 the Chortitza and Molotschna settlements had a total of 73 motor- and steam-driven mills, 26 factories of agricultural machinery, 38 brick factories, and 20 other industries, making a total of 157. In addition there were 105 flour mills and 54 other smaller enterprises, making a total of 316 industries. In addition there were 69 industries in the other Mennonite settlements of the Ukraine and an estimated 200 in the eastern provinces of Russia, making a total of about 585 industries. Of this total nearly 60 were located in the Chortitza and Molotschna settlements. The milling industry was the largest among the large-scale industries of the Ukraine (51.8 per cent). The next largest was the production of agricultural machinery. This indicates that before World War I there was a definite trend toward industrialization among the Mennonites of Russia, particularly in the older settlements. The number of industries and large farm estates on one hand and the constantly growing laboring class on the other hand were indications of a shift in process which endangered the predominant rural pattern of life among the Mennonites of Russia. According to Ehrt one third of all Mennonite capital was invested in capitalistic enterprises (for profit) and two thirds in the traditional smaller farm and home industry. Two and eight-tenths per cent of the population had 34 per cent of the total capital in their hands. The average property ownership among the Mennonites of the Ukraine was 8,000 rubles per person, and in the later settlements 3,300 rubles. In Siberia it was only 1,400 rubles.

In connection with the industrial development among the Mennonites of Prussia and Russia it should be stated that many inventions were made by industrial leaders. Naturally in most cases the industrialist used patterns of western European agricultural machinery. Their inventions were possibly more or less limited to the adaptation of these machines to their particular environment and needs. Originally many of the industries developed from smaller home industries. Later the characteristics of the modern capitalistic developments became more evident. Many of the sons of the industrialists who had started on a small scale went to schools of engineering in Germany, Switzerland, and Russia in order to be better qualified to continue the enterprise of their fathers. During the last decades the Mennonites of Russia had numerous engineers in various branches of industry. (See also **Agriculture** *Among the Mennonites in Russia* and **Business.**)   C.K.

H. G. Mannhardt, *Die Danziger Mennonitengemeinde* (Danzig, 1919); Horst Quiring, "Die Auswanderung der Mennoniten aus Preussen, 1788-1870," *Menn. Life*, April 1951, 36 f.; A. Ehrt, *Das Mennonitentum in Russland* (Berlin, 1932) 89 ff.; Cornelius Krahn, "Agriculture Among the Mennonites of Russia," *Menn. Life*, January 1955, 14 ff.; "Mennonite Industry in Russia," *Menn. Life*, January 1955, 21 ff.; Jakob J. Niebuhr, "Jakob G. Niebuhr Fabriken," *Menn. Life*, January 1955, 25 ff.; A. Bonwetsch, *Der Handel mit landwirtschaftlichen Maschinen und Geräten in Russland . . .* (Berlin, 1921) 35 ff.; D. H. Epp, "P. H. Lepp," *Bote* (Rosthern, Sask., 1928) Nos. 10-13; David Rempel, "The Mennonite Colonies in New Russia" (unpublished Stanford University thesis, 1933) 275 ff.; B. H. Unruh, *Die niederländisch-niederdeutschen Hintergründe der mennonitischen Ostwanderungen* (Karlsruhe, 1955).

Infant Baptism. Protests against the church institution of infant baptism had been almost completely silenced by persecution before the Reformation period. The sparse and somewhat unclear information on the opponents of infant baptism seems to show that many did not oppose it as such, but only because it was performed by officials unworthy of the office and was therefore invalid.

When the reformers shouted the watchword of the sole authority of the Scriptures, and defended this principle tenaciously against the Roman Church and its claims of authority, it was inevitable that along with other usages of the Roman Church, also its method of baptism would be subjected to a serious examination in the light of the Scriptures. Diligent study of the Bible led many to the apparently new discovery of the fact that the New Testament not only knows nothing of all the ceremonies in which the rite of baptism came gradually to be clothed, but also that it does not even mention infant baptism or cite an instance of such baptism, indeed that infant baptism could not be made to agree with the teachings of the apostles.

The fact that there is no trace of infant baptism in the New Testament is recognized today almost unanimously by theologians. Even Schleiermacher (p. 1) said openly, "All traces of infant baptism presumably found in the New Testament must first be put into it."

Paul always saw faith and baptism together. "Naturally Paul and with him the original church could not conceive of baptism without faith. The question of the effect of baptism on an unbeliever did not enter his field of vision" (Stromberg, 27). If it is a fact that faith is a prerequisite for baptism, then infant baptism has no meaning. Only a sacramental conception can consider it necessary for salvation.

Catholic theologians rest their case for infant baptism on tradition. But the Protestants demand Scriptural evidence. J. A. Möhler (*Symbolik,* Par. 30) comments: "That infant baptism is in the Protestant view of the sacraments a totally incomprehensible act, there is no doubt; if the sacrament is effective only through faith, of what value may it be to an unconscious child? The Anabaptists, about whom Luther was so excited, drew from the premises he had given, very simple demands, and he was therefore unable to refute them without sacrificing his own views." Schleiermacher admits that the symbolic books of the Protestant churches "view infant baptism apart from all historical aspects and undertake to justify it in and for its own sake, but inadequately and on mutually contradictory grounds (*Der christliche Glaube* II, Par. 138).

Similarly Luther's proofs for the justification of infant baptism are not unified, but show a clearly discernible uncertainty. Since Luther in his controversy with the feared Anabaptists found himself compelled to base his arguments on Scripture, he utilized the passages which are still cited today and which seem to justify infant baptism.

At first Luther based his proof on the creed (Sermon, 1518) or on the faith of those who present the child (Jan. 13, 1522). But in 1522 he already began to claim faith on the part of the child. No one could prove the opposite. Children were more receptive than adults (as in his exposition of Galatians in 1519). In addition to reference to circumcision Luther also uses New Testament references. Above all, Matt. 19:14 seems to him a principal argument. See his elucidations in the sermon for the third

Sunday after Epiphany in the *Kirchenpostille*. He very positively defends his claim that children have a faith of their own. In his booklet, *Von der Wiedertaufe an Zwei Pfarrherrn* (1528), he says, "No one is saved through the faith of others, but only through his own. . . . Baptism helps nobody and should be given to none unless he believes for himself." That children without faith of their own receive grace through baptism is "a dream." That the faith of the church can substitute for the faith of the individual is only the opinion of Sophists and without foundation in the Scriptures. The idea that the child is baptized on his own future faith is rejected by Luther as early as 1523. "Faith must be present before or at the baptism, otherwise the child is not rid of sin and the devil." The concept that by baptism the child is merely received into "Christendom," is "made up out of the imagination." A baptism in which the same presuppositions cannot be made for the children as in adult baptism, and in which the child does not receive the same as an adult, is no baptism at all, but rather only a "play and mockery of baptism."

In answer to the question how a faith of their own comes into being in infants, Luther has various answers. He says the petitions of the godfathers secure it to the child. Or, the priest acts in Christ's stead and gives the children faith and the kingdom of heaven. In addition to the "strong" and "firm" Scriptural references (Matt. 19:13-15; Mark 10:13-16; Luke 18:15, 16), Luther also cites I John 2:13: "I write to you, little children." He also points to the baptism of entire households; then again to circumcision, which made believers of Abraham's children. How much more should this apply to baptism. John the Baptist's leaping in his mother's womb is incredible without presupposing faith (Luke 1:41).

In reply to Rom. 10:17, that faith comes from preaching, Luther asserts that children, precisely because they are without reason, are so much the more able to believe. Therefore if a baptism is to be safe, infant baptism is safest of all. Historical proof is also employed at times by Luther, by referring to the long existence and generality of the practice of infant baptism. Then he points to the gifts and achievements of men baptized in infancy as evidence that infant baptism is pleasing to God.

In contrast to this strong emphasis on the objective effect of the sacrament of baptism, which to be sure cannot be imagined without faith on the part of the child, Zwingli saw in baptism only a symbol of the obligation the candidate assumed. Zwingli was at first an opponent of infant baptism. In his book on baptism (1525) he confesses, "The error led me astray a few years ago, that I thought it would be much better not to baptize children until they had arrived at good faith." Hubmaier (*q.v.*) mentions in his *Gespräch von der Kindertaufe* (Nikolsburg, 1526) that when he and Zwingli had conferred together in May 1523, in Zürich, Zwingli had granted that infants should not be baptized. Felix Manz (*q.v.*) confirms this in his *Schutzschrift* (letter of defense) to the city council: "I am certain that Master Ulrich understands this idea of baptism, that is, that infants should not be baptized,

much better than we, but I do not know for what reason he does not announce it openly."

In his conflict with the Swiss Brethren Zwingli changed his opinion completely. In his writing to the Strasbourg theologians on Dec. 16, 1524, he already defended infant baptism, comparing it with circumcision, which was replaced by baptism according to Col. 2:11. When in I Cor. 7:10 the apostle calls the children "holy," baptism is presupposed! As an example of the baptism of infants he cites the baptism of John the Baptist, which was not at all different from Christian baptism. He calls untrue the assertion that the apostles inquired into the faith of candidates before baptizing them. Sometimes it had been done, sometimes omitted.

In his book, *Welche Ursach geben zu Aufruhr und wer die wahren Aufrührer sind* (1524), Zwingli grants that there is in the New Testament no clear command for infant baptism; but since it contains no clear prohibition either, we must refer back to the Old Testament; and thus he speaks of circumcision again. In the book, *Vom Tauf, vom Wiedertauf, und vom Kindertauf* (1525), Zwingli expresses himself thus on the baptism of infants: "The children of Christians are no less God's children than their parents, just as in the Old Testament. And if they are God's children, who will object to their being baptized?" Circumcision was a symbol of what baptism is to us. As the former was given to the children, the latter should be also.

With convincing and striking arguments Hubmaier refutes the ground Zwingli presents for infant baptism. Col. 2:11 speaks of the circumcision not made with hands. Thereby baptism is not made the equivalent of circumcision, but its higher position is brought out. It is not a mere outward act, but an inward process. The "shadow" of the Old Testament is wiped out. The word "baptize" is not used in Scripture in the sense of "teach," as Zwingli asserts. The baptism of John is not identical with the baptism of Christ. The former signified confession of sin, the latter faith in pardon. Baptism assumes the confessing faith and the obligation to live in accord with God's will. When Zwingli points out the Greek word "disciple" and asserts that teaching follows baptizing, Hubmaier replies that one can become a disciple of Christ only through teaching and faith. Only when teaching and faith precede does one receive baptism, without thereby putting an end to teaching; Christian understanding must continue to grow. As further evidence for infant baptism Zwingli cites Mark 10:14: "Suffer the children to come unto me." Hubmaier makes it clear that this does not mean they should be baptized (Usteri, 256).

Calvin's concept of infant baptism is peculiar. He considers the children of Christian parents sanctified by their descent and in God's covenant; hence they are entitled to the sign of the covenant.

Schleiermacher (d. 1834) made an attempt in his teaching on faith to hold to infant baptism as a church custom, of course abandoning Luther's position. He declares infant baptism to be an imperfect baptism, the effect of which is suspended until the recipient has become a personal believer. He says, "Infant baptism is a complete baptism only when, after instruction is completed, the confession of faith is considered the last act belonging to it."

But Schleiermacher admits openly: "But we cannot maintain the necessity of a baptism thus divided into two parts, which, however, happens when one damns the Anabaptists and Mennonites for assuming that children who die unbaptized can be saved. . . . Therefore it would have been very reasonable to abandon infant baptism at the time of the Reformation, in order to approach more closely to the institution by Christ, and we could still do so. . . . It would then be normal to leave it to every Protestant family to decide whether they want to present their children for baptism in the customary way, or not until they have confessed their faith, and we should explain that we repeal the old condemnation pronounced on the Anabaptists on this point and that we are willing to maintain church communion with the Mennonites, if they will only not declare simply invalid our completed infant baptism; on this point it should be easy to reach an agreement." This generous attitude is held today by not a few theologians, and they act accordingly.

In the first edition of HRE the statement is made, that "there is no trace of infant baptism to be found in the New Testament may be considered a fact in scientific exegesis." In the third edition Dr. Feine says, "The practice of infant baptism in the apostolic and post-apostolic period is not demonstrable" (Vol. XIX, 403). In the same volume (446) Drews declares, "There is complete absence of evidence that children were baptized in apostolic times. Whenever the attempt has been made to offer Scriptural proof for infant baptism, it has been a waste of effort."

In fact, the "strong and firm verses" of Luther do not speak for, but against infant baptism. For they (Matt. 19:14; Mark 10:14; Luke 18:16) show that the Lord loved the children without baptism. For He caressed and blessed them, but did not baptize them nor command that they be baptized.

The five instances in Acts of the baptism of entire households leave, on careful exegesis, no room for the baptism of small children. As Tobias Beck says, "All the baptized households, according to circumstances mentioned in the account, consisted of responsible persons."

The verse in I Cor. 7:14, on which Luther once requested Melanchthon to enlighten him as to whether it might be used in favor of infant baptism, is definite evidence against any apostolic practice of infant baptism. "Paul would not have used that argument if infant baptism had been customary at that time. Infant baptism is certainly not apostolic" (Olshausen on I Cor. 7:14).

Beyschlag comments on this verse: "Of infant baptism there is in (Paul's) writings as in the entire New Testament no mention; rather, the manner in which he argues in I Cor. 7:14 on the subject of the children of Christians—that, if the non-Christian spouse were unclean and not sanctified by his life with his Christian spouse, then the children of Christians would also be unclean—is striking proof that there was then no thought of sanctifying children through baptism. Hence only those came for baptism who were compelled by a personal faith.

In their rejection of infant baptism the Anabaptists of the Reformation built their case solely on the Bible, than which they recognized no other authority. Their assertion that there is no trace of infant baptism in the New Testament, neither directions nor an example, and further that the teaching of the New Testament on faith completely excludes infant baptism, they defended with great positiveness and with more or less skill by citing examples and passages from the Bible.

Thomas von Imbroich (1558) opposes infant baptism with unusual skill on Biblical grounds. In Matt. 28 he points out that teaching and faith must precede baptism; teaching should be given before and after baptism; teaching is followed by repentance and faith. By Christian baptism faith is confessed and sealed. But baptism must be followed by godly living. This is the order of Christ and His apostles. His Biblical refutation of the argument that baptism is the same as circumcision and that the baptism of entire households speaks for infant baptism, is really exhaustive. (Güldene Aepfel in Silbern Schalen, q.v., 48-121.)

Servaes (q.v.) likewise clearly shows the incorrectness of infant baptism in his first epistle (Güldene Aepfel, 53), and in the second (ibid., 73).

Pilgram Marpeck (q.v.) in his Vermahnung discusses the subject at great length. He shows the invalidity and error of infant baptism, and strikingly refutes with Biblical and historical proofs the arguments arrayed in its behalf. Next to Hubmaier's booklet, Marpeck's Vermahnung is the most important presentation of the teaching and practice of baptism by the Anabaptists (Gedenkschrift, 213-50; Loserth, Quellen).

Since the Anabaptists of the 16th century viewed infant baptism as being contrary to the New Testament, they logically considered those baptized as infants as not baptized at all. In his booklet Von der Christlichen Tauff der Gläubigen (1525) Hubmaier writes that the Anabaptists stated quite openly that they had not been baptized as infants, and must therefore be baptized now (Sachsse, 17). Against the favorite proofs for infant baptism Hubmaier argues to the point as follows.

(1) There is a complete absence of Scripture for baptizing children upon their future faith. It is the same as like planting a grapevine at Easter, hoping for future grapes, when the vine may die.

(2) To interpret infant baptism as a symbol of initiation, whether of beginning faith or of the new life, is contrary to Christ's institution of baptism.

(3) The vicarious faith of parents and godfathers is not known in the Scriptures. The candidate for baptism must believe for himself.

(4) The children of believers are not ipso facto believers, for they have not yet heard God's Word. They are on the same plane as other unbelievers. Otherwise there would be two kinds of baptism.

Hubmaier continues that many recognize the erroneousness of infant baptism, but were afraid of "rebaptism." But such baptism is not rebaptism, since they were not baptized as infants. In the sixth chapter of this book Hubmaier discusses the question, "Does the Scripture forbid infant baptism?" He says, "Yes, indirectly, for it commands believers' baptism. If one says: What is not expressly forbidden is permitted, one re-establishes the whole papal system."

Hubmaier also offers historical proofs. The claim that infant baptism had been customary since apostolic times he refutes by referring to the numerous papal edicts which clearly presuppose adult baptism.

To the question whether unbaptized children are saved, Hubmaier points to God's love, for if God dealt only according to justice, no one would be saved. But no definite answer could be given. Matt. 19:14 Hubmaier explains from the Greek to mean not the children themselves but the humble.

In his book of 1526 (*Der Uralten und gar neuen Leerern Urteil, das man die jungen Kindlein nit taufen solle bis sy im Glauben underricht sind*) Hubmaier replies to Zwingli's arguments for infant baptism. Here historical proofs are given much room. Statements of numerous Church Fathers are mustered for adult baptism and against infant baptism. In the foreword Hubmaier condemns the abuse of letting infants partake of communion. On the same plane is the abuse of administering baptism to children who do not yet believe. In addition to the proofs he adduced from Scripture in his last book, he would here bring human testimony.

The material was without doubt assembled with great pains. But Hubmaier often cites inexactly and on unreliable sources, frequently errs in dates, so that many of his historical proofs do not stand historical scrutiny. But in his assertion that church history affords protests against infant baptism and certain evidence for the continuance of the baptism of believers in old Christian families, Hubmaier was entirely correct. Modern historical research has confirmed these facts. The fact, for instance, that among the many pictorial sketches of baptisms in the catacombs of the first centuries not a single infant baptism is depicted, is important archaeological evidence.

The practice long continued, precisely in Christian families, of not baptizing infants, can only be explained on the basis of established custom. The rise of doctrines on baptism in contradiction to tradition, and in all parts of the Roman empire, without evoking sharp objection on the part of leading theologians and councils, is a psychological impossibility. Even bishops did not baptize their own children. These cannot have been isolated instances. They would have attracted attention and been attacked if there had existed a firm tradition of infant baptism. The omission of infant baptism in many Christian families of the third and fourth centuries cannot have been a matter of innovation, but of holding to an old practice.

Among the well-known men of that time Ambrose must be mentioned, who was born in Trier about 340, as the son of a Roman prefect of Gaul. The family had adopted Christianity a century before. Among their progenitors was the martyr Sotharis. After his father's death, his mother moved to Rome. Ambrose was not baptized until his thirty-fourth year. Jerome, the Christian scholar and translator of the Bible, was born in Dalmatia (*ca.* 340) of Christian parents. He was baptized in Rome by Pope Liberius in 360. Augustine, the son of the pious Monica, was not baptized until 387, when he was 33 years old. Gregory (d. 390), bishop of Nazianzus in Cappadocia, was baptized in his thirtieth year, after he had completed his studies. His brother Caesarius and his sister Gorgona, both certainly Christians, were baptized shortly before their death. Their mother, Nonna, was descended from an old and respected Christian family. She dedicated her son Gregory to the Lord with prayer, placing his infant hands on the Bible. Basil (d. 379), bishop of Caesarea in Cappadocia, belonged to an old Christian family known for its many martyrs, but he was not baptized as an infant. The same is true of the patriarch Nectarius (d. 398) and of Ephraem Syrus (d. 373). Chrysostom, whose mother Anthusa prayed and read the Bible with him, was baptized after he was a lawyer and after three years of instruction, by bishop Meletius of Antioch.

The oldest writings of the post-apostolic period contain no evidence of infant baptism. The oldest certain evidence of the rise of this practice is found in Tertullian (*q.v.*) in his *De baptismo*. He, however, objects to it, and advises postponing baptism until after the candidate has received instruction. Hubmaier is correct in maintaining that the views of the Pelagians or of Cyprian prove nothing, for the utterances of the Church Fathers are authoritative only if they coincide with those of the Scriptures (1527, *Von dem khindertauff*); Origen did not declare himself in favor of infant baptism; furthermore he was frequently in error too. This is correct. Origen's alleged testimony for infant baptism comes from the free Latin translation of Rufinus, who was interested in fitting Origen's teaching to the later orthodox dogma (Heussi).

The rise of the practice of infant baptism is shrouded in darkness. There is neither any information of the beginning of the practice nor any synodal resolution to introduce it. Neander (214 ff.) finds several elements in the spirit of the post-apostolic period that were favorable to the introduction of infant baptism; e.g., the idea of the magical effect of baptism and of its necessity for salvation. Von Stromberg (162) points out the fundamental religious mood, which found expression in the mystery religions. "Surely none of the Christians of the first and second generations were free of mystery-piety."

"Progressive materialization of the sacred" and the "concept of mysteriously working forces in the act of baptism disconnected baptism from the personal experience of salvation, and faith in baptism was emptied of its most valuable content" (Stromberg, 166). A complete reversal had taken place in the primitive Christian idea of salvation. Its beginnings can be noticed early in post-apostolic literature. Hermas says, life is given by the baptismal water, and the forgiveness of all past sins, therefore it is necessary to salvation. Barnabas teaches that in baptism the Christian enters into possession of salvation and the indwelling of God. Similar expressions are found in Justin, Clement of Alexandria, and others.

When the mysterious effect of the objective means of grace known as sacraments is assumed, then an important premise for infant baptism has been given. Nevertheless the generalizing of the practice was slow. Tertullian (*De baptismo,* 18) is still an opponent when he declares, "To be sure, the Lord says: and forbid them not to come unto me. Then indeed they may come when they are grown, when they learn, when they are taught there where they are coming. They may become Christians when they can know Christ. Why does the age of innocence hasten to have its sins forgiven? In temporal affairs more care is taken. Should heavenly possessions be entrusted to one to whom earthly goods cannot be entrusted? Let them first understand how to request salvation, that it may be granted them at their request."

In Cyprian (*q.v.*) infant baptism finds a zealous defender. He too sees in baptism the means of the new birth, release from the devil, death, and hell, and of the granting of the Holy Spirit. Under Cyprian's influence 66 bishops declared themselves in favor of infant baptism in 253. They should be baptized as early as possible (Ep. 64, 2; see *De baptismo*); they receive the Holy Spirit (Ep. 64, 3). In the crying and wailing of infants Cyprian heard the request for the grace of baptism (Ep. 64, 6).

After Cyprian the baptism of infants became current practice in North Africa. A similar resolution was passed in 305 by a synod at Elvira in Spain. Logically infants also participated in communion (*De lapsis; Const. Apost.* VIII, 12, 13; *Dionysius, Areopagiticus. De hierarch. eccl.* VII, ii; *Augustine's epistles,* 23, etc.). This custom remained in vogue for centuries in the West, and in the Greek Orthodox church has continued until today, immediately connected with confirmation.

Augustine, in his controversy with the Pelagians, found it necessary to strongly emphasize infant baptism. Pelagius sponsored infant baptism in rejecting original sin, Augustine promoted it because of the sinfulness of children. Without baptism, says Augustine, there is no rebirth and no salvation.

The retention of infant baptism is in the final analysis an ecclesiastical matter. Those who consider the church of believers on the basis of voluntary membership the correct form cannot favor infant baptism. Those who favor a church including as nearly as possible the entire population or at least the masses, will consider infant baptism as the act of accepting them into Christendom and the means of relieving all the descendants of church members of the necessity of making the decision. The principle of the mass-church demands infant baptism. From this standpoint the practice still has many zealous defenders, who freely admit that it was not an early Christian practice, but only a later church custom.

Among the Anabaptists the question of the meaning and use of baptism only in the total framework of church life became of such great importance that to the outsider it usually seemed the main point of their doctrine. Today as well, the question of infant baptism gains or loses its significance and interest in connection with the questions of the nature of the Christian Church.

The question of infant baptism has received serious attention recently again in continental state church circles, particularly because of the open repudiation of infant baptism by Karl Barth in 1943 in his pamphlet, *Die kirchliche Lehre von der Taufe.* His son Marcus Barth published in 1951 a large work, *Die Taufe ein Sakrament?* in which he took basically the same position, as did Johannes Schneider's *Die Taufe im Neuen Testament* a year later. Both latter works give an exhaustive exegetical discussion of all New Testament passages dealing with baptism. Many pastors in the Swiss, German, and Dutch state churches openly followed Karl Barth's lead, although it was difficult for any of them to put into practice their convictions and to refuse to baptize the infants brought to them. The strongest counterattack against Barth was that by Oscar Cullmann, also professor at Basel, in 1948 in his booklet, *Die Tauflehre des N.T.,* although H. Grossmann had already attacked Barth's position in his booklet *Ein Ja zur Kindertaufe* in 1944. Cullmann sought to prove that the early church must have practiced infant baptism. J. Jeremias, professor at the University of Göttingen, had already attempted this proof in 1938 in his earlier booklet, *Hat die älteste Kirche die Kindertaufe geübt?* Both Cullmann and Jeremias rely more upon historical evidence than exegetical proof. B. H. Unruh in 1950 carefully examined and refuted the arguments for infant baptism in his "Zur neuesten Literatur über die christliche Taufe," followed by Paul Schowalter in 1953, "Noch einmal: Die Tauffrage."   J.WA., H.S.B.

A. Seeberg, *Die Taufe im Neuen Testament* (*Bibl. Zeit- u. Streitfragen,* 1913); W. Heitmüller, *Taufe und Abendmahl im Urchristentum* (*Rel. Volksbücher* 1, 22-23, 1911); A. v. Stromberg, *Studien zur Theorie und Praxis der Taufe* (Berlin, 1913); E. Händiges, "Taufe, die Lehre der Mennoniten" in *RGG;* C. Sachsse, *D. Balth. Hubmaier als Theologe* (Berlin, 1914); John Horsch, *Menno Simons* (Scottdale, 1916); *idem, Infant Baptism* (Scottdale, 1917); J. Warns, *Die Taufe* (2d ed. Cassel, 1922); *idem, Staatskirche? Volkskirche? Freikirche?* (Homburg, 1919); Schleiermacher, *Der christliche Glaube* II, 138; P. Althaus, *Die Heilsbedeutung der Taufe im Neuen Testament* (Gütersloh, 1895); J. A. Möhler, *Symbolik* (Mainz, 1832 ff.); J. Usteri, "Darstellung der Tauflehre Zwingli's," *Theol. Stud. u. Krit.* XXV (1882); *Gedenkschrift zum 400-jährigen Jubiläum der Mennoniten . . .* (Weierhof, 1925); J. Loserth, *Quellen und Forschungen zur Gesch. der oberdeutschen Taufgesinnten im 16. Jahrhundert* (Vienna and Leipzig, 1929); Karl Barth, *Die kirchliche Lehre von der Taufe* (Zürich, 1943); *Was ist Taufe?* ed. F. Gruenagel (Stuttgart, 1951); Marcus Barth, *Die Taufe ein Sakrament?* (Zürich, 1951); Johannes Schneider, *Die Taufe im Neuen Testament* (Stuttgart, 1952); H. Grossmann, *Ein Ja zur Kindertaufe* (Zürich, 1944); O. Cullmann, *Die Tauflehre des N.T.* (Zürich, 1948); J. Jeremias, *Hat die älteste Kirche die Kindertaufe geübt?* (Göttingen, 1938); B. H. Unruh, "Zur neuesten Literatur über die christliche Taufe," *Menn. Gesch.-Bl.* VII (1950) 31-42; P. Schowalter, "Noch einmal: Die Tauffrage," *Menn. Gesch.-Bl.* X (1953) 33-36; *ML* II, 488-94.

Ingalls Mennonite Brethren Church, located in Gray Co., Kan., five miles north of Ingalls, a member of the Southern District, is the outgrowth of an original union or mission church founded in 1923. It now (1954) has a membership of 57. D. W. Siemens, B. C. Willems, G. G. Wiens, Wm. Neufeld, D. J. Wiens, and (at present) J. W. Fast have been leaders in the congregation.   J.W.Fa.

Ingenheim, Jörg von, with Hans Schmidt wrote the song, "O Herre Gott vom Himmelreich, Merck auff und sieh die Nothe," found in the *Ausbund* (*q.v.*).

Particulars about Jörg are not available. Hans Schmidt (*q.v.*) and four companions, all Hutterite missionaries, suffered martyrdom at Aachen, Germany, in 1558. Apparently Jörg was the man not named by van Braght who recanted and was set free. But soon he repented his apostasy and returned to a loyal and faithful life among the brotherhood in Moravia. (Wolkan, *Lieder,* 146; *Mart. Mir.* D 209 ff., E 588 ff.) vDZ.

Ingolstadt, a city (pop. 40,270) on the Danube in Upper Bavaria, Germany, became the residence of the dukes of Bavaria-Ingolstadt in 1392. The university, founded in 1472, transferred to Landshut in 1800 and then to Munich in 1826, played an important role during the Reformation period through the activity of several of its professors of theology. Some of them were active opponents of the Anabaptist movement, as Dr. Johann Eck (*q.v.*), Luther's well-known opponent, and Urban Rhegius (*q.v.*), who later became the Lutheran preacher in Augsburg. The later Anabaptist leader Balthasar Hubmaier (*q.v.*) earned his doctor's degree here; he was called in 1512 as professor of theology, and in 1515 was made Prorector of the university; in addition he preached at St. Mary's. Another prominent Anabaptist who studied here was Hans Denk (*q.v.*); he was matriculated on Oct. 29, 1517, and was given the bachelor's degree in 1519.

In 1543 a Hutterite from Allgäu by the name of Damian (Thaman) was seized in Ingolstadt as he was about to leave for Moravia, and was burned at the stake when he would not recant. His courage and steadfastness aroused admiration among the spectators (Beck, 154).

The death of a second Anabaptist martyr executed in Ingolstadt, Michel Fischer, is commemorated in a Hutterite song. After a 12 weeks' imprisonment he was beheaded on Aug. 7, 1587, after a vain attempt by the Jesuits to convert him (*Die Lieder der Hutterischen Brüder,* 785).

The first settlement of Jesuits in Bavaria took place at Ingolstadt in 1549; they took over a chair of theology at the university. When the Hutterian martyr Christian Gasteiger (*q.v.*) was thrown into prison here on May 30, 1586, the Jesuits visited him by two's (for the purpose of converting him) during the 12 weeks of his imprisonment as well as after his transfer to Munich, where he was executed on Sept. 13. Opposition to the Anabaptist movement also took literary form at Ingolstadt. Thus in 1576 Dr. Kaspar Franck published here his catalog of heretics, which pays special attention to Hubmaier and Denk. Here too the propaganda of Christoph Erhard (*q.v.*) and Christoph Andreas Fischer (*q.v.*) was printed; they were Jesuits of Ingolstadt (Jöcher's *Gelehrten-Lexikon*).

When Elector Max Joseph, who became King Maximilian I Joseph of Bavaria in 1799, took over the government he eliminated the Jesuit control of government under his predecessor Karl Theodore and proclaimed complete religious liberty in Bavaria. The country was now open to the Mennonites. The ruler, being acquainted with their agricultural achievements in his home at Zweibrücken in the Palatinate, welcomed them. They settled in various places between the Danube and the Alps, where representatives of their faith had been martyred in the 16th century.

A number of Amish families settled near Ingolstadt. The first family to settle here, the Suttors from St. Goar on the Rhine, acquired the former monastic estate Hellmannsberg about 1810. From Hesse and Alsace followed families by the name of Oesch, Oswald, Ingold, and Güngerich, of the Amish branch. They organized a congregation about 1810 and held services in their homes.

In the middle of the 19th century other Mennonites from the Palatinate and at the turn of the century from Lower Franconia and Baden, settled in the vicinity of Ingolstadt. They joined the Eichstock-Singern (*q.v.*) church and were served by the preachers of that congregation: Michael Landes and Daniel Lichti from Au. In 1891 a new Mennonite congregation was formed, known as Rottmannshart (near Manching) where Michael Landes (served as elder at least from 1902 to his death in 1927) later lived, which later moved its seat to Ingolstadt. At the death in 1912 of preacher Güngerich of the Amish branch the two congregations united. In 1930 it had 90 baptized members. It held the meetings in a rented hall in Ingolstadt, until a meetinghouse was built in 1952, and also in Rottmannshart and Niederfeld. The elder in 1925-49 was Michael Horsch of Hellmannsberg; since then Eduard Landes and Hellmut Horsch serve as elders. The membership in 1955 was 135, including 40 unbaptized children.

The members lived scattered as far as 55 miles apart. Therefore those living up the Danube formed a separate church in 1912 at Donauwörth (*q.v.*), which was transferred in 1926 to Augsburg. HEGE.

Beck, *Geschichts-Bücher; Die Lieder der Hutterischen Brüder* (Scottdale, 1914); *ML* II, 414 f.

Ingolt, Friedrich, an Anabaptist of Strasbourg, participated in the disputation with Hans Denk (Dec. 22, 1526) and stated that he felt justified in not leaving Hans Denk, and in loving him sincerely. The name Ingold is still found among South German and American Mennonites.

F. P. Gelbert, *Magister Johann Baders Leben und Schriften* (Neustadt a.d.H., 1868); *ML* II, 415.

Inheritance, Right of (*Erbrecht*). In the 16th century and later the Anabaptists were restricted in their rights to hand their possessions down to their children. Since their marriages were not solemnized in the church they were not legally valid, and the children were consequently not entitled to inheritance. This was the case in the canton of Bern in Switzerland (Müller, 134). The opinion of a Protestant divine, Dec. 8, 1701, saw in this attitude an unjust punishment and a sign of intolerance. On May 17, 1721, the Bern government passed a regulation that the children of Mennonite women, whose fathers were living in exile, should not be considered Swiss, but be sent to their exiled fathers. A government rescript of May 17, 1722, provided that Reformed parents had the right to disinherit their children if they became Mennonites; but if they returned to the Reformed Church, their inheritance should be given them without interest. "Lateral lines entitled to inheritance may claim half of the legacy of an Anabaptist, whereas according to a decree of March 17, 1729, the entire estate of a deceased Anabaptist falls to the Church if there are no direct heirs" (Müller, 355).

In Russian Mennonite circles it was often the practice to leave cripples, the deaf, the blind, mental defectives, and epileptics twice as large an inheritance as healthy members of the family.

As to the Netherlands: during the period of persecution (1530-75) the property of the martyrs was usually confiscated, but there are a few cases in Amsterdam (Grosheide, *Bijdrage,* 260) and elsewhere, when the families of the executed inherited the possessions of their parents. These cases were exceptions.

Later on until 1795 some limitations were placed on the rights of inheritance for Mennonites. These limitations were not the same in all the provinces. In the city of Groningen in 1601 a resolution was passed that Mennonites (and others) who did not perform their marriages in Reformed churches, and unbaptized children, would be deprived of hereditary possessions. In Deventer the congregation was not permitted to receive an inheritance in 1662 because it was "an illicit society" (Blaupot t. C., *Groningen* II, 70-71), and in 1705 the congregation of Molkwerum had to give up a large bequest to the Reformed Church for the same reason (Blaupot t. C., *Friesland,* 204). But these limitations were not always strictly enforced, and so Mennonite congregations often received bequests. In some congregations it seems to have been the custom that members assigned 10 per cent of their property to the church, or that after their decease relatives made this arrangement. In some churches where there were seamen, especially whale-hunters as in De Rijp and Workum, these people, either by letter, or orally with the deacons, made an arrangement to assign a part of their property to the church, with the condition that the deacons would provide for their children in case they should not return from an expedition.   NEFF, vDZ.

Friesen, *Brüderschaft,* 654; Müller, *Berner Täufer;* N. van der Zijpp, *Gesch. der Doopsgezinden in Nederland* (Arnhem, 1952) 124; G. A. Wunkes, *De Geref.-Kerk in de Ommelanden . . .* (Groningen, 1904) 21; E. Teufel, "Die Beschlagnahme und Verwaltung der Täufergutes durch den Fiskus im Herzogtum Württemberg im 16. und 17. Jahrhundert," in *Theologische Ztscht* VIII (1952) 296-305; *ML* I, 603.

Inman, Kan. (pop. 650), a village located in McPherson County in the central part of the state, was founded in 1887, soon after the Rock Island railway was built, and was called Aiken. This was changed to Inman the following year.

Approximately 1,500 Mennonites live near and in Inman, perhaps 25 per cent of them in town. They own and operate about half of the businesses. The groups represented are the Church of God in Christ Mennonite, G.C.M., K.M.B., M.B., and M.C. There are six Mennonite churches in the community. Cooperatively they sponsor a home for the aged in Inman with rooms for 18 residents.   P.T.N.

Inman Mennonite Church (GCM), located in Inman, McPherson Co., Kan., a member of the Western District Conference, dates back almost to the coming of the Mennonites to Kansas and the establishment of the Hoffnungsau (*q.v.*) congregation, its mother church. Because of the large area of settlement, Sunday schools were soon started in various schoolhouses in the outlying areas of the settlement. In 1909 the mother church erected and dedicated a small church building in Inman as a home mission project, supplying it with ministers. In 1921 this group organized as the Inman Mennonite Church with 106 charter members and Abraham Albrecht as pastor. Nine ministers have served as pastor, with Ben Rahn the present pastor. The 1953 membership was 206. A new modern church was dedicated on March 3, 1955.   B.R.

Inn Valley (German, *Inntal*). There are three long river valleys in Tirol which have become important in Anabaptist history because to them the Anabaptists fled during the worst persecutions to eke out an existence; viz., the valleys of the Inn, the Adige, and the Puster.

In the Inn Valley the oldest Anabaptist territory was that of Rattenberg-Freundsberg. At Rattenberg Anabaptists were found in 1527. From the time Leonhard Schiemer (*q.v.*) was beheaded and his body burned (Jan. 14, 1529), followed by 70 other martyrs, to the end of the Anabaptist movement in Tirol there was no period of any length in which they were not found here. This is also true of the mining city of Schwaz, where a booklet was put on sale "in which Anabaptism is drawn (in pictures) for those who cannot read." In Schwaz the Anabaptists were already pursued by placards. Besides secret members there were said to be five or six leaders (*Vorsteher*). This was the situation in the entire region between Schwaz and Rattenberg. Villages named in the court records are Brixlegg, Ratfeld, Kramsach, Breitenbach, Puch, and Inning. The number of Anabaptists executed in Schwaz is given in the list of 1581 as 20, the best known being Hans Schlaffer (*q.v.*).

In Kufstein measures were instituted against the Anabaptists during this time. Sixteen martyrs are listed. In 1533 the contention was made by authorities that in the domain of Rattenberg, Kufstein, and Kitzbühel no one was left who was "stained with Anabaptism," and that in Kufstein "their eradication is so vigorously pursued that their leaders and other sectarians can find no shelter." But this does not correspond with fact. The recantation of Jakob Portner, a clergyman who had joined the Anabaptists, reveals that he had preached with extraordinary success in Kitzbühel, Rattenberg, and Kufstein, baptizing many who "persisted to the end, when they were sentenced from life to death."

An appendix to the Anabaptist mandate of Ferdinand I of March 26, 1534, warned all towns and magistracies in which boatmen lived who sailed the Danube, to see to it that no Anabaptists were accepted as passengers. This mandate includes also the Inn River, which was part of the route to Moravia.

In Hall Anabaptists were pursued as early as 1528; it was an important Anabaptist center. "At Hall," says Schwyger's *Chronik*, "many persons, men, women, and maidens, young and old, have come into the sect of the Anabaptists." Among the Anabaptists tried there, two sisters, outstanding for their steadfastness, Annele Malerin and Urschl Ochsentreiberin, who were baptized in Hall, are celebrated in song and in the chronicles. They were "drowned in the water."

One of these songs reveals that Mils near Hall was also an Anabaptist center. The register of 1581 lists the number of martyr executions as eight. Anabaptist propaganda had already begun in 1528, as is inferred from the inquiry made by the government at Innsbruck as to why Anabaptist preachers had been allowed to preach so long in the towns, including Innsbruck. The most significant and most famous of all the martyrs of Tirol was Jakob Hutter (*q.v.*), who was burned at the stake here after "terrible torture" on March 3, 1536. In Calzein and Rothholz there were Anabaptists as early as 1527; two ended their lives at the stake.

As in the lower valley, the Anabaptist movement was active for many decades in the upper Inn Valley, especially after Hutter's death. From Pfunds to Innsbruck they can be traced, and in certain localities, like Imst and Landeck, they were particularly strong at times. From its list of martyrs, as important as that of Innsbruck, it is seen that some of the executions took place in the late 1520's. Hearings took place at Imst in 1538, to which Dr. Gallus Müller (*q.v.*) was sent to convert the accused. But Müller's efforts were in vain. There Sebastian Hubmaier and Hans Grünfelder, later "the aged Oswald," lay in prison. Griesinger reported to the brotherhood in Moravia that they testified to God's Word and the truth; their joy could not be described; a crowd of 1,000 witnessed the execution of Bastl and Hansl. A fourth Anabaptist, Jakob Zängerle, was executed in Imst in the same year. In 1561 Anabaptists fled from Imst to Moravia; in the 70's they still had contacts with the Anabaptists of Moravia. An execution is listed at Landeck. Anabaptists from Landeck also fled to Moravia. In Telfs there were several in 1537.

In the upper Inn Valley Griesinger was active for a time; it was the home of Ursula Hellrigl, whom Gall Müller tried to convert. In lower Engadine (Grisons) the movement was active, and propagated itself to the upper Inn (Tirol); Anabaptists were still found there in 1533. In Stams three were executed, and in Petersberg two. Thus the entire Inn Valley, as far as it lies in Tirol, was in the 16th century the home of Anabaptism. The greatest number lived in Kitzbühel (*q.v.*), which also shows the largest number of blood witnesses. LOSERTH.

Loserth, *Anabaptismus;* Beck, *Geschichts-Bücher;* Wolkan, *Geschicht-Buch;* Zieglschmid, *Chronik;* ML II, 421 f.

Inner Light: see **Spiritualism.**

Inner Word: see **Spiritualism;** also **Bible: Inner and Outer Word.**

Inquiry Meeting (*Umfrage*): see **Counsel Meeting.**

Inquisition, a religious court of the Roman Church for the extermination of sectarians and heretics. The old Catholic Church knew no such institution. Athanasius held it to be a sign of the true church that she forced no one, and persecution to be an invention of Satan. Chrysostom thought likewise. Augustine was the first to advocate corporal punishment of the heterodox, through his false exegesis of Luke 14:23, "Compel them to come in," though even he opposed capital punishment. The death penalty was not reached until the 11th century, when Rome was beginning to subjugate the entire religious life and thought of Western Europe.

Since the ninth century there had been episcopal courts, whose duty it was to investigate and remove all abuses in the church, including false doctrine. Since in the opinion of the popes these courts dealt too leniently with the rise of the Waldensians, Cathars, etc., Pope Gregory IV, continuing the work of Lucius III and Innocent III, organized the Inquisition (inquiry or investigation) and committed its leadership to the Dominicans, who, responsible only to the pope, proceeded without pity in carrying out its program.

An institution of this kind, unparalleled in history, can be understood only as the practical result of the doctrine developing at the time, that the pope as God's representative had absolute power of life and death in his hands. In the final analysis it was a product of the rigid Roman law of the time of the Caesars. The innovation was, to base the execution of heretics on the Bible. From the Bible's symbolic designation of heretics as thieves and wolves, Thomas Aquinas concluded that thieves are hanged and wolves clubbed to death. The verse in Titus 3:10, that one who causes divisions should be avoided, he construed thus: avoidance is best carried out through execution. There have been few times in history when Christian doctrine was so completely misunderstood as at this time of the rise of the Inquisition.

In general the Inquisition took the following course: The trial was initiated by denunciation through anyone, including corrupt persons. The confession of the accused, which was required for execution, was often forced by merciless torture; it was then repeated, thus obtaining the "free" confession. The penitent had to recant, and after satisfying the required punishment was received back into the church. The inquisitors frequently made honest attempts to win the accused to the church. But if he was recalcitrant, he was committed to the temporal authorities for execution at the stake. Tens of thousands thus fell victims to the external unity of the church. The few more familiar examples of inquisition trials make it clear that in addition to arbitrariness, rank injustice often prevailed (as in the case of Conrad of Marburg, who after two years of effective work was slain by German knights). After 1542 the Inquisition became a terrible weapon in the service of the Counter Reformation.

The Inquisition was first successfully used in Italy. The court records of Venice show 35 Anabaptist(?) trials in the 16th century, and four in the 17th century. France saw its most terrible operation in the Albigensian war 1209-29 and following. Because of its involvement with the interests of the king the Inquisition was "successful" against the Albigenses in spite of popular revolt against its cruelties. In Spain, where it became a state institution, it operated with similar cruelty against Waldensians, Cathars, and especially Jews and the descendants of the Moors.

Whereas the Inquisition was successful in stamping out all Protestant movements in the above three countries, it failed in the northern Netherlands in its struggles against the Beguines and Beghards, the Brethren of the Common Life, and the Reformation movements. Under Charles V (1519-56) some thousands were executed, most of them Anabaptists. He said the guilt of the Anabaptists was as great as that of other heretics, and they must therefore suffer the same penalties; however, if they showed themselves penitent before their death, one might proceed more leniently with them: if men, such penitents should be beheaded; if women, buried alive. For the introduction of the Inquisition into Germany an indisputable legal basis was laid in the imperial edicts. In spite of its defective organization and the resistance of all classes it seems to have been even bloodier than in the Romance countries. In Germany it finally terminated in a general witch hunt, which cost many more lives.

Although modern times have put an end to the Inquisition, the Catholic Church has not abandoned it. The congregation of cardinals is today still predominant, nor has a single decision been made declaring the Inquisition contrary to the spirit of Christianity.

The reformers had no such institution. Nevertheless Calvin stood entirely on the platform of the medieval Inquisition in trying the anti-Trinitarian Servetus and turning him over to the temporal authorities to be burned (1553). Luther was on the same ground, when he, after having considered banishment adequate punishment (q.v.) for Anabaptists until 1528, from that time on also sponsored capital punishment for them. Nor did Melanchthon, Zwingli, and Calvin correct this error of the great reformer. In the question of the burning of heretics they exceeded Luther, when they applied to the Anabaptists the old laws of the Jewish theocracy concerning the bloody extirpation of Baal-worship (Deut. 13:7-11). Thus the Lutheran estates could also sanction the terrible mandate of the Diet of Speyer of April 23, 1529, which advocated that "each and every Anabaptist and rebaptized man or woman of an age of understanding shall be judged and brought from life to death with fire and sword or the like according to the occasion, without previous investigation by the clergy." In the following important addition lies Luther's contribution to the theory of the Inquisition, which supersedes the Middle Ages: "The government punishes the heretic for the sake of public peace, and not for the sake of the church; i.e., ecclesiastical power is no longer to be higher in authority than temporal power" (Köhler, 36).

On the whole it may be said that the Reformation prepared the way for religious liberty, though it did not itself take that way. It is to the credit of the Anabaptists that they rejected the use of force in religious matters and demanded unconditional toleration as an outcome of their understanding of faith. Unfortunately they were then unable to prevail. The gradual elimination of the Inquisition came in the period of the Enlightenment.   H.Q.

P. Flade, *Das römische Inquisitionsverfahren in Deutschland* (1902); H. Hermelink, *Der Toleranzgedanke im Reformationszeitalter* (Leipzig, 1908); P. Fredericq, *Geschiedenis der Inquisitie in de Nederlanden* (2 vv. 1892); P. Wappler, *Inquisition und Ketzerprozesse in Zwickau zur Ref.-Zeit* (Leipzig, 1908); W. Köhler, *Reformation und Ketzerprozess* (Tübingen, 1901); Ign. v. Döllinger, *Kleinere Schriften* (1890); H. C. Lea, *A History of the Inquisition in the Middle Ages* (3 vv., New York, 1888); Frid. Hoffmann, *Geschichte der Inquisition* (2 vv., Bonn, 1878); *HRE* IX, 152 ff.; *ML* II, 422.

Institute Monthly, official organ of the Elkhart Institute (q.v.), was intended as a means of keeping former students in touch with the school. The first issue was printed in October 1898 and the last in May 1903. In the June-July number, 1903, it became the *Goshen College Record.* The format, eight three-column pages 8¼ x 11¼ in., was changed after the first year to 16 two-column pages 7 x 9½ in. The first editorial staff was W. K. Jacobs, editor, and I. R. Detweiler, business manager. Beginning with the sixth issue F. S. Ebersole served as editor. He was succeeded by C. K. Hostetler. The Mennonite Historical Library at Goshen College has a complete file.   J.S.U.

Instrumentum publicum *wegen desjenigen, was bey denen Churfl. Pfaltzischen Herrn Commissarien gegen die Protestante Mennoniste zu Rheydt in Anno 1694 in facta vorgenohmen vnd sich zugetragen* (1696) is the title of a printed protocol giving detailed information on the expulsion of the Mennonites from Rheydt, which was published in Crefeld in 1801. This booklet of 25 pages octavo is an important source for the history of the Anabaptists in the Rhineland. A copy is found in the Mennonite Library at Amsterdam. The library also contains a manuscript copy of a Dutch translation made by Godschalk Godschalks in 1771. This latter was translated into English by N. B. Grubb and published in the *Mennonite Yearbook and Almanac* for 1910 (Philadelphia, Pa.) and as a separate pamphlet under the erroneous title *Pro Copia Instrumentum Publicum* (1909) along with the English translation of two letters of 1708 (Germantown) and 1745 (Skippack) to Amsterdam, found in the Amsterdam Mennonite Archives. The German edition was reprinted in *Gem.-Kal.* 1933, 126-31. (Rembert, *Wiedertäufer,* 530 f.; *ML* II, 426.)   NEFF.

Insurance is the practice of distributing the economic risks of an individual or a group among an entire group or at least among a large number of individuals willing to bear their portion of the risk. This method of seeking protection against hazards may cover losses resulting from damage to, or destruction of, life, property, or almost any type of economic wealth. In buying insurance the purchaser gets a contract which sets forth the obligations and benefits falling upon or accruing to the parties involved.

The principle of sharing losses is an old one among Christians. Mennonites from their earliest history have practiced it as an integral part of brotherhood life. Sharing was, however, not thought of in terms of systematic and selective risk-bearing modern insurance. The forerunner of present-day insurance was the mutual aid society, which has replaced the informal, spontaneous, and unorganized expression of bearing one another's burdens in the primary group relations of the Anabaptist and Mennonite brotherhoods.

As early as 1623 the Mennonites of West Prussia, Germany, organized the Tiegenhöfer Privat-Brandordnung for the purpose of rendering systematic aid to members in cases of loss from fire, storm, or other emergencies. It will be noted that this organization did not cover losses due to death but rather losses of property resulting from accidental or natural causes. Such organizations as the above in time became integral parts of Mennonite life and culture when the Prussian Mennonites migrated to Russia and later to the United States and Canada. Toward the latter half of the 19th and early 20th centuries the other Mennonites in America organized a number of similar aid organizations. There are now (1956) approximately 70 mutual aid societies among the Mennonites in the United States and Canada. The majority of these societies protect their members against total losses from fire, storms, hail, and natural disasters. Two societies, however, are simple assessment death benefit societies, and a half dozen are burial aid societies. In more recent years, three mutual auto aid societies have been formed, also a number of prepayment health and hospital aid societies.

All of the Mennonite aid societies originally accepted only members of Mennonite churches in good standing as participants in their programs, and this is still true in about three fourths of the societies. However, a number of the organizations have slowly accepted non-Mennonites. This change in policy was often brought about as a result of intermarriage. Several of the aid societies no longer require Mennonite church membership as a condition of joining, and one of the oldest and largest Mennonite insurance societies has dropped the name "Mennonite" and is no longer under Mennonite direction.

The size of the aid societies ranges in membership from the smallest with 130 members to the largest society, which takes in non-Mennonites, with over 10,000 members. The average for 26 societies in 1955 was 2,500 members. All of the regular mutual aid casualty insurance societies are operated on the simple assessment plan. Although economic reason is not the major one for the existence of the Mennonite societies, the cost of the insurance to the members of the societies is from 25 per cent to 75 per cent lower than in many of the straight commercial insurance companies.

Mennonites have traditionally been opposed to commercial insurance companies, and specifically to the principle of life insurance and the companies selling it. (See articles **Life Insurance** and **Mutual Aid**.) J.W.F.

Intercontinental Company, Limited, a Canadian corporation chartered Nov. 19, 1925, with chief office at Winnipeg, Man., by General Samuel McRoberts, chairman of the board of the Chatham-Phenix National Bank in New York, and Edward Robinette, president of Stroud & Co. of Philadelphia, invest-

ment bankers. The purpose of the corporation, as set forth in the minutes of its first meeting, Dec. 16, 1925, was to carry through "a plan for promoting and assisting the emigration to Paraguay, South America, of certain religious sects [Mennonites] now residing on farms in Northwestern Canada [chiefly Manitoba] and recolonizing the farms so vacated by placing new settlers [new Mennonite immigrants from Russia] thereon." The stock of the company consisted of 10,000 shares of common stock owned by McRoberts and Robinette and ultimately 5,000 shares of preferred stock with par value of $100. Additional funds were raised by sale of first-mortgage bonds, called Farm Lien Bonds, to the value of $1,000,000 (?), secured by the land holdings purchased from the emigrating Mennonites of Manitoba. Later (1930) second-mortgage bonds to the value of more than $100,000 were sold to Mennonite and Amish buyers through A. J. Miller, former director of American Mennonite Relief in Russia, with endorsement of MCC officials. Because of the farming difficulties in 1927 ff., the depression of 1929 ff., and the relative financial failure of the Paraguayan project, the holders of the first-mortgage bonds (chiefly the National Trust Co. of Toronto and Winnipeg, but also the American Corporation Bond and Share Co. of Delaware with $240,000 holdings, the Interprovincial Trading Corporation of Canada with $96,000, and lesser holders) foreclosed the company. As a result the Mennonite second-mortgage bond holders lost all their equity. The foreclosure apparently took place in 1931, since no further records of the IC could be found.

A complicated financial and corporate structure was set up to handle the entire Manitoba-Paraguay operation. The Corporacion Paraguaya was organized at Asuncion in April 1926 to purchase from the Carlos Casado Co., an Argentine corporation, the land in the Chaco needed for resale to the Manitoba Mennonites. The American Continental Co., C. par A., was organized in July 1926 at Santo Domingo, Dominican Republic, to hold the stock of the Corporacion Paraguaya. In 1929 the AC held $763,000 of IC gold bonds, while the CP also held $237,000 of the IC gold bonds, which had been issued to pay the CP for the land purchased from it by the IC for sale to the Manitoba emigrants. When the relative financial failure of the CP became clear, the MCC finally purchased the entire stock of the CP and its assets for $57,000, with a net value to the sellers of less than $25,000. This was done in 1937.

Thus practically the entire assets of McRoberts and Robinette in their Paraguay venture were wiped out. A rather grandiose scheme motivated originally, largely on the part of General McRoberts (q.v.) at least, by a humanitarian concern for the Mennonites (together with, of course, hope for financial gain) failed. But in the course of the 12 years (1925-37) in which it was in operation, the McRoberts-Robinette project made possible the entire Mennonite colonization in Paraguay, both Menno and Fernheim, as well as aiding the new immigrants to Manitoba in securing land for settlement.

The Intercontinental Company purchased a total of 43,998 acres from the Manitoba Mennonite emigrants for an over-all price of $902,900.39, of which approximately $308,000 was paid out in cash, and the rest in Chaco land, 137,920 acres at five dollars per acre. The company sold its Manitoba land in turn to new Mennonite immigrants from Russia on long-term crop payment contracts, and from its Winnipeg office aided the purchasers in many ways with further small loans and advice on crops and farm management. Under the pressure of farm depression conditions the sale contracts were renegotiated to easier terms in order to save the situation.

H.S.B.

The records of the IC are deposited in the Archives of the Mennonite Church at Goshen College. See also W. Quiring, "The Canadian Mennonite Immigration into the Paraguayan Chaco," *MQR* VIII (1934) 32-45.

Intercourse Mennonite (MC) Mission outpost, now extinct. In 1897, ten years after Hershey Sunday School was started in the Pequea District, Lancaster Mennonite Conference, Mahlon Buckwalter and Henry H. Hershey opened a Sunday school in the schoolhouse east of Intercourse. The enrollment was 75. In 1904 this school could no longer be used, and the outpost was closed.

I.D.L.

Intermarriage: see Mixed Marriage.

Inter-Mennonite Relations. *A. Europe.* The development of sectors of the Anabaptist movement in distinct linguistic and geographical areas (Switzerland, South Germany, Netherlands, Moravia, Vistula Delta) and the emergence of the Hutterite brotherhood in Moravia as a variant communistic type resulted in a lack of close relations between the distinct Anabaptist groups already in the middle of the 16th century. · The tensions became very serious between the Hutterites and the Swiss Brethren, as well as between the Dutch-Northwest German followers of Menno and the High Germans (and Swiss Brethren). As a consequence brotherly relations were completely severed in both cases, and in the latter case Menno Simons excommunicated the entire opposite party. Close relations, however, were maintained between the Dutch Mennonites and those of the Vistula Delta. A relatively harmonious relationship was also achieved among all the South German and Swiss Anabaptists, of which the general Anabaptist conferences of 1555, and 1557, and 1568 at Strasbourg are a testimony. For a time there were two distinct groups of Anabaptists in the South, viz., the Swiss Brethren (more in Switzerland), and the followers of Pilgram Marpeck (*q.v.*). As the recent doctoral dissertation, *Pilgram Marpeck, sein Kreis und seine Theologie* (University of Zürich, 1955), by J. J. Kiwiet has shown, it was Marpeck who, after strenuous endeavor (1540-54), succeeded in bringing the two groups together in 1555. Kiwiet even holds that the remnants of the Melchiorites in South Germany were included in this union.

The account of the tragic divisions, in Dutch Mennonitism, beginning in 1566, which were not fully overcome in the Netherlands until the forming of the A.D.S. in 1811, is better given in the article **Netherlands,** although these divisions penetrated all the Anabaptist-Mennonite communities in North Germany from Emden to Königsberg, and even had significant consequences in the earlier stages of Mennonite history in Russia. The attitudes of certain of these schismatic parties were often very harsh toward the other groups, including general excommunication and the requirement of rebaptism for transfer of members. This was particularly true of the Flemish versus the Frisians. The Frisians and particularly the third major group, the Waterlanders (who were not transplanted outside the Netherlands), were milder in their attitudes.

The Hutterites went their own way completely until the early 19th century when they settled in the Ukraine near the Molotschna Mennonite settlement, and were aided by Johann Cornies (*q.v.*). There was some friendly correspondence in the 18th century between them and the Dutch Mennonites. No close relations resulted from their settlement in 1874-77 near the Mennonite settlements in South Dakota. However, a considerable number of Hutterites in South Dakota joined the G.C.M. and K.M.B. groups, no doubt in part because of the memory of Cornies' assistance.

The Swiss Brethren continued relatively isolated (the South German Anabaptists having practically died out by the time of the Thirty Years' War, 1618-48). However, the great tribulations of the mid-17th century in Bern resulted in repeated intervention in their behalf by the Dutch Mennonites, and the ultimate settlement of some Swiss Mennonites in Holland, where they were finally absorbed. The Swiss Brethren settlers in the Palatinate in the time of their suffering from the French invasions at the end of the 17th and beginning 18th centuries received from the Dutch Mennonites substantial financial relief, and aid in emigration to Holland and Pennsylvania. Considerable correspondence between Palatinate Mennonite leaders and the Dutch Mennonite relief agency lies in the Amsterdam Mennonite Archives. The Dutch Mennonites were also generous in their aid to the West and East Prussian Mennonites suffering from floods or persecution in the 17th and 18th centuries. The attempted settlement of the Lithuanian Mennonites from the Memel area in Holland in the early 18th century was a failure.

Apart from the above-noted relations the Mennonites of the Netherlands and the rest of Europe developed no intimate relations or co-operative effort until the 19th century, when the Dutch Mennonite mission in the Dutch East Indies (beginning in 1847) enjoyed considerable support from the Mennonites of Russia and Germany. The mission, representing the evangelical fraction of the Dutch, became an inter-Mennonite bond which transcended the negative effect of the rise of modernism in the Dutch church. In Germany the *Mennonitische Blätter* (*q.v.*, founded in 1854) and the Vereinigung der Mennonitengemeinden im Deutschen Reich (*q.v.*, a conference founded 1886) both contributed much to bringing the various and widely scattered Mennonite communities together as well as mediating good relations with the Dutch Mennonites.

The development of the Mennonite World Conference (first meeting in Basel in 1925) under the leadership of the German pastor, Christian Neff (*q.v.*), was the first extensive inter-Mennonite relationship developed in Europe. In the post-World

War II period (1945-) a series of international Mennonite co-operative organizations has arisen, which have multiplied and intensified good inter-Mennonite relationships in Europe. The list includes the International Mennonite Peace Committee (1936, 1949), European Mennonite Bible School (1949), European Mennonite Evangelizing Committee (EMEK, 1952), European Mennonite Relief Committee (1954), Mennonite Voluntary Service (MFD, 1954), and *Der Mennonit* (1948, its inter-Mennonite publishing committee created in 1957). All of these organizations include representatives of all Mennonite national groups in Europe (Dutch, Swiss, French, and German) except the Bible school and *Der Mennonit,* which have no Dutch representation. The North American Mennonites are represented through the Mennonite Central Committee (MCC) in all of them except EMEK. The European groups are also all represented along with North America in the Preparatory Commission for the Mennonite World Conference, and take part in its sessions. Since 1950 the MCC has been operating out of Basel, Switzerland, a Christian education materials project (CEMO) with the co-operation and later direct management of the Mennonite Publishing House of Scottdale, the latter publishing at Basel through the Agape Verlag (est. 1955) German and French materials for summer Bible schools. An Advisory Council representing four of the European national Mennonite groups (except Holland) co-operates in the project.

The schisms which caused so much trouble and difficulty in Holland and on through to West Prussia and Russia (1565-1811), and the Amish schism (1697) in Switzerland, France, and South Germany, have all been overcome in Europe. The only remaining schism is that of the Mennonite Brethren and Mennonite Church in Russia (1860), which still persists in Russia. This schism caused much bitterness at the beginning, and resulted in long-continued tensions.

B. North America. The successive migrations from Europe to North America (1683-1860), i.e., from Switzerland, France, and Germany to Pennsylvania and further west, including Ontario, resulted in the formation of a new North American Mennonitism which maintained no connections with its European homeland. (Mennonite and Amish groups at first remained separate in the New World.) The same was true also of the successive waves of immigration from Russia to the prairie provinces and states of Canada and the United States (1874, 1922, 1930, 1947 ff.) and to South America (1930, 1947 ff.) in Paraguay, Brazil, and Uruguay. The Mennonite Brethren-Mennonite schism has been perpetuated in all these settlements and lands, although there has been a varying amount of co-operation between the two groups, both in Russia and in North and South America. The Allianz-Gemeinde, founded in 1907 in the Ukraine, was a vain attempt to bridge the gap between the two major groups. In Russia (from 1910), in Paraguay (1930), and in Brazil (1930) a valuable co-operative organization was established in the form of the KfK (*q.v.,* Commission for Church Affairs), which represented both major groups and the Allianz-Gemeinde (*q.v.*). In Russia,

under the pressure of conditions, a general conference was formed in 1910, including both the M.B. and Mennonite groups, which has also had a beneficent influence on intergroup relations in the new settlements in Paraguay and Brazil (1930 ff.), where there has been considerably closer co-operation than in North America.

Most of the Mennonite immigrants from Europe to North America in the first 190 years (1683 to 1860), being of relatively homogeneous Swiss-South German background (including Alsace-Lorraine), naturally formed one common brotherhood, uniting in the group known as the Mennonite Church (MC), overriding even the Amish schism, although half of the Amish, the Old Order and the Conservative Amish, remained outside this fold. The only exceptions were the smaller Swiss and South German groups arriving in the second quarter of the 19th century, which, though akin to the earlier immigrants of this group, shared in the formation of the General Conference Mennonite Church (begun in 1860), whose first nucleus was a dissident block (1847) from the Eastern Pennsylvania area of the Mennonite Church (MC). The large first Russian and Prussian Mennonite immigration groups of 1874-80 in their prairie state settlement joined the General Conference Mennonite group.

The formation of the "General Conference of the Mennonites of North America" in 1860 was the first attempt at a deliberate over-all union of all Mennonite congregations. The vision was that of John H. Oberholtzer, who conceived of it as co-operation of autonomous congregations working together in the fields of missions, publication, and education. The beginning was inauspicious, securing the adherence of only a few congregations at the outset, but gradually one third of all the Mennonites of North America was brought under its wing, including most of the large Swiss settlements in Indiana and Ohio, and ultimately the Central Conference composed largely of regional Illinois Amish. By no means all of the Russian Mennonite immigrants, however, joined the General Conference, even outside the K.M.B. and M.B. groups, the Peters-Wall churches (later E.M.B.) and the large Old Colony group in Manitoba remaining outside. It has been successful in bringing together into one working fellowship a great number of congregations of divergent origins and backgrounds.

Since the Mennonite Brethren and smaller splinter groups from Russia also continued their separate life, and the conservative "Old Colony" groups in Manitoba (1874-80 arrival) did the same (not joining even the General Conference group), and since several new schismatic groups (E.M., E.M.B., M.B.C., and Central Conference) were formed in the period 1855-90, both from the older M.C. group and the G.C.M. group, the ranks of the North American Mennonites were by 1900 rather badly broken. The effects of the Oberholtzer division of 1847 in Pennsylvania, of the M.B. division of 1860 in Russia, of the M.B.C. division of 1874 in Indiana and Ontario, and of the smaller Egly (1866) and Stuckey (1871) divisions in Indiana and Illinois, had left deeper wounds than is sometimes realized, and augmented the already existing distance between the various

Mennonite groups due to differences in European background and to differing emphases developed in America. Hence it was that inter-Mennonite relations in North America were largely negative or even polemic in the period before World War I (1914-18).

However, some welcome exceptions to the general negative American status before 1914 should be noted, the chief being the co-operative inter-Mennonite effort to aid the often very needy Russian immigrants of 1874-80. The Mennonite Board of Guardians (*q.v.*), founded in 1873 for this purpose, though not an official co-operative effort of conference bodies, was composed of representatives from the M.C. and G.C.M. groups and rallied support from almost all sections of Mennonitism in America. To support this work Union Aid committees (*q.v.*) were formed in Eastern Pennsylvania and Ontario. J. F. Funk (MC) with his Mennonite Publishing Co. at Elkhart, Ind., became and remained for many years the chief publisher for the Russian Mennonites in Manitoba. For over 40 years, for instance, the *Mennonitische Rundschau* (*q.v.*) was published by him and his later successors at Scottdale. The Mennonite Aid Plan (*q.v.*), founded in 1882 at Elkhart in the M.C. group, soon secured a clientele among the Russian Mennonites, especially in Minnesota and South Dakota, and ultimately became chiefly their agency. The Home and Foreign Relief Commission (*q.v.*, MC) founded in 1897 at Elkhart, Ind., for famine relief in India, was a quasi inter-Mennonite organization with widespread support from several Russian Mennonite groups in the prairie states, and with D. J. Jantzen, a "Russian" Mennonite, as a leading co-worker and one-year secretary. M. S. Steiner (*q.v.*, d. 1911), the president of the Mennonite Board of Missions and Charities (*q.v.*), had a vision of an inter-Mennonite mission organization, which he attempted but failed to achieve. The Congo Inland Mission (*q.v.*, 1911) was the first and only successful inter-Mennonite mission organization, with official representation at first from two conferences (Evangelical Mennonite and Central) and later of three, the General Conference Mennonites being added later.

Significant inter-Mennonite co-operation in North America did not begin until 1913, had only a slow growth between the two world wars, and came to full growth only after 1940, particularly with the remarkable development that has taken place since World War II. An attempt at drawing all Mennonites of North America closer together was made through the All-Mennonite Convention (*q.v.*, meetings held usually triennially 1913-36), but with little permanent success. Bluffton College (*q.v.*), enlarged in 1913 from "Central Mennonite College," together with the Mennonite seminary, later (1921) called Witmarsum Theological Seminary (*q.v.*), carried for a time the inter-Mennonite idea, having a board unofficially representing three Mennonite bodies (G.C.M., E.M., and Central Conference), and hoping to unite all branches of Mennonites in a common educational effort. This vision also did not come to fruition and Bluffton finally became a straight G.C.M. school, while Witmarsum was discontinued in 1931. One other joint institution, the Meadows

Mennonite Home (*q.v.*) at Meadows, Ill., was established in this period (1923) by the Central and Defenseless (E.M.) conferences.

The major event in inter-Mennonite co-operation in the period between the wars was the founding of the Mennonite Central Committee (*q.v.*) in July 1920 as the official agency of six Mennonite bodies for famine relief in Russia. Fortunately it was not disbanded upon the completion of this work in 1925, but only remained moribund, to begin its real career with the colonization of Russian refugees in Paraguay in 1930. Almost simultaneously the Canadian Mennonite Board of Colonization (*q.v.*) was organized (1922, preceded by Canadian Central Committee in October 1920), representing most Mennonite groups in Canada, to aid in the great migration of Russian Mennonites to Canada. Both the MCC and the CMBC have continued to be vital service organizations on an inter-Mennonite basis, though with different fields of work, and have furnished the background and stimulus for many subsequent inter-Mennonite activities and organizations. The Mennonite Colonization Board (*q.v.*), organized about the same time (1924) in Kansas on an inter-Mennonite basis, accomplished little and finally was absorbed by the MCC in 1947.

The experience of co-operation in the extensive and long-continued MCC program of service to the new Mennonite settlements in South America, in which all the North American Mennonites have joined, has had an important and wholesome influence on inter-Mennonite relations, both within North and South America.

World War II gave the greatest impetus to inter-Mennonite co-operation through the joint effort of all major Mennonite bodies to define a common peace position in the United States and to administer Civilian Public Service (*q.v.*). The Mennonite Central Peace Committee (*q.v.*), organized in March 1939 as the official agency of seven Mennonite bodies to work in this field, turned over its work to the MCC and its Peace Section in January 1942. The Peace Section has continued as a vital inter-Mennonite organization in this field. The good success of the MCC in its relief, colonization, and peace work, gradually led all Mennonite bodies in the United States and Canada, except the most isolated smaller ones, to support its work and to join its membership, so that it has become the one truly all-Mennonite inter-Mennonite organization. As such it has continued to enjoy immense prestige and good will.

The scope of MCC activities was gradually increased to include Voluntary Service (1946), though to a somewhat limited extent; Menno Travel Service (1947); Mental Health Service (1947) now (1957) administering three mental hospitals; European Farm Trainee Program (1950); I-W Services (1952); co-ordination of Mennonite Disaster Service (1955); Ailsa Craig, Ont., Boys' Farm (1955); Mennonite Indemnity, Inc. (1957), which is a reinsurance company to serve over 60 Mennonite mutual aid societies; and the joint delegation to Russia (1956). All these MCC activities serve on an inter-Mennonite basis, either through representation from various Mennonite bodies or by service to them. The MCC was also the carrier of the Mennonite World Conference in 1948 and represented the North American groups in the planning of the Conference for 1952, though now replaced by the North American Committee of Reference and Counsel for the Sixth Mennonite World Conference, which represents seven Mennonite bodies.

A series of inter-Mennonite agencies in the field of relief and nonresistance was also set up in Canada, all now affiliated with the MCC. They are the Nonresistant Relief Organization (*q.v.,* November 1917) in Ontario, the Conference of Historic Peace Churches (*q.v.,* July 1940) in Ontario, the Mennonite Central Relief Committee (*q.v.,* March 1940) in Western Canada, and the Canadian Mennonite Relief Committee (*q.v.,* December 1940) in Manitoba.

In the United States quite a significant number of new inter-Mennonite organizations have been set up since World War II. They include the Association of Mennonite and Affiliated Colleges (1944), the Mennonite Research Fellowship (*q.v.,* 1946), the MENNONITE ENCYCLOPEDIA (published by a joint publishing committee of the three major Mennonite publication boards set up in 1947), the Association of Mennonite Hospitals and Homes (*q.v.,* 1951), the Association of Mennonite Aid Societies (*q.v.,* 1955), and the Associated Mennonite Biblical Seminaries (*q.v.*), set up in 1956. The last is a grouping of Biblical seminaries with center at Elkhart, Ind. (Mennonite Biblical Seminary, GCM, and Goshen College Biblical Seminary, MC, at Goshen, with hoped for adhesions of certain other groups later). In 1956 the Mennonite Publishing House (MC) and the Mennonite Publication Office (GCM) began the joint preparation and publication of a graded Sunday-school lesson series. The *Mennonite Quarterly Review* (founded 1927) and *Mennonite Life* (founded 1946) have from the beginning had inter-Mennonite editorial boards, though published by single agencies. *The Mennonite Weekly Review,* reaching as it does a large readership in all branches and having an all-Mennonite news coverage, has been a wholesome influence. The latest inter-Mennonite project is the Inter-Mennonite Ministerial Study Conference, sponsored by the Inter-Mennonite Ministerial Study Committee, which in turn was sponsored by the North American Committee of Reference and Counsel for the Sixth Mennonite World Conference, and which is composed of representatives of five North American Mennonite conferences.

Local inter-Mennonite meetings of various kinds have been held in several Mennonite communities, such as the Mennonite Teachers Association (Kansas), Sunday-school conferences, ministerial meetings, and conferences of former CPS men. Disaster Service agencies have been set up on an inter-Mennonite basis across the United States (1954-56), and in more than one case inter-Mennonite groups have co-operated in actual disaster work. In the area of Kitchener-Waterloo, Ont., an inter-Mennonite ministerial meeting is held (annually since 1950) and in another area (central Illinois) one such meeting was held in 1956. In Chicago for some years an inter-Mennonite meeting of city missions has been held annually (since 1940). In New York, Chicago, To-

ronto, Philadelphia, and Iowa City, inter-Mennonite student group meetings have been held occasionally and in Philadelphia the Mennonite Student Center has been established (1953), open to all Mennonites though operated by one group alone.

The Conference on Mennonite Cultural Problems met annually 1942-47, since then biennially, sponsored by the Association of Mennonite Colleges. Since 1947 this association has also sponsored annual summer tours of Mennonite students and alumni to Europe. It also sponsors the Inter-Collegiate Mennonite Peace Society, which has been active since 1950.

A considerable number of educational institutions were established on an inter-Mennonite basis from 1886 on, sometimes with only two groups co-operating officially, sometimes without official group co-operation but on the basis of a private board of control with unofficial representatives from two or more groups. Among these have been Mountain Lake (Minn.) Bible School (1886); Mennonite Collegiate Institute at Gretna, Man. (1890); Freeman Junior College, Freeman, S.D. (1903); Immanuel Bible School (now Academy) at Reedley, Cal. (1927); Lustre Bible School at Frazer, Mont. (1928); Elim Bible School at Altona, Man. (1928); Steinbach Bible School at Steinbach, Man. (1936); Bethany Bible School (now Academy) at Munich, N.D. (1938); and Grace Bible Institute at Omaha, Neb. (1943).

A number of Mennonite hospitals have also been established on an inter-Mennonite basis, chiefly in Manitoba, such as Concordia at Winnipeg (1930), Bethania at Altona (1936), Bethel at Winkler (1935), and Bethesda at Steinbach (1937).

The remarkable growth of inter-Mennonite activities since 1940 reflects a growing mutual understanding and enlarging good will among Mennonites of the several distinct denominational organizations. Recently mergers of several Mennonite groups have taken place, or are in process: G.C.M.-Central Conference in 1945; Evangelical Mennonite and Evangelical Mennonite Brethren in 1953 (not fully merged as yet); K.M.B. and M.B. planning to merge in 1957. Earlier the Mennonite (MC) and Amish Mennonite district conferences (MC) had merged in stages in 1916-25, and in 1956 the Conservative Mennonites had to all intents and purposes merged with the Mennonite Church (MC). One related group, the Brethren in Christ, originally branching off from Lancaster County (Pa.) Mennonites in 1770, but with little or no connection to Mennonites since then, has drawn very close to the Mennonite denominational family through its membership in the MCC, in the Council of Mennonite and Affiliated Colleges, and in the Mennonite World Conference. On the other hand, the Mennonite Brethren in Christ (United Missionary Church) has drawn almost completely away from the Mennonite family even dropping the name Mennonite except in Pennsylvania.

Through numerous channels also the relations between European Mennonites and North American Mennonites have been growing closer and warmer. Chief of these channels has been the MCC relief work in Europe in 1945 ff., which has directly served Mennonites in all European countries, and brought some 300 workers from America to Europe often in direct contact with European Mennonites in various local areas. These workers and MCC executive committee members have often attended Mennonite congregational and conference meetings in Europe, as well as numerous special meetings designed to provide for fellowship between European and American Mennonites. MCC area directors have been charged with liaison responsibilities, and in 1950 a direct Liaison Committee was established in Germany composed of representatives of the MCC and the three German Mennonite conferences. The Student Exchange Program sponsored by the Association of Mennonite Colleges has brought over 100 European Mennonite students to American Mennonite colleges since 1946, and the MCC Exchange Trainee Program likewise has brought over 150 young Mennonites to America. The Mennonite World Conference in 1948 brought some 25 European delegates to America, many of whom toured American and Canadian Mennonite congregations afterwards. And the two world conferences in Europe since then, at Basel (1952) and Karlsruhe (1957), have brought over 500 different American Mennonites to Europe. The MCC brought Elder Samuel Gerber from Switzerland on a tour of North American churches in 1951. Ernst Crous of Göttingen, Germany, served as exchange professor at Goshen, Bethel, and Bluffton colleges in 1948-49.

Closer relations between the older European and American bodies and the young churches established in Asia, Africa, and South America by mission efforts are cultivated not only by the regular visits of mission board secretaries to the several foreign fields, but also by the MCC relief operations in these areas and by visits from leaders of the younger churches to the West as well as attendance by some of them in Mennonite colleges and seminaries in the States and Canada, and at the World Conference sessions. The MCC centers in Sao Paulo, Montevideo, and Asuncion in South America also contribute to closer relationships.

Closer intergroup relations among the mission areas of the several boards on the foreign mission fields, especially in India and Japan, have been fostered through the creation of area co-operating relief committees through MCC stimulus. Such committees have been created in India (Mennonite Relief Committee for India, 1948) and Japan.

The only inter-Mennonite institution established in the areas outside Europe is the Mennonite Biblical Seminary founded in Montevideo, Uruguay, in April 1956, supported by the M.C. and G.C.M. mission boards in North America and administered by an inter-Mennonite board of directors representing Brazil, Paraguay, Uruguay, and Argentina.

Thus inter-Mennonite relationships are growing on an intercontinental as well as an interdenominational and international basis, and give good prospect of continuing to grow closer and more fruitful.
H.S.B.

International Mennonite Peace Committee (IMPC) was organized at Fredeshiem, Netherlands, July 4, 1936, immediately following the Mennonite World Conference meeting held at Amsterdam and Elspeet, with Jacob ter Meulen, librarian of the Hague Peace Palace Library, as executive secretary. The purpose of the committee was to promote the peace principle among the Mennonites everywhere and to render assistance to conscientious objectors who might become involved in difficulties because of their refusal to do military service. The committee issued a "Manifesto" to all Mennonites, but apart from rendering some aid to the Hutterites who were forced out of Germany by Hitler, did not accomplish much, partly because activity was suspended by World War II. It became moribund and was superseded by a reorganized committee in 1949.

The IMPC was reorganized in 1949 at Elspeet, Holland. The members of the new committee represented Holland, France, Switzerland, Germany, United States, and Canada, the North American members being appointed by the MCC Peace Section. The first officers were H. S. Bender (United States) chairman, Chr. Schnebele (Germany) vice-chairman, C. F. Brüsewitz (Holland) secretary, Pierre Widmer (France) fourth member; they have continued with little change to date (1957). The stated purpose of the IMPC is (a) to maintain contact between the Mennonite peace groups in the various countries; (b) to furnish a channel for cooperative action by these groups as may be desirable; (c) to publish a news bulletin to serve the international Mennonite peace cause; (d) to provide international Mennonite peace conferences at regular intervals; (e) to support those Mennonites in various countries who suffer for conscience' sake because of their nonresistant convictions; (f) to aid in clarifying, deepening, and applying fundamental convictions in regard to Biblical nonresistance; (g) to aid in a more effective nonresistant witness.

The committee has carried on its work in line with the above purpose, holding a number of international conferences at Belfort, Basel, Karlsruhe, Heilbronn, and Heerewegen, and beginning in 1955 the publication of a newsletter.   H.S.B.

International Refugee Organization (IRO) was the official agency of the United Nations Organization (UNO) for the maintenance and resettlement of European refugees. Although it was first officially organized on Aug. 20, 1948, through the Preparatory Commission of IRO it actually began work July 1, 1947, the date of expiration of the UNRRA (United Nations Relief and Rehabilitation Agency) and the Intergovernmental Committee for Refugees. By the time it had terminated operations on Jan. 31, 1952, it had provided care and maintenance for more than 1,000,000 refugees in camps in Europe, moved 1,038,750 in resettlement to overseas countries, and repatriated 72,834 to their countries of origin, at a cost of slightly more than $400,000,000.

Many Russian Mennonite refugees were helped by IRO, both in maintenance in camps in Germany, as well as in free transportation to Canada and South America. In 1948 four major transports (*Volendam* twice, *General Heinzelmann, Charlton Monarch*), all IRO except the first (for which MCC later received $160,000 from IRO), transported a total of 5,499 refugees to South America, chiefly to Paraguay. The first *Volendam* (*q.v.*) transport of Jan. 28, 1947, actually initiated the IRO resettlement program. The MCC through C. F. Klassen (*q.v.*), its

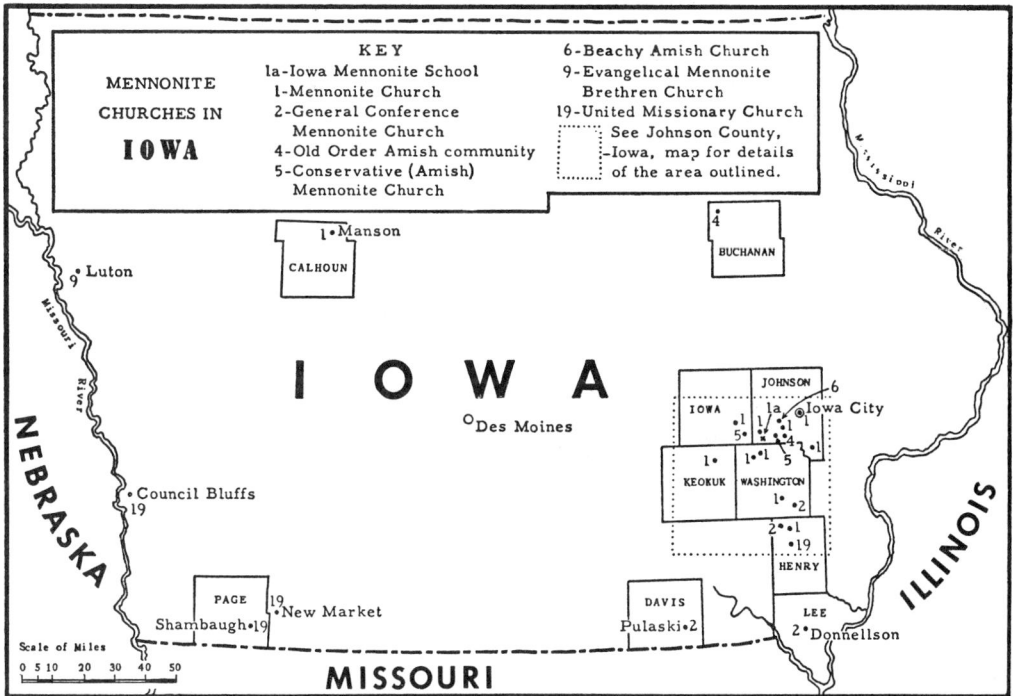

KEY

MENNONITE CHURCHES IN **IOWA**

1a-Iowa Mennonite School
1-Mennonite Church
2-General Conference Mennonite Church
4-Old Order Amish community
5-Conservative (Amish) Mennonite Church
6-Beachy Amish Church
9-Evangelical Mennonite Brethren Church
19-United Missionary Church

See Johnson County, Iowa, map for details of the area outlined.

commissioner for refugees, co-operated closely with the IRO, with whom it had excellent relationships.

When IRO was discontinued, part of its work was assumed by the Office of the High Commissioner for Refugees established by UNO in December 1950, and part by the Intergovernmental Committee for European Migration, organized in late 1951 on the initiative of the United States.

Before IRO took over, UNRRA, which had been established by UNO on Nov. 9, 1943, took on the refugee problem and established refugee camps, beginning this work on Sept. 1, 1944. However, its service was limited to citizens of member states of the United Nations. The Intergovernmental Committee for Refugees, established in 1945, assumed responsibility for the relief of refugees in Western European and neutral countries where the MCC was not operating. The constitution of IRO was actually adopted by UNO in December 1946, but the required 15 signatory nations were not secured until 1948. The Preparatory Commission in IRO was set up on July 1, 1947, by 20 nations (including some that had not yet formally adhered to IRO) as a stopgap until the full official activation of IRO could take place.

The MCC co-operated with IRO also by lending, beginning June 27, 1949, a team of three (or more) workers for welfare service in IRO-operated Displaced Persons (DP) camps. When the IRO program was discontinued in January 1952, and Church World Service (CWS) continued a welfare service program in the DP camps, the MCC-IRO team was transferred to CWS, continuing this service until 1954. H.S.B.

Intzinger, Franz, an Anabaptist at Leoben, Styria, Austria, was to be arrested in March 1530, but left the country a week before the order was to be carried out. In 1535 the note is made, "Franz Intzinger has become an Anabaptist, is being sought." He was apparently among the iron-dealers in Leoben at that time. (Archives of the city of Styria, *Faszikel* 18315; *Ztscht des. hist. Vereins für Steiermark,* No. 20, p. 268.)

Intzinger is probably identical with Franz Intzinger of Leiben in Styria, who emigrated from Nikolsburg with other nonresistant Anabaptists in 1528 and was made deacon together with Jakob Mändl, and then preacher at Austerlitz. It is thought that he lived for a time in Linz and baptized there (Wappler, 73, 187 f.). In 1530 complaint was voiced concerning their bookkeeping. The dissatisfaction over his management of church property may have been the cause for his return to his former home. HEGE.

Beck, *Geschichts-Bücher;* Wolkan, *Geschicht-Buch;* P. Wappler, *Inquisition und Ketzerprozess in Zwickau* (Leipzig, 1908); *ML* II, 427.

Iowa, an agricultural state in the upper Mississippi Valley, in 1953 had nine Mennonite communities, with approximately 5,200 members. Of these, 2,814 are members of the Mennonite Church (MC), while 817 are Old Order Amish, 754 General Conference Mennonites, 470 Conservative Amish Mennonites, 230 United Missionary Church, 52 Beachy Amish, and 26 Evangelical Mennonite Brethren.

By 1839 the wave of Mennonite westward migration had reached Iowa, when John C. Krehbiel from the Palatinate settled in West Point Twp., Lee

County. By 1845 enough settlers had located there to make it possible to organize a church (GCM), but this was postponed until 1849 because of the murder of their minister. In 1850 they completed the building of their new church, the first Mennonite meetinghouse in Iowa. Later a new one was built in West Point, but for the past several decades no services have been held in it, and the West Point congregation has been dissolved. During the 1850's large numbers of Mennonites from the Palatinate and from Bavaria moved into Franklin Township, and organized the Zion congregation, which is now located in Donnellson. As their numbers increased, a third congregation was organized in Franklin Center, but when their members moved to Kansas in the seventies their church declined in membership, and the building was finally torn down. Only one congregation of Mennonites is left in Lee County, but through the influence of their German parochial school, which they maintained until World War I, they have preserved much of their German background and their philosophy. Members of the Lee County church moved to Washington County, where they organized the Salem Church in 1865, but after 1875 the members began to move to Kansas and the church became extinct.

The Christian Raber family, who reputedly settled in Lee County in 1840, were very likely the first Amish to live in Iowa. The Rabers were followed by other Ohio families, so that by 1846, when Bishop Joseph Goldsmith arrived from Butler Co., Ohio, there were enough Amish for the organization of a church. By 1855 the church membership reached 55, its largest number. At that time, the Amish began to move to Henry and Davis counties, and in 20 years their Lee County settlement had completely disappeared. The first Amish to settle in Davis County bought land there in 1854, but did not organize a church until 1861. At that time they had 32 members and in 1954 they had 121. By 1890, when the Pulaski Mennonite Church joined the Middle District Mennonite Conference (GCM), they had discarded all of the distinctive teachings of the Amish branch.

The settling of Joseph Roth in Jefferson County in 1843 was the beginning of the Jefferson-Henry-Washington County Amish community. During the next decade Amish settlers moved into Henry County, and in 1851 they first bought land in Marion Twp., Washington County. These settlers, originally from Alsace and Switzerland, had migrated from Wayne Co., Ohio. Their church (MC) was organized in 1852-53 by Joseph Goldsmith of Lee County. After he moved to Henry County in 1855, he became its resident bishop. At first there was only one church organization, but later the church was divided into the Trenton Township and the Marion Township congregations, with Goldsmith in charge of both. In 1862 Benjamin Eicher was ordained preacher of the Washington County group and in 1866 he became bishop. The two congregations gradually drew apart, and after 1874 the Washington County or "Eicher" church no longer co-operated with the Henry County congregation, which came to be known as the Sugar Creek Church. The Eicher church developed along more

liberal lines than its sister church, and in 1892 it joined the General Conference of Mennonites (GCM). In 1900 the Eicher congregation established a branch church in Wayland, which since 1927 has been an independent congregation. The Sugar Creek Mennonite Church (MC) outgrew its building and so in 1949 the Bethel church was built north of Wayland to accommodate the members living in that area. The combined membership of the two churches (1955) is over 600.

By far the largest Iowa Amish and Mennonite settlement, established in 1846, is the one in Johnson and the bordering counties of Iowa and Washington. Their church was organized with 27 members by Joseph Goldsmith of Lee County in 1851. The 16 congregations of the settlement in 1953 had over 2,850 members. At first the Johnson County group adhered strictly to the Amish discipline, but during the late seventies a more liberal element withdrew from the Old Order. Since then, a majority have joined the more liberal Amish Mennonite or Mennonite (MC) churches, and the Johnson County Old Order membership in 1953 was only 464. (See map of Johnson County.)

Settlements established in several other Iowa counties were not permanent. Among these were the Mennonite settlement established in Mahaska County in 1852 (MC), the Page County Mennonite colony of 1864 (MC), and the Polk County group of 1856 (GCM). The Amish Mennonite settlements established in Pocahontas and Wright counties during the nineties have also disappeared, and the church established by the Stauffer (*q.v.*) Mennonites from Pennsylvania in Osceola County lasted only from 1887 to 1911. These groups were so small that it was difficult to maintain a community life. Other causes for their failure were the lack of leadership and disagreements among the ministers.

The Shambaugh, Iowa, Mennonite Brethren in Christ Church was organized first as a Brethren in Christ congregation, but joined the Mennonite Brethren in Christ conference after 1883. Near by is the New Market Mennonite Brethren in Christ Church, incorporated May 12, 1894. Their third church is the one at Trenton in Henry County. This latter church, organized during the eighties, became one of the first members of the Mennonite Brethren in Christ Conference, founded in 1883. More recently another congregation was established in Council Bluffs and very recently the Grace Missionary Church (UMC) was organized in Iowa City.

During the Civil War Mennonite families from Virginia settled in Keokuk Co., Iowa. When S. B. Wenger moved to the community in 1879 he hoped to establish a Mennonite church there, but not until 1898 was a congregation organized at that place. In 1953 this Mennonite (MC) church had a membership of 92. In 1892 and after, Amish Mennonite families from Illinois moved into Calhoun Co., Iowa. Five years later their congregation, now known as the Manson Mennonite Church (MC), was organized. In 1953 it had 273 members. Dissatisfied Old Order Amish Mennonites of Johnson County established a settlement in Buchanan County during 1914. Since that time others have moved in from Kansas, Indiana, and Ohio, and in 1953 their total membership was 353. Other Old Order Amish organized a Beachy Amish church in Johnson County in 1946, now known as the Sharon-Bethel church (*q.v.*). Others leaving the Amish in recent years joined the Conservative Amish Upper Deer Creek Church (*q.v.*), which has led to its expansion into the second congregation, Fairview, the two having a combined membership of 470. Missionary activity of the Johnson County churches brought about the establishment of congregations in Iowa City and at Iowa Valley. The most recently established Mennonite community in Iowa is the one founded near Luton (*q.v.*) in the western part by the Evangelical Mennonite Brethren. A mission (MC) was started in Des Moines in 1956.

The Mennonites in Iowa are mostly rural although a shift to small town business has gained momentum among them during the last two decades. The chief towns in which Mennonites live, either as retired citizens or as businessmen, are South English, Wellman, Kalona, Iowa City, Wayland, Donnellson, Pulaski, and Manson. Many Mennonites are engaged in specialized agriculture, especially in the turkey industry. The Maplecrest turkey industry, which began in the Johnson County Mennonite community, is nationally known.

The only Mennonite church institution in the state is the Iowa Mennonite School (*q.v.*), northeast of Kalona, founded by the local churches (MC and CAM) in 1945. In 1878 Samuel D. Guengerich (*q.v.*) of Johnson County launched *Der Christliche Jugendfreund*. In 1912 S. D. Guengerich and four other Amish leaders, three of whom lived in Iowa, organized the Amish Mennonite Publishing Association (*q.v.*), which has been an important influence in the life of the Amish through the past four decades.

The General Conference Mennonite Church had its origin in a conference meeting in the West Point Mennonite Church in May 1860. Among the prominent Mennonite leaders in Iowa have been Christian Schowalter (1828-1907, GCM), Benjamin Eicher (1832-93, GCM) Joseph Goldsmith (1796-1876, MC), Sebastian Gerig (1839-1924, MC), Jacob Swartzendruber (1800-68, OOA), Jacob F. Swartzendruber (1851-1924, OOA), and Samuel D. Guengerich (1835-1929, CAM).

During World War I many Mennonite young men were assigned to Camp Dodge, near Des Moines. In World War II Mennonite Civilian Public Service camps and units were located at Denison (No. 18) and Mount Pleasant (No. 86). A Mennonite dairy herd tester unit also operated in the state. Under the draft law which followed World War II Mennonite I-W men were in units located in Des Moines, Mount Pleasant, and Iowa City.   M.G.

In 1953 the Iowa Mennonite churches had the memberships given below.

Northwestern Iowa
Luton (EMB)	26
Manson (MC)	273

Northeastern Iowa
5 OOA districts, Buchanan Co. area	353

Southwestern Iowa
New Market (UMC)	50
Shambaugh (UMC)	49
Council Bluffs (UMC)	12

Southeastern Iowa
Davis County
Pulaski (GCM)	121

Lee County
Donnellson (Zion, GCM)	223

Henry-Washington County
Sugar Creek (MC)	462
Bethel (MC)	152
Wayland (GCM)	285
Eicher-Emmanuel (GCM)	125
Trenton (UMC)	89

Keokuk County
Liberty (MC)	92

Iowa-Johnson-Washington Counties
6 Kalona area OOA districts	464
Sharon-Bethel Beachy Amish	52
Upper Deer Creek and Fairview (CAM)	470
Grace Missionary (UMC)	30
Iowa City (MC)	93
Iowa Valley (MC)	27
West Union (MC)	381
Wellman (MC)	345
Daytonville (MC)	55
Lower Deer Creek (MC)	369
East Union (MC)	565

M. Gingerich, *The Mennonites in Iowa* (Iowa City, 1939); E. G. Swartzendruber, *Amish and Mennonite Church Centennial near Wellman and Kalona, Iowa* (Wellman, 2d ed., 1953); *Documents Relating to Bishop Jacob Schwarzendruber (1800-1868)* (reprinted from *MQR*, July 1946, Vol. XX); M. Gingerich, "A Century in Iowa," *Menn. Life* II (January 1947) 24; Emma K. Bachman, "From the Krehbiel Family Album," *Menn. Life* X (July 1955) 135; Vernon Neufeld, "Mennonites Settle in Lee County," *Menn. Life* VIII (October 1953) 170; *Haus und Handbuch für die Familie David Ruth, zu Eichstock, 1852* (at BeCL); *ML* II, 436-38.

Iowa City, Iowa, is the county seat (pop. 27,212) of Johnson County (*q.v.*) and the home of the University of Iowa, which has attracted many Mennonite students, partly because of its proximity to the large Mennonite settlement southwest of the city. Nine members of the faculty of Goshen College, five of Hesston College, and three of Bethel College have received degrees from the University of Iowa. In the 1951-52 school year Mennonite students in Iowa City organized a fellowship which has remained active. In 1953 a I-W unit of conscientious objectors was established at the University of Iowa hospital. The Iowa City Mennonite Church (*q.v.*) consists of a membership of approximately 100, comprising largely the Mennonites who have moved to the city. Mennonites of the county regularly patronize the stores of Iowa City.   M.G.

Iowa City (Iowa) Mennonite Church (MC), formerly Iowa City Gospel Mission, began as the Mennonite Sunday School on Nov. 27, 1927, in the old Cartright schoolhouse on Orchard Street on the west side of the Iowa River in Iowa City. The work began as a result of the vision of Will Guengerich, Chris Hershberger, Joe C. Brenneman, and others, in part to provide a church home for Mennonites who had moved to the city. The present meeting-house was erected in the summer of 1939 at 614 Clark Street (corner of Clark and Seymour) on the east side of the Iowa River. The present member-ship (1954) is 100 and the pastor is Virgil J. Bren-neman. As a mission it was operated by the Iowa-Nebraska District Board of the Mennonite Church. In January 1952 Norman Hobbs, who was then pastor, left the Mennonite Church. Taking about 20 members with him, he organized a new congre-gation (Grace Missionary) which is now affiliated with the United Missionary Church. In October 1954 the Mission became an independent congrega-tion assuming almost the entire support of the pro-gram and its pastor. At that time it was also de-cided to change the name to Iowa City Mennonite Church.   V.J.B.

Iowa County, Iowa, located in the southeastern part of the state, is bounded on the east by Johnson County (*q.v.*) and on the south by Keokuk and Washington counties, all of which contain Men-nonite settlements. Amish Mennonites settled in adjoining Johnson County in 1846 and by the next decade the settlement had spread westward into Iowa County. The Upper Deer Creek Conservative Mennonite Church (*q.v.*), the West Union Men-nonite Church (MC) (*q.v.*), and the Parnell Mission sponsored by the West Union Church, are located in the southeastern part of the county. Approxi-mately 500 Mennonites live in the county.   M.G.

Iowa Mennonite Benevolent Association, Inc., was organized in March 1956, at Kalona, Iowa, to build and operate a Mennonite home for the aged, to be erected in 1957 at Kalona to accommodate about 40 guests. The association is composed of 33 members representing six of the seven Mennonite (MC) con-gregations, the three Conservative Mennonite con-gregations, and the one Beachy Amish congregation in the general Kalona-Wellman area, and elected by them. The board of directors consists of six mem-bers chosen by the association.   H.S.B.

Iowa Mennonite Historical Society: see Mennonite Historical Society *of Iowa.*

Iowa Mennonite School (MC), Kalona, Iowa, is a Christian high school established to counteract through Christian education the secularism of the public schools and to offer high-school training to a considerable number of youth who would otherwise not have received such training. It serves the compact Kalona-Wellman Mennonite settlement in Johnson, Iowa, and Washington counties.

The school was founded in the fall of 1945, offer-ing the 9th and 10th grades. Grades 11 and 12 were added in succeeding years. The school is lo-cated about eight miles northwest of Kalona and the same distance northeast of Wellman, directly south across the road from the Lower Deer Creek Church. It is operated under the direction of the Iowa-Nebraska Conference, with a Conference-appointed board, originally of six members. Other governing groups of the school are a local board composed of lay members, and a religious welfare board composed of personnel from the other two boards.

Ministers who led in organizing the school were Amos Gingerich, J. Y. Swartzendruber, and S. J. Horst. The charter faculty was S. J. Horst, Samuel B. Nafziger, and Esther Detwiler. Administrative officers of the school have been S. J. Horst, principal 1945-49, Paul T. Guengerich, principal 1949- , Samuel B. Nafziger, dean 1945-52, Alvin J. Blough, asst. principal 1952- . The enrollment in 1954-55 was 184.

The physical plant consists of a nine-acre campus with a 50 x 72 ft. three-story brick building (erected in 1948) for classrooms and administration, and an 80 x 140 ft. brick and glass block auditorium-gymnasium with supplementary classrooms and farm shop (erected in 1954). The auditorium has a seating capacity of 1,800.

Spiritual benefits already being harvested are obvious as the youth find, in addition to their secu-lar training, an added sense of loyalty to Christ and the church. Among the 182 alumni are quite a number who are in further preparation for a posi-tive service to the program of the church. P.T.G.

Iowa-Nebraska Conference (MC) came into being in 1920 as a result of a merger of the Western Am-ish Mennonite Conference and the Mennonite con-ference west of Indiana. All congregations belong-ing to the above-named conferences within the states of Iowa, Nebraska, and Minnesota, and one congre-gation located at Thurman, Col. (16 in all), were designated as one section or district and formed into the new conference.

The Merger Committee also appointed the follow-ing executive committee, whose duty it was to ar-range for the first meeting of the new conference: S. C. Yoder, D. G. Lapp, J. E. Zimmerman, P. J. Blosser, C. J. Garber, and Simon Gingerich (Lapp, Blosser, and Garber represented the Mennonites; Yoder, Zimmerman, and Gingerich the Amish Men-nonites). The first session of the conference was held at the Lower Deer Creek Church, Kalona, Iowa, on Sept. 14 and 15, 1921. Officers of confer-ence elected were: Moderator, S. C. Yoder; Asst. Moderator, D. G. Lapp; Secretary, Simon Gingerich; Asst. Secretary, Allen Good (a guest from Carstairs, Alberta). Bishop J. S. Shoemaker, Dakota, Ill. (also a guest), preached the conference sermon. Com-mittees were appointed to draft constitutions for the conference and the mission board to be presented at the next regular meeting. Several revisions and re-prints have been authorized, the latest of which bears the date of 1949.

The preamble of the constitution states the object of conference in the following words: "For the purpose of promoting the cause of Christ and unify-ing and strengthening the church in our field." The constitution provides that all regularly ordained bishops, ministers, and deacons who are in full fel-lowship in their respective congregations in the dis-trict shall be members of conference. The first re-port of congregations to the conference listed 15 congregations reporting (one having failed to report) a total membership of 2,924; bishops 7; ministers 29; deacons 13. The latest (1955) report available lists the membership as being 4,386; bishops 12; ministers 36; deacons 16.

J. D. Graber and wife were the first from the conference to enter the foreign mission field. At present there are missionaries from this district in Puerto Rico, South America, India, and Japan. The Iowa City Mission was opened in 1927. A number of congregations are sponsoring Sunday schools and preaching points in the outlying districts. Young men and young women from this district have been working with the Mennonite Central Committee in the homeland and in the foreign fields.

The Iowa-Nebraska School Committee was organized by the conference in 1944 and a high school launched in 1945 with Silas Horst, South English, Iowa, as principal. The school is known as the Iowa Mennonite School (*q.v.*), and is located near Kalona. Its initial enrollment was 38, and at this writing it is approximately 176. It offers a full four-year high-school course together with a high-school Bible course. Members from this district are also found on the faculties of Goshen College, Hesston College and Bible School, and the Mennonite Nurses Training School. (*ML* II, 438.) S.Gɪ.

Iowa-Nebraska (Mennonite) District Mission Board (MC) was organized in September 1922 upon the adoption of its constitution by the Iowa-Nebraska Conference. Its first officers were J. C. Brenneman, Kalona, Iowa, president; D. B. King, Parnell, Iowa, treasurer; and Peter Kennel, Strang, Neb., secretary. The board is composed of the executive committee of five members and one member elected by each of the 23 congregations, making a total of 28 members. Members of the executive committee hold office for three years and are elected by the conference. Its current annual budget is approximately $3,000, with which it carries on the work of the Thurman, Col., rural mission and continues to give some support to the Iowa City congregation, which is now independent. Beginning in 1948 the board has published *Missionary Challenge,* which is now a 24-page quarterly, edited by Fred Gingerich, Chappell, Neb. In 1954 the officers of the board were Ammon Miller, Milford, Neb., president; Leroy V. Miller, Kalona, Iowa, vice-president; Silas Horst, South English, Iowa, secretary; and Ira Wenger, Mt. Pleasant, Iowa, treasurer. S.J.H.

Irapuato, a city in the state of Guanajuato, Mexico, about 220 miles northwest of Mexico City, where under the leadership of H. P. Krehbiel of Newton, Kan., some of the Mennonite refugee families settled who had come to Mexico and had settled first in Rosario (*q.v.*). In Irapuato the refugee settlers attempted to earn a living by means of irrigation farming. After two years of discouraging experiences most of the families left. Some went to El Trebol in the state of Durango to try for the third time to found a successful settlement; others moved to Cuauhtemoc, and still others decided to emigrate to Canada. This was possible because after two years in Mexico they could secure citizenship and over-

come illnesses which had earlier prevented them from entering Canada. (See **Mexico.**) C.K.

Irle, Tilmann, b. May 14, 1848, at Anstoss near Freudenberg, Germany, d. Nov. 25, 1922, at Velbert (Rhineland), was a German missionary in the service of the Dutch Mennonite Missionary Association 1880-87 at the station of Pakanten in Sumatra, Indonesia. He found a church with about 100 members, which he increased with 17 baptisms. In his further work under the Rhenish Missionary Association of Barmen he became very well acquainted with the difficulties involved in mission work among Mohammedans; nevertheless he remained at his post as long as he was able (1921). (*ML* II, 438; *DB* 1893, 110-20.) Neff.

Irnsum, a town in the Dutch province of Friesland, about eight miles south of Leeuwarden. Mennonites were found here at an early time, at least before 1600. In the 17th century there were in Irnsum two congregations, one of which died out about 1740; nothing more is known about it. The other congregation, with a baptized membership of about 75, joined the Mennonite Conference of Friesland in 1695. Shortly before, in 1684, it acquired a meetinghouse with some stained glass windows, which was an exception in Mennonite meetinghouses. In the 18th century it united with the Poppingawier (*q.v.*) congregation. In 1838 the membership of Irnsum and Poppingawier numbered 83; in 1871, the membership having increased to about 160, it was decided that each congregation should be independent, but served by the same preacher. The old church of Irnsum was remodeled in 1837, 1848, 1866, and 1940. The last lay preachers of the congregation were Sipke Jelles van Teerns, serving 1804-29, a baker, who received a small remuneration, and Durk Gerbens Visser, a retired farmer, in 1829-36. The first trained minister, educated at the Amsterdam Mennonite Seminary, was Izaak Molenaar, who served here 1837-78. The later ministers were J. Pottinga Hz. 1880-86, H. J. Elhorst 1887-88, J. S. Pekema 1889-91, M. L. Deenik 1892-97, R. van der Veen 1897-1902, Iz. Hulshoff 1903-14, H. J. Woelders 1915-17, P. A. Vis 1918-30, M. van der Meulen 1935-39, A. J. Snaayer 1940-44, H. R. Keuning 1948-50, Miss J. W. Zuidema 1951-54, and H. Annema since 1954. The parsonage was built in 1838 and enlarged in 1852. The baptized membership of Irnsum is now (1954) 114 and Poppingawier 41. Church activities include a Sunday school for children, *Menniste Bouwers* (youth association), young members' group, and a ladies' circle. vᴅZ.

Inv. Arch. Amst. II, 2, No. 221; Blaupot t. C., *Friesland,* 168, 189, 247, 306; *Naamlijst 1829,* 54 f.; *DB 1870,* 139-60; *1872,* 190 f.; *ML* II, 438.

Isaac (Isaak, Isac) is a Mennonite name of Prussian background appearing early in the church records of Tiegenhagen, Ladekopp, Rosenort, Heubuden, Elbing, and other congregations. From Prussia this name was transplanted to the Mennonite settlements of the Ukraine. Franz Isaac (*q.v.*) was the author of *Die Molotschnaer Mennoniten* (Halbstadt, 1908). From the Ukraine the name was spread over Russia and also transplanted to the United States in the 1870's and to Canada and South America after World War I.

Outstanding representatives were F. J. Isaac, b. Aug. 9, 1888, who was a G.C.M. missionary to India; John P. Isaac, b. Aug. 5, 1872, who was physician in Freeman, S.D., and Glendale, Cal.; Susan Isaac, physician and surgeon, Moundridge, Kan., b. Aug. 23, 1859, d. July 8, 1938.   C.K.

Isaac, Franz (d. 1899), of Tiege, Molotschna, Russia, was a farmer, teacher, and after 1850 minister of the Ohrloff-Petershagen Mennonite Church. His chief contributions were his championship of tolerance, easing the lot of the oppressed, and writing the book *Die Molotschnaer Mennoniten* (Halbstadt, 1908), in which he presents mostly documents pertaining to the economic, religious, and cultural life of the Molotschna Mennonites. His father started the collection of documents which he continued and which his son Franz Isaac, Jr., prepared for publication, the latter stating in the preface "that a certain bias in the presentation cannot be denied." His struggle and "bias," according to P. M. Friesen (p. 703), finally led him to withdrawal from the ministry and his congregation.

Isaac became a member of the Commission for the Landless (*q.v.*), in which capacity he wrote many applications and represented the growing number of landless Mennonites of the Molotschna settlement (*Molotschnaer Mennoniten,* 27-86). His efforts along these lines were not in vain. In the documents pertaining to the religious development of the Mennonites of the Molotschna settlement we find his name attached to many applications in behalf of groups separating from the main body of the Mennonites, such as the Mennonite Brethren and the Friends of Jerusalem. In paragraphs between the documents in his book he freely expressed his convictions, particularly in the concluding chapter (pp. 333-52). The following sentence is characteristic: "One is astonished and wonders how it is possible among Mennonites for the stronger group with their spiritual leaders at the helm, again and again to attack smaller groups as if they alone had the right to exist, not realizing that all Mennonites are merely a tolerated sect" (p. 345). He considered the "failure to recognize the line between the religious and the civil authorities and responsibility" as the crux of this problem (p. 348). Again and again he reproached the religious leadership for appealing to civil authority to achieve its goals; he believed that a spiritual leader must achieve his goal by setting an example of true piety and Christian living.

When the Mennonites of Russia confronted compulsory military conscription during the 1870's, Isaac was repeatedly delegated to represent the Molotschna Mennonites, together with men like Leonhard Sudermann and H. Epp. In contrast to those who thought that migration to America was the only solution, he was satisfied with the institution of forestry service and expressed his "Russian patriotism" similarly to P. M. Friesen. Isaac championed an enlightened, educated, and democratic Mennonitism in Russia and was spiritually akin to

the Friends of Jerusalem who separated from the main Mennonite body during the days of his activity. As a Mennonite historian, Isaac's chief contribution lies in his making available documents pertaining to the Molotschna Mennonites, most of which would otherwise be entirely inaccessible today. (*ML* II, 438.)   C.K.

Isaachs (Isaac, Isaks, Izaaks), **Jacob,** was a preacher of the Groningen Old Flemish congregation of Przechowka (German, *Wintersdorf*) (*q.v.*), Poland. He lived at Schönsee (*q.v.*) on the Vistula. On July 13, 1719, when the Dutch elder Hendrik Berends (Hulshoff) (*q.v.*) visited the congregation he was chosen as preacher (*dienaer in't woordt*). About 1722 he visited Holland and conferred with Herman Schijn (*q.v.*), the elder of the Amsterdam Zonist congregation, concerning the needs of a number of Mennonites in Lithuania. His letters (found in the Amsterdam Archives) give much information on the situation and emergency of the Lithuanian and Polish Mennonites of the Culm district. In a letter of June 18, 1737, he wrote that he was severely ill, that he expected his death in the near future, bidding a last farewell to his friends and benefactors in Holland, but in August 1738 he was still alive; indeed his name is still found in the *Naamlijst* of 1743. (*Inv. Arch. Amst. I,* Nos. 1105 f., 1594, 1596, 1602 f., 1606, 1608, 1612, 1621, 1637, 1661; II, 2, Nos. 738, 763.)   vDZ.

Isaak, Franz F., was born in Tiege, Molotschna, South Russia, Sept. 27, 1876. He taught school in the Don area ten years, in Nikolaifeld, Bezabotovka, and Millerovo. In 1898 he was converted and joined the M.B. Church by baptism. He married Aganetha Dörksen in 1899. He was elected to the ministry in the M.B. Church and ordained in 1911 and served as minister in Millerovo. He emigrated to Canada in 1925 and settled in Winnipeg, where he served the M.B. Church as minister for many years and for some time as leader and on the M.B. Canadian Conference city missions committee. For many years he was employed by the British and Foreign Bible Society in its Bible House in Winnipeg. He died May 14, 1944.   A.J.I.

Isaak, John Phillip (1861-1918), a Russian Mennonite Brethren businessman and minister, was born Feb. 20, 1861, in Tiege, Molotschna, in the province of Taurida, Russia, the oldest son of Phillip and Margaret (Toews) Isaak. He was followed by three brothers and two sisters. He graduated from the Zentralschule in Orloff. In 1881 (or 1882) he was married to Catherine Jantz. To this union were born 13 children, several of whom died in infancy, with John, Phillip, James, Margaret, Elizabeth, and Marie surviving. Several of these became physicians. Dr. J. J. Isaak was chairman of the Relief Committee in Harbin, Manchuria, *ca.* 1930, and helped many refugees to the United States and to South America. Elizabeth, also a physician, succeeded him in this field and is still in China. Margaret, the first Mennonite woman to attend the University of St. Petersburg, married a Baptist preacher, I. V. Neprash, and with him now directs the Russian Missionary Service with headquarters at Philadelphia, Pa.

J. P. Isaak with his wife joined the Mennonite Brethren Church in its early years and held many important church offices, including the leadership of a congregation for about 20 years. He served for about the same period of time as a member of the school board and Agricultural Association board in the province of Taurida, participating actively in relief work for native Russians in 1905-6 near the Volga River.

J. P. Isaak gave great encouragement to P. M. Friesen (*q.v.*) in writing his historical book (*Brüderschaft*) and assisted substantially in financing this work. He also contributed to missionary enterprises. His life was one of constant activity as a landowner, farmer, Christian businessman, and minister of the Gospel. He died in 1918 and was buried in the cemetery of the village of Tiege. He resided at various places including Adamovka and Zhitlova Balka, Ekaterinoslav; Rückenau and Tiege, Taurida.   J.J.T.

Friesen, *Brüderschaft;* J. F. Harms, *Geschichte der Mennoniten Brudergemeinde* (Hillsboro, Kans.).

Isenbaert, Joost (d. Aug. 25, 1673), was an elder of the Flemish congregation of Middelburg, Dutch province of Zeeland, after 1637. He was a man of conservative principles and in 1659 fell into disharmony with his colleagues Adriaan van Eeghem and Pieter Baart, whom he accused of Socinianism (*q.v.*). In 1665 he brought a charge before the city government against Adriaan van Eeghem and Thomas van Eeghem (who in 1663 had succeeded Pieter Baart after the latter had moved to Vlissingen). Both preachers were suspended and only Isenbaert was allowed to preach. But most members took the side of the van Eeghems. A schism in the congregation threatened but was prevented by the conciliatory attitude of Adriaan van Eeghem in December 1665.   vDZ.

C. P. van Eeghen Jr., *Adriaan van Eeghem* (Amsterdam, 1886) 20 f., 25-81 *passim*.

Isolley (Iseli), **Rudolph**, from the Tannental, Switzerland, a martyr of the Swiss Brethren, executed at Bern in 1538. (*ML* I, 171; II, 438; *Mart. Mir.* E 1129.)

Israels, Ben, pseudonym of the author of *Tractaet der Buytengetrouwden* (Amsterdam, 1628). The author, who rejects the severe practice of forbidding intermarriage, is either Anthony Jacobsz (Roscius, *q.v.*) of Hoorn, or Yeme de Ringh (*q.v.*) of Harlingen, both preachers of the Dutch Waterlanders. (*Biogr. Wb.* IV, 471.)   vDZ.

Issoli, Verena, of Schülbach, Signau territory, Switzerland, an Anabaptist martyr executed at Bern in 1537. (*ML* II, 438; *Mart. Mir.* E 1122.)

Italy. Sixteenth-century sources contain many references to Anabaptism in Italy, and later observers, among them Karl Benrath (*q.v.*), have assumed an organic connection between Swiss or German Täufer and Italian congregations. Critical study of the extant evidence, however, fails to reveal such a relationship. Italy provides, therefore, a classic example of the misunderstandings that may result when loosely defined terms like "Anabaptism" are used freely for polemical purposes.

Lutheran ideas penetrated Italy in the 1520's, leading Cardinal Caraffa, the later Pope Paul IV (in office 1555-59), to publish an edict against Protestants in 1530. By 1542 the Evangelical movement had grown to such proportions that Pope Paul III (1534-49) reorganized the Roman Inquisition, which quickly took steps to liquidate heresy. Many Italians then fled to the Swiss cities, to the back-country regions of Graubünden (Grisons, *q.v.*), and to some territories now in northern Italy (viz., the Valtelline and the counties of Chiavenna and Bormio) which were at that time in political dependency upon the three Raetian Leagues. The free-thinking ideas of some of the refugees, reflecting a rationalistic approach to the fundamentals of Christianity, drew the attention of Swiss reformed leaders to them. Camillo Renato of Sicily was the most troublesome of these Italians. He was active in Chiavenna in 1546 and succeeding years and became embroiled in controversy over the sacraments and other subjects with the Reformed pastor Mainardi. The struggle dragged on for several years and during its course Renato was condemned by synods and by Bullinger himself. Mainardi called Renato an "Anabaptist" and listed his heresies: he rejected infant baptism and held unorthodox opinions concerning the nature of Christ, salvation, the existence of hell, and the sleep of souls. Another man, Tiziano by name and a friend of Renato, professing to be guided only by the Spirit, combined anti-Trinitarian views with rejection of infant baptism. Although he opposed the magistral use of the sword by Christians, neither he nor Renato was associated with any northern Täufer community. Both Renato and Tiziano are best thought of as "spiritual reformers." There are scattered references to later Italian "Anabaptist" activities in these border regions, but they are careless polemical accusations.

In northern Italy around 1550 there flourished an evangelical movement, often called "Anabaptist," whose radical teachings closely resemble those found in the Leagues. Tiziano, expelled from the Leagues in 1549, returned to Italy, and in Florence met one Pietro Manelfi (*q.v.*), a former priest. He converted Manelfi and others to that brand of spiritual religion which he had himself learned from Renato. Manelfi believed Tiziano responsible for the Italian "Anabaptist" movement, and thought he had some link with the northern Täufer. Internal evidence belies the latter connection; and the origin of the movement can hardly be ascribed to Tiziano, for the anti-Trinitarian teachings of Servetus had been preparing the soil in Italy at least since 1539. But Tiziano certainly played a leading part in the growth of a number of small clandestine communities which existed in Venetia by 1550. In that year Christological disputes disturbed the congregation at Vicenza. Manelfi, who defected in 1551 and exposed details of the movement to the Inquisition, described a synod which met at Venice in September 1550 to consider these matters. Although the assembly contained delegations from congregations in Switzerland as well as Italy itself, all of the participants were Italian, the implication being that there was no connection with northern Anabaptists. This synod agreed upon a set of anti-Trinitarian principles. It seems indubitable that Renato and Tiziano, representing the indirect influence of Servetus, were responsible in large measure for this radical orientation. However, some members of the sect refused to go along with the majority, notably the congregations of Cittadella and Verona. This moderate element, whose origin and teachings are obscure, seems to have had an independent origin despite similarities to the Täufer in their conception of baptism.

Following the synod Manelfi and Tiziano worked for a year as missionaries, but then late in 1551 Manelfi exposed the whole situation to the Inquisition at Bologna. In the flurry of prosecutions that followed, some individuals named by Manelfi abjured and their depositions confirm the anti-Trinitarian character of the movement. Others remained true to their faith and fled their homeland. Among these fugitives are to be found not only representatives of the anti-Trinitarian viewpoint who constituted a majority of those fleeing to Moravia and Poland but also the only Italians about whom we have evidence of association with genuine Täufer; for several of them eventually found their way to the Moravian Hutterite communities. When these men learned of the Hutterites they were greatly surprised and pleased: this is convincing evidence that the Italian sect had developed independently, at least of the Hutterites. One of these men, Antonio Rizzetto (q.v.), went first to Thessalonica and only after several years joined the Hutterites. Giulio Gherlandi (q.v.) and Francesco della Sega (q.v.; also Saga) evidently stayed in hiding in Italy several years before making the trip to Moravia and joining the Hutterites. These three men stand out because they later undertook missionary trips to Italy for the Hutterites and were there arrested and put to death by the Inquisition at Venice in the 1560's. The net result of Inquisitorial activity in this whole period was the liquidation of the Evangelical movement in north Italy.

Venetian anti-Trinitarianism had connections with a similar movement in Naples. A deposition made to the Venetian Inquisition by Lorenzo Tizzano, who may be identical with Tiziano, classified heretical opinions in Neapolitan circles into "Lutheran," "Anabaptist," and "diabolical," but this testimony reveals that Tizzano meant "anti-Trinitarian" when he said "Anabaptist." There is no evidence connecting the movement in Naples with the Täufer.

The evidence given in this article invalidates much of the material in the following *ML* articles: *Ferrara, Italien, Manelfi, Mantua, Negri, Padua. Camillo Renato, Pietro Manelfi,* and *Franciscus Negri* can no longer be considered as Anabaptists, and the meeting at Venice in 1550 was not an "Anabaptist Synod."   DeWIND.

L. Amabile, *Il Santo Officio della Inquisizione in Napoli* I (Citta di Castello, 1892); K. Benrath, *Geschichte der Reformation in Venedig* (Halle, 1887); idem, "Wiedertäufer im Venetianischen um die Mitte des 16. Jahrhunderts," *Theologische Studien und Kritiken* LVIII (1885) 9-67; D. Berti, "Di Giovanni Valdes e di taluni suoi discepoli secondo nuovi documenti tolti dall'Archi-

vio Veneto," *Atti della R. Accademia dei Lincei: anno CCLXXV,* serie terza, memorie della classe di scienze morali, storiche e filologiche II (1877-78) 61-81; *Bullingers Korrespondenz mit den Graubündnern,* ed. T. Schiess, XXIII-XXV of *Quellen zur Schweizer Geschichte* (Basel, 1904-6); D. Cantimori, *Eretici italiani del cinquecento* (Florence, 1939); F. C. Church, *The Italian Reformers, 1534-1564* (New York, 1932); E. Comba, *I nostri protestanti* II (Florence, 1897); idem, "Un sinodo anabattista a Venezia anno 1550," *Rivista cristiana* XIII (1885) 21-24, 83-87; H. A. deWind, "'Anabaptism' and Italy," *Church History* XXI (1952) 20-38; idem, "Italian Hutterite Martyrs," *MQR* XXVII (1954) 163-85; C. Renato, "Trattato sul battesimo e sulla eucaristia di Camillo Renato," in *Per la storia degli eretici italiani del secolo XVI in Europe,* ed. D. Cantimori and E. Feist, No. 7 of Reale Academia d'Italia (1937) 47-54; F. Trechsel, *Die protestantischen Antitrinitarier vor Faustus Socin,* Book II, *Lelio Sozzini und die Antitrinitarier seiner Zeit* (Heidelberg, 1844); E. M. Wilbur, *A History of Unitarianism: Socinianism and its Antecedents* (Cambridge, Mass., 1947); *ML* II, 438 f.

Ittlingen, a village (pop. 1,307, with 31 Mennonites) in the Sinsheim district of Baden, Germany. The first Mennonites, refugees from Switzerland, settled here in 1655. In the 19th century the village was the seat of a Mennonite church, whose members came from the Bockschaft and Streichenberg congregations. In 1841 Christian Hege placed his newly built house in Ittlingen at their disposal for services. In Bockschaft and Streichenberg services continued to be held alternately for two years longer. For many years Ulrich Hege (d. 1896) of Reihen, founder of the *Gemeindeblatt der Mennoniten* (q.v.), served as their elder. In 1913 the congregation merged with that at Immelhausen (q.v.), with their seat at Sinsheim (q.v.). (Mannhardt, *Jahrbuch* 1888, 31; *ML* II, 439.)   HEGE.

I-W Service. When the 1948 Selective Service law was passed by the United States Congress conscientious objectors were deferred from all service obligations. The amendment to the law passed in 1951, however, required conscientious objectors, in lieu of induction into the armed forces, to perform "civilian work contributing to the maintenance of the national health, safety, or interest" for a period equal to that required for men inducted into the armed forces, that is, for a period of twenty-four consecutive months.

In anticipation of some such required period of service, the Selective Service System had prepared and recommended to Congress a system of government-operated camps for conscientious objectors similar to those operated under the former Civilian Public Service program. This plan was specifically rejected by Congress, and it was clearly stated that no "camps" were to be set up under the new law. As a result of further study by the Selective Service System in consultation with other government agencies and with church agencies representing conscientious objectors, the present service plan was devised and set up.

Under this new service plan conscientious objectors may be assigned to public agencies and to approved nonprofit private agencies for the performance of their required two years of service. Working conditions, pay, and leave arrangements for conscientious objectors are expected to be the same as for other employees in the same grade and class in the same employing agency. (In a few states conscientious objectors were engaged in state institutions at rates lower than those for other employees, but these discriminatory practices have been gradually reduced.) Conscientious objectors are permitted to volunteer for approved work, and are usually assured of assignment to the work of their choice if it is within the approved category. About 85 per cent of the men who entered I-W service have exercised the privilege of volunteering and thus of choosing their place of employment. Those who do not volunteer may be ordered to service by their local boards if they have reached the age at which men are being called for the armed services and if the local board has found an employing agency which is willing to hire them. Assignments may be made to church agencies engaged in relief and other welfare services at home and abroad, and the men so assigned may be used in foreign as well as domestic service. While dissatisfaction with service assignments has occurred in some instances, Selective Service statistics show that out of a total of 6,000 persons assigned to I-W service only 25 had deserted their job, thus becoming delinquent. This may be compared with about 600 delinquents in the CPS period. The much better record is attributed to greater general satisfaction as a result of the much wider range of opportunities of service, and the liberal choices provided.

More than 1,700 governmental and private nonprofit agencies have been approved by Selective Service for the employment of conscientious objectors, but assignments have been made to less than half of this number. Assignments to public agencies are not approved if their employee needs may be filled from the ranks of unemployed persons in the surrounding locality, and other limiting factors have entered into some situations. Most of the openings have occurred in mental hospitals, general hospitals, and tuberculosis sanatoriums. In spite of unemployment in some parts of the country, there have usually been more openings for conscientious objectors than qualified persons available to fill the openings.

The regulations establishing this new plan of service were issued in February 1952, but the first assignments were not made until July 1952. Because of a large backlog of available men, assignments continued at an accelerating rate so that in the period of October 1952 to September 1953 the average monthly rate was more than 300. With the backlog of men taken up, the rate of assignments has dropped considerably and is not likely to exceed 100 per month and may be lower, depending on the rate at which men are called for the armed services. A peak was reached in September 1954, when almost 5,000 men were in service. Since that time, while assignments have continued at a reduced rate, large numbers have completed their two years of service, thus reducing the total in service. Approximately 6,400 men were assigned during the first three years of the program's operation.

At the peak there were about 3,400 men in service from the churches of the MCC constituency, of whom about 45 per cent were of the Mennonite Church (MC), 15 per cent Old Order Amish, 14 per cent General Conference Mennonite, 5 per cent Conservative Mennonite, 5 per cent Church of God in Christ, 4 per cent each Mennonite Brethren and Brethren in Christ, 9 per cent from the other groups, including independent congregations, in the MCC constituency.

In October 1954, 1,794 Mennonite and Brethren in Christ I-W's answered a questionnaire circulated by J. S. Schultz of the Mennonite Central Committee. The following information was compiled by Schultz.

Mental and general hospitals employ more than two thirds of the men. If Veterans Administration Hospitals, tuberculosis sanatoriums and boys' training schools are added, 80 per cent of the men are accounted for. Over half of the Mennonite and Brethren in Christ men are employed in government-controlled institutions, either state, municipal, or federal. During the first three years of operation, an average of 8 per cent of the Mennonite and Brethren in Christ I-W's chose to work in projects administered by their own church agencies. 75 per cent of I-W's are 20-24 years of age.

Nearly 45 per cent of the men are hospital attendants. The next largest group, consisting of only 14 per cent, work on maintenance crews. Following closely in size are groups such as kitchen workers or janitors performing housekeeping duties, and those in specialized fields such as medical laboratory technicians or personnel directors. Only 5 per cent are doing farm work.

About 70 per cent of the men work in urban centers of more than 50,000 population. Mennonite and Brethren in Christ I-W's are employed by about 300 of the more than 1,700 approved institutions. They are serving in 37 states and 20 foreign countries. Fifty per cent are employed in Kansas, Indiana, Ohio, and Pennsylvania. Over 36 per cent are in the larger metropolitan areas of Los Angeles, Cal.; Denver, Col.; Chicago, Ill.; Indianapolis and Westville, Ind.; Kansas City and Topeka, Kan.; Cleveland, Ohio; Norristown, Pa.

Sixty-five different denominations are represented in the ranks of I-W men. I-W men from the MCC constituency make up 67 per cent of the total. This compares with approximately 40 per cent in the CPS period. Selective Service statistics show 8,500 conscientious objectors who are either at work or will be assigned out of a total of 16,153,861 registrants (eighteen years and over). According to their statistics the percentage of conscientious objectors in the total population (.005) has remained constant as compared with the proportion during the World War II period.

As in the World War II period, the Mennonite Central Committee has been asked by its constituent churches to assume over-all responsibility for the I-W program administration. All representation to Selective Service officials is channeled through the MCC. Services to the men themselves are administered by or co-ordinated through the MCC. The Mennonite Relief and Service Committee (MC),

Elkhart, Ind., and the Civilian Public Service Committee (CGC), Galva, Kan., share in this administration, particularly to the men of their own conferences. In addition to these well-organized efforts, numerous pastors, both on their own and at conference request, make periodic calls on I-W men at their places of employment. Organization among the men themselves wherever they can be grouped is encouraged to provide opportunities for worship and fellowship and the strengthening and extension of their Christian witness.

The cost of administering the I-W Service is borne by voluntary contributions from the constituency. The administrative office for this department at the MCC headquarters has been headed continuously by W. T. Snyder to date (January 1956).   J.HA.S.

Ixheim, a village south of Zweibrücken, Palatinate, Germany, now a suburb of the city, the seat of a former Amish congregation which had some members living in the adjacent province of Lorraine, France. Until 1814 Zweibrücken was the capital of a duchy. After the Thirty Years' War (1618-48) the dukes of Zweibrücken, in order to rebuild their sorely devastated land, accepted persons who were suffering religious persecution. Thus in 1648 Swiss Mennonites were already finding their way to Zweibrücken. In 1712, when Louis XIV expelled the Mennonites from Alsace, some of the expellees came to Lorraine and to Zweibrücken, most of them from the principality of Rappoltstein. From that time on, the Zweibrücken congregation was an independent organization. It was represented at the conference in Essingen in 1759 by Jakob Steinmann and Uli Bachmann, in 1779 by Andreas Leyenberger, Jakob Bachmann, and Jakob Dettweiler. In the records of both conferences it is called the Zweibrücken congregation but in several issues of the *Naamlijst* (e.g., 1769, 1784) it is called Hirschberg-Kirschbach (*q.v.*), possibly after certain villages in which the meetings were most frequently held in the homes of members. When the Palatinate passed into French hands in 1797 many of the Ixheim people emigrated to Bavaria, and with them some from Lorraine and Lower Alsace. The prefect of the Moselle region writes in 1803: "The emigration of these Anabaptist farmers would be disastrous, for they are the most competent, and in general they are very obedient to the law. Several families from the region of Zweibrücken have already been lured to Bavaria by the elector, their

former ruler, and he is planning to bring as many as possible into his new state."

In the course of the 19th century emigration continued. Many went to the interior of France; many a French Mennonite family of today stems from Zweibrücken. Others went to America. In spite of all this, the church maintained itself. Meetings were held in the scattered homes on both sides of the border. In 1844, when a division took place in the congregation, one party of 17 families built a small church at Ixheim, while the remaining families met on the Stuppacherhof near Hornbach, and later rented a hall in Zweibrücken (*Menn. Bl.,* 1859, 15), where they continued to meet until the death of their last elder, Christian Stalter, in 1909. After that they all met together at Ixheim. About this time several families joined them from the Bitscherland (*q.v.*) congregation in Alsace which had been dissolved about 1902. After World War I the remnants of the latter congregation formed a new organization at Saargemünd. The Ixheim congregation was incorporated in 1912.

The Ixheim Amish long maintained their distinctive practices: lay preachers, beards, strict shunning, footwashing (some of the older members until 1932). And although hooks and eyes were discarded by 1880, the Ixheim members were long called *Häftler* (*q.v.*) and the near-by Ernstweiler Mennonite members *Knöpfler* (buttoners). In 1859 Ixheim had 141 members; the preachers were Christian Oesch, Christian Stalter, and Christian Gingerich, and the deacon was Georg Guth. The congregation was fully organized as Ixheim in 1884. In 1937 the baptized membership was 134, with Christian Guth as elder (since 1907), and Otto Schertz and Georg Nafziger as preachers; the congregation was at that time called Ixheim-Saar, since it included the remnant of the Saar congregation. On Jan. 17, 1937, the Ixheim and Ernstweiler congregations met jointly, agreed to merge the proceeds from the sale of their properties, and established a single congregation called "Mennonitengemeinde Zweibrücken." Hugo Scheffler, pastor of Ernstweiler, served as pastor until the appointment of Theo Hotel of Kaiserslautern in 1952. This was the last Amish Mennonite congregation to merge with the South German Mennonite Conference. The Ixheim meetinghouse still stands as a private dwelling. (Hugo Scheffler, "Vereinigung Ixheim-Ernstweiler," *Gem.-Kal.* 1939, 71-81; *ML* II, 448 f.)

P.So., J.A.H.

J

Jaarboekje, Doopsgezind (Dutch Mennonite Yearbook): see **Doopsgezind Jaarboekje**.

Jaarboekje voor de Doopsgezinde Gemeenten in de Nederlanden (Yearbook of the Mennonite Congregations in the Netherlands), usually cited as *Muller's Jaarboekje,* was published by Samuel Muller at Amsterdam, first issue in 1837. In the foreword Muller explained that it was to be a new edition of the *Naamlijst* (*q.v.*), a list of European Mennonite congregations and their ministers, which at first had been published annually, then at longer intervals, the last issue being that of 1829. The new *Jaarboekje,* under the title "Doopsgezinde Mengelingen" (Miscellanies), presents an extremely valuable series of historical articles.

The second edition of the *Jaarboekje* appeared in 1840, covering the years 1838-39, and in addition to the lists and news of the congregations also contained valuable historical material, especially the articles by Leonhard Weydmann (*q.v.*) on the Palatinate. The third and last issue, for the years 1840-50, appeared late in 1850. Its principal contents were an extensive account of the history of theological instruction among the Dutch Mennonites, written by Muller.

The Jaarboekje was in a sense continued in the three editions of D. S. Gorter's (*q.v.*) *Godsdienstige Lectuur voor Doopsgezinde,* 1854, 1856, and 1858, followed by the *Doopsgezinde Bijdragen* (*q.v.*) of 1861-1919. (*ML* II, 385.)　　　　NEFF.

Jaarsma, Frederik, was a Dutch Mennonite preacher, serving the Waterlander congregation at Leeuwarden (*q.v.*) ca. 1710-26; here he became involved in a quarrel with some members of the church who insisted on baptism by immersion. In 1726 he moved to Vlissingen, where he served until about 1752 (he did not die in 1726 as is stated in *DB* 1874, 73). His son Hermannus Jaarsma, after studying at the University of Franeker and the Amsterdam Theological Seminary, served as minister in the Mennonite congregations of Gouda 1740-44 and Emmerich, Germany, 1744-83. (*DB* 1874, 60-73, 95, 111; *Naamlijst* 1743.)　　　　vDZ.

Jacob Antheunis (Jacob de Schoenlapper, i.e., cobbler), an Anabaptist martyr, who was executed by burning at the stake at Antwerp, Belgium, on May 22, 1575, the evening before Pentecost. Van Braght relates that he was put to death with tongue screws to prevent his speaking to the bystanders. Van Braght also states that Antheunis' pregnant wife was executed after her confinement; but P. Génard, who studied the sources, did not find any record of her. Jacob was sentenced on the charge of frequenting forbidden meetings and possessing forbidden books. He is said to have written some letters from prison, which were lost during the revolt at Antwerp on Nov. 4, 1576.　　　　vDZ.

Mart. Mir. D 693, E 1007; *Antw. Arch.-Blad* XIII, 193, 200; XIV, 96 f., No. 1082; *ML* II, 386.

Jacob of Antwerp (Jacob van Antwerpen, Jacob van Herwerden, Gosen van Winterswijk, Wolter), a Dutch Anabaptist leader, was beheaded at Deventer, Dutch province of Overijssel, on May 17, 1535. He was born in the Dutch Betuwe district, had formerly been an organist of the Catholic Church, had been baptized in March 1534 at Emden, East Friesland, by Tasschenmaker (Dirckgen Tasch, *q.v.*) and joined the revolutionary wing of Anabaptism as a co-worker of the Münsterite leader Jan van Geelen (*q.v.*), who sent him to Deventer to take a letter to van Geelen's wife Fenne. Jacob also baptized her and her servant (Feb. 9, 1535). A few days later he was arrested, tried, and put to death.　　vDZ.

Inv. Arch. Amst. I, No. 96; *DB* 1899, 9; 1917, 116, No. 58; 1919, 8 f.; Mellink, *Wederdopers,* see Index.

Jacob Bul, an Anabaptist martyr, is identical with Arent Block (*q.v.*). (*DB* 1912, 36, 42.)　　vDZ.

Jacob van Campen (Kampen), or *Jacob Jansz van IJsselmuiden,* also called Coomans, born 1505, a bishop of the Dutch Anabaptists and a martyr, executed at Amsterdam on July 10, 1535. He was a native of IJsselmuiden, was a cloth shearer by trade, but sometimes he worked as a peddler. He was married to Aeff Petersdochter of North Holland. It is rather strange that this important leader is not found in the martyrbooks. The reason for the omission may be that in his early period he had many contacts with revolutionary leaders.

Jacob van Campen was one of the 12 apostles sent out by Jan Matthysz van Haarlem (*q.v.*) in the fall of 1533. His trips extended unto Münster in Westphalia and Emden in East Friesland; he also visited the Dutch provinces of Groningen and Friesland; his activity in the towns of Kampen and Rotterdam is known and in the provinces of North Holland and Utrecht he baptized a number of persons. He himself was baptized and ordained a bishop by Pieter de Houtzager (*q.v.*). From early 1534 he mostly stayed at Amsterdam, then already the seat of a considerable Anabaptist congregation. In February 1534 Jacob van Campen and Pieter de Houtzager baptized a large number of persons at Amsterdam and van Campen held regular meetings there near the Jan Rodenpoorts tower. The assertion made by some authors, e.g., L. Hortensius and G. Brandt, that Jacob van Campen was sent from Münster by Jan van Leyden to be a bishop at Amsterdam is not correct. He warned against the revolutionary Münsterite principles, especially against polygamy, and opposed acts of violence and revolt. In a meeting of Dutch Anabaptist leaders held at Spaarndam near Haarlem in December 1534 or January 1535, where the question was discussed whether the Anabaptists of Holland should take up arms and go to Münster, van Campen argued that the coming of the Lord should be patiently awaited; when Jan van Geelen (*q.v.*) planned an attack on the city of Amsterdam (May 1535), Jacob van Campen "did not consent to this proposal." The accusation of some authors like Vos and Mellink that van Campen belonged to the revolutionary wing of Anabaptism is not true. He was a follower of Melchior Hofmann (*q.v.*) and a man of peaceful principles.

As to his interpretation of the Bible van Campen was of the opinion (like Cornelis Pietersz wt den Briel, while Obbe Philipsz was opposed to this view) that the Scriptures "stand on two hoofs" (see **Gespauwde Klauw**), i.e., he defended the doctrine that "all that is written in the Old Testament is also found in the New Testament and will take place either spiritually or literally." This opinion gave rise to much unsound interpretation of Old Testament prophecies.

Jacob van Campen was an important leader, whose activity was well known to the government. As early as Feb. 23, 1534, a mandate of the imperial stadholder of Friesland indicated van Campen as a principal Anabaptist, together with Melchior Hofmann, Obbe Philipsz, and Pieter de Houtzager, and on March 2, 1534, it was announced in Amsterdam that anyone who delivered Jacob van Campen or Jan Matthysz to the officials of justice would be rewarded. In May 1535 van Campen was arrested in Amsterdam. A widow who had given him shelter was hanged with her son before her own door. Van Campen was tried several times and also tortured. He did not forsake his faith. On July 10, he was sentenced to death and executed that very day. First his tongue "by which he has disseminated his false teachings" was cut off, then his right hand "by which he has rebaptized." Thereupon he was beheaded and his corpse burned.

His confession during the trials, containing a number of valuable facts about the Anabaptist movement in Amsterdam, was published by Grosheide.   vDZ.

Inv. Arch. Amst. I, No. 97; Grosheide, *Verhooren*, 94-105, 193 f.; Kühler, *Geschiedenis* I, *passim*, see Index; *DB* 1917, 85, 98, 101 f.; Mellink, *Wederdopers, passim*, see Index.

Jacob Claesz of Landsmeer (Dutch province of North Holland), an Anabaptist martyr who was burned at the stake at Amsterdam on Nov. 9, 1549, after cruel torture. His property was confiscated. His wife Cecilia Jheronymusdochter (*q.v.*) was also put to death at Amsterdam in 1549. Jacob Claesz is apparently identical with Jacob van Wormer (*q.v.*).   vDZ.

Mart. Mir. D 85, E 485; *Inv. Arch. Amst.* I, No. 351; *DB* 1917, 173; Grosheide, *Bijdrage*, 158; *ML* I, 358.

Jacob Claesz van der Veer, a Dutch Anabaptist martyr who lived at Utrecht outside the St. Catharine's Gate. In 1533 he had received (re)baptism, but in July 1534 before the Court he retracted his "error" in order to save his life; yet he remained in contact with the Anabaptists. For this fact, and especially because he read heretical (i.e., Anabaptist) books which he had bought in Amsterdam, he was sentenced to death and beheaded at Utrecht on March 13, 1535.   vDZ.

Inv. Arch. Amst. I, No. 106; *Berigten Hist. Genootschap, Utrecht* 1851, IV, 2, p. 129; *DB* 1917, 122, No. 163.

Jacob Cremer (*Cramer, Kremer*), a Dutch Anabaptist, a native of Winsum, Dutch province of Groningen. He belonged to the revolutionary wing of Anabaptism; with Antonius (Anthonie) Kistemaker (*q.v.*) he was active in the province of Groningen in 1534-35; in East Friesland he had been in prison for a while; he also had visited Münster (*q.v.*) in 1534. He was arrested during the Anabaptist assault on the St. Johns monastery at Warfum in the province of Groningen and brought to the city of Groningen, where he was beheaded in April 1535.   vDZ.

BRN VII, 362, 369 f.; *DB* 1906, 31; 1917, 119, No. 100; Mellink, *Wederdopers*, see Index; *ML* II, 179.

Jacob Daneels (Jacob de Metselaar, i.e., mason), an Anabaptist martyr, who was burned at the stake on the market square at Antwerp, Belgium, on Feb. 5, 1558, because he had been rebaptized and even after much suffering refused to recant. He was gagged to prevent his addressing the crowd of bystanders. Jacob was a native of Komen (Commines) in Flanders. His name is found in the song "Aenhoort Godt, hemelsche Vader" (Hear, O God, heavenly Father), found in the *Lietboecxken van den Offer des Heeren*, No. 16.   vDZ.

Mart. Mir. D 201, E 583; *Antw. Arch.-Blad* VIII, 443, 445; XIV, 22 f., No. 253; Wolkan, *Lieder*, 63, 72; *ML* II, 386.

Jacob Dirks (Diericsens), a native of Wageningen, Dutch province of Gelderland, an Anabaptist martyr, a tailor of Utrecht, Dutch province of Holland. About to be seized as a Mennonite, he fled to Antwerp. His wife, not a Mennonite, joined him later and died there. But Jacob and his two grown sons, Andries (or Adriaen) and Hans (or Jan), were seized and condemned to death. On the way to the place of execution his youngest son, Peter, met them and threw his arms around his father; he was rudely torn away. Standing at the scaffold the father asked, "How is it, my dear sons?" Each replied, "Very well, my dear father." They were hanged and then burned on March 17, 1568. Andries' fiancee and her sister looked on from a distance with sad hearts. Jacob's property was confiscated and realized a considerable amount.   NEFF, vDZ.

Mart. Mir. D 370, E. 724; *Antw. Arch.-Blad*, X, 13, 67; XII, 477; XIV, 54 f., No. 630; *ML* I, 450.

Jacob Elberts, a martyr: see **Jacob de Geldersman**.

Jacob van Emden, a Dutch Anabaptist, a follower of the Münsterite leader Jan van Geelen (*q.v.*), took part in the Anabaptist revolt at Amsterdam, May 10-11, 1535. He was bestially executed at Amsterdam on May 14, 1535. (Grosheide, *Verhooren*, 62-64.)   vDZ.

Jacob Fredriks, a Dutch Mennonite, who went with Dirk Jansz Cortenbosch (*q.v.*) on a visit to the Mennonites along the Rhine, and then in April 1572 paid a visit to Prince William I of Orange at his castle at Dillenburg, Germany. They were asked by the Prince to collect money among the Mennonites of Holland for the purpose of liberating this country from the Spanish yoke. They promised to do so, but because Fredriks, of whom nothing further is known, had no opportunity to visit the congregations, Cortenbosch and P. W. Bogaert (*q.v.*) collected the money.   vDZ.

Inv. Arch. Amst. I, No. 421; Blaupot t. C., *Holland* I, 84; *DB* 1873, 4, 8.

Jacob de Geldersman, an Anabaptist martyr, a native of Harderwijk, Dutch province of Gelderland, died at the stake at Amsterdam, May 24, 1546, with Dirk Pieters Smuel. In the sentence he is called Jacob Elberts van Harderwijk. Both lived in Edam and on March 12 were seized at home by the court procurator of The Hague and the sheriff of Amsterdam and taken to prison. Smuel was a preacher who had for several years been preaching secretly, and rejected the confessional, purgatory, and the Mass. Jacob had refused to honor the host when the priest approached him with it. He attended Smuel's sermons. The *Martyrs' Mirror* indicates that a fourth man (Andries Smuel) had apparently also been arrested; but there is no verdict concerning him. The two were sentenced at The Hague, but executed in Amsterdam. Van Braght gives a part of the sentence, Smuel's will to his wife Wellemoet Claes, and a letter to the brotherhood. They stated that they owned no books by Menno Simons or David Joris; but in addition to the Bible they possessed a "booklet on the faith." His letters are very well written, with an abundance of Biblical citations; but they contain no special information. The execution lasted more than 24 hours.   K.V.

Inv. Arch. Amst. I, No. 338; *Mart. Mir.* D 75, E 475; *DB* 1887, 114-16; Grosheide, *Bijdrage,* 108 f.; *ML* II, 47.

Jacob van Gershoven, an Anabaptist martyr, was drowned at the Steen castle at Antwerp, Belgium, on Oct. 17, 1562, together with his brother Aert van Gershoven. He was a native of Tongeren, Brabant, and had lived for some time at Breda, Dutch province of North Brabant, and was a confectioner by trade. (*Antw. Arch.-Blad* IX, 142, 149; XIV, 32 f., No. 366.)   vDZ.

Jacob Ghysbertszn van Gameren, a native of the Dutch duchy of Gelderland, had on the instigation of the Münsterite leader Jan van Geelen (*q.v.*) partaken in the Anabaptist assault on Amsterdam, May 10-11, 1535, and was therefore brutally executed on May 14 at Amsterdam. (Grosheide, *Verhooren,* 61, 63 f.)   vDZ.

Jacob de Goudsmid: see **Jacob Schot.**

Jacob Heymans Tollincx, a brother of Gosen Heymans (*q.v.*), was beheaded at Utrecht, Netherlands, on July 5, 1569, because he had been present at heretical meetings. He may have been a Mennonite. Jacob and Gosen had been arrested on Sept. 20, 1568.   vDZ.

I. M. J. Hoog, "Onze Martelaren," in *Ned. Arch. v. Kerkgeschiedenis,* n.s. I (1902) No. 172.

Jacob Jansz Scheedemaker (also called Jacob Jansz Kist), a Dutch Mennonite leader, a preacher at Emden, East Friesland, who was banned in 1555 or 1556; he was probably excommunicated by Leenaert

Bouwens (*q.v.*) for being too lax in the practice of shunning (see **Ban**). But a considerable number of Mennonites agreed with Scheedemaker and they were then called the "Scheedemaker" group. At the same time and for the same reason Hendrik Naeldeman (*q.v.*) and Joriaen Heynsz were excommunicated; both were leaders at Franeker in Friesland; they also had many followers, who were called "Franekeraars." Soon after his excommunication Scheedemaker moved from Emden to De Rijp in the Dutch province of North Holland; in this Waterland district most Mennonites rejected rigorous shunning, being inclined to somewhat milder practices. From then on, the names "Franekeraars" and "Scheedemakers" disappeared, and were replaced by the general term "Waterlanders" (*q.v.*), who separated from the main body in the fall of 1556. An attempt made by Menno Simons early in 1557 to reconcile the Waterlanders with Leenaert Bouwens and the supporters of rigorous shunning miscarried. Jacob Jansz Scheedemaker became a Waterlander leader. In September 1577 he drew up the first Dutch confession (Waterlander Confession) with Hans de Ries, Simon Michiels, Simon Jacobs, and Albert Verspeck. On Nov. 28, 1578, he and Hans de Ries debated with D. V. Coornhert (*q.v.*) on the question whether there could be a true Christian church on earth. In 1581 Scheedemaker was appointed elder and moved to Haarlem. Here he became involved in a quarrel with Hans Doornaert (*q.v.*), a Flemish immigrant and a preacher. The quarrel was settled during a meeting at Haarlem, Sept. 14, 1587, which Coornhert, then a notary at Haarlem, also attended. A debate between Scheedemaker and Coornhert was held at a meeting of Waterlander leaders at Alkmaar on Nov. 29, 1587, when they agreed that persons who had not been baptized should also be admitted at the communion. Scheedemaker was still active in, 1596. On March 3 of that year he preached at Rotterdam, using silent prayer criticized by the Reformed Minister Franciscus van Lansbergen (*q.v.*). He must have died soon after.

In 1591 Scheedemaker was attacked by Pieter Cornelisz, a Reformed pastor at Alkmaar, in a booklet, *Argumenten ende Bewysredenen,* in which he proved that it is permissible for a Christian to hold government office. Scheedemaker, supported by Hans de Ries, his fellow preacher, answered with *Nootwendighe Verantwoordinge der Verdruckter Waerheyt* (probably published in 1597), in which he also defended silent prayer against van Lansbergen. In 1590 he was elder of the Waterlander congregation at Amsterdam; on Oct. 22 of this year some young Frisian leaders such as Lubbert Gerritsz (*q.v.*) and Hoyte Renix (*q.v.*) wrote a letter to Scheedemaker concerning a merger of the Frisians and the Waterlanders, which had been proposed by Scheedemaker and his co-ministers, but which the Frisians considered premature.   vDZ.

Inv. Arch. Amst. I, 714; *BRN* VII, 55; Blaupot t. C., *Holland* I, 46, 114, 119, 123 f.; K. Vos. *Menno Simons* (Leiden, 1914) 132, 135, 191; Kühler, *Geschiedenis* I, 317 f., 350, 353, 359, 363 f., 368-74; *DB* 1863, 114; 1864, 2, note 20 f., 32 f., 35; 1877, 79-91; 1894, 34; 1897, 78 f., 92-105; 1904, 142-58; 1909, 145 f.; 1917, 29; *Biogr. Wb.* IV, 525 f.; *N.N.B.Wb.* IX, 449.

Jacob de Keersgieter, a martyr: see **Jacob de Rore.**

Jacob Lowys, an Anabaptist martyr executed at Gent, Belgium, on Nov. 22, 1570 (method unknown). The Dutch martyrbook *Historie der Warachtige getuygen Jesu Christi* . . . (Hoorn, 1617) contains two accounts on this martyr and Joris van Meersch, executed with him. Both accounts are incomplete; the second was used by van Braght in the *Martyrs' Mirror.*
The exact year and date of execution (not given by van Braght) were found in the records by A. L. E. Verheyden. Jacob and Joris are celebrated in a hymn, "Broeders en susters al ghemeyn, fondeert alleen op Christum den Steijn" (Brethren and sisters altogether, build only on Christ, the stone, as a foundation). The hymn is found in the *Tweede Liedenboeck* of 1583.   vDZ.
Mart. Mir. D 506, E 845; *Bibliographie* II, No. 489; Verheyden, *Gent,* 57, No. 199; Wolkan, *Lieder,* 72; *ML* II, 696.

Jacob van Meppel, a Dutch Anabaptist martyr, beheaded on Sept. 16, 1534. He had taught in Anabaptist meetings. Further particulars are unknown (*DB* 1917, 122, No. 154).   vDZ.

Jacob (or Jaques) **Mesdag** (Mestdach, Mesdach), a Dutch Anabaptist martyr, burned at the stake at Kortrijk (Courtrai), Belgium, on Nov. 8, 1567, with Joos Casteels, Willem Aertsz (Aertsen), and Karel Hannebeel. They had been arrested at Zwevegem on March 1, 1566. They all remained steadfast and died valiantly. Jacob Mesdag was born at Langemarck and had lived at Capelle near Ieper; he was a weaver and a miller; in 1563 he had been (re)baptized and joined the congregation.
The *Martyrs' Mirror* contains a letter written by Jacob Mesdag in prison on Sept. 9, 1567, after he had been in prison for 18 months, addressed to S. I. H. or Suzanneken, who was his sister and also a member of the church. Jacob Mesdag was a member of the Dutch Mennonite Mesdag (*q.v.*) family.   vDZ.
Mart. Mir. D 358-66; E 715-21; Verheyden, *Courtrai-Bruxelles,* 36 f., No. 17; *ML* III, 116.

Jacob de Metselaer, a martyr: see **Jacob Daneels.**

Jacob van Os(s)enbrug (Ossenbroich), not a native of the German town of Osnabrück as has been supposed, but probably originally from the duchy of Jülich. By trade he was a farrier (shoeing smith). He was an Anabaptist leader and confessed (according to the record) that he had been baptized at Münster (*q.v.*) on Jan. 6, 1534, by Jan van Leyden. But this must be an error; on that date Jan van Leyden was not yet in Münster. Soon after he returned to the territory of Jülich to win recruits for Münster. He promised to show them all the miracles which God had performed in Münster and threatened that God would punish the wicked world about Easter, when only those who were in Münster could be saved, because Münster was the New Jerusalem. He succeeded in rounding up a number of persons, including Gillis (Gys) van Rothem (*q.v.*), with whom he marched to Münster. It is very remarkable that they are said to have traveled un-

armed. At Neuss they crossed the Rhine; upon arrival at Düsseldorf the whole group was arrested and tried on Feb. 28, 1534. The outcome of this trial is not known and further information about Jacob van Ossenbrug was not available.   vDZ.
Rembert, *Wiedertäufer,* 372-77; W. Bax, *Het Protestantisme in het Bisdom Luik* I (The Hague, 1937) 70-72; Mellink, *Wederdopers,* 28 f., 291; *ML* III, 314.

Jacob, de Oude (Old Jacob), an Anabaptist martyr, executed in the castle of Berchem near Antwerp, Belgium. Bartel (*q.v.*) and Jacob had come from Antwerp to Berchem to comfort Hans van Monster (*q.v.*), who was in prison here. Both were then arrested and after much temptation executed. The date of execution is unknown; van Braght (*Mart. Mir.*) places it "about 1550." All three remained loyal to their faith. Jacob's judges thought he was a preacher and elder, but he was not. He is said to have been very eloquent and well versed in the Scriptures.   vDZ.
Mart. Mir. D 102, E 500; Blaupot t. C., *Groningen,* II, 18; *ML* II, 385.

Jacob Peeters (in the official records Jacob Peeters Aertssone), by trade a cooper, was burned at the stake at Antwerp, Belgium, on Oct. 22, 1551. (The *Offer des Heeren* and later martyrbooks, including van Braght's *Martyrs' Mirror,* give the date as Oct. 2.) No particulars are known about this martyr, except that he admitted that he had been (re)baptized and he was not willing to recant. He died with Pieter (Peter) Bruynen and three other brethren. Van Braght does not report the name of Jacob Peeters, but states that on the same day still "another brother" was executed. This unknown martyr must have been Jacob Peeters.   vDZ.
Offer, 177, note 1; *Antw. Arch.-Blad* VIII, 405, 415; XIV, 18 f., No. 207; *Mart. Mir.* D 128, E 498.

Jacob Pouwels, an otherwise unknown Dutch Anabaptist, who was the leader of the Anabaptist group in Groningen in the spring of 1534, when the elder (bishop) of Amsterdam, Jacob van Campen, visited that city. The statement that the group of Anabaptists in the city of Groningen then numbered 1,100 must be an exaggeration. (*DB* 1917, 114, No. 41; Mellink, *Wederdopers,* 254.)   vDZ.

Jacob Rederwijn, an Anabaptist martyr, burned at the stake on the Vrijdagsmarkt at Gent, Belgium, on April 13, 1557, together with two other martyrs. (Verheyden, *Gent,* 24, No. 53.)   vDZ.

Jacob Remmes, a Dutch Anabaptist preacher, active in 1534, and a follower of the revolutionary Münsterite (*q.v.*) principles. Particulars are lacking. (*DB* 1909, 11; 1917, 119, No. 93.)   vDZ.

Jacob (Jacques) de Rore (also called *Jacob de Keersgieter,* i.e., chandler, his father's trade), an Anabaptist martyr, executed with Herman van Vlekwijk by burning at the stake at Brugge, Belgium, on June 8, 1569. Jacob de Rore was a preacher (probably an elder) and one of the most prominent Mennonite leaders in Flanders. He was born at Kortrijk (Courtrai) in Flanders in 1532 or 1533 and was a weaver by trade. In 1551 he left the Catholic

Church and in 1554 he was one of five persons baptized by Gillis van Aken (*q.v.*) in the forest of Marken near Kortrijk. Soon after, he became a leader in the Kortrijk (*q.v.*) congregation. When Leenaert Bouwens (*q.v.*) baptized here in 1557, Jacob de Rore was present. In 1559 he married a member of the congregation at Armentières; the wedding was performed at Armentières by Adriaen Termentiers. In 1560 Jacob became a preacher. Up to 1566 he was especially active in the south of Flanders; he preached at Armentières, Kortrijk, Meenen, Wervik, Poperinge, Roesselare, Ieper, Thielt, Gent, St. Andries, and Brugge. He performed a large number of marriages. In 1566-68 he mostly lived in Brugge. On Feb. 1, 1567, he attended a conference at Harlingen, Dutch province of Friesland, which was called to settle the Frisian-Flemish schism (see **Flemish Mennonites**). Jacob de Rore took the side of the Flemish.

In 1569 he visited Gelre and the territory of Cleve. In April of the same year, having returned to Brugge with Herman van Vlekwijk, both were arrested. They were severely cross-examined (the Franciscan monk Broer Cornelis was one of the Inquisitors) and tortured. They died steadfast.

In prison Jacob de Rore wrote 19 letters. Letters 1, 7, 10, and 14-19 are undated. They are addressed to his wife (Nos. 1, 8, 18), to his children (Nos. 3, 4), to his sister G. F. (Nos. 6, 15, 17), to his brother (No. 9), to his congregation at Brugge or Kortrijk (Nos. 2, 10, 16), to the congregation of Hondschote (No. 5), to Elder Paulus van Meenen (*q.v.*) (No. 7), to a brother of the congregation (Nos. 11, 13), to the ministers of the Flemish congregations (No. 12), to the congregation of Armentières (No. 14), to Adriaen Olieux, who was in prison at Armentières (No. 19).

These 19 letters are found in a book published in 1577 (n.p.), entitled: *In dit teghenwoordighe Boecxken zijn vele schoone ende lieflijcke Brieven van eenen ghenaemt Jacob de Keersmaecker die hy wt zijnder ghevanchenisse ghesonden heeft,* etc. There is a reprint of 1584 (n.p.). Of both editions a copy is found in the Mennonite Library at Amsterdam. There must also have been an edition of 1571, which has been lost. The book also contains the disputation between Jacob de Rore and Broer Cornelis, and two songs: (*a*) "Aenhoort ghy Christen schaer voorwaer, Hier int openbaer" (Hear, ye host of Christians, here publicly), (*b*) "Seer minnelijc gegroet zijn moet alle die doet het goet" (Kindly greeted should be all who do the right). These songs are found in Wackernagel, *Lieder.*

The Dutch martyrbooks have inserted a number of these letters of Jacob de Rore. The 1615 edition contains Nos. 1, 2, and 3; the editions of 1617 and 1626 and 1631 Nos. 1, 2, 3, 4, 7, and 12; van Braght's *Martyrs' Mirror,* editions of 1660 and 1685, both have Nos. 1, 2, 3, 4, 7, 11, and 12. The book of Jacob de Rore was very popular among the Mennonites. Joos de Tollenaere (*q.v.*) wrote 1589 from prison to his daughter (see *Mart. Mir.* D 777, E 1080) that after his death her mother should give her the booklet by Jacob de Keersgieter, "because therein are found fine exhortations." vDZ.

Mart. Mir. D 424-37, 452-75; E 371, 774-818; Verheyden, *Brugge,* 58-60, No. 63; *Bibliographie* I, 305-18; *DB* 1893, 44; Wackernagel, *Lieder,* 200-2.

Jacob de Schoenmaker (the cobbler), an Anabaptist martyr: see **Jacob Antheunis.**

Jacob (Jacques) **Schot** (Jacob de Goudsmid, i.e., Goldsmith) was drowned in a tub in the Steen castle prison at Antwerp, Belgium, on Feb. 1, 1560, with Gomer de Clercq (Gomer de Metselaer) and Pedro de Soza (Pieter van Spagnien). The names of these martyrs are celebrated in a hymn "Aenhoort Godt, hemelsche Vader" (Hear, O God, heavenly Father), No. 16 of the *Lietboecxken van den Offer des Heeren,* where they are called Gommer Metser, Peter van Spaengen, and Jacob Goutsmit. vDZ.

Offer, 567; *Mart. Mir.* D 270, E 640; *Antw. Arch.-Blad* IX, 6, 11; XIV, 28 f., No. 309; *ML* II, 386.

Jacob Spillebout (Spilboot or Spillebont), an Anabaptist martyr, was burned at the stake on Aug. 7, 1559, at Gent, Belgium, together with five other martyrs. He was a native of Nukerke (Nijpkerke) in Flanders and a serge weaver. His name is found in the song "Ick moet een liet beginnen" (I must begin a song), No. 14 in the *Lietboecxken van den Offer des Heeren.* vDZ.

Offer, 348, 556; *Mart. Mir.* D 246, E 620; Verheyden, *Gent,* 25, No. 65; Wolkan, *Lieder,* 62, 71.

Jacob de Swarte (Zwarte), an Anabaptist martyr, was born at Nukerke (Nijpkerke) in Flanders, a son of Jan de Swarte (*q.v.*). He lived in Oostende and Hondschoote, in which town he was baptized upon his faith in 1557. In the spring of 1558 he moved to Brugge, and soon united with the Mennonite congregation. In vain he tried to win his Catholic wife and his son-in-law to the faith. During a meeting of the congregation a number of members were arrested including Jacob and his cousin Jan Vervest. He did not forsake his Lord and died loyally at the stake on Aug. 15, 1558, at Brugge, Belgium. (*Mart. Mir.* D 202, 583; Verheyden, *Brugge,* 41, No. 24.) vDZ.

Jacob Symonsz of Delft, a Dutch Anabaptist preacher of whom not much is known. He is said to have been a learned man. In March 1534 he was arrested at Bergklooster (*q.v.*) as a leader of the 3,000 Anabaptists who had arrived there en route to Münster, having sailed from Amsterdam. He was beheaded at Amsterdam on March 30, 1534. A hymn written by Jacob Simonsz is found in the *Geestelyck Lietboecxken van D(avid) J(oris).* vDZ.

Inv. Arch. Amst. I, No. 745; *DB* 1917, 121, No. 125; Mellink, *Wederdopers,* 107, 210, 353.

Jacob Tyettye of Goënga, Dutch province of Friesland, is listed among the Anabaptist preachers in a proclamation of the Frisian Stadholder of Feb. 23, 1534, but about his activities nothing is known. (*DB* 1917, 116, No. 61; Mellink, *Wederdopers,* 243.) vDZ.

Jacob van der Weg(h)e, an Anabaptist martyr, was burned at the stake at the Vrijdagsmarkt of Gent, Belgium, on July 28, 1573. Jacob was born at Ronse

(Renaix) in Flanders. After having been hunted for a long time by the inquisitors in the south part of Flanders, he went to Gent, where he joined the congregation and lived quietly for three years. Then he was arrested and put to death with three other martyrs. During this execution, which took place at eleven o'clock in the morning, the crowd of bystanders, sympathizing with the martyrs, interfered with the executioner and the priest-confessor, and the execution could not be carried out until the police arrived and the victims were gagged to prevent their speaking to the crowd. Like many martyrs in Flanders, Jacob does not seem to have accepted the doctrine of incarnation (q.v.) as taught by Menno Simons. A brother of Jacob, Hans van der Weghe (q.v.), had also died at the stake at Gent on Nov. 7, 1570. (Mart. Mir. D 61, E 969; Verheyden, Gent, 63, No. 224.)   vDZ.

Jacob of Wormer, Dutch province of North Holland, an Anabaptist martyr, who according to van Braght, Martyrs' Mirror, was burned at the stake at Amsterdam in 1542, together with his wife Seli. They are obviously identical with Jacob Claesz (q.v.) of Landsmeer and his wife Cecilia Jeronymusdochter (q.v.), both executed at Amsterdam in 1549. Van Braght himself suggests this identity. (Mart. Mir. D 61, 85, E 464; ML II, 386.)   vDZ.

Jacob van Yperen (also called Jacob van Houte), an Anabaptist martyr, who was burned at the stake at Antwerp, Belgium, on May 22, 1557. (Van Braght in the Mart. Mir. says he was beheaded and does not give exact date.) His name is found in the song "Aenhoort Godt, hemelsche Vader," No. 16 of the Lietboecxken van den Offer des Heeren.   vDZ.

Offer, 564; Mart. Mir. D 185, E 569; Antw. Arch.-Blad VIII, 434, 438; XIV, 22 f., No. 246.

Jacobs, Antonius, an otherwise unknown Anabaptist leader, who in prison at Haina, Hesse, Germany, wrote a letter with Melchior Rinck (q.v.), which is found in Brüderliche Vereynigung etzlicher Kinder Gottes, 1534, Dutch translation 1560. (BRN V, 599 f., 642.)   vDZ.

Jacob's Creek Valley in Fayette and Westmoreland counties in Southwestern Pennsylvania was the site of what seems to have been the first Mennonite settlement west of the Allegheny Mountains and the second oldest in the Allegheny Conference District. The pioneer settlers came to Jacob's Creek Valley in the period prior to 1789 on to 1800 from Lancaster Co., Pa., and Washington Co., Md. Early names were Strickler, Stauffer, Shallenberger, Sherrick, Shank, and Rist. The settlers south of Jacob's Creek built a meetinghouse near Pennsville before 1800, and this group was sometimes called the congregation of Jacob's Creek Valley. Those north of the creek built a place of worship at Stonerville in about 1800. These two congregations were later merged into one with a meetinghouse in Scottdale, Pa.
                                         J.L.H.

E. Yoder, "The Mennonites of Westmoreland County, Pa.," MQR XV (1941) 155-87.

Jacobs, Eduard (1833-1919), born at Crefeld, Germany, archivist and librarian of the Prince of Stolberg at Wernigerode a.H., author of the treatise "Die Wiedertäufer am Harz" in Zeitschrift des Harzvereins für Geschichte und Altertumskunde (Wernigerode, 1899), 423-536 and 631-33. The work constitutes a valuable addition to research in Mennonite history, giving much source material (from the court records in the Magdeburg archives) and a thorough presentation of the life and faith of the Anabaptists in the Harz.

Jacobs, in co-operation with Gustav Kawerau and Julius Köstlin, founded in 1883 the Verein für Reformationsgeschichte, which after World War I made plans to publish all the hitherto unpublished court records, government and church protocols, mandates, letters, regulations, etc., relating to the Anabaptist movement of the 16th century in a single comprehensive collection of source material (see **Historiography**). Since 1948 this Verein has in conjunction with the Mennonitischer Geschichtsverein been publishing and preparing for publication these new source materials of Anabaptist history.
                                     NEFF, H.S.B.

H. S. Bender, "Publication and Research Projects in Anabaptist-Mennonite History," MQR (January, 1949); ML II, 101; Die Heimat (Crefeld) XI (1932) 99; ML II, 386.

Jacobs, Heinrich, an Anabaptist martyr, was beheaded in Bergheim, Rhineland, Germany, in 1536 because he would not give up his faith. (Rembert, Wiedertäufer, 523; ML II, 386.)   NEFF.

Jacobs, Joris, an elder of the Janjacobs (q.v.) group, ordained in 1639, who baptized 302 persons in 1640-47 in the Dutch province of Friesland. (Inv. Arch. Amst. II, 2, No. 9a; DB 1889, 4.)   vDZ.

Jacobs, Rijk, author of Een schriftelycke waerschouwinge voor valsche leere. Ghemaeckt door R. J. en voor sijne kinderen tot een Testament naeghelaten om daerdoor te onderscheyden het thegenschrijven van J. R. [Jacques van Reineghem, i.e., Jacques Outerman, q.v.] gedaen thegen dat heylsaem schriftmatige getuygenisse der gesonder leere Jesu Christi schriftelick ende mondelick betuycht door A[rent] B[arentsz] en H[endrick van Gulik] (n.p., 1612). In this booklet Jacobsz accuses Outerman of Socinianism (q.v.). This Rijk Jacobs is probably identical with the Rijck Jacobsz who was a physician at Baambrugge, province of Utrecht, and from 1614 a preacher of the Waterlander congregation at Staveren, Friesland, who disagreed with Hans de Ries (q.v.) and other Waterlanders in insisting that persons coming from the Reformed Church should be rebaptized. He also published De predicatien der namen Gods (Amsterdam, 1624). W. J. van Douwen's surmise (Socinianen en Doopsgezinden) that he later became a Reformed pastor is not very probable.   vDZ.

Inv. Arch. Amst. I, Nos. 545-53; DB 1897, 164; N.N.B. Wb. IX, 443 f.; Biogr. Wb. IV, 485 f.

Jacobs, Wouter, a Mennonite preacher of Ameland (q.v.), who in 1714 copied the "Dooplijst" (list of baptisms) of Elder Leenaert Bouwens (q.v.). This copy, acquired in 1855 by Pastor K. S. Gorter of Ameland (*DB* 1889, 3), is now in the Amsterdam Mennonite archives (*Inv. Arch. Amst.* II, 2, No. 9). The Wouter Jacobs copy, which is more accurate than the Appingedam copy used by Blaupot ten Cate, was used by Karel Vos in his study on the "Dooplijst" in *Bijdragen en Mededeelingen van het Hist. Genootschap* XXXVI (1915) 39 ff.   vpZ.

Jacobs(z), Anthoni (Anthony, sometimes called Roscius after the friend and teacher of Cicero), b. 1594 probably at Amsterdam (according to Schijn in Hoorn), d. 1624, was a Dutch Mennonite elder in the Waterlander congregation at Hoorn. In January 1624 he was skating from Hoorn to Amsterdam, where he was to preach a sermon, pushing the sled in which his wife Jannetje Jansdochter was sitting with their child, and fell through a hole in the ice. The child drowned and Jacobsz with much trouble saved his wife, who, however, died soon after. Two weeks later Jacobsz also died. This tragic accident made a deep impression. Joost van den Vondel (*q.v.*), Holland's greatest poet, then still a member of the Amsterdam Waterlander congregation, celebrated the family in a poem, and Jeme de Ringh (*q.v.*) of Harlingen published a sermon for Anthoni's funeral. Anthoni Jacobsz was a grandson on his mother's side of the well-known Elder Lubbert Gerritsz (*q.v.*) and a son of Jacob Thonis (Theunissen), a deacon of the Waterlander congregation of Amsterdam; his brother Lambert Jacobsz (*q.v.*) was an elder of the Waterlander congregation of Leeuwarden. Anthoni studied medicine, obtained his doctor's degree, and was appointed elder at an early age, being much appreciated by his congregation. He published *Wederlegginghe des Kinder doops . . . teghen Robertum Puppium, dat deselve niet uit God is* (n.p., 1617, reprinted Amsterdam 1636). After Herman Faukelius (*q.v.*), a Reformed divine, had attacked the Mennonites in *Babel, dat is Verwerringhe der Wederdooperen onder malkanderen* (1621), and Claes Claesz (*q.v.*) of Blokzijl had defended the Mennonites, Anthoni Jacobsz also wrote a refutation entitled *Babel, d.i. Verwerringe der Kinderdooperen onder malcanderen* (n.p., 1626), which was published after Jacobsz' death. He is also thought to have been the author of a booklet published at Amsterdam in 1628 under the pseudonym of Ben Israels, *Tractaet der Buytengetrouwden sonder onderscheijt.* vpZ.

Schijn-Maatschoen, *Geschiedenis* III, 270-89; *Biogr. Wb.* IV, 480-82; Kühler, *Geschiedenis* II, 44, 59, 64, 66-69, 77, 142 f.; *DB* 1883, 7; *ML* II, 386.

Jacobsz, Claes, a Mennonite bookdealer at De Rijp, Dutch province of North Holland, who published the well-known book by Pieter Pietersz, *Wegh na Vreden-stadt* (1624), and in the same year two sermons of the same author, *Twee Eenvoudighe Stichtelijcke Predicatiën.* This volume also contains a booklet by Claes Jacobsz himself, *Een Christelijcke Sendtbrief aen een bedruckte Weduw,* of 1622. The letter by Claes Jacobsz was reprinted at De Rijp in 1644.   vpZ.

Jacobs(z), Jan, a Dutch Mennonite elder, b. May 25, 1542, at Harlingen, d. July 17, 1612, at Leeuwarden,

who founded a group called the *Janjacobsgezinden.* Jan Jacobsz was a preacher and elder of the Frisian Mennonites. He was appointed to the ministry about 1562, became an elder about 1580. He visited a large number of congregations, always traveling about and until his death preaching and baptizing, sometimes in mortal danger. He was a man of austere principles, requiring that the members of the church avoid the "world" in every way, not marrying outside the group, nor carrying on business with nonmembers. In 1589, when the Frisian Mennonites were divided into *Zachte Vriezen* (Mild Frisians) with Lubbert Gerritsz as leader and *Harde* or *Oude Vriezen* (Severe or Old Frisians), Jan Jacobsz was one of the leaders of the latter and in 1599, when a quarrel arose among the Old Frisians he separated with a number of adherents, forming the Janjacobs group, which banned Pieter Jeltjes (*q.v.*) and his followers. About 1603 he was probably involved in a quarrel with the followers of Tijs Gerrits (*q.v.*), which caused a new schism.

In the meanwhile Jan Jacobsz was exiled from Friesland by the government because of his great activity (April 1600); he then turned first to Medemblik, and soon after to Hoorn, where he had many followers. In the course of time he was allowed to live in Friesland, though forbidden to preach. When this restriction was lifted in 1611, he and his wife returned to Harlingen, and he again began to travel about. Arriving at Anjum (*q.v.*) in June 1612, he fell ill and was unable to preach; he went to Leeuwarden, and feeling his end drawing near he called his coelders for a last farewell, soon after dying at the home of his sister Griet Jacobs at Leeuwarden.

Jan Jacobsz composed 46 hymns, which are found in a songbook published after his death, entitled *Eenighe Gheestelijcke Liedekens, gemaeckt aen verscheyden personen door Jan Jacobszoon van Harlingen . . . Ende ten Druck bestelt door P. W.* (Amsterdam, Nicolaes Biestkens, 1612). Loosjes's assertion that Jan Jacobsz was a son of Jacob de Heere, or Scheltema, who was born at Aalst, Flanders, and that Jan Jacobsz was the Dutch ancestor of the de Heere family has been proved false. His father was Jacob Hayesz, a native of Harlingen where Jan Jacobsz was born.   vpZ.

J. Loosjes, *Jan Jacobs en de Jan Jacobsgezinden* in *Ned. Archief voor Kerkgesch.* XI (The Hague, 1914) number III, 183-209; *Biogr. Wb.* IV, 482-84; *N.N.B.Wb.* VIII, 911; *Ned. Patriciaat* XXVII (1941) 218; *BRN* VII, 67 f., 213 ff., 527, 554; *DB* 1867, 65; 1876, 30-35; 1889, 6-10; 1894, 31; 1900, 74, 98.

Jacobsz, Lambert, b. *ca.* 1598 in Amsterdam, d. June 27, 1636, at Leeuwarden, a grandson on his mother's side of the noted Mennonite leader Lubbert Gerritsz (*q.v.*), a son of the deacon Jacob Teunis, and a brother of Anthoni Jacobsz (*q.v.*), was an elder of the Waterlander Mennonite congregation at Leeuwarden (*q.v.*), Dutch province of Friesland. During his ministry there was some difficulty with the city government because of the building of a new meetinghouse in 1630-31, and Lambert Jacobsz was fined twice, apparently because he had preached in the new church, which was forbidden by the government.

In 1620 Lambert Jacobsz married Aeghtje Theunisdochter, a daughter of a Mennonite preacher and flax trader. Vondel (*q.v.*) wrote a poem for this occasion. In the fall of 1633, after the death of Aeghtje, he married Hillegont, daughter of Dirk Velius of Hoorn. He was a close friend of Dirk R. Camphuyzen (*q.v.*). In 1636 Lambert Jacobsz died as a victim of the plague. A son of Lambert Jacobsz was Abraham van den Tempel (*q.v.*), a well-known Dutch painter. The artist Govert Flinck was a pupil of Lambert Jacobsz.

Lambert Jacobsz was not only a Mennonite minister but also carried on a business in paintings, being himself also a painter. About 1618 he had visited Italy. Until very recently Lambert Jacobsz was quite unknown as a painter. None of his paintings were discovered before 1918. Now there are 25 pictures known to have been made by him. The Mennonite congregation of Leeuwarden possesses three of them. In 1936 a memorial exhibition of his pictures was held in Leeuwarden and Amsterdam. Most of his pictures show an Italian landscape, after a drawing he obviously made in 1618, and in this landscape a Biblical scene, such as Joseph sold by his brethren, Isaac and Rebecca, Ruth and Boaz, or the question of paying tribute (Matt. 22:16-21). His most impressive painting is that of the Apostle Paul.   vDZ.

Biogr. Wb. IV, 484 f.; Friesch Museum, Leeuwarden, *Herdenkings-Tentoonstelling Lambert Jacobsz. 27 Juni-27 September, 1936, Catalogus;* H. L. Straat, "Lambert Jacobsz, Schilder," *De Vrije Fries* XXVIII, 1 (Leeuwarden, 1925); DJ 1937, 67-72; *Oud Holland,* 1930, 145; 1934, 241 ff.

Jacobsz, Mattheus, a Dutch book printer, who in 1557 published the New Testament in the Dutch language, reprinted in 1558, 1559, and 1562. These editions were especially used by the Dutch Mennonites before the Biestkens Bible (*q.v.*) was printed in 1560.   vDZ.

Jacop Pierin, an otherwise unknown Anabaptist martyr, executed about 1559 at Hondschoote (*q.v.*) in Flanders. (Verheyden, "Mennisme in Vlaanderen," ms.)   vDZ.

Jacquemijne de Wilde, an Anabaptist martyr, widow of the martyr Gillis Rooze (*q.v.*), was imprisoned in February 1568 at Brugge, Belgium, together with 13 other Mennonites, when their meeting was surprised by the police. Nine of them recanted, but Jacquemijne remained faithful to the end and died as a martyr at the stake between April 13 and July 28, 1568. (Verheyden, *Brugge,* 54, No. 54.) vDZ.

Ja(c)ques d'Auchy (Dauchi, Dosie, Doussy), an Anabaptist martyr, secretly executed on March 14, 1559, in prison at Leeuwarden. He was a merchant who was basely betrayed to the police by a van der Waal at Harlingen. In prison he was visited by his wife, who "would have liked to die with him and inherit the blessed life." He comforted her with the words, "Do not let it dismay you that I must go a little ahead of you; that is the Lord's will." It was revealed in the trial that he was baptized by Leenaert Bouwens in Emden. Nothing else is known

of his activities. He was a man of considerable education, unequaled by any other Dutch martyr. Before his conversion he may have been a lawyer. In the discussion with the inquisitor he cites the church fathers Eusebius, Tertullian, and Cyprian. The French language was his mother tongue. His confession was translated from the French into the Dutch language and at least one song he composed was French. So we may assume that northern France or French Flanders was his native country.

Of great importance is his confession, a detailed transcription of his trial by the inquisitors, which he wrote from memory, since it offers an extremely valuable insight into the doctrine and life of the Anabaptists of that period. More than 20 times he was ordered to appear before the inquisitor and again and again the painfully detailed examination about the most important questions of faith was begun anew. Quite surprising is the spiritual superiority of the Anabaptist over his theologically trained opponents in keen understanding and extensive acquaintance with the Scriptures. He met them most skillfully.

Most of the arguments were about baptism and communion. Adroitly he refuted the arguments for infant baptism with superior Biblical grounds. When, for instance, his opponent pointed out that whole households were baptized and that they probably included small children, he replied that the Bible says nothing of them, but rather states expressly that all the members of the households had heard and believed the word, which could surely not be said of small children. With equally convincing force, and with clever, most fitting Scriptural replies he disputed the bodily presence of Christ in the communion, and rejected the doctrine of the Mass as un-Biblical. To the reproach that he rejected the word of the holy Church Fathers, he replied, "I do not reject them, but leave them where they are; for I find enough material in the Word of God for a firm foundation, and enough water of life in the pure fountain, so that I do not need to drink from creeks and pools, which are usually murky and foul." On one occasion he denounced David Joris as "a heretic who destroys the breaking of bread"; i.e., rejects the Lord's Supper.

When asked if he was a follower of Menno Simons' doctrine, he answered, "I believe that Jesus was entirely the Son of God in flesh and spirit; but the question of the origin of His flesh I leave to . . . God; the apostles did not argue about it." His view of the Old Testament is also interesting: it is to be appraised only according to the testimony of Jesus and His apostles. "We are no longer under the law, but under the Gospel." Finally he pointed out the immoral conduct of the bishops and priests, and challenged his opponent to name a single one in the great number who lived a morally clean life, so that he might follow after him. The "heresy master" was now silent, and at length remarked that wicked can also have faith, pointing to Judas and Demas. But the Anabaptist replied aptly, "Then a thief who admonishes his fellows not to steal will also secure results. They would much more probably say, 'If it is evil, why do you do it? You hypocrite, take the beam from your own eye; then you will be able to see the mote in mine.'" His "Confession" is a significant document for the understanding of Mennonite history.

Jacques d'Auchy also composed a number of songs, at least three of which are known: (a) a song translated from the French into the Dutch and included by Carel van Mander (q.v.) in his hymnbook De Gulden Harpe, which begins "Tot Leeuwarden op eenen dag"; (b) a song beginning "Ghy Borgers Jerusalem, aensiet," found in the Nieu Liedenboeck of 1562 and later hymnbooks; (c) a song beginning "Och siet hoe droeve dingen," found in the Lietboecxken van den Offer des Heeren (1563 and following editions), No. 24 (Offer, 608-11).

The oldest martyrbook, Het Offer des Heeren of 1562, contains the following by and about Jacques d'Auchy: (1) his confession of faith; (2) accounts written by himself of his confessions made before the commissarius and the inquisitors; (3) a song on his capture, suffering, and death, beginning: "Seer wonderlijck, o Heere, sijn U wercken vermaert." All of these, the song in prose, are found in the later martyrbooks including van Braght, Martyrs' Mirror. Van Braght contributes two accounts on this martyr, once calling him Jaques Dosie and once Jaques d'Auchy. Of Jacques' confession there is also a French edition, titled Confession de Foy . . . (n.p., 1626). NEFF, vDZ.

Inv. Arch. Amst. I, No. 746; Offer, 268-323, 608-11; Mart. Mir. D 101 f., 212-36; E 498, 591-611; BRN VII, 173 ff., 197 ff., 225; Wolkan, Lieder, 64, 67, 70; Wackernagel, Lieder, 198; F. C. Wieder, Schriftuurlijke Liedekens (The Hague, 1900) 187; ML I, 89 f.; III, 394.

Ja(c)ques Bostijn (Coppin Bostijn), an Anabaptist martyr, burned at the stake on July 16, 1562, at the Vrijdagsmarkt at Gent, Belgium, with Laurens Allaerts, Pieter van Maldegem, and Pieter van Male. His name is celebrated in the song "Als men schreef duyst vijfhondert Jaer," in the Lietboecxken van den Offer des Heeren, edition of 1578 and following. He was a native of Kortrijk (Courtrai) in Flanders. Members of the Mennonite Bostijn family were found in the Amsterdam "Lam, and Toren" congregation in the 17th and 18th centuries. They may be related to this martyr. (Offer, 650; Mart. Mir. D 289, E 656; Verheyden, Gent, 28, No. 88.)
vDZ.

Jacques van Hulten (Verhulten), an Anabaptist martyr, burned at the stake at Antwerp, Belgium, on Jan. 28, 1573, together with Grietken van den Steene and Janneken Croecx. Jacques' wife Lynken Ghysseleers (q.v.) died as a martyr on Feb. 20, 1573. Jacques is charged with the crimes of having left the Catholic Church, being rebaptized, having partaken in forbidden meetings in Antwerp and elsewhere. (Antw. Arch.-Blad XIII, 99 f., 171; XIV, 88 f., No. 1001.)
vDZ.

Jacques (Jacob) van Maldegem, a Mennonite preacher: see Maldegem.

Jacques van der Mase, an Anabaptist martyr from Brussels, was burned at the stake in 1536 or 1537 at Kortrijk (Courtrai), Belgium. He probably had belonged to the revolutionary wing of Anabaptism and he had relations with Münsterite Anabaptists in

a number of towns in the Netherlands, as The Hague, Delft, Rotterdam, Dordrecht, Gorinchem, and Geertruidenberg. After the fall of Münster (q.v.) in July 1535 he went to Flanders. He is one of the rare instances of revolutionary principles among the Anabaptists in Flanders and at the same time an indication of early occurrence of Anabaptism at Kortrijk. (Verheyden, Courtrai-Bruxelles, 31, No. 1.)
vDZ.

Jacques Mergaert, an Anabaptist martyr, burned at the stake at Antwerp, Belgium, with Hans Corneliszoon de Ruytere and Hans Bret on Jan. 4, 1577. Jacques was born at Gent and was sentenced to death for attending forbidden meetings of the Anabaptists, being rebaptized, and persevering in this "heresy." (Antw. Arch.-Blad XIII, 210; XIV, 98 f., 1119.)
vDZ.

Jacques (Jacob) Semou, perhaps identical with Jan de Schaper (q.v.), an Anabaptist martyr, born at Béthune, French Flanders, a weaver, 38 years of age, living at Borgerhout near Antwerp. He had been (re)baptized at Gent about 1558 by Joachim Vermeeren, and was arrested while attending a meeting in the house of Jan Poote (q.v.) at Antwerp in February 1569. Twice he was severely tortured, but refused to tell the inquisitors who had preached the sermon. On March 19, 1569, he was burned at the stake at Antwerp together with Jan Poote, Hans Vermandele, and Joos van Beeke. (Antw. Arch.-Blad XIII, 344, 368, 398, 440; XIV, 64 f., No. 714.)
vDZ.

Jacques de Stremont (d'Estremont), a martyr, was burned at the stake at Brussels, Belgium, on March 28, 1571, together with Hans van der Straten. It is likely, though not quite certain, that he was a Mennonite. (Verheyden, Courtrai-Bruxelles, 102, No. 148.)
vDZ.

Jacques Verbruggen, an Anabaptist martyr, burned at the stake on Jan. 31, 1573, at Antwerp, Belgium, together with Hans der Weduwe and Jenneken Beaucoup. Jacques was charged with rebaptism and attending the meetings of the Anabaptists. (Antw. Arch.-Blad XIII, 101 f., 173; XIV, 88 f., No. 1004.)
vDZ.

Jaecxken van Hussele, an Anabaptist martyr, who on Dec. 22, 1569, was burned at the stake on the Vrijdagsmarkt at Gent, after having been strangled, together with Tanneken van der Meulen and Jaecxken Teerlings. Particulars are not available. Their names are found in a song "Als men schreef duyst vijfhondert Jaer," of the Lietboecxken van den Offer des Heeren, edition of 1578 and following. (Offer, 653; Mart. Mir. D 407, E 759; Verheyden, Gent, 55, No. 185.)
vDZ.

Jaecxken Teerlings, an Anabaptist martyr, executed at Antwerp, Dec. 22, 1569 (Verheyden, Gent, 55, No. 186), together with Jaecxken van Hussele (q.v.).
vDZ.

Jaepgen Maertensd, an Anabaptist martyr of Ouddorp, who was drowned at Alkmaar in Holland on

July 14, 1537, on a charge of sacrilege, together with Kathryn Willemsdr. (*DB* 1909, 20 f.)   vDZ.

Jagdeeshpore Mission, a station and the hub of the General Conference Mennonite Christian work in the Phuljhar and Deori area of India, and the most recent station in this work. Jagdeeshpore is located south of the great Mahanadi River, about 60 miles south of Champa. E. B. Steiner and P. J. Wiens with their families had visited this area off and on since 1916, and baptized a number of persons. In 1923 the Moyers were asked to go to this area and search out a plot for a mission station. A plot, 5½ miles north of Basna, near the little village of Jagdeeshpore, in a dense oriental semitropical jungle was chosen. Christians from all around this jungle plot came to help in clearing it and building the first buildings. Growth came with almost breath-taking speed. By the end of 1924 several buildings were finished. By the end of 1928 Dr. Dester had a complete hospital established. By the end of 1948 John Thiessen had a complete high school established with a 28-acre school farm, poultry establishment, dairy, carpentry shop, weaving shop, tailoring shop, print shop, etc. The Christian community has increased from a few hundred to some three thousand in 1949, scattered in some 130 villages, all around Jagdeeshpore. Jagdeeshpore has grown in a quarter of a century from an obscure village hidden in the jungles of India to one widely known and appreciated.   J.T.

Jager, de, a family name, borne by a number of Dutch Mennonite ministers. Besides Hendrik de Jager (*q.v.*) and his son Jan de Jager (*q.v.*), both of whom served at Hamburg, Germany, there were Pieter de Jager, serving at Vlissingen 1663-71, Leiden 1671-79, and later at Schiedam 1692-? (concerning this man and the troubles he caused at Leiden and Rotterdam, see *Inv. Arch. Amst.* I, Nos. 809, 815-17; *DB* 1909, 160; and *De Zondagsbode,* 1898, Sept. 18 and 27), Henrik Teunis (Hendrik Theunis de Jager) who was a preacher at Harlingen, Holland, in the last decades of the 17th century, and Wigger Thomas de Jager, who served at South Giethoorn 1749-ca. 98.   vDZ.

Jager, Henrick de (Hendrik Teunis de Jager) (1690-1749), an outstanding preacher of the Hamburg-Altona Mennonite Church in the first half of the 18th century, was born Feb. 23, 1690, the son of the preacher Henrik Teunis of Harlingen, Holland. He was given an education unusual at the time in science and linguistics, mastered Latin and the Oriental languages, thus becoming after Hoekstra (*q.v.*) the "first learned preacher of the church." Because of his talents and education much attention was early centered on him, especially in view of the current shortage of ministers. Following Hamburg custom he prepared himself for business as a vocation. At the age of 21 he was chosen preacher, and nine years later, in 1720, elder. His strength of character enabled him to overcome his physical weakness.

The congregation was in a period of fermentation and change, having just come through the Socinian storms raised by Galenus Abrahamsz de Haan. The foe was no longer the external one of government

oppression, such as de Jager's predecessor, Gerrit Roosen, had struggled against in his booklet, *Unschuld und Gegenbericht,* but internal in the freer flow of spirit within the congregation. At the same time the church reached new cultural and economic prosperity, in spite of the heavy war levies and the burning of Altona in the war between Sweden and Denmark. Nevertheless de Jager maintained the traditional doctrine; indeed, in opposition to contrary opinion he held it the more carefully. But the inner relationship between congregation and pastor relaxed. A symbol of this change was the transition to a paid ministry. Thus de Jager stands at the threshold of the period in which a new type of minister was developing, with a new awareness of his calling.

De Jager led the church with a firm hand. After his ordination orderly church records were kept again, church discipline was exercised, and baptismal instruction prepared for life. Unfortunately there are no printed sermons from his pen. The speaker at his funeral, Karsdorp the Elder, gives this general characterization: "He preached Jesus Christ the Crucified as the foundation of salvation. He pointed constantly to the Word of God and sound doctrine." We can assume that he remained true to the irenic and practical views of Philippus of Limburg, his theological teacher, and that pietistic coloring, except in a few turns of phrase, cannot be found in him, in spite of the resemblance to Zinzendorf seen by Roosen.

With de Jager's collaboration, perhaps at his instigation, the first church school was established in Altona. The occasion for it was the fact that the Dutch language, used in preaching, writing, and church business, was being gradually replaced by German in the home and secular life, so that the oncoming generation scarcely understood Dutch. The schedule was not ambitious; it provided for the three R's, the main subject being Bible, with its adjunct, the singing of hymns. In connection with the school de Jager carried on extensive correspondence with Holland, Danzig, and Friedrichstadt. He was the founder of the church library at Altona, leaving to it much of his personal library.

De Jager's frailness and the death of five children caused him to live with his own demise in view. He died at the age of 59, on April 10, 1749. Gerrit Beets (*q.v.*), in his introduction to Karsdorp's funeral address, called him a "pillar of the church." He is the author of *Lykdicht ter heuchelyke nagedachtnisse van den Godzaligen Gerrit Roosen in zyn Leeven oudste Leeraar der Gemeente.*   O.S.

Gerrit Karsdorp, *Over de doot van den eerwaarden H. T. de Jager* (Hamburg, n.d.-1749); B. C. Roosen, *Gesch. d. Menn.-Gem. zu Hamburg und Altona* (Hamburg, 1886-87); E. H. Wichmann, *Geschichte Altonas* (Altona, 1865); Bolten, *Historische Kirchennachrichten; ML* II, 387.

Jager, Jan de, a minister of the Hamburg-Altona Mennonite Church, b. March 10, 1719, d. May 12, 1802, the oldest son of Henrick de Jager (*q.v.*), who gave him an excellent education in the "learned languages," astronomy, anatomy, and botany. From his twelfth to his twenty-second year he lived with his uncle, in order to be introduced into "trade."

Three years after his first marriage he was chosen as a probationary minister, having been in a sense bequeathed to the church, together with Karsdorp, Jr., by the "dying lips" of his father. It was even harder for the son to accept the office than it had been for the father. He did not preach a sermon until a year later, and his installation as a full preacher was postponed repeatedly until a year after the death of his first wife. He had meanwhile refused remuneration in order not to be bound. He was too adventuresome to be suited to a permanent pastorate. He spent much time in Friedrichstadt, the home of his second wife, so that the congregation had to have several ministers at the same time. Nevertheless Hoekstra stated in Jager's funeral sermon that his preaching was stirring and appealing, based on the conviction that faith is profitable, disbelief harmful, because on them depend life and death.

Extant are the following sermons preached by him: a sermon in verse, "Vaderlijke Ontboezeming aan myne kinderen," and the following printed funeral addresses: (1) "Die Aufmerksamkeit einer Gemeinde auf den Tod ihrer Lehrer bei dem seligen Absterben des . . . G. Karsdorp" (1750); (2) "De zalige hope en verwachting eener godvruchtige Ziele in Leven en in Sterven ter gelegentheid von het zalig overlyden van . . . J. Ris over Ps. 39, 8" (Hamburg, 1784).   O.S.

G. Karsdorp and S. Hoekstra, *Stand- en Gedachtenisrede*, 1802; *Biogr. Wb.* IV, 488; *Naamlijst* 1804, 70; *ML* II, 387.

Jäger, Philip: see **Philip Weber.**

Jahrbuch der altevangelischen Taufgesinnten *oder Mennoniten-Gemeinden*, published by H. G. Mannhardt (Danzig, 1888), is a continuation of the *Jahrbuch der Mennoniten-Gemeinden in West- und Ostpreussen*, published by the same author in 1884. The latter contains first a New Year's sermon of the author, then statistics of the churches in East and West Prussia of 1852 and 1882, showing that there had been a decline of 655 in membership. It is followed by the essays: "Die Mennoniten in der dramatischen Literatur," and "Ein Beitrag zu den Rechtsverhältnissen der Mennoniten," which deals with a suit against the Danzig Mennonite Church, which was decided in favor of the church. In conclusion he presents a brief chronicle of events in the Mennonite churches.

The yearbook of 1888 is richer in content. It contains exact statistics of the Mennonites in the various countries: Germany, Switzerland, France, Holland, Russia, and some from America, reporting the date of origin, membership, names of preachers and elders, and the institutions. The second part of the booklet is entitled *Verschiedenes aus der Tätigkeit und den Einrichtungen der Mennoniten,* and presents articles on (1) the home and foreign mission work of the Mennonites; (2) the *Vereinigung der Mennoniten-Gemeinden im Deutschen Reich* and its origin; (3) instruction among the Mennonites of Russia, with an interesting account of their school for the deaf in Blumenort; (4) the school at the Weierhof near Marnheim (Palatinate);

and (5) the text of several laws and regulations concerning the Mennonites. Ludwig Keller (*q.v.*) gives a list of books important to the history and doctrine of the Mennonites; the book closes with a recommendation of Mennonite books and periodicals. (*ML* II, 388.)   NEFF.

Jahrbuch, Mennonitisches: see **Mennonitisches Jahrbuch.**

Jakob, Hans, a co-worker with Pilgram Marpeck (*q.v.*), a High German Anabaptist elder. The only fact known about his life is that he participated in the composition of the extensive defensive booklet, *Antwort auf Kaspar Schwenckfelds Beurteilung des Buches der Bundesbezeugung von 1542,* written by the South German and Swiss Brethren 1544-46 under Marpeck's leadership.

The esteem in which the High German and Swiss Mennonites held the document can be estimated by a comment written by Walpurga, the Marshalck of Pappenheim, the original owner of the copy now in the central library of Zürich: "If God should call me (i.e., to eternity), this book shall be handed out only to the true believers, and those who have a zeal for God shall see the salvation of their souls therein; it shall not go into the world, for I prefer to give it to the God-fearing." (*ML* II, 388.) HEGE.

Jakob Heinrich, an Anabaptist writer of hymns, author of the hymn, "Ick roep tot u wt dieper noot" and probably also of "Ick moet eens gaen vertellen." Nothing else is known of him. (Wolkan, *Lieder,* 80; *ML* II, 279.)   NEFF.

Jamaica Mennonite Church (MC) was organized with 26 members on July 10, 1955, at Constant Spring, Jamaica, by Bishop Truman Brunk, Moderator of the Virginia Mennonite Conference, who baptized 11 persons and received by transfer from other denominations 15 persons. Warren and Erma Metzler were appointed missionaries to Jamaica in November 1955 by the Virginia Board of Missions and Charities, which is administering the work in cooperation with the Mennonite Board of Missions and Charities (Elkhart, Ind.). This work had a unique origin. Mr. and Mrs. D. H. Loewen of Manitoba (GCM) went to Jamaica in October 1954 to investigate the possibilities of mission work and soon began a private work. Unable to continue because of poor health, and failing to secure the support of their own conference mission board, they appealed to the MCC for help, which passed on the appeal to the Virginia board. The Loewens and a group of Jamaican Christians with whom they had found fellowship then formally invited the Virginia board to take over the work. Jamaica is a small British island in the West Indies, 95 miles southeast of Cuba, about 145 miles long (4,450 sq. mi.) and very mountainous, with a population (1943) of 1,237,391. H.S.B.

Mary Slabaugh, "Let's Visit Jamaica," and "Farewell for the Metzlers," *Gospel Herald* XLVIII (1955) 1214-16.

Jamerau (Jamrau), a village situated near the Vistula River in West Prussia, belonging to the territory of Culm (*q.v.*). Jamerau was settled by Dutch Mennonite farmers as early as 1597. The oldest lease was not preserved; in the lease of 1626 the following names are found (some of them may have been garbled): Joachim Rothe, Joachim Leskau, Hans Fott, Steffen Baltzer, Michel Decker, Hans Zimmermann, Ertman Stubbe. The Mennonites of Jamerau belonged to the Schönsee (*q.v.*) congregation. In 1752 the burgomaster and city council of Culm renewed a lease with the tenants Cornelis Frans, Johan Voet, Johan Nagtigal, Jakob Wedel, Peter Sievert, and Andreas Kurk, which obligated these tenants to keep the dikes along the Vistula in good condition. These tenants were all Mennonites, who (or whose parents) had fled from Lithuania (*q.v.*) about 1732. Abraham Nickel of Jamerau, a deacon of the Schönsee congregation, in 1806 presented a gift of 30,000 Talers to King Frederick William III and Queen Louise of Prussia, then fleeing before Napoleon, as a proof of the loyalty of the Mennonites in this district.   vɒZ.

F. Szper, *Nederl. Nederzettingen in West-Pruisen gedurende den Poolschen tijd* (Enkhuizen, 1913) 147 f.; Herbert Wiebe, *Das Siedlungswerk der niederl. Mennoniten im Weichseltal* (Marburg a.d. Lahn, 1952) 36, 57, note 16, 82, 94; J. A. Duerksen, "Przechowka and Alexanderwohl," *Menn. Life* X (April 1955) 76-82.

James, Epistle of, is generally attributed to James, the brother of Jesus, in Jerusalem. Luther called it an "epistle of straw," because it does not "promote Jesus." Menno criticized Luther severely for this statement. But even though the name of Jesus is mentioned only twice, His teachings meet us throughout, as they are given in the Gospels, particularly in the Sermon on the Mount. His earnest admonition to endure suffering and trial in patience, his opposition to an unfruitful theology, his warning against sins of the tongue, against the secularization of the church, against the injurious influence of wealth and opulent living, the command against swearing, and his insistence upon a life of prayer make of the Epistle of James a classic exponent of a practical Christianity which permeates everyday life. No wonder that it has always been highly regarded in Anabaptist circles.   NEFF.

C. Krahn, *Menno Simons* (Karlsruhe, 1936) 56, 109; *ML* II, 388.

James River United Missionary Church, organized in 1936, is located one mile south and 1½ miles west of James River, Alberta. In June 1941 a meetinghouse was erected with seating capacity of 75. In 1955 the church had 14 members with G. W. Dedels serving as pastor.   M.L.B.

James Valley Hutterite Bruderhof, four miles south of Elie, Man., was founded in Canada in 1918 because of Canada's more liberal provisions for conscientious objectors to military service. It was established by several families of the Milltown Bruderhof, 12 miles southeast of Huron, S.D., with David Hofer their preacher. David Hofer was also one of the founders of Milltown, was chosen to the ministry there on June 2, 1907, and confirmed in the office on Oct. 10, 1909. He died on April 6, 1941, in the James Valley Bruderhof at the age of 64. Peter Hofer was chosen preacher on Aug. 24, 1919, and confirmed on Sept. 8, 1935. In 1950 the colony had a total population of 128.   D.D.

Jamesville Hutterite Bruderhof, Utica, S.D., was founded in 1884 by several families from the Wolf Creek Bruderhof. Their preacher Elias Walter, Sr., was chosen to the ministry in 1889 in Wolf Creek. In 1918 the Bruderhof sold its possessions and moved to Alberta, founding the Springvale Bruderhof near Rocky Ford. In 1937 the Jamesville site was bought by Hutterian Brethren from Manitoba. Their preacher Friedrich Waldner was chosen in the Roseisle Bruderhof. In 1950 the Jamesville settlement numbered 107 souls.   D.D.

Jamnitz, Oswald von, an Anabaptist martyr, who was arrested at Vienna, Austria, in 1545 and because he remained steadfast in his faith was drowned there in the Danube. (*Mart. Mir.* D 71, E 473; *DB* 1899, 115.)   vɒZ.

Jan, an Anabaptist martyr who was executed at Antwerp, Belgium, on Oct. 2, 1551. This martyr, named in a letter by Peter Bruynen (*Offer,* 180, 182 and *Mart. Mir.* D 129 f., E 498), is identical with Jan de Oude Kleerkoper (*q.v.*).   vɒZ.

Jan, an Anabaptist martyr, reported by van Braght (*Mart. Mir.* D 288, E 655), executed at Antwerp, Belgium, in 1561, is Jan van Lyere (*q.v.*).   vɒZ.

Jan, an Anabaptist martyr, was executed in 1561 at Cologne, Germany, by drowning in the Rhine, together with Orvel and Pleun (Pleunis). (*Mart. Mir.* D 286, E 654; *ML* II, 389.)   NEFF.

Jan van Ackeren (Akeren, Akkeren), an Anabaptist martyr, born at Kortrijk (Courtrai) in Flanders, a serge weaver, was executed on April 2, 1569 (not 1573, as van Braght states), at Antwerp, Belgium, together with Jan de Timmerman and Balthasar de Rosières. Jan van Ackeren, who was 63 years of age, declared during his trial that he had been (re)baptized "six or seven years ago" by Pauwels van Tielt in a wooded spot near Halewijn, Flanders, in the presence of about 50 persons shortly after midnight. Jan, whose wife and two daughters were still living at Kortrijk, had moved to Antwerp only two weeks before he was arrested. He was tortured on March 9, and refusing to recant was sentenced to death, which he underwent with cheerfulness. The letters which he wrote in prison have been lost.   vɒZ.

Mart. Mir. D 644, E 965; *Antw. Arch.-Blad* XII, 361, 370, 399, 440; XIV, 64 f., No. 722; *ML* II, 389.

Jan Aertsz, an Anabaptist martyr, a joiner from Oesterhout (Oosterhout, Dutch province of North Brabant?), was beheaded at Delft, Dutch province of South Holland, with 10 others on Jan. 7, 1539. Apparently he was a follower of David Joris (*q.v.*). In 1534, when living in the territory of IJsselstein, he organized meetings in which the Scriptures (or other books?) were read.   vɒZ.

Inv. Arch. Amst. I, No. 749; *DB* 1899, 158-60; 1917, 160-67; Mellink, *Wederdopers,* 233.

Jan (Johan) **Andries,** a Mennonite preacher of Utrecht: see Aken, Jan Andries van.

Jan Arends (Arents, Arnts), an unknown Anabaptist martyr, executed at Amsterdam on May 11, 1532.   vɒZ.

C. A. Cornelius, *Geschichte des Münsterischen Aufruhrs II* (Leipzig, 1860) 385.

Jan van Bemelen, an Anabaptist martyr of Maastricht, Dutch province of Limburg. When persecution arose there, Jan and his wife fled, but afterwards returned and were arrested. Jan was beheaded there in April 1538 on the Vrijthof square. His wife was released because she was not (re)baptized. vDZ.

W. Bax, *Het Protestantisme in het Bisdom Luik* I (The Hague, 1937) *passim,* especially 141 f.

Jan Berne, a shoemaker, one of the four leaders of the Anabaptist congregation in Maastricht, Dutch province of Limburg, in whose home Hendric Slachtscaep (*q.v.*) van Tongeren stayed in 1533, writing "letters and other things," according to a letter written by the Duke of Jülich to the city of Maastricht, July 16, 1533. In 1527 Jan Berne had been in court for "Lutheranism"; he was reading (said the charge) forbidden books. He was released upon a public church confession. One and one-half years later he was again in prison, with Jan van den Bosch. In 1532 he had been charged with blasphemy against the holy sacrament; in March 1533 he was accused of holding secret conferences. In 1535 he fled from the city with his wife. Nothing more is known of him. NEFF.

W. Bax, *Het Protestantisme in het bisdom Luik* I (The Hague, 1937) 79-81 and *passim,* see Index; Rembert, *Wiedertäufer,* 76, 78, 358; *ML* I, 197.

Jan Beukelsz (Bokelszoon, Bockelszoon), the revolutionary Anabaptist leader and "King of Münster": see **Jan van Leyden.**

Jan (Johan) Block, an Anabaptist martyr, had as a rich young man led a frivolous, pleasure-seeking life. The conversion of one of his former drinking companions made such an impression on him that he also became a believer and joined the Mennonites. When the government heard of this they confiscated all his lands and set a reward of 70 guilders on his seizure. He fled, but returned when he found no refuge anywhere, to support himself by the work of his hands. He was betrayed and in 1569 (not 1572, as van Braght erroneously states) was arrested in Nijmegen. He was held in the city prison for 53 days, and racked three times. During his imprisonment he wrote a letter to his fellow believers, in moving words bidding his friends a last farewell in the hope of a reunion in eternal joy. Before the courts he remained steadfast in his faith, and was therefore sentenced to die at the stake and was executed outside the Molenpoort on July 23, 1569. He endured his martyrdom with the same joyful submission. O.H., vDZ.

P. C. G. Guyot, *Bijdragen tot de Geschiedenis der Doopsgezinden te Nijmegen* (Nijmegen, 1845) 26-28; *Mart. Mir.* D 562, E 894; *ML* I, 237.

Jan Blo(c)k, a linen weaver of Gent, an Anabaptist martyr, was executed by burning at the stake at Vught, Dutch province of North Brabant, on Sept. 9, 1538, with a gag in his mouth to prevent his speaking or calling. He had been arrested in August at 's-Hertogenbosch (*q.v.*), together with seven others, including his wife Lysken (*q.v.*), who was

burned at the stake the next day, and Paulus van Drunen (*q.v.*), the bishop of the congregation, who was executed on the same day as Jan Block. (*Mart. Mir.* D 42, E 447; *DB* 1917, 189.) vDZ.

Jan Bosch van den Berge, a martyr: see **Jan Durps.**

Jan Boulin (Boullyn), an otherwise unknown Anabaptist martyr, born at Hasselt in the Belgian province of Limburg, was burned at the stake on July 13, 1553, at Antwerp. (*Antw. Arch.-Blad* VIII, 421, 423; XIV, 20 f., No. 223.) vDZ.

Jan van Capel(le), a native of Flanders, an Anabaptist martyr, was burned at the stake at Vught, Dutch province of North Brabant, on Sept. 11, 1538. (*Mart. Mir.* D 42, E 448; *DB* 1917, 189.) vDZ.

Jan Christiaenz (in van Braght, *Martyrs' Mirror,* Jan N.), an Anabaptist martyr. He was a native of Zeebrugge in Flanders and lived in Brugge (*q.v.*). In the fall of 1561 a severe persecution befell the congregation and a large number of members were arrested. Jan Christiaenz was among them. He was burned at the stake on Dec. 11, 1561, together with six others, while on the previous day five had already suffered martyrdom. These martyrs are celebrated in a song, "Genade en Vrede moet Godvresende sijn," found in *Veelderhande Liedekens* of 1569, reprinted by Wackernagel. vDZ.

Mart. Mir. D 288, E 655; Verheyden, *Brugge,* 49, No. 37; Wackernagel, *Lieder,* 130.

Jan Claesz (John Claess in the English *Mart. Mir.*), an Anabaptist martyr, born at Alkmaar, baptized by Menno Simons, for whom he rendered valuable service as a bookdealer. In Antwerp he had 600 copies of Menno Simons' books printed; 200 he sold in the province of Holland and the rest he shipped for distribution to Friesland. He was a Mennonite preacher in Amsterdam; in his house religious services were held. Betrayed by Reynier Willemsz, a follower of David Joris, he was imprisoned and on Jan. 19, 1544, he was beheaded at Amsterdam with Lucas Lamberts van Beveren (*q.v.*), surnamed Bestevaer. Van Braght presents six testaments made by him, three to his wife, one each to his children, to his "brethren and sisters according to the flesh," and "to his entire generation," which bear witness to his faithful brotherly love and the faith of the Mennonites of that period. This is also true of the brief, moving courageous confession given before his cruel execution. The *Offer des Heeren* contains a song written on the death of these two men (p. 65), beginning "Het waren twee gebroeders goet, seer lieffelijck van zeden." It is also found in the *Ausbund* of 1583 and following editions: "Es waren zwei Brüder gut, sehr lieblich auch von Sitten." NEFF.

Inv. Arch. Amst. I, Nos. 257-59; *Offer,* 78-90; *Mart. Mir.* D 66-70, E 468; *DB* 1864, 144-46; 1899, 77; 1903, 17; 1906, 56-73 *passim;* 1909, 26 f.; Wolkan, *Lieder,* 65, 128; *ML* I, 359.

Jan Claesz, a cloth shearer of Gouda, Dutch province of South Holland (not of Grouw, Friesland), an otherwise unknown Anabaptist martyr, was beheaded at Leeuwarden, capital of Friesland, together with four others, on Feb. 8, 1539, charged with (re)baptism and "contempt of the holy sacrament and the institutions of the Holy Church." vDZ.

Inv. Arch. Amst. I, 746; F. H. Pasma, *De Doopsgez. te Grouw* (Grouw, 1930) 5, note 1.

Jan Claesz, an Anabaptist martyr, a native of Weesp, an unmarried man who lived at Rarop in the Dutch province of North Holland. He cheerfully confessed his faith and was therefore burned at the stake at the Muiden castle near Amsterdam in 1569 together with Thijs Jeuriaensz. (*Mart. Mir.* D 480, E 823; *ML* II, 389.) vDZ.

Jan Claesz Cock (Jan de Cock), a Dutch Anabaptist leader, executed at The Hague on March 24, 1535, by being torn to pieces. Though not much is known about his activities, he must have been a man of great influence, for Reinier Brunt, attorney general of the Court of Holland, called him "a bishop, being a great preacher of the new sect." He was living at Delft, Dutch province of South Holland, and about the spring of 1534 adopted the Anabaptist-Münsterite principles. He not only baptized a large number of persons, but was also involved in revolutionary activity, such as an assault planned on Amsterdam. He was arrested at Terheide near The Hague and before his judges named a large number of leading Anabaptists. Maybe it was for this reason that David Joris (*q.v.*), also betrayed by Cock, left Delft. vDZ.

Inv. Arch. Amst. I, Nos. 213, 745; *DB* 1917, 112, No. 27; Mellink, *Wederdopers*, 77, 85, 213-18, 371.

Jan Cleeren, of Gortsleeuw, Flanders, an Anabaptist martyr, by trade a *hertekens-maker*(?), was drowned at the Steen castle at Antwerp, Belgium, on Aug. 9, 1560. He is probably identical with Jan de Tasmaker (*q.v.*), found in the *Offer des Heeren* and later martyr books, including the *Martyrs' Mirror*. (*Antw. Arch.-Blad* IX, 111, 121; XIV, 30 f., No. 330.) vDZ.

Jan de Cock: see Jan Claesz Cock.

Jan Cooman (*Koopman,* i.e., merchant), an Anabaptist martyr, burned at the stake at Antwerp, Belgium, on May 5, 1569, together with Jan Hasebroek, Hans Moens, and Herman de Timmerman. Jan Cooman was sentenced to death because he had been rebaptized and held meetings in his house, in which he had exhorted those present. From this fact we may suppose that he was a preacher. (*Mart. Mir.* D 415, E 766; *Antw. Arch.-Blad* XII, 382, 400; XIV, 66 f., No. 755.) vDZ.

Jan Cornelisz (called *Oude Jan*) of Hazerswoude (*q.v.*), Dutch province of South Holland, an Anabaptist martyr, beheaded on March 26, 1534, at Haarlem. He is called one of the principal Anabaptist leaders. Nothing more is known. vDZ.

Inv. Arch. Amst. I, No. 745; *DB* 1917, 121 (No. 124) 151; Mellink, *Wederdopers*, 176, 189.

Jan Cornelisz (Jonge Jan Cornelisz) of Hazerswoude (*q.v.*), Dutch province of South Holland, an Anabaptist martyr, burned at the stake at The Hague on April 15, 1534. He had been among the

Anabaptists who were taken prisoner at Bergklooster (*q.v.*) en route to Münster (*q.v.*). Together with him five others suffered martyrdom. (*DB* 1917, 121, No. 135, 171.) vDZ.

Jan de Cudse (also *de Kudse* or *van Cussegem*), an Anabaptist martyr, burned at the stake on Sept. 4, 1556, at the market place of Antwerp, Belgium. His name is mentioned in a song, "Aenhoort Godt, hemelsche Vader," found in the *Lietboecxken van den Offer des Heeren,* No. 16. vDZ.

Offer, 564; *Mart. Mir.* D 167, E 554; *Antw. Arch.-Blad* VIII, 432, 435; XIV, 22 f., No. 235.

Jan Damasz, a cobbler of Monnikendam or Noordwijk, an Anabaptist martyr, was beheaded at The Hague on April 10, 1535. He was one of the principal Dutch Anabaptist leaders, apparently of the revolutionary wing. (*Inv. Arch. Amst.* I, No. 745; *DB* 1917, 113, No. 33.) vDZ.

Jan Davion, an Anabaptist martyr, beheaded at Antwerp, Belgium, in February 1545. He was a merchant at Rijssel (Lille) in France, and an adherent of David Joris (*q.v.*). He was arrested at Antwerp in September 1544. (Mellink, *Wederdopers,* 413.) vDZ.

Jan van Delft, of Amsterdam, a fuller, was one of the first Anabaptists in the Netherlands. With nine others he was arrested and sentenced to death because of heresy and rebaptism. Like most of this group, Jan recanted. He was beheaded at The Hague on Dec. 5, 1531. The other victims were Jan Volkertsz (Trypmaker) (*q.v.*); Evert Jansz, a cobbler from Coesfeld in the territory of Münster, Germany; Frans Willems; Gerrit (Geryt) Meynerts, a goldsmith; Jan Hermansz (Lange Jan Houtstapelaer), born at Haarlem; Jan Gouweszn, a fuller; Thomas Janszn; Jan Thomaszn; and Vranck Willemszn. (*Inv. Arch. Amst.* I, No. 6; *DB* 1917, 159 f.; Grosheide, *Bijdrage,* 50, 302.) vDZ.

Jan Diericxsone (alias *de Cammere*), born at Kortrijk (Courtrai) in Flanders, a cordmaker, was arrested at Brugge, Belgium, and beheaded there in 1568, exact date unknown, because of Anabaptism. The fact that he was not burned at the stake seems to indicate that he had recanted. (Verheyden, *Brugge,* 56, No. 57.) vDZ.

Jan Dirck Volbrechtsz, of Leiden, an Anabaptist martyr, beheaded at The Hague in the Netherlands on Aug. 16, 1544. He had been baptized in 1534 at Leiden by Cornelis Pietersz wt den Briel (*q.v.*). He is supposed to have been an adherent of the revolutionary Anabaptist leader Jan van Batenburg (*q.v.*). (*Inv. Arch. Amst.* I, Nos. 288, 745; Mellink, *Wederdopers,* 192, 410.) vDZ.

Jan Dircksz (Jan Dircxs, Dirks, Dirksz). There are a number of Anabaptist martyrs in the Netherlands bearing this name:

(1) *Jan Dirks* (Dircxszoon), of Alkmaar, Dutch province of North Holland, who was among the Anabaptists sailing from Amsterdam to Bergklooster (*q.v.*) en route to Münster; arrested in Bergklooster, he was sentenced to death by the Court of

Holland and executed at The Hague on April 10, 1534 (*Inv. Arch. Amst.* I, No. 745; *DB* 1905, 173). According to Vos (*DB* 1917, 170) this Jan Dircksz is identical with Jan Walen (*q.v.*), the date of execution being April 15, 1534. Another Anabaptist from Alkmaar, a locksmith also called Jan Dircx, who had also sailed to Bergklooster, but who had not yet been baptized, was tried April 25, 1534, and was sentenced to ask the sheriff and the alderman of Alkmaar for pardon for his trespass. (*DB* 1909, 14.)

(2) *Jan Dirksz,* of Aalsmeer, Dutch province of North Holland, in whose house Jacob van Campen (*q.v.*), bishop of the congregation of Amsterdam, had preached before March 1534. He was burned at the stake at The Hague on April 10, 1534.

Inv. Arch. Amst. I, Nos. 744 f.; *DB* 1917, 121, No. 127; Grosheide, *Verhooren,* 97; Mellink, *Wederdopers,* 185 f.

(3) *Jan Dirksz,* also of Aalsmeer, a blacksmith. He was arrested before Feb. 23 and burned at the stake on April 10, 1534, the same day as the above Jan Dirksz. (Bibliography immediately above.)

(4) *Jan Dirks de Lapper* (cobbler), executed Oct. 29, 1538, at The Hague by beheading, being charged with heresy and Anabaptism. (*Inv. Arch. Amst.* I, Nos. 198, 475.)

None of these martyrs is found in the Mennonite martyrbooks.   vdZ.

Jan van Doornik, an Anabaptist martyr, burned at the stake in 1569 at Antwerp and named by van Braght (*Mart. Mir.* D 415, E 766), is identical with Jan Poote (*q.v.*).   vdZ.

Jan Dries, from Lier in Brabant, Belgium, an Anabaptist martyr, was burned at the stake at the Vrijdagsmarkt at Gent, Belgium, on April 3, 1557. (Verheyden, *Gent,* 23, No. 51.)   vdZ.

Jan Droochscheerder (cloth shearer, his official name being Jan Deels), an Anabaptist martyr, was burned at Antwerp, Belgium, on Aug. 27, 1555. Particulars are not known. He is named in the song "Aenhoort Godt, hemelsche Vader" (Hear, O God, heavenly Father), No. 16 of the *Lietboecxken van den Offer des Heeren.*   vdZ.

Offer, 564; *Mart. Mir.* D 161, E 550; *Antw. Arch.-Blad* VIII, 426, 429; XIV, 20 f., No. 288; Wolkan, *Lieder,* 63, 72.

Jan Durps (Jan Bosch van den Berge, Berghe), an Anabaptist martyr, a weaver, was burned at the stake at Maastricht, Dutch province of Limburg, on Sept. 23, 1559. He served the congregation "by reading as well as admonition," and thus came to the attention of the government. He was arraigned as a heretic and Anabaptist. Before the clergy, who tried to lead him to recantation, as well as before the government, he openly confessed his faith. In order to bring Durps back to the Catholic Church in spite of all, the affair was turned over to the Inquisition. This attempt was also futile. In spite of torture he remained steadfast until his death at the stake, Sept. 23, 1559, at Maastricht, having just before his death spoken to the assembled crowd

about his faith. (*Mart. Mir.* D 258, E 630 f.; *DJ* 1939, 59-61; *ML* I, 248.)   O.H., vdZ.

Jan Echtwerken (Egtwerken, Egtwarken), from "Krommeniersdijk in Waterlandt" (Dutch province of North Holland), an Anabaptist martyr, who was burned at the stake at The Hague in April 1534. (Van Braght, *Mart. Mir.* D 62, E 465, erroneously gives the date as 1542.) K. Vos suggests that Jan Echtwerken is identical with Jan Walen (*q.v.*), who is the same person as Jan Dirksz (*q.v.*), burned at the stake at The Hague on April 15, 1534. (*DB* 1917, 170; *ML* I, 501.)   vdZ.

Jan van Eenhoorne, born at Landegem, Flanders, an Anabaptist martyr, was burned at the stake at Gent, Belgium, on March 12, 1562. (Verheyden, *Gent,* 27, No. 81.)   vdZ.

Jan Everts, an Anabaptist martyr, a shoemaker by trade, born at Deventer, was seized with his wife Anneken at Arnemuiden, not far from Middelburg, capital of the Dutch province of Zeeland. He confessed that he had been baptized at The Hague by a weaver, Meynart (probably Meindert of Emden). For four years he had neither been at the confessional or at communion; he had no intention of going, for he disregarded the commands of the Catholic Church. Concerning the sacrament of the altar, he did not believe that God was in it, but that it served only as a memorial of the suffering and death of our Lord. Any ordinary person who had been baptized upon his faith could distribute it. The Son of God received no flesh from Mary, for whatever is of the flesh is sinful, and God's Son was without sin. He confessed that he had, to be sure, heard of Jan Beukelszoon van Leyden, who was in Münster, "but what he is or does there is unknown to him except that he has heard tell that he is king there." On the rack Jan Everts betrayed a number of Anabaptists in Amsterdam, The Hague, and Delft. After he had been baptized he traveled about, going first to Amsterdam, where he was arrested, but was released upon recanting; then he lived in the bishopric of Münster and afterwards in the city of Deventer, Dutch province of Overijssel, where he married Anneken "only with a promise, giving her half of a broken coin, not marrying her according to the ordinance of the Church, which seemed to him to be of no value." He died faithful, only 26 years of age. The execution took place at The Hague on April 19, 1535, by beheading.

His wife Anneken, also called Tanneken, who had been baptized at Delft, Dutch province of South Holland, by Obbe Philips (*q.v.*), was pregnant when she was arrested; she had to stay in prison until the birth of the child. What happened to her is not known.   NEFF, vdZ.

K. R. Pekelharing, *Bijdragen voor de Gesch. der Hervorming in Zeeland,* in *Archief Zeeuwsch Genootschap* VI (Middelburg, 1866) 19-24; *DB* 1908, 5-7; Mellink, *Wederdopers,* 91, 207-11, 319 f.; *ML* I, 616.

Jan Evertsz van Wij, of Amsterdam, an Anabaptist martyr, beheaded at Amsterdam on Dec. 31, 1534. He had been baptized by Jacob van Campen (*q.v.*) after he had not attended the Catholic Church for a number of years. He was in prison for about six weeks. The city government tried to protect him from capital punishment, but they were apparently compelled by the Court of Holland to put him to death. He seems to have belonged to the revolutionary type of Anabaptism. (Grosheide, *Verhooren*, 13, 35-43.)   vDZ.

Jan-Evertsvolk, followers of Jan Evertsz (*q.v.*), preacher of the Flemish congregation at Haarlem (*q.v.*), Dutch province of North Holland, numbering 728 baptized members, who in 1681 formed a separate congregation, at first holding services at the Bakenessergracht, and after 1684 in a new meetinghouse at the Kruisstraat. In 1747 the Jan-Everts group, who had especially in the first decades been very conservative, dissolved, its members joining the main Flemish congregation. (*DB* 1863, 147 f.)
                                                  vDZ.

Jan Fasseau, an otherwise unknown Anabaptist martyr, a native of Griory in the Belgian province of Hainaut (*q.v.*), was beheaded in 1555 or 1556 at Bergen (Mons), capital of Hainaut. (*ML* II, 284.)
                                                  J.L.

Jan Fransz, from Calcar, Germany, an Anabaptist martyr, was beheaded at Amsterdam on Sept. 15, 1534, because he had participated in the journey to Münster, having been arrested at Bergklooster (*q.v.*). (*Inv. Arch. Amst.* I, No. 745.)   vDZ.

Jan van Geelen (Jan van Geel, Johan van Geyl, Hansken van Gelen, once called Hansken Lukener), a partisan of Jan van Leyden (*q.v.*), a former soldier, a resident of Deventer, went from there to Münster early in 1534 and became the doorman of Queen Divara. On Dec. 24, 1534, he left the city with three companions, equipped with money and a thousand copies of Rothmann's *Van der Wraecke* (revenge) for distribution. In the Netherlands he propagandized for the cause of the Münsterite kingdom and everywhere handed out money for the purchase of arms. For he was sent to the Netherlands by Jan van Leyden specifically to create revolution there in order to detract attention from Münster. Early in January 1535 he came to Amsterdam. Here the "banner of justice" was to fly, i.e., the signal for revolution given. But among the Anabaptists he met resistance. Their bishop, Jacob van Campen (*q.v.*), would not be persuaded. Also the conference at Spaarndam, where 32 Anabaptist preachers met in the middle of December 1534 or early in January 1535, rejected his plans. At the end of January 1535 he was in Antwerp, Belgium, where he had a number of adherents; then he became active in the Dutch provinces of Friesland, Groningen, and Utrecht, where he succeeded in stirring up sedition (Olde Klooster near Bolsward, Warfum, and in the territory of IJsselstein). At Amsterdam he even contacted Pieter van Montfoort, a young priest, who was the ambassador of the Spanish government of Brussels (April 1535), and through deceit and cunning he obtained safe conduct from him to continue his criminal activity. He sent word to his wife Fenneken at Deventer that unless she had herself baptized he would disown

her. She complied, and on April 17 suffered a martyr's death by drowning in the IJssel. Van Geelen's efforts to create revolution throughout the Netherlands had but small success. He was partially successful in Friesland, where the Oldeklooster (*q.v.*) was taken by a band of revolutionaries, but in Groningen at Warfum (*q.v.*) a similar attempt failed. In South Holland, where van Geelen had a number of followers, especially in the small town of Benschop (*q.v.*), plans were continued to attack Woerden, Oudewater, and Leiden, but both because of lack of organization and insufficient numbers these grand revolutionary plans completely failed. He planned a major attack on Amsterdam, secretly calling the Anabaptists from everywhere in the Netherlands. But most of the Anabaptists were not revolution-minded, and stayed at home. Van Geelen, in bitter disappointment, nevertheless pressed the attack. On the night of May 10, 1535, followed only by 32 men, he assaulted the city hall of Amsterdam. Jan van Geelen himself was killed in the storm of the city hall, and the survivors were all executed.
                                            NEFF, vDZ.

C. A. Cornelius, *Historische Arbeiten* (Leipzig, 1899); *Inv. Arch. Amst.* I, No. 96; Grosheide, *Verhooren*, 15-21, 59-64; *DB* 1875, 63; 1899, 1-19; 1919, 5, 9; Kühler, *Geschiedenis* I, *passim*, see Index; Mellink, *Wederdopers*, *passim*, see Index; C. A. Cornelius, *Die Niederländischen Wiedertäufer während der Belagerung Münsters 1534 bis 1535* (Leipzig, 1869); *ML* II, 41.

Jan Geertsz (Geers, Gheerts, Gheertszoen, Gheertsen, Gerritsz, Gerritsen, and after his trade also Jan Ketelaer), a Dutch Anabaptist martyr, a native of Delft, province of South Holland. He was a coppersmith living on the island of Texel, where he was baptized in 1559. His wife was able to visit him in prison at The Hague. On Dec. 15, 1564, he was burned at the stake in The Hague. In 1566 a booklet appeared containing letters written by Maeyken Boosers and Jan Gerrits' testament to his brethren (he was evidently a preacher) and the first part of his letter to the "Lutheran pope." A copy of this very rare booklet is found in the Library of the University of Gent, Belgium. The second part was printed in the martyrbook of 1617, known as the *Groot Martelaersboek*. The booklet of 1566 was reprinted in *Het Offer des Heeren* of 1570 with a letter "to his acquaintances" and a song about him, "Tis een periculose tijt" (It is a perilous time). He knew Latin. His letter to the Lutheran preacher is very rude in tone. His will reveals that he was married and his mother was still living. From prison he sent nutshells, spices, and cloves to be used in his memory. From his third letter it is seen that he was tortured in prison, that he attended school in Delft during the great fire there (May 3, 1536), and that he owned a copy of Menno Simons' *Van de nieuwe Creature*, as well as of Dirk Philips' *Van de geestelijke Restitution*.   K.V.

Inv. Arch. Amst. I, Nos. 407, 744 f.; *Offer*, 393-410; *Mart. Mir.* D 317, E 680; Wolkan, *Lieder*, 68; *ML* II, 83.

Jan van Genck (van Ghenck, van Gink), an Anabaptist martyr, was executed at Amsterdam. This martyr is the same person as Jan van Ghenck Jr., who lived at Maastricht, Dutch province of Limburg, in 1528 and was fined there because he had some heretical books. Henric Rol (*q.v.*) stayed in his house in September 1534. At this time meetings of the newly founded congregation of Maastricht, as of heretics before, were held in his house and sometimes baptism was administered here. Jan van Genck seems to have been a deacon. By trade he was a shoemaker. At the end of 1534 or the beginning of 1535 Jan and his father, also called Jan, and a brother Frans, all with their wives, fled from Maastricht. Apparently they went to Amsterdam. Nothing further is known of the father or of Frans. Jan van Genck Jr. was arrested in February and beheaded on March 6, 1535, at Amsterdam, with a number of others, among whom was Hendrik Biesman (*q.v.*), also from Maastricht.   vDZ.

Mart. Mir. D 412, E 763; Grosheide, *Verhooren,* 53; W. Bax, *Het Protestantisme in het Bisdom Luik* I (The Hague, 1937) 84 f.; *ML* II, 389.

Jan (Jehan) **van Gendtbrugge,** an Anabaptist martyr, beheaded before the Gravensteen castle at Gent, Belgium, on July 19, 1535. Particulars are lacking. (Verheyden, *Gent,* 2, No. 4.)   vDZ.

Jan Gerrits, an elder of Emden: see **Gerrits, Jan.**

Jan Gerritsz, an Anabaptist martyr: see **Jan Geertsz.**

Jan Gerroltsma, an Anabaptist martyr, was executed on April 14, 1533, at Leeuwarden, Dutch province of Friesland, because he had been rebaptized. His daughters Griete and Femme were executed there for the same reason on the following day. (K. Vos, *Menno Simons,* Leiden 1914, 229.)   vDZ.

Jan Ghyselinck (Jan de Lapper, i.e., cobbler), an Anabaptist martyr, died on March 15 or 16, 1569, at the Steen castle at Antwerp, Belgium, during his torture. (The records say "Op den Steen doot gepijnt.") His corpse was hanged as a deterrent example.

Jan, born at Brugge and previously living at Dambrugge, had been in Antwerp about one year when he was arrested with other members at a meeting of the congregation held in the house of Jan Poote (*q.v.*). Jan then was 38 years of age and a widower. He had been baptized upon his faith four years before by Elder Hendrik van Arnhem (*q.v.*). He played an important part in the congregational life at Antwerp, being a *weetdoener,* i.e., the man who announced to the members the place and hour of the meetings. The meetings were held at irregular times and different places, in order to evade (as far as possible) being surprised by the police. (*Antw. Arch.-Blad* XII, 353, 367, 414; XIV, 64 f., No. 718.)   vDZ.

Jan Gouwensz: see **Jan van Delft.**

Jan Grendel, an Anabaptist martyr, born at Kortrijk (Courtrai), Belgium, came from Oudewater to Goes, Dutch province of Zeeland, in 1562. He was arrested the day after his arrival and put to death after a long imprisonment, the execution taking place before Easter 1563. Neither the exact date nor the manner of execution is known, nor are any other particulars about him is known. (*Mart. Mir.* D 298, E 663; *ML* II, 172.)   vDZ.

Jan van Gulik (Johann von Jülich), an Anabaptist leader, of whose activities nothing is known, was present in 1536 at an Anabaptist meeting in Bocholt (*q.v.*) in Westphalia, Germany. The field of his activity was Gelre (*q.v.*). (*DB* 1919, 193; *ML* II, 239.)   vDZ.

Jan van Halteren, an Anabaptist martyr, was beheaded June 2, 1539, at Haarlem, Dutch province of North Holland. Here he was arrested in the house of Lambrecht Duppijns (*q.v.*). He was originally from the Dutch province of Utrecht and obviously an adherent of David Joris (*q.v.*).   vDZ.

Bijdr. en Mededeelingen Historisch Genootschap Utrecht XLI (Amsterdam, 1920) 200 f., 208, 210 f., 218.

Jan van Hasebroek (Haesbrouck), an Anabaptist martyr, apparently a native of Hasebrouck in French Flanders. He was burned at the stake at Antwerp, Belgium, on May 5, 1569, because he had been rebaptized. While in prison he wrote three letters to his wife, which reveal his great love for his family, as well as his strong faith. From the wealth of his knowledge of the Bible he comforted his wife and admonished her to be faithful unto death, which is followed by eternal joy. He urged her to take good care of their two small children and teach them the way of truth, that at the judgment they might stand at God's right hand. He told her that a letter coming to them fell into the hands of the prison master and caused them much grief. He gave her a sign to use in writing to him to indicate that she had received his letter. He sent greetings from his fellow prisoners Jan Koopman and his servant Hansken.   NEFF.

Mart. Mir. D 415, 419-24; E 766, 770-74; *Antw. Arch.-Blad* XII, 382, 401; XIV, 66 f., No. 756; *ML* II, 262.

Jan van Hasselt, an Anabaptist leader of Amsterdam, who had much influence in a group called after him the Jan van Hasselt Sect. He was apparently also active in Rotterdam and Antwerp. (Grosheide, *Bijdrage,* 115.)   vDZ.

Jan Helleman, an Anabaptist martyr, burned alive at Brugge, Belgium, on Jan. 16, 1552. Particulars are lacking. (Verheyden, *Brugge,* 36, No. 17.)   vDZ.

Jan Hendricks (Heyndricx), an Anabaptist martyr, strangled and burned at the stake on Feb. 21, 1559, at Middelburg, Dutch province of Zeeland, together with Mayken Daniels and Andries van Laerbeke. They had all three fled from Flanders because of their faith and were arrested July 15, 1558. The city government of Middelburg questioned the Catholic priest at Roesselare, Flanders, about them, indicating that they had lived there. Jan was a native of Waert (Weerden) and was by trade a locksmith.   vDZ.

K. R. Pekelharing, *Bijdr. voor de Gesch. van de Hervorming in Zeeland,* in *Archief Zeeuwsch Genootschap* VI (1866) 38-40.

Jan Hendricksen (Hendriksz), from Zwartewaal, Dutch province of South Holland, an Anabaptist martyr, living at Delfshaven near Rotterdam, the steersman of a herring-drifter, was burned at the stake at Delft, Dutch province of South Holland, on Feb. 5, 1572, with Maerten Jansz Corendrager. He was held in prison for more than a year. While in prison he wrote a moving letter of farewell to his wife, urging her to continue faithfully in the doctrine. He wrote in a similar vein to Maerten Jansz, his fellow prisoner, and also to his brother and sister. His report of his repeated cross-examinations shows an amazing knowledge of the Bible and a firmness of faith not usual in an unlettered man. His death is the subject of the hymn "Verhoort ons droevich claghen" (Hear our sad lament), which is found in the *Lietboecxken van den Offer des Heeren*, 1578 and later editions. (*Offer*, 558-62; *Mart. Mir.* D 606, E 932; Wolkan, *Lieder*, 69; *ML* II, 282.)   NEFF, VDZ.

Jan Hendriks (Heynricxz), a mason from IJsselstein (*q.v.*), an Anabaptist martyr, beheaded on March 12, 1535, at Utrecht in the Netherlands. He admitted that he had often lodged Anabaptist bishops in his house. He was familiar with the revolutionary plans to make an attack on Amsterdam.
                   VDZ.
 Inv. Arch. Amst. I, No. 104; *Berigten Hist. Genootschap Utrecht* IV, 2 (1851) 1; *DB* 1917, 122, No. 162; Mellink, *Wederdopers*, 76, 81, 200, 235.

Jan Hendriksz of Utrecht, a Dutch Anabaptist martyr, who had been baptized by Leenaert Bouwens (*q.v.*), was at the age of 28 sentenced to die at the stake on March 28, 1558, at Rotterdam, with Pieter van Eynoven (*q.v.*), Evert Nouts (*q.v.*), and two women, Annetgen Antheunisdochter and Stijntgen Jansdochter. The execution, however, miscarried. Its slow and horrible progress caused the crowd of spectators to become so greatly excited that they violently freed the victims. Jan Hendriksz, unconscious, was taken to a house near by and escaped. A song commemorating this execution, beginning "In den jare vijfthienhondert, En achtenvijftig claer," is found in *Veelderhande Liedekens* of 1569. The Rotterdam court records show that three days after this event Guert Willemszoon, who had taken part in the liberation of the above victims of persecution, was sentenced to death. NEFF, VDZ.
 Inv. Arch. Amst. I, Nos. 384-86; *Mart. Mir.* D 192-96, E 575; I. M. J. Hoog, *De Martelaren der Hervorming in Nederland* (Schiedam, 1885) 31-33, 237-41; Wackernagel, *Lieder*, 135; *ML* II, 282.

Jan Henricxz of Delft, an Anabaptist martyr, was beheaded on Nov. 8, 1544, at Delft, Dutch province of South Holland, because of Anabaptism. He was a follower of David Joris (*q.v.*) and had received from Cleve two booklets written by David Joris. (*Inv. Arch. Amst.* I, Nos. 744 f.; Mellink, *Wederdopers*, 217, 414.)   VDZ.

Jan Hermansz (Jan de Houtstapelaer, or Lange Jan): see **Jan van Delft**.

Jan Hesselsz, a cooper from Dokkum, Dutch province of Friesland, an Anabaptist martyr, was beheaded at Leeuwarden, Friesland, on Feb. 11, 1539. Particulars are not known.   VDZ.
 J. Reitsma, *Hondert jaren uit de Gesch. der Hervorming . . . in Friesland* (Leeuwarden, 1876) 63.

Jan Heyndricx, a cabinetmaker of "Yertsele by shertogenbosche," an Anabaptist martyr, likely a follower of David Joris, was beheaded on Jan. 7, 1539, at Delft, Dutch province of South Holland, together with ten others. (*Inv. Arch. Amst.* I, No. 749; *DB* 1899, 158-60; 1917, 160-67.) VDZ.

Jan Hulle, an Anabaptist martyr, burned at the stake in 1561 at Ieper (Yperen) in Belgium. The information of van Braght (*Mart. Mir.*), who states that he died faithfully, does not contain any particulars. Apparently Jan Hulle was a victim of the inquisitor Titelman (*q.v.*), who in 1561 severely persecuted the congregation of Ieper and other Flemish towns. If the name should be Jan *van* Hulle, this martyr very likely belonged to the Mennonite van Hulle family, which was found in Gent and Antwerp in Belgium, and whose descendants in the 17th and 18th centuries lived at Haarlem in the Netherlands (see **Denys van Hulle**) (*Mart. Mir.* D 288, E 656.)   VDZ.

Jan Jacobsz, a martyr: see **Hans Jacopsens**.

Jan Jacobsz (Jacobssen) of Amsterdam, called *De Noorman*, an Anabaptist martyr, was beheaded on May 15, 1535, at Amsterdam, because he had been rebaptized.   VDZ.
 Mart. Mir. D 412, E 764; Grosheide, *Verhooren*, 70-72; Mellink, *Wederdopers*, 144.

Jan Jacobs(z) of Benschop (*q.v.*), Dutch province of Utrecht, an Anabaptist martyr in whose house baptism had been administered and who persevered in his "heresy," was burned at the stake on May 11, 1534, at Amsterdam. (*DB* 1917, 121, No. 141; Mellink, *Wederdopers*, 233.)   VDZ.

Jan Jacobsz Hayesz, a Dutch elder and leader of the Janjacobsgezinden: see **Jacobs(z), Jan**.

Jan Jansz, surnamed Ghyphen(?), a tailor from Hamm near Wesel, Germany, an Anabaptist martyr, was beheaded on Jan. 7, 1539, at Delft, Dutch province of South Holland, because of rebaptism. He was probably a follower of David Joris (*q.v.*). (*Inv. Arch. Amst.* I, No. 749; *DB* 1899, 158-60; 1917, 160-67.)   VDZ.

Jan Jansz van den Berg (Berch) from the territory of Cleve, Germany, an Anabaptist martyr, executed at Amsterdam on July 8, 1539. He had been baptized at Delft, Dutch province of South Holland, in 1538 by Claes "with the crippled hand." VDZ.
 Inv. Arch. Amst. I, No. 211; *Mart. Mir.* D 415, E 766; Grosheide, *Bijdrage*, 143, 307.

Jan Jansz Brant, an Anabaptist martyr, who in his youth had led a dissolute life. After his conversion both he and his wife joined the Mennonite Church. They were natives of Zuidland on the South Holland island of Putten, and were arrested on Nov. 9, 1559, at Geervliet on the same island. Jan Jansz remained steadfast and was sentenced to death on Nov. 29, 1559. The execution did not take place immediately after the sentence. Apparently this delay was caused by negotiations for a ransom, which, however, were fruitless. The date of the execution is not known. It took place at the castle of Geervliet (not at The Hague as *Bibliographie* and also *ML* report). Jan Jansz was bound in a sack and thrown from the bridge of the castle into the moat. When the sack burst open, the executioner pushed him under the water with a pole. This cruel death is celebrated in a song found both in the *Lietboecxken van den Offer des Heeren* (1563 and following editions) and the *Tweede Liedeboeck* (1583) beginning "Hoort Vrienden, ich schenck u een liet" (Hear, friends, I give you a song). The account found in the later martyrbooks, including van Braght, *Martyrs' Mirror,* is taken from this song. It is not clear what happened to Jan Jansz's wife. She was still in prison when the song was written after her husband's death.   NEFF, VDZ.

Offer, 550-52; *Mart. Mir.* D 243, E 617; Wolkan, *Lieder,* 62, 71; *ML* I, 256.

Jan Jansz van Calckeren, a native of Calcar, territory of Cleve, Germany, an Anabaptist martyr, was beheaded on March 12, 1535, at Utrecht in the Netherlands. He was a barber and surgeon and belonged to the revolutionary wing of Anabaptism. (*Inv. Arch. Amst.* I, No. 103; *DB* 1917, 122, No. 161; Mellink, *Wederdopers,* 85, 234.)   VDZ.

Jan Jansz Schot (Jan Jansz Schilder, i.e., painter) was an influential leader of the Anabaptists at Rotterdam (*q.v.*). He had been baptized in December 1533 by Jan van Leyden. After much activity he was apprehended and imprisoned at The Hague. Forsaking his faith, he was not burned at the stake but beheaded. This execution took place on April 10 at The Hague (not Rotterdam as de Hoop Scheffer suggests). After his death his widow Maryken continued to lodge Anabaptists. According to K. Vos, Schot was originally from Brussels, and his wife, also of Brussels, was an illegitimate daughter of Johanna van der Gheenst and Emperor Charles V.   VDZ.

Inv. Arch. Amst. I, 744 f.; de Hoop Scheffer, *Gesch. der Kerkhervorming* (Amsterdam, 1873) 532; K. Vos, *Gesch. der Doopsgez. gemeente te Rotterdam* (Rotterdam, 1907) 5; *DB* 1905, 169-75; 1917, 115, No. 49.

Jan Jansz de Timmerman (Jan Pouwelszn van Dircxhorn), an Anabaptist martyr, was beheaded at Amsterdam on May 8, 1534, together with Gheryt van Campen because of revolutionary Anabaptist activity. (Grosheide, *Verhooren,* 26; Mellink, *Wederdopers,* 108-10, 160.)   VDZ.

Jan Jansze (Hansken Schalijdecker) from Tongeren in Belgium, an Anabaptist martyr, baptized Feb. 9, 1535, by Damas (*q.v.*) at Middelburg, Dutch province of Zeeland, was beheaded in 1536 at Zierikzee, same province. Particulars were not available. (*Inv. Arch. Amst.* I, 744 f.; Mellink, *Wederdopers,* 317.)   VDZ.

Jan Jantsz of Benschop (*q.v.*), Dutch province of Utrecht, an Anabaptist martyr, sentenced March 11, 1534, by the Court of Holland to be executed by burning at the stake because he had been rebaptized and had been among the Anabaptists who sailed from Amsterdam en route to Münster (*q.v.*). The

execution took place on March 24, 1534. (*Inv. Arch. Amst.* I, 744 f.)   VDZ.

Jan Joosten van Goedereede (Jan Jooste) of Goeree, Dutch province of South Holland, an Anabaptist martyr, who was beheaded at The Hague Feb. 10, 1534. He had previously been a Catholic priest in the Dutch province of Zeeland, joined the Anabaptists, being baptized by Gerrit Boeckbinder in 1531 and lived in Amsterdam three years. Here he married and was ordained a preacher by Jacob van Campen. With eight fellow believers he was arrested. At this cross-examination he admitted that Gerrit Boeckbinder had baptized him; he then was sent with Jan Matthys from Haarlem and Jacob van Campen to Wormer and Westzaan, where he preached and baptized seven or eight persons. When he was asked whether the Anabaptists kept a list of baptized persons, he replied that he knew nothing of it; their promises were Yea and Nay; they called themselves *Bondgenoten* (*q.v.*), the name of the adherents of Melchior Hofmann.   NEFF.

Inv. Arch. Amst. I, Nos. 11, 744 f.; *DB* 1907, 41; 1917, 115, No. 53; L. Keller, *Geschichte der Wiedertäufer . . .* (Münster, 1880) 153; C. A. Cornelius, *Geschichte des Münsterischen Aufruhrs* (Leipzig, 1865) 383, 387; Mellink, *Wederdopers,* 105, 156, 207, 351 f.; *ML* II, 130 f., 432.

Jan Kanneghieter of Coesfeld in Westphalia, Germany, an Anabaptist martyr, was beheaded on June 1, 1535, at Amsterdam, on the charge of being rebaptized and having partaken in the attack on the Amsterdam town hall, May 10-11, 1535. He was tried on May 11 and 24. Jan admitted that he had been at the place before the town hall when the attack was launched, but he had not joined and had no weapon. Seeing what was taking place, he had left. Jan had been baptized by Obbe de Vriess, i.e., Obbe Philips (*q.v.*) outside the town of Dokkum in Friesland. Before he came to Amsterdam, he had stayed in Groningen. Severe torture "with rope and rod" on May 28 did not succeed in bringing forth new particulars. He apparently did not approve the use of weapons. (Grosheide, *Verhooren,* 65 f.)   VDZ.

Jan Kerbusch, an otherwise unknown Mennonite preacher, who in 1566 preached and baptized at St. Winnoxbergen and other towns in the south of Flanders in Belgium. (Verheyden, "Mennisme in Vlaanderen," ms.)   VDZ.

Jan (de) Koopman (merchant), an Anabaptist martyr: see **Jan Cooman.**

Jan van Leyden, also called Jan (Johan) Beuckelsz or Bockelszoon, Anabaptist leader at Münster (*q.v.*) in Westphalia, Germany. He was born at Leiden, Dutch province of South Holland. He was at first a tailor, then a merchant, and later an innkeeper; as a rhetorician he liked to act the part of King David. He was in many ways a highly gifted man, but his conceit and his self-love betrayed him. Because he became an influential man with a large and devoted following, he founded an Anabaptist government at Münster, became king of this New Jerusalem, reigning there with absolute supremacy more than a year. Jan van Leyden, whose character was a mixture of shyness, ambition, and maniacal wickedness and yet not without germs of religious feeling, has been an enthralling mystery to the present. Certainly he was much more than an ordinary adventurer. His conduct and acts, his fanaticism, and his immorality did great harm to the growing Anabaptist movement of 1534 and the following years, first because he misled a large number of peaceful Anabaptists, especially of the Netherlands, winning them over to his revolutionary view that the kingdom of God was to be established on earth by the uprooting of the "ungodly," which included the use of weapons; secondly, because the world and especially the rulers of that time and later turned away with horror from Anabaptism, ignoring all distinctions between the outrageous disciples of Jan van Leyden and the peaceful followers of Obbe Philips and Menno Simons. Until the end of the 16th century the Dutch government was filled with fear that the Anabaptists might repeat the revolution of Münster, and non-Mennonite authors, Roman Catholic as well as Lutheran and Reformed, even in the 17th century insisted that the governments take action against the Mennonites in order to save the world from the horrors of Münster; the legend that Anabaptism and Mennonitism is derived from Jan van Leyden and Münster continues to this day, even in the books of serious historians. All this is the consequence of the deeds of Jan van Leyden, the evil genius of early Anabaptism.

In November 1533 Jan van Leyden joined the Anabaptists, being baptized by Jan Matthijsz of Haarlem (q.v.). Soon his house in Leiden became a center of Anabaptist activity. Cornelis Pieters wt den Briel (q.v.) and other leaders preached and baptized there. In December 1533 Jan van Leyden was sent out by Jan Matthysz as an apostle to preach the Gospel, and first visited Alkmaar, Hoorn, Enkhuizen, then Den Briel and Rotterdam. Until this time the Anabaptist views of Jan van Leyden did not much differ from those of other Dutch leaders, who preached the coming of the kingdom of God, which the faithful had to wait and pray for, but under the influence of Jan Matthysz he abandoned the peaceful principles.

On Jan. 13, 1534, he arrived in Münster, where he had paid a short visit in July 1533. He soon obtained much influence in Münster, though then other leaders like Rothmann (q.v.) and especially Jan Matthysz, who came to Münster in February 1534, predominated. But after the death of Jan Matthysz at Easter 1534, Jan van Leyden's influence increased and before July 1534 he reigned with absolute power. He organized the defense of the city against the army of Franz von Waldeck, Bishop of Münster, who had laid siege to the city. Communism of goods had been practiced since February 1534; in July of this year polygamy was introduced and in early September Jan van Leyden was appointed King of Zion (or New Jerusalem). In the meanwhile Jan van Leyden tried to strengthen the defense forces also by inviting the Anabaptists of the Netherlands and elsewhere, first by promises, then by threats that the world would perish and only those in the holy city of Münster would be saved. With much exertion and a surprising skill he defended the city against the episcopal army until the city was taken on June 25, 1535.

Jan van Leyden, who had hidden in a cellar, was found and arrested. For a few months he was sent from one German dynastic residence to another as a curiosity. Then he was sentenced to death and executed in a very cruel way at Münster on Jan. 22, 1536. There is a portrait of Jan van Leyden in copper engraving by H. Aldegrever, and an oil painting of both Jan and Queen Divara made by Herman tom Ring (now in the Museum of Schwerin, Germany).   vDZ.

Some of the abundant literature dealing both with Jan van Leyden and the Münster period of Anabaptism in general is recorded in the article on Münster (q.v.); see also H. Detmer, *Johann von Leiden, seine Persönlichkeit und seine Stellung im Münsterischen Reiche* (Münster, 1903); Kühler, *Geschiedenis* I, especially 78-185, *passim*; Mellink, *Wederdopers, passim*, see Index; *Inv. Arch. Amst.* I, Nos. 52, 82, 141; H. v. Schubert, *Der Kommunismus der Wiedertäufer in Münster und seine Quellen* (Heidelberg, 1919); C. A. Cornelius, *Berichte der Augenzeugen über das Münsterische Wiedertäuferreich* (Münster, 1853). The numerous novels and dramas which have been written on this subject are surveyed by W. Rauch, *Johann von Leyden, der König von Sion, in der Dichtung* (Münster, 1912), and Hugo Hermsen, *Die Wiedertäufer zu Münster in der deutschen Dichtung* (Stuttgart, 1913); *ML* I, 240.

Jan Lievensz of Gent, an Anabaptist martyr, burned at the stake on Aug. 18, 1550, at Antwerp, Belgium. This Jan Lievensz, of whom no further particulars were available, is not the same person, also called Jan, to whom reference is made in the song "Ick sal met vreugden singen" (I will sing with joy), of the *Lietboecxken van den Offer des Heeren,* as *Bibliographie* II, 707, No. 338 reports. The Jan celebrated in the song is likely Jan de Oude Kleerkoper (q.v.). (*Antw. Arch.-Blad* VIII, 389, 392; XIV, 18 f., No. 191.)   vDZ.

Jan de Lindwercker, a martyr: see **Jan van de Walle.**

Jan Lubberts, an otherwise unknown Dutch Mennonite elder, who (according to Carel van Gent) was ordained by Dirk Philipsz. (*BRN* VII, 558.)
                    vDZ.

Jan Lucas: see **Luies, Jan.**

Jan-Lucasvolk, a group of Mennonites in the Netherlands in the 17th century, followers of Jan Lucas or Luies (q.v.). They were the forerunners of the Groningen Old Flemish (q.v.).   vDZ.

Jan van Lyere, from Lier in the Belgian province of Brabant, an Anabaptist martyr, was drowned Sept. 6, 1561, at Antwerp in the Steen castle. His wife Lijntgen (Lijnken van Dale) (q.v.) was drowned at Antwerp on Nov. 14, 1562. Jan, a native of Brussels and a carpet weaver by trade, served the congregation as a deacon. A song celebrating Jan and Lijntgen is found in *Nieu Liedenboeck* of 1562 and inserted in Wackernagel, *Lieder*. It begins: "Lieve broeders, ick groet u met sanghen" (Dear brethren, I greet you with songs).   vDZ.

Mart. Mir. D 288, E 655; *Antw. Arch.-Blad* IX, 124, 133; XIV, 30 f., No. 344; Wackernagel, *Lieder,* 140; Wolkan, *Lieder,* 72.

Jan (Jehan) **Maes,** an Anabaptist martyr, was burned at the stake on March 16, 1565, at Rijssel (Lille) in France. Jan, who was born at Bollezeele in Flanders and lived in Hondschoote (*q.v.*), was arrested on March 7, 1563, at Halewijn (*q.v.*), while he was visiting the preacher Jan de Swarte (*q.v.*). A number of the Mennonites of Halewijn, including Jan de Swarte, were also arrested by the inquisitor Titelman (*q.v.*). They all suffered martyrdom at Rijssel. (*Mart. Mir.* D 299, E 664; *ML* II, 711.) vDZ.

Jan Matthijsz van Haarlem (Matthys, Matthyssen, Mathis), an Anabaptist leader, originally a baker of Haarlem, Dutch province of North Holland. He had been baptized by Melchior Hofmann (*q.v.*), but left the way of love and peace preached by Hofmann to enter upon a course of hatred and violence against the ungodly. He did not follow Hofmann's command to wait two years before baptizing, but proclaimed himself a prophet sent by God to establish the kingdom by force. He left his wife and took another, Dieuwertgen, who after his death became the chief spouse of Jan van Leyden (*q.v.*) at Münster. She was then called Queen Divara. In 1533 he appeared in Amsterdam and won some followers there, whom he sent out two by two as apostles to proclaim to the world that Enoch had appeared and that the millennium was near its fulfillment. Two of them, Gerrit Boeckbinder (Gerrit tom Kloster) and Jan van Leyden (Johan Bockelson), who had been baptized by Jan Matthijsz, arrived at Münster in Westphalia on Jan. 13, 1534. This city now became the New Zion, elected to initiate the kingdom of God. In February Matthijsz also arrived, and the rebellious reign of the Dutch adventurers began. On April 5 Matthijsz met an adventurous death. In the midst of a merry company he arose, allegedly seized by divine inspiration, and cried, "Father, not as I will, but as Thou wilt." He immediately left the festivities; it had been revealed to him that he should go out to meet the enemy. On the next day (Easter) he chose ten or twenty companions and marched out of the city to its besiegers. He was surrounded and died fighting bravely. (See also **Münster.**) NEFF.

C. A. Cornelius, *Historische Arbeiten vornehmlich zur Ref.-Zeit* (Leipzig, 1899); *Inv. Arch. Amst.* I, No. 47; Kühler, *Geschiedenis* I, *passim*; Mellink, *Wederdopers, passim*; *DB* 1919, 213-17; *ML* III, 60.

Jan Matthijsz (Matthijsz) **van Middelburg** (also called Jan Matthijsz Blaeuwaert), a native of Middelburg, Dutch province of Zeeland, a goldsmith, was an Anabaptist leader and martyr. As a preacher he was active in 1534 in Middelburg and the island of Walcheren; then he disappeared from Zeeland, where his possessions were confiscated. In the first half of 1535 he stayed in Amsterdam, where he and Jacob van Campen were the principal leaders of the large congregation. Here he forsook the peaceful Anabaptist view to become a follower of the Münsterite principles of Jan van Leyden. Together with Jan van Geelen (*q.v.*), the Münsterite ambassador, he prepared the attack on Amsterdam, May 10-11, 1535; the assault miscarried and a large number of Anabaptists were apprehended; Jan

Matthysz, however, was not among those imprisoned; he must have escaped. In a revolt at Hazerswoude, Dutch province of South Holland, on Dec. 31, 1535, a Jan Matthijsz was found, who likely is identical with Jan Matthijsz van Middelburg. In early 1536 he lived in England. In the summer of 1536 he attended a meeting of Anabaptist leaders at Boekholt (Bocholt in Westphalia, Germany), where he defended the peaceful principles of Obbe Philips against the Münsterite leaders. Hence he must have been converted from his revolutionary views to his former peaceful grounds. Returning to England, he was arrested there and put to death on Nov. 29, 1538, at London. vDZ.

Inv. Arch. Amst. I, Nos. 97, 145; Grosheide, *Verhooren,* 48, 193; Mellink, *Wederdopers, passim; DB* 1909, 17, 25; *ML* III, 60.

Jan van der Mersch, an Anabaptist martyr, a native of Kortrijk (Courtrai), was burned at the stake on June 7, 1569, at Kortrijk (Courtrai), Belgium. He had been present at two meetings held in early 1569 in the vicinity of Kortrijk and had been a member of the congregation since 1566. His imprisonment lasted for 152 days. Jan van der Mersch, whose property was confiscated, apparently belonged to the van der Meersch (van Meersch, van der Mersch) family, some Mennonite members of which emigrated to the Netherlands in the following decades. (Verheyden, *Courtrai-Bruxelles,* 40, No. 30.) vDZ.

Jan Mudder, an Anabaptist living at Appingedam, Dutch province of Groningen, a merchant, whose house in early 1534 was a center of Anabaptism, where a number of Anabaptists were baptized. Here Obbe Philips (*q.v.*) ordained his brother Dirk Philips (*q.v.*) elder in 1534. vDZ.

P. G. Bos, "De Wederdopers in Groningerland," *Groningsche Volksalmanak* 1909, 161.

Jan N., an Anabaptist martyr: see **Jan Christiaenz.**

Jan de Nayer, a nickname of Jan van Leyden (*q.v.*), found in V.P., *Successio Anabaptistica* (*BRN* VII, 86). The word *Nayer* means "stitcher," because the later king of Münster had originally been a tailor. vDZ.

Jan Neulen, a citizen of Visscherswert, south of Roermond in the Dutch province of Limburg. The village belonged at that time to the Montfort district of the duchy of Gelre (*q.v.*). A circle of Anabaptists lived here, to whom Menno Simons preached in 1544 or 1545. On the morning following the preaching Jan Neulen took Menno by boat down the Maas to Roermond. About the same time Theunis van Hastenrath (*q.v.*), visiting the Mennonites in this region, preached in Jan Neulen's home. Neulen was seized and tried at Montfort on Nov. 10, 1550. His house was confiscated, but he apparently escaped with his life. vDZ.

Nederl. Archief v. Kerkgesch. (n.s.) X (1913) 255, 264-66; *DB* 1890, 54; Vos, *Menno Simons* (Leiden, 1914) 2, 86 f., 242; W. Bax, *Het Protestantisme in het bisdom Luik* I (The Hague, 1937) 307, note 1, 328, 330 f.; *ML* III, 306.

Jan (Hans) **van Ophoorn** (Ophooren, Ophoren, Ophorn), a Mennonite elder of Antwerp, Belgium, fled from the city and was then banished forever on

April 10, 1570 (*Antw. Arch.-Blad* XII, 448, 451). By this time he was already living at Emden, East Friesland, Germany, from where he traveled to Cleve and Cologne in October 1569 to settle a schism in the Cleve congregation (*Inv. Arch. Amst.* I, No. 466). He was a fanatic and at the conferences of Mennonite leaders held at Emden and Hoorn in 1578 he opposed the plan to make peace among the Dutch Mennonites, who were divided by schisms. By his stubbornness he prevented the "Humstervrede" (*q.v.*), a partial reconciliation achieved in 1574, from evolving more widely. He was so severe in keeping "the church without spot or wrinkle," that he is said to have banned not only all other Flemish and Frisian congregations, but also the members of his own congregations with the exception of his wife and himself. Ophoorn died in poverty at Norden.   vdZ.

Inv. Arch. Amst. I, No. 466; V. P., *Successio Anabaptistica; BRN* VII, 69 f., 551 f.; Kühler, *Geschiedenis* I, 428, 433; *ML* III, 306.

Jan de Oude Kleerkoper, an Anabaptist martyr, was burned at the stake at Antwerp, Belgium, on Oct. 21 or 22, 1551 (van Braght, *Martyrs' Mirror,* erroneously reports October 2), together with Peter Bruynen, Pleunis van Hoevele, Martin du Petitz, and Jacob Peeters. About their imprisonment we are informed by two letters of Pieter Bruynen, found in the *Offer des Heeren.* Their names are celebrated in a hymn, "Tot lof des Vaders, soons, heyligen geest" (To the glory of Father, Son and Holy Ghost), found in the *Offer* and included in the *Ausbund* (*q.v.*). The confession of Jan de Oude Kleerkoper is found in the *Offer* and following martyrbooks, including the *Martyrs' Mirror.* From the records published by P. Génard in *Antwerpsch Archievenblad* it appears that his official name was Jan van der Wouwe(re)n, born at Westerloo, Flanders; he was charged with the crime of rebaptism and persisting in his "heresy."   vdZ.

Offer, 177-86; *Mart. Mir.* D. 128, 130 f., E 500; *Antw. Arch.-Blad* VIII, 405, 415; XIV, 18 f., No. 208; *ML* II, 389.

Jan Paeuw (Pauw, Pou), an Anabaptist martyr, a maker of blocks for ships. He was a deacon in the Amsterdam congregation, preached nonresistance, condemning all use of force, as opposed to Münsterite teaching. In his home meetings were often held and baptism administered, even after his arrest, which occurred at the end of December 1534. On the rack he betrayed what he wanted to withhold. On March 6, 1535, he was beheaded at Amsterdam with eight brethren.   vdZ.

Mart. Mir. D 212, E 763; Grosheide, *Verhooren,* 45-53; Kühler, *Geschiedenis* I, 89, 137, 151, 177; *ML* III, 338.

Jan (van) Parijs, an Anabaptist martyr, burned at the stake on March 30, 1568, on the Veerle square at Gent, Belgium, together with Pieter Aelbrechts (Pierken van Cleve), Hendrik Maelschap, and Laurens Pietersz, while at the same time seven non-Mennonite iconoclasts, who had destroyed the icons of saints in the Catholic churches, were hanged at the Veerle square. Jan van Parijs was born at Kortrijk (Courtrai) in Flanders, in 1565 or 1566;

he had received baptism on his faith; by profession he was a weaver. His name is found in the song "Als men schreef duyst vijfhondert jaer, ende twee en tsestich mede" of the *Lietboecxken van den Offer des Heeren*. (*Offer*, 652; *Mart. Mir.* D 367, E 723; Verheyden, *Gent,* 42, No. 136; *ML* II, 389.)
                                                    vdZ.

Jan Pennewaerts, from Leuven, Belgium (or Loenen, Dutch province of Utrecht), an Anabaptist martyr, burned at the stake at Amsterdam on March 20, 1549, together with five brethren and two sisters. The names of these martyrs are celebrated in the hymn "Tis nu schier al vervult ons broeders getal" (the number of our brethren now is nearly complete), found in *Veelderhande Liedekens* of 1566 and later Dutch hymnbooks. Jan had been baptized by Gillis van Aken (*q.v.*). (*Mart. Mir.* D 82, E 483; *ML* III, 342.)   vdZ.

Jan Pieter Eggesz, of Krommeniedijk, Dutch province of North Holland, an Anabaptist martyr, beheaded on March 26, 1534, at Haarlem, Dutch province of North Holland. In the sentence he is called "one of the principal preachers and baptizers." He was one of the Anabaptists who had sailed from Amsterdam to Bergklooster (*q.v.*) en route to Münster. (*Inv. Arch. Amst.* I, No. 744 f.; *DB* 1917, 115, No. 54, 151.)   vdZ.

Jan Pietersz (Jan Pieterssen, Jan Piers), an Anabaptist martyr, burned at the stake in 1572 at Breda, Dutch province of North Brabant. Jan Pietersz was a weaver. In 1563 he was baptized during a night by Leenaert Bouwens (*q.v.*) at Leiden, where he then lived. Later he had stayed at Vlaardingen and then at Klundert near Breda. Anabaptist meetings were held in his house. A meeting of Aug. 5, 1571, where about 50 persons were present, was surprised and a number of persons arrested, including Jan Pietersz. He refused to take an oath and died steadfast. (*Mart. Mir.* D 603-5, E 629-31; *DB* 1912, 30-35; *ML* III, 372.)   vdZ.

Jan Pieters(z) Vleyshouwer, a butcher from Alkmaar, Dutch province of North Holland, participated in the meeting of Anabaptist preachers held at Alkmaar on Jan. 19, 1534, when the question of Münster (*q.v.*) was discussed, joined the party going to Münster, and later united with the Batenburgers (*q.v.*), lodged Anabaptists in Leiden, then joined the David-Jorists, and was finally sentenced to death. He was beheaded on Aug. 7, 1544. (*DB* 1909, 12-30; *Inv. Arch. Amst.* I, Nos. 744 f.; *ML* III, 372.)   E.C.

Jan Pietersz Wagenmaker (John Wielmacker), an Anabaptist martyr, was burned at the stake on July 22, 1575, at Smithfield in London, England. Jan Pietersz, who was a wagon builder, had emigrated, obviously because of persecution and also on account of lack of work, from Flanders, Belgium. Probably he had lived at Gent, where his first wife was put to death because of her Anabaptism. Jan Pietersz and 21 Flemish Anabaptist immigrants were apprehended when they held a meeting at Easter of 1575 in London, outside the Aldersgate. They were all

arrested and after much tribulation Hendrik Terwoort (q.v.) and Jan Pietersz were put to death.
In a letter to Queen Elizabeth they stated that they
could not believe otherwise than that "they feel in
their conscience." They remained steadfast and died
loyally. When Jan Pietersz was led to the execution
place, he said, "This way went all the pious prophets, and also Christ our Saviour."

Two letters of Hendrik Terwoort and Jan Pietersz
are found in van Braght, *Martyrs' Mirror,* where
also detailed information is given about their fate
and confession.

These two martyrs are celebrated in a hymn,
"Aenhoort met neerstichden (neerstichheden), menschen verstaet wel mijn" (Hear attentively, ye people, understand me well), which is found in the
very rare *Confessio* of Thomas van Imbroich, printed at Gent in 1579. Some fragments of songs composed by Jan Pietersz are found in the *Martyrs'
Mirror.* (*Mart. Mir.* D 694-712, E 1008-24.) vDZ.

Jan Pipart, an Anabaptist martyr, burned at the
stake at Brussels, Belgium, on March 31, 1568. Jan
confessed that he had regularly attended Mennonite
meetings at Borgerhout and Antwerp, and loyally
refused to recant. (Verheyden, *Courtrai-Bruxelles,*
74, No. 41.)   vDZ.

Jan Pompmaker, an adherent of Jan van Batenburg
(q.v.), was (according to the confession of the latter in 1537) one of the principal Anabaptist leaders
in the Netherlands. About Pompmaker and his activities, however, very little is known. (*Inv. Arch.
Amst.* I, Nos. 188 f.; Mellink, *Wederdopers,* 343,
398.)   vDZ.

Jan Poote (Poeten; Jan van Doornik in van Braght,
Mart. Mir.), an Anabaptist martyr burned at the
stake on March 19, 1569, at Antwerp, Belgium. He
was born near Hasselt in the territory of Liége, Belgium, and was a tailor by trade. During his trial he
confessed that he was about 50 years of age, that he
had not attended the Catholic Church for 13 or 14
years. He had been baptized in the woods between
Kortrijk and Doornik in Flanders, but did not
name the elder who had baptized him. He had
married his wife in a meeting of the congregation.
Living at Dambrugge near Antwerp, he held Mennonite meetings in his house. He was apprehended
with a number of members when such a meeting,
attended by about 30 persons, was surprised. Even
in torture Jan refused to inform his judges who
were the preachers and members of the congregation, and what elders had come from abroad to perform baptism and marriages. He died as a true
Christian. His confiscated property realized a considerable amount of money.   vDZ.

Mart. Mir. D 415, E 766; *Antw. Arch.-Blad* XII, 338,
367, 397, 440, 477; XIV, 64 f., No. 712.

Jan Portier, born at Komen (Commines) in Flanders and by trade a fuller, an Anabaptist martyr,
was burned at the stake in November 1568 at Mee-
sen (Messines), Flanders. Several times he was cruelly tortured, but did not recant, dying loyally for
his Lord. (*Mart. Mir.* D 367, E 722.)   vDZ.

Jan Pouwelsz, an Anabaptist martyr: see **Jan Jansz
de Timmerman.**

Jan Quirijnsz (Krijns): see **Quirijn Jansz.**

Jan (van) Raes, a weaver, born at Lauwe and living
at Meenen, Flanders, was arrested there and burned
at the stake April 30, 1569, at Kortrijk (Courtrai)
Belgium, together with Fransoois de Timmerman,
Pieter den Ouden, Jan Wattier, Wouter Denijs, and
Kalleken, the widow of Anpleunis van den Berge.
Jan had received (re)baptism in 1565. His property
was confiscated. (*Mart. Mir.* D 408, E 759; Verheyden, *Courtrai-Bruxelles,* 39, No. 25; *ML* III, 425.)
                                                  vDZ.

Jan van Reenen, a heretic in Amsterdam, who gave
the inquisition much to do, was very active in revolutionary Anabaptist circles of Amsterdam, though
he denied (November 1534) that he was an Anabaptist himself. His wife Leentgen and his daughters Adriana and Lysbeth died as Anabaptist martyrs.   vDZ.

Inv. Arch. Amst. I, No. 57; Grosheide, *Verhooren,* 29-
33; Mellink, *Wederdopers,* 110-13, 145.

Jan Reynerszoon, an Anabaptist martyr, a schoolteacher at IJlst in the Dutch province of Friesland,
who, according to tradition, suffered martyrdom at
Leeuwarden, Friesland, probably in 1556 (information from H. J. Busé).   vDZ.

Jan Rosensvolk, a congregation at Leiden, Holland,
named after their leader or elder Jan Ro(o)se (q.v.).
This small group, which was also called "Huiskopers" and had probably split off from the Flemish
congregation in the early 17th century, probably
merged with the Flemish congregation in 1663.
                                                  vDZ.

L. G. le Poole, *Bijdr. tot de kennis van . . . de Doopsgez. te Leiden* (Leiden, 1905) 11, 26 f.

Jan de Ruytere, an Anabaptist martyr: see **Hans
Corneliszoon.**

Jan van Ryssele, an Anabaptist martyr, burned at
the stake on Aug. 14, 1571, at Antwerp, Belgium.
Particulars are lacking. Jan was charged with rebaptism and having attended forbidden meetings.
(*Antw. Arch.-Blad* XIII, 71, 76, 161; XIV, 86 f., No.
969.)   vDZ.

Jan de Schaper, an Anabaptist martyr, according to
van Braght (*Mart. Mir.* D 415, E 766) burned at the
stake in 1569 at Antwerp, Belgium. Génard, who
studied the documents of Antwerp, did not find the
name of Jan de Schaper. We suggest that Jan de
Schaper is identical with Jacques Semou, not mentioned by van Braght, and burned at the stake at
Antwerp on March 19, 1569.   vDZ.

Jan van Schellingwou (Scellinckwoude), a Dutch
heretical leader, active in Amsterdam in 1534-35; he
belonged to the revolutionary wing of Anabaptism;
it is rather curious that this man who had so much
to answer for was not sentenced to death, but only
banished from the territory of Amsterdam for five
years.   vDZ.

Inv. Arch. Amst. I, Nos. 61, 80, 113, 121 f., 138; Grosheide, *Verhooren*, 13, 38; *idem, Bijdrage* 41, 47; Mellink, *Wederdopers*, 112, 150-52, 369, 380 f., 385.

Jan-van-Schellingwous-Gezinden, a group of Dutch Mennonites: see **Jan van Schellingwou.**

Jan van Schoonhoven, an otherwise unknown Dutch Anabaptist, who was present at a meeting of Anabaptist leaders in 1536 at Bocholt (*q.v.*) (Boekholt) in Westphalia, Germany. He may be identical with Johan van Utrecht, a former Catholic priest, who stayed in Münster in 1534. (*DB* 1919, 194; *ML* I, 239.)   vDZ.

Jan Schut (Schutte), an Anabaptist martyr. A hymn composed by him, "O heer God ick magh wel clagen met suchten so menichfalt" (O Lord, I may well lament with many sighs), is found in the *Lietboecxken van den Offer des Heeren*, 1563 and following editions. This hymn in German translation, "Ach, Gott, ich muss dir klagen," is found in *Ein schon gesangbüchlein Geistlicher Lieder* of about 1565. This hymn shows that he held Menno's doctrine of the Incarnation. A song, "Godt, wilt ons salveren, het lijden coemt ons aen" (O God, wilt Thou save us, for suffering is near), commemorating the suffering of Jan Schut, is found in *Veelderhande Liedekens* of 1569. This song relates that Jan was tortured and put to death at Vreden, in the territory of Münster, Germany. The Dutch martyrbook of 1615 adds that he died in 1561 and the martyrbook of 1617 reports that he was executed by beheading. He had been baptized in 1543 by Leenhart Munsels. Both songs are inserted in Wackernagel, *Lieder*.   vDZ.

Offer, 611-14; *Mart. Mir.* D 287, E 654; Wackernagel, *Lieder*, 144, 146; *DB* 1909, 106 f., 117; Wolkan, *Lieder*, 64, 78, 99, 104.

Jan Smeitgen (Smeiken, official name Jan Hoetz, also called Jan van Tricht, Johan (Jan) van Maastricht, Janne Sme(e)kens), a Dutch Anabaptist leader, bishop, and martyr, burned at the stake at Antwerp, Belgium, on May 24, 1537. At first Jan, who was a blacksmith, lived at Maastricht (*q.v.*), Dutch province of Limburg. Here he became the leader of the congregation after the death of Henric Rol (*q.v.*), September 1534. Soon after he seems to have been interested in the revolutionary Anabaptist views, for in the meetings of the congregation shortly after Christmas 1534 he read the booklet *Van der Wraecke,* sent from Münster. He is also said to have read from "a book of St. Paul," obviously one of the epistles in the New Testament. During this time he baptized in attics, in cellars and other hidden places, also outside the city in neighboring towns like Born, Dieteren, and Sittard. He is even said to have baptized at Leuven, Belgium, the center of most fanatical Catholicism. About his baptizing we are informed by the martyr Metken (*q.v.*), who was baptized by him. "With a cup he took water from a cask and poured it on her head."

During the persecution of the Maastricht congregation in January and February 1535, Jan succeeded in escaping and moved to Antwerp, Belgium. Here his activity in preaching and baptizing is testified

to by the declaration of many martyrs. In 1536, at a conference of Anabaptist leaders at Bocholt (*q.v.*), Germany, he abandoned the Münsterite principles, for he and Jan Matthijsz van Middelburg are said "to have vehemently attacked" the Münsterite doctrines of polygamy and the visible reign of Christ on earth. Concerning his suffering and death no information was available.   vDZ.

W. Bax, *Het Protestantisme in het Bisdom Luik* I (The Hague, 1937) 135-38 and *passim; Antw. Arch.-Blad* VII, 434; XIV, 16 f., No. 163; *DB* 1864, 148; 1917, 113 (No. 36); 1919, 194; Kühler, *Geschiedenis* I, 201; Mellink, *Wederdopers, passim:* see Index.

Jan de Smet (Smit) of Gent, Belgium, by trade a yarn twister, an Anabaptist martyr, was burned at the stake on May 25, 1568, at Gent. His name is celebrated in the song "Als men schreef duyst vijfhondert jaer ende twee en tsestich mede," found in the *Lietboecxken van den Offer des Heeren,* edition of 1578 and later editions. Van Bracht, who calls this martyr Jan de Smid, does not mention the date of execution. (*Offer*, 652; *Mart. Mir.* D 370, E 726; Verheyden, *Gent*, 45, No. 147.)   vDZ.

Jan Smit, an Anabaptist martyr, executed in 1572 by hanging near Haarlem, Dutch province of North Holland. Through the intermediation of Simon Fytsz, Mennonite preacher on the Dutch island of Texel, van Braght was enabled to give a number of particulars concerning Jan Smit: he was born in the earldom of Marck near Cologne, Germany, but later lived at Monnikendam, Dutch province of North Holland. Here he was arrested but liberated by a Protestant officer. Soon after, while he was in a boat on the Zuiderzee, he was apprehended again by a Spanish soldier, and brought to Amsterdam, where he was urged to assist the Spanish army, then besieging Haarlem, to fight their enemies; he refused to do so "because he had no enemies." He was sentenced to death by Don Frederick, son of the Duke of Alba (*q.v.*), and suffered martyrdom as a true disciple of Christ. (*Mart. Mir.* D 641, E 962.)   vDZ.

Jan van Sol, of Danzig, West Prussia, came to Brussels, Belgium, in 1550, and visited Viglius van Aytta, chief president of the (Spanish-Catholic) Privy Council, and suggested a policy of combating Anabaptism, in which he would assist by checking that the newborn children were baptized and that no one in the Netherlands be allowed to move to another town unless provided with a certificate issued by the priest of his home church. If this project had been adopted, Mennonitism would have had a hard struggle, but Viglius distrusted van Sol. So he was put on trial. Van Sol was found to have at his disposal valuable information about the Mennonites. The Court of Holland, whose advice had been asked, opposed the project, fearing that it might seriously injure Dutch trade. So van Sol's plan miscarried. Moreover Jan van Sol proved not to be very reliable. It was revealed that he had lived at Dordrecht, Dutch province of South Holland, where he had kept an inn. In 1530 he fled to Danzig, Prussia, for safety because of his many debts. At Danzig, where he called himself Johann (Jan) Solius, he had a prosperous business. In 1536 he left

Danzig and bought the "Robitten" estate near Bardeyn in East Prussia. For a time he seems to have been a Melchiorite (*q.v.*) and even perhaps a member of the Danzig congregation. He later returned to Danzig and to Holland to win converts, and was apparently successful. But he had little influence among the Mennonites, who considered him untrustworthy. By 1550 he was no longer a Mennonite. He may have spent his last years from about 1556 in the territory of Preussisch-Holland. Mannhardt's assumption that he was a physician is probably untenable. vDZ.

H. van Alfen, "Documenten betreffende Jan van Sol en zijn voorstel tot vervolging van de Wederdopers," in *Ned. Archief v. Kerkgeschiedenis*, n.s. XXIV (The Hague (1931) 205-36; *DB* 1917, 136-38; H. G. Mannhardt, *Die Danziger Mennonitengemeinde* (Danzig, 1919) 39-41.

Jan (Johan, Janne, Jannes) **Specke** (or Johan Speckart, apparently identical with Hans Speck), a former Dominican monk of Groningen in the Netherlands, who about 1534 joined the Anabaptists and soon became a leader of the Batenburgers in the Netherlands (followers of the revolutionary Anabaptist Jan van Batenburg). Specke often stayed at Strasbourg in Alsace and was active in Groningen and Deventer. In 1537 he was apprehended at Antwerp, Belgium, and burned at the stake there in 1537, probably on May 24. vDZ.

Mellink, *Wederdopers*, 133, 264, 266, 286, 396; *Antw. Arch.-Blad* VII, 434; XIV, 14 f., No. 162.

Jan Stevens, born at Saiffelen, was a custodian of the Catholic Church at Hoingen near Sittard, Dutch province of Limburg; he was won for the Reformation probably by Dionysius Vinne (*q.v.*) and soon joined the Anabaptists. On Aug. 23, 1533, he was imprisoned at Maastricht, Dutch province of Limburg. He escaped from prison on Aug. 10, 1534, but was arrested again; about his further life nothing is known. By his preaching he had much influence in the eastern part of the duchy of Jülich and the bishopric of Liége. Theunis van Hastenrath (*q.v.*) in his confession in 1551 called him a deacon, assigned to take charge of the money of the congregation and to provide for the poor. vDZ.

Rembert, *Wiedertäufer*; W. Bax, *Het Protestantisme in het Bisdom Luik* I (The Hague, 1937) 64-70; Mellink, *Wederdopers*, 298-300; *DB* 1909, 124.

Jan Stevensz: see **Stevensz, Jan**, of Nijeveen.

Jan Styaertsz and his cousin Pieter, Anabaptist martyrs, beheaded in 1538 at Vinderhout, near Gent, Belgium. They lived first at Meredor (Merendrée) in Flanders. Because they were dissatisfied with the Catholic Church and its doctrines, they traveled to Germany (to Münster?), because they had heard that there was "a better faith." They were baptized in Germany, but soon were disappointed and returned to Flanders. Shortly after their return they were arrested. Their prison was a filthy pit full of vermin which ate their food and their clothes.

Van Braght, *Martyrs' Mirror*, also reports that Jan, falling ill, was allowed to go home for nursing. He did not flee, but after his recovery obediently returned. (*Mart. Mir.* D 44, E 449; Verheyden, *Gent*, 4, No. 9-10.) vDZ.

Jan (Janne) **de Suyckerbacker**: see **Joachim Vermeeren.**

Jan de Swarte (de Zwarte), an Anabaptist martyr, burned at the stake in March 1563 at Rijssel (Lille) in France. Jan was a weaver, originally from Belle (Bailleul) in Flanders, chosen deacon and preacher by the congregation at Nijpkerke. He often moved, apparently because of persecution. Successively he lived at Hondschoote, Rijssel, Wervik, Meenen, and then in Halewijn, in all these towns serving the congregation. At Halewijn (Halluin), Belgian province of East Flanders, he was arrested in the night of March 7, 1563, together with his wife Claesken and their four sons, Claes, Christiaen, Hans, and Mahieu, besides two men who were staying with them and other members of the congregation of Halewijn. They were brought to Rijssel and all remained steadfast but Jacomijntgen, the wife of Pieter the Shoemaker. Jan de Swarte was executed on March 16, on the same day as his son Claes and his guests Jan Maes and Perceval van den Berge and also Pieter the Shoemaker and Hendrik Aertsz. A few days later his wife Claesken, Christiaen, Hans, and Mahieu suffered martyrdom. (*Mart. Mir.* D 299, E 664; *ML* II, 389.) vDZ.

Jan Tade (Jan Taet, also Jan Hermenss or Jan de Buidelmaker) was called "one of the principal Anabaptist leaders" by van Batenburg (*q.v.*) during his trial at Vilvoorde in 1538. Tade, born at Kampen, Dutch province of Overijssel, and living at Alkmaar, Dutch province of North Holland, was arrested at Utrecht in 1539, together with a number of Anabaptists, including Derckgen, the wife of David Joris (*q.v.*). By his persistent denial that he was ever rebaptized or belonged to the Anabaptists he was set free. A number of places are known in which he was active. vDZ.

J. de Hullu, *Bescheiden betr. de Hervorming in Overijssel* I (1899) 246 ff.; *DB* 1909, 23, 27.

Jan-Tammes-volk, a branch of Dutch Mennonites, followers of Jan Tammes of Groningen, who in 1688 was excommunicated from his congregation (Old Flemish) because he was a champion of baptism by immersion and free preaching by all members of the church, as practiced by the Collegiants (*q.v.*). He was also said to have believed that the Old Flemish branch was not the only true Christian church. Besides this, he was charged with laxity in shunning those who had married outside the group (*buitengetrouwden*).

It is not known whether Jan Tammes had many adherents. A small congregation of Jan-Tammes-volk was found at Harlingen, Dutch province of Friesland, of which Jan Jansen Blaauw was chosen preacher in 1709. (*DB* 1877, 129; 1883, 75-85; *ML* II, 389.) vDZ.

Jan de Tasmaker, named in the song "Aenhoort Godt, hemelsche Vader" of the *Lietboecxken van den Offer des Heeren,* and still in prison at Antwerp, Belgium, when this song was made (1560), is not found in the martyrbooks nor in the official records. Maybe he is identical with Jan Cleeren (*q.v.*), executed at Antwerp on Aug. 9, 1560. (*Offer*, 568.) vDZ.

Jan Thielemansz (Tilemans, Thielsz, or Johan Tielens), an Anabaptist martyr, burned at the stake on Dec. 18, 1568, at The Hague in the Netherlands. Jan was a preacher and is said to have preached at Dordrecht, Dutch province of South Holland. He may have lived there. (*Mart. Mir.* D 377, E 731; *DB* 1912, 39.) vⅮZ.

Jan Thomaszoon: see **Jan van Delft.**

Jan Thymansz (alias *Dapper*), an otherwise unknown Anabaptist martyr, was beheaded on Sept. 15, 1534, at The Hague in the Netherlands. He had participated in the journey from Amsterdam to Münster in March 1534. (*Inv. Arch. Amst.* I, No. 745; *DB* 1917, 122, No. 152.) vⅮZ.

Jan de Timmerman. This Anabaptist martyr, not found in van Braght, *Martyrs' Mirror,* is likely identical with Jan Wiljoot (*q.v.*), named by van Braght but not found in official records. Jan de Timmerman was burned at the stake on April 2, 1569, at Antwerp. He was born at Kortrijk (Courtrai) in Flanders and was 26 years of age. He lived at Borgerhout, a suburb of Antwerp, and was a weaver. His two little children had not been baptized, because, as he confessed, "in the Scriptures nothing is found of children's baptism and (he) is of opinion that one should not baptize children." Jan had been baptized seven years before, at the age of about 19, by Elder Hans Busschaert (*q.v.*) in a hamlet near Armentières in Flanders. He had been apprehended at a meeting of the Antwerp congregation held in the house of Jan Poote (*q.v.*). (*Antw. Arch.-Blad* XII, · 355, 370, 399; XIV, 64 f., No. 719.) vⅮZ.

Jan van Tricht: see **Jan Smeitgen.**

Jan Vaetz, from Sittard, Dutch province of Limburg, an Anabaptist martyr, was drowned on Sept. 6, 1561, at the Steen castle at Antwerp, Belgium, on charge of being rebaptized and persisting in this "heresy." (*Antw. Arch.-Blad* IX, 124, 133; XIV, 30 f., No. 343.) vⅮZ.

Jan van den Velde, an Anabaptist martyr, beheaded on June 11, 1539, at Utrecht in the Netherlands, because he had been rebaptized. He was a native of Antwerp, Belgium, and a painter by profession. Further information was not available. vⅮZ.

Berigten Hist. Genootschap (Utrecht, 1851) IV, 2, p. 139; Mellink, *Wederdopers,* 237.

Jan Vervest (or van der Veste), an Anabaptist martyr, died in prison at Brugge, Belgium, on Aug. 24, 1558. He was a native of Gent, where he apparently made contacts with the Anabaptists in 1551. In this year because of persecution he fled with his family to the Netherlands, living at Amsterdam and Dordrecht. Being a rhetorician, he had no opportunity to earn his living in the Netherlands. So he returned to Gent, where he was baptized by Gillis van Aken in 1553. When a new persecution arose Jan and his family moved to Brugge. Here he regularly attended the meetings of the congregation; during one of these meetings he was apprehended together with his wife Livine Verwee and two other Mennonites, Jacob de Swarte and Hans van den Broucke. He refused to recant, even though he became dangerously ill, and died in prison. His wife also died in prison (September 1558). They had eight children. The oldest of them, a son of 18, Lievin, who had broken with the Catholic Church, was persuaded by the inquisitor to return penitently to the Church. The second, Hansken, a son of 15, refused to become a Catholic. He succeeded in escaping from the Gravensteen prison. Even little Betken of 13 was tried and forced to give particulars about the life and friends of her parents. (Verheyden, *Brugge,* 42, No. 25.) vⅮZ.

Jan de Vlascoper, an Anabaptist martyr, named in H. Alenson's *Tegenbericht op de Voorreden van 't groote Martelaer Boek* (Haarlem, 1630, reprint *BRN* VII, 248), who was in 1576 in prison with Hans Bret (*q.v.*) at Antwerp, Belgium. From the records studied by P. Génard and published in *Antwerpsch Archieven-Blad* it appears that this Jan de Vlascoper is identical with Hans (Jan) Corneliszoon de Ruytere (*q.v.*), a preacher of the Antwerp congregation. vⅮZ.

Jan Volkertsz Trypmaker (Tripmaker; he was a maker of "trips," a kind of wooden shoes), born at Hoorn, Dutch province of North Holland, a Dutch Anabaptist leader, who founded the Amsterdam congregation. In 1530 Trypmaker was in Emden (*q.v.*), East Friesland, where Melchior Hofmann (*q.v.*) had founded an Anabaptist congregation, which he put under the care of Trypmaker when he left Emden; a few months later, about November 1530, Trypmaker also had to leave Emden, driven away by the intolerance of the Reformed preachers. Trypmaker then moved to Amsterdam, where he was active about one year. There is only scarce information about his activities. He is said to have baptized "many persons"; he also performed marriages; apparently his field of activity was also outside Amsterdam. In Amsterdam he was not much hindered by the city magistrates. So he could found and build up the congregation in the peaceful Anabaptist principles which he had learned from Melchior Hofmann. In the fall of 1531, when the Court of Holland at The Hague learned of his activities, the city magistrates of Amsterdam were summoned to arrest Trypmaker. Jan Hubrechts (*q.v.*), then a burgomaster of Amsterdam, had to obey the order from The Hague, but being opposed to persecution, he tried to save Trypmaker, but Trypmaker gave himself up to the police, confessing that he was rebaptized. Trypmaker was sent to The Hague and tried there. During his trial he reported the names of more than 50 Anabaptists in Amsterdam; seven of them then were arrested and also sent to The Hague. Here they died together with Trypmaker, being beheaded on Dec. 5, 1531. Their heads were afterwards sent to Amsterdam and exhibited there as a warning. Shortly before his execution Trypmaker had recanted as had all the seven other prisoners. For this reason they have not been included in the martyrbooks. vⅮZ.

C. A. Cornelius, *Gesch. des Münsterischen Aufruhrs* II, 404 f., 409; *Inv. Arch. Amst.* I, No. 6; *DB* 1917, 111, 159 f.; 1919, 135-39; Kühler, *Geschiedenis I,* 64-68.

Jan Walen, an Anabaptist martyr, who (as can be stated on the basis of official records) was burned at the stake on April 15, 1534, at The Hague in the Netherlands, with Cornelis Luytgensz and Dirk Gerritz, all three from Krommenierdijk, Dutch province of North Holland. They had been among the Anabaptists who sailed from Amsterdam en route to Münster (q.v.), but were arrested at Bergklooster (q.v.). Van Braght (*Mart. Mir.* D 13, E 424) erroneously states that this execution took place in 1527, and in another place (*Mart. Mir.* D 62, E 464) an account is found of the martyrdom in 1542 of a number of Anabaptists from Krommenierdijk. Obviously, as K. Vos has shown (*DB* 1917, 168-70), all these accounts belong together, Jan Echtwerken, Jan Dirksz, and Jan Walen being one and the same person. vDZ.

Jan van de Walle (Jan de Lintwerker), an Anabaptist martyr, burned at the stake on Feb. 26, 1571, at Antwerp, Belgium. Jan, a ribbon maker, was born about 1531 at Eecke near Gent in Flanders. In 1553 or 1554, because of persecution, he fled to Antwerp, where in a wood near the city he had been baptized by Elder Leenaert Bouwens (q.v.). In 1555 he fled to Gent, about 1557 to Holland, but after 1560 he lived again in Antwerp. He was chosen as preacher and deacon of the congregation in 1565 by the congregation at a meeting held in an attic in the city. He had not baptized "because he had not been chosen to this end," but sometimes he performed marriages. He refused to take an oath. In January 1571 he was arrested at Antwerp and several times tried and severely tortured. On the rack he gave some information about the congregation, which then numbered 200-300 members. The meetings usually were attended by about 50 persons. Obviously meetings were held in different quarters of the town. He also gave some information about some elders and leaders like Hans Busschaert and Herman de Timmerman. Jan van de Walle died loyal to his faith as did his wife Calleken Meevels on the same day as her husband. Calleken was his third wife; his first and second also had been Mennonites. A brother of Jan, Martin van der Walle, had suffered martyrdom at Brugge in 1558. In Jan's house two letters were found written by Hans de Wever, i.e., Elder Hans Busschaert, and one written from Emmerich, Germany, signed by Joost Janszen, August 1570. Van Braght gives only a short account on this martyr. vDZ.

Mart. Mir. D 506, E 846; *Antw. Arch.-Blad* XII, 449, 451, 456; XIII, 3, 11-13, 33, 35, 43, 62; XIV, 72 f., No. 843; Verheyden, *Brugge,* 46 f.; K. Vos, "De Doopsgez. te Antwerpen," in *Bulletin de la Commission Royale d'Histoire de Belgique* LXXXIV (Brussels, 1920) 349-51; the letters found in Jan's house are reprinted here, pp. 382-86; *ML* II, 389.

Jan Wattier (Watier) **de Jonge,** an Anabaptist martyr, burned at the stake on April 30, 1569, at Kortrijk (Courtrai) in Belgium, with four other martyrs. Van Braght, *Martyrs' Mirror,* who gives the year of their martyrdom, but not the exact date, relates that they were arrested in Meenen and brought to Kortrijk, where they were kept incommunicado in prison for about three weeks. They were cruelly tortured on the rack, in order to obtain information

for the magistrates, but the Lord gave them strength and they did not betray their fellow members. They died steadfast.

Verheyden has contributed some particulars to the general account by van Braght. Jan Watier had been born at Komen (Commines) in Flanders; he was a weaver living at Meenen. At the end of 1565 or at the beginning of 1566 he had received baptism upon his faith. (*Mart. Mir.* D 408, E 759; Verheyden, *Courtrai-Bruxelles,* 39, No. 26.) vDZ.

Jan Wermbouts (Jan de Coster), an Anabaptist martyr, beheaded at The Hague in the Netherlands on July 30, 1544. Jan was a revolutionary Anabaptist, an adherent of Jan van Batenburg (q.v.). (*Inv. Arch Amst.* I, No. 280.) vDZ.

Jan de Wever, a Mennonite elder in Flanders, named in the *Martyrs' Mirror* (D 765, E 1070), is identical with Hans Bouwens Busschaert (q.v.). vDZ.

Jan (van) Wijnssen: see **Johan van Wynssem.**

Jan Wiljoot, an Anabaptist martyr, according to van Braght (*Mart. Mir.* D 415, E 766) burned at the stake in 1569 at Antwerp, Belgium, together with 10 other martyrs. Van Braght does not give any particulars about this martyr. P. Génard, who studied the records of Antwerp, did not find the name of Jan Wiljoot. Perhaps he is to be identified with Jan de Timmerman (q.v.), burned at the stake at Antwerp on April 2, 1569. vDZ.

Jan Willems(z) (Wilhems), of Roermond (also said to be of Cleve), a revolutionary Anabaptist, "in whom Jan van Leyden seemed to have returned," as Kühler writes. His headquarters were near Wesel, Germany, but he was also active in the eastern part of the Netherlands. In 1574 he was arrested and imprisoned at Wesel. By bribing the jailer, he was able to lead his followers even while in prison, for a period of five years. On March 12, 1580, he was put to death at Wesel by burning at the stake. With him the Münsterites and Batenburgers (q.v.) died out. Charles de Nielles (q.v.), the Reformed minister at Wesel, in 1695 published a French translation of Obbe Philips' *Bekentenisse* at Leiden, adding an account of Jan Willemsz' career in order to alert the government against "the pernicious doctrines of the Anabaptists." vDZ.

BRN VII, 66 note, 101; *DB* 1900, 200; Kühler, *Geschiedenis* I, 208-11.

Jan Willemsz (1583-1660), a minister of the Waterlander congregation at De Rijp, Dutch province of North Holland: see **Willemsz, Jan.**

Jan Willemsz (1533-88), of Hoorn, Dutch province of North Holland, a well-known Dutch Mennonite leader and elder. His father, living between Hoorn and Enkhuizen, turned from the Catholic Church to the Mennonites and then moved to Hoorn where the magistrates were tolerant and where he was safe. Jan Willemsz was appointed elder at Hoorn in 1557. After the outbreak of the Flemish-Frisian schism he joined the Frisian Mennonites (q.v.). Both Jan Willemsz and Lubbert Gerrits (q.v.), also a preacher of the Hoorn congregation, were invited in December 1566 to come to Friesland to settle the Frisian-Flemish quarrel. Jan Willemsz presided at the decisive meeting of Feb. 1, 1567, which, however, did not reconcile the divided body. In 1568, while he was on the way to visit Dirk Philips, who was then staying at Emden, Germany, Jan Willemsz and all the Frisians were excommunicated by Dirk Philips, who took the side of the Flemish. Jan Willemsz was rather moderate; he much deplored the schism that had arisen among the Dutch Mennonites and during his life he did as much as he could to maintain peace among the Frisians and succeeded in keeping them in one united body, but soon after his death the Frisians too divided into a moderate and a conservative group. Of the private life and special activities of Jan Willemsz almost nothing is known. De Hoop Scheffer (*DB* 1867, 58-65) gives some information about his descendants (see **Sleutel** family), many of whom were active in the Mennonite Church.   vDZ.

BRN VII, 62 ff., 67 f., 340 f.; *DB* 1893, 26-79, *passim;* Kühler, *Geschiedenis* I, *passim,* see Index.

Jan Woutersz van Cuyck, an Anabaptist martyr, burned at the stake on March 28, 1572, at Dordrecht, Dutch province of South Holland, together with Adriaenken Jansdochter van Molenaersgraef. The account of van Braght, *Martyrs' Mirror,* about these martyrs is very detailed; obviously van Braght, born about 50 years after their execution in the same town of Dordrecht and living there, had at his disposal firsthand information.

Jan Woutersz was an artist, both a painter and etcher of glass. He was born at Dordrecht. Here he was arrested in February 1572; when the sheriff came to his house and asked him whether Jan van Cuyck was living there, he answered, because a Christian should always tell the truth, that he himself was Jan van Cuyck. He was imprisoned at the Vuylpoort. After some trial and torturing, both Adriaenken and Jan were sentenced to death and suffered martyrdom in faith and peace. The Amsterdam Mennonite Library has a rare booklet, *Sommige belijdinghen, schriftelijcke Sentbrieven ende Testamenten geschreven door Jan Wouterszoon van Cuyck . . .* (1579, n.p., but likely Gillis Rooman at Haarlem published this book). It contains the confession and eleven letters by Jan Woutersz, all found in the *Martyrs' Mirror.* The letters of Jan Woutersz in the booklet are followed by a letter by Adriaenken and a letter from her husband to her. Finally the volume has two songs, one with a puzzle title "Babel 8 my niet, veel min 8 x"; this means *Babel acht mij niet, veel min acht icks* (Babel, i.e., the Roman Catholic Church does not respect me; no more do I respect it); the other song begins, "Uut de woestijn roepen wy heer tot dy, die ons in ald' noot staet bi" (From the desert we call, Lord, to Thee, who helpest us in all distress). The author of the second hymn and maybe of both is Jan A. van Dort, Adriaenken's husband. Jan Woutersz' letters are addressed as follows: (1) to his brother-in-law and his sister; (2) to his brother and his sister; (3) to the congregation of Dordrecht; (4) to his wife; (5) to his wife and his daughter; (6) to his

only daughter; (7) to his parents; (8) to his sister-in-law, who was still a Catholic; (9) to his three youngest sisters; (10) to his oldest brother-in-law and his sister; (11) to his youngest brother-in-law P. I. These letters are all written in an exquisite style; obviously Jan Woutersz was a man of good education. The letters to his wife and to his little daughter (only seven years old) are very striking; the letters to his brother and sisters, especially to his Catholic sister-in-law, who was a Mother Superior in a convent, are evangelistic, full of Christian love, pressing to conversion. Every letter gives a testimony of a strong, sound Biblical faith. When during the trial the sheriff proposed to Jan Woutersz that he should return to the old Catholic faith and be set free and live with his wife—he had been married only nine years—he replied that he would not recant. Then the sheriff asked him: "Don't you want to live?" and Jan answered: "Sure, I do, but not for anything in the world would I renounce my faith." (*Mart. Mir.* D 566-600, E 897-926; *Bibliographie* I, 93-107.)   vDZ.

Jan (Janne) **van der Wouwen** (van den Wouwe), an Anabaptist martyr, is identical with Jan de Oude Kleerkoper (*q.v.*).   vDZ.

Janjacobsgezinden, a branch of Dutch Mennonites, the followers of Jan Jacobsz (*q.v.*), who in 1599 separated from the Old Frisians (*q.v.*). This schism is described in *Noodwendighe Verclaringhe van 't verscheel ende Questie geresen tusschen Ian Iacobsz van Harlinghen met sijne medehulpers ende tusschen Pieter Ielties van Collum met sijne medestanders.* The Janjacobs group was a conservative, austere group, who did not allow their members to have contact, either in trade or in private conversation, with "worldly" people. They were severe in banning and for this reason they often had difficulties with the magistrates (Leeuwarden, Bolsward, Ameland, Terschelling). As in the days of Menno Simons their elders traveled around to administer baptism and communion. The names of most of them have been preserved: first Jan Jacobsz himself, then Zille Douwes, Hans Janssen, Seerp Sybrands, Cornelis Jarichs, Jacob Theunis, Laurens Jansen, Jacob Claassen, Jacob Gerrits, Sikke Tjerks, Jan Tjerks, Joris Jacobs, and Jacob Jansen. The baptismal lists of some of them, in which they noted down the number of persons they baptized in each congregation, have been preserved; Cornelis Jarichs baptized no fewer than 1,040 persons. Some of the elders also visited Prussia and baptized there, but it is not yet known which Prussian church belonged to the Janjacobs group. The Janjacobsgezinden adopted their own hymnbook in 1613: *Eenighe Gheestelijcke Liedekens* (*q.v.*) made by Jan Jacobsz, and a sequel to it, *Eenighe Nieuwe Gheestelijcke Liedekens.* This hymnbook was used until the 18th century. The Janjacobs group numbered at first about 20 congregations, all but two, Hoorn and Amsterdam, in the province of Friesland. Most of them were always small in membership, except Ameland, which as late as 1804 numbered 432 members. The total number of male baptized members in 1666 in Friesland is said to have been 643. By 1700 eight of their congregations had disappeared, and in the 18th century, when the Jan-jacobsgezinden were usually—erroneously—called Old Flemish Mennonites, all their congregations were dissolved but Ameland, which did not unite with the other Mennonites on this island until 1855.

vDZ.

J. Loosjes, "Jan Jacobsz en de Jan-Jacobsgezinden" in *Ned. Archief voor Kerkgeschiedenis* XI (The Hague) 1914, issue 3, 185-240; Blaupot t. C., *Friesland*, 311; *BRN* VII, 213-15; *DB* 1861, 87; 1874, 59; 1889, 6-13, 16, 18 f., 28-50; 1890, 1-38; S. F. Rues, *Tegenwoordige Staet* (Amsterdam, 1745) 71; *Menn. Bl.,* 1890, 125 ff.; *ML* II, 389.

Janjgir Mennonite (GCM) Mission Station is located on the southeastern edge of the village Janjgir, in Bilaspur District, Madhya Pradesh (formerly Central Provinces), India. It was opened by J. F. Kroeker, who visited this spot with P. A. Penner in April 1901. He procured land in December 1901, after which first buildings were erected. The Kroekers served only one term. In 1906 Annie C. Funk arrived from Hereford, Pa., served a term, started the first girls' school, sailed for furlough, perished on the *Titanic*. In 1909-37 (except for 1916-21) P. W. Penner served here, extensively developed the work, erected many buildings. Other missionaries who made distinctive contributions were the E. B. Steiners, Miss M. R. Burkhalter, Miss H. E. Nickel, Miss A. Schmidt, and the W. F. Unruhs. Unruh started the Bible School here in 1929. More recent workers included the S. T. Moyers, the F. J. Isaacs, and the J. R. Duerksens. The name of the Indian pastor M. Rufus Asna, who served 45 years, beginning 1903, will long be associated with Janjgir. The congregation was organized in 1912. The meetinghouse was erected 1909, replaced by a larger one in 1926. The present Indian pastor is Philip Lader. The baptized membership in June 1949 was 160.

Types of work include the A. C. Funk Memorial School for girls, the Chhattisgarhi Bible School, a small medical dispensary, a coeducational primary school. The Girls' School has in residence about 130 girls, with work up to VIIIth Standard. The enrollment of the Bible School is about 60. An extensive evangelistic work in 360 surrounding villages has been a feature of the work during the years.

S.T.M.

Janjgir (India) **Union Bible School** was opened on July 3, 1930, as a training school for native pastors, evangelists, teachers, and Bible women of the Hindustani congregations of the General Conference Mennonite Church in central India, with a three-year course. The school began with six months of classroom work, conducted in the Sunday-school wings of the Janjgir Church, and two months of village evangelism, but soon increased to nine months of classroom work with one-month village evangelism. The first term had 14 students, with W. F. Unruh as principal. Succeeding principals were Martha Burkhalter, S. T. Moyer, J. R. Duerksen, and Curt Claassen. Under J. R. Duerksen the school became an inter-mission school, though the administration and staff remained G.C.M. In 1955 only 21 of the 47 students were of the General Conference Church; the remainder being distributed as

follows: Churches of Christ 16, Mennonite Church (MC) in India 4, Mission Bands 2, Evangelical Christian Church (Allahabad) 2.

H.S.B.

Jan(ne) de Hane, an otherwise unknown Anabaptist martyr, burned at the stake at Antwerp in 1537. (*Antw. Arch.-Blad* VII, 434; XIV, 14 f., No. 161.)

vDZ.

Janne de Snijdere (alias Jan Rotterdamme), an Anabaptist martyr burned at the stake on May 5, 1571, at Brussels, Belgium, together with his wife Elisabeth Bruyne. Janne was a native of Brouwershaven, Dutch province of Zeeland. Their six children were baptized in the Catholic St. Gudule cathedral at Brussels on the day their parents were executed. This Janne de Snijdere is probably not identical with Jan Snijder, an Anabaptist who (Mellink, *Wederdopers,* 217, 414) lived at Cleve, Germany, and who in 1544 sent two books by David Joris to Delft, Holland. (Verheyden, *Courtrai-Bruxelles,* 102, No. 154.)

vDZ.

Janneken, an Anabaptist martyr who was drowned in a tub in the Steen castle at Antwerp, Belgium, in 1558, together with Noële (*q.v.*). The identity of this martyr could not be established. (*Mart. Mir.* D 202, E 583.)

vDZ.

Janneken, an Anabaptist martyr, who while in prison wrote the song "Verhuecht verblijt groot ende cleijn" (Be glad and rejoice, both ye great and small), found in the *Lietboecxken van den Offer des Heeren,* 1563 and following editions, also *Tweede Liedeboeck* of 1583 and mentioned by Wolkan (*Lieder,* 62, 71). A notice in the margin of the page reports that the poet was a young woman called Janneken, who was drowned at the Steen castle at Antwerp. It is not clear which Janneken is meant, either Janneken van Aken (Jenneken Eghels) (*q.v.*) or Janneken van Houtte (*q.v.*). Probably it was the latter.

vDZ.

Janneken, daughter of Anneken Botson, burned at the stake about 1585 in St. Veit, in the duchy of Luxembourg, together with her mother and Mayken Pieters. (*Mart. Mir.* D 753, E 1,060; *ML* I, 250.)

vDZ.

Janneken: see **Janneken van Hout(t)e.**

Janneken, an Anabaptist martyr, the wife of Dirk van Wesel (*q.v.*), was arrested with him and ten others March 11, 1571, at Deventer, Dutch province of Overijssel, where she was burned at the stake between May 24 and June 16, 1571. (*Mart. Mir.* D 552 ff., E 885; *DB* 1919, 29-37.)

vDZ.

Janneken, the widow of Melchior Simonsse: see **Janneken Mels.**

Janneken, the widow of the martyr Pieter Freerks (*q.v.*), was drowned at Leeuwarden, Dutch province of Friesland, on Dec. 19, 1537.

vDZ.

J. Reitsma, *100 jaar uit de Gesch. der Hervorming . . . in Friesland* (Leeuwarden, 1876) 63.

Janneken van Aken (*Jenneken Eghels*), an Anabaptist martyr, drowned in a wine-cask, April 3, 1560, inside the Steen castle (prison) at Antwerp,

Belgium, together with Lenaert Plovier and Mayken de Hont. Particulars about this martyr are
lacking. We only know that she was born at Haerlebeke near Kortrijk in Flanders. Her name is celebrated in the hymn "Aenhoort Godt, hemelsche
Vader" in the *Lietboecxken van den Offer des
Heeren;* she may be the author of the song "Verhuecht verblijt groot ende cleijn" of this *Lietboecxken.*   vDZ.

   Offer, 552 f., 567; *Mart. Mir.* D 270, E 641; *Antw.
Arch.-Blad* IX, 7, 12; XIV, 28 f., No. 316; *ML* II, 389.

Janneken Botson: see **Janneken,** daughter of Anneken Botson.

Janneken du Boys, wife of André Vanneaux, an
Anabaptist martyr, drowned at Antwerp, Belgium,
on April 22, 1558. Particulars are unknown. See
also **Janneken Walraven.** (*Antw. Arch.-Blad* VIII,
444 f., 469; XIV, 22 f., No. 256.)   vDZ.

Janneken Cabeljaus, wife of the martyr Hendrik
Aertsz (*q.v.*), an Anabaptist martyr, burned at the
stake in 1564 at Rijssel (Lille) in France. The execution probably took place on Feb. 22. She was
born at Ieper, and lived with her husband in Halewijn (*q.v.*), Flanders, when they were arrested in
the night of March 7, 1563, at the same time as a
number of Mennonites. She remained steadfast in
trial and died loyally. (*Mart. Mir.* D 299, E 665.)
                                                         vDZ.

Janneken Croecx, an Anabaptist martyr, burned at
the stake on Jan. 28, 1573, at Antwerp, Belgium,
with Grietgen van den Steen and Jacques van Hulten, because she had been rebaptized and had attended forbidden meetings. (*Antw. Arch.-Blad* XIII,
100 f., 172; XIV, 88 f., 1003.)   vDZ.

Janneken op Dextelaer, an Anabaptist martyr,
drowned July 5 or 6, 1557, at the Steen castle at
Antwerp, Belgium, together with Klaerken (Claerken Boucket) and Margriete (Margriet Vanneau).
Afterwards their naked corpses were thrown into
the Scheldt River. Janneken, whose name is celebrated in the song "Aenhoort Godt, hemelsche
Vader" (Hear, O God, heavenly Father) of the
Lietboecxken van den Offer des Heeren, is apparently identical with Janneken van Hout(t)e (*q.v.*),
who is found in the official records. (*Offer,* 565;
Mart. Mir. D 185, E 569.)   vDZ.

Janneken Dhanins, wife of Lievin van Booxtale
and daughter of Jan van Sleidingen, an Anabaptist
martyr, burned at the stake on Aug. 19, 1573, on
the Vrijdagsmarkt at Gent, Belgium, together with
two other women, Martinken Meere and Olyverynken 's Keizers. All three were gagged to prevent
their speaking to the bystanders. The crowd, indignant at this precaution, assumed a threatening attitude against the executioner and his aids, so that
the soldiers were charged to clear the market place,
which measure nearly caused a revolt. (Verheyden,
Gent, 64, No. 231.)   vDZ.

Janneken van Hout(t)e, an Anabaptist martyr, not
found in van Braght, *Martyrs' Mirror,* but likely

identical with Janneken op Dextelaer (*q.v.*), named
by van Braght. She was born at Antwerp, Belgium,
and belonged to the Mennonite congregation in this
town. Janneken, a *jonckmeyssen* (a young or unmarried woman), was bound in a sack and drowned
at the Steen castle at Antwerp on July 5 or 6, 1557.
This martyr may be the author of the song "Verhuecht verblijt groot ende cleyn" (Be glad and rejoice, both great and small) found in the *Lietboecxken van den Offer des Heeren.* (*Offer,* 553;
Antw. Arch.-Blad VIII, 434, 438; XIV, 22 f., No.
250.)   vDZ.

Janneken van Hulle, an Anabaptist martyr, was
burned at the stake on Nov. 7, 1570, on the Vrijdagsmarkt at Gent, Belgium, together with Janneken van Rentegem and Hans van der Weghe, because she had been rebaptized and partaken in the
meetings of the Mennonites. Two years before,
both Janneken van Hulle and her sister Cateline, of
whom nothing is known, then fugitives, had been
banished forever from the territory of Gent, as
Mennonites. Van Braght reports that Janneken was
unmarried, and that with a gag in her mouth she
died peacefully. (*Mart. Mir.* D 528, E 864; Verheyden, *Gent,* 56, No. 193; *ML* II, 365.)   vDZ.

Janneken de Jonc(k)heere, an Anabaptist martyr,
burned at the stake on July 21, 1562, at Gent, Belgium, together with her sisters Vyntgen and Goude-
ken and two other Mennonites. She was born at
Merendree in Flanders. She was about 26 years of
age. Further particulars were not available. Van
Braght, *Martyrs' Mirror,* mentions this martyr twice,
once in 1562, without exact date and once in 1569,
which is wrong. Janneken is celebrated in a song,
"Als men schreef duyst vijfhondert jaar, ende twee
en tsestich mede," found in the *Lietboecxken van
den Offer des Heeren,* 1578 and following editions.
                                                         vDZ.

   Offer, 650; *Mart. Mir.* D 289, 407, E 656, 759; Verheyden, *Gent,* 29, No. 93; *ML* II, 432.

Janneken Kinderkens, an Anabaptist martyr, beheaded on March 24, 1562, inside of the Gravensteen (castle and prison) at Gent, Belgium. She was
a daughter of Adriaen Kinderkens, was born at
Moerbeke near Geeraardsbergen in Flanders, and
was 24 years of age. Further particulars are lacking.
(See also **Verkindert;** Verheyden, *Gent,* 28, No.
83.)   vDZ.

Janneken Mels (Janneken Melchior Simonsse or
Simonsdochter), from Brielle, Dutch province of
South Holland, and baptized there in 1536 by Cornelis Pieters (Cornelis wt den Briel), an Anabaptist
martyr, was beheaded on Sept. 4 at Zierikzee, Dutch
province of Zeeland. Janneken and three other Anabaptists were apprehended early in the morning of
July 20, 1536; after imprisonment, trial, and torture
all four died loyally. During the trial one of the
burgomasters had snarled to them: "We care not
for your Word of God, but hold to the mandate of
the Emperor, and shall ignominiously exterminate
all those who act contrary to it." (*Mart. Mir.* D 38,
E 445; Mellink, *Wederdopers,* 227, 317.)   vDZ.

Janneken van Munstdorp, who in the documents is called Jenneken van den Velde(n), a native of Ieper, Flanders, wife of the martyr Hans van Munstdorp (*q.v.*), was burned at the stake on Oct. 6, 1573, at Antwerp, Belgium, together with Maryken (Maeyken van Dissenbeke) and Lysken Luchtens. Van Braght's *Martyrs' Mirror* relates that Janneken was pregnant when she was arrested and in prison gave birth to a daughter, whom she named Janneken. Before the officials could take away the child, the baby was secretly given to "friends," i.e., members of the congregation, to bring her up. Janneken wrote a testament to her infant daughter Janneken, and two letters, one to her parents, who had not yet come to the true faith, and one to her sister. To her little daughter she wrote that they had been married only a short while when the martyr's death for the Lord's sake overtook them; she should not be ashamed of them, but follow them and live a godly life. The mother could not give her much earthly goods, but a good name; she should be industrious and good and fear God. In the letters to her parents and sister she thanks them for what they have done for her, and commends her little daughter to her sister. "Oh, that it had been the will of the Lord, that I could have brought her up, in what great regard I should have held her for my dear husband's sake; though I should have suffered want with her, I should not have parted with her; but the will of the Lord be done." She regrets that her long imprisonment has caused such great expense. She affectionately urges her parents to seek their salvation. She will precede her sister to the heavenly city, where they will be united.

Hans and Janneken van Munstdorp (according to van Braght) are commemorated in the hymn "Och vrienden al te samen, hoort, hoe wy op Bamisdagh verstoort" (O hear, all ye friends, how we were disturbed on St. Bavo's day), found in the *Rotterdamsche Lied-boeck*. This hymnal is no longer extant.   NEFF, vDZ.

Mart. Mir. D 664, E 983; *Antw. Arch.-Blad* XIII, 129 f., 179; XIV, 92 f., No. 1037; *ML* III, 183.

Janneken van Rentegem, an Anabaptist martyr, burned at the stake on Nov. 7, 1570, on the Vrijdagsmarkt at Gent, together with Janneken van Hulle and Hans van der Weghe. She was charged with the crimes of rebaptism and attending the Mennonite meetings. According to van Braght, *Martyrs' Mirror,* she was unmarried. (*Mart. Mir.* D 528, E 864; Verheyden, *Gent,* 56, No. 194.) vDZ.

Janneken Roelandts (in *Lietboecxken,* Roolants), an Anabaptist martyr, executed in 1569 at Gent, Belgium (manner of execution and exact date unknown). She was the wife of Peter Stayaert, who was executed at the same time. She is celebrated in the song "Als men schreef duyst vijfhondert jaer, ende twee en tsestich mede," found in the *Lietboecxken van den Offer des Heeren,* 1578 and following editions. This martyr is not found in official sources at Gent. The *Bibliographie* statement that she was probably the wife of Roelandt Stayaerds is wrong. (*Offer,* 653; *Mart. Mir.* D 407, E 759; *Bibliographie* II, 760, No. 666.)   vDZ.

Janneken Walraven, listed by van Braght as an Anabaptist martyr who was executed in 1557 at Antwerp, Belgium. Van Braght writes: "In the year 1557 on Pentecost eve there was burnt alive at Antwerp . . . Janneken Walraven, the mother of Jacques Walraven, who was a minister of the Word at Amsterdam among the Mennonites." Here van Braght is wrong, confusing two martyrs, Tanneken (Anneken) Walraven (*q.v.*), widow of Jan Verschelt, burned at the stake on May 22 (Pentecost), 1557, at Antwerp, who may have been the mother of the afore-mentioned preacher, serving 1588-1617, and Janneken du Boys (*q.v.*), wife of André Vanneaux, drowned at Antwerp on April 22, 1558. Thus Janneken Walraven did not exist. (*Mart. Mir.* D 178, E 563.)   vDZ.

Jannes van Romershoven, an Anabaptist martyr, who was apprehended on May 31, 1538, and burned at the stake on June 14, 1538, at Curingen, Belgian province of Limburg (then bishopric of Liége). He was unmarried. In the accounts of his martyrdom he is called a Lutheran, and two "Lutheran" books which he possessed were burned with him. But Lutheran here does not mean adherent of Martin Luther, but heretic in general. The word Lutheran in this period often was used, even in cases of Anabaptism. From the account it is clear that Jannes was an Anabaptist, because he is said to have been the principal "Lutheran" of Gorsleeuw, that he had rebaptized many persons, not only at Gorsleeuw, but also at Antwerp, and that he died in his heresy (*luthery*) refusing to be converted and unwilling to renounce his rebaptism.   vDZ.

W. Bax, *Het Protestantisme in het bisdom Luik* I (The Hague, 1937) 161 f.

Jannetgen Hendricxdochter, from Amsterdam, wife of Peter Dircxzn, had been among the Anabaptists who sailed from Amsterdam March 24, 1534, en route to Münster. She was arrested on the boat, but either was released or managed to escape. Jannetgen was arrested again in Amsterdam in August or September 1539, whereas her husband was imprisoned in The Hague, where he was put to death on Nov. 6, 1539. Jannetgen was sentenced to death on Nov. 4, 1539; since she was pregnant, the execution was to be postponed until after the birth of the child. It is not known whether the execution took place. (Grosheide, *Bijdrage,* 103 f.)   vDZ.

Jannetgen (Jannetje) **Jansdochter,** from Utrecht in the Netherlands, an Anabaptist martyr, was drowned on May 21, 1535, at Amsterdam, together with ten other women. She was married to Willem Dircxzn Tymmerman, and confessed that she had been baptized by Gerrit Ghijsen van Benschop (*q.v.*) in his house at Benschop. She did not repent this baptism.   vDZ.

Mart. Mir. D 413, E 445, where the date of execution is given as May 15; Grosheide, *Verhooren,* 67, 70.

Jannetgen (Janneken) **Matthijsdochter,** an Anabaptist martyr of whom there is only scarce and questionable information. She is not found in van Braght, *Martyrs' Mirror.* According to the sentence books, Jannetgen Matthijsdochter was sentenced at

Leiden, Dutch province of South Holland, on Nov. 21, 1552, to be drowned because of Anabaptism, but it is strange that her name is not found in the song "Eylaes, ick moch wel suchten Dat nu buert so groot ellent" (Alas, I must lament that now comes about so great misery), written by Adriaen Cornelisz (*q.v.*) to celebrate the death of some martyrs, who according to the sentence book were sentenced to death at the same date as Jannetgen Matthijsdochter. Nor is she found in another hymn celebrating some martyrs of Leiden of 1552, "Ick mag wel droeflijck singen, in desen tijt van noot" (I must sadly sing in this time of distress). Both hymns are found in the *Lietboecxken van den Offer des Heeren* of 1563 and following editions. Perhaps the puzzle of Jannetgen Matthijsdochter can be solved in assuming that her execution was for some reason postponed. (*Offer,* 578, note 1.)   vDZ.

Jannetje Matthysdochter, from Medemblik, Dutch province of North Holland, an Anabaptist martyr, was drowned on Nov. 25, 1539, at Leiden, Dutch province of South Holland. Details about this martyr were not available. Mellink supposes that she had fled from Haarlem, where there had been a recent persecution, to Leiden, and that she was an adherent of David Joris (*q.v.*). She was arrested together with two other Anabaptist women while reading Anabaptist books in an attic. Daniel Jansz, a schoolteacher, who had given them shelter in his attic, was banished from the city of Leiden. (Mellink, *Wederdopers,* 204.)   vDZ.

Jannetje Thijsdochter, 35 years of age, wife of Pieter Thoniszn, a carpenter at Amsterdam, belonged to the Anabaptist congregation of Amsterdam. She had been baptized about Pentecost 1534 by Jacob van Campen (*q.v.*), the Anabaptist bishop of Amsterdam, in the house of the deacon Jan Paeuw (*q.v.*). She was apprehended, apparently at The Hague, on Jan. 22, 1535, when she was on a business trip to Delft. She recanted and renounced her faith, and for this reason she was not included in the martyrbooks. Apparently she was set free after her trial of Jan. 23. The report of this trial is very interesting, because Jannetje gave much and detailed information about the Amsterdam Anabaptist congregation and its leaders; between Pentecost 1534 and January 1535 more than 300 persons were baptized in the house of Jan Paeuw (*q.v.*). The total number of Anabaptists in Amsterdam was about 3,500; preachers from abroad always were lodged with members of the congregation; some preachers had come from England; a plan to capture the city of Amsterdam by weapons, toward Christmas 1534, of which Meynart van Emden (*q.v.*) was one of the promoters, was condemned and thwarted by Jacob van Campen; in a meeting of 32 Anabaptist leaders, held in December 1534 at Spaarndam, near Haarlem in the Dutch province of North Holland, the majority had rejected the revolutionary principles.   vDZ.

Inv. Arch. Amst. I, 79; Grosheide, *Verhooren,* 179-84; Mellink, *Wederdoper, passim,* see Index.

Jannijn Buefkijn (Hans Keeskooper), an Anabaptist martyr, born in Werwik, unmarried, baptized in 1547 by a certain Christiaen, burned at the stake on July 9, 1551 (van Braght erroneously gives the date as 1550), in Gent, Belgium. His death is sung in the hymn, "O Heer u wil ick loven" (O Lord, I will praise Thee), in *Het Offer des Heeren* and in the *Ausbund* in German, "O Herr dich will ich loben." It has 13 stanzas of eight lines. It is based on a letter written by the martyr in prison, stating the confession he made before his judges, especially on baptism and communion. He also describes how a young man who had not yet been baptized because he was not well enough established in the Christian life, joyfully witnessed to his faith and suffered death for it. Hans van Overdamme (*q.v.*) was also executed at the same time as Jannijn. They had arranged between them that Jannijn, when he reached the site of execution, would remove his stockings, in order to give Hans more time to address the crowd.   NEFF.

Offer, 121-26; Wolkan, *Lieder,* 66, 127, and 147; Verheyden, *Gent,* No. 26, p. 14; *Mart. Mir.* D 95 f., E 493; *ML* I, 289.

Jans: see also **Jansen** and **Jansz.**

Jans, Cornelis: see **Mandemaker, Cornelis Jans.**

Jansen, Neb., a village (1950 pop. 244) in Jefferson County, in the southeastern part of the state, was named in honor of Peter Jansen (*q.v.*), one of the Mennonite pioneers. Today Jansen has one Mennonite church (Evangelical Mennonite Brethren) with 73 members.

The first major settlement in the Jansen community, the Kleine Gemeinde, came from Russia in 1874-75, and settled in Cub Creek Precinct in seven small, somewhat isolated "line villages" of Rosenort, Rosenhof, Rosenfeld, Rosental, Neuanlage, Heuboden, and Blumenort. The Jansen community at one time had six different Mennonite churches operating: Kleine Gemeinde (150; 1874-1908); E.M.B. (150; 1879 to present time); K.M.B. (50; 1880-1916); G.C.M. (popularly called Peter Jansen's Church, comprised largely of the personnel on P. Jansen's ranch, 6 to 8 families, 1890-1909); M.B. (50; 1901-47); Reformed Mennonites (four or five families who held services in homes were never formally organized. Some of this group still live in the vicinity of Jansen today). The community was predominantly Mennonite until shortly after the turn of the century when mass migrations away from Jansen began, which resulted in a sharp decline in Mennonite population and the eventual closing down of all but one of the Mennonite churches. The last Mennonite church to close was the M.B. in 1947.

Today (1953) the town of Jansen has five places in which alcoholic beverages are sold, in sharp contradiction to the "clause" which Peter Jansen was responsible for having inserted into the original deed of each town lot in Jansen which prohibited the sale of liquor in the town of Jansen. D.P.M.

Cornelius J. Claassen, "Peter Jansen—Pioneer, Leader and Philanthropist," *Menn. Life* II (October 1947) 41-

43; G. E. Reimer and G. R. Gaeddert, *Exiled by the Czar; Cornelius Jansen and the Great Mennonite Migration, 1874* (Newton, 1956); D. Paul Miller, "An Analysis of Community Adjustment: A Case Study of Jansen, Nebraska" (Ph.D. thesis, Nebraska, 1953).

Jansen (Neb.) Evangelical Mennonite Brethren Church is a congregation of 73 members (1954) belonging to the Evangelical Mennonite Brethren Conference of North America. It began in 1879, with the first services in the homes of the members. The first pastor was John Fast, the minister serving the longest was B. O. Kroeker; the present minister is Paul F. Goossen (1956). A church built in 1891 on the northwest corner of Jansen was destroyed by a tornado in 1929, and was replaced by a new building on the north edge of Jansen. This is the only Mennonite congregation in the area. E.R.

Jansen (Neb.) Kleine Gemeinde Mennonite Church was established after the arrival of 36 families of Kleine Gemeinde (*q.v.*) Mennonites from Russia in Jefferson Co., Neb., in 1874 under the leadership of Abraham Friesen. After meeting in homes for a time they constructed a church two miles west and three miles north of the present site of Jansen. Because of the infiltration of other Mennonite groups and the scarcity of land, the entire Kleine Gemeinde, as far as its members had not joined other groups, migrated to Meade, Kan., in 1906-8. (See also **Meade** Kleine Gemeinde.) C.K.

D. Paul Miller, "The Story of the Jansen Churches," *Menn. Life* X (1955) 38; C. Krahn, "From Russia to Meade," *Menn. Life* VI (1951) 18 f.; G. E. Reimer and G. R. Gaeddert, *Exiled by the Czar; Cornelius Jansen and the Great Mennonite Migration, 1874* (Newton, 1956).

Jansen (Neb.) Krimmer Mennonite Brethren Church was founded in the Kleine Gemeinde Mennonite settlement after a group of Krimmer Mennonite Brethren had come to this community from Russia in 1877. Originally this group associated with the Evangelical Mennonite Brethren founded by Isaac Peters (*q.v.*). But in 1880 they withdrew and under the leadership of J. A. Wiebe founded the Jansen Krimmer Mennonite Brethren Church. In 1905 or 1906 a brick church was built one mile east of Jansen. The membership never exceeded 75. By 1950 only three families were left in the community, who attended the M.B. church. C.K.

D. Paul Miller, "The Story of the Jansen Churches," *Menn. Life* X (1955) 39; G. E. Reimer and G. R. Gaeddert, *Exiled by the Czar; Cornelius Jansen and the Great Mennonite Migration, 1874* (Newton, 1956).

Jansen (Neb.) Mennonite Brethren Church, now extinct, was organized in 1890 by Elder J. J. Regier. At that time Isaac Wall was chosen minister and leader. An old saloon was purchased and remodeled into a meeting place. Later a church was built. Through revivals the congregation grew and for some time numbered more than 100 members. Later most of these members moved to newer settlements, and the congregation at present consists of only two families. Other ministers who served the church are Adam Ross, G. H. Jantzen, Waldo Hiebert, and P. V. Balzer. H.E.W.

Jansen, Arrien, a member and in 1719-20 a deacon of the Waterlander Mennonite congregation at Leeuwarden, Dutch province of Friesland, who, after 1674, promoted the idea in this congregation that baptism should be administered by immersion and thus caused much dissension in the congregation. In 1720 he left the congregation with a number of adherents, but in 1725 he was again admitted into the congregation. (*DB* 1874, 60, 64-73.) vDZ.

Jansen, Claes (Klaas, Klaus, Nicholas) (1658-1745), one of the first Mennonite settlers in the United States, came to Germantown, Pa., from Crefeld, Germany, in 1685. Later he lived in the Skippack area where he became a trustee in the Mennonite congregation in 1708 and a preacher in 1717. The assertion (*DB* 1884, 75) that he was appointed minister in 1692 or shortly after to serve together with Rittenhouse (*q.v.*) is not attested by the old documents. It is very probable that Claes Jansen was the ancestor of the Johnson family which was very prominent in the Lower Skippack congregation in the 19th century furnishing three Henry G. Johnsons as ministers in succession and leading to the nicknaming of the congregation as the "Johnson Mennonites" (*q.v.*). vDZ.

H. S. Bender, "The Founding of the Mennonite Church in America at Germantown, 1683-1708," *MQR* VII (October 1933) 231, 234 f.; J. G. de Hoop Scheffer, "Het Tweede Eeuwgetijde van de Vestiging der Duitschers in N.-Amerika," *DB* 1884, 75.

Jansen, Cornelius (1822-94), a leader in the Mennonite emigration from Russia to the prairie states in 1873, was born at Tiegenhof, West Prussia, on July 2, 1822, the son of Daniel and Anna Buhler Janzen. He lost his mother at the age of ten, and then lived with his uncle Gerhard Penner, elder of the Heubuden (*q.v.*) congregation, who helped him in his training as a merchant. He was baptized at Tiegenhof. He married Helena von Riesen on May 4, 1848. They were the parents of six children: Margaretha, Peter (*q.v.*), Anna, Johannes, Helena, and Cornelius. In 1850 the family emigrated to Berdyansk, Russia, returned to Schidlitz, a suburb of Danzig, in 1852, and went back to Berdyansk in 1856. He served as "the founder and for many years the representative of the Prussian and Mecklenburg Consulate" at Berdyansk. In the early 1870's when the Mennonites felt their way of life threatened by the new conscription law, Jansen was a tireless leader in the move of immigration to America, and was consequently banished from Russia on May 26, 1873. After visiting friends in Prussia and Quakers in England, he with his family arrived at Berlin (now Kitchener), Ont., on Aug. 13, 1873. They moved to Mount Pleasant, Iowa, in 1874, and then to their permanent home in Beatrice, Neb., in 1876. Here they joined the church founded by immigrants from Prussia under Elder Andreas.

In the United States Cornelius Jansen and his son Peter continued their work in behalf of the brotherhood by petitioning the United States government for permission to settle the Russian Mennonites in compact groups and by helping the immigrants find new homes. He also influenced his Quaker friends to give financial aid to the poorer settlers. He was also an active crusader for temperance both in Europe and America. His published works (pamphlets) were: *Sammlung von Notizen über Amerika* (Danzig, 1872), *Gedanken englischer und deutscher Friedensfreunde, Gedanken über die Pflichten der Christen, Gedanken über den indirekten Militärdienst, Ausschluss der American Paper als gegen Krieg zeugend, Gedanken über Religionsfreiheit.* All were published at the author's expense by the printer Paul Thieme at Danzig, the first in April 1872, the others in August 1872. In 1873 appeared *Adressen an die Christenheit,* Edwin Groening, printer. Pamphlets three and four were also translated into English.

Cornelius Jansen died on Dec. 14, 1894, at his home in Beatrice and was buried in the near-by Mennonite cemetery. Some 112 letters and telegrams received by the family at this time indicated what he meant to his neighbors, friends, and the Mennonites whom he had helped. Through his deep convictions he became the Moses who led his people from Prussia and Russia to the "promised land" and inaugurated a migration movement to North America in magnitude far beyond his anticipation.   G.R.G.

Cornelius Jansen Collection (Bethel College Historical Library); Gustav E. Reimer and G. R. Gaeddert, *Exiled by the Czar; Cornelius Jansen and the Great Mennonite Migration 1874* (Newton, 1956); *Memoirs of Peter Jansen* (Beatrice, 1921); C. H. Smith, *The Coming of the Russian Mennonites* (Berne, 1927); C. Krahn, ed., *From the Steppes to the Prairies* (Newton, 1949); Georg Leibbrandt, "Emigration of the German Mennonites from Russia to the United States and Canada in 1873-1880," *MQR* VI (October 1932) 205-26, and VII (January 1933) 5-41.

Jansen (Jantzen), **Hans** (b. 1690), preacher of the Mennonite church at Dannenberg (*q.v.*) in Prussian Lithuania, in August 1732 because of persecution moved to the Netherlands with a number of Mennonites. They were enabled (11 families) by the Dutch Mennonite Committee of Foreign Needs (*q.v.*) to settle on farming land at Wageningen, Dutch province of Gelderland. Here Jansen, also a farmer, became the preacher. In the next year his son Christian also moved from Prussia to Wageningen. Hans Jansen, like many of his members, dissatisfied with the quality of his land, moved to the island of Walcheren, province of Zeeland, in February 1735, where also a number of Prussian Mennonites had been settled by the committee. He then settled at Oostkapele, and stayed there until 1744. At this time most of the colonists, both at Wageningen and at Walcheren, had returned either to Königsberg or Danzig, conditions having improved in Prussia. Hans Jansen also returned to Prussia (June 1744). His son Christian had returned in 1743. Of Hans Jansen, who gave the Dutch Committee much trouble by his stubbornness and his slanderous letters, a large number of which are still found in the Amsterdam archives, nothing further is known after he left the Netherlands. vdZ.

Inv. Arch. Amst. I, Nos. 1924-73 *passim,* 2074, 2110, 2213, 2226, 2228 f., 2233 f., 2241; *DB* 1905, 122-58; 1906, 94, 98, 116-38.

Jansen (Jansz, Janse), **Jacob:** see **Job Janze.**

Jans(en), Michiel, who played a part in the Flemish-Frisian schism 1566: see **Michiel Jans(en).**

Jansen, Peter, a son of Cornelius (*q.v.*) and Helena (von Riesen) Jansen, was born in Berdyansk, South Russia, on March 21, 1852, died on June 6, 1923. In 1873 he emigrated to America, settling in 1876 on a ranch near Jansen (*q.v.*), Neb., a town named in his honor. In 1909 he sold the ranch and retired to Beatrice, Neb. He married Gertrude Penner on May 4, 1877, and had seven children: Helen, John, Anna, Katherine, Gertrude, Cornelius, and Margaret. Soon after his arrival in America he became a representative of the railroad companies in the midwest. He was a pioneer, farmer, rancher, politician, diplomat, and traveler. He and his father were instrumental in bringing many Mennonites from South Russia to Nebraska, had an interview with President Grant and General Custer in 1874 regarding the settlement of Mennonites in the West, and took an active part in the early development of the state. He started one of the first large-scale sheep farms in Nebraska, feeding 15,000 to 25,000 sheep a year; he founded the town of Jansen and organized the Jansen Bank, which has operated continuously since 1887. In 1884 he was chosen as alternate delegate to the Republican National Convention; in 1888 he was Justice of the Peace in Jefferson County; in 1896 was delegate at large to the Republican National Convention; in 1898 elected to the Nebraska State Legislature representing the 34th district; in 1899 named by President McKinley as U.S. Commissioner to the Paris Exposition; in 1901 represented Nebraska at McKinley's funeral; in 1904 represented Nebraska at the Louisiana Purchase Exposition in St. Louis; and, in 1910 was elected to the Nebraska State Senate. He was urged to run for governor, but declined because of (in his own words) "my pronounced opposition to war and all that is military."

Although he became prominent in local, state, and national affairs he always remained a friend to people in the common walks of life and was a member of the Mennonite Church until his death. He was listed in *Who's Who in America* in 1913, and in 1921 published an autobiography entitled *Memoirs of Peter Jansen.*   D.P.M.

Memoirs of Peter Jansen. A Record of a Busy Life (an autobiography, Beatrice, 1921); Cornelius J. Claassen, "Peter Jansen—Pioneer, Leader and Philanthropist," *Menn. Life* II (October 1947) 41-43; G. E. Reimer and G. R. Gaeddert, *Exiled by the Czar; Cornelius Jansen and the Great Mennonite Migration, 1874* (Newton, 1956); D. Paul Miller, "An Analysis of Community Adjustment: A Case Study of Jansen, Nebraska" (Ph.D. thesis, Nebraska, 1953); *ML* II, 391.

Jansen, Reinier, a Quaker of Sneek, Netherlands, a lace worker, emigrated to America after 1700, and founded a printing house at Germantown, Pa. He was not a Mennonite, as has been asserted. vdZ.

DB 1884, 76; W. I. Hull, *William Penn and the Dutch Quaker Migration to Pennsylvania* (Swarthmore, 1935) 108-16.

Jansen, Wiger, author of the Dutch Mennonite hymnbook, *De geestelijke Goudschaale* (*q.v.*) (Leeuwarden, 1751).   vdZ.

Janson, Abraham (1754-1823), the son of Gerhard Janson, was an outstanding Mennonite farmer, living at Harxheim, Palatinate, Germany. On June 17,

1782, he presented a vigorous petition to the University of Heidelberg for a reduction of his protection fee from 12 fl. to 6 fl. annually, threatening that he might be compelled to change his place of residence, and join his relatives at Crefeld, Neuwied, or Monsheim, "where the Mennonites are less burdened," especially since the university was also greatly benefited by his efficient farming. The petition was granted, and extended to the other Mennonite subjects of the university in the Zellertal. A formal statement by the university issued on April 11, 1785, gives him great praise and compares him to David Möllinger (q.v.) of Monsheim.

With his father Gerhard Janson (1702-61), who had leased half the Geispitz estate in Harxheim, Abraham Janson laid the foundation for the prosperity of the Janson families in Harxheim, Dirmstein, and Bockenheim (Palatinate). During the French occupation he served ably as mayor of the three towns, Harxheim, Zell, and Niefernheim. (*ML* II, 391.)   NEFF.

Janson, Jean (1823-96), grandson of Abraham Janson (q.v.), was a farmer in Harxheim, and was for nearly 25 years a member of the Palatine legislature at Speyer and 1881-86 a delegate to the Reichstag. His service to the cause of agriculture was recognized by Bismarck in a letter dated Jan. 18, 1879 (found in *ML* II, 392). Jean Janson was the possessor of the Bavarian Order of St. Michael, second class.   NEFF.

Jansoon, Claes, tot Haserswoude, obviously a preacher of the (former) Mennonite Flemish congregation of Hazerswoude, Dutch province of South Holland, published *Een cleyn Tractaetgen van den val Adam,* followed by two hymns (n.p., 1625), and *Een Belijdenisse des Gheloofs, dat door de Liefde werckt* (n.p., 1627). This book is a devotional work in which are included a number of hymns, apparently composed by the author himself.   VDZ.

Janssen, Dirk, after 1719 a Mennonite elder of the Old Flemish congregation (called *Klerkschen* or *Huiskopers*) at Danzig, West Prussia, a brother of Elder Anthony Janssen (d. 1725), who in 1725, after the death of the Dutch Elder Adriaan van Gammeren, at the request of the Danzig Old Flemish congregations of Amsterdam and Rotterdam, moved with his family from Danzig to Amsterdam, where he served as an elder September 1725-November 1, 1733. Then he returned to Danzig, serving there until his death in 1750.   VDZ.

H. G. Mannhardt, *Die Danziger Mennoniten-Gemeinde* (Danzig, 1919) 89 f.

Jans(z), Arent, b. May 28, 1610, at Groningen, d. there Oct. 6, 1679, a Dutch Mennonite elder of the Groningen Old Flemish Mennonites, serving in his home town from about 1636 until his death. He was a rather wealthy merchant and in 1636 was one of the founders of the Groningen Old Flemish congregation, then usually called *Arent Jansgemeente.* In 1677 he bought a plot behind his house "de Block" in the Boteringestraat, on which a meetinghouse was built for the congregation, which still stands (rebuilt in 1813-15); in 1678 he contributed

liberally for this building. In 1664 at his expense a new edition of *Veelderhande Liedekens* was printed by I. van Wesbusch at Haarlem. This was used as a hymnbook in the Arent Jans congregation. Arent was married to Albertje Jans Mabé; he was a son of Jan Arents in't Block, and a grandson of Arent Cornelis, a Catholic priest who had left the Catholic Church about 1580 to join the Mennonites. Both Arent Jansz's father Jan Arents and his father-in-law Jan Jansz Mabé of Groningen were preachers or deacons in the Flemish congregation, and had attended the debate held at Middelstum (q.v.) in 1628 on the question whether the Flemish congregation should unite with the other Mennonites. Arent Jansz's daughter, Albertje Arends Blok, was married to Willem Hesselink (1648-1720), a preacher of the Groningen Old Flemish Mennonites at Enkhuizen and later at Groningen.   VDZ.

H. Dassel Sr., *Menno's Volk in Groningen* (Groningen, n.d.) 24 ff., 33; *Catalogus Amst.*, 267; *Groningsche Volksalmanak* 1921, 103.

Jansz, Cornelis, author of *Nootwendigh bewijs, dat sij tegen die waerheit handelen, alle die daer leeren datter niemandt eenich Doopsel ofte sacramentelijck teecken der ghenaden Christi gebruycken ofte bedienen mach, tenzij dat hij eerst bij haer in hare Ghemeynten daertoe vercoren ende verordineert is* (n.p., 1603, which was an answer and a refutation of a book by C. G., entitled *Een grondich bewijs uyt der Goddelycken Schriftueren . . .* , n.p., n.d.). In this remarkable book Jansz defends the opinion that every brother of the church is authorized to administer baptism and communion. About the author, who belonged to a tolerant branch of Mennonitism, either Frisian, High German, or Waterlander, no further information was available. He may be identical with Cornelis Jansz (*Inv. Arch. Amst.* I, No. 483), to whom Lubbert Gerritsz (q.v.) wrote a letter in 1592 promoting the union of Waterlanders with the High Germans and the Frisians. Obviously the Cornelis Jansz (*Inv. Arch. Amst.* I, Nos. 576, 590) who was in 1630 an elder in the Dutch province of Groningen is not the same person.   VDZ.

Jansz, Geleyn (d. about 1668), a Mennonite printer and bookseller at Vlissingen, Dutch province of Zeeland, who, like his son Jan Geleynsz, published a number of Mennonite books, including *'t Nieuw Geestelijck Kruyt-Hof,* 1665, a hymnbook, and in 1666, *Handelinge* (q.v.) *der Ver-eenigde Vlaemse en Duytse Doopsghesinde Gemeynten gehouden tot Haerlem in 1649,* and also in 1666, *Het Concept van Ceulen, De Belijdenis des Geloofs* by Outerman, and *Eenige Aanteyckeningen uyt de Ernstige Aenporringhe tot de Gemeynschap der Heyligen.* VDZ.

Jansz, Hero, preacher of the Old Flemish Mennonite congregation of Amsterdam, serving 1610-(?), who as appears from L. de Buyser's (q.v.) *Verklaringe van den droevigen handel . . .* (Amsterdam, 1616), was censured by the congregation because of his idea that the Flemish branch was not the only true church of Christ. After confession before the congregation he was maintained as a preacher. De Buyser, who was not satisfied with the decision and wanted Jansz to be excommunicated, indicates that Jansz was a spiritualist, who laid more stress upon the "inner word" than upon the Scriptures. (*DB* 1896, 99-107.)   vpZ.

Jansz, Klaas, a Dutch preacher: see **Man, Klaes Jansz.**

Jansz, Mees (Meys), a Dutch Mennonite elder, serving in the 17th century in the Flemish congregation of Huisduinen (*q.v.*), Holland. He was one of the most conservative leaders of the Flemish Mennonites, later of the Zonists (*q.v.*). In June 1660 he attended a Flemish conference at Leiden (see **Leidsche Synode**), where he represented the Zaandam congregation, having in April of that year been in Hamburg, Germany, where he performed baptism and probably ordained the preachers Dr. Werner Jansz Colombier and Gerrit Roosen (*q.v.*). Particulars about his life were not available.   vpZ.
Verhaal van't gene verhandelt ende besloten is in de By-eenkomste tot Leyden (Amsterdam, 1661) 7, 8, 11, 21, 23, 33; B. C. Roosen, *Gesch. der Menn.-Gemeinde Hamburg* I (Hamburg, 1886) 46, 60; *Inv. Arch. Amst.* II, 1310-12.

Jansz, Pieter, a Dutch elder and author: see **Twisck, Pieter Jansz.**

Jansz, Pieter, a Dutch Flemish Mennonite elder of Leiden and Amsterdam: see **Mo(o)yer, Pieter Jansz.**

Jansz, Pieter, in the 17th century an elder of the Waterlander congregation of Wormerveer, Dutch province of North Holland, who published a new edition of Hans de Ries' Confession of Faith, which he revised and provided with a large number of Scripture texts. There are three editions of Pieter Jansz's edition, of 1654, 1660, and 1686, all published at Krommenie (*Biogr. Wb.* IV, 526 f.). The Pieter Jansz who was about the same time a Waterlander Mennonite elder at Harlingen, Friesland (*DB* 1901, 74, 77), was apparently not the same person as Pieter Jansz of Wormerveer.   vpZ.

Jansz, Pieter, "van den Busch" (a hamlet near Krommenie), from 1665 a preacher and from 1675 until his death an elder of the Frisian Mennonite congregation of Wormerveer, Dutch province of North Holland (he was moderator of the North Holland Frisian Conference in 1698), proprietor of a paper mill, traveled to Friedrichstadt (*q.v.*) in Holstein, Germany, on business and also served the congregation there, which had no minister, with preaching, baptism, and communion. He died on this trip at Friedrichstadt in 1698.   vpZ.
N.N.B.Wb. IX, 455; J. Aten, *De Doopsgez. Krommenieër Zeildoekfabrikeursfamilie Kuyper* (n.p., n.d. 1953) 25 f.

Jansz, Pieter (1820-1904), the first missionary of the Dutch Mennonite Missionary Association at Amsterdam, was born Sept. 25, 1820, in Holland, taught at Delft until 1851, when he was sent to the mission in Java (May 1851). At first he took a position as tutor on the estate of an Armenian, and there carried on evangelization; in 1854 he settled in Japara. After two and one-half years of work he baptized the first five natives. Slowly with great difficulty the work expanded. The mission stations Kedung-Pendjalin (*q.v.*) and Bondo were opened. In 1875

he wrote a booklet, *Landontginning en Evangelisatie op Java,* in which he suggested that Christian settlements be established, because young Christians living among Mohammedans were always in danger of losing their Christian principles, for in Mohammedan villages religious and social life are closely interwoven. The Dutch Missionary Association, however, did not at this time accept this proposal.

In 1881 Jansz resigned from the work on account of ill health, giving it over to his son P. A. Jansz (*q.v.*), and entered the employment of the London Bible Society; in 1888 he published the New Testament in Javanese, and in 1892 the Old Testament. In 1895 he published the second edition of the whole Bible, as well as several Javanese readers and a very valuable Javanese dictionary in two volumes, with the titles *Practisch Nederlandsch-Javaansch Woordenboek* and *Practisch Javaansch-Nederlandsch Woordenboek,* both published at The Hague. These literary efforts won him the distinction of the Order of the Knight of the Dutch Lion. The last years of his life (1902-4) he spent at Kaju-Apu (*q.v.*), at the home of his son-in-law, missionary Johann Fast, where he died June 6, 1904.   NEFF.
Biogr. Wb. IV, 527-29; *Uit Verleden en Heden der Doopsgezinde Zending* (n.p., 1947) 12-18; *DB* 1885, 59, 61-63; 1886, 73, 82, 85; 1887, 41 f.; 1891, 31; 1892, 37, 39, 41 f.; 1904, 236 f.; *ML* II, 392.

Jansz, Pieter Anton (1853-1943), a Dutch Mennonite missionary in Indonesia, son of Pieter Jansz (*q.v.*), was born May 29, 1853, in 1881 took over his father's work and carried out the idea his father had expressed in his booklet in 1874; namely, to form a settlement and integrate all activities such as instruction, clearing of the land, school, evangelization, community and church, in founding the mission colony Margaredjo (*q.v.*). The colony prospered, and in 1936, when P. A. Jansz resigned, the congregation numbered nearly 800 members. The school has also been blessed in its work, especially in training native teachers. After his resignation he left his beloved Margaredjo and lived in Ungaren, giving his full time to the revision of the Javanese Bible. He died in January 1943 during the Japanese occupation of Java.   NEFF.
"Levensbericht van den Zendeling P. A. Jansz," in *De Kleine Medearbeider,* 1910; *Uit Verleden en Heden der Doopsgezinde Zending* (n.p., 1947) 18 f., 35 f.; several *Jaarverslagen* (annual reports) of the Dutch Mission Association; *DB* 1892, 42-45; *ML* II, 392.

Jantz, Peter, was born at Jeziorka, Schwetz (at that time German; now Polish), June 3, 1744, and died Sept. 2, 1810. His parents were among the original settlers of Franzthal, Neumark, near Driesen. In 1765 he married Ancke Wedel. Jantz served the Przechovka Flemish Mennonite Church and the Brenkenhoffswalde Mennonite Church 48 years as minister and the latter as elder for a period of 34 years. He was instrumental in obtaining the land and the money to build the church in 1778, having appealed to the Mennonites in Holland for aid (see **Alexanderwohl** Mennonite Church). (*Inv. Arch. Amst.* II, 2, No. 853.)   JA.A.D.

Jantzen, Hermann, elder of the Flemish congregation at Elbing, published a book in 1741 with the title, *Konfession oder kurzer Glaubensbericht, derer bekannten taufgesinnten Gemeinden in Preussen zur Erbauung der Jugend herausgegeben.* It contains 92 questions and answers. (*Menn. Bl.*, 1857, 62; *ML* II, 392.)

Janz, Heinrich Tobias, Elder of the Landskrone Mennonite Church in the Molotschna settlement, Taurida, South Russia, was born Jan. 17, 1887, at Landskrone, the son of Tobias Benjamin and Margarethe (Enns) Janz. In January 1912 he married Katharina Reimer (1893-1923) in Schönau, Zagradovka. Six children were born to them. In 1923 he married Käthe Ediger, to whom were born three children. Janz was educated in the Zentralschule at Gnadenfeld and the normal school at Halbstadt, and devotedly served his home village as a teacher from 1913 to 1922, when the Soviet government made this work impossible. Janz was a member of the Margenau-Landskrone Mennonite congregation. He was chosen as minister in 1922, and as elder in 1926. Janz was a clear thinker, an exceptional teacher, and a good leader. For a time he served on the executive committee of the Association of Citizens of Dutch Extraction (*Verein Bürger holländischer Herkunft*). His work as elder was fruitful, particularly during the periods of the great famine, when revivals were taking place in the congregations. But this activity was unfortunately of short duration. Janz performed his last baptism in 1931. He had baptized 56 young people. In 1932 he was banished with his family from the village; two years later he was compelled to flee to Caucasia, and spent the rest of his life homeless. In 1935 he was arrested there and after a long trial sentenced to death as a political criminal. For 99 days he awaited his execution in the death cell. Then came pardon and a review of his case. His son Heinrich was present when Janz and other Mennonite preachers were led out. Janz, though only a shadow of his former self, was the only one to defend his faith and religious work. He was then sentenced to ten years of hard labor in Siberia. The last word received from him came in 1940, saying that he was partially paralyzed by a cerebral hemorrhage and was facing death by starvation in a camp in the North. The date of his death is not known.   J.J.Th.

Janzen (Jantzen, Janssen, Jansson, Jansen, Johnson, Jansz, Janz, Jantz, Jans), one of the most widespread Mennonite family names of Dutch-Prussian background, derived from Jan (Johann, John) a given name, to which is added "zon" (zen, sen, etc.), the combination meaning "son of John." The name was very common among the Dutch Mennonites and found its way into the congregations bordering the Netherlands such as Crefeld, Gronau, and East Friesland; also in Schleswig-Holstein and Prussia, where it was represented in the congregations of Elbing, Königsberg, Tiegenhagen, Ladekopp, Rosenort, Fürstenwerder, Heubuden, Tiensdorf, Orloffer-felde, Schönsee, Jeziorka, Deutsch-Kazun, etc. The name appears first on record in Danzig in 1568. From Prussia it was transplanted to Russia and later to North America, where it is found in most of the settlements started after 1874, and to South America.

A branch of this name was transplanted from the Lower Rhine to Pennsylvania, where it was changed into Johnson. For outstanding leaders of the name check the various forms of the name listed in the *Mennonite Encyclopedia, Who's Who Among the Mennonites* (1943), and the ministerial lists of Mennonite yearbooks. (Reimer, *Familiennamen,* 111.)
                      C.K.

Janzen, Heinrich (b. 1869), a teacher of the deaf at Tiege, South Russia, a son of Johann Janzen, the minister of the Gnadenfeld Mennonite Church, and son-in-law of P. M. Friesen (*q.v.*), the Mennonite historiographer, b. Sept. 11, 1869, at Gnadenfeld. In the spring of 1892 he passed the elementary teachers' examination at Melitopol. That winter he spent in Frankfurt, Germany, as an apprentice to Johann Vatter, the most renowned teacher of the deaf and director of the Frankfurt school for the deaf. In the fall of 1893 he was employed by the school for the deaf at Tiege, where he remained until 1924. Meanwhile he continued his own education, especially in the handicrafts, such as work in wood, metal, and basket weaving, so that in addition to the regular school subjects his 23 years of pedagogical service included training his pupils in practical arts. Incorruptible conscientiousness in carrying out his duties, persistence in articulation, and skill in preparing visual materials so vital in the education of the deaf, and his long experience made him an invaluable asset. Later, after he had retired from active school life because of his health, he kept up close connections with the institution, serving as corresponding secretary, treasurer, bookkeeper, teacher, and promoter of the school. (*ML* II, 392.)   H.J.

Janzen, Heinrich Johann (1844-1904), a teacher and minister of the Gnadenfeld Church (Molotschna), born at Ladekopp (Molotschna), Jan. 25, 1844. He was employed as a teacher at a small school on an estate at Hochfeld. In 1865 he took over a school with 175 pupils at Waldheim, married Maria Dirks, a daughter of Heinrich Dirks (*q.v.*), a missionary in Sumatra. For reasons of health he resigned his position early in 1868. He was one of the first Mennonite teachers to pass the city teachers' examination, and he learned surveying. He conducted the Gnadenfeld village school 1880-84. In 1880 he was ordained as a minister by the Gnadenfeld church. He remained an active preacher here to the end of his life, though he was absent from the congregation for extended periods: 1884-91 he served as preacher at the Vladimirov forestry camp, and 1891-93 as housefather of the Tiege school for the deaf. He died in November 1904.

As an adviser he was much sought after. He was interested in science and art; his sketches and an oil painting have some artistic merit. His literary efforts include these extant works: detailed (fragmentary) autobiography, collected sermons, devotional material, poems, hymns, and a conversion story, *Ein Gnadenwunder* (published by P. Neufeld, Halbstadt). (*ML* II, 393.)   H.J.

Janzen, Jacob H. (1878-1950), a Mennonite teacher, preacher, elder, and author, a man of rare gifts and rich understanding, and influential in the General

Conference. He was born on March 19, 1878, in Steinbach, South Russia, and died on Feb. 16, 1950, at Waterloo, Ont. He was educated in the Zentralschule at Gnadenfeld, and by industrious private study he acquired a teachers' certificate in Melitopol and Kharkov; and in 1913-14 he studied philosophy and natural sciences at the universities of Jena and Greifswald in Germany. He served in Russia first as a village schoolteacher; in 1908-21 he was head teacher of the Girls' School at Tiege, Molotschna. He was ordained to the ministry on Nov. 19, 1906, at Gnadenfeld. Because he was a minister he was compelled by the Red government to give up his teaching position in 1921. From that time until his emigration he served the congregations with preaching and lecturing, and also represented the interests of the Mennonite Church to the government as a member of the *KfK* (*q.v.*). In the fall of 1924 he arrived in Canada and settled in Waterloo, Ont., where he was ordained as elder on Feb. 14, 1926, and where he lived until his death with the exception of 1935-37, when he was the head of the Girls' Home in Vancouver and elder of the United Mennonite Church in British Columbia. In Ontario he did a great work in gathering and organizing the new immigrants from Russia in 1924 and the following years into congregations, especially in the Kitchener-Waterloo area. In addition he did much work as a traveling evangelist and as a writer. At least 38 published writings have come from his pen. Bethel College, where he lectured repeatedly, awarded him a doctor's degree in 1944 in recognition of his services for the Mennonite brotherhood. Particulars about his life and work, as well as a list of his writings, are found in *Mennonite Life* (July 1951) and also in *Der Bote* (April 12, 1950). He was a pioneer Mennonite writer, his articles and short stories appearing in many European and American Mennonite papers and yearbooks. (The J. H. Janzen collection is located in BeCL.)   N.N.D.

Janzen, Jakob W., leading minister of Sergeyevka-Alexandertal Mennonite Brethren Church of the Fürstenland Mennonite settlement in Russia. Janzen was ordained to the ministry in 1892 and had had charge of the congregational church records since 1889. The statistics of 1905 (H. Dirks) and the address book of Mennonite ministers (D. H. Epp) of 1913 list him as a minister of this congregation. Nothing is known about his later activities. (Friesen, *Brüderschaft,* 239, 404, 449.)   C.K.

Janzen, Johannes Heinrich (1868-1917), a teacher at the Ohrloff Zentralschule in the Molotschna Mennonite settlement of South Russia and minister of the Gnadenfeld Mennonite Church, b. Jan. 6, 1868, at Waldheim (Molotschna), the eldest son of Heinrich Johann Janzen (*q.v.*). After studying for three years at the normal school in Theodosia (Crimea), he taught at the Ohrloff Zentralschule until his death in 1917, a period of 28 years. His pedagogical methods led away from dry teaching in the direction of real life situations, and his literary work, *Das goldene Zeitalter der Zukunft,* clearly shows his leaning toward technical schools. In religious matters he was a doubting seeker and a rationalist

until 1906, when he was converted to a somewhat pietistic view. From that time on he was an active and fruitful worker in the Mennonite churches, enjoying unusual popularity and respect.

Like his father, he was an amateur artist; although his work is imperfect in technique it reveals a deep love and understanding for the Molotschna landscape. His sketches, not yet published, form a valuable contribution to the study of the Russian Mennonite milieu. Some have found their way to Canada.

His literary works are for the most part also unpublished. Among them are children's stories like "Das Märchen vom Weihnachtsmann," "Die Geschichte van Miez, Mauz, Murr, und Hinz," lyric poems and prose, pedagogical and philosophical essays and articles. In addition, a few stories have been published in periodical literature—"Der David," and "Das Falkennest." He also kept a diary.   H.J.

H. Goerz, *Die Molotschnaer Ansiedlung* (Steinbach, 1950); *ML* II, 393.

Janzen, Peter (1857-1918), elder of the Memrik Mennonite Church, was born in the village of Rudnerweide in the Molotschna settlement in South Russia, the son of Wilhelm Janzen and Agnes Siebert. He was the second child in the family and had two brothers and two sisters. Peter Janzen married Margaretha Isaak and became the father of three sons and five daughters.

In 1885, when the Memrik Mennonite settlement was founded in the province of Ekaterinoslav, Peter Janzen was one of the settlers, locating in the village of Michailovka. In August 1885 Janzen was one of four preachers elected by the settlers, and two years later he was chosen as leading minister of the Memrik Mennonite Church. On June 28, 1888, Peter Janzen was ordained as elder by Elder Goerz. His oldest son Peter became a preacher in the Memrik church in the later 1920's but he emigrated to Mexico.

Peter Janzen served his church faithfully and was loved and respected by his congregation until his death by typhoid fever on Nov. 17, 1918. Because of the civil war raging in Russia, the funeral had to be conducted under great difficulty in the school building of his home village Michailovka, interment taking place in the cemetery of the same village.   J.A.D.

Japan. Japan proper is composed of an archipelago of four main islands and hundreds of smaller ones. Honshu, the largest and centrally located, is also culturally and economically the center of the country. Tokyo, ranking third in world population, is located centrally in this island, and is the very heart of Japan. To the south of Honshu lie the larger island of Kyushu and the smaller Shikoku. These two islands and the southern two thirds of Honshu are caressed by the warm Kuroshio currents from the south, making these areas subtropical in climate. Intense tropical typhoons sweep up from the south and lash these areas in late summer and early fall, often bringing intense suffering and destruction from strong winds, floods, and tidal waves. Hokkaido lies

MENNONITE MISSIONS IN
JAPAN

MENNONITE CHURCH (MC)
1. Nakashibetsu
2. Kushiro
3. Hombetsu
4. Kamishihoro
5. Obihiro
6. Taiki
7. Tokyo

MENNONITE BRETHREN CHURCH (MB)
8. Osaka (3 centers)

GENERAL CONFERENCE MENNONITE CHURCH (GCM)
9. Kobe
10. Hyuga
11. Miyakonojo
12. Miyazaki
13. Kobayashi-shi
14. Nichinan-shi

Scale of Miles

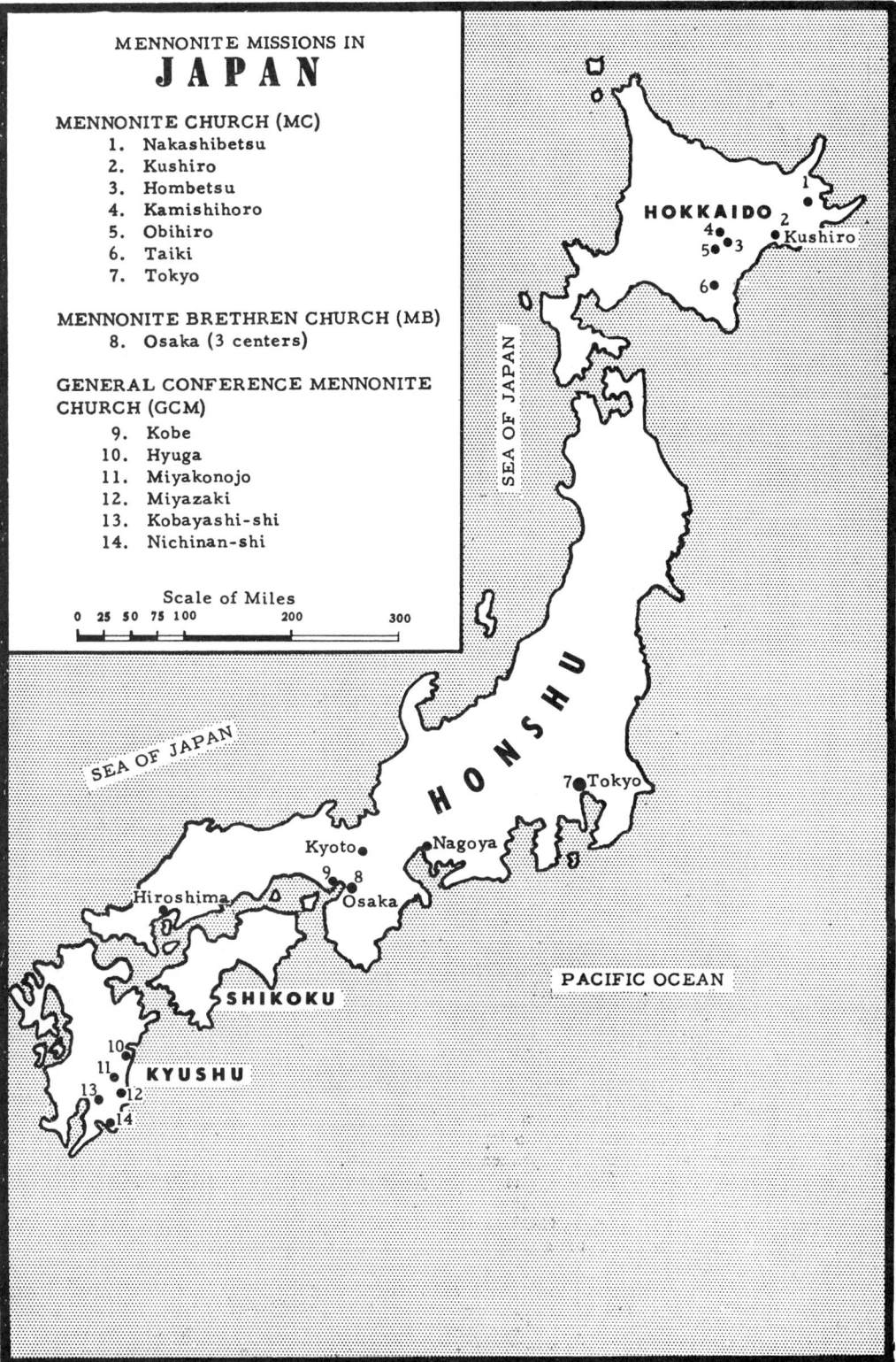

0 25 50 75 100   200   300

SEA OF JAPAN

HOKKAIDO

Kushiro

HONSHU

SEA OF JAPAN

Kyoto

Nagoya

Tokyo

Hiroshima

Osaka

PACIFIC OCEAN

SHIKOKU

KYUSHU

far to the north, separated from the main island by the Tsugatu Straits. Hokkaido's shores are swept by the chill currents originating in the Arctic, and its prevailing winds are northwesterly, sweeping down across the vast Siberian and North Manchurian plains, so that climate in Japan varies more than her 1300 miles from north to south would indicate.

Into this archipelago, comprising only 147,707 square miles (a little less than the state of California) and lying just off the coast of the Asiatic mainland, are crowded over 80 million people. Since farming is still the main occupation, and since the country is extremely mountainous, only 17 per cent of the country being arable, farm land is at a premium and farms are of necessity small, varying from ¾ of an acre in the south to as high as 40 acres in the newly settled northern island of Hokkaido. Though rich in gold, copper, and sulphur, Japan lacks the basic natural resources for modern heavy industry, and so finds her economic life dependent largely on the often not too considerate whims of the western world.

Japanese history loses itself in old, prehistorical legend. Jimmu Tenno, the semihistorical founder and first emperor of the Japanese nation, supposedly lived about 600 B.C. He is said to have been a direct descendant of the sun-goddess, and the direct ancestor of a long line of two and one-half centuries of emperors, culminating in the present Emperor Hirohito. The Japanese are proud of this old history, and much of the religio-patriotic fervor that made possible the recent and terrible Pacific conflict grew out of this semi-mythology.

The Mennonite witness to this ancient land is not old. Though modern Protestant missions in Japan will soon be 100 years old, the Mennonite participation numbers only seven summers. After an exploratory trip by J. N. Byler, the MCC sent its first workers, Henry and Lydia Thielman, to Japan in April of 1949. With the help of Ruth and Rhoda Ressler, who arrived later in the same summer, a relief and rehabilitation work was established in the completely devastated Konohana-ku section of the city of Osaka. In December of the same year the Mennonite Board of Missions and Charities (MC) sent two missionary families to Japan, the Carl Becks and the Ralph Buckwalters. A year later, in August 1950, the Mennonite Brethren Church sent their first missionary, Miss Ruth Wiens. Later that same winter the General Conference Mennonite Church's first representative, Miss Lenore Friesen, arrived also to begin language study. In the summer of 1953 the Brethren in Christ Church sent their pioneer couple, Peter and Mary Willems, to Japan.

These four groups have worked independently, yet with a very close sense of fellowship and cooperation. The M.C. missionaries went to the northernmost, neglected island of Hokkaido, G.C.M. missionaries to the southernmost tip of the southern island of Kyushu, the Brethren in Christ to the Yamaguchi prefecture in the southwestern part of the main island of Honshu, and the M.B. group stayed in and around the city of Osaka, where they have absorbed the plant and program of MCC in that city. The MCC has moved to Tokyo, where it hopes to become more active in a direct peace witness and in literature production, and where it has the Norman Wingerts and the Melvin Gingerichs as workers.

American personnel now in Japan numbers as follows: M.C. 17, G.C.M. 18, M.B. 12, and Brethren in Christ 2. A Mennonite church has arisen from the native soil of Japan which now numbers approximately 250 active members. Though many of these are young in years and all of them are young in Christian experience and come out of a religious culture foreign to Christianity, many of them seem willing and anxious to give themselves to the work of the church. Almost the entire burden of the Sunday schools is borne by the national church. Home and hospital visitation, street evangelism, Bible study, summer Bible camp, winter Bible school, village tent evangelism, personal witnessing, and a variety of other activities depend largely on this young church for personnel and support. A number of young men from the various missions are now away in Bible schools and seminaries in preparation for giving a fuller ministry to their local congregations.   C.C.B.

Japara, a district of the Indonesian island of Java, formerly the center of the Dutch Mennonite missions, since 1940 an independent congregation (membership in 1953, 27 baptized, 42 children): see **Java.**   vdZ.

Jaques Mesdagh, an Anabaptist martyr: see **Jacob Mesdag.**

Jasper de Schoenmaker (shoemaker), official name Gaspard Deken or de Decke, an Anabaptist martyr, was burned at the stake at Hondschoote (q.v.) in Flanders, Belgium, on April 4, 1562. Six other persons suffered martyrdom with him. Jasper was born at Hasebroeck (French Flanders). (*Mart. Mir.* D 298, E 663; *Bibliographie* II, No. 688; *ML* II, 394.)
                                          NEFF, vdZ.

Jasper de Taschringmaker (official name Jaspar Hermansz), an Anabaptist martyr burned at the stake at Antwerp, Belgium, on June 22, 1569. He was living at Borgerhout near Antwerp and was a *weetdoener* of the congregation; i.e., he had to announce the place and time of the meetings. His property was confiscated and sold, realizing a rather considerable amount. His wife Maeyken Janssens van der Goes (q.v.) and his youthful daughter Nelleken Jaspers (q.v.) both died as martyrs.
                                                        vdZ.

Mart. Mir. D 406, E 758; *Antw. Arch.-Blad* XII, 365, 370, 385, 402, 405, 477; XIV, 66 f., No. 730; *ML* II, 394.

Jasper Church of God in Christ Mennonite Church, now extinct, located about four miles east of Jasper, Mo., was organized in 1883 with about 20 members when Elder John Holdeman and Preacher Frank Seidner moved to that place from New Pittsburg, Ohio. During its time of about 15 years, services were held in the homes and in the Mayflower school. The racial background of the members was Pennsylvania German. John Holdeman was the elder, and later Amos Seidner was ordained to the ministry. About 1898 John Holdeman moved to

JATER—JAVA

Moundridge, Kan. Nearly all the members soon afterward moved to other organized congregations.

A.L.Y.

Jater, an Anabaptist martyr, was burned at the stake on Aug. 9, 1550, at Arnhem, Dutch province of Gelderland. In the sentence this martyr is called Jater Willem Libresdochter, wife of Goirt Raeymakers. She was 40 years of age. From about 1529 to 1547 she had lived at Maastricht, Dutch province of Limburg. She had been baptized about 1542 at Maastricht by Lenart (Lenaert van IJsenbroeck, *q.v.*). One of the principal charges against her was that she possessed a book written by Menno Simons. She frankly confessed her faith and even tried to win over the judges to her principles. She stated that true Christians are obliged to live according to "the way and doctrines of the apostles"; they do not defend their faith with worldly weapons, and in the congregation they aid one another and do not let any starve. Jater was arrested by the bailiff of Montfort at Illikhoven (*q.v.*) in the duchy of Upper-Gelre, where she had been living for three years, and from where she was brought to Arnhem.

vDZ.

Vos, *Menno Simons* (Leiden, 1914) 86, 242; W. Bax, *Het Protestantisme in het bisdom Luik* I (The Hague, 1937) 328-30; the trial and sentence are published in *Nederl. Archief v. Kerkgeschiedenis* X (The Hague, 1913) 261-63, 268; *ML* II, 394.

Jaussling (Jaussle, Jausel), **Ulrich** (1573-1621), was the successor of Sebastian Dieterich (*q.v.*), as the leader of the total Hutterite community in Moravia and Hungary. Concerning Jaussling's origin nothing is known. Bossert surmises that he came from Grossgartach near Heilbronn, where there were several Josslin families after 1570. By trade he was a coppersmith. On March 14, 1599, he was made a preacher, on Feb. 24, 1602, an elder, and on Dec. 18, 1619, leader of the total brotherhood. As such he had by no means an easy position. At that time the Thirty Years' War was raging in the country, causing the brotherhood enormous losses by murder, plundering, and arson. Jaussling fled to Hungary with many helpless brethren. The strains and responsibilities of the care of the brotherhood apparently undermined his health. At the age of 48 he died at the Pränitsch castle in Hungary, April 8, 1621, 22 years after his first ordination and a little more than two years after becoming leader. The chronicles describe him as a God-fearing, zealous, and faithful leader, who left many good teachings to the brotherhood. His successor, Rudolf Hirzel (*q.v.*), was chosen on May 9, 1621; he was, however, not equal to the strenuous task, and was deposed a few months later.   HEGE.

Beck, *Geschichts-Bücher;* Wolkan, *Geschicht-Buch;* G. Bossert, "Wiedertäuferbischöfe aus Württemberg," *Schwäbischer Merkur,* June 19, 1920; *ML* II, 394.

Java, the second largest island of Indonesia with 50,000 square miles and approximately 40 million inhabitants, is the seat of a century-old Dutch Mennonite mission work and two organized Mennonite conferences. The island is divided into 23 districts, of which one of the smallest, Japara, lying on the north coast, is one of the most thickly populated,

and is the center of the Mennonite work on the island. After June 1898 the Mennonite mission was the only mission in this territory since the Dutch Reformed mission turned over to the Mennonite board the stations of Pati and Kaju-Apu.

The Javanese people are almost exclusively Mohammedans. Originally they were Animists, but about the time of Christ they accepted Buddhism as their national religion. In the 13th century the first Mohammedan missionaries arrived and in a short time they had overthrown the Hindu religion. Though outwardly the Javanese people accepted Mohammedanism, in their real nature they remained Animists. To this day they offer sacrifices to the spirits, whose number is reckoned at more than one thousand. The outward formality of the Mohammedan religion and its moral indifference correspond more with the Javanese character than the moral earnestness of Christianity. With their indifferent, somewhat dull character, and being given to the gross sins such as lying, stealing, and immorality, they are difficult to win for the Christian faith, which demands a more earnest, moral manner of life. The missionaries have had a hard task and have secured fruits from their labors only slowly and after much difficult and sacrificial work.

After the Mennonite Mission Society in Amsterdam decided in 1847 to establish a mission in the Dutch East Indies, the first missionary, Pieter Jansz (*q.v.*), sailed in August 1851 to Java. At first he located in Semarang, but in 1854 moved to Japara, a city which was not far from Semarang on the north coast. Jansz had earlier been prepared as a teacher and missionary by learning the Javanese and Malay languages and by studying the anthropology and culture of the Dutch East Indies. His work under the Mohammedan Javanese turned out to be very difficult. The first converts were baptized in 1854. In addition to preaching, he devoted himself to teaching the children of the natives. In 1856 a second missionary was sent out, H. C. Klinkert, who remained only a short time in Java. In 1857 Th. Doyer followed him, but died in 1861. Thereafter N. D. Schuurmans came out to the field in 1863 to work with Jansz. Schuurmans then took over the teaching work, while Jansz devoted himself to literary work, translating various writings into Javanese which were very useful in evangelization and teaching. In 1877, after 30 years of work, the church had only 39 members, and only 8 to 20 persons took part in the Sunday services. In 1875 the first stone school building was erected and five pupils of Schuurmans were at work as teachers in the neighborhood of Japara. In 1881 Jansz resigned from the mission field but remained in Java and translated the Bible into Javanese for the British and Foreign Bible Society. He died in 1904 at Kaju-Apu near Japara.

In 1878 P. A. Jansz (*q.v.*), the son of Pieter Jansz, began a new epoch of work. He had come to the Netherlands in 1867, where he secured his license as a teacher in 1871, and was appointed missionary in 1878. He inaugurated new methods of work on the mission field, basing his work on the insight that the religious and economic life of the natives was very closely related. It is almost impossible for the Javanese to be Christians within the Mohammedan cultural pattern, so Jansz combined the development of new land for agriculture with evangelization. On Aug. 26, 1881, he secured a tract of land in permanent possession (hereditary lease) for the yearly payment of 2 guilders per acre. This tract had 192 Javanese acres (one Javanese acre equals 1.9 American acres) and was later enlarged to 233 (433 U.S.) acres. The whole annual rental therefore was about 500 guilders. Jansz moved the congregation to this tract after he had established conditions which the settlers agreed to submit to. The chief requirements were the following: (1) only those who had good moral character would be accepted; (2) those who transgressed morally after acceptance would be expelled; (3) the smoking of opium as well as its ownership and sale were forbidden; (4) strong drink was also forbidden, both in use and in sale; (5) all idolatrous and superstitious practices had to be given up; (6) polygamy was forbidden, and gambling or similar practices would not be tolerated; (7) all inhabitants were obliged to attend the Sunday services faithfully, to send their children to school, and to observe Sunday as a rest day; (8) all inhabitants were to maintain their land, roads, bridges, and waterways themselves and pay regular contributions into the colony treasury; (9) the only requirement which they had to deliver to the government was a part of the rice harvest and a small annual cash payment for the land. Jansz had described these methods in a book entitled *Evangelization Through Colonization in Java* (*Landontginning en Evangelisatie op Java,* 1877). The first actual occupancy of the colony was in February 1881, which may be taken as the date of founding. The first colony (village) was given the name of Margaredjo, which means "the way to happiness." In 1901 a second colony was established with the name Margokerto, with 320 acres (608 U.S.). In 1910 a third colony was established with the name Bumiardjo, with 47 (89 U.S.) acres. And in 1925 another tract was secured with 197 (374 U.S.) acres, called Pakkies. These colonies became strong centers of Christianity in a Mohammedan land. They were the home base from which the neighboring villages could be evangelized.

Jansz devoted himself also with great consecration to teaching. When he began his work in 1878 the mission school had only 19 pupils. In 1932 the school program included a normal school, 5 intermediate schools, and 15 elementary schools, with a total of 1,264 pupils. In addition, there was established at Kudus a Chinese school with 151 pupils. A "seminary" for the training of native teachers was established at Margoredjo, which was given financial support by the government beginning in 1903, and in 1931 was designated as a normal school.

After 1878, additional missionaries were sent out to Java to work with Jansz. All of them, with the exception of a few Germans, were of Russian origin. Among them were Johann Fast who went out in 1888, Johann Hübert in 1893 (d. 1944), and Johann Klaassen in 1899 (died 1950), all from Russia. Daniel Amstutz from Switzerland served 1934-46. Hermann Schmitt and Otto Stauffer, who served in 1929-41,

and Maria Klaassen, 1929-50, were all from Germany. Schmitt and Stauffer died in 1942.

The Japara mission field was divided into four districts. (1) Kedung-Pendjalin, near Japara, was the location of the first congregation. To this district belonged the colonies of Margokerto and Pakkies. In 1932 the number of Christians in this territory was 627 adults with 649 children. (2) The second district was Margoredjo, together with Bumiardjo, with 1,203 Christians and 1,189 children in 1932. (3) The third was Kaju-Apu, a location which was taken over from the Rotterdam Reformed Missionary Society in 1899. In this district, with 159 Christians and 91 children in 1932, are also located the towns of Kudus (since 1929) and Pakkies. (4) The fourth district is Kelet, where the central hospital and the leper asylum of Donorodjo are located; it had 145 Christians and 94 children in 1932. The total of the four districts was 2,130 Christians and 2,023 children. The congregation of Margoredjo was made independent in 1928, with its own native preacher named Roebin.

A third new kind of mission work was medical missions. In 1894 a hospital was built at Margoredjo, and in 1902 another at Kedung-Pendjalin. Dr. H. Bervoets, who had been sent out in 1894 as the first missionary doctor in the service of the Dutch Missionary Society, was transferred to Java in 1908 and attached to the Mennonite Mission field. He was given by the government a tract of about 50 acres of oak forest lying between Margoredjo and Kedung-Pendjalin which he was allowed to use tax-free for the medical mission program. Kelet lies some 2,000 feet above the sea level and has a pleasant climate and much natural beauty. A hospital was built here which contained four halls and numerous apartments and side buildings including a school and a church. It also had a laboratory, a drug department, two operating rooms, and a darkroom. It had good equipment, including an X-ray. The hospital also served the leper colony of Donorodjo and maintained policlinics at Keling, Bangsri, Wedaridjaska, Taju, and Pati. The hospital itself had 50 beds and was normally staffed by 4 native helpers. In 1931 it had a total of 408 patients with 12,040 days of occupancy. At the Kedung-Pendjalin hospital there were 38 beds with 3 native helpers with a total in 1931 of 280 patients and 8,204 hospital occupancy days. In Kelet, the hospital had 367 beds, 2 European doctors, 2 European nurses, 64 native helpers, and in 1931 had 1,748 patients with 108,495 occupancy days.

The leper colony of Donorodjo was opened in 1916. It was established with the help of a considerable sum of money which had been collected in 1909 on the occasion of the birthday of Princess Juliana, from people living in the Dutch East Indies, and which was granted by the queen to be used for the leper work. The name Donorodjo actually means "gift of the princess." It is a leper village in which each leper has the free use of a piece of ground which he cultivates. The patients can establish their dwellings where they wish. They have their own coinage and a store in which everything can be purchased. They also have their own administration and their own organizations under their own leadership. There is here also a school and a church. The celebration of the Lord's Supper, in which many lepers are not able to take the bread in their own badly damaged hands, is a very impressive service. Donorodjo was always under the leadership of European directors.

The mission reached deep into the life of the natives. The appearance of a Christian village is very different from that of a Mohammedan village. An official report prepared under the direction of the Dutch Minister of Health and Welfare before 1931 reported five points in which the influence of the mission could be observed, and where it had reached very deeply into the life of the people. These were, housing and house furniture, clothing, cultivation of the fields, livestock, and payment of taxes and all financial obligations. In eleven other aspects of the life of the people various favorable results were noticed as the consequence of the influence of the mission, such as the establishment of permanent marriage relationships, the resistance to native fanatics, the elevation of womanhood, better teaching and attendance at the schools, more industriousness and economy, less spending of money for worthless purposes, less gambling and less use of opium, prostitution and polygamy, and more concern for the cultivation of gardens and fields. It is generally known that the native Christians have practically nothing to do with the police, that they always perform their obligations punctually whether financial or otherwise, that they remain in their locations permanently and therefore cause very little trouble to the authorities.

The financial support of the mission program included a subsidy from the government, which in 1928 amounted to approximately 35,000 guilders. The contributions to the mission treasury from the various Mennonite countries of Europe in that year were as follows: Holland 23,000 guilders, Germany 14,500 guilders, France and Switzerland together 2,000 guilders.

World War II led to catastrophe for the Dutch Mennonite Mission in Java. When the German army occupied the Netherlands in May 1940 contact with the congregations and missionaries in Java was broken. Two German missionaries, Hermann Schmitt and Otto Stauffer, were interned. After the Japanese attack on Indonesia in 1942 they were to be taken with other internees to Singapore. On the way the boat was torpedoed by a Japanese U-boat and both missionaries lost their lives. The remaining missionaries, Daniel Amstutz and Dr. K. P. C. A. Gramberg, reached an agreement with the Javanese Mennonite leaders that all the congregations should now become completely independent of the mission. In Kelet a union of Javanese Christian congregations in the Muria area was founded on May 30, 1940, with the name "Brotherhood of the Javanese Evangelical Christian Churches in the Vicinity of Pati, Kudus, and Japara," directed by a committee of five Javanese together with Amstutz and Gramberg. The eleven autonomous congregations later elected a synod for the general management of the church with Soehadiweka Djojodihardjo, the son of Sardjoe Djojodihardjo, a former student at the University of

Djahathas (Batavia) and pastor of the Pati congregation, as chairman. The church is founded on the Bible and the Apostles' Creed. Baptism upon confession of faith and the rejection of the oath, as well as congregational autonomy, are Mennonite characteristics. In November 1940 five competent Javanese preachers were ordained. Each congregation usually has an elder, several preachers, and several meeting places.

Supervision of the schools was made the responsibility of Sardjoe Djojodihardjo, and the direction of the colonies was given over to Soemjar. In Donorodjo P. J. Bouwer was replaced as director by H. C. Heusdens, a missionary formerly in the Celebes. Since it was not possible to send money from the Netherlands, some financial support was given by Dutch Mennonites in Java and the Emergency Committee of the Reformed Mission in Batavia.

In 1942, when Java was occupied by Japan, terrible disorders broke out, especially in the Muria area. Fanatical Moslems waged a "holy war." They attempted to destroy all mission property and compel all Christians to accept the Mohammedan religion. The mission hospital at Taju and the Gramberg home were completely destroyed, as were also the churches in Margoredjo and Tegalambo; several schools and churches were partly destroyed. The leper establishment at Donorodjo was plundered and the inmates fled, but Heusdens, refusing to become a Moslem, was bestially killed. Kelet was liberated after a sort of siege. Unfortunately several Javanese Christians in their distress became Mohammedans, but they later returned to the Christian church. Others, like Sardjoe Djojodihardjo and Roebin, held unwaveringly to their Christian faith.

During the Japanese occupation there were many difficulties for the congregations. Europeans were no longer permitted to work with the Javanese. The Japanese took over responsibility for the Germans on the island, and in time transferred the Schmitt and Stauffer families to Tsingtao, China, from where after the war, with the help of the Mennonite Central Committee, they were taken to Reedley, Cal. The church union took upon itself all the responsibility for as well as the possession of the former mission properties. The schools could again be opened on condition that the teachers swear an oath of loyalty. This the teachers refused to do, and the schools remained closed. Donorodjo and Kelet were supervised by the Japanese; the German Mennonite head nurse, Maria Klaassen, was allowed to remain. Without the assistance of a physician she managed the hospital with extraordinary skill until 1950. On a return trip to Germany in June 1950 her father Johann Klaassen (q.v.) died at Djakarta. Maria Klaassen is now living in California with the family of Hermann Schmitt. Gramberg tried to continue his work in Djuwana, but he was interned in Kudus. Amstutz worked for a time in secret, but he was then also interned in Kudus with his family. In 1943 the aged missionary Jansz died and in 1944 Hübert's wife died, all of whom had remained in Java. Fast had died in 1941.

The Christian churches worked on under difficult circumstances, especially because the Japanese favored the Mohammedans. Famine resulted when the Japanese confiscated all the supplies of rice. In August 1945 came fortunately the Japanese surrender and liberation. Meanwhile Indonesian nationalism awakened, and after the revolution and the declaration of independence from Holland all contacts with Europeans became impossible. The Mohammedans considered themselves the true nationalists; they did not trust the Christians because they belonged to a "western religion." Therefore the Javanese Christians organized a Christian political party, which declared itself in favor of an independent state of Indonesia.

Because of the political confusion in Java and two military missions of the Netherlands, there was for a long time not a single contact with the Dutch Mission Society. To be sure, the Amstutz and Gramberg families returned (1946) to their home countries from the concentration camps. Mrs. Gramberg had died in the internment camp after long suffering. Not until 1949 was it possible to re-establish contact.

Meanwhile a group of workers of the Mennonite Central Committee appeared in Java in 1949, which did much relief work "in the Name of Christ," first in Djakarta, and soon also in Pati and vicinity, with headquarters later in Kelet. Amstutz went back to Java as an MCC worker 1949-50. Beside direct relief the MCC program included a medical clinic, financial aid to the Bible school, and to the local churches. It became clear that the congregations had well survived the emergency. The congregation in the Muria area had endorsed a resolution which had been proposed at a Kwitang conference in Djakarta in 1947. The larger Javanese congregations had all declared themselves independent, and had said that the proclamation of the Gospel in Indonesia was in the first place the task of the national congregations; foreign churches including the Dutch could carry on missions in co-operation with the Indonesian churches; since the national churches were not yet in a position to assume all the responsibilities for the work they had to ask the foreign churches to assist them with workers and with money; but these churches were to understand that the situation in the new state was entirely changed: the missionaries were no longer as formerly to be the leaders of the congregations and of the work, but should rather work in more specialized vocations as needed by the Javanese congregations. In this manner the Muria congregation also asked for help. It had established in Pati a secondary theological school in 1950 to train its preachers. This school was to be the center of spiritual work, for example, for the training of church workers and for the Sunday schools and the spread of Christian literature. For this purpose they asked for three workers. In 1951 Jan F. Matthijssen and his wife went from Holland to Java, Matthijssen becoming a teacher in the theological school and an adviser of the synod. Mrs. Matthijssen organized Sunday-school work. At a synod held at Kelet in December 1951 the foundation was established for medical work, with the hope that it would receive from the Indonesian government the right to administer one or more hospitals. A missionary council was also appointed, with Matthijssen as secretary. In 1952 a second missionary, R. Kuitse, was called by the Pati congregation as a teacher in the theological school. The director of the school is Pastor S. Djojodihardjo. It has now been decided to combine the Pati school with the theological school of the Reformed Church of East Java in Malang in 1955 under a combined board and with Reformed and Mennonite (Kuitse) teachers. For the medical work the Muria church appointed the French Mennonite physician Dr. Marthe Ropp, who with a German Mennonite nurse, Liesel Hege, has already worked in Java for several years under the MCC. Daniel Amstutz is engaged as an itinerant preacher in Europe in the interest of the mission.

The theological school at Pati has proved a real center for evangelization, for example, through contact with Javanese intellectual circles and library work. An evangelistic periodical, *Kabar Baik,* is published in the Javanese and Indonesian languages. The Muria church is a member of the ecumenical council of Indonesia.

Since 1951 the Dutch Missionary Society and the Mennonite conferences of France, Germany, and Switzerland have been working together in support of the work in Java in the organization known as the European Mennonite Evangelization Committee (EMEK). In 1953 EMEK spent 30,887.79 guilders for the work in Java. For the work in New Guinea in co-operation with the Dutch Reformed Church the Dutch Mission Association contributed an additional 34,525.06 guilders. The chairmen of the mission association, now called the Doopsgezinde Vereniging tot Evangelie-verbreiding, since the death of Pastor Nijdam (1946) have been Mrs. A. J. Meerdink-van den Ban until 1952, W. F. Golterman 1952-54, and since 1954 Pastor H. Bremer. The present secretary is C. M. Roggeveen, and the treasurer S. J. Keyzer.

In 1953 the Malay Mennonite Church had 11 congregations, 2,410 members (plus 2,850 children), and 19 ministers, of whom 11 were elders. Following are the statistics by congregations:

| | Membership | |
Names	Baptized	Children
1. Pati	176	122
2. Margoredjo	970	1144
3. Kelet	167	262
4. Bandungardjo	100	91
5. Margokerto	132	229
6. Bondo	103	172
7. Kedung-Pendjalin	451	469
8. Japara	27	42
9. Petjanga'an Ngeling	84	100
10. Kudus	124	132
11. Kaju-Apu	76	107

The Chinese Mennonite Church in Java, which in 1954 had approximately 1,500 members in 9 congregations, arose independently from the Dutch mission program and the Malay church, but as a result of the influence of the mission. It was organized in 1921 and has always been independent. Its center has always been Kudus (*q.v.*). Whereas the Malay churches are composed of 95 per cent of small farmers and laborers, relatively poor, the Chinese church is composed more of urban people who are relatively well-to-do.

Both Malay and Chinese churches were represented at the Fifth Mennonite World Conference in August 1952 at Basel, Switzerland, by their respective presidents, S. W. Djojodihardjo for the Malay church, and Tan King Ien for the Chinese church. Both men toured the Mennonite churches in Europe and North America before and after the World Conference. Herman Tan, Jr., and his wife of the Chinese church spent three years in theological study at North American Mennonite institutions in 1952-55.   C.N., W.F.G.

Annual reports of the Dutch Mennonite Mission Board, called *Jaarsverslag*, 1848 ff.; T. Kuiper gives a condensed history of the mission in *DB* 1885 (54-67), 1886 (73-87), 1887 (32-48), 1889 (54-63), 1890 (39-52), 1891 (30-41), 1892 (30-45), 1893 (106-20); S. Coolsma, *De Zendingseeuw voor Ned. O. Indie* (Utrecht, 1901); J. Klaassen, *De Doopsgezinde Zending op Java* (Wolvega, n.d.); C. Nijdam, *De Doopsgezinde Zending* (Wolvega, 1931); D. Amstutz et al., *Verslagen van het Doopsgezind Zendingsveld op Java* 1940-1947 (n.p., n.d.); A. Mulder, "A Century of Mennonite Missions," *Menn. Life* III (January 1948) 12-15; Daniel Amstutz, "Dutch Mennonite Missions During the War," *Menn. Life* III (January 1948) 16-19; Robert Miller, "Mennonite Churches in Java," *Christian Living* III (August 1956) 16 f.; *Uit Verleden en heden van de Doopsgezinde Zending 1847-1947* (n.p., n.d.); Gerhard Hein, "Johann Klaassen, Das Lebensbild eines Missionars," *Gem.-Kal.* 1952, 19-40; *ML* II, 395-97.

Jay County (Ind.) Old Order Amish Mennonite settlement, near Portland, established in the spring of 1937 when seven Amish families, including Bishop Isaac E. Gingerich, moved there from Buchanan Co., Iowa. Recently several families have left the settlement, Preacher Enos Bontrager and Jacob Mast with their families moving to Tennessee in 1946, and Preacher Jacob Miller and family moving to Missouri in 1947. The 1953 membership was approximately 58; Isaac E. Gingerich was the bishop. His adopted son (ord. 1948), Perry Gingerich, is serving as a minister.   N.Z.

Jazykovo: see **Yazykovo** Mennonite Settlement.

Jebba, a city of 12,000 located on the Niger River, Nigeria, West Africa, in which the United Missionary Church is conducting missionary work. A station was opened at Jebba in 1910 under A. W. Banfield, F.R.G.S. On May 17, 1913, C. T. Homuth held the first baptismal service, baptizing 22 converts. The present church, completed in 1926, seats 500. The station includes a Bible college, a four-room dispensary, and a school which occupies three buildings; it has 16 teachers and an enrollment of 420 (1957). There are five outstations.   E.R.S.

Jedelshauser, Hans, a needlemaker from Ulm, who in 1579 had joined the Hutterite brotherhood in Moravia (most likely in Nikolsburg) together with his wife and children, but who five years later, in 1584, left this group together with his family and turned Catholic, probably under the influence of Christoph Erhard (*q.v.*), then a priest in Nikolsburg. He signed a *Widerruf* (Recantation) in which he gave 12 reasons why he could no longer tolerate the Anabaptist way. This writing, very

slanderous and artificial, is in the main the work of Erhard himself, who, although well familiar with the Hutterites from personal contact, did not hesitate to accuse them of the worst vices. Three years after the event, Erhard published a small pamphlet entitled *Zwelf wichtige und starke Ursachen Hansen Jedelshauser . . . warumb er mit seinem Weib . . . von den Widertäuffern, so man Hutterischen Brüder nennt, sey abgetretten . . . sich aber zu der Catholischen Kirche bekehrt habe . . .* (Ingolstadt, 1587, about 100 pp.). The name of Erhard appears only in the dedicatory preface. The *Zwelf Ursachen* covers only the first 28 pages; the rest is a similarly venomous slander against Luther, who is made mainly responsible for the origin and rise of Anabaptism. The pamphlet served a propaganda purpose in the fight of the growing Counter Reformation (*q.v.*) against both the sectarians and the Lutherans (copy in GCL). (*ML* I, 607.)   R.F.

Jedwilleiten, a village in the Memel district of East Prussia, formerly Prussian Lithuania, where Mennonites settled in the early 18th century. The tradition that Mennonites from Switzerland settled here in 1713 has not been proved, but by 1722 Mennonites from West Prussia were found here. In this year a man called Berend Jenson (Jansen), who had been a member of the church, but had been banned because of his bad life, made a complaint about the Mennonites of this village to Frederick William I, King of Prussia, accusing them of having persuaded a number of Lutherans to join their Mennonite congregation. Thereupon the king issued a decree forbidding them to proselytize among the members of the Lutheran Church.   vDZ.

H. Wiebe, *Das Siedlungswerk niederl. Mennoniten im Weichseltal* (Marburg a.d. Lahn, 1952) 43, 69, notes 1, 5, 6, 8.

Jeens, Wytze: see **Brouwer, W. J.**

Jehan de la Beecke, an Anabaptist martyr, who was burned at the stake after having been strangled at Brugge, Belgium, on Oct. 15, 1558. Jehan was born at Komen (Commines) in Flanders and had married at Wervik. By trade he was a *mutsenscheerdere,* but when he was unemployed he worked on farms. He was 24 years of age; in 1557 he had been (re)baptized. He was put to death with Pauwels Vermaete, Martin van de Walle, and Hansken van den Broecke. A man called Jan van de Beke from Komen, burned at the stake at Gent in March 1557 because of heresy (Verheyden, *Gent,* 23, No. 46), may have been a relative of Jehan de la Beecke. (Verheyden, *Brugge,* 47, No. 23.)   vDZ.

Jehan Bertheloot, an Anabaptist martyr, a native of Cassel, Flanders, was burned at the stake at Brugge, Belgium, on Dec. 10, 1561. He is not mentioned in van Braght's *Martyrs' Mirror.* He may be identical either with Hansken Parmentier (*q.v.*) or Hans Lisz (*q.v.*), both found in the *Martyrs' Mirror* (D 288, E 655). (Verheyden, *Brugge,* 51, No. 43.)   vDZ.

Jehan (Hans) Cant, an Anabaptist martyr, a native of St. Winnoxbergen, Flanders, burned at the stake at Brugge, Belgium, on Dec. 11, 1561, is not named

in van Braght's *Martyrs' Mirror*. He is perhaps identical either with Hansken Parmentier (*q.v.*) or Hans Lisz (*q.v.*), both found in the *Marytrs' Mirror* (D 288, E 655). (Verheyden, *Brugge,* 50, No. 42.)
                                                      vdZ.

Jehan (Jan) (van) **Moyaert,** a rather unknown Mennonite leader, was active in Flanders about 1564. He was then about 40 years of age and a textile merchant at Rijssel (Lille) or Doornik (Tournai). Was he a relative (or ancestor) of the Dutch Flemish Moyer family, to which the elder Pieter Jansz Mo(o)yer (*q.v.*) belonged? (Verheyden, "Mennisme in Vlaanderen," ms.)   vdZ.

Jehan Toulet, an otherwise unknown Mennonite preacher, who about 1564 was active in Armentières, Brugge, and other towns in Flanders. According to a letter from the margrave of Antwerp to the regent Margaret of Parma, he was a native of Armentières, a middle-aged merchant, who attended the fair at Frankfurt, Germany. (Verheyden, "Mennisme in Vlaanderen," ms.)   vdZ.

Jehanne du Boys, wife of Andries Vanneaulx, an Anabaptist martyr, drowned at Antwerp, Belgium, on April 22 (or 25), 1558. She was born at Antwerp and lived at Doornik (Tournai). From there she fled to Antwerp because of persecution. She was charged with "the crime of being rebaptized and persisting in the error of the sect of the Anabaptists." Her husband, also a member of the congregation, was fugitive. Probably the martyr Janneken Walraven, found in van Braght's *Martyrs' Mirror* (D 178, E 563), is the same person as Jehanne du Boys. (*Antw. Arch.-Blad* VIII, 444 f., 469; XIV, 22 f., No. 256.)   vdZ.

Jehring, Joachim Christian (1691-1729), a Lutheran preacher at Reepsholt in East Friesland, author and editor of a book which is an important source of Mennonite history, *Gründliche Historie von den Begebenheiten, Streitigkeiten und Trennungen, so unter den Tauffgesinnten oder Mennonisten von ihren Ursprung an, bis auf das Jahr 1615 vorgegangen, anfänglich von einem Mennonisten selbst, der sich I. H. V. P. N. genennet, in holländischer Sprache beschrieben, jetzund aber . . . übersetzet und mit einigen Anmerckungen, Zugaben und Vorbericht, worinnen von denen nachhero gefolgten Streitigkeiten und jetzigen Zustande derselben gehandelt wird, vermehrt von Joachim Christ. Jehring mit einer Vorrede von Jo. Francisco Buddeo* (Jena, 1720). (See **Buddeus.**)

This book of 336 pages has the following contents: pp. 1-73 are an introductory account of the history and doctrine of the Mennonites, in which Jehring defends them against false charges; pp. 74-188 give a German translation of the book named in the title of Jehring's book, which was written by the anonymous I. H. V. P. N., *Anfang und Fortgang der Trennung der Tauffgesinnten* (original title, *Het beginsel der scheuringen . . .* , reprinted in *BRN* VII; see **Beginsel**); pp. 189-221, Obbe Philips' Confession; pp. 222-26, Menno Simons' letter to the church at Franeker; pp. 226-29, Menno Simons' letter to the church at Emden; pp. 230-32, closing

comments of Carel van Gent; pp. 232 and 233, *Wahrhaftiges Geschichts-Register;* pp. 234-36, additions which serve to explain Mennonite history and doctrine: (1) Doctrinal statements of Uko Walles; (2) Verdict of the consistorium at Groningen concerning Uko Walles; (3) Reply of Uko Walles and his followers to the council of Groningen; (4) Baptism and communion among the Ukowallists; (5) Baptism among the Mennonites (with brief catechism and formulary); (6) Information concerning a dispute of the Mennonite church at Emden (1691); (7) Public prayers of the Mennonites; (8) Formulary for the installation and ordination of preachers among the Mennonites; (9) Agreement and union reached by the Mennonites in 1664; (10) Intercessory letter written by the States General to the canton of Bern in 1710; (11) Information concerning disputes in the church at Amsterdam and Rotterdam; (12) Concerning the Münsterites (in Latin); it is the pamphlet by A. Corvinus (*q.v.*). This view of the contents indicates its importance, which has not lost its significance even today. (*ML* II, 401.)   NEFF.

Jelis de Backer, an Anabaptist martyr, seized with Adriaen Jansz, a fellow believer, because of his faith. Because they refused to leave the brotherhood they were burned at the stake in 1571 at Rijssel (Lille). (*Mart. Mir.* D 549, E 884; *ML* I, 102.)   O.H.

Jelis (Gillis, Gieles, Michiel), **Bernaerts** (Gielis van Gent), an Anabaptist martyr, was imprisoned and suffered martyrdom at Antwerp, Belgium, on June 18, 1559, with Adriaen Pan (*q.v.*). He was a native of Thielt, Flanders. He had been a preacher in Gent (*Offer,* 379). In 1556 a price of 100 Caroliguilders was placed on his head. He apparently then moved from Gent to Antwerp. His will, two letters to his wife, and a letter which he wrote to his brothers and sisters after he had been sentenced to death are found in the *Martyrs' Mirror*. These letters testify to his courage and constancy, indeed to the spirit of the Anabaptists of the time. In the *Offer des Heeren* (1562) there is a hymn of seven stanzas which commemorates his death: "Gebenedyt God in des hemels pleyn, Verbreyt zijn wercken goet." (See also **Gielis van Gent.**)   O.H., vdZ.

Offer, 373-92; *Mart. Mir.* D 251, E 624; *Antw. Arch.-Blad.* IX, 2, 8; XIV, 26 f., No. 291; Wolkan, *Lieder,* 68; *ML* I, 196.

Jelis Claversz, an Anabaptist martyr found in van Braght's *Martyrs' Mirror* (D 536, E 871) with the information that he was executed at Antwerp, Belgium, in 1571 with a large number of fellow martyrs. This martyr is, however, not found in the Antwerp records. *Bibliographie* suggests that Jelis Claversz is identical with Gillis van Havre, executed at Antwerp on May 9, 1571. This may be true. He may have been the same person as Jelis de Metselaer (*q.v.*), who (according to *Mart. Mir.* D 506, E 846) was burned at the stake at Antwerp on May 2, 1571. (*Bibliographie,* No. 148; *ML* I, 360.)   vdZ.

Jelis Matthijsz, a martyr: see **Gielis Matthysz.**

Jelis de Metselaer (mason), an Anabaptist martyr, found in van Braght (*Mart. Mir.* D 506, E 846) with the information that he was burned at the stake at Antwerp, Belgium, on May 2, 1571. Apparently the information by van Braght is not correct. This martyr is not found in the official records. He may have been identical with Jelis Claversz (*q.v.*), officially called Gillis van Havre. If this is true, the date of execution was May 9, 1571. vɒZ.

Bibliographie, No. 540; *Antw. Arch.-Blad* XIV, 70 f., No. 899; *ML* II, 402.

Jelis (Gielis) **Outerman** (Aefterman), an Anabaptist martyr who was seized with eleven other Anabaptists while they were assembled for a religious service. After a lengthy imprisonment the others were executed on Dec. 10, 1561, and he on the next day, at Brugge, Flanders. Jelis was a native of Dixmuide, Flanders. His name is found in the hymn "Genade en Vrede moet Godvreesende sijn," found in *Veelderhande Liedekens* of 1569. vɒZ.

Mart. Mir. D 288, E 655; Verheyden, *Brugge,* 50, No. 39; Wackernagel, *Lieder,* 130; *ML* III, 330.

Jelis Potvliet, an Anabaptist martyr, was beheaded at Wervik, Flanders, with Jelis Strings and his brother Pieter Potvliet (*q.v.*). They were all weavers, originally from Thielt in Flanders. They were sentenced to die at the stake, but because heavy rains had made the wood too wet to burn, they were beheaded. (*Mart. Mir.* D 289, E 656; *ML* III, 386.)
vɒZ.

Jelis Strings (Strinx), an Anabaptist martyr, beheaded at Wervik, Flanders, with Jelis and Pieter Potvliet. For particulars see **Jelis Potvliet.** vɒZ.

Jelles, Jarich, a native of Friesland, apparently from Harlingen, was a member of the Amsterdam Lamist Mennonite congregation. He was unmarried and the well-to-do owner of a grocery store in Amsterdam. About 1650 he retired from business to devote himself to "acknowledging the truth which is after godliness" (Titus 1:1). He was a deacon in the Lamist church from 1653. He died in 1683. After his death his *Belydenisse des Algemeenen en Christelyken Geloofs* was published at Amsterdam in 1684. In the appendix to this confession is found a short biographical sketch of Jelles, probably by the editor and printer of the book, Jan Rieuwertsz (*q.v.*). This confession is deeply influenced by the principles of Spinoza and Descartes, of whom Jelles was a devoted adherent. vɒZ.

Biogr. Wb. IV, 535 f.; C. B. Hylkema, *Reformateurs* II (Haarlem, 1902) 212-42; K. O. Meinsma, *Spinoza en zijn kring* (The Hague, 1896).

Jellys Ballam, a follower of the revolutionary Anabaptist leader Jacob van Antwerpen (*q.v.*), was beheaded on Feb. 17, 1535, at Deventer, Dutch province of Overijssel. (*DB* 1919, 8-10.) vɒZ.

Jena, a city in Thuringia, Germany (pop. 82,722). Here the preacher Martin Reinhard, supported by Gerhard Westerburg (*q.v.*), opposed infant baptism without, however, ceasing to practice it. In March 1524 Reinhard had republished a book of A.D. 1430 with the title, *Anzeigung, wie die gefallene Christenheit wiedergebracht mög werden in ihren ersten Stand;* it contains the demands made by the Bohe-

mian Brethren "who held to the evangelical doctrine" at the Council of Basel in 1430 (Keller, 202). After Luther's dispute with Carlstadt at Jena, Reinhard was banished in 1524. He went to Nürnberg, whence he was again banished on Dec. 17, 1524 (Keller, 227).

Several years later some events took place which were to be decisive in the suppression of the Anabaptists in Thuringia. On Nov. 20, 1535, 16 Anabaptists were seized at a meeting in Kleineutersdorf. Four men of this group, Hans Peissker, Heinz Kraut, Jobs Möller, and Lorenz Petzsch, were taken to Jena; Petzsch had not yet been baptized, and since he seemed inclined to recant he was separated from the others. The cross-examinations were begun on Dec. 1 by the city pastor and several councilors; Kaspar Cruciger and Philip Melanchthon also took part; but all attempts to make them recant failed. Melanchthon reported to Elector John Frederick the fruitless course of the investigation and advised him to apply serious penalties against the prisoners. He wrote on Jan. 19, 1536, "Although some may not in other respects be obstinate people, yet the dangerous sects must be resisted in which is so much terrible, shameful error" (*Corpus Reformatorum* III, 16). The three prisoners were then put on the rack. Since nothing could be pressed from them beyond what they had already said, they were sentenced to death on Jan. 26, 1536, on the strength of an opinion of the law school of the University of Wittenberg, which had been transferred to Jena because of the plague. They were executed on the same day. Lorenz Petzsch, who had been kept alone in a cell, escaped before the execution.

At the urging of Melanchthon, John Frederick issued a mandate on April 10, 1536, in which the statements of the executed were compiled and proved erroneous, unchristian, and deserving of punishment. At the same time Melanchthon wrote a booklet, *Verlegung etlicher unchristlicher Artikel, welche die Wiedertäufer vorgeben,* which was sent to every pastor in their jurisdiction, with orders that it be read from the pulpit and explained every third Sunday, so that every one might avoid severe punishment. It was published in Wittenberg in 1536.

HEGE.

P. Wappler, *Die Stellung Kursachsens und des Landgrafen Philipp von Hessen zur Täuferbewegung* (Münster, 1910); idem, *Thüringen;* Ludwig Keller, *Johann Staupitz und die Anfänge der Reformation* (Leipzig, 1888); *ML* II, 403.

Jenneken de Beaucoup, an Anabaptist martyr, was burned at the stake on Jan. 31, 1573, at Antwerp, Belgium, together with Jacques Verbruggen and Hans der Weduwe. Particulars about this martyr are lacking. She was sentenced to death because of having been rebaptized and having attended forbidden meetings. (*Antw. Arch.-Blad* XIII, 102 f., 172; XIV, 88 f., No. 1006.) vɒZ.

Jenneken de Cantere, an Anabaptist martyr, was burned at the stake on May 28, 1573, at Antwerp, Belgium. She was a native of Brussels. During the trial she at first denied, but later admitted that she had attended the forbidden meetings of the Mennonites. For this crime she was sentenced to death.

Apparently she was not (yet) a member of the congregation. Lynken Groffels was put to death with her. (*Antw. Arch.-Blad* XIII, 119 f., 178; XIV, 90 f., No. 1031.)   vDZ.

Jenneken Jan Diericx (Jenneken van Diericx), an Anabaptist martyr, drowned on Jan. 31, 1573, at the Steen castle of Antwerp, Belgium. P. Génard, who studied the documents at Antwerp, found the following note, the meaning of which is not quite clear: "was condemned to the stake, but since she was not willing to go to the fire, she has been executed with water" (i.e., has been drowned). (*Antw. Arch.-Blad* XIII, 102 f., 173, 188; XIV, 88 f., No. 1007.)   vDZ.

Jenneken Peeters, an Anabaptist martyr, was burned at the stake at Antwerp, Belgium, on Aug. 14, 1571, with Jan van Rijssele and two Calvinists. She was an unmarried woman, apparently rather young. She was charged with the crimes of "having joined the sect of the Anabaptists, having attended their meetings, and persisting in her heresy." (*Antw. Arch.-Blad* XIII, 71, 73, 161; XIV, 86 f., No. 968.)   vDZ.

Jenneken Pots, an Anabaptist martyr, executed on Jan. 28, 1576, at Antwerp, Belgium. It is unknown how this martyr and Lynken Clercx, who was executed on the same day, were put to death. Jenneken was sentenced for rebaptism, attending forbidden meetings of the Mennonites, and possessing a number of heretical books. (*Antw. Arch.-Blad* XIII, 198; XIV, 98 f., No. 1104.)   vDZ.

Jenneken van den Velde(n), an Anabaptist martyr, is identical with Janneken (van) Munstdorp (*q.v.*).

Jensma, a Dutch Mennonite family of farmers, found in the Bildt area in the province of Friesland since the 17th century; many members of the family have served as deacons in the St. Anna Parochie congregation.   vDZ.

Jenyn (Viviaen) **Reechove** (van Redichove), an Anabaptist martyr, beheaded on June 12, 1536, in front of the Gravensteen castle at Gent, Belgium. No further information was available. (Verheyden, *Gent,* 2, No. 6.)   vDZ.

Jeroen Tinnegieter, a Mennonite, probably from the Belgian province of Henegouwen (Hainaut), who had emigrated from Belgium because of persecution, and lived at Franeker, Dutch province of Friesland, after about 1560. As a member of the congregation he was chosen preacher, but in this capacity he was not accepted by the elders of Franeker, Harlingen, Leeuwarden, and Dokkum, who had ratified the *Verbond* (*q.v.*) *van de vier Steden* (Pact of the Four Towns). At first Jeroen respected this decision, but soon after, supported by his fellow immigrants from Flanders, he took up his office and severely attacked Ebbe Pieters (*q.v.*), the elder of Harlingen. A complicated quarrel arose in 1566, which in 1567 ended with a schism between the Flemish and Frisian Mennonites. (*DB* 1893, 12-80, *passim.*)   vDZ.

Jeronimus (Jeronymus van der Capellen or Jerosme de la Chapelle), an Anabaptist martyr, burned at the stake at Antwerp, Belgium, on May 22, 1557. Jeronimus was a native of Brussels; by trade he was a maker of tin pots. He lived at Gent, Belgium, with his wife Margriete (*q.v.*). Here in 1555 their marriage was performed "according to the customs of the Mennonites." From Gent they fled to Antwerp, where, both being Mennonites, they hoped to live more safely. But soon they were arrested and both sentenced to death, Margriete being executed about six weeks after her husband on July 5. They died loyally; their names are celebrated in the hymn "Aenhoort Godt, hemelsche Vader" (Hear, God, heavenly Father), found in the *Lietboecxken van den Offer des Heeren.* Jeronimus' property was confiscated and sold.   vDZ.

Offer, 564; *Mart. Mir.* D 185, E 569; *Antw. Arch.-Blad* VIII, 433, 437, 469; XIV, 22 f., No. 242; Verheyden, "Mennisme in Vlaanderen," ms.

Jeronimus Cleermaker, an Anabaptist belonging to the revolutionary wing of Anabaptism. He was a native of Egmond aan Zee, Dutch province of North Holland, and was involved in a revolt at Poeldijk near The Hague (Netherlands), where he was beheaded on March 14, 1536.   vDZ.

E. van Bergen, "De Wederdoopers in het Westland," in *Bijdrage voor de Geschiedenis van het Aartsbisdom Haarlem* XXVIII (Leiden, 1903) 275 f.

Jeronimus Pael, an Anabaptist martyr, one of the first to die at Antwerp, Belgium, where he was beheaded on Feb. 17, 1535. He seems to have agreed with the revolutionary principles of the Münsterites (*q.v.*).   vDZ.

W. Bax, *Het Protestantisme in het Bisdom Luik* I (The Hague, 1937) 137; *Antw. Arch.-Blad* VII, 316; XIV, 12 f., No. 129.

Jeronimus Schepens, an otherwise unknown Anabaptist martyr, a shipbuilder, was burned at the stake July 14, 1576, on the Veerle square at Gent, Belgium, together with Raphael van de Velde (*q.v.*). The proceeds of his goods sold after confiscation indicate that he was well-to-do. (*Mart. Mir.* D 715, E 1026; Verheyden, *Gent,* 66, No. 237.)   vDZ.

Jeronimus Segersz (Jeronimus Woutersz), an Anabaptist martyr, burned at the stake at Antwerp, Belgium, on Sept. 1, 1551. His wife Lysken Dirks (*q.v.*), who had been arrested at the same time, was executed on Feb. 19, 1552, after she had given birth to a child. All the Dutch martyrbooks, from the *Offer des Heeren* of 1562 to van Braght's *Martyrs' Mirror,* contain several letters which the pair exchanged while both were imprisoned at the Steen castle of Antwerp. Ten letters were written by Jeronimus, three by his wife. These letters give a striking presentation of both martyrs' fate and piety. They also contain considerable information about congregational life in those days as well as about the practices of the inquisitors. No other documents give us such a deep impression of the "faith of our fathers" as these letters. In the *Offer des Heeren* the letters are followed by a hymn to commemorate the steadfastness of this couple, beginning "God de Heere is ghetrouwe, hij troost de zijne vroech en spaey" (God the Lord is faithful, He comforts His own early and late). Jeronimus by trade was a tinker or coppersmith. One of his descendants was Herman Zegers, Mennonite preacher at Utrecht, Netherlands, who in 1632 signed the Dordrecht Confession. vɒZ.

Offer, 126-76; *Mart. Mir.* D 107-27, E 504-22; *Antw. Arch.-Blad* VIII, 402, 414, 417; XIV, 18 f., No. 202; *DB* 1864, 82-102.

Jersey City (N.J.) Mennonite Brethren in Christ Church was organized Dec. 15, 1940. In 1953 the congregation had 62 members with H. D. Yarrington serving as pastor. D.E.T.

Jerusalem, New, or the *New Zion (Sion),* a name given to the city of Münster (*q.v.*) in Westphalia, Germany, after Jan van Leyden (*q.v.*) had founded here his Anabaptist "kingdom." vɒZ.

Jesse, Willem, a Dutch Mennonite pastor, was born on Nov. 1, 1833, at Rotterdam, and died on Feb. 23, 1912, at Amsterdam. After studying at the Mennonite Theological Seminary at Amsterdam Willem Jesse served the congregation of Giethoorn 1858-62 and Zaandam-Oost 1862-99. He also was a permanent delegate on the board of the A.D.S. (Dutch Mennonite General Conference) and trustee of the Mennonite Seminary. During his pastorate Jesse turned to radical liberalism. After he had resigned he gave catechetical instruction for a number of years in the "Vrije Gemeente" (non-confessional liberal congregation) founded by his friend P. H. Hugenholtz at Amsterdam. He was one of the compilers of the hymnbook of the Dutch Protestant Union, which was much used also in Mennonite congregations. The Jesse family were among the pillars of the Rotterdam Mennonite congregation; Adrianus Arnoldus Jesse (1834-1900), a brother of Pastor Willem Jesse and owner of a drugstore, served the church of Rotterdam for many years as a deacon and as moderator of the church board. vɒZ.

Biogr. Wb. IV, 541-43; *DB* 1901, 215; 1912, 209-12; *De Zondagsbode,* 1911-12, 70, 72.

Jesuits, members of the Society of Jesus (abbreviated "S.J.," always found after the name of a member), a Catholic order founded by Ignatius of Loyola (1481-1556), a Spanish nobleman who during an illness experienced a conversion and founded this order in 1534. Its main purpose was to assist the papacy in the fight against all foes of Catholicism, first Lutherans, later Calvinists, and all sectarians generally called "heretics." Absolute obedience to the pope was a major point of this new order, which distinguished itself from the older monastic orders in that its members did not necessarily live in monastic houses but could be active at any place where their work was needed. In 1540 the pope confirmed this new "Society," which from then on was the very spearhead of the reform of the Roman Church and of the fight by all kinds of means to regain those areas which had been lost to Protestantism and (to a lesser degree) Anabaptism (see **Counter-Reformation**). By 1560-70 Jesuit activity began to show some success, and 17th-century Europe was definitely shaped, at least in part, by the activities of the Jesuits.

The Jesuit activities were manifold: they were representatives of the new type of dedicated parish priests, the lack of which had worked in favor of Protestantism and Anabaptism; they found entrance to many princely courts in France, Spain, Austria, and later Poland (but were forbidden in England, the Netherlands, Sweden, and Russia), where they became father confessors of the rulers and their families, and thus exerted a definite political influence. The same holds true for smaller courts such as those of Catholic dignitaries (archbishops, bishops, etc.). Then we find Jesuits in the entire educational program of many states, from the elementary grades up to universities.

From the point of view of Anabaptist-Mennonite history only a few countries require attention: the Rhineland (Cologne, Jülich), the bishopric of Speyer, Bavaria (always a pillar of the Catholic faith), and above all the Hapsburg countries—Austria, Tirol, Moravia, and from the 18th century on also Hungary. Poland, too, was an important field of Jesuit activities but here, besides Lutherans, the Socinian or Unitarian Church was their main target.

(A) *The Sixteenth Century.* The Jesuits had considerable success in converting Anabaptists on the Lower Rhine, especially in Cologne, from 1557 to 1566. The details are given in a book by Joseph Hansen (*q.v.*), *Rheinische Akten zur Geschichte des Jesuitenordens 1542-1582* (Bonn, 1896). They "converted" some, delivered many to the executioner, and had most of them expelled from the land (Rembert, 536-41). Ernst Müller reports (*Berner Täufer,* 195) that the Swiss Brethren who settled in Jülich-Berg in 1653 were driven out by the Jesuits.

As to the bishopric of Speyer we hear of the imprisonment (1568) of the Hutterite missionary Hans Arbeiter (*q.v.*), formerly a "Swiss brother" of the Rhine area congregation. From the Hutterite *Geschicht-Buch* (Wolkan, 327) we know of the vain attempts of a Jesuit preacher of the cathedral church (*Domprediger*), Dr. Lamprecht, to convince the brother of his errors and to bring him back to the old church. The story is most dramatically told by Hans Arbeiter himself. After seven months, the brother was released. The *Geschicht-Buch* reports once more of such an incident in Speyer. In 1612 two brethren were caught and imprisoned in Kierweiler castle, where again Jesuits worked upon them but to no avail. After having passed through much tribulation, they were finally freed (Wolkan, 506-10).

As to Bavaria, we know very little about Jesuit activities during the 16th century, although such work might be assumed. Since 1549 Jesuits were teaching at Ingolstadt (*q.v.*), where later a great center of Jesuit activities developed with a great university and a Jesuit press. But Anabaptism had already been weak here in the second half of the century, and died out completely around 1580-90. We know of one Hutterite brother, Christian Gasteiger, who was imprisoned in Ingolstadt in 1586, and again worked upon by Jesuits, but his final martyrdom came not in Ingolstadt but in Munich. "The Jesuits pressed hard" to achieve his death sentence (Wolkan, 423-24). In Ingolstadt also a number of polemical books against the Anabaptists were published, such as the books by Christoph Erhard (*q.v.*), Christoph Fischer (*q.v.*), Caspar Franck, and Jacob Gretser, although Erhard was not a Jesuit.

A real life-and-death struggle was experienced by the Hutterian Brethren in southern Moravia under the growing influence of the Jesuits who promoted the Counter Reformation there as strongly as possible. When the Dietrichsteins (*q.v.*) bought the manorial estate of Nikolsburg in 1575, hard days for the brethren were ahead. Adam Dietrichstein for the first time installed a Jesuit, Michael Cardaneus (1541-90) of Vienna, as parish priest in Nikolsburg 1579. He was called "the Nikolsburg apostle." It was the time of the papacy of Gregory XIII (d. 1585), who took a particular interest in the Jesuit activities in the Hapsburg lands as they put an end to the tolerant period under Maximilian II (d. 1576). Cardaneus also published a polemical booklet, *Orthodoxa Solatiique plena nova . . .* (now lost) against the heretics. Yet in spite of complaints (see Wolkan, *Geschicht-Buch,* 391-92) the pressure was still bearable and the "golden period" of the Brethren continued for another ten or fifteen years (Loserth, 186-88). Cardaneus' successor was the more aggressive Erhard (*q.v.*), himself no Jesuit, who, however, published his books in Ingolstadt. His time in Nikolsburg was 1583-89. By far the most dangerous of all was Christoph A. Fischer, S.J. (*q.v.*), parish priest at Feldsberg 1595-1607, whose venomous polemics hurt the Brethren so much that from that time on a serious decline set in. Among other sources Fischer quotes another work of Jesuit origin, the *Postilla in Festis Trinitatis,* by George Scherer, S.J. (written in 1586 or 89; printed at the monastery of Bruck in Moravia about 1604).

The Hutterite decline is also due to the activities of the head of the Counter Reformation in Moravia, Cardinal Franz von Dietrichstein (*q.v.*), active from 1599 on. He was strongly supported by both pope and emperor. It is interesting to learn that his official historiographer and biographer, Georg Dingenauer, S.J., was also a Jesuit and most likely of great influence upon the course of action in Moravia. He was the Cardinal's father confessor. His report of the fight against the Hutterites and of their final expulsion in 1622 is called *Memoria piarum rerum gestarum a dilatione religionis catholicae in Moravia ab anno MDCXXI* (1631). It was never printed, and the manuscript finally came into the Vatican Library at Rome (*Bibl. Ottobononia,* No. 827). In 1628 the Cardinal had asked Dingenauer to prepare a report concerning the restoration of all of Moravia to the Roman faith, in which the expulsion of the Hutterian Brethren should become the very climax, since the Cardinal was particularly proud of this his achievement (Hruby, 103-4).

(B) *The Eighteenth Century.* In this century the Palatinate had as its only Catholic ruler the prince elector Karl Theodor (*q.v.*) (ruled 1742-99), who had been educated by Jesuits and who now tried to carry out their principles. Of some renown is the case of the three children of a Mennonite widow Maurer who were taken away from their mother, baptized in a Catholic church, and kept in a Catholic orphanage. One child died there, but the others,

having been released after confirmation, soon thereafter were baptized into the Mennonite (Amish) Church by the Bishop Johann Nafziger. Thereupon the children were again put into jail; an opinion of the University of Heidelberg even advised the death penalty. After prolonged actions back and forth, they were eventually released, but the minister Nafziger was exiled forever (*Gem.-Kal.* 1906, 54-78).

The effect of missionary activities of the Jesuits had wider repercussions again in Hapsburg territories, this time in Slovakia and Transylvania. Here the Hutterites had been able to survive on a rather reduced scale (community of goods had been given up in 1685 or 1695), as long as the government in Vienna had not singled them out as an obnoxious segment of the population. When Empress Maria Theresa (reigned 1740-80) eventually consolidated her empire, she gave special orders to Jesuit missionaries to convert the Anabaptists still extant in her realm. We read in the *Geschicht-Buch* and in archive records published by Beck what happened. An elaborate confiscation of books took place (Beck, 563-642), which books then were transferred to Jesuit houses in Skalitz, Tyrnau (Trnovo), and Bratislava, Slovakia, whence they were taken over by Budapest (University Library), Esztergom, and Bratislava. Actually the earliest confiscation had taken place already in 1692: the codex A b 18 of the University Library of Budapest, bearing an *ex libris* "Coll. Soc. Jesu Posonii," i.e., Bratislava.

Much more dangerous was the enforced "conversion" to the Catholic faith. Children were taken away and put into orphanages, men were removed into Jesuit houses either to change their minds or to die there eventually. Catholic services were held on the Bruderhofs, and everyone was compelled to attend. To all this the Empress had given her consent, and Jesuits carried out the orders, using both harsh and mild methods. One advice was to put all stubborn men into the army, but that was not carried out. In Sobotiste, Slovakia, the Jesuit missionary Emerich Rotari was active around 1760; in Levar (Velky Levary) the priest Heinrich (Henricius), a former Jesuit, was active around 1780 (the Society of Jesus having been suppressed in 1773). Even the general of the Society of Jesus himself expressed interest in this work and ordered the dispatch of more missionaries into this field in 1760 (Beck, 584-86, 587, 601, and *passim,* also *Klein-Gesch.-Buch,* 233-34). The final result was a complete conquest in Slovakia (see **Habaner**). Those few who still opposed tried emigration; only very few succeeded in it.

In Transylvania it was the ill-famed Father Delpini or Delphini, S.J., who carried out similar activities among the old Hutterites around Alvinc and the new Hutterites (from Carinthia) around Kreutz and Stein in 1760-67. Here the story of the *Klein-Geschichtsbuch* is most detailed, since Johannes Waldner, the writer, remembered it from his own youth. While Delpini's work at Alvinc was somewhat successful (e.g., conversion of Märtl Roth, the former *Vorsteher*), it was without any result at Kreutz and Stein (among the Carinthian newly converted brethren). *"Nun steht es freilich nit in der Wölfen Gnaden, dass noch Schaf leben, also stund es auch nit in der Jesuiten Macht mit den Schäflein des Herrn nach seinem tyrannischen Herzen zu handeln"* (*Klein-Gesch.-Buch*, 295). Delpini traveled to Vienna (taking Märtl Roth with him) to receive special permission from the Empress to use all means deemed necessary for his "conversion" work. In 1767 he established the ill-famed Catholic orphanage in Hermannstadt (today Sibiu, Rumania), and prepared to send all Anabaptist children to this place. When the Brethren recognized this ultimate danger (some adults were at that time in prison, but the brotherhood would accept that as part of their fate as a suffering church), they decided to risk a nearly desperate step—the flight from Transylvania across the mountains, uncertain of their goal and future state. Thus the intended conversion never took place. In 1767 the brotherhood moved quietly away at night. Some years later those jailed in Hermannstadt were able to reach the rest of the brotherhood in Russia, having been finally released.

In the Netherlands there was little Jesuit activity against the Mennonites, and that only in literary form. Franciscus Costerus, S.J. (*q.v.*), wrote a polemic on the calling of Mennonite ministers, *Toetsteen van de Versierde Apostolische Successie eens Wederdoopers Jacob Pieterssen van der Molen* (Antwerp, 1603).

The transfer of membership by a number of Dutch Mennonites to the Catholic Church in the 17th century, particularly at Amsterdam, including Joost van den Vondel (*q.v.*), was not due to secret Jesuit activity, as was assumed by some writers, e.g., H. J. Allard, in his *Vondels Gedichten op de Sociëteit van Jezus* ('s Hertogenbosch, 1868, pp. 3 ff.). Reyer Anslo, however, a nephew of the Waterlander preacher Cornelis Anslo, was converted by the Jesuits.

In recent times one Jesuit priest-scholar, Dunin-Borkowsky (*q.v.*), has made early Anabaptism the object of an erudite study claiming that the greater part of the first generation Anabaptists tended toward anti-Trinitarianism (*q.v.*). He has been fully refuted in that point by more recent research.

R.F.

H. Boehmer, *The Jesuits* (Philadelphia, 1928); R. Fülop-Miller, *Power and Secret of the Jesuits* (1931); Rembert, *Wiedertäufer;* Loserth, *Communismus;* F. Hruby, *Die Wiedertäufer in Mähren* (Leipzig, 1935); also the works by Beck, Wolkan, and the *Klein-Gesch.-Buch;* ML II, 403-5.

Jeugd-oefening *in de ware Gods-dienst. Zo als de zelve onderwezen werd in de gemeente Christi (die men de Waterlandsche Doops-gesinde gemeente noemd) binnen Leiden.* Of this Dutch Mennonite catechism there have been four editions: Leiden, 1675, 1683, 1704, and Alkmaar, 1726, the last with the note that it was reprinted for the Mennonite congregation of de Rijp. The titles of several editions have a somewhat modified spelling. This catechism in a modified and augmented edition was also reprinted under the title *Jeugd-oeffening voor de Kinderen der Christenen, gelijk als de zelfde onderwezen worden in de vereenigde Doops-gezinde Gemeente tot Haerlem* (Haarlem, 1683, 1691, 1726), the last edition much modified. vDZ.

Jeuriaens (Joriaensz), **Thys:** see **Thijs Joriaensz.**

Jever, a district in Oldenburg (*q.v.*), Germany. The Anabaptist movement in Jever is very closely connected with that in adjacent East Friesland (*q.v.*). With varying success Lutheranism vied with Zwinglianism for supremacy after 1525. The religious convictions of Count Enno (*q.v.*) were determined by many motives, least of all by religious motives, and swung back and forth between Luther and Zwingli. Carlstadt's great influence in the region about 1530 led Enno to take decisive steps against the Sacramentists, to expel Carlstadt, and to adopt a Lutheran church order based on the Marburg articles. But the vacillation continued.

Anabaptists from East Friesland and Holland were probably in Jever at a very early period. It is difficult now to determine what was meant by the term Anabaptist; they all agreed, however, on the rejection of infant baptism. At any rate, after the fall of Münster in 1535 and the appearance of Menno Simons they formed the main stock of the Mennonites, which fact shows that there were among them not only extreme spiritualists, but also real *Täufer*. Because of the confusion of confessions they did not find it too difficult to maintain their position upholding simplicity and apostolic Christianity.

Maria, who was for many years the regent of Jever (1515-75), advised by Remme of Seedieck, made several attempts to resist the Anabaptists, but never completely gained the upper hand over them. In contrast to the edicts, the measures actually adopted were very mild, expulsion being the highest penalty. The attitude of the city preachers shows the same spirit; the strong conflict of religious movements among the free Frisians did not remain fruitless. The *Erklärung der Prediger Jeverlands zum Interim* (1549) and the undated and anonymous *Confessio Jeverensis* contain Anabaptist ideas to a greater degree than do the *Augustana* and *Apologie.*

Yet the Anabaptist movement cannot have been strong. The village of Jever was, to be sure, an open town (until 1536) and as such offered transit, but probably no more, since police supervision intentionally gave this aspect emphasis. At any rate, in 1576 only six Anabaptists are mentioned, in part with their residences, at the colloquium held with them and the Calvinists, which resulted in the expulsion of the Anabaptists from Jever. (See also **East Friesland.**) O.S.

C. A. Cornelius, *Der Anteil Ostfrieslands an der Reformation* (Münster, 1852); L. Schauenburg, *Die Täuferbewegung in der Grafschaft Oldenburg-Delmenhorst und der Herrschaft Jever* (Oldenburg, 1888); *idem, Beiträge zur Kunde der Ref.-Geschichte* (1888, popularized version of the above); H. Reimers, *Die Gestaltung d. Reformation in Ostfriesland* (Aurich, 1917; No. 20 of *Abhandlungen und Beiträge zur Gesch. Ostfrieslands); ML II*, 405.

Jeyesz, Jeye (Jaye Jayesz), a preacher of the Amsterdam Mennonite Lamist church, 1648-71. After at first having opposed the progressive views of Galenus Abrahamsz (*q.v.*), a preacher of the same congregation, he soon became his friend and follower and sided with him during the quarrel and schism between the moderates or Lamists and the conservatives or Zonists.   vdZ.

H. W. Meihuizen, *Galenus Abrahamsz* (Haarlem, 1954) *passim,* see Index.

Jeziorka (German, *Kleinsee*), a village near the Vistula in the district of Schwetz, former territory of Polish Prussia (*q.v.*). Some 13 Mennonites of Dutch origin, from Przechovka (*q.v.,* Wintersdorf), settled there in 1727 to cultivate the land which had been laid waste by soldiers. The Mennonite group increased in 1732, when 12 families of the territory of Culm, persecuted by the Catholic bishop of Culm, also moved to Jeziorka. Like their mother church in Przechovka the Mennonite group of Jeziorka belonged to the Groningen Old Flemish branch. Apparently they never formed an independent congregation, but were in one congregation with their brethren in Przechovka and Konopath, although a church was built in Jeziorka in 1743. They sometimes were financially supported by the Dutch Mennonite Committee of Foreign Needs at Amsterdam. Though in the land leases of 1727 and again 1767 freedom of religion was granted to them, there were many difficulties with the Roman Catholic officials. Besides this the soil was too wet for profitable agriculture. For these and other reasons some of the Mennonites in 1765 moved to Brenkenhoffswalde (*q.v.*) and Franzthal (*q.v.*) in Neumark. In an official list of inhabitants of Jeziorka the following family names are found: Nagtigal (4), Ratzlaw (3), Becker (2), Unrau (2), Baller (1), Fott (1), Schmidt (1), Schultz (1), Pantzer (1). Again about 1813 a number of them emigrated to Deutsch-Wymysle (*q.v.*) in Poland. In the 19th century nearly all Mennonites disappeared from this territory.   vdZ.

Herbert Wiebe, *Das Siedlungswerk niederl. Mennoniten im Weichseltal . . .* (Marburg a.d. Lahn, 1952) 30 f., 42, 45, 47, 71 note 6, 81; *Inv. Arch. Amst.* I, Nos. 1091, 1601, 1607, 1702, 1713-36.

Jheronimo Droochscheerder (cloth shearer), an otherwise unknown Anabaptist martyr, born "bij Colm" (near Cologne?), was executed at Antwerp, Belgium, in 1535 (date unknown), by burning at the stake after he had been beheaded. He is called "one of the principal Anabaptists." (*Antw. Arch.-Blad* VII, 366; XIV, 14 f., No. 144.)   vdZ.

Jisp, a village in the Dutch province of North Holland near Krommenie (*q.v.*). The existence of an Anabaptist congregation here at a very early date is attested by the fact that in 1533 there were a number of Anabaptists in the town and that in 1581 the Jisp congregation was represented at a conference meeting at Amsterdam. It belonged to the Waterlander (*q.v.*) branch. In 1673 it seemed to be united with the Waterlander congregation of Wormer; it may later have been independent, for in 1833 a new union was made with Wormer. In 1793 the membership was so small that a decision had been made to sell the meetinghouse and to dissolve the congregation; but these plans were not carried out. The membership was 2 in 1825, 13 in 1847, and about 30 in 1900. Now (1954) the membership together with Wormer numbers 104, of which about

one fifth live at Jisp. Until about 1850 services were held both at Wormer and Jisp, from then on only in Wormer, the meetinghouse in Jisp having been sold. In 1923 the congregation of Wormer-Jisp made a union with that of Krommenie (*q.v.*) and has since then been served by the pastor of Krommenie.

From about 1637 until the 19th century Jisp was an important whaling center. Many whaling boats were owned by Mennonites of Jisp, particularly by members of the Mol (*q.v.*) family; Jan Jacobsz Mol was from 1728 one of the directors of the Dutch Greenland fishery. In the 17th and 18th centuries cod-liver oil rendering and biscuit baking (for the whalers and other ships) were important Mennonite industries at Jisp. Some members of this Mol family served as preachers, elders, and deacons in the 17th and 18th centuries.   vdZ.

Inv. Arch. Amst. I, Nos. 10, 98, 253, 708, 896; *DJ* 1837, 16; 1941, 40; *DB* 1877, 80; *ML* II, 406.

Jo Daviess County, Ill., the northwesternmost county in the state, to which came a few immigrant German Mennonite families with the names Baer, Duerrstein, Heer, Musselman, and Neuenschwander, beginning about 1840. Johannes Baer, ordained minister and bishop in Europe, served the congregation until his death about 1863 and was succeeded as minister by Michael Musselman. Services were held in a schoolhouse until a small church building was erected south of Scales Mound near the present Hammer Cemetery, which was originally a Mennonite cemetery. Soon after 1878 the congregation became extinct.   N.P.S.

Herald of Truth XV (December 1878) 211; H. F. Weber, *Centennial History of the Mennonites of Illinois* (Goshen, 1931) 94 f.

Joachim of Floris (Joachimus Calaber) (*ca.* 1132-1202), founder and first abbot of the Cistercian monastery in Calabria, an Italian mystic, the originator of the prophecy concerning the approach of the age of the Spirit (in 1260), which was to follow upon the age of the Father in the history of Israel and the age of the Son in the history of the Catholic Church, as the third and final era, and bring about a renewal of the Spirit in secularized Christendom. Joachim's ideas became widely spread. In some respects he prepared the way for the Reformation and Anabaptism; for the former in his antipapal attitude, which became more and more pronounced among the rigorous Franciscans, and for the latter in his demand for the renewal of life and his apocalyptic view of history and of the Bible.

Thus apparently Melchior Hofmann (*q.v.*) was influenced by Joachimite ideas in his exegesis of Revelation, in which he has the two witnesses of Rev. 11 appear before the dawn of the new age and oppose the anti-Christian papacy, and prophesy for 1,260 days in the spirit of Elijah and Enoch. The Joachimites understood these witnesses to be St. Francis and St. Dominicus, whereas Hofmann's followers saw their Elijah in Hofmann himself. Hofmann's analysis of history deviates from Joachim's in that he divides the period after Christ into three ages. A division of world history into three parts is again encountered in the exegesis of the High German Anabaptists, who call the Old Testament time yesterday, New Testament time today, and future time tomorrow, but here all extra-Biblical speculation is absent. G.H.

E. Benz, *Ecclesia Spiritualis* (Stuttgart, 1934); H. Bett, *Joachim of Flora* (London, 1931); G. Arnold, *Kirchen- und Ketzer-Historie* (Frankfurt, 1703) XII, 3, 5; XIII, 2, 3, c. 3, 2; F. O. zur Linden, *Melchior Hofmann, ein Prophet der Wiedertäufer* (Haarlem, 1885) 93 and 195 ff.; J. Loserth, *Quellen und Forschungen zur Geschichte der oberdeutschen Taufgesinnten im 16. Jahrhundert* (Vienna, 1929) 583; *ML* II, 427.

Joachim Ooms (Janssens), an Anabaptist martyr, was drowned in the Steen castle at Antwerp, Belgium, on Nov. 9, 1560, with Joris Leerse (*q.v.*). Joachim was a native of Curingen in the bishopric of Liége. There is little information about these martyrs. They were pious men; after the trial they sang. Standing at the stake Joachim said, "O Father, forgive them that they inflict this suffering upon us; but we thank Thee that Thou hast made us worthy to suffer for Thy name; therefore, O Lord, assist us, and succor us with Thy help in this last extremity." At the end they sang together a farewell. In commemoration of their death the hymn was written, "O Heere God eeuwich Vader verheven," found in the *Lietboecxken van den Offer des Heeren* of 1563 and in *Nieu Liedenboeck* of 1562. NEFF.

Offer, 560; *Mart. Mir.* D 275, E 644; *Antw. Arch.-Blad* IX, 115, 121; XIV, 30 f., No. 334; *ML* II, 427.

Joachim Vermeeren (Joos or Hans or Janne), called "(de) Suyckerbacker," a Mennonite elder who lived at Antwerp, Belgium, and who baptized there as well as at Gent and other Flemish towns a large number of people, and also performed many marriages. From which year Joachim was active could not be ascertained, but in 1557 he was already an elder. He also visited the Dutch province of Zeeland and in 1565 he was in Cologne, Germany. Here, apparently together with Matthys Servaes (*q.v.*), he was arrested. Under the persuasion of the Catholic priest Georg Cassander, who visited him in prison, Joachim recanted. About his further fate nothing is known.

Joachim's wife was also a Mennonite; Elder Dirk Philips (*q.v.*) wrote a letter to her, presumably in 1559, while she was in prison at Antwerp (this letter is found in *BRN* X, 675-88). According to van Braght's *Martyrs' Mirror* D 269, E 639 the name of this woman was Adriaentgen (Jochem's Wijf). In the letter by Dirk Philips her exact name is not found. Shortly after, this woman with four other Anabaptists succeeded in escaping from the Steen castle prison. It is not clear whether she was later rearrested and put to death (as the superscription of Dirk Philips' letter suggests) or not. No documents about her are available. vDZ.

K. Vos, "De Doopsgezinden te Antwerpen," in *Bulletin de la Commission Royale d' Histoire de Belgique* LXXXIV (Brussels, 1920), reprint 338-43; Mellink, *Wederdopers*, 310, 399; Verheyden, "Mennisme in Vlaanderen," ms.

Job (Jacob) **Janze** (Jansen, Jansz), an Anabaptist martyr of Harlingen, Dutch province of Friesland. He left Harlingen in May 1567 and settled in a village near Den Briel, Dutch province of South Holland. Here he lived quietly for some months, but in the fall of that year he was arrested and taken to The Hague, where he died at the stake on Dec. 18, 1568, with Jan Thielemansz (*q.v.*). He played a role in the Flemish-Frisian schism as one of the six men who banned Ebbe Pieters (*q.v.*). But later he asked Ebbe's pardon, adding, "How we poor human beings have let ourselves be misled to examine the Scripture in a spirit of discord and dissension instead of love, peace, and unity." Before his death he wrote a letter to Jan Willemsz (*q.v.*) and Lubbert Gerritsz (*q.v.*) concerning his part in the "Compromise." A letter he wrote was published in 1609 (n.p.) with a letter by Thijs Joriaens (*q.v.*). NEFF, vDZ.

Mart. Mir. D 377, E 731; *BRN* VII, 542; *DB* 1893, 48 f.; *Catalogus Amst.*, 100; *ML* II, 390.

Jobs, Jacob, a Dutch Mennonite elder, serving the congregation of the Jan-Jacobsz group (*q.v.*) on the island of Ameland (*q.v.*). In 1765 he was chosen preacher, in 1769 appointed elder, serving until his death in 1804. He was a lay preacher, having received no special theological training and governing the congregation "according to God's Word and the Mennonite usage," maintaining the old principles and even the ban, which was then quite unusual in Dutch congregations. By this maintenance of old customs he sometimes came into conflict with his congregation, especially with his coelder Cornelis Pieters Sorgdrager (*q.v.*), who introduced some new practices in the congregation like the "audible prayer," only silent prayers then being usual. Jacob Jobs was one of the last elders in the Netherlands who strictly maintained the Mennonite principles and customs of the 17th century. (*DB* 1889, 18, 31-43; 1890, 1-30.) vDZ.

Jobst, an otherwise unknown Anabaptist, who became a Hutterite elder and baptized Elisabeth, the wife of Hans Beck (*q.v.*), among others, apparently in South Germany about 1533. (Wolkan, *Lieder*, 30.) vDZ.

Jochem (Joachim) **Joosten,** an otherwise unknown Dutch Anabaptist martyr, beheaded on March 5, 1545, at The Hague, is said to have been the author of some Anabaptist books, which, however, have been lost. vDZ.

Inv. Arch. Amst. I, 745; L. Knappert, *Anabaptistica* (Leiden, 1905) 149 f.

Joes Mennonite Brethren Church, located 1½ miles east of Joes, on Highway 36, Yuma Co., Col., a member of the Southern District Conference, was organized in 1892 in a schoolhouse. A sod church was built in 1893 under the leadership of Henry Bergthold, replaced in 1918 by the present building which seats 200. The present (1953) membership is 61, with Eldo Ratzlaff as pastor. Ministers who have served are Henry Bergthold, Elder David Dyck, Jacob Friesen, Abraham Heinrichs, David Strauss, Peter Fleming, and Roland Wiens. P.C.H.

Joest Jacops (Jacopssoen), author of some hymns of the Dutch Mennonite hymnary *Het Tweede Liedeboeck* of 1583, viz., "Jubileert met vreuchden te samen" (Jubilate with joy all together), "Ick ben seer bedroeft int herte mijn" (I am much afflicted in my heart), and perhaps also of "In druck lijden en groot torment" (In distress, suffering, and great oppression). No further information about him was available. (Wolkan, *Lieder,* 70, 79 f.; *ML* II, 386.)   NEFF, vDZ.

Johan Andries(sen): see **Aken, Johan Andries van.**

Johan van Essen, an Anabaptist of Maastricht, Dutch province of Limburg, who is said to have been handed over by the city magistrates to the Supreme Court in 1542, apparently was executed for the fact that he had been rebaptized.   vDZ.

W. Bax, *Het Protestantisme in het Bisdom Luik* I (The Hague, 1937) 224.

Johan Lubelei (Loebeleie), an Anabaptist belonging to the revolutionary Münsterites (*q.v.*), was beheaded on Feb. 6, 1535, at the Brink square at Deventer, Dutch province of Overijssel. (*DB* 1919, 7 f.; Mellink, *Wederdopers, passim,* see Index.)   vDZ.

Johan (Jan) van Utrecht: see **Jan van Schoonhoven.**

Johan (Jan) van Wynssem (called Johan de Jonge), an Anabaptist belonging to the patrician van Wynssem (*q.v.*) family at Deventer, Dutch province of Overijssel, who like some other members of this family joined the Anabaptists and shared the revolutionary principles of Jan van Leyden (*q.v.*), who baptized Johan at Münster about Feb. 17, 1534. Johan van Wynssem was arrested on Jan. 28, 1535, and after a trial beheaded at the Brink square at Deventer on Feb. 6, 1535. (*DB* 1919, 5, 7 f.; Mellink, *Wederdopers,* 25, 28, 79, 272 f.)   vDZ.

Johann von Jülich: see **Jan van Gulik.**

Johann von Maastricht, an Anabaptist leader, who was present at the Anabaptist conference at Boekholt (Bocholt) in Westphalia, Germany, in 1536, is obviously identical with Jan Smeitgen (*q.v.*). vDZ.

Johann Nikolaus, an Anabaptist martyr, who was beheaded at Amsterdam in 1544: see **Jan Claesz.**

Johann, Sankt (*Johanniskirchen*), a former Mennonite congregation in the Rhenish Palatinate, which embraced the localities of Queichhambach, Böchingen, Ramberg, and Flagelstock, where services were held in rotation. In 1840 the congregation still had a membership of 100. It was greatly weakened by emigration to America, and has died out. (*ML* I, 74; II, 428.)   NEFF.

Johann von Schoenhofen: see **Jan van Schoonhoven.**

Johanna van Kent, an Anabaptist martyr: see **Boucher, Jane.**

Johannestal Mennonite Brethren Church, now extinct, located 15 miles from McClusky, N.D., was founded in 1904. In 1906 a meetinghouse was built. Early ministers and leaders were George Sattler and Ludwig Seibel. The latter was the leader of the Mennonite Brethren Church at McClusky. In 1924 the membership was 24. Its members have joined other Mennonite Brethren churches in the vicinity and in California.   C.K.

J. F. Harms, *Die Geschichte der Mennoniten Brüder-Gemeinde* (Hillsboro, n.d.,-ca.1924).

Johannestal Mennonite Church (GCM), located at Hillsboro, Kan., was organized in 1882 by Mennonites who had come from the Deutsch-Wymysle (*q.v.*) and Deutsch-Kazun (*q.v.*) congregations near Warsaw, Polish Russia. They began worshiping in private homes and in schools after their arrival and officially organized in 1882, joining the General Conference Mennonite Church in 1896. The first building was erected in 1884 three miles north of Hillsboro. In 1898 a new church was built which was later enlarged and replaced by a new one in 1922, to which a brick addition was added in 1951. The congregation was first served by John S. Hirschler. In 1886 John Gerbrandt and John Ewert were elected ministers. Gerbrandt (*q.v.*) was ordained elder in 1890.

There was a schism and for a time there were a First and a Second Johannestal Church, the latter being served by John D. Bartel as elder. Both groups used the same church. When John D. Bartel moved to North Dakota in 1897 John Plenert was elected elder, having been ordained to the ministry in 1893. After John Gerbrandt moved to Saskatchewan in 1905 the two groups reunited under Elder Plenert, who was succeeded by S. M. Musselman in 1937; Musselman died in 1938 and was succeeded by J. M. Regier, who served the congregation 1939-51. Roy Henry became the elder in May 1951 and was succeeded in 1954 by Delton W. Franz, and in 1956 by Esko Loewen. In 1956 the congregation had a membership of 199.   C.K.

Sixtieth Anniversary of the Johannestal Mennonite Church (Hillsboro, Kan., 1952).

John Casimir (1543-92), Count Palatine at Rhein, administrator of the Palatinate 1583-92. He was the fourth son of Elector Palatine Frederick III. After the death of his brother, the Lutheran-minded Elector Louis VI, he assumed the rule of the Palatinate as the guardian of his minor nephew, who later became Elector Frederick IV, in accord with the testamentary provision. It was his aim to win the populace to the Calvinist faith, which his father was the first German prince to enter. Since the Lutheran church council did not bow to his demands, John Casimir had it removed from office; the Lutheran preachers who refused voluntarily to join the Calvinist church were also dismissed.

The Anabaptists were also required to accept the Calvinist creed, but they resisted the demand. A tense struggle ensued, which affords an interesting glance into the religious life of the populace. John Casimir saw in the Anabaptists "poor straying people," who must find their salvation in the Reformed Church. They, on the other hand, pointed out to him the corrupt conditions in his own church, which prevented their joining it.

In 1583 John Casimir then issued a severe mandate against the Anabaptist leaders as "obstinate, misleading, and seditious corner preachers," who spread an "offensive, poisonous, treacherous doctrine, harmful to eternal and temporal welfare." Their preaching and meeting were severely interdicted under threat of stiff penalty. If an Anabaptist was found out, he would have to state the grounds of his separation before the magistrate

(*Amtmann*), and in the presence of the Reformed preacher. Whoever would not be instructed in church doctrine would be thrown into prison and put on a meager diet. The pastors must from time to time try to convert them and must meanwhile baptize their as yet unbaptized children. Anyone who still persisted in his faith would then be exiled, and his property would be managed by the city; his wife and children would receive the income from it.

The mandate admits that the Anabaptist movement was strongest where no sound doctrine was preached and where the people lived wicked lives. This fact was also the reason for the Anabaptist refusal to attend church. In the future they must have no occasion to take offense at the manner of life of a fellow citizen. The pastors were urged to "live a Christian life" and to refute and overthrow Anabaptist doctrine with arguments from the Holy Scriptures. Officials and persons in authority must support the pastors by urging the Anabaptists to go to state church services and by giving a good example in word and deed, "so that it might be said in truth that by their conduct our Father in heaven is praised." Officials were obliged to attend the sermons; special chairs should be assigned to them in the churches. No citizen would be permitted to neglect church attendance without good reason. Whoever disobeyed this injunction would be punished by imprisonment. Officials must diligently seek out Anabaptists.

But outward compulsion did not bring about the desired inward change. Five years after the mandate was enacted, the Anabaptist movement was still not suppressed, but had even spread. Banishment from the country could no longer be carried out because it harmed the state economically. Government pressure relaxed.

The state church council tried the more zealously to suppress the movement, but in 1588 confessed that without the outward political compulsion and the support of temporal authorities they could accomplish nothing. This was easy to understand in view of the offensive conduct of the people, as the pastor of Wiesloch, Nussloch, and Leimen reported to the church council; there was no hope of winning the Anabaptists into the church. They would see in the members "nothing but what pains the heart and causes offense, namely, a free, unrestrained epicurean manner with swearing, cursing, gluttony, drinking, dancing, quarreling, fighting, fornication, immorality, and the like."

In the last years of John Casimir's life, the Palatinate was hard pressed by foreign powers. A part of the population was drafted for military training in 1588; thus Johann Casimir was one of the first rulers to introduce a popular militia. Death put an end to his goal of setting up a Protestant emperor. In the last years of his reign only one act of government is mentioned that deals with the Anabaptists. In 1591 his subjects were forbidden to employ them for money.   HEGE.

Chr. Hege, *Die Täufer in der Kurpfalz* (Frankfurt, 1908); Martha Brandt, *Johann Kasimir und die pfälzische Politik in den Jahren 1588-1592* (Berlin, 1909); ML II, 430.

John II, Casimir, King of Poland 1648-68, confirmed the privileges of the Mennonites in a document of June 16, 1650 (found in Mannhardt, pp. LXIII-LXV), which states that the Mennonites were not to be suppressed for their religion, that they should be released from the obligation of paying a protection fee, and remain in "full possession of their property, rights, privileges, justice, and all their customs."

When the Mennonites were later made suspect of Arianism in order to have them expelled from the country, the king again protected them ("in order that our income may not suffer serious loss") in an order dated Nov. 20, 1660, for "the law of 1558 against Arians cannot be applied to the Mennonites, who are farmers, and whose religious services are not public, but are held as the religious dignitaries permit them. We promise for ourselves and our successors that we intend to preserve in freedom these subjects and Mennonites in Tiegenhagen together with their descendants, and we command our officials to protect the Mennonites in accord with this order and to see that they are protected by others."
                        NEFF.

W. Mannhardt, *Die Wehrfreiheit der Altpreussischen Mennoniten* (Marienburg, 1863); ML II, 431.

John III, Duke of Jülich, Cleve, and Berg, 1511-39, a vacillating prince, who especially in the regulation of religious matters was led by his advisers. In 1529 he gave the delegates from his cities strict orders to carry out the imperial mandate, which commanded that all "Luthryanen" who ventured to baptize anew should be "without hesitation punished, burned, beheaded, or drowned" (Rembert, 19). In 1533 he had a church inspection (Cornelius, 216-48) made, which was to pay particular attention to the sects, inquiring into the residence and activities of "corner preachers," time, place, and organization of their meetings, and the nature of their books. The results revealed that there were Anabaptists in many places, and strict measures were undertaken to combat them. On March 14, 1534, John issued an edict against the Anabaptists, ordering that "the leaders and inciters be brought to suitable punishment; . . . those who persist in their error be executed with fire, and those who recant, with the sword; but those simple ones who have been misled and will take upon themselves penitence and public confession shall receive grace" (*Monatshefte*, 161 ff.).   NEFF.

Rembert, *Wiedertäufer*; C. A. Cornelius, *Geschichte des Münsterischen Aufruhrs* I (Leipzig, 1855); *Monatshefte für rheinische Kirchengeschichte*, 1917; Otto R. Redlich, *Jülich-Bergische Kirchenpolitik am Ausgange des Mittelalters und in der Reformationszeit*, 2 vv. (Bonn, 1907-11) in *Publikationen der Gesellschaft für rheinische Geschichtskunde* XXVIII; ML II, 428.

John Frederick I, the Magnanimous, Elector of Saxony, 1532-54, the elder son of John the Steadfast (*q.v.*), followed closely in the steps of his father. He demanded of Philip of Hesse that he execute Fritz Erbe (*q.v.*), the Anabaptist prisoner at Eisenach, and obtained the verdict of the Leipzig jurists, which also required Erbe's death. Nevertheless Philip was reluctant to carry out this sentence (a letter dated May 22, 1533, to John Frederick). In the reply of May 25, John Frederick insisted that Fritz Erbe be punished by death, supporting his opinion on the imperial mandates and on the opinion his father had received from the Wittenberg theologians. Still Philip did not yield; on May 28 he replied that he could give his consent only to further imprisonment or expulsion. The dispute nearly ended in a rupture between the two princes, for John Frederick intended to have Erbe executed on his own responsibility (letter of July 28, 1544); nevertheless consideration for Philip saved Erbe from a martyr's death; he died in prison.

The 19 Anabaptists imprisoned at Berka (Hausbreitenbach district), who were cross-examined on June 19-21, 1533, were treated better. In this case also, John Frederick wanted to apply the death penalty according to the imperial mandate; the chancellor Brück agreed. But Philip refused, and out of respect for him the prisoners were released.

On Jan. 26, 1536, John Frederick had three Anabaptists sentenced to death and executed upon the advice of Melanchthon (report to the elector of Jan. 19, 1536) and the opinion of the legal scholars at Jena (q.v.) (Wappler, Stellung, 149). Two additional executions followed. On April 10, 1536, John Frederick issued a new mandate against the Anabaptists, drawn up by Melanchthon. The first part repeated the mandate of Jan. 17, 1528. Then as a warning to all, and pointing out the recent executions, follow the Anabaptist articles of faith, by which they were misleading and poisoning the soul and body of the simple populace. At the same time the elector sent to every parson in the electorate of Saxony a copy of Melanchthon's book, *Verlegung etlicher unchristlicher Glaubensartikel, welche die Wiedertäufer fürgeben* (Wittenberg, n.d.) to be read and explained on every third Sunday.

In 1543 John Frederick had the steadfast Peter Erbe executed (Wappler, Inquisition, 90). In 1545 he wished to apply the imperial mandate to some Anabaptists in Mühlhausen. In a joint letter with Duke Maurice of Saxony (July 24) he tried to gain Philip's consent. But the latter made a decisive reply (Aug. 19, 1545), which is a beautiful memorial to his religious tolerance and magnanimity. At the end of January 1530 the court of Wittenberg had two Anabaptists put to death, causing an unfavorable reaction.   NEFF.

P. Wappler, *Die Stellung Kursachsens und des Landgrafen Philipp von Hessen zur Täuferbewegung* (Münster, 1910); idem, *Inquisition und Ketzerprozesse zur Reformationszeit* (Leipzig, 1908); *ML* II, 429.

John Frederick II (1529-95), Duke of Saxony, the son of Duke John Frederick the Magnanimous. After the capture of his father in the Battle of Mühlberg in 1547, he shared the government of Saxony with his brother John William and in behalf of his minor brother, John Frederick III; when the latter died childless in 1565, John Frederick II became the ruler of Gotha.

Like his father John Frederick II fought the Anabaptists. But after the Battle of Mühlberg his father became more lenient; on Sept. 15, 1551, he wrote

from prison to his son John Frederick II: "To threaten heretics with the fear of fire and not to instruct them in the Scriptures, we cannot consider Christian or right" (Schmidt, 135). And on March 7, 1559, Philip of Hesse wrote to the duke, "We should not look only upon ourselves, but also upon other Christians, that they also may fare well, and if they perhaps err in one article, they should not therefore be consigned to the slaughtering bench" (*Corpus Reformatorum* IX, 759).

But these admonitions made no impression on John Frederick II. Soon after the opening of the University of Jena, which he had founded in 1558, he had his Lutheran theologians work out a confessional statement, known as the Weimar Refutation, in which he damns without differentiation all the sects: Servetus, Schwenckfeld, the Antinomians, Sacramentists, Osiandrists, Stankarists, Majorists, Adiaphorists, as well as the "Anabaptists who are an unchristian sect." The Refutation appeared in 1559, a booklet of 84 pages with the title, *Des Johans Friderichen, Hertzogen zu Sachsen, für sich selbs und von wegen seiner Brüder, Hertzog Johan Wilhelm und Hertzog Johan Friderich in Gottes Wort prophetischer und apostolischer Schrift gegründete Confutationes, Widerlegungen und Verdammung etlicher Corruptelen, Secten und Irrtumen.*

Duke John Frederick II was placed in the imperial ban in 1563, and arrested in 1567 at the surrender of Grimmenstein near Gotha. He died May 9, 1595, in a castle at Steyr in Upper Austria. HEGE.

P. Wappler, *Die Stellung Kursachsens und des Landgrafen Philipp von Hessen zur Täuferbewegung* (Münster, 1910); G. L. Schmidt, *Justus Menius, der Reformator Thüringens* II (Gotha, 1867); *ML* II, 429.

John Miller's Mennonite Church, former name of the River Corner Mennonite Church (q.v.).

John III, Sobieski, King of Poland 1674-96, protected Mennonite privileges and rights. When the *voivode* of Pomerelle promoted the expulsion of the Mennonites in the Marienburg parliament (1676) and in the Polish parliament, the provincial judge reported to the king the injury that would accrue to the economic welfare of Marienburg if this should happen. The king was convinced, and commanded that the constitution which had already been passed opposing the Mennonites, be destroyed, and in a rescript of 1678 gave them special protection. In addition to their original lands, others were now assigned to them. In 1694 the king reaffirmed all these rights, expressly designating that all the privileges granted by earlier kings should be extended to all the Mennonites living in the Werder. The regulation of Aug. 22, 1694, reads, "Since the Mennonites have shown great zeal to prove themselves deserving, it is fitting and proper to preserve to them all their rights, privileges, and customs, . . . and we will grant the free exercise of the Mennonite religion." In 1681 he saved the lace makers from oppression by the Danzig magistrates by reaffirming their former privileges.   NEFF.

W. Mannhardt, *Die Wehrfreiheit der Altpreussischen Mennoniten* (Marienburg, 1863) 87 ff.; *Inv. Arch. Amst.* 11, 2, No. 697; *ML* II, 431.

John the Steadfast, Elector of Saxony 1525-32, an ardent friend and patron of Luther, headed the evangelical estates in Germany and was an active promoter of the Reformation. On Feb. 26, 1525, he issued a public order for Koburg, "that no one, be he citizen, peasant, or whoever, except regular pastors, preachers, and chaplains who have charge of pastoral work at each place and are authorized to do so, shall be permitted to preach, baptize, or perform other offices of the kind at his home or anywhere else." This regulation was extended to Thuringia and Franconia on March 31, 1527.

On Jan. 17, 1528, the elector issued a new mandate against the Anabaptists (Wappler, 165), extending the scope of the previous one. All who, without office, preach or baptize, shall be arrested. Likewise all writings and books of the Anabaptists, sacramentists, and enthusiasts shall be confiscated. This mandate was to be posted on the church doors and announced every Sunday at the close of the services.

As early as February 1527, the first Anabaptists in the electorate of Saxony were seized, racked, and beheaded. They were Beutelhans (*q.v.*) of Königsberg, and Wolf Schreiner (*q.v.*). Hence it is not surprising that John the Steadfast readily gave his assent to the decree of Charles V, April 23, 1529, condemning Anabaptists to death with fire and sword. This position he stubbornly maintained in opposition to Philip of Hesse (*q.v.*). On Dec. 4, 1529, he wrote Philip, demanding that he have Melchior Rink (*q.v.*) executed, and if he could not agree to do it, he should at least have him banished, lest he lead other subjects astray. Thus he managed to have Rink exiled from Hesse and Saxony. He also wrote a warning to Count Günther of Schwarzburg, on March 27, 1530, concerning the Anabaptists, requesting that he arrest Valentine Ickelsamer (*q.v.*) and deliver him to Gotha. On Jan. 18, 1530, he had six Anabaptists executed at Rheinhardsbrunn, an act which caused considerable unrest.

On Oct. 9, 1531, some Anabaptists seized in Hausbreitenbach were brought to Eisenach and tried on the rack. What should be done with them? John requested an opinion of the Wittenberg theologians, which was sent in late October. It recommended the death penalty. Since the Anabaptists were no doubt revolutionary, the elector might with a clear conscience apply the death penalty against them. But though John agreed, he lacked authority to do so, for Hausbreitenbach was held in joint jurisdiction with Hesse. Thus a long-continued quarrel arose between John of Saxony and Philip of Hesse. The suggestion was made that all the Anabaptists under joint jurisdiction be equally divided between them, allowing each to proceed as he saw fit. But there were serious objections to this course.

The matter was then presented for discussion to the League of Schmalkalden in session at Nordhausen (early December 1531), but without result. Saxony insisted on the death penalty; Hesse resisted. Meanwhile Rink had again been seized. John insisted on the supreme penalty; in a letter dated Dec. 21, 1531, he expressed the hope that Philip would now have the dangerous prisoner executed in accordance with the law of April 23, 1529. But the landgrave refused. Instead he sentenced him to "eternal imprisonment." He informed John of this fact and stated that he could not sentence anyone to death by the sword for a matter of faith. The elector, defeated in the case of Rink, in a letter of Jan. 15, 1532, begged the landgrave to come to an agreement with him in the punishment of the Hausbreitenbach Anabaptists; the laws should be strictly obeyed. But the landgrave was unwilling to accede, and the earlier suggestion of dividing the Anabaptists in the area was carried out. Of the Anabaptists falling to Saxony three were killed (1532). NEFF.

G. Berbig, "Die Wiedertäuferei im Ortslande zu Franken . . ." in *Deutsche Zeitung für Kirchenrecht* XII, 386-88; XIII, 337-41 (contains the mandates issued by John); *ML* II, 428.

John William (1658-1716), Elector Palatine 1690-1716 was a strongly Catholic ruler, who was not interested in the needs of his non-Catholic subjects. Not until eight years after the death of his father, Philip William, was the "concession" granted the Mennonites renewed. Repeated petitions were ignored, largely because of the distress caused by the war Louis XIV made on the Palatinate. On Feb. 10, 1698, the Mennonites presented their petition again, and were heard. On Feb. 18 the elector issued an order to his magistrates to grant the request and carry out its requirements. On Nov. 3, 1698, followed the decree renewing the concession.

In John William's reign occurred the forcible evacuation of the Mennonites from Rheydt (1694), which attracted much attention. At the intervention of the Dutch Mennonites the States-General and King William III of England each wrote a letter of intercession (*q.v.*) to the elector, requesting not only that the Mennonites be granted complete freedom to carry on trade and crafts, but also that their confiscated property be restored. The States-General also wrote to Emperor Leopold, requesting his intervention with the elector to have the persecution of the Mennonites ended. Reluctantly John William yielded to the pressure of the States-General, the emperor, and the king of England. On April 12 and Aug. 17, 1697, he decreed that the Mennonites should be permitted to carry on free trade and that their property and books be restored to them at once (Rembert, *Wiedertäufer,* 530-33).

On the whole the Mennonites were given reasonable consideration under John William. The request of a Mennonite named Schnebely to settle in Mannheim was refused, although the mayor had approved it (May 10, 1706). On the other hand, the petition of all the Mennonites in the Palatinate to be released from all military service was granted (Jan. 27, 1712). Two years later the fee they were paying the state was increased by a considerable sum. Their request to have it reduced, supported by the Dutch Mennonites (Jan. 15, 1715), was rejected. NEFF.

A. Brons, *Ursprung, Entwickelung, und Schicksale der Taufgesinnten oder Mennoniten* (Norden, 1884); *Inv. Arch. Amst.* I, Nos. 1427 f., 1749-53, 1755; *ML* II, 431.

Johns, Daniel J. (1850-1942), one of the outstanding leaders in the Indiana-Michigan Amish Mennonite Conference and later of the entire Mennonite Church (MC). He was a great-grandson of Joseph

Schantz (*q.v.*), a Swiss Amish immigrant to America of about 1765, who first located in Berks Co., Pa., but later removed to Somerset Co., Pa., where he laid out building lots for the city of Johnstown, which was named in his honor. Daniel J. Johns was born in Somerset County on Sept. 8, 1850, the son of John Johns. In 1865 John Johns removed to Lagrange Co., Ind., with his family, partly because he had been elected sheriff of Conemaugh Township, an office which he could not accept because of his faith —although he felt that his brethren in the faith had helped elect him. Daniel taught school successfully for seven years. He married Nancy Yoder in 1875. Two of their six children are Bishop O. N. Johns of Louisville, Ohio, and Ira S. Johns (d. 1956) of Goshen, Ind. D. J. Johns united with the Amish Mennonite Church in 1876, and six years later was ordained preacher on the basis of a congregational vote, by the visiting bishop, Joseph Stuckey (*q.v.*) of Illinois. In 1887 Isaac Schmucker, who was the first Amish Mennonite bishop in Indiana, ordained D. J. Johns to the office of bishop. He was a vigorous and progressive leader. He helped organize the Indiana-Michigan A.M. Conference in 1888 and served for more than 25 years in the united conference after it merged with the Indiana-Michigan Mennonite Conference in 1916. He helped arrange for the first Sunday-school conference (MC) in 1892, helped organize the Elkhart Institute Association in 1895, helped arrange for the first session of the Mennonite General Conference in 1898, and helped organize

the Mennonite Board of Missions and Charities in 1906. As a bishop he was rather mild in his discipline as a middle-aged leader, but became more strict in his later years. He died May 22, 1942, about 60 years after his ordination as preacher.   J.C.W.

Johns, Joseph (Schantz) (1749-1813), a Swiss Amish immigrant of 1769 who located in the angle formed by the converging Stony Creek and Conemaugh River on the present site of Johnstown, Pa., in 1793. In a charter of Nov. 3, 1800, he deeded most of his farm, together with a plot of 141 lots (with instructions for public buildings including a school and courthouse), for a town, Conemaugh. The name was later changed to Johnstown in his honor, made legal in 1834. The city now has a population of 67,000. Johns, like other Amishmen, moved away from the growing town to a farm nine miles south, near the present village of Davidsville (named after Amishman David Stutzman), in 1807, where he and his descendants, including his son John and grandson, also named Joseph Johns (Amish members), are buried. A statue of Joseph Johns (by J. Otto Schweizer) was erected on the town square in 1913 on the occasion of the first centennial of Johnstown.   J.A.H.

Somerset County Deed Book II, 246-47; Maurice A. Mook, "Amishman Who Founded a City," *Christian Living* II (July 1955).

John's Lake Mennonite Brethren Church, a member of the M.B. Central District Conference, formerly

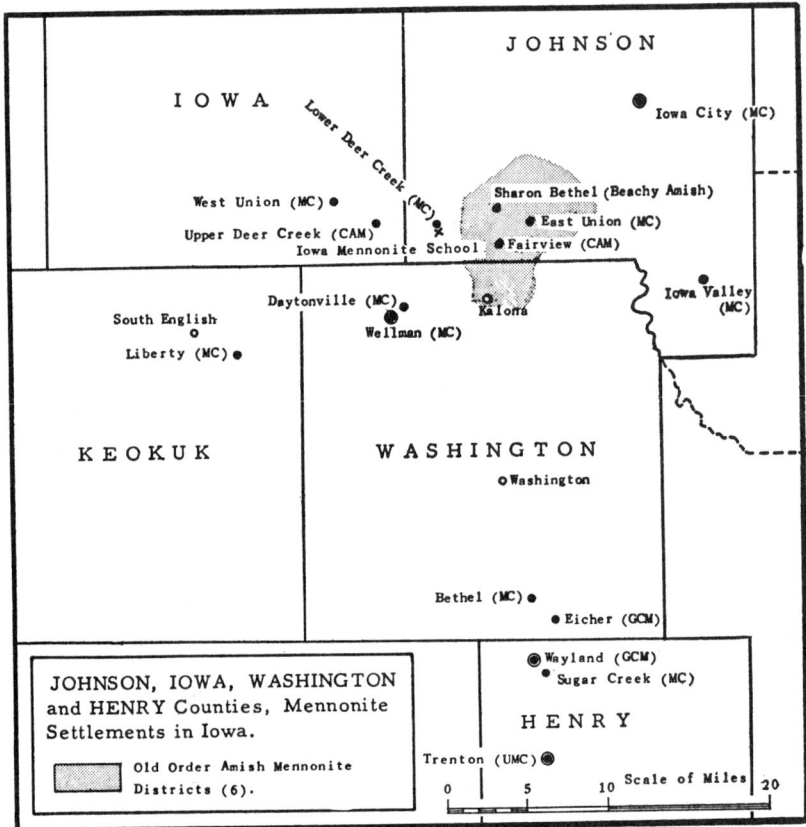

JOHNSON, IOWA, WASHINGTON and HENRY Counties, Mennonite Settlements in Iowa.

☐ Old Order Amish Mennonite Districts (6).

known as Johannesthal, located at Regan, Burleigh Co., N.D., was organized by Ludwig Seibel. A church was built in 1916. The congregation is affiliated with the McClusky M.B. Church, and has been served by its pastors. The membership of 24 was listed under McClusky only in the 1954 Central District Conference *Yearbook*. Lillian Schafer, missionary to Colombia, South America, and Elsie Schafer, a Christian worker, have come from this church. **A.A.D.**

Johnson County, Iowa, in the eastern part of the state, lies approximately 50-70 miles west of Davenport. It is an agricultural county with only one large city, Iowa City (*q.v.*), within its borders. Located within the county are six Mennonite churches; East Union, Lower Deer Creek, Iowa Valley, and Iowa City are members of the Iowa-Nebraska (MC) Conference, while Fairview is Conservative Amish Mennonite and Sharon-Bethel is Beachy Amish. All but Iowa City and Iowa Valley are located in the southwest corner of the county. In the same general area are six Old Order Amish districts with 464 members, most of whom live in Johnson County. The Johnson-Iowa-Washington county settlement contains 2,821 Amish and Mennonite church members in 16 congregations of whom approximately 1,800 live in Johnson County. Of the 2,821 members, 1,835 belong to the Mennonite Church (MC), 470 to the Conservative Amish Mennonite Conference, 52 to the Beachy Amish, and 464 to the Old Order Amish.

The first Amish to move into the county came from Ohio and Pennsylvania in 1846. The settlement was one of the most successful established by the Amish in the central states and has grown steadily during the past century. As the home of three generations of Swartzendruber bishops—Jacob, Frederick, and Jacob F.—as well as of Samuel D. Guengerich (*q.v.*) and his publishing enterprise, the community has been unusually influential in Amish Mennonite circles. Recently the Iowa Mennonite School (*q.v.*) was established in the heart of the Johnson County Mennonite community. Unusual also is the fact that from this Amish community have come at least nine Mennonites who have earned the doctor of philosophy degree. At least 12 Elkhart Institute and Goshen College faculty members were born in this settlement. **M.G.**

M. Gingerich, *The Mennonites in Iowa* (Iowa City, 1939); E. G. Swartzendruber, *Amish and Mennonite Church Centennial near Wellman and Kalona, Iowa* (Wellman, Iowa, 1953).

Johnson County, Mo., approximately 50 miles southeast of Kansas City, with Cass County (*q.v.*) on its western border, at one time contained an Amish Mennonite settlement, located in the southwestern part of the county near Holden. The first Amish settlers in the community were Joseph Gerber and his family, who moved here from Indiana around 1870. The first church was built in 1889 and was located six miles southwest of Holden. By 1893 the congregation, named Pleasant View, had 53 members, who were served by the preachers David Morrell and Andrew Miller, both old men. Later in this decade Henry Rychener was ordained to

serve the church. Under his leadership the church changed from German to English services. At its highest membership, the congregation numbered approximately 100. After Rychener moved to Ohio, D. B. Raber was ordained to serve the congregation. About 1908 members began to move from the community to Cass Co., Mo., Aurora, Ohio, and other places. When Raber moved to Portage Co., Ohio, in 1911 the church was without a minister and eventually became extinct. **M.G.**

Johnson, Francis, born at Richmond, England, in 1562, died at Amsterdam, Netherlands, Jan. 10, 1618, was a Puritan minister banished from England in 1590 because he had offended the queen. He then successively was a pastor of an English emigrant group at Middelburg, Dutch province of Zeeland, converted to Brownism (*q.v.*) in 1592, became pastor of the Brownist congregation of Islington near London, England, in 1592, was in prison at London 1593-97, and after 1598 served as pastor of a Brownist congregation at Amsterdam with Thomas Ainsworth (*q.v.*), with whom he fell into discord, so that Ainsworth and a large number of members separated from Johnson and his followers, called Johnsonians or Francisites, in 1610. In 1612 Johnson was ordered by the magistrates of Amsterdam to leave the city; he then moved to Emden, Germany, but soon was back in Amsterdam, where he died. Johnson, an ambitious and a quarrelsome man, is of interest for Mennonite history, because he, in the period in which there were many contacts between Mennonites and Brownists and a number of Brownists had intended to join the Mennonites (see **Smyth, John**), fervently tried to prevent this union. Some of his other writings were: *A Brief Treatise Containing Reasons Against Two Errors of the Anabaptists* (n.p., 1609-10, reprinted 1645) and *A Christian Plea, Conteyning Three Treatises Touching the Anabaptists and Others* (n.p., 1617). **vDZ.**

J. G. de Hoop Scheffer-W. E. Griffis, *History of the Free Churchmen* (Ithaca, N.Y., n.d.-1922) *passim; N.N.B.Wb.* IX, 461-63.

Johnson, Nicholas (1787-1873), a resident of Fayette County, Pa., near Masontown, ordained deacon in 1809, then minister and finally bishop in 1840 in the Masontown Mennonite (MC) Church. A progressive leader, he has the credit of introducing in 1842 the first Mennonite Sunday school. **H.S.B.**

Johnson Mennonites. The original Skippack Mennonite congregation and meetinghouse were located in what was then Bebber's (now Skippack) Twp., Montgomery Co., Pa. The Mennonite settlement was begun there in 1702. The first meetinghouse, erected about 1725, was replaced by a new meetinghouse in 1844. Three years later came the Oberholtzer schism in the Franconia Conference, and a portion of the congregation seceded with him. The other portion of the congregation, which remained in the Franconia Conference, rather than to resort to litigation withdrew and erected the Upper Skippack meetinghouse in 1848. The old Skippack meetinghouse and congregation then came to be called

Lower Skippack. The Lower Skippack congregation passed through some trials after the division of 1847, one of which was the lack of harmony between its preacher, Henry G. Johnson, and the new Oberholtzer Conference. For instance, Johnson wished to promote the observance of footwashing, whereas the conference wished to allow congregational freedom on the matter. As a result the Lower Skippack group ceased attending the sessions of the conference. The conference then passed a resolution on May 15, 1859, declaring the ministers and delegates of the group to be out of order, since they had ceased to attend the conference. Most of Johnson's congregation stood by him and withdrew from the conference, the group retaining the ownership of the meetinghouse. A small part of the congregation, however, maintained connections with the conference and conducted separate services in the meetinghouse until they were denied the use of the building in 1865. By resolution on May 4, 1886, the conference officially declared that the congregation had ceased to exist. Among the ministers ordained by the Johnson group were Johnson's son, Henry H. Johnson, in 1878, and his grandson, Henry M. Johnson, in 1915. The group was therefore commonly known as the "Johnson Mennonites." It has continued as a congregation with a membership (1954) of 300, with Henry M. Johnson as bishop, Frank Crall as minister, and Warren B. Anders as deacon.   J.C.W.

J. C. Wenger, *History of the Mennonites of the Franconia Conference* (Telford, 1937) 96-99, 359, 360.

Johnstown, Pa., is a city (pop. 67,000) in Cambria County, adjacent to a large Mennonite (MC) settlement in northern Somerset County and southern Cambria County. Johnstown was named after Joseph Johns (*q.v.*), an Amishman who settled here in 1793 and platted part of his farm for a town in 1800. The Mennonites (MC) settled in this area about 1790. The area has a membership of 850 with eight churches, one of them a mission church located in the city, all belonging to the Allegheny Conference. Only a small percentage of the membership ever lived in the city before 1939, when the mission was started there. Johnstown is the shopping center of this area. Johnstown is known as the "flood city," having been destroyed in 1889 by the breaking of a dam near South Fork about 13 miles above the town. It has large steel mills, and large coal workings in the surrounding area, making it an important industrial city.   A.Ka.

Johnstown Bible School, Johnstown, Pa., a six-week winter Bible school, held annually in January and February in the Stahl Mennonite (MC) Church near Hollsopple, Pa., was begun in 1922, as a result of urging by S. G. Shetler, the minister of the Stahl church. It is controlled by an autonomous board of ten, including three Allegheny Conference appointees. Its enrollment has never been large, in 1955 being 24 for the day school, 70 in the evening school. The principals have been S. G. Shetler 1925-35 and 1940-42, E. C. Bender 1937-39, Lloy Kniss 1942-44, Sanford G. Shetler 1944-47, Paul Roth 1947-54, Har-

ry Y. Shetler 1954-56. The day school was discontinued in 1956.   H.S.B.

C. Y. Fretz, "A History of Winter Bible Schools in the Mennonite Church," *MQR* XVI (1942) 51-81, 178-96.

Johnstown First Mennonite Church (MC) was founded in 1939 as a mission under the district mission board of the Southwestern Pennsylvania Mennonite Conference (now Allegheny Mennonite Conference), which still sponsors it. The services were held in rented dwelling houses until 1949. In 1945 a lot with house was purchased close to the center of the city; the house was converted into a parsonage. A brick meetinghouse was built on an adjoining lot, and dedicated in 1949. The membership was 66 in 1955, with John E. Gingrich as pastor and bishop (ord. 1955).   J.E.G.

Johnstown (Col.) Mennonite Brethren Church, now extinct, had its origin in 1906, when a number of Mennonite Brethren families who had moved from Kirk to Loveland, Col., organized a congregation with Henry Nickel as leader. By 1924 the membership numbered 37. In 1926 the Loveland church was relocated in Johnstown, Col. In the following years attendance ran as high as 100; however, being unable to buy or rent land, more and more people left for other Mennonite areas, especially in California. By 1943 the membership had dwindled to 21. After several years the remaining members joined the Evangelical Free Church and the Baptist Church in Greeley. At the 1948 Southern District Conference the church was officially dissolved.   O.Ha.

Johnstown Mennonite (MC) **School,** a church high school located at Hollsopple, Pa., five miles south of Johnstown, founded in 1944, is operated by an independent board representing chiefly the Mennonite (MC) congregations of the immediate vicinity. In 1955 it had four teachers, with an enrollment of 39. Operated as a part of the same institution is an eight-grade elementary school with an enrollment of 67, and a total of six teachers, including the high-school staff. Sanford Shetler has been principal from the beginning.   H.S.B.

Jonas, Justus (1493-1555), a humanist and theologian, co-worker with Luther. In 1521 he was appointed professor of canon law at the University of Wittenberg, accompanied Luther to the Reichstag at Worms, and supported him in his translation of the Bible and in church inspection. He introduced the Reformation at Halle in 1541.

In his views on the Anabaptists, Jonas shared fully the view prevailing at Wittenberg. When Emperor Charles V issued his edict against the Anabaptists on Jan. 4, 1528, which became the pattern for similar laws in many countries making adherence to an Anabaptist group punishable by death, and Melanchthon published his booklet, *Adversus Anabaptistas Judicium,* Jonas at once translated this attack on the Anabaptists into German, with the title: *Unterricht Philip. Melan. Wider die Lere der Widerteuffer aus dem latin verdeudschet, durch Just. Jonas.* He dedicated the book to Michael Meienburg, city secretary of Nordhausen, to whom Jonas wrote on Feb. 3,

1538, that he hoped it would aid many pious hearts and consciences disturbed by such false doctrine, and that lovers of the Gospel would gladly read it and thank God for such powerful, gracious preservation of the pure doctrine and divine truth (Kawerau, 118). In 1539 he was one of the instigators of the church inspection in Saxony and wrote the local *Kirchenordnung*.

Melanchthon's arguments were not accepted in all theological circles. The Swabian reformer Johannes Brenz (*q.v.*) wrote a reply to the book, which denies the government the right to punish the Anabaptists with death for their faith.

Jonas did not play an important part in the further opposition to the Anabaptists. HEGE.

G. Kawerau, *Der Briefwechsel des Justus Jonas* I (Halle, 1884); A. Weingarten, *Zeittafel zur Kirchengeschichte* (1905) 117; Th. Pressel, *Justus Jonas* (Elberfeld, 1862); *ML* II, 432.

Joncker, Roelof Agge, a Dutch Mennonite preacher (d. 1730), who served at Oldemarkt (*q.v.*) 1699-1712 and at Cadzand (*q.v.;* also called Nieuwvliet) 1712-30. Joncker published his *Mennoniste Vrageboeck* (Steenwijk, 1708), and in 1709 a hymnbook with the title: *Eenige psalmen des propheten Davids. Op sodainige wijsen als bij de Boeren en Zeeluy veel bekent zijn; nieuwelijcks in dicht gestelt.* His conduct caused offense. VDZ.

Inv. Arch. Amst. II, Nos. 1642-56, 2184; II, 2, Nos. 595, 598; *DB* 1878, 12; 1889, 110 f.; *ML* II, 432.

Jonckhans, Dirck, a martyr: see **Dirck, Cleynen.**

Jong, Arnoldus de, a Dutch Mennonite pastor, b. April 14, 1802, at Leeuwarden, d. May 22, 1854, at Dantumawoude, studied at the Amsterdam Mennonite Seminary and served the congregation of Surhuisterveen 1826-27 and Dantumawoude 1827-54. He is the author of some poetical works. He was married to Anna Fontein of Harlingen. His son Dirk Fontein de Jong was a promoter of the Frisian dairy industry, having also a keen interest in church matters; in 1896 he was president of the Friese Sociëteit (Mennonite Conference in Friesland). A grandson of Arnoldus de Jong, also called Arnoldus de Jong (1873-November 1946), was a Mennonite minister of the following congregations: Noordhorn 1898-1910, Hindeloopen 1910-14, and Broek op Langendijk 1914-38. VDZ.

Jong, Pieter Claesz de, a manufacturer of canvas, who was about 1740 a Mennonite preacher of the Waterlander congregation of Krommenie, Dutch province of North Holland, published *Kort Begrip van de Christelyke godsdienst* (Amsterdam, 1742; this work formerly was ascribed to R. Buitenpost, *q.v.*), and *Godvruchtig levensgedrag van Trijntje Klaasd. Heynes* (Amsterdam, 1743). De Jong was an ardent Collegiant (*q.v.*) and often attended the meetings of this group at Rijnsburg. He addressed these meetings a number of times in 1738-80. VDZ.

DB 1877, 130; *Biogr. Wb.* IV, 558; *N.N.B.Wb.* IX, 470; S. Lootsma, *Het Nieuwe Huys* (Zaandam, 1937) 70.

Jonge Vlamingen, formerly a branch of the Dutch Mennonites: see **Flemish Mennonites.**

Jonge Vriesen (Friezen), formerly a branch of the Dutch Mennonites: see **Frisian Mennonites.**

Jongejan Cornelisz: see **Jan Cornelisz.**

Jongerenbond: see **Doopsgezinde Jongeren-Bond** and **Friese Doopsgezinde Jongeren-Bond.**

Jooris (Joost) de Backere, a Mennonite of Gent, Belgium, who, at the age of 80, died in prison at Gent on June 10, 1573. By trade he was a threadtwister. (Verheyden, *Gent,* 63, No. 222.) VDZ.

Joos: see also **Joost.**

Joos Baten, an Anabaptist martyr beheaded on Jan. 26, 1536, at Antwerp, Belgium. He is said to have been one of the leading Anabaptists. He was a weaver of satin, originally from Nyenhoven (?). (*Antw. Arch.-Blad* IX, 381, 426, 428; XIV, 14 f., No. 150; Mellink, *Wederdopers,* 388.) VDZ.

Joos van Beke, an Anabaptist martyr, burned at the stake at Antwerp, Belgium, on March 19, 1569, together with Hans Vermandele, Jan Poote, and Jan Semou. Joos was unmarried, 32 years of age, and a native of Denterghem in Flanders. He was a belt maker, and had lived at Antwerp since 1563, the last two years in the house of Jan Poote. Twice he was tortured. He had been baptized at Antwerp by Joos de Cruysere (*q.v.*). He said that infant baptism was idolatry. (*Antw. Arch.-Blad* XII, 336, 368, 398, 440, 477; XIV, 64 f., No. 710.) VDZ.

Joos Casteels (or Josse van den Casteele, called Joost Kasteel by van Braght, *Martyrs' Mirror*), an Anabaptist martyr, burned at the stake at Kortrijk (Courtrai) in Flanders, Belgium, on Nov. 8, 1567, together with Jaques (Jacob) Mestdach, Willem Aertsz, and Karel Hannebeel. Joos, born at Reckem, was arrested at Zwevegem in Flanders. He had been a member of the church since 1563. (*Mart. Mir.* D 358, E 715; Verheyden, *Courtrai-Bruxelles,* 37, No. 18.) VDZ.

Joos de Cruysere, an Anabaptist elder and martyr: see **Joos Verbeek.**

Joos de Hoymaekere (Hatmaker), an Anabaptist martyr, was burned at the stake on June 22, 1569, at Antwerp, Belgium, with Jasper Hermansz. He had been rebaptized, attended Mennonite meetings, and participated in their communion service six months before he was arrested. (*Antw. Arch.-Blad* XII, 385, 401; XIV, 66 f., No. 763.) VDZ.

Joos Inghelbijl, an otherwise unknown Anabaptist martyr, burned at the stake on Sept. 26, 1569, on the Vrijdagsmarkt at Gent, Belgium. (Verheyden, *Gent,* 55, No. 181.) VDZ.

Joos Jansz, an Anabaptist martyr, beheaded at Zierikzee, Dutch province of Zeeland, on Oct. 11, 1561 (van Braght, *Mart. Mir.,* erroneously 1563, without further date). Joos, who was born at Krabbendijke, was arrested at Somerdijk (probably Sommelsdijk, *q.v.*). (*Mart. Mir.* D 301; E 666; *Bibliographie* II, No. 374.) VDZ.

Joos Kint (Joos Kindt, Jooskint, Joos Kind, Josse 't Kindt), an Anabaptist martyr, burned at the stake at Kortrijk (Courtrai), Belgium, on July 16, 1553 (van Braght, *Mart. Mir.*, does not mention the date). Joos was a citizen of Kortrijk. He was charged with the following heresies: Jesus Christ did not assume His human nature from the Virgin Mary (doctrine of Incarnation as also believed by Menno Simons); the sacrament is not the true flesh and blood of the Saviour; confession of sin to the priests is not necessary; denying all doctrines of the Catholic Church.

Joos was tried five times and tortured several times. He died loyal to his faith, which he had fairly and cleverly defended against the inquisition officials. An account of his trials is found in his own letters written from prison. These two letters are found in the Dutch martyrbooks, from the *Offer des Heeren,* edition of 1570, until van Braght's *Martyrs' Mirror.* A song composed to celebrate this martyr, "De meeste vruecht coemt door Godts woort" (Most gladness emanates from the Word of God), is also found in the *Offer des Heeren,* and inserted in some later hymnbooks.   vDZ.

Offer, 219-37; *Mart. Mir.* D 150-56, E 540-46; Verheyden, *Courtrai-Bruxelles,* 31, No. 2; *BRN* VII, 166-68; Wolkan, *Lieder,* 66, 128; *ML* II, 432.

Joos Meeuwens, an Anabaptist martyr, burned at the stake at Obignies near Doornik (Tournai), Belgium, with five other martyrs. For particulars see **Adriaen van Hee.** (*Mart. Mir.* D 203, E 584.) vDZ.

Joos de Suyckerbakker: see **Joachim Vermeeren.**

Joos (Josse) de Tollenaere, an Anabaptist martyr, was executed at Gent, Belgium, on April 13, 1589, with Michiel Buyse and Joosyne Swyntz (Sijntgen Wens). The execution took place secretly in the Gravensteen castle at Gent, where the victims were strangled; their corpses then were hanged outside the gate. Joos was a prominent member and deacon of the congregation at Gent. He corresponded with the congregation of Haarlem, Holland, which had sent money for the poor members of the church at Gent. He had received baptism on faith about 1563. When he was arrested on Jan. 13, 1589, in a house on the Corenmerct at Gent, he was about 50 years of age. The Dutch martyrbooks (first, *Offer des Heeren,* edition of 1599) contain some letters Joos wrote in prison. As early as 1599 a collection of his letters had been published at Harlingen: *Sommige Brieven ofte Belijdingen . . . .* Van Braght (*Mart. Mir.,* ed. of 1660) prints the same collection, three letters, two obviously to the congregation of Gent and one to his daughter, Betgen, born in 1574. In this striking letter he writes that after his death her mother should give her as a keepsake a "testament," a "Dirick Philips Fondament-boeck," a "Liedboeck" (hymnbook), and a booklet of Jacob de Keersgieter (*q.v.*), which books obviously had belonged to Joos himself. He commends her to diligent reading of these books "because there are fine exhortations in them." Joos died faithfully as he had loyally served the congregation.   vDZ.

Mart. Mir. D 764-77, E 968-1080; Verheyden, *Gent,* 68, No. 246; *BRN* II, 622, 625; *Bibliographie* I, 395-403.

Joos Vermeer(en): see **Joachim Vermeeren.**

Joos de Vinck(e), an Anabaptist martyr, burned at the stake on March 2, 1580, on the Vrijdagsmarkt at Gent, Belgium, with four others. Joos was born at Poperinge in Flanders and was 27 years of age. (Verheyden, *Gent,* 26, No. 68.)   vDZ.

Joos (de) Vlaminck, an Anabaptist martyr, burned at the stake on March 2, 1560, on the Vrijdagsmarkt at Gent, Belgium, with four others. Joos was 21 years of age and a native of Brugge, Flanders. (Verheyden, *Gent,* 26, No. 69.)   vDZ.

Joos van de Walle, an Anabaptist martyr, burned at the stake on the Vrijdagsmarkt at Gent, Belgium, on March 2, 1560, together with four others. Joos was a citizen of Gent, and was 32 years of age. It could not be ascertained whether Joos van de Walle belonged to that van de Walle (*q.v.*) family of which a number of members died as Anabaptist martyrs. (Verheyden, *Gent,* 26, No. 71.)   vDZ.

Joost Ewouts, one of the leaders of the Old Frisian Mennonites in the Netherlands, who, together with Jan Jacobsz (*q.v.*) and others, banned Lubbert Gerritsz in 1589. Joost Ewouts was the son of Ewout Pieters, who was a mayor of Hoorn. (Blaupot t. C., *Holland* I, 38; *BRN* VII, 67 f.)   vDZ.

Joost Goethals, an Anabaptist martyr, executed at Gent, Belgium, in 1569. There are no particulars about this martyr, neither the exact date of execution nor the way in which he was put to death. Verheyden, in his study of the sources at Gent, did not find this martyr. His name is found as No. 31 in the song "Als men schreef duyst vijfhondert jaer, Ende twee en tsestich mede," in the 1578a edition of the *Lietboecxken van den Offer des Heeren.* (Offer, 653; *Mart. Mir.* D 407, E 759; *ML* II, 134.)   vDZ.

Joost (Josse) Joosten, an Anabaptist martyr, executed at Veere, Dutch province of Zeeland, in December 1560. He was born at Goes, same province. A student familiar with Latin, 18 years old, he was seized, cruelly racked, and burned at the stake "on Monday before Christmas" in 1560. At his death he sang the last stanza of a hymn he had composed; it begins, "Och Heere Ghi staet altijt in mijnen sinne" (Lord, Thou art always in my mind). The song is found in a number of old Dutch Mennonite hymnbooks. The confession of faith he wrote has unfortunately been lost.   NEFF.

Mart. Mir. D 282, E 651; Blaupot t. C., *Holland* I, 73; F. C. Wieder, *Schriftuurlijke Liedekens* (The Hague, 1900) 178, 196; *ML* II, 432.

Joost Meerssenier, an Anabaptist martyr, was executed in Gent in Flanders in 1569 with two brethren and a sister. "But in all this they courageously persevered, and could in no wise be induced to apostatize, so that they finally had to lay down their lives for the name of Christ." The exact date and manner of execution are unknown. Verheyden, who studied the documents at Gent, did not find this martyr. Joost's name is No. 37 in the song "Als men schreef duyst vijfhondert jaer, Ende twee en tsestich mede," found in the appendix of the *Lietboecxken van den Offer des Heeren.* (*Offer*, 653; *Mart. Mir.* D 407, E 759; *ML* III, 65.)   vdZ.

Joost van Pecuwe (Pecuven), an Anabaptist martyr, beheaded in 1535 at Haarlem, Dutch province of North Holland. While being tortured he confessed having been rebaptized. Further particulars were not available. (*DB* 1917, 153; Mellink, *Wederdopers,* 179.)   vdZ.

Joost (Josse) **van der Straten,** an Anabaptist martyr, burned at the stake at Antwerp, Belgium, on Shrove Tuesday of 1571. At first he had lived at Kortrijk (Courtrai) in Flanders; later he lived at Antwerp as a chairmaker. He was arrested outside Antwerp by Spanish soldiers and without trial or sentence cruelly put to death by the soldiers on the market place of Antwerp in front of the town hall. This irregular execution makes clear why his name was not found in the documents of Antwerp studied by P. Génard (*q.v.*). According to Verheyden (*Gent,* 60), Joost van der Straten was an old man of about 70 years. Van Braght mentions that his wife and his daughter did not belong to the brotherhood. At least two of his sons died as martyrs, Hans van der Straten (*q.v.*) at Brussels on March 28, 1571, and Martin van der Straten (*q.v.*) at Gent on Dec. 4, 1572. (*Mart. Mir.* D 540, E 1010.)   vdZ.

Joost Verbeeck (Joos de Cruysere, i.e., Kruisheer), also called Meester Joos, an Anabaptist martyr, burned at the stake at Antwerp, Belgium, on June 21, 1561. He had been arrested at Antwerp on June 7, at eleven o'clock in the evening. He was tortured several times, even twice in four days, and as a result of this severe torture he could not write with his right hand because this hand was broken. Of his private life it is only known that he was a native of Asperen, Dutch province of South Holland. In prison he wrote a short letter to his wife. Van Braght (*Mart. Mir.*) mentions that he was a *dienaer* of the Word of God and of his congregation. This means that he was a preacher or an elder. It is known that he baptized at Utrecht (Netherlands) in February or March 1561, and also at Antwerp. In the old documents he is often confused with the Elder Joachim Vermeeren (*q.v.*).

Joost, who during his trials and tortures refused to betray his brethren, also steadfastly went to his cruel death. When he was conducted to the little house of straw in which he was to be burned to death, four brethren out of the crowd cried to him, "Fight valiantly, dear brother!" While burning in his little hut of straw, the bystanders heard him pray: "O heavenly Father, into Thy hands I commit my spirit." Of his suffering and death a song was composed, beginning "O God, ick moet u claghen mijns herten droevich leyt" (O God, I must complain to Thee the sad affliction of my heart). This hymn is found in the *Nieu Liedenboeck* of 1562, in the *Lietboecxken van den Offer des Heeren* of 1563, and other old Dutch Mennonite hymnbooks. In Joost Verbeeck's trial recognition is given to Mennonite trustworthiness, even by their enemies, the judge saying to Joost, "I know that your people are telling the truth."   vdZ.

Offer, 538-44; *Mart. Mir.* D 283 f., E 651 f.; *Antw. Arch.-Blad* IX, 137; XIV, 32 f., No. 360; K. Vos, "De Doopsgez. te Antwerpen," in *Bulletin . . . d'Histoire de Belgique* LXXXIV (Brussels, 1920) 333, 344-49; Wackernagel, *Lieder,* 136; Wolkan, *Lieder,* 62, 70.

Joost (Joos, Josse) **Verkindert** (Ver Kindert, Verkinderen), an Anabaptist martyr, burned at the stake at Antwerp, Belgium, on Sept. 12 or 13, 1570, with Laurens Andries, after they had been arrested there during the night of May 30-31. In prison Joost wrote 28 letters, which have been collected in *Sommige Brieven, Testamenten ende Belijdingen geschreven door Joos Ver Kindert,* and published in 1572 (likely printed by Gillis Rooman at Haarlem, Holland); a copy of this 1572 edition is found in the Library of the Leiden University. The volume was reprinted 1577 (no place nor name of printer); a copy of this second edition is found in the Amsterdam Mennonite Library. The first letter is dated June 3, 1570, the last Sept. 12, 1570. Eighteen letters were written to his wife, eight to his mother or his brothers and sisters, one to his congregation of Antwerp, and one to all the brethren and sisters in (the congregation) of Harlingen and Franeker (Dutch province of Friesland).

Of these letters only the following eleven were included in the Dutch martyrbooks, including van Braght's *Martyrs' Mirror:* No. 3 (to his wife, mother, brethren and sisters), No. 7 (to the church of God at Antwerp), No. 10 (to his brother Willem), No. 12 (to his wife), No. 15 (to his mother), No. 19 (to his wife), No. 21 (to his brother W.), No. 22 (to his wife and to all the brethren and sisters in the Lord), No. 23 (to his wife), No. 26 (to his brothers and sisters), No. 28 (farewell-letter to his wife, after he had been sentenced to death).   vdZ.

Mart. Mir. D 509-27, E 844-63; *Antw. Arch.-Blad* XIII, 11, 61; XIV, 76 f., No. 866; *Bibliographie* I, 447-61.

Joost de Wielmaker (wheelwright), an Anabaptist martyr, was seized at Antwerp, Belgium, in 1570 with his wife and four other Anabaptists. Joost and Jan de Posamentwerker were executed there in the same year. Van Braght (*Mart. Mir.* D 506, E 846) states that his wife was executed with him. This is a mistake, as Génard found in his study of the sources. (*Antw. Arch.-Blad,* 74 f., No. 827; *ML* II, 432.)   vdZ.

Joosyne Swynts, an Anabaptist martyr: see **Sijntgen Wens.**

Jordan, a small village in Louth Twp., Lincoln Co., Ont., on the east bank of Twenty Pond, near the present Highway 8, where services were held probably in 1840-70 by the Mennonites (MC) when they were strongest in this county. It never was an organized congregation. The Moyer church three miles west was the central church. Early ministers near the Jordan church were Daniel Hoch (1806-78), who after 1850 led the Canada-Ohio (GCM) movement; Abraham Rittenhouse (1840-1919), ordained in 1871, and Daniel Honsberger (1835-1914), ordained in 1875. Early deacons were Christian Honsberger (1781-1831) and Philip Wismer (1810-97).   J.C.F.

Jörg Friese (Juriaen Friesen, Jurriaen Lademaker): see **Friesen, Georg.**

Jörg vom Hause Jakob: see **Blaurock.**

Jorg vom huss Jacob (not the same person as Jörg Blaurock, *q.v.*), an Anabaptist preacher, who was active in Schaffhausen (*q.v.*), Switzerland, in 1535. He is identical with Marti(n) Lingg (*q.v.*), also called Mathi Weniger. (Paul Peachey, *Soziale Herkunft*, 47.)   vDZ.

Jörg of Ingersheim: see **Leserlin.**

Jörg, Josef Edmund (1819-1901), a Catholic writer, publisher of *Historische politische Blätter,* and author of *Deutschland in der Revolutionsperiode von 1522-1526* (Freiburg i. Br., 1581); and *Geschichte des Protestantismus in seiner neuesten Entwicklung* (2 vv. Freiburg, 1858), in which he discusses the Anabaptists. This is especially true of the former book, which contains much valuable, authentic archival material, but which he evaluates uncritically and one-sidedly. He considers the Anabaptists to have been the logical representatives and defenders of Luther's doctrine of Christian liberty. Their cardinal doctrine, viz., "be taught only by God," they took from Luther. The right of free investigation and interpretation of the Bible must lead to unrestrained arbitrariness. Also their common possession of property and wives could be traced to this doctrine. The most peculiar charge Jörg makes is that they made a treaty with the Turks to destroy the German government, but that this was averted by the withdrawal of Soliman II from Vienna; for the Anabaptists this was a severe defeat. Jörg bases his assertions on statements forced on the rack. The historical value of his work cannot be rated high. (*ML* II, 433.)   NEFF.

Jörg von Passau: see **Nespitzer, Georg.**

Joriaen van Goor: see **Joriaen Ketel.**

Joriaen Heyns of Franeker, Dutch province of Friesland, was a partisan of Hendrik Naeldeman (*q.v.*) against Leenaert Bouwens and Menno Simons, and insisted on lenience in maintaining the ban and avoidance.   vDZ.
    BRN VII, 54 f., 460, 464 f.; K. Vos, *Menno Simons* (Leiden, 1914) 132 note.

Joriaen (Jurriaen, Jurrien, Jurjen) **Ketel** (Ketelaer), an Anabaptist martyr, beheaded on Aug. 9, 1544, on the Brink square of Deventer, Dutch province of Overijssel. He was born about 1511. Joriaen had been an Anabaptist since 1533, when he was rebaptized. His first wife, Elsken (*q.v.*), also an Anabaptist, was drowned at Utrecht, Netherlands, on June 18, 1539.

Joriaen Ketel, a tailor by trade (or a cloth or silk merchant), is said to have been of high rank, his father being a nobleman and he himself being educated in the upper circles. During or soon after the Münsterite (*q.v.*) troubles he joined the Anabaptist leader Jan van Batenburg (*q.v.*). At that time Joriaen was called Joriaen (Hendricksen) van Goor. After Batenburg's death (1538) Joriaen was convert-

ed from his profligate life by David Joris (*q.v.*), whose loyal follower he remained until his death. On the order of David Joris he visited the Landgrave of Hesse; he also accompanied David Joris to Antwerp, Belgium, and to Basel, Switzerland. He provided for the printing of David Joris' *Wonderboeck,* which had appeared in 1542 without mentioning place and printer; he also had intermediated in the publishing of other books by David Joris since 1539. At Pentecost of 1544 he was arrested at Deventer. Four or five times he was tortured; he confessed that he did not approve the revolutionary principles of Batenburg; he frankly confessed his following of David Joris, saying that this leader had taught him nothing but good things. In his last hour he wrote a striking letter to his wife.

Joriaen is the author of the following booklets: (1) *Heilsame Leere* (n.p., n.d.) followed by a song, "In lijden end noot heb ick, o Godt, Dijn guede ende Genede ervonden" (In grief and distress I have experienced, O God, Thy goodness and mercy). This book was reprinted at Groningen in 1634. (2) *Ein edel Duerbaer Testamenth;* (3) *Belijdinghe, Een Brief tot sijnder Huysfrouwen geschreven;* and (4) *Ein Suyverlijcke Schone Korte Leeringe.* (All of these are found in the AML; the last three are extant only in a manuscript of about 1700.)   vDZ.

    Inv. Arch. Amst. I, Nos. 209, 211, 263, 271 f., 276; *DB* 1917, 141; 1919, 20-22; L. Meihuizen, "Overzicht van de Geschiedenis der Doopsgezinden te Arnhem," in *Een eeuw Doopsgez. Gemeente* (Arnhem, 1952) 19-23; Mellink, *Wederdopers, passim,* see Index; *Bibliographie* I, 233-46; *Catalogus Amst.,* 58.

Joriaen Simonsz, an Anabaptist martyr, burned at the stake at Haarlem, Dutch province of North Holland, on April 26, 1557, together with Clement Dirksz (*q.v.*). Mary Joris (*q.v.*), who had been imprisoned with these two men, died in prison. Joriaen was a native of "Hallmen uyt Vrieslandt," which obviously means Hallum (*q.v.*). According to *Bibliographie* Joriaen was a weaver, but van Braght (*Mart. Mir.*) calls him a bookseller, which is more likely. For it is related that after Joriaen had been executed the officials also intended to burn his books. But this plan could not be carried out because the assembled crowd eagerly took possession of the books. Joriaen and Clement died faithfully as may be seen from two songs composed to celebrate their death: "Hoort vrienden al, hier in dit aertsche dal" (Hear all ye friends, here in this earthly dale), inserted in the *Lietboecxken van den Offer des Heeren* of 1563 and other Dutch hymnbooks, and "Hoert toe, gy Christen scharen" (Hear ye Christian hosts), found in the *Nieu Liedenboeck* of 1562. The oldest edition of the Dutch martyrbook *Het Offer des Heeren* of 1562 contains a "testament" and three short letters and a song, composed by this martyr. The song begins "O Vaders, wilt ghy eenen schat, U kinderen nalaten" (O fathers, if you would leave a treasure to your children). Joriaen also composed at least two other songs, both found in *Veelderhande Liedekens* of 1566: "Hoort vrienden altesamen, ghy die daer vreest den Heer" (Hear ye friends all together, who fear the Lord) and "Hoort doch nu al te samen, die te Haerlem binnen woont" (Now hear ye all who live in Haarlem).   vDZ.

Offer, 257-67, 586-91; *Mart. Mir.* D 178, E 563; *Bibliographie* II, 767; Gorter's *Doopsgezinde Lectuur* II (1856) 336-50; Wolkan, *Lieder,* 63, 78; Wackernagel, *Lieder,* 133.

Joris, an Anabaptist martyr: see **Goris Cooman.**

Joris (Joris Christiaensz), an Anabaptist martyr, drowned in a tub in the Steen castle prison at Antwerp, Belgium, on Jan. 27, 1560, with Jan (Hans) Gielis (or de Backer), Anthonis Cleys (Claesz), and Thielman Naeberchs. Van Braght's *Martyrs' Mirror* does not mention Joris Christiaensz or Thielman Naeberchs, but gives an account on Hans de Backer, Anthonis Claesz, and Joris Tielemans. Obviously van Braght has confused Joris Christiaensz and Thielman Naeberchs, making of these two persons only one martyr. The facts are made clear by P. Génard in *Antwerpsch Archievenblad.* Joris is celebrated in the hymn "Aenhoort Godt, hemelsche Vader" (Hear, O God, heavenly Father), which is found in *Lietboecxken van den Offer des Heeren* (No. 61 of the 16th hymn).   vdZ.

Antw. Arch.-Blad IX, 5, 10; XIV, 26 f., No. 305; *Bibliographie* II, No. 774; *Offer,* 567; *Mart. Mir.* D 270, E 640; Wolkan, *Lieder,* 63, 72.

Joris, David: see **David Joris.**

Joris Leerse (called only *Joris* in the *Martyrs' Mirror*) an Anabaptist martyr, who was drowned at the Steen castle at Antwerp, Belgium, on Nov. 9, 1560, with Joachim Ooms *(q.v.).* When they were being led to the execution site they sang: "O Heere, gy staet altijd in mijnen sine" (Lord, Thou art always in my mind). At the stake they began to sing the farewell hymn, "Oorlof aen broeders en susters gemeyn" (Farewell to all the brethren and sisters). Joris said, "Lord, Thou knowest that I have sought Thee and my salvation; and for this cause I must now die. Therefore, O Lord, receive me graciously." He also said, "Citizens of Antwerp, fear not; though we die for the truth, Christ our Lord went before and we must follow Him." To commemorate their death the song "O Heere God eeuwich Vader verheven" (O Lord, our God eternal and mighty Father), was written, which is found both in the *Lietboecxken van den Offer des Heeren* of 1563 and the *Nieu Liedenboek* of 1562. This song and also the Dutch martyrbooks, including van Braght's *Martyrs' Mirror,* state that these martyrs were burned at the stake, but the official documents say they were drowned. Joris Leerse was a native of Lier in the Brabant, Belgium.   NEFF, vdZ.

Offer, 560-62; *Mart. Mir.* D 275, E 644; *Antw. Arch.-Blad* IX, 115, 121; XIV, 30 f., No. 333; Wolkan, *Lieder,* 62, 72; *ML* II, 435.

Joris van (der) Meersch (in van Braght's *Martyrs' Mirror* van Meesch), an Anabaptist martyr, executed at Gent, Belgium, on Nov. 22, 1570 (method of execution unknown), with Jacob (Jacop) Lowijs. The *Martyrs' Mirror* states that they were executed "about 1570." Particulars are lacking. The Dutch martyrbook *Historie der Warachtige getuygen Jesu Christi* (Hoorn, 1617) contains two accounts on these martyrs, both incomplete; the second account was used by van Braght. Joris and Jacob are celebrated in a hymn, "Broeders en susters al ghemeyn,

fondeert alleen op Christum den Steijn" (Brethren and sisters all together, build only on Christ, the Stone, as foundation), found in the *Tweede Liedeboeck* of 1583. (*Mart. Mir.* D 506, E 845; Verheyden, *Gent,* 57, No. 198; Wolkan, *Lieder,* 72; *ML* III, 65.)   vdZ.

Joris Oud-Kleer-kooper, an Anabaptist martyr, was burned at the stake at Antwerp, Belgium, on Jan. 30, 1557, with Pieter de Backer. They faithfully suffered their cruel fate. Joris' name is found in the hymn "Aenhoort Godt, hemelsche Vader" (Hear, O God, heavenly Father), included in the *Lietboecxken van den Offer des Heeren* of 1563. In the official records this martyr is called Joris van Koevoorden; he was a secondhand clothes dealer.   vdZ.

Offer, 564; *Mart. Mir.* D 184, E 568; *Antw. Arch.-Blad* VIII, 433, 436; XIV, 22 f., No. 237; *ML* III, 330.

Joris from Paris, an Anabaptist martyr, burned in England on April 24, 1551. He was a Dutchman. Further particulars are not available.   vdZ.

De Hoop Scheffer and Griffis, *History of the Free Churchmen* (Ithaca, N.Y., n.d.-1922) 175 f.

Joris Tielemansz, according to van Braght, *Martyrs' Mirror,* an Anabaptist martyr, drowned in a tub in 1560 at Antwerp, Belgium. Here van Braght has made a mistake; by incorrect reading of a song in the *Lietboecxken van den Offer des Heeren (Offer,* 567) he confused two martyrs who were executed at Antwerp on Jan. 27, 1560, viz., Joris Christiaensz *(q.v.)* and Thielman Naeberchs *(q.v.).*   vdZ.

Joris (Joostenszoon) Wippe, an Anabaptist martyr, drowned at Dordrecht, Dutch province of South Holland, on Oct. 1, 1558. He was a native of Meenen in Flanders, Belgium. Van Braght's statement that he had formerly been a burgomaster of Meenen has proved incorrect; in the list of burgomasters of Meenen his name is not found. After his conversion he emigrated to Dordrecht in the Netherlands, adopting the trade of cloth-dyeing. He was a charitable man who dealt generously with the poor, widows, and orphans. On April 28, 1558, he was arrested at Dordrecht and soon sent to The Hague for trial. After some time he was returned to Dordrecht, where he was sentenced to death by drowning on Aug. 4, 1558. The execution was postponed because the executioner refused to put to death a man who was renowned for his goodness. Not until October, after much hesitation, was he secretly drowned in a wine cask. The Dutch martyrbooks have preserved three letters by Joris Wippe: the first two were written to his wife from prison in The Hague; the third, a striking letter to his children, was written from the Vuylpoort prison at Dordrecht after he had been sent back to Dordrecht. All the letters are undated. (*Mart. Mir.* D 203, E 551, 584, 926; Verheyden, "Mennisme in Vlaanderen," ms.)   vdZ.

Jorists, followers of David Joris *(q.v.):* see **Davidjorists.**

Joss, Gottlieb, Protestant pastor at Herzogenbuchsee, Switzerland, author of the book, *Das Sektenwesen im Kanton Bern* (Bern, 1881), in which he gives the Mennonites friendly treatment, though not always with historical accuracy. The rise of the *Neutäufer (Fröhlichianer)* is carefully recounted. (*Gbl.*, 1885, 38 ff.; *ML* II, 435.)

Josse Tam, an otherwise unknown Anabaptist martyr, burned at the stake at Hondschote in Flanders, Belgium, on Oct. 20, 1571. (E. de Coussemaker, *Troubles religieux* IV, 211 f.)   vDZ.

Jossine Andries, an Anabaptist martyr: see **Stijntgen Vercoilgen.**

Jösslin, Philipp, an Anabaptist participant in the disputation at Frankenthal (*q.v.*), Palatinate, in 1571; he, however, was not active as a speaker. He came from Heilbronn, Württemberg, and was apparently the representative of the Württemberg Anabaptists. (*Menn. Bl.*, 1894, 89; *ML* II, 435.)
                                                  HEGE.

Jost, Lienhard, of Illkirch, an Anabaptist of Strasbourg, a follower of Melchior Hofmann. He proclaimed himself a prophet; his first wife, Ursula, was also a prophetess in the group. Their history has not yet been uncovered.   NEFF.

F. zur Linden, *Melchior Hofmann, ein Prophet der Wiedertäufer* (Haarlem, 1885) 310 ff.; A. Hulshof, *Geschiedenis van de Doopsgezinden te Straatsburg van 1525-1557* (Amsterdam, 1905) 173, 199, note 204; *ML* II, 436.

Josyne Schricx, an Anabaptist martyr, burned at the stake on Aug. 20, 1538, at Brugge, Belgium. Josyne, who was born at Brussels, was the widow of Jacob van der Mose. She had been baptized upon her faith in 1534. Her children had not been baptized. When Josyne was arrested, one of her children had died; the other, four years of age, was immediately baptized by order of the magistrates. Josyne was given a good testimony of Christian living by the Anabaptists of Gent; obviously she had lived there before she moved to Brugge. She was the first Anabaptist woman to suffer in Brugge. She was burned alive without the usual mitigation of being previously strangled, a method of execution seldom applied to women. (Verheyden, *Brugge,* 31, No. 5.)
                                                  vDZ.

Josyne Steeghers, an Anabaptist martyr: see **Sijntgen.**

Jouckes, Age, preacher of the Groningen Old Flemish Mennonites at Knijpe (*q.v.*), Dutch province of Friesland, was excommunicated in 1687 because of "his strange opinions and his disobedience," which consisted in his view that other Mennonites like the "Twiskers" (followers of P. J. Twisck: Old Frisians) and others were good Christians just as well as the Groningen Old Flemish. This opinion, differing from the general views of the Groningen Old Flemish, who thought their brotherhood to be the only true Christian church, originated from Collegiant (*q.v.*) principles, to which Age Jouckes was won over. The ban was pronounced after a vote by the brethren. Age Jouckes now joined the Waterlander Mennonite congregation of Heerenveen-Knijpe, in which congregation he soon became a

preacher. The year of his death is unknown. In 1706 he was still a preacher. (*DB* 1870, 108-18; 1879, 2; 1883, 76, 82.)   vDZ.

Joure, a village in the Dutch province of Friesland, has since earliest times been the seat of a Mennonite church. Leenaert Bouwens baptized 9 persons here in 1551-54 and 8 in 1563-65, a total of 17 at Joure. It can be assumed that a congregation was established here then, though its existence is not mentioned until the end of the century. In the 17th century there were two congregations: the one belonging to the Old Flemish (*q.v.*) branch was extinct by 1700, when the two remaining members, Wolter Beerends and his wife, moved to Sneek and joined the Old Flemish at IJlst, to which they handed over the treasury of the dissolved church. The only congregation remaining, which took a rather moderate position, built a new meetinghouse in 1664. It seems to have had a stained glass window, probably a memorial of the founding.

In 1760 a division occurred in this church on the question of choosing a new preacher. Eight brethren and sisters left the church, formed the "small congregation," and soon built a church on Botersteeg, called "Nieuwe Huis," previous meetings having been held in the homes of members, most of whom lived in Broek, a hamlet near Joure. Their first preacher, untrained, was Barre-Hiddes (Gorter) from 1763 until his death in 1804. He was followed by a trained and salaried preacher, Govert Jan van Rijswijk, serving 1808-17. In 1817, with a membership of 52, it returned to the mother church. On August 24 the first sermon was preached in the "Oude Huis" to the combined congregation. Until then the "Oude Huis" congregation had been served by lay preachers, like Gjoldt Hylkes (Brouwer) 1743-1804, and Inne Wouters (Cath) 1780-1814. The last lay preacher, the strict but also sensitive Ulbe Durks Bakker, who had served the church since 1780, felt himself too old to serve the combined church. He was succeeded in 1818 by Abraham Doyer of Zwolle. In 1823 K. Ris of Makkum followed. The old church became too small for the growing membership; the new one, built on the same site and dedicated on Sept. 26, 1824, is still in use; a pipe organ was added in 1858. A new parsonage was acquired in 1919 and again in 1946. K. Ris served until his death in 1852. The following ministers have served the congregation since that time: J. Hartog 1853-54, F. Born 1854-86, J. Pottinga 1886-90, M. L. Hartog 1891-1928, N. van der Zijpp 1928-40, J. Meerburg Snarenberg 1941-47, A. G. van Gilse 1947-51, and J. Krijtenburg 1951- . The baptized membership in 1695 was about 100; in 1817, when the congregations merged, 210; in 1861, 239; 1900, 356; 1916, 384; 1955, 250. Members live in town (pop. about 4,000), and a number of surrounding villages, even at a distance of 16 miles. Members in town are mostly businessmen or workingmen; members in the vicinity are usually farmers. In winter services are also held monthly in Langweer (*q.v.*). Church activities include a Sunday school for children; *Menniste Bouwers* (youth group 12-18 years); weekly church services of the youth 12-16 years; young members' group 18-35 years; ladies' circle. The congregation possesses six large silver communion cups of about 1770 in rococo style of high artistic value. vdZ.

Archives of the congregation; Blaupot t. C., *Friesland, passim,* see Index; *Naamlijst* 1829, 50 f.; *DB* 1879, 2; 1890, 88 note 1; 1892, 90 f.; 1895, 12, 24; 1910, 21; *Inv. Arch. Amst.* II, 2, No. 222; *ML* II, 436.

Judenplan, the name given by the Chortitza Mennonites to an agricultural Jewish settlement attempted by the Russian government in the Kherson province. In order to give the Jewish settlers thorough training in agriculture, German farmers, mostly Mennonites, were settled among them. The settlement comprised six villages: Novopodolsk, Novovitebsk, Kamenka, Izluchislaya, Novokovea, and Novo-Zhitomir.

The position of the master farmers in the Jewish villages was very unfavorable. They were usually in the minority in the ratio of 1 to 5, and were therefore completely subject to the arbitrary will of the village in cultivating the fields. The fields of the master farmers were scattered among those of the Jews. To the right and left of well-cultivated fields there were neglected fields. Furthermore, the Jews let the Russian peasants pasture their cattle on these uncultivated fields, and consequently the cultivated fields of the Mennonites were trampled. Not until 30 years later was the land of the Mennonites separated from the rest.

At the head of the Jewish settlement was a Mennonite superintendent; in 1851 Dietrich Epp, a young man of 32, took over this task. At his death, April 3, 1900, at the age of 80, the Jewish author Zinov described his work as follows in a graveside address: When Dietrich Davidovitch was appointed superintendent of the Jewish settlement he at once undertook to organize the settlement put in his care. The villages had just been established and the residents were completely inexperienced in agriculture. The superintendent spared no pains or energy in his benevolent instructions. While they were working on the steppes, he was continually riding from one to the other, directing the Jewish farmers by precept and example, showing them how to cultivate their land; he also taught them how to plant trees around their houses. His work received repeated grateful recognition from the government. (ML II, 439 f.) D.H.E.

Judicium, a polemic written by Caspar von Schwenckfeld (*q.v.*) in reply to Pilgram Marpeck's (*q.v.*) *Vermahnung,* which had appeared anonymously in 1542. Marpeck's booklet, called the *Taufbüchlein,* since it is an exposition and guide to the churches for the proper observance of baptism and communion, rejects all mystical interpretation of these two signs of union, but demands the highest standards of faith and life on the part of the members. The *Vermahnung,* of which only two copies exist, in libraries in London and Stuttgart, but which was reprinted in the *Gedenkschrift zum 400-Jährigen Jubiläum der Mennoniten oder Taufgesinnten* (Ludwigshafen, 1925, 178-282), was used by Schwenckfeld in attacking Anabaptist teaching. (He had for many years been in friendly intercourse with them.) He presented his views in a writing to

the Anabaptists which contains 100 "talks" and carries the title, *Über das neu Büchlein der Taufbrüder im 1542 Jahr ausgangen Judicium;* there is a manuscript copy in the library at Wolfenbüttel.

In Anabaptist circles the *Judicium* produced great disquiet. Marpeck said it contained untrue charges, false interpretations and inferences, "as if we did not properly understand and observe communion with Christ, baptism, ban, and communion, did not know God nor Christ, made a god of the creature and a creature of God, confused one thing with another, and finally did not know ourselves where we stand." These charges created deep concern among the Anabaptists with their striving for holiness; to the external pressure of persecution by church and state was added misunderstanding on the part of hitherto like-minded circles. The seriousness of this worry is indicated by Walpurga of Pappenheim, who said 30 years later that "Schwenckfeld had caused great anxiety among the believers."

The *Judicium* discusses dogmatic questions on which the views of the Anabaptists, now in written form, differed from those of Schwenckfeld; they did not agree on the Incarnation, baptism, or church organization. Schwenckfeld was of the opinion that believers no longer had the power to keep unity in the Holy Spirit, in baptism, ban, discipline, and communion, but that the sending of a prophet was needed; also that the O.T. fathers, the patriarchs, prophets, etc., had also been Christians. On other questions previous discussions had already proved fruitless.

Lutheran divines also took note of the *Judicium.* Matthias Flaccius wrote a reply to it with the title *Matthiae Flacii Antwort auf das Stenckfeldische Büchlin, Iudicium genannt,* a copy of which is said to be in the library of Count Palatine Ottheinrich (Schottenloher, 38).

The opposite conceptions of these questions, which had not been so clearly evident until they were written down, led the elders of the South German and Swiss Brethren under the leadership of Pilgram Marpeck to reply in a comprehensive statement, which circulated among the Brethren in manuscript form, a copy also being given to Schwenckfeld. He did not reply. The *Verantwortung,* as Pilgram Marpeck called this reply, is still extant in various libraries (Munich, Zürich, and Olomuce) and was published in 1929 by Johann Loserth (in *Quellen und Forschungen zur Geschichte der oberdeutschen Taufgesinnten im 16. Jahrhundert*). It had previously been only occasionally mentioned in the literature. It is today considered the most important source for the evaluation of the doctrine and views of the High German and Swiss Brethren in the middle of the 16th century. (*ML* II, 440.)

HEGE.

Jugendwarte: see **Mennonitische Jugendwarte.**

Jülich. The territory of Jülich between the Meuse and the Lower Rhine, including a part of what is now the Dutch province of Limburg, was in the 14th century united with the territory of Berg east of the Rhine and the smaller and more remote territory of Ravensberg (the area of Bielefeld) and in the early

16th century also with that of Cleve (*q.v.*), which had been since the 14th century united with that of the Mark (more to the east). The united territories —large and influential in Northwest Germany— were governed by the dukes John III (1511/1521-39), William V the Wealthy (1539-92), and John William (1592-1609). From 1614, Cleve-Mark-Ravensberg belonged to the Elector of Brandenburg, Jülich-Berg to branches of the Palatine Wittelsbachs. Jülich itself was divided into 29 districts (*Aemter*), whose bailiffs were called "Amtmann" or "Drost," and besides included a number of small subordinate territories (*Unterherrschaften*). These magistrates as well as the owners of these small subordinate territories belonged to the hereditary nobility and were rather independent, especially in church affairs, often combining legal jurisdiction and church patronage. Ecclesiastically the duchy of Jülich-Berg-Cleve belonged in the 16th century to the Catholic bishoprics of Cologne and Liége.

Exiled preachers or adherents of non-tolerated churches could easily find shelter here. This fact was of benefit to the Anabaptists, who had come here very early. As useful workers and craftsmen as well as competent farmers they often found protection from persecution on the estates of the nobles. Especially in the north and west of the country there were many of these nobles. Among them Werner von Pallant (*q.v.*), bailiff of Wassenberg, is prominent, who sheltered the Wassenberg preachers (*Predikanten*) (*q.v.*).

Also the indecision of Duke John III (*q.v.*) favored the rise of non-Catholic tendencies. He tried to preserve the unity of the church by way of individual regulations. After publishing the *Kirchenordnung* of 1532 he called a meeting of the councillors of his territories. Here it was explained to him that it was necessary to have the help of the temporal sword to put an end to the "abuses that plunge the country into insurrection"; to that end a church inspection should be ordered. This inspection, held the following year, revealed that Anabaptism had numerous followers in the country. Three tracts of Anabaptist origin were confiscated: a treatise on communion and baptism, a letter of consolation, and an open epistle (Rembert, *Wiedertäufer*). Sometimes the councillors argued with those who did not attend church services. But finally with ruthless severity the authorities began the work of eliminating them. The prisons were filled.

Jülich became a mission field for the Münsterites. They were in 1535 planning to "let the banner fly" at four places in Holland, Friesland, Limburg, and Jülich (here at Eschenbroich near Wassenberg) at once. But after the suppression of the kingdom of the Anabaptists in Münster in the same year 1535 a general Anabaptist persecution flared up in the duchies of Jülich, Berg, and Cleve. Without regard for religious or social position the victims were committed to the executioner; until the middle of 1536 he carried out his bloody office in the various districts. "Justified" is the laconic comment at the edge of a long list of names. In Born 30 persons, mostly men, were executed after September 1534. In Bergheim the case was similar. In 1537 (not 1532, the date given in the *Martyrs' Mirror*) Veit tho Pilgrims

was executed in Gladbach. The *Martyrs' Mirror* records executions at Born, Linnich, and Sittard in 1550-52.

"The mandate of Speyer was applied in its full severity: the obstinate were burned, the recanters killed with the sword" (Rembert, 422). But church inspections of 1550 and 1559-60 showed that the movement persisted through all the storms of persecution. When certain places and districts were declared free of Anabaptists, they had increased in others, as in Dremmen, Hückelhoven, Susteren, and Millen. Lambrecht Kremer (called Lembgen) and Hermes of Aachen were now their leading preachers. (As to the duchy of Cleve, an edict of Duke William issued to the officials of Cleve and Mark on March 9, 1560, ordered that Anabaptists should be taught by orthodox clergymen to bring them back to the church. The obstinate should be brought to trial and await sentence by the duke. The old local and imperial laws were to be renewed and enforced; offenders were to be expelled from the country. On July 10, 1560, Duke William issued further orders that all pictures and books held for sale which represent the party of Anabaptists or the Sacramentists should be confiscated. This edict was repeated on Feb. 25, 1562. On Jan. 23, 1565, a sharp decree was issued against Anabaptists, Sacramentists, Davidjorists, etc.) The magistrate of Brüggen and Tegelen was severely reprimanded in 1567 for tolerating Anabaptists and giving them shelter. In 1574 the abbot of Gladbach lamented that the Anabaptists numbered no less than 150 families. (As to the duchy of Cleve: On Aug. 30, 1577, objection was made to a proposed church inspection by the representatives of all the towns of Cleve meeting at Rees; the group, however, admitted that the secular government must see to it that false sects would not slip into the country; but the present inspection seemed to them to have the character of an Inquisition, especially since it was managed by such as seemed questionable to the adherents of the true and blessed doctrine. The Landtag decided on Sept. 26, 1577, that the inspection should be dropped except against obvious Anabaptists. A list of 1622 shows 151 families; a list of 1654, 38 families; it may be assumed that they numbered 500-600 souls.) The Concept of Cologne (1591) was signed by Theunis Comes as the representative of the church at Gladbach, Diderich Verwer for all congregations in the country of Millen and at the Meuse (i.e., country of Born), Franz of Rheinbach for the congregation at Flamerse (Flamersheim), and by several other representatives of churches on the Lower Rhine. In 1611 the preachers of the church at Gladbach wrote a letter to Holland (*Catalogus Amst.*, No. 536).

For a time the Anabaptists enjoyed a certain degree of toleration. An edict of Count Palatine Wolfgang in 1610 to the magistrate of Sittard ordered him henceforth not to molest them for their faith. The situation was reversed when Count Palatine Wolfgang William, who had turned Catholic, came into power in 1614. On Feb. 19, 1619, Anabaptist meetings were prohibited. (As to the duchy of Berg: On April 19, an edict was sent to the magistrate of Löwenburg to arrest all the Anabaptists who attended their forbidden meetings. On Sept. 1, 1622, followed a strict command to all magistrates and the clergy, not to allow any Mennonites to live in the country; their schools or churches should be torn down and their property confiscated. A further edict of Feb. 20, 1624, softened some of the provisions; nevertheless negligent officials were reminded of their duty, and the Mennonite meetinghouses continued to be razed.)

The Mennonites, who made their living mostly by weaving, spinning, the linen trade, selling thread, making spinning wheels, and the like, had excessive levies made on them, frequently amounting to one fourth of their income. Their expulsion from Rheydt (q.v.) in 1694 evoked much adverse comment. In spite of patriotic love of their country, a sense of duty, and willingness to sacrifice they were not tolerated; they decreased in number and finally the churches became extinct. Most of the refugees settled in cities like Crefeld (q.v.) and Dutch towns like Maastricht (q.v.) and particularly Nijmegen (q.v.). A large number of weavers from Jülich, most of whom had formerly come from Gladbach, were allowed to settle in Nijmegen in 1642-57. For the Mennonites of Jülich the Dutch Mennonite Committee for Foreign Needs organized some collections. In 1694 William III of Orange (q.v.), stadholder of the Netherlands and king of England, at the instance of the Dutch Mennonites wrote a letter of intercession to John William (q.v.), Elector of the Palatinate and Duke of Jülich, requesting full toleration for the persecuted Mennonites in Jülich, but not until the beginning of the 18th century were the few remnants in Jülich given recognition.

NEFF, E.C.

W. Bax, *Het Protestantisme in het bisdom Luik* I (The Hague, 1937) 37-75, 300-23; Heinrich Forsthoff, *Rheinische Kirchengeschichte* I. *Die Reformation am Niederrhein* (Essen, 1929); L. Keller, *Die Gegenreformation in Westfalen und am Niederrhein*, Part I (Leipzig, 1881); Otto R. Redlich, *Jülich-Bergische Kirchenpolitik am Ausgange des Mittelalters und in der Reformationszeit* I and II, 1, 2 (Bonn, 1907-11) *(Publikationen der Gesellschaft für rheinische Geschichtskunde 28)*; Rembert, *Wiedertäufer;* W. Risler, "Täufer im bergischen Amt Löwenburg, Siebengebirge," *Gesch.-Bl.* XII (1955); E. Crous, "Auf Mennos Spuren am Niederrhein," *Der Mennonit* VIII (1955) 155, 170 f., 186 f.; IX (1956) 10 f., 26; idem, "Von Täufern zu Mennoniten am Niederrhein," *Der Mennonit* IX (1956) 74-76, 90 f., 106-8, 122-24; W. Risler, "Duisburg," *Gesch.-Bl.* VIII (May 1951); *Inv. Arch. Amst.* I, Nos. 536, 1141, 1146, 1194 f., 1205, 1305, 1400-4, 1419, 1427, 1432, 1749; *DB* 1909, 120-26; P. C. G. Guyot, *Bijdr. tot de Gesch. der Doopsgez. te Nijmegen* (Nijmegen, 1845) 13-19, 43-75; *ML* II, 445 f.

Julius, a Swiss Anabaptist elder, otherwise unknown, baptized in South Germany about 1530. (Wolkan, *Lieder,* 30.) vDZ.

Junge Gemeinde is a 16-page, 6 x 8 in. monthly periodical, edited by Gerhard Hein and published by the Youth Commission of the South German Mennonite Conference, first issue January 1948. It appears as a supplement to the biweekly *Gemeindeblatt der Mennoniten* (q.v.). Alexander Prieur became the editor in January 1957. H.S.B.

Jungheim of Geyssen, called "young John," a Hessian Anabaptist, who with Peter Tasch (q.v.) and others signed the "Bekenntnis oder Antwort etlicher Fragstücke oder Artikel der gefangenen Täufer und anderer im Lande Hessen," of December 1538. Nothing more is known of him. (*ML* II, 447.)

NEFF.

Jung-Stilling, Johann Heinrich (1740-1817), Pietist, physician and economist, b. Sept. 12, 1740, in Grund near Hilchenbach, Westphalia, Germany, the son of a tailor and schoolmaster. At the age of 15 he became a schoolteacher at Litzel, where he came in contact with religious separatists, and worked as teacher and tailor, learned the treatment of the eye from a Catholic priest, and studied this science at Strasbourg (1770-72), where he made the acquaintance of Goethe and Herder, practiced medicine in Elberfeld, acquired fame for his operation on cataracts (1773-78), lectured on technical subjects in the Kameralschule at Kaiserslautern (1778-84), and became professor at Marburg, then at Heidelberg (1784-1803), was made councilor of Charles Frederick, Grand Duke of Baden, in Heidelberg (1803-7), and was finally pensioned by the duke and spent his last years at Karlsruhe (1807-17). Throughout his life his first interest lay in serving the kingdom of God.

Through his numerous writings, his extensive correspondence, and frequent journeys, Jung-Stilling left traces of his influence in many places, including the Mennonite communities. Among his works, his *Lebensgeschichte,* particularly *Jugend* and *Wanderschaft,* the novel *Heimweh,* the periodical *Der graue Mann,* *Biblische Erzählungen,* and the novel *Theobald oder die Schwärmer,* were read widely in Mennonite families, especially in the Palatinate. In his autobiography, *Heinrich Stillings Wanderschaft* (Berlin and Leipzig, 1778, 47 f.), he relates that he worked for a tailor Isaak (I. Becker) at Rade vor dem Walde (Waldstätt) and was beneficially stimulated in religious thought by him. This man was apparently a Swiss Mennonite emigrant (*Menn. Bl.,* 139; *Heimweh* I, 77). Jung-Stilling speaks in some detail about the Mennonites in his *Taschenbuch für Freunde des Christentums,* publishing a picture of Menno Simons, defending them against unjust accusations, and praising their Christian foundation and character (*Menn. Bl.,* 1890, p. 62; *Gbl.,* 1899, p. 83).

He also makes an interesting remark about the Palatinate Mennonites in *Heimweh:* "The pastor in Kaiserslautern (q.v.) was called to account, because he had permitted a Mennonite woman to be buried in the churchyard, and had attended the funeral." Obviously these words refer to the case of religious intolerance described in detail in *Gem.-Kal.* 1909, 63 ff. In this allegorical novel, *Heimweh,* he pays a tribute to the Swiss Mennonite way of life by having his hero Eugenius meet his bride-to-be in a Swiss Mennonite home, where he also receives his most impressive lessons on faith.

In May 1785 Jung-Stilling and his wife visited the Mennonite David Möllinger (q.v.), the "father of clover culture in the Palatinate," at Monsheim, whose album contains the following entry in verse: "Certainly the man does not live in vain, who always knows his intentions, himself, and his duty.

In memory of Salome Jung, nee St. George" (d. May 25, 1790).

"Friend Möllinger! Here I cannot make verses; for my heart is too full of thanks to the heavenly Father, too full of bliss to think of rhymes; Möllinger and Stilling, two brothers whom the Lord has raised from the dust, should be filled with nothing but thanks and praise to their Creator and Preserver." Jung-Stilling signs himself "Möllinger's brother, Dr. Johann Heinrich Jung, grand ducal councilor and professor at Heidelberg, Monsheim, May 2, 1785."

With the Palatine Mennonites, Johann Risser of Friedelsheim, B. Eymann of Kindenheim, and Jakob Krehbiel of Weierhof, Jung-Stilling carried on an extensive correspondence. The occasion for the correspondence was probably the conversion of a young Jew, Heinrich Wilhelm David Hamann, who was won for Christianity by his contacts with the Mennonites. Jung-Stilling became interested in him and arranged his journey to England, where he was trained as a missionary to the Jews (in Basel, 1844-73).

Jung-Stilling's hymn, "Vater, deines Geistes Wehen," was adopted in the hymnal of the South German Mennonites of 1910 (No. 170).

Jung-Stilling also had some influence on the Mennonites of Russia. Some of the Mennonites in Russia were so impressed by his description in *Heimweh* (to some extent also by other similar literature) of an imaginary oriental theocracy near the Aral Sea that they founded a colony there, expecting to find in it the refuge from the antichrist pictured allegorically by Jung-Stilling. Franz Bartsch (*Unser Auszug*, 8) says: "The reading of Jung-Stilling's writings, e.g., his *Heimweh,* had given the first impetus [to the idea]." (See also Epp, Claasz.)   NEFF, E.H.B.

HRE XIX, 46 ff.; RGG III, Col. 468; G. Stecher, Jung-Stilling als Schriftsteller (1913); A. Vömel, Briefe J.-St. an seine Freunde Wiegand und Grieber (1905); H. R. G. Günther, Jung-Stilling (1928); E. H. Correll, Das schweizerische Täufermennonitentum (Tübingen, 1925) 112 ff.; Chr. Neff, "Jung-Stilling über Menno Simons" (contains 3 letters from J.-St. to Johannes Risser) in Gem.-Kal. 1937, 49-53; idem, "Jung-Stilling und die Mennoniten," Menn. Jugendwarte XVIII (1938) 36-45, 56-66, 80-88 (contains letters from J.-St. to David Möllinger, J. J. Becker, and Jacob Krehbiel); Fr. Bartsch, Unser Auszug nach Mittelasien (Halbstadt, 1907) 8; ML II, 446 f.

Juniata, a county in central Pennsylvania having four Mennonite congregations, two M.C., one G.C.M., and one Old Order Amish. Among the Mennonite settlers to locate here in 1774 were the Krehbiels from central Europe by way of Lancaster and Franconia districts. One of the M.C. congregations worships alternately at Cross Roads and Lauver, the other at Lost Creek and Delaware. These two congregations have 300 members. Near-by Susquehanna and Locust Grove (a mission) in Snyder County and Buffalo in Union County are part of the same settlement. All Mennonite (MC) congregations are affiliated with the Lancaster Mennonite Conference. The General Conference Mennonite congregation at Richfield was organized in 1884; its membership is 312. A few Amish families came to the county as early as 1760, and there were

three congregations in the 19th century, but they all moved away by 1890. Amish families from Mifflin County and from adjoining states again moved into the county in 1950, establishing one congregation. Juniata County is the birthplace of several noted leaders; Daniel Kauffman (1865-1944) (*q.v.*) was born here.   J.A.H.

Junior Messenger, a children's paper of the General Conference Mennonite Church, began publication as a biweekly on Jan. 1, 1939, changed to a weekly in 1943, and enlarged to its present size, 8 pages, and further enlarged to 7½ x 10½ in., in 1951. In 1956 it was enlarged to its present size, 9 x 12 in. It is printed by the Mennonite Press, North Newton, Kan., for the Board of Education and Publication and is an official organ of the General Conference Mennonite Church. Editors have been Mrs. H. J. Andres, Mrs. T. A. van der Smissen, Mrs. Arnold Regier, Mrs. Henry Funk, and Griselda Shelley. The circulation of the paper is approximately 4,000.   W.C.

Junius, Jacobus, author of *Eenige Zedige doch korte aanmerkingen over de Broedertwist van vier Doopsgezinde leeraren . . .* (Amsterdam, 1717). This pamphlet gives some information about a conflict between two preachers of the Amsterdam Zonist congregation, Harmen Reynskes van Overwyk and David van Heyst, and the preacher Douwe Douwensz Muys, of Hindeloopen in Friesland, who were accused by Cornelius van Huyzen (*q.v.*) preacher of Emden, of being followers of Spinoza and perverting the Christian truth of salvation. Jacobus Junius (likely a pseudonym) took the side of van Huyzen.   vDZ.

Jura, a system of mountains and faults in Central Europe, which reaches the height of 5,600 ft. in France. This forest-covered ridge with its many gorges was the most favorable possible place of refuge for persecuted Mennonites. Of the Swiss Jura mountains, it is the Bernese Jura and the Neuchâtel Jura that were principally used in this way. Solothurn and the Basel Jura sheltered them in passing through. In the French Jura Mennonite refugees from Bern and Alsace began to settle at the beginning of the 18th century.

A large part of the Swiss Jura belonged to the prince bishopric of Basel. In 1528 the bishop transferred his seat to Pruntrut. When the Bernese government persecuted the Mennonites they found refuge on the heights of the Jura in his domain. For economic advantages to the country the Mennonites were tolerated here. There was, of course, no lack of complaints on the part of the native population against the Mennonites, or of orders banishing them. But these orders were at first laxly carried out. Since the south Jura was in the political sphere of Bern, and under its influence accepted the Reformation, Bern demanded of the prince bishops that they pursue the Anabaptists more vigorously. Continued disturbance drove many Mennonites to further emigration to the French Jura, and finally to America. When the bishop was driven out by the French in 1792, the bishopric became a part of the Republic of

France as Departement Mont Terrible. A petition presented by the Mennonites asking exemption from military service was denied.

In 1815 most of the bishopric was incorporated in the canton of Bern, which at that time valued its woods less highly than its "granary" (canton of Aargau) and its "wine cellar" (canton of Waadt or Vaud). Thereby the Jura Mennonite congregations suffered the same lot as the Emmental churches (*q.v.*). In the course of time several churches became extinct through emigration, as Tscharner, Vanne, Monto, Chaluet, Münsterberg, and La Ferrière. Here and there fragments of masonry and neglected fruit trees indicate the former Mennonite settlements (*viz.,* on the south slope of Monto). These places have for the most part become pasture. Other congregations endured and are today active: Sonnenberg, Kleinthal, Cortébert-Berg, Chaux d'Abel-berg, Porrentruy-Courgenay, Lucelle (Grosslützel), and Les Bulles. The total baptized membership is about 1,000.

The religious development of the Jura Mennonites is like that in other regions. Originally their services were held in concealed clefts and caves. The "Geiss Chilchli" in the Kleinthal congregation, a small cave along the road to the present church in Perceux, recalls those days. Later they met in private homes; at the end of the 19th century meetinghouses were built everywhere. Faithful ministers maintained contact with the scattered members, admonishing and strengthening them in the faith. Contact with the Emmental church, the *Evangelische Gesellschaft,* and the "Free Churches" kept spiritual life awake, and about 1910 brought forth new life.

In economic life the Mennonites in the Jura have been proverbial for faithfulness in word and deed, industry and frugality. Thus they have again and again as renters won the good will of the owners and thereby that of the prince bishops. Even the government at Bern appreciated their pioneer work. Toward the end of the 19th century they began to acquire ownership of the land. This trend was promoted by the prosperity of World War I.

Whereas the German-speaking members of the Reformed Church who settle here lose their German completely in the second and third generation, the Mennonites have throughout the centuries retained it, constituting little islands of German in the French-speaking region. The reason for this lies in their religious isolation and their private schools. The great distance to the public schools justifies the government in supporting private schools on these isolated farms. Nevertheless these schools have repeatedly led to heated debates in the Grand Council at Bern as well as in the newspapers. The number of schools is decreasing, and the larger ones are trying to become state schools. (See **Bern.**)   A.-T.

Müller, *Berner Täufer;* S. Geiser, *Die Taufgesinnten-Gemeinden* (Karlsruhe, 1932); H. L. Lehmann, *Das Bisthum Basel* (Leipzig, 1798); P. Bridel, *Chourse de Bâle à Bienne, par les Vallées du Jura* (Basel, 1789); C. F. Morel, *Abrégé de l' histoire et de la Statistique du ci-devant Evéché de Bâle* (Strasbourg, 1813); V. Rossel, *Histoire du Jura Bernois* (Geneva, 1914); P. O. Bessire, *La Question Jurasienne* (Porrentruy, 1919); C. Junod, *L'ancien Evéché de Bâle à l'époque napoléonienne 1800-1813* (Tavannes, 1918); *Emmentaler Blatt,* No. 42-43 (1909), No. 33 (1914), No. 31 (1923); *Der kleine Bund* (literary supplement of *Der Bund* in Bern) 1928, No. 21; *Der Sonntag* (supplement of *Neue Berner Zeitung*) 1929, No. 30; *Gem.-Kal.* 1924 and 1925; D. Gratz, *Bernese Anabaptists* (Scottdale, 1953); S. Gerber, "Die Mennonitengemeinden im Berner Jura," *Der Mennonit* I (1948) 36 f., 47 f.; S. Gerber, "Swiss and French Mennonites Today," *Menn. Life* VII (April 1952); *ML* II, 447 f.

Juriaen Friesen: see **Friesen, Georg.**

Juriaen Libich, a martyr: see **Liebich (Lübich) Jörg.**

Juridical Procedures Relating to the Anabaptists (German, *Rechtsprechung*). I. *General.* Legal action against Anabaptists developed in a natural way out of the juridical practice concerning heretics in general. In the 12th century when ecclesiastical defection or nonconformity led to the rise of Albigensian and Waldensian sectarianism, the Roman Church undertook stern measures of repression. Pope Gregory IX, 1227-41, creator of the first compilation of Canonical Law, established the Inquisition (*q.v.*), and Emperor Frederick II, 1220-50, in his Sicilian Law Code put the temporal arm of imperial law at the disposal of the church in all cases against heretics. In the 15th century, when the old Roman Law was assimilated into the German Law, the Civil Code of the Holy Roman Empire renewed the old laws of the emperors Gratian, Valentinian II, and Theodosius I (all of A.D. 380) concerning the exclusive right and authority of the Catholic Church, and that of the emperors Honorius and Theodosius II (A.D. 413) concerning the capital crime of rebaptism, punishable with death (*Corpus Juris Civilis* I, 1 and VI, 2). In criminal law, trials by torture (to obtain confessions incriminating to the accused) had been in use for various crimes against general security ever since the 13th century. In the trials of Anabaptists in particular the questionnaire set up before cross-examination was easily manipulated in such a way that it would influence the outcome of the trial. The first Anabaptist to die thus as a "heretic" on Catholic soil was Eberli Bolt (*q.v.*), executed in the canton of Schwyz on May 29, 1525, the first on Reformed soil was Felix Manz (*q.v.*) at Zürich on Jan. 5, 1527, and the first on Lutheran soil were two men and four women at Reinhardsbrunn (*q.v.*) on Jan. 18, 1530 (see also **Gotha** for names).

In the course of the persecution of the Anabaptists a double change is evident on the part of the government, due to a considerable extent to the Peasants' War; the charge shifted more and more from heresy to sedition; and on the part of the Reformers the sentencing of heresy grew more bitter to the extent that in heresy they were no longer attacking a hostile church, but defending their own.   E.C.

II. *Jurisdictional Practices of Ferdinand I in all of Austria, Bavaria, and the Territories of the Swabian League.* Ferdinand I (*q.v.*), Archduke of Austria, King of Bohemia and Hungary, and later also Emperor of the Holy Roman Empire, "the prince of darkness" as Jakob Hutter called him in his epistle of 1535, the "tyrant and enemy of divine truth who has had many of ours innocently and mercilessly murdered," was a staunch fighter for the undisturbed integrity of the Catholic Church. With the mandate of Aug. 20, 1527, he ushered in a systematic persecution in his domain by publishing a list of heretical doctrines, adherence to which would lead to capital punishment (see **Mandates**). The Anabaptists were charged with only two obnoxious articles: rejection of infant baptism and abuse of the Sacrament of the Altar. In the Ordinance of Feb. 26, 1528, to the Austrian Government he complained about laxity in the proceedings against Anabaptists (see **Austria**). But very soon he transformed these heresy-proceedings into extraordinary proceedings against "rebels."

South German influence on Ferdinand's mandates is very probable. Bavaria (*q.v.*) had already proclaimed martial law (*Standrecht*) against Anabaptists. "The ducal secretary Pernöder testified that no proper court session was held for the prisoners but that the sentence was simply read to them, whereupon they were led to execution" (Wiswedel, II, 55). The Swabian League (*q.v.*) with its practice of martial law shows again the governmental ideas regarding those who deviated from the old church. Many were sentenced to death without recourse to any juridical process, e.g., Eitelhans Langenmantel (*q.v.*). On March 7, 1528, the Swabian League issued a mandate against the Anabaptists which expressly said that "it can easily be estimated even by a simple Christian with little understanding" to what an extent Anabaptism will lead to "new revolts and rebellions," unless torture is undertaken and earnest punishment (Klüpfel, II, 319).

The specter of the Peasants' War (1525) was constantly in Ferdinand's mind. Like other princes of the time he too saw in Anabaptism a real threat to governmental authority. To be sure, this was not the only reason for his ruthless persecution of the Anabaptists; another was the presumed Christological heresies. Blasphemous words against "the Mother of God," for instance, were to be punished "in body, life, and property according to the occasion and the degree of guilt." Anyone who administered Holy Communion without having been consecrated as a priest was to be punished with "fire, sword, or water according to the judgment of the judges" (Nicoladoni, 259). Ferdinand argued that since seditious acts would surely ensue from heretical teachings (considered even more serious than a criminal act), extraordinary procedures should be pursued in all such cases, disregarding general legal practices. Ferdinand's policy concerning Anabaptists had, no doubt, also a significant influence upon the ill-famed mandate against Anabaptism of the Diet of Speyer, passed April 22, 1529. On the basis of this mandate Anabaptists were to be condemned to death by fire and sword, "without previous inquisition by spiritual judges." As it is generally known, the Reformers (Luther, Melanchthon) gave their consent to this basic mandate. The motivating force behind Ferdinand was no doubt his confessor, the Court Preacher Johann Faber (*q.v.*), who also played an important role at the Diet of Speyer. It was he who one year earlier cross-examined Balthasar Hubmaier (*q.v.*) and otherwise engaged in literary activities against the Anabaptists.

III. *Luther and Melanchthon.* Luther's (*q.v.*) views on heretics and their punishment have been thoroughly investigated by Sohm (*q.v.*), Köhler (*q.v.*), Wappler (*q.v.*), Paulus (*q.v.*), and more recently by John Oyer (see *Bibliography*). Until about 1524, Luther definitely rejected the idea of governmental intervention in matters of faith. In his letter "To the Christian Nobility of the German Nation" (1520) he states that heretics should be conquered "with Scripture not with fire, as the forefathers did. If it were an art to overcome heretics with fire, then the executioners would be the most learned doctors on earth." He urged lenience toward the Zwickau Prophets, and did not even want them to be imprisoned (Luther's Correspondence, ed. De Wette, Letter of Jan. 17, 1522, II, 135). In his book *Von weltlicher Obrigkeit* (1522) he sharply opposed government interference in spiritual matters. Also in a letter to his Prince of Saxony he admonished that the office of the Word should not be resisted. "Just let them preach confidently and vigorously what they can and against whom they will, for . . . there must be sects" (Luther's letters, *ibid.,* Aug. 21, 1524 (?), II, 547).

In 1525, however, a change took place in Luther's opinion. In a letter dated March 4, 1525, to Spengler, the city clerk of Nürnberg, concerning the "three ungodly painters" (against whom the city council was conducting a trial) the concept of "blasphemy" occurs for the first time. For this particular offense it was necessary for the temporal powers to step in automatically. As to punishment, Luther does not express himself yet. In the years 1526-28, the concept of "sedition" takes the more prominent place. This idea had been drilled into the national consciousness during the Peasants' War, mainly by the weight of Lutheran publicity. Now, on Feb. 9, 1526, Luther declared to the Prince Elector that in order to prevent sedition and a mob spirit, "there shall be one kind of preaching only at one place" (Luther's Letters, *ibid.,* III, 88 ff.). The word "sedition" was also utilized in connection with the newly established Lutheran church inspections (the Electoral Instructions for the inspectors of June 16, 1527, use this term expressly. Sehling, I, 142 ff.). Hence, anyone who did not agree with the Lutheran Church on a point of doctrine, was subject to the temporal authorities also on the suspicion of sedition. It should be emphasized, however, that with the by far greatest number of Anabaptists there was no evidence of seditious tendencies whatever to justify the intervention of the government, even though great divergencies existed in points of doctrine. The task of church organization, however, made it imperative now to find a justification for proceedings against all those who showed any anti-Lutheran mind. Since, as was generally assumed, the suspicion of sedition was not a sufficient ground for proceeding against deviators, it became necessary to find a new weapon. That was the concept of "blasphemy," used by Luther for the first time in the above-mentioned letter to Spengler of 1525.

Apparently Melanchthon (*q.v.*) was the first to draw the logical conclusions from this situation and demanded of the government that it punish false teachings. The occasion for this was given first by the exceedingly embarrassing results of the church inspections in Saxony which seemed to indicate a threat to the very existence of the new church (*Corp. Reform.; Opera Melanchthoni,* I, col. 941). It was also Melanchthon who became instrumental in the formulation of the official "Opinion" of the theological faculty of the University of Wittenberg concerning the legal aspects of the punishment of deviations in all matters of church discipline. Here the idea of blasphemy is clearly stated as the main argument for the death penalty. According to the study by Meissner, the Wittenberg theologians seemed to have arrived at this idea of blasphemy as the most serious criminal fault by all opponents by pointing to the concept of "ingratitude to the Gospel" (Luther's letter of Nov. 22, 1526, *loc. cit.* III, 135) as well as by reference to the Electoral Instructions of June 16, 1527 (Richter, I, 78). In a letter of Feb. 15, 1530, Melanchthon promoted the idea that blasphemous articles of faith, even if they have nothing to do with sedition, must be punished with the sword. By this procedure an extraordinarily effective legal device was now found for the persecution of all "heretics" and at the same time for the defense of the new church.

Luther bestowed his sanction upon this device in his *Exposition of the 82d Psalm.* The background of it is as follows: Around 1530, a new party had arisen in Nürnberg which advocated toleration and liberty of conscience in matters of religion. Thereupon, on March 17, 1530, Spengler wrote to Veit Dietrich at Wittenberg asking him to persuade Luther—then just working on an Exposition of Psalm *Deus Sedet in Synagoga*—to put into this new booklet a condemnation of the new party and its philosophy, all the more as this party defended its stand by reference to the "booklet by Doctor Luther addressed to the Elector of Saxony, against the fanatical Thomas Müntzer." Veit Dietrich then looked Luther up and expounded to him the principles of the prevailing criminal law of the time. Luther then developed these ideas further in his *Exposition of the 82d Psalm* (Hausdorff). In this Exposition Luther stressed first of all the high dignity of all authorities (or magistrates), which at one place he calls outright "gods." Seditious heretics are to be "punished straightway and without compunction." But likewise also those who teach only contrary to a published article of faith should be punished as open blasphemers who "are not to be tolerated." Against them he recommended quick justice, on the basis of Lev. 24:16 and also the Church Fathers, who had no more patience with false doctrines than Moses.

That Luther's *Exposition of the 82d Psalm* was actually considered as a declaration of principles to guide legal practices can be proved by numerous references (see **Meissner**). The courts of Saxony only too willingly concurred with the suggestions and opinions of the Wittenberg theologians. "They followed the opposite course from Ferdinand's juridical practice, namely, turning from the persecution of sedition to a secular trial of heretics" (Meissner). One might also mention the Imperial Cities of Germany, which followed in general also the direction of the Wittenberg theologians in their administration of justice in all cases of Anabaptism.

IV. *Brenz.* Johann Brenz (*q.v.*) of Württemberg for many years had defended toleration as a matter of principle. In his booklet, *Ob eine weltliche Obrigkeit mit göttlichem und billigem Recht möge die Wiedertäufer durch Feuer und Schwert vom Leben zum Tode richten lassen* (1528), he taught that mere heresy not associated with revolt should be fought only with the spiritual sword, the Word of God, inasmuch as it does not belong to the concern of the temporal powers. Furthermore this booklet proved that the accusation against the Anabaptists was definitely unjustified. Through this booklet Brenz' influence on the juridical practice in Württemberg and elsewhere was quite beneficent: there were at least no death sentences in Württemberg. But later on, unfortunately, Brenz drifted into the current of Luther and Melanchthon. In 1557, he became a signatory of the declaration of several theologians entitled *Prozess wie es soll gehalten werden mit den Wiedertäufern, durch etliche Gelehrt so zu Worms versammelt gewesen, gestellt* (see **Bedenken**). This gloomy document deals in patricular with juridical questions concerning the proper course of trials of "heretics." The heads and seducers were to be put to death as blasphemers, for God had clearly commanded secular authorities to punish blasphemy. For that reason it had been right to punish Servetus [the Anti-Trinitarian, 1553]. The concept of blasphemy, as developed by Luther and Melanchthon, is interpreted as formal only (as Meissner has shown), i.e., it does not define particular non-orthodox teachings but in general means simply opposition as such; i.e., rebellion against the new church. It should, however, be mentioned that in the Stuttgart copy of this document (here called "Bendenken, etc.") the passage about Servetus' execution as well as another passage advocating death penalty for heresy is crossed out. Gustav Bossert, Jr., assumes that either the Duke of Württemberg or Brenz deleted these passages, and concludes accordingly that both the duke and the Württemberg theologians agreed basically with Brenz' earlier stand opposing the shedding of blood (*Blätter,* 25).

V. *Bucer and Capito.* These two reformers of Strasbourg were entirely dependent on Wittenberg. In a document called *Reformationsprogramm* (Program for the Reformation) of 1535 sent in the name of the Strasbourg clergy to the Count Palatine Rupprecht, the establishment of a formal inquisition, ruthless intervention of the government in family life with respect to the baptism of children, and the sharpest measures against all foes or deprecators of the Gospel are demanded (original copy of this document in the State Library in Munich). Bucer believed that the government had the right to introduce Christianity among its subjects and to eradicate any false worship. "Unorthodox teachers are to be punished by body and life." . . . "The power of the government over the conscience of its subjects is most harshly represented by Bucer" (Hagen).

VI. *Zwingli and Calvin.* Like Luther also Zwingli (*q.v.*) went through a certain change in his ideas concerning the punishment of heretics. In the earlier period of his reformatory activities he was possessed by the same optimism as Luther that the pure Gospel would renew everything and turn it to the good. But when in 1525 Anabaptism appeared in Zürich and tried to establish congregations on a New Testament pattern, he lost more and more the feeling that the norm of the Gospel and the new "Christian State" do not absolutely coincide. He began teaching the identity of Christianity and civil order, and committed to the "Christian" government of Zürich not only the supervision of general morality but also the care for the particular discipline of the new reformed church. He is said to have recommended the beheading of Anabaptists "on the strength of imperial law," as Balthasar Hubmaier claimed (*Ein Gespräch Balthasar Hubmörs von dem Kindertauff*, 1526). The Swiss authorities only too willingly acted upon his advice and opinion in all Anabaptist trials.

Calvin (*q.v.*) at first intended to have the spiritual office exclusively take charge of church discipline without any participation by the state. But soon developments in Geneva (*q.v.*) likewise went far beyond this initial program; the state police now also began to become involved in matters of church discipline. "We have sharpened the sword that they may accomplish their blood work" (*Corp. Ref., Opera Calvini*, VIII, 477). He expected from the state unconditional subjugation of all heretics and deviators. The execution of Michel Servetus in 1553 is a clear illustration of Calvin's enormous influence upon the temporal authorities of Geneva. (See also article **Punishment of Anabaptists**.) W.W.

G. Bossert, Jr., "Aus der nebenkirchlichen religiösen Bewegung der Reformationszeit in Württemberg," in *Blätter für württembergische Kirchengeschichte* XXVIII (1929) 1-41; *Corpus Reformatorum, Opera Melanchthoni; Corpus Reformatorum, Opera Calvini;* Carl Hagen, *Deutschlands literarische und religiöse Verhältnisse im Reformationszeitalter* (Frankfurt, 1886); Urban Gottlieb Hausdorff, *Lebensbeschreibung eines christlichen politici Lazari Spengler's* (Nürnberg, 1741); Heinrich Hermelink, *Der Toleranzgedanke im Reformationszeitalter* (1908); K. Klüpfel, *Urkunden zur Geschichte des Schwäbischen Bundes 1488-1533,* Part 2 (Stuttgart, 1853); Walter Köhler, *Reformation und Ketzerprozess* (Tübingen and Leipzig, 1901); Robert Kreider, "The Anabaptists and the Civil Authorities of Strasbourg, 1525-1555," *Church History* XXIV (1955) 99-118; Wilhelm Martin Leberecht de Wette, ed. *Martin Luther, Briefe, Sendschreiben und Bedenken* II and III (Berlin, 1826-27; Erich Meissner, "Die Rechtsprechung über die Wiedertäufer und die antitäuferische Publizistik" (Ph.D. dissertation, Göttingen, 1921; this dissertation forms the basis for the material in the present article): A. Nicoladoni, *Johannes Bünderlin von Linz und die oberösterreichischen Täufergemeinden in den Jahren 1525-1531* (Berlin, 1893); John Oyer, "The Writings of Melanchthon Against the Anabaptists," *MQR* XXVI (October 1952); idem, "The Writings of Luther Against the Anabaptists," *MQR* XXVII (April 1953); Nikolaus Paulus, *Protestantismus und Toleranz im sechzehnten Jahrhundert* (Freiburg i.Br., 1911); A. L. Richter, *Die evangelischen Kirchenordnungen des 16. Jahrhunderts,* 1, 2 (Weimar, 1846); Emil Sehling, ed. *Die Evangelische Kirchenordnungen des 16. Jahrhunderts* I, Part 1 (Leipzig, 1902); Paul Wappler, *Inquisition und Ketzerprozesse in Zwickau zur Reformationszeit* (Leipzig, 1908); Wiswedel, *Bilder* I, II, and III; Horst Schraepler, "Die rechtliche Behandlung der Täufer in Württemberg, Hessen, Baden, Kurpfalz und der deutschen Schweiz in den Jahren 1525-1618" (Tübingen doctoral dissertation, 1956); *ML* III, 433-39.

Jurjen-Thomas-volk, a branch of Dutch Mennonites, followers of Jurjen Thomas (*q.v.*), who in 1637 was excommunicated by the Groningen Old Flemish Mennonites, because of his conflict with Jan Luies (*q.v.*) and Uko Walles (*q.v.*). The small group of Jurjen Thomas' followers, which was found only in the province of Groningen, and was still in existence in 1681 (*DB* 1870, 114), may soon thereafter have merged either with the original Groningen Old Flemish from which they had separated, or with some other group. (*N.N.B.Wb.* III, 800.) vDZ.

Jus retractus (*Auslösungsrecht*), the right of redemption, used against the Mennonites in the Palatinate. By this phrase is meant the right of all Catholic and Protestant subjects in the Palatinate, for all time, to buy back from the Mennonites at the original selling price any piece of land which the Mennonites bought. On Jan. 18, 1726, the elector issued the decree "that the *jus retractus* was to be applied against the Anabaptists, in favor of Catholic and Protestant subjects, and that from now on Anabaptists were to yield without any further delay the above-mentioned property upon receipt of the original purchase price." Upon a moving petition from the Mennonites a further electoral decree followed on April 25, "whereby the right of redemption would apply only to future purchases," and was therefore not retroactive. By an electoral decree of April 1, 1737, the right of redemption was limited to three years. It remained at this stage until it was repealed by Elector Max Joseph IV, on April 17, 1801. (*Gem-Kal.* 1912, 120-34; *ML* II, 98.) NEFF.

Juschanlee: see **Yushanlee.**

Just, Martin M. (1866-1919), elder and conference leader of the M.B. Church, was the oldest of the 12 children of William and Wilhelmine Leitke Just. The parents, of German-Lutheran background, lived in a settlement in the Don River Valley, South Russia, where Martin was born July 14, 1866. In 1873 the family joined the Mennonite Brethren Church, and in 1880 emigrated to America, settling on a farm three miles west of Aulne, Marion Co., Kan., where their children grew up. After his elementary schooling Just attended a Bible School during the winter 1885-86 at Canada, Kan., which J. F. Harms (*q.v.*) was conducting.

On Oct. 27, 1887, Just married Anna Schapanski and established a farm home. After her death he married Hannah Patzkowski Aug. 22, 1894. Of the nine children born to the family, the two sons died in infancy and the seven daughters survived him. The family moved to a homestead at Isabella, Major Co., Okla., in 1895 where they lived for the rest of Just's life.

In 1888 Just was converted and joined the Ebenfeld M.B. Church. When he settled in Oklahoma he joined the South Hoffnungsfeld M.B. Church southeast of Fairview. He at once became active in the church, was elected deacon in 1896 and a year later to the ministry. In 1900 he was ordained as minister and in 1905 as elder. In addition to his effective ministry in the local church, which extended over a period of 22 years, he was much used in the churches of the M.B. Conference, especially in Oklahoma.

Just rendered a remarkable service in the M.B. General Conference. He was secretary of the Home Missions Committee, 1903-9, and served on the Foreign Mission Board, 1909-19. He was moderator of the Conference from 1915 until his death in 1919. In the Southern District Conference he was also very active from its beginning in 1909, serving as secretary of the Home Mission Board for ten years. The Conference elected him moderator for three consecutive one-year terms. Just also showed keen interest in the educational efforts of the M.B. Church, serving on its educational committee for some time. After the establishment of Tabor College, he was also a member of its Board of Directors.

Elder Just died at his home at Isabella, Aug. 22, 1919; interment was at the South Hoffnungsfeld M.B. Cemetery.   J.H.L.

Justice Mennonite Brethren Church, fomerly called Brookdale, a member of the Canadian Conference of the M.B. Church, was organized by Jacob A. Loewen in 1930 with 8 members. In 1940 a church was built 3½ miles northeast of Justice, Man. The membership in 1952 was 57. Jacob J. Loewen has been its leader and minister since 1937.
                                                   J.J.L.

Jut, a former Dutch Mennonite family, found from the 17th century at Amsterdam, where some of the members were deacons of the Zonist (*q.v.*) congregation. An important member of this family was Pieter Nicolaas Jut van Breukelerwaard (Amsterdam 1786-Laag Soeren 1874), at first a stock dealer at Amsterdam. Staying at Hanau, Germany, for recovery from a serious disease, he was won over to nature cure, and after his return to Holland bought a country place at Laag Soeren, which was later set up as a nature cure establishment. He translated a number of books and pamphlets on nature cure. He willed a sum of money to the Mennonite conference of Friesland (F.D.S.), which is administered as the Fund-Jut van Breukelerwaard.   vDZ.

Jutte Eeuwouts, a Dutch Anabaptist martyr, who was hanged at The Hague on March 17, 1536. Jutte Eeuwouts was a wealthy lady living at Poeldijk in the Dutch province of South Holland near The Hague. Her house was a center of Anabaptist activity; here a number of fanatical and revolutionary Anabaptists used to meet, among whom was Adriaen Adriaensz, known as "the king of Israel." On March 8-9, 1536, the magistrate surprised a meeting of about 40 persons in the house of Jutte Eeuwouts;

some were killed, including Adriaen Adriaensz; others, including Jutte, were arrested. The whole group was put to death at The Hague. Jutte was executed in a specially cruel way.   vDZ.

Kühler, *Geschiedenis* I, 118 f.; E. van Bergen, "De Wederdoopers in het Westland," in *Bijdragen v.d. Geschiedenis v.h. Bisdom Haarlem*, 1903, 269-88; Mellink, *Wederdopers*, 218 f., 221.

Jutzi (Judtzi, Judzy, Yutzy), a Mennonite family name, originally found in Switzerland. Some members of this family migrated to France (Alsace) and Germany (Baden and Palatinate) in the 17th and 18th centuries because of oppression. Both from Alsace and Baden some Jutzis emigrated to America in the late 18th and early 19th centuries, chiefly to Ontario.

Peter Judzy was a preacher of the Gerolsheim (*q.v.*) congregation in the Palatinate from 1765 until after 1802, and Jacob Jutzi served as an elder at Neuwied (*q.v.*), Germany, 1759-92 (or 93) and from then until after 1802 as elder of the Mannheim congregation. In America the family has been exclusively Amish or only recently turned Mennonite (MC). D. S. Jutzi of Tavistock, Ont., has long been a bishop in the Ontario Amish Mennonite Conference, while Rufus Jutzi of Elmira, Ont., is secretary of the Ontario Mennonite (MC) Conference. Three men bearing the name Yutzy are serving as Mennonite ministers in Michigan, Iowa, and Kansas.

Jutzi, George (1800-81), one of the few Amishmen who wrote a book. He was born in France, came to America as a young man, and settled in Pennsylvania. Later he moved west to Stark Co., Ohio, and died in Wilmot Twp., Waterloo Co., Ont. In 1853 Alexander Stutzman of Somerset, Pa., published a volume with Jutzi's *Ermahnung an seine Hinterbliebenen,* together with his poetry and other material. The "Letter of Exhortation to his Posterity," originally written in 1842, covers the first 88 pages; then follow 237 pages of rhymed verses, again addressed to his children and containing admonitions, warnings, and instructions in the proper Christian conduct of life. The concluding rhymed *Abschieds Wunsch* covers not less than 55 pages. Generally speaking the spirit of these writings is very characteristically Amish: the sturdy and concrete Biblical faith without much emotion, but with the determination to carry out this faith in all fields of practical life. The rest of the book is taken up by a brief history of the Mennonites and Amish, partly taken from Gerhard Roosen (*q.v.*) and written by Sam (Shem) Zook of Mifflin Co., Pa.   R.F.

K

Kaaden, Peace of, a treaty of peace signed at Kaaden on the Eger in Bohemia on June 29, 1534, by Philip of Hesse and King Ferdinand of Austria, by which Duke Ulrich of Württemberg regained his land. This treaty was of great importance to Lutheranism by sanctioning for Württemberg the achievements of the peace of Nürnberg; "but all Sacramentists, Anabaptists, and all other new unchristian sects . . . shall not be tolerated in the land." Thereby Anabaptists were for several centuries prohibited from living in Württemberg, although this law was not strictly enforced.   NEFF.

J. Witte, *Philipp der Grossmütige von Hessen und die Restitution Ulrichs von Württemberg 1526-1535* (Tübingen, 1882) 205; Bossert, *TA* I: *Württemberg*, 11 and 37; Fr. Thudichum, *Die deutsche Reformation* II (Leipzig, 1909) 415-29; *Ztscht für Kirchengesch.* XI, 215 ff.; *ML* II, 449.

Kaan, a Dutch Mennonite family, numerous representatives of which are found from at least the 17th century in a number of congregations in the province of North Holland, such as Barsingerhorn-Kolhorn, Wieringerwaard, and Zijpe. They usually were farmers. Many of them served as deacons. Now they are scattered all over North Holland.
                                                                                 vDZ.

Kaars, a Mennonite family found in the Dutch province of North Holland. The earliest representatives of this family are found in the small congregation of Krommeniedijk, where in the late 17th century they were manufacturers of canvas. Some of them were deacons of the church. A lateral branch of this family is the Kaars Sijpestein family of Krommenie (*q.v.*), where they were manufacturers of canvas and where now are found the world famous linoleum and oil manufacturing plants of the Kaars Sijpesteins. The founder of this big business was Hendrik Sijpestein (1773-1835), married to Bregje Kaars (1775-1803). He was a son of the (non-Mennonite) schoolteacher, later public notary, Willem Sijpestein. Most members of the Kaars Sijpestein family have been Mennonites. Willem Kaars Sijpestein of Krommenie is at present a member of the Algemeene Doopsgezinde Sociëteit (General Dutch Mennonite Conference). (*Ned. Patr.* XVIII, 1927, 339-44.)
                                                                                 vDZ.

Kaaskooper (Caeskooper), a Dutch Mennonite family, found in the province of North Holland. Jan Janse Kaeskooper (1627-99), whose family was living at Alkmaar by 1580, was a preacher of the Flemish congregation at Alkmaar 1654-74 and from then until his death of the Alkmaar Waterlander congregation. He was commemorated by his colleague Jan Bosch in *Zedige Redenvoering* (Alkmaar, 1699). Claas Arentse Kaaskooper, a member of the Koog-Zaandijk (*q.v.*) congregation, was active in behalf of the persecuted Swiss Mennonites in 1710. In the 18th century some members of the Kaaskooper family were active in the Collegiant (*q.v.*) movement.   vDZ.

J. de Lange CJzn, *Beknopte Geschiedenis der Doopsgezinde gemeente te Alkmaar* (n.d., 1927) *passim*, see Index; *Inv. Arch. Amst.* I, No. 918, II, No. 1909.

Kaege (Kaegy, Kaegi), a Mennonite family name. Klaus Kaegi, of Wald in the canton of Zürich, Switzerland, was subjected to a cross-examination on Jan. 30, 1616, in which he definitely acknowledged himself to be an Anabaptist. Apparently he was expelled because of this. In 1683 Felix came from Switzerland to the Palatinate and settled on the Bolanderhof near Kirchheimbolanden, Palatinate, Germany. He had six sons and a daughter (who married a Neef). His son Philipp remained on the Bolanderhof, which is now in the possession of the eighth generation of descendants. At present the name is found only here, at Weierhof, and at Ibersheim. Jakob Kaegy (1861-1940), Bolanderhof, was an agricultural expert and for many years the principal of the Weierhof (*q.v.*) school.

In 1715 Hans (John Rudolf) Kägy migrated to Lancaster Co., Pa., where he located in the Conestoga settlement. He was married to a daughter of Martin Kendig. One of his sons, Henry, migrated to Page Co., Va., in 1768, and in the following year to Shenandoah County. Two other Kägy families, all of whom can be traced back to Switzerland, emigrated to Lancaster Co., Pa. A Johannes Keagy arrived in 1739; a Rudolph Kägy arrived in 1764. The family, however, never became prominent in American Mennonitism, and apparently early transferred to other denominations, among which the Dunkard (Church of the Brethren) Church was prominent. A grandson of Hans, John Keagy, was a Dunkard preacher, one of the earliest of that group in western Pennsylvania.   NEFF, P.S.

C. Bergmann, *Die Täuferbewegung im Kanton Zürich bis 1660* (Leipzig, 1916) 92; Franklin Kaegy, *A History of the Kägy Relationship in America from 1715 to 1900* (Harrisburg, 1899); *ML* II, 449.

Kaege, David (1767-1846), an outstanding Mennonite farmer of Offstein, Rheinhessen, Germany. With great ingenuity he increased his paternal inheritance (Backhaushofgut), by raising anise, rape, and cabbage, besides grain, potatoes, and clover, by distilling whisky and vinegar, and by purchasing farms in the vicinity. He also owned ten *Morgen* of vineyard, which he cultivated by advanced methods. He was always ready to help his neighbors, friends, and relatives with advice and deed, always striving to raise the agricultural level. He urged the raising of cattle and horses. He was known for his benevolence, and was respected by all. Though he was open to the world socially and intellectually, in church affairs as deacon of the church at Heppenheim a.d.W., he opposed all innovations and with Johannes Galle he resisted the progressive course of the churches in the Palatinate and Hesse, including the employment of trained, salaried preachers. (*Gem.-Kal.* 1925, 39-63; *ML* II, 449.)
                                                                                 NEFF.

Kaerl (van Yperen): see **Laurens van de Walle.**

134

Kager (Kag), **Hans,** a revolutionary in Augsburg, Germany, who was executed there in August 1524 with Hans Speisser. G. Uhlhorn writes, "It is characteristic that the martyr lists of the Anabaptists include these two men, though with some difference in spelling, among their blood witnesses, perhaps an indication of the type of elements now beginning to stir in Augsburg." There were, however, no Anabaptists before 1525. Nor does Uhlhorn cite an Anabaptist martyr list, but quotes Ottius, *Annales Anabaptistici,* who in turn does not list Kager. Kager does not appear in the Anabaptist martyr lists. Their identity is not clear. (See **Koch, Hans.**)
HEGE.
G. Uhlhorn, *Urbanus Rhegius* (Elberfeld, 1861) 62.

Kager (Karger), **Man(n)g** (van Bragt, *Mart. Mir.,* has *Mankager*), a journeyman shoemaker of Füssen, Bavaria, a Hutterite martyr, was seized in 1529 with two brethren and four sisters in Fill (*q.v.*) in the Adige, Austria. On Nov. 19 they were cross-examined and then executed. Mang Kager confessed that he had been baptized by George Blaurock (*q.v.*); he considered the Mass, infant baptism, transubstantiation, worship of the saints, and the confessional worthless. Christ is the mediator between God and man. "What he confessed with his mouth he would also testify to with his blood; he would not abandon his faith, but would persist in it to the end."
NEFF.
Wolkan, *Geschicht-Buch,* 55; Beck, *Geschichts-Bücher,* 89; Zieglschmid, *Chronik,* 74, 76; *Mart. Mir.* D 27 f., E 435 f.; *ML* II, 449 f.

Kai Chow, one of the six counties on the southern tip of Hopei province, China, where the General Conference Mennonite Church conducted mission work. Kai Chow is more commonly known by the name "P'u-yang," which is the proper government designation. This county is the largest of the six counties occupied by the mission and is central geographically. It has a population of approximately one-half million and an area 1,000 square miles. Besides the county seat there were some 50 larger market towns and hundreds of small villages. In 1911 H. J. Brown and his wife purchased property in Kai Chow and started independent mission work, which in 1914 was taken over by the General Conference Mennonite Mission Board. In 1916 the first boys' school buildings were completed, and in 1918 a large church building, seating 800, was erected and a girls' school begun. In 1940 the mission property consisted of about 20 acres of land in the city and east suburb, on which were located two church buildings, five missionary homes, two primary schools, a coeducational middle school, and a Bible school. The total student enrollment exceeded 500. There was also a hospital with 80-bed inpatient capacity and a daily outpatient count of about 100. The total church membership in the six counties was 2,273 in 1940, organized into 24 congregations. Thirteen of these, as well as nine preaching places, were in P'u-yang County. With the Japanese occupation, schools and hospital were overcrowded and relief work among refugees taxed all resources. By 1941 the missionary families with children left the station and the following year the

five who remained were interned. Attempts were made to reopen the work after the war but the renewal of civil war between the Communist and Nationalist sides made this impossible. (*ML* II, 450; *ME* I, †.)
S.F.P.

Kaiser, Appolonia, an Anabaptist martyr of Mühlhausen in Thuringia, Germany, baptized in 1535 by Peter Reusse (*q.v.*), was drowned in the Unstrut on Nov. 8, 1537, with Jakob Storger and seven other Anabaptists between Mühlhausen and Ammern. (Wappler, *Thüringen,* 158, 162, *et passim; ML* II, 451.)

Kaiser (Käser, Keser, Kayser, Keyser), **Leonhard,** a Lutheran martyr, a former chaplain, was burned at Schärding on the Inn on Aug. 16, 1527, because he would not recant. The trial and execution caused much excitement in Germany. Reports concerning his death grew in the manner of legends. The publication of the execution was very painful to Johann Eck (*q.v.*), who had participated as prosecutor in the trial at the orders of Bishop Ernest of Passau (a younger brother of dukes William and Louis of Bavaria). He therefore replied in his booklet, *Warhafftige handlung, wie es mit her Lenhart Käser zu Schärding verbrandt, ergangen ist.* Luther published a counterreply.

In the older accounts Leonhard Kaiser is called an Anabaptist martyr. But this was an error. The steadfastness of the martyr made a deep impression on the bystanders. The judge who pronounced the death sentence was so moved that he soon resigned his position. His assistant, Leonhard Mittermaier, emigrated to Moravia and joined the Hutterian Brethren. The Hutterite chronicle states that he reported the execution to them and apparently took Kaiser to be an Anabaptist. It is very likely that he did not know the difference, since the charge was presented in Latin, and Kaiser answered in German; it is also strange that the chronicles of the Moravian Hutterites record only the outward events, and do not discuss his faith.

Two Anabaptists died later as martyrs in Schärding: in 1529 Vigilg Plattner (*q.v.*), who had also been a priest, and in 1571 Wolf Binder (*q.v.*).

As the heirs of his considerable estate Kaiser named his brothers and the schoolmaster Ulrich. The latter he admonished to continue to teach the boys; but if he could not stay there because of tyranny, then one of his relatives should take him and his boys to some place where "the Word of God is preached pure" (Roth, p. 27). Only four days after this execution Ferdinand I issued his first mandate against Zwinglians and Anabaptists for his Austrian hereditary lands, which threatened severe penalties for all who deviated from the Roman church on any point. Therefore schoolmaster Ulrich probably had occasion to leave the country with a relative and his charges.

A Dutch family tradition has it that the descendants of Leonhard Kaiser fled to Holland, and called themselves Keyser (*q.v.*) there.
HEGE.
Fr. Leeb, *Leonhard Käser, Ein Beitrag z. bayr. Ref.-Gesch.* (Münster, 1929); Fr. Roth, *Leonhard Kaiser, ein evangelischer Märtyrer aus dem Innviertel* (Halle, 1900); Th. Wiedemann, *Dr. Johann Eck* (Regensburg, 1865);

V. A. Winter, *Geschichte der Schicksale der evangelischen Lehre in und durch Baiern* (München, 1809); Beck, *Geschichts-Bücher*, 25; Wolkan, *Geschicht-Buch*, 42; Zieglschmid, *Chronik*, 58; *Mart. Mir.* D 9 f., 47, E 420-22; *ML* II, 104, 451.

Kaiserslautern, the second largest city (pop. 80,000) in the Palatinate, Germany, since 1896 the seat of a Mennonite congregation which in 1954 numbered 67 baptized members. It is united into a single church with Zweibrücken (*q.v.*), Kühbörncheshof (*q.v.*), and Saarland (*q.v.*).

In Kaiserslautern there were Mennonites in the 16th century. In 1566 the preacher Sylvanus notified the council that some Anabaptists had slipped into the city, especially a master cooper, Balthasar Bender, who should be questioned. In the hearing Bender refused to take the oath, and said he would not take part in war. He had also taken a wife who did not attend church here. They were banished from the city. "He thanked God that he must suffer somewhat for His name, and would leave the city" (Küchler, 11 and 12). On April 18, 1595, the Anabaptist Barthel Lorch said he would let himself be hanged on a tree before he would go to church. In 1730, in the procession through the city forest, some Anabaptists from Aschbacherhof, Christian Knebel, Hannsz Jacob Hirsch, and Clauss Ochsel, were lashed by the city authorities. In 1740 Kaiserslautern was instructed to raise a troop of militia to serve six years; but the city was to send no Anabaptists, Jews, "or other rabble," for such would not be accepted (Küchler, 615).

The Mennonite lists in the Karlsruhe archives state that in 1724 a Mennonite was living as owner at the city mill. In 1738 Heinrich Jordan, Ulrich Gindelsberger, and Jakob Guth were living in the city, but nothing more is said about them. They were perhaps from the near-by Eselsmühle, where there was an Amish congregation until the middle of the 19th century. The Dutch *Naamlijst* (1775 ff.) mentions a congregation near Kaiserslautern with Christian Schenck and Christian Imhoff Jr. as preachers. The Amish congregation held services alternately at Obermehlingen, Willensteinerhof, Horterhof, Ingweilerhof, and Schallodenbach; in the 50's they rented a hall at Eselsfurth, in which they held services every three weeks. The elders were Johann Maurer of Obermehlingen (d. 1850) and Johann Imhof of Willensteinerhof near Trippstadt (d. 1857). The preachers were Jakob Ehresmann of Dörrmoschel and Daniel Schönbeck of Ingweilerhof. In 1772 the Mennonite Christian Raque acquired the Lichtenbrucherhof near Kaiserslautern for 115 guilders (Zink, 272).

The families of Jakob Oswald, Lorenz Walter, Joh. Chr. Höfli, Jakob Latscha, and Hans Joder were living on neighboring farms as for instance the Mückenhof, and Christian Lichti in Rothselberg near Wolfstein.

In 1744 the administration still ruled that no public service or permission to marry be granted them, and that they should not be permitted to stay in Kaiserslautern (Küchler, 642).

In 1780 the council inquired by what plan the dead of the three Christian creeds were buried in the common cemetery. The answer was given that all the dead were laid strictly in the order of their death and that there were no separate plots. But that there were exceptions is shown by the magistrate's order that the exhumed Mennonites were to be reburied at once in the original place (Küchler, 745). This probably refers to the following shocking instance of intolerance in 1780. Among the laborers in a yarn spinnery were two Mennonites, J. Dietrich and Johann Strohm. The wife of the former died and was buried in the common cemetery. When the Catholic clergy learned that an Anabaptist had been buried there with the honors of the church, they set all wheels in motion to punish this crime. They managed to have the body exhumed at night and buried outside the cemetery. All efforts of the management of the factory and their attorney to have the deceased given an honorable burial were futile (*Gem.-Kal.*, 1900, 63-78).

In 1878 the three congregations in the neighborhood of Kaiserslautern (Neudorferhof, established in 1700, meetinghouse 1866; Kühbörncheshof 1832, meetinghouse 1832; and Ernstweiler 1680), which until that time had been independent congregations with lay preachers, united to employ a trained and salaried preacher, who assumed pastoral care of the three groups as a circuit and preached at the three places in rotation. Although none of these older congregations was located in the city, they jointly assumed the name Kaiserslautern for their circuit of three groups. In 1896, however, a congregation was organized in Kaiserslautern and added to the group, enlarging it to four units. The Ernstweiler group united with Ixheim in 1936 and took the congregational name of Zweibrücken. In 1949 the remnants of the former independent Saargebiet congregation organized themselves into a "Saarland" congregation and affiliated with the Kaiserslautern circuit. In 1951 Neudorferhof detached itself from this circuit and affiliated with the Sembach congregation. The circuit was served by the following ministers: S. Blickensdörfer 1878-80; Abraham Hirschler 1880-1931; A. Harder 1931-37; Hugo Scheffler 1937-51; Theo Hotel 1951- . The baptized membership of the four units of the circuit in 1954 was as follows: Kaiserslautern 67, Kühbörncheshof 159, Zweibrücken 201, Saarland 61; total 488, plus 163 unbaptized children. The meeting places were rented halls in the cities of Kaiserslautern and Zweibrücken, and the rural meetinghouse of Kühbörncheshof.

The Mennonite Central Committee began a relief program in Kaiserslautern in early 1947, which has developed into permanent social welfare work. In gratitude for this help, the city government named one street "Mennonitenstrasse" and donated a plot of ground in the center of the city, on which in 1955 the MCC erected a permanent building containing administrative offices, a residence for workers, and a meeting room for church services. The MCC program in Kaiserslautern began with child-feeding, added a home for the temporary care of undernourished children from Berlin, and in 1949 a neighborhood center (*Nachbarschaftsheim, q.v.*) in a building supplied by the city.   NEFF, H.S.B.

J. Küchler, *Chronik der Stadt Kaiserslautern aus den Jahren 1566-1798* (Kaiserslautern, 1905); Th. Zink, *Kaiserslautern in der Vergangenheit und Gegenwart* (1914); *Menn. Bl.*, 1859, 15; *ML* II, 452.

Kaju-Apu, one of the three oldest stations of the former Dutch Mennonite mission in Java, Indonesia. It is located south of Mt. Muria, four miles from Kudus. Some Javanese Christians on an evangelizing tour found at Kaju-Apu some persons desirous of instruction. On July 26, 1853, four men were baptized by Hoezoo, a missionary working at Semarang under the Dutch (Reformed) mission board. By 1875 this beginning had increased to 92 members. After Hoezoo's death in 1896 the Dutch Mennonite Missionary Society took over the station on July 1, 1898. By that time there had been some loss of members to the Catholic Church and also by members moving away. The remaining 54 members were served alternately by Johann Hübert and Pieter Anton Jansz. In December 1901 Johann Fast took charge of the mission and built a residence, a school, and a dispensary in addition to the chapel which was built by Hoezoo. Outstations were built at Pati (15 miles away) and Taju (30 miles away). When Fast returned to Europe for his health in 1909, the stations were served by Johann Klaassen (*q.v.*) until he had to return to Europe for his health. The work was then in charge of J. Siemens, who was also compelled to return to Europe in 1914. Meanwhile the congregation had grown to 105 souls, with 55 baptized members. The mission school had three teachers and 100 pupils. The dispensary served 80-100 patients daily.

In 1904-21 Kaju-Apu was unoccupied, the work being carried on by N. Thiessen from Margoredjo. This period was the time of the revival among the Chinese in Kudus (*q.v.*). It was continued when Fast returned in 1921 and established a subsidiary station in Karangrava. In 1928, in his fortieth year of service, Fast was compelled to leave for a cooler climate.

In June 1929 Hermann Schmitt took over Kaju-Apu, living in Kudus, since there were greater opportunities for work there. Kaju-Apu became a subsidiary with extensive autonomy. Gersom, who had faithfully assisted in the work for more than 40 years, retired in 1932. Most of the members are poor farmers. Since the voluntary contributions of the members and the small income from the rice fields bought by the missionaries at a former time were insufficient to cover the essential expenses, the congregation received aid from the mission treasury.

In 1933 the Kaju-Apu congregation had a membership of 70 adults and 84 children. Sunday services were attended on an average by 66 adults and the Sunday school by 68 children, and the catechetical instruction by 34 young people. Shortly after 1930 this congregation became to some extent independent. Excellent native teachers and preachers, like Tirtoadi, Radija Nitiardjo (until 1936), Wigeno Mororedjo (since 1936), had charge of the congregation, which became completely independent on Nov. 24, 1940. World War II, the Japanese invasion (1942), and the political alterations in Indonesia put the congregation to a severe test, but it stood the test. In 1949 the membership numbered 65 baptized members and 146 children. In 1955 these figures were 76 and 107. The preacher (now elder) of the congregation since 1941 is W. Mor-

oredjo. (Reports of the Dutch Mennonite Mission Association; *ML* II, 450 f.)   H.Sc., vDZ.

Kalamazoo State Hospital Civilian Public Service Unit, No. 120, Kalamazoo, Mich., was operated by the Mennonite Central Committee. It was approved Nov. 3, 1943; closed June 22, 1946; had a capacity of 30 men; and assisted in the care of the mental patients. A unit of I-W men was assigned to the Kalamazoo hospital under the new draft law following World War II.   M.G.

M. Gingerich, *Service for Peace* (Akron, Pa., 1949) 239.

Kalamazoo (Mich.) United Missionary Church had a membership of 81 in 1953. F. I. Rouse was serving as pastor.   M.G.

Kalamba, a former station of the Congo Inland Mission in Africa, was established in 1912 among the Baluba-Lulua people, located on the Kasai River about 150 miles south from Charlesville. The work at this place went forward with good results for many years, but in time factors developed which hindered the work so that in 1946 the Board granted the request from the field to terminate the work and establish a new station at a point some distance westward. The new station was named Mutena. The statistics for Mutena in 1949 were: missionaries, 8; native pastors, 2; baptisms, 86; church members, 967; awaiting baptism, 400; communities where services are conducted regularly, 106; native leaders in training, 14; rural schools, 43; rural teacher-evangelists, 45; average attendance of all schools, 1,103; native medical helpers, 4; new cases treated, 3,327.   R.L.H.

Kaldenkirchen, a town (pop. 5,700), earlier called Kaldekerk, in the Brüggen district of Jülich, Germany. In 1533 there was much disputing in the vicinity concerning the Mass and communion. A hatter named Venlo preached. When *Herr* Anthonius preached in Bracht the bells rang. In 1550 the *Merchenarius* Johann Backhuys was deposed from his position in the church by the bishop of Liége. There were a number of Anabaptists in the Brüggen district: in 1638 seven in Dülken and seven in Kaldenkirchen; in 1652 six in Dülken, one in Bracht, and eight in Kaldenkirchen. Shortly after this last listing they had to leave the district. We meet a number of them again in Crefeld, from where they emigrated to Pennsylvania in 1683. Of particular interest is the fate of Theisz Dohr (Doermans or Peterschen), which is given at length in the records contained in the state archives at Düsseldorf, Jülich-Berg II, 252. His sons and sons-in-law were in the group that emigrated to America in 1683. Kaldenkirchen was also the home of the brothers Jan and Willem Streypers, who played a role in the emigration to Pennsylvania. They had originally been Reformed, but became Quakers and were Quakers in Germantown. The Quaker church was established by English missionaries at Kaldekerk as early as 1680. Jan Streypers returned to Kaldekerk permanently in 1706.

H.S.B.

W. I. Hull, *William Penn and the Dutch Quaker Migration to Pennsylvania* (Swarthmore College, 1935).

Kalender, a Dutch Mennonite calendar, which appeared under different names: *Doopsgezinde Kalender, Zendings-Kalender, Broederschapskalender,* containing a page for every day of the year, was issued for the first time in 1937. For the years 1943-47 no *Kalender* appeared. In 1956 the calendar for the first time does not contain a page for each day, but has a page with a picture for every 14 days.   vDZ.

Kalff (Calff, Kalf), a Dutch Mennonite family of Zaandam, province of North Holland, which played an important part in the economic prosperity of this town. They were merchants and shipowners, often engaging in whaling as far away as Greenland. Cornelis Michielsz Calff (1652-1721), who was a shipbuilder and equipped a number of boats for his own business in whaling grounds near Greenland, and who was consulted by Peter the Great of Russia when he visited Zaandam in 1717, was a preacher of the Flemish congregation of Zaandam from 1680, and of the United Flemish and Waterlander Nieuwe Huys congregation 1687-d. 1721. His son Nicolaas Kalf (Claes Cornelisz Calf, 1677-1734), who was a wholesale dealer, shipowner, and manufacturer of Zaandam, and was known for his excellent collection of coins and other art treasures, was a promoter of the founding of the West Zaandam Mennonite orphanage in 1713-14. J. Kalff, a lawyer, was one of the founders of the congregation at The Hague in 1880-81.   vDZ.
S. Lootsma, *Het Nieuwe Huys* (Zaandam, 1937) 31, 35 f., 48, 65, 115 f., 141, 186; *DB* 1896, 64, 69 f.

Kalker (Calcar, Kalker), **Hendrik Jans van** (1683-?), a Dutch Mennonite of Deventer who left the Old Flemish congregation of his home town to join the Swiss Mennonite congregation of Sappemeer. He published at Groningen in 1744 a Confession drawn up by his father-in-law, Jan van Komen, and wrote a preface for this book. It is not clear whether an appendix to this book, entitled: *Korte Redengevinge van den dienst der Oudsten,* which contains a number of particulars about the Swiss Mennonite ministry in the Netherlands, was written by van Komen or by van Kalker. Van Kalker was married 1703 to Grietje van Komen. (*DB* 1919, 75; *Biogr. Wb.* IV, 645; *N.N.B. Wb.* IX, 487; *Inv. Arch. Amst.* I, No. 1887.)   vDZ.

Kalker (Calcar), **Izaak van,** of the old van Calcar (*q.v.*) family of Deventer, b. there about 1678, d. in August 1756 at Zaandam, was 1712-56 a (lay) preacher, of the Old Flemish congregation of Zaandam Oost. He is also said to have preached for the New Swiss (*q.v.*) Mennonite congregation of Sappemeer (*q.v.*), who met in a small private house on the former Sapmeer (reclaimed lake). Van Kalker published *Belijdenis en Lofgezangen* (1737), *Zedelijke en Stichtelijke Gezangen* (Zaandam, 1737), *Geestelijke Lofzangen* (Zaandam, 1739), and *Israels Verdrukking en Verlossing in Egipten* (Zaandam, 1739).   vDZ.
Biogr. Wb. IV, 644 f.; S. Lootsma, *Het Nieuwe Huys* (Zaandam, 1937) 21.

Kalker, Jan van, b. 1760, d. 1834 at Heerenveen, a Dutch Mennonite lay preacher, who served the congregation of Noordbroek 1776-83, Neustadt-Gödens 1783-88, and Heerenveen 1788-1821. He was not the same person as the Jan van Calcar (*q.v.*) who was preacher of the New Swiss (*q.v.*) Mennonites of Groningen and Sappemeer in 1755-78.   vDZ.

Kalkwijk, a canal near Hoogezand in the Dutch province of Groningen, Netherlands, where there are a number of small farms. This hamlet, originally called Oude Friesche Compagnie (Old Frisian Company), was founded in 1631 by some peat-farmers, mostly Mennonites, who had come from the environs of Heerenveen, Friesland. During the 17th century, about 1670, a number of Mennonites from the Palatinate, Germany, are said to have settled here, but concerning these "Palsters" no further information was available. The name Kalkwijk, according to an old tradition, is derived from the Swiss Mennonite Kalken family, which settled here in 1711. Others are of opinion that the name Kalkwijk originated from a lime (Dutch: *kalk*) kiln found here, which was owned by a Mennonite family, later called Calkema. It was at Kalkwijk, too, that the Swiss emigrant Samuel Peter (Maihusen), the ancestor of the Dutch Mennonite Meihuizen (*q.v.*) family, settled in 1714.   vDZ.
Müller, *Berner Täufer,* 322; J. Huizinga, *Stamboek van Samuel Peter (Meihuizen) en Barbara Fry* (Groningen, 1890) 43, 54 f.; *DJ* 1932, 71.

Kalleken: see also **Calleken.**

Kalleken, widow of Anpleunis (*q.v.*) van den Berge, an Anabaptist martyr, was burned at the stake on April 30, 1569, at Kortrijk (Courtrai) in Flanders, Belgium, where her husband had suffered martyrdom on Nov. 17, 1568. Kalleken, whose official name was Cathelijne Saelins, or Calleken Stalins, had been (re)baptized in the fall of 1567 or in the spring of 1568 and was arrested at Meenen, Belgium, to which town she apparently had moved after her husband's arrest. She died faithful. Her goods were confiscated. With her were executed Pieter den Ouden (Oudeghodt), Fransoois de Timmerman, Jan van Raes, Jan Wattier, and Wouter Denys. (*Mart. Mir.* D 408, E 759 f.; Verheyden, *Courtrai-Bruxelles,* 40, No. 28.)   vDZ.

Kalleken Claes, an Anabaptist martyr: see **Cathelijne Claes.**

Kalleken N., an Anabaptist woman who was arrested in July 1592 at Gent, Belgium, together with Bartholomeus Panten and Michiel de Cleercq. The two men suffered death at Gent on Sept. 15, 1592. Van Braght's statement (*Mart. Mir.* D 779, E 1082) that Kalleken was put to death with the two men is an error; Verheyden (*Gent,* 70, note 1) found in the documents that Kalleken did not suffer death but was released after she had renounced her faith. (*ML* II, 453.)   vDZ.

Kalleken Strings (Strincx, Stryngs), an Anabaptist martyr, was burned at the stake at Ieper (Ypres) in Belgium on Oct. 18, 1561. She was arrested with some other members of the Ieper (*q.v.*) congregation. Kalleken is celebrated in the song, "Als men schreef duyst vijfhondert eenentsestich Jaer" (No. 21 of the *Lietboecxken van den Offer des Heeren*).

This song informs us about her strong faith, but does not give any particulars about her. Somewhat more instructive is another song, "Geroert ben ick van binnen" (I am moved in my heart), No. 23 of the *Lietboecxken,* which is also found in the *Nieu Liedenboeck* of 1562. On the basis of this hymn the Dutch martyrbook of 1615 gives an account of this martyr, which is repeated in the following martyrbooks, including van Braght's *Martyrs' Mirror,* which states that Kalleken was a young and well-educated woman, who, notwithstanding a number of attempts to make her renounce her faith, remained steadfast. She was executed secretly because the officials feared a revolt of the populace. This execution took place some time after the death of her fellow members of Ieper.   vDZ.

Offer, 591, 605; *Mart. Mir.* D 285, E 652; Wolkan, *Lieder,* 64, 72; Wackernagel, *Lieder,* 141.

Kallenberg, Hans, a priest, was in 1526 among the first *Täufer* (Anabaptist) group at Aarau (*q.v.*), Switzerland. Further information about Kallenberg is lacking, Kallenberg apparently soon having left the Anabaptists.   vDZ.

P. Peachey, *Die soziale Herkunft der Schweizer Täufer in der Reformationszeit* (Karlsruhe, 1954) 24-26, 90, 109, No. 9.

Kalona, Iowa, is situated in the eastern part of the state, in northern Washington County, 19 miles southwest of Iowa City. It has a population of 1,015, a considerable number of whom are Mennonites (MC). Amish and Mennonite farmers live in the areas surrounding the town, although the center of their community lies to the northwest. The nearest Mennonite church, East Union (MC), is located two miles north of Kalona, and the nearest Conservative Mennonite church, Fairview, is a mile farther north and two east. Six Old Order Amish congregations are located near the town. A considerable number of the members of the Lower Deer Creek Mennonite Church (MC) have a Kalona address. See map of Johnson County.   A.L.S.

Käls (*Kels*), **Hieronymus** (Jeronimus, Jerome), a Hutterite martyr of Kufstein, Tirol, Austria, a schoolmaster of the "church in Moravia." That there were still numerous Anabaptists in Lower Austria, especially in Vienna, in spite of the severe persecution resting on them in the 1530's is revealed in the trials conducted in Vienna in 1536. The men involved were Jerome Käls and his comrades, Michael Seifensieder of Wallan in Bohemia and Hans Oberecker of Affers in the Adige Valley, Upper Austria.

The trials are of more than ordinary interest, for here it can be seen that the continuous executions were a horror to the judges as well as to the population, and that the unheard-of courage of their faith and their readiness to die amazed the judges. The judge's attitude to these three men is outspokenly friendly; their brethren have access to them, bring them letters of consolation from the churches, and carry their epistles back to the churches; indeed, the prisoners are engaged in so lively a correspondence that the guards must have

closed their eyes to it. We are not surprised when Hans Käls wrote that it "would be a comfort if the Brethren had a woman living here who could bring us a good letter of comfort, even if she did it as if she were bringing us food or wine."

The course of the trial against the three Brethren was as follows: In the first days of 1536, Hans Amon (*q.v.*) had sent the three to the church in the Adige. But they did not get beyond Vienna, for they were seized there. On Feb. 3 Käls wrote to Hans Amon, who had just sent him a letter of consolation: "When we had come into the horrible sodomitic city of Vienna, we turned in at an inn where the Neustadt coaches have their lodging. While we were eating, the people wanted us to drink, as is their devilish custom. We showed them that we would have no communion with such abominations. Thereupon they began to slander your name, but we fearlessly defended your piety. Then one who sat at the table asked for paper and ink; he wrote a Latin note: *Sunt hic tres personae. Videntur mihi esse Anabaptizatores.* (Here are three persons who I think are Anabaptists.) He did not know that I knew Latin. I told this to the brethren, and we agreed in God's name to await what might come.

"After about two hours the bailiffs came and led us bound to the judge. When he learned that we were from Jakob Hutter's church, he said we were probably the right ones. We answered, Yes, thank God, we are the right ones. Then he had us put into a common prison. There we had to suffer much disgrace and shame. To us this was a great joy; we were only pained when they slandered you. After seven days we were summoned before the judge, who admonished us to desist. We declared that we wanted to confess the truth to our death and admonished the judge to desist from his unbelief.

"In a week the judge summoned us again. Serpents were sitting with him: three selected, treacherous, learned priests. When these made light of our calling, mocked our faith, and said they were sent to lead us away from our error, I replied joyfully: We are on the right way and have our calling from God. He has taught us not to listen to the voice of strangers. We are all willing to give an account, but not to such monks and priests who are sent by the pope, the true antichrist."

For two and one-half hours Käls now defended "his teachings on hereditary sin, infant baptism, the call, and the idolatrous sacrament." The kindly admonition of the judge of his life and body to think of his wife and children was in vain. The prisoners could not complain about the severity of the judge: "We heard," writes Käls, "two days ago that the judge told some of the councilors and men high in this world, that we were too obstinate, and he was sorry. He praised us before them. He will question us once more with kind and friendly words, but then deal with us in severity."

In his second letter to Amon Käls says, "We have learned that many pious Christian hearts here in Vienna have bravely witnessed the truth to the Lord—brethren and sisters who remained steadfast and undismayed in the greatest tribulation." He is referring here to some Austerlitz brethren, from whom the Hutterites had separated in 1531.

The prisoners even succeeded in winning new members to their faith. Käls writes, "A man came to us in prison, bade us the peace of God, and brought us gifts. To him we wrote that we are surprised that he could live a Christian life in this idolatrous, cruel, and bloodthirsty city. We begged him to go to you at once and give an account to you. When he comes to you, instruct him in a friendly spirit; for he risked his life for us, brought us paper and writing materials, and did good to us."

Amon is requested to take the members of the church who are still living in Tirol at once to Moravia. "May Oberecker's wife and child," writes Käls, "be commended to your care. His wish to be imprisoned either with me or with Hutter is now fulfilled." He asks in conclusion that his mother and brother be taken to Moravia; they are willing to suffer all things, but alone they cannot stand. Among those to whom he sends greetings are Hutter's widow and Jörg Fasser.

In view of the fact that the Hutterite group had separated from the Austerlitz group, Käls's testimony concerning members of the Austerlitz group who sealed their faith with death at about the same time as he, is noteworthy. "I know the Austerlitz group very well, and know that they do not live according to the command of Christ. Nevertheless I must report that many pious Christians have bravely testified to the truth here in Vienna. We hear only good of them, and testify that through them God has given great Christian signs."

In prison Käls was apparently quite noisy. "To the priest I cried out, how long would he blaspheme with his unprofitable yelling. Then Huetstöck came to me in prison and said, Jerome, you must stop your yelling. I said I would not, for then the stones in the wall would cry out. To the priest who came to indoctrinate me I said: You ungodly fellow, throw away your fool's cap, take a hoe and work." All three of the prisoners finally handed the judge an account (*Rechenschaft*) of their faith. They wrote, "We are compelled to write to you, since we are unworthy to speak to you, and not skillful enough. We have now appeared before you many times and have answered your questions and requests with the truth as we want to answer for it before God; thus we still stand and will persist therein until our death. Therefore we beg you, for God's sake not to trouble yourself any further."

Like Käls, Seifensieder (Hans Mändl) and Oberecker also sent letters to their fellow prisoners or to the brotherhood in Moravia. Seifensieder (or Behaim as he is called here) explains that he had at first been with many sects and false brethren "now and again in Beheim," all of whom boast and have a good outward appearance, until God finally drew him out of this terrible darkness.

The last letter Käls wrote to his wife, "his dearest Treudl," has moving tones: "I send you a hymn. I sang it in my prison through God's Spirit with a sincere heart. May the Lord also teach you to sing it to His praise and glory. I send it to you with sincere love. Remain God-fearing and faithful and constant in the truth. I thank God, who gave you to me in mercy. I pray God that He may preserve you to your children. Always be obedient to the dear brethren and sisters, be of lowly, humble heart, always esteeming others better than yourself. . . . Greet my son David. Ask my brother Lienhard Sailer (Lanzenstiel) to teach you the tune, greet him for me and tell him to learn it too and sing it for my sake."

Among his brethren Käls had the reputation of being an excellent, learned schoolmaster, who wrote many good teachings and prayers for the children. In prison he wrote in addition to the song mentioned above also: "Ich freu mich dein, o Vater mein"; "Ich reu und klag den ganzen Tag"; "Ich will dich Herr und mein Gott loben" (*Die Lieder*, 61-71).

The *Rechenschaft* of these three brethren is important if for no other reason than that they contain the earliest testimony to Hutter's teaching, "to whom Jerome was an intimate brother." Strangely there is no reference to the community of goods, which was the center of Hutter's doctrinal edifice.

On March 31, 1536, the three prisoners were burned in Vienna.	LOSERTH.

Wolkan, *Geschicht-Buch*, 106, 118-22, 296; Zieglschmid, *Chronik*, 143, 158, 390 f.; Beck, *Geschichts-Bücher*, 128; R. Friedmann, "Die Briefe der österreichischen Täufer," *ARG* XXVI (1929) 80; Lydia Müller, *Glaubenszeugnisse oberdeutscher Taufgesinnter* I (Leipzig, 1938); *Mart. Mir.* D 39, E 445; *ML* II, 453-55.

Kaltern, a town (pop. 4,000) in southern Tirol, Austria, on the right side of the Adige Valley, 10 miles south of Bozen. In the vicinity of Kaltern Jörg Zaunring worked in 1528; in 1533 he suffered martyrdom near Bamberg (*q.v.*). According to a register of the Hutterite congregations of 1581, four Anabaptists were executed for their faith in Kaltern.	HEGE.

Wolkan, *Geschicht-Buch*, 64, 73, and 182; Zieglschmid, *Chronik*, 89, 233; *ML* I, 613; II, 455.

Kalva-Kurthy, a Mennonite Brethren mission station in India, was begun by Mr. and Mrs. J. H. Lohrenz in 1922. Sanction for land and for building a mission station near Kalva-Kurthy village, 60 miles due south of Hyderabad, Madhya Pradesh (formerly Central Provinces), was procured in 1933. Mr. and Mrs. J. A. Wiebe were the first resident missionaries and erected a dwelling house and several smaller buildings. Other missionaries who have worked in this station are Mr. and Mrs. J. J. Dick, and Mr. and Mrs. J. N. C. Hiebert; Mr. and Mrs. Herman H. Warkentin and Mary Doerksen were in charge in 1949. The work done from this station as center includes mainly itinerating evangelism in the villages. The field has an area of 1,000 square miles and a population of 160,000. The native church numbers 800 members. A primary school has at times been conducted on the station.

J.H.L.

Kalverboer, Simon (d. March 1892), was a lay Mennonite preacher of Krommeniedijk (*q.v.*), Dutch province of North Holland, serving 1786-1829. He wrote a history of this congregation, which is found in manuscript in the Amsterdam Mennonite Library. Because of his conservatism and his obstinacy many

members left the congregation during his ministry to join either the Mennonite congregation of Krommenie or the Reformed Church. (*Naamlijst* 1829, 28; *DJ* 1837, 17; *Inv. Arch. Amst.* II, 2, No. 224.)
vdZ.

Kamenka, a village in the Orenburg Mennonite settlement in northeast Russia, founded in 1894. The M.B. Church of Orenburg in the Urals was founded in 1895 as a subsidiary of the M.B. Church of Einlage in the province of Ekaterinoslav. On Dec. 17, 1901, it became an independent congregation with its seat at Kamenka, where in 1894, four of the 41 families were members of this church; by 1926 there were only six families in the village who were not members. A church was built in 1900. In 1905 Kamenka was organized as a subsidiary of the Orenburg M.B. Church. In 1901 Kornelius DeFehr was ordained as elder of the congregation, succeeded as minister in 1918 by David D. Päthkau. DeFehr died in 1919 or 1920. The congregation was actively engaged in evangelization among the Russians of the vicinity. The following ministers were exiled after 1929: Abram Teichröb, Jakob D. Rempel, Gerhard D. Rempel, Isaak D. Redekopp (all of Kantserovka), Aron J. Heyde and David D. Päthkau of Kamenka, and Abram D. Rempel of Petrovka. Also about 18 Sunday-school teachers and the choristers Abram Falk (Kamenka), Bernhard Falk (Kantserovka), and Hermann Neufeld (Kamenka) were exiled. (Friesen, *Brüderschaft,* 473 ff.; *ML* II, 455.)
W.Q.

Kamensky, Peter Valerioanovitch, a Russian nobleman living in the district of Bachmut, province of Ekaterinoslav, Russia, a member of the Second Duma, chairman of the Legislative Commission on Religion of the Third Duma, member of the Imperial Council, who unselfishly defended the Mennonites in word and writing during the end of the 80's and beginning of the 90's of the 19th century, when the Moscow newspaper *Novoye Vremya* (with its special reporter Velitsyn) and other prominent Russian newspapers attacked the German colonists in Russia. He knew the Germans in the Bachmut district where he was their neighbor and maintained constant relationship with them.

In 1895 he published his book *Problem or Misunderstanding, Regarding the Foreign Settlements in Russia,* which brought him into serious disrepute in the highest circles and called forth many opponents. In the book he proved that the many accusations against the colonists were based on ignorance, misunderstanding, or wrong interpretation. He acted as a true nobleman, seeking only justice. In the matter of the working out of the new law on the sects as well as in the matter of the liquidation of the German landholdings the accused always found in Kamensky a faithful friend, representative, and supporter of all legal and just right and claims. (*Menn. Bl.,* 1896, p. 74; *ML* II, 455.)
D.H.E.

Kämmerli (or in some Pennsylvania-German congregations "Schtüvli," and known in English as the "anteroom") is the small room inside and near the entrance to many Mennonite (MC) or Amish Men-

nonite meetinghouses, formerly more common than now since the change from a plural to single ministry makes the room now unnecessary. It is usually the room at the right, another at the left being reserved for mothers caring for their infants. The Kämmerli provides a meeting place for the ministers before the opening of the regular worship service. Here they plan for the morning service—who is to read the Scripture, who is to preach. On occasion they also discuss disciplinary problems before entering the auditorium to begin the service. Another function of the Kämmerli is to serve as a place for taking the counsel of the congregation. After explaining the matter on which the ministers desire the counsel, advice, or opinion of the members, they retire to this room while the members come in one by one to report their wishes. The Kämmerli also is used for the half-hour instruction period for the class being prepared for baptism. The instruction periods usually begin in late winter and continue until summer. In Old Order Amish congregations which hold their services in a private home the ministers usually use an upstairs room for these purposes. The use of the Kämmerli gradually declined at the turn of the century in those congregations which adopted the open counsel. It then became a cloakroom and Sunday-school classroom.

A similar function was performed by the *Ohm-Stübchen* (*q.v.*) in the Dutch, North German, and Russian Mennonite groups.
J.S.U.

Kampen, a city (1947 pop. 23,025, with 251 Mennonites) in the Dutch province of Overijssel. Soon after 1530 there were many Anabaptists here. Since many Flemish fled from their homes for the sake of their faith and settled in Kampen, the church here developed into a flourishing congregation in the second half of the 16th century. Between 1584 and 1620 the government issued a number of public notices against the "secret conventicles of the Anabaptists," thus indicating their numerical strength. Banishment was the penalty for attending their meetings. But on the whole the Kampen authorities were more tolerant toward the Mennonites than toward Remonstrants, Catholics, or Lutherans. In 1625 a notice was posted that Mennonites could be married only in Reformed churches, or the marriage would be considered void. In 1658 this notice was changed to read that the Mennonites could perform their weddings before the mayors. In the meantime (1644) they had furnished a house on Boven-Nieuwstraat as a meetinghouse. It was rebuilt in 1677.

Release from military service met with fewer obstacles here than elsewhere. In 1665 (war with England) the Mennonites were assigned to the extinguishing of fires. Repeatedly the government inquired into the finances of the church.

At the beginning of the 18th century there were in Kampen two congregations, the larger one Flemish (Waterlander), which in 1674 joined the Zonist (*q.v.*) conference, the other (Groningen) Old Flemish. In 1711 a new congregation was formed by a number of Swiss refugees (others at Groningen, Sappemeer, and Deventer). Not only because of the language, but also because of the strict discipline of the Swiss Mennonites, they wanted their own organization. The Swiss Mennonites (86 persons arrived here on Aug. 24, 1711, most of whom were farmers living near Kampen) at first held their meetings in the homes of the members, but in 1768 they acquired a meetinghouse Achter de Nieuwe Muren in town. Their elders were Daniel Ricken 1712-36, Jacob Staalen (Stähly) 1736-57, Peter Teune (Thöne) 1736-63, Hans Hupster 1769-92, and Jan Jans Hoosen (q.v.) of Giethoorn 1805-22. The Old Flemish congregation, which had only 23 male members in 1710, was soon dissolved, and in 1767 had only a few members left. In 1781 these joined the Flemish. The Swiss church, though it had at first been strengthened by many new arrivals, gradually declined, and in 1822 the 25 remaining members joined the other congregation. After the merger the Nieuwestraat meetinghouse was too small; therefore a new church in the Broederstraat was rented in 1823, and purchased in 1847. This church is still in use by the congregation; it is a historic building, erected about 1480; until the Reformation it had been the chapel of St. Anna convent and later a Walloon Reformed Church. The congregation possesses two beautiful engraved silver communion cups from the 18th century. Its pulpit, kept from the Walloon church, dates back to 1611.

The membership numbered 104 in 1834, 110 in 1861, 173 in 1900, 127 in 1956. During the last century the congregation was served by the following ministers: J. Sybrandi 1851-86, H. Ens 1886-1909, Corn. Vis Jzn 1909-30, F. van der Wissel 1932-37, A. F. L. van Dijk 1938-47, Miss H. C. Leignes Bakhoven 1947- . The church activities include Sunday school for the children, and a ladies' circle.
                                                        vDZ.

Inv. Arch. Amst. I, Nos. 69, 84, 147, 267, 886, 1180, 1225, 1350, 1366, 1903-20; II, Nos. 2016-31; II, 2 No. 223; *DJ* 1840, 44; 1850, 37-39; *DB* 1875, 57; 1881, 78-105; 1882, 117; J. Huizinga, *Stamboek van Samuel Peter (Meihuizen) en Barbara Fry* (Groningen, 1890) 65-68 and *passim; ML* II, 455 f.

Kampen, van, a Mennonite family at Leer (*q.v.*), East Friesland, Germany, which had two (lay) Mennonite ministers, e.g., Kornelis van Kampen, at Leer, who served his home church from 1729-d. 63, and his son Kornelis van Kampen Kornzn, who was a minister at Emden 1739-56, and in the Zon (*q.v.*) congregation at Amsterdam 1757-d. 81. In the northeast of the Dutch province of Groningen there is also a Mennonite van Kampen family, many members of which have served the congregation of Mensingeweer (*q.v.*) as deacons.   vDZ.

Kampen, Johann Jakob van, the last unsalaried minister of the Danzig Mennonite Church, b. 1803 in Schottland near Danzig, d. Nov. 8, 1867. He stemmed from an old Mennonite family in Elbing (*q.v.*). Jost van Kampen, who acquired citizenship there in 1585, placed a plot of land at the disposal of the congregation, on which the first chapel was erected in 1590. In 1835 Johann van Kampen was made a director of the Danzig church, and in 1861 was chosen minister to support Jakob Mannhardt (*q.v.*). He served faithfully in this capacity until his death. He arranged the archives, collected books

for the church library, and conscientiously continued the church records begun by Anton Schreder; after his death Wilhelm Mannhardt (*q.v.*) continued them. For several years van Kampen was a member of the city council and chairman of the city Poor Commission (*Armenkommission*) as well as of an orphanage in Danzig.   NEFF.

H. G. Mannhardt, *Die Danziger Mennonitengemeinde* (Danzig, 1919); *ML* II, 456.

Kampen, Nicolaas Godfried van (b. 1776 at Haarlem, d. 1839 at Amsterdam), was a Dutch Mennonite, a son of Willem van Kampen and Maria Stetius (of Crefeld). Young Nicolaas was intended to continue the florist business of his father and his grandfather near Haarlem. After his father's accidental death in 1783 and his mother's remarriage, Nicolaas was educated by his uncle at Crefeld and at the Mühlheim Commercial School. In 1795, when the florist business was about to be liquidated, Nicolaas moved to Leiden, intending to go into the book business. But instead he became an editor of the *Leidsche Courant* in 1801. In 1798 he had been baptized, and in 1805 he married Jacoba van Duuren of Leiden. For many years van Kampen lived in impoverished circumstances, earning his living by giving private lessons. In the meantime he became a student of literature and history and published a large number of writings, including a history of the French domination of Europe (1810-23, eight volumes). In 1829 van Kampen, who had never been a university student, was honored by a call to teach Dutch literature and history at the Athenaeum (university) of Amsterdam. He was frequently given awards by learned associations such as Teyler's foundation at Haarlem. During his Leiden period he was a deacon of the Mennonite congregation 1812-15, 1818-19, 1821-29.   vDZ.

S. Muller, *Levens- en Karakterschets van N. G. van Kampen* (Haarlem-Leiden, 1840); *N.N.B.Wb.* III, 661-63.

Kampen, Willem Abraham van (b. 1811 at Leiden), a son of the foregoing, was a preacher of the Dutch Mennonite congregation of Wormer and Jisp. In 1841 he resigned to go into business. He published a collection of sermons (*Leerredenen*) (Amsterdam, 1841). (*DJ* 1850, 22; *Biogr. Wb.* IV, 656.)   vDZ.

Kamphuyzen, Dirk R.: see **Camphuysen, Dirk Rafaelsz.**

Kampner, Agatha and **Elizabeth,** Anabaptist martyrs, natives of Braidenberg in the Adige Valley, Austria, who were seized in 1529 with three brethren and two sisters in Fill (*q.v.*) in the Adige, and executed on Nov. 19, 1529. Agatha confessed that she had been baptized before Christmas, 1528, by a preacher named Töbich, in a village near St. Gall, Switzerland; she did not consider infant baptism valid; for even if children die without baptism, they die in innocence and are the Lord's. The Mass she considered nothing; for Christ had not said to His disciples: Go ye and hold Mass, but go ye and preach the Gospel. Concerning communion she said, because one confesses in the faith that He is seated at the right hand of the heavenly Father, whence He will come to judge the quick and the dead, she did not believe that He permits the priests to put Him into the host. Concerning holy days she said no day is holier than another; Sunday was ordained in order that people may meet, preach, and speak about the Gospel; it is now misused for gluttony and other evil. With the help and grace of God she would stand by her faith.

Elizabeth confessed that she had been baptized by Georg Blaurock (q.v.) in the summer of 1529, in accord with the command of Christ in the name of the Father, Son, and Holy Ghost. On other points she expressed herself like her sister.

With them were executed two other women, Christine Tollinger of Penon and Barbara of Thiers (q.v.), and four men, Wolfgang von Moss of Teutsch-Noffen, Thoman im Waldt from Aldain, Georg Frik of Wirtsburg, and Mang Kager (q.v.) of Füssen.   NEFF.

Wolkan, Geschicht-Buch, 65; Beck, Geschichts-Bücher, 64 f., 89; Zieglschmid, Chronik, 74, 77 f.; ML I, 325; II, 456.

Kanagy (Kenagy, Kenege, Gnaeg, Gnaegi, Gnagy, Gnagey, Genegy), an Amish Mennonite family name found in Pennsylvania, Maryland, Ohio, Michigan, Indiana, Iowa, Missouri, Colorado, Oregon, and other states. Hans Gnaegi was a member of the Amish Mennonite church at Montbéliard, France, in 1723. Johannes Gnaeg arrived in Philadelphia in 1742 with a group of Amish immigrants. Barbara Kenege arrived in Pennsylvania from Switzerland in 1749. Christian Gnaegi from Switzerland came to Pennsylvania between 1750 and 1760 and settled in Somerset County, where many of his descendants still live. Joseph Kenegy with his five sons, Ulrich, John, Yost, Joseph, and Jacob, migrated from Switzerland to America in 1770 and settled in Berks Co., Pa. The *Mennonite Cyclopedic Dictionary* is authority for the statement that "later John and Yost moved to Somerset Co., Pa., and from there to Ohio, and still later Yost moved to Illinois. From these five brothers, there came a numerous family, scattered from coast to coast." Joseph had a brother John who came to America in 1754, whose descendants live in Ohio. An Ulrich Keneagy, born in Berks Co., Pa., settled in Lancaster County in 1795. His Amish ancestors came from Switzerland.

Among the church leaders bearing this family name were Jacob C. Kenagy (1821-94), a bishop (MC) at East Lynne, Mo., and S. M. Kanagy (1869-1941), teacher at Hesston College, superintendent of the Mennonite Home Mission in Chicago, and bishop in the Wanner Church (MC) at Blair, Ont. Nelson Kanagy is a minister in the Oak Grove Mennonite Church (MC), West Liberty, Ohio. J. Forrest Kanagy, Biglerville, Pa., is secretary of the Mennonite Board of Education (MC).

M.G.

E. Gnagey, *A Complete History of Christian Gnaegi* (printed at Elkhart, Ind., 1897).

Kansas, central state of the United States, pop. (1950) 1,905,229, organized as a territory in 1854, admitted to the Union in 1861, has a larger Mennonite population than any other state west of the Mississippi, most of whom came to America during the great Mennonite migration of the 1870's from Russia, Poland, and Prussia. The first Mennonites, however, to settle in Kansas came from the eastern states at an earlier date. M. W. Keim and his friends from Pennsylvania in 1869-70 purchased from Case and Billings 5,000 acres near Marion Center. Attracted by the Homestead Act of 1862, Daniel, Christian, and Margaret Kilmer of Elkhart Co., Ind., settled in the southeastern part of McPherson County in 1871. This became the nucleus of the Spring Valley Mennonite Church (MC), located on the western end of the "twenty-three mile furrow," which connected the scattered farms of the Pennsylvania-German Mennonites of this area. The east edge of the twenty-three mile furrow bordered on the Brunk farm and cemetery located on Highway 50 between Hillsboro and Marion. Here R. J. Heatwole and Henry G. Brunk located, coming from Virginia. Soon others followed from Ohio, Indiana, Illinois, and Missouri. The beginnings of this settlement preceded the great Mennonite migration to the prairie states and provinces from Russia by two years. Later Pennsylvania Mennonites (MC) established the following congregations: Catlin (q.v.) in Marion County in 1877, West Liberty (q.v.) in McPherson County in 1883, Pennsylvania (q.v.) in Harvey County in 1885, and Pleasant Valley (q.v.) in Harper County in 1897. The Amish of Yoder and Partridge in Reno County near Hutchinson came to Kansas starting in 1883, and an Amish Mennonite congregation was established at Crystal Springs (q.v.) in Harper County in 1904.

The Beginning of the Settlements of Mennonites from Russia, Poland, and Prussia. When the Mennonites settled in Russia in 1789 and the following years they were given written guarantees by the Czars that they could settle in solid communities, conduct their own schools, and have their own administration and also that they would be exempted from any form of military service. When rumors regarding a general conscription law came into circulation among the Mennonites in Russia around 1870 they were alarmed. Soon for some individuals of deep-rooted convictions, America appeared on the horizon. Among them was Cornelius Jansen (q.v.). He was in touch with Russian and foreign authorities at Berdyansk, from whom he received information regarding Canada and America. Benjamin Warkentin and three friends came to the United States in 1872, making their headquarters at Summerfield, Ill. Railroad agents tried to interest Warkentin in various settlement possibilities. Faithfully he reported all his experiences and findings to David Goerz (q.v.) of Berdyansk, who circularized the information among the Mennonites of the Molotschna settlement.

The first settlement by Mennonites from Russia in Kansas took place in 1873 when Peter and Jacob Funk bought land from the Santa Fe Railroad near the present site of Marion for $2.50 per acre. Christian Krehbiel, who was present at the time of the purchase, reports: "With this land purchase the die was cast for Kansas" (*From the Steppes*, 31). This was the beginning of the Brudertal Mennonite Church (q.v.).

Meanwhile the Summerfield Mennonites also became interested in the land of the prairies. As a

MISSOURI

NEBRASKA

K A N S A S

OKLAHOMA

Kansas City (GCM)
Argentine (MC)
Mennonite Children's Home (MC)

Topeka (GCM) ⃝

•Anderson Co. district (OOA)

Fredonia First (GCM)
•Emmanuel (CGC)

Hillsboro
Hesston
•First (GCM)
•Eden (CGC)

Tampa
•Tampa (MB)

Friedensteal (GCM)•
Logan (CGC)•

McPherson•

Wichita
Lorraine Avenue (GCM)
Wichita (MB)•
Eureka Gardens (MC)

Newton

Mennoscah Camp (GCM)•
•Sumner Co. district (OOA)

Plainview (CM)•
•First (GCM)

Wichita (MC)
Zion (GCM)

Bethany (MC)•
•Pleasant Valley (MC)
Harper

Sterling (EM)•
Hutchinson(OOA)•
Arlington (GCM)

Kingman

Partridge district (OOA)•

•Bergtal(GCM)

Dorrance
•Dorrance (MB)

Greensburg
Calvary (MC)•Kiowa County Memorial Hospital(MC)
Bethel (CGC)•• Faith (GCM)

•Crystal Springs (MC)•

•Protection (MC)

Ransom
•First (GCM)

•Banston (GCM)

•Russel Springs (CGC)

Scott (CGC)•

Shallow Water
•Shallow Water (MC)

•Ingalls (MB)

•Cimarron (CGC)
Montezuma•
Ebenfeld (GCM)
Montezuma (CGC)
Bethel Home for the Aged (CGC)

Salem (CGC)•

Spring Valley (MB)•

oMeade
•Emmanuel (Ind.)
Meade (EMB) •oMeade Bible Academy (EMB)

Pleasant Valley (GCM)•

•Meadow (GCM)

Kansas

Scale of Miles
0 5 10 20 30 40 50 60 70 80 90 100

result of investigation trips they chose land near Halstead, Kan. For $2.00—$15.00 the Santa Fe reserved for the Summerfield Mennonites land in townships 21, 22, 23, and 24, in McPherson and Harvey counties. Warkentin built a mill on the Arkansas River near Halstead. The first Summerfield Mennonites moved to Kansas in the spring of 1875, where the Halstead Mennonite Church (q.v.) was organized March 28, 1875.

Although the official delegates did not favor Kansas, and even Cornelius Jansen, who initiated the imigration to America, chose Nebraska, Kansas became the preferred state by most of the immigrants, in spite of the fact that Warkentin was not considered a delegate and was not specifically consulted by the delegation. One reason why some Mennonites preferred Canada above any of the prairie states was the fact that they were offered large compact areas such as the East Reserve (q.v.) and the West Reserve (q.v.) on the Red River, on which they could live just as they had in Russia, with their own schools and self-government. This none of the states could offer. After debating this question, the U.S. Congress felt that Mennonites would have to be satisfied with settling on alternate sections of land offered by the railroads. Regarding nonresistance the Canadian promises were also more specific than those of the United States.

While Congress was still debating the petitions the movement of the Mennonites from Russia, Poland, and Prussia to the United States set in. Wilhelm Ewert, the Prussian delegate, arrived in Peabody May 16, 1874, accompanied by a number of Prussian Mennonites. He joined the Funk brothers of Brudertal near Marion Center. Elder Jacob A. Wiebe and Johann Harder leading the Krimmer Mennonite Brethren, crossing the Atlantic with their group on the City of Brooklyn, arrived in New York on July 15, 1874. They settled on 12 sections of land in Marion County, establishing Gnadenau village and the Gnadenau Krimmer Mennonite Brethren Church (q.v.).

In the midst of the Mennonite migration from Russia to Kansas A. E. Touzalin, land commissioner for the Santa Fe, became agent of the Burlington and Quincy Railroad. In this capacity he made considerable effort to divert to Nebraska the immigrants which he had solicited for Kansas, since the Burlington ran through Nebraska. The Santa Fe secured C. B. Schmidt (q.v.) as agent, who immediately contacted the Mennonites.

Meanwhile the movement from Russia continued. The large Alexanderwohl group arrived in New York aboard the Cimbria on Aug. 27, 1874, and the Teutonia on Sept. 3, 1874. It was met by David Goerz, Wilhelm Ewert, and C. B. Schmidt of the Santa Fe, all boosters for Kansas. The Teutonia group with Dietrich Gaeddert and Peter Balzer as leaders followed them to Kansas, while Jacob Buller and his group proceeded to Nebraska. Jacob Buller had refused to see Kansas as a delegate. Now he and his group soon went from Lincoln, Neb., to Kansas, where they bought land in Marion and McPherson counties north of Newton. This became the large Alexanderwohl (q.v.) settlement and church. The immigrants settled in villages similar to those they had left behind in Russia. The settlers who had come on the Teutonia under the leadership of Dietrich Gaeddert chose to settle 20 miles west of the Alexanderwohl settlement, purchasing about 35,000 acres of railroad land in the adjoining corners of Reno, McPherson, and Harvey counties. This settlement and church became known as Hoffnungsau (q.v.). The town of Buhler was founded in the heart of the settlement.

Another group of some 109 families from Russian Poland arrived in Topeka about the same time. During the middle of the winter of 1874-75, 265 more families followed. These were Swiss Volhynian Mennonites under the leadership of Jacob Stucky, one of the delegates, who settled along Turkey Creek in McPherson County in the vicinity of the present Moundridge. They organized the Hoffnungsfeld congregation, the mother church of the Eden (q.v.) and other congregations.

The "Polish" Mennonites, led by Tobias Unruh, a delegate from Ostrog, Poland, left Antwerp late in November on three ships, Nederland, Vaderland, and Abbotsford. The group consisted of 265 families. The poorest 50 families remained in Pennsylvania for the winter while the others continued their trip to Kansas. The Mennonite Board of Guardians (q.v.) gave them aid and distributed them for the winter in the vicinity of Newton, Florence, and Great Bend. Most of them were settled on small farms in the spring, in the vicinity of Canton, later joining the Church of God in Christ, Mennonites (q.v.), founded by John Holdeman. The Emmanuel Church (q.v.) and the Pawnee Rock Bergtal Mennonite Church (q.v.) also belong to this group. Later others moved to Oklahoma. Still others never came to Kansas but settled in Dakota. Only some 1,400 persons came to Kansas during 1875, the migration to Manitoba being much greater during this year.

C. Henry Smith reports that 1,275 families arrived in the United States and Canada during 1874. Of these, 600 families came to Kansas. In addition to these, 150 families temporarily remained in the east, some in Pennsylvania, some in Ontario. Thus about half of the total number of immigrants of 1874 came to Kansas. The next largest group went to Manitoba, after which followed the group to the Dakotas. The passengers used the Inman, Allen, Red Star, Hamburg-America, and Adler lines. Some arrived in New York and others in Philadelphia. C. B. Schmidt, the most enthusiastic agent, who secured some letters of introduction from Mennonites who had arrived in Kansas, left New York on Feb. 1, 1875, and went to Russia to win more immigrants for Kansas. Yet 1874 remained the peak year for Mennonite immigration to Kansas. According to Shipley, the total number of Mennonites immigrating to North America in 1874 was 6,402, of whom it was estimated that about 5,300 came to the United States, with nearly 3,000 coming to Kansas (p. 87).

The Prussian Mennonites, founding the Emmaus Mennonite Church (q.v.), the First Mennonite Church of Newton, and the Zion Mennonite Church at Elbing, began to come to Kansas in 1876 and the following years. Among them was Leonhard Sudermann of Berdyansk, who had originally not been impressed by Kansas. Only smaller numbers reached Kansas after this. The steamer *Strassburg,* arriving in New York on July 1, 1878, carried 35 families headed for Kansas. The steamer *Switzerland,* arriving in June 1879, brought 42 additional families to Kansas. Of the Swiss Galician Mennonites 22 families came to Kansas, settling near Arlington and Hanston. By 1880 the immigration had dwindled down to a few families per year. Again in 1884 some Central Asian Mennonite families reached Newton. Abraham Schellenburg arived in Kansas in 1879 with some Mennonte Brethren, settling at Buhler and Hillsboro.

The first Brethren in Christ (*q.v.*) reached Abilene, Kan., in 1879, coming from Harrisburg, Pa. This denomination also developed settlements and congregations in Brown and Dickinson counties and elsewhere.

Of the approximately 18,000 Mennonites that came to North America from Russia in 1873-84, about 10,000 came to the United States, of whom possibly 5,000 settled in Kansas. No one has yet attempted to establish the exact figures. According to T. R. Schellenburg, the census schedule of 1880 revealed that 7,000 persons (German-speaking) were settled in Marion, Reno, McPherson, and Harvey counties, of whom 74 per cent were from Russia, 17 per cent from Poland, and 9 per cent from Germany. Most of them were Mennonites.

Kansas was a competitor to Manitoba. The Old Colony, Bergthal, and other conservative groups were won for Manitoba because the Canadian government promised them what they asked for; i.e., land for compact settlements, self government, and their own schools. Kansas received a large portion of the Molotschna, the Prussian, the Swiss Volhynian, the Swiss Galician, and the Polish Mennonites. No Old Colony Mennonites from Chortitza, with the exception of those few who had joined the Mennonite Brethren, came to Kansas.

There were a number of factors influencing the decision of so many Mennonites from Russia to settle in Kansas. The Kansas railroads were great boosters and competitors. Christian Krehbiel and Bernhard Warkentin, who advised and counseled many of the Mennonite leaders, were Kansas boosters from the beginning. Through Warkentin, David Görz, who was still in Russia, advertised and spread the good news about Kansas. He continued this promotion in his paper *Zur Heimath,* which he edited and published in Halstead, and through his booklet *Die Mennoniten-Niederlassung auf den Ländereien der Atchison, Topeka, und Santa Fe Eisenbahn.* Most important, however, was very likely the fact that Kansas was located geographically very much the same as the Ukraine whence the Mennonites came. The weather, the crops, and the general conditions were very similar to those of the Molotschna settlement. Winter wheat and even watermelons could be expected to grow here just as in Russia. The water level could easily be reached. Many feared the severe winters of Manitoba, Minnesota, and Dakota.

The following sections apply primarily to the Mennonites who came from Russia:

Economic Life. The economic status and background of the Kansas Mennonite farmers differed greatly. Some had been successful and prosperous farmers, and brought a considerable amount of money; others were poor and had to borrow money. They needed the aid of the Mennonite Board of Guardians and others. Generally speaking, the Mennonites of Prussia and the Molotschna were prosperous and advanced in culture. The economic status and the educational level of the Mennonites coming from Poland was considerably lower. All of them seemed to intend to continue their accustomed way of life. The Alexanderwohl (*q.v.*) immigrants settled in villages north of Newton. Noble L. Prentis has given us a vivid portrayal of Mennonite life in that community in 1874-77. In "The Mennonites in Kansas," "The Mennonites at Home," and "A Day with the Mennonites" (see *From the Steppes*) he describes their life at home, their dress, their food, how they farmed, and their qualities as farmers, such as patience, endurance, skill, and success in spite of pioneer difficulties and grasshopper plagues.

Against the advice of Warkentin the settlers brought with them all kinds of furniture, tools, and implements, even wagons and plows. If they had forgotten anything they wrote to relatives to bring it along; e.g., gooseberry sprouts or tulip bulbs. They transformed the prairie by erecting their homes on their quarter sections or in villages surrounded by rows of shade trees, mulberry trees, and fields of waving grain. Mulberry hedges were planted to provide food for the silkworms, an industry which they brought from the Ukraine and intended to continue on the Kansas prairies. A silk mill was established in Peabody, Kan., but it did not prosper. Some of the typical furniture (*q.v.*) gradually disappeared. Threshing stones and other implements used in the early days can be seen today in the Kauffman Museum of Bethel College. Mulberry hedges, Russian olive trees, thistles, and bindweeds can still be found in Kansas. Even Russian watermelons have responded to the "survival of the fittest."

The most important economic contribution of the Mennonites was the introduction of hard winter wheat. In 1874 the Mennonites from Russia sowed the first winter wheat seed which they had brought with them. After experimenting with different varieties they found that the hard red Turkey winter wheat was best suited to the soil and the climatic conditions of Kansas. It gradually spread into the neighboring non-Mennonite counties of Kansas. Warkentin, whose father had been a miller in the Ukraine, and who had established a mill in Halstead, ordered a large shipment from the Crimea in 1885-86 for distribution among the farmers of Kansas, and established the Newton Milling and Elevator Co., using steel rollers instead of stone burrs to grind the hard wheat. Warkentin also continued to experiment with different varieties of wheat on his own experiment station in Halstead. In 1900 the Kansas State Millers Association and the Kansas Grain Dealers Association asked Warkentin to import a large shipment of seed wheat from the Ukraine. As a result 15,000 bushels were imported and distributed to farmers the next year. In 1896 Mark A. Carleton of the United States

Department of Agriculture came to Warkentin to inquire about his experiments with wheat. Carleton went to the Ukraine in 1898 to study the Turkey wheat in its native country. Warkentin located a plot for him near Halstead where he could experiment with some 300 varieties of wheat from Russia. Numerous varieties of wheat have been developed since. Kansas still raises the wheat the Mennonites introduced 80 years ago, although other newer varieties have now taken precedence over the Turkey variety. The Mennonites of Kansas were pioneers in transforming the prairies into wheat fields and thus helped make Kansas a bread basket for the world.

The great handicap in the economic life of the Mennonites of Kansas is the fact that the prairie states from time to time experience a cycle of drought. Farming has undergone many changes, but basically it remains the same. Grain and dairy farming are found everywhere.

Unlike the Mennonites of Russia, the Kansas Mennonites, with the exception of the milling industry in which Warkentin and Rudolph Goerz were prominent, never played a very significant role in the production of machinery or in industry. At present the activities of the Mennonites along this line are confined mostly to feed mills and grain elevators, some of which are co-operative enterprises. The Buller Manufacturing Company of Hillsboro and the Hesston Manufacturing Company produce some agricultural machinery. In Newton the Mennonites have been leaders in the banking business. Most of the Mennonite communities have banks and businesses operated by Mennonites. The following table of Mennonite businesses for 1924 is probably still true with the exception of the milling industry in Newton, which is now almost entirely in non-Mennonite hands. In other cases there might be an increase in Mennonite business in these towns.

TOWNS IN KANSAS

Showing Mennonite Population and Businesses, 1924

(From C. C. Janzen, p. 50)

Name	Established	Population 1924	Per cent controlled by Mennonites
Buhler	1887	600	75
Goessel	1893	100	100
Halstead	1873	1,200	13
Hesston	1886	600	50
Hillsboro	1879	1,574	85
Inman	1886	432	75
Lehigh	1879	395	30
Moundridge	1886	800	60
Newton	1872	10,000	5
			90 of the flour milling; 50 of the banking.

In addition to these towns the following have a predominately or strong Mennonite population: North Newton, Elbing, Whitewater, Canton, Walton, Marion, McPherson, Peabody, and Yoder. The large cities, like Wichita, Hutchinson, Topeka, Lawrence, and Kansas City, have a constantly increasing Mennonite population; some of these Mennonites have established congregations.

Cultural Life. One of the reasons why the Mennonites came to America was their insistence on maintaining their religious and cultural life as they had inherited it. To promote this, schools and churches were immediately erected everywhere. In both of them the use of the Bible and the German language prevailed for many years. Gradually the parochial schools were replaced by public schools, but some of them continued, supplementing the education of the public schools with instruction in Bible and the German language. Some of these schools, like the Emmatal (*q.v.*) school, became secondary schools patterned after the traditional Russian Mennonite Zentralschule. The Halstead Seminary, the forerunner of Bethel College, founded in 1882, was the first step toward collegiate education. Preparatory schools (*q.v.*) were established in all larger Mennonite communities such as Hillsboro, Goessel, and Moundridge. A Kansas Conference (*q.v.*) was organized in the interest of education. The Teachers' Association (*q.v.*) (*Lehrerverein*) played a very significant role in the promotion of education. Bethel College (*q.v.*) was established at its present location in 1887 as the successor to the Halstead Seminary, serving primarily the General Conference Mennonite Church constituency of the prairie states and provinces. Tabor College (*q.v.*) at Hillsboro, founded by the Mennonite Brethren, was established in 1908. Hesston College of the Mennonite Church (MC) was established in 1909 to serve the congregations of that group west of the Mississippi. Each of these three schools, located within a radius of 30 miles, maintained an academy which offered high-school subjects, and Hesston College still does. The curriculum of the colleges has grown and changed in accordance with the trends of education and the demands of the constituencies.

In all the Mennonite communities nearly all the young people attend high schools. In some of them religious instruction is given. Zoar Academy (*q.v.*), sponsored by the Krimmer Mennonite Brethren, was recently discontinued. New secondary parochial schools were established in the Berean Academy (*q.v.*) at Elbing and the Central Kansas Bible Academy (*q.v.*) at Hutchinson.

The pattern of the cultural life of the Mennonites of Kansas has changed considerably. Not only have the walls which separated the various ethnic and cultural groups, such as the Swiss Volhynian, Low German, Prussian, and Polish background Mennonites, been torn down, but also the walls between all groups and their environment. The former practice of nonconformity has either received an entirely new interpretation or has been nearly forgotten. The barrier of language and customs has been almost completely removed, with the exception of some of the more conservative groups. As a rule, Mennonites fulfill their obligations as citizens in voting. Some of them even choose the legal profession as a vocation. It was formerly said that Mennonites stay out of court and that there are no divorces in Mennonite communities. This is no longer completely true.

Religious Life. Out of the Kansas Conference came the Western District Conference (*q.v.*) of the General Conference Mennonite Church. Of the 66 congregations of the Western District, 53 are located in Kansas, which is by far the largest number of General Conference congregations in any of the states or provinces. The membership was 11,118 in 1955 and the total population including children, 15,552. The Mennonite Brethren have 10 congregations in Kansas (2,000 members, 1951); the Krimmer Mennonite Brethren 3 (449 members, 1955); the Church of God in Christ Mennonite, 14 (1,917 members, 1954); the Evangelical Mennonite Brethren 2 (297 members, 1955); Mennonite Church (MC) 13 (1,575 members, 1954); the Brethren in Christ 5 (240 members, 1955); the Evangelical Mennonite Church 1 (143 members, 1955); the Old Order Amish have 6 districts (386 members, 1954); the Conservative Mennonites 1 (113 members, 1954). Regarding the more conservative groups it can be said that through the contact with other Mennonite groups in Civilian Public Service and in relief projects, their spiritual life and their forms of worship have been revitalized and as a rule they have developed an active program of missionary and evangelistic outreach. Interest in education is growing continually. Kansas, with its three Mennonite colleges and many secondary schools, is not only the center for the Mennonites of the prairie states as far as education is concerned, but also a center for Conference organizations and publications. The General Conference headquarters are located in Newton, where the various boards of the Conference do their business. The Conference maintains a bookstore in Newton, and together with Bethel College, a Mennonite Press in North Newton. In North Newton there is also a clothing center of the MCC for the prairie states. At Newton is the Prairie View Hospital, a mental hospital operated by the MCC.

Hillsboro, located some 28 miles north of Newton in Marion County, has become the national headquarters for the Mennonite Brethren. It is the location of the largest Mennonite Brethren congregation east of California, the Mission Board of the Mennonite Brethren, the Mennonite Brethren Publishing House and bookstore, and Tabor College. Hesston and Hesston College, six miles northwest of Newton, has become a center for the Mennonite Church (MC) in Kansas. All three college campuses are being used extensively by their constituencies for conferences, and religious and cultural programs sponsored by the respective colleges. Bethel Deaconess Home and Hospital (*q.v.*) at Newton, Bethesda Hospital at Goessel (*q.v.*), and Salem Hospital at Hillsboro (*q.v.*), as well as the Mercy Hospital (*q.v.*) at Moundridge, and a number of homes for the aged are Mennonite-sponsored institutions. The Hertzler Clinic of Halstead was originally also sponsored and supported by the Mennonites. Midland Mutual Fire Insurance, the oldest fire insurance of Kansas, was originally a Mennonite organization, founded by David Goerz.

The total Mennonite church membership of Kansas is 18,294 (1955). This should make a total Mennonite population (including children) of about 30,000. Many Kansas Mennonites have migrated to Oklahoma and the Pacific Coast to establish settlements of various Mennonite branches in these areas.   C.K.

C. C. Janzen, "A Social Study of the Mennonite Settlement in the Counties of Marion, McPherson, Harvey, Reno, and Butler, Kansas" (Ph.D. thesis, Chicago, 1926); Helen B. Shipley, "The Migration of the Mennonites from Russia, 1873-1883, and Their Settlement in Kansas" (M.A. thesis, Minnesota, 1954); Ed. G. Kaufman, "Social Problems and Opportunities of the Western District Conference Communities of the General Conference of Mennonites of North America" (M.A. thesis, Witmarsum Seminary, 1917); Gideon G. Yoder, "The Oldest Living American Mennonite Congregations of Central Kansas" (M.A. thesis, Phillips University, 1948); C. Henry Smith, *The Coming of the Russian Mennonites* (Berne, 1927); Gustav E. Reimer and G. R. Gaeddert, *Exiled by the Czar: Cornelius Jansen and the Great Mennonite Migration, 1874* (Newton, 1956); Cornelius J. Dyck, "Kansas Promotional Activities with Particular Reference to Mennonites" (M.A. thesis, Municipal University of Wichita, 1955); G. D. Bradley, *The Story of the Santa Fe* (Boston, 1920); Ernst Correll, "The Congressional Debate on the Mennonite Immigration from Russia, 1873-74," *MQR* XX (February 1946) 174-88; G. Raymond Gaeddert, *The Birth of Kansas* (Lawrence, 1940); *Herold of Truth*, Elkhart, 1873 ff.; *Herold der Wahrheit*, Elkhart, 1871 ff.; Cornelius Krahn, "Some Letters of Bernhard Warkentin Pertaining to the Migration of 1873-1875," *MQR* XXIV (July 1950) 248-63; Georg Leibbrandt, "The Emigration of the German Mennonites from Russia to the United States and Canada in 1873-1880," I, *MQR* VI (October 1932) 205-26, and II, *MQR* VII (January 1933) 5-41; Abraham Albrecht, "Mennonite Settlements in Kansas" (M.A. thesis, Kansas, 1924); James C. Malin, *Winter Wheat in the Golden Belt of Kansas* (Lawrence, 1944); Arthur E. Hertzler, "What Kansas Mennonites Have Produced," *Kansas Magazine*, 1939, 87; Alberta Pantle, "Settlement of the Krimmer Mennonite Brethren at Gnadenau, Marion County," *Kansas Historical Quarterly* XIII (February 1945) 259-85; L. L. Waters, *Steel Trails to Santa Fe* (Lawrence, 1950); P. P. Wedel, *Kurze Geschichte der aus Wolhynien, Russland, nach Kansas ausgewanderten Schweizer-Mennoniten* (n.p., 1929); *Zur Heimath*, Halstead, 1876-81; Cornelius Krahn (ed.), *From the Steppes to the Prairies* (Newton, 1949); see also articles on Kansas in *Mennonite Life; ML* II, 458 f.

Kansas City, a city of over 585,000 population, located at the junction of the Kansas and Missouri rivers, approximately three fourths of which is situated in Missouri and one fourth in Kansas. Mennonites (MC) opened the Mennonite Gospel Mission (*q.v.*) at 200 South 7th St. (Kansas City, Kan.) in May 1905. Later extension work was carried on in Argentine, a section of southern Kansas City, Kan. A building at 3105 Strong Avenue was purchased and used for a mission hall. As a result of mission activity in this area the Kansas City Argentine Mennonite Church (*q.v.*) was built in 1924 at the corner of 37th and Metropolitan Avenue and dedicated in 1925. Previous to this the 7th Street building was sold. In 1946 the Argentine Mennonite Church was organized out of the original Mennonite Gospel Mission congregation. This congregation now has a membership of 102. An outgrowth of Mennonite mission activity in this area was the Mennonite Children's Home (*q.v.*) in 1917. It is located at 1620 South 37th Street. In 1946 the Mennonite Gospel Center (*q.v.*) was established. It is located at 1238 Washington Street and has a membership of 25. All of these institutions were established by the Mennonite Church (MC). A Voluntary Service program (MC) known as the Kansas City Hospital Unit is located at 2512 Holmes St.,

Kansas City, Mo. This is also the I-W center for men doing their alternative service in Kansas City. In 1956 the Western District (GCM) purchased a church at 40th and Rainbow Streets, Kansas City, Kan.; it is used by the Mennonite fellowship, which has been meeting in Kansas City.   M.G.

Kansas Conference of Mennonites *(Kansaskonferenz)* was the forerunner of the Western District Conference of the General Conference Mennonite Church, founded through the initiative of David Goerz in 1877, who proposed in *Zur Heimat* (Aug. 15, 1877) to have a meeting with teachers pertaining to their profession. The meeting took place in the home of Heinrich Richert *(q.v.)*, Alexanderwohl, at which teachers, ministers, and elders were present. W. Ewert was chosen chairman and David Goerz secretary. A committee was elected to work out a plan by which the conference could successfully conduct an educational program.

The first official Kansas Conference meeting took place Dec. 14-15, 1877. In the invitation it was suggested that all congregations were entitled to send one delegate for every 30 members. Ten congregations (including the Mennonite Brethren of Marion County) sent delegates totaling about 70 persons. On the agenda were chiefly educational matters, such as the establishment of a secondary school *(Zentralschule)* and also questions pertaining to songbooks, home missions, foreign missions, and relief. It was recommended that Mennonites aim to establish their own school districts and if there were sufficient Mennonites in a community, to establish a Mennonite parochial school. Questions pertaining to curricula and textbooks were discussed in detail. The minutes of this and the following meetings were regularly published in *Zur Heimat.*

At the second meeting (Nov. 6-7, 1878) the school committee presented a report. David Goerz was sent as a delegate to the Middle District Conference (at the time Western District Conference) meeting in Berne, Ind., and to the General Conference meeting at Wadsworth, Ohio. At the third session (Oct. 27-29, 1879) such questions were discussed as to whether it is sufficient for a congregation to maintain its numerical strength by having the children join the church or whether a congregation should demonstrate its spiritual life by reaching out into communities where the Gospel is not preached. This session was also attended as guests by Jakob Wiebe and Johann Harder of the Gnadenau Krimmer Mennonite Brethren and Abraham Schellenberg of the Mennonite Brethren. The fourth conference (1880) was also attended by delegates from the Salem Mennonite Church, South Dakota. At the sixth conference the school committee presented the constitution of the proposed secondary school *(Fortbildungsschule)*.

The regular reports of the conference deal with questions pertaining to education, home missions, and publication efforts, for all of which committees had been created. Numerous problems of a general nature and those pertaining to congregations and individuals were discussed in brotherly and orderly manner. The meetings were held in various congregations. At the sixteenth session, held Oct. 26-

27, 1892, the Kansas Conference was dissolved and its work and business transferred to the newly organized Western District Conference *(q.v.)*. This name had been in use by the present Middle District Conference until 1888. The chief concern of the Kansas Conference had been matters pertaining to education on the elementary and secondary level. Bethel College *(q.v.)*, organized at this time, was one of the results of these efforts. The interests in education were now in the hands of the German Teachers' Association *(q.v.)* and a special education committee of the Western District Conference. Until then the Fortbildungsschulen, first at Emmatal *(q.v.)* and later at Halstead *(q.v.)*, were supported and owned by the Kansas Conference. With the closing of this school and the founding of Bethel College this relationship was modified.   C.K.

Die Entstehung der Kansaskonferenz der Mennoniten-Gemeinden 1877-1892 (official Kansas Conference minutes and reports), in Bethel College Library.

Kansas-Nebraska Mennonite (MC) **Conference** (1879-1920). As early as 1871 a few Mennonites had settled in central Kansas. In 1872 several families settled in Marion and (eastern) McPherson counties; they were served by Bishop Henry Yother *(q.v.)* of Blue Springs, Neb. Within the next few years Mennonite settlements were also started in Adams Co., Neb., and Osborne, Ness, Harvey, and McPherson counties, Kan. As early as April 1876 a church was built on the land of Bishop Daniel Brundage *(q.v.)*, known as the Spring Valley Mennonite Church, located near Canton, Kan.

The first conference met on the forenoon of April 14, 1876, in this church. Besides the bishops Yother and Brundage, two ministers, one deacon, and a delegated layman attended the conference. Singing and Scripture reading were in both English and German. Six resolutions were discussed and approved as follows: (1) Members should not seek protection in lightning rods; (2) Members should take no part in worldly insurance; (3) It was considered inconsistent with nonresistant doctrine to go to the polls to vote; (4) It was not considered advisable for brethren to hold the office of Road Overseer; (5) Attendance at worldly amusements is not in accordance with the Word of God; (6) Brethren moving in from abroad should bring a church letter.

It was decided that conference should meet again on the fourth Friday of April 1877 at the same place. Brundage was for 15 or more years very active in encouraging and organizing the Mennonite settlers who came to Kansas. R. J. Heatwole *(q.v.)* served as secretary of the first conference and as moderator of a number of sessions. From 1879 to 1890 the conference met for both a spring and fall session; from 1892 on there was only an annual session of conference which was usually held in October. Brethren from Nebraska attended the conference for the first time in 1879; that is perhaps the reason why 1879 is given as the beginning year of the Kansas-Nebraska Conference.

The conference of 1907 took action requesting the Mennonite Board of Education to take steps to establish a school "in which Bible work is made a specialty somewhere in the west." As a result of this action Hesston College and Bible School was established in 1908-9. The conference of 1912 appointed D. S. Weaver and L. O. King to meet with persons from other interested conferences to consider establishing a home for the homeless. Out of this interest the Kansas City Children's Home was established in 1917.

Beginning apparently with only a few churches in central Kansas in 1876 and adding the church in Adams Co., Neb., the conference continued to grow by adding churches in other states. By 1895 mention is made of the churches in Oklahoma. In 1900 churches in Idaho and Oregon were added. In 1904 Colorado was added, in 1908 the congregation at Plainview, Tex., and in 1911 the congregation at Las Vegas, N.M. The conference of 1905, held in Oregon, decided to divide the conference, making the Rocky Mountains the dividing line. The western congregations, three in number, were organized into the Pacific Coast Conference on Nov. 1, 1906. From the small beginning of five ordained men in 1876, by 1908 there were 7 bishops, 21 ministers, and 8 deacons. By 1909 the reported membership had increased to 949, and in 1920 to 1,204 with 6 bishops, 30 ministers, and 16 deacons.

The redistricting in 1920 of all Mennonite and Amish Mennonite conferences west of Indiana resulted in the reorganization of the Kansas-Nebraska Mennonite, Missouri-Iowa Mennonite, and Western Amish Mennonite conferences into the Missouri-Kansas (q.v.) Mennonite, and Iowa-Nebraska (q.v.) Mennonite conferences, with the Illinois A.M. congregations assigned to the Illinois (q.v.) Mennonite Conference, and those in Oregon assigned to the Pacific Coast (q.v.) Conference. In 1920 (last session of the Kansas-Nebraska Conference, Aug. 2-4, 1920) the following 18 congregations (with membership) constituted the conference: Kansas—12 congregations with 797 members (Spring Valley at Canton, 72; Pennsylvania at Newton, 102; West Liberty at Windom, 125; Catlin at Peabody, 35; Protection, 62; Hesston, 111; Yoder, 70; Pleasant Valley at Harper, 155; Larned, ; Mennonite Gospel missions at Kansas City, 48 and Argentine, 17); Colorado—3 congregations with 228 members (La Junta, 109; East Holbrook at La Junta, 111; Limon, 8); Texas—1 congregation at Plainview, 42 members; Oklahoma—1 congregation, Milan Valley at Jet, 37; Nebraska—1 congregation at Roseland, 100.

The conference also had a district mission board, organized in October 1905, composed of the representative elected by each congregation in the conference. When the conferences were reorganized in 1920, the mission board was also reorganized to conform to the new boundaries of the Kansas-Nebraska Conference.   H.A.D.

Conference Record Containing the Proceedings of the Kansas-Nebraska Mennonite Conference 1876-1914.

Kanselboek, the liturgical manual of the Dutch Mennonites, drawn up by a committee appointed by the A.D.S., of which S. H. N. Gorter (q.v.) was president. It was published in 1948: *Kanselboek ten dienste van de Doopsgezinde Gemeenten in Neder-* *land,* and offered to the congregations in order to secure more unity in the order of church services. It contains liturgies (orders) of ordinary services as well as of special services (baptism, communion, induction of new preachers, funerals, etc). Many of the Dutch congregations did not appreciate the *Kanselboek,* considering it a contradiction of the Mennonite concept of congregational autonomy. Notwithstanding this aversion, the *Kanselboek* proved to be very helpful, especially to young ministers.   vDZ.

Kaplanbek was an estate some 14 miles northwest of the city of Tashkent (q.v.) in Turkestan (q.v.), Central Asia, where the first and second groups of the chiliastic Mennonites from Samara, inspired by Claas Epp (q.v.), found a temporary shelter after their arrival on Oct. 15 and Nov. 25, 1880, respectively. When the successor of Governor Konstantin von Kaufmann, with whom they had made arrangements for settlement, did not honor the promise, the group proceeded to Bokhara (q.v.) and from there to Khiva (q.v.). (See Asiatic Russia, Ak-Metchet, Aulie-Ata.)   C.K.

Kaplaneihof, a small settlement of six farms, two miles southeast of Bergzabern, Palatinate, Germany, one-half mile east of Deutschhof (q.v.), has been occupied by Mennonites since 1787. In that year Elector Karl Theodor sold to the Mennonite Joseph Schowalter of Klein-Bundenbach near Zweibrücken (originally from Geisberg) the entire estate, which was then divided into six separate small farms of about 25 acres each. Additional families which came included Christian Lehmann of Niederrödern (q.v.) a son-in-law of Schowalter, and two other Schowalter families, originally from Geisberg and Schafbusch. In 1957 the six families on the Kaplaneihof included two Hege and four Schowalter families. Otto Schowalter, pastor of the Hamburg Mennonite Church, and Paul Schowalter, pastor of Weierhof, stem from Kaplaneihof. The Kaplaneihof families are members of the Deutschhof congregation and attend the services there.   L.W.

Karaganda: see **Soviet Central Asia.**

Karaguy, a village in the Orenburg (q.v.) Mennonite settlement of Russia, was founded in 1908. In 1910 it became the seat of a subsidiary congregation of the Kamenka M.B. Church. The Karaguy center included Chernoozernoye, Kamyshevo, Zelenoye, Karaguy, Pretoria, and Zuvorovka. The earlier meetinghouse, which had been built in Kamyshevo in 1899, was sold and torn down when the larger church in Karaguy was built in 1914. Ministers of the Karaguy M.B. Church were Wilhelm Giesbrecht (leader 1898-1905), Jakob Bergen (leader 1905-9), David Janz, Gerhard Neufeld, Daniel Friesen, Kornelius Janzen, Franz Heier, and Abram Janzen. After 1914 David Janz of Zagradovka in the Ukraine was ordained as elder of the Karaguy congregation.

The Mennonites of Karaguy belonged to the Orenburg (q.v.) Mennonite Church, with a center at Deyevka (q.v.). (*ML* II, 459.)   W.Q.

Karassan Mennonite Church, Simferopol District, Crimea, Russia, was founded in 1862 by Mennonites from the Molotschna settlement, who established villages in the area at this time. Jacob Wiebe (*q.v.*) was the first elder (1862-80). He was succeeded by Heinrich Unruh (1880-83), Abr. Friesen (1884-   ), G. A. Rempel, and Jakob Lötkemann, who was exiled under the Soviets. The elders were assisted by many ministers, some of whom joined the Mennonite Brethren Church of the Crimea. Originally the Ettingerbrun, later Busau, Mennonite Church was a part of the Karassan church. In 1905 the Karassan church with its branches Spat, Pasha-Tchakmak, and Dyurmen had a membership of 846 and a total population of 1,928. The main place of worship was Karassan.   C.K.

Friesen, *Brüderschaft*, 709; *Statistik der Mennonitengemeinde in Russland Ende 1905*, p. 63.

Karel van Gent (Carel van Ghendt), the reputed author of *Het Beginsel en voortganck der geschillen, scheuringen, en verdeeltheden onder de gene die Doopsgesinden Genoemt worden (q.v.)*, written in 1615 but first published in 1658 at Amsterdam. W. J. Kühler considers him to be the author and calls him "the best historian among the old Doopsgesinden" (*Geschiedenis* I, 365). De Hoop Scheffer held him to be the author, Karel Vos flatly denies the authorship, while N. van der Zijpp and Cornelius Krahn are uncertain. A certain Carel van Ghendt was one of the two secretaries who wrote the *Protocol* of the Emden disputation of 1578 (printed in 1579), but no trace of a Carel van Gent has been found among the Doopsgesinden of the first century. For the details of the life of the author of *Het Beginsel,* who might be Carel van Gent, see the article **Het Beginsel.** The most thorough discussion of the identification problem is that by Samuel Cramer in *BRN* VII, 491-500.
H.S.B.

Karel Halling, an Anabaptist martyr, a native of Steenwerck, Flanders, who was burned at the stake in 1567 at Armentiéres in Flanders. (*Mart. Mir.,* D 345, E 704; *ML* II, 237.)   vDZ.

Karel (*Chaerle*) **Hannebeel,** an Anabaptist martyr, called simply Karel by van Braght (*Mart. Mir.*), was burned at the stake on Nov. 8, 1567, at Kortrijk (Courtrai) in Flanders, Belgium, together with Joos Casteels, Willem Aertsz, and Jaques Mesdag. Karel, who was a native of Nederwaestene, and was arrested in Zwevegem, had been a member of the church since 1563. He frankly confessed his faith and died steadfast.   vDZ.

Mart. Mir. D 358, E 715; Verheyden, *Courtrai-Bruxelles*, 36, No. 16.

Karel (Kaerle) **de Raed(t),** an Anabaptist martyr, was burned at the stake at Tillegem near Brugge, Belgium, on May 18, 1570 (van Braght, *Mart. Mir.,* erroneously 1568, without exact date). With him Hansken in 't Schaeck and Willem de Snijder suffered martyrdom, while Karel's wife Grietgen was executed some days after. Karel, who was born at Whyngene in Flanders, and was a shepherd, had been a member of the congregation of Brugge since 1564. On Ascension Day (May 4), 1570, he was arrested with a number of other members of the congregation at a meeting held in the woods of Tille-

gem. (*Mart. Mir.* D 654, E 725; Verheyden, *Brugge,* 60, No. 64; *ML* III, 425.)   vDZ.

Karel (Kaerle) **Tankreet** (Tancreet, Tanghereet), an Anabaptist martyr, burned at the stake on July 5, 1559, on the Vrijdagsmarkt at Gent, Belgium, with three other martyrs, while a number of others, including Proentgen, the wife of Karel Tankreet, were executed on Aug. 7. All these martyrs, who had been arrested on Friday after Pentecost of 1559, have been celebrated in a hymn, "Ick moet een liet beginnen" (I must begin a song), which is found as No. 14 in the *Lietboecxken van den Offer des Heeren* of 1563. Karel Tankreet originally was from Nijpkerke (Nieukerke) in Flanders; by trade he was a cobbler.   vDZ.

Offer, 348, 556 ff.; *Mart. Mir.* D 246, E 620; Verheyden, *Gent,* 25, No. 61.

Karel (*Charles*) **van Tiegem** (*Thieghem*), an Anabaptist martyr, steadfastly suffered martyrdom at the stake on Dec. 20, 1560 (van Braght, *Mart. Mir.,* erroneously has 1559 without exact date), at Kortrijk (Courtrai) in Flanders, Belgium. Karel was a native and citizen of Kortrijk. At first he was a shoemaker, then a weaver. His few possessions were confiscated. (Supersedes **Carel van Tiegem,** *ME* I, 517.)   vDZ.

Mart. Mir. D 242, E 617; Verheyden, *Courtrai-Bruxelles,* 35, No. 11.

Karel van de(n) Velde, an Anabaptist martyr, burned at the stake at Hondschote (*q.v.*) in Flanders, Belgium, on April 20, 1562. Six other martyrs with him suffered martyrdom, all dying faithful. He was a native of Gent. (*Mart. Mir.* D 298, E 663.)

Karg, Georg (1512-76), a German Lutheran theologian. He studied theology at the University of Wittenberg, in 1547 he became pastor in Schwabach, and in 1553 general superintendent at Ansbach. In the following years his position with the Wittenberg theologians was very influential. He was often, second to Melanchthon, spokesman for the group in making declarations. In 1557 he participated in the theologians' disputation at Worms (Sept. 11-Oct. 7). Here he signed with Johann Brenz, Johann Marbach, Michael Diller, Johann Pistorius, Jakob Andreae, and Jakob Rungius an opinion drawn up by Melanchthon at the request of the elector Palatine Ottheinrich (*Corpus Reformatorum* IX 1842, col. 521, No. 6501) for the suppression of the Anabaptists (see **Diller, Michael**). It was printed at Worms in 1557 under the title, *Prozess, wie es soll gehalten werden mit den Wiedertäufern,* by Paulus and Philip Köpflein. It gives the German authorities suggestions for dealing with the Anabaptists, in order to lead them back into the church. Any of the Anabaptist leaders who did not comply with this demand were to be killed with the sword as insurrectionists and blasphemers.   HEGE.

G. Bossert, *TA* I: *Württemberg,* 161-68; R. Friedmann, "Eine dogmatische Hauptschrift der hutterischen Täufergemeinschaften in Mähren," *Archiv f. Ref.-Gesch.* XXVIII (1931) 104 and 111 (see also 1920, 118); *Menn. Bl.,* 1893, 108; K. Schornbaum, "Markgraf Georg Friedrich von Brandenburg und die Einigungsbestrebungen der Protestantischen Stände 1556-1559," *Archiv f. Ref.-Gesch.* XVII (1920) 105 ff.; *ML* II, 459.

Karl Theodor (Charles Theodore) (1724-99), Elector of the Palatinate, Germany, head of the Sulzbach line, who inherited the Palatinate in 1742 upon the death of Charles Philip (*q.v.*), the last of the Neuburg line. In 1777 he also inherited the territories of the Bavarian line. He was a Catholic, educated by the Jesuits, and made it very hard for the Mennonites of his domain throughout his reign.

On Feb. 18, 1743, the Mennonites presented a petition to Charles Theodore for confirmation of the concession (*Privilegium*) of 1664 and a reduction of the annual per capita protection fee from 12 to 6 florins. They repeated the petition on Dec. 10, 1743, and on March 30, 1744, offered to make a free contribution of the 10,000 florins which they had loaned the ruler in 1741, in return for the proposed reduction of the annual fee. Charles Theodore granted the petition on condition that the limit of 240 families in the country be gradually reduced to 200. Mennonite sons would have to receive a special governmental permit to remain in the country after marriage, and new Mennonite immigrants would need the same.

An official inquiry of Oct. 22, 1752, revealed that the number of families had risen to 250, the increase being chiefly in the districts of Alzey, Heidelberg, and Neustadt, since many families had harbored relatives arriving since 1744 who had no official permits, and others also had likewise come into the country illegally. A legal opinion requested by the prince objected to expulsion of the surplus Mennonites, giving as the reason that "no more industrious and capable subjects could be found, who, apart from error in religion and customs and intense zeal, should serve as models for other religious groups." The prince refused, however, to follow this advice and decreed that the previous rulings should be strictly enforced, including the reduction to 200 families. A corresponding decree was issued to all district officials on Dec. 23, 1763. The Mennonites of the Zellertal, who were under the jurisdiction of the University of Heidelberg, did not succeed in getting their annual protection fee reduced until 1769 after a long struggle.

In 1784 the entire Mennonite population addressed a petition to the prince for a cancellation of the special "retract" law, which permitted sellers of land to Mennonites to repurchase it within three years at the original sale figure without regard to any increase in value or improvements. The princely chancellor Raubisson supported the petition, stating that he had always considered the law a harsh one. However, the prince rejected the petition in his decision of Sept. 27, 1787. After Charles Theodore's death the renewed petition of the Mennonites for cancellation of the "retract" law was granted by Elector Max Josef IV on March 28, 1801, for the right bank of the Rhine, after the French authorities had canceled it for the left bank as early as 1793. The Mennonites of the Palatinate were then gradually treated as full citizens and freed from the payment of the annual protection fee. (*ML* II, 463 f.) G.H.

Karlin, an Anabaptist of Zürich, probably identical with Karl Brennwald (*q.v.*).

Karolswalde, during 1801-74 the seat of a congregation of West Prussian Mennonites, located near Ostrog, Volhynia, Russia. Coming from Graudenz, Culm, and Thorn along the Vistula River (some authorities say 1780-85) a small group of West Prussian Mennonites settled at Michalin near Machnovka in the province of Kiev. Due to a disagreement with the government the majority of the Michalin group migrated to Karolswalde in 1801. The group spread to surrounding villages as Antonovka, Karolsberg, Jadvinin, Dossidorf, and Fürstendorf. Benjamin Dircks was ordained elder of the group in 1817, Tobias Unruh in 1853. Names of common occurrence were Becker, Buller, Decker, Dirks, Goertz, Koehn, Schartner, Siebert, Thomas, and Unruh.

In 1874 the entire group emigrated to America as part of the larger Mennonite emigration from Russia of that year. Tobias Unruh had taken an active part in the negotiations prior to the emigration of the Russian Mennonites, and was one of the 12 delegates sent to America on the exploratory trip of 1873. The Karolswalde emigrants left Volhynia in several groups: July 28, 1874, 25 families; Oct. 24, 1874, 40 families; and Nov. 3, 1874, 27 families. The leaders Tobias Unruh and Ben Buller left on Nov. 11, 1874.

Because of poor economic conditions in Volhynia the group had made little economic progress there and consequently required considerable financial aid to make the journey to America. Arriving in Kansas in the middle of January 1875, without resources, the group was given considerable aid by American Mennonites. The majority of the group settled near Canton, Kan. The present Emmanuel Mennonite Church (*q.v.*) near Moundridge as well as most of the members of the Church of God in Christ, Mennonite, congregations in the Canton area are from this group. The Bergthal Mennonite Church (*q.v.*) near Pawnee Rock, Kan., is also from this group. The settlements at Montezuma, Kan., and Meno, Okla., are largely of Karolswalde background. Tobias Unruh and a few others settled in South Dakota, establishing the Friedensberg (*q.v.*) congregation near Avon. E.C.

H. G. Mannhardt, *Jahrbuch,* 1888, 79; *Menn. Bl.,* 1888, 128; Ernst Crous, "Mennoniten in Wolhynien und den benachbarten Gouvernements Kiew und Tschernigow," in *Gesch.-Bl.* XIII (1956); Cornelius Krahn, ed., *From the Steppes to the Prairies (1874-1949)* (Newton, 1949); *Das Namensverzeichnis der Aeltesten, Lehrer und Diakonen oder Vorsteher der Taufgesinnten Mennonitischen Gemeinden* (Elbing, 1843, Danzig, 1857); Abe J. Unruh and Verney Unruh, *The Tobias A. Unruh Biography, Diary and Family Record 1819-1950* (Pulaski, 1950); Walter Kuhn, "Deutsche Täufersiedlungen im westukrainischen Raume," *Ztscht für Ostforschung* IV (1955) No. 4; *ML* II, 468.

Karpfis, Jörg, an Anabaptist martyr drowned at Zürich, Switzerland, in 1532 with Hans Herzog of Stadel. As far as the records go, he was the fifth Anabaptist victim of the persecution in Zürich.

E. Egli, *Die Züricher Wiedertäufer zur Ref.-Zeit* (Zürich, 1878) 91; *TA Zürich,* 280, 283, 285, 287; *ML* 468.

Karsdorp, a former Dutch Mennonite family name, especially found at Leiden, where Jan Karsdorp was a deacon of the Flemish congregation 1695-97, and of the (in 1700) united Mennonite congregation 1714-17; Nicolaas Karsdorp was five times a deacon of this congregation during the period 1725-62 and Anthony Karsdorp four times in 1747-77. The Karsdorps were rather well-to-do merchants. Gerrit Karsdorp (*q.v.*) and Gerrit Karsdorp, Jr. (*q.v.*), both preachers at Hamburg, Germany, were members of this family. Another member of this family, Abraham Karsdorp, a carpenter at Dordrecht, Dutch province of South Holland, was custodian of the meetinghouse and the last member of the Dordrecht congregation when it died out about the middle of the 19th century. After his death his nephew J. Karsdorp considered himself private owner of the properties of the congregation, as did after his death in 1865 his heirs, who sold the meetinghouse and appropriated the funds of the congregation. Harmen Karsdorp, Jr., from Hamburg, apparently belonging to the same family, emigrated to Pennsylvania in 1700, with his wife Adriana de Vos and their children, and became a preacher of the Germantown congregation. Isaac Karsdorp (d. before 1708), who also went to Germantown in 1700, probably also emigrated from Hamburg. The Prussian Mennonite name Kasdorf, found in Prussia, Russia, and America, is probably of the same origin as Karsdorp.   vdZ.

DB 1862, 109-12; 1867, 156 f.; 1868, 145-56; 1869, 3, 126; MQR VII, 1933, 46 f., 230 f., 236.

Karsdorp, Gerrit, a minister belonging to an old Mennonite family of Leiden, several branches of which lived in North Germany. He was a minister at Friedrichstadt a. d. Eider and then at Hamburg, serving the church there 1718-50. He was the first salaried minister of the Hamburg Mennonite Church, receiving 1200 marks annually. He was zealous in promoting the instruction of the children, and had 60 Dutch question-and-answer books sent from Holland for this purpose. He died on Sept. 19, 1750. His colleague Gerrit Beets delivered his funeral sermon, *De vrolyke gesettheyd eenes Christen tegens de verschrikkingen des doods* . . . (Hamburg, n.d.).   R.Do.

R. Dollinger, *Geschichte der Mennoniten in Schleswig-Holstein* (Hamburg and Lübeck, 1930); Pieter Beets, *Gedächtnisrede auf Gerrit Karsdorp;* ML II, 468.

Karsdorp, Gerrit, Jr., son of the above, minister of the Hamburg-Altona Mennonite Church, b. May 23, 1729, d. Oct. 11, 1811. He studied history and church history (Mosheim) independently. To learn merchandising he was apprenticed to Isaac Stokman, a Mennonite, whose daughter Sara he married in 1758. In 1750, at the age of 21 years, he became a ministerial candidate; in 1753 he became a preacher of the congregation, and in 1764 he was ordained to the ministry. He served the church nearly 61 years. He refused a salary because being in business he did not need it. During his long service he ordained many preachers.

He was well-read, and owned a library of over 9,000 volumes. Theologically he showed no particular stamp, except that he is an illustration of how the practical Mennonite traditions and beliefs were easily adapted to the religious language of the time. He was a member of the Hamburg Society

for the Promotion of the Arts and Useful Crafts, in which his love for humanity and his tolerance could find expression outside the church, so that he could be called an "enlightened spirit" in this regard.

A portrait of Karsdorp adapted from an etching by L. Wolf is contained in *Gesammelte Denkmäler der Liebe und Achtung* (Altona, 1812). His published works are *Jubelpredikatie ter gelegenheid der 50 jarige Amtsbediening 27. Juli 1800* (Altona); *Redevoering over het noodzaakelyk verband tuschen de prediking van het goddelyk woord en tuschen een geregeld christelyk gezang* . . . (Altona, 1802); funeral sermons for Frederick V of Denmark, Gerrit Beets, Pieter Beets, Berend Roosen, Reinh. Rahusen, Jan de Jager, and Abr. Wynands.   O.S.

Nemnich, *Verzeichnis der Bibliothek Karsdorps* (Hamburg, 1812); *Gesammelte Denkmäler der Liebe und Achtung* (Altona, 1812); B. C. Roosen, *Gesch. der Menn.-Gem. zu Hamburg und Altona* II (Hamburg 1887); ML II, 468.

Kartels, Joseph (1872-1931), a German Catholic historian, for a time city archivist at Fulda. In 1906-15 he taught at the Realgymnasium at Ahrweiler; in 1920 he entered a Capuchin monastery, and in 1921 he became a priest in Mainz. He inaugurated the *Fuldaer Geschichtsblätter* in 1902 with an address, "Die Wiedertäuferbewegung im ehemaligen Hochstift Fulda" (pp. 3-20), which he delivered to the historical society of Fulda on the Anabaptist movement (1529-87) in Grossenbach near Hünfeld, based on records in the Marburg state archives. (*ML* II, 468.)   E.C.

Kasai, a district in the Belgian Congo, which is the location of the Mennonite Brethren Kasai district mission field. The area covered by the mission has approximately 35 villages with an estimated 12,000 population. The mission is generally referred to as the Bololo (*q.v.*) field. See map of Belgian Congo.   A.E.J.

Kaspar, the name of an Anabaptist of Graz, Austria, a painter by profession, who, the court records say, not only joined the Anabaptists, but also instructed and baptized others therein. He was seized and instructed by the clergy, but "would not desist from his error." He finally pretended to do so, but later withdrew his recantation, and left the city in 1529. Where he went is not stated.

In accord with the decree of Ferdinand I his house was now torn down, and the building site sold to a citizen by the name of Stephan Kirchbacher; the money was used to repair the "burned" castle at Graz. Kaspar's children, Caecilie and Franz, presented a petition to the authorities that the building site be given them. The manager of the princely estates denied the request, on the ground that it would give the impression that the painter had been mistreated, though he had in reality deserved a far more severe punishment; if the prince wished to show the children mercy, he could order the mayor to pay out the value of the land. The site was a good one, near the church, fronting on two streets. The painter's relatives twice protested (document of July 11, 1535), but Kirchbacher retained possession. It is not known whether the children received any compensation.

The original of the above record is in the Vienna state archives, division *Oesterreichische Akten Steiermark*. For details see **Graz**, which this article supplements. (*ML* II, 469.)   LOSERTH.

Kaspar of Schöneck, an Anabaptist martyr: see Caspar.

Kassel, a Mennonite family: see **Cassel.**

Kat, a Dutch Mennonite family name, especially found on the island of Ameland, where some of them were deacons of the church; Jan Jacobs Kat (d. 1803) was a preacher 1762-77. They were usually members of the Foppe Ones congregation; Pieter Jacobs Kat (d. 1864) was a preacher from 1829 and an elder from 1843 to 1851 of the Jan-Jacobsz congregation. (*DB* 1889, 18 f.) Many of them were captains of boats. Hidde Dirks Kat, of Hollum, Ameland, was the author of an interesting book: *Daghboek eener reize ther Walvisch- en Robbenvangst gedaan in de jaren 1777 en 1778 door den Kommandeur H. D. Kat* (Haarlem, 1818). (*De Zondagsbode* III, 1, Nov. 3, 1889.) Some of the members of this family lived in Workum, Hindeloopen, and Amsterdam. Hidde Abesse, of Hindeloopen, was in 1697 the skipper of the *Barbara,* a boat owned by the Mennonite van Eeghen (*q.v.*) family. Probably the preacher Jacob Kat (*q.v.*) also belonged to this family. Jan Lammertsz Kat (or Kadt), who was a preacher of Wormer and Jisp in 1697 (*DB* 1898, 79 ff.), was apparently not a member of this family.   VDZ.
Wanda Oesau, *Hamburgs Grönlandsfahrt* (Glückstadt-Hamburg, 1955) 194 ff.

Kat, Jacob Jansz (d. 1748), a Dutch Mennonite preacher at Amsterdam (Old Frisians) 1704-48, published *Kort begrip van de Leere der Waarheyt . . . ,* of which are extant a 2nd edition of 1736, a 3rd edition of 1747, and a 4th (erroneously indicated 3rd) edition of 1762, all published at Amsterdam. This catechism was used in the Amsterdam Zonist (*q.v.*) congregation until 1801. (*DB* 1868, 109; 1869, 103; 1898, 16 f.; *Biogr. Wb.* IV, 670.)   VDZ.

Kate, ten, a Dutch Mennonite family name. Many members of the ten Cate (*q.v.*) family spelled their name "ten Kate" after the close of the 17th century; e.g., Jan ten Kate, d. 1679 at Amsterdam. He was a preacher of the United Flemish-Frisian-High German-Waterlander congregation of Amsterdam from 1677, publisher of some sermons and two volumes of religious poems. In the 19th century two unmarried brothers, Rijkle (1770-1855) and Keimpe ten Kate (1775-1856), sons of Lammert ten Kate, bequeathed their considerable properties (*DB* 1917, 66-73) to the Mennonite congregation of IJlst (*q.v.*), where they had lived.   VDZ.

Kate, Lambert Hermansz ten, b. Jan. 23, 1674, at Amsterdam, d. there Dec. 14, 1731, the son of Herman ten Kate and Sara Blaupot. He was baptized in the Lamist (*q.v.*) church on April 18, 1706. Like his father he was a grain dealer in Amsterdam. He was one of the educated and generally gifted men, of whom the Amsterdam Mennonite Church had a

great many at the time. He was a linguist, a forerunner of Jakob Grimm, who understood the value of his work (Kalff, 436). In his main work, *Aenleiding tot de kennisse van het verheven deel der Nederduytse sprake* (Amsterdam, 1723), his basis was not the written language and grammar, but the living speech; he gives a number of conversations in various dialects, which he sees in a remote connection, and for which he drew up a table of sounds. This work proves him to have been a man with a sense of reality, and makes him the originator of the science of comparative languages in the Low Countries.

He also published two devotional books: *Drie gewichtige Bedenkingen des Gemoeds; benevens den Weg tot Heil* (Amsterdam, 1728) and *Het Leven van onzen Heiland Jezus Christus* (Amsterdam, 1732).   VDZ.
J. te Winkel, *Ontwikkelingsgang der Nederlandsche Letterkunde* III, 392-96; G. Kalff, *Gesch. der Nederl. Letterkunde* VI (Groningen, 1910) 554; *Biogr. Wb.* V, 670 f.; *N.N.B.Wb.* V, 295 f.; *ML* II, 469.

Kathelijne (*Calle*) **van Lokerhoute** (Loorehoute), an Anabaptist martyr, was beheaded in the Gravensteen Castle at Gent, Belgium, on March 24, 1563, together with two other victims. She was the wife of Loys Allaerts and 40 years of age. (Verheyden, *Gent,* 28, No. 84.)   VDZ.

Katherijn of Lier: see **Catharina.**

Kating, a village in Germany in the south of the Eiderstedt (*q.v.*) region below Tönning a.d. Eider, Schleswig-Holstein, where several Mennonite families lived in the last half of the 17th century and the first half of the 18th; e.g., David Lourensen, a smith who belonged to the Frisian congregation at Friedrichstadt. Mennonites from the Rhenish Palatinate also settled here, among them the Strichler family. Through mixed marriages and emigration Mennonitism here soon became extinct. (*ML* II, 474 f.)   R.Do.

Katlijk, Dutch province of Friesland, where Leenaert Bouwens in 1563-65 baptized 20 persons. Since there was never a congregation in this town it is assumed that the newly baptized members joined a congregation in the neighborhood of Katlijk, viz., Mildam, Knijpe, or Heerenveen.   VDZ.

Katrijn Huyghendochter, widow of Jacob Pieterszn, of Rotterdam, was drowned on Feb. 6, 1539, at Delft, Dutch province of South Holland, because she had been rebaptized.   VDZ.
Inv. Arch. Amst. I, No. 749; K. Vos, *Geschiedenis der Doopsgezinde Gemeente te Rotterdam* (1907) 6.

Katrijn Witten, from Lierichuysen (?), an Anabaptist martyr, was drowned on Jan. 17 or 23, 1539, with three other women at Delft, Dutch province of South Holland, because of rebaptism. Probably she was a follower of David Joris (*q.v.*). (*Inv. Arch. Amst.* I, No. 749.)   VDZ.

Katwijk aan Zee, a town in the Dutch province of South Holland, where Leenaert Bouwens (*q.v.*) baptized 27 persons in 1563-65. From that time it was seat of a small Mennonite congregation which later belonged to the Flemish branch. In 1649 the congregation had no preacher. It must have died out soon after, because no mention is made of this congregation at the Flemish conference at Leiden, June 1660. (Blaupot t. C., *Holland* I, 330.)   vDZ.

Kauenhowen (Kauenhoven, Kaunhowen, Kauenhofen; Dutch *Couwenhoven*), the name of a Mennonite family originally of Danzig, first appearing in the records there in 1656 and living there until 1945. There are two Kauenhowen lines, the relationship of which is probable, but could not yet be established by records.

The origin of the family is in the Netherlands where the place name Kouwenhoven (Couwenhoven) is to be found in a number of regions, e.g., near Amersfoort, Bunnik, and Leiden. From which of these places the Danzig Kauenhovens came, cannot be stated definitely. They must have emigrated from the Netherlands to the mouth of the Vistula about the first part of the 17th century, settling at Danzig and its suburbs, especially Altschottland, Schidlitz, and Stolzenberg. From there the Kauenhoven family spread over a large area during the following centuries. Since 1732 the family name is mentioned in the records of Königsberg in Prussia, where members of the family resided until 1908. In 1732-53 four members of the Danzig Kauenhoven family went back to the Netherlands, where descendants are living today at Heemstede, Amsterdam, and Utrecht. Between 1784 and 1855 several members of the Danzig and Königsberg Kauenhoven families emigrated to Russia. One of them, Bernhard Kauenhoven (1786-1841), settled shortly after 1809 at Rosenthal near Chortitz, Ukraine. He later on moved to Bergthal from where his descendants emigrated to the East and West Reserve of Manitoba in 1875. In 1922 some of the Canadian Kauenhovens went to Mexico, settling near Cuauhtemoc, Chih., and in 1927 others settled in the Menno Colony in the Paraguayan Chaco. In 1840 Heinrich Peter Kauenhoven (Henry P. Cowenhoven, 1814-96) left West Prussia for the United States and became one of the Colorado pioneers at Aspen, Col. In 1880 Theodor Kauenhoven (1853-1918) went from Königsberg to London, England, where some of his descendants adopted the family name Carton. It has not yet been ascertained whether there is any connection between the Mennonite Kauenhoven family of Crefeld (1755-1802) and the members of the van Kouwenhoven-Conover family of New York whose forefathers came there from Amersfoort in 1626.

With very few exceptions up to 1815 all members of the two Danzig Kauenhoven lines belonged to the Danzig Flemish Mennonite congregation or to the Königsberg Mennonite Church. After that date the Kauenhovens living at Danzig and Königsberg in Prussia more often than not left the Mennonite church and became members of the Reformed, Lutheran, or Baptist churches by marrying outside the Mennonite church. In the 20th century, however, some of them returned to the Mennonite church. On the other hand, the Kauenhovens who emigrated to Russia and consequently to America have always remained members of the Mennonite church, most of them belonging to the Sommerfeld church of the "Old Colony." The name Kauenhoven is now comparatively rare among Mennonites. There are about 9 Kauenhoven families in Europe now, and about 6 each living in the Mennonite settlements of Manitoba (Canada), Cuauhtemoc (Chih., Mexico), and Menno (Paraguay). Among the members of the two Kauenhoven lines several have rendered outstanding service to their congregations and in public life. In the period from 1678 to 1830 eleven members of the Danzig Kauenhovens were deacons of the Danzig Flemish Mennonite Church, three of whom were also ministers besides. Two of the Kauenhoven women were elected deaconesses in 1758 and 1804. Of the Königsberg Kauenhovens two were deacons, one of them later on a minister of the Königsberg Mennonite Church.

Special mention should be made of the following persons of the older branch: Arend Kauenhoven (1712-92), a brandy distiller, vinegar brewer, and spice seller at Altschottland near Danzig, willed to the Danzig Flemish Mennonite Church 11,000 guilders; Abraham Kauenhoven (1674-1731), in 1720 "Vorsteher" of the Danzig Flemish Mennonite Church. Of the members of the younger Danzig Kauenhoven family should be mentioned Cornelius Kauenhoven (1683-1756), a lacemaker in the city of Danzig (?) chosen "Vorsteher" in 1718 and preacher in 1720 of the Danzig Flemish Mennonite Church; Berend Kauenhoven (1707-63), a brewer at Schönfeld near Danzig, in 1743 chosen "Vorsteher," 1749 preacher in the Danzig Flemish Mennonite congregation; Isaak Kauenhoven (1714-94), a dyer of silk, citizen of Königsberg, West Prussia, "Vorsteher," preacher, and benefactor of the Königsberg Mennonite congregation; Johann Kauenhofen (1892-1935), a preacher, orphan supervisor, and Schulze (*q.v.*) of the Neuenlage Mennonite settlement at Cuauhtemoc, Chihuahua, Mexico.   K.K.

Kurt and Walter Kauenhowen, ed., *Die Kauenhowen* (No. 1, Verden/Aller, 1926); Kurt Kauenhowen, ed., *Mitteilungen des Sippenverbandes der Danziger Mennoniten-Familien Epp-Kauenhowen-Zimmermann* (Göttingen, 1935-40), continued as *Mitteilungen des Sippenverbandes Danziger Mennoniten-Familien* (Göttingen, 1941-43), again continued as *Nachrichtenblatt des Sippenverbandes Danziger Mennoniten-Familien* (Göttingen, 1943-44); Kurt Kauenhowen, "Stammfolge Bernhard Kauenhowen zur Ausbreitung einer russlanddeutschen Siedlerfamilie 1600-1938," in *Der Wanderweg der Russlanddeutschen* (Stuttgart, 1939) 137-40.

Kaufbeuren, a city (pop. 19,738) in Swabia, southwest Bavaria, Germany, once an imperial city, which passed to Bavaria in 1803. It opened very slowly to the Reformation. Anabaptists soon came here from Augsburg; among them Hans Kraft and Gallus Fischer were influential. At first the Protestant pastors tried with partial success as in other imperial cities to win them by friendly persuasion. Then the Swabian League (*q.v.*) in 1528 hunted down the Anabaptists with a squadron of 400 horsemen. In Kaufbeuren 40 persons were seized, of whom five were beheaded (May 13, 1528) and seven had their cheeks burned through. These events intimidated the council, and Catholicism won control for the next 15 years.

But Anabaptist ideas continued to influence the

populace, and after 1535 Schwenckfelders (*q.v.*) and Zwinglians obtained a firm footing. The progress of the various branches can no longer be traced. In any case, by 1543 the council was apparently completely under Schwenckfeld influence. It is worth noting that Catholic services were at this time in no way encroached upon. Religious developments in Kaufbeuren were discussed by the Protestant estates at the Diet of Worms in 1545. Delegates from various cities were sent there, who with great difficulty succeeded in pushing out these quiet "confessors of the glory of Christ." But in secret their influence continued. During the Schwenckfeld period the council passed many measures against the Anabaptists, causing many to emigrate. A letter written by Ferdinand I to the council of Kaufbeuren, dated Sept. 5, 1545, contains the court records of the trials of the Kaufbeuren Anabaptists, Hans Staudach (executed at Vienna in 1546), a baker of Kaufbeuren, his wife Ursula, and his cousin Blasius Staudach (baker), Hans Hofmayr (weaver), Hans Feuerbach (apparently a preacher), Anna Zacharias, the widow of a butcher, Katharina Losch, and Anna Stangel (Alt, 9-24). Alt (37) prints the sincere letter of comfort and admonition written by a Kaufbeuren Anabaptist woman named Katharina.

In the 17th century there were still some Anabaptists in Kaufbeuren; the court records repeatedly note that citizens go to the Anabaptists in Moravia, stay a while, and return, or that they have given lodging to Anabaptists.   H.Q.

F. Stieve, *Die Reichsstadt Kaufbeuren* (1870); Th. Keim, *Schwäbische Reformationsgeschichte bis zum Augsburger Reichstag* (Tübingen, 1855); K. Alt, *Wiedertäufer in und aus Kaufbeuren* (Kempten, 1930); *ML* II, 475.

Kauffman (Kaufman, Kaufmann, Kauffmann, Coffman, Cauffman), a prolific Mennonite and Amish family, originating apparently in Steffisberg, canton of Bern, Switzerland. One of the early Mennonite settlers in Lancaster Co., Pa., was Andrew Kauffman, who came in 1717 from Friesenheim, Palatinate, to which place he had earlier come from Steffisberg. The Palatinate Mennonite census lists of the late 17th and early 18th century contain a number of Kauffman families, and as late as 1936 there were as many as 44 Kaufmanns in nine congregations in South Germany. Another line of Swiss Kauffmanns emigrated to Alsace and Montbéliard about the same time, of which there were still in 1954, 20 Kauffmann families in seven congregations in France, including a preacher at Belfort. Around 1800 several of these Kauffmann families (Amish) joined the migration to Galicia and Volhynia (1803) (Michelsdorf, Eduardsdorf, Horodisch) and finally came from there to Kansas (Moundridge) and South Dakota (Freeman). P. R. Kaufman's *Unser Volk und seine Geschichte* (1931) tells the story of this group. From this group stem Ed. G. Kaufman (1891-), president of Bethel College (1932-52), R. C. Kaufman (1910-), dean of the same college (1949-56), and Charles Kauffman, curator of the Kauffman Museum (all GCM).

The direct immigration of Kauffmans from the Palatinate to America began with Isaac and Andrew Kauffman, who settled in Lancaster Co., Pa., in 1717. From this line came such leading figures in the Mennonite Church (MC) as David D. Kauffman (1827-96), first Mennonite bishop in Missouri (Versailles), and his son Daniel Kauffman (1865-1944), a long-time bishop and editor of the *Gospel Herald,* living most of his active life at Scottdale, Pa. A branch of this Lancaster County line located early in western Virginia (Page Co.) where Michael Kauffman was the first Mennonite minister. Here the name was changed to Coffman. Bishop Samuel Coffman (1822-94), his son J. S. Coffman (*q.v., 1848-99*), the noted evangelist of Elkhart, Ind., and the latter's son Bishop S. F. Coffman (*q.v.,* 1872-1954) of Vineland, Ont., were noted bearers of this name.

The progenitor of the Amish Kauffmans, Jacob Kauffman, came to Berks Co., Pa., in 1754 from the Palatinate. Many Kauffmans are still found among the Old Order Amish (10 preachers by that name in 1955), chiefly in Pennsylvania, Ohio, and Illinois. Those families who have joined the Mennonite group have produced a number of outstanding leaders in the Mennonite Church (MC), among them Milo Kauffman (1895-), president of Hesston College (1933-50) and leading bishop in Kansas; Nelson Kauffman (1904-), bishop at Hannibal, Mo., and president of the Mennonite Board of Education (1948-); J. N. Kaufman (1880-), long-time missionary in India and bishop near Peoria, Ill. There were in 1955 in the Mennonite (MC) Church 25 ordained men bearing the name Kauffman. Sister Frieda Kaufman (*q.v.,* 1883-1944) was a prominent leader in deaconess work in the General Conference Mennonite Church. Her parents came from Switzerland.   H.S.B.

C. F. Kauffman, *A Genealogy and History of the Kauffman-Coffman Families of North America 1584-1937* (York, Pa., 1940) 775 pp.; J. C. Beachey, *Family Record of Moses and Katie Kauffman and Their Descendants* (Arthur, Ill., 1941) 65 pp.; M. A. Kauffman, *Abraham Kauffman Family History* (Fresno, Ohio, ca. 1950) 100 pp.; Mrs. Abe Gingerich, *Family Record of Jacob Kauffman and His Descendants* (Arthur, Ill., 1952) 16 pp.

Kauffman, Daniel, son of Bishop David D. and Elizabeth (Winey) Kauffman, b. June 20, 1865, in Juniata, Pa., d. Jan. 6, 1944, near Parnell, Ia. The family moved to Elkhart, Ind., in 1866, and to Morgan Co., Mo., in 1869. He secured the degree of Principal of Pedagogics at the Missouri State University, taught school in Missouri 1883-97, and served as county commissioner (superintendent) 1887-90. For a time he conducted a private business college at Garden City, Mo. He was married in 1887 to Ota J. Bowlin, who died in 1890. There were two children, James A., and an infant daughter who did not live. In 1902 he married Mary C. Shank. There were six children, three of whom are living: Homer M., Alice (Mrs. Fred Gingerich), and Fannie (Mrs. Michael Sarco). He lived in Missouri, most of the time at Versailles, until 1909, when he moved to Scottdale, Pa. One year, 1922-23, he lived at Goshen, Ind. His closing months were spent in the Iowa home of his daughter Alice.

Under the preaching of J. S. Coffman he was converted in 1890, and joined the Mennonite Church (MC). He was ordained minister in 1892 and bishop in 1896. His natural gifts as speaker, teacher, writer, and leader soon made him the outstanding leader of the Mennonite Church and for over 40 years he made an impact on the church not even approached by any other person. A born organizer, he led in the setting up of the organizational patterns which still are in effect. He was at one time a member of 22 committees and boards. He was a prime mover in the organization of Mennonite General Conference, and its first moderator at the age of 33. He is the only man to have been moderator four times. Three times he preached the conference sermon, seven times was chairman of the Resolutions Committee, and at some time served as chairman of most of the other important committees. He also served as moderator of the Missouri-Iowa and the Southwestern Pennsylvania conferences. Able to transcend all bounds of sectionalism and factionalism, he was a church statesman, serving often as mediator and conciliator.

Kauffman urged the establishment of Hesston College, taught in the Bible School at Alexandria, Va., which proved to be the beginning of Eastern Mennonite College, and served one year (1922-23) as president of Goshen College. He taught winter Bible terms at all the Mennonite (MC) colleges, and was widely used as an instructor when the Bible Conference movement was at its height.

Kauffman was a prolific writer at a time when the church was poor in writers. He was the author of the following books and booklets: *Manual of Bible Doctrine* (1898), *One Hundred Lessons in Bible Study* (1899), *A Talk with Church Members* (1900), *Life Insurance* (1903), *A Talk with Our Boys and Girls* (1906), *Bible Doctrines Briefly Stated* (1908), *One Thousand Questions and Answers* (1908), *The Conservative Viewpoint* (1918), *The Message and the Message-Bearer* (1919), *The Christian Worker* (1922), *The Gospel Mirror* (1922), *The Mennonite Church and Current Issues* (1923), *The Way of Salvation* (1923), *The Two Standards* (1923), *Mennonite History* (1927), *My Vision of the Future* (1938), *Fifty Years in the Mennonite Church* (1941), *The Devotional Side of Life* (1942). He served as editor of *Bible Doctrine* (1914) and as editor and chief writer of *Doctrines of the Bible* (1928) and *Mennonite Cyclopedic Dictionary* (1937). He was coauthor with J. S. Hartzler of *Mennonite Church History* (1905) and with J. L. Stauffer of *Helps for Ministers* (1930).

His greatest work was as editor of the *Gospel Witness* (1905-8) and of the *Gospel Herald* (1908-43). Through wise editorial policies and capable editorial writing he used his position through 39 years to mold the life and thought of the church. Both as preacher and writer he came to be recognized as the spokesman of the church. His emphasis on doctrine made him the interpreter of the Mennonite Church to itself.

He helped to launch *Beams of Light*, was joint editor of the *Sunday-School Teachers' Quarterly* (1907-14), and editor for many years of tracts and the *Family Almanac*.

His biography, *Life and Times of Daniel Kauffman* (Scottdale, 1954), was written by his daughter Alice. He was buried in the Alverton cemetery north of Scottdale.†   P.E.

Kauffman, John D. (1847-1913), was born in Logan Co., Ohio, lived most of his life in Elkhart Co., Ind., but moved to Shelbyville, Ill., in 1907, where he died. He was an unordained self-appointed "preacher" until 1911, when he was ordained bishop by Bishop Peter Zimmerman of the Linn Township A.M. Church (*q.v.*). The group which followed Kauffman from Indiana in 1907 was organized into a congregation (Mt. Hermon) and built a meetinghouse near Shelbyville in 1912, where they continued with a maximum membership of 85 (1930), which in 1954 was down to 45, with Joseph Reber as bishop, who was ordained in 1914 as Kauffman's successor. Preacher S. E. Yoder of Delafield, and Peter Zimmerman of Roanoke sided with the group.

The Kauffman group, with the two congregations at Mt. Hermon and Linn Township, became known as the Sleeping Preacher (*q.v.*) group because of Kauffman's strange custom of going into trances for several hours at a time, during which he conducted a religious service and preached a full sermon.   H.S.B.

Pius Hostetler, *Life, Preaching, and Labors of John D. Kauffman* (Shelbyville, Ill., 1916).

Kauffmann, Mathys, of Kriegstetten, Solothurn, Switzerland, was one of the Anabaptist preachers held in chains in the newly built penitentiary and orphanage in Bern, who were considered "the most important preachers and ringleaders" (see **Bern**). From March 3, 1659, to Sept. 10, 1660, Kauffmann was there. Efforts of the council and the clergy to convert him were in vain. On Jan. 20, 1660, the appointed persons "betook themselves to the Anabaptist business" in the penitentiary to give the Anabaptists an examination. On 16 points the prisoners had to give an account, covering doctrine, communion, baptism, and attitude to government. All remained true to their convictions. Kauffmann had been seized at Koppingen in the canton of Bern, at his daughter's home. Now he besought the council to release him because he wanted to go to Solothurn. According to a decision of the council of June 15, 1660, the prisoners were to be banished. On Aug. 27 they were again cross-examined, but they still "persisted in their opinion, no matter what one tried with them." Kauffmann was then taken to the border via Brügg with the others on Sept. 10, 1660, and banished.   S.G.

A. Fluri, *Beiträge zur Gesch. der bernischen Täufer* II: *Das Waisenhaus als Täufergefängnis* (Bern, 1912); S. Geiser, *Die Taufgesinnten-Gemeinden* (Karlsruhe, 1931) 398 ff.; *ML* II, 475.

Kauffman Mennonite Church (MC), a member of the Lancaster Conference, is located on the Kauffman farm on the Manheim Pike in Lancaster Co., Pa. The congregation had formerly (prior to 1860) met at Sun Hill, several miles from the present location, but when it moved it adopted the name of its benefactor, Abraham Kauffman, who gave his farm of 97 acres to the church. The first meeting-house here was built in 1860, enlarged in 1891, and recently remodeled. It was earlier a part of the Hernley-Erb circuit, but today has its separate ministers. Homer D. Bomberger is the bishop, William Heisey is minister, and Ernest Bauman, deacon. The membership in 1954 was 72.   I.D.L.

Kauffman's was formerly a Mennonite (MC) congregation of the Lancaster Conference about two miles north of Annville in Lebanon Co., Pa. The community was settled by the Myers, Shirks, Ellenbergers, Lights, and Brightbills. In 1773 Frederick Kauffman was the Lebanon County bishop. The meetinghouse, which was built on the lands of Benjamin Bowman before 1768, was used until 1851, when the United Brethren claimed the building. The Mennonites then, under their bishop Jacob Dohner, moved east to the present site of Dohner's (*q.v.*) meetinghouse, the congregation now bearing that name being the lineal descendant of Kauffman's.   I.D.L.

Kaufman, David S., was born near Davidsville, Pa., Sept. 7, 1834, son of Samuel Kaufman, d. July 17, 1918. He married Lydia Kaufman and moved to Lagrange Co., Ind., some years later, where he was ordained to the ministry. In the spring of 1877 he was ordained bishop in the North Barrens district of the Old Order Amish Mennonite Church. Bishop Kaufman was very successful in leading his flock. Although he also had his troubles and sometimes a few adversaries, still he always succeeded in preserving peace in the church. His services and advice were much sought in other states. He was called and let himself be used in church work in more different places than any other bishop of his time. He was always very successful in working for peace and harmony wherever he was called. His field of service covered the entire country from Pennsylvania to Oregon and from North Dakota to Mississippi. Although he was lenient toward other leaders who could not quite agree with his views, he was firm in his convictions and adhered strictly to what he thought was right where he himself had to take the lead.   E.J.B.

Kaufman, Isaac (1807-86), an Amish Mennonite philanthropist of northern Somerset County near Johnstown, Pa., who owned considerable stock in the Pennsylvania Railroad and was one of the directors of an early bank in Johnstown. He was widely sought for his sound financial advice and the large number of private loans he made to Amish settlers in this area. The Kaufman Amish Mennonite Church near Davidsville, Pa., was named in his honor. He died Oct. 17, 1886, aged 79. (Register of Wills, Somerset County courthouse.)   J.A.H.

Kaufman, Sister Frieda Marie, b. Oct. 23, 1883, at Haagen in Wiesental, Baden, Germany, the daughter of Johannes and Marie Egle Kaufmann, citizens of Switzerland. In July 1892 the parents and three daughters, Anna, Elizabeth, and Frieda, came to Halstead, Kan. From early childhood until she entered the public school of her native village, she

had attended kindergarten conducted by Lutheran deaconesses. For a year the family lived in a Catholic community, and the seven-year-old girl spent much of her time in the home of a group of nuns who lived just across the street from the Kaufmanns. They were very kind to the little neighbor and gave her many coveted privileges of helping with the tiny tots in the kindergarten section of the parochial school. Under these influences she decided to become a sister, a desire she never lost.

She was educated in the Bethel College Academy 1900-2; the Deaconess Hospital Training School, Cincinnati, Ohio, 1902-4; graduate nurse Aug. 8, 1904; ordained deaconess June 11, 1908; registered nurse July 16, 1913; Doctor of Humane Letters, Bethel College, 1942.

Sister Frieda served as deaconess nurse in private homes, 1904-8; sister in charge of Bethel Deaconess Home and Hospital, Newton, Kan., 1908-38; Deaconess Mother, Bethel Deaconess Home and Hospital, Newton, 1908-43. She shared in the organization and building of Bethel Hospital, Mountain Lake, Minn., and Bethel Home for the Aged, Newton. She was editor of *In the Service of the King* 1941-44. In 1934 Sister Frieda made a trip to Europe, which she recorded in her book *Auf Wanderwegen* (Newton, 1935). She was a member of the First Mennonite Church (GCM) of Newton. She died on Aug. 7, 1944, at Newton and is buried there.
                    L.M.S.

Kaufman Amish Mennonite Church, now extinct. Among the first settlers of Conemaugh Twp., Somerset Co., Pa., were some Amish Mennonites who began to come about 1790. Christian (Schmidt) Miller (d. 1845) was one of the first and became the first Amish bishop in the township. Others kept moving in until there were possibly several hundred members around Johnstown. The advent of the steel mills into Johnstown caused many of them to move westward. They adhered strictly to the German language, which caused a general decline in membership. In 1880 they built two meetinghouses, one near Davidsville, Somerset County, known as the Kaufman Church, because it was built and financed by Isaac Kaufman and because more than half the members have the name Kaufman, and another near Geistown, Cambria County. After the death of Bishop Moses B. Miller in 1902, services at the Geistown church (sometimes known as the Miller church) were discontinued, while the Davidsville church continued with ministerial help supplied by the Mifflin County churches until 1916, after which all Amish worship was discontinued and the church dismantled. The few surviving members united with the Mennonite Church (MC).
                    A.KA.

Kaufman Mennonite Church (MC), located two miles east of Holsopple, Pa., is the youngest of the congregations of what was once a united Johnstown bishop district. The other congregations in the district were, with date of first meetinghouse, Blough (1836), Weaver (1855), Thomas (1874), Stahl (1882), and Elton (1899). These congregations constituted in effect a single congregation, called in the conference minutes the Johnstown congregation, with one bishop, which in 1900 was listed as having about 500 baptized members. Bishops were Jacob Blough (d. 1849), Samuel Blough, Sr. (d. 1877), Samuel Blough, Jr., Jonas Blough (d. 1906), James Saylor (ord. bishop 1903). About 1940 the district was divided and the individual congregations given different bishops. The Kaufman congregation apparently was organized as a separate body about 1912, when the first meetinghouse was built and 94 members were listed. It had no minister of its own until 1917, when A. J. Blough was chosen. In 1955 the membership was 162, with Harry Y. Shetler and Irvin M. Holsopple serving as ministers. The remnant of the old Kaufman Amish (q.v.) Mennonite congregation, which had been located in the same area, joined the new Kaufman Mennonite congregation (*History of the Southwestern Pennsylvania Conference*). H.S.B.

Kaunitz, Ulrich von, a ruler in Moravia, in whose territory Austerlitz (q.v.) was located, was kindly disposed to the Reformation, though he was a Catholic. Thus in 1528 he allowed the nonresistant Hutterite Anabaptists, called *Stäbler* (q.v.), who had separated from the *Schwertler* (q.v., Anabaptists who did not share the principle of nonresistance), to move from Nikolsburg to Austerlitz.   vDZ.

Kautz, Jakob (1500-?), for two years a Lutheran preacher at Worms, Germany, joined the Anabaptists in 1526. In his later public work he expressed some ideas similar to Hans Denk's (q.v.). In the spring of 1527 Denk and Ludwig Haetzer (q.v.) finished translating the Prophets from Hebrew to German at Worms, a task which had not yet been done because of linguistic difficulties. Thus Kautz had a considerable period of contact with Denk beginning in January 1527. Denk did not appear in public in Worms, but after his expulsion from Strasbourg used this retirement to devote himself to his scholarly work.

In the free imperial city a lively religious movement was in progress, the consequence of the struggles of the citizenry with the bishop. The courage and eloquence of the gifted young preacher Kautz had soon won a considerable following. He urged a spiritual Christian life, and union with God, placing no value on cult forms. He felt himself akin to Wolfgang Capito (q.v.), who also laid the chief stress on the spirit, and who, of all the reformers, was most like the Anabaptists in position. Thus it is easy to understand Denk's influence on him.

Kautz at first worked quietly for the movement. In January 1527, his colleague Hilarius joined the Anabaptists. For a while they continued to practice infant baptism, so that the government would have no cause for action against the parents. But on Jan. 27, 1527, the Elector Palatine, Louis V, to protect the rights of his brother, the bishop of Worms, demanded that the council take steps against these two preachers. The council hesitated, urging the bishop instead to have the pure Gospel preached in the churches; then peace and quiet could be kept among the citizens.

The elector, however, insisted, and on March 31, 1527, Kautz and Hilarius had to answer before the council. Kautz refused to preach contrary to his convictions, and continued to preach them. His following increased from day to day. Karl Hagen says one hundred peasants, followers of Kautz, were executed because they would not recant. On Thursday, June 13, he challenged his opponents to a public disputation. He outlined his views in seven theses (*ML* I, 158), and attached them to the door of the Predigerkirche in Worms. In them he stresses the inner life, which forms the core of religious striving. The "external," which for him includes the written and spoken word, communion, and infant baptism, has no power to comfort the inner man or assure him of salvation. Even the physical suffering of Christ would not be a true reconciliation with God without inner obedience. The Christian must be a disciple and follow the Father's commands like the Son.

Fr. Zorn, the chronicler of Worms, says Haetzer, Denk, and Melchior Rink were invited to participate in the disputation, but their names are not given in any publications (zur Linden, 174); the replies to the seven theses also name only Kautz as their author. Nor do the Kautz views as a whole coincide with Denk's. Denk's statements on these points, where they are found in his writings, are clearer and more mature. It is therefore most unlikely that Denk co-operated in drawing up the theses, or even that he gave his consent to their publication (Hege, 38-42).

Kautz's theses brought an immediate response. The two Lutheran preachers in Worms, Ulrich Preu and Johann Freiherr, wrote seven counter theses, which they posted on the church doors and put into print at once. At the advice of Johann Cochlaeus, who was also replying to some theses published in both Latin and German, the council decided on July 1, 1527, to banish the two preachers from the city. On July 2 the Strasbourg reformers issued a publication titled, *Getrewe Warnung der Prediger des Evangely zu Strassburg vber die Artickel, so Jakob Kautz, Prediger zu Wormbs, kürtzlich hat lassen aussgehen,* concerning which Röhrich says the preachers here defend "several of the debated doctrinal statements with arguments that careful exegesis would hardly consider valid; and other reasons are presented so strikingly and convincingly that they would not be without effect on the less prejudiced" (Röhrich, *Reformation* I, 339). Zwingli also attacked the Kautz theses.

After his expulsion from Worms Kautz sought refuge in South Germany. He seems to have gone first to Rothenburg on the Tauber, where he worked with Wilhelm Reublin (q.v.). Then he went to Augsburg, where on June 22 a new edition of the translation of the prophets had just come off the Ottmar press. He took part in the martyrs' synod on Aug. 20, 1527 (Keller, *Reformation,* 427). In June 1528 he went to Strasbourg (Cornelius, II, 274). Here the reformers tried again to convert him. He left the city, but returned in August, and was seized on Oct. 22, 1528, at a meeting, with Wilhelm Reublin and other attendants. In prison he had frequent talks with the reformers, but his request for a public debate was denied when the council learned that Worms had expelled him (Röhrich, "Strassburgische Wiedertäufer," 43). Kautz and Reublin now drew up a statement of their faith: they knew only adult baptism; infant baptism was not in accord with Christ's command; they compared the Strasbourg theologians to unskilled carpenters, who tear down more than they can build up (Röhrich, 44). In prison Kautz and Reublin again complained that they were not permitted to present their teaching openly or to the magistrate. The magistrate still refused public debate; they must limit themselves to written expression (Röhrich, 47). Not much is known of the content of their written statements, for they are lost (see **Bucer;** Schiess, I, 169).

The authorities asked the advice of various preachers and councilors as to how to proceed with the prisoners. One opinion has been preserved; it recommends the death penalty for Kautz and exile for the others (Hulshof, 84).

In prison Kautz became ill and declared himself willing to renounce Anabaptism. He was expelled, and then attached himself to Peter Schöffer, the printer who had published several editions of the translation of the Prophets by Denk and Haetzer in 1527 and 1528 (Hege, 22-31). In the same year, 1529, Kautz published the first complete German Bible based on the original text, five years before Luther's Bible. The Worms Bible was built on Luther's, as far as it had appeared. The rest is based on the Zürich Bible. The apocryphal books are attributed to Kautz, who made use of Leo Jud's translation of 1529 (Metzger, 75).

Kautz tried to earn a living as a tutor. Seriously ill, he sought (Oct. 14, 1532) medical aid in Strasbourg; but the magistrate refused him entry on the ground that it was not clear that he had renounced Anabaptism, and asked the opinion of the Strasbourg reformers (Cornelius, 279). In a second petition for toleration Kautz, broken in body and spirit, wrote that he had renounced it in prison, and now "knew nothing but Jesus the Crucified, that He is Lord; but no lover of God can abstain from proclaiming the virtue of Him who has called us to His wonderful light" (Röhrich, "Strassburgische Wiedertäufer," 63). His petition for toleration in the city was denied on the counsel of the reformers on Oct. 16 (Röhrich, 60; Cornelius, 277).

Little is known of Kautz's further fate. He died soon afterward, and his wife seems to have followed him in death a little later. His father's brother Peter took care of their children in Worms.

According to Calvary, *Mitteilungen aus dem Antiquariate* I (1870, supplement 5, 6, p. 52), the following works by Kautz have appeared: *Von der evangelischen Mess. Mit schönen christlichen Gebetten vor und nach der entphahung der Sacramente* (Hagenau, 1524), and *Wie man die Kranken und sterbenden Menschen ermanen . . . sol* (n.p., 1574).   HEGE.

J. Böshenz, "Jacob Kautz, ein Grossbockenheimer Volksprediger der Reformationszeit," in *Neue Leininger Blätter* I (October 1926); A. Brecher, "Jakob Kautz," in *ADB* XV, 510-11; Chr. Hege, *Die Täufer in der Kurpfalz* (Frankfurt, 1908); C. A. Cornelius, *Gesch. des Münsterischen Aufruhrs* II (Leipzig, 1860); F. O. zur Linden, *Melchior Hofmann, ein Prophet der Wiedertäufer* (Haarlem, 1885); A. Hegler, "Jakob Kautz," in *HRE* X, 192-94; A. Hulshof, *Geschiedenis van de Doopsgez. te Straatsburg van 1525 tot 1557* (Amsterdam, 1905); J. J. Metzler, *Gesch. der deutschen Bibelübersetzungen in der schweizerisch-reformierten Kirche* (Basel, 1876); T. W. Röhrich, *Gesch. der Ref. in Elsass* I (Strasbourg, 1830); idem, "Zur Gesch. der Strassburgischen Wiedertäufer," in *Ztschr f. d. Hist. Theol.,* 1860; L. Keller, *Die Reformation und die älteren Reformparteien* (Leipzig, 1885); Georg Baring, "Die Wormser Propheten" (reprint from *Archiv für Ref.-Gesch.* XXXI, 1934, 23-41); idem, another article with the same title in *Deutsches Bibelarchiv, Dritter Bericht* (Potsdam, 1933); *ML* II, 476-78.

Kazakhstan: see **Soviet Central Asia.**

Kedung-Pendjalin, a former mission station of the Dutch Mennonite missionary association in Java (*q.v.*), established in 1869 by members of the church founded in and about Japara by Pieter Jansz, the first missionary sent by the association. These members were living in several villages south of Japara, but since land was too scarce to assure them a living they settled north of Japara on land covered by virgin forests given them free of charge by the Dutch government, and built the village Kedung-Pendjalin.

Almost at the same time Pasrah, an assistant of Pieter Jansz, founded a small Christian congregation. It was served in turn by Jansz, Schuurmans, and Pieter Anton Jansz. In 1893 Johann Hübert came to the field and located at Kedung-Pendjalin in 1895. A church seating 400 was built in that year. In 1896 two evangelists, Tresno and Martakarija, were appointed, and gave devoted service for many years. In 1906 a 40-bed hospital was erected, which was later enlarged. In 1908 Hübert built a school, which in 1933 employed five teachers for a student body of 199.

In 1931 Hermann Schmitt took over the schools of this station, so that Hübert could devote all his time to the church. In 1933 it had a membership of 1,317, including the 649 unbaptized school children, five assistants and evangelists, two Sunday schools, and seven schools. In 1954 the baptized membership was 451, with 459 children.

The following subsidiary churches belong to Kedung-Pendjalin: Bondo, established in 1897, church dedicated in 1899, school built in 1895; Balongkodak, founded in 1904, church built in 1908, and a school in 1911; Puladjati, founded 1896, dissolved 1908; Japara, founded 1852, and reopened for the third time in 1924; Margokerto, founded 1900, church dedicated 1928; Tembelang, founded 1907, school 1910; Poring, founded 1921; Pakis, founded 1925. Missionary Johann Hübert was in charge of this congregation until 1936; he was followed by Otto Stauffer (*q.v.*), who served until 1940. On Nov. 24, 1940, this congregation became independent, with S. Jogopranoto as its pastor. In 1949 the congregation numbered 373 baptized members and 511 children; in 1955 the figures were about 450 and 500. (Reports of the Dutch Mission Association; *ML* II, 478.)   J.H., vDZ.

Keersgieter, Jacob de: see **Jacob de Rore.**

Keescooper, Hans: see **Jannijn Buefkijn.**

Keessen, a Dutch Mennonite family of Aalsmeer (*q.v.*). Since the 18th century usually occupied in fruit and tree raising, the family now owns one of the famous flower, nursery, and export businesses of this town. Many of its members were deacons. Gerrit Cornelis Keessen served 1798-*ca.*1830 as a preacher of the Nieuwe Vermaning congregation, as did also Dirk Aldert Keessen 1826-56, Willem Keessen 1832-*ca.*60, and Willem Dirks Keessen, Jr., 1861-66. D. W. Keessen Azn published *De vermaningen te Aalsmeer in den ouden tijd* (Aalsmeer, 1932) and *De Doopsgezinde Gemeenten te Aalsmeer 1642-1942* (n.p., n.d.—Aalsmeer, 1942).   vDZ.

W. Tsj. Vleer, *De Aloude Aalsmeerse Familiën* (De Kaag, n.d.-1953).

Keest, Jacob, a deacon of the Flemish Mennonite congregation at Franeker (*q.v.*), Dutch province of Friesland, who in 1586 opposed Elder Thomas Byntgens and soon became the principal leader of the Contra-Huiskopers (*q.v.*), Byntgens being the leader of the Huiskopers. Jacob Keest is thought to be identical with Jacques Outerman (*q.v.*), who about 1600 was a well-known preacher at Haarlem.

Perhaps earlier traces of Jacob Keest can be found if we assume that he is the same person as the Jacob Keest mentioned by Verheyden (*Courtrai-Bruxelles,* 20) who in 1553 was a cloth merchant living at Kortrijk (Courtrai) in Flanders, Belgium, near the (Cloth) Hall, and who was suspected as to his religion. (*BRN* VII, 553; Kühler, *Geschiedenis* I, 430 f.)   vDZ.

Keg, a Dutch Mennonite family, since the early 17th century found at Zaandam, North Holland, where this family was engaged in shipbuilding during the 17th and early 18th centuries. After a period of economic decline the family became prominent again about 1830 in oil milling, the cheese trade, and cheese export, particularly to England. Many members of the Keg family have served as deacons in the West Zaandam Mennonite congregation and in a few other congregations. Pieter Keg, of Zaandam, was a trustee of the A.D.S. (Dutch Mennonite general conference) in 1873-81.   vDZ.

Keim, Anthoni (called *Kleyn* by van Braght, Dutch *Martyrs' Mirror,* and *Klein* in the German edition of 1780), a Hutterite martyr, a tailor of Gunzenhausen (Middle Franconia), Bavaria, Germany, was seized with Hans Staudach (*q.v.*) and two companions when they were about to go to Moravia, and taken to Vienna (Aug. 2, 1546), and after a long, severe imprisonment and several cross-examinations, in which they victoriously attested their faith, they were beheaded on Nov. 22, 1546. To commemorate their death Wolf Sailer (*q.v.*) and Hans Gurtzham (*q.v.*) each wrote a song; both are found in *Die Lieder der Hutterischen Brüder.*   NEFF.

Wolkan, *Geschicht-Buch,* 205 f.; Beck, *Geschichts-Bücher,* 165-67; Zieglschmid, *Chronik,* 260, 265 f.; *Die Lieder der Hutterischen Brüder* (Scottdale, 1914) 133, 136; *Mart. Mir.* D 74, E 475, where the name is Antony Keyn; *ML* II, 478, 507.

Keim, Karl Theodor (1825-78), a German research scholar in church history, professor of theology at the University of Giessen. He contributed to the study of Anabaptist history in his works, *Reformation der Reichsstadt Ulm* (Stuttgart, 1851); *Schwäbische Reformationsgeschichte bis zum Augsburger Reichstag* (Tübingen, 1855); *Reformationsblätter der Reichsstadt Esslingen* (Esslingen, 1860); and his article "Ludwig Hetzer. Ein Beitrag zur Charakteristik der Sektenbewegungen in der Reformationszeit," in *Jahrbücher für deutsche Theologie* (1856, pp. 215 ff.). (*ML* II, 478.)   NEFF.

Keim Meetinghouse (MC) was built in 1859 in St. Paul, several miles from Salisbury, Somerset Co., Pa. The building was of simple frame construction, 30 x 35 feet in size, and cost $535. It was also known as the Mennonite Union, because although it was largely in the hands of the Mennonites, the Lutheran and Reformed congregations also shared in its use, the latter having contributed $200 to the building project. It was sold to the Lutherans in 1893.

The Mennonite congregation which was served by the Keim Meetinghouse was established in 1780 near Meyersdale, Pa., and was the first Mennonite body to be organized in the Casselman Valley District. The first minister was Jacob Seiler or Saylor (1715-93), a former Amish minister from Germany who was ordained by a Lancaster County bishop in eastern Pennsylvania for the purpose of serving in the Meyersdale area. At the time of the building of the Keim Meetinghouse, H. H. Blauch was the minister (served 1853-1904). His activity and vision as pastor and leader of the group so encouraged an increase in numbers that by 1859 it was no longer feasible to meet in schoolhouses and the First Baptist Meetinghouse of West Salisbury, as had been the custom of the group for some years. It was at this point that the Keim Meetinghouse was constructed. In 1878 the Mennonites erected their own meetinghouse at Springs (*q.v.*) some five miles southeast, called the Folk Meetinghouse. The group worshiping in the Keim Meetinghouse was in effect the later Springs congregation. It was probably called Keim's because of David Keim (1832-1915), preacher 1870 and bishop 1875-1915.   A.E.S.

Keiser: see Keyser.

Kelet, a hospital in Java located on the highway leading from Taju to Japara on the north side of Mt. Muria in the former province of Central Java. Kelet was established by the former Dutch Mennonite mission on Java, built under Dr. H. Bervoets and opened in 1915. It has beds for 142 patients, has a children's ward, a fully equipped surgery, laboratory, and electrotherapy. Dr. Bervoets was replaced in 1921 by Dr. K. P. C. A. Gramberg, who was assisted after 1930 by Dr. F. C. van der Horst; in addition there was always a government physician in service there. The first nurse was Helene Goossen of Russia, who served 1920-22; she then married Dr. Gramberg. Other nurses (deaconesses) were Panman 1922-25, Spannenburg 1927-29, and Maria Klaassen 1931-51.

The indigenous personnel, 40-50 nurses, some of whom had midwife certification, were with few exceptions trained at Kelet. The leper colony at

Donorodjo (*q.v.*) (eight miles north of Kelet) was also established by Dr. Bervoets and belongs to Kelet. The head physician of Kelet officiates at Donorodjo. Kelet also maintains two subsidiary hospitals, Taju with 22 beds and Bangsri with 10 beds, besides the dispensaries at Pati, Juvana, and Vedarijeska. Soon after the opening of the hospital a mission school was built at Kelet. The teachers were trained in the mission school in Margoredjo.

The extent of the hospital services is indicated by the following 1932 statistics: a total of 2,105 patients was admitted, with 117,142 days of nursing care; in Kelet alone, 1,481 patients with 48,481 days of care. The clinics gave 54,485 treatments to 9,769 patients. The total expenses were 112,820 guilders, of which the government contributed 78,586 guilders.

The development of the hospital also gave rise to a thriving congregation living in and around Kelet. The staff became the center of a live youth group. Pastoral care from 1915 was in the hands of a native assistant, Pariman Martosentono (elder since 1950), directed by Hermann Schmitt in Kudus. At the end of 1932 the church had 92 members and 125 children. Average attendance at church was 128 adults. In 1930 a church was built; meetings had previously been held in a room of the hospital. Among the lepers in Donorodjo there was also a Christian group, with a leper preacher. The head of the colony, P. Bouwer, assisted with the preaching, and missionary N. Thiessen of Margoredjo had the spiritual oversight over the colony. In 1954 the Kelet congregation had 167 baptized members and 262 children. It had become fully independent on Nov. 24, 1940.

Maria Klaassen, missionary nurse, was able to continue at Kelet throughout the vicissitudes of World War II, the Japanese occupation, and the guerrilla warfare afterwards. She operated the hospital successfully singlehandedly until she left the field in 1951. The MCC relief program in this area, which had been begun in 1949 at Pati, moved its headquarters to Kelet in 1953. (Reports of the Dutch Mission Association; *ML* II, 479.) K.P.G., vDZ.

Keller, Gottfried (1819-90), a Swiss literary figure, one of the most important writers in German literature. His best-known work is probably the novel, *Der grüne Heinrich;* but his *Züricher Novellen* are also widely read. One of these *Novellen, Ursula,* takes the reader into the Reformation in Zürich. Zwingli is engaged in a struggle with the Catholics and Anabaptists. A soldier just returned from the Italian wars attaches himself faithfully to Zwingli. He finds that his sweetheart has become a follower of the fanatical Anabaptists. What the author presents is a caricature. Excesses, some of which occurred in St. Gall, are here ascribed to the Zürich Anabaptists in unpleasant exaggeration. Finally Ursula finds her lover seriously wounded on the battlefield of Kappel, saves him from death, is cured of her madness in the distress of war, and as his wife follows him to his house. NEFF.

Elizabeth Bender, "Portrayal of the Swiss Anabaptists in Gottfried Keller's *Ursula,*" *MQR* XVII (July 1943) 136-50; *ML* II, 479.

Keller, Ludwig, b. March 28, 1849, at Fritzlar, Germany, d. March 9, 1915, in Berlin, attended school at Rinteln, studied classical philology at the universities of Leipzig and Marburg, and then specialized in archives. In 1874 he began his work in archives for Prussia. Until 1895 he was state archivist in Münster. Intensive study of the archives here led to the publication in 1885-87 of *Die Gegenreformation in Westfalen und dem Niederrhein* (see also his articles, "Zur Geschichte der Wiedertäufer nach dem Untergang des Münsterischen Königreichs," *Westdeutsche Ztscht* I, 1882, 429-68; and "Zur Kirchengeschichte Nordwestdeutschlands im 16. Jahrhundert," in *Ztscht des bergischen Geschichtsvereins* XV, 1879, 106-42) and to his realization that the religious brotherhoods outside the church organizations had been given a completely false evaluation in traditional presentations of church history.

In succession Keller published his epoch-making writings, vindicating Anabaptism, and giving the initial impetus to an entirely new judgment and to most zealous inquiries into this religious movement. In 1880 his *Geschichte der Wiedertäufer und ihres Reiches zu Münster* appeared; in 1882, *Ein Apostel der Wiedertäufer* (Hans Denk); in 1885, *Die Reformation und die älteren Reformparteien;* in 1886, *Die Waldenser und die deutschen Bibelübersetzungen;* in 1887, *Zur Geschichte der altevangelischen Gemeinden* (a lecture given in Berlin on April 20, 1887); in 1888, *Johann von Staupitz und die Anfänge der Reformation.* In addition to these he wrote a series of articles for the *Mennonitische Blätter,* 1883, 1885-90; for the *Gemeindeblatt,* 1885-89; and in the *Allgemeine Deutsche Biographie.*

He was an ardent exponent of the idea that there was a direct connection between the Waldenses and the Anabaptists (*Gbl.,* 1886, 70), and that their principles, doctrines, and institutions continued to live in the Christian church from its beginnings through the centuries in brotherhoods which he named "altevangelische Brüdergemeinden" (see *Menn. Bl.,* 1890, 113; *Gbl.* 1890, 85).

Keller was violently attacked. Nevertheless he continued undismayed on his way, which led him to a far-reaching syncretism. He had a vision of an ideal Christian brotherhood of humanity above the dogmatic ecclesiastical or materialistic, naturalistic view of the world. To bring about this brotherhood he won friends for it among the Baptists and Mennonites and other extra-church groups, including the Free Masons. On Oct. 10, 1892, he instigated the organization of the Comenius-Gesellschaft (*q.v.*), which published the *Monatshefte der Comenius-Gesellschaft;* in 1895 a pedagogical supplement was added, called *Comeniusblätter für Volkserziehung.* The former included a series of valuable informative articles and treatises from the past and present of Anabaptism (e.g., *Monatshefte,* 1897, 131-76, "Grundfragen der Reformationsgeschichte"; 1912, 115, "Zwei Jubiläen. Ein Beitrag zur religiösen Zeitgeschichte").

In 1897 Keller became a Mason. But his hope of finding in this organization fighting allies for his ideas was not fulfilled. Nevertheless he remained faithful to it. His prize-winning book, *Die geistigen Grundlagen der Freimaurerei und das öffentliche*

Leben (1911), and *Die Freimaurerei* (1914) in the Teubner Collection, *Aus Natur und Geisteswelt,* were unusually successful.

Ludwig Keller rendered the Mennonites a meritorious service by his historical research, which obligates them to lasting gratitude. Among the historians much influenced by him were not only the Mennonites John Horsch, Christian Neff, and Christian Hege (*q.v.*), but also Karl Rembert and Friedrich Thudichum (*q.v.*). J. H. Kurtz pays the following tribute to Keller in his widely used *Lehrbuch der Kirchengeschichte* (14th ed., 1906, Vol. II, 55): "It is Keller's achievement to have brought out into the forefront of scholarly consideration the great significance of Anabaptism in the history of the Christian spirit in the 16th century, and to have called emphatic attention to the rich religious literature and remarkable organizational activity of the Anabaptists as well as the primitive Christian elements in their movement." NEFF.

"Geisteskultur," *Monatshefte der Comeniusgesellschaft,* 1913, 78-86; Amalie Keller, "Ludwig Keller—Scholar with a Mission," *Menn. Life* VIII (October 1953) 159 f., 192; *DB* 1903, 151-63; 1911, 98-100; *ML* II, 480.

Keller, Ludwig, and the Mennonites. Ludwig Keller had significant relations with the German Mennonites and certain Mennonite scholars, and exerted a tangible influence upon them. Around 1880 the Mennonites in Germany were not very historically minded, and took the attitude more of the "Stillen im Lande" than feeling a mission to the society around them. In this situation Keller's book, *Ein Apostel der Wiedertäufer,* appeared in 1882, centering attention upon Hans Denk (*q.v.*). It was a real eye opener for Mennonites, and many were willing to accept Hans Denk (the "spiritual reformer") as the finest and most original expression of the "Anabaptist" genius. (Today scholarship has learned to make a distinction between the spiritualists such as Denk, and the regular Anabaptists.) Between 1882 and 1892 (when Keller founded the Comenius Gesellschaft) Keller sought closer contacts with Mennonites and tried to promote his idea of the "old evangelical brotherhood" among them. He began to publish articles of this nature in the *Mennonitische Blätter* beginning in 1883, and in the *Gemeindeblatt* in 1885. He also had personal contacts with German and Dutch Mennonite preachers whom he wanted to win over to his vision. In 1885-93 a lively correspondence developed between Keller and John Horsch (*q.v.*)—after 1887 in America—and in 1885-91 between Keller and Christian Neff (*q.v.*), as well as with other men of influence in the Mennonite church.

Keller's letters reveal much about his intentions. He claimed that "the best and purest tradition of Anabaptism" goes back to the period of 1517-34. Since there was no Anabaptist in the strict sense before 1525, this contention needs explanation. Keller equated the teachings of mystics and spiritual reformers with those of Anabaptists proper. Thus he included in his list of "early Anabaptists" men like Johann von Staupitz (Luther's superior in the monastery at Erfurt), Sigmund Salminger, Jacob Dachser, Christian Entfelder, and above all Hans Denk. They all taught a free semimystical and individualistic interpretation of the Scriptures (over against Luther's solid Biblicism and ecclesiasticism), but they had little to do with the essential idea of Anabaptism. Keller urged his Mennonite friends to study Denk, the *Theologia Deutsch,* also Tauler and other mystics. It is known that in those years the father of John Horsch published the *Deutsche Theologie* together with comments by Denk (1886), and John Horsch published Denk's *Von der Wahren Liebe* at Elkhart, 1888. The *Mennonitische Blätter* and the *Gemeindeblatt* published long excerpts from these authors, and so did the *Herold der Wahrheit* (1888-91) and the *Kirche unterm Kreuz* (1885-89) in America. W. Molenaar, a leader of the Berlin Mennonites, wrote to Keller in 1886, "We are definitely espousing your program but believe that the moment has not yet come for general action," which meant for the promotion of the idea that the Mennonite congregations should reconstitute themselves as an aggressive "old evangelical brotherhood."

Keller's letters to John Horsch are particularly revealing. Horsch was a young man full of enthusiasm and willing to risk money and more for the propagation of such ideas. At first the *Gottesfreunde* (among them the *Theologia Deutsch* had originated in the 15th century) attracted both Keller and Horsch more than the Anabaptists, but soon also the latter moved into the focus. In 1883 Joseph Beck (*q.v.*) had published his *Geschichts-Bücher der Wiedertäufer in Österreich und Ungarn,* which provided rich material for the student of Anabaptism. Keller also called attention indiscriminately to Sebastian Franck and Caspar Schwenckfeld. In spreading the ideas of all these men he saw the "German mission" of the Mennonites. Its goal should be the overcoming of prejudices among the Lutherans against Anabaptism, a goal eventually reached, to a large extent thanks to Keller's efforts.

When in 1887 young Horsch moved to Elkhart, Ind., the correspondence became even more intense. Keller hoped that Horsch could perhaps help in reshaping also the Mennonite church in America according to his ideas, but he warned Horsch to proceed slowly, with circumspection and greatest care. The *Herold der Wahrheit* of these years (1887-91) abounds in reprints of the above-named authors, together with reprints from Johannes Arndt, Matthias Claudius, Michael Hahn, and—at long last—also some genuine Anabaptists, taken from newly discovered Hutterite sources. Strangely enough, Menno Simons is somewhat neglected and his authority even opposed. (Keller: "By cleaving to Menno Simons the goal of the brotherhood has been narrowed down too much.") In 1891 John Horsch published his *Kurzgefasste Geschichte der Mennoniten,* quite in line with Keller's ideas; Hans Denk appears here as the most important early spiritual leader of Anabaptism.

But then, all of a sudden this trend came to an end. Keller lost interest in making the Mennonite church the mouthpiece for his ideas, and turned to other pursuits (Christian humanism and Freemasonry). And so the correspondence stopped. The same was true in Germany: the Keller period was definitely over by 1893.

Looking back we may say that it is easier to understand the issues today than it was in the 1880's. Keller had been thinking of the Mennonites as an open society of inspired Christians, while the Mennonites understood themselves as a closed brotherhood with strict discipline. Keller, who was always a staunch individualist with some inclination toward mysticism, had very little appreciation for this type of church life, and his association with the Mennonites inevitably had to come to an end. And yet his idea of "old evangelical brotherhoods" was widely accepted even long after the 1880's. The Langnau-Emmental Swiss congregation accepted this name for their church and on the title page of P. M. Friesen's book on the Mennonites in Russia (1911) we meet this term again. It is still used now and then in Mennonite writings, and has, no doubt, also a grain of historic truth in it. (See **Altevangelische** Wehrlose Taufgesinnten-Gemeinden for a discussion of Keller's influence on the use of this term by Mennonites.) The Keller letters to John Horsch are preserved in the Goshen College Library. His letters to Christian Neff are preserved at the Weierhof. R.F.

R. Friedmann, "John Horsch and Ludwig Keller," *MQR* XXI (July 1947) 160 ff.; Elizabeth H. Bender, "The Letters of Ludwig Keller to John Horsch, 1885-1893," *ibid.*, 175-204; R. Friedmann, *Mennonite Piety Through the Centuries* (Goshen, 1949) 257; *ML* II, 480.

Kell(n)er, Wenisch (Köhler), a Hutterite, was ordained in Moravia as a preacher in 1578, and as elder in 1580; in 1584 he and six other Brethren were sent out as missionaries; and on May 6, 1593, he died at Lewar (Levary) in Hungary. He is the author of the song, "Wach auf, ihr Kinder Gottes all" (Wolkan, *Lieder*, 233). In Gottmading near Schaffhausen he wrote letters to Matthias Binder (*q.v.*), Michael Veldthaler (*q.v.*), and Claus Braidl (*q.v.*), on Aug. 12 and 14, 1584, reporting on his work and success in the neighborhood of Zürich. NEFF.

Loserth, *Communismus*, 176 ff.; Beck, *Geschichts-Bücher*, 319; Wolkan, *Geschicht-Buch*, 388 *et passim*; *Die Lieder der Hutterischen Brüder* (Scottdale, 1914); Zieglschmid, *Chronik*, 501, 520, 567; *ML* II, 480.

Kelowna (B.C.) Mennonite Brethren Church, a member of the Canadian Conference of the Mennonite Brethren Church of North America, was organized with 36 members on June 8, 1947, under the leadership of J. J. Unger as minister. The first meeting place was a private house, then a rented hall until 1948, when the new church 60 x 40 ft. was built. The 1953 membership was 72, with J. J. Unger still serving as pastor. Kelowna is an isolated congregation, located 200 miles east of the Fraser Valley churches, in the Okanagon Valley about 80 miles north of the Washington state border in a city of 10,000 population. The small congregation at Oliver, 70 miles south of Kelowna, in charge of J. J. Klassen, is a subsidiary of Kelowna. J.J.U.

Kemp, Franciscus Adriaan van der, was born May 4, 1752, of Dutch Reformed parents, at Kampen, Netherlands, and prepared for a military career. At the University of Groningen (1770-73) he heard lectures on the most varied subjects. In 1773 he entered the Mennonite seminary in Amsterdam, and the next year became a member of the Mennonite church. He became a ministerial candidate in 1775 and served the congregations of Huizen 1775-77 and Leiden 1777-87. His effervescence and his radical ideas were the cause of many difficulties. Yet a severe illness made it apparent that a large proportion of his congregation was attached to him. But this affection grew cool as van der Kemp became more and more involved in politics, and threw all the force of his character. into the cause of democracy on the side of the Patriot movement. In 1775 the Patriots sympathized with the Colonies in the American struggle for independence against England, and van der Kemp openly espoused their cause. He became a close friend of John Adams, the American commissioner in Holland 1780 ff. He published a number of sermons: *Het gedrag van Israel en Rehabeam, ten spiegel van Volk en Vorst,* followed by *Staatkundige Aanmerkingen* (Leiden, 1782), *Elftal kerkelijke Redevoeringen* (Leiden, 1782), *Viertal Leerredenen, op Bedestonden gehouden* (Leiden, 1783).

In 1785 he was granted a leave of absence to travel. In Wijk-bij-Duurstede he joined the secret military society *Pro pace et bello* and soon resigned his pastorate to become captain of a militia company. In June 1787 he was arrested in Amersfoort, and released in November on the condition that he leave the country.

On May 4, 1788, van der Kemp landed in New York. His reception by eminent Americans included an invitation by George Washington to Mount Vernon. He became a farmer, and acquired American citizenship. He lived for six years near Kingston, N.Y., and then established a home at Oneida Lake, and finally at Barneveld. He found old and new friends, and inner quiet. His love for preaching revived, his political fervor subsided. In 1803 he assisted in forming a union for church services in his home town, Olden Barneveld; Sunday school was held in his home.

He continued to write devotional and learned articles, using the English language from now on. Harvard awarded him the LL.D. degree. In 1817 he wrote an account of his romantic life for his only son. He died on Sept. 7, 1829. vDZ.

Helen Fairchild, *Franciscus Adrian van der Kemp 1752-1829: An Autobiography* (New York and London, 1903); *Dictionary of American Biography* XIX (N.Y., 1936); *DB* 1907, 99-151; *N.N.B.Wb.* VIII, 953-58; *Biogr. Wb.* IV, 706-18; L. G. le Poole, *Bijdragen tot de Kennis van het kerkelijk leven onder de Doopsgezinden . . . te Leiden* (Leiden, 1905); *ML* II, 481.

Kempe, Adriaan, b. about 1710 at Norden, d. 1779 at Medemblik, was baptized at Norden, Germany, on Feb. 13, 1729; in 1731-79 he was preacher of the United Frisian and Waterlander congregation at Medemblik, Dutch province of North Holland. In 1739 he was married to Cornelia Metschaart (Messchaert) of Hoorn. He published *Jesus Christus de Paerl en Pronk van 't Geslachte der Menschen* and seven other sermons (Medemblik, 1740). (*Biogr. Wb.* IV, 724; *Ned. Patriciaat* XVI, 218.) vDZ.

Kempen, a town (pop. 10,000) in the former Prussian Rhine Province, six miles west of Crefeld. Here the Anabaptists found adherents in the middle of the 16th century. Under Archbishop (of Cologne) Hermann, who had Protestant leanings, the authorities apparently did not concern themselves greatly about them, for, as the preacher Hardenberg reported to Theodor von Buchell, the privy councilor of the archbishop, they were quiet and orderly, and he hoped by indoctrination to win them; if they resisted he would use "other means," and that the Anabaptists threatened no danger. About 1550 many prominent families of this town were Anabaptists. Even some burgomasters of Kempen in 1560 and following years belonged to the Anabaptists. But from 1569 Bishop Salentin of Cologne gradually succeeded in suppressing Anabaptist influences in Kempen, though Mennonites were found in the town until after 1648.

Kempen and the adjacent Aldekerk (*q.v.*) were the source of the first Mennonite migration to Crefeld (1609). There had been even earlier connection with Crefeld. The pastors of Kempen, Anrat and Hüls, reported that an old preacher from Crefeld by the name of Wolter had appeared in their district; he had previously been the pastor at Odenkirchen, and had there adopted Anabaptist ideas.

HEGE, VDZ.

Rembert, *Wiedertäufer, passim;* Ernst Crous, "Von Täufern zu Mennoniten am Niederrhein," *Der Mennonit* IX (July 1956) 107; *ML* II, 481.

Kempen, Gerhard (Gerrit) **von,** an Anabaptist martyr who died at the stake at Wiesen (?) in 1550 "for the testimony of Jesus Christ." (*Mart. Mir.* D 99, E 497; *ML* II, 481.)

Kemper, Freule Christine de Bosch, b. at Amsterdam, Holland in 1840, and died May 12, 1924, at Amersfoort, daughter of Professor Jeronimo de Bosch Kemper and Maria Hulshoff, was baptized in 1861 by J. G. de Hoop Scheffer, then Mennonite pastor at Amsterdam. Soon after, in 1867, she broke with her idle, luxurious life to devote herself to the education of young women. In 1880 she moved from Amsterdam to Amersfoort, where she opened her house to all kinds of young women. Being very well-to-do she asked nothing for herself but was charitable to others. Like her sister Jeltje she was also a champion of women's rights, but she did not proclaim her ideas beyond her home circle. She bequeathed her stately residence to an old people's home and her other property to the "Christine-Stichting" (*q.v.*), a foundation, administered by Mennonite directors, for the improvement of the material condition of women. (*DJ* 1926, 21-33, with portrait.)

VDZ.

Kempsville Amish Mennonite Church (Beachy Amish) is located a half mile northeast of Kempsville, Va., in the southeastern part of the state. An Old Order Amish community had been established here near the beginning of the present century by settlers, many of whom came from Somerset Co., Pa. In 1940 some of the later arrivals in the community led a movement to allow ownership of automobiles by members of the congregation. This produced a schism and the formation of the Kempsville church. After this event, most of the Old Order who did not join the progressive group moved out of the community. In 1955 the congregation had 150 members, with Jacob J. Hershberger and Ezra N. Troyer serving as ministers and Paul Brenneman as bishop. The congregation operates a parochial school, fully organized in 1946. A Conservative Mennonite church was organized here in 1952, with Simon Coblentz as bishop. Some 15 families left the community in 1953 to found a new congregation at Montezuma, Ga.

M.G.

A. J. Beachy, "The Rise and Development of the Beachy Amish Mennonite Churches," *MQR* XXIX (April 1955) 118 ff.

Kempten, a Swabian town (pop. 40,000) in Bavaria, Germany, on the Iller River. In the Middle Ages it consisted of two towns, the old and the new. The former adopted the Reformation in 1527; the latter was the center of the Kempten district and of a Benedictine abbey, whose abbots had been princes of the empire since 1360.

In the middle of the 16th century Anabaptists were found here, for three decrees were passed against them dated Sept. 8, 1544, Sept. 8, 1551, and Sept. 7, 1562. The first points out that the "blind, offensive, and damned sect" of the Anabaptists is making inroads and growing, and commands the people to abstain from it and conduct themselves in accord with the old, true faith. Whoever was not willing to do so should sell his goods and leave Kempten, or be punished with life imprisonment or other penalty of property or body. The second adds that the imperial "recess" of Augsburg of Feb. 14, 1551, applies to them. The third mentions the imperial law of April 23, 1529, and stipulates that no special burial ground can be given the Anabaptists, who bury their dead in secret, that anyone dying outside the Catholic faith without confession or the sacrament should be buried only under the nearest gallows.

From these decrees it may be inferred that the Anabaptist movement in and around Kempten was strong and maintained itself for a long time.

NEFF.

W. Koehler, "Zur Gesch. der Täufer im Stift Kempten," in *Festschrift zum 70. Geburtstag von Dr. Christian Neff* (Weierhof, 1933); *ML* II, 481.

Kengel, Benjamin (Beniam), a Hutterite, a tailor in Sobotiste, Hungary, left the brotherhood in June 1645, because he thought outward usages were not necessary to a Christian. He won a following, but after his death most of his adherents returned to the brotherhood. Against him Ehrenpreis (*q.v.*) wrote *Antwort und Widerlegung der irrigen, verführerischen und falschen Meinung des Benjamin Kengels und seines Anhangs etlicher Articul.*

NEFF.

Wolkan, *Geschicht-Buch,* 630 f.; Zieglschmid, *Chronik,* 841 ff.; *ML* II, 481 f.

Kennel, a Mennonite family name of Swiss origin. In 1759 a von Kennel from Reichenbach is named among the Anabaptists of Montbéliard, France. In 1940 the name was still found among the South German Mennonites, in the Frankfurt congregation. In 1955 there were still numerous Kennel families among the French Mennonites, including a preacher in Montbéliard and seven out of eight preachers in the Haute Marne congregation.

The Kennel family was represented in the Hessian Mennonite congregation in Butler Co., Ohio. Peter Kennel served as a minister in the Apostolic Mennonite Church (GCM), Butler County, 1847-96. He came to America with his parents in 1830. John Kennel settled in Woodford Co., Ill., in 1833. John J. Kennel, who was ordained a minister in the Central Conference Mennonite Church in Tazewell Co., Ill., in 1912, was a nephew of Peter Kennel of Butler Co., Ohio. The Linn Amish Mennonite Church (q.v.) near Roanoke, Ill., is sometimes known as the Kennel church because Joseph J. Kennel served as its minister for a number of years and John Kennel as its bishop.

Among the early settlers in the Wellesley Amish Mennonite congregation of Ontario was Christian Kennel. Peter Kennel migrated from France to Ontario in 1881, and later moved to Milford, Neb. In 1905 he was ordained as minister of Salem (MC) at Shickley, Neb. In 1913 he was ordained bishop and served in that office until his death in 1923. His son Peter Kennel, Jr., is now bishop of this church, and a grandson, Leroy Kennel, is pastor of the Lombard Mennonite Church in a western suburb of Chicago. The Kennel family has also been prominent in the Amish Mennonite community of eastern Pennsylvania. John A. Kennel is a bishop in the Millwood congregation at Gap, Pa. At the present time, five ministers with the Kennel family name are serving Mennonite (MC) churches in eastern Pennsylvania.   M.G.

Kent County, Del., Old Order Amish Mennonite settlement consists of four districts having about 250 members, located west of Dover. Amish families from various states moved to Kent County. The first to come were the families of Bishop David Y. Miller and Jacob K. Miller in 1915. Others came from Geauga Co., Ohio, Oscoda Co., Mich., Lancaster Co., Pa., Somerset Co., Pa., and Ford Co., Kan. The original settlement was divided into two districts in 1928, and the west district of the original settlement was divided in 1933. In 1946 several Byler families with others consisting of about 18 families moved to Catlett, Faquier Co., Va. In 1947 a more progressive congregation was organized under the leadership of Bishop Seth Byler of Stark Co., Ohio. The present (1956) bishops are John D. Hochstetler, D. Leroy Nissley, Eli S. Miller, and Simon W. Byler.   J.A.H.

Kent County, located in southern Michigan and including the city of Grand Rapids, has been the seat of two Mennonite (MC) churches, Caledonia (q.v.) and Bowne (q.v.). The Caledonia settlement was located some 12 miles west of the Bowne settlement. The first settlers in the Caledonia area came in 1864. Those locating at Caledonia came partly from Ontario, and partly from such states as Indiana, Ohio, and Pennsylvania. The first meetinghouse was erected in 1865 and replaced by another in 1881; the latter burned down in 1923. Only the cemetery now remains to mark the location of the building. The congregation seemed to prosper at first, there being 40 members at Caledonia by 1867. But internal differences over religious practice led to the weakening of the congregation and its ultimate death by

1910. The Bowne settlers located in Kent County in 1865, coming from Somerset Co., Pa., and from Ontario. The first meetinghouse was a log structure and was erected jointly by the Church of the Brethren and the Mennonites (MC) about 1870, being used for seven years on alternate Sundays by the two groups, after which the Brethren built their own separate house of worship. The present building of the Bowne congregation (also called Elmdale) was erected in 1901. The present membership (1956) of the congregation is 104.   J.C.W.

Kent, Johanna of, an Anabaptist martyr: see **Boucher, Jane.**

Kentucky is one of the southern states, bounding Illinois, Indiana, and Ohio on their southern borders. Until recently (1943) Mennonites have by-passed the state, very likely because the chief routes of Mennonite westward migration lay north of the Ohio River. There are now eleven Mennonite missions and churches in the state with a total membership of 143. Seven of these are churches and missions of the Mennonite Church (MC) with a membership of 90, and three of the Conservative Mennonite Church, with a membership of 53. These churches are located in two areas of the state. Morgantown, with a membership of seven, is located in the west central part of the state, and is sponsored by the Berea Mennonite Church (MC) of Montgomery, Ind. The other nine stations are located in the eastern part of the state. Teges and Wildcat, with 25 and 37 members respectively, situated south of Booneville, are sponsored by the Pike Mennonite Church (MC), Elida, Ohio. Approximately 15 miles northeast are the three Conservative Mennonite stations named Turners Creek, Bowlings Creek, and Gays Creek, with memberships of 25, 8, and 11. Northeast of these stations, and near Highway 15, southeast of Jackson are the two mission stations Caney Creek and Talcum, the latter with four members. The first is sponsored by the Indiana-Michigan Mennonite District Mission Board (MC) and the latter by the Clinton Frame Mennonite Church (MC), Goshen, Ind. Approximately 30 miles northeast of Jackson are two Mennonite missions sponsored by the Virginia Mennonite Board of Missions and Charities (MC). These are Crockett and Relief, with seven and eleven members. The first of the ten missions was Relief, established in 1943. It was followed by Turners Creek in 1946, Bowlings Creek in 1947, and Wildcat and Crockett in 1949. The later stations were begun in 1950-52. Big Branch, near Talcum, was added in 1956.   M.G.

Keppel (Kepfel, a parish in the duchy of Berg, Germany), **Wilhelm von,** an early Anabaptist, a former Catholic priest. He may have been a preacher (ML II, 482), but there is no proof for this assertion, nor is there information as to the time of his uniting with the Anabaptist congregation. While he was a member he worked at his trade of buckle-making (Krampenmacher) in the duchy of Berg, now in the Rhine-Wupper district. In 1561 he was arrested ("a priest, Wilhelm Keppel by name") with a large number of the Anabaptist congregation of Cologne (*q.v.*). Only those were punished who refused to recant. Wilhelm von Keppel was arrested the second time in 1562, and must therefore have been released after the first arrest, which indicates that he had recanted. After his second arrest he was imprisoned in one of the towers of Cologne, where he was subjected to torture before he was transferred to the dungeon in September 1562, which was the prison of the Supreme Court of Cologne. He was placed into a cell already occupied by the Anabaptist Georg Friesen (*q.v.*). Both were tortured here in an attempt to convince them of the correctness of infant baptism. In his cross-examination Wilhelm declared that "he did not regard the ceremonies of the church as anything, considered the Catholic worship useless, the devil was the teacher of the Catholics, only God's Word, and by no means the doctrines of men should be obeyed." But neither the rack, threats, nor any other attempts at conversion induced him or Georg Friesen to recant, and they were consequently sentenced to death by drowning. After the waters of the Rhine had closed over Georg Friesen, Wilhelm declared himself willing to recant. Thereupon he was banished from the city and region (*Turmbuch* No. 2, p. 98; Ennen, 815, note 2): "Wilhelm Krampenmacher of Monheim banished and condemned by the *Grefen* and bailiffs of the city and the archbishopric of Cologne; because he would be submerged in a boat with Georg, and feared death, he said that he would desist from his error."

Their imprisonment and the martyrdom of Friesen Keppel later described in a song which is found in the *Ausbund* (No. 22, p. 131 ff.), but which is true to fact only in so far as it refers to Georg Friesen, since he denies the recantation he made. Another account of these men is found in the *Martyrs' Mirror,* which in some respects contradicts the account given in the poem. The reason for the errors in the reports is not yet clear.

In the song Wilhelm von Keppel closes with admonitions to his brethren and sisters, poses as their defender, who "has fought with lions wild and with wolves" (stanza 34), and in stanza 35 he cries out to them—ambiguously—"Therefore, dear brethren and sisters mine, prepare yourselves with diligence, that you may also be qualified to fight with such a foe." Was he alluding to the qualifications of Georg Friesen or his own? Why did he not rather maintain a humble silence? A.R.

Turmbücher (found in the Historical Archives of the City of Cologne) No. 2, pp. 59 and 98; No. 5, p. 48; Leonhard Ennen, *Geschichte der Stadt Köln* IV (Cologne and Neuss, 1875) 814 f.; Wackernagel, *Kirchenlied,* 817 ff.; Wolkan, *Lieder,* 101; *Mart. Mir.* D 295, E 661; *ML II,* 482.

Kerber (Körber, Kerwer, Körffer), a Mennonite family of West Prussia, Germany, recorded as early as 1586. Especially in the Montau-Gruppe and Deutsch-Kazun congregations they were found from the early 17th century. Steffen Kerber was (1737) a preacher of the Montau Frisian (sometimes also called Waterlander) congregation. Another Steffen Kerber (1734-1800) served this congregation as preacher from 1767 and as elder from 1781; Peter Kerber (1759-1814) served as preacher from 1795,

elder 1801; Peter Kerber (1782-1821) as preacher in 1801, elder 1814. Others served as deacons. They were apparently all farmers. In 1940 there were 42 bearers of the name in East Germany. The name has not spread into other countries. C.K.

L. Stobbe, *Montau-Gruppe, ein Gedenkblatt* (Montau, 1918) 83-89; Reimer, *Familiennamen,* 111.

Kerbert, a Mennonite family, formerly found at Koog aan de Zaan, Dutch province of North Holland. Jan Kerbert, b. 1820 at Koog, d. April 11, 1890, at Arnhem, studied at the Mennonite seminary at Amsterdam and thereupon served as Mennonite pastor at Rottevalle 1845-46, Hoorn 1846-67, and Zwolle 1867-84, retiring in 1884. Coenraad Kerbert (Koog, 1816-57), a physician in his home town, was a noted botanist. vDZ.

Kerckhove, van de (Kerhoven), a Mennonite family from Flanders which emigrated to the Netherlands. One branch moved to Haarlem as early as about 1590 and became related by marriage to other Mennonite families such as Meevels, Teyler, and Snep. Another branch settled about 1630 near Aardenburg in Dutch Zealand Flanders. Here Tanneken van den Kerckhove was married about 1632 to Christoffel Hebberecht (*q.v.*). Both branches have died out. vDZ.

Kerkgezangen, Christelijke, a Dutch Mennonite hymnbook, published at Haarlem, Holland, in 1851 and used by the Haarlem congregation and a few others. It contains 176 hymns with notes, mostly borrowed from other Mennonite hymnals. This hymnbook, commonly called *Oude Haarlemsche Bundel,* was in use at Haarlem until 1895, when it was replaced by the *Doopsgezinde Liederen* (*q.v.*). (*DB* 1861, 159 f.; 1865, 76 ff., 91 ff.) vDZ.

Kern, Ruepel: see **Gellner, Rupp.**

Kerssenbroick, Hermann von (b. *ca.* 1520), attended the cathedral school in Münster in 1533, and remained there until the Anabaptist kingdom was set up there; and after the city had been taken he returned to the same school. He lived a while in Cologne and Hamm; for 25 years (1550-75) he was rector of the cathedral school at Münster, and died July 5, 1585, as rector of the cathedral school at Paderborn. His two books, *Belli Monasteriensis contra anabaptistica monstra gesti descriptio, auctor Hermanno a Kerssenbroick* (Cologne, 1545), and *Anabaptistici furoris Monasterium inclitam Westphaliae metropolim evertentis historica narratio, autore Hermanno a Kerssenbroick,* are source materials for Anabaptist history in Münster.

The former is a lengthy poem in hexameters, of no value in content, which he himself rejected as immature in his later years; the latter of greater importance, though not faultless critically, since it was written from the Catholic point of view and is prejudiced. In 1573 it was given for publication to the Cologne printery of Gervinus Calenius, but the Münster city council prohibited its publication. The council could, however, not carry out its intention to suppress it, for manuscript copies were already in the hands of several persons. In 1730 and 1750 an inadequate edition was printed. A German translation published in 1771 (2nd ed. 1881) is full of errors (Löffler). In 1900 H. Detmer (*q.v.*) published a thorough edition of the work in two volumes at Münster (Cornelius, p. xxiv and p. xxix). In 1929 the Aschendorf publishers at Münster printed another edition in German translation based on a different manuscript copy, with an introduction by S. P. Widmann.   NEFF.

C. A. Cornelius, *Die Geschichtsquellen des Bistums Münster* II (Münster, 1853); C. Löffler, *Die Wiedertäufer zu Münster* . . . (Jena, 1923); H. Detmer, *Hermann von Kerssenbroch's Leben und Schriften* (Münster, 1900); *ML* II, 483 f.

Kesselflicker (Kesselbusser, Ketelbueter), **Johannes,** a deacon and active leader of the Anabaptist congregation (*Christliche Brüder*) at Maastricht, Netherlands, baptized in 1541 by Leonhard Fälber (*q.v.*), was haled several times (1559, 1566) before the court in Jülich. He testified that he did not attend the state church services because idolatry was practiced there, that he held only baptism on confession of faith to be true baptism, the communion only a symbol. (Rembert, *Wiedertäufer,* 433, 450.)
                                                    H.S.B.

Kesselsdorf (also *Gesselsdorf,* Czech, *Kostolna*), a village in Slovakia (formerly Hungary) between Tyrnau (Trnava) and Trencin (Trentschin). Here the Hutterian Brethren began a Bruderhof in 1622, after they had been expelled from Moravia, on the estate of the manorial lord Hans Palffy (Wolkan, 572). Most of the Brethren there came from the Bruderhof Gostal (*q.v.*), Moravia. During the Thirty Years' War, the Brethren had much to suffer also in Slovakia; in 1626 the Kesselsdorf Bruderhof was plundered and partially destroyed (Wolkan, 604; Beck, 431). Later Turkish Wars again brought misery to this Bruderhof: on Sept. 6, 1665, Turkish troops plundered and destroyed it to a large extent. Forty-six persons were either killed or dragged away. One sister, Susanna, returned after 15 years of imprisonment in Turkey, after the Brethren had paid a ransom of 150 guilders (Beck, 532). The survivors were lodged for over a year in a near-by castle, during which time 26 brethren died. On Aug. 8, 1665, Count Nicolas Palffy gave them his ruined house at Schatmansdorf near Bratislava (Beck, 520).

During the era of the overseer Andreas Ehrenpreis (*q.v.*) Kesselsdorf reached a certain fame. It was here that a great number of written sermons and sermon-collections were drawn up (see **Sermons, Hutterite**). It was almost as if Kesselsdorf had been made a sort of official center of preaching. Here the preachers H. F. Küntsche (*q.v.,* d. 1659), Andreas Binder (d. 1662), Michel Mildner (d. 1660), and Tobias Bersch (*q.v.,* d. 1701) were active. There may have been several other preachers, whose names are not given. The *Klein-Geschichtsbuch* contains on pp. 204-14 and 218-21 excerpts from 26 such sermons, usually introduced as "by a pious and inspired teacher at Gesselsdorf." No names are given, partly on purpose to stress the collective nature of this material, and partly because the authors were actually not known. (Hutterite literature in general is to a large extent anonymous.) But the frequent reference to Kesselsdorf is at least significant. Ap-

parently these men were supported by the bishop Ehrenpreis who wanted to create henceforth an official tradition as to the how and what to preach. It so happened that a number of very good preachers were in residence at Kesselsdorf, and thus this new type of devotional literature came into being. It is still used today; in fact it represents more than anything else present-day Hutterite piety. HEGE, R.F.

Beck, *Geschichts-Bücher;* Wolkan, *Geschicht-Buch;* Zieglschmid, *Klein-Geschichtsbuch; ML* II, 484.

Kessler, Johannes (1502-74), reformer and chronicler of St. Gall, Switzerland. On his way to the University of Wittenberg at the inn "To the Black Bear" in Jena he met Martin Luther, who was returning from the Wartburg disguised as a knight. Upon his return to St. Gall, Kessler conducted Bible study classes, which were attended by the Anabaptists. A difference arose between them on the question of infant baptism, which finally led to a division. Kessler is the author of the *Sabbata,* a cultural and church history, in which he treats the Anabaptists with gratifying objectivity, though not with full understanding. It was published in 1866-68, edited by Ernst Götzinger, and in 1902 by Emil Egli and Rudolph Schoch. A new edition appeared in 1945 (Zollikofer, St. Gall). (*ML* II, 484.)
                                                    NEFF.

Kessler, Moritz, an Anabaptist martyr, is no doubt identical with "a tinker from the Emmental" in Switzerland. Moritz was a native of Sumiswald, and is frequently mentioned in the court records of the Emmental. On Oct. 12, 1532, he promised to desist from Anabaptism, but did not keep his promise, and was expelled with his family in February 1533 for perjury. Two years later he returned to Bern and was put to death in the first half of 1535. The record of the wages paid the sexton uses the words, "to bury Kessler, who was executed." Kessler's wife returned to the state church and had her child baptized on April 1, 1535. But later she again joined the Anabaptists and was banished with her children.   HEGE.

Th. de Quervain, *Kirchliche und soziale Zustände in Bern unmittelbar nach der Einführung der Reformation* (Bern, 1906); *Mart. Mir.* E 1129; P. Peachey, *Die soziale Herkunft der Schweizer Täufer in der Reformationszeit* (Karlsruhe, 1954) 45, 117, No. 177; *ML* II, 484.

Kestenholz: see **Chatenois.**

Ketelaer, Jan Geers, an Anbaptist martyr: see **Jan Geertsz.**

Ketelbueter, a family in Maastricht, Dutch province of Limburg, many members of which were active in early Anabaptism. The most prominent of them was Lenart (Leonard, Lentgen) Ketelbueter, who was baptized in September 1534 by Henric Rol (*q.v.*) and was a deacon of the Maastricht congregation. His son Simon was also an Anabaptist. In early 1535, when persecution arose in Maastricht, Lenart fled from Maastricht to Antwerp with a number of members of the congregation, among whom were a daughter and his son Jan, who was baptized at Antwerp. Here too Lenart was active, but soon all trace of him is lost. Lenart's wife

Anna was in prison at Maastricht in 1537; she was released, apparently because she had recanted. Another member of this family was Jan Ketelbueter, Lenart's brother, in whose home at Maastricht the Anabaptists sometimes met in 1534. Ruth Ketelbueter was also a deacon at Maastricht. On Jan. 28, 1535, he was arrested with other members of the congregation; he denied his faith and was beheaded on Feb. 13, 1535. His wife, also an Anabaptist, was put to death in 1539 at Nijmegen, Dutch province of Gelderland. Lysken Ketelbueter, a sister of Lenart and Jan, also a member of the congregation, had been Henric Rol's housekeeper; in the records it is suggested that she was Rol's wife.

Thoenis Ketelbueter and his wife of Maastricht still adhered to Anabaptism in 1545, when the congregation had been wiped out. Also a Jacob Ketelbueter is named as an Anabaptist. Probably Johann Kesselflicker (Ketelbueter), who was baptized in 1541 by Leonard Fälber (*q.v.*), also belonged to this family. vDZ.

W. Bax, *Het Protestantisme in het Bisdom Luik* I (The Hague, 1937) *passim*, see Index; Mellink, *Wederdopers, passim*, see Index; *DB* 1917, 120, Nos. 110-11.

Kettler, Johann Dietrich, a magistrate at Norden, East Friesland, Germany, who successfully defended the Mennonites in a debate before the imperial court at Vienna in 1705. Five years later the East Frisian government asked him for a "detailed report" on another dispute. Thereupon he drew up a detailed account covering 48 folio pages, which is of historical value. (*Menn. Bl.*, 1906, 21; *ML* II, 484.)
NEFF.

Kettner, Friedrich Gottlieb (1670-1739), a Lutheran theologian. During his last years he was the second pastor at St. John's in Magdeburg, Prussia, Germany. As *praeses*, with Karl Gottlob Zeidler as *respondens,* according to contemporary academic custom, he treated the life, doctrine, and writings of Menno Simons, as well as the confessions and teachings, diffusion, and customs of his followers, after a brief reference to Müntzer and Münster (in the series *Lipsiae, literis Christiani Scholvinii*), titled *Historiam Mennonis ejusque asseclarum* (1696). (*ML* II, 485.)
E.C.

Ketzer-Historie and **Ketzer-Lexikon.** The 16th century produced a special literary type, the "Catalog of heretics," created out of the utmost hostility against all non-orthodox, primarily non-Catholic Christian groups (including the Lutherans and Reformed). These often voluminous and most uncritical enumerations of heretics were intended to fight all those stigmatized as heretics and if possible to eradicate them. The public should be warned, and to dramatize the danger, the encyclopedic technique of listing all the hundreds of "false" teachers and "damnable" groups of heretics was used. One should remember that liberty of conscience (*q.v.*) and toleration were yet generally unknown ideas, abhorred and considered as being against all common sense.

Only a few exceptions to this attitude are known: a few humanists (like Sebastiano Castellio), then the Anabaptists whose idea of a believers' church presupposed voluntarism and a free decision of each individual, and finally the lonely figure of Sebastian Franck, the "spiritual reformer," whose *Chronica, Zeytbuch und Geschichtsbibel* (*q.v.*, 1531) for the first time dared to justify, if not actually to glorify, the otherwise greatly slandered "heretics" as persons who genuinely sought and found their own answer in matters of theology and doctrine. The intolerance of the century, however, prevailed and the heretics were persecuted all the same.

This spirit or attitude changed altogether toward the end of the 17th century, in the period commonly called the "age of reason" or from the point of view of church history the "age of Pietism" (*q.v.*). Christianity now became a matter of subjective experience (*Innerlichkeit*) while all questions of doctrine were submitted to a rational scrutiny and considered of secondary significance. Thus the picture changes almost to the opposite of the earlier century. Rationalists and pietists alike devaluate orthodoxy (and with it the "traditionalist" viewpoint of the church, e.g., the position of a Luther or Calvin), and discover so to speak the particular attraction of all sectarians, medieval and modern, and vindicate the "heretics" as the true orthodox (i.e., right believers), and vice versa.

The man who more than anyone else achieved this change of historical viewpoint is Gottfried Arnold (*q.v.*), mainly through his justly renowned *Unpartheyische Kirchen- und Ketzer-Historie* (Frankfurt, 1699). Erich Seeberg devoted a 600-page study to this book (see Bibliography) in which he traces the major roots of this historical viewpoint or historical evaluation. They are in the main threefold: (*a*) humanistic-rationalistic (example, Castellio), (*b*) legalistic: natural-law school (example, Grotius), and (*c*) mysticism and mystical theology (example, Jacob Böhme). Arnold himself stands halfway between mystical theology and Pietism, the religion of subjectivity. All these trends have one trait in common: the idea that the Church has fallen ever since Emperor Constantine became the very patron of the church in A.D. 312 or 313. Seeberg contraposes the "idea of tradition" (both in Catholicism and Protestant orthodoxy) to that of the "Fall" (*Verfallsidee*) of all sectarians, spiritual reformers, and the three afore-mentioned groups. According to the latter interpretation of church history, the "heretics" are the true representatives of the church of the spirit, who continue the genius of both Jesus Christ Himself and the apostles, but they are persecuted by the representatives of the "Anti-Christ," be they officials of the Roman or of the new Protestant state churches. Here the idea of vindication of what in recent times has often been called "the Left Wing of the Reformation" is the great theme of rewriting the history of the church. Like Jacob Böhme, Arnold considers as the "true heretics" not the poor sectarians but all those whom he calls "the non-regenerated nominal Christians" (Seeberg, 391). Arnold characterizes his own historiography by the new term *unpartheyisch,* that is non-partisan, by which he means the direct outlook at the Master Jesus Christ Himself, not through the eyes of any theological faction but straight through the eyes of the "pure spirit" as it is experienced in the rebirth of the soul. That Arnold actually was anything but "non-partisan" in his writing needs hardly to be mentioned. His sympathies lie clearly with the "Left-Wing" people, the Anabaptists and related groups.

There is of course no dependency of Arnold upon Franck, but we might agree with Seeberg's remark that one cannot help feeling "as if Arnold stretches out his hand to his lonely brother in the spirit across a period of one century and a half" (Seeberg, 517). Arnold's technique in writing his *Ketzer-Historie* "unpartheyisch" is to quote profusely from the writing of all "heretics," including the Anabaptists, thus letting them plead for themselves, and paying little attention to the usually cited opinions and reports of the official churchmen who naturally were biased against all these nonconformists. The fact that the book by Johann Heinrich Otte (*q.v.*) or Ottius, *Annales Anabaptistici* (Basel, 1672), had been published not long before might point to the renewed interest in Anabaptist source publications and their general evaluation. Arnold got his material, however, from many different sources, and one is amazed how much factual knowledge was available for the searching scholar already at the end of the 17th century; it needed but to be read with a friendly understanding.

Only as a footnote to this discussion on Arnold it should also be remarked here that Arnold's famous contemporary, Christian Thomasius, jurist and philosopher, in many regards depended on Arnold. Otherwise a lover of the "natural-law" idea, he published in 1697 a tract with the characteristic title, *Ob Ketzerey ein strafbares Verbrechen sey,* quite in line with Arnold's position, namely, that heresy is no crime at all but the personal right of each individual, upon which no government should infringe.

After Arnold this literary type of *Ketzer-Historie* flourished for almost a century, but the spirit of the 18th century changed the emphasis again, this time in favor of greater "objectivity" (not yet present in Arnold) and historical relativism. The good church historian, thus the opinion now runs, should not judge at all but collect and in a matter-of-fact fashion present the sources and facts just as they are. Needless to say that in this "age of enlightenment" the appreciation for the sectarians, above all for the "primitive-Christian" Anabaptists, was rather poor and inadequate. But the same was also true for the understanding by orthodoxy. In any case, at long last the term *Ketzer* lost its sting and received more the character of a technical term (somewhat like today's term "Left Wing of the Reformation"). But it should also be stressed that all the authors presently to be quoted were equally opposed to both the defenders and the accusers of the "heretics." In no case can they be called their friends or sympathizers as Arnold and some of his friends had been.

Here is the list of books related to this type of church-historiography:

(1) Anonymous: *Gottfried Arnold, Fortsetzung und Erläuterung der Unpartheyischen Kirchen- und Ketzer Historie,* Frankfurt, 1715, i.e., vol. II, part 3, and vol. III (also new editions 1729 and 1740). (Arnold had died in 1714.)

(2) Johann Georg Walch, *Historische und Theologische Einleitung in die Religions-Streitigkeiten, welche sonderlich ausser der evangelisch-lutherischen Kirche entstanden.* 5 vv., 1724-36 (some of the volumes saw a 3rd edition).

(3) Johann Lorentz von Mosheim, (a) *Versuch einer unpartheyischen und gründlichen Ketzergeschichte* (Helmstädt, 1746, 2nd ed. 1748), treating only the history of the Ophites and the Apostel-Brüder, and

(b) *Anderweitiger Versuch einer vollständigen und unpartheyischen Ketzergeschichte* (Helmstädt, 1748), treating exclusively the history of Servetus in great detail.

(4) Johann Conrad Füsslin, (a) *Neue und unpartheyische Kirchen und Ketzer Historie der Mittleren Zeit.* 3 vv. (Frankfurt and Leipzig, 1770-74) and

(b) *Beyträge zur . . . Kirchen . . . Geschichte des Schweitzerlandes.* 5 vv. (Zürich, 1741-53). Its subtitle states: *Enthaltende authentische bishero zum theil ungedruckte, zum theil gantz rare Urkunden . . . darinnen die Zwistigkeiten der Römisch-Catholischen, der Lutheraner, und der Reformirten, wie auch der Wiedertäuffer und anderer Sectierer . . . an den Tag gelegt werden*—a truly nonpartisan program.

To this list of objective Ketzer-Historien belong also several more encyclopedic works of that kind and period, namely,

(1) John M. Mehlig, *Historisches Kirchen- und Ketzerlexicon,* 2 vv. (Chemnitz, 1758)

(2) J. G. H., *Compendieuses Kirchen- und Ketzer-Lexicon* (Schneeberg, 1733, 1734, 1744, and 1756). A fifth edition came out in 1789 at Stendal under the title, *Kurtzgefasstes Kirchen- und Ketzer-Lexicon.* The initials J. G. H. stand for Johann Gottfried Hering (M. Holtzmann, *Deutsches Anonymen Lexikon* VI, 1911, No. 6159). Either out of modesty or for the fun of anonymity, J. G. H. disclaims any credit for the compilation of this seemingly popular encyclopedia; he claims only to be the editor concerned with the publication as such. (*ML* II, 496, erroneously gives 1731 as the date of the first edition, and takes Schneeberg, the place of publication, for the name of the editor.)

(3) *Ketzer-Lexicon, oder: geschichtliche Darstellung der Irrlehren, Spaltungen und sonderbaren Meinungen im Christenthume . . . ,* translated from the French of V. de Perrodil and edited by Peter Fritz (3 vols., Würzburg, 1828-29), had the French title, *Memoires pour servir à l'histoire des égarements de l'esprit humain par raport à la religion chrétienne: on Dictionnaire des Hérésies, des Erreurs et des schismes . . .* (Paris, 1764). The first part of this encyclopedia deals with the "heresies" from the beginning of the church to the 16th century. The second part treats all "heresies" in an alphabetical order. Among them are found the Anabaptists (Vol. II, pp. 67-90), Mennonites, Carlstadt, Müntzer, etc. The presentation is biased and from a Catholic point of view.

(4) *Ketzer-Lexicon . . .* (Würzburg, 1828) is an alphabetical treatment in three volumes of all groups

which had separated from the main body of the Catholic Church throughout the centuries. It first appeared in the French language and was translated into German by Peter Fritz. The treatment is from a Catholic point of view and includes the Anabaptist and Mennonite groups.

Again as in the case of church historiography also these volumes represent the complete reversal of the spirit of the "Ketzer-Catalogs" of former centuries. Now a sort of curiosity prevails; one just wants to get information about these strange outsiders and their peculiarities. That the general theme of the "Fall of Christianity" since Constantine found sympathetic ears in this century may be easily understood.

This spirit, however, did not continue for too long. With the coming of the period commonly called "Romanticism," the pendulum swings again in the opposite direction. Traditionalism and orthodoxy become dominant again, and with them that kind of church historiography which condemns (and even slanders) sectarianism, and in particular Anabaptism. When one hundred years later (20th century) a more sober viewpoint eventually succeeded, the old term *Ketzer* was dropped altogether. The book by Walter Nigg, *Das Buch der Ketzer* (Zürich, 1949), is too broadly conceived to be of value for the present discussion.   R.F.

Walther Köhler, "Kirchengeschichtsschreibung" and "Philosophie der Kirchengeschichte" in *RGG* III (1929) with ample bibliography; Erich Seeberg, *Gottfried Arnold, die Wissenschaft und Mystik seiner Zeit, Studien zur Histographie und zur Mystik* (Meerane i. Sa., 1923) a work of outstanding value; E. Troeltsch, *Social Teaching of the Christian Churches* (1930, in particular p. 788), a volume which emphasizes the idea of natural law in relation to the judgment concerning the heretics; likewise also the several writings by Wilhelm Dilthey (not available in English); R. Friedmann, "Conception of the Anabaptists," *Church History* IX (1940), in particular 349; also Roland H. Bainton, "The Left Wing of the Reformation," *Journal of Religion* XXI (1941) 124-34; Horst Quiring, article "Mennonisten-Lexikon," *ML* III, 95; for the 16th-century heretic-catalogues see also Henry DeWind, "A Sixteenth Century Report on the Religious Conditions in Moravia," in *MQR* XXVIII (1955).

Keulen, Pieter van: see Peter van Coelen.

Keurlis, Pieter, one of the first German immigrants to America (13 families from Crefeld), who landed in Pennsylvania on Oct. 6, 1683, and founded Germantown. He acquired 200 acres of land from J. Telner (*q.v.*), and was the first German bartender in America. He was a Crefeld Quaker, formerly a Mennonite.

Fr. Nieper, *Die ersten deutschen Auswanderer von Krefeld nach Pennsylvanien* (Neukirchen, 1940); W. J. Hull, *William Penn and the Dutch Quaker Migration to Pennsylvania* (Swarthmore, 1935) 231; *ML* II, 486.

Keuter, Albert, b. Jan. 7, 1892, at Blokzijl, Dutch province of Overijssel, d. March 10, 1945, at the concentration camp of Bergen-Belsen, Germany. He studied theology at the University and the Mennonite Seminary at Amsterdam and served as pastor in the Mennonite congregations of Oost- and West-Graftdijk 1917-20, Twisk and Medemblik 1920-25, Akkrum 1925-28, and The Hague 1928 until Jan. 4, 1944, on which date he was arrested by the German Nazi officials, the Netherlands then being occupied

by the Germans. It was his Christian conviction that he should fight the pseudo-religious ideas of National Socialism and support the victims of Hitlerism in the Netherlands. After his arrest he was at first imprisoned at Scheveningen near The Hague, then at Vught, Dutch province of North Brabant, where he found his oldest son, who had been arrested at Amsterdam; in September 1944 he was transported to the camp of Heinkel in Germany, where he for some time shared his bunk with A. du Croix, Mennonite pastor of Winschoten and also imprisoned by the Germans; later on he was transported to a camp near Sachsenhausen and finally to Bergen-Belsen, where he died five days after his son. Like a true Christian he was a blessing even in prison; when it was possible he preached or comforted his fellow prisoners. The strong faith and the cordial friendliness of this "modern martyr" remain in grateful memory of many members of The Hague congregation. vDZ.

H. W. Mcihuizen, *Een dader des Woords* (Amsterdam, n.d.-1946); idem, *"Laat Uw werk aan Uwe knechten gezien worden,"* memorial service, held in the Mennonite church of The Hague, July 1, 1945 (The Hague, 1945)

Keyn, Antony: see Keim, Anthoni.

Keyser, a Mennonite family name in the Netherlands. According to a Dutch family tradition the relatives of Leonhard Kaiser (*q.v.*), a Lutheran martyr (van Braght, *Mart. Mir.,* erroneously lists him among the Anabaptists), burned at the stake in 1527 at Schärding, Austria, moved from Austria to the Netherlands, where they spelled their family name "Keyser." In Holland they joined the Anabaptists. The tradition of the Austrian ancestry of the Dutch Keyser family, however, is not very likely true. Keyser is a rather common Dutch family name, both Mennonite and non-Mennonite.

At Amsterdam the Keysers were manufacturers and businessmen. Mattheus Keyser, a member of the Waterlander congregation at Amsterdam, had some disagreement with Jan Theunisz (*q.v.*) in 1612, and in 1613 he and some others left the Waterlander group of the Bevredigden (*q.v.*) to join the Afgedeelden (*q.v.*). Another Keyser of Amsterdam, Dirk Gerritsz Keyser was married to a daughter of Tobias Govertsz van de Wyngaert (*q.v.*), preacher of the Flemish congregation of Amsterdam, one of the Amsterdam representatives to sign the Dordrecht Confession of 1632. Dirck Keyser, b. 1635, d. Nov. 30, 1714, the oldest son of Dirk Gerritsz, emigrated from Amsterdam, where he was a silk merchant, to Pennsylvania in 1688 and was an active member of the Germantown Mennonite congregation. His son, Peter Keyser, who came with his father to America, left the Mennonite Church in 1719 to join the Dunkards (*q.v.*).

As early as 1534 Obbe Philips (*q.v.*) administered baptism in the house of a broker, called de Keyser(e) at Delft, Dutch province of South Holland, and in 1539 Arent Jacobssen Keyser (*q.v.*), of De Rijp, was drowned at Monnikendam in the Dutch province of North Holland. Since the 16th century the family name of Keyser (Keyzer) is very common on the Dutch island of Texel, all being Mennonites; Albert Dirksz Keyser was a preacher of the

Waterlander congregation of Burg on the island of Texel 1713-55, succeeding his father, Dirk Pietersz Keyser, while many members of this family served here as deacons. Albert Pieters Keyzer (Keyser) (d. 1731) was preacher of the Frisian congregation of Wieringen, province of North Holland 1690-1700; Dirk Cornelisz Keyser was preacher of the Frisian congregation of Langedijk and Koedijk in the province of North Holland 1723-ca. 68, and his brother Willem Cornelisz Keyser was preacher in the same congregation 1727-d. 60, and Dirk Keyser in the early 18th century was a preacher of the Frisian congregation of Wormerveer. S. L. Keyser of Amsterdam, a descendant of this family, is now (1955) treasurer of the Dutch Mennonite Mission Association.   HEGE, vDZ.

DB 1884, 74; 1891, 43, 57; Mellink, *Wederdopers*, 211; *Naamlijst* 1731 ff.; Chr. S. Keyser, *The Keyser Family* (Philadelphia, 1889); H. S. Bender, "The Founding of the Mennonite Church in America at Germantown, 1683-1708," *MQR* VII (October 1933) 227-30, especially 230-33; *ML* II, 451.

KfK: see **Kommission für Kirchenangelegenheiten.**

Kharkov, a province and city in the Ukraine, South Russia, area 12,000 square miles, population (1946) 2,500,000. According to the evaluation of 1909 there were in the province of Kharkov, especially in the district of Izyum, 1,386 settlers of Mennonite origin, divided in two groups of colonies, Naumenko and Zamoilovka. The valuation amounted to over 10 million rubles.

The Naumenko settlement (established in 1889) was grouped around the station of Barvenkovo of the Lozovaya-Rostov Railway. It included the villages of Grigoryevka, Petrovka, Elenovka, Vassilyevka, and the factory and mill owners in Barvenkovo. Their founders emigrated from the Mennonite Brethren group at Einlage (Kitchkas), and their villages formed a subsidiary of that church. An exception was Grigoryevka, which was composed of settlers from New York, the Chortitza daughter colony. The individual settlements had good school buildings, and Barvenkovo had a school of commerce supported principally by Mennonites. There were M.B. church buildings in Barvenkovo and Petrovka. Inadequate connections with the mother colony, together with economic deterioration caused some loss of religious and intellectual life. Sharp opposition to the local authorities and to the Mennonites at first had an unfavorable effect. The group had about 16,200 acres of land, besides important industrial establishments, and numbered over 600 souls.

The second group, Zamoilovka, near Bachmetyevka was founded by emigrants from the Molotschna and consisted of several villages founded in 1888 and after. They were Zamoilovka, Shostakovo, Novo-Stepeno, Ryskovo, etc. The villages were laid out on land which they had bought.

Besides these villages there were several settlements of German Lutherans (Elizavetovka near Barvenkovo, Ivanovka, etc.) and Baptists.

After the Russian Revolution there were Mennonite students attending the schools of higher learning in the city of Kharkov. After 1922 the Verband

Bürger holländischer Herkunft (*q.v.*) had its headquarters in Kharkov. (*ML* I, 339.)   C.B.

Kharkov, capital (pop. 833,000) of the Ukraine, Russia, a railroad and industrial center, founded in 1654, played a significant role for the Mennonites of the Ukraine. A number of small settlements were established in the province of Kharkov (*q.v.*). Some Mennonites found their way to the city before World War I. N. H. Hildebrandt was instructor of German in the high school of Kharkov (1898-1918). All of his children received a very good education. Käte was a physician. His son-in-law, J. L. Festa, was a tutor of many Mennonite teachers. The firm Braun and Epp, Mennonites originally from Tiegenhof, Danzig, had the agency of the Mercedes cars, etc., there. J. S. Ediger was a successful practicing homeopathic physician until 1917. Kharkov usually had a number of Mennonite students. Among them were Eliesabet Isaak and J. Dick, both of whom studied medicine.

After World War I, B. B. Janz and A. Dick resided for a time (1922- ?) in Kharkov. Both represented the Mennonites and were active in the *Verband Bürger holländischer Herkunft* (*q.v.*). In addition, Kharkov was always a stopping place for Mennonites traveling through. Evidently, however, the Mennonites did not organize a congregation here. Some attended the Lutheran Church and others worshiped with the Baptists. (A. H. Dueck, "Memorien," ms.)   C.K.

Khartch, a village of the Mennonite settlement in the district of Khassav-Yurt (*q.v.*), Russia, in the Terek region, founded in 1901 on the left bank of the Sulak River, which flows into the Caspian Sea, and is crossed by the Talma Canal. It comprised 30 farms of 108 acres each. The inhabitants, who were immigrants from the Mennonite Molotschna settlement in Taurida, were engaged in agriculture and sheep-raising; a small mercantile business also developed. Khartch had a church in which the Mennonites of the western part of the colony met for services. The village supported an elementary school, which was attended exclusively by Mennonite children. (*ML* I, 339.)   HEGE.

Khassav-Yurt: see **Terek Mennonite Settlement.**

Kherson, a city (1939 pop. 97,186) in the Ukraine, Russia, on the right bank of the Dnieper, 15 miles before its opening into the Black Sea. The province of Kherson (1946) numbers 700,000 inhabitants and with its 10,000 square miles it was formerly one of the largest in the country, bounded by the Dnieper and Dniester rivers and the Black Sea. Its soil is fertile and adapted to wheat raising. The population was mixed, made up of immigrants, including a large number of Germans, who in 1804, 1808, 1817, and later established more than 150 villages, with 810,000 acres of land.

In 1871 the Molotschna Mennonite volosts, Halbstadt and Gnadenfeld, purchased over 54,000 acres situated north of the opening of the Vizan into the Ingulets, where they established the Mennonite daughter settlement of Zagradovka with 16 villages, which for the most part had the names of Molotschna villages (Ohrloff, Tiege, etc.). In 1918 the settlement owned over 86,400 acres not including the very important private farms. There were also several daughter villages of this settlement in the province of Kherson, partly on their own land, and partly on rented land. The Mennonite population numbered 5-6,000 souls, of whom one fifth belonged to the Mennonite Brethren, with a meetinghouse in Tiege, and the others to the Mennonite Church, with a church in Nikolaifeld, where a central school was also built for the district in 1895. Near this colony was located one of the forestry services on which the Mennonites satisfied requirements for military duty. In addition the settlement founded a daughter colony in 1894 near Tempelhof in the province of Stavropol and in 1909 the larger one near Barnaul (q.v.). (ML I, 340.)   C.B.

Khiva, a former khanate in Central Asia, conquered by the Russians in 1873. All possessions of Khiva on the northern side of the Amu Darya became Russian and the rest was also subject to Russia although ruled by the khan. Under the Soviets Khiva became a part of the Turkmen SSR.

A group of Mennonites from the province of Samara under the leadership of Claas Epp (q.v.) in 1880 sought refuge in Central Asia to escape military conscription and to prepare to meet Christ at His Second Coming. After unsuccessful attempts to settle near Tashkent, they proceeded in the direction of Khiva where they settled in 1882 on the Amu Darya River. Since they were constantly attacked by the surrounding native population, some 20 families returned to Samara in 1884 in order to set out for America.

The remainder under the leadership of Claas Epp settled on the oasis of Ak-Metchet (q.v.) in the vicinity of the city of Khiva. During the pioneer days numerous families left the settlement to go to America. After the economic hardships had been overcome, and after the death of Claas Epp in 1913 their chiliastic views gradually disappeared and the settlement attained the status of a normal religious and economic life. During the Soviet regime it was dissolved and the group exiled.   C.B., C.K.

Claas Epp, *Die Entsiegelung des Propheten Daniel* (Alt-Tschau, 1878); Franz Bartsch, *Unser Auszug nach Mittel-Asien* (Halbstadt, 1907); J. Janzen, "Mennonite Colony in Turkestan," *MQR* IV (October 1930) 282-89; *ML* I, 347.

Kicin, a small village near Vola-Vodzinska, not far from Warsaw, Poland, was established by German Mennonite and Lutheran settlers on the estate of Count Kicinski around 1842. Evidently the Mennonite settlers came from the Deutsch-Kazun Mennonite settlement near Warsaw. Peter Ewert (q.v.) of this community took a large number of the Mennonites with him into the Baptist Church, which was started here in 1855. Mennonites of this community were probably members of the Vola-Vodzinska Mennonite Church (q.v.), which in turn was a subsidiary of Deutsch-Kazun (q.v.)   C.K.

Eduard Kupsch, *Geschichte der Baptisten in Polen* (Lodz, 1932) 59 ff.

Kidron Mennonite Church (GCM), now extinct, was located three miles southeast of Taloga, Okla. It was represented for the first time in the General Conference session of 1911, although three years earlier it had had a membership of 25. The minister in 1911 was Heinrich Reimer, and in 1945, the last time the church was listed in the official minutes of the General Conference, H. U. Schmidt was the pastor.   M.G.

Kidron Mennonite Church (MC), located in Kidron, Wayne Co., Ohio, a member of the Ohio-Eastern Conference, was organized Oct. 18, 1936, with 332 members, under the leadership of bishops Aaron Mast of Belleville, Pa., and A. J. Steiner of North Lima, Ohio, who had been appointed by the Ohio-E.A.M. Conference to organize the group which was withdrawing from the Sonnenberg (q.v.) independent (Swiss) congregation, founded in the community in 1817 by immigrants from the Swiss Jura congregations. The membership in 1954 was 491, most of whom were rural people with a Swiss background. The meetinghouse, a brick structure with a seating capacity of 800, was erected in 1937. On Nov. 15, 1937, Allen Bixler was ordained minister, and Reuben Hofstetter deacon. On May 24, 1938, Isaac Zuercher was ordained minister. On Dec. 21, 1941, Hofstetter was ordained as bishop and has the oversight of the congregation. All three men were still serving in 1956. A mission outpost was started at Dillonvale, Ohio, in 1942, and with several workers stationed there had a membership of 23 in 1956.   A.Bix.

Kief Mennonite Brethren Church of Kief, McHenry Co., N.D., a member of the Central District Conference, was organized in 1911 by Ludwig Seibel with 25 members of Russian racial background. This congregation affiliated itself with M.B. congregations of Russian-speaking people in Canada. The present church building was erected in 1911. Ministers who have served this congregation are E. Lushenko, who served until 1923, and Daniel Rerekrestenko until 1943. These have been assisted by Ed Simbalenko 1923-44 and after that by Levi Simbalenko for three years. The membership in 1953 was about 35.   A.A.D.

Kieferndorf, Philipp, a preacher of the Mennonite church at Monsheim, Hesse, Germany, 1889-94, a native of Leistadt (Palatinate), was the first minister whose theological education was sponsored by the *Vereinigung* of Mennonite churches in Germany. He studied at the universities of Basel, Jena, Heidelberg, and Berlin. In 1892 he wrote a treatise on the oath, *Der Eid* (Worms, 1892), the first systematic treatment of the question. Later Kieferndorf migrated to Jerusalem, and died there. (*ML* II, 486.)   Hege.

Kiel, in Schleswig Holstein, Germany, population (1950) 253,857, is the seat of a Mennonite congregation, founded in 1948 by refugees from the Danzig area who settled in this region. In 1956 it had 332 baptized members, with Hans Rempel as pastor, who was at the same time serving as pastor of a Lutheran congregation in the city. Most of the members live outside the city in surrounding towns and villages.

In December 1946 the MCC relief program in this area was begun with headquarters in Kiel, continuing until the summer of 1950. Until the summer of 1948 Kiel was also the MCC headquarters for the entire British Zone, with C. J. Dyck as director.

H.S.B.

Kielstra, Tjepke, b. April 27, 1852, at Bolsward, d. Feb. 4, 1936, at Zeist, was one of the most active and prominent Mennonite ministers in the Netherlands in the late 19th century. He was trained at the University of Groningen and the Mennonite Theological Seminary at Amsterdam. Appointed ministerial candidate in 1876, he first served the small congregation of Zwartsluis, at the same time being in charge of the Mennonites living in the neighboring town of Meppel (*q.v.*). Through his work in Meppel a congregation was founded in 1879, and a church was built there, dedicated by Kielstra on Jan. 11, 1880. In 1885 he was called as minister of the congregation at Middelburg (*q.v.*). During his Middelburg period (1885-1901) Kielstra's great gifts, both of heart and intellect, came to full development. In this time he served not only the Middelburg congregation, but until 1899 also Vlissingen and Goes. All these congregations experienced a period of spiritual prosperity; in all three towns Kielstra dedicated new churches. His book *Het godsdienstig leven, eene schets der Christelijke geloofs- en zedeleer,* published at Amsterdam in 1883 (reprinted in 1890, 1901, and 1914), is evidence of his thorough catechetical instruction. (This book was translated by Kielstra into German; this translation appeared shortly after his death: *Das religiöse Leben, Skizze einer christlichen Glaubens- und Sittenlehre,* Bern-Leipzig, 1936.)

During his Middelburg period Kielstra, who had already given the impulse to the publication of the Dutch Mennonite weekly *De Zondagsbode* (*q.v.*), in 1894 (after failing in 1890) successfully insisted on the formation of a committee to care for those Mennonites who were living in towns where there was no Mennonite congregation (Commissie voor de Doopsgezinden in de Verstrooiing, *q.v.*). He himself took an active part in the work of the committee and even after he had resigned continued to visit the Mennonites in the diaspora.

In 1901 (farewell sermon on Feb. 17) he left the congregation of Middelburg, and at the same time the ministry, to be a district public school inspector (until 1927). In the meantime he was also a teacher of Hebrew, having already taught Hebrew in the Gymnasium of Middelburg, and continued to teach in Amersfoort until 1930. He did not return to the ministry. In 1910 he seriously considered accepting a call to the congregation of Hallum, Friesland, but finally rejected it. Nevertheless his love for the church was unfailing; he was a beloved guest-preacher in many congregations. In Zeist, where he lived after 1916, there was no Mennonite congregation, but Kielstra, with the help of some others, succeeded in founding one in 1921, and the

new church of Zeist was dedicated in 1933 by Kielstra, who was then 81 years old.

Besides his *Het godsdienstig leven* of 1883, Kielstra also published some booklets on Mennonite history; e.g., *Hans Denck* (No. 3 of the set of booklets for the Mennonites in the diaspora), *Het oproer te Munster* and *Over oud Evangelische gemeenten.* He also published some sermons, among them *De vreugde van den godsdienstigen mensch* (Zwartsluis, 1880), a dedication sermon of the Meppel church, and a larger number of articles in the *Zondagsbode*. A commemorative sermon preached in 1926 to celebrate his fiftieth year in the ministry was published under the title *Na Vijftig Jaar, 1876-1926.*

Kielstra, being a highly gifted teacher, perhaps more than preacher, had a keen interest in the social problems of his time. With his warm heart he did much for the welfare of the common people, not only during his pastorate, but also in later years; he also wrote a number of papers to insist on better living conditions and pensioning of the working classes. But Kielstra in the first place was a pious man; he was a moderate liberal, but he was not a rationalist like many of his contemporaries, considering the assurance of a heart enlightened by the Holy Spirit of greater value than the acquisition of intellectual knowledge. His whole life was a plea for ethical holiness. In 1890, when a meeting was held to discuss the question whether Mennonites should go into the army if compulsory military service should be introduced (this indeed happened in the Netherlands in 1898), Kielstra declared that the New Testament is a strong testimony against force and that he was not willing to act contrary to the clear statements of the New Testament, for "conscience must not yield to any claim of society."

Kielstra was married twice: in 1876 to H.C.W.A. Eger (1853-92), who bore eight children, and in 1894 to Maria P. Fak Brouwer (1877-1934).

His oldest son was Johannes Coenraad Kielstra (1878-1951), who studied law, then became a government official in the Dutch East Indies, and successively rose to high military ranks. He was later a professor at the universities of Utrecht and Wageningen in the Netherlands, teaching agrarian law. In 1933-42 he was governor of the Dutch territory of Surinam and afterwards ambassador of the Netherlands to Mexico. Like his father he was a loyal member of the church. On the matter of military service, however, he largely differed with his father. In a booklet, *Geweld en Rechtshandhaving* (Assen, n.d.), he controverted the views of unilateral disarmament and refusal of military service.

One of the daughters of Tjepke Kielstra, Henriëtte Charlotte Kielstra, b. 1882 at Zwartsluis, performed no mean achievements in behalf of the schooling of the deaf. She also inherited her father's love for the Mennonite Church, being for more than 25 years, until 1954, a deaconess and a member of the church board of the congregation of Rotterdam.

vD Z.

DJ 1937, 25-33, with portrait; *De Zondagsbode,* Feb. 9, 1936; *DB* 1882, 3, 5; 1883, 43-66; 1891, 101; 1894, 75; 1895, 144; 1901, 214; 1905, 193; 1910, 231; *ML* II, 486.

Kien, Johannes, preacher of the Mennonite congregation of Middelburg, Dutch province of Zeeland, and author of *Den Honigraet der Godgeleerdheid* (Middelburg, 1704) and other theological treatises, in 1710 left the Mennonite Church and joined the Reformed. His reason for this step was "that the Reformed Church knows only one way to salvation, i.e., faith in Jesus Christ, and the Mennonites three ways; i.e., nature, the law of Moses, and the Gospel of Jesus Christ." After his transfer to the Reformed Church Kien tried to be appointed pastor of the Reformed church at Essequebo in the Dutch West Indies, but he seems not to have obtained this office since in 1725 he was still living in the province of Zeeland. For his leaving the Mennonites and his theological views Kien was attacked by his former Mennonite colleague Gerardus de Wind in *Johannes Kiens redenen des geloofs onderzocht* (Vlissingen, 1711). Johannes Kien was born at Middelburg ca. 1670. (*DB* 1891, 63 f.; 1895, 121; *Biogr. Wb.* IV, 747 f.)

vDZ.

Kiernica, a Ruthenian village in Galicia (*q.v.*). In 1848 Peter and Magdalene Kintzi (*q.v.*) of Einsiedel bought the 3,000-acre estate Kiernica, and laid it out in farms for their eight married children. Settling them on individual farms rather than in a village was an innovation among the Galician Mennonites. From this beginning a congregation developed which owned a church building by 1862, and employed Johannes van der Smissen of Altona as their minister. He served until 1868. After the merger of all Mennonite settlements in Galicia into one organization, Kiernica was for a long time the seat of the leading minister, Johann Klein (*q.v.*). In the constitution (1909) of the Galician Mennonite Church it had the name Kiernica-Lemberg, but the official center was transferred to Lemberg.

The founders had intended that Kiernica remain a Mennonite settlement, and specified in their will that it should not be sold to others; but this clause was declared illegal, and many Mennonites sold their land and moved away. In 1934 there were six families resident there, with the names of Kintzi, Ewy, Müller, and Schmidt. The meetinghouse was sold after World War I.

J.Ru.

P. Bachmann, *Mennoniten in Kleinpolen* (Lemberg, 1934) 220-27; Artur Miller, "Mennonitengemeinde Kiernica-Lemberg," *Unser Blatt* (Gronau i.W.) III (1949) No. 54 (Nov. 1), No. 55 (Nov. 15), No. 56/57 (December), IV (1950) No. 58 (Jan. 1), and No. 59 (Feb. 1); *ML* II, 486.

Kiesling, Johann Rudolf (1706-78), a Lutheran theologian and Orientalist. In addition to many other works, some in Latin and some in German, he published (Reval and Leipzig) in 1776 *Das Lehrgebäude der Wiedertäufer, nach den Grundsätzen des Martin Czechowitz, eines der ältesten Bestreiter der Kindertauf und seiner Nachfolger, zur Vertheidigung der Kindertaufe.* After his death and without his name another title was published in 1779: *Historische Untersuchung der anabaptistischen Streitigkeiten, nebst einer exegetisch-dogmatischen Prüfung der alten und neuen Einwürfe wider die Kindertaufe.*

The book by Martin Czechowic (d. 1613), a Pol-ish Socinian, which Kiesling attacked, had the title, *De paedobaptistarum errorum origine et de ea opinione, qua infantes baptizandos esse in primo nativitatis eorum exortu creditur* (Lublin, 1575, copies were in the state and university libraries at Königsberg). Czechowic attacked 14 errors of the advocates of infant baptism, and, in an appendix, also the Socinian idea that baptism is unnecessary for those who believe and have grown up in Christianity.

Kiesling, in 31 paragraphs, answers the most important assertions of the old book, following its order. But he forgets to say that paragraph 16 concerns the ninth error, paragraphs 21-23 the twelfth error, paragraphs 26 and 27 the fourteenth error, and paragraphs 28-30 concern the appendix; and the approximately 40 excerpts from Czechowic are by no means *verbatim;* indeed, one might think Kiesling had a different version, or that he was making up his own Latin extracts. (For bibliography, see *ML* II, 486 f.)

E.C.

Kiessling, Hans, one of the leading personalities of the Augsburg Anabaptists, holding the office of deacon. His activity ended with the martyrs' synod, which met in Augsburg the last week of August 1527 (see **Augsburg**), and in which he participated. He was seized before the week had passed. On the rack information on other members of the congregation was expressed from him. Other arrests followed. On Oct. 18, 1527, he was banished from the city as an Anabaptist ringleader with Eitelhans Langenmantel (*q.v.*), Endres Widholz, Gall Fischer, and Peter Scheppach. The exiles met in surrounding villages for mutual comfort and strength. Langenmantel was repeatedly visited in Göppingen by Kiessling, Widholz, and Fischer; he was living in the house of Laux Lang, a brother of the archbishop of Salzburg and Cardinal Matthias Lang (*q.v.*). In 1529 Kiessling was permitted to return to Augsburg. Nothing is known about his further activity.

HEGE.

Keller, *Reformation;* Chr. Meyer, "Zur Geschichte der Wiedertäufer in Oberschwaben," in *Ztscht des Hist. Vereins für Schwaben* (1874); Fr. Roth, "Zur Geschichte der Wiedertäufer in Oberschwaben," *loc. cit.,* XXVII and XXVIII (1900, 1901); *idem, Augsburgs Reformationsgeschichte* (Munich, 1901); *ML* II, 487.

Kill Creek Mennonite Church (MC), now extinct, located in Osborne Co., Kans., took its name from a near-by creek and the township in which it was located in Osborne Co., Kan., took its name from a vania, arrived about 1875, and the congregation was organized soon afterwards by Bishop Abraham Newschwanger. A church was built in Kill Creek Township about 15 miles southwest of Osborne, the county seat. The membership of the congregation was never large. It was composed of such names as Newschwanger, Winey, Bickel, Graybill, and Shellenberger. Because of crop failures and also because of dissension the congregation died out about 1910. The church building was sold to the Presbyterians.

G.G.Y.

Killig, Andreas, concerning whom nothing is known except that he was a Hutterite and the author of the song, "Mein Geist lässt mich nicht ruhen." It bears the heading, "A new, sad song of the persecution that took place in Gross-Schitzen in the year 1725." The story is told in 80 stanzas.

NEFF.

Die Lieder der Hutterischen Brüder (Scottdale, 1914) 879 ff.; *ML* II, 487.

Kimedoncius (Kimdonck), **Jacobus,** b. *ca.* 1550 at Kempen near Cologne, d. 1596 at Heidelberg, Germany, was for some time a Reformed pastor at Gent, Belgium, and at Middelburg in the Netherlands. He attacked Dirk Philipsz (*q.v.*) in his book *Van der Doope onses Heeren Jesu Christi, bekentenisse door Dierick Philips, metgaders een beandtwoordinghe derselver bekentenisse* (Middelburg, 1589). (*Biogr. Wb.* IV, 835 f.; *DB* 1908, 26 f.)

VDZ.

Kimswerd, Dutch province of Friesland, where Leenaert Bouwens in 1551-82 baptized 125 or 132 persons; in 1563-65 he baptized here no less than 65. This large number suggests the existence of a congregation, of which, however, nothing is known. The newly baptized members may have joined the congregation of near-by Arum.   VDZ.

Kinderbote, a periodical (GCM) published at Rosthern, Sask., was founded in 1887. Carl van der Smissen (*q.v.*) was editor of the *Kinderbote* for many years. Since he was opposed to fairy tales and fiction the *Kinderbote* had a rather sober viewpoint. After World War I, since the German language was banned from the lower schools and the children began to speak English, the *Kinderbote* contained an English section, which grew larger and larger.

When the great immigration to Canada started in 1923, the General Conference at Saskatoon in 1938 agreed that there should be an English paper for the United States. Accordingly the *Junior Messenger* appeared, in addition to the *Kinderbote*. J. G. Rempel of Rosthern was the editor of the *Kinderbote* 1940-56. He was followed by Cornelia Lehn.

In 1953 the *Kinderbote* had 2,400 subscribers, about 750 of them in South America, chiefly in Paraguay. The *Kinderbote* appears on the first and 15th of the month, i.e., 24 issues per year, 4 pages, 9½ x 12½ in.   J.G.R.

Kinderliedekens, ofte Jeugdsboecxken was a Dutch booklet of an anonymous compiler containing religious songs for children. It was published at Hoorn in 1630 and was much in use among Mennonites. The compiler or author was probably a Mennonite.   VDZ.

DJ 1837, 65; M. Schagen, *Naamlijst van Doopsgezinde schrijveren* (1745) 59.

Kindert, Pieter van der: see Verkindert, Pieter.

King (Koenig, Kinig, Konigh, König), a Swiss Mennonite family name found in the Palatinate Mennonite census lists as early as 1717 when Hans König was registered in the district of Alzey. In 1770 another Hans König was the preacher of a Mennonite congregation in the territory of Waldeck. In 1940 there was one Mennonite named König living in Northwest Germany and seven in South Germany.

On Dec. 22, 1744, Jacob, Christian, and Samuel König arrived in Philadelphia from Rotterdam. These are the ancestors of many Mennonites with this name scattered through Pennsylvania, Ohio, Illinois, and Kansas. Between 1732 and 1806, 38 persons bearing the name König arrived in Philadelphia, although it is not known how many of these were Mennonites.

Nicolas King (Koenig) (1814-76) was born in Switzerland and came to America in 1832, moved to Wayne Co., Ohio, and later to Fulton County. He was ordained minister in 1844 and bishop in 1871. John P. King (1827-87) was born in Mifflin Co., Pa., moved to Champaign Co., Ohio, in 1849, and later to Logan Co., Ohio. He was ordained deacon in 1859 and in 1872 was ordained bishop. In 1886 he moved to Coffee Co., Kan. He traveled extensively and exerted a commanding influence in the Mennonite Church (MC). Three brothers, L. O. King, Hutchinson, Kan.; B. B. King, now Scottdale, Pa.; and John Y. King of West Liberty, Ohio, were ministers in the Mennonite Church. Henry J. King, Arthur, Ill., is a Mennonite bishop and evangelist. S. M. King was a missionary to India. Christian B., Christian L., Joel, and John King, all of Ronks, Pa., and Joshua and John King of Uniontown, Ohio, are ministers in the Old Order Amish Church. J. H. King (b. 1861) was a leading bishop in the Central Conference Church.   H.H.HAR.

Isabelle King Yoder, *Centennial Memoir of Abraham and Mattie King* (Harrisonburg, Va., 1949).

King, Joseph H., was born May 2, 1861, son of Daniel and Mary Hotler King, who came to Central Illinois from Butler Co., Ohio. He lived his entire life in the vicinity of Carlock, Ill. He married Salina A. Lantz, also of Carlock, Oct. 16, 1883. There were three children. He died March 5, 1935. He was ordained to the ministry in the North Danvers Mennonite Church (GCM) by Bishop Joseph Stuckey, April 17, 1892. Later he shepherded a group of the members living in Carlock, from which grew the Carlock Mennonite Church, of which he was the first pastor, 1916-22. He served for extended periods as a member of the Central Conference Mission Board, field secretary of the conference, and secretary of the (Bloomington) Mennonite Hospital Board.   R.L.H.

King Ranch Hutterite Bruderhof near Lewistown, Mont., founded in 1935 by Preacher Joseph Stahl and several families from the Huron commune. Their population in 1947 was 65, with 25 baptized members.   D.D.

Kingman County, Kan., is known for its fertile red soil and rolling hills. Its principal crop is wheat and there is also a considerable amount of grazing land. The total population of the county is over 12,000.

There are two General Conference Mennonite churches in Kingman County—Bethany Mennonite Church (*q.v.*), southeast of Kingman, organized in 1907, and the Zion Mennonite Church in Kingman (*q.v.*), which was organized in 1929. In addition, the camp of the Western District young people, Camp Mennoscah (*q.v.*), is located there, on the Ninnescah River west of Murdock.   H.J.S.

Kings View Homes, the second of Mennonite Central Committee mental hospitals, located 2½ miles southwest of Reedley, Calif., resulted from the 1947 MCC assignment to erect three such hospitals. The Kings River, which forms the northwest border of the 43-acre ranch, has given its name to the hospital. The ranch provides fruit and vegetables to the hospital and also an avenue of therapeutic work.

The plant consists of the main building with 8,500 sq. ft. and an activity building with 1,800 sq. ft. Personnel are housed in Reedley. Kings View Homes was opened on Feb. 11, 1951. It now (1955) has three psychiatrists, a psychiatric social worker, psychologist, and four nurses on the total staff of 30. Arthur Jost was appointed administrator in 1950 and he continues to direct the business and public relations program. Kings View Homes has utilized many volunteers from the community in its recreational, devotional, and educational program for patients and staff alike. A number of patients have been placed in foster homes in the community.

The present services include full psychiatric care, medical workup in conjunction with local general medical facilities, outpatient care, and foster home care. All types of mental patients are admitted. The ultimate program is to include facilities for 100 patients. At this writing, a study committee is being appointed to study the steps for its further development. (*ME* II, †.)   A.Jo.

Kingwood Bible Church of the Mennonite Brethren Conference of North America, located at 1125 Elm St., Salem, Ore., was organized as the Mennonite Brethren Church of West Salem on Oct. 13, 1940, by 27 members of the M.B. Church of Dallas, Ore., who felt the need of a place of worship in Salem. In 1944 the church was enlarged to provide room for the newly organized Salem Bible School and Academy. In order to reach more people the present name was adopted. Pastors who have served the church are Abe A. Loewen, Albert Fadenrecht, Alex Sauerwein, and Frank Wiens. The membership in 1957 was 185.   P.Pa.

Kingwood Reformed Mennonite Church is located in Wellesley Village, Stratford, Waterloo Co., Ont. Established in 1850, it had a membership of 27 in 1948.   J.L.K.

Kinsinger (Kenzinger, Kentzinger, Kinnzinger, Kinzinger, Kitzinger), a Swiss Mennonite family name occurring in the Palatinate Mennonite census lists under various spellings in 1717, 1724, 1743, and 1759. A Christian Kentzinger, whose name appears in 1724, was the ancestor of those carrying this family name in South Germany. In the 1940 census of Mennonite families in South Germany, 14 Kensingers were members of the Sembach Mennonite Church. Peter Kinzing, the noted mechanic and clockmaker at Neuwied, Germany, whose collection was admired by Goethe, Lavater, and Basedow in 1774 (*MQR* XXV, 1951, 252), no doubt belonged to this Kinzinger family.

In 1729 an Abraham Kensinger arrived in Philadelphia. Joseph Kensinger, a native of the Palatinate, came to America and settled in Butler Co., Ohio, in 1826. He was ordained as minister in the Amish congregation in 1844 and served until his death in 1857. Peter Kinsinger, a distant relative of the above Joseph, born in the Palatinate in 1827, was ordained to the ministry of the Butler Co., Ohio, Amish congregation in 1867 and served there until his death in 1888. Joseph Kinsinger from the Palatinate, a brother of the above Peter, settled in Butler Co., Ohio, in 1850. He was ordained there in 1861 and served the Amish congregation until he moved to Wayne Co., Ind., in 1868.

Bertha Kinsinger Petter observed the sixtieth anniversary of her work among the Cheyenne Indians of Oklahoma and Wyoming in 1956. She was one of the first Mennonite women to graduate from a college (Wooster).

Members of the Butler County Kinsinger families moved to central Illinois as early as 1837. Here Michael Kinsinger was ordained to the ministry in 1862 and died in 1895. John Kinsinger from Butler County was ordained in 1881. Michael Kinsinger, an immigrant from Germany, was ordained in 1889 and died in 1912. Joseph Kinsinger was ordained in 1891 and died in 1925. These served in the Central Conference of Mennonites.

At least as early as 1842 Kinsinger families from Butler Co., Ohio, were living in the Lee Co., Iowa, Amish settlement. Later, members of these families moved to the Amish Mennonite settlement of Davis Co., Iowa.

Jacob Kinsinger migrated to America from Hesse-Kassel, Germany, in 1832, and finally settled near Springs, Pa. A son, Peter Kinsinger, served as a bishop (1884-1923) in the Old Order Amish church of Johnson Co., Iowa. His relatives and descendants are still found in this community. Other members of the family remain in the Grantsville, Md., Amish Mennonite community.   M.G.

Kint (*Kind, Kindt*), **Joos** (*Josse*): see **Jooskint.**

Kinthis, Jobst, of Freinsheim, Palatinate, Germany, the otherwise unknown author of the *Gesprächbüchlein* (*q.v.*), which has a certain significance for the history of the Mennonites in the Palatinate. (*ML* II, 494.)

Kintzi, Peter, b. Oct. 18, 1802, at Einsiedel in Galicia, d. Feb. 15, 1874, at Kiernica (*q.v.*), was a wagoner by trade, became a farmer, and worked himself up from a very modest beginning to the possession of the large Kiernica estate. He was the founder of the Mennonite church at Kiernica by creating a fund to which he contributed 3,000 florins. For all the efforts of the Mennonite brotherhood he had a warm interest and an open hand. He liked to help wherever there was need. He supported such institutions as the school at Weierhof and the Dutch Mennonite missionary association with sizable gifts. Of his 16 children, nine were living when he died.   Neff.

P. Bachmann, *Mennoniten in Kleinpolen* (Lemberg, 1934); *Menn. Bl.,* 1874, 29; *Gbl.,* 1874, 3 and 45; *ML* II, 494.

Kinzer Mennonite Church (MC), located in the small thriving town of Kinzers on the Lincoln Highway, Lancaster Co., Pa., is a member of the Lancaster Conference. In 1897 a meetinghouse was built here for the benefit of retiring farmers. Until 1916 the quarterly mission meetings were held alternately at Kinzer and at Paradise. The 1955 membership was 143. G. Parke Book was bishop, the Paradise-Kinzer ministers served, and Clarence V. Groff was deacon.   I.D.L.

Kiowa County, Kan. (pop. 4,730), is located in the south central part of the state. The Mennonites in the community are largely farmers living in the south half of the county. There are three branches of Mennonites in the area. The Church of God in Christ Mennonites were the first group of Mennonites to come to the county, coming from Marion and McPherson counties in 1906. They have a country church of approximately 80 members.

The Mennonite Church (MC) in Greensburg was organized in 1932 by various Mennonite families who came to this community around 1908 and after. Its membership of 75 comes from seven different denominational backgrounds. The Mennonite Board of Missions and Charities (MC) of Elkhart, Ind., operates a 24-bed general hospital in Greensburg, which is the only Mennonite institution in the county. The Faith Mennonite Church (GCM) was organized in 1948 and has a membership of 31 (1955).   S.J.

Kipfer (Küpfer), a family name found among the Mennonites in Switzerland since the rise of Anabaptism. Elizabeth Kipfer (*q.v.*) died as martyr in 1538. Johannes Kipfer of Langnau, where the family has been resident since 1680, was long the editor of the *Zionspilger,* the weekly periodical of the Mennonites in Switzerland. To this family also belonged Ulrich Kipfer (*q.v.*) and another Ulrich Kipfer, of Frittenbach, preacher of the Emmental (*q.v.*) congregation from 1825, who in 1852 left the Emmental with a number of other Mennonites to settle in Adams County, Ind., where he was a minister until he died in 1866. The name is also found among Swiss Mennonites in Ontario. In Perth County, near Newton, Ont., an Amish congregation of 125 members is known as the Kipfer group.

vDZ.

Delbert Gratz, *Bernese Anabaptists* (Scottdale, 1953) 135, 153 f.; Samuel Geiser, *Die Taufgesinnten-Gemeinden* (Karlsruhe, 1931); Paul Peachey, *Die soziale Herkunft der Schweizer Täufer in der Reformationszeit* (Karlsruhe, 1954); *Mart. Mir.* E. 1129; Th. de Quervain, *Kirchliche und soziale Zustände in Bern 1528-36* (Bern, 1906); *ML* II, 494.

Kipfer (Küpfer), **Elisabeth,** a Swiss Brethren martyr of Sumiswald in the canton of Bern, Switzerland, was executed at Bern for her faith in 1538. (*Mart. Mir.* E 1129; *ML* II, 494.)

Kipfer, Johann, an elder of the Mennonite congregation of Langnau in the Emmental, Switzerland, was born Oct. 15, 1858, at Oberfrittenbach in the Raingut not far from Langnau. As a youth he was converted by the preaching of the German revival-

ist Elias Schrenck. As a means of spreading the Gospel, Kipfer and some others founded the *Zionspilger* (*q.v.*) in 1882, which has been published in Langnau continuously since that time. Kipfer was also an instigator in building the meetinghouse and parsonage (Vereinshaus) at Kehr near Langnau in 1888. Kipfer became the editor of the *Zionspilger* following the death of Samuel Bähler, the first editor in 1890, holding this position until 1943, with the exception of 1898-1900, when Matthias Pohl served as editor.

In 1884 he was ordained as preacher of the Langnau Mennonite congregation. His deepest interest was, however, the promotion of the Evangelical Alliance, more than the development of the Mennonite congregations on the principles of their fathers. He therefore stressed Luther's doctrine of justification rather than that of discipleship as stressed by the fathers. This explains the dropping of articles on Mennonite history from the *Zionspilger* during Kipfer's editorship, contrary to Bähler's editorial policy.

In the 1890's Kipfer was ordained as elder of the Emmental congregation. In this office he sought especially to implant the message of salvation into the hearts of his catechumens. On the one hand his good judgment against extremist movements was greatly appreciated. On the other hand, he was sometimes intolerant toward other brethren in the conference. Mennonite tradition was for Kipfer a thing of the past; he sought so much the more after fellowship with believers of other circles, especially in the Free Churches, but also in the state church. The content of his theological thought can be summarized as "faith and grace." This was the keynote of the *Zionspilger,* which contained mostly articles written by non-Mennonites, e.g., Wilhelm Meili and Heinrich Kurz. For 60 years Kipfer worked along these lines, impressing this stamp on the Emmental congregation. Mennonite principles were given only partial consideration. This was true of the Confession of Faith of the Emmental congregation which Kipfer wrote in 1937. He presented this document for adoption by the other Swiss Mennonite congregations, but it was rejected on the ground that it went too far in involvement with the state church and in the recognition of infant baptism as being "in the spirit of the Scriptures." In 1943 Kipfer retired as editor, moved with his family from Kehr to Langnau, and died on March 15, 1944.

S.G.

Kipfer, Ulrich, deacon of the Mennonite congregation in the Emmental, canton of Bern, Switzerland, was born near Langnau in 1772. He passed through the changes of the 1830's in the Emmental churches, and wrote an exact, detailed account of the division of 1835 (see **Bern, Samuel Fröhlich,** and **Neutäufer**). For a long time he corresponded with the Mennonites living in the Palatinate. In March 1810 Ulrich Kipfer, Nikolaus Gerber, Christian Gerber, and Christian Brand made a futile appeal to the cantonal government of Bern requesting the observance of the rights granted the Mennonites in 1799 by the "Act of Toleration." In 1850 Kipfer helped to draw up the petition to the government at Bern for military exemption for the Mennonites, and was one of the signatories.   S.G.

S. Geiser, *Die Taufgesinnten-Gemeinden* (Karlsruhe, 1931) 467, 474; Delbert L. Gratz, *Bernese Anabaptists* (Scottdale, 1953) 100; *ML* II, 494.

Kirche unterm Kreuz, Die (The Church under the Cross), a religious periodical published in the German language by John G. Stauffer (*q.v.*) of Quakertown, Pa., from April 1885 to September 1891. The subtitle reads as follows: *Botschafter des Heils in Christo (Den Wehrlosen Christen in Amerika gewidmet).* The masthead carried the motto, *"Christum vermag niemand recht zu erkennen es sei denn dass er ihm nachfolge im Leben, Hans Denk,"* apparently as so-to-speak the editor's program or intention with this paper. In December 1885, the term *Kirche* in the title was changed to *Gemeinde* (congregation, brotherhood) which seemed to Stauffer nearer to his ideal than the former term. In 1885 the paper came out monthly; from January 1886 on it was published only bimonthly, until November 1888 (altogether 27 issues, 432 pages). Then in January 1889, Stauffer "dropped the denominational" and again changed the title, now the former subtitle as the main title as follows: *Botschafter des Heils,* adding as something new: *Und Zeichen der Zeit,* indicating the search for the signs of the second coming of Christ. In this new dress 17 issues of the magazine appeared (272 pages), after which it was discontinued quite abruptly.

The journal was in many regards similar in tone to the contemporary European German and Swiss Mennonite papers (*Mennonitische Blätter, Gemeindeblatt der Mennoniten,* and *Zionspilger*) but never had any official connection with the Mennonite church. In fact, Stauffer was rather conscious of his independence from any organized church life. "Wherever I meet men who love the Lord Jesus Christ I keep brotherhood with them" (letter to John Horsch). In many regards this journal was also similar to the *Herold der Wahrheit* after John Horsch had taken over its editing in 1888, with the difference that the latter paper was strictly "denominational" in its intention, serving the Mennonite church (MC) as a real church paper. But otherwise both Stauffer and Horsch (as well as Ulrich Hege in Germany) had at that time one great idea in mind: to revive the church (or brotherhood) in the spirit of the forefathers of the 16th century, or should we better say in the spirit of the "old evangelical brotherhoods," as Ludwig Keller (*q.v.*) saw and propagated them in his many books ever since the publication of his *Hans Denk* in 1882. Keller's influence in the 1880's was very strong. Everywhere among Mennonites Stauffer wanted to assist in the "great awakening" on his own initiative by publishing a magazine in which all these publications and sources should be made known to a wide public, first of Mennonite background and later of a general Christian interest. Stauffer never had any official backing, although he addressed himself many times to his Mennonite readership (both of the old church and the new General Conference congregations). His paper had a good circulation, and was also welcomed outside his church.

Stauffer's first program was to reprint the entire book by Anna Brons of 1884 (*Ursprung . . . der Taufgesinnten oder Mennoniten*), which he actually concluded in the fall of 1888. Besides this he reprinted material from the recently published *Geschichts-Bücher der Wiedertäufer,* by J. Beck (*q.v.*), 1883, which was certainly a service for the American readers who then did not know anything about the Hutterites; next he planned to reprint from Keller's books, from W. Mannhardt's *Die Wehrfreiheit der . . . Mennoniten,* 1863, and from M. Klaasen, *Geschichte der wehrlosen Taufgesinnten Gemeinde,* 1873. He also published a radical Christian essay by Heinrich Balzer (*q.v.*), the well-known minister of the Kleine Gemeinde (*Verstand und Vernunft,* 1833), and a fine article by Leonhard Sudermann, *Von der Wehrlosigkeit und dem Leiden.* Stauffer's own editorials were usually of a high standard and well able to awaken sensitive souls. He was also interested in a strong revival of the Deknatel (*q.v.*) sermons, as e.g., a comparison between the Mennonite church and the church at Laodicea (IV, 129 f.). But then—almost suddenly—he discontinued this kind of work. He reports his disappointment in his endeavor, which was so incongruous to the prevailing American mind. In any case, from 1889 on, he shifted the tenor to the "Signs of the time," i.e., to eschatological ideas concerning Christ's second coming. Once more, in September 1891, he published a fine tract (or sermon) of his own, "Philadelphia and Laodicea," in which he admonished his readers: turn away from Laodicea and enter Philadelphia, the city of the open door. It was his last message. We do not know what went on behind the scenes, but it was (as far as it is known) the last issue. Stauffer, who had lost his inner ties with the Mennonite church (of any branch), had become a solitary man, and both his name and his work have been almost forgotten.

                                                 R.F.

R. Friedmann, *Mennonite Piety Through the Centuries* (Goshen, 1949) 258-60; Bender, *Two Centuries,* 99 f.; and a short autobiography by Stauffer himself in J. H. Battle, *History of Bucks County, Pa.* (Philadelphia, 1887) 1067-69.

Kirchen-Gemeinden, *Kirchliche Mennoniten, Kirchliche* are terms used occasionally among Mennonites from Russia. The origin of the term *Kirchen-Gemeinden* can be traced back to the early history of the Mennonites in Russia when there were two *Gemeinden* (communities) in existence in each settlement. The civil and the ecclesiastical communities were integral parts of solid Mennonite settlements. In order to distinguish between the civil community or *Gemeinde* and the ecclesiastical body or *Gemeinde,* the distinction between *Gemeinde* as a civil organization and the *Kirchen-Gemeinde* came into usage. One can find this distinction in early records and writings pertaining to the Mennonites of Russia.

A different meaning and connotation was given to this term by members of the Mennonite Brethren Church after 1860, when they began to refer to the members of the Mennonite Church of Russia as *Kirchliche* and their congregations as *Kirchen-Gemeinden.* The above-mentioned term was taken over and given new meaning. Among those using the term it implied that those to whom this name was given were meeting for worship in a "church building" (*Kirche*), while the Mennonite Brethren met originally in private homes and later in a *Versammlungshaus* (meetinghouse), which was not spoken of as a church. Among those using the term, it may have—it still does—implied many other things in which the new Mennonite Brethren movement differed from the traditional Mennonite Church. This distinction can be compared with the terms in use among Pennsylvania-German Mennonites when they speak of "old" Mennonites and "new" Mennonites.

Although the term *Kirchen-Gemeinden* or *Kirchliche* has become obsolete among the Mennonites of the United States who use the English language, it is still being used among the Mennonite Brethren in Canada and South America and occasionally also by other Mennonite groups. Not only is there no justification for the use of this name in the Americas, but there was also none in Russia, with the possible exception of the time when a confusion between the ecclesiastical body and the civil organization in Mennonite communities could take place. *Kirchliche Mennoniten* are simply "Mennonites" and the *Kirchen-Gemeinden* are just Mennonite churches or congregations and should be referred to in these terms. No confusion is possible with other Mennonite groups of Russian background since they all added a distinguishing name to their traditional name "Mennonite" (Mennonite Brethren, Evangelical Mennonite Brethren, etc.). (*ML* II, 500.) C.K.

Kirchenkonvent, one of the various names used by the Mennonites of Prussia and Russia to designate the body of deacons, ministers, or elders of a congregation or settlement. Very common were "Lehrdienst," "geistlicher Vorstand," "Konferenz," and "Kirchenkonvent." The latter gradually became accepted among the Chortitza Mennonites (see **Chortitzaer Mennonitischer Kirchenkonvent**) and also among the Molotschna Mennonites (see **Molotschnaer Mennoniten-Kirchenkonvent**). The Kirchenkonvent was not a board with executive authority and it had no power to pass regulations for various congregations. Resolutions passed were subject to the approval of the various congregations represented in the Kirchenkonvent. During the second half of the past century, the Kirchenkonvent grew into a conference organization which included all congregations and settlements and later on even congregations of other Mennonite branches. Lay delegates became common. (See **Allgemeine Bundeskonferenz** *der Mennonitengemeinden in Russland*.)
C.K.

Kirchenkonvent (Church Convention) was the name given the church authorities in Bern, Switzerland, in earlier centuries. It was a sort of consistorial or synodal council. The designation was derived from Catholicism, were "convent" means a congregating of monks or nuns. It is a purely local board, and not to be confused with the *Kirchenrat* (church council), in which the large and small councils (of the government) were also represented. The members of the *Kirchenkonvent* presented to the government several official opinions on the solution of the Anabaptist problem, demanding violent measures which led to cruel persecution. Characteristic of their ideas are the opinions of the clergy of 1585 and the divided opinion of the *Konvent* in 1670. Under the date of Feb. 13, 1693, a government order was sent to the *Konvent* to suggest in writing "the cause of this leaven," and to recommend measures to counteract the rapid spread of Anabaptism.   S.G.

Berner Ratsmanual; Prediger Ordnung (Bern, 1824); S. Geiser, *Die Taufgesinnten-Gemeinden* (Karlsruhe, 1931) 207-9, 404, 414; *ML* II, 496 f.

Kirchenordnungen (Church Regulations), the name of the government regulations issued by the civil authorities of the several German states, areas, or towns and cities, or at times by the church administrative office, to regulate church affairs, beginning with the time of the Reformation. Each Kirchenordnung usually began with a doctrinal section, then followed with directions for the conduct of worship including a detailed liturgy, the church offices, organization of the general church administration of the land, salaries of church officials, administration of church property, alms administration, church discipline, marriage, school affairs, etc. Frequently it contained directions regarding the combating of heresy (other confessions). The oldest Kirchenordnung was that adopted by the synod of Homberg in Hesse in 1526, which is noteworthy in that it calls for a church of "believers only," but which never was put into effect by any civil authority. The first effective Lutheran Kirchenordnung was that of Braunschweig of 1528.

Most of the Kirchenordnungen had paragraphs prescribing how the Wiedertäufer (Anabaptists) were to be dealt with, usually calling for turning them over to the authorities as enemies of church and state. Others were milder in their requirements, such as that of Philip of Hesse in 1537, which required "each superintendent to deliver a good sermon, especially in those areas where the Anabaptist ferment has become noticeable, so that the people shall be held by clear preaching to stand by pure doctrine, the fear of God, and obedience." Since the specifications of the Kirchenordnungen had much weight and influence, their bearing on Anabaptist history is not negligible. (For further details see article in *ML* II, 499 f.) The full text of the German Kirchenordnungen has been published by Emil Sehling in the six large volumes of his *Die evangelischen Kirchenordnungen des XVI. Jahrhunderts* (Leipzig and Tübingen, 1907-55). (*ML* II, 499 f.)
NEFF.

Kirchheimerhof in the duchy of Zweibrücken, Germany, is mentioned in Dutch *Naamlijst* of 1769 and following issues, as a Mennonite center, being one congregation together with Freudenberg and Hombach. Johannes Schönny (Schöny), elder after 1745, lived at Kirchheimerhof. Other elders were Joseph Schnebele, preacher 1762, elder 1767 until after 1802, Christian Wels(?), preacher 1774, elder 1781-84; preachers were Johannes Lehmann 1745-*ca.* 80, Rudolf Schmidt 1755-*ca.* 83, Peter Boër 1755-*ca.* 80,

Georg Finger 1783 until after 1800, and Ulrich Lehmann 1783 until after 1802. (See also **Zweibrücken**.)

vᴅZ.

Kirchliche Mennoniten: see **Kirchen-Gemeinden**.

Kirianov Mennonite Brethren Church was a congregation in the province of Tobolsk, Siberia, under the leadership of Hermann Peters (*q.v.*), commonly known as the *Apostolische Brüdergemeinde* (*q.v.*).

Kirrweiler, a village (pop. 1,500) in the Rhenish Palatinate, Germany, mostly Catholic, near Neustadt a.d.W., where according to Hutterian tradition two Hutterian Brethren, Hans Arbeiter (*q.v.*) and Heinrich Schuster (*q.v.*), lay in prison 29 weeks in 1568. "Thus at Kirweiler Arbeiter was put into a dark dungeon, where one is deprived of the light of day, and Heinrich into the common prison" (Wolkan, *Geschicht-Buch,* 327). This prison was evidently the Hambach castle (formerly known as the Kästenburg, now the Maxburg). The fortress, which belonged to the see of Speyer until 1789, was destroyed in the Peasants' War and rebuilt by feudal service in 1525, was seriously damaged by Albrecht Alcibiades of Brandenburg, and in the Thirty Years' War demolished. (*ML* II, 500 f.)   Neff.

Kirschgartshäuserhof, a hamlet near Mannheim, Germany, on the road to Lampertheim, was occupied in the 18th century by ten Mennonite families, which formed a congregation and held services every Sunday. A register of April 10, 1742, lists the following names: Abraham Strickler, Stephan Brennemann, Johann Jakob Hackmann, Christian Danner, Christian Krafft, Jakob Schaub, Johannes Landes, Jr., Rudolph Schneider, Adam Danner, Diether Kieferndorf, and Jakob Landes.

It is not known when they settled here. In 1740 they were charged the protection fee, "not only the sum due for the past years, but also the increased sum for the future"—a sum they could not possibly raise. Vainly the owner of the land, Anna Sophie, widowed Countess of Sayn and Wittgenstein, appealed to the court in their behalf. They had to move out—nobody knows where they went (records in the *Generallandesarchiv* in Karlsruhe). (*ML* II, 501.)   Neff.

Kiss. In conformity with the New Testament command that Christians greet each other with the holy kiss (Rom. 16:16; I Cor. 16:20; II Cor. 13:12; I Thess. 5:26) or the kiss of love (I Pet. 5:14) considerable use has been made of the kiss as a symbol of love and fellowship in the history of the Christian Church. This spontaneous and pure expression of the love for the brethren within the fellowship was originally a part of every corporate act of worship. It was not the same as the common kiss among friends in the Roman world, nor the common Jewish salutation among friends, for it was a "holy" kiss and observed only among members of the church. In his description of the worship services of the Christians of the second century, Justin Martyr reported that the kiss was regularly used. The *Apostolic Constitutions* state: "Then let the men apart, and the women apart, salute each other with a kiss in the Lord." Origen connected the kiss of the Christians with the apostolic injunction of Rom. 16:16. Cyprian reported that the one baptizing a convert, as well as the entire church, greeted the newly baptized with the holy kiss. The evidence is clear that the kiss was uniformly used at both baptism and communion in the early church, and it is found in all the ancient liturgies. Gradually it disappeared from common use, from the fourth century on, and became restricted to liturgical and ritual ceremonies. It continued to be practiced in the early medieval church in baptism, ordination, consecration of bishops, absolution of penitents, marriage ceremony, and the Lord's Supper. In the liturgical churches, particularly Roman Catholic and Greek Orthodox, it has continued to the present day with little modification in the ceremonies of ordination and consecration of bishops. In the medieval period such a conception of the kiss developed as involved the kissing of inanimate objects associated with the sacraments and services of the church as well as the vestments and rings of the higher clergy. These have also continued to the present day. It was renewed again somewhat in its original sense in monasticism and in some of the medieval sects such as the Albigenses and Waldenses. The Anabaptist movement of the 16th century, apparently of all countries, Switzerland, Germany, and Holland, revived and maintained the observance of the holy kiss in the common fellowship of the brotherhood on a widespread if not universal basis.

In a fellowship such as the Anabaptists with an emphasis on a literal following of the commands of Christ and His apostles, with a stress on the infallibility, unity, and authority of the Bible, with a conscious attempt to re-establish the church on its apostolic foundations, it is not surprising to find the same spirit of love within the fellowship which characterized the early church, nor to find love's most intimate and Biblical expression, the holy kiss. Their heartfelt love for their fellow believers caused them to adopt the terminology of the family in speaking of one another, referring to one another as brothers and sisters, just as the earliest Christians (and later the Waldenses) had referred to one another. The letters of persecuted Dutch Anabaptists or Mennonites abound in examples of this familial denotation; e.g., "We would inform our most beloved brethren and sisters in the Lord, and all who seek to fear the Lord with the whole heart, that we are all (the Lord be praised forever) of very good cheer, and hope to adhere to the word of the Lord." "Herein rejoice now with us, O you holy brethren and sisters in the Holy Spirit of truth." "In the same year, on the first Friday after St. Martin's Day, brother John Korbmacher, a minister of the Word of God and of His church (who was frequently sent out into the work of the Lord), was apprehended for the faith and the Word of God" (*Mart. Mir.* D 181, 488, 276, E 566, 830, 645).

In this environment of love and affection the injunctions of Paul to "greet the brethren with a kiss of love," and that of Peter to "salute one another with a kiss of love" were readily accepted by the Anabaptists as directly applying to themselves as a sign and seal of the love and brotherhood which existed among brethren and sisters.

Menno Simons mentions the kiss at least twice in his writings. With his strict emphasis on a disciplined and pure church it is not surprising to find his emphasis on the relation of the kiss to the disciplined brotherhood. "If some deceiver should come to us who has left the doctrine of Christ . . . we should not receive such an one into our houses, lest he deceive us; and . . . we should not greet him as a brother lest we have communion with him. . . . But the greeting or kiss of peace signifies the communion." "We certainly know that there is but one excommunication in the Scriptures, which does not only extend to the spiritual communion, such as the Lord's Supper, and the hand and kiss of peace; but it also extends to the bodily communion, such as eating, drinking, daily actions and conduct . . ." (Writings, 480, 971).

Thus we find that as early in the Anabaptist movement as Menno Simons the kiss was accepted as a normal Christian practice. Moreover we are sure from this that it was one of the instruments of discipline and of defining the brotherhood in that it was practiced only among the brethren and sisters and that it was denied those brethren and sisters who because of sin were in a state of excommunication.

The kiss had an early emphasis among the early Dutch Anabaptists as evidenced by the writing of Menno Simons; did it also have early acceptance by the Swiss-South German Anabaptists? As will be shown there are a few references in the Martyrs' Mirror to the use of the kiss by Anabaptists in Austria as early as 1528, and again in 1546, and by Alsatian Anabaptists in 1558. The kiss is not mentioned in the Schleitheim Confession, the earliest of the Anabaptist statements of faith, which was formulated in 1527 near the border of Switzerland and Germany. However, in 1568, after a series of conferences held to come to an agreement on faith and practice, a discipline of 23 articles was adopted by a group of South German and Swiss Anabaptists at Strasbourg. The eleventh article of this discipline states the use of the kiss and its restriction to the brotherhood. The fact that the kiss is limited as to sex in this discipline is also significant. "11. The brethren and sisters, each to each, shall greet each other with a holy kiss; those who have not been received into fellowship shall not be greeted with a kiss, but with the words, 'the Lord help you'" (MQR I, 1927, 65).

Another early confession is one appearing in the Martyrs' Mirror under the title "Confession of Faith According to the Holy Word of God" and reputed to have been written about the year 1600. In this confession the kiss is twice alluded to, once in connection with footwashing and once in relation to excommunication. Article XXIII: Of the footwashing of believers. When their fellow believers, out of love, visit them, they shall with heartfelt humility, receive them with the kiss of love and peace into their houses, and as a ministration of their neighbors, according to the humility of Christ, wash their feet. . . . Article XXIX: Of the withdrawing from and avoiding of apostate and separated members is confessed: As separation is commanded by God for the reformation of sinners, and the maintenance of the purity of the church; so God has also commanded and willed, that in order to shame him to reformation, the separated individual is to be shunned and avoided. . . . This withdrawing extends to all spiritual communion, as the Supper, evangelical salutation, the kiss of peace, and all that pertains to it. This withdrawing extends likewise to all temporal and bodily things . . . (Mart. Mir. D I, 439, 445; E 399, 405).

After having been stated so strongly in the earlier statements of faith it is rather startling that the kiss is not mentioned in the important Dordrecht (1632) and Cornelis Ris (1747) confessions, which have become the official statement of faith of the majority of contemporary North American Mennonite churches; the Mennonite Church (MC) and the Amish churches holding to the Dordrecht Confession, and the General Conference Mennonite Church holding to the Ris Confession. Nor is the kiss mentioned in the catechisms of the early Mennonites (Shorter Catechism, 1690, Waldeck Catechism, 1778, Roosen's Catechism, 1702).

There is no extended discussion of the holy kiss by the early Anabaptists. As has been pointed out, it signified communion to them and was observed as a symbol of fervent Christian love. However, how often the Anabaptists practiced this greeting or on what occasions we do not know. Nonetheless, we do have some clues. As has been pointed out, the "Confession of Faith According to the Holy Word of God" associated the kiss with the washing of the saints' feet, which shows antiquity in that use of the kiss by many Mennonite groups today. The kiss also obtained a place as the ordinary salutation among brethren and sisters as will be shown later. Thus is preserved, or rather revived, the apostolic twofold use of the holy kiss—ritualistic and salutatory.

The letters and incidents recorded in the Martyrs' Mirror are the important primary sources for our knowledge of the uses of the holy kiss as the salutation of love between Christians. Since the book deals exclusively with the persecutions of the brethren and sisters, the accounts of the kiss are in some relation to the events of their persecution. This does not mean that the salutation was observed only by those undergoing persecution, but rather it implies that it was a common observance by all the brethren and that it quite naturally carried over to their periods of trial and suffering, becoming a source of comfort and an expression of their unquenchable love.

There is one account of the kiss being given in prison. The early date of this account, 1546, makes it especially significant. This incident occurred in Styria, a province of Austria, and Vienna, showing that the kiss was practiced by the South German-Swiss group of Anabaptists as well as the Dutch followers of Menno. "They were then led in iron chains through Styria, and delivered into the bailey, at Vienna, to the jailer who said, 'Come, I will bring you into a vault where others of your brethren are'" (Mart. Mir. D 73, E 474). In the prison were Hans Stautdach and three fellow prisoners.

When they met, they embraced and kissed each other and praised God, who had brought them together for the glory of His name.

One account records the kiss being given by two brethren at their trial: "When John Claess and Lucas Lamberts, an old man of eighty-seven years, called grandfather, came to court they greeted one another with a kiss" (*Mart. Mir.* D 69, E 471).

A number of accounts of the kiss being given at the time of execution also appear in the *Martyrs' Mirror*. The first is another account of Austrian Anabaptists, this time having occurred at Bruck on the Mur, in Styria. The date of this account is even earlier, 1528, just three years after the Zürich Brethren broke with Zwingli, and just one year later than the Schleitheim Confession. "A circle having been formed, they all knelt down (Acts 7:60; 20:36) and earnestly prayed to God that they might finish this their evening sacrifice. They then arose and submitted to the sword. The executioner was sad; for he did not like to do it. The youngest of them all entreated his brethren, that since he felt of good cheer and bold, they should let him suffer the first pain; he then kissed them, and said, 'God bless you, my beloved brethren; today we shall all be together in Paradise'" (*Mart. Mir.* D 19, E 429).

The next account is also of early date, 1544, but occurred in the province of Overijssel, Netherlands: "When the time of suffering drew nigh, Maria said: 'Dear sister, heaven is opened for us; for what we now suffer for a little while we shall forever be happy with our bridegroom.' Then they gave each other the kiss of peace. Thereupon they prayed together to God . . ." (*Mart. Mir.* D 66, E 467). Note the interesting tendency to refer to the kiss as the "kiss of peace," which is not Biblical, but a denotation which arose in the early church. This use of the term "kiss of peace" by the early Anabaptists must be either a carry-over from the Roman Church or a result of reading the early Church Fathers. There is an account of the kiss being given by Gotthard of Nonnenberg and Peter Kramer, of the duchy of Berg on the Lower Rhine, at their execution in 1558. "When the time had come for them to die, they rose to their feet, called upon God in heaven, and as brethren in Christ, and as a token of brotherly love and unity, kissed each other with the sweet kiss of peace, as those that were united with God, and thus were beheaded standing" (*Mart. Mir.* D 208, E 591).

The next account concerns two men apprehended in Cologne and executed in 1562: "And thus George was compelled to be the first one to be made ready for an offering. When he was ready for death, he took brotherly leave from William and they kissed each other with a holy kiss of love. Then George was thrown overboard" (*Mart. Mir.* D 296, E 662).

The fervent love and unmistakable Christian witness of the Christian martyrs motivated their persecutors to attempt to prevent their witness of love at Deventer in the Netherlands in 1571. "Thus Claes was brought upon the scaffold first and he fell upon his knees to prayer, but the executioner lifted him up, for the Spaniards would not tolerate it, and cried, 'Villains, villains!' But the six preceding ones, who had been offered up first, had performed their prayers, and had not been prevented from it; for they had been allowed to come together and also to kiss one another; but since the people said so much about it, how they had prayed, and so lovingly kissed one another, they had resolved to bring only one at a time on the scaffold. Now when Claes stood at the stake, they also brought Ydse upon the scaffold and he forced his way to Claes and kissed him. Hence the Spaniards clamored again and were enraged" (*Mart. Mir.* D 554, E 887).

In reading the accounts of the holy kiss among the early Anabaptists there arises the problem of whether it was practiced promiscuously between the sexes. In some accounts one cannot be sure from the text whether the kiss is exchanged between men and women, in a few promiscuity is certain, and in others the kiss is definitely limited to members of the same sex as it is today in Mennonite groups (*Mart. Mir.* D 106, 548, E 503, 882).

Besides being referred to in the narration of the martyrdoms of the Anabaptist Christians, the kiss is often alluded to in the letters of the martyrs to their relatives and fellow Christians. Sometimes the kiss is referred to directly; at other times, while the word "kiss" itself does not occur, its meaning is readily inferred. The holy kiss is described in eleven narrations in the *Martyrs' Mirror*, in 16 letters the word "kiss" appears, while in at least 95 letters the kiss is alluded to by some term other than "kiss." Two letters from Hans Bret dated 1576 and written at Antwerp illustrate the use of the kiss as the Christian salutation in correspondence: "Thus dear brother, I would write you more, but I have no more paper now. Farewell, the Lord be with you and I greet you now, dear brother, with a holy kiss, for I think that you will see my face no more" (*Mart. Mir.* D 734, E 1043). In this letter Hans's use of the "holy" kiss would seem to be somewhat out of line with its general connotation given by Menno and the Strasbourg Discipline of 1568 as signifying the communion of the brotherhood, since as the title of this letter indicates, his brother "had not yet come to the knowledge of the truth." The other letter is addressed to his mother: "My dear mother, I greet you with a holy kiss of love (I Pet. 5:14), for I think that you will see me no more in this flesh nor I you, my mother."

The following two illustrations of the kiss used in correspondence are more orthodox in their brotherhood dimension, being limited to the household of faith. The first is from a letter entitled "A Letter from Jerome Segers to the Brethren and Sisters" (Antwerp, 1551): "Greet one another with a holy kiss of peace. Jude 21, 24, 25; I Cor. 16:20." The second is from a letter written from Cologne in 1558 by Thomas von Imbroich: "Greet all the saints with the kiss of love, and all who love the Lord Jesus, and tell them to be kind; for God is the Hero and Captain, who so faithfully succors in time of need" (*Mart. Mir.* D 115, 200, E 511, 581).

A characteristic of the strong emphasis on the definition of the brotherhood and the fervent love within it is that members of the same family saw their heavenly relationship just as important or more important than their earthly relationship.

Thus when Joris Wippe salutes his wife with the kiss he refers to her both as wife and as "sister in the Lord" (The Hague, 1558): "Everlasting joy, grace, and peace from God our heavenly Father, through Jesus Christ our Lord and Saviour, and the joy of the Holy Spirit, in your heart and conscience, be with you, my beloved wife and sister in the Lord; I wish it to you as an affectionate salutation in the Lord and to all our dear children whom God has given to us; to Him be praise forever and ever. Amen" (*Mart. Mir.* D 205, E 586).

The form of the greeting in these letters very often follows very closely the Biblical texts from which its use is drawn. Sometimes the Biblical references are even given by the authors: "I greet all believers with a holy kiss. Greet one another with a kiss of love." "Receive one another with a holy kiss of love." "Greet one another with a kiss of charity: Peace be with you all that are in Christ Jesus. Amen. I Pet. 5:14" (*Mart. Mir.* D 338, 341, 366, E 697, 700, 711).

It is then evident that among the early Biblical Anabaptists or Mennonites the holy kiss was frequently practiced both as the common salutation among Christians and as a part of certain rituals, among which footwashing was one. It is further evident that this kiss of peace was the sign or symbol of the communion or brotherhood, that, in essence, its use defined brotherhood.

The history of the kiss from the time of the early Anabaptists until the last century is difficult to trace because of the scruples of many groups against keeping written records. However, it was brought with the early Mennonite immigrants to America and has been preserved, so that today it is still practiced to a greater or less degree by a large portion of the North American Mennonites.

The main body of American Mennonites, the Mennonite Church (MC), composed largely of South German and Swiss immigrants, seemingly has always held to the practice of the kiss. In fact, toward the end of the 19th century, Mennonite ministers were speaking of seven ordinances having been enjoined by the Bible, of which the holy kiss was one. In 1921 the General Conference of the Mennonite Church (MC) declared the kiss an ordinance to be observed by all believers, in a statement of faith entitled "Christian Fundamentals."

One early reference to the kiss by American Mennonites occurs in a letter from three ministers of Eastern Pennsylvania, Andreas Ziegler, Isaac Kolb, and Christian Funk, to several ministers of Crefeld, Germany, and Utrecht, Netherlands, dated 1773. The kiss is here mentioned as one of the privileges denied those who are disciplined for marrying outside the church: "Concerning marriages, it is not approved nor permitted that any one should marry outside the community, and in the case it occurs, the person, whether brother or sister, is notified to withdraw from the fellowship, the brotherly council, the kiss of peace, and the Lord's Supper, until they have made expiation to the community" (*MQR* III, 1929, 230).

A further proof that the withholding of the brotherly kiss from transgressors was a part of church discipline in the Mennonite Church (MC) is found in an interesting decision of the committee of bishops called in to deal with the problem of Jacob Wisler in the Yellow Creek Church, Elkhart Co., Ind., dated Oct. 17, 1871, as follows: "John M. Christophel is asked to acknowledge that he erred in greeting with the kiss one who had been set back from full fellowship by the counsel of the brotherhood."

In the Mennonite Church (MC) today the kiss is observed in a number of situations. It accompanies the footwashing service, the reception of members into the church by baptism or reclamation, and the ordination of ministers, and is the salutation among believers in general. In all cases it is practiced only by members of the same sex. In the footwashing service the men and women are separated, and after each brother (sister) has washed his neighbor's feet the kiss is exchanged. Restriction of sex in the kiss is maintained in the reception of sisters into the church by a sister, often the bishop's wife, taking the newly baptized or restored sister by the hand and giving her the kiss. The salutatory kiss which originally was the ordinary salutation among all the brethren has declined somewhat in its use until in some congregations its practice is limited to the ministers and deacons, who observe it at every church service.

The Mennonite Church (MC) through its periodicals (*Herald of Truth*, 1864-1905; *Gospel Witness*, 1905-8; *Gospel Herald*, 1908 until the present) has constantly and consistently held the ordinance of the kiss before its members and defined its meaning for them and their duty to the brotherhood and to Christ to practice it. Most of the volumes of the *Gospel Herald* contain at least one article on the kiss. Undoubtedly this fact coupled with constant preaching on the subject from the pulpit and in Sunday schools has been a determining factor in the continuance of the use of the kiss in the Mennonite Church today. The kiss is emphasized (1) as a command of the apostles, and (2) as the sign and symbol of brotherhood. The first emphasis stresses obedience to Scripture and discipleship, the legal aspect of the Gospel. The emphasis on the kiss as the sign and symbol of brotherhood stresses the freedom and spontaneity of the fellowship of the Gospel.

There has been a tendency especially in the more liberal conferences of the Mennonite Church (MC) for the salutatory holy kiss to be limited to the ministers, for the lay members to observe it less often among themselves, and for ministers to observe it less often when meeting lay members than when meeting other ministers. Because of this the kiss is accused of having become "ceremonial" and having lost its original spontaneity. The secular greeting has taken the place of the holy kiss where the latter has been dropped, aiding the breakdown of the concept of the brotherhood which led to the dropping of the use of the kiss as the common salutation. "In this age when the love of many shall wax cold, it is becoming more and more common to omit the kiss . . . and how cold and formal the words of the greeting, the shallow 'hello' of the world being substituted for the hearty 'God bless you,' or 'Peace be with us!' And, oh how much encouragement we miss" (*Gospel Herald* XXI, 1928, 498).

In contrast to the Mennonite (MC), the "conservative" conferences such as Old Order Amish Mennonites, Old Order (Wisler) Mennonites, Church of God in Christ Mennonites (Holdeman), Reformed Mennonites, and Conservative (Amish) Mennonites have maintained either an absolute or a greater relative separation from all other groups and influences. In general they have placed a greater emphasis on the Mennonite heritage and tradition, opposing almost all advances and thus manifesting a tendency toward maintaining a distinctive and separate culture. In this separate and controlled environment it has been much easier for the brotherhood to maintain such practices as the kiss. In these groups the kiss is practiced universally in its ritualistic sense at baptism and footwashing. As the Christian salutation it is practiced almost universally among all members, lay as well as ministers, except in the Conservative (Amish) Mennonite Conference where it is only practiced between brethren and ministers at the invitation of the ministers. There is a tendency arising even in such a conservative group as the Church of God in Christ, Mennonite, toward weakening in the practice of the kiss. In general this group of churches has not been active in publication, nor has it attempted to maintain its heritage in this manner; they have relied, as has been stated, on a strict separation and discipline to maintain their heritage and tradition. One striking exception to this statement is the well-written summary of doctrine published by the Reformed Mennonites entitled *Christianity Defined*. This book contains a well-written three-page discussion of the holy kiss, as well as discussion of a number of other areas of faith and practice.

In the General Conference Mennonite Church the practice of the kiss is very rare. No mention is made of the holy kiss in either the *Handbuch für Prediger* (1893) or the new *Minister's Manual* (1950). The Eastern District which broke away from the Franconia Mennonite (MC) Conference in 1847 has but two congregations which practice the kiss, both of which left the Mennonite (MC) communion rather recently: The Richfield, Pa., congregation which joined the Eastern District of the General Conference in 1941, and the Stirling Avenue, Kitchener, Ont., congregation which joined in 1947. Both these churches observe the holy kiss at footwashing.

When the kiss was dropped in the Eastern District is uncertain, but it is significant that the kiss is not mentioned in the *Ordnung der Mennonitischen Gemeinschaft,* which was drawn up at the time of the break with the Franconia Conference (MC) in 1847.

The practice of the salutatory brotherly kiss among the Mennonites of Dutch-Prussian-Russian background has not been investigated. There are indications that this practice was observed quite generally during the first centuries, but was gradually confined to the ministers and such occasions as baptismal services. The final stage is that the use of the brotherly kiss is given up. This stage was reached by all Mennonites of Holland and the urban churches of Germany. Among the rural churches of Prussia, Poland, and Russia the second stage, that is, the use of the kiss among the ministers, was generally still in use. This is to some extent still the case among the Mennonites who have come from Russia and have settled in South America and Canada. Occasionally an old practice along these lines can be noticed among the Mennonites of the United States. A few years ago when the deacons of the Friedenstal Mennonite Church at Durham, Kan., which originated in Poland, extended a call to a minister, they bade him farewell following their visit by giving him the brotherly kiss. This was no doubt an old tradition among this group, going back to the early centuries. In the Bethel Mennonite Church, Inman, Kan., male members were kissed by the minister when they were received into the church by baptism or church letter until some ten years ago, when this practice was dropped.

In Russia the common use of the brotherly kiss was reintroduced, retained, and re-emphasized among the Mennonite Brethren, who originated in 1860. Among the Mennonite Brethren in America as well as the Evangelical Mennonite Brethren, the Krimmer Mennonite Brethren, and Church of God in Christ Mennonites, the practice of the salutatory brotherly kiss is still in use although not as generally as formerly.

The Central District Conference of the General Conference is the result of a split in the Amish Mennonite Church in Illinois, begun in 1871 and completed in 1899. With its conservative Amish background the Central District has maintained footwashing and the kiss in connection with it. The holy kiss as the Christian salutation has also been maintained until recently. However, due to lack of teaching on the subject, its use is declining among many people, especially the young people.

The Evangelical Mennonite Conference is another Mennonite body which arose through a split in the Amish Mennonite Church, in 1864. In this conference the kiss is practiced at footwashing by those who participate, but the salutatory use of the kiss has been lost.

In the Mennonite Brethren Church in the United States the kiss is not the general Christian salutation, but it is observed in footwashing services. However, in Canada, where footwashing has been dropped, it is observed in the communion service.

Among the European Mennonites the observance of the kiss has completely died out in Holland and Germany, but persists in France and Switzerland, though only as a salutatory kiss (not universal however), footwashing having almost completely died out where it was practiced (Amish background congregations in France) and never having been practiced in Switzerland and South Germany (except scattered congregations of Amish background). In Holland the kiss was observed by conservative groups like the Groningen Old Flemish into the 18th century.   J.RE.

Mart. Mir., passim; Menno Simons, *Writings, passim; Christianity Defined* (third edition, Lancaster, 1940); A. E. Crawley, "Kissing," *Encyclopaedia of Religion and Ethics* VII (N.Y., 1920); E. Venables, "Kiss," *Dictionary of Christian Antiquities,* edited by W. Smith, II (London, 1888); J. Moffatt, *Love in the New Testament* (N.Y., 1930).

Kist, Jacob Jansen: see Jacob Jansz Sche(e)demaker.

Kistenmaeker, Wilhelm: see **Willem de Kistenmaker.**

Kitchener-Waterloo, Ont., twin cities with a population of 35,657 and 9,025 respectively, is the center of the largest community of Mennonites in Ontario. The first Mennonites came to Waterloo County from eastern Pennsylvania in 1800 and soon occupied a large part of the virgin land of the county, particularly in Waterloo and Woolwich townships. In 1824 an Amish community was established in the western part of the county, Wilmot Township. In 1872-75 a schism occurred in the Mennonite community which resulted in the establishment of the Ontario Conference of the United Missionary Church, a large congregation (Bethany) being established in the city of Kitchener, and several smaller ones in county towns. In 1889-90 a conservative schism occurred in which much of the Woolwich district withdrew to form the Old Order Mennonite group. In 1925 the large Stirling Avenue group withdrew from the First Mennonite (MC) congregation, and later joined the General Conference Mennonite Church. The immigration from Russia in 1922-25 (supplements of 1930-31 and 1947-50) led to the formation of strong General Conference and Mennonite Brethren congregations. Thus the Kitchener-Waterloo community in 1955 represents a variegated pattern of Mennonitism.

In the city of Kitchener proper are located the following congregations. First Mennonite (MC) 1807, 579 members; Stirling Avenue (GCM) 1925, 445; Mennonite Brethren 1925, 375; Bethany (UMC) 1877, 323; Evangel United Mennonite Church (UMC) 1949, 45. In Waterloo are located Waterloo Mennonite (MC) 1854, 281; Waterloo-Kitchener (GCM) 1925, 390. Thus the total membership of the seven churches in the twin cities is 2,439. In addition there are 15 other MC churches in the county with 1,894 members, a large Old Order Mennonite community with 1,730 members in 14 meeting places, and three other U.M.C. churches with 297 members; at least one of the Amish Mennonite churches with 521 members can be reckoned in the Kitchener-Waterloo area. The total of 6,881 baptized members, of whom probably 2,300 live in the twin cities, constitutes one of the largest compact urban-rural Mennonite communities in North America.

In Kitchener are located two Bible schools: the Ontario Mennonite Bible School and Bible Institute (MC) and Emmanuel Bible College (UMC), the Golden Rule Book Store (MC), a branch of the Mennonite Publishing House at Scottdale, and Rockway Mennonite (MC) School, a church high school.

The Mennonite population has made a major contribution to the Kitchener-Waterloo community over the 150 years of its settlement there. Not many industries have been established by Mennonites, the largest possibly being the Hallman Organ Co. (MC) manufacturing electric organs. Earlier Jacob Y. Shantz (MBC; 1828-1909) had been a leading industrialist and city builder. The excellent agricultural production of the county has been largely due to the Mennonites, who continue to be a major element in the rural area. (*ML* II, 501 f.)　　　　H.S.B.

Kitchener First Mennonite Church (MC), a member of the Ontario Conference, located at 800 King Street East, Kitchener, Ont., had its origin in the log church built by Benjamin Eby in 1813 in the southeast corner of the large cemetery adjoining the present building. This was the first building erected solely for religious worship in Waterloo County. Known simply as "Ben Eby's," it stood until 1854, when the "Christian Eby" frame church replaced it. In 1902 this structure in turn was replaced by a brick building which still forms the main part of the present edifice, known until 1917 as the Berlin Mennonite Church. In 1928 and 1949 this church was enlarged, and can now seat 1,000 persons.

This congregation was the second to be organized in Waterloo County and has remained the central and strongest congregation in the Ontario Conference. The peak population in the Ontario Conference in the early period was 2,500 souls in 1840. How many of these the "Ben Eby" church could claim is uncertain, but the log church with its frame annex might have held 250. The low point in membership was reached just before the J. S. Coffman revivals of the early 1890's. In 1898 the membership of the congregation was 195. In 1924, following the division which resulted in the founding of the Stirling Avenue Mennonite Church (GCM), the membership was 123, but by 1956 had risen to 587. (The Stirling Church, which also had 123 in 1924, had 457 in 1954.) The causes of this division were differences of opinion on polity, church government, and the regulation of attire, the new Stirling group desiring congregational church government rather than conference authority. Both churches have prospered and relations between them are cordial.

A serious division had occurred two generations earlier (1872-75) which resulted in the formation in 1877 of the Bethany United Missionary Church, which had a membership of 323 in 1953, and which has always been the central and largest congregation of the Ontario U.M.C. conference. Thus in 1953-54 there were three Kitchener congregations with a total membership of 1,347, all of which sprang from the original Benjamin Eby congregation.

The leading ministers of First Church and dates of ordination are as follows: Benjamin Eby, Nov. 27, 1809; Abraham C. Weber, 1850; Christian Eby, 1854; Daniel Wismer, 1860; Samuel S. Bowman, 1878; Eli S. Hallman, 1897; Urias K. Weber, 1907. In 1924 C. F. Derstine, already a minister and bishop, became pastor, a position he still holds (1954). John H. Hess served as associate pastor 1949-56 and Edgar Metzler 1957- . Outstanding deacons have been Benjamin Shoemaker 1890-1911, George . Weber 1911-41, John Kehl 1942- . Isidore B. Snyder was chorister 1882-1922, and Titus L. Kolb 1914-49. M. C. Cressman (*q.v.*) was a Sunday-school teacher for 57 years and an active lay leader.

Before 1890 all services had been in German.

Up to 1870 German was no handicap to the growth of the church, but in 1870-90 it undoubtedly had much bearing on the decline in membership. The decline in the use of German began with the Coffman revivals of 1890-91, which were all in English. With the ordination of E. S. Hallman in 1897 all evening services were in English, though morning services were chiefly in German. After 1907 the decline in German was most pronounced and German was then preached only in alternate Sunday morning services until the termination of German preaching in 1924.

Revivals have long been and still are a feature of the work of this church. The Coffman revivals furnished most of the leaders for this congregation for the ensuing 30 years. In 1907 Bishop S. F. Coffman began a winter Bible school in this church which has grown into the large and flourishing Ontario Mennonite Bible School (q.v.). In 1928 a vacation Bible school was begun in this church. It was the first summer school both in this city and among Canadian Mennonites. It has greatly flourished, drawing pupils from all denominations. The membership is 70 per cent urban and 30 per cent rural. The racial background is chiefly Pennsylvania German. J.B.C.

J. B. Cressman, "History of the First Mennonite Church of Kitchener, Ontario," *MQR* XIII (July and October 1939); Ezra Eby, *History of Waterloo Township* (Kitchener, 1895).

Kitchener Mennonite Brethren Church, located in Kitchener, Waterloo Co., Ont., a member of the Canadian Conference of Mennonite Brethren churches, was organized on May 25, 1925, under the name "Molotschna Mennoniten-Brüder-Gemeinde," with Jacob P. Friesen as leader. On Nov. 20, 1932, the church was reorganized under its present name with H. H. Janzen as pastor. The membership in 1954 was 375; most of the members live in the city. For a number of years the congregation used a rented hall for its meetings, but later bought a church which is still being used. The following ministers have served the church: J. P. Friesen, J. W. Reimer, J. P. Wiens, P. Klassen, H. Konrad, H. H. Janzen, D. Klassen, I. Ewert, J. Sudermann, H. Thielmann, Frank C. Peters, and J. J. Toews, the present pastor. (*ME* I, †.) H.H.J.

Kitzbühel, a town (pop. 2,000) in Tirol, Austria. Few places in Tirol had as many Anabaptists as Kitzbühel, in the archbishopric of Salzburg. To be sure, the Tirolean government had on Nov. 28, 1527, demanded that the archbishop assist in eliminating the sect, and had issued orders to the subordinate authorities to that effect; but these public servants lacked either the interest or the power to halt the movement. Instead, refugee Anabaptists from Salzburg and other parts of Tirol met here.

A number of them were seized in March 1528; by April 200 had been arrested. Many were dismissed when they recanted; but 110 refused to do so. An order of April 2 promised pardon to all but the preachers and those who had talked about Christian liberty, community of goods, or against the sacraments; the houses where they met and observed communion should be burned and torn down, unless it involved innocent persons.

At the same time strict orders were sent out to catch "the priest" Paul, who was preaching in the community, and his disciple, Hans Rott, who was preaching in the mountains of Reutte and in the castle of Helene von Freiberg at Münichau. Proceedings were started against this lady, and on May 5, 1528, 106 persons "spotted with Anabaptism" were ordered to appear in the cemetery of Kitzbühel to make a solemn recantation and receive the penance they must pay. Thirty-six were doubtful, and were treated "kindly and painfully"; 13 were easily persuaded, the others only after long torture.

On May 9 the iron-miner Hans Schwaighofer and Hans Platzer of Aschlberg were tried, and on Aug. 12 executed. While they were on the road to the site of the execution "Thomas Herrmann (q.v.) of Böhmisch-Waidhofen spoke some sharp words," and was himself called before the court and condemned to death. At this trial the jurors said it was hard for them to try such a case, "for they did not know whether the verdict would be accepted by the people." The consequence of this was that the judge was instructed to get jurors from a distance for such cases. This may have been the occasion for the mandate of Feb. 5, 1529, stipulating that the verdict should not be pronounced according to personal opinion, but according to regulations.

Since the burning of Anabaptist houses caused damage to others, a notice was sent to Kitzbühel on April 30, 1529, that henceforth only houses in the country should be burned.

The care of the children of fugitive Anabaptists became a problem. In Kitzbühel alone there were 40 to 50. They were kept in a special home until they were able to take care of themselves.

One such fugitive, who forsook wife, child, and goods, was George Grünwald (q.v.) of Kitzbühel, the author of the song, "Kommt her zu mir, spricht Gottes Sohn," which can be found in many Anabaptist manuscripts (Wackernagel, *Kirchenlied* III, 128). In September 1529 Grünwald was at Lackstatt in Bavaria, Germany, and was seized there and executed in 1530.

Some of the Anabaptists who had recanted at the cemetery had again joined the group; they were seized with some others who had assembled for worship on the wooded mountain slopes, and dealt with in accordance with the mandates. Many of them had been won by a former chaplain, Jakob Partzner; he himself escaped to Augsburg. Seized there, he was returned to Kitzbühel, and confessed that he had worked as an Anabaptist in Kitzbühel, Rattenberg, and Kufstein, and was now sincerely sorry. He recanted on Aug. 29, 1530, thereby saving his life.

Helene von Freyberg (q.v.) was also involved with Anabaptists; she was considered "at the bottom of the matter, that so many persons had been baptized and put to death." After long hesitation she recanted in 1534. Christina Häring (q.v.), on the contrary, remained steadfast and was executed in 1533.

In order to instruct those Anabaptists who had been found in and around Kitzbühel in May 1530, the Franciscan monk Tonauer of Schwaz preached missionary sermons for four weeks. Then on July 30 the orders of the government for the discovery and eradication of the Anabaptists throughout the country were announced. These were the days in which Hutter began his extensive work in Tirol and Moravia. One of the questions the government asked local authorities was: why were suspected preachers allowed to preach so long at some places like Kitzbühel?

On June 19, 1533, the authorities reported to the ruler that the Anabaptists in the Kitzbühel region had been wiped out; but they erred. In autumn of 1533 it was reported that a priest, Paul Kessler, in Kitzbühel was taking a wanton attitude on infant baptism. Of course, the Anabaptists were no longer numerous in Tirol; but persecution in Moravia drove many Tirolean Anabaptists back to Austria, and even Hutter's death in 1536 did not end the movement.

On Feb. 22, 1544, the government reported to Brixlegg that the Hutterian Brethren in Moravia were planning to lead the Anabaptists to Moravia the following spring, and that a large number had reported for emigration in Kitzbühel. But the next few years were relatively quiet. In May 1557 a native of Kitzbühel, Hans Kräl (*q.v.*), was seized in Taufers and brought to judgment. For two years he lay in a dungeon, until he won his freedom. In 1561 he was again in Kitzbühel, and reported to the brotherhood in Moravia the death of Mändl, Rack, and Kotter. The fear inspired by these executions did not last long.

Soon other Anabaptists from Kitzbühel were taken to court. They reported that Kräl was their leader. He writes, "There is not an hour that we are safe from their bloodthirsty hands. They search and spy day and night, where they might seize us." Hence in the next year it is Hans Kräl and Leonhard Dax (*q.v.*) on whose capture the authorities were bent. Well-to-do persons from Kitzbühel migrated to Moravia in 1564.

Thus in spite of all the measures passed, the Anabaptist movement in Kitzbühel did not die out. The more freely they were allowed to move in Moravia, the stronger the train of immigrants became. Hans Kräl, having won a reputation for bravery on his bold missionary journeys in the highlands, was chosen leader of the thriving church in Moravia. In 1592 the Anabaptist Georg Pintlechner from the territory of Kitzbühel was reported "unwilling to be corrected of his error. If he remains obstinate, proceed according to the mandates."

In the 1590's the movement continued to grow weaker, nor is there any mention of Anabaptist propaganda in Kitzbühel. The number of those who testified to their faith with their blood in Kitzbühel, according to a manuscript of 1581 found in the metropolitan library in Gran, was 68, certainly a stately number for so small a town. Loserth.

Beck, *Geschichts-Bücher*, 55, 107; Wolkan, *Geschicht-Buch*, 41 f., 64, 183; Zieglschmid, *Chronik*, 57, 89, 154, 234; Loserth, *Anabaptismus*; *ML* II, 502-4.

Klaar Vertoog *dienende tot wederlegginge van de ongefondeerde beschuldigingen van Franciscus Elgersma* . . . (n.p., 1689). This anonymous book refutes the objections of F. Elgersma (*q.v.*), a Dutch Reformed minister, who had attacked the Mennonites and especially Foecke Floris, accusing them of Socinianism (*q.v.*). As to the author, C. B. Hylkema and W. J. Kühler took Galenus Abrahamsz (*q.v.*) to be the author, but H. W. Meihuizen thinks that Claes Stapel (*q.v.*) is the author. vDZ.

H. W. Meihuizen, *Galenus Abrahamsz* (Haarlem, 1954) 162.

Klaas Tigler-Leen, a foundation for the financial support to be given to young people, descendants of Klaas Tigler, who might wish to study at a Dutch university. All branches of study can be chosen, except training for the Roman Catholic priesthood and military science. The founder was Klaas Tigler (*q.v.*) (1724-1811) of Leeuwarden, a preacher of the Mennonite congregation in his home town. In 1832-1920 the Leeuwarden Mennonite church board administered the foundation. Among about 50 beneficiaries there have been eight Mennonite theological students, whose educational expenses have been paid by the fund. vDZ.

Gedenkboek Honderdjarig bestaan Klaas Tigler Leen te Leeuwarden, 1832-1932.

Klaasen, Gerrit, an elder of the Old Flemish Mennonite congregation of Danzig, West Prussia, Germany, whose years of serving are unknown, stayed 1627-29 in the Netherlands, especially at Amsterdam and Rotterdam, to arbitrate in disputes within the congregations. (*Inv. Arch. Amst.* II, 2, Nos. 423 f.) vDZ.

Klaassen (Klassen, Klaeszen, Klasen), a Mennonite family: see **Claassen.**

Klaassen, Eije: see **Clasen, Eje.**

Klaassen, Jakob Abramovitch, a Mennonite teacher, b. Aug. 3, 1847, in the Bergtal settlement, Ekaterinoslav, South Russia, the son of Abram Klaassen, the volost secretary, d. Dec. 16, 1919, in Rosental near Chortitza. In 1875 he married Agnes Sudermann, to whom were born six children. In the history of Mennonite education in the Ukraine he occupies a prominent place. He taught for 46 years. At the age of 17, upon completion of the course in the Chortitza Zentralschule, he began his career as a teacher in the elementary school, and 16 years later transferred to the Chortitza Zentralschule (*q.v.*), where he taught in 1881-95.

Klaassen was a man of unusual capacity for work and self-discipline, continuing his own education until he was at the head of the teaching profession among the Russian Mennonites. He was an earnest Christian, rooted deeply in Mennonitism in thought, feeling, and deed. He was an ardent advocate of girls' schools, and helped to establish them among the Russian Mennonites. The rapid growth of the Chortitza Mädchenschule (*q.v.*), where he taught the last 18 years of his life, was principally his achievement. His teaching subjects were religion, German, Russian, history, and drawing. (*ML* II, 504.) H.E.

Klaassen, Johann, b. March 17, 1872, in Ladekopp, district of Halbstadt, Taurida, Russia, d. June 25,

1950, at Djakarta (Jakarta, formerly Batavia), Indonesia, a Mennonite missionary. Initially he was trained as a businessman, but in 1893 he began his missionary studies, first at St. Chrischona near Basel, Switzerland, then at Rotterdam in the Netherlands. In the meanwhile he had been ordained as a preacher in Russia (June 9, 1896). After he had finished his studies, being appointed missionary by the Dutch Mennonite Mission Association, he sailed for Java, now Indonesia, then Dutch East Indies, where he arrived on the field in March 1899. He was active in Margaredjo until June 1905 when he returned to Europe because of illness. In his first Indonesian period he had been married July 6, 1903, to Magdalena Horsch from Gelchsheim, Germany, sister of Michael and John Horsch. He remained in Europe until August 1908. The European period was devoted to medical studies and trips in Holland, Germany, Switzerland, and Russia to arouse interest in missions. Back at Java he was in charge of a large field, serving Margaredjo, Kedung-Pendjalin, Kaju-Apu, and Pati. After 1910, when missionary Johann Hübert had come back from Europe, he served only at Kaju-Apu and Pati. Here he worked with much blessing as an evangelist, as a teacher, and also doing some medical work. From 1913 to 1923 he lived in Europe, at first at Lautenbach, then mostly in Heilbronn, Germany. But though far from the mission field, he did not forget his "brown brethren" and traveled widely to preach and to collect money for the mission work. Because of the war and political changes in Russia after 1914 he was unable to enter his native country and lost touch with its congregations. He became a German citizen in 1915.

From April 1923 to Jan. 8, 1925, Klaassen again was on the Java mission field, now serving Margaredjo and the leper colony of Donorodjo. In the spring of 1925, after having visited the Dutch Mennonite mission of Pakanten on the island of Sumatra, he returned to Germany. The following years were devoted to mission promotion until he returned to the mission field for the fourth time in 1939. On the mission field he found his children: Helene, a nurse, married in 1926 to the missionary Hermann Schmitt (q.v.), Maria, also a nurse, and Martha, married to the missionary Otto Stauffer (q.v.). He re-entered Java as a widower, his wife having died in 1929. He now lived mostly in the home of Hermann Schmitt in Kudus. After a year of happiness and blessings among his relatives, bitter years followed. At the outbreak of the war between Germany and the Netherlands both Schmitt and Stauffer, being German subjects, were interned in a camp and in 1942 both perished when their ship, transporting them from Java to India, was torpedoed. Other calamities followed: hostilities of the Mohammedans, the Japanese invasion in 1942, and 1945 the troubles which accompanied the political movement of independence of the republic of Indonesia loosed from the Dutch motherland, the communistic disturbances, the attacks of fanatical Mohammedan bands against missionaries and native Christians, and the guerrilla wars of 1948-49. In all these troubles and disasters Klaassen remained loyal to his faith and continued to serve his Lord as much as he could. On Jan. 6, 1950, he took leave of his beloved mission field, delivering a short address in the church of Kelet. It was his intention to go to his daughter's home in California, but while in Djakarta he had a stroke and died there on June 25, 1950.

Klaassen was a man of steadfast simple piety, whose preaching and life was able to strike many hearts and to win over for the church of Christ a large number of Javanese natives. vDZ.

"Johann Klaassen," Gem.-Kal. 1952, 19-39, Part I autobiographical, Part II by Maria Klaassen, Part III by Gerhard Hein; reports of the Dutch Mennonite Mission Association.

Klaassen, Martin, a teacher in the village of Köppenthal near Saratov, South Russia, wrote the book, *Geschichte der wehrlosen taufgesinnten Gemeinden von den Zeiten der Apostel bis auf die Gegenwart* (Danzig, 1873), when exemption from military service was at issue in Russia. His purpose was to follow nonresistance as a Christian principle through the history of the church, and by giving a connected historical account of nonresistant brotherhoods who remained true to the Gospel of Jesus, to encourage the Mennonites of his day to hold fast to the principle. He divides the history of these brotherhoods into three periods: The first period begins early in the third century, when the first "Anabaptists" opposed the secularized church, and extends to Peter Waldus; the second period extends to Menno Simons, and the third to 1873. He did not believe, however, that these various groups belonged together. Their stamp of connectedness derives from their adherence to the Word of God. This book was written with warm devotion and was not without its effect. (*ML* II, 504.) H.Q.

Klaassen, Michael (1860-1934), a Mennonite (GCM) minister, the son of Martin Klaassen (q.v.), was born Aug. 26, 1860, in Köppenthal, Trakt settlement, Russia. He received his secondary education under Jacob Penner, was baptized by David Hamm in 1877, and followed his parents to Central Asia in 1880. Here he married Margaretha Janzen. In 1885 they came to America, spending the first years in Beatrice, Neb. In 1894 they moved to Bessie, Okla., where he was elected minister of the Sichar Mennonite (GCM) Church in 1896. In 1901 he was elected elder of the Herold Mennonite Church, which had been organized in 1899. For 17 years he taught German and Bible in the elementary school there. He was active as an itinerant minister in Oklahoma. Because of the hardships during World War I he went to Morden, Man., with a number of his church members in 1918, and there organized another Herold Mennonite Church. He died at Morden on Oct. 18, 1934. C.K.

J. G. Rempel, *Fünfzig Jahre Konferenzbestrebungen, 1902-1952* I (1954) 128.

Klaasz (Klaese, Klaase), **Jacob** (d. February 1658), was elder of the Frisian congregation of West-Zaandam 1609-58 and also served the Frisian congregation of Westzaan; in 1640 he had some difficulties at the conference of Frisian churches in North Holland because contrary to the conservative views of most Frisian congregations, he was willing to promote a union with the Flemish Mennonites, whom he esteemed as good Christians just as well as the Frisians.   vDZ.

Inv. Arch. Amst. I, No. 865; S. Lootsma, *Het Nieuwe Huys* (Zaandam, 1937) 83 f., 99, 102, 191.

Klaasz, Jan, also called Jan Klaasz (Klaaszen, Claessen) van Grouw, because he lived at Grouw, or Jan Claesen Backer, apparently because he was a baker, was a Mennonite preacher of the congregation at Grouw (*q.v.*), Dutch province of Friesland, where he served 1680 until at least 1702. He was a man of fragile health but of a strong spirit, and notwithstanding his poor education he was versed in theological problems. Jan Klaasz was a champion of rather liberal ideas and is not without reason called a Socinian (*q.v.*). He enthusiastically participated in the meeting of the Collegiants (*q.v.*) in his home town, where he met Mennonites, Reformed, and non-church men, all of a liberal trend. In his home church his ideas caused a schism; a group of more conservative members in 1696 separated from the main body and founded a congregation, called the Flemish congregation. The other and larger group was at first called the Jan Claesen congregation, later mostly the Waterlander congregation. Jan Klaasz's ideas are best known from his book *De Leere der Doopsgezinden verdedigd* (Amsterdam, 1702). The gist of his theological ideas is the view that the Holy Scriptures are secondary to the immediate action of the Spirit of God in the heart of the believers. Only when enlightened by the Spirit of God can one truly read the Scripture. Though Jan Klaasz does not deny the deity of Christ, he is more interested in His example than in His death. The doctrine of salvation by the satisfactory death of Christ is not a substantial part of his doctrines. With an astonishing knowledge of the old Mennonite literature he shows that among the early Anabaptists personal faith as a trust in God was more emphasized than the creed of the congregation; the well-known confessions are not to prescribe the faith, as is the opinion of some Mennonites, but they are merely directives for the members of the church. In these ideas of Jan Klaasz one will easily recognize the spiritualistic teachings of Galenus Abrahamsz, and indeed Galenus greatly influenced the preacher of Grouw, but the latter goes further and admits that some of his ideas agree with those of Socinus, which Galenus never did.

Not only in his home congregation but also elsewhere Jan Klaasz's opinions were opposed. Sometimes this happened in a peaceful way as in the correspondence which Jan Klaasz conducted with E. A. van Dooregeest (*q.v.*) after 1695.

Klaasz's book, *De Leere der Doopsgezinden,* was directed against the "strange and false notions" (*vreemde misduidingen*) of Douwe Feddriks (*q.v.*), Mennonite preacher of Harlingen, who had called him an irascible troublemaker, breaker of peace, Socinian, Arian, and Spinozist, but who, according to Jan Klaasz, had more likeness to a Reformed (Calvinistic) than to a Mennonite preacher.

Some of his members at Grouw in 1695 lodged a complaint of Socinianism against him with the Re-formed Classis at Leeuwarden, but apparently it did not result in a trial.   vDZ.

Inv. Arch. Amst. II, No. 2946; *Biogr. Wb.* II, 56 f.; F. H. Pasma, *De Doopsgezinden te Grouw* (1930) 8-11 with a facsimile of a letter of Jan Klaasz; Blaupot t. C., *Friesland,* 193, 226, 235 ff.; *idem, Groningen* I, 189; J. C. van Slee, *De Rijnsburger Collegianten* (Haarlem, 1896) 216 ff.; H. W. Meihuizen, *Galenus Abrahamsz* (Haarlem, 1954) 183 f., 186.

Klaasz, Klaas, of Blokzijl: see **Claesz, Claes.**

Klaerken, an Anabaptist martyr: see **Claerken Boucket.**

Klaes: see also **Claes.**

Klaesken, an Anabaptist martyr: see **Claesken.**

Klampferer, Bernhard and **Marx,** brothers, who were sent by the Hutterian Brethren in Moravia to Vienna "to purchase the tools for their trade." When they were about to return they were imprisoned by the baron of Roggendorf on April 1, 1573, after a long argument with him on infant baptism; they proved from the Scriptures that children should not be baptized. When he saw that his preaching did not change their mind, he summoned the preacher from Krems (*q.v.*), Master Gangolf Wanger (Beck, 263); Wanger's efforts were equally futile. After an imprisonment of eleven weeks they were released and permitted to return to Moravia. Their dispute on baptism is recorded in a manuscript in the archives at Brno, "Verantwortung Brueder Marx vnd bernharts Klampffrern, zu wien in irer gefenckhnus vmb der warhait willen 1573." NEFF.

Beck, *Geschichts-Bücher,* 261 f.; Wolkan, *Geschicht-Buch,* 362-65; Zieglschmid, *Chronik,* 471; *ML* II, 504.

Klampferer (Klampherer), **Julius:** see **Gherlandi, Giulio.**

Klassen, a Mennonite family: see **Claassen.**

Klassen, Cornelius Franz, b. Aug. 3, 1894, as the oldest of 13 children of Franz F. and Justine Wiebe Klassen in the New Samara, Russia, Mennonite settlement, d. at Gronau, Germany, May 8, 1954, an active lay worker in the Mennonite Brethren Church of Canada after 1928, an outstanding leader and administrator in Mennonite relief and colonization work in Russia, Canada, and Europe, and from 1945 to his death director of the refugee and resettlement service of the Mennonite Central Committee in Europe in behalf of the Russian and Danzig refugees. His early schooling was in the village school at Donskaya, Neu-Samara, where the family lived from 1900 on (his father operated a store there until 1918), and in the Zentralschule at Karassan, Crimea, 1907-10. After his baptism into the M.B. Church at Lugovsk in the summer of 1911, he entered (1912) the office of the Otto Deutz Co. of Moscow. His plan to study medicine was blocked by induction into the Mennonite forestry (CO) service 1915-17. Meanwhile he studied (1913-14) in Education under A. Tcheriyayev in St. Petersburg and then served a year as private tutor.

Klassen's first representative service for the Mennonite brotherhood was in 1917 as delegate to the All-Mennonite Congress at Ohrloff, and also to the Bundeskonferenz at Halbstadt, representing the Mennonite forestry service men. With Peter Froese he was delegated by the Congress to negotiate the release of Mennonites held in prison in Moscow by the Kerensky government, where his outstanding gifts of diplomacy and determination were demonstrated. With Froese he was chosen again at Ufa in 1920 to represent the Mennonites of East Russia and Siberia at Moscow, after having served as elected representative of the settlement of New Samara and Orenburg both at Moscow and to the Bashkir Republic at Sterlitamak (1918-19). He worked in Moscow in 1920-21 in the United Council of Religious Bodies and the Russian Relief Committee, and aided A. J. Miller in the negotiations with the Kremlin which laid the foundation for the American Mennonite Relief (AMR) of the MCC in Russia. He was active in the AMR program 1921-23, then shared in the organization (1923) and administration (vice-president) of the all-Mennonite organization, A.M.L.V. (*Allrussischer Mennonitischer landwirtschaftlicher Verein,* Peter Froese, president), which rendered great service both in the great emigration of 1922-25 to Canada, and in taking over the representation of the Mennonites of Russia after the church conference organization was suppressed by Moscow. In 1928 he left Russia, arriving at Winnipeg in December of that year.

In Canada Klassen entered the service of the Canadian Pacific Railway (1930-) and became the effective leader of the great work of paying off the entire transportation debt of those emigrants of 1922-25 whose trip from Russia to Canada had been financed by the loans from the C.P.R., over $1,000,-000. He was also an active and intimate collaborator with David Toews (*q.v.*), of Rosthern, in the work of the Canadian Mennonite Board of Colonization. He helped to organize the Mennonite Central Relief Committee of Western Canada (1940), and served as its first secretary-treasurer. He served on the board of trustees of the Gretna (Man.) Mennonite Collegiate Institute and the Mennonite Brethren Bible College in Winnipeg. He was a member of the Committee for General Welfare and Public Relations of the M.B. General Conference 1936- , and secretary of the Military Problems Committee of the Mennonite Churches of Western Canada 1941- . With David Toews he served as Canadian delegate to the Mennonite world conferences at Danzig (1930) and Amsterdam (1936), also as delegate and speaker at the succeeding world conferences at Goshen-Newton (1948) and Basel (1952). From 1944 he was a member of the Mennonite Central Committee, and a member of its Executive Committee from 1946.

Klassen's greatest work was as European Commissioner for Refugee Aid and Resettlement under the MCC in Europe from December 1945 until his death, during the last year serving also as general director of MCC work in Europe. He was the MCC representative on the important Liaison Committee with the German Mennonites, also on the Board of Trustees of the European Mennonite Bible School at Basel. He carried through with outstanding success the arduous and difficult assignment of negotiating with various governmental and international agencies (UNO, IRO, etc.) for the exit permits, transportation, and migration for over 10,000 Russian (plus several thousand Galicians and Danzigers) Mennonite refugees to Canada, Paraguay, and Uruguay. He was the father of the resettlement housing program for Danzig Mennonite refugees in Germany (Niederbiber, Espelkamp, Backnang, Enkenbach, and Wedel), which he administered to his death, and a prime figure in the establishment of the service of old people's homes at Leutesdorf (where he is buried), Enkenbach, and Pinneberg. During the difficult postwar period in Europe, particularly in Germany, he rendered a great service as a counselor and helper in the revival of Mennonite church life, in the establishment of such institutions as the *Foyer Mennonite* at Valdoie-Belfort, France, the Basel Glaubenskonferenz, and *Der Mennonit,* of which he served as editor during the last year before his death. Throughout his service he remained a devout, simple Christian of deep faith and dedicated life, an inspirer to thousands, both young and old, in both Europe and America. Through his tireless labors and extensive speaking tours on behalf of relief, he became not only the symbol of Mennonite relief and refugee service to Mennonites in general but a strong influence for better mutual understanding and co-operation among Mennonites across denominational lines. This found expression also in his participation in the work of the MENNONITE ENCYCLOPEDIA, of which he served as an associate editor from the beginning to his death.

He was survived by his wife Mary (nee Brieger) and four children, Harold, Walfried, Herbert, and Irmgard. His residence in Canada was in Winnipeg until 1948 when the family moved to Abbotsford, B.C.†
                                                                H.S.B.

Der Mennonit VII (1954) 83-87; *Mennonitische Rundschau* LXXVII (May 19, 1954) No. 20, pp. 1-5.

Klassen, Jakob Jakovlevitch, b. April 7, 1856, d. Oct. 8, 1919, executive secretary (*Kanzleiführer*) of the Chortitza (Russia) Mennonite administration (*Gebietsamt*) after 1888. The volost administration was a sort of cabinet in miniature, headed by the volost elder, who was elected for a term of three years, assisted by an aide and an executive secretary. They had executive power to carry out orders and directions from the legislative body, the volost meeting, and from the Russian government. This executive organ had to look after nearly all the social aspects of life in the Mennonite villages, like the purchase of land for the landless, management of the "communal land," and provide for the orphans' care, fire insurance, tax for forestry service, and in a sense the higher schools of the settlement. Thus an executive secretary of the *Gebietsamt* who conducted the work for 34 years, with frequent changes of volost elders, was a very influential leader. Rich in experience, familiar with psychology of his people, progressive and democratic in temperament, Jakob Jakovlevitch Klassen gave direction and worked constructively for the Chortitza Mennonite community.

As a zealous promoter of education, Klassen took a leading part in all the educational efforts of his time. With his co-operation the Chortitza Mädchenschule (*q.v.*) was founded. With his support the Zentralschule was enlarged, and the normal school built. Thanks to his initiative, the daughter settlements joined Chortitza in the support of the normal school. He was one of the founders of the public library of Chortitza.

Klassen's death was a tragic one. During the period of terror from the Machno bands in 1919, he was sent by the community to Ekaterinoslav to seek aid to meet the violence of the bandits. Unsuccessful he returned to Chortitza, was seized by the bandits and shot near Alexandrovsk. (*ML* II, 504 f.)

Klassen, Johann J. (1872-1942), was active as teacher and minister of the Chortitza settlement, both in the city of Ekaterinoslav, South Russia, and later as minister and elder in Canada. Born in the village of Kronsgarten in the vicinity of Ekaterinoslav, he completed the Zentralschule with its pedagogical course at Chortitza. For a year he taught in the elementary school at Chortitza, only to leave as the first student from Chortitza to study at the Theological Seminary at Basel, Switzerland. This was made possible through the scholarship founded by a Mennonite industrialist. After his return he taught for several years in the village of Schönhorst near Chortitza. In Schönhorst he was elected to the ministry in 1902. In 1905 he was called to teach in the Chortitza Zentralschule. After a few years he went to Ekaterinoslav (*q.v.*), where he replaced the well-known minister and editor of the *Botschafter,* David H. Epp (*q.v.*), who had moved with his paper to Berdyansk, as teacher and minister (1912-18). Again he returned to Chortitza, and as a minister in the congregation and teacher in the Zentralschule, he shared with his contemporaries the first severe postwars year with their anarchy, robberies, typhus, and hunger.

In 1923, when the doors were opened for emigration, Klassen with many others went to Canada. A large number of these immigrants established their homes on newly acquired farms, first in Saskatchewan, then also in the other provinces. J. J. Klassen soon began to gather these scattered groups in Saskatchewan into a congregation. The Nordheim congregation with its main station at Dundurn, about 30 miles from Saskatoon, was the first organized church of the immigrants, and J. J. Klassen was the first elder of these Mennonites to be ordained in Canada. The ordination was performed by David Toews (*q.v.*). Due to the sickness of his wife, J. J. Klassen spent the last years of his life in British Columbia. In an auto accident on Jan. 29, 1942, he here came to a tragic death.

Because of his deeply spiritual disposition, his unwavering faith on the one hand, and his calm unbiased judgment on the other hand, as well as his enormous Bible knowledge, he already in the old country and even more in the new country left a permanent influence on the Mennonite congregations.　　J.G.R.

Klassen, Johann Peter (1868-1947), a leading elder and writer of the Russian and Canadian Mennonites (GCM), was born May 27, 1868, at Schönwiese near Alexandrovsk (Saporozhe), Ukraine, Russia, the son of Peter and Agenetha Klassen. He was married twice: first to Katharina Wieler (7 children), and in 1911 to Katharina Dyck (2 children). After completing the Chortitza Zentralschule he served as village schoolteacher for five years. He served the Kronsweide (*q.v.*) Mennonite congregation as preacher from 1904 and as elder from 1907 until his emigration to Canada in 1923, with residence however in Schönwiese. In 1928 he founded the Schönwiese (First Mennonite) church in Winnipeg, serving as its elder until his retirement in 1939. He died at Vancouver on May 25, 1947, and is buried at Winnipeg.

Klassen was a rather prolific writer, chiefly of poems. J. H. Janzen calls him "the most productive and most natural of [the Russo-Canadian Mennonite] poets." He adds, "he writes mostly for existing melodies, so his poems at the moment they appear are already songs . . . . An inexhaustible and unconquerable joy speaks out of all his poems . . . , even though he has suffered much from an infirmity." His published booklets of poems include *Aehrenlese* (Winnipeg, n.d., 73 p.), *Brocken* (Winnipeg, 1932, 32 p.), *Dunkle Tage* (Scottdale, 1924? 32 p.), *Krümlein* (Scottdale, 1924? 43 p.), *Meine Garbe* (Vancouver, n.d., 102 p.), *Nohoaksel* (Yarrow, 1946, 87 p.), *Roggenbrot* (Vancouver, 1946, 134 p.), *Wegeblumen* (Scottdale, 1924? 52 p.), *Der Zwillingsbruder von "Meine Garbe"* (Vancouver, n.d., 100 p.). In addition he also published *Reiseskizzen über die Auswanderung im Jahre 1923* (Scottdale, 1924? 37 p.).　　H.S.B.

J. H. Janzen, "The Literature of the Russo-Canadian Mennonites," *Menn. Life* I (January 1946) 23 f.; *Fünfzig Jahre Konferenzbestrebungen 1902-1952* I, 183 f.

Klassen, Peter Abraham, elder of the Kronsweide Mennonite Church near Chortitza, son of Abraham Klassen and Justina Hildebrand, was born in 1825 on the island Chortitza, South Russia. His first wife was Anna Janzen, and his second wife Aganeta Schulz, each of whom had four children. One son, Johann Peter Klassen, later also became the elder of the Kronsweide Mennonite Church, emigrated to Canada, and became one of the leaders there. He served his church as a minister 1851-1902, and from 1867 also as elder. He died 1905 and was buried at Neu-Schönwiese.　　J.H.En.

Klassen, Peter J. (1889-1953), a minister (GCM) and outstanding Mennonite poet and literary artist, was born June 7, 1889, at Ohrloff, Molotschna, Russia. He attended the secondary school at Spat, Crimea, and taught school. On Jan. 3, 1910, he married Liese Löwen and entered business. During 1916-24 he was again a teacher. He made numerous trips to Moscow to represent the Mennonite constituency. He was active as a youth leader and choir director. On July 3, 1923, he was elected minister of the Ebenfeld Mennonite Church and ordained by P. Wiens. After teaching a year at Arkadak he emigrated to Canada in 1925. For a while he lived in Rosthern and Saskatoon, Sask. In 1928 he purchased a farm at Superb, Sask., and lived there until 1948, when he went to Yarrow, B.C., where he spent the last years of his life. He died at Abbotsford on July 19, 1953.

Peter J. Klassen, although struggling with sickness and want nearly all his life, was an outstanding writer. J. H. Janzen said of him, "He is the one who is most widely known in German literature and is the only [Mennonite] poet who has received high honors and an income for his literary work." In 1951 the Canadian Mennonite Conference published 5,000 copies of his *Verlorene Söhne* because of its significance in promoting the Mennonite peace principles. Many of his stories appeared in installments in *Der Bote*. He was also a constant contributor to *Der Kinderbote* for the column "Onkel Peters Ecke."

Among Klassen's writings are the following: *Der Peet. Geschichten vom Peet und seinen Kameraden* (Superb, 1943-49, 4 vv.); *Die Heimfahrt* (Superb, 1943); *Heimat einmal—Eine Erzählung aus Russlands jüngster Vergangenheit*, 2 vv. (n.p., n.d.); *Die Geschichte des Ohm Klassen* (Regina, n.d.); *Fünfunddreissig Fabeln* (Superb, 1944); *Grossmutters Schatz und andere Geschichten, Gedichte und Fabeln* (Superb, 1939); *Als die Heimat zur Fremde geworden, wurde die Fremde zur Heimat* (Winnipeg, n.d.).   C.K.

J. G. Rempel, *Fünfzig Jahre Konferenzbestrebungen, 1902-1952* II, 344 f.; J. H. Janzen, "The Literature of Russo-Canadian Mennonites," *Menn. Life* II (January 1946) 24; *Der Bote*, Aug. 19, 1953, 6.

Klatt, Johann Karl, one of the outstanding schoolmen among the Mennonites of South Russia. As a young man he was a teacher on the country estate of Johann Cornies II, son of the well-known Johann Cornies (*q.v.*), and later became the son-in-law of the former. He studied systematically, Cornies' rich library offering a good opportunity for such study. Frequent contact with the Russian nobility and high government officials, and his service on the board of the Melitopol Realschule, as well as various other non-Mennonite institutions, gave him vision and social security, which served him well in representing the cause of Mennonite schools to the authorities.

In 1883 Klatt was elected to the school council by the conference (*Kirchenkonvent*), the head of the district (*Gebietsvorsteher*) of Halbstadt and Gnadenfeld, and the functioning member of the school council. In 1884 he was elected president of the school council, served in this capacity until 1887, when he resigned to serve as a regular member of the council. P. Heese (*q.v.*) succeeded him as president.

Klatt and Heese did many things together, such as school visitation, conferences, and examinations. Both also promoted schools financially. Under their influence the school system in the Molotschna took a long forward stride. On Sept. 4, 1884, Klatt received the silver medal "For zeal" in his services to the cause of education. Klatt also served on the board of the Ohrloff Zentralschule in 1880-90. He was a member of the Gnadenfeld Mennonite Church, and as a youth had been a pupil of Heinrich Franz.   A.B.

P. Braun, "Der Molotschnaer Mennoniten-Schulrat" (ms.); Friesen, *Brüderschaft*, 595, 650; *ML* II, 505.

Klaus, Alexander, a Russian of German extraction, in 1889 published a book in Russian with the title *Nashi Kolonii* (Our Colonies), which will always be important for the history of foreign colonies in Russia. To the Hutterites and Mennonites he devotes 128 pages. In 1887 the *Odessaer Zeitung* published a German translation of the book, done by its editor, Jakob Töws, under the title *Unsere Kolonien*. (*ML* II, 505.)   D.H.E.

Klausen (Italian, *Chiusa*), an ancient village of Tirol, Austria, which became Italian after World War I. It lies narrowly confined by the Säben Mountain and the Eisack River. Until the 10th century it was an episcopal see, which was transferred to Brixen. Towering over the town is the Säben abbey (Roman camp Sabiona) and the castle of Branzoll.

In Anabaptist history Klausen is important. It was the scene of the last labor of several Anabaptist leaders. Here Georg Blaurock (*q.v.*), one of the founders of the movement in Zürich in 1525, was burned to death. Several years later Jakob Hutter (*q.v.*) was put into the dungeon of Branzoll, and then burned at the stake at Innsbruck. Seven Anabaptists were executed for their faith in Klausen (Beck, 278).

For a long time the Anabaptists were the only evangelicals in this area. To be sure, Andreas Carlstadt (*q.v.*) was here for a time in 1525 at the invitation of the mine owners of Villander (one mile southwest of Klausen), but he soon returned to Saxony (Loserth, 448; Pitra, 89). This invitation, however, indicates that the Klausen area was ready for evangelical teaching. The first Anabaptist preacher in the Eisack Valley was Jörg Zaunring, who later accompanied Hutter on some of his journeys. He baptized Michael Kürschner (Klesinger) in June 1528 in Vells; Kürschner (*q.v.*) later became the leader of the Anabaptist group around Klausen. In Klausen and Gufidaun (one mile east of Klausen) Kürschner was apparently especially active, since in February 1529 the government charged the officials with laxity in their suppression of the Anabaptists. On April 25 he was seized with seven others at a meeting in Kitzbühel and taken to Innsbruck, where he was condemned to death and burned at the stake across the bridge on June 2. He himself confessed to having baptized over 100 persons (Loserth, 470 f.).

When Georg Blaurock, who had just been banished from Switzerland, heard of the desire for the Gospel in Tirol, he was at once willing to take charge of Kürschner's orphaned congregation. In May 1529 he came to Klausen with Hans Langegger. His success did not remain concealed from the government. To avoid capture he went to other places to work, but in August he returned to Klausen and Gufidaun, and was betrayed by the authorities. On Aug. 14 he and Hans Langegger fell into the hands of Hans Preu, the magistrate, and were burned Sept. 6, 1529, at Klausen.

The effect of Blaurock's preaching was so deep that many of the members of the group followed his example and were faithful unto death. On the Breitenberg ob Leifers near Bozen several persons were surprised at a meeting and seized, among them Simon Kob of Breitenberg and his wife. The monk Gardian of Bozen tried for three weeks to persuade them to return to the church; but most of them remained steadfast and were put to death. During the night of Nov. 16, 1529, four men and four women of Blaurock's group were seized at Vill near Neumarkt. They were also given instruction by a priest on government orders, and the steadfast were executed (Loserth, 487 and 500).

In Klausen Ulrich Müllner was beheaded on Oct. 2, 1531, because he belonged to the Anabaptist group (Beck, 105).

Jakob Hutter was also working around Klausen during these years. A part of Blaurock's group was sent to Moravia by Hutter, after he had established connections with the Anabaptists there. After his return he worked principally in Klausen. A reward of 40 guilders was offered by an order of July 8, 1529, for reporting an Anabaptist leader. In a cave near Gufidaun he held a meeting attended by 150 persons, most of them from Teys and Villnöss (northeast of Klausen), and held a communion service. In Albeins (two miles north of Klausen) and at Prugg 50 to 60 persons met at night (Loserth, 502).

The government was seriously intent on seizing Hutter, as well as Christoph Gschöll and Hans Amon (Loserth, 507). On Dec. 13, 1532, orders were sent to judge Flamm to try to find where the three leaders, Jakob Hutter, Hans Amon, and Offerus Griesinger, could be caught, "since now in winter they cannot live in the woods and forests." Hutter and Amon were given shelter by Peter Binder in Klausen. In January 1533 Hutter had held a meeting in Villnöss, attended by about 70 persons from the Puster Valley. The meeting was not noticed, for the episcopal councilors in Brixen rebuked the authorities of Klausen for not catching Hutter, "who was trying to mislead the community," and who was so often seen in Klausen (Loserth, 508 f.). In August 1533 Hutter went to Moravia again, where as the chroniclers relate, "he put the true brotherhood in pretty good order by the help and grace of God" (Beck, 114), and in 1534 returned to Klausen. In the meantime he had married. On Nov. 25, 1535, he and his wife and three other women were seized in the house of the former sexton Hans Steiner on the other side of the Eisack bridge, and taken to Burg Branzoll. Katharina Hutter was cross-examined on Nov. 3 in Klausen by the city judge Lienhard Mair at Creuz, and imprisoned in Gufidaun castle, from which she made her escape (Loserth, 556 f.). Jakob Hutter died at the stake on Feb. 25, 1536, at Innsbruck.

The Anabaptist movement in Klausen was now destroyed. Ferdinand's wish was fulfilled; he had written to the authorities at Innsbruck on Dec. 24, 1535, "We are confident that the capture of Hutter will do much to wipe out the Anabaptist sect" (Loserth, 562). Raw force had won.   LOSERTH.

Loserth, Anabaptismus; Wolkan, Geschicht-Buch, 41, 55, 64, 118, 182; Zieglschmid, Chronik, 76, 89, 157, 233; F. Pitra, Klausen und Umgebung (Brixen, 1910); ML II, 505-7.

Kleef (Cleve), **Pieter van,** an Anabaptist martyr: see **Pieter Aelbrechts.**

Kleefeld, a common Mennonite village name transplanted from Russia to America. The name appeared in the following Mennonite settlements: Molotschna and Barnaul, Russia; West Reserve, Man.; Cuauhtemoc, Mexico; Menno and Fernheim, Chaco, Paraguay.   C.K.

Kleefeld, a village in the Molotschna Mennonite settlement in the Ukraine, Russia, situated on the left bank of the Yushanlee River, was founded in 1854 by 40 families, and was the second youngest village of the Halbstadt volost. The village comprised 8,300 acres of land.

In 1929 the name Kleefeld was also given a village in the Fernheim settlement in Paraguay. In 1950 it had 104 inhabitants.   HEGE.

Neuer Haus- und Landwirtschafts-Kalender XLIII (Odessa, 1911) 108; J. W. Fretz, Pilgrims in Paraguay (Scottdale, 1953) 31; ML II, 507.

Kleefeld (formerly Gruenfeld) Church of God in Christ Mennonite Church, located at Kleefeld, 30 miles southeast of the city of Winnipeg, Man., was organized in 1881. Most of the members are descendants of the first settlers of 1874-75, immigrant Mennonites from Russia, and until 1881 were a part of the Kleine Gemeinde (q.v.) group. One of the first ministers, Abraham Isaac, was actively in charge from 1881 until his death in 1938. In 1902-11 most of the congregation moved west to Swalwell, Alberta. Among them was Peter Toews, the first leader. John I. Penner, present leading minister, and Deacon Jacob I. Bartel were ordained in 1924. Later Joseph Isaac was ordained as minister and Peter I. Bartel as deacon. A meetinghouse was erected in the early eighties. The present church was built in 1907 in Hochstadt and moved to its present site in 1917. Its seating capacity is 250. Low German is spoken in the homes. The majority of members are farmers. The church activities in both the German and English language include weekly Sunday morning worship services, Sunday school, midweek Bible classes, and singing practice, with Christian Endeavor every third Sunday evening. The sewing circle aids in MCC relief, hospitals, and home mission work. The membership in 1956 was 181.   J.I.P.

Kleefeld (Man.) Evangelical Mennonite (Kleine Gemeinde) Church is located eight miles west of Steinbach. Its first meetinghouse was built in 1940. The Kleefeld church had a baptized membership of 140 in 1955. The church has a weekly Sunday school and a monthly *Jugendverein*. This is the smallest district in membership in Manitoba of the Kleine Gemeinde. The ministers are John R. Friesen and Peter K. Bartel. Gerhard S. Fast is deacon. Between 1874 and 1940 services were held in the village schools and later in a near-by church. Arnold Fast was ordained as minister of the Kleefeld church in 1955.   D.P.R.

Kleermaker, G., whom van Braght in his *Martyrs' Mirror* (D 644-46, E 965-67) lists as an Anabaptist martyr, executed at Antwerp, Belgium, in 1573 (exact date and method of execution not given). A letter written by G. Kleermaker in prison to "J.H.," a sister of the congregation, is found in the *Martyrs' Mirror*. But this information is incomplete and probably incorrect. No martyr by this name was found among the victims in Antwerp. G. Kleermaker may be identical either with Coenraad Cleermaker or with Gillis Glercq, Nos. 1044 and 1052 of Génard's list in *Antw. Arch.-Blad* XIV, who were both banished from the city and not put to death.

vDZ.

Klei-Oldambt: see **Oldambt.**

Klein Eicholzheim: see **Adelsheim.**

Klein Hoopjen (Little Heap, Group); by this name the Groningen Old Flemish congregation of Zaandam in the Netherlands is indicated in 1723. Formerly the name was also usual in other towns in the Netherlands for small conservative groups.

vDZ.

S. Lootsma, *Het Nieuwe Huys* (Zaandam, 1937) 20.

Klein, Johann (1836-1910), a prominent elder in the Galician Mennonite Church, near Lemberg, then Austria-Hungary, and the last lay-preacher in the church, to whom (according to Bachmann, *Kleinpolen*, 324-5) is to be attributed the survival of the entire Galician group as a Mennonite brotherhood since the other elder, Jacob Müller (1834-1914, ordained elder in 1883), had withdrawn from active service.

Klein was born in 1836 at Einsiedel, the son of Johann (1814-75) and Maria Ewy Klein, grandson of Friedrich Klein (1776-1831), who came to Galicia from the Palatinate in 1785. Johann married Christine Müller in 1857; they had 10 children. He started farming in 1864, in 1870 acquired possession of the estate Dobrovlany (*q.v.*) near Stry, but lived at Kiernica from 1883 on. He was ordained preacher in 1860, and elder in 1877. He died Aug. 9, 1910, at Kiernica.

H.S.B.

P. Bachmann, *Mennoniten in Kleinpolen 1784-1934* (Lemberg, 1934); ML II, 507.

Klein Lubin, a village in West Prussia on the Vistula in the territory of Schwetz, then Polish, was settled by Dutch colonists as early as 1525. In 1595 they obtained some privileges, including free transportation of goods along the Vistula and later also freedom from military levies. A land lease of 1632 shows that at this time the farmers of Klein Lubin were all Mennonites. They were probably members of the Montau (*q.v.*) congregation. Some of the Mennonite families living here in the 17th and 18th centuries were Schultz, Janzon (Jantzen), Görtz, Vogt, Baltzer, Schroeder, and Rosenfeldt.

vDZ.

Felicia Szper, *Nederlandsche Nederzettingen in West-Pruisen* (Enkhuizen, 1913) 133; Herbert Wiebe, *Das Siedlungswerk niederländischer Mennoniten im Weichseltal* (Marburg a.d. Lahn, 1952) 22 f., 79.

Klein Nembschitz (Czech, *Nemcic*), a village near Upper Bayanovic, east of Auspitz (Hustopece) in Moravia, where the Hutterian Brethren had a Bruderhof which they had to abandon in 1559. They moved to Pellertitz (Polehraditz), and again set up a Bruderhof, from which they were driven in 1563 (Beck, 210 and 214).

In 1562 the Hutterian Brethren also founded a Bruderhof in Klein Nembschitz near Pralitz on the right bank of the Jihlava and acquired a mill from Sigmund von Zastrizel, Baron of Kaunitz. In 1565 the brotherhood chose Leonhard Dax (*q.v.*) as preacher, who served temporarily as a missionary to the Palatinate. When they were driven out of their households in the Thirty Years' War, they settled in Farkeshin, a village on the Dudwaag, southeast of Tyrnau (Trnava). (Beck, 214 and 410.)

HEGE.

Beck, *Geschichts-Bücher*, 210 *et passim*; Wolkan, *Geschicht-Buch*, 302, 314-16, 404, 427, 494 f.; Zieglschmid, *Chronik*, 397, 408, 412, 521, 551, 646, 647; ML II, 508.

Kleine Afrika-Bote, Der, was a monthly periodical published by the Afrika-Missions-Verein from June 1936 through January 1944. In all, 80 issues were published. Its editor was F. C. Thiessen, a Mennonite Brethren minister, and its place of publication was the Rundschau Publishing House of Winnipeg.

The Afrika-Missions-Verein was an independent mission society organized to sponsor the mission at Bololo in the Belgian Congo where Mr. and Mrs. Heinrich Bartsch had established a mission field. The major support of this mission society came from Mennonite Brethren churches and individuals. Since the mission field was incorporated in the missionary program of the Mennonite Brethren Church in 1943 *Der Kleine Afrika-Bote* discontinued its publication.

J.F.S.

Kleine geistliche Harfe, Die, the first Mennonite hymnbook produced in America, prepared by a committee of the Franconia Mennonite (MC) Conference (*q.v.*) in Eastern Pennsylvania, and used in that conference district as the official hymnbook for over a century. It was printed at Germantown in 1803, with further editions as follows: Germantown 1811, 1820; Northampton 1834; Doylestown 1848; Lancaster 1870; Elkhart 1904. The full title of the first edition is as follows: *Die kleine geistliche Harfe der Kinder Zions, oder auserlesene geistreiche Gesänge, allen wahren heilsbegierigen Säuglingen der Weisheit, insonderheit aber allen Christlichen Gemeinden des Herrn zum Dienst und Gebrauch mit Fleiss zusammen getragen, und in gegenwärtiger Form und Ordnung gestellt; nebst einem dreyfachen Register. Erste Auflage. Auf Verordnung der Mennonisten Gemeinden. Germantaun: Gedruckt by Michael Billmeyer, im Jahre 1803.* This title covers only the first 40 pages, which contain only psalms, 30 in number. The second title, covering the main part of the book (412 pages with new pagination), reads as follows: *Sammlung alter und neuer Geistreicher Gesänge, zur öffentlichen und besondern Erbauung und Uebung in der Gottseligkeit, insonderheit aber den Gemeinden des Herrn, auf Begehren guter Freunde, zum Dienst und Gebrauch mit Fleiss zusammengetragen in gegenwärtiger Form und Ordnung. Nebst einem dreyfachen und darzu nützlichen Register. Erste Auflage, Germantaun: Gedruckt bey Michael Billmeyer, 1803.* This section includes an appendix (373-412), and contains a total of 475 hymns. It is followed by three un-paginated indexes 18 pages in length. All editions are identical in content (40, 412, 18 pages) except that a *Zugabe einiger auserlesener Lieder* of 20 pages containing twenty hymns was added in the second edition, which grew as follows: 1820, 21 hymns; 1834, 23; 1840, 24; 1870, 34. The 1870 and 1904 editions have a short title, *Zions Harfe,* pasted as a label on the spine.

The preface to the first edition explains the reason for its publication. "Since the Psalms of David were in use in most of the meetings, and still were not available everywhere, and since in many meetings two or three hymnals were in use, it was thought useful to print a hymnal so that there could be more uniformity in the praise and worship of God our Saviour, Jesus Christ. Therefore a selection of spiritual songs was taken out of various spiritual songbooks, most of which can be sung to the melodies of familiar hymns. In the selection we were primarily concerned to choose such hymns as are needful and useful, in the light of the present dubious state of the Christian Church, for the encouragement and warning of souls desirous of salvation. For this reason the book is sincerely recommended to all evangelical churches in this land for their kind acceptance and profitable use."

Since the Lancaster Mennonite (MC) Conference (*q.v.*) was also preparing a hymnal at the same time, an attempt was made to have the two groups unite in the publication of a joint hymnal. A meeting was held in Lancaster for this purpose, but the laudable intention failed. (See letter of Martin Möllinger of Lancaster, Feb. 20, 1821, in *MQR* V, 1931, 55-57.) The Franconia delegation at the session reported having already brought together enough hymns for a complete hymnbook and having 3,000 subscriptions in advance, for "they have a large and strong church as well as a large district and are well-trained in singing." The Franconia delegates also reported that "their hymns had been handed in by so many brethren and dared not be omitted"; so they thought it best for the two groups to proceed with separate hymnbooks, the Lancaster group also having received many selections submitted by individual members. These comments give light on the method of selection of the hymns, a very democratic procedure.

The sources of the selections can no longer be determined. Most probably a considerable number of contemporary European and American German language hymnals were used. The 30 psalms were obviously adapted from Lobwasser's popular collection. Only two of the *Harfe* hymns are also found in the *Ausbund* and these are standard parting hymns: "Lebt friedsam, sprach Christus unser Herr," and "Muss es nun sein gescheiden." The remarkable similarity (three-fourths identity) of the title-page text with that of *Das kleine Davidische Psalterspiel* (2nd ed., Baltimore, 1797) might suggest a borrowing of many hymns from that hymnal, but this is not the case. The same is true of the short hymnal of 56 pages, *Die kleine Harfe* (Chestnuthill, 1792) bound with the *Psalterspiel*. Clearly the editors of the new hymnal used the wording of the two title pages, and probably the very title itself

was half-borrowed, but there is no evidence of dependence upon the hymnal itself for much hymn selection. The Franconia Mennonites were eclectic in compiling their hymnal, using standard German hymns and ignoring the only hymnal of their own heritage, the *Ausbund*. The Lancaster *Unpartheyisches Gesangbuch* used 64 hymns of the *Ausbund*. The Franconia and Lancaster hymnals had about half of their hymns in common.

Seidensticker's listing (*The First Century of German Printing in America,* Philadelphia, 1893, p. 40) of an edition of the *Kleine geistliche Harfe* in 1753, which he calls "Hymnbook for Mennonites," is a manifest error. (*ME* II, †.)   H.S.B.

Kleine Gemeinde, since 1952 called Evangelical Mennonite Church (Canada), originated in 1814 in the Molotschna Mennonite settlement in Russia (founded in 1804), when Klaas Reimer (*q.v.*) assumed the role of leader of a small group of dissatisfied members of the Mennonite Church. Before coming to Russia, Klaas Reimer had been elected minister at the Neunhuben Mennonite Church near Danzig on Sept. 1, 1801, to become co-minister with his father-in-law, Elder Peter Epp. Klaas Reimer's autobiography reveals that he began to study the Bible, the *Martyrs' Mirror,* and other books diligently after he had been elected to the ministry. Encouraged in the thought by his dying father-in-law, he too came to the conclusion that there was no future for the Mennonites in the Danzig area; thus he left with some 30 members of his congregation and arrived in the Old Colony (Chortitza) settlement in 1804, where he became acquainted with a like-minded minister by the name of Cornelius Janzen, who was elected to the ministry at Chortitza in 1805 during Reimer's stay there.

From the Old Colony Klaas Reimer and his group proceeded to the Molotschna settlement where they settled permanently in 1805. Here Reimer soon found that the Mennonites were, in his judgment, too lax in church discipline and rather low in moral standards. He was opposed to contributions made to the Russian government during the Napoleonic War and he objected to coercion in punishing evildoers of the Mennonite community, and to other "worldly" practices. Reimer's unpleasant relationship with the Elder Jacob Enns was another significant factor in a separation of some families from the main church. Reimer's group began to hold special meetings in private homes in 1812. Cornelius Janzen, who had followed Klaas Reimer and his group, co-operated along these lines. The group elected Klaas Reimer as elder in 1814 in the presence of Elder Heinrich Janzen of the Schönwiese church of the Old Colony who, however, hesitated to ordain him formally. Thus Klaas Reimer assumed the functions of an elder without ordination. Cornelius Janzen, his co-minister, preached an installation sermon, and the group of some 18-20 members considered itself organized as a church. Janzen left the Kleine Gemeinde in 1822 and returned to the old church, but three other preachers left the old church to join the Kleine Gemeinde; namely, Heinrich Wiebe 1830, Heinrich Balzer 1834, and Peter Penner 1835.

One of the basic characteristics of this small group was its radical attempt to save a small remnant of children of God from the disastrous influence of the world. It had very strong ideas on nonconformity, humility, and church discipline. On the positive side diligent reading of the Bible, the writings of Menno Simons, Dirk Philips, and Peter Peters, as well as the *Martyrs' Mirror,* foot-washing, strict discipline, honesty, etc., were zealously practiced. The Molotschna *Oberschulze* (1842-48), A. Töws, declared that in 14 years none of the members of the Kleine Gemeinde had been punished for any civil offense. Their preaching was an "admonishing" to live in repentance and in the fear of God. Catastrophes were interpreted as means of preparation for the Judgment Day and were narrated in primitive ballads. Among the practices especially condemned were card-playing, smoking, drinking, higher education, musical instruments, mission work, and marrying one's sister-in-law. Any worldly act, or even an expressed worldly sentiment, was punished with excommunication followed by·shunning. The group vigorously objected to all possible forms of resistance. It was not permissible to help the police in apprehending violators. Children were taught to take life seriously and, therefore, laughing and joking was frowned on. Swearing or the use of vain words was not tolerated. Some of these things were carried to such an extreme that their whole conception of a religious life became narrow and cramped. For this reason the movement remained very small for almost a century. It was not an attractive church to join and was called in derision "De Kleen-gemeenta" (Low German for "Little Church"), in German, "Kleine Gemeinde." In contrast the rest of the Mennonites in the Molotschna were called "die grosse Gemeinde," the big church. Outside persecution by the "big church" probably strengthened these people in their principles, but inside dissensions among leading characters weakened them considerably from time to time. Jealousies and unhealthy rivalries developed, due in part to too strict discipline.

Klaas Reimer died on Dec. 25, 1837. When Abraham Friesen was elected as his successor on April 3, 1838, the number of male members entitled to vote was 61. An elder of the Mennonite Church in the Molotschna, Bernhard Fast, was asked to ordain Abraham Friesen as an elder. He met with his coelders, Peter Wedel, Wilhelm Lange, and Benjamin Ratzlaff, inviting representatives of the Kleine Gemeinde to meet with them. Since the latter were not willing to agree to the conditions under which Abraham Friesen could be ordained as elder, Friesen simply assumed the functions of an elder without ordination. Through the intervention of Johann Cornies the elders of the Mennonite Church were compelled by the civil authorities to recognize the Kleine Gemeinde and the functions of its unordained elder as valid. This was done through a decree issued Jan. 28, 1843, by the Russian Government Board of Guardians at Odessa (*Fürsorgekomitee*). On June 10, 1847, Johann Friesen was elected elder, succeeding Abraham Friesen who died on July 1, 1849. The number of voting male members at this time was 91. At an election on Nov. 21,

1864, it had increased to 122. The entire group emigrated to North America in 1874, Cornelius Töws and David Klassen having been the Kleine Gemeinde delegates in the study group of 12 sent ahead "to spy out the land."

In 1834 Heinrich Balzer, a well-educated Mennonite minister of Tiege, joined the Kleine Gemeinde, expressing his reasons for this action in a lengthy treatise on "Faith and Reason" (*Verstand und Vernunft*). He died on Jan. 1, 1846.

An interesting episode in the history of the Kleine Gemeinde in Russia was its connection with the origin of the Krimmer Mennonite Brethren (*q.v.*) group, founded in 1869 by Jacob A. Wiebe (*q.v.,* 1839-1921). A group of Mennonite families from the Molotschna (Wiebe himself was from Ohrloff) about 1860 bought a Mohammedan village in the Crimea, which they named Annafeld. Through a spontaneous religious revival most of the families in the villages began to seek a more earnest Christian life and experienced conversion, Wiebe among them. Since Wiebe had become acquainted with a leader of the Kleine Gemeinde during a period of work as a hired hand in the Molotschna, he invited the Kleine Gemeinde elder, Johann Friesen, to visit the Annafeld group and organize them as a Kleine Gemeinde congregation, which the latter did in 1867. Wiebe and a P. Berg were ordained as preachers, and Wiebe soon thereafter as elder. Friesen had refused to accede to the request by the Annafeld group for rebaptism, but the group remained dissatisfied on this point and finally proceeded to have one of their members (Kornelius Enns was chosen) rebaptize Elder Wiebe, who in turn on Sept. 21, 1869, rebaptized 18 others. This is considered by the K.M.B. group as their founding date. Immersion was adopted as the mode. The group chose the name "Brüdergeminde" but was soon called "Krimmer Mennoniten Brüdergemeinde" to distinguish it from the Mennonite Brüdergemeinde founded in the Molotschna in 1860, with which it had nothing to do. The act of rebaptism constituted in effect a withdrawal of the Wiebe group from the Kleine Gemeinde with which it had had fellowship for only a few years, although it was not a true schism of a fraction from the historic Kleine Gemeinde group. However, much of the ultraconservative spirit of the Kleine Gemeinde was combined with an emphasis on conversion, assurance, and experience in the K.M.B. group. There was little further connection between the K.M.B. and the Kleine Gemeinde, but in the United States a Kleine Gemeinde preacher, Abraham Klaassen, joined the K.M.B. group in Kansas about 1879.

In 1866 internal dissension in the Kleine Gemeinde in the Molotschna became so serious that signs of disintegration appeared, and the group divided into two parts. Elder Johann Friesen excommunicated two preachers, Abraham Friesen and Peter Friesen, and two deacons, Jacob Friesen and Klaas Friesen. There was a reconciliation on May 6, 1869, through the help of Elder Jakob Wiebe. The group adhering to the excommunicated men (26 male members) then organized themselves into a congregation and on May 4, 1869, elected Abraham Friesen as elder. He was ordained to the office by Elder Johann Harder of the Blumstein Mennonite Church. In the Johann Friesen group Peter Toews had been ordained preacher in 1868, and was ordained elder in 1870.

Elder Jakob Wiebe was sent to the Molotschna at the time of these troubles to attempt reconciliation. He also visited the Kleine Gemeinde group at Berezenko. His diary reports having achieved reconciliation in a meeting at Fischau, no date being given. Franz Isaac (*Molotschnaer Mennoniten,* 93) reports that the entire Molotschna Kleine Gemeinde group moved to the district of Ekaterinoslav "in the sixties," but fails to state exactly when or where the migration took place. Presumably the place of settlement was Berezenko.

[The handwritten church record of Klaas Reimer and successors, now in possession of Elder D. P. Reimer of Giroux, Man., states: "The congregation divided into two parts in January 1866, held an election, and Heinrich Enns was chosen elder of the one part by majority vote, and as deacon Abr. Löwen, and as preachers Peter Töws and Gerhard Goossen. . . . On Jan. 6, 1868, Cornelius Töws was chosen deacon, then preacher, and following him Joh. Goossen as deacon. But Töws did not preach because he had earlier been under the ban. There was disunity about this matter, and Elder Heinrich Enns was removed from his office in 1868. In the spring of 1869 Preacher Jakob Wiebe was chosen elder in the Crimea on May 6. With the help of the latter with God's help, the congregation which had earlier belonged to Enns was reunited with a part of the congregation belonging to Joh. Friesen, with the preachers Abraham Friesen, Isaak Friesen, and Gerhard Schellenberg, and deacon Peter Wiebe." Additional notes written at the same place in the record by Peter Töws give the information that Gerhard Schellenberg was chosen preacher Nov. 23, 1866, and removed from that office Aug. 29, 1871. Another writer states that Preacher Isaak Friesen was removed from office in April 1870 for improper conduct and that Peter Töws had been ordained elder on Oct. 10, 1870. It is impossible to clear up satisfactorily what actually happened.]

Nebraska. The Kleine Gemeinde emigrants to North America in 1874 settled in three groups, the two larger ones in Manitoba, the smaller one of 36 families at Jansen, Jefferson Co., Neb., led by Elder Abraham Friesen. Here seven distinct villages were organized: Rosenort, Rosenhof, Rosenfeld, Rosental, Heuboden, Neuanlage, and Blumenort. In the same year this group was organized into a congregation and built a meetinghouse two miles west and three miles north of the present site of Jansen. By 1879 Isaac Peters, elder of the E.M.B. church at Henderson, had come into the community and organized an E.M.B. congregation (officially fully organized in 1890) out of dissatisfied Kleine Gemeinde families. John Holdeman's attempt to organize a ‘Church of God in Christ congregation here in the next few years failed (he won only a few families), in contrast to his success in Manitoba.

A few families also joined the Reformed Mennonites (Herrites), although no congregation was ever organized here. The K.M.B. congregation organized here in 1880 was composed of K.M.B.

families coming from Russia. This group, as well as the M.B. congregation organized in the 1890's, won a few Kleine Gemeinde families. In spite of these losses the Kleine Gemeinde congregation grew, but in 1906-8 the entire settlement migrated to Meade, Kan., to secure cheaper land and more isolation.

Kansas. The U.S. Census report for 1916 shows three Kleine Gemeinde congregations in Kansas at that date, all near Meade, with 171 baptized members, and three Sunday schools with 66 pupils. Apparently the settlement made in 1906-8 by that time had three meeting groups. By 1926 the census reports four congregations with 214 members, and three Sunday schools with 150 pupils. In 1936 the census shows two congregations, with 275 members, and two Sunday schools with 92 pupils. There were two meetinghouses in 1937 at the time of the important Kleine Gemeinde conference held here, but actually only one congregation. In 1944 the congregation dissolved, part joining the local E.M.B. congregation, while 124 charter members formed (on April 30, 1944) the independent Emmanuel Mennonite (*q.v.*) congregation which took one of the two meetinghouses. Elder Jacob F. Isaac continued with an unorganized small group, which in 1954 had 25 members.

Manitoba. The larger part (60 families) of the Kleine Gemeinde migration of 1874 to North America located in Manitoba in two parts. The smaller one located in the West Reserve in two villages (Rosenort and Rosenhof) near Morris, and a much larger group in five villages (Blumenhof, Blumenort, Grünfeld—Kleefeld, Steinbach, Rosenfeld) in the Steinbach area. The two groups (congregations) were under one elder, a moderately progressive and able man, Peter Toews, who had been ordained preacher in the Molotschna in 1866, and elder in 1870. In the first years in Manitoba the group enjoyed a healthy normal development. Then Peter Toews, becoming concerned about the spiritual condition of the church, sought contact with John Holdeman, who had broken away from the Mennonite Church (MC) in 1859 in Ohio and led a small group of followers called the Church of God in Christ, Mennonite. He had a small congregation in Lone Tree Twp., McPherson Co., Kan., organized in 1878 among the Russian Mennonites in this community. Toews corresponded with Holdeman who then visited the Manitoba Kleine Gemeinde group in 1879. In June 1881, Toews himself visited the Lone Tree Church of God congregation in Kansas, and becoming convinced that he should join the group, invited Holdeman to come to Manitoba. This he did in the fall of 1881, accompanied by a fellow minister, Mark Seiler. As a result of their work Elder Peter Toews, three of the other six ministers, and 165 members (about half; some say one third) of the Kleine Gemeinde in Manitoba were rebaptized and joined the Holdeman group. The reordination of the ministers took place in January 1882. By 1954 this ex-Kleine Gemeinde group had 1,367 baptized members in Manitoba and Alberta.

The Holdeman schism was a major disaster for the Kleine Gemeinde. It was probably the more progressive element that left, so that the more conservative and leaderless remnant, discouraged by what had happened, withdrew into a stricter conservatism and isolation from all other religious groups. In the next 30 years the group remained small and static, with a constant loss of more progressive-minded families to other groups. A number joined the E.M.B. congregation which had been organized in Steinbach in 1897, and which has been built up largely out of Kleine Gemeinde transfers.

With World War I and after, change began to come. In 1920 the first automobiles were permitted. In 1926 the first Sunday school was organized in the Steinbach Kleine Gemeinde congregation, followed by choir singing and young people's meetings. The country Kleine Gemeinde churches soon followed the example of the Steinbach town church to some extent. By the middle thirties they also had Sunday schools, young people's meetings, and later choir singing. In 1935 a church paper, *Der Familienfreund*, was established here. The Steinbach Bible Academy (*q.v.*), a private inter-Mennonite school, was established in Steinbach in 1936 largely by the Steinbach Kleine Gemeinde congregation. The mission interest also developed about this time. In 1954 the Kleine Gemeinde had about 25 missionaries serving in the Belgian Congo, French West Africa, Bolivia, Panama, Mexico, and Northern Canada. Relief work was undertaken in co-operation with other Mennonite groups in Manitoba through the Canadian Mennonite Relief Committee and the MCC, during and following World War II. The Kleine Gemeinde has been an active member of the Canadian Mennonite Relief Committee of Manitoba. In 1946 an invalid home was taken over from a private group in Steinbach.

During the years of progress following World War I, the growth of the group was remarkable, with an approximate tripling of membership. In 1954 the Manitoba membership was 1,805 in seven congregations. In 1896 their ancient organizational pattern (one elder over all) was broken by the establishment of two elder districts, each of the two congregations (Blumenort near Giroux, Rosenort at Morris) being given its own elder. In 1947 the final move was made to give each of the other three (Kleefeld, Prairie Rose, Steinbach) the right to elect one of its ministers as leader or pastor. All the congregations continued together as a "conference." Blumenort, Steinbach, and Kleefeld had been from the beginning sub-districts of the one Blumenort congregation, each with its own meetinghouse.

Mexico. The experiences of World War I and the new Manitoba school law of 1919-20 created much dissatisfaction among the Manitoba Kleine Gemeinde, as it did among the Old Colony and Sommerfeld Mennonites. Delegates were sent to Mexico to prospect for colonization possibilities, and others were sent to northern Quebec. Since both reports were negative, plans were dropped. After World War II, however, the idea of emigration was renewed. In 1948 a colony (called "Quellenkolonie") was founded at Las Jagueyes, Chihuahua, Mexico, where 35,000 acres were bought at $7 per acre, this being two thirds of a ranch, of which the other third was bought by Old Colony Mennonites from Saskatchewan. By the fall of 1949 about 15 per cent (*ca.* 100 families with *ca.* 700 souls) of the Manitoba Kleine Gemeinde group had moved on to the tract, most of them from the Blumenort and Morris congregations. Of the 23 Kleine Gemeinde preachers in Manitoba, four joined the colony, plus four deacons. The elder who went along was P. P. Reimer, who died in 1949. C. R. Reimer was ordained in his place. In Mexico the following villages were established: Springstein, Talheim, Eichenbach, Grünland, Wiesenheim. In 1954 the baptized membership in Mexico was 323.

The Kleine Gemeinde has remained until recently one of the more conservative and traditional of the Russian Mennonite groups which settled in North America. They have maintained strict nonresistance and nonconformity, the practices of footwashing and the wearing of the prayer shawl (cap) by women, the unsalaried and untrained ministry, and in the main the use of German in worship.

P. M. Friesen (*Brüderschaft,* 111), basing his report in part on Abraham Friesen's *Einfache Erklärung* (1845), states that the Kleine Gemeinde members liked to read the old Dutch Mennonite writers such as Menno Simons, Dirk Philips, P. J. Twisck, and T. J. van Braght, as well as the Danzig confessions of Hans van Steen and Georg Hansen, and that they translated many old Anabaptist works into German and promoted them (*Weg nach Friedenstadt, Die wandelnde Seele*). It is possible, though not proved, that the *Wandelnde Seele* edition published at Stuttgart in 1860, and the edition of Peter Peters' *Ausgewählte Schriften* published at Stuttgart in 1865 were both sponsored by the Kleine Gemeinde. However, Friesen errs in ascribing the translation of the *Wandelnde Seele* to the Kleine Gemeinde, since the translation was done earlier by B. B. B. (Benedict Brackbill), as the preface indicates. The 1901 (Elkhart) reprint of the 1865 Peter Peters' works may have been sponsored by the Manitoba Kleine Gemeinde; the preface is signed by A. L. F. Gerhard Cornelsen of the Molotschna settlement was the translator of the third part of Peter Peters' works and the sponsor of the 1865 edition. A Gerhard Cornelson was head of a family living in Gnadenau, the K. M. B. village in Marion Co., Kan., in 1875.

The present (1955) Kleine Gemeinde congregations, all in Manitoba, with membership, are as follows: Rosenort at Morris (1874) 479, Blumenort (1874) 446, Steinbach (1874) 400, Prairie Rose (1918) 260, Kleefeld (1874) 142, Riverton, 90 miles north of Winnipeg (1950) 46, and McGregor, 90 miles west of Winnipeg (1952) 32. The total baptized membership is thus 1,805, plus 2,293 unbaptized children. Including Mexico and Kansas the total membership is 2,153. Riverton was founded by K. G. members from other districts. McGregor was the result of union of members of the Sommerfelder, Bergthaler, and Rudnerweider churches, which then joined the K.G.   H.S.B.

Friesen, *Brüderschaft,* 106-13 (includes a reproduction of Klaas Reimer's manuscript account of the origin of the Kleine Gemeinde); C. Krahn, "From Russia to Meade," *Menn. Life* VI (July 1951) 18 f.; D. P. Miller, "The Story of Jansen, Nebraska," *Menn. Life* IX (1954)

73-75; *idem*, "The Story of the Jansen Churches," *Menn. Life* X (1955) 38-40; D. J. Classen, "Meade, a Changing Community," *Menn. Life* VI (July 1951) 14-17, 19; P. J. B. Reimer, "From Russia to Mexico, the Story of the Kleine Gemeinde," *Menn. Life* IV (October 1949) 28-32; J. W. Fretz, "The Mennonite Community at Meade," *Menn. Life* VI (July 1951) 8-13; P. A. Wiebe, *Kurze Biographie des Bruders Jakob A. Wiebe* (Hillsboro, 1924); D. Paul Miller, "An Analysis of Community Adjustment. A Case Study of Jansen, Nebraska," unpublished Ph.D. thesis at the University of Nebraska, 1953; J. M. Penner, *A Concise History of the Church of God* (n.p., 1951); R. Friedmann, "Faith and Reason," *MQR* XXII (1948) 75-93; Abraham Friesen, *Eine Einfache Erklärung über einige Glaubenssätze der sogenannten Kleinen Gemeine. Wohlmeinend aufgesetzt von einem treuen Diener am Wort des Herrn im Jahre 1845* (Danzig, n.d., 40 pp.); reprint at Quakertown, Pa., in the "Himmelsmanna" Druckerei, 1901; G. E. Reimer and G. R. Gaeddert, *Exiled by the Czar* (Newton, 1956). The diaries of Klaas Reimer and Abraham Friesen have been preserved, also the record book containing the report of the elections of all ordained men; *ML* II, 507.

Kleine Zon, name of a congregation at Amsterdam, Netherlands, which separated in 1670 from the *Zon* (*q.v.*) congregation, holding its meetings in the "Arke Noachs (Noë)" on the Prinsengracht until it merged again with the mother congregation in 1679. The little congregation of Het Sterretje (*q.v.*) split off from the Kleine Zon. In 1720-52 the Frisian congregation of Amsterdam held its meetings at the Kleine Zon meetinghouse, thus usually called Arke Noachs (*q.v.*). (*Inv. Arch. Amst.* II, Nos. 1393-1404; *DB* 1895, 5.)   vDZ.

Kleines Hand-Büchlein, *darinnen Morgen- und Abend Gebeter, wie auch zur Tauf und Communion, und mehr andere etc. enthalten sind. Nebst verschiedenen Märtyrer und andern Liedern,* the last Swiss Mennonite prayer book (*q.v.*); a small size (2x3 in.) pocket companion apparently intended for everyday devotional reading although its contents are not quite in accordance with this idea. It seems to have been and still is a rather popular book, as six European and two American editions prove. The oldest edition of 1786 apparently comes from the Palatinate although the title page does not indicate any place of publication. Later European editions are: 1801 Basel (von Mechel publishing house, *q.v.*); 1816 Römhild (Thuringia); 1837 Basel (von Mechel), this and all following editions changed by omission of several prayers and a new 53-page appendix; 1867 Biel (Switzerland); 1930 Meiringen (Switzerland). The two American editions are: 1835 Osnaburg, Stark Co., Ohio (Heinrich Kurz); and 1872 Elkhart, Ind. (John F. Funk). When American Mennonites shifted to the English language this prayer book lost its former value. No German Mennonite prayer book has ever been translated into English.

The first three editions contain 16 prayers, and 10 hymns and brief rhymes; all later editions contain only 12 prayers in the first part, with the same hymns, and in the second part (called *Anhang*) 11 hymns and 3 prayers. The entire work is very sentimental and a typical product of Pietism (*q.v.*) with its strong emphasis upon melancholy (*Schwermütigkeit*), sickness, and dying. And yet, the book is rather a combination of old Dutch Mennonite prayers of a quasi-formal nature (see **Clock, Leenaert**) together with certain hymns known from the *Ausbund,* plus non-Mennonite material apparently borrowed from prayer books and hymnbooks of the territorial state churches (Lutheran) of the 18th century. Of the 16 prayers of the earlier editions 13 are lifted verbatim either from the 1664 manual of van Sittert (*q.v.*), called *Christliches Glaubensbekenntnis der waffenlosen . . . Christen* (see **Confessions**), or perhaps from the 1702 *Güldene Äpfel* (*q.v.*), which contains about the same collection (namely, morning and evening prayers, prayers for the ordinances such as baptism and Lord's Supper, also for weddings, prayers before and after sermons, and one "to be spoken before a sick person"). To this are added new, non-Mennonite prayers, such as "Prayers of a sad and sorrowful person in the throes of death" (this prayer was later added to all 19th-century editions of the *Ernsthafte Christenpflicht, q.v.*), a general prayer directed to Jesus ("Der Du, oh Herr Jesu, uns so teuer erkaufet und erlöset hast," highly characteristic of the pietistic mood), and one "In the agony of death," concluding with "Sighs in times of dying" ("Darum allein auf Dich, Herr Christ, verlass ich mich").

The new form of the book after 1837 omits the prayers "before and after the sermons," and adds three prayers, viz., "Of those present at the passing away of a person, also good for funerals," another funeral prayer, and one "for persons in melancholy and inner troubles" (*Anfechtung*), a rather strange assemblage for a pocket devotional reader.

Among the hymns are the "Haslibacher Lied" (*q.v.*), the song describing the visit of three Christians from Thessalonica to Moravia (published as a pamphlet for the first time in 1695), the hymn by Hans Reist, likewise of 1695, entitled "Es ist eine wunderschöne Gab," and several of non-Mennonite origin. The 1837 appendix has eleven hymns dealing with dying and the futility of life ("Bedenke Mensch, das Ende"; "Wohl dem der stets ans Ende denkt"; "Ach wie kurz ist unser Leben"; etc.), also a song of penitence (*Buss-Lied*), "Denket doch, ihr Menschenkinder," headed "Thomas à Kempis Nachfolge Christi, in der Melodey des 42. Psalmes."

R.F.

R. Friedmann, "Mennonite Prayerbooks" in *Mennonite Piety Through the Centuries* (Goshen, 1949); Wolkan, *Lieder,* 161-64; *ML* II, 246.

Kleinhäufler. Concerning the origin of this word, to which others like *Stäbler, Gemeinschafter, Schwertler,* and *Sabbater* should be added, the chronicles of the Hutterian Brethren relate: In 1528, because the group in Nikolsburg was growing and a large number adhered to Jakob Widemann and Philip Jäger, Spittelmaier commanded his people to have nothing to do with them. The difference was still that which had existed between Hubmaier and Hut (*q.v.*). Widemann and Jäger held their meetings in the homes, received pilgrims, guests, and strangers from other countries, and united into a brotherhood (*Gemeinschaft*). Spittelmaier, on the other hand, taught that war, the sword, and levies should be maintained, hence the name Schwertler. The other group was called "Kleinhäufler" and "Stäbler" by the Spittelmaier group. The Schwertler, the chronicles add, were also called Sabbater.

The names Kleinhäufler, Stäbler, and Gemeinschaftler thereafter referred to those Anabaptists who separated from the Nikolsburg group in 1528, and later also from the Rossitz Anabaptists, and who in 1530 were divided into two groups, the Hutterites and the Austerlitz group. The Stäbler taught "that a Christian should not take part in war, therefore do not carry a sword, but only a staff." (ML I, 507 f.) LOSERTH.

Kleinsasser, a common family name among the Hutterian Brethren. Its progenitor was Johannes Kleinsasser (q.v., d. 1779 at Vishenka, Russia) of Aemlach, Carinthia, Austria. He was a leader of the group of Lutherans expelled from Carinthia and taken to Transylvania by Maria Theresa when they refused to return to the Catholic Church. In 1755 the group went to Alwinc, where a number, including Kleinsasser, joined the Hutterian Brethren. He was baptized and appointed as leader on probation in 1762 (*Vorsteher in der Versuchung*) and ordained in 1763. The name is now found in South Dakota, Montana, Manitoba, and Alberta. See also **Waldner, Johannes.**) D.D.

Kleinsasser, Johannes, of Aemlach in Carinthia, Austria, was the leader of the Protestants who were persecuted in their homeland and were by compulsion settled in Transylvania in the 1750's. By this time the heterodox were not simply banished from the country, for the refugees might then strengthen a hostile power, but were sent to a crown land, which enjoyed certain freedoms. Kleinsasser took his family with him: his wife Barbara, and four children, Stephan, Mathis, Joseph, and Christina.

In Transylvania Kleinsasser united with the group of his compatriots who refused to give the oath of allegiance to Maria Theresa, believing the oath to be forbidden by the New Testament, and thus deprived himself of the right to a home and land (see **Carinthia**), and united with the Hutterites at Alwinc (q.v.), which entailed privation, hardship, and want. His son Stephan died the first year in Transylvania. The following year he and his family were transferred to Kreuz. A pious man, he held his brethren to continued prayer.

When the small group took steps to order its life in spiritual and temporal affairs, the vote for leader in 1761 fell on Kleinsasser, and after he had been baptized with Joseph Müller in 1762, and received instruction on the essential doctrines, such as baptism, communion, marriage, exclusion from the group and reception, he was installed as leader (*Vorsteher in der Versuchung*) on April 27, 1762, and confirmed in that position in January 1763. The Alwinc colony gave him the necessary books for study. Thus the congregation had a shepherd. His position was an extremely difficult one, not wanting in mistreatment and chains.

It was therefore decided to try to find a place where they could live more peacefully. They found such a place in Wallachia, and in 1775 established themselves there. But peace was shattered by the Russo-Turkish war with its terrible consequences. Kleinsasser's suffering at the hands of Turkish and Tatar robber bands was described by Johannes Waldner (q.v.), who later became the leader and chronicler of the brotherhood. "I prayed," he writes (he was an eyewitness), "to the Lord in this distress: O Lord, wilt Thou thus make an end of Thy church, and quench Thy truth and Thy light and let it perish? That is impossible!"

The offer of Count Rumyantsev to give the plundered brotherhood a peaceful home on his lands was very welcome. In Vishenka Kleinsasser used his talents to develop the colony. Weaving made a good start the first year; pottery was successful by 1773, a smithy and mills were built. A room was built for the meetings of the elders, and also a cold pantry. In 1778 they built the big and little schools, and in 1779 a chapel, which was later turned into a nursery.

Waldner reports that God granted blessed years with good crops; the brotherhood recovered from the extreme poverty of previous years. "Hänsel" Kleinsasser, elder and leader of the entire brotherhood, died at Vishenka on Oct. 16, 1779, in his fifty-third year, having served the brotherhood with the utmost devotion for 18 years. (Zieglschmid, *Klein-Geschichtsbuch; ML* II, 508 f.) LOSERTH.

Kleinsasser, Joseph, chosen preacher March 12, 1901, by the Milltown Hutterite Bruderhof in South Dakota, confirmed Dec. 2, 1902. He was a schoolteacher more than 17 years. On Feb. 11, 1934, he was chosen as elder of the "Schmiedeleut" (q.v.). He died April 16, 1947, at the Milltown Colony, Bernard, Man. D.D.

Kleinsee: see **Jeziorka.**

Kleinste Hoopjen, Het (the Smallest Heap), a name formerly sometimes given to the Ukowallist (q.v.) or Groningen Old Flemish congregations in the Netherlands. (*DB* 1876, 39, note 2.) vDZ.

Kleintal, a Mennonite church in the Bernese Jura, Switzerland, sometimes called Moron. The congregation embraces the Mennonites scattered over the county of Moutier with small overlappings into bordering districts. The region is sometimes called the Münstertal, and the French name Moutier refers to the same political and geographical district as Münster.

The name Kleintal is used to designate the following areas: the source and upper reaches of the Sorne (Bellelay, Châtelat, Monible, Sornetan) and the little valleys of the Fontaines (Souboz, les Ecorcheresses) and the Chaliere (Perrefitte). This general valley region is surrounded in the north by the mountain chain of Béroie-Droit Mont-Perceux-Montagne de Moutier, and in the south by the elevation of Monbautier-Moron. This is the Kleintal district with its numerous scattered Mennonite farm homes. But in the territory of the congregation are also included the "Grosstal" and the Münstertal. The Mennonites gave to the upper end of the Birstal the name "Grosstal" or Dachsfeldertal (Vallée des Tavannes), in which the most important towns are Tavannes, Reconvilier, Malleray, Bévilard, Sorvilier, and Court. In the side valley of the Trame are located Le Fuet, Saicourt, and Saules, with Champoz near the Moron elevation. The side valley of Chaluet near Court was earlier a great place of refuge for the Anabaptists and the seat of the extinct congregation of Tscheiwo.

The rocky mountain slopes of the region are covered with firs, and in the meadowlands on the summits are numerous separate farms. The soil is not fertile, and yields sparsely what industrious farmers can eke from it. The Moron chain reaches a height of 4,460 ft. On the plateau-like west foot of the chain stands the hamlet of Moron (el. 3,400 ft.) with its school and chapel. Whereas in former times Chaluet (Tscheiwo) and Montagne de Moutier (Münsterberg) were the focal points of the Swiss Brethren in this community, Moron has now become the center.

The Moutier region, belonging to the prince-bishopric of Basel, was allied with Bern in 1486. Under Bern's protection the French-speaking population accepted the Reformation, and Bern controlled it in matters of religion and marriage. Thus the Moutier Valley had a Catholic spiritual prince, and a Protestant ally.

The Bernese government and the prince-bishop persecuted the Swiss Brethren on similar principles. But political considerations led the bishops to a more tolerant and lenient treatment, in spite of Bern's protests. The Swiss Brethren gradually earned the favor of the bishops and their officials by their quiet industry and competence. Even though the populace demanded the expulsion of the Swiss Brethren on economic grounds, orders of conscription were laxly enforced.

The territory of the Kleintal church was probably the first region of the Jura to be settled by persecuted Swiss Brethren. In April 1535 the prince-bishop of Basel notified the council of Solothurn (which was allied to Bern) that Anabaptists were moving into the mountains. An agreement was reached which permitted each canton to pursue Anabaptists into the other's territory. In 1538 a meeting was held between Bern and the bishop of Basel "for the extermination of this unchristian, damned sect." In March 1538 a disputation was held in Bern, at which the local Anabaptists were represented by Hans Heinrich Schneider of Moutier. In 1540 Bern sent orders to the bishop and the Moutier authorities, "that the Anabaptists be punished and stopped." There must have been a large number here. In 1596 the prince-bishop demanded of the provost and chapter of Moutier, that they clean out "the filth of the sect of Anabaptism highly damned in the Holy Roman Empire, in the Seehof." In 1622 Solothurn urged the persecution of certain Anabaptists, naming them. In 1693 the prince-bishop issued an edict of proscription. Though in the canton of Bern "looking through the fingers" was severely punishable, the prince-bishops officials were very lax in carrying out the edict. In 1720 a report on church conditions stated that there were many Swiss Brethren in the region.

In 1729 the landowners raised objections to the numerous orders of expulsion, saying that the native renters did not know how to utilize milk, and that the Swiss Brethren work brought much more money into the country. In 1731 the towns of Roche, Perrefitte, and Montagne de Moutier presented a petition for the banishment of the Anabaptists from the Moutier Valley, because they were in possession of many of the estates, while the natives were unemployed and roofless. A letter from Solothurn supported the petition, saying that the Swiss Brethren met on the "Brächbiel, by the old hut, Monteau, Schiltsberg." In 1732 these towns renewed their petition. Thus it is very unlikely that the orders of 1730 were painstakingly carried out.

In 1732 the prince-bishop demanded of Georg Moschard, "Bannerherr" of Moutier, a report on the Swiss Brethren. The report says, "They bring money into the land, they work land which without them yields no income; they live extremely modestly, visit no inns, give no occasion for complaint, pay twice as much rent as the natives could, and the landowners cannot be deprived of the right to choose their own workers."

In 1733 Swiss Brethren affairs took a dubious turn. On Jan. 15 all the communities collectively demanded expulsion. Jan. 20 brought a presentation in their favor from Court. In the Chaluet Valley in the district of Court, the Anabaptists of the 17th century had "as faithful and submissive subjects of the bishop peacefully made the hitherto untilled land usable." (*Geographisches Lexikon der Schweiz* I, 440.) On Jan. 26 came the petition for expulsion from Moutier Grandval, and Jan. 27 one from the 19 communities in the Prévôté of Moutier Grandval. On the same day the prince-bishop issued an edict of banishment, giving owners three months and renters a year to leave. The commune of Court demanded a longer period of grace. The mayor of Moutier and the magistrate of Delémont were to give their opinion; these were very favorable to the Swiss Brethren. At this time Peter Ramseier (b. 1706) was chosen preacher of the Kleintal church in 1730, and elder in 1732. In 1734 the Court community declared its opposition to exile and praised the 20 Swiss Brethren families living there.

The economic struggle continued. New complaints against the Swiss Brethren brought the reply from the prince in 1767, that no objective charges could be raised against these people, and that the interests of sound politics required an increase in the population of the state.

Thus they remained in the canton, even through the period of French domination. The story is still told on the Mennonite (leased) farm of Béroie, that when the French troops marched through in December 1797, they took possession of the monastery of Courtine de Bellelay and the 30 monks had to flee. The famous monastery school, which had been honored in 1784 by a visit of Prince Henry of Prussia and the duchess of Bourbon, was dissolved, the monastery sold, most of the land to Frenchmen, and new lands put up for lease. Nearly all of these lands were occupied by Swiss Brethren. Besides the Emmental cheese of their homeland they also manufactured the specialty of the monastery farm, the Bellelay cheese called Tête de moine.

From that time on this region became more and more prominent in the life of the Mennonites of modern Moutier. By emigration to America, Tscheiwo and Münsterberg lost in strength and in importance. A register of Mennonite families in 1832 in the Moutier district lists 126 households. Among them there were fifteen families named Moser, nine Lehmann, nine Bichsel, seven Burkhalter, seven Nussbaum, six Amstutz, six Baumgartner, six Boegli, six Neuenschwander, six Liechti, four Gerber, four Sprunger, four Kläy, three Augsburger, three Geiger, three Studer, three Oberli, three Steiner, three Wälti, and three Widmer.

In 1815 the entire region fell to the canton of Bern. The Bernese government did not molest the Mennonites of Kleintal (nor in the Jura in general), for which they sent the government a letter of thanks signed by Ulrich Röthlisberger, Jakob Engel, and Michael Gerber. In the 19th century the military question caused some unrest among the Swiss Mennonites. Until then they had been exempt from military service. The new federal constitution, however, brought universal conscription. In 1850 several brethren presented a petition for exemption, signed for Moutier by Peter Studer (Malleray), David Nussbaumer (La Côte, Souboz), and Peter Sommer (Vion near Tavannes, belonging to Sonnenberg). The famine years, 1819 and 1833, and the military question in 1850 and 1874 caused many families to emigrate to America. Their names disappear from the church records. After these emigrations the congregation of Kleintal numbered only 112 baptized members and 97 children in 1887. (Mannhardt, *Jahrbuch*, 1888, 39.)

The Kleintal region was also the home of the popular nature doctor Hans Moser in Champoz. "His house was constantly filled with patients seeking help, from dawn to dawn" (*Abrégé*). "At that time the Mennonites were easily recognized by their gray clothing with hooks and the beard" (Ellenberger, 53). In the second half of the 19th century the religious life of the community had a peaceful course. Faithful ministers tried to prevent religious lethargy or deadness. A census of 1874 counted 390 Mennonites, including children, in the Moutier Valley.

Toward the end of the 19th century, three men became prominent in the church: Christian Gerber (see **Gerber**), d. Oct. 3, 1928, in Emmenholz (see *Zionspilger*, 1928, No. 43; *Schweizer Bauer*, 1928, No. 120), Gottlieb Loosli (*q.v.*), a teacher in Moron, and Jakob Amstutz, b. April 25, 1866, in Montbautier, and ordained elder on Sept. 9, 1917.

In 1881 Christian Gerber leased a farm in Bellelay. With his vigorous and fiery temperament he at once set about securing a church building for the Kleintal congregation. With some financial aid from the German Mennonites the Kleintal church built a chapel in Moron in 1893. In 1899 Christian Gerber moved to Emmenholz and founded there a subsidiary of the Kleintal church. The church work was looked after by the quiet and retiring elder Peter Bögli, with Gottlieb Loosli and Jakob Amstutz as preachers. On July 28, 1908, the house of Amstutz in Les Cerniers was struck by lightning and burned to the ground, destroying all the manuscript church records.

This period was a very active one. A revival went through the church, bringing much blessing, awaking spirits. But perfectionism and fanaticism also sought entry, for a time completely destroying inner peace. From 1908 to 1913 members' meeting were not held. Through the conciliatory efforts of Gottlieb Loosli and the election of new elders and preachers on Sept. 6, 1917, the difficulties were cleared away, and the church has grown.

In 1934 the elders in service were Jakob Amstutz, Le Fuet; and Hans Geiser, Combe de Peux; the preachers were Samuel Geiser, Châtelat; Abraham Gerber, Emmenholz; and Eugen Burkhalter, La Côte (Souboz). In addition to the Moron chapel, which has a school in the ground floor, the church built a school-chapel at Perceux and at Montbautier. At the state (public) school in Moron Walter Loosli was the teacher; at the state school in Montbautier, Alfred Amstutz, and at the private school in Perceux, Katharina Sprunger. All three schools have nine grades. The enrollment at Moron was usually 30, at Montbautier and Perceux 25. The schools have a good reputation, and use the German language. Moron, Montbautier, and Perceux have Sunday schools and choruses. Two additional places have Sunday schools. Evangelistic meetings are held annually in Moron and Perceux, usually three or four days in January.

In 1934 the membership was 281 baptized members, and over 150 children, with about 65 families. In 1954 it had declined to about 250 baptized members. A section held its meetings at Reconvilier near Tavannes, another section held services in Biel. Both these groups were under the leadership of Elder Samuel Geiser, for many years elder at Moron and secretary of the Swiss Conference.

In 1954 the elders at the Moron center were Samuel Amstutz, Jacob Hirschi, Abr. Gerber, and Theo Loosli, with Eugen Burkhalter as preacher and Walter Loosli as deacon. Loosli was still teacher of the Moron school.   A.-T., H.S.B.

Müller, *Berner Täufer;* S. Geiser, *Die Taufgesinnten-Gemeinden* (Karlsruhe, 1932); J. Ellenberger, *Bilder aus dem Pilgerleben* (3 vv. n.p., 1878-83); M. Fallet-Scheurer, "Berner Bauer im Jura," in *Schweizer Bauer,* 1929, Nos. 146, 149, 152, 153; *Abrégé l'histoire de la statistique du ci-devant de Bâle par Charles Ferd. Morel* (Strasbourg, 1813); *ML* II, 509-11.

Klein-Werder: see **Marienburger Werder.**

Klemperer (Klampherer), **Julius:** see **Gherlandi.**

Klercken (*Clercquen, Clerckschen*), a term used in the 18th century to denote a West Prussian Mennonite group. According to H. van der Smissen it refers to the Huiskopers (*q.v.*). It is not unlikely that the name is identical with the *Clarichen* (*q.v.*) named in the Confession of Faith by Georg Hansen (*q.v.*). In that case, it refers to the Flemish Mennonites, known as the "Danzigers." A fuller discussion of the problem is found in the article **Clarichen.** (*Menn. Bl.,* 1910, 62; *ML* II, 511.)
                                                                    NEFF.

Klesinger, Michael: see **Kürschner.**

Kleyn Hoorns Liet-boeck was formerly one of the most popular Dutch Mennonite hymnals. It derives its name from the town of Hoorn, where the first editions were printed and published. Its first editor was Jan Jansz Deutel (*q.v.*). Most of the hymns found in this book are borrowed from older Dutch hymnbooks. It contains 30 Psalms in the rhymed version by Dathenus (*q.v.*), 15 *Lofsanghen,* 106 *Gheestelycke Liedekens.* Then follow an *Aenhangsel* (supplement) of 21 hymns (former edition 11), *'t Vermeerdert Aenhangsel* of 33 *Stichtelycke Gesangen* (previous editions had 61). The 1736 and following editions add a *Nieuw Aenhangsel* of 5 *Stichtelycke Gesangen.* The earliest edition now extant is that of 1644-45, but there were some older editions. Schagen (*Naamlijst der Doopsgezinde schrijveren*) mentions editions of 1630, 1638, and 1661, of which no copy seems to be extant. The Amsterdam Library has editions of 1644-45, 1649, 1657, and 1685, all printed at Hoorn, 1736 at Amsterdam, and 1814 at Sneek. Besides these Blaupot ten Cate (*Holland* II, 212) lists editions of 1656, 1661, and 1685, all printed at Amsterdam. The 1814 edition was printed for the congregation of Balk, Friesland, who used this hymnal until a large part of the congregation emigrated to the United States in 1853-54; in the Uiterweg Oude Vermaning (old church) of Aalsmeer the *Kleyn Hoorns Liet-boeck* was used until 1862. A copy of an edition of 1646, bound with *Twee korte Vermaen Brieven van wijlen Dirck Gerritsz* which contains some songs by Gerritsz and was published in 1648 is found in BeCL. (*ME* II, †.) (*DB* 1862, 147; 1887, 86-112; 1892, 56, 65; *ME* II, †.)   vDZ.

Kliewer, a widespread Mennonite family, originally from Holland, where they are called Kluiver (Kluyver, Cluyver). Some members of this family migrated from the Netherlands to West Prussia. In 1629 Dutch farmer Peter Kliewer was among the Mennonite land-leasers of the village of Klein Wolz near Graudenz. In Danzig the Kliewer family is also found since the 17th century. The first representatives of the family in Danzig were five brothers, Jakob, Cornelius, Paul, Conrad, and Heinrich; but nothing is known of any except Jakob Kliewer (1669-1728). He was received into the congregation on Oct. 29, 1694, and chosen deacon in the Frisian church in 1714. His first wife was Lucia van Dühren, his second Sophia Arentz. There were eight children from his first marriage, among them Jakob (1704-75) and Heinrich (1709-62). The former was a preacher and elder in the Frisian Mennonite congregation in Neugarten-Danzig from 1742. In 1748 Heinrich moved to Tiegenhof.

Heinrich's oldest son, Jakob Kliewer (1743-1826), was chosen head of the Frisian Mennonite church at Neugarten in 1786, preacher in 1797, and elder in 1798, serving during the difficult period of the war. When this church merged with the Flemish in 1808 he remained an elder in the united Danzig Mennonite church, which had 900 members. During his co-operative work with Peter Thiessen, Jr., the Mennonites lost two meetinghouses in the sieges of 1807 and 1813; a spacious new one was built in 1819. These two elders died only a few days apart. They were the last ones chosen from the congregation (pictures in Mannhardt, *Die Danziger Mennoniten-Gemeinde*). From this time on the church was served by trained ministers; Jakob van der Smissen had been called shortly before their death.

Jakob Kliewer was married twice. From his marriage with Deborah Jantzen (b. Dec. 1, 1742, d.

March 17, 1796) he had ten children; from his second marriage with Sara van Dühren (b. Dec. 23, 1773, d. Dec. 19, 1820) four children. Two of the sons of his first marriage, Heinrich (b. Dec. 24, 1770, d. Jan. 10, 1847) and Abraham (b. Feb. 10, 1778, d. Sept. 6, 1859), were copperplate engravers; the descendants of the former continued the art in Berlin, the son of the latter in Danzig. The youngest son of the second marriage, Gustav Kliewer (b. July 18, 1803, d. Feb. 29, 1872), was *Vorsteher* of the Danzig Mennonite church 1836-62, and a city commissioner 1836-48; he also served on the boards of various charitable institutions. His oldest son, Paul Kliewer (b. Feb. 14, 1851), became head of the sales department of the sugar refinery in Riesenburg, and was a member of the board of directors until 1923; he was a city commissioner of Riesenburg (1904-15), and was named a city elder when he left. In 1915 he moved to Danzig.

Members of the family who lived in East Prussia, Poland, and Russia all stemmed from Danzig. Many families emigrated to America when universal military training was introduced in the 18th century and settled largely in Kansas. Several missionaries to the Indians belonged to this family, as Henry J. Kliewer and Peter A. Kliewer to the Cheyennes (*q.v.*) and John J. Kliewer to the Arapahoes (*q.v.*). The chairman of the Foreign Mission Board of the General Conference Mennonite Church was for 25 years John W. Kliewer, who was also president of Bethel College (*q.v.*) 1911-20 and 1925-32.

In Paraguay members of the Kliewer family are also found. In 1930 Kornelius Kliewer instigated the founding of the village Rosenfeld in the Gran Chaco; the inhabitants had previously been members of the church at Wymysle in Poland. The population of the village in 1934 included four Kliewer families with 31 persons. Dr. Fritz Kliewer (d. 1956) was for a time principal of the Zentralschule in Filadelfia, and in 1954 a teacher in the new Witmarsum Colony in Brazil. Besides these there are two Kliewer families in the Fernheim Colony who come from the Waldheim settlement in South Russia, which was settled by Mennonites from Poland.   HEGE.

H. G. Mannhardt, *Die Danziger Mennoniten-Gemeinde* (Danzig, 1919); *Gem.-Kal.* 1934, 101; *MQR* VIII (1934) 69; *ML* II, 512 f.

Kliewer, Johann, was one of the last elders of the Deutsch-Wymysle Mennonite Church in Poland. He was ordained elder in 1885 and joined the local newly established Mennonite Brethren congregation on July 17, 1893, where he continued his service as a minister. On Nov. 4, 1895, he was ordained co-elder of the congregation. The Deutsch-Wymysle Mennonite Church chose Johann Schmidt as his successor. He also joined the Mennonite Brethren. (H. G. Mannhardt, *Jahrbuch* 1888, 77; Friesen, *Brüderschaft,* 479; see also **Deutsch-Wymysle.**)   C.K.

Kliewer, John Walter, was born June 8, 1869, in the German Mennonite community of Michalin (*q.v.*), Russian Poland, the son of John P. and Aganetha Foth Kliewer. In 1874 his parents migrated from Poland to Kansas with their entire family, locating about 10 miles east of Newton, Kan. He was married in 1902 to Emma Ruth of Halstead, Kan. Three children were born to this union. Kliewer attended high school in Newton, and after graduation from the Halstead Seminary in 1890 taught for a few years. Later he attended Bethel College and Garrett Biblical Institute, where he received the Bachelor of Sacred Theology degree in 1901. In 1925 Garrett Biblical Institute and Bluffton College both conferred the honorary Doctor of Divinity degree upon him.

As a young man Kliewer united with the Gnadenberg Mennonite Church (GCM). He served as pastor of the Mennonite Church in Wadsworth, Ohio, in 1901-3, and the Berne Mennonite Church in 1903-11.

In 1911 Kliewer was called to the presidency of Bethel College and resigned in 1920. In 1925 he again became president of Bethel College and directed the administration of the college until 1932. His greatest contribution was made as president of Bethel College. His administration came in a period of transition of the college and so was difficult and stormy, but the school made great progress under his leadership.

Kliewer was a great conference leader. For a number of years he served on the Board of Trustees of Bluffton College. He was elected to the Home Mission Committee of the Middle District Conference while serving the Wadsworth Church and later became president of the Middle District Conference. He served as secretary of the General Conference in 1905-8. In 1908-35 he served on the Foreign Mission Board, and was sent to the Orient to visit the Mennonite mission fields in China and India. On this tour he also visited Mennonite churches in Europe. Upon his return he spent one year in visiting and reporting to Conference congregations. He also served on the Peace Committee of the General Conference during World War I.

On Oct. 16, 1932, Kliewer suffered a stroke, but recovered sufficiently to keep up his preaching duties until after the death of his wife in 1935. His remaining years he spent in retirement in the Bethel Home for the Aged writing his *Memoirs*. On Feb. 9, 1938, he died at Newton, Kan.

Kliewer was the author of two books: *Letters of a World Tour* (Bethel College, 1936) and *Memoirs of J. W. Kliewer* (Bethel College, 1943). E.G.K.

A published obituary of J. W. Kliewer may be found in *Memoirs of J. W. Kliewer*. Published biographies are found in A. Warkentin's *Who's Who Among the Mennonites* (1937) and Eva Sprunger's *The First Hundred Years* (Berne, 1938); P. J. Wedel, *The Story of Bethel College* (Newton, 1954).

Klinkert, a Dutch family, found in the 17th and 18th centuries in a number of rural congregations in the province of North Holland, e.g., De Rijp and Graft, and also found at Amsterdam, in the Lamist and Zonist congregations, where some of them were deacons. Claas Klinkert, a sailor of Graft, was captured as a slave by the Turks; a collection for his liberation was taken in his home church in 1709. Theunis Klinkert was from 1738 a (lay) preacher of the Beverwijk congregation. Bastiaan Klinkert (1794-1854) of Amsterdam was sent to England by

his father at the age of 14 to escape military service. This Bastiaan Klinkert, a wealthy ship broker like his father, in his spare time studied literature; his studies on William Shakespeare were epoch-making (*N.N.B.Wb.* III, 695). His uncle Hendrik Klinkert Bast.zn (d. 1824) was a regent of the Collegiant-Mennonite Orangeappel (*q.v.*) orphanage at Amsterdam in 1813-24. Another member of this family was Hildebrand Cornelis Klinkert, who follows.

vDZ.

Klinkert, Hildebrand Cornelis, b. June 11, 1829, at Amsterdam, d. Nov. 20, 1913, at Leiden, was at first a surveyor; he was educated for the missions by D. Harting (*q.v.*), pastor at Enkhuizen, and the Mission School of Rotterdam; in 1857 he entered the service of the Dutch Mission Association. He worked at first with Pieter Jansz (*q.v.*) at Japara, but in 1861 transferred to Semarang, his principal task being to translate the New Testament into the Malay language. In 1862 he settled on the island of Chianjur (Tjiandjur) as a missionary. In 1863 he entered the service of the Dutch Bible Society and later became an instructor of the Malay language at the University of Leiden. NEFF.

Annual reports of the Dutch Mission Association; *Biogr. Wb.* V, 20 f.; *DB* 1885, 60-63; 1886, 82 ff.; 1887, 32 ff., 37; 1890, 39 ff., 44 ff., 46, 48; 1891, 34; *ML* II, 513.

Klinkhamer, a Mennonite family of Amsterdam, found in the Lamist congregation from about 1650. Barent Klinkhamer, a well-to-do silk merchant, married to Cecelia Looten, was a deacon of the Lamist Church. He was known for his liberality toward the poor, both Mennonites and others. Govert Klinkhamer (Amsterdam, 1702-74), a son of the foregoing, was a (mediocre) poet; in 1725 he published at Amsterdam *De Kruisgezant, of het Leeven van den Apostel Paulus* (two volumes). vDZ.

Biogr. Wb. V, 25 f.; Blaupot t. C., *Holland* II, 162; M. Schagen, *Naamlijst der Doopsgezinde schrijveren* (Amsterdam, 1745) 57.

Klinkhamer (Klinckhaemer), **Laurens** (1626-87), a physician of Leiden, Dutch province of South Holland, where he was born and died. Though from a Mennonite family and married in 1667 to the Mennonite Deliana van Hoogmade, and a Mennonite himself, he did not have much contact with his home church, but devoted himself ardently to Collegiantism (*q.v.*), which taught that there is no true Christian church on earth. He wished "to raise badly torn Christianity to the level of the apostolic period." He was much distressed over all who thought that their own church was the only true Christian church. Galenus Abrahamsz (*q.v.*), a Mennonite minister at Amsterdam, at first a follower of the Collegiants, but later somewhat critical of their principles, was for this reason called by Klinkhamer "the pest of the Collegiants." By his books, especially *Vryheydt van spreecken in de Gemeynte der geloovingen* (Leiden, 1655), he had wide influence on the Dutch Mennonites. vDZ.

J. C. van Slee, *De Rijnsburger Collegianten* (Haarlem, 1895) *passim*, see Index; C. B. Hylkema, *Reformateurs* I, II (Haarlem, 1900, 1902) *passim*, see Index; *Biogr. Wb.* V, 21-25.

Klippenfeld, a village in the Molotschna settlement in the Ukraine, Russia, founded in 1862 on the Tokmak, a small tributary of the Molochnaya River three miles from Stulayevo, the railway station. The village comprised 2,300 acres; in 1917 it had a population of 310. (*ML* II, 513.)

Klock, Leonhard: see **Clock, Leenaerdt.**

Klomp, Pieter, b. about 1760, d. Aug. 19, 1832, at Groningen, studied at the Mennonite Seminary at Amsterdam and became one of the outstanding ministers among the Dutch Mennonites of his time. He first served t. Staveren 1784-98; in 1798 he was called to the Groningen Old Flemish congregation in the city of Groningen. By his activity and his tolerant views he succeeded in achieving a union of his Old Flemish congregation with the Flemish-Waterlander congregation at Groningen in November 1809. It was Klomp, who on Dec. 10, 1809, preached the first sermon for the united congregation. He also promoted the merging of the independent congregation of Swiss Mennonites of Groningen with the united congregation, which happened in 1824. Klomp, who in 1807 had been appointed *commissaris* (elder and leader) of the Conference of Groningen Old Flemish Mennonites, presided at the last meeting of this conference in 1815. In 1826 he became the moderator of the Groningen Sociëteit (Conference), founded in that year. Klomp served at Groningen until his death in 1832. vDZ.

Blaupot t. C., *Groningen* I, 136, 148, 152, 195; H. Dassel Sr., *Menno's volk in Groningen* (Groningen, n.d.) 35, 43, 48; *Inv. Arch. Amst.* II, No. 2261.

Kloosterburen, a hamlet in the Dutch province of Groningen, formerly the seat of a Mennonite congregation which also included the neighboring hamlets of Leens and Vliedorp. (It was also called the Marne Brotherhood (*q.v.*) for the district in which these hamlets are situated.) This congregation belonged to the Old Flemish branch. The congregation is mentioned in 1616 and still existed in 1683, but had died out before 1731, for it does not appear in the first *Naamlijst* of that year. vDZ.

Inv. Arch. Amst. I, Nos. 562, 571; *DB* 1879, 4; 1906, 46.

Klopfenstein, an Amish Mennonite family originally from Switzerland. In the 18th century some members of this family were found in the Normanvillars (*q.v.*) congregation in Alsace, where Peter Klopfenstein was a preacher in the early 18th century. In the 1830's, when most Mennonites left Normanvillars for the United States, most of the Klopfenstein family remained. They gradually left the Mennonite church. J. Klopfenstein was the editor of an almanac for Mennonite farmers, *l'Anabaptiste ou le Cultivateur par expérience,* on the title page of which is found a curious picture of a Swiss Mennonite farmer in ancient costume with a plow, published at Belfort, France, 1812-21. vDZ.

Delbert L. Gratz, *Bernese Anabaptists* (Scottdale, 1953) 92-94, 135, note 83; *Catalogus Amst.,* 23; J. H. Yoder, "Mennonites in a French Almanac," *Menn. Life* IX (1954) 154-56.

Klöpfer, Hans, of Feuerbach near Stuttgart, Württemberg, Germany, was baptized about 1540 by Martin Fesser at Esslingen (*q.v.*), and then went to Moravia. Here he was a preacher of the Swiss Brethren at Polaw on Magdeberg (Meyberg) until 1543; at a meeting at Tasswitz he solemnly left them, giving four defects as the reason: (1) community of goods was not practiced; (2) they paid taxes which were used for war and bloodshed; (3) the preachers were not convinced of their authorization; (4) they punished adultery, thievery, and the like among themselves instead of through the government, and thus kept impure spirits and unclean hearts in their midst. With four companions he joined the Hutterian Brethren in Schäckowitz and was sent to Württemberg in 1543 by Leonhard Sailer and Peter Riedemann, to warn Hans Gentner (*q.v.*) and Michael Kramer of false doctrine and summon them home. About 1550 he became a Hutterite preacher and died in 1562 at Nikolsburg, where he was greatly respected. G.Bo.

Beck, *Geschichts-Bücher,* 153, 214; G. Bossert, *TA* I: *Württemberg* (1930) 199; Wolkan, *Geschicht-Buch,* 189 ff., 192, 306, 314; Zieglschmid, *Chronik,* 242, f., 246, 409; *ML* II, 513.

Klopper, a Mennonite family at Amsterdam. Members of this family were found in the Zonist congregation, and some also in the Lamist congregation. Two members of this family served as pastors of Mennonite churches. Reinier Klopper from Amsterdam, who studied at the Amsterdam Zonist (*q.v.*) Mennonite Seminary in 1736-41, was preacher at den Ilp 1742-45 and Almelo 1745-54. He was called to Almelo in May 1745, but could not preach his first sermon before Nov. 20, 1746, because the Baron of Almelo refused to approve the appointment. Nicolaas Klopper (d. *ca.* 1812 at Amsterdam) attended the Zonist seminary at Amsterdam for a time, but was dismissed because he did not accept the strict Zonist (*q.v.*) doctrines. He then served as preacher of the Goes congregation until 1752. In 1754-58 he studied at the Lamist seminary, and then served the congregations of Bolsward (until 1764) and Harlingen 1764-86. He was an ardent Patriot (*q.v.*) against the oligarchy of the old Reformed governing families. His radicalism (*DB* 1905, 23 f.) caused so much discord with his congregation that he was forced to resign. After his resignation he lived at Amsterdam. vDZ.

Uit het Verleden der Doopsgez. in Twenthe (Borne, n.d.) 24-28; *Inv. Arch. Amst.* II No. 1738.

Klopreis (Kloprijs), **Johann,** one of the outstanding Wassenberg (*q.v.*) preachers, b. in Bottrop parish near Recklinghausen, Westphalia, Germany, studied theology at the University of Cologne 1518-21, became a vicar at Wesel, Bislich, and Büderich, where he became a friend of Clarenbach (*q.v.*), was summoned to court on account of his evangelical sermons and forced to recant. When he nonetheless continued his Protestant preaching, he was summoned to Cologne the second time. Clarenbach accompanied him. Both were imprisoned. Klopreis was sentenced to "eternal prison" and Clarenbach to death; he was executed on Sept. 28, 1529. Klopreis escaped on New Year's night with the aid of Theodor Fabricius (*q.v.*) and found refuge in Wassenberg on the Roer with bailiff Werner von Pallant who employed him as chaplain. Later the gates of the city church were opened to him; here he served a large congregation in an evangelical manner, using bread and wine during the observance of the Lord's Supper. In the surrounding territory he found numerous like-minded preachers, one of whom was Heinric Rol (*q.v.*), who exerted a great influence on Klopreis. Through him he was led beyond the initial Lutheran influence to some Zwinglian and early Anabaptist views. For four years Klopreis labored here without disturbance. When Pallant lost his office through the Cleve government on account of his evangelical innovations, he sent Klopreis to Philip of Hesse about Christmas of 1532 to intercede for him.

Klopreis went first to Büderich and proceeded to meet his friend Rol, who had meanwhile gone to the city of Münster. In February 1532 Klopreis arrived in Münster at the moment when this city was going through a significant transformation. The evangelical movement had been victorious and had reached an agreement with the bishop and ruler regarding the Reformation in the city. Klopreis was urged to stay. He accepted the position as minister and had his wife and children join him. With the transformation of Münster from an evangelical city to an Anabaptist Jerusalem, Klopreis underwent some additional changes. He was baptized on Jan. 5, 1534, and became an Anabaptist evangelist. The book *Bekentnisse van beyden Sacramenten Doepe und Nachtmaele,* published Nov. 8, 1533, was signed by Rothmann, Rol, Klopreis, Vinne, Staprade, and Stralen. This fact puts Klopreis in the front line of the early Anabaptist movement in Münster. C. A. Cornelius says that Klopreis opposed some of the radical developments such as polygamy.

With Gottfried Stralen, Klopreis was sent as an "apostle" to Warendorf (*q.v.*) on Oct. 13, 1534, to preach and baptize. The council of the city accepted the Anabaptist message. On Oct. 21, 1534, the bishop besieged the city and the council had to turn the "apostles" over to him. The co-workers were put to death while Klopreis was sent to the archbishop of Cologne. On Jan. 29, 1535, he was subjected to an examination on the rack. His "confessions" were published by J. Niesert (102 pages). On Feb. 1, 1535, he was burned at the stake at Brühl.

Klopreis was no doubt one of the most significant of the "Wassenburg predikanten." His association with and a letter he wrote to Clarenbach during his imprisonment reveal that he was a deeply religious, evangelically minded, and well-educated man, and worthy of a better fate. The stages of his development demonstrate that he was willing to accept the full truth and that in Münster he was unable to stop the development of a movement which was taking a course which he did not approve. What his attitude would have been when the city of Münster was defended by the sorely oppressed radical wing of Anabaptism is hard to tell. He died as a peaceful witness to the truth he had received. He greeted the stake at which he was to die with a prayer of praise.   NEFF, C.K.

Ernstliche handlung zwischen den hochgelerten Doctorn inn der gotheyt . . . unnd eynem gefangnen genant, Adolph Clarenbach . . . (1528) (BeCL); J. Niesert,

Münsterische Urkundensammlung I (Coesfeld, 1826); Mellink, *Wederdopers* (Groningen, 1954); *ADB* XVI, 209; *Ztscht des Bergischen Geschichtsvereins* IX (1873) 144 ff.; Rembert, *Wiedertäufer,* 311 ff.; C. A. Cornelius, *Geschichte des Münsterischen Aufruhrs* (Leipzig, 1855); W. Bax, *Het Protestantisme in het bisdom Luik I* (The Hague, 1937) 46 ff.; *ML* II, 513.

Klubnikovo, a village in the Ural Mts. of Orenburg, Russia, was the seat of a subsidiary congregation of the M.B. Church of Kamenka. It included the villages of Aliessovo, Stepanovka, Klubnikovo, Kubanka, Kitchkas, Rodnichnoye, Dolinovka, and Dobrovka. In 1906 a large church was built in Klubnikovo, which was closed by the Soviets in 1931 and used for grain storage. The leading ministers of Klubnikovo were Jakob Friesen (Kitchkas) to 1911, Heinrich H. Kröger (Aliessovo) to 1921, and Peter P. Funk (Kubanka). Preachers were Johann J. Block (Dolinovka), d. 1912, Johann D. Rempel (Rodnichnoye), David H. Kröger (Kubanka), Jakob J. Martens (Rodnichnoye), Gerhard D. Rempel (Rodnichnoye), and Heinrich Brucks (Kubanka).
W.Q.

Klundert, a hamlet in the Dutch province of North Brabant where a number of Mennonites were found about 1570. With their brethren at Breda (*q.v.*) they held meetings on the "Buursteedse heide" near Princenhage or in the homes of the members in Breda or also on the "Niervaert," i.e., Nieuwervaart near Klundert in the homes of Elsken Deeken (or Deckers) and Jan Peetersz. A meeting in the house of the latter, on Aug. 5, 1571 (van Braght, *Mart. Mir.,* erroneously 1572), attended by about 50 members, was surprised by the police and a number of them were arrested, most of whom were executed at Breda. After this disaster no Mennonites were found there.   vDZ.

DB 1912, 29-48; *Mart. Mir.* D 603-6, E 929-31; *Ned. Archief v. Kerkgesch., Nieuwe Serie* XXXVIII (1951) 23.

Kluyver, Dutch Mennonite family, many members of which were living at Koog aan de Zaan, Dutch province of North Holland, in the 18th and 19th century, where they were merchants and oil-millers. From this family numerous descendants, who spell their name Kliewer (*q.v.*), are found in Prussia, Russia, and America.   vDZ.

Knapp, Albert (1798-1864), a German Protestant theologian, educated at the theological seminary at Maulbronn and the University of Tübingen, in 1820 was made vicar in Feuerbach, where his contacts with Ludwig Hofacker produced a deep change in him. As pastor at Kirchheim unter Teck he published the *Christoterpe,* a yearbook, 1833-53. In 1836 he became a pastor in Stuttgart, where he died on June 18, 1864. He is known as a writer of church songs. His *Evangelischer Liederschatz für Kirche und Haus* (1837), which was found in many Mennonite homes, contains 3,590 hymns, 1,200 of which he wrote himself. Johannes Molenaar (*q.v.*) secured his aid as a collaborator on the *Gesangbuch zum gottesdienstlichen und häuslichen Gebrauch in Evangelischen Mennoniten-Gemeinden* (Worms, 1854). He wrote three songs especially for this book; it contains in addition 24 others of his hymns. Of these, 20 were kept in the 1910 revision, and a new one adopted. His *Christliche Gedichte* (Basel, 1829) and *Herbstblüte* (Stuttgart, 1859) were also familiar in the South German homes. Thus through his hymns he exerted a lasting influence on the Mennonites of South Germany.   NEFF.

M. Knapp, *Albert Knapp als Dichter und Schriftsteller* (Tübingen, 1912); *Gbl.*, 1911, 38 f., 42 f., 47 f.; *ML* II, 513 f.

Knel, Johan (Büchner), an Anabaptist martyr, was burned at the stake in London on May 2, 1550, with Anna Cantiana, because they believed "with Menno Simons . . . that the Son of God . . . did not receive His humanity from Mary." (*Mart. Mir.* D 99, E 498; *ML* II, 514.)   vDZ.

Kneutzinger, Jörg: see **Kreutzinger.**

Knijpe, a village in the Dutch province of Friesland, about five miles from Heerenveen. Mennonites living at Knijpe often belonged to the congregation which had its meetinghouses at Heerenveen (*q.v*). Mennonites were found at Knijpe by the 17th century. The history of Mennonites and their congregations in Knijpe is very complicated. In the 18th century there was a Frisian congregation at Knijpe, which had a meetinghouse at Bovenknijpe. This congregation merged with the Waterlander congregation of Heerenveen-Knijpe in 1741. In 1780 this united church was divided into two independent congregations: (*a*) Heerenveen, (*b*) Bovenknijpe (*q.v*.), both still existing.

In Knijpe there was also a Groningen Old Flemish congregation, sometimes called Heerenveen-Knijpe, Knijpe-Mildam, Nieuw-Brongerga, or Mildam. In 1710 the membership stood at about 30, in 1733 at 68, in 1754 at 22. After merging with the Mildam (*q.v*.) congregation the baptized membership numbered 60 in 1767. The preachers were Jan Jochems, mentioned in 1681, Jeyp Annes in 1683, Age Jouckes (*q.v*.) until 1687, Sjoerd Annes mentioned in 1685, Reitse Cobes (Koops) serving 1720-68, Jacob Sikkes chosen 1731, banned 1749, Anne Johannes serving 1769-83(?), Jan Tjerks (Vermanje) 1784-1805. The congregation died out in 1805. (See also **Heerenveen, Bovenknijpe,** and **Mildam.**) vDZ.

Blaupot t. C., *Friesland*, See Index; P. Veen, *De Doopsgezinden in Schoterland* (Leeuwarden, 1869); *DJ* 1840, 43; *DB* 1870, 108 ff.; 1879, 2, 90; 1890, 94; *Naamlijst;* *ML* II, 514.

Knipperdolling, Bernt (Bernhard) (*ca*.1500-36), a leader of the Anabaptists in Münster, Westphalia, Germany. He was a prosperous clothing merchant. His home was located near St. Lambert's Church. He is first mentioned in 1527 when he helped to free Tonies Kruse, who had been imprisoned by the bishop. When the evangelical movement spread in Münster he joined it, particularly in supporting B. Rothmann. When the bishop and the city council lost their influence through the democratic Anabaptist movement, he was elected mayor in February 1534. He became a staunch supporter of Jan Matthys (*q.v*.) and Jan van Leyden (*q.v*.) when they arrived. Both were guests in his home. Jan van Leyden married Knipperdolling's daughter. After the 12 elders appointed by Jan van Leyden took over the government, he lost his office as mayor but remained

the special representative of Jan van Leyden. When Jan van Leyden proclaimed himself king, Knipperdolling was opposed but finally yielded. After the defeat of Münster he was found in a hiding place and shared the fate of Jan van Leyden and Bernhard Krechting, who were cruelly tortured to death on Jan. 23, 1536. The corpses were hung in the tower of St. Lambert's Church. Numerous portraits of Knipperdolling—paintings, woodcuts, etchings, etc.—were produced by artists like H. Aldegrever and Ch. van Sichem (Geisberg). (See also **Münster Anabaptists.**)   C.K.

C. A. Cornelius, *Historische Arbeiten vornehmlich zur Ref.-Zeit* (Leipzig, 1899) 99-101; idem, *Berichte der Augenzeugen über das Münsterische Wiedertäuferreich* (Münster, 1853); L. Keller, *Gesch. der Wiedertäufer und ihres Reichs zu Münster* (Münster, 1880) *passim;* Kühler *Geschiedenis* I, see Index; *ADB* XVI, 293; M. Geisberg, *Die Münsterischen Wiedertäufer und Aldegrever* (Strasbourg, 1907); Mellink, *Wederdopers* (Groningen, 1954); *ML* II, 514.

Knipscheer, a Dutch Mennonite family. Jan Knipscheer (1836-1927), married to Wilhelmina Johanna Meihuizen, was at first a teacher at Weesperkarspel; he then founded a private school at Amsterdam, serving at the same time as catechist of the Amsterdam Mennonite congregation. His son Jacob Frederik Knipscheer (May 22, 1865—Feb 20, 1954) studied at the University and the Mennonite Seminary of Amsterdam 1881-87, and then served the congregations of Baard 1888-90 and Knollendam 1890-1930. For many years he was secretary of the *Zaansche Emeritaat en Invaliditeitsfonds.* His brother Frederik Samuel Knipscheer, born at Amsterdam in 1871, who studied at the Mennonite Seminary 1890-96, joined the Reformed Church in 1898 and was pastor at Akersloot 1898, Grosthuizen 1903, and Zaltbommel 1911. He died in 1955. He published, among other historical books and papers, "Geschiedenis van het stil en het stemmelijk gebed bij de Nederlandsche Doopsgezinden" in *DB* 1897 and 1898, "Abdias Widemarius twistgesprekken met de Mennisten" in *DB* 1907, and "De Nederlandsche gereformeerde synoden tegenover de Doopsgezinden, 1563-1620" in *DB* 1910 and 1911. Leendert Dionys Geerten Knipscheer (b. 1903), son of J. F. Knipscheer, after having studied at the Amsterdam University and Mennonite Seminary, served at Oudebildtzijl 1926-31, Dantumawoude 1931-35, and since 1935 at Groningen. He has been the editor of the *Doopsgezind Jaarboekje* (*q.v*.) since 1949, and published (together with H. Bremer) *Wie zijn wij?* (Groningen, 1947) and *Verhalen uit de Doopsgezinde Geschiedenis* (Amsterdam, n.d.-1953). vDZ.

Knobloch (*Knoblauch*), **Georg** and **Greta.** Greta was an Anabaptist martyr, the first wife of Georg Knobloch, a resident of Emseloh in Thuringia, whom she had married as a widow. She was seized with him, and after a valiant confession of her faith was beheaded in April 1534 at Sangerhausen. On the scaffold Greta declared before the crowd of spectators that she was dying for the sake of the Word of God; she had never harmed anyone. Her courage was greatly admired by the crowd.

Georg, who had not yet been baptized, saved his life by recanting. But he must have repented of his recantation, for on Oct. 6, 1534, he was baptized with Greta's three grown children of her first marriage. He is probably identical with Georg Meurer. Greta's sons-in-law, Jobst and Heinrich Möller, soon followed her in martyrdom. (See **Möller, Jobst**, for extended account.)   NEFF.

E. Jacobs, "Die Wiedertäufer am Harz," in *Ztscht des Harzvereins für Gesch.* . . . XXXII (1899) 433 ff.; Wappler, *Thüringen*, 108 ff.; *idem, Inquisition und Ketzerprozess in Zwickau* (Leipzig, 1908) 100; *ML* II, 515.

Knodsenburg, J. C. van, a Dutch Mennonite of Amsterdam, an opponent of the Lamist minister Galenus Abrahamsz (*q.v.*). He published *Eenige Extracten uyt verscheyden Mennoniste Autheuren, Martelaren en Belijdenissen* (Amsterdam, 1663), defending the doctrine of salvation by the death of Christ and combatting Galenus' views of perfectionism. Concerning the author no further information was available.   VDZ.

Knollendam, a village in the Dutch province of North Holland. When the government in 1535 in consequence of the Münster catastrophe passed sterner measures against the heretics, Knollendam was one of the places named, "where the Anabaptists stayed most." At the end of 1535 special police appeared from the court to seize them. But they had already fled. Four houses in which Anabaptists had lived were razed, and one was burned as an abhorrent example. On April 10, 1535, Claesz Matthijs of Knollendam confessed his faith in The Hague with death by fire.

In Knollendam and the adjoining villages, Marken-Binnen, Krommeniedijk, and Uitgeest, congregations were soon formed, which united to a greater or lesser degree with Knollendam. In 1672-78 and 1726-33 these churches revealed a spirit of sacrifice for the sake of exemption from military service and aid to brethren in other countries.

The congregation at Uitgeest died out about 1750. The Krommeniedijk congregation united with Knollendam in 1804. The few members of Marken-Binnen joined the Knollendam congregation in 1828. In the 18th century this congregation usually was called West-Knollendam. Originally meetings were held in the homes of the members. In the early 17th century a frame church was built, renovated in 1745 and 1753 and replaced by a brick church in 1842; an organ was added in 1897.

The membership always was small, numbering 70 in 1772, 36 in 1804, 77 in 1861, 130 in 1900, and 35 in 1956. During the last century the following ministers served here: D. Lodeesen 1855-56, H. de Boer 1857-59, R. Brouwer 1860-63, G. A. Hulshoff 1864-89, and J. F. Knipscheer 1890-1930. The pulpit has been vacant since 1930; in 1934-47 and again since 1955, the congregation has been served by the pastor of Wormerveer (*q.v.*).   VDZ.

Inv. Arch. Amst. I, 98; *DJ* 1850, 25; *DB* 1883, 72; 1907, 37 f., 41 f., 72-76; Blaupot t. C., *Holland* I and II, *passim,* see Index; *ML* II, 515.

Knonau, a magistracy in the canton of Zürich, Switzerland, in which there were many Anabaptists in the 16th century. Complaints about their numbers produced renewed sharp mandates to punish them. On April 3, 1589, the Anabaptists presented to the magistrate of Knonau a document drawn up by Andreas Gut of Affoltern with the request to send it to the council and theologians of the city of Zürich. In it they give the reasons for their attitude toward the government and their views on the institutions of the church. Soon afterward they presented a second, very detailed "Supplication to the burgomaster and the council of the city of Zürich by a few Anabaptists," which they call a "simple confession." In it they discuss five questions: the reasons for the great division, the evaluation of the Old Testament in comparison with the New, their position on government and on accepting worldly office, and baptism. This was evidently a very important document (Bergmann, 62-64).

On Aug. 17, 1636, a disputation was held in Knonau, which was attended by 36 of the 58 Swiss Brethren living under the jurisdiction of Knonau. It was futile. The Swiss Brethren were then to send in individual answers in a short time. This happened on Sept. 26, 1636. The document was drawn up by the Swiss Brethren preacher, Rudolf Egli, and carried 20 signatures. The signers were seized, but were released by the wife of the magistrate. Yet the pressure was not eased. Their property was confiscated, causing great consternation and resistance. The Swiss Brethren emigrated, many of them to the Palatinate. In a short time Anabaptism was completely suppressed in Knonau.   NEFF.

C. Bergmann, *Die Täuferbewegung im Kanton Zürich bis 1600* (Leipzig, 1916); *ML* II, 515.

Knox County, Ohio, Amish lived for less than 20 years (between 1830 and 1860) in a fairly compact group about one mile north of Martinsburg. Preacher (later bishop) Isaac Schmucker (*q.v.*) was ordained to the ministry here in 1838 but moved to Noble Co., Ind., in 1841.   J.S.U.

Knuyt, Francois de, a Mennonite elder at Zierikzee in the Dutch province of Zeeland in the first third of the 17th century, was a lover of peace and possessed great gifts. Repeatedly he disputed with Reformed preachers; in 1617 he debated with Abraham Stamperius at Sommelsdijk on infant baptism. By trade he was a fuller. He traveled much; on one of his journeys he was arrested in April 1615 and imprisoned at Aardenburg, because he had contacted the Mennonites here, preaching against the express interdiction of the city government. De Knuyt seems to have been influenced by the Flemish elder Jacques Outerman, while he in turn to some degree influenced Galenus Abrahamsz, who was a native of Zierikzee, where de Knuyt lived.

De Knuyt was a convinced exponent of silent prayer (*q.v.*), which was then in the process of being replaced by audible prayer by the preacher. Hans de Ries was an influential and ardent advocate of audible prayer. De Knuyt opposed it publicly, and wrote against it in his book, *Onder Verbeteringhe. Een corte bekenntnisse onses geloofs* (1618 and reprinted in 1623, 1635, 1642, 1648, 1684, and 1709). In the later reprints the confession is supplemented by his devotional hymns.

Outside his own circle de Knuyt found an opponent, Godefridus Udemans, a Reformed preacher at Middelburg, who felt obliged to publish a 380-page book against him (*Noodige Verbeteringhe . . .* 1620). Later Aernout van Geluwe, a Catholic bookseller in Gent, opposed him with a book titled *Een onverwinnelijcke schriftmathige roomsch catholijcke belijdenisse des geloofs . . . teghen de onschriftmathighe belijdenisse der nieuwgesinde Wederdooperen . . .* (Antwerp, 1654).   vdZ.

Biogr. Wb. V, 69-72; Blaupot t. C., *Holland* I, 194 f., 216; *DJ* 1837, 65; *DB* 1876, 86; 1877, 25 f., 42, note; 1897, 106-9, 114 f.; 1898, 57, 73-76; 1908, 106; H. W. Meihuizen, *Galenus Abrahamsz* (Haarlem, 1954) 12-15, 18, 25; *ML* II, 516.

Kob (Gobl), **Simon,** an Anabaptist martyr, was a member of Georg Blaurock's (*q.v.*) congregation in the Eisack Valley of Tirol, Austria. He was seized at a meeting near Bozen in the autumn of 1529, with his wife and her sister Margarete as well as other participants. In Bozen the monk Guardian tried for three weeks to bring them back into the Catholic fold. Most of the prisoners did not yield and were put to death in Bozen, among them Kob and his wife. Their property was given to their children upon orders of King Ferdinand. (Loserth, *Anabaptismus,* 487, 500; *ML* II, 516.)   Hege.

Kob(e)litz (Kobelic; Czech, *Kobyli*), a village between Auspitz (Hustopece) and Chaykovitz in southern Moravia, where the Anabaptists began to live on Lipa territory (see **Kromau**) in 1589. In the Bocskay war this Bruderhof as well as the one in near-by Paraditz was burned down by the invading enemy (July 1605). In 1616 a spark set fire to the rebuilt house and reduced to ashes the part used by the coopers, masons, and carpenters. Kobelitz suffered more than other Hutterite settlements in the rebellion. By mid-October it had been plundered six times. Dampierre's troops lodged here two days (Oct. 11 and 12), broke down all the doors, chests, and drawers, chopped up the filled wine barrels, stole the brewing pans and the kettles as well as all the tools, even the smiths' bellows, and dragged away all the bedding, linens, and cloth supplies in addition to the big clock and bells, a total of 70 wagonloads of booty. Finally they killed a brother and burned down the school. In March 1620 Polish troops again plundered the scarcely rebuilt house, and in December all the inhabitants had to flee to escape the inhuman cruelties of the passing troops. They had scarcely returned, when they were again robbed by the imperial troops; this was repeated so often in a short time that "nothing was left in the house." In October the imperial troops dug up all the money and other goods the Hutterites had buried. The expulsion of 1622 put an end to this martyrdom, as well as to the settlement itself.
P.De.

Beck, *Geschichts-Bücher,* 302 *et passim;* Wolkan, *Geschicht-Buch,* 487, 517, *et passim;* Zieglschmid, *Chronik,* 636, 659; *ML* II, 516.

Koch, Elise, an Anabaptist martyr, was burned at the stake at Bamberg, Bavaria, Germany, on Jan. 30, 1528, with two men and two other women for their faith.

P. Wappler, *Die Stellung Kursachsens und des Landgrafen Philipp von Hessen zur Täuferbewegung* (Münster, 1910); *ML* II, 516.

Koch, Hans, a martyr, probably Waldensian, who was put to death with Leonhard Meister at Augsburg, Bavaria, Germany, in 1524. He is the author of the oldest song in the *Ausbund,* "Ach Gott, Vater im höchsten Thron." His further identity has not yet been clarified. Samuel Cramer identifies Koch and Meister with Hans Kag (see **Kager, Hans**) and a Speiser or Pfoster, both of whom were beheaded as revolutionaries at Augsburg in 1524 (Uhlhorn). But such an identification is today considered dubious. None of these names is found in the Hutterite Chronicle.   Neff.

Fr. Roth, *Augsburgs Reformationsgeschichte* (Munich, 1901) 189 ff.; Wolkan, *Lieder; Mart. Mir.* D 1 f., E 413 f.; S. Cramer, "De geloofwaardigheid van *van Braght,*" *DB* 1899, 65-164, especially 116 f.; G. Uhlhorn, *Urbanus Rhegius* (Elberfeld, 1861) 62; *ML* II, 516.

Koch, Konrad (Coenraet, Conrad), an Anabaptist martyr of Honnef on the Rhine, in the Löwenberg (*q.v.*) area of the duchy of Berg, Germany, was beheaded there on Nov. 26, 1565, after he had remained true and steadfast through a long imprisonment. From prison he wrote two short letters describing his life and asserting his determination to suffer death for his faith. He asks his friends' intercession, that the Lord might give him the strength to do so, to God's glory and his own salvation. The book *Güldene Aepfel in silbernen Schalen* (*q.v.*) prints his letters (pp. 132-36) and says that he came from Leuenburch (Löwenberg). With Heinrich Koenen of Breidtbach (of whom nothing else is known) he wrote the song, "Hört zu, ihr Christen alle."   Neff.

W. Risler, "Täufer im bergischen Amt Löwenburg," *Gesch.-Bl.,* 1955 and 1956; Wolkan, *Lieder,* 100; *Mart. Mir.* D 324-26, E 686-88; *ML* II, 516.

Koch, Margarete, a widow, known as "die alte Garköchin," was banished on account of her faith from her home in Hersfeld, Hesse, Germany, and later also from Vacha, and was arrested with Fritz Erbe (*q.v.*), who had taken her in, was released, and seized again. For years she languished in prison. She had to undergo many cross-examinations, through which she remained faithful. Her fate is not known.   Neff.

P. Wappler, *Die Stellung Kursachsens und des Landgrafen Philipp von Hessen zur Täuferbewegung* (Münster, 1910); *ML* II, 516.

Kodarma, a town in the Hazaribagh District, Bihar Province, India, and the first mission station of the Bihar Mennonite (MC) Mission (*q.v.*). It is the most important center of the world's leading mica mines. It is located on a double track trunk line of the East Indian Railway running between Calcutta and Delhi, and connected by a black top road with the Grand Trunk Road, the most important Calcutta-Delhi highway. Kodarma is in the eastern end of the Mennonite mission field. It was transferred to the Mennonites by the Methodists, who formerly worked it, and was first occupied by the Mission when the S. J. Hostetler family arrived there Jan. 29, 1940, from Dhamtari, M.P. (*q.v.*). In January 1941 the M. C. Vogt family also came here from the Dhamtari area, and one or both of these families worked here until March 1947. The work done was direct evangelism, village school work, work with high-school boys, establishing and nurturing groups of believers, and medical aid. About 25 were baptized, mostly of the Turi caste, and several Mohammedans. Social ostracism and threats triggered by a remarkable case of healing scattered most of the Christians. When the Palamau field (q.v.) opened, the missionaries moved to Latehar, because it is a much more promising field. However, the Kodarma field is still visited at intervals to keep contact with the Christians there. Dhan Masih Lakra and Anand Masih Topono and their wives were also workers in Palamau field. S.J.Ho.

Koedijk, a hamlet in the Dutch province of North Holland, where there was formerly a Mennonite congregation of the Frisian branch, always served by the same preachers as the near-by congregation of Langendijk, now Broek op Langedijk (q.v.). The congregation of Koedijk, always small, declined during the 18th century; the last services in the little meetinghouse were held in December 1805. (Naamlijst 1806, 75; 1808, 87.)   vdZ.

Koehn (Könn, Koen, Kuehn, Kien, Kane) is an old Prussian Mennonite name first recorded in 1681, which was found in the church records of Danzig, Tragheimerweide, Deutsch-Kazun (Poland), and other places of the Vistula Delta. The Alexanderwohl church record before the migration to Russia also lists the name as one of the early members of the congregation. From Prussia and Poland the name spread to Russia. Today it is, however, most frequently found in Kansas and Oklahoma among the Mennonites that have come from Karolswalde, Poland, many of whom have joined the Church of God in Christ, Mennonite. This group has eleven preachers with the name Koehn.   C.K.

Koekebakker, a Dutch Mennonite family, found at Wormerveer, province of North Holland, from at least the early 18th century. They are members of the Waterlander Mennonite congregation and at the same time in the 18th century ardent Collegiants (q.v.) as well as ardent Patriots (q.v.). Hendrik Koekebakker (1809-88), married to Guurtje Prins, ran an oil mill and was a stock dealer at Wormerveer. His son, also called Hendrik, b. Feb. 5, 1847, d. Oct. 8, 1890, at Zwartsluis, studied at the University of Utrecht and the Mennonite Theological Seminary of Amsterdam. He became a ministerial candidate and served the following congregations: Burg on Texel 1871-74, Ouddorp 1874-78, Berlikum 1878-81, Giethoorn 1881-86, and Zwartsluis-Meppel 1886-90. He was liberal in theology, being called "a sage," whose papers on ethics, such as "De ontwikkelingstheorie en de Zedeleer" in De Gids (1881) and Het godsdienstig zedelijk belijden (Amsterdam, 1878), are of importance. Pastor Hendrik Koekebakker also was the first editor of the Dutch Mennonite weekly, the Zondagsbode. He was married in 1873 to Sina Huizinga (d. 1901). (Biogr. Wb. V, 89 f.; N.N.B.Wb. X, 474 f.)

Two of Hendrik's sons also went into the ministry: Jacob Koekebakker (b. 1875), who served the congregations of Den Ilp-Landsmeer 1899-1903, Aardenburg 1903-19, and Middelburg-Goes 1919-40, was active in behalf of the Russian Mennonites in 1921, visiting Russia in that year. He also was the first president of the board of trustees of the Elspeet (q.v.) Broederschapshuis. He published De Droom (three sermons, Middelburg, n.d.-1924). Willem Koekebakker (1878-1954) was Mennonite pastor at Zwartsluis 1904-9 and Dordrecht-Breda 1909-45. He was editor of De Zondagsbode 1930-42, and published De Zelfstandigheid der Gemeente (n.p., 1926); Ons Belijden (Wolvega, 1928); Tot geloof bewegen en bewogen worden (Utrecht, 1948). DJ 1922, 83 ff.; 1955, 16 f.)   vdZ.

Koenen, an important Mennonite family in Hamburg and Friedrichstadt a.d.Eider, Germany. The progenitor of the family was Jan Koenen of Haffkrug near Lübeck, who later operated a sugar refinery in Altona. Isaac Koenen (later a member of the Hamburg-Altona Mennonite Church) and several other Mennonites had previously been living in the immediate dominion of Wickrath (Kreis Grevenbroich, south of München-Gladbach) of the Reformed Baron Wilhelm Thomas von Quadt (1632-70, censured by Emperor Leopold I in 1663 for having Mennonites in his dominion, but nevertheless confirmed as baron in 1667). In Friedrichstadt there were the merchant Jan Koenen, whose son Abraham (1697-1778) was a preacher for 50 years at the Friedrichstadt Mennonite Church, and the councilor and merchant Lukas Koenen (ca. 1690), whose son Lukas, chairman of the church, moved into the "ferry-house" in Tönning in 1742, and according to a royal contract leased the ferry to Norderdithmarschen, for which he paid an annual sum of 226 Talers.   R.Do.

B. C. Roosen, Gesch. der Menn.-Gem. Hamburg-Altona (Hamburg, 1886); R. Dollinger, Gesch. der Menn. in Schleswig-Holstein (Hamburg and Lübeck, 1930); ML II, 517.

Koenen, Abraham, in 1725-ca.67 a preacher of the Dutch Mennonite congregation of Hazerswoude (q.v.), was asked to intermediate in the United Flemish, High German, and Frisian congregation of Danzig, West Prussia, where a schism had arisen between its elder Hendrik van Duren (van Dühren) and some of his fellow preachers supported by a large part of the congregation. Koenen stayed in Danzig from September 1740 until May 1741 and succeeded in restoring peace. Called to be elder of the Danzig congregation (November 1740), Koenen refused the call, preferring to return to his home congregation. (Inv. Arch. Amst. II, Nos. 2657-59, 2661-71, 2674; II, 2 No. 812.)   vdZ.

Koers, a mimeographed periodical, published as an occasional journal for leaders of the Dutch Mennonite youth work, normally seven numbers annually, 20 pages per number, 8½ x 11.   H.S.B.

Koffler, Philip, an Anabaptist martyr of Vill in Tirol, Austria, seized in Kaltern at the end of 1532. In the face of death he begged for mercy, but refused it at the price of recantation, and was condemned to death. He is frequently mentioned in Jakob Hutter's (q.v.) letters. In his house Georg Frick (q.v.), who was later put to death for his faith, and others were baptized by Benedict (Gampner), a former chaplain of Bruneck in Tirol, who joined the Anabaptists in the middle of 1529, and who took charge of George Blaurock's (*q.v.*) group in Vill and Tramin when Blaurock was captured.   Hege.

Loserth, *Anabaptismus in Tirol*, 487; Zieglschmid, *Chronik*, 75; ML II, 518.

Koffmane, Gustav (1852-1915), a Lutheran theologian, educated at the University of Breslau, Germany, became pastor in Kunitz, received the doctorate in 1902 and was appointed as Church Superintendent in Krischnitz, where he died. He is the author of the valuable work on the Anabaptists in Silesia (*q.v.*), "Die Wiedertäufer in Schlesien," which was published in the *Correspondenzblatt des Vereins für Geschichte der evangelischen Kirche Schlesiens* III (1887) 37-55. (*ML* II, 517.) Neff.

Kofler (Koffler), **Andreas,** a martyr of the Hutterian Brethren, from the Adige, Tirol, Austria, was arrested at Ibbs (Ybbs) near Amstetten in Lower Austria and beheaded in 1545 "for the sake of the Gospel and divine truth."

Mart. Mir. D 72, E 473; Beck, *Geschichts-Bücher*, 163; Wolkan, *Geschicht-Buch*, 209; Zieglschmid, *Chronik*, 260; *ML* II, 518.

Kofler, Hans, an Anabaptist martyr, one of the first Anabaptists in Tirol, Austria. He was seized in 1528, but was pardoned. At the end of February 1529 he was again captured in Rattenburg, Austria, and executed several weeks later at Sterzing, Austria. (Loserth, *Anabaptismus,* 472, 477; *ML* II, 518.)   Hege.

Köhler, Georg, an Anabaptist martyr, an illiterate day laborer of Mülsen St. Michall near Zwickau, Germany, was baptized with Georg Knobloch (*q.v.*) on Oct. 6, 1534. He at once became a zealous propagandist for his faith, making a deep impression. He was seized at Riestedt near Sangerhausen, Sept. 2, 1535, and was soon afterward executed at Sangerhausen with Georg Möller and an Anabaptist woman.   Neff.

P. Wappler, *Die Täuferbewegung in Thüringen von 1526-1584* (Jena, 1913) 166 ff.; E. Jacobs, "Die Wiedertäufer im Harz," in *Ztscht des Harzvereins f. Gesch. u. Altertumskunde* XXXII (1899) 440 ff.; ML II, 518.

Köhler, Hans, an Anabaptist martyr, stemmed from Heyerode, a village near Mühlhausen in Thuringia, Germany, was seized in November 1537, while he and Hans Scheffer were conversing on matters of faith with Fritz Erbe, who was a prisoner at Eisenach. After long cross-examinations which he had to endure under Justus Menius (*q.v.*) he was put to death at the end of January 1538. (Wappler, *Thüringen*, 172-74; *ML* II, 518.)   Neff.

Köhler, Walther, a Lutheran church historian, b. Dec. 27, 1870, at Elberfeld, Germany, d. Feb. 18, 1946, at Heidelberg. He was professor of church history at the universities of Giessen (1904-9), Zürich (1909-29), and Heidelberg (1929-46). He was an outstanding research scholar in the history of the Reformation. His works on Luther and Zwingli are of superior importance, especially *Luther und die Kirchengeschichte* (1900), *Luther bis 1521* (1921), *Luther und die deutsche Reformation* (1917), *Zwingli als Theologe* (1919), *Ulrich Zwingli und die Reformation in der Schweiz* (1919); *Huldrych Zwingli* (1923), *Zwingli und Luther; ihr Streit über das Abendmahl* (1924 and 1953), *Das Buch der Reformation H. Zwinglis* (1926).

In the field of Anabaptist history he was an authority. His unprejudiced, objective presentation deserves special mention. Some of his works in this field were *Reformation und Ketzerprozess* (1901); article "Menno und die Mennoniten" in *RGG,* first edition (1908); edition of the Schleitheim *Brüderliche Vereinigung* (1908); "Die Züricher Täufer," in *Gedenkschrift zum 400-jährigen Jubiläum der Taufgesinnten oder Mennoniten* (1925); "Zur Geschichte des Täufertums in Kempten," in *Beiträge zur Geschichte der Mennoniten, Festgabe für D. Christian Neff* (1938). In the second edition of *RGG* (1927-32) he wrote among others the articles "Denk," "Grebel," "Hofmann," "Hubmaier," "Hut," "Joris," "Manz," and "Sattler." He published an extensive annotated Anabaptist bibliography in the *Archiv für Reformationsgeschichte* (1940-48) under the title, "Das Täufertum in der neueren kirchenhistorischen Forschung."

His contributions in the *Mennonitische Geschichts-Blätter* include "Das Täufertum in *Calvins Institutio*" (1937, pp. 1-4); "Der Verfasser des *Libellus confutationis*" (1938, pp. 1-10); "Die Verantwortung im Täufertum des 16. Jahrhunderts" (1940, pp. 10-19). His *Dogmengeschichte* (Volume II, Zürich, 1951) is the first work of its kind to give due recognition to the Anabaptists. For the *Mennonitisches Lexikon* he wrote the articles **Luther** and **Catholicism.**

Köhler was a close friend of Christian Hege and Christian Neff, a member of the executive committee of the *Mennonitischer Geschichtsverein,* and chiefly responsible for the bestowal of the honorary doctor's degree upon Neff in 1925 by the University of Zürich. Three Mennonite historians took their doctor's degrees in church history under him at Heidelberg in 1935-36—Horst Quiring, Harold Bender, and Cornelius Krahn. On his deathbed he is reported to have said, "Ich möchte am liebsten als Mennonit sterben" ("I would like best to die as a Mennonite").   Neff, H.S.B.

E. Crous, "Walther Köhler," in *Menn. Gesch.-Bl.,* 1949, 31-33; Rudolf Wihr, *Die Rehhütter Chronik* (Ludwigshafen, 1937); *ML* II, 518.

Kohlhof, a hamlet in the Palatinate, Germany, between Speyer and Ludwigshafen. It has existed since the middle of the 17th century, and belonged to the electoral family. It was originally called Kohlloch, for it made charcoal from the wood of the forests. Mennonites have been leasing it as hereditary lessees since 1713.

In that year Ulrich Schneider took it over, and on Feb. 12, 1716, he gave half of it over to Jakob Blickensdörfer and the other half to Joseph Burgholder, the son-in-law of Hans Gochnauer. The Mennonite register in the national archives at Karlsruhe lists five names in 1717: Ulrich Schneider, Hans and Jakob Gochnauer, Matth. Stauffer, and

Hans Jakob Blickensdörfer; the register of 1768 names two families, Georg Wagner and a Blickensdörfer widow. Descendants of these families are still living on the Kohlhof, though the Wagners are no longer Mennonites. In 1806 it became the property of the inhabitants.

As a congregation Kohlhof is first mentioned in 1790, when permission was asked at Neustadt to meet for worship and to build a church. Permission was granted in a government rescript of Nov. 5, 1790, with the stipulation that the building should not look like a church and should not have a bell. But the building could not be erected until 100 years later, with gifts from other Mennonite churches and a grant of 500 marks from the local government. It was dedicated Aug. 12, 1888.

Before 1888 meetings had been held in a specially furnished room in the home of a member. The earliest information dates back to 1791; Georg Blickensdörfer, who was the preacher at both Kohlhof and Neuwied (*q.v.*), wrote soon after permission for meeting had been granted, "On Feb. 20, 1791, the first meeting was held on the Kohlhof with seventy souls."

Live connections existed at that time with the Moravian Brethren; several Kohlhof Mennonite families moved to Neuwied and joined them there. That is probably the reason why the Moravian Brethren still meet annually for a conference at the Kohlhof. These meetings were at first called *Gehilfenkonferenz*. The first one of which there is record took place on June 13, 1826, and was attended by 28 brethren. Others were held on June 19, 1833, Sept. 16, 1835, and May 24, 1836, on the Kohlhof and in 1827 and 1828 also in Hassloch.

In 1833 the Kohlhof church made an agreement with the Friedelsheim (*q.v.*) church, whereby they would be served by the Friedelsheim minister, but maintain their congregational independence. Kohlhof early had its own cemetery, and made a new one in 1840. It has been incorporated since 1890. The membership in 1934 was 47, of whom 32 were living on the Kohlhof. In 1953 it was 65. Johannes Foth, pastor of the Friedelsheim Mennonite Church, has been serving the congregation since 1904. J.F.

Menn. Bl., 1888, 101; *Gbl.*, 1888, 91; *Gem.-Kal.*, 1894, 118 with picture; *ML* II, 518 f.

Köhn, Peter, a Mennonite minister, born at Waldheim near Gnadenfeld in the Molotschna settlement in the Ukraine, Russia. He was educated at St. Chrischona in Basel, Switzerland. About 1903, at the age of about 30, he was called as minister to the new Mennonite Brethren congregation at Alexandertal, province of Samara (now Kuibyshev), which had a meetinghouse in Mariental, to help the congregation over some difficulties. Peter Köhn soon saw that it could not survive as an M.B. congregation, and therefore tried to make an *Allianz-Gemeinde* of it. In this change the principle of rebaptism was sacrificed, so that members of the Mennonite Church could join it. Köhn was a highly esteemed preacher, and was invited to preach in many Mennonite churches. Since the small M.B. congregation was unable to support him, he returned to Waldheim after four years of fruitful

service. Nothing is known of his further life, except that in 1936 he wrote a letter to Bernhard Harder in Germany, requesting an artificial leg to replace one he had lost in an accident.   B.H.

Kohnert, a Mennonite family, formerly found both in East and West Prussia. This family is of Dutch descent, the name Kohnert being the same as the Dutch Christian name Koenraad (Conrad). Salomon Kohnert was a preacher of the Waterlander congregation of Lithuania (Memel-Niederung, *q.v.*) in 1743-1800. Andreas Kohnert served as preacher at Schweinsgrube (congregation Stuhmsche Niederung) 1764-d.88; in the same congregation, then called Tragheimerweide, David Kohnert, of Klein Schardau, was a preacher in 1859-*ca*.90. (*Naamlijst*.)   vdZ.

Koker, de, a former Dutch Mennonite family, originally from Flanders, Belgium, many of whose members are found after about 1640 in the Flemish Mennonite congregation of Rotterdam. Among the first of this family found in the Rotterdam records were Gillis de Koker and his son Daniel de Koker. Sara de Koker (1702-58), Daniel's daughter, was married to Petrus Smidt, preacher of the Zonist (*q.v.*) congregation of Amsterdam and professor at the Zonist Seminary. Johannes and Gillis de Koker of Rotterdam, visiting Jülich, Germany, in 1719, intervened in behalf of some Dompelaars from Crefeld (*q.v.*), who were imprisoned (*DB* 1861, 77 f., 80). Three members of this family, viz., Peter (Pieter), Yellis (Gillis), and Michael (Michiel) de Koker, were about 1725 among the proselytes and adherents of Alexander Mack (*q.v.*), the leader of the Dompelaars or Church of the Brethren; they remained, however, in the Netherlands and did not join the exodus of the Brethren to Pennsylvania in 1729. Members of the de Koker family were also found at Haarlem. Whether the Mennonite Abraham de Koker, who lived near Aardenburg (*q.v.*) and in 1730 married Tanneken Slock, was related to this family could not be decided.

Nearly all the de Koker family in the 18th century favored the Collegiant movement; some of them, like Pieter de Koker, Sr., Gerrit de Koker, and Gillis de Koker, often delivered addresses at the Collegiant center at Rijnsburg (*q.v.*). Most of them left the Mennonite Church; e.g., Gerrit de Koker, who in 1786 founded the old people's home "Hofje van Gerrit de Koker" at Rotterdam, and Alida de Koker, died 1794 at Rotterdam, who founded another Hofje there, called "Uit liefde en Voorzorg." A Joris de Coocker (*Inv. Arch. Amst.* I, 539) was a member of the Mennonite congregation of Harlingen, Friesland, in 1612.   vdZ.

Martin Grove Brumbaugh, *A History of the German Baptist Brethren in Europe and America* (Mount Morris, 1899).

Kolb, a Mennonite family, probably of Swiss origin. Caspar Kolb, a peasant of Walkringen in the canton of Bern, attended the disputation at Bern in 1538 as a leader of the Swiss Brethren. Barbara Kolb(in) was in prison at Zürich with three other Anabaptist women in 1639 because of their faith. However, not all the Kolbs in Switzerland were Swiss Brethren.

One of the representatives of the Reformed Church with whom Hans Pfistermeyer (*q.v.*) had to debate in the prison at Bern on April 19, 1531, was Franz Kolb. In the late 17th and early 18th centuries the Kolbs are found also in the Palatinate; some were preachers and elders in the congregations at Mannheim, Kriegsheim, and other places, among them Peter Kolb, elder at Mannheim.

This family, of slight importance in Europe, has produced numerous leaders in the Mennonite (MC) Church in America, particularly in Eastern Pennsylvania. In 1707 four children of Dielman Kolb (1648-1712) of Wolfsheim in the Palatinate came to Germantown as the very first forerunners of the large migration from that region to Eastern Pennsylvania, and one Dielman came in 1717. They settled early in Skippack (1709). Peter (1671-1727), the oldest of the children, remained in Mannheim where he was a Mennonite preacher. Martin (1680-1761) was ordained preacher at Germantown in 1709, but served at Skippack. Henry (d. 1730) was a preacher at Skippack. Dielman (1691-1756, *q.v.*) was a preacher at Salford and an associate with Henry (Henrich) Funck (*q.v.*) in the supervision of the publication of the Ephrata edition of the *Martyrs' Mirror*. Other prominent leaders in the Franconia Conference (MC) have been: Isaac (1711-76), first bishop of Rockhill; Amos (1879-), bishop at Vincent (Spring City); Elias W. Kulp (1880-), preacher at Bally. A total of 15 Kolbs have served as ordained men in the Franconia Conference. Most of the members of the Vincent congregation are direct or related descendants of Jonathan Kolb (1825-97), long-time deacon at Vincent. Jacob Kolb (1769-1858), preacher, was the founder of the Kolb's and Longenecker's congregation in Holmes Co., Ohio. A. B. Kolb (1862-1925), of the Waterloo Co., Ont., Kolb line, was a prominent layman at Elkhart, Ind., and an editor for many years of church publications in J. F. Funk's Mennonite Publishing House there. J. Z. Kolb (1836-1921), his father, was a long-time influential deacon in Waterloo Co., Ont. His younger brother, A. C. Kolb (1871-1937), who lived at Elkhart in 1888-1904, was the first secretary of the Elkhart Institute (*q.v.*) and of the Home and Foreign Relief Commission (*q.v.*).   J.C.W., vDZ.

D. K. Cassel, *A Genealogical History of the Kolb . . . Family* (Norristown, 1895); R. B. Strassburger, "The Kolb Family," 391-413 in *The Strassburger and Allied Families of Pennsylvania* (Geweynedd Valley, Pa., 1922); Delbert Gratz, *Bernese Anabaptists* (Scottdale, 1953); H. S. Bender, "The Founding of the Mennonite Church in America at Germantown, 1683-1708," *MQR* VII (October 1933) 227-50.

Kolb, Andreas and **Katharina**, a married couple who suffered death for their faith. With several like-minded persons they were baptized at Zella Sankt Blasii, Ohrdruf district of Sachsen-Gotha, Germany, on June 7, 1528, by Volkmar of Hildburghausen. Volkmar at this service prepared them for future suffering: whoever would be a true Christian must leave everything he has and suffer persecution unto death. His predictions were promptly fulfilled. The authorities set up a vigorous search for those who had been baptized in Zella. Most of them were young married couples. They fled, leaving their children with relatives. But after only a few weeks

some were discovered and brought back. An official list of arrests with its sober figures gives a shocking picture of the suffering that broke upon these families. There were six couples, who had left sixteen children behind, the oldest of whom was thirteen years old and blind. Their names were Andreas Kolb and wife, two children aged one and five; mayor Hans Fock and wife, one child aged two; Balthasar Armknecht and wife, four children aged two, three, five, and nine; Georg Unger (called Bader) and wife, four children aged four, ten, twelve, and thirteen; Kaspar Komel and wife, four children aged one, three, five, and seven; and Kunz Eigeler and wife with one child.

Andreas Kolb was the first arrested. He was sent to Reinhardsbrunn (a former monastery, and later a resort palace of the dukes of Sachsen-Gotha) near Gotha; Elector John (*q.v.*) of Saxony was notified of the arrest. Kolb confessed that he had been baptized, and at his urging his wife had also been baptized. He asked for instruction; if he had erred he would return to the church. By recanting he won his release, but later returned to the Anabaptists; his wife likewise.

A year later both were again arrested with seven other Anabaptists and taken to Reinhardsbrunn. Here each one was informed on Jan. 10, 1530, that he had forfeited his life and goods, since he had not kept his word to abstain from false doctrine.

After these admonitions they were given time to reflect and to receive further instruction. Andreas Kolb declared that he would stand by his faith. His wife, who had decided to recant, was unable to move him, and withdrew her own recantation. Christoph Ortlep and three women, Elsa Kunz, Barbara Unger, and Katharina König, also remained steadfast. One week later, on Jan. 18, 1530, they were put to death at Reinhardsbrunn. Only two men, Valentin Unger and Balthasar Armknecht, and one woman, Osanna Ortlep, probably some of them related to the above, begged for mercy and recanted (Wappler, *Kursachsen,* 12, 133-37).

The sentence of death passed on four women and two men who valued their faith above their life stirred up much comment, and resulted in the Wittenberg theologians taking a definite position in regard to the forcible suppression of the Anabaptists. Not only in letters did they express their views, but also in books.

The Gotha superintendent, Friedrich Myconius, had some doubts, because the condemned prisoners had not been convicted of sedition. He wrote to Philip Melanchthon about it, who was at that time making a conspicuous change, "a gradual letting go of the impression of the commands of the Sermon on the Mount" (Lüthje, 518). Melanchthon replied (February 1530) to Myconius that he was in full sympathy with the Reinhardsbrunn verdict. "Anabaptists, even though they are otherwise blameless, reject some of their civic duties. But even if they have no seditious, but obviously blasphemous articles, it is my opinion that it is the duty of government to kill them" (Wappler, *Kursachsen,* 14). This view was shared by Luther now too. In his exegesis of Psalm 82, two months after the verdict of Reinhardsbrunn had been carried out, he said emphatically that heresy should be punished by the government.

Shortly after this event Myconius and Justus Menius, the general superintendent of Eisenach, decided to refute the Anabaptist teachings in a book. The manuscript was presented to Luther for his opinion; on April 12, 1530, he expressed the desire to add a paragraph on the call to preach. The book appeared soon afterward under Menius' name with the title, *Der Widdertauffer lere und geheimnis aus heiliger Schrifft widderlegt;* it contained a foreword by Luther and a dedication to Philip of Hesse, dated May 4, 1530.   HEGE.

Wappler, *Thüringen,* 185, 303 f.; *idem, Die Stellung Kursachsens und des Landgrafen Philipp von Hessen zur Täuferbewegung* (Münster, 1910); H. Lüthje, "Melanchthons Anschauung über das Recht des Widerstandes gegen die Staatsgewalt," in *Ztscht für Kirchengesch.* XLVII (1928); *ML* II, 519 f.

Kolb, Dielman, preacher of the Mennonite Church at Salford, Pa., b. Nov. 10, 1691, at Wolfsheim, Palatinate, Germany, the youngest of six children, d. Dec. 28, 1756, at Skippack, Pa. His father, Dielman Kolb, b. 1648 in Wolfsheim, d. Oct. 13, 1712, in Mannheim, Germany, was married to a daughter of Peter Schumacher (a Quaker), who was one of the first Palatines to settle in Germantown in 1685. The son, and also his older brother Peter (d. 1727), who was a preacher at Mannheim, took a warm interest in his brethren who had been banished from Switzerland, sheltered them, and in general did much for them. He continued his correspondence with the Committee for Foreign Needs at Amsterdam after his arrival in America. In 1714 he married Elisabeth Schnebeli of Mannheim. On March 21, 1717, he emigrated to America with his family. They arrived in Philadelphia on Oct. 10. From there Dielman Kolb went to Salford (in Montgomery County), where he bought about 500 acres of land. With Heinrich Funck (*q.v.*) he founded the Salford congregation (MC) in 1738, and with him supervised the translation of the *Martyrs' Mirror* (*q.v.*) from Dutch into German 1745-48. It was through his influence that his close friend Christopher Dock's (*q.v.*) *Schulordnung* was written and later (1770) published. In the struggles and needs of a pioneer Mennonite settlement his work and influence were of lasting benefit to the brotherhood. His only child Elizabeth was married to Andrew Ziegler (1707-97), preacher (1746-) and bishop (1762-) at Skippack.   HEGE, H.S.B.

D. K. Cassel, *A Genealogical History of the Kolb, Kulp or Culp Family* (Norristown, 1895); R. B. Strassburger, *The Strassburger and Allied Families of Pennsylvania* (Gweynedd Valley, 1922); S. W. Pennypacker, "A Noteworthy Book," *Penn'a. Mag. of Hist. and Biog.* V, No. 3 (1881); J. D. Souder, "The Life and Times of Dielman Kolb, 1691-1756," *MQR* III (January 1929) 33-41; *Dictionary of American Biography* X (N.Y., 1933); *ML* II, 520.

Kolb, Franz, reformer of Bern, Switzerland, a native of Lörrach, Baden, Germany. He studied at the University of Basel, acquiring a Master's degree. After working three years in Bern (1512-14) he moved to Nürnberg. Through Berchthold Haller's (*q.v.*) mediation he came back to Bern, and became a fiery promoter of the Reformation. Kolb helped

Haller compose the ten *Schlussreden,* which served as the basis for the disputation in Bern (1528), which ended in a decisive victory for the Reformation.

In Anabaptist history Kolb is of importance for his debates with some of the Swiss Brethren. The first one took place on May 21, 1527, with Hunger, Peter Breyt, the "Seckler" Math. Han, Bastian Hammer, and Steffan Haffner. In early February 1530 Kolb and Kaspar Grossman (*q.v.*), in the presence of the Council, tried to convert the Swiss Brethren leader, Konrad Eichacher, by means of Romans XIII, but was not successful. He also took part in the discussion with Hans Pfistermeyer (*q.v.*) in Aarau on April 19, 1531, where the preachers had better success. Franz Kolb died in Bern on Nov. 11, 1535.   S.G.

S. Scheurer, *Mausoleum* (Bern, 1742); *Endliche Bekanntnus der widertöffer . . . 21 tag may im 1527 jar* (*Unnütze Papiere* LXXX, No. 1); Steck and Tobler, *Aktensammlung zur Gesch. der Berner Ref.,* No. 2718; *Ein Christenlich Gespräch, gehallten zu Bernn zwischen den Predicanten vnn Hansen Pfyster Meyer von Arouw, den Widertouff, Eyd, Oberkeyt, ond andere Widertöuferische Artikel Betreffende* (1531); Müller, *Berner Täufer,* 74; *ML* II, 520.

Kolb, Martin (b. 1680), the third of the seven children of Dielman Kolb, who emigrated from Wolfsheim, Germany, to Germantown, Pennsylvania, in the spring of 1707. He took with him three younger brothers, Johannes, Jakob, and Heinrich, and on May 19, 1709, he married Magdalena van Sintern, a daughter of Isaac van Sintern, the Germantown deacon, who had emigrated from the Hamburg-Altona church to Germantown in 1700. In 1709 he was among the first settlers of Skippack, 15 miles north of Germantown, where he lived until his death in 1761. He was the first preacher of Skippack, the first rural congregation in America. He had been ordained on April 20, 1708, perhaps by Elder Jakob Godschalk. There are no records of his 53 years of service at Skippack. With his brother Dielman he wrote a letter, Oct. 9, 1745, to the *Commissie voor buitenlandsche nooden* in Holland.   H.S.B.

A. Brons, *Ursprung, Entwickelung und Schicksale der . . . Mennoniten* (3rd ed., Norden, 1912); *ML* II, 520 f.

Kolb, Peter (Petter, Petrus), was in the first half of the 18th century elder of the Kriegsheim Mennonite congregation in the Palatinate, Germany. In 1709 he visited the Netherlands; presumably was the confidential agent of the Dutch Mennonite Committee of Foreign Needs of Amsterdam. In 1731 he was invited to give information to the Amsterdam Committee concerning the needs of the congregations in the Palatinate. (*Inv. Arch. Amst.* I, 1430, 1439, 1443, 1470; *ML* II, 521.)   vDZ.

Kolb's and **Longenecker's** Mennonite (MC) churches, in Holmes Co., Ohio: see **Longenecker's.**

Kolde, Theodor Hermann Friedrich (1850-1913), Lutheran church historian, professor of theology at the University of Erlangen, Germany, was an opponent of Ludwig Keller (*q.v.*). His works are valuable in the field of church history (see *Beiträge zur bayrischen Kirchengeschichte* XX, 1914, 97-166).

Bearing on Mennonite history are *Johann Staupitz, ein Waldenser und Wiedertäufer* (1885); *Zum Prozess des Johann Denk und der drei gottlosen Maler* (Leipzig, 1887); "Hans Denk und die gottlosen Maler in Nürnberg," in *Beiträge zur bayrischen Kirchengesch.* VIII; and *Andreas Althamer, der Humanist und Reformator in Brandenburg-Ansbach* (Erlangen, 1895).   NEFF.

H. Jordan, *Theodor Kolde, ein deutscher Kirchenhistoriker* (Leipzig, 1914); *ML* II, 521.

Koldershofje, a former Mennonite old people's home at Haarlem, Holland. It was closed before 1700, apparently by merging with another similar institution. (*DB* 1876, 116.)   vDZ.

Kolhorn, a village in the Dutch province of North Holland. Anabaptism here is of a very early date. On March 6 or 7, 1534, during a raid on the Anabaptists eleven of them from Nieuwe Niedorp were apprehended on the dike near Kolhorn. Leenaert Bouwens (*q.v.*) baptized 32 persons here in 1563-65. At that time or soon after there was a Frisian congregation here, forming a unit with that of Barsingerhorn. The (lay) preachers of this congregation were Jacob Jacobsz Teeke (1714-57), Frans Albertsz Vrijer (1721-*ca.* 1756), and his son Albert Fransz Vrijer (1741-55). The preacher Daniel Hovens, who served here 1755-57, had many difficulties with the Reformed ministers and government officials because he had given catechetical instructions to a Reformed girl. The old meetinghouse was restored in 1759. On Sept. 15, 1788, when nearly the whole village of Kolhorn was destroyed by fire, the meetinghouse also burned down. In 1790 the small congregation, numbering hardly 20 members, erected both a meetinghouse and a parsonage. A large number of preachers served here between 1757 and 1784. In this year Claes Stuurman accepted a call; he was the last preacher of the Frisian congregation of Barsingerhorn and Kolhorn. His dedication sermon of the rebuilt church, Dec. 19, 1790: *Leerreden ter inwying van de nieuwgebouwde Doopsgezinde Kerk te Kolhorn,* was published at Alkmaar in 1792. In 1826 Stuurman died, and in 1827 the congregation, then numbering 14 members, merged with the Waterlander congregation of Barsingerhorn and Wieringerwaard.   vDZ.

Inv. Arch. Amst. I, No. 937; II, Nos. 1535-37; Kühler, *Geschiedenis* I, 174; *DB* 1880, 81-96; *Naamlijst* 1829, "Kerknieuws," 31; *ML* II, 521.

Kollum, a village in the northeast of the Dutch province of Friesland, where in the 16th and 17th centuries Mennonites were very numerous. Leenaert Bouwens (*q.v.*) baptized four persons here in 1551-54, 21 persons in 1563-65, and 201 persons in 1568-82, totaling 226; besides these, in 1563-65 eight others in the Kollumer Nieuwland.

In the early 17th century there were at Kollum at least three Mennonite congregations: (*a*) A Waterlander congregation which was represented at the Waterlander conference of 1647 at Amsterdam and in 1695 joined the Sociëteit of Friesland. Its membership then was already very small, probably not more than 30. Its members were for a large part poor and were almost continuously supported

by other Mennonites; e.g., in 1658 by the Mennonites from the southwestern part of Friesland and in the 18th century by the Sociëteit of Friesland. Often the pulpit was vacant. Of its meetinghouse at Kollum nothing is known. In 1745 this Kollum congregation united with that of Buitenpost (*q.v.*) and was then called Kollum and Buitenpost. In 1835 the united congregation, then numbering only 10 members, merged with that of Surhuisterveen (*q.v.*) and the name of Kollum disappeared. (*b*) A Groningen Old Flemish congregation called Kollum and Visvliet (*q.v.*) or also Visvliet and Kollum. This congregation died out before 1700. (*c*) An Old Frisian, also called Jan Jacobsz (*q.v.*) group, congregation of which nothing is known but the fact that it died out in the early 18th century, its meetinghouse having been sold before 1729. There may even have been a fourth congregation at Kollum (*d*) of Pieter-Jeltjes-volk (followers of Elder Pieter Jeltjes, *q.v.*) of Kollum, who was banned by Jan Jacobsz in December 1599.

In 1932 Mennonites living at Kollum formed a "Menno Simonsz-Kring," which belongs to the congregation of Zwaagwesteinde (*q.v.*). The membership of this group amounted to 38 in 1955. vDZ.

Blaupot t. C., *Friesland, passim,* see Index; *DB* 1874, 107 f.; 1879, 3; 1892, 71 f.; 1895, 12, 20; 1903, 81, 91, 105; 1905, 29; 1907, 79; 1912, 66, 68; *ML* II, 522.

Kollumerzwaag, a hamlet in the Dutch province of Friesland, formerly the seat of a Mennonite congregation about which only scarce particulars are available. The various issues of the Dutch *Naamlijst* mention this congregation, which often was without a preacher. It is supposed to have been founded about 1600, the membership then numbering about 100. In 1695, when the Sociëteit of Friesland was founded, Kollumerzwaag also joined, having then about 50 members. It often was subsidized by the Conference of Friesland. In 1815 its meetinghouse had become dilapidated and was out of use, and in 1816 was transferred to Zwaagwesteinde (*q.v.*) rebuilt there, being dedicated May 6, 1816, by H. A. Bosma, the last (untrained) preacher of Kollumerzwaag. In 1844 the congregation of Kollumerzwaag was dissolved, the remaining members joining the congregation of Dantumawoude (*q.v.*).   vDZ.

DB 1895, 12, 20; 1903, 165; *Naamlijst* 1829, "Kerknieuws," 47; H. J. Buse, *De verdwenen Doopsgezinde Gemeenten in Friesland,* reprint from *De Vrije Fries* XXII (1915), 11 f.

Köln: see **Cologne.**

Köln, Peter von: see **Peter van Coelen.**

Komander (Dorfmann), **Johann** (1484-1557), the reformer of the canton of the Grisons (*q.v.*), Switzerland, studied with his friend Zwingli under Wittenbach in Basel, and in 1524 became pastor of St. Michael's in Chur. Komander achieved prominence as Protestant spokesman at the disputation in Ilanz, Jan. 7-9, 1526, for which he had drawn up 18 theses, which clearly betray Zwingli's influence in form and content. The adherents of the old faith, the abbot of St. Lucius and Theodor Schlegel, tried to sabotage the disputation, but Komander persisted unshakably in defending the Protestant doctrine, so effectively that soon after the disputation at Ilanz the Reformation took great forward strides in the Grisons.

Beginning in 1525 the activities of the Swiss Brethren leaders, Blaurock, Manz, Grebel, and Castelberger, made themselves felt in the Grisons (q.v.), especially in Chur (q.v.). The success of these men not only caused Komander great concern; he thought the progress of the Reformation threatened, since the Anabaptists were being actually supported by the Catholics. The struggle was particularly difficult for Komander for the reason that the Swiss Brethren as a matter of principle based their doctrine on the authority of the Holy Scriptures.

In his distress Komander wrote to Zwingli on Aug. 8, 1525, lamenting (free translation): "In the first place I inform you that the Anabaptists fill us with care and sorrow. People in the Grisons no longer want to hear the pure Gospel. They draw to their sect many of the best-instructed in the Bible, so that they no longer attend our services. Innumerable accusations are made against me. Those citizens who have not signed themselves away to the Anabaptists are waiting in indecision and amazement. The Gospel seems to many to be vain babbling, indeed as something repugnant. As the third party that has the advantage when the other two are engaged in conflict, the Papists rejoice in the schism. They pour oil into the fire and feed it to a mighty flame. The abbot of St. Lucius, for instance, supports our city scribe, whose wife is an Anabaptist and was therefore banished from the city, with word and deed, procures books and other aid for him, and in general promotes the spread of the sect, in order to give the misled ones over to mockery as soon as I am brought to a fall. The city scribe is preparing for a disputation, which is to try me severely, and he is boasting in advance of victory. Then, of course, everything will take a most splendid course: the exiles will return to the family circle, will feel comfortable at home, and I shall have a heavy burden in the turn of events. But as God will. In Zürich the Anabaptists have been defeated, and as long as they are not successful there, other victories will do them no good. I am opposed to a disputation in our town. But if the council should decide in favor of one, then I demand that it be conducted in writing, so that our arguments, the scribe's and mine, can be proved at leisure. Help me, faithful Zwingli, in distress, that the Gospel may not be smothered in Grisons."

In the meantime the struggle against the Anabaptists had become a federal affair. The burgomaster and the council sided against the Anabaptists. To what extent this step was due to Komander's influence is not clear. In connection with a federal diet in Chur, a considerable number of "Anabaptists, iconoclasts, and other disobedient obstinate ones" were seized and tried. At the Davos Diet in May 1526, the Catholic and Zwinglian creeds were accepted as equally valid, but Anabaptist teaching was forever prohibited.

In the spring of 1528, Komander complained again about the difficulty of his position. He told Zwingli that he had to use all his strength to combat the "Catabaptists." They had their meetings in

Chur, and there were many among the citizens, who secretly or openly adhered to them. Castelberger (q.v.) was also carrying on his propaganda in the city; many citizens were being confused by him. He (Komander) had to work and worry more about these people than if twice the number of Papists attacked him. Some had been seized, and now people were crying that the pastor was to blame; that it was he who urged expulsion and that he thirsted for innocent blood. Indeed, their death did not please him at all. But he was sorry that they did not stop misleading the people.

For the disputation planned for the day after Easter in 1531, Komander had formulated 12 theses, the last of which stated, "Anabaptism is an error and an enticement against God's Word and doctrine."

In the long dispute and wearisome negotiations with Camillo Renato, the leader of the radical movement in northern Italy, Komander was also involved; but he refused to decide the issue, referring them to Zürich and Basel, "where there are learned men, who are better qualified to mediate between them."

Komander carried on a regular correspondence with Bullinger. In 1550 he fell ill of the plague. His co-worker Johann Blasius was taken by death, but he recovered, though he probably did not regain his vitality. He died in 1557. His successor was Johann Fabricius Montanus of Zürich. S.G.

"Kommander" and "Camillo Renato" in *HRE*; E. Camenisch, *Bündner Ref.-Gesch.* (Chur, 1920; J. C. Füsslin, *Beiträge zur Erläuterung der Kirchen-Ref.-Gesch.* I (Zurich, 1741); J. Stumpf, *Chronika vom Leben und Wirken des Ulrich Zwingli* (Zürich, 1932) 76; *Zwingli's Werke* VIII (Leipzig, 1914) 341 f.; *ML II*, 525 f.

Komejannen, Komejansche Doopsgezinden, or **Komen Jans-Volk,** name given in the Netherlands to a group of Dutch Mennonites. The name is found in some letters of Jan Theunisz of 1627 and in an old booklet of 1628, now lost, in which Hans Arentsz (H. Alenson, q.v.) is called a bishop among the *Koomen-Jannen* or *Hansijtten* (see BRN VII, 143). From this notice it is clear that the Komejannen were a kind of Waterlander Mennonites, whose leader was Hans de Ries. The name was rather common in the province of North Holland. According to J. Adrsz. Leeghwater (q.v.), a preacher Comen (i.e., merchant) Jan preached in De Rijp (q.v.) in this province about 1572, from whom the name may have been derived. vDZ.

BRN VII, 143; S. Lootsma, *Het Nieuwe Huys* (Zaandam, 1937) 14-16; *DB* 1896, 18; 1917, 15, 30.

Komen (*Commines*), a town in Flanders, Belgium, southwest of Kortrijk (Courtrai), where Mennonites were found about 1550 and there may have been a congregation. Guillaume van Robays died here as a martyr 1552, an unknown blacksmith in 1551. vDZ.

Komes (Comes, Commerts), **Teunis** (*Tönis*) (1535-after 1607), owner of the Gatherhof at Rheydt, in 1591 signed the Concept of Cologne (q.v.) as a representative of the Mennonite congregation at München-Gladbach, Rheinland, Germany. He was an ancestor of the Jacob Gottschalk (*q.v.*) who emigrated to Pennsylvania and was a preacher of the church of Germantown. The family name of Komes, spelled in different ways: Kommes, Komms, Kohmsen, was also found in West Prussia before 1700. They may have been related to the Rhineland branch of this family.   vDZ.

Reimer, *Familiennamen*, 112; Walter Risler, "Das München-Gladbacher Mennonitenverzeichnis von 1654," in *Beiträge zur Gesch. rhein. Mennoniten* (Weierhof, 1939) 94-130, especially 109; W. Niepoth, "Jakob Gottschalk and His Ancestry," *MQR* XXIII (January 1949) 35-47.

Kommerau (Polish, *Osiec*), a hamlet on the left bank of the Vistula River in the district of Graudenz, where on Polish territory (after 1772 German) Dutch Mennonites founded a settlement about 1570. Land leases of 1604, 1656, 1684, and 1773 have been preserved. In 1623 the Mennonites of Kommerau obtained exemption from military taxes and quartering of soldiers. (See **Montau**.)
                                                                              vDZ.

Herbert Wiebe, *Das Siedlungswerk der Niederl. Mennoniten . . .* (Marburg a.d.Lahn, 1952) 23, 80.

Kommission für Kirchenangelegenheiten — KfK (Committee for Church Affairs) was an organization among Mennonites of Russia (also transplanted to the Mennonite settlements in South America), which contrary to previous practices, represented all Mennonite groups in Russia. In 1910 a *Glaubenskommission* was appointed at Schönsee by the *Allgemeine Bundeskonferenz der Mennnonitengemeinden in Russland* (*q.v.*) to deal with the tremendous problems of that time. The Russian parliament had issued a new law regarding religious groups by which the Mennonites were stripped of their former privileges and treated as a "sect." The KfK became an effective agent in these emergency situations. At the conference at Nikolaipol in 1912, the name *Glaubenskommission* was changed to *Kommission für Kirchenangelegenheiten*. This commission became the executive committee of the conference (*Bundeskonferenz*) to carry out its decisions in so far as they did not conflict with the local autonomy of the congregations and also to represent the collective Mennonite body to the government.

The first committee consisted of Elder Abr. Goerz of Ohrloff; Heinrich Braun (Mennonite Brethren), and D. H. Epp. In 1911 D. H. Epp was appointed chairman and K. Unrau was added as treasurer. Later Wilhelm Dyck took the place of Heinrich Braun. In 1912 the KfK was also charged with the responsibility for arranging the programs and obtaining governmental permission to hold conference sessions. At a meeting of the *Allgemeiner Mennonitischer Kongress* (*q.v.*) in Ohrloff in 1917, it was decided that the chairman of the KfK devote his full time to the work of the conference and that he should receive a salary. During the time of the Revolution and the confusion following it, all activities came temporarily to an end. At the first conference after the Revolution, held in Chortitza in October 1922, a new committee was elected composed of Elder Johann Klassen of Schönwiese, Elder Jacob Rempel of Grünfeld, Heinrich Wiebe of

Steinfeld, and Jakob Janzen of Tiege. The functions of the committee remained the same with special authorization for action in cases of emergency. The committee chosen in 1925 consisted of Elder Alexander Ediger of Schönsee, Aaron Dyck of Margenau, and Cornelius Martens of Grossweide. Later representatives from Siberia and the Crimea were added. The activities of the KfK in Russia came to a close in 1926-27 when all organized religious activities became impossible.

The Mennonites of Brazil and Paraguay continued the practice of having an inter-Mennonite KfK to take care of all common religious problems of the settlements. The KfK in Brazil had the same name *Kommission* as the corresponding Russian Mennonite KfK, and continued until 1947, when the withdrawal of the Mennonite Brethren group rendered it moribund. For the Paraguay KfK, see the article **Kommission für kirchliche Angelegenheiten**. (For bibliography see **Allgemeine Bundeskonferenz** der Mennonitengemeinden in Russland; *ML* II, 526.)   D.H.E., C.K.

Kommission für kirchliche Angelegenheiten—KfK (Commission for Church Affairs), located in Colony Fernheim of the Paraguayan Chaco, was organized in late 1930 by the leading ministers of the three newly formed Mennonite churches there— Mennonite Brethren, Mennonite, and Evangelical Mennonite Brethren, as a result of earnest counsel on the part of the German and North American Mennonite leaders, especially in order to be better able to cope with the rigors of pioneering and its effect upon the spiritual life of the settlers, to guide the establishment of schools, and in general to counsel the colony on all cultural and spiritual matters. The purpose of the KfK was the same as that in Russia (see **Kommission für Kirchenangelegenheiten**). Considerable difficulty was experienced in the early days of organization. Whereas the first commission consisted of six members, two from each of the three churches (denominations), the new commission, reorganized on Aug. 30, 1932, consisted of eleven members, four from the Mennonite Brethren Church, four from the Mennonite Church, and three from the Evangelical Mennonite Brethren Church, which in turn organized its own executive committee of three ministers: Nicolai Wiebe (EMB) as chairman, Johann Teichgraef (GCM) as secretary, and Gerhard Isaak (MB) as vice-chairman. Statutes drawn up and accepted at that time, but modified and rewritten in 1945, provided a basis upon which the KfK could work, both on internal colony problems and in representing the churches' concerns to the government and foreign organizations. The KfK has proved itself a great blessing to the colony churches at all times, especially in times of common difficulties and in the churches' struggle for a higher cultural and spiritual level within the colonies. It seems indispensable, especially since members of different Mennonite groups are pioneering together and are dependent upon one another daily. The statutes of the KfK follow:

1. *Membership:* The Commission for Church Affairs is composed of representatives of all existing

churches (denominations) in Fernheim. Each church (denomination) has the right to have one representative on the KfK for every hundred members or any part thereof, the denominational leaders automatically becoming these representatives.

2. *Method of Procedure:* The routine work of the KfK is done by the Executive Committee, consisting of the leaders of the respective churches. In special or emergency cases and at the close of every church year, the larger KfK is present at the meeting.

3. *Assignment of the KfK:* (*a*) First, the KfK is to represent the churches to the outside world, i.e., to the Paraguayan government and to the Mennonite and like-minded churches of foreign lands. (*b*) It is the guardian of the spiritual and cultural values of our Mennonite brotherhood. By this is meant that it is the responsibility of the KfK to guide and supervise the education of our youth and the training of our children on the basis of our Christian Mennonite faith, by virtue of which we receive the *Privilegium* (privileges) from the Paraguayan government. (*c*) To co-ordinate and mediate between the churches: (1) In questions of common concern that need clearance. (2) In questions concerning the furthering of cultural and spiritual life and the building of the kingdom of God. (3) In questions concerning the customs and habits of our brotherhood. These questions can be submitted by the churches or raised directly by the KfK.

Internal questions of the individual congregations are not dealt with by the KfK, in so far as they do not adversely affect the total brotherhood. The KfK always works in co-operation with the churches and in contact with the colony administration. J.I.

Konferenz-Jugendblatt *der Mennoniten Brüdergemeinden in Kanada* is a 32-page, 9 x 12 in. illustrated quarterly periodical published by the Youth Work Committee of the M.B. Conference of Canada, first number July 1944. Until May 1954 it was printed at Winnipeg and edited by H. F. Klassen. Beginning in May 1954 it was printed at Yarrow, B.C., and edited by H. H. Voth. Since it is distributed free to the youth of the church its periodicity and size has been irregular. To the end of 1956 a total of 67 numbers had appeared for an average of five numbers per year. The first four numbers were published by the Manitoba M.B. Committee for Youth Work. H.S.B.

König: see King.

König, Katharina, an Anabaptist martyr, was executed at Reinhardsbrunn in Sachsen-Gotha, Germany, with three other women and four men (see **Kolb, Andreas**). This sentence of death caused Friedrich Myconius, the superintendent of Gotha, some uneasiness, which Melanchthon tried to dissipate in a letter dated February 1530. NEFF.

P. Wappler, *Die Stellung Kursachsens und des Landgrafen Philipp von Hessen zur Täuferbewegung* (Münster, 1910) 12, 127, 135, 137; *ML* II, 537.

Königsbach, a village (pop. 3,399) in Baden, Germany, mostly Protestant. There were Anabaptists here already in the 16th century. Around Bretten

(*q.v.*) and Maulbronn they found temporary refuge about 1530. The wooded border regions of Württemberg, Baden-Durlach, and the bishopric of Speyer were favorable to the spread of the Anabaptist movement during the period of persecution, for they offered some security. In 1531 from 200 to 300 persons met in the forests of Bretten and Reibsheim (Bossert, LIX, 59, 77). Later on, when the group was greatly reduced by emigration to Moravia, it was served by Hans Schoch (Schochhans), who lived in Königsbach. About 1555 he was seized for conducting these meetings, but managed to escape from prison in the tower at Cannstadt (Bossert, *Württemberg,* 530 and 1021; LIX, 76). Further arrests were made in a forest not far from Königsbach, as reported on Feb. 11, 1572 (Bossert, *Württemberg,* 346).

After the Thirty Years' War Swiss Mennonites settled in Königsbach. On Aug. 24, 1661, these Mennonites requested that the margrave of Baden confirm their former "privileges." A congregation was organized; a church book has been preserved, giving information dated 1766, besides entries on births, weddings, and funerals for the period 1815-69. Of frequent occurrence are the names Ehrismann, Kempf, Täuscher, Wagner, and Wolber; there are references to families by the name of Egli, Eyer, Funk, Katz, and Oesterle. The church book is in the possession of the local Protestant pastor. The number of Mennonites in Königsbach decreased during the 20th century because of emigration. The census of 1910 enumerated 33, five of whom lived on the Johannestalerhof; in 1925 only ten Mennonites were counted. HEGE.

TA Baden-Pfalz; TA Württemberg; Gustav Bossert, "Beiträge zur badisch-pfälzischen Reformationsgeschichte," in *Zeitschrift für die Geschichte des Oberrheins* LIX (1905; *Mitteilungen der bad. hist. Kommission,* No. 27 (1905) 197; *ML* II, 537.

Königsberg, a town (pop. 1,500) in Lower Franconia, northern Bavaria, Germany, formerly belonging to the duchy of Sachsen-Koburg, and an enclave in the bishopric of Würzburg, 15 miles east of Schweinfurt, today a resort town in a wooded region.

For Anabaptist history the city and its vicinity is important, for from it the Anabaptist movement soon spread over Middle Germany. The first Anabaptist preacher there was Hans Hut, a native of this region. Until 1524 he was a sexton at Bibra, seven miles south of Meiningen, but was expelled when he refused to have his child baptized. He went to Königsberg in Franconia (Meyer, 241). In the spring of 1526 he joined the Anabaptists, and became very active in Königsberg and the vicinity. In his sermons he moved away from the social revolutionary ideas of Thomas Müntzer, under whose spell he had been for a time; he sought instead to prove that the peasants had been in the wrong in the revolt, in that they had sought their own advantage, and not the glory of God (Wappler, *Thüringen,* 31).

Hut's words fell on receptive soil. In a short time he had won a stately following. The sparsely populated region around Königsberg, which was then an enclave of the electorate of Saxony, offered good opportunities for undisturbed meetings. Besides Hut, also the cabinetmaker Eucharius Binder and Joachim Mertz served as evangelists here for a time; but they soon went into other regions. They devoted themselves completely to the service of the new doctrine, "moved up and down the Main and its tributaries, and everywhere challenged the people to attend their conventicles, which they usually held at night and behind barred doors in remote mills, farms, or suburban homes" (Wappler, *Thüringen,* 29).

This extensive work could not long remain concealed from the authorities, who scented new calamities everywhere since the bad experiences of the Peasants' War. In the middle of January 1527 the bailiff of Königsberg, Kuntz Gotsmann, received word from the bailiff of Würzburg concerning Anabaptist activities in the Königsberg district with the request that he suppress them, "that no revolt may arise therefrom." Gotsmann accordingly had had three men arrested, among them Hans Beutel (Beutelhans), a Königsberg citizen, who was preaching to the peasants without the knowledge of the government, "in the pretense, as if they were proclaiming God's Word." If such meetings continued, he reported to Koburg, another revolution could be feared. With Hans Beutel another Königsberg citizen, Wolf Schreiner (also called Wolf Schominger) was named, arrested because of the new baptism, furthermore a smith of Friesenhausen, who was returned to Würzburg because he had been seized in the bishopric.

The bishop's representative wished to be present at the cross-examination of the Königsberg prisoners, and after the questioning by the bailiff of Königsberg, with the use of the rack applied by the Koburg executioner, he would also ask the prisoners some questions. Although it had never before been the custom to admit a representative of the bishop to a trial of a Königsberg peasant with torture, the Koburg government acceded to his wish (Berbig, 305 f.). The bailiffs agreed that both would apply the rack. The prisoners were evidently tortured until they admitted that they were planning a rebellion.

At a new hearing without torture, in the presence of the assistant magistrate, Georg von Hassberg, the mayor, and several councilors of Königsberg, they recanted some of their previous statements, saying that they had made them "out of lack of understanding and for fear of the rack." Their statement about the approaching end of the world only meant that "when God comes to judge the world at the end of time and would judge all men, they, as specially chosen Christians, if they remained true to the end, would help Christ judge the survivors, when He comes in His divine majesty in the clouds" (Berbig, 299, 335).

The reports were placed before Elector John of Saxony (*q.v.*), who decreed in an edict of Feb. 27, 1527, that the accused, Beutelhans and Wolf Schreiner, had, to be sure, forfeited their lives by making pretended baptism a sign of rebellion; but if the prince-bishop of Würzburg, Konrad von Thüngen (governed 1519-40), would not have the prisoners in his realm put to death, he would also show mercy

to the poor mortals and grant them their lives. Otherwise, if the two prisoners persisted in their faith they should be killed with the sword. In addition he decreed: In the entire Franconian territory no one is permitted to preach and perform the sacraments except the pastors and preachers ordained for the purpose (Berbig, 297).

Suspects, if someone gives security for them, should perform church penance according to the following stipulations: "Every Sunday before the sermon they shall come to Königsberg, report to the bailiff, stand in a row before the church door, without shoes, with a sack hung about each one, all speaking prohibited. At the beginning of the sermon they shall be called before the pulpit and here again stand in a row with downcast eyes and bowed heads. After the sermon a public confession is to be made by the culprits. The people are to be instructed on the error by skillful preachers. The property of the principal offenders shall be described, evaluated, and confiscated, but the offenders shall have the use of the income for their sustenance. All who are subjected to the 'shame punishment,' shall be put into prison one or two days every month and then renew their promise. Obstinate persons are to remain under arrest and be further prosecuted" (Berbig, 297).

Other arrests had meanwhile been made, including women with small children and pregnant women, from the territories of Königsberg, Münnerstadt, Königshofen, Hassfurt, and Staffelstein. The prisons were overflowing (Berbig, 333). In Königsberg, Hans Forster, the son-in-law of Hans Beutel; Thomas and Kaspar Spiegel, brothers from Ostheim; and the miller of Aurach, whose mill was in the bishopric, were seized.

The council of Königsberg at once began the instruction of the prisoners, securing the Koburg preacher Balthasar Düring, a native of Königsberg. He preached there on April 7, 1527 (Berbig, 336), but was apparently not too successful (Wappler, 34).

The death sentence was pronounced on them in spite of a lack of evidence of an intended revolution (all the racked prisoners instead stressing their nonresistance), and in spite of the fact that the burgomaster and council of Königsberg praised their previous conduct, rejected all suspicion of revolutionary plans, and asked that their lives be spared, and that the council of Koburg gave a similar testimonial for Wolf Schreiner. The bishop had Kaspar Spiegel and the miller of Aurach beheaded; thereupon the elector had Beutelhans and Wolf Schreiner put to death (Wappler, *Kursachsen,* 4, 129-31).

Many families fled before the persecution, but the movement could not be suppressed in Franconia or Saxony. In spite of the newness of the movement and the short time the adherents had belonged to it, their primitive Christian ideals were so deeply implanted that they would not yield it up to violence. As in Zürich, fugitives spread the movement to adjacent countries. Through Hans Hut and his group it spread south to Upper Austria; in the north and west it penetrated into Thuringia as far as the Harz and into Hesse. Even though some excitable spirits became guilty of selfish deeds, for which the leaders were not at all responsible, the religious goals of the original movement remained immovably the basis of the movement. Wappler, the historian of the Anabaptist movement in Thuringia, reaches the following conclusion on the basis of existing government records: "Their ideal is holiness. Therefore there is among them more or less withdrawal from the state and its institutions, a quiet acceptance of suffering as the cross of Christ, and a simple, purely Biblical devotional worship conducted by preachers of their own choice" (Wappler, *Thüringen*, 221).   HEGE.

G. Berbig, "Die Wiedertäufer im Amt Königsberg . . . 1527-28," in *Deutsche Ztscht für Kirchenrecht* XIII, 291-353; H. Böhmer and P. Kirn, *Thomas Müntzers Briefwechsel* (1931); Chr. Meyer, "Die Anfänge des Wiedertäufertums in Augsburg," in *Ztscht des hist. Vereins f. Schwaben u. Neuburg* I (1874) 211-53; K. Schulz, "Thomas Müntzers liturgische Bestrebungen," in *Ztscht für Kirchengesch.* XLVII (1928); P. Wappler, *Die Täuferbewegung in Thüringen* (Jena, 1913); idem, *Die Stellung Kursachsens und des Landgrafen Philipp von Hessen zur Täuferbewegung* (Münster, 1910); E. Kipp, *Kurze Lebensabrisse von Königsbergs (in Franken) berühmten Männern* (1924); E. Jacobs, "Die Wiedertäufer am Harz," in *Ztscht des Harzvereins . . .* XXXII (1899) 466; *ML* II, 539-41.

Königsberg (now Russian *Kaliningrad*), the capital (1931 pop. 372,000) of the former German province of East Prussia, a Baltic seaport on the Pregel River. The first official record of Mennonites is of 1579, when they presented a petition to Margrave George Frederick for permission to settle in Königsberg and other towns. The reply was the order of expulsion, later frequently repeated, but apparently never enforced. It is probable that there were some here earlier, for in 1554 the Academy of Königsberg added to its rules the stipulation that every professor must swear neither to consent to nor to defend Anabaptist doctrine.

But the first Mennonite congregation in Königsberg did not come into being until 1722. In 1716 Johann Peter Sprunk (his original Dutch name was Jan Pietersz Spronck) and Heinrich van Höfen, and soon afterwards Jakob Schröder and Isaak Kroecker, were given permission to settle in Königsberg because they could distill rye whiskey "in the Danzig manner." Their skill brought the city considerable revenue, since it was now not necessary to import whiskey from Danzig; thus the Mennonites were permitted to stay in spite of the violent protest of the Lutheran clergy. In 1720 there were at a meeting in the home of the merchant Vos "six Manists and nine women" present. These meetings were allowed to be held only in the family circle. For communion they had to make the long journey to Danzig or Elbing. They therefore asked for permission to hold their services "in all quietness."

Frederick William I granted this request on April 2, 1722, not only because he found nothing dubious in the confession of faith presented by Sprunk, but especially because the Mennonites had paid 6,190 talers in taxes in five years. The practical king exploited their prosperity by requiring an annual fee of 200 talers to be paid to the recruit treasury for permission to organize as a congregation.

Thus the Mennonites could worship very quietly "because they everywhere endeavor to live a pious, quiet, and honorable life, . . . and especially they have tried to fulfill each and every duty of faithful and obedient subjects." The lively commercial connections between Königsberg and Danzig, Elbing, and Holland gradually brought a small congregation into being. The guarantee of freedom from military duty also brought several families from Polish territory. Nevertheless the Königsberg church never had more than 17 families; Sprunk was their first elder. The only knowledge we have of him is that he interceded for the Mennonites in the Tilsit lowlands when they were threatened with exile in 1723; his intervention was fruitless.

In the following years we hear of the attempts of the Mennonites to be admitted to the trades; the border weavers, Jakob Schroeder (of Danzig), Cauenhowen, and Bulert, did not succeed; only Bernd Claassen van Dyck obtained citizenship. A general regulation was passed on Dec. 10, 1730: Mennonites are excluded from citizenship; they may practice their trades upon payment of a protection fee in addition to the regular taxes.

In the midst of the negotiations, the edict of Feb. 22, 1732, was passed, banishing all Mennonites from the country within three months. The reason was their nonresistance. In their place the king wished to settle other Christians (Salzburg exiles; see **Carinthian Exiles**). Besides, the Sämland consistorium, in an unfavorable report, had charged that the Mennonites, along with the Unitarians, Jews, and Arians, had held public services and conducted their funerals "with a public show with funeral sermons," which was allowed only the three established churches. The Kriegs- und Domänenkammer of East Prussia protested the expulsion, pointing out the profit brought the state treasury by their crafts. The economical king was persuaded to let the Mennonites stay, provided they would establish woolen and cloth mills. Thereupon most of them returned to Königsberg. Frederick the Great gave them citizenship soon after his coronation. From that time on the congregation developed undisturbed, and dedicated its first meetinghouse in 1770.

In 1767 the first Mennonite hymnal in German was published in Königsberg. The publication of a hymnbook in German shows that the Dutch language of the first generations of Mennonites had fallen into disuse. About the Dutch origin of the first Mennonites of Königsberg not much is known. Most of them went to Königsberg after having settled first in West Prussia. Contacts with the Dutch Mennonites, especially with Amsterdam, were still strong in the 18th century. Some Mennonites of Königsberg had moved directly from Holland to Königsberg, as for example Jan Bruinvis(ch), a merchant from Amsterdam, who founded a large business here about 1710, and who, in his capacity of intermediary between the East Prussian (ex-Lithuanian) Mennonites and the Dutch Mennonite Committee of Foreign Needs at Amsterdam, wrote a large number of letters to Amsterdam, the first of which is dated Aug. 12, 1711, and the last June 23, 1744. Bruinvis' letters are found in the Mennonite Archives of Amsterdam. Of great interest is a letter dated May 16, 1735, written by Spronck (or Sprunk) to the Committee at Amsterdam, which states that there were two congregations in

Königsberg and seven poor families. Spronck also complained that Bruinvis had married outside the church and neglected the congregation (*Inv. Arch. Amst.* II, 2, No. 796; No. 799 is another interesting letter from Spronck, dated July 5, 1737). It is not quite clear which two branches of Mennonites were meant by Spronck, nor when these two congregations merged. The Dutch *Naamlijst* of 1743 and following editions mention only one congregation, which belonged to the Old Flemish. The following ministers are named for this church in the 18th century: Jan Pietersz Spronck (elder) serving from 1727, Cornelis Claasen 1731 (or 1738), Lammert van Dijk 1744, Willem Reynke 1751, Pieter Spronck 1758, Izaac Kreker (d. 1786) 1758, elder in 1767, Izaac Kauenhoven 1763-89, Jacob Kreker 1766, Zacharias Schröder 1766, Willem Temerman (or Zimmerman) 1778, Abraham Olffers 1782, Heinrich Penner 1786, and Johann Wieler 1789, elder in 1795.

When universal military service was introduced in Prussia in 1814, and was apparently to include the Mennonites, the church board appealed to the king. The immediate nearness of the Königsberg philosopher Kant is felt in this petition (given in Mannhardt, pp. 176 ff.): "Violation of nonresistance would mean to a Mennonite, who keeps the religion of his fathers and his conscience faithfully, the ruin of the moral person. For only in unwavering faith in the doctrines of his group and in conscientious obedience to them can a man be moral. It is therefore not merely a civic obstacle, it is religion itself which imposes upon us the impossibility of participating in war." This petition brought results.

The church secured a competent minister in Karl Harder (*q.v.*), who was born in Königsberg in 1820. After the completion of his theological studies he preached in the Elbing (*q.v.*) and Königsberg churches. On the basis of his Easter sermon at Elbing in 1845, 24 families left the Elbing-Ellerwald church, built a meetinghouse of their own in Elbing, and united with the Königsberg congregation. Harder served the Königsberg congregation until 1857, when he went to Neuwied. Adolf Siebert was pastor at Königsberg in 1898-1938. Josef Gingerich, last chairman of the church council, took pains to develop a feeling of cohesion and to draw the Mennonite youth studying in Königsberg into church life by instituting social evenings with lectures. In 1934 the church had 65 members, including children; in 1941 the same number was reported.

After Siebert's retirement in 1938 the congregation was served by Erich Göttner and Horst Quiring, the Danzig and Berlin Mennonite pastors. The attack and capture of the city by the Russians in 1945 put an end to the congregation, although its last chairman, Josef Gingerich, did not leave the city until 1946.

The congregation belonged to the Vereinigung of the Mennonite churches in Germany. On April 13, 1899, it gave the Vereinigung a sum of 125,000 marks, 60 per cent of the income to be applied to the Elbing and Königsberg churches, and the remaining 40 per cent to be used by the Vereinigung. In 1929, 75 per cent of the income was to be applied

to Königsberg; the obligation to pay a certain annual sum to Elbing was canceled.   H.Q., vDZ.

W. Mannhardt, *Die Wehrfreiheit der Altpreussischen Mennoniten* (Danzig, 1863); Christine Hege, *Kurze Geschichte der Menn.* (Frankfurt, 1900); E. Randt, *Die Mennoniten in Ostpreussen* (Königsberg, 1912); J. Gingerich, "Die Mennonitengemeinde Königsberg und ihr Ende," *Mennonit* II (1949) 22; H. Penner, "The Anabaptists and Mennonites in East Prussia," *MQR* XXII (1948) 212-25; W. J. Schreiber, *The Fate of the Prussian Mennonites* (Göttingen, 1955); *ML* II, 538 f.

Koninck, Isaac Hendriks de, a Dutch Mennonite preacher of the Flemish congregation at Dordrecht, who promoted a union of this congregation and the Old Flemish congregation of Adriaan Cornelisz in this town, which in 1632 led to a fusion of most Flemish and Old Flemish congregations in the Netherlands on the basis of the Dordrecht Confession (*q.v.*). The de Koninck (Coninck) family was also found at Rotterdam, where David de Koninck was a deacon of the Flemish congregation 1652-55. (*Inv. Arch. Amst.* I, Nos. 569, 583, 588; *DB* 1862, 103.)   vDZ.

Konopat(h) (Deutsch-Konopath), near Przechowka (Wintersdorf) in the district of Schwetz (*q.v.*), on the Vistula River, a village where Mennonites lived (in 1772 one third of the population was Mennonite), who, together with those of Przechovka (*q.v.*), formed a congregation of the Groningen Old Flemish branch. Two elders from the Netherlands, Alle Derks (*q.v.*) and Hendrik Berends (Hulshoff) (*q.v.*), who visited the Mennonites of Konopath shortly after 1700 and 1719, made a list of all the names of the members. In this list well-known West Prussian names are found, such as Raatslof (Ratzlaf), Tesmer, Nagtegaal (Nagtigal), Voet (Foth), Smit (Schmidt), Jans, Jansen, Boeler (Buhler), Isaachs, Onrouw (Unruh). In 1719 the group of Mennonites at Konopath (in the Dutch sources called Kunpad or Koenpat) numbered 52. This congregation, regularly found in the Dutch *Naamlijst,* emigrated to the Molotschna (*q.v.*) Mennonite settlement in South Russia in 1819-20 and 1823-24.

"Bezoekreis van Hendrik Berends Hulshoff," in *Bijdragen en mededeelingen v. h. Hist. Genootschap.* LIX (1938) 75, 79; J. A. Duerksen, "Przechowka and Alexanderwohl," *Menn. Life* X (April 1955) 76-82.

Konrad von Neuenstadt, an Anabaptist from Neuenstadt near Heilbronn a. N., Württemberg, Germany, who was a prisoner in the Oberhaus at Passau in 1535. In his trial he testified that he had been baptized two years earlier by a Swiss Brother named Julius. He refused to recant. (*ML* II, 544.) W.W.

Kontenius (Contenius), **Samuel** (1749-1830), member extraordinary of the *Fürsorge-Komitee* (*q.v.*) of the foreign settlers in South Russia. He earned the gratitude of the foreign settlements in Russia for his important services. At the age of 25 he came to Russia from Silesia, in 1785 entered Russian state service, in 1799 received the commission to inspect the foreign settlers in South Russia. In 1800 was appointed chief judge of the *Neu-Russische Vormundschafts-Comptoir der Ausländer.*

After 1803 Kontenius was occupied with the settlement of many foreigners coming into New Russia: Germans, Bulgarians, Greeks, Swedes, and French. In 1803-5 he directed the founding of 120 villages in the vicinity of Odessa, in the Crimea, and on the Molochna River, and the erection of the necessary buildings. He arranged for fruit culture and supervised the silk and wine industries. He laid the foundation for the future prosperity of the German settlements, especially that in the Molotschna, conscientiously giving his attention to all the branches of business. The founding of the Agricultural Association (q.v.) in 1830 is attributed to his initiative. Johann Cornies was a great admirer of Kontenius. In 1818 poor health compelled him to resign.

On his journey to the Crimea, Alexander I, passing through the Mennonite villages and impressed by the achievements of 15 years in beautiful orchards, splendid woods, and cultivation of the soil, asked Kontenius to continue his aid to the settlers as far as his health permitted. He devoted himself to this task until his death. His small capital he left to the building of schools and churches.

D.H.E.

A. M. Fadeew, *Kontenius-Biographie* (1831); *ML* II, 545.

Konteniusfeld (Conteniusfeld), a Mennonite village of the Molotschna settlement in the Ukraine, Russia, founded in 1821, named for Samuel Kontenius (q.v.) (located 10 miles from Stulayevo, a railway station, comprised 6,356 acres of land before the Revolution; the population before World War I was 507. The principal industries were the culture of wheat, cattle, fruit, and bees. The village had an elementary school. Formerly there was a large shop which manufactured farm machinery. (Concerning the disintegration of the village see **Molotschna** and **Ukraine**; *ML* II, 545.)

Kontz, an Anabaptist martyr, who was executed in Brixen in Tirol, Austria, in the autumn of 1533. Jakob Hutter (q.v.) mentions him in an epistle written in Auspitz, Moravia, Nov. 21, 1533. (Loserth, *Anabaptismus,* 500; *ML* II, 545.)   HEGE.

Konvent: see **Kirchenkonvent.**

Kooch, Jacob Pietersz van de(r): see **Pietersz, Jacob.**

Koog (Coogh). According to the minutes (*Handelinghe*) of the meeting of representatives of Flemish congregations held at Haarlem in 1649, a Flemish Mennonite congregation existed here, which, being vacant at that time, was to be served by Huisduinen (q.v.). Obviously by Koog is meant Valkkoog, not far from Huisduinen in the Dutch province of North Holland. Of this congregation no further information was available; it must have died out in the 17th century.   vDZ.

Koog (aan de Zaan), a town about 10 miles north of Amsterdam, in the Zaan district, with a Mennonite congregation, the official name of which is Koog-Zaandijk (Zaandijk being a town adjacent to Koog). Because sources are lacking, it is impossible to state when the congregation of Koog-Zaandijk was founded, but at an early time Anabaptists were already found here. About 1600 the Mennonites comprised the great majority of the inhabitants, both of Zaandijk and Koog. In this time most of them belonged to the Waterlander (q.v.) branch, some were Flemish (q.v.), and a few Frisian. None of these groups formed an independent congregation and only a primitive Flemish meetinghouse was found at Koog. The Waterlanders belonged to the congregation of Westzaan and Oost-Zaandam, the Flemish to the Flemish congregation of West-Zaandam, and the Frisians to the congregation of Zaandam and Westzaan-Zuid. In course of time most Frisians joined the Flemish group, and both Flemish and Waterlanders obtained meeting-houses at Koog and became independent congregations. A Flemish meetinghouse was rebuilt in 1645. Until 1648 the Flemish Mennonites of Zaandam also used to worship in the Koog meetinghouse, but in 1648 a Flemish meetinghouse was built at Zaandam, and the Koog-Zaandijk group including that of Wormerveer (q.v.) became somewhat independent.

A Waterlander meetinghouse was built in 1637 in the northern part of Koog, and in 1646 the Waterlander group became a fully independent congregation. This Waterlander congregation seems to have been more conservative than Waterlander congregations usually were. About 1673 the preacher Pieter Pietersz was dismissed because he tried to introduce the tradition of "free speaking" (i.e., that lay members also be allowed to deliver addresses) as was usual among the Collegiants (q.v.). In 1680 the Waterlander and Flemish congregations of Koog-Zaandijk merged. The Flemish meetinghouse was sold and the Waterlander meetinghouse became a home for poor members. A new meetinghouse was erected on the Hoogstraat. This characteristic frame building of 1680 is still in use. It was largely renovated in 1873 and again in 1931. An organ was installed in 1870. The congregation possesses six silver communion cups, which date from the late 17th century, and which were probably given to the congregation when the new meetinghouse was built in 1680. At the time of the merger in 1680, there were 68 members of the Flemish branch and about 200 Waterlanders. The preachers at that time were Symen Aarjans (Adriaansz) and Dirk Simonsz Moeriaen (q.v.) (of the Waterlanders) and Aris Pieters of Zaandijk and Aris Cornelis Caeskoper (of the Flemish).

The united congregation witnessed a period of prosperity. In 1701 the membership numbered 584, the highest number ever reached. An orphanage was built in 1697, and in 1698 Abraham Verduin (q.v.), who had been trained by Galenus Abrahamsz (q.v.) of Amsterdam, was called to serve the congregation as preacher. He served until about 1752. The congregation was a member both of the Rijper Sociëteit (Waterlander Conference of North Holland) and of the Zonist Conference.

Among the families of Koog-Zaandijk who promoted Mennonitism was the Honig (q.v.) family; members of this family, who founded the large and well-known Honig grocery factories, are still found here as members of the Mennonite congregation.

In the last part of the 18th and the first decades of the 19th century there was a decline both of activity and of membership. The membership decreased in one century by about 200; but in the 19th century there was a considerable growth: 1808, 417; 1833, 470; 1861, 506; 1900, 516. From then a decrease took place, to 399 in 1955. The congregation always was rather well-to-do. In the early 18th century it contributed liberally to the needs of the Mennonites in Prussia (1727-36 a total of 2,840 guilders). From this time on the congregation was served by the preachers Sjoerd Pietersz van Dokkenburg 1750-75, his son Pieter van Dokkenburg 1770-1811, Jan Visser 1788-1831, Jan Bruin 1827-?, Jan van Gilse 1834-37, Christiaan Muller 1838-68, Jochem Boetje 1868-72, A. W. Huidekoper 1873-77, S. Lulofs 1877-89, P. S. Bakels 1889-1907, J. P. Smidts 1908-22, J. M. Leendertz 1923-27, J. E. van Brakel 1928-45, and E. H. Boer 1946- .

The congregation has an old people's home called the Johanna Elisabeth Stichting. Church activities include ladies' circle, young members' association, Sunday school for children, youth group Elfregi.

vᴅZ.

Inv. Arch. Amst. I, No. 708; II, 2032 f.; Blaupot t. C., *Holland* I and II; S. Lootsma, *Het Nieuwe Huys* (Zaandam, 1937) 13, 23, 25, 32, 75, 82, 226; *DB* 1870, 180; 1874, 144; 1895, 180; 1900, 99; 1918, 65 f., 146; *De Zondagsbode* XXIV (1910) No. 21; *ML* II, 547.

Kooiman, a Dutch Mennonite family, mostly farmers on the island of Texel (*q.v.*); Pieter Kooiman, who was then an old man, is mentioned in 1731 as a (lay) preacher of the Waterlander Mennonite congregation of Den Burg, Texel. (In the *Naamlijst* of 1743 he is listed as a retired minister.) A descendant of this family is Jan Kooiman (1865-1934), who served as pastor of the Mennonite congregations of Oudebildtzijl 1891-93, Barsingerhorn 1893-1911, Workum 1911-14, Akkrum 1914-23, and Ternaard 1923-30. (*Inv. Arch. Amst.* II, No. 1632; *De Zondagsbode* XLVII, Nos. 42-43.)   vᴅZ.

Kool, a Dutch Mennonite family name. Pieter Kool, a brewer of Amsterdam, was married to Anna Roskam of Beverwijk. Soon after his marriage Kool took over his father-in-law's vinegar factory at Beverwijk. Their son was Agge Roskam Kool, b. Oct. 16, 1714, at Amsterdam, d. March 23, 1789, at Beverwijk. This Agge Roskam Kool was a remarkable man. He not only ran the vinegar factory with much ability and profit, but also made a number of useful inventions, for example, the breeches buoy, an apparatus to rescue the shipwrecked. He was the inventor of an improved method of vaccination for a cattle plague. He also made maps of the Dutch coast and low-tide zone. For a large number of years Kool served the Mennonite congregation of Beverwijk as a deacon. At the same time he was an ardent Collegiant (*q.v.*). He often stayed at Rijnsburg (*q.v.*), the Collegiant center in the Netherlands, where he delivered many addresses and also performed baptism by immersion after 1753. In 1760 he baptized Aagje Deken (*q.v.*).

In 1736 Agge Roskam Kool was married to Trijntje Jansd. Honig of Zaandijk. One of their eleven children was Jan Kool, b. 1741 at Beverwijk, d. 1816 at Zaandijk, who in 1766 was married to Stijntje Gerritsd. Honig of Zaandijk and who ran a well-known paper mill at Zaandijk.

Some Kool descendants were later found at Alkmaar, where both Jacob Pieter Kool Jzn and Jacob Pieter Kool Pzn were cheese exporters and also deacons of the congregation 1869-84 and 1881-91, 1894-1919 respectively. P. Schuckink Kool, a descendant of Agge Roskam Kool and like his ancestor a resident of Beverwijk, served his home church as a deacon from 1857 for more than 25 years. A branch of this family lived in Amsterdam. (*N.N.B.Wb.* IV, 855 ff.; *DB* 1903, 186; 1909, 100.)

vᴅZ.

Koolaert, Elisabeth, a Dutch Mennonite poet: see Hoofman.

Koolaert de Kuyper, an Anabaptist martyr, who was seized in 1561 at Hondschooten in Flanders and burned at the stake at St.-Winox-bergen (Bergues-St.-Winox) "for the sake of the testimony of our Lord Jesus Christ."

Mart. Mir. D 283, E 651; *Bibliographie* II, No. 438; *ML* II, 547.

Koolman: see **Coolman.**

Ko(o)men, Jan van, author of *Belydenisse des Geloofs onder de Doopsgezinde Christenen . . .* (Groningen, 1744), which confession was used by the Swiss Mennonites whose ancestors had migrated from Switzerland to the Netherlands in 1711. The confession was edited after the death of van Komen by his son-in-law Hendrik van Kalker (*q.v.*). It is not clear whether the appendix following the Confession entitled *Korte Redengevinge van den dienst der Oudsten* was also written by van Komen or by van Kalker. Jan van Komen (*ca.* 1680-1742) originally belonged to the Groningen Old Flemish congregation of Deventer (*q.v.*), where he lived. About 1721, together with some other members, he left this congregation because it had, in their opinion, become too much conformed to the world; they moved to Hoogezand in the province of Groningen and joined the congregation of the Old Swiss Brethren at Sappemeer (*q.v.*), in which congregation van Komen became a preacher (*DB* 1919, 75).

Jan van Komen was married to Grietje van Calkar, a granddaughter of the Deventer Old Flemish Elder Abraham Willems Cremer (*q.v.*). A daughter of Jan van Komen named Trijntje was married to Hendrik van Calkar (Kalker), editor of the *Confession.*

The family name of van Komen (van Koomen, van Coomen, van Comen) whose ancestor originally may have been an inhabitant of the Belgian town of Komen (Commines) is also found among the Flemish Mennonites of West Prussia. vᴅZ.

Biogr. Wb. V, 205 f.; J. Huizinga, *Stamboek . . . van Samuel Peter (Meihuizen) en Barbara Fry* (Groningen, 1890) 59-61, 63, 75, 82; *DB* 1918, 75, 77, 109.

Koop, A. J., of Chortitza, South Russia, a leading Mennonite industrialist, received his training as an apprentice in the workshop and factory of P. H.

Lepp (*q.v.*), who helped him to get started in industry. Koop established his own factory in Chortitza in 1864. He was so successful that additional factories were built at Einlage and Alexandrovsk. In 1908 they had an output of 610,000 rubles. At Alexandrovsk during that year 288 workers were employed, at Chortitza 81, and at Einlage 100. The factories produced the usual agricultural machinery used by the Mennonites and the Russians of the Ukraine. When, in 1914, Koop's enterprise observed its fiftieth anniversary it was listed as the second largest of the Mennonite industries in Russia. During the Russian Revolution the factories were nationalized but continued their work. Little is known about the personal life of the founder. (See also **Agriculture** *Among the Mennonites in Russia* and **Industry** *Among Mennonites in Russia*.)   C.K.

D. Rempel, "The Mennonite Colonies in New Russia" (doctoral dissertation, Stanford University, Cal., 1933); "Mennonite Industry, Russia," *Menn. Life* X (January 1955) 21.

Koopman, Jan, an Anabaptist martyr: see **Jan Cooman.**

Koopmans (formerly often Coopmans, *q.v.*), a Dutch Mennonite family. Besides Klaas Koopmans and his son Rinse Klaasz Koopmans (*q.v.*), there have been at least three other preachers of this family. Gerbrand Koopmans, b. 1779 at Leeuwarden, d. 1836 at Koudum, studied at the Amsterdam Mennonite Seminary 1801-5 and served the congregations of Zaandam "Oude Huys" 1805-14, Oostzaandam 1814-21, and Bolsward 1821-31 (*Naamlijst* 1815, 82-84; 1829, 29, 44). Dirk Koopmans, b. 1792 at Leeuwarden, d. 1849 at Amsterdam, served the congregation of Kampen 1818-22. In that year he resigned to move to Amsterdam, where he founded an insurance business (*Naamlijst* 1829, 39). Lieuwe Koopmans has been the pastor of the De Rijp congregation since 1954.   vDZ.

Koopmans, Rinse, the son of Claes Rinses Coopmans (*q.v.*), a butter merchant, who in 1722-d.92 was a lay preacher of the Mennonite congregation of Leeuwarden. Rinse Koopmans was born March 9, 1770, at Grouw in Friesland; after completing his study at the Mennonite Seminary in Amsterdam in 1794 he was a ministerial candidate and served successfully in Blokzijl (September 1794), Dokkum (April 1795), and Amsterdam (February 1796). This career bears witness to his excellent preaching ability; his skill as a pastor and a comforter of the sick was equally highly praised. In 1812 he was chosen to succeed Hesselink (*q.v.*) as professor at the Mennonite Seminary in Amsterdam, but could not give his speech of acceptance until two years later when French dominion was overthrown (June 8, 1814). Characteristic of Koopmans is the theme of this address: "To the application of the divine authority of revealed doctrine against those who, while they elevate human speech, the excellence of the Gospel, as well as the wisdom and character of Jesus Christ by their words of praise, reject the divine authority of revelation, especially that of Jesus Christ." Koopmans had the ability to unfold to his students without partiality the views and opinions of others. Hearty and cheerful as he was, he was rather the type of a pious father—he had a large family—than of a scholar. His *Redevoeringen en Verhandelingen* (2vv., Amsterdam, 1819) treat literary as much as philosophical subjects. As a theologian he acquired fame by a prize-winning (*Teylers Godgeleerd Genootschap* award) treatise, "De zoenoffers des Ouden Verbonds en den dood van Christus met derselve vergeleken." In 1797 he married Janke Cnoop (d. 1823) of Bolsward.

On Sept. 5, 1826, Koopmans died at his country home "Bovenburen" near Koudum in Friesland.   vDZ.

Biogr. Wb. V, 206-10; *Naamlijst* 1815, 58-63; 1829, 24; *Inv. Arch. Amst.* I, Nos. 688, 691-93, 696; *DJ* 1850, 124 146-53; *DB* 1892, 86; 1898, 21; 1901, 18; *ML* II, 547.

Koopmans, Wopko Cnoop, b. Sept. 23, 1800, in Amsterdam, a son of the above. At first he applied himself to literary study. The University of Utrecht awarded him a doctorate in philosophy and *de humane Letteren*.

Meanwhile Koopmans became interested in theology; in 1823 he became a ministerial candidate at the Mennonite Seminary in Amsterdam. He served the Utrecht congregation 1823-27. In 1827 he was appointed as a professor at the Mennonite Theological Seminary in Amsterdam with Samuel Muller. He lectured on criticism, hermeneutics, and New Testament exegesis, later on Christian ethics. It was a great pity that during his entire career Koopmans felt overshadowed by his colleague Muller. This feeling was so serious an obstacle for one whose demands upon himself were high, that he never published his theological works. He died March 4, 1849.   vDZ.

Biogr. Wb. V, 210-16; *N.N.B.Wb.* IX, 546 f.; *Naamlijst* 1829, 24, 36; *DJ* 1850, 15, 156-68; *DB* 1885, 55; 1897, 59; 1901, 19, 144 f.; *ML* II, 547 f.

Kopf, Daniel, an Anabaptist martyr, mentioned by van Braght (*Mart. Mir.* D 27, E 435), is identical with Daniel Kropf (*q.v.*). This Kropf was put to death in 1536, not in 1529, as *Martyrs' Mirror* states.   vDZ.

Kopijn (*Copijn*), **Jan,** of Amsterdam, who died in 1711 at Dordrecht, living after 1675 at Middelburg, Dutch province of Zeeland, was a deacon of the Mennonite church and thereupon a preacher at Middelburg 1680-1706. In this year he moved to Zuilen near Utrecht. Not much is known about Kopijn. He wrote a number of poems, one of which celebrated his fellow preacher Adriaen van Eeghem (*q.v.*). Another familiar devotional poem by Kopijn was *Eenvoudige Samenspraak over het Leeven en Lyden van Kristus,* two volumes (Utrecht 1708 and 1736). Kopijn was married in 1690 to Janneken Terwen, of Middelburg. (*Biogr. Wb.* V, 236 f.) vDZ.

Köppental, a village of the Trakt Mennonite settlement in the province of Samara, Russia, founded in 1855 by Mennonites from Prussia who settled on both banks of the Malyshevka River, was named after the Russian state councilor von Köppen, who promoted the settlement. The village originally consisted of 25 families each farming 175 acres. In 1897 it had 56 farms and a population of 174 and in 1914 there were 168 inhabitants. In 1880-81 some of the settlers followed Claas Epp (q.v.) to Central Asia (q.v.).

The administration of the Trakt settlement (Malyshinskaya Volost, later Köppental Rayon) was located in Köppental. Köppental also built a church in 1866, and had a secondary school (Zentralschule) which was erected before World War I and was the center of many of the organizations and activities of the Trakt settlement. At the beginning of World War II its population with that of the entire Trakt settlement was evacuated to Asiatic Russia. (See also **Trakt** Mennonite Settlement. **Trakt** Mennonite Church; *Am Trakt*, North Kildonan, 1948; *ML* II, 548.)   C.K.

Köppental-Orloff Mennonite Church: see **Trakt Mennonite Church.**

Kopper, a Mennonite family of West Prussia, Germany, particularly in the Montau-Gruppe (q.v.) congregation. They were mostly farmers living in the adjacent villages of Klein Sanskau and Dragass. Some of them served the church as preachers and elders; e.g., Hans Kopper, preacher 1774 until after 1802; Isaak Kopper (1809-56), preacher from 1831, elder 1850-56; Gerhard Kopper (b. 1840), preacher from 1871, elder from 1881; Bernhard Kopper (1851-1916), preacher 1880-1916; Bernhard Kopper (b. 1893), preacher 1924, elder 1934, serving until the catastrophe of 1945, and since then in West Germany.   vDZ.

L. Stobbe, *Montau-Gruppe, ein Gedenkblatt* (Montau, 1918); several issues of *Gem.-Kal.*

Kops (Cops), a Dutch Mennonite family originally from the Rhineland, Germany. Wolter Kops (q.v., ca. 1520-1602 or later), who lived at München-Gladbach in the duchy of Jülich, was the ancestor. His son was Claes Wolters Cops (q.v.), who served as preacher of the München-Gladbach Mennonite congregation and later at Haarlem. Two of Claes Wolters Cops' sons were Goedschalk Cops (1586-1636), a merchant of yarns and linen at Goch, Germany, and Willem Kops, b. 1619 at München-Gladbach, d. 1665 at Haarlem. He also was a linen merchant, living at Nijmegen (q.v.), where he obtained citizenship in 1652, not by swearing an oath of allegiance, but "bij Mannen waerheyt," i.e., by simply making an affirmation of loyalty. He was a deacon of the Nijmegen congregation. About this time Wyand Kops, a deacon, moved from Gladbach to Nijmegen. In 1669 he returned to Gladbach. Descendants of Goedschalk and Willem Kops since the 18th century were especially found at Haarlem, where they often were deacons and trustees of the Mennonite orphanages, and in Amsterdam, where they also served the congregation as deacons. In Amsterdam most of them were members of the Zonist (q.v.) congregation. Jacob Kops, a merchant, lived at Hamburg about 1675. Willem Kops (1724-76), a merchant of Haarlem, was also a man of letters; he is considered the author of *Het Leeven van Pieter Langendijk*. In 1774 he published the poems of Elisabeth Koolaart-Hoofman (q.v.), with a biography, and in the same year *Schets eener geschiedenis der Rederijkeren*. The

preachers Jan Kops (q.v.) and his grandson Jan Kops were members of this family. In the 19th century there are also a number of descendants by the name of Bruyn Kops, descended from Pieter Kops (Haarlem, 1746-1803), owner of a yarn factory and also serving in some governmental offices, and M. C. van Oosten de Bruyn. Their son Cornelis Johannes de Bruyn Kops (1791-1858) was a mayor of Haarlem. Three sons of this Cornelis de Bruyn Kops, viz., Jacob Leonhard (1827-87), Alexander Louis (1827-92), and Cornelis Johannes (1830-91), occupied prominent places in the Netherlands, the first two as engineers, the last as a political economist. vDZ.

Ned. Patriciaat X (1919) 1920-2000; XL (1954) 206-28; *DB* 1874, 6, 13 f., 20; *N.N.B.Wb.* III, 714-16; IV, 861; B. C. Roosen, *Geschichte der Mennoniten-Gemeinde zu Hamburg und Altona* I (Hamburg, 1886) 74.

Kops (Cops), **Claes Wolters** (1559-July 1641). He was the son of Wolter Kops (named above). He was a weaver and after 1593 lived on the Aldenhof at ‹München-Gladbach, duchy of Jülich, Germany, but was frequently at Haarlem in connection with his trade or in consequence of persecution. In 1581 he married Grietgen Comes (d. 1616) at Cologne. He was twice remarried. Kops was a Mennonite preacher at München-Gladbach, and for some time also of the High German congregation at Haarlem, Holland, where he became involved in a dispute (about 1610) with his colleague Leenaerdt Clock, apparently concerning marriage with non-members of the group (*buitentrouw*), Kops taking the more conservative position. Kops thus obstructed the merging of his High German group with the Young Frisians and Waterlanders, a movement initiated by the Concept of Cologne in 1591. In 1619 he was again living at München-Gladbach, where he had a considerable business in yarn and linen. In 1622 he is said to have been a wealthy man, living on a great estate, and was censured for this by Abraham Rietmaker of Aachen. After 1622 there is no further information about Claes Wolters Kops, except the date of his death. His followers were called Claes-Woltersvolk. There was a Claes-Wolters congregation in Friedrichstadt, Germany, as late as 1632.   vDZ., W.N.

Inv. Arch. Amst. I, No. 554 f.; II, Nos. 1195, 2626 f.; 2789; *DB* 1874, 6; Kühler, *Geschiedenis* II, 92; Ernst Crous, "Von Täufern zu Mennoniten am Niederrhein," *Der Mennonit* IX (1956) 91, *ML* I, 364.

Kops, Jan, b. March 6, 1765, at Amsterdam, d. Jan. 9, 1849, at Utrecht. His parents, Jacobus Kops, a yarn merchant, and Hillegond Schotvanger, belonged to the conservative Old Frisian Mennonite congregation, but Jan Kops joined the progressive Lamist congregation. He studied at the Amsterdam Theological Seminary 1781-87, and then served as pastor of the Leiden congregation 1787-1800. He became much interested in politics and was an ardent Patriot (q.v.), and in 1795, when the Dutch Mennonites obtained equal political rights with the members of the Reformed Church, Kops became a member of the city government at Leiden. In 1799 he was appointed director of agriculture in the Netherlands, whereupon he resigned from his ministry and moved to The Hague. In 1815 he became professor of botany and agricultural economics at the

University of Utrecht. In 1816-43 he preached in the Utrecht Mennonite congregation. He published a number of books and papers on agricultural economy, but no theological books, except two sermons. One of his outstanding publications in the field of botany (in collaboration with J. C. Sepp, *q.v.*) is *Flora Batava* (first vol. at Amsterdam, 1800). In 1830 he became a trustee of the A.D.S. (Dutch General Mennonite Conference and a curator of its seminary.

Kops was married to Johanna Daams of Haarlem. Albertus Kops, who was one of the children of Jan Kops, b. 1814 at Amsterdam, d. 1874 at Utrecht, married Grietje Cleyndert of Zaandam. Their son Jan Kops, b. 1846 at Utrecht, d. 1872 at Tjalleberd, studied theology at the Amsterdam Mennonite Seminary, and became pastor of the Tjalleberd congregation in September 1872. He served only a few months before an untimely death. His daughter Geertruida Kops (1853-1941) was married to W. J. Leendertz (*q.v.*).   vDZ.

Ned. Patriciaat XL (1954) 209; *Biogr. Wb.* V, 232-36; L. G. te Poole, *Bijdragen tot de kennis . . . van de Dg. te Leiden* (Leiden, 1905) *passim; Naamlijst* 1829, 35 f.; *DJ* 1850, 37; *DB* 1875, 55; J. Baert, *Jan Kops, pionier van Hollands Landbouw* (The Hague, 1943); J. M. G. van der Poel, *Heren en Boeren* (Wageningen, 1949) chapters III-VIII; an autobiographical manuscript by Kops, "Levensbericht," is found in the Utrecht University Library.

Korba Mission Station, one of the five main stations of the General Conference Mennonite Mission in India, is situated 25 miles north of Champa, Madhya Pradesh (formerly Central Provinces), India. It was opened by C. H. Suckau in 1915. The area of the Korba field covers 2,200 square miles, with a population of 230,000, and over 1,000 villages. There are four outstations. The first church was organized on Dec. 1, 1915; and the first meetinghouse was dedicated in February 1920. The church has not grown very rapidly; some of the first members have reverted to Hinduism. The membership in 1954 was 146, but there are prospects of many children of Christian families being gathered in. The church was served by the Indian pastor, J. R. Singh, for some 15 years, and is now (1955) served by the Indian pastor, Malachi Chawbey.

The station has no institutional work except a primary school and a dispensary. District evangelism has been chiefly emphasized. The most encouraging feature of this work is the increasing interest in literature, a large amount of which, including Bibles, Testaments, Bible portions, tracts, and handbills, is sold and distributed each year. (*ML* II, 548; *ME* I, †.)   P.W.P.

Korbmacher, Hans, an Anabaptist martyr: see **Mändl.**

Kornelis and **Kornelisz,** variant Dutch spellings of *Cornelis* and *Cornelisz* (*q.v.*).

Kort-Adriaentgen van Gent, an Anabaptist martyr: see **Adriaen de Hoedemaker.**

Kort Onderwys des Christelijke Geloofs (Short Catechism of the Christian Faith) was drawn up by Jan Maarensz Mol (*q.v.*) of Wormer at the request of the Zonist (*q.v.*) conference. It was edited at Amsterdam in 1697 by E. A. van Dooregeest, Herman Schijn, and Pieter Beets (reprints 1698, 1710, 1723, 1740, 1753, all at Amsterdam). The *Kort Onderwys* in all editions is followed by *Korte Schets van onderwys voor de aankomende Jeugd* (Short Outline of Instruction for the Older Youth), of which there were separate editions at Alkmaar (n.d.) and De Rijp, 1740.   vDZ.

Kort Verhael *van de Vereeninghe tusschen de Doopsgesinde Ghemeynten, die aen d'eene zijde ghenoemt worden Vlamingen, aen de ander zijde de Vereenigde Vriesen ende Hoogduytschen, Vreedsaem geschiet binnen Amsterdam, den 26. April, des Dingsdaeghs near Paesschen, Anno 1639* (Amsterdam, 1639). This booklet of 42 pages gives a complete account of the service held in the Amsterdam Lamist church to celebrate the union of the Flemish and the Frisian-High German congregations. Speakers at this meeting, which lasted for more than five hours and was attended by more than 3,000 persons, were Pieter Jansz Moyer, Joost Hendricksz, Tielemann Tielen (van Sittert), and Tobias Govertsz (van de Wyngaert).   vDZ.

Kort Verhael ende Belijdenisse *der ware Religie . . .* (Haarlem, 1622) is a Dutch Mennonite confession with a large preface. The author I. P. was probably Jacob Pietersz van der Meulen (*q.v.*) with his copreachers.   vDZ.

Kort Verhael *van het Leven ende Daden van Hans de Ries* (De Rijp, 1644): see **Ries, Hans de.**

Korte Belydenis *der Waterlandsche Gemeenten* (Rotterdam, 1740): see **Besluyt** *der Voornaemste Waterlandsche leeraren.*

Korte Belydenisse des Gheloofs, *mitsgaders de voornaemste zeden, wetten ende kerckelycke Discipline in de Christelycke Vlaemse Doopsgezinde Ghemeente.* This Dutch Mennonite book, mentioned by M. Schagen, of which there seems to be no copy extant, was printed at Haarlem in 1644 and reprinted 1684 and 1685 at Hamburg, Germany, for the Flemish congregation of Hamburg-Altona.   vDZ.

M. Schagen, *Naamlijst der Doopsgezinde schrijveren* (Amsterdam, 1745) 60.

Korte Beschrijving, *Hoe het met de Doopsgezinden gegaan is van 't begin af (1522) tot dezen tijd toe (1647).* This account, written in 1647 by an unknown author, probably belonging to the Waterlander branch of the Dutch Mennonites and already 70 years of age, is only extant in an 18th-century manuscript by J. B. (?), found in the Amsterdam Mennonite library. It was published and commentaried by J. G. de Hoop Scheffer in *DB* 1876. The *Korte Beschrijving* is written with strict impartiality and is a valuable source of information on the history of the Dutch Mennonites. (*DB* 1876, 13-41.)   vDZ.

Korte History *der protestante Christenen, die men Mennoniten of Doopsgezinden noemt . . .* (Amsterdam, 1711): see **Schijn, Herman.**

Korte, Maeyken de, an Anabaptist martyr: see **Maeyken de Corte.**

Kortrijk (*Courtrai*), a town (1949 pop. 40,825) in Flanders, Belgium, was in the 16th century a center of cloth and linen weaving and the seat of a Mennonite congregation. Anabaptists were found here as early as 1533. In this year Jacques van der Mase (*q.v.*), who had read Rothman's booklet *Van de Wrake,* traveled to Münster (*q.v.*) and visited a large number of Anabaptist groups or congregations in Holland. After the fall of Münster (July 1535) he returned to Belgium, apparently cured of his revolutionary ideas. After spending some time in Brugge (*q.v.*) he returned to Kortrijk in 1537 or 1538. Through the activity of van der Mase and the mysterious Pieter van Gelder (*q.v.*) a congregation arose in Kortrijk, of which, however, very little is known. In 1553 Kortrijk is said to have been the most infected (with Anabaptism) town of Flanders. In 1553 Joos Kindt (*q.v.*) was arrested here and put to death. In 1556-61 a number of other victims followed. In 1568-69 other martyrs died, most of them weavers. The total number of Anabaptist-Mennonite martyrs executed at Kortrijk was 24, and one died in prison. A number of Anabaptists from Kortrijk died as martyrs in other towns of Flanders; seven of them suffered death at Gent. In addition to the information concerning the Kortrijk congregation given by its martyrs it is also known that Leenaert Bouwens baptized 14 persons here in 1554-56, and 11 or 18 in 1557-61. Jacob de Rore (*q.v.*) in his first letter of 1561 greets "the friends of Kortrijk." It is not clear whether the congregation died out or was dispersed in 1569, when on April 30 six Mennonites were put to death here. In any case its activity declined and nothing is heard any more of a congregation in this town. Yet it may have led a hidden existence, since shortly after 1600 some Mennonites from Kortrijk, among whom were members of the de Hauterive (van Outrijve) and the Steenkiste families, moved to Aardenburg in the Dutch province of Zealand and to Haarlem, North Holland.					vDZ.

Verheyden, *Courtrai-Bruxelles,* Introduction, 15-30 f.; Kühler, *Geschiedenis* I, 439; *ML* II, 553.

Kortrijk, *an unknown Anabaptist martyr from,* executed on July 27, 1553, on the Vrijdagsmarkt at Gent, Belgium. He was burned at the stake and his corpse hanged outside the Mudepoorte (Verheyden, *Gent,* 18, No. 37). Van Braght (*Mart. Mir.* D 150, E 540) erroneously identifies this unknown martyr with Joos Kindt, but this latter martyr was put to death at Kortrijk on Jan. 20, 1553. vDZ.

Kortrijk, Adriaen van (*Adriaen van Cuertrycke*), a deacon (or preacher) of the Mennonite congregation of Gent, Belgium. About 1545 he wrote, in the name of the congregations of Gent, Meenen, Roesselare, Hondschoote, Nijpkerke, and Waastene, a letter to the congregation of Antwerp requesting that an elder might be sent to these congregations because "they are in trouble and young and they do not receive enough visits from elders." No answer to this letter is known.					vDZ.

A. L. E. Verheyden, "De Doopsgezinden te Gent 1530-1630," in *Bijdrage tot de Geschiedenis en de Oudheidkunde van Gent,* 1943, 105-7.

Korver family: see **Corver.**

Korzeniecer Kämpe was until 1909 an island in the Vistula River on the left bank, opposite Thorn, Germany. In the early days its population was probably exclusively Mennonite (five families: Adrian, Ewert, Funk, Gerbrandt, and Nickel). At the turn of the 20th century there were only three Mennonite families there (widow of Gerhard Dirks, H. Foth, and Nickel). All of these were members of the Obernessau (*q.v.*) Mennonite Church. In the first decade of the 20th century, a part of Korzeniecer Kämpe was taken to build a stately harbor; the inhabitants had to leave their homes and move to Thorn. (*Menn. Bl.,* 1905, 29, 39; *ML* II, 553.)					NEFF.

Kosciusko, Marshall, and Elkhart County (Ind.) Old Order Amish settlement was started *ca.* 1850 by families moving from Holmes Co., Ohio, and also from the Amish settlement in eastern Elkhart County-Lagrange County.

In 1954 it consisted of 10 districts (congregations) with a total of 607 members, Nappanee being the largest trading center. In 1940 Bishop Burkholder led a schism which joined the Beachy Amish group, but which has failed to secure more than a small following.

About 1875 a progressive Amish congregation was formed from Old Order Amish background with a meetinghouse erected in 1877 on West Market St. in Nappanee, now G.C. Many of the present members of this congregation as well as of the North Main St. Mennonite (MC) congregation are of Amish background. In 1940 a Beachy Amish congregation (Burkholder) was formed near Nappanee, and in 1954 a Conservative Mennonite congregation (Bethel), also near Nappanee. H.S.B.

Kossen, a Mennonite family name, found in the north of the Dutch province of North Holland, formerly all farmers. Descendants of this family are Dirk Kossen (b. 1865 at Barsingerhorn, d. 1934 at Driehuis), who studied at the university and Mennonite Seminary at Amsterdam and then was pastor of Mennonite congregations of Den Helder 1891-95, The Hague 1895-97, Akkrum 1898-1913, and Bolsward 1913-32. He was a trustee of the A.D.S. (Dutch General Mennonite Conference) in 1905-31 and the promoter of the "Dienstjarenfonds" (*q.v.*) in 1911, of which he was president 1924-34. His son Hendrik B. Kossen, b. 1923 at Bolsward, studied at the Amsterdam university and seminary, and served the IJlst congregation 1950-56, and Berlikum 1956- . (*Zondagsbode* XLVII, Nos. 24-25; *DJ* 1935, 17-25 with portrait.)					vDZ.

Kota Nopan, a station of the former Dutch Mennonite mission in Sumatra, Indonesia, the capital of (Klein-) Mandailing, and the seat of Dutch government officials, 15 miles north of the mission station Pakanten (*q.v.*), amid a strictly Mohammedan population. About 1923 this station was opened by P. Nachtigal. Several years later some Tobanese

Christians settled here, reinforcing the young church. In 1934 it had 53 members. A church was built in 1938. About 1942 this congregation joined the Batak Christian Church. (*ML* II, 553.) J.KL.

Kotlyarevo Mennonite Brethren Church, Memrik, Russia, was founded in 1885 as a subsidiary of Rückenau Mennonite Brethren Church. Its first meetinghouse, acquired in 1887, was replaced by a new structure in 1897. In 1900 the congregation became independent and in 1902 its minister Isaak Fast was ordained elder. In 1909 he died and was succeeded by Jakob Dörksen, who retired in 1926, when Johann M. Janzen, who was exiled in 1934, became the leader.

In 1887 the membership of the congregation was 52. In 1905 it was 345, with a total of 670 worshipers including children. In 1934, when the elder was exiled, the congregation had to discontinue functioning. In addition to the elders the congregation was served by preachers Tobias Voth (from 1895), Franz Fröse (from 1900), Gerhard Berg (from 1901), Kornelius Klaassen (from 1904), Franz Goossen (from 1900), Kornelius Isaak (from 1900), Abraham Pätkau (from 1904), and Peter Rogalsky (from 1908). C.K.

H. Goerz, *Memrik* (Rosthern, Sask., 1954) 29 ff.

Kotozufka: see Neumannovka.

Kotte (Cotte, Codt, Coodt), **Johann Clausen** (Jan Claesz), also called Rollwagen (Rolweghen, Rolwaghen), a prominent leader of the Mennonites of Eiderstedt (*q.v.*), Holstein, Germany, the son of the Flemish Nikolaus Peter Kotte at Oldenswort in the region of Eiderstedt, whence he was banished in 1588. Then he moved to the Netherlands. About 1590 he lived at Amsterdam as a broker and obtained citizenship there. In collaboration with Caspar Coolhaes, a progressive Reformed clergyman, and like Kotte a defender of religious freedom, he wrote in 1601 *Tsamenspreeckinge van dry personen over het rigereus Placcaet van Groeningen* (n.p., 1601; revised ed.; n.p., 1602), in which they attacked the mandate issued in 1601 by the States of Groningen (*q.v.*) against the Mennonites. This pamphlet by Coolhaes and Kotte (here called Rolwaghen) caused a literary conflict with the Calvinists. Rolwaghen was sharply attacked by a number of Calvinists, including a certain Wijnant Kras. He defended himself and the Mennonites in *Corte Bestraffingh* (n.p., 1602) and *Tegenbericht* (n.p., n.d.). Rolwaghen also attacked the Reformed minister Johannes Acronius (*q.v.*).

Kotte, who during his stay in the Netherlands called himself Jan Claesz Rolwaghen, seems to have left Amsterdam soon after 1602, and settled in Tönning in Holstein, Germany. Here he was appointed as supervisor of the ocean dike by Duke Johann Adolf of Holstein-Gottorp. He composed a confession of faith in Flemish, "but in such a style that it concealed more than it revealed the Mennonite faith by using dark and ambiguous words."

In the disputation with the Anabaptists held at Tönning on Aug. 31, 1607, he was their spokesman. They were requested to present a clearer statement of their faith. Kotte did this on July 22, 1608. Then on Sept. 14, 1608, a new disputation lasting three days was held in the castle at Schleswig. Very thoroughly Kotte defended the religious principles of his group against Fabricius (*q.v.*). Kotte was in great favor with the Duke. On Nov. 1, 1614, he achieved a moderation of the edict which had banished the Mennonites from Holstein territory.

The information concerning the origin of the name Rollwagen in the periodical *Die Heimat* of March and July 1934 (published by Karl Wachholtz, Neumünster) is incorrect. The question has not yet been clarified. In the *Nordfriesisches Jahrbuch* (Husum, 1934, 93-99) Albert Vlamynck published a letter written by the dike engineer C. J. Rolweghen in Tönning, July 2, 1611, in which Rolweghen encloses the plan for a dike, and refers to the dike builder Jan Claas Coott. (*N.N.B.Wb.* II, 1227; *Catalogus Amst.*, 193 f.; *ML* II, 553 f.) NEFF, vDZ.

Kottenem, Matthijs van: see Matthias Servaes.

Kotter, Eustachius (Eustace Kuter), a Hutterite martyr, a stone mason, who was seized with Hans Mändl (*q.v.*) and Georg Rack (*q.v.*) in 1560 near Rosenheim in Bavaria, Germany, and sent to prison in Innsbruck. He was a native of Tirol, Austria. On November 22-24 he was cross-examined on the rack; he gave an excellent confession of his faith which was taken down "word for word" and has been preserved by the Hutterian Brethren (Wolkan, 308). From it we learn that he was baptized by Leonhard Lanzenstiel (*q.v.*) in 1540, had been captured four or five years before in the Puster Valley and taken to castle Neuhaus, later was captured again, but obtained his freedom once more.

The pastor of Hall attempted to win the three prisoners to the Catholic faith, but had no success. On June 5, 1561, Kotter and Rack wrote an epistle to the brotherhood in Moravia, stating that they were to be executed on Tuesday after Corpus Christi. "We are paying God our vow. We do this with joy and are not sad, for this day is holy unto the Lord" (Loserth, 206).

On June 13 all three were sentenced to death. When the imperial mandate was read to them, according to which they merited death, Eustachius Kotter said, "What concern of ours is the imperial mandate, that you read it to us? Read our confession, to which we have testified with holy, also divine and Biblical writing, that it is the real truth of God, for which we must suffer today."

At the execution site they prayed earnestly and commended body and soul to the Lord. "First Kotter was beheaded because he was sick or weak in the flesh." Their martyrdom is commemorated in the song, "Hört nun, alle Fromme," in 81 stanzas (*Die Lieder der Hutterischen Brüder*, 415-22).

Eustachius Kotter is the author of two hymns (Loserth credits him with three), which he wrote in prison: (1) "Mein Gott und Herr, dir sei viel Ehr," 25 stanzas; in acrostics it reads, "Mein lieber Bruder Hans Mändl, ich Stächl, schicke dir ein Lied, schau, obs recht sei, wo nicht, tus aus. O Gott, erlös die Gefangenen." (2) "Stärk uns, O Gott, in dieser

Not," 17 stanzas, the first 13 of which contain the acrostic "Stachius Koter."   NEFF.

Die Lieder der Hutterischen Brüder (Scottdale, 1914) 3, 636-39; Wolkan, *Lieder*, 228; J. Loserth, *Der Anabaptismus in Tirol* (Vienna, 1892) 206; Wolkan, *Geschicht-Buch*; Zieglschmid, *Chronik*; *Mart. Mir.* D 276, E 645; *ML* II, 554.

Kotzenbüll, a village in the south of the Eiderstedt (*q.v.*) region, west of Tönning, Germany, early settled by Mennonites because of its favorable location for the Dutch Mennonites; the first proscription took place in 1566. In 1577 other Mennonites were examined by the provost. The "privilege" of 1623, which applied also to residents of the region, gave them peace. Yet they never grew strong; there were only individual families. In 1738 there were still four families. Later Mennonitism disappeared from the region because of families dying out and mixed marriages. (*ML* II, 554.)   R.Do.

Koudum, a village in the Dutch province of Friesland, had two small Mennonite congregations soon after 1600, one of them a Waterlander congregation, which merged in the course of the 17th century, and in 1695 had a combined membership of 80. It was always served by lay preachers. After the departure of its last preacher, Tjalling Tjallingius, in 1803 it was served by the neighboring Molkwerum; but when this pulpit also became vacant about 1813, the few remaining members joined Hindeloopen (*q.v.*). In 1867 an independent congregation was again established at Koudum, chiefly through the efforts of Pastor Lodeesen of Hindeloopen, which, since 1870, has had a hall of its own for meetings. The congregation was served by the Hindeloopen (*q.v.*) ministers until 1942, and since then by those of Workum (*q.v.*). A new room for a meetinghouse was acquired in 1899 and rebuilt in 1903. The membership was 31 in 1900, 36 in 1932, 26 in 1955. Church activities include a ladies' circle and Sunday school for children.   vDZ.

DB 1869, 156; 1870, 32-44, 177; 1874, 87; 1890, 137; 1903, 82, 189; *ML* II, 554.

Kouwer, a Mennonite family, found in the Zaan district, Dutch province of North Holland, living at Zaandam, Wormerveer, and Koog aan de Zaan. Some members of this family have served the church as deacons. Benjamin Jan Kouwer (b. 1861 at Wormerveer, d. 1933 at Utrecht), a noted physician at Haarlem and later professor of gynecology at the University of Utrecht, was a member of the church.   vDZ.

Kraak-Mennisten, a name given in the 18th century in the Dutch province of Groningen to the conservative Mennonites or "Fijne Mennisten," whereas the progressive Mennonites sometimes were called "Balder Mennisten."   vDZ.

K. Vos, *Het honderdjarig bestaan van de Sociëteit van Doopsgez. Gemeenten in Groningen* (Groningen, 1926) 6.

Kraen (Craen, Kranen), a Mennonite family living in Antwerp, Belgium; from this town Peter Kraen (Kranen), a button maker, had a narrow escape in 1571. His wife was for a while in prison at Antwerp. Peter Kraen moved to Cologne, Germany, where his daughter Sara, b. 1566 at Antwerp, in 1585 married Joost van den Vondel, a hatmaker, also of Antwerp, who had also fled from there to Cologne because of his Mennonite conviction. This Joost van den Vondel and Sara Kranen (Kraen) were the parents of the famous Dutch poet Joost van den Vondel (*q.v.*, b. 1587). In 1596 the van den Vondel family moved to Amsterdam. Sara Kranen died here in 1638; she belonged to the Flemish congregation of Amsterdam. Whether the West-Prussian Mennonite Krahn (*q.v.*) family (Kraan, Kran) is related to the Antwerp Kraen family could not be ascertained. It is not very likely that Huyge Jacob Kraen (*q.v.*), who died as an Anabaptist martyr in 1534 at The Hague, belonged to this family. vDZ.

Krafft, Adam (1493-1553), Hessian reformer, became acquainted with Luther at the Leipzig disputation (1519), became a Lutheran preacher at Erfurt, returned to Fulda in 1521, then worked in Hersfeld, came in contact with Landgrave Philip (*q.v.*), who appointed him court preacher in 1525. As such he accompanied the prince to Speyer, where he preached almost daily during the session of the diet (1526), participated in the Homburg Synod (Oct. 20, 1526), and with Lambert von Avignon he drew up the Homburg liturgy (*Kirchenordnung*), became chief inspector of the church in Hesse (1526-27), and was the spiritual counselor at the Hessian criminal court, where he also had to deal with the Anabaptists. He took a lenient attitude on the Anabaptist question, and observed that "a conversion of the Anabaptists can be expected when the vices of adultery and drunkenness and the like are removed." In 1527 he was appointed professor of theology at Marburg, and continued to work for the promotion of the Lutheran Reformation until his death. (*ML* II, 555.)   NEFF.

Krafft, Hans, a knifesmith of Eismersberg near Augsburg, Germany, and his wife Apollonia were among the first Anabaptists cross-examined by the Augsburg city council. Both declared in October 1527 that they would not "desist from their position" and were then permanently expelled from the city. Hans Krafft, however, returned and was again "put out" on Jan. 13, 1528. In that summer he came back again. In the meantime he had lived for a time in Esslingen a.N., according to a letter from Esslingen dated Jan. 23, 1528. He was again examined in Augsburg in April 1528, when he admitted that he had wanted to settle in Alt-Hegenberg, but had been driven out with other Anabaptists by the Bavarian rulers. He was twice examined in Strasbourg in 1528, once in the presence of Bucer and Capito. He admitted that he had baptized four persons at Mundelsheim near Strasbourg, and declared that he "would stay with Christ" and refused instruction.   E.T.

T. W. Röhrich, "Zur Geschichte der Strassburgischen Wiedertäufer in den Jahren 1527 bis 1543," in *Ztscht für die historische Theologie*, 1860, 36.

Kraggehuis, a Dutch Mennonite recreation center on the lake near Giethoorn (*q.v.*), formerly much used for youth camps.   vDZ.

Krahn (Kran, Kraan, Kraen, Kranen) is a Dutch-Prussian Mennonite name which occurred among the Mennonites of the Lower Rhine (Joost van den Vondel's mother was a Kraen) and is still found among the Dutch Mennonites. In the Danzig Mennonite Church record the name is first mentioned in 1689. Representatives of this family were found in Tiegenhagen, Rosenort, and Heubuden. Franz Crous's study shows that there were only a few Mennonites by this name in Prussia after World War I.

Among the first six families who went from Danzig to the Ukraine in 1787 was a bachelor, Abraham Krahn. Others followed. This name did not occur in the Molotschna settlement. A number of sons and daughters of Cornelius Krahn went to Manitoba during the migration of 1874, and spread to Saskatchewan, North Dakota, Minnesota, Mexico, and Paraguay. Among those remaining in Russia, Georg I. Krahn (*q.v.*) should be mentioned. Cornelius P. Krahn is a minister in Reinland, Man., and Peter B. Krahn, his brother, is a teacher and church worker near Altona, Man. Cornelius Krahn is the editor of *Mennonite Life* and director of the Bethel College Historical Library, North Newton, Kan. (Reimer, *Familiennamen;* see also **Kraen.**) C.K.

Krahn, Isaak Georg, was born Oct. 21, 1882, in Schönhorst, a village in South Russia. He attended the Chortitza Zentralschule and pedagogical courses. After passing the teachers' examinations he went to the Orenburg Mennonite settlement, where, with a few interruptions, he served as a generally respected teacher for 20 years. On June 27, 1911, Krahn was ordained as minister of the Deyevka Mennonite congregation. Equipped with a thorough knowledge of the Bible and the gift of fluent speech, he had good attendance at the services he conducted. The confidence of the congregation is shown by the fact that they chose him as elder by a large majority and ordained him in 1926. With great devotion he performed the duties of this office until 1930, when he was sent into exile for a period of ten years. He did not return home.

Elder Krahn was a very decisive character. In his native village he was loved and respected by the young people as well as the congregation. In his private life he went through many a difficult experience. In her prime his wife was taken by death, leaving him in impoverished circumstances with nine young children. His son Peter was later exiled from the village with his wife, and died of starvation near the home village. His second wife was also sent into banishment. "These are they that have come out of the great tribulation and have washed their garments white in the blood of the Lamb." J.P.P.

P. P. Dyck, *Orenburg am Ural* (Clearbrook, B.C., 1951) 62 f., with portrait.

Kraichgau, formerly a part of the Palatinate, later a part of northern Baden, Germany, a fertile region, devastated in the Thirty Years' War, where many Swiss Mennonite exiles settled in 1652 on estates of the imperial knights. Some of their descendants are still living there, especially in the Sinsheim district. HEGE.

Bossert, *TA* I: *Württemberg,* 682, 818; "Der Kraichgau Adel," in *Ztscht f. Gesch. des Oberrheins* VIII (1857) 391-92; *ML* II, 555.

Kräl, Hans, the head of the collective Hutterian brotherhood in Moravia 1578-83. The chronicles designate him: "who is usually called the Kitzbüchler." The records of his trial indicate that he stemmed from the "Brichsental." He was one of the most active itinerant preachers until the spring of 1557, when he was seized in Taufers (*q.v.*) in the Puster Valley. The *Geschicht-Buch* gives an extremely graphic and detailed description (from his pen) of his capture and of his severe imprisonment, first in the dungeon of the castle tower, where his clothing rotted from his body and he nearly perished in filth and vermin, and then 37 weeks in the Block. He also described in a poem these sufferings as well as his steadfastness proved in "kindly" and in "racked" examinations. His imprisonment lasted 23 months. Since his conversion was apparently out of the question, and since he had furthermore won the admiration of Hans Fünger, who was holding him for the government, by his faithful and brave attitude, Fünger appealed to the emperor to have Kräl sentenced not to death, but to the galleys. Ferdinand granted this request on Jan. 19, 1559, on condition that expenses be paid by Kräl's relatives or the judges. On the transport Kräl escaped, when the guards became intoxicated at an inn at Niederdorf: he went to Moravia, where he was chosen *Diener der Notdurft* in 1560, and *Diener des Evangeliums* in 1561, confirmed the following year (Beck, 24).

In spite of the risks he had undergone in Tirol, Kräl again ventured several times into that area, and was one of the most courageous Hutterite preachers. He was an eyewitness of the execution of Mändl at Innsbruck in 1561. The following year the government learned that he had held meetings, preaching and baptizing in Kitzbühel around Götzens and Schwaz. In 1562 Kräl was again in Moravia, where he was made preacher. He went back to Tirol several times without being caught.

After the death of Peter Walpot the Bruderhof at Neumühl elected him as their leader on Feb. 5, 1578. He held office in the "golden time of the brotherhood" in Moravia. Except for the temporary clouding of his relations with John, Lord of Zierotin, at Ludenburg (*q.v.*) and the temporary closing of the household at Sobotiste as well as the evacuation of Wostitz there was only progress to record, in spite of heavy taxation in the country. In Frischau and Porlitz and (for the third time) in Schäckwitz new Bruderhofs were set up.

On Nov. 9, 1583, Kräl became seriously ill; he summoned the elders once more to his deathbed, admonished them to hold fast to the brotherhood and to be faithful in performing their duty. He also charged them especially with the care of widows and orphans. At the age of about 63 he died at Neumühl, Nov. 14, 1583. The *Väterlied* characterizes him thus: "Constantly kind, of peaceful bearing, meek, also inclined to gentleness, well preserved in stocks and chains, in which he lay a long time, a man with whom good counsel could always be found, gifted with modesty." His particular merit lies in his continuation of the chronicle begun and carried to 1542 by Kaspar Braitmichel (*q.v.*), the *Geschicht-Buch,* which he undertook with Haupprecht Zapff.   P.DE.

The epistle written by Kräl to Melchior Platzer was published in the *Familien-Kalender* (Scottdale, 1928) 20-26; R. Friedmann, "Die Briefe der österreichischen Täufer," in *ARG* XXVI (1929); XXVIII (1931); Beck, *Geschichts-Bücher*; J. Loserth, *Der Anabaptismus in Tirol* (Vienna, 1892); R. v. Lilienkron, *Zur Liederdichtung der Wiedertäufer* (Munich, 1875) 158-66; Th. Unger, "Ueber eine Wiedertäuferhandschrift des XVII. Jahrhunderts," in *Jahrbuch der Gesellschaft f. d. Gesch. d. Prot. in Oesterreich* XVIII (Vienna, 1897); Loesche, *Tirolensia; ML* II, 555 f.

Krall Mennonite Church (MC), the second oldest meetinghouse in the Lancaster Conference still in use, is located in Lebanon Co., Pa., near Buffalo Springs. When Lebanon Township was a part of Lancaster County the Mennonites settled in this area, but later were largely absorbed by the Church of the Brethren. Within the last 15 years in particular, due to the high prices of land in Lancaster County, part of the overflow is going to Krall. The membership (1954) is 84. Simon G. Bucher is bishop, Martin E. Weaver and Sidney B. Gingrich ministers, and Norman G. Shue deacon.   I.D.L.

Kralltown Mennonite Mission (MC), located in York Co., Pa., was built in 1888 as a union house. The membership, never numerous, had all passed away or moved out, and all services were discontinued. The East Petersburg congregation, following a summer Bible school in 1950, reopened the church. James B. Siegrist has located here as minister. Although no membership is claimed here as yet, the average Sunday-school attendance is 48 and the summer Bible school averages 179.   I.D.L.

Kramer, a Mennonite family of Hamburg, Germany, now extinct. They were a wealthy mercantile family, probably originally from Holland. Lourens Kramer (d. 1714), married to Adriana de Vos(z), and his brother Lucas Kramer (d. 1719), married to Sara de Vos(z), were important Greenland whalers. Lucas Kramer and Elisabeth and Susanna Kramer supported the building of a new meetinghouse at Altona in 1796. Pieter Kramer (d. 1796), three times a deacon of the church, bequeathed it 1,000 Marks.   vDZ.

B. C. Roosen, *Geschichte der Menn.-Gemeinde Hamburg-Altona* II (Hamburg, 1887) 6, 82, 84.

Kramer (Krämer, Kremer), **Peter,** an Anabaptist martyr, "a servant (minister) of the church and a deacon in Jülich-Berg," Germany, who was seized in 1558 with Gotthard (*q.v.*) of Nonnenberg, and, when all attempts to convert them proved futile, beheaded at Windeck castle. Their brave death made a deep impression. "The common people were amazed, and said: 'What a marvelous thing behold we here! These men so willingly to go to death, when they could easily obtain their liberty.' . . . The executioner said with fear and trepidation that he would never execute such men again." A song of 15 stanzas was written about their death, No. 21 in the *Ausbund*: "Merkt auf, ihr Völker überall" (Wolkan, *Lieder*, 101, 136). John Horsch (*Kurzgefasste Geschichte*, 130) says: "Kramer, Hein-

rich, Three epistles to the brethren imprisoned with him, 1558." This is obviously Peter Kramer. NEFF.

Mart. Mir. D 207, E 590; Wolkan, *Lieder*, 101, 136; John Horsch, *Kurzgefasste Geschichte der Mennoniten-Gemeinden* (Elkhart, 1890); *ML* II, 556.

Kranewetter, Peter (Pieter Kraneweter), a Hutterite martyr, was executed in 1536 with Christian Alseider (*q.v.*) and four companions at Gufidaun (*q.v.*), Austria. In prison they wrote two epistles: one to Jakob Hutter and the brotherhood in Moravia, and the other to the brotherhood in the Adige.   NEFF.

Wolkan, *Geschicht-Buch*, 75; Beck, *Geschichts-Bücher*, 108 f.; Zieglschmid, *Chronik*, 104; *Mart. Mir.* D 38, E 444; *ML* II, 556.

Kratz, Clayton (1896-1920), a Mennonite relief worker who gave his life in the service of the Mennonite Central Committee in the relief program for the Mennonites of South Russia following World War I. He was born Nov. 5, 1896, at Blooming Glen, Pa., he was an outstanding student of Goshen College, and was president-elect of the student religious organization (Y.P.C.A.) when he accepted appointment of the first relief team, with Orie O. Miller, Arthur W. Slagel, which was sent out by the newly organized MCC (*q.v.*). After arrival at Constantinople Sept. 27, 1920, Miller and Kratz pressed on to the Molotschna settlement in the Ukraine, which was at that time under General Wrangel and the White (anti-communist) Army. After an inspection tour Kratz was left at Halbstadt to set up a headquarters while Miller returned to Sevastopol to arrange for the transport of the supplies which Slagel was to bring from Constantinople. Before the relief program could get started the Red Army overran the Ukraine, forcing Wrangel into precipitous retreat into the Crimea. The Russian Mennonites urged Kratz to flee, but he chose to stay as long as possible, believing that American relief workers as neutrals would be safe. He planned to leave the day before the White Army withdrew from Halbstadt but was trapped by an overnight advance of the Reds, who at first arrested him and then released him upon the pleas of the Mennonite leaders. Two weeks later he was again arrested, having been last seen in Fürstenwerder.

G. A. Peters, who gives the only firsthand account of Kratz's disappearance (*Die Hungersnot*, 11-16), reports that his endeavors to discover what had happened produced only the information that the Red Commander for Halbstadt had sent him by way of Bachmut to Kharkov, from where he would probably be sent to Moscow and home to the United States by way of Sweden. Peters believes that in view of the manner of his arrest and the attitude of the officials, Kratz was not executed but probably died of some disease before being released.

Endeavors of the following year by A. J. Miller, then director of the MCC relief program in Russia, to determine what happened to Kratz, which included inquiries in Kharkov and Moscow (Foreign Office), were completely fruitless. He deposited a memorandum on Oct. 10, 1921, on the case, with Foreign Minister Litvinov, and later a similar memorandum with Minister Rakovsky in Kharkov, but neither brought any results. Miller investigated the case thoroughly locally and speculates that the arrest may have been instigated by the highest volost official, Bagon, a Lett who had previously worked in a Halbstadt printing plant. At this time of disorganization it was impossible for the central government officials to properly control the local underlings, many of whom were of a hoodlum type and were a disgrace to the party they pretended to represent, and it is quite possible that the arrest was a purely local blood-lust matter. It is known that Kratz was struck brutally on the occasion of his final arrest.   H.S.B.

In Memoriam, Clayton H. Kratz (n.p., ca. 1945) a 4-page leaflet; P. C. Hiebert, *Feeding the Hungry* (Scottdale, 1929); G. A. Peters, *Die Hungersnot in den mennonitischen Kolonien in Süd-Russland* (Scottdale, 1923); *ML* II, 556.

Kratz, Maxwell H. (1875-1939), was born at Frederick, Pa., on Nov. 17, 1875. His early years were spent there and in Philadelphia, Pa. He studied at Sumneytown Academy, Perkiomen Seminary, and at Princeton University, where he was graduated in 1899 with honors. Later he served as Vice Principal of Perkiomen Seminary. From 1905 to 1908 he attended the University of Pennsylvania Law School, was admitted to the bar, and practiced law until his death. In the last ten years of his life he conducted his own private law course, and it is estimated that about half of the 5,000 law candidates in Pennsylvania attended his school. He was a deep thinker and he served more as an adviser and interpreter of the law than as a practitioner. His emphasis was always on the essentials of the law and the righteousness of the law. To him law was a sense of divine justice. He was a legal theologian. He was baptized in the Schwenksville Mennonite Church (GCM) and became an active member in the Second Mennonite Church, Philadelphia. He was a fervent speaker and promoter of the work of the church. Throughout the Mennonite church he will be best remembered as one of the three men elected to the first Mennonite Central Committee on Sept. 27, 1920. He was active in the leadership of the MCC during its first projects of Russian relief, the purchase of land in Paraguay, and its incorporation. He was also one of the pioneers of laymen's work in the Mennonite church (GCM), being one of the founders of the Brotherhood in the Eastern District Conference in the early 20's. He died Nov. 19, 1939.   J.H.F.

Obituary in G.C.M. *Yearbook* for 1941, p. 31; J. D. Unruh, *In the Name of Christ* (Scottdale, 1952).

Kratzer, a Mennonite family, originally found at Aeschi in the Bernese Oberland, Switzerland. In 1711 members of this family emigrated to the Netherlands because of persecution and settled near the town of Groningen. Anthony Kratzer (Krätzer, Kratser), who was born in Switzerland, was an elder of the Nieuwe Zwitsers (*q.v.*) congregation near Groningen 1740-79. Others served as deacons both in the Nieuwe and Oude Zwitsers church.   vᴅZ.

Delbert L. Gratz, *Bernese Anabaptists* (Scottdale, 1953) 49; J. Huizinga, *Stamboek van Fiepke Foppes* (Groningen, 1887) *passim*, see Index.

Krauel, a former colony of Russian Mennonites located in the district of Alto Krauel, Santa Catarina, Brazil, was founded in 1930, dissolved in 1952 after a gradual disintegration. The colony was more commonly known as Witmarsum, after the name of the central village. The name Krauel is derived from a small river which flows into the Itajahy some distance above Blumenau. Alto Krauel is a deep valley lying about 40 miles from the railhead at Hansa Hammonica, about 12 miles long and 1½ to 4 miles wide. The sides of the valley rise to a maximum of 2,300 ft. above sea level, the ridges of the low mountains being 500-1,000 feet above the valley floor. However, the valley floor itself is not flat but rolling, and covered with thick forest. Hence, although the climate is good and rainfall plentiful, agriculture is not very profitable because of the cost of clearing the land, the distance from the markets, and the medium quality of the soil. It takes 6-8 years to make the land cultivable with horse-drawn implements. The chief crops are corn, aipim (a starch-bearing tuber which must be converted to starch for profitable sale), and sweet potatoes. Attempts at dairying and logging were not too successful. After a few years beginning in 1934, families began to leave because of the poor economic prospects, cultural isolation, and internal social and ecclesiastical weakness of the colony. By 1952, practically all had left, and the history of the colony came to an end. The earlier emigration had been to Curitiba (*q.v.*). At the end about 70 families, chiefly M.B., left to found a new colony at Bage (*q.v.*) north of Curitiba city.

The reason for the now clearly mistaken location of the Krauel colony is to be sought in the difficult situation in which the refugees from Russia found themselves in the camps in Germany November 1929-January 1930. The German government had generously granted temporary asylum in Germany but was pressing for early resettlement. Since Canada at that time had very strict health requirements for immigrants and barred completely those who had had trachoma, and the United States was even stricter, these two destinations were impossible. The arrangements for Paraguay which the MCC was making were not yet complete in January 1930, and in any case Paraguay was not attractive because of its poverty and isolation. The Hanseatic Colonization Co. of Hamburg, a close ally of the German government in colonization matters, owned land in Santa Catarina which it was willing to sell on credit, but the only tract available for sale in a compact area such as the Mennonites sought was the Krauel tract, hence the choice. The Krauel tract was not large enough to accommodate the entire group which wanted to go to Brazil; so the remainder, some 130 families with 500 souls, was settled on a small high plateau (2,300 ft. above sea level) some 20 miles from the Krauel, an almost criminally impossible location, which was soon abandoned.

The original Krauel settlement consisted of 152 families ranged along both sides of the river, each family owning and living on 40 to 100 acres of land with a frontage of 700 feet on the river. For administrative purposes the colony was divided into three villages (civil districts: Witmarsum with 70 families, Waldheim with 46, and Gnadental with 36). Each village had a Schulze and a school. An Oberschulze was the colony leader. The colony had no civil autonomy; this organization handled only internal social, educational, and economic matters. The "town" of Witmarsum was in effect the capital of the colony. David Nikkel was the long-time Oberschulze.

The Krauel colony had two Mennonite churches, M.B. with 200 baptized members in 1934, and the Mennonite Church with 65 members. Church meetings were held in the schoolhouses, until in the last years (1950) a commodious meetinghouse was built by the Mennonite Church in Witmarsum.

In 1934 the settlement was relatively complete and at the high point in population—159 families, mostly from Siberia, with 846 souls, distributed as follows among the three "villages": Witmarsum 341, Waldheim 290, Gnadental 202. (For further information see the article **Brazil**.) (*ML* II, 556-58.)   H.S.B.

Kraut, Heinz, an Anabaptist martyr, a tailor of Esperstedt near Frankenhausen in Thuringia, Germany, was baptized by Alexander, the Anabaptist leader of Thuringia, whose position he fell heir to when Alexander was put to death. In 1530 he was seized, purchased his freedom by recanting, but immediately joined them again, becoming a very successful "apostle." He traveled as far as Moravia to visit the believers (Jacobs, 440). On Nov. 20, 1535, he was captured in the home of Hans Peisker, a miller. Peisker, Kraut, and Jobst Möller (*q.v.*) were given several hearings before Cruciger (*q.v.*) and Melanchthon (*q.v.*), and were beheaded at Jena on Jan. 26, 1536. (See **Möller, Jobst**, for extended account.)   NEFF.

Wappler, *Thüringen;* E. Jacobs, "Die Wiedertäufer am Harz," in *Ztscht des Harzvereins* XXXII (1899) 445 f.; *ML* II, 558.

Krautschlögel, Jörg, an Anabaptist martyr of Austria, was put to death at the stake with his wife at Melk, a town near St. Pölten in Lower Austria in 1527 (Loserth, 151). From the cross-examinations it is known that he was a toll collector at the Danube bridge in Vienna. He was one of the first Anabaptist preachers in Austria. He lived later in Melk and was very zealous for the spread of the movement in that region. In 1526 he won Leonhard Lochmaier (*q.v.*), who had been a Catholic priest for eight years, to his faith.   HEGE.

A. Nicoladoni, *Johannes Bünderlin von Linz* (Berlin, 1893); Loserth, *Anabaptismus; ML* II, 558.

Kraybill Mennonite Church (MC), located in the fertile Donegal Valley, Lancaster Co., Pa., first met in the homes of members and Kraybill's Mill. In 1810 Jacob Kraybill donated the ground for a building and cemetery. The third church is now on the site. In 1908 a church was built in Mt. Joy and gradually the congregation was moving that way, until by 1949 the building was turned over to the Kraybill Christian School Board for a school (ten grades). Ministers who served here are Jacob Hershey, the two Peter Nissleys, and Kraybills. The cemetery is still used by the congregation. I.D.L.

Krebs (Kreps), a Swiss Mennonite family, originally from Reutigen in the Bernese Oberland, a number of whom moved to the Netherlands because of the harsh measures of the Bern government against the Mennonites. Some of them settled near Kampen, others near Groningen. In the Netherlands as in Switzerland they were engaged in farming. Peter Krebes (Pieter Kreps) (d. 1741) was a deacon of the Oude Zwitsers (*q.v.*) near Groningen. Hans Krebs, a deacon of the Swiss Mennonite congregation of Kampen, promoted the merging (1822) with the local Mennonite congregation in this town.   vDZ.

Delbert L. Gratz, *Bernese Anabaptists* (Scottdale, 1953) 49, 65; J. Huizinga, *Stamboek van Derk Pieters* . . . (Groningen, 1883) see Index.

Krechting, Bernd (Bernhard), a brother of Hinrich Krechting (*q.v.*), was a Catholic priest and educator at the court of the Count of Bentheim, Westphalia, Germany, and later a priest at Gildehaus. Here he began to preach Anabaptist views and consequently had to leave. He proceeded to Münster in 1534 and began to take an active part in the establishment of the Anabaptist kingdom, functioning as a minister and member of the council of Jan van Leiden. When the city was conquered by the bishop's troops he was tried, cruelly tortured, and put to death on Jan. 22, 1536, together with Jan van Leyden and Bernhard Knipperdolling.   C.K.

Gerhard de Buhr, "Der Wiedertäufer Hinrich Krechting und seine Sippe" (ms in BeCL); C. A. Cornelius, *Berichte der Augenzeugen über das Münsterische Wiedertäuferreich* (Münster, 1853) 375 ff., 405 ff.

Krechting, Hinrich (1501-80), a leader in the Münsterite "kingdom," born at Schöppingen, Westphalia, Germany, and later a priest at Gildehaus. (*q.v.*). In 1533 Krechting was appointed administrator of the territory of Sandwelle near Ahaus by the Bishop of Münster. In this capacity he received an order to arrest Arnd Belholt, who was a supporter of Bernhard Rothmann at Münster. When Jan van Leyden came to Schöppingen in 1533 he stayed in Krechting's home. Krechting resigned from his office because he refused to comply with the bishop's orders to execute Johann van der Wiek, a Lutheran minister. Summoned by the Bishop, he fled to Münster, arriving there on Feb. 15, 1534. His brother Bernd Krechting (*q.v.*) was already there. Both became outstanding leaders in the religious and political development of the city. Hinrich became the chancellor of the Münsterite kingdom and the supreme chancellor of "King" Jan van Leyden. The other relatives and friends he had brought with him from Schöppingen also received special positions.

When the decisive battle between the forces of Jan van Leyden and the Bishop took place, Hinrich Krechting received the opportunity through Johann von Raesfeld, an acquaintance of his, to escape with a small remnant. For a while he remained at Lingen, Westphalia, then fled to Oldenburg, where he continued to promote the cause of the Anabaptists as a follower of David Joris. In May 1538 he took part (opposite side) in the debate with David Joris in Oldenburg, emphasizing the significance of the Bible against Joris's visionary views. Because of the insecurity of his position Krechting left Oldenburg after 1538 and settled in Gödens, Friesland, on the land of the Count Hero von Oldersum. Under the influence of John á Lasco he became Reformed, and in 1545 became the *Vorsteher* of the Reformed

Church at Dykhausen, where he died June 28, 1580. He was probably the only leader who survived the Münster catastrophe. The Münsterites were sometimes called the "Crechtingsvolk" after the Krechting brothers. C.K.

Gerhard de Buhr, "Der Wiedertäufer Hinrich Krechting und seine Sippe" (ms in BeCL); C. A. Cornelius, *Bericht der Augenzeugen über das Münsterische Wiedertäuferreich* (Münster, 1853) 379 ff., 405 ff.; Mellink, *Wederdopers,* see Index; *ML* II, 558.

Krefeld: see **Crefeld.**

Krehbiel (Krehbill, Krebell, Kraybill, Krayenbuhl, Crayenbühl, Craybill, Grabill, Graybill), a name of frequent occurrence among the Mennonites of Germany and America, originally Krayenbühl. The family stems from the parish of Grosshöchstetten at a place near Signau, in the canton of Bern, Switzerland (*Gem.-Kal.,* 1905, 143).

The first member of this family known to have been an Anabaptist was one Hans Krähenbühl from Signau who attended the Anabaptist disputation in the city of Bern in March 1538. In a list of Anabaptists living in the vicinity of Langnau, canton of Bern, in 1621, one Anna Krayenbühl is mentioned. The following members of the Krähenbühl family were brought before the Bernese authorities in the 17th century because of their Anabaptist beliefs: Barbara 1645, Peter 1655, and Margredt 1678.

The Krehbiel family has figured in practically all of the migrations in which Bernese Anabaptists have taken part. The first of which we have record who left Bernese territory was Jost Krähenbühl, who with others went to the Palatinate, Germany, in 1671. In 1709 he purchased the Pfrimmerhof near Sippersfeld in the Palatinate. In 1682 Peter Krehbiel settled on the Weierhof near Bolanden. In 1770 a member of this family migrated to Galicia (*q.v.*) and 15 years later to Russia. This family as well as a number of members from the families in the Palatinate migrated to America in the 19th century. They first settled in New York and Ohio but are now located mostly in Iowa and Kansas. The family name is still well known among Mennonites in the Palatinate today.

The family was found in Ste.-Suzanne, Montbéliard, and Allenjoie in the Princely County of Montbéliard as early as 1719. Most found their way to America in the following century.

In Germany the following Krehbiels were of note. Adam Krehbiel (*q.v.*, 1766-1804) was a preacher in the Weierhof congregation (*q.v.*), who influenced and was influenced by Tersteegen. Jakob Krehbiel (1835-1918) was a deacon and an active leader in the Sembach congregation (*q.v.*). J. J. Krehbiel (1841-95) was a farmer at Weierhof and a leader in the church, who helped to found the South German Conference.

In 1851 a descendant of Jost, John Krehbiel, migrated to America; he was the father of Christian (*q.v.*), who was in turn the father of Henry P. (*q.v.*) and Christian E. (*q.v.*), the latter being the father of Olin Krehbiel. All of these men were prominent leaders in the General Conference Mennonite Church, Christian E. and Olin being presidents of the conference. In 1770 a grandson of Jost emigrated

to Galicia, and 15 years later to Russia, and his descendants went on to Marion and McPherson counties in Kansas 1874 ff.

Jacob Krehbiel (1781-1860), Pfrimmerhof, a descendant of Jost and minister of the Weierhof congregation, emigrated to Clarence, N.Y., near Buffalo in 1831, where he became a bishop (1839) in the Ontario Mennonite (MC) Conference. He prepared an account of the Krehbiel family (extended to 1880 by J. C. Krehbiel), which was translated and reprinted in W. J. Krehbiel's *One Branch of the Krehbiel Family* (McPherson, 1950). He was somewhat of a historian and wrote a pamphlet which was published at Speyer, Germany, under the title *Letter from America and a Report About Conditions There* (1832). His valuable manuscript, "A Few Words About the Mennonites in America in 1841," was published in the *MQR* VI (1932) 43-57, 110-21. J. C. Krehbiel (1811-86) moved to Lee County, Iowa, in 1839 and became a prominent minister in the G.C. Mennonite Church, being one of the original promoters of the organization of the conference in 1859-60. His son J. J. Krehbiel (1838-1921) of Newton, Kan., was a prominent layman (GCM) and for 20 years president of the Bethel College board of trustees. Another scion of Jost Krehbiel, also of Lee County, Iowa, was Henry J. (*q.v.*, 1865-1940), a prominent G.C.M. minister and president of the conference. Daniel Krehbiel (1812-88, *q.v.*) of West Point, Iowa, and Cleveland, Ohio, was a prominent worker in the General Conference Mennonite Church. A Krehbiel family from Alsace settled in Allen Co., Ind., in the mid-19th century, where they changed their name to Grabill. The town of Grabill north of Ft. Wayne was named after a member of this family.

For the branch of the family that settled in Lancaster Co., Pa., and became prominent in the Mennonite Church (MC), see **Grabill.** D.L.G.

J. J. Krehbiel, *Jost Krehbiel auf dem Pfrimmerhof* (Moundridge, Kan., 1903) a genealogical chart; D. L. Gratz, *Bernese Anabaptists* (Scottdale, 1953) 190; *ML* II, 565.

Krehbiel, Adam (1766-1804), a Mennonite farmer-preacher at the Weierhof, Palatinate, Germany. He was a personal friend of Gerhard Tersteegen (*q.v.*), exchanged letters with him and visited him at Mülheim. Tersteegen called him "a man after God's own heart." One of his letters was printed in Tersteegen's *Weg zur Wahrheit* (Cologne, 1865, 12-14). In this letter of Aug. 30, 1766, Adam Krehbiel expresses his gratitude for Tersteegen's writings, for now he sees that "rest is to be found . . . in self-denial, love, dying, and conquering in God's will and favor." He asks for Tersteegen's prayers, that he may be completely turned away from everything material and be led into sweet fellowship with God (*Menn. Bl.,* 1875, 42).

Krehbiel's childlike faith and sincere piety are clearly shown in his correspondence with P. Weber (*q.v.*) of Hardenburg, whom he thanks (1771) for the stimulation and encouragement he had received from the books, *Lebensbeschreibung heiliger Seelen* and Swedenborg's *Offenbarung von der gemeinschaftlichen Liebe und deren herrlichen Früchten.* On March 25, 1773, he sent him a note to be forwarded to Johannes Deknatel (*q.v.*). The last years of his life were saddened by the distress of war. The French used his beloved chapel as a barracks, and meetings had to be held in his modest living room. The weaknesses of age gradually prevented him from performing the duties of his office. He died in 1804. (*ML* II, 565.)   NEFF.

Krehbiel, Christian (1832-1909), the son of John and Katharine (Krehbiel) Krehbiel, was born Oct. 18, 1832, at Weierhof, Germany. He was the third child in a family of twelve children of which six boys and four girls grew to maturity. His ancestry traces back to Switzerland. About 1671 Jost Krähenbühl, under the pressure of persecution, left that country and settled in South Germany. Christian attended school in the Palatinate for five years and then three more years in Bavaria, his family having moved to Kleinschwabhausen, Bavaria, in 1844. He continued to receive religious instruction until the age of 17 as required by law, but was baptized at the age of 15.

When Christian's older brother Jacob was drafted into the army, the parents were anxious to shield their sons from military service. So they sold their farm at a great loss, paid 1,000 guilders for Jacob's release, and made preparation to go to America. In 1851, after some difficulty in getting the necessary papers, the family sailed for America, taking 35 days for the ocean voyage. They landed at New York, then continued to Buffalo, Cleveland, and Ashland, Ohio. That fall Christian with another young man took a river boat down the Ohio and up the Mississippi to St. Louis and Iowa to prepare the way for a group of families to come west in the spring. Christian was a strong young man and well able to do hard pioneer work such as cutting trees and helping build a log house and barn on the 100 acres of land which his parents bought for $800. He also became an expert at butchering and an amateur veterinarian.

On March 14, 1858, he married Susanna A. Ruth, the daughter of David Ruth, and to them were born 16 children. Nine sons and three daughters grew to adulthood. Two sons were listed in *Who's Who*. Three sons became ministers. For two years he lived with his father-in-law. During this time he was afflicted with an eye trouble and it was feared he would become permanently blind. In 1860 he moved to Summerfield, Ill., which at that time offered better farm advantages. In 1864 by election and lot he became a minister and soon after was made elder of the Summerfield Mennonite Church. In addition to the local church work he had much to do with conference. He promoted the starting of the Western District Conference (now Middle District) in 1868, and then later in 1877 helped organize the Kansas Conference (now Western District). At the sixth General Conference he was asked to be one of three traveling ministers for the Conference. He took an interest in the Wadsworth School development and delivered one of the dedicatory sermons at the opening of this school. Through his guidance, S. S. Haury, a member of his congregation preparing for mission work, was led to offer himself to the conference. This led to the creation of the Foreign Mission Board in 1872 with Krehbiel elected as president, which position he held for 24 years.

Along about 1869 he advocated the idea of colonization farther west and this brought him in contact with the Russian Mennonites who came in 1873 to look for land. He played an important part in assisting that large body of Mennonites to make the shift from the steppes of Russia to the plains of Kansas. In order to help the settlers the Mennonite Board of Guardians was formed with Christian Krehbiel, president; David Goertz, secretary, and John F. Funk, treasurer.

In 1879 he moved his family to Halstead, Kan., where four years before an offspring church of the Summerfield congregation had been organized.

In connection with the foreign mission work among the American Indians, Krehbiel conducted an Indian Industrial School on his farm in Kansas 1887-96. When this had to be discontinued, he initiated an Orphan and Children's Aid Society (*q.v.*) and operated its orphanage in his home 1896 —?. He promoted the plan of a school for Kansas and this developed into the Halstead Seminary which was later moved to Newton and became Bethel College. He was instrumental in organizing the Mennonite Charité which aided Dr. Arthur E. Hertzler (the *Horse and Buggy Doctor*) to build his hospital. Besides farming, he was interested in other business enterprises, helping his sons get started in the flour milling and in the book and publishing business.

He served as pastor of the Summerfield and Halstead congregations for 45 years without a salary. When on his 70th birthday the church took a love offering of $400.00 for him, he turned it over to missions. He died April 30, 1909, and is buried at Halstead.   O.A.K.

"Autobiography of Christian Krehbiel" (manuscript translated by Edward Krehbiel and Mrs. Elva K. Leisy); Margaret Krehbiel Goerz, "Christian Krehbiel" (in manuscript form); H. P. Krehbiel, *History of the General Conference of the Mennonites of North America* I (n.p., 1898) 428-35; Ed. G. Kaufman, *The Development of Missionary and Philanthropic Interest Among the Mennonites of North America* (Berne, 1931); C. Krahn, ed. *From the Steppes to the Prairies* (Newton, 1949); M. Gingerich, *The Mennonites in Iowa* (Iowa City, 1939); *ML* II, 565 f.

Krehbiel, Christian Emmanuel (1869-1948), b. Sept. 25, 1869, at Summerfield, Ill., was the seventh of the 16 children of Christian and Susanna Ruth Krehbiel, who came from the Palatinate, Germany. C. E. Krehbiel received his training at the Mennonite Preparatory School at Halstead, Kan., and the Kansas State Normal at Emporia. After teaching a year he entered Presbyterian Theological Seminary at Bloomfield, N.J. He attended the University of Berlin, Germany, 1899-1901. He married Mary A. Wirkler of Newton, Kan., on July 27, 1902, and two children, Olin and Florence, were born to them.

In 1901-20 Krehbiel was secretary of the Western Book and Publishing Company (later the Herald Book and Publishing Company) and did editorial work for several German periodicals. He started and edited *The Sower*, the young people's section of the *Mennonite*. He also served as the secretary of the Mennonite Charité 1908-31, and superintendent of the Leisy Orphan Aid Society 1901-48.

About 1921 Krehbiel retired from business to devote the rest of his life to Christian work. He served as field secretary for the General Conference Mennonite Church 1921-30. In 1922-23 he was in Russia in relief work for the MCC. He was ordained as minister on Dec. 2, 1923, and held many offices, both in the Western District Conference and the General Conference. He was General Conference statistician in 1923-38, chairman of the Board of Publication 1923-26, secretary of the General Conference 1926-38, president of the General Conference 1938-45, member of the Mennonite Biblical Seminary Board 1941-47, of the Home Mission Board 1945-47, and editor of the *Christlicher Bundesbote* (*q.v.*) 1930-46.

Krehbiel was a member of the Bethel College Mennonite Church at North Newton, Kan., where he served as deacon for many years. He organized the Lorraine Avenue Mennonite Church of Wichita, Kan., and was its pastor in 1931-35. He served as supply pastor of the Eden Mennonite Church, Moundridge, Kan., while their pastor was doing relief work in Europe.

Krehbiel wrote the following: *Historical Sketch, First Mennonite Church, Halstead, Kansas* (Newton, 1925); the chapter on clothing in the book *Feeding the Hungry* (Scottdale, 1929); numerous articles, short stories, and some poems.

Following several heart attacks, he died on June 9, 1948, at Newton, and was buried in the Halstead cemetery. O.A.K.

Krehbiel, Daniel (1812-88), the son of Jakob and Elizabeth Kapp Krehbiel, was born at Weierhof, Germany, April 22, 1812. He received the usual education of that day and took up the saddler trade. In 1832, because of his convictions that a Christian should have no part in military service as required in Germany, he came to America.

At first he located in western New York where he had relatives and worked at his trade. He started in business for himself near Buffalo in 1836. He was married to Mary Leisy of Cleveland, Ohio, July 18, 1841, and five years later they moved to that city. Although Krehbiel's business prospered he missed the blessings of a Mennonite church, and after an unsuccessful attempt to gather the scattered Mennonites of the city together into a church, he moved to West Point, Iowa, in 1856, where some of his brothers from Germany had recently settled.

Daniel united with the Mennonite church at West Point. Nine miles away was the Zion Mennonite Church where his brother Jacob was pastor. Observing that these congregations had little in common, he was concerned that isolated and scattered Mennonites be brought together. At his suggestion the two congregations met in 1859; he expressed his ideas on union to do mission work and so a call was issued for a general conference in 1860.

In 1862 he returned to Cleveland, but he continued active in the new organization which he had founded. The Conference placed him on the building committee and in 1872 elected him as treasurer

of the mission board, which office he held until 1881. He died at his home in Cleveland, on Jan. 4, 1888. O.A.K.

M. Gingerich, *The Mennonites in Iowa* (Iowa City, 1939); H. P. Krehbiel, *History of the General Conference of Mennonites of North America* I (n.p., 1898) 401-6; *ML* II, 566.

Krehbiel, David (1849-1908), a teacher in the Realschule at Weierhof, Palatinate, Germany, b. May 17, 1849, at Ramsen, d. July 7, 1908. He attended the Gymnasium at Basel and the normal school at Schiers in Switzerland, and then the universities at Neuchâtel and Basel, accepted a position at the Realschule at Weierhof in 1873, which he resigned in 1900 because of ill health. He won enduring merit by his long service as bookkeeper of the Mennonite school association, by his warm advocacy of the principles of the Mennonite brotherhood, and by his well-written articles in *Mennonitische Blätter* and clever stories in *Pilgerleben* and *Christlicher Gemeindekalender*. His deeply felt religious verses, one of which, "Ja, liebster Jesu, Dein sind wir," is found in the South German Mennonite hymnal, were collected and published by his son under the title *Religiöse Gedichte*. (*ML* II, 566.) NEFF.

Krehbiel, Henry J. (1865-1940), a leading minister of the General Conference Mennonite Church, was born at Franklin, Iowa, Sept. 8, 1865, the son of Jacob and Katherine Ruth Krehbiel. His father served many years as pastor of the Summerfield, Ill., Mennonite Church. Henry was baptized in 1880. His education included attendance at McKendry College at Lebanon, Ill., and graduation from the Evangelical Theological Semiary (now Eden Theological Seminary) at St. Louis, Mo. He served two pastorates—Trenton, Ohio, 1892-1907, and Reedley, Cal., 1908-38. He served as president of the conference 1920-26, on the Board of Publication for 42 years, part of the time as president, and as the only American delegate to the first Mennonite World Conference of 1925 at Basel, Switzerland. *A Trip Through Europe, A Plea for the Abolition of War, and A Report of the 400th Anniversary of the Denomination* (Newton, 1926) was the fruit of the European trip. He was active in the founding and promotion of Bluffton College and received the honorary D.D. from it in 1930. He was married to Lydia Ruth in 1893; they had four sons and one daughter. He died on Oct. 5, 1940, and is buried at Reedley. W.H.KR.

Krehbiel, Henry Peter (1862-1940), was born at Summerfield, Ill., on April 13, 1862, the third child of Christian and Susanna Amalie Ruth Krehbiel. He had three living sisters and eight brothers, of whom three preceded him in death. His parents immigrated from the Palatinate. On Nov. 21, 1887, he was married to Matilda Emelia Kruse of Halstead, Kan. To this union two children were born, Elva Agnes (Leisy) of Dallas, Tex., and Ariel Kruse, deceased in infancy. In 1878 he and his brother J. W. Krehbiel went to Kansas to break prairie for the coming of the Christian Krehbiel family to Kansas. In 1881 Henry attended Emporia Normal at Emporia, Kan., then taught the Quaker School in Harvey

County for one year, after which he attended Kansas University for a year. For five years he was manager of a hardware store in Halstead. Then in 1892, feeling called to the ministry, he took his family to Oberlin, Ohio, and in 1897 received the B.D. degree from the Oberlin Theological Seminary.

During the years at Oberlin he was supply pastor for the Mennonite churches in Sterling and Wadsworth, Ohio. In 1897-1900 he was pastor of the First Mennonite Church at Canton, Ohio, continuing to serve the church at Sterling. While here he also founded and edited a Mennonite paper, *The Review* (*q.v.*). He also was active in promoting Bluffton College, at Bluffton, Ohio. In October 1900 the family returned to Newton, where he took over the management of the bookstore later known as The Herald Book and Publishing Co. He also published and edited the German Mennonite newspaper *Post und Volksblatt,* later named *Der Herold.* In 1923 he established *The Mennonite Weekly Review.*

In 1905 he began his regular trips to Burrton, Kan., where he organized a church at the request of the Home Mission Board of the Western District Conference. Later he was ordained as elder of the church. In 1912 he started a mission church in Hutchinson, Kan.

Krehbiel held many offices and committee posts in various conferences. He was secretary of the Home Mission Board of the General Conference, 1914-23; member of the Mennonite Immigration Bureau which he helped organize in 1906; member of the special committee on merger of Bethel College with the Western District Conference, 1916; member of the Committee on Exemptions for both the Western District and General Conferences, 1917; member of Committee on War Exemptions for All Mennonites, 1918. In 1917 he was elected Conference representative for Bethel College. He organized the Mennonite Settlers' Aid Society in 1918. From 1908- he was statistician for the General Conference, and from 1913 the American representative for the *Mennonitisches Lexikon.*

Among his publications are numerous pamphlets. *War Being Inconsistent with the Teachings and Spirit of Christ* won first prize in a Quaker contest in 1895. Others were: "How Can Mennonite Doctrines Receive More Recognition," *Bundesbote,* 1895; "Mennonite Settlements in Kansas," *Mennonite Yearbook,* 1896; "Our Position Toward Secret Societies," Conference paper, 1896 (Mennonite Book Concern, 1898); "History of Education Among the Mennonites" (Herald Publishing Co., 1925), a paper read at the Bethel College Bible Course; "What Is a Pacifist?" (Herald Publishing Co., 1931), a paper read at the Quaker-Mennonite-Brethren Conference at Mount Morris, Ill.

He further wrote: *History of the Mennonite General Conference,* Vol. I, 1898 and Vol. II, 1938 (Vol. III of the history was projected but not completed); *War, Peace, Amity,* 1937.

His activities were varied. In 1896 he invented an endless sickle; in 1900 a newspaper file for libraries. In 1909 he was a member of the Kansas Legislature as representative from Harvey County. In 1914-18 he interested himself in Mennonite expansion by opening a colony in Wyoming. During World War I he concerned himself with the position of the conscientious objector and traveled with a committee to Washington, D.C., for conferences with the Secretary of War, and also visited Mennonite boys in military camps. After the war he turned his energies to helping refugee Mennonites abroad. He opened two colonies, one near Spokane, Wash., and the other at Cuauhtemoc, Mex. He was greatly interested in the historical background of the Mennonites. In 1927 he and his wife undertook a trip around the world which carried them to many Mennonite churches in Europe, and to Mennonite missions in India.

In 1931 he lost his wife. In 1936 he married Katie A. Friesen of Burrton. On Dec. 2, 1940, he passed away at his home in Newton. He lies buried in the mausoleum at Halstead, Kan.   E.K.L.

Krehbiel, Jakob, a Mennonite farmer on the Randeckerhof near Alsenborn, Palatinate, Germany, b. Jan. 5, 1835, at Obersülzen, d. July 26, 1918. Besides being a very successful farmer, he also did considerable writing. He wrote various stories, "Der Engel Wacht," "Die Werber," "Der Bubendieb," "Aus dem Kavalleristenleben," "Ein passiver Soldat," "Der Rote," and "Wer mag's deuten?" which were published in *Jugendblätter* (1865-69). Without formal education, he was well informed in several intellectual fields, as history, religion, politics, etc. He was also active in the Sembach (*q.v.*) church, serving as its president after 1885 with great devotion, and attended and took part in the south German Mennonite conferences. As a citizen he was always ready by word or deed to serve any cause for the common good (*Gem.-Kal.,* 1920, 37-50). Worthy of mention is his energetic rejection of the brochure by pastor Helferich (*q.v.*) on infant baptism (*Menn. Bl.* 1865, 78 f.). (*ML* II, 566.)   NEFF.

Krehbiel, Johann Jakob (1841-95), a Mennonite farmer on the Weierhof, Palatinate, Germany, b. April 10, 1841, became chairman of the Mennonite Educational Association in 1882; in 1886 he was appointed the first Palatine member of the curatorium of the Vereinigung (*q.v.*). At the Palatine-Hessian conference at Eppstein (May 27, 1886), he urged closer union with the Baden Mennonites; this union resulted in the establishment of the Badisch-Pfälzische Konferenz, which was later called the Conference of the South German Mennonites. With sacrificial devotion and deep understanding he shared in all the endeavors to gather and preserve the brotherhood, as well as in many branches of charitable work in the Protestant church. Still in the prime of life, he was snatched away by pneumonia on June 10, 1895. (*Gem.-Kal.,* 1897, 1-37; *ML* II, 566.)   NEFF.

Kreider (Kreiter, Greider), a Mennonite family which migrated from the Palatinate to Pennsylvania in the early 18th century. Jacob Kreider (d. 1751) came in 1716 to Lancaster County, settling south of the city of Lancaster. The family spread from Lancaster County to a few other communities in

Ohio (Wadsworth), Indiana (Elkhart Co.), Illinois (Sterling), and Missouri (Palmyra). A number of ordained men have borne the name. In the Lancaster Conference (MC) there were Tobias (d. 1791), deacon at Mellinger's; Tobias, preacher at the same place 1847-64; Frank (1868-   ), preacher at East Petersburg since 1908. Jacob M. Greider (1835-1931) was a prominent deacon at Salunga. Jacob's brother, Bishop John M. Greider (1823-91), served as bishop 1872-91 in the Medway church, Montgomery Co., Ohio. Daniel Kreider (1782-1860) served as a minister, first in York Co., Ont., from about 1825 on, then moved to Wadsworth, Ohio, where a relative, Jonas M. Kreider (1857-1933), was a long-time preacher. One of the latter's grandsons, Robert (1919-   ), served as preacher in the same congregation since 1943; and another, Carl, is serving as dean of Goshen College 1944-   . Amos E. Kreider, a prominent minister in the General Conference Mennonite Church, came from the Sterling, Ill., congregation (MC). His son Robert is dean of Bluffton College 1954-   Bishop J. M. Kreider (1869-1946) was a long-time minister (MC) in northeastern Missouri, preacher from 1898 and bishop from 1912 to his death. His son John F. (deacon since 1928) and grandson Harold (preacher since 1950) serve the same district.   H.S.B.

Kreider, John Mellinger (J. M.) was born May 24, 1869, at Soudersburg, Lancaster Co., Pa., the oldest of the 12 children of George and Anna Mellinger Kreider. He received all his formal education in the Soudersburg public elementary school. On Nov. 24, 1890, he was married to Hettie Elvina Buckwalter and became the father of nine children. He was a member of the Paradise Mennonite Church, Lancaster, and as a young man was very active in Sunday-school work. He lived in Lancaster County until 1898, when he was ordained to the ministry and moved to Palmyra, Mo., to be the pastor of the Mennonite church there. He was ordained bishop for the Northeast Missouri churches in 1912. He served as a member of the Mennonite Board of Education for many years, conducted evangelistic meetings throughout the United States and Canada, and served on many committees of the church.

He supported his family on a dairy farm at Palmyra, on which he lived till his death on Feb. 28, 1946.   N.E.K.

Kremer, Lubbert Janz: see Cremer.

Kremper and Wilster Marsch, the marshy region to the right of the lower Elbe near the villages Krempe and Wilster; the nearest city is Glückstadt, Prussia, Germany. In the middle of the 16th century Mennonites were already located in the "royal wilderness"; the pastor of Wilster requested the king to watch the "Hollanders" suspected of Anabaptism. Nevertheless they established themselves in such numbers that they brought about a change in agriculture from mere cattle raising to dairying that gradually spread to the east coast of Holstein. Great quantities of cheese were shipped to Lübeck around 1600.

Gradually sharper measures were taken against the Mennonites. The provost of Itzehoe complained in 1635 about the great "applausum" they were winning, and ordered that citizens who had given the oath of loyalty to state and church should see to it that none charged with false doctrine stayed in the parishes. Christian IV decided that the "Manists" should cease their "exercise of baptism and other ceremonies" and "turn to our religion," or leave the country. The alarmed immigrants claimed the (see **Glückstadt**) Privilegium of 1631, asking for three years' grace on account of flood damage and the building of expensive dikes. This request was refused. But by 1642 it was again reported that Mennonites had again entered the country, and were ordered out of the Steinburg district within four weeks. In August 1643 Christian IV again directed the authorities to "keep a watchful eye on sects like Anabaptists, Mennonites, and others in the marshes." Now it became quiet. Most of them likely took refuge in Glückstadt.

A possible attempt to settle in the adjacent Süderdiethmarschen is inferred from a prohibition of such settlement issued by the king in 1637.

They were more leniently treated in the parishes of Brockdorf and Wewelsfleth, where a Mennonite applied for a teaching position. These two parishes belonged to the same district (Steinburg) as the Kremper and Wilster Marsch.   R.Do.

E. George, "Die wirtschaftlichen und kulturellen Beziehungen der Westküste Schleswig-Holsteins zu den Niederlanden," in *Nordelbingen* I; *Heimatbuch des Kreises Steinburg* II; W. Jensen, *Die Wilstermarsch;* ML II, 566 f.

Krems, a city (pop. 20,359) in the Wachau region of the Danube Valley in lower Austria. Anabaptists appeared here as early as 1527. On Nov. 15, 1527, the magistrate of Krems inquired of the government what attitude he should take toward the Anabaptists staying at Gedersdorf; six days later he ordered them all arrested. In its ensuing report the council stated that there were respected citizens among the Anabaptists; that Jörg Krautschlögel (*q.v.*) had been known to be one. Among those seized were some illiterates, who were therefore less responsible, and some pregnant women and mothers of infants. A backslidden monk from Gleink together with his wife and child were arrested on suspicion of this doctrine. The government ordered on Dec. 13 that the pregnant women and nursing mothers be released on bail; the council asked grace for the citizen Joh. Ernst, stated that the trial would demand much effort and money, and inquired what further steps should be taken. The government ordered on Feb. 8, 1528, that the council should proceed according to the mandates and the degree of responsibility of the prisoners. The register of martyrs lists three executions in Krems.

Since Krems lay on the route most travelers took from Tirol or Switzerland to Moravia (and the Moravian Anabaptist brotherhood was augmented for decades chiefly by additions from Tirol) they are often mentioned here. Although special mandates had been issued to the boatmen strictly forbidding the transport of Anabaptists, the refugees continued to prefer the Danube trip, leaving the boat at Stein, opposite Krems. In the village of Hohenwart (*q.v.*) near Krems several Anabaptists lay in prison in 1534. Hutter addressed an epistle to them. After some time they were taken to Egginburg, where their cheeks were burned through and they were released. The feet of one had been in the stocks so long that they had to be amputated in Moravia.

In the 1540's especially large numbers of Tyrolese migrated to Moravia via Krems. In spite of the watchfulness of the authorities, most of them arrived safely in Moravia. Nevertheless some were seized. A group led by Sebastian Leutner, a binder from the Adige, who had led four transports safely, was caught in Stein. He recanted, but died of the plague before he could be released by penance. Konrad Heinzemann, however, who was seized there two days later leading a Swabian group, was more steadfast (1558). He was taken to Vienna with Christel Kircher, who had been Leutner's traveling companion, where he was released in the following year through the intervention of Pfauser, the Lutheran court preacher of Archduke Maximilian, before the bishop of Vienna, Anton Brus, could initiate the trial.

Magister Gangolf Wagner, the preacher of Krems, was called to Vienna in 1573 by the Lower Austrian *Landmarschall,* Hans Wilhelm, Baron of Rogendorf, to convert the brothers Marx and Bernhard Klampferer (*q.v.*), but to no avail.

In the 1580's several Swiss groups touched Krems en route to Moravia. The Zürich council complained about the emigration of so many people, especially about the Moravian emissaries, who lured them with small gifts, especially with little knives of their own production. In 1608, when a Swiss group was arrested by the magistrate in Krems, who took from them their possessions and sent them into the community for forced labor, the Moravian authorities, including Cardinal Dietrichstein, protested this act to the emperor on Oct. 17, and demanded their immediate release; they declared that because of war there was in many localities a shortage of inhabitants and that the immigration of the Swiss was very desirable (*Pamatkenbuch,* 1601 ff., Brno, State archives).　　　　　　　　　　　　　　　　P.DE.

Ottius, *Annales Anabaptistici* (Basel, 1672); J. Kinzl, *Chronik der Städte Krems und Stein* (Krems, 1869); Beck, *Geschichts-Bücher;* Loserth, *Communismus;* Wolkan, *Geschicht-Buch;* Zieglschmid, *Chronik; ML* II, 567.

Kress, Simon, of Gündelbach, Maulbronn district of Württemberg, Germany, the home of Bartholomäus Riegel (*q.v.*). Simon Kress was an unusually zealous missionary for the Hutterian Brethren in Moravia, preaching in his home town and vicinity (1574) and in the region of Schorndorf, was seized in Oberurbach near Schorndorf and taken to Wittlingen on Nov. 12, 1582.

In 1589 it was reported in the *synodus,* which was a conference of the consistory, the church council, and the general superintendent, that the bailiff of the castle was permitting Kress to go about freely and work outside the castle grounds. Although the magistrate and superintendent of Urach had

protested, it remained thus. In 1596 Pastor Tobias Fetzer in Wittlingen admitted that the two Anabaptist prisoners, Simon Kress of Gündelbach and Hans Dauber of Illingen, conducted themselves modestly, kindly, and friendly, and had asked to be permitted to go to church. They actually came to church, accompanied by the bailiff of the castle, sang the psalms with the rest, listened to the sermon, by nods and gestures indicated their approval of the pastor's words, and indicated disapproval by shaking their heads. This confused the congregation; it seemed to them that something contrary to Scripture was being said. Therefore the permission to attend church was withdrawn. The bailiff thought the prisoners ought to cut down some willow thickets into pasture. With pick and hoe it would be easier to convert them than with the Bible.

Their imprisonment continued. The Urach *Pfarrelationen* of 1603 state that Kress has become quieter, less defiant than Hans Dauber. In 1605 Kress received a visit from his wife and son, who persuaded him to present a petition: if he could return to his home, he would promise not to enter into a discussion with anyone, but attend quietly to his business. It is not known whether or not he was released. In any case, by 1617 he had died.　　　　　　　　　　　　　　　　　　G.Bo.

Beck, *Geschichts-Bücher,* 198; Wolkan, *Geschicht-Buch;* Zieglschmid, *Chronik; ML* II, 567 f.

Kretz, Matthias (1480-1543), a Catholic theologian, cathedral deacon in München, did not (contrary to information from the antiquariat of Calvary) expressly and specifically attack the Anabaptists in his frequently reprinted sermon on the Mass (1524).　　　　　　　　　　　　　　　　　　E.C.

ADB IX, 645 ("Gretz"); Calvary, *Verzeichnis seltener und wertvoller Werke* (Berlin, 1869) 29 and 53; *ML* II, 568.

Kreutzinger, Jörg, a baker's assistant, an Anabaptist martyr, was killed with the sword and then burned with seven brethren at Wels (*q.v.*) in Upper Austria, June 28, 1528. Three days later two women were drowned, and six persons who recanted were pardoned, subject to public penitence (see **Penance** and **Haslinger**).　　　　　　　　　　　NEFF.

A. Nicoladoni, *Johannes Bünderlin* (Berlin, 1893) 100, 187; *ML* II, 568.

Kreuzenstein (*Grätzenstein*), a castle in Lower Austria near the Manhartsberg, has a long, involved history extending back to 1000.

On March 22, 1523, Archduke Ferdinand, the brother of Charles V, assigned the management of the castle, the criminal court, and the money for their upkeep from the income from districts of Korneuburg, to his councilor, Count Niklas von Salm. Two years later Niklas distinguished himself in the army of Charles V at Pavia, in the capture of the French king, Francis I, and as a reward received the castle as a hereditary fief. To it belonged the outlying villages, Gerasdorf, Leobendorf, Perzendorf, and Kleinkötz.

This was about the time, the end of 1527, when Balthasar Hubmaier (*q.v.*) was arrested and imprisoned in Kreuzenstein. Imprisonment in the dilapidated rooms was particularly hard. Here Hubmaier received visits from distinguished men, and had his famous interview with Johannes Fabri, who had been a fellow student, and who later became bishop of Vienna, in a futile attempt to persuade him to recant; the only concession Hubmaier made was to leave the decision to a general council. His fate took its course, and he died at the stake on March 10, 1528, in Vienna.

The castle remained in possession of the family of Count Niklas von Salm und Neuburg am Inn until 1585, when it was sold to Count Ferdinand von Hardegg, and finally to the Count of Wilczeck.

The old castle in which Hubmaier lay imprisoned so long has long since become a ruin, and has been replaced by a splendid edifice put up by Count Johann von Wilczek in 1879. In 1928, at the formal commemoration of the quadricentennial of Hubmaier's death, visitors from many nations made an excursion to Kreuzenstein. They found in a window nook an old etching: the familiar picture of Hubmaier. On the original there are two sketches beside his head, one depicting the burning of Hubmaier, the other depicting the drowning of his wife (*Menn. Bl.,* 1928, 38). LOSERTH.

The literature on Kreuzenstein is best found in the *Topographie von Niederösterreich* IV, 490-98. A picture of the old castle is found in Vischer, *Topographia archiducatus Austriae, 1672;* a picture of the new castle by Camillo Sitte, in *Monatsschrift des Oesterreichischen Museums* I; *ML* II, 568 f.

Kreuznach, a city (pop. 26,557) in the southern Rhine Province of Prussia, formerly under Palatine jurisdiction, where in 1529 the Anabaptist, Philip of Langenlonsheim, was beheaded. There seems to have been an Anabaptist congregation here very early, but no particulars are known before 1556, when a division occurred. The Hutterite chronicle records the following account:

Several members of the group around Kreuznach, who were called the Swiss, had left it because of sin and transgression within the group, and were won to the Hutterian brotherhood by Hans Schmidt (*q.v.*). The reasons for this step were: (1) Although they have taught and learned that one should give himself completely to God, with all that he has, they have granted that each may use his own goods for himself and give to the poor what will benefit them. (2) Although they have taught that no one should call anything his own, but that what one has is also one's neighbor's, nevertheless if anyone needs anything he has to buy it of the other. (3) Because they do not teach the truth on original sin, pay taxes for war, and secretly discipline misdeeds, so that they may not become public. (4) Because they are not truly separated from the people of the world, but in many regards mingle with them, and because their preachers disagree and quarrel among themselves. Diebold (Winter) and Farwendel (*q.v.*) are named.

Among those dissatisfied with the group were Lorenz Hueff (*q.v.*) of Sprendlingen, a preacher; Rupp Gellner (*q.v.*) or Kern, Matthes Stroh, and Wilhelm Henchen. Thoman Neuman of Wolfsheim, a cobbler, journeyed to Moravia to get acquainted with the Hutterian Brethren. He brought back a favorable report. These men then decided to join the Hutterian brotherhood. After long oral and written negotiations an agreement was reached on Nov. 26, 1556, on various points (marriage, war taxes, separation, support of preachers, purchase of houses and land, and moving to Moravia). In Moravia Lorenz Hueff was accepted as a preacher.

The Concept of Cologne was signed in 1591 by a representative of the Kreuznach congregation. Nothing further is known of it, but it is inferred that remnants survived the Thirty Years' War, for right after the war ended, Swiss Mennonite refugees settled here and a new congregation was formed, which existed a long time under the name of Rheingrafenstein (*q.v.*), more recently called Neudorferhof. NEFF.

Wolkan, *Geschicht-Buch,* 270-78; Zieglschmid, *Chronik,* 357-60; *ML* II, 569.

Kriegsheim, a village near Worms in Rheinhessen, Germany, which until 1815 belonged to the Alzey district of the Palatinate. It was the seat of a Mennonite congregation until 1820; since 1821 the adjacent Monsheim is its center.

The origins of the congregation here presumably lie in the early period of the Anabaptist movement. For the period 1588-1608 there are sparse official records, which afford a glance into the lot of an oppressed, long-established Anabaptist group (reports of the local Reformed pastor and his inspector to the church council, measures passed by the Burgrave of Alzey and the government at Heidelberg), which is typical of the suppressive attitude of the Palatinate, especially in the Alzey district. In 1600 there were 13 couples in Kriegsheim; in 1601 a report mentions 66 persons. Cross-examinations by the Burgrave of Alzey on Dec. 29, 1601, and Jan. 11, 1602, were fruitless. The Anabaptists did not have the local clergy marry them, were designated as "despisers of the holy sacraments" by the state church, were even said to have mocked churchgoers. They were by trade craftsmen and peasants (weavers, farmers, saw filers, glaziers, cobblers, and vinedressers).

The following family names are listed: Strohm, Zunich, Moroldt, Meyer, Schmidt, Labach, Scherer, Bidinger, Herstein, Bekker, Mezger, Brosam, and Bischoff. Among the citizens they seem to have been respected, since they were apparently given public office "before other subjects" (in the list of 1608 a field-keeper was arrested). "Subjects" even married the children of Anabaptists, which is the more remarkable because the Burgrave of Alzey had in 1588 reckoned the Kriegsheim heretics among the serfs. This group of Anabaptists apparently did not disapprove of mixed marriages or holding civil office; in this respect the original Palatine Anabaptists differed from the stricter Swiss Brethren, who came after the Thirty Years' War. They had a leader (*Vorsteher*) and held their meetings at night. In a house between Kriegsheim and Pfeddersheim a well-attended meeting was surprised on Aug. 13, 1608, and two *Vorsteher* who preached were arrested. The Kriegsheim congregation appears to have survived the storms of the Thirty Years' War which devastated the Palatinate; it was augmented by Swiss Brethren who began to arrive in 1650.

About 1657 a group of Kriegsheim Mennonites joined the Quakers through the influence of Ames (*q.v.*). But this Quaker group emigrated to Pennsylvania in 1685; thus members of the Kriegsheim group were a part of the early German settlement at Germantown. The brief period during which there were Quakers at Kriegsheim was marked by a series of conflicts with the church and the state. There was also tension between them and the Mennonites, as a letter written by Hinrich Cassel, a Mennonite preacher of Gerolsheim, in 1679 shows. The Quaker writings breathe the spirit of the English Revolution, in sharp contrast to the "devoted subject" style of Mennonite petitions. In contrast to the Mennonites, the Quakers refused all payment of taxes to church or state, the large or small tithe, or even congregational fees. "It seems strange to us that money is required of us to pay for our liberty of conscience." Confiscation of crops, cattle, furniture, and wine, as well as arrest and imprisonment were the order of the day. It is to be feared, writes the "entire poor congregation at Kriegsheim" to the *Oberamt* in 1680, that "the best inhabitants will leave the village and settle elsewhere."

The Quakers were strengthened in their radical position by emissaries from England, who reported back to the Quaker annual conference in London— William Penn was also in Kriegsheim in 1667; nevertheless in 1664 they succeeded in obtaining an investigation of events in Kriegsheim, probably by means of a letter written by the village schoolmaster, John Philley, to the elector, which resulted in negotiations with the Quakers and Mennonites in the presence of the author of the letter. In consequence the Mennonites were granted toleration on Aug. 4, 1664, which also applied to the Quakers, who were frequently officially called "Manists." In 1669 the government decided "that the Quakers either pay money for their religious freedom as the Anabaptists did or be put out of the country." In 1685 they were expelled.

In 1710 the Mennonites of Kriegsheim were compelled to do military service, not only to be a guard under arms, but even to join the regular militia. Their protest to the government at Heidelberg in 1711 resulted in their release from these duties the following year.

The size of the Kriegsheim church can be estimated from the tables drawn up for the electoral cabinet for the levy of the protection fee. According to these lists of Mennonites, Kriegsheim had 52 persons in 1680, and 41 in 1773. In 1738 the following family names were registered: Voldt, Bäcker, Strohm, Kühn, Krämer, Janson, Müller, Hüthwohl. A protocol of 1768 shows that the Mennonites of the Zeller Valley (Lichti and Linscheid of Harxheim) were members of the Kriegsheim church. The same is true of Monsheim; for this protocol is signed by David Möllinger (*q.v.*) as the president of the Kriegsheim church. The Kindenheim Mennonites were also counted as part of Kriegsheim. In 1803 Preacher Christian Eymann signed the Ibersheim Resolutions for Kriegsheim.

Peter Kolb (*q.v.*) was an elder of the Kriegsheim congregation in the early 18th century; in 1728 he was succeeded by Christian Weber, who served until about 1770. The Dutch *Naamlijst,* which always lists Kriegsheim as "Griesheim," names the following ministers of the 18th century: Wilhelm Krämer, Johann Schörger, Henrich Müller, all serving until about 1769, Henrich Strohm 1758-90, Peter Müller until about 1775, Michel Stiess, preacher from 1766, elder from 1772 until after 1802, Jacob Krehbiel 1763-*ca.* 84, Jacob Kägy 1771-*ca* 84, Christian Eymann from 1774, Peter Weber 1778-81, Johann Dettweiler from 1784, Heinrich Krämer from 1788.

A complete list of the localities belonging to the Kriegsheim church at the beginning of the 19th century is found in a register drawn up for the erection of a new church about 1820. When the first theologically trained minister in South Germany, Leonhard Weydmann, was employed (1818-36 at Monsheim, then at Crefeld), he was promised a new church building. The villages enumerated are Biedesheim, Bockenheim, Bubenheim, Dirmstein, Kindenheim, Kriegsheim, Monsheim, Niederflörsheim, Pfeddersheim, and Offstein; and the family names were Bühm, Christoffel, Dettweiler, Eymann, Geber, Hahn, Hüthwohl, Hirschler, Hiestand, Janson, Krehbühl, Kieferndorf, Neef, Krämer, Möllinger, Kaege, Rupp, Seitz, Stauffer, Strohm, Schneider, Vogt, Weis, Weber, Wiehner.

The Kriegsheim Mennonites had their own cemetery; the Catholic church now stands on the site. The hall in which they had held their meetings being in need of repair as well as being too small, it was sold in May 1820, especially since it was exposed to floods of the Pfrimm. The proceeds were applied to the new building at Monsheim (*q.v.*).

W.F.

Chr. Neff, "Geschichtliches aus der Gemeinde Monsheim," *Menn. Bl.,* 1892, Nos. 1-4; Chr. Hege, *Die Täufer in der Kurpfalz* (Frankfurt, 1908); E. Correll, *Das Schweizerische Täufermennonitentum* (Tübingen, 1925); W. Hubben, *Die Quäker in der deutschen Vergangenheit* (Leipzig, 1929); W. Fellmann, "Kriegsheimer Mennoniten und Quäker in ihrer religiösen Verschiedenheit," *Beiträge zur Geschichte der Mennoniten (Festgabe für D. Christian Neff,* Weierhof, 1938) 19-24; *ML* II, 572 f.

Krimmer Mennonite Brethren Church had its origin in the village of Annafeld near Simferopol, Crimea, Russia, on Sept. 21, 1869, as a group of 19 persons, with Jacob A. Wiebe (1839-1921) as the actual founder. A group of Mennonite families from the Molotschna (Wiebe himself was from Ohrloff) about 1860 had bought a Mohammedan village in the Crimea, which they named Annafeld. Through a spontaneous religious revival most of the families in the village began to seek a more earnest Christian life and experienced conversion, Wiebe among them. Since Wiebe had become acquainted with a leader of the Kleine Gemeinde during a period of work as a hired hand in the Molotschna, he invited the Kleine Gemeinde elder, Johann Friesen, to visit the Annafeld group and organize them as a Kleine Gemeinde congregation, which the latter did in 1867. Wiebe was ordained as preacher, and soon thereafter as elder. Elder Peter Bärg, who had transferred to the Kleine Gemeinde as preacher, was also accepted by the new group as their preacher. Friesen had refused to accede to the request of the Annafeld group for rebaptism, but the group remained dissatisfied on this point and finally proceeded to have one of their members (Kornelius Enns was chosen) rebaptize Elder Wiebe, who in turn on Sept. 21, 1869, rebaptized 18 others. This is considered by the K.M.B. group as their founding date. Trine immersion forward in a flowing stream was adopted as the mode. The group chose the name "Brüdergemeinde" but was soon called "Krimmer Mennoniten Brüdergemeinde" to distinguish it from the Mennoniten Brüdergemeinde founded in the Molotschna in 1860, with which it had no connection. (Krim is the German name for Crimea.) The act of rebaptism constituted in effect a withdrawal of the Wiebe group from the Kleine Gemeinde, with which it had had fellowship for only a few years, although it was not a true schism from the historic Kleine Gemeinde group, since the entire Annafeld group continued under Wiebe's leadership. However, much of the ultraconservative spirit of the Kleine Gemeinde was transmitted into the K.M.B. group, in combination with the new K.M.B. emphasis on conversion, assurance, and experience. There was little further connection between the K.M.B. and the Kleine Gemeinde, but in the United States a Kleine Gemeinde preacher, Abraham Klaassen, who had been ordained in 1869 in Russia, joined the K.M.B. group in Kansas about 1879.

The new church grew slowly, and when they left for America in 1874 numbered only about 40 baptized members. All of the group emigrated except three families, a total of 20 families, the vanguard (the K.M.B. group were the first to receive passports) of the great emigration of Mennonites from Russia 1874-80 to the prairie states of the United States and to Manitoba. Their leaders on arrival were Elder Wiebe and Preacher Johann Harder (1836-1930), earlier from the Ohrloff Mennonite congregation at Blumstein in the Molotschna settlement, who had been elected minister in 1871 before the departure from Russia.

The K.M.B. group arrived in New York on July 15, 1874, and after some delay incurred in searching for land, during which the group as a whole remained at Elkhart, Ind., they arrived at this new home, 14 miles northwest of Peabody, Marion Co., Kan., on Aug. 16. Accustomed to village type settlement in Russia, the entire group settled as one village called Gnadenau, destined to become the most perfect of the few communal villages organized by the Mennonites in Kansas, although even it lasted only two or three years. The village never had a post office, and when in 1879 a branch of the Santa Fe railroad went through the north edge of the settlement, and Hillsboro was built on the line two miles north of the village, Gnadenau lost its future. The Gnadenau K.M.B. group was very strict in various ways and this together with its variant practice of immersion (forward) prevented two M.B. families which settled in the community in 1875 from joining it and led to the foundation of the Ebenfeld M.B. congregation.

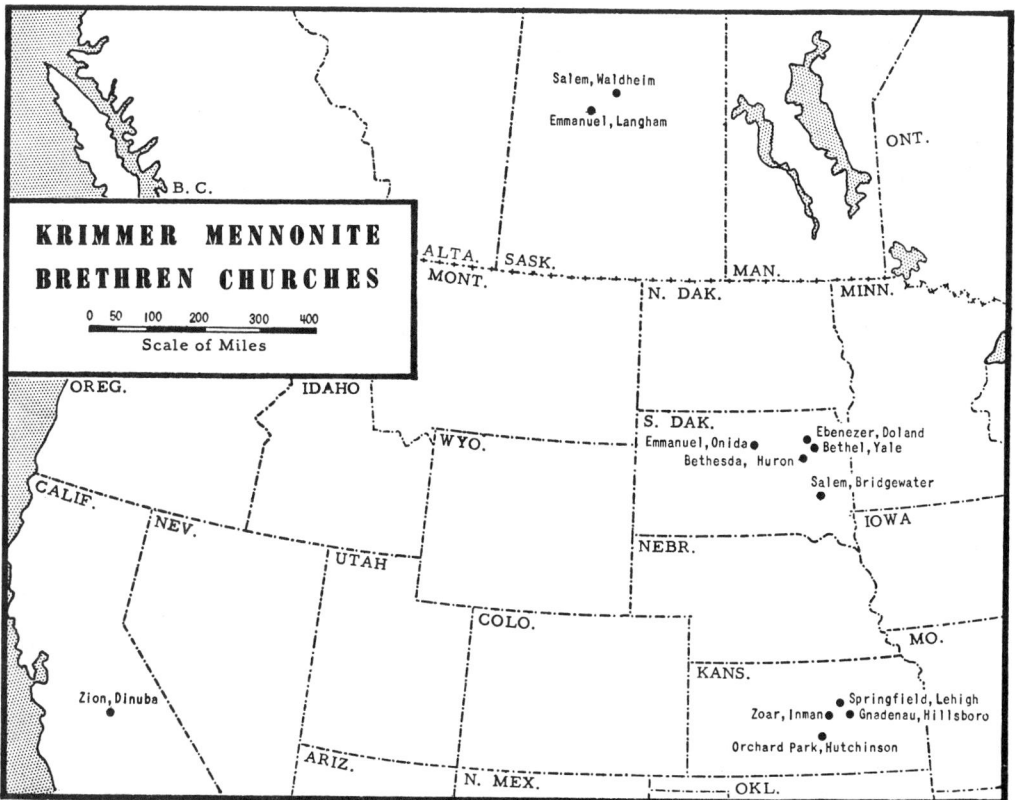

KRIMMER MENNONITE
BRETHREN CHURCHES

0 50 100   200   300   400

Scale of Miles

The first Gnadenau church building, erected in 1874 of adobe walls with thatched roof, did not stand the weather; so a frame building was erected in 1877. On Feb. 15, 1877, the congregation was incorporated as the "Gnadenau Mennonite Church." On March 30, 1899, the name was changed in the charter to "Crimean Mennonite Brethren Church," but popularly the name remained "Krimmer M.B." In 1895 a new building was erected 2½ miles south of Hillboro, and is still in use.

Elder Jacob A. Wiebe served until his resignation in 1900, then was succeeded as elder by his brother Henry (1900-10), and he in turn by John J. Friesen (1910-37). The group suffered a heavy loss in membership when Elder Wiebe resigned. On July 12, 1917, the "Krimmer Mennonite Brethren Church of North America" was incorporated at Hillsboro.

Four additional K.M.B. congregations were established in Kansas: Springfield at Lehigh (1902), Zoar at Inman, Lyons in Rice County, and one in Butler County. The last two did not survive long. Additional congregations were established as follows: South Dakota (Bridgewater 1886, Yale 1902, Doland 1919, Onida 1920, Huron 1947); Saskatchewan (Waldheim 1899, Langham 1901); California (Dinuba 1911). The following further congregations did not survive: Oklahoma (Bethel near Hooker 1907-19, and Bethel near Weatherford 1897-1937); Kansas (Emmanuel near Garden City 1918-36); North Dakota (Emmanuel near Chasely 1921-32). A small congregation was established at Jansen (near Fairbury, Neb.) in 1880, largely out of converts from the Kleine Gemeinde, which continued until 1930. In the same year 1880 John Holdeman attempted to win the K.M.B. group at Gnadenau to his views, but failed. In that year or 1879 Abr. Klassen, a Kleine Gemeinde preacher from Jansen, joined the K.M.B. group.

The K.M.B. Conference counts its first regular session to have been held in 1880, although records were not kept before 1882. It has met annually ever since.

On Sept. 15, 1890, the K.M.B. Conference was granted a charter for the "Industrial School and Hygenic Home for Friendless Persons," an orphans' home which was built just north of the original Gnadenau village site in 1894. It was operated for about 20 years, then was converted into the Salem Home for the Aged and Helpless. In 1918 the K.M.B. group joined with the M.B. group to establish the Salem Hospital in Hillsboro.

In 1886 the K.M.B. Conference opened mission work among the colored people at Elk Park, N.C., the first Mennonite Negro work. The conference has never had a foreign mission board but has supported foreign missionaries at work under other boards. Its Foreign Missions Committee represents the mission interests of the conference. In 1940 the K.M.B. Conference officially joined in the support of Tabor College (M.B. Church) by appointing a member on the Tabor board.

Always deeply religious in nature and emphasizing a deep inner experience, regeneration, assurance of salvation, and holy living, the K.M.B. group has stood for an intensely serious and strict manner of life. The group was very conservative and very slow to make changes in outward forms in dress and in general habits and customs, insisting upon maintaining the customs brought along from Russia and resisting Americanization and worldliness. Clothing was made of good materials but no lace or ornamentation was allowed. For many years the women were not allowed to wear hats to church but wore kerchiefs, shawls, or bonnets on their heads, and always wore white aprons to church. Children were dressed like their parents. The wearing of neckties and detachable collars by the men was banned. Since about 1900, however, the K.M.B. have adopted the common dress of the American community.

In worship the simple older practices were long observed. Musical instruments and choirs were introduced only about 1940. Part singing was long forbidden. Other prohibitions included life insurance, voting at elections other than school elections, taking photographs, and serving on juries. Shunning of excommunicated was practiced. All these practices have now been dropped, although a certain heritage of strictness, earnestness, and warmth characterizes the religious spirit of the group.

In recent years negotiations have been carried on looking toward a merger with the M.B. group on the basis of an overture of 1951 from the M.B. group. These plans were finally dropped at the 1954 conference, but the original Gnadenau congregation withdrew from the K.M.B. Conference in that year and merged with the near-by Lehigh M.B. congregation. But plans have been made for a complete conference merger with the M.B. Conference in July 1957.

Before the Gnadenau withdrawal the 1954 conference statistical report revealed the following membership figures: Kansas, 3 congregations, Gnadenau (1874) 120, Springfield at Lehigh (1902) 90, Zoar (1879) 349; California, 1 congregation, Zion at Dinuba (1911) 262; South Dakota, 5 congregations, Bethel at Yale (1902) 315, Salem at Bridgewater (1886) 222, Emmanuel at Onida (1920) 92, Ebenezer at Doland 105, Bethesda at Huron (1947) 52; Saskatchewan, 2 congregations, Salem at Waldheim (1899) ca. 100, Emmanuel at Langham (1901) 52. The reported membership in the eleven congregations was 1,791. In addition there were nine mission points, not including the work among the Negroes in North Carolina.

D. M. Hofer and J. W. Tschetter were joint founders of the K.M.B. city mission at 2182 Lincoln Ave., Chicago, and also joint publishers of the periodical *Der Wahrheitsfreund* (q.v.), which served as the conference organ 1915-47. Since then the *Christian Witness* (1941-) has been the conference organ.

Among the outstanding leaders of the K.M.B. group in the first third of the 20th century were David E. Harder (1872-1930), son of the noted preacher Johann Harder, who has also served on the faculties of three Mennonite colleges: Tabor, Bethel, and Freeman; P. A. Wiebe, D. M. Hofer, and J. W. Tschetter. H. C. Barthel founded and led for many years the first Mennonite mission in China (1901-49), which was largely staffed and supported by the K.M.B. Church, though never officially conducted by the board.   H.S.B.

J. A. Wiebe, *Das Entstehen der Krimmer Mennoniten Brüder Gemeinde in Süd-Russland im Jahre 1869* (Elkhart, 1905) (7 pp.); P. A. Wiebe, *Kurze Biographie des Bruders Jakob A. Wiebe, Seine Jugend, Seine Bekehrung, und wie die Krimmer Mennoniten Brüdergemeinde gegründet wurde* (Hillsboro, 1924) (27 pp.); Friesen, *Brüderschaft*; Albert Pantle, "Settlement of the Krimmer Mennonite Brethren at Gnadenau, Marion County" (Kan.), *Kansas Historical Quarterly* XIII (1945) 259-85; L. L. Waters, *Steel Trails to Santa Fe* (Lawrence, Kan., 1950) contains (229-31) an account by Elder Jakob Wiebe of the early years of the Gnadenau village written in Wiebe's old age for A. E. Case of the Santa Fe Railway and deposited in manuscript in the possession of the company; *Konstitution der Krimmer Mennoniten Brüdergemeinde von Nord-Amerika nebst Freibrief* (n.p., 1927); *Yearbook of the Krimmer Mennonite Brethren Church of North America; Die Geistreiche Lieder-Auswahl für Familien und öffentliche Erbauungen mit Sorgfalt gesammelt von der Krimmer Mennoniten Brüdergemeinde. Erste Auflage* (Elkhart, Ind., Mennonite Publishing Co., 1884); *Konferenzbeschlüsse der Krimmer Mennoniten Brüdergemeinde von Nord-Amerika, zwischen den Jahren 1882 bis 1940* (Inman, Kan.); *Bericht über die zwei Beratungen, die am 21. Oct. und 11. Nov. 1895 stattfanden.* (Hillsboro, Kan., 1895); *Der Wahrheitsfreund* contains scattered historical articles (1944, Nos. 13 and 15; 1946, Nos. 9-14 and 18-21; No. 22); *ML* II, 574 f.

Krimmer Mennonite Brethren *Publications Committee* was created at the 36th annual conference session, which met in 1915, to meet the need of printing a conference periodical and to supervise conference publications. The Committee is composed of six members elected by the delegates at the annual conference session for a term of three years. The editor of the Conference periodical is usually called in in an advisory capacity for the Publications Committee meetings. The current budget of the Committee is $4,200.00.

Since its establishment the Committee has functioned in publishing the Conference Yearbooks, Articles of Faith, the Constitution, a résumé of Conference recommendations and decisions under the title *Konferenzbeschlüsse,* and the Conference periodicals, *Wahrheitsfreund* 1915-47 and *Christian Witness* 1941- .   W.O.E.

Krimmer Mennonite Brethren *Publishing House,* Chicago, Ill. At their annual session in 1914 the K.M.B. Conference elected a committee and authorized it to proceed in establishing a conference paper and if possible a publishing house to be owned and operated by the Conference. D. M. Hofer and J. W. Tschetter provided the necessary funds for the purchase of a building at 2812 Lincoln Ave., Chicago, and the needed printing equipment, on the condition that a city mission could be conducted in a part of the building housing the publishing activities. The first issue of the K.M.B. Conference paper *Der Wahrheitsfreund* (*q.v.*) appeared on July 28, 1915. It was discontinued in 1947 after the *Christian Witness* (*q.v.*) had become the official Conference paper. Meanwhile the printing equipment was sold to John H. Klassen and moved to Inman, Kan., where he continued to print for the K.M.B. Conference for several years.   M.S.H.

Kripp zu Krippach und Prunberg, Johann Nepomuk von (1821-82), a historian. He was educated at the Gymnasium at Hall and the University at Innsbruck, Tirol, Austria. From 1850 to 1881 he was a teacher of geography and history at the Innsbruck

Gymnasium. In connection with the history of his local community he wrote "Ein Beitrag zur Geschichte der Wiedertäufer in Tirol" (*8. Programm des k. k. Staatsgymnasiums zu Innsbruck,* Innsbruck, 1857, 3-60). As sources he used manuscripts in the Innsbruck archives and in the *Stiftsregistratur* in Brixen. By way of introduction he gives a detailed account of the Hutterian Brethren in Moravia. E.C.

33. Program des k. k. Staatsgymnasiums zu Innsbruck (1882) 51-53; *ML* II, 575.

Kristkovo (*Christkovo*; German, *Christfelde*) and the neighboring hamlet of Kossovo, situated in the Polish territory of Schwetz (*q.v.*) near the left bank of the Vistula River, were in the 17th and 18th centuries occupied by Mennonite farmers of Dutch descent. In 1650 the Mennonites of Kristkovo and Kossovo obtained a charter of protection granted them by King Johann II Casimir of Poland. They were granted freedom of religion and the privilege of choosing their own *Schulze* (magistrate) and conducting their own schools. They also had an economic privilege, permitting them to transport their grain without paying taxes to Danzig, in order to sell it there. A congregation of Kristkovo is not known; these Mennonites may have belonged to a congregation of a neighboring town. (See Przechovka.)   vDZ.

F. Szper, *Nederl. Nederzettingen in West-Pruisen gedurende den Poolsche tijd* (Enkhuizen, 1913) 143 f.

Kroeker (Kroecker, Kreker, Kröckert, Krueger, Kröger), a Prussian Mennonite name, first recorded in Tiegenhagen in 1627. The name occurred in the following congregations and communities: Danzig, Ladekopp, Rosenort, Fürstenwerder, Heubuden, Elbing, and Königsberg, and from here spread to Poland, Russia, and North and South America. In 1940 there were only about 40 Mennonite bearers of this name in its various forms in East Germany. Outstanding representatives of this name were Isaac Kroeker, elder (1767-87) of the Königsberg Mennonite congregation, Jakob Kroeker, elder of the Elbing Mennonite Church (1808-46), Jakob Kroeker (*q.v.*) of Russia and Germany, Abraham J. Kroeker (*q.v.*) of Russia and Mountain Lake, Minn., and M. A. Kroeker, M.B. minister at Mountain Lake and Hillsboro, Kan. (Reimer, *Familiennamen,* 112.)   C.K.

Kroeker, Abraham Jakob (1863-1944), a minister and writer of the Mennonite Brethren Church, was born in Rosenort, Halbstadt District, Molotschna Mennonite settlement, South Russia, on Dec. 11, 1863, the son of Jakob and Sarah Wiens Kröker. He received some secondary education by private instruction, and at 17 began his teaching service in Mennonite village schools, 1881-88. He was converted at 19 and joined the M.B. Church. In 1891 he went to Rumania for three years as a missionary. He married Agatha Langemann on Sept. 10, 1892. To them nine children were born. In 1894 he established his home at Spat, Crimea. Here his chief occupation for ten years was farming. He moved to Halbstadt in 1904.

In 1897 Kroeker entered publication work, in part with his cousin, Jakob Kroeker (*q.v.*). From 1897 to 1918 he published the *Christlicher Familien-*

Kalender (*q.v.*), 1900-5 the *Christliches Jahrbuch,* and 1899-1917 the *Christlicher Abreisskalender* (*q.v.*), all of which were widely circulated among Mennonites in Russia as well as in America. From 1903 to 1920 Kroeker edited and published the *Friedensstimme,* the organ of the M.B. Church in Russia, which had, however, a much wider circle of readers. In 1904 he was one of the founders of *Raduga* (*q.v.*), a publishing house at Halbstadt, Molotschna, of which he was manager until 1920.

Kroeker left Russia in 1921, came to America in April 1922, by way of Constantinople, lived in Winnipeg, Man., a year; then moved to Mountain Lake, Minn., his family following in 1924. Here he established and operated a bookstore a number of years and also for some time was joint editor of *Der Mithelfer* (*q.v.*) with N. N. Hiebert.

He wrote the following books: *Für freie Stunden* (Odessa, 1902); *Pfarrer Eduard Wüst* (Hillsboro, 1903); *Meine Flucht* (1922), enlarged as *Jehova Hilft* (Mt. Lake, *ca.* 1925), English as *My Flight from Russia* (Scottdale, 1932); *Bilder aus Sowiet Russland* (Hillsboro, *ca.* 1922); *Unsere Brüder in Not* (Striegau, 1930); *Auf dunklen Pfaden* (Striegau, 1933, in collaboration with a fellow minister); *Als die Sterbenden* (in collaboration with his daughter Margaret). *Meine Flucht* and *Bilder* went through numerous editions. He also compiled and published a revised (1927?) edition of the songbook *Heimatklänge,* first published in 1889 at Halbstadt, Russia, compiled by Isaak Born.

Kroeker died at Mountain Lake on Nov. 22, 1944, and was buried there.   J.H.L.

Friesen, *Brüderschaft;* M. Kroeker, *Ein reiches Leben* (Wüstenrot, 1940); "Abraham J. Kroeker—Writer and Publisher," *Menn. Life* VII (1952) 165; *ML* II, 575.

Kroeker, Jakob, a leading Mennonite theologian and writer, b. Oct. 31, 1872, in Gnadental, Molotschna, in South Russia, d. Dec. 12, 1948, near Stuttgart, Germany. After passing the state examination he spent two years as a teacher at a Mennonite school at Menlarstchick, near Spat (Crimea). He was married to Anna Langemann on July 18, 1894. Then he spent four years at the Baptist theological seminary at Hamburg, and upon his return to Russia was ordained preacher and elder by David Schellenberg, Aug. 18, 1898. He and David Dürksen (*q.v.*) served as traveling evangelists. In 1906 Kroeker settled at Halbstadt; with Abraham Kroeker (*q.v.*) he published *Die Friedensstimme* (*q.v.*), the first Mennonite church paper in Russia, and a widely used *Christlicher Abreisskalender* (*q.v.*). He was also one of the founders of *Raduga,* the first Mennonite publishing concern, and the deaconess home in Halbstadt.

About that time he was deeply impressed by the revivalist Dr. Baedeker and through him made contacts with the flourishing evangelical circles in St. Petersburg, which extended into the circles of the nobility, and with the Alliance movement in Germany and the Baltic states. He attended the Alliance Conference at Blankenburg almost every year, and was a member of its committee. In addition he worked with great success at Bible conferences in Russia, an activity he continued even after

he moved to Wernigerode a.H., Germany, in July 1910. This extensive service was interrupted by the first World War.

Now Kroeker devoted himself to theological study, particularly of the Old Testament; the mature fruit of this study is the series *Das lebendige Wort,* planned to comprise 14 volumes of 400 pages each, eight of which had appeared in 1934. Other smaller works by Kroeker have been published: *Allein mit dem Meister; Der verborgene Umgang mit Gott; Gottes Segensträger; Licht von seinem Lichte; Verhüllte Segenswege des Glaubens; Weltstaat und Gottesreich; Vom Heimweh der Seele;* and *Er sprach zu mir.* His *Römerbrief-Kommentar Kapitel 1-8, Ein Handkommentar,* was published after his death in 1949. Some books went through numerous editions.

In collaboration with Pastor Jack he served Russian prisoners of war in camps through the distribution of Bibles and preaching, and called the missionary society *Licht im Osten* (*q.v.*) into being in 1918, which for years educated Russian preachers at a seminary in Wernigerode, gave relief to the needy in Russia, published a missionary paper, *Dein Reich komme* (*q.v.*), and conducted an annual conference (*Glaubenskonferenz*). In addition Kroeker was a speaker at many Bible conferences and recognized as a theologian by leaders of the German, Swiss, and Dutch, Lutheran, Reformed, and free churches. He exerted lasting influence upon the Mennonites of Germany, Switzerland, and North America by his lecture tours.

During World War II the Kroekers celebrated their golden wedding anniversary. After the German collapse they had to leave Wernigerode because it was in the Russian zone. The aging couple and ailing husband found a home near Stuttgart, where he died in 1948. Some of the children have meanwhile emigrated to Canada, while Mrs. Kroeker and some of the children remain in Germany.†
                                          NEFF., C.K.

Friesen, *Brüderschaft,* pp. 468, 659, and 671; M. Kroeker, *Ein reiches Leben* (Wüstenrot, 1949); *ML* II, 576.

Kroeker, Johann F., missionary (GCM) at Janjgir (*q.v.*) India, was born in Gnadenfeld, Russia. He attended St. Chrischona Bible School, Switzerland, and Bethel College, North Newton, Kan., graduating from the academy in 1899. He married Susanna Schowalter of Mühlhausen, Germany. He, his wife, and the P. A. Penners were the first General Conference missionaries to India, arriving at Bombay on Dec. 9, 1900. The Kroekers opened the mission station at Janjgir, erected the first buildings, organized the school, and opened evangelistic work. Because of ill health they returned to Russia in 1909, where he served as itinerant evangelist of the Gnadenfeld Mennonite Church among the Mennonites of Siberia. The date of his death is not known.   C.K.

Friesen, *Brüderschaft,* 708, 718, 149 ff.; *Twenty-five Years with God in India* (Berne, 1929) 185.

Krohn, Barthold Nikolaus (1722-95), a German Protestant theologian, was employed as a tutor in the home of the Mennonite Hermann Goverts of

Hamburg and later became a preacher in the church of St. Mary Magdalene in Hamburg. He is the author of a book titled *Geschichte der fanatischen und enthusiastischen Wiedertäufer vornehmlich in Niederdeutschland. Melchior Hofmann und die Secte der Hofmannianer* (Leipzig, 1758). The book is based on sound scholarly research and for its time represents a notable achievement. But it has been far overtaken by the writings of M. L. Leendertz and F. O. zur Linden.

Of particular interest is the promise of the author to continue his work in the form of a general history of the Anabaptists and Mennonites in the following series: The second book, *Jan Matthys, Jan van Leyden, Johann Theodorici Batenburg, oder die Sekten der aufrührerischen Wiedertäufer und sogenannten Schwerdtgeister in den Niederlanden und in Westphalen;* the third book, *Ubbo Philipps oder die Sekte der Ubboniten;* the fourth book, *Menno Simons oder die Sekte der Mennonisten, das ist der wehrlosen und waffenlosen Taufgesinnten in den Niederlanden und in den von ihnen an andere Orte gepflanzten Gemeinen.* But he did not get beyond gathering the material. In 1782 he gave his entire collection of manuscript notes to the city library of Hamburg, consisting of 36 volumes folio and 22 volumes quarto. This material was destroyed during World War II. Most of it was taken from Ottius (*q.v.*). The Amsterdam Mennonite library has a paper by Krohn, copied by A. M. Cramer from the original manuscript, "Allgemeine Geschichte der Taufgesinnten oder Mennoniten in den Niederlanden." (*ML* II, 576.)   NEFF.

Kromau, a town (pop. 3,500) in western Moravia, of German and Czech stock. During the Reformation it was the center of the domain of Berthold von Lipa, who also possessed the Göding domain. In both domains he favored Anabaptism, so that several Bruderhofs arose here. By orders from Vienna he was compelled to expel them in 1534; but in 1545, 46 new settlements were made at Kromau, Rackschitz, Schackwitz, Gurdau, Kobelitz, Pavlovitz. During the persecution of 1550 they had much to endure, and some had to leave temporarily, but later were permitted to develop undisturbed. In 1622 the Bruderhofs here suffered severely at the hands of imperial troops; 500 men of the Löbel regiment were quartered in Kromau and Eibenschitz (Ivancice). The confiscated domain became the property of Gundakar von Liechtenstein.

The Bruderhof at Kromau was paid a visit in 1620 by King Frederick of the Palatinate on his way to Brno. He writes about it to his consort on Feb. 6, saying that the Brethren had given him specimens of their artistic products, including a splendid iron bedstead, a quantity of knives, and beautifully stitched gloves; for the queen they had given him very lovely china (see **Ceramics**); if they were living nearer Prague he would visit them frequently.   P.DE.

J. Schmidl, *Hist. soc. Jesu prov. Boh.* III (Prague, 1754); C. Aretin, *Beiträge zur Gesch. der Lit.* VII (Munich, 1806); Beck, *Geschichts-Bücher;* Loserth, *Communismus;* P. Dedic, "Die religiösen und kirchl. Verhältnisse in Mahren," ms.; Wolkan, *Geschicht-Buch; ML* II, 576.

Kromayer, Hieronymus (1610-70), a German Lutheran theologian, professor at the University of Leipzig, wrote a series of books frequently reprinted on exegetical, dogmatic, and ethical subjects, often quite polemic in nature. In his late years he produced a church history (*Ecclesia in politia*), which also mentions the Anabaptists and Mennonites, and a *Theologia positivo-polemica,* which deals in objective order with the controversies of the Lutherans with the Catholics, Calvinists, and Remonstrants, Socinians, Anabaptists, Weigelians, Jews, etc. In 1670, posthumously, his *Scrutinium religionum tum falsarum, Paganismi . . . tum unice verae et orthodoxae, Luteranismi* was published for the first time. He treats each religion by first presenting it and then refuting it. It is interesting to note that in obviously ascending order he ranks "Catabaptism and Quakerism" immediately after "Paganism, Islam, and Judaism," and before "Weigelianism, Rosicrucianism, Socinianism, Arminianism, Calvinism, Abyssinism, Anatolicism, Papism," and "the only true and orthodox Lutheranism." Of the *Quinque Disputationes selectiores,* at least the first, *De satisfactione Christi* (1642), refers once more to the Anabaptists. (*ADB* XVII; *RGG* III; *ML* II, 577.)
E.C.

Kromhorn: see Krummhörn.

Krommenie, a town (pop. 7,000) in the Dutch province of North Holland. There were Anabaptists here very early. Dirk Gerritsz van den Busch from the vicinity of Krommenie was burned at the stake as a martyr in The Hague on April 15, 1534. Just as in the neighboring villages, a congregation no doubt was also formed here at Krommenie. Of its history not much is known. It belonged to the Waterlander wing. It is said to have numbered 300 members in 1675, but this may be exaggerated. Already by that time the congregation was rather liberal, most members being under Collegiant (*q.v.*) influence. On July 22, 1702, many homes were burned down; the church also fell a victim to the flames. In its place a beautiful new frame church was built. It was dedicated on May 17, 1703 (Ascension Day), by C. van Diepenbroek of Haarlem. It is still in use. It has an oak pulpit, old benches and a cabinet organ from the 18th century. The meetinghouse is to be renovated in the near future. In the 18th century the membership decreased. In 1826 it numbered only 73; then it increased: 104 in 1836, 126 in 1861, 197 in 1900, 248 in 1927; from then there has been a decline: 170 in 1955. Since 1923 the pastor of this congregation has been also serving Wormer and Jisp (*q.v.*). The first minister of Krommenie who was educated at the Amsterdam Mennonite Theological Seminary was Jan Walig, serving here 1821-64; he was followed by Jeronimo de Vries 1865-70, J. W. van der Linden 1870-73, J. P. van der Vegte 1874-80, J. de Stoppelaar 1881-85, J. G. Boekenoogen 1885-1922, R. C. de Lange 1923-27, F. Kuiper 1928-32, J. Maarse 1932-47, J. H. Hylkema 1949- . Church activities include a ladies' circle and Sunday school for children.

Krommenie, whose population numbered about 2,000 in 1700, 3,050 in 1867, and about 7,000 in 1957, has always been an industrial town. Formerly it was known for its manufacture of canvas (in 1725 as much as 33,271 pieces); at present it has a number of factories, one of which is the widely known linoleum factory owned by the Mennonite Kaars Sypesteyn (*q.v.*) family.   vDZ.

Blaupot t. C., *Holland* I and II, see Index; Kühler, *Geschiedenis* I. 87, 108; *Inv. Arch. Amst.* I, No. 708; II, Nos. 2036-38; II 2, Nos. 267, 324; J. C. van Slee, *De Rijnsburger Colleginten* (Haarlem, 1895) 194-96; *DB* 1863, 97; 1883, 72; *Contactbrief van de Doopsgez. Gemeente Krommenie*, 1953; *DJ* 1955, 18-20; *ML* II, 577.

Krommeniedijk, a hamlet in the Dutch province of North Holland, was in the earliest times the home of numerous Anabaptists. In 1534 no fewer than 69 persons of this community were accused of "Anabaptism." In that year Jan Dirks Walen (or Walig) and Cornelis Luytgens of Krommeniedijk suffered a martyr's death by burning at The Hague. A congregation was organized here early, belonging to the Waterlander branch, but it always remained small and soon joined the neighboring church at Knollendam (*q.v.*) in supporting a minister, Simon Kalverboer, who served 1786-1828; in 1804 the two congregations formally merged. The combined congregation had only 14 members at that time. In 1847 a new meetinghouse was built in Krommeniedijk; it acquired an organ in 1897. Services were held here by the Knollendam pastor until 1921, when the building was sold.   vDZ.

Inv. Arch. Amst. I. Nos. 14, 17, 20, 892, 896, 1180; II, 2, Nos. 225, 243; Kühler, *Geschiedenis* I, 108; *DJ* 1850, 25; *DB* 1902, 244; 1907, 36 f., 40-42, 72-76; *Naamlijst* 1806, 68; *ML* II, 577.

Kromwal was once a Mennonite church in the Dutch province of Friesland. It was a hamlet situated between Witmarsum and Sneek on a high sandy plateau, surrounded at that time by swamps. Here the Anabaptists met at night in the olden times, coming from the neighboring localities; for example, from Hennaard, where Leenaert Bouwens baptized 110 persons. According to the Frisian historian Schotanus, who was born in the vicinity, there was a meetinghouse here as early as 1615. Little is known of the fate of this congregation. When the Frisian Sociëteit was established (1695) it had a membership of 50. In 1835 the number was 65; in 1861, 98. Since Kromwal was no longer the center of the congregation, the members took over a new church and parsonage at Ytens (*q.v.*) in 1865, and changed their name accordingly. Since 1923 this church has united with Baard (*q.v.*) for its pastoral service. The area covered by the charge of the minister of Ytens and Baard is the most extensive in the province of Friesland. (See **Ytens.**)   vDZ.

Blaupot t. C., *Friesland*, see Index; *DJ* 1840, 21 f., *DB* 1864, 75-81; 1865, 161; *ML* II, 577.

Kronsfeld, a common Mennonite village name transplanted from the Chortitza settlement of South Russia to Canada and South America. The name appeared in the following settlements: Neu-Rosengart, Ukraine; West Reserve, Man.; Cuauhtemoc, Mexico; and Neuland, Paraguay.   C.K.

Kronsfeld, a Mennonite village in the Chortitza settlement in South Russia, founded in 1880 by Heinrich Rempel. The first settlers were Johann Rempel, Julius Wall, Jakob Ketler, Heinrich Wall, and Wilhelm Wieler. The lease contract covered a period of 25 years; the rental amounted to about one ruble per acre. In 1900 a school was built. In 1907 the land was purchased through a Farmers' Bank, each settler receiving a farm of 32-37 acres. (*ML* II, 577.)   D.H.E.

Kronsgart Mennonite Brethren Church, near Winkler, Man., had its beginning in 1896 when some members of the Winkler M.B. Church bought farms 8-12 miles northwest of Winkler. The congregation was organized in 1896 with 13 members and Jacob Heide as pastor. J. B. Penner was ordained as minister in 1917. After using schools for meeting places, a church building was erected one-half mile north of the station of Kronsgart. Ministers who have served the congregation were J. Heide, B. Penner, leader, J. J. Buller, P. Shultz, G. Klassen, John J. Neufeld, and A. A. Hyde. The membership in 1955 was 174. The church is a member of the Manitoba Provincial Conference of the M.B. Church.   H.H.R.

Kronsthal, a Mennonite village of the Chortitza settlement in the province of Ekaterinoslav, South Russia. When the original Chortitza settlement was founded in 1789-1802, the government purchased an adjacent area of 5,400 acres to be added to it. On this land the village Kronstal was settled in 1809, and at the west end of Kronstal a sister village, Neu-Osterwick, was settled in 1812. The first 12 farmers came from Kronsweide and Rosental. In addition to agriculture the villagers engaged in wagon building and cabinet making, for which there was a good demand. In the first decades crop failures and diseases of the cattle made progress difficult. But gradually the village achieved prosperity, especially in the two decades before World War I. During the Revolution, and especially from Sept. 21 to Dec. 31, 1919, Kronstal suffered just as severely as the other villages at the hands of the Machno robber bands. Most of the stables were robbed of the last colt and the last cow. The Mennonite population at this time was 460. The typhus epidemic brought by the Machno bands attacked 406 persons between November and the following April; 66 died; only 80 did not contract the disease. Two persons were murdered, four died of starvation (1922). By Jan. 1, 1927, a total of 151 Mennonites had emigrated to Canada from here. In 1929-41, 70 persons were exiled and during the outbreak of the war between Germany and Russia (1941) 21 were evacuated eastward. Those remaining were evacuated to Germany (1943), whence some were returned to Russia by the Russian Army and others proceeded to America. (K. Stumpp, *Chortitza*, Berlin, 1943; *ML* II, 577 f.)   C.K.

Kronsthal, like many village names in Russia, was transplanted to Mennonite settlements in the New World, among them to the West Reserve in Manitoba and to the Hague settlement in Saskatchewan.   C.K.

Kronsweide, a village in the Chortitza Mennonite settlement, Ukraine, South Russia, was founded in 1790 by Frisian Mennonites near Einlage, and was first called Alt-Kronsweide (*q.v.*). Shortage of water compelled its abandonment in 1833; only five or six farmers remained. About four versts away, in a deep valley, Neu-Kronsweide was built, which in the course of 85 years grew into a thriving colony. Here was located the central church of the Kronsweide congregation; a second one was built in Schönsee in 1862. In October 1919, while the revolution was raging, Neu-Kronsweide was destroyed by fire and sword; 14 men were murdered; only the bare walls were left of the church. In 1925 the village began to be slowly rebuilt by returning fugitives, but it was as laborious as 130 years earlier. No village in the Kronsweide congregation suffered so disastrously as Neu-Kronsweide and Andreasfeld (*q.v.*), which was also wiped out. (*ML* II, 578.)

D.H.E.

Kronsweide Mennonite Church in the Chortitza settlement of South Russia had its principal church in Neu-Kronsweide; the congregation also met in churches at Schönwiese (*q.v.*), Kronsgarten (*q.v.*), and Einlage (*q.v.*), and in schools in the villages of Insel Chortitza (an island in the Dniepr), Neu-Schönwiese, and Jakovlevo. The Kronsweide Mennonite Church represented the Frisian (*q.v.*) Mennonites, while the Chortitza Mennonite Church was of Flemish (*q.v.*) background. The first elder of the congregation was (?) Klassen, who died in 1794. In that year a preacher (or elder?) was chosen at a meeting in charge of Cornelius Warkentin, an elder of the Prussian brotherhood. It is, however, not known who was at the head of the congregation before 1800. Since that time the elders were Heinrich Janzen 1800-24; Jakob Hildebrand (son of Peter Hildebrand, *q.v.*) 1825-67; Peter Klassen 1867-1902; Jakob Wiebe 1902-7; Johann Klassen 1907-23; Johann Martens, who was chosen in 1924, was exiled in the Ural territory 1930-36, returned and was exiled again in 1938. During this time public worship and religious activities were made impossible.

In 1887 (Mannhardt, *Jahrbuch,* 67 f.) the Kronsweide congregation numbered 750 baptized members and 765 children. Meetinghouses then were found at Neu-Kronsweide and Schönwiese (*q.v.*), and in all seven villages schools of good quality were being conducted.

In 1905 the Kronsweide Mennonite Church had a population of 1,925, of whom 900 were members. *Unser Blatt* reported in 1928 that the total population was 860 and the membership was 489. This apparently refers to the Kronsweide congregation and does not include the other Frisian branches. If it does, it would indicate that many of the members had emigrated to Canada. The same statistics reveal that the congregation had five ministers, four ministerial candidates, four deacons, in addition to the Elder Johann Martens. The majority of them had a secondary school training. Of the total congregation, 686 had Zentralschule education, 10 normal training, 52 secondary, and 3 university training.

Of the 80 families of Kronsweide who were taken

to Germany by the German army in 1943, some 350 persons were sent back to Russia by the Russian army. (H. Dirks, *Statistik,* 1905; *Unser Blatt* III, May 1928, 193.)

J.H.En., C.K.

Kropf, Daniel, an Anabaptist martyr, claimed by the Hutterian Brethren in their songs and chronicles as one of their number.

In 1533, when the persecution of Anabaptists grew more and more severe in Tirol, Austria, many fled into adjacent regions, spreading the movement into new territory. On June 4, 1532, a strict command was sent to Styria to hunt out the Anabaptists who might be there, for it had been reported that several had been seen in the Enns Valley.

But there was no need of orders to Styria. The Lutheran authorities were no less intent than the Catholics on preventing Anabaptist infiltration, and refugee Anabaptists, like Jakob Hutter, went to Moravia instead of Styria. Styrian authorities, however, succeeded in apprehending an outstanding Anabaptist preacher and writer of hymns, Daniel Kropf. All that is known of his life is found in the *Geschicht-Buch,* p. 48, in an entry of 1534: "Daniel Kropf, a servant of the truth, was seized in Styria at Graz with six others; with the two men he was sentenced to die by the sword, but the four women were drowned. Have testified with their body and life. Of this Daniel there are four songs which he made; also other writings on baptism and other points."

The *Märtyrertafel* (*Geschicht-Buch,* 182) also names the seven who testified to their faith with their blood. Of the writings mentioned in the *Geschicht-Buch,* the only ones known are the songs and his confession of faith, which he composed in prison in the name of his fellow prisoners to present to the council of Graz, and which is here summarized: To know the articles of our faith, for which we have left wife, children, goods, and been imprisoned by you and held and tortured a long time as evildoers. The Apostles' Creed follows, which is nearly identical with the Catholic version, except that the prisoners said. "We believe also, that there is a Christian church, in which the Holy Spirit has His work." He rejects water baptism and infant baptism. Of the communion he says that Christ is present in it figuratively; for those who eat of the Lord's bread and drink the cup, and thereby proclaim the Lord's death with humble thanksgiving and in faith of the body and blood of Christ. We do not believe like Antichrist (the pope), who with his following has desecrated the Lord's Supper and thinks he has conjured the physical Christ into the bread. In water baptism we see only a symbol of the bond which unites God with man through Christ. Salvation cannot lie therein, for it does not "stand in baptism," but alone in faith in Him whom God has sent. Herein the Antichrist has taken the liberty of mingling poison with His word.

Only three of the four songs mentioned by the *Geschicht-Buch* are known; they are printed in *Die Lieder der Hutterischen Brüder* (pp. 59-67). One song of 26 stanzas forms an acrostic of his name, thus identifying him as the author. It begins, "Das Himmelreich sich nahet, freut euch, ihr Christen, sehr." The second song begins, "Wer da christlich leben will, der heb' sich auf, setz ihm (sich) kein Ziel." It is a didactic poem of 33 stanzas with five lines in each. The last song, 19 stanzas of eight lines each, begins, "Wohl auf, O Gott vom Himmel, schweig jetzt nicht länger still"; it laments the sorrows the people of God now suffer. "Herr, stärk Herz und Sinnen dem armen Häuflein klein." LOSERTH.

Wolkan, *Geschicht-Buch*, 48; Beck, *Geschichts-Bücher; Die Lieder der Hutterischen Brüder* (Scottdale, 1914); J. Loserth, "Die Wiedertäufer in Steiermark," in *Mitteilungen des hist. Vereins für Steiermark*, No. 42, pp. 142 ff.; *ML* II, 578 f. Kropf's confession of faith is found in Codex 190 at Bratislava (Pressburg) in a copy made by Beck in the archives at Brno.

Krufft, Heinrich (von), a capmaker, a preacher of the Anabaptists at Cologne (*q.v.*). As early as 1560 the council of this city had learned that the Anabaptists numbered 40, and that their head was Heinrich Krufft, "a small squat man, who also dispenses baptism outside the city." Little is known of him; nothing concerning his death. His wife, Anna Derenbach, was expelled from Cologne in August 1565. Perhaps he is identical with Johann Krufft, who was baptized in the fall of 1534, by Gerhard (or Arnold) Westerburg. Ludwig Keller surmises that he is Pastor Johann at Rodenkirchen (Rembert, 475, note 1). Heinrich Krufft was a close friend of Matthias Servaes (*q.v.*). With him he traveled to München-Gladbach, preaching and baptizing. Servaes wrote him two letters from prison. Heinrich Krufft wrote two songs: "Herr Gott, ich muss nun klagen," and "Hinweg ist mit genommen," which name him acrostically. (Wolkan, *Lieder,* 100; Rembert, *Wiedertäufer,* 475 ff.; *ML* II, 579.) NEFF.

Kruikjes, bij de (at the jugs, i.e., near a house where the stone tablet in the facade showed six jars or stone bottles), name of a Mennonite congregation of Amsterdam, Holland, belonging to the Old Flemish branch, also called "Huiskopers" (*q.v.*), or "Dantsikers" (Danzig Old Flemish), meeting here from 1620 to 1788. They merged with the Amsterdam Zonist (*q.v.*) congregation on Jan. 1, 1789. The last preachers of the congregation "bij de Kruikjes," Cornelis Focking, serving after 1767 (d. 1791), Jan Christiaan Sepp (*q.v.*) after 1781 (d. 1811), Abraham Tieleman after 1786 (d. 1820), became the preachers of the Zonist congregation at the time of merging. Before this congregation began to meet here in 1620, this meetinghouse had apparently been used by another Old Flemish congregation from 1586 on. (*Inv. Arch. Amst.* II, 117-30; *Naamlijst* 1789, 57 f.) vDZ.

Krumau: see Kromau.

Krummhörn (Dutch, Kromhorn) is a district of East Friesland, Germany, located northwest of Emden (*q.v.*), between Emden and Greetsiel west of the line Emden-Wirdum, which in former times had a large Anabaptist-Mennonite population. In 1551-61 Leenaert Bouwens (*q.v.*) baptized in the village of Wirdum (1 baptism, 3 baptismal candidates),

Hinte (1 baptism), Groothausen (1 baptism, 2 candidates), and especially in Hamswehrum (3 baptisms, 9 candidates), making a total of 6 baptisms and 15 baptismal candidates. In 1563-65 he baptized in Wirdum (5 baptisms, 28 candidates), Woquard (1 baptism, 2 candidates), Wybelsum (4 baptisms, 9 candidates), and Pewsum (3 baptisms, 5 candidates), a total of 13 baptisms and 44 candidates. In 1633 there were in the Krummhörn, from north to south along the west bank, the following numbers of families: Greetsiel 1, Hauen 4, Pilsum 3, Manslagt 1, Groothusen 5, Hamswehrum 9, Upleward 3, and Heiselhusen 1; further inland, Wirdum 2, Visquard 1, Eilsum 5, Dykhausen 2, and Syhlmönken 2.

In 1622 the separation of the Groningen Old Flemish under the influence of Uko Walles (*q.v.*) becomes stronger here. In the newly reclaimed land at Wirdum lived Abraham Nannings, the preacher of the Eilsum congregation, which met in the home of Rottger Rolef. He had at first been of a different mind, but was later rebaptized in the Dutch province of Groningen. He officiated at marriages, but for baptism an elder came from Leer, and after this elder's death, someone from Groningen. All the Mennonites registered in the Greetsiel area had probably been rebaptized in the previous decade. In official questionings the authorities sought information concerning the relations with other Mennonite groups and concerning any proselytizing in the recognized churches. Nannings replied by referring to their letter of protection.

In the following 125 years the trend to the city became effective among the Mennonites. In 1769 there were in Eilsum 3 baptized members, in Greetsiel 5, and in Wirdum 1; they united at that time with the larger Norden congregation. In the following years the preacher of Norden held three or four sermons annually at Krummhörn until there were no members left (about 1780). The *Naamlijst* does not mention Krummhörn (Kromhorn) in 1731 ff. E.C.

Blaupot t. C., *Groningen, Overijssel en Oost-Friesland* I; J. P. Müller, *Die Mennoniten in Ostfriesland vom 16. biz zum 18. Jahrhundert* (Emden and Borkum-Amsterdam, 1887); Leonardus Hesta, "De laatste bladzijde van de geschiedenis der oud-vlaamsche gemeente te Norden," *DB* 1895, 74-100, especially 82, 85, 88; *ML* II, 577.

Krüsi, Johannes, one of the first martyrs of the Anabaptist movement. Concerning his life and work little is known. In the middle of 1525 he was arrested in St. Gall, but released upon oath not to return to the city (see **St. Gall**). In the canton of Appenzell he won the Reformed congregation at Teusen to himself. In the abbey of St. Gall he also had some success; but all evangelization was forbidden him by a decision of the four protectorates of the abbey (Zurich, Lucerne, Schwyz, and Glarus). The abbot Franz von Gaisberg gave orders to seize every Anabaptist who came into his realm preaching (Götzinger, 407). On June 3, 1525, Krüsi was still preaching in the vicinity of Tablat; when the magistrate and his servants ordered him to stop preaching, the large crowd listening protested (*Eidgenössische Abschiede*). Krüsi was soon afterward seized at night in bed in his native town, St. Georgen, and was later taken secretly (as Kessler says, contrary to custom) to Lucerne. The council of Lucerne asked St. Gall for instructions on Aug. 11, 1525, relating what was reported about him, that Krüsi urged disobedience to the government, rejected infant baptism, advocated adult baptism and community of goods, rejected the holy Sacrament, instead of which he invented the breaking of bread and observed it in his own way (Strickler, 399).

The reply from St. Gall seems to have been lost. Krüsi was condemned to death at the stake, and was put to death in 1525 (Kessler). He was the second blood witness of the Swiss Brethren known by name. The first martyr was Eberli Bolt (q.v.), who was burned at the stake in Schwyz on May 29, 1525.

Some later historiographers have confused Johannes Krüsi with Anton Kürsiner of Schwyz (or Roggenach; see *Zwingliana* I, 139); Nitsche (64) considers the two to be the same person (see also Egli, 26, who states that Krüsi was also called Hans Kern of Klingnau).

In Teufen the Anabaptists persisted for some time after Krüsi's death. About Christmas 1528 an Anabaptist council was held here, attended by representatives of other countries (Beck, *Geschichts-Bücher*, 64). Not much is known about it, but it seems to have been held for the purpose of purging the brotherhood of impure elements. One of the visitors was Augustine Bader (q.v.), whose fantastic ideas were rejected by the hundred or more representatives at the council, whereupon he left the brotherhood and went his own way. Teufen seems to have been important in the further history of the Swiss Brethren. In November 1529 the Appenzell clergy, including Walter Klarer and Matthias Kessler, held a disputation with the Swiss Brethren here (*Zwingliana* I, 367; IV, 58).   HEGE.

H. Bullinger, *Ref.-Gesch.* I (Frauenfeld, 1838); E. Götzinger, *Joachim v. Watt: Deutsche Historische Schriften* II (St. Gall, 1877); J. Kessler, *Sabbata* (St. Gall, 1902); R. Nitsche, *Gesch. der Wiedertäufer in der Schweiz* (Einsiedeln, 1885); J. Strickler, *Aktensammlung zur Schweiz. Ref.-Gesch.* I (Zürich, 1878); idem, *Eidgenossische Abschiede* IV, Part Ia (1873) 672, 692, 705, 734; *ML* II, 579 f.

Kruydt-Hofken, a Dutch hymnbook: see **Gheestelijck Kruydt-Hofken.**

Kuban, a Mennonite settlement in the Kuban district of the Northern Caucasus, Russia, on the Kuban River, which flows from the east into the Black Sea. This region had previously been inhabited by Nogais, who had emigrated to Turkey. In connection with the organization of the Mennonite Brethren in the parent settlements, the Mennonites in the Molotschna and Chortitza requested an additional grant of 17,500 acres of the government, through Johann Claassen (q.v.) of Liebenau, for a new settlement on the Kuban. On this tract the villages Wohldemfürst (later Velikoknyazheskoye) and Alexanderfeld (later Alexandrodar) were founded in 1862 and 1866. In 1866 the settlement, which throughout its brief history consisted predominantly of Mennonite Brethren, had its Mennonite privileges confirmed.

The early settlement was confronted with serious difficulties. Only 67 of the 100 families for whom land had been granted settled there by 1866. In part the difficulties were internal, caused by Templers (q.v.) and Adventists (q.v.), and were removed to a large extent when these elements withdrew. Then there were also economic difficulties. From the neighboring natives (Tatars, Circassians) with their primitive methods, they could get no help in agriculture. They had to learn by trial and error; gradually cattle raising and fruit culture proved most successful. There was a ready market for the Mennonite bred Red cow; and horses were bought by the army.

Fruit culture was brought to an even higher state of development. Well-developed nurseries distributed millions of improved strains of fruit trees, berries, and ornamental trees. Industry related to these occupations was also thriving: there were two factories which made farm implements, mills of various kinds, and stores. There was a co-operative for cheese making and grape growers (since 1890), a credit union, a grain storage elevator, and an association of consumers.

In 1910 there were ten landless day laborers, 150 landless craftsmen and factory workers, eight small farms, 22 half farms and 57 full farms; the owners of the full farms often owned several; and 15 owners of larger farms outside the settlement, who kept their connection with the villages by owning land there too.

Intellectual and spiritual life were also maintained on a high level. Their schools with eight-year courses (ages 7-15) and excellent teachers, were unique for their high standards even among the Mennonites. In addition there was a music club, which owned a hall, and a library club. Each wing had its own church, Mennonite Church (see **Wohldemfürst-Alexandrodar** Mennonite Church), Mennonite Brethren, and the Jerusalemsfreunde. All Mennonite groups had their own *volost* administration in Velikoknyazheskaye; here the district administrative center common to all groups was also located.

The settlement achieved great prosperity. The outstanding success of the Mennonites in the Kuban in the fields of pedagogy and agriculture was repeatedly given recognition by the Czarist government, even to the extent of granting titles of personal nobility, more than in any other Mennonite settlement. "The Kubans were unusual workers" and "savers." Here the "intelligent village," "the combination of intellectual and physical work," the ideal of the sociologists, became a reality. Their highly developed economic system was destroyed by Communism, through no fault of their own. The number of Mennonites in the Kuban in 1904 was about 2,000 (Friesen, 455); in 1914 it had declined to 1,500, and in 1926 to 1,400 (Ehrt, 78 and 152).

During the Revolution the settlement suffered like the others. A small group left the Kuban for Canada in 1924-25. During the following years many were exiled, particularly 1937-38. Gradually the settlement disintegrated. During the Russo-German War (1941) all remaining Mennonites were sent to

Kazakhstan. A few refugees who had escaped to the Ukraine have reached Canada.   T.B.

A. Ehrt, *Das Mennonitentum in Russland;* Friesen, *Brüderschaft;* K. Lindmann, *Von den deutschen Kolonisten in Russland* (Stuttgart, 1924); *Die Kubaner Ansiedlung* (North Kildonan, 1953); *ML* II, 580.

Kudus (*Koedoes*) is the largest city (1954 pop. 55,000) of the former Dutch Mennonite mission field in Java, Indonesia; the population in 1930 was distributed as follows: 43,697 Javanese, 4,386 Chinese, 180 Arabians and other Asians, and 381 Europeans. Kudus is the government center of the province, covering 295 sq. miles, and comprising 147 villages, total population (1930) 305,942. The principal industry is the manufacture of cigarettes. The native population is Mohammedan.

The interest of the mission turned to Kudus when work in the city of Japara seemed unfruitful, and work was opened in the villages. Some Chinese, who had been converted by the Salvation Army, refused the oath of citizenship, and as a result of Bible study desired to be baptized. Since Kaju-Apu was then unoccupied, they called N. Thiessen, stationed at Margaredjo, to baptize them. This was the beginning of a revival that soon reached the villages of Tandjung and Majong. At Kudus, Tandjung, and Majong mission schools were opened in the Malayan language, but could not long be maintained because of the increasing demand for schools using the Dutch language.

In 1921, after Johann Fast returned to Kaju-Apu from Europe, there were 49 baptized Chinese in Kudus. Besides the missionary, a native Christian, Tee Siem Tat, did much to develop the congregation. It was incorporated in 1927, and in the same year Tee Siem Tat received permission from the Dutch colonial government to preach and establish churches. The church, with a membership of about 200, became independent of the mission. In 1928 it built its own meetinghouse. To the subsidiary congregations in Tandjung and Majong a third was added in Japara. When new missionaries came to Kaju-Apu, it was decided that Hermann Schmitt should locate in the city of Kudus (*Jaaresverslag,* 1928, 17).

The mission work in Kudus consisted of evangelization, colportage, and a school. Evangelization and pastoral care were in the hands of the pastor and a native helper for Kudus and its subsidiary, Pendo-Rabajan, which came into being in 1931 chiefly through colportage. The combined membership at the end of 1932 was 51, besides 34 children. Services were attended by an average of 59 persons. From Kudus as a center other stations were served: Kaju-Apu (*q.v.*); Pati (*q.v.*), a city 15 miles from Kudus, with a native helper (Albonese) and 28 baptized members and 30 children, and an average attendance of 62. The hospital at Kelet (*q.v.*) also belonged to the Kudus field. Kudus was the colportage center for the entire field. There were five colporteurs who sold about 200 Bibles a month and distributed more than 1,000 tracts.

The Dutch language school for Chinese children was built in 1924 by Fast and his niece, Miss Jansz. In 1927 its enrollment was 57. In 1932, when Tjen A.

Kwoei from the Mennonite Brethren mission in Surinam was made head of this school, it increased to 160 pupils, with several additional teachers. Besides the Chinese, Javanese children also attended this school. It was the only Christian school of its kind on the Mennonite field, preparing for secondary schools, and was therefore of great importance to the community.

The small Javanese congregation of Kudus was until 1940 conducted by Hermann Schmitt (*q.v.*) and some native assistant preachers and teachers. On Nov. 24, 1940, the congregation became independent. Then Sastroadi became its preacher. In 1949 the total membership of this Javanese congregation numbered 78 baptized and 63 children, in 1955, 130 and 150.

In Kudus there is also a Chinese Mennonite congregation with a membership in 1955 of about 450. Tan King Ien is its pastor. (*ML* II, 516 f.)
          H.Sc., vDZ.

Kuesen, Cathrijn, an Anabaptist martyr: see **Trijnken Keuts.**

Kufstein (Kofstein), a city (pop. 11,844) in the Inn Valley of Tirol, Austria, played an outstanding role in Anabaptist history. The number of executions was given as 16 in the record of 1581, placing it fourth among the 13 towns and villages of the valley.

Leonhard Schiemer's writings indicate that there were Anabaptists in Kufstein as early as 1527. Three are named in 1528: the knifesmith's wife, Jörg Held, and his wife. In spite of all the harshness of the suppressive mandates and the vigor of their application there were Anabaptists in and around Kufstein in 1529-30; the bloody trial of Georg Grünwald (*q.v.*) and 15 other Anabaptists was brought to its conclusion here. The teacher of these persons, the former chaplain of Kitzbühel, Jakob Portzner, escaped with his life by recantation. Anabaptists who fled lost their property by confiscation; among these were Wolfgang of Elmau, Michael of Weissenbach, Lienhard Hofer, and Paul Frauenhofer.

The mandates brought results. In June 1533 the government reported to the king "that in the three domains of Rattenberg, Kufstein, and Kitzbühel no one is known to be contaminated with Anabaptism, or that it is making inroads," welcome news to Ferdinand, who had just sent further admonitions to the archbishop of Salzburg to wipe out the Anabaptists at Kufstein.

Since Hutter's death in 1536 there had indeed been a weakening in Anabaptist propaganda, but it was by no means extinguished. In 1540 "Black Lindl" of the Puster Valley lay in prison at Kufstein. Special care was taken to apprehend the Anabaptists traveling up and down the Inn to Krems (*q.v.*) en route to Moravia. When a group of these was imprisoned in Wasserburg, the judge of Kufstein was told the boatmen should also have been arrested.

In later decades there is only occasional reference to Anabaptists in Kufstein; in 1577 caution is again urged to prevent their traveling down the river to go to Moravia, and an order was issued on June 10, 1578, strictly forbidding the transport of Anabaptists on the river. As at the turn of the century the situation of the Anabaptists in Moravia also became precarious, immigration from the Inn became less frequent, and finally stopped. LOSERTH.

Beck, *Geschichts-Bücher;* Loserth, *Anabaptismus;* Wolkan, *Geschicht-Buch;* Zieglschmid, *Chronik; ML* II, 581.

Kühbörncheshof, a Mennonite church in the northwest of the Rhenish Palatinate, Germany, which is united with Zweibrücken (*q.v.*), Kaiserslautern (*q.v.*), and Saarland (*q.v.*) into a single congregational circuit.

The estate where once "a pure wilderness" reigned was returned to agriculture by Hans Heinrich Latscha, a Swiss Mennonite refugee. In 1717 Latscha acquired 220 acres of field and woods from the Palatine government, for which he paid an initial sum of 85 florins, and a rental of eight malters of oats to the secretariat at Kaiserslautern, in addition to eight florins as an annual fee. He had as capital four oxen, two cows, and two steers (*Karlsruher Generallandesarchiv Akten: Mennoniten-Verzeichnis*). Johannes Risser (*Menn. Bl.,* 1855, 50) states that Latscha and his wife Maria came from Maasmünster in Upper Alsace in 1715. The Latscha family has remained on the farm to the present. Other Mennonite families, for instance, Rink, settled there too.

The neighboring Stockborn was also settled by Mennonites; especially the Koller family is represented here. A record of Jan. 27, 1727, shows that the inhabitants of Kühbörncheshof were permitted by the government to have private worship services. They joined the Sembach congregation and in spite of the great distance, did not form an independent congregation until 1832, when the new chapel was dedicated (*Gem.-Kal.,* 1901, 108 with picture). Their first preacher was Heinrich Koller (1832-46), who until then had served the Sembach congregation. On May 10, 1852, a conference was held at the Kühbörncheshof, which passed a resolution to publish and use the *Pfälzisch-hessisches Formularbuch.*

In 1802, according to Frey's *Statistik der Pfalz,* there were in Erfenbach 16 Mennonites, Stockborn 7, Rodenbach 12, Kühbörncheshof 28, and Otterbach 7; in 1834, Stockborn 36, Trippstadt 37, Weilerbach 15, Kühbörncheshof 48. In 1934 there were on the Kühbörncheshof 11 families with 53 souls; Stockborn 7 families with 35, Olsbrücken 2 families with 6, Horterhof 2 families with 8 (the register of 1752 lists Jakob Borckholder at Horterhof with 7 members in the family), Schallodenbach one family with 13, Kottweiler one family with 11, Rodenbach one family with 3, Oberstaufenbach one family with 4, Katzweiler 2 persons: a total of 26 families with 128 souls.

In 1878 Kühbörncheshof was united into a single preaching charge with Ernstweiler and Neudorferhof, called Kaiserslautern (*q.v.*). The last lay preacher of Kühbörncheshof was Jakob Rinck (d. 1891), who served until 1877. The first salaried minister (after the union) was Samuel Blickensdörfer, who served 1878-80. He was followed by Abraham Hirschler 1880-1931, Abraham Harder 1931-37,

Hugo Scheffler 1937-51, and Theo Hotel 1951- . In 1954 the Kaiserslautern circuit consisted of the congregations of Zweibrücken and Saarland, in addition to Kaiserslautern and Kühbörncheshof. The 1954 membership of Kühbörncheshof was 159 baptized, plus 56 children. The congregation is a member of the Vereinigung of Mennonite Churches in Germany, the Palatine-Hessian Conference, and the Conference of South German Mennonites. (*ML* II, 581 f.)   NEFF.

Kühler, Wilhelmus Johannes (1874-1946), a Dutch Mennonite church historian, professor at the Mennonite Seminary of Amsterdam and the University of Amsterdam, was born at Amsterdam on Dec. 8, 1874. Like his cousin Karel Vos (*q.v.*) he was descended on his mother's side from the Wybrands family, which had already produced two Mennonite church historians (Aemilius Willem and Christiaan Nicolaas). His father, Paulus Frans Kühler, a businessman of Amsterdam, was a member of the Walloon Reformed Church. W. J. Kühler was educated at the Amsterdam seminary and university, studying under Samuel Cramer (*q.v.*) and I. J. de Bussy (*q.v.*) in 1892-97.

In 1897 W. J. Kühler entered his first position as a minister, serving the Terschelling (*q.v.*) congregation until 1902, when he accepted a call to the congregation of Meppel-Assen in the province of Drente, and in 1905 to the Leiden congregation. He made use of the facilities of the University of Leiden for research into history, and in 1906 published in the *Doopsgezinde Bijdragen* an article on *Het Offer des Heeren* (*q.v.*), the oldest Dutch martyrbook, which had just been republished. He had previously published studies in the *Theologisch Tijdschrift* on the *Confessio Tetrapolitana* and on D. R. Camphuyzen.

Then Kühler turned his attention to the Middle Ages, especially G. Groote and his following. He published an article, "De prediking van Geert Groote," in *Teyler's Theologisch Tijdschrift.* Then he made himself responsible for the publication of Horn's *Vita Gerardi Magni* (*Archief voor Kerkgeschiedenis*) and the *Biographien van devote zusters te Deventer* (*Archief voor de geschiedenis van het Aartsbisdom Utrecht*). In further research he discovered that the *Vita Gerardi Magni* was not an original work by Thomas à Kempis, but was a propagandistic excerpt from an older work, which was then intentionally destroyed. His chief contribution in this field was his dissertation, *Johannes Brinckerinck en zijn klooster te Diepenveen* (Rotterdam, 1908). This study was very favorably received, also by Catholic scholars. Hensen, who later became the director of the Dutch Historical Institute at Rome, wrote, "I know of no Protestant writer who has penetrated so deeply into delicately developed Catholic religious life." Kühler's next important work was *Het Socinianisme in Nederland* (1912), which includes the relations between Socinianism and the Dutch Mennonites in the 16th-18th centuries.

When Samuel Cramer retired from his professorship at the Mennonite Seminary, W. J. Kühler succeeded him on Sept. 1, 1912, in Mennonitica and practical theology and on Feb. 10, 1913, in church history at the University of Amsterdam. His installation lecture was on "De beteekenis der Dissenters in de Kerkgeschiedenis van Nederland." In 1913 he also became the librarian of the Mennonite Library of Amsterdam; with great care he had many of the old unbound books bound in bindings suited to the age of the book. In 1916 he became the editor of the *Doopsgezinde Bijdragen,* which he was unfortunately unable to publish beyond 1919.

In addition to several minor studies, Kühler now devoted more and more interest to the history of the Dutch Mennonites. The church history written by Blaupot ten Cate having become antiquated, Kühler published the first volume of his painstaking history, based on the sources, *Geschiedenis der Nederlandsche Doopsgezinden in de zestiende eeuw* (Amsterdam, 1932).

In 1940 Kühler published at Haarlem the first part of the second volume of his lifework, entitled *Geschiedenis van de Doopsgezinden in Nederland, Tweede helft 1600-1735, eerste helft.* When he died only one chapter of the sequel was ready. This was printed under the title *Gemeentelijk Leven* (Haarlem, 1950), followed by a biography of Kühler by Chr. P. van Eeghen. In the *Doopsgezinde Bijdragen* Kühler published the following papers: "Gesprek met Menno" (1905), *Het Offer des Heeren* (1906), "Het vrouwtje van Gouda," a short story (1907), "S. Cramer," a biography (1916), "De strijd om de belijdenis in de vereenigde Vlaamsche, Friesche en Hoogduitsche gemeente te Utrecht" (1916), "De vier tijdvakken van de geschiedenis der Doopsgezinden in Nederland" (1917), "De oprichting der Amsterdamsche Kweekschool in 1735" (1918), and "Het Nederlandsche Anabaptisme en de revolutionnaire woelingen der zestiende eeuw" (1919). Mention should be made besides of a large number of articles in the field of Mennonite history published in *De Zondagsbode,* and also of his important paper, "Het Anabaptisme in Nederland" in *De Gids* (1921), in which he defended the peaceful character of Anabaptism in the Netherlands against the views of Karel Vos.

W. J. Kühler's son Paulus F. Kühler has been a treasurer of the A.D.S. (Dutch Mennonite General Conference) since 1951. C.K.

Biographical sketch of W. J. Kühler by Chr. P. van Eeghen, in Kühler's *Geschiedenis van de Doopsgezinde in Nederland; DB* 1912, 201, *Verslag A.D.S.* 1944, 16; *Algemeen Doopsgezind Weekblad* 1946, Nos. 7 and 8; *DJ* 1949, 38 f.; *ML* II, 582.

Kuhn (Kaumuff, Khumbauf), **Blasius** (Blasy), was one of the early Anabaptist preachers of the bishopric of Speyer on the right side of the Rhine and in adjacent regions. When persecution grew more violent he led the group around Bruchsal (*q.v.*) and Bretten, which had gained about 500 adherents by 1530 and 1531, to Auspitz (*q.v.*) in Moravia. (*ML* II, 582.) HEGE.

Kühn, Johannes, author of *Toleranz und Offenbarung, eine Untersuchung der Motive der Toleranz im offenbarungsgläubigen Protestantismus* (Leipzig, 1923, 473 p.), perhaps the first book to present an adequate and fair interpretation of Anabaptism in general. Kühn posed the question of the motivation of the different denominations within Protestantism which accept the revelation of the Holy Scripture as the final authority (*offenbarungsgläubig* is his term) for toleration or the opposite. In this field the book is a valuable contribution to the history of ideas in the 16th and 17th centuries. Kühn discovered that the groups were by no means uniform in their spiritual attitudes, and thus he had to develop a typology of his own to make the attitudes for or against freedom of conscience understandable. He was of course familiar with the typology of Troeltsch (church and sect) and the latter's term "spiritual reformers," and F. Heiler's typology of prophetic and mystical religion; but he found such a condensation into polar groups wanting in the face of the many-sidedness of the real history of ideas. Thus he developed a five-point typology which surprised many but which is fairly generally accepted today.

Kühn proposes five types: (1) the prophetically preached religion of revelation, Martin Luther being an example. The Word of God has been revealed to us, hence we have but to preach it (*verkündigen*) and cannot permit any deviation from it. No room is left for effective toleration (except in the private sphere of unspoken thoughts). (2) The spiritualistic motive (this term Kühn borrowed from Troeltsch). As an example Schwenckfeld is named, and for the Anglo-Saxon world Roger Williams, the Baptists, Congregationalists, and John Milton (whom Kühn describes as half way between Luther and the rational idealists of type 5). This type of Protestantism has no objective (formulated) creed; it believes in a "concrete" spiritualism and in figurative interpretation of the Scriptures. The church concept is accordingly loose and without much obligatory discipline. (3) The motive of Anabaptist discipleship (*täuferische Nachfolge*), where the teachings of Jesus and His message of the kingdom overshadow the doctrinal formulations of Paul. Two representatives are discussed: the Anabaptists for Central Europe, and the Quakers for the Anglo-Saxon world. Both emphasize the intention of active sonship of God (*tätige Gotteskindschaft*) which issues in a sacred communal life (*heiliges Gemeinschaftsleben*). The two great symbols of such a discipleship Christianity are (*a*) love and (*b*) the cross. For the Anabaptists the cross (i.e., the suffering church) is almost more significant than love since the principle of separation from the world restricts the latter to their own group. Quakers, who are more open to the world, do not emphasize the cross so much (although they knew it only too well in the 17th century) but prefer to teach love in action. It implies also toleration, as the church concept is one of voluntary association (*Freiwilligkeitskirche*).

Kühn effectively defends the Anabaptists against the reproach of "legalism" and stresses their Biblical concreteness, namely, to actually live the way which Jesus has shown. Here the difference from the basic theological structure of the great reformers becomes particularly evident (224). Love assumes the connotation of nonresistance and nonvengeance; faith is considered a free gift of grace which cannot be constrained (hence liberty of conscience). The fight for the kingdom of God is exclusively done with the "sword of the spirit."

It was not until 20 years later that H. S. Bender introduced the idea of discipleship into the discussion of the essence of Anabaptism again; since that time it has become more and more evident that this is perhaps the most adequate interpretation of the spirit of Anabaptism which can be formulated. To be sure, however, it does not yet exhaust the theological basis of this orientation.

(4) The next type is the mystical form of Biblical Protestantism. Actually and strangely, there are very few mystics within Protestantism (over against Catholicism). Apparently Protestantism does not lend itself easily to this type. Kühn discusses as an example David Joris (was he really a mystic?) and Jacob Boehme (in whom, incidentally, Rufus M. Jones recognizes a forerunner of Quakerism). In Joris the motives are rather mixed but the idea of dying (to the world) and resurrection (to celestial vision) is present in any case. The final *unio mystica* with the divine is the very goal of all meditation. This type of Christianity dissolves to a large extent the idea of Scriptural revelation (over against the spiritual reformers), and is little interested in group or church life, thus working strongly for individualism.

(5) The last type: ethical and rational religion, actually a form of Christian "idealism" (or, in the 19th century, liberal Protestantism), has finally lost all concreteness of the Scriptural revelation, reducing Christianity to a sort of ethical reasonableness or humanism. It is a cool and intellectual affair with Sebastian Castellio (Switzerland) and Arminius (Netherlands) of the 16th century, and with Hugo Grotius and Chillingworth of the 17th century, and similar forerunners of rationalism and enlightenment as examples. Strangely enough Kühn includes in this type also Philipp Spener, the "father of Pietism," known for his emphasis upon emotional inwardness and subjectivism. But a finer analysis proves that his roots were of the same kind; revelation is now dissolved (hence toleration promoted) and emphasis is shifted to the ethical aspect.

Needless to say, this typology, like all other typologies, is not always fitting. Historic realities do not exactly match given categories, and most persons and movements cut across different types. Also the concept of the "spirit" within the many Christian groups of modern times is oscillating and many sided. Still, a framework like the one described helps much toward a clearer picture of the development of ideas, and in particular its interpretation of Anabaptism may be called new and highly acceptable.   R.F.

Kuhr (Gor), **Joseph**, a Hutterite preacher at Alwinc (*q.v.*) in Transylvania during the reign of Maria Theresa, and the leader of the group which in the face of severe persecution and augmented by the refugees from Carinthia fled to Walachia (*q.v.*) and thence to Vishenka (*q.v.*) in Russia; in Walachia he was chosen as head of the brotherhood, serving thus 1779-94.

From the pen of his successor, the historiographer Johannes Waldner (1749-1824), we learn many facts concerning the unparalleled energy of this man, who saved this Alwinc and Carinthian group from threatening extinction and led it to great prosperity in Russia. Before they left he was ill six months of the plague, which killed many of the Brethren at Alwinc and took its toll in his own family. On Aug. 15, 1774, he was chosen as a preacher and confirmed the following year.

In 1762 began the struggle of the Transylvanian authorities to compel the Hutterian Brethren to sacrifice their faith. Only the leaders were to be banished from the country. Their chief opponent was the Jesuit Delpini (called "Delphini" in the chronicles), who placed himself at the disposal of the government for this very purpose. An imperial mandate was issued in 1762, that the Brethren would be tolerated in the country only on the condition that they would abandon their faith and join one of the three established churches. The Brethren replied that they preferred to leave, but the government refused to permit this, insisting on conversion instead.

The initial steps were taken by the Catholic bishop; if they would not comply voluntarily, they would be forced to do so. Kuhr undertook to defend the Hutterites before the bishop. In the spring of 1763, the government had Kuhr and the head of the brotherhood imprisoned; but in September they were released.

Six weeks later Delpini appeared, and made daily visits among the Brethren. First they had to give up their books. Then the elder, Mertl Roth, and the brotherhood were officially ordered to transfer to the Catholic faith. He, Delpini, would instruct them. On Sunday Delpini came to their chapel and preached on John 16: "I have yet many things to say unto you." At the close of the sermon he asked how they had liked his sermon. All were silent. Kuhr arose and said: "What you have said from the Gospel I know as well as you do; what you have said about the many saints I do not believe; and what you said about the Jesuit who moved a mountain is a Jesuit lie. The meaning of this part of the Gospel is quite different: Jesus means the rulers of the world, who like a mountain stand in the way of the truth, they shall be moved by the firm faith of the God-fearing." Then began an argument on infant baptism, in which Kuhr refuted Delpini. "You have made no Catholic of me," said Kuhr in conclusion.

But what followed was ominous. When the Jesuit rose to go, Kuhr cried out that he would not attend any more of his sermons: "He who still calls himself a brother or sister, let him decide to follow me!" But not a person, not even his son, went. Not a person, not even an elder, said a single word against the Jesuit. But the Jesuit, meeting Kuhr on the street, said, "Just wait; I'll teach you!" Kuhr replied, "You can teach me nothing; you can not do more to me than God permits."

Delpini recognized that if he was to achieve his end he must render Kuhr innocuous. Kuhr was imprisoned in Klausenburg three years. Continued attempts were made to convert him, but to no avail. Waldner repeats some of the conversations between Kuhr and his adversaries, and they are indeed evidence of courage and talent. "He did not find it difficult to forsake his wealth and worldly possessions . . . yea, even his children for Christ's sake, for he loved God above all things." After three years he was released. He was asked to promise not to escape. "I am not a rogue nor an evildoer, and will await what God sends me."

The resistance of the Alwinc Anabaptists grew weaker. Mertl Roth, the elder of the group, was persuaded to recant, and the others followed. Roth's excuse for his step was, "We do not observe our faith right, and community of goods has disappeared. Even if we resist a long time, we must finally become Catholic. God may still turn the tide; a war may come, and then we may live for our faith under another government."

Kuhr proved that a brotherhood does not have to perish unless it gives itself up. Kuhr made an essential contribution, not only in the fact that the Hutterian Brethren still exist, but also that they are growing and thriving. He organized the resistance and persuaded the brethren who still had a spark of resistance in them to flee from Alwinc to Kreuz, where with the help of the Carinthian emigrees a new brotherhood was set up in the old spirit, in which Kuhr was the active ferment. With him went Johannes Stahl with wife and four children, Anna Wipf with five children, Jakob Stutz with his mother, a weaver named Joseph with his mother, and Lorenz Tschetterle. But of these some were seized. When Kuhr was informed that the entire brotherhood in Alwinc had confessed the new faith and fallen on their knees before the bishop, and Kuhr was urged to let himself be taught too, he said. "What shall I do? Each must carry his own burden and answer for himself on the Last Day."

Since Kuhr's presence in the country constituted a threat to the new Catholics, he and Johannes Stahl were conducted to the Polish border. Thus ended the Alwinc brotherhood. A total of 19 persons, whose names Waldner has recorded, escaped.

Who should know better than Kuhr that Transylvania would be no home for a new brotherhood? They found no favor in the eyes of Joseph II, who issued the Edict of Toleration for the two Protestant churches.

Kuhr and Stahl wandered through Poland to Moldavia and on to Walachia, seeking a suitable site to set up their religious brotherhood. Walachia seemed favorable. There was land, no religious compulsion, and German settlers welcomed. And so the Hutterites of Kreuz, increased by the Alwinc remnant, migrated in October 1767 over the Transylvanian Alps. It was a very difficult journey with women and children on rough paths. Many a one, says Waldner, discovered that a sleeper can walk and a walker sleep. In Walachia Kuhr helped to establish the colony on a sound basis, for he understood the native tongue.

But the fortunate beginnings were interrupted by the Russo-Turkish war. Turkish robber bands plundered the Bruderhof and mistreated the people in a barbarous way. Then the colony accepted the offer of the Russian field marshal, Count Romyanzov, to settle on his estates in Vishenka on the Desna. They spent several decades in Russia, making rapid progress. Kuhr introduced all the old institutions of the brotherhood, which had been lost during the migratory years. But to him his most important task was to return to Transylvania and get his three children who were still living in Alwinc; he brought two out, his son Joseph and his daughter Gretel; but his son Michel had married a Hungarian wife and could not leave then. He promised to come the following year, but he died in 1786.

Kuhr held the office of preacher for many years, until old age compelled him to turn it over to Johannes Waldner, the historian, retaining, however, the headship of the brotherhood. He died May 2, 1794, at the age of 80. A week before his death he delivered his last *Rede und Vermahnung* to the assembled elders. He had been a preacher for 46 years; the entire brotherhood was under his care 15 years. (From the "Denkwürdigkeiten Johannes Waldners," kindly loaned to the author by Elias Walter, Macleod, Alberta.) LOSERTH.

Zieglschmid, *Klein-Geschichtsbuch;* J. Loserth, "Decline and Revival of the Hutterites," *MQR* IV (1930) 93-112; *ML* II, 582-84.

Kuinre (De Kuinder), a town in the Dutch province of Overijssel, formerly the seat of a Mennonite congregation belonging to the Groningen Old Flemish branch. Apparently this congregation, of which Jan Gerts, a carpenter, was chosen preacher in 1648, died out soon after. (*DB* 1879, 7, 90.) vDZ.

Kuiper (Kuyper, Cuiper, Cuyper), a common Dutch family name, both Mennonite and non-Mennonite. Since Kuiper means cooper, the 16th-century Anabaptist leaders, such as Dirck Cuper (*q.v.*) and Frans Reines Kuiper (Frans de Kuyper, *q.v.*), may have been coopers. On the Mennonite Kuyper family which has been living at Krommenie, Dutch province of North Holland, since the last quarter of the 18th century a history was published by Jan Aten, titled *De Doopsgezinde Krommenieër Zeildoekfabrikeursfamilie Kuyper* (n.p., n.d., 1953). They were usually manufacturers of canvas, and played an important part both in the history of the town and the Krommenie Mennonite Church.

One Kuiper family is of special importance to the Dutch Mennonites. This family originally lived at Leeuwarden. Tako Kuiper was the first of this family to study theology and to become a Mennonite minister. He was born at Leeuwarden, and died at Blokzijl on Sept. 7, 1813, studied at the Amsterdam Lamist Seminary 1784-89, and served as minister of the following congregations: Grouw (Groote Huys) 1790-99, Neustadt-Gödens 1799-1804, Midwolda 1804-7, and Blokzijl 1807-13. His son Jan Kuiper, b. Jan. 4, 1794, at Blokzijl, d. Sept. 24, 1882, at Sneek, studied at the Amsterdam Mennonite Seminary 1813-19, and was pastor at Emmerich 1819-20, Dantumawoude 1820-27, and IJlst 1827-70 (he also served the Old Flemish congregation at Sneek

1835-38). He published *Lijkrede op Uilke Reitses* (Leeuwarden, 1823) and *Tweetal Voorlezingen* (Sneek, 1835). Taco Kuiper's grandson was Tako Kuiper (*q.v.*); his great-grandson was Abraham Kornelis Kuiper (*q.v.*), and his great-great-grandson (son of A. K. Kuiper) Frederik (Frits) Kuiper, b. 1898 at Amsterdam, pastor of Amersfoort 1924-28, Krommenie, Wormer, and Jisp 1928-32, Alkmaar 1932-45, and Amsterdam since 1947. Frits Kuiper is the author of "Karl Barth en de Kinderdoop," in the *Zondagsbode* 111, Nos. 22-25, and reprint; *De Opstanding* (Assen, 1928); *Sovjet-Rusland en het Christendom* (Amsterdam, 1937); *De Gemeente in de Wereld* (Haarlem, 1941); *Gelooft het Evangelie* (n.p., n.d.-1945); *De ware Vrijheid, Paulus' Brief aan de Galaten* (Haarlem, 1947); *Ontmoeting met het Oude Testament* (Haarlem, 1950); *Israel en de Goijem* (Haarlem, 1951); *Wij en ons erfdeel* (Amsterdam, 1952). Johanna E. Kuiper (1896-1956), a daughter of A. K. Kuiper, wrote *Bijbel voor de Jeugd* (1948); she died unexpectedly while visiting the former Dutch mission fields in Java. To this family also belonged Koenraad Kuiper (1854-1922), a brother of A. K. Kuiper, professor of Greek literature at the University of Amsterdam, who served the church as deacon and was for a number of years a trustee of the A.D.S. and curator of its theological seminary. Gerrit T. J. Kuiper of Rotterdam (where his father, Koenraad Kuiper, was director of the zoo and president of the Mennonite church board), a member of the same family, is an architect, one of whose creations is the new Mennonite church of Rotterdam, built 1950-51.   vDZ.

Kuiper, Abraham Kornelis, a Dutch Mennonite minister, the son of Taco Kuiper (*q.v.*), b. Sept. 20, 1864, at Amsterdam, d. June 29, 1944, at Amsterdam. He studied at the University of Amsterdam and the Mennonite Seminary under Hoekstra and de Hoop Scheffer. On Jan. 5, 1890, he preached his introductory sermon at Rottevalle and Witveen, Friesland. In 1893 he married Henriette Sophia Muller, the youngest daughter of the noted Frederik Muller, who in turn was the son of Samuel Muller (*q.v.*).

On Feb. 19, 1894, he received his doctorate from the University of Amsterdam with a dissertation on Zechariah 9-14. He served the congregations of Rottevalle until 1895, Warga 1895-99, Wormerveer 1899-1901, Amsterdam 1901 until his retirement in 1930. He died on June 29, 1944. His sermons, like those of his father, drew large audiences even outside the Mennonite fold. He published three volumes of sermons: *Als ziende den Onzienlijke* (Amsterdam, 1923), *In de schuilplaats des Allerhoogsten* (Amsterdam, 1926), and *Vernieuwd van dag tot dag* (Amsterdam, 1930). He also wrote *Industrie en persoonlijkheid* (Haarlem, 1915), *Het toevertrouwde goed* (n.p., n.d.), *Geschiedenis van het volk Gods in het Oude Testament* (Amsterdam, 1933), *Geschiedenis van het volk Gods in het Nieuwe Testament* (Amsterdam, 1934), *Heilig onze gedachten* (Amsterdam, 1938). Numerous devotional contributions appeared in the magazine *Overdenkingen,* of which he was coeditor. Kuiper was active in the *Gemeentedagbeweging* (*q.v.*), and promoted the cause of

missions among the Dutch Mennonites. From 1914-24 he was chairman of the Doopsgezinde Zendingsvereniging. He was also active in the peace movement and was for some time a member of the executive committee of *Kerk en Vrede*. Frits Kuiper, a minister in Amsterdam, is his son. (*ML* II, 584 f.).   C.K.

Kuiper (Cuiper), **Egbert,** was an elder of the Mennonite church of Harlingen, Dutch province of Friesland, who played a part in the Frisian-Flemish schism 1566-69. (*DB* 1893, 54, 57, 65, 79.)   vDZ.

Kuiper, Jacob, a Dutch Mennonite pastor, b. at Koog aan de Zaan, d. 1825 at Deventer. After studying at the Amsterdam Mennonite Seminary, he served Makkum 1773-75 and Deventer 1775-1820. He was an ardent Patriot (*q.v.*), who in 1788 had to leave the town of Deventer for some time because he was threatened by the wrath of the Orange party. Kuiper published three philosophical treatises, all awarded prizes and published by the Teyler Society at Haarlem: *Over Gods byzondere Voorzienigheid* (1782), *Over de onverschilligheid en den verstandigen ijver voor Godsdienstige waarheden* (1788), and *Over de grondregel der Protestanten of het regt op en de verpligting tot eigen oordeel in den Godsdienst* (1791). (*Biogr. Wb.* V, 317.)   vDZ.

Kuiper, Taco, a Dutch Mennonite minister, b. Nov. 17, 1824, at Bolsward, Friesland, d. Oct. 15, 1906, at Haarlem. Like his grandfather Taco Kuiper he chose the ministry as his life's vocation after having been graduated from the Mennonite Seminary and the Athenaeum of Amsterdam in 1849. He served the congregations of Zuid-Zijpe until 1850, Warga, Zaandam-Westzijde 1852-59, and Zwolle 1859-62. He then was called to the Amsterdam Mennonite Church which he served until his retirement in 1890. Kuiper was an outstanding preacher, the large Singelkerk always being filled when he preached. In his theological views he adhered to a Biblical and ethical orthodoxy in a time when modernism was the trend among the Dutch Mennonite brotherhood. For some time he served as a member of the Executive Committee of the A.D.S. and secretary of the Doopsgezinde Zendingsvereniging (mission society). He published some sermons, *Tiental Leerredenen* (Zwolle, 1893) and translated Uhlhorn's *Der Kampf des Christentums mit dem Heidentum,* which appeared under the title *Strijd en overwinning* . . . of which the third edition appeared in 1879. Some articles by Kuiper are found in *Doopsgezinde Bijdragen* (1877, 1880, 1885, 1886, 1887, 1889, 1890, 1891, 1892, 1893). Taco Kuiper was a son of Esgo Taco Kuiper, a notary at Bolsward, and Neeltje Feenstra, daughter of Pastor P. W. Feenstra of Sneek. He was married to Elizabeth Hovens Greve, a daughter of Pastor K. H. Hovens Greve of Steenwijk. Kuiper died on Oct. 15, 1906, at Haarlem. (*Biogr. Wb.* V, 318-20; *DB* 1901, 36; 1907, 177-83; *ML* II, 585.)   C.K.

Kükenbieter, Joachim, a Lutheran divine of Schwerin, Germany, wrote a letter to Pastor Johann Garthe at Hamburg in 1539 about Obbe Philips (*q.v.*). He says that Obbe had in that year moved to the territory of Mecklenburg in Germany, where he had a large following called "Obbiten," and intended to go to Rostock. This letter, which states emphatically that Obbe was a peaceful Anabaptist leader, is important for our knowledge of Obbe's activities shortly before he left the Mennonites. (*DB* 1884, 15 f.)   vDZ.

Kulenkamp, Gerardus (Bremen, 1700-Amsterdam, 1775), was a Reformed minister from 1725, serving Amsterdam in 1733-75. He attacked the Moravian Brethren in three books; in the first of these, *De naakt ontdekte enthousiasterij, geest-driverij, en bedorven mystikerij der zo genaamde Hernhuthers* (Amsterdam, 1739-40, 2 vv.), he also accused the Mennonites of heterodoxy. In a paper published by Kulenkamp in the periodical *De Boekzaal* of October 1740 he sharply accused Joannes Deknatel, the Mennonite minister at Amsterdam, of having forsaken the basic creed of the Mennonites as summarized in the *Oprecht Verbondt van Eenigheyd* (*q.v.*) of 1664, and of teaching Socinian (*q.v.*) heresies. Many Mennonites, including Deknatel (*q.v.*), were at this time much in sympathy with the Moravians. Kulenkamp's charges against the Moravian Brethren and the Mennonites were refuted in a *Brief aan een Vriend* (Amsterdam, 1740) by an anonymous author, who signed his work as "Irenophilus," and who was apparently a Mennonite. vDZ.

Chr. Sepp, *Johannes Stintra en zijn tijd* (Amsterdam, 1865-66, 2 vols.), *passim; Biogr. Wb.* V, 322-27; *DB* 1868, 57.

Kulm: see **Culm.**

Kunders, Thones, head of one of the first 13 German Quaker-Mennonite families from Crefeld who arrived at Philadelphia on Oct. 6, 1683, beginning the German immigration to America. Kunders, who later called himself Anthony Conrads and still later Cunard, and was also called Dennis Conrad, was born in Gladbach, and was a citizen of Crefeld. He was Quaker, but had formerly been a Mennonite. In his house in Germantown (*q.v.*) were held the first German services in America, attended by both Mennonites and Quakers. (Pastorius says Kunders and his wife were Mennonites, as was also her brother, William Streypers, who had immigrated with them, but Hull has shown this to be an error.) It was in Kunders' home that the first protest against slavery in America was signed in 1688. Kunders was one of the eleven citizens to whom Penn granted the charter of Germantown in 1689, and was appointed as one of the first burgesses, a proof that he could not have been a Mennonite. He died in 1729.

A descendant of Thones Kunders in the fifth generation was Sir Samuel Cunard (1787-1865), who founded the first steamship line between England and America, known as the Cunard Line.   HEGE, H.S.B.

D. K. Cassel, *Gesch. der Menn.* (Philadelphia, 1890); *Die Heimat* X (Crefeld, 1931) 86; W. I. Hull, *William Penn and the Quaker Migration to Pennsylvania* (Philadelphia, 1935) 218 *et passim;* C. Henry Smith, *The Mennonite Immigration to Pennsylvania* (Norristown, 1929); *ML* II, 585.

Künigl, Master Wolfgang, a royal procurator in Austria. It is not known whether he belonged to the noble house of that name. From the court records of the Anabaptists in Austria on and below the Enns we learn that in the persecution of the Anabaptists in 1527-28 he played a role which was not pleasant to him, as court prosecutor.

King Ferdinand was shocked by the increasing Anabaptist movement in his Austrian hereditary lands. From all sides came word that the authorities were lax toward the ecclesiastical innovations, and that Austria was the hotbed of sectarianism. Therefore Ferdinand issued not only the general mandate of Aug. 28, 1527, but also many special mandates, obliging the officials to persecute the Anabaptists.

In October 1527 Wolfgang Künigl received instructions to cross-examine the Anabaptists imprisoned in Steyr (*q.v.*) and Freistadt (*q.v.*) and to proceed according to the mandates. On Oct. 29 he began his work in Styria. The case was to be tried in the presence of representatives of the five cities. Of unusual interest is the report he sent three days later to the governor and regents of the cantons of Lower Austria. He related what had taken place in Steyr, and recommended for persons of their type a fine instead of the penalty of Horb (*q.v.*) and Rottenburg, which was degrading, and would cause many prisoners to escape, deserting their families. There were, to be sure, people who deserved a more severe sentence than that of Horb, people who say the sacrament is mere bread and disregard baptism. There were Anabaptists held secretly, not yet put into prison, by abbots, noblemen, and prelates. At Melk it was no better; two Melk citizens had conducted Hans Hut to Steyr.

Two days later he reported that more Anabaptists were reported every day. If he would proceed with the Horb penalty they would all run away, and a great insurrection might take place. This could be avoided by levying a fine. With the Horb penalty he would not be sure of his life. In other words, he hoped to be able to persuade the prisoners to recant, and earn the lighter penalty; the obstinate would be punished in accord with the mandates. But the king disagreed. One could be lenient only in the case of the young and simple.

On Nov. 16 Künigl came to Freistadt. There the magistrate had not made the necessary provisions, for he thought he did not have the right to take steps against Anabaptists, not having the "regalia." Künigl was quite annoyed by his dealings with these Upper Austrian citizens. Here in Freistadt all had recanted. He requested that the Horb penalty be lightened.

Since the authorities inferred from Künigl's letters that many Anabaptists had fled, a special mandate was sent out on Dec. 23, 1527, making it a crime to shelter or feed fugitive Anabaptists. Not until February 1528 was the case against the Freistadt Anabaptists continued, and Künigl was again appointed to conduct the prosecution. On April 8 the accused swore to leave the country. LOSERTH.

J. Jäkel, *Zur Geschichte der Wiedertäufer in Oberösterreich* (Report 47 of the Francisco-Carolinum, Linz, 1889); *ML* II, 585 f.

Kunpad: see **Konopat(h).**

Kunstbuch, Das, a codex of about 740 pages, 22 x
16 cm, in the Bürgerbibliothek at Bern, Switzerland,
containing a collection of 42 letters and documents
of 1527-55. The editor and copyist was Jörg Maler
(*q.v.*) of Augsburg, who signed his work on Sept.
4, 1561. The following writers and writings are
represented in the codex: Pilgram Marpeck (*q.v.*)
fifteen letters and one tract, Leopold Scharnschlager
(*q.v.*) three letters and three tracts, Leonhard Schiemer (*q.v.*) two letters and two tracts, Jörg Maler
(*q.v.*) two letters and one tract, Sigmund Bosch
(*q.v.*) two letters; Hans Hut (*q.v.*), Hans Has,
Cornelius Vech, Helena Freiberger (von Freyberg,
q.v.), Hans Bichel (Büchel, *q.v.*), Christian Entfelder (*q.v.*), Valentin Eckelsamer (Ickelsamer, *q.v.*),
and Hans Schlaffer (*q.v.*) represented by one document each; two anonymous tracts; one letter from
the churches in Moravia to Marpeck. None of these
documents are known from any other printed or
manuscript source except the one by Han Hut and
two of those by Schiemer. The codex was first
reported to the learned world in July 1955 by
Heinold Fast and Gerhard Goeters, who noticed
it in the Bürgerbibliothek. It is of extraordinary
importance, throwing new light on South German
and Swiss Anabaptism particularly of the period
of 1540-60. A detailed analysis and evaluation of
the *Kunstbuch* is given by Heinold Fast in the
Archiv für Reformationsgeschichte for 1957, No. 1.

H.S.B.

Kuntersweg, a part of the ancient route from Italy
to Germany in the scenic mountain valley of the
Eisack in southern Tirol (formerly Austrian, now
Italian). The localities in or above this valley to be
considered here are Atzwang in the jurisdiction of
Ritten, and Völs and Blumau in the jurisdiction of
Kastelruth.

In most of its copies the Hutterite Chronicle
lists eight blood witnesses "on the Kuntersweg";
some say nine without specifying the localities.
Martyrs' deaths are listed in the persecution period
of 1529; but 1528 is probably correct. On May 9,
1528, Augustin Heurling informed the government
that in Lower Atzwang several Anabaptists who
had recanted and had assumed the prescribed penance were again obstinately holding to their old
error. Four days later the government at Innsbruck
ordered that they be prosecuted and appointed the
Altenburg judge to take charge. Jurors were to
be chosen from other localities, since many of those
to be sentenced had a large, influential relationship
in the local region. Proceedings against Margaret
Köblin were to wait until after the birth of her
child.

Among those sentenced at this time was Matthes
Kerschbaumer. His wife Margaret, who had not
asked for pardon at the proper time, had her
sentence commuted on June 3 from burning at the
stake to drowning. When the judge, Jakob Fuchs
von Fuchsberg, twice postponed the execution because relatives and even clergy wanted to ask the
government for clemency, he was reprimanded
and ordered to execute the death sentence at once.

The official of Spaur on the Ritten was given orders
to rebuke the clergy for intervening in a "matter
of faith."

It can be assumed that most of the executions
occurred at Völs, in which village the *Kopialbuch,
causa Domini,* preserved in the archives at Innsbruck
(vol. II, fol. 226 f., 229, 232 f., 240 f., 320, 330, 370 f.,
420, 518) mentions Anabaptists several times. In
June 1528 Jörg Zaunried was operating in Völs, who
baptized the local historiographer, Michel Kürschner
(*q.v.*), and appointed him head of the brotherhood; Kürschner was very active in the Adige. On
Dec. 5, 1528, Augustin Heurling and the judge of
Bozen were charged with sentencing the Anabaptists imprisoned at Völs. Several days later the
captain on the Adige set the date for calling the
jurors on Dec. 18, 1528. Several names are known:
Magdalena, wife of Hans Bair; Elisabeth, sister of
Wolfram; Lienhard Fundnatscher, and Hans Voll
persisted in their faith and were put to death.

Fundnatscher's wife, Christoph Mesner, and Melchior Schneider repented and were pardoned to
blows with a rod on the public square. It also
happened that Melchior Schneider's brother offered
to try to catch the "Anabaptist principals," Michel
Kürschner, Matthias Waldner, and the wife of Gall-
büchel, if he were pardoned. These people were
very active in the region, and the government was
employing all the means at its disposal to apprehend
them. The Adige authorities agreed. Kürschner
was imprisoned in Innsbruck and executed on June
2, 1529.

In April 1529 two young shepherds of Völs were
arrested, but they were pardoned because they repented and because of their youth and lack of understanding. In 1532 several persons were seized at
Völs on a suspicion of Anabaptism, but the outcome of the case is not known.   P.DE.

Beck, *Geschichts-Bücher;* Loserth, *Anabaptismus;* Wolkan, *Geschicht-Buch;* Zieglschmid, *Chronik;* Loesche,
Tirolensia; ML II, 586 f.

Küntsche (Küentsche), Hans Friedrich, originally
of Württemberg, Germany (according to Bossert
the name must have been *Kündscher* or *Kündscheer,*
named in the records of 1609), a Hutterite brother,
from 1641 preacher, d. 1659 in Kesselsdorf (*q.v.*),
Slovakia. He was the most outstanding author of
(written) sermons, usually called *Vorreden* and
Lehren by the Hutterites (see **Sermons, Hutterites**).
He more than anyone else promoted the system of
writing down sermons for each Sunday and other
occasions. The *Klein-Geschichtbuch* mentions
frequently "pious and inspired teachers at Gesselsdorf" who produced sermons, excerpts of which
Johannes Waldner (*q.v.*) inserted in his chronicle
(Zieglschmid, 204-21). The modern Hutterites in
Canada still have some of the original sermon-note-
books signed "H. F. K.," containing sermons on
Isaiah 9 (no year), Isaiah 11 (1650), Isaiah 49
(1655), Isaiah 58 (1658), Matt. 5 (1659), Luke 3
(1652), Acts 2 (1659; this is a set of sermons for
the celebration of Pentecost, still in use today), and
Rom. 8 (1656). Both "teachings" on Acts 2 and
Romans 8 are actually voluminous books, copied
and recopied ever since. It is not impossible that

many more of the existing sermons go back to this preacher, or *Lehrer* as he is often called. During the first period of the Hutterite stay in the Ukraine (about 1770-1810) all these numerous sermons were collected anew and put together into "sermon-collections," still extant today in western Canada and still in use. Most of them are anonymous, but one finds also not infrequently at the end notes such as "H. F. K.," or "Kesselsdorf," and a year, usually between 1650 and 1660.   R.F.

Wolkan, note in the *Geschicht-Buch*, 646; Zieglschmid, *Klein-Geschichtsbuch; TA Württemberg*.

Kuntz (Cuntz), **Elsa,** an Anabaptist martyr, was put to death at Reinhardsbrunn near Gotha, Germany, with five companions on Jan. 18, 1530, because she refused to recant. The execution attracted much attention. Melanchthon (*q.v.*) tried to defend her, and Justus Menius (*q.v.*) in this connection published his book, *Der Widdertauffer lere* (1530), with a foreword by Luther, in which he takes a position of opposition to the Anabaptists (see **Kolb, Andreas** and **Katharina**). (*ML* II, 587.) HEGE.

Küntzi, Hans, and his son **Kleinhans** (or *Junghans*), both wool weavers of Oberglatt, canton of Zürich, Switzerland. They were natives of Klingnau in the canton of Aargau, and in 1526 were among the Anabaptists there. Kleinhans Küntzi was active in the canton of Zürich, from which he was banished between 1526 and 1529. He baptized many Anabaptist converts. He was executed at Liechtenstein before Dec. 26, 1529. A Paul(li) Küntzi from Stalden in the canton of Bern was named as Anabaptist in 1535.   VDZ.

TA Zürich; P. Peachey, *Die soziale Herkunft der Schweizer Täufer in der Reformationszeit* (Karlsruhe, 1954) 45, 117, No. 181 f., 131, No. 502.

Kunz, an Anabaptist who died as a martyr between Christmas 1536 and April 10, 1537, at Bozen, Austria (now Italy). Particulars are not known. The cross-examination of his traveling companion, Kaspar Huber, under Christoph Ochs in Michelsburg (*q.v.*) in the Puster Valley, revealed that both had come into Tirol from Moravia. Huber had been baptized at Auspitz by Jakob Hutter in 1535, was imprisoned at Schöneck in Tirol, and was likewise put to death for his faith. (Loserth, *Anabaptismus,* 141; *ML* II, 587.)   HEGE.

Künzelsau, a town (pop. 5,559) on the Kocher, in the Jagst district of Württemberg, Germany, where Anabaptism found adherents soon after its inception (see **Hohenlohe**). (*ML* II, 587.)

Kuonle, Lienhard, an Anabaptist of Oberschlechtbach, a village near Rudersberg in Württemberg, Germany, confessed at his trial at Schorndorf (*q.v.*) on March 21, 1613, that "eighteen years previously he had regularly attended church. But when he was elected burgomaster and was required to swear an oath, he refused; for he considered it a sin. For that reason he was arrested and kept confined at Schorndorf for four weeks. Then he began to associate with the Anabaptists; he joined the Swiss brotherhood and was baptized in a woods near

Frankenstein (in the Palatinate) belonging, he supposed, to some nobleman, because he did not consider his first baptism in infancy valid." On April 16 he was again questioned. He had been persuaded to be baptized by a brother from Moravia. Then he bought a New Testament and found his faith therein. He had been at Aschhausen near Oehringen nine of the eighteen years. Orders came from Stuttgart to deal leniently with him; he was banished. Nothing more is known of him. (*TA Württemberg,* 841-43; *ML* II, 587.)   NEFF.

Kürnbach, a town in the Bretten district of Baden, Germany, with (1933) 1,202 Protestant inhabitants. In 1525 the pastor Wendel Ziegler used German in baptizing and at the insistence of the congregation distributed communion in both kinds. After the Peasants' War the Austrian government suppressed Protestantism in Stuttgart. Consequently the evangelically-minded went to the adjacent villages of the Imperial Knights for their spiritual food, thereby coming in contact with the Anabaptists.

About 1530 Michel Jungmann, approximately 45 years old, was baptized by Blasius (Kuhn, *q.v.*) of Bruchsal at Zaberfeld (in the jurisdiction of the barons von Sternenfels zu Ochsenburg) in the home of Stratz Bernhard, together with Bernhard's wife, Bastian N., and Hans Lemmer of Ochsenburg (the last two deserted the movement later on) and Bärbel Bender of Sulzfeld, who died in Moravia. As his motive for joining the Anabaptist movement Jungmann stated that he had heard in sermons, "He who believes and is baptized shall be saved." Also the offensive life of the priests repelled him.

Not long after, Jungmann was arrested by the mayor of Güglingen. With the executioner at his side he was commanded to go to church, hear Mass, and accept the papacy. In the face of fire, Jungmann consented and was released. But when he was to swear to leave the town forever he could not commit such an "abomination and idolatry," and fled to Moravia, where he lived in "Augsten" (Auspitz?). When he heard that Duke Ulrich had returned he hastened home. About 1543 he was again banished, but soon returned, only to be banished once more.

During the interim the Anabaptist movement spread. The Brethren easily found shelter in the many localities owned by the Imperial Knights. They met in the forest of Bretten near Flehingen, where Schoch Hans of Königsbach (*q.v.*) preached and baptized, also a Bastian of Dinglingen from Strasbourg. There was no need of a special "sign" by which they could recognize each other. They soon learned to know each other. From Durlach there were Martin Schneider; Margaretha, wife of Matheis Starcker; a farm hand, Simon N., from Alsace; Katharina, the wife of Augustin N.; and Jakob Hartmann; from Knielingen (near Karlsruhe), Cyriakus N. and Wendel N.; from Eggenstein (near Karlsruhe), Matheis N.; from Kürnbach, Michel Zainer and Heinrich Bierer, who had however not been baptized; and one from Diefenbach (Maulbronn district), who recanted.

Michel Jungmann also took part in these meetings.

But as he was once coming to Kürnbach he was seized and taken to Güglingen. He was cross-examined three times; viz., on March 18, March 25, and June 14, 1555. With warmth he confessed: he placed his salvation on Christ our Lord, and wanted to become a partaker in it, by believing His words and living according to them. On the questions in which he differed from the church, he at first evaded the issue, but then he said concerning infant baptism: he knew nothing to say about it, knew no Scripture for it, and therefore let it stand on its own merit. Concerning the Lord's Supper he said in reply to the question whether he believed that the true body and blood of Christ were distributed in the sacrament: No, the bread and wine were rather symbols and remembrances. He had not preached or baptized, because he had not been called to do so. At the third hearing, when the executioner placed the rack beside him, he also gave the names of the leaders and the brethren and the place of meeting. To the magistrate he said he was a weak old man, not a sectarian, and only wanted to please God and his neighbor. He promised that if he was freed he would attend church; as God gave him warning and light he would live; but one must live according to Protestant doctrine. Upon the signed promise to leave the country he was permitted to return to Durlach.

About two years later Jungmann was again at Kürnbach in spite of his promise, together with his son Hans and Margarete Bierer of Pfaffenhofen, who were mentioned several times in previous hearings. They were all arrested. Michel was again cross-examined, and said he "would have all things in common." The magistrate banished him again. This time Hans Jungmann knew the appropriate Scripture passages and argued with the pastor nine weeks in prison. Finally he declared he was willing to go to church. Margarete Bierer agreed with him. They went to church, even took communion and attended the baptismal service of an infant, and were then set free. Jungmann died soon afterward in the Palatinate; Margarete stayed in Durlach three years, returned to Pfaffenhofen, and in 1562 was once more among the Anabaptists.

In 1572 new trials were held for Anabaptists whose names are not known. In 1576 two new adherents were baptized: Michel Jungmann, probably a son of Hans and grandson of the older Michel, and Joachim Roth. They were questioned in Stuttgart. Roth promised to join the church and leave the Anabaptists. a formal trial was arranged for Jungmann. But he apparently submitted too; for in 1583 he was again held in Kürnbach, as well as the backslidden Roth, Katharina, the wife of Jakob Ludwig, the gatekeeper and the riding servant and other subjects of Bernhard von Sternenfels. Jungmann seems to have persisted in his faith and been banished, but was protected by von Sternenfels who needed him as a builder. In 1586 Sternenfels was still employing the gatekeeper, and also Reichardus Reichart of Endersbach (near Stuttgart) as cooper. The duke demanded that proceedings be initiated against all of them because they adhered to Anabaptist doctrine.

In 1602 a servant at the castle was called a "Wiedertäufer." Then all trace of the Anabaptist movement disappeared from Kürnbach. The revelations made in the trials concerning the piety of the Anabaptists are a pleasant picture; they wanted to live for their faith as God-fearing people, resisted the government only when it violated their conscience (oath, war); the judgment of the officials varied, but generally there was a feeling of human pity for their destruction.   E.BE.

G. Bossert, "Die Ref. in Kürnbach bei Eppingen," in *Ztscht f. d. Gesch. des Oberrheins* LI (1897) 83-107; *TA Württemberg; TA Baden-Pfalz;* E. Becker, "Die Wiedertäufer zu Kürnbach," in *Beitr. zur Hess. Kirchengesch.* I (1903) 113-39; *ML* II, 587 f.

Kurpfalz: see **Palatinate.**

Kürschner (Kirsner, Kirschner, Klesinger), **Michael,** an Anabaptist martyr, was baptized in June 1528 in Eisack Valley of Tirol, Austria (now Italy), by Georg Zaunring (*q.v.*), who was later the traveling companion of Jakob Hutter (*q.v.*), and was appointed by Zaunring as the head of the local Anabaptist group. His mission field after August was the Eisack and Adige Valley, especially around Teutsch-Noffen, Gufidaun, Kurtatsch, Kaltern, Leifers, and Klausen, where he baptized over 100 persons. Before his conversion to Anabaptism he had been court recorder at Völs. The authorities kept a sharp lookout for him and caught him and seven others at a service on the night of April 25, 1529, at Kitzbühel. He was taken to Innsbruck and imprisoned in the Kräuter tower. He refused all attempts to convert him, and died at the stake on June 2, 1529, at Innsbruck. The authorities were in such haste with this execution that they did not even wait for word from Ferdinand, to whom the case had been reported (Loserth, 468, 470 f.).

Georg Blaurock (*q.v.*), one of the founders of the movement, took charge of the orphaned congregation. He arrived here in May 1529, accompanied by Hans Langegger of Ritten in the Eisack Valley, and after a brief period of work also died at the stake in Klausen (*q.v.*). (See **Kuntersweg.**)   HEGE.

Loserth, *Anabaptismus;* Beck, *Geschichts-Bücher,* 90; Zieglschmid, *Chronik,* 74; *ML* II, 602.

Kürschner, Wolf (Laupt, Hussbecken), was one of a group of Anabaptists who under the pressure of persecution went from Bretten (*q.v.*), Germany, to Moravia; but when government pressure made it difficult for the barons to tolerate them on their lands he returned to his old home. Before he reached his family he was seized on Nov. 14, 1535, by spies of the magistrate Ulrich Winzelhäuser of Güglingen, Württemberg, Germany, with a married couple from Knittlingen, and was placed in the tower of Güglingen. Leonhard Eheim, pastor of Pfaffenhofen, was assigned to work with them, discussing with them especially infant baptism and the oath, but to no avail.

The ensuing trial by the magistrate revealed that Wolf Kürschner and several women had been baptized at Oberacker by Hans Beringer of Knittlingen. His statements give a picture of the religious views of the once stately congregation around Bretten, concerning which there is little other information. The prisoners placed no value on infant baptism. They did not hold that the sacrament contained the flesh and blood of Christ, and opposed the oath, warfare, and capital punishment. A Christian might hold a public office in government if the government were Christian and acted accordingly. They did not believe that the devil and all the damned would ultimately be saved. They accepted as completely true the teaching of the Protestant Church on the person and the work of Christ.

The prisoners were released from the tower on Dec. 2, 1535, by their brothers, who were not Anabaptists. The brothers were later found out and arrested, but released upon the request of the nobility, officials, relatives, and neighbors; the petition stressed the brotherly love that bade them do this. They had also taken great pains to make Kürschner change his views, with success. His fellow prisoners had to attend the torture and beheading of a murderer, whereupon they declared they would do all that they were shown and taught.
HEGE.

G. Bossert, "Wolf Kürschner, der Täufer von Bretten," in *Ztscht f. d. Gesch. des Oberrheins* (1910) 431-52; *TA Baden-Pfalz; TA Württemberg*, 46, 995; *ML* II, 602.

Kürssner, Mathis, an Anabaptist martyr, apparently a member of the congregation at Horb on the Neckar, was seized with Michael Sattler (*q.v.*) after the meeting at Schleitheim in which the first Anabaptist-Mennonite confession of faith was formulated. After Sattler's execution on May 21, 1527, on the evening of the same day, Kürssner was put to death with Stoffel Schuhmacher, Michel Lenzi, and the aged Geiger, at Rottenburg am Neckar, Germany.
HEGE.

W. Köhler, *Brüderliche Vereinigung etzlicher Kinder Gottes sieben Artikel*, in *Flugschriften aus den ersten Jahren der Reformation* II (Leipzig, 1908) 303; *ML* II, 602.

Kurtatsch, a locality in the Eisack Valley in Tirol, Austria (now Italy), a scene of Georg Blaurock's (*q.v.*) activity after his exile from Zürich. Here he took the place of the leader Michael Kürschner (*q.v.*), who was in prison in Kitzbühel. In Kurtatsch Anabaptism had spread as early as 1528; in 1529 its adherents, with the exception of the leaders, were punished for leaving the church by being publicly beaten and banished (Loesche, 36). Blaurock proclaimed the Gospel here in July 1529 with outstanding success. But in August he was caught by bailiff Preu, held prisoner in Gufidaun (*q.v.*) castle (Loserth, 486), and burned at the stake on Sept. 6 at Klausen.
HEGE.

G. Loesche, *Archivalische Beiträge zur Gesch. des Täufertums und des Protestantismus in Tirol* (1926); Loserth, *Anabaptismus; ML* II, 602 f.

Kurtz, Jonathan, b. July 8, 1848, near Lancaster, Fairfield Co., Ohio, d. July 10, 1930, in Mishawaka, Ind., was a leading bishop in the Indiana-Michigan Amish Mennonite Conference, and the merged Mennonite (MC) Conference. He was ordained preacher in 1882, and bishop in 1888, serving the Maple Grove congregation near Topeka, Ind. He was an early and active supporter of progressive

activities of all kinds, and helped in establishing missionary and educational work (Goshen College) in the activities of the church. He was married to Lizzie Byler on March 19, 1878, who with their five children survived him.   H.S.B.

Kurtzville, Ont., a small village six miles northwest of Gowanstown in Wallace Township, where a Mennonite church (MC) and cemetery were located about 1865. A German Sunday school is known to have been conducted there in the 1880's under the Mennonite Conference of Ontario. (See the **Wallace** Mennonite Church.)   J.C.F.

Kusters, Paulus (d. 1707), emigrated from Crefeld, Germany, to America with his wife Gertrude Streypers and three sons Arnold, Hermanus, and Johannes, all Mennonites, and settled at Germantown, Pa., about 1693.   VDZ.

H. S. Bender, "The Founding of the Mennonite Church in America at Germantown, 1683-1708," *MQR* VII (October 1933) 232, 235.

Kutter, Eustachius: see Kotter.

Kuyper (Cuyper, Kuiper), **Cornelis (de),** a Dutch Mennonite elder of the Flemish congregation at Haarlem, who died before 1617. He was a partisan of the well-known Dutch elder Jacques Outerman (*q.v.*) of Haarlem. He defended the doctrine of the Incarnation (Christ did not receive His flesh from Mary) as taught by Menno Simons. He was attacked by Pieter Matthysz and two Reformed ministers of Middelburg, Johannes Seu and Herman Faukelius, on a charge of Socinian views. In September 1609 de Kuyper, Francois de Knuyt, Mennonite preacher of Zierikzee, and Jan van Voorden, elder of Utrecht, had a disputation at Zierikzee with Reformed ministers. De Kuyper published *Eenvuldighe verantwoordinge met corte Verklaringhe onses Geloofs van den Eenighen God . . . als oock van de Heylige Menschwerdinge onses Salichmakers . . .* (n.p., n.d., ca. 1604).   VDZ.

Biogr. Wb. V, 408-10; W. J. Kühler, *Het Socinianisme in Nederland* (Leiden, 1912) 92, 101; *DB* 1908, 23-26.

Kuyper (Cuypers), **Frans (de)** (1629-ca. 1691), became a Remonstrant (*q.v.*) preacher at Vlaardingen, Dutch province of South Holland, in 1652, but resigned in 1653, because he did not agree with infant baptism. He moved to Amsterdam and later to Rotterdam and became a book printer. Among the most important publications by Kuyper are *Bibliotheca Fratrum Polonorum, quos unitarios vocant,* i.e., the Socinians (*q.v.*). In the Dutch Collegiant movement Kuyper was a prominent member, though his stubbornness caused discord with many of them, especially with Joannes Breedenburg, whom he accused of Spinozism. Through his adherence to the philosophical principles of Spinoza he had a wide influence on the growing liberalism of his time. In the Collegiant movement he met with numerous Mennonites; he had some sympathy for Mennonite principles, especially for nonresistance; the booklet *De recht weereclooze Christen of verdeediging van het gevoelen der eerste Christenen en gemartelde Doops-gezinden,* published by Kuyper (Rotterdam,

1678), however, was not written by him, as has sometimes been supposed, but by Joan Hartigveldt (*q.v.*). De Kuyper published *Broederlijke Onderhandeling van de Waterdoop tusschen Klaas Stapel en Frans Kuyper* (Rotterdam, 1680), and is supposed to be the author of *Den Philosopheerende Boer* (1676).   vdZ.

Biogr. Wb. V, 332-43; *N.N.B.Wb.* IV, 868; J. C. van Slee, *De Rijnsburger Collegianten* (Haarlem, 1895) see Index; C. B. Hylkema, *Reformateurs* I (Haarlem, 1900) II (Haarlem, 1902) *passim*, see Index; W. J. Kühler, *Het Socinianisme in Nederland* (Leiden, 1912) 246; *DB* 1900, 184 ff.

Kuyper, Teunis Dirksz, of Huisduinen, dates of birth and death unknown, was a Dutch Mennonite preacher, at first on the island of Texel, then of the congregation of Huisduinen, of Haarlem (from 1668) and from 1670 of the Flemish congregation at Alkmaar. Here a quarrel arose in 1672, when Gerrit Jansz Veerom, who had been banned in Amsterdam, was called to the ministry at Alkmaar. In 1674 Kuyper with a number of followers separated from the main body, opening a "preeckhuys" near the Oude Veste, where Kuyper promised to allow "freedom of speech" according to Collegiant practice. But this separate group soon declined, chiefly because of the stubbornness of Kuyper. In 1683 he moved to Friesland, probably to Harlingen. Before his departure from Alkmaar, Kuyper published *Verzoenschrift dienende om de Vereenigde Waterlanders en Vlamingen op de Koningswegh tot versoeninghe te brengen met de Waterlandsche Doopsgesinde op de Oude Veste tot Alckmaer* (n.p., 1683).   vdZ.

Biogr. Wb. V, 343 f.; *DB* 1891, 4-6, 8; (J. de Lange C. Jzn) *Beknopte Geschiedenis der Doopsgez. Gemeente te Alkmaar* (1927) 24-27, 156.

Kwango Mennonite Brethren Mission in the Belgian Congo is one of the M.B. mission fields in Africa. The other, the Kasai (*q.v.*) field, is located near by. The Kwango field, embracing the district capital of Kikwit, extends 110 miles east and west and 150 miles north and south. The population of the Kwango field is approximately 500,000, living in approximately 1,000 villages and several hundred company posts. The chief mission stations are located at Kafumba, Matende, Kipungu, Lusemvu, Kajiji, Panzi, and Belle Vue. Kajiji and Panzi were taken over in 1954 from the liquidated Unevangelized Tribes Mission. In 1955, 12 missionaries were located at Kafumba, 4 at Matende, 7 at Kipungu, 5 at Lusemvu, 6 at Kajiji, 6 at Panzi, and 6 at Belle Vue, where the school for missionary children is located. The native church in the Kwango area numbers around 6,000.   A.E.J.

Kweekschool *tot opleiding van Doopsgezinde leraren* (Seminary for the training of Mennonite ministers): see **Amsterdam Theological Seminary**.

Kymäus (Kymeus), **Johann** (1498-1552), a Protestant minister at the time the Ziegenhain church discipline (*Zuchtordnung*) was introduced in Hesse. He was at first a Franciscan monk, then pastor at Homburg, Hesse, Germany, and later superintendent at Kassel. Kymäus was one of the theologians appointed to reply to the *Restitution* sent to Philipp of Hesse by the Münster Anabaptists in 1534 (Rembert, 296). In 1537 he published a booklet on the synod of 355 held at Gangra (60 miles northeast of Angora) with the title, *Ein Alt Christlich Concilium fur 1200 jaren zu Gangra jnn Paphlagonia gehalten, wider die hoch genante heiligkeit der Mönchen vnd Wiederteuffer . . . verdeutscht und ausgelegt,* for which Martin Luther wrote a preface. The booklet attacks especially the Anabaptists and their "false doctrines"; an evil tree cannot bear good fruit (Keller, 163).

After the trial of the Anabaptists at Marburg, which led to the introduction of confirmation (*q.v.*) in the Protestant churches, he was a coauthor of the opinion titled *Bekenntniss oder Antwort etlicher Fragestücke oder Artikeln der gefangenen Täufer und Anderer im Land zu Hessen,* which led to the conclusion "that they would gladly forgive these brethren in the Lord" (Hochhuth, 612-26; **Hessen**).

                                    Hege.
K. W. H. Hochhuth, *Ztscht f. d. hist. Theol.*, 1858; L. Keller, *Johann von Staupitz und die Anfänge der Reformation* (Leipzig, 1888); Rembert, *Wiedertäufer*; *TA Hessen*; *ML* II, 603.

L

La Ferrière: see **Ferrière.**

La Glace Mennonite Brethren Church, located two miles south of La Glace in the Peace River area of northwest Alberta, was organized about 1928 when newly arrived Mennonite immigrants from Russia settled here. Its largest membership was well over 100 but in 1955 it numbered only 52. A Bible school has been conducted by this congregation on the church premises for a number of years. The following ministers have served this church: G. Wiens, J. Schmidt, M. Hamm, N. Siebert, and A. Janz.

A.A.T.

La Gloria Mennonite Church (MC), located along Highway 281, 2½ miles south of Premont, Jim Wells Co., Tex., until recently known as the Falfurrias Mennonite Church, was organized March 18, 1928. It is a member of the South Central Mennonite Conference. The membership in 1955 was 21, with H. F. Reist as bishop and Samuel C. Swartz as minister.

H.F.R.

La Junta (Col.) Mennonite (MC) Church was organized May 4, 1903. J. M. Nunemaker, a minister of Roseland, Neb., decided on this location in the irrigated land of eastern Colorado as the place of settlement for a Mennonite farm colony after several investigative trips through eastern Colorado in 1902. Two congregations were finally established, East Holbrook (q.v.) in the country and La Junta in the city. A few of the original settlers came from Roseland, but most came from Elida, Ohio, led by a minister, D. S. Brunk, and his son J. M. Brunk, later made a minister at La Junta, who arrived at Pueblo in December 1902 and joined forces with Nunemaker. A few others came from Harrisonburg, Va., including the Rhodes and Heatwole families. The Holbrook settlement, 12 miles northeast of La Junta, was begun by Nunemaker on Feb. 17, 1903. The J. M. Brunk family started the Fairmount settlement four miles west of La Junta in the same month. On May 4, 1903, the La Junta Mennonite Church was organized with 20 charter members living in two settlements, among them two ministers, J. M. Nunemaker and George Ross. The first La Junta meetinghouse was an old Presbyterian church given by the city and occupied on March 6, 1905. On Dec. 31, 1916, a new brick church was dedicated. The congregation at once joined the Kansas-Nebraska Conference (q.v.) and received S. C. Miller of Jet, Okla., as its first bishop. Later bishops were ordained from the congregation—J. A. Heatwole, who served 1910-40, and Allen Erb 1939- . In 1954 the membership was 168, with Wilbur Nachtigall as pastor 1954-

The La Junta congregation was the mother church of Mennonites (MC) in Colorado. From it were organized East Holbrook in 1904, Denver in 1941, Pueblo in 1949, and a Spanish (Mexican) congregation in La Junta in 1941, which in 1954 had 42 members, with David Castillo as pastor.

Because of the healthful dry climate and the (former) belief that tuberculosis could best be treated in such climates, local Mennonites established a sanitarium in 1908, located 4½ miles west of La Junta, and operated until 1927. In 1920 the city of La Junta asked the Mennonites to take over the hospital, which they did, and operated it until 1927, when a new Mennonite hospital and sanitarium were erected. A school of nursing was operated in connection with the hospital in 1915-58.

H.S.B.

La Junta *Mennonite* (MC) *School of Nursing.* The Mennonite Sanitarium Training School for nurses was founded in 1915 by the Mennonite Board of Missions and Charities, under whose general control it operated until the fall of 1949, when it was transferred to the Mennonite Board of Education, whose primary purpose is to administer the educational institutions of the church. Until 1946 the school was an integral part of the Mennonite Hospital and Sanitarium. At this time the organizational pattern was revised, the school being set up as an independent institution under the direct supervision of a school board of control. The name was then changed to its present form. Since its beginning the purpose of the school has been to "give Christian young women training in the care of the sick in such an environment that they may develop in Christian life and character." The motto of the school, "Not to be ministered unto, but to minister," is the basis for the formulation of the philosophy which underlies its total program. The school has been fully accredited by the Colorado State Board of Nurse Examiners since its beginning and received temporary accreditment by the National Accrediting Service in 1951.

The program covers a period of 39 months: 9 months in an accredited college, where the prenursing sciences are studied, and 30 months in the nursing school, where the clinical instruction and practice is secured. Clinical practice in medical and surgical nursing, maternity, operating room, tuberculosis, and diet therapy are obtained in the Mennonite Hospital and Sanitarium at La Junta. Pediatric and Psychiatric Nursing is obtained by affiliation with the Children's Hospital in Denver and Colorado University School of Nursing at the State Hospital in Pueblo. An elective in Public Health Nursing is also available through the University.

A total of 343 nurses have been graduated to date. The current enrollment is 51. Lydia Heatwole, a graduate of the first class, director 1918-32, and Nora Mae Miller, of the class of 1923, director of education 1925-50, were the guiding personalities in the history of the school. Maude Swartzendruber has been director since 1943 and Edna Amstutz director of education since 1950. Because of a decline in the patient census at the Mennonite Hospital it has been decided to discontinue the School of Nursing with the class graduating in 1958. (See also **Mennonite Hospital and Sanitarium.**)

M.Sw.

La Junta (Col.) Mennonite Hospital (MC) had its beginning on Jan. 1, 1920, when control of the previous city hospital was granted to the Mennonite Board of Missions and Charities. Before that the Board had owned and operated the Mennonite Sanitarium (tuberculosis), located 4½ miles east of La Junta, which had been acquired on March 19, 1906, from the Mennonite Sanitarium Association, although the building was not completed until Oct. 25, 1908. After 1920 the combined institution was called Mennonite Hospital and Sanitarium (*q.v.*).
H.S.B.

La Maie, in France, north of Belfort, the seat of a former Mennonite congregation, marked on the map (*ME* I, 67) as an extinct Mennonite congregation.

La Mesa, Cundinamarca, Colombia, South America. Mission work was begun in this center by the General Conference Mennonite Church in 1953. Miss Alice Bachert, then living in near-by San Javier, and LaVerne A. Rutschman were instrumental in gathering a formerly disorganized group of believers and organizing them into a church in November 1953. A lot and building on Calle 6a, #21-69 were purchased in July 1954, and the building was remodeled to serve as a chapel and day school. The day school was named Colegio Meno and was opened in 1955. Lic. Luis Rodriguez is the minister-in-charge of preaching and teaching. The baptized membership numbers 23.
G.S.

La Plata, Puerto Rico, was the location of a unit in Civilian Public Service Camp No. 43, which was approved in June 1942 and closed in March 1947. Operated jointly by the Brethren Service Committee and the MCC, it served under the Puerto Rican Reconstruction Administration in the area of public health. In April 1943 the MCC, upon the invitation of the Brethren, approved the establishment of its own service unit under CPS No. 43 in Puerto Rico and in the following month sent its first workers to this assignment. Co-operating with the P.R.R.A., the Mennonites first undertook medical work, opened a clinic in December, and in August opened the 24-bed La Plata hospital which they had built. In addition the Mennonite unit opened clinics in four outlying districts and offered dental services. The second part of the work consisted of community service, particularly the direction of recreational activities. When in 1947 the P.R.R.A. liquidated its program in the La Plata area, the Mennonte Board of Missions and Charities, Elkhart, Ind., purchased the property. The Mission Board is now not only operating the La Plata hospital but has built churches and other institutions. In 1955 there were 267 members in 12 Mennonite churches and missions on the island, all an outgrowth of the work begun by the MCC in 1943.
M.G.

M. Gingerich, *Service for Peace* (Akron, 1949) 263-70; J. Holsinger, *Serving Rural Puerto Rico* (Scottdale, 1952).

La Salle, originally a town on the southern limits of Niagara Falls, N.Y., now a part of the city, is the location where Jacob Krehbiel (1835-1917), who affiliated with the G.C.M. Church about 1880, held services for a small group of followers. Situated in Niagara County and near the Sanborn Mennonite Church (*q.v.*), it was neighbor to Preacher David Habecker. Habecker's grandchildren moved into this urban center. There have been no members here since early in the 20th century.
J.C.F.

La Salle Mennonite Brethren Church, of the municipality of MacDonald, Man., was organized by 17 families of La Salle and Osborne on Sept. 19, 1926. Its church building was erected in 1930, the lumber having been given by a friend of the Mennonites. In 1954 the baptized membership was 58. It is a member of the Manitoba Provincial and the Canadian District Conferences of the Mennonite Brethren Church. Jacob Pauls is the minister.
H.NE.

La Voz Menonita (*The Mennonite Voice*) is the official monthly organ (16 pp., 7 x 10½ in.) of the Argentine Mennonite Church. The first issue appeared in March 1932 with Albano Luayza as editor. Ernesto Suarez succeeded him in January 1949. Its purpose is to present the message of salvation and to expound Mennonite doctrines and practices.
L.S.W.

Laakeman (Laekeman, Lakeman), **Melis Pietersz,** b. about 1670, d. Jan. 9, 1699, at Zaandijk, where he was a blacksmith, was preacher of the Mennonite congregation (Frisians) at Oosthuizen about 1691-93 and of Wormerveer (Frisians) 1693 until his death. Laakeman, a blacksmith's servant at Purmerend, was baptized in 1691 in the Frisian congregation of Oosthuizen; later he worked in Hoorn. He was married twice; both times his wife died only one year after marriage. Laakeman was a pious man, who had to struggle with poverty.

After his death a volume of his sermons was published: *XXXVI Predicatiën* (Amsterdam, 1700). These sermons were very popular; the book was used in the congregation of Balk, Friesland, until the middle of the 19th century (*DB* 1892, 76). Other members of the Lakeman family served also as preachers at Wormerveer. Some members of this family were found at neighboring Krommenie, and later also at Amsterdam.
vDZ.

Het Leven en sterven van M. P. Laakeman (Amsterdam, n.d.—about 1700); *Biogr. Wb.* V, 434 f.; *ML* II, 604.

Laan, a Dutch Mennonite family found in the province of North Holland. Originally they were farmers at Middelie. Remmelt Laan (1645-1731) moved from Middelie to Wormerveer about 1720. His grandson Jan Dirksz Laan (1719-64), not a farmer like his ancestors, but a grocer, was preacher of the Frisian Mennonite congregation of Wormerveer 1746-64. He adopted Hartog (*q.v.*) as his family name. Also Remmert Laan, b. 1775 at Enge Wormer, d. 1831 at Wormerveer, went into business. He became a partner in the Wessanen en Laan factories (flour, cocoa, etc.) at Wormerveer, which had been founded in 1765 by his uncle Dirk Remmeltsz Laan. Like this uncle Remmert Laan was at the same time a deacon of the Wormerveer Frisian congregation, as were his sons Jan Laan (1803-91) and Adriaan Laan (1810-51). His grandson Dirk Laan (1843-1905), also director of the Wessanen en Laaen factories, was a senator 1897-1905. Reyer Laan, who belonged to the same family, was an untrained preacher of the congregation of Middelie-Axwijk 1746-81. Jan Jansz Laan of Amsterdam, d. 1738, apparently of the same family, was a member of the Lamist Mennonite congregation, being at the same time an active Collegiant (*q.v.*) and in 1712-38 serving as a "regent" (trustee) of the Oranjeappel Collegiant orphanage, as was his wife Agatha Bruin from 1718-d. 49. Some members of this family are still farmers in North Holland.   vdZ.

J. C. van Slee, *De Rijnsburger Collegianten* (Haarlem, 1895) 173, 175, 289, 291; *Ned. Patriciaat* XII (1921-22) 71-86; *Naamlijst* 1755 ff.

Labadists, the followers of Jean de Labadie (1610-74), a native of Boury, near Bordeaux, France. De Labadie had a Jesuit education. After his withdrawal from the order he preached on the freedom of the will and on grace as against the merit of works, and in 1650 he joined the French Reformed Church. Sixteen years later he was a preacher at Middelburg (Holland). Removed from office in 1668 because of his attacks on the secularized church, he founded a separatist church in Amsterdam, with well-attended meetings. When the magistrate forbade outsiders to attend worship in a home, the group found asylum with Princess Elisabeth, abbess at Herford, Westphalia, Germany, until they were banished as "sectarians, Anabaptists, and Quakers." Then they settled in Altona. After Labadie's death the group with 162 members returned to Holland, and located at the castle of Wieuwerd. The colony was dissolved in 1732. There were several points of ideological contact between the Labadists and the Mennonites, since the Labadists tried to realize the ideal of the early Christian Church, requiring community of goods and a serious, holy life; but there is no evidence of any specific connections between the two groups. Labadie's ideas are best known from his book *Le discernement d'une veritable église selon l'Ecriture* (Amsterdam, 1668); in this book concerning the practice of free prophecy especially his pietism appears. His *Manuel de piété* (Middelburg, 1668), translated into German by G. Terstegen under the title *Handbüchlein der wahren Gottseligkeit,* was once popular among the American Mennonites.   NEFF, vdZ.

Biogr. Wb. V, 456-67; C. B. Hylkema, *Reformateurs* I and II (Haarlem, 1900, 1902) *passim*; H. Heppe, *Geschichte des Pietismus* (Leiden, 1879) 241-374; R. Friedmann, *Mennonite Piety Through the Centuries* (Goshen, 1949) 59 f., 218; Wilhelm Goeters, *Die Vorbereitung des Pietismus in der Reformierten Kirche der Niederlande bis zur Labadistischen Krisis 1670* (Leipzig, 1911); Friedrich Nieper, *Die ersten deutschen Auswanderer von Krefeld nach Pennsylvanien* (Neukirchen, 1940); *ML* II, 603.

Labor Unions. The official attitude of the Mennonite Church (MC) to labor unions is described as follows in a report (1954) of the Committee on Economic and Social Relations (*q.v.*) of its General Conference: "In a manner analogous to that of the state, labor organizations as we know them serve a useful purpose for the maintenance of justice and a balance of power in a sub-Christian society. For this reason the Christian may co-operate with the union (as he does with the state) in so far as doing so does not conflict with his Christian testimony.

Since they are power organizations, however, placing the demand for justice above the way of love, most unions reserve the right to use methods out of harmony with the Christian testimony, the strike, which violates the principle of nonresistance, being an obvious example. For this reason it is believed that the Christian must find the place where he can most consistently draw the line between co-operation and non-co-operation with the union." This is the general position of the more conservative American Mennonite groups, including the Brethren in Christ Church. It has come to explicit formulation in the past 20 years.

Continuous witness over a period of more than two decades has resulted in a rather general, and sometimes surprisingly sympathetic understanding of the Mennonite (MC) position by organized labor. One result of this has been a series of formal understandings with numerous unions in which the conscience of the nonresistant employee is recognized, he being excused from union membership and activity with the understanding that in case of conflict between employees resulting in a strike he maintains a position of neutrality, taking part on neither side of the conflict. The nonresistant employee accepts the conditions of work as determined by the union and management, and he pays to the union the equivalent of union dues, which in numerous cases are specified as a contribution for the benevolent and welfare services of the union. By 1956 the Committee on Economic and Social Relations had signed general understandings of this type with six international unions, the agreements applying to every local of these internationals. In the case of numerous other unions regional and local understandings had been entered into with the support of the international office, as well as many local understandings which did not necessarily have such support.

Although in 1956 hundreds of members of the church (MC) were working in union shop industries under the terms outlined above, and although this solution was generally considered satisfactory, the practice within the brotherhood with respect to labor relations was not uniform; and there was a general recognition that as in the case of the Christian's relation to the state so likewise his relation to the changing economic order requires continuous study in order that his witness concerning social justice, love, and nonresistance be kept clear, and that he be enabled to make a positive contribution toward harmonious human relations in the industrial world.

In line with this conviction the Committee on Economic and Social Relations was giving special attention to the responsibility of Mennonite industrial managers and their employees for mutual co-operation in the development of management-labor relations on the basis of Christian brotherhood, rather than by means of power in which management and labor are pitted against each other. Thus it was believed that the brotherhood would not only be giving a witness through the manner of its own economic relations, but would also be in a position to make a contribution to the achievement of harmonious management-labor relations in general.

After 1950 occasional meetings of Mennonite industrial employers and employees were held under the sponsorship of this committee looking toward this end, and a special study conference for the further examination of the Christian's relation to labor organizations was being planned for the autumn of 1957.

In other Mennonite groups having a considerable number of men employed in industry, no similar explicit position has been formulated, although similar basic concerns are present. In groups which are exclusively rural there has been no need for a clear position. In Europe, where Mennonites have not maintained a clear position on nonresistance, no particular position on labor unions has been taken.

G.F.H.

Lachmann, Johann (*ca.* 1492-1538), reformer of Heilbronn (*q.v.*), Württemberg, Germany, studied at the University of Heidelberg, became a priest in Heilbronn in 1514, sided with the Reformation in 1524, led it safely through the conflict with powerful opponents, tried with some success to lead the peasant movement along more moderate paths, and took a lenient attitude toward the Anabaptists.   NEFF.

HRE II, 197 f. *RGG* (3d ed.) II, Col. 1447; M. von Rauch, *Johann Lachmann, der Reformator Heilbronns* (Heilbronn, 1923); *ML* II, 603.

Lachmund, a woman of Wintershausen, Thuringia, Germany, was seized in March 1543, at the instigation of Justus Menius (*q.v.*), with Franz Erbe and the wife of Betzenhans (*q.v.*), on the suspicion of having joined the Anabaptists. At the cross-examination conducted by Menius on July 16 at Eisenach, she declared that she confessed Anabaptist doctrine and would stay by it. The electoral councilors gave as their opinion that she was not to be subjected to a painful hearing (i.e., on the rack), because she had neither baptized nor been baptized, and recommended banishment. Elector John Frederick imposed this sentence on July 18, because "she would not desist from her unchristian and offensive errors on baptism, the sacrament, and other points." The same sentence with the same argument was also passed on Betzenhans's wife.   HEGE.

P. Wappler, *Die Stellung Kursachsens und des Landgrafen Philipp von Hessen zur Täuferbewegung* (Münster, 1910) 94 f., 213 f.; idem, *Thüringen,* 179; *ML* II, 603.

Ladekopp, an ancient village in the Free State of Danzig, in the middle of the Vistula-Nogat delta. It is known to have existed in 1255. A Mennonite church was organized here in 1735 with the same name. In 1935 it had 537 baptized members and 213 children. The members were mostly farmers, owning 545 ha. of land, some merchants, industrialists, and retired persons. The Flemish Mennonites who settled in Ladekopp and surrounding localities belonged to the Grosswerder church, while the Frisian Mennonites united with the Orlofferfelde church. In 1735-40, when the Grosswerder congregation was divided into four parts, Ladekopp became the Orloff Quarter. They had their own preachers and deacons, but the elder served all four quarters. The *Naamlijst* of 1743 names as preachers of Ladekopp (Flemish church) Jakob Wiebe, Abraham Wiebe, Hans Penner, and Pieter Klaassen (Clasen). They were followed by Gillis Wiens, Jakob Suckau, Cornelis Suckau 1753-*ca.*83, Abraham Konrath 1759, Peter Wiebe 1758-before 1800, Cornelis Wall 1762-before 1800, Isaak Teeuws (Töws) 1762-after 1802, Hans Wall 1762-before 1780, Peter Klaassen 1777-after 1802, Cornelis Klaassen 1782-*ca.*96, Johann Töws Jr. 1787-after 1802, Johann Wall 1787-*ca.*97, Hans Wall 1798-?, Peter Regier 1799-?, Abraham von Riesen 1801-? In later years Ladekopp was served by its own elder, six preachers, and two deacons. The later elders of Ladekopp with year of ordination were Jakob Wiebe 1833, Johann Töws 1853, Johann Wiens 1873, Johann Neufeldt 1905, and Johann Penner 1919.

In 1768 the congregation, with the consent of the bishop of the state church, built a meetinghouse in Ladekopp which seated 600 persons. For the members living in the southwest a church was built at Pordenau in 1800, with a seating capacity of 250. Both churches had adjoining cemeteries for their members. The home for poor members, built in 1800, was sold in 1894; needy members were by that time supported in their homes. Church records were kept from 1775 to the end of World War II (*q.v.*). The baptized membership of Ladekopp-Pordenau was 564 in 1852, 400 in 1882; that of Ladekopp-Pordenau-Orlofferfelde 707 (1,114 souls) in 1888; 1,141 souls in 1928; 1,021 souls in 1941 (739 baptized members). The last elders were Johann Penner of Prangenau (preacher 1903, elder 1919-d. 43) and Johannes Dyck II (preacher 1919-?).

In 1882 the congregation was incorporated. Since the members of the Ladekopp congregation and the Frisians of the Orlofferfelde church lived side by side in the same village, and since to obtain corporation rights it was necessary to define limits, these congregations merged for business purposes. Their leaders met for the discussion of common problems.

The Ladekopp church belonged to the Conference of the East and West Prussian Mennonite Churches, and from 1892 was a member of the Vereinigung (*q.v.*). In the fighting at the end of World War II in 1945 the meetinghouses at Ladekopp and Pordenau were burned down. The members were all evacuated westward into Denmark and Germany. (*ML* II, 604.)   A.J., vDZ.

Ladekopp, a village on the left bank of the Tokmak River of the Molotschna Mennonite settlement, Ukraine, Russia, named after a Mennonite village in West Prussia, was established in 1806 by 26 Mennonite families from Prussia, being one of the oldest villages of the Molotschna settlement. In 1914 it had 100 Mennonite families with 460 inhabitants. The village had a school and was primarily occupied with agriculture. Most of the inhabitants belonged to the Petershagen Mennonite Church (*q.v.*).

In 1929-30 the collectivization of agriculture took place and the first families were sent to Siberia as kulaks. In 1941 only one third of the population was Mennonite. At the outbreak of the war some men were drafted into the army and some had to dig trenches. Soon all men above 16 years of age were sent east. The women and children were gathered at the station of Gross-Tokmak on Sept.

30, 1941, to be transported east. When the Germans approached they returned to their homes. On Sept. 12, 1943, the Mennonite population of the village, some 140 persons, was evacuated to Germany. Only about 25 persons succeeded in going to Canada and two to Paraguay; the rest were returned to Russia. (*ML* II, 604.) C.K.

Laer, van, an aristocratic Dutch Mennonite family of businessmen. Jan van Laer, a deacon of the Flemish congregation of Amsterdam, was excommunicated in 1623 by the Flemish Elder Jan Luies (*q.v.*), because van Laer did not agree with his strict ideas (*Inv. Arch. Amst.* I, No. 562; *N.N.B.Wb.* III, 709). Willem van Laer, originally from Amsterdam, then living at Hamburg, Germany, married Levina Coppenol (about 1700) of Amsterdam. Their son Cornelis van Laer of Amsterdam in 1746 joined the Moravian Brethren in the Netherlands and became treasurer of their Mission Association. Some of the van Laer family were deacons at Amsterdam. A side branch of this family has the name Blo(c)k van Laer. There are some descendants in the United States who spell their name Black van Lear. vDZ.

Lafayette First Mennonite Church (EMC), South 26th and Kossuth Streets, Lafayette, Ind., was organized on Aug. 2, 1942, with 24 members under District Superintendent N. J. Schmucker. The first pastor was Reuben C. Cantrell. The concrete block building was erected in 1941 and the auditorium enlarged in 1951. E. G. Steiner served as pastor 1946-51, Paul A. McCoy 1951-55, and Owen Haifley 1956- . The membership was 70 in 1956.

The congregation is actually the direct successor to an older congregation, whose meetinghouse, built in 1885, was located about eight miles east of Lafayette, north of the village of Perth, and was sold in 1941. The community here was started in the 1850's by Amish settlers from Butler Co., Ohio, and some direct from Germany. The chief family names were Gingerich, Ehresman, Imhoff, Zimmerman, Amstutz, Mellinger, and Gerber. Earlier ministers were Christian Zimmerman, John Zimmerman, and Christian Gerber, in that order, all of whom are buried in the Mennonite cemetery just south of Edna Mills. E.G.St.

Lagrange County, Ind., which lies directly east of Elkhart County, on the Michigan border, is an integral part of the Elkhart-Lagrange County Mennonite and Amish settlement. The first to arrive here were a group of Amish families from Somerset Co., Pa., and Holmes Co., Ohio, who settled first in Clinton Twp., Elkhart Co., in 1841, a portion of this group moving 15 miles further east to Newberry Twp., Lagrange Co. The descendants of this group divided about 1860 into the Old Order Amish and the more progressive element who later became a part of the Indiana-Michigan Mennonite Conference, largely in the Forks congregation, whose meetinghouse lies just east of the Elkhart County boundary. A second group of Amish, progressive from the beginning, came from Fairfield Co., Ohio, to organize the Maple Grove Mennonite Church at Topeka about 1855. This group suffered two divisions, one before 1900, and one in 1923, which resulted in the Topeka Mennonite (GCM) Church.

The Townline Conservative Mennonite Church was formed out of former Old Order Amish about 1885, with its meetinghouse just across the eastern border of Elkhart County. Mennonite settlers from Somerset Co., Pa., near Johnstown, were the majority element in the settlement made about 1860, which led to the formation of the Shore Mennonite Church (1874) near Shipshewana, later the Emma Mennonite Church (1901), the Marion Mennonite Church (1947), and the Plato Mennonite Church (1950). All these churches are west of the city of Lagrange, except the latter which is five miles east of Lagrange.

In 1954 there were the following congregations in Lagrange County: Old Order Amish, 17 congregations with *ca.* 1,000 members; 6 Mennonite (MC) congregations with 1,132; one Conservative Mennonite with 120; one General Conference Mennonite with 235. The total Mennonite and Amish baptized membership in Lagrange County in 1954 was thus *ca.* 2,500 in 25 congregations. H.S.B.

Lahoma Mennonite Brethren Church, now extinct, located in Lahoma, Garfield Co., Okla., was founded about 1906 as an affiliate of the Sued-Hoffnungsfeld congregation of Fairview, Okla., a member of the Southern District Conference. The congregation built a church and chose John Schneider as its leader. The largest total membership (baptized) was about 30 (1914).

Among the reasons for its disbanding in 1923 were that some families moved away, others found other church homes, and lack of a leader, although several ministers of the near-by M.B. congregations upon request from the Southern District Conference tried hard to keep it going.

The members of the Lahoma M.B. congregation, together with members of the North Enid M.B. Church that had meanwhile settled in Enid, began to gather in the city for services and organized as the Enid-Lahoma M.B. Church. The name is now Enid City Mennonite Brethren Church (*q.v.*). P.C.G.

Laird is a district of the large Rosenort Mennonite (GCM) Church of Saskatchewan, centering in the town of Laird (pop. 400), about 50 miles north of the city of Saskatoon. The Rosenort Mennonite Church, established in 1894 by the newly arrived Elder Peter Regier from Prussia, contains eleven church districts and has over 1,400 baptized members. Laird was one of the first organized districts of this congregation. It has had a church building since 1910. The first ministers were Heinrich Warkentin, Jacob Janzen, Cornelius K. Ens, David Epp (1953). Among the ministers now living are C. F. Sawatzky and Arthur Friesen, the leader of the church. At present four ministers and one deacon are serving the Laird district, which has over 100 members. The elder (1954) is J. G. Rempel, who lives in the main district of the congregation, Rosthern. The town also has an M.B. church. J.G.R.

Laird (Sask.) Mennonite Brethren Church is a member of the Canadian M.B. Conference. The Laird congregation was organized in 1898 with approximately 60 members under the leadership of Jacob B. Wiens, apparently the first organized M.B. church in Saskatchewan. The meetinghouse was first built in the country and later moved into town. Men who have served as ministers and leaders of the church are Jacob B. Wiens, Elder David Dyck, P. A. Penner, D. D. P. Epp, Jacob Wieler, J. B. Fischer, and the present leader Henry Speiser. The 1954 membership was 47. J.H.E.

Lake Charles (La.) Mennonite Church (MC), now extinct, began in 1898, when the first settlers moved down from the northern states. A few families came from Austell, Ga., in 1905. The largest membership was about 40. The bishops serving have been Andrew Shenk, J. M. Kreider, J. N. Durr, and E. S. Hallman. The ministers have been Jonas Nice, Clarence Bontrager, and John E. Wenger. At present (1954) the E. G. Leidig family alone remains in the community. E.S.H.

Lake Region Mennonite Church (MC), a member of the North Central Conference, was organized in May 1928, nine miles from Detroit Lakes in Becker Co., Minn. This is predominantly a dairy section and cheap land has been a major attraction. There are 412 lakes in a radius of 25 miles from Detroit Lakes, and the land is quite hilly and covered with second growth timber except where farmers have cleared it and built homes.

The J. B. Stehman, J. D. Stoll, and J. C. Gingerich families moved to the Detroit Lakes community in the fall of 1926; the first family was from South Dakota, and the last two from Ulen, Minn. Later others came from Cass Co., Mo., South Dakota, Iowa, Nebraska, Montana, and Pennsylvania. Nineteen families from Nebraska represent the greatest influx from any one state.

The seven rural mission (MC) stations in northern Minnesota sprang up following work started at White Earth in a schoolhouse as a branch Sunday school of the Lake Region Mennonite Church. The Lake Region meetinghouse was dedicated on July 1, 1936, and enlarged in 1948. In 1954 the membership was 87, with Elmer D. Hershberger as bishop and Menno Erb as preacher. J. C. Gingerich was minister 1926-53. E.D.HE.

Lakenbereider, een (a cloth manufacturer), an unknown person, was burned at the stake on Aug. 18, 1550, at Antwerp, Belgium. The *Antwerpsch Chronykje* (quoted by Génard in *Antw. Arch.-Blad*) relates that when an Anabaptist baker of Gent was burned at the stake on the market place of Antwerp, this Lakenbereider approached the victim and kissed him, exhorting him to remain steadfast. He was at once arrested and executed a few days after, because he was "unwilling to abandon his error." This martyr could not be identified. (*Antw. Arch.-Blad* VIII, 390, 393.) vDZ.

Lakeside Hutterite Bruderhof, located near Cranford, Alta., was founded in 1935. Their preacher Peter Hofer, who was chosen in the Wolf Creek, S.D., Bruderhof in 1926, moved to the Wolf Creek commune near Stirling, Alta., and from there went with several families to found the Lakeside Bruderhof. Joseph Wipf was chosen to the ministry here in 1944. In 1947 the commune numbered 162 souls, with 64 baptized members. D.D.

Lakeside Hutterite Bruderhof, located nine miles west of Headingly, Man., was founded in 1947 by Preacher Jörg Wipf and ten families from the Maxwell Bruderhof six miles west of Lakeside. The Brethren bought land and built houses and stables. In 1947 the Bruderhof numbered 78 souls, 28 of them being baptized members. D.D.

Lakeview Mennonite Church (MC), a rural congregation, located at Wolford, Pierce Co., N.D., a member of the North Central Conference. The first preaching service was held on Nov. —, 1913. In July 1916 a series of meetings was held by I. S. Mast and 22 members were received into the church. A congregation was then organized, a church was built, and a Bible conference was held. In May 1916 J. C. Gingerich of Missouri was ordained and given charge of the congregation, serving until he moved to Ulen, Minn. In 1919 Eli G. Hochstetler was ordained deacon, 1923 minister, and 1926 bishop; he is still (1955) serving the congregation. In 1926 Calvin Ringler was ordained a minister, serving until he moved to Colorado for his health. In 1931 John Stoll was ordained minister. Summer Bible school has been held each summer since 1939. The congregation came largely from an Amish background. The membership in 1955 was 112, with Rufus Beachy as minister. F.E.K.

Lambach: see **Lembach.**

Lambert (John Nycolsen), an Anabaptist martyr, burned at the stake on Nov. 22, 1538, at Smithfield in London, England, together with three unknown martyrs from Flanders. (Verheyden, "Mennisme in Vlaanderen," ms.) vDZ.

Lambert Dirks, an Anabaptist martyr, executed Jan. 1, 1539, at Alkmaar, Dutch province of North Holland. (*DB* 1891, 1; *ML* I, 451.) vDZ.

Lambert van Doornick, an Anabaptist martyr, was seized with five brethren, Adriaen van Hee, Joos Meeuwens, Willem de Hoedemaeker, Goossen de Hoedemaecker, and Egbert de Hoedemaecker, as they were holding an evening service near Doornik (Tournai) in Flanders in 1558, and burned at the stake in a forest on Hennegau territory. (*Mart. Mir.* D 202, E 584; *ML* II, 606.) NEFF.

Lambert, Sidenham (1855-1937), a minister in the Mennonite Brethren in Christ Church, was born in Northampton Co., Pa. He was ordained in 1876. He was married to Emma Hosller in 1876, who died in 1903. Among their eight children was Mrs. J. A. Huffman. He was later married twice more, to Amanda Long in 1905, and to Anna Flatter in 1915. He held pastorates in Fleetwood, Pa., Bethel Church in Elkhart Co., Ind., Potsdam, Ohio, and Beech Grove, Darke Co., Ohio. He served as presiding elder in the Indiana and Ohio Conference for a number of years; was president of the General Conference Executive Board for eight years, treasurer of the Indiana and Ohio Conference for six years, and a member of the General Conference for many years as well as its chairman in 1900.   J.A.Hu.

Lambert Mennonite Church (MC), located 7½ miles west of Job, in Dry Fork District, Randolph Co., W. Va., is operated by the Home Mission Board of the Middle District of Virginia Conference. Work was begun here in 1900. The meetinghouse was built in 1949. The church serves the people of Middle Mountain and Lambert Hollow. Services had been held in the Wymer and Lambert schoolhouses for 50 years. The membership in 1956 was 35, with Paul Good serving as minister.   H.A.B.

Lambrecht (Lambert) **Duppijns** of Haarlem, an Anabaptist martyr, beheaded on June 2, 1539, at Haarlem, Dutch province of North Holland. Duppijns was arrested in his own house on May 23, with his wife and a few other Anabaptists. When the house was searched about 500 copies of unbound books by David Joris (*q.v.*) were found and confiscated. On May 24 Duppijns was tried; he refused to admit the stay of David Joris at his house. Thereupon the officials took recourse to a trick. Adriaen Adriaensz, an Anabaptist who had recanted, was imprisoned with Duppijns, pretending to Duppijns that he was still a loyal member. So the officials learned the secret. On May 28 Duppijns was tortured a second time. Duppijns, who was a native of the bishopric of Münster, Westphalia, Germany, was a David-Jorist, as were also his wife and the whole company meeting in his house.   vDZ.

Bijdr. en Mededeelingen Hist. Genootschap, Utrecht XLI (Amsterdam, 1920) 199-201, 208 f., 211, 217 f.

Lambrecht Henricx, an Anabaptist martyr, executed on Dec. 16, 1575, at Antwerp, Belgium, with Augustijn de Vuelpere. Lambrecht was sentenced to death because he had attended Mennonite meetings and possessed "heretical" books. (*Antw. Arch.-Blad* XIII, 197; XIV, 96 f., No. 1102.)   vDZ.

Lambrecht Jacobs (Grootboot) of Purmerend, Dutch province of North Holland, an Anabaptist martyr, had sailed in March 1534 from Amsterdam en route to Münster, but was arrested at Bergklooster (*q.v.*). He obviously was set free here but was rearrested in 1540, and sentenced to death on Sept. 22, 1540, by the Court of Holland. The execution by the sword took place at The Hague. Lambrecht belonged to the revolutionary wing of Anabaptism, being a follower of Jan van Batenburg (*q.v.*). (*Inv. Arch. Amst.* I, Nos. 232, 744 f.)   vDZ.

Lambrecht Linthermans, an Anabaptist martyr, was burned at the stake in 1537 (exact date unknown) at Antwerp, Belgium. Linthermans was a wool weaver. (*Antw. Arch.-Blad* VII, 434; XIV, 14 f., No. 159.)   vDZ.

Lambrechts-Vos, Anna (b. 1876 at Rotterdam, d. 1932 at Soest), was a Dutch Mennonite musician and composer of cantatas and songs, and 1894-1928 organist of the Rotterdam Mennonite Church. She was a sister of Karel Vos (*q.v.*), a Mennonite minister and outstanding historian. (*Zondagsbode* XLV, 1931-32, No. 13.)   vDZ.

Lame Deer Mennonite Mission Church (GCM): see **Petter Memorial** Mennonite Church.

Lamist Mennonite Church (*Kerk bij 't Lam*) in Amsterdam, now known as the Singelkerk. In 1607 Harmen Hendricks van Warendorp, a native of Aachen, Germany, purchased a lot on the Singel for 5,000 gilders, beside the brewery "'t Lam" (i.e., at the sign of the Lamb). There he had a church building erected (1608) that cost him 7,800 gilders, "out of love to God and the church." It became the place of worship of the Flemish branch of the Mennonites. The church was completely remodeled in 1639-40. It remained the property of the van Warendorps until 1740, when the congregation bought it with the adjacent houses for the sum of 29,573 gilders. In 1777 an organ was put into the church. In 1840 it was remodeled again. It is still the meeting place of the Mennonites of Amsterdam. Thorough and costly repairs were made in 1953-54, when the decaying wooden pillars of 1609 on which the church was built were replaced by concrete pillars.

The Flemish group in Amsterdam was given the name "bij 't Lam" in 1608. It was a large, important congregation. In 1632, on the basis of the Dordrecht Confession, part of the Old Flemish joined the Lamist congregation; in 1639 it was still further augmented by its union with the United Frisians and High Germans. It had a membership of about 1,000 at this time. In 1664 a split occurred in consequence of a dispute between Galenus Abrahamsz (*q.v.*) and Samuel Apostool (*q.v.*), when the latter withdrew with 500 members and henceforth met in a house with the sign of the sun (see **Zonists** and **Lammerenkrijgh**). Four years later, June 1, 1668, the Waterlander congregation "bij den Toren" united with the "Lamb" congregation. The united church (*vereenigde Gemeente*) used both church buildings until 1812; after this the church "bij den Toren" was no longer in use. In 1728 the small Old Frisian (or Jan Jacobs group) congregation, meeting in the Bloemstraat, joined the Lamist congregation. In 1801 the Zonist congregation united with the Lamist and Toren groups.

The church known as "van 't Lam en Toren" assumed responsibility for the Amsterdam Mennonite Seminary (*q.v.*) in 1735, thus laying the foundation for the A.D.S. (1811). It had at an earlier period helped poor congregations to engage trained ministers. Thus the Lamist church has been a great blessing to the Mennonites, not only in Amsterdam, but also in all the Netherlands.   vDZ.

DB 1863, 1-42; 1898, 1-54; *Naamlijst* 1802, 59-68; *Inv. Arch. Amst.* II, Nos. 131-228, 1243-1343; *ML* II, 606.

Lamistische Sociëteit (Lamist Conference): see **Zuid-Hollandsche Sociëteit.**

Lamists (also called *Galenists* after their leader Galenus Abrahamsz de Haan) was the name of the group of 1,500 left in the Mennonite church at Amsterdam after Samuel Apostool in consequence of the *Lammerenkrijgh* (*q.v.*) separated from the Flemish "bij 't Lam" group in 1664 with 500 members, and met for worship in a house with a gable sign "to the sun." Hence the Apostool group were known as Zonists (*q.v.*). The division extended to almost all the Mennonites of Holland. In the new names, Lamist and Zonist, the old distinctions between Flemish, Frisian, etc., were swallowed up. The Lamist, the more liberal wing, was the larger. Even today one can see on the weather vane on many a Dutch Mennonite church a sketch of a lamb. By the end of the 18th century the gulf between the Zonists and Lamists was largely bridged over. At the beginning of the 19th century union was achieved everywhere. Nevertheless throughout the 19th century traces of the division were still perceptible. (*ML* II, 606.)   vDZ.

Lammerenkrijgh (War of the Lambs), the name of the dispute which broke out soon after 1650 in the Flemish Lamist congregation (bij 't Lam) in Amsterdam on the question whether the Flemish was the (only) true church and whether or not a confession is essential to salvation. The older party in the church was opposed to Galenus Abrahamsz (*q.v.*) and his Collegiant ideas. While Galenus and his followers stressed "life" rather than doctrine, the conservative party held to the unabridged confession of faith. Thus the lamentable strife ensued, which first split the Amsterdam church and then burst apart the recently won unification of the Mennonites in all Holland (see **Amsterdam** *Mennonite Church*). Conflicts at Rotterdam and Utrecht, like the Amsterdam quarrel, had as early as 1660-61 ended in a victory of the conservatives.

This quarrel has become known in history as the "Lammerenkrijgh." The name is a derisive epithet for the unpleasant bickering of the lambs of God, borrowed from one of the innumerable polemics of the time.   vDZ.

H. W. Meihuizen, *Galenus Abrahamsz* (Haarlem, 1954) 54-98; W. Kühler, *Het Socinianisme in Nederland* (Leiden, 1912) 149-75; *DB* 1901, 1-37; 1916, 145-95; *ML* II, 606.

Lammertsz, Lammert, living at Haarlem, Holland, about 1644 (biographical data not available), participated in the controversy between Petrus Bontemps (*q.v.*), Joost Hendriksz (*q.v.*), and Passchier de Fijne, by publishing in 1644 two pamphlets in which he attacked both Bontemps, who had combatted the Mennonites, and the liberal ideas of Hendriksz and de Fijne, who had defended the Mennonites. (*Biogr. Wb.* V, 507; *Catalogus Amst.,* 201.)   vDZ.

Lamotte (Mich.) United Missionary Church had a membership of 28 in 1953. Its pastor was B. H. Surbrook.

Lampeter Music Hall, located in Lampeter, Lancaster Co., Pa., has this foundation marker: "Lampeter Music, Lecture and Bible School lovingly dedicated to the memory of the early settlers of Lancaster County 1898." To Henry B. Herr belongs most of the credit for this structure. It became a preaching point for the Brick Mennonite (MC) congregation, two miles away. In November 1905 A. D. Wenger conducted here one of the first revivals held in Lancaster Conference, following approval of such work in the fall Conference. Amos Geigley and others

held continued meetings here and it was a preaching point, somewhat under Henry B. Herr's supervision. By about 1915 this mission moved back to the Brick church. Later the local school board bought the building, and it is still being used as a school.   I.D.L.

Lancaster, Pa. (pop. 64,000), the "Hickory Town" laid out in 1730, was the first inland town of William Penn's backwoods, almost 70 miles west of his Philadelphia settlement of 1681. James Hamilton, whose family named Hamilton, Ont., had earlier circumscribed a hickory tree at George Gibson's Tavern, a frequent Indian rendezvous. This tavern was near a fine spring, and was the only house in Lancaster. The log courthouse was built on the square in 1730. The town soon became a shopping center for a strong Mennonite community. By 1752 the population was 311. It was the seat of the Continental Congress of the Thirteen Colonies, meeting from Oct. 1, 1777, for nine months. It was the state capital 1799 to 1812, when Harrisburg permanently claimed this honor. It was the home of President James Buchanan. The Mennonite community in this agricultural Eden and this rapidly growing inland metropolis in the heart of Lancaster County were mutually benefited. It is the home of Armstrong Linoleum, RCA, Alcoa, Hamilton Watch, of silks and New Holland farm machinery. One Mennonite (MC) church, the Chestnut Street church, built in 1879, has spread so that today there are eight missions in and on the borders of this city. In addition there is one Reformed Mennonite, one General Conference Mennonite, and one Mennonite Brethren in Christ church here. The total Mennonite membership in the city in 1956 was about 600.

Lancaster city is the head and trading center of the largest compact Mennonite and Amish community in North America, and since the dissolution of the Mennonite settlements in Russia, probably of the world, with a total of over 25,000 baptized members living within a radius of 25 miles, in over 150 congregations. (*ML* II, 606.)   I.D.L.

Lancaster Christian Street Mission (MC), a mission for colored, was opened in 1933 as an outpost for the E. Vine Street Mission, Lancaster Mennonite Conference. It opened on Howard Street, moved to 460 Rockland Street, but since 1939 has been located in a new meetinghouse at S. Christian and Locust Street. Joseph S. Lehman was superintendent of the work from the start and was also pastor 1935-55. In 1955 D. Stoner Krady was bishop and Lester T. Weaver minister. The membership in 1956 was 51.
                               I.D.L.

Lancaster County, Pa., was carved out of Chester County and incorporated as the fourth in Pennsylvania in 1729. Named after Lancashire in North England, this county of the Indian country had but a few explorers and Indian exploiters before the Swiss and Palatine immigrants of 1710 arrived, who settled along Pequea Creek for 20 miles. Large influxes of Mennonites (1717-56) from the Palatinate (some from Switzerland direct) followed, with contingents of Lutherans and Reformed. By 1738

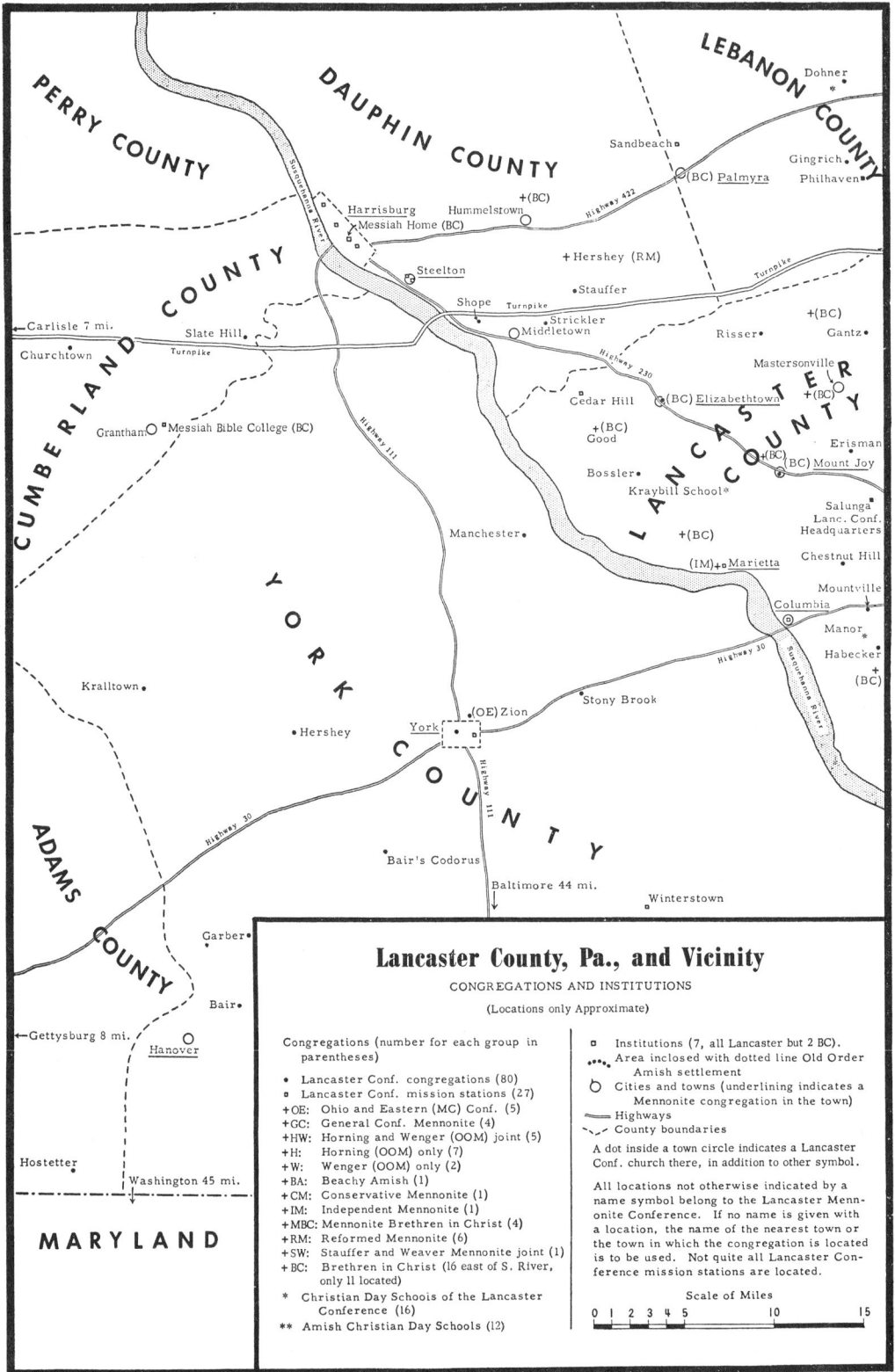

PERRY COUNTY

DAUPHIN COUNTY

LEBANON COUNTY

Dohner

Sandbeach□

Gingrich

(BC) Palmyra   Philhaven

Highway 422

CUMBERLAND COUNTY

Susquehanna River

Harrisburg
Messiah Home (BC)   Hummelstown   +(BC)

+ Hershey (RM)

Turnpike

Steelton

Stauffer

Shope   Turnpike

+(BC)

←Carlisle 7 mi.

Slate Hill   Strickler
Middletown

Risser•   Gantz•

Churchtown

Turnpike

Highway 230

Mastersonville

Grantham○ ■Messiah Bible College (BC)

Highway 111

Cedar Hill

+(BC)
Elizabethtown   +(BC)

LANCASTER COUNTY

+(BC)
Good

Erisman

Bossler•

+(BC)
(BC) Mount Joy

Kraybill School*

Salunga
Lanc. Conf.
Headquarters

Manchester•

+(BC)

Chestnut Hill

(IM)+▲Marietta

Mountville

Columbia ◎

YORK COUNTY

Manor

Habecker

+
(BC)

Highway 30

Kralltown•

Susquehanna River

•Hershey   York   (OE) Zion   Stony Brook

Highway 30

Highway 111

Bair's Codorus

Baltimore 44 mi.

Winterstown

ADAMS COUNTY

Garber•

←Gettysburg 8 mi.

Bair•

○
Hanover

Hostetter•

Washington 45 mi.

MARYLAND

Lancaster County, Pa., and Vicinity

CONGREGATIONS AND INSTITUTIONS

(Locations only Approximate)

Congregations (number for each group in parentheses)

- • Lancaster Conf. congregations (80)
- ▫ Lancaster Conf. mission stations (27)
- +OE: Ohio and Eastern (MC) Conf. (5)
- +GC: General Conf. Mennonite (4)
- +HW: Horning and Wenger (OOM) joint (5)
- +H: Horning (OOM) only (7)
- +W: Wenger (OOM) only (2)
- +BA: Beachy Amish (1)
- +CM: Conservative Mennonite (1)
- +IM: Independent Mennonite (1)
- +MBC: Mennonite Brethren in Christ (4)
- +RM: Reformed Mennonite (6)
- +SW: Stauffer and Weaver Mennonite joint (1)
- +BC: Brethren in Christ (16 east of S. River, only 11 located)
- * Christian Day Schools of the Lancaster Conference (16)
- ** Amish Christian Day Schools (12)

□ Institutions (7, all Lancaster but 2 BC).
•••• Area inclosed with dotted line Old Order Amish settlement
○ Cities and towns (underlining indicates a Mennonite congregation in the town)
═ Highways
╲╱ County boundaries

A dot inside a town circle indicates a Lancaster Conf. church there, in addition to other symbol.

All locations not otherwise indicated by a name symbol belong to the Lancaster Mennonite Conference. If no name is given with a location, the name of the nearest town or the town in which the congregation is located is to be used. Not quite all Lancaster Conference mission stations are located.

Scale of Miles

0 1 2 3 4 5   10   15

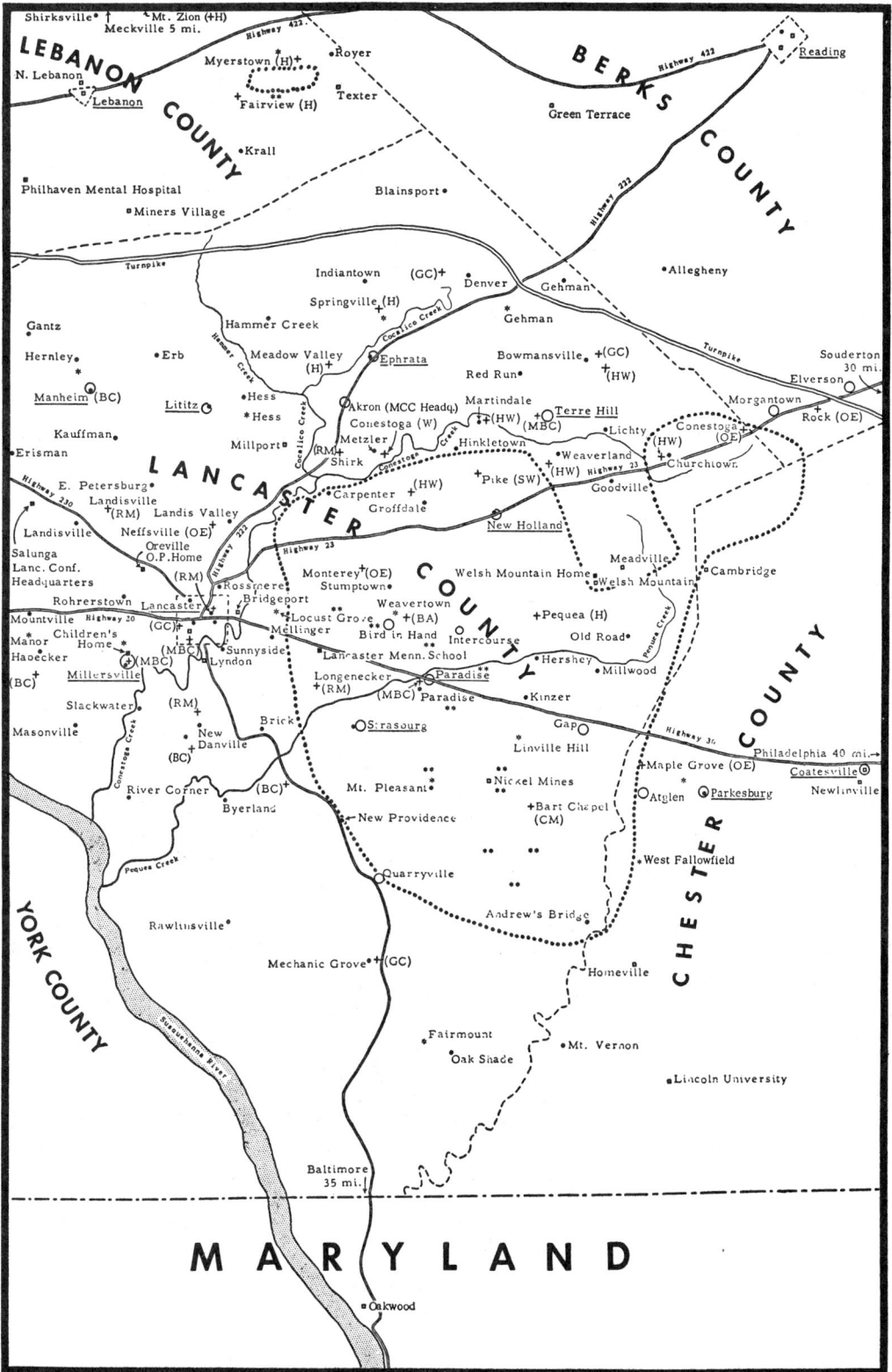

LEBANON COUNTY

Shirksville • ↑ Mt. Zion (+H)
Meckville 5 mi.
Myerstown (H)+ • Royer
N. Lebanon
Lebanon
Fairview (H) • Texter
Krall

Highway 422

BERKS COUNTY

Highway 422 • Reading

Green Terrace

Philhaven Mental Hospital
• Miners Village
Blainsport •

Highway 222

Turnpike
Indiantown (GC)+
Denver
Gehman • Allegheny
Gantz
Springville (H)
Hammer Creek
Gehman
Hernley •
• Erb
Meadow Valley (H)
Cocalico Creek
Bowmansville +(GC)
Red Run •
+(HW)
Souderton 30 mi.
Manheim (BC)
Lititz
• Hess
Ephrata
Martindale
+(HW)
Terre Hill (MBC)
Lichty
Conestoga (OE)
Morgantown
Elverson
Rock (OE)
Turnpike

Kauffman.
• Hess
Akron (MCC Headq.)
Conestoga (W)
Metzler
Hinkletown
Weaverland
(HW)
Churchtown.
Erisman •
Millport
(RM)+
Shirk
Conestoga Creek
+(HW)
Weaverland (HW) Highway 23
Goodville

LANCASTER COUNTY

E. Petersburg
Landisville (RM)+
Landis Valley
Carpenter (HW)
Groffdale
Pike (SW)
Highway 230
Neffsville (OE)
Oreville O.P.Home
(RM)
New Holland
Meadville
Welsh Mountain Home
Cambridge
Landisville
Salunga
Lanc. Conf. Headquarters
Rossmere
Bridgeport
Highway 23
Monterey (OE)
Stumptown
Welsh Mountain Home
Welsh Mountain
Rohrerstown
Lancaster
(GC)
Mellinger
Weavertown
Locust Grove +(BA)
Bird in Hand
Pequea (H)
Mountville Highway 20
Manor
Children's Home
(MBC)
Sunnyside
Lyndon
Intercourse
Old Road
Haecker
(BC)+
Millersville
(MBC)
Lancaster Menn. School
Hershey
Millwood
Longenecker +(RM)
Paradise
(MBC) Paradise
Kinzer
Slackwater
(RM)
Brick
Strasburg
Gap
Highway 30
Philadelphia 40 mi.
Masonville
New Danville (BC)
Linville Hill
Maple Grove (OE)
Coatesville
Mt. Pleasant
Nickel Mines
Atglen
Parkesburg
Newlinville
River Corner (BC)+
Byerland
New Providence
Bart Chapel (CM)
West Fallowfield

CHESTER COUNTY

Pequea Creek
Rawlinsville
Quarryville
Andrew's Bridge
YORK COUNTY
Mechanic Grove +(GC)
Homeville
Susquehanna River
Fairmount
Oak Shade
Mt. Vernon
Lincoln University
Baltimore 35 mi.

MARYLAND

• Oakwood

the population was 2,560; by 1752, 3,977; by 1850, 98,944; and by 1954, 241,000. From the first settlement, which was made at Lampeter, the Mennonites went north to the city and then branched over the county, leaving the south for the Scotch-Irish and Friends, and the east for the Welsh. Postlethwaite was the first seat of local government, but by 1730 it was moved to "Hickory Town" (Lancaster), where it has remained. The Mennonites, so strongly entrenched as farmers in the county, for decades played a strong role in the county's prosperity. The United Brethren, Reformed Mennonite, Evangelical Church, and Brethren in Christ groups started here, and the Church of God had very early essential support in the county.

In Lancaster County there are about 12,600 Mennonites (MC) in 80 congregations or preaching points, 3,100 Old Order Amish in 30 congregations, 2,900 Old Order Mennonites in 17 congregations, 318 Stauffer, Reidenbach, and Weaver (a type of Old Order) Mennonites. The Beachy Amish have two congregations with 269 members. The Ohio and Eastern Conference has eight congregations with 1,400 members in this area, although part of the membership is in the bordering territory of Berks County and Chester County. The General Conference Mennonites have three congregations, in Lancaster, Bowmansville, and Denver, with 207 members. The Reformed Mennonites (Herrites) have 225 members in this area, their original starting point having been near Lancaster city. The Mennonite Brethren in Christ have two congregations, Lancaster and Terre Hill, with 110 members, also a mission point at Paradise. Thus these eight distinct groups of Mennonites had in 1954, 21,300 baptized members in over 150 congregations. This is the largest concentration of Mennonites in such a compact area anywhere in North America, and since the dissolution of the compact Mennonite settlements in Russia, anywhere in the world.

Two related peace church groups, the Church of the Brethren and the Brethren in Christ, also have numerous strong congregations in the county, the former having 21 congregations with 7,500 members, the latter 12 congregations with 1,200 members.

Lancaster County Mennonites have several institutions in addition to a number of elementary schools. These are all under the Lancaster Mennonite (MC) Conference: Lancaster Mennonite School (1942, Lancaster), two homes for the aged, i.e., Mennonite Home (1903, Lancaster) and Welsh Mountain Samaritan Home (1898, New Holland), the Mennonite Children's Home (1911, Millersville), and Philhaven Hospital (1952, Lebanon, Pa., for mental and nervous diseases). A headquarters center for the Lancaster Mennonite Conference and its mission board is being developed at Salunga. The Mennonite Central Committee's headquarters have been at Akron since 1937.

The Lancaster County area is noted for its outstanding agricultural production, in which the Mennonites and Amish have always played a major role. It has often ranked in the first three counties in the United States for total value of agricultural production and is justly called the "Garden Spot." It also presents a beautiful landscape with its gently rolling valleys and well-kept farms and countryside.

I.D.L.

Ira D. Landis, "Mennonite Agriculture in Colonial Lancaster County, Pennsylvania," *MQR* XIX (1945) 254-72; H. M. J. Klein, *Lancaster County, Pennsylvania, A History* (N.Y., 1924) 4 vols.; H. Roddy, *Physical and Industrial Geography of Lancaster County, Pennsylvania* (Lancaster, 1916); I. D. Rupp, *History of Lancaster County* (Lancaster, 1844); *Proceedings of the Lancaster County Historical Society, 1895-* (Lancaster); W. Kollmorgen, *The Old Order Amish of Lancaster County, Pennsylvania* (Washington, D.C., U.S.D.A., 1942); *ML* II, 607 f.

Lancaster County (Pa.) **Amish** first settled in that part of the county which in 1752 was organized as Berks County (*q.v.*). Some Palatine Amish settled north and west of the present site of Reading as early as the second decade of the 18th century. They were joined later by Amish from Switzerland. Settlement within the present boundaries of Lancaster County began in 1759 when John Hertzler and his wife Veronica moved south from the northern frontiers of the county in consequence of Indian raids and the massacre of some Amish settlers during the French and Indian War. The Hertzlers were joined in 1760 in the Conestoga Valley (*q.v.*) near Morgantown by the family of Jacob Mast, also his father-in-law, Michael Hoelley (Hooley), and John Lapp.

Jacob Mast seems to have been the first Amish minister to serve the new congregation, but Christian Stoltzfus, son of Nicholas Stoltzfus, a Palatine immigrant who arrived in 1766, is said to have been the first ordained Amish minister to settle within the present bounds of Lancaster County. Family names which occur most frequently among the Amish in the county are Beiler, Fisher, Glick, Kauffman, Hertzler, Mast, King, Zook, Stoltzfus, Lantz, Lapp, Esh, and Blank.

Jacob Hertzler, living in the northern part of what is now Berks County, served the Conestoga group as bishop until his death in 1786. He was succeeded by Jacob Mast, ordained bishop in 1787. He in turn was followed by Peter Blank and John P. Mast. From the beginning of Jacob Mast's service as bishop the colony flourished. He was a prosperous farmer but he found time to visit and help build the other Amish settlements in Berks, Chester, and Lancaster counties. He is said to have visited also the congregations in Cambria and Somerset counties. His 12 children all married Amish mates and reared families in the Amish church. By 1850 nearly the entire membership of the large congregation was related to this Mast family by marriage or direct descent. A large percentage of the 6,000 descendants of Nicholas Stoltzfus are known for their conservatism and have remained loyal to the Amish or Amish Mennonite Church. David Beiler of Gap held firmly to the old order when western congregations began to erect meetinghouses in 1862 and to introduce other innovations. On the other hand, the Millers, Kurtzes, Zooks, Hertzlers, Reichenbachs, and others have hundreds of descendants in the Lutheran, Reformed, and United Evangelical denominations of Berks County and throughout the nation. There is always the possibility, to be sure, that many of these are the descendants of early non-Amish Swiss and Palatine settlers. Since the Amish rarely receive any non-Amish into their congregations, and since those who "marry out" very rarely remain in an Amish congregation, the Lancaster County Amish have remained an almost purely Swiss-Palatine racial group within the bounds of their adopted country and retain the cultural mores of their ancestors.

The Amish by natural increase and immigration have spread over a large part of the eastern and southeastern part of Lancaster County. Camp meetings and revival meetings by pietistic groups have swept away a considerable number of the Amish from their quiet, less emotional denominational heritage. Failure to provide service opportunities for the young people caused scores of Amish young people to unite with other denominations. One Amish family produced three Methodist ministers.

After some Amish congregations in states farther west began to erect meetinghouses, the Lancaster Amish gradually (1877-82) divided into two main groups: the "Church Amish," which adopted the name Amish Mennonites (q.v.), and the "Old Order Amish" (q.v.). But in spite of numerous defections Lancaster County still has the second largest number of Amish congregations in any one county in America, next to Holmes County, Ohio. Ohio now surpasses Pennsylvania in the total number of congregations.

Some family names listed among the early Lancaster County Amish immigrants have disappeared to a large extent. The Hershbergers and Hostetlers, for instance, moved to Mifflin Co., Pa., and are now numerous in Holmes Co., Ohio. The Yoders also are much more numerous in Ohio and Indiana than in Lancaster County, although a certain Barbara Yoder and her children were among the first Amish settlers in what is now Berks County.

In 1955 there were in Lancaster County or the immediately adjacent Berks and Chester County borders 30 Old Order Amish congregations with 3,100 baptized members. The following additional congregations descend directly from O.O. Amish origins by schism: Conestoga A.M. (1877) and its daughter congregations of Zion, Oley, and Rock, with a total of 664 members; Maple Grove (1882) and its daughter congregations of Media Chapel and Sandy Hill, with a total of 580 members. Both of these groups are in the Ohio and Eastern Conference. The Millwood congregation broke off from the Maple Grove congregation in 1945 to join the Lancaster Conference; it has 431 members with its five daughter congregations. One small congregation, Bart, with 31 members, left the O.O. Amish ca. 1950 to join the Conservative Mennonites. Two congregations, Weavertown and Maple Grove A.M., with 269 members, formed from the O.O. Amish ca. 1925, have joined the Beachy Amish group.

Thus the original pre-Revolutionary Amish immigrants, less than 200 souls in total number, according to C. H. Smith's estimate, have now grown to over 5,000 baptized members with some 10,000 souls, still adherents to the Amish-Mennonite faith.

J.S.U.

C. G. Bachman, *The Old Order Amish of Lancaster County* (Norristown, 1942); C. Z. Mast and R. E. Simpson, *Annals of the Conestoga Valley in Lancaster, Berks, and Chester Counties, Pennsylvania,* (Elverson, 1942); M. L. Montgomery, *Historical and Biographical Annals of Berks County, Pennsylvania I* (1909); C. H. Smith, *The Mennonite Immigration to Pennsylvania in the Eighteenth Century* (Norristown, 1929); G. M. Stoltzfus, "History of the First Amish Mennonite Communities in America," *MQR* XXVIII (October 1954) 235-62.

Lancaster Mennonite Conference. The Lancaster (Pa.) Mennonite Conference (MC) first convened in 1711, a few months after the Swiss-Palatine immigrants had established themselves in their new home, to select by lot one of their number to return to Europe. Hans Herr, their bishop and general adviser, was chosen, but Martin Kendig actually returned. In 1725 five representatives, Martin Baer, Hans Burkholtzer, Christian Herr, Benedikt Hirsche, and Johannes Bowman, attended the first general Mennonite Conference, held probably in Manatawny, when the historic Dordrecht Confession was translated into English and signed by 16 leaders, for all American Mennonites. The Conference always established peaceful relationships with the Indians, so that within the confines of the central county no blood was spilled on either side.

The Christian Herr house, built in 1719 on the Conestoga Road, connecting Indiantown, Brandywine, and Germantown, is the oldest meetinghouse-dwelling still standing in the county. The John Herr house, built in 1740, for 60 years provided a large room on the second floor as a place of worship. Abbeyville and Weaverland were built before 1750, the members having previously met in private houses and barns. Hernley (1745), Habecker (1760), and Bair's Hanover (1774) were built on Penn grants. The Byerland house (1747) is preserved as a sample of the simplicity and miniature size of the meetinghouses in the woods of that day. Today many are about 50-60 ft. x 100 ft. They still are conservative in architecture, economically built with considerable free labor by the members, simple but practical, of brick or substantial blocks, with a raised pulpit at one end, and the floor sloping toward it, and furnished with basements for religious education and meals for all-day meetings.

Fifteen years after the first settlement in Lampeter, the Mennonites were located throughout Lancaster County and ready to overflow. The Conference nurtured some of the scattered daughter colonies until full-fledged in the Ontario, Virginia, Washington County (Md.)-Franklin County (Pa.), and the Southwestern Pennsylvania Conferences. The Conference gave not only Benjamin Eby to Ontario, but most of the pioneers of both Waterloo and Woolwich Townships (Ont.), to establish two strong Mennonite communities in Upper Canada. It sent Ebersoles, Lehmans, Horsts, and Martins to people Franklin Co., Pa., and Washington Co., Md., mostly in 1790 and later. It gave Weavers, Abraham Brubaker, Rhodes, Stricklers, Heistands, etc., first to the northern Shenandoah Valley, Va.; then by 1790 David Heatwole, Joseph Wenger, Peter Burkholder, and others to Rockingham Co., Va. John Graybill went to Juniata County in the early 1770's, followed by Brubakers and Shellenbergers; they in turn peopled Blair County and Freeport, Ill. John Brubaker started Rockton, Pa. J. A. Ressler opened the India Mission in 1899. The Snyders and Abram Metzler established the church at Martinsburg in Morrison's Cove, Blair Co. Bishop Michael Horst went from here to Stark County, Ohio, the Metzlers to Columbiana County, John M. Greider to Clark County, William Westheffer and Henry Martin to Martin's Church, Wayne Co., Ohio. Christian Snavely went to Sterling and Simon Graybill to Freeport, Ill. David B., John M. R., and Reuben M. Weaver, Daniel A. Diener, Tillman Erb, J. D. Charles, and Abram Hess went to Hesston and elsewhere in Kansas. John M. Kreider went to Palmyra, Mo.

They were always thrifty, with large families earlier, and of the middle class of Americans, preferring independence of one another, but in times of stress and strain, ready for the necessary relief. As pioneers they had more extensive barns than houses, so that both in this area are considerably larger than in most other large American communities. The best agricultural practices are followed. Some hemp and flax were raised in the first century. Dairying, beef fattening, and now poultry raising, including broiler production, was a big factor in preserving the fertility of the soil. This with industry, diversification, and crop rotation has always placed Lancaster County as the first in America in agricultural wealth. The land values, increased from 35 cents to $1,800 per acre, would mean smaller farms, but the cost of building mostly offsets this trend. At first the parents retired on the farm, but in later times in towns. There were town meetinghouses in Lancaster (1879), Elizabethtown (1905), Lititz (1906), and Mt. Joy (1908). Others were built later. Now 60 per cent of the members are still dependent upon agriculture. The rest are in industry, domestic employment, and the professions, especially teaching.

During the German ferment period, 1729-ca. 90, their preachers were not permitted to perform marriages. They became naturalized beginning with 1729, under the British Crown. By 1742 Hans Tschantz called a conference to reprimand Martin Meylin for his large, extravagant sandstone house, to hold to simplicity and allay any undue suspicions among the neighbors concerning their prosperity. On Sept. 7, 1758, a committee was sent to Holland to obtain aid for the suffering Virginia brethren. On Nov. 7, 1775, they appealed to the Colonial Assembly for recognition of their conscientious scruples, which resulted in favorable legislation.

It was during the Revolutionary days that the United Brethren Church started here, when a Mennonite bishop, Martin Boehm, and a Reformed minister, Philip W. Otterbein, met in 1767 in Isaac Long's barn. The former was excommunicated in 1777 and the new church began 1780, and was revived by another ex-Mennonite, Christian Newcomer, at the turn of the century. The Brethren in Christ in Conoy Twp., Lancaster Co., started about 1780. The Reformed Mennonites came later but officially started in 1812. The Stauffer division oc-

curred in 1845, the Martinite (Old Order Mennonite) in 1893, which in turn suffered the Joseph Wenger division in 1926. The Ridenbach division in the Stauffer group occurred in 1946.

Semiannual conferences have been held at the Mellinger meetinghouse in the fall and at one of the three Rohrerstown meetinghouses in the spring as far back as records are extant, about 1740. (Beginning in 1953 the latter was moved to East Petersburg.) Here all Conference decisions were made and approved or rejected. This was the practice up to 40 years ago, with no long meeting of the Bishop Board prior to the session, at which the actual decisions are made for the Conference, with only nominal ratification by the total conference body. Now the bishops meet monthly or oftener for a day or more before the meeting of Conference.

The moderators of Lancaster Conference in order were Hans Herr, Hans Burkholder, Hans Tschantz, Bentz Hirschi, Christian Burkholder, Jacob Brubaker, Samuel Nissley, Peter Eby, Jacob Hostetter, Benjamin Herr, Jacob N. Brubacher, Benjamin Zimmerman, Benjamin Weaver, Noah L. Landis, W. W. Graybill, and Henry E. Lutz. By 1912 Peter R. Nissley became the first secretary. The present officers are H. E. Lutz, Moderator, Noah W. Risser, Assistant Moderator, Amos S. Horst, Secretary, Richard Danner, Assistant Secretary, and Mahlon Witmer, Treasurer. Until very recently the senior bishop in order of service served as moderator. Henry Lutz was the first elected moderator.

The Conference with more than 150 preaching points includes within Lancaster County (q.v.) 78 churches from Blainsport to Oak Shade, from Churchtown to Elizabethtown, with 640 and 621 members in the two largest, Weaverland and Mellinger, both distinctly rural. Then there are eight in Lebanon County, three in Cumberland County, ten in York and Adams, five in Dauphin, three in Berks, seven in Juniata, Snyder, and Union Counties, with many more scattered (see missions below).

These are divided into 19 bishop districts. Weaverland, the largest, has 18 preaching points, 1,897 members, 17 Sunday schools with an enrollment of 3,012 and an average attendance of 2,520, and 19 summer Bible schools with 2,925 and 2,477 respectively, and two young people's Bible meetings with 180 in attendance. Bishop J. Paul Graybill is assisted by 20 ministers and 10 deacons. The total membership in 1954 was 15,166, with 23 bishops, 193 ministers, and 102 deacons.

The Spring Conference in 1871 sanctioned the Sunday-school movement and today in 148 schools, there is an enrollment of 22,706 and an attendance of 18,175. Following the first (1927) summer Bible school at Norris Square, Philadelphia, the movement has grown until in 1953 there were in the Conference 165 with 26,116 enrolled and an average attendance for the ten nights of 23,312. The young people's Bible meetings started almost 50 years ago and the number is slowly increasing, with 6,724 attending, meetings customarily held on Saturday evenings.

In this, the largest and second oldest conference, close communion is observed with unfermented wine. Adult baptism by pouring is generally held in the meetinghouse (now). Anointing with oil is a bit more prominent than a few decades ago. Divorce is not sanctioned and weddings within the church are encouraged; in either home or church they are to be held with simplicity. The holy kiss is still practiced. The devotional covering is conscientiously and continuously worn. A distinct garb, both for the men and women, is strongly advocated and observed by most. The plain garb is required of the women for membership, and of the men for active participation in church work, though not for membership.

The ministers have other vocations; formerly they were all farmers. They receive no salary and frequently no support. There are five ministers who can still preach German; the transition to English was at its peak by 1900. For two centuries the types and figures and the sufferings of our Lord were rehearsed at communion time. At the semiannual counsel meeting, Matt. 18:1-22 is the Scriptural basis of the sermon. At preparatory services, generally on the Saturday before communion, Matt. 6:1-18 is used; at the ordination of a deacon Acts 6:1-7, of a minister Luke 10:1-20, and of a bishop John 21:15-17. The ministers are chosen by lot in the established congregation, unless there is but one candidate. When the votes are to be taken, the qualifications in I Tim. 3, Tit. 1, etc., for the office are stressed. The congregation is given the opportunity to present their choices to the bishops present. One vote for the offices of deacon and minister and five for the bishop place the recipient in a class for examination. The ordination then follows in two to seven days.

Since October 1905 a revival meeting has been held annually or biennially in each congregation. At Elizabethtown in early 1906 there was a class of 130 converts. There have been numerous large classes, but the largest were in the first two decades. While the number in classes is low generally, the revival does much to revive a congregation and is an additional blessing to our ministers.

The Mission Movement beginning in the mid-1890's received real impetus from this Conference. With John Mellinger and the Paradise district we have not only what was necessary to crystallize and establish local and foreign missions here, but as a spur into other areas. With the organization in 1916 of the present mission board (Eastern Mennonite Board of Missions and Charities, q.v.), the earlier missions in many cases took on new life, but the work also spread, so that today there are six missions in central Maryland, a large field developed on the Alabama-Florida border, three missions each in Tampa (Fla.), New York, Philadelphia, and Reading, two in Coatesville, one each in Lebanon and Harrisburg. In addition to the eight in and around Lancaster, there are numerous other missions in and within driving distance of the central county. Some are also in prospect in central and northern Pennsylvania and rural New York. In 1934 the first foreign missionaries were sent to Tanganyika, in 1948 to Ethiopia, in 1950 to northern Honduras, in 1951 to Luxembourg in Europe,

and to Somalia in Africa in 1953. On Jan. 1, 1954, there were 86 missionaries attached to the foreign mission fields and about 67 stations with 360 missionary workers in America, besides the established congregations and their work.

In the early day the children were given all their schooling in their homes. At the turn of the 18th century the school and church were often under one roof. Our home township had four of these— Landis, Lehn, Rudy, and Frick. Then with the enactment of the public school laws in 1834 and 1835, the Mennonites were opposed to sending their children to such schools, for the blessings of education in their schools under their own supervision would be lost. At Erisman, Risser, Hammer Creek, Stumptown, Cross Roads, Bossler, Chestnut Hill, Metzler, and Weaverland, the school was then placed on the adjoining grounds. Now again with the school far removed geographically and spiritually from the church, there is a retrenchment in the present Christian Day School movement. The first school of this kind was opened at Locust Grove in 1939. Now there are 19 in the area, exclusive of Old Order Amish and the Shaeffer Private School, with 45 teachers and about 1,228 pupils.

Although requested in 1922, the first Ephrata Winter Bible school was held in 1938, and after five terms the Lancaster Mennonite School opened in the fall of 1942, with a special Bible term added in 1953. It is a full high school, operated by a board of trustees appointed by the conference. The enrollment in 1954-55 was 303, with a faculty of 18. Some of the above elementary schools have ninth and tenth grades. In Tanganyika there are 60 bush schools with a thousand pupils, with some primary and middle schools started.

The winter Bible schools were placed at pivotal points in the Conference, beginning in 1943, meeting Tuesday and Thursday evenings for six weeks in January and February, until now there are 13 such, with an additional day school of two weeks at Millwood. These reach 2,200-2,500 of our constituency. They include book study, the Bible, missions, Christian education, Christian ethics, theology, and pedagogy, using chiefly our own literature as texts. Like the Sunday school they reach all ages.

There are now three old people's homes in this Conference. Oreville in 1903 was the first. The Welsh Mountain Mission (1898) gradually developed into the Good Samaritan Home. In 1953 the Philadelphia Colored Home was opened. Together about 185 are provided for within these three institutions. A girls' home for Mennonites working as domestics in Reading has been serving for many years. A children's home in Millersville in 1911 began to invite unfortunate children of all ages into its sphere, with Levi Sauder serving as superintendent until his death in October 1940. 1,215 children have received physical and spiritual nurture here.

In loving appreciation of what God through the Dutch Foreign Relief Committee accomplished in bringing the Mennonites to America, they aided wherever possible, not only in the early years when it was a case of mutual survival, but throughout the years. In the 1870's and 1922 they did their part in settling the Russian Mennonites on this continent. Following World War I Orie O. Miller, the Myers, Zimmermans, and others served in France and Near East Relief. The MCC has been a channel for immigration and relief funds from the Conference since 1920, aggregating in 1949-52 alone more than $224,500. The Conference has always had a member on the MCC, first John Mellinger, and more recently Henry F. Garber. The sewing circles were a substantial aid in giving materials in kind over the years. The movement began in 1895 in the Paradise district, developing into a general circle by 1911. Many tons have moved out from and through the Ephrata Clothing Depot, into overseas relief distribution. The Mary Mellinger cutting room at Paradise (1948) is serving an ever-enlarging constituency and service both local and world-wide.

Through itinerant evangelism and Voluntary Service, the summer Bible schools have not only spread over the southeastern states, central Maryland, and northern Pennsylvania, but have exceeded the Sunday-school figures by 3,400; they have reached the unreached, not only in isolated places, but in migrant work camps the year round and among the Puerto Ricans in the Lancaster County area and have established missions and congregations.

The Peace Problems Committee, earlier the Bishop Board, helped to steer the church through the war years, promoted nonresistance teaching, provided for the pastoral care of men in CPS and I-W service, and represented the church in its peace testimony.

The Lancaster (Mental) Hospital was opened in 1952 on the north edge of Mt. Gretna, with a maximum capacity of 35 patients, with one doctor, two nurses, and numerous helpers. A large farm is attached. It is called Philhaven (q.v.).

The historic German *Martyrs' Mirror* (1748), with the Ephrata prints of *Ernsthafte Christenpflicht* of 1745, 1770, 1785, and 1808, and the 1769 *Christliches Gemüthsgespräch*, following the English translation (1727) of the historic Dordrecht Confession, adopted by the 1725 Conference, were the known extent of our Mennonite publications for this century. But in the next 15 decades this changed. The *Ernsthafte Christenpflicht* appeared in Lancaster in 1826, 1841, 1852, 1862, 1868, 1875, 1876, 1892, 1904, and 1927, and the *Gemüthsgespräch* there in 1811, 1836, 1869, and 1892, English 1857, 1870, 1878, 1892, and at Union Grove in 1921. The *Ausbund* was reprinted at Lancaster eight times, 1815, 1834, 1846, 1856, 1868, 1880, 1908, and 1912. The *Unparteyisches Gesangbuch* (1804-1923) appeared in 17 editions as the official conference hymnbook. The Ehrenfried *Martyrs' Mirror* was published in 1814 and the Lampeter edition of I. D. Rupp in 1836. Menno Simons' *Fundamentbuch* appeared in German at Lancaster in 1794, 1835, 1853, and 1876, in English in 1835, 1863, and 1869. *Christian Spiritual Conversation in Saving Faith* (1857, 1870, 1878, 1892, and 1921), a translation of *Christliches Gemüthsgespräch*, included Christian Burkholder's *Counsel for Youth*, a translation of *Anrede an die Jugend*, which appeared in two editions in Ephrata in 1804, and was added to the

Gemüthsgespräch in its editions of 1839, 1848, 1868, 1869, and 1873, but had a separate edition at Allentown in 1829. *The Wandering Soul*, which appeared in 8 German and 10 English editions in Pennsylvania 1768-1919, appeared in English in Lancaster in 1874. In 1787 the Froschauer New Testament was published in German at Ephrata.

One of the first original writings known aside from Christian Burkholder's was a series of three *Question and Answer Booklets for the Sunday School*, prepared by Amos Herr and other leaders with John F. Funk in 1880 and 1881. Earlier was the Conference Meeting Calendar in 1854, prepared by Abraham Martin. The other Calendar editors for the century were Abraham Brubaker, John W. Weaver, and since 1940 Ira D. Landis.

The Rules and Discipline of Lancaster Conference was put into a printed leaflet in 1881 and has appeared since in numerous revisions, the last in 1954. In the same decade (1880) appeared Jacob N. Brubacher's *Brubaker Genealogy* and in 1896 John Hess's second *Hess Genealogy*. In 1902 A. D. Wenger's *Six Months in Bible Lands* was published and in 1931 M. G. Weaver's *Lancaster Mennonite Conference,* the first conference history attempted by any Mennonite.

Since 1924 the *Missionary Messenger* is the official organ of the Mission Board and since 1941 the *Pastoral Messenger* of the Conference. The *Mennonite Youth Service* (1951) is a monthly, *Victory Calls* (1949), an annual, and now many congregations have weekly or fortnightly bulletins.

The Christian Nurture Committee has revised the weekday Bible school manuals of the late thirties, so that by 1955 there will be new courses from kindergarten I to grade VIII, with two for high-school grades. This committee has prepared *Youth Faces Life* and *Making Our Homes Christian,* two smaller publications for religious education. It has a ten-year program of Bible Memory work for school and Sunday school, and a Bible reading program for family altars, beginning with the whole New Testament in 1954.

The *Hershey Genealogy* by Henry Hershey appeared in 1929, the *Missionary Movement Among Lancaster Conference Mennonites* in 1937, *Faith of Our Fathers on Eschatology* (1946), *The Landis Family Book,* Sections I-IV (1950-54), and *I Must See Switzerland* (1954) by Ira D. Landis. *Africa Calls* (1936) by Catherine Leatherman and Ada Zimmerman, *Africa Answers* (1951) by Merle Eshleman, *Noah Mack, His Life and Times* (1952) by Graybill, Landis, and Sauder, and *Christian Manhood* (1948) by Eshleman and Mack were other publications by Lancaster authors.

The Conference has had outstanding leaders in Hans Herr (1639-1725), Benedict Brackbill (1665-1720), Bentz Hirsche (1697-1789), Christian Burkholder (1746-1809), Peter Eby (1766-1843), Jacob Hostetter (1774-1865), Jacob N. Brubacher (1838-1913), and layman John H. Mellinger (1858-1952). With their foundations and links in co-operation with every member, today on nonconformity, including apparel, the Conference is conservative, on nonresistance officially solid, considerably opposed to

Calvinism and eternal security, but slightly colored by fundamentalism and pietism. I.D.L.

M. G. Weaver, *Mennonites of Lancaster Conference* (Scottdale, 1931); Ira D. Landis, *The Missionary Movement Among Lancaster Conference Mennonites* (Scottdale, 1938); *idem, The Lancaster Mennonite Conference History and Background* (Lancaster, 1956); ML II, 608.

Lancaster Mennonite Mission (MC), often called the "Vine Street Mission," located in a former Baptist church at 112 E. Vine Street, Lancaster, Pa., was opened on North Street on July 4, 1896, following the organization of the Lancaster Sunday School Mission. B. F. Herr and David Lantz served as the first superintendents. By 1899 the mission was located at 462 Rockland Street, and by 1908 at the present address. The John Mosemanns, D. Parke Lantz, D. Stoner Krady, and others received valuable missionary experience here. For a time Weaver's Book Store and Printery was housed in the basement. The 1954 membership was 85, with Frank M. Enck as pastor. I.D.L.

Lancaster Mennonite School (MC) is a secondary school opened in September 1942 by the Lancaster Conference and operated by a board of directors elected by that body. It is located on the Lincoln Highway (Route 30), four miles east of Lancaster, Pa. The buildings, built for use as a mill and farm, and the grounds had been used earlier by the Yeates School, which was a boys' preparatory school operated by the Episcopal Church. The property includes about 88 acres of land, about half of which is under cultivation, the rest in pasture, woods, and stream. A strong spring supplies the water. There is at present a large barn for the farm, in addition to seven buildings used for school activities.

Grades nine to twelve are offered in college preparatory, commercial, home economics, and Bible curriculums. A two-year Bible course is offered for those who do not want or need the four-year course and are interested in taking Bible courses until they can legally leave school. A six-week winter Bible school offers short courses in Bible on the school campus. The school emphasizes Christian service, missionary interests, and evangelism. The school maintains high scholastic standards to assure equality with comparable public high schools and admission to colleges and professions. Its monthly student publication is called *The Mill Stream*.

In addition to the local young people who come as day students there are also some from such areas as Delaware, Maryland, Ohio, and New York, also a few foreign students and missionaries' children. Though the school has been Mennonite in emphasis and attendance, pupils of all denominations are welcome and each year there are some students from other denominational groups.

Principals have been J. Paul Graybill (1942-54) and Amos W. Weaver (1954-). Noah Good has been dean from the beginning. The enrollment in 1956-57 was 385. N.G.

Lancaster (Pa.) Reformed Mennonite Church secured its first meetinghouse in 1855 by purchasing a building which was used until 1905. Its present meetinghouse, located at the corner of E. James and Cherry Streets, was erected in 1904. J.L.K.

Landau (pop. 22,870), formerly a free city, under French occupation 1648-1816, then a fortified city in the Palatinate, Germany. There was very probably an Anabaptist group here as early as 1526, to whom Hans Denk (*q.v.*) brought a letter of recommendation from the Strasbourg Anabaptists after his banishment from Strasbourg. Johannes Bader (*q.v.*), the reformer of the city, was probably not aware of their presence before his disputation with Hans Denk.

At Bader's advice the council decided to expel the Anabaptists from the city. Early in January 1527 an order was issued to all the guilds, making it a criminal offense to harbor Anabaptists. In the same month the mayor notified the authorities that "Jakob Kremer has a maid who was baptized at Rott near Weissenburg [Alsace] about three years ago." On April 26, 1528, Georg Brauner, Wolf Hitschler's son-in-law, Master Lorenz, Peter Hammer, and Stoffel Lauinger with his wife and children were banished.

Shortly before Pentecost in 1528 many men, women, servants, and maids were questioned by the council. Most denied any Anabaptist leanings; they were admonished to abstain "from Anabaptism and secret mutiny." Those who confessed Anabaptist connections were ordered to leave the city. The banishments continued. Johannes Bader wanted to hold a disputation with them, but was refused.

After Bader's death the suppression continued. In 1556-58 all Schwenckfelders and Anabaptists were banished from the city. In 1582 again they were driven out. Yet the Anabaptist movement succeeded in maintaining itself in secret. In 1591 the Landau congregation signed the Concept of Cologne (*q.v.*). Nothing further is known of it. NEFF.

J. P. Gelbert, *Magister Johannes Baders Leben und Schriften* (Neustadt, 1868) 181 ff.; E. F. H. Medicus, *Gesch. der evangelischen Kirche der bayrischen Rheinpfalz* (Erlangen, 1865), supplementary volume 25 and 27; Chr. Hege, *Die Täufer in der Kurpfalz* (Frankfurt, 1908) 15-21; ML II, 608.

Landeck, a town (pop. 5,534) in the Upper Inn Valley, Austria, one of the centers of the Anabaptist movement in northern Tirol. In 1529 Bartlmä Has was examined on a charge of Anabaptist inclinations; he was probably put to death. At least the martyr list in the *Geschicht-Buch* mentions a blood witness in Landeck. In 1539 a group of Anabaptists including a widow were questioned on the rack.

An indication of the strong growth of the movement is the series of Anabaptists imprisoned during the following years; they were "safely kept in the dark dungeon with warm water or goat soup made with little fat, otherwise fed once a day on bread and water." In 1543 some escaped; one of these was Hans Prugger, who was to be taken to the galleys via Hungary; in 1544 Hans Mändl (*q.v.*) escaped after 22 weeks of imprisonment with frequent trials on the rack, by beating his foot-chains with stones until he could slip out of them, and letting himself down on the rope used to bring up his food. In the 1540's several groups from Landeck migrated to Moravia; their property was secured by the government for the use of the children they left behind. In 1556 there was a larger emigration. In 1574 the Moravian Hutterites sent a special epistle to Landeck. Up into the 1580's there is mention of Anabaptists at Landeck.   P.De.

Beck, *Geschichts-Bücher;* Loserth, *Anabaptistmus;* Wolkan, *Geschicht-Buch;* Zieglschmid, *Chronik; ML* II, 608 f.

Landersheim (Landesheym), in the Lower Rhine district, Germany, was in the 16th century the seat of a Mennonite congregation. Klaus (Claes) von Landerschrift(?) in 1591 signed the Concept of Cologne in the name of this congregation. Further particulars about this congregation were not available.   vdZ.

Landes (Landis), a widely ramified Mennonite family in South Germany and in the United States. It stems from the canton of Zürich, Switzerland, where it is found (spelled Landis) in Pfäffikon on Lake Zürich in 1417, Hirzel in 1438, and Menzingen in 1454.

Horgenberg near Hirzel was the birthplace of Hans Landis (*q.v.*), a Mennonite preacher who died as a martyr on Sept. 29, 1614, in his seventieth year. He left a large family. His wife Margaretha Hochstrasser was 60 years old and stood loyally at his side. The father's steadfastness engraved itself deeply into the hearts of his children, who preserved his spiritual legacy for the most part, resisting the pressure of the government on their faith. His son Felix (*q.v.*) died in prison in 1642 in consequence of inhuman treatment, but Felix's wife Adelheid Egli managed to escape after four years. Another son, Hans, married to Elisabeth Erzinger, was also a preacher; his daughter Margaretha lay in prison with him for 60 weeks. The martyr's daughter Verena was married to the weaver Jacob Suners of Holland(?); she died in prison at Zürich in 1643 at an advanced age in consequence of maltreatment (*Mart. Mir.* D 822, E 1121), one of the last victims of the persecution of the Zürich Swiss Brethren. Through Hans Suner, probably a son of Jacob Suner, frequent relief offerings of the Dutch Mennonites passed to the Swiss Brethren.

After the execution of Hans Landis the Zürich council decided to confiscate Anabaptist property without respite. On Oct. 22, 1614, it ordered the confiscation of the property of exiles. The property left by Hans Landis was indeed promised to his wife and children on Feb. 23, 1615, but only on the condition that they join the state church within two weeks. Otherwise they could expect only exile and loss of property. Since the sorely tried widow could not make such a promise she was "laid in bonds" on May 24. The Reformed preacher tried to win her to his church in prison. It is not known how long she was held. Her children were at first intimidated, but finally most of them decided to stay with the Swiss Brethren. The government then confiscated the property and put dependent members of the family among strangers. About 1640 the property of Rudolf, Hans, and Felix Landis, all sons of the martyr, was sold.

The descendants of the martyr Hans who were loyal to the faith of their fathers left the country. Some of them settled in Alsace (especially in the Rappoltstein region). The first mention of the family in the Palatinate occurred on March 2, 1661, when a group of 50 persons was surprised at an evening meeting at Steinsfurt near Sinsheim on the Elsenz; they were heavily fined (see **Hasselbach**). Among them were Hans Heinrich Landes of Rohrbach, his son Rudolf Landes of Weiler, and his mother and sister.

In the 18th century there were Mennonite members of the Landes family in the Palatinate at Steinsfurt, Zuzenhausen, Schatthausen, Richen, Bockschaft, Kirschgartshausen, Ibersheim, Heppenheim, Hochheim, and Herrnsheim. In Monzernheim near Alzey a member of the Landes family (his Christian name is not stated; it was probably Johann Jakob Landes who was at this time a renter of the Dalberg estate near Herrnsheim) wanted to purchase an estate owned by a merchant living in the Dutch province of Groningen. He had already paid, but the Catholic renters (Roll and Walldorf) objected and demanded that the sale be nullified; they also demanded a decision as to whether a Mennonite in the Palatinate could buy land at all and own it like a Catholic citizen. On Jan. 24, 1726, an electoral decision compelled Landes to yield the land to the plaintiffs upon repayment of the purchase price and other expenses. On Jan. 18 a decree was issued by which any member of the three established churches could require a Mennonite purchaser to return it for the original sale price. This regulation remained effective until 1801, with the modification in 1737 limiting the right of redemption to three years (see **Jus Retractus**).

In the 19th century the family produced personalities whose influence on the Mennonite churches in Baden, Württemberg, and Bavaria was very beneficial. Heinrich Landes (d. 1886) of Ehrstädt, later at Lautenbach near Heilbronn (*q.v.*), was one of the leading elders (see **Baden** and **Hege**). In a similar spirit his sons worked, Christian Landes (d. Oct. 10, 1933) and Heinrich Landes (d. June 24, 1918) at Lautenbach. The former was a cofounder of the Mennonite deaconess work taken up in 1904 in Baden and Württemberg, and was for many years the director of this charitable work (see **Deaconess**, and *Gem.-Kal.,* 1933, 36-38), and a cofounder of the Heilbronn branch of the Evangelical Alliance (*q.v.*). A son of Heinrich, Walter, is elder of the church at Heilbronn, and another son, Christian, is a preacher there.

The task of visiting minister among the Mennonites of Baden was undertaken by Michael Landes of Albertshausen in 1872 after completing his training at St. Chrischona. He was the first full-time visiting preacher (*Reiseprediger*) in Germany. In his later years he preached for the congregations at Eichstock and Ingolstadt (d. July 13, 1926). His deep piety and humility won him honor and appreciation even on the part of the Catholic clergy of his vicinity (*Gem.-Kal.,* 1928, 63-74). Emanuel Landes served the congregations of Munich, Regensburg, and Eichstock as pastor for many years until his retirement in 1954 at the age of 74.

The members of the family expelled from Switzerland who did not settle in the Palatinate, emigrated to America in the 18th century, retaining the Swiss spelling of their name. In 1717, with the first German mass immigration, three brothers, Benjamin, Felix, and Johannes Landes of Mannheim, landed in Pennsylvania. American immigration lists of 1727, 1732, 1734, 1736, and 1745 contain the names of other members of the family. The towns Landisville and Landis Valley were named for them, in which large Mennonite churches were established. The name is of frequent occurrence among the Mennonite preachers in Pennsylvania. The Dutch *Naamlijst* names Jacob Landis as a preacher at Indian Creek in the late 18th century, and Abraham Landis from about 1790 at Deep Run.

John Landis settled at Quakertown in Bucks Co., Pa., Franconia Conference (MC) district. Jacob, who settled in Lancaster County, had one son Benjamin (1700-81), ordained to the ministry before 1746, who became the progenitor of the widespread Lancaster Landis line. Among the prominent Lancaster Conference (MC) ministers have been John B. Landis (1820-1902) of East Petersburg, John L. Landis (1832-1914) of Mellinger's, Sanford B. Landis (1869-1926) of Mellinger's, and Noah L. Landis (1857-1940) of Landis Valley, preacher from 1898 and bishop from 1905, moderator of the conference 1928-40. His son Ira D. Landis (1899-), also of Landis Valley, preacher since 1921, is the historian of the Lancaster district. Noah E. Landis (1893-) is a bishop at Alpha, Minn. In 1954 eight ministers in Eastern Pennsylvania bore the name Landis.   HEGE.

C. Bergmann, *Die Täuferbewegung im Kanton Zürich bis 1660* (Leipzig, 1916); E. Correll, *Das schweizerische Täufermennonitentum* (Tübingen, 1925); D. B. Landis, *The Landis Family* (Lancaster, 1888); C. Henry Smith, *The Menn. Immigration to Pennsylvania* (Norristown, 1929); M. G. Weaver, *Mennonites of Lancaster Conference* (Scottdale, 1931); Ira D. Landis, *The Landis Family Book*, 4 vv. (Lancaster, 1950, 1952, 1953, 1954); Henry S. Landes, *Descendants of Jacob Landes of Salford Township, Montgomery Co., Pennsylvania* (Souderton, 1943); Jakob Landes, "Hans Landes und seine Kinder," a manuscript in Goshen College Library; *ML* II, 609 f.

Landis Derry Meetinghouse, located in Derry Twp., Dauphin Co., Pa., on the north edge of Hershey, was erected probably as an "Unpartisan Mennonite Meetinghouse" as was Shirk's in East Hanover Twp., Lebanon Co., which by 1854 was transferred to the United Brethren. This Spring Creek Meetinghouse tract came from John Landis (1753-1829), a great-grandson of Felix Landis, a pioneer of East Lampeter, Lancaster Co. Henry Landis (1764-1844), another great-grandson of Felix, was a minister of the Landis congregation. There is a small cemetery here, in which are the graves of John Landis and others bearing this family name. The United Brethren absorbed most of the Mennonite membership. Henry's son Henry Jr. (1794-1885) founded the Landis Meetinghouse (congregation) at Palmyra, Lebanon Co., Pa.   I.D.L.

Landis, Felix, a son of the martyr Hans Landis (*q.v.*), a member of the Anabaptist congregation at Horgerberg, canton of Zürich, Switzerland, was held with his wife Adelheid Egli in the Ortenbach prison

in Zürich with inhuman treatment until death released him from his suffering about 1642. His wife languished in prison for four years before she managed to escape. But her household had been destroyed, her children given to strangers, house and furniture sold, and the proceeds of 5,000 florins confiscated. (*Mart. Mir.* D 821, E 1120; *ML* II, 612.)
NEFF.

Landis, Hans, a Swiss Brethren martyr, a preacher from Wädenswil in the canton of Zürich, Switzerland, was imprisoned in the Wellenberg in 1608; after a few months his fellow prisoners managed to release him from the chains, and all escaped. The others were soon captured, but Hans reached his native village. Another attempt was made to indoctrinate the Anabaptists to win them to the state church. On Jan. 21, 1613, the first disputation of the government with them took place at Wädenswil. It was fruitless, as was also the second one, held on Feb. 23. Thereupon Hans Landis was again put in prison with five other Brethren. In early August negotiations were begun. Landis remained "stiffnecked." He refused to emigrate, saying that the earth was the Lord's; no one had authority to send them away out of the country; they were going to stay in the country.

On Aug. 25, 1613, all six Brethren were condemned to galley service and were to be delivered to the French minister at Solothurn on the next day. Once more they were given permission to emigrate, with a week's time to decide. Three wavered and consented; the others encouraged Landis to be faithful. These three (Hans Landis, Galli Fuchs, and Stephan Zehnder) were taken to Solothurn and lodged in prison to await transport. In three days they escaped.

In December 1613 Hans Landis, having returned to minister to his flock, was again seized. In prison he wrote to his church and his friends. He asked his wife for the *Doms-büchli* (the *Confessio* of the martyr Thomas von Imbroich, *q.v.*). He was questioned on the rack. On Sept. 29, 1614, he was sentenced to death and was beheaded the next day. This was the last Anabaptist execution in Zürich.

Hans Landis had a stately figure (*Mart. Mir.* D 804-6, E 1103-51), "a long black beard mixed with gray and a manly voice." The executioner asked his pardon for what he was about to do; Landis replied that "he had already forgiven him; may God also forgive him; he knew very well that he must carry out the government's orders." When his wife and children came to the place of execution with "sorrowful crying and mourning, to bid him at the end an eternal good night," he asked that they leave him, so that "his good resolution and his good courage for the death facing him might not be moved or hindered." In the *Ausbund* (*q.v.*), No. 132, is a song of 46 stanzas commemorating his death. It begins "Ich hab ein schön neu Lied gemacht."
NEFF.

C. Bergmann, *Die Täuferbewegung im Kanton Zürich* (Leipzig, 1916) 82 ff.; S. Geiser, *Die Taufgesinnten-Gemeinden* (Karlsruhe, 1931) 372 ff.; P. Kläui, "Hans Landis of Zürich," *MQR* XXII (1948) 203-11; idem, *Geschichte der Gemeinde Horgen* (Horgen, 1952); *ML* II, 612; *Inv. Arch. Amst.* II, 2, No. 865a.

Landis Valley, a town (pop. 1,200) on the Reading Road, four miles northeast of Lancaster, Pa., was started by "Schmidt Jacob" Landis (1780-1848), a blacksmith, a son of John of Dauphin, Pa. It is in Landis Valley, named for Benjamin Landis (1730-87), a grandson of the pioneer Jacob Landis (1667-1730), who moved on to the Snavely holdings in 1750. The Landises of this area are of the latter line. "Smith Jacob" Landis Jr. (1813-61) built the first hostelry in 1855, and when the post office was established in 1872, the older name was adopted and long after the post office of the stagecoach days, it is still Landis Valley. The Reading Road Mennonite meetinghouse (MC), now also called Landis Valley (*q.v.*), is in this village.   I.D.L.

Landis Valley Mennonite Church (MC), Lancaster Co., Pa. The first Mennonites in this valley, who came about 1718, worshiped at first with their brethren at Lampeter, but by 1728 in the homes of John Jacob Snavely and John Long. The Benjamin Landis house, formerly the Snavely dwelling on the Reading Road, and Isaac Long's spacious buildings, were frequent meeting points. The latter was also the scene of the meeting in 1767 when the United Brethren Church originated. By 1814 there were four combined church-school houses at Lehn, Landis, Rudy, and Frick. Since these schools were functioning well, they opposed the 1834 Pennsylvania School Law. In fact the central meetinghouse was not built until 1847, leaving the former for school purposes. This church, called "Reading Road" for 60 years, was built of logs in the present cemetery near the Eden Road. In 1884 a brick meetinghouse, 40 x 60 ft., was built on the present site through the courtesy of Isaac S. Landis. This served the congregation until 1928, when the present 54 x 96 ft. church was built. Valentine Metzler (*q.v.*) was an early bishop. In 1832 it became a part of the Hammer Creek Bishop District, with Noah L. Landis (1857-1940), the only bishop ever chosen from the congregation. The first Sunday school, held in 1888, led to a Christian and Missionary Alliance schism in 1892. Amos S. Horst and Mahlon Zimmerman are the present bishops, Ira D. Landis and Levi M. Weaver ministers, and Norman L. Hess deacon. The 1953 membership was 256. Until the seventies, services were held every four weeks in the morning, then until three decades ago every two weeks, at first in the evenings, but for the last eleven years in the morning. The Sunday school started in the afternoon fortnightly (warmer months only), then in the morning before church, then weekly in the morning, whether "church Sunday" or not. Since the gas rationing of the early forties, both Sunday school and church services have been held weekly in the morning.   I.D.L.

Landis, Verena, a daughter of the martyr Hans Landis (*q.v.*), was placed in house arrest in her home near Zürich, Switzerland, in 1643, at an advanced age, because she was too sick to be transported to prison. The shock and the rough treatment caused her death soon after. (*Mart. Mir.* D 822, E 1121.)

Landisville, Lancaster Co., Pa., is a small village, settled first by retired farmers. Jacob Minnich in 1798 built the first house on the Harrisburg Pike, six miles northwest of Lancaster, and in 1808 a hostelry. In 1809 his brother-in-law built the second dwelling near by, which John Landis (Jr.) purchased to be used as a store. The village was named Landisville in his honor; he also became the first postmaster. The town, in East Hempfield Township, has three meetinghouses—Mennonite (MC), Reformed Mennonite, and Church of God. I.D.L.

Landisville Mennonite Church (MC). Herman Long's home mentioned in a deed of 1787 had by about 1752 been the home of the Landisville congregation. This was on the south side of the town near the camp meeting woods. By 1790 a log meetinghouse, still extant as a dwelling, was built. The third church was built of brick near by in 1855, and was replaced in 1912 by the present 54 x 96 ft. structure, also of brick. The unrest of 1834 gave the Church of God a start. The congregation almost died out. Salunga became a preaching point also 1893-1953, but Landisville is now the only meetinghouse. It was a part of the Erisman-Hernley-Kraybill District since John Lehman's bishop district was organized, and since then its bishops always served here. Henry E. Lutz is (1954) the bishop, Christian Frank and Barton Gehman ministers, and Christian E. Charles deacon. The 1954 membership was 212. The Sunday school started in 1878, but it was not "evergreen" nor continuous at first. The young people's Bible meeting is in a four-week district circuit, with 350 in attendance.   I.D.L.

Landisville (Pa.) Reformed Mennonite Church is located in Lancaster County. Its meetinghouse was erected in 1869.   J.L.K.

Landless (*Landlose*). Among the Russian Mennonites the landowners and farmers were called *Wirte* in contrast to those who had no land and who were known as the *Landlose* or *Anwohner* (*q.v.*), but who lived in the villages alongside of the *Wirte*.

The plan of settlement in the Mennonite colonies in South Russia such as the Chortitza and Molotschna colonies was village (*q.v.*) settlement, rather than scattered individual farms. The government grants of 176 acres (65 dessiatines) to each settler (Wirt) were so located as to form compact village blocks, each block having a narrow frontage on the village street. Once the immediately available space was parceled out, new families formed by marriage had no land. These had to earn their livelihood as farm hands, by renting land, by trade, industry, etc. Small remnant parcels of land at the end of the village were sold by the landowners to these landless families, about one acre for 100 rubles ($50). Such families were called Anwohner. In the village organization, the landless Anwohner had no vote, but had to pay their share of the taxes, etc., which were levied per capita on the basis of population. And so it was very likely that in many cases a large landless family had to pay more than a farmer with 176 acres.

About 1865 there were in the Molotschna 1,384 landed families and 2,356 landless families (of whom 1,063 were Anwohner); besides these about 490 families were living on farms, owned or rented, outside the villages and in towns. The land-owners therefore comprised less than one third of the population, but had all the rights, while the other two thirds had no rights. To rectify this condition a Committee for the Landless (*Landlosen-Kommission, q.v.*) was formed, consisting of both the landed and the landless. The landless worked for the right to vote, and for the division of the 43,000 acres which at that time belonged to the Molotschna but had not been parceled out, besides the 21,500 acres of unapportioned land attached to some of the villages. This would have been enough land to give 25-30 acres to each Anwohner. The landowners, on the other hand, wanted to lay out new villages with half farms of 88 acres, but this would not have helped all the families. The landless appealed to St. Petersburg, and after another investigation the government ordered that the available land should be distributed among the Anwohner, 40 acres to each family. After this was done there were in the villages owners of full farms (176 acres), half farms (88 acres), and small farms (40 acres), all having a voice in the government. Some of the "small farmers" of course had the inconvenience of owning land up to 12 miles from their homes.

But this expedient did not solve the problem permanently. It was therefore decided to establish a fund for the purchase of new land for the oncoming generations, into which an annual sum of 13 cents per acre (10 kopeks) was to be paid. In addition the large roads, "Tchumackonwege," which were originally a mile wide, were reduced; this yielded another 35,100 acres, which were, however, not apportioned to the landless, but remained the common property of the whole settlement. This land was rented out, and the proceeds put into a settlement fund from which new land could be bought again and again for the oncoming generation. In 1874, when universal military service was introduced in Russia, and as a result about 15,000 Mennonites emigrated to America, the settlement of new lands was discontinued for about ten years, since the land vacated by the emigrants was now available. The settlement fund, however, continued to grow since the 10 kopek tax was not suspended. After this interval new settlements were made more frequently than ever, financed largely by the fund.

The new settlers were granted five interest-free years of grace in making payments on their land purchases. During the next five years the purchase price was to be refunded with a little interest. Any land not paid for at the end of ten years was mortgaged. The payments flowed back into the settlement fund. In this manner some 45 daughter settlements had been formed by 1930 by the Molotschna (*q.v.*) settlement in conjunction with Chortitza (*q.v.*), Am Trakt (*q.v.*), and Alt-Samara (*q.v.*), the four original mother settlements.   A.B.

A. Klaus, *Unsere Kolonien* (Russian) (St. Petersburg, 1869); Franz Isaak, *Die Molotschnaer Mennoniten* (Halbstadt, 1908); A. Ehrt, *Das Mennonitentum in Russland von seiner Einwanderung bis zur Gegenwart.* (Langensalza, 1932); ML II, 612 f.

Landlosen-Kommission or *Kommission der Land-losen* was a commission which originated in the

Molotschna Mennonite settlement in 1863 as the result of the fact that two thirds of the Mennonite population was without land (see **Anwohner**). After 150 of these landless (*q.v.*) Mennonites had appealed to the *Fürsorge-Kommitee* (*q.v.*) to remedy this situation, Franz Isaac, Johann Fast, Johann Dörksen, and Isaak Fast were appointed to the *Landlosen-Kommission* to represent the landless Mennonites in negotiations with the government and with the Mennonite civic authorities. On March 18, 1865, this commission presented a "project or proposal" as to how the surplus land was to be distributed among the landless. Considerable opposition had to be overcome on the part of the local Mennonite authorities and the prosperous Mennonite farmers who rented this land. Through the sympathetic understanding of the Russian government, the *Fürsorge-Kommitee,* and the Agricultural Association, the cause of the landless was given a hearing and the land was finally distributed among them. Franz Isaac (*q.v.*) was an outstanding champion of this cause. At the end of his life he could say, "The mother settlement, although it cannot solve all problems which are connected with the settlement of the landless, now recognizes its obligation and is purchasing land for growing families. Although the initial steps were difficult, conditions have improved, and the result is general welfare." He credited the general welfare to the fact that provision had been made for developing a system by which the landless were provided with land (p. 86). The *Landlosen-Kommission* played a significant role in this achievement.   C.K.

Franz Isaac, *Die Molotschnaer Mennoniten* (Halbstadt, 1908) 27-86.

Landon, Camp, *Voluntary Service Unit,* near Gulfport, Miss., sponsored by the Mennonite Central Committee Voluntary Service Section, had its beginning with Civilian Public Service Camp #141. The Civilian Public Service camp was opened in February 1945, to assist in the control of environmental diseases. In 1946 with the aid of a summer unit of eight girls and a number of year-round volunteers such additional projects as community recreation, Bible school, and home welfare were undertaken. The transition in March 1947 from CPS to Voluntary Service was therefore effected without difficulty. A few months following the close of CPS the unit was requested to vacate Camp Bernard, the CPS unit site. To provide a new site the Mennonite Central Committee secured a 25-year lease on six acres of land, purchased surplus government buildings, and moved them on this acreage. The unit was renamed Camp Landon because of its location in the Landon community.

Following the transition from CPS to VS additional projects undertaken included home, school, and church building and repair, and the building of church and Sunday-school equipment. About 60 families, 15 churches, and 15 schools received volunteer help. Shop and sewing classes were conducted for white and colored children for a number of summers. A program of weekly religious instruction and recreation was launched in most of the Negro schools of the county. The total enrollment in these classes in 1954 was approximately 1,000 pupils. The summer Bible school program was expanded, the enrollment in 1954 reaching over 1,200.

In the summer of 1953 the first retreat for Negro children was held, with 30 in attendance. In the fall a community center was opened for Negroes in the North Gulfport community.

The unit was well received by the community from the beginning. It has been able to maintain good community relationships while working with both white and colored people. The contribution to improved race relations is difficult to measure but has been appreciated by the Negroes. The summer Bible schools, which now are largely conducted in co-operation with existing churches, have been highly appreciated. The work with the young people in the retreat, the schools, and the community center has promise of making a significant contribution to the young people and youth organizations in the churches.   O.K.

Landsdienaren, a name used by the Dutch Mennonites who were united in the Frisian Conference (Friesche Sociëteit) of the province of North Holland and given to the elders in charge of the conference. After the 18th century the name, sometimes also used in the Flemish groups, is no longer found.
                                                    vDZ.

Landshut, a city (pop. 36,000) on the Isar in Bavaria, Germany, 1255-1504 the principal residence of the dukes of Lower Bavaria. In 1800-26 the Bavarian state university, previously at Ingolstadt and now at Munich, was located at Landshut.

In the spring of 1528 August Würzlburger (*q.v.*), the leader of the Regensburg Anabaptist congregation, preached and baptized in the territory of Landshut. In a brief visit he won a number of converts, among them Hans Sedlmaier with his wife and their sons Paul and Willibold and daughter Katharina, also Hans Frank, a weaver of Oberhain. Hans Sedlmaier and Hans Frank were soon discovered; Sedlmaier said he would remain in his faith, while Frank begged for mercy (Winter, p. 26 ff.). On May 26 the council of Regensburg wrote to the council of Augsburg, stating that a few days previously a man had been beheaded in Landshut, whom Würzlburger had baptized (Nestler, 74). This was probably Sedlmaier. Duke Louis wrote on June 2 that all other persons baptized by Würzlburger were put to death, regardless of willingness to recant—a total of nine persons (Nestler, 77).

Somewhat later the same lot befell some Hutterian Brethren. On April 2, 1560, Klaus Felbinger (*q.v.*), a Hutterite preacher, and Hans Leitner were seized in Neumarkt in Lower Bavaria, and put into the tower at Landshut on April 7. By this time Bavaria no longer simply inflicted the death penalty in spiritual matters, but first undertook to convert the heretics. Sometimes they held formal disputations; theologians from Landshut and Munich took pains to induce Felbinger to change his faith. In the course of 15 weeks, he was dealt with ten times on questions of faith; in addition he was given 18 articles to answer in writing. Detailed records of these conversations have been preserved, which Fel-

binger, in chains and with poor illumination, wrote out. They were published by J. Loserth, as an epistle to the brotherhood in Moravia in his book, *Der Communismus der mährischen Wiedertäufer* (Vienna, 1894) 292-310, and as an epistle to Leonhard Lanzenstiel (*q.v.*) in *Ztscht für allgemeine Geschichte* I (1884) 451-54. Since both Felbinger and Leitner remained steadfast in their faith they were beheaded on July 19, 1560. This execution raised the number of Anabaptist executions in Landshut to 12.   HEGE.

H. Nestler, *Die Wiedertäuferbewegung in Regensburg* (Regensburg, 1926); V. A. Winter, *Gesch. der baierischen Wiedertäufer im 16. Jahrhundert* (Munich, 1908); *ML* II, 613 f.

Landshut (Czech, *Lanzhot*), a town (pop. 3,000) in the jurisdiction of Lundenburg in Czechoslovakia, on the Moravian-Slovak border. Hutterian Brethren began to settle here in "the good time," establishing a Bruderhof in 1565. In 1608 the thriving community suffered badly at the hands of Hungarian troops, who burned down the Bruderhofs in Landshut and Bilowitz and killed four Brethren at Bilowitz. The brotherhood fared still worse in 1619, when Dampierre invaded Moravia. On Sept. 20 the Bruderhof in Landshut was plundered and burned, the rough soldiery tortured the provision master and another brother, and raped three sisters, tearing the child from the breast of one of them. In 1622 Landshut was evacuated.   P.DE.

Beck, *Geschichts-Bücher;* Loserth, *Communismus;* Wolkan, *Geschicht-Buch;* Zieglschmid, *Chronik; ML* II, 613.

Landskrone, a village name of the Molotschna settlement, Russia, was transplanted to Barnaul, Siberia; East Reserve, Man.; and Fernheim and Friesland, Paraguay.   C.K.

Landskrone, a village of the Molotschna Mennonite settlement, Ukraine, South Russia, founded in 1839 by Mennonites coming from Prussia. In 1869 Landskrone had 36 families with standard farms and 52 with smaller places or no land, with a total of nearly 10,000 acres. In 1914 it had a population of 600. The nearest railroad station was Stulnevo on the Tokmak line. Landskrone belonged to the Gnadenfeld district of the province Taurida. The principal occupation was farming and cattle raising. The village had a few business enterprises and an elementary school. For several years after World War I there was also an intermediate school (*Fortbildungsschule*). Some of the teachers were H. T. Janz (1913-24) and Heinrich Willms.

During and after the Revolution the village gradually disintegrated. Many of the men were sent to exile. When the German Army approached in 1941 all men of 16 to 60 were sent on foot to Kharkov and from there were shipped to Siberia. Soon all women and children were sent from Stulnevo to Siberia. Only a few individuals escaped and have found their way to America to tell the story of the tragic end of Landskrone.

Landskrone built a church in 1910, a subsidiary of the united Margenau-Alexanderwohl-Landskrone

Mennonite Church (*q.v.*). In 1918 it was host to the General Conference, which convened here.

H.J., C.K.

A. A. Töws, *Mennonitische Märtyrer* II (Abbotsford, 1954) 425; *ML* II, 614.

Landsmeer, a hamlet in the Dutch province of North Holland. Anabaptists were found here at an early period. Jacob Claesz (Jacob van Wormer) and his wife Celi (Seli), executed as martyrs at Amsterdam in 1549, probably were natives of Landsmeer (*Mart. Mir.* D 61, E 464). In 1554-65 Elder Leenaert Bouwens (*q.v.*) baptized here on several occasions a total of 27 persons. From then on a congregation must have existed here, which later sided with the Frisian Mennonites. Information concerning this congregation is scarce. In 1660 a member of this church, Gerrit Pieters Boon, who had been appointed sheriff of Landsmeer, was exempted from this appointment because he had religious scruples against holding a governmental office (*Inv. Arch. Amst.* I, No. 449). The congregation of Landsmeer in 1673, during the war, contributed some 150 guilders to the general collection of the North Holland Mennonites, which the government had asked them to organize with the aim of providing the soldiers with good clothes. At least since the end of the 17th century the congregation of Landsmeer seems to have been served by the preachers of neighboring Den Ilp (*q.v.*). Gerrit Dirksz, preacher of Landsmeer, died in 1701. The *Naamlijst* of 1808 (82 f.) states that the congregation of Landsmeer no longer existed, only that of Den Ilp remaining.

The assertion of Hendrik Berends Hulshoff (*Bezoekreis,* 35) that a congregation of Huiskopers (i.e., Danzig Old Flemish, *q.v.*) existed at Landsmeer has not been proved.   vDZ.

Blaupot t. C., *Holland* I, 251; M. J. Harp, *Lyk- en Pligt-predicatie op Gerrit Dirksz, leeraar tot Landsmeer* (Amsterdam, n.d.–1701); *Inv. Arch. Amst.* I, Nos. 357, 449; *ML* II, 614.

Landtsperger, Johannes, a Carmelite monk at the monastery of St. Anna in Augsburg, Germany, whose writings were of no slight influence during the Reformation. Of his origin and early life nothing is known, and his personality is still cloaked in mystery. He was often confused with the Carthusian monk, Johann Justus Lansperger in Cologne (d. 1539), and especially with the parson of Landshut, Johann Müller alias Landtsberger of Eggenfelden in Lower Bavaria (d. *ca.* 1544). This has been thoroughly proved by Max Martin in his book, *Joh. Landtsperger, Die unter diesem Namen gehenden Schriften und ihre Verfasser* (Augsburg, 1902). According to his study, Landtsperger was closely akin to the Anabaptists in Augsburg. When severe persecution broke upon them in 1527 Landtsperger went to Switzerland. He attended the great disputation of 1528 in Bern and died there probably at the end of 1529 or the beginning of the next year.

Ottius mentions his book, *Ein wahrhafte, kurtze underwysung, wohär man zinsz und zehenden schuldig seye. Zur erhaltung des Christlichen fridens und ufrur zu vermyden* (1528). From this inclusion it was inferred that Ottius considered him an Anabaptist. But this is no doubt an error, for

Landtsperger attacks the Anabaptists in this book. V. A. Winter most definitely considered him an Anabaptist, confusing him with the city pastor of Landshut. Ludwig Keller took it for granted that he was an unusually "influential Anabaptist writer." S. Calvary, who lists eleven of Landtsperger's writings, four being given in full, says (p. 130): "We believe that he actually had Anabaptist inclinations, because in his booklet, *Ein Christliche underrichtung wie die Göttlich geschrifft vergleycht soll werden,* he confesses himself to be one." Dr. Martin has on valid grounds attributed this booklet to Hans Hut (*q.v.*); Johannes Landtsperger is the publisher. In his book, *Eine kurtze erinnerung etlicher geschrifft, daraus man die kindertauff nit zimmlich sein beweisen will* (1528), Landtsperger defends infant baptism and reveals himself to be a sharp opponent of the Anabaptists, as also in an earlier book, *Ein gründtlicher Bericht: vom christlichen Tauff und seyner Kraft und notdürfftigkait* (1526).

Although it is possible that there were connections between Landtsperger and the Anabaptists in Augsburg concerning which we are not informed, he cannot be considered one of them. At any rate he soon gave up these connections and championed Zwingli and Oecolampadius, as his books on communion show.   NEFF.

J. H. Ottius, *Annales anabaptistici* (Basel, 1672) 47; V. A. Winter, *Gesch. der Wiedertäufer im 16. Jahrhundert* (Munich, 1908) 54-56; Keller, *Reformation,* 434; *Mitteilungen aus dem Antiquariat von S. Calvary & Co. in Berlin* I (Berlin, 1869) 131-255; K. Schottenloher, *Philipp Ulhart* (Munich, 1921) 60-64; *ML* II, 614.

Lang, Jörg, an Anabaptist, one of the group of Swiss Brethren returning from Moravia who were seized at the border and put into the subterranean dungeons of the castle at Passau (*q.v.*). On Aug. 25, 1535, he was cross-examined with some others in the presence of Schröttinger, the cathedral preacher, and the pastor of St. Paul's. But he did not yield. He was probably one of those who "rotted" in these terrible holes in the earth. His wife Eva went the same road of suffering, remaining steadfast at her trial. Their son John presumably suffered the same fate, for the records say he did not give up his faith. (*ML* II, 615.)   W.W.

Lang, Laux, a citizen of Gögingen near Augsburg (*q.v.*), Bavaria, Germany, in whose home Eitelhans Langenmantel (*q.v.*) stayed after being banished from Augsburg in October 1527, and where he was visited by many well-known Anabaptists. Here occurred the baptism of the wife of his servant Hermann Anwald, who always accompanied him on his journeys, and who had also joined the brotherhood in the autumn of 1527. All three of them, together with two other Anabaptists of Gögingen, Bernhard Zirgkendorffer and Hans Pfefferlein, fell into the hands of Diepold von Stein, the captain of the Swabian League (*q.v.*) on April 24, 1528, and were put to death at Leitheim on May 11, 1528, by the executioner of Memmingen. Laux Lang, at whose house Langenmantel moved so freely, was the brother of the Archbishop of Salzburg and Cardinal Matthäus Lang (*q.v.*), who had large numbers of Anabaptists in his bishopric put to death, and also communicated with Augsburg in November 1527 in the matter of prosecuting the Anabaptists. HEGE.

Fr. Roth, "Zur Gesch. der Wiedertäufer in Oberschwaben," in *Ztscht des Hist. Vereins f. Schwaben und Neuburg,* 1900 f.; *ML* II, 615.

Lang von Wellenberg, Matthäus (1468-1540), Cardinal and Archbishop of Salzburg, the son of poor Augsburg citizens, a Humanist, Master's degree from Tübingen in 1490, privy secretary of the imperial chancellor Berthold von Henneberg, who was the secretary of Emperor Maximilian II, and who won the emperor's highest favor. As archbishop of Salzburg he was unpopular because of his dictatorial, sometimes violent nature; nevertheless the country owed its increased prosperity to his rule.

Against the Anabaptists Lang was all harsh severity. Since he, as a temporal prince in Salzburg, combined the supreme temporal authority with the spiritual, he was able to conduct his struggle with Anabaptists with all his force. As early as 1523, before the Anabaptists had appeared, he charged his inspection commissioners to pay special attention to heretical maneuvers. There is no specific evidence of the presence of Anabaptists in Salzburg; the beginning of the movement here seems to have been Hans Hut's brief preaching. Hut had come from Linz, and when he departed from Salzburg he left behind him as apostles two men whom he had baptized in Steyer, namely, Hieronymus of Mansee, a former monk from the abbey Ranshofen, and Eucharius Binder, a cabinetmaker from Koburg. In Augsburg Hut kept up his connections with the Salzburg Anabaptists, who were at both places called "Gärtnerbrüder" (gardener brothers, but the real word was "Gartbrüder," from "gartenn"—wander).

In July 1527 Lang complained about the rapid growth of the movement in his territory and ordered his officials to proceed against them with all severity. A polemic leaflet appearing in 1528, the *Newe Zeytung,* gave information about the doctrines of the Anabaptists in Salzburg and comments that they assembled in homes or solitary places, that the members gave their money and possessions to the leaders and promised never again to enter the "temples of stone"; that they would consider the sacrament nothing but bread and wine. Naturally the slander was heard, that if there were a sufficient number of them, they would establish themselves by violent means.

On Oct. 18, 1527, Lang issued the first mandate against the Salzburg Anabaptists, forbidding their meetings and their doctrine in general, and ordering the pastors to bring the erring ones back into the church by indoctrination, but at the same time also ordering the officials to scout for Anabaptists, and report on the number they seized. Especially in his Tirol domain of Kitzbühel (*q.v.*) they were causing him trouble; on Nov. 28, 1527, the Austrian government reminded the cardinal to be on the lookout there and to commission his administrator Hans Finsterwalder to conduct the persecution. As evidence of their spread the government sent him on Dec. 12 the statements made by Leonhard Schiemer (*q.v.*), who was a prisoner in Rattenberg.

A few days after the mandate was issued, five armed men managed to arrest a group of 32 Anabaptists in Salzburg, certainly including Hieronymus of Mansee and Carius Binder. Since none of them would desist, these two together with Wolfgang Winter, a tailor of Mistelbach, were burned at the stake on the Fornhof in Salzburg on Oct. 22, 1527. Then they beheaded five brethren "who had acknowledged their error" before committing their bodies to the flames. A woman and a beautiful girl of 16, the daughter of the goldsmith Georg Steiner, a friend of Hans Hut, who remained steadfast, were sentenced to death by drowning. When the executioner carried the girl to the watering trough in which her life was to end, she laughed at the water. . . . Both corpses were burned, as were also four others of persons beheaded, one of whom was the judge, one a nobleman, and one a boxmaker of Salzburg. A lacemaker and girdlemaker who would not recant were burned alive. "They lived a long time during the execution, and cried much to God, so that it was pitiful to listen to." In November Lang also sent the court records of ten Anabaptists to Augsburg, most of whom had been put to death; all but two confessed that they had been baptized by Hans Hut.

In the meantime Lang's police had the fortune of arresting a meeting of 11 women and 16 men, whose leader was a former priest. On Nov. 5, 1527, ten women and one man recanted and were expelled from the country. Six remained firm, including the preacher, the city scribe, and a girdlemaker, "a handsome fellow." These three and a locksmith were taken to his house near the park, in which they had held their meetings, and since they remained steadfast, they were burned together with the house. Two other houses which had served the same purpose were also reduced to ashes. In 1528, 41 Anabaptists lay in prison in Salzburg. The martyr list of the Hutterite chronicles lists 38 persons executed in Salzburg, two in Loser, one in Abtenau, and three in the Kucheltal, besides a few in the region now belonging to Bavaria.

In order to block the movement, Lang on Nov. 14, 1527, issued a charge to the priests at Hallein, Radstadt, Laufen, and Tittmoning, to win the erring ones back with convincing sermons, but to report obstinate ones at once. Several formularies were issued for the procedure in the cross-examinations. The questions asked were whether the accused had baptized adults, or had merely been recently baptized, whether voluntarily or through persuasion or force, what they thought of community of goods, of the government, the sacrament, of the deity of Christ, where they had held their meetings, how many persons had attended them, and who, etc.

In order to prevent any addition from without, Lang directed his magistrate in Salzburg to pay close attention to travelers to and through the city. On Jan. 24, 1528, a new police order was issued, which prohibited the employment of strangers in the trades; in the inns no conversations were permitted, especially with strangers, about Luther or the Anabaptists. To the administrator of Passau, Lang gave instructions for combating the Anabaptists. For his archdiocese he issued a severe "instruction" on April 18, 1528, defining the procedure from this time on: preachers, leaders, instigators, and propagators of Anabaptist doctrines, if they remained steadfast, were to be burned alive; if they recanted, they should be beheaded and their corpses burned. Misled ones and those who had sheltered Anabaptists should be drowned if they remained steadfast. The less guilty and the fellow travelers were to be punished with prison and whippings, particularly the servants and the young. To these punishments, which were already employed, there were added for the treasurers and the "announcers," the razing of their homes, fines, and exile. This procedure became a pattern for many a neighboring region. In 1529, for example, Scheurl recommended it to Nürnberg.

Under the pressure of this severe persecution the Anabaptist movement in Salzburg died relatively rapidly, many adherents emigrating to Tirol. Here Lang pursued them doggedly in his Kitzbühel domain; but since he confiscated the possessions of the victims into his own hands, he came in conflict with the Innsbruck chamberlains, who demanded them for King Ferdinand as the ruler of Tirol. In accord with the customary practice they wanted to grant Lang only as much of the property of the victims as was required to cover the costs of the trial and execution. Ferdinand ordered the Austrian government at Innsbruck on Nov. 27, 1530, to mediate between Lang and the councilors. The latter were annoyed because the church prince had already confiscated numerous estates without first coming to an agreement with them; the covetous cardinal insisted that since the territory was his possession and not a pledge, he was within his rights, comparing it to his practice in Salzburg. The dispute ran on for years; on Feb. 8, 1532, the council still held to its view (records in the archives of the court in Vienna, section court finance).

Nevertheless in June 1533, the king made a new appeal to the cardinal to take earnest steps against the Anabaptists in Kitzbühel, Kufstein (q.v.), and Rattenberg (q.v.). At the provincial synod held in Salzburg in May 1537, in preparation for the Council of Mantua, the pastors of Tirol complained again about the increase of the Anabaptists, whereas one hears nothing of the sort concerning Salzburg. Konrad Siebenbürger, who was charged two years later in St. Johann in the Pinzgau with Anabaptist sympathies, was declared innocent.   P.DE.

Newe Zeytung von den Wiedertauffern vnd yhrer Sect, newlich erwachsen im stifft zu Salzburg vnd an anderen enden mer etc., leaf 4, o. 10. (Salzburg, 1528, 2d ed., Dresden, 1528); Beck, *Geschichts-Bücher;* F. A. Datterer, *Des Kardinals und Erzbischofs von Salzburg, Matthäus Lang Verhalten zur Reformation* (Freising, 1890); W. Hauthaler, "Kardinal Matthäus Lang und die religiöse und soziale Bewegung seiner Zeit," in *Mitteilungen der Gesellschaft für Salzburgische Landeskunde* XXXV (Salzburg, 1895); J. Schmid, "Des Kardinals und Erzb. von S. Matth. Lang Verhalten zur Reformation," in *Jahrbuch der Gesellschaft für die Geschichte des Prot. in Oesterreich* XIX (Vienna, 1898 ff.); J. Loserth, *Anabaptismus in Tirol* (Vienna, 1892); idem, "Zur Gesch. der Wiedertäufer in Salzburg," in *Mitteilungen der Ges. für Salz. Landeskunde* III (Salzburg, 1912); H. Widmann, "Zur Beurteilung d. Salzb. Eb. M. L." *op. cit.* LV (Salzburg, 1915); Wolkan, *Geschicht-Buch;* G. Loesche, *Geschichte des Protestantismus im vormaligen und im neuen Oesterreich* (3d ed., Vienna and Leipzig, 1930); *ML* II, 615-17.

Lange, de, a common Dutch family name, of which there is also a Mennonite branch. This is found at Zaandam from the late 18th century, although in the 19th century some of its members also lived at Alkmaar. Fourteen members of this family have served as deacons in the congregation of Zaandam-West. At Alkmaar Timon Henricus de Lange was 1849-81 a deacon and Jan de Lange Corn. Jzn (1852-1940) served as deacon and president of the church board 1877-1940, i.e., for nearly 63 years, 37 of which he was president of the church board. In commemoration of the fiftieth anniversary of Jan's service his historical study *Beknopte Geschiedenis der Doopsgezinde Gemeente te Alkmaar* was published by the church board in 1927.

R. C. de Lange (b. 1891) is a Mennonite minister, serving at Woudsend 1915-19, Leermens-Loppersum 1919-23, Krommenie *ca.* 1923-27, and Aalsmeer 1927-56. He is active in behalf of West Hill Sunday schools for children, editing a number of periodicals for instruction in Sunday-school matters.   vDZ.

Lange Lillo (Langelille), a hamlet in the Dutch province of Friesland, formerly the seat of a Mennonite congregation (Frisians), which was combined with the Frisian congregation of Heerenveen (*q.v.*), but must have died out about 1740. (*Naamlijst* 1731.)   vDZ.

Lange, Friedrich Wilhelm, related to Wilhelm Lange (*q.v.*), became a member of the Gnadenfeld Mennonite Church, South Russia, in 1837 and was elected minister in 1838 and elder in 1841. Lange was an unusually successful teacher and had taught in Prussia. Heinrich Franz I (*q.v.*) was his pupil. Lange favored a warm piety and was a personal friend of Eduard Wüst (*q.v.*). Hermann Lenzmann related, "Wüst, who came to our church, was throughout his life in close brotherly contact with my father and his predecessor, Elder Fr. W. Lange, and frequently preached in their congregation just as they preached in his." Lange performed Wüst's marriage ceremony (*Menn. Jahrbuch* 1904-5, 78). He was a great promoter of evangelism, missions, abstinence, and music. Because of personal difficulties, he resigned in 1849 and accepted a position as teacher and assistant minister in the Swedish Lutheran Church at Schlangendorf on the Dnepr River, Ukraine. (Friesen, *Brüderschaft,* 83 f.; *ML* II, 617.)
        C.K.

Lange, Johannes, a relative of Wilhelm Lange (*q.v.*), was sent by the Gnadenfeld Bruderschule (secondary school) of the Molotschna Mennonite settlement, Ukraine, Russia, to the Kirschenhardthof school of Württemberg, Germany, to take a teacher training course. The brilliant young man not only received a very good training but also came under the influence of Christoph Hoffman and Christoph Paulus, the leaders of the Templer (*q.v.*) movement of the Friends of Jerusalem. After his return in 1861, he became a teacher in the Gnadenfeld Bruderschule. He was joined by his brother Friedrich who had received his training in the same school. Since the Langes not only exposed the children but also the adults in private meetings to the teachings of the

Templer group, the matter was investigated by the authorities. When Johannes Lange began to advocate the cause of the landless (q.v.) his case became more complicated. For seven months he was kept in custody as the Halbstadt Gebietsamt after his arrest on Jan. 25, 1863. This was during the time that the Gnadenfeld Evangelische Mennonitengemeinde was founded (Friends of Jerusalem). In 1866 Johannes and Friedrich Lange went to St. Petersburg to defend the cause of their newly founded church. As a result in 1868 the group was permitted to settle on the estate of Orbelyani in the vicinity of Pyatigorsk in the Kuban River in the Caucasus where the Mennonite Brethren had settled. They established there the settlement Tempelhof (q.v.). Next to Nikolai Schmidt (q.v.), Johann Schmidt, and Isaak Fast (q.v.), Johannes Lange and his brothers Friedrich and Benjamin played a significant role in the founding of the Templer Church and in laying its religious and educational foundations. Their educational standards remained high.　　　　　　C.K.

Heinrich Sawatzky, *Templer Mennonitischer Herkunft* (Winnipeg, 1955); Franz Isaac, *Die Molotschnaer Mennoniten* (Halbstadt, 1908); H. Görz, *Die Molotschnaer Ansiedlung* (Steinbach, 1951).

Lange, Wilhelm, outstanding elder of the Mennonite Church at Brenkenhoffswalde (q.v.) and Gnadenfeld (q.v.), was a Lutheran from the Wartebruch near Landsberg, and came to Brenkenhoffswalde in 1790 (1788). Soon he was received into the Mennonite Church, and was elected minister in 1802 and elder in 1810 (1812). He was a very popular and successful minister, through whose efforts many non-Mennonites joined the congregation, including such names as Lenzmann, Klatt, and Johann Lange. Through him the congregation was in close touch with the Moravians of the community, who influenced the Mennonites very strongly.

Lange was a leader of the emigration from the Neumark to Russia in 1834. He obtained special permission from Czar Nicholas I for 40 families to settle at the Molotschna, South Russia, where they established the Gnadenfeld (q.v.) settlement and congregation. Here he died in 1840 at the age of 76. Wilhelm Lange's correspondence, dating back to the time of the immigration to Russia, presents a picture of the religious and cultural life of that day. (Found in BeCL.)　　　　　　C.K.

B. H. Unruh, "Die Mennoniten in der Neumark," *Gem.-Kal.*, 1941; Friesen, *Brüderschaft*, 80 f.; ML II, 617.

Langedijk, De, a North Holland region north of Alkmaar, where there have been Anabaptists since at least 1535 (*Inv. Arch. Amst.* I, No. 101), has been the seat of a Mennonite congregation, until about 1800 called Langedijk and Koedijk, now called Broek op Langendijk (q.v.).　　　　　　vDZ.

Langedult, Pieter, b. 1640 at Haarlem, Holland, d. there 1677, was a physician and preacher of the Flemish Mennonite congregation of Haarlem. Langedult, who was a champion of Collegiant (q.v.) principles, wrote the following books: *De Apostolice Outheyt van de Vryheyt van Spreken in de Vergaderingen der Christenen, tegens Ds A. van Dalens Alleen-spreken verdedigt* (Haarlem, 1672)

(Anton van Dale, q.v., his co-preacher of the Haarlem Flemish congregation, had published a book against the Collegiant practice of "free speaking" in the congregation), and *De nietigheyd der Chiliastery* (Haarlem, 1676), in which Langedult attacked the chiliastic ideas of the Collegiant leader Daniel de Breen (q.v.). He further published a Dutch translation of J. L. Wolzogen, *De werelose Christen* (Haarlem, 1676), a tragedy entitled *Christus lydende en verheerlykt, het allerheylsaamste Treurspel* (3 vv., Haarlem, 1684; 3d ed. Amsterdam, 1714), *Christelyke Sedekonst ofte beoefeninge der Godsaligheyd* (Leiden, 1684), and *Aanteekeningen ofte Verklaaringen over de Klaagliederen van Jeremias* (Amsterdam, 1687). The last three books were published by his friend after his early death. Laurens Klinkhammer (q.v.) edited his *Sedekonst*.　　　　　　vDZ.

Biogr. Wb. V, 537-39; N.N.B.Wb. V, 309; C. B. Hylkema, *Reformateurs* (Haarlem, 1900-2) I, 142; II, 105, 155; J. C. van Slee, *De Rijnsburger Collegianten* (Haarlem, 1896) *passim*, see Index; ML II, 670.

Langegger (Langecker), **Hans** (*Hans von der Reve*), a weaver on the Ritten, an Anabaptist martyr of Tirol, Austria (now Italy). All that is known of him is that he accompanied Georg Blaurock (q.v.) on his wanderings in the Tirolean Alps, when he came into the Eisack Valley to take over the orphan congregation of Michael Kürschner (q.v.), who had been put to death at Innsbruck on June 2, 1529. Langegger assisted Blaurock, one of the founders of the Zürich brotherhood, with his knowledge of the rugged Tirolean terrain. It may have been due to his skill that Blaurock, who had a large following everywhere, was able to elude the authorities for nearly four months. On Aug. 14, 1529, both were discovered and arrested; and since they persisted in their faith they were burned at the stake at Klausen (q.v.) in the Eisack Valley. HEGE.

J. Loserth, *Der Anabaptismus in Tirol* (Vienna, 1892) 486; *Mart. Mir.* D 22, E 430-32; ML II, 617.

Langenbach, Velten, from Nieuwstadt near Sittard, now Dutch province of Limburg, author of the song written in the middle of the 16th century, "Von Herzen muss ich singen," which gives his name in acrostic. Nothing else is known of him. (Wolkan, *Lieder,* 100, 104; ML II, 617.)

Langendijk, Pieter, a Dutch poet, whose parents, Arent Pieters van Langedijk and Anneke Luykes Nieuwenhuysen, were Mennonites. He was born July 25, 1683, at Haarlem, died there July 9, 1756. He lost his father early. His mother opened a linen shop, but was unable to give her six-year-old son a proper education. Pieter learned some Latin and French in a school at Amsterdam conducted by a Quaker, but had to leave because of poverty. In The Hague he was employed as a designer in a weaving mill, and in 1722 he moved to Haarlem. On his deathbed he was baptized as a member of the Mennonite church. He acquired fame through his comedies. Besides these Langendijk published *Levensloop der Aartsvaders,* an illustrated rhymed version of the lives of the Patriarchs (Haarlem, 1740), some poems, *Op de Afbeeldingen van Doopsgezinde Leeraars,* and a remarkable poem, published in 1713 at Haarlem, entitled *Zwitsersche Eenvoudigheid, klaagende over de bedroven zeden veeler Hollandse Doopsgezinden of Weerloze Christenen* (Swiss plainness, lamenting the depraved morals of many Dutch Mennonites or defenseless Christians), in which he severely criticizes the worldliness of the Dutch Mennonites, interpreting the ideas of the Swiss Mennonites, who had emigrated to the Netherlands in 1711. With Claas Bruin he wrote *Tafereelen der eerste Christenen*. Kalff says Langendijk's opposition to ambitious clergymen as shown in his works is due to his Mennonite principles. F.H.K.

N.N.B.Wb. II, 764-68; Blaupot t. C., *Holland* II, 162; *Zondagsbode* XLVI (July 23, 1933);*DB* 1897, 168, note 1; G. Kalff, *Geschiedenis der Nederlandsche Letterkunde* V (Groningen, 1910) 469-77; Irvin and Ava Horst, "Simplicity Laments Corrupted Manners," *Menn. Life* X (July 1955) 129; *ML* II, 617, 679.

Langenfeld, a village in Bavaria (Middle Franconia), Germany, located near Scheinfeld, between Würzburg and Nürnberg, where the Anabaptist movement found followers in the 16th century just as in the adjacent villages of the Steigerwald (Iphofen, Sulzfeld near Kitzingen, and Diespeck near Neustadt a.A.). Jörg von Passau (also called Nespitzer), who was sent out as an evangelist by the Anabaptist synod (see **Martyr Synod**) at Augsburg (Aug. 20, 1527), worked here as a preacher 1527-30. According to Jörg, he was not executed in Bamberg (*ML* I, 115), but recanted in Ansbach in the face of an expected death sentence. HEGE.

K. Schornbaum, *TA* II: *Brandenburg*, 112, 197; J. E. Jörg, *Deutschland in der Revolutionsperiode 1526-1528* (Freiburg, 1851); *ML* II, 617.

Langenlonsheim, Philip of, an Anabaptist martyr, who was beheaded in 1529 in Kreuznach, a town not far from the village of Langenlonsheim. (*Mart. Mir.* D 30, E 438; *ML* II, 617.)

Langenmantel, Eitelhans (Hans), a member of the Anabaptist congregation of Augsburg (*q.v.*), Bavaria, Germany, descended from the patrician Langenmantel family of Augsburg, called "vom Sparren" because of the chevron in their coat of arms. He was a son of Hans Langenmantel, who had held the office of mayor in Augsburg 14 times, had been captain of the Swabian League for many years, and died in 1505. One of his brothers was the gallant George Langenmantel, who fell in the battle of Pavia as the leader of the Black Knights in the service of France. Eitelhans ruined his health and squandered his money traveling through France and Italy.

Like his relative, councilor Christoph Langenmantel, Eitelhans favored the Reformation, but became an Anabaptist when he became acquainted with the nature of the movement. He associated with Ludwig Haetzer (*q.v.*); Hans Hut (*q.v.*) baptized him in the presence of Jakob Dachser (*q.v.*) and Eucharius (see **Binder, Eucharius**) of Koburg in March 1527 in the Langenmantel home, which became a place of meeting for the Augsburg Anabaptists. Langenmantel, as a "learned and well-read man," promoted their interests in word and deed. The council warned him to "keep clear of the Ana-

baptists," and ordered the expulsion of nonresistant Anabaptists.

On the basis of information given by the Anabaptists seized on Sept. 15, 1527, Eitelhans was arrested, but because of the influence of the family in the city he was treated much more leniently than the others; the preacher of the city held a disputation with him which resulted in his withdrawal from the Anabaptists and his recognition of infant baptism as "the Christian church teaches it." He was released from prison on Oct. 15 and banished from the city. He went first to Göggingen, but when the Anabaptists thronged about him, he went on to Langenneufnach and finally bought a house in Leutershofen.

On April 24, 1528, as Sender relates, he was seized at night by Diebold von Stein, captain of the Swabian League (*q.v.*), with his maid and a half-grown servant, and taken in chains to Weissenhorn. After several days Langenmantel and his servant boy were beheaded, and the maid was drowned. The captain "did all this without law, for . . . no sentence had been pronounced on them; the captain said the League had commanded it. For having previously been an Anabaptist he had been banished from Augsburg, and so he was tried twice for one offense, which is contrary to all law and reason."

But he seems after all to have remained an Anabaptist, for while his relatives offered 3,000 gilders for his release, the pastors of Weissenhorn, Oberhausen, and Wellenhausen tried to direct him on the right path. The pastor Johannes Schneid stood by him as he was executed by the executioner of Memmingen on May 11, 1528. On account of severe gout he was beheaded seated in his armchair.

Eitelhans Langenmantel is the author of the following tracts: (1) *Ain kurtzer begriff von den Alten und Newen Papisten auch von den rechten und wahren Christen* (1526, Weller, No. 3832); (2) *Dies ist ain anzayg: ainem meynem, etwann vertrauten gesellen über seine hartte widerpart, des Sacrament und anders betreffend* (Nürnberg, 1526; Weller, No. 3831); (3) *Ain kurtzer Anzayg, wie doctor M. Luther ain zayt hör hatt etliche schrifften lassen ausgeen vom Sacrament, die doch straks wider einander* (January 1527); (4) Ott and Veesenmeyer credit him with *Ein göttlich und gründlich offenbarung von dem warhaftigen Widertauffern mit gottlicher warheit anzaigt* (1527), but Schottenloher (*Philipp Ulhart*) has shown that Jakob Dachser was the author. This is replied to in the book by Urban Rhegius, *Notwendige Warnung wider den newen Tauforden an alle Christglaubigen durch die diener des Evangelii zu Augsburg* (1527).

Among the manuscripts of the Anabaptists of Moravia and Hungary are two treatises by Eitelhans Langenmantel (Cod. VIII g. 27, Cod. VIII g. 25 at Budapest and Cod. Lyc. at Bratislava of 1618) which present the Swiss view of communion. They are (5) *Von Nachtmahl des Herren durch den getreuen Zeugen Gottes Hannss Langenmantel,* and (6) *Ein ander prüff: vom Sakrament auch durch Hanns Langenmantel gemacht.*

Langenmantel has also been considered the author of a hymn found in the *Ausbund* (*q.v.*), reprinted by Wackernagel. It has 16 stanzas and begins "Kom

Gott Vatter vom Himmel mit der Kraft deines Geists"; but it is actually the work of Peter Riedemann, was written in 1529 at Gmünden, and was dedicated to the memory of Langenmantel by the publishers of the *Ausbund*. It is found in Codex VIIIc at Budapest with Riedemann's name.

A further writing ascribed by John Horsch to Langenmantel, *Eine Auslegung des Vater Unser,* is found in a booklet published by Horsch at Elkhart, Ind., in 1888, in combination with Hans Denk's *Von der wahren Liebe.* Horsch says the *Vater Unser* was written in 1527 and is found in manuscript form in the Hutterite *Epistel-Buch* of 1566 (Horsch, 21). Ludwig Keller states further that this *Vater Unser* had already been published in a booklet in 1527 together with a sermon presumably by Hans Denk, but gives no indication of the author of the *Vater Unser.* The codex which Horsch used is a copy done in 1888 by Elias Walter, now in the Pibrock Bruderhof in Alberta. It contains the Langenmantel tract, expressly ascribed to him, under the title *Eine hüpsche Erklärung des Vater Unser.*   LOSERTH.

K. Schottenloher, *Philipp Ulhart, ein Augsburger Winkeldrucker und Helfershelfer der "Schwärmer" und "Wiedertäufer"* (Munich, 1921); *Gasparii Annales* in *Menken S. S. Rerum Germ.* I; Clemens Sender, *O. S. B. Hist. Relatio;* G. Veesenmeyer, "Nachricht von Eitelhanns Langenmantel, einem Augsburgischen Wiedertäufer," in *Beiträge zur Gesch. der Literatur* (Ulm, 1782); *Die Weissenhorner Historie* in Fr. L. Baumann, *Quellen zur Geschichte des Bauernkrieges in Oberschwaben* (Tübingen, 1876) 1-240; G. Uhlhorn, *Urbanus Rhegius im Abendmahlsstreite* (1861); L. Keller, *Johann von Staupitz und die Anfänge der Reformation* (Leipzig, 1888) 325; Fr. Dobel, *Memmingen im Reformationszeitalter nach handschriftlichen und gleichzeitigen Quellen* (Memmingen, 1874); Fr. Roth, *Augsburgs Reformationsgeschichte 1517-1527* (Munich, 1881); Beck, *Geschichts-Bücher,* 35 f.; *Mart. Mir.* D 20 f., E 429 f.; *MQR,* Jan. 1948, pp. 40-42; *ML* II, 618.

Langezwaag, a village in the Dutch province of Friesland, where there was formerly a Mennonite congregation of the Flemish branch. Probably a congregation existed here already in the 16th century. About 1620, at a meeting of Flemish leaders held at Langezwaag, a quarrel arose between the elders Jan Luies (*q.v.*) of Groningen and Jacques Outerman (*q.v.*) of Haarlem. Soon after this the congregation of Langezwaag joined the Groningen Old Flemish group. In 1648 Meinte Sjoerds and Cornelis Jeltes were preachers here. Though figures are not available, the membership must have been very small. Meetings were held in a private home "In de Wyngaart." It seems that about 1645 the congregation of Langezwaag was united with that of Knijpe (*q.v.*). After 1655 there is no further information. The congregation must have died out before 1710, because it is not found in a list of the Groningen Old Flemish congregations drawn up in this year. (*DB* 1879, 3, 90; *N.N.B.Wb.* III, 797.)   vDZ.

Langham (Sask.) Evangelical Mennonite Brethren Church was established in 1912. The church, rebuilt after it was totally destroyed by fire in 1929, seats 250. Its 1955 membership was 110. Jacob Hiebert has been the pastor of the church since 1954. M.G.

Langnau, a beautiful village in the Emmental (Emme Valley), the main village of the Signau district, the largest village (pop. 8,726) in the canton of Bern, Switzerland. It has a number of industries. It was once the center of pottery and linen weaving in the Emmental; in the 18th century it became the center of the "Emmentaler" cheese industry. The village is mentioned for the first time in A.D. 850.

On March 13, 1525, the preacher at Langnau was threatened by Bern, because his preaching "is producing discord, revolt, and disobedience" to the government. By a decision of the council of Feb. 28, 1527, two men of Langnau were put in "neck irons" for destroying an image. On Oct. 25, 1526, Bern demanded that "the priests at Langnau and elsewhere, who do not wish to hold Mass, must continue to hold Mass." Three days later Langnau replied, citing the mandates of Bern which ordered that the Word of God be taught on the basis of the Holy Scriptures of the Old and New Testaments (*Aktensammlung*).

Thus the people of Langnau, even before the Reformation was introduced there, showed independence in religious thinking and religious life, as well as a desire for freedom. These traits are also responsible for the persistence of Anabaptism in the Emmental. Langnau was always an Anabaptist center and today has the oldest Mennonite congregation in the world. The local clergy often had to cope with the Swiss Brethren, as the baptismal registers of Langnau report. The *Chorgerichtsmanuale* of Langnau omitted the Anabaptist persecutions and showed that the populace was not hostile to the Swiss Brethren. On May 6, 1934, the citizens of Signau elected an Emmental Mennonite to the Great Council of the canton of Bern. The Mennonite meetinghouse is located at Kehr, on the outskirts of Langnau.

In Langnau Ernst Müller, the author of the authoritative history of the Mennonites of Bern, was the pastor of the state church from 1884 to 1927. Langnau is the meeting place of the Swiss Mennonite conference every fall. Here also the *Zionspilger* (*q.v.*) is published. (See **Bern** and **Emmental.**)   A.-T.

Müller, *Berner Täufer;* S. Geiser, *Die Taufgesinnten-Gemeinden* (Karlsruhe, 1931); Hs. Käser, "Ausserkirchliche christliche Versammlungen im Unteremmental in früherer Zeit," *Brosamen,* 1926, Nos. 1-9; *idem,* "Chorgericht und Landvogt in Behandlung der Täufergeschäfte," in *Blätter für bernische Gesch. und Altertumskunde* (1928, No. 2); D. L. Gratz, *Bernese Anabaptists* (Scottdale, 1953); *ML* II, 619.

Language Problem. Problems caused by language have repeatedly arisen among the Mennonites because of their migrations from one language-and-culture area to another, often because of persecution, but at times also of desire for economic betterment. The maintenance of the language of the motherland has aided in maintaining separation from the surrounding culture in the new homeland and thus strengthened the sense of nonconformity to the world. This has often made it easier to maintain the distinctive Mennonite principles and intensify the feeling of group solidarity. On the other hand, the language breach has usually prevented a program of active evangelism and outreach, and has imposed a necessary system of private or parochial schools. As long as the breach with the surrounding culture and language was complete and continuous, problems of adjustment, either of the group with the outside world, or of individuals to individuals within the group, seldom arose. However, when the breach has been only partial, or when individuals or a subgroup within the larger group become wholly or partially assimilated to the "outside" language, serious problems of internal adjustment have arisen. At times this has been a problem of adjustment between the generations, so that youth has come into conflict with age, and usually large numbers of the youth have been lost to the group and its faith and way of life. At other times factionalism has arisen, resulting in serious schisms. Conservative groups attempting to hold the language line have died out because of failure to adjust to the new environment. Successful maintenance of small language enclaves detached from any larger language culture body has resulted in cultural and intellectual impoverishment, frequently with attendant religious losses. The battle to maintain the language has usually been fought with religious sanctions which have at times gone to the extreme of claims of higher spiritual values for the mother tongue as compared with the new tongue and of forfeiture of group principles and even faith in God in case of surrender of the language. Usually the transition from one language to another has required two or more generations of confusion and turmoil with considerable loss of membership en route, as well as the diversion of much energy from constructive work. The effect in literary production and consumption by the group is also usually very detrimental.

The following cases of serious problems caused by language transition may be noted: (1) Dutch to German for the Anabaptist-Mennonite refugees from Holland settling in northwest Germany (Emden, Crefeld, Hamburg, Lübeck) and the area of East and West Prussia (Danzig, Elbing, Königsberg, Graudenz). The transition was completed everywhere but Emden by the end of the 19th century. (2) German to English for the Mennonite immigrants to Pennsylvania from Switzerland and the Palatinate, Germany, in the 18th century (including daughter settlements in Ontario, Virginia, western Pennsylvania, and Ohio). A similar problem faced the immigrants from Switzerland, Alsace, and South Germany to the area west of the Allegheny Mountains as far as Illinois. Both of these immigrant groups made the transition largely in the second half of the 19th century. The stress and strain of the transition, complicated with other factors of course, played a large role in the schisms among the Amish (Old Order Amish) 1850-80 and the Mennonites (Old Order or Wisler Mennonites 1870-1900). (3) The transition from German to English among the immigrants from Russia to the prairie states and provinces (1874-88). In the United States this transition occurred in the first quarter of the 20th century. In Canada it is still in progress, where it is delayed and intensified by the arrival of very large further contingents of immigrants from Russia in 1922-25, 1930-32, and 1947-50, and is now in its most intense phase.

Other cases of language problems are: (1) the Swiss Mennonite German-speaking enclaves in the French-speaking Jura area of the canton of Bern, Switzerland, which though small in quantity is just as serious as in other cases of larger extent. (2) The German-speaking Mennonite communities in inner France, and the less serious but similar situation in Alsace. (3) The German-speaking Mennonite communities established in Paraguay and Uruguay in Spanish language areas, and in Brazil in a Portuguese language area.

The case of the German-speaking Mennonite settlements in Russia is unique. Until after 1920 they, with other German immigrant groups, had been permitted linguistic and cultural as well as religious autonomy, and with the aid of large block settlements, foreign language schools, and cultural superiority, they successfully maintained the German language and avoided cultural deterioration. The attempt of the Czarist government in 1870-80 to russify these groups contributed heavily to the great emigration to North America at that time. The final destruction of the block settlements and the autonomous Mennonite educational and cultural institutions (1929-39) thrust Russian Mennonitism into a crisis. The present generation of Mennonites in Russia now faces the language problem in an acute form. The coming generation will perforce become Russian in language. This need not, however, be fatal to Mennonitism in Russia, any more than the transition to English has been in the United States.

A particular case of the language problem is that of the Old Colony Mennonites in Manitoba, who thought they had a governmental guarantee dating from the time of their settlement in 1874-77, of school and language autonomy. Losing this in the strenuous period of World War I, large blocks emigrated to Mexico and Paraguay, where they were promised school and language autonomy, and where they have recreated through block settlement and German schools the desired state of language maintenance. In both areas, however, the Old Colony groups suffer from considerable cultural deterioration.

The language problem has been further complicated for the Mennonites by the maintenance of dialects or sublanguages, e.g., the Plattdeutsch among the Russian Mennonite immigrants in North and South America and the Pennsylvania-Dutch among the Old Order Amish. In such groups where the dialect has displaced the High German, at least relatively, the people have lost almost all touch with the literary German language except Bible reading, and therefore have largely stopped reading serious literature of either religious or secular character, with resulting cultural and religious impoverishment.

Sometimes the theory of the cultural value of using two languages has been propounded to support retention of the "mother tongue." Actually it is probable that only highly intelligent persons who diligently pursue both languages on a literary level profit from this dualism. More common outcomes are the failure to master either language adequately, confusion of vocabulary and ideas, undesirable carryover of idioms from one language to the other

(Germanisms in English and Anglicisms in German), and undesirable foreign accents which handicap individuals in their speaking and other expression as they move in public life.

The language problem has often become acute in the pulpit. Without diligent effort few preachers acquire the ability to preach well in a second language after middle age is reached, and they may be unwilling to pay the necessary price to do so. Consequently congregations have suffered in pulpit leadership because of preachers able to use only the older language. With the older generation of members unable or unwilling to accept a new language in the pulpit, they have denied their children and youth the privilege of religious teaching and worship in the new language, the only one which the latter fully comprehend.

Language problems are characteristic of all immigrant religious groups who find themselves in a new and strange language-culture situation. But these problems have been intensified among Mennonites by their distinctive emphasis upon nonconformity and nonresistance.   H.S.B.

Langweer, a village in the Dutch province of Friesland, seat of a Mennonite circle (*Kring*) since 1950, whose members (28 in 1955) belong to the Joure (*q.v.*) congregation. During the winter services are held once a month by the pastor of Joure.   vDZ.

Lansbergen (Lansberghe), **Franciscus van** (d. 1626), a native of Gent, a Reformed preacher successively at Kortrijk, Brugge, and Gent, fled to Leiden, and studied medicine there. In 1593 he was called to Rotterdam to preach for the Reformed Church; he joined the Remonstrants and gave up his position in 1619. Before coming to Rotterdam he had attacked the Waterlander idea, as presented by Hans de Ries and Jacob Jans Scheedemaker, that the institutions given by God in the Old Testament have no validity for the New. In 1596 he attended a sermon by Jan Jansz; then he wrote an attack on silent prayer in church in his books, *Van de vremde en onschriftmatighe manieren der Wederdoopscher Leeraren heymelijcke ghebeden,* and *Een grondelijcke wederlegginghe van Jacob Jansz* (Rotterdam, 1596).   vDZ.

A Mennonite van Lansberge(n) family, found at Haarlem, Holland, in the 17th and 18th centuries, was apparently not related to this Franciscus van Lansbergen.

Biogr. Wb. V, 555 f.; *N.N.B.Wb.* II, 772 ff.; *DB* 1864, 34; 1897, 78-82, 88 f., 97-105; *ML* II, 619.

Lanoy, de, a Mennonite family, probably originally from Flanders, Belgium, or Northern France, which moved to Leiden in the Netherlands. Branches of this family were later found in Amsterdam, Holland, and Hamburg, Germany. In Hamburg Jan de Lanoy (b. *ca.* 1654 at Leiden, d. March 10, 1722, at Hamburg), a cloth-dealer, served the Hamburg-Altona Mennonite congregation as a preacher from 1681 until his death. He is said to have been in sympathy with the Lamist teachings of Galenus Abrahamsz (*q.v.*), while his three fellow preachers were more conservative. This caused some discord in the congregation shortly after 1690, which ended only with

Lanoy's death. He was a wealthy man; in 1717 he contributed 1250 Marks to the building of the new meetinghouse at Altona, while his son Jan de Lanoy, Jr., contributed 600 Marks. His daughter Ida was married to Ernst Govers, a Mennonite merchant, owner of whalers, and also a deacon.

At Amsterdam the de Lanoys were also merchants and often deacons of the (Lamist) Mennonite Church. Some of them sympathized with the Collegiants (*q.v.*) and were governors of the Oranjeappel (*q.v.*) Collegiant orphanage. Karel de Lanoy (b. 1827 at Amsterdam, d. 1918 at Haarlem) was a Mennonite pastor at Oldeboorn Nieuwe Huis 1852-56 and Haarlem 1856-90. For many years he was a trustee of the A.D.S. (Dutch General Mennonite Conference) and a curator of the Amsterdam Mennonite Seminary.   vDZ.

B. C. Roosen, *Geschichte der Menn.-Gemeinde zu Hamburg-Altona* I (Hamburg, 1886); II (1887) *passim;* church records of Leiden and Amsterdam.

Lansdale Mennonite Church (MC), in Lansdale, Pa., was established as a mission in 1935. It was under the direction of the Franconia Mennonite Board of Missions and Charities until 1951, when it became a church. In 1954 it had a membership of 60, with Jacob Rittenhouse as pastor.   M.G.

Lanzenstiel (*Lantzenstiel;* often called *Seiler,* i.e., ropemaker), **Leonhard** (d. 1565), a native of Bavaria, Germany. Little is known of his early life and conversion. In 1529 he was with the Anabaptist congregation at Kromau with Hans Amon (*q.v.*), and from there he went to Austerlitz in Moravia, where he was called to the ministry.

At the end of 1536, he and his companion Jörg Fasser (*q.v.*) left Austerlitz, arriving at Windorf in Lower Austria on April 27, where they found several sisters and "some other kindhearted people"; but in the inn there was a "very indecent Sodomitic group." They looked around for another inn and found it with the tollkeeper of the village. The gang from the inn followed them. "As far as we were concerned," they wrote to Hans Amon, "it was easy and slight. But when we heard them blaspheme the name of God, our hearts were greatly stirred to point out their sin and evil. Indeed, God has not without reason permitted this wicked, sinful people to be destroyed by the Turks; He will within a short time reveal Himself in a different way in grim anger."

The two were arrested and put into the local prison. On the next day they were taken to Mödling and questioned on the rack before the judge and the council. "We gave testimony to the truth in such a way that they were all terrified and didn't say a single word against it."

They were imprisoned "with many ungodly, shameful people," whose company was abhorrent to them. From May 8 to June 1 they wrote Hans Amon at least six letters, to which he replied with rich comfort. The first letter says a dear brother from Vienna was with them. In the second letter they say, "The town in which we are imprisoned belongs with the government of Vienna to the terrible Babylon, and the judge is now at the Landtag, so we think he will bring us a message which will not terrify us, for we desire with our whole hearts to be dissolved." The judge and the council had visited them and told them that all would end well. "As our dear brethren have complained that they lay in a prison into which all kinds of wickedness was thrown, so it also goes with us. But we have great joy in departing from this world and joining the multitude that rests and worships." Lanzenstiel warned the brethren in Moravia that they should be cautious, for some of their names were known to the government. With a fourth letter he sent Amon "Jakob's washcloth," apparently a possession of Hutter, concerning whose death Amon had told them. The fifth letter the prisoners thought would probably be the last; the judge and the council were urging them to desist and threatening exile and terrible torture.

In the next letter they say, "If we hadn't said that the men from Vienna were our brethren (viz., Jeronymus Käls and his companions), they would gladly have released us." But now they had to act in accord with the king's commands. An important man had been with them and had told them that if they wished to be freed they must desist from several articles; soon the priests from Vienna would be sent to them. Eight days previously (May 25) the wife of a wealthy merchant had visited them and told them of Hutter's death.

The news of the capture of two such valiant brethren caused sorrow in the brotherhood, since within a short period they had been deprived of their most capable men. Amon comforted the prisoners, "Fight to the end. For you are waiting in Paradise our beloved Jakob (Hutter) and Jeronymus (Käls) with a mighty host of the elect. Testify to the truth and warn men of the coming judgment."

In another letter Amon admonished the prisoners to remain true. "Think of dear Jakob. Did he not remain true in all torture, and was God not with him? Likewise Jeronymus, Michel, and Hänsel. Think of Peter Riedemann and Hans von Lichtenfels. Are they not faithful witnesses? I might name hundreds who are an example to us for honesty, piety, and faith."

After nearly a year in prison, facing death with the courage of "young lions," they were somehow released without violating their conscience. Particulars are not known. Scarcely released, Fasser assembled a congregation at Peckstal in Austria, was seized here in 1537 and executed. His followers escaped to Moravia.

Lanzenstiel had a great future before him. He went to Trässenhofen on the Moravian border in Lower Austria and then apparently on to Tirol. His wife Apollonia was seized in 1539 on the road toward Brixen and drowned.

In that year Lanzenstiel was chosen preacher and went to the Adige and from there to Switzerland. Although his journey had been betrayed to the authorities, spies had been posted, and notices had been issued against him, he managed to evade their pursuit.

Three years later (1542), after the death of Hans Amon, Lanzenstiel was entrusted with the leadership of the entire brotherhood. The chronicles say

that he was a "pious, honorable man and faithfully looked after the church of God." His leadership began under the most favorable auspices. He had a very competent assistant in Peter Riedemann, "who helped him carry the burden of the church."

Year after year groups continued to come to Moravia from all sides. There was economic progress. Some of the later additions were weavers and developed a flourishing craft in Moravia. They seem to have imported from Hungary the wool they needed, for the Moravian estates, to protect the domestic market, issued an order in 1544 prohibiting the purchase of wool anywhere other than in the royal cities or the baronial estates. The Hutterites were all the more willing to obey, for the barons showed increasing interest in protecting them and in 1545 and 1546 granted them new households in Rackschitz, Kromau, Eibenschitz, Gobschitz, Bisentz, Bapayedl, Pawlowitz, Altenmarkt, Göding, Schaikowitz, Paraditz, Pochtisch, Bupschitz, Wesseli, Gurdau, Puslawitz, and Frätz.

This increase of Anabaptism brought great concern to the government and new tests and persecutions to the Anabaptists. In the spring of 1545 an order was issued in Prague that the Hutterites be expelled, and the estates complied to the extent that they required them to give up their communal life. Since the Landtag of this year also threatened them with expulsion, they presented a solemn protest to the barons. They give an account of their doctrines and institutions and defend themselves on all the charges raised against them. Only to serve God had they come to Moravia; for at other places they had not been able to do so. Since evil accusations were being raised against them by thoughtless people, they felt it necessary to explain that there must be governments, for they were instituted by God.

The following years of Lanzenstiel's direction are recorded in the chronicles as the time of the great persecution in Moravia, Austria, and Hungary. Repeatedly Ferdinand I requested the estates to expel them, threatening severe penalties. In addition the Bohemian revolt of 1547 and its suppression by Ferdinand gave him the opportunity he was looking for to increase the Catholic power in political as well as in religious affairs, and to carry out his intention to re-establish the religious status of 1526.

This was the beginning "of sorrow and tribulation, the time of the cross, and severe persecution" from one country to another. Fortunately the Hutterites found support in the Moravian barons, who insisted upon their right to improve their constitution according to their own custom, judgment, and conscience. The principle of imperialism did not succeed in Moravia as in Bohemia; and so better days came for the Hutterites. In 1550 and 1553 they set up three new households. And so the period of Lanzenstiel's direction also marked the beginning of the "good time of the brotherhood," which continued until his death, giving way then to a still better one, the "golden time."

Among the leaders of the brotherhood Lanzenstiel was not outstanding for his talents. The chronicles, however, say of him that he gave his brethren many wholesome teachings, comforting epistles, and explanations of the Holy Scriptures. To his credit is also the fact that he permitted a man to work beside him who far surpassed him in intellectual gifts, Peter Riedemann. His special field seems to have been economic organization. The *Väterlied* credits him with many beneficent regulations. Unfortunately, most of these have been lost, for the oldest regulations that have been preserved stem from the time of Klaus Braidl. Only the regulation for shoemakers dates back to Lanzenstiel (1561).

At any rate, under Lanzenstiel's careful guidance the brotherhood prospered; old Bruderhofs were provided for, new ones established, and missionary work carried on with vigor. New members were added and groups which had split off joined the brotherhood again. Their songs also commemorate the growth of the brotherhood under Lanzenstiel's guidance.

After a life rich in difficulty and endeavor Lanzenstiel died on March 3, 1565, at Klein-Nembschitz in Moravia. Of his writings there have come down to us the six letters which he wrote with Jörg Fasser in prison in Mödling, and his "Schusterordnung." The "Rechenschaft," which was written by Peter Riedemann, may also be in part a result of his influence.

LOSERTH.

Beck, *Geschichts-Bücher*, 216 f.; Zieglschmid, *Chronik*, 164 *et passim*; Loserth, *Communismus*; ML II, 619-21.

Lapine Civilian Public Service Camp No. 60 was located about 18 miles west of Lapine, Ore. It was opened in December 1942. A Bureau of Reclamation camp, its chief project was the building of an irrigation dam on the upper Deschutes River. Because of its excellent buildings capable of housing 600 men and the immensity of the project Selective Service changed it into a government-operated camp. The MCC ended its operation of CPS No. 60 on Dec. 31, 1943, the day before it became government camp No. 128.   M.G.

M. Gingerich, *Service for Peace* (Akron, Pa., 1949).

Lapp (Lappe, Lape, Lap), a Mennonite family name. The first settler by this name to come to America was Johannes (L) Lap, who arrived in Philadelphia on Sept. 29, 1733, on the *Pink Mary,* which sailed from Rotterdam via Plymouth. He settled in Bucks Co., Pa., and became the progenitor of the Lapp family in the Mennonite Church (MC). One of his descendants was Deacon Samuel W. Lapp of the Line Lexington, Pa., congregation, who moved to Nebraska in 1879 and is better known as the father of four sons who became bishops, and two of them foreign missionaries in the Mennonite Church. They are Daniel G. (1867-1952), who spent the greater part of his life at Roseland, Neb. He was a widely traveled and an outstanding bishop in the western part of the church in the United States and served on a number of church-wide committees and boards; Samuel G. (1869-1916), who served the South English, Iowa, congregation; Mahlon C. (1871-1923), who was a pioneer missionary to India 1901-23; and George J. (1879-1951), who served five terms as a missionary to India and was also a widely known and much-used speaker in the churches in America. Other descendants of this first settler include two deacons of the Line Lexington congregation, Abra-

ham (1777-1855) and Henry B. (1853-1931); and John E. Lapp (1905-), bishop in the Plain congregation, Lansdale, Pa. John Lapp (1798-1878) was bishop at Clarence, N.Y.

The progenitor of the large Lapp family in the Old Order Amish Church is thought to have been Michael Lapp (b. April 6, 1737), who likely arrived in Philadelphia on Sept. 22, 1752. This family greatly outnumbers in size the family in the Mennonite Church. The *Family Almanac* (Scottdale, Pa., 1954) lists 17 ordained men by this name among the Amish, whereas the Mennonite Church lists but one.

J.E.L.

Perkiomen Region (Pennsburg, Pa.) X, No. 2 (April 1932); *Ancestry of Abram Clemmer*; C. L. Lapp, *Genealogy of the Descendants of Isaac and Barbara Lapp* (n.p., 1941).

Lapp, Daniel G., b. April 29, 1867, at Line Lexington, Pa., d. Dec. 15, 1951, at Sterling, Ill., a son of Samuel W. and Sarah Gross Lapp, a prominent bishop and general church leader in the Mennonite Church (MC), who spent 48 years as pastor of the Roseland, Neb., congregation of the Iowa-Nebraska Conference district. He was ordained preacher in 1903 and bishop in 1915. He was an active evangelist for 7 years, vice-president of the Mennonite Board of Missions and Charities for 16 years, vice-president of the Mennonite Board of Education for 10 years, and long a member of the Board. His last six years he spent as pastor of the West Sterling, Ill., congregation. He was married to Ida M. Good on Feb. 22, 1898. He had seven children, one of whom is Mrs. Wilbur J. Hostetler, a former missionary to India.   H.S.B.

Lapp, George Jay, b. May 26, 1879, at Juniata, Neb., one of the eight children of Samuel W. and Sarah Gross Lapp, d. Jan. 25, 1951, at Goshen, Ind., was an outstanding foreign missionary of the Mennonite Church (MC), having served nearly 40 years (1905-45) in the Central Provinces of India. He was ordained to the ministry in 1905, and as bishop in India in 1928. He served as interim president of Goshen College February 1918-June 1919. He attended Elkhart Institute one year in 1901, then Northwestern University two years 1901-3. His degrees were: B.A., Goshen College (1913); M.R.E., Bethany Biblical Seminary (1930); B.D., Goshen College Biblical Seminary (1947). He was married twice: (1) Esther Ebersole, June 25, 1905; (2) Fanny Hershey, April 14, 1920. Mrs. J. Lawrence Burkholder (Harriet) and Mrs. Ezra Camp (Lois) are daughters. In India he was the founder and director of the Mennonite Bible School from 1910 to its merger with the Dhamtari Christian Academy in 1931. He was a member of the National Christian Council of India and under its direction made a study of rural life, which was published as *The Christian Church and Rural India* (Calcutta, 1938). He wrote and published in Hindi *Menno Simons and the Mennonite Church* (Jubbulpore, 1929) and *Fundamental Doctrines of the Bible* (Jubbulpore, 1933).   H.S.B.

Lapp, Mahlon Cassius (1872-1923), a Mennonite (MC) missionary and bishop, was born in Line Lexington, Bucks Co., Pa., on Feb. 4, 1872, the son of Deacon Samuel Whistler and Sarah Gross Lapp, the eighth generation of the Lapp immigration from Europe. "Tradition has it that John Lapp, who landed in Philadelphia Sept. 29, 1733, was raised Amish, fell in love with and married a Mennonite girl, and they became the progenitors of Bucks County branch of the Lapp family" (*Mennonite Cyclopedic Dictionary*, p. 204). Mahlon was the fourth of five children in the Lapp family. The oldest child was the only girl. In February 1878, at the age of six years, he moved with his parents to Roseland, Neb., where he grew to manhood. As a boy he attended grade school at Roseland and later helped his father and brothers on the farm. For several years he worked as a constructionist in a bridge gang. After his conversion at the age of 21 he assisted Jacob Burkhard in conducting an extension Sunday school at Antioch, about 30 miles distant from their home, traveling the distance each week by horse and buggy.

In 1899 Mahlon went to Chicago to serve as a missionary in the Mennonite Home Mission located at that time on West 18th Street. His city mission service continued until 1901, during which time he took a short business course at the Elkhart Institute, Elkhart, Ind. On June 10, 1901, at the Home Mission he was united in marriage to Sarah Hahn of Clarence Center, N.Y. In the same month the Mennonite Evangelizing and Benevolent Board (now the Mennonite Board of Missions and Charities) appointed Mahlon and Sarah Lapp missionaries to India. Before they sailed Mahlon was ordained to the ministry and to the office of bishop by Bishop Albrecht Schiffler in the Mennonite church at Roseland. They arrived in India in October 1901. He resided in that country until his death in 1923. He had no children.

During his missionary service in the American Mennonite Mission at Dhamtari, Central Provinces (now Madhya Pradesh), India, Mahlon served as cobishop of the Mennonite Church with Bishop J. A. Ressler until the latter left India in 1908. Then he was the only bishop until the ordination of Peter A. Friesen on April 2, 1916. He continued his bishop responsibilities until his death. He also served for a short time as treasurer of the Mission and later as assistant superintendent until Ressler left in 1908, when he became superintendent and served in that capacity until about 1920. During his terms as superintendent he also served as agent of the Mennonite Board of Missions and Charities. He was the first moderator of the India Mennonite Conference when it was organized in 1912 and was frequently elected to that office afterwards.

The missionary life of Mahlon Lapp "was busy and strenuous from the beginning. A many-sided, able man placed in a land of many and urgent needs, he was constantly sought out for help and advice by Europeans and Indians of all classes. He was farmer, doctor, builder, and minister. He became all things to all men that he might by all means save some. He loved the people and was loved by them" (annual report of the American Mennonite Mission, 1923). Although he was not a trained physician, one of his major contributions to India was along medical lines. Hundreds of people traveled many miles on foot and by cart to be treated at his clinic.

Mahlon Lapp's death occurred in Calcutta, India, on May 30, 1923. He was interred in the Sunderganj Mennonite cemetery at Dhamtari. (*Gospel Herald,* July 26, 1923; *Christian Monitor,* June 1932.) J.N.K.

L.A.R.A. (Licensed Agencies for Relief in Asia) was established in March 1946 by the American Council of Voluntary Agencies for Foreign Service, Inc., New York, N.Y., as special commission for conducting relief activities in Japan, Korea, and Okinawa. It is a federation of 13 U.S. relief agencies and was licensed by the U.S. government to ship relief supplies in bulk to Asia for distribution to the needy. It was the sole U.S. agency through which welfare shipments in bulk received exemptions and priorities provided by military government. The contract between L.A.R.A. and the Japanese government was not signed until March 23, 1950, and was to "be effective from April 1, 1950, until the activities of L.A.R.A. in Japan are fully terminated." Supplies began to arrive in Japan in November 1946.

The distribution of relief supplies was done through Japanese welfare agencies on the basis of need without respect to birth, religion, or political affiliation and at no cost to the recipient. Most of the supplies were distributed to individuals in institutions recommended by the prefectual departments of welfare. Three Americans served L.A.R.A. in Japan as liaison to the supreme commander for the Allied Powers. They also served as a central coordinating committee for the distribution of contributed supplies.

During the five and one-half years of L.A.R.A. operation in Japan a total of 33,477,122 pounds of food, clothing, soap, and medicine was channeled through the organization. In addition 2,036 goats and 45 milk cows were also among the L.A.R.A. gifts.

The Mennonite Central Committee became a member of L.A.R.A. in March 1947. J.N.B.

L.A.R.A.—A Friend in Need, published by the Ministry of Welfare of Tokyo, 1953 (a report on the activities in Japan); *Thanks to L.A.R.A.,* published by the Social Bureau-Ministry of Welfare-Japanese Government (a pictorial report on the distribution of L.A.R.A. supplies); Minutes and Reports of L.A.R.A. meetings at the American Council of Voluntary Agencies for Foreign Service, Inc., New York, N.Y.

Laren-Blaricum, Dutch province of North Holland. Mennonites living here on Sept. 21, 1950, organized a Mennonite circle, which in 1956 numbered 70 baptized members. The pastor of the neighboring congregation of Hilversum, to which the members of the circle belong, is in charge of this group. vDZ.

Lark, The, a yearbook, first published as part of the *Hesston Academy Journal* in 1915. Occurring as the last issue of each school year, it was variously known as the "Commencement Issue" and the "Senior Number." In 1924, when it became a separate publication, the yearbook was named *The Lark*.
W.E.O.

Larslan Mennonite Brethren Church, located in Valley Co., Mont., a member of the Central District Conference, began as a subsidiary of the Lustre,

Mont., congregation in 1917, when a number of families from Lustre located here. J. F. Thiessen was, therefore, their pastor until 1943. In 1945 the Larslan church was organized with 29 members. Other ministers who served the congregation were A. A. Dick, J. J. Toews, H. C. Quiring, and Karl Dick. In 1929 a basement was constructed and used as a church, and remodeled in 1945. Kathryn Lentzner, a missionary in Colombia, S.A., came from this church. In 1954 the membership was 38, with Walter Schlichting as pastor.   A.A.D.

Las, Virgile de, translated some Dutch Mennonite writings into the French language: Théodore Philippe (i.e., Dirk Philips, *q.v.*), *Enchiridion ou Manuel de la Religion Chrétienne* (n.p., 1626). This work also contains a translation of Menno Simons' *Van de nieue creature* and some letters and confessions by the martyrs Jaques d'Auchy, Thys Joriaensz, Hans Alewijnsz, and Jacob de Rore. Las was a native of Lyon, France, and probably a Protestant clergyman. (*DJ* 1840, 64 f.)   vDZ.

Lasco (Laski), **John á** (1499-1560), an important Reformation leader, was born at Lask, Poland (hence the name), studied in Rome 1514-17 and in Basel in 1524, where he was a pupil of Erasmus and bought the latter's library. In 1527 he became priest at Gnesen. In 1538 he went to Holland, where he joined the Reformation. In 1542, at the request of Countess Anna, ruler of East Friesland, he went to Emden and assumed the leadership of the church in that territory, using the Calvinist pattern. In 1548 he was compelled to give up his post because of the Interim and went to London, where he became the pastor of the Walloon congregation there. In 1553 he and his congregation were forced to flee to escape the persecution of "Bloody Mary," the new Catholic queen. He came to Warnemünde, but forced by Lutheran pressure from here as well as Rostock, Lübeck, and Hamburg, finally went to Frankfurt. In 1556 he returned to Poland, where he was active in the leadership of the Evangelical Reformation until his death in 1560.

Lasco's relationship to the Anabaptist movement and particularly to Menno Simons deserves attention, especially during his stay in Emden 1542-48. Until 1544 the Anabaptists had been tolerated by Countess Anna, but now as a result of imperial pressure, they were to be expelled. Lasco reports (in a letter of July 26, 1544, to Hardenberg, *Opera* II, 574) that the church was to be cleansed, not on God's account, but on the emperor's, and so harshly, the innocent along with the guilty, that he felt compelled to request the Countess not to expel all foreigners but only those who could be proved to be heretics after an examination by Lasco and his assistants. He probably hoped, like Calvin in Strasbourg, to win the Anabaptists to his side. Menno Simons and David Joris gladly accepted the invitation to a disputation, hoping thereby to win toleration, but with no thought of joining Lasco's church.

The disputation between Menno and Lasco, which took place at Emden Jan. 28-31, 1544, in the former Franciscan monastery, dealt with the following five points: (1) the incarnation of Christ, (2) infant baptism, (3) original sin, (4) sanctification, (5) the calling of preachers. Menno reports (Menno's *Opera*, 519) that he was treated in a friendly manner and was allowed to leave the city in peace, even though no agreement was reached on points (1), (2), and (5).

In accord with a promise which he had made, Menno delivered to Lasco three months later a written statement of faith covering points (1) and (5) and promised to send him later a treatise on point (2), which latter apparently never was done. The confession of faith bears the title: *Een korte ende klare belydinge ende schriftelycke aenwysinge, Ten eersten: Van der Menschwerdinge onses lieven Heeren Jesu Christi; Ten tweeden: Hoe dat beyde de Leeraers ende Gemeynte Christi, nae Schrifts vermeldinge sullen ende moeten geaert zijn; Geschreven aen de Edele ende Hooghgelarde Heeren, H. Johan a Lasco, met t'samen sijne Mede-hulperen binnen Emden, Anno 1544. Door Menno Symons. Joan. 8, 31; I. Cor. 3, 11. (Opera,* 517-42.) The confession was printed by Lasco and used as evidence against Menno and not for him, as Menno had expected. Menno denied Lasco's charge that he had first distributed the confession among his followers, saying that he had shown it only to a certain W. H. G., a burgomaster (Menno's *Opera,* 356a and 356b).

Lasco was disappointed in his hope of winning over the Anabaptists. With all his tolerance, he certainly did not intend to permit an Anabaptist church to exist beside his own. This is evident from an edict of the Countess Anna of 1545 (*Kirchen- und Polizeiordnung*) which Lasco certainly helped to draft. According to this edict, the "Davidian and Batenburger sects" were not to be examined by the superintendent (Lasco) but to be "executed by the neck" if they did not leave the country. The "Mennists," however, were to be examined first and then expelled from the country if they did not accept instruction from the Scriptures (Müller, 24 f.).

Soon after delivering the confession to Lasco, Menno left East Friesland, for Lasco says in the above-mentioned letter to Hardenberg, "I know that at present Menno is living mostly in the bishopric of Cologne and has led many astray there." Lasco did not let Menno rest, however, even in foreign parts. Although Menno had accepted invitations to disputations at Bonn and Wesel, Lasco and Hardenberg prevented him from attending, by means of charges which, though not mentioning Menno specifically, deeply offended him. The Wesel authorities wrote Menno that they would let the executioner debate with him (Menno's *Opera,* 515b, 235a). During Menno's residence in the Rhineland Lasco twice visited his friend Hardenberg as well as Hermann von Wied, the Archbishop of Cologne, who was friendly to the Reformation. It is possible that on these occasions he used his influence against Menno.

Lasco's polemical booklet against Menno's confession of faith was published at Bonn in 1545 under the title: *Defensio verae semperque in ecclesia receptae doctrinae de Christi Domini incarnatione, adversus Mennonem Simonis* (a Lasco, *Opera,* 1-60).

It was not until 1553, after Menno had been reminded of Lasco as a result of the latter's arrival there on his flight from London, that he replied to Lasco's *Defensio*. Lasco with his several shiploads of refugees (his London congregation) was stuck in the ice in Wismar harbor. The Anabaptists of Wismar, under Menno's leadership, rendered brotherly assistance to the Lasco refugees. Menno's reply of 1554 bears the title: *Een klare onwederspreekelyke Bekentenisse en Aenwysinge, . . . dat de geheele Christus Jesus, Godt en Mensche, Mensche en Godt, Gods eengeboren en Eerstgeboren eygen Sone is, niet gedeylt noch gestuckt, maer een eenig ongedeylt Persoon, Soon ende Christus, Godts Woord in der tijd vleesch geworden. Met een grondelijke Confutation . . . van Johanne a Lasco . . . Door Menno Symons (Opera,* 350-82). The unpleasant personal attacks which so often appear in the polemics of this time are absent in this booklet, since Menno's chief concern was to present once more before his death, which he expected soon, his doctrine of the incarnation (*q.v.*). C.K.

Johannis a Lasco, Opera tam edita, quam inedita rec., ed. A. Kuyper (Amsterdam, 1866); Menno Simons, Opera Omnia (Amsterdam, 1681); H. Dalton, Johannes a Lasco (Gotha, 1881); K. Hein, Die Sakramentslehre des Johannes a Lasko (Berlin, 1904); C. Krahn, Menno Simons (Karlsruhe, 1936); J. P. Müller, Die Mennoniten in Ostfriesland (Amsterdam, 1887); ML II, 621 f.

Latehar, Palamau District, Bihar Province, India, is the Latehar subdivision headquarters, and a station of the Bihar (*q.v.*) Mennonite Mission (MC). It is in the southwestern part of the field. It was first occupied in March 1947 by S. J. and Ida Hostetler, but was not finally acquired until Feb. 16, 1949. It had previously been occupied by the British Disciples of Christ Church who offered it to the Mennonites. The western part of the Bihar field extends over 5 of the 20 thanas of Palamau District, and the eastern part over 9 of the 32 thanas of Hazaribagh District. Kodarma (*q.v.*) was the headquarters of the work in the latter area.

In the Palamau field there are three stations: Latehar, Chandwa, 17 miles to the east, and Bathet, 20 miles north of Chandwa. In this Palamau area live over 30,000 Oraons and 3,000 Mundas. Several hundred thousand of these two tribes in the adjoining Ranchi District are Christians, and those in the Palamau area are also receptive to the Gospel. Since the opening of work Latehar has been occupied principally by the Henry D. Beckers, S. J. Hostetlers, and S. Allen Shirks; Chandwa by the John E. Beachys and the M. C. Vogts; and Bathet by the Paul Knisses. In 1955 there were 110 church members reported in the field. (*We Enter Bihar*, Elkhart, 1951.) S.J.Ho.

Latscha (Latschar, Lachat, Lörsch, Lörtscher, Latschaw, Leutscher, Lötscher), a Mennonite family name, originally Lötscher (*q.v.*), from Latterbach near Erlenbach in the Simmental, canton of Bern, Switzerland. The first member of this family known to have been an Anabaptist was Hans Lötscher, who was born at Latterbach in 1601. He wrote a hymn of 41 stanzas entitled "Ein schön new geistlich Lied." In 1633 he married Anna Kammerer from Latterbach. The three oldest of their five children,

Hans, Melchior, and Anna, were brought before the *Täuferkommission* (*q.v.*) in Bern because of their Anabaptist beliefs. They remained true to their faith and were imprisoned. The brothers Hans and Melchior escaped in 1667 but were soon returned to prison. After four years in prison at Bern they were sentenced to galley service with four other Anabaptists in 1671-73. They returned to claim their inheritance from their father, who had died while they were away, but were refused it. In 1667, while imprisoned at Bern, Hans Lötscher wrote a letter which is preserved in the *Martyrs' Mirror* (E 1129-30), in which he lists some 40 persons who met death at Bern because of their Anabaptist faith. Abraham Lötscher, youngest brother of Hans and Melchior, emigrated to Holland in 1711, where the name soon became Leutscher (*q.v.*) A number of his descendants have been Mennonite leaders in that country.

The family name takes the form Latscha and Latschar in the Palatinate and America. About 1714 Hans Heinrich Lötscher emigrated from the Simmental to Alsace, and later to the Palatinate, Germany, where he settled on Kühbörncheshof near Katzweiler. His children settled in various Palatinate Mennonite communities. One son, Johannes Franz, emigrated to Pennsylvania. The chief homes of the family in America are Berks Co., Pa., and Waterloo Co., Ont. The Latschar Mennonite Church is located near Mannheim, Ont. Among the outstanding personalities bearing the name were: Jacob Latscha (1849-1912), a merchant in Frankfurt a. M., where he built a chain of 134 stores, and was active in YMCA work; and John B. Latschaw (1804-87) who served the Franconia Conference (MC) as minister for 44 years, including 15 as bishop. In 1940 there were still 37 members of the family in three Mennonite congregations in South Germany —Kaiserslautern, Sembach, and Ludwigshafen. D.L.G.

Adolf Fluri, "Die Lötscher von Latterbach," in Beiträge zur Geschichte der bernischen Täufer (Bern, 1912); J. Latscha, Der Mann und sein Werk (Frankfurt, 1932); ML II, 625, 694 f.

Lauber Hill Mennonite Church: see **Archbold**, Ohio, Reformed Mennonite Church.

Lauingen, a city on the Danube in Bavaria, Germany, where two Anabaptists were put to death for their faith, one before 1531 by beheading, the other before 1581. (Beck, *Geschichts-Bücher,* 279, 310; ML II, 625.)

Laurelville Mennonite Camp (MC) is a 52-acre mountain tract on the western slope of the western range of the Allegheny Mountains, 42 miles east of Pittsburgh, 10 miles northeast of Scottdale, Pa. The 17 buildings include a tabernacle, dining room, large lounge, and cottages and dormitory facilities for about 250 guests. Recreational facilities include a large concrete swimming pool. The activities during July and August include eight to ten church camps and conferences of one week each designed for various ages from juniors to adults. The camp is owned by the Mennonite (MC) Campground Association, composed of 29 members from Ohio,

Pennsylvania, Maryland, and Virginia, and incorporated under a charter in the state of Pennsylvania in 1944. The original site and part of the present facilities were purchased from the Methodists, which had earlier operated it as a camp. Additional improvements and facilities represent a total investment of approximately $80,000.   A.J.M.

Lauren, Bartel: see **Louwer, Bartel.**

Laurens: see also **Laureys, Lauwereyns,** and **Lourens.**

Laurens (Lauwerens) Allaerts (Loys Alaert), an Anabaptist martyr, burned at the stake at Gent, Belgium, on July 16, 1562, with Pieter van Maldeghem, Jacques Bostijn, and Pieter van Maele. Laurens was a citizen of Gent, a maker of bags (*taschmaker*), and 30 years of age. His wife Kathelijne van Lokerhoute had suffered martyrdom at Gent on March 24, 1562. The names of Laurens and his three fellow martyrs are found in the song, "Als men schreef duyst vijfhondert jaer ende twee en tsestich mede," found in the supplement to the *Lietboecxken van den Offer des Heeren* (No. 1).   vDZ.

Offer, 649; *Mart. Mir.* D 289, E 656; Verheyden, *Gent,* 28, No. 86; *ML* I, 29.

Laurens van Gelder (Lauwereyns Cruwele or Cruele), an Anabaptist martyr, burned at the stake (*Mart. Mir.* says beheaded) on May 22, 1557, at Antwerp, Belgium, with Jeronymus, Pieter de Meulenaer, Jacob van Yper, and Martin de Wael. Their names are found in the song, "Aenhoort Godt, hemelsche Vader" (Hear, O God, heavenly Father), No. 16 of the *Lietboecxken van den Offer des Heeren.* Laurens was a native of Kortrijk (Courtrai) in Flanders. His trade is not mentioned. K.V., vDZ.

Offer, 564; *Mart. Mir.* D 185, E 569; *Antw. Arch.-Blad* VIII, 434, 438; XIV, 22 f., No. 244; Wolkan, *Lieder,* 63, 72; *ML* II, 47.

Laurens, Hendrik: see **Hendriks, Laurens.**

Laurens (Lauwerens) van der Leyen (Verleyen), an Anabaptist martyr, beheaded on Nov. 9 (or 4?), 1559 at Steen Castle at Antwerp, together with Mattheus de Pottebakker and Andries Langedul. Their names are found in the song, "Aenhoort Godt, hemelsche Vader," No. 16 of the *Lietboecxken van den Offer des Heeren,* where Laurens is called Lauken. He was a native of Gent and probably belonged to the van der Leyen (*q.v.*) family, of which a number of members suffered martyrdom. Van Braght included in the *Martyrs' Mirror* four letters by Laurens van der Leyen, which he wrote in prison on May 25, July 10, undated, and Oct. 25. The first letter is addressed to the congregation at Emden, Germany, where two of his brothers lived; the second to the congregation of Antwerp, to which apparently also the third is written; the fourth to a brother of this congregation. These letters contain a number of important facts. Laurens was arrested on May 21, 1559. He was tried several times, but apparently not tortured. The inquisitors who interrogated him were a man named Claes, then the "Dean of Ronse," i.e., Inquisitor Titelmann (*q.v.*), and the margrave of Antwerp. Laurens defended his faith with a

strong conviction and much ability. "When I used to gamble and get drunk, and to follow the world," Laurens said, "I was left unmolested; but now that I truly confess the name of God, I am persecuted." He had also been arrested some time before, because he had sung *geestelycke Liedekens* (spiritual hymns); why he then was released is not stated. The inquisitor threatened him several times with cruel death and said to him: "You certainly know . . . that I caused your sister (i.e., Tanneken van der Leyen, *q.v.*) to be thrown into the Scheldt River." But neither threats nor supplications could make Laurens renounce his faith, which he strongly confessed. He had not yet received his baptism on faith. "I was," he said, "not yet good enough." The *Martyrs' Mirror* also contains his confession of faith, delivered on July 4, 1559. In this confession he defends the doctrine of Incarnation as taught by Menno Simons. A number of members of the congregation of Antwerp were in prison with Laurens, the names of whom he gives in the third and fourth letters, and many of whom faithfully suffered martyrdom after Laurens had been put to death. They could observe how Laurens was executed and died as a true follower of his Lord.   vDZ.

Offer, 567; *Mart. Mir.* D 262-70, E 633-40; *Antw. Arch.-Blad* IX, 5, 10; XIV, 26 f., No. 304; Wolkan, *Lieder,* 63, 72; *BRN* VII, 158, 170; *ML* II, 648.

Laurens Pietersz (Lauwereins Peters), an Anabaptist martyr, was burned at the stake on March 30, 1568, on the Veerle square at Gent, Belgium, with Jan van Parys, Pieter Aelbrechts (Pierken van Cleve), and Hendrik Maelschap. They were executed in a barbarous manner. They had not yet been baptized on their faith. Their names are found in a hymn, "Als men schreef duyst vijfhondert jaer ende twee en tsestich mede," No. 1 of the supplement to the *Lietboecxken van den Offer des Heeren.* Laurens was (according to the records) a native of de Kempen, a region northwest of Antwerp.   vDZ.

Offer, 652; *Mart. Mir.* D 367, E 723; Verheyden, *Gent,* 43, No. 139; *ML* III, 372.

Laurens de Schrijnwerker, an otherwise unknown Anabaptist leader, apparently from the Dutch province of Zeeland, was active in Middelburg, Zeeland, where he baptized in 1535. (Mellink, *Wederdopers,* 321.)   vDZ.

Laurens Tiettyezoon, an Anabaptist martyr, beheaded on Dec. 7, 1549, at Leeuwarden, capital of the Dutch province of Friesland, together with Tiyttye Douwes, because he had been rebaptized and "had a false opinion of our holy Christian faith." vDZ.

J. Reitsma, *Honderd jaren uit de Geschiedenis der Hervorming* (Leeuwarden, 1876) 63; *Inv. Arch. Amst.* I, No. 746.

Laurens Verkamer (Loureys van den Camere), an Anabaptist martyr, burned at the stake on April 26, 1569, at 's Hertogenbosch, Dutch province of North Brabant. Verkamer, who was a citizen of Antwerp and well-to-do, had joined the local Mennonite congregation, but fled with many other Mennonites because of persecution. He intended to go to Nijmegen in the Dutch province of Gelderland, but en route was arrested at 's Hertogenbosch on Jan. 5, 1569, and loyally suffered martyrdom.   vᴅZ.

Mart. Mir. D 386, E 740; *Bibliographie* II, No. 806; *Antw. Arch.-Blad* XII, 421, 424, 472, 478; XIV, 70 f., No. 789.

Laurens van de Walle (Lauwers van der Walle), an Anabaptist martyr, being a weaver by trade, was arrested at Ieper (Ypres) (*q.v.*) in Flanders and burned there at the stake in 1561 (exact date unknown) with Maeyken Kocx, Calleken Strings, and Anthonis Schoonvelt. They are celebrated in a hymn beginning, "Geroert ben ick van binnen" (Inwardly I am moved), found in the *Lietboecxken van den Offer des Heeren,* No. 24. This hymn, slightly modified, is also found in *Een Nieu Liedenboeck* of 1562, and is given in Wackernagel, *Lieder.* From this song, which was the principal source of the later Dutch martyrbooks, including van Braght's *Martyrs' Mirror,* it is known that this group, driven from their homes by persecution, had shortly before arrived in the neighborhood of Ieper, where they lived as artisans, apparently as weavers. They were surprised by the officials and all arrested but a few who escaped. In the hymn the name of Laurens van der Walle is not found. The song also names Kaerl (van Yperen), who apparently is identical with Laurens van de Walle. There are other martyrs named van de Walle (*q.v.*), to whom Laurens van de Walle may have been related.   vᴅZ.

Offer, 603-7; *Mart. Mir.* D 285, E 652; *Bibliographie* II, No. 832; Wackernagel, *Lieder,* 141.

Laurensz, Hendrik (d. before 1770), a son of preacher Laurenz Hendriks (*q.v.*), was *ca.* 1714-59 a minister of the Mennonite congregation at Nijmegen, Dutch province of Gelderland. In 1715 he was ordained as an elder by Jan Kroes (Crous) of Crefeld. He proved to be a good shepherd in the time the Nijmegen congregation had to endure many hardships. Together with his colleague Pieter Hendriks (Eger) he was the last untrained and unsalaried minister of Nijmegen. (*DB* 1875, 78 f.; *Inv. Arch. Amst.* II, No. 2154.)   vᴅZ.

Laurensz, Jan, a Mennonite from Rotterdam, Holland, a follower of Spener, who often visited in Pietistic circles at Frankfurt, Germany, together with Jacob van de Velde and Abraham Hazevoet, who were also Mennonites. Jan Laurensz in May 1683 bought a tract of land from William Penn with the intention of emigrating to Pennsylvania (*DB* 1884, 72). Laurensz and the other Mennonites are, however, not found among the early Mennonite immigrants to North America.   vᴅZ.

Laurentie Jans, wife of Wouter Heyne, an Anabaptist martyr, born at Gapinge, Dutch province of Zeeland, was burned at the stake on Aug. 24, 1538, at Brugge, Belgium. Further particulars are not known except that she had been (re)baptized in 1536. (Verheyden, *Brugge,* 33, No. 9.)   vᴅZ.

Laurents (Lauwerens) **Andriesz** (Andriessen), an Anabaptist martyr, burned at the stake at Antwerp, Belgium, on Sept. 12 or 13, 1570, with Joost Verkindert. Van Braght in the *Martyrs' Mirror* gives a

letter Laurents wrote on Sept. 9, 1570, to Joost's wife, which contains an admirable testimonial to their faith: "It is still the purpose of us both to adhere to the eternal truth by the great help of the Lord, without whom we can do nothing, and to whom we must also constantly look for help and comfort." The Biblical references from the New Testament are excellently assembled and arranged. The letter closes with these words: "Hence, my dear Sister, be content and do not grieve immoderately . . . . We must part here once. Thus, hasten, that we may all meet together when men shall not be able to part us any more. May the good and almighty Lord full of grace and truth make us fit thereto." Laurents was unmarried.   NEFF.

Mart. Mir. D 509, 527, E 848, 863; *Antw. Arch.-Blad* XIII, 11, 62; XIV, 76 f., No. 867; *ML* I, 71.

Laurents de Schoenmaker, an Anabaptist martyr: see **Schuster, Lorenz.**

Laus deo, salus populo (Glory to God, Salvation to the People) was the motto of a society that made a new and improved translation of the Psalms into Dutch verse in 1759 (here and there retaining the translation by Peter Dathenus), which was used in many Dutch Mennonite churches, first in the Zonist congregation at Amsterdam in 1762, in 1768 in the Lamist congregation. In a few congregations (Ameland, Beverwijk, Dantumawoude, Franeker, Koog-Zaandijk, Wormer-Jisp) it was in use until the early 20th century. There have been following editions of the *Laus Deo* version: 1760 without notes, 1761 with notes, 1765, 1883, and 1896 all at Amsterdam. (*DB* 1865, 72 f., 81-83; 1900, 99.)

The society (*genootschap*) Laus Deo Salus Populo was composed of eight Dutch poets, most of whom were Mennonites: Lucretia Wilhelmina van Merken and her husband Nicolaas Simon van Winter, Lucas Pater, Pieter Meyer, Bernardus de Bosch, Anthony Hartsen, Henry Jean Roullaud, and Hermanus Asschenberg. Thirty-nine Psalms were rhymed by van Merken, twenty-five by van Winter, nineteen by Pater, nineteen by Roullaud, sixteen by Hartsen, fifteen by Asschenberg, eleven by de Bosch, and six by Meyer.   vᴅZ.

W. J. B. Serfontein, *Die Psalm as Kerklied* (Nijkerk, 1956) 67 f.; *ML* II, 625.

Lausoms-Gemeente, the name of the Flemish group on the Dutch island of Ameland, which was named for Laus Hendricks of Nes, one of its first elders, who served here 1683-*ca.*1745. It was also called the Foppe Ones (*q.v.*) congregation. It must have been originated in the early 1660's. The names of many of its preachers and elders have been handed down. In 1804 it joined with the Jan Jacobsz group, a group of Old Frisian Mennonites, but usually called Old Flemish. (*DB* 1889, 5, 12, 17, 20; *ML* II, 625.)   vᴅZ.

Lautenbach (*Lautenbacherhof*) near Heilbronn, Germany: see **Lobenbach.**

Lauver Mennonite Church (MC), located between Richfield and Cocolamus in Juniata Co., Pa. The first church was built in 1867 on the farm of Jacob

Lauver. This brick building served the congregation until 1928, when a larger brick church replaced it along the improved highway. The congregation is a part of the Juniata-Snyder Bishop District of the Lancaster Conference, with Boyd Kauffman and Jacob G. Brubaker, ministers. The membership for Cross Roads-Lauver in 1956 was 153.   I.D.L.

Lauwereinse Huutgheers (Ootgheers), widow of Ancelmus Baers, an Anabaptist martyr, was arrested in February 1568 at Brugge, Belgium, with 13 other members of the Mennonite congregation in this town. She was one of the four who remained steadfast and was burned at the stake at Brugge between April 13 and July 28, the exact date being unknown. (Verheyden, *Brugge,* 53, No. 51.)   vDZ.

Lauwereyns Claesz, an Anabaptist martyr, who was burned at the stake with two other Anabaptists on June 28, 1553, at Leeuwarden, capital of the Dutch province of Friesland. Lauwereyns was sentenced to death because he was (re)baptized and persisted in his "heresy"; he was of the opinion "that all which is done in the (Catholic) Church is idolatry." vDZ.

J. Reitsma, *Honderd jaren uit de Geschiedenis der Hervorming in Friesland* (Leeuwarden, 1876) 63; *Inv. Arch. Amst.* I, No. 746.

Lauwereys (Laurens) **van Rentergem,** an Anabaptist martyr, who was executed at Gent, Belgium, in 1569 with four other Anabaptists. The exact date and method of execution are not mentioned in the martyr books; Verheyden (*Gent,* 56) did not find this martyr in the official records. This martyr is named in the hymn "Als men schreef duyst vijf-hondert jaer, ende twee en tsestich mede," in the *Lietboecxken van den Offer des Heeren. (Offer,* 653; *Mart. Mir.* D 407, E 759.)   vDZ.

Lavater, Johann Caspar (1741-1801), a Reformed minister of Zürich, Switzerland, who attained a wide sphere of influence through his devotional sermons, his prolific writing, and his extensive pastoral correspondence. His keen ability to observe enabled him to find in a human profile the key to the character. He developed his system, founding the modern study of physiognomics. In his *Physiognomische Fragmente* III he has a picture of Menno Simons and describes it as follows: "Menno Simons —like his teaching and his brotherhood. Simple and sincere. Not hard; not soft; quietly searching with a thirst for the truth; quietly active with gentleness and loyalty. Calm, tinted with melancholy. Calm observation with devouring sympathy. In the outline of the nose, especially at the top—how much loyalty, wisdom, capability! Mouth and chin, as much as can be seen of them, faithfulness, humility, and silence" (*Menn. Bl.,* 1910, 86). However, since the picture has no historical basis, the analysis, of course, had no significance.

With Basedow and Goethe he also visited the Mennonites in Neuwied on July 19, 1774. In his diary are these notes: "Visited the Mennonites Friedenreich (*q.v.*) and Kinzing(er)—splendid faces, full of simplicity and honor, and round about them— many boys, daughters, mothers, faces, equally noble,

innocent, affectionate, went into their church without tower or bell, spoke of their worship, looked into their orthodox catechism—Basedow asked: would they accept one who did not believe in the Trinity? Got this reply: not to communion. Looked at their artistic musical clocks" (*Menn. Bl.,* 1930, 107.)   NEFF.

J. C. Lavater, *Physiognomische Fragmente zur Beförderung der Menschenkenntnis* III (Leipzig, 1778) 267; *Goethes Rheinreise mit Lavater und Basedow im Sommer 1774. Dokumente herausgegeben von Adolf Bach* (Zürich, 1923) 119; *ML* II, 625 f.

Lawrence County (Pa.) Old Order Amish settlement. Lawrence County was organized in western Pennsylvania in 1849. A Mennonite (MC) congregation and an O.O.A. settlement of four church districts with 250 members (1954) are located in the county, near New Wilmington. The origin of the settlement dates back to 1847, when Amishmen from Mifflin Co., Pa., located there. Christian Yoder purchased 200 acres on April 1, 1847, and Abraham Zook purchased 200 acres on May 8, 1847. A large number of Beilers, including Jacob Byler, son of Hans Beiler, the first Amish bishop of Mifflin County, moved soon after the settlement began. The early settlers often traveled to and from Lawrence and Mifflin counties on foot. Other settlers who followed were Adam Hostetler, John Knepp, John Kanagy, Shem King, and Jonathan Lantz. The new settlers were without ministers until Dan, son of Jacob Byler, and Christ Byler were ordained with the help of outside ministers, probably from Holmes Co., Ohio. Christian Byler was the first resident bishop. He was succeeded by his son Jonas Byler, Yost J. Byler, and Gideon Wengerd, the present bishop.

There are three church districts (East, East North, South East) in the New Wilmington area with a membership of about 300. These three districts have a combined ordained ministry of 12 members. The East North district extends over the border into Mercer County. The original settlement was first divided into the East and West districts in 1916, and in 1947 the East was divided again, making a total of three districts.

About 1850 a number of families withdrew from the Amish Church. The new group with Preacher John Kanagy and Bishop Shem King as leaders worshiped in homes for 22 years (until 1872), when a meetinghouse, the present Maple Grove Mennonite (MC) Church (*q.v.*), was built.

In 1924 about eight families moved from the New Wilmington settlement to the vicinity of Enon Valley, in the southwest part of Lawrence County. This group was led by Reuben Byler and son Jacob S. Byler, who organized a congregation. The Enon Valley settlement was supplemented by families from Mifflin Co., Pa., and from Ohio, so that the settlement now consists of 32 families. The Byler families outnumber by far all others. The Mausts are numerous also, having come from Holmes Co., Ohio. Other families who have lived there include Hostetler, Sommers, Detweiler, Plank, Knepp, Kurtz, Kaufman, King, Shetler, Swartzendruber, Kanagy, Miller, Yoder, Lantz, Petersheim, Spichear, Lapp, and Moose.   J.A.H.

Lawrence County (Tenn.) Old Order Amish settlement was begun by settlers who came to Ethridge, Lawrence Co., Tenn., in January 1944. First settlers were Jacob P. Gingerich, Joe E. Yoder, and Dan M. Yoder from Lumberton, Miss. Others from Wayne Co., Ohio, joined the group in the fall of 1944. A congregation was started with Joseph F. Zook as the first preacher. Dan M. Yoder and Levi J. Hostetler have since been ordained preachers. Levi J. Swartzendruber of Wayne Co., Ohio, has bishop oversight of the two congregations here, which in 1954 had 84 members. S.E.Y.

Lawton View Mennonite Brethren Mission, located at Lawton, Okla., is an outgrowth of the Post Oak Indian and Mexican Mission at Indiahoma. Missionary A. J. Becker began this work among Mexicans in the eastern part of the city in 1935. A mission chapel was built and dedicated in 1937. The mission workers who have served at this location are Mr. and Mrs. A. J. Becker, Mrs. Anna Gomez, J. A. Gonzales, Mr. and Mrs. J. J. Reimer, Salvador Rivera, and Walter Gomez. After a number of converts from the Mexicans and the white population had been baptized, a local church was organized.

In 1946 the mission was shifted to the southwestern part of the city, where it is located at present. Here the church continued to grow for some time; but later, due to migrations, the Mexican element of the congregation began to decrease. The congregation now consists mainly of the "poor whites." Becker has continued to assist in this work, and Harry Bartel has also been stationed here for a short time. The present mission workers are Mr. and Mrs. Frank P. Nickel. A new church building was erected in 1946. The Mission is under the supervision of the Foreign Mission Board of the M.B. Church. J.H.L.

Lay Preachers, the designation for preachers who without theological education are chosen out of the congregation to the office of preaching, and receive no fixed remuneration. In Holland and Germany they were called "love preachers" (Dutch *Liefdepredikers,* German *Liebesprediger*), i.e., those who preach for love's sake, or lay preachers (Dutch *Leeken-predikers,* German *Laienprediger*), which in the Netherlands meant men without special training, who nevertheless received some remuneration.

In the primitive church all the male members were "brethren"; each had the right to serve according to his gifts as evangelist, preacher, or teacher. Preaching was not yet attached to a special office. There was as yet no privilege for proclamation of the Gospel. Only as ecclesiastical offices became more sharply defined was this right reserved to the priest. Even as late as the third century laymen were permitted to preach occasionally, although it was considered improper to do so in the presence of the bishop without his express request. Soon afterward lay preaching ceased entirely; it was forbidden. Vainly did small groups such as the Cathars, Waldenses, and Lollards from time to time seek to re-establish lay preaching within the bounds of the Roman church of the Middle Ages. The Lateran Council of 1179 (Pope Alexander III) forbade the Waldenses to preach; but they continued

their preaching with the greatest success and joyfully endured the bloodiest persecution and most inhuman suppression. This was also true of other groups such as the Cathars and the Lollards (*q.v.*).

During the Reformation lay preaching was revived. Luther at first granted the right of preaching to every Christian; but in his struggle with the Anabaptists he abandoned the principle, severely attacking "corner preaching." Zwingli, too, opposed the right of free preaching; preaching he considered a privilege of church office.

In Anabaptism, however, lay preaching attained its full right, and the principle is still firmly held in the Mennonite churches in various countries and continues to be widely practiced in more than one group. In fact in the first quarter of the 20th century at least three fourths of all Mennonite congregations were served by lay preachers, and in 1955 at least half.

In the earliest times the Mennonites were averse to theology, considering it unnecessary or actually harmful. God's Word was the only foundation to build upon. To understand and explain it, no learning or worldly wisdom was required, but only a faithful, honest, untiring seeking and searching in the Scriptures (Acts 17:11). Every Christian should know the Scriptures. Scriptural knowledge was in fact very comprehensive among the Anabaptists. It was said of them, "It seemed as if they had eaten the entire Bible," or "They had the Bible on their thumbs" (*DJ* I, 89; see **Formantijn**).

The change from lay preaching to a trained and salaried ministry began first in Holland. There the Mennonites began as early as the late 16th century to call educated men into the ministry; they were usually physicians, who in addition to their own vocation also preached, receiving little or no compensation for their preaching, and who had little formal theological education. There were important men among these preachers, especially in the first half of the 17th century and later, like Anthoni Jacobs Roscius (*q.v.*), Galenus Abrahamsz de Haan (*q.v.*), Antonius van Dale (*q.v.*), Gerardus de Wind (*q.v.*), and Herman Schijn (*q.v.*). After the Mennonite Seminary was established in Amsterdam (*q.v.*) in 1735 theological study became the common custom in Holland. By 1830 nearly all the Dutch churches employed theologically trained preachers. Only a few churches like Ameland (*q.v.*) and Balk (*q.v.*) held to the old custom of lay preaching, until about the middle of the 19th century. The lay preachers supported themselves, receiving only some small remuneration for the time they could not work on their farms or in their business. In the country this system lasted until the early 19th century, but in most cities untrained preachers received a salary from 1680 on. The few untrained preachers (10 out of 114 in 1955) who still serve in Dutch congregations are salaried like those trained.

In Germany the city churches have all had trained and salaried preachers for a long time, whereas the country churches in West Prussia (extinct since 1945), Baden, Württemberg, and Bavaria (*Badischer Verband*) faithfully retain the old practice. In the Palatinate and Rheinhessen the transition to a salaried ministry was made early in the 19th century.

A small circle of four congregations led by Johannes Galle (see **Jakob Galle**) vehemently attacked it as a ruinous innovation. But a scant generation later all opposition had disappeared. All of the six churches of the Palatinate-Hessian Conference have single salaried pastors. The Munich-Regensburg circuit also followed this practice about 1910-53, but has now reverted to the older practice. The two churches in the South Palatinate, Deutschhof and Branchweilerhof, and since 1945 also Berlin, have the lay ministry.

It is of interest to note that as recently as 1898 Eduard Dyck, the preacher of the Rosenort church near Elbing in West Prussia, was to be penalized for preaching a graveside sermon as a lay preacher, thereby breaking a police regulation of Feb. 13, 1852. But he was declared not guilty by the court at Tiegenhagen; the state attorney appealed, but the appeal was rejected (*Menn. Bl.,* 1898, 67; 1899, 3).

In Russia the lay ministry was retained throughout the entire history of the Mennonite Church there, although a few men did secure theological training in Germany and Switzerland beginning about 1900. However, when such men became ordained preachers they usually also held a teaching position as a means of livelihood.

Among the French Mennonites the lay ministry is still universal, while in Switzerland three of the largest congregations now (1955) have trained and salaried ministers.

In North America the lay ministry has been maintained exclusively to the present (1955) in all the more culturally conservative groups, such as the Old Order Amish, Old Order Mennonites, Church of God in Christ Mennonites, Conservative Mennonites, Kleine Gemeinde, etc. In the largest of the American groups, the Mennonite Church (MC), only recently has there been any appreciable increase in the use of trained and fully salaried ministers. In 1955 not more than 10 per cent of these congregations employed pastors with training and salary. On the other hand practically all of the congregations of the remaining groups in the United States— General Conference, Mennonite Brethren, Evangelical Mennonites, Evangelical Mennonite Brethren, and most of the Krimmer Mennonite Brethren— employed trained and salaried pastors, though by no means did all of them have full seminary training, many having training only in Bible institutes or colleges. The General Conference Mennonite Church was the earliest to adopt the salaried ministry (quite general from 1900 on) and has the most universal practice. In Canada, however, the number of salaried (and trained) ministers is still very small in any of these conference groups. In Mexico and South America salaried ministers are unknown except in the indigenous Argentine Mennonite Church.

The reasons for the increasing surrender of the lay ministry in the United States are varied. In some cases it is the desire for better preaching and more effective pastoral service. The increasing pressure of the surrounding secular culture, and the competition of other religious groups, have called for more full-time religious leadership, which cannot well be had without paying salaries. Untrained men feel themselves increasingly inadequate and refuse to accept the call to the pastorate. Mechanized farming and urban living make it difficult for men to carry the dual load of a full secular occupation and the pastor-preacher assignment.

The demands for theologically and Biblically trained preachers have forced the larger Mennonite conferences and national groups to establish theological seminaries or Bible training schools. Where this has not been done because of the inability of the group to maintain a school because of small size, the preachers have secured their training in theological schools of other denominations. At times the outside influences channeled into the Mennonite brotherhood through such training have been significant and beneficial, but also at times harmful. The most notable case of this latter has been the incursion of theological liberalism and modernism into the Dutch and Northwest German churches in the late 19th and early 20th centuries. It is a general fact that those groups which have maintained the lay ministry have remained more theologically and traditionally conservative. On the other hand the lay ministry has at times not been strong enough to resist successfully the inroads of strange doctrines and certain influences hostile to the historic Mennonite faith. It is impossible to establish a general rule that the change from a lay ministry to a trained and supported ministry has always been harmful. It has been and can be a source of strength and progress. This change-over in the Palatine-Hessian congregations in the early part of the 19th century has been given credit for saving these congregations from serious decay and even extinction. (See also **Ministry, Elder,** and **Bishop;** *ML* II, 605.)

NEFF, H.S.B.

Le Heux, Jan Willem Nicolaas (1880-1952), was a professor of the Military Academy at Breda, Netherlands, and for many years a deacon of the Mennonite congregation of Breda. Under the pseudonym of David Tomkins he published a number of sketches and poems in various Dutch Mennonite periodicals. The drawing of the Old Menno Simons meetinghouse at Witmarsum, Friesland, found on the cover of the *Doopsgezind Jaarboekje* was made by Le Heux in 1931.   vdZ.

Algemeen Doopsgezind Weekblad **VI** (1951-52) No. 39; *DJ* 1953, 10 f.

Le Poole, a Dutch Mennonite family: see **Poole, le.**

Leaman, Amos Hershey (1878-1950), a Mennonite (MC) city missionary, was born near Gordonville, Lancaster Co., Pa., on Feb. 18, 1878, the third of the eight children of Jacob B. and Anna Barbara Hershey Leaman. On June 22, 1902, he was married to Amanda Eby. They were the parents of four children.

Hershey was educated at the Millersville State Normal School, Moody Bible Institute, and Chicago Theological Seminary, receiving a degree of Bachelor of Divinity in 1915. He attended the Mennonite Church at Paradise, Pa. In the fall of 1896 under the preaching of J. S. Coffman (*q.v.*) he was converted, and in November of that year he assisted the Chicago Mennonite Home Mission, then at 639 W. 18th Street, later becoming superintendent of the mission, serving until 1920. He was ordained to the ministry in the spring of 1902. As the work grew, Leaman raised funds for a new building, which was dedicated at 1907 S. Union Avenue on Jan. 5, 1919. In 1920-32 he served in Moody Bible Institute in Evangelism and Practical Work, for several years as Director of Practical Work. In 1930 he traveled to England and Scotland under the auspices of the Institute.

Leaman was a promoter of various city-wide Christian lay activities; he helped to institute the Chicago Easter Sunrise Service, the first of which was held at Soldier Field in 1933. He also led in the founding of the Christian Business Men's Committee of Chicago, which sponsored noonday services in a theater in the Loop and a related radio broadcast. In 1944 he became superintendent of the Lydia Children's Home in Chicago, helping to restore its finances and get its license renewed.

Leaman was active in the Illinois Mennonite Conference and Mission Board, serving as field worker of the latter for several years. He challenged many young people to Christian service.

Leaman served as pastor of the Mennonite Church (GCM) at 73rd and Laflin Streets for approximately ten years during the 1940's. He died in Chicago on May 27, 1950, and was laid to rest in Irving Park Cemetery, Chicago. H.Z.

Leamington Mennonite Brethren Church, located in Leamington, Essex Co., Ont., a member of the Canadian Conference of the M.B. Church, was organized on Nov. 20, 1932, under the leadership of Isaak Tiessen, the first minister. The membership stood at 178, the majority of whom were rural people. For a number of years the congregation held its meetings in a rented hall, together with the members of the United Mennonite Church. Then a church was built by the Mennonite Brethren, which is still in use. The following ministers have served the church: I. Tiessen, G. Reimer, J. F. Dick, W. Toews, A. Huebert, J. Kroeker, and P. Friesen. The pastor (1956) is David Derksen. H.H.J.

Leatherman (Ledermann, Ledterman, Letherman), a Mennonite family which is represented chiefly though not exclusively in the Franconia Conference (MC) congregations, particularly of Bucks County, Pa. It has died out among the Mennonites of Germany. The progenitor of these Bucks County Leathermans was Jacob Ledterman, who came to America from Europe in 1741 (d. 1769) at the age of 32, with his wife and sons Jacob and Abraham. He settled at Deep Run in Bucks County, at which place the Mennonites built their first meetinghouse in 1746. Most of his children were born in America. Among the Leathermans who have served in the ministry of the Franconia Conference congregations were Samuel Leatherman (1815-1904), Line Lexington, ordained preacher in 1843 and bishop in 1876; John M. Leatherman (1845-1924), Deep Run, ordained preacher in 1889; John E. Leatherman (1909-), since 1936 a missionary in Tanganyika; Quintus Leatherman (1903-), since 1952 a missionary in London. In 1878 the Mennonite Publishing Co., of Elkhart, Ind., published a 32-page book-

let for children entitled *Bible Lessons,* written by Daniel S. Leatherman. Many of the non-Mennonite Leathermans of North America are descended from other immigrants than the Jacob Ledterman described above. J.C.W.

John Letherman & Emma Leatherman Candler, *All Leatherman Kin History* (Nappanee, Ind., 1940).

Lebanon County, Pa. In 1729 Lebanon Township was a part of Lancaster County. In 1813 it united with a part of Dauphin County to form Lebanon County. Lebanon is its county seat. Numerous Mennonite families moved into the area. The United Brethren schism, again broken by the United Christian Church, preyed much upon them; others moved into Juniata County and communities farther west. The Church of the Brethren later absorbed them, so that most of the present membership is the result of 20th-century colonization. The earliest meetinghouse was built at Shirksville in 1775, the home of Caspar Shirk of Chestnut Hill. Other early houses of worship were located at the site of the present Gingrich, Krall, and Dohner churches, and also the Kauffman, Shirk, and Light (in Lebanon) churches. More recently Meckville, Miners Village, Royer, Texter, and North Lebanon were opened. The Mennonite membership in the ten congregations is 521; Krall with 77 is the highest. I.D.L.

Lebanon County Amish. A group of Old Order Amish families of Lancaster Co., Pa., moved to adjacent Lebanon County, in 1941, locating near Myerstown. In 1954 there were two congregations with three preachers and one deacon and a membership of 40. Bishop oversight is supplied by the Lancaster congregations. J.A.H.

Lebanon (Pa.) Mennonite Brethren in Christ Church, organized in 1910, had 58 members in 1953, with E. J. Rutman as pastor.

Lechfeld, Bavaria, Germany, a Mennonite refugee camp and temporary settlement (1921-25), located on the former military drill ground of the same name about 10-12 miles directly south of Augsburg. The *Mennonitische Flüchtlingsfürsorge (q.v.,* founded Nov. 12, 1920), a German Mennonite organization, sought in various ways to aid Mennonite refugees from Russia who had come to Germany before the major emigration movement from Russia to Canada in 1923-25. A small colonization attempt in Mecklenburg *(q.v.)* in 1921 had failed. A similar attempt at Camp Lechfeld, although on a much larger scale, beginning in April 1921, also failed and by 1926 was completely abandoned for lack of funds. In 1923 a separate transit refugee camp was established at Lechfeld for Russian Mennonites who were temporarily held back from emigration to Canada because of trachoma or other health reasons. From July 27 to Aug. 19, 1923, a total of 658 Mennonites were successfully treated. By Oct. 31, 1924, the camp had given a total of 85,000 days of nursing care. The remnant still at Lechfeld when the camp was closed were transferred to the Ueberseeheim, a refugee home in Hamburg.

The Lechfeld colonization scheme was an extensive one and failed in part because of lack of the necessary capital. The German government made

2,000 acres available, together with barracks and other buildings. The M.F.F., having little capital, could not handle the project alone, hence arranged a working agreement, whereby it (M.F.F.), the relief agency Christenpflicht (q.v.) of Ingolstadt, and the Conference of German Baptists were to co-operate in the plan. Loans were secured, an agricultural director was appointed—Michael Horsch of Hellmannsberg, then Philipp Lichti of Herrlehof, under whom Philipp Hege had the direct management. Place was to be provided for 60 families. By Christmas of 1921 there were 180 Mennonites present. Schools were established (Jakob Ewert was one of the teachers) and other religious and cultural activities undertaken. Home industry was established, particularly basket weaving and a small clothing factory. For three years, 1921-23, the farm was operated successfully, but the burden of supporting too many refugees who could not work became too great. The German government refugee commission had intended Lechfeld to be a temporary project of five years, while the Mennonites tried to make it a permanent settlement with the intent to sell the land in smaller parcels to the refugee families. However, the success of the great movement from Russia to Canada, the inflation in Germany, the lack of unity among the three relief agencies and with the German government, led to the abandonment of what had once been a promising venture. The only large attempt at a permanent Russian Mennonite settlement in Germany had failed. The M.F.F. changed its name on May, 1922, to "Deutsche Mennoniten-Hilfe" (q.v.). H.S.B.

Deutsche Mennoniten-Hilfe, ihre Entstehung und Arbeitsgebiete (Oberursel, 1924); *ML* III, 208, article *Mennonitische Flüchtingsfürsorge;* M. Horsch, "The Mennonite Colony on the Lechfeld," *Gospel Herald* XIV (July 7, 1921) 267 f.; J. Horsch, "A Mennonite Relief Work for Russian Fugitives," *Gospel Herald* XIV (June 9, 1921) 203 f.; "Das Lechfeld Siedlungsland," *Menn. Bl.,* LXIX (1922) 12 f.; *ML* II, 626.

Lectureships. Two Mennonite scholarly lectureships have been est. in the United States, the Menno Simons Lectureship (q.v.) at Bethel College (GCM), est. in 1953, with a focus on Anabaptist-Mennonite history, and the Conrad Grebel Lectureship under the Mennonite Board of Education (MC), est. in 1952, with a scope including theology, ethics, and general church concerns and work. Holders of the latter lectureship have been Paul Mininger (1952), "Foundations for Christian Education"; Milo Kauffman (1953), *"Christian Stewardship in the Mennonite Church"; G. F. Hershberger (1954), "The Way of the Cross in Human Relations"; Paul Erb (1955), *"The Alpha and the Omega"; Gideon G. Yoder (1956), "The Evangelism and Nurture of Children"; C. K. Lehman (1957), "The Holy Spirit in Christian Experience"; J. D. Graber (1958), "A Philosophy of Missions"; H. S. Bender (1959), "This Is My Body." The lectures are to be published as books; those marked * having already appeared. H.S.B.

Lectuur, Godsdienstige, *voor Doopsgezinden, verzameld,* in the second and third volume called *Doopsgezinde Lectuur tot bevordering van christelijke kennis en godzaligheid,* is the title of a Dutch Mennonite periodical published by D. S. Gorter

(q.v.) with several of his colleagues in 1854, 1856, 1858. It contains valuable devotional and historical articles. It was similar in spirit to the *Doopsgezinde Bijdragen* (q.v.), which can be considered a continuation of the *Lectuur.* (*Menn. Bl.,* 1856, 37-41; *ML* II, 635.) NEFF.

Lee County, Iowa. The first area in Iowa Territory to receive white settlers was Lee County, located in the southeastern tip of the territory along the Mississippi River. The first Mennonites to settle in Iowa were John C. Krehbiel, wife, and son, of Butler Co., Ohio, who arrived in Fort Madison, Lee County, on Nov. 1, 1839. The first Mennonite child to be born in Iowa was the Krehbiel daughter Johanna Maria (Jan. 26, 1840), who became the wife of Daniel Hertzler and the mother of the famous "Horse and Buggy Doctor" Arthur E. Hertzler. In 1849 Krehbiel was chosen minister of the West Point Mennonite Church (Bush Church), where he preached until his death in 1886. Mennonite settlers followed Hertzler, locating near his home a few miles south of West Point. In 1849 these settlers organized the West Point (q.v.) Mennonite Church and elected two ministers, Krehbiel and Jacob Ellenberger. They then built the first Mennonite church in Iowa, 1½ miles east of the present town of Franklin, and held their first service in it on Pentecost 1850. Eventually the Bush church was abandoned and a new building was constructed in West Point. In time this church was abandoned as most of the members moved to other communities.

In the early fifties Palatinate Mennonites moved to Franklin Twp., Lee County, about eight miles from West Point, and there organized a church. Their first church, built two miles northwest of Donnellson in 1855, came to be known as Zion (q.v.), and was rebuilt in 1880. In 1909 their third church was erected in the town of Donnellson (q.v.). The Mennonites decided that their two churches were too far apart and so they constructed a third one in the town of Franklin (q.v.) in 1868. This church began to decline a few years later when members moved away, and became extinct.

The West Point and Zion churches are important for the part they played in the organization of the General Conference Mennonite Church. In 1853 the two congregations had held a conference in which they agreed to work together in harmony, and in a second conference in 1859 they agreed to invite other Mennonite churches to join their union. As a result, the delegates of four churches met at West Point on May 28 and 29, 1860, in a meeting that is regarded to be the beginning of the General Conference Mennonite Church. In 1954 the Lee County G.C.M. membership was 233.

Probably the first Amish Mennonites to move to Iowa were the members of the Christian Raber family, who came to Lee County from Hamilton Co., Ohio, in 1840, and settled near Charleston. Christian is the ancestor of several Rabers who became ministers in the Mennonite church. The Rabers were joined by other families: Rogie, Kinsinger, Werey, Hauder, Reese, Fordemwalt, Augspurger, Goldsmith, Schwartzentruber, Plank, von Gunden, Wagler, Shantz, Lehman, Schrock, Musser, King,

Klopfenstein, Miller, Schlotter, Bechler, and Roth. The date of the organization of the church is uncertain, but since Christian Raber was an ordained Amish preacher, services may have been held in the early forties. Christian Schwarzentruber, an Amish bishop, moved to Lee County very likely in 1845. It is probable that the church was organized in the year of his arrival. The most influential Amish leader was Bishop Joseph Goldsmith (*q.v.*), who settled there in 1846. John Fordemwalt, another Amish preacher, located there in 1849. The largest membership of the church may have been 50. In 1855 the church began to decline as members moved to Davis and Henry counties and other places. This was caused in part by the faulty land titles held by some of the Amish settlers.   M.G.

M. Gingerich, *The Mennonites in Iowa* (Iowa City, 1939); W. J. Krehbiel, *History of One Branch of the Krehbiel Family* (McPherson, 1950); Vernon Neufeld, "Mennonites Settle in Lee County, Iowa," *Menn. Life* VIII (October 1953) 170.

Leeghwater, Jan Adriaensz, b. 1575 at De Rijp, Dutch province of North Holland, d. February 1650 at Amsterdam, a Dutch architect noted for his mills and dikes. In the drainage and reclaiming of several lakes in North Holland between 1608 and 1635 he was an important figure. He engaged in similar work in Prussia, Denmark, France, and England. In his *Haarlemmermeerboeck* (1641) he published a plan for the drainage of this lake, which was carried out in 1845-52. One of his buildings was the beautiful little town hall of his native town. Leeghwater was also a clockmaker, cabinetmaker, and engraver. In 1605 he obtained a patent on a diving bell which he had invented, in which he could stay under water for some time. In 1642 (reprint Saerdam, 1688) he published *Een cleyn chronycke ende voorbereydinge van de afkomst ende 't vergrooten van de dorpen van Graft en de Rijp*. This book contains some information on the Mennonites of these villages. He was a Mennonite, probably a member of the Waterlander congregation. A Laurens Leegwater was a preacher of the Mennonite congregation of Koog-Zaandijk in the early 17th century.   vDZ.

J. G. de Roever, *J. A. Leeghwater, het leven en werk van een 17de eeuwse waterbouwkundige* (Amsterdam, 1944); *N.N.B.Wb.* VI, 909-11; *DB* 1917, 12 f., 15; *ML* II, 626.

Leenaert van Antwerpen: see **Lenaerdt (Lenart) Boeckbinder**.

Leenaert Bouwens, an important early Dutch Anabaptist elder, was born in Sommeldyk in 1515 and died at Hoorn in 1582. He probably originally followed some trade or profession which involved ocean travel. In his youth he was a member of the "Rederyker" (a political oratory club).

After he had been an active Mennonite preacher for some time and as such had participated in the conference in Lübeck in 1546, he was ordained elder at Emden by Menno Simons in 1551. He lived in the neighboring village of 't Falder. He undertook various trips, at first in East Friesland, Groningen, and Friesland, visiting also the islands of the North Sea, in order to administer baptism and communion. His wife was dissatisfied because of the danger attending his journeys. In the 1681 edition of

Menno's work there is a letter Menno wrote to Leenaert's wife, trying to persuade her to consent to her husband's trips.

Bouwens's activity extended farther and farther; he made a journey to North Holland and from there into Flanders (Belgium). He kept records of his trips and of the number he baptized at each place. He baptized in five distinct periods: in 1551-54, 869 persons; 1554-56, 693 persons; 1557-61, 808 persons; 1563-65, 4,499 persons; and 1568-82, 3,509 persons, making a total of 10,378 baptisms. There is perhaps an error in his report on Gent in the third period; if so, the number is decreased by 126, making a total of 10,252. This baptismal list was published (there are two extant copies) in the *Bijdragen en Mededeelingen van het Historisch genootschap in Utrecht* (XXXVI, 1915, 39-70). The beginnings of many congregations can be found by this list.

Bouwens played an important part in various important events in early Mennonite history. He was present at the meeting in Wismar in 1554, where several church regulations were passed by the assembled elders. In 1556 he was removed from his office for a while in consequence of the violent quarrel over the ban in Waterland and Emden, where Leenaert was the leader of the stricter party in the debate. With the aid of Dirk Philips by means of a threat he managed to win Menno to his side at a meeting in Harlingen. From this dissension a division ensued which began in Waterland, caused Hendrik Naeldeman (*q.v.*) in Franeker to separate from the brotherhood, and brought about a complete division between Menno and the High Germans, whose leaders were the elders Zylis (*q.v.*) and Lemke (*q.v.*) in the lower Rhine area.

Immediately after Menno's death Leenaert Bouwens was accused by the church of (1) domineering ambition, (2) accepting 50 talers for spiritual services as elder, (3) wine drinking. On this account he was inactive for several years, even though he was not removed from office. But four years later (1565) Dirk Philips deposed him together with six fellow elders. This caused deep dissatisfaction in Friesland, where he had baptized thousands, and where the division was felt with bitterness. Then Bouwens settled in Harlingen. This event is one of the decisive factors in the great split which arose in 1566 in Franeker and Harlingen and led to the great division between the Flemish and Frisians in 1567. Right after the death of Dirk Philips in 1568 Bouwens resumed his office of preaching, now siding with the Frisians (*q.v.*).   K.V.

Inv. Arch. Amst. I, No. 383, 416; II, 2, Nos. 9, 9a; K. Vos, *Menno Simons* (Leiden, 1914); Kühler, *Geschiedenis* I, *passim*; *DB* 1863, 94; 1864, 76 f.; 1873, 141; 1876, 22; 1878, 4, 6; 1881, 75; 1887, 116; 1889, 3 f.; 1890, 92; 1891, 1, 42; 1893, 13-16, 75, 79 f.; 1894, 30-36, 40-46, 59; 1895, 106; 1896, 37, 40; 1899, 33, 35; 1900, 98; 1903, 3 f., 14, 146; 1905, 172; 1908, 61, 106; 1909, 31, 156; 1910, 123 f.; K. Vos, "De Dooplijst van Leenaert Bowens," *Bijdr. en Mededeelingen v. h. Hist. Gen.* (1915) 36, 39 ff.; Cornelius Krahn, *Menno Simons* (Karlsruhe, 1936) 39, 65, 79, 85, 117, 133, 156, 159, 164; *ML* I, 250 f.

Leendertz, an old Mennonite family which emigrated at the end of the 16th century from the Palatinate, Germany, to Cleve (*q.v.*) in the Lower Rhine territory. The first representative of this family found at Cleve was Pieter Leendertz (1609-83) whose son was Leendert Leendertz (d. 1691 at Cleve) who was married to Billeken Wilms. A son of Leendert Leendertz, Willem Leendertz, was a preacher of the Mennonite congregation of Cleve 1720-ca.45 (*Naamlijst* 1731); he may be identical with Willem Leendertz, who (*Inv. Arch Amst.* II, No. 2580) is said to have been *voorlezer* (reader) of that congregation and resigned in 1743 because of old age and illness.

In the early 17th century some members of this family moved to Rees (*q.v.*), where Jan Leendertz became the ancestor of the Rhineland branch of the Leendertz family, which still exists. Harmen Leendertz, a son of Jan Leendertz, was a preacher of the congregation at Rees 1707-ca.40 (*Naamlijst* 1731). Other members of the family in the 18th century moved to Emmerich (*q.v.*) and to the Netherlands, especially to Nijmegen and Haarlem. At Nijmegen Willem Leendertz (1721-1810), who had come from Cleve about 1738, was at first a baker and then a merchant. In 1757-1810 he was a deacon of the Mennonite congregation (*DB* 1875, 80 f.). He was married in 1750 to Elisabeth van Eger, a daughter of Petrus van Eger, preacher of the Nijmegen Mennonite congregation, and remarried twice; he had 17 children.

In the Netherlands a large number of members of this family were Mennonite preachers, all trained at the Amsterdam Mennonite Seminary. Cornelis Leendertz, b. July 31, 1784, at Nijmegen, d. June 7, 1857, at Amsterdam, married to Antje Rotgans, served at Zuidveen 1808-10, Steenwijkerwold 1810-14, and Zaandam-West 1814-54. He published *Leerrede bij de herdenking van mijn 25 jarige Predikdienst* (Amsterdam, 1839) and together with his co-preacher B. van Geuns, *Leerredenen* (n.p., 1841). He also published some poems. His son Jacobus Leendertz, b. Jan. 30, 1809, at Zuidveen, d. June 5, 1877, at Leer, was married to Engelina Mesdag of Groningen and served at Mensingeweer 1832-37, and Leer, Germany, 1837-77. A son of this Jacobus Leendertz was Cornelis Leendertz, b. May 7, 1843, at Leer, d. Dec. 23, 1928, at Middelstum, pastor of Staveren 1866-73, Zwartsluis 1873-75, Noordhorn 1875-98, and Middelstum 1898-1908. Mennonite ministers were also Pieter Leendertz (1817-80) (*q.v.*) and Abraham Cornelis Leendertz, b. Nov. 4, 1822, at Kampen, d. Dec. 25, 1899, at Cleve, serving at Cleve 1850-95, whose son Willem Isaac Leendertz (*q.v.*) and grandsons Willem Leendertz (b. 1883) and Johannes Matthias Leendertz (b. 1885) were Mennonite ministers, as were two other sons of Abraham Cornelis Leendertz, one of whom was also called Abraham Cornelis Leendertz (*q.v.*), and Cornelis Abraham Leendertz, b. Oct. 19, 1861, at Cleve, d. May 1, 1939, at Norden, serving the congregation of Norden, Germany, 1889-1931.

Whether Jan Leendertz, about 1650 a Mennonite preacher at Zutphen, Dutch province of Gelderland (*DB* 1881, 46), belonged to this Leendertz family could not be ascertained. Tjepke Leendertz, d. 1816, preacher of Ameland from 1767, apparently did not.
                                                              vDZ.

Stammbaum der Familie Leendertz, bearb. von Kommerzienrat Friedrich August Leendertz (n.p., 1907);

Nederl. Patriciaat XIX (1930) 120-42, 290 f.; W. Niepoth, *Zur Geschichte des Geschlechts Leendertz in Rees* (1941); *ML* II, 626.

Leendertz, Abraham Cornelis, b. March 18, 1854, at Cleve, Germany, d. April 30, 1930, at Budel, Dutch province of North Brabant, a son of Pastor Abraham Cornelis Leendertz of Cleve, was a Mennonite minister, serving at Warns 1880-82. Then he resigned because of illness and resumed his ministry in 1886, serving the Holwerd congregation 1886-93. In this year he published *Voor Hart en Huis,* a guide for family worship (Leeuwarden, 1893). In the same year he left the Mennonites and became a Reformed Church minister, serving at Sappemeer 1893-99, Leiden 1899-1903, Stolwijk 1903-6, Coevorden 1906-14, St. Jacobi-Parochie 1914-17, and Budel 1917-30. (*Biogr. Wb.* V, 679 f.)   vDZ.

Leendertz, Pieter, b. Nov. 17, 1817, at Amsterdam, d. Sept. 10, 1880, at Dortmund, Germany, on a vacation trip, married to Janke Wagenaar of IJlst, was a son of the Mennonite merchant Willem Leendertz (b. 1779 at Nijmegen, d. 1837 at Kampen). He was educated at the Amsterdam Mennonite Seminary and served as preacher at Woudsend 1840-55, Den Ilp 1855-64, and Medemblik 1864 until his death. He was very influential even beyond Mennonite circles. In addition he was an outstanding specialist in medieval literature and language. From 1864 he co-operated with his friend de Hoop Scheffer (*q.v.*) in editing the works of P. C. Hooft, which appeared in two volumes in 1875. In 1856 he and de Hoop Scheffer assumed the editorship of the genealogical paper *De Navorscher,* raising it to a high level. He owned a valuable library, specially rich in manuscripts and songbooks, and also a rare collection of works of music. Nearly everything, including his valuable notes, was destroyed in a fire on Feb. 5, 1863, which destroyed the church and parsonage of Den Ilp. He took this blow, which annihilated the work of a lifetime, with Christian composure, and preached on Job 2:10 in the school at Den Ilp on Feb. 15, 1863. In *Doopsgezinde Bijdragen* of 1861 he published a paper on "De Naam Doopschgezinden." (*Biogr. Wb.* V, 673-76; *N.N.B.Wb.* VI, 914-18; *DB* 1881, 122; *ML* II, 626.)   vDZ.

Leendertz, Willem Isaac, b. Nov. 25, 1850, at Cleve, Germany, d. Oct. 19, 1917, at Amsterdam, married to Geertruida Kops of Utrecht. He was a son of Abraham Cornelis Leendertz, pastor at Cleve, and like his father a Mennonite preacher. He was educated at the Amsterdam Mennonite Seminary, and served the congregations in Wormer-Jisp in 1875-78, Ouddorp 1878-81, Veenwouden 1881-88, De Rijp 1888-90, and Amsterdam 1890-1912. Urged by de Hoop Scheffer he wrote a treatise on Melchior Hofmann, which won a prize given by the Teyler Theological Society; it was published in 1883. He was closely attached to the Mennonite brotherhood, but also liked to work with other groups. From 1887 to 1914 he was editor of *Geloof en Vrijheid,* a Protestant quarterly, in which all kinds of articles from his pen appeared. The ministry in Amsterdam with its varied tasks, especially with his many hours of instruction (sometimes 24 in a week), did not leave him much time for historical studies. In *Geloof en Vrijheid* XXIII (1889) he published an important paper, "Johannes Deknatel, een piëtist onder de Doopsgezinden." Nevertheless he devoted much time and interest to the Dutch Mennonite Mission Association, serving as its secretary 1895-1917, and in this capacity carried on an extensive correspondence with the missionaries in Java and Sumatra, his German education serving him well. In 1912 he resigned his ministry for reasons of health.   J.M.L.

Biogr. Wb. V, 676-79; *Zondagsbode* XXX, 1916-17, No. 52; XXXI, 1917-18, No. 2; V. Loosjes Az, *Levensbericht* (Leiden, 1918); *ML* II, 627.

Leenhart Munsels, an Anabaptist elder, who about 1543 baptized Jan Schutte in Bocholt, Westphalia, Germany (*DB* 1909, 106, 117 f.), may be identical with Leonard Fälber (*q.v.*).

Leens, a town in the Dutch province of Groningen, in the Marne region, where since the 16th century there were numerous Mennonites who belonged to the very conservative Groningen Old Flemish branch. The congregation of Leens, of which Jacob Melles (b. 1649, d. February 1683) and Ary Aris were preachers in the 17th century, may have merged with a neighboring church, probably that of Rasquert (*q.v.*), at the close of the 17th century or in the early 18th. (*Inv. Arch. Amst.* I, No. 562; II, No. 2039; *DB* 1879, 4.)   vDZ.

Leentgen, wife of Jan van Rheenen (*q.v.*), an Anabaptist martyr, was drowned on May 21 (van Braght, *Mart. Mir.,* erroneously May 15), 1535, at Amsterdam, with a number of other Anabaptist women, including her daughter Adriana Jans, while another daughter, Lysbeth Jans, had been put to death on May 15. Leentgen had been (re)baptized early in December 1534 in her own house at Amsterdam by "a man of Benschop," who is obviously Gerrit Ghysen of Benschop (*q.v.*). (*Mart. Mir.* D 413, E 764; Grosheide, *Verhooren,* 67-70.)   vDZ.

Leentgen, an Anabaptist martyr, was put to death in 1564 in the Sint Pieters cloister at Gent, Belgium, together with her daughter Pieryntgen Ketels. Exact date and method of execution are unknown. The names of these martyrs are found in the hymn, "Als men schreef duyst vijfhondert jaer ende twee en tsestich mede," found in the *Lietboecxken van den Offer des Heeren* (Supplement, No. 1). (*Offer,* 651; *Mart. Mir.* D 301, E 666; Verheyden, *Gent,* 30, No. 101.)   vDZ.

Leentgen Hendricxdochter, an Anabaptist martyr, a native of 's Hertogenbosch, Dutch province of North Brabant, was baptized at 'Dordrecht about May 1534 by Bartholomeus Boeckbinder (*q.v.*). She was arrested in Amsterdam in May 1535 and put to death with a large number of other Anabaptist women by drowning on May 21 (not May 15, as *Mart. Mir.* states), 1535.   vDZ.

Mart Mir. D 413, E 764; Grosheide, *Verhooren,* 67-70; Mellink, *Wederdopers,* 145, 229, 312; *ML* II, 282, 627.

Leer, a town (pop. 15,000) in East Friesland, in the province of Hannover, Germany, the seat of a Mennonite church which originated in the early years of the Anabaptist movement. Its founders were probably refugees from Holland and Flanders. It is known that the martyr Elisabeth (*q.v.*) found temporary asylum here. The family names van Hoorn and Bavink occur in the earliest period. Other Mennonite family names were Alringh, Lulofs, Vissering, Zytsama, and later also Rahusen. Covering the years 1635-1768 there is a *Grootboek* (financial record) which gives some information on the history of the period. The congregation did not attract much outside attention. It had only a lay minister; for communion, which was called "unity" after I Cor. 10, and baptism, the elder of Emden was called in. During the time of the difficulty with the government concerning letters of protection, etc., nothing is heard of the Mennonites at Leer, perhaps because they had nothing to be extorted from them.

The congregation was said to be Flemish, and as such presumably represented the moderately strict wing in church discipline. Besides this group, there was in Leer also a (Groningen) Old Flemish or Ukowallist congregation, concerning whose rise and historical development there is no information, but which was in existence by 1660. The two groups united on Aug. 24, 1767. The Old Flemish group had a church at the Kolleweg; this chapel, called "De Schollenberg," which had been the property of the deacon David Joosten (Vissering) was purchased in 1771. It was razed in 1825, and a new church erected with a pleasant garden on the Wörde. A wing was added to accommodate a sexton's apartment and rooms for the church council and for catechism. Two years later an organ was installed. Leer was probably one of the first German Mennonite churches to have an organ. For some years it accompanied only Dutch singing. In fact the services were conducted in Dutch until the 1870's. Untrained preachers of the Old Flemish congregation were Lubbert Alberts ca. 1680, Harmen Geerts ca. 1685, Jan Hendriks 1713-ca.40, Jan Warners 1721-ca.42, and Harmen Berentsz Alringh 1742-ca.58.

The last lay preacher of the Flemish congregation at Leer resigned in 1728. For a few years the church was served by Dutch preachers (*DB* 1896, 147). Then Cornelius van Campen, also an untrained preacher, was called and ordained as an elder. In the meantime the East Frisian churches centered more and more around Leer, especially in negotiating with the government in financial matters (Müller, 159 ff.). Van Campen introduced a church register, having received government permission to do so. At the same time Norden was also ordered to keep a church record (Müller, 1710). After van Campen (1729-63) the following served the congregation as pastor: Reinhard Rahusen of Hamburg 1763-85; P. Beets 1785-89; Hendrick Janssen 1789-1829; P. Feenstra 1829-36; J. Leendertz 1837-77; A. G. van Gilse 1878-90; and S. F. van der Ploeg 1891-1920.

The membership of both the Old Flemish and the Flemish congregations always was small. The Old Flemish congregation numbered about 50 baptized members in 1710, 40 in 1733, and 29 in 1754. Of the Flemish congregation there are no figures available before the merger of 1767. The united congregation numbered about 50 baptized members in 1780, 59 in 1840, 73 in 1861, 57 in 1898, *ca.* 20 in 1935, and 43 in 1955.

After 1920 the pulpit was not filled, and the congregation affiliated with the Mennonite church at Emden, A. Fast serving as pastor here as well as at Emden. After the destruction of Emden in World War II, Pastor Fast made his residence in Leer for a time. The Leer church was incorporated in 1908 and is a member of the Vereinigung. Earlier it had become a member of the Dutch A.D.S. and other Dutch Mennonite associations, and drew its preachers largely from Holland.   vDZ.

J. P. Müller, *Die Mennoniten in Ostfriesland* (Amsterdam, 1887); Blaupot t. C., *Groningen* I and II, *passim*, see Index; *Inv. Arch. Amst.* II, Nos. 2794 f.; G. ten Cate, *Geslachtslijst van de familie Vissering* (n.p., 1903); *DB* 1879, 8; 1902, 226; *DJ* 1840, 46; *Naamlijst* 1731 ff.; *ML* II, 627 f.

Leermens, a village in the Dutch province of Groningen (*q.v.*), where there have always been Mennonites since the earliest times. Obbe Philips worked here and won many followers. A congregation was organized, which like most in this province later joined the Old Flemish branch. After a period of decline it united in 1783 with another small congregation at Loppersum. The church is now listed as the Leermens-Loppersum congregation. The membership was always small. Before the merging with Loppersum the baptized membership numbered about 75 in 1710, 70 in 1733, 50 in 1754, and 30 in 1767. It was long served by lay preachers: Klaas Tonnys until about 1754, Pieter Jans 1719 until his death in 1760, Sievert Pieters 1739 until his death in 1778, Pieter Klaassen 1752 until his death in 1760, Jacob Tietes (Huizinga) after 1763. After the union it was also served by lay preachers, Jacob Tietes of Leermens serving until his death July 29, 1821. Then the pulpit was vacant until 1836, when Claas Bakker, trained at the Amsterdam Mennonite Seminary, became pastor. He served until his death in 1884 and was followed by Alje Muller 1888-1905, Frederik ten Cate 1907-12, L. G. Holtz 1914-18, R. C. de Lange 1919-23, A. P. van de Water 1925-28, F. J. de Holl 1929-34, Miss H. C. Leignes Bakhoven 1934-40, H. A. M. den Herder 1942-46, S. J. Bouma 1946-53, H. J. Witteveen since 1953.

The membership of the united Leermens-Loppersum congregation was about 35 when the two congregations merged in 1783, 42 in 1836, 91 in 1898, 90 in 1956. Originally meetings were held both in Leermens and Loppersum, later in Leermens only, where there was a simple meetinghouse. This was abandoned in 1848 after a new meetinghouse—improved in 1927 and still in use—had been built in Zeerijp, now the center of the congregation, where a parsonage was built in 1835. An organ was not installed until 1908. In 1834 the Leermens-Loppersum congregation received the property of the neighboring congregation of Appingedam (*q.v.*), which was then dissolved. In 1912 the female members were given the same rights as the male. Church activities now (1956) include a Sunday school for children.   vDZ.

Blaupot t. C., *Groningen* I and II, *passim*; see Index; *Inv. Arch. Amst.* II, Nos. 2040 f.; *Naamlijst* 1829, 64; *DJ* 1837, 32 f.; 1840, 42; 1850, 58; *DB* 1877, 108; 1879, 4; *ML* II, 628.

Leetonia Mennonite Church (MC), in Leetonia, Columbiana Co. (*q.v.*), Ohio, is one of three Mennonite churches lying within a 7-mile radius and extending across the boundary line of Columbiana and Mahoning counties. All are members of the Ohio Mennonite and Eastern Conference (MC). For the first three quarters of a century the three meetinghouses—Metzler's or North Lima and Oberholser's or Midway three or four miles southwest, both in Mahoning County (*q.v.*), and Nold's or Leetonia three or four miles south of Midway—served as meeting places for church services for one congregation. This Mennonite settlement was one of the oldest as well as one of the largest in Ohio. Services were held at each church once a month. The fourth Sunday was kept open for visiting. Metzler's was erected in 1824, Oberholser's in 1825, and Leetonia in 1828. Jacob Oberholser, a Mennonite minister, his family of 21 children were among the first settlers to arrive in 1807 from Bucks Co., Pa. He donated a plot of ground for the first log church. Jacob Nold, also from Bucks County, settled in the southern part of the settlement, organized services there in 1819, and donated the land on which Nold's was erected in 1828. Metzler and other settlers from Lancaster County settled in the northern part, where he donated a plot of ground for Metzler's near North Lima. Bishop Nold and his friends from eastern Pennsylvania were not accustomed to practice the ordinance of footwashing. But wishing to have fellowship with the other Ohio ministers, Nold made strenuous efforts to persuade his friends to practice the ordinance. He made many visits to the Mennonite settlements extending across northern Ohio and western Pennsylvania, preaching, ordaining ministers, and administering communion.

Beginning in 1892 services were held at Midway every other Sunday for the entire settlement and on the intervening Sundays at both North Lima and Leetonia. More recently for a number of years Leetonia had a separate Sunday-school organization and met every Sunday. North Lima and Midway each had its own Sunday-school officers but the entire Sunday school met at the two churches on alternate Sundays. Since about 1950 each of the three has been considered as a separate congregation with not only its own Sunday-school officers and its own ministers but also its own bishop. Following Jacob Nold, Joseph Bixler served as bishop, then John Burkholder, then for many years A. J. Steiner. In recent years he assisted in the ordination of Paul Yoder, bishop at Midway, his son David at North Lima, and Stephen A. Yoder at Leetonia. Communion services were customarily held at Midway in the fall but in 1946 by vote of the Leetonia congregation communion was held there for the first time. The present membership at Leetonia (1954) is 113, at Midway 159, and at North Lima 149.   J.S.U.

Leeuw (Leeu, Leu), a Mennonite family, originally from the Rhineland, Germany, since the 17th century found as businessmen in Haarlem and Amsterdam, where they were members of the

Flemish congregations and became quite wealthy. Members of this family married into the de Bosch, Rutgers, de Flines, Block, van Lennep, van der Heyden, and van Heyst families. Ameldonck Leeuw, a Mennonite preacher or elder at Cologne, signed the Concept of Cologne of 1591 for this congregation. Already in 1569 he seems to have been a preacher at Cologne (*Inv. Arch. Amst.* I, No. 466). Some of his grandchildren lived at Emmerich, from where they moved to Haarlem, Holland. This family was also found in Nijmegen, Dutch province of Gelderland, where Thomas Ameldonck Leeuw and his son Jan Ameldonck Leeuw were preachers, Thomas until his death in 1689, Jan 1690-*ca*. 1714. After the early 18th century the family name disappears from the Mennonite records, the descendants apparently having gone over to the Reformed Church. An Ameldonck Leeuw (d. after 1674) published in 1670 a musical tragedy entitled *De Toveres Circe, treuerspel met Kunst en Vliegwerken, Nieuw muzyk en Baletten.* vDZ.

Leeuwarden, capital (1953 pop. 79,960; 1,898 Mennonites in 1947) of the Dutch province of Friesland, is the seat of a large Mennonite congregation (1,020 baptized members in 1956), which is the oldest congregation of Friesland and one of the oldest in the Netherlands. This congregation can be traced back to Melchior Hofmann (*q.v.*), who preached here in 1532 among a group of adherents, among whom was Obbe Philips; Hofmann's followers mostly belonged to the middle classes. Undoubtedly the Anabaptist group at first led a hidden existence. In the fall of 1533 two apostles of Jan Matthijsz (*q.v.*) of Haarlem, viz., Bartel Boeckbinder (Bartholomeus van Halle) and Dirck Cuper (Kuiper), visited the group and baptized Obbe Philips and Hans Scheerder, 14 or 15 persons being present. The next day both Obbe and Hans were ordained as elders. In the following years there were at Leeuwarden only slight traces of Münsterism. Menno Simons often visited the congregation, the last time in 1557. Elder Leenaert Bouwens baptized here as follows: 1551-54, 26 persons; 1554-56, 34; 1563-65, 198; 1568-82, 247; a total of 505.

Both the first and the last Anabaptist martyr put to death in the Netherlands were executed at Leeuwarden. The first was Sicke Freerks Snyder on March 20, 1531, the last Reytse Aysesz on April 23, 1574. The martyr Elisabeth Dirks (*q.v.*), who was executed on May 27, 1549, was a member of the Leeuwarden congregation and is said "to have seduced many persons."

The congregation of Leeuwarden played a part in the Frisian-Flemish schism in 1566-67. About 1560 the elders, preachers, and deacons of four congregations (Leeuwarden, Dokkum, Franeker, and Harlingen), without the knowledge of the members, made a secret agreement of 19 articles (*Verbond der Vier Steden,* see *DB* 1893), which was one of the causes of the Frisian-Flemish quarrel.

In Leeuwarden there were at the close of the 17th century at least three congregations:

(1) A Flemish congregation meeting near the "Waag" (municipal weigh-house). Of this congregation there is not much information; it is said to

have numbered about 200 members in 1695, being at that time the largest Mennonite group in the city. On June 21, 1705, it merged with the Waterlander congregation.

(2) An Old Frisian (Janjacobsz group) congregation (in *Naamlijst* erroneously called Old Flemish), meeting at the "Zwitsers waltje"; it was founded about 1600, and greatly prospered in the early 17th century. (In 1603-12 Elder Jacob Theunisz baptized 97 persons here.) In 1695 its membership numbered only 21, and in 1758 the few remaining members joined the United Waterlander-Flemish congregation. Their last preachers were Jan Gerbens until about 1740, Siebrand Douwes 1715-*ca*.50, Hendrik Benedictus *ca*.1750, Meinert Daniels 1741-58, who still served the United congregation after the merger until he resigned in 1769, and Pieter Cornelis van 't Veer 1752-58.

(3) A Waterlander congregation, which met at the Wirdumerdijk, which had about 100 baptized members in 1695. The oldest meetinghouse has disappeared; a new frame meetinghouse was built in 1631; it was completely renovated in brick in 1760, rebuilt in 1760, and again rebuilt and enlarged in 1850 as may be seen by a commemorative stone tablet. Other renovations took place in 1889 and later. The old pulpit and organ of the Amsterdam Toren (*q.v.*) meetinghouse, which had been in the Amsterdam Zonist church, were bought by the Leeuwarden congregation and installed on June 20, 1813.

(4) There probably was also a Frisian congregation, although nothing is known about it.

(5) Of a High German congregation there is only one literary trace. It must have merged with the Waterlander congregation before 1647.

(6) A congregation of Pieter Jeltjes-volk (*q.v.*) is also mentioned here.

The Mennonites of Leeuwarden had much trouble with the city magistrates until the 18th century. In 1596 the Reformed preacher Ruardus Acronius (*q.v.*) obtained permission from the magistrates to enter the meetings of the Mennonites "op het Niewland" (i.e., of the Waterlanders on the Wirdumerdijk) to interrupt the preacher. This led to the Leeuwarden disputation (*q.v.*) of 1596. Especially Johannes Bogerman, who was a Reformed minister at Leeuwarden 1604-26 and professor at the Franeker University 1636-37, opposed the Mennonites. He succeeded in setting the magistrates against the Mennonites. In 1631 Lamberts Jacobs (*q.v.*), the Waterlander preacher, was fined twice because he had ventured to preach in the new church against the will of the government. Especially the Janjacobsz group occupied the attention of the authorities. They were exhorted by the magistrates in 1670 and 1675; perhaps their strict practices of banning and shunning gave the government a justifiable reason to take action. In 1687 Jacob Jansen Voogt, preacher of the Waterlander congregation, was banished because of Socinianism (*q.v.*), but residing in the city was permitted and even preaching, on condition that he be examined beforehand by the Reformed ministers. There is also evidence that the city government was kindly disposed to the Mennonites. Marcelis Goverts, a Mennonite, was appointed city architect and when he and his wife, Mayke Marcus, founded a Hofje (home for old women) on Dec. 11, 1658, which was presented to the deacons of the Waterlander congregation on Aug. 16, 1659, the Court of Friesland gave its approval notwithstanding the fact that the Reformed Church of Leeuwarden contested the right of the Mennonites to administer the old people's home.

Since 1758 there has been only one Mennonite congregation in Leeuwarden. In that year the baptized membership may have numbered about 370. In 1834 it had decreased to 270, but from then there has been a considerable growth: 533 in 1861, 941 in 1898, 1,020 in 1956.

In the 17th and 18th centuries Collegiantism (q.v.) had a rather strong influence on the Mennonite congregation. Arrien Jansen in 1682 disturbed the congregation by his ideas that baptism be administered only by immersion, and that the Lord's Supper should not be held in the morning, as was usual, but during the night. Those who favored baptism by immersion built a large stone tub in the floor of the meetinghouse, in which baptism was administered by immersion a few times. The appearance of the tub was a source of unrest in the congregation and a schism threatened. The provincial government of Friesland on Feb. 15, 1720, ordered the tub removed. However, this did not happen before 1850, although baptism by immersion had dropped out of use and peace had returned. But Arrien Jansen and his followers, who had separated from the main body in August 1720, were not reaccepted as members until January 1726.

During the years following the French Revolution there was another conflict in the congregation. Its preacher Abraham Staal, who served beginning 1788 (before this time he had been a Lutheran minister), and who was a fanatical Patriot (q.v.), was dismissed from his position in 1792 because the majority of the members did not share his views. On July 14, 1797, he was received again into the ministry on the order of the city government, but soon afterwards the congregation and Pastor Staal came to an agreement, the latter voluntarily resigning. Other ardent Patriots in this city were the Mennonites Oene K. Gorter and Dirk Zeper.

For a long time the Leeuwarden congregation was served by lay ministers. Among them were Claes Karsten Tigler 1680-1725, his son Djurre Clases Tigler (years of service unknown), Here Fedes Tigler 1716-ca.50, Dirk Uptes Oldersma 1726-ca.51, Uilke Wytzes de Vries 1726-62, Heert Michiels 1726-ca.80, and Claas Koopmans 1772-ca.1800. Usually there were four or five ministers. The first minister of the Leeuwarden congregation to be educated at the Amsterdam Mennonite Seminary was Klaas Tigler (q.v.), a grandson of Claes Karsten Tigler and son of Djurre Clases Tigler. He served 1750-85. In 1753 two other trained ministers were called; viz., Siebolt (van) Abbema 1753-66, and Jacobus Hesseling 1753-91. They were followed by Jan Menalda 1764-71 and Pieter Brouwer 1785-87.

Until about 1800 there were in the congregation, besides the trained preachers, also two or three lay preachers chosen from the congregation. Jan Brouwer, called in 1793, was the only preacher

from 1805 until he resigned in 1822. He was followed by Cornelis S. van Geuns 1822-27, Jan Pol 1827-49, Abraham Allard Hulshoff 1845-70, Matthijs van Geuns Cornszn 1849-88, P .W. Feenstra 1870-97, P. K. Bijl 1888-92, P. Zondervan 1892-1924, M. L. Deenik 1897-1931, J. D. Dozy 1926-33, J. IJntema 1931-36, L. Bonga 1934-52, F. van der Wissel 1937-57, Th. van Veen 1953- , J. T. Nielsen 1957- . The congregation has an old people's home, called the Marcelis Goverts-gasthuis, and in 1925 acquired a room for youth meetings and other church activities in the Ruiterskwartier. In 1952 the room for the church board, in which are found three beautiful paintings by the artist Lambert Jacobsz, who was preacher of the Leeuwarden congregation until 1636, and also the rooms for catechetical classes were rebuilt. Church activities in 1956 included a choir, women's circle, men's circle, young members' group of the 18-30 years, youth group, and Sunday school for children. In 1954 two stained glass windows by Joep Nicolas were installed in the church, representing the miraculous draught of fish (John 21) and the footwashing incident (John 13).   J.Y., vDZ.

Blaupot t. C., Friesland, passim, see Index; Inv. Arch. Amst. I, Nos. 5, 237, 241 f., 356, 375, 493; II, Nos. 99, 2042-47; II, 2 No. 252; Naamlijst 1815, 97 f.; DJ 1850, 44; DB 1861, 138; 1874, 59-76; 1893, 1 ff., passim; 1900, 90; 1917, 125; 1918, 110, note I; W. Eekhoff, Geschiedkundige beschrijving van Leeuwarden II, 111; ML II, 628-30.

Leeuwarden Disputation. By 1572 the northern Netherlands had in large part cast off the Spanish yoke. This event opened a new chapter in Mennonite history. The time of blood-witnessing was past. The last martyr in the northern Netherlands, Reytse Aysesz (q.v.), died on April 23, 1574, in Leeuwarden.

The epoch of tolerance gradually opened. The government usually closed an eye and permitted the Mennonies to meet unmolested. This tolerance is to a great extent the merit of William of Orange, who had learned to know the Mennonites as industrious citizens and several times came to their defense (see **Middelburg**). His son, Prince Maurice, followed his father's example. This attitude also accorded with the Utrecht Union (1579), which stipulated that "every one shall be free in his religion, no one shall be arrested or examined on account of his faith."

Nonetheless this position was not everywhere adhered to. Calvinism, which had grown powerful in its resistance of Spain, was by nature intolerant. The Reformed Synod of Dordrecht had already in 1574 taken up the struggle with the Anabaptists; they decided to request the government not to tolerate anyone who would not swear to obey the government and to demand that all children be baptized; that the Reformed preachers should be permitted to attend the meetings of the sectarians in order to convert them. Marnix van St. Aldegonde (q.v.) even favored capital punishment for them.

The Mennonites suffered much at the hands of the Reformed clergy. The resolutions of synods against them are innumerable. Even in Friesland, where the census of 1586 revealed that one fourth of the population was Mennonite, the Reformed Church created many difficulties for them. The government edict of Harlingen (April 7, 1581), that no religion should be practiced except the Reformed, gave them a certain right to suppress the Anabaptists. The government was little inclined to yield to the demands of the preachers to close the Mennonite meetinghouses. Peter van Coelen (*q.v.*) confesses in the Leeuwarden disputation, that "this praiseworthy government has hitherto granted us religious liberty in all kindness and courtesy" (*Protocol,* p. 17), and that "we may live in liberty according to our conscience under our praiseworthy government" (*Protocol,* p. 438).

Nevertheless the provincial States of Friesland had consented in 1584 that all ministers should have free entry into the meetings of the sects, and the sectarian preacher was obliged to reply to everything that was refuted with God's Word.

Ruardus Acronius (*q.v.*), Reformed preacher in Cornjum and assistant preacher in Leeuwarden, a hothead, acrimonious and implacable, who was often in conflict with his own party, made use of the edict mentioned above. In 1594 he entered a Mennonite meeting at Nieuwland near Leeuwarden to dispute with them but the congregation rose and left. Then he tried it in Cornjum. He entered the house of Jelmer Simons, where the brewer Isbrand Isbrands of Leeuwarden was preaching. This time derisive words met him. Acronius, thoroughly angered, complained openly that the Mennonites were rapidly expanding and would not dispute. Isbrand Isbrands, called to account, replied that he was not capable of disputing, and did not expect any results from it anyway.

Thereupon Acronius published a report on this meeting (July 1, 1595). His charges were answered by Peter van Coelen in writing (Aug. 19, 1595), who although he was nearly 70 years old, offered himself for a disputation.

The disputation was held in the Galilean church at Leeuwarden (*q.v.*) Aug. 16-Nov. 17, 1596 (see article **Disputations**, where the eleven points of debate are given). The two speakers officially had equal rights; Peter was permitted to state his terms, and some of them were accepted. He was permitted to choose a secretary. Only his request that some Mennonites should be among the chairmen was refused.

The manner in which the debate was carried on by both sides was rude. The request of the chair to avoid all acrimoniousness was not observed. Acronius began to speak of Münsterite descent and paid little attention to Peter's ideas. Peter spun his speeches out much too long, and his tone was usually hostile. In the 54th session the chair limited the speeches on both sides, and in the 107th he urged them to refrain from unfriendly words. But especially Acronius continued to speak with great bitterness. Nor was the chair quite neutral, although Peter in his thanks at the conclusion of the disputation said the chairmen conducted themselves properly and not like those parties (the Reformed). The outcome was that each was still of the same opinion as before. But the Reformed proclaimed themselves the victors.

The *Protocol,* a stately volume of 502 pages, was printed by Gillis van den Rade (Aegidius Radaeus) at Franeker. It was provided with a foreword of 52 pages, in which the Stadholder and the Frisian States expressed their opinion about the debate and its results. This foreword is a very biased and libelous piece of writing. Acronius is called " our dear, valued, and very faithful servant of the Word of God," and Peter's speeches are "long-winded discourses." Peter was "completely, faithfully on the basis of God's Word" refuted. The foreword closes thus:

"Because it is well known that the Anabaptists plant and cherish nothing but shameful and terrible errors, which overthrow the foundation of our eternal salvation and destroy the well-being of the churches, we wish to ask each of our dear and faithful subjects and other lovers of the truth . . . that they be on their guard against the sect and doctrine of the Anabaptists as a ruinous evil. Even though they are everywhere tolerated for special reasons, they are still like those who in hypocrisy speak lies (I Tim. 4:2), whose doctrine eats like a cancer (II Tim. 2:17)."

An immediate consequence of the debate was the decision by the Frisian States that Mennonite religious services were forbidden in Friesland. When the prohibition was violated in Leeuwarden, the Mennonite preachers were severely fined and many were forbidden to engage in business. Jan Jacobsz of Harlingen was banished from Friesland in 1600.

In the following period, however, the Mennonites were tolerated in spite of many complaints by the synods. Early in the 17th century many Mennonite churches were built. Now and then the spirit of persecution flared up. But with few exceptions, the government no longer interfered. An official disputation like that at Leeuwarden was not held in Holland again. (*ML* II, 630 f.)   vdZ.

Leeuwe (Leeuwen), **Claes van,** was a rector of the Latin school at Zutphen, Dutch province of Gelderland, where he died in 1549. When it became known that he had been a Mennonite, having been baptized upon his faith, his corpse was exhumed and buried in unconsecrated earth. His wife Cornelia (*q.v.*) died as a martyr. (*DB* 1881, 42, note 1.)   vdZ.

Legal Status. The legal right of Mennonites to the free exercise of their religion as expressed in decrees of rulers, or legislation by the political units in which they lived, is treated in the article *Religious Liberty.* The following discussion relates solely to the legal rights of the Mennonites as ecclesiastical bodies to hold property and function under the law as legal persons. The discussion as it relates to Mennonites in Europe is based on the article *Körperschaftsrechte* in the *Mennonitisches Lexikon.* In that article Christian Hege reports the historical development of the legal status of Mennonite churches in Prussia on the basis of the pamphlet by Gustav Reimer, *Sind die Mennoniten-Gemeinden in Preussen und in der freien Stadt Danzig Körperschaften des öffentlichen Rechts?* (Heubuden, 1920), while J. Yntema reports only briefly on the situation in the Netherlands.

Since the Anabaptists never enjoyed full legal toleration anywhere in Europe there never was any possibility for their congregations to have a juridical legal status or to hold property. The Mennonites did not enjoy full legal toleration and a corresponding legal status in any country in Europe until the turn of the 18th-19th century. This came first in Holland in 1795 as a result of the French Revolution when the state church was disestablished and all religious groups were given equal rights. Since then every Dutch Mennonite congregation can become a legal entity. At first, permission and approval of the congregation's constitution was necessary, but now only the delivery of a declaration to the proper governmental office is necessary. The congregations are autonomous and have full power to hold property, to receive and administer all funds including legacies, and in general to function as juridical persons. The A.D.S. (*q.v.*) and other conferences, though not incorporated, have the rights of a legal person.

In Switzerland and France the development was similar to that in the Netherlands. The French Revolution finally brought a large measure of freedom although full legal status did not come until later in the 19th century.

In Germany the legal status of Mennonite congregations was long confused. In practice the grants and permissions given to Mennonite congregations by rulers or state authorities meant that the congregations could in reality hold property (own meetinghouses) and receive legacies, etc., as the fully recognized state churches did. However, full legal recognition did not come until quite late, for instance, in Prussia in 1874 when a special law was passed, called "The Law of June 12, 1874, Pertaining to the Conditions of the Mennonites." Even here incorporation was not a right, but could be "granted by joint agreement of the Minister of Justice, the Minister of the Interior, and the Minister of Religious Affairs"; and certain conditions had to be met. In the other German states the granting of full legal status, including the right of incorporaton, proceeded in a variable fashion, some earlier and some later than in Prussia. The right to become a registered association (*Eingetragener Verein*), which carried much the same privileges as the incorporated body (*Körperschaft des öffentlichen Rechts*) enjoyed, including ownership of property, came earlier and more easily than the right of incorporation. A basic change was brought about by the Constitution of the Republic of 1919, which placed all religious bodies on the same legal footing. Basically in Germany today only an associated group of congregations can become an incorporated body, while individual congregations remain registered associations. The conference known as the *Vereinigung der Deutschen Mennonitengemeinden* (formerly *Vereinigung der Mennonitengemeinden im Deutschen Reich*) was the first German Mennonite incorporated body (Nov. 8, 1922, in Hamburg). The Bavarian Mennonite congregations were incorporated as a Vereinigung Aug. 31, 1926, and each separate congregation received the right to incorporate on March 16, 1928. All did this except Ingolstadt. The South German Conference called the *Badisch-Württ.-Bayerischer Gemeindeverband* has remained a registered association.

In the United States and Canada the legal status of churches is regulated by the laws of the several states and provinces, not by national federal legislation. The common practice has been for such congregations not to become incorporated. Congregational property and money are usually held by trustees (commonly three in number) who can usually act as a legal person. On the other hand church boards (mission, education, publication, etc.) and institutions (schools, homes for the aged, hospitals, etc.) are usually incorporated with boards of trustees. The general conferences of the separate branches are sometimes incorporated, e.g., those of the General Conference Mennonite Church and the Mennonite Brethren Church, but not that of the Mennonite Church (MC). The Mennonite Central Committee (*q.v.*) was not incorporated until 1937 (in Pennsylvania) and then chiefly in order to hold property.

In the United States and Canada churches, church boards, and institutions of the nonprofit type, whether corporated or unincorporated, are exempt from taxation, and are usually incorporated under nonprofit corporation acts.   H.S.B.

Legeder, Mathes, an Anabaptist of Tirol, Austria (perhaps from Klausen; a citizen of Klausen named Martin Ledeger migrated to Moravia in 1542), who was chosen deacon at Steinabrunn in 1537. Probably on his way to Tirol with a message from Moravia, he was seized and imprisoned in Sterzing in 1541. In December 1542 he was sentenced to galley service; but he had already escaped and returned to Moravia. In 1551 he was ordained preacher at Schackwitz. He wrote two songs in prison with Christel Lissner (*q.v.*). One begins, "Nun hört, ich will euch singen, wie es vor Augen ist," 22 stanzas (*Die Lieder,* 303-5); the other begins, "Nun hert, was ich euch singen will, die Frommen miessen leiden viel," 24 stanzas (Wolkan, *Lieder,* 229; *Die Lieder der Hutterischen Brüder,* 313-18). Legeder died in 1552 at Bergen near Nikolsburg. He is said to have foretold his death a week before.   P.DE.

Beck, *Geschichts-Bücher;* Zieglschmid, *Chronik,* 181, 227, 340, 342; Loserth, *Anabaptismus;* Wolkan, *Geschicht-Buch; Die Lieder der Hutterischen Brüder* (Scottdale, 1914); *ML* II, 631 f.

Legemeer, a hamlet in the Dutch province of Friesland, not far from Joure, where Elder Jakob Theunis baptized 14 persons in 1603-18. The minutes of the Frisian Sociëteit show that in 1700 there were 33 members here not in need of support. In 1726 Legemeer was still giving a small annual sum for foreign relief. About 1725, after the pulpit had been vacant for nearly half a century, partial union was made with the neighboring congregation of Sloten (*q.v.*); about 1755 this union was dissolved, the preacher of Legemeer then also serving at Sloten. A merger of the two congregations was brought about in 1775, but in 1789 the few remaining members of the Sloten-Legemeer congregation joined the Balk (*q.v.*) congregation.   vDZ.

Blaupot t. C., *Friesland,* 164, 189, 306; *Naamlijst* 1808, 83; *DB* 1895, 12, 20; *ML* II, 632.

Lehigh, a town (pop. 200) in Marion Co., Kan., where State Highway 15 crosses U.S. Highway N. 50. About 80 per cent of the population are Mennonites, belonging to the G.C.M., M.B., and K.M.B. branches. The Seventh-Day Adventist, Lutheran, and M.B. churches have discontinued in recent years, leaving only the Lehigh Mennonite Church (GCM) in town. Lehigh is in the midst of Mennonite settlements, with M.B. headquarters (Hillsboro) 6 miles to the east and G.C.M. headquarters (Newton) 23 miles to the south. Unique in Lehigh are its streets, which were laid out according to early wagon trails and the Santa Fe Railroad.   P.W.G.

Lehigh County (pop. 198,207), located in eastern Pennsylvania, has approximately 1,400 Mennonites, who live mainly in the southern part of the county. The settlement extends into Northampton and Bucks counties. Two thirds of the Mennonites (Allentown, 2 congregations, Coopersburg, Emmaus, Macungie, and Zionsville) are members of the six congregatons of the Mennonite Brethren in Christ Church, the rest being members of the three congregations (Allentown, Saucon, Upper Milford) of the Eastern District Conference (GCM), and of one congregation of the Franconia Conference (MC), the Allentown Mission.

The first settlers arrived sometime before 1735, building a church near Coopersburg in 1738 and one near Zionsville in 1740. The first M.B.C. church was built near Zionsville in 1858. The M.B.C. Church maintains a home for the aged in Center Valley, the Berean Bible School in Allentown, and Mizpah Grove, a campmeeting grounds.   M.S.

D. K. Cassel, *Geschichte der Mennoniten* (Philadelphia, 1890) 126-28; J. A. Huffman, *History of the Mennonite Brethren in Christ Church* (New Carlisle, 1920) 68 f.; E. R. Storms, *Mennonite Brethren in Christ Handbook* (Kitchener, 1948); J. C. Wenger, *History of the Mennonites of the Franconia Conference* (Telford, 1937) 20, 224, 337.

Lehigh Mennonite Brethren Church at Lehigh, Marion Co., Kan., a member of the Southern District Conference, was organized Aug. 27, 1884, under the leadership of David Dick. The membership fluctuated from 100 in 1890, 23 in 1892, 42 in 1897, 100 in 1928, to 52 in 1953. Miss Anna Enns, a missionary to Africa, was ordained in 1945. Ministers who have served the congregation are Jacob B. Wiens, Cornelius Knaak, Jacob J. Harder, A. J. Boese, Gerhard Bartel, John A. Nickel, John A. Harder, Jacob J. Kroeker, G. A. Flaming, William Neufeld, and P. R. Lange.

In 1955 the Lehigh congregation was amalgamated with the Gnadenau congregation of the K.M.B. Conference; the combined congregation is now operating as the Gnadenau Mennonite Brethren Church, with a membership of about 200. Franklin Jost is the pastor.   P.C.H.

Lehigh (Kan.) Mennonite Church (GCM) is a member of the Western District Conference. There were a few Mennonite families living in and around Lehigh before 1890, who met for worship in an old frame school building. On Dec. 12, 1900, the congregation was organized, and in 1906 the first church was built. In 1901 evangelists P. J. Krause and C. C. Heidebrecht were ordained as ministers. The latter resigned soon afterward; Krause served until his death in 1917. He was followed by F. G. Pankratz,

who served until 1925, Gustav Frey, who served for six years, Gerhard Friesen, and B. H. Janzen. In 1947 the present pastor, Peter W. Goering, accepted the charge. The church was enlarged in 1926, remodeled in 1945. The 1954 membership is 227.
P.W.G.

Lehighton Mennonite Brethren in Christ Church, located in Carbon Co., Pa., was organized in 1895. In 1953 the congregation had 68 members with J. B. Layne serving as pastor.   E.W.B.

Lehman (Lehmann, Layman, Leemann, Leeman, Leaman), a Mennonite family name originating in the Emmental, canton of Bern, Switzerland. The name means a person living on a gentle slope (*Lehn*). Near Langnau, the original home of most of the Mennonite Lehman families, there is a farm named Lehn, because of its topography. Wilhelm Lehman of Afterleen near Hassli in the Emmental is the earliest Anabaptist of this family of whom we have record. He was imprisoned in October 1566 because he refused to take the oath of allegiance. He testified to his faith when questioned as did also his wife. He was sentenced to death by the sword. After eleven days of anxious waiting for his execution he did take the oath and was pardoned. During the difficult times of the first two decades of the 18th century most of the Lehmans left their Emmental home. Some went to the Palatinate, others to Alsace or the Bishopric of Basel, and some to Pennsylvania. Felix Lehman, a peasant of Hirslanden-Zürich, Switzerland, was rebaptized by Heinrich Winckler as early as 1526 (*TA Zürich,* 134).

The Dutch *Naamlijst* names Hans Lehmann, preacher from 1761, elder from 1772, and Peter Lehmann, preacher from 1750, both in Switzerland, Jacob Lehmann (d. *ca.* 1780), preacher of the Schafbusch congregation in Lower Alsace, Johannes Lehmann, preacher 1745-*ca.* 80, and Ulrich Lehmann, preacher 1783 until after 1802, both of the Freudenberg congregation in the duchy of Zweibrücken, and Johannes Lehmann, elder of the Heppenheim congregation (Palatinate) from 1782 until after 1802.

Hans Lehman landed in Philadelphia on Sept. 27, 1727, and settled near Lititz, Lancaster Co., Pa. His descendants are numerous in Lancaster County and adjoining counties and have representatives in many of the Mennonite congregations in the eastern United States and Canada. Many of his descendants have served as leaders in the church.

As early as 1718 a Lehman family found its way to the Jura from the Emmental settling near Münster, and a short time later members of this family settled at Vion on the Sonnenberg, where descendants live to this day. Hans Lehmann, a bishop in the Jura from 1772 on, with four other Jura bishops journeyed to the Palatinate in 1782 to bring peace to the divided church there.

In 1819 Peter Lehmann (1776-1843) came to America to help form the first 19th-century Swiss Mennonite settlement in this country in Wayne Co., Ohio, naming it Sonnenberg after the old home in the Jura. Two years later a bishop, Hans Lehman, came to join this settlement. In the following years many others of this family came to this community. The family came to be found in the other Swiss

Mennonite communities, especially Berne, Ind., where it is today one of the most numerous families of that community.

Daniel Lehman (1742-1801) was the first Mennonite (GCM) minister and bishop in Franklin Co., Pa. Joseph S. Lehman (1847-1936) was business manager for the Mennonite Publishing Company, Elkhart, Ind., and also served as an evangelist. Peter Y. Lehman (1847-1925) was a minister and bishop at the Clinton Brick and Shore congregations (MC) in Indiana. He was influential in the Indiana-Michigan (MC) Conference. Peter S. Lehmann (1821-99) was a minister in Jura, Switzerland, who came with a large portion of his congregation to found Berne, Ind., in 1853. He later lived in Hickory Co., Mo., where he shepherded a small flock of Swiss Mennonites (GCM). When this community dissolved he returned to the Berne community, where he spent his last days. A. H. Leaman (1878-1950) was a mission worker (MC) and evangelist in Chicago. Daniel N. Lehman (1852-1925) was a minister and bishop at the Millersville Mennonite (MC) Church, Lancaster Co., Pa., and an energetic worker in the Lancaster Mennonite (MC) Conference. The following three ministers were his sons. Christian K. Lehman (1881-) has been a minister since 1917 and a bishop since 1938 in the Millersville district of the Lancaster Conference (MC). Chester Kindig Lehman (1895-) is a minister (MC), dean of Eastern Mennonite College 1922-56, and the author of several books and pamphlets on the Christian faith. Daniel Webster Lehman (1893-) is professor of education and psychology at Eastern Mennonite College since 1921 and a bishop in the Virginia Conference (MC) since 1947. Japhet F. Lehman (q.v., 1860-1932), of Berne, Ind., was a prominent layman in the General Conference Mennonite Church, a leader in conference publication activities, for 34 years manager of the Mennonite Book Concern of Berne. His son Gustav Adolf Lehman (1886-) taught music and directed choirs at Bluffton College and Colgate-Rochester Divinity School. Martin Clifford Lehman (1883-) was a minister (MC) and missionary to India for 24 years. J. Irvin Lehman (1895-) has been a minister since 1922 in the Marion, Pa., Mennonite (MC) Church.

In 1940 there were still 55 persons in Mennonite families in Germany, all in the south, bearing the name Lehmann. They were found in the congregations Dühren, Ernstweiler, Frankfurt, Friedelsheim, Kaiserslautern, Deutschhof, Kühbörncheshof, Möckmühl, Monsheim, and Sembach, with 23 of them in Ernstweiler. (ML II, 632.)   D.L.G.

Lehman, Japhet F. (1860-1932), a Mennonite (GCM) leader, was born June 8, 1860, at Berne, Ind., the only son and fifth of the eight children of Peter S. and Verena Sprunger Lehman, who were of Swiss birth. In February 1883 he married Elizabeth Neuenschwander of Berne. They were the parents of six children. Though Lehman's formal education was limited to 18 months in the subscription schools in Hickory Co., Mo., and three months at Moody Bible Institute in Chicago, he rendered outstanding service in many offices on church, Sunday-school, and educational boards. He was a lead-

ing member of the First Mennonite Church of Berne, and very active in the "saloon fight" at Berne. For 34 years he was the manager of the Mennonite Book Concern which was located at Berne, developing it into an important servant of the Conference. For 30 years he served on the Board of Publication of the General Conference Mennonite Church. He was always actively interested in the education of young people. In 1900 he was elected to the first Board of Trustees of Bluffton College, and remained on the Board until his death. From 1868 to 1880 the family lived in Hickory Co., Mo. He died at Berne on Nov. 13, 1932, and was buried in the M.R.E. cemetery west of Berne.   A.H.S.

Lehman, a "preaching appointment" (MC) in Ellice Twp., Perth Co., Ont., named for Jacob Lehman, a Mennonite who immigrated with his family from Alsace about 1850 and settled in Ellice Twp., southwest of the Wallace Mennonite Church (MC) at Kurtzville (q.v.). At first services were held here at three-month intervals. From 1865 appointments were every eight weeks, then later alternated with Wallace. Ministers were supplied. Communion was served from the earliest date until the membership decreased. The community consisted of Jacob's family and in-laws by the name of Weber and Shellenberger. Jacob and his wife, a Showalter, were buried at Martin's meetinghouse south of St. Jacobs; his son Christian at Wallace, and his wife, Mary Graybill, at Geiger's in Wilmot township. Cheaper land attracted these pioneers to Ellice. The close of the Mennonite testimony was due to intermarriage and some returning to organized congregations. J.C.F.

Lehner (Leener, Leenert, Leenders, Leenderts, Lienders), **Peter,** b. 1677 in Switzerland, d. 1755 at Sappemeer, Dutch province of Groningen, married to Elisabeth Rustener (or Rogener), was a farmer at Oberhofen, north of Lake Thun, Switzerland, and a preacher of the congregation. In July 1711 he was forced to emigrate to the Netherlands, where he settled on a small farm near Sappemeer. Here too he was a preacher, serving the Swiss Mennonites and after the schism of 1720 the New Swiss Brethren until his death in 1755. Poverty-stricken because of the cattle plague and other calamities, too weak by old age to administer the farm, he left it to his oldest son Christian, who succeeded in keeping his head above water by extra earning from weaving. Peter Lehner's grandson, Pieter Pieters Leenerts (Sappemeer 1750-1807), adopted the family name of van Calcar (van Calker). This Pieter van Calcar was also a preacher of the Swiss Brethren congregation (years of serving unknown). He founded a distillery at Hoogezand.   vDZ.

J. Huizinga, *Stamboek van Samuel Peter (Meihuizen) en Barbara Fry* (Groningen, 1890) 155; introduction to the *Stamboek,* 61, 115.

Lehrdienst, derived from *Lehre* (teaching) and *Dienst* (service), was a term used to designate the body of ministers of a congregation, particularly by the Mennonites of Prussia and Russia. The origin of this designation very likely goes back to the Netherlands. The chairman of the Lehrdienst was the elder (Aeltester, Oudste), who was assisted by the other ministers of the congregation. The Lehrdienst was not only responsible for the preaching in the various meetinghouses of the congregation but also in matters of discipline and business functions which are now in America taken care of primarily by the church council. The Lehrdienst of a number of congregations of one settlement was sometimes organized in the Kirchenkonvent (q.v.). At times the name Kirchenkonvent seems to have carried the same meaning as Lehrdienst. In America, where the congregations of Prusso-Russian background have adopted the one-minister system, the functions and the term Lehrdienst have become obsolete. (See also **Elder, Minister.**) C.K.

Franz Isaac, *Die Molotschnaer Mennoniten* (Halbstadt, 1908).

Lehrer (Dutch, *Leraar*), translated "teacher," the name commonly used for minister or preacher in the earlier days of the Anabaptist-Mennonite movement in Europe, and on down well into the 19th century. Its use is based on Eph. 4:11, and came into currency among the pre-Reformation sects. It was probably intended to clearly repudiate the sacerdotal and clerical concept of priest (Catholic) or official pastor (Protestant) and to emphasize the basic teaching function of the minister, who was

also commonly called *Diener des Wortes* (servant of the Word), and who was not primarily to administer sacraments but to expound, interpret, and apply the message of God's Word. H.S.B.

Lehrerkonferenz: see **Mennonite Teachers' Association.**

Lehrerleut, one of the Hutterite kinship groups, so named because their founder, Jacob Wipf, was a teacher in Russia and also in South Dakota. His group of thirteen families (a few joined the other two groups in South Dakota on arrival) was the last to come from Russia to South Dakota, arriving in 1877, the other two, the Dariusleut (q.v.) and the Schmiedeleut (q.v.), having come in 1874-75. The Lehrerleut families all came from the village of Johannisruh, Molotschna, where they had not lived in community. In South Dakota they founded the Old Elmspring Bruderhof near Parkston, which they occupied until 1932. From this original single Bruderhof twenty-two colonies had sprung by 1950, for which statistics are given below. Although the Lehrerleut are organized as a unit with their own leader (*Vorsteher*), they differ from the other two kinship groups only in very minor points, such as the wearing of buttons by the men in place of hooks and eyes. H.S.B.

Census of Lehrerleut Bruderhofs—July 1, 1957

Lehrerleut Bruderhofs in Alberta

Name of Colony	Address	Founded	Population	Head Preacher
Acadia Valley	Oyen	1952	86	Peter J. Entz
Big Bend	Woolford	1920	127	John J. Waldner
Crystal spring	Magrath	1937	97	Peter A. Entz
Elmspring	Warner	1929	122	Michael J. Mändel
Handhill	Hanna	1956	85	Samuel S. Kleinsasser
Hutterville	Magrath	1932	115	John J. Waldner
MacMillan	Cayley	1937	84	Jacob J. Wipf
Miami	New Dayton	1924	128	Peter P. Hofer
Milford	Raymond	1918	95	John P. Wipf
New Dale	Queenstown	1950	92	Samuel S. Decker
New Elmspring	Magrath	1918	85	John J. Entz
New Milford	Winfred	1951	99	John J. Hofer
New Rockport	New Dayton	1932	102	John J. Wipf
O. K. Colony	Raymond	1934	153	Jacob J. Waldner
Old Elmspring	Magrath	1918	98	Andrew J. Wurz
Rockport	Magrath	1918	125	John D. Hofer
Rocklake	Wrentham	1935	115	John A. Gross
Rosedale	Etzekom	1952	89	Michael M. Hofer
Springside	Duchess	1955	100	Joseph J. Waldner
Sunnyside	Warner	1935	135	Jacob M. Hofer

Total 2132

Lehrerleut Bruderhofs in Saskatchewan

Benck	Shaunavan	1949	95	Jacob J. Wipf
Cypress	Maple Creek	1950	50	Jacob J. Entz
Slade	Tompkins	1952	80	Andrew A. Wipf

Total 225

Lehrerleut Bruderhofs in Montana

Name of Colony	Address	Founded	Population	Head Preacher
Birch Creek	Valier	1947	125	Jacob A. Waldner
Glacier	Cut Bank	1950	115	Michael J. Entz
Hillside	Sweet Grass	1950	129	Andrew A. Wurz
Miami	Pendroy	1948	145	John P. Wipf
Milford	Augusta	1945	150	Joseph Kleinsasser
Miller Ranch	Choteau	1949	162	David D. Hofer
New Rockport	Choteau	1948	90	Peter D. Hofer
Rockport	Pendroy	1948	127	Joseph J. Waldner
		TOTAL	1043	Overall Total pop. 3,400

Thus the present (1957) total of Lehrerleut Bruderhofs is 31, and the total population is 3,400. The elder of the Lehrerleut is (1957) Peter D. Hofer.

Lehrerverein (Russia): see **Mennonite Teachers' Association.**

Leiden, a town in the Dutch province of South Holland (1953 pop. 91,632, with 626 Mennonites), where Anabaptists have been found since the earliest period, who apparently at first mostly belonged to the revolutionary branch. Unemployment and poverty among the weavers, who were numerous in this city, were a fertile matrix for revolutionary teachings, which the Anabaptist elder Cornelis Pieters of den Briel (*q.v.*) proclaimed here soon after 1530. He was active in Leiden at several times. Pieter Pietersz, alias Borrekieck, tried and executed at Amsterdam in July 1535, reports a number of names of Anabaptists at Leiden in 1534 who had been baptized by Cornelis Pietersz. In 1533 Jan Beuckelszoon (Jan van Leyden, *q.v.*) lived here. In April 1534 an attack on the city was contrived but not carried out and in January 1535 a new attack was planned but prevented by treason. At that time a number of Anabaptists were apprehended and put to death. After Münster had fallen (July 25, 1535) there were still some traces of Münsterism at Leiden, but gradually this declined and after a number of followers of Batenburg (*q.v.*) had been arrested in May 1544 the revolutionary Anabaptists disappeared. Apparently at that time a congregation of peaceful Anabaptists already existed, of whose earliest history not much is known. In 1544 Reyer Willemsz of Leiden is said to have circulated books by Menno Simons. There were some martyrs in 1552, and Leenaert Bouwens baptized 27 persons here in 1563-65. About this time or shortly thereafter a number of Mennonites came from Flanders. About the circumstances of the Mennonites during the siege of the city by Spanish soldiers in 1574, no information is available.

In the last decades of the 16th century the schisms among the Dutch Mennonites caused a number of different branches at Leiden also. About 1600 there existed four congregations: Flemish, Waterlander, Frisian, and High German. Perhaps there was also a French-speaking Waterlander congregation. Only about the Waterlander and the Flemish is there adequate information. In both the Flemish and the Waterlander congregations a number of names are found which show that its members were refugees from Flanders and especially from French Flanders: Christian names, such as Jacques, Gilles, François, family names like Hennebo, Marville (Marvilje), Tavenne, des Mulliers, du Forest, Casier (Cesaer), Le Poole, van de Walle, de Pla (le Pla), Viane, Calvaert, Bossu, le Leu, and Roynaert.

Although no figures are available, it is known that the Flemish congregation was rather small. In 1626 its preachers Francois van Achterson, Joost Cassier, and Hendrick Ongena signed the Outerman confession, while in 1632 Christiaan de Koninck and Jan Weyns of Leiden signed the Dordrecht confession. This caused a schism in the Leiden Flemish congregation. A small number, following Elder Jan Rose (*q.v.*), separated from the main body and did not return before 1663, after Rose had died. In 1639 the Frisian congregation, which had been joined by a number of High German Mennonites, merged with the Flemish church. In 1660 an old people's home, called De Hoeksteen, and intended for aged women of the congregations, was founded on Het Levendael. The congregation was conservative and a champion of strict Mennonitism. In 1660 together with the congregations of Rotterdam, Dordrecht, and Gouda, it arranged a meeting of Flemish elders and preachers, held at Leiden, June 18-23, presided over by Tieleman Jansz van Braght (*q.v.*), in which a number of church regulations were made and a strict attitude was stipulated against Galenus Abrahamsz (*q.v.*) and his followers. And after the Lammerenkrijg (*q.v.*) the Leiden Flemish congregations took the side of the Zonists (*q.v.*). On Feb. 13, 1701, it merged with the Waterlander congregation. At this time the conservative views seem to have disappeared, since in the stipulations of the union a clause is found in the formula of "benodiging" (*q.v.*) (invitation to the Lord's Supper) which is rather liberal, also admitting non-members to the communion service. The Flemish meetinghouse in the Boogaardsteeg was sold in 1726.

Of the history of the Waterlander congregation, always numbering a larger membership than the Flemish, there is more detailed information. In the early 17th century it was usually called "Duitsche en Walsche Gemeente," i.e., Dutch and Walloon congregation. It is not clear whether there was an independent Walloon (French-speaking) Waterlander congregation at Leiden; a document of 1613 was signed in French by Jean (Jan) de Mortier as bishop of the congregation of the "Valons" at Leiden, by Jan des Mulliers as preacher, and by Joost Cesaer as deacon. Possibly the French-speaking did not form an independent church, but met separately as long as the French-speaking refugees did not understand the Dutch language. There is a nearly complete list of elders, preachers, and deacons of the Leiden Waterlander congregation from 1613. Figures about the number of members are not available, except those of 1675, when the number of baptized members was 165. After that year there was a considerable decrease of membership. Most members were rather well-to-do, as is proved from legacies made to the congregation. In 1630 one of the members, Gerrit van Hoogmade, a deacon, founded an old people's home, the "Hofje" called Bethlehem. This institution, located on the Levendaal, consisted of 16 small houses facing a court, in which the inmates had separate residences. These houses and also the old gate of 1631 are still standing. The congregation was represented in 1647 at the large Waterlander meeting at Amsterdam. Since 1638 it had its meetinghouse in the Pieterskerkstraat, which, though totally rebuilt, is still in use by the Leiden congregation. From 1675 the congregation, which had joined the Lamist conference of South Holland, insisted on thorough training of ministers. When the Waterlander and Flemish congregations had merged in 1701, the total membership numbered about 300. The hoped-for growth expected from the union was not realized. In 1737 the membership was 201, in 1799, 105, and in 1847 only 43. From then on there was a considerable increase: 115 in 1861, 455 in 1902, 442 in 1934, 500 in 1955.

The two old people's homes, De Hoeksteen and Bethlehem, were merged and in 1811 the Bethlehem house was sold. The Hoeksteen-hofje was henceforth called Bethlehem. Formerly the church board was supreme in governing the church. From 1701 until about 1914 only two congregational meetings (in 1810 and 1882) were held in which the brethren of the congregation were called to give advice to the church board. The preachers were chosen by the church board, while the board, assisted by the "Groote Kerkeraad," was self-perpetuating.

In 1774 a pipe organ was built in the meetinghouse, one of the first in a Dutch Mennonite church. In 1859 the meetinghouse was completely rebuilt. In 1752 the congregation took over the care of the property of the dissolved Mennonite congregation of The Hague, administering it and caring for Mennonites living at The Hague until a new congregation was formed there in 1882. Pastor Sepp of Leiden, who had given catechetical instruction at The Hague from October 1879, also preached from then until the new congregation called its own pastor in 1883. In 1777-87 François Adriaan van der Kemp (q.v.) was preacher at Leiden. By his patriotic sympathies and his aversion to nonresistance he caused some dissension in the congregation. He was followed by Jan Kops 1788-1800, Jan van Geuns 1789-1814, Abr. de Vries 1801-3, Matthijs Siegenbeek (at the same time professor at the University of Leiden) 1804-29, Isaac Molenaar 1814-18, Anthony Doyer Thz. 1818-53, Christiaan Sepp 1854-82, Aemilius W. Wybrands 1882-86, Salvus Kutsch Lojenga 1887-1904, W. J. Kühler 1905-12, J. Wuite 1912-25, L. Bonga 1926-34, F. ten Cate 1935-43, A. J. Snaayer 1944-54, and S. L. Verheus from 1955. The members of the

Leiden congregations are found in the city of Leiden and surrounding towns Oegstgeest, Leiderdorp, Voorschoten, Katwijk, Noordwijk, Sassenheim, Rijnsburg, and Alphen aan de Rijn. Church activities include a ladies' circle, young members group, Sunday school for children. The Leiden church has four large silver communion cups of 1705 and three pewter communion pitchers of about 1750.   vdZ.

Inv. Arch. Amst. I, Nos. 82, 104, 162, 257, 261, 269, 288, 372, 613, 708, 781, 827, 907, 1081, 1126, 1415, 1562; II, Nos. 2048-72; II, 2, Nos. 253-58; Mellink, Wederdopers, 186-207; L. Knappert, De opkomst van het Protestantisme in eene Noord-Nederlandsche stad, 1908, passim; Offer, 195, 526, 578 f.; L. G. le Poole, Bijdragen tot de kennis van het Kerkelijk leven onder de Doopsgezinden te Leiden (Leiden, 1905); Verhaal van 't gene verhandelt ende besloten is in de By-eenkomste tot Leyden (Amsterdam, 1661); Blaupot t. C., Holland I and II, passim, see Index; DB 1875, 27-31; 1876, 62; 1892, 103-27; 1896, 60 f., 71; 1900, 15-19; 1907, 114, 116-20, 128-33; 1917, 149; 1918, 49, 53 f.; ML II, 634.

Leiden, een Liedeken van IIIJ *vrienden, van,* a Dutch hymn composed by Adriaen Cornelisz (q.v.), commemorating the martyrdom of Willem (Willem Matthijsz), Mariken (Marijtgen Adriaens) Dieuwertgen Jans, and Mariken Jans. These four martyrs were executed at Leiden (q.v.) in the Dutch province of South Holland. They were not put to death in 1550, as is stated in *Groot Offerboek* of 1615 and van Braght, *Martyrs' Mirror,* but in the fall of 1552. The song beginning "Eylaes ick mach wel suchten, dat nu buert so groot ellent" (Alas, I should sigh because now occurs such great misery) is found in the oldest edition of the *Lietboecxken van den Offer des Heeren* of 1562-63, of the *Nieu Liedenboeck* of 1562, and later Dutch hymnbooks. It has been republished by Wackernagel. A prose version of this hymn is found in the 17th-century Dutch martyrbook, including the *Martyrs' Mirror.* vdZ.

Offer, 578-80; Wackernagel, Lieder, 194; Wolkan, Lieder, 63, 70 f.; F. C. Wieder, De Schriftuurlijke Liedekens (The Hague, 1900) 107.

Leidsche Bundel, a Dutch Mennonite hymnbook, which took its name from Leiden where it has been printed. The official name was *Liederen ten gebruike in doopsgezinde gemeenten.* It was compiled by two Dutch Mennonite ministers, J. Sepp of Beverwijk and H. Boetje of Hengelo, who in this hymnbook published 198 hymns from other hymnaries. The first edition appeared October 1897, followed by four other editions, 1899, 1903, 1911, 1919. In 1900 an anthology of Psalms, according to the version of the Dutch Reformed Church, was added, reprinted in 1906. Besides a few old Mennonite hymnals and the hymnal of the Dutch Protestant Union (see **Protestantenbond**) the *Leidsche Bundel* was the most used hymnal until 1944. In 1900 the *Leidsche Bundel* was used by 14, in 1925 by 53 congregations.
DB 1897, 249; 1902, 15-22.)   vdZ.

Leidsche Synode (Synod of Leiden), a name sometimes used for a meeting of Flemish Mennonite elders, preachers, and deacons held June 18-23, 1660, at Leiden, Dutch province of South Holland. Of this meeting, for which the congregations of Rotterdam, Dordrecht, Gouda, and Leiden had taken the initiative, T. J. van Braght (q.v.) of Dordrecht was moderator and Bastiaan van Weenighem (q.v.) of

Rotterdam secretary. Forty-two men, representing twenty-two congregations, were present. It decided that vacant pulpits should be cared for by neighboring congregations; a plan was made to compose one confession to replace the collection of *Algemeene Belijdenissen* (this plan was never carried out), and measures were taken against progressive preachers such as Galenus Abrahamsz (*q.v.*) who were judged to have forsaken the basic doctrines of the church. The account and the resolutions of this meeting are found in *Verhaal van 't gene verhandelt ende besloten is in de Bij-eenkomste tot Leyden door eenige Doops-gezinde Leeraren en Diaconen, die men Vlamingen noemt,* published at Amsterdam, 1661.

vdZ.

Leiningen, a family of the Palatinate, Germany, which is mentioned already in the Carolingian period. From the 12th to the 19th century it controlled a large part of the Palatinate. Emich II founded the Augustinian monastery of Höningen, where Mennonites settled after the Thirty Years' War, whose descendants (Hirstein) still live there. Frederick I, progenitor of the Altleiningen line, built the castle Neuleiningen and Battenberg; Battenberg is the home of several Mennonite families (Hartmetz, Rings, Hirstein). He lived in Altleiningen castle, today a stately ruin on top of a mountain, at the foot of which the Altleiningen Mennonite church stands. Ibersheim was also for a time in the possession of the counts of Leiningen. The Friedelsheim (*q.v.*) castle, today the Mennonite parsonage, was loaned to the counts of Leiningen by the abbey of Limburg. Philip I, founder of the Leiningen-Leiningen line, introduced the Reformation in 1555. On Dec. 1, 1565, he and his brothers issued a Lutheran liturgy. The Mennonites under the rule of the counts of Leiningen enjoyed undisturbed tolerance. They were not burdened by oppression, and were not obligated to pay the protection fee required of them in the electorate. (*ML* II, 635.)

Neff.

Leisy, Isaac, August, and **Henry,** all Mennonites and brothers from Friedelsheim, Palatinate, Germany, who came to the United States in 1852, founded the Leisy Brewery in Keokuk, Iowa, in 1862. In 1872 the family purchased the brewery of Fred Haltnorth in Cleveland and transferred operations to that city. In 1935 after the repeal of prohibition, the Leisy Brewing Company was reorganized and Herbert F. Leisy, grandson of Isaac Leisy, became and still is its president. The family has not been Mennonite for several generations.

C.K.

Leisy Orphan Aid Society was incorporated in 1884 as the result of a $5,000 bequest by Jacob and Mary Strohm Leisy, of Halstead, Kan. The Society is under the control of four G.C.M. churches—First Mennonite Church (Halstead), First Mennonite Church of Christian (Moundridge), West Zion Mennonite Church (Moundridge), and Garden Township Mennonite Church. Leisy bought the present "Orphan Farm" for $3,000, one and a half miles south of Halstead. Christian Krehbiel (*q.v.*), under whose council the bequest was made and the foundation created, was in charge of handling the

benefaction. The income from the Leisy Foundation was to be used to support orphan children within the confines of home missions. The orphans were not to be over 13 years old and were to be placed with Christian families.

In order to offer a wider circle of opportunities to share in this Christian service to children and to extend the aid to homeless children, another auxiliary organization, The Mennonite Orphan and Children's Aid Society (*q.v.*), was incorporated on Oct. 4, 1893, with 35 individuals and congregations in seven states as members who contributed $5 or $100 annually, which entitled them to vote and to life membership. Membership certificates to the number of 426 were issued. Later the two societies united. In addition a Mennonite Charité (*q.v.*) was incorporated at Halstead in 1908.

There were always 12-20 children in the Society Home coming from Chicago, Kansas City, and the state of Kansas, who were gradually distributed primarily in Mennonite homes. In the 20 years, 1914-34, $8,789.60 was expended in aiding orphans. After World War I the Leisy Orphan Aid Society aided Mennonite orphans in Russia and Canada, and after World War II help was extended to Mennonite orphans in South America. The Society is still active. Most of the files have been preserved in the BeCL.

C.K.

C. E. Krehbiel and P. P. Wedel, *Fiftieth Anniversary of Leisy Orphan Aid Society* (Halstead, 1934).

Leitfaden *zum Gebrauch bei gottesdienstlichen Handlungen zunächst für die Aeltesten und Prediger der Gesamt-Mennoniten-Gemeinde in Baden und anderer mit ihr verbundenen Gemeinden* (Sinsheim, 1921). This is the title of the Minister's Manual (*q.v.*) now in use in the Mennonite churches of Baden and Württemberg. It is an almost unchanged new edition of the formulary compiled by Ulrich Hege (*q.v.*) and published in 1876 (Sinsheim), for which the Palatine formulary and the manuscript notes of Elder Christian Schmutz (*q.v.*) were used. The first part of the book contains the Apostles' Creed, Biblical benedictions, and greatly abbreviated prayers for public worship. The first section of the second part deals with the choosing and ordination of a preacher with or without the lot, the second section with the choice and dedication of a deacon, the third with baptism, including the case of persons transferring their membership from another denomination, the fourth with visiting preachers, the fifth with church discipline, the sixth with communion, the seventh with marriage, the eighth with funerals and funeral prayers. A brief appendix gives the forms of the oath valid in the German states of Prussia, Baden, Württemberg, and Bavaria. (*ML* II, 635.)

Neff.

Leitgen, a Mennonite elder, active in the Dutch province of Limburg, who died about 1545. He is named in the trial of Theunis van Hastenrath (*q.v.*). In the beginning, about 1535, he had some leaning toward Münsterite (*q.v.*) principles, but later he was a peaceful Anabaptist. He was probably a native of the city of Jülich (*q.v.*). (*DB* 1890, 58; 1909, 120; Rembert, *Wiedertäufer,* 390.)

vdZ.

Leitner (Leutner), **Hans**, a Hutterite martyr, was captured with Klaus Felbinger (*q.v.*) on April 2, 1560, at Neumarkt, Lower Bavaria, Germany, and imprisoned at Landshut (*q.v.*), where they were repeatedly cross-examined and terribly tortured. When all these attempts to convert them proved futile, they were beheaded on July 19, 1560.

NEFF.

Beck, *Geschichts-Bücher*, 234-36; Wolkan, *Geschicht-Buch*, 304-6; Zieglschmid, *Chronik*, 400-2; *Mart. Mir.* D 274, E 643; *ML* II, 635.

Leitstern, Der, a 4-page monthly periodical, 8 x 11 in., is the official organ of the Rudnerweide Mennonite Church, published at Altona, Man., and edited by the elder, W. H. Falk. The first number appeared in January 1943.

H.S.B.

Lely, a Dutch Mennonite family of Hoorn, where Cornelis Tymons Lely in 1686 and his brother Gerrit Tymons Lely in 1689 were called to the ministry of the Frisian congregation (*DB* 1867, 81, 84), and of Amsterdam, where its members were found in several Mennonite congregations. To this family belonged the preacher Cornelis Lely (*q.v.*), while Cornelis Lely (*q.v.*) is also a descendant of this family.

vDZ.

Lely, Cornelis, b. 1686 at Hoorn, d. 1758 at Amsterdam, married to Maria Salm of Amsterdam, was a son of Pieter Tymonsz Lely of Hoorn. He was a surgeon in Amsterdam and in 1718-52 a preacher and elder of the Old Frisian congregation (Arke Noachs) at Amsterdam. He published a sermon to commemorate his late co-preacher Jan Dirksz Schotvanger (d. 1735), entitled *Paulus leven en zalige verwagting* (Haarlem, 1735).

vDZ.

Biogr. Wb. V, 727; *Inv. Arch. Amst.* II, No. 1411; *DB* 1881, 107.

Lely, Cornelis, b. Sept. 23, 1854, at Amsterdam, d. Jan. 14, 1929, at The Hague, was a Dutch engineer and a member of the Second, and later of the First Chamber of the Dutch States-General, governor of Surinam 1902-5, and three times Minister of Public Works (1891-94, 1897-1901, 1913-18). In 1918 a law was passed to reclaim the Zuiderzee. To this gigantic task, which has proved to be of great national importance and which was begun in 1923 and by now (1955) not yet entirely finished, Lely had given both the impulse and the plans by his *Nota's over de afsluiting en droogmaking van de Zuiderzee* (Leiden, 1887-91). Lely stemmed from an old Mennonite family and was a member of the church, being for some time also a member of the church board at The Hague.

vDZ.

K. Jansma, *Lely, de bedwinger der Zuiderzee* (Amsterdam, 1948).

Lembach, a government district and village in the Rohrbach area, Upper Austria. Anabaptist meetings are mentioned here in 1527. Matthias Dorsauer, who was arrested in 1528 at Passau, baptized here. Then there is no further mention of Anabaptists. Probably none of the three places in Lower Austria having this name is meant in the Hutterite records, but rather (Neu) Lengbach (*q.v.*) in the Vienna Woods (Wienerwald). (*ML* II, 636.)

P.DE.

Ritter, *Geograph.-statistisches Lexikon* II (Leipzig, 1895); A. Nicoladoni, *Johannes Bünderlin von Linz und die oberösterreichischen Täufergemeinden* (Berlin, 1893); *ML* II, 636.

Lembach, a village west of Wissembourg in Lower Alsace, near the border of the Palatinate. The region is mountainous and picturesque with many old ruins. There were once many Mennonite families here. At the close of the Thirty Years' War Swiss Mennonite refugees settled here, welcomed by the barons of Fleckenstein to rebuild their extensive lands in Lower Alsace. They held their meetings on the Froensburg, an estate at the foot of Froensburg castle; some of the Palatine Mennonites met with them. The membership steadily declined. Emigration to Bavaria, Poland, and America took large numbers; the fact that they lived widely scattered hastened the decline. When Froensburg passed into other hands the congregation met in a rented hall at Hirschtal in the Palatinate, and finally on the Fleckensteinerhof (*q.v.*) in Alsace. When this farm also passed into non-Mennonite hands the members no longer met. There were only a few families left. The Palatine families went to Ixheim (*q.v.*) (Zweibrücken), the Alsatians to Geisberg (*q.v.*). The last elders of Lembach were Peter Jordy of the Fleckensteinerhof and Joseph Guth of the Bärenbrunnerhof near Busenberg. (*ML* II, 636.)

P.So.

Lemberg (Lvov), a city (pop. 330,000) formerly in Poland, now in Russia. In the 15th century Lemberg had a strongly German stamp. Decrees were issued in the German language and German was the language of church services. In the next century the awakening nationalistic spirit made Lemberg a bulwark of Polish thought. After the first division of Poland in 1772 Lemberg was ceded to Austria. In spite of the attempt to Germanize it Lemberg remained Polish, with a strong Ruthenian element.

The Mennonite community in Galicia (*q.v.*), which had been established in 1784, was located at first in three villages about three miles southwest of Lemberg, the capital of the province, with Einsiedel as the center and the seat of one of the congregations. In 1830 a subsidiary settlement (Neuhof) was made in a village about 10 miles northwest of the villages, which also became a daughter congregation. Further settlements were made on scattered larger estates, of which Kiernica—5 miles east of Grodek, 10 miles west of Lemberg—became (1860) the seat of a congregation. Gradually the older settlements dissolved and the families scattered, so that by 1914 the 400 baptized members were living in over 100 places. In 1909 the previous congregations were united in one and the name Kiernica-Lemberg given to it, with Lemberg the seat. In 1936 only 57 (souls) Mennonites were living in the city of Lemberg.

In 1911 a one-story building at 23 Koshanovski Street was purchased in which a chapel, a parsonage, a council room, and a janitor's apartment were housed. In 1925 a second floor was built to furnish quarters for students and houseparents, called a *Schülerheim*.

In 1939-40, as a result of an agreement between Germany and Russia, all Germans were evacuated from this region and the Galician Mennonites were resettled in the region of Thorn and Posen. Thus the Lemberg congregation came to an end. Lemberg became Russian.　　　　　　　　　　H.S.B.

P. Bachmann, *Mennoniten in Kleinpolen* (Lemberg, 1934); *ML* II, 636 f.

Lemke (Lemken, Lemmeken), an elder in the High German Anabaptist congregation, probably a native of Upper Gelre. He was married to Fyken Gerlacx van Megen. He was a deacon at Illikhoven about 1550 and after the martyrdom of Theunis van Hastenrath in 1551 took over the eldership in Jülich. He is apparently identical with a man called Lemken Bruerren, a maker of bags, also called Cremers (peddler), who was a resident of Maastricht, Dutch province of Limburg, and arrested there in March 1533 because he had received "Lutherans," i.e., heretics, obviously Anabaptists, in his house. Lemken then was pardoned and did penance. In 1538 he is said to have left the city. In 1545 he was present at the baptism of the martyr Liisken (*q.v.*) at Visschersweert; he then lived in this hamlet until 1547, when his house was razed by the officials of the duchy of Jülich because it was the house of a heretic and had harbored forbidden meetings. He then moved to the neighboring hamlet of Illikhoven. About this time Menno Simons stayed at his home in Illikhoven. He was very active in both preaching and baptizing; e.g., at Lichterwald in 1553, Susteren 1557, Born 1558, and also at Aachen, where he had a number of followers.

With Zylis, Herman van Tielt, and Hans Sikken he went to Wüstenfelde, in May 1556, and held a two-day discussion with Menno Simons and other elders on the application of the ban in marriage. After the others had left, Lemke remained and explained to Menno Simons that he was in complete agreement with him, but did not wish to admit this in the presence of the brethren, because he was afraid of losing his influence. But he made up his mind to conquer the resistance of his brethren against the ban in marriage, and if he succeeded he wanted one or two Dutch elders to come to them, and introduce the ban among them. But this did not take place; Lemke sided entirely with Zylis, who rejected the ban in marriage as an abomination.

Menno Simons complained that Lemke denied having ever "fraternised" with him, and that he answered all the pleas of the elders with the "very unfriendly and stubborn words," that he "had not come for their sake."

After the Strasbourg conference in 1557 Zylis and Lemke wrote a friendly letter urging peace and unity (*DB* 1894, 47-53). Menno Simons replied on June 11, 1558, in a pamphlet, *Grondelijk Onderwijs ofte bericht van de excommunicatie,* rejecting their plea. Thereupon Zylis and Lemke wrote an extremely violent reply, in which Lemke boasted that aside from the doctrine of church discipline he differed from Menno in three or four additional articles, and that he would rather be excommunicated by the Dutch elders than to grant that they were right. Then Menno put the High German preachers

under the ban and published his *Antwoort aan Zylis und Lemmeken,* in which he repudiated brotherhood with them. Nothing more is known of Lemke. In a letter found in van Braght's *Martyrs' Mirror* (D 329, E 690) written by Matthias Servaes (*q.v.*) to Heinrich Krufft, Servaes warns him of a brother named "L." If this brother is Elder Lemken, as Bax supposes, he was still living in 1565.　　　NEFF.

W. Bax, *Het Protestantisme in het Bisdom Luik* I (The Hague, 1937) 142, 302; *DB* 1890, 55, 61; 1894, 36 f., 42, 44 f., 51 f., 58, 60 f.; *BRN* VII, 56, 61, 87, 207, 222; K. Vos, *Menno Simons* (Leiden, 1914) *passim*, see Index; Kühler, *Geschiedenis* I, 323-25, 327; C. Krahn, *Menno Simons* (Karlsruhe, 1936) 94-97; *ML* II, 637.

Lemlin, Konrad, of Sintelfingen (called Angelfingen in the Passau records), an Anabaptist martyr, had baptized the wife of Michel (Khumbauf) of Bruchsal, Baden, Germany, at Barnbach in 1530 and Hans Steuber (Stöber) of Durlach, Baden, in 1531. At the end of 1531 he was seized with his wife Ursula Spanner of Gmünd and put into the prison in Vaihingen on the Enz, Württemberg, because of his Anabaptist convictions. Because he would not recant he was burned at the stake. His wife, who also remained true to her faith, was also to have been executed, but because of her unborn child she was spared; she had to swear that she would leave Württemberg and never return. (*TA Württemberg,* 256; *ML* II, 637.)　　　　　　　　G.Bo.

Lemmer, a town in the Dutch province of Friesland, where Leenaert Bouwens in 1551-54 baptized 4 persons and in 1563-65, 22 more. There must have been a congregation here at that time, of which, however, nothing is known. In the 18th century it was still in existence, though very small in membership. In 1748 the few remaining members joined the neighboring congregation of Sloten (*q.v.*).
　　　　　　　　　　　　　　　　　　　VDZ.

H. J. Busé, "De verdwenen Doopsgezinde Gemeenten in Friesland," reprint from *De Vrije Fries* XXII, 14.

Lenaerdt (Lenart) **Boeckbinder** (*Leenaert van Antwerpen*), a Dutch Anabaptist sent out as an apostle in the fall of 1533 by Jan Matthysz (*q.v.*) of Haarlem. He was a native of Antwerp, Belgium, and was active in preaching and baptizing in a number of towns; in early 1534 at Gorichem; in the fall of 1534 at Zierikzee and Schiedam; in December 1534 at Delft and Rotterdam, and shortly thereafter in Antwerp. He is likely identical both with the Lenaert van Kampen, who is said to have been the leader of a congregation of 400 members in the town of Kampen, Dutch province of Overijssel, and with Lenaert van Emden. He must have been an influential member of the revolutionary branch of Anabaptism. After December 1534 all trace of him is lost. (*DB* 1917, 100, No. 104; Mellink, *Wederdopers, passim,* see Index.)　　　　　　VDZ.

Lenaert Aerntsz, an Anabaptist from Naaldwijk in the Dutch province of South Holland, who was arrested at Poeldijk (*q.v.*) and beheaded and broken on a wheel at The Hague on March 14, 1536. Lenaert belonged to the revolutionary wing of Anabaptism. (*Inv. Arch. Amst.* I, No. 745; Mellink, *Wederdopers,* 220 f.)　　　　　　　　　　　VDZ.

Lenaert van Emden, a Dutch Anabaptist leader: see Lenaerdt (Lenart) Boeckbinder.

Lenaert van Kampen is identical with Lenaerdt (Lenart) Boeckbinder (q.v.).

Lenaert Plovier (Plouvier, Pluvier, Plumer), an Anabaptist martyr, who on April 4, 1560 (*Offer* 1559, but this means by the old calendar), was executed at Antwerp, Belgium, with Janneken Eghels and Maeyken de Hont. They were put in a sack and drowned in a wine cask at the Steen castle at Antwerp. The *Offer* contains his testament, a letter to his children, and a hymn, "Testament van Lenaert Plovier." The *Groot Offerboek* of 1615 and following martyrsbooks, including van Braght's *Martyrs' Mirror,* give a number of particulars, procured by his son. Lenaert was a native of Meenen (Menin) in Flanders (according to the records of Antwerp he was born at Wervik, Flanders). Living in Meenen, he was a well-to-do cloth merchant. In 1555 he united with the Mennonite congregation of Meenen (q.v.); he refused his reappointment as assayer of cloth, because the office required him to take an oath. Shortly after, he moved from Meenen to Antwerp, where he started a silk business. Knowing that persecution also threatened him in Antwerp he intended to move to the Netherlands. He had already sent his wife Maeyken with their four little children to the Dutch province of Friesland and had put his property in safety, when he was arrested, and being unwilling to deny his faith, was put to death. In vain his parents tried to have him released. During the night of execution two friends, Kerstine van Damme and Joost Noe, who later lived at Franeker, Dutch province of Friesland, had secretly listened at the wall of the castle, that they might hear some last word of Lenaert. The name of this martyr is also found in the hymn "Aenhoort Godt, hemelsche Vader" (Hear, O God, heavenly Father), No. 16 of the *Lietboecxken van den Offer des Heeren.* In prison he wrote six letters, but only one of these has been preserved. It is found in van Braght's *Martyrs' Mirror.* In the 17th and 18th centuries a number of Ploviers were members of the Flemish congregation at Haarlem, Holland. Their relationship with Lenaert Plovier could not be ascertained. vDZ.

Offer, 367-73, 567, 667; *Mart. Mir.* D 270-72, E. 641-43; *Antw. Arch.-Blad* IX, 7, 11; XIV, 28 f., No. 315; Wolkan, *Lieder,* 67; *ML* III, 379.

Lenaert de Schoolmeester (i.e., schoolteacher, because he formerly had been a schoolteacher at Alken in the territory of Liége, Belgium) was a Mennonite elder. The Dutch martyr Jater (q.v.) told during her trial in 1550 that she had heard him preach in 1540 at Maastricht, Dutch province of Limburg. He impressed upon his hearers that they should live "after the way and doctrines of the apostles" and that they would be persecuted because of the name of God. Lenaert had also baptized Jater. He may have been identical with Lenhard van Maastricht, Leenaert van Yzenbroek, and Leonhard Fälber (q.v.). (*DB* 1890, 57; 1909, 117 f.) vDZ.

Lenaert Willemsz and his wife Beatrix Jansdochter, from Terheide near The Hague, Dutch province of South Holland, Anabaptist martyrs, drowned on March 17, 1535, probably at The Hague. Particulars are lacking. (*Inv. Arch. Amst.* I, No. 745; Mellink, *Wederdopers,* 217.) vDZ.

Lenart Kerstenzoon, an Anabaptist martyr, burned at the stake on July 1, 1569, at Utrecht in the Netherlands. Lenart, a native of Venlo, confessed during trial that he had often attended Anabaptist meetings; he and his wife Trijntgen (q.v.) had been (re)baptized; he was not willing to recant his faith, and died steadfast. vDZ.

I. M. J. Hoog, "Onze martelaren," in *Ned. Archief voor Kerkgeschiedenis* I (1902) No. 118; *DB* 1903, 5.

Lenart Ketelbueter: see Ketelbueter family.

Lenart van Ysenbroeck (Lenhart van Yzenbroek, Eschenbroich, Eyssenbrouk), also called Leonhard van Tongeren and Leonhard van Maastricht, an Anabaptist elder, whose activity can be traced in a number of towns in what is now the Dutch province of Limburg (Born, Dieteren, Maastricht, Sittard) beginning in 1535. He baptized the martyrs Mente Heynen and Jater. He was still active in the Dutch Limburg area in 1561; his meetings were attended by people from near and far; sometimes 200 or 300 persons are said to have been present. Rembert considers him to be identical with Leonhard Fälber. For particulars see the article Fälber. vDZ.

DB 1909, 117 f.; 1917, 119, No. 106; W. Bax, *Het Protestantisme in het bisdom Luik* I (The Hague, 1937) 72 f., 349 f.; Rembert, *Wiedertäufer,* 450-53; Mellink, *Wederdopers,* 306.

Lengbach, Austria, located in the Wienerwald. The first mention of Lengbach appears in an apology of the government councilors to an accusation made by the king, dated March 4, 1528, which says that they were holding several Anabaptists in Lengbach, awaiting instructions from the king on what was to be done with them. Persecution in Moravia was bringing many Anabaptists to Lower Austria, where the marshal Dietrich von Hartitsch (q.v.) was hunting them down. It was, however, not the marshal but the clerk of Neulengbach, the knight Blasius Notlitsch (d. 1547; his tombstone is still near the altar of St. Sebastian in the Ansbach church) who succeeded in capturing them. On June 3, 1528, he reported to the government that with the aid of Gryss, master of the hunt, he had brought to Lengbach 33 newly baptized persons, who had been living for three weeks in the forest "on a high mountain," 16 men and 17 girls and women. Most of them were very young; only four were past 40. There was among them a furrier who had assumed the priestly role of baptizing. As much as he had been able to understand "in haste," none would desist from his error. In conclusion the knight requested, "Since other people draw a salary for annihilating and crushing the new sect," he should also be rewarded.

The king decided that the cost must be borne by the magistracy, but the prisoners must be turned over to Hartitsch, who soon afterward executed 18 men and women. Although the court records are silent on this point, there must have been other Anabaptists here, for the chronicles list 45 executions in Lengbach, of a total of 105 for all of Lower Austria, Vienna included.   P.DE.

J. Loserth, "Die Wiedertaufe in Niederösterreich von ihren Anfängen bis zum Tode Hubmaiers (1525-28)," in Blätter des Vereins für Landeskunde von Oesterreich XXXIII (1899) 417-35; Wolkan, Geschicht-Buch; Zieglschmid, Chronik, 232; ML II, 636.

Lengua Indian Mission in the Paraguayan Chaco was considered by the Mennonite immigrants to the Chaco in 1932, two years after their arrival there; the project was, however, prevented for two years by the war between Paraguay and Bolivia. In 1935 a missionary association called *Licht den Indianern* (q.v.) was organized by 48 members of the various Mennonite groups (G.C., E.M.B., and M.B.). The first missionaries sent to the field were Abraham Unger, Abraham and Anna Ratzlaff, and Gerhard and Katharina Giesbrecht. The first convert, Sepe Thama (i.e., a son), was baptized after ten years of work. In 1951 the congregation had 28 members, of whom 15 were baptized on Jan. 22, 1950.

The language of the Lengua Indians is a very difficult one to learn; there was at first no written matter in the dialect used at the station. The language consists of only 17 letters, the sounds of which include a peculiar lisp which is very difficult to acquire. Besides receiving spiritual service, the Indians are also encouraged to give up their nomadic way of life and make permanent settlements. As yet the Catholic Church has put no obstacles in the way of the work.

In 1946 the Mennonite Brethren Mission Board (Hillsboro, Kan.), by agreement with the missionary society, took over the Chaco Mission Field. The missionary society continues to serve as the representative of the Chaco Mennonites and shares in the operation of the Mission by counseling with the M.B. Board, also raising funds in Paraguay. However the administrative and financial responsibility remains in the hands of the North American Board, which furnishes most of the finances. In 1949 the name of the Chaco Mission was officially changed to "Chaco Amerikanische Mennonitenbrüder Mission Licht den Indianern." (See **Paraguay Mennonite Brethren Mission**.)   G.B.G.

Survey of the Mission Fields of the Conference of the Mennonite Brethren Church of North America Located in India, Africa, Brazil, Paraguay, and Colombia, made by A. E. Janzen, Executive Secretary and Treasurer of the Board of Foreign Missions During December 1948 to June 10, 1949 (Hillsboro, April 1950) 86-116; ML II, 637 f.

Lenhard van Maastricht, a Dutch Anabaptist leader, apparently identical with Lenart van Ysenbroeck (q.v.) and Leonhard Fälber (q.v.).   vDZ.

Lenhart (Leonhard) **von Fritzlar: see Fälber, Leonhard.**

Lenige, Dirk Pieters (1722-98), a Mennonite merchant at Makkum, Dutch province of Friesland, a friend of the Mennonite ministers J. Stijl and Matthias van Geuns, and had a keen interest in Mennonite church matters. In 1778-92 he wrote a number of poems in the Frisian language, some of which were published by G. A. Wumkes in the periodical *Yn ús eigen Tael* (1915), 61-74. His daughter Cynthia (Kynke) Lenige (1755-80) was an artist; she did some remarkably good drawings. A volume of her poems in the Dutch language entitled *Mengeldichten* was published in Amsterdam in 1782 after her death.   vDZ.

N.N.B.Wb. IV, 901 f.; G. A. Wumkes, Bodders yn de Fryske striid (Boalsert, 1926) 377-83; DJ 1943, 68-78.

Lennep, van, a very old family, mentioned already about 1000 and at that time living at the country seat of Linepe (Lennepe) near Düsseldorf, Germany. In the Middle Ages a branch of this family produced a number of magistrates at Emmerich, Germany. From this branch proceeded the Dutch Mennonite van Lennep family, whose ancestor was Warner van Lennep, a merchant, born in 1597 or 1598 at Emmerich and died in 1644 at Amsterdam. He moved from Emmerich to Amsterdam, where he married Sara van Halmael. His son Jacob van Lennep (1631-1704) and his grandson Aernout van Lennep (1658-1728), a son of Jacob, were both deacons of the Amsterdam Mennonite Lam-en-Toren congregation. Both were silk merchants and were appointed by the burgomasters of Amsterdam as directors of the silk market at Amsterdam. The van Lennep family, by their excellent commercial ability —they mostly traded with the Levant, especially Smyrna—by their wealth and their reliability, were highly respected and were among the influential citizens of Amsterdam. By marriage they became related to a number of other well-known Amsterdam Mennonite families, such as van Halmael, van der Meersch, Block, Leeuw, Rutgers, de Veer, Looten, de Neufville, Roeters, de Wolff, and Bierens.

The aforementioned Jacob van Lennep, a silk merchant and manufacturer of a famous gold and silver cloth and of linen damask, had built a splendid house on the Herengracht, where the mercantile aristocracy of Amsterdam at that time lived; he moreover owned the country home "Roosenberg" in Watergraafsmeer. His son and successor Aernout van Lennep in 1699 bought the country home "Het Paradijs" at Heemstede near Haarlem.

In the 18th century some members of this family went over to the Reformed Church, probably because they wished to hold high state offices, from which the Dutch Mennonites were excluded until 1795, or to enter the army. The first of this family to leave the Mennonite Church was David van Lennep (1721-71), who joined the Reformed Church in 1745. Other branches of the family remained Mennonite and served the Amsterdam congregation as deacons until recent times, among whom was Jacob Abraham van Lennep, who in 1775 took the initiative in building a pipe organ in the Amsterdam Singel church. There is only one Mennonite minister from the family, viz., Egbert David van Lennep, b. Jan. 2, 1787, at Almelo, d. June 1, 1851, at Doetichem, a son of Jacob Roeters van Lennep and Catharina Coster, who, after studying at the Amsterdam Seminary, served the congregations of Zutphen 1810-11 and Almelo 1811-38. To this family also belonged H. S. van Lennep (q.v.).   vDZ.

F. K. van Lennep, *Verzameling van oorkonden betrekking hebbende op het geslacht van Lennep* I (Amsterdam, 1900); *Ned. Patriciaat* IX (1918) 232-52; *Jaarboek Amstelodamum* XXXIX (1942) 45 ff.; *DB* 1863, 22; 1912, 105; Kühler, *Geschiedenis* II, 131, note 2.

Lennep, Henrick Samuel van, b. Feb. 10, 1832, at Amsterdam, d. Oct. 24, 1914, at Heemstede, a jurist and well-known legal authority in Amsterdam and director of the Vesta Life Insurance Company. He served the A.D.S. as a trustee from 1869 until his death, and as treasurer from 1872 until his death. He was elected chairman of this conference (A.D.S.) three times. He also served for a long time as chairman of the Dutch Mennonite Mission Association, and for 12 years as a deacon of the Amsterdam congregation. He was married to Anna Cecilia van Eeghen. NEFF.

DB 1903, 132-35; 1911, 133; *Zondagsbode* XXVI (1911-12) No. 15; XXVIII (1914-15) No. 1; *ML* II, 638.

Lenoir, North Carolina, the center of Krimmer Mennonite Brethren work among the Negroes. In 1951 Mr. and Mrs. P. H. Siemens reported that the following churches had been built in North Carolina and Tennessee since the time they arrived on the field: Beach Bottom (1926), Heaton (1928), Shell Creek (1931), Bushtown (first church 1932, second church 1936), Cove Creek (1939), Elk Park (1939), Laytown (1940), Lenoir (1945), Boone (1948), and Darley (1950). A 1952 report indicated that a five-month Bible school had an average attendance of 90; the daily vacation Bible school held two weeks in each church had an enrollment of over 300 children; child evangelism classes were conducted; the Pioneer Boys, the Home Builders, and the men's Bible Club met regularly; revival meetings were held in all of the churches, resulting in nine conversions. The membership in 1955 was 235, with four ordained ministers. M.G.

Lensen, Jan, was the head of one of the 13 Crefeld families (Mennonite and Quaker) who immigrated to Pennsylvania, arriving in Philadelphia on Oct. 6, 1683, on the "Concord" (*q.v.*), who were therefore the forerunners of German immigration to America. He came from Rheydt, was a linen weaver by trade and settled in Germantown, where he was naturalized as a citizen in 1691. His family was (according to Hull) the only one of the 13 original settler families to be and remain Mennonite. HEGE.

Wm. I. Hull, *William Penn and the Dutch Quaker Migration to Pennsylvania* (Swarthmore College, 1935); *ML* II, 638.

Lenz, Paul, was one of the judges in Tirol, Austria, who in 1561 had to pronounce sentence against Hans Mändl (*q.v.*), Eustachius Kotter (*q.v.*), and Jörg Rack (*q.v.*). He was a native of Götzens and as a representative of the Sonnenburg district had been called with three others from this diocese to Innsbruck. The jurors refused the request of the government to be put under oath again and because it was a religious matter put the responsibility for the trial on the spiritual authorities, refusing to have anything to do with it. In spite of all the pressure they produced a written "excuse."

In order to find the perpetrators of this refusal, which was considered disobedience, the Innsbruck

regents required everyone to declare whether he would or would not obey the will of the prince and his mandates. All the jurors yielded except Lenz and two others. The emperor favored lenience, and suggested that the trial be dropped and the three prisoners sent to the galleys. But the local government of Tirol disagreed and begged him to act in accord with the mandates; they finally carried out the decisions against the Anabaptists passed in Speyer in 1529. Under the threat of removal from office, imprisonment, and loss of citizenship, Lenz and the two others yielded and pronounced the death sentence. Though they were not punished, they were put under police supervision.

The valiant martyrdom of the three executed Anabaptists moved Lenz to join the Anabaptists himself and win others in Götzens. When the magistrate at the request of the government began to investigate this matter, Lenz had already gone to Moravia; his estate was confiscated. (Loserth, *Anabaptismus* 119-210; *ML* II, 638.) P.DE.

Lenzburg, a district (*Amt*) in the Swiss canton of Aargau (*q.v.*), where soon after its rise Anabaptism seems to have spread quietly. In the public discussion with some Protestant preachers, held at Bern, March 11-17, 1538, two Anabaptists of the Lenzburg district were present. Soon after more rigorous measures were adopted, which caused most Anabaptists of Lenzburg to move to Moravia (*q.v.*). vDZ.

Lenzes (Lensens), Goitze, author of a private songbook entitled *Nuttige tytkortinge of Stichtelyke gezangen* (Leeuwarden, 1757). Lenzes was an untrained preacher of the Mennonite congregation of Drachten, Dutch province of Friesland, 1744-*ca*.83. vDZ.

Lenzi, Michel, an Anabaptist martyr of whom nothing is known except that on May 21, 1527, a few hours after the execution of Michael Sattler (*q.v.*) at Rottenburg, Germany, he also died as a martyr, having refused to return to the Catholic Church. At the same time Mathis Kürssner, Stoffel Schuhmacher, and "the aged Geiger" were also put to death. Fourteen other Anabaptists saved their lives by recanting. HEGE.

W. Köhler, *Brüderlich Vereinigung etzlicher Kinder Gottes* (1527) in *Flugschriften aus den ersten Jahren der Reformation* II (Leipzig, 1908) 303; *ML* II, 638.

Lenzmann, August (1823-77), an influential Mennonite leader and elder at Gnadenfeld, Russia, was born Jan. 29, 1823, in Brenkenhoffswalde (*q.v.*), Prussia, Germany, of Lutheran parents, but joined the local Mennonite congregation before it emigrated to Gnadenfeld under the leadership of Elder Wilhelm Lange (*q.v.*). Lenzmann was baptized on May 27, 1834, chosen as minister in 1851 and as elder in 1854. He was a cofounder of the Gnadenfeld Bruderschule; he was an intimate friend of Eduard Wüst (*q.v.*), of whom he says, "The memories of the brotherly fellowship which he enjoyed with the dear Pastor Wüst until his departure from the struggling to the triumphant church will always remain a blessing for me" (Friesen, 171). Hermann

Lenzmann, his son, also speaks of the close and fraternal contact between his father and Wüst (*Menn. Jahrbuch* 1904-5, 78).

Lenzmann was the elder of the Gnadenfeld Mennonite Church at the time when the Mennonite Brethren Church originated. He was the one whom the brethren approached before their separation with the request that he administer the Lord's Supper to them privately; but he refused to do this because he considered it contrary to Mennonite practice and likely to disturb the unity within the brotherhood (Friesen, 319). Lenzmann tried to direct those favoring a separatist movement. Johann Claassen, the leader of this group, was a member of his church and had been the cofounder of the Bruderschule. The experience of failing to reconcile various extremes within his congregation and the entire Molotschna Mennonite settlement disappointed Lenzmann. His later relationship with the Mennonite Brethren and also the Friends of Jerusalem was somewhat influenced by these bitter experiences, which are also reflected in the account which he published in the *Mennonitische Blätter* (No. 6, 1863). He states that it was a falsification of facts to claim that "the brethren who had left the church were the real and genuine children and followers of Pastor Wüst and that they were persecuted primarily because of this; a rude blasphemy against the deceased who cannot defend himself. . . . Wüst did not hesitate to admonish them according to Scripture and asked them to give up their pride and to humble themselves before the Lord" because they had emphasized the "free grace" of God in a wrong manner (Friesen, 318). Many of the official communications (published by Isaac) bear Lenzmann's signature. Lenzmann objected particularly to the Mennonite Brethren claims that before Wüst there had been "neither a vital religious life nor any mission festivals" among the Mennonites, for such activities had been an old practice at Gnadenfeld and Rudnerweide.

Lenzmann also had to deal with another controversial question pertaining to the Friends of Jerusalem, when Johann Lange (*q.v.*), who taught at the Bruderschule, spread views of this group to which Lenzmann objected. Lenzmann was an outstanding leader promoting an active and vital Christianity among the Mennonites of the Molotschna. It was unfortunate that he and others did not manage to keep all forces and movements in one fold. He probably suffered more under it than anyone else. His account and role in the religious developments of 1850-60 is very significant and deserves careful study and analysis, particularly since he and his congregation were by background and development related most closely to the revivalistic and pietistic views emphasized by Wüst.   C.K.

Friesen, *Brüderschaft,* 171, 317 ff., 743; *Menn. Blätter,* March 16, 1863; *Menn. Jahrbuch* 1904-5, 78; Fr. Isaac, *Die Molotschnaer Mennoniten* (Halbstadt, 1908); *ML* II, 638 f.

Lenzmann, Hermann A., the son of August Lenzmann, an outstanding educator and printer. He received his secondary education under Heinrich Franz, whose daughter he married, taught elementary school at Berdyansk, and attended the Theological Seminary at Barmen, Germany, in 1868-72, after

which he spent some time at the Normal School of Neuwied. In 1873-81, with the exception of 1875, he taught at the Gnadenfeld Zentralschule. In 1875 Lenzmann studied at the University of Tübingen under J. T. Beck. During the years 1881-98 he taught at the Halbstadt Zentralschule. For 1898-1907 he returned to the Gnadenfeld Zentralschule.

In 1907 Lenzmann established a printing press at Gross-Tokmak, Molotschna, where numerous Mennonite books were published. The first issues of *Mennonitisches Jahrbuch* (1903-6) were printed and published by Lenzmann. In the issue of 1903-4 he published an appeal for support of the *Jahrbuch*. During the following years (1904-5 and 1906-7) he presented a lengthy biography of Johann Tobias Beck in the *Jahrbuch*. Görz says of him that he was "one of our best educated teachers" (p. 163).   C.K.

H. Görz, *Die Molotschnaer Ansiedlung* (Steinbach, 1951); H. Dirks, "Aus der Gnadenfelder Gemeindechronik," *Menn. Jahrbuch* 1911-12, 28 f.; Friesen, *Brüderschaft,* 602.

Leo Mennonite Church (MC), located in Leo, Ind., a small rural town eleven miles northeast of Ft. Wayne, Ind. The first meetinghouse, built on the bank of the St. Joseph River about 1½ miles southeast of Leo in 1887, was used until 1917, when a church was purchased in the town of Leo. This congregation was without conference affiliation until 1905, when it united with the Indiana-Michigan Conference, and Jonathan Kurtz of Topeka, Ind., was given bishop charge. From 1906 to 1910 this church had no local minister. In 1910 Andrew S. Miller was ordained minister, and John Lugbill was deacon. In 1944 S. J. Miller was appointed pastor, and in 1947 the church was remodeled. The baptized membership in 1954 was 237, with S. J. Miller (ordained 1950) as bishop and Ben Graber as deacon.   S.J.M.

Leoben, the "iron city" (pop. 12,000) of Styria, Austria, in the upper Mur Valley. The first emissaries of the Anabaptists arrived here in the autumn of 1528 and at once found followers. On Sept. 18, the magistrate Siegmund von Dietrichstein (*q.v.*), one of the most notable names among the Lutherans in Styria, gave orders to the mayor, judge, and council of Leoben to arrest Peter Schuster, who was suspected of being an Anabaptist, with his wife and children, and to make an inventory of his property. Three days later came an order to look for other Anabaptists. On Sept. 27 the command was issued to question him, if necessary on the rack, to learn who preached for them, who had taken part in their meetings, and in whose houses they had met. All those reported should be arrested at once. The examination apparently brought nothing important to light, for Dietrichstein gave instructions on Oct. 20 to release Schuster and his family, and to return their property to them, but only in exchange for an oath to be on call at all times.

Schuster, however, was actually at that time an Anabaptist, for on New Year's Day of 1529 the vice-regent of Styria, Seifried von Windischgrätz, issued an order to the authorities of Leoben to apprehend the fugitive brethren Grinzinger and Schuster, if they had not already done so. The importance of quick action is indicated by the thrice repeated *cito!* (quickly). Meanwhile both had escaped.

On the other hand, Dietrichstein reported to the king on Jan. 7 that his magistrate in Kammerstein had arrested an Anabaptist fugitive from Upper Austria en route via Krems (*q.v.*) to Leoben, where 30 to 40 Anabaptists, among them many peasants, had met weekly. He had the prisoner taken to Graz. In order to cope with the constantly spreading movement toward adult baptism, the Vienna government in the name of the king delegated the provost Hieronymus Wüst to take special charge of the situation in Bruck and Leoben.

Dietrichstein also asked his brother-in-law, Wolf von Stubenberg auf Kapfenberg, to see to the arrest of the "many bad fellows" who wandered secretly about Bruck and Leoben and in the Kapfenberg jurisdiction, "persuading the poor populace to Anabaptism." Two days later the king himself authorized Dietrichstein to have the Anabaptists hunted by secret spies, and to seize all who were suspect. He also informed Dietrichstein that he had asked the archbishop to send skilled and competent preachers to the regions most seriously threatened. By the end of January the council of Leoben reported that eight Anabaptists had been seized, and asked for instructions in handling both those who would recant and those who would be obstinate. Dietrichstein put the case into the hands of the provost, and commissioned him to be lenient to the penitent.

But by March 18 a new command came from Vienna to Dietrichstein to seize several citizens of Leoben, who were reported to be Anabaptists. Four weeks later an order came to deal severely with two of the captured Anabaptists, unless they were very young. The confiscation of the property of fugitive Anabaptists continued; on April 21, 1529, Ferdinand (from Speyer) sent to his councilor and chamberlain Veit Zollner the property of the two Anabaptists, Franz Intzinger (*q.v.*) and Peter Schuster, with the obligation to pay 200 guilders to Pruner, the clerk of the provincial court, who had been promised a share in such estates.

The flight of individual Anabaptists from Leoben continued; for on May 3, 1529, Dietrichstein ordered Leoben to seize the wife of Jörg Schlesinger, who had escaped to Moravia and had asked her to come to him. The report of the council that she had already gone brought severe censure upon the magistrate. Her departure could not possibly have been accomplished so secretly that no one noticed it! Let him immediately find those who knew of it! Three weeks later the magistrate of Freienstein managed to capture an Anabaptist, who was sent to Graz and imprisoned on the Schlossberg, where several of his brethren already lay. On June 2 the magistrate of Leoben was ordered by the government to ask the wife of the fugitive Anabaptist Wieser, under oath, whether she was not also "contaminated by this sect."

In 1530 Intzinger apparently returned to his home for a short time; he was recognized and pursued, but not captured. The magistrate of the Frauenburg in the upper Mur Valley reported on March 20 that he had arrived too late. Intzinger and his family had already moved on.

The Anabaptists from Leoben and other places in Upper Styria, who were imprisoned in the Schlossberg at Graz, lay there a long time. The new magistrate, Hans von Ungnad, who considered them "pious and simple people" and would soonest have let them go, received orders from the king on July 19 to spare the penitent, the young, and the simple, but to put to death the obstinate. It is Baron von Ungnad, of whom Antoni Erfordter said in the epistle he wrote when he left Klagenfurt (September 1538), "that he would rather give up all his honor than kill a man because of his faith"; among the nobility of the four hereditary lands there was not another who was marked by "such manly honesty, valid before God."

Until 1533 there is occasional mention of Anabaptists who were trying to gain adherents in secret. But they were no longer strong. According to the register of martyrs in the chronicles, there were none at Leoben. The *Geschicht-Buch* relates that in 1539 Christoph Gschäl traveled from Moravia through Upper Styria, but his very dangerous work brought no results. Among the prisoners in the Falkenstein prison there was a Brother Peter Schuster, who was perhaps the fugitive from Leoben.

P.DE.

Beck, *Geschichts-Bücher*; J. Loserth, "Zur Gesch. der Wiedertäufer in der Steiermark," in *Mitteilungen des hist. Ver. f. Steiermark* L (1903) and *Ztscht des hist. Ver. f. Steiermark* X (1913); Wolkan, *Geschicht-Buch*; Zieglschmid, *Chronik*; P. Dedic, *Der Protestantismus in der Steiermark im Zeitalter d. Ref. u. Gegenref.* (Leipzig, 1930); ML II, 639 f.

Leonhard, Grand Master of the Teutonic Knights: see **Dorfbrunner, Leonhard.**

Leonhard the Schoolmaster, whose true name was Leonhard Eleutherobios, brother of Christoph Eleutherobios (*q.v.*), was a schoolmaster at Linz, Austria, who joined the Anabaptists in 1527, probably being baptized by Hans Hut. Little is known of him. He published a German translation of Johann Bugenhagen's booklet, *Was und Welches die Sünde sei in den Hl. Geist.* (See **Eleutherobios.**) H.S.B.

Leonhard van Tongeren: see **Lenart van Ysenbroeck.**

Leopold, Joh., a martyr: see **Leupold.**

Leopold I (1640-1705), Emperor of the Holy Roman Empire 1658-1705, the son of Emperor Ferdinand III. His reign covered a long period of 47 years. He was a friend of the sciences and of music, a composer, and a lover of books; personally fond of splendor and full of the joy of living, his morals were above reproach. The influence of his Catholic education was felt in the severe and unjust treatment of Protestants, which sometimes resulted in revolts, especially in Hungary. Through the good fortune of having able generals, he raised Austria to the status of a great world power.

The struggles "with Turks and Tartars" resulting from his interference in Transylvania caused the Hutterian Brethren at Alwinc much suffering. In Slovakia (then belonging to Hungary), where they had become a cultural factor, the emperor granted them a letter of protection (*Protektionsschreiben und Privilegium*) on Jan. 29, 1659 (the only one ever granted by a Hapsburg ruler), for the districts of Neutra, Pressburg, and Trentschin, directing the authorities there to give them full protection. But this did not prevent the quartering of troops and the burning of parts of these Bruderhofs as well as that at Alwinc in the first Turkish war in 1663-64. A copy of the "privilege" is kept in the Imperial Chancellery at Vienna; Beck reprints it in his *Geschichts-Bücher* (496).

The imperial government at that time took a hostile attitude to the Mennonites of Germany. In 1672 it protested the settlement of 300 to 400 Mennonites in Hamburg (*q.v.*), calling their admission a violation of the *Instrumentum* of the Peace of Westphalia. The Hamburg senate nevertheless warmly defended them, declaring that the Mennonites "are peaceful and also capable citizens, who have nothing to do with the Anabaptists of Münster, but have instead taken the government into their church prayer."

The severity of Leopold's enforcement of the Counter Reformation led to a revolt and to the second Turkish war. Four years previously the Jesuits, accompanied by soldiers, had entered the Bruderhof in Sobotiste and had made a futile attempt to convert the Hutterian Brethren; now another attempt was made by summoning the leaders Poley and Milder (*q.v.*) to court. But the steadfastness of the Brethren, and the lenience of Archbishop Kollonitsch, president of the Hungarian chancellery, put an end to the oppression of the Hutterites. Against Lutherans and Calvinists, however, it continued unabated; members of their clergy were sent to the galleys.

The Brethren suffered very severely in 1683 at the hands of Turkish and Hungarian troops overrunning the country after the Turkish defeat. The victory at Munkacs and Belgrade strengthened the imperial rule. In 1688 Kollonitsch ordered that the Hutterite children in Velke Levary (*q.v.*) be baptized. Some obeyed, thus making the first breach in the brotherhood. The Brethren at Alwinc put an end to the demoralization and reorganized their Bruderhof in 1694.

In Jülich the emperor also intervened in favor of the Anabaptists in 1694. Elector John William (*q.v.*) had (through a band of peasants and soldiers, led by three commissioners) attacked the Mennonites in Rheydt, especially those settled as tenants on the estates of the nobles. This band plundered and destroyed much on these estates, and kidnaped about 30 persons, including women and children, mistreating some of them. The Crefeld Mennonites redeemed them at great cost. This disgraceful persecution evoked intervention by foreign powers. King William III of England wrote a letter to the elector on Aug. 11, 1694, requesting that the persecution be stopped, the property be restored, and that protection be granted them in the future. The Dutch States-General on Sept. 16 made an earnest protest to the emperor himself, with the same demands, pointing out the bad precedent set here in John

William's attitude toward peaceful and quiet subjects like the industrious and competent Mennonites. Thereupon the emperor actually appealed to the latter to spare them, admitting that the Peace of Westphalia declared "three religions permissible in the empire," and that "said Minists were not included" among them; but he asked the elector to consider the weight and importance of the foreign intercessors. John William replied that the Mennonites had been settled in his territory without his knowledge by avaricious officials, but finally yielded, and on Aug. 17, 1697, restored the possessions of the refugees, including the confiscated books and printed matter, gave them permission to sell their property, and promised to grant them free "commercium" in his domain.

There is no record of further oppression of the Mennonites before the death of Leopold I in 1705.

P.DE.

K. V. Wurzbach, *Biogr. Lexikon d. Kaiserl. Oesterr.* V. (Vienna, 1859); Beck, *Geschichts-Bücher;* K. L. v. Heigel, "Neue Beitr. z. Charakteristik Leopolds I.," *Sitzber. d. bayr. Akad. d. Wiss.* II (München, 1890); F. v. Krones and K. Uhlirz, *Oesterreich Gesch.* III (Leipzig, 1915); K. Uhlirz, *Handbuch d. Gesch. Oesterreichs* (Graz, Vienna, Leipzig, 1927); Wolkan, *Geschicht-Buch;* Zieglschmid, *Chronik;* G. Loesche, *Gesch. des Prot. in Oesterreich* (Vienna, Leipzig, 1930); Rembert, *Wiedertäufer;* A. Brons, *Ursprung, Entwickelung und Schicksale der . . . Mennoniten* (3d ed., Norden, 1912); *ML* II, 240, 640 f.

Lepers, Paraguay Mission to, was projected by the Mennonite Central Committee in co-operation with the Fernheim (*q.v.*) Colony in 1945 as an expression of appreciation to Paraguay for its reception of the Mennonites from Russia in 1930. The assistance of the American Leprosy Mission was secured, which pays two thirds of the cost of the buildings and current operations, the rest coming from the MCC budget for work in Paraguay with a small support from the Mennonites in the Chaco. Dr. John Schmidt of Mountain Lake, Minn., was appointed director of the work in 1950, which is located east of Barrio Grande, 50 miles east of Asuncion, on land purchased by the MCC. Originally one clinic was conducted here, and two others at Coronel Oviedo and Kilometer 81. The latter was the only one in operation in 1956; it treated 180 patients during the year. Emphasis is put on ambulatory treatment, the doctor going out to the grass huts where the people live. A territory of about 5,000 sq. mi. is registered with the Paraguayan government as the area of MCC work, within which the mission tries to find and treat all leprosy cases. The Paraguayan Mennonites help with voluntary service workers. Paraguay has an incidence of about 3-5 per thousand, one of the highest incidences of leprosy in South America.   H.S.B.

Lepp (Loep, Leepp, Lipp, Lippe), a common Mennonite name of Prussian or Dutch background. The name apeared in Heubuden, Tiegenhagen, Ladekopp, Rosenort, Neunhuben, etc. It is first recorded in Orlofferfelde in 1601. From Prussia the name spread to Russia and North America. It is likely that the name Leppke found in Mennonite Brethren circles in the United States is of different background. Outstanding was Peter H. Lepp (*q.v.*), the pioneer Mennonite industrialist of Chortitza. Aron Lepp (*q.v.*) was an elder of the Mennonite Brethren Church at Einlage. Eduard H. Lepp (*q.v.*) was a significant member of the Mennonite church of Danzig. Hermann P. Lepp is pastor of the Mennonite church at Harrow, Ont. (Reimer, *Familiennamen,* 113.)   C.K.

Lepp, Aron, an elder of the Mennonite Brethren at Einlage, South Russia. He had been baptized by immersion on April 22, 1862. In consequence he was accused of being an "Anabaptist" by the *Fürsorgekomitee* in Odessa, and was dismissed from his office of civil and economic supervision of the Jewish settlement (see **Judenplan,** *ML* II, 439 f.). In 1866 he was put in charge of Andreasfeld, a subsidiary congregation, by the Baptist preacher August Liebig (*q.v.*); at a conference in 1868 he was chosen to the ministry, and on Oct. 18, 1869, ordained by the Baptist Elder Oncken of Hamburg. Although Lepp had received a Baptist ordination, he was reordained by the Mennonite Elder Janz of Friedrichsfeld, when he was chosen to fill the place of Elder A. Unger in 1876.

Lepp was a determined opponent of the union of the Mennonite Brethren with the Baptists. He argued that the Mennonites would jeopardize their rights, and that the confessions of faith were too divergent. It is therefore largely due to his influence that the Mennonite Brethren did not merge with the Baptists. Lepp served in the office of elder until an advanced age. In 1901 he retired. (Friesen, *Brüderschaft; ML* II, 641.)   A.B.

Lepp, Eduard Hermann (1850-1926), a merchant and chairman of the Danzig (*q.v.*) Mennonite Church, was born June 26, 1850, at Tiegenhof in the Danzig Werder, and served from 1894 until his death as a member of the church board and as treasurer of the mother deaconess house and the Augusta Victoria foundation, and was also a city councilman and president of the Danzig merchants' association. He worked long for the welfare of his church, cooperating with his friend H. G. Mannhardt (*q.v.*). On Dec. 8, 1926, he died. (*ML* II, 641.)   O.W.

Lepp, Peter Heinrich (1817-71), a pioneer Mennonite industrialist of Russia, was born in Einlage near Chortitza Dec. 29, 1817. His father, Heinrich Lepp, was a carpenter and died when Peter was 13 years old. Since Peter had no inclination to follow agricultural pursuits, to which his stepfather encouraged him, he was permitted at the age of 15 to go to Prussia to learn clockmaking from one of his relatives. Having mastered this, his desire to continue the study of machinery led him to visit German industries. His relatives, fearing that such unsteady life would not be conducive to good character building, sent him back to Russia. Soon after his return he married.

P. H. Lepp bought a home in Chortitza and began to make the typical Mennonite wall clocks, as a rule with two apprentices. Through German book dealers he obtained many books on mechanics and industries and gained an unusual knowledge of science and the manufacture of machinery. Com-

pelled by poor eyesight to discontinue watch- and clockmaking, he acquainted himself with foundry work and the building of machinery in Lugansk. In 1853 he produced his first threshing machine in Chortitza and sold it to a large estate owner. By 1861 more of the Russian large estate owners were attracted by his work. His small factory obtained parts from a foundry in Ekaterinoslav, which were often faulty. In 1860 Lepp erected his own foundry to be able to supervise the production of all parts himself. However, his machinery met very strong competition through British import. Since Lepp was able to guarantee his product and replace parts directly at any time, and could also instruct people in the operation of machines, it gradually came to be preferred to the imported machines. It took a long time for him to win the confidence of the banks so that they would lend him the necessary funds to develop his enterprise.

In 1867 the factory produced 115 threshing machines, 50 winnowers, 175 iron horse rakes, 125 chaff cutters, 12 reapers, and 8 trieurs. With the invention of the *lobogreyka* (reaper) the factory rapidly expanded. Lepp now took as his partner Wallmann, who possessed some capital. During the early 1880's the new concern became known as Lepp and Wallmann. A branch factory was established in Schönwiese, a suburb of Alexandrovsk, now Zaporozhe. In 1889 the firm employed 250 men in its two factories. During that year 1,200 reapers, 220 threshing machines, 500 winnowers, 15 steam threshers, and 15 boilers were sold. In 1908 the capital stock was 1,200,000 rubles, the output was 900,000 rubles, and 270 men were employed. By 1911-12 the number employed was 700, and by 1914 the capital stock had mounted to 2,400,000 rubles. The Lepp and Wallmann business was the largest of the eight large Mennonite factories in Russia. During the Russian Revolution the factories were nationalized but continued their work.

P. H. Lepp, who died in Prussia while visiting his brother in 1871, did much to revolutionize and improve agriculture in the Ukraine. His descendants continued his work. (See also **Agriculture** *Among the Mennonites in Russia,* **Business** and **Industry** *among the Mennonites of Russia.*)   C.K.

"Mennonite Industry in Russia," *Menn. Life* X (January 1955) 21 ff.; D. H. Epp, "P. H. Lepp," *Der Bote* (Rosthern, 1928) No. 10 ff.; D. Rempel, "The Mennonite Colonies in New Russia" (doctoral dissertation, Stanford University, 1933).

Leraar (*Leeraar*), designation given in the Netherlands to Mennonite preachers: see **Lehrer** and **Ministry.**

Leserlin (Leslin), **Georg** (Jörg), of Ingersheim, Besigheim district of Württemberg, Germany, an Anabaptist preacher, had very early—the Passau records say in 1535 at the age of ten, which is impossible—baptized Margarete, the wife of Hans of Schüchtern, and together with Hans Schmidt (*q.v.*) he wrote the song, "O Herre Gott vom Himmelreich, Merkt auff und sich die worte," which deals with the persecution of the believers. Leserlin was imprisoned in Stuttgart in 1533, because he had been misled by "perverted people and cunningly devised booklets," but in consideration of his youth, simplicity, and his willingness to recant, he was released after instruction by experienced and learned men, and most humbly thanked all who had helped in his conversion. Young Leserlin was probably the son of the Leserlin who had died in prison. According to the Passau court records Georg also died in prison; hence it must be assumed that he again joined the Anabaptists, was put into prison, and died there.   G.Bo.

TA Württemberg; 179, 198; Wackernagel, *Kirchenlied* V, No. 1070; K. Steiff and G. Mehring, *Geschichtliche Lieder und Sprüche Württembergs* (Stuttgart, 1912) 1076 f.; *ML* II, 641.

Letters of Protection (*Schutzbriefe*) were given the Mennonites in Altona (now Germany) by Duke Ernst von Schaunburg in 1601 (in 1604 by King Christian IV of Denmark and confirmed by all the succeeding kings of Denmark). As a rule they were granted free exercise of their religion and release from the oath and military service. The Mennonites in Eiderstedt and Friedrichstadt received a letter of protection from Duke Friedrich of Gottorp on Feb. 13, 1623; the Mennonites were given such letters by Countess Anna (*q.v.*) and Count Carl Edward in East Friesland in 1738, and the Mennonites of Danzig on Feb. 12, 1792, etc. (See the concession of Charles Louis in the article on him.)   NEFF.

Lettonitz (Lettnitz), a village (pop. 1,000) northeast of Austerlitz in Moravia. Little is known of the Bruderhof of the Hutterian Brethren set up here. In 1619-20 it was plundered by Polish troops of the imperial army which had surprised Pruschan and Kobelitz (*q.v.*), murdering five Brethren and shooting a child at its mother's breast.   P.DE.

Beck, *Geschichts-Bücher,* 381; Wolkan, *Geschicht-Buch;* Zieglschmid, *Chronik,* 725; *ML* II, 642.

Leubel, Michel, an Anabaptist martyr, who recanted in 1532 and then bitterly repented his deed; "he stumbled like Peter and did it against God; his flesh had been weak; but he had acquired grace. Let no man persuade him that water without faith has any value; the covenant and the water must be together, as Peter says; on this faith he would die." On the night of Jan. 30, 1533, he was drowned in the Rhine (court records of Speyer). (*ML* II, 642.)   NEFF.

Leupold, Hans (Hans Schneider, i.e., tailor), one of the first Anabaptist martyrs in South Germany, not to be confused with Hans Seibold. He came from Kleinaitlingen near Augsburg, Bavaria, Germany, and early in the summer of 1527 he joined the Anabaptists there. He was baptized by Jakob Dachser (*q.v.*) and served as a deacon. He took part in the Martyrs' Synod (*q.v.*) on Aug. 20, 1527.

In those days Urban Rhegius (*q.v.*) wrote his book, *Wider den neuen Tauforden, notwendige Warnung an alle Christgläubige,* dated Sept. 6, 1527. At the same time a systematic persecution of the Anabaptists in Augsburg began. On Aug. 28 several members were arrested and tortured, among them the preacher Jakob Dachser. On Sept. 15, 1527, others were arrested, including Hans Hut (*q.v.*)

and Jakob Gross (*q.v.*); and soon afterwards Eitel-hans Langenmantel (*q.v.*) and Siegmund Salminger were seized. Now all the Anabaptist preachers in Augsburg lay in prison; the plan was to make them recant together with a considerable number of the Anabaptists of the city, after instruction by the city parsons.

One of those arrested was Hans Leupold. He refused to confess that the doctrine of the Anabaptists was erroneous and was therefore, with eight others, expelled from the city on Oct. 1, 1527, on the pledge never to return. On the following days further exiles followed. The preachers, however, remained under arrest, since they would not recant. The congregation, robbed of its preachers, at once chose Hans Leupold to be their leader at Bobingen near Augsburg. Fearlessly he proclaimed the Gospel, strengthened and consoled the harassed brethren and made contacts among the South German Anabaptist groups. For several weeks he preached in Esslingen, and with a letter from the Esslingen Anabaptists he visited the Worms congregation; with a letter of consolation from Worms to the brethren at Esslingen, he returned to the vicinity of Augsburg. The members of the Augsburg congregation who had not yet been discovered had been visited by preachers traveling through, especially by Leonhard Dorfbrunner (*q.v.*), who baptized about 100 persons in Augsburg in 1527.

On the evening of March 26 Hans Leupold managed to reach Augsburg undetected. On April 2 he assembled about 60 persons in a narrow cellar to observe communion and to choose leaders for the growing congregation. The choice fell on Claus Schleiffer of Vienna and Peter Ringmacher. The latter was at once sent to Regensburg to preach for the Anabaptist brotherhood. Under the leadership of Hans Leupold and Jörg of Passau, the Augsburg brethren met on Easter (April 12) morning in the home of the sculptor Adolf Doucher. Some of the members, seeing armed guards near by, had become suspicious and returned to their homes; those at the service were restless and fearful of an attack. Leupold invited the timid to leave while there was still time, and some escaped. But the remaining 88 were seized and expelled from the city, some having holes burned through their cheeks.

Leupold was questioned with and without the rack. He confessed whom and where he had baptized, and added that he was always glad when someone was converted. He declared that the Anabaptists were not planning an attack, as some seemed to fear. At their meetings they considered God's Word, principally the Gospels and the Prophets, which had recently been translated into German by Hans Denk, who had likewise been baptized in Augsburg, and Ludwig Haetzer. The brotherhood, Leupold continued, was very watchful to keep out false doctrine, and if a member erred he was instructed. Nor did they wish to have all things in common; they did not want anybody to be deprived of his possessions by violence. But aid should be voluntarily given the needy, regardless of whether or not he belonged to the brotherhood. He taught that one should acknowledge God, live according to His commands, and strive to attain the truth. Members who did not live a proper life, and did not show a deep interest in love and the truth, were warned several times and then put out of the brotherhood if the warning was fruitless. He had taught repentance and that the end time was at hand, without indicating when it would begin or end (Roth, 60-65).

Although the trial of the 88 prisoners (Roth, 71 f.) revealed no unchristian attitude or doctrine, Hans Leupold was condemned to die. The sentence was based on the mandate of Oct. 11, 1527, which prohibited on penalty of death, imprisonment, or fine, joining the Anabaptists, withholding baptism from infants, feeding their preachers, or taking part in any mob (Meyer, 251). He had secretly come to the city, had held meetings in pits, cellars, and other unsuitable places at suspicious times in the city and its vicinity, rejected infant baptism, preached adult baptism and other evil doctrines under the guise of the good, had also baptized a number of persons within and without the city, and also carried letters for the Anabaptists. He was beheaded on April 25 at Augsburg. Leupold was survived by his wife and two children, the youngest of whom was five months old.

When the verdict that he was to be sentenced from life to death was read to him from the Rathaus, he cried out, "No indeed, gentlemen of Augsburg, but from death to life!" causing great amazement among the spectators (Beck, 37). This mood also pervades the song, "Mein Gott Dich will ich loben," which he wrote in prison shortly before his execution. It reveals the "singleness" of his mind and the genuineness of a faith that he not only taught, but also lived. He admonishes his brethren to trust in God, and prays for his persecutors. This hymn is the only written record left by him. It was printed in the *Ausbund* (*q.v.*) and by Wackernagel in his collection, *Das deutsche Kirchenlied* (III, 478).

For the Augsburg Anabaptist brotherhood Leupold's death was a devastating blow; their surviving leaders (Dachser, Gross, and Salminger) were in prison or expelled from the city. But the spirit permeating them lived on.   HEGE.

Beck, *Geschichts-Bücher*; Chr. Hege, *Ein Rückblick auf 400 Jahre mennonitischer Geschichte* (Karlsruhe, 1935); Chr. Meyer, "Die Anfänge des Wiedertäufertums in Augsburg," in *Ztscht des Hist. Vereins für Schwaben und Neuburg* I (1874) 207-53; Fr. Roth, "Der Höhepunkt der wiedertäuferischen Bewegung in Augsburg und ihr Niedergang im Jahre 1528," in *loc. cit.* XXVIII (1901) 1-154; idem, *Augsburgs Ref.-Gesch.* (Augsburg, 1901 and 1904); *ML* II, 642 f.

Leutscher, a Dutch Mennonite family, descending from the Swiss Mennonite family of Lötscher (*q.v.*), Latscha (*q.v.*). Among the Swiss emigrants forced to leave the country and moving to the Netherlands in 1711 was Emanuel Lörtscher (Leutscher), a farmer from Erlenbach (Berner Oberland) and his family. They settled on the farm of Vinkhuizen, near Hoogkerk, about five miles from the city of Groningen. Numerous descendants are still living in the Netherlands. Some of them were preachers and elders of the Swiss Mennonites: Rudolf Leutscher, who according to *Naamlijst* served 1755-61, but according to other information was already a preacher in 1741, Izaak Jannes Leutscher, b. 1740, d. Nov. 20,

1826, a farmer first at Noorddijk, then at Noordhorn near Groningen, serving 1791-1811, and Christiaan Jacobs Leutscher, a farmer at Hoogkerk, d. Aug. 8, 1824, serving 1812-24 at Groningen. After Rudolf's death the Swiss congregation at Groningen merged with the United Mennonites; in Sappemeer the Swiss congregation had united with the Dutch Mennonites some time before. The son of preacher Izaak Jannes Leutscher, Jannes Izaak Leutscher (1772-1866), a farmer, at Noorddijk, Noordhorn, and Hoogkerk until his death, even after the Swiss congregation had dissolved, faithfully held to the Swiss simplicity of dress and style of living.   vDZ.

J. Huizinga, *Stamboek . . van Samuel Peter (Meihuizen) en Barbara Fry* (Groningen, 1890) *passim*, see Index, 124; *Ter Nagedachtenis van C. Leutscher* (n.p., n.d.); *Naamlijst* 1829, 61; *ML* II, 694 f.

Leuvenig (Leuvenich, Leuvenigh), **van,** a Dutch Mennonite family, a branch of the Crefeld von Loevenich (*q.v.*) family, is found at Amsterdam, where they usually were cloth merchants. They joined the Amsterdam Zonist (*q.v.*) congregation. Deacons of this congregation were Sander Hans van Leuvenich 1670-74, 1682-86, Abraham van Leuvenigh 1684-8, 1703-6, Steven van Leuvenigh 1722-26, Hendrik van Leuvenigh 1758-62, 1768-72, Gerrit van Leuvenigh 1763-66, 1773-76, and Pieter Johan van Leuvenigh 1782-86, 1791-1806. Other members of this family, including the preacher B. van Leuvenig (*q.v.*), belonged to the Amsterdam Lamist congregation.   vDZ.

J. Rogge, *Het Handelshuis van Eeghen* (Amsterdam, 1948) *passim;* Church records of Amsterdam.

Leuvenig (Leuvenigh, Loevenigh), **Bartholomeus van,** b. April 15, 1691, at Burtscheid, Germany, d. Dec. 18, 1759, at Amsterdam, was a son of Bartholomeus van Loevenich, a cloth merchant at Burtscheid and a member of the well-known von Loevenich (*q.v.*) family. Bartholomeus van Leuvenig, who received his theological training at the Amsterdam Athenaeum and from the Remonstrant professors Clericus and van Limborgh, and who was married to Joanna de Clercq, of Amsterdam, in 1713 became an assistant preacher of the Amsterdam Lamist congregation, being its pastor 1716-39, in which year he resigned because of his health. He was a member of the Dutch Mennonite Committee of Foreign Needs, and frequently corresponded with the West Prussian churches; a number of these letters are found in the Mennonite Archives at Amsterdam. He published *Lykreden ober het Afsterven van D. Eekens* (his Amsterdam colleague) (Amsterdam, 1732); *Gods Tugtles aen Jerusalem* (Amsterdam, 1734); *Stichtelyke Gezangen* (Amsterdam, 1744); and *De Brief aan de Gemeente van Laodicea verklaard en toegepast* (13 sermons) (Amsterdam, 1746). G. van Heyningen delivered his funeral sermon, published at Amsterdam in 1759.

F.A.E., vDZ.

Biogr. Wb. V, 770-72; *Zondagsbode* III, No. 43 (Aug. 24, 1890); *Inv. Arch. Amst.* II, No. 2641; *ML* II, 686.

Levellers, an important political and religious movement in England (1647-49) at the time of Cromwell, which, obviously influenced by Anabaptism, demanded absolute civil and religious liberty and the complete separation of church and state, but which finally degenerated into a passionate attack on the state and was therefore gradually suppressed. Pieter Cornelisz Plockhoy (*q.v.*) was associated with the Levellers.   NEFF.

H. Weingarten, *Die Revolutionskirchen Englands* (Leipzig, 1868); E. Troeltsch, *The Social Teachings of the Christian Churches* (N.Y., 1931); D. Robertson, *The Religious Foundations of Leveller Democracy* (N.Y., 1951); E. Bernstein, *Cromwell and Communism* (London, 1930); T. C. Pease, *The Leveller Movement* (Amer. Historical Association, 1916); L. and M. Harder, *Plockhoy from Zurik-zee* (Newton, 1952); *ML* II, 644.

Levina, an Anabaptist martyr, who was burned at the stake at Gent, Belgium, on Feb. 14, 1554, together with David (David van der Leyen, *q.v.*). These martyrs are celebrated in two hymns, one found in the *Lietboecxken van den Offer des Heeren* (No. 7) beginning "Ghy Christen al te samen" (You Christians all together), and one inserted in the Dutch hymnary, *Nieu Liedeboeck* of 1562, beginning "Och Heere ic moet u claghen" (O Lord, I must complain to Thee). The information in later Dutch martyrbooks, including van Braght's *Martyrs' Mirror,* is a prose version of the first hymn. Levina said that she would rather die and leave her six children than to fail Christ; so she died steadfast. The scarce information from the hymns and the martyrbooks has been amplified by A. L. E. Verheyden with a number of particulars from the official records. Here this martyr's name was Lievine Ghyselins; she was the widow of Willem van Leuven (*q.v.*), a shoemaker, who was executed at Gent because of Anabaptism on Feb. 17, 1553. When he was put to death, Lievine was already in prison. Her execution was apparently postponed because she was pregnant. Lievine was the mother of Frans (Franchoys) van Leuven, who suffered martyrdom at Gent on July 28, 1573. The crowd attending the execution of David and Levina is said to have been greatly affected by their cruel death.   vDZ.

Offer, 531-35; *Mart. Mir.* D 160, E. 549; Verheyden, *Gent,* 20, No. 40; Wackernagel, *Lieder,* 132, Wolkan, *Lieder,* 61; *ML* II, 646.

Lewär: see **Velké Levary.**

Lewellen (Neb.) United Missionary Church, located eight miles north of Lewellen, was founded in 1928, and its building erected in 1929. It had 33 members in 1955 with J. P. Tschetter as pastor.   J.P.T.

Lewis County (N.Y.) is located in the north central part of New York State bordering the Adirondack Mountains on the east. The Mennonites are found in the central part of the county in and around the villages of Lowville and Croghan. There are approximately 800 Mennonites in Lewis County and about 50 members living near Woodville in Jefferson County, an adjoining county. The First Mennonite Church (MC), organized in 1941, is located at New Bremen (*q.v.*) and had 193 members in 1954. The two older Conservative Amish Mennonite churches with a combined membership of about 600 are located near Croghan and Lowville. The first Amish Mennonite settlers came to Lewis County from Alsace-Lorraine in June 1833. One of the first to

arrive was Michael Zehr. Among the families who arrived soon after were Martin, Moser, Steria, Nafziger, Lehman, Farney, Virkler, and Kennel. For a history of the Amish Mennonite community, see **Lowville** Conservative Mennonite Church. B.F.Z.

Lewis County, Tenn., Old Order Amish settlement was founded in the spring of 1946 when the Amish families of P. M. Bontreger, Jacob Mast, and Alvin Mast of Jay Co., Ind., moved to near Hohenwald, Lewis Co. A congregation of 20 members meets regularly for worship in homes. The minister in charge is Jacob D. Mast, the deacon P. M. Bontreger, and the bishop Christ M. Bontreger of Buchanan Co., Iowa.   S.E.Y.

Lexington Mennonite Church (MC), located at Line Lexington, Bucks Co., Pa., in the Delaware Valley, 25 miles north of Philadelphia, a member of the Franconia Mennonite Conference, dates back to colonial times. There is a record of land purchased by four trustees in 1752, with a log meetinghouse as the first church building. The first known minister and bishop was David Ruth, 1796. The church was incorporated in 1836-37. It has gradually changed from a rural to an urban status. The membership in 1956 was 194; the bishop was Arthur D. Ruth, and Claude B. Meyers and Merle R. Ruth the ministers.   A.D.R.

Lexmond, a small town in the Dutch province of South Holland, where Leenaert Bouwens (*q.v.*) baptized eleven persons. There is no information that a congregation ever existed here. The newly baptized may have joined the congregation of Vianen (*q.v.*).   vDZ.

Ley, Evert Jacobs, a Mennonite preacher of Emden, East Friesland, Germany, where he delivered a funeral sermon, *Lykreden op Wytse de Vries* (published Amsterdam, 1727). This shows that he was a preacher, though his name is not found in the Emden list of preachers. In 1730-*ca.* 37 he was a preacher at Kampen, Dutch province of Overijssel (*DB* 1881, 90). Further information was not available.   vDZ.

Ley, van der, a Dutch Mennonite family, formerly at Zaandam and Koog aan de Zaan. Symon Aarjans van der Ley (Simon Adriaansz) was a preacher of the Koog-Zaandijk Waterlander congregation (year of calling unknown) and from 1680 of the United Flemish and Waterlander congregation of Koog-Zaandijk. He lived at Zaandijk, and died before 1700. His cousin Jan Pietersz van der Ley (1671-1750) married to Mary Claesd. Kaaskooper, and their son Aris (Jans) van der Ley (1708-1800), both of Zaandijk, were noted manufacturers of paper, operating the de Bonsem, de Wever, and 't Fortuyn mills. The van der Ley family has now died out.   vDZ.

Leydecker, Jacobus, a Dutch Reformed minister of Middelburg, province of Zeeland, who wrote a treatise against the Mennonites, accusing Adriaen van Eeghem (*q.v.*), Mennonite preacher of Middelburg, of Arianism (Unitarianism). The (shortened) title of Leydecker's book reads: *De Sake van den Sone Gods verdedigd* (Middelburg, 1701). vdZ.

Leyden, and **Leydse Synode:** see **Leiden** and **Leidsche Synode.**

Leyen, van der, a Mennonite family in Flanders, Belgium. In 1534 Lievin van der Leyen was tried at Gent for heresy; in 1551 he was arrested again, this time at Merelbeke near Gent; though he was convicted of heresy and his property confiscated, he was not executed but released, as was (his brother?) Jan van der Leyen, after both had abjured their heretical opinions. David van der Leyen (*q.v.*) of Gent was burned at the stake there on Feb. 14, 1554. Tanneken van der Leyen (*q.v.*), an unmarried woman of Gent, was drowned in 1555 and Laurens (Laureys) van der Leyen (*q.v.*) was beheaded at Antwerp in 1559. Frans (Franchoys) van der Leyen (*q.v.*) suffered martyrdom at Gent in 1558. Tanneken, Laurens, David, and Frans were children of Mennonites. Their father, whose name is not mentioned, is said to have also been a Mennonite who escaped martyrdom because he was seriously ill (Verheyden, *Gent,* 21). vdZ.

Leyen, von der, a Mennonite family of Crefeld, Germany. To this enterprising family Crefeld owes its rise to prosperity. Adolf von der Leyen from Rade vorm Walde in the duchy of Berg in Germany acquired citizenship in Crefeld in 1679.

Adolf began the manufacture of silk thread and velvet ribbon and on the side sold silk ribbon and embroidery silk, imported foods, Nürnberg trinkets, Bibles, calendars, etc. After his death in 1698 his son Wilhelm became the soul of the business; he manufactured silk ribbon and velvet yard goods, selling most of his products at the fair at Frankfurt. He purchased the raw silk from Zürich and had it spun and twisted in Milan and Turin. Later the East India Company delivered the Asiatic raw silk direct to Crefeld. In spite of unfavorable conditions of transportation von der Leyen's business increased in his own sales outlets in Frankfurt, Cologne, Strasbourg, Zürich, and Geneva. In 1724 he established a dyeing plant. Soon his business was limited to the manufacture and sale of his own silk and velvet wares.

Although in competition with Lyons, the Netherlands, and Cologne the von der Leyens achieved an unusual prosperity, so that in the span of a century Crefeld had to extend its walls five times. The four sons of Wilhelm von der Leyen added three supplementary firms. But the firm of the Brüder Friedrich and Heinrich von der Leyen, established in 1731 with a capital of only 18,900 Reichsthaler, soon overtook it, creating a world business of hitherto unheard of dimensions in silk goods, which increased from year to year (by 1740 the turnover was 206,000 Rt., and by 1756, 520,000 Rt.).

In 1738 King Frederick William I visited Crefeld, inspected the factories and warehouses, having previously ordered the exemption of the von der Leyen workmen from military duty. The introduction of machinery from the Netherlands hastened the growth. The old silk center of Cologne, with its tradition- and guild-bound silk industry, now sought to prevent the importation of the cheaper and better wares from Crefeld, but the royal council declared that if that was done, a duty would be placed on Cologne wines passing down the Rhine. The prohibition was therefore abandoned.

Although with the commission system prevalent at that time thousands of hand weavers living as far away as Cleve earned their living by working for the Crefeld firm, and subsidiaries were established in Geldern, Xanten, and Aldekerk, the city itself continued to grow through the influx of master weavers from Italy, France, and the Netherlands. In the course of a century the population increased twentyfold; it grew from 1,499 in 1722 to 4,576 in 1740, 6,082 in 1763 (2,700 of whom were directly employed by the firm), and 7,896 in 1787.

In 1755 Frederick the Great bestowed on Friedrich and Heinrich von der Leyen the title of *Kommerzienrat* for their great service to their workers, and later also upon their three nephews Conrad, Friedrich, and Johann. This title released the bearer from the jurisdiction of the city, making him subject directly to the king. But in spite of this the Crefeld products were barred from many places "east of the Weser." Even the wares destined for Poland and Russia by way of the Frankfurt a.d.O. fair were charged duty for crossing the country. On this point King Frederick was adamant, in order not to threaten his favorite Brandenburg silk industry. Nevertheless the Crefeld industry continued to grow, employing 3,400 workers in 1786, the year of King Frederick's death. Since this industry had grown to maturity without help from the state, the government avoided interfering with its internal affairs. In 1751 and 1763 the king was in Crefeld and made his headquarters with the von der Leyens. His expressions of satisfaction are found in the *Acta Borussica.* In 1763 he notified the government of Cleve that the Crefeld firm was not to suffer competition from small industries which would be unable to maintain themselves, by the luring away of workers, and by having their machinery, invented by themselves, copied.

In their wills the brothers Friedrich (d. 1778) and Heinrich (d. 1782) erected a modest monument for themselves (*ML* II, 572). By this time the firm was exporting goods to all parts of Europe and to America. The three nephews, Friedrich (d. 1787), Conrad (d. 1797), and Johann (d. 1795), continued to increase it. The new king, Frederick William II, recognizing at once the importance of Crefeld, bestowed on the three men a title of hereditary nobility. Johann built the magnificent house on Friedrichstrasse, which later became a bank, and Conrad built as his residence the "castle," which became the city hall.

The confusions of 20 years of war 1794-1814 caused the firm to decline. Johann von der Leyen purchased for his residence the Kieckhorst estate in the Moers district. Conrad's son Friedrich Heinrich (b. 1765) was still a manufacturer from tradition, but his interests lay in intellectual and aesthetic pursuits. As a friend of Fr. Ad. Krummacher, noted as a preacher and writer of parables, he and his highly educated mother lived in the intellectual world of

Rousseau and Kant. Friedrich Heinrich von Conrad von der Leyen exercised his Kantian sense of duty in his interest in the industry and the people of Crefeld. Selflessly he devoted himself to the interests of the city, while the generals of the French army were comfortably quartered in his home. Later he exchanged friendly letters with the prince who became Frederick William IV. His cousin Friedrich Heinrich, a son of Friedrich von der Leyen, united with the Reformed Church and turning to rural life purchased the Moers feudal estate and Bloemersheim castle, as well as the monastery land of Meer (Neuss district).

Difficulties increased during this period, the most severe being the continental blockade and the change from rococo fashions to English fashions. The period 1797-1805 brought serious losses, some of which were regained in 1810. Competition with the Berg industry was too severe to permit further expansion. Nevertheless the firm of Friedrich and Heinrich von der Leyen continued until its dissolution to be the greatest industrial undertaking of the Rhineland and probably the greatest silk industry of the entire western world in its period.

The owners of the firm always regarded their position and their wealth as entailing responsibility to the people. They considered their income only as the just reward of their management of property belonging to God, to whom they must give account. Benevolent works were the necessary outcome of their faith, which was turned not to comfortable mysticism and contemplation, but to adventurous action. Their business was conducted as a large family affair. Workers employed in good times were not discharged in bad times. Even in 1780, when there was already a great surplus of manufactured goods, no workers lost their jobs, whereas in Lyons and Rouen 17,000 silk weavers were discharged. In 1794, 200 workers were given a sort of old-age retirement pension.

As Mennonites the von der Leyens were tolerant. Frederick William I in 1738 praised their tolerance when he learned that people of all creeds were employed by them. As the house of Orange had in 1695 permitted the Mennonites to build a church, Frederick the Great now allowed the Catholics to build one. The von der Leyens then built the "Siebenhäuser," the income of which was to be used for the poor, and provided a considerable fund for the employment of well-educated Mennonite ministers. The spirit of the von der Leyens, which considers wealth as an obligation, still prevails in Crefeld.   K.R.

W. Kurschat, *Das Haus Friedrich & Heinrich von der Leyen in Krefeld* (Frankfurt, 1933); W. Niepoth, "Zur Frühgeschichte der Familie von der Leyen," in *Die Heimat* XXI (1950) 156-58; *Inv. Arch. Amst.* I, No. 1380; Gerhard von Beckerath, "Die wirtschaftliche Bedeutung der Krefelder Mennoniten und ihrer Vorfahren im 17. und 18. Jahrhundert" (dissertation, Bonn, 1951); Walther Risler, "Mennonites of Krefeld," *Menn. Life* VI (April 1951) 26; *ML* II, 645-48.

Leytner, Hans, a martyr: see **Leitner.**

Lezius, Friedrich (b. 1859), a Protestant theologian, lecturer at the University of Greifswalde, Germany, then (1901) professor of church history at the University of Königsberg, Prussia, retired in 1925. In his book, *Der Toleranzgedanke Lockes und Pufendorfs* (1900), he discusses at length the part of the Anabaptists in the spread of religious toleration. (*Menn. Bl.,* 1907, 88; *ML* II, 648.)

Liberalism *in the Dutch Mennonite Church.* Liberalism is a concept found both in politics and theology. In politics Liberalism is the opposite of all kinds of totalitarianism; on the one hand it rejects absolutism and conservatism, on the other hand socialism and communism. Religious liberalism is the antithesis of fundamentalism and orthodoxy. What has been the attitude of the Mennonites toward Liberalism?

(*a*) *Political Liberalism.* Before the end of the 18th century Mennonites hardly had any opportunity to influence political life of the countries in which they lived. In most countries they lived more or less as closed groups, which were merely tolerated and were completely dependent on the favor of the rulers. Only in the Netherlands and in some German cities like Hamburg and Crefeld conditions were somewhat better, but even here political freedom and equality with the members of the state church was not acquired until about 1800. Even at the present time Mennonites are in many countries still only tolerated groups; in others, like America, they take little interest in politics. Only in the Netherlands and the North German cities like Emden, Hamburg, and Danzig have the Mennonites been engaged in the political life since the early 19th century. As to the Netherlands, in the course of the 19th century there were a striking number of Mennonites holding office as city councillors, provincial councillors, members of both the first and the second chambers of the legislature, and ministers of state. With one or two exceptions they were all (political) liberals, opposed to too much state interference, upholders of religious and political tolerance, and in many ways opposing the Calvinistic political parties. Though at present many Dutch Mennonites are attached to or vote for the Labor Party and occasionally also for some Christian political parties, many Mennonites in politics are still adherents of liberal principles.

(*b*) *Religious Liberalism.* On the whole the Mennonites in the past and present have been attached to orthodoxy and even to fundamentalism, though there have been exceptions from the very beginning of Anabaptism; e.g., Hans Denk (*q.v.*) and Jacob Kautz (*q.v.*) in Germany in some respects differed from their coreligionists as to the orthodox Biblical doctrines. In the Netherlands the martyr Herman van Vlekwijk (*q.v.*) was an anti-Trinitarian; the elder Adam Pastor (*q.v.*) denied the deity of Christ and the doctrine of satisfaction and was excommunicated because of it; a number of early Dutch leaders, especially among the Waterlanders, such as Hans de Ries (*q.v.*) were less orthodox than most other Mennonites. But in general Mennonitism was orthodox until about 1860, when most of the Dutch Mennonites and many in the city congregations of North Germany turned to Liberalism. It should be emphatically pointed out that in Holland and Germany Liberalism has a somewhat different meaning from the usual meaning of this term in America. In America Liberalism usually means free thinking and even atheism or agnosticism, i.e., a complete rejection of faith, while in Western Europe Liberalism means a critical conception of the Bible. Although there have been and still are great differences within liberal theology and between its adherents, it may be asserted that all liberals are unanimous in the following views: (1) the Bible is not the word of God in a strict sense, but contains the word of God; (2) Jesus Christ is not *the* son of God, but *a* son of God in the sense that all men are; His birth was not supernatural, but natural, His death was not expiatory, but exemplary; (3) man on earth is not a victim of Adam's sin and fall in Paradise, to be justified only by the atoning blood of Christ, but a natural creature, gifted with free will and the possibility of serving God in following Christ's example; (4) doctrines like the inspiration of the Scriptures, satisfaction, trinity, and hell are denied.

When Liberalism, then mostly called Modernism, arose about the middle of the 19th century, most Dutch Mennonites were soon won over to its ideas. It was largely due to the influence of S. Hoekstra Bzn (*q.v.*), then professor of the Amsterdam Mennonite Seminary, that Liberalism among the Mennonites did not assume as radical a form as it took elsewhere. The turn of the Dutch Mennonites to Liberalism was not unexpected nor accidental; it was in a sense rather self-evident, being the consequence of Dutch Mennonite piety of especially the 17th and 18th centuries. During these centuries and even before gradually more stress had been laid upon personal (individual) conviction and practical Christianity than upon church doctrines, which, though accepted in a traditional way, became more and more "dead capital" (Hoekstra). Besides this the spiritualistic tendency, found already in the early Dutch Anabaptist martyrs (see **Spiritualism**) and in the 17th century among the Waterlanders and the Lamist Mennonites, created a type of individualistic piety, which though it does not necessarily lead to Liberalism (neither Hans de Ries nor Galenus Abrahamsz was liberal), easily opens the door to Liberalism by its conception that the inspiration of man by the Holy Spirit is more basic than the "written word of God." Moreover influences from outside, like the strong contacts of the Mennonites with Collegiantism (*q.v.*) and the teachings of Socinianism (*q.v.*) in which Liberalism is already found as *in nuce,* made them receptive to Modernism. Foecke Floris (*q.v.*) and particularly Jan Klaasz (*q.v.*) van Grouw (*De leer der Doopsgezinden,* 1702) in their time were almost complete liberals. Doctrines such as original sin, satisfaction by the atoning suffering and death of Christ, were even in the 17th century a tradition for the Mennonites, rather than a part of their real faith, and the doctrine of the Trinity never was part of their essential creed. These doctrines were easily lost after new views came into prominence. But this came not only because Liberalism in the Mennonite congregations produced the new trend of criticizing the Scriptures by rationalistic human understanding; it was particularly the religious pathos of Moralism in Liberalism that appealed to the Mennonites, who by their preference for practical Christianity always had laid much stress upon "Christian ethics."

Liberalism not only changed the type of faith, but being opposed to galling bonds also criticized church practices, leading to the practice not only of admitting members of other denominations to the Lord's Supper, but even heartily welcoming unbaptized persons to the communion services. It is also due to Liberalism that in a few congregations baptism was abolished, or that at least some persons were admitted into the church without adult baptism. Only in one congregation (Franeker) was the Lord's Supper abolished (but has since been restored). The background of these measures is the radical liberal idea that a Christian church is in fact like other human organizations, being a union of people for the sake of religion, and not a church of God strictly speaking. This radicalism, however, was far from being generally adopted in Dutch Mennonite congregations. Thus, for example, in 1867, when the preachers Straatman and Corver of Groningen suggested that church services be modernized by abolishing prayers and Scripture readings and by speaking "on general actual cultural problems," the church board and the majority of the members did not consent, and both preachers retired.

Since its rise, about 1860, Liberalism in Holland has undergone great changes. The words "Liberalism" and "Modernism" have nearly all dropped out of use. At present liberals call themselves *vrijzinnigen.* This *vrijzinnigheid* has grown less self-confident, leaning less on the results of modern science (e.g., the theory of evolution), and subjective philosophy; less optimistic too as to a gradual development of God's kingdom from within by the natural goodness of man; Liberalism now is undoubtedly more religious and more Biblical than a century ago, open for the mystery of God's mercy to man, not natural to man's own mind. And though it maintains its critical conception of the Bible, it is more disposed to accept the exceptional signification of the Scriptures and the particular essence of Jesus Christ.

The rise of Liberalism in Holland and its adoption by most Mennonites brought about the co-operation of the Mennonites with liberals from other churches; e.g., with some of the Reformed Church and the Remonstrants. An interchurch organization for the promotion of liberal Christianity was the *Nederlandse Protestantenbond* (*q.v.*), founded in 1880, in which a large number of Mennonites have been active until the present. Its hymnals have been used in many Mennonite congregations. Dutch Mennonites also co-operate in the "Central Committee of Liberal Protestantism" and are largely interested in the VPRO (liberal Protestant broadcasting organization).

In the foregoing exposition it has been repeatedly said that most Dutch Mennonites have embraced liberal ideas. There have, however, always been a number of Mennonites who did not accept Liberalism. The congregations of Ouddorp and Blokzijl never tolerated liberal preaching. Against the growing influence of Liberalism some members of the Amsterdam Mennonite congregation in 1892 founded a union "for the maintaining of God's infallible Word in the Mennonite Church of Amsterdam."

This group supported its own preacher (C. P. van Eeghen, Jr.) and its own Sunday school for children until 1912. In 1892, when Hoekstra retired from his professorship at the Amsterdam seminary, a number of representatives in the A.D.S. made a strong attempt to have an orthodox professor appointed. Some Mennonites, unhappy with Liberalism, joined the Reformed, or sometimes the Baptists. Orthodoxy at present, though still in the minority, is more influential than it was half a century ago. This is partly due to the *Vereniging voor Doopsgezind Broederschapswerk* (see **Broederschapswerk**), founded in 1917, in which, especially in its first two decades, orthodox Mennonites found an opportunity to assert themselves. The orthodox views of such professors of the Amsterdam seminary as W. Leendertz and W. F. Golterman have also influenced a number of younger Dutch Mennonite ministers. Some of them co-operate in the "Ecclesiologische werkgroep" (ecclesiological unit), publishing their views in 1954 in *Doopsgezind Belijden Nu.*

Notwithstanding these differences, orthodox and liberal members of the Dutch Mennonite brotherhood wholeheartedly live together aand co-operate in church activities.   vDZ.

Liberty of Conscience: see Religious Liberty.

Liberty Mennonite Church (MC), located in Liberty Mills, eleven miles south of Jackson, Mich., on U.S. 127. The meetinghouse is a former Methodist church built in 1867 with a seating capacity of about 150. It was closed in 1936, but was opened in 1946 under the direction of the Indiana-Michigan Mission Board. The congregation was organized in March 1950 with 13 charter members under the leadership of T. E. Schrock, bishop, and Oscar Leinbach, minister. In 1956 the membership was 21, mostly rural.   O.L.

Liberty Mennonite Church (MC), located near South English, Keokuk Co., Iowa, a member of the Iowa-Nebraska Conference, was organized in 1898 by L. J. Heatwole and Daniel Driver with nine members. The membership in 1954 was 84. S. B. Wenger was one of the charter members and a chief promoter of the work at this place. Services were held in a schoolhouse until the autumn of 1900, when a new meetinghouse was dedicated. The first resident minister was S. G. Lapp, later ordained bishop. Serving with him was P. J. Blosser as minister from 1907, serving as bishop since 1929. Silas J. Horst was assistant pastor in 1955.   S.J.H.

M. Gingerich, *Mennonites in Iowa* (Iowa City, 1939).

Libraries: see Historical Libraries.

Licht den Indianern (Light to the Indians), a missionary association organized on Sept. 17, 1935, in the Fernheim Colony, Chaco, Paraguay, by 48 members of the various Mennonite groups. It took up work at once among the Lengua Indians (*q.v.*) with G. B. Giesbrecht as the missionary, who was assisted in the course of the years by others. Later work among the Chulupies was added. The association, feeling itself inadequate to carry the growing program alone, finally requested the Mennonite

Brethren Mission Board of Hillsboro, Kan., to take over the work, which it did in November 1945. However, the association has continued in existence, representing the participation of the Chaco Mennonites in the Lengua Mission and contributing financial and other support to the work.   H.S.B.

Licht im Osten, a missionary association for the spread of the Gospel among the people of the East, was founded Feb. 6, 1920, with its seat in Wernigerode am Harz (Germany). Its leaders for many years were Jakob Kroeker (*q.v.,* d. 1948) and Walter Jack (d. 1939). As a matter of principle, the association has established no new congregations, nor sent out or ordained missionaries and preachers. It has always promoted and supported spiritual life in existing churches, congregations, and fellowship centers through the education of ministers, distribution of Bibles, and relief work in times of need. The association is based on the principle of the unity of all of God's children (John 17:21). Wherever its service is desired it serves the people and brotherhoods of East Europe, in all churches and races. It was initially principally connected with "Evangeliums-Christen" of the revival in Russia, but it has also aided Baptists, Mennonites, Reformed, Lutherans, and Greek Orthodox in many different ways. The work of the association has had to adapt itself to the changing religious policies of Soviet Russia. In 1927 it closed its Bible school, and only until the end of 1928 was it possible to send Bibles and concordances to Russia. Since 1930 its services have been largely caritative.

Of the literature published by the association in the Russian language, the new Bible concordance (1,277 pp., 10,000 terms) must be mentioned, of which 10,000 copies were printed in 1925. Of these, 1,500 were sent to Russia, and the rest to various countries of Europe, America, and Asia. More and more the association turned its attention to the countries on the fringes of Russia and to Russian emigrants (promotion of the Ukrainian translation of the Bible by Ohienko, support of preachers, orphanages, etc., in Europe, Asia, and America). After World War II the work was reorganized as the *Missionsbund zur Ausbreitung des Evangeliums* (Missionary Association for the Spread of the Gospel) in Stuttgart-Mühlhausen, with extensive distribution of Bibles and Christian literature in the language of displaced persons and German refugees from the East, as well as the sending of relief parcels to sufferers in East and West Germany. This distribution of relief was made possible by friendly organizations in America (including Mennonites) and in Europe (Sweden, Switzerland, and Holland; in Sweden the organization is called "Slaviska Missionen"). The work of the association is supported by voluntary contributions from friends in many lands. The organ of the association, *Dein Reich komme,* appears bimonthly and is sent free of charge to friends as a means of giving information.
                                                             Ja.D.

Lichtenau, a Mennonite village name of the Molotschna settlement, Russia, transplanted to the East Reserve, Man., and Neuland, Paraguay.   C.K.

Lichtenau Mennonite Church (GCM), located near St. Elizabeth, Man., was organized in 1925, and is composed almost entirely of immigrants from Russia of 1924-26. Services were held in a rented church until 1930, when a new meetinghouse was built. In 1956 the membership was 118, with N. H. Unruh as leading minister, assisted by Heinrich Friesen and Arndt Lehn.　　　　　　　　　　　　N.H.U.

Lichtenau-Petershagen Mennonite Church, situated in the Molotschna settlement, Taurida, South Russia, and known as the "Reinflämische Gemeinde," originated as the result of a division in 1824 in the Ohrloff-Petershagen (q.v.) congregation, which was the first and only congregation at the beginning of the Molotschna settlement except for the Kleine Gemeinde (q.v.) which separated in 1812. It was also called "Grosse Gemeinde," since about three quarters of the population of the Molotschna belonged to it, 430 families in contrast to the 142 which remained at Ohrloff. Its first elder was Jakob Warkentin, who served from 1824 to 1842, when because of differences with the colonial administration (Johann Cornies) he was deposed from his duty as elder by the Fürsorgekomitee (q.v.) in Odessa on the charge of unauthorized interference in civil affairs. After this event the large Lichtenau congregation was divided into three smaller ones: Lichtenau-Petershagen, Margenau-Schönsee (q.v.), and Pordenau (q.v.), each with its own elder. This was also an order from Odessa.

After the division of 1842 the greater part of the population of the following villages belonged to the Lichtenau-Petershagen congregation: Altonau, Münsterberg, Blumstein, Lichtenau, Lindenau, Fischau, Schönau, Tiegenhagen, Petershagen, Ladekopp, some from Ohrloff and Tiege, making a total of approximately 5,000. The first meetinghouse at Lichtenau was built in 1826, a second and larger one, of brick, in 1860. In later years it was surrounded by mighty chestnut trees. There were also meetinghouses at Petershagen (built in 1831), Schönfeld, Rosenhof, and Blumenfeld. After Jakob Warkentin the following elders served the Lichtenau-Petershagen congregation: Dirk Warkentin 1842-69, Jakob Töws 1869-1908, Bernhard Epp 1908-22, David Epp 1922-26, and Peter Nickel 1926-31. In 1887 the total baptized membership numbered 2,388, and 2,496 children.

In former times only Sunday morning services were held, but in later years, before and after World War I, church life became more varied. Song festivals and Bible conferences attracted many visitors, especially under the last two elders, D. H. Epp and P. Nickel. Sunday school was also introduced, as religious instruction had been banished from the schools. As in most other Mennonite churches in Russia there was no instrument to accompany the singing. Services were conducted in German. Church discipline was limited to temporary expulsion for moral misconduct.

In the early 1920's the church building and everything in the church became property of the state, but services still continued although they became more and more difficult because of ever-increasing

church taxes. In 1931 Elder P. Nickel was compelled to leave and the church was closed.

In 1905 the total membership, including children, was about 4,000, and in 1926 it was 5,000. The General Mennonite Conference (Allgemeine Mennonitische Bundeskonferenz) met three times in the Lichtenau church: 1889, 1899, and 1918. On Oct. 31, 1926, the congregation observed its centennial.
　　　　　　　　　　　　　　　D.H.E., H.G.
D. H. Epp, "Hundertjahresfeier der Lichtenauer Gemeinde," Unser Blatt II, 75, 79; H. Görz, Die Molotschnaer Ansiedlung (Steinbach, 1951); Friesen, Brüderschaft; Mannhardt, Jahrbuch 1888, 70 f.; ML II, 648 f.

Lichtenstein, Ludwig, an Anabaptist martyr, beheaded in 1530 at Esslingen (q.v.), Württemberg, Germany.

Lichtfelde, Molotschna, Ukraine, the village in which the Molotschna Evangelische Mennonitenbruderschaft (q.v.) (Evangelical Mennonite Brotherhood) originated. On May 16, 1905, a church was founded with the above name, advocating the spiritual nurture of all believers, participation in the Lord's Supper by all baptized believers, irrespective of the form of baptism, and refusal of fellowship at communion with unbelievers. No one was compelled to be baptized by immersion, but by 1935 few remained who had not been baptized by immersion. (See also Evangelische Mennoniten-Gemeinden).

Organizationally the church had a council of elders, with one man as leader. In order of their terms they were A. Nachtigal (died in Canada), A. A. Toews (residing in British Columbia), and J. Becker (exiled under Soviet rule in 1935).

The early antagonism of the Mennonite Brethren Church gradually changed to mutual understanding and respect, and the church spread to outlying villages and churches in many areas of Russia. Church membership stood at 450 in 1935.　　　　H.P.T.
H. Görz, Die Molotschnaer Ansiedlung (Steinbach, 1951).

Lichtfelde (Lichterfelde), a Mennonite village name of Prussian origin, transplanted from the Molotschna settlement to Barnaul, Siberia; West Reserve, Man.; Cuauhtemoc, Mexico; and Fernheim, Paraguay.
　　　　　　　　　　　　　　　　　C.K.

Lichti (Liechty, Lichdi, Lichty, Leichty, Leighty, Leichti, Liechti), a Mennonite name, likely deriving from Lichtgut, a farm that gets much sun located at the end of a valley near Signau, in the Emmental, canton of Bern, Switzerland. The first known home of the family was near Landiswil in the Bowil district of the canton of Bern. The name appears in the earliest records of the area, dating back to the latter part of the 14th century. The earliest known Anabaptist in the family was Jacob Liechti, who was born about 1540 near Landiswil, where he was a farmer.

Georg Lichti (q.v.) was one of the leaders of the Swiss Brethren who left Switzerland for the Palatinate in 1671. He settled at Grossbockenheim. There was also an Ulrich Liechti (b. 1640), who settled on the Ibersheimerhof in 1676. These families have numerous descendants in Bavaria and the Palatinate. Branchweilerhof, near Neustadt a.d.W., Palatinate, is the home of a large family, the minister of the congregation being Adolf Lichti. Kurt Lichdi, owner of a large retail grocery chain in South Germany, is a minister in the Heilbronn (Württemberg) Mennonite Church. Steffen Lichti also came to the Palatinate from Switzerland soon after 1670.

Each migration of Mennonites from Switzerland has had representatives of the Liechti family in it. The Ulrich Liechti family settled in Montbéliard about 1710. Many of their descendants have found their way to America, settling especially in Wayne and Fulton counties, Ohio, near Berne, Ind., eastern Iowa, and Ontario. The first of the family who found their home in America arrived about 1750 from France, settling in Lancaster Co., Pa. A church named Lichty's is in the Weaverland District of the Lancaster Conference (MC). Early in the 18th century some Liechtis found their way from the Emmental to the Jura, where they established homes for a century, many migrating to the Ohio and Indiana Swiss Mennonite settlements in 1830-75. Today the family is especially numerous around Berne, Ind. Abraham Lichti (Lichty), b. 1793 on the Branchweilerhof, near Neustadt, Palatinate, married to Elisabeth Möllinger, a farmer at Friedelsheim (q.v.), immigrated to the United States in 1883 and died at Cleveland, Ohio, in the same year.

Among the American church leaders bearing the name have been John C. Lichti (1869-1951), a long-time minister in the G.C.M. Church (serving 1894-1948), long pastor of the Deer Creek (GCM) and Medford (GCM) churches in Oklahoma, and long-time member of the Emergency Relief Board, also secretary, and chairman; J. A. Liechty (1864-1947), minister of the Beech Mennonite (MC) Church at Louisville, Ohio; Willard Leichty (1906-   ), minister in the Sugar Creek (MC) Mennonite Church at Wayland, Iowa.

In 1940 Lichti was the seventh most numerous Mennonite family name in South Germany, with 94 representatives, 28 of them in the Branchweilerhof congregation, the rest scattered among Adelsheim, Heilbronn, Sinsheim, Augsburg, Durlach, Munich, and Weierhof.

In the early 18th century some members of the Lichti family emigrated from Switzerland to the Netherlands; their descendants are still found there, spelling their name Leegte. About 1900 Izaak Leegte, of Hoogkerg, was a member of the church board of the congregation at Den Horn, Dutch province of Groningen.   D.L.G.

Malinda Liechty and Delbert Gratz, *Liechty Family History* (1955) (in preparation); *Inv. Arch. Amst.* I, No. 1248; Müller, *Berner Täufer,* 200-4; Fritz Braun, "Nineteenth Century Emigrants from the Mennonite Congregation of Friedelsheim in the Palatinate," *MQR* XXX (April 1956) 133-54, especially 145.

Lichti, Georg, one of the leading Swiss Brethren preachers who, expelled from Switzerland, settled in the Palatinate, Germany, in 1671. With Valentin Hüthwohl he visited all the localities where the refugees had found shelter and set up a register of names which he sent to the Dutch Mennonites. He stayed for a time in Kriegsheim (q.v.), and then settled in Grossbockenheim. (*Inv. Arch. Amst.* I, Nos. 1248, 1409; *ML* II, 649.)

Lichti Old Order Amish congregation, located in Wellesley Twp., Waterloo Co., Ont. About 1911 Bishop Jacob F. Lichti, ordained minister in 1898 and bishop in 1901, and John Gascho, ordained minister in 1913, separated from the Mapleview Amish Mennonite congregation. There was no doctrinal dispute. The group led by Jacob F. Lichti was inclined to be more liberal than the Old Order, but more conservative than the Mapleview congregation. About 1912 they built a new meetinghouse one-half mile east of the other church. Jacob F. Lichti continued as bishop and John Gascho was ordained minister in 1913. Their membership has increased from an earlier probable 150 to a present membership of 236 with 82 families and 360 worshipers. They use the German language entirely and continue to use the *Ausbund.* They have no Sunday school and are not affiliated with any conference. Services are held every Sunday. The present ministers are Samuel Roth, Samuel Lichti, and Noah Gerber. Since the death of Jacob F. Lichti in 1944 they have called upon Bishop Moses Nafziger of Mornington to perform the bishop's functions.   J.C.F.

Lichty (or Smoketown) **Mennonite Church** (MC), a congregation of the Weaverland circuit, Lancaster Conference, first worshiped in the farm homes of Christian Lichty and Peter Shirk, until the meetinghouse was built in 1849 a mile southeast of the present site. In 1889 the present stone meetinghouse was erected. (This was the church where the introduction of a pulpit aided the Old Order Mennonite schism.) This was earlier also called Zimmerman, and the cemetery in a field a half mile southwest of the present sector still carries the name. The bishop Christian Zimmerman lived hereabouts. This was also Preacher John W. Weaver's home church. J. Paul Graybill is bishop and the Weaverland ministers are in charge. The membership in 1956 was 92.   I.D.L.

Lick Creek Mennonite Church (MC), affiliated with the South Central Conference and located in Camden Co., Mo., was organized on Jan. 10, 1939, with 20 members. The present (1955) membership is 18. Summer Bible schools have been conducted each year since 1936. The first and present pastor is J. P. Brubaker. The work was started just before World War I under the direction of J. R. Shank and H. A. Diener. The first bishop was J. C. Driver; at present J. R. Shank is in charge. Services are held occasionally in adjoining communities.   J.P.Br.

Liebe, Christian, a Mennonite preacher in the Palatinate, Germany, who made a trip to Switzerland in 1714 to visit the brethren there, to comfort them in their persecution, and, if necessary, to baptize. But he was seized and condemned to galley service. A letter he wrote in Palermo with two surviving companions in suffering, dated Sept. 16, 1715, describes their sad situation. His mother in the Palatinate presented a petition to the authorities at Bern for his release. Finally, on Jan. 10, 1716, he was set free and at once returned to his home in the Palatinate.

NEFF.

Inv. Arch. Amst. I, Nos. 1375, 1377 f.; Müller, *Berner Täufer*, 226 ff.; *DB* 1908, 121 f.; *ML* II, 649.

Liebich (Lübich, Liebig), **Jörg**, was one of the group of Anabaptists in Tirol, Austria, who caused the government at Innsbruck great difficulties. Some strange stories are recorded about him. Liebich was sent by the brotherhood in Moravia to Tirol in 1538. Captured in the Inn Valley, he was put into the Vellenburg (near Innsbruck) "into a bad tower." Hans Mändl (*q.v.*), who was imprisoned there in 1560, describes it thus: "It is very deep. I have heard of six fathoms. But it has a little window at the top, and the sun shines in awhile, so that it is light. The tower is of course full of vermin. The bats fly about the prisoner with a rustle, and the mice eat his food."

It seems the prisoner suffered hallucinations. Liebich thought he was being tempted by the devil. Some of the current stories of his hallucinations were collected in *Ein kurze History, was sich verlaufen mit unserem lieben Bruder Georg Liebich in seiner Gefängnis.* The fiend tempted him in various forms, as a virgin, or as a youth, or perhaps as an armed soldier, and told Liebich all kinds of tales of happenings in the brotherhood, and the evil committed by one or the other. When he was not successful in turning the prisoner's mind he flew out, leaving a stupefying stench behind. And since the devil had not been successful he sent his assistants.

One of these was Dr. Weber, the pseudonym of the noted Dr. Gallus Müller (*q.v.*), to whom the government had assigned the task of converting the Anabaptist prisoners. Müller also related to Liebich that the brotherhood in Moravia was dispersed, so that no brother knew where another was. In this Liebich recognized the tempter, accused him of deception, and rejected him with earnest reproof. To complete the temptation the "children of Satan" chained a beautiful maiden named Ursula Hellriegel to his foot. What the devil would have liked to see is easily imagined, say the chronicles. But the prisoner did not fall.

Liebich's trial brought the judges a reproof from the king. After Liebich had been in prison for two years without being affected by Müller's persuasion, the authorities asked King Ferdinand whether the prisoner should not be sent to the galleys of Andrea Doria. The king gave his consent; but because of the expense of transporting a single prisoner, he was not sent.

After two more years Liebich was placed before the jurors. The judges of the district of Sonnenburg realized that Liebich should be expelled from the country. He was, to be sure, an Anabaptist, but neither a backslider nor a preacher, had misled only a few, and had furthermore been converted. To their inquiry as to what further steps should be taken, the king replied that they should send Liebich to Vienna to be taken to the galleys to fight against the infidels.

But Liebich stayed in the Vellenburg until April 24, 1544, when he was banished. "Liebich made

several songs in prison, which the brotherhood still has and sings," say the chronicles. Beck comments that they cannot be found under his name; but the above account of his imprisonment is found in Codex 234 of the Pressburg cathedral chapter.

LOSERTH.

Beck, *Geschichts-Bücher*, 155-57; Loserth, *Anabaptismus*, 53 f.; *Mart. Mir.* D 64 (where he is called Juriaen Libich, his prison Filleburg, and the year of his imprisonment is given as 1544), E 466; *ML* II, 649 f.

Liebig, August, Baptist preacher of Hamburg, Germany, who gave valuable assistance in the Mennonite Brethren movement in Russia. He went to Chortitza in the spring of 1866, was arrested by the district court (*Gebietsamt*) after a brief period spent in organizing the group, was taken to Ekaterinoslav and Odessa, and deported as an undesirable person. In June 1871 he returned in response to an urgent appeal by the Russian Mennonite Brethren and settled in Andreasfeld. He succeeded in leading the group into a quiet and orderly status. Among other things he arranged for annual Bible courses for preachers to continue a month. He did not touch the Mennonite confession of faith, and always advocated the parallel existence of Mennonites and Baptists. In 1875 he accepted the pastorate of the Baptist Church in Odessa, and later emigrated to America, keeping up his Mennonite contacts. (Friesen, *Brüderschaft; ML* II, 650.)

NEFF.

Liebur (*Liebersche Gemeinde*), a congregation in the Lower Rhine area, Germany, was one of the Mennonite congregations which favored the Concept of Cologne (*q.v.*) in 1591. Hendrick Frinch-Winckel (?) signed the Concept in the name of this congregation.

vDZ.

Liechtenstein, a tiny sovereign principality bounded by Switzerland and Tirol (area 62 sq. miles, pop. 11,218). In the Vaduz area a Hutterite Bruderhof was formed in 1934, modeled on those of the Hutterian Brethren in the 16th century. It was an offshoot of the Rhönbruderhof near Neuhof (Fulda district), was set up near Triesenberg above Vaduz (elevation 5,170 ft.) and was called the Almbruderhof (*q.v.*) Silum, which was moved to England in 1938. (*ML* II, 650.)

HEGE.

Liechtenstein, John VI (Hans) (1500-52). In religious matters Hans Liechtenstein's position was identical with that of his uncle Leonhard (see **Liechtenstein, Leonhard von**). At the death of his father Wolfgang he was only 20. In 1535 he married Anna, daughter of George VI of Liechtenstein; after her death he married Esther von Dietrichstein; he had seven children. Hans entered early into the service of Ferdinand I in the Turkish wars and on diplomatic missions. Politically he sided with the Moravian nobles for Ferdinand, in opposition to the majority of the Bohemian estates, when they prepared their revolt against the emperor and Ferdinand in the Schmalkaldian war. In consequence he occupied a respected position in public affairs.

Like his uncle Leonhard he was a Protestant. Hubmaier (*q.v.*) dedicated his book on infant baptism to John and Leonhard. It may therefore be inferred that they were friendly to the Anabaptists. There is no indication in the Hutterite chronicles that he was baptized. John died in 1552 as an imperial councilor and chief syndic of Moravia, and was buried at Eisgrab. (*ML* II, 650.)

LOSERTH.

Liechtenstein, Leonhard von, lord of Nikolsburg (1482-1534), a member of the Anabaptist brotherhood in southern Moravia, the son of Christoph III, who founded the Nikolsburg line of this famous Moravian noble house, and his wife Amalia von Starhemberg. On July 25 Leonhard took part in a tournament in Vienna. He was married to Katharina von Boskovitz. Like most of the Moravian nobility he was an avowed champion of the Reformation.

When Balthasar Hubmaier (*q.v.*) fled from his home it was on Leonhard's estates that he found asylum; in his own words, he found the light of evangelical clearness burning more brightly here than anywhere else on earth. There was a Lutheran congregation here in 1524; its preacher was Hans Spittelmaier (*q.v.*) of Bavaria, assisted by Oswald Glait (*q.v.*), also of Bavaria, and supported by Martin Göschl, provost of Kanitz. Under the protection of the house of Liechtenstein Hubmaier carried on an active propaganda for the Anabaptist cause, which attracted his brethren from all sides to this haven. His extensive polemic writings were printed by Froschauer (*q.v.*).

There can be no doubt that Leonhard von Liechtenstein was baptized in Nikolsburg "besides much people." Two of Hubmaier's polemic booklets carry Leonhard's name. The very first of them, *Ein Gesprech Balthasar Hubmörs von Fridberg, doctors, auff Mayster Ulrichs Zwinglens zu Zürich Taufbüchlein von dem kindertauff,* and also *Ein einfeltiger unnderricht auf die wort: Das ist mein Leib in dem Nachtmahl Christi,* are dedicated to him. In the preface to the latter Hubmaier says of Leonhard: "I marvel not a little that such high and powerful names are collected in one person." Leonhard was, the preface continues, a manifestation of the strength, truth, and resistance of mankind, so that even the fierce lion of this world could not terrify him; and Liechtenstein said the light had come into the world which the good love and the wicked hate. The "Stein" is the rock upon which the wise man in the Bible built his house. Nikolsburg was Nicopolis, which the cosmographers called Emmaus. This should remind the reader how Christ met the two disciples on the road to Emmaus as it became evening.

The thronging of the Anabaptists into southern Moravia and the adjacent parts of Austria evoked the sternest countermeasures on the part of Ferdinand I, especially since after the battle of Mohacs Moravia fell to the house of Hapsburg. His failure to eradicate the Anabaptists completely was due to the protection given them by the nobles. But even Liechtenstein, who had tried to mediate between Hubmaier and Hut, was unable to save Hubmaier. Ferdinand summoned Leonhard to Vienna, and Balthasar Hubmaier and his wife were at once seized and put into Kreuzenstein (*q.v.*) castle. It is prob-

ably a fact that Hubmaier's arrest in 1527 and his subsequent execution were the result of his political agitation in Waldshut, rather than his Anabaptist faith; for the persecution in Moravia did not take place until the following year (1528).

Hubmaier's death was a severe blow to the Anabaptists in Moravia, as was also the severity of the persecution that followed in Moravia and Austria. Nevertheless they were not wiped out, but rather grew, because the growing threat of Turkish invasion occupied the populace and the police. In Nikolsburg the hostility between the followers of Hut and Hubmaier on the "sword and war" and on "tax and communal living" grew more and more divisive.

Leonhard von Liechtenstein held to the party of the "Schwertler" (*q.v.*) as opposed to the "Stäbler" (*q.v.*). The Schwertler were the group who were later generally called the Swiss Brethren, and lived in several villages around Nikolsburg. The Stäbler were those who held that a Christian could not with a good conscience bear arms. Leonhard von Liechtenstein made several futile attempts to unite the brethren, and finally expelled the Stäbler from the country. To the very last he befriended them, however; when they were about to go he told them they might have stayed in Nikolsburg. They replied that their consciences had testified against his preachers. He accompanied them to Unterwisternitz, "furnished them a drink and took no toll." In Austerlitz they were received by the lords of Kaunitz.

It is assumed that Leonhard died in 1534. He was survived by two minor sons, Christoph IV and Leonhard II.

LOSERTH.

Jakob von Falke, *Gesch. der fürstl. Häuser Liechtenstein* II (Vienna, 1877); Beck, *Geschichts-Bücher; ML* II, 650-52.

Liechty: see **Lichti.**

Liedeken, Een, *van XII vrienden van Gent,* Dutch Anabaptist hymn: see **Gent, Een Liedeken.**

Liedeken, Een, *van ses vrouwen binnen Antwerpen gedoot . . . in't jaer 1559.* This hymn of 25 stanzas begins with the words "Babels Raets mandementen worden aldus volbracht" (the orders of Babel [the Catholic Church] are thus executed); it celebrates the death of six Mennonite women, who died for their faith at Antwerp in Belgium. Their names are not found in this song. As can be concluded from the official records they are Maeyken Cadts (de Catte), Magdaleentgen Andriesdochter, Aechtken van Zierikzee (see **Aechtken Joris Adriaensdochter**), all three executed on July 18 or 19, 1559, and Oude Maeyken (Maeyken Sprincen), Margriete van Halle (Grietgen Bonaventuers), and Maeyken de Corte, executed on Oct. 11 or 12, 1559. The author of this hymn, which is the most beautiful of all the hymns of the *Offer des Heeren,* had known these martyrs personally, visiting them in prison, as the second stanza indicates. In this hymn he tells how they were betrayed by a "Judas" into the hands of the margrave, and were arrested in a house outside Antwerp, where the Mennonites used to hold their meetings. In this raid the leaders of the congregation and most members escaped, only the six women being taken to prison. They were tried and tortured, but "the Lord well preserved their mouths" and they did not reveal the names of their fellow members. After much tribulation and suffering they were put to death; they died valiantly for their Lord.

This hymn was composed only one year after the death of these martyrs. It is found in the Dutch hymnals, *Nieu Liedenboeck* of 1562, *Lietboecxken van den Offer des Heeren* of 1563 and following editions, and *Tweede Liedeboeck* of 1583. (*Offer,* 581-86.)   vDZ.

Liedeken, Een, *van LXXII vrienden,* is a Dutch Mennonite hymn of 25 stanzas by an unknown poet written to celebrate 72 martyrs who were executed at Antwerp, Belgium, in 1555-60. It begins with the words "Aenhoort Godt, hemelsche Vader, ons clagen in deser tijt" (Hear, O God, heavenly Father, our lamentation in this time). The martyrs mentioned here are all found in the publications by Génard (*q.v.*) in the *Antwerpsch Archievenblad,* but while Génard usually gives the names of the victims according to the records with their place of birth, the hymn mostly names them after their trades. The first of the 72 martyrs is Tanneken van der Leyen, executed on Oct. 5, 1555, and the last one is Maeyken van Aken (Maeyken de Hont), who suffered death on April 4, 1560. The hymn, which has proved to be very accurate, was composed before Aug. 9, 1560, for Jan de Tasmaker, who is obviously identical with Jan Cleeren (executed on this date), was still in prison—as the author expressly mentions—when the hymn was written. The hymn is found in the Dutch hymnbooks, *Nieu Liedenboeck* of 1562, *Lietboecxken van den Offer des Heeren* of 1563 and following editions, *Tweede Liedeboeck* of 1583. (*Offer,* 563-68.)   vDZ.

Liedekens and **Liedboeck** (*Liedenboeck, Liedtboeck, Lietboeck*): see **Hymnology.**

Liedekens, 42, a collection of 42 Dutch Mennonite hymns, published together with *Een Vermaen-Boeckjen* by Jan Gerritsz (*q.v.*). Only the third edition (Amsterdam, 1655) is extant. The hymns are without notes.   vDZ.

Lieder der Hutterischen Brüder, Die (Scottdale, Pa., 1914, 894 pages, large size). Until the publication of this big hymnal, the Hutterites had nothing that would compare with the *Ausbund,* the hymnal of the Swiss Brethren, in fact no printed hymnal of any sort. It is true that prior to the 18th century the Hutterites had a great number of manuscript hymnals in which their innumerable *Lieder* were collected. Rudolf Wolkan (*Lieder,* 165-69) describes 21 such codices in European libraries, to which he adds three more which he could not reach. In America the Brethren have a few such codices too, some of which have become extremely difficult to read with the passing of time. But no hymnal was ever declared "official" and nothing had ever been printed. It must be assumed that in former centuries most of the hymns sung at Hutterite services were learned by rote and handed on to the next generation by

word of mouth. It was therefore almost a daring enterprise when Elder Elias Walter (1862-1938), then of South Dakota but later of Standoff Colony, near Macleod, Alberta, decided to prepare a printed hymnal. When he received the approval of the brotherhood the publication became a semiofficial undertaking.

In his preface Elias Walter reports briefly about the sources from which he compiled the book: (1) a codex with 165 hymns, written sometime before 1600 (275 leaves, well preserved, title page missing); (2) another codex with 140 hymns, written about 1650 in Slovakia (400 leaves, again title page missing); (3) a third codex of 390 leaves, of which the first 60 are missing, containing 80 hymns (the time is that of Ehrenpreis, 1650-60, the writing good but the paper slowly falling apart). Many of these hymns are incomplete, although a century earlier they were said to have been known in full to the Brethren. Most likely even today many more codices are available than these three, but they are hidden in some of the 120 Bruderhofs in America and not easily found. Elias Walter arranged his book chronologically, though he did not always keep this plan, and the order is often quite confusing. The book begins with a hymn by Felix Manz (martyred in Zürich in 1527), *Mit Lust so will ich singen,* present in two of the sources named. Next follow hymns by Jörg Wagner (martyred 1527), Michael Sattler (1527) (a hymn of 50 stanzas), Leonhard Schiemer (1528), Hans Schlaffer (1528), Balthasar Hubmaier (1528), of whom one hymn is printed, a supposed second was not available; two hymns go back to Jörg Blaurock (whom Walter reports as martyred in 1529, although the *Geschicht-Buch* gives 1527 as the date of his martydom); five hymns come from Ludwig Haetzer (d. 1529). Of special interest is the discovery that the hymn, *Sollst du bei Gott dein Wohnung han,* which was customarily ascribed to Haetzer, is here (28-9) printed as deriving from Schiemer. It is this hymn whose fifth stanza was often quoted, *Ja, spricht die Welt, es ist ohn Not dass ich mit Christo leide* .... We may trust the manuscript and assume that the tradition was incorrect (see *ML* II, 230). Of Hans Hut's known four hymns two are printed here.

And so the volume proceeds through the hymn collections of the early times year by year. Elias Walter wrote a brief biographical sketch for each hymn writer, sometimes also listing his other works. Many of these hymns are extremely long (over 100 stanzas). Some of the Brethren were very productive, writing 30, 40, and even 50 hymns. Many of these hymns are anonymous; they could be identified only by reading the acrostic (where the initials of each stanza put in order reveal a name or message, a technique used mainly by brethren in prison). Walter points to this device whenever he decodes it. Three fourths of all hymns could thus be ascribed to individual authors; the rest may be assumed to have been composed collectively by groups of Brethren.

Rather famous among these hymns is the *Väterlied,* describing the work of the forefathers, the *Vorstehers* of the brotherhood. It was begun by Georg Pruckmaier (d. 1585), who wrote 75 stanzas, and then continued by others until 1639, with a total of 105 stanzas. On page 877 it is still later continued by other loyal writers up to the year 1734, with a total of 18 more stanzas. At the year 1605 the *Botschkai Lieder* attract our attention (author unknown), describing all the horror of the attack of Turks, Magyars, and Tatars on the South Moravian colonies (158 stanzas, 804-12). The last part of the hymnal contains a number of hymns by the last great bishop of the brotherhood, Andreas Ehrenpreis (*q.v.*, d. 1662); one hymn is about his death. Close to 100 hymns are versifications of Biblical stories, which, however, are not quite as popular as the more personal hymns.

Not all these hymns are strictly of Hutterite origin. In fact A. J. F. Zieglschmid discovered that at least one is of Jesuit origin. But the Brethren are used to all of them, accept them, and are loath to change anything.

The *Lieder* has become "the" hymnal of the brethren. It is used daily at the prayer hour, and at all services on Sundays, holidays, and other occasions. One is amazed that these stanzas, often quite unwieldy, can actually be sung. Often they bear little connection with the worship service as such, and even their original meaning of three or four centuries ago is not always understood. But they are sung in many cases simply out of deference to tradition. The preacher "lines" the hymns, that is, he reads one line at a time, then the congregation sings it according to melodies familiar to all. (There is no notation.) Only the preacher has a hymnal at the service, but most brethren know the texts by rote.

The singing of these hymns also deserves a few remarks. All hymns are sung in unison, not in parts, and they are overloud, almost shrill, with strained vocal chords. Zieglschmid, who discusses this kind of communal singing in a footnote in the *Klein-Geschichtsbuch* (580, n. 3), points out that according to an old report the Mennonites in the Molotschna also used to sing "über alle Massen grell und laut aus der Kehle gepresst." It is possible that this (not too appealing) method has its origin in 16th-century conditions when Brethren imprisoned for their faith wanted to communicate with other brethren in the same place but in different rooms. At least some sources mention such overloud singing at a quite early date (1536). A reference is also made to Isa. 58:1, "Cry aloud, spare not, lift up thy voice like a trumpet" (*Lasst uns schreien, dass uns der Hals kracht*, in the Denk-Haetzer translation).

In recent years some brethren expressed dissatisfaction with some parts of the *Lieder* book, and a new edition was brought out in 1953, in which 75 hymns were omitted, mainly those which contained versifications of Bibles stories. There is some grumbling, however, by others, since many liked the book as it was composed originally.

In the meantime, the late A. J. F. Zieglschmid (*q.v.*) began a thorough study and revision of this book. He found a great number of mistakes, inaccuracies, and false readings. Many hymns had been "zersungen," i.e., the words were changed and the meaning was lost, often even a whole line

was omitted, and so forth. Moreover, he distinguished between genuine Anabaptist hymns and others which were adopted from outside, as was mentioned above (a Jesuit hymn). Thus he compiled a new, revised, purified and corrected edition, to which he added a number of Hutterite songs unknown at the time of Elias Walter, for instance, the versification of the entire Psalter by Wolf Seiler (d. 1550). The *Lieder* contains 48 of his hymns (see Wolkan's note 1 in *Geschicht-Buch*, 257). The result of this scholarly work is a manuscript of nearly 4,500 sheets, still unpublished and deposed at the Mennonite Historical Library of Goshen College. It is yet uncertain whether the Hutterian Brethren will accept this "revision" or not, when a need for a new edition arises.

Elias Walter edited a smaller hymnal, the *Gesang-büchlein, Lieder, besonders zum Auswendiglernen für die Jugend in der Schule geeignet, meistens aus alten Handschriften gesammelt und herausgegeben von Elias Walter* (n.p., 1919, 525 pp., octavo). In 1930 a second edition of this hymnal was produced, printed in Macleod, Alberta, with 480 pages. In 1940, after Elias Walter's death (1938), a third edition was brought out under the title, *Gesang-büchlein, Lieder für Schule und häuslichen Gebrauch, herausgegeben von den Hutterischen Brüdern in Kanada* (n.p., 1940, 591 pp., octavo). In neither of these editions is any reference made to sources, authors, or historic backgrounds. Thus the *Gesangbüchlein* has become more a popular hymnbook for school and family singing, and as such is a real favorite. Among other hymns it contains also the old (most likely not Hutterite) song, "Das goldene A-B-C." It contains Lutheran and pietistic hymns, but no old Hutterite hymns. (See also **Hymnology.**)   R.F.

Wolkan, *Lieder;* Wolkan, *Geschicht-Buch;* Zieglschmid, *Klein-Geschichtsbuch; ML* II, 89.

Liederen bij de Doopsgezinden in gebruik (Hymns used by the Dutch Mennonites) is a small hymnary, published at Amsterdam in 1791, which was a reprint of the *Oude Liederen* (*q.v.*) of 1684, but which was much altered in this new edition.   vDZ.

Liederen, Christelijke, a Dutch Mennonite hymnbook in two volumes, published at Amsterdam in 1870 by the church board of Amsterdam, and for this reason usually called "Amsterdamsche Bundel." These two volumes of hymns were introduced to replace the "Groote Bundel" (*q.v.*) of 1796 and the "Kleine Bundel" (*q.v.*) of 1791. The *Christelijke Liederen* were also used in a number of other Mennonite congregations besides Amsterdam. The first volume contains 153 hymns, taken from the *Groote Bundel,* the *Kleine Bundel,* and the *Uitgezogte Liederen* (*q.v.*). The second volume has 132 hymns, borrowed from the Reformed *Evangelische Gezangen,* the *Vervolgbundel,* and the hymnary of the Lutherans. In 1916 an appendix of another 48 hymns was added, being numbered 133-81. This appendix, published at Amsterdam, contains 18 Psalms from the Dutch Reformed hymnary and 30 classical Christian hymns by Luther, Gustaf Adolf, Paul Gerhard, and Tersteegen.   vDZ.

Liederen en Gezangen, or *Opwekkende Gezangen,* a small volume of hymns published at Haarlem, Holland (n.d., 2d ed. Haarlem, 1763). There is also an edition of Amsterdam 1793 (and a much altered version of 1791) (see **Liederen bij de Doopsgezinden in gebruik**). This hymnary is a reprint of the *Oude Liederen* (*q.v.*), consisting of 12 hymns of the Lamist-Toren congregation of Amsterdam from 1684.   vDZ.

Liederenbundel *ten dienste van de Doopsgezinde Broederschap*: see **Doopsgezinde Bundel.**

Liedtboecxken genaamt het Otterken, a Dutch Mennonite hymnary compiled by Maeryn den Brauwer. As far as known no copy is extant. According to M. Schagen (*q.v.*) there were two editions, 1616 and 1642, both at Haarlem.   vDZ.

Liedtjes, Christelijcke: see **Jan Stevens.**

Liefde, Jan de, b. Dec. 25, 1814, at Amsterdam, d. there Dec. 6, 1869, "author, preacher, poet, composer, humorist, and theologian," entered the Amsterdam Mennonite Seminary in 1832, attended the lectures of Muller, who considered him an excellent student, and of Koopmans, was called to preach at Woudsend in 1837, and two years later at Zutphen. He was converted in the revival movement "Réveil," and became one of its ardent advocates. He stirred up animosity by his polemic, *Gevaar, gevaar en geen vreede* (1844), which exposed and attacked the weaknesses of the Mennonite Church. His position became untenable, and he resigned on Oct. 26, 1845, leaving the brotherhood and joining a group of apostolic Separatists. A year later, on the advice of van der Brugghen, he entered the normal school at Mörs in Germany with the intention of preparing himself for the teaching profession. Before the completion of the course, however, he served for a short time as director of the Rhine missionary association at Barmen, and in 1848 returned to Holland. He worked at a collection of "folk writings." Poverty caused him to decide to go to America. Wealthy friends of the Réveil movement held him back and gave him an evangelistic position in Amsterdam, and built him the church "Eben-Ezer." He had a seminary of his own to train evangelists. He took an especial interest in the poor and initiated an organization called "For the welfare of the People," the object of which was to raise the social and economic level of the very destitute.

De Liefde's hostility to the (Reformed) church at the conference of the "Friends of the Truth" at Amsterdam in 1854 obliged him to resign this position. He founded a free brotherhood, which after a brief growth disintegrated. This unhappy experience consumed his vitality and put an early end to a life of great blessing. He lived temporarily in Utrecht and Amersfoort. To acquire the necessary funds he made frequent trips to England. For some years he had his home there. His brother-in-law, Johannes Molenaar (*q.v.*), pastor at Monsheim, translated some of his folk writings: "Der Schiffbrüchige aus dem fernen Lande," "Die Diligence oder die Reise nach der Stadt der Erbschaft," "Des Christen Einnahme und Ausgabe," "Der Sträfling,"

and "Allgemeine Geschichte für das Volk" (*Menn. Bl.,* 1865, 63). They were read in Mennonite circles in South Germany. In 1857 a few Mennonites at Hollum, Ameland (*q.v.*), who were followers of de Liefde, left the Mennonite congregation to found a "Free Evangelical Congregation."   NEFF.

F. J. de Holl, "Jan de Liefde, zijn denkbeelden over de gemeente en zijne vroomheid," in *DB* 1901, 133-95; S. Coolsma, *J. de Liefde in zijn leven en werken geschetst* (Nijkerk, 1917); *Biogr. Wb.* VI, 1-14; *DJ* 1840, 19, 22; 1850, 37; *DB* 1861, 37, 146; 1881, 55-61; 1896, 27, 35; *ML* II, 653 f.

Liefdepredikers (German, *Liebesprediger*), a term designating those ministers in Dutch and German Mennonite congregations who did not receive special training (see **Lay Preachers**), and who preached for "love's" sake, i.e., without remuneration.   vDZ.

Liége (Dutch, *Luik*), a city in Belgium (1949 pop. 156,200), where some Anabaptists were found in the 16th century. Wilhelm Stupman (Mottencop) from Aachen, Germany, is said to have founded an Anabaptist congregation here in 1533. Of this congregation, however, almost nothing is known. Two "Lutheran" (i.e., heretical) women, who in 1544 were thrown from Pont des Arches (arched Bridge) into the Meuse River, were apparently Anabaptists. Their names are unknown. In 1570 a Mennonite woman, Lyntgen Kemels (*q.v.*), suffered martyrdom at Liége, but there is no evidence of a congregation there at that time.   vDZ.

W. Bax, *Het Protestantisme in het bisdom Luik* I (The Hague, 1937) 74, 163; II (1941) 313; H. E. Halkin, *Le Réforme en Belgique sous Charles-Quint* (Brussels, n.d.-1957) 53, 81, 83, 84 f.

Lienz, a city (pop. 10,000) in eastern Tirol, Austria, in the Drau Valley, where there were Anabaptists especially around 1530, so that the magistrate was ordered by the government in 1533 to pursue them with all diligence, to offer rewards of 60 to 100 florins for information leading to the capture of their leaders, and to spare no effort or money in their extermination. Two years later orders came from Innsbruck to block the migrations to Moravia in Lienz. In 1576 the bishop of Salzburg called the attention of the Innsbruck government to the increase of the Anabaptists in Lienz; thereupon the government sent the Lienz authorities orders to act aggressively. The Hutterite Jakob Platzer fell into the hands of the authorities here in 1585, who had him and four companions instructed in the Catholic faith for four weeks in prison. In order to win his release Platzer recanted at a public service in the church of St. Andrew, but immediately returned to the brotherhood, was seized again in near-by Sillian in 1591, and beheaded after a long imprisonment. In 1588, the magistrate passed new measures against the Anabaptists.   P.DE.

Beck, *Geschichts-Bücher;* Wolkan, *Geschicht-Buch;* Zieglschmid, *Chronik;* Loserth, *Anabaptismus;* Loesche, *Tirolensia; ML* II, 654.

Lier (*Lierre*), a city (1950 pop. 29,136) in the Belgian province of Antwerp (formerly Brabant), not far from the city of Antwerp, important in the 15th and 16th centuries for its many looms. It served as a refuge to the exiled Danish King Christian II and his wife who espoused the Lutheran faith. Christian was suspected of connections with the Lutherans at Antwerp. His servants held Protestant meetings and made proselytes. His quartermaster Willem van Zwolle refused to recant his evangelical faith and was executed by burning at Mechelen on Oct. 20, 1529.

For a long time nothing is heard of the innovations in Lier. In January 1550 or 1551 (*BRN* II, 246, 569) four persons were taken prisoner on the charge of holding conventicles. They were Govert Mertens (*q.v.*), a street-maker of Maastricht, about 33 years of age; Marie Vlaminx of St. Truijen, 75 years old; Anneken (Tanneken) van Roosbroecke (*q.v.*), about 34 years old; and Gielis (*q.v.*) van Aerde, a weaver, 32 years old. Anneken and Gielis were born at Lier. On Jan. 30 they were examined. They freely and valiantly confessed that they had been baptized on their faith, and rejected the offer of mercy. They spent their last night in prison singing psalms. In the morning they were burned on the market square. Among the spectators Govert discovered some brethren and encouraged them with a few words. The executioner of Antwerp had been called to put them to death. A song in commemoration of their death was written by Hans van Overdam, and is found in *Het Offer des Heeren*. The other Anabaptists evidently fled after these executions. Some were betrayed and seized at Gent— Joris, Wouter, Grietken, and Naentken, all of Lier— and burned in 1551.   vDZ.

A. Bergmann, *Gesch. der Stad Lier* (Lier, 1873) 174-78, 200-4, 216-33; *Offer*, 568-77; *ML* II, 654.

Lier, een liedeken *van IIIJ vrienden van,* is a hymn composed by Hans van Overdam (*q.v.*) to commemorate four martyrs executed at Lier (*q.v.*) in 1551. It begins "Als men schreef duyst vijfhondert, en daartoe nog vijftich Jaer." It is found in *Veelderhande Liedekens* of 1565 and 1569, and was included in the *Lietboecxken van den Offer des Heeren* (*q.v.*) and some later hymnbooks. (Wackernagel, *Lieder,* 126; Wolkan, *Lieder,* 63, 78.)   vDZ.

Liesveldt, Jacob van, a printer at Antwerp, boosted the Reformation by printing Testaments and Bibles in the Dutch language; in 1522 the Gospels according to the Vulgate, in 1526 the complete Bible, following Luther's as far as it went, and the rest after the Vulgate. In the sixth reprint (1542) there are several pictures: for Matt. 4:3 a picture of Satan in the form of a monk; with I John 5 the note, "Salvation comes alone through Jesus Christ." In 1536 the executioner of Antwerp was summoned to burn "the Bible and other (!) heretical books" printed by van Liesveldt. A second charge was brought against him in 1542 because he had published "Troostinge der Goddelycker Scryft" (Consolation from the Holy Scriptures), but this time he was acquitted. Van Liesveldt was noted for printing heretical books. Because of this he was executed on Nov. 27, 1545. Although it cannot be proved, it may be assumed that the first Anabaptist martyrs used the Liesveldt Bible before their own translation, the Biestkens Bible (*q.v.*), was published. Many Bible quotations in the old Anabaptist writings have the wording of the van Liesveldt version.   vDZ.

Antw. Arch.-Blad. VII, 428, 457, 460, 463-66; **VIII,** 347-53; XIV, 14 f., No. 155; *BRN* V, 587; *DJ* 1837, 54; *DB* 1890, 61, 64; *ML* II, 655.

Lietboeck, *inhoudende Schriftuerlijcke Vermaen Liederen, Claech Liederen, Gebeden, Danck Liederen, Lofsanghen, Psalmen ende ander stichtelijcke Liederen, de welcke gheoeffent ende ghesongen worden onder de medeleden der Ghemeenten Christi,* with notes (Rotterdam, 1582), is a Dutch Mennonite hymnal composed by Hans de Ries (*q.v.*). It contains a preface by de Ries, an introduction on how to sing hymns, and the hymns in six parts: (1) "Leerachtige Vermaen-Liederen" (20 hymns), (2) "Claech-Liederen ende Gebeden" (22), (3) "Danck-Liederen ende Lof-Sanghen" (10), (4) "Sommighe Cruys-Liederen" (10), (5) "Verscheyden Schriftuerlijcke Liedekens" (11), (6) "Veerthien van de Heyligen Propheets Davids Psalmen" (14 Psalms).

The second edition (Alkmaar, 1604) has the same title and shows only a few slight alterations. A number of hymns were added, the first part now numbering 24; second part 32; the third part 30; the fourth part 10; the fifth part 14. In this edition the hymns and psalms are followed by some "schriftuerlijcke spreucken" (verses from the Scriptures).

The third edition (De Rijp, 1624) is entitled *Het Boeck der Ghesangen.* It contains the introduction and parts 2, 3, and 5 of the first and second editions, and besides these all of the 150 Psalms in the rhymed version of Dathenus (*q.v.*). Moreover it has the confession of faith of 1610 by Hans de Ries and Lubbert Gerritsz.

In the fourth edition (De Rijp, 1648) the introduction is omitted; otherwise the fourth edition is nearly the same as the third; a few hymns have been added, and the title of this edition reads *Gesanghboeck.* The fifth and the sixth editions (1658 and 1681, both at De Rijp) are exact reprints of the fourth edition under the same title, except that in the fifth edition the psalms are not found. There was an edition of 1643 at Hoorn, of which there is no complete copy extant.

These hymnals, used by the Dutch Waterlander congregations until the end of the 18th century and very popular, from which a number of hymns were adopted in the later Dutch Mennonite songbooks, were commonly called "'t Gesangboek van de Ries." The hymnbook *Het Boek der Gesangen* (Hoorn, 1619) is a shortened version of the 1604 edition, augmented with the complete collection of psalms.   vDZ.

Lietboecxken, Een, *tracterende van den Offer des Heeren, int welke oude en nieuwe Liedekens, wt verscheyden copien vergadert zijn, om by het Offerboeck geuoecht te worden,* is a collection of 25 hymns; the oldest known edition is dated 1563. These songs, some of which have genuine poetic feeling and merit, commemorate the men and women who died as martyrs to their faith; many were written by eyewitnesses. Some were printed on loose leaves and distributed soon after the execution had taken place. The influence of these hymns was enormous. They acquainted the populace with the faith and courage of the martyrs, and also gave strength to the imprisoned Anabaptists. How often we read that they sang a hymn on their way to the execution. The songs were adopted into hymnals.

The *Lietboecxken* was always published with the old martyrbook *Offer des Heeren;* only the year of the first edition of the *Offer* is 1562, that of the first *Lietboecxken* 1563. This first edition apparently was printed at Emden by Nicolaes Biestkens (*q.v.*). There are eleven editions known of the (*Offer* and) *Lietboecxken*: (1) 1562-63; (2) 1566, n.p.; (3) 1567, n.p. (apparently printed by Biestkens); (4) 1570, n.p., probably also a Biestkens publication; (5) 1578, n.p., probably also by Biestkens; (6) 1578, n.p. (same year as edition 5), probably printed at Delft by Aelbrecht Heyndricksz; (7) 1580, n.p., probably by Biestkens; (8) 1590, published by Willem Jansz Buys at Amsterdam; (9) 1592, n.p. (printer unknown); (10) 1595 at Amsterdam by Willem Jansz Buys; (11) 1599 at Harlingen by Peter Sebastiaenszoon. Editions 1, 3, 4, 5, 7, 8, 9, 10, and 11 are found in the Amsterdam Mennonite Library; Nos. 4, 5, 7, and 10 in the Goshen College Library; Nos. 2 and 6 in the Library of the University of Gent; Nos. 5 and 6 in the Library of the University of Utrecht. Editions 1-4 and 7 contain 25 hymns; No. 5 has 26; Nos. 8, 10, and 11 have 28; the only existing copy of No. 9 is incomplete. Fourteen of the hymns published in the *Lietboecxken* had been published before in Dutch hymnbooks. Three of these hymns are also found in the *Ausbund*. A new edition of the *Lietboecxken* and the *Offer* was published in 1904 at The Hague, with introduction and notes by S. Cramer in *BRN* II. (*ML* II, 652.) vDZ.

Lieven Claus (Claes), beheaded on Sept. 27, 1549, at Gent, Belgium. He was the father of the Anabaptist martyrs Cathalijne and Suzanneke Claes (*q.v.*), executed on Dec. 3, 1573, at Gent. It is not clear whether Lieven was a Calvinist or a Mennonite. (Verheyden, *Gent,* 65, 12, No. 19.) vDZ.

Lieven (Lievijn) Jansz (Liefken de Keyser, or Liefken van Gent), an Anabaptist martyr, burned at the stake on Aug. 6, 1552, at Amsterdam together with five co-martyrs. Lieven Jansz, who was a native of Gent, Belgium, and a weaver by trade, had been baptized by Gillis van Aken. (*Mart. Mir.* D 142, E 535; Grosheide, *Bijdragen,* 309.) vDZ.

Lieven van de Walle, an Anabaptist martyr, was beheaded on June 5, 1536, in front of the Gravensteen castle at Gent, Belgium. In the records of the bailiff he is called a "Lutheran," but this is merely the general indication of heresy. In fact he was an Anabaptist, having received (re)baptism in his faith. By trade he was a barber. Willem van de Walle (a brother of Lieven?) had already on Aug. 4, 1535, been banished from Gent because of his Anabaptist opinions. Many members of the van de Walle (*q.v.*) family were Mennonites, some of whom died as martyrs. (Verheyden, *Gent,* 2, No. 5.) vDZ.

Lievens, Antonette, a Dutch Anabaptist poet who composed the hymn "Aensiet o Heer onsen strijt groot" (Regard, O Lord, our great struggle), found in *Het Tweede Liedeboeck* (1583). The name of the composer can be read from the first letters of the 16 stanzas. Nothing is known of her life. (Wolkan, *Lieder,* 70; *ML* II, 655.) vDZ.

Lievijn van Gent, an Anabaptist martyr: see **Lieven Jansz.**

Lievin Verreken, a fish-hawker at Gent, Belgium, who was burned at the stake on the Vrijdagsmarkt at Gent on Sept. 15, 1553, was probably a Mennonite. (Verheyden, *Gent,* 19, No. 38; *idem,* "Mennisme in Vlaanderen," ms.) vDZ.

Life Insurance (or Assurance), commonly a contract insuring the payment upon the death of a person of certain benefits to a surviving relative or friend. In modern times it has taken on other forms beyond simple death benefit, including endowments and annuities, but in any case the contingencies requiring payment of benefits are always in some way dependent upon human life. Such benefits are in no way related to need, as is the case in other forms of insurance, such as fire, theft, or accident, but only to the amount of money paid in by the policyholder. True life insurance began first in England in 1720, although scientific life insurance did not begin until 1764 with the foundation of the Equitable society in England in that year. On the European continent and in America life insurance developed much later, e.g., the first successful company in France in 1819, in Germany in 1828, and in the United States in 1843 (a few small and short-lived companies had begun earlier, the first in 1812). The Mutual Life Insurance Company of New York was the first permanent large modern company. Life insurance has had its greatest development in the United States and several British dominions, certain of the great companies of the United States constituting the largest aggregates of capital in the world, with tremendous financial power.

At first practically all American Mennonites were radically opposed to life insurance, as were many other Christian denominations. The more conservative Mennonite groups, including the Mennonite Church (MC), forbade their members all forms of life insurance from the beginning, usually making excommunication the penalty. Applicants for membership were required to surrender their insurance policies before being received. At first there was similar opposition to all forms of insurance. By the beginning of the 20th century, however, opposition to fire and auto accident insurance had greatly diminished. The introduction of compulsory workmen's compensation insurance about this time by the several states created serious problems for conservative Mennonites at first, but ultimately this was generally accepted. Gradually the opposition to life insurance diminished, so that by the middle of the 20th century in the Mennonite Church (MC) the absolute prohibition of holding life insurance was being modified in many areas, although a considerable block of opposition remains where it is still prohibited. In the General Conference Mennonite Church, the Mennonite Brethren Church, and certain related groups, whatever minor opposition there may once have been has completely disappeared, although such opposition apparently never was very strong.

Many weighty arguments have been offered against life insurance, among them the following: it reflects trust in man rather than in God; it means becoming "unequally yoked together with unbelievers"; it is equivalent to merchandising in human life; it is putting a monetary price on human life, which is considered unscriptural since man is the "temple of the Holy Ghost." These objections to insurance were bolstered by a powerful practical argument, namely, that the commercial insurance companies did not really help the needy, but sought only to protect the healthy and rejected as poor risks the weak and the ill who really needed protection. Many Mennonites also objected to taking out life insurance because it was contrary to the spirit of genuine mutual aid and brotherhood. Finally the corrupt practices of many earlier life insurance companies were often cited as objections to all life insurance; and truly the history of life insurance has been marked by many and large scandals, so much so that rigid legislative control was necessary to curb the greed and the fraudulent practices which appeared. The first such law was the Life Assurance Act of 1774 in England, commonly called the Gambling Act since speculation in the lives of other people, particularly public men, had become a public scandal. Numerous American life insurance companies went bankrupt in the 19th century, and frequently policies were so drafted as to trap the unwary and deprive them of their equities. Penalties for nonpayment of premiums were harshly enforced. The evil repute of commercial life insurance among Mennonites was fostered by these indubitable facts, which greatly fortified the theological arguments.

A form of mutual brotherly aid insurance has developed among Mennonites in North America in recent decades in the form of death and burial benefit associations, which are in effect life insurance arrangements. They differ substantially from commercial life insurance, however, in several respects: (1) the benefit payments are small, intended to cover only the cost of burial, or also medical bills attendant upon the last illness; (2) the system is entirely and truly mutual; (3) salary payments to officials are nonexistent or very low; (4) no agents' premiums are paid; (5) membership is limited to church members.

The earliest of these burial aid organizations was the Mennonite Aid Society of Mountain Lake, Minn., founded in 1897, followed by the Menno-Friendly Beneficial Association of Philadelphia, Pa., in 1908, and the Mennonite Burial Aid Association of Altona, Man., in 1910. Ten other similar societies were organized in 1934-52 as follows: Niagara Mutual Funeral Society, Niagara-on-the-Lake, Ont., 1934; Vineland Beerdigungskasse, Vineland, Ont., 1934; the Mennonite Mutual Supporting Society of Arnaud-St. Elizabeth, St. Elizabeth, Man., 1934; Beerdigungs-Verein zu Leamington, Ont., 1935; Mennonite Burial Aid, Halbstadt, Man., 1940; Mutual Burial Fund, Montezuma, Kan., 1940; Pacific Mennonite Aid Society, Reedley, Cal., 1941; Mennonite Aid, Inc., Goshen, Ind., 1949 (the only such society operating under a conference [MC] authorization); West Abbotsford and Clearbrook Mennonite Church, Funeral Aid, Abbotsford, B.C., 1952; and Alberta Mennonite Relief Society, Coaldale, Alberta.   H.S.B.

Light's Meetinghouse was built in Lebanon, Pa., in 1817, wl en Felix Light was one of the ministers of the local Mennonite congregation. His grandfather, Johannes, an immigrant of 1718 (d. 1759), was also a preacher. Felix' home was the meeting place for the Mennonites from the first until this church was built. This home, with a stockade around it, served also as a shelter for the community during the French and Indian Wars, harboring as many as 30 families at one time. This was the Light Fort, still partially intact. About 1830 Felix Light defected to the United Brethren and claimed the meetinghouse. The Mennonites went to country churches thereafter. Not until the present decade, when a mission was opened, has there been a Mennonite church in Lebanon. The meetinghouse erected at Shirksville in 1775, seven miles north of Lebanon near Fredericksburg, was formerly called "Light's," but has long gone by the name Shirksville.   I.D.L.

Ligny (Meuse), the name of a French Mennonite congregation in the general area of the Departement of the Meuse, before 1933 called Vaucouleurs, and appearing in the *Gemeinde-Kalender* beginning with 1951 as Meuse (Ligny). In the 1941 *Gemeinde-Kalender* it was still called Ligny; no issues of the *Gemeinde-Kalender* appeared 1942-50. The *Gemeinde-Kalender* notes in 1933-41 that it was not a member of the French conference. The membership is listed as follows: ca. 75 souls in 1926, 50 souls in 1933, ca. 40 souls in 1951, and ca. 70 souls in 1955. Elders were J. Kennel 1927-35, P. Kennel 1938-55.   H.S.B.

Liiske(n), an Anabaptist martyr, burned at the stake on Aug. 10, 1550, at Montfort, in the territory of Upper Gelre, now Dutch province of Limburg. Her trial of July 21, 1550, at Arnhem, Dutch province of Gelderland, gives many interesting particulars. Liisken was the wife of Aerken Snyder (tailor); she was born about 1520 at Groote Spawe near Maastricht and had been (re)baptized about 1545 by Theunis van Hastenrath (*q.v.*) in the house of Jan Neulen (which was therefore demolished). Lemken (*q.v.*) and the martyr Metken (*q.v.*) were present at the baptism. After a sermon by Theunis, he baptized her with water which had been drawn from a well. During the trial she also confessed that she had heard Gillis van Aken (*q.v.*) preach and once on an evening Menno Simons, when he was preaching in a meadow. She further gave interesting information about the greeting used by the Mennonites by which they recognized one another. Liisken, being examined concerning her faith, was accused of agreeing with Menno Simons and his followers.   vDZ.

Ned. Archief v. Kerkgeschiedenis X, issue 3 (The Hague, 1913) 252-57; *DB* 1890, 60; K. Vos, *Menno Simons* (Leiden, 1914) 86, 241.

Lijnken and **Lijntgen:** see **Lynken** and **Lyntgen.**

Lijnslager, Floris Jacobsz (1721-78), was an aristocratic merchant at Alkmaar, Dutch province of North Holland, much renowned for his important collection of drawings. He was a good friend of

Elder Doornbos (*q.v.*) of Wormerveer and a member of the Frisian Mennonite congregation at Alkmaar, which he served as a deacon 1765-78. His father, Jacob Florisz (d. 1743), had been a deacon of the same congregation 1731-43, and his grandson Abraham Lijnslager Moeriaen 1815-25 of the united congregations of Alkmaar. (*N.N.B.Wb.* II, 860.)
vDZ.

Lijntgens (Lijns, Lijntjes), a Mennonite family at Zaandam, Dutch province of North Holland, members of the Oude Huys or Frisian Mennonite congregation. Hendrik and Cornelis Lijntgens in 1628 contributed liberally to a new meetinghouse at Zaandam. Pieter Lijntgens (*q.v.*) may also have been a member of this family.
vDZ.

S. Lootsma, *Het Nieuwe Huys* (Zaandam, 1937) 80.

Lijntgens, Pieter, d. after 1605, a Mennonite, the leader of an important trading house at Amsterdam. Lijntgens had invested more than 100,000 guilders in the East India Company, founded in 1602, but since this trading company dealt with privateers, Lijntgens sold his shares as most Mennonites did, because such illegal profits did not agree with their moral principles. Lijntgens intended to found a new company for the trade with the Dutch East Indies, whose ships would be unarmed, but the Dutch States-General, fearing the competition and wishing to support the monopoly, decided that only ships of the old East India Company would be allowed to trade with the East Indies. Thereupon a Compagnie-Lijntgens was founded, which tried to obtain a license from France to carry on trade from France to the Indies. This plan, however, was never carried out, probably because of the death of Lijntgens.
vDZ.

R. Fruin, *Verspreide Geschriften* II (The Hague) 400-2; *N.N.B.Wb.* VII, 819 f.

Lijsabeth, wife of Claes de Vries, an Anabaptist martyr, burned at the stake at Antwerp, Belgium, in 1571. She died steadfast with a tongue-screw in her mouth, preventing her from speaking to the crowd gathered around the execution place. The identification of Lijsabeth and the exact date of her execution is not clear, since this martyr is not found in the official records of the Antwerp executions. (*Mart. Mir.* D 536, E 871.)
vDZ.

Lijsbeth and **Lijsken:** see **Lysbeth** and **Lysken.**

Lijsken, wife of Jeronimus Segersz: see **Lysken Dirks.**

Lileva Mennonite Church, Ostrog district in the province of Volhynia, is listed by Heinrich Dirks, with Johann Janz as leading minister, Johann Nachtigall as cominister, and Johann Dekkert as deacon. No particulars are given about membership, etc. P. M. Friesen also lists the congregation without any additional information. Both sources state that this congregation was a branch of the Alexanderwohl (*q.v.*) Mennonite Church of Russia. This fact indicates that these two congregations had a common background. (Dirks, *Statistik,* 1905, p. 39; Friesen, *Brüderschaft,* 719.)
C.K.

Liliencron, Rochus von (1820-1912), a theologian, scholar in Germanics and composer of music, a native of Plön, Holstein, Germany, was introduced into Old German literature and research in folk music by Karl Simrock. His opus magnus, *Die historischen Volkslieder der Deutschen vom 13. bis 16. Jahrhundert* (five volumes), appeared in 1865-69. In his study of the sources he chanced upon the manuscript copies of the Hutterian Brethren in Moravia in the library at Wolfenbüttel, and published a number of them under the title "Zur Liederdichtung der Wiedertäufer" in *Mitteilungen aus dem Gebiet der öffentlichen Meinung in Deutschland während der zweiten Hälfte des 16. Jahrhunderts (Abhandlungen der k. bayer. Akademie der W. III. Cl., vol. 13, section I).* In it he briefly characterizes the Anabaptist martyr hymns, in which the sanctification of men and its preservation in life and death is nearly the sole subject and content. "Love is the great and inexhaustible theme of these songs; for love alone is the distinguishing mark of the children of God" (p. 124). In conclusion he asserts: "The total of the songs reproduced here amounts to 65, a gruesome total of bloody inhumanity and religious aberration" (p. 140). This result of his research awakened his interest in Anabaptist history, which led to further publications. The great reference work, *Allgemeine Deutsche Biographie,* 45 volumes of which appeared under his editorship with 23,273 biographical sketches, included sketches of outstanding personalities in Mennonitism, as Georg Blaurock, Matthias Servaes, Hans Denk, Conrad Grebel, Georg Grünwald, Melchior Hofmann, Balthasar Hubmaier, Hans Hut, Jakob Hutter, Thomas von Imbroich, David Joris, Jakob Kautz, Eitelhans Langenmantel, Felix Manz, Pilgram Marpeck, Michael Sattler, Menno Simons, Hans Raiffer, Hermann von Beckerath, Balthasar Denner, Wilhelm Mannhardt, etc. Individual articles contain a few errors, since the author used material which has been outdated by recent research. But the fact that Liliencron made an attempt to present objective pictures is shown by his co-operation with men who were recognized authorities on Anabaptist history. A considerable number of articles were furnished by Ludwig Keller (*q.v.*). (*ML* II, 655.)
HEGE.

Lille (*Ryssel*), a city (pop. 179,778) of France. In the 16th century it belonged to Flanders. At least 17 Calvinists and 16 Anabaptists died here as martyrs. A surgeon of Lille was drowned in the Moselle at Metz in 1538.

In 1563 a large number of Anabaptists were arrested, of whom at least 13 suffered a martyr's death, including Jan de Swarte of Nijpkerken (Nieppe) with his wife Klaesken and four sons, Klaes, Christiaen, Hans, and Mathieu. Jan was a deacon and preacher. He practiced his weaver's trade at various localities in Flanders, finally at Halewijn (Halluin). In his house Perceval van den Berge of Swevegem and Jan Maes of Hondschooten were caught. Through betrayal by the pastor of Halluin, N. van den Kasteelen, the inquisitor Pieter Titelman van Ronse, accompanied by many policemen from Lille, took them prisoner in addition to Pieter Schoenmaker and his wife Jacomijntje (who, however, recanted), Hendrik Aerts, a hatmaker, his wife Janneken Cabeljaus, and a sister Calleken Steens, married to a brother Augustijn, who was not captured. The two younger sons of Jan de Swarte could have escaped, but they refused to forsake their parents. Several brethren tried to comfort the prisoners by shouting to them; Jan lay in a hole called "paradise." One of them, Herman, was caught and imprisoned. These 13 were burned in three groups.

In 1567 five wealthy merchants of Lille were seized at Antwerp. The wealthiest was Christiaen Jansens Langedul (q.v.). They were caught at a meeting. Several managed to escape when Christiaen began a conversation in French with the captain. His wife was Mayken Raets, perhaps a sister of the mathematician Wilhelm Raets at Maastricht. His letters record his terrible tortures and his disputes with a "thin little Jesuit." He was burned on Sept. 15, 1567, with Cornelis Claes, Mattheeuws de Vick, and the preacher Hans Symons, who was one of the delegates sent to smooth over the friction in Friesland in 1556 (Vos, 52 f.).

In 1570 Maerten Karettier of Bousbecque was put to death. In 1571 Adriaen Jans Hoedemaker (q.v.) and Jelis de Backer (q.v.) died at the stake. Frossard mentions 1556 as the first year in which Anabaptist martyrs were executed at Lille, but their names have not been transmitted. The total number of martyrs who died at Lille is 95, 31 of whom are found in the martyrbooks.   K.V.

Ch. I. Frossard, *l'Eglise sous la croix pendant la domination espagnole* (Paris, 1857); *Mart. Mir., passim*, see Index; K. Vos, "De Doopsgezinden te Antwerpen in de Zestiende Eeuw," in *Bulletin de la Commission Royale de Belgique* LXXXIV (Brussels, 1920) 52 f.; *ML* II, 655 f.

Lima First Mennonite Church (GCM), located in Lima, Allen Co., Ohio, was organized Oct. 1, 1935, as a mission, and as such is functioning today. It is a member of the Middle District Conference. The present meetinghouse, erected in 1936, is a brick structure with a seating capacity of 125. The membership in 1955 is 76; the pastor is Sylvan Lehman.   S.Le.

Lima Mission (MC) was organized in the southeastern part of the city of Lima, Ohio, in January 1910 as a result of mission interest at the Pike and Salem congregations (q.v.). E. E. Troyer and C. D. Brenneman were the first superintendents. Later in the year Preacher B. B. Stoltzfus and family of West Liberty were invited to locate at the mission. Several years later Mennonites were invited to assist in a Sunday school conducted on North Jefferson Street by the Presbyterian Board. The brotherhood in Allen, Logan, Champaign, and Fulton counties assisted B. B. Stoltzfus and his family in remodeling the church and building a home for the workers, completed in 1917. As part of the building fund Stoltzfus donated his share of an oats crop which he had raised in North Dakota. The congregation was organized in 1922 by the Eastern A.M. and Ohio Mennonite conferences. The two conferences had ordained Henry Müller, a mission convert, as deacon the year before. After Stoltzfus' health declined in 1924, the Board appointed Earl Miller and his

wife Fern as workers, who left in 1926 to take charge of the Peoria, Ill., mission (q.v.). In 1926 Maurice O'Connell and his wife Geneva, converts of the Ft. Wayne, Ind., mission (q.v.), were appointed superintendent and matron. O'Connell served as licensed preacher until 1928, when he was ordained to the ministry. S. E. Allgyer ordained him bishop in 1940. After his death in 1946 he was succeeded by Glenn Martin of North Dakota. Since 1953 Darwin O'Connell, assistant pastor, is serving as pastor. The membership in 1954 was 73.   J.S.U.

Limborgh (Limborg, Limborch, Limburg), **van,** a former Dutch Mennonite family found both at Leiden and Amsterdam, where a number of them served the congregations as deacons in the 17th and 18th centuries. This family may have originated from the Dutch province of Limburg or adjacent parts of Germany. Isaac van Limburgh published *Vrede presentatie aan G. Abrahamsz en zyne Medestemmers* (Amsterdam, 1664). Pieter van Limburg, who at the end of the 17h century was a preacher of the Mennonite congregation at Burtscheid-Maastricht, had a quarrel with a Pieter Frenken, and published *Noodig verhaal, dienende tot waerschouwinge van den onbehoorlijken handel van zekeren Pieter Frenken* (Amsterdam, 1703).   vDZ.

M. Schagen, *Naamlijst der Doopsgezinde Schrijveren* (Amsterdam, 1745) 62; *Inv. Arch. Amst.* II, 2074; II, 2, Nos. 259, 646.

Limborch, Philippus van, b. at Amsterdam in 1633, d. there in 1712, was a Remonstrant (q.v.) minister at Gouda (1657-67) and Amsterdam (1667-68) and from 1668 until his death professor at the Remonstrant Theological Seminary at Amsterdam. Van Limborch, who published a large number of theological books in Latin, is of interest for Mennonite history because of the fact that after the death of Galenus Abrahamsz (q.v.) in 1706 he trained a number of Mennonite preachers and also because of the influence of his books and his theological ideas, such as rejection of predestination, emphasizing practical Christianity, and his aversion to infant baptism.   vDZ.

B. Glasius, *Godgeleerd Nederland* II ('s Hertogenbosch, 1853) 376-80; *Biogr. Wb.* VI, 41-47; *DJ* 1850, 105; *DB* 1882, 78; 1918, 70.

Limburg, a province of the Netherlands. In the 16th century the northern part belonged to Gelderland, the middle part to the duchy of Jülich (q.v.), whereas the southern part together with Maastricht (q.v.) was subject to the prince-bishop of Liége as well as to the emperor.

Even before 1530 there are indications of the spread of "heretical books." In Hoengen near Sittard the priest Dionys Vinne preached evangelical sermons in April 1530. In 1534 a group of Maastricht people went to Susteren, to hear the sermons of a "suspicious and infamous preacher." Hoengen as well as Susteren are in Jülich territory, where Duke John III paid very little attention to the work of the reformers. It is not certain whether the preachers in these cases were Sacramentists or Anabaptists. Others who preached Protestant doctrine were Dionys Vinne of Diest, Gillis von Rothem (whom Vos confused with Gillis of Aachen, *ML* I, 2), Johann Klopreis (*q.v.*), Hendrik Slachtscaep (of Tongeren), Gottfried Stralen, and Hendrik Rol (see also **Wassenberg Preachers**), who were very influential, but went to Münster one after the other (Gillis von Rothem was captured before he reached Münster).

In the following years, probably through the influence of these men, the Münster movement increased in Limburg; Rol or Slachtscaep wrote an epistle to them; there must have been a congregation in Maastricht of more than a hundred members, in which there was some trend to revolutionary ideas in 1534. Forty Limburg Anabaptists led by Jacob van Ossenbrugge started out for Münster but were stopped at Düsseldorf on Feb. 20, 1534. Henric Rol (*q.v.*), who was active in Maastricht (*q.v.*) for some time until he was arrested there on Sept. 2, 1534, and executed shortly after, had a beneficent influence upon the congregation, which, however, was nearly wiped out by persecution in January 1535. There were also Anabaptists in other places, e.g., in Venlo and near Roermond; in the villages Visschersweert and Illikhoven they were numerous. Menno Simons preached in the vicinity of Roermond in 1545. Also Elder Theunis van Hastenrath worked here with great success. Van Braght named several nonresistant blood witnesses of Maastricht, two in 1559 and four in 1570.

On Nov. 30, 1652, Wolfgang Wilhelm of Pfalz-Neuburg put up a notice announcing that the Anabaptists who would not join the Catholic Church would be expelled from the duchy of Jülich. Many went away and settled in Nijmegen and Maastricht. From this time there was a congregation in Maastricht, which existed until 1823. In Vaals on the German border there was a church which was used by the Mennonites of Aachen until 1785.

Now there is only one congregation in the province of Limburg, called Zuid-Limburg or Heerlen (*q.v.*), where Mennonites living in this coal-mining district founded a circle in 1926 and an independent congregation in 1936. The meetinghouse and parsonage are located at Heerlen. To this congregation also belong the Mennonites living at Maastricht, Geleen, Sittard, etc. The few Mennonites scattered through the northern part of the province are regularly visited by Mennonite ministers sent out by the committee for the Mennonites in the diaspora (see **Verstrooiing**). The total number of Mennonites in the province of Limburg in 1859 was 16; 1889, 69; and 1947, 285. (See also **Lower Rhine.**)   vDZ.

Jos. Habets, *De Wederdoopers in Maastricht tijdens de regeering van Keizer Karel V* (Roermond, 1877); *Gedenkboek der Hervormde Gemeente van Maastricht* (Maastricht, 1932); W. Bax, *Het Protestantisme in het bisdom Luik en vooral te Maastricht* (The Hague, I, 1937; II, 1941); K. Vos, *Menno Simons* (Leiden, 1914) 85-87; *DB* 1894, 89; 1902, 135; 1909, 120-26; K. Vos, "Anabaptisten in Limburg," *Zondagsbode* XXII (1908-9) No. 21; *ML* II, 656.

Limburg, a town in the Belgian province of Limburg, near the German border, where a number of Anabaptists were found shortly after 1530, followers of Melchior Hofmann (*q.v.*). On March 7, 1536, five Anabaptists from the villages of Montenaken and Heukelom in the duchy of Vroenhoven were arrested and brought to Limburg, where after trial and torture they were burned at the stake about March 17, 1536. They were Johan Bevers, Heine Krokarts (called Vastarz), and the wife of Sevrin Raermakers with her son and daughter. All these martyrs had been baptized by Jan Smeitgen (*q.v.*) of Maastricht. A congregation founded here in the course of time had to endure persecution several times. In 1566 it numbered about 30 members. It held its meetings in a forest near Limburg. Soon after 1566 it may have dissolved either because of persecution or because the members moved elsewhere.   vDZ.

F. Lemaire and A. L. E. Verheyden, "Une enquête sur le Protéstantisme au duché de Limbourg en 1569," in *Bulletin d'Histoire* LXVIII (1953) 139, 147 f.; *et passim;* L. E. Halkin and F. Lemaire, "Un procés d'anabaptistes à Limbourg en 1536," in *Bulletin d'histoire* CXXI (1956) reprint.

Limmen, a hamlet south of Alkmaar in the Dutch province of North Holland, about 1534 a center of Anabaptism, mostly of revolutionary character. A meeting held in February 1534 was attended by 20 persons. (*Inv. Arch. Amst.* I, No. 11; Mellink, *Wederdopers,* 170 f.)   vDZ.

Limon (Col.) Mennonite (MC) Church, a member of the South Central Conference, was organized on Sept. 10, 1922, with 19 charter members, and grew in nine years to 118 members (1931). Thereafter the membership declined, due in part to drouth conditions, until in 1954 the membership was only 36, with Valentin Swartzendruber serving as pastor. Until 1925 the congregation met in a schoolhouse eight miles southwest of Limon. In that year a new church was dedicated a mile north of the schoolhouse, but more recently (*ca.* 1947) the building was moved into the town of Limon.   L.C.M.

Linck (Link), **Wenzeslaus** (b. 1483), one of the leading German theologians of the Reformation period. He was born at Colditz, Saxony, took his doctorate in theology in 1511, in 1520 he succeeded Johann von Staupitz as vicar general of the Augustinian order in Germany; on Jan. 28, 1523, he became a Protestant preacher in Altenburg, in 1525 became chaplain at the abbey of St. Catherine at Nürnberg. He was one of the first Lutheran clergymen called by the council of Nürnberg to introduce the Reformation there.

In Nürnberg Linck opposed the Anabaptists. In connection with the orders previously issued by the mayor and the council he published a pamphlet without stating the year or his name with the title, *Grundtliche Unterrichtung eines erbarn Rats der Statt Nürmberg,* in which he gives warning of the seductive doctrine of the Anabaptists and also instructs the pastors in the town and in the country how they "shall most faithfully admonish and instruct the people in their sermons from the Holy Scriptures." Since this pamphlet mentions the death of Hans Hut, which took place on Dec. 6, 1527, it was probably printed early in 1528; it contained 40 pages. A revised and enlarged edition followed. In it the author tries to defend infant baptism and several other doctrines of his church against the objections of the Anabaptists. His method of proof is often quite naive. The booklet is a graphic example of the nature of the struggle the theologians of the 16th century waged against the Anabaptists.

On the question of punishment of the Anabaptists Linck was uncertain when his colleague Andreas Osiander advocated their execution to the council of Nürnberg. He therefore turned to Luther, who advised against capital punishment on July 14, 1528, "even if the punishment was well-deserved." He was frightened by the conclusion which might be drawn from the application of such procedure. The Protestants would also be hit by it, "as we see before our eyes, that the papists in abuse of their spiritual right have shed innocent blood which they called guilty." But Luther considered exile from the country as an appropriate punishment.   HEGE.

H. Rotermund, *Fortsetzung und Ergänzung zu Chr. Gottl. Jöchers allgem. Gelehrten-Lexikon* III (1810) Col. 1854; a reprint is found in G. A. Will's *Beyträge zur fränkischen Kirchen-Historie* (Nürnberg, 1770, pp. 229-320), as well as in the stereotype edition of this book in 1773, with the title, *Beyträge zur Geschichte des Anabaptismus in Deutschland; ML* II, 656 f.

Lincki, Martin: see **Lingg.**

Lincoln, a town in England, the seat of a Separatist congregation which called itself "Anabaptist" but was apparently Baptist, which in 1626 joined the "Anabaptist" congregations of London, Sarum, Coventry, and Tyverton in writing a letter to the Dutch Mennonites with the idea of joining the Waterlander Mennonites. This union, however, did not come into being (see **Coventry**). On Sept. 5, 1630, the Lincoln congregation wrote a letter to the Waterlanders in Amsterdam defending the strict maintenance of church discipline, which was neglected by the Waterlanders. (*Inv. Arch. Amst.* II, Nos. 1372-77.)
vDZ.

Lincoln, Neb., the location of two Mennonite-operated Civilian Public Service camps during World War II. The first was the Lincoln Experiment Station Camp No. 106, under the state College of Agriculture. The camp was approved in May 1943, and closed in October 1946. The men worked in the dairy division, agronomy department, horticulture, animal husbandry, and poultry departments. A farm and community school, with evening classes and lectures, was operated by the MCC for the men in the unit during a two-year period beginning in October 1944.

In September 1944 CPS Camp No. 138 was established at Lincoln, with two units, one of which was located on an MCC-owned farm 1½ miles east of College View, a suburb southeast of Lincoln. Unit 2 was located 10 miles northwest of Lincoln, on a farm owned by the Peace Problems Committee of the Mennonite Church (MC). Both of these units did work for the U.S. Soil Conservation Service. Both conducted farm and community schools similar to that in camp No. 106, although each of the three schools had its own educational director. In November 1944, the MCC sponsored a two-day conference at Lincoln of all their farm and community school leaders. Camp No. 138 was closed in October 1946. Since Lincoln is a center of a number of Mennonite communities and the state uni-

versity is located here, numerous Mennonites reside in the city. However, no fellowship or congregation has thus far been organized.   M.G.

M. Gingerich, *Service for Peace* (Akron, Pa., 1949) 181-86; J. E. Lehman, editor, *Mennonite Farmunity; 1st Anniversary* (Malcolm, Neb., 1946).

Lincoln Avenue Gospel Mission (KMB), located at 2812 Lincoln Ave., Chicago, Ill., was officially opened Oct. 24, 1915, with David M. Hofer as superintendent and Joseph W. Tschetter as associate superintendent. The first meetinghouse, a two-story brick structure with a seating capacity of about 125, full basement for Sunday school, and living quarters for the workers on second floor, is still used for regular services. John S. Mendel succeeded David M. Hofer and is the present (1954) superintendent.
J.S.M.

Lincoln (Neb.) United Missionary Church was organized with 19 charter members in 1952. The church now (1955) has an attendance of 100. The new meetinghouse is known widely in Lincoln as "the church with the lighted steeple." The pastor is Walter Stump.   M.G.

Lind (Lint), **Esaias Arentsz de,** was the son of Arent de Lind of Brielle and his wife Anneken Jans, the well-known martyr, who was drowned at Rotterdam, Netherlands, on Jan. 24, 1539. After the sentence was passed, Anneken in prison wrote a "Testament" (farewell letter) to her little son Esaias, then nearly six years old. This testament is found in *Offer des Heeren*, 70-75. The *Martyrs' Mirror* relates that Anneken, on the way to the place of execution with the little boy on her arm, asked the bystanders to take pity on the child; thereupon Lenert Jansz, a baker of Rotterdam, took up the boy (see the engraving in Dutch *Mart. Mir.*). Esaias de Lind, who later belonged to the Reformed Church, became a wealthy man, who occupied high offices; he was burgomaster of Rotterdam 1580-81 and 1589-90. He was a good friend of the Dutch statesman Johan van Oldenbarnevelt. In later years his business failed and de Lind was reduced to poverty. He died in 1602 or shortly after. Esaias' son Michiel (d. 1645) also went into the magistracy at Rotterdam; another son Pieter Esaiasz, who apparently died before 1618, went into the navy. It was Esaias, the son of Michiel de Lind, who gave the information on Anneken and Esaias Arentsz to van Braght, which is found in the *Martyrs' Mirror*.   vDZ.

N.N.B.Wb. II, 823; *DB* 1905, 170; *Mart. Mir.* D 143; the English edition omits pp. 143-45 of the Dutch.

Lind, Thijs (Tijs) **van,** an Anabaptist martyr: see **Matthijs van Lind.**

Lindal Mennonite Brethren Mission, located near Morden, Man., began as a result of work done by students of the Winkler (Man.) Bible School. In 1935 H. S. Voth baptized 32 persons and in 1938, 10. Soon after this a mission church was organized under the M.B. conference of Manitoba. J. P. Braun supervised this church for six years in addition to his ministry at the Morden M.B. Church. A small church building was erected in 1939. The church membership represents various nationalities —Polish, English, German, etc. J. Kehler served as minister for five years. A number of the members have moved to other places so that at present (1954) the membership is 25. Wilmer Kornelsen is the pastor. The church is located 7 miles west and 8 miles south of Morden. H.H.R.

Lindale Mennonite Church (MC), located one mile north of Edom, Linville, Rockingham Co., Va., is a member of the Virginia Conference. Largely because of a shift of the membership of the Brenneman (*q.v.*) church, it was decided in 1898 to build a church one mile north of Edom on land adjoining the original Brenneman cemetery. This church soon absorbed the membership of the old Brenneman congregation and in 1919 the Brenneman meetinghouse was sold and the proceeds placed to the credit of the Lindale church. In 1900 George R. Brunk conducted in this church the first series of meetings held in the Northern District of the Virginia Conference. At this time 16 were added to the church. Three years later A. D. Wenger held another series of meetings, when 22 were received. The church, being centrally located, has served as a gathering place for teachers' meetings, and more recently a weekly prayer meeting for the district.

The large influx of members from other places to the vicinity of the Eastern Mennonite College has in the last few years largely increased the membership, so that it became necessary in 1948 to enlarge the meetinghouse. The membership in 1954 was 178, with J. R. Mumaw serving as pastor and Moses Slabaugh as assistant pastor. T.S.

Lindanus, Wilhelmus (Willem Damasz van Lindt), b. 1523 at Dordrecht, Dutch province of South Holland, Dutch inquisitor and bishop, was educated at the University of Leuven (Louvain), Belgium, received a doctorate in theology and was made dean at The Hague. As vicar of the Bishop of Utrecht he was made spiritual commissar (*geestelijk commissaris*), charged with the control of heresy in Holland, Friesland, and Zeeland. Although he was energetic and thorough in the assigned task, his calmness distinguished him favorably from his colleague Tapper and others. "He listens well and is not easily angered" (*Mart. Mir.* D 222, E 600). In 1556 he went to Friesland. Victims of his activity were the high-ranking Jacques d'Auchy (*q.v.*), Claesken, and her husband Hendrik Eeuwesz, all of whom were executed at Leeuwarden in 1559. When the new bishoprics were established in 1561 Lindanus was made bishop at Roermond, then at Gent, where he died on Nov. 2, 1588. He also wrote numerous books admonishing the Catholic Church to improve the life of its members; e.g., *Oprecht Tryakel teghen 'tvenijn alder dolinghen onses tijdts* . . . (Antwerp, 1567). vDZ.

Glasius, *Godgeleerd Nederland* II ('s Hertogenbosch, 1853) 380-83; J. Reitsma, *Hondert jaren uit de Geschiedenis der Hervorming . . . in Friesland* (Leeuwarden, 1876) 94-106; DB 1872, 32, 91-94; 1899, 45, 52; 1906, 68, 84-86; ML II, 657.

Lindbrook (Alberta) Mennonite Brethren Church was organized in 1928 with 14 members. Its first presiding minister was A. Froese. The meetings were held in the homes of members until 1940, when the first church building was erected. In 1944, when

the membership had grown to 70, the building was enlarged. At present (1954) the church has a membership of 55. The pastor is Peter J. Warkentin, assistant pastor Peter Goertz. P.J.WA.

Linde, Antonius van der, b. 1833 at Haarlem, Holland, d. 1893 at Heidelberg, Germany, was educated at the expense of the Haarlem Mennonite congregation, of which his parents were members. While he was a schoolteacher he started to study philosophy. At first he was a rationalist, then a follower of Hegel. About 1855 he left the Mennonite Church and joined a strictly orthodox Reformed group who had separated from the main Reformed Church, and served for a short period as a preacher. He soon had left it, and studied philosophy at the University of Göttingen, Germany, obtaining his Ph.D. degree in 1862. Later he was employed in the Royal Prussian Library in Berlin. He wrote a large number of books and papers on very different subjects; for Mennonite history his bibliographical study on David Joris (*q.v.*), published at The Hague in 1867, is of interest. (*Biogr. Wb.* VI, 51-56.) vDZ.

Linden, Friedrich Otto zur (1857-1927), a Protestant pastor at Neuwied, Germany, and church historian. His biography of Melchior Hofmann (*q.v.*), *Melchior Hofmann, ein Prophet der Wiedertäufer* (Haarlem, 1885), 477 pp., inspired by Friedrich Nippold (*q.v.*), which was accepted in 1882 as a prize-winning treatise by Teylers Godgeleerd Genootschap, is of great importance for the history of Anabaptism. This work—to use zur Linden's own words—"is in that class of presentations which show Anabaptism in an essentially more favorable light than has been customary on the part of traditional historiography. It strives to do justice to Anabaptism without at the same time overrating this important movement at the expense of the Reformation" (*op. cit.*, p. XVI). Zur Linden considers Mysticism the determining feature of Anabaptism in general and of Melchior Hofmann in particular. It is not quite clear whether he means to indicate that this is a difference in principle from the reformers. This treatise is a veritable mine of historical and statistical material for the study of Anabaptist history. (*ML* II, 657 f.) D.C.

Linden, Hendrik Antonieszoon van der: see **Antonides, Henricus.**

Linden, Jan Willem van der (b. 1846 at The Hague, Holland, d. there 1923), was a Dutch Mennonite pastor, serving the following congregations: Krommenie 1870-73, Barsingerhorn 1873-83, Hoorn 1883-84, and Harlingen 1884-1912. He published a large number of philosophical-dogmatical writings, including *Beknopte godsdienstleer* (Groningen, 1902), in which he presents a liberal dogmatics, and a number of sermons. (*Biogr. Wb.* VI, 77 f.) vDZ.

Linden Church of God in Christ Mennonite Church, located west of Swalwell, Alberta, began in 1902 when Samuel Boese, a preacher from Oregon, took up one of the first homesteads in the district. In 1904 he was joined by Preacher Peter Baerg from Manitoba, under whose leadership the congregation prospered greatly. The members have come from Oregon, North Dakota, Manitoba, and Kansas. The first church building was built in 1904, enlarged twice, and replaced by new buildings in 1920 and 1951. Samuel Boese in 1944 deeded to the church some land and a large house, now called the "Linden Home." Since 1922 seven preachers and four deacons have been ordained. The church has the regular services, Christian Endeavor programs, a sewing circle, etc. The membership in 1955 was 368. (See **Swalwell.**)   J.W.T.

Linden (Alberta) Evangelical Mennonite Brethren Church (now M.B.), formerly called Swalwell, was organized in 1930 out of members of the E.M.B., M.B., Allianz-Mennonite, G.C.M., and C.G.C. groups which had settled in this district as follows: three C.G.C. families from Oregon in 1902-3, a number of families from Manitoba in 1903 ff., and 15-18 families from Russia 1923-25, many of these from what was in Russia known as the "Allianz" group. Since there was no congregation of any of these groups in this region, the Mennonites of the various branches met together occasionally for worship in private homes and schoolhouses. One of the leaders, N. A. Rempel, was later ordained as an M.B. minister. In 1926 J. R. Barkman, E.M.B., a schoolteacher, came into the community and influenced the group toward the E.M.B. (then called Bruderthaler) Conference. This trend was helped by successful revival meetings held in 1926 by G. P. Schultz of Chicago, an E.M.B. evangelist. In 1930 the group unanimously applied for membership in the E.M.B. Conference, but when the E.M.B. representative came, only about half of the group actually joined the E.M.B.; the rest, mostly M.B., refused to go along, although they continued to worship with the E.M.B. congregation. In 1933 a meetinghouse was erected at Linden, and also one at Namaka, where the members were chiefly Allianz (*q.v.*) from Russia, and this group joined the E.M.B. in 1934, with A. A. Toews as leader. (In 1942 Namaka withdrew from the E.M.B. Conference and joined the M.B. Conference.) In 1934 the M.B. members fully joined the Linden E.M.B. Church. In 1947-48 finally the Linden congregation also joined the M.B. Conference, with Sam Ratzlaff as leader.   C.W.T.

Linden Mennonite Brethren Church, located about eight miles north of Acme, Alberta, formerly affiliated with the E.M.B. Conference, but since 1948 a member of the Canadian M.B. District Conference, began when Mennonite immigrants from Russia settled in this area. The meetings were at first held in a public school, but later a church building was erected near Linden. N. A. Rempel has been the presiding minister of the church nearly 20 years. The membership in 1954 was 93; Peter J. Doerksen was the pastor, and J. A. Froese assistant pastor.
                                                    A.A.T.

Lindenau, a Mennonite village name transplanted from Prussia to the Molotschna and Trakt Mennonite settlements of Russia; West Reserve, Man.; and Menno and Chaco, Paraguay.   C.K.

Lindenau, a village of the Molotschna settlement, eight miles from Halbstadt, Ukraine, South Russia, was established on July 15, 1804, by eleven Mennonite families from West Prussia. Before World War I there were 350 Mennonite inhabitants. The next railroad station was Svelodolinskaya, three miles away. The occupation of the village was mostly agriculture, principally small grains. Before the Revolution the village had 21 farms of 173 acres each, later 75 farms of 87 acres each. Before the Revolution about half of the population were craftsmen, such as carriage makers, upholsterers, smiths, and dyers.

During and after the Revolution the village suffered severely. The collectivization was accomplished in 1929. Many of the farmers were sent to Siberia as kulaks. This continued till the outbreak of World War II. In 1941, when the Germans approached, most of the male population was sent to Siberia. The remaining families continued farming in groups of four to five until they were evacuated westward when the Germans retreated in 1943. Some of them reached Canada, but most of them were returned to Russia. (*ML* II, 658.)   C.K.

Lindenhofje, a former Mennonite home for aged women at Amsterdam, which was founded in 1614 by the Waterlander congregation for its poor members. In 1801 it was closed and the inmates were moved to other homes of the Amsterdam Mennonite congregation. (*Inv. Arch. Amst.* II, Nos. 427-30.)
                                                    vDZ.

Lindental, a small Mennonite settlement in South Russia near the railway station Sinelnikovo, the inhabitants of which joined the Kronsweide Church after the confusions of World War I. In Lindental there were once splendid buildings and parks. Before the war there was no lack of motorized machinery on any farm; there were shops on a large scale, such as iron works and factories for the production of farm machinery. In the postwar period the thriving village decayed, in the destruction that met so many other settlements. The inhabitants fled, returned, and had to flee again. One front after another passed over small Lindental, one band of robbers followed another, and so the inhabitants were robbed of all their possessions. It can be gratefully stated that no one died a violent death. But typhus claimed a number of victims here. (*ML* II, 658.)   D.H.E.

Lingg (Lincki), **Martin,** an Anabaptist leader of Schaffhausen, Switzerland, who is identical with "Marti Weniger called Lincki" and is called one of the "principal baptizers and ringleaders of the sect." In the difficult struggles of the beginning Anabaptist movement in Zürich until he was banished from the country after the disputation in Zürich on Nov. 6-9, 1525, together with Ulrich Teck of Waldshut and Michael Sattler (*q.v.*), he was an active leader.

But this zealous Swiss Brethren preacher was not intimidated in his successful work. We find his traces in Lostorf, canton of Basel, and in the cantons of Solothurn and Bern. An Anabaptist named Flückinger confessed before the court in Bern in

July 1531 that he had been baptized on the past Easter Day by the Anabaptist leader Lincki of Schaffhausen.

Lincki played the chief role in the disputation at Zofingen (q.v.) in July 1532 as spokesman for the Anabaptists. Bern had demanded that the authorities of Solothurn should see to it that at least the Anabaptist preacher Lincki, who preached openly, take part in the disputation. Lincki defended the Anabaptist principles at Zofingen with skill. According to the court records he was again preaching in the canton of Zürich at Andelfingen and Ossingen in October 1532. But his period of activity as an Anabaptist preacher did not last much longer. Having returned home, this zealous advocate of Anabaptism gave up the struggle and made a public recantation at Schaffhausen. "God be thanked," said the lords of Bern, that this "outstanding leader" has recanted.   S.G.

Müller, *Berner Täufer;* P. Burckhardt, *Die Basler Täufer* (Basel, 1898) 44; E. Egli, *Aktensammlung,* Nos. 863 and 1887; S. Geiser, *Die Taufgesinnten-Gemeinden* Karlsruhe, 1931) 139, 173, 175, 179, 343; C. A. Bächtold, *Die Schaffhäuser Wiedertäufer in der Reformationszeit* in *Beiträge zur Vaterländischen Geschichte,* (Schaffhausen, 1900) 71-118, especially 97-115; *ML* II, 658.

Linggenscher, Peter, an Anabaptist martyr, a native of Geneva, Switzerland, lived in destitute circumstances at Rümlingen, supported by the wealthy brother Ulrich Madlinger; he had been expelled from the canton, but returned and was probably threatened with drowning and expelled the second time. When he appeared again and took part in the meetings of the Swiss Brethren at Lostorf or Ettingen, he was drowned in a brook near the Homburg castle together with Hans Madlinger (q.v.) on Feb. 11, 1531.   NEFF.

P. Burckhardt, *Die Basler Täufer* (Basel, 1898) 41; *ML* II, 658.

Link, Johannes (d. 1545), a Franciscan monk, was born at Nürnberg, Bavaria, Germany, died at Bamberg, where he was ordained to the priesthood in 1525 and zealously opposed the Anabaptists. Several of his sermons in manuscript form have been preserved in the Munich state library (*cod. germ.* 4264). They come from the Franciscan monastery at Freising and were copied in 1532 in the Franciscan monastery at Bamberg by Jacob Angst. The original has been lost. The arguments seem to have served as a basis for Franciscan sermons to combat the Anabaptists. Copies of Link's sermons have also been found among the court records of the Würzburg state archives.

One sermon has the heading, "Eine tröstlich Unterweisung wider die neue Ketzerei auferweckt von den verkehrten Wiedertäufern im Anfang des 1524. Jahres bis hier-her." It was written in 1531 and from the Catholic point of view it condemns 15 articles of the Anabaptist faith as false doctrine. Another copy, also of 1531, ends with the challenge that heretical doctrines must be combated with sermons and sword; he gives ten reasons. Then he gives directions for winning backsliders back into the Catholic Church if they are approachable to indoctrination by learned men while they are in prison. But he has learned that this is usually not the case with the Anabaptists, wherefore he advises against the "instruction of that kind of obstinate persons."

The hopeless conditions in the Catholic Church which gave occasion to falling away are admitted by Johannes Link. He enumerates no less than 100 abuses, which he deplores.   HEGE.

P. Minges, "Johannes Link, Franziskanerprediger († 1545)," in *Beitr. z. Gesch. d. Renaissance und Reformation, Joseph Schlecht zum sechzigsten Geburtstag* (Freising, 1917) 250-54; D. Clauss, "Der Bamberger Franciscaner-Prediger Hans Link," in *Ztscht f. bayer. Kirchengesch.* VIII (1933) 159-69; *ML* II, 659.

Linken, Mattheus van, an Anabaptist martyr: see **Mattheus Bernaerts.**

Linn Township Amish Mennonite Church, unaffiliated, located seven miles northwest of Roanoke, Ill., was organized about 1910 with 45 members under the leadership of Peter Zimmerman, who had earlier been a minister in the Roanoke Mennonite (MC) Church. The present meetinghouse was built in 1916. Former ministers include Peter Zimmerman, John W. Kennell, and Joseph J. Kennell (bishop). The membership in 1954 was 169, with D. M. Hostetler serving as bishop, John E. Hostetler as minister, and S. E. Unzicker as deacon.

The congregation is sometimes locally called the "Kennell" church, after Bishop J. J. Kennell. It does not belong to the Conservative Mennonite Conference, but remains unaffiliated. Its origin goes back to 1904, when Peter Zimmerman and 40 members withdrew from the Roanoke (MC) congregation because they wished to adhere to the rigid Amish practice of "shunning," which Roanoke refused to do. Zimmerman later came under the influence of John D. Kauffman (q.v.) of the "Sleeping Preacher" group at Shelbyville, Ill. (Mt. Hermon congregation), which had been begun there about 1907, and was ordained bishop by Bishop John R. Zook of New Wilmington, Pa.   D.M.H.

Linnigh (Linnich), a Mennonite family, apparently originally from Linnich on the Ruhr, duchy of Jülich, Germany, where Mennonites were found as early as 1551. The Linnigh family lived at Amsterdam from the early 17th century, engaged in business, and were members and sometimes deacons of the Waterlander congregation. Jacob Linnigh was a preacher of the Amsterdam Waterlander, later of the united Waterlander and Lamist congregation from 1661 until he resigned in 1684.

A branch of this family is found in Eiderstedt and Hamburg, Germany. Andreas Linnich was a brewer at Eiderstadt about 1650 (*ME* I, 41). He may have been identical with Andreas Linnich, who about 1640 moved from Rade (q.v.) near Düsseldorf, Germany, to Friedrichstadt. Jacob Linnich, probably a son of Andreas, was a merchant at Hamburg, where he and his descendants served the Mennonite congregation as deacons.   vDZ.

Linsenbuch, Hans, an Anabaptist martyr, a subject of the lords of Hacke zu Brücken on the Helme in North Thuringia, Germany, made some derisive comments on infant baptism and was therefore arrested and compelled to recant. But he again joined the Anabaptists and after a long imprisonment was sentenced to death by fire by verdict of a court at Leipzig, and was beheaded on Dec. 4, 1537, at Brücken.   NEFF.

Wappler, *Thüringen*, 165; E. Jacobs, "Die Wiedertäufer am Harz," 1899, 492; *ML* II, 659.

Linz on the Danube. The extent of the Anabaptist movement in Upper Austria in the late 1520's can be learned from the records of the cross-examinations given the imprisoned Anabaptists in 1527-28 in several cities in Germany, and also from the reports sent to the government by various authorities. We learn that after the dispersal of the congregation founded at Steyr by Hans Hut, Linz became a center for the Upper Austrian Anabaptists "ob der Ens."

According to the court records of Passau, Kasper Weinberger, a linen weaver, had moved to Linz from Freistadt, where he was baptized by Jakob Portner, the chaplain of the baron von Roggendorf, and with him a cobbler named Wolfgang and his sister. Hans Stieglitz and his brother Leonhard were baptized in an inn at Linz at Michaelmas in 1527.

Ambrosius Spittelmaier, a relative of Hans Spittelmaier of Nikolsburg in Moravia, made some significant statements. Ambrosius "stemmed from Linz where his father lived." "His name which he received in baptism as an infant he was keeping, but not the baptism." Expelled from Linz he had gone to Augsburg. Then he was arrested in Kadolzburg and tried in Erlangen. His principal teacher he said was Hut. In addition there was also the German secretary Leonhard Freisleben (*q.v.*), also known as the schoolmaster of Wels, and his brother Christoph, and also Hans Kirchner of Wels.

The Anabaptist group at Linz included also Jakob of Meissen, who was serving as an "apostle" near Freistadt, and especially Wolfgang Brandhuber (*q.v.*), "the preacher of Linz," and Hans Schlaffer (*q.v.*) also "sometimes called the parson ot Linz," Hans Fischer former secretary of the baron of Stahremberg, also Thomas of Grein, usually called Waldhauser, who was burned at the stake at Brno two days before Easter 1538.

The Linz Anabaptists also include Johannes Bünderlin (*q.v.*), of whom the *Vergichtbuch* of Strasbourg makes the comment for the year 1529: "was baptized in Augsburg, spiritually akin to Denk" (*q.v.*). Little is known about his life. It is not even known whether he died a natural death or was burned as a sacrifice to his convictions.

Brandhuber was condemned to death in 1529 "as a preacher and a ringleader of the seducing sect," together with the preacher Hans Niedermaier and 70 others. According to the account in the chronicles of the Hutterian Brethren, Brandhuber faithfully taught Christian brotherhood above all, one of the main principles of this group of Anabaptists, "that one should have all things in common which serve to the glory of God."

But the stern orders of Ferdinand I against the Anabaptists had not accomplished what he expected of them. On May 11, 1532, he wrote to the magistrate of Upper Austria: in spite of serious mandates the

sect keeps on increasing in our principality under your jurisdiction. The best way to conclude the affair with the Anabaptists imprisoned in Linz, Wels, Garsten, and other places would be by instruction. For that purpose four honorable, clever men, two clergymen, and two secular, should be commissioned to indoctrinate them. Those who are penitent shall receive mercy; ringleaders, preachers, and backsliders shall be treated according to the regulations which have been issued.

In consquence of this decree several of the Anabaptists in Linz offered to abstain from their doctrine. The government then passed suitable measures. After that time there was a rapid decline of the Anabaptist movement in Upper Austria. LOSERTH.

Beck, *Geschichts-Bücher;* J. Jäkel, "Zur Frage über die Entstehung der Täufergemeinden in Oberösterreich," *25. Jahresbericht des Staatsgymnasiums in Freistadt,* 1895; *idem,* "Zur Gesch. d. Wiedert. in Oberösterreich und speziell in Freistadt," *47. Bericht über das Museum Francisco Carolinum* (in Linz) (Linz, 1889); *idem,* "Kirchliche und religiöse Zustände in Freistadt während des Reformationszeitalters," *19. und 20. Jahresbericht des Staatsgymnasiums in Freistadt, 1889-90;* A. Nicoladoni, *Johannes Bünderlin von Linz und die oberösterreichischen Täufergemeinden in den Jahren 1525-1531* (Berlin, 1890); *idem,* "Johannes Bünderlin von Linz und seine Stellung zu den Wiedertäufern," *46. Bericht des Museums Francisco Carolinum, 1888;* J. E. Jörg, *Deutschland in der Revolutionsperiode* (Freiburg, 1851); *ML* II, 659 f.

Lioren, Pieter Jans, son of the noted Elder Jan Willems (*q.v.*), born at Hoorn and a member of the Frisian Mennonite congregation, was made magistrate at Hoorn in 1597, a member of the admiralty in 1612, and mayor 1614-16. In the coup d'etat of Prince Maurice against Oldenbarnevelt in 1618 he was thrown out of the senate. In 1595 he designed a new model for a sailboat on the proportions of Noah's Ark—the "Hoornsche gaings" or "fleutschepen" (120 ft. long, 20 ft. wide, 12 ft. deep). In a short time quite a number of these boats were in use. Half a century later the boats in the fleet were modeled on different proportions. (*DB* 1867, 65-70; *ML* II, 660.)   K.V.

Lippenhuizen, a village in the Dutch province of Friesland, where there is said to have been a Mennonite church in the early days. By 1686 it had already been incorporated into the neighboring congregation of Gorredijk (*q.v.*), which is still known as Gorredijk-Lippenhuizen. The Lippenhuizen meetinghouse, built in 1802 and rebuilt in 1875 (*DB* 1876, 128), was used until Sept. 14, 1947, and then sold. (*ML* II, 660.)   vDZ.

Lippijntgen (Lippinkin) **Roetsaert** (Roetzaerts), an Anabaptist martyr, a daughter of Jan Roetsaert, living at Bellem near Gent, Flanders, was beheaded on July 19, 1576, inside the Gravensteen castle at Gent with Barbele Pieters and Kreupel Sijntgen (Sijntgen Bornaige), while on the same day Michiel Willems was burned at the stake. Lippijntgen had been (re)baptized in 1565. This martyr is not found in van Braght, *Martyrs' Mirror,* but is apparently identical with Lippijntgen Stayaerts (*q.v.*), who van Braght says was executed in 1569; this must be an error. (Verheyden, *Gent,* 67, No. 240.)   vDZ.

Lippijntgen Staeyaerts (Stayerts), found in van Braght's *Martyrs' Mirror* as an Anabaptist martyr. This martyr is included twice by van Braght; once (*Mart. Mir.* D 388, E 740) as Lippijntgen Stayerts, wife of Pieter Stayert, executed at Gent, Belgium, in 1569; again (D 648, E 968) as Lippijntgen Stayaerts, executed at Gent in 1573, together with Kreupel Sijntgen. These statements by van Braght are not exact; no Lippijntgen Staeyaerts (Stayerts) has been found in the official documents and Kreupel Sijntgen (*q.v.*) did not die in 1573 but in 1576. Verheyden (*Gent, 67*) solved the problem by assuming that Lippijntgen Stayaerts (Stayert) is identical with Lippijntgen Roetsaert (*q.v.*), executed at Gent in 1576.   vdZ.

Lissner (Lisner), **Christian** (Christl), a Hutterite who was seized at Sterzing in Tirol, Austria (now Italy), with Matthias Legeder (*q.v.*), but who returned "uninjured" to the brotherhood after a long confinement in chains. He and Legeder together wrote two songs: "Nun hört, ich will euch singen, die frommen miessen leiden viel," and "Nun hert, was ich euch singen will." Nothing else is known about him.   NEFF.

Wolkan, *Lieder*, 229; idem, *Geschicht-Buch*, 178; Zieglschmid, *Chronik*, 227; *Die Lieder der Hutterischen Brüder* (Scottdale, 1914) 303; *ML* II, 660.

Literary Societies, community organizations for the cultural, literary, and social development of their members, were a common feature of the American cultural scene in the 19th century and after. They have, however, practically died out and been replaced by other community clubs, such as women's clubs, men's fellowship groups of various kinds, etc. They were introduced into American Mennonite life primarily as young people's clubs, first in academies and colleges and then in local congregations. Elkhart Institute (*q.v.*) founded in 1894, and its successor Goshen College, have always had such societies, which for a long time played a major role in student life, although they have now become relatively minor factors on the campus. Eastern Mennonite College and Hesston College have also always had such societies.

Literary societies were common in Mennonite (MC) communities from about 1920 on. One of the first was organized in the Yellow Creek-Holdeman congregation near Wakarusa, Ind., about 1900, but it soon died out. The first permanent society was organized in the Forks Mennonite Church near Middlebury, Ind., in 1910, followed by one in the Middlebury congregation in 1912, and three more in 1913 at Elkhart, Nappanee, and Clinton Frame near Goshen. By 1924 a state convention of literary societies within the Indiana-Michigan Mennonite Conference district was organized which met annually thereafter. The development in Ohio and Illinois was similar, state conventions also being organized. Later, with the organization of Mennonite (MC) Youth Fellowship on a national scale, with its emphasis on religious activity, the role of the literaries declined somewhat, and they were often displaced by local MYF organizations. State MYF conventions also tend to displace the state literary conventions. Some literary societies have, however, continued.

The literary societies furnished avenues for expression and social fellowship which often contributed much to personal growth and development through their monthly meetings in the homes of members. At times they lost some of their literary character and became largely social gatherings. In order to promote high quality of work and experience the Young People's Problems Committee of the Mennonite General Conference (MC) arranged the publication of the *Young People's Literary Society Manual* (Scottdale, 1934, 148 pp.), written by C. F. Yake. The Illinois state organization, the Mennonite Literary Society of Illinois, in 1925 began the publication of the *The Literary Helper* (Vol. I, Sterling, Ill., 17 pp.), designed to aid local societies in their work of organization and programs; only one number appeared. In 1937 (?) Raymond Yoder, traveling secretary for the Indiana-Michigan Literary Convention, published a history of all Indiana literary societies under the title *Indiana Literaries* (pp. 184). Literary societies were apparently chiefly characteristic of the midwestern Mennonite (MC) Church. Few similar organizations developed elsewhere in this group, and apparently none at all in other Mennonite branches, except in their schools and colleges.

The Phalo Club of Goshen is a unique women's literary club, founded *ca.* 1915, whose members are taken chiefly from the Eighth St. (GCM) and the College (MC) congregations.   H.S.B.

General Conference Mennonites and Mennonite Brethren. Literary societies in these groups found their chief support and field of activity in connection with the schools, particularly the colleges, Bethel College, Tabor College, Freeman College, Gretna Collegiate Institute, Rosthern Junior College, Mennonite Brethren Bible College, and Canadian Mennonite Bible College. Similar societies were found at Bluffton College in the early days. Later on the societies specialized in debating.

At Bethel College there were in the earliest days a German Schiller-Verein and an English Platonian Society. During the seventh school year they were replaced by the Belles Letters Society, Germania Verein, the Juvenile Society, and the Parliamentary Law Club. The emphasis was placed on reading, writing of essays, and music. In the college papers many of the results of the societies were published. Tabor College and Freeman College had similar organizations. The old type of literary society has now been replaced by modern clubs, such as the Deutscher Verein in Canada and similar organizations. In general, modern forms of entertainment have made the old literary society obsolete.   C.K.

H. P. Peters, *History and Development of Education Among the Mennonites of Kansas* (Hillsboro, 1925).

Literature, Mennonites in. The following series of seven articles presents a survey of the Anabaptist-Mennonite theme in the belletristic literature of the Netherlands, Germany, France, Russia and Russo-German emigrés, and North America, in that order. At the same time the surveys include belletristic literature produced by Mennonites on whatever theme. Literature of less than high quality is also included. Only in the literature produced by Mennonites outside of Holland is an attempt made to be somewhat exhaustive, including even material of slight quality. The bibliography of the major article on Germany lists a number of titles which are not treated in the text of the discussion. For additional material on literature by Mennonites, see **Catechisms, Confessions of Faith, Devotional Literature, Historiography, Hymnology, Religious Literature,** and **Sermons.**

I. *Netherlands.* The role which the Mennonites and other groups spiritually related to them have filled in Dutch literature has been a dual one, on the one hand active and on the other hand passive. On the one hand numerous poets and writers of varying significance have come from their circles, and on the other hand the group has constituted on the passive side an object of discussion in literature, a discussion which has consisted chiefly of contumely and derision.

1. *Writings by Mennonites.* The creative literary activity of Dutch Mennonites begins with the very earliest Anabaptist documents from the times of persecution and martyrdom in the 16th century. In these stirring, at times deeply moving, and always very personal testimonies of human suffering, of devotion to husband and wife and children, of the torturing concern of the future of loved ones, and of the calm and unshakable devotion to faith and readiness to suffer which rises high above all suffering and thinking, we often come suddenly upon a childlike-pure, ingenuous beauty which the writer did not consciously strive for and of which he very likely was wholly unconscious. Consider for instance the letters of Hendrik Verstralen (1571) and Maeyken Wens (1573), or the little song by the former, or the warlike, somewhat heavy, trumpet song of Anneken Jans (*q.v.*), the impetuous, passionate pupil of David Joris, or the song by Margriet and Janneken, who were cast into the Scheldt River after they had been brought secretly to Antwerp and condemned to death, or many of the martyr stories and martyr hymns. The ancient documents produced by these martyrs (letters, testaments, farewells, confessions of faith, etc.) were collected and published in a volume called *Het Offer des Heeren* (*q.v.*) which appeared in 1562 for the first time, and to which a *Lietboecxken* (*q.v.*) was added beginning with the edition of 1563. The entire volume was reprinted in 1904 by Samuel Cramer (*q.v.*) as the second part of *Bibliotheca Reformatoria Neerlandica.* The *Offer des Heeren* is not only a collection of valuable historical material, not only a worthy and precious monument to the suffering of the first Anabaptists; it also contains a treasury of literary beauty, concerning which literary historians such as Kalff and Prinsen and the severe critic Busken Huet, as well as the theologians de Hoop Scheffer, Cramer, Kühler, and Knappert, are quite agreed. The large *Martelaers-Spiegel (Martyrs' Mirror)* by T. J. van Braght, which appeared in 1660, was a continuation and expansion of the older martyr book.

Of the multitude of songbooks the following should be mentioned as the most significant and best known: the *Geestelijck Liedt-Boecxken* by David Joris which contains songs of 1529-36 and in particular the song, already mentioned, by Anneken

Jans (the only extant copy is in the royal library in The Hague); the *Lietboeck* (1582) by Hans de Ries (*q.v.*), the Waterlander preacher of Alkmaar, in which appeared a translation of "Ein feste Burg ist unser Gott" which is praised by Kalff; *Een nieu Liedenboeck* (1560, 1562) and *Veelderhande Liedekens* (1560, 1569), both thoroughly discussed by Kalff.

The songbooks which were intended for use in specific congregations are one or more levels lower in literary quality. Such as *'t Groot Hoorns Liedtboeck* and *'t Kleyn Hoorns Liedtboeck* (both of 1644) and *Het Rijper Liedt Boecxken* (1669), the *Middelieër Liedboeck* (1651), *'t Gheestelijck Bloem-Hofken* (Haarlem, 1637), *'t Gheestelijck Kruydt-Hofken* (Amsterdam, 1637), Claes Stapel's *Lusthof der Zielen* (Harlingen, 1681, 1686), and Alle Derks' *Lusthof des Gemoets* (Groningen, 1732) and *Agter-Hofje* (Groningen, 1736).

The first Mennonite in the field of belles-lettres proper was Carel van Mander (*q.v.*, 1548-1606). Having fled for conscience' sake from the southern Netherlands to Holland, he settled in Haarlem in 1583, where as a painter he became the close friend of the noted artists Cornelis Corneliszn van Haarlem, Hendrick Czn. Vroom, and Hendrick Goltzius, and where he is also supposed to have been the instructor of Frans Hals. In 1604 he moved to Amsterdam, where he died and was buried in the "Old Church." His famous work, the *Schilder-Boeck* (1603, 1604, new ed. 1946), in which he fused psychological and novelistic matter with biographical and historical data after the fashion of Vasari, still has value in the field of the history of art, especially for the history of the Dutch and German schools. As a poet he participated zealously in the movement to transplant the Italian Renaissance to Dutch soil. In 1597 he published translations of Virgil's *Bucolica* and *Georgica* with a sonnet to Goltzius as an introduction. Later he published a commentary on Ovid's *Metamorphoses* with an abundance of mythological detail, afterwards published as an appendix to the *Schilder-Boeck.* As a Christian poet he wrote "Gheestelycke Liedekens" as a booklet entitled *De Gulden Harpe* (1605, 1613; the first edition, 1599, bore the title *De Harpe oft des Herten Snarenspel* attached to the *Hooghe Liedt Salomo*); he also wrote the hymns in the booklet entitled *Bethlehem, dat is het Broodhuys, inhoudende den Kerstnacht . . . Liedekens of Leysen, die de Herderen . . . 's nachts, hun vee wakende, singen met verlangen na de comste Christi* (1613). Among his writings is an attempt at an epic poem entitled *Olijf-Bergh ofte Poema van den laetsten Dagh,* which likewise did not appear until after his death (1609). Several of his poems also appeared in the *Nederduytsche Helicon* (1610).

Another writer belonging to the same literary period of the rhetoricians (*Rederijkers*) who has often been classed as a Mennonite was Roemer Visscher (1547-1620), the author of *Brabbelingh* and *Sinnepoppen* (both 1614), which are neither poetic nor ingenious, but are only moralistic pieces in prose to accompany a series of symbolical copper etchings by Claes Jzn. Visscher. There is, however, no adequate ground for his classification as a Mennonite. Some consider him to have been a liberal Catholic while others hold that he was a Calvinist with a tendency toward libertinism.

Pieter Pietersz (q.v., 1574-1651), a Mennonite minister at De Rijp and later at Zaandam, was the author of a noteworthy book, *Wegh na Vredenstadt* (Road to the City of Peace). Among the "travels to eternity" of which Bonaventura's *De Septem Itineribus Aeternitatis* may have been the archetype, Pietersz' book is an interesting specimen. This book, published first *ca.* 1625 and followed by seven other Dutch editions, has also been translated into German. Gerrit Honig and Robert Friedmann are of the opinion that John Bunyan's famous *Pilgrim's Progress* (1678) was largely influenced by *Wegh na Vredenstadt*. David Joris and Hendrick Niclaes (q.v.), *Dat geestlicke Landt der Beloften,* dealt with the same theme.

Joost van den Vondel (1587-1679), the great master of the Golden Age of Dutch literature, was of Mennonite ancestry, both from his father's side and his mother's side. His father, a milliner (*hoedstoffeerder*) by trade, had been persecuted in Antwerp because of his Mennonite faith, like the parents of Vondel's mother, and had fled to Cologne, where the poet was born. Later the father with his family migrated by way of Bremen to Holland, settling in Amsterdam in 1597 as a hosiery merchant. His gifted son, at first a faithful Mennonite and even in 1616-20 a deacon in the Waterlander congregation which met in the church "bij den Toren" (tower), and a close friend of many of its preachers, united with the Catholic Church in 1641. The grounds for this spiritual migration are to be sought perhaps first of all in the very human longing for a religion with compelling and unshakable authority, but also in the desire of the poet for mystical experience, and probably as well in the deep disillusionment which he experienced as the result of the unedifying quarrel between Hans de Ries (q.v.) and Nittert Obbesz (q.v.) which confused the Mennonite church in Amsterdam in 1624-27, and against which he wrote his poem "Antidotum" (1626). Vondel's drama *Gijsbreght van Aemstel* (1637) was a harbinger of this inner change, for it is already full of Catholic atmosphere. Many of his later works can be considered a literary defense of his new-won faith; for instance, the dramas *Maeghden* (1639), *Peter en Pauwels* (1641), *Maria Stuart* (1646), the poems *Brieven van der Heilighe Maeghden* (1642) and *Eeuwgetij der Heilige Stede te Amsterdam,* and an ecclesiastical-didactic, rather prosaic poem in three books, entitled *Altaergeheimenissen* (both written in 1645), *Johannes de Boetgesant* (1662, 6 books), and *De heerlyckheit der Kercke* (1663, 3 books). Vondel wrote two beautiful poems for the dedication of the Remonstrant church in Amsterdam (1630). Unfortunately very little evidence appears in Vondel's writings of his earlier faith, concerning which he says in his poem *Toetssteen* (1650) that he was bound to it in his youth only because it was an inherited doctrine for him (*door errefleer*). A few traces however are found, chiefly in the scattered verses which he composed for the etched portraits of several well-known Mennonite preachers, Hans de Ries, Cornelis Anslo, both of whom he esteemed highly (the latter etching was one by Rembrandt of 1641), Lubbert Gerritsz, and Antonius Roscius, to whom he dedicated two poems.

Another Mennonite literary figure who, like Vondel, became a Catholic, was Reiner (or Reyer) Anslo (1626-69), a poet of average ability with some outstanding moments, and a nephew of the abovenamed preacher Cornelis Anslo. He lived for many years in Italy and died in Perugia. *Roomsche Lier* is the title of his collected poems, in which Vondel's influence is very evident. When the poet Pieter Czn Hooft died, Anslo wrote a long poem as an introduction to the 1671 edition of Hooft's works. Pastor Dirk Rafaelsz Camphuysen (q.v., 1586-1626), although not a Mennonite but rather inclined to the Remonstrants, should be mentioned in passing as a meritorious pious poet who was highly esteemed by the Collegiants, and whose version of the Psalms was sung by them for many years, even as late as the closing of the Collegium at Rotterdam on Jan. 11, 1788. Joachim Oudaen (q.v., 1628-92) was of a similar type in religious as well as in literary respects. He also, like his father, joined the Collegiants, and he also composed a version of the Psalms entitled *Uytbreiding der Psalmen* (1680-81). He had for a time been a deacon in the Waterlander Mennonite Church in Rotterdam. He composed a short poem for the portrait of Menno Simons (*DB* 1916). He cultivated in his lyric poems a type which was seldom used in the Dutch poetry of that day, namely, the description of landscape paintings.

Among the numerous Mennonite composers of hymns, whose songs, usually of little literary value, are found in several Dutch Mennonite hymnbooks, are (besides de Ries, Vondel, and Oudaen, mentioned before) Menno Simons, Dirk Philips, Leenaert Clock, Jan Jacobsz, Claes Ganglofs, Pieter Jans Twisck, Marijn den Brauwer, Abraham van Gherwen, Jan Jansz Deutel, Jan Claesz Schaap, Alle Derks, H. A. Hoejewilt, Bernardus de Bosch, Anthony Hartsen, Galenus Abrahamsz, Jan Luyken, Adriaan Spinniker, Reinier Rooleeuw, Aagje Deken, Adriaan Loosjes Pz., A. H. van Gelder, J. Lugt Dz., Assuerus Doyer, Klaas Sybrandi, Jan de Liefde, Herman Boetje, A. A. Sepp.

Anthoni Janssen (van der Goes) published several volumes of poetry: *Christelyck Vermaeck, Bestaende in Verscheyden Stichtelycke Rymen en Gesangen* (1645), *Zederymen* (1656), and *'t Doolhof te Versailles, met Vaerzen verrykt* (n.d., repr. 1733); his son Joannes Antonides (q.v.) van der Goes (1647-84), in his time a famous poet, admired and eulogized by no less a person than Vondel, wrote a number of poems and tragedies, e.g., *Trazil of Overrompelt Sina,* and particularly *De Ystroom,* 1671. Some of his poems were posthumously edited and published by his father (*Gedigten,* 1685, repr. 1704, 1715). Tieleman Jansz van Braght (q.v.) wrote *Anghstig Swanen-Gesangh of Troostelooze Vreede* (1647), and Jan Philipsz Schabaelje (q.v.) wrote *Lusthof des Gemoeds,* the most popular Mennonite book ever published, from 1645 on in numerous Dutch, German (*Die wandelnde Seele*), and English (*The Wandering Soul*) editions.

The physician and theologian, Pieter Langedult (q.v., 1640-77), a member of the Flemish Mennonite congregation in Haarlem, composed several

Christian dramas, including what might be called a passion play.

The gifted poet and etcher Jan Luyken (*q.v.*, 1649-1712), the son of an educated schoolteacher and an independent thinker who had connections with both the Remonstrants and the Mennonites as well as later with the Collegiants, and who finally joined the Mennonite group in Amsterdam of which Galenus Abrahamsz de Haan was the leader, was the creator of the best Dutch lyric poetry after Vondel, Bredero, and Hooft, particularly in his youthful poems which were published in 1671 under the title *De Duytse Lier*. His very effective love poems, often filled with the most fervent love of nature, are among the best of such poetry of the 17th century. However, here and there among these poems there is evidence of a certain melancholy which forecast a later spiritual change. After a silence of seven years he published a work called *Jezus en de Ziel* (1678), which reveals the influence of Jacob Böhme. This fine poetic work portrays the heaven which may be found in the human spirit when the light of God shines in and when the voice of God is heard. His work entitled *Voncken der Liefde Jesu* (1687) is likewise full of the same quiet bliss, the same mystical submergence in God, the same fellowship with the Lord. Other of his religious poetry was published later in *Spiegel van het menselijk bedrijf* (1694) containing poetic comments on trades and professions of all kinds, which are represented in a long series of etchings by his own hand. On the other hand *Zedelijke en Stichtelijke Gezangen* (1704), *Beschouwing der Wereld* (1708), *De Onwaardige Wereld* (1710), *Het leerzaam huisraad* (1711), and *Des menschen Begin, midden en einde* (1712) are chiefly of didactic character. Luyken's etchings which accompany his poems, and probably still more those which appeared in van Braght's *Martelaers-Spiegel* (1685) and his great series of etchings called *Icones Biblicae of Afbeeldingen der merkwaardigste geschiedenissen van het Oude en Nieuwe Testament* (1708, 1729), contributed much to his unusual popularity among Dutch Protestants of the most varying views, which lasted more than two centuries. Under the impression of the great and often entrancing beauty of Luyken's best religious poetry, even the most strictly orthodox forgot that the poet had gradually withdrawn from all external forms of the church in religion. In 1673 he joined the Mennonite church in Beverwijk, where he lived for some time after his marriage, and in the following year he transferred to the Mennonite church in Amsterdam, after his settlement in that city. He seems earlier to have had strong leanings toward the Collegiants, like his father and his brother Christoffel. For a short time in 1699 he withdrew from the city and from the world of men to a quiet country place near Haarlem. Later (1703) he went to Schellinkhout, not far from Hoorn, but soon thereafter he was living again in Amsterdam. There he lost his wife and his three children (his son and pupil Caspar, the etcher, died in 1705) by death and in 1712 he followed them to the land which he had long since sought in his pious Christian faith.

The good Claas Bruin (*q.v.*, 1670-1732), an honorable bookkeeper in Amsterdam, is a part of the comfortable, somewhat commonplace literary provincialism of the time. He was the diligent author of several minor moralistic and historical dramas and poems and moreover of *Kleefsche en Zuid-Hollandsche Arcadia* (1716), *Noordhollandsche Arcadia* (1732), and *Speelreis langs de Vechtstroom op de uitgegeevene Gezichten van de Zeegepraalende Vecht* (1719), in which he endeavored to praise the beauty of the landscape in certain districts in a pastoral, erotic, and materialistic style.

Elisabeth Koolaert—Hoofman (1664-1734) was one of the first Dutch women to write poetry. Some of her verse was published by Willem Kops in 1774.

Achior van den Abeele (*q.v.*), a Mennonite preacher at Haarlem from 1712, published besides theological books *Eens Jongelings pelgrimagie, of wandelweg, Bepland met Gedichten en Gezangen* ... (1718) and *Den Uyterlyken Boogaard, bestaande in Hof- en Landgezigten, Overgebracht op de inwendige Gestalten des Gemoeds* (1730). Abraham Heems, a well-to-do silk merchant at Haarlem, wrote *Antipater, of de Dood van Alexander* (1723), *Bybelpoëzy* (1729), and *Absolon, of de gestrafte Heerszucht* (n.d.); his daughter Femina Hugaart-Heems (1724-81) also published a number of poems. Roelant van Leuve published *Mengelwerken* (3 vv., 1723) and *Doorluchte te Voorbeelden der Ouden, Zinnebeelden ... en Gedigten* (1725). Herman van Logchem, a Mennonite merchant, was the author of a few comedies and tragedies, including *Krispijn ... of Erfgenaam door List* (1725) and *Sirena, veldheer der Parthen* (1738). T. J. van Braght, probably a relative of the author of the *Martyrs' Mirror*, published *De Gewiekte Kruiwagen, ter opvoering der onoverwonnen keizerlijke Stad Dordrecht* (1717). These publications are all mediocre and have passed into complete oblivion.

Hendrik Rintjes, a Mennonite preacher and bookseller at Leeuwarden, published *Gedachten op den Jongsten dag* (1681, repr. 1684) and *De Morgenstond in haar Somersche Vermakelijkheden vertoont* (1684, repr. 1690).

The wealthy merchant Sybrand Feitama (1694-1758), likewise an Amsterdam Mennonite, actually undertook to climb to the summit of Parnassus. However, after the publication of his first and only tragedy, entitled *Fabricius* (1720), he limited himself to translations of French dramas. His teacher in grammar was the Mennonite Lambert Hermansz ten Kate (*q.v.*, 1674-1731), a grain dealer in Amsterdam, a many-sided and gifted dilettante in art and learning of all sorts, the author of *Gemeenschap tussen de Gottische sprake en de Nederduytsche* (1710), later of *Aenleiding tot de kennisse van het verhevene deel der Nederduytse sprake* (1723) and of *Oeffen-Schets over het vereisch der Dichtkunst* (1724). He was in this period a versatile connoisseur of languages, and his learned studies are still a subject of scholarly study. The *Aenleiding* contains a study of the development of sounds and the voice, and a method of phonics and prosody. He had earlier (ms. dated 1699) written *Verhandeling over de Klankkunde* in connection with a study of versification. He was a deacon in the Haarlem Mennonite Church.

Pieter Langendijk (*q.v.*, 1683-1756), the ingenious and prolific composer of several comedies which often approach the farcical, came from a Mennonite family although he did not actually join the brotherhood until his deathbed. His best-known works are those in which he portrays and satirizes the weaknesses of rich, speculating, self-satisfied merchants and their relatives. These works are *'t Wederzijds huwelijksbedrog* (1712), *De Zwetser* (1712), *Krelis Louwen* (1715), *De Wiskunstenaars* (1715), and *De Spiegel der vaderlandsche Kooplieden* (1756). From 1722 to his death he lived in Haarlem.

Another literary figure of the 18th century was Christina Leonora de Neufville (1713-81), who composed moralistic-theological observations in metrical form. The two brothers Cornelis and Petrus Loosjes (1723-92 and 1735-1813), both pastors of Mennonite churches with final pastorates in Haarlem, founded the rationalistic periodical *De Vaderlandsche Letteroefeningen* in 1761 (ceased publication December 1876). Other Mennonites were connected with this periodical such as Jeronimo de Vries, Sr. (1776-1853), who was a literary historian and critic and also a member of the A.D.S. (Mennonite General Conference) and a curator of the Seminary in Amsterdam, and the bookseller Jacob Wybrand Yntema (1779-1858), also of Amsterdam, who was for a time publisher and editor of the periodical. Adriaan Loosjes (1761-1818), a son of Petrus Loosjes, a bookseller and publisher of Haarlem after the completion of his theological studies, a friend of the Enlightenment and a poet of moderate ability, is known as the author of a historical novel *Maurits Lijnslager* (1808), which was widely read both then and later, and which like his earlier work, *De Historie van Mejuffrouw Suzanna Bronkhorst*, reveals the influence of the novels of Elisabeth Wolff-Bekker. The latter writer, who was a much more gifted, clever, and productive author (1738-1804), preferred, although she was of the Reformed faith and the widow of a pastor of this church, to attend the Mennonite churches with her Mennonite friend and co-worker Agatha (Aagje) Deken (*q.v.*, 1741-1804), who had been reared in the Collegiant orphanage in Amsterdam. Aagje Deken, a faithful Mennonite, composed several hymns for the Haarlem Mennonite Church. After 1777 the two women lived together for a time in De Rijp and Beverwijk, then several years in France, and finally in The Hague.

Govert Klinkhamer (1704-74), of Amsterdam, a moderately gifted poet, published *De Kruisgesant, of het Leeven van den Apostel Paulus* in 1725. Willem Kops (1724-76), a textile merchant at Haarlem, wrote a number of poems; he was the anonymous author of *Leeven van Pieter Langendijk* (*q.v.*). He also published a study on the Dutch rhetoricians, *Schets eener geschiedenis der Rederijkeren*, and a linguistic study, *Oude woorden en spreekwijzen*. He also edited some of the poems of Elizabeth Koolaert-Hoofman. Bastiaan Klinkert (1794-1854), a wealthy ship broker of Amsterdam, published a number of epoch-making studies on Shakespeare.

Another writer who should be mentioned was Simon Stijl (1731-1804), a physician in Harlingen, who is noted for the clear and powerful prose style

of his historical work, *De opkomst en bloei der Vereenigde Nederlanden* (1774), and who treats the state of the dramatic arts and literature of his time in his biography of an actor, *Leven van Jan Punt* (1781). Because of his distaste for all churchly connections and his urge toward unconditional independence, he never joined a church, although he belonged to a Mennonite family. Further there is the Amsterdam merchant and city historian Jan Wagenaar (1709-73). The Harlingen pastor Johannes Stinstra (1708-90), who was deposed from his office for many years because of his Socinian views, devoted himself to the translation of Richardson's novels. A number of other well-known Mennonites had connections with the literature of the time either as linguists or as critics, such as the philologist Matthys Siegenbeek (*q.v.*, 1774-1854), pastor in Dokkum where he brought about the union of Mennonites and Remonstrants, after 1797 professor of the Dutch language and literature at the University of Leiden. Siegenbeek's successor, Matthias de Vries (1820-92), was also a Mennonite. Siegenbeek and de Vries were the creators of a new Dutch orthography. Anthony Winkler Prins (*q.v.*, 1817-1908), a Mennonite pastor in Tjalleberd and Veendam, a Freemason and widely known as the editor of a widely used Dutch encyclopedia, was a co-worker on the magazine *Braga* with the Reformed pastor and poet J. J. L. ten Kate, which in 1842-44 published exclusively a sharp and often satirical versified critique of contemporary romantic literature. Also to be named are J. G. de Hoop Scheffer, professor at the University and Mennonite Seminary of Amsterdam (1819-93), P. Leendertz Wzn. (1817-80), pastor in Medemblik, and D. Harting, pastor in Enkhuizen.

In concluding the first part of this survey mention should be made of Simon Gorter (1838-71), a friend of de Hoop Scheffer, pastor in Aalsmeer and Wormerveer, journalist and author of excellent literary essays (*Letterkundige Studien*, 1871) and novels; Christiaan Nicolaas Wybrands, pastor in Enschedé, author of a history of the Amsterdam stage from 1617 to 1772 (1873), *Tooneelstudien* (1889), and of a valuable and richly documented study entitled *Het Menniste Zusje* (*Zondagsbode*, 1902-3, 1914, second edition); the latter's gifted brother Aemilius Willem Wybrands (1838-86), pastor at Edam, Hoorn, and Leiden and church historian, noted for his research in the ecclesiastical drama of the Middle Ages (1861); the Haarlem pastor and religious poet, Jeronimo de Vries Jr. (*q.v.* 1838-1915), highly esteemed for his gifts as a preacher; the pastor and author Johannes Dyserinck (1835-1912), who published numerous articles and several books dealing primarily with Dutch writers and artists of the 18th and 19th centuries (Wolff and Deken, Bellamy, Beets, Bosboom-Toussaint, Pierson, Winkler Prins), G. J. Boekenoogen (1870-1930), the author of a study of the portraits of Menno Simons (*DB* 1916).

Among recent Mennonite authors of short stories, all dealing with Mennonite history, are to be mentioned Pastor Hermanus Schuurmans (1867-1942), author of *Van de Oude Garde* (1907), Leendert Hansma (*q.v.*, 1861-1940), who published a number of sketches in several issues of the *Doopsgezind*

Jaarboekje, W. J. Kühler (*q.v.,* 1874-1946), whose fine tales, "Gesprek met Menno" and "Het vrouwtje van Gouda," are found in *Doopsgezinde Bijdragen* of 1905 and 1907, Herman Bakels (*q.v.,* 1871-1952), who in four papers published in the *Doopsgezinde Bijdragen* of 1900, 1901, 1902, and 1904, later collected in book form, *Het Volk van Menno* (1908), well mingled history and fiction, and Pastor R. Schuursma (b. 1870), author of *Van Elisabeth, die een bagijntje was* (1921). David Tomkins (pen name of J. W. N. le Heux, *q.v.*) wrote sketches and poems for Dutch periodicals. Some Mennonite pastors, e.g., J. D. van Calcar and Miss W. C. Jolles, published a number of Biblical plays; J. E. Tuininga is the author of a Christmas play. Miss J. E. Kuiper's *Bijbel voor de Jeugd* (3rd ed., Amsterdam, 1951) is an outstanding work giving the essential Bible content in paraphrasing adapted to adolescents. Note also her *Van Gods Geslacht, Karakters uit den Bijbel* (Amsterdam, 1926, in collaboration with Prof. Ph. Kohnstamm). Her *De Zangers van den Prins* (Amsterdam, 1951) is a story for youth from the time of the beginning of the Eighty Years' War.

Pastor Lykele Bonga (1892-1952) published a volume of poems *Als Glas in Lood* (1938) and Pastor Andries Lucas Broer (b. 1900) three collections: *Open Vensters* (1929), *Langs Uwe wegen* (1936), and *Er Staat een Ploeg* (1942).

2. The Mennonite Theme in Literature. Allusions to the Mennonites and related groups are numerous in the older Dutch literature. They are quite naturally found for the most part in authors of other faiths, and in so far as they were written at the time of the beginnings and first progress of the Anabaptist movement are filled with a great earnestness and seriousness. Among the writers of this type we must mention first of all Dirk Volkertsz Coornhert (*q.v.,* 1522-90), the writer and poet, philosopher and theologian, the socratic-platonic Christian who, although he belonged to the Catholic Church, sought quite independently his own way to the highest truth, and who was the courageous defender of absolute freedom of conscience, whom Kühler calls "the friend and at the same time the enemy of the Anabaptists," and to whom he attaches the title of "the Dutch Sebastian Franck" (*Geschiedenis* I, 359). In addition to his theological and polemic writings dealing with the new teachings, such as *Van de bejaerden Doope, Uytroedinghe van des Verderfs plantinghe* (dedicated to Hans de Ries), *Van de sendingh der Lutheranen, Swinglianen en Mennonieten* (1583), *Opperste Goedts nasporinghe,* in which he has de Ries appear in a conversation, and his *Kleijn-Munster* (1590), written against David Joris, he produced also an altogether different type, a satirical dialogue ("samenspraak") entitled *Aertzney der sielen* (1570), in which the pope, Luther, Calvin, as well as Menno Simons, "de duysterlingh," are subjected to bitter mockery. His friend, the faithful Catholic Hendrick L.zn. Spieghel (1549-1612), mentions Jan van Leiden and Melchior Hofmann in his *Kerktwistsjaarlied* of 1601. Carel van Mander portrays with deep sympathy the industry, the strict and quiet manner of life, the peacefulness and piety of the Anabaptists, in his *Olijf-Bergh. Vondel's* verses attached to the pictures of Mennonite preachers have already been

mentioned. The very meritorious poet Jan Jansz Starter (1594-1626), whose parents belonged to the little group of Brownists who had fled from England and joined the Waterlander Mennonite church in Amsterdam in 1615, wrote among other lyrical and comic poems (*Friesche Lusthof,* 1621) the well-known and fetching parody entitled *Menniste Vrijagie* (courtship), which, however, as A. E. H. Swaen has shown, is an almost literal translation of an English parody on the prudishness of the young Puritan woman (*Tijdschr. Mij. v. Ned. Letterk., nr.* 16). Jan Zoet (1614-74), the rhyming innkeeper, Collegiant, pietist, chiliast, and later Labadist and polygamist, is more pungent and uncouth in his digs at the Old Frisian Mennonites, whose painful soberness in clothing he attempted to ridicule, perhaps confusing the clothing of the Mennonites with that of the Quakers. In his satire *Het groote Vischnet* the Mennonites as well as all other ecclesiastical bodies of the time were subjected to attack (*zoo quaad te grijpen als een aal*).

The highly talented lyric poet Gerbrand Adr.zn. Bredero (1585-1618) refers to the uprising of the Anabaptists in Amsterdam in 1535 in his notable drama *Het Moortje* (1616), which is characterized by vivid action, ingenious portraiture, and a free use of the vernacular with a rich spicing of all sorts of humorous expressions. The same drama also refers to the supposed weakness of Mennonites for rich food and drink. One of the characters, a young man, mentions among other fine food "een benistekoeck" (Mennonite cake), and at another place a drunken fellow tells of a drinking bout in which he emptied glass after glass of a "beniste boortje," i.e. (according to F. A. Stoett), glasses filled to the brim. These two expressions as well as similar ones are also found in several farces of the same period such as those by Pers, Breughel, and Fokkens. Other farcical pieces mention "Menniste streken," "treken," and "knepen" (tricks and dodges) and "schijnheiligheid" (sanctimoniousness), while Quakers and Labadists suffer the same contumely (Noseman, H. v. Halmael, P. de la Croix). The collected writings of Jeroense (1684), C. Tuinman (1726), and P. J. Harrebomee (1858) contain expressions, phrases, ironical verses, and the like, which attempt to paint pictures of Mennonites in the same unpleasant colors. However, out of the midst of this gay company of authors, for the most part without gifts and often without name, the brilliant Thomas Asselijn (1620-1701) with his well-known trilogy, *Jan Klaaz of De gewaande Dienstmaagd* (1682), *'t Kraambedt of Kandeelmaal van Saartje Jansz* (1684), and *De Echtscheiding van Jan Klaaz en Saartje Jansz* (1685), stands out. The presentation of the first drama with its bubbling humor, its powerful realism, and its living local color was a tremendous success. Great agitation however was occasioned by the abundance of references to Mennonites of various groups, to Collegiants, Socinians, and Quakers, to occurrences in their eventful history, and to all kinds of peculiarities in their faith, their clothing, their manner of life, their speech, and their style of speaking. Trouble was stirred up, particularly by the pointed allusions; which were easily understood by the public, as they were meant to be, to noted persons, families, and business concerns. These persons attacked were so highly indignant and agitated that the magistrate was drawn into the matter and forbade further presentation of the play. The outcome was a bitter battle of pamphleteers. The second and third play in Asselijn's trilogy also contained a multitude of obvious allusions to Mennonite and related themes. On "Thomas Asselijn en De Doopsgezinden" H. W. Meihuizen wrote four papers in *Algemeen Doopsgezind Weekblad* IX (1955).

The Amsterdam Anabaptist uprising of 1535 was also the subject of a tragedy by Pieter Adriaensz Codde, *Herdopers Anslagh op Amsterdam* (1641), which was often performed in the Amsterdam theatre "with great approval."

None of the comedies of Pieter Langendijk (*q.v.*, 1683-1756), who was mentioned above, treats the Mennonites in this fashion, but a poem of his does. It bears the title "Zwitsersche eenvoudigheid, klaagende over de bedorven zeden veeler Doopsgezinden of Weerlooze Christenen," and deals with simple Swiss Mennonite farmers who emigrated from their homeland to the Netherlands in 1711 because of persecution. The Swiss Mennonites are represented as being highly astonished at the great luxury which they found among the rich Mennonite merchants of Amsterdam where they spent a few weeks, particularly the luxury which they observed in their stately homes on the canals.

Similar comments on the same theme, although in a quieter and more sensible tone, are to be found by Justus van Effen in the *Hollandsche Spectator* (1731-35), a weekly journal treating of various subjects, which was patterned after the English *Spectator,* also in the later *Nederlandsche Spectator* (which had Mennonites among its contributors), as well as in other similar periodicals. Of course not all the accusations and condemnations found in the above-mentioned works are to be taken at face value, although not everything dare be assumed to be fiction. All types of life, certainly of churchly and sectarian life, develop ridiculous and obnoxious perversions. However, the various groups were often confused with one another, much to the disadvantage of the better types. Furthermore it must not be forgotten that it was easy for those who were critical to mock and condemn the Mennonites who had always manifested somewhat singular behavior in society because of their semi-isolation, particularly as they gradually came to greater and greater prosperity in the course of the 17th and 18th centuries and gradually at the same time surrendered much of their traditional Mennonite simplicity. But the more the Mennonites mingled with the rest of the population, and the more they secured the same legal privileges and rights, the more they dropped out of the eye of the outside world and the more they lost their attractiveness for literary writers, at least as an object for criticism and satire. In the letters and novels of Elisabeth Wolff and Aagje Deken, particularly in *Willem Leevend* and *Cornelia Wildschut,* which reflect the spirit of a later age, the Mennonites are treated in quite a different fashion. Good-natured jokes are made at their expense, or their human weaknesses and foibles are held up in an objective and kindly, often comical, frankness, but at the same time praise and recognition are given for their good qualities. And soon after the death of these two authors who were so kindly disposed toward the Mennonites, the Mennonites disappear out of Dutch literature as an easy prey for the critics.

Although the Dutch Mennonites had been granted equality with the Reformed, partly in 1796 and completely by the constitution of 1848, even in the second half of the 19th century something of the former disrespect for the Mennonites occasionally echoes in the literature, as in the novel *Klaasje Zevenster* by Jacob van Lennep (1st ed., 1865, IV, p. 74) and in *Camera Obscura* by Hildebrand (1839).

In the Dutch literature of the 20th century certain periods or persons, particularly of the oldest and preferably of revolutionary Anabaptism, have been treated by Dutch authors. In 1920 P. H. van Moerkerken (1877-1951) wrote his novel *Het nieuwe Jeruzalem;* Jef Last published *Het eerste schip op de Newa* (1945); Muus Jacobse (pseudonym of K. H. Heeroma, b. 1909) composed the poems *Het Offer des Heeren (ca.* 1930) and *De drie Kooien* (1946); J. de Jonge wrote *Anna Holmer* (1949); Jan Mens wrote a novel on Wendelmoet Claesdochter (*q.v.*) entitled *De witte Vrouw* (1952); Ypk fan der Fear (pseudonym of L. Post-Beuckens) published a novel in the Frisian language, *De Breugeman komt* (Drachten, 1953), of which a translation in Dutch is *De bruidegom komt* (Baarn, 1956); the book by Paul Dietz, *Sterrenzaaisel van Brahma,* contains a chapter on Jan van Geelen (*q.v.*); B. Stroman wrote *Obbe Philips, oudste der Dopers* (1953); G. J. Hoogwerf wrote *De profeet* and *De zwaardgeesten;* and Marja Roc wrote *Een koning verleid* (The Hague, n.d., 1954). The writers Theun de Vries (b. at Veenwouden, Friesland, 1907) and Jef (Josephus C. F.) Last (b. at The Hague, 1898), both well-known Dutch novelists, are of Mennonite descent, but in their numerous novels they only incidentally deal with Mennonite subjects. H. A. Lunshof wrote a novel on the Mennonite preacher Antony Winkler Prins (*q.v.*), entitled *Leven zonder Demon* (Amsterdam, 1950).

Dirk Coster in *Verzameld Proza* (1927), 182 f., paid attention to the Mennonites in Dutch literature, while the Reformed K. H. Heeroma, now professor of Dutch literature at the University of Groningen, published thorough studies on Mennonite poets.

In 1915 H. P. G. Quack, a noted professor of Amsterdam University, wrote in his engrossing *Herinneringen* (1915) about the highly esteemed Mennonite family of Jelle Hingst, formerly at Harlingen, later at Amsterdam, whose son Sybrand Jan Hingst (*q.v.*) was his close friend. H.F.W.J., vDZ.

G. Kalff, *Geschiedenis der Nederlandsche Letterkunde* (1906-12); J. Prinsen: J. Lzn., *Handboek tot de Nederlandsche letterkundige geschiedenis* (1916); J. te Winkel, *Ontwikkelingsgang der Nederlandsche Letterkunde* (1908); Cd. Busken Huet, *Het Land van Rembrand* (2nd ed., 1886); Kühler, *Geschiedenis* I, II, and III; Robert Friedmann, *Mennonite Piety Through the Centuries* (Goshen, 1949); J. G. de Hoop Scheffer, "Onze Martelaarsboeken," in *DB* 1870; L. Knappert, *Van der vaderen lijdensmoed (Geschriftjes t. beh. v. d. Doopsgez. i. d. verstrooiing,* No. 23, 1906); K. Vos, *Menno Simons* (Leiden, 1914); G. J. Boekenoogen, "De portretten van Menno Simons," in *DB* 1916; S. Cramer, "Bijdrage tot de geschiedenis van ons kerklied," in *DB* 1900, 1902; *idem,* "Het eigenhandig laatst adieu van Maeyken Wens aan haar kind," in *DB* 1904; P. Leendertz, Jr., *Het leven van Vondel* (1910); G. Kalff, "Vondel's leven," in *De Gids*, 1896, II; F. A. Stoett, *Nederlandsche spreekwoorden, spreekwijzen, uitdrukkingen en gezegden* (1901); P. J. Haarebomee, *Spreekwoordenboek der Nederlandsche Taal* (1858, 1861, 1870); C. Tuinman, *De oorsprong en uitlegging van dagelijks gebruikte Nederduitsche spreekwoorden* (1726); J. A. Worp, *Geschiedenis van het drama en van het tooneel in Nederland* (1904); L. A. Rademaker, *D. Camphuysen* (1898); D. Rzn. Kamphuyzen, *Uitgelezen stichtelijke rijmen, met eene inleiding . . . door Dr. J. van Vloten* (1861), *Klassiek Letterk. Pantheon;* D. Rzn. Camphuysen, *Bloemlezing uit zijn gedichten, met inleiding door Dr. J. C. van der Does* (1934); Th. Asselijn, *Jan Klaaz of Gewaande Dienstmaagd,* ed. by F. Buitenrust Hettema, N. A. Cramer and K. Poll (1900) *(Zwolsche Herdrukken); Algemeen Doopsg. Weekblad,* IX (1955), Nos. 18-20, 22; P. van Eeghen and J. Ph. van der Kellen, *Het werk van Jan en Caspar Luyken* (1905); Jan Luiken, *Duitsche Lier,* ed. M. Sabbe *(Klass. Letterk. Pantheon); Stichtelijke verzen van Jan Luyken,* collected and with an introduction by C. B. Hylkema (1904); C. B. Hylkema, "De nieuwlichter Jan Luyken," in *De Gids* IV, 1904; *idem, Reformateurs* (1900-2); J. C. van Slee, *De Rijnsburger Collegianten* (1895); Galenus Abrahamsz de Haan, *Verdediging der Doopsgezinden* (1699); J. Hartog, "Iets van de publieke openie over de Doopsgezinden in het midden der 18de eeuw," in *DB* 1867; *idem,* "Uit het leven van een tijdschrift," in *De Gids* (1877); *idem, De spectatoriale geschriften van 1741-1800* (2nd ed., 1890); L. Knappert, "De Doopsgezinden in den Franschen Tijd," in *DB* 1912; A. van der Hoeven, *Lambert ten Kate* (1896); W. Brom-Struick, "Stemonderzoek door Nederlanders," in *Tijdschr. der Vereen. v. Nederl. Muziekgeschiedenis* XIII, No. 4; P. Langendijk, *De Spiegel der Vaderlandsche kooplieden,* new edition with notes and introduction (with biography) by C. H. Ph. Meyer, 1929 *(Klass. Letterk. Pantheon);* M. G. de Boer, "De uitwijking van Zwitsersche Doopsgezinden naar Nederland," in *De Zondagsbode,* May 29 and October 2, 1932; Jan ten Brink, *De roman in brieven* (1889); J. Dyserinck, *Brieven van Betje Wolff en Aagtje Deken* (1904); *idem, Hulde aan Betje Wolff* (1884); *idem,* "Van en over Betje Wolff," in *De Gids* III, 1884; *idem,* "Wolff en Deken," in *De Gids* IV 1892; *idem,* "In de Beemster pastorie," in *De Gids* I, 1903; H. P. G. Quack, *Herinneringen* (1915); W. A. P. Smit, "Vondel en zijn Bekering," in *Nieuwe Tallgids* XXIX (1935); D. Coster, *Verzameld Proza* (1927); N. van der Zijpp, *Geschiedenis der Doopsgezinden in Nederland* (1952); *idem,* "Wolff en Deken in de kerkelijke situatie van hun tijd," in *Boeket voor Betje en Aagje* (1954); K. H. Heeroma, *Poëzie van de 16de en 17de eeuw (Bibl. der Nederl. Letteren,* 1940 and 1950); *idem,* "Dopers Dichterschap," in *Tijdschrift Ned. Taal en Letteren* LXVIII, 1 (1950) and *Maandblad v. Socialism en Democratie* for February 1953; H. F. W. Jeltes, "Mennonites in Dutch Literature," *MQR* XI (1937) 142-55; H. W. Meihuizen, *Galenus Abrahamsz* (Haarlem, 1954); T. A. Rompelman, "Lambert ten Kate als Germanist," *Mededelingen Kon. Ned. Akad. van Wetensch;* 1952, section *Letterkunde; ML* II, 669-72.

II. *Germany, Austria, and Switzerland to 1937.* The actual literary discovery of Anabaptism was made in the second half of the 19th century, when research was stirring up a more general interest in Anabaptist problems. The literature dealing with the Mennonites in the first half of the 19th century, whether in the nature of biography or monograph, has the character of personal reaction of the author rather than a general interest in the history and principles of Anabaptism as such. Nevertheless there were earlier literary depositions, though rare.

Seventeenth and Eighteenth Centuries. The oldest literary mention concerns the Anabaptists in Moravia and stems from the pen of one no less important than the author of *Simplicius Simplicissimus,* Johann Christoph Grimmelshausen *(q.v.),* and occurs in 1669. In Book V, Chapter 19, Grimmelshausen describes as if he had seen them in person the institutions and the peaceful life of the Hutterian Brethren *(q.v.).* Their puritanical and pious living makes a deep impression on the hero of the novel, but he finally rejects the Hutterite pattern as the solution of his life-problem, especially since he must view these people as heretics. The question arises here, from what source the author derived his knowledge of the Anabaptists. He was never, as far as is known, in Moravia, nor is it possible, as some have suggested, that he became acquainted with them "in the valleys of the Black Forest"; his whole manner of presentation indicates that he must have read about them. The chapter on the Anabaptists in Moravia is a unit in itself, as well as a purely descriptive essay, making the assumption that it is a reproduction, perhaps from memory, appear a fact. For the structural development of the novel the Anabaptist chapter is significant in that it supplies the motivation for the hero's return to religion.

The pleasure in travel incipient in the 18th century, the century of realism; the eye for detail schooled by the great journeys of discovery; and on the other hand, toleration of the Mennonites and their becoming settled—all these factors helped to place their cultural and religious life before a more objective lens than in the Reformation and post-Reformation periods.

Timidly the distinction between the Münsterites and the Mennonites was winning its way to the fore. The chapter "In Reimen kurtz gefasste Ketzer-Geschichte" in *Der Alten und Neuen Schwärmer Widdertäufferischer Geist* is evidence of this; it presents Menno Simons as a gentle but positive Reformer.

The travel journals of the time offer many references to the Mennonites. The widely read Uffenbach, in *Merkwürdige Reisen durch Niedersachsen, Holland und Engelland* (1780), mentions the churches of the Amsterdam "Mennists," stressing their simplicity, and (so early) states his opinion that there is no observable difference between their worship and that of the Reformed, "except that they, as is well known, baptize no infants. . . ." With respect he describes the character of the Mennonites as "very clean and inwardly excellent." In Philipp Wilhelm Gercken's *Reisen durch Schwaben, Bayern,* Parts III and IV, covering the years 1786 and 1788, there is a description of the farm of the hereditary Mennonite leaseholder of the Donnersbergerhof in the Palatinate. Mention must also be made of the *Reise nach Danzig* by the painter and engraver Chodowiecki *(q.v.),* although it was originally written in French. It has fixed in word and picture the nature of the Danzig Mennonites as somewhat parsimonious but honest.

We are taken into an altogether different world by the Pietist Jung-Stilling *(q.v.)* in his *Heimweh* (1794). Jung-Stilling knows and respects the South German Mennonites. With affection he sketches the life of a Mennonite family in the Palatinate, the cleanliness and industry, and above all the unemotional and unsentimental piety. This Mennonite family the author uses allegorically for the place where the soul is prepared for the struggle of life, and he has thereby correctly caught the significance of the Mennonite character.

Nineteenth Century. The first author who was a personal friend of the Mennonites was the Prussian official and educator Ludwig von Baczko (*q.v.*). In his *Familiengemälde in drei Aufzügen: Die Mennoniten* (Königsberg, 1809) he becomes the champion of a small group of people upon whom the verdict still lies which permits certain "liberties" toward them. In opposition to this idea Baczko presents reality, which will shatter all defamation and will bring to victory the selflessness of the Mennonite to aid a thoughtless landowner and his daughter back to the right way. Baczko was the first to write an independent work about the Mennonites. Franz Sonnenfeld published *Der Wiedertäufer von Weisskirch* (1818), one of his beautiful stories of the people. Weisskirch is an estate in Alsace in the Sundgau, near the French border.

In the case of Jens Jakob Eschels also it was personal contact with Mennonites that produced a living picture. In his *Lebensbeschreibung eines alten Seemannes* (1835) he catches the commercially correct, but humanly warm tone of the Mennonite mercantile houses in his characterization of the van der Smissens, fathers and sons. Johanna Schopenhauer, the mother of the philosopher Arthur Schopenhauer, in her memoirs makes an entry, brief but objective, of her acquaintance with the Mennonites of Danzig (1842). Julian Heins' *Menno Simonis, Ein dramatisches Gedicht* (1844) is a slight poetic production (46 pp.) of no literary value, though sympathetic. Agnes von Möller (d. 1879), a teacher in Königsberg, published in 1851 *Die Mennoniten,* a popular story whose hero was a young Danzig Mennonite who had joined the Prussian army in 1813, the same person as Wildenbruch's *Menonit.*

It is not until the second half of the 19th century that literary material on the Mennonites grows out of historical reflection. At its beginning stands Achim von Arnim's fragment, *Die Kronenwächter* (1817), with its romantic historico-philosophic interpretation of the events in Münster as a stage in the purification of the German spirit and the idea of empire. Münster is bound up with the fate of the Empire. The crown is in Münster! Thus the *Kronenwächter,* had it been completed, would have been the first attempt to emerge from a purely sectarian and polemic judgment of Münster. It was written in anticipation of the results of the work of individual scholars, and produces its fruit intuitively, as literature frequently does.

The invigorating air of a more realistic period, which is beginning to move in Arnim's work, we inhale deeply in the Novelle by Adolf Stern (*q.v.*), written nine years later, *Die Wiedertäufer* (1866). Stern stands within the problems of history. The degree of dependence of Anabaptism upon, and its independence from, Münster becomes evident. Stern's work presupposes that of the historian Cornelius (*q.v.*), whose scholarly presentation of the course of events in Münster in his works is given a psychological and artistic interpretation in the figure of the penitent Bernt Rothmann. The contrast between Rothmann and the other leading figure is used to clarify inherent possibilities in the Münster development, but at the same time to lead in the definite direction of the verdict that Münster

and "the other Anabaptists" belong in two different categories. In the penitent Anabaptist Rothmann, Stern has created a unique character.

Between Stern's Novelle and Keller's *Ursula* (*q.v.*) not much was published; it consists only of the popular tales of the Alsatian Margarethe Spörlin and a poem by Johann Gabriel von Seidl, *Der Wiedertäufer* (1876), both historically true to reality. The motif of Seidl's poem is supported by the *Martyrs' Mirror*. Spörlin knows the Alsatian Mennonites at first hand and pictures their practical charity and moral strength, and has the tolerant reformers of Strasbourg do them justice, decrying the intolerant attitude which entered the city later. The three tales of her *Elsässische Lebensbilder* (1875), "Das Waldhaus," "Mein Kuckuck," and "Der Heimgang," deal with Anabaptists or Mennonites.

With Gottfried Keller's *Ursula* (1878) we are taken for the first time into the period of the origin of Anabaptism on Swiss soil. An unlucky star seems to have hovered over the literary interpretation of this part of Anabaptist history; the old biased polemic sources, Bullinger and Kessler, and the overpowering patriotic warrior characteristics of Zwingli control the field. Keller in particular uses as the background of his story only the excrescences occurring in the "fringe areas" of Anabaptism. His heroine Ursula becomes entangled in these aberrations, and demands that her lover, just returned from the Italian wars, also become an Anabaptist. He refuses. At this point reality and fantasy become strangely confused. In this dubious light the incident of the escape from the "Wellenberg" is portrayed. Ursula is finally brought to her senses by the events of the war in which her lover is fighting. She follows him to the battlefield and finds him seriously wounded in the evening after the battle. From now on they live "as worthy members of society." In this Novelle Keller was trying to portray not history, but an idea. Anabaptism, he means to convey, passed away, as it had to, like any transitional phase in any human evolution finding its true nature. This judgment of Anabaptism is meant to represent a judgment on the Christian religion, and not Anabaptism alone. Behind it is the atheistic humanism of Feuerbach. It is a matter of removing the husks from the real character of religion and thus cleansing it of its aberrations (Meumann).

Wilhelm Heinrich Riehl (*q.v.*) views Anabaptism with more historical truth. In his Novelle *Mein Recht* (1875) he treats the problem of nonresistance with special understanding; the idea of nonvengeance wins. The author reveals the weight of this problem not only for the historical situation in which it was set, but for the entire wretched world. It can cause one to lose his mind. Very clearly the springs are brought to light from which the moral content of Anabaptism and of non-Anabaptism are built up; Anabaptism lives from the Bible; non-Anabaptism, in spite of its attachment to the church, finds its moral norms in the folk mores. Riehl has left no doubt but that society needs the Bible.

The Mennonites were cited before the forum of a saber-rattling theatrical world by the dramatist Ernst von Wildenbruch (*q.v.*). His "tragedy" *Der Menonit* (1882) is a sad play, from the point of view of artistry as well as of content. The deep conviction of nonresistance in the old sense has been turned by Wildenbruch into a theatrical affair of honor, and the Mennonites branded as cowardly traitors. Wildenbruch had no inkling of the meaning of nonresistance; he did not take the pains to examine his characters, or he would not have permitted himself to be swept into such an insult. The "hero" of the drama, who abandons his Mennonitism, staking all on his honor, forgets to save his "honor" as soon as he can exchange it for a petticoat. The author has rendered a poor service both to the concept of honor and to the Mennonites. Gysbert von Vincke (*Ein kleines Sündenregister,* 1882) has severely criticized the dramatic qualities of the tragedy and has shown that it did not contribute a page of honor to the history of German literature.

The third work of higher quality and a new type on the basis of research is Taylor's *Klytia* (1883). *Klytia* is the work of a theologian, and Taylor the pseudonym of Adolf Hausrath (*q.v.*). His portraiture of Anabaptist character is on the main based on contemporary research, chiefly that of Ludwig Keller, and by his own thought on the philosophy of history creates a peculiar view of Anabaptism, which does not, however, do justice to historical fact. To be sure, his Anabaptist Werner is a religious and moral personality, in pleasant contrast to the theologians involved in disputes, a man of unselfish charity. But in the first place his personality is not developed in the story, but plays the role of an "apparition" in moments of danger; he is the good spirit or bad conscience according to the need. From the literary point of view he is merely a motive. In the second place, he lacks historical effectiveness. He remains an isolated figure. Besides, his aversion to dogma does not, like that of the real Anabaptists, stem from a sound Biblicism, but from the modern antithesis between religion and faith, between dogma and life. He has neither church nor brotherhood behind him. He is therefore seen from the modern point of view of "progressive" Protestantism as opposed to the reactionary forces. The Anabaptist Werner is the handyman of enlightened Deism of the 19th century. Hausrath did not create an ideal historical figure, but rather a historical ideal. Interestingly, *Klytia* was reprinted at Newton, Kan., in 1929 by the Herald Publishing Co., called the sixth edition, having been run as a serial in *Der Herold*.

Judging from the literary products, the battle for genuine Anabaptism fluctuates, with more turbulence and indecision than in the research itself. Since Wildenbruch there is no historical thread to follow. Sympathy alternates with antipathy. An exception is found in the presentations that know something of the questions posed by history. Marie Loeper-Hoesella's *Der Mattenbauer* (1890) follows not long after Wildenbruch; of this story Mannhardt could say it was a vindication of the Mennonites.

A year later (1891) Theodor Fontane sets the American Mennonites in a rather dubious light in *Quitt* (1891). The picture, though friendly, is a mixture of truth and fiction. Fontane was never in America. But although the name of the Mennonite settlement, Nogat-Ehre, is his invention, the story is based upon an actual Mennonite community at Darlington, Okla., as Zieglschmid has shown. The Mennonite Hornbostel, who in some respects resembles a Biblical patriarch, through the course into which Fontane has forced the story for the sake of artistic unity, falls into the schism between love and justice when he receives Lehnert, a murderer who has fled to America, into his home, sees through him, finally accepts him into the church, but still refuses him the hand of his daughter. Fontane's moral strength was not adequate to the task of finding a solution. This inadequacy is shared by the Mennonite. At the end Lehnert loses his life in the same manner as the man whom he has killed; then all is "quits." In the novel there are, in confusion, an element of Calvinistic predestination, the idea of justice, and a general sentimentally Christian background. What caused Fontane to intertwine the Mennonites into this "machinery" of fate?

Family recollections and other oral reports must be the source of Bernhardine Schulze-Smidt's acquaintance with the Mennonites; for her knowledge is on the one hand too definite to have been invented, and on the other too inexact to be the result of her own observation. In both stories, *Weltkind* (1896) and *Eiserne Zeit* (1898), the protagonist is a physician, so that an inner connection may be safely assumed. The problem, clearly presented, is Mennonitism versus the world or culture, and it cannot be said that the presentation is wrong. For such students really exist, who, having viewed a completely different world, have outgrown the tradition-bound and narrow circles of the paternal homestead, or even become estranged from it. The author does not describe his physician-hero as an apostate, but shows that the Mennonite heritage can retain its effectiveness even under new circumstances. In the deeds of the selfless doctor, who at the same time understands human nature, the moral strength of Mennonitism lives on. Even though the historical basis for the motif of the repudiation in *Eiserne Zeit* may not be demonstrable, yet there is a great deal of truth in the way the repudiated one finds his church in the end, and may serve another dying man as a priest.

Twentieth Century before World War I. The period 1900-14 produced a series of literary works of the greatest variety. In 1904 a Protestant minister of Württemberg, Wilhelm Stähle, under the pseudonym of Philipp Spiess, wrote a historical novel on the early Anabaptist period of his own country, basing it on the person of the provost Aichelin (*q.v.*), and titling it *Der Reichsprofos.* Spiess knows the history and the sources, and in a large measure he does justice to the earnestness of the Anabaptist concept of life. He has an Anabaptist exercise Christian love to his enemy, the monster Aichelin (*q.v.*). To this extent Spiess considers Anabaptism a legitimate branch of the Reformation. But by having his Anabaptist gradually develop "a quiet attachment to Protestant doctrine," he makes the purely historical effect in this one Anabaptist a principle of negative judgment on Anabaptism in general and fails to recognize the independence of the Anabaptist type.

In *Hungerjahr* (1907) Heinrich Bechtolsheimer presents a graphic picture of the well-ordered Mennonite farm in the Palatinate or Hesse and of the people who operate a farm of this kind. As Baczko had done long ago, Bechtolsheimer shows how the Mennonite interprets brotherly love—as the act of assistance.

Written from the viewpoint of the established Protestant church, though with an understanding of Anabaptism, are the two books, *Die drei Brüder vom Brockhof* (1908?) by Peter Cürlis, and *Zwei Häuser, zwei Welten* (1911) by Ernst Marti. Cürlis takes a portion of the history of the Reformation in the Rhineland and describes the struggle between the creeds as it determines the fate of the three brothers of the Brockhof. The Reformed Church is finally the victor. Anabaptism and Menno Simons are also involved in this conflict. Menno is presented as a congenial person. He, of course, stands somewhat aside; this is stylistically shown by not weaving him into the narrative in person, but by excerpts from his writings as if he were giving a historical report. This stylistic defect is at once also a defect in the inner critique. For according to Cürlis the Reformed Church became the heir of Anabaptism by the adoption of church discipline and in the fate of martyrdom it shared with Anabaptism. Thereby two points of view of the decline of Anabaptism in the Rhineland are stated. But there are still enough other differences remaining between the Reformed and the Anabaptist faith, precisely the decisive ones, which do not fit into this sort of explanation.

Ernst Marti, with his story of Swiss Anabaptists in the Emmental about 1700, treats the inner structure of the two groups, those belonging to the state church and the Anabaptists. He understands both. Not only the socially rooted church-consciousness of the peasant belonging to the large church, but also the brotherhood-consciousness, deriving from the opposition between the kingdom of God and the world of the Mennonite weaver, has its recognized strong points. But they are "two worlds," which can never be united: when the Anabaptist maiden finally receives the ring of her lover from the Sonnenhalde, it is the greeting of one who has died.

Lotte Gubalke's *Das Marienbild der Nonne Zeitlose* (1911) is a product of phantasy. It presents a modern caricature of Hans Denk. A supernatural libertinism is falsely ascribed to him, of which there is no trace in history. The entire terminology of Denk's language is a clumsy distortion of his deep thoughts into decadent sentimentality.

Ferdinand von Wahlberg's *Mennoniten* (1912) places the Russian Mennonites near to Tolstoy. It must be called a novel of propaganda even though some of the description is accurate. Out of the problematics of the concept of nonresistance Wahlberg evolves great future tasks for the Mennonites, which become the tasks in behalf of a new humanity. In it "humanity is the mature fruit for which the Mennonites have been the seeds." However flattering it sounds, in this analysis of the problems the future task of the Mennonites is misunderstood. The concept of nonresistance, which with the Anabaptists is obedience to the Scripture, is here harnessed to the secularized idea of pacifism after the model of Tolstoy: an economic utopia.

Taking up the idea of nonresistance and coupling it with the discipline of the ban, Lu Volbehr in *Kathrin* (1916) treats the spiritual problems of a soul on an unhistorical—and historically impossible—background (the Mennonites had unceremoniously seized possession of some vacant lands!), in which the "laws" of the Mennonites are played against the spiritual attitude, heightened to tragic proportions, of a woman who becomes a Mennonite through marriage. It is at once ridiculous and dangerous, since, written during the war as it was, it might have caused the peculiarities of the Mennonites to create a cleft between them and society—if the sentimentality were not so obvious. It is a counterpart to Wildenbruch's *Menonit,* where the victim of Mennonite "doctrine" is the man; with Volbehr it is the woman.

After World War I, personal and therefore historical memoirs or sometimes narrative presentation on the basis of personal acquaintance are given in the following works: Herman Sudermann, *Bilderbuch meiner Jugend* (1922); Elisabeth Bartels, *Doch hängt mein ganzes Herz an dir, du kleine Stadt!* (1920); Ferdinand Pont, *Wir wollten* (1921); Agnes Miegel, *Geschichten aus Alt-Preussen* (1926); Paul Fechter, *Das wartende Land* (1931); Marie Gallison-Reuter, *Aus meinem Leben in zwei Welten* (1927).

Sudermann, of Mennonite descent, offers a slightly ironically tinted description of the "sectarians from whom I stem," the religious services in the Elbing-Ellerwald Mennonite church, the somewhat narrow spirit, which, for instance, prohibited the wearing of "white blouses." Sudermann is glad to have outgrown Mennonitism.

The congregation at Friedrichstadt furnishes the subject matter for the books of Elisabeth Bartels and Pont. In the one by Bartels the congregational life is restored by Pastor Neufeld. Impressions of the activities in the city, instruction from the pastor and the stern sisters, the joys of a trip to Hanerau, the estate acquired by the Mannhardt family through marriage with the van der Smissens are recounted. Ferdinand Pont goes back into the history of Friedrichstadt. He shows the hopelessness of the attempts to develop the city. The Mennonite spirit is an unintentional impediment; its oscillation between love of the world and rejection of the world prevents an energetic course of action. Pont is a rationalist; consequently he does not grasp the seriousness of the problem of harmonizing Christianity and culture. Agnes Miegel mentions Mennonite character only casually, but correctly recognizes its solidity. Paul Fechter's strongly realistic style of description, like Sudermann's, portrays usually the accidental traits of character. His Elbing Mennonites are presented in their domesticity and in their jargon, to be sure; but on the whole they are not very clearly seen.

In his historical novel of propaganda, *Albrecht Dürer, ein deutscher Heiland* (1924), Hermann Kosel deals with the conflict with the "ungodly painters," and thus also comes to speak of Hans Denk. According to Kosel, Denk is the originator of all evil, a "phantast and inciter." This designation sounds very strange, coming from the mouth of a man whose conception of Christianity is far more "phantastic" than the faithful attainment of faith through self-discipline in Hans Denk.

The Zwingli memorial year, 1931, brought forth several novels about Zwingli. The forerunner of these was Wilhelm Schäfer's *Zwingli-Volksbuch* (1926). The poet's intention to make Zwingli prominent prevents the artistic utilization of the results of modern research on Anabaptism; the ancient picture of the Anabaptists is instead restored. In his careless simplification of events Schäfer makes use of Anabaptism as a foil for Zwingli's sound sense. The Anabaptists are pictured only in their confused extremes; in Grebel's eyes the fire of fanaticism also glows. The work is based, like Emanuel Stickelberger's *Zwingli* (1930), on the ancient polemic sources. Stickelberger goes into greater detail, but nevertheless makes Anabaptism into an affair of the beer table and the street rather than an evangelical movement. He assumes a meeting of Grebel and Manz of Zürich with Thomas Müntzer, which has deeply influenced Grebel. This personal contact never existed; the assumed influence of Müntzer is beyond the realm of probability. Stickelberger gives no clue as to the means by which such a planless movement could have had the strength to form a brotherhood and to create an exemplary manner of life.

A peculiar mixture of the deepest sympathetic comprehension of the problem and the worst selection of material is found in Ludwig Huna's *Kampf um Gott, ein Roman aus der Zeit der Wiedertäufer* (1923). Huna takes the reader into the midst of the ferment in Reformation times, into the process of the rise of the creeds. The scene is chiefly Hesse and Münster; the leading characters are Philip of Hesse on the one hand, and Balser, the disciple of Denk, and his wife Lukardis, on the other. The theme is toleration. Its champions are the Anabaptists and Philip, who is under their influence. The Anabaptist movement is viewed in its historical results. Denk's line of thought is on the whole repeated correctly; the readiness of the Anabaptists to sacrifice is nicely portrayed. The distinction between them and the Münsterites is clearly brought out. Denk's disciple wants to save Münster and makes a strenuous effort to do so. He tells the Münsterites that their sin exceeds all papist and Lutheran sins. But the book has a flaw; Huna completely overlooks the fundamentally Biblicistic character of Anabaptism. Instead he makes Denk the decisive figure. This is unhistorical. There is propaganda in this evaluation. It is clearly expressed in Philip's becoming the forerunner of the concept of a free and democratic state; for so Huna interprets Denk and places him as a statesman into his world. The toleration of these Anabaptists with their freedom of religion and conscience is only a stage on the road of the progressive evolution of the birth of the "real" person, until finally "spirit and faith are mightier than the will of the prince." The book bears the stamp of its time. The state finally enters into the inheritance of the church, as the "amen" at the end of Philip's address is spoken not by the theologians but by the secular chancellor.

A very different spirit permeates *Wilhelmus von Nassauen* (1932?) by Wilhelm Kotzde-Kottenroth. It is of the people. The Netherlands with inexpressible sacrifice are in the throes of their struggle with Spain. In the enormous sea of blood that flowed there, the fate of the Anabaptists is only a droplet. But even this droplet is a testimonial of evangelical confession. It is thus that the author sees the Mennonites, "whom the Frisian Menno Simons had won with his gentle teaching." As the example of a Mennonite whose father had been burned at the stake is to show, the Dutch abandoned nonresistance in the horror of the age and because of insight into the process of growth as a nation (*Volk*).

To the extent that Werner Kortwich's *Friesennot* (1935) applies to the Russian Mennonites at all—the story claims to deal with them—the problem of nonresistance is again unfolded, but is diverted into the special case of obedience to a Bolshevik government. The background of the story is unhistorical; the course of events is unhistorical. With his alternative, "Bible or gun!" the argument is directed against Christianity in general, although it is not intended to be so pointed, for that would mean that Christianity would be shattered by the question of nonresistance. But it is clear that this argumentation is not developed from the idea of nonresistance so much as out of the aggressive Christianity of the opponent to the leader of the settlement. The author's concept of Christianity bears features of bias. The steadfastness of the leader who, as long as he does not have the most valid reason for interfering, controls himself out of obedience, acquires an aura of weakness as over against the attitude of the other. In reality the continuing fanatical challenge is as unnatural as it is unnecessary; for the leader is also capable of action. No Lutheran Christian would have shot down the band at once, but only when it was necessary. And so the fundamental idea, to show that the Christian has no alternative in his attitude toward Bolshevism than to take a gun, is not clearly developed. There is a lack of ability to show Bolshevism as it is; the subject matter of the story is merely an incident of undisciplined soldiery, and the action an episode. *Friesennot* was also made into a commercial motion picture in Germany.

A different approach to the problem is made by Alexander Schwarz in his book, *In Wologdas weissen Wäldern* (1934). (Alexander Schwarz is the pseudonym of Hans Harder.) From the lines of this book somewhat suggestive of a diary, we see the true face of Bolshevism, the inhuman systematic brutality, and the satanic hate against all who believe in God. The reader feels as if he were standing on the verge of an abyss. Madness lies beyond. And yet God lives. This is the experience of these Christians, these Mennonites. Only in one respect is its characterization too "literary": in the way the young Mennonite students parry fate with sarcasm.

The Mennonite refugee camp at Mölln (1930) also found its novelist in Ernst Behrends. All the strength of conquering obstacles which he has observed in these people Behrends concentrated in the figure of *Beata* (1935). To be sure, the conflict which he experiences—a deeply conceived problem of marriage —is a romantic conception, but it is kept within the framework of faith and is a real problem and thus becomes an experience of reality. This same genuineness characterizes also those aspects of the story which the author had not himself personally observed, especially the Mennonite settlements in Russia. In no previous work have the Mennonite principles, as they deviate from the Lutheran creed, been presented so impartially and with so little distortion as here. In this respect *Beata* is a modest foundation stone in the understanding of the *una sancta*.

The migrations of the Mennonites from Russia have also revealed some significance for the Germans in other countries. This is a new point of view. It was used the first time by Maria Veronika Rubatscher in her novel *Das lutherische Joggele* (1936), significantly called in the subtitle "a novel out of the martyrbook of the German soul." One might think that the Anabaptism of Tirol, that most unfortunate of all Anabaptist groups, has found its singer. With loyalty to the sources their fate is related, historically attested characters appear; in the sparse strokes with which the life of the brotherhood is fixed, a sure historical line has been drawn and the effect of the life of the Anabaptists upon the people receives due consideration. But in the epic flow of the narrative there are cliffs. The standpoint of the author as representing "Auslandsdeutschtum" makes her treat Anabaptism first as a German popular movement and only secondly an evangelical movement. The Anabaptists are the religious reaction against the estrangement of the German populace from church politics. Therefore the reason for the existence of Anabaptism is not given full consideration. The reasons for the terrible persecution by the church remain completely unclarified. Like the burning of witches the persecution of Anabaptists is a part of the tragedy of the life of the German spirit. This is an evasion of the bare facts. In the second place, the Anabaptist heritage in Tirol is won by the "Old Church, eternally victorious." The hero of the novel finally joins the saints as a saint in the popular faith. The historical process of the disappearance of Anabaptism from Tirol is only apparently given. The silence on the actual reason for the extermination as a fault of the church, in connection with the other idea of the popular character of the movement, makes room for a clever interpretation: the church had managed to create a substitute for the specific religious needs which were met in Anabaptism, and thus has in the end incorporated this "popular movement." In a similar manner the church also absorbs the nationality of the people with their customs and powers; the natural piety of the heart with the "paganism still in its blood" which is portrayed here is no compliment for the Deutschgläubige," but only a requisition of the *anima naturaliter christiana* for the church (Roman Catholic). The book is the product of a Catholic who loves Germany. But in spite of good foundations Anabaptism does not receive due justice. O.S.

Johann Christoph Grimmelshausen, *Der abenteuerliche Simplicissimus* (Montbéliard, 1669); *Anabaptisticum et enthusiasticum Pantheon* (1712); Daniel Chodowiecki, *Reise nach Danzig 1773* (first ed. French, German ed. in 1923); Zacharias Conrad von Uffenbach, *Merkwürdige Reisen durch Niedersachsen, Holland und Engelland* III (1780) tells of Balthasar Denner; Philipp Wilhelm Gercken, *Reisen durch Schwaben, Bayern* III, IV (1786-88)

tells of the Donnersberghof; Johann Heinrich Jung-Stilling, *Das Heimweh* (Marburg, 1794); Ludwig v. Baczko, *Die Mennoniten: Ein Familiengemälde in 3 Aufzügen* (Königsberg, 1809); Franz Sonnenfeld, *Der Wiedertäufer von Weisskirch* (1818); Achim von Arnim, *Die Kronenwächter* (Berlin, 1817), dramatized in 1844; Jens Jacob Eschels, *Lebensbeschreibung eines alten Seemannes* (Altona, 1835); Johanna Schopenhauer, *Jugendleben und Wanderbilder* (Braunschweig, 1842); Julian Heins, *Menno Simonis* (Danzig, 1844); K. J. Clementi, *Reise durch Friesland, Holland, . . .* (Kiel, 1847); Adolf Stern, *Die Wiedertäufer* (Leipzig, 1866); Margarethe Spörlin, *Elsässische Lebensbilder* (Basel, 1875); Johann Gabriel von Seidł, *Der Wiedertäufer* (Vienna, 1876 ff.); Gottfried Keller, *Urusla* (Zürich, 1878); Wilhelm Heinrich Riehl, *Mein Recht* (1875) (Stuttgart, 1880); Ernst v. Wildenbruch, *Der Menonit* (Berlin, 1882); George Taylor (Adolf Hausrath), *Klytia* (Leipzig, 1883); Gisbert Vincke, *Ein kleines Sünden-Register* (Freiburg, 1883); Natalie von Stackelberg, *Aus Carmen Sylvas Leben* (Heidelberg, 1886), tells of Karl Harder; *Die alte Lehmann, Phantasien einer alten Danzigerin* (Danzig, 1886); Samuel Keller, *Sein Erbe* (Meiringen and Leipzig, 1889); Marie Loepet-Hoesella, *Der Mattenbauer* (Gera, 1890); Theodor Fontane, *Quitt* (Berlin, 1891); Bernhardine Schulze-Smidt, *Weltkind, eine Idylle aus dem Rheingau* (Bielefeld, 1896); Berend Goos, *Erinnerungen aus meiner Jugend* (Hamburg, 1896-97); Bernhardine Schulze-Smidt, *Eiserne Zeit, Familiengeschichte aus den Befreiungskriegen* (Bielefeld, 1898); Emma Dina Hertz, *Die Urgrosseltern Beets* (Hamburg, 1899); Philipp Spiess (Wilhelm Stähle), *Der Reichsprofos* (Heilbronn, 1904); H. S. Burrage, *Getreu bis ans Ende* (translated from the English) (Kassel, 1905); Berend Goos, *Erinnerungen aus meiner Jugend, Auswahl* (Hamburg, 1907); Heinrich Bechtolsheimer, *Das Hungerjahr* (Wiesbaden, 1907); Peter Cürlis, *Die drei Brüder vom Brockhof* (Neukirchen, n.d., ca. 1908); Carmen Sylva, *Mein Penatenwinkel* I (Stuttgart, 1908); Lotte Gubalke, *Das Marienbild der Nonne Zeitlose* (Stuttgart, 1911); Ernst Marti, *Zwei Häuser, zwei Welten* (Frauenfeld, 1911); Ferdinand v. Wahlberg, *Mennoniten* (Vienna, 1912); Lu Volbehr, *Kathrin* (n.p., 1916); Rudolf Stratz, *Du reichst mir deine Hand* (Stuttgart, 1920), treats Russian Mennonites; Elisabeth Bartels, *Doch hängt mein ganzes Herz an dir, du kleine Stadt* (Hermannsburg, 1920); Ferdinand Pont, *Wir wollten* (Erlangen, 1921); Hermann Sudermann, *Bilderbuch meiner Jugend* (Stuttgart, 1922); Agnes Miegel, *Geschichten aus Alt-Preussen* (Jena, 1926); idem, *Kinderland* (Leipzig, n.d.); Hermann C. Kosel, *Albrecht Dürer, ein deutscher Heiland* (Stuttgart, 1923-24); Wilhelm Schäfer, *Huldreich Zwingli* (Munich, 1926); Marie Gallison-Reuter, *Aus meinem Leben in zwei Welten* (Kaiserswerth, 1927); Anita Iden-Zeller, *Wo ich in Kanada Romantik fand* (in *Reclams Universum*); Mathilde Jung, "Rund um den Donnersberg" in *Die Pfalz am Rhein* (ca. 1930); August Becker, *Die Pfalz und die Pfälzer;* Friedrich Blaul, *Träume und Schäume vom Rhein, aus den Papieren eines Müden* (reprinted, Kaiserslautern, 1923); Emanuel Stickelberger, *Zwingli* (Stuttgart, 1930); Ernst Müller, *Sonne über dem See* (1931); Paul Fechter, *Das wartende Land* (Stuttgart and Berlin, 1931); Ludwig Huna, *Der Kampf um Gott* (Leipzig, 1931); Wilhelm Kotzde-Kottenrodt, *Wilhelmus von Nassauen* (Stuttgart, ca. 1932), tells of Dutch Anabaptists under Alba; Werner Kortwich, *Friesennot* (Leipzig, 1935); Ernst Behrends, *Beata* (Heilbronn, 1935); Alexander Schwarz (Hans Harder), *In Wologdas weissen Wäldern, ein Buch aus dem bolschewistischen Bann* (Altona n.d.-1935); Marie Gerbrandt, "Die alte Liese," in *Ostdeutsche Monatshefte,* 1935; Maria Veronika Rubatscher, *Das lutherische Joggele* (Heilbronn, 1936); J. Ellenberger, *Bilder aus dem Pilgerleben,* 3 vv. (1878-83); David Krehbiel, *Religiöse Gedichte* (Landau, n.d.); Jakob Landes, *Licht im Fensterlein, Gedichte und Lieder* (Karlsruhe, 1925); Elsa Löwenberg, *Gedichte.*

Critical discussions: Hedwig Meumann, *Entstehung und Aufbau von Gottfried Kellers Ursula* (Bonn, 1916, dissertation); Harry Maync, "Theodor Fontane," in *Deutsche Dichter* (Frauenfeld, 1928); E. Petzet, *Briefwechsel zwischen Theodor Fontane und Paul Heyse* (Berlin, 1929); Albert Soergel, *Dichtung und Dichter der Zeit* (20th ed., Berlin, 1928); F. Ostarhild on F. v. Wahlberg in *Die evangelische Diaspora,* 1936; E. Ermatinger, *Weltdeutung in Grimmelshausens Simplizissimus* (Leipzig, 1925); H. G. Mannhardt, "Die Mennoniten in der dramatischen Literatur," in *Jahrbuch der Mennoniten-Gemeinden für West- und Ostpreussen* (Danzig, 1883); Chr. Neff, "Die Mennoniten in der Literatur," in *Mennonitisches Gemeindeblatt für Oesterreich,* 1913 (Lemberg, 1913); Otto Schowalter, "Die Mennoniten in der allgemeinen deutschen Literatur. Bibliographie," in *Beiträge zur Geschichte der Mennoniten* (Weierhof, 1938) 83-88; Elizabeth Horsch Bender, "Mennonites in German Literature" (unpublished master's thesis, University of Minnesota, 1944); the following articles by Mrs. Bender in *MQR:* "The Portrayal of the Swiss Anabaptists in Gottfried Keller's *Ursula*" (XVII, 1943, 136-50); "Ernst von Wildenbruch's Drama, *Der Menonit*" (XVIII, 1944, 22-35); "The Anabaptist Novellettes of Adolf Stern and Wilhelm Heinrich Riehl" (XVIII, 1944, 174-85); "Jung-Stilling and the Mennonites" (XX, 1946, 91-97); Ernst Correll, "Theodor Fontane's *Quitt*," *MQR* XVI (1942) 221 f.; A. J. F. Zieglschmid, "Truth and Fiction and Mennonites in the Second Part of Theodore Fontane's Novel *Quitt:* The Indian Territory," *MQR* XVI (1942) 223-46; *ML* II, 667-69.

III. *Germany, Austria, and Switzerland, 1937-57.* Since 1936, the date of the last work in the previous article, the Anabaptist theme has been used in numerous works, including several by major authors. In 1937 Ricarda Huch, a gifted and versatile author, included an unusually understanding treatment of the Anabaptists in her belletristic history, *Das Zeitalter der Glaubensspaltung.* In the same year E. G. Kolbenheyer's three volume fictionized biography of Paracelsus was published in which he also discussed the Anabaptists with understanding. In 1939 Lulu von Strauss und Torney, a writer of high quality, whose work springs to a large extent from a love for her native Westphalia and its history, wrote a novel entitled *Der jüngste Tag,* which is generally considered her best work. In it one of the major characters is a mentally ill Westphalian weaver, inspired to prophecy by the Münsterites, who is accused of setting fire to a village when the millennium does not come on the date he has predicted, and is stoned to death. It is a fine character study.

David Joris is the subject of one novel, written by Rudolph Stickelberger, editor of the Lucerne (Switzerland) *Neue Nachrichten.* Stickelberger entitled his story "Schwarmgeister," and published it with a biography of Bernhardin von Ochino in a volume called *Narren Gottes* (1945). The only purpose of the book appears to be entertainment, and Stickelberger distorts the facts of Joris' life to increase its entertainment value. He considers the followers of Joris to be Anabaptists per se, and all Anabaptists to be unbalanced "Schwarmgeister."

One novel and one Novelle having as their theme the Dutch-North German Anabaptists have appeared since World War II. Neither has much literary value. The novel, Heinrich Specht's *Heil'ge Feuer* (n.d.), was written during the war. Based on the Reformation legend of Anna Holmer, which Arnold Fokke put into writing in Dutch in 1876, it treats Münster, the North German Anabaptists, and political conflict on the Frisian-German border. The Novelle is "Die Geburt der Liebe," a romanticized story of Menno Simons by the popular former Swiss author and Hollywood director Hans Müller-Einigen, which makes Menno out to be a champion of 19th-century religious liberalism. It is published with two other

historical Novellen in a volume entitled *Die Menschen sind alle gleich* (1946).

The Swiss-South German Anabaptists appear in fiction more frequently than does the Dutch-North German group. In his biography of Sebastian Franck, entitled *Sebastian* (1952), Hans Franck, a good writer, treats Hans Denk and the Nürnberg Anabaptists associated with the "gottlose Maler" ("the ungodly artists"). His work is based on inaccurate sources, such as Will-Erich Peuckert, and although he is sympathetic with the Anabaptists and portrays them as redeeming some weaknesses of the state church, he dismisses them ultimately as "Schwärmer." He gives no indication of understanding that there is an Anabaptism different from the mystic fanaticism which he pictures in Nürnberg.

A large proportion of the writers interested in Anabaptism at the present time are Swiss. In 1945 Erich Diebold, a Swiss journalist, wrote a novel on the Anabaptists of the canton of Zürich entitled *Folge dem Licht.* It is a poorly written book, lacking as much in historical understanding as in depth of character portrayal and convincing plot development. The author's thesis seems to be that the Anabaptists had excellent ideas, of which he mentions "conversion to righteousness and brotherly love, self-denial, and discipleship to Christ" (Foreword, 8), but that they were wrong in trying to overthrow the existing government (as he maintains they did) in order to introduce those ideas by force into a society not yet ready for them.

Two Swiss dramas of unequal value, Caesar von Arx's *Brüder in Christo* (1947), and Heinrich Künzi's *Barbara* (1948), were published almost simultaneously. *Barbara,* a Bernese dialect drama produced by the Berner Heimatschutz Theater, portrays an Anabaptist girl who clings firmly to her faith in the face of persecution by church and state. It is pro-Anabaptist; the love and strength of Barbara put her accusers to shame. The play has dramatic weaknesses and errors in historical interpretation, especially in the final act, in which the Anabaptists escape en masse to the Jura Mountains. The drama by von Arx, on the contrary, is a tragedy strong from the standpoints of both idea and execution. Its hero, Zürich city councillor Falk, a friend of Zwingli, becomes convinced of the correctness of the Anabaptist position, but because of a chain of tragic circumstances considers himself unworthy of becoming an Anabaptist and thus remains in the state church, his sensitive spirit broken because he does so. Von Arx treats this genuinely tragic motif not only with penetrating understanding of the human problem involved, but also with astounding insight into the nature of Anabaptism as well as of the Reformed tradition, and he portrays the essential conflict between the two with magnificent clarity. His knowledge of the historical setting is also exceptionally good. Von Arx, whose works are primarily historical tragedies of the nature of *Brüder in Christo,* is generally considered to be Switzerland's leading modern dramatist, and *Brüder in Christo* is probably his best. It is also possibly the best literary production ever written with an Anabaptist or Mennonite theme.

Willi Schäferdiek's *Rebell in Christo* (1953), which has Thomas Müntzer as its hero, incidentally brings the Zürich Anabaptists (Grebel and Manz) into contact with Müntzer, erroneously of course, since the movement had no connection with Müntzer or the Peasants Revolt. The representation of the Anabaptists is sympathetic, apparently based largely on Grebel's letter to Müntzer. He also brings Hans Denk into his story. Schäferdiek was for some time dramatic director of the Berlin radio, and is a leading German author.

Only five works appearing after 1935 use the later Mennonite theme. They are all novels. Walther Laedrach's *Passion in Bern* (1938) is a sympathetic and historically accurate novel based on the persecution of the Bernese Anabaptists in the first two decades of the 18th century. *Der Frondeur* (1945), an excellent novel in the Bernese dialect by Rudolf van Tavel, an outstanding Swiss novelist, discusses incidentally the Mennonites of the Emmental after the Thirty Years' War. The last of the major novels on the Mennonites is Eva Caskel's *Marguerite Valmore* (1948), the story of a French emigré's entrance into the Mennonite community at Danzig during the time of the French Revolution. One of Ilse Schreiber's novels on Canada, *Vielerlei Heimat unter dem Himmel* (1949), has as its main theme the Russian Mennonite emigrants to Canada. A second, *Canada, Welt des Weizens* (1951), mentions them incidentally.

Among the South German Mennonites several short story writers have appeared, whose tales have been published chiefly in the *Christlicher (Mennonitischer) Gemeinde-Kalender*, particularly Mathias Pohl (1860-1934), long pastor in Sembach (Palatinate), who also published religious verse, Martha Händiges, the wife of Pastor E. Händiges, now at Enkenbach (Palatinate), and Charlotte Hofmann-Hege. The *Gemeinde-Kalender* has also carried some religious verse by Pastor Gerhard Hein of Sembach. M.E.B.

Ricarda Huch, *Das Zeitalter der Glaubensspaltung* (Berlin, 1937); E. G. Kolbenheyer, *Paracelsus*, 3 vv. (Munich, 1937); Walter Laedrach, *Passion in Bern; ein Täuferroman um den Schultheissen Johann Friedrich Willading* (Zürich, 1938); Lulu von Strauss und Torney, *Der jüngste Tag* (Jena, 1939); Erich Diebold, *Folge dem Licht* (Zürich, 1945); Rudolf Stickelberger, *Narren Gottes* (Zürich, 1945); Rudolf von Tavel, *Der Frondeur* (Bern, 1945); Hans Müller-Einigen, *Die Menschen sind alle gleich* (Bern, 1946); Friedrich Reck-Malleczewen, *Bockelson; Geschichte eines Massenwahns* (Berlin, 1946); Caesar von Arx, *Brüder in Christo* (Zürich, 1947); Friedrich Dürrenmatt, *Es steht geschrieben* (Basel, 1947); Heinrich Specht, *Heil'ge Feuer* (Nordhorn, n.d.); Eva Caskel, *Marguerite Valmore* (Hamburg, 1948); Heinrich Künzi, *Barbara* (Bern, 1948); Erich Müller-Gangloff, *Vorläufer des Anti-Christ* (Berlin, 1948); Ilse Schreiber, *Vielerlei Heimat unter dem Himmel* (Hamburg, 1949); idem, *Canada, Welt des Weizens* (Munich, 1951); Hans Franck, *Sebastian* (Gütersloh, 1952); Willi Schäferdiek, *Rebell in Christo* (Hattingen; 1953); Helmut Paulus, *Die tönernen Füsse* (Antwerp, 1954); Franz Theodor Csokor, *Der Schlüssel zum Abgrund* (Hamburg, 1955).

IV. *Germany: The Münster Theme.* Until the late 18th century the only significant mention of the Anabaptists occurs in some contemporary didactic and satirical poems. Understandably, the period of storm and stress found the Münster theme attractive, and in the last 25 years of the 18th century three dramas on the Münster rebellion, all of poor quality, appeared in Germany. In 1777 Christoph Bernhard Schücking, an uncle of the noted Levin Schücking and himself a citizen of Münster, wrote a drama on Elizabeth Wandscherer, Bockelson's wife, entitled *Elisabeth* (Münster). Although the drama is freighted with excesses, which are explained not only by the period in which it was written but also by the youth of the author, and although it lacks any finished artistry, it foreshadows the presentation of personality conflict in Jan of Leyden as tragedy which is more fully developed in later works. In his *Jan von Laiden* (Münster, 1786) Baron von Nesselrode senses the dramatic possibilities in the Münster episode, although his characters behave with too much flattering dramatic nobility to be in good taste. A drama by Christian August Vulpius (Goethe's brother-in-law), *Johann von Leiden* (Leipzig, 1793), portrays von Leyden as a titan.

In 19th-century Germany the Münsterites appear as a literary theme with relative frequency, and their treatment is adapted to the century's changing moods. The only work of literary value to mention them, however, is Achim von Arnim's romantic novel *Die Kronenwächter* (Berlin, 1817). Arnim places the imperial crown in Münster, and considers the Münster episode a positive step in the development of the German concept of empire. Despite his fantastic main theme, Arnim strives for historical accuracy of detail and may well have set the trend, growing especially in the second half of the century, toward greater historical objectivity regarding the Anabaptists.

As a result of the 19th-century interest in historical fiction, five historical novels on the Münsterites, all distinctly inferior from a literary point of view, appeared in the first half of the century. Van der Velde's *Die Wiedertäufer* (1821; Leipzig, 1851) is a superficial bit of entertainment literature. Under the influence of the English Romanticist Walter Scott, Karl Spindler, in *Der König von Zion* (1834; Stuttgart, 1854), the novel which more than any other awakened the interest of the Germans in the Münster episode, attempts to view the characters of his story in the light of their historical situation. He does not really succeed, however, since he considers all Münsterites to be either evil or insane and has no insight into the tensions of the Reformation reflected in Münster. Adolf Görling, in *Die Wiedertäufer*, attempts to give a picture of the entire Reformation. The fifth work is J. D. Mallmann's *Johann von Leyden, Eine Geschichte fürs Volk* (1844). Meyerbeer's opera, *Le Prophète* (1845), in which Jan of Leyden, the hero, is praised and his failure blamed on "the times," strongly affected the German attitude toward the Münsterites in its German translation (1846). The text of the opera was by Scribe.

Five works on Münster appeared in the third quarter of the 19th century. In 1854 Adolf Mützelburg published (at Berlin) *Der Prophet,* a novel of 1,100 pages based to a large extent on Spindler's work. *Johann von Leyden* (Münster, 1855) by Heinrich Brinckmann is a meaningless drama in blank verse. In his long and once popular poem, *Der König von Zion* (Hamburg, 1868), Robert

Hamerling, an active promoter of German democracy, makes Leyden a representative of modern social problems, a champion of freedom. The influence of Hebbel is shown in Ernst Mevert's drama, *Der König von Münster* (Hamburg, 1869), in that Leyden's downfall is attributed to the fact that he is not in line with the "general laws of events in the world." Mevert is the first to exploit to any real extent the tragic potential in Münster, and Hugo Hermsen considers his to be the best of the 19th-century dramas on the Anabaptists. Ludwig Schneegans, in *Jan Bockhold* (Munich, 1877), sees Leyden as an emotionally sick man. Also in 1877 (Bielefeld and Leipzig) Rudolf Weber published an exceedingly poor historical novel, *Die Wiedertäufer von Münster,* borrowed mostly from Mützelburg.

During the last quarter of the century, the Münsterites receive only programmatic treatment. Herman Tiemann's novel, *Die Wiedertäufer in Münster* (Braunschweig, 1892), is a Victorian warning to the German people not to abandon the traditional virtues. Tiemann tried to interpret Jan of Leyden psychologically, but he could not comprehend the spirit of the Reformation and succeeded only in comparing him with enthusiasts of his own time. The politically fraught atmosphere of the era in which he wrote is evident in his attempt to make the naive Münsterites represent sophisticated political ideas, an attempt which of course fails. Victor Hardung's drama, *Die Wiedertäufer in Münster* (Glarus, 1895), is a naturalistic picture of "the baseness of the great human rabble" (*die Niederträchtigkeit des grossen menschlichen Gesindels*), paradoxically in verse, which is completely unsuccessful in its attempt to create in Jan a tragic hero. Hardung calls his characters "cattle" (*Viecher*). Two equally unsuccessful works were written by A. J. Cüppers: a drama, *Der König von Sion* (Berlin, 1900), so weak from both dramatic and psychological standpoints that it was never performed, and a historical novel, *Im Banne der Wiedertäufer* (Berlin, 1892).

The 20th century produced a remarkable number of works, both novels and dramas, using the Münster theme. The first was Hans Hartmann's drama, *Von Krone und Ehre* (Strasbourg, n.d.—1914). In 1915 Wilhelm Schmidtbonn, depressed because of the war, wrote his rather raw drama on Münster, entitled *Die Stadt der Besessenen.* Jan Freimark's novel, *Johann von Leiden* (Berlin, 1919), is worthy only of mention. *Das Tausendjährige Reich* by Hermann Rehm (Rothenfelde, 1925) is a revision of Spindler's novel. In 1935 Bernhard Kellermann wrote a drama on Münster, *Die Wiedertäufer* (Berlin), which is fairly similar to Schmidtbonn's. His interest in the Anabaptists, however, comes from a rather romantic fascination with the long ago and the far way, coupled with an interest in social problems. *Der König im Käfig* by Ludwig Webmann (Münster, 1935) is a short novel of no consequence. Although it was published with the help of societies interested in Westphalian history and culture, it exploits the sensational, is designed to paint the Münster episode in the darkest colors possible, and is little more than an adventure story. The following lesser novels should also be noted: Hugo Strauch, *Die tolle Stadt*

1926; Eugen von Sass, *Johann von Leiden* (Dresden, 1930); Josef von Lauff, *Elisabeth Wandscherer, die Königin, Scherenschnitt aus der Geschichte der Wiedertäufer* (Leipzig, 1931); Anna von Krane, *Die Verfehmten. Roman aus der Wiedertäuferzeit* (Köln, 1935); and Käthe Lübbert-Griese, *Der Teufel in Münster* (Berlin, 1937). Gerhard Hauptmann's intended novel, *Die Wiedertäufer,* begun in February 1916, remained a fragment of 25 pages, which was published in the *Gerhard Hauptmann Jahrbuch* I (Breslau, 1936).

Since World War II, three noted contemporary authors, Friedrich Dürrenmatt (Swiss), Franz Theodor Csokor (Austrian), and Helmut Paulus (German), have written major works on the Münsterites. Dürrenmatt, a young Zürich dramatist, has won much acclaim, especially among students, for his experimental dramatic techniques. At its premiere in Zürich *Es steht geschrieben* (1947), his drama on Münster, which is quite daring technically, was greeted with excitement mingled with catcalls. It combines admiration for the firm faith of the Münsterites and their obedience to it under stress with the realization that this faith was also immeasurably dangerous to its adherents. Dürrenmatt's drama is original in idea as well as in technique. The Austrian Franz Theodor Csokor has gained recognition both as a novelist and as a dramatist. His novel on the Münsterites, *Der Schlüssel zum Abgrund* (1955), is a serious effort to see the Münster episode as an expression of the turmoil of the Reformation and thus to understand the Reformation itself more fully. However, in spite of moments of insight and artistic power, it is disturbing in its unconvincing exploitation of some of the more sensational tales that have grown up concerning Münster. Helmut Paulus, although not strikingly original in technique or idea, is a master storyteller and a popular author. The motif of his work is didactic; his most common theme is that only a life for others is fruitful. This is the import of *Die tönernen Füsse* (1954), his novel on the tragic disillusionment caused by the selfishness of Jan of Leyden.

In 1937 Friedrich Reck-Malleczewen, a physician who was a member of the East Prussian aristocracy and who suffered spiritually under the Nazi regime, published a biography of Jan of Leyden which he entitled *Bockelson—Geschichte eines Massenwahns* (Berlin), and which was intended as a warning to the Germans against the mass hysteria under Hitler. During the war his book was passed from hand to hand in the underground. Reck-Malleczewen himself was executed at Dachau in 1945. His book was republished in 1946, with additional material including a biography by his wife and an introduction by Paul Zöckler. In 1948 Erich Müller-Gangloff, a friend of Reck-Malleczewen, now the director of one of the institutes known as Evangelische Academien in Germany, published a series of sketches of tyrants under the title, *Vorläufer des Anti-Christ,* which he dedicated to his martyred friend. He includes members of the violent wing of the Anabaptists, especially Bockelson, whose portrait he bases on that of Malleczewen; and he calls the Anabaptists the "Rattenfänger der Reformation." His attempt to find a recurring pattern among tyrants which might aid in an understanding of Hitler is interesting, but his treatment of the Anabaptists is seriously in error. He is unable to distinguish between genuine and spurious Anabaptism, and he maintains that Jan of Leyden denied his position under torture at the end. Following is a typical sentence from his book: "Die Täuferbewegung war ja von vornherein eine weit über die Stadt Münster hinaus verbreitete Erscheinung, die in vielen Landschaften des damaligen Reiches unter der Oberfläche gärte, und explosionsartige Ausbrüche ähnlich dem des Bauernkrieges erwarten liess" (96). M.E.B.

Wilhelm Rauch, *Johann van Leyden, der König von Sion, in der deutschen Dichtung* (Borna-Leipzig, 1912, 129 pp.); Hugo Hermsen, *Die Wiedertäufer zu Münster in der deutschen Dichtung* (Stuttgart, 1913, 161 pp.), containing a complete list of all titles published, with bibliographical data.

V. *France*. In France the Mennonites were practically unknown; hence they are rarely mentioned in French literature, and then only as Anabaptists. In addition to Marquis de Pezay, Michiels, and Grandidier, who are discussed in the article **Alsace**, Emile Erckmann (d. 1889) and Alexandre Chatrian (d. 1890) used Mennonite subjects. In several novels which they wrote conjointly, especially in *L'Ami Fritz,* the Mennonites receive mention, though of a superficial kind. They are presented as honest people whose word is reliable; their farms are described as exemplary; there is occasional reference to peculiarity in dress and doctrine.

There are also some essays in travel literature, almanacs, and yearbooks which mention them very favorably. Some of these are *Une excursion dans les vosges* by A. Benoit (Nancy, 1860) and *Turquestein* by H. Lepage (Nancy, 1886). Benoit writes of the Mennonites in the White Saar, "They are traditions rather than people. Their meetings held in this house or that in the valley show the severity of their principles. Listen to these psalms and songs in the German language, these sermons, as long as they are monotonous; look at these attentive faces, these serious rites, in which the body of Christ is represented by a loaf of bread which is broken into small strips, and the blood by wine in a plain pitcher; observe the complete absence of church decoration, of all religious show, and tell me whether there is not something great and noble in such a religion, whose adherents have been so hard hit by fate, but who have preserved their old principles as a precious possession in their unshakable entirety."

Voltaire (d. 1778) in his novel *Candide* (1759) takes his hero through all sorts of incredible adventures around the world. In Holland he meets an Anabaptist, "a man who has not been baptized, a good Anabaptist named Jacques." This "best man in the world" is interested in all the unfortunate and is positively opposed to all violence. He comes to a sudden end in trying to save the life of a man who has previously without any cause given him a terrible beating.

G. Meyerbeer's opera *Le Prophète,* using the Münster theme, appeared in Paris in 1845.

J. B. Muller, a preacher in the Mennonite congregation at Toul, has been publishing numerous short stories of religious character in *Christ Seul,* the French Mennonite organ. P.So., H.S.B.

VI. *Russia and Russo-German Emigrés*. This section treats the literature in the German language by or about the Mennonites living in Russia or as emigrés in Germany, United States, and Canada. With the improvement of education among the Mennonites of Russia a greater interest in literature became noticeable during the second half of the 19th century. Small home and school libraries were started by the turn of the 20th century. Some Mennonite teachers took up writing. Bernhard Harder (*q.v.*), a well-known minister and evangelist of Russia, wrote many poems for practically every occasion, which were collected and edited by Heinrich Franz, Sr., and published in 1888 under the title *Geistliche Lieder und Gelegenheitsgedichte.* J. H. Janzen says that Bernhard Harder was "our first significant poet," whose songs breathe "a warm, lifelike piety of the heart out of which joy radiates, many of them having the essence of folk songs." Peter B. Harder (*q.v.*), a son of Bernhard Harder, also a teacher, was one of the pioneer novelists of the Mennonites of Russia. Best known is the novel *Die Lutherische Cousine.* In *Lose Blätter,* a collection of short stories and poems which appeared in 1910 in *Aufwärts* (*q.v.*), he portrays Mennonite life in Russia with great ability and power of observation. J. H. Janzen says that because of his writing about Mennonites he "was regarded almost as an outsider," in spite of his being a very good teacher and the son of the widely known and recognized Bernhard Harder. About *Lose Blätter* Janzen says that they "enjoyed kind reception" although they caused the author much criticism from those who felt exposed.

Heinrich J. Janzen (*q.v.*), the father of J. H. Janzen, wrote poetry under the title "Erzeugnisse schlafloser Nächte," of which several appeared in H. Dirks' *Mennonitisches Jahrbuch* (Halbstadt, 1905-13) and some were taken into the *Gesangbuch.* J. H. Janzen says about his father's poems that he fears "they will never become real folksongs." They have depth and thought but lack elasticity.

J. H. Janzen (*q.v.*) published his first fiction in the form of short stories under the pseudonym J. Zenian and the title *Denn meine Augen haben Deinen Heiland gesehen, Erzählungen von J. Zenian* (Halbstadt, n.d., 1910). Two parts of this book were reprinted in Canada in 1925 and 1927 as *Du hast Dich meiner Seele herzlich angenommen* and *Dein Blut.* The author states that his book "was reviewed favorably in most German papers of Russia, America, and also Germany." Arnold Dyck, another Mennonite writer, describes vividly in "Jacob H. Janzen—Writer" (*Menn. Life,* July 1951, 33) what an overwhelming impression this book made on him and others when at last a gifted Mennonite writer wrote about Mennonite life in the form of fiction. J. H. Janzen himself states that he, Martin Fast, and Gerhard Loewen formed a "league of young poets" at that time. Although they could not meet because of distance they sent each other poems and encouraged and criticized each other in chain letters. Gerhard Loewen (*q.v.*), also a teacher and minister, published a collection of poems under the title

Feldblumen. Arnold Dyck, who republished this volume in North Kildonan, Man., in 1940, says, "His poems are flawless in form and diction. In this category they belong to the best that the pen of our writers has left us." He quotes Linde, the German literary critic, who speaks of his poems as "not being overwhelmingly beautiful but very lovely" (*Menn. Life,* January 1948, 23). Martin Fast of Muravyevka, Samara, also wrote poems. Unfortunately, little information is available about his life and writings. These were the pioneers of Mennonite fiction and poetry in Russia. Those of the younger generation who were inspired by them produced their writings primarily in Canada.

The Russian Revolution interrupted a phase of cultural development and brought it to a sudden halt. It can be expected that some literature and poetry was produced under Communism but it is too early to make a study of it. Jacob Sudermann, an artist and poet, died in a concentration camp. Signs of literary efforts are found in *Unser Blatt* published in Russia in 1925-27.

Germany: The sufferings and experiences of 1914 and later produced an unusual crop of young Mennonite writers, most of whom left Russia to settle, at least temporarily, in Germany. Theodor Block published *Hungerlieder* (Bad Homburg, 1922); A. B. Enns, a book of poems, *Die Hütte* (Emden, 1924); Dietrich Neufeld, *Ein Tagebuch aus dem Reiche des Totentanzes* (Emden, 1921; also printed in the United States in English 1930 at Claremont as *Russian Dance of Death* with the author's pen name Dirk Gora); also by Neufeld are *Mennonitentum in der Ukraine* (Emden, 1922), and *Zu Pferd 1000 km durch die Ukraine* (Emden, 1922). His writings reveal literary qualities. Later in Canada he continued along these lines by writing, under the name Novokampus, *Kanadische Mennoniten* (Winnipeg, 1925). Gerhard Fast's *Im Schatten des Todes, Erlebnisbericht aus Sowjetrussland* (Wernigerode, 1935) is a moving report, historical in fact, but powerfully and imaginatively written and of high literary quality.

More recently Hans Harder, a teacher in the pedagogical school at Wuppertal, Germany, has devoted a number of novels to the Mennonites of Russia. His *In Wologdas weissen Wäldern* (Altona, 1934) describes the suffering of the Mennonites of Russia sent to the concentration camps of northern Russia. In *Das Dorf an der Wolga* (Stuttgart, 1937) he portrays in fiction the beginning, flowering, and decline of a Mennonite village of the Volga area. In his novel *Das sibirische Tor* (Stuttgart, 1938) he treats the Orenburg Mennonites, portraying the German Mennonite culture in the Russian environment. *Die Hungerbrüder* (Heilbronn, 1938) is the account of a family of German settlers in Russia, possibly Mennonites, who in the horrors of famine and starvation make their way to the East to escape from Russia. When they cross the river into China only the two boys are left, penniless, and are found by a relief organization, obviously the MCC, and sent to South America. These are the major novels in which he treats Mennonites. Of the many Mennonite writers who have written on the Mennonites of Russia no other has found as much recognition in the German press as Harder, and he is probably the best writer of fiction produced as yet by the Mennonites anywhere. He hopes to complete a cycle of Mennonite novels, which would include the American aspect. Harder's writings rarely mention Mennonites, presenting his characters as Germans, but those who know their background can readily identify it as Mennonite. Other novels by Harder, all with non-Mennonite but Russian themes, are *Wie Lukas Holl seine Heimat suchte* (1938), *Der deutsche Doktor von Moskau* (1940), *Klim: ein russisches Bauernleben* (1940), and *Die vier Leiden des Adam Kling* (1942).

United States: Among the Mennonite writers who were educated in Russia and came to the United States after World War I and have made significant contributions using the German language is Peter G. Epp (*q.v.*), whose outstanding novel is *Eine Mutter* (Bluffton, 1932). He also published *Das Wunder* (Newton, 1926), *Die Erlösung* (Bluffton, 1930), *Johanna,* and *Das Geisslein.* Several chapters of his large manuscript "An der Molotschna" were published in *Der Bote* (Rosthern). Epp had an unusual gift for portraying Mennonite culture.

Canada: The Mennonites of Canada who had come from Russia after World War I have been much more productive in the field of literature than the earlier immigrants, whose only significant product was Isaac Friesen's two volumes of religious verse, *Im Dienste des Meisters* (Constance, Germany, ca. 1910). J. H. Janzen, who came to Canada in 1924, continued his writing and became one of the most productive authors. Of his approximately forty books and booklets published in Canada many are short stories and plays (complete list in *Menn. Life,* July 1951, p. 42). Well known are his Low German one-act plays, *De Bildung* (Blumenort, 1912; Waterloo, 1945), *De Enbildung* (n.p., 1913), *Daut Schultebott* (n.p., 1913), *Utwaundere* (n.p., 1931), and his collection of poems *Durch Wind und Wellen* (Waterloo, 1928). In *Wanderndes Volk* (3 vols., n.p., 1945-49) the author relates incidents from his family history in fictional form. *Tales from Ancient and Recent Mennonite History* (1948), his only writing in English, is a popularized and fictionized narrative, a translation of his *Erzählungen aus der Mennoniten-Geschichte* (1943). Unfortunately in his later years Janzen had to depend on his own mimeograph to spread his writings. The limited editions of his writings, the sale being largely limited to the Mennonite market, made it impossible to have them printed without financial loss.

One of the most significant Canadian writers has been Arnold Dyck, who has written High German as well as Low German fiction and plays. He introduced himself to the Mennonite reading public as the editor of the *Mennonitische Warte* (1935-38) and of a series of booklets on Russian Mennonite history published by the Echo Verlag (*q.v.*). During the war he wrote the novel *Verloren in der Steppe,* which he illustrated himself, and which was published in five volumes (Steinbach, 1944-48). In this story he relates the experiences of Hänschen who was "lost" in the steppes of the Ukraine. Like Peter Epp in *Eine Mutter,* Dyck succeeds in depicting Mennonite village life and the culture in general in a masterful way. In *Meine Deutschlandfahrt* (North

Kildonan, 1950) the author relates his experiences during a revisit in Germany after World War II, where he finally settled in 1954. However, Dyck will probably remain best remembered for his Low German writings. His two-volume *Koop enn Bua op Reise* (Steinbach, 1943) has been reprinted repeatedly. This was followed by *Dee Millionäa von Kosefeld* (Steinbach, 1946) and the two-volume *Koop enn Bua faore nao Toronto* (North Kildonan, 1948 f.). In *Dee Fria* (Steinbach, 1947) Dyck presents a Low German one-act play, of which he soon published a new edition with an added twenty-fifth scene. This was followed by two one-act plays dealing with the forestry service program among the Mennonites of Russia, entitled *Wellkaom op'e Forstei* (North Kildonan, 1950) and *De Opnaom* (1951). *Onse Lied en ola Tiet* (Steinbach, 1952) contains a collection of humorous Low German stories and skits. The Low German plays by Dyck have been presented in many Mennonite communities and schools of Canada and the United States and always find a receptive audience.

G. A. Peters wrote a number of books and other prose dealing with the experiences of the Mennonites of the Ukraine during and after the Revolution which are of some literary significance. Among them are *Menschenlos in schwerer Zeit* (Scottdale, 1924?), and *Wehrlos?* (Scottdale, 1924?). He also published two volumes of his poems, entitled *Gedichte* I, II (Scottdale, 1924?). G. H. Peters published a collection of his poems entitled *Blumen am Wegrand* (North Kildonan, 1946).

One of the most productive writers was Peter J. Klassen who presented his experiences among the Mennonites of Russia and Canada in numerous volumes of which the following should be mentioned: *Grossmutters Schatz* (Superb, 1939), *Die Geschichte des Ohm Klaas* (Yarrow, n.d.), *Heimat einmal* (two volumes, Yarrow, n.d.), *Die Heimfahrt* (Superb, 1943), *Der Peet* (four volumes, Superb, 1943-49), *Verlorene Söhne* (Winnipeg, 1952), *Als die Heimat zur Fremde geworden,* and *Fünfunddreissig Fabeln* (Superb, 1944), the last largely a translation of the Russian Krylov.

Johann P. Klassen wrote many poems, of which J. H. Janzen, who calls him "the most productive and most natural of our poets," says, "An inexhaustible and an unconquerable joy speaks out of all his poems." Some of his poems were published in the following volumes: *Wegeblumen* (Scottdale, 1924?), *Dunkle Tage* (Scottdale, 1924?), *Krümlein* (Scottdale, 1924), *Brocken* (Winnipeg, 1932), *Meine Garbe* (Vancouver, 1946), *Der Zwillingsbruder von "Meine Garbe"* (Vancouver, n.d.), *Nohoaksel* (Yarrow, 1946), *Roggenbrot* (Vancouver, 1946), and *Aehrenlese* (Winnipeg, n.d.).

Gerhard Toews (Georg de Brecht) wrote *Heimat in Trümmern* (Steinbach, 1936) and *Die Heimat in Flammen* (Regina, ca. 1922). Gerhard Johann Friesen (Fritz Senn) published, like most of the Canadian writers, many of his poems and other contributions in the *Mennonitische Warte* (1935-38). This was also the case with G. G. Wiens, who wrote very unhappy reminiscences about the American Mennonites under the name "Jan Friesen" (*Mennonitische Warte,* 1938).

Heinrich Görz published a collection of poems, *Gedichte* (North Kildonan, n.d.). Abram Johann Friesen wrote a short story *Prost Mahlzeit* (Grünthal, 1949) and a drama, *Gott grüsse Dich!* (Grünthal, 1952). Karl Fast in *Gebet der Wahrheit die Ehre* (three volumes, North Kildonan, 1950-52) relates in an autobiographical narrative the last years of his experience in Russia before World War II and after the war as a prisoner of war. He is the only Canadian Mennonite writer thus far who has described these experiences in fiction.

These are only representative of the writers among the Mennonites of Canada originally from Russia who wrote fiction, poetry, and drama dealing with their own heritage and experiences, among which the catastrophic years of the Russian Revolution and Communism are outstanding. Not all writers and writings could be mentioned here. Many of the writers will be forgotten but some will survive. Much fiction and poetry can be found in the German Mennonite papers published between World Wars I and II, particularly in *Die Mennonitische Welt* (Winnipeg, 1948-52), *Der Bote* (Rosthern, Sask., 1924-), *Der Herold* (Newton, Kan.), and *Mennonitische Rundschau* (Winnipeg, Man.). Many of the writers wrote under pseudonyms.

One question that involuntarily arises in reviewing these many writers is why the Russian Mennonites as a rule produced so few literary and artistic works and what caused the sudden emergence of so many writers at one time. The preliminary answer could be that the Mennonites of Russia had reached an economic, religious, and educational level by about 1910 in which reflection and literary production could be anticipated. The terrible experiences during the Russian Revolution and under the Communistic regime brought about a fruition along these lines in a way unprecedented except possibly in the Netherlands during the Golden Age after the period of martyrdom. This Russo-German Mennonite literary output is at times fully conscious of the religious background and mission of the Mennonites, but above all in most cases it is representative of a German culture of which the educated Mennonites of Russia became more fully aware at the turn of the 20th century. The climax of this literary movement seems to have now been reached and passed. Because of the gradual adjustment of the Mennonites to the Canadian environment the future is not hard to predict; the prospects for a continuation of the Russo-German literary tradition in Canada are not bright, particularly with the inevitable transition to the English language. The writings in the High German language will remain a monument of a literary achievement, but increasingly less read. On the other hand, the Low German fiction and particularly the dramas by Arnold Dyck will probably be enjoyed for years to come. C.K.

Elizabeth Horsch Bender, "Mennonites in German Literature" (unpublished master's thesis, University of Minnesota, 1944); Elmer F. Suderman, "The Russo-German Mennonite Theme in the American Novel" (unpublished master's thesis, University of Kansas, 1948); Cornelius J. Dyck, "How Literary Critics Have Evaluated Mennonite Writers of the Twentieth Century" (unpublished paper, Bethel College, 1953); Bertha Fast, "Low German Literature for Children" (unpublished collection, 1948, BeCL); J. H. Janzen, "The Literature of the Russo-Canadian Mennonites," *Menn. Life* I (January 1946) 22-25; "Books by J. H. Janzen," *Menn. Life* VI (July 1951) 42; Arnold Dyck, "Jacob H. Janzen—Writer," *Menn. Life* VI (July 1951) 33; Horst Quiring and Cornelius Krahn, "Mennonites in German Literature—1940-1950," *Menn. Life* VII (April 1952) 85; Cornelius Krahn, "Hans Harder—A Mennonite Novelist," *Menn. Life* VIII (April 1953) 78; Wilhelm Schneider, *Die auslanddeutsche Dichtung unserer Zeit* (Berlin, 1936); H. Langenbucher, *Volkhafte Dichtung der Zeit* (Berlin, 1937); K. K. Klein, *Literaturgeschichte des Deutschtums im Ausland* (Leipzig, 1939); Albert Soergel, *Dichtung und Dichter der Zeit* (Leipzig, 1928).

VII. United States and Canada (in English). Little of the literature about the Mennonites written in America comes to grips with any doctrinal or ethical questions inherent in the Mennonite faith. In fact, even in regard to entertainment, which is the obvious objective of much of it, it is not on a high plane. Only recently have attempts been made, usually by the Mennonites themselves, to deal with such problems; they have produced a number of good stories, but most of them are on an adolescent level as literature in its narrower sense.

The earliest fiction written in America on the Anabaptists-Mennonites concerns the Swiss Brethren of the Reformation period. It is *True to the End* (Philadelphia, *ca*. 1895) by Henry S. Burrage, a Baptist church historian. It follows history closely—perhaps too closely to result in good fiction. It is, however, a sympathetic treatment. The only liberty the author has taken with the facts of history is to have the first Swiss Brethren have themselves rebaptized by immersion upon discovering from further study of the Bible that their first baptism as adults, namely by pouring, was invalid. It was published in a German translation as *Getreu bis ans Ende* (Cassel, Germany, 1905 and 1920; 5th ed. 1922).

A less sympathetic, but prolific writer was Helen R. Martin, whose favorite subject was ridicule of the Pennsylvania Dutch. Among her novels are several dealing with the Mennonites and Amish of Pennsylvania. *Tillie, a Mennonite Maid* (N.Y., 1904), *Sabina, a Story of the Amish* (N.Y., 1905), and *The Betrothal of Elypholate* (N.Y., 1907; a collection of short stories) have Mennonites or Amish as their principal characters; in *The Schoolmaster of Hessville* (N.Y., 1920) the Mennonites play a minor role. In all of these works Mrs. Martin treats the stricter branches of the Mennonite family, viz., the Amish and the "New" Mennonites (Herrites). In Mrs. Martin's writings the Mennonite faith, indeed whatever savors of Pennsylvania Dutch, is something to be sloughed off in the process of personal growth and development. Some of her books are sheer melodrama.

Two early serialized attempts at fiction appeared in Mennonite periodicals. One was *Jake, a Story of Plain People,* by S. M. Grubb (*q.v.*), published in the *Mennonite* in 1911, which deals with the Mennonites of Eastern Pennsylvania, though not very happily. In 1922-24 the *Christian Monitor* published *The Clemen Family* by John Horsch (*q.v.*), which is a fictional narrative of events among the early Swiss Brethren. It is, however, not a literary success, since the characters are lost in the mass of historical facts.

The novels by B. Mabel Dunham, of Kitchener,

Ont., herself a descendant of Mennonites, are highly sympathetic and effective treatments of the early Mennonite settlers of that area. *The Trail of the Conestoga* (Toronto, 1924) deals with the immigrants to Waterloo County, Ontario, from Pennsylvania, and their early settlement in Canada. *Toward Sodom* (Toronto, 1927) gives a picture of the religious problems created later in the same settlement by isolation from and nonconformity to the "world" and the consequent loss of many young people to other creeds and faiths. Her point that the trend toward the city ("Sodom") is fatal to Mennonitism is debatable. *Kristli's Trees* (Toronto, 1948) is a charming novel for adolescents, also dealing with the Mennonites of Ontario. Miss Dunham's *Grand River* (Toronto, 1945) is a wider descriptive and historical account of the settlement of this section of Ontario, and includes the Mennonite contribution to the total development of the province.

In 1925 Elsie Singmaster's volume of short stories *Bred in the Bone* (N.Y.) appeared, with an Eastern Pennsylvania locale. Many of these stories deal with the stricter branches of the Mennonites and Amish, but in a very different way from Mrs. Martin. Miss Singmaster is one of America's great short story writers, hence her stories have an artistic finish. Furthermore her interpretation, though often amused, is never derisive, and always gentle. Her "juvenile" novel, *I Heard of a River* (Phila., 1948) dealing with the Palatine German immigrants to Pennsylvania, including the Mennonites, touches on Mennonite nonresistance.

A most unfriendly interpretation of the Amish of Northern Indiana is given by Ruth Lininger Dobson in her novel *Straw in the Wind* (N.Y., 1937). Even from a stylistic point of view this novel is far inferior to Miss Dunham's works. J. W. Yoder, himself a Mennonite of Amish descent, has presented an idyllic account of the Amish in Pennsylvania in his two semifictional books, *Rosanna of the Amish* (Huntingdon, 1940) and *Rosanna's Boys* (Huntingdon, 1948). Though adults also find pleasure in the freshness and charm of the picture, the books must be classified as juveniles because of the absence of any serious problems.

The Mennonite immigrants from Russia, specifically the Gnadenau (KMB) Mennonite settlement in Kansas, are the subject of two novels in the second quarter of the 20th century. *The Flamethrowers* (Caldwell, 1936) by Gordon Friesen, a son of the settlement, is highly inimical, and written from a "leftist" point of view; its characters are not typical. On the other hand, *The Locusts* (N.Y. and London, 1943), by Otto Schrag, is an important novel; the sections dealing with the Mennonites are sympathetic to them, although some of the author's interpretations of their way of life may be questioned. It was also published later in German as *Die Heuschrecken* (Munich, 1948). Helen Clark Fernald's treatment of the same community in *Plow the Dew Under* (N.Y., 1952), and Catherine Nickel's *Seed from the Ukraine* (N.Y., 1952) are not on an adult plane as literature.

Elizabeth A. Schroeter's slightly fictionized autobiography, *From Here to the Pinnacles, Memories of Mennonite Life in the Ukraine and America*

(N.Y., 1956), is an interesting account of the experiences and problems of a Mennonite Brethren immigrant of 1913 from the Ukraine to California, which includes not only episodes "as nearly as possible as they took place," but also "the ceremonies exactly as they were practiced." It is based upon a diary begun at the age of seven. All but the last 60 pages deal with Russia.

Travelogues and semi-autobiographical writings have been produced by a considerable number of American Mennonites. H. J. Krehbiel's *A Trip Through Europe* (Newton, 1926), Frieda Kauffman's *Auf Wanderwegen, Plaudereien über eine Europareise* (Newton, 1935), and Arnold Dyck's *Meine Deutschlandfahrt, Eine Reiseplauderei* (North Kildonan, 1950) tell about trips to Europe. S. C. Yoder's *Down South America Way* (Scottdale, 1943) and *Eastward to the Sun* (Scottdale, 1953) tell of a journey to Europe and India visiting Mennonites and their missions, and of one to the Mennonite missions and colonies in lower South America. Three MCC relief workers, Willard and Verna Smith in *Paraguayan Interlude, Observations and Impressions* (Scottdale, 1950) and Samuel A. Yoder in *Middle-East Sojourn* (Scottdale, 1951), relate experiences and observations, the former in Paraguay, Argentina, and Brazil, and the latter in Egypt, Ethiopia, and Palestine. Autobiographical reminiscences are related by Hillegonda van der Smissen in *Bilder aus meinem Leben* (Newton, ca.1935, English as *Sketches from My Life,* Newton, ca. 1935), S. C. Yoder in *Horse Trails Along the Desert* (Scottdale, 1954), and Dorothy McCammon, *We Tried to Stay* (Scottdale, 1953). The last of these, a moving account of the experiences of a missionary couple in Communistic China, was rated as one of the ten best religious books of the year by the *Saturday Review.*

In Canada Frederick Philip Grove, who was a teacher at Winkler, Man., and married Katherine Wiens, a Mennonite, touches on Manitoba Mennonite life in his novels *Our Daily Bread* (Toronto, 1929) and *In Search of Myself* (Toronto, 1946). Paul Hiebert's novel *Sarah Binks* (Toronto, 1947) deals with pioneer conditions in Western Canada and is a satire on self-important literary criticism.

The scene of *High Bright Buggy Wheels* (N.Y., 1951), by Luella Creighton, is in Ontario among some of the stricter Mennonites, possibly Brethren in Christ. Miss Creighton shows an appreciation of the idyllic aspects of their rural religious life, but little understanding for their faith.

In recent years a number of young Mennonite (MC) women have been writing Christian fiction for young people, several of their works dealing with Mennonite life or doctrine. *Not Regina* (Scottdale, 1954) by Christmas Carol Kauffman, is a novel on Swiss Anabaptist beginnings and persecutions. Eunice Shellenberger's *Wings of Decision* (Scottdale, 1951) has nonresistance as its theme. Helen Brenneman's *But Not Forsaken* (Scottdale, 1955) is an interpretation of refugee experiences based on the author's experiences as an MCC relief worker in the refugee camp at Gronau, Germany, after World War II, and is of superior quality, probably the best fiction produced as yet by an American Mennonite writer. In addition to her historical novel,

Mrs. Kauffman has written a number of religious novels for adolescents, not specifically on Mennonite themes, including *Lucy Winchester* (Scottdale, 1945), *Light from Heaven* (Scottdale, 1948), *Dannie of Cedar Cliffs* (Scottdale, 1950), and *Life with Life* (Scottdale, 1952). Edna Beiler has written many good juvenile stories which have been published in the *Youth's Christian Companion* and *Words of Cheer.* Ten of the *Words of Cheer* stories were reprinted as *Ten of a Kind* (Scottdale, 1953). She also writes stories in *Christian Living.* Esther Eby Glass has many good stories for adolescents to her credit appearing in the *Youth's Christian Companion* since about 1947.

Other books on a late adolescent level are Marcus Bach's *Dream Gate* (Indianapolis, 1949), which gives insight into the life of a boy in a Hutterite settlement in North Dakota, and *Blue Hills and Shoofly Pie* (Philadelphia, 1952) by Ann Hark, which contains some valuable descriptions of Amish life.

Some of the most delightful books on the Amish are those written for children; usually they have charming illustrations. Among these are *Henner's Lydia* (N.Y., 1937), *Skippack School* (N.Y., 1939), and *Yoni Wondernose* (N.Y., 1942) by Marguerite de Angeli; *Little Amish Schoolhouse* (N.Y., 1939) and *Amish Moving Day* (N.Y., 1942) by Ella Maie Seyfert; and *Lovina, A Story of the Amish* (N.Y., 1940) and *Appolonia's Valentine* (N.Y., 1954) by Katherine Milhous. *Plain Girl* (N.Y., 1955) by Virginia Sorensen is the pleasant story of an Amish girl in a public school, intended for older children.

Barbara (Mrs. Don.) Smucker, a Mennonite author, wrote the thoughtful and impressive *Henry's Red Sea* (Scottdale, 1955), relating the escape of a group of Russian Mennonite refugees from Berlin in 1948 on their way to final settlement in Paraguay. It is meant for children. Elizabeth (Mrs. Harold) Bauman's *Coals of Fire* (Scottdale, 1954) contains eighteen fictionized true stories for youth illustrating nonresistance, six of them Mennonite.

The recent American stage has had one play with a Mennonite theme and two musical comedies based on Amish life and customs. *Papa Is All* (N.Y., 1942) by Patterson Greene makes an average comedy of the universal theme of the overly strict father, using a conservative Mennonite group to carry it. It has no value beyond entertainment. *Plain and Fancy* (N.Y., 1955), by Joseph Stein and Will Glickman, was a very successful musical comedy on the stage, and gives a sympathetic interpretation of the Amish. *By Hex* (1956), written by John Rengier, was little more than a weak reworking of some of the ideas in *Plain and Fancy.*

A number of American Mennonites have written successful religious lyric poetry. Jacob Sudermann, Joanna (Mrs. Herman) Andres, and Miriam (Mrs. Millard) Lind have published poetry in various Mennonite periodicals. Mrs. Lind has to her credit a volume, *Such Thoughts of Thee* (Scottdale, 1952), containing excellent poems, most of which are on religious subjects.

Leo Beachy (1874-1927), of Grantsville, Md., wrote familiar essays on nature and people from his vantage point on Mount Nebo in the Allegheny

Mountains, which were published as a series in the *Christian Monitor* and then in booklet form as *Letters and Pictures for Isabelle* (Scottdale, 1915).

E.H.B.

Earl F. Robacker, *Pennsylvania German Literature* (Philadelphia, 1943); Elizabeth Horsch Bender, "The Mennonite Theme in Contemporary American Fiction," *Proceedings of the Fourth Conference on Mennonite Cultural Problems* (Newton, 1945) 107-34; idem, "Three Amish Novels," *MQR* XIX (1945) 273-84; idem, "The Dream Gate," *MQR* XXIV (1950) 289 f.; Mary Royer, "The Amish and Mennonite Theme in American Literature for Children," *MQR* XV (1941) 147-49; J. B. Cressman, review of *The Trail of the Conestoga* and *Toward Sodom*, *MQR* V (1930) 68-72; John Umble, review of *Rosanna of the Amish*, *MQR* XV (1941) 143-47 and of *Rosanna's Boys*, *MQR* XXIII (1949) 115-17; Elmer Suderman, "The Russo-German Mennonite Theme in the American Novel" (master's thesis, University of Kansas, 1948, unpublished); G. Berg, "Mennonites in Fiction—Gnadenau," *Menn. Life* II (October 1927) 23 f., a review of *Flamethrowers*; Victor Peters, "Frederick Philip Grove," *Manitoba School Journal* IX (October 1948); J. R. Clemens, "Pennsylvania Mennonites in Print 1940-1950," *Menn. Life* VII (1952) 83-85; Charles Burkhart, "The Amish Theme in Recent American Theatricals," *MQR* XXXI (1957) 60-62. Reviews of practically all of the above titles will be found in either *MQR* or *Menn. Life*. The complete text of *Plain and Fancy* was printed in *Theatre Arts* for July 1956, 33-63. Recordings of the complete performance are also available on disks. The text was also published as a libretto in *French's Musical Library* as *Plain and Fancy. A Musical Comedy. Book by Joseph Stein and Will Glickman, Music by Albert Hague, Lyrics by Arnold B. Horwitt* (Samuel French, Inc., New York, 1956).

Lithuania, the name of the district of East Prussia which was called "Gumbinnen" (*q.v.*) from 1918 on. In its northern part, near Tilsit, Mennonites had been living since 1711, known until 1925 as the Lithuanian congregation, later as Memelniederung. Its varied fate has been sketched in the article **Gumbinnen**; its inner history shall be considered here.

The Swiss Mennonite families who had been expelled from the canton of Bern and who settled in the village Jedwilleiten in 1711 must have without exception moved away in the following years, for by 1723 there was no trace left of them (contrary to the view expressed in the pertinent literature, W. Mannhardt, *Die Wehrfreiheit*, 116; E. Randt, 8 f.). Even the rental contracts made out with the Swiss Brethren have been lost or never existed. Furthermore all the Mennonite settlers of the village of Jedwilleiten about 1723 were of West Prussian origin, as their names clearly show: Tobias Barthel, Jacob Janson, Johann Schröder, Peter and Hans Quapp, Heinrich and Peter Jansen, and Peter Rhod.

The West Prussian Mennonites who settled here after 1713 stem almost exclusively from the congregations of Montau, Schönsee, and Thorn; they suffered very severely in their home country of the plague, war, special taxes, and were compelled to emigrate. On the basis of a guarantee of freedom of conscience and exemption from military service given by the King of Prussia, they traveled by the more comfortable sea route to their new home in the Kukernese area, very close to the supposed (or short-lived) Swiss settlement. They did much toward draining this piece of the countryside.

Their stress upon a moral way of life attracted many persons to them from other creeds. A series of transfers of membership occurred, especially of servants who had moved to Lithuania with the Mennonite farmers and who were repelled by the excessive drinking among the members of their faith. This is the only Mennonite church in East and West Prussia in which a considerable number of such transfers took place.

This thriving congregation was granted only eleven years of peaceful existence. In 1724 the king's recruiting officers forcibly broke into the Mennonite homes. To their protests the king replied with the order that they leave the country. And so the 160 Mennonite families moved back into the Werder. Their homes, some of them newly built, had to be abandoned in haste and sold below their value. For their labor in building dikes and ditches they were remunerated by the government. Though the conditions of the sale were just enough, the loss of their new home was painful. Relatives and brethren in the Werder offered them a place to stay, especially in the Thiensdorf church, where each owner of a "hide" of land obligated himself to take in a family and furnish pasture for two cows; but there were no funds to make a new settlement in Polish Prussia. As in all times of need, the Dutch brethren were appealed to for aid.

The refugees acquired 88 hides of land by sale and lease in several localities: in Dierungshof, two miles from Elbing and two miles from Marienburg; in Rudnerweide opposite Mewe; in Klein-Montau, one and one-half miles from Marienburg; in Kamincke, one mile from Marienburg. About 90 families settled in these places. About 24 well-to-do refugee families had already bought land in the Werders and in Schönsee and Montau. There were about 40 destitute families left. These families were offered a favorable opportunity to return to Lithuania, to settle on the Rautenburg estates of Count von Waldburg. Two Mennonite families were already living there, who called them and soon had a total of 47 families together. Although all of them were without funds, they began to drain the land, dig ditches, build houses, and even erected a mill.

Again a Mennonite colony was taking form—they called themselves the Dannenberg church—when the king's command to leave the land unexpectedly struck them. He preferred the Salzburg refugees who would bear arms. All the objections of the count and of the Ministry of War, pointing out the extraordinary capability of the Mennonites, were of no avail. The Mennonites had to leave at once or be liable to "cart punishment"—to be taken to the fortification in a cart; so they left the country that had for six years again been their home.

This time they did not turn to their friends in Polish Prussia, but sailed to Holland. About half of them, 24 families, went to Holland; the rest probably went to the Werders (e.g., Isaak Sperling) and north to Polish Lithuania. The former group, who were evidently planning to return permanently to the home of their origin, were the families of Hans Smit, Tomas Funk, Giels Ewert, Andries, Simon and Hans Krayer, De Jonge Hans Krayer, Jacob Weedler, Daniel Weedler, Heinrich Voet, Jonas Nachtigael, Willem von Steen, Isaac Abraham, George Grubert, Christoph Block, Jan Geerds, Henrich Gronau, Abraham Geerds, Gillis Voot, Hans and Dirk Janssen, David Unrouw, Jacob Abraham; also later, Georg Pauls, Bartel Kruss from Königsberg, Pieter Tietken from Danzig, and Hendrik Lucht from Lithuania.

The Dutch did not welcome this immigration. Their fears were realized. The Lithuanian families —110 persons arrived at Amsterdam after a stormy voyage of three months' duration—were settled in Wageningen and Walcheren at great expense (the offering amounted to 65,000 florins). But after three years there was trouble. It was probably good for both sides that the colonists of Wageningen betook themselves homeward by sea in 1736. The Walcheren settlers followed the next few years.

At the beginning of the reign of Frederick the Great in 1740, West Prussian Mennonites again went to Lithuania, namely, 60 families from the Elbing region. They were joined by some returning from Holland. Although this settlement had to be abandoned on account of the frequent floods, the "Mennonite dam" is evidence of their colonizing work. They were followed in 1758 by 12 Mennonite families who settled in Plauschwarren (on the right bank of the Memel). Gradually more settled.

By 1776 the Lithuanian church numbered 387 souls, and with some variations maintained this number to World War II. The first Dutch *Naamlijst* to mention the congregation of Lithuania is that of 1743. The congregation was then said to belong to the Waterlanders, which may also mean Frisians. The elders were Adrian Sievert and Hans Vooth (Foth), and preachers Hendrik Dirksz and Hendrik Casper. Later *Naamlijsten* name as preachers Salomon Kohnert 1743-*ca*.95, Andries Ewert from at least 1750-*ca*.60, Hendrik Janzen 1754 (elder in 1769-94, Abraham Gerzen 1762-*ca*.75, Jan Rosenfeldt 1762-74, Dirk Jantzen 1769-? (elder 1791), Steffen Baltzer 1771-*ca*.90, Heinrich Roosenvelt 1774-?, Peter Janzen 1787-?, Jacob Evert 1792-?, Franz Janzen 1793-?, and Abraham Rosenfeldt 1799-?. Many of the names on the oldest extant membership list (1774) are those of the settlers of 1713-32, of whom many returned: Ewert, Eckert, Ediger, Gertzen, Ketler, Krause, Kreyger, Lucht, Pauls, Penner, Schmidt, Szepanske, Vodt. Some of the names later disappeared; those who remained to the end are Ewert, Voth, Götzke, Janz, Rosenfeld, Göritz, Hübert, Mertins, Scheffler, Wohlgemuth (the first six names indicate origin in the Graudenz marsh).

This vanishing of names is largely explained by their adherence to nonresistance. The amount of land free of military duty granted to the 64 Mennonites was fixed and could not be exceeded; young people who bought other land obligating them to military service were put out of church. The Mennonites who accepted military service tried unsuccessfully to form an organization of their own in 1855. Thus they were lost to the church. This changed in 1868 when service in the medical and transport corps was permitted, and at the same time the restriction on land ownership was removed. But though the church had always been very strict on nonresistance, during World War I only three or four members took advantage even of the noncombatant service privilege. The government lamented the emigration of so many capable and well-

to-do persons. An opinion of the *Oberpräsidium* of Königsberg in 1842 says, "The outward and moral conduct of the Mennonites . . . is exemplary. Their intellectual training is in general higher than that of the other inhabitants. Their energy and intelligence is conspicuously above that of the other inhabitants . . . . They maintain friendly intercourse with their neighbors, but never take part in the disorders occurring frequently in the lowland. . . . In this way they have had the greatest and most salutary influence directly and by example on the moral and nutritional state as well as on the culture and civilization of their neighbors."

The first little meetinghouse was built in 1767 in Plauschwarren; 120 years later it was completely rebuilt, but in ten years, 1893, it was sold and turned into a dwelling because most of the Mennonites had moved away from Plauschwarren. For most of the members Plauschwarren was too far away, and so they built a chapel on the estate of Grigolienen. It was soon too small, and in 1831 the manor house of Adlig Pokraken was remodeled to serve as a church, and the *Gem. Kal.* 1926-27 lists the congregation by this name.

As to the membership there is only scarce information: there were 233 members in 1774, 239 in 1788, 287 in 1851, 499 in 1882, and 521 in 1887. In 1940 the baptized membership stood at 326. During the last years of its existence the following elders served: Heinrich Foth 1882-1910, Heinrich Pauls 1910-32, and Bruno Götzke 1932-45. H.Q., vDZ.

Inv. Arch, Amst. I, Nos. 1021, 1070 f., 1080, 1085, 1141, 1163, 1165, 1174, 1180, 1237, 1347, 1571-95, 1921-2243; II, 2, Nos. 704 f., 707-37, 739, 743-49, 752 f., 755-62, 764-75, 778, 782, 784-86, 792; Erich Randt, *Die Mennoniten in Ostpreussen und Litauen bis zum Jahre 1772* (Königsberg, 1912); W. Mannhardt, *Die Wehrfreiheit der Altpreussischen Mennoniten* (Marienburg, 1863); H. Pauls "Geschichte unserer Gemeinde Adlig Pokraken in Ostpreussen," *Gem.-Kal.*, 1921; W. Kühler, "Helfende Bruderliebe in der Vergangenheit seitens der holl. Bruderschaft," in Chr. Neff, *Mennonitische Welthilfskonferenz* (Weierhof, 1930); A van Gulik, "Een mislukte kolonisatie te Wageningen," in *DB* 1905, 112-63; 1906, 93-138; G. L. von Reisswitz, *Beiträge zur Kenntnis der Mennonitengemeinden* II (Breslau, 1829) contains an interesting table of members and the land they owned; *ML* II, 660-62.

Litigation is a legal process by which claims are brought before a court and a decision is rendered by a judge with or without the aid of a jury. Although there are variations in Mennonite faith and practice with respect to litigation, in a general way it may be said that the historic Mennonite view on this question, as well as the current attitude of those Mennonites holding most consistently to the principle of nonresistance, is substantially as follows: (1) Members of the Christian brotherhood may not settle differences among themselves by means of litigation in the civil courts. (2) It is inconsistent for the Christian to be the aggressive party in a suit at law against another person, even when legal justice is on his side. (3) When a Christian is summoned to court, charged with violation of the law, he may employ the services of an attorney in his behalf. (4) In case a civil suit is brought against a Christian it is not necessarily inconsistent with the principle of nonresistance for him to defend his case before the court by legal means, although every effort should be made in the spirit of love to make settlement out of court even in case of an unjust plaintiff. (5) Purely routine actions, so-called friendly suits, are allowable.

The basic principle at stake in this position is that of Christian love. The Christian is called to a ministry of reconciliation, entering into the work of Christ, reconciling men unto God. Suits at law directed by one individual against the person of another involve an "offense," condemned in Matthew 18:6 because it creates a barrier between the offender and the offended. If the latter is a fellow Christian, the result is a schism in the body of Christ. If he is a non-Christian, the Christian who brings suit renounces his ministry of reconciliation to those outside the body of Christ. I Corinthians 6:1-7 requires Christians to settle disputes among themselves without resorting to courts at law, whereas the spirit and teaching of the entire New Testament is that the Christian should be ready to suffer wrong rather than to offend another by taking vengeful or punitive action against him.

In case of action brought against the Christian by the state for alleged violation of the law, the principles outlined above would indicate that the accused may not use legal procedures for the denial of an act which has been committed. Legal counsel may be employed, however, to establish the truth in the case; to plead one's guilt and to pray for clemency when this is in order; to establish one's innocence when such is the case; and to claim the supremacy of God's higher law when the latter is in conflict with the laws of men. In case of such defense before the court, however, the procedure must be with the spirit of love and reconciliation, the objective being not personal interest but rather obedience to the will of God, as in the case of Paul and others of the apostles before the authorities who were defending not primarily themselves but the cause of Christian liberty. The same spirit of reconciliation is even more important in case of defense in a civil suit where action is brought by another individual, for here personal relationships are involved and offense must be avoided lest the Christian's ministry of reconciliation be made of none effect. Here the minimum requirement would be that the Christian make every possible effort to settle the case in a peaceable manner outside of court.

It is also clear that in the complex economy of the 20th century more details of the life of the individual Christian are affected by the state and the law than was formerly the case. This has had the effect of greatly enlarging the above-mentioned nonlitigious category of routine legal procedures, including so-called friendly suits. This may include such varied procedures as the clearance of title to real estate, the settlement of estates, the determination of tax responsibilities, the settlement of claims before various civil boards such as workmen's compensation boards, rent control boards, and public utility commissions, appeals in the draft procedures of the Selective Service System, land damage cases involving the right of eminent domain, perhaps even the claims of one corporation against another, and many other types of cases. While these need not involve any conflict of personal relationships there may well be cases

where there is such involvement. A recent conference sponsored by the Peace Problems Committee of the Mennonite Church (MC) for the study of this question recognized this fact and registered its concern that the brotherhood exercise great care to employ only such legal procedures as in any given case will harmonize with the principles of love, nonresistance, and reconciliation outlined above, and which above all do not involve the element of personal offense. The conference also called attention to such procedures as the making and processing of wills, mechanics' liens, mortgages, and many others which may or may not be used in harmony with this spirit, depending on the attitudes and the purposes of those who employ them.

Because of their attitude on litigation Mennonites historically have seldom entered the legal profession, except in those groups which have changed their position or who no longer hold to the principle of nonresistance. Some of Holland's leading attorneys, for example, have been Mennonites, and the current president of the A.D.S. (Dutch General Conference) is a lawyer. There have been a number of lawyers within the membership of the General Conference Mennonite Church in America and there is one lawyer who is a member of the Mennonite Church (MC) and an active layman in the Lancaster Conference. He as well as certain G.C.M. lawyers serve primarily as counsel in nonlitigious matters as the term has here been defined, having a concern to assist their clients in an understanding of the law as it affects their affairs, as well as to direct their legal and business relationships along lines which harmonize with the way of love, nonresistance, and reconciliation.

A notable case of litigation among the American Mennonites in violation of their own principles, and recognized as such by the court, occurred following the Oberholtzer (q.v.) schism when the Boyertown Mennonite meeting was divided, one group following Oberholtzer and the other remaining in the Franconia Conference. For some years both groups used the same meetinghouse, but when the trustees, who were of the Franconia group, in erecting a new meetinghouse specified certain conditions for its use by the Oberholtzer group, the latter filed suit claiming rights in common with the Franconia group. When their petition was denied (1879) they appealed the case and won a decision in their favor (1882). The Franconia trustees now appealed this decision, whereupon the court reversed itself (1883). The Boyertown groups now built two meetinghouses and the Franconia trustees were disciplined by their Conference for having appealed the case, the appeal being interpreted as an aggressive action, whereas no discipline was administered for having appeared as defendants in the first instance.

The court's clear understanding of the Mennonite position on litigation, and of its violation in the Boyertown case, is seen in the judge's statement following his decision in favor of the plaintiff in 1882. The statement follows: "It is to be regretted that the members of this religious organization should have such differences which they cannot harmonize. The Mennonite Church is world-wide renowned for peace, brotherly love, and good will to all, and for the amicable settlement of all their difficulties among themselves in a Christian spirit. The court is the last place to which they should resort, and indeed never should until all other amicable modes at an honest method of adjustment have failed. Once in court, immaterial how it may terminate, feelings of discord are often engendered, that many years will not allay. Neighbors who before were friends are parted forever." (See *Samuel H. Landis, et al. vs. Henry S. Borneman, et al., Supreme Court of Pennsylvania, Eastern District, January Term, 1883, Paper Book of Appellants,* Reading, 1883, XLVIII, XLIX.) In the Mennonite Church (MC) and more conservative groups, members are disciplined for violation of the above standards, and may even be excommunicated. In the remaining groups in America lawsuits are forbidden, except in the G.C.M. group, which discourages them; but discipline is not always strictly applied. In the more conservative congregations in Germany, as well as in France and Switzerland, tradition has remained very strong against members being the aggressive parties in lawsuits. In the remainder of European Mennonitism the tradition has long since ceased to function. G.F.H.

Elvin Souder, "Problems of a Conscientious Objector in Legal Practice," *Proceedings of the Seventh Annual Conference on Mennonite Cultural Problems* (North Newton, 1949) 101-12; Paul Erb, "Nonresistance and Litigation," *MQR* XIII (1939) 75-82.

Lititz Mennonite Church (MC) is located in the center of a strong Mennonite community in Lancaster Co., Pa. Fifty members of the Hess and Hammer Creek congregations appealed for a meetinghouse in the borough (then Warwick). In 1906 this house was built. Jacob H. Hershey (1862-1947), ordained at Olathe, Kan., but a native son, became the first pastor, but it was still part of the Hess-Hammer Creek District. Ephraim N. Eby (1852-1937) served as deacon, and Noah L. Landis (1857-1940) as bishop from the start. Amos S. Horst and Mahlon Zimmerman are the present (1956) bishops, John S. Hess and Melvin Lauver pastors, and Lester B. Wenger deacon. The membership is 203. The church was remodeled in 1952. I.D.L.

Little Eden Camp, a Mennonite (MC) campground of 10 acres, located on the north shore of Portage Lake 1½ miles west of Onekama, Mich., and 1½ miles east of Lake Michigan, 240 miles almost due north of Goshen, Ind. Some 30 years earlier a lumber camp had been established on the plot, which was later sold to the Church of the Brethren for a recreation camp site, who in turn sold it to a group of Mennonites from Archbold, Ohio, in 1944.

The Mennonite group in 1945 organized a non-profit corporation known as "Little Eden Camp Ground Association Inc.," with 53 charter members. Association membership in 1955 totaled 84, made up of members of the Mennonite Church (MC) from Illinois, Indiana, Ohio, and Pennsylvania. The association is governed by a board of directors elected annually. Its assets totaled $37,100 in 1955.

Little Eden operates on a summer schedule beginning the last week in June and closing the first week in September, usually set up for nine groups of one week each. The 1955 season included five weeks for children including high-school age. The four weeks for adults included: Church Music and Young People, Christian Business and Professional, Christian Fellowship—Family, Farmers, and the Goshen College faculty retreat of two days. Facilities include a hotel building housing the administrative office, kitchen and dining room, social room, auditorium, second-floor sleeping rooms, and a third-floor dormitory, 17 cabins, a number of which house more than one family. The total capacity of the camp is approximately 125, although at times children's camps have enrolled as many as 200. L.A.B.

Little Visitor, an illustrated eight-page paper for children, published experimentally for the Christmas season of 1878 by H. B. Brenneman, Elkhart, Ind. Brenneman was the "Brother Henry" whose articles appeared frequently in the Children's Department of the *Herald of Truth.* There were no further issues. N.P.S.

Littlefield (Tex.) Church of God in Christ Mennonite Church, now extinct, was organized in the summer of 1917 with 60 members under the leadership of J. K. Esau and C. W. Toews. The first members came from Kansas, North Dakota, and Manitoba in 1915. A meetinghouse was built in 1917. Pioneer hardships and pressure of World War I drove many of these to their former localities. The remaining six or seven families continued worship and Sunday school in their homes after the church building was sold and moved. Visiting ministers from various places in Kansas, Oklahoma, and Texas came occasionally to give pastoral care. Ben T. Koehn moved here in 1938 to assume the pastorate for several years. The congregation was dissolved on Feb. 3, 1942, its members having moved to various congregations in Kansas and California. A.R.T.

Littlefield (Tex.) Mennonite Brethren Church was organized in 1915. The church building was erected in 1916. The first permanent pastor was J. J. Wiebe, followed by A. L. Schellenberg. When Schellenberg was called to lead the M.B. Publishing House in Hillsboro, Kan., the congregation was without a minister and gradually disintegrated, the members moving to other M.B. communities. The highest membership was 100. P.C.H.

Liturgy: see **Order of Service.**

Litwiller (Litwiler), a Mennonite family mentioned in the Palatinate Mennonite census lists in 1685, where the name of Hans Leutweyler appears. Peter Litwiller (1809-78) of Alsace migrated to Ontario in 1829, where he became a bishop in the Wilmot Amish Mennonite Church. His son Christian (1848-1924) and his grandson Peter (1869-1930) were ministers in the Ontario A.M. Church. A great-grandson Nelson (1898-) and the latter's son John are Mennonite (MC) missionaries in Uruguay. Between 1834 and 1850 the Litwiller family came to central Illinois near Metamora. Later the family also settled near Hopedale and Gridley, Ill. Among the ministers in Illinois have been Joseph Litwiller (1836-1914) of the Hopedale Church (MC), Jonas

Litwiller (1865-1944) of the Pleasant Grove (MC) Church, and John W. Litwiller (1874-1955) of the Boynton Central Conference Mennonite Church. Simon Litwiller (1880-1956) was the bishop of the Hopedale (*q.v.*) Mennonite Church (MC) since 1925. John W. and Simon were grandsons of Joseph Litwiller. The Illinois Litwillers have their background in Butler Co., Ohio. Several Litwillers are preachers in the Church of God in Christ Mennonite congregation at Ithaca, Mich.   M.G.

Livermore, Cal., the location of Mennonite Civilian Public Service unit No. 150, which served in the United States Veterans' Hospital at that place, an institution for tubercular patients. On Dec. 1, 1945, a total of 117 CPS men arrived at the hospital, but the number declined in the following months because of transfers and demobilization. The unit was closed in December 1946.   M.G.

M. Gingerich, *Service for Peace* (Akron, Pa., 1949) 273 f.

Liverpool Mennonite Church: see **Manchester.**

Livine (Vincken) **Verwee,** wife of Jan Vervest (*q.v.*), died in prison at Brugge, Belgium, on Sept. 20, 1558. Probably born at Gent in Flanders, she wandered about with her husband, living for some time in Gent, Amsterdam, Dordrecht, and other towns and from about 1554 on at Brugge. After attending Mennonite meetings for a number of years she was baptized on her faith in 1555 at Brugge by Elder Gillis van Aken (*q.v.*). In the summer of 1558 a meeting she was attending was surprised and a number of members of the congregation, including Livine and her husband, were arrested. Livine died in prison, her husband having also died in prison about a month before. (Verheyden, *Brugge,* 44, No. 26.)   vDZ.

Livingston County, Ill., Mennonite churches were the result of the expansion movements of the Amish Mennonites beginning about 1860 from the timberstream areas to the "Gridley Prairie." The Waldo Mennonite (MC) Church was the mother church in the area; the Flanagan (GCM) and Meadows (GCM) and the Salem Defenseless, now Evangelical Mennonite, congregations were formed largely from dissatisfied elements from the Waldo group. The Salem Orphanage and the Meadows Old People's Home were initiated by the Defenseless group, but now receive support from all the Mennonite groups. Today there are approximately 1,000 Mennonites in Livingston County. The Meadows Church and the Meadows Old People's Home, which are part of the Gridley Prairie settlement, are just across the line in McLean County.   T.R.S.

Livingston Church of God in Christ Mennonite Church, located at Livingston, Merced Co., Cal., was organized in 1943 after the Winton church became too crowded. A meetinghouse was built with a seating capacity of 200. In 1953 the church had a membership of 110 with ministers Jesse Koehn, John A. Koehn, and S. A. Nichols.   J.A.K.

Livingston (Cal.) Mennonite Brethren Church was organized on June 9, 1922, with A. Z. Sawatzky as temporary leader. In May 1927 the church attendance was around 100. J. M. Ens then became the leader. In the following years the people that had moved to Livingston settled more in the direction of Winton, and the two groups then organized as the Winton M.B. Church (*q.v.*), discontinuing Livingston.   P.C.H.

L. K., author of a Dutch hymnbook (Wolkan, *Lieder,* 113 ff., 155), is Lenaert Klock or Clock (*q.v.*).

Lo, Peter (b. 1530), a Protestant theologian, born at Elberfeld, Germany, where his father was a schoolteacher and secretary of the council. In 1552 he was made chaplain in his native town. Charged with "Anabaptism" and threatened with imprisonment, he fled to Francis II, Count of Waldeck at Beyenburg. When he attempted to return to Elberfeld he was arrested. But he managed to escape from prison, and in March 1558 he moved to Beyenburg and entered the service of the count.

In 1565 William, Duke of Jülich-Cleve-Berg, asked Lo to "convert" the Anabaptists held in Blankenberg and Bensberg. Lo disputed with them on June 23-24 in Blankenberg and June 28-July 2 in Bensberg. Not only ducal councilors and other persons of the court, but the duke himself took an active interest in these conversations. In order to induce "poor Martin," an Anabaptist preacher, to recant, the official called his attention to the great interest of His Highness in the salvation of his soul. On the question of the salvation of unbaptized infants Lo agreed with the Anabaptists but he tried to justify infant baptism "in a sort of continuing proof" and stated that those who despise the sacrament are doomed to eternal damnation, "since they made God a liar and mistreated Christ, and destroyed the symbol of the new covenant." But the Anabaptists stood by their position: little children cannot believe, and without faith baptism is an empty form. Martin Wilach declared that the prevailing church was "no longer a church of Christians but a church of heathen," and "matters of faith are not the concern of the temporal ruler." Lo is said to have won some of them over, but most of them remained true to their convictions. In 1650 there were still some Anabaptists the Blankenberg area.   W.W.

K. W. Bouterwek, "Die Reformation in Wuppertal und P. Lo's Anteil an derselben," in *Ztscht des Berg. Geschichtsvereins* IV (1867) 273-336; Nebe, "Drei Briefe über Peter Lo's Verhandlungen mit den Wiedertäufern in Blankenberg 1565," *loc. cit.* XXXIV (1899) 1-15; Schönneshofer, *Geschichte des Bergischen Landes* (Elberfeld, 1895) 202; H. Niemöller, *Peter Lo* (1907); *ML* II, 674.

Loag's Corner Mennonite Mission (MC), located in a schoolhouse on the Elverson-Honey Brook Road, Chester Co., Pa., was conducted by the Weaverland Missions Committee under the Lancaster Mennonite Conference. It was opened early in July 1922 and continued with some interest until October 1931, when it closed. The Weaverland ministers supplied the preaching mission, and members from the surrounding churches, some of whom lived near by, supplied the workers.   I.D.L.

Lobach, Johannes, was arrested on Feb. 26, 1717, with Jacob and Willem Grahe (*q.v.*) and four other Mennonites in Solingen and taken to Düsseldorf, Germany, where they languished in prison for three years, until they were released at the intervention of Holland (*DB* 1861, 50-85). The name Lobach was also found in the Mennonite congregation of Kriegsheim (*q.v.*) in the 17th century. In the 19th century there was in the Crefeld Mennonite Church a respected mercantile family with this name. (*ML* II, 674.) NEFF.

Lobenbach, a hamlet near Stein on the Kocher River in Baden, Germany, the seat of a Mennonite congregation in the 19th century which met alternately here and in Lautenbach near Neckarsulm. Lobenbacherhof is first mentioned as a congregation in A. Huntzinger's *Religions-, Kirchen- und Schulwesen der Mennoniten* (Speyer, 1830) as having 3 families with 20 persons. In 1857, according to J. Mannhardt's *Namens-Verzeichnis,* it had 40 baptized members, with Christian Funk of Kochendorf as preacher. In 1888 Mannhardt's *Jahrbuch* calls the congregation Lautenbach-Lobenbach with Heinrich Landes as elder (1885-1918) with 52 baptized members. By 1904 it is called Lobenbach-Heilbronn in the *Gemeinde-Kalender,* and by 1915 Heilbronn (*q.v.*) alone. (*ML* II, 674.) H.S.B.

Lober, Julius, a South German Anabaptist preacher; little is known about his work. We have only his statements as given in the records of his trial in 1531, which are however important, because they form the basis for theological and legal opinion concerning the punishment of Lober and his fellow prisoners. They are important for an evaluation of the Anabaptist movement in Franconia, for their examination corrected many false assertions. For example, the Anabaptists of that region had been considered revolutionary and it was thought that they had their women in common; but this was out of the question in view of the strictness of the South German Anabaptist morals. They had been put on a plane with the "Puschenhamern," a small group of misguided people who based their manner of living on the dreams of their leader Hans Schmied, and practiced divorce and remarriage as well as community of goods (Wiswedel, II, 31). They did not baptize persons joining their circle (*TA* 224-28). Nevertheless they were counted Anabaptists. This furnished a legal basis, in addition to religious separation, for the suppression of the Anabaptist movement. In his cross-examinations Lober was therefore expressly questioned on these points. But there was no evidence of the truth of these charges.

Thanks to Lober an important document has been preserved for Anabaptist history which was taken away from him at the time of his arrest; viz., a list of the places in which Anabaptists had been executed for their faith in 1527-31 along the Rhine and the Danube. It gives the number of martyrs for a series of towns and is one of the few sources which give summarizing information about Anabaptist martyrdoms, though it cannot be considered exhaustive (reprinted in Beck, 310-12; see also **Palatinate**).

Lober was a tailor in Zürich. In Strasbourg he came in contact with the Anabaptists, when a journeyman reproved his sinful life and instructed him from the Bible. After several years of association with the Brethren he was baptized by Wilhelm Reublin (*q.v.*). Then he went to Bruchsal (*q.v.*), an Anabaptist center in the Kraichgau. Here Lober was chosen leader of the congregation of about 500 members. But he led them only a short while. Five members of his congregation had already died as martyrs. Many families were planning to move to Moravia. Lober had been there previously and was sent by his congregation to visit the Brethren in Moravia with a letter in 1531. On the way he visited Anabaptists in Franconia. His wife during this time stayed in the home of Ulrich Hutscher (*q.v.*) in Tief (Oberntief) and was imprisoned with him at Hoheneck near Windsheim. When Lober learned this he went there on April 8 to find out the reason for the seizure. The bailiff Albrecht Gailing questioned him and arrested him too.

On April 10, 1531, the bailiff reported the case to George, Margrave of Brandenburg, and on April 16 the prisoners were cross-examined by three clergymen, by Andreas Althamer (*q.v.*), who had already attacked the Anabaptists in several widely distributed pamphlets, by Sigmund Schneeweis, and by Johann Rürer. The main topic of discussion was infant baptism. Lober could not be convinced that it was Scriptural; nor did he accept the statements of the theologians that a child could believe. He declared that he would stay by his conception of baptism which had been administered to him as an adult. Nor could he accept Luther's teaching on communion; the body of Christ had come for his comfort, and through the blood of Christ he had been saved from his sins. Obedience and taxes are due the government. But he could not swear an oath. Of community of women he knew nothing. "If anyone should teach him such a thing he would say that this doctrine was of the devil and not of God." Nor did he advocate community of goods, but he was ready to aid his brother who was in need, without compulsion, from brotherly love. The punishment of the wicked belongs only to God.

After the conclusion of the cross-examination and the attempts to convert them Lober stated that he would not desist from his faith; likewise spoke his fellow prisoner Ulrich Hutscher. An additional attempt by the clergymen to make the prisoners yield their faith was fruitless, whereas the third prisoner, Bernhard Weik of Bruchsal, begged for mercy and declared that he was ready to join the state church (*TA* 217-29).

Margrave George was undecided as to the further steps to take with these prisoners, and asked advice of Nürnberg. The theologians and jurists of Nürnberg, of whom the council had requested an opinion, were unanimous "that this sect of the Anabaptists is doubtless a public error and a seduction," but they did not agree on the punishment. The lenience of the theologians' opinion is surprising. But as Jörg pointed out it was based on regard for the emperor and the imperial cities. Since it was impossible to punish Catholic error, as Andreas Osiander explained to the council, it would "be unbecoming to punish one part with the sword and the other part not at all; for it is well known and badly spoken of what the papists do in the corners, one knows it and yet will not punish it" (Jörg, 706).

The opinion of the theologians, dated April 29, 1531, advised that error in the Christian faith should be wiped out through indoctrination in the Word of God and not with the sword. The government should not interfere in matters of faith unless there is sedition in addition to false doctrine. Some of the theologians were also of the opinion that the imperial laws and the regulations of the Swabian League against the Anabaptists were in many points contrary to the Word of God and too tyrannical. Community of goods was no reason for inflicting severe punishment on the Anabaptists, since it could be carried out in a Christian spirit and had even been introduced by the apostles for the alleviation of distress. If the Anabaptists act as they say, their words would be blameless. But if they should attempt compulsory sharing of goods, then it would be the duty of the government to interfere. Lober and Hutscher should be banished from the country as obstinate and separated members of the church. Several theologians also favored detaining them for a while longer and giving them opportunity to be converted. But the other theologians did not consider prison a means to compel return to the church; knowledge of the truth must come freely and without terror, alone through the Word. Imprisonment would make these people more obstinate.

The jurists said the imperial law which prohibited Anabaptism on penalty of death was much too sharp for Christians, but the government could decree lifelong exile. If one then returned, he could be punished corporally for transgression of the law. Lober, because he was a priest and practiced community of goods which would certainly give rise to revolt and civil war, and likewise Hutscher, should be asked on the rack who their brethren were, where they lived, what they thought of possessions, whether they should be shared forcibly, and whether they did not believe that the government should be destroyed. If they had that kind of opinions they should be punished accordingly. But if they did not, they should still be branded with some kind of physical sign, either with an iron or by having their ears cut off and be driven out of the country with a lash. Longer imprisonment was not recommended.

The Ansbach (margravate) government was not adverse to the counsel of the Nürnberg lawyers. Lober and Hutscher were questioned again. Religious questions were scarcely touched. An attempt was made to charge them with sedition, and to make them say that it was their goal to lead the people into "a false appearance of a pretended good life, to form a big army, and to destroy all government" (*TA* 236).

On May 6, 1531, Lober was confronted with ten questions relating to these points. He denied having deviated from the pure teaching of the Gospel. They reproached him with misunderstanding the commandment of Christ to baptize and demanded that he desist from his "error," but he refused. Then the charge was made, that behind the "favorable and hypocritical front" something else lurked, namely, the elimination of all government and the com-

munizing of all goods, which Lober denied. There must be governments, he declared; one must obey the state whether good or bad. He would undertake nothing against the government; only in matters of faith it was better to obey God than man. To the question, who their heads were, he answered that he knew of no head but God in heaven; those who teach them the Word of God they call shepherds, teachers, preachers, and leaders; they are considered no different from other brethren and among them there was no respect of person.

Since Lober refused to recant he "was tortured three times." The records say that he prayed God to give him grace to overcome the torture and to be true to his belief. His tormentors apparently pitied him, for he called out to them that they should continue to carry out their orders; for their superiors did not know what they were doing (*TA* 239).

On May 12 he was told that Christ had not taught baptism, but repentance; he replied that he had repented, and been baptized upon his faith, adopted a life meet for repentance and now he was in God's mercy. Luther and other Christian preachers did not preach baptism as it had been taught at the time of the apostles; nor did they carry out apostolic discipline, since they did not apply the ban and tolerated the wicked in the church. He would not desist from his faith. He knew that he could stand before God only if he relied on Christ the Lord and not on men (*TA* 245).

The Ansbach government then asked Nürnberg for another opinion on the punishment of Lober and Hutscher. The theologians taking part in formulating this opinion were Friedrich Pistorius, Georg Pesler, Hektor Pomer, Dominicus Schleuper, Andreas Osiander, Blasius Stöckel, and Sebastian Fürnschilt; and the jurists were Dr. Scheurl, Dr. Hepstein, Dr. Gugel, Dr. Mullner, Christoph Coler, and Hans Rider. The theologians called attention to the wide dissemination of Anabaptism. Therefore they urged caution. The consultations dealt only with questions of faith. If they wanted to act in accord with the Word of God, they must consider the prisoners as persons "who had temporarily erred and had committed no other deeds." They should be instructed kindly, since they neither understood nor interpreted the Bible correctly. They were not guilty of sedition. But if they should not be amenable to instruction, but persisted in their error, they should be expelled from the country, since in that case they would be openly resisting the government. Osiander considered it questionable to punish these poor people whose intentions were of the best; but on the other hand this error could not be tolerated.

The lawyers also dealt only with questions of faith and stated that there could be no talk of sedition or of the suppression of the government. Scheurl declared that the prisoners had "let themselves be baptized against the command of God." Since they persisted in their error, they had also "acted to the offense of the government and of Christian love." One could therefore say with a good conscience that they had forfeited their life. But because this error was greatly on the increase it was necessary to treat these prisoners accordingly. If they could be made to recant, they should be branded on the cheek or forehead because of disregard for the transgression of the law, and then be expelled from the country. Gugel and Mullner concurred in this opinion. As a punishment for rebaptism they recommended branding or cutting off the ears. Mullner states that since Lober did not reject the government nor did the Anabaptists wish to compel anyone to give up his goods, the prisoners should be penalized only as misguided, erroneously baptized persons (*TA* 259-62). On the same day the mayor and the council of Nürnberg wrote to Ansbach that it was difficult to take action against the Anabaptists. If they were only misguided Nürnberg would, if the case were theirs, punish them by exile.

The Ansbach government was not satisfied with Nürnberg's advice. Now the Schmalkaldian League meeting, which was about to be held at Frankfurt, was to make the decision. The Ansbach emissaries tried to secure a resolution which would forbid the toleration of Anabaptists in the regions under its jurisdiction and which would leave it open to each government to penalize Anabaptists who after instruction by the clergy would not desist from their faith. But the League declared itself on June 9, 1531, not authorized to give advice on the punishment of Anabaptists. Finally the case was taken under advisement by the Landtag committee of Brandenburg. In a decision at Kosten on March 21, 1532, they agreed on exile; "only the very obstinate should be punished" (Schornbaum, *Politik,* 500, 516).

What the Ansbach government finally did with Lober is not known. Nor do we hear anything more of him.   HEGE.

Beck, *Geschichts-Bücher; J. E. Jörg, Deutschland in der Revolutions-Periode 1522-1526* (Freiburg, 1851); *TA Bayern* I; Karl Schornbaum, *Zur Politik des Markgrafen Georg von Brandenburg* (Munich 1906); W. Wiswedel, *Bilder* II; *Ztscht für die Geschichte des Oberrheins* LVIII, 81; *ML* II, 675-77.

Lochem, van (van Loghem, van Loghum), a Mennonite family of the Netherlands, living at Enschedé, province of Overijssel, since before 1572. Until about 1700 it was also found at Burgsteinfurt, Westphalia, Germany, which apparently was its original residence. Later branches of this family are also found at Almelo, Deventer, Winterswijk, Amsterdam, and other Dutch towns. It could not be ascertained when this family turned from Catholicism to Mennonitism, but at least in 1626 Dries van Lochem of Enschedé was a Mennonite, as were his children and their descendants. They usually were businessmen and textile manufacturers. The sons of Lambert van Lochem, Herman (1695-1782) and Jan van Lochem (1691-1766), were the founders, in 1728, of a large textile plant at Enschedé (half-linen and later cotton). Some members went into the magistracy, e.g., Hendrik van Lochem (1774-1843), who published some volumes of poems, and his son Hendrik van Lochem (1808-81), both of whom served as town clerk of Deventer. Jan van Lochem of Enschedé (1774-1829), a textile manufacturer, was burgomaster of Enschedé 1818-29. Many members of the van Lochem family served the Mennonite Church as deacons. By marriage they became related with a number of well-known Mennonite families, such as Stenfort, Warnaars, Blijdenstein, Willink, Hofkes, Paschen, Naber, ten

Cate, Bavink, Nieuwenhuis, Eppenhoff, van Delden, van Dalen.   vDZ.

G. Heeringa, *et al., Uit het verleden der Doopsgezinden in Twenthe* (Borne, n.d.) 32-46; P. Beets, *Stamboek der Willingen* (Deventer, 1767); J. H. Warnaars, *Het geslacht Warnaars* (Amsterdam, 1920); *N.N.B.Wb.* I, 1278; VI, 960.

Locher, Hans, of Munich, Germany, author of the tract, *Ein tzeytlang geschwigner christl. Bruder,* etc., 1523, who chastises the evils prevalent in the Catholic Church, and also the "traitor" Luther, and who presents views that resemble those of the Anabaptists. Nothing else is known of him. (Rembert, *Wiedertäufer,* 103; *ML* II, 677.)   NEFF.

Lochmaier, Leonhard, a Hutterite martyr. After the death of Hutter it was clear that Moravia and not Tirol was the center of the Austrian Anabaptist movement. But this does not mean that there were no men of energetic action for the Anabaptist cause left in Tirol. One such man was Leonhard Lochmaier. He stemmed from Freising, had been a Catholic priest eight years, was baptized in 1526 by Jörg Krautschlögel (*q.v.*), who was burned at the stake in 1527 with his wife; then he served the brotherhood in Moravia, Lower Austria, and the adjoining parts of Slovakian Hungary.

In 1538 he was in the upper valley of the Inn, in the valleys of the Oetz and Pitz at the side of Offrus Griesinger (*q.v.*), where he gathered a congregation. But in the last days of April he with nine companions, George Übel of Lenbach near Brixen, Hans Nass of Tirdl-Meran, Ruepp Haas, Cyprian, and Veit Kuhn of Hueb, Veronika Klasen, Manhart's wife Ursula Hellriegel, Anna Mark, and Margareta Kofer, fell into the hands of Eitelhans Gienger, magistrate of St. Petersburg. Veit Kuhn declared himself to ready to recant immediately and was pardoned. The rest were taken for trial to Petersburg. Because Lochmaier was a priest, and had been seized in the bishopric of Brixen, he was turned over to the ecclesiastical court.

By this time the cantonal government of Tirol had come to the conclusion that the barbarous methods being used were not producing the desired results, and that more could be done to convert the Anabaptists by persuasion. In Dr. Gallus Müller (*q.v.*), court preacher in Innsbruck and city pastor in Tirol-Meran, they had a well-qualified person for this task.

The efforts of Gallus Müller and the suffragan Albrecht of Brixen were successful, for on July 18, 1538, the government was asked to pardon Lochmaier. The government, believing that pardon would make the best impression on the populace as well as on the Anabaptists, complied. Indeed the vice-governor and chancellor of Brixen announced that Lochmaier had made his recantation "sincerely and devoutly" in the local church and had given undoubted signs that he meant it, and "if he were pardoned he would do much good for the eradication of this sect." Ferdinand made the request that Lochmaier be detained in Brixen another year, so that the constancy of his character and conduct could be tested. This information was given to the councilors in Brixen with the request that they henceforth use Lochmaier for the conversion of his former companions.

But in the meantime a change had taken place in Lochmaier. When the suffragan and vicar Jörg Stemmler read him the letter from the government he replied that he had not requested Dr. Gallus Müller to trouble himself on his account with the king and would not be in a position to thank him for it. When they showed him his recantation he said "he had done this out of fear and terror foolishly, he himself didn't know how; he had repented twice as often as the number of hairs upon his head." When he was told that he should now go out and convert the Anabaptists, he replied, "he would not only not deflect them from their faith, he would stay with it himself." At the same time he attempted to make contact with Griesinger who was imprisoned there. Perhaps it was the news of the imprisonment of this Anabaptist leader that moved Lochmaier's heart so powerfully.

The government was informed about this incident on Sept. 6, 1538. It was reported that Lochmaier made an attempt to free himself by removing his chains. Dr. Müller immediately sent a report to King Ferdinand; and the king replied that they should halt the pardoning of Lochmaier. The government wrote that since only worse things were to be feared from Griesinger and the other prisoners, they should not hesitate to take the necessary steps. The Brixen authorities wrote to Ferdinand that they knew no other course but to commit them both to the flames.

On Sept. 16 the Brixen council discussed whether Griesinger and Lochmaier should be executed publicly or quietly. They decided that "Griesinger, who is gentle and quiet in speech, would move many of the people. Therefore we are planning to let the law take its course in all secrecy." Dr. Müller remained interested in Lochmaier to the last moment and tried again to persuade him to recant. That displeased the chancellor Han. "Good Dr. Gall is deceived by Lochmaier's hypocrisy and patience, which is not usual with the Anabaptists. In reality he is a malicious preacher, who has for nearly ten years been casting pious folk into misfortune. If he should get out again, he would do worse than Hutter, who did a great deal of damage. If he is let out again nothing else can be believed but that he will return to the Anabaptists where his pregnant wife is." To his wife Bärbel, Lochmaier had Griesinger write a letter thanking her for her love. "God has helped me again; I know that I have sadly grieved you; pardon and forgive me!" And Griesinger wrote, "Leonhard, to be sure, fell in weakness; but God be praised he is confessing the Lord again." In a second letter he said, "We were supposed to have been executed before this but something suddenly interfered."

Griesinger was put to death on Oct. 31, 1538. In his last letter to the brotherhood in Moravia Lochmaier wrote, "Why I am so long imprisoned only God knows. I have consoled myself to die with pious Offerus, but God the Lord has denied it to me; I am waiting every day like a poor lamb. But the preachers must have their arbitrary way and

take off my priestly robes and only then deliver me to the hangman."

The conclusion of the degradation was delayed; for only a bishop may perform it. On Oct. 8 the suffragan had died and Prince-bishop Georg was outside the country. Not until Lochmaier's degradation was complete was he put to death with a sword, "several days after Offerus." The principles he defended against Dr. Gall and the other Catholic clergy were those of the Hutterian Brethren.

Lochmaier left two letters written in prison; one to his wife Bärbel, and the other to the brotherhood in Austria and Moravia. These letters reveal the location of the Bruderhofs in Moravia, "where they might serve each other without hindrance." These were at Tischnowitz (leader Brother Oswald), Rohrbach (Brother Matthes), Butschowitz (Brother Ulrich) at Austerlitz, Auspitz, Schackwitz, Rackwitz, Pilgram, Kostel, Znaim, and Popitz; in Lower Austria at Nannsgarten and Walltersdorf.

Two songs written by Lochmaier have been preserved: a devotional hymn of ten stanzas, "Lobt Gott den Herrn, ir fromme Kindt," and "Verlass mich nicht o Herr, mein Gott."   LOSERTH.

Beck, *Geschichts-Bücher*, 137; Wolkan, *Geschicht-Buch*, 139-42; Zieglschmid, *Chronik*; Loserth, *Anabaptismus; idem*, "Zwei biographische Skizzen aus der Zeit der Wiedertäufer in Tirol," in *Ztscht der Ferdin. für Tirol und Vorarlberg* III, No. 39, pp. 288 ff.; *Mart. Mir.* D 42, E 448; *ML* II, 677-79.

Lochy. In many localities in Moravia, especially in the southern part of the country, there are subterranean passages and rooms made by human hands, called "lochy" by the Slavic population. They are, however, by no means peculiar to Moravia; for similar ones are known in western Slovakia, in southern Bohemia, and also in Bavaria and Alsace. They are especially common in Upper and Lower Austria where they are called "earth stalls" or "earth holes."

The interest in these subterranean buildings has continued for more than half a century and the results of investigation to clarify their origin, the time of their creation, and their purpose has been written down in numerous essays and in two separate volumes. The greatest credit in the investigation of these holes in Austria and Moravia is due P. Lambert Karner, a Benedictine monk of Lower Austria, who investigated personally nearly all the more important ones known in his time, and described, measured, and sketched them minutely. More than 25 years of his life he devoted to this strenuous study; he wrote the results in the comprehensive work, *Die künstlichen Höhlen aus alter Zeit*. For future investigation Karner's work is of special value for its exact and very detailed descriptions.

But this is not the case with the conclusions which Karner deducted from his information and experiences. Scholarship, in this case represented by the noted archaeologist Oswald Menghin, has shown Karner's views on the age and purpose of these passageways to be wrong. In opposition to Karner, who considered the holes as prehistoric or at least very early historical places for a mysterious religious cult, Menghin believes that they are medieval or modern creations, which served the populace as a hiding place in times of war and distress.

This sober view, which is shared by M. Hörnes, R. Much, and the Moravian archaeologist J. L. Cervinka, has since been adopted by nearly all scholarly investigators. Nevertheless the romantic view of these holes has persisted to the present, especially through the efforts of Franz Kiesslinger, who, in his work *Ueber das Rätsel der Erdställe,* goes even further than Karner. Kiessling thinks them to be the work of a prehistoric race of dwarfs inhabiting Central Europe.

But even the sober view of the subterranean passages can be criticized. Menghin and his followers explain their origin by the assumption that they were built by the people for security in times of war. But it has been shown that the Moravian, Austrian, Bavarian, and Alsatian passages agree in their general layout as well as in typical details, so that one can speak of a unified system. It is hard to assume that people living so far apart would have built hiding places which agree even in measurements. On the other hand some of the holes are by no means primitive creations, but give evidence of greater knowledge, imagination, and skill than can be attributed to the medieval peasants. Contrary to all previous explanations of the rise, origin, and purpose of these passageways it can be said with assurance that at least those in Moravia were made by the Hutterian Brethren, who appeared there as early as the second third of the 16th century, lived here nearly a century, remnants maintaining themselves there until almost the middle of the 17th century. More than any of the religious brotherhoods in Moravia at that time, they were persecuted because of their religious faith. The first great persecution, which was to banish them, indeed to eliminate them from the country, was begun at the command of King Ferdinand, and was so severe that nothing was left for them but to flee into the mountains and forests or in the truest sense of the word to disappear below the earth into the holes they had created as a shelter.

For this idea there are evidences in their chronicles in which I shall cite only several of the more important which can be found in the books by Rudolf Wolkan (*Geschicht-Buch*), Joseph Beck (*Geschichts-Bücher*), and Zieglschmid (*Chronik*). Thus in the description of the persecution of 1548 it is said that the Brethren "made holes and pits in the earth like foxes for their home. However hard it is for a person to endure, they would have accepted it with great thanks if it had only been permitted and granted them. But they could not stay for any length of time, they were spied out and pursued." In Popice (near Auspitz), "where they also stayed below the earth in pits, there came godless persons who made a fire before the hole and wanted to suffocate them with the smoke or smoke them out. But they were driven away and prevented. Especially around the Meyberg (in the Pollau Mountains in south Moravia), they had in many places pits and holes in which they stayed for a while with their children; also in the clefts of the rocks . . . of the Meyberg, and also in other localities in the country where they were able" (Wolkan, 249; Beck, 186 f.). During the persecution of 1550 the lord of Liechtenstein learned that "the Brethren were living in caves and holes on his land" in his Nikolsburg domain. But while he was preparing to get them out they vanished (Wolkan, 251 f.; Beck, 189 f.). Another place in the Hutterian chronicle states that during the six years of the persecution they lived in "holes of the earth" (Beck, 184 and 191), which is confirmed by other chronicles. In later times, when the Hutterites already had many established settlements, even as late as the first decade of the 17th century, thus not long before their exile into Slovakia, enemies attacking their houses discovered their "concealed holes in the earth" (Wolkan, 561, 556, 558, etc.). These references prove that during the persecution in Moravia the Hutterian Brethren built subterranean hiding places which they described as "holes in the earth," pits, and "secret archways" (the holes really are arched).

It would be difficult to deny the great probability that these passageways are identical with the modern "lochy," as the name "Löcher" suggests. But in addition there is a tradition still current among the people which connects these holes with the Anabaptists. The individual volumes of the topographical Moravian geography published in Brno show that the inhabitants of Syrovin assert that the "lochy" were hiding places of the Anabaptists. Also the holes in Lanzhot (Landshut) as well as in Nykolcice (Nikelschütz), where the holes exist precisely at the places where the Hutterites had their Bruderhofs, and also in Tynec (Teinitz) tradition calls the holes Anabaptist. In Tvrdonice (Turnitz), where the people still relate that the persecuted Anabaptists had lived in long cellars, some of which still exist, these cellars are doubtless holes. Hence local tradition completely corroborates the Hutterian chronicles.

If we then assume that the Anabaptists were the originators—this does not mean of all the holes—we can explain much that has hitherto defied explanation. For instance, knowing that the Anabaptists did not meet the enemy with a weapon, not even when their life was threatened, we can more easily understand the complicated and sometimes apparently irrational plan of the holes. Thus when a passage keeps changing its direction and when a pit is interrupted and continues on a higher level which can be reached only by a special tunnel and when the same passage in a great arc returns to its original point of entry, all of this serves to give time to the victim to escape from his pursuers, and obviously to confuse the opponent.

The assumption of an Anabaptist origin for these passages explains a number of particulars of the internal arrangement, such as the various chambers in which the passages always end, the niches for watchmen and lights, and especially the clever foresightedness with which these passages were planned and executed. It is known that there was among the Hutterites a concentration of skilled craftsmen and highly intelligent personalities. Since we know that the Hutterian Brethren had a strongly centralized organization which regulated every activity according to unified lines, we understand the source of the unity of the subterranean passages. And these passages occurring from Alsace to Slovakia are located in precisely those places where the Anabaptists had their settlements for a long time.

These explanations by no means constitute a complete solution of the problem of the subterranean passage called lochy or earth stalls and earth holes, but they bring concrete evidence of Anabaptist origin for at least the Moravian holes, and thereby point to possibilities which may yet lead to the final solution of this interesting question.   K.C.

L. Karner, *Künstliche Höhlen aus alter Zeit* (Vienna, 1903); F. Kiesslinger, *Ueber das Rätsel der Erdställe* (Vienna, 1923, 2d ed., 1925; discussed by H. Mötefindt in *Wiener Prähistorische Ztscht* XI, 1924, 154); O. Menghin, "Ueber das Alter der Erdställe und Hausberge," in *Wiener Präh. Ztscht* III (1916) 101-10; J. L. Cervinka, "Loch," umole, jeskyne na Morave in *Casopis morav. musea zemskeho* (Periodical of the Museum of Moravia in Brno, V, 1905) 266-78; K. Cernohorsky, "Novokrtensky puvod moravskych lochu" (The Anabaptist Origin of the Moravian Holes) in *Lidove noviny* (Brno) Sept. 27, 1934; *ML* II, 679-82.

Lockport Mennonite Church (MC), located three miles north of Stryker, Williams Co., Ohio, a member of the Ohio and Eastern Conference, had its beginning in 1834-36, when a group of Amish settlers from Alsace and France settled in the Fulton County area. The most common names were Short, Stuckey, Graber, Beck, and Aschliman. At first, in accord with Amish practice, they met in homes for services. In 1870 the Central meetinghouse was built and served the entire Fulton-Williams County settlement. Even after other meetinghouses were built at Lockport and West Clinton, the group was organized as a single congregation until 1943. The Lockport church was built in 1908 and remodeled in 1930. It is located at the western end of the Mennonite community. In 1955 the membership was 382, with Walter Stuckey as bishop, and Simon Stuckey and Earl Stuckey as ministers. In 1951 the Lockport congregation established the Pinegrove Mennonite Church (*q.v.*).   W.S.

Locle-Bressels, an Amish Mennonite church in the canton of Neuchâtel, Switzerland, on the French border, formerly called the Neuenburg church. The severe persecution of the Mennonites by Bern, continuing into the 18th century, induced many old Bernese peasants in the Jura to seek refuge in the mountains of Neuchâtel. A few may have gone to this canton as early as 1671 and 1693-95, when the Mennonites were compelled to leave with all their possessions. But the principal immigration took place in the first quarter of the 18th century, when several old Bernese families settled in Val de Ruz, Chaux-de-Fonds, and Le Locle. At the demand of the political communities of the Jura, the Prince Bishop of Basel ordered the evacuation of all Mennonites from his domain in the Jura in 1730-31. Though this order was not carried out, a number of families went to Neuchâtel. One of these immigrants was Christian Hummel (Ummel) of Buchholterberg near Thun.

These immigrants, who settled on farms around Le Locle and the hamlet of Bressels (La Sagne), constituted the Locle-Bressels congregation. The earliest information about it states that in 1785 Abraham Kocher, his sister Bäbi Kocher, and Susanna Frutiger, who were on the farm of Abraham Ramseyer, a preacher, were received into the congregation. These brethren were Amish, and kept close contact with the sister congregation at Montbéliard, France.

Services were held on the scattered farms. In the second half of the 19th century many of the members emigrated to America, and the congregation, which was always small (in 1887 only 31 baptized members, 14 males besides 46 children), continued to decline. In 1923 the group merged with Chaux d'Abel (*q.v.*). Jacob Müller was elder 1881-1911, and Alexander Stähly elder 1902-23 (preacher from 1867). David Geiser appears in the yearbook as preacher 1902-23, 1902 being the first volume containing Swiss congregational reports. (*ML* II, 682.)   S.G.

Locren, Pieter van, was preacher of the Amsterdam Mennonite Lamist congregation 1662- ? . By his radicalism, his Collegiant (*q.v.*) principles, his Socinianism (*q.v.*), and his pugnacity he contributed to the schism in the congregation between the Galenists (followers of Galenus Abrahamsz, *q.v.*) and the *Apostoolsen* (adherents of Samuel Apostool, *q.v.*), which became definite in June 1664.   vDZ.

H. W. Meihuizen, *Galenus Abrahamsz* (Haarlem, 1954) 80, 84 f., 97, 111; W. J, Kühler, *Het Socinianisme in Nederland* (Leiden, 1912) 160.

Locust Grove Conservative (Amish) Mennonite Church, located in Union Twp., Mifflin Co., Pa., one-fourth mile west of Belleville, organized in November 1898 under the leadership of Bishop Abraham D. Zook. The congregation worshiped at first on alternate Sundays at the Belleville and Allensville A.M. meetinghouse, and six months later in the home of David Z. Yoder one mile north of Belleville. A new meetinghouse was built in 1899, and enlarged in 1927 and 1948. The congregation is a member of the Conservative Mennonite Conference. Brethren ordained in the congregation include Samuel T. Yoder, John L. Mast, Jonas D. Yoder, Benjamin Glick, John B. Zook, Emanuel B. Peachey, and Louis Peachey. The 1954 ministers include senior Bishop John L. Mast, junior Bishop Emanuel B. Peachey, preachers John B. Zook and Louis Peachey; the 1954 membership was 405.   J.J.Y.

Locust Grove Mennonite Church (MC), located five miles northwest of Burr Oak, St. Joseph Co., Mich., a member of the Indiana-Michigan Conference, was started as a mission station by the Shore congregation near Shipshewana, Ind., about 1940. On Nov. 18, 1945, the church was organized with 61 charter members, and Orvin H. Hooley was ordained as pastor. Lee J. Miller, bishop of the Shore congregation, serves as bishop. The 1954 membership was 190. The first meetinghouse was built in 1941 and enlarged in 1950.   O.H.H.

Locust Grove Mennonite Church (MC), located five miles southwest of Elkhart, Ind., a member of the Indiana-Michigan Mennonite Conference, developed out of a Sunday-school mission operated by students of Goshen College and was organized with its own pastor (Russell Krabill) in 1945. In 1948 Ralph Stahly was ordained as pastor, and in 1954 as bishop. The membership in 1956 was 54. The meetinghouse was built in 1950.   R.ST.

Lodenstein, Jodocus van, a Dutch theologian, b. Feb. 6, 1620, at Delft, d. Aug. 3, 1677, at Utrecht, a man of profound influence on the Dutch Reformed Church by his earnestness, sincere piety, and untiring effort. He was an outstanding hymn writer; some of his hymns were adopted into the Mennonite hymnals. NEFF.

N.N.B.Wb. IX, 614-16; G. Kalff, *Gesch. der Nederl. Letterkunde* IV (Groningen, 1910) 468-73, 505; *DB* 1900, 90 f.; *ML* II, 682.

Loder, a Dutch family, some of whose members are Mennonites. Christiaan Lodewijk Loder I.Mz., a merchant at Amsterdam, married to C. W. Cardinaal, was a deacon of the Amsterdam Mennonite church 1840-44 and 1856-60. His son Christiaan Lodewijk Loder (1843-1908), an engineer, was appointed to the State Wharf at Amsterdam in 1863; in 1873-1906 he was managing director of state shipbuilding and as such he designed a number of warships. One of the most prominent Dutch jurists in the Netherlands was Bernard Cornelis Johannes Loder (1849-1935), who was a member of the Mennonite church board at Rotterdam from 1874. At first he was a lawyer, particularly renowned for his knowledge of maritime and international law. He filled important posts and high offices: after World War I he was a Dutch representative in the peace conference of Paris in 1919; in 1908-22 he was a member of the Dutch State Council; he also was the first president of the International Court of Justice. vDZ.

N.N.B.Wb. VI, 321 f.; J. Kosters, *In Memoriam Mr. B. C. J. Loder* (Amsterdam, 1935).

Lodi, Cal., a town (pop. *ca.* 20,000) in the Central Valley, San Joaquin County, 40 miles south of Sacramento, the state's capital, is one of the Mennonite communities in the valley noted for their fine fruits and diversified farming, located in one of California's fine cherry-growing areas. Nearly all of the 200 Mennonites in and around Lodi are of the Mennonite Brethren group and are employed in cereal processing, the steel industry, and the building trades.

The first Mennonites came to Lodi in 1907 from Harvey, N.D. The Mennonite element grew rapidly and in the early 1920's the Mennonite Brethren church, with a capacity of 350, was overflowing. Optimism ran high and a site was purchased for the possible location of a Mennonite Brethren college on the West Coast. Congregational difficulties, however, gave the Mennonites in Lodi some severe setbacks. At present, the Mennonite Brethren church, the only Mennonite institution in Lodi, has a membership of 110 and shows signs of growth.

The second Mennonite institution in the vicinity is the Victor Community Chapel, located three miles west of Lodi, a project of the Mennonite Brethren Home Mission Board of the Pacific District Conference. This work began in 1946 and attendance today is 75-100. The Victor community was originally owned and planned by Jacob Knoll, a prosperous Mennonite of Lodi. L.R.J.

Lodi (Cal.) Mennonite Brethren Church, a member of the Pacific District Conference, had its beginning in 1907, when Jacob Knoll, George Bechtold, and

Ludwig Reimche arrived in Lodi from Harvey, N.D. For three years these families attended the Evangelical Church in Victor, a hamlet four miles east of Lodi. In 1911 they rented a private home in Victor and held regular services there. In 1912 they moved to Lodi locating in another rented house, and organized a congregation under the leadership of John Berg. The first meetinghouse was erected in 1912, the second in 1920 at the corner of Flora and Garfield streets, 40 x 22 ft. in size. In 1955 an additional educational unit was erected, 60 x 30 ft. Many of the people of this congregation as well as of the community in general are of German background. Many have come from the German Lutheran and Baptist villages in Russia. In the early 1920's the church was filled to capacity, but due to internal difficulties and people moving south the church spent a number of years with a small membership. The first pastor was John Berg, followed by John H. Richert, Peter Rempel, Fred Just, F. F. Wall, J. M. Schlichting, George Reimche, George Sattler, Christ Reimche, John S. Dick, George Warkentin, A. A. Smith, H. D. Wiebe, and Henry H. Epp. In 1956 the pastor was Henry H. Dick, with a membership of 118 and an average attendance of 200. HE.H.D.

Lodovicus, martyr, who (*Mart. Mir.* D 23, E 433) was beheaded in 1529 with two brethren at Costnitz on Lake Constance, Germany. He was a learned man and a Waldensian preacher. vDZ.

Loesche, Georg Karl David (1855-1932), meritorious Austrian church historian, studied at the universities of Bonn, Tübingen, and Berlin, in 1880 became pastor of the German church in Florence, Italy, in 1885 instructor at the University of Berlin, 1887 professor of church history on the Protestant faculty of the University of Vienna. Among his numerous publications his *Geschichte des Protestantismus in Oesterreich* (3d edition, 1930) deals especially with the Anabaptists, as do also his articles "Zur Geschichte des Protestantismus in Oberösterreich" and "Tirolensia" in Nos. 45 and 47 of the *Jahrbuch der Gesellschaft für die Geschichte des Protestantismus im ehemaligen und im neuen Oesterreich.* For 40 years he was the editor of this periodical, which became very important for the study of the history of Protestantism in Austria. He also published articles by other authors on the Anabaptists in Austria. He made a lasting contribution to the study of the Austrian Anabaptists. P.DE.

K. Völker, "Georg Loesche, Ein Beitrag zur Geschichte der Wiener evangelischtheologischen Fakultät," in *Jahrb. der Gesellschaft für die Geschichte der Protestanten in Oesterreich* LIV (Vienna and Leipzig, 1933); *ML* II, 682.

Loevenich, a town in the duchy of Jülich, Germany, Lower Rhine area, where there have been a few Mennonites since the 16th century. Elder Theunis van Hastenrath (*q.v.*) baptized someone from Loevenich about 1550. Apparently the von Loevenich family found at Burtscheid near Aachen, Germany, and van Leuvenigh, at Amsterdam, Holland, derived its name from this town. (*DB* 1909, 121.) vDZ.

Loewen (Löwen, Loewens, Leewen, Leewens, Liewens, Lieuens), a Prussian Mennonite name of Dutch or Flemish background, appeared in the church record of Danzig as early as 1676. This name was found also in Tiegenhagen, Ladekopp, Rosenort, Fürstenwerder, Heubuden, Elbing, and Königsberg. From Danzig and Prussia the name was transplanted to Russia, the United States, Canada, and South America. Peter Löwen (*q.v.*) was a missionary from Russia serving in Sumatra. Anton Löwen (Ukraine and Siberia) was an outstanding teacher and minister. Outstanding leaders in Russia and Canada were Daniel J. Loewen (*q.v.*), Gerhard Loewen (*q.v.*), and Jacob A. Loewen. Heinrich Loewen and Wilhelm Loewen were leaders in Russia and South America. (Reimer, *Familiennamen.*)   C.K.

Loewen: see also **Löwen.**

Loewen, Daniel Jakob (1872-1951), an elder of the Mennonite (GCM) Church, was born Sept. 16, 1872, at Yazykovo, South Russia, the son of Jakob and Maria Klassen Löwen. In 1898 he was married to Anna Ketler; they had one son and five daughters.

When Daniel Loewen was 16 years old the family moved to Borissovo in the Bachmut settlement, this being the first of at least six pioneering experiences. About 1905 he was ordained to the ministry. In 1910 the family moved to Davlekanovo in the province of Ufa, where Daniel and two brothers owned a thriving mill. After the Revolution following World War I the family went on to the Omsk settlement in Siberia. In 1924 they came to Canada and settled at first on a farm near Harris, Sask. He served as a minister in the Westheim Mennonite Church at Rosemary, Alberta, and as elder of the Hoffnungsfeld Mennonite Church at Rabbit Lake, Sask., 1936-42, until he was compelled by his health to resign. He, however, continued to serve as assistant elder in the Schönwiese Mennonite Church of Manitoba. On March 14, 1951, he died at North Kildonan, Man.   J.H.En.

Loewen, Gerhard (1863-1946), a Mennonite educator, writer, and minister, b. March 19, 1863 (Russian Calendar), Chortitza, South Russia, d. June 2, 1946, Stuartburn, Man. He was the son of Gerhard G. and Sara Wiebe Löwen, attended the Zentralschule, and the normal school of Chortitza, after which he received a certificate for elementary teaching. After some additional training under A. A. Neufeld he received at Ekaterinoslav a private tutor's diploma with German as his major. At the age of 18 he began his teaching career, serving at Einlage (two years), Neuhorst (three years), Neu-Osterwick (eight years), Rosental Ratzyn, Chortitza (1903), again Einlage (nine years), and Arkadak (three years). In 1896 he received a silver medal with a red Alexander ribbon "For outstanding Service." In 1912 he joined the new settlement at Arkadak, Saratov, living in the village of Leonidovka. In 1884 Loewen married Maria Derksen. They had 13 children.

In 1925 Loewen emigrated to Canada, where he taught at the Mennonite Educational Institute at Altona, Man., for two years. In 1927 he joined his children at Stuartburn, Man., devoting his time to the instruction of the children of the community in German and Bible.

In 1896 the Chortitza Mennonite congregation, of which he was a member, elected Loewen as a minister. In addition to his work as teacher and minister, Loewen was a poet and writer. His articles and poems were published in numerous periodicals in Russia, Germany, and Canada. In 1895 he published a collection of poems, entitled *Feldblumen* (Halbstadt). After this followed in collaboration with M. Fast and Penner a volume *Fröhliche Weihnachten* (Halbstadt), a collection of plays and poems for use in school Christmas programs. In 1906 he published *Eine Ferienreise* (H. Lenzmann, Gross-Tokmak) and in 1946 followed a second enlarged edition of *Feldblumen* (Steinbach, Man., 1946).   Ar.D.

Arnold Dyck, "The Poet Gerhard Loewen," *Menn. Life* III (January 1948) 22 f.

Logan County, Ohio, located in west central Ohio, is primarily an agricultural area with rolling terrain. Amish Mennonites, largely from eastern Ohio and Mifflin Co., Pa., settled in the southern part of the county beginning about 1840. West Liberty (1950 pop. 1,397), at the southern border of the county, is central to the present Mennonite settlement which spills over into Champaign County to the south. In 1954 there were three Mennonite (MC) churches in the community, including about 1,000 persons. Two of the churches, Bethel and South Union, and about two thirds of the Mennonite population in the area are located in Logan County. The Mennonite Orphans' Home, established 1898, is located in West Liberty.   J.H.Ka.

Logan County, Ohio, Mennonite (MC) congregation, now extinct, was founded in 1832 in Union Township several miles northwest of West Liberty by families from Rockingham Co., Va. Henry Kulp brought his family to Union Township in a three-horse wagon in 1831. His brother-in-law Daniel Funk followed in 1832. Daniel Funk was ordained to the ministry about 1840 and sometime later bishop. The congregation never prospered. Some of the first families returned to Fairfield Co., Ohio, and later joined the group that helped found the Salem Mennonite settlement in Allen Co., Ohio. Others moved to Clay and Owen counties (*q.v.*), Ind., where some of their descendants have become ministers in the Methodist and United Brethren churches. Those who remained in Logan County united with the German Baptist congregation southwest of Bellefontaine.   J.S.U.

Logan Church of God in Christ Mennonite Church, located near Durham, Marion Co., Kan., was organized in the late 1880's. The meetinghouse was built in 1904. The 1955 membership was 71, with Claude Unruh as minister. The congregation is sometimes known as Durham.   C.C.W.

Loghem (Loghum, Lochem) van, a former Dutch Mennonite family: see **Lochem, van.**

Lohrenz, Henry W. (1878-1945), minister, educator, and prominent leader in the Mennonite Brethren Church, was born near Moundridge, Kan., Feb. 2, 1878, the third of the ten children of Heinrich and Elizabeth (Wiens) Lohrenz, who emigrated from the Molotschna Mennonite settlement in South Russia in 1874. Henry was converted and baptized into the M.B. Church in 1896. For two years he taught school in the vicinity of Inman, Kan. In the fall of 1900 he enrolled in the German Department School which the M.B. Church at that time conducted in connection with McPherson College, McPherson, Kan. After completing this course he continued in the college, graduating with the A.B. degree in 1908. He married Anna M. Friesen on Dec. 26, 1906. Of the six children born to them four died in infancy; a daughter and a son survive.

In 1904 the Ebenfeld M.B. Church near Hillsboro, Kan., of which Lohrenz was a member, elected him to the ministry and ordained him three years later. He was a gifted public speaker and for 41 years preached extensively and effectively and was much in demand to speak at conferences, festivals, and at other important occasions.

Lohrenz performed the greater part of his life's service in connection with the educational efforts of the M.B. Church, taking a leading part in the establishing of Tabor College at Hillsboro in 1908, and serving for 23 years as the president of the College. During most of this time he taught natural science and Biblical subjects in addition to the administrative duties. During these years of teaching Lohrenz continued his graduate studies, receiving the M.A. degree from Kansas University in 1911. He also attended Columbia University. When it became apparent that his work would be in the theological college, he prepared himself through further study at Southern Baptist Theological Seminary, Louisville, Ky., Princeton Theological Seminary, Princeton, N.J., and Presbyterian Theological Seminary, Chicago, Ill. The Northern Baptist Theological Seminary, Chicago, granted him the D.D. degree in 1929. Beginning with September 1932 Lohrenz taught Bible and biology in Bethel College for two years, then Bible in the Corn (Okla.) Bible School and Academy for one year. Beginning in 1935 he served as dean of the Theological College of Tabor College for six years and continued as professor of New Testament four years more.

Lohrenz rendered valuable service in the conference activities of the M.B. Church. In his early years he was much used as secretary. For some time he wrote and edited the M.B. Sunday-school quarterly. The conference found in him an able leader and a useful worker, electing him to various boards and important committees. He was elected moderator of the General Conference for four three-year terms and served the Southern District Conference as moderator nine one-year terms. He served as chairman of the Board of Foreign Missions of the M.B. Church 1919-36 and as executive secretary-treasurer 1936-45. In connection with these duties he traveled extensively, representing the cause of missions at churches and conferences. He edited a number of booklets on missions and wrote many articles for the *Zionsbote*.

Lohrenz died at Hillsboro on March 16, 1945, and was buried at the local M.B. Cemetery. ("Nachruf" in *Zionsbote*, May 16, 1945.)   J.H.L.

Loisten, followers of Eloy (Loys) Pruystinck (*q.v.*) in Antwerp, Belgium, and elsewhere. They are men-

tioned in Luther's letter "An die Christen zu Antorff" (Antwerp) of 1525. Here they are said to embrace the following heresies: every man possesses the Holy Spirit; the Holy Spirit is nothing but man's own mind; hell and reprobation do not exist; the carnal body of man is damned, but every soul has everlasting life. The Loists exerted some influence on the extreme left wing of the large and complicated movement of Anabaptism in the Netherlands. David Joris (*q.v.*), who lived in 1524 in Antwerp before he joined the Anabaptists (and also later), may have been influenced by them. Rembert calls them "Freigeister." The Loist movement was suppressed before 1545. Eloy Pruystinck himself was executed at Antwerp on Oct. 23, 1544.   vDZ.

Rembert, *Wiedertäufer*, 165-75; *Inv. Arch. Amst.* I, No. 276; J. Fredericks, *De Secte der Loisten of Antwerpsche Libertijnen* (Gent, 1891); Mellink, *Wederdopers*, 413.

Loman Mennonite Church (MC), formerly called the Northern Light Gospel Mission, located about four miles south of Loman, which is on the Canadian border in Koochiching Co., Minn., is a member of the North Central Conference. It has (1954) a membership of 20, all rural people. The mission was started in July 1938, by two couples, the Groffs and the Schantzes, of Pennsylvania. This is a work of faith with no promise of support by any board, church, or individual and with no solicitation. The workers of the area have also started work at White Earth, Menahga, Leader, Cass Lake, and Graceton, with two families at all but the latter two places, Cass Lake having two single workers, and Graceton one family to date. This group of workers conducts services regularly at eleven different places. In 1943 Irwin Schantz was ordained minister for the Loman church. The present minister is William Kurtz.   I.S.

Lombard Mennonite Church (MC), located 18 miles west of Chicago in the suburb of Lombard, was organized on Oct. 23, 1954. For over two years previous to this Mennonite families that had moved to the Chicago area for vocational interests had met in homes for Bible study and fellowship. The charter membership, beginning with 14 members, was closed a year later with 51 members. This included associate members from the Evanston and Elgin I-W units and members of the General Conference Mennonite Church living in the area. Services are held at the church parsonage at 1012 Whitmore Lane, Lombard, and the East Lombard Civic Club Building, Westmore and Division, Lombard, until there is a regular church building. The church is affiliated with the Illinois (MC) Mennonite Conference. Le-Roy Kennel is the pastor.   L.E.K.

London, the capital of Great Britain, was in the early years of the Reformation the scene of Anabaptist activity, especially of the followers of Melchior Hofmann, who came to England in the 1530's from the Netherlands. About 1535 the authorities arrested four Englishmen in London for their part in the distribution of an Anabaptist confession of faith. They had connections with Flemish Anabaptists. At the house of one of them, John Raulinges in London, "many of the sayd faction dyuers tymes assembled," and their "bishop and reder" was a Fleming by the name of Bastian. The foreign Anabaptists in England were the chief victims of persecution under Henry VIII. On May 25, 1535, 25 Dutch Anabaptists were examined at St. Paul's for erroneous views regarding the incarnation, the mass, and baptism, with the result that 14 were condemned. Two of this number were burned at Smithfield on June 8, 1535, and the others sent to various English towns for a similar death. On Oct. 1, 1538, the king appointed an ecclesiastical commission, including Archbishop Cranmer and three other theologians, "to search for and examine Anabaptists . . . and destroy all books of that detestable sect." On Nov. 24 four Dutch Anabaptists recanted by bearing fagots at St. Paul's, while on Nov. 29 three were burned at Smithfield. One of these was Jan Mathijsz van Middelburg (not to be confused with Jan Matthys van Haarlem), the well-known leader at Amsterdam and elsewhere in the Low Countries; the other two were Peter Franke and his wife, a young couple from Brugge in Flanders. On May 3, 1540, three Anabaptists were executed at Southwark, of whom two were foreigners and one an Englishman.

Since about 1535 Anabaptists had been escaping from Holland and Flanders to London. In June 1535 David Joris, intending to go to London to save his life, sailed from Vlissingen (Flushing), Dutch province of Zeeland, but learning that the Anabaptists were also persecuted in London, he gave up his plan when his ship was forced by a storm to return to Vlissingen (Kühler, *Geschiedenis* I, 199). A. L. E. Verheyden in *Mennisme in Vlaanderen* gives the following information: On Nov. 22, 1538, "Lambert, alias John Nycolsen, was burned in Smithfield and the same day two Flemings and the wife of one of them were adjudged to death. A third man abjured. They were Anabaptists." (Quoted from *Letters and Papers, Foreign and Domestic, of the Reign of Henry VIII*, vol. XIII, 2, 1893, p. 374.) On April 10, 1540, a Mennonite named Barnes "has been put in the Tower with his two accomplices, accompanied by 10 or 12 burgesses of this town and 15 or 20 (?) strangers, mostly from Flanders and all Anabaptists." (Quoted from *loc. cit.*, vol. XV, 1896, p. 205 f.)

After the death of Henry VIII in 1547 the Anabaptists in England appeared more in the open. In 1549 John Hooper complained that the Anabaptists flocked to his lectures in London and disputed on the doctrine of the incarnation. One of their leaders, Henry Hart, held a public debate with John Reynolds at St. Margaret's Church in London, likely about 1553. Joan Boucher (see **Boucher, Jane**) was tried before Archbishop Cranmer and other ecclesiastics on April 12, 1549, and was condemned and burned at the stake May 21, 1550, as an Anabaptist, particularly for holding the Melchiorite view of the incarnation. At her trial she declared "a thousand in London were of her sect." John (Johan) Knel (*q.v.*) and Anna Cantiana were also martyred in this year by burning at the stake (*Mart. Mir.* D 99, E 498).

In Elizabeth's reign 20 Dutch Anabaptists were arrested in London at the time of a meeting on Easter, April 3, 1575. Of this group 14 were banished, two escaped from prison, and two, Jan Pieters and Hendrick Terwoort, were burned at Smithfield on July 22 of the same year (*Mart. Mir.* D 694-712, E 1008-24). These Anabaptists "were Menno's people." The elders of the Austin Friars Church in London, the congregation for foreigners, were severely accused, particularly by Protestants in Antwerp, for their implication in this affair. This was one part of a long chapter of controversy about Anabaptists in London in connection with Austin Friars, which resulted in 1562 in the expulsion and banishment of Adrian van Haemstede, one of the ministers, for holding tolerant views.

London and Norwich were strong separatist centers during Elizabeth's reign, and it was at London that the Barrowist wing of Independency had its rise. The separatist leaders, Henry Barrow, John Greenwood, and John Penry, were executed at London in 1593, and the congregation led by Francis Johnson to Amsterdam in the same year came from London. The first congregation of separatists holding to believers' baptism to be established on English soil, to which the General Baptists owe their origin, was founded at London in 1612 when Thomas Helwys and his followers returned to England from Amsterdam.

In the Mennonite archives at Amsterdam (*Inv. Arch. Amst.* II, 1367-75) are found a few letters of a correspondence in 1624-30 between Elias Tookey (*q.v.*) of London and the Dutch Mennonites (Hans de Ries and Reinier Wybrantsz) concerning a union to be made between some evangelical congregations in England (London, Lincoln, Sarum, Coventry, and Tyverton), who called themselves Anabaptists, but obviously were Baptists, and the Dutch Waterlander Mennonites, which union, however, did not come to pass.   I.B.H.

J. S. Brewer and J. Gairdner, *Letters and Papers, Foreign and Domestic, of the Reign of Henry VIII* (London, 1920-32, Vol. XIII, Addenda I); D. Wilkins, *Concilia Magnae Britanniae et Hiberniae* (London, 1737, Vol. IV); *Mart. Mir.;* J. Hessels, *Ecclesiae Londino-Batavae Archivum* I-III (Cambridge, 1887-97); C. Burrage, *The Early English Dissenters* I-II (Cambridge, 1912); B. Krohn, *Gesch. der fanatischen und enthusiastischen Wiedertäufer* (Leipzig, 1758); ML II, 687.

Lone Tree Church of God in Christ Mennonite Church, located 5½ miles north and one mile east of Moundridge, Kan., was organized in 1878, when 70 persons were baptized by John Holdeman, one of the first congregations of the denomination in Kansas. As the congregation increased the original sod meetinghouse was replaced by a larger building in 1880, which was in turn replaced in 1890 and 1906, and enlarged in 1925, with a seating capacity of 900. Benjamin Schmidt and Henry Koehn were the first residing ministers. Other ministers who have served the church previous to the present ministers are Tobias A. Unruh, John Holdeman, and Jesse Johnson. The church has a membership of 540 (1955). Most of the members are of Dutch descent and many still speak Low German at home, but the services are conducted in English. Since this is the largest congregation of the denomination, it has been host to nine conferences. About 1,200 persons have been baptized here since the beginning of the congregation.   J.Jo.

Long Bay United Missionary Church, now extinct, on Manitoulin Island, Ont., was organized about 1892. It was called Bethesda. E.R.S.

Long Green, Md. The Amish Mennonite congregation in Baltimore County, Md., began when Moses Miller moved from Lancaster County, Pa., to Long Green valley in 1833. Others from Mifflin County, Pa., and from Lancaster County followed in 1834. By about 1849 the following families had arrived: Christian Hertzler, Isaac Hertzler, Jacob Hertzler, John Kennel, John Mast, Daniel Nafzinger, Peter Nafzinger, Christian Neuhauser, Aaron Smoker, John Smoker, Jacob Waltz, David Warfel, and Solomon Yoder. The first church officers were Daniel Nafzinger, deacon; John Mast, minister; and Solomon Yoder (d. 1880), bishop. Andrew Miller was ordained later, but moved to Union County before 1875. Solomon Yoder's son Lewis was ordained minister in 1880. He died June 16, 1893. Isaac D. Hertzler was ordained in 1894, but moved to Warwick County, Va., in 1897. Following this the congregation was left without a resident pastor until 1909.

In 1894 the congregation was temporarily accepted by the Indiana Amish Mennonite Conference. Membership was transferred to the Ohio and Pennsylvania Amish Mennonite Conference in 1899. Ministers from these areas visited Long Green about once a month. For years Bible study was held in the homes each Sunday afternoon. Though the congregation had dwindled to 20 members, a frame meetinghouse was built and dedicated on Christmas Day of 1898. The first Sunday school was opened about 1895, and soon was held weekly the year round. In 1909 John M. Hartzler moved to Long Green as pastor. For a time the congregation seemed encouraged, and a few members were added to the group. But the meetinghouse burned down in 1915, the Hertzlers moved to Belleville, Pa., and other families moved away. Some of the young people united with other church groups. The last surviving member died in 1953. The cemetery is cared for by a permanent committee of five descendants of former residents, who now live in Pennsylvania and Virginia. (Diary of Isaac D. Hertzler, 1875; *Herald of Truth,* April 1880, p. 77; December 1880, p. 221; July 1, 1893, p. 214; June 15, 1899, p. 186; Feb. 1, 1899, p. 42; Jan. 6, 1910, p. 649.) SI.H.

Long, Izaak le, b. April 19, 1683, at Frankfurt, Germany, d. in 1762 at Hanau, Germany, lived at Amsterdam 1718-44. He was a collector and translator of books, especially on church history. Le Long was a member of the Reformed Church, but in 1738 he joined the Moravian Brethren. He published a large number of books in the Dutch language, including *Boekzaal der Nederduytsche Bijbels* (Amsterdam, 1732, 2d ed. Hoorn, 1764), which is of interest because of Mennonite Bibles and New Testaments reviewed in this book. It is, however, not complete; for example, an edition of the Bible in folio, published by the Mennonite Jacques van der Schuere in 1649 at Amsterdam, is not mentioned. vDZ.

N.N.B.Wb. VIII, 1023-28; W. Lütjeharms, *Het Philadelphisch-oecumenisch streven der Hernhutters* (Zeist, 1935) *passim,* see Index.

Longdale Mennonite (GCM) Mission Church is located one-half mile southwest of Longdale, Blaine Co., Okla., and seven miles north of Canton. The Cheyennes living in this district formerly attended church at Cantonment. The Cantonment church was taken down, rebuilt near Longdale, and dedicated on Dec. 19, 1926. The work of Longdale has been in charge of the missionaries G. A. Linscheid 1926-38 and Benno Toews 1938-40 from Cantonment, Arthur Friesen 1940-47, Alfred Wiebe 1947- . For church membership see **Fonda.** A.WI.

Longenecker's and Kolb's Mennonite (MC) congregations in the northwestern part of Holmes Co., Ohio, were organized in 1830 as one congregation with two meeting places by settlers from Bucks Co., Pa., including such families as the Longeneckers, Kolbs, Freeds, Beidlers, Barkeys, Hauns, Mumaws, Weldys, Moyers, and Shoups. The first meetinghouse, Kolb's, was built of logs in 1833, Longenecker's of hewn logs in 1834. The congregation, originally a member of the Ohio Mennonite Conference (q.v.), is now a member of the Ohio and Eastern Conference (q.v.). Paul Lantz is the pastor and the reported membership (1954) 64. The congregation has never had a resident bishop. In the early years overflow crowds met at the church at communion partly to hear the excellent singing. Later, conditions resulted in decline in membership —the moving away of more active families, the unfaithfulness and silencing of three ministers over the years, and proselyting by the German Methodists. Sunday-school workers from the Walnut Creek congregation succeeded in keeping alive the little congregation at Longenecker's. Kolb's meetinghouse has been abandoned and razed, while Longenecker's was recently rebuilt, so that the congregation is now called Longenecker's. Nearly all of the church members in the neighborhood are now members of a thriving Reformed Church. J.S.U.

Longenecker's Reformed Mennonite Church is located in Lancaster Co., Pa. This was the original meeting place when the Reformed Mennonite Church was established in 1812. J.L.K.

Lont, a Mennonite family name found in the Dutch province of North Holland, especially in the congregations of Niedorp and Wieringen, where members of this family have served as deacons. vDZ.

Loon, van, a Dutch Mennonite family, which furnished a number of Mennonite deacons and preachers. Apparently this family lived at Rotterdam, where Herman van Loon, baptized 1695 in the Waterlander congregation, was appointed preacher of the (1700) united congregation in March 1705 but resigned on March 31 because of dissension in the congregation concerning his call. He resumed his ministry on March 11, 1706, served until his death on Nov. 4, 1710. His son Isaac van Loon was a deacon at Rotterdam 1710-14. To this family also belong the preachers Abraham van Loon (q.v.) and his son Petrus van Loon (q.v.). Another Abraham van Loon, a physician at Amsterdam, also of this family, was interested in theology, publishing, besides medical books, Frederik Toger's (q.v.) *Samenstel der*

Godgeleerdheid (Leiden, 1726) and (translated from English) W. Derham's *God-geleerde Natuurkunde* (Leiden, 1728 and 1739). It is not certain whether also Jochem van Loon (d. 1692), a leather merchant and preacher of the Waterlanders at Dordrecht from 1667 (*N.N.B.Wb.* VIII, 1071), belonged to this family.   vᴅZ.

Loon, Abraham van (1656-1725), married to Jannetje Tirion of Gouda, was a physician and preacher of the Mennonite congregation of Gouda from about 1690 until his death. He was of some renown for his eloquence and delivered an address at Rotterdam on June 6, 1700, when the Flemish and Waterlander congregations in this town merged. A sermon entitled *Christelijke Vredewensch* was published at Rotterdam in 1700. Besides this he published *De Jongeling onderwesen tot Doop en Avondmaal* (Gouda, 1713). Before this he published the exegesis of the Gospel of Matthew by Hugo de Groot (Gouda, 1685). As a member of the progressive Lamist (*q.v.*) group he combated the conservative Zonist leader Herman Schijn, who had attacked the church board of Rotterdam, accusing it of admitting non-Mennonites to the Lord's Supper, in two booklets—(*a*) (with W. Suderman and Adriaan van Alkmaar): *Verklaring en Verdediging van de Aanspraak voor het Avondmaal bij de Doopsgezinden te Rotterdam,* and (*b*) (with Adriaan van Alkmaar) *Twee brieven tegen H. Schijn.* (*Inv. Arch. Amst.* II, Nos. 1765 f., 1769.)   vᴅZ.

Loon, Petrus van, b. *ca.* 1690 at Gouda, d. Oct. 28, 1754, at Veenendaal, a son of Abraham van Loon, was a Mennonite preacher at Veenendaal (or Rijnsche Veen) in the Dutch province of Utrecht, Holland, from 1719 until his death, having previously served the congregation at Schiedam. He had at the same time assumed the care of a settlement of Mennonites who had left East Prussia because they had been deprived of their nonresistant privilege. With aid from the Dutch Mennonites 45 persons arrived in Wageningen at Christmas 1732. His son Isaacus van Loon, who studied at the Amsterdam Mennonite Seminary 1742-48, was appointed assistant to his father. Jacobus van Loon, another son of Petrus, served from 1755 for some years as preacher of the Mennonite congregation of Middelharnis.   vᴅZ.

Inv. Arch. Amst. I, Nos. 1953, 1961, 1964, 1971, 1975, 1982, 1984; II, Nos. 2321-36; *DB* 1905, 124 f., 149 f., 1906, 96; 98, 103 f., 108; 1909, 161; *ML* II, 687.

Loop (Ohio) United Missionary Church had 71 members in 1954, with J. Sabo, Jr., serving as pastor.

Loos, a Mennonite family, particularly living at Blokzijl, Dutch province of Overijssel. They usually were lumber dealers and some of them were deacons of the Mennonite congregation. One of them was Jacob Loos Bzn (1839-90), who served for 30 years as treasurer of the Blokzijl church board.   vᴅZ.

Loosjes, an old Dutch Mennonite family, whose ancestor, as far as is known, was Aryan (Adriaen) Jacobs Loosjes (1550-1635), living on the Molenbuurt at Zaandam, Dutch province of North Holland. This family has produced a large number of Mennonite preachers, first of whom was Krelis

Aryanse (Cornelis Adriaensz Loosjes) (1660-1720), a grandson of Aryan Jacobs, who from 1693 until his death was a preacher of the Frisian congregation at West-Zaandam. His son Adriaan Loosjes, his grandsons Cornelis and Petrus Loosjes, as well as a number of other descendants, are mentioned in the following articles. Some members of the Loosjes family were ardent Collegiants (*q.v.*), e.g., Herman Loosjes of Zaandam, who in 1706-8 spoke occasionally at the Collegiant center at Rijnsburg. Another outstanding member of the family was Cornelis Overbeek Loosjes (1785-1841) (*Naamlijst 1829,* 54; *DB* 1881, 54 f.), a son of Vincent Overbeek, a plumber at Haarlem, and Engeltje Loosjes, a daughter of Cornelis Loosjes (*q.v.*), who served the congregation of Zutphen 1818-38, resigning because of bad health. (*Ned. Patriciaat,* XIV, 1924, 180-88; *ML* II, 687.)   vᴅZ.

Loosjes, Adriaan, b. April 15, 1689, at West-Zaandam, d. there March 24, 1767, was a lumber dealer at Zaandam, who was chosen as preacher of the West-Zaandam Frisian congregation in 1714. He served until 1762. Because this office demanded so much time—Loosjes had not received a special training and gave much time to the study of Latin, Bible, and history—he retired from business to devote himself entirely to the ministry. In 1747, during a visit of the Dutch stadholder William IV of Orange, Loosjes addressed him in the name of all Mennonites of North Holland. Loosjes published a funeral sermon for his colleague Klaas Jacobsz Nen, *De gezegende naagedachtenis des Rechtveerdigen* (West-Zaandam, 1755). He co-operated with others in producing a translation of the Latin works of Flavius Josephus, which was published at Alkmaar in 1732 and 1736. His son Petrus Loosjes (*q.v.*) edited his interesting historical notations on the region in which he lived: *Beschrijving der Zaanlandsche Dorpen* (1794). Loosjes is also said to have published an address on the Acts of the Apostles, and some papers on comets and on Palestine. Adriaan Loosjes was married in 1714 to Guurtje Klaasd. Visser and after her death to Trijntje Louwe in 1725; both were of Zaandam.   vᴅZ.

DJ 1837, 99; S. Lootsma, *Het Nieuwe Huys* (Zaandam, 1937) 57-59, 65-68, 104; M. Schagen, *Naamlijst der Doopsgezinde Schrijveren* (Amsterdam, 1745) 64; *Inv Arch. Amst.* II, No. 3145.

Loosjes, Adriaan, a son of Petrus Loosjes (*q.v.*) and Sijtje Oudt, b. May 13, 1761, at Den Hoorn on the island of Texel, and d. Feb. 28, 1818, at Haarlem. He studied theology at the Amsterdam Mennonite Seminary, but never went into the ministry; after finishing his studies he prepared himself for the book business, opening a bookstore in Haarlem in 1782 and soon after a publishing house, which still exists under the name of Erven Loosjes. He took a prominent place in the cultural life of his town and his times. Loosjes wrote a large number of novels, of which *Het leeven van Maurits Lijnslager* (1808) and *Hillegonda Buisman* (1814) are the best known. Particularly his *Maurits Lijnslager,* which because of its patriotic spirit was the favorite book of the youth during the life of its author and even after, was highly appreciated. He also published some volumes of poems and a number of plays. Loosjes was president of the Teyler Society (*q.v.*). In his quality of moderator of the Mennonite church board he held an address in 1809 to commemorate the union of the two Mennonite congregations of Haarlem in 1784; this paper, *Bij Gelegenheid van het Vriedenmaal* was also published (n.p., n.d.). For a few years he was manager of the Mennonite orphanage at Haarlem.

Loosjes, who about 1790 was an ardent Patriot (*q.v.*), also held some political offices, being a member of the Haarlem "Weeskamer" (Orphans' court) and the provincial government of Holland in 1796.

He was married to Cornelia Johanna Herdingh (1765-1841) of Leiden.   vdZ.

N.N.B.Wb. IV, 929-31; M. H. de Haan, *Adriaan Loosjes* (Utrecht, 1934); G. Kalff, *Geschiedenis der Nederl. Letterkunde* (Groningen, 1910) VI, 436-41; VII, 131 f.; *DJ* 1850, 143; *ML* II, 687.

Loosjes, Adriaan, b. Aug. 4, 1828, at Haarlem, d. June 21, 1902, son of the book dealer Vincent Loosjes. At the age of 17 he wrote the devotional articles for the *Christelijk Album* (1846), which was widely read. After completing his study at the Amsterdam Mennonite Seminary 1846-51 he was called as pastor to the congregation at Rottevalle-Witveen. The next year (1852) he moved to Akkrum. In 1854, at the age of 26, he accepted a call to the Mennonite church at Amsterdam and served this congregation for 39 years.

Of Adriaan Loosjes' preaching Feenstra remarked, "His capability bordered on genius." Loosjes himself said, "I know of no higher title of honor than to have been a preacher in the 19th century." His Biblical orthodox point of view did not interfere with his high regard for people who differed with him. His extensive pastoral work was probably the reason for his long literary silence. Not until his later years did he again appear before the public. In addition to treatises in the *Stemmen voor waarheid en vrede,* another study must be mentioned, *De gedachten van Pascal en zijne kleinere geschriften vertaald en toegelicht* (Haarlem, 1889). He also published a funeral sermon to his colleague P. van der Goot (*q.v.*), entitled *Jezus Christus altijd dezelfde* (Amsterdam, 1877), and *Voor ruim een halve eeuw* (Haarlem, 1897); his son Vincent Loosjes (*q.v.*) published a number of his father's sermons, *Uit de Prediking van A. Loosjes* (Haarlem, 1905).

Adriaan Loosjes' services were recognized by bestowal of membership in the *Maatschappij der Nederlandse Letterkunde* and the provincial society of Utrecht. He was married twice, 1852-62 to Margaretha van Geuns, and 1864-1902 to E. H. Bavink. On Sept. 24, 1893, he resigned his pastorate and died nine years later at Bloemendaal near Haarlem. He gave his rich library to the Amsterdam Mennonite Church.   vdZ.

P. Feenstra Jr., "Levensbericht", in *Levensb. My. Ned. Letterk.* 1903-4; *DB* 1904, 66-114; 1902, 242; *ML* II, 670, 688.

Loosjes, Cornelis, a son of Adriaan Loosjes (*q.v.*) and Guurtje Klaasd. Visser, was b. Jan. 28, 1723, at West-Zaandam and d. Jan. 5, 1792, at Haarlem. He was trained for the ministry at the Amsterdam

Mennonite Lamist Seminary 1742-44 and served as a preacher of the congregations of Gouda 1744-51, Oost-Zaandam 1751-63, and Haarlem, Peuzelaarsteeg 1763-84, and the united Haarlem congregation 1784 until his death. During his Oost-Zaandam period there was some excitement because of his rather liberal ideas. Especially the fact that in 1785 he had baptized and introduced into the ministry at Beverwijk Anthony van der Os (*q.v.*), a former Reformed minister who was excommunicated from the Reformed Church because of his liberal tendencies, caused quite a stir and resulted in a large number of pamphlets against both van der Os and Loosjes. Loosjes was keenly interested in Dutch literature; he was a good friend of the well-known authors Betje Wolff and Aagje Deken (*q.v.*), and in 1761 founded the *Vaderlandsche Letteroefeningen,* a literary periodical which soon became very influential, particularly by its book reviews. Loosjes was married to Fijtje van Wummenum. (*Inv. Arch. Amst.* II, No. 1800; *DB* 1897, note 2, 1909, 101.)   vdZ.

Loosjes, Jacob, son of Adriaan Loosjes (*q.v.*), b. Jan. 17, 1874, at Amsterdam, d. Oct. 17, 1935, in Bussum; studied Dutch language and literature, passed his doctoral examination, then studied law and earned his doctorate with a dissertation, *De algemeene waterstaatsreglementen onderling vergeleken.*

After serving for several years in the department of "waterstaat," he began his study at the Amsterdam Mennonite Seminary, in 1908 becoming a ministerial candidate. In May 1909 he was called to the Mennonite church in Hollum on Ameland. During his service for the "waterstaat" he wrote a historical treatise, *Waterstaatswetgeving voor 1813.* Now he turned his attention to church history, especially that of his own brotherhood. In addition to many articles in the *Mennonitsches Lexikon,* his book *De Gereformeerde Kerk van Ameland* (1912) is particularly important. Of great interest for Mennonite history is his paper "Jan Jacobsz en de Jan-Jacobsgezinden," published in *Nederl. Archief voor Kerkgeschiedenis* of 1914.

In those days there was little possibility for an orthodox Mennonite preacher to be called to a pulpit, Jacob Loosjes therefore found himself obliged to join the Lutheran Church. In 1914 he accepted the call to Tiel and in 1918 to Bussum. After 1920 he was also a lecturer on history at the Lyceum at Bussum. To the historian a new field of work was opened, the history of the Lutheran Church in the Netherlands. The results of his study are in part found in the *Biografisch Woordenboek der Protestantsche Godgeleerden in Nederland,* which is published under his coeditorship with J. P. de Bie. In addition Loosjes published his *Geschiedenis der Luthersche Kerk in de Nederlanden* in 1921; *Luthersche weldadigheid* in 1924; *Naamlijst van predikanten enz. der Luthersche Kerk in Nederland,* 1925.

In 1925 Loosjes was called to the professorship at the Lutheran seminary in Amsterdam and in the following year he made his speech of acceptance on the subject, "Lutherschen en remonstranten in den tijd van de Dordtsche Synode," but remained a lecturer at Bussum at the same time. He was an untiring worker. Again and again scholarly works flowed from his pen, as in 1932 the *History of the Christ Church (English Episcopal Church)*. Loosjes was actually not a theologian but a historian, who worked very exactly and sought to fathom the history in his various fields of work, at first in the work of the "waterstaat," then Mennonite history on Ameland, and finally Lutheran history. (*ML* II, 688 f.)

W.LE.

Loosjes, Petrus, a son of Adriaan Loosjes (*q.v.*) and Trijntje Louwe, half brother of Cornelis Loosjes (*q.v.*), b. Nov. 20, 1735, at West-Zaandam, d. Jan. 12, 1813, at Haarlem. Having been trained at the Amsterdam Mennonite Lamist Seminary 1754-59, he served as preacher in the congregations of Den Hoorn on the island of Texel 1759-62, Monnikendam 1762, and Haarlem 1762-1811 (congregation of the Klein Heiligland until 1784 and when this congregation merged with that of Peuzelaarssteeg, of the united congregation until he resigned in 1812). Together with his half brother Cornelis, also a preacher of Haarlem, he edited the *Vaderlandsche Letteroefeningen,* a literary periodical founded by his brother, of which after the death of the latter he was the only editor. He wrote a sequel to the well-known Dutch history of Jan Wagenaar, *Vaderlandsche Historie,* to which he added 24 volumes, published anonymously 1786-1811.

Petrus Loosjes was married to Sijtje Oudt. Their son Adriaan (*q.v.*) was a well-known bookseller and founder of the Loosjes publishing house. Their daughter Agatha (b. 1766) was married to François Bohn, a Mennonite of Leiden, who founded at Haarlem a publishing company, which is still in existence. (*N.N.B.Wb.* VIII, 1072 f.; *Naamlijst* 1815, 72 f.; *DB* 1909, 101.)

vDZ.

Loosjes, Vincent, only son of Adriaan Loosjes (*q.v.*) and Cornelia Johanna Herdingh (Haarlem, 1786-1841), succeeded his father in the book and publishing business of Erven Loosjes. Both he and his wife Suzanna van Westerkappel were managers of the Haarlem Mennonite orphanage. In memoration of the second centennial of the founding of the orphanage, Loosjes in 1834 delivered an address which was published: *Toespraak aan de kinderen in het Oude Weeshuis* (Haarlem, 1834). In 1828 he became a trustee of the A.D.S. (Dutch Mennonite General Conference) and curator of its theological seminary.

vDZ.

Loosjes, Vincent, a son of Adriaan Loosjes and Margaretha van Geuns, b. Nov. 24, 1855, at Amsterdam, d. Sept. 19, 1932, at Amersfoort, a preacher and author like his father. After the completion of his study at the University of Groningen and the Amsterdam Mennonite Seminary he served as pastor of the Mennonite congregation of St. Hippolytushoef en Stroe on Wieringen 1879-81, Blokzijl 1881-86, Beemster 1886-90, Sneek 1890-1912, and in his last years, 1912-21, the large Amsterdam church. On April 3, 1921, he resigned from the ministry and enjoyed eleven years of rest. He always showed an earnest and sincere piety, also in his sermons, of which he demanded high aesthetic quality. Theologically he was certainly not modernistic, nor was

he strictly orthodox. He wished "to hold himself only to the Bible as the authoritative document; the revelation of the sacred love of God to man made perfect in the Gospel and in the life of Jesus demands the love of men in exchange." Vincent Loosjes wrote a great deal; of his five novels, *Rinske Sonnema,* published in 1896 (a third edition in 1923), is probably the best known. In addition he wrote a number of poems, some of which have been published in collections of folk songs. He was fond of making aphorisms, many of which have been collected in two booklets, *Bitter en Zoet* (1909) and *Prikkels en Pluimen* (1919). In his literary works, which rarely surpass mediocrity, we are struck by his keen observation of people and his disturbingly blunt expressions, which also characterized his sermons. His sharp, ruthless honesty repelled some listeners. Nevertheless he was a faithful shepherd and a good friend to many. In addition to his imaginative works he also published a study on Louis Bonaparte, King of Holland (1888). In addition he published a sermon, *Des Tempels vergankelijke luister* (Sneek, 1892), and *Enkele opmerkingen over de zelfstandigheid onzer gemeenten* (Haarlem, 1902).

In his Sneek period he took part in social life, but his actual metier was his study. In 1879, shortly before he took on his first preaching position, he married Wilhelmina Willers, who died before he moved to Amsterdam.

vDZ.

P. Feenstra Jr., Levensbericht" in *Levensber. My Ned. Letterk.* (Leiden, 1933); P. B. Westerdijk in *Zondagsbode* Sept. 25, 1932; *idem, DJ* 1934; *ML* II, 689.

Loosli, Gottlieb (1868-1931), teacher of the school at Moron, Switzerland, in the Jura district, and elder of the Kleintal (*q.v.*) Mennonite Church, was born Jan. 27, 1868, in Eriswil in the Emmental, Switzerland, the youngest of ten children. Frail from birth, he became seriously sick and spent a half year in the hospital in Basel. A deaconess nurse helped him in his Christian life. In 1888 he entered the normal school at Beuggen. On Nov. 1, 1892, he took over the private school at Bellelay. In the autumn of 1893 teacher and pupils migrated to Moron into the schoolroom on the first floor of the new chapel. In 1895 he married Rosa Frutiger. Until 1919 Mrs. Loosli conducted the class in needlework at Moron.

At Christmas in 1900 the Looslis joined the Mennonite Church in the Moron chapel. In 1911 the Kleintal church put him in charge of the baptismal instruction. In 1917 upon a majority decision of the population of Châtelat the Moron private school was turned into a German language school. In the same year he was chosen preacher of the Kleintal church, and in 1929 he was made elder. In 1927 a son replaced him as a teacher and on March 5, 1931, he died in the circle of his wife and eight children with the words, "I am glad to depart, but am saved only through grace. I am glad that I always stressed this." The school at Moron and its good reputation are his achievement. In the brotherhood he bridged over many a difference, and devoted his whole being to the welfare of the brotherhood. (*Berner Schulblatt,* 1931, No. 2; *Zionspilger,* 1931, No. 15; *ML* II, 689 f.)

A.-T.

Looten (Lootens, Loten), a Dutch Mennonite family. A branch of this family emigrated from Flanders, Belgium, in the early 17th century, and is found at Aardenburg (*q.v.*), Dutch Zealand Flanders. David Looten, a Mennonite, born at Bellem near Brugge, but a citizen of Aardenburg, died at Leiden in 1626. Laurens Looten (d. after 1688), a well-to-do farmer, and his family contributed generously to the building of a new meetinghouse in 1655. His descendants joined the Reformed Church. Other branches of the Looten family are found in Leiden and Amsterdam. Laurens Jansz Looten, a cloth merchant, moved from Leiden to Amsterdam in 1612. His son Jan Looten (b. 1618 at Amsterdam), married to Cathalijntje Harmansdochter, of Jülich, was a painter of landscapes. He lived in England for some time, and probably died there in 1681. Karel Loten in the first decades of the 17th century was a wealthy merchant of Amsterdam, who owned a stately country home in De Beemster (*q.v.*). By marriage the Amsterdam Lo(o)ten family, which belonged to the Waterlander Mennonite congregation, and after its merger in 1668 to the united Waterlander-Lamist Church, was related to other well-known Mennonite families such as Rutgers, Verhamme, Roeters. Some members of this family served as deacons. The Looten family died out in the 18th century. (*N.N.B.Wb.* IX, 623; church records of Amsterdam.) vDZ.

Lootsma, Sipke (1888-1940), a schoolteacher and later a professor at the Lyceum at Zaandam, Netherlands, who wrote a number of historical papers. He also published some books, including *De Zeildoekweverij te Krommenie* (1928) and *Bijdrage tot de Geschiedenis der Nederlandsche Walvischvaart, meer speciaal Zaansche* (Wormerveer, 1937). Of great interest for Mennonite history is the memorial volume which he wrote on the occasion of the 250th anniversary of the meetinghouse of Zaandam-West (*q.v.*). This book, entitled *Het Nieuwe Huys 1687-1937, Friesch-Doopsgezinde Gemeente West-Zaandam* (Zaandam, 1937), was published by the church board. Lootsma was a deacon of this congregation from 1935 until his death. vDZ.

Lopes, Willem Klaasz, published *Ontleding der Christelyke Kerken-order ende deszelfs Ampten, waar in het Gebruyk en Misbruyk der zelver wert aangewezen* (Amsterdam, 1699). In this book and in his *Antwoord op eenige Vragen, die op myn Ontleding zyn voorgekomen* (Amsterdam, 1699) he attacked the Reformed views on the church and its offices, as defended by D. Bakkamude and Johannes Smetius, the latter (1636-1704) being a Reformed minister at Amsterdam. Of Lopes there was no further information available. He probably lived at Amsterdam and belonged to the Zonist congregation. The Amsterdam Mennonite Archives possess a manuscript copied by Marten Schagen (*q.v.*) which contains a philosophical debate between W. Reimarus and Lopes. Lopes also seems to have written a number of pamphlets published in 1664-65 during the *Lammerenkrijg* (*q.v.*), in which he took the side of Apostool and the Zonists against Galenus Abrahamsz and the Lamists. vDZ.

M. Schagen, *Naamlijst der Doopsgezinde Schrijveren* (Amsterdam, 1745) 64; *Inv. Arch. Amst.* I, No. 754 g.

Loppersum, a town in the Dutch province of Groningen, formerly the seat of a Mennonite congregation. Soon after 1530 Anabaptism is said to have had adherents at Loppersum. In 1557-61 Leenaert Bouwens baptized some persons here (4 or 7, the exact number could not be ascertained). About 1569 the Mennonites living at Loppersum and surrounding towns were severely molested by the district governor Imel van Lotteling, who planned to obtain their property by having it confiscated. Shortly after 1584 they suffered much under de Mepsche, provost of Loppersum, but it seems that no one lost his life. In the 17th century a congregation of Groningen Old Flemish existed here. The names of its preachers have come down from about 1680; they all were untrained and mostly farmers. In 1659 a meeting of Groningen Old Flemish leaders was held at Loppersum, where a statement was drawn up concerning clothing, furniture, etc., which the members of the Old Flemish congregations were allowed to have. (This statement is found in Blaupot ten Cate, *Friesland,* 307 f.) In the 18th century the congregation became very small: 1710 about 50 members; 1754, 17 members. In 1783 it merged with the congregation of Leermens (*q.v.*), forming the Leermens-Loppersum congregation. For the history of the united congregation, see **Leermens.** Of a meetinghouse of Loppersum nothing is known; the members presumably met in private homes. Now the meetinghouse of the congregation of Leermens-Loppersum is at Zeerijp (*q.v.*). vDZ.

Blaupot t. C., *Groningen* I, 15, 52, 86, 125, 127, 142, 198; *DJ* 1840, 43; *DB* 1879, 4, 111; *Oud-Archief,* Groningen, No. 145.

Lorch on the Rhine, a town in the Wiesbaden district of Hesse, Germany, at the confluence of the Wisper into the Rhine, was at the beginning of the 16th century a thriving village, inhabited by weavers who made use of the abundant water power of the Wisper and carried on trade with their cloth as far as the Netherlands. At that time Lorch was the seat of a strong Anabaptist group, under the leadership of a "bishop," Peter Nyerup of Calcar. On May 10, 1537, fire broke out in the city destroying several houses. Arson was suspected. A maid questioned on the rack threw suspicion on the Anabaptists. Several of them, including the bishop, left the city; their property was confiscated. Many were taken prisoner.

"They confessed on the rack that their doctrines were: Christ is not the true God, His body did not come from Mary but from heaven, only personal piety could accomplish justification, there is no original sin, contacts with non-Anabaptists are prohibited, the oath is forbidden as blasphemy, all goods are common, each one has a free will in spiritual matters, infant baptism is evil, state and government are evil institutions, and service in war a grievous sin." Albrecht, Elector of Mainz, demanded the greatest severity of punishment. By the end of 1537 there were 240 persons under arrest. Eustachius Pohl, Konrad Heftrich, both of Lorch, Sebastian Köhler of Geisenheim, and Wendel Lill of Rüdesheim, were hanged as "heretics, sectarians, perjurers"; Konrad Mohr and Sebastian Röhrig of Lorch were beaten and branded, and many others were banished from the country. Eighty-two citizens of Lorch were punished with a fine of 20 guilders and neck irons. Most of the exiles settled in the area of Katzenellenbogen. The movement was completely suppressed. Most of the Anabaptists became Protestants. (*Menn. Bl.,* 1893, 89-91; *ML* II, 690.)   NEFF.

Lord's Supper, interpretation among Anabaptists. The Anabaptists, being followers neither of Luther nor of Zwingli nor of Rome, had to develop their own understanding of the ordinance of the Lord's Supper and its meaning. That it was a ceremony for the remembrance of the death of Christ brings the Anabaptists somewhat in the neighborhood of Zwingli's interpretation. But beyond that, the Brethren developed quite an original viewpoint elsewhere little appreciated in Protestant circles, which emphasized the idea of fellowship or brotherhood in connection with the Lord's Table or the Supper. It meant to the Anabaptists not only the memory of the Lord's supreme sacrifice, but also a new dedication of the idea of *Gemeinschaft,* that is, living and, if need be, suffering together as a fellowship of dedicated disciples. This interpretation perhaps goes back to the words of the Apostle Paul in I Cor. 10:17. The eating and drinking together in a solemn meal was to them a symbol of their perfect togetherness in which the individual fuses with the group as a whole, foregoing self-will of any kind.

To illustrate this idea, the Anabaptists revived an old parable of the early church which runs somewhat as follows: "As the grain-kernels are altogether merged and each must give its content or strength (*Vermögen*) into the one flour and bread, likewise also the wine, where the grapes are crushed under the press, and each grape gives away all its juice and all its strength into one wine. Whichever kernel and whichever grape, however, is not crushed and retains its strength for itself alone, such an one is unworthy and is cast out. This is what Christ wanted to bring home to His companions and guests at the Last Supper as an example of how they should be together in such a fellowship" (Andreas Ehrenpreis, 1652).

The story of this parable is quite interesting. We find it for the first time in the "Teaching of the Twelve Apostles" (in Greek called *Didaché*), of about A.D. 120 when primitive Christian brotherhood was still strong in the churches of the Near East. We find the same parable again in the 63rd Epistle of Cyprian (A.D. 250). How it was handed down to the Reformation period is not known; perhaps it was through Eusebius (*q.v.*). It is true that of a rather early date even Martin Luther quotes it in his "Sermon about the most venerable sacrament of the Holy Corpus Christi," of 1519; but obviously he could not follow up this idea when he began to develop his own new theology.

Among the Anabaptists, however, we meet it time and again. A random sampling of Hutterite literature yielded at least three references in this area: Claus Felbinger's Confession of Faith of 1560, Peter Walpot's Epistle to the "Swiss" Brethren at Modenbach on the Rhine, 1577, and also Andreas Ehrenpreis in his great *Sendbrief* of 1652 (printed) quotes this parable in full. In each case the Brethren want-

ed to emphasize that self-giving or self-denial, renunciation of self-will, for the sake of the brotherhood, is the very essence of discipleship, to which every brother should rededicate himself ever again at the solemn occasion of the Lord's Supper.

However, not only the Hutterites, but also Menno Simons taught the same ideas, perhaps drawing from the same sources as the Hutterites (Eusebius?). This is what Menno Simons had to say about the Lord's Supper: "Gelijck als dan een natuurlijck brood van veel korens in de meulen gebroocken met water gekneet/ van des vyers hittigheydt tot een broodt gebacken wordt/ alsoo wordt oock de gemeynte Christi uyt veel geloovingen/ met de meulen des Godlijcken woordts in have herten gebroken/ met dat water des Heyligen Geests/ en met dat vyer der reynder ongeverweder liefden in een lichaem gedoopt" (Krahn, 142).

It was perhaps from Menno Simons (or from some other, not yet known tradition among the Brethren) that the Amish later borrowed this parable, to be used at their communion services. It is still used as a sermon topic (referring to I Cor. 10:17) on communion Sunday. To be sure, the emphasis with the Amish is slightly different from that of the Hutterites, yet in both cases the parable is to illustrate the meaning of the meal as a symbol of a closely knit brotherhood and as a collective rededication to the path of discipleship. (See **Communion.**)   R.F.

Lydia Müller, *Der Kommunismus der mähr. Wiedertäufer* (Leipzig, 1927) 66; C. Krahn, *Menno Simons* (Karlsruhe, 1936) 142; R. Friedmann, "The Epistles of the Hutterian Brethren," *MQR* XX (1946) 169; "Claus Felbinger's Confession," *MQR* XXIX (April 1955).

Loreburn Mennonite Brethren Church, now extinct, located near Loreburn, Sask., was organized in 1927 with 13 members and F. F. Wiens as leader. It belonged to the Herbert District Conference.   J.I.R.

Lörrach, a town (pop. 19,294) in Baden, Germany, seven miles northeast of Basel. The castle of Rötteln, formerly the residence of the counts of Hachberg and of the margraves of Baden, was destroyed by the French in 1678 but was rebuilt in 1867.

In the vicinity of Lörrach Anabaptist doctrine coming from Basel early found adherents. For a long time the Anabaptists were able to hide from their persecutors in this border region. They held their meetings usually at night in isolated places in the woods. They also performed some baptisms in Lörrach in the house of Friedrich Ludi. In 1582 the congregation was discovered. Ten members were subjected to cross-examination by the pastors of Lörrach and the neighboring villages in the presence of the magistrate Konrad von Ulm. The record was sent to Durlach and is found in the *Generallandesarchiv* at Karlsruhe. It affords a good insight into the religious position of the South German Anabaptists. Those being questioned had to explain first their nonattendance at regular church services and then their views on communion, baptism, oath, and government. Most of them had only a few years previously joined the group. The reason given for leaving the state church was that they were dissatisfied with moral conditions within the church.

Their Christian earnestness is expressed especially

in their concept of communion. Valentin Roser of Lörrach declared that only he who does the right and abstains from sin is worthy to receive communion. He had intended to go to communion at Easter, but had not done so, because someone had slandered him and he was undecided as to whether he should call him to account. Communion in the big church was participated in by many who did not repent or correct their lives. Hans Ludi of Lörrach, whom the local pastor called an Anabaptist preacher, stated that he did not go to communion in the church because there was no serious attempt made by its members to correct their conduct. A similar answer was given by Friedrich Ludi of Lörrach, a former judge. He pointed out that the partakers of the communion in the Lörrach church lived an offensive life through excessive drinking. He could not therefore attend church and communion. The pastor added in the report to the government, that Ludi desired nothing but to do what pleases God; he would separate himself from the ungodly. None of them wished to hurt anyone and were willing to obey the requirements of the government in all points.

The brotherhood seems to have been rather widespread. Evasive answers were given to questions about their preachers; they gave the name of a dead one, but they would not name the living ones. Clara Kreysin declared that she would betray no one, but finally admitted that their preacher came from Basel and his name was Marx. Leonhard Mayer, whose home town is not named, admitted that one was called Friedle and lived on the other side of the Rhine, and another was from Riehen and others from Stetten.

The magistrate ordered the persons under trial to attend church in Lörrach henceforth or to be subject to a serious command from Durlach. For several Sundays they would be watched to see if they attended the sermon; if they did not come their possessions would be inventoried for later confiscation. A report of the magistrate to the government dated Aug. 23, 1583, reveals that the accused did not attend the sermon, "but appeared disobedient." Their possessions were thereupon listed; but because of the plague prevalent in Lörrach nothing could be done against the Anabaptists. The pastors were instructed to admonish them.

Several men promised to go to church and to take communion. One of them, Germain Bertschin, added that the Anabaptists were pious and God-fearing, that they prayed earnestly, did not swear, and injured no one. But the rest stayed with their opinion and their brotherhood. Of Leonhard Dietrich in Oetlingen the local parson Franz Gut reported that he would pray God to show him the right way to salvation. Pastor Paul Cherber of Binzen reported concerning the widow M. Kreysin of Rümmingen, that "with the exception of disregard for going to church and the holy sacrament he knew nothing about her but love and goodness, uprightness and loyalty toward the poor."

Nonresident Anabaptists were banished from the town; there is no information on the fate of residents. Nor is there any later mention of the movement at Lörrach. The name Ludi (*q.v.*) (and Ludin) is still found in Lörrach. Hege.

Mühlhäusser, "Die Wiedertäufer in Lörrach im Jahre 1582," in *Studien der evangelisch-protestantischen Geistlichen des Grossherzogtums Baden* I (1875) 24-33; *TA Badenpfalz; ML* II, 690 f.

Lorraine. Little is known of an Anabaptist movement in Lorraine. Refugees from Flanders, including a surgeon of Lille, came to Metz in 1538, and judging from a letter Calvin wrote to Farel, they must have won some converts. But their work was of short duration. They were taken prisoner; two were drowned in the Moselle, and one was branded and expelled.

In the 18th century considerable numbers of Mennonites settled in the duchy of Lorraine, whom Louis XIV had expelled from Alsace in 1712. From the Leber Valley (Ste-Marie-aux-Mines) they migrated over the mountains into the Saar Valley, and spread over the Lorraine plateau as far as the duchy of Zweibrücken. In the mountains they formed the Hang and Salm congregations, farther north the Welschland, the German-Lorraine, and the Bitscherland congregations.

When the rest of Lorraine came to France in 1766, Louis XV made inquiries about the Mennonites, but did not disturb them, since the reports were favorable. Some years previously he reprimanded an official who had wanted to compel the Mennonites living in the bishopric of Metz to have their children baptized.

In the 19th century the Mennonites moved westward, forming congregations that gradually adopted French as their language; some of the churches in the German-speaking area in northern Lorraine remained. In the four départements of Lorraine there were in 1935 some 800 Mennonites, in eleven congregations. In 1955 there were only eight congregations with some 750 souls.

The largest number of Mennonites are in the département of Moselle. Here in the German-speaking area there are two congregations: Sarreguemines, formerly Bitscherland, and Diesen, descended from the German-Lorraine congregation. On the linguistic border is Sarrebourg, derived in part from the Welschland and in part from the German-Lorraine congregations.

In the départements Meurthe and Moselle there are three congregations: Baccarat, Lunéville, and Toul, which originated chiefly from the Welschland and Salm congregations, with some additions from German-Lorraine and Zweibrücken.

In the Vosges département the Vosges (Darney) congregation was organized from the above congregations. In the département Meuse is the Meuse (Ligny) congregation, with the same origin as the above. The Salm (now Bénaville) and Hang congregations were made a part of Lower Alsace after the Franco-Prussian War, and are in the French-speaking area. (*ML* II, 694.) P.So.

Lorraine Avenue Mennonite Church (GCM), located at S. Lorraine and East Gilbert, Wichita, Kan., is a member of the Western District Conference. In June 1928 C. E. Krehbiel gathered some interested people to consider the formation of a General Conference Mennonite church in Wichita. A year later

Arnold Funk was placed here as a worker under the mission committee. In 1932 a house was built and dedicated to serve as a church, and a congregation was organized with 17 charter members. In 1951 a stone and brick church was built, the first building having been converted into a parsonage. In 1954 the church had 311 members. Pastors who have served the church are Arnold Funk, C. E. Krehbiel, Olin Krehbiel, S. M. Musselman, E. D. Schmidt, P. E. Frantz, J. H. Langenwalter, and George S. Stoneback (1954).   G.S.S.

Lörsch, a Swiss Mennonite family name: see **Latscha** and **Lötscher.**

Los Angeles, Cal., a city (pop. 2,243,910) located in the county by the same name, has eight Mennonite congregations as follows: E.M.B.—The Church of the Bible, 8004 Vineland, Sun Valley, Cal., with 80 members; G.C.M.—Community Mennonite Church (in process of organization) and Immanuel Mennonite Church, 10335 Paramount Boulevard, Downey, with 271 members; Independent—35th Street Mennonite Church, 35th and Normandie, with 35 members; M.B.—City Terrace Mennonite Church, 1441 North Herbert, with 31 members; Hoover Boulevard M.B. Church, with 61 members, and Valley M.B. Church (in process of organizing), 14162 Van Nuys Boulevard, Pacoima, Cal., with 20 members; M.C.—Calvary Mennonite Church, 147 West 73rd St., with 74 members. The total Mennonite membership in the area in 1956 was probably about 700. Mennonites began to settle in Los Angeles about 1902. (See also **Upland.**)   D.D.E.

Los Angeles (Cal.) Mennonite Brethren Church located at 8109 S. Hoover St., a member of the Pacific District Conference, was organized on June 22, 1924, with an initial membership of 41 persons, and met in rented locations until the first meetinghouse was erected, dedicated Feb. 18, 1940. The first leader was A. C. Friesen, followed by P. P. Rempel in September 1924 and a series of other ministers. The membership in 1957 was 41, with Peter Klassen as part-time pastor. There has been a considerable transient membership, with no large permanent M.B. residential group in Los Angeles.   P.F.W.

Los Jagueyes, *Mexico, Mennonites.* Early in 1948 a group of Kleine Gemeinde (*q.v.*) Mennonites from Manitoba and a smaller group of Old Colony and Sommerfelder Mennonites from Saskatchewan and Manitoba purchased a ranch of 52,700 acres at Los Jagueyes, Chihuahua, Mexico, at $7.00 per acre, for the purpose of settlement. Two thirds of this land was fit for cultivation and one third was mountainous and partly wooded. It is located about 80 miles northwest of Cuauhtemoc and 12 miles southwest of the Sommerfelder Mennonite settlement at Santa Clara. The northern two thirds of the land was set aside for the Kleine Gemeinde and the southern third for the Old Colony Mennonites. The aim of these people was to preserve the German language for their children, and escape the social and religious changes taking place in Canada.

In July 1948 the first seven families of the Kleine Gemeinde arrived at Los Jagueyes, "the place of springs," hired a large caterpillar and put into the virgin soil nearly 1,000 acres of oats. It being a dry late season, only feed was harvested in November, which, however, was of great help to the numerous settlers arriving that fall, most of whom brought their machinery and some stock along from Manitoba. By March 1952 the final group of about 12 families left Manitoba to conclude the movement. This brought the total Kleine Gemeinde group to about 90 families, or over 600 souls, which, however, comprised only 15 per cent of the church in Manitoba. Elder Peter P. Reimer was the spiritual leader of the emigrating group until his death in April 1949. In March 1951 Cornelius R. Reimer was ordained elder of the group, now called the Kleine Gemeinde of Mexico. In 1954 the baptized membership was 323.

Within a radius of about five miles from the center of the settlement, where a large adobe church has been built, six villages have been established: Morgental, Talheim, Grünland, Wiesenheim, Ebenfeld, and Eichenbach. Five of the villages have schools, the teachers being elected from the membership of the church. The language of instruction is German with a little English to assist in keeping contact with the relatives and friends in Manitoba.

There is a planing mill, a cheese factory, a garage, two stores, a hatchery, a sawmill, a machine shop, and a shoemaker's shop. Thus the settlement in four short years (1948-52) established itself as an agricultural, economic, and religious unit, though its members have come from five different congregations and districts in Manitoba. There is almost constant economic contact with Chihuahua, the capital of the state, which is only 100 miles away.

Early in 1949 an MCC emergency health clinic was established 12 miles from the settlement under the directorship of Peter J. B. Reimer, which proved to be of great help, since the nearest hospital was 80 miles away. About two years later this clinic was moved by request of the settlers directly into the center of the settlement.

The southern third of the ranch was settled at the same time by about 30 families of Old Colony Mennonites from Saskatchewan and some Sommerfelder Mennonites from Manitoba. The former were mostly poor and the latter were somewhat better off economically. This factor and probably a different social and religious background led to considerable friction among the group, so that their spiritual leader, Bishop John Leppky, returned to Saskatchewan, where he soon died. A number of other families of this group have also returned to Canada. They have had two other leaders who apparently have also left the settlement. However, the group has established three villages. The ground is higher in this settlement, the soil better, and the countryside more attractive than in the northern area. The Kleine Gemeinde group has lately purchased a part of this land to help the Old Colony group financially, and may possibly have to take over most of it because of the apparent economic and cultural disintegration of the Old Colony group.   P.J.B.R.

P. J. B. Reimer, "From Russia to Mexico," *Menn. Life* IV (1949) 26-33.

Löscher, Kaspar (1836-1718), a German Lutheran divine, educated at the University of Leipzig. He became church superintendent in Sondershausen in 1668, first pastor at Erfurt in 1676, superintendent at Zwickau in 1679, and general superintendent and professor at Wittenberg in 1687. His oldest son was the noted Valentin Löscher. In 1688 the following work was published in Wittenberg: *Secta Mennonitarum, quoad ortum, progressum et mataeologiam, elencho, qua potiora religionis capita, notatam, delineata; praeside Dn. Casparo Loescher . . . autor Johannes Vaget, Bremensis.* In general in the older dissertations the *praeses* is considered the author. The list of Kaspar Löscher's works, expressly excluding the *Disputationes a respondentibus elaboratae,* does not contain this title; and the wording of a foreword of the *praeses* to the *respondens* explains why it is sometimes attributed to Löscher, and sometimes to Vaget.

It contains 56 pages quarto with many sources. The booklet first discusses the various names for the Mennonites and then gives a historical sketch. A second section treats *Formam sectae huius externam* and particularly *Hodomoriam mennonianam eiusdemque confutationem;* nine *phantasmata* are presented and rejected.   E.C.

G. Wernsdorf, *Collegium pietatis Davidicum . . .* (Wittenberg, 1718, a funeral sermon with a biographical sketch and a list of his writings, called by Jöcher an independent work of the young Löscher); F. Blanckmeister, *Der Prophet von Kursachsen, Valentin Ernst Löscher und seine Zeit* (Dresden, 1920); ML II, 691.

Lose, Peter, of Gemünden, Hesse, Germany, Anabaptist, was seized at Wolkersdorf with nine Anabaptists, including Jörg Schnabel (*q.v.*) and Leonhard Fälber (*q.v.*), imprisoned at Marburg, and signed the *Bekenntnis oder Antwort etlicher Fragestück oder Artikel der gefangenen Täufer und anderer im Lande zu Hessen.* On Dec. 10, 1538, he was cross-examined. "He gave Bucer such loose and frivolous answers that the listeners laughed heartily, and therefore, because he answered so mockingly and disrespectfully nothing special was talked with him." Nothing further is known about him. (*Ztscht f. d. hist. Theol.,* 1858, 610 f.; *TA Hessen; ML* II, 687.)   NEFF.

Losea, Abraham de (1619-90), a Reformed theologian, born at Murten, Switzerland, stemmed from a family of Arles, Provence, France, whose progenitor, the canon Jean, joined the Reformation and came to Geneva in 1523. Abraham de Losea received his first pastorate in 1641 in Könitz near Bern, and in 1647 he was made third assistant at the cathedral in Bern. This office gave him citizenship in the city. In the following years he rose in ecclesiastic position. In 1662 he was made the second pastor at the cathedral. Above him there was only one position, that of first pastor, which was usually associated with the deanship of the Bernese clergy.

In January 1659 de Losea was appointed by the government to the newly constituted Anabaptist committee (*Täuferkommission*), and conducted many examinations of Anabaptists confined in the orphanage and penitentiary. As a member of the *Kirchenkonvent* (*q.v.*) he helped to formulate several opinions on the Anabaptists. In them he always advised tolerance and a more lenient and just judgment, and opposed measures of violence. Evidence of this attitude is found in the opinion of the *Kirchenkonvent* ("first opinion") of 1670 (reprinted in Müller, 140-43), in which only five of the clergymen of the city advocated lenience. The majority ("second opinion") favored intolerance, increasing the government mania for persecution. De Losea died in 1690 as pastor in Thun.   S.G.

"Bernische Pfarrer 16.-19. Jahrhundert," ms., Archives of the Canton of Bern; "Kirchenwesen" II D. 85, E. 86, and F. 87, Archives of Bern; "Miss. Hist. Helv." III 272, in City Library of Bern; *Historisch-Biographisches Lexikon der Schweiz* II, "Delosea" (Neuenburg, 1924); Müller, *Berner Täufer;* S. Geiser, *Die Taufgesinnten-Gemeinden* (Karlsruhe, 1931); *ML* II, 691 f.

Losenegger, Moritz, an Anabaptist martyr of Bern, Switzerland, a native of Thun, was banished from the canton on Dec. 20, 1532, but returned and was arrested. He was sentenced to die for breaking the exile, but was pardoned on Jan. 8, 1533, and was then banished again under threat of death if he should return once more. He nevertheless came back. In the autumn of 1535 it was learned that he was staying at Trachselwald; on Oct. 28 the government ordered his arrest, but he was not seized until May 2, 1536. He was then executed at Bern. No particulars are known concerning his work, except that he was a zealous preacher. In van Braght's list of martyrs in the *Martyrs' Mirror* Losenegger was the eleventh Anabaptist martyr in Bern.   HEGE.

Th. de Quervain, *Kirchliche und soziale Zustände in Bern, 1528-1536* (Bern, 1906); *Mart. Mir.* E 1,129; *ML* II, 692.

Loserth, Johann (1846-1936), Austrian historian, was born Sept. 1, 1846, at Fulnek in Moravia, whither his ancestors had fled as refugees from Silesia in the 17th century. They were weavers. Since machinery encroached upon their industry, his father opened a cereal business, the proceeds of which, however, did not cover the expenses of long illness in the family. Under such circumstances there could be no thought of university training for the six sons.

Johann was then to learn cabinetmaking. A kindly relative made it possible for him to attend the gymnasium in Troppau and Kremsier. Because of inadequate support these were years of bitter privation. By private teaching he earned the necessary money for study. In the autumn of 1866 he went to the University of Vienna. The professors to whom he owed most were Ottokar Lorenz and Theodor Sickel; the latter admitted him in 1869 into the Institute for Research in Austrian History. After the completion of his study he taught at a realgymnasium in Vienna. He received his doctor's degree at Tübingen (1871), and later also in Vienna (1874) for his work on the sources for the history of Kremsmünster. This publication led to a scholarly dispute with the famed historian Georg Waitz, which ended in victory for Loserth.

In 1875 Loserth was called as professor to the newly founded University of Czernowitz in Bukowina. In 1893 he was called to the University of Graz, Austria, and in 1917 he retired. In 1896 he became a member of the Academy of Vienna. He continued his writing with studies on the sources of Königsaal history, which led him into research on

Cosmas of Prague and other old Bohemian sources. In this connection he published a series of critical works on the older history of Bohemia. His studies on the spiritual roots of Hussite doctrine were determinative. As a fruit of this research he published the book *Huss und Wiclif* (1884, second edition 1925), which proves the complete independence of the Hussite doctrines from Wycliffe's writings. These studies brought Loserth into contact with the Wycliffe Society, which began the publication of Wycliffe's Latin works in 1883. Of the 40 volumes which were published by 1922, 14, all of them first editions, were edited by Loserth. These publications are all accompanied by many critical individual inquiries, most of which were published in the writings of the Vienna Academy.

Studies in Moravian archives directed Loserth's attention to the Anabaptists, who had spread over Nikolsburg, southern Moravia, and Austria, and had carried on a live correspondence with their brethren in neighboring countries. These studies brought Loserth into connections with Joseph von Beck (*q.v.*), whose literary legacy he took over and completed with additional archival work. Works on the history of Anabaptism in Moravia, Lower Austria, Styria, Salzburg, Tirol, and Switzerland followed; also a biography of Balthasar Hubmaier (*q.v.*), biographical sketches of Georg Blaurock (*q.v.*), Pilgram Marpeck (*q.v.*), and others. At an advanced age Loserth published other important works on the history of the Anabaptist movement. Among them was Pilgram Marbeck's *Verantwortung* (1929), a book replying to Schwenckfeld.

What Loserth discovered on the history of Anabaptism in Styria was also significant. It was shown that there were not only isolated Anabaptists there, as had previously been supposed, but that until 1530 the country was literally flooded with them. This information we owe to Dingauer, a Jesuit who was an official and father confessor in the Dietrichstein (*q.v.*) family and wrote a history of the house of Dietrichstein. He used the archives of Sigmund von Dietrichstein, who was for his part not a severe opponent of the Anabaptists, but incurred the reproach of Ferdinand for his lenience.

Finally Loserth uncovered a very valuable source on the decline of the Anabaptists in Moravia and Hungary and their restoration by the Carinthian emigrants, who were expelled to Transylvania in 1755, there became acquainted with the last remnants of the Hutterites, and finally accepted their teaching. Since they could not remain in Transylvania, they migrated to Wallachia and then to Russia; in the middle of the 19th century they went to North America (see **Kuhr, Joseph**).

Loserth's call to Graz opened further fields of study in the history of the Reformation and the Counter Reformation in Inner Austria with sources and thorough treatment. This resulted in inspiration for other historical studies of the country, of history of the noble families, of economics, and of Austrian history in general. His familiarity with the intellectual currents of the 13th and 14th centuries qualified him to write the history of the late Middle Ages for the *Handbuch der mittelalterlichen und neueren Geschichte von Below-Meinecke.*

Loserth died in Graz on Aug. 30, 1936, two days before the completion of his ninetieth year.

In the *Zeitschrift des Historischen Vereins für Steiermark,* vol. XXII (1926) appeared: W. Erben and A. Kern, "Johann Loserth als Geschichtsforscher. Eine Uebersicht seiner wissenschaftlichen Werke." The table of contents lists 286 articles, omitting book reviews and articles in current papers; for the history of Bohemia 65 titles, for the Wycliffite and Hussite movements 63 titles, for the history of the Anabaptists 25 titles, for the history of the Reformation and Counter Reformation in Austria and adjacent countries 68 titles, miscellaneous 62 titles.

For the history of the Anabaptists the following should be named: "Zur Geschichte der Wiedertäufer in Mähren, in *Zeitscht für allgemeine Geschichte, Kultur-, Literatur- und Kunstgeschichte* I (1884) 438-57; "Die Stadt Waldshut und die vorderösterreichische Regierung in den Jahren 1523-26," in *Archiv f. österr. Geschichte* LXXVII (Vienna, 1891); "Deutschböhmische Wiedertäufer," in *Mitt. d. Vereins f. Gesch. d. Deutschen in Böhmen* XXX (1892); "Der Anabaptismus in Tirol von seinen Anfängen bis zum Tode Jakob Huters (1526-36). Aus den hinterlassenen Papieren des Josef R. von Beck," in *Archiv f. österr. Geschichte* LVIII (1892); "Der Anabaptismus in Tirol vom Jahre 1536 bis zu seinem Erlöschen," *loc. cit.* LXXIX (1893); *Doctor Balthasar Hubmaier und die Anfänge der Wiedertaufe in Mähren* (Brno, 1893) VIII, 217; "Wiedertäufer in Steiermark," in *Mitt. d. Hist. Ver. f. Steiermark* XLII (1894) 118-45; "Der Kommunismus der Huterischen Brüder in Mähren im 16. und 17. Jahrhundert," in *Ztscht f. Sozial- und Wirtschaftsgeschichte* III (1895) 61-92; "Der Communismus der mährischen Wiedertäufer im 16. und 17. Jahrhundert. Beiträge zu ihrer Geschichte, Lehre und Verfassung," in *Archiv f. österr. Geschichte* LXXXI (1895) 135-322; "Die Wiedertaufe in Niederösterreich von ihren Anfängen bis zum Tode Balthasar Hubmaiers, 1525-28," in *Blätter des Ver. f. Landeskunde von Niederösterreich* XXXIII (1899) 417-35; "Georg Blaurock und die Anfänge des Anabaptismus in Graubünden und Tirol," in *Vorträge und Aufsätze aus der Comenius-Gesellschaft* VII (1899); "Zur Geschichte der Wiedertäufer in Steiermark," in *Mitt. des Hist. Ver. f. Steiermark* I (1903) 177 ff. and *Ztscht des Hist. Vereins f. Steiermark* X (1912) 267 ff.; "Zur Geschichte der Wiedertäufer in Salzburg," in *Mitt. d. Gesellschaft f. Salzburger Landeskunde* LII (1912) 35-60; "Studien zu Pilgram Marbeck," in *Gedenkschrift zum 400-jährigen Jubiläum der Mennoniten oder Taufgesinnten, 1525 bis 1925,* 134-78; *Pilgram Marbecks Antwort auf Kaspar Schwenkfelds Beurteilung des Buches der Bundesbezeugung von 1542, Quellen und Forschungen zur Geschichte der Oberdeutschen Taufgesinnten im 16. Jh.,* J. Loserth, ed. (Vienna and Leipzig, 1929) XII, 592 pp. In the *Mennonitisches Lexikon* he published over 100 articles, which also appear in the MENNONITE ENCYCLOPEDIA.

See also *Akten und Korrespondenzen zur Geschichte der Gegenreformation in Innerösterreich unter Erzherzog Karl II. und Ferdinand II.* (Vienna, 1898-1907) (*Font. rer. Austr.,* 2. Abt., vols. 50, 58,

60); *Die Reformation und Gegenreformation in den innerösterr. Ländern im 16. Jh.* (Stuttgart, 1898) VIII, 614 pp. A.Ke.

M. Uhlirz, "Johann Loserth zum 80. Geburtstage, 1. Sept. 1926," in *Ztscht des dt. Vereins f. d. Geschichte Mährens u. Schlesiens* XXVIII (1926) 1-8; Karl Völker, "Der Historiker des innerösterreichischen Protestantismus," in *Christliche Welt*, 1936, No. 16; Paul Dedic, "Johann Loserth zum Gedächtnis," in *Der Säemann*, No. 10; Christian Hege, "Johann Loserth," in *Menn. Gesch.-Bl.* I (1936) 36-40; *ML* II, 692-94.

Lost River Mennonite Church (GCM), located near Bethany in northeastern Saskatchewan, is a member of the Canadian District. Lost River is a small stream that disappears underground. The Lost River community is about 30 miles distant from the Carrot River and Petaigon areas, each of which also has a congregation. The first settler at Lost River was probably Cornelius Ens, who came from Manitoba in 1912. The first pastor was Cornelius Ens, who retired after 25 years of service, and was succeeded by Jacob H. Ens, the present (1956) pastor. The membership, at one time 300, was 150 in 1954, and is not given in the 1956 Yearbook. J.G.R.

Lostadt, Elsa van, wife of Gysbrecht van Baeck, Lord of Varik, bailiff of the town of IJsselstein, Dutch province of Utrecht, was much in sympathy with the Anabaptists, whom she soon after 1530 largely favored. Later she joined the Anabaptist-Münsterite sect of the Batenburgers (*q.v.*). In August 1544 she was imprisoned at The Hague, but was released without trial, probably in February 1545, against a security of 1,000 caroli-guilders; on Oct. 3, 1548, she was acquitted by the Court of Holland, which had ordered the imprisonment in 1544. This favorable arrangement concerning a notorious heretic was due to the fact that Elsa van Lostadt was a noble lady of high rank and especially because the influential Maximiliaan van Egmond, Count of Buren, had appealed to the Emperor Charles V. vdZ.

Inv. Arch. Amst. I, 283 f., 311, 314, 325, 350; *DB* 1917, 142; Kühler, *Geschiedenis* I, 99, 175, 208; Mellink, *Wederdopers*, 234, 241, 341, 415.

Lot, a method for the selection of church officials. Although there is no documentary evidence of the use of the lot by Anabaptists in the selection of church officials (elders, bishops, preachers, deacons), and although the lot is not mentioned in any Mennonite confessions of faith, there is inferential evidence that it came into use fairly early among the Swiss Mennonites and was generally in use among them and their descendants in France, South Germany, Galicia, Volhynia, and North America throughout the 17th-19th centuries. It has been uniformly used in the following groups in North America since the beginning of settlement here: Mennonite Church (MC), Old Order Mennonite, Old Order Amish, and Conservative Mennonite, but by no other North American groups. Although the practice is rapidly fading out in many districts of the Mennonite Church (MC), it is still almost universally used in the Franconia, Lancaster, and Washington-Franklin conferences. It remains in unchanging use in the remaining three above-mentioned groups. Apparently the lot was never used in any of the Dutch, North and East German, and Russian Mennonite groups in Europe, or in any of their descendant groups anywhere else in the world. The Hutterian Brethren have long used the lot in the selection of preachers, but not in the selection of Vorsteher and other officials. In the General Conference Mennonite Church the lot was used only in the congregations of Swiss background (not much after the 1870's) and the Eastern District. W. S. Gottschall claims that he was the last to be ordained by this method (1904).

N. van der Zijpp reports that although there is probably no direct evidence that the lot was used for the selection of ministers by the Dutch Anabaptists and Mennonites, there is reason to believe that it was used on occasion. The pamphlet *Lammerenkrijgh* (1655) contains the following: "Then three preachers and three deacons had to be chosen, which among us is always done by a majority of votes of the entire brotherhood." Cornelius Krahn quotes Menno as saying, "Servants of the holy Word shall be duly called either by the Lord Himself, or by means of the pious" (*Writings*, 665). "Others, born of the unblamable church of Christ, were chosen by lot as was Matthias" (*Writings*, 443).

The lot is customarily used in the following manner in the selection of men to be ordained. The vote of the congregation or district is first taken for candidates, one or more votes being required for admission to candidacy, the number of required votes being determined from time to time by conference rules or tradition, or local congregational decision. Thereupon the bishop in charge, usually assisted by one or more visiting bishops, places on a table in the sight of the congregation a number of hymnbooks or Bibles equal to the number of candidates, in one of which he or an assistant has hidden a thin slip on which is written the following verse from Proverbs 16:33: "The lot is cast into the lap; but the whole disposing thereof is of the Lord." A special prayer for divine action is then offered. Each candidate in succession now takes one of the books, which the bishop then opens in turn until he finds the lot slip. It is assumed that the one in whose book the slip is found is the one whom God has chosen. The chosen one is then usually immediately ordained. In the Franconia Conference (MC) each book contains a slip, all being blank but the one "bearing the lot."

The practice of the use of the lot is grounded primarily on the example of the choice of Matthias to take the place of Judas in the company of the twelve apostles as recorded in Acts 1:23-26. There the apostles prayed, "Thou, Lord, . . . shew whether of these two thou hast chosen." Those who use the lot believe that God operates through it to select the right person for the vacant office. The use of the lot usually goes with a high concept of the ministerial office as one conferred by God and not by men. It accordingly serves to elevate the chosen person above the congregation and gives him considerable prestige and authority. It also usually effectively eliminates factionalism and partisanship in the selection and later relationship of the chosen one to the congregation, since the choice is clearly not by vote. It also gives the chosen one a strong sense of direct call by God. In the older times one vote was enough to place a man in the lot for any office, although in more recent times some groups have required at least two or more votes for minister, one for bishop, or at least five from the entire bishop district.

Ordination by lot usually is a dramatic experience for a congregation. The service is loaded with tension, expectancy, and uncertainty. It is one of the few times when direct divine action can be visibly experienced, at least for those who sincerely believe that God acts through the lot, and it therefore intensifies the religious experience of the group practicing it. It is to be distinguished sharply from a mere drawing of straws or lots to break a tie.

The history of the use of the lot among Mennonites has as yet not been thoroughly studied. It was used in 1711 in Lancaster (Conestoga) to determine who should go to Europe to report to the brotherhood about the new colony. It was used in 1805 to determine the assignment of individual farm tracts to the purchasers of the Waterloo Township Mennonite settlement tract. It has been used in other Christian groups, among them in the Moravian Church in colonial Pennsylvania. In the first period of Moravian history at Bethlehem and other early settlements the lot was used for various decisions, among them the choice of marriage partners. In Lititz it was used for this purpose down into the 19th century.   H.S.B.

H. S. Bender, "The Historical Background of Our Present Ministerial Offices," Gospel Herald XLII (1949) 1051, 1061.; W. S. Gottschall, "The Lot," The Mennonite, 1928, p. 3.

Lötscher is the name of a widely ramified Mennonite family stemming from the Simmental in the Bernese Oberland of Switzerland. The progenitor was Hans Lötscher (see **Leutscher** and **Latscha**) of Latterbach near Erlenbach, born 1601, a pious man, author of the song, "Schön new Geistlich Lied" (41 stanzas), in which he gives examples from the Bible to warn his descendants and contemporaries of the spirit and confusion of the world. On Jan. 21, 1633, he married Anna Kammerer of Latterbach. The three oldest of his five children, Hans, Melchior, and Anna Lötscher, were taken to the Anabaptist prison in Bern in 1666. The clergy on the Anabaptist Commission, including Abraham de Losea (q.v.), were instructed to visit them diligently, teach them, and take away "their whims." Considering their youth, there was hope that "they might be led on the right way." But they persisted steadfastly in their faith.

Hans and Melchior escaped from prison in August 1667, but were soon recaptured and put into the orphanage in Bern. After four years of imprisonment they were put in irons and taken to Venice on March 16, 1671, with four other Mennonites as galley-slaves. Then they were lost sight of, except that in 1673 they were again in the canton of Bern to take over the inheritance from their father. They were refused.

In 1711 members of the family of the youngest brother Abraham were among the Mennonites emigrating to Holland, where the name was soon spelled "Leutscher." Several of his descendants became Mennonite preachers in Holland. One of them,

Jan Isaak Lotscher, who died in September 1866 at the age of 94 years, had carefully kept the Swiss costume of his fathers.   S.G.

A. Fluri, "Die Lötscher von Latterbach," in Blätter für bern. Gesch., Kunst und Altertumskunde (Bern, 1912); Müller, Berner Täufer; S. Geiser, Die Taufgesinnten-Gemeinden (Karlsruhe, 1931); ML II, 694 f.

Lotzer (Loytzer), **Sebastian** (1490-?), a writer of the Reformation era, the son of a church official in Horb, Württemberg, Germany. He was a furrier, a trade which brought him into contact with the educated and wealthy. His brother Johann was the personal physician of Bishop Wilhelm of Strasbourg and of Elector Louis V (q.v.) of the Palatinate and a friend of Erasmus (q.v.). On his journeys Sebastian came to Memmingen, became a citizen, married, and took over his father-in-law's business; hence he was also called Weyenlin Bamer. He early became a Protestant, and the intimate friend of the learned preacher Christoph Schappeler. He was most deeply influenced by Eberlin's Fünfzehn Bundesgenossen.

It is very likely that Lotzer formulated the petition of the Memmingen peasants to the council on Feb. 24, 1525, which became the basis for the famous Twelve Articles of the Peasant Revolt (q.v.), which are not the work of an individual, as A. Götze assumes, but which constitute the official program of the peasants agreed upon by the peasants at a meeting on Feb. 27, which was initiated by Lotzer. Lotzer was appointed "field secretary" or chancellor by Ulrich Schmid, the leader of the Baltringen peasants. The articles (which appeared in print on March 19, 1525) epitomized what had been current in Upper Swabia, basing the peasant demands on "divine law," and combining the social revolution with the religious problem; but on the whole they were quite moderate. Lotzer was also the author of the beautiful, courteous, and altogether irenic letter of the peasants' committee to the Swabian League which had refused peaceable negotiations (Vogt, Correspondenz des Ulrich Arzt, Nos. 115 and 137).

The greater the peasant host grew, the less were Schmid and Lotzer able to assert their peaceful intentions. A rebellion took place against Schmid (April 12-17). The Battle of Wurzach was a complete defeat for the peasants. Schmid and Lotzer fled to St. Gall, Switzerland, Schappeler's home town, where Lotzer met Kessler, who gives a very valuable report on him in his Sabbata. The Swabian League ordered the Memmingen council to arrest Lotzer, but he was safely concealed and no longer heard of. His brother Johann presumably aided him under an assumed name.   G.Bo.

G. Bossert, "Seb. Lotzer und seine Schriften," in Blätter für württembergische Kirchengeschichte, 1887, 25-78 (reprint Memmingen, 1906); Günther Franz, Der deutsche Bauernkrieg (Munich, 1933) 196 ff.; Alfred Götze, Seb. Lotzers Schriften (1902); idem, "Die Artikel der Bauern," Hist. Vierteljahrsschrift, 1901, 1-12; idem, "Die zwölf Artikel der Bauern," op. cit., 1902, 1-32; Fr. L. Baumann, Die zwölf Artikel der Bauern (1896); ML II, 695.

Loucks, Aaron (1864-1945), for many years a prominent leader in the Mennonite Church (MC), was born at Scottdale, Pa., Nov. 20, 1864, where he lived all his life with the exception of 13 months' residence in Riverside, Cal. He died at Scottdale Aug. 20, 1945. Interment in Alverton cemetery. He was the son of Jacob Stauffer and Mary Saylor Loucks of Somerset Co., Pa., who were the parents of eleven children. The progenitor of the American branch of the Loucks family was Peter Loucks, who was born in Germany in 1706 and came to America in 1738, settling in Bucks Co., Pa. Aaron Loucks was twice married. His first wife was Amelia Medsgar, and to this marriage his three children were born. His second wife was Sadie Saylor, who preceded him in death about a year. He became a member of the Mennonite Church (MC) in the spring of 1887, and was a charter member of the Scottdale congregation when it was incorporated in January 1898. He was ordained to the ministry at Stonerville (now Alverton), Pa., and as bishop at Scottdale in 1893.

As one of a number of men who were active in the Mennonite Church in its "great awakening" in the years previous to and following the beginning of the 20th century, he was active in establishing various organizations which grew up in that time. He was the founder of the Mennonite Publishing House and largely instrumental in beginning the publication of the *Gospel Witness* in 1905, which in 1908 was merged with the *Herald of Truth*, published in Elkhart, Ind., to become the *Gospel Herald*. He helped to organize the Mennonite Publication Board in 1907. When this organization took over the Publishing House and all its publications in 1908, Scottdale became the official publication headquarters of the Mennonite Church (MC).

Aaron Loucks was also interested in the other organizations of the church and was active in the work of the Mennonite General Conference, the Mennonite Board of Missions and Charities, and the Mennonite Board of Education, of which he was treasurer for a number of years. As chairman of the Mennonite Relief Commission for War Sufferers he made a trip to the Near East in 1918. He was a leader in the peace work of the church during World War I and was especially active in contacting government officials and in visiting brethren detained in camps.

Loucks was active in the Southwestern Pennsylvania (now Allegheny) Conference and the Sunday-school conference of the same district, which he helped to organize in 1895. He was also in part the originator of the Bible conference movement which for a number of decades was widely used as a means of giving Bible instruction to the rank and file of the Mennonites. Through his leadership, the first Bible conference held in a Mennonite congregation was conducted at the Scottdale church for two weeks, beginning Dec. 28, 1896.   P.E.

Louis XIV (1638-1715), king of France 1643-1715, intended to make France an absolute monarchy. Although he was strictly Catholic, he did not permit the pope to interfere in any political affairs. Very energetically he defended Catholic customs and usage, which were called freedoms of the Gallic church. He was also a zealous promoter of religious unity in France. There were in the kingdom many Protestants, to whom Henry IV had guaranteed freedom

of conscience and certain political rights in the Edict of Nantes (1598). Richelieu, the minister of Louis XIII, had withdrawn these political rights. Now Louis XIV proceeded to restrict their freedom of conscience. What was not expressly promised in the Edict was prohibited. All means were used to convert the Protestants. The most terrible of these was the compulsory quartering of troops, who were guilty of all sorts of violence, upon the unfortunate ones, until they declared themselves ready to recant. The large numbers of conversions were announced and celebrated with great rejoicing. Finally the Jesuits persuaded the king that there were practically no Protestants left in France and that the Edict was therefore meaningless. It was repealed in 1685. The remaining Protestants were forbidden to leave the country on threat of being sentenced to the galleys. Nevertheless hundreds and thousands of them fled over the borders and brought their fund of knowledge, particularly in industry, to their new home.

Although Alsace had been French since 1648, it was not affected by the Edict of Nantes, since the Peace of Westphalia had assured it freedom of conscience. But there were many Mennonites in Alsace. Against them the king was particularly prejudiced. In France the name Anabaptists had the effect of a bogey; it suggested only the Peasant Revolt and the revolt of Münster. But the Alsatian Mennonites were quiet, and the government of the newly acquired province was so complicated that they escaped notice for many years. The attention of the king was directed to the Mennonites when he came into conflict with the Dutch States-General. But here he heard only favorable reports about them. Sometime previously General Turenne had met with the Dutch Ambassador M. van Beuningen. Turenne censured the States-General for tolerating so many sects, especially the Anabaptists. The statesman replied: "Why should we not tolerate the Anabaptists? They are such good people and so easy to get along with. They do not seek honor and regard, so they are in nobody's way. We do not fear revolt from a sect which has as one of the articles of its faith a prohibition against carrying arms. The Mennonites pay their share of all public taxes, and that suffices us. With their taxes we pay mercenaries who are more useful to us in the army than they could be. They build us up by the purity of their morals. They carry on agriculture, industry, and trade without wasting what they earn in luxury or gluttony. People of other creeds frequently do not act thus but by their excesses are a public offense and a great injury to the state. To be sure they refuse to render an oath, but that is of no significance, for their promise to speak the truth binds them like an oath" (Michiels, 104 f.).

In 1672, when the French army marched into Holland, Louis XIV sent Raymond Formantyn (*q.v.*) to get information about the Mennonites and make a report. The learned man went to Emmerich to the bookdealer van Beughem. Since they did not understand each other's language they conversed in Latin. Van Beughem summoned the Mennonite preacher Heinrich van Voorst and served as interpreter for him. Formantyn was amazed at the Biblical knowledge of the Mennonite. He looked up in a

French Bible the references cited and underlined them. After a two days' discussion they departed on friendly terms and Formantyn promised to give a favorable report. But the effect of this report was not evident, for Louis XIV had to withdraw from the country. The French troops retreated to Alsace via the Palatinate, doing a great deal of damage (1674). The unfortunate Palatinate, to which many Mennonites from Switzerland had fled, was devastated again in 1689.

But the hour of persecution was also to strike for the Alsatian Mennonites. There were many of them in the gravure Rappoltstein and especially around Ste.-Marie-aux-Mines, where they had achieved a certain economic position through their industry, rousing the envy of their neighbors, especially since they were exempt from military service. Complaints reached Versailles. In the name of the king, de la Houssaye issued a circular on Sept. 9, 1712, requiring that all Anabaptists be expelled from the kingdom. They turned to the gravure of Montbéliard, which at that time belonged to Württemberg, to the duchy of Lorraine, to Zweibrücken, and to the Breisgau in Baden.

The count of Rappoltstein at that time was Christian II von Birkenfeld, a captain in the French army, a favorite of the king. Although it meant a great loss to his country, he had to carry out the king's command exactly, whereas other lords in Alsace were more lenient. It seems that the numerous Mennonites living in Upper Alsace and especially in the Sundgau (south of Altkirch) were not molested. Also in Rappoltstein they were again tolerated on a petition by the count, at least a certain number of families.

Louis XIV died in 1715. Under his successors the Mennonites again enjoyed relative peace on the condition that they would draw no public attention to themselves. In 1766, when Lorraine became French, inquiries were made about them; but since the reports were favorable they were tolerated until finally the French Revolution brought religious freedom to all.   P.So.

Alfred Michiels, *Les Anabaptistes des Vosges* (Paris, 1860); *ML* II, 697 f.

Louis V (1478-1544), Elector Palatine 1508-44, conservative in church matters, and not averse to Protestantism. He frequently strove to mediate between religious factions. He did not leave the Catholic Church, in part because four of his brothers were bishops (Ried, 57).

The Anabaptist movement became rather widespread in his realm beginning in 1527. Immediate countermeasures were passed, involving the death penalty. Apparently the elector was opposed to its infliction in matters of faith, as can be inferred from the fact that he asked opinions of jurists at 21 places (Wiswedel, 23).

In 1527 the Palatine chancellor Florenz von Venningen composed a legal document which advocated the death penalty for persons who were baptized on their faith, and which was sent to the juristic faculties of ten universities for criticism (Krebs, 568). Replies rejecting the death penalty did not influence the elector, for he did not wish to

irritate the emperor. On Jan. 4, 1528, the notorious mandate of Charles V was published, which ordered the death penalty for Anabaptists. In this connection Louis issued a mandate on March 5, 1528, in order, as he stated, "to live out most obediently the command and edict of the Roman Imperial Majesty," forbidding baptism on faith on penalty of death and confiscation of goods, offering high rewards for information on a baptized person (Hege, 58 f.; see **Palatinate**). The Hutterite chronicles report that 350 Anabaptists were executed under Louis V (Beck, 279). Other reports give lower figures. But that they were numerous enough to cause some uneasiness is implied in the opinion of the Nürnberg scholars on the punishment of the Anabaptists dated April 29, 1531, which states that Louis "had caused a large number to be sentenced from life to death" (*TA Bayern* I, 226).

This severe procedure against the Anabaptists brought Louis many a reproach (Krebs, 570 and 574). The Hutterite chronicles report that he rued the many executions (Beck, 32). In fact after 1529 there is no record of an Anabaptist execution in the Palatinate. A confirmation of the Hutterite assertion can be seen in his request of March 23, 1529, in the consultations concerning the imperial law against the Anabaptists April 22, 1529; though he declared himself in agreement with its specifications on punishment, he wished "that only those be punished by death who refused to abstain from Anabaptism" (Ney, 138). The law then specified that those who recanted should be pardoned.   HEGE.

Beck, *Geschichts-Bücher*; Chr. Hege, *Die Täufer in der Kurpfalz* (Frankfurt, 1908); Manfred Krebs, "Beiträge zur Geschichte der Wiedertäufer am Oberrhein," in *Ztscht f. d. Gesch. d. Oberrheins* LXXXII (1931); J. Ney, *Geschichte des Reichstages zu Speyer im Jahre 1529* (Hamburg, 1879); Karl Ried, *Moritz von Hutten, Fürstbischof von Eichstätt (1539-1557) und die Glaubensspaltung* (Münster, 1925); *TA Bayern* I; *TA Baden-Pfalz*; Wiswedel, *Bilder* II; *ML* II, 699.

Louis, Duke of Bavaria, conjoint ruler with his brother William IV 1515-45. Both were violent opponents of the Anabaptists. Even before the edict of Charles V they issued a mandate on Nov. 15, 1527, which declared the Anabaptists to be criminals who deserved corporal and capital punishment (Winter, 170-76). On Dec. 5, 1527, the inquisitor Martin Pasensner of Jesenwang was given supreme authority to ferret them out (Winter, 177). Whoever joined them and was caught must die; recantation did not save them from death (Nestler, 77). Louis carried on a correspondence with the council of Regensburg concerning the Anabaptist preacher Würzlburger, and had him sentenced and executed in Regensburg (Nestler, 76-78).   HEGE.

Hermann Nestler, *Die Wiedertäuferbewegung in Regensburg* (Regensburg, 1926); V. A. Winter, *Geschichte der baierischen Wiedertäufer im 16. Jahrhundert* (Munich, 1809); *ML* II, 697.

Louis (1554-93), Duke of Württemberg 1568-93, son of Duke Christoph, until 1558 under the guardianship of the privy councilor Melchior Jäger and later completely dominated by him, was very good-natured, strictly Lutheran, musical, somewhat given to drink. To check the spread of Anabaptism the official *Landhofmeister,* chancellor, and councilors, in 1584 insisted on the death penalty and torture in certain cases for Anabaptist leaders and for exiles who kept returning. But Louis, under the influence of the court chaplain Lukas Osiander, who pointed out that the Catholics would then also apply torture and the death penalty to Protestants, decided that for a while he would wait and use the more lenient method.   G.Bo.

Stälin, "Das Rechtsverhältnis der religiösen Gemeinschaften und der fremden Religionsverwandten in Württemberg nach seiner geschichtlichen Entwicklung," in *Württembergische Jahrbücher für Statistik und Landeskunde* (1868) 170; *ML* II, 699.

Louisiana, a southern state bordering on the Gulf of Mexico. It is probable that the first Mennonites to visit this state were immigrants from Alsace-Lorraine, who landed at New Orleans, a seaport and the chief city of the state. Thus in 1839 Christian Reeser and his two brothers and sister from France arrived in that city. In 1874 John F. Funk had correspondence with Mennonites who were residents of New Orleans (*Menn. Hist. Bulletin,* July 1954). In 1898 Mennonites settled near Lake Charles (*q.v.*), about 200 miles due west of New Orleans, and founded a church (MC) which at one time had 40 members. By 1955 only one family was left in the community, the others having moved away because rice farming did not become as successful a venture as expected. In 1918 a Mennonite congregation was organized at Allemands, 30 miles west of New Orleans, but it existed only a few years, the families all moving away. In 1936 three families from the Franconia Mennonite Conference moved to Allemands (*q.v.*) and established a Mennonite (MC) church which now has 45 members. An outgrowth of this church is the one at Akers (*q.v.*), 40 miles north of New Orleans. It was built in 1942 and in 1955 had 20 members, all natives of Louisiana, largely French-speaking.   M.G.

Louisville, Ohio, a town (pop. 4,000) in a farming community in east central Stark County. Five miles northeast of Louisville a Mennonite (MC) settlement worships at the Beech Church, which has 369 members, 7 per cent of whom live in the town. Probably all live within shopping distance of Louisville. Mennonites (Amish from Alsace) came to this community in 1823.   N.O.

Lourens Janssen (*Louwereyns Jansz Nooddruft*). This Anabaptist martyr is named twice by van Braght, once (*Mart. Mir.* D 726, E 1036) as Lourens de Schoenmaker, and again (D 747, E 1055) as Louwerens Jansz Nooddruft. He was a shoemaker of Delft, Holland. He was arrested at Antwerp in August 1576 and after a severe imprisonment was burned at the stake on Jan. 18, 1577. Since no writing materials were available to him, he wrote two letters to his friends by scratching them with a pin on pewter spoons, which show a deep piety. One of them says, "Grace and peace from God the Father and our Lord Jesus Christ be with you my very dear and in God beloved sister in the Lord, Weyndelken and her daughter M.; this I wish you from the depths of my heart before God, who searcheth

the hearts and reins, that you may walk before Him unharmed and unhindered in His truth, to which He has called you; and always look to Christ and to all the righteous. Adieu, in this time, adieu." (*Antw. Arch.-Blad* XIII, 211; XIV, 98 f., No. 1120; *ML* III, 265.)   NEFF.

Lourens (Laurens) **de Schoenmaker,** an Anabaptist martyr: see **Laurens Janssen.**

Lourents de Schoenmaker, an Anabaptist martyr: see **Schuster, Laurenz.**

Lourys Lourisz, a Dutch Anabaptist martyr of Leiden, beheaded on July 28, 1534, at The Hague. He was active in preaching and baptizing at Leiden, Dutch province of South Holland, probably in the spring of 1534. The assertion of Knappert that Lourisz practiced polygamy and left behind "two widows" has been disproved by Mellink, who suggests that Lourys Lourisz was a brother of the martyr Adriaen Lourisz (*q.v.*).   vDZ.

Inv. Arch. Amst. I, Nos. 47c, 744 f.; Mellink, *Wederdopers,* 191 f., 194, 229, 353; L. Knappert, *De opkomst van het Protestantisme in eene Noord-Nederlandsche stad* (1908) 139; *DB* 1917, 112, No. 25.

Louwe (Louw), a Dutch Mennonite family living at Zaandam, province of North Holland. Some of them were owners of whaling boats and were well-to-do businessmen. Already in 1628 they were members of the Frisian congregation (Oude Huys). A large number of them served the Mennonite congregation of Zaandam-West as deacons. Louwrens Jansz Louwe (b. Feb. 2, 1657, at Zaandam, d. there Jan. 30, 1723) was preacher of the Zaandam-West congregation from 1681 until his death. In 1697 he was among the four *buitenleraren* (preachers or elders from other congregations) who were at Wormer (*q.v.*) to decide concerning Jacob Pieters Banning, preacher of Wormer who had enunciated "new opinions"; e.g., that there are no angels or devils (*DB* 1898, 77-97, *passim*). Cornelis Louwrens Louwe in 1781 bequeathed to the Mennonite orphanage of Zaandam-West 2,000 guilders and a beautiful clock, which is still in possession of the Zaandam congregation. Jan Hendriksz Louwe, of Krommenie, was a member of the Waterlander congregation and at the same time an ardent Collegiant (*q.v.*). In the period 1691-1712 he often delivered addresses in the Collegiant center at Rijnsburg.   vDZ.

S. Lootsma, *Het Nieuwe Huys* (1937) 80, 121 f., 186, 192 ff.

Louwer (Lauren, Louren, Louwers), **Bartel** (Bartholomeus), born at Goch, Germany, about 1580, d. at Amsterdam after 1670, in his youth traveled over many countries and lived in 1617 for some time at Vilna, Lithuania, was from 1642 preacher (later elder) of the Flemish congregation of Amsterdam until about 1660. He published *Kort Verhael, eens Gesprecks, voorghevallen in der Wildae oft Vylnae* (Amsterdam, n.d.; 2nd ed., n.p., 1655; 3rd ed. Amsterdam, 1664). An extract of this booklet and some biographical notes on Louwer are found in Maatschoen's *Aanhangzel.* Louwer, who was a champion of strict Mennonite principles, was a representative of the Amsterdam congregation in the Flemish conferences at Haarlem in June 1649 and Leiden in June 1660. He was a friend of T. J. van Bracht, to whom he gave a letter from Zürich, Switzerland (*Mart. Mir.* D 805, E 1104), containing particulars about the martyr Hans Landis.   NEFF, vDZ.

Schijn-Maatschoen, *Geschiedenis* III, 249-69; H. W. Meihuizen, *Galenus Abrahamsz* (Haarlem, 1954) 35, 71-73; *Biogr. Wb.* V, 621-23; *ML* II, 695.

Louwerens Jansz Nooddruft, an Anabaptist martyr: see **Lourens Janssen.**

Louwys de Wever (official name Loys Luycx) of Laerne near Gent, Flanders, was beheaded on April 22, 1558, at Antwerp, Belgium. He was threatened with burning at the stake, but after recanting he was beheaded. The martyrbooks, not knowing this fact, have listed him among the martyrs. Hence his name is found in a hymn "Aenhoort Godt, hemelsche Vader" (Hear, O God, heavenly Father), No. 16 of the *Lietboecxken van den Offer des Heeren.* Van Bracht states that Louwys was beheaded at Antwerp in 1558 (without exact date) because of his true confession and his steadfastness.   vDZ.

Mart. Mir. D 201, E 583; *Antw. Arch.-Blad* VIII, 444 f., XIV, 22 f., No. 255.

Love (Greek, *Agape*). *Agape as Primary and Sacrificial.* Agape is the deepest and truest fact of the Christian faith. To Jesus love to God and to neighbor constituted those commandments on which depend all the law and the prophets. To Paul it is the greatest in his faith, hope, and love trilogy and the crucial ingredient of all relations and realities.

The sacrificialists are right (to use the typology of sacrificialist-mutualist of Dan Williams) in stressing agape as a gift from God and as a reality bestowed on the unworthy, the ugly, and the downtrodden rather than the lovely. On the other hand, Nygren strains unduly in trying to force the whole Biblical presentation of agape through the narrow definition of uncaused agape. And, moreover, the sacrificialists have not adequately developed the concrete incarnational reality of agape in Jesus Christ, the supreme response to whom is discipleship. Following Christ is the key to Christian ethics even though it operated dialectically with forgiveness. The mutualists are correct in stressing community as the crucible in which love operates and toward which it moves. Just as discipleship saves agape from being a philosophical abstraction, community saves it from individualism. Against the mutualists' (MacMurray and Wieman) question the affirmation is to be questioned that self-realization is the cause or effect of community. Rather the truly Christian foundation is: self-realization through self-sacrifice in Christian community.

Amos Wilder writes that ". . . the claims of the Kingdom take the forms of claims of discipleship to Jesus in the accomplishment of his errand." Thus our Lord seeks a response: vertically in worship and obedience; horizontally in service to the neighbor. In human history there is no guarantee of this response; indeed, there is a basic dimension of tragedy expressed in alienation, separation, hostility, conflict, and martyrdom. Here the eschatological dimension of love enters since there is never a fully temporal realization. God in Christ is a suffering lover whose love is never fully returned. Christ suffered for us on the cross; Christ suffers with us in discipleship living; Christ suffers because of us in sin and rebellion. In all this, divine love is revealing itself. And in all this divine love seeks a response.

Agape as Brotherhood and Mutuality. God's love is socially creative—thus producing fellowship, community, and church. The primary meaning of community is the Christian community which, in turn, effects the larger human community. The church is a brotherhood of love, and this is a superior view to the church as an impersonal station dispensing grace, or to the church as a static intellectual depository of truth, or to the church as a link in the chain of historical continuity, or to the church as the chaplain of culture values. Therefore, as a corporate society the church is originated, sustained, and characterized by agape.

The tension between the Anabaptist understanding of agape as creative of community and other Protestant and Catholic views is the issue of direct or indirect influence in the larger secular community. The Anabaptist tradition developed in the context of rigorous Bible study and severe persecution. This suggested that the Anabaptists ought to be willing to sacrifice universality for intensity. The world observes the love, the voluntary, filial obedience, and the cultural creativity of the Christian community, and finds this suggestive and stimulating to its own life. There are strong voices advocating a more direct way of influencing the secular community, but thus far this view has floundered on the dilemma of pacifism and power.

To the Anabaptists one of the sure fruits of love is mutual aid. In recent years this has had a real renewal in theory and practice. On the other hand, there is the Niebuhrian claim that the essence of mutual love is reciprocity, a fact that introduces prudential considerations where agape is compromised by ego-claims. Patterns of institutional mutual aid (hospitals, homes for aged, fire insurance) tend to provide specified kinds of care and service for specified amounts of financial contribution. An element of reciprocity enters in here and, unchecked, can be destructive of agape. But, fundamentally there is unlimited liability for the brother regardless of the ego-claims he can make. And, in addition, sacrificial love on all the Jericho roads of history has the obligation to help the neighbor outside of the Christian brotherhood.

In the Anabaptist tradition communities are of two types: the communal or communistic as in the Hutterites, and the semi-communal. The semi-communal has been normative, calling for private property in the form of home and business yoked to a radical doctrine of stewardship in a brotherhood-centered existence with common liability for all risks as well as duties of Christian witness and work.

The real enemy of love in modern society is atomistic individualism, which has no doctrine of community, and which, when it enters the church, views love as subjectively inward.

Within Anabaptist community there has been a regular peril in the rejection of the outgoing missionary thrust in order to preserve mutuality in the

Christian brotherhood. While there is a rich inner life in the church, it is precisely the reality of Christ's saving love which sends Christians out into witness and service.

Agape and Justice. The Cross is the symbol of sacrificial love, the Golden Rule is the symbol of mutuality, and an eye-for-an-eye and a tooth-for-a-tooth doctrine is the symbol of justice. The *Lex Talionis* of the Old Testament is confirmed in the *suum cuique* of classical jurisprudence. The latter refers to the rendering to each man that which is due him whether in punishment or damages.

Once again the problem for agape is raised by the ego-claims of justice. The first degree murder is punished by death or life imprisonment, and the speeding driver by a $10.00 fine. What is even more painful, the state enforces these claims of the law with policemen, militia, and armies. Ultimately, it poses the problem of war itself, which is the collective denial of agape.

Love and justice are dialectically related. Love, even perfectly nonresistant love, can do many things which justice wants to do: give equal care to the lowly, help people to secure the help they deserve, and create the integrity, order, and character, without which society is impossible.

But love is also the contradiction of justice and the law. There are times, especially in periods of danger and upheaval, when the counsel of love cannot be made plausible mundane common sense and fulfillment; it may appear to be treason, folly, and naive religious zeal. To the disciple of Christ in such moments love must then rest its case on the foundation of Truth. Love is Biblical. Love is in the will of God. Any Christian convinced that he is abiding in the love of God, the will of God, and the truth of God obviously would be foolish to abandon this for prudential considerations of justice. Perhaps Emil Brunner has caught the strange relationship here when he said, "There is an antithesis between love and justice. The antithesis does not sever the bond between them nor the bond sever the antithesis."

To be truly loving the Christian ought to be nonresistant. Yet, in the years ahead, it would appear that the English and Greek words for love might be better terms in describing the peace testimony than the valid but more limited term of nonresistance. I John 4:8 declares that God is love. Our response to His love is the central fact of the Christian life.   D.E.S.

Loveland (Col.) Mennonite Brethren Church, now extinct, was organized in 1906 with Heinrich Nikkel as leader, succeeded by Conrad Burkhart in 1914. The membership never exceeded 37. By 1924 most of the members had moved away and the congregation became extinct.   P.C.H.

Lovendegem, a village between Gent and Brugge in Belgium, where in 1629-30 the Mennonites held some meetings in the home of a farmer Zegher Clays, son of Gheerolf. These Mennonites also attended the meetings at the Biezen near Aardenburg (*q.v.*) in Dutch Zeeland, Flanders. The names of some Mennonite families living here are known (among them Coppens, Claeys, Dobbelaere). Some Mennonites formerly living in Gent seem to have joined this group. A lawsuit was opened against the Mennonite Samuel Pitts and his mother (outcome unknown). After 1630 no meetings seem to have been held at Lovendegem, most Mennonites then having moved away to the Netherlands, especially to Aardenburg.   vDZ.

DB 1876, 96, 101, 103-6; F. K. van Lennep, *Verzameling van Oorkonden betr. het geslacht van Eeghen* (Amsterdam, 1918) 134 ff., 140, note 2; A. L. E. Verheyden, "Mennisme in Vlaanderen," ms.

Low German *language:* see **Plattdeutsch.**

Löwen, Peter (1882-1955), a Mennonite missionary and elder, was born at Muntau, Ukraine, South Russia, on April 2, 1882, the son of Peter and Maria Löwen. He taught the elementary school at Spat, Crimea, and at the age of 22 went to the Mission School of Neukirchen near Mörs, Germany, after which he continued his education at Leiden, the Netherlands. On July 8, 1911, he married Emilie Fellmann. They had eight children.

On Sept. 11, 1911, Löwen was ordained as elder and missionary and worked for three years in the Dutch Mennonite mission of Sumatra (*q.v.*), after which he returned because of the ill health of his wife. For forty years he served as a minister promoting missions among the Mennonites of South Germany. He served primarily at Donauwörth, Augsburg, Nürnberg, and Würzburg, where he died on Feb. 13, 1955.   C.K.

Obituary in *Gbl.,* May 1, 1955, p. 43; *Der Mennonit* IX (April 1955) 63.

Löwenberg, a Mennonite family found principally in the Palatinate and in the United States. The progenitor of the family was Johannes Löwenberg, born 1775, a weaver of Bolanden. He was originally Protestant, but married Elisabeth Hahn, a member of the Mennonite congregation at Weierhof, and joined the Mennonite Church there and also settled there. A son with the same name emigrated to the United States in 1850 with his family and a group of relatives and friends and settled in Donnellson, Iowa. The present members of this family in the United States are his descendants. The progenitor of the branch remaining in Germany was Michael Löwenberg (1821-74), a minister of the Weierhof congregation and the founder of the school at Weierhof (*q.v.*).

One of Michael's sons was Thomas Löwenberg, b. Feb. 26, 1849, at the Weierhof, married first to Kathi then to Sophie Göbel, d. March 23, 1928. He received his pedagogical training in the normal school at Schiers, Switzerland, and his theological training in the mission school at Barmen, Germany. In 1873 he accepted the position of minister in the Weierhof-Uffhofen congregation and after his father's death for a time was the head of the Weierhof school. In 1882 he was called as minister of the Mennonite congregation at Ibersheim-Eppstein-Ludwigshafen, and served them until 1917. He spent his period of retirement at the Weierhof. All the present members of this family in Germany are descendants of Thomas and his brother August.

Some members of this family settled in Iowa, from where the name spread over other states.

NEFF, P.S.

"Einiges aus dem Leben des Michael Löwenberg," *Gem.-Kal.* 1896, 2-20; Christian Neff, "Thomas Löwenberg, ein Lebensbild," *Gem.-Kal.* 1929, 106-11; *ML* II, 695 f.

Löwenberg, Michael (1821-74), preacher of the Mennonite church at Weierhof (*q.v.*), Palatinate, Germany, founder of the Realschule at Weierhof, b. Nov. 8, 1821, at Weierhof, d. there Dec. 13, 1874. He married the widow of Johannes Dahlem in 1848. Löwenberg received his training at the normal school in Beuggen. In 1848 he opened a private elementary school at Weierhof. In 1849 he was called to the ministry of the congregation there, serving until his death in 1874. In 1868 he published in the *Mennonitische Blätter* an appeal to "the Mennonites in Germany, South Russia, and Holland" to establish a Christian school, the principal purpose of which would be to train preachers. On Dec. 2, 1867, the school was opened on a modest scale, and under the direction of Ernst Göbel (*q.v.*) it became the largest private school in the Palatinate. (See **Real-Anstalt am Donnersberg.**) It was first located in the Weberhäuschen, which had been built in 1810 by the original Johannes Löwenberg. One of Michael's sons, Thomas (1849-1928), was pastor of the Weierhof congregation 1873-82, and 1882-1917 pastor at Ibersheim. (*Gem.-Kal.* 1896, 2-20; *ML* II, 695.)

NEFF.

Löwenberg (Löwenburg), a government district (*Amt*) of the former grand duchy of Berg, in the Siebengebirge, Rhineland-Westphalia, Germany. In the 16th century and the first half of the 17th numerous Anabaptists were living here. In 1564 the duke gave orders to keep a close watch for Anabaptists and rebaptized persons, and to hunt them up in the woods, ravines, heaths, and similar lonely places. In 1565 the pastor of Honnef denied that he was a follower of the Anabaptists; he had, on the contrary, converted a number of those who had followed after the Anabaptists for one to six years. On Nov. 26, 1565, Konrad Koch (*q.v.*) was beheaded in Honnef. On May 1, 1591, the Concept of Cologne was signed for the Löwenberg congregation by "Jan Koch, on behalf of the church in Hauffen (i.e., Honnef) and Caspar of Dollendorf." On April 9, 1619, a decree was issued by the Count Palatine that he, the count, perceived with displeasure that the Anabaptists were greatly increasing in the Löwenberg district and were secretly meeting. All the Anabaptists caught at such meetings were to be punished. Following new decrees by the government against the Anabaptists lists of the Anabaptists were turned in to the authorities. On Dec. 30, 1562, the decree was issued that the Anabaptists who were carrying on important trade or possessed considerable estates were to leave the country within two years; those who had no possessions, within six months. From the Löwenberg area some went to the gravure of Wied, south of the Siebengebirge, in 1654-56, and became the founders of the Neuwied Mennonite congregation. Others (especially the Schumacher family) went to the Palatinate around

Kriegsheim, from where they later emigrated to the United States. The later fate of most of the Anabaptists of the Löwenberg area has not yet been investigated. The last information about the Mennonites in this area is a report of 1670 that the Mennonites had all left the country, but were still owners of estates.

W.N.

State archives of Düsseldorf, Jülich-Berg II, 244, 255, 256; Rembert, *Wiedertäufer*, 444, note 2; W. Risler, "Täufer im bergischen Amt Löwenburg," *Gesch.-Bl.* XII (1955) 6-21; XIII (1956) 31-46; W. Niepoth, "Die Wanderungen und Wandlung der Mennonitenfamilie Schuhmacher," *Der Mennonit* X (1956) 27 f.

Lower Deer Creek Mennonite Church (MC), Kalona, Iowa, is located four miles north and four west of Kalona, in the neighborhood of the first Amish Mennonite settlement in Johnson County in 1846. After an influx of settlers, their first church was organized in 1851. Sometime before 1863, the church had become large enough to make necessary its division into two congregations, the Deer Creek district and the Sharon Township district. In 1877 the former district was divided into Upper Deer Creek and Lower Deer Creek. Although these two churches were Old Order Amish Mennonite, contrary to custom they discontinued holding services in their homes and in 1890 built churches. In 1917 Lower Deer Creek erected a large frame structure, which was destroyed by fire in January 1956. A new church was constructed a short distance north of the former site during the same year (1956). Following the severance of fellowship with the Old Order churches in 1917 after a controversy and a division over the issue of the installation of telephones in the homes of members, the Lower Deer Creek congregation followed an independent course until it joined the Western District Amish Mennonite Conference in 1919. Jacob F. Swartzendruber (*q.v.*) for many years served as bishop of the church (1887-1913). In 1955 the bishop was John Y. Swartzendruber, having been ordained to that office in 1919. The membership was 364. In 1945 the Iowa Mennonite School (*q.v.*) was established across the road from the church.

M.G.

M. Gingerich, *The Mennonites in Iowa* (Iowa City, 1939); E. G. Swartzendruber, *Amish and Mennonite Church Centennial Anniversary* (Wellman, Iowa, 1953).

Lower Mennonite Church (OOM), located four miles southwest of Wadsworth, Medina Co., Ohio, is a member of the Ohio-Indiana Conference. A minister by the name of Abraham Rohrer moved into this area from Maryland in 1832 and was ordained as bishop in 1836. Therefore it is probable that the church was organized under his leadership about 1832. Other ministers who have served the congregation were Michael Rohrer, Henry Beery, Bishop Isaac L. Good, Jacob Newcomer, and Edwin Koppes. The first meetinghouse was probably a frame structure built between 1835 and 1840. The present (1954) congregation numbers 27 members and is in charge of Moses G. Horst as bishop and Abram Good as minister.

When the Wisler (Old Order) Mennonite division occurred in Elkhart Co., Ind., in 1871, the Lower congregation, including Bishop Rohrer (1788-1878) and the other ordained men, and all but a half-dozen families, sided with Wisler. The small minority who remained with the other Mennonite Conference withdrew from the congregation, though still using the meetinghouse part of the time, and ultimately built the Bethel meetinghouse in 1893 hence are called the Bethel Mennonite Church (q.v.). They had no minister until 1881. Ab.G.

Lower Rhine, the section of the Rhine from Cologne to its mouth in the North Sea, 117 miles of which lie in Germany. In Mennonite history this section of the river and the area extending as far as Andernach played an important role. It was a part of the route which connected Switzerland, the cradle of the Anabaptist movement, to Holland, the home of Menno Simons.

Even before the Reformation the division of the country into many small religious and political regions facilitated the rise of separatist groups. Of lasting influence on circles of practical Christianity were "Master" Johannes Eckhart (q.v.), who died in 1327 while he was on trial for heresy before the Court of Inquisition under the Archbishop of Cologne, and Thomas a Kempis, the author of the devotional book *De imitatione Christi*. Thus the soil in the region of the Lower Rhine was well prepared for the reception of the Upper German Anabaptists.

As in the Netherlands, the Anabaptists were until the middle of the 16th century the only Reformation party in this region. Contributory to the spread of the movement, in addition to the urge to proclaim the Gospel, was also the wretched spiritual care of the people, which caused frequent complaint on the part of the Catholic populace. A church inspection ordered by the duke in 1533 revealed that many of the clergy "administered the sacraments only in return for payment, and many had subsidiary businesses, such as the sale of intoxicating beverages," with a train of evil consequences, as the criminal records of the time show. The revelations of the inspectors concerning the educational level of the clergy were quite shocking. Real theologians were the exception. "No wonder that the clergy and with them the church fell into popular disrepute and that the itinerant preachers of the new doctrine found favorable soil" (Scheibler, 13).

Furthermore, the Jülich Declaration of April 8, 1533, admits that there had always been things in the Catholic Church which should have been corrected, but which had been tolerated and overlooked for the sake of peace. The chaplains and priests were conspicuous for their immorality. In Jülich all moral laws seemed "to have been dissolved in the communities in which Anabaptist congregations were later formed" (Rembert, 52 and 60).

Thus the Anabaptists found entry all along the Lower Rhine, especially in the largest state, the duchies of Cleve-Mark and Jülich-Berg, which were united in 1521, but had separate jurisdiction, also in the county of Mörs, in the archbishopric of Cologne (q.v.), as well as in the imperial cities of Aachen (q.v.) and Cologne (q.v.). Because of the mandates (q.v.) isued against them they conducted their meetings in secret.

On the origin and development of Mennonite congregations little is known. Congregations arose at first in the Jülich districts of Wassenberg, Heinsberg, Millen, and Born, from which numerous martyrs are reported. The first martyr in the duchy of Jülich was Vit to Pilgrams, who died at München-Gladbach in 1537 (not as *Martyrs' Mirror* says in 1532). Congregations were also formed in Aachen in 1533, in Cologne in 1531, which had over 100 members in 1562, and in München-Gladbach (see **München-Gladbach**) in 1532, where the congregation numbered 151 families in 1622, most of them weavers (names in Keller, II, 224-29; a register of 1654 with 114 names is given by Walter Risler in *Beiträge,* 97-107). In 1534 there was also a congregation in Emmerich (q.v.), which soon after the one in Cleve (q.v., 1895) expired in the early 20th century. In the second half of the 16th century other congregations were formed, the period 1589-1609 being remarkable in "that the laity here kept the leadership in religious matters in their own hands" (Keller, 6). Anabaptists were also found at many places in the duchies of Cleve, Jülich, and Berg.

The growth of the Anabaptist movement in the region of the Lower Rhine gave the governments cause for a second church inspection in 1550. In Jülich (q.v.) it was hoped that this church inspection would bring about an improvement in this respect, so that complaints about evil conditions would cease (Rembert, 425). Church reforms could, however, be carried out only gradually (Keller, 10). On March 9, 1560, Duke William III issued an edict to the officials of Cleve and Mark, ordering that "Sacramentists and Anabaptists" should be instructed by orthodox preachers and an attempt be made to bring them back to the Catholic Church.

In 1563 the Catholic priest Georg Cassander (q.v.) was assigned to convert to Catholicism the Anabaptist teacher Johannes Campanus (q.v.), who had for years been a prisoner; but he was not successful. Later Protestant preachers were also called to convert arrested Anabaptists. In the districts of Blankenberg and Bensberg in the duchy of Berg, where the Anabaptists were numerous, William arrested many participants in nocturnal worship services in the open fields; with these prisoners Peter Lo (Lohe), the Protestant parson of Elberfeld, disputed in the presence of several councilors June 13-24, 1565, in the castle of Blankenberg on the Sieg, and June 28-July 2, 1565, in Bensberg, principally on questions which had been discussed at the disputation of Frankenthal (q.v.). Several of the prisoners joined the Protestant Church; the others persisted in their opinion or escaped further oppression by flight. Lo was rewarded for his efforts by honorable recognition by the duke (Bockmühl, 296-301).

On Jan. 23, 1565, William issued a further order to eliminate abuses in worship. But at the same time he demanded that "Anabaptists, Sacramentists, followers of David Joris, Menno Simons, and others" should be reported, so that orthodox pastors could convert them; in case they refused to become Catholic, their goods should be confiscated (Keller, I, 114). A mandate of Oct. 1, 1585, against religious groups not included in the religious peace of 1555 gave the officials orders to extirpate the Anabaptists (Keller, I, 75 f.).

In spite of this sharp measure the Anabaptists spread along the Lower Rhine. Some Protestants also joined the Anabaptist groups. The pastors were to prevent this. A decision of the third Reformed synod of Berg, at Elberfeld on Jan. 3, 1590, required the preachers to explain to the people the "coarse and great error" by personal admonition, intercession, and prayer in the churches (Keller, II, 102, 180; Rembert, 439).

The seriousness of the Anabaptist profession of faith is shown in the agreements they made in Cologne on May 1, 1591, with the Mennonites on the Upper Rhine and in Holland under the name of the "Concept of Cologne" (*q.v.*), which formed a unifying bond between widely scattered Anabaptists (Hege, 149-52). The document was signed by several congregations in the Lower Rhine region: Cologne, Flammersheim, Odenkirchen, Rees, and Lieber, and also by all the congregations in the duchy of Berg, at Millen, and on the Maas (Rembert, 618).

Under Johann Sigismund, Elector of Brandenburg, and Wolfgang, Count Palatine of Neuburg, an era of tolerance dawned in 1610; the old restrictions which limited the religious faiths in the country to the three recognized by the Empire were over. But when Wolfgang's successor adopted the Catholic faith in 1614, new persecutions began in Jülich-Berg (in 1619). Persons caught at Anabaptist religious services were to be punished (Rembert, 445). On Sept. 1, 1619, all officials and clergymen received orders to exterminate the Anabaptists (Keller, III, 257). But this decree was not radically carried out.

After 1652 the pressure increased, when an edict was issued by Philip William ordering compulsory conversion or exile, so that the Mennonites began to emigrate from Jülich and Berg to Crefeld, where the Mennonites had been preaching in public since 1634 and considered themselves an independent congregation. From Gladbach 70 families moved to Crefeld after emigrations to Nijmegen had already taken place. In 1653 the Elector of Cologne expelled the Mennonites, 70 families finding reception in and around Crefeld (Nieper, 18 and 30).

With the emigration of Mennonites from Crefeld to America in 1683 the old imperial law against the Anabaptists was silently abandoned. It had been passed in 1529 by the Diet of Speyer, and brought unspeakable woe to the Anabaptists. Since none of the treaties recognized the Mennonites as a body to be tolerated, the old imperial law was invoked again and again. As late as 1694 Elector John William of the Palatinate, the regent of Jülich and Berg, had 40 Mennonites at Rheydt (*q.v.*) arrested at night, and rejected a petition of the Dutch government on their behalf on the ground that he would have to bear the wrath of the entire empire if he should release the prisoners; but for a consideration of 8,000 Talers he would be willing to release them. William III of England and Emperor Leopold I (*q.v.*) also intervened on their behalf. Finally after three years they were released, their property restored, and they were permitted to live in peace and pursue their trades (Nieper, 24-36). Since that time no German government has based a decision on the imperial law against the Mennonites.

The Mennonite congregations of the Lower Rhine area were Crefeld, Cleves, Goch, Emmerich, and Rees. All except Crefeld died out at the end of the 19th or the beginning of the 20th century.

In economics the later Mennonites in the region of the Lower Rhine occupy a special place. To them Crefeld owed its rapid development and Germany owed a new means of income, namely, the velvet and silk industry, which has its center in Crefeld. (See **Crefeld** and **Jülich**.)   HEGE.

L. Keller, *Die Gegenreformation in Westfalen und am Niederrhein* (3 vv., 1881-95); Rembert, *Wiedertäufer;* Chr. Hege, *Die Täufer in der Kurpfalz* (Frankfurt, 1908); Fr. Nieper, *Die ersten deutschen Auswanderer von Krefeld nach Pennsylvanien* (Neukirchen, 1940); W. I. Hull, *William Penn and the Dutch Quaker Migration to Pennsylvania* (Swarthmore, 1935); *Beiträge zur Geschichte Rheinischer Mennoniten* (Weierhof, 1939); W. Risler, "Mennoniten in Duisburg," *Menn. Gesch.-Bl.* VIII (1951) 2-17; W. Scheibler, *Geschichte der evang. Gemeinde Monschau* (Aachen, 1939); M. Goebel, *Gesch. des chr. Lebens in der rhein.-westphäl. evang. Kirche* I (Coblenz, 1849); P. Bockmühl, in *Monatshefte für Rheinische Kirchengesch.* (Mörs, 1910); Otto Redlich, *Jülich-Bergische Kirchenpolitik (Publikationen der Gesellschaft für Rheinische Geschichtskunde)* XXVII I, II (1), II (2) (Bonn, 1907, 1911, 1915); Ernst Crous, "Auf Mennos Spuren am Niederrhein," in *Der Mennonit* VIII (1955) 155, 170-71, 186-87; IX (1956) 10-11, 26; *idem*, "Von Täufern zu Mennoniten am Niederrhein," in *Der Mennonit* IX (1956) 74-76, 90-91, 106-8, 122 f.; W. Risler, "Täufer im bergischen Amt Löwenberg, Siebengebirge," *Gesch.-Bl.* XII and XIII; Gottfried Buschbell, *Geschichte der Stadt Krefeld* I (Krefeld, 1953); Gerhard von Beckerath, "Die wirtschaftliche Bedeutung der Krefelder Mennoniten und ihrer Vorfahren im 17. und 18. Jahrhundert" (dissertation, Bonn, 1951); *ML* III, 249-51.

Lower Skippack Mennonite Church, an independent congregation in Skippack Twp., Montgomery Co., Pa. The Mennonite settlement in this township was made in 1702, and the first house of worship for what was called the Skippack congregation was erected about 1725. A new meetinghouse was built in 1844. Three years later the Oberholtzer division occurred in the Franconia Conference (MC) to which the congregation then belonged, and the portion of the Skippack congregation which seceded from the conference to join the Oberholtzer group took possession of the new meetinghouse. The portion of the congregation which remained in the Franconia Conference finally in 1848 built what came to be called the Upper Skippack meetinghouse, and as a consequence the meetinghouse of 1844 came to be called Lower Skippack. By 1851 there was disharmony in the Lower Skippack congregation which a committee of the new (Oberholtzer) conference failed to resolve. Three ordained men of the congregation withdrew from both congregation and conference, namely, Bishop Abraham Hunsicker, and preachers Henry A. Hunsicker and Abraham H. Grater. Trouble and dissension continued, partly because Preacher Henry G. Johnson, who had been ordained in 1847, insisted strongly on a literal observance of footwashing (John 13:1-17). In 1861 the Oberholtzer Conference expelled Johnson, who retained the support of most of his congregation. The small remnant of the congregation that stayed with the conference under the leadership of Preacher David Bergey died out by 1886. Johnson's son, Henry H. Johnson, was ordained in 1878 as a preacher in the now independent Lower Skippack Church, and the latter's son, Henry M. Johnson, was ordained preacher in 1915. Because of three generations of Johnson preachers the group has often been called Johnson Mennonites (*q.v.*). Amos K. Bean was ordained in 1873 and bishop two years later. The congregation still observes footwashing, and is a bit more conservative in discipline than are the General Conference Mennonite congregations of eastern Pennsylvania, although less strict than the churches of the Franconia Conference (MC). The membership of Lower Skippack stood at about 300 for the last twenty years. In 1954 Henry M. Johnson was serving as bishop, and Frank Croll as minister.

J.C.W.

J. C. Wenger, *History of the Mennonites of the Franconia Conference* (Telford, 1937).

Lowville-Croghan Conservative Mennonite Church in Lewis Co., N.Y., had its beginnings in 1833, when the Mennonites of Alsace-Lorraine, looking toward America for new opportunities and to escape compulsory military training, were approached by a land agent who came to them in search of settlers for a large plot of ground in northeastern New York. In 1833 the first three Mennonite families came. They were the preachers Michael Zehr and Rudolph Virkler, and Bishop Joseph Farney. Other settlers followed the first pioneers and by 1836 the first Amish Mennonite congregation of Lewis County was organized. They met in the homes until 1912 when the first meetinghouse was erected at Croghan.

In 1847-52 a number of the members, including all of the ministers but Michael Zehr, left to form a new group, the Apostolic Christian Church (*q.v.*), because they felt that immersion was the correct mode of baptism. This group, fully organized in 1852 by Benedict Wyeneth, who was sent out from Switzerland by Fröhlich, at the request of the Virkler family, is now known as the Evangelical Baptist Church.

In 1909 the settlement had enlarged so much that several families felt it advisable to move to Lowville, about 20 miles away from the earlier settlement; a meetinghouse was built near Lowville in 1914. In 1914 the congregation joined the Conservative Amish Mennonite Conference that had been organized in 1910. Then the first Sunday school began in 1915. The present church was built in 1934.

The second church schism came in 1941 because several church workers refused to wear the required Amish Mennonite garb. The 68 members who left formed the First Mennonite Church of New Bremen, which in 1954 had 193 members.

In 1939 several families moved to Woodville (*q.v.*), about 50 miles from Croghan. From 1944 services were held once a month until 1947, when Andrew Gingerich was ordained as pastor to serve this group, later organized as a separate congregation with Gingerich ordained as bishop in 1952, and 53 members in 1954.

Lowville and Croghan continue as one congregation with a membership in 1954 of about 600, including the Pine Grove Mission at Glenfield.

Christian Nafziger (1861-1953) was ordained to the ministry in 1896 and long served as bishop. Bishop Lloyd Boshart (1913-   ), ordained bishop

in 1945, was in charge of the congregation in 1955, assisted by preachers Elias Zehr, Richard Zehr, and Leon Martin.

M.G.S.

Loy Pruystinck: see **Eloy Pruystinck.**

Loys de Clercq (de Visschere), an Anabaptist martyr, burned at the stake in 1537 at Antwerp, Belgium. Further information was not available. (*Antw. Arch.-Blad* VII, 433; XIV, 14 f., No. 157.) vDZ.

Loys Luycx: see **Louwys de Wever.**

Loyse de Coucq, an Anabaptist martyr, burned at the stake on May 26, 1573, at Antwerp, Belgium, with three others. She was sentenced to death because she had attended the forbidden meetings of the Mennonites. Apparently she had not yet received (re)-baptism. (*Antw. Arch.-Blad* XIII, 116 f., 178; XIV, 90 f., No. 1028.) vDZ.

Loysen (Loisen, Loytzen), a former Polish banking house, to whom is due the credit for the settling of Dutch Mennonites in the lowlands of the Vistula in the second half of the 16th century. Hans, Simon, and Steffen van Loysen had possession of Tiegenhof as security for a loan made to the King of Poland. It was at that time a marsh, most of it covered with reeds and brush. In 1562 they persuaded the Dutch Mennonites to build a new home here; the offer was gladly accepted, for in Holland they were not tolerated, whereas in Tiegenhof they would not be subject to oppression. In a short time the land was made arable; and after the expiration of the free period the Mennonites took it on lease. The lease contracts promised them exemption from certain fees and from military burdens. The contracts were repeatedly renewed and confirmed by the Polish kings. The *Privilegium* which Ladislas IV (king 1632-48) gave the Mennonites on Dec. 22, 1642, stressed the cultural achievement of their ancestors, and stated that the Mennonites had been called into the country by the Loysen family with the consent of King Sigismund August. The area was at first called the "Neue Hof," later Loytzenhof, though it was only a short time in the possession of the Loysen family; in 1581 it was taken over by Ernst von Weiher, and was then called "Weihershof." After 1760 it was known as Tiegenhof.

There have been some Dutch Mennonites by the name of Loysen. They apparently came to the Netherlands from Flanders, Belgium. Joos Loysen, a Mennonite of Middelburg, a wood dealer and owner of a sawmill, and a certain Maillart in 1593 wrote a letter to Prince Maurice of Orange in the name of the "nonresistant Christians" (i.e., Mennonites) of Middelburg in order to plead for freedom from the oath, which had been granted by his father William of Orange (*DB* 1908, 40). HEGE, vDZ.

A. Brons, *Ursprung, Entwicklung und Schicksale der Mennoniten* (3d ed., Norden, 1912); W. Mannhardt, *Die Wehrfreiheit der Altpreussischen Mennoniten* (Danzig, 1863); Ernst Regehr, "Geschichtstabelle d. Gemeinde Rosenort," in *Menn. Bl.*, 1937, 2; Felicia Szper, *Nederl. Nederzettingen in West-Pruisen gedurende den Poolschen tijd* (Enkhuizen, 1913) 95 f., 199; *ML* II, 696.

Lubberden (Lubberde), an old Mennonite family of Aalsmeer (*q.v.*), Dutch province of North Holland.

Klaas Jacobs Lubberde (1769-Nov. 1849) was a preacher of the "Oude Vermaning" of the Frisians on the Uiterweg, Aalsmeer 1804-49, and Pieter Jans (Lubberden) (1815-88) was from 1847 a deacon of the "Nieuwe Vermaning" on the Uiterweg, and preacher 1858-66; in 1866 he resigned, when the congregation merged with the Zijdweg Waterlander congregation, which had a trained minister. Pieters Jans Lubberden then served the united congregation as a deacon until his death.   vDZ.

W. Tsj. Vleer, *De aloude Aalsmeerse familiën* (De Kaag, n.d.-1954) 32.

Lubbert Gerritsz, a Dutch Mennonite elder: see Gerritsz, Lubbert.

Lubbert-Gerritsz-volk or *Lubbertisten,* name given to a Dutch branch of Mennonites, the followers of Lubbert Gerritsz (elder 1559-1614, *q.v.*), which originated in a schism in 1589 in Amsterdam (Kühler, *Geschiedenis* I, 432; *DB* 1864, 25; 1872, 56). This group was more usually called *Jonge* or *Zachte* or *Slappe Vriezen* (young, moderate, or lax Frisians, *q.v.*).   vDZ.

Lubbertsdochter, Judith, b. Dec. 21, 1601, at Amsterdam, d. there about 1670, was baptized in 1618 upon confession of faith in the Amsterdam Waterlander congregation. She was an unlettered and simple woman, earning her living by darning hose. About 1628 she moved to Alkmaar and became engaged to Jan Philips Schabaelje (*q.v.*), but this engagement was broken off about a year later. Judith returned to Amsterdam, left the Mennonite Church, and became a member of the Roman Catholic Church by rebaptism. She was a poet, her poems showing a somewhat mystical trait. A number of her poems are found in Mennonite hymnaries, e.g., in *Gheestelijck Kruydthofken* (De Rijp, 1629), *Rijper Liedtboecxken* (2d ed., De Rijp, 1636), and *Gheestelyck Bloem-hofken* (Haarlem, 1637). (*N.N.B.Wb.* X, 529-31; *Jaarboek Amstelodamum* 1937.)   vDZ.

Lübeck, a city (pop. 238,000) in Schleswig-Holstein, Germany, an important Baltic seaport. As early as the middle of the 16th century a wave of the Anabaptist movement was felt in East Holstein (see **Holstein**). Until 1700 there was a group of Mennonites in Lübeck, although they were never "privileged," nor did they have a church or school. No records written by them have been preserved. Refugees from the Jülich district settled there after 1532 as renters and tanners, and even as manufacturers of gunpowder. Mayor Jürgen Wullenwever seems to have favored them.

In 1535 and again in 1553 and 1555 the theologians of the "Wendic cities," of which Lübeck was one, passed unified measures against them. The Anabaptists, "with whom God has scourged the world," were to be expelled from all the localities; sheltering them was made punishable; anyone who was not accepted in one city should not be taken into another of the group; for the sake of caution the preachers of the state church were to be examined in the Augsburg Confession and its "Apology." Outsiders should announce themselves to the spiritual and secular authorities before taking lodging; never-

theless they repeatedly found reception and **work** without announcement or questioning. Repeated renewals of the mandates did not have the desired result. In spite of exiles on a week's notice, "Netherlanders tainted with all kinds of suspicious religions" kept appearing within and outside the city. In 1546 Menno Simons (*q.v.*) had a discussion in Lübeck with N. M. van Blesdijk (*q.v.*), the son-in-law of David Joris (*q.v.*), which did not lead to unification, and in 1552 an equally fruitless discussion with Adam Pastor (*q.v.*) on the deviating doctrines.

The Thirty Years' War brought new accretions from Fresenburg (*q.v.*) and the rest of Holstein, which however apparently did not disturb the council. The Mennonites were summoned and examined by the clergy, with scant results. The people liked the strangers; in 1671 a Menist woman was employed as a "Bademutter." About 1690 a preacher held the forbidden "conventicula" even during divine services. This time the council interfered, and promised the church authorities that they would prevent the sectarian baptism of Lutherans and sectarian marriages. The protest of the accused that they had nothing to do with the dangerous fanatics of Münster did not carry any weight. In 1735 there were only two or three Mennonite families counted in the city. In 1700 there had been seven. Hans Hermansz (d. *ca.* 1722) was the preacher of the congregation.

We learn some particulars about the economic importance of the Mennonites "in the office of lacework and ribbon making"; Isaak von Eken, one of its founders, was accused of having made forbidden propaganda for his sect and having changed the pledge with an addition that avoided the oath. But his reference to the punctual payment of his taxes as well as to the toleration Mennonites were receiving in other places had the intended effect.

The decline of the little congregation was chiefly the result of Lutheran propaganda; they watched carefully to see that the children were baptized, sometimes baptizing them without the knowledge of their parents.

Little is known of internal conditions among the Lübeck Mennonites. They held their meetings in the neighboring Ovendorf, observed communion twice a year, or else went to Fresenburg for this purpose. The visit of outside preachers was welcome. Jakob Denner of Hamburg is said to have obtained permission to hold quiet church services (1687-94, 1700). Ministers had, in general, no fixed salaries; an exception may have been the noted Hamburg preacher Gerhard Roosen. The rites forbidden in Lübeck (baptism, etc.) were usually performed in Hamburg. In the second half of the 17th century twenty persons from Lübeck were baptized in the Hamburg-Altona congregation. In the 19th and 20th centuries there were still a few Mennonites there.

In 1950 a new congregation was organized at Lübeck out of Danzig-West Prussian refugees who had been meeting in an unofficial way in the city since 1945. In 1954 the baptized membership was 144. The congregation was under the pastoral oversight of the Hamburg Mennonite congregation.

R.Do.

C. H. Starcke, *Lübecker Kirchenhistorie* (1724); B. C. Roosen, *Geschichte der Mennoniten-Gemeinde zu Hamburg und Altona* (Hamburg, 1886-87); Robert Dollinger, *Geschichte der Mennoniten in Schleswig-Holstein, Hamburg und Lübeck* (Neumünster, 1930); C. Krahn, *Menno Simons* (Karlsruhe, 1936); *ML* II, 696 f.

Lubin: see **Gross-Lubin.**

Lucas County (Ohio) Reformed Mennonite Church, located 1½ miles east and one-half mile north of Whitehouse, Ohio, was organized by Frederick Bucher in 1864. In 1838 John Moser, who with his family had come from the Emmental, Switzerland, and settled in Putnam Co., Ohio, in 1834, moved with his wife and two children to the Whitehouse community, followed by the Geiger, Bösiger, Neuenschwander, and Bucher families from Switzerland, and several families from Pennsylvania Mennonite and others of Alsatian Amish background. These were the families who left their former Mennonite affiliation to follow Bucher in 1864.

From the beginning they used a small building near the site of the present church, which was built in 1892, but which is no longer in use. Ministers who have served the church include Nicholas Roth, John K. Myers, Benjamin Bucher 1889-1923, Joseph Bucher 1898-1928, and Herbert Bucher 1923-51. The membership at present is six, who attend the Fulton County Reformed Mennonite Church.   D.L.G.

Lucas-Filips-volk or *Borstentasters,* a name given to a group of Mennonites at Haarlem, Dutch province of North Holland. They were adherents of Lucas Filips (Philips), a preacher of the Old Flemish (Huiskopers) congregation, meeting at the Helmbrekersteeg. In 1620 a quarrel arose between Filips and his co-preacher Vincent de Hondt (*q.v.*), who was offended by Filips' defense of a young man who had behaved improperly with his fiancee and by Filips' refusal to "ban" the young man. De Hondt banned not only the young man, but also Filips and his adherents, who, however, kept the meetinghouse, though the minority of the members sided with Filips. The Vincent de Hondt group obtained a new meetinghouse elsewhere. The Lucas-Filips-volk died out soon after 1700. (*DB* 1863, 135 f., 156.)   vDZ.

Lucas Hendricks (Heindricx), an Anabaptist martyr, was seized at an Anabaptist meeting at Brugge in Flanders, and burned at the stake on Dec. 10, 1561, with Adriaen Brael (*q.v.*) and four other companions; they died with the confession of Paul on their lips: "I have fought a good fight, I have finished the course, I have kept the faith: henceforth there is laid up for me the crown of righteousness, which the Lord, the righteous judge, shall give to me at that day" (II Tim. 4:7, 8). Lucas Hendricks was a native of Landegem in Flanders. His name is found in the hymn "Genade en Vrede moet Godvreesende sijn" (Mercy and peace must be to the God-fearing), found in *Veelderhande Liedekens* of 1569 and later editions. It was reprinted by Wackernagel.   NEFF, vDZ.

Mart. Mir. D 288, E 655; Verheyden, *Brugge,* 49, No. 36; Wackernagel, *Lieder,* 190; *ML* II, 282.

Lucas de Groot, an Anabaptist martyr, born at Oostende, Belgium, was executed there in 1568 by hanging. Particulars are lacking. (*Mart. Mir.* D 367, E 722; *ML* II, 187.)   vDZ.

Lucas Lambertsz van Beveren (Bestevaer), an Anabaptist martyr, beheaded at Amsterdam on Jan. 19, 1544, with Jan Claesz (*q.v.*). Lucas Lambertsz is the oldest of all the martyrs, being 87 years of age. No particulars are known about him except that he had been baptized by Menno Simons. The statement in the *Mennonitisches Lexikon* that he was a preacher, is not correct. Jan Claesz and Lucas Lambertsz are celebrated in a hymn found in *Offer des Heeren,* beginning "Het waren twee gebroeders goet" (There were two good brethren).   vDZ.

Offer, 78, note 86, 88; *Mart. Mir.* D 66, 70; E 471; *Inv. Arch. Amst.* I, No. 259; *DB* 1864, 145 f.; *ML* I, 214.

Lucas (Luckes) Michielsz, an Anabaptist martyr of Dordrecht, Dutch province of South Holland, by profession a glass-blower or a painter on glass, who was burned at the stake with seven other martyrs on March 20, 1549, at Amsterdam. He had been baptized by Gillis van Aken (*q.v.*). These martyrs are celebrated in the hymn "Tis nu schier al vervult ons broeders getal" (The number of our brethren is now nearly full), found in *Veelderhande Liedekens* of 1556 and later editions. (*Mart. Mir.* D 82, 84; E 483, 484; Grosheide, *Bijdrage,* 308; *ML* III, 124).   vDZ.

Lucelle, Grand (German, *Grosslützel*), a group of houses on both sides of the border between Switzerland and Alsace near the source of the Lucelle in a charming wooded region. The civil seat of government is on the Alsatian side of the border. It has been the seat of a Mennonite congregation since the end of the 19th century.

Very early some Anabaptists persecuted by the government of Bern, Switzerland, must have sought protection on the isolated farms around Lucelle in Pleigne (Pleen), Bourrignon (Bürgis), and Develier (Dietwiler), all in the Delémont (Delsberg) district. In 1731 the officials of Delémont appealed to the bishop, for the landless were demanding the expulsion of the Mennonites, while the landed offered them protection. In 1732 the people of Delémont asserted that the Mennonites were there to the advantage of the wealthy and the ruin of the poor. It is therefore likely that the mountain estates were pretty well settled by Mennonites about 1732.

In 1874 services were held in Bourrignon, Develier, and Roggenburg in the various homes; the brotherhood called itself the Delsbergtal church, as it is still often called today. Mennonites also settled the Alsatian border farms, and to meet the need for a common, centrally located church building, Abraham Bögli of Scholis, and David Neuenschwander, on May 26, 1891, bought the "Glashütte," an inn on the Alsatian side of Lucelle. In 1901 after a serious fire it was completely remodeled, and on Nov. 24 the new chapel was dedicated. During World War I it became so difficult to cross the border that the Swiss members began to hold their services in private homes again. By the end of the war some of the families on the Alsatian side had moved away. In 1955 only two member families were living on the Alsatian side out of about 80 members.

The elders of the Lucelle congregation have been Michael Nussbaumer ? -1902, Peter Allemann (preacher only), David Gerber 1924-38, and Christian Schmutz now (1955) serving. With the death of Elder David Gerber in 1938 Christian Schmutz, preacher and later elder of the Pruntrut congregation at Courgenay, took over and has continued the ministry at Lucelle alone. When the dissolution of the Courgenay (q.v.) congregation took place at the death of the last elder, Peter Ramseyer, in 1933, the former members of this Amish congregation living on the Swiss side joined either Lucelle or Porrentruy, while those on the Alsatian side went to the Birkenhof (q.v.) church. Porrentruy and Lucelle were Mennonite, not Amish. (Note: The article **Courgenay** is in error in that since 1933 there has not been a congregation bearing the name Courgenay; it is called Porrentruy.)

Around 1850 emigration to America was extensive. Later the congregation suffered further losses to the new congregation at Porrentruy (q.v.) (Pruntrut). In 1928 it had 62 baptized members (and 52 children) living on individual farms in the Delémont district, in 1955 about 80 members. The most common family names were Amstutz, Gerber, Bögli, Klay. The members are all farmers. The congregation belongs to the *Konferenz der altevangelischen Taufgesinnten Gemeinden der Schweiz.* (ML II, 188.)   A.-T., H.S.B.

Lucerne, a canton in Switzerland (pop. 223,409), predominantly Catholic. The Reformation found no entry here. Lucerne headed the Catholic cantons and in the religious wars it led the Catholic party.

The Lucerne Council took severest measures to suppress the Anabaptist movement. In 1525, the year of the birth of the brotherhood, Johann Krüsi (q.v.) died at the stake at Lucerne as the second blood witness of the Swiss Brethren, Eberli Bolt (q.v.) having been executed a few months previously in Schwyz. Julius Lober (q.v.) in his list mentions two martyrdoms in Lucerne in 1531 by drowning (Beck, 311). Orderly court procedures in religious matters were excluded in Lucerne; a decision of the Catholic cantons of June 10, 1532, decreed that Anabaptists in their territory, if they did not desist from their false doctrine, were without ado to be put to death (Strickler, 589). How many Swiss Brethren became victims of this decree is not known. At the Lucerne Assembly of the Catholic cantons it was decided on April 30, 1560, to take steps against the Swiss Brethren at Appenzell, and the meeting in Baden in 1567 confirmed the resolutions of 1532 (Bergmann, 42).   HEGE.

Beck, *Geschichts-Bücher;* Bergmann, *Die Täuferbewegung im Kanton Zürich* (Leipzig, 1916); Joh. Strickler, *Actensammlung zur Schweizerischen Reformationsgeschichte in den Jahren 1521-1532* IV (Zürich, 1881); *ML* II, 709.

Lücken, Jan (Johann): see **Luykens, Jan.**

Lücken, von, established a Mennonite church on his estate Zahrensdorf, one mile from Boitzenburg in Mecklenburg, Germany, *ca.* 1850, thereby arousing the opposition of the government, leading to his arrest and a prison sentence. His final plan was to sell his estate and emigrate to Australia, in order to establish a large Mennonite church there. He had negotiated with the British government for an extensive tract of land, but died suddenly in 1852. (*Menn. Bl.,* 1883, 6; *ML* II, 697.)   NEFF.

Lüdemann, Hermann (1842-1933), a German Protestant theologian, professor of theology at the University of Bern, Switzerland, in 1884, retired in 1928, author of the book, *Reformation und Täufertum in ihrem Verhältnis zum christlichen Prinzip* (Bern, 1896), in which he expresses a surprisingly unfriendly attitude to the Mennonites, and particularly to the views of Ludwig Keller (q.v.).   NEFF.

Menn. Bl., 1897, 1 and 89; *Vorträge und Aufsätze aus der Comeniusgesellschaft* V, Nos. 1 and 2; *ML* II, 697.

Ludi, Hans, the first Anabaptist martyr in the canton of Basel, Switzerland, from Bubendorf in the Waldenburg district, joined the Swiss Brethren in 1528, destroyed the images of the saints in the local church, and was therefore whipped, and later, on Jan. 12, 1530, beheaded at Basel. By trade he was a mason. He may have belonged to the Swiss Lüthi (q.v.) family.   NEFF.

P. Burckhardt, *Die Basler Täufer* (Basel, 1898) 26, 33, and 37; *ML* II, 697.

Ludwigshafen, the largest city (pop. 122,329) in the Rhenish Palatinate, Germany, founded in 1843 by Louis I, King of Bavaria, elevated to a town in 1853. Since 1891 it has been the seat of a Mennonite church which was previously known as Friesenheim (q.v.). The oldest parts of the present city (Ankerhof, Hemshof, Rohrlacherhof, and Gräfenau) were settled by Mennonites soon after the Thirty Years' War. They were all hereditary leaseholders on lands owned by nobles and monasteries. At first they belonged to the Mannheim (q.v.) congregation. The origin of the congregation really goes back to 1702, according to the *Gemeinde-Kalender.* In the beginning it was united with Eppstein and Ruchheim.

The Ludwigshafen-Friesenheim congregation is in a circuit with Ibersheim (q.v.) and Eppstein (q.v.), which together employ a common pastor who lives in Ibersheim. The baptized membership in 1954 was about 80. The members are farmers, officials, merchants, and laborers. The congregation has a meetinghouse, which was dedicated on Sept. 9, 1903. The Conference of the South German Mennonites met here annually for many years, until the church became too small; then larger halls were rented. The location of the city makes it a center for the Mennonites of South Germany. The city was badly damaged in the bombings of World War II. NEFF.

Valuable information is found in *Heimat-Blätter für Ludwigshafen a. Rh. und Umgebung,* 1922, 1923, 1928, 1930, and 1933; also in *Pfälzische Familien- und Wappenkunde* (Ludwigshafen a. Rh.), since 1952; *ML* II, 699.

Lugovsk Mennonite Brethren Church was located in the Buzuluk area of the province of Samara, Russia. The area was of somewhat rolling contour but promised new hopes for the landless class which had settled here under the auspices of the mother settlements.

Johann Löwen was among the first settlers. Abraham Martens and Bernhard Bergen were two of the first ministers. Other ministers were Cornelius Klassen, Jakob K. Wieler, N. Töws, Jakob Wiens, and Tobias Voth. In 1926 most of the leading men were sent into exile and the church was used as a public school; thus the church ceased to exist. J.J.T.

Lugt, a Dutch Mennonite family, found from about 1600 at Aalsmeer, province of North Holland, where they were shipbuilders; from about 1700 they were shipbuilders and tar brokers and later in insurance at Amsterdam; some of them are now lawyers or bankers. This family has produced two preachers: Pieter Evert Lugt (b. Jan. 10, 1841, at Amsterdam, d. June 1, 1908, at Amersfoort, married to Welmoet Tideman), who served at Noordeinde van Graft 1865-71, Noordbroek and Nieuw-Scheemda 1871-74, IJlst 1874-78, and Winterswijk 1878-1908; and Paul J. Lugt, b. 1916, pastor of Wieringen 1941-45. (*Ned. Patriciaat* XXIX, 1943, 291-318; *DB* 1908, 209.)

vDZ.

Luies (Lues, Luyes, Lucas), **Jan,** date and place of birth unknown, d. Jan. 21, 1637, was a farmer, apparently at Kloosterburen, Dutch province of Groningen (not Noordbroek as has been suggested both by Blaupot ten Cate and Kühler). He was at the same time preacher and elder of the Flemish Marne (*q.v.*) congregation, and founder of the Groningen Old Flemish branch of Mennonites.

Jan Luies was a stubborn and very intolerant man, who opposed the attempts at unity between the different branches of Dutch Mennonites. He especially condemned the *Harlinger Vrede* (Peace of Harlingen, 1610) between the Frisian and Flemish congregations of Harlingen, Friesland. In 1617 he was at Haarlem, where he banned Jacques Outerman (*q.v.*), elder of the Flemish congregation. Again about 1620 at a meeting at Langezwaag (*q.v.*) in Friesland, he denounced Outerman as the "most awful heretic he had ever met." On April 13-16, 1622, he disputed at Hoorn with P. J. Twisck, elder of the Frisians, and prevented a union with the Frisians. In 1623 Luies went to Blokzijl to ban the Flemish elder Claes Claesz (*q.v.*), who according to Luies was too lenient in maintaining the old principles of banning and shunning. Claesz defended himself against Luies in *Onschult ende Bestraffinghe des onschriftmatighen oordeels,'t welck by Jan Luyes ende sijne medestanders gegeven ende uytgesproocken is* (2nd ed. Amsterdam, 1627). Likewise in 1623 Luies stayed at Amsterdam, where a part of the Flemish were planning to merge with the Frisians, and prevented the union by his obstinacy, banning a number of members including the preacher of the Amsterdam Flemish congregation, Abraham Dirksz (Bierens). For this act he was blamed by his former adherent Jan Gerritsz in a booklet *Een Spieghel des Geloofs* (printed not before 1641, Amsterdam). He also was active in Blokzijl, Giethoorn, and Deventer (all in 1627).

The question of unification was fully discussed at a meeting on Sept. 18-21, 1628, at Middelstum (*q.v.*).

Here Jan Luies, assisted by Elder Uko Walles (*q.v.*) from Noordbroek, opposed a number of tolerant Flemish leaders, such as Claes Claesz of Blokzijl, Pieter Jans Moyer of Amsterdam, and Joost Hendriks of Harlingen. Here the rupture between Jan Luies and his intolerant adherents on the one side, who presumed that only the Flemish church was the visible church of the Lord, and on the other side the more lenient elders, led by Claes Claesz, who wished to make peace and union with other groups of Mennonites, became definite.

The followers of Jan Luies, who were numerous in the province of Groningen and who were at first called Jan-Lucas-volk, but soon were given the name of Groningen Old Flemish (*q.v.*) Mennonites, broke off all intercourse with the Flemish. After the death of Jan Luies, his coelder Uko Walles became their leader, for whom they have also been called Ukowallists (*q.v.*). vDZ.

Inv. Arch. Amst. I, Nos. 558 I, II, VI, 571, 606; II, 1232-40; II, 2, No. 66; *N.N.B.Wb.* III, 797-800; Blaupot t. C., *Groningen* I, 60, 64-67; Kühler, *Geschiedenis* II, 83 f., 133-35; *ML* II, 389.

Luik: see **Liége.**

Luiken: see **Luyken.**

Luikinga, Willem (1879-1928), a Dutch Mennonite pastor, who after study at the University of Groningen and the Mennonite Seminary at Amsterdam, became a ministerial candidate in 1906, thereupon serving the congregations of Aalsmeer 1907-15 and IJmuiden 1915-28. In the *Doopsgezind Jaarboekje* 1920 he published the paper "Langs een oude Vermaning," an interesting study of old Mennonite life at Aalsmeer. His son Hendrik Luikinga, b. 1916, is also a Mennonite pastor, serving at Veendam-Pekela 1943-47, Almelo 1947-49, and since 1949 at Zaandam.

vDZ.

Luirts, Luirt, a preacher (already serving in 1645) and elder of the Groningen Old Flemish Mennonites, being a farmer near Westeremden in the Dutch province of Groningen. From 1645 until 1663 he repeatedly traveled about to visit the Groningen Old Flemish congregations in the Netherlands and North Germany. He was present at the delegates' meeting at Loppersum (*q.v.*) in 1659, where a number of restrictions were made concerning plain clothing and furnishings for the members of the Groningen Old Flemish group. Luirt Luirts died on Oct. 6, 1674. He was a member of the Huizinga (*q.v.*) family, but did not yet bear this family name. (*DB* 1879, 5, 9 f., 86, 89 ff., 111.) vDZ.

Lulofs, a Mennonite family, living at Leer, East Friesland, Germany, since the 17th century. A branch of this family in the early 18th century moved to Amsterdam, where Warner Lulofs became a deacon of the Lamist congregation in 1735. A descendant of this family was Sicco Lulofs (b. 1849 at Amsterdam, d. 1927 at The Hague), who was a Mennonite pastor for more than 55 years, serving at Broek op Langendijk 1872-75, Winterswijk 1875-77, Koog-Zaandijk 1877-89, Deventer 1889-1901, and The Hague 1901-27. For many years he was a trustee of the A.D.S. (Dutch General Mennonite Conference) and a curator of the Amsterdam Mennonite Seminary. He published only a number of sermons. His colleague G. Wuite Jz of The Hague wrote his obituary in *Doopsgezind Jaarboekje* of 1929. vpZ.

Lundenburg (Czech, *Breclav*), a city (pop. 10,371) on the border between Moravia and Lower Austria. The whole vicinity of Lundenburg, in the possession of the barons of Zierotin, who were friendly to the Anabaptists, became one of the most important Anabaptist settlements. Some of the chronicles give the year 1543, others 1545 as the year of the founding of the Lundenburg Hutterite Bruderhof. It was set up in a house purchased from the barons and in the shoemaker's house "where the bath (barbershop) is." The Lundenburg barber-surgeons soon enjoyed a wide reputation.

At about the same time Bruderhofs were set up in the immediate neighborhood in Altenmarkt, Kostel, Bilowitz, Schaikowitz, Saitz, Paulowitz, and other places. The prosperity of Lundenburg industry made it possible after a short time to purchase a second house near the Meierhof, which Bartholomäus von Zierotin gave over to the Hutterites.

Johann Jr. von Zierotin, who expelled them from his land in 1579 for refusing to pay taxes, recalled them after three days, and in 1580 even gave them a park and forest belonging to the Catholic prebend of Kostel, thereby involving himself in some difficulty with Pawlowsky, bishop of Olmütz. The Brethren of Lundenburg, Kostel, and Landshut (*q.v.*) greeted their new lord, Ladislaus Welen von Zierotin, with a gift of knives and majolica produced by their shops; the majolica was so beautiful that he sent it to his teacher Dr. Grynäus in Basel.

During the revolt this region suffered particularly severely; on Sept. 19-20, 1619, imperial troops under Dampierre burned down the Bruderhofs, including the one in Lundenburg, having first plundered it and murdered about 20 men and women. On Nov. 10 the army returned, plundered the castle, into which the Brethren had put some things for safekeeping, and the mill and brewery belonging to them; they stole the cattle and kidnaped the leaders. In 1621 new misfortune struck the Bruderhofs which had with great toil been partly rebuilt: destruction, robbery, compulsory military service, especially on Wallenstein's orders, were the order of the day.

The expulsion of the Hutterites in 1621 annihilated the splendid settlements in this domain. The wish of Gundakar von Liechtenstein to employ a few Anabaptists was refused in 1624 by Cardinal Dietrichstein. P.DE.

Beck, *Geschichts-Bücher;* Loserth, *Communismus;* Wolkan, *Geschicht-Buch;* Zieglschmid, *Chronik;* L. Preuss, *Geschichte Lundenburgs (Progr. des Lundenb. Gymnasiums 1903-04); ML* II, 701.

Lüneburg, an area of Braunschweig in the former Prussian province of Hanover, Germany, with Celle as its capital, which was made Protestant by resolution of the Landtag on April 18, 1527. At the head of the church system Duke Ernest placed Urban Rhegius (*q.v.*) in 1531, as superintendent general, an office which had not previously existed in the

Lutheran Church. Rhegius had been called to Celle in September 1530 from Augsburg, where he had just finished a severe struggle with the Anabaptists and had finally had them suppressed by force. In Lüneburg the movement had not won a foothold, but Rhegius used the influence of his position to injure them in other countries.

In an opinion delivered to Philip of Hesse by the Lüneburg clergy on June 5, 1536, on the question "whether it was fitting that a government compel Anabaptists and other heretics to accept the true faith, and to punish with the sword those who persist in their heresy," they advocated capital punishment. They compared the task of the government with that of a physician who cuts off a bad limb when medicine fails to cure, lest it contaminate the entire body. Secular authority could with a good conscience put to death all persistent heretics, just as it has power to kill adulterers, thieves, murderers, and revolutionaries. As evidence several Old Testament Scriptures were cited.

Philip did not follow these suggestions, but many theologians found the arguments convenient. Bullinger (*q.v.*), for instance, used them in a letter to Calvin on June 12, 1554, to weaken the opposition to the burning of Servetus (Paulus, 221). The opinion was widely read. In the 16th and 17th centuries it was reprinted several times under Rhegius's name; in 1537 at Hamburg, 1538 Strasbourg, 1562 Nürnberg in *Die Deutschen Bücher von Urban Rhegius* (Vol. IV, pp. 211-15); and 1608 in Frankfurt, in J. Bidenbach, *Consiliorum theologicorum Decas* (Vols. III and IV, pp. 201-18). (Hochhuth, 266-578.)

In 1555 Lüneburg joined in the decision of the Hansa cities to prevent Menno Simons from baptizing among his brethren in the Baltic Sea region (Mannhardt, 84). HEGE.

K. W. H. Hochhuth, "Mitteilungen aus der protestantischen Sekten-Geschichte in der hessischen Kirche," in *Ztscht für die hist. Theol.,* 1858; Mannhardt, *Jahrbuch,* 1883; N. Paulus, *Protestantismus und Toleranz im 16. Jahrhundert* (Berlin, 1911); Gerh. Uhlhorn, *Urbanus Rhegius* (Elberfeld, 1861); Johs. Warns, *Die Taufe* (Cassel, 1922); *ML* II, 701 f.

Lunéville, a city (pop. 19,065) in northeastern France, known as the residence of Stanislaus Leczinski, King of Poland, when he was Duke of Lorraine. Peace was concluded here in 1801 between Austria and France. Lunéville is the seat of a small Mennonite church. The Mennonites living here in the 18th century belonged to the Welschland (*q.v.*) congregation. On account of the distance between the members they divided, the local Mennonites formed the Lunéville-Dieuze church (Mannhardt, *Jahrbuch,* 1888, 42), which met twice a month at the homes of the members. The congregation then consisted of fifteen families, with Christian Schweitzer as elder.

The Franco-Prussian war divided the congregation politically, but they continued to meet together until 1893, when border difficulties made it advisable to separate. The French families joined the congregation at Nancy. The German families continued to meet once a month in Dieuze. The number declined because of emigration and a low birth rate. Finally they joined the congregation at Morhange.

After World War I the Nancy church died out. The Lunéville-Dieuze group joined Gerbéviller (*q.v.*), a subsidiary of Baccarat (*q.v.*); together they organized the Lunéville congregation. It had then a membership of about 40 souls, and met once a month in a rented hall in Lunéville. There were smaller meetings and prayer meetings in the various homes. In 1954 the membership was *ca.* 30 souls, with no elder, and with a meeting only once a month. The preacher is Emile Muller, living in Herbéviller. (*ML* II, 702.)   P.So.

Luray (Va.), the name generally applied to the Shenandoah National Park Civilian Public Service Camp No. 45. It was operated by the Mennonite Central Committee under the National Park Service. Opened in August 1942, by December it had an enrollment of 152 men. The camp was located approximately 15 miles southeast of the town of Luray, near the center of the Shenandoah National Park and a stone's throw west of the Skyline Drive. Among the jobs assigned to the men were the conducting of wild life surveys, blister rust control, construction of lookout towers, maintenance of the National Park headquarters, clearing the highways of snow, emergency farm work, and fire fighting. Two special schools, directed by the MCC, were held at Camp No. 45, an arts and crafts school and a cooking school. The camp was closed in June 1946.
M.G.

M. Gingerich, *Service for Peace* (Akron, Pa., 1949) 150-7.

Lüsen (Lisen), a village (pop. *ca.* 300) in the Lüsental, a subsidiary valley of the Rienz in southern Tirol, Austria (now Italy). Although it was close to Brixen, it was open to the Anabaptist movement. In 1532 Hutter (*q.v.*) baptized seven persons here according to a statement made by Friedrich Brandenberg, his companion, who was put to death soon afterward. In 1534 Offerus Griesinger (*q.v.*), one of the boldest and most adept Anabaptist apostles in Tirol, won many adherents here. In 1535 the judge of Brixen came to Lüsen, called the people together, and announced to them the severe Anabaptist mandates of the Brixen government, and threatened that anyone who in the future sheltered an Anabaptist would be executed, and his house burned down. He took ten unsubmissive persons with him to Brixen, of whom seven recanted but only apparently, in order to escape to Moravia. In 1536 Hans Grünfelder (*q.v.*) was leader and treasurer in Lüsen, and held a "big meeting" in March. Sigmund Han, the chancellor of the prince-bishop, informed the bishop that Hans Amon (*q.v.*) was active around Lüsen, and that 17 persons had left their homes to go to Moravia, including some who had once "sworn off" their error. The Brixen authorities raided the region, combing it for certain persons. Grünfelder escaped, but was later caught in the Oetztal and executed at Imst. Griesinger again took up the work here; in the meantime he had taken several groups to Moravia, returned as a missionary to Moravia, been imprisoned, and escaped. Now he was captured again at Lüsen in April 1537 and imprisoned in Brixen, whence he managed again to escape.

Anabaptists of Lüsen en route to Moravia in 1542 were stopped in Kropfsberg and sent to Brixen for judgment. Lüsen was also the home of Balthasar Dosser, "a particularly dangerous agitator," who was cruelly put to death with several companions at Innsbruck in 1562. Even in the 1580's, indeed in 1604 there are in the court record still some traces of the Anabaptists.   P.De.

Beck, *Geschichts-Bücher;* J. Loserth, *Der Anabaptismus in Tirol* (Vienna, 1892); J. V. Zingerle, *Schilderungen aus Tirol* (1877); Wolkan, *Geschicht-Buch;* Zieglschmid, *Chronik;* Loesche, *Tirolensia;* ML II, 702.

Lusthof des Gemoeds, a Dutch Mennonite devotional treatise: see **Schabaelje, J. Ph.**

Lusthof des Gemoets (Pleasure Garden of the Heart), a Dutch Mennonite hymnary, published in 1732 at Groningen, with an introduction by Alle Derks (*q.v.*). This hymnbook, which was to replace an older songbook, was used by the Groningen Old Flemish until about 1830. It contains 139 "schriftuirlycke liedekens" (Scriptural songs) borrowed from other hymnaries and without notes, being intended for public meetings and also, as is said in the title and in the introduction, "to be read to refresh the souls." It is followed by an appendix, called *Agter-Hofje* (Back Yard), of which two editions 1732 and 1736 are known, both at Groningen. This *Agter-Hofje* contains 51 hymns with notes; it has a short preface by Alle Derks.   vDZ.

Lusthof der Zielen, a Dutch hymnary: see **Stapel, Claes.**

Lusthofje des Gemoeds (Little Pleasure Garden of the Heart), a Dutch Mennonite booklet, only 2 x 3 inches, containing 31 devotional songs by J. H. Deutel (*q.v.*), arranged alphabetically and without notes. There is extant only a 2d edition, published at Hoorn in 1663.   vDZ.

Lusthofje Sions, 't, a Dutch Mennonite hymnal, was published in 1668 at Hoorn and contains on 533 pages 239 hymns (27 psalms and 212 "geestelijke liedekens"), all without notes. It was published, and very probably also edited, by Jan Jansz Deutel (*q.v.*). The full title reads: *'t Lusthofje Sions, Bestaande in eenige Psalmen Davids, Lofzangen ende Geestelijke Liedekens. Zeer bequaam om in de Christelijke Vergaderingen der Geloovigen, ofte elders ter eeren Godts, ende tot onderlinge stigtinge met aandacht gezongen te werden.* (Copy in AML.)
vDZ.

Lustprieel der Zeeden, *om te dienen tot vermaek en stichting der zeedige sanglievende gemoeden,* is a Dutch Mennonite hymnal, of which as far as is known no copy is extant. Blaupot ten Cate (*Holland* II, 213) mentions an edition of 1685 published by Hendrik Rijntjes (*q.v.*) at Leeuwarden.   vDZ.

Lustre, Valley Co., Mont., is the center of one of the most recent Mennonite colonization successes. The community, which now contains three Mennonite congregations, the Lustre E.M.B. (1917) with 103 members, the Bethel G.C.M. (1924) with 71 members, and the Lustre M.B. (1917) with 132 members, for a total of 306, was started about 1917 on virgin prairie. The nearest other churches are the Larslan M.B. congregation with 38 members, 20 miles northwest, and the two G.C.M. congregations at Wolf Point (Bethel and United) 37 miles southwest with 129 members. Wolf Point, a town of 2,500, is the business center for the Lustre community. The Lustre settlement is located in the Fort Peck Reservation region, the Fort Peck Dam on the Missouri River being 50 miles to the south. The three Mennonite churches of Lustre, all clustered closely together, unite in the support of Lustre Bible Academy (q.v.), which was established in 1928. From the beginning there has been the closest co-operation in various matters between the Mennonites of all branches in the community.   H.S.B.

Lustre Bible Academy, located at Lustre, Mont., is an outgrowth of the Lustre Bible School, which was begun in 1928. In 1947-48 a two-year high-school course was added. In 1948-49 the Academy was accredited as a regular 4-year high school by the state of Montana. In addition to the high-school curriculum Bible subjects are also taught. In 1954 a new school building with gymnasium was erected. The girls' dormitory, two teacherages, and the old and new school buildings stand on a spacious campus.

The school is located in the heart of this Mennonite area, with the M.B. Church of Lustre, the Bethel (q.v., G.C.M.) Lustre Church, and the E.M.B. Church, all within two or three miles of the Academy, and draws its support completely from the interested local Mennonite constituency. Leo Goertzel has been serving as principal for 6-7 years, with three additional teachers on the staff. The enrollment for 1954-55 was 40-45.   H.P.W.

Lustre Evangelical Mennonite Brethren Church, located near Lustre, Mont., was organized July 7, 1917, the first of the three Mennonite congregations in this prairie community. The first meetinghouse, 16 x 28 ft., was built the same year, and replaced in 1928 by a new church, 40 x 60 ft., with a seating capacity of 300. In 1954 the membership was 103, with Henry P. Wiebe as pastor.   H.P.W.

Lustre Mennonite Brethren Church, a rural church located at Lustre, Valley Co., Mont., 25 miles north of Frazer, was organized by Heinrich Voth on Nov. 17, 1917, with 47 members. The congregation met in a schoolhouse until 1923, when a building was erected. J. F. Thiessen, its first pastor, served for 26 years. He was assisted by Benjamin Redekopp until 1922, by A. A. Dick until 1943, and by J. J. Toews. These ministers also served the Volt and Larslan M.B. congregations. Arthur Flaming served from 1944, assisted by J. J. Toews. This church is strongly missionary-minded, having sent four of its members to the foreign field. In 1954 the membership was 132, with Leo S. Wiens as pastor.
                A.A.D.

Lüthard, Christoph (1590-1663), professor of philosophy at the University of Bern, Switzerland, from 1618, professor of theology from 1628 until his death.

In high esteem for his work in training the pastors of Bern, he also merited praise for his contribution to the school system. On Jan. 4, 1659, he was appointed on the newly organized Anabaptist Commission, and with his colleagues interviewed the "Anabaptists in the penitentiary." About this time Dutch intervention in behalf of the Mennonites was begun. Abraham Heidanus (q.v.), professor of theology at the University of Leiden, and Hans Vlamingh, an Amsterdam merchant, wrote long letters to Lüthard (printed in Müller, 173-79), advocating a free exercise of religion. In his reply Lüthard as a member of the Anabaptist Commission tried to present the condition of the Mennonites in a favorable light and to justify the attitude of the Bern theologians and the government.   S.G.

"Bernische Pfarrer im 16.-19. Jahrhundert," a manuscript in the state archives of the canton of Bern; Müller, *Berner Täufer; ML* II, 702 f.

Luther, Martin (1483-1546), reformer and founder of the Lutheran Church, was born Nov. 10, 1483, at Eisleben, Germany; died there on Feb. 18, 1546. The subject of Luther and his relations with Anabaptism (Luther, with other opponents of Anabaptism, called them "Wiedertäufer") naturally falls into two parts; viz., a purely theological inquiry into his concept of baptism in general and infant baptism in particular, and an inquiry into the punitive measures against the Anabaptists desired or sponsored by Luther in connection with his basic position on the persecution of heretics.

1. *Luther's Concept of Infant Baptism.* Concerning baptism Luther expressed himself at some length for the first time in 1519 in his "Sermon on the Holy, Worthy Sacrament of Baptism" (*WA* II, 4 ff.). Infant baptism was not yet a problem here, but was taken for granted as premise; here Luther opposed the practice prevalent "at many places," of sprinkling with the hand, and wished that "the child be completely submerged in the water and pulled out again," to correspond with the meaning of baptism, "that the old man and sinful birth of flesh and blood is to be completely drowned through the grace of God"—only thus is it possible to satisfy the meaning of baptism and give "a true complete symbol." Baptism is furthermore a mark by which the people of Christ are recognized and which separates us from "all unbaptized human beings." This idea later became important for the idea of the mass church.

In contrast to the Catholic magical and sacramental view which soon (in the growing Christian life) replaced baptism with one's own works of repentance, or thought that "there was no longer any sin left, became lazy" and negligent, Luther stressed the obligation which baptism places upon the entire life—"therefore all of life is nothing but a spiritual baptism without cease until death"—in confidence in God's assurance, who in the sacrament "unites Himself with you and becomes one with you in a merciful comforting bond." For Luther the baptized person is in principle ("sacramentally") "entirely pure and innocent," but not in fact, since he is still living in the sinful flesh, and is now to become clean in the strength of the Holy Spirit, who is guaranteed in baptism. But it must never become "a false security," as if in trusting in the grace imparted by the sacrament one might live according to his own will: "See to it, if you so wickedly and willfully sin upon grace, that judgment does not seize you!" Faith is religious strength; when Luther designated it as "the most necessary of all and the foundation of all comfort," he interpreted faith in this connection as the sustaining foundation of life in baptism, and faith is thus seen not from the point of view of the child but of the adult, mature Christian.

This is different from the accents in *De captivitate babylonica ecclesiae* (Concerning the Babylonian Captivity of the Church) in 1520 (*WA* VI, 526 ff.). Here is found right at the beginning the statement that baptism is "most beneficial to children"; they are "initiated" thereby and "are sanctified by the most simple faith in the word of God." If this sacrament had been given to adults it would have lost its strength, since the devil would surely have had it sold for money as he then did the indulgences. According to the promise of Mark 16:16, faith is an absolute necessity for the proper working of baptism, to the extent that "faith can save even without the sacrament"; without faith baptism is harmful. Since this faith must accompany one throughout his entire life, it begins in the act of the baptism of the child as the "justifying" faith. Luther here logically deals with the objection that this faith is impossible in children "who do not grasp the promise of God and cannot have the faith of baptism." He solves this problem in harmony with tradition ("because all say it"; thereby he is thinking of the guarantee of the godparents) by stating that the faith of the person bringing the little child to the act of baptism comes to the assistance of the child. This is not to be understood to mean that this faith of another has a substitutionary effect but rather that it is evaluated as the prayer of the believing church which affects God so that the word of God works upon the child, just as it is also capable of transforming the heart of an ungodly man, "which is no less deaf and incapable than any little child." Thus the child is "transformed and renewed by a faith infused into him." The sacrament is capable of bursting even "the most obstinately opposed bar," especially here where it works through the strength of faith and of the prayer of the church.

In order to understand this view of Luther, the following must be observed. "As the sacrament of baptism is a gift of God, it is He who does something here, not man. This completely precludes the idea that baptism is to be considered an act of presentation of the child to God by the parents and the church as Zwingli thought of it. Faith too, however necessary, must be considered purely as an act of God, not as an act of expression of man; all subjective psychological anchorage is missing." Since it is a work of God, not of man, as Paul teaches (Eph. 2:8), Luther rejected the concept of the baptism of children upon their future faith as adults as the Waldenses and Bohemian Brethren held it. And for this very reason infant baptism was religiously valuable to Luther because by it in his view children are put into right relationship with the sacramental activity of God, "not concerned to do any kind of effort or any kind of work, completely free, sure and blessed alone through the glory of their baptism." Little children are thus the perfect example for correct baptism. Furthermore as the sacrament of initiation and the supporting foundation of faith baptism can only be infant baptism.

2. *Luther's Reasons for Infant Baptism and Infant Faith.* Luther founded infant baptism and the faith of children on Matt. 19:14 or Matt. 2:16 (innocent children are "holy and blessed"), on John the Baptist who leaped in faith in his mother's womb (Luke 1:41), on the example of circumcision in the Old Covenant, on the baptism of whole families by the apostles (Acts 10:48; 16:33; I Cor. 1:16), and on Christian tradition "since the times of the apostles in all the world by all of Christendom," which God would surely not have allowed to continue if it had not been right, especially since all other heresies perished. But he admitted that there is in the New Testament no particular command to baptize children; they are included in "all the heathen" (Matt. 28:19). Just as the faith of a Christian remains with him in his sleep, unaware to him, so also faith can begin in children though they are unaware of it (*WA* 17, 2, 86).

3. *Luther's Opposition to Anabaptism.* These above principles as held by Luther show that any understanding with the Anabaptists was for Luther theologically impossible. He remained true to his concept of baptism expressed in 1520 and only stiffened in the objectivization of his doctrine of the sacrament in his dispute with Carlstadt and Zwingli, in which he became more and more unyielding. God's word of promise remained for him superior to the symbol, the water. "It is more important to teach God's word than to baptize" (*WA* 26, 164). Baptism is also subordinated to faith; "even if someone had never been baptized but did not know any better or firmly believed that he has been properly and surely baptized, such faith would still be enough for him, for as he believes, so he is before God" (*WA* 26, 171). But the effectiveness of the word is so immediately put into the symbol that this symbol, i.e., the water, becomes its bearer and is therefore taken away from the profane. It is no longer "simple water"; but it is "with" and "by" the water that baptism carries the strength of the word of God, of the promise of the forgiveness of sin.

At the same time the baptism of children "is the surest baptism of all" (*WA* 26, 157), precisely because the child "cannot deceive" but possesses the true passivity and receptivity of the believer. These two facts together make the act of baptism appear as an *opus operatum* and of magical Catholic nature, which was not at all Luther's intention. His religious interest lay in making the sacrament independent of human wishes, in the working out of the pure objectivity of God's work of grace. But Luther's formulation is theologically unsatisfying. His error lies in the impossibility of giving faith the theological significance here ascribed to it as a matter of principle. It is strange that this theologian of faith was unable to do this. He always feared "works," i.e., human self-righteousness, if faith should become "personal" in the modern sense.

4. *Disputes with the Anabaptists.* Luther disputed

theologically with the Anabaptists only in literary form, and principally in four writings: (1) his booklet *Von der Wiedertaufe an zwei Pfarrherrn* of 1528 (*WA* 26, 137 ff.); (2) the foreword to the book by Justus Menius, *Der Wiedertäufer Lehre und Geheimnis* of 1530 (*WA* 30, 2, 209 ff.); (3) his *Von den Schleichern und Winkelpredigern* of 1532 (*WA* 30, 3, 510 ff.); and (4) his sermons of February 2, 9, 16, and 23, 1528 (*WA* 27), as well as in the *Kirchenpostille* of 1523 for the Gospel on the third Sunday after Epiphany (*WA* 17, 2, 72 ff.), also separately published under the title *Von der Kinder Tauf und fremdem Glauben* in the introductions to Urbanus Rhegius' *Widerlegung des Bekenntnisses der Münsterischen neuen Valentinianer und Donatisten und zur Neuen Zeitung von den Wiedertäufern zu Münster 1535* (*WA* 38, 336 ff.). In addition there are his letters, his official opinions, and the expressions in his *Table Talks*.

Luther apparently did not have exact information on Anabaptist writings, however certainly he has "heard" and "read" and "knows" all manner of things (*WA* 26, 140). All individualization is missing, especially since Luther lumps the Anabaptists together with the Sacramentists (Zwingli, Carlstadt, Schwenckfeld, etc.), not entirely without justification, of course, to the extent that the Anabaptist doctrine of the communion was the same as that of Zwingli or Oecolampadius. It is of no significance that he declared "the error of the Anabaptists more tolerable than that of the sacramentists in this matter" (baptism), "for the Sacramentists completely destroy baptism, but they [the Anabaptists] make it new" (*WA* 26, 173); Anabaptists and Sacramentists remained for him still Pilate and Herod, who were united as one over and against Christ.

In the divisions of Anabaptism Luther sees a sign of its ungodliness. The Anabaptist limitation of baptism to the believer he considers entirely impossible, since the baptizer cannot look into the heart of a man to see whether he really believes. Such a baptism is a "baptism upon adventure" (Mark 16:16), even if there is talk of "the sure faith"; for the confession of the one to be baptized proves nothing, since he too is not "sure" of his faith since he is of course not free of temptation. (One is impressed with Luther's rejection of all anchoring of the grace of baptism in a human or emotional activity such as "trusting and building upon oneself and not upon the word of God alone.")

The Anabaptist practice of preaching in secret (in actuality the consequence of persecution) was to Luther "a certain sign of the devil," especially since they had no "call" to preach. The eschatological hope of certain Anabaptist circles for an earthly kingdom with the murder of all the ungodly (e.g., Müntzer) was to him an unchristian, seditious, and vengeful spirit (Luke 22:26). In Christology he accused the Anabaptists of Münster of teaching "that Christ did not receive His body from Mary, as they call it [but in Mary], although He was called the seed of David" (*WA* 38, 349). The claim of the Anabaptists to have authorization to speak because of the "Sitzrecht" (I Cor. 14:30, "If a revelation is made to another sitting by, let the first be silent") he definitely rejected with the interpretation that

Paul was speaking of prophets, i.e., "teachers who have the office of preaching in the churches" (*WA* 30, 3, 522).

Luther rejected the whole idea of rebaptism (which was among the Anabaptists merely the practical consequence of their demand for adult baptism, and not a principle) with the argument that the person who performs the act of baptism is irrelevant; baptism "under the papacy" was also right, and Augustine had opposed the Donatists (*WA* 27, 42 ff.). "It was a mistake to build baptism on the faith of the baptizer; I base baptism on God's Word." Luther was here referring to the Donatists of the fourth century who rejected the baptism of a bishop who had recanted under persecution and then was restored to office.

In the moral demands of the Anabaptists, based on the ethics of the Sermon on the Mount (rejection of the oath and holding magisterial office, stress on the holy living of the believing Christian), Luther saw legalism, sedition, and the denial of ineradicable human sinfulness. His entire polemic here is however completely doctrinaire in rejecting realism and individual differentiation.

But it is undeniable that there were unbridgeable theological differences between the two sides; and just as Luther failed to try to understand the Anabaptists, so also did the Anabaptists fail to understand him when they pointed out the ineffectiveness of infant baptism. This last argument in particular was not fair to Luther, since he had from the beginning attacked the inadequacy of the bare act of infant baptism as such and pointed out its ineffectiveness for the whole of life. (See also p. 421.)

5. *Luther and the Catholic Heresy Laws.* The manner of the proceedings against the Anabaptists by both church and secular authorities which Luther advocated and desired, is rightly to be seen as a part of the whole question of Reformation and "heresy." Anabaptism offered the principal practical occasion for his consideration of the question of what legal procedures were to be applied to heretics.

To be sure, the first basic statements by Luther on this question were made in regard to his own case and were against the existing Catholic heresy laws. "The burning of heretics is contrary to the will of the Holy Spirit," says one of the paragraphs of the 95 theses of 1518 (*WA* I, 624; see 391 f.), and in the *Address to the Christian Nobility of the German Nation* in 1520 he said, "Heretics must be overcome with the Scriptures, not with fire; if it were an art to overcome heretics with fire, then the executioners would be the most learned doctors on earth" (*WA* 6, 455). Spiritual things must be judged spiritually (I Cor. 2:13); the government is not lord of the conscience, but has only to do with temporal, not with spiritual order. On the other hand, the church has its own means of discipline by the norm of Matt. 18:16 ff., i.e., by brotherly admonition and finally the ban, which may, however, not extend into the civil sphere (see *Sermon on the Ban* of 1518, published in 1520, *WA* VI, 61 ff.).

Luther's sharp differentiation between the Gospel and the world works itself out logically here. "The soul's thoughts and feelings can be known to none but God; therefore it is . . . impossible to command

and compel anyone with force to believe thus or so; another approach is needed for this; force will not do it" (1523, *WA* 11, 264). This "other approach" was to fight with the word of the Bible, and Luther was firmly convinced that it would win the day with everyone in the one true understanding comprehensible to all. "God's Word illumines the hearts, and thereby all heresy and error will vanish from the heart" (*WA* 11, 269). Luther's strength of faith was able here to demonstrate splendid strength and confidence in the purely spiritual conquest of heresy; only lack of faith doubts the effectiveness of the Holy Scriptures. "I believe that the idea of burning heretics comes from the fear of being unable to overcome them with the Word" (1520, *WA* 6, 582). "Let the spirits burst and clash one with the other. If some meanwhile are misled, very well, that is what happens in the real course of war; where there is strife and battle, there some must fall" (*WA* 15, 219). Heresy appears, entirely within the sphere of faith, as an aspect of divine leading of history; heresy is necessary from this point of view (Matt. 18:7; I Cor. 11:19). "It is a plague of divine wrath" over sin; heretics admonish to alertness, "cause the faith and the doctrine of the church to be practiced," thereby promoting it directly. "If Cerinthus had not been, then John the Evangelist would never have written his Gospel." Indeed, there is truth concealed in heresy—"There has never been a heresy that has not stated some truth" (1525, *WA* 14, 694). All these are verdicts of faith.

These verdicts in part fall into the period when Anabaptism had already entered in the field of Luther's vision. In Part II of the booklet *Of Worldly Government, to What Extent Obedience Is Its Due* (1523) the statement is defended in the sharpest imaginable manner that "Heresy can never be resisted with fire" (*WA* 11, 268); if there is heresy, let it be overcome, as is proper, with God's Word (*WA* 11, 270), even though Luther is not here referring to the Anabaptist movement, but was led to this formulation of the issue by Melanchthon. In his writing, *A Letter to the Princes of Saxony Concerning the Seditious Spirit* (1524), which is concerned directly with Müntzer, but indirectly with Carlstadt and the "Schwarmgeister," Luther writes, "Just let them preach as they like and with confidence; for, as I have said, there must be sects and the Word of God must go to the battle field and fight" (*WA* 15, 218). But now, disturbed by the violent iconoclastic seditious aggression of Müntzer (*WA* 15, 200 f.), he drew a sharp line: "But if they want to do more than fight with the Word, and also want to break and strike with the fist, there your Excellency shall attack, be it we or they, and let them be at once expelled from the country" (*WA* 15, 219), i.e., then they are to be punished by the government as rebels, for they then themselves overstep the Christian area of action and enter into the secular area which is the concern of the government.

6. *Fighting the Anabaptists with Secular Power.* Unfortunately in Luther's mind the Anabaptist movement came more and more into the category of sedition, partly because of civil disturbances connected with the movement (e.g., *WA* 30, 3, 513),

partly because of radical utterances on the part of certain Anabaptists, and partly because of more or less biased reports. Consequently Luther was never able to recognize the quiet, purely religious Anabaptism. It was to him not a matter for spiritual weapons, since he was unable to differentiate them, and no longer saw any of them as purely spiritual opponents. In the foreword to the *Instruction of the Inspectors to the Pastors in the Electorate of Saxony* (1528, *WA* 26, 200) Luther speaks of the duty of the government to see that "dissension, partisan spirit, and sedition do not arise among their subjects." This statement concerned the prohibition of all Anabaptist literature in Saxony. For Luther the Anabaptists were no longer "sinners primarily against religion," but rather "against the essence of the state" (Wappler, *Kursachsen,* 15).

In the punishment of Anabaptists as revolutionaries Luther, in an official opinion to Philip of Hesse, gave the ruler the right to decide. According to the occasion of the incidents he might pardon, expel, or—in the case of obstinate transgressors against the ruler's mandates—execute with the sword. To be sure, in a letter of July 14, 1528 (Enders VI, 299 ff.), he wrote, "I hesitate to pass the death sentence, even when it has been amply merited; their expulsion is sufficient." And in 1530 in his *Exposition of Psalm 82 (WA* 30, 1, 192 ff.) he warned the state not to abuse its power and sought to protect and retain the moral character of the governmental "majesty." Nevertheless, in practice he became more and more inexorable, recommending that "corner preachers," Anabaptists, etc., be commended to the executioner. Luther's judgment became definitive for Saxony's treatment of the Anabaptists, even though he cannot be held accountable for particulars. He approved the imperial mandates against the Anabaptists of 1529 ff.

A second line of thought plays a part in Luther's attitude. In the letter to Lazarus Spengler, Feb. 4, 1525 (Enders V, 117), Luther wrote that he did not yet consider Anabaptism (*Schwärmertum*) blasphemous. After about 1528, in connection with his opinion that Anabaptism was essentially seditious and in view of the fact that the preaching of the Word, which he had hitherto believed would always be victorious, was failing here, he changed his mind and demanded a ruthless application of the penalty for blasphemy, as found in natural law (equivalent to the second commandment), in the Old Testament (Lev. 24:16), and in the Justinian Code. The objectivity of the fact of blasphemy seemed to Luther so compelling that in 1530 in his *Exposition of Psalm 82* and in 1531 in his concurrence with Melanchthon he said that heretics (Anabaptists) should be condemned even without trial and process of law. Even if the potentate acts too hastily, he is still right (*WA* 31, 1, p. 309 *Corp. Ref.* IV, 740).

7. *Luther Favors the Execution of Anabaptists with the Sword.* From this point of view Luther's famous official opinion of 1531 (not 1541!) in cooperation with the Wittenberg theologians must be understood (*Corp. Ref.* IV, 737 ff.). It repeats his views in a more or less classical form and must not be weakened. His addition to the decision of his colleagues is explained by the fact that John

of Saxony had requested an opinion of the theological faculty as a whole and of Luther in particular. The opinion was formulated by Melanchthon, but Luther added the words "I approve," and expressly sanctioned the executions of heretics, "although it is terrible to view." He did this for four reasons: (1) They condemn the office of preaching the Word. (2) They have no definite doctrine. (3) They suppress true doctrine. (4) They want to destroy the kingdom of this world.

All four points, even the condemnation of the office of preaching and their false doctrine, were included in the category of sedition and blasphemy, and were therefore, on the basis of the second commandment, to be punished by the government. This was not at all a matter of interference by the state in the inner realm of faith; it was a question of the preservation of public order, which lies in the hand of the sword of government. Anabaptism was punished as a crime against the public, not because its faith was different, but because it (in Luther's opinion) disturbed public order through sedition and blasphemy.

Luther often replied to objections to this view, raised in part by himself and in part by others. He did so especially in his *Exposition of Psalm 82* in 1530 (*WA* 31, 1, pp. 183 ff.), where he replied to the charge by Lazarus Spengler, of Nürnberg, that he (Luther) contradicted himself. He held to the principle that "no one should or can be compelled to believe"; but if one is punished for teaching contrary to the creed, he is not punished as a "simple heretic," but as a "public blasphemer, subject to secular penalties. Personally one may believe what he will; on inner matters of faith no judge passes sentence," but teaching and blaspheming are prohibited, "unless the teacher goes where there are no Christians." The Papists, who confess the Apostles' Creed, were logically not included among the blasphemers.

The congregating of nonconformists who cannot be compelled to believe is to be punished by the government for the reason that "corner preaching" foments disturbance and sedition; here too it was not the heretical belief that was punished. Luther also forbade Protestant clergymen to preach to the congregation of "a Papist or a heretic," seeing sedition in the very act of preaching without an official call. But why were not the Jews, who blaspheme against Christ, not punished as blasphemers? Luther replied: they were already punished in their "staying outside Christendom, and furthermore are not admitted to public office." Furthermore, they would be punished if they blasphemed openly or by "corner preaching" in Christian homes. But on these principles, would it not be possible for "the tyrants who persecuted the Gospel," i.e., the Catholics, to punish the Evangelicals in whom they see blasphemers? "Answer: what difference does that make?" The kings of Israel killed some true prophets also, nevertheless the command to stone the false prophets remained in force.

Furthermore, a citizen is obliged to report to the magistrate and to the pastor any case of a corner preacher that might come to him. Should he not do this, he would be acting contrary to his oath of loyalty to the magistrate, and would be acting as a despiser of the pastor, to whom he owes the honor, and would be against God, and would be guilty along with the corner preachers of causing trouble.

8. *Luther's Distinction in the Matter of Heresy.* Luther's Sermon on Matt. 13:24 ff. (the tares among the wheat) of Feb. 7, 1546, thus shortly before his death (*EA* XX, 2, 2nd ed. pp. 540 ff.) maintained this position and is not to be construed as moderation due to old age. One should remember that by this time the threat which Luther saw in Anabaptism and *Schwärmertum* no longer existed; no more sedition (*Aufruhr*) and no more blasphemy was in evidence. The tares, it is true, still included heretics, conspiracies, and sects (*Ketzer, Rotten und Sekten*) but these were "within the church" (*ibid.,* 555, 558), and were not to be considered as disturbers of public order or as blasphemers. Hence the severest penalty was to be only the ban of the church, not governmental punishment, "no human power and might." Here the heretic is "only a heretic."

The much-debated question whether Luther sought to establish the death penalty for heresy is therefore to be answered thus: a distinction is to be made between two kinds of heretics, i.e., those who are "only heretics," namely, those who diverge from the official doctrines of the church only in purely internal churchly matters which have no public significance, and those whose divergent teaching occasions public unrest or blasphemy of God. This latter kind of heresy is a public crime and as such falls into the sphere of the state authorities, who punish such cases in accord with the existing laws on rebellion and blasphemy, usually with the death penalty. Such cases of heresy were to be reported, although the reporting was to be not only to the civil authorities but also to the pastor; the pastor was to be considered in this case not as representative of the church but as the state-appointed guardian against blasphemy.

On the other hand, the other type of heretics, the "only heretics," did not fall within the sphere of the state, but were subject only to church discipline (Matt. 18:16 ff.). Of course it is true that in practice this type seldom occurred any more since the failure of the earlier disputations to win them (although disputations were not completely abandoned). This was not due to any inconsistency on Luther's part or any abandonment of his principles, but to the fact that in those days (quite differently from the present time) the state and society were understood to be controlled by Christian principles.

The Apostles' Creed was at that time, so Luther understood, the fundamental constitution of Christian society, and consequently the state and the public were under a creed which included particularly the whole of Christian theology, and which accordingly required that the state punish in the civil courts the holding of doctrines which no longer concern the modern state. A Christian government would have to consider as blasphemy against God (and punish appropriately) any offense against the Gospel, and that included the rejection of infant baptism. And in a consciously Christian society divergences in church matters could scarcely be distinguished in practice from civil disorders and conflicts. The state was the "custodian of the two tablets," i.e., it was also the guardian of order in the church, was sensitive to sedition in this area, and punished accordingly. As a result the heretic who was "only a heretic" practically ceased to exist.

But in this respect Luther did not belong to the Middle Ages (as N. Paulus claimed), nor is therefore the Reformation type of heresy trial, which was based upon Luther's ideas, to be rated as a Catholic inquisition trial. The Catholic-medieval principle that the church investigates, while the state executes, was absolutely not Luther's concept. He dissolved the connection of church and world at this point. In him there could be no church-state heresy trial, but rather two theoretically sharply distinct trials, one the ecclesiastical trial against the heretic, as a pure heretic, and the other the state trial against rebels and blasphemers.

9. *Elimination of the State Heresy Trial after the Separation of Church and State.* According to Luther's concept then, the executions of Anabaptists took place only on the basis of the second type of civil heresy trial, not on the basis of the first type of ecclesiastical trial. The result was of course the same as it was in the Middle Ages; the heretics were persecuted and as much as possible wiped out. But the above distinction [of two types of heresy trial] is therefore not to be considered as superficial or a piece of sophistication. It became highly important when the "Christian" character of the state and society vanished. As the obligations of the state to punish the heretic ceased, the ecclesiastical heresy trial against the "pure heretics" was all that remained, and the Protestant church never demanded that the "pure heretic" should be punished by the state. It was just because the church was not interested in this matter that she unreservedly endorsed the development of the modern state. Such was not the case in Catholicism—think of Spain, for instance. Wherever in Catholicism the bond between church and state was dissolved in the matter of heresy trials, it was dissolved by the state and not by the church. This important difference in the general development of culture and ideas was the result of Luther's position.

The tragedy is to be seen in the fact that as a result of the interrelationship of the most diverse circumstances from which the self-responsibility of certain individual Anabaptists cannot always be excluded, Anabaptism was not evaluated by Luther on the basis of its own religious quality and depth. There were, to be sure, isolated instances when Luther spoke words of recognition for the martyr courage of Anabaptists (Enders 6, 263), but to the end Anabaptism remained for him the "seditious spirit" (*aufrührerische Geist*). Even after the bloody persecutions ceased, Anabaptism suffered severely in the public mind because of Luther's verdict. Current Reformation historiography is successfully trying to correct Luther's verdict. W.K.

Köhler makes it clear that Luther's recommendation of harsh action against the Anabaptists, including the death penalty, was based upon his belief, shared by Melanchthon, that they were guilty of sedition and blasphemy. It is difficult, however, to avoid the feeling that a major cause for the severity was the simple fear that the Anabaptists might gain sufficient influence to threaten the success of the Reformation by winning too many adherents to their cause and thus breaking the monopoly of the church which Luther and Melanchthon were establishing. In the earlier period of his activity, as Köhler points out, in the high confidence which Luther had in the victory of the truth he was proclaiming, Luther was quite willing to let others speak, in the confidence that the true Word of God would overcome all heresy. Later, shaken by the Peasants' War and the ensuing reaction, as well as by general evidence that the support of the populace for true spiritual religion was not all that he expected or considered necessary, he leaned more and more on the arm of flesh, the ecclesiastical and political power, to guarantee the success of the evangelical movement. At that point it was safer to call on force than to risk the free contest of ideas. In addition to this, the general fear of revolutionary uprisings evoked by the Peasants' War and Thomas Müntzer, as well as by other minor incidents related to the Anabaptists, makes it easy to understand that Luther's insecurity could intensify the appeal to force.

But on what just background could Anabaptists, who did not deny the Apostles' Creed or any article of it more than did the Roman Catholics, be accused of blasphemy? The common and standard meaning of blasphemy is abandoned if rejection of infant baptism is blasphemy. Was any major deviation from the established faith to be rated as blasphemy?

The charge of sedition is likewise very suspect, no matter how sincerely it may have been believed. Philip of Hesse did not take the charge seriously, neither did Johannes Brenz and others who could be mentioned. Bainton has pointed out that "Luther construed mere abstention from public office and military service as sedition" (*Here I Stand,* 376). The Anabaptists were arrested as disturbers of the peace, but actually because Luther considered the introduction of a second and rival religion into a locality to be a disturbance of the public order. The greatest irony, however, is the repeated condemnation of the Anabaptists by Luther and other reformers as "corner-preachers," i.e., as conducting private and not public services. But when did the authorities or Luther ever offer or permit the Anabaptists the privilege of public preaching? Anabaptist preachers were discredited by Luther also because they had no proper call, i.e., because they were not appointed by his official state church, regardless of the call from their own brotherhood church.

Luther and Melanchthon can be understood as children of their time, but they can not be excused from rising above it as others did, notably the Strasburg authorities and Philip of Hesse, who, like others, saw that the better answer to the Anabaptists was not to execute them but to improve the life and character of the preachers and church members and thus remove a major ground of Anabaptist criticism.

Köhler makes baptism the chief point of difference between Luther and the Anabaptists. An adequate understanding, however, calls for the recognition of other major points of difference. The most important of all was the concept of the church. The

Anabaptists called for a brotherhood composed of adult and responsible believers only, committed to full discipleship, a voluntary, free and holy church. Baptism on confession of faith was one of the symbols of this church and the only mode of entrance. Luther, who understood well this vision, rejected it as impracticable and chose to maintain the traditional concept of the mass church with the entire population included in it by compulsory infant baptism. This was the real break of the Anabaptists with the Reformation. With this concept of the church it is easy to understand why the Anabaptists, as Albrecht Ritschl says, "considered themselves to be the ones who were bringing to its true conclusion the work of restoration of the church which Luther and Zwingli had begun" (*Geschichte des Pietismus*, p. 7), . . . "the more thorough, decisive, and complete Reformation which Luther surrendered in 1522 and Zwingli in 1524" (p. 22, Ritschl summarizing the view of Max Göbel). Here lies a vast difference in basic central position, and not just a disagreement in the meaning of baptism.   H.S.B.

WA—Weimar edition of Luther's Works, D. Martin Luthers Werke, kritische Gesammtausgabe (1883-1932); EA—Erlangen edition of Luther's Works (2nd ed. 1863-1932), Dr. Martin Luthers sämmtliche Werke; E. L. Enders, Luthers Briefwechsel, Dr. Martin Luther's sämmtliche Werke, 15 vv. in Erlanger-Frankfurter Ausgabe (2nd ed., Leipzig, 1884-1932); J. Gottschick, Die Lehre der Reformation von der Taufe (Tübingen, 1906); H. Hermelink, Der Toleranzgedanke im Reformationszeitalter (Leipzig, 1908); Walter Köhler, Reformation und Ketzerprozess (Tübingen, 1901); J. Köstlin, Luthers Theologie (2nd ed., 2 vv., Stuttgart, 1901); J. Küstlin-Kawerau, Martin Luther (5th ed., 2 vv., Berlin, 1903); Th. Kolde, Martin Luther 2 vv.. (Gotha, 1884, 1893) 89; N. Paulus, Luther und die Gewissensfreiheit (Munich, 1905); idem, "Luther und die Todesstrafe für Ketzer, neue Rettungsversuche" in Histor.-Politische Blätter (145) 1910, 177-89, 243-55; R. Sohm, Kirchenrecht I (Leipzig, 1892) 546 ff.; K. Völker, Toleranz und Intoleranz im Zeitalter der Reformation (Leipzig, 1912); Paul Wappler, Die Stellung Kursachsens und des Landgrafen Philipp von Hessen zur Täuferbewegung (Jena, 1913); idem, Thüringen; Johannes Warns, Die Taufe, Gedanken über die urchristliche Taufe, ihre Geschichte und ihre Bedeutung für die Gegenwart (Cassel, 1913, 2nd ed., 1922); John Horsch, Infant Baptism, Its Origin Among Protestants and the Arguments Advanced for and Against It (Scottdale, 1917); Roland H. Bainton, Here I Stand, A Life of Martin Luther (N.Y., 1950); Hans-Werner Gensichen, Damnamus. Die Verwerfung von Irrlehre bei Luther und im Luthertum des 16. Jahrhunderts (Berlin, 1955); John Oyer, "The Writings of Luther Against the Anabaptists," MQR (1953) 100-10; H. S. Bender, The Anabaptist Vision, (Goshen, 1944, repr. of MQR XVIII (1944) 67-88; ML II, 703-8.

Lüthi (Luthi, Lüthy) is a well-known Swiss Mennonite family name. Hans Lüthi, of Eggenwil, canton of Aargau, was present at the Anabaptist debate at Bern in 1538. In the 17th century members of this family were found near Rauperswil in the Emmental (*q.v.*). In the last decades some Lüthis moved from Switzerland to Alsace (*q.v.*); about 1800 some of them were living in the valley of Ste-Marie aux Mines, Alsace, now in the Montbéliard congregation. To this family also belonged the preacher Hans Lüthi (*q.v.*) of Sumiswald, and perhaps also the Anabaptist martyr Hans Ludi (*q.v.*), executed at Basel in 1530.   vDZ.

D. L. Gratz, *Bernese Anabaptists* (Scottdale, 1953) 38, 48, 87, 190, 191, 200.

Lüthi, Hans, a Mennonite preacher of Schaufelbühl near Sumiswald, in the Emmental (*q.v.*), Switzerland, was shipped to the galleys with four other Mennonites in 1714 at the age of 54. Because they had frequently been banished, but kept returning home, and because they spread Mennonite doctrine, "helping to fill the country with such stubborn rabble," the government inflicted this severe penalty. They were taken to Sicily and forged to the galleys. A letter dated Nov. 16, 1715 (printed in Müller, *Berner Täufer*, 226), written by the three comrades in suffering, Christian Liebe, Peter Wüthrich, and Joseph Probst, stated that of the five Mennonites, Niklaus Baumgartner had died at Turin and Hans Lüthi on the galleys. (*Inv. Arch. Amst.* I, No. 1377; *ML* II, 708.)   S.G.

Lutkegast, a hamlet in the Dutch province of Groningen, formerly seat of a Groningen Old Flemish Mennonite congregation. It must have been dissolved before 1700. (Kühler, *Geschiedenis* II, 138; *DB* 1879, 4.)   vDZ.

Luton (Iowa) Evangelical Mennonite Brethren Church was founded in February 1941 by about a dozen families emigrating from the dried out areas of Jansen and Henderson, Neb., and a few families who came later from Colorado. Church services were held in the larger farm homes for a year; then a modest church was built. Lay members and guest speakers supplied the pulpit until September 1941, when John R. Dick was called as pastor. In 1953 Frank C. Wiens was pastor and the membership was 45.   J.R.D.

Luxembourg, an independent constitutional grand duchy with an area of 999 square miles (about the size of Lancaster Co., Pa.) and a population (1947 census) of 290,992, of whom 283,273 are Roman Catholics.

The Reformation made little headway in this strongly Roman Catholic country. Relatively few individuals accepted the new teaching, which was vigorously suppressed by both church and state authorities. There were no Anabaptists here, as far as is known, until recent times, when Amish Mennonites migrated here from near-by countries. On Oct. 13, 1843, the farm estate called Spittelhof, near Flaxweiler, canton of Grevenmacher, Luxembourg, was rented by Daniel Oesch (b. 1795 in Alsace). In the spring of 1844 he with his wife Elise (nee Beller) and children moved here from Rehlingerhof, near Wincheringen, Germany, and took up residence on this farm. So began the little Mennonite congregation in this little country, with 13 baptized members and 17 children.

In 1876 Joseph Schertz from the Saar married the youngest daughter of Daniel Oesch and took up residence near Berdorf, canton of Echternach. In 1892 the Peter Nafziger family migrated here from Liessem, Germany. The present Luxembourg Mennonites consist largely of descendants of the three immigrants—7 Oesch families, 2 Schertz families, and 4 Nafziger families—a total of 13 families numbering 65 souls, of whom 46 are counted as members of the congregation. A Nafziger family in

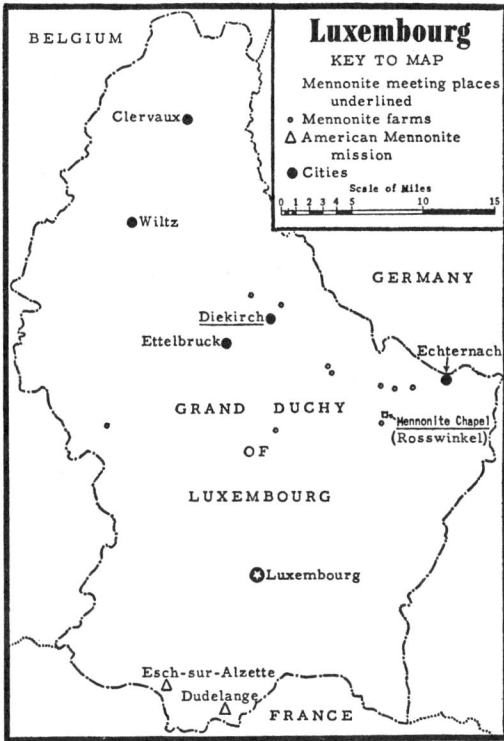

Liessem and a Guth family in Jägershof in near-by Germany are also associated with this congregation. Most of the Luxembourg Mennonites are farmers, located on farms scattered across the north-central part of the country.

Elders of the congregation have been Nicolas Oesch (1841-1906, son of pioneer Daniel), Nicolas Nafziger (1849-1922) of Liessem, Germany, Peter Nafziger (1858-1944, the immigrant), and Joseph Oesch (1905-54), who served as elder from 1939 until his accidental death in 1954. The congregation belongs to the Alsace Mennonite Conference in France.

Sunday morning services are held on the second, third, and fourth Sunday of each month. Sunday school is conducted for the children. A *Bibelkurs* (Bible Conference) has been held each winter since 1946. A spring youth day was held in 1939 and several times since.

Services were held in the homes of the members until 1948, when a wooden barracks was rented in Diekirch. In 1953-54 a stone building for worship was built at Rosswinkelhof near Consdorf, canton of Echternach in the eastern part of the country, so that the congregation now has its own chapel, dedicated Sept. 26, 1954.

In the latter 1940's the Eastern Mennonite Board of Missions and Charities (Pa.) took steps to find a location for launching mission work in Europe. Because of spiritual need discovered in the industrial area extending from the southern part of this country to Metz, France, it was decided to begin work in Esch-sur-Alzette, the industrial center of southern Luxembourg. The first missionaries sent were

Clarence and Lela Fretz, who arrived in the country on Sept. 13, 1951. Accompanying them were Harvey and Mildred Miller, missionaries sent by the Conservative Amish Mennonite Mission Board, which was also co-operating in this undertaking. The Fretzes were stationed in Esch-sur-Alzette and the Millers in Dudelange, six miles away. Gospel services, literature distribution, Bible camps, and boys' and girls' crafts clubs are among the activities carried on to give a Gospel witness in this area.

C.Y.F.

Josef Meyers, *Geschichte Luxembourgs* (Luxembourg, 1940) 149-53; Mannhardt, *Jahrbuch* 1888, 35; *ML* II, 708.

Luyck, Petrus de, a Dutch Reformed minister at Groede, Zeeland, Flanders, who published *Het eerste deel van den Spiegel der Waerheyt, waerinne duydelick ghesien wort, dat de Mennisten, aennopende de H. Schrifture, zijn een verwardt Babel ende Midianitisch ghevecht onder malcanderen* (Vlissingen, 1633); there is also an edition published at Rotterdam in the same year. In this rare book, containing seven dialogues, a number of Mennonite leaders are attacked by the author, including Menno Simons, Dirk Philips, Jacques Outerman, Claes Claesz of Blokzijl, François de Knuyt, Anthoni Jacobsz, Jacob Pietersz van der Meulen, and Cornelis de Kuyper. This book is valuable not for the strict Calvinistic views and arguments, which are almost all borrowed from H. Faukelius (*q.v.*), *Babel der Wederdoperen* of 1621, but for the fact that some Mennonite writings are named in it, which have since been lost. vpZ.

Luyken, a Dutch family. Caspar Christoffel Luycken moved from Essen, Germany, to Amsterdam. In 1633 he married Hester Coores from Middelburg, Dutch province of Zeeland. Caspar Luycken, at first a clothmaker, later became schoolteacher. He felt keenly existing "social disorder," the contrast between the poor and the wealthy shipowners and crew, and employers who took advantage of the miserable situation of the employed. He joined the Remonstrant congregation at Amsterdam, but in later years he participated in the meetings of the Collegiants (*q.v.*). Being a friend of Galenus Abrahamsz (*q.v.*), preacher of the Flemish Mennonite congregation of Amsterdam, Luycken defended him against the calumnies and falsehoods of his antagonists in a booklet, *Ondersoeck over den inhout van twee boecxkens, genaemt de ontdekte Veynsinge* (Amsterdam, 1655). A son of Caspar Christoffel Luycken was Jan Luyken (*q.v.*), the noted artist. In the late 17th and early 18th centuries some Luykens were members of the Amsterdam Lamist Mennonite congregation. Jan Luykens (*q.v.*), who emigrated from Crefeld to Germantown in 1683, may have been a member of this family. It could not be ascertained whether Andries Lucken, who signed the Dordrecht Confession for the Rotterdam congregation in 1632, belonged to this family or not. vpZ.

N.N.B.Wb. VI, 974; H. W. Meihuizen, *Galenus Abrahamsz* (Haarlem, 1954) 55, 64.

Luyken (Luiken, Luycken), Jan, famous engraver and poet, especially of devotional poems, b. April 16, 1649, at Amsterdam, d. there April 5, 1712. He became an apprentice in the atelier of Martinus Saeghmolen, and moved in a frivolous anti-church society. This is the period of his bombastic book of poems, *Duytse Lier* (1671), and his acquaintance with Maria de Oudens (1646-82), whom he married in 1672. Four of his five children died young. The oldest son, Caspar Luyken (1672-1708), was also trained as an engraver by his father, and supported his father during his last years. His work was chiefly in illustrating books. Of Caspar's work 1,187 pieces are extant.

In 1673 Jan Luyken was baptized in the Lamist Mennonite Church at Amsterdam, and shortly after joined the Mennonite congregation at Beverwijk, about 16 miles northwest of Amsterdam, though he was probably attracted by the Collegiant views of Paulus Bastiaensz of Beverwijk, where he stayed for a time. But the great change in his life came at a later period. The book *Kort Verhaal van het Godvrugtig leven en Zalig Afsterven van Joannes Luiken* (1712) reports, "In the twenty-sixth year of his life the Lord appeared in his heart in a powerful manner" (1675), whereupon, "afire with the love of God, he forsook his old bad company," to join the God-fearing. These were the followers of Jakob Böhme. There was at that time a colony of Böhme's disciples, under the leadership of Coenraad van Beuningen, a noted statesman, Professor Allardt de Raedt, and especially Johann Georg Gichtel (see **Gichtelianer**), a lawyer who had been expelled from Regensburg. Galenus Abrahamsz, Mennonite preacher and physician, must have had some influence upon Luyken's conversion.

After his conversion Luyken withdrew from the church. In solitude he continued his etching and his contemplation; closely attached to a few kindred spirits, he wrote mystical poems tinged with pantheism. In the course of time these poems were considered orthodox and were held in high esteem in pietistic circles in the first half of the 19th century. With the publication of Hylkema's book *Reformateurs* (1900-2) a new light was shed on these devotional poems, revealing their anti-church and heterodox character. Since then these poems have been even more admired.

A number of volumes of these lyrics, with artistic steel etchings, appeared in the course of time: *Jesus en de Ziel* (1678), *Voncken der Liefde Jesu* (1687), *De Spiegel van het Menselijk bedrijf* (1694), *Zedelijke en Stichtelijke Gezangen* (1704), *Beschouwing der Wereld* (1708), *De Bykorf des Gemoeds* (1709), *Het Leersaam Huisraad* (1709), *De onwaardige Wereld* (1710). After Luyken's death there appeared: *Schriftuurlijke Geschiedenissen en Gelijkenissen* (1712), *Des menschen Begin, Midden en Einde* (1712), *Geestelijke Brieven* (1714), *Verzameling van Geestelijke Brieven* (1741), *Het Overvloeiend Herte* (1767). A number of his poems are found in former Dutch hymnbooks, and even in the present *Doopsgezinde Bundel.* (See **Literature, Netherlands**.)

Ten years after Luyken's death the widow of Barend Visscher published a collection of ninety-two Luyken engravings, professedly among his best, illustrating events from early church history. Beneath each plate is a verse of six lines by Claas Bruin (1671-1732), who was a member of Luyken's circle of devotional poets. Opposite each plate is a poem by Pieter Langendijk (*q.v.;* 1683-1756).

C.B.H.

A complete bibliography on Luycken (1712-1889) is found in Dr. Maurits Sabbe, *Joan Luykens Duytse Lier* (Zutphen); articles by C. B. Hylkema in *De Gids* XIV (1904) p. 28, by J. C. van der Does in *Stemmen des Tijds* (1928, Nos. 137 and 264; 1929, Nos. 147 and 508; 1931, No. 621); and in *Nieuwe Taalgids* (1929, No. 197; 1930, No. 245); J. Luycken, *Tafereelen der eerste Christenen* (Amsterdam, 1722) "Voor-bericht"; *N.N.B.Wb.* II, 223.

*

Jan Luyken was a very important, versatile, and creative Dutch engraver and etcher in the period after Rembrandt; 3,275 works are known to be his. His favorite field was the illustration of books. In addition to travel literature and historical works he used many Biblical subjects. He made his own preliminary sketches; many of them can be seen in Amsterdam (Prentenkabinet and Museum Fodor), Haarlem (Teyler Museum), and Rotterdam, as well as in London (British Museum) and Vienna. A collection donated to Amsterdam contains 897 leaves.

His work is distinguished for its clarity, especially in group studies. His best illustrations are found in his own books of poems. For the second edition (1685) of van Braght's *Martyrs' Mirror* he furnished 104 copper etchings, illustrating the martyrdom of Anabaptists and Mennonites of the 16th century. These plates with eleven additional plates from J. L. Gottfried, *Historische Kronyck* (Leyden, 1698), were reprinted at Leiden without van Braght's text, with French and German captions, and called *Théatre des Martyrs.* A Dutch edition was published in 1738 by Marten Schagen at Alkmaar. They also appeared in the 1780 edition of the *Martyrs' Mirror* printed at Pirmasens, but not in any succeeding German or American editions. After the printing of this edition the plates were supposedly lost; in 1925 they reappeared in South Germany in private possession.

HEGE.

N.N.B.Wb. VI, 974-76; DB 1890, 71; 1900, 90 f.; 1902, 99 f.; G. Kalff, *Geschiedenis der Nederl. Letterkunde* IV (Groningen, 1910) 467, 522-37, 543-47; *Bibliographie des Martyrologes* II, 417-28; P. van Eeghen, *Het Werk van Jan en Casper Luycken* (Amsterdam, 1905); M. D. Henkel, "Jan und Caspar Luyken," in *Allgemeines Lexikon der bildenden Künstler* (ed. Hans Vollmer) XXIII (Leipzig, 1929) 488-89; Chr. Hege, "Ein kurpfälzisches Bücherverbot," in *Menn. Gesch.-Bl.* I (1936) 26; *ML* II, 700.

Luykens (Lücken), **Jan,** head of one of the 13 Crefeld families who landed in Philadelphia on Oct. 6, 1683, and settled in Germantown. He was a Quaker, a citizen of Crefeld, but was a native of Wesel. When the land was divided among the Germantown settlers by lot on Oct. 25, 1683, Luykens as a farmer acquired 200 acres. Jan served as constable of Germantown in 1691-95, as sheriff in 1694-95, and died in 1744. HEGE.

Daniel K. Cassel, *Geschichte der Mennoniten* (Philadelphia, 1890) 36-44; W. I. Hull, *William Penn and the Dutch Quaker Migration to Pennsylvania* (Philadelphia, 1935); W. Niepoth, *Die Eltern und Voreltern des Johann Luyken* (1935 and 1948); *ML* II, 697.

Luyt Jansz, b. at Amsterdam, a citizen of Alkmaar, Dutch province of North Holland, an Anabaptist martyr, was beheaded on May 6, 1531, probably at The Hague. Concerning this martyr, among the first Anabaptist martyrs in the Netherlands, no further information was available. (Grosheide, *Bijdrage,* 49, 302.) vdZ.

Luytgens, Walig Dirk: see Waechlink Dirks.

Luytjes, Cornelis, a member of the Waterlander congregation at Barsingerhorn, Dutch province of North Holland, who published the following books: 1. *Godt verheerlykt in den Zondaar* (Hoorn, 1757; of this book there is an edition of Amsterdam, n.d., of which only the title page is changed, then reading *God in den Sondaar verheerlijkt*); 2. *Beoeffenend Onderwys voor de Jeugd tot Doop en Avondmaal* (Hoorn, 1761), a catechism; 3. *De Gangen Gods in Zyn Heyligdom ontdekt* (Amsterdam, 1765), which contains an account of the life of Jesus. Concerning Luytjes there is no further information; apparently he was not a preacher, since his name is not found in the *Naamlijsten.* vdZ.

Luyttyen Dircxzoen, an Anabaptist martyr, of whom there is no further information, was executed at Leeuwarden, capital of the Dutch province of Friesland, because he had been rebaptized. The sentence is dated April 10, 1535. vdZ.

K. Vos, *Menno Simons* (Leiden, 1914) 228.

Lydens-Geschiedenisse van den Zaligmaker, De, is a book, particularly for young people, in the Dutch language by an anonymous author. It deals with Christian martyrs, describing their lives and sufferings. It contains many Mennonite martyrs both Dutch and Swiss. The book is of no special value for Mennonite history. The 51 pictures found in it were taken from J. B. (Bout, *q.v.*), *'t Merg van de Historien der Martelaren.* There are three known editions, all rather rare: Amsterdam 1778, Haarlem 1791, and Rotterdam 1820. (*Bibliographie* II, 407-16.) vdZ.

Lynken, the wife of Jan van de Walle, an Anabaptist martyr: see **Calleken Meevels.**

Lynken (Lijnken) Baillaerts, an Anabaptist martyr, was burned at the stake on Feb. 28, 1573, at Antwerp, Belgium, with Henry Hannon, because she had been rebaptized, had attended forbidden meetings, and had refused to deny her faith. (*Antw. Arch.-Blad* XIII, 109 f., 176; XIV, 90 f., No. 1017.)

Lynken (Lijnken) Claesdochter, an Anabaptist martyr, beheaded on Aug. 14, 1561, inside the Gravensteen castle at Gent, Belgium, with Tanneken Delmeere. Lijnken, who was a daughter of Claes Ghijselbrechts, was born at Maren near 's Hertogenbosch, Dutch province of North Brabant. (Verheyden, *Gent,* 27, No. 78.) vdZ.

Lynken Clercx, an Anabaptist martyr, executed (manner unknown) on Jan. 28, 1575, at Antwerp, Belgium, with Janneken Pots. She had deviated from the Roman Catholic Church and though she had not yet been baptized upon her faith, she was

eager to receive this baptism. (*Mart. Mir.* D 693, E 1008; *Antw. Arch.-Blad* XIII, 198; XIV, 98 f., No. 1105.) vdZ.

Lynken (Lijnken) Ghysseleers (or Ghyssels), a native of 's-Hertogenbosch, Dutch province of North Brabant, wife of the martyr Jacques Verhulten, an Anabaptist martyr, was burned at the stake on Feb. 21, 1573, at Antwerp, Belgium, together with Willem Huyberts and Lysken Pennaerts. She was charged with the crime of having been rebaptized. (*Antw. Arch.-Blad* XIII, 107 f., 175; XIV, 90 f., No. 1014.) vdZ.

Lynken (Lijnken) Groffels (Groffelaers), of Brussels, an Anabaptist martyr, who was burned at the stake on May 28, 1573, at Antwerp, Belgium, with Jenneken de Cantere. She had twice attended a Mennonite meeting. Apparently she was not (yet) a member of the congregation. (*Antw. Arch.-Blad* XIII, 119, 178; XIV, 90 f., No. 1030.) vdZ.

Lynken (Lijnken) Jacops, an Anabaptist martyr, drowned at the Steen castle at Antwerp, Belgium, on Dec. 31, 1558. Van Braght calls this martyr Lijntgen, and gives only the year of execution, not the exact date, giving only brief information. From the records it is known that she was born at Dilsen, in the territory of Liége, Belgium, the daughter of a boatman. According to *Lietboecxken van den Offer des Heeren* she was "Hendricks Joncwijf," i.e., she was married to Hendrick shortly before. Together with Lynken three other martyrs died. The four women, each of them crookedly bound with ropes, died steadfastly and peacefully. Lijnken is celebrated in the hymn "Aenhoort Godt, hemelsche Vader" (Hear, O God, heavenly Father), No. 16 of the *Lietboecxken van den Offer des Heeren.* vdZ.

Offer, 566; *Mart. Mir.* D 202, E 655; *Antw. Arch.-Blad* VIII, 456, 466; XIV, 24 f., No. 275; *ML* II, 709.

Lynken de Meyere (Smeyers), an Anabaptist martyr, beheaded on March 24, 1562, inside the Gravensteen castle at Gent, Belgium, together with Janneken Kinderkens and Kathalyne van Lokerhoute. Lynken, who was 26 years of age, was the wife of Pieter van Male, who was put to death at Gent on July 17 of the same year. She is said to have been a native of Zandbergen and a daughter of Jan de Meyere. The name of De Meyere (*q.v.*) is often found among the Flemish emigrants who fled about 1630 to the Dutch town of Aardenburg. (Verheyden, *Gent,* 28, No. 82.) vdZ.

Lynken Pieters (*Lynken van Heercke*), an Anabaptist, secretly beheaded on Nov. 20, 1560, inside the Gravensteen castle at Gent, Belgium, together with Soetken van den Houtte and Martha Baets. After the execution their corpses were thrown into a pit outside the Muide Gate. Soetken and Martha are named by van Braght, *Martyrs' Mirror,* but Lynken is not. Lynken was a daughter of Pieter Cornelis; she was born at Hamme near Dendermonde in Flanders, was unmarried and 25 years of age. (Verheyden, *Gent,* 27, No. 77.) vdZ.

Lynn (Mich.) United Missionary Church had 10 members in 1953. Bruce W. Pearson was its pastor.

Lyntgen (Lijntgen), the name of a number of martyrs: see **Calleken Meevels, Lynken Clercx, Lynken Jacobs, Lyntgen van Dale.**

Lyntgen, "a young maiden," an Anabaptist martyr, who was executed at Antwerp, Belgium, on Jan. 28, 1575, obviously is identical with Lynken Clercx (*q.v.*). (*Mart. Mir.* D 693, E 1008.) vDZ.

Lyntgen (Linken) **van Dale** (van Braght, *Mart. Mir.* only *Lijntgen*), wife of Jan van Lyers, an Anabaptist martyr, was drowned at the Steen castle at Antwerp, Belgium, on Nov. 13, 1562 (not Aug. 15, 1561, as *Mart. Mir.* says; see **Bastiaen,** *ME* I, 247), with some other Anabaptist martyrs. They are celebrated in a hymn "Lieve broeders, ick groet u met sanghen" (Dear brethren, I greet you with hymns), found in the *Nieu Liedenboeck* of 1562. The hymn is included in Wackernagel, *Lieder.* vDZ.

Mart. Mir. D 288, E 655; *Antw. Arch.-Blad* IX, 143, 150; XIV, 32 f., No. 370; Wackernagel, *Lieder,* 140.

Lyntgen (Lijntje) **Joris** (Goris), an Anabaptist martyr. Lijntgen and her daughter Trijntgen were among the 12 Anabaptists arrested by Spanish soldiers on March 11, 1571, at Deventer, Dutch province of Overijssel. Notwithstanding the effort of the judges to make her renounce her faith, Lijntgen remained steadfast and suffered death by being burned at the stake at Deventer on June 16, 1571, together with her daughter and some other Anabaptists. (*Mart. Mir.* D 552 ff., E 885 ff.; *DB* 1919, 30-38.) vDZ.

Lyntgen Kemels, an Anabaptist martyr, burned at the stake in 1570 at Liége, Belgium. Besides the brief account by van Braght no particulars were available about this martyr. (A Bartel Kemels was in 1566-67 among the Calvinists at Hasselt in the bishopric of Liége; see W. Bax.) vDZ.

W. Bax, *Het Protestantisme in het bisdom Luik* II (The Hague, 1941) 213, 215, 225, 311; *Mart. Mir.* D 509, E 848; *ML* II, 481.

Lyntgen Wendelyn, an Anabaptist martyr from Flanders, drowned on Sept. 5, 1562, at Antwerp, Belgium, with Mariken van Meenen. (*Antw. Arch.-Blad* IX, 141, 149; XIV, 32 f., No. 363.) Lyntgen had been baptized and persisted in this baptism. vDZ.

Lysanderhöhe, a village of the Trakt Mennonite settlement (*q.v.*) in the province of Samara, Russia, founded in 1864, consisting in 1897 of 22 farms, with a population of 119. A part of the population joined the trek to Turkestan in 1891, while others emigrated to America. In 1914 the population was 146. Franz Bartsch (*q.v.*), the author of *Unser Auszug nach Mittelasien,* was the teacher of the village school. After the Revolution of 1917 the cultural and economic level of the village began to decline. Some of the inhabitants went to Canada and others were exiled. Little is known about the fate of those who remained and the present status of the village. C.K.

Am Trakt, Eine Mennonitische Kolonie im Mittleren Wolgagebiet (North Kildonan, Man., 1948); *ML* II, 709.

Lysbet van Dulmen (Dülmen in Westphalia, Germany), an Anabaptist martyr, was drowned on June 11, 1539, at Utrecht in the Netherlands with 10 other women. They were apparently Davidjorists (*q.v.*). vDZ.

Berigten Hist. Genootschap Utrecht IV, 2 (1851) 139; Mellink, *Wederdopers,* 237.

Lysbeth, the wife of Amel Jacobs, from Koog on the Dutch island of Texel, an Anabaptist martyr, was executed in 1537; place, exact date (before April 21), and manner of execution are unknown. Her property was confiscated. (*Inv. Arch. Amst.* I, 185.) vDZ.

Lysbeth (Lysbette, Elisabeth Piers(s)ins; van Braght, *Mart. Mir.,* only Elisabeth), an Anabaptist martyr burned at the stake on July 21, 1551, on the Veerle square at Gent, Belgium, with Gilles de Gusemme. Standing on the place of execution, the executioner treated her indecently, the only case of indecency which is related in the literature concerning the martyrs. Gillis and Lysbeth are celebrated in a song "Als men schreef vijftienhondert jaer en een en vijftich daer toe voorwaer," No. 8 in the *Lietboecxken van den Offer des Heeren.* Both had been (re)baptized by Gillis van Aken. Lysbeth Piersins may have belonged to the Pierson family later found in the Netherlands and the Pearson family of England. vDZ.

Offer, 535-37; *Mart. Mir.* D 105, E 502; Verheyden, *Gent,* 17, No. 33; *ML* I, 552.

Lysbeth Bouwes and **Lysbeth Diricxdochter** participated in the revolt at the Oldeklooster (*q.v.*) in the Dutch province of Friesland; they were arrested and brought to Leeuwarden on April 7, 1535, where on April 14, 1535, they were sentenced to death by drowning. vDZ.

K. Vos, *Menno Simons* (Leiden, 1914) 229.

Lysbeth Dirksdochter, an Anabaptist martyr: see **Elisabeth Dirks.**

Lysbeth Hermansdochter, a native of the bishopric of Münster, Germany, an Anabaptist martyr, was drowned on Jan. 31, 1539, at Delft, Dutch province of South Holland. She declared that her first baptism was false and regretted having not yet received (re)baptism. She was probably a Davidjorist (*q.v.*). (*Inv. Arch. Amst.* I, No. 749.) vDZ.

Lysbeth Jansdochter, an Anabaptist martyr from Benschop, Dutch province of Utrecht, probably a sister of Adriana Jans (*q.v.*), was drowned on May 15, 1535, at Amsterdam with six other women. They were in prison already on March 1 of that year. (*Mart. Mir.* D 413, E 764; Mellink, *Wederdopers,* 144.) vDZ.

Lysbeth Smeets, an Anabaptist martyr, who was drowned on March 16, 1535, in the Scheldt River at Antwerp. Her husband Mattheus Sauvaige had been put to death as an Anabaptist on March 3 of the same year. Particulars are lacking. Mattheus and Lysbeth are among the first Anabaptist martyrs of Antwerp. (*Antw. Arch.-Blad* VII, 319; XIV, 12 f., No. 139.) vDZ,

Lysbeth Somerhuys of Deventer, an Anabaptist martyr, burned at the stake on June 16, 1571, at Deventer, Dutch province of Overijssel, together with her sister Catharina and others. For particulars see **Catharina Somerhuys.**   vDZ.

Lysken (Lijsken, Lysken or Lynken Vermeulen, wife of Maerten van Wijk or Maerten Thomaessen), an Anabaptist martyr who was burned at the stake on May 5, 1571, at Antwerp, Belgium, with her husband and Gillis van Havere. Van Braght gives the date of execution as May 2, and states that Lysken was in prison for about one year. (*Mart. Mir.* D 506, E 846; *Antw. Arch.-Blad* XIII, 53, 63; XIV, 76 f., No. 900.)   vDZ.

Lysken, an Anabaptist martyr, burned at the stake on Sept. 11, 1538, at Vught near 's Hertogenbosch in the Dutch province of North Brabant. Lysken and her husband, Jan Block of Gent, belonged to the small congregation of 's Hertogenbosch, of which Paulus van Drunen (*q.v.*) was the bishop. Eight members of this congregation were apprehended and, remaining steadfast, were burned at the stake at Vught on Sept. 10-11, 1538. Van Braght (*Mart. Mir.* D 41 f., E 447 f.) gives an account from an old manuscript which he received from Friesland. In the account of the trial and execution, van Braght mentions twelve martyrs but names only four of them (Paulus van Drunen, Jan Block, Michiel Stevensz, and Adriaen of The Hague), not including Lysken.   vDZ.

Lysken (Lysken Luchtens or Lichtens), an Anabaptist martyr, was burned at the stake on Oct. 6, 1573, at Antwerp, Belgium, with Maeyken Goossens, Jenneken van den Velde, and Maeyken van Dissenbeke. Particulars are lacking except the information that Lysken was a native of Tongeren in the bishopric of Liége, Belgium. Lysken and her fellow martyrs are celebrated in a hymn, found in the *Rotterdamsch Lied-Boeck:* "Och vrienden al te samen, hoort" (Ye friends all together, hear).
                                                    vDZ.

Mart. Mir. D 664, E 983; *Antw. Arch.-Blad* XIII, 130, 180; XIV, 92 f., No. 1039; *ML* II, 709.

Lysken, wife of Jan van de Walle, an Anabaptist martyr: see **Calleken Meevels.**

Lysken (Elisabeth) **Dirks** (Dirk Andries Dochter,

Lisken Aerts, Aertssen), wife of Jeronimus Segersz, an Anabaptist martyr, drowned in the Scheldt River at Antwerp, Belgium, on Feb. 19, 1552, after she had given birth to her child in prison. The old record says, "Because of her heresies and because she has confessed to have been rebaptized she was sentenced to be put alive into a sack and to be drowned." Her husband had been burned at the stake at Augsburg on Sept. 2, 1551. The *Offer des Heeren* and later martyrbooks, including van Braght, *Martyrs' Mirror,* have preserved a correspondence between Jeronimus and Lysken, while both were in prison. Jeronimus wrote eight letters to Lysken, Lysken three to Jeronimus. These letters give a striking testimony of her strong Biblical faith and a warm love to her husband. They are among the most moving pieces of martyr literature. By her faith Lysken comforted her husband and by singing devotional hymns she is said to have heartened and strengthened her fellow prisoners. Lysken and Jeronimus have been celebrated in a hymn, "God de Heere is getrouwe" (The Lord is faithful), found in the *Offer des Heeren.*
                                                    vDZ.

Offer, 126-76; *Mart. Mir.* D 107-28, E 504-22; *Antw. Arch.-Blad* VIII, 409, 416; XIV, 20 f., No. 215; Wolkan, *Lieder,* 66; *DB* 1864, 100; *ML* II, 635.

Lysken van Linschoten was lashed and expelled from the country upon orders by Duke Johann of Witgenstein, Germany, in 1601. (*Mart. Mir.* D 803, E 1103; *ML* II, 709.)

Lysken Pennaerts, an Anabaptist martyr, burned at the stake on Feb. 21, 1573, at Antwerp, Belgium, with Lynken Ghysseleers and Willem Huyberts. Particulars are lacking. (*Antw. Arch.-Blad* XIII, 107 f., 175; XIV, 90 f., No. 1015.)   vDZ.

Lysken Smits, an Anabaptist martyr, who (according to *Offer des Heeren* and later Dutch martyrbooks, including van Braght, *Mart. Mir.*) was executed in 1560 at Antwerp, Belgium, by being drowned in a tub. Lysken Smits is likely identical with Elisabeth Christiaens (*q.v.*) (Kerstiaens), who according to the records was drowned in a tub at the Steen castle at Antwerp on March 16, 1560. The name of Lysken Smits is found in a hymn, "Aenhoort Godt, hemelsche Vader" (Hear, O God, heavenly Father), No. 16 in the *Lietboecxken van den Offer des Heeren.* (*Offer,* 567, No. 69; *Mart. Mir.* D 270, E 640.)   vDZ.

M

Maakal, Wolter Martens (*ca.* 1760-1846), was the last lay preacher of the congregation of Warns, Friesland, Netherlands, serving there in 1810-16. He was unmarried and had formerly been the captain of a ship. Some sermons which he used to read in the meetings have been preserved. (*DB* 1900, 40-46, 51-54, 57, 60 f.)   vdZ.

Maarse (Maarsse, Maarsen), a Dutch Mennonite family of Aalsmeer, province of North Holland, found there from about 1700. Many members of this family were deacons of the various congregations found at Aalsmeer. A member of this family was Jan Maarse, b. 1886 at Amsterdam. He earned his doctorate in chemistry at the University of Amsterdam in 1913, served as a professor of chemistry 1914-30. During this time he began the study of theology at the University and the Mennonite Seminary of Amsterdam. Becoming a ministerial candidate in 1932, he served the congregations of Krommenie-Wormer-Jisp 1932-47 and Edam-Monnikendam 1947-51. In this year he retired. In 1936 he obtained his Th.D. degree (thesis: *Een psychologische en zedekundige studie over de begrippen eer en eergevoel*). Besides this and a number of papers in chemical and theological periodicals, he edited in 1939 and 1947, together with N. Westendorp Boerma (*q.v.*), two posthumous works of I. J. de Bussy (*q.v.*) and in 1955 a psychological-ethical study, *Toorn, haat en zelfbeheersing* (Anger, Hatred, and Self-control).   vdZ.

Maarseveen, a former Mennonite church in the Dutch province of Utrecht. According to the report of a conference held at Haarlem in 1649 by the Frisians, High Germans, and Flemish congregations, the Maarseveen congregation belonged to this union. It has disappeared without a trace. (Blaupot t. C., *Holland* I, 330; II, 43; *DB* 1863, 101; *ML* II, 710.)   vdZ.

Maartensdijk, Sint, a town on the island of Tholen, Dutch province of Zeeland. Mennonites living in Tholen in the early days met in a private house at Sint Maartensdijk; in 1647 Elder Jacques van Maldeghem (*q.v.*) of Aardenburg performed a marriage here. This troubled the Reformed church board of Sint Maartensdijk and caused the board in 1633-48 to make repeated complaints to the magistrates, which, however, seem to have been without result. It is not clear whether there was a Mennonite congregation at Sint Maartensdijk. At any rate nothing is known about this congregation.   vdZ.

J. Was, "De Doopsgezinden op het eiland Tholen, voornamelijk te St-Maartensdijk in de XVIIe eeuw," in *Jaarboek Zeeland*, 1852, 35-50.

Maartje Medinx of Alkmaar, Dutch province of North Holland, an Anabaptist martyr, who is listed by Boomkamp as having been executed at Amsterdam on May 15, 1536. The list of persons executed at Amsterdam, however, does not name her. vdZ.

G. Boomkamp, *Alkmaar en deszelfs Geschiedenis* (Amsterdam, 1747) 92.

Maaslandsluis: see Maassluis.

Maassluis, a town in the Dutch province of South Holland, about 10 miles west of Rotterdam, where there was a Mennonite congregation in the 17th century, belonging to the Flemish branch. It was subsidized by the Rotterdam congregation in 1635; and at the delegates' meetings, both at Haarlem in 1649 and Leiden in 1660, it was reported to have a vacant pulpit. There was in the 17th century also a very small Waterlander congregation at Maassluis, of which however there is no further information. The Flemish congregation, which owned a simple meetinghouse, died out in 1691. In 1731 the neighboring church of Rotterdam received the sum of 183 guilders, which was the remnant of the possessions of the Maassluis Flemish congregation and administered until then by someone at Maassluis.   vdZ.

Blaupot t. C., *Holland* I, 330; K. Vos, *Geschiedenis der Doopsgezinde Gemeente te Rotterdam* (Rotterdam, 1907) 13; *De Zondagsbode* XXXII (1918-19) No. 4.

Maastricht, capital (1951 pop. 80,000) of the Dutch province of Limburg (*q.v.*). The soil had been well prepared for the Anabaptist movement, for the city had been a center of the Beghards and Beguines (*q.v.*) in the Middle Ages.

As in the duchy of Jülich, there was in Maastricht a separatist brotherhood at least by 1527, which called itself the "Christian Brethren"; the arrest of a member is reported in that year. It is possible— Habets considers it very probable —that this was an Anabaptist group. In doctrine they were at least closely related to the Swiss Brethren. They avoided public church services, observed communion in its primitive form, and gathered to study the Bible; they did not make use of the courts. But there is no record that they practiced adult baptism. When they were noticed by the authorities they were accused of "Lutheran heresy"; this of course does not prove that they were Lutheran. They were more likely Sacramentists (*q.v.*). The brotherhood had a strong following in the guilds. Their leaders were Jan Berne, Merten Goltsmeth, Meess Droegescherer, Paes Tymermans, and Jan van Genck.

About 1530 there were Anabaptists in Maastricht. The group grew rapidly, numbering over 100 by 1533. It was visited in 1533 by Hendrik van Tongeren (also called Slachtscaep), a traveling Anabaptist preacher. In the same year Gys van Rotheim and other Anabaptist leaders from abroad visited the Anabaptist group at Maastricht, of which Jan Smeitgen (*q.v.*) and Ruth Ketelbueters were the leaders. Of greater importance to them was Henric Rol (*q.v.*), a preacher who had left Münster, and now led them, quietly and intelligently, as a "bishop." Though he worked very quietly, he did not escape the authorities. He was taken prisoner on September 2, 1534, and burned at the stake in Maastricht shortly after. Then Jan Smeitgen took his place. In January 1535 a severe persecution broke upon them, and 16 persons were executed. Only three of them, Lysken Ketelbueters, Bartholomeus van den Berge, and his wife Mente Jan Heynendochter, remained steadfast, and were burned at the stake; the other 13 recanted and were beheaded. The peaceful principles preached by Rol obviously were not maintained, since the Münsterite booklet *Van der Wrake* had been read during the meetings of the congregation. It is known that 54 fled, some of them to Antwerp (among them Jan Smeitgen), and the congregation became extinct, though there were some Anabaptists in the city later on. Jan van Bemelen was executed at Maastricht in 1538; Lenaert de Schoolmeester (*q.v.*) preached here in 1540 and the elder and martyr Theunis von Hastenrath (*q.v.*) baptized two women here before 1551. Van Braght names as martyrs from Maastricht Trijnken Keuts and Jan Durps, a weaver in 1559; Arent van Essen and his wife Ursel, and the aged Neeltgen and her daughter Trijnken in 1570. And in 1573 Marie Kerckhoffs, not named by van Braght, suffered martyrdom here.

Because of the mandate (Nov. 30, 1652) issued by Wolfgang Wilhelm, Duke of Jülich, the Mennonites found themselves compelled to leave the duchy. Some of them settled in Maastricht, where they more or less in concealment formed a brotherhood. The name of the congregation varied; sometimes it was known by the name of Maastricht, sometimes Burtscheid (Botschert), or Vaals. In Vaals, in the extreme southeast near the German border, there was a meetinghouse. The congregation was served by the following preachers: Pieter van Limburg *ca.* 1684-97, Jacobus van Hoorn ? -1710, Joannes Helgers 1711-d.1714, Pieter Staal 1747-87, Cornelis de Haan 1787-91, and Bernardus Cremer 1792-95. When the preacher Pieter Staal moved away from Burtscheid to Maastricht in 1768, the Burtscheid-Vaals group separated and soon expired. By 1795 the meetinghouse in Vaals was no longer in use. Nothing is known of a meetinghouse at Maastricht.

The congregation at Maastricht was also small. After 1795 it had no preacher. Their considerable capital was managed by a notary. In 1828 only one member was left. In 1864 the property was taken over by the Dutch government. All attempts to prevent the confiscation as well as later attempts to regain the property failed. The Mennonites now living in Maastricht have no connection with the earlier congregation and belong to the congregation of South Limburg (*q.v.*), also called Heerlen.

vDZ.

Inv. Arch. Amst. I, Nos. 235, 1468 f.; II, Nos. 2073-88; II, 2, Nos. 259-60; *DB* 1861, 178-80; 1909, 122; *Gedenkboek Ned. Herv. Gemeente Maastricht* (1932) 9-18 and 379-85; Jos. Habets, *De Wederdoopers te Maastricht ten tijde van Keizer Karel V.* (1877); Rembert, *Wiedertäufer; Monatshefte für rheinische Kirchengesch.*, 1914, 66; 1919, 60; L. Keller, *Gesch. d. Wiedertäufer . . . zu Münster* (Münster, 1880) 155 ff.; W. Bax, *Het Protestan-*

tisme in het Bisdom Luik en vooral te Maastricht (The Hague, I, 1937; II, 1941); E. Crous, "Auf Mennos Spuren am Niederrhein," *Der Mennonit* IX (1956) 10; *ML* II, 710.

Maatschappij tot Nut van 't Algemeen, a Dutch association for the public welfare, usually called "Het Nut," was founded on Nov. 16, 1784, on a plan made by Jan Nieuwenhuizen, the pastor of the Mennonite Church of Monnikendam, and his son Martin Nieuwenhuizen, a physician at Edam. The objective of "Het Nut" was to promote education among the poorer classes by means of the publication of good but inexpensive books, and also to improve the school system and the education of youth. To this end independent chapters of the organization were founded in various places in the Netherlands under the leadership of the central management at Amsterdam. Article I of the first constitution of the association stated, "Everyone, of any rank or religion, wherever he may live, and at any time shall be eligible for membership on the Association and its chapters." This principle of toleration has been preserved to the present by the stipulation of Article II, "The Association strives to attain its goal independently of any ecclesiastical or political party."

In the first years of its existence the Association had a great influence on the improvement in instruction, especially by means of building model schools and publishing good schoolbooks. The first school law of 1806 incorporated to a large extent the principles that the Association had presented to the "National Convention" of 1796 as "General Thoughts Concerning National Education," and which were already practiced in their schools.

In 1791 the Association began its work in the field of libraries. The first library was opened in Haarlem. By 1956 the Association had 205 public libraries, in addition to 45 libraries for young people.

The Association also gave the impulse for the establishment of the first savings banks in 1817; the number of savings banks had grown to 133 by 1956.

Taking its work seriously, the Association has sought to extend its field of activity by paying an increasing amount of attention to social work. It also supports the promotion of preparatory and "continuation" instruction, guarantee of pension for kindergarten teachers, instruction in handicrafts, establishment of specialized libraries, arranging library reading, lectures, refining popular entertainments, physical exercise, sport, leasing of garden plots, founding of savings banks and people's banks.

In 1918 the Association created a professorship of pedagogy at the University of Amsterdam, with which is connected a seminar and an office for research in problems of organization and pedagogy. Since 1919 it has been publishing the periodical *Volksontwikkeling*.

The Association has about 300 chapters in the same number of localities. From the very beginning the Mennonites have taken a large interest in the activities of "Het Nut." Both in the head board and in the boards of the chapters Mennonites often were leading. H. Craandijk, now (1957) moderator of the A.D.S. (Dutch general Mennonite conference), is at the same time president of the Maatschappij tot

Nut van 't Algemeen. In 1927 it had 40,000 members. (*Gedenkboek 1784-1934; Het Nut Nu*, 1953; *ML* II, 102 f.)   K.Ho.

Maatschoen, Gerardus (d. 1751), was an apothecary and in 1726-50 the preacher of the Zonist Mennonite congregation in Amsterdam. He is known for his Dutch translation of the *Historia Christianorum, qui in Belgio Foederatione inter Protestantes Mennonitae appellantur* (2 vv., 1723 and 1739) by Herman Schijn (*q.v.*), his friend and colleague. The translation—a previous one had been made by Matthys van Maurik—he completed with the addition of the foreword, notes, illustrations, and a third volume (Amsterdam, 1743-45). The title of Maatschoen's translation reads: *Geschiedenis dier Christenen welke in de Vereenigde Nederlanden onder de Protestanten Mennoniten genaamt worden,* and the third volume, composed by Maatschoen himself, is entitled *Aanhangzel, Dienende tot een Vervolg of Derde Deel van de Geschiedenisse der Mennoniten;* this contains 19 additional biographies and bibliographies of outstanding Dutch Mennonite ministers. Maatschoen also published *Eeuwigdurende Gedagtenis der Rechtvaardigen* (Amsterdam, 1728), a funeral sermon for Herman Schijn (*q.v.*), and *Lyk-reden op Dirk Cornelisz* (Amsterdam, n.d.-1741). Maatschoen was attacked by G. van Hemert (*q.v.*) in *Brief aan G. Maatschoen* (Middelburg, 1744), in which this Reformed pastor censured Maatschoen for denying the descent of the Mennonites from the Münsterites. The catalog of his library, "containing 278 pages," is evidence that he knew Mennonite history.   C.K., vDZ.

M. Schagen, *Naamlijst der Doopsgezinde Schrijveren* (Amsterdam, 1745) 65; Blaupot t. C., *Holland* II, 136; Glasius, *Godgeleerd Nederland* ('s Hertogenbosch, 1853) 423; *N.N.B.Wb.* VII, 829; *DJ* 1837, 100; *DB* 1891, 66; *ML* II, 710.

Mabé, a Dutch Mennonite family, apparently of Flemish descent, whose members lived particularly in Groningen and Haarlem, and belonged to the Groningen Old Flemish branch. Jan Jansz Mabé, of Groningen, who likely was a preacher, was present at a Flemish conference at Middelstum (*q.v.*) in 1628 (*Groningsche Volksalmanak* 1921, 103). At Haarlem, Evert Mabé was a preacher of the Groningen Old Flemish congregation from 1711 until his death about 1754; Pieter Mabé was a merchant or factory-owner, and in 1743-d.81 a preacher in the same congregation. Cornelis Mabé (1696-*ca.* 1760) was at first a preacher, then an elder of the Danzig Old Flemish group at Haarlem, as was his son Cornelis Mabé de Jonge 1753-*ca.* 58. In the 19th century some of the descendants of Cornelis Mabé served as deacons in the Haarlem Mennonite church. Femina Mabé (1784-1870), of Haarlem, was married to Samuel Muller (*q.v.*).   vDZ.

Naamlijst 1731 ff.; *DJ* 1840, 40 ff.; *DB* 1879, 7; 1892, 94; *Inv. Arch. Amst.* I, No. 677; Blaupot t. C., *Groningen* I, 65, 133.

Mabel Memorial Chapel is located three miles southeast of Harrisonburg, Va. It was built and endowed by Dr. Lucian Heneberger, a naval officer, as a memorial to his wife Mabel who had died many years before the building of the chapel in 1898. The congregation is a branch of the Harrisonburg Presbyterian Church. Moses Wenger, a Mennonite, donated the land for the church, school, and cemetery. This gift likely gave the Mennonites a right to hold services here once a month for the benefit of the Wenger, Good, and Landis families who lived near by. These services were discontinued in the 1920's.   H.A.B.

McClusky (N.D.) Mennonite Brethren Church, a member of the M.B. Central District Conference, was organized in 1903 by Ludwig Seibel, who became the first pastor and served this congregation for 27 years. A small church was built in 1914 and later enlarged. Other ministers who have served for brief periods are John Siemens, Peter Wiens, David Fast, Herman D. Wiebe, LaVern Loewens, and G. W. Schroeder. Gothilf Winter, an ordained deacon, was the leader of the congregation at intermittent periods. The pastor in 1954 was Ernest T. Schafer, followed by Alvin Ysker, who was serving in 1956, with a membership of 22.   A.A.D.

McCook County, in southeastern South Dakota, adjoins the two heavily Mennonite populated counties of Turner and Hutchinson. The one Mennonite church (GCM) in the county is located in Bridgewater. This town with population of less than 1,000 is an important trading center for Mennonites and has a number of business establishments operated by them. The total Mennonite population of the county is approximately 300, of whom less than 100 live in Bridgewater.   J.D.U.

Maccovius (Makovski), **Johannes** (1588-1644), a Reformed theologian, came from Poland to Franeker in the Netherlands in 1613 as tutor of some young Polish noblemen who were students at the University of Franeker. In 1615 Maccovius was appointed professor of theology in this university. He was an ultra-orthodox follower of Calvin, who continually came into conflict with other Calvinistic theologians, and who at the Reformed synod held at Dordrecht in 1618-19 took a rigid attitude against all kinds of religious toleration. Maccovius attacked the Mennonites in a few writings, particularly in *Proton Pseudos Anabaptistarum,* a bitterly prejudiced book.

Maccovius was married three times; his first wife was Antje van Uylenburgh (d. 1634), a sister of Saskia van Uylenburgh, known as Rembrandt's (*q.v.*) wife.   vDZ.

A. Kuyper, *Joh. Maccovius* (Leiden, 1899); *N.N.B.Wb.* IX, 637-39.

McDougal Flat United Missionary Church, located 3 miles west of Sundre, 27 miles west of Olds, Alta., was organized in 1934. Its membership in 1955 was 15, with G. W. Dedels as pastor. A new church is in process of building.   G.W.D.

Machiels, Simon: see **Simon Michielsz.**

Machno, Nestor, commander of an army of anarchists in South Russia during the revolution of 1918-21, at a time when various Russian armies of divers political inclinations were contending for the possession of the Ukraine. Since this movement rejected every form of government (on their flags was the inscription: anarchy is the mother of all order), their hostility was directed not only toward the rightist parties, but also against the communists, who were not sufficiently radical. This army that at one time is supposed to have numbered 100,000 men was recruited chiefly from the ranks of the poor Russian peasantry. Every estate holder, industrialist, in short every owner of property, was considered an enemy of the working masses. They recognized only one verdict—execution.

This army, consisting almost exclusively of Russian peasants, naturally had a strong nationalistic attitude despite the fact that the contrary was maintained by their leaders. Thus a great gulf existed between these and the generally well-to-do Mennonite population, who had sympathized with the Germans during the occupation after 1917. This accounts for the severe suffering endured at the hands of the bandits by this group. When in the late summer of 1919 Batyko Machno (Little Father Machno, as his devoted adherents called him) broke through the army front of the loyalists with General Denikin near Umany in the Western Ukraine, he stormed with his horses back into the Ukraine. From Gulyay-Pole, his home, he directed the reign of terror as long as it was safe for him there. In this region there were wealthy Mennonite landowners on whose estates Machno in his youth had been a cattle herder. The Machno troops preferred to stay in the Mennonite villages, and stole great quantities of horses, wagons, produce, clothes, and whatever they could carry with them. Local bandits united with this army to take their share in the loot of furniture, agricultural machinery, etc. What they could not take away they simply destroyed.

All the Mennonite colonies which had the misfortune of being under the temporary yoke of Machno had very difficult experiences. The greatest sufferings, however, were experienced by the settlements Borzenkovo, Zagradovka, and Chortitza with its daughter settlement of Nicolaipol. Two hundred forty names appear on a list of November 1919 of those murdered in Zagradovka. In Borzenkovo in the village of Ebenfeld alone 63 persons were murdered, and in Steinbach of the same settlement 58 persons. The army stationed in the Chortitza settlement Sept. 21-Dec. 22, 1919 (the Mennonites had already left the island of Chortitza at this time), inflicted great suffering. There was hardly a village that was not mourning at least several who had been murdered by the band (see **Chortitza**). In the village of Eichendorf in the Nicolaipol settlement 81 men and 4 women were murdered during the night of Nov. 26, 1919. With the other villages, such as Hochfeld, Petersdorf, and Nicolaipol, the number murdered exceeds 100. It must be added, however, that the murders in the Nicolaipol settlement were committed mostly by local bands rather than the Machno army. The Self-Defense Corps (*q.v., Selbstschutz*), which had been organized and drilled by German occupation army officers before the withdrawal of the German troops, was ineffectual in a military sense and only provoked worse reprisals.

In addition to the violence committed by the Machno troops, an epidemic of typhus broke out among them affecting over half of the troops, including Machno himself. Since these troops were lodging in the Mennonite homes, scattering a vast amount of vermin, practically the entire adult population of the Chortitza settlement contracted the disease. As many as 11-15 per cent of the colony's population died. These were with few exceptions all adults.

The ideal Anarchists (the Russian noble Peter Kropotkin may be considered the father of Russian Anarchism) remained aloof from this movement and therefore it had no foundation upon which to build its future. The result was that it deteriorated into banditry such as Russian history had experienced in adventurers like Pugachev or Stenka Razin. Machno was frequently wounded in battle and finally fled to Rumania and from there to Poland. After a lengthy prison term in Warsaw, he was tried and condemned to death. Thus his career came to a violent end. According to other reports, however, he died in Paris, France.   J.G.R.

P. Arschinow, *The History of the Machno Movement, 1918-1921* (published by a "group of anarchists in Germany," in the Russian language, Berlin, 1923); Dirk Gora, *Russian Dance of Death* (Claremont, Cal., 1930); Gerhard Lohrenz, *Sagradowka* (Rosthern, Sask., 1947); C. Henry Smith, *The Story of the Mennonites* (Newton, 1950); Heinrich Toews, *Eichenfeld-Dubowka* (Karlsruhe, n.d.).

Machnovka is a town on the western edge of the province of Kiev in Russia and of significance to Mennonite history as the point of identification for the Deutsch-Michalin settlement, 1791-1874, which was located a few miles south of Machnovka.

M.H.S.

Machnovka Mennonite Church (Polish Russia): see **Michalin** Mennonite Community and Church.

Machtelt Dieric Jansdochter, an Anabaptist martyr, drowned in a wine cask on Aug. 26, 1539, at Delft, Dutch province of South Holland, together with Marritgen Jansdochter from Deventer. Machtelt, who was apparently a follower of David Joris (*q.v.*), is said to have been a native of "Luynen uit het Sticht van Monster"; this may mean either Schelluinen near Monster, Dutch province of South Holland, or Löhne in the Bishophic of Münster, Westphalia, Germany. (*Inv. Arch. Amst.* I, No. 749; *De Navorscher* X, 1860, 349.)   vDZ.

McGlothlin, William Joseph (1867-1933), an outstanding American Baptist church historian, was born in Sumner County, Tenn., served as professor of church history in the Southern Baptist Theological Seminary in Louisville, Ky., and from 1919 until his death as president of Furman University. In addition to his studies on the history of the Baptists in the United States his research extended to the Anabaptists of the 16th century. One of the fruits of this work was his doctoral dissertation (University of Berlin) on the origins of the Anabaptist movement in Bern, Switzerland. He found an abundance of material in the archives of Strasbourg, Basel, Bern, Zürich, and St. Gall, and in the research done by Ernst Müller (*q.v.*), who had been the first to use this material in his book *Geschichte der bernischen Täufer*, and was able to add to the information in this book. The last two chapters of McGlothlin's work were published as his thesis under the title, *Die Berner Täufer bis 1532*. Under the same title the entire work was published in 1906. He also wrote articles on the 16th-century Anabaptists for Hastings' *Dictionary of Religion and Ethics*. In 1915 he published the book *Infant Baptism in History*. He died on May 28, 1933, as the result of an automobile accident. (*ML* III, 64.)   Hege.

Mack, Alexander, Sr. (1679-1735), chief founder of the Church of the Brethren, eighth child of Johann Philipp and Christina Philbrunn Mack, was born July 27, 1679, in a mill on Bergstrasse in Schriesheim, near Heidelberg, then in the Palatinate (now Baden), Germany. He married Margaretha Kling, a daughter of Velten Kling, a councilor of Schriesheim, on Jan. 18, 1701. The Macks had three sons and two daughters. The daughters died in Germany and one record says the mother also died there. The sons, John Valentine, Johannes, and Alexander, Jr., came to America with their father in 1729. Alexander Mack, Jr. (1712-1803), served the early Brethren church in Pennsylvania as minister for over 50 years.

Mack grew up in the Calvinist faith and was Reformed until about 1705, when he came to know some Baptists and Hochmann of Hohenau. With Hochmann he did some preaching along the Rhine and in Switzerland. In 1708 with seven others he founded at Schwarzenau, Wittgenstein, then in Hesse, the "Brüder Gemeinde," which was the beginning of the Church of the Brethren. He lived in Schriesheim until the fall of 1706, when he was expelled on account of his faith and fled with his family to Schwarzenau in Wittgenstein, where he lived until 1720. Then because of persecution he led most of the group from Schwarzenau to Westerveen, Dutch province of Friesland, a hamlet in the neighborhood of Surhuisterveen (*q.v.*). Here they stayed 1720-29, and from here went to Germantown, Pa., to join the group of Brethren who had emigrated from Crefeld to Germantown in 1719 under the leadership of Peter Becker. Mack died at Germantown on Jan. 31, 1735, and was buried in Axe's burial ground at that place. In 1894 his remains were moved to the cemetery just behind the Germantown Church of the Brethren, 6611 Germantown Ave., Philadelphia, Pa.

During his stay in the Netherlands a few Dutch Mennonites, including some members of the de Koker (*q.v.*) family of Rotterdam, were won to ideas of Mack, who baptized them by immersion. This sympathy, however, seems to have been only temporary, for they did not join the Brethren emigration to the States.

Mack's writings consist largely of answers to questions about his faith. *A Conversation between Father and Son,* and *Ground Searching Questions.*
                                          L.W.Sh.

James Quinter, "Memoir of Alexander Mack, Senior" in *Brethren Encyclopedia*, 7-14 (published by Henry Kurtz, Columbiana, Ohio, 1867); Freeman Ankrum, *Alexander Mack the Tunker and His Descendants* (Scottdale, 1943); H. Brunn, "Alexander Mack, The Tunker," in L. W. Shultz, *Schwarzenau Where the Brethren Began in Europe* (Milford, Ind., 1954); Martin G. Brumbaugh, *A History of the German Baptist Brethren in Europe and America* (Elgin, Ill., 1906).

Mack, Andreas (Andrew) (1836-1917), a prominent leader in the Franconia Mennonite Conference (MC), the son of Jesse M. Mack and Susanna Stauffer, was born Oct. 16, 1836, in the Bally district of Berks Co., Pa., where he lived all his life. His family of six children included a bishop, Noah H. Mack (*q.v.*) of New Holland, Pa., and a preacher, Jesse, of Providence-Skippack. He was ordained preacher at Bally on Sept. 25, 1863, and, by the unanimous consent of the district, was ordained bishop on Nov. 6, 1875. He was a man of sterling character, a born leader of men, and a successful farmer. He favored missions before the Franconia Conference did, and approved the organizing of the Mennonite General Conference, even though the majority of his conference did not. He aided in the 1874 Russian immigration to Kansas, and followed the fortunes of this group with interest for his entire life. He was moderator of the Franconia Conference for many years while the German-English transition was occurring and also the transition from no missions to the organization of the Franconia Mennonite Mission Board in the year of his death. He was probably the strongest leader of his day in the Conference. He died Oct. 29, 1917.   I.D.L.

John C. Wenger, *History of the Mennonites of the Franconia Conference* (Scottdale, 1938).

Mack, Noah H. (1861-1948), an outstanding leader in the Lancaster Conference (MC), born at Niantic, near Bally, Pa., on Feb. 1, 1861, was a son of Bishop Andreas Mack and Elizabeth P. Haldeman. He grew up in the Bally community and was baptized in the Hereford (MC) congregation in Bally. In 1881 he came to Lancaster County to teach school. Early he associated himself with the Sunday schools of Groffdale and Metzler and mission work on the Welsh Mountain, of which he was superintendent 1899-1910. He was married on Dec. 23, 1882, to Elizabeth S. Sensenig Weber. There were no children. Mack was ordained preacher for the Groffdale-Metzler district on Aug. 30, 1900, and assistant bishop for this district on Jan. 23, 1919. By his own request he was transferred to the York-Adams district in 1926, although he continued to live in New Holland. He was a charter member of the Eastern Board of Missions and Charities, a member of the Examining Committee of that Board, and for a time secretary of the Lancaster Conference. He was very active in many aspects of church life. He died Oct. 31, 1948; he was buried at Groffdale.   I.D.L.

J. Paul Graybill, Ira D. Landis, and J. Paul Sauder, *Noah H. Mack, His Life and Times, 1861-1948* (n.p., n.d.).

Mackinaw, one of the nine original congregations of Amish Mennonites in central Illinois, along the Mackinaw River in southern Woodford County. In the 1830's Amish families settled along the river. As more settlers located in this area it became known as the "Mackinaw Meeting." In 1840 Christian Ropp was ordained preacher and in 1846 bishop of this congregation. The church was one of those that participated in the General Amish Conference (*Diener-Versammlungen, q.v.*). Later the congregation became part of the Amish Mennonite movement which organized the Western District Amish

Mennonite Conference. After 1872 the southern portion of the Mackinaw Meeting began to use the old church of the Rock Creek congregation, while the other portion continued meeting in homes. This led to the creation of two congregations, Roanoke (*q.v.*) and Goodfield, both later members of the Illinois (MC) Conference. M.G.

H. F. Weber, *Centennial History of the Mennonites of Illinois 1829-1929* (Goshen, 1931).

McKinley Mennonite Church (GCM) in McKinley, near Mio, Oscoda Co., Mich., is a mission sponsored by the Central Mennonite Conference Board of Home and Foreign Missions. In 1951 the chapel was built to strengthen the work that had been started a few years previously by the Comins (*q.v.*) church. Lowell Troyer became pastor of the mission in 1951.
M.G.

McLean County, Ill., is the largest county in the state and ranks as one of the four leading agricultural counties in the United States. It is located in the north-central part of Illinois. Bloomington is the county seat. Most of the land is of the rich prairie type, broken only here and there by the more rolling wooded sections along the streams. Leading agricultural products are corn and soybeans as cash crops, besides dairying. The first Mennonite (Amish from Ohio, Alsace, etc.) immigrations to this section began about 1829, but did not reach sizable proportions until about 1850. Mennonites settled entirely in the northern and western parts of the county, except for one small settlement in the eastern part near Anchor, which has since largely disintegrated. The northern and western settlements extend also into Livingston, Woodford, and Tazewell counties. Total Mennonite population of the county is approximately 900, almost all of whom belong to the Central Conference, now a district of the General Conference Mennonite Church. Mennonite congregations in the county are Meadows, Carlock, Normal, and North Danvers, with about 800 members. Mennonite institutions are the Mennonite Hospital (*q.v.*) in Bloomington, and the Meadows Mennonite Home (for the Aged) (*q.v.*) at Meadows.

Peter Maurer, the first Mennonite settler in Illinois, located in McLean County in 1829, near Rock Creek, five miles north of Danvers. The major migration to the area came in 1832-50. However, the first two congregations, organized in 1833 and 1836, were both located across the border in Woodford County. The first congregation organizing in McLean County was the Rock Creek or Yoder Mennonite Church, organized in 1851 (meetinghouse 1853). From this church, later called North Danvers, three other congregations developed—South Danvers (1859), East White Oak (1892), and Carlock (1914). The Meadows Mennonite Church (1892) and the Anchor Mennonite Church (1894, dissolved 1953) on the far north and far east borders of the county had other origins. A mission congregation and also a bookstore were established in Bloomington in 1956 by the Mennonite (MC) Church. R.L.H.

W. B. Weaver, *History of the Central Conference Mennonite Church* (Danvers, 1926).

McMillan Hutterite Bruderhof near Caley, Alberta, was founded in 1937 by members of the Big Ben Bruderhof near Wolford, Alberta. Their preachers are Jakob Wipf, chosen in 1921, and Samuel Kleinsasser, chosen in 1939. In 1947 the colony numbered 145 souls with 58 baptized members. D.D.

McMinnville, Yamhill County (Ore.), Old Order Amish settlement, located near McMinnville, consisting of 60 members, dates back to 1895, when the families of David Schrock, Amos Schrock, Tobias T. Yoder, Joseph Christner, and Jacob K. Miller moved there from the neighborhood of Hubbard, Marion Co., Ore. The congregation was organized in 1896 with Tobias Yoder as bishop and David Yoder as minister. Other ordained men who have served the congregation are David Y. Miller, Daniel E. Miller, David D. Schlabach, and Daniel Coblentz. The settlement died out twice, 1904-6 and 1927-28, but was reorganized in both cases. In 1955 the membership was 35, with Menno Swartzentruber serving as bishop and Samuel Weaver as minister. D.E.M.

McPherson, the county seat of McPherson County, Kan., was founded in 1872. It became a trading center for the Mennonites who settled in the county (*q.v.*) in the early 1870's. From 1898 to 1905 the German Department of McPherson College operated by the Church of the Brethren was staffed by the Mennonite Brethren in return for the use of the college facilities by Mennonite Brethren students, 249 of them attending the college in this period. This experience later led to the founding of Tabor College (*q.v.*) in Hillsboro.

W. J. Krehbiel (GCM), the son of J. J. Krehbiel of Newton, Kan., bought the *McPherson Daily Republican* in 1899 and operated it until 1944. His son Kenneth has since taken over this publication. In 1906 John J. Wall and Herman Rogalsky, who had operated a mill in Buhler since 1897, founded the Wall-Rogalsky Milling Company in McPherson, transferring their interests from Buhler. This concern was still doing business in 1957. The First Mennonite Church (GCM) is the only Mennonite church in the city limits. It was at first a home mission project of the Western District Conference and was organized as a church on July 29, 1945. In 1955 it reported 142 members. Pastors have been Roland P. Goering and Henry Goossen. The church building was dedicated Oct. 30, 1949. J.F.S.

Louis R. and Harold M. Regier, "The Buhler Mill and Elevator Company," *Menn. Life* VIII (April 1953) 82; H. P. Peters, *History and Development of Education Among the Mennonites in Kansas* (Hillsboro, 1925); W. J. Krehbiel, *History of One Branch of the Krehbiel Family* (McPherson, 1950).

McPherson County, Kan., is located immediately south and east of the center of Kansas. This county of 895 square miles was organized in 1870. A year later the first Mennonites (MC) arrived from Elkhart Co., Ind., settling in the southeastern part of the county. In December 1872 Bishop Henry Yother of Nebraska held communion services with the group in McPherson County, which became the West Liberty congregation near Windom and the Spring Valley congregation near Canton. The total membership was 163 in 1955.

The Mennonite migration from Russia in 1873 ff. resulted in several settlements in the eastern and southeastern areas of the county. General Conference Mennonite congregations established at this time were Friedenstal near Roxbury, Emmanuel south of Canton, Hopefield-Eden west of Moundridge, Christian immediately south of Moundridge, Hoffnungsau southeast of Inman, and Bethel south of Inman.

In the early 1880's the John Holdeman family moved to McPherson County from Missouri and promoted among the Polish Mennonite settlers between Canton and Moundridge the new group which he had founded in 1859, the Church of God in Christ, Mennonite. The result was the establishment of the Meridian congregation east of Moundridge, and the Lonetree congregation north of Moundridge. The Zion church at Inman is also of this group. The total membership of these three congregations in 1955 was 885. In the last decade Mercy Hospital has been established in Moundridge by the Church of God in Christ, Mennonite.

The Zoar Mennonite Church southwest of Inman was established by the Krimmer Mennonite Brethren group when the General Conference group established the congregations named above. In 1955 it had 335 members. The Zoar church established the Zoar Academy and Bible School in 1915, maintaining it until it was discontinued soon after World War II.

Present General Conference churches in McPherson County include Eden, Hopefield, West Zion, First of Christian, and Emmanuel, all of Moundridge; Inman, Hoffnungsau, and Bethel, of Inman, First of McPherson, and Friedenstal near Roxbury, with a total of 2,625 members. Of a total population of 23,670 in the county in 1950 more than one fifth were Mennonites, most of whom lived in the southeastern half of the county, and the total Mennonite membership of all branches was 4,005.   J.F.S.

McRoberts, Samuel (1868-1947), a leading American banker, who was the key figure in the coming of the Canadian Mennonites to Paraguay in 1926-27. Born in Malta Road, Mo., Dec. 20, 1868, his education completed with B.A. and M.A. degrees from Baker University (1891, 1894) and an L.B. from the University of Michigan (1893), he entered into the banking business in 1909 as vice-president of the National City Bank of New York (1909-19), continuing as president of the Metropolitan Trust Company of New York (1921-25) and chairman of the Board of the Chatham-Phenix National Bank of New York (1925-32). During World War I he was chief of the division of procurement of the Ordnance Department of the United States Army and was made Brigadier General on Aug. 26, 1918, hence was commonly called General McRoberts. He died Sept. 9, 1947.

McRoberts was enlisted to help the Mennonites by a visit in 1919 of a committee of four from the Old Colony settlement near Hague, Sask., who must have learned of him through a Canadian banker friend. He refused aid but was won for the Mennonite cause by his wife (Harriet Skinner), a devout Christian, Fundamentalist, daughter of a Presbyte-

rian minister, who was convinced the Mennonites were outstanding Christians fighting God's battle in an unbelieving world, and therefore should be helped. With characteristic thoroughness McRoberts undertook the Mennonite case and became the chief promoter and financier (losing a considerable amount in the course of time) of the Canadian colonization in the Paraguayan Chaco, operating through the Intercontinental Land Company (organized in 1925; q.v.) and the Corporación Paraguaya (organized in 1926; q.v.). Details of McRoberts' operations are given in the articles on the above two corporations. McRoberts engaged Fred Engen (q.v.), an experienced land agent, who studied a wide range of locations throughout the world (Manchuria, Africa, Mexico, South America), keeping in mind the Mennonite terms, which were complete freedom of religion, language, and schools, military exemption, local autonomy, good soil, and isolation from the world. They decided on Argentina, but soon discovered that Argentina refused the Mennonite terms. An accidental meeting with president-elect Gondra of Paraguay en route to Argentina led ultimately to the choice of the Chaco for the Mennonite colonization project. McRoberts personally negotiated with Paraguayan government and civic leaders for the Mennonite privileges. He also persuaded the Catholic authorities, including the papal nuncio and the archbishop, to approve the project.

Without this personal intervention of McRoberts the Mennonite colonization (first Menno Colony in 1926, and later Fernheim, and other Russian Mennonite colonies 1930 ff.) would probably never have been established.   H.S.B.

John Bender, "Paraguay Calling," Part II, "The Mennonite Colonies in Paraguay," pp. 9-35, gives further details of McRoberts' activities. (Copy in GCL.)

Macungie Mennonite Brethren in Christ Church in Macungie, a town in Lehigh County, Pa., seven miles southweast of Allentown, was founded in 1902. In 1956 it had 27 members and was part of a circuit with Zionsville and Emmaus, of which W. W. Hartman was the pastor.   H.S.B.

Madera County, Cal. (pop. 36,904), is located in the central part of the San Joaquin Valley. The county seat and principal city of 14,000 (1953 estimate) carries the county's name and is known as the gateway to Yosemite National Park.

The Mennonite population of Madera County is made up of approximately 15 families, mostly rural, and almost entirely Mennonite Brethren, with several G.C.M. families who attend the M.B. services. The M.B. congregation is the only Mennonite institution in the county, having 34 members.

The first Mennonite congregation (GCM) in Madera County was organized in 1914. The Co-operative Land Company built a church for it in the Mennonite community 10 miles northwest of Madera, which was taken over by the Mennonite Brethren in 1919, who finished paying for the church property. During the first few years of settlement, the General Conference group largely moved away because of poor economic conditions. The present Mennonites are predominantly cotton and dairy farmers, with some working for wages in the city of Madera. Several families of Mennonite origin attend the Baptist and Assembly of God churches in Madera.

Economic opportunities for the Madera County Mennonites are relatively limited, and prospects for the future, as has always been the case, are not too encouraging. Over the years, many young people have left the county in search of a more favorable economy.   L.R.J.

Madera Mennonite Brethren Church, located in Madera Co., Cal., formerly the Fairmead Mennonite Brethren Church, is a member of the Pacific District Mennonite Brethren Conference. It changed its name when the town and post office of Fairmead were discontinued. The church was organized with Cornelius Wittenberg as pastor when a number of Mennonite Brethren families from Russia settled in the district in 1911-12. Together with General Conference Mennonites they erected a temporary church building, but the group dissolved when the settlers were unable to meet payments on the land they had purchased. On Oct. 19, 1919, they reorganized with Peter Wall as leader and reopened the church. Bernard Wall, a brother of Peter Wall, served the church as leader for 25 years, from 1928 until his retirement in 1953. The membership rose to 36 in 1924, but later declined to about 20. On Nov. 5, 1939, a new church building was dedicated. In 1954 the membership was 34, with Jacob R. Quiring as pastor.   I.G.N.

Madison and Union County (Ohio) Amish Community. The present (1954) Old Order Amish settlement of three districts and 267 baptized members near Plain City dates back to 1896. Amish Mennonites who lived in Champaign County traveled through Madison County en route to their former home in Holmes County. They told of the opportunity, the fertile black land, and of the attractiveness of the Darby Plains in Madison County. The Amish among the hills of Holmes County became interested, and the three men who first investigated the possibilities for settlement in 1885 in Madison were Mose Slabaugh, J. J. Miller, and Benjamin Frey. The first permanent Amish settlers, J. J. Miller, Moses M. Kaufman, Eli J. Miller, Dan J. Miller, Moses Slabauch, David Farmwald, and Albert Spesinger, moved there in the spring of 1896. The first ordained men came in 1897; they were Benjamin Frey, a deacon of Holmes County, and Benjamin Troyer, a preacher from Kansas. Other settlers in 1887 were Moses Hostetler, Pete J. Kramer, John Hostetler of Holmes County; Jonas Gingerich from Geauga Co., Ohio; David Kauffman and John Troyer from Kansas.

Ministers from Holmes County came to preach for the group about every four weeks, until the ordained members, Frey and Troyer, took regular charge in 1897. In 1898 Eli P. Beachy was ordained minister, and in 1899 Jacob Farmwald. In 1900 Bishop C. S. Beachy with Preacher Christ Swartzendruber of Virginia moved to Madison County. In 1904 Preacher Moses Troyer from Geauga County moved to Madison County.

By 1904 the settlement had grown considerably, and with the influx of ministers it was thought best

to divide the settlement into two church districts, North and South. In 1906 Moses Miller was ordained bishop in charge of the South district, while C. S. Beachy had charge of the North. In 1925 the North district was divided again, this time forming the East and West districts. Bishop C. S. Beachy had charge of both the East and West districts until 1930, when Jacob Farmwald was ordained bishop for the East district. Succeeding and present (1954) bishops in charge of the three districts (242 members) are John Plank and Noah L. Troyer.

Beginning in 1916 a few of the Amish here transferred their membership to the Oak Grove Mennonite Church (MC) at West Liberty, Ohio. During the early twenties a considerable number of Amish did this. At the request of the group Bishop S. E. Allgyer of West Liberty in 1924 came to Plain City for the first preaching service, which was held in the home of John B. Yoder. With the increasing demand for services at Plain City a Sunday school was organized on July 11, 1926, in an old abandoned church building at Resaca until the Sharon Mennonite (MC) congregation was organized in 1933, when Abram Kaufman was ordained minister. Sharon (q.v.) had 179 members in 1954.

During the years of gradual transition from the Amish to the Mennonite, the Amish worked out an agreement with S. E. Allgyer concerning the transfer of memberships. Amish persons who were expelled from the church were received by the Mennonite church upon confession of faith. The Amish agreed to lift the ban (*Meidung*) upon Amish expelled members after they were received into the Mennonite church.

On Oct. 8, 1939, under the leadership of Bishop M. M. Beachy of Salisbury, Pa., the Canaan Amish Mennonite congregation was organized (Beachy Amish). Emery Yutzy and Robert M. Kauffman were ordained to serve that congregation, which had a membership of 52 in 1954.

On Sept. 10, 1944, the United Bethel Conservative Amish Mennonite Church was organized by Elmer Swartzendruber, who had ordained Andrew Farmwald to the ministry. The 1954 membership was 140.

Thus the total Madison-Union County community of Amish background in 1954 had 613 members in 6 congregations of 4 distinct groups.

                                                      J.A.H.

John E. Beachy, "History of the Sharon Mennonite Church," *Christian Monitor*, November 1948, 342.

Madlinger, Hans, an Anabaptist martyr of Häflingen in the canton of Basel (*q.v.*), Switzerland, and his wealthy brother Ulrich, were among the first Anabaptists in Basel. Hans probably took part in the third disputation in Basel on Dec. 29, 1529, was arrested, "lay in prison over ten weeks and also had to suffer torture until he recanted" in 1530. But he returned to the Anabaptists and in December 1530 recanted a second time. In January 1531 he was arrested again as a backslider, was submerged three times, and because he would not leave the country, was drowned in a brook at the Homburg castle on Feb. 10, 1531, with Peter Linggscher (*q.v.*). Both Hans and Ulrich (Uli) were peasants.   NEFF.

P. Burckhardt, *Die Basler Täufer* . . . (Basel, 1898) 30-41; Paul Peachey, *Die soziale Herkunft der Schweizer Täufer in der Reformationszeit* (Karlsruhe, 1954) 52, 53, 70, 132, Nos. 520-22; *ML* II, 711.

Madschidl, Michael: see **Matschidl.**

Maelbouts: Pieryntgen, an Anabaptist martyr: see **Pieryntgen** (van Male).

Maeren (Maren), **Hendrik van** (Hinrich or Heyndrick van Goch), a former Catholic priest who became an active Sacramentist (*q.v.*) preacher at Warendorf, Westphalia, Germany, in the summer of 1533. On Jan. 5, 1534, he joined the Anabaptists by baptism at Münster (*q.v.*) together with Rothmann, Rol, Stapraet, and other Münster preachers. Then he again was active at Warendorf, baptizing a number of persons, with whom he went to Münster on Feb. 17, 1534. In October he was one of the apostles sent out to convert the world, but a few days after leaving Münster he was arrested at Soest, Westphalia, and beheaded there on Oct. 23, together with Dusentschuer, Slachtscaep, and five others. (Mellink, *Wederdopers,* 22, 26-28, 48 f., 85.)
vDZ.

Maerten (Martin) **Bossier,** an Anabaptist marytr, arrested in 1558 at Wervik in Flanders, Belgium, and burned at the stake, apparently also in Wervik. Particulars are lacking. (*Mart. Mir.* D 200, E 582; *ML* I, 249.)
O.H., vDZ.

Maerten Cornelisz (Marten de Schoenmaker), an Anabaptist martyr, was burned at the stake at The Hague, Holland, on July 7, 1558, with Waechlink Dirks (Walig Dirk Luytgensz) and Adriaen Pietersz (Adriaen Pier Trappers). All three were natives of Winkel, Dutch province of North Holland. Particulars about these martyrs are lacking. (*Inv. Arch. Amst.* I, Nos. 391, 744 f.; *Mart. Mir.* D 202, E 583.)
vDZ.

Maerten van Delft, an Anabaptist martyr: see **Maerten Jansz** (Corendrager).

Maerten Dirksz, of Limmen near Alkmaar, Dutch province of North Holland, an Anabaptist martyr, was burned at the stake on April 25, 1534, at The Hague or at Haarlem in the Netherlands. He had been with the Anabaptists who sailed from North Holland on March 24, 1534, en route to Münster (*q.v.*), but was arrested at Bergklooster (*q.v.*). (*Inv. Arch. Amst.* I, No. 745; *DB* 1917, 121, No. 138.)
vDZ.

Maerten Jansz (Jansen) **Corendrager** (Maerten van Delft), an Anabaptist martyr, was burned at the stake at Delft, Dutch province of South Holland, on Feb. 5, 1572, with Jan Hendriksz (Jan Hendricksen, *q.v.*). Their death was commemorated in the song "Verhoort ons droevich claghen, o Heer in dese noot" (Hear, O Lord, our sad complaint in this distress). Both this hymn, found in the *Lietboecxken van den Offer des Heeren,* and also the detailed account found in the Dutch martyrbooks of 1615 and later, including van Braght's *Martyrs' Mirror,* give substantial information about these two martyrs, who had to endure many cruelties and died loyal, Maer-

ten Jansz with the words, "O Lord, be merciful to me, poor sinner, who am not worthy to suffer for Thy name; but Thou hast made me worthy." Maerten Jansz was a citizen of Delft, a grain porter (hence the name) of the market place. The official sentence of these martyrs is found in the *Martyrs' Mirror.* (*Offer,* 658-62; *Mart. Mir.* D 606 f., E 931; *ML* II, 549.)
NEFF, vDZ.

Maerten Karrettier, an Anabaptist martyr of Bousbecque (Busbeke), put to death for his faith in 1570 at Rijssel (Lille) in France. Particulars are lacking. (*Mart. Mir.* D 509, E 848; *ML* II, 468.)

Maerten Luykensz (Luycx), of Beveren in Flanders, Belgium, an Anabaptist martyr, was beheaded on June 4, 1539, at Alkmaar, Dutch province of North Holland. Particulars are lacking; according to Mellink, Maerten was an adherent of David Joris (*q.v.*). (*Inv. Arch. Amst.* I, No. 748; *DB* 1909, 22; Mellink, *Wederdopers,* 173.)
vDZ.

Maerten Pieters, an Anabaptist martyr from Maasland, near Den Briel, was beheaded at Den Briel (Brielle) on the Maas, Dutch Province of South Holland, on June 25, 1569, with Grietgen Jans. (*Mart. Mir.* D 388, E 740; *ML* III, 372.)
NEFF, vDZ.

Maerten Saey-Wever, an Anabaptist martyr, burned at the stake at Antwerp, Belgium, with some other martyrs on Jan. 30, 1557. His name is found in hymn No. 16, "Aenhoort, Godt, hemelsche Vader" (Hear, O God, heavenly Father) of the *Lietboecxken van den Offer des Heeren.* His official name was Maerten (Martin) van Steertegem; he was a native of Wervik in Flanders and a weaver of serge. He left behind some furniture, which was confiscated.
vDZ.

Offer, 564; *Mart. Mir.* D 184, E 568; *Antw. Arch.-Blad* VIII, 433, 437, 469; XIV, 22 f., No. 240; Wolkan, *Lieder,* 63, 72.

Maerten Schoenmaker: see **Marten Cornelisz.**

Maerten van der Straten: see **Martin van der Straten.**

Maerten de Wael (official name Martin le Josne), an Anabaptist martyr, burned at the stake at Antwerp, Belgium, on May 22, 1557. His wife, Claerken Boucquet (*q.v.*), suffered martyrdom at Antwerp on July 6 of the same year. Maerten was a native of Douai in France. His name is found in the hymn "Aenhoort, Godt, hemelsche Vader" (Hear, O God, heavenly Father), No. 16 of the *Lietboecxken van den Offer des Heeren.*
vDZ.

Offer, 564; *Mart. Mir.* D 185, E 569; *Antw. Arch.-Blad* VIII, 434, 437; XIV, 22 f., No. 243; Wolkan, *Lieder,* 63, 72.

Maerten van Wijk(e) (Maerten Thomassen), an Anabaptist martyr, was burned at the stake at Antwerp, Belgium, on Feb. 26, 1571, together with Calleken Meeuwels and Jan van de Walle. Concerning this martyr van Braght's *Martyrs' Mirror* is incomplete and not quite accurate in stating that he was executed in 1570 (without exact date). The records published by Génard give a number of particulars. Maerten was a tailor, a native of Wijk bij Duurstede,

Dutch province of Utrecht. He was 25 or 26 years of age; Hans Busschaert had baptized him four years previously at Antwerp one evening after dark. During his trial Maerten rejected infant baptism and refused to take an oath. He signed the trial with his name: Merten Thomassen. His marriage with Lysken (Calleken Meeuwels) had been performed in the Anabaptist congregation. (*Mart. Mir.* D 506, E 846; *Antw. Arch.-Blad* XIII, 30, 42, 62; XIV, 76 f., No. 872.) vDZ.

Maertsz, Willem, a Dutch Mennonite preacher of Hoorn, who published *Twaalf Predicatien over verscheyden Plaetsen der Heyliger Schriftuer* (Hoorn, 1679). (Schijn-Maatschoen, *Geschiedenis* II, 655 f.) vDZ.

Maes, Hans van der: see **Hans Vermeersch.**

Maes Sc(h)oenmaker: see **Matthijs van Balk.**

Maeyken, an aged Anabaptist martyr, "an honorable widow deserving double honor," was seized with five sisters of her faith at Antwerp, Belgium, and after steadfastly confessing her faith drowned on Oct. 11, 1559. (*Mart. Mir.* D 249, E 623, 639; *ML* II, 711; see also **Oude Maeyken.**) NEFF.

Maeyken, 't Oude (Old Maeyken), an Anabaptist martyr: see **Oude Maeyken.**

Maeyken, an Anabaptist martyr, was taken prisoner with Hans van Munstdorp, his wife, and two other women, as they had met to hear the Word of God, and imprisoned at Antwerp, Belgium. In September 1573 Hans van Munstdorp was burned at the stake. Since his wife was pregnant, the four women were not delivered to the stake until Oct. 6, after "they had valiantly withstood the many terrible threats, the arguments of the worldly learned men and other means used against them." Their death is mourned in the song, "Och vrienden al te samen hoort," included in the *Rotterdamsch Liedboek* (now lost). This martyr is apparently identical with Maeyken Goossens (*q.v.*). (*Mart. Mir.* D 644, E 983; *ML* II, 711.) NEFF, vDZ.

Maeyken van Aken: see **Maeyken de Hont.**

Maeyken Boosers, an Anabaptist martyr, a descendant of the Alard de Boosere family, magistrates of Doornik (Tournai, Belgium), was burned at the stake there, Sept. 18, 1564. A song written for her, "Die op den Heere betrouwen" (Those who trust in the Lord), is found in *Offer* and later martyrbooks. Van Braght's *Martyrs' Mirror* prints seven short letters written to her parents, children, brothers and sisters, that testify to her clear religious understanding, her strong faith, and her great joy in suffering and dying for her conviction. During her trial Maeyken was disrobed and tortured to compel her to name her fellow believers; the attempt was futile. The 1566 edition of *Offer des Heeren* also contains a short letter of her children to her, which, however, was not inserted in later editions; it is also missing in the *Martyrs' Mirror.* Maeyken's letters, and the one written by her children were published in a separate edition of 1566 (n.p.), together with *Testament ghemaecket by Jan*

Gheertsen. This short letter was published by Cramer in *BRN* II (*Offer des Heeren*) 626. Maeyken Boosers, who was a wealthy woman and only twenty-four years old when she was executed wrote in a graceful style. On one of the visits of her children to her cell she gave her son a pear. The boy did not eat the pear, but saved it; it is now in Amsterdam. This son Hans (Jan) (b. 1559) escaped to Emden and attended the disputation with the Reformed in 1578. He lived at the "Groote Veen" near Oldersum, East Friesland, where he died on May 20, 1652. This is known through the van Geuns family, which is descended from the de Boosers. K.V., vDZ.

Offer, 411-20; *Mart. Mir.* D 302 ff., E 667-69; *Bibliographie* I, 705-8;; *DB* 1898, 114-16; 1902, 168-70; 1906, 56, 64, 69, 79; Wolkan, *Lieder,* 68; *ML* I, 245.

Maeyken (Mayken) Cadts (Kats, de Catte), a daughter of Joos de Catte, an Anabaptist martyr of Wervik, Belgium, was seized on May 20, 1559, by the margrave of Antwerp with five other Anabaptist women and was drowned in the Steen castle after a courageous confession of faith on July 19 or 29, 1559 (not during the night of June 18 as related by van Braght). Maeyken and the five other women who were to die with her are celebrated in a hymn "Babels Raets Mandamenten worden aldus volbracht," found in the *Lietboecxken van den Offer des Heeren* (No. 19); her name is also found in hymn No. 16, "Aenhoort, Godt, hemelsche Vader." vDZ.

Offer, 566, 581 ff.; *Mart. Mir.* D 249, E 623; Wolkan, *Lieder,* 63, 71 f.; *Antw. Arch.-Blad* IX, 3, 9; XIV, 26 f., No. 296; *ML* II, 475.

Maeyken (Mayken) Christiaens, an Anabaptist martyr, burned at the stake on April 30, 1569, at Antwerp, Belgium. The account in van Braght's *Martyrs' Mirror* concerning this martyr, here only called Maeyken, is rather brief, but Génard published some particulars from the official records. Maeyken Christiaens was born about 1539 at Nypkerke (Nukerke, Nieppe) in Flanders; she was married to Willem de Clercq (Willem van Poperinghe, (*q.v.*), also of Nypkerke. Adriaen, a Mennonite elder, had performed the ceremony at Nypkerke in 1561. Their daughter of four years had not yet been baptized. Maeyken had received (re)baptism only one year before. She did not know the man who baptized her. The ceremony took place in a wood. Maeyken was apprehended with many other members of the congregation when a Mennonite meeting in the house of Jan Poote (*q.v.*) near Antwerp was surprised. She was tortured on March 5, but did not betray the names of her fellow members and died steadfast. vDZ.

Mart. Mir. D 661-64, E 979-82; *Antw. Arch.-Blad* XII, 360, 376, 400; XIV, 64 f., No. 721; *ML* II, 711.

Maeyken (Mayken) de Corte (Korte), an Anabaptist martyr, who was burned at the stake (*Mart. Mir.* erroneously beheaded) with Grietge Bonaventuers and "old Maeyken" on Oct. 11, 1559, at Antwerp, Belgium. Van Braght's *Martyrs' Mirror* prints a letter she wrote, giving striking testimony to her strong Biblical faith and her joy in dying. She says her two sisters visited her and tried by all means to save her life; if she would only say she had erred;

but she resisted, and would gladly seal her faith with death.

"I feel," she writes, "that the more I humble myself, the more the mighty God works in me, and pours His grace into me. Then I cry most bitterly, fall upon my knees, and thank my God, and say: O my Lord and God, what am I, child of Adam, that Thou art mindful of him, Thou hast given him dominion over all Thy works .... What shall we render unto Him, my dear sister, but a penitent and contrite heart,... with love and great gratitude .... Let us love one another fervently, for God is love, and constantly exhort each other, lest we wax cold through the deceitfulness of sin; so that God may be glorified in us, and we may be delivered from pride, and from unreasonable and wicked men; for all men have not faith. The Lord is faithful; He will strengthen and keep us." Maeyken was a native of Gent, Belgium. She is commemorated in two hymns, "Babels Raets Mandamenten" and "'Aenhoort, Godt, hemelsche Vader," both found in the *Lietboecxken van den Offer des Heeren.*

NEFF, vDZ.

Offer, 566, 581 ff.; *Mart. Mir.* D 249, E 623; Wolkan, *Lieder,* 63, 71 f.; *Antw. Arch.-Blad* IX, 4, 10, 16; XIV, 26 f., No. 301; *ML* II, 553.

Maeyken Daniels (Mayken uyt Waes van Ghendt), an Anabaptist martyr, was strangled and burned at the stake on Feb. 21, 1559, at Middelburg in the Dutch province of Zeeland. Being a native of Roesselare in Flanders, Belgium, she was held in prison for a long period, while the magistrates of Middelburg sought information about her from the Roman Catholic priest of her native town.   vDZ.

K. R. Pekelharing, "Bijdragen voor de Geschiedenis der Hervorming in Zeeland," in *Archief Zeeuwsch Genootschap* VI (1866) 38-40.

Maeyken van Deventer, an Anabaptist martyr, who is said to have been executed in Rotterdam, Dutch province of South Holland, in 1573 (*Mart. Mir.* D 657, E 977-79). This is, however, rather questionable (*DB* 1905, 173), for in 1573 Rotterdam was no longer in Spanish hands, and her bequest to her four children is almost identical with that of the martyr Anneken van Rotterdam (*q.v.*). (*ML* II, 432.)   NEFF.

Maeyken Deynoots, an Anabaptist martyr, executed at Rijpermond (i.e., Rupelmonde, Belgium), in 1571. The method and exact date of execution are unknown. With Hendrik Verstralen (*q.v.*) she was imprisoned in the castle of Rupelmonde and chained with iron shackles. The *Offer des Heeren* (1578) and the later Dutch martyrbooks, including van Braght's *Martyrs' Mirror,* contain short letters by Maeyken addressed to the congregation. They were farewell letters, in which she admonished them to remain steadfast in the faith. She was apparently acquainted with the writings of Menno Simons or Dirk Philips. Maeyken's letters had been published separately before they were included in the *Offer des Heeren.* (*Offer,* 646-48; *Mart. Mir.* D 548, E 880-82; *DB* 1899, 83; *ML* II, 432.)   vDZ.

Maeyken van Dissenbeke, an Anabaptist martyr, burned at the stake on Oct. 6, 1573, at Antwerp,

Belgium. Particulars about this martyr are lacking (*Bibliographie* II, No. 841). She may be identical with Maeyken Wens (*q.v.*). (*Antw. Arch.-Blad* XIII, 130 f., 180; XIV, 92 f., No. 1040; *DB* 1904, 127 f.)   vDZ.

Maeyken Doornaerts, an Anabaptist martyr, who with two other Anabaptist women was subjected to horrible torture and, still true to her faith, burned at the stake at Belle (Bailleul), Flanders, in 1556. (*Mart. Mir.* D 166, E 553; *ML* I, 467.)   NEFF,

Maeyken Filiers (Filgiers), an Anabaptist martyr: see **Mariken Fransse.**

Maeyken Floris (Flours), an Anabaptist martyr, burned at the stake at Gent, Belgium, on Aug. 7, 1559. Van Braght's account, which follows the account in the *Offer des Heeren,* is incorrect. He states that Maeyken was executed with 11 comartyrs and does not relate the exact date of the execution. Maeyken was a native of Nukerke (Nypkerke, Nieppe) in Flanders. She was one of a group of 12 Mennonites whose stay had been reported to the magistrates by treachery, and who were all apprehended. Baudin (Baudynken), Maeyken's 12-year-old sister, was also examined; but notwithstanding the severe threats of the officers, she resolutely refused to reveal the place where her parents were staying. Of the group arrested four victims were burned on July 5, and six more, including Maeyken, on Aug. 7. Two members either escaped or abjured their faith. Maeyken died steadfast. The execution took place on the Vrijdagsmarkt at seven o'clock in the morning.

Maeyken and the other martyrs are commemorated in a hymn, "Ic moet een liet beginnen" (I must begin a song), No. 14 of the *Lietboecxken van den Offer des Heeren;* this hymn is also found in the *Nieu Liedenboeck* of 1562. Another hymn, "Een eeuwighe vruecht, die nieten vergaet" (An eternal joy, which does not pass away), is found in *Veelderhande Liedekens* of 1569. This hymn is more accurate than that of the *Lietboecxken;* it also gives the information that the group of 12 Mennonites was betrayed to the attorney-general of Gent by a Beguine, and that they were apprehended that very evening while they were eating together.   vDZ.

Offer, 348, 556 ff.; *Mart. Mir.* D 246, E 620-22; Verheyden, *Gent,* 25, No. 67; *ML* I, 656.

Maeyken Goossens, an Anabaptist martyr, burned at the stake on Oct. 6, 1573, at Antwerp, Belgium. Van Braght's *Martyrs' Mirror* names her twice, once with her full name, and once calling her only Maeyken, both times giving 1573 as the year of execution, once giving the exact date. The records published by Génard give the information that she had previously lived in the Dutch province of Zeeland, and that she was married to Hans van Obbergen, who is identical with Hans van Munstdorp (*q.v.*).   vDZ.

Mart. Mir. D 644, E 965; *Antw. Arch.-Blad* XIII, 130, 179; XIV, 92 f., No. 1038; *ML* II, 139.

Maeyken Groffelaers, an Anabaptist martyr, burned at the stake with three other martyrs at Antwerp, Belgium, on May 26, 1573. She was a native of

Brussels, had often attended the Mennonite meetings, but was not yet (re)baptized, though she would have liked to receive baptism upon her faith "if she had only had an opportunity." (*Antw. Arch.-Blad* XIII, 115 f., 177; XIV, 90 f., No. 1025.)   vD Z.

Maeyken de Hont (Hondt), an Anabaptist martyr, drowned in a tub or wine-cask on April 4, 1560, within the Steen castle at Antwerp, Belgium, with Janneken Eghels (Janneken van Aken) and Lenaert Plovier. She was a daughter of Jan de Hont. In the Dutch martyrbooks, where no exact date of the execution is given, she is called Maeyken (Mayken) van Aken. Her name is found in the hymn "Aenhoort, Godt, hemelsche Vader" (Hear, O God, heavenly Father) of the *Lietboecxken van den Offer des Heeren* (hymn No. 16).   vD Z.

Offer, 567 f.; Mart. Mir. D 270, E 641; Antw. Arch.-Blad IX, 7, 12; XIV, 28 f., No. 317; ML II, 711.

Maeyken (Mayken) **Jans**, an Anabaptist martyr, the widow of Frans Laureysz, was burned at the stake in Middelburg, Dutch province of Zeeland, in 1569 (probably May 2). She was a native of Middelburg and about 40 years of age. (*DB* 1908, 17; *ML* II, 390.)   vD Z.

Maeyken Janssens van der Goes, an Anabaptist martyr, was a fellow captive of Abraham Picolet (*q.v.*) and his friend Hendrick van Etten (*q.v.*) of Breda, with whom she was burned at the stake in Antwerp, Nov. 22, 1569. Her husband Jasper de Taschringmaker (*q.v.*) had suffered a similar death on June 22. Her 18-year-old daughter Neelken (*q.v.*) (Nelleken) was also burned at the stake for her faith, on June 27, 1570. Maeyken was apparently a native of the town of Goes in the Dutch province of Zeeland. (*Mart. Mir.* D 475, E 818; *Antw. Arch.-Blad* XII, 425, 453; XIV, 70 f., No. 792; *ML* II, 133.)
                                                    K.V., vD Z.

Maeyken Kocx, an Anabaptist martyr, was seized at Ieper (Yperen), Flanders, Belgium, in 1561 with four others, and "loving God above all, and, out of love to Him, adhering to the truth known and accepted," she was publicly burned at the stake. Her name is celebrated in a hymn, "Geroert ben ick van binnen" (I am inwardly stirred), which is found in the *Nieu Liedenboeck* of 1562, as well as in the *Lietboecxken van den Offer des Heeren* of 1563 (No. 23) and *Tweede Liedeboeck* of 1583. In this hymn she is called only Maeyken (Mayken). vD Z.

Offer, 603 ff.; Mart. Mir. D 285, E 654; Wackernagel, Lieder, 141; Wolkan, Lieder, 72; ML II, 519.

Maeyken Pickelin, an Anabaptist martyr, a simple, pious woman, who suffered a martyr's death in 1590 after much suffering. In his account van Braght (*Mart. Mir.*) does not relate particulars nor the place and exact date of her execution. Notwithstanding her Dutch Christian name it is unlikely that she was a native of the Netherlands. She may have been German and put to death in Germany. (*Mart. Mir.* D 777, E 1080; *ML* III, 371.)   NEFF, vD Z.

Maeyken Pieters, an Anabaptist martyr, who was burned at the stake at St. Veit in Luxembourg in

1585 together with Anneken Botson (*q.v.*) and her daughter Janneken Botson. (*Mart. Mir.* D 753, E 1060; *ML* III, 371.)   NEFF.

Maeyken Pieters, a Mennonite woman, wife of the martyr Willeboort Cornelisz (*q.v.*), was arrested on Jan 19, 1562, at Gent, Belgium, and imprisoned in the Gravesteen castle of Gent. Here she gave birth to a child, which immediately was baptized in a Catholic church. Maeyken, who had been arrested with many other Mennonites, a number of whom were put to death, was released during the riots which arose at Gent. Later, when the magistrates intended to rearrest her, she had fled.   vD Z.

K. R. Pekelharing, "Bijdr. tot de Geschiedenis van de Hervorming in Zeeland," in *Archief Zeeuwsch Genootschap* VI (1866) 44-46.

Maeyken Sprincen, an Anabaptist martyr: see **Oude Maeyken**.

Maeyken Trams, an Anabaptist martyr, burned at the stake at Brugge, Belgium, on Dec. 11, 1561. She was one of a group of members of the Brugge congregation who had been apprehended on Nov. 10, 1561, when they were holding a meeting in a house outside the town. Five of them suffered martyrdom on Dec. 10; the other seven, including Maeyken, were executed on the next day. These martyrs are celebrated in the hymn "Genade ende vrede moet Godvresende zijn" (Mercy and peace should be to the God-fearing), found in the Dutch hymnal *Veelderhande Liedekens* of 1569, reproduced by Wackernagel. This hymn has been the principal source for the account in the martyrbooks. In the records she is called Maykin, wife of Bertram de Raedt, born at Wynne in Flanders. In the index to the 1685 Dutch edition of van Braght's *Martyrs' Mirror* she is listed as Maeyken Frans, but this must be an error. (*Mart. Mir.* D 288, E 655; Verheyden, *Brugge*, 49, No. 38; Wackernagel, *Lieder*, 130.)   vD Z.

Maeyken Truyens, an Anabaptist martyr, executed at Antwerp, Belgium, on Jan. 19, 1577, because she had been (re)baptized and frequented Mennonite meetings. Particulars about this martyr are lacking. With her Geertruyt Faes and Laureys Janssen suffered martyrdom. They were the last Mennonites to die in Antwerp. (*Antw. Arch.-Blad* XIII, 211; XIV, 98 f., No. 1121.)   vD Z.

Maeyken Wens, an Anabaptist martyr, burned at the stake at Antwerp, Belgium, on Oct. 6, 1573. The Dutch martyrbooks following the *Historie der Martelaren* of 1615 contain five letters by Maeyken, which are also found in van Braght's *Martyrs' Mirror*. Two of these letters are addressed to her husband Mattheus Wens, two to her son Adriaen, and one to Jan de Metser, a preacher or a deacon of the congregation. These letters are among the most moving parts of the martyr literature, both in the firmness and purity of Maeyken's faith and in the care she shows for her children. "The Lord be forever praised for the great grace He has shown me, who have feared so much. My dear brother in the Lord, always watch, for the Lord will come like a thief in the night," she wrote to Jan de Metser after she had been sentenced to death. And to her husband: "O my very dear and beloved husband, pray to the Lord heartily in my behalf, to remove the conflict from me; for it is in His power, if it is His pleasure." To her son Adriaen, only 15 years old: "Write me a letter as to what your heart says, whether you desire to fear the Lord; this I should like to know. But you must write it better than the last two letters were written; the one which Maeyken Wils brought, however, was good." In the second letter to her son, a farewell letter of Oct. 5: "Adieu once more, my dear son Adriaen; ever be kind, I pray you, to your afflicted father all the days of your life, and do not grieve him. . . . I have written this since I was sentenced to die for the testimony of Jesus Christ."

Maeyken had been arrested in April 1573. She was imprisoned in the Steen castle of Antwerp, where her husband and her children sometimes visited her; they also wrote some letters. One of these letters, written by her husband, has been preserved, and is now found in the Amsterdam Mennonite archives. This rare piece is the more precious, because on the back of the paper is written Maeyken's farewell letter of Oct. 5 to her children, the only existing autograph letter of a martyr.

Maeyken was executed on the morning of Oct. 6, with a tongue screw to prevent her from addressing the crowd as martyrs often did. Her son Adriaen watched the execution, but when his mother was tied up to the stake he fainted. When he regained consciousness he looked for the tongue screw in the ashes where his mother had been burned, and took it as a memento of his mother.

There has been some question on the identity of this martyr. Since Génard did not find her name in the records of Antwerp, the *Bibliographie* even suggests that she may never have existed, the account in the martyrbooks being merely a phantasy. But this is not the case. It has been clearly shown, as the *Bibliographie* reluctantly admits, by Samuel Cramer (*DB* 1904, 127 f.) that Maeyken, the wife of the mason Mattheus Wens, being a native of Dissenbeke in Flanders, was in the official Antwerp records called Maeyken van Dissenbeke (*q.v.*) and in the martyrbooks Maeykens Wens. In 1566 about 50 persons of Antwerp, suspected of Anabaptism, were summoned to answer to the magistrates for their heresy; among them were besides Janne de Weese (i.e., the preacher Jan de Metser, to whom Maeyken wrote her letter in prison) also "Mattheus Wens, mason, and Maeyken his wife," having been living "in den oudenaertschen ganck" (Oudenaerde lane). They did not appear to answer, apparently because they had fled from the city. They later must have returned.

The autograph letter by Maeyken was acquired by the Amsterdam Mennonite archives in 1902 at a public auction.   vDZ.

Mart. Mir. D 661-64, E 979 f.; *Antw. Arch.-Blad* IX, 291, 294; XIII, 130 f., 179 f.; XIV, 92 f., No. 1040; *Bibliographie* II, No. 841; *DB* 1898, 114; 1899, 104, 108, 121; 1904, 115-33.

Maeyken Wouters (Wauters, Wolters), an Anabaptist martyr, drowned at Liege (Luik) in Belgium, together with Aeltjen Baten. On the same day they were thrown from a bridge into the Maas River. According to van Braght this happened on July 24, 1595, after the women had stayed in prison for ten weeks. The statement of Daris (Bax II, 344) that the execution took place on Oct. 29, 1593, is not very tenable, since Maeyken's letter is dated 1595. Aeltgen was a rather aged woman, Maeyken rather young and unmarried. Both were natives of Zonhoven in the territory of Vogelsanck, Belgian province of Limburg. The accurate and detailed account in the *Martyrs' Mirror* portrays their firm faith in trial and even in torture. In prison Maeyken wrote a letter to her parents and further to "all the believers (i.e., members of the congregation) and all who love the truth." These martyrs are celebrated in the hymn "Voorwaer 't dient niet versweghen, dees werelts blintheyt groot" (The great blindness of this world should not be concealed) found in *Veelderhande Liedekens* of Lenaerdt Clock (Haarlem, 1598) and other Dutch hymnals.   vDZ.

Mart. Mir. D 789-92, E 1091-93; W. Bax, *Het Protestantisme in het Bisdom Luik* II (The Hague, 1941) 344-47.

Magdaleene Jans, an Anabaptist martyr "belonging to the sect of the Mennonites," wife of Matheeux Maurisz of Middelburg, Dutch province of Zeeland, was burned there at the stake on March 13, 1572. Particulars are lacking.   vDZ.

W. te Water, *Kort Verhaal der Reformatie van Zeeland* (Middelburg, 1766) 148; *DB* 1908, 17.

Magdaleentken (Magdalena) **Andriesd**, an Anabaptist martyr, was taken prisoner with five sisters of the faith by the margrave of Antwerp, Belgium, on May 20, 1559, condemned to death with two of them on June 18, and after a courageous confession of their faith they were drowned in the same night in the Steen prison at Antwerp. The name of Magdalena, who was a native of Maastricht, Dutch province of Limburg, is found in two hymns: "Aenhoort Godt, hemelsche Vader" (Hear, O God, heavenly Father), of the *Lietboecxken van den Offer des Heeren* (No. 16) and *"Babels Raets Mandamenten"* (The mandates of the Council of Babel are thus executed), which hymn is found both in the *Nieu Liedenboeck* of 1562 and in *Lietboecxken van den Offer des Heeren* of 1563.   vDZ.

Offer, 566, 581 note 1; *Mart. Mir.* D 249, E 623; Wolkan, *Lieder*, 63, 71 f.; *Antw. Arch.-Blad* IX, 3, 9; XIV, 26 f., No. 297; *ML* II, 711.

Magdalena, an Anabaptist martyr from Waterland, i.e., the district north of Amsterdam, Holland, was executed about Aug. 14, 1544, at Vught, Dutch province of North Brabant, on the charge of being a follower of David Joris (*q.v.*). (*Inv. Arch. Amst.* I, No. 287).   vDZ.

Magdalena de Vos, a daughter of Willem de Vos of Oost-Vleteren in Flanders, an Anabaptist, was arrested at Brugge, Belgium, in July or August 1538. Though she recanted she was punished for forsaking the Roman Catholic Church by being buried alive at Brugge on Aug. 21, 1538, which was very unusual. (Verheyden, *Brugge*, 32, No. 7.)   vDZ.

Magistracy: see State.

Mahaska County, Ia., in the southeastern part of the state, was the location of a Mennonite (MC) settlement which was established in 1852 some distance west of Oskaloosa, when the Peter Beutler family of Ashland Co., Ohio, located there. Beutler was a Mennonite preacher. Among the original settlers were three Beutler families and the Jacob Gehman family. Sometime after 1863 Peter T. Beutler was ordained to the ministry and Jacob K. Beutler served as deacon. After 1863 the *Herald of Truth* reported several visits to this community by Mennonite (MC) ministers from the east and occasionally communion services conducted in the small congregation. At no time was there a Mennonite meetinghouse in the county. Meetings must have been discontinued sometime before Jacob K. Beutler's death in 1892. Descendants of these families are no longer Mennonites. Now known as the Butlers, members of the family have been prominent in Oskaloosa, Iowa.

M.G.

M. Gingerich, *The Mennonites in Iowa* (Iowa City, 1939) 138-45.

Mahbubnagar, a Mennonite Brethren Mission station in India, located in the district center, Mahbubnagar, 50 miles southwest of Hyderabad, Madhya Pradesh (formerly Central Provinces), built by the American Baptist Telugu Mission about 1890. In 1937 the American Mennonite Brethren Mission purchased the property and took over the field, the indigenous church uniting with the Andhra M. B. Church.

Resident M. B. missionaries have been Mr. and Mrs. J. A. Wiebe and Mr. and Mrs. A. A. Unruh; the present (1953) missionaries are Mr. and Mrs. J. N. C. Hiebert and Mr. and Mrs. Ernest E. Schmidt. The spacious mission compound contains a missionaries' residence, church, school, hostels for school boys and school girls, a building housing the printing press, and some smaller buildings. An adjoining compound contains a building formerly used as hospital.

The activities include the regular services in the station church, extensive evangelistic and church work in the town and in villages, the conducting of a middle and primary school for many years but which was changed in 1949 to a high school and primary school, publication and the operation of a printing press, and the work of a dispensary for some time. The station field, having an area of 1,400 square miles and 200,000 population, has several village churches, and the total church membership of the field (1953) is 900. J.H.L.

Mahieu Antheunis (Antoine), called Dupla, an Anabaptist martyr. Van Braght names him after his home and birthplace Mahieu van Halewijn, a village in the Belgian province of Flanders. He was imprisoned, and the authorities tried all sorts of means to dissuade him from his belief. But these efforts were without results. On Feb. 18, 1559, he was burned at the stake at Kortrijk (Courtrai) in Belgium with Jelis (Gilles) de Groot. His possessions were confiscated. An investigation carried out in his house at Halewijn by the prosecutor revealed that Mahieu owned Mennonite books (we are not informed what books they were) and an extensive correspondence. (*Mart. Mir.* D 242, E 616 f.; Verheyden, *Courtrai-Bruxelles,* 33, No. 7.) vDZ.

Mahieu van Halewijn, an Anabaptist martyr: see **Mahieu Antheunis.**

Mahieu (Hieu) de Swarte, youngest son of the martyr Jan de Swarte (*q.v.*), an Anabaptist martyr, was burned at the stake probably on April 27, 1563, at Rijssel (Lille) in France. He had been arrested at Halewijn (*q.v.*), Flanders, on March 7, 1563, together with his parents, his brothers Claes, Christiaen, and Hans, and other members of the congregation. These Mennonites and also his father were put to death on March 16 at Rijssel (Lille) in France, while his mother and his three brothers suffered martyrdom with him, all remaining steadfast. Mahieu was only 16 years of age when he died. (*Mart. Mir.* D 299 f., E 664 f.) vDZ.

Mahieu Waghens, an Anabaptist martyr, burned at the stake on Aug. 15, 1538, on the Vrijdagsmarkt at Gent, Belgium. He was a peddler and the leader of the early Anabaptist congregation of Gent. This congregation used to meet in his home, and when no preacher was present Mahieu delivered an address. He held some revolutionary views; e.g., the believers should be ready to clear away evils and abuses in Gent, when necessary even by force. These ideas were very rare among the Belgian Anabaptists and if the congregation of Gent may have shared the principles of its leader at this moment, it soon chose the way of peaceful nonresistance, following the footsteps of its Lord. On the scaffold before the execution took place Mahieu was placed on show with a placard on which was found the inscription, "Archdeacon of the Anabaptists." After the execution his carbonized corpse was hanged on the gallows together with this placard. (Verheyden, *Gent,* 4, No. 11.) vDZ.

Mahoning County, Ohio, located in eastern Ohio adjacent to the Pennsylvania state line and formed from Columbiana (*q.v.*) and Trumbull counties in 1846, is the home of two Mennonite churches (MC), Midway (*q.v.*) with a membership of 159 and North Lima (*q.v.*) with 149, and one Wisler congregation (OOM), Pleasant View (*q.v.*), with a membership of 94. The first Mennonites in the county came from Bucks Co., Pa., in 1807 and were later joined by others from Canada. The Leetonia congregation (*q.v.*), located a few miles to the south in Columbiana County and organized ten years later, is part of the settlement. Early bishops were Jacob Oberholzer (*q.v.*) and Jacob Nold (*q.v.*). Until recently, when a bishop was ordained for each of the three M.C. congregations, A. J. Steiner (*q.v.*) had served as their bishop. The town of North Lima is the trading center of the community. Youngstown, 11 miles to the north, is the county seat. J.S.U.

Maidstone Mennonite Brethren Church, at Maidstone in northern Saskatchewan, a member of the Canadian Conference, was organized in 1926 with 12 members. At present (1954), there are 8 members, with W. W. Martin as leader. J.H.E.

Maillaert de Grave, of Leisele, near Veurne in Flanders, Belgium, was a member of the Mennonite congregation in his native village, together with his wife Valentyne Ryckele. Paulus van Meenen (*q.v.*) was for a time the elder of this congregation. Later Maillaert, who was a cabinetmaker, moved to Brugge and participated in the life of the congregation there; meetings were held in his home. In February 1568 he, his wife, and their three children were arrested. Though they recanted, their petition to the Duke of Alba (*q.v.*) was rejected and both Maillaert and Valentyne were burned at the stake at Brugge in July 1568. (Verheyden, *Brugge,* 55 f., Nos. 56 and 58.)   vDZ.

Main Centre Mennonite Brethren Church, Saskatchewan, was organized in 1904 under the leadership of Bishop Benjamin Janz. The meetinghouse was built in 1907, enlarged in 1922, and improved in 1945. The 1954 membership was 221. The following have been ordained: as leader, Benjamin Janz; as preachers, Jacob J. Martens, John P. Wiebe, Heinrich P. Janz, Klaas Ewert, Jacob F. Redekop, John Siemens, John D. Goertzen, and Arthur F. Martens. The following have been the leaders of the church at Main Centre: Benjamin Janz, Jacob Ewert, John P. Wiebe, Klaas Ewert, Jacob A. Martens, Abram P. Janz, and Abram D. Rempel. The pastor in 1956 was Abe Goertz; the preachers were John Siemens and John Goertzen, the latter serving as assistant pastor.   J.I.R.

Mainz (Mayence), the capital (pop. 87,000) of Rheinland-Pfalz, Germany, situated on the Rhine, opposite the confluence with the Main. In the eighth century Boniface made it an archbishopric. The city long remained a center of Christian Germany. In Mainz and Bingen the Waldenses had a considerable number of adherents; they were severely persecuted during the Inquisition (Haupt, 9).

The first years of the Reformation also saw the establishment of Protestant congregations in the archbishopric. In 1524 a pamphlet was published titled *Trostbrief der Christlichen Kirchendiener zu Wormbs an die frommen Aposteln und bekenner Jesu Christi, so itzt zu Meintz, Ringaw, und allenthalben im Bistum gefangen liegen, iren lieben Brüdern* (copy in the city library of Mainz), containing serious charges against the Catholic clergy, and admonishing the prisoners to be steadfast in faith, since they cannot count on human aid. Which wing of Protestantism they adhered to is not clear. Archivist F. W. E. Roth thinks they were "Anabaptists" (*Menn. Bl.* 1893, 89 and 105); he bases his assumption on the use of the terms "bishops" and "elders." Hermann Haupt supposes that they were Lutherans (Haupt, 26), while Ludwig Keller and Friedrich Thudichum consider them to have been organized Moravian Brethren congregations (*Monatshefte,* 49-51 and 134 f.). At any rate they cannot have been Anabaptists of the Swiss Brethren type, since that movement did not arise until the following year.

Concerning the fate of these prisoners there is no record, but it may be safely assumed that they lost their lives; for the clergy of Mainz were determined persecutors of all non-Catholics. At the end of December 1525 the cathedral of Mainz sent a delegation to Pope Clemens requesting him to use his influence with Charles V to have the heretics annihilated (Friedensburg, 101). The mandates passed by the emperor substantiate this idea. Meanwhile the Anabaptist movement reached the bishopric; there are records, though sparse, of the punishment of its adherents (Bossert, 4).

Elector, cardinal, and archbishop Albrecht of Mainz, archchancellor of the Holy Roman Empire, known for his trade in indulgences which occasioned the posting of Luther's theses, issued a severe mandate on Jan. 31, 1528, threatening his subjects with loss of life and property if they joined the Anabaptists, but promised immunity to the Anabaptists if they would give themselves up and become informers on their brethren (Wappler, 227). The movement was not so easily suppressed, however, for the electoral law (*Strafordnung*) of 1594 still stipulates that "anyone who defends Anabaptism, calls secret meetings, preaches, or . . . belongs to a sect shall at once be reported to the government" (*Menn. Bl.* 1894, 74). There is no information on later regulations or penalties.   HEGE.

G. Bossert, *TA* I: *Württemberg;* W. Friedensburg, *Zur Vorgeschichte des Gotha-Torgauischen Bündnisses der Evangelischen 1525-1526* (Marburg, 1884); H. Haupt, *Beiträge zur Ref.-Gesch. der Reichsstadt Worms* (1897); P. Wappler, *Die Stellung Kursachsens und des Landgrafen Philipp von Hessen zur Täuferbewegung* (Münster, 1910); Rembert, *Wiedertäufer,* 111; *Monatshefte der Comenius-Gesellschaft* VII (1898) 49-51, 134 f.; *ML* III, 1.

Mair (Mayr), **Baltasar** (Walser), a Hutterite martyr, a preacher in the brotherhood, was beheaded at Walsburg in Carinthia, Austria, with two other Brethren in 1531. A song that he wrote has been lost.   NEFF.

Wolkan, *Geschicht-Buch,* 48; Beck, *Geschichts-Bücher,* 105; Zieglschmid, *Chronik,* 67; *Mart. Mir.* D 33, E 440; *ML* III, 1.

Mair, Matthias, a Hutterite martyr, a native of Tirol, Austria, chosen deacon in 1551; betrayed by a priest, who sent his cook after him to detain him under the pretense that she wanted to become an Anabaptist, he fell into the hands of the Catholic peasants at Wier near Vienna, was taken to Baden, and after six days of imprisonment, during which the priests tried in vain to convert him, he was drowned on July 27, 1592. Three or four times the executioner pulled him out of the water to ask him whether he would recant, but he refused as long as he could speak. His death produced excitement and disappointment among the people, for he was known as a good and upright man. He and Thoman Haan (*q.v.*) are mourned in the song (20 stanzas), "Trost, Fried und Freud, Standhaftigkeit im Herren."   NEFF.

Beck, *Geschichts-Bücher,* 317; Wolkan, *Geschicht-Buch,* 437 f.; Zieglschmid, *Chronik,* 565 f.; *Die Lieder der Hutterischen Brüder* (Scottdale, 1914) 797; Wolkan, *Lieder,* 236; *Mart. Mir.* D 788, E 1089; *ML* III, 1.

Mair, Wolf (Wolfgang), a Hutterite martyr, was seized with Wolf Huber (*q.v.*), near Tittmoning, Austria, in 1559, taken to Salzburg, and cruelly tortured to force him to name those who had given him shelter; but he betrayed no one. Then the monks and priests tried to make him abjure his faith. "They put them all to shame with the Word of God, and their testimony and with their steadfastness, and showed that their faith was the way of divine truth to eternal life in Christ Jesus, on which they would stay with God's help." Then they were taken back to Tittmoning and condemned to die there on Nov. 10, 1559. They sang joyfully on their way to execution. At the site Wolf Mair cried out to the people, "Today I will offer unto my God a true burnt sacrifice, pay my vows, and testify with my blood to the divine truth." In prison he wrote to his wife, describing the two examinations on the rack, relating his conversation with the officials, and assuring her that he would die cheerfully, knowing that his family was provided for. Van Braght's *Martyrs' Mirror* states that he was executed at Luxembourg. He is known as the author of two songs: "Wo soll ich mich hinkehren, Mein Gott, in dieser Frist" (12 stanzas), "Wo soll ich mich hinkehren, Mein Gott, in diesem Zwang" (12 stanzas). NEFF.

Beck, *Geschichts-Bücher*, 221; Wolkan, *Geschicht-Buch*, 303 ff.; Zieglschmid, *Chronik*, 398 f.; *Die Lieder der Hutterischen Brüder* (Scottdale, 1914) 623-26; *Mart. Mir.* D 243, E 617; *ML* III, 2.

Maisbrunn, an estate in the Dachau district of Bavaria, Germany. The former owners of this land had set aside a field to be used as a burying ground, before the Mennonite chapel and cemetery were built at Eichstock (*q.v.*). After the Hartmetz and Hirschler families left, the estate passed into the possession of a Catholic, who broke down the cemetery fence and used the gravestones to improve his buildings. The appeals of the previous owner to purchase the cemetery in the name of the Mennonite Church of Eichstock were not recognized, since the congregation was not incorporated and could therefore not acquire property. (*ML* III, 2.)   D.M.

Maisch, Gottlob (1825-1908), a German writer of historical and theological works. In his book *Religion und Revolution* (1892) he discusses Anabaptism. Maisch is one of the modern scholars who find the roots of Anabaptism in the peaceful Swiss Brethren. Not until the leaders had been wiped out by the cruel persecution were the radical elements able to win the upper hand as in Münster. But even in Münster he sees at first a good Protestant movement under Rothmann, until the radical elements won out and destroyed the work begun in a truly religious spirit. The book, to be sure, presents no new material on the Anabaptist movement, but Maisch gives it a positive evaluation. (*ML* III, 2.)   H.Q.

Major County, Okla., in the northwestern part of the state, is the seat of six Mennonite churches with a total membership of 1,153, as follows: 3 G.C.M. with 507 members: Saron in Orienta, 6 miles north of Fairview, New Hopedale in Meno, and West New Hopedale north of Ringwood; one M.B. Church in Fairview with 411 members; one Church of God in Christ, Mennonite (Fairview), with 235 members. A small group, called the Penner Church, related to the Church of God in Christ, Mennonite, but independent, worships about 6 miles north of Fairview. Fairview is the county seat. The Meno Bible Academy (*q.v.*) is located in Meno in the northeast corner of the county.   H.U.S.

Makkum, a town in the Dutch province of Friesland close to the dike which shuts off the former Zuiderzee, the seat of a Mennonite congregation, founded here (according to Blaupot ten Cate) in 1550-80, but possibly of a still older date. About 1600 there were three congregations here:

(*a*) A Jan Jacobsz group, sometimes also, though incorrectly, called Old Flemish. This congregation was founded before 1599; for on July 22 of this year representatives of the Makkum congregation were called to Dokkum, Friesland, to settle the dispute between Jan Jacobsz and Pieter Jeltjes. In the early 17th century this congregation must have been rather large; in 1603-18 Elder Jacob Theunisz baptized a large number of persons here. Its meetinghouse was found in the Wijde Steeg. From about the middle of the 17th century there was a decline: in 1755 the congregation had no preacher and was served by those of Ameland and Baard. In 1785 the last member of the Makkum Jan Jacobsz congregation died; then Baard and Ameland, the two remaining congregations of this branch, divided the property of the Makkum congregation, each receiving 1600 guilders, and in 1788, when the old meetinghouse was sold, another small amount.

(*b*) A Waterlander congregation, the history of which is entirely unknown. The existence of this congregation is proved by the fact that mention of it is made at the large Waterlander conference at Amsterdam in 1647. It must have merged with the Flemish congregation before 1695.

(*c*) A Flemish congregation, on which there is only scanty information. In 1695, after it had merged with the Waterlanders, it joined the Friesche Sociëteit (Mennonite conference of Friesland). At this time the baptized membership numbered about 260. Among the first trustees of the Friesche Sociëteit were representatives of the Makkum congregation, in the 18th century called United Flemish and Waterlander congregation. Of this congregation a book of members baptized since 1690 has been preserved and also a book of births in the families of the members from 1740-1816. In the course of time its membership decreased: 167 baptized members in 1740, 90 in 1808, 115 in 1861, 77 in 1900, 48 in 1957. This decrease is partly caused by the fact that the town of Makkum, like most little towns on the Zuiderzee, declined in the late 17th and in the 18th century because of the wars of the Netherlands with England; also in the 19th century many inhabitants moved elsewhere. A curious circular of 1771 by the church board, in which the members were encouraged to make larger contributions to the church, clearly shows the decline of the congregation. (This letter was published in *De Zondagsbode* XLVI, 1932-33, No. 33.) Until 1790 the congregation had been served by untrained preachers. The first minister trained at the Amsterdam Mennonite Seminary was Pieter van der Bij, serving here 1792-1814. He was followed by Reitze de Vries 1814-19, Klaas Ris 1820-23, H. L. Bauman 1824-34,

A. Doyer van Cleef 1835-76, J. A. Oosterbaan 1878-1901, F. C. Fleischer 1902-9, Jacob Hulshoff 1909-20, P. J. Keuning 1921-25, and Miss J. M. Eelman 1925-32. In 1933 the Makkum congregation made an arrangement with the near-by congregation of Witmarsum-Pingjum to be served by the same minister. These ministers were W. F. Golterman 1933-36, H. P. Tulner 1936-39, A. H. van Drooge 1940-46, and Miss S. E. Doyer 1946-57.

The Makkum meetinghouse of the former Flemish congregation was a plain building. About 1850 it was modernized and in 1909-10 entirely rebuilt (dedicated April 17, 1910). The congregation of Makkum has a youth group. In the town of Makkum is found the well-known Dutch pottery owned by the (Mennonite) Tichelaar (*q.v.*) family. vDZ.

Inv. Arch. Amst. II, Nos. 2089-92; Blaupot t. C., *Friesland, passim*, see Index; J. Loosjes, *Jan Jacobsz en de Janjacobsgezinden* (1914) reprint, p. 49 f.; *DB* 1890, 15-18; 1899, 211; 1909, 186; 1910, 190; *ML* III, 2.

Malcolm, Neb., the address of Unit 2 of CPS Camp No. 138: see **Lincoln.**

Maldegem, Jacques (Jacob) **van,** a Mennonite preacher born about 1580 at Hansbeke near Zomergem, in the bishopric of Gent, Belgium, was banished from the bishopric because of his successful work for his brotherhood. In 1614 he was made elder of the church at Aardenburg (*q.v.*) in Dutch Zeeland-Flanders and on April 12, 1615, he was taken prisoner at a church service. He was a cattle breeder by trade and in addition he faithfully served the Mennonite church. He preached not only at Aardenburg, but also at Sint Martensdijk (*q.v.*) and, braving the mandate of the magistrates, in 1630 at Zomergem (*q.v.*). He was active especially in trying to win over to the Mennonites the Protestant refugees from Flanders. By this activity he incurred the displeasure of the Reformed magistrates of Aardenburg. In 1634 he was seized by the Spaniards and was held in Brugge and later in Damme, but acquired his freedom on Sept. 16, 1635. He preached several times more and then, probably by government orders, resigned his ministry. From 1636 there is no further record of his work in Aardenburg; in 1647 he was still active, for in that year he officiated at a marriage at Sint Martensdijk. (*DB* 1876, 81, 86, 98 f., 108, 109-15; 1883, 4-6; 1884, 59; *ML* III, 2.) NEFF, vDZ.

Male, van, family name of Mennonites in Flanders and at Amsterdam. Cornelis Jansz van Male was a preacher and elder of the Old Flemish congregation meeting at "de Kruikjes" (*q.v.*) at Amsterdam. He died about 1620 at a very advanced age. Among the Mennonite martyrs found in *Offer* and *Martyrs' Mirror* are Pieter van Male and Marijntgen and Pierijntgen van Male, all of Gent, Belgium, and executed there in 1562 and 1564. vDZ.

DB 1896, 104-7; Kühler, *Geschiedenis* II, 131 f.; *Mart. Mir.* D 289, 301, E 656, 666.

Maler, Gregor, an Anabaptist preacher of Chur (*q.v.*), Switzerland, stopped for a time in Augsburg, Germany, to baptize several persons who wished to join the brotherhood. He took part in the Martyrs' Synod of Aug. 20, 1527 (Keller, *Ref.*, 428), and was one of the evangelists sent out by that body. According to a statement made by Jakob Gross (*q.v.*), who was imprisoned at Augsburg soon after the synod, Maler was assigned with Hans Denk (*q.v.*), Ulrich Trechsel (according to the statement of Hans Hut, who was also seized, Trechsel was sent to Worms), and Hans Beck (*q.v.*) to the Cantons of Basel and Zürich; the council of Augsburg passed this information on to the council of Strasbourg with the request that they keep close watch on these men, and report back (Röhrich, 33). While Denk and Beck went first to Ulm, and from there had to move on soon, Gregor remained a while longer in the vicinity of Augsburg (Keller, *Apostel,* 221). On Oct. 15, 1527, he visited Eitelhans Langenmantel (*q.v.*), who had been banished from Augsburg, at Göppingen.

He also visited Strasbourg (exact date unknown) and is also said to have been in Basel. In April 1528 he was arrested at Feldkirch in Vorarlberg, Austria. Because it could not be proved that he had been rebaptized (he refused to answer this question) he was released. There is no further trace of him.

HEGE, vDZ.

L. Keller, *Ein Apostel der Wiedertäufer* (Leipzig, 1882); idem, *Die Reformation und die älteren Reformparteien* (Leipzig, 1885); T. W. Röhrich, "Zur Geschichte der strassburger Wiedertäufer," in *Ztscht für die Historische Theologie,* 1860; Fr. Roth, "Zur Geschichte der Wiedertäufer in Oberschwaben," in *Ztscht des Historischen Vereins für Schwaben* XXVII (1900); Paul Peachey, *Die soziale Herkunft der Schweizer Täufer* (Karlsruhe, 1954) 42, 89, 113 No. 89; *ML* III, 3.

Maler, Jörg, a South German Anabaptist of the Marpeck circle, the copyist and compiler of the *Kunstbuch:* see **Marpeck, Pilgram.**

Maler, Martin: see **Zehentmayer.**

Malerin, Anna, an Anabaptist martyr: see **Anna Malerin.**

Maliapen, an epithet given the Mennonites around Hoorn in West Friesland, Netherlands, "because of their enormous stupidity," according to the statement of the notorious heresy judge W. D. Lindanus (*q.v.*), in his book, *Dubitantius de vera certaque,* etc. The term is probably derived from "malle apen" or "japen" (dull monkeys, or stupid fellows). (*DB* 1872, 32; *ML* III, 3.) vDZ.

Malsch, two villages in Baden, Germany, in which the Anabaptist movement found a number of adherents in the 16th century, one situated south of Karlsruhe, and the other north. Malsch, in the Ettlingen district, with about 5,000 predominantly Catholic inhabitants, belonged formerly to the abbey of Reichenbach, but was annexed by Duke Frederick of Württemberg in 1595, and in 1603 fell to Baden. The earliest records concerning Anabaptists are dated 1543. The village chronicle records that Count Palatine John had an illegal regulation announced, expelling Anabaptists. Nevertheless it is known that there were Anabaptists in the city for many decades. They maintained connections with the Hutterian Brotherhood. In 1559-81 many families fled to Moravia, abandoning their property. That this amounted to a considerable sum may be inferred from the fact that in 1610 Baden and Württemberg fell into a dispute concerning it.

In Malsch in the Wiesloch district, a village of about 1,600 predominantly Catholic inhabitants, a number of persons, taking offense at the conduct of the local priest, joined the Anabaptists (see **Baden**). In March 1539 three men, five women, and three girls were arrested and imprisoned in the fortress of Rotenberg. They had recently been baptized by Wendel Metzger of Heidelsheim (Bruchsal district) and Hans Gentner of Sulzfeld (Eppingen district); the latter went to Moravia and died in 1548 at Schäkowitz as "a faithful evangelical servant of Christ, after many sorrows and many a struggle, which he endured for Christ's sake." Two preachers as well as the Bishop of Speyer sought to indoctrinate the prisoners and win them back to the Catholic Church. Of Barbara Decker it was said that she vigorously resisted the demand to recant, but the others yielded. Some of the Malsch Anabaptists went to Moravia. Among the 150 Hutterian Brethren imprisoned in the Falkenstein Castle (*q.v.*) in 1539 who were to be sent to the galleys there were several Anabaptists of Malsch (Wolkan, 157). HEGE.

TA Württemberg; Bossert, "Beiträge zur badisch-pfälzischen Reformationsgeschichte," in Ztscht für die Gesch. des Oberrheins LIX, 71-88; B. Schwarz, "Wiedertäufer in Malsch," in Mitteldeutscher Courier (1904) No. 21; Wolkan, Geschicht-Buch; Zieglschmid, Chronik, 200 f.; Beck, Geschichts-Bücher; ML III, 3 f.

Malysch District (Malyschner Bezirk), a Mennonite settlement in the Volga region of Russia, about 60 miles southeast of Saratov, named for the creek Malysch, which flows into the Tarlyk, a tributary of the Volga. It was settled in 1854-59 by Mennonites from West Prussia, led by Claas Epp, the former mayor of the village of Fürstenwerder (*q.v.*), and comprised 10 villages: Hahnsau, Köppental, Lindenau, Fresenheim, Valuyevka, Hohendorf, Lysanderhöhe, Orloff, Ostenfeld, and Medemtal. The oldest village, Hahnsau, passed into Little Russian possession at the end of the 19th century. North and west of the Mennonite settlement German Lutherans and Catholics were settled. (*ML* III, 4.) F.B.

Man, Klaes Jansz, usually called only Klaes Jansz, was a Dutch Mennonite preacher at Uithoorn (of moderate ability, years of service unknown) and published a funeral sermon, *Lykpredicatie over het salig Afsterven van J. G. Buyser* (Amsterdam, 1697) delivered for Buyser (*q.v.*), an elder at Emden. Klaes Jansz was a follower of Buyser. vDZ.

Schijn-Maatschoen, Geschiedenis II, 657; N.N.B.Wb. IX, 455; Biogr. Wb. IV, 526; J. Hartog, Geschiedenis der Predikkunde (Amsterdam, 1865) 229 f.

Manatant, an 18th-century geographical designation for a territory which covers a portion of the eastern section of Berks County, Pa. The term is evidently a variant form of Manatawny, the name of a huge tract of land of more than 20,000 acres, sold by William Penn to John Henry Sprogel. By 1715 Sprogel had set aside about three acres within the limits of the present borough of Pottstown for burial purposes, and in this Sprogel cemetery many Mennonites were buried in the 18th century, including

Bishop Martin Bechtel (1710-86). The term Manatawny is still used in Berks County as one of the four groups of townships which comprise the county: there are fifteen townships in the Manatawny district. Part of the area, at least, is drained by the Manatawny stream, a part of the Schuylkill River system. But Bally, the village where the Hereford Mennonite Church (*q.v.*) is located, is also in the Manatawny district, although located in the Perkiomen Valley, another branch of the Schuylkill. Mennonites settled in what were later the townships of Colebrookdale (created 1741) and Hereford (created 1753) as early as 1720; the present Washington Township of Berks County, in which the Hereford congregation is located, was not created until 1839. When the Mennonite ministers of eastern Pennsylvania met to adopt the Dordrecht Confession in 1725 two of them signed as representing the "Manatant." One of these was Daniel Langenecker of near Royersford, who served the Coventry congregation across the line in Chester County, and the other was Hans Jacob Bechtel, who lived near Pottstown, but who preached, at least in part, at Hereford. The term Manatant was therefore loosely employed by the Mennonites to designate the area from the present town of Bally (established 1860) to Pottstown, and even down the Schuylkill Valley to the Coventry area. J.C.W.

Cyrus T. Fox, Reading and Berks County, Pennsylvania I (New York, 1925) 273-94; J. C. Wenger, History of the Mennonites of the Franconia Conference (Telford, Pa., 1937) 15, 19, 45, 93, 113, 206, 251, 280, 403.

Mancelona, Mich., a town about 40 miles south of Petoskey, the location of a small settlement of Mennonites (MC), where J. S. Coffman held several services in July 1881, and where he hoped a congregation would soon be organized. One of the Coffman meetings was held in the house of David Garber. One must have been organized soon, since on Sept. 22, 1883, "two young persons were received into the church by baptism," and "on the 23rd communion services were held." Nothing further could be learned about this early group. In 1948 a mission was established here called Cold Springs. In 1956 Willard Bontrager was the pastor, with 22 members. (*Herald of Truth,* 1881, 139; 1883, 314.) H.S.B.

Mancelona (Mich.) United Missionary Church had 25 members in 1954. E. R. Sims was serving as its minister. M.G.

Manchester Mennonite (MC) Church (formerly called Liverpool), a member of the Lancaster Conference, is located eight miles north of York, in York Co., Pa. The Mennonites in this community, the Keller, Leib, Reiff, and Rodes families, worshiped in private homes and in the Hoover Union Church until 1810. In that year a yellow sandstone meetinghouse was built on land given by Christian Keller one-half mile north of the town of Manchester. It was regularly used until 1850 when the congregation in effect had died out. Thereafter it was occasionally used by the Stony Brook congregation as an additional preaching point. In 1948 it was reopened as a mission station in the old building, the oldest meetinghouse still in use in the

Lancaster Conference. In 1949 Joseph H. Martin was ordained as pastor and in 1954 Lloyd L. Hollinger as assistant pastor. In 1955 the membership was 50.   I.D.L.

Mandach, Sophie von, mother of the owner of the Hohenegg castle in Tirol, Austria (now Italy). Loesche reports that she gathered a group of Anabaptist women about her and took no taxes from the Brethren. Nothing further is known concerning her relations with the Anabaptists. Her son joined the Schwenckfelders.   W.W.

G. Loesche, *Die Gesch. des Protestantismus in Oesterreich* (3rd ed., Leipzig, 1930) 374; *ML* III, 4.

Mandailang, Groot, a territory on the Indonesian island of Sumatra (*q.v.*), where a mission station among the Tobanes immigrants was opened in 1925 by the Dutch Mennonite Mission Association, on the special instigation of Pastor J. E. van Brakel (*q.v.*) of Koog-Zaandijk. This mission, generously supported by the congregation of Heubuden (*q.v.*), West Prussia, was successful (two small congregations soon arose at Bonandolok and Sihipeng) but in 1930 had to be transferred to the German Rheinland Mission Society because of lack of Mennonite missionaries. (*Jaarverslag,* reports of the Mennonite Mission Association 1925-30.)   vDZ.

Mandates were the laws of the Holy Roman Empire which gave instructions to the higher officials. In the German territories the regulations passed for their own domain in the 15th-18th centuries were often also called mandates. In addition the term "edict" was used for regulations meant for general knowledge, for commands as well as for prohibitions. Such laws were passed during the Middle Ages against religious brotherhoods which arose beside the Catholic Church. For the Holy Roman Empire Frederick II introduced a general church regulation in 1232, decreeing that persons condemned and delivered to the secular courts by the church must be put to death. This applied first of all to extra-church reform groups.

For the suppression of the Anabaptists and the Mennonites mandates were issued in amazingly large numbers. Persecution began in Zürich immediately after the initiation of the Anabaptist movement in 1525 with the passing of a decree that introduced a long series of mandates announcing the severest penalties. Whatever violence fanaticism could invent for the annihilation of a separatist group was precipitated into these mandates. In harshness these mandates differed very little from the heresy laws of the Middle Ages.

The organization of independent congregations was strictly prohibited by the mandates, and accordingly their preachers were denied the right to perform any official functions. Children were forcibly baptized by preachers of the established state churches; the Swiss Anabaptists were obliged to participate in state church communion services, and had to be married in the state church at a time when this regulation was not yet mandatory for the people in general. Their devotional literature was confiscated in all countries, and most of it destroyed; in some

states the very buildings in which they met were torn down.

Every member of a congregation was personally hit by the ruthless stipulations of the mandates. They were thrown into prison, deprived of their property; it was made a criminal offense to shelter them, employ them, feed them; high rewards were offered for their capture; they were subjected to cruel torture; their bodies were mutilated by cutting off limbs or by branding them with hot irons on forehead or cheek, and finally those who persisted in their faith were killed by drowning, hanging, beheading, and even by burning or burying alive— not at all because they were accused of some heinous crime, but because they did not agree with all the doctrines and institutions of the established churches.

But it was not only the difference in doctrine that gave the Anabaptists occasion to separate themselves from the church, but frequently also the offensive conduct of members of those churches. This can be seen not only in the mandates on morals of the 16th century, but also by the various regulations passed against the Anabaptists, which stress these unworthy conditions, thereby trying to influence officials and clergy (Müller, 87, 116; Hege, 141; Bergmann, 53; Loserth, *Communismus,* 318).

A summary of the numerous mandates issued against the Anabaptists and Mennonites does not exist. Nevertheless the laws published in the recent collections of sources afford a dependable view of the proceedings against the movement which seized wide circles of the population and found followers in nearly all of the German territories. The following table is an attempt on the basis of available sources to give a survey of a struggle which the governing powers ruthlessly waged with secular means against spiritual forces for several centuries, without, however, obtaining their goal, which was the universal eradication of their opponents. (Symbol * indicates that a copy of the original mandate is found in GCL; symbol ** indicates that the mandate is printed in *TA Württemberg,* pp. 1-10.)

1525

Jan. 18. Zürich orders unbaptized children to be baptized and expels foreign Anabaptists.

Feb. 1. Zürich forbids infant baptism in private homes.

Feb. 26. Elector John of Saxony forbids preaching and officiating at marriages, baptisms, etc., by persons not called by the church.

March 1. Zürich forbids baptism on faith on penalty of fine and exile.

April 26. St. Gall forbids baptism on faith.

Nov. 30. Grüningen (Zürich) penalizes baptism on faith with fines.

1526

March 1. Zürich threatens the death penalty for baptism on faith.

May 20. Grisons forbids all extra-church brotherhoods on penalty of corporal and capital punishment.

June 2. Basel forbids adult baptism on penalty of exile.

July 14. Basel inflicts corporal punishment and confiscation of property for attendance at Anabaptist preaching services.

Nov. 19. Zürich announces the death penalty for listening to Anabaptist sermons.

1527

March 1. The mandate of Bishop Weigand of Bamberg.

March 26. The Nürnberg edict against Hans Hut.

March 31. John of Saxony extends the decree of Feb. 26, 1525, to other districts.

July 6. Basel orders corporal punishment and confiscation for baptism of adults, omission of infant baptism, and sheltering Anabaptists.

July 27. Strasbourg prohibits the sheltering and feeding of Anabaptists.

*Aug. 14. Concordat of the cities Zürich, Bern, and St. Gall.

Aug. 20. General mandate of Ferdinand I against all Protestants.

Oct. 11. Augsburg threatens membership in an Anabaptist group with corporal and capital punishment.

Oct. 18. Cardinal Matthias Lang of Salzburg forbids Anabaptist preaching and orders raids to hunt them out.

Oct. 23. Mandate of Ferdinand I for Upper Austria.

Oct. 27. New mandate issued by Cardinal Lang.

Nov. 1. Regensburg announces severe corporal punishment for adult baptism and for sheltering Anabaptists.

Nov. 5. Dukes William and Louis of Bavaria require all Anabaptists to be seized.

Dec. 15. Margrave Philip of Baden forbids adult baptism on penalty of corporal and capital punishment.

Dec. 16. Zürich mandate sharpened.

Dec. 19. Mandate of Bishop Weigand of Bamberg renewed.

Dec. 23. The prince-bishop of Brixen orders the seizure of Anabaptist preachers.

Dec. 31. Duke George of Saxony proclaims severe punishment for adult baptism.

1528

*Mandate of Duke Christoff of Württemberg, issued at Stuttgart.

**Jan. 4. Mandate of Emperor Charles V (Speier).

Jan. 6. Margrave George of Brandenburg orders corporal and capital punishment and confiscation as a penalty for adult baptism or giving Anabaptists shelter and food.

Jan. 7. The mandate of Bern is extended to the canton.

Jan. 16. Mandate of Ferdinand for Upper Austria.

Jan. 17. John of Saxony orders those to be seized who function as preachers without ecclesiastical calling.

Jan. 22. Bern mandate sharpened.

Jan. 23. Mandate of the city of Biel (Switzerland).

**Jan. 26. Mandate of Ferdinand I for Württemberg permits execution without court procedure.

Jan. 28. Mandate of Dukes Ottheinrich and Philip of Pfalz-Neuburg.

Jan. 31. Cardinal Albrecht of Mainz forbids joining the Anabaptists on penalty of corporal punishment and confiscation, but promises pardon for those who will betray Anabaptists.

Feb. 4. Mandate of Ferdinand I for Lower Austria.

Feb. 22. The Swabian League decides to send out scouts to hunt out the Anabaptists.

*Feb. 24. Mandate of Ferdinand I for Austria.

Feb. 26. Order of regent to officials of Stuttgart, Cannstatt, etc., to watch for Anabaptists.

Feb. 27. Ferdinand I stipulates that rebaptized persons be put to death in spite of recantation.

March 5. Louis V of the Palatinate decrees the death penalty for adult baptism.

March 24. New general mandate of Ferdinand I orders death by fire for Anabaptist preachers and beheading for the penitent.

March 24. Mandate of Frankfurt.

*April 1. Ferdinand decrees a mandate for Upper Austria, promising pardon for Anabaptists who voluntarily recant, accept church penance, and betray their preachers.

April 5. Mandate of the Bishop of Speyer.

April 18. Cardinal Lang of Salzburg decrees the death penalty for Anabaptist preachers.

July 28. Decree of Ferdinand I to the local courts in Lower Austria.

Aug. 1. Mandate of Ferdinand I for Silesia.

1529

Jan. 26. Styria orders the seizure of Anabaptists and the burning of their houses.

April 1. A regulation in the reformation of Basel demands that Anabaptists join the state church or be sentenced to life imprisonment, with the death penalty for apostates.

April 7. Mandate of the Bishop of Bamberg.

**April 22. Imperial law at Speyer.

**April 23. Mandate of Emperor Charles V.

May 18. Mandate of Ferdinand I for his hereditary lands decrees death by fire for the Anabaptists.

May 24. Mandate of Ferdinand I for the Austrian possessions in Alsace.

1530

Jan. 18. Edict of banishment by Enno I of East Friesland.

*March 2. Mandate of Ferdinand I ordering the officials to carry out the prescribed punishments of Anabaptists without pity.

March 26. Zürich orders the death penalty for sheltering Anabaptists.

April 27. Sharpened mandate of Bavaria decrees death penalty even with recantation.

Sept. 27. Strasbourg renews the mandate of July 27, 1527.

Nov. 17. Basel joins the concordat of Aug. 14. 1527.

**Nov. 19. Imperial recess at Augsburg.

Nov. 23. Basel pardons the Anabaptists who recant after their first imprisonment, otherwise they are banned, and those who return are to be drowned.

1531

March 22. Mandate of Ferdinand I for Lower Austria decrees the execution of Anabaptists who do not recant and the burning of their meetinghouses.

June 20. George of Brandenburg warns against the Anabaptists, demands that they be found, and threatens a severe penalty for arguing about or defending their doctrine.

July 31. Bern threatens the death penalty for exiles who return.

Dec. Philip of Hesse deprives the Anabaptists of their hereditary possessions if they do not join the state church.

1532

May 7. Mandate of Ferdinand I for Carinthia.

June 10. Decision of the cities of Lucerne, Uri, Schwyz, Unterwalden, and Zug to abolish court procedures for Anabaptists.

1533

March 2. Bern threatens steadfast Anabaptists with life imprisonment.

1534

Feb. 12. A Dutch proclamation orders the seizure of all Anabaptist preachers.

March 3. Strasbourg orders the installation of "Täuferherren."

May 9. Sharpened edict of Ferdinand I proclaiming the death penalty for all who promote Anabaptism and severe punishment for lax judges.

**June 29. Imperial law against the Anabaptists (Kadan).

Nov. 8. Bern orders marriages to be solemnized by the pastors and participation in communion in the churches.

Dec. 23. George of Saxony orders that every Anabaptist be put to death and his property confiscated.

Dec. The council of Mühlhausen (Thuringia) forbids joining the Anabaptists.

Dec. The council of Erfurt warns against the Anabaptists and demands that they be reported.

1535

March 13. Bern threatens returning Anabaptists with beheading (instead of drowning).

April 22. In the Bishopric of Passau the sheltering of Anabaptists is prohibited.

**April 25. Imperial recess at Worms against Münster.

April 28. Strasbourg orders the compulsory baptism of infants.

May 26. Repetition of the mandate of May 24, 1529, for the Austrian possessions in Alsace.

June 11. Regensburg enforces former mandates and orders submission to church doctrine.

June 18. Ulrich of Württemberg promises recanting Anabaptists mercy, and to backsliders the death penalty.

Aug. 14. New decree of the Dukes of Bavaria.

Oct. 23. Proscription by Duke Albrecht of Prussia.

1536

April 10. Mandate of John Frederick of Saxony in part repeating the mandate of Jan. 17, 1528.

July. Ulrich of Württemberg promises pardon for recantation, exile for steadfastness, and death for preachers and apostates.

Oct. 24. Friesland threatens the death penalty for anyone who shelters Menno Simons.

1537

Dec. Philip of Hesse threatens foreign Anabaptists with exile, and the death penalty in case of return.

1538

March 23. The Strasbourg mandate of exile: upon return four weeks in prison, upon second return fingers cut off and cheeks burned, upon third return drowning.

July 18. Edict of Rostock.

Sept. 6. Bern threatens all Anabaptist leaders with death.

1539

**April 19. Anabaptists are not to be tolerated (Frankfurt).

June 13. A sharp new mandate of Ferdinand I.

Nov. 18. Mandate of Ferdinand I for Tirol orders the razing of Anabaptist meetinghouses and the quartering of troops on the villages until the Anabaptists are eradicated.

Nov. 27. Ferdinand I demands that Regensburg suppress the Anabaptists.

Dec. 2. Regensburg mandate threatens anyone joining the Anabaptists, sheltering them, or giving them food with the extreme penalty.

Dec. 10. The Bishop of Brixen offers a reward of 100 guilders for an Anabaptist preacher brought in alive and 50 for one brought in dead.

1540

**Generalkonstitution of Charles V.

April 9. Sharpened Strasbourg mandate; corporal and capital punishment upon refusal to take an oath, corporal punishment and confiscation for sheltering Anabaptists.

July 25. Edict of Heilbronn.

1541

July 24. New mandate of the Dukes of Bavaria.

1542

Dec. 21. Command of Ferdinand I to the judges not to pronounce sentence according to their conscience, but to proceed according to the mandates.

1543

Feb. 12. Duke Albrecht of Prussia orders exile.

1544

**June 10. Imperial recess at Speyer.

Aug. 31. Edict of Charles V against Menno Simons.

Sept. 8. Regulation of Kempten stipulates exile or eternal punishment for Anabaptists.

Nov. 10. Federal decree of Switzerland.

Dec. 10. Sharpened mandate of Ferdinand I for the Austrian possessions in Alsace.

1548

Jan. 25. Groningen orders the Anabaptists to leave the city on penalty of death.

May 5. Ferdinand I orders exile of Anabaptists from Austria.

June 15. Ferdinand I orders the exile of the Ana-
bapists from Hungary.

1549

April 6. Countess Anna of East Friesland forbids
sheltering Anabaptists.

1551

**Feb. 14. Imperial recess at Augsburg.
Aug. 26. Inquisition in Venice.

1553

Sept. 6. Mandate of Ferdinand I to find Anabaptist preachers.

1554

Oct. 22. Edict of Ferdinand I for Tirol against those
returning from Moravia.
Edict of Cologne announces strict execution of
imperial laws.

1555

July 10. Renewed edict of Cologne.
Aug. 1. Mandate of the Wendic cities (Lübeck,
Hamburg, Lüneburg, Wismar, Rostock, Stral-
sund, Greifswald) against Menno Simons.
Sept. 25. Imperial recess at Augsburg.

1556

April 23. Mandate of the Count Palatine Wolfgang
of Pfalz-Zweibrücken.
May 9. Mandate of Ottheinrich in Pfalz-Neuburg.

1557

July 9. Renewed order of exile from Moravia.

1558

*June 25. Duke Christoph of Württemberg decrees
severe punishment for teaching extra-church
doctrines.
Jan. 25. Ottheinrich of the Palatinate forbids Anabaptist meetings of their preachers.
Sept. 29. Mandate of Archbishop Michael Khünberg
of Salzburg.

1561

July 5. Sharpened mandate of Ferdinand I for
Austria.
Aug. 7. Mandate of the Prince-Bishop of Brixen.

1563

Oct. 2. Renewed mandate of Ferdinand I for Tirol.

1564

Feb. 16. Bern threatens Anabaptists with penalties
of property and body.

1565

Jan. 23. Duke William of Jülich orders the razing
of the meeting-houses, separatist brotherhoods,
and the punishment of the steadfast.

1566

April 28. Bern orders the church to find the Anabaptists.
May 30. Imperial recess at Augsburg (against sects
and erroneous opinions).
Sept. 16. First mandate of Ferdinand II which does
not tolerate non-Catholics.

1567

June 8. Resolution at Baden (Switzerland) stipulates drowning for those who do not recant and
apostates.
Aug. 12. Ferdinand II renews the mandate of
Ferdinand I of July 5, 1561.

1573

April 26. Expulsion of Mennonites from Danzig;
they are received in the suburbs.
July 1. Mandate of the Archbishop of Salzburg.

1578

Oct. 8. Mandate of Ferdinand II for the Tirol.
Oct. 30. Mandate of Johann Thomas, Bishop of
Brixen.
Dec. 10. Mandate of Cologne threatening Anabap-
tists with death.

1579

Jan. 8. George Frederick orders the expulsion of
the Mennonites from the duchy of Prussia.
Dec. 30. Bern renews the threat of confiscation of
goods and death.

1581

Feb. 1. Mandate of Ferdinand II for Tirol.

1582

Aug. 13. Count Edzard II of East Friesland prohibits the sale of real estate to Mennonites.

1583

Feb. 16. Edict of exile of Mennonites in the duchy
of Prussia. Severe edict of Johann Kasimir for
the Palatinate ordering the seizure of Anabaptists and the compulsory baptism of their children.

1584

Sept. 20. Duke William of Bavaria gives a reward of
40 or 50 guilders for information concerning
an Anabaptist passing through. Renewal of the
edict of exile against the Mennonites of Prussia.

1585

July 1. Mandate of Ferdinand II for the Tirol and
part of Austria.
Sept. 3. Bern threatens the Anabaptists with expulsion and with death in case of return.

1586

Nov. 12. Renewal of the edict of exile against the
Mennonites of Prussia.

1587

Feb. 28. Duke William V of Bavaria rewards the
capture of an Anabaptist with 25 to 100 guilders.

1591

Jan. Johann Kasimir of the Palatinate prohibits the
employment of Mennonites.
July 20. New mandate of Ferdinand II for Tirol.

1592

April 15. Mandate of Bern against the migration of
Anabaptists to Moravia.

1593

July 1. Archbishop Wolf Dietrich of Salzburg orders the execution of every Anabaptist without previous inquisition, by fire and sword and confiscation of property.

1595

Renewed mandate of the council of Cologne.
June 11. Basel orders confiscation of property of all expelled Mennonites.

1596

June 11. The bishop of Basel orders the expulsion of the Anabaptists in the Münstertal.

1597

Feb. 10. Bern mandate of Sept. 3, 1585, renewed.

1598

May 27. The Frisian States forbid Mennonite worship services.

1599

March 10. Bern declares confiscated Mennonite property to be a state possession.

1601

Groningen forbids Mennonite church services and excludes unbaptized children from inheritance.
March 23. Mandate of exile of Rudolf II for Lower Austria.
April 30. Cologne order of expulsion on penalty of death.

1612

Dec. 30. Zürich imposes a fine for nonattendance at state church services and orders the imprisonment of Mennonite preachers.

1613

Nov. 24. Count Enno II of East Friesland forbids Mennonite religious services on penalty of a fine of 5,000 Reichstaler and the loss of the meetinghouse.

1614

Sept. 9. Mandate of expulsion by the city of Aachen.

1619

Feb. 19. Jülich forbids Mennonite religious services.
Sept. 1. Jülich mandate of expulsion.

1620

Prohibition of meeting in Deventer on penalty of expulsion.

1622

Sept. 17. Mandate of expulsion by Ferdinand II for Moravia.
Sept. 25. Count Enno III of East Friesland orders the seizure of attendants at Mennonite service.
Sept. 28. Order of expulsion by Cardinal Franz von Dietrichstein against the Hutterian Brethren in Moravia.

1624

Feb. 11. Bern demands marriage in the state church on penalty of imprisonment.

1625

March 3. Mandate of Ferdinand II for Lower Austria.

1628

Dec. 4. Ferdinand II requires Cardinal Franz von Dietrichstein to impose fines on the Moravian nobles who do not expel the Hutterites.

1637

Zürich decides on expulsion of Anabaptists who will not join the state church and orders confiscation.
Sept. 12. Count Palatine Wolfgang Wilhelm commands the expulsion of Mennonites from Jülich, Cleves, and Berg.

1641

March 10. Ulrich II of East Friesland revokes the rights of the Mennonites, but they are restored in 1647.

1644

April 11. Bern orders the imprisonment of Anabaptists who do not join the state church.
Dec. 26. Renewal of the Bern mandates of Sept. 3, 1585, and Feb. 10, 1597.

1648

Jan. 10. Bern decides to send Anabaptists to the galleys.

1650

Nov. The diet of Brno orders the expulsion of the Anabaptists who are still in the employ of the nobles.

1652

Nov. 30. Mandate of Wolfgang Wilhelm of Jülich that induces the Mennonites to emigrate.

1658

Dec. 20. Mandate of Bern orders the expulsion of Anabaptists who do not join the state church and seizure of their preachers.

1659

Jan. 4. The appointment of a committee for Anabaptist affairs in Bern.
Aug. 9. Bern commands expulsion of the Anabaptists with whipping and branding.

1669

Feb. 1. Bern offers a reward of 30 Kr. for the arrest of an Anabaptist.

1670

Sept. 8. Bern imposes heavy fines for sheltering Anabaptists and offering them meals.

1671

Jan. 7. Bern requires an oath of allegiance in order to discover the Mennonites.
Aug. 24. Bern demands 2 or 3 hostages from localities that are lax in expelling the Mennonites.

1690

March 6. Bern disinherits children of marriages not solemnized in the state church.

1691

March 16. Bern mandate of expulsion for refusing the oath and military training.

1693

March 10. Mandate of expulsion by Bishop Johann Konrad of Basel.

April 6. Bern offers a reward of 25 to 50 thalers for the arrest of a Mennonite preacher.

May 31. Bern forbids the sale of "Täufer Testamente."

July 10. Reprint of the Bern mandate of Aug. 9, 1659.

1694

April 25. Bern forbids the employment of any who do not have papers from officials or pastors.

1695

Feb. 22. Bern declares all legal business of Mennonites as invalid, prohibits the burial of Mennonites in the cemeteries, pays 100 Reichstaler for a Mennonite preacher, threatens young women with expulsion, older women with life imprisonment if they do not join the state church.

March 28. Bern threatens to arrest all who do not take part in communion at Easter.

1699

May 19. Institution of "Täuferjäger" (Anabaptist hunters) in Bern.

1707

June 7. Bern orders that persons who do not take communion be reported to the Täuferkammer.

1709

April 26. Bern renews its prohibition against giving Mennonites a room for meeting.

Dec. 28. Bern offers 30 Kr. for reporting the return of an expelled Mennonite.

1711

Feb. 11. Bern permits the Mennonites to leave for Holland and Prussia.

Sept. 30. Bern renews its former mandates against the Mennonites.

Dec. 11. Mennonites remaining or returning to Bern are threatened with life imprisonment if they do not join the state church.

1712

Aug. 13. Louis IV orders the expulsion of Mennonites from France.

1714

May 23. Bern again threatens to send Mennonite preachers to the galleys.

1718

Aug. 29. New Bern mandate.

1720

March 12. Bern threatens Mennonites who return with whipping and branding.

1731

Feb. 5. Prince-Bishop Johann Konrad of Basel again commands the expulsion of the Mennonites.

1733

Hungarian mandate orders the Hutterian Brethren to have their newborn children baptized by Catholic priests.

1734

July 10. Bern imposes a fine of 50 to 100 Thaler for furnishing the Mennonites a room for meeting.

1743

Dec. 4. Bern dissolves the Täuferkammer, whose duty it was to excute the mandates.

1761

Jan. 8. The Hutterian Brethren in Hungary are placed under the local priests, their preachers are removed, and their books confiscated.

The dates of the mandates reveal the rapidity of the spread of the Anabaptist movement when its leaders were compelled to leave the canton of Zürich. Very soon it made itself felt in central Germany and in the Austrian Alps; for by 1527 a number of mandates had been issued threatening the severest penalty upon joining the Anabaptists. The mandate of Charles V of Jan. 4, 1528, extended the persecution to the whole empire. It was supported by further mandates by princes, bishops, and cities. With the greatest zeal a hunt was instituted for the Anabaptists, resulting in numerous deaths. At the Augsburg session of the Swabian League which decided to send a military division of 400 horsemen to scout for Anabaptists, the Bamberg chancellor Georg Tessinger reported on Feb. 28, 1528, that Bishop Weigand was having many Anabaptists executed, and it was said that Duke Wilhelm of Bavaria was at the same time having a large number (*grosse mechtige somm*) of Anabaptists put to death including two noblemen, the barons of Perwangen (Kühn, 239). When the Diet of Speyer in 1529 assented to the imperial mandate of the previous year, persecution reached its ultimate severity. Since the populace and the judges frequently felt sympathy with the persecuted, the Diet of Speyer of 1544 made it the duty of everyone to give information of Anabaptists, and the imperial recess at Augsburg of 1551 threatened judges who tempered their judgment with mercy with deposition, fines, and imprisonment.

It is amazing that the Anabaptists were able to maintain themselves under this long continued use of violence. Without the inner security which their trust in God afforded them in hours of decision, they would certainly have been defeated by this violent attack. They were, to be sure, greatly weakened numerically in this unequal battle, but contrary to the wish of their oppressors they could not be wiped out, and proved what confidence in faith is able to achieve in suffering.

It is characteristic of the attitude of former historiographers that until the 19th century only the individual aberrations were considered as typical of Anabaptism, whereas they completely ignored the serious striving for a life of discipleship as well as the dangers and suffering the Anabaptists endured. For the history of the Anabaptist-Mennonite movement and for the history of modern civilization the mandates furnish significant source material which has hitherto received little notice.

With few exceptions the mandates were directed against religious opinions. The early mandates frequently expressed a fear that ignoring the church doctrines might lead to political revolution. That argument had been used in all periods for the suppression of doctrines that deviated from the established church. For instance, in the edict passed by Dukes William and Louis of Bavaria on March 5, 1522, the statement was made in prohibiting Lutheran doctrine that "there is no more certain consequence than the destruction of all divine and human laws, order, and government; through it an irreparable, troublesome misunderstanding would rend the Christian faith, if anyone would take the liberty to explain the holy Gospels and Scriptures according to his own head and understanding, and thereby the unity of the Christian church would be destroyed." Many of the mandates against the Anabaptists likewise resulted from this fear, and therefore condemned separation, and designated the Anabaptists as a seducing sect and as tares that must be weeded out (Bern mandate 1527).

The intention of these severe measures against separatist religious groups in the Reformation period was, as it had been in the Middle Ages, to preserve the unity of the church. Therefore no exposition of Scripture was tolerated which did not agree with established church doctrines. Most of the mandates promised immunity upon return to the church and the recognition of its doctrines, above all of infant baptism, making it clear that it was not a question of civil transgression.

Questioning the doctrine of infant baptism was interpreted as a criminal offense (mandate of Jan. 4, 1528). Rejection of this doctrine and the introduction of adult baptism initiated the persecution. The change in the views of the theologians on infant baptism and adult baptism in the course of centuries can be seen in the history of the church. At the fifth council of Carthage in 401 the resolution was passed: he who does not know definitely that he has been baptized shall be baptized again (Sachsse, 37); in March 413, Roman law penalized rebaptism with death. The church council of Switzerland, in spite of the fact that religious freedom had been legally established in Switzerland since April 12, 1798, favored the compulsory baptism of Mennonite children as late as 1809, and would leave it to the children to decide when they were grown whether they wished to be baptized again (Müller, 376); the church council brought it about that in the canton of Bern Mennonite children born between 1799 and 1810 were baptized in the state church on command of the government (Müller, 382).

This course of action and this concept of the law of Rome that baptism on confession of faith should be punished by death if it was preceded by infant baptism has long been outgrown. The Mennonites had to pay enormous sacrifices before this tolerant concept, for the recognition of which they had struggled for so long, became the commonly accepted idea. The Mennonites share in the credit for the fact that a free personal conception has replaced the medieval compulsion of the state church, as it is expressed once again in the mandates listed above. Thereby one of the Mennonite requirements has been fulfilled, namely, that the power of the state should not exert a determinative influence in religious questions, nor should the church mingle in politics, and that a strict separation between church and state should be maintained, which leads to the toleration of various religious brotherhoods.

In the *Netherlands* the execution of the mandates is not clear, because in the Reformation period the supremacy of the emperor was not everywhere established there, with the consequence that mandates issued for the entire empire were not strictly enforced in some of the provinces.

There were fourteen imperial mandates that concern the Reformation in general. They were known as "Placcaten" there, and popularly as "Bloedplaccaten" (blood-mandates). The mandate of June 10, 1535, was issued expressly against Anabaptism. Those who had preached and baptized, borne the name of prophet, apostle, or bishop, and refused to recant were to be punished by fire; those who were rebaptized or harbored a rebaptized person were to be put to death, the men by beheading, and the women by drowning. The one who revealed an Anabaptist to the authorities was to receive one third of his property; the one who failed to reveal him was to be put to death.

In addition to the imperial mandates others were issued by the regent and the stadholders; these were often repetitions of the imperial mandates in shorter form. Besides these there were also decrees that were intended only for some province, like the one issued in Friesland on Dec. 7, 1542, against Menno Simons, which offered a reward of 100 guilders and the pardon for any crime to the one betraying him to the authorities. Schwarzenberg lists 18 further edicts issued against the Anabaptists in Friesland.

After the war of liberation against Spain when the governments of the northern Netherlands had become almost entirely Calvinist, mandates still continued to be issued. Most of these were issued by the provincial and city governments. Thus the Frisian States forbade all Mennonite services in the province in an edict of May 27, 1598. In Groningen a severe mandate was published in 1601, which not only prohibited Mennonite services, but also disinherited all baptized children. In the same province mandates were issued against Uko Walles (*q.v.*) and his followers on Aug. 30, 1637, and March 16, 1661. In 1722 the States of Friesland forbade all Mennonite services unless the preachers would sign a formulary of agreement with the orthodox creed. Though two mandates against Socinians, Quakers, and "Dompelaars," published by the States of Friesland in 1622 and 1687, did not directly concern the Mennonites, they were sometimes used against Mennonite preachers, as for example in 1687 in the case of Foecke Floris (*q.v.*). City edicts against the Mennonites contained similar penalties as late as the 18th century, though in general they were no longer strictly enforced.   HEGE, vDZ.

Beck, *Geschichts-Bücher;* Zieglschmid, *Chronik;* Wolkan, *Geschicht-Buch;* C. Bergmann, *Die Täuferbewegung im Kanton Zürich* (Leipzig, 1916); *TA Württemberg; TA Bayern* I; *TA Zürich;* E. Egli, *Actensammlung zur Geschichte der Zürcher Reformation* (Zürich, 1879); A. Fluri, *Beiträge z. Gesch. der bernischen Täufer* (Bern, 1912); S. Geiser, *Die Taufgesinnten-Gemeinden* (Karlsruhe, 1931); Chr. Hege, *Die Täufer in der Kurpfalz* (Frankfurt, 1908); J. Kühn, *Deutsche Reichstagsakten unter Kaiser Karl V.* VII (Leipzig, 1935); Loserth, *Anabaptismus; idem, Communismus;* Chr. Meyer, "Zur Gesch. d. Wiedert. in Oberschwaben," *Ztscht d. Hist. Vereins f. Schwaben u. Neuburg* I, 1874; Müller, *Berner Täufer;* H. Nestler, *Die Wiedertäuferbewegung in Regensburg* (Regensburg, 1926); A. Nicoladoni, *Johannes Bünderlin von Linz und die oberösterreichischen Täufergemeinden* (Berlin, 1893); Rembert, *Wiedertäufer;* T. W. Röhrich, "Zur Gesch. der strassburgischen Wiedertäufer," *Ztscht f. d. historische Theologie* XXXI (1860); C. Sachsse, *D. Balthasar Hubmaier als Theologe* (Berlin, 1914); *Theologische Studien und Kritiken* LXI (1888) 503 f.; K. Schottenloher, *Die Buchdruckertätigkeit Georg Erlingers in Bamberg* (Leipzig, 1907); E. Staehelin, *Das Buch der Basler Reformation* (Basel, 1929); J. Strickler, *Actensammlung zur Schweizerischen Reformationsgeschichte* IV (1881); P. Wappler, *Die Täuferbewegung in Thüringen* (Jena, 1913); *idem, Inquisition und Ketzerprozesse* (Leipzig, 1908); *idem, Die Stellung Kursachsens und des Landgrafen Philipp von Hessen zur Täuferbewegung* (Münster, 1910); V. A. Winter, *Geschichte der baierischen Wiedertäufer* (Munich, 1809); Richard Tester, "Die Religionsmandate des Markgrafen Philipp von Baden 1522-1533," *Ztscht für Kirchengeschichte* (1890) 307-29; *Catalogus Amst.,* 19, 20, 60, 101; W. Schreiber, *Geschichte Bayerns* I (1889) 476; *Mart. Mir.* D 35 f., 64, 104, 163-65, 802 f., 806-8; E 442 f., 466, 501, 551-53, 1102 f., 1105 f.; I. M. J. Hoog, *De Martelaren der Hervorming in Nederland* (Schiedam, 1885) 67-86; Blaupot t. C., *Friesland,* 63-70, 142 f., 312 f.; *idem, Groningen* I, 285-87; II, 32 ff., 167-84; *DB* 1870, 22; *Inv. Arch. Amst.* I, Nos. 19, 26, 35, 38, 59, 130, 136, 164, 231, 299 f., 308, 316 f., 327, 335 f., 339, 341, 366, 381, 398, 405 f., 414, 419 f., 444, 446, 448, 450 f.; *ML* III, 4-11.

Mandemaker, Cornelis Jans, a Dutch Mennonite preacher, belonging to the Flemish branch, who about 1630 was ordained as elder of the Arnhem congregation by Adriaen Cornelis, elder of Dordrecht. Mandemaker was one of the moderate Flemish and in 1632 signed the Dordrecht Confession (*q.v.*) both personally and in the name of his congregation. He lived at Arnhem on Ketelstraat and apparently was a basketweaver, from which trade he or his father derived his name. The congregation met as early as 1607. Cornelis Jans died before 1649, since in this year the congregation of Arnhem had no preacher.   vDZ.

Kühler, *Geschiedenis* II, 195; *Een Eeuw Doopsgezinde Gemeente* (Arnhem, 1952) 26-28.

Mander, Karel (Carel) **van** (or **Vermander**), was a Mennonite painter and poet. He was born in 1548 in Meulebeke in Flanders, Belgium. After a short period in Rome and Vienna he married Ludovica Buyse, painted in Kortrijk (Courtrai) and Brugge, left Flanders in 1583 for the sake of his conscience (it is not known when he joined the Anabaptists), and became the head of the Haarlem School of painting. He was the teacher of some noted Dutch painters, including Cornelis Cornelisz van Haarlem, Hendrick Vroom, and Hendrick Goltzius. He lived in Amsterdam from 1604 until his death on Sept. 11, 1606; "he was buried with the laurel wreath." Van Mander was a man of versatile gifts. In re-

sisting foreign influence he added to the development of the Dutch language. Although he was under Renaissance influence (in 1597 he published a Dutch translation of Virgil's *Bucolica* and *Georgica,* and later a commentary on the *Metamorphoses* of Ovid), he was opposed to the pagan influences in the world of art. His poetry, which is of slight literary merit, clearly portrays this conflict. His collection of poems, *De Gulden Harpe, inhoudende al de geestelycke Liedekens* (Haarlem, 1599; reprints Alkmaar, 1605; Enkhuizen, 1607; Amsterdam, 1613, 1620, 1626; Haarlem, 1627; Rotterdam, 1640, 1656; Enkhuizen, 1709), shows typical Mennonite traits. Van Mander, however, played no important role in the church. He belonged to the Old Flemish branch. His *Gulden Harpe* was used as a hymnal in some of the Old Flemish congregations. Mention should be made also of van Mander's volumes of poems, *Tafel-boecxken, inhoudende voor en nae den eten verscheyden dankseggingen en tafelredenen, in rijm gestelt* (Alkmaar, 1603), *Olyf-Bergh ofte Poëma van den laetsten Dagh* and *Bethlehem, dat is het Brood-huys,* both published in 1609 after his death. *Bethlehem* was reprinted in all the editions of the *Gulden Harpe,* from 1613.

Few of van Mander's paintings have been preserved. His fame today rests chiefly on his *Het Schilderboeck,* which he began in 1597 and published in 1604 (reprints 1764, 1936, 1946). It contains the biographies of Dutch artists, and constitutes the chief source for the study of early Dutch painting. There are also French (1884 f.) and German (1906) versions of the *Schilderboeck.*   vDZ.

Thieme-Becker, *Künstlerlexikon* XXIII (1929) 606-7; Kalff, *Gesch. der Nederl. Letterkunde* III, 387-413; R. Jacobsen, *Carel van Mander* (Rotterdam, 1906); Kühler, *Geschiedenis* II, 117-24, 130; *N.N.B.Wb.* I, 1295-98; *DB* 1900, 79-83; Blaupot t. C., *Holland* II, 210; H. E. Greve, *De Bronnen van Carel van Mander* (The Hague, 1903); Helen Noë, *Carel van Mander en Italië* (The Hague, 1954); *ML* II, 669; III, 1.

Mändl (Mendel), the name of several Hutterite brethren of different origin and descent. The first of this name is Jakob Mändl, formerly an administrator of the Lord of Liechtenstein at Nikolsburg, Moravia, who had joined the earliest Anabaptist group, there led by Jakob Wideman (*q.v.*), and was appointed Diener der Notdurft (*q.v.*) at Austerlitz in 1529. Perhaps the best-known brother of this widespread name is Hans Mändl (*q.v.*) or Klein Hänsel, of Guffidaun, Tirol, whose courageous stand at his trial and martyrdom at Innsbruck in 1561 won him abiding high regard among the Brethren. Another Mändl, apparently of no relationship to the former, is reported by the Hutterite Chronicle for 1582. He was Jakob Mändle, who, while accompanying a Hutterite missioner to Switzerland, was apprehended by the authorities and shortly thereafter drowned in the Limmat River near Baden, Aargau, Switzerland. A schoolmaster Wilhelm Mändl was active around Nikolsburg before 1621, but no further details are given. The *Klein Geschichts-Buch* reports also a brother Paul Mändelig of Czech origin, who had joined the brotherhood in Slovakia late in the 18th century and in 1783 migrated together with 56 other brothers and sisters to Vishenka (*q.v.*) in the Ukraine to be reunited with the remnants of the brotherhood. His name quite probably was later changed into Mändl or Mendel, and it is he who became the ancestor of all Mendels of today who live on Hutterite Bruderhofs in North America, or have become members of the G.C.M. or K.M.B. groups. (See **Hutterite Family Names.**) (Zieglschmid, *Chronik* and *Klein-Geschichtsbuch.*)

R.F.

Mändl (Korbmacher), **Hans,** official name Hans Reichenberger, also called "Der kleine Mändl," a Hutterite martyr, was after Blaurock (*q.v.*), Hutter (*q.v.*), and Amon (*q.v.*) the most important of the Hutterite leaders in Austria. A native of Albeins near Gufidaun, a basketmaker by trade, he was won for the Anabaptists by Offerus Griesinger (*q.v.*) and was baptized by him in the Weissenbach Valley near Pens in the summer of 1536. Shortly afterward, while he was attending a meeting with a number of recent converts in the Sarn Valley, at which Griesinger preached, he fell into the hands of a band of scouts sent out by the district judge Joseph Grebmer. He lay in chains for 26 weeks at Sterzing. Wearied by his long imprisonment and the continued attempts to convert him, he escaped from the tower. "God helped him out," say the Hutterite chronicles.

Nothing is heard of his work until 1544 in connection with his second arrest. He was staying at Freiwald near Kortsch in a congregation of about 50 persons, to whom he presented Gilg Federspiel as leader. Not long afterward he was taken prisoner; after 22 weeks in chains at Landeck he escaped "with an unspotted conscience," but four years later, in November 1548, he again fell into the hands of his adversaries, and was held in prison 11 weeks in the company of Hans Gregenhofer, a Hutterite preacher of Nikolsburg. The priests of St. Lorenzen and Brixen received orders to instruct the two prisoners, but they escaped before any attempt could be made to convert them. Their jailers were surprisingly sympathetic with them; the priests raised the complaint that the prisoners were being treated with too much lenience, that they had been told that they were in prison not because of doctrine, but for disobedience, and they were given Bibles and other books according to their wish.

The escaped prisoners may have gone to Moravia, for many Anabaptists arrived there in the next year from Landeck, Schwatz, and Petersberg. In Moravia, Mändl was made a preacher in 1551, serving with vigor until his death. His particular assignment was to travel as a missionary. Thus he appeared almost year after year in Tirol and sent one little group after another to Moravia, most of them from the Vintschgau and the Puster Valley. To be sure, some fell into the hands of scouts, but most of them reached the Canaan they longed for. All attempts to seize Mändl failed; for the people protected this emissary in spite of all the mandates. During this period of roving evangelism he wrote **three** epistles, which have been preserved: (1) To **the** brethren in the Lord who live here and there in **the** Adige; (2) To the zealous in the Oberland; and (3) To all the good of heart, who have a zeal for God and His truth, sent in 1554 by us brethren and

followers of Christ and His divine truth, we whom you know well and request that you become God-fearing.

Since the authorities did not manage to catch Mändl, who had so often been in the country and had baptized so many and was there again now, they were ordered "that they should henceforth keep a better watch on water as well as land." The government had made the discovery that the doctrines of the Anabaptists were making inroads in the Vintschgau, at mines in Scharl, at Matray, Salurn, etc., and that the Anabaptists were selling their goods and leaving the country by day and night secretly and openly by land and on the Inn. So much the more zealously did the authorities look for Mändl. On Jan. 19, 1560, they sent orders to Gufidaun, Steinach, and Axams to find out whether Mändl had property in Ableins, and whether he had a wife and child. They made the unhappy discovery that in Schlanders alone there were about 1,000 Anabaptists. So much the more pleasant was the news that Mändl had been captured near Rosenheim on Nov. 15, with Jörg Rack (*q.v.*) and Eustachius Kotter (*q.v.*).

Mändl was taken to Tirol and imprisoned in a deep tower on the Wellenberg, the other two in the Kräuterturm in Innsbruck. The priest Jörg Schiechl, "a clever and learned" man, was given the task of examining and converting them, "found that they were attached to Anabaptist doctrine and were completely obstinate therein and not open to his Christian instruction," and that more serious and severe measures were required. Mändl was cross-examined on Jan. 2, Kotter on Jan. 22, 23, and 24, Rack on Jan. 26 and 27, with and without the use of the rack. Several articles were presented to them which they were required to answer point by point. To the question whether they believed that one must obey the church, they replied that "of the present church they were not able to acknowledge that it was the true one. Only these who walk consistently in faith, doctrine, and life are true Christians." Baptism is a true sacrament. They denied that the sacrament of the altar is the true body of Christ. Concerning marriage, the wife is not obliged to obey the ungodly husband. Also it is not godly to marry for money or for fleshly lust. Their faith is not a "damned sect." They refused to recant; they thanked God that they were in the true faith and would stay in it to their end. Mändl's confession of faith has been preserved. It has the title, "Glaubensbekenntniss dreier Mannspersonen mit Namen Hans Mändl, Eustachius Kotter and Jörg Rack," and is found in the manuscripts at Pressburg, Gran, and Budapest.

The trial was prolonged because of jurisdictional disputes. Hans Mändl described his situation in a letter to his fellow prisoners. "They have put me into the tower where our dear brother Jörg Liebich lay for a long time. It is probably very deep, I have heard 6 fathoms, but it has a tiny window at the top, and when the sun comes around that it shines in a while, so that is is light. When the new year was past the authorities came with a new order." He received the articles mentioned above (a total of 46), which he had to answer. "I went to the torture as unfraid as if it had been no torture. After they had dealt with me three days, they put me back in the tower. At times I hear the worms in the wall. Bats buzz around me at night, and the mice rustle around me, but God makes everything easy for me. The second time they dealt with me one day because there were only six articles." The confession given by Mändl and his fellow prisoners coincides with the *Rechenschaft* by Peter Riedemann (*q.v.*), which appeared in print four years later. The death sentence—some of the judges evidently suffered qualms of conscience—was pronounced on June 10 and was carried out on the same day.

The chronicles record that a great multitude of people was there. On their way to execution, Dax pressed their hands, making them very happy. At the site of execution their statements and the sentence were read to the crowd. The spectators accused the judges and jury of shedding innocent blood. They explained that they had to obey the imperial commands. "O blind world," said Mändl. "Each one ought to judge according to his own heart and conscience. But you judge us according to the imperial mandates." He made a lengthy address to the witnesses; what he said was the divine truth, say the chronicles. Even when the judge said, "Hans, stop a little," he kept on talking until he was hoarse. Eustachius, "who was weak in the flesh," was first beheaded; then Jörg bowed his head to the sword; the executioner bound Hans Mändl to a ladder and threw him alive into the flames with the corpses of the other two (Codex 235, Pressburg).

Besides his epistles Mändl left four songs: "Dein Wunsch und Gab empfangen hab," 6 stanzas (*Die Lieder der Hutterischen Brüder*, 630); "O Gott in deinem Himmelsthron," 13 stanzas (of the year 1548; *op. cit.*, 631 f.); "O Vater mein, ein Kindlein dein" (*op. cit.*, 632-34); and "Gott Vater, in deinem Reich" (manuscripts 203 and 232 at Pressburg, Domkapitel). Kotter and Rack each also left three songs (manuscripts 203, 232, and 194 at Pressburg).

LOSERTH.

Beck, *Geschichts-Bücher*, 222-25; J. Loserth, *Anabaptismus;* for this article a manuscript by Beck was also used, "Hans Mändl und die Rechtsprecher des Landgerichts Sonnenburg," which coincides with the chronicles and the above book; *Mart. Mir.* D 276, E 645; Wolkan, *Lieder*, 228; Wolkan, *Geschicht-Buch;* Zieglschmid, *Chronik; ML* III, 11-13.

Mändl, Jakob, an Anabaptist martyr, was arrested with Heinrich Summer at Zurzach in Switzerland, and after five weeks of imprisonment in the town of Baden drowned there on Oct. 9, 1582. Twenty-four priests had vainly tried to convert the two men. Some of the judges hesitated to pronounce the death sentence on a matter of faith. Finally the majority voted for the death penalty, which the Brethren suffered joyfully. They admonished the great crowd of spectators to leave their sinful life and turn to God, and sang a song of praise. Their death made a deep impression on the spectators. Three songs were written on their death: "Merkt auf, ihr gliebten Gottes kindt, Die ir hie im Jammertal sindt," 42 stanzas; "Wir haben lust, Ein liedt zu singen, Könens nit vnderlon," 38 stanzas, found in Wolkan,

Lieder, 234 f.; *Die Lieder der Hutterischen Brüder* contains the first and also "Aus tiefer Not schrein wir zu dir, Herr Gott, hör unser Bitten." NEFF.

Wolkan, *Geschicht-Buch*, 428; Zieglschmid, *Chronik,* 527 ff.; Beck, *Geschichts-Bücher*, 272 f.; *Mart. Mir.* D 749, E 1057; *ML* III, 11-13.

Manelfi, Pietro, of San Vito, Italy, a Catholic priest, became a leading figure in the north Italian anti-Trinitarian "Anabaptist" movement of the late 1540's until he relapsed and exposed the sect to the Inquisition at Bologna in October 1551. Instructed in Lutheran teachings around 1540-41 at Ancona by the Capuchin Fra Girolamo Spinazola and by Bernardino Ochino, after about a year he gave up his priestly duties on the advice of another ex-Capuchin, one Master Giulio. Some three years later he left for Padua where he was installed as a Lutheran minister. He then traveled about for some time in northern Italy visiting evangelical communities.

In 1548 or 1549 in Florence Manelfi met Tiziano (*q.v.*), who had recently been expelled from the Rhaetian Leagues on account of radical doctrines he had probably acquired from Camillo Renato. Tiziano and two companions, Iseppo of Asolo and Lorenzo of Modiano, acquainted him with the "Anabaptist" doctrines; to wit, (1) infant baptism is not Scriptural, (2) Christians cannot be magistrates, (3) the sacraments are only signs, (4) the Scriptures are the sole standard of truth, (5) the Catholic Church is diabolical and its baptism is not Christian. Some months later in Ferrara a former canon Iseppo of Vicenza converted him to these beliefs, upon which Manelfi, along with four companions, was baptized by Tiziano.

Manelfi now went to Vicenza with these men and soon Christological questions were brought up in the congregation. To settle the disputed points it was decided to call a council of leaders of the sect, two from each congregation in Italy and Switzerland, plus other interested parties. Tiziano and Iseppo of Asolo recruited the delegates in northern Italy, the Rhaetian Leagues, and the Swiss cantons. Manelfi had part of the responsibility for seeking funds and providing housing for delegates. Some 60 persons, all Italians and representing around 30 places, including Basel, Chiavenna, and St. Gall, gathered at Venice in September 1550. They met for 40 days and reached nearly unanimous agreement on several points which may be summarized as follows: Jesus was a man but filled with the virtue of God; there are no angels, and there is no devil or hell; only the elect shall be raised at the Judgment Day, the souls of the wicked dying with their bodies; salvation is by election alone and not by good works or by the sacrifice of Jesus. Manelfi claimed to have been instrumental in getting these points discussed and adopted. There was agreement on the other "Anabaptist" views mentioned above, special emphasis being laid on the teaching concerning magistrates.

At the conclusion of the council several men were designated as "apostolic bishops" to bring the conciliar decisions to the member congregations. Manelfi, as one of these, traveled to Vicenza, Padua, Treviso, and Istria with Marcantonio of Asolo.

Their labors brought about a separation between the congregations willing to accept the radical doctrines and those which held to the more moderate course, a division that was already in evidence at the council when the delegates from Cittadella refused to accept its conclusions. Manelfi named Lorenzo Niccoluzzo of Modiano and Pasqualino of Asolo as other companions on these visits, especially to the Romagna, Ferrara, and Tuscany. In September 1551 Manelfi was called to Verona to explain his doctrines. At a Sunday meeting attended by around 25 persons in a secluded spot not far from the city he found acceptance for his teachings on baptism and the incarnation of Christ but the meeting broke up in disagreement when he asserted that Christ was a man, born of the seed of Joseph.

October 1551 found Manelfi and a friend en route from Vicenza to Tuscany, when near Ravenna he decided to return to the Catholic Church. He told his companion of his decision, proceeded to Bologna and turned himself over to the Inquisition. On Oct. 17 he made his first deposition, wherein, after describing the circumstances of his conversion, he revealed the story of the Venetian Council. The authorities saw the vital importance of this information and transferred the case to Rome, where Manelfi prepared three more statements. In a deposition made on Nov. 12, 1551, he added details of his work as apostolic bishop and of what he knew about Tiziano. He also discussed the beliefs of his sect, stressing its teaching on magistrates, and pointed out that the unorthodox Christological doctrines did not form a part of the Anabaptist teaching until the council's meetings. He asserted that the only authority recognized by the sect was the Bible, excepting the first two chapters of Matthew and the first two chapters and part of the third of Luke: these passages, he said, were believed to have been inserted into the Gospels by St. Jerome. On Nov. 13 Manelfi provided more information about the council and named several men who attended it. He summarized the arrangements made for accommodating delegates and described the character of the proceedings. He named some of the other men who were selected as apostolic bishops: Nicola of Treviso, Tiziano, Iseppo of Asolo, Marcantonio of Asolo, Paolo of Treviso, Iseppo of Vicenza, Hieronimo Speranza of Vicenza, Bartolomeo of Padua, Giacometto of Treviso. Manelfi also listed as many members of the sect as he could recall and added the names of a number of Lutherans in Venetia. On Nov. 14 in his final deposition he described several occasions on which he and others had narrowly escaped capture and how they had more than once effected entrance to prisons to comfort fellow believers and even to win new converts. Thus in 1549 with Benedetto of Asolo, Manelfi had bribed the guards at a prison in Venice and had persuaded Pietro Speziale of Cittadella, a Lutheran prisoner, to undergo rebaptism at their hands. In some other cases they actually helped prisoners to escape. It is evident that the sect had a well-organized underground network and communication system. Finally, after telling of his attempt to win over the Veronese community to anti-Trinitarianism, Manelfi concluded his evidence

by listing the names of several more Anabaptists in Vicenza.

About Manelfi we have no further knowledge. Presumably he was received back into the Roman Church, but his fate is of less interest than that of the people on whom he informed. The Inquisition moved swiftly. In December 1551 orders for the arrest of the persons named by Manelfi were sent to the political authorities at Padua, Vicenza, Treviso, and Asolo, and arrests and recantations followed. Many persons were forced to hide or flee the country; some went as far as Thessalonica, while a few years later some found refuge in Moravia with the Hutterites. The fate of the remainder is obscure, but this much is clear: Manelfi's treachery was substantially responsible for the exposure of the movement to destruction, even though the last symptoms of evangelical religion did not disappear from north Italy for about two decades.   DeWind.

K. Benrath, *Geschichte der Reformation in Venedig* (Halle, 1887); *idem*, "Wiedertäufer im Venetianischen um die Mitte des 16. Jahrhunderts," *Theologische Studien und Kritiken* LVIII (1885) 9-67; E. Comba, *I nostri protestanti* II (Florence, 1897); E. Comba, "Un sinodo anabattista a Venezia anno 1550," in *Rivista cristiana* XIII (1885) 21-24, 83-87; ML III, 13 f.

Mang, Hans, an Anabaptist martyr, a hatter by trade, was taken prisoner at Sonthofen in Swabia, Germany, and died in prison in 1567 after a severe imprisonment; he kept the faith to the end.

Mart. Mir. D' 344, E 703; Beck, *Geschichts-Bücher,* 252; Wolkan, *Geschicht-Buch,* 324; Zieglschmid, *Chronik,* 423; ML III, 14.

Mangold, Stephan, a weaver by trade, a member of the Anabaptist congregation of Augsburg, Germany, baptized by Jacob Gross. Soon after the Martyrs' Synod his membership in the group became known to the Augsburg City Council, and he was arrested on Sept. 17, 1527. He refused to recant, but finally agreed "to swear himself out of the city," and was consequently expelled with five other members of the congregation including the stonemason Sebold Peuthelin (Roth, 235) and the wife of the preacher Sigmund Salminger. He sought refuge in Strasbourg, where he participated in a public hearing held in the presence of the reformers Capito and Bucer with several Anabaptists from Augsburg and many "others of all sorts of trades" (Röhrich, 36). But like all the rest, he refused to desist from his faith, and was therefore probably liable to the decision of the council expelling all Anabaptists (Gerbert, 56). There is no information concerning his further course.   Hege.

C. Gerbert, *Gesch. der Strassburger Sectenbewegung* (Strasbourg, 1889); T. W. Röhrich, "Zur Geschichte der strassburgischen Wiedertäufer," in *Ztscht für historische Theologie,* 1860; Fr. Roth, *Augsburgs Ref.-Gesch.* (2d ed., Augsburg, 1901); ML III, 14.

Manheim, a town (pop. 4,246) on the Big Chiques, 10 miles northwest of Lancaster, Pa., was laid out in 1762 by Henry W. Stiegel, and named after Mannheim, Germany. The noted Stiegel glassware was manufactured here in colonial times. In 1756 over 100 of the 118 families in the surrounding township of Rapho were of German-Swiss extraction. Two Mennonites, Stauffer and Eby, made grandfather clocks here in the early 1800's. Peter Longenecker about 1763 and Abraham Hostetter in 1839, both Mennonites, built gristmills near by. The Manheim (q.v.) Mennonite Church has its meetinghouse in the town, built in 1896. A large and thickly populated Mennonite community surrounds the town.   I.D.L.

Manheim Mennonite Church (MC) was organized and its meetinghouse built in 1896 for the convenience of the members from the surrounding churches who had moved to town. After the East Chestnut Street meetinghouse in Lancaster it was the next town church built in the conference district. In 1955 the active ministers were Homer D. Bomberger, bishop, and Ira B. Huber, minister, with 170 members. The regional winter Bible school for this district is held here.   I.D.L.

Manitoba, a province of central Canada, area 219,723 sq. mi., pop. 729,744, with 44,667 Mennonites (1951), divided into 16 civil units, called municipalities, bounded on the south by Minnesota and North Dakota, on the west by Saskatchewan, and the east by Ontario; chiefly an agricultural province, wheat being the main crop. Winnipeg is the capital. Its many lakes and rivers drain to Hudson Bay. The principal rivers are the Red, the Winnipeg, and the Saskatchewan. The Red River settlement was established by Selkirk in 1811 and was the nucleus of the province when it was organized in 1870. Beginning in 1874 Mennonites from Russia settled in Manitoba on both the east and west of the Red River between Winnipeg and the United States boundary. This area still constitutes the main concentration of Mennonites in the province. The great change that has taken place is that whereas they were originally confined to the rural areas, they are found today in all the surrounding towns and cities and particularly in Winnipeg (q.v.), which had 5,751 baptized Mennonites in 1951, and over 7,000 in 1955.

The Coming of the Mennonites. The Mennonites of Manitoba are of Prusso-Russian background; they began to come to Manitoba in the 1870's as a result of the introduction of universal military conscription in Russia. The second and third waves of Mennonite immigrants came to Manitoba after World Wars I and II. By far the largest of these three was the second migration, when nearly 21,000 Mennonites came to Canada. In contrast with the immigrants settling in the prairie states of the United States in 1874-80, who were primarily from the Molotschna settlement of Russia, Prussia, and Poland, the Manitoba settlers of the same period were with a few exceptions from the Chortitza (q.v.) or Old Colony (q.v.) settlement and its daughter settlements Bergthal (q.v.) and Fürstenland (q.v.). That this group and some of the Kleine Gemeinde Mennonites chose Manitoba is not accidental. The delegates of these groups were interested in the most liberal guarantees which would safeguard the future of their traditional economic, cultural, and religious life in a foreign environment as they had known it in Russia. Most of the Mennonites settling in the United States, par-

ticularly those of Molotschna and Prussia, were willing to adjust themselves to a much greater degree to the environment of the chosen land. They had already adjusted themselves to the economic and cultural life of their Prusso-Russian homelands to a larger degree than the conservative Old Colony groups.

After delegates from the Chortitza and Molotschna settlements had repeatedly tried in vain to obtain from the Russian government a guarantee to the effect that they would continue to be exempt from any form of governmental service to the country some of the leaders listened to voices stating that the only alternative would be emigration to a country which would offer them the "Privilegium" which the Russian government had given them and was now withdrawing. Cornelius Jansen and Leonhard Sudermann promoted this idea. Many meetings took place in the Chortitza and Molotschna settlements. The Bergthal and Fürstenland Mennonites took an active part in these meetings and watched the development with apprehension. Under the influence of Cornelius Jansen, Elder Gerhard Wiebe of Bergthal became interested in emigration to North America. When a delegation of 12 was sent to North America in 1873 to investigate settlement possibilities, the Bergthal group sent Jacob Peters and Heinrich Wiebe. The Old Colony (Chortitza) itself and Fürstenland had no official representatives in the delegation. The Kleine Gemeinde was represented by David Classen and Cornelius Toews. Meanwhile John Lowe, Secretary of the Canadian Department of Agriculture, sent William Hespeler to Russia, who met Cornelius Jansen at Berdyansk on July 25, 1872, and promised the Mennonites "fullest assurance as to freedom from military service."

The Bergthal delegates, Peters and Wiebe, arrived in Berlin, Ont., in March 1873, where they were guests of Jacob Y. Shantz (q.v.), who was a great booster of Manitoba. Together they investigated Kansas, Texas, Colorado, and Nebraska, finally proceeding to the Red River Valley of Manitoba to meet the other delegates. Here the 12 delegates were introduced to the governor by Hespeler. A group of 24 persons on five wagons drove 40 miles southeast of Winnipeg to inspect the land which became known as East Reserve (q.v.). Before the group had seen all the eight townships of the East Reserve they returned to Winnipeg; most of them, being disappointed, went to the United States. Hespeler accompanied the four Bergthal and the Kleine Gemeinde delegates to the West Reserve (q.v.) located north of the boundary and west of the Red River extending toward the Pembina Mountains.

After this inspection four of the delegates proceeded to Ottawa, where they received on July 26, 1873, a statement regarding the conditions under which the Canadian government would accept and settle the Mennonites who desired to come to Manitoba. These "privileges" were briefly the following: (1) complete exemption from military service; (2) a free grant of land in Manitoba; (3) the right to conduct their own traditional schools (with German and Bible as the main subjects); (4) the privi-

Name of the Church — **Location**

MENNONITE BRETHREN

1. Alexander — Alexander
2. Arnaud — Arnaud
3. Ashern (Mission) — Ashern
4. Boissevain — Boissevain
5. Elmwood — Winnipeg
6. Elm Creek — Elm Creek
7. Gnadenthal — Gnadenthal
8. Grossweide — Grossweide
9. Holmfield — Holmfield
10. Justice — Justice
11. Kronsgart — Kronsgart
12. Domain (La Salle) — La Salle
13. Lena — Lena
14. Lindal (Mission) — Lindal
15. Manitou — Manitou
16. Marquette — Marquette
17. Morden — Morden
18. Newton Siding — Newton
19. Niverville — Niverville
20. North Kildonan — North Kildonan
21. South End — Winnipeg
22. Springstein — Springstein
23. Steinbach — Steinbach
24. Winkler — Winkler
25. Winnipegosis (Mission) — Winnipegosis
26. Gospel Light Mission — Winnipeg

GENERAL CONFERENCE MENNONITE

27. Arnaud — Arnaud
28. Altona B. — Altona
29. Arden B. — Arden
30. Gladstone B. — Gladstone
31. Graysville B. — Graysville
32. Gretna B. — Gretna
33. Halbstadt B. — Halbstadt
34. Homewood B. — Homewood
35. Kane B. — Kane
36. Lowe Farm B. — Lowe Farm
37. MacGregor B.
38. Morden B. — Morden
39. Morris B. — Morris
40. Plum Coulee B. — Plum Coulee
41. Rosenfeld B. — Rosenfeld
42. Spencer B. — Spencer
43. Steinbach B. — Steinbach
44. Winkler B. — Winkler
45. Bethel Mission — Winnipeg
46. Blumenort — Gretna
47. Carman B. — Carman
48. Elim — Grunthal
48a. General Mennonite Mission — Winnipeg
49. Glenlea — Glenlea
50. Lichtenau — Ste. Elizabeth
51. Niverville — Niverville
52. Nordheim — Winnipegosis
52a. North Kildonan — North Kildonan
53. Sargent Ave. — Winnipeg

54. Schoenfeld — Headingly
55. Schoenwiese — Winnipeg
56. Springstein — Springstein
57. Steinbach — Steinbach
58. Whitewater — Whitewater
58a. Crystal City W. — Crystal City
58b. Lena Group W. — Lena
58c. Manitou Group W. — Manitou
58d. Ninga Group W. — Ninga
58e. Rivers Group W. — Rivers

Manitoba

- • Mennonite Congregations
- ○ Towns
- ＊ Mennonite Institutions
- B. Bergthaler congregations
- W. Whitewater congregations

(See also East Reserve and West Reserve maps)

Scale of Miles

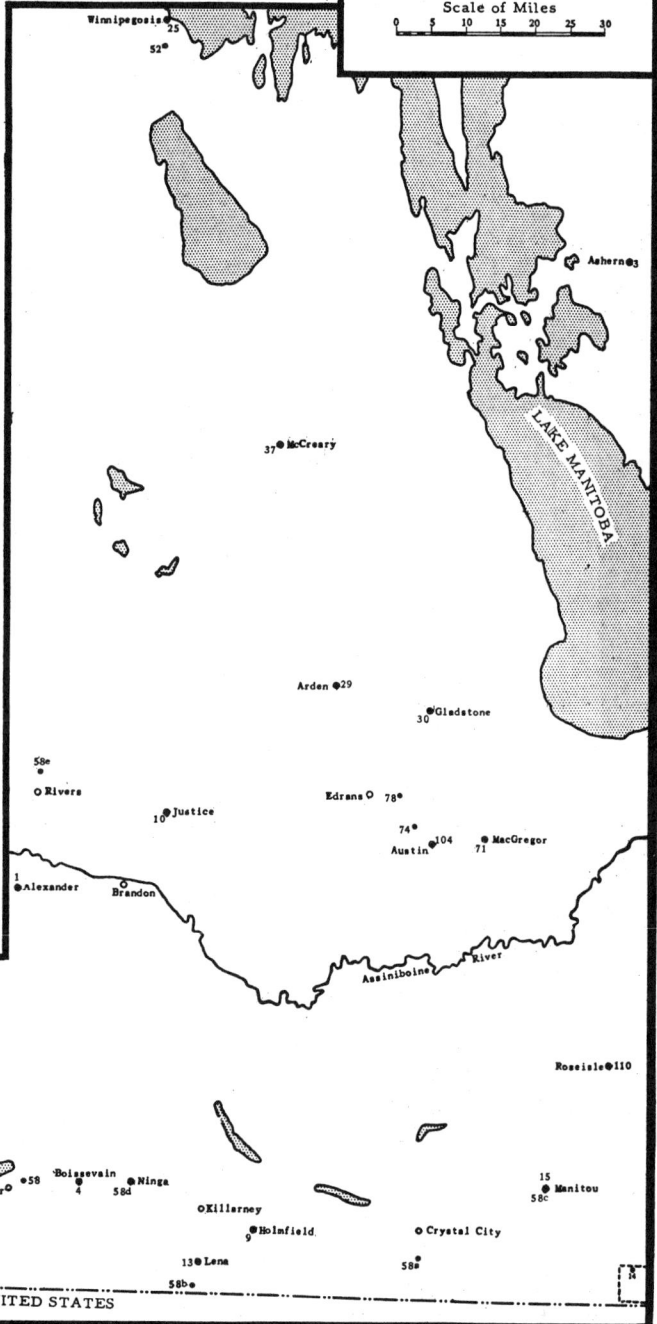

UNITED STATES

CHURCH OF GOD IN CHRIST MENNONITE
59. Greenland (Ste. Anne) 62. Sinclair (Ewart)
60. Kleefeld 63. Steinbach
61. Rosenort 64. Whitemouth

EVANGELICAL MENNONITE (KLEINE GEMEINDE)
65. Rosenort (Morris) 69. Prairie Rose
66. Blumenort 70. Riverton
67. Steinbach 71. MacGregor
68. Kleefeld 72. Winnipeg (Mission)

RUDNERWEIDE MENNONITE
73. Altona 80. Neubergthal
74. Austin 81. Plum Coulee
75. Bergfeld 82. Reinland
76. Eigenhof 83. Rosefarm
77. Glencross 84. Rosenfeld
78. Mayfield 85. Winkler
79. Morden 86. Winnipeg (Mission)

OLD COLONY MENNONITE
87. Chortitz 89. Rosenort
88. Blumenfeld 90. Reinfeld

CHORTITZ MENNONITE
91. Chortitz 95. Grunthal
92. Silberfeld 96. Weidenfeld
93. Niverville 97. Steinbach
94. Rosengart 98. Winnipeg (Mission)

EVANGELICAL MENNONITE BRETHREN
99. Steinbach 101. Christian Fellowship
100. Stuartburn Chapel (Winnipeg)
102. Winnipeg (Mission)

SOMMERFELDER MENNONITE
103. Altona 110. Roseisle
104. Austin 111. Rudnerweide
105. Inwood 112. Schoenthal
106. Kronsweide 113. Silberfeld
107. Osterwick 114. Sommerfeld
108. Plum Coulee 115. Stuartburn
109. Reinland 116. Winkler

INDEPENDENT
117. Emmanuel Mennonite Mission Church Steinbach

MENNONITE INSTITUTIONS
118. Can. Menn. Bible College (GCM) Winnipeg
119. M. B. Bible College Winnipeg
120. M. B. Collegiate Institute Winnipeg
121. Menn. Collegiate Institute (general) Gretna
123. Steinbach Bible Institute (general) Steinbach
124. Winkler Bible School (MB) Winkler
125. Elim Bible School (GCM) Altona
126. Invalid Home (EMC, KG) Steinbach
127. Concordia Hospital (GCM) Winnipeg
128. Bethesda Hospital (general) Steinbach
129. Bethel Hospital (general) Winkler
130. Bethania Home for the Aged (GCM) Winnipeg
131. Tabor Home for the Aged (MB) Morden
132. Home for the Aged (MB) Winkler
133. The Christian Press, Ltd.,
     M. B. Publishing House Winnipeg
134. D. W. Friesen & Sons, Ltd.,
     Publishing Company Altona

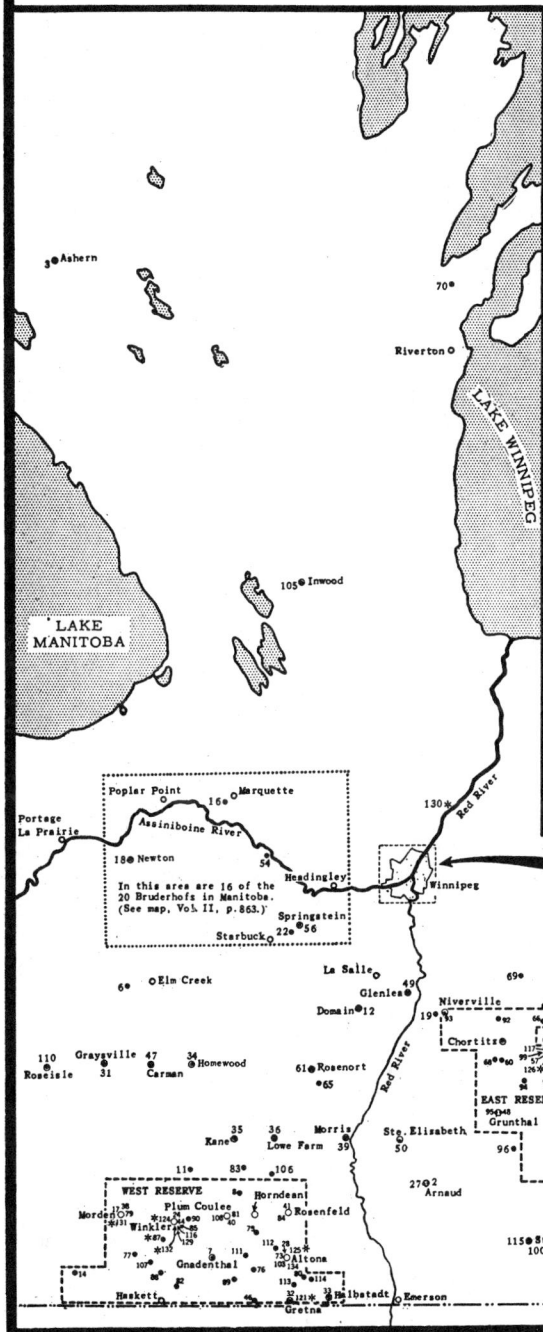

LAKE WINNIPEG

LAKE MANITOBA

3 Ashern

70

Riverton O

105 Inwood

Poplar Point
16 Marquette
Portage La Prairie
Assiniboine River
18 Newton
54
Headingley
Winnipeg

In this area are 16 of the 20 Bruderhofs in Manitoba. (See map, Vol. II, p. 863.)
Springstein
Starbuck 22 56

Whitemouth O
64

130

Red River

Enlargement of Winnipeg
72
52
20
26
21
55
5 133
120 119 86
53
98
101
127
45
118
102
48

La Salle
Glenlea 49
Niverville
Domain 12
19
Chortitz
La Salle
6 Elm Creek

69
Ste. Anne
Giroux
117 Steinbach
44 60 99 57 128 42
126 126 43 123
97 57
124

110 Graysville 47 34 Homewood
Roseisle 31 Carman
61 Rosenort
65

EAST RESERVE
95 48 Grunthal
96

35 36 Morris
Kane Lowe Farm 39
Ste. Elisabeth
50

11 83 106
WEST RESERVE Horndean
Morden 79
124 90 108 81
Winkler 85
87 116
77 107 Gnadenthal
7 111
112 28 125
108 134 Altona
76
14
113
121 33 Blbstadt
Gretna
Haskett

27 2
Arnaud

115 Stuartburn
100

lege of affirming instead of taking the oath in court; (5) a cash grant for passage from Hamburg to Ft. Garry (Winnipeg) of $30 per adult, $15 per child under eight years, and $3 per infant.

After the return of the delegation to Russia the Bergthal group, consisting of five villages, went in a body to the East Reserve of Manitoba. Elder Gerhard Wiebe reports about the choice as follows: "The congregation chose Canada because it is under the protection of the Queen of England and, therefore, we believe that the principle of nonresistance will be maintained there for a longer period of time and also that the school and the church will be under our own administration." The last point was made possible because the Canadian government set aside the East Reserve and West Reserve tracts for the Mennonites to establish compact settlements with their own schools and local administration. Although the Mennonites probably misunderstood the extent and duration of some of these "privileges," the United States could not match this offer.

The first Bergthal immigrants arrived in Winnipeg on July 31, 1874, on the steamer *International* by way of Chicago, St. Paul, and the Red River. Immigrant houses had been erected for them at the place where Niverville is located today. During 1874, 780 Bergthal Mennonites arrived, who were joined by members of the Kleine Gemeinde (*q.v.*). The largest number of Bergthal immigrants came in 1875, followed by the last group in 1876, making a total of about 500 families consisting of nearly 3,000 persons who were transplanted from Bergthal in Russia to the East Reserve in Manitoba.

The Kleine Gemeinde also came to America as a group, being the conservative wing of the Molotschna Mennonites, organized by Klaas Reimer (*q.v.*). About half of the members of the group went to Jansen (*q.v.*), Neb., and the other half to Manitoba, where they established Steinbach (*q.v.*) on the East Reserve and Rosenhof and Rosenort on the West Reserve. The total number of this group that went to Manitoba was about 800 persons. They were the only Molotschna Mennonites to settle in Manitoba.

In 1877 the East Reserve consisted of 38 villages occupied by 700 families with some 3,500 people. The majority had come from Bergthal and had been joined by a few families from the Chortitza settlement and the small Kleine Gemeinde group. Some of the original 38 villages still in existence today are Steinbach, Grünthal, Chortitz, and Schönsee. The villages are patterned after those which the Mennonites had left in Russia and received the same names. The advisers and sponsors of the settlements on the East Reserve were William Hespeler of the Department of Agriculture and the Ontario Mennonite Jacob Y. Shantz. When Lord Dufferin visited the East Reserve on Aug. 21, 1877, he praised very highly the progress made by the settlers. In Winnipeg he reported that he had seen "village after village, homestead after homestead, furnished with all conveniences and incidents of European comfort," and he had seen "cornfields already ripe for harvest and pasture populated with herds of cattle stretching away to the horizon." The Canadian government loaned the Mennonite immigrants

nearly $100,000, guaranteed by the Mennonite Aid Committee (*q.v.*) of Ontario, to which the latter added some of its own funds.

Apparently the Bergthal Mennonites reserved for themselves the East Reserve, leaving the West Reserve for the Mennonites from the Old Colony and Fürstenland. Fürstenland, the daughter colony of Chortitza, had its own elder in Johann Wiebe, but did not have its own Oberschulze. Administratively it was a part of the Chortitza settlement, at the time of migration. The leadership of the Chortitza or Old Colony settlement was more progressive. Elder Gerhard Dyck and his cominister Heinrich Epp of Chortitza had been in St. Petersburg repeatedly but they did not favor emigration to America. Elder Gerhard Dyck and Elder Gerhard Wiebe of Fürstenland, and Elder Johann Wiebe of Bergthal, were related and in contact with each other. In spite of the fact that the Chortitza settlement had no intellectual leaders and delegates as promoters of the emigration, a great number of the Mennonites from this settlement were ready to go to Canada. They attached themselves to the spiritual leadership of Johann Wiebe of Fürstenland. Some 300 families or 1,600 persons settled on the West Reserve in Manitoba during 1875. The West Reserve, consisting of 17 townships comprising an area of 612 square miles, was located west of the National border between the Red River and the Pembina Mts. and reaching to the United States border. During the summer of 1875 the first arrivals were living in immigration houses while villages were laid out and homes constructed.

Jacob Y. Shantz, who kept a list of all Mennonites passing through Ontario on their way to Manitoba (this list has been preserved in the Bethel College Historical Library), reported that 258 families came to Manitoba in 1874, and 621 families the following year, making a total of 879 families or some 5,000 persons. The total number of immigrants to Manitoba from 1874 to 1880 was (according to Shantz) 7,442 persons. D. H. Epp (*Die Chortitzer Mennoniten*) reported that 3,240 of them came from the Chortitza and Fürstenland settlements. Shantz lists a total of 799 persons from the Kleine Gemeinde. Adding these two lists we have 4,039, which leaves 3,403 as coming from the Bergthal settlement. The question left open is how many of the total of 3,240 listed by Epp came from Fürstenland and how many from Chortitza. E. K. Francis (*In Search of Utopia,* 89), who thought that all the Mennonites of the West Reserve came from Fürstenland, and for this reason refers to the Old Colony Mennonites of the West Reserve as "Fürstenländer," has evidently overlooked Johann Wiebe's statement that 1,009 persons were ready to leave Fürstenland, and also Epp's report that a total of 3,240 went to Manitoba from Chortitza and Fürstenland. Fürstenland (*q.v.*) had 154 farms. On the assumption that there were 154 families consisting of 7 members each the total is 1,078. This would mean that nearly the total population is included in Johann Wiebe's figure of 1,009, and that it was impossible that all 3,290 had come from Fürstenland. We can thus conclude that the Bergthal group was slightly larger than the Chortitza-Fürstenland group together, and that of the Chortitza-Fürstenland group about one third came from Fürstenland, while the other two thirds came from Chortitza. The term "Old Colony" Mennonites referring to the conservative group of the West Reserve is therefore appropriate.

By 1877, 25 villages had been established on the West Reserve. Most of the names are repetitions of those in use in the Chortitza or Old Colony settlement in Russia: Rosengart, Neuendorf, Blumengart, Kronsthal, Chortitza, Osterwick, Schönwiese, etc. In the two reserves together some 110 villages were established in the first decade. Some gradually disintegrated, others were transplanted to other localities. When the East and West Reserves were finally set aside "for the exclusive use of the Mennonites from Russia" by Order-in-Council of April 25, 1876, they included 25 townships or over a half million acres, which was about 6 per cent of the total area of Manitoba at that time (Francis, 62).

Adjustment to the New Environment. The Chortitza-Fürstenland people had scarcely all arrived when a shift of the Bergthal people from the East Reserve to the West Reserve set in. Around 1880 Hespeler reported that some 300 families of the East Reserve had moved to the West Reserve, leaving 400 families in the East Reserve. The reason he gave for this was that the East Reserve suffered more during the wet years since it lay lower than the West Reserve. Also, the Dominion Lands Acts made it possible for those in the East Reserve to acquire a second homestead in the West Reserve. Some of the villages established by the Bergthal people on the West Reserve were Gnadenfeld, Schönhorst, Sommerfeld, Halbstadt, Altonau, Bergfeld, and Schönthal. Already at this time departure from the traditional village settlement pattern was becoming common among the Bergthal people; a similar departure soon became apparent in other areas of life. Thus the Bergthal Mennonites of the East Reserve introduced a disrupting element into the fixed pattern of the Old Colony Mennonites of the West Reserve. Innovations introduced by Bergthal Mennonites were, however, as a rule followed and accepted by some of the Old Colony Mennonites.

The Bergthal Mennonites of the East Reserve continued as an ecclesiastical unit under the name Bergthal Mennonite Church, while the Chortitza-Fürstenland group on the West Reserve was organized as the Reinland Mennonite Church (named after Reinland municipality), which later became known as the Old Colony Mennonite Church. They had all come from the same background, but had developed slight differences which increased from year to year. Now that the large group of the Bergthal Mennonites had moved into the heart of the Old Colony Mennonite settlement the differences were accentuated by innovations and personality clashes. The Chortitza-Fürstenland group of the West Reserve became the custodian of tradition, while the newcomers from the East Reserve, the Bergthal Mennonites, became champions of progress and adjustment to the new environment. For the Old Colony Mennonites of the West Reserve the village pattern was the only way of life permissible and deviation was punishable. There was also disagreement regarding singing and the use of songbooks. Thus the Bergthal Mennonites from the East Reserve who had located in the West Reserve could not worship and have fellowship with the Old Colony group of the West Reserve. Since 1880 they had had their own elder in Johann Funk. Elder Johann Wiebe of the Reinland or Old Colony Mennonite Church of the West Reserve called a Bruderschaft (general meeting of male members) on Oct. 5, 1880, at which it was decided that those who were willing to adhere to the traditional principles and practices of the church should renew their membership, thus eliminating those who were lukewarm. The "lukewarm" members actually preferred to join the Bergthal Church of the West Reserve and did so. Thus the differences between Old Colony and Bergthal Mennonite groups were in various respects intensified.

In 1880 the provincial government intended to replace the Mennonite self-government of the Schulze and Oberschulze as based on old practices in Russia by the regular Canadian civic government. In the East Reserve the change met little opposition. The Bergthal Mennonites of the West Reserve were also ready to accept this change, particularly since the Mennonite government was in the hands of the previously established Old Colony Mennonite authority. For the Old Colony Mennonites to give up their self-government with the Schulze and Oberschulze and to yield to the Canadian municipality system meant not only forfeiting a practical and cherished tradition, but also the infiltration of practices and directives coming from a government beyond the jurisdiction of the elders and the discipline of the congregation. In spite of this opposition the municipality of Reinland was organized in 1883. The civic offices were usually filled by members of the Bergthal Church or by those expelled from the Old Colony Church. The Old Colony Mennonites approved of the *Waisenamt* (a mutual aid system centering around the care of orphans), but refused to co-operate in the *Brandordnung* (a mutual fire insurance) of the Bergthal Mennonites. Excommunication and the ban were used for those who adjusted themselves by wearing the clothing of the Canadian environment and by introducing other innovations such as bicycles.

One of the greatest problems arose from the school question. The Old Colony Mennonites of the West Reserve wanted to have their own teachers (without special preparation) teaching the children during a short term for a few years according to their own curriculum. The Kleine Gemeinde and the Bergthal Mennonites were more progressive and willing to avail themselves of government aid to improve teaching, and in a number of Mennonite villages established district schools. The first inspector of the Mennonite district schools was Jacob Friesen. H. H. Ewert (*q.v.*), principal of the Gretna Mennonite School, did much to improve the educational system and practices of his day, particularly after he was appointed government inspector. This only antagonized the conservative Old Colony element. (The problems regarding the school question are discussed in detail in the article **Old Colony Mennonites.**)

Economic Life. By 1907 the West Reserve was encircled by a network of railroads, supplied with grain elevators and business places. Winnipeg became an accessible market for butter, cheese, cream, poultry, eggs, and livestock. The tendency to abandon the traditional village and to settle on one's own land increased after 1880. First it was noticeable in the outskirts of the Reserve from Winkler south to the international boundary and from there east to Gretna. By 1898 the West Reserve had only 24 villages left. This involved changes regarding the traditional community land which had to be parceled out to those who left the village. Three-year rotation of crops gradually gave way to the Canadian practices. Great changes came about through the purchase of modern American machinery. The Mennonites are credited with the introduction of the mulberry tree, flax, and sunflowers to Manitoba. Until the turn of the century the Mennonites of Manitoba and Ontario had a kind of monopoly on Canada's flax production. Grain was brought along in bags by the immigrants, especially wheat. But this hard winter wheat, which had made Kansas famous, proved to be a failure in Manitoba. Spring wheat, oats, and barley became staple crops. Vegetables and fruits were cultivated. Jacob Y. Shantz helped the Mennonites along these lines. Mennonites made use of milling facilities wherever they were provided commercially by outsiders, and built their own mills only when such services were not available. Windmills were located in a number of villages. Feed mills were found in Blumenort, Altona, and Gretna. Steinbach of the East Reserve also had its own mills. Cheese making became important among the Mennonites, who generally operated on a co-operative basis. The early Mennonite cheese factory disappeared when milk and cream could be sent to the market in Winnipeg.

On the favorable soil of the West Reserve wheat and cash crop farming soon became prevalent, while most of the East Reserve with its inferior soil was for many decades limited to dairy farming. A middle-sized farm was 100 acres. In the East Reserve the tendency was to increase the size. The West Reserve soon began to suffer from overpopulation, partly because the young people were kept close to home, until an opportunity to found daughter colonies arose. Because of the rapid increase of the Mennonite population it became necessary to subdivide standard-size homesteads. This was handled through the Waisenamt (*q.v.*). The Mennonites had not immediately occupied all the land of the two reserves. Later the ban against non-Mennonite settlers was lifted and non-Mennonite population moved into the unoccupied areas of the reserves. On the other hand the Mennonites later extended their own landholdings in other directions beyond the limits of the reserves. The Old Colony Mennonites took the initiative in creating a new reserve in the Rosthern-Hague district of Saskatchewan, where by 1897, 200 Mennonite families from Manitoba were residing in villages just as they had been in Manitoba. Another settlement was made in Swift Current, Sask., in 1904, also by the Old Colony Mennonites. Other settlements were established in Didsbury, Alberta, Drake, Sask., and other places. According

to the church record of the Old Colony Mennonite Church (J. P. Wall) the total number of Old Colony Mennonites in Canada in 1912 was 8,166 souls, of whom 4,358 lived in Saskatchewan. This shows that more than half of the Old Colony Mennonites were at that time located in Saskatchewan. In 1911 the number of the Mennonites in Manitoba was 14,498 (according to the census given by Dawson) and for Saskatchewan 6,542, which makes a total of 21,040. The Old Colony group was thus about 40 per cent of the entire Mennonite population.

Religious Life. The religious and cultural life of the Manitoba Mennonites was marked by very conservative attitudes. With the exception of the small Kleine Gemeinde group, they were all of the same Old Colony background. The Bergthal group had been established as a daughter colony only a few decades earlier in Russia. The Fürstenland daughter settlement had been established only about ten years before the departure to Canada. Although it furnished in Johann Wiebe the elder for the West Reserve, it was only a small segment of the total. The real differences in religious and cultural views originated in Canada and were possibly to a large extent due to personalities. The immigrants coming from the Bergthal settlement in Russia settled under the leadership of Gerhard Wiebe on the East Reserve. This was the nucleus for the Bergthal Mennonite Church. The Old Colony or Chortitza and Fürstenland Mennonites settled on the West Reserve, establishing the Reinland Mennonite Church, better known since as the Old Colony Mennonites (*q.v.*), under the leadership of Elder Johann Wiebe from Fürstenland. These two groups were apparently getting along well with each other. Through the infiltration of the Bergthal element on the West Reserve differences and difficulties arose, most of them relating to the retention of the religious and socioeconomic practices of the old country or sacrificing them for new practices of the Canadian environment. The question arose whether a member of the church could withdraw from the village and settle on his quarter of land, and exchange furniture, implements, clothing, etc., which he had brought along, for those in use in Manitoba. Of great significance was the matter of accepting government-sponsored schools and government administration of the settlements. Gradually, however, the Schulze and Oberschulze were replaced by the reeve, and Mennonite church schools by district schools. All this was alarming for the Mennonites, who remembered that they had come to Manitoba not only because of their objection to a government-prescribed service but also out of opposition to the Russianization program and the introduction of Russian into their schools. Now they faced the same problem in the Canadian environment in spite of the guarantees they had received.

In 1880 Elder Johann Wiebe through a brotherhood meeting reorganized the Reinland Mennonite Church of the West Reserve, making adherence to the old principles and practices a test of church membership. Many of the Old Colony Mennonites at this time joined the Bergthal group of the West Reserve, which had moved in from the East Reserve and had organized under the leadership of Elder

Gerhard Wiebe of the East Reserve an independent church with Johann Funk as elder. However, Johann Funk was too progressive for some of the Bergthal Mennonites of the West Reserve. In 1890 most of the group rejected his leadership and organized what became known as the Sommerfeld Church (*q.v.*), since its elder, Abraham Dörksen, lived in the village of Sommerfeld. Elder Johann Funk and his following continued under the name Bergthal Mennonite Church (*q.v.*). In the East Reserve the Bergthal church became known as the Chortitz Mennonite Church (*q.v.*), since its elder resided in the village of Chortitz. Thus by the turn of the century the descendants of the original Chortitza settlement in Russia had divided into the large Old Colony Mennonite Church of the West Reserve, with a less conservative Sommerfeld Church and a rather progressive Bergthal Mennonite Church near by, and a Chortitz Mennonite Church of the East Reserve which was spiritually and culturally most closely related to the Sommerfeld group. In addition to this there was the Kleine Gemeinde of Molotschna background represented in both East and West Reserve as a minority group. Although conservative in comparison to the Molotschna Mennonites in their attitude toward education and other questions which confronted the Manitoba Mennonites, they could be compared with the progressive Bergthal group led by Johann Funk.

In addition to the divisions caused by internal differences, new divisions occurred also because of the infiltration of new religious ideas and practices brought in from the outside. In 1882 representatives of the Church of God in Christ, Mennonite (Holdeman group), from Kansas to Ohio caused a break among the Kleine Gemeinde of the East Reserve which led to the organization of a Holdeman Church in the East Reserve which was joined by the Kleine Gemeinde elder and nearly half of the total group. By 1890 the Mennonite Brethren, who originated in Russia in 1860, had started a fellowship in the West Reserve at Winkler which became the nucleus of the various Mennonite Brethren congregations in Manitoba. The Evangelical Mennonite Brethren, originating at Henderson, Neb., and Mt. Lake, Minn., won followers at Steinbach among the Kleine Gemeinde and others, which led to the organization of a congregation of the group there at the turn of the century. In 1937 the Rudnerweide Mennonite Church (*q.v.*) was organized by Wilhelm H. Falk through the separation of a group from the Sommerfeld Mennonite Church, which was more evangelistic and more progressive. The migration of the most conservative element from Manitoba to Mexico and Paraguay, after World War I, and the coming of Mennonite immigrants from Russia after World Wars I and II, greatly affected and changed the spiritual and cultural life of the Mennonites in Manitoba.

The Bergthal Mennonite Church, which originated under the leadership of Johann Funk in 1890, spearheaded educational progress and helped H. H. Ewert (*q.v.*) in the establishment of the Mennonite Collegiate Institute (*q.v.*) at Gretna and the organization of the Canadian Mennonite Conference (*q.v.*) in 1902, which most of the non-M.B. immigrants coming to Canada after World War I and World War II joined. Most of the congregations of this conference are members of the General Conference Mennonite Church (*q.v.*), but the large Bergthal Church with almost 4,000 baptized members, has remained outside the General Conference thus far.

The following were the elders of the various groups. After the turn of the century Johann Wiebe, the leader of the Old Colony Mennonite Church, who was assisted by 12 ministers, was succeeded by Elder Johann Friesen, later in Mexico by Isaac M. Dyck. Jacob Froese became elder of the Old Colony Mennonites remaining in Manitoba. Elder Abraham Dörksen of the Sommerfeld Mennonite Church was assisted by 11 ministers. Elder David Stoess of the Chortitz Mennonite Church of the East Reserve, who had succeeded Elder Gerhard Wiebe, was assisted by seven ministers. The Kleine Gemeinde had Abraham Dyck on the East Reserve and Jakob Kroeker of Rosenort as elders, each assisted by five ministers. Peter Toews, a former elder of the Kleine Gemeinde, was elder of the Church of God in Christ, Mennonite. David Dyck was elder of the Mennonite Brethren group at Winkler. Johann Funk, elder of the Bergthal Mennonite Church, was succeeded by Jacob Hoeppner in 1903. He was succeeded by David Schultz in 1926, who since 1953 has had a coelder in Jacob M. Pauls.

Migration and Population Shifts. During World War I the school question and the resistance of the Old Colony Mennonites and other conservative groups of Manitoba to adjustment to the Canadian environment came to a showdown. The School Attendance Act passed in 1916 did not prohibit the attending of private schools, provided they conformed with the standard set up by the school administration, but once a private school was condemned, a public school was established with compulsory attendance. C. B. Sissons summarized the situation as follows: "When the war spirit got hold of the West, and to poor equipment were added the dual sins of pacifism and German speech, . . . recourse was had to compulsion." It was at this time of "persecution" that the thought of a migration into another country was born. Repeated delegations sent to the provincial and dominion Canadian governments were without success. The government was determined to break the resistance of the conservative Mennonites. Public schools were established in all Old Colony districts, and teachers were hired to hoist the flag each morning and lower it again each evening, but not a single child attended the schools. Thereupon attendance at public schools was made compulsory and punishment was administered when children did not attend the school. When repeated petitions to give the Mennonites the right to conduct their own schools were of no avail, a decision was reached to look for another country.

In 1919 two delegations went to South America, visiting Brazil, Argentina, and Uruguay. Even Alabama and Mississippi were considered as places to settle. In 1920 the Old Colony Mennonites sent a delegation to Mexico. A second one followed in January 1921. They obtained a "Privilegium" very similar to that which they had once received from the Canadian government, which they presented to their constituency in Canada. On March 1, 1922, the first train left Plum Coulee, Man., followed by three from Haskett, Man., on March 2-11. Two more trains left Swift Current. All of these settled near Cuauhtemoc, Chihuahua, Mexico. The Old Colony Mennonites from Hague, Sask., settled in Durango, Mexico. By 1926, of the 4,926 Old Colony Mennonites of Manitoba 3,340 had moved to Cuauhtemoc. Only a few more than 1,000 of the approximately 3,250 Old Colony Mennonites of Swift Current, Sask., and only 946 of the 3,932 of the Hague, Sask., Old Colony Mennonites moved to Mexico. This indicates that the willingness to migrate to Mexico was much weaker among the Old Colony Mennonites of Saskatchewan than in Manitoba where about three fourths of them participated in the migration. A smaller group of the Sommerfeld Mennonites of the West Reserve under the leadership of Abraham Derksen settled in Mexico in 1922 at Santa Clara, not far from the Old Colony Mennonites. During 1926-27, 1,744 Sommerfeld and Chortitz Mennonites from Manitoba went to the Chaco, Paraguay, where they established the Menno settlement, the first one of a number of settlements established by Mennonites in that country, the later settlements being made by Mennonites from Russia. After World War II Chortitz and Sommerfeld Mennonites from Manitoba also went to Paraguay, establishing a settlement near Villarrica in the eastern part of the country. Of the 1,650 persons who first settled there about one third returned to Manitoba. After World War II, Old Colony Mennonites from Manitoba, Mexico, and Saskatchewan also established a settlement in the Peace River Valley of Alberta, near Fort Vermilion. Kleine Gemeinde Mennonites from Manitoba established a settlement near the Old Colony settlement at Cuauhtemoc in 1948, called Quellenkolonie (q.v.).

Thus the most conservative element of the North American Mennonites located in Manitoba and Saskatchewan became trail blazers of Mennonite settlement in a wholly new cultural environment. They sought out an environment to which it would be least tempting to adjust themselves. This was Latin America. Probably 5,000 to 6,000 Mennonites left Manitoba after World Wars I and II for the new settlements. In the case of the Old Colony Mennonites a minority was left in Manitoba without leadership. In the case of the Sommerfeld and Chortitz Mennonites the majority in Manitoba stayed, which is also the case with the Kleine Gemeinde. The most conservative element of Mennonites was thus removed from Manitoba. This in itself was significant for the later development of the Mennonites of that province. However, the most important fact was that an almost equal number of Mennonites from Russia settled in Manitoba after World Wars I and II. Thus far Mennonites of Manitoba had been rural; many believed that to give up rural life for city life would mean to give up the Mennonite faith. With the coming of the Mennonites from Russia after World War I and the depression this was completely altered. Of the 2,000 Mennonite families which came to Manitoba in 1922-30 about four fifths settled on farms, some of which had been left behind by the conservative element moving to

South America and Mexico, while about one fifth located in Winnipeg. After World War II about 3,000 Mennonites from Russia came to Manitoba, mainly to Winnipeg. In the city the Mennonites are employed as laborers and have established businesses, factories, etc. A number of Mennonite schools and congregations have been established in Winnipeg, and the present Mennonite population in the city makes it, next to Amsterdam, the largest Mennonite city population in the world.

In the rural areas Manitoba has been significant for the spread of the co-operative movement. By 1946 the Federation of Southern Manitoba Co-operatives, with 26 affiliated organizations, covered territory with a total population of about 20,000, which was almost exclusively Mennonite. The co-operative tended to replace the old institution of mutual aid which had served the Mennonites in decades past. Altona in the West Reserve became the center of numerous co-operative enterprises. In 1944 the Co-operative Vegetable Oils Limited was organized by some 800 farmers and businessmen in the Altona area. Less successful were the co-operatives on the East Reserve, where private enterprise prevailed.

CANADIAN MENNONITE CONFERENCE CHURCHES IN MANITOBA, 1954-55

Churches	Members	Total Population	Families	Ministers	Elders	Places of Worship
Arnaud	124	244	45	3	0	1
Bergthal	2,089	3,390	944	24	2	20
Bethel	269	384	120	3	2	1
Blumenort	368	684	146	9	2	5
Elim	250	472	111	2	1	1
Glenlea	55	87	19	2	0	1
Lichtenau	132	201	55	3	0	1
Niverville	139	366	62	1	0	1
Nordheim	117	195	41	2	1	1
Schönfeld	154	253	61	4	1	1
Schönweise (Winnipeg)	1,477	2,249	478	7	1	8
Springstein	194	354	83	1	1	1
Steinbach	208	354	86	5	0	1
Whitewater	568	1,103	230	12	1	6
Winnipeg	224	325	80	6	1	0
St. Vital	59	100	21	1	0	1
Scattered	30	50	15	1	0	1
	6,457	10,811	2,597	86	13	51

All except Bergthal are members of the General Conference Mennonite Church. The Bergthal Mennonite Church worships at the following places: Morden, Winkler, Plum Coulee, Rosenfeld, Altona, Gretna, Halbstadt, Morris, Lowe Farm, Kane, Homewood, Carman, Graysville, St. Vital, MacGregor, Gladstone, Arden, Neu Bergthal, Steinbach, and Spencer.

(Statistics are based on reports by B. Ewert, "Die Mennoniten in Manitoba," *Mennonitisches Jahrbuch*, 1951; reports of 1955; *Jahrbuch der Konferenz der Mennoniten in Canada* 1955; and other records.)

MANITOBA MENNONITE CONFERENCES AND CHURCHES

Church	Year Founded	Location
Chortitza Mennonite Church	1874	East Reserve
Kleine Gemeinde Mennonite Church	1874	East and West Reserves
Old Colony Mennonite Church (Reinland)	1875	West Reserve
Bergthal Mennonite Church	1880	West Reserve
Church of God in Christ, Mennonite	1882	East and West Reserves
Sommerfeld Mennonite Church	1890	West Reserve
Mennonite Brethren	1890	East and West Reserves
Evangelical Mennonite Brethren	1894	East Reserve
Canadian Mennonite Conference	1902	East and West Reserves
Rudnerweide Mennonite Church	1937	West Reserve
Hutterian Brethren	1918	West of Winnipeg

STATISTICS OF MANITOBA MENNONITE CHURCHES, 1950

Name	Location	Baptized Members	Total Population	Families	Ministers	Congregations
Chortitza	East Reserve	1,684	3,516	800	12	6
Kleine Gemeinde (EM)	Steinbach and Morris	1,920	3,800	1,000	20	6
Old Colony	West Reserve	638	1,465	360	5	4
Bergthal	West and East Reserve	2,089	3,390	944	24	20
Church of God in Christ	East Reserve and Morris	773	1,500	350	12	4
Sommerfeld	Manitoba	4,120	7,944	1,900	16	10
Mennonite Brethren	East and West Reserve	3,512	7,100	1,750	80	30
Evangelical M. B.	Steinbach, Stuartburn, Winnipeg	400	800	200	3	2
Canadian Mennonite Conf. (including Bergthal)	East and West Reserves	6,457	10,811	2,597	98	43
Rudnerweide	Rudnerweide	1,716	3,400	853	24	20
Emanuel Mission	Steinbach	300	600	590		
Hutterian Brethren	West of Winnipeg		1,990			18

The flow of Mennonites from the country to the city increased rapidly with the coming of the Mennonites from Russia after World War I. During the days of depression many of the daughters went to the city to do housework. They had to make a living and to pay off debts for their transportation from Russia to Canada. One of the settlements of Mennonites, North Kildonan on the outskirts of Winnipeg, has grown to a modern suburb with numerous enterprises as well as two Mennonite churches. Winnipeg has a factory established by J. Klassen, the C. A. DeFehr and Sons' Importing and Sales Company, and numerous other enterprises. There is also the Concordia 50-bed hospital, and the Bethania Old People's Home on the bank of the Red River operated by the Mennonite Benevolent Society. Winnipeg is also the home of the Mennonite Brethren Bible College, and the Canadian Mennonite Bible College, established in 1947 and 1948 respectively. The Old Colony Mennonites were not permitted to go to Winnipeg, and if they did they were considered to have left the fold. Today Winnipeg with its 7,000 Mennonites has a larger Mennonite population than any other North American city. According to the census of Canada the Mennonite population of Winnipeg was 114 in 1921,

909 in 1931, 1,285 in 1941, and 5,751 in 1951. Other towns with a predominant Mennonite population in the East Reserve are Steinbach, Niverville, Grünthal; and in the West Reserve Winkler, Altona, Gretna, Plum Coulee, Rosenfeld, Lowe Farm.

During World War II approximately 2,453 Manitoba Mennonites served their country in Alternative Service as conscientious objectors. Almost an equal number served in the regular army. In addition to this a great number of men were exempted from service because they were farmers or teachers. During this time all the Mennonite congregations in Manitoba organized the Mennonite Peace Committee. The elders of the Sommerfeld, Chortitz, Bergthal, Rudnerweide, Kleine Gemeinde, Church of God in Christ Mennonite, E.M.B., and Old Colony Mennonites organized a Council. The executive committee of this Council had authority to negotiate with the government pertaining to all CO matters.

During World War I the Hutterites in the United States living on Bruderhofs underwent some hardships which led to their migration to Canada. Of the 17 Bruderhofs of South Dakota, 15 went to Canada in 1918-25. In 1955 there were 23 Bruderhofs in Manitoba located west of Winnipeg, named as follows: Blumengart, Sturgeon Creek, Barrickman,

Maxwell, Iberville, Rosedale, James Valley, Riverdale, Waldheim, Bon Homme, Milltown, Huron, Poplar Point, Elm River, Sunnyside, New Rosedale, Lakeside, Riverside, Rock Lake, Springfield, Bloomfield, Crystal Spring, and Oak Bluff. The total population of these 23 Bruderhofs was 2,600 in 1955.

C.K.

Cornelius Krahn, "Adventure in Conviction. Russia, Canada, Mexico" (manuscript); E. K. Francis, *In Search of Utopia. The Mennonites in Manitoba* (Altona, 1955); E. H. Correll, "Mennonite Immigration into Manitoba," *MQR* XI (July and October 1937); and Carl Dawson, *Group Settlement. Ethnic Communities in Western Canada* (Toronto, 1936); E. K. Francis, "Mennonite Contributions to Canada's Middle West," *Menn. Life* IV (April 1949); Cornelius Krahn, ed., *From the Steppes to the Prairies* (Newton, 1949); Heinz Lehmann, *Das Deutschtum in Westkanada* (Berlin, 1939); George Leibbrandt, "Emigration of the German Mennonites from Russia to the United States and Canada in 1873-1888," *MQR* VI f. (October 1932 and January 1933); Paul J. Schäfer, *Die Mennoniten in Canada* (Altona, 1947); Walter Schmiedehaus, *Ein feste Burg ist unser Gott* (Cuauhtemoc, 1948); J. J. Thiessen, "Present Mennonite Immigration to Canada," *Menn. Life* IV (July 1949); Paul J. Schaefer, *Heinrich H. Ewert. Lehrer, Erzieher und Prediger der Mennoniten* (Gretna, 1945); C. Henry Smith, *The Coming of the Russian Mennonites* (Berne, 1927); J. G. Rempel, *Fünfzig Jahre Konferenzbestrebungen 1902-1952* (Steinbach, 2 volumes); *Erfahrungen der Mennoniten in Canada während des zweiten Weltkrieges 1939-1945;* Benjamin Ewert, "Die Mennoniten in Manitoba," *Menn. Jahrbuch,* 1951; Don E. Totten, "Agriculture of Manitoba Mennonites," *Menn. Life* IV (July 1949) 24; J. N. Hoeppner, "Early Days in Manitoba," *Menn. Life* VI (April 1951) 11; P. J. Schaefer, "Heinrich H. Ewert—Educator of Kansas and Manitoba," *Menn. Life* III (October 1948) 18; J. J. Siemens, "Sunflower Rebuilds Community," *Menn. Life* IV (July 1949) 28; J. W. Fretz, "The Renaissance of a Rural Community," *Menn. Life* I (January 1946) 14; Gerhard Wiebe, *Ursachen und Geschichte der Auswanderung der Mennoniten aus Russland nach Amerika* (Winnipeg); *Jahrbuch der Konferenz der Mennoniten in Canada 1955* (Didsbury); David Janzen, "A Sociological Study of the Mennonites of Winnipeg" (manuscript); D. H. Epp, *Die Chortitzer Mennoniten* (Chortitz, Russia); H. H. Ewert, "Die Mennoniten in Manitoba," *Bundesbote Kalender,* 1903, 31-35; J. F. Galbraith, *The Mennonites in Manitoba, 1875-1900* (Manitoba, 1900); Karl Götz, "Bei den russlanddeutschen Mennoniten in Manitoba, Kanada," *Mitteilungen des Sippenverbandes der Danziger Mennoniten-Familien . . .* 1939, 28-31; *Journals of the House of Commons of the Dominion of Canada . . . Session 1886,* printed by order of the House of Commons; Klaas Peters *Die Bergthaler Mennoniten & deren Auswanderung aus Ruszland & Einwanderung in Manitoba* (Hillsboro); W. Rempel, "Die Mennoniten in Süd-Manitoba," *Bundesbote Kalender,* 1898, 36; J. Shantz, *Narrative of a Journey to Manitoba, Together with an Abstract of the Dominion Lands Act and an Extract from the Government Pamphlet on Manitoba* (Ottawa, 1873); C. B. Sissons, *Bi-lingual Schools in Canada* (London, 1917); *Sixty Years of Progress. Diamond Jubilee, 1884-1944* (Altona, 1944); Walter Quiring, *Russlanddeutsche suchen eine Heimat* (Stuttgart, 1938); *Waisenverordnung der Reinländer Mennoniten Gemeinden . . .;* J. B. Hedges, *Building the Canadian West: The Land Colonization Policies of the Canadian Pacific Railway* (New York, 1939); S. C. Yoder, *For Conscience Sake* (Goshen, 1940); Johann P. Wall, "Diary, 1919"; Johann P. Wall, "Statistics of the Old Colony Mennonites from 1910 ff." (both microfilm, BeCHL); "Old Colony Mennonites and Hutterites," Record Groups No. 85; Records of the Bureau of Immigration . . . , Files 54623/130 and 54623/13OH, April 21, 1919-Nov. 10, 1931, The National Archives of the U.S., 1934 (microfilm, BeCHL); David Harder, "Von Kanada nach Mexiko" (manuscript, BeCHL); various yearbooks and conference reports; Victor Peters, "Manitoba Roundabout, a Pictorial Survey," *Menn. Life* XI (July 1956) 104-9; *ML* III, 14-16.

Manitoba Conference *of the Mennonite Brethren Church,* called in the Act of Incorporation "The Mennonite Brethren Church of Manitoba." The M.B. Church of Manitoba had its beginning on May 30, 1886, when Henry Voth baptized two couples. The place of beginning was Burwalde, near Winkler, where a little chapel was constructed. In 1898 this chapel was moved to Winkler. Then other churches sprang up around Winkler. A large influx of new immigrants arrived in 1922-25, most of them settling in or near Winnipeg. Today the M.B. Church is spread over the southern portion of the province, with a membership of 3,462 in 22 congregations.

On April 5, 1940, it was decided to incorporate the Mennonite Brethren Church of Manitoba, which was done. "The objects of the corporation are to promote, engage in and carry on the Christian Religion and Christian Worship and religious education according to the religious belief of the members of the corporation." The doctrines of the church are the fundamental teachings of the Bible about God the Father, Jesus Christ, and the Holy Spirit, as given in the *Glaubensbekenntnis* of the M.B. Church. At present there are 22 local churches in Manitoba, including five missions. The following institutions are owned by the Manitoba M.B. Church: one Bible school, one high school, one old folks' home, five mission stations, one Bible college (owned and supported by the whole M.B. Church of Canada). The Conference met twice annually until 1942, since then only once annually.

The M.B. Church of Manitoba is a member of the Northern District (Canadian) Conference, which holds its meetings once annually in one of the provinces of British Columbia, Alberta, North Saskatchewan, South Saskatchewan, Manitoba, and Ontario. The Northern District Conference is a member of the General Conference of the M.B. Church of North America.

Outstanding personalities of the Manitoba Conference have been H. S. Voth, A. H. Unruh, J. G. Wiens, H. H. Janzen, D. D. Derksen, and G. D. Pries.

H.H.R.

Manitoba Mennonite Mutual *Insurance Company* was established at Steinbach, Man. (its present head office), in 1874, and incorporated in 1940. It serves all branches of Mennonites in Manitoba, and in 1955 had 2,800 policy holders with $18,000,000 of property covered.

H.S.B.

Manitoba Mennonite settlement, the largest Old Colony Mennonite settlement in Mexico, located on the outskirts of Cuauhtemoc, Chihuahua, 70 miles west of the city of Chihuahua, was established in 1922 by Old Colony Mennonites from Manitoba, Can. The land consists of 23,000 acres and was purchased from Zuloaga in the San Antonio Valley in 1921 for $8.25 per acre by two companies founded for this purpose (Heide-Neufeld und Reinländer Waisenamt and Rempel-Wall und Reinländer Waisenamt). Charles Newman and J. F. Wiebe were the mediators in the purchase. The settlement occupies a strip about 75 miles long (north-south) and several miles wide.

The Manitoba Mennonite settlement forms a civic and ecclesiastical entity. The civic leader is the Oberschulze (*q.v.*) and the spiritual leader is the elder (Isaac M. Dyck). The affairs of this settlement are handled independently of the Swift Current Mennonite settlement (*q.v.*) located to the north, and the Durango Mennonite settlement (*q.v.*) located in the neighboring state. In 1926 the Manitoba settlement consisted of 3,340 persons; in 1949 the number had grown to 7,706, and in 1953 the number was 8,768. The settlement consists of some 45 villages stretching from Cuauhtemoc to Rubio. Very few of the settlers live in Cuauhtemoc (*q.v.*). (See also **Old Colony** Mennonites, **Mexico**, and **Cuauhtemoc** Mennonite Settlement.) C.K.

Manitoba School Commission *(Schulkommission)* was organized in 1913 through the initiative of H. H. Ewert for the purpose of encouraging the instruction of German and Bible in all Mennonite district and parochial schools. It was composed of representatives of the Sommerfeld and Bergthal Mennonites and the Mennonite Brethren. The Commission reported annually to its constituencies. A special task was the negotiation with the authorities when the Mennonites were in danger of losing their privilege to continue their own schools in the German language. When the Commission failed in its efforts along these lines it was discontinued. A newly created Mennonitische Schulvorsteher-Konvention assumed the other tasks of the Commission. C.K.

Paul J. Schaeffer, *Heinrich H. Ewert* (n.p., 1945) 85 ff.

Manitou (Man.) Mennonite Brethren Church, a member of the Northern District Conference, was organized in 1927 under the leadership of Anton Berg, with 44 members. All of these were at that time new immigrants from Russia. A church building was erected in 1931. The following have served the church as ministers: Abram Friesen, Heinrich Goosen, and Gerhard Klassen. Many of the members moved to British Columbia in recent years. The membership (1954) is 84; John Wiebe is the pastor and John Lepp assistant pastor. J.P.F.

Manitou (Col.) Mennonite (MC) Church, at 206 Deerpath Ave., Manitou Springs, Col., a member of the South Central Conference, was organized in 1920, the meetinghouse having been dedicated on Aug. 15, 1920. The first pastor was Kore Zook, followed by L. C. Miller. The highest membership was 106 in 1946. Later more of the members lived in Colorado Springs, hence in 1948 the congregation was renamed First Mennonite Church of Colorado Springs (*q.v.*), with a meetinghouse in that city, which had 148 members in 1954, with Jess Kauffman as pastor. Near by is the Rocky Mountain Mennonite (MC) camp. L.C.M.

Manna, The, a 4-page doctrinal and inspirational monthly, edited by John G. Stauffer and published at Milford Square 1879-80, and at Quakertown, Pa., 1881-1909. Until 1906 it appeared as an English edition of *Das Himmelsmanna* (*q.v.*), first published in 1876. Bluffton College Library has a complete file. N.P.S.

Mannhardt, a German family, a part of which became Mennonites at the turn of the 19th century. Several members of the family were important in the development of the Danzig Mennonite Church and for German Mennonitism in general.

Johann Wilhelm Mannhardt (1760-1831), was born Feb. 14, 1760, the son of a teacher in Klein-Heppach in Württemberg, became a ministerial candidate in the Lutheran seminary in Tübingen, and was employed as private tutor in the home of the pietistically inclined Mennonite merchant, Jakob Gysbert van der Smissen (*q.v.*) at Altona on the Elbe. There he became the teacher of Anna van der Smissen, a niece of his employer, who later (1790) became his wife. With the assistance of his father-in-law, Hinrich III van der Smissen, he acquired possession of Hanerau, an estate near Neumünster in Holstein in 1798, and lived there until his death on Nov. 20, 1831. Er.G.

Heinz Münte, *Das Altonauer Handlungshaus van der Smissen 1683-1824* (Altona, 1932).

Jakob Mannhardt (1801-85), the fourth son of the above, was born Oct. 4, 1801, completed the Gymnasium course at Lübeck, living in the home of the father of the poet Emanuel Geibel, studied theology at the universities of Tübingen (the first Mennonite student of theology) and Bonn, became Mennonite pastor at Friedrichstadt in 1828, and at Danzig in 1836, and died there on May 12, 1885. In 1854 he founded the first German Mennonite periodical, the *Mennonitische Blätter,* which he published until 1874, at first bimonthly and later monthly, supported by his colleagues B. C. Roosen, Johannes van der Smissen, Johannes Risser, Johannes Molenaar, and Heinrich Neufeld. As a preacher his pious faith and unfailing charity won him the highest regard, which was given rarely beautiful expression on the occasion of the fiftieth anniversary of his ordination (*Menn. Bl.,* 1878, 42). NEFF.

Johann Wilhelm Mannhardt (1831-80), a Germanistic specialist, the oldest child of Pastor Jakob Mannhardt and Adriana Margaretha (nee Thomsen), was born at Friedrichstadt on March 26, 1831. The stories of his great-grandmother and of his mother, who was reared by her, stirred the interest of the boy in folk tales and philology, and especially mythology and folk ways and Germanic legend. He studied at the universities of Tübingen and Berlin 1851-54. In 1858 he settled in Berlin as a private lecturer at the university. In several larger works, *Germanische Mythen* (1858), *Die Götter der deutschen und nordischen Völker* (1860), and *Weihnachtsblüte in Sitte und Sage* (1864), Dr. Wilhelm Mannhardt contributed to the scholarly development of folklore. He was also an active co-worker on the *Zeitschrift für Mythologie und Sittenkunde.* He continued his study along this line when his frail and misshapen body compelled him to return to his paternal home in Danzig, where he was city librarian. By sending out questionnaires, by private research in folk tradition, by visiting the internment camps in the wars of 1864, 1866, and 1870, he unceasingly gathered material for an *Urkundenbuch der Volksüberlieferungen* he was planning. He also published some smaller works as the fruit of his research: *Roggenwolf und Roggenhund, Die Korn-dämonen, Wald- und Feldkulte.*

To German Mennonitism Mannhardt rendered an essential service in the time when the final struggle of the Mennonites of East and West Prussia for the preservation of their freedom from military service was in progress. In 1863 he published the valuable book, *Die Wehrfreiheit der Altpreussischen Menno-niten,* in which he presented a reliable, authenti-cated understanding of the historical development of the Mennonite principle of nonresistance and of the effort to preserve freedom from military service.

Wilhelm Mannhardt also devoted a great deal of energy to the service of the Danzig Mennonite Church. After 1869 he was frequently asked by the church to take the place of his aged father and read a sermon. This congregation owes to him its chron-icle covering the years 1862-73, which he worked out with conscientious truthfulness and insight into the problems of the decisive period when nonre-sistance was dropped and mixed marriages were per-mitted. On Dec. 25, 1880, a heart attack put a sud-den end to the life of this humbly pious and modest scholar with his rich knowledge and clear vision and honest search for the truth.   ER.G.

H. G. Mannhardt, *Die Danziger Mennonitengemeinde. Ihre Entstehung und ihre Geschichte von 1569-1919* (Dan-zig, 1919) 289-94; *ADB* XX, 203-5.

Hermann Gottlieb Mannhardt (1855-1927), the successor of his uncle, Pastor Jakob Mannhardt, in the office of elder in the Danzig Mennonite Church, was born Jan. 14, 1855, on the family estate of Hanerau in Holstein. His father, Hermann Gottlieb Mannhardt, the youngest son of Johann Wilhelm Mannhardt, was manager of forests on the estate. His mother, Bertha Weihe, was the daughter of a pastor in Westphalia. His intellectual development was influenced by his residence with his uncle Jakob and his daily association with his cousin Wilhelm Mannhardt during the last years of his attendance at the Gymnasium (1871-75). He studied theology at the universities of Strasbourg, Berlin, and Kiel 1875-78, adopting a mildly liberal theological posi-tion. Because of a dislike for the state church sys-tem he prepared himself for teaching and then taught German and history at the girls' school con-ducted by his cousin Louise Mannhardt in Danzig until 1900.

After the autumn of 1878 he frequently took the place of his aged uncle in the pulpit of the church. He became a member of the church, and on Nov. 30, 1879, he was ordained a minister by his uncle, and later also elder. H. G. Mannhardt served his congregation nearly 48 years, with lasting results. On Oct. 20, 1880, he married Elise Dyck of Einlage.

H. G. Mannhardt's work in his congregation was fraught with blessing. His sermons, born of per-sonal faith, intellectually clear, his earnest baptismal instruction, his personal contacts with many of the members, his regular pastoral visits, and his readi-ness to help both as pastor and as friend, bound him closely with his congregation. During the dec-ades of his service the church grew; members of the rural churches moved into the city, and members of other denominations joined his church. A new parsonage was built in 1884, corporation rights were

acquired in 1887 on the basis of a constitution draft-ed by him, a new church hospital was erected in 1902, a new songbook was issued in 1908—which unfortunately suffers from a too rationalistic text and melodic weakness—and the organ was rebuilt in 1914. High points of his period of service were the celebration of the quadricentennial of Menno Simons' birth on Nov. 6, 1892, for which he pub-lished a widely distributed *Festschrift;* the impor-tant eighth general conference of the German Con-ference, the Vereinigung der Mennonitengemeinden im deutschen Reich, which met in his church on April 28-30, 1908; and the celebration of the three hundred fiftieth anniversary of the congregation at Danzig as well as the centennial of the present church building on Sept. 14, 1919, for which he wrote the thoroughly authenticated, lively book, *Die Danziger Mennonitengemeinde. Ihre Entstehung und ihre Geschichte von 1569-1919.* In 1905 he pub-lished and distributed to his members and to others who attended his church *Predigten und Reden aus 25 jähriger Amtszeit.*

Beyond the limits of his own congregation H. G. Mannhardt served German Mennonitism with his knowledge, experience, and energetic action. He always took an active part in the conferences of the West Prussian Mennonites, sometimes as secretary, later as treasurer of the mission board, and as a member of the committee of elders. He was equally interested in the formation of a union of the Men-nonites of Germany, to be based on the Gospel of Jesus Christ and the common heritage. The visit of Pastor S. Cramer (*q.v.*) of Enschedé, Holland, in the summer of 1884 gave the impetus for the found-ing of the Vereinigung (*q.v.*) in 1886. The initial step was taken by the Danzig, Hamburg-Altona, and Crefeld congregations. Until his death Mann-hardt served as the farsighted, competent moderator of its conferences, as a member of the curatorium, as assistant moderator and secretary, on the publication committee, as pastor of the students, and as special speaker at the celebration of the twenty-fifth anni-versary of the organization of the Vereinigung in Crefeld on May 3, 1911. He published an excellent account of the creation of the Vereinigung in his *Jahrbuch* of 1888, and a series of annual reports un-til after the beginning of the first world war. The rise of the Berlin Mennonite Church is closely as-sociated with that of the Vereinigung. Pastor Mann-hardt gave this organization a boost by delivering an address at the first meeting held to prepare for it on Oct. 3, 1884, in Berlin. Several times every year he held services, administered baptism, and made pastoral visits in the Berlin congregation.

On a journey to the conference of the Palatine and Hessian Mennonites he became acquainted with the brotherhood in South Germany in Kaiserslau-tern in 1906. He also took part in the centennial of the A.D.S. (Dutch General Conference) in Amster-dam in September 1911.

His pen he also devoted to the interests of the Mennonite Church. In the promotion of Mennonite publication he saw a means of strengthening Men-nonite group consciousness. From Jan. 1, 1888, to his death in July 1927, he was an associate editor of the *Mennonitische Blätter;* during his lifetime he wrote for it many articles on historical and literary subjects, and on a wide variety of questions relating to Mennonite church life. To the *Christlicher Gemeindekalender* he contributed historical articles and two original stories. The publication of the *Mennonitisches Lexikon* he greeted with pleasure and wrote for it several articles on the West Prussian and Danzig Mennonites. Of his longer works mention should be made of his *Jahrbuch der Mennoniten-Gemeinden in Ost- und Westpreussen* (1883) and his *Jahrbuch der altevangelischen Taufgesinnten oder Mennoniten* (1888). Articles on Mennonite statistics in various countries and on the origin of the *Vereinigung* give these yearbooks their special value.

In addition to his manifold service to his church and to Mennonitism in general, H. G. Mannhardt made many public appearances in Danzig, giving addresses at various celebrations and theological and literary lectures; for many years he directed the "Literaria," a scholarly literary club in Danzig. He retained his physical and mental vigor until a few days before his death. When he died on July 16, 1927, his congregation, German Mennonitism, and many of his fellow citizens thought with honor and affection of this man, characterized by a living faith and moral earnestness as well as great intellectual gifts, yet withal retaining modesty and simplicity of character. Er.G.

H. G. Mannhardt, *Die Danziger Mennonitengemeinde. Ihre Entstehung und ihre Geschichte von 1569-1919* (Danzig, 1919); *Menn. Bl.*, 1927, No. 9, 73-80; *Gem.-Kal.*, 1929, 36-47; *ML* III, 16-18.

Mannheim, most populous (pop. 254,000) city of Baden, Germany, situated at the confluence of the Neckar with the Rhine, founded by Elector Palatine Frederick (*q.v.*) IV in 1606. The builder was Barthel Janson, a Dutch citizen. The city was destroyed by Tilly in the Thirty Years' War, and rebuilt in 1653 by Elector Charles Louis (*q.v.*), who developed it into the chief commercial center of his domain. By settling Walloons and Huguenots there he made it a haven of religious toleration and liberty. On Nov. 13, 1688, it was seized by the French and burned the following March. Elector John William (*q.v.*) engaged Franz Timmermann, the Dutch teacher of Peter the Great, to rebuild it. Mannheim was the capital of the Palatinate 1720-78; in 1803 it fell to Baden.

In 1655 two Hutterite emissaries from Sobotiste, Jakob Amssler (*q.v.*) and Christoph Baumhauer (*q.v.*), obtained permission to establish a Hutterite Bruderhof here. The terms agreed upon stipulated that (1) their house or houses should be built of stone, be roofed with tile, and be two stories in height; (2) they should enjoy all the privileges of citizens, could receive foreigners into the brotherhood, but citizens only with the previous knowledge of the authorities; (3) they should have penal authority over their own members; (4) they were exempt from all service in the army or court, or any other pertaining to the sword; but (5) they should pay their annual rental fee and other taxes, according to the regulations; (6) for five years they should be exempt from payment of a protection fee, and beginning in 1661 pay an annual sum of 50 florins;

(7) concerning civic obligations they should come to an agreement with the city authorities; (8) each of the contracting parties might terminate the agreement upon a half year's notice; in that case the Brethren should be permitted to sell their property and take their goods with them (Beck, *Geschichts-Bücher*, 492 f.). Each member over fifteen years of age was to pay a recognition fee of ten florins per year (Walter, I, 292).

According to Struve they were "poor but industrious people, who would not have agreed with all Anabaptists, especially not with those who doubt the divinity of Christ. They practiced community of goods, engaged in all sorts of handicrafts except the manufacture of instruments of war, and did not marry outside their brotherhood" (Walter, 292; from a letter written by Heinrich Clignet in 1672 to Prof. Joh. Heinrich Ottius of Zürich, author of the *Annales Anabaptistici, q.v.*).

According to the records of the council of Nov. 23, 1664, the Hutterian Brethren built their first houses in 1652. In 1666 there were eight families. Probably in consequence of the plague their number decreased, for in 1670 there were only four families left: Moses Wirtz, a cooper and their preacher and leader (*Vorsteher*), Joseph Grütmann, a potter, Abraham Zahn, a knifesmith, and Heinrich Weinwurm, a tailor. There was also a blacksmith among them. (Liselotte, the daughter of Elector Charles Louis, as a child frequently visited the Bruderhof and at an advanced age in 1718 still recalled clearly having watched them at work, "of whom one made handsome knives of fragrant wood, another was a potter, and another swung the smith's hammer.") After his death they let the smithy to an outsider, but reclaimed it in 1671, for additional brethren had arrived from Hungary. Like the Jews and the Polish Brethren (Socinians who had settled there at the same time as the Hutterites, but had remained only three years), they were not drafted for statute labor or guard duty, but instead paid an annual redemption fee. From the record of the council determining the amount of this fee, dated January 1674, we learn that there were at that time 13 families in the Hutterite settlement. In June another family moved in. Their leader was now Joseph Grütmann. The council records say of him that the brotherhood in Hungary put him in charge of the settlement, to see that the buildings were kept in good repair until they could be sold. Several members joined the Reformed Church; in 1684 Jakob Grütmann also took this step. The city records state that on Dec. 9, 1684, the brotherhood was dissolved and the property divided; its value amounted to 1,332 guilders (*Mannheimer Geschichtsblätter* II, 56).

It is possible that the Swiss Brethren settlement in Mannheim was older than that of the Hutterian Brethren. Definite information is lacking. Risser, the minister of the Sembach congregation, asserted that "from 1650 on, Mennonite families from the Palatinate and new ones from Switzerland moved into the depopulated city and in inconspicuous quiet formed a small congregation led by their elder; their life and civic industry was by no means a deterrent to the reviving city" (*Menn. Bl.*, 1855, 40). The earliest Mennonite lists of the *Landesarchiv* at

Karlsruhe do not mention any Mennonites living in Mannheim. It is possible that they were at first exempt from the redemption fee. Heidelberg reported on Feb. 12, 1662, that there were no Mennonites in its territory, since most of them were living in Mannheim. From Dirmstein (*q.v.*) it is learned (May 17, 1682) that occasionally a preacher came to Obersülzen from Mannheim to hold a meeting. This is proof that there was a Mennonite church in Mannheim at that date. Ernst Müller (p. 315) mentions a letter sent by Peter Lehmann and Rudy Heusser from Mannheim to the Swiss Brethren dated Dec. 23, 1697. (In June 1697 a very destructive fire raged in Mannheim.)

On March 10, 1701, the city council received an inquiry asking whether the Mennonites were considered citizens or mere residents. The reply, dated May 6, stated that five families were granted citizenship, partly because of the substantial houses they had built and partly on the basis of their peaceableness; but since the council was aware that this procedure was displeasing to the elector they had admitted no more Mennonites the last two years.

On May 9 the city mayor inquired of the elector whether the request of another Mennonite for citizenship should be granted. He said further that the six families living there now and the twenty families living there earlier had not only built well, but had in all respects conducted themselves honestly and compatibly. In June 1702 the Mennonites of Mannheim sent a petition to the elector, requesting that Mennonites moving into the city be permitted to become citizens as heretofore without having to obtain a special concession. This petition also states that before the destruction of the city in 1689 there had been twenty families living there. On July 4, 1702, Jakob Snebly, a Mennonite citizen of Mannheim, requested and received certification of their status from the French occupation authorities, which stated that the Mennonites had complied with all their civic obligations such as statute labor and guard service. On April 27, 1706, at the request of the city authorities, Christian Blüm drew up a list of members: there were 11 families, Christian Blüm, Johann Jakob Schnäbele, Ulrich Mayer, Hans Müller, Christian Eicher, Matth. Bonn, Paulus Enger, Martin Meule (Meile or Mellinger?), Christian Stauffer, Johann Hassert, and the widow of Johann Schüler (?). On May 14, 1706, the mayor sent this list to the elector, and asked whether more should be admitted, since they were making frequent application; also whether preference should be given those who had money to build at once. The reply was that the Mennonites now living in Mannheim should be gradually put out of the city, since they were not to be tolerated in the province. From this time on the Mennonites appear regularly in the registers, which give some interesting testimony concerning their life and status.

In 1717, 19 Mennonite families lived in Mannheim: Hans Jakob Schnebele, Ulrich Mayer, Hans Neukumet, Paulus Engers, Chr. Stauffer, Valentin Christophel, Joh. Christophel, Heinrich Christophel, Matthias Bonn, Christian Blüm, Ulrich Stauffer, Johannes Fried, Andreas Berg, Jak. Schnebele's widow,

Martin Meyli (Möllinger?), Jakob Hauter, Peter Heuffendorf, Chr. Fischart's widow, Philip Noldt, Jakob Hunzinger(?).

In 1738, 23 families: Joh. Hunzinger, Christian Schuhmacher, Andreas Berg's widow, Jakob Schnebele, Konrad Geber, Matth. Baumann's widow, Peter Pletscher, Jakob Cetti, Andreas Hackmann, Jakob Eicher(acker), Jakob Graf, Konrad Gerhard's widow, Joh. Stauffer, Jakob Dahlem, David Bechtel, Nikolas Blüm, Joh. Heeussert, Sr. and Jr., Joh. Borckholder, Joh. Kohler, Peter Holl, Jakob Blüm, Karl Krämer's widow.

In 1743, 15 families: Joh. Adam Hunzinger, Joh. J. Graf, Joh. Heussert, Joh. Jak. Pletscher, Susanna Berg (a widow), Margarethe Bonn (widow), Agnes Geber (widow), Abraham Mossimann, renter on Mühlau, David Bechtel, Jakob Eichacker, Joh. Keller, Joh. Burkholder, Christian Schuhmacher, Nicolaus Bonn, Jakob Graf.

In 1752, 18 families: Jak. Pletscher, Chr. Schuhmacher, Jak. Gräf, Joh. Bühler, Joh. Borckholder, Joh. Hassert (these 6 families before 1744), David Bechtel, Adam Hunzinger, Jak. Eichacker, Chr. Eicher, Friedrich Möllinger, Mathias Bonn, Abraham Deutsch, Martin Möllinger, Chr. Neukumeter, Joh. Hunzinger, Jakob Hackmann. Most of them were distillers.

In 1759, 18 families: Joh. Georg Bechtel's widow (weaver since 1726), Chr. Neukumeter's widow, Heinrich Mayer, Joh. Hassert, Martin Möllinger, Friedr. Möllinger, Christian Schuhmacher, Joh. Schuhmacher, Jakob Hunzinger, wine merchant, J. Hunzinger's widow, Geber's widow, Matth. Bonn, Josepf Graf, Abraham Deutsch, Joh. Keller, Joh. Graf, Jak. Pletscher (artisan), Jak. Hackmann.

In 1768, 20 families: Chr. Schuhmacher, Martin Möllinger, Jak. Pletscher, Abraham Deutsch, Joh. Hassert, Joh. Keller, Joh Schuhmacher, Jak. Hunzinger, Jak. Neukumet, Jak. Hackmann, Joh. Hackmann, Dan Geber, Jak. Geber, Matth. Bonn, Friedrich Bergthold, Jak. Bechtel, Joh. Schmidt, Peter Graf, Jak. Hunsinger's mother (a widow), Dan. Pletscher's widow.

In 1732 the Mennonites numbered 35 families: there were Mennonites living outside the city on the Kirchgarthäuserhof (*q.v.*), Gräfenau, and Hemshof (see **Friesenheim**). In the early 18th century Hans Jacob Schnaebele (Schnäbeli) was preacher. Martin Möllinger was elder 1761-*ca.*72; the preachers were Johann Huntzinger, Heinrich Pletscher, Christian Schumacher until about 1772, Jakob Plätscher 1741-?, Jakob Hackmann 1741-?, and Jacob Gerber 1775-? (*Naamlijst*). The deacon was David Bechtel (Müller, 221).

For a long time Mannheim was a center of the congregations in the Palatinate, both East and West. Here the letters and petitions to Holland were written and the petitions to the Palatine government drawn up (Oct. 2 and 30, 1730; March 7 and May 5, 1740; May 2, 1742; Dec. 10, 1743; March 30, 1744; May 14, 1784). On Jan. 6, 1708 (*Inv. Arch. Amst.* I, No. 1254b; Müller, 255), the elders of the Mannheim congregation wrote a letter to Amsterdam, telling of the visit of one of the brethren to Switzerland. A letter of March 30, 1710, relates that 56 Swiss Mennonite prisoners had arrived at Mannheim from

Switzerland on March 28, many of whom remained there because of sickness when the rest moved on (see **Bern**). (*Inv. Arch. Amst.* I, 1258.)

Great anxiety came upon the leaders of the congregation in 1742, when they were ordered to pay the withdrawal fee for some brethren who had moved out of the city. The petition they sent to the government for release from this burden states that Pletscher had gone to Eppstein in 1737, Peter Holl to Eppstein and on to Crefeld in 1741, Johann Stauffer also to Crefeld, and Jakob Cetty to Kirchheim near Heidelberg in 1738. Abraham Mossemann had settled in Mühlau near Mannheim; on Jan. 12, 1742, he was assessed the protection fee from the middle of October 1741.

By 1774 the congregation of Mannheim had apparently fallen into decline, having neither an elder nor a preacher. Preachers of neighboring congregations occasionally served at Mannheim (*Naamlijst* 1786).

In 1782 a certain Count Bock described a visit he paid to the Mennonites in Mannheim. Their place of meeting was a large hall. In the background was an armchair, elevated somewhat above the benches filling the room. Before this chair stood a table with a Bible on it. This was all there was in furnishings. At the entry were the words, *Zum Haus des grossen Vaters.*

On June 11, 1792, the leaders presented a petition to the government, requesting that the impoverished Daniel Möllinger be excused from his protection payment. On it the mayor remarked that the Mennonites never made a petition of this nature without serious cause. One of the outstanding preachers was Martin Möllinger (*q.v.*) (for his correspondence with Steen in Danzig, etc., see *Menn. Bl.,* 1854, 30 and 44 f., and *Gem.-Kal.,* 1935, 112-20). Finally the congregation was served for a time by Weydmann, the Monsheim minister. About 1830 it was dissolved. Its capital, which amounted to several thousand guilders, was given to the city poor fund and to the Protestant Church. The few members who had remained true to the faith of the fathers transferred to Friesenheim (*q.v.*) and other congregations.

The archives of the Reformed Church in Mannheim contain four Mennonite church record books, which are of great interest to students of family history. NEFF.

Inv. Arch. Amst. I, Nos. 1254, 1258, 1266, 1268, 1270, 1342, 1374, 1440, 1472, 1475-82; Beck, *Geschichts-Bücher,* 492 f.; A. Brons, *Ursprung, Entwicklung und Schicksale der . . . Mennoniten* (Emden, 1912) 200; *Gbl.* 1904, 17; M. Göbel, *Gesch. des christl. Lebens in der rhein. Kirche* (1849) I, 591; II, 696; *Mannheimer Gesch.-Bl.* II (1901); A. Medicus, *Gesch. der evangelischen Kirche in Königreich Bayern, supplement* 1865; *Menn. Bl.,* 1855, 40; Müller, *Berner Täufer,* 211, 315; Nüssle, *Bilder und Beiträge aus und zur Kirchengesch. der Stadt Mannheim;* B. G. Struve, *Ausführlicher Bericht von der Pfälzischen Kirchenhistorie* (Frankfurt, 1721) 692; K. F. Vierordt, *Gesch. d. evangelischen Kirche in dem Grossherzogtum Baden* IV (*Karlsruhe,* 1856) 507; W. Fellmann, "Vier Mannheimer mennonitische Kirchenbücher im Pfarrarchiv der reformierten Gemeinde Mannheim," in *Gesch.-Bl.* IV (1939) 57 f.; Fr. Walter, *Mannheim in Vergangenheit und Gegenwart* III (1907); J. Ellenberger, *Bilder aus dem Pilgerleben* III (n.p., 1883) 28; *DB* 1895, 68; *ML* III, 19-22.

Manson (Iowa) Mennonite Church: see **Cedar Creek.**

Mantelhof, a farm in the Aalen district of Württemberg, Germany, the site of numerous martyrdoms. On Jan. 1, 1531, the horsemen of Württemberg and of the provost of Ellwangen, led by provost Aichelin (*q.v.*), surprised Mantelhof and seized the resident farmer and his son besides 20 other persons, all of them Anabaptists. The farmer and his son were hanged on a linden tree in the neighboring village of Essingen. The farmer was let down three times, and was offered his life if he would be converted, but to no avail. The son was probably similarly treated. The others were given a chance to recant and save their lives; few did so. Fourteen of them lost their lives by being burned together with the house they were in. Beck states that 23 persons were burned at Mantelhof. The saying was current that if they had waited another day or two a large crowd of Anabaptists, perhaps 200, would have been caught at Mantelhof, for there were many of them in the desolate places of the Aalbuch. Some of them were seized by Wolf von Rechberg at Hohenrechberg and released upon payment of a fine. G.Bo.

F. L. Baumann, "Weissenhorner Historie von Nikolaus Thomä," 170 ff., in *Quellen zur Gesch. des Bauernkriegs in Oberschwaben* (*Bibliothek des Literarischen Vereins* CXXIX); *Beschreibung des Oberamts Aalen* (1854) 321; Beck, *Geschichts-Bücher,* 311; Zieglschmid, *Chronik,* 54; *ML* III, 22.

Manuscripts from ancient and modern times form the most important source material for the study of Anabaptist-Mennonite history. Only a little of this material is privately owned; most of it has been preserved in archives (*q.v.*) and libraries. After archivist Ludwig Keller had given the impetus by his books on Anabaptism, a beginning was made in collecting and examining this valuable material.

That found in Zürich, as far as it concerns the 16th and 17th centuries, has been published and utilized in the works of Emil Egli (*q.v.*) and by Cornelius Bergmann in his book, *Die Täuferbewegung im Kanton Zürich bis 1660.* A volume of Zürich *Täuferakten* was published in 1952, extending, however, only to 1533.

The State Archives of Bern contain court records of extraordinary scope and value. Ernst Müller has worked through most of it in his book, *Die Bernischen Täufer,* and more recently Delbert Gratz for his book, *Bernese Anabaptists.* Much that is of importance for research is contained in Vol. 80 of the so-called *Unnütze Papiere,* an enormous folio volume of manuscripts; likewise the volume *Kirchenwesen* II, 131, *De Anabaptistis Varia,* and the three large manuscript volumes, *Kirchenwesen* II, D 85, E 86, and F 87 of Abraham de Losea (*q.v.*). A mass of manuscript material on Anabaptist matters is contained in the *Turmbücher,* the *Mandatenbücher,* the *Missivenbücher,* the *Täufer-Urbar,* as well as the *Rats- und Chorgerichtsmanuale.* Various volumes of manuscripts (*Kontrollbücher,* etc.) and a bundle of court records from the 19th century report on the Anabaptists of that period. Much valuable material for the history of the Anabaptists is also located in the Fascicles *Misc. Hist. Helv.* I, II, III, VII, VIII, XI, XIII, and XIV. Much of the Bern material has been microfilmed by the Bluffton College Historical Library.

The manuscripts in the city archives of Basel have been worked through by Paul Burckhardt in his book, *Die Basler Täufer*. There is here a large bundle of court records, *Criminalia*, which deals with Anabaptist history in the 16th and 17th centuries. The materials concerning the 18th and 19th century Edward Thurneysen has covered in a general historical survey in "Die Basler Separatisten im 18. Jahrhundert," in *Basler Jahrbuch*, 1895 and 1896. (See also the article **Basel.**) The manuscripts of more recent times were copied by the theological student Peter Dirks in 1914 for the archives of the *Mennonitisches Lexikon*. Their value lies chiefly in the line of family history.

In 1920 the directors of the *Verein für Reformationsgeschichte* decided to have all the *Täuferakten* (court records concerning Anabaptists) published, which have been preserved in the archives and libraries of German-speaking Europe. This is being done in the series, *Quellen zur Geschichte der Wiedertäufer* (since World War II *Täufer*), which is publishing the court records of Württemberg, Bavaria, Alsace, Baden, Palatinate, Switzerland, Thuringia, Saxony, Silesia, and the Lower Rhine. The first volume was published in 1930: *Herzogtum Württemberg*, by Gustav Bossert, Sr. (Leipzig, 1930, XVI and 1199 pages). Later volumes have appeared as follows: *Markgraftum Brandenburg* (Bayern I) by Schornbaum 1934; South German and Hutterite documents in *Glaubenszeugnisse* I by Lydia Müller 1938; *Baden-Pfalz* by Krebs 1951; Imperial Cities (Bayern II), by Schornbaum 1951. By these publications the rich treasures in Anabaptist manuscripts preserved in various archives and libraries in these countries will be made easily accessible. This will give opportunity and occasion to thoroughly investigate the manuscripts of the last decades of the 16th century as well as those of the 17th and 18th and will make them available for proper research. Those that have been preserved in the *Generallandesarchiv* in Karlsruhe, have been copied by Christian Neff and are now in the archives of the *Lexikon*. The records of the 16th century were utilized by Christian Hege in his book, *Die Täufer in der Kurpfalz* (Frankfurt, 1908). The Hesse manuscripts were published in 1951 by the Historical Kommission für Hessen und Waldeck. The Swiss documents are being published by L. von Muralt in a series called *Quellen zur Geschichte der Täufer in der Schweiz; Zürich* appeared as Vol. I in 1952.

The exceedingly rich manuscript source material of Austrian Anabaptism was treated and listed by Robert Friedmann in a very valuable work (*Archiv für Reformationsgeschichte* XXVI, 1929). The manner in which he describes and evaluates the peculiar importance of these Anabaptist manuscripts, found in "books" and letters or lost, deserves the profoundest respect.

The library of the Mennonite Church in Amsterdam contains an uncommonly rich collection of important manuscripts (letters) and court records on the history of the Dutch, Swiss, and German Mennonite congregations. They are carefully listed in the *Inventaris der Archiefstukken*, Vols. I and II (1883-84). The records of Germany and Switzerland are contained in Vol. I, Nos. 1248-1745, Vol. II, Pt. I, Nos. 2571-2862, and Pt. II, Nos. 680-867. Their publication is earnestly desired in the interest of historical exploitation. The Historical Committee of the General Conference Mennonite Church has microfilmed most of these materials and made them available for research in America.

Some valuable manuscripts on the history of the Swiss Anabaptists and Mennonites are found in private possession. The task of collecting them and preserving them for the brotherhood has been undertaken by the Swiss Mennonites. A large part of their collection has been published by M. Pohl in the *Christlicher Gemeindekalender*, 1906-11, and by Christian Neff, 1929-30, under heading, "Geschichtliche Beiträge aus den Mennoniten-Gemeinden."

There is also some manuscript material of historical importance among the Mennonite families in Hesse and the Palatinate. It has in part been published in the *Christlicher Gemeindekalender*, 1925 ("Lebensbild von David Kaege von Offstein"), and in the *Mennonitische Blätter*, 1907, p. 51 f.; 1912, p. 2 f.; and in the *Gemeindeblatt*, 1929; most of it, reposing in the archives of the *Lexikon*, still awaits publication. (*ML* II, 247 ff.)   NEFF, H.S.B.

Manz, Felix, one of the founders and first martyr of the original Swiss Brethren congregation in Zürich, Switzerland, was born about 1498, the son of a Zürich canon, acquired a thorough knowledge of Latin, Greek, and Hebrew. When Zwingli came to Zürich in 1519, Manz joined him enthusiastically and became a regular attendant at Zwingli's Bible classes.

Differences of opinion soon arose when he and his associates demanded the abolition of tithes and interest. Zwingli hesitated, although he could not entirely close his mind to the Biblical basis for this demand (see his noted sermon on divine and human righteousness on June 24, 1523). Even more insistently the Brethren demanded the abolition of the Mass. When Zwingli left the decision in this matter in the hands of the Zürich city council the Brethren broke with him and henceforth held their own meetings in the home of Felix Manz's mother.

The question of baptism at once arose. Several fathers refused to have their children baptized. They were fined. On Jan. 17, 1525, a public disputation was held in the city hall of Zürich to decide the issue, with Conrad Grebel and Felix Manz representing the Brethren. Zwingli was pronounced the victor. In consequence an order was issued on Jan. 18, threatening those who would not have their children baptized within eight days with banishment from the city. Grebel and Manz were to desist from their arguing and submit to the opinion of "my lords (of the city council)."

This the Brethren refused to do. On Jan. 21 they performed the rite of adult baptism and held a communion service among themselves, thereby making their break with the Zwingli church final and establishing their brotherhood as a distinct Christian body. The movement spread rapidly through the city and the canton of Zürich. Felix Manz was among the most zealous in proclaiming the new doctrine. He was repeatedly arrested. He earnestly requested an opportunity to express himself in writing on the points in dispute, since it was impossible to do justice to the matter in oral debate. But the council refused.

The second disputation in Zürich took place on March 20, 1525. The result was again negative. The Brethren (14 men and 7 women) were imprisoned in the Hexenturm on bread and water. On April 5 they managed to escape. But they were soon captured and subjected to a severe cross-examination. Felix Manz testified that he had never rejected government, interest, and tithes. If he had taken the liberty to preach in other pastorates, he had only done what a disciple of Christ must do. Capital punishment he had denounced, as well as the use of the sword; community of goods he had not taught, but only willingness to share with the needy. Two weeks after his escape from the Hexenturm he had baptized in Embrach, and would continue to do so.

After his release Manz went to the Oberland of Zürich, especially to Grüningen (q.v.). But he did not stay here long. By the middle of May we find him with George Blaurock at Chur in the canton of Grisons, Blaurock's home. On July 18 he was seized and taken back to Zürich. The letter which the magistrate of Chur sent to the Zürich council on July 13, 1525, states:

"For a long time we have had among us one who calls himself Felix Manz. The same has created much trouble and discord among our people by baptizing old people and corner preaching, to such an extent that we ordered him to leave the city. After he returned and did as before, disregarding the public proclamation in the church forbidding adult baptism on penalty of death, loss of honor and loss of property. Therefore we arrested him and held him a few days. But because he is an obstinate and recalcitrant person we released him from prison and because he is one of yours we have sent him to you, with the friendly request that you look after him and keep him in your territory, so that we may be rid of him and our people remain quiet, and that in case of his return, we are not compelled to take severe measures against him."

In Zürich Manz was confined in the Wellenberg for several months and then released on Oct. 7. On the next day he was already with Grebel taking part in a meeting of the Anabaptists at Bezholz. Here they were surprised by the magistrate. Grebel was seized, but Manz escaped until Oct. 30, when he was also put in prison. At the suggestion of the magistrate the third public Anabaptist disputation was held in Zürich on Nov. 6 and 8 in the Grossmünster of the city. Grebel and Manz were again the spokesmen of the Brethren. The outcome was that on November 18 the council sentenced Blaurock, Grebel, and Manz to prison on bread, water, and "Mus," forbidding all contact with the outside, "as long as my lords should see fit."

This imprisonment was not of long duration. Soon afterward we find the three leaders of the Brethren

again in the highlands of Zürich, where they promulgated their doctrines more vigorously than ever. They were again arrested and subjected to a severe questioning. They held to their faith and were ready to die for it. Again they requested permission to present their case in the matter of baptism in writing, as Zwingli had already done in his book, *Vom Tauff, vom Wiedertauff und vom Kindertauff* (at the end of May 1525). Manz expressly stated that he had never disputed, but had only testified to his faith; the Scriptures alone had led him to his position on baptism; no Christian could strike with the sword, nor does he resist evil.

The council now resorted to severer measures. On March 7 the sentence was pronounced: "Manz, Grebel, and Blaurock, besides 15 other Anabaptists including six women, shall be placed on straw in the new tower on bread and water until they die and decay. No one may visit them or have power to change their condition, be they well or sick, without the consent of my lords." Repetition of the offense would be punished without mercy by drowning. Sooner than the severity of the verdict would indicate, the prison doors were opened. At any rate, by April 1526 the three Brethren leaders were assisting their harried brethren in Grisons and Appenzell.

In the fall of 1526 it was learned that Manz and Blaurock were in the region of Grüningen baptizing. To put an end to this activity the council applied the edict of March 7, which made adult baptism punishable by drowning. On Dec. 3, 1526, Manz and Blaurock were surprised at a meeting of the Brethren, seized, and taken to Zürich, where they were placed in the Wellenberg prison. It was Manz's final imprisonment. On Jan. 5, 1527, he was sentenced to death, "because contrary to Christian order and custom he had become involved in Anabaptism, had accepted it, taught others, and become a leader and beginner of these things because he confessed having said that he wanted to gather those who wanted to accept Christ and follow Him, and unite himself with them through baptism, and let the rest live according to their faith, so that he and his followers separated themselves from the Christian Church and were about to raise up and prepare a sect of their own under the guise of a Christian meeting and church; because he had condemned capital punishment, and in order to increase his following had boasted of certain revelations from the Pauline Epistles. But since such doctrine is harmful to the unified usage of all Christendom, and leads to offense, insurrection, and sedition against the government, to the shattering of the common peace, brotherly love, and civil co-operation and to all evil, Manz shall be delivered to the executioner, who shall tie his hands, put him into a boat, take him to the lower hut, there strip his bound hands down over his knees, place a stick between his knees and arms, and thus push him into the water and let him perish in the water; thereby he shall have atoned to the law and justice. . . . His property shall also be confiscated by my lords."

He was taken bound from the Wellenberg over the fish market to the boat. As he was being taken between the shops he praised God with a loud voice and cheerfully testified to the people that he was about to die for the truth. Meanwhile the dismal procession had reached the place of execution. It was three o'clock in the afternoon. "As he stood there with the depths of Lake Zürich below him, the blue sky over him, and the mountains with their snowy peaks in the sunshine, around him, his soul in the face of death looked out above these. As a preacher at his side spoke sympathetically to him encouraging him to be converted, he hardly heard him; but when he perceived his mother's voice on the opposite bank, together with his brothers admonishing him to be steadfast, he sang with a loud voice while he was being bound, *'In manus tuas, Domine, commendo spiritum meum,'* and the waves closed in over his head." He was buried in the St. Jakobs cemetery in Zürich. The *Ausbund* (*q.v.*), No. 6, has a song written by him: "Mit Lust so will ich singen." While he left no published writings, the *Protestation und Schutzschrift* of December 1524 addressed to the Zürich Council, attributed to Conrad Grebel by Egli, Köhler, and Bender, has been shown by W. Schmid to have been written by Manz.

NEFF, H.S.B.

E. Egli, *Die Züricher Wiedertäufer zur Reformationszeit* (Zürich, 1878); *Mart. Mir.* D 3, E 415; A. Brons, *Ursprung, Entwickelung und Schicksale der . . . Mennoniten* (Emden, 1912); Wolkan, *Lieder,* 8 f., 141; *Menn. Bl.,* 1888, 9; 1894, 4; J. C. Füsslin, *Beiträge zur Erläuterung der Kirchen-Ref.-Gesch. des Schweizerlandes* I-V (Zürich, 1741-53); *Zwingliana* IX (1950); H. S. Bender, *Conrad Grebel* (Goshen, 1950); *TA Zürich; ML* III, 22-24.

Maple Glen Conservative Amish Mennonite Church, Grantsville, Md.: see **Casselman River** congregation.

Maple Grove Mennonite Church (MC), located less than a mile north of Atglen, Pa., a member of the Ohio and Eastern Conference, was organized as the Millwood congregation in 1882 with a membership of 124. The Maple Grove meetinghouse was built in 1909. The original church at Millwood, a frame structure, was enlarged in 1935 to the present seating capacity of 450. The Millwood and Maple Grove churches continued to function as one congregation until 1945, when the Millwood part withdrew to join the Lancaster Conference, while the Maple Grove Church continued under the Ohio and Eastern Conference. On Oct. 1, 1954, the membership of the Maple Grove congregation was 418, with Aaron F. Stoltzfus, Abner G. Stoltzfus, and Calvin S. Kennel serving as ministers.   A.G.S.

Maple Grove Mennonite Church (MC), five miles east of Gulliver, located in Schoolcraft Co., Mich., a member of the Indiana-Michigan Conference, began as a mission outpost in 1942. It was organized as a congregation on Jan. 11, 1948, with 15 charter members. The first services were held in homes, then in the township hall and in the local schoolhouse. On May 21, 1950, a meetinghouse was dedicated. In 1955 the membership was 45, with Norman Weaver serving as bishop-pastor.   N.WE.

Maple Grove Mennonite Church, Ashtabula Co., Ohio: see **Ashtabula County** Mennonite Church.

Maple Grove Mennonite Church (MC), located about one mile east of Belleville, Pa., was organized by "meetinghouse" Amish as a congregation in 1863

under the leadership of Bishop Solomon Byler. Services in the new building were held for the first time on Aug. 9, 1868. The congregation affiliated itself with the Eastern Amish Mennonite Conference, but is now affiliated with the Allegheny Conference. Samuel Yoder served as bishop 1864-84. Succeeding bishops were David Zook 1884-86, Michael Yoder 1886-89, Abraham D. Zook 1889-98, Michael Yoder assisted by John E. Kauffman 1898-1910, Eli H. Kanagy 1910-?, Aaron Mast 1935- . The membership (1954) is 278, with Aaron Mast as bishop and Jacob Weirich as minister.

In 1936 the Maple Grove congregation started a mission outpost at Barrville, five miles north of Belleville. It was organized as a separate congregation in 1956.   A.KA., J.L.H.

Maple Grove Mennonite Church (MC), near Ellicott City, Howard Co., Md., about 20 miles southwest of Baltimore, is a member of the Lancaster Conference. The Cottage City, Md. (*q.v.*), congregation had begun contact in this area in 1934. In 1935 and 1937 tent meetings were held, which resulted in 15 converts. A meetinghouse was built soon thereafter. The membership in 1957 was 33, with Walter Shank as pastor and Lloy S. Kniss as bishop. Mount Airy, a former mission point of the Maple Grove church, has become an independent congregation.   I.D.L.

Maple Grove Mennonite Church (MC), located two miles south of New Wilmington, Lawrence Co., Pa., was organized about 1850 by a group that had withdrawn from the Old Order Amish Church under the leadership of their first minister and bishop John Kanagy. They built the first meetinghouse (25 x 35 ft.) in 1872, remodeled in 1902 and finally removed; the present meetinghouse (36 x 56 ft.) was built in 1930. This rural church, which had a membership of 68 in 1955, belongs to the Ohio and Eastern Conference and is under the leadership of Nathan Nussbaum as pastor, and Roy Kaufman.

N.N.

Maple Grove Mennonite Church (MC), located in Topeka, Ind., a member of the Indiana-Michigan Conference, was organized with 18 charter members in May 1854 under the leadership of Bishop Isaac Smucker (1810-93). Smucker was followed by Jonathan Kurtz (1848-1930) and Edwin Yoder (1889-), who is the present bishop and senior minister. Others who have served as associate ministers were David F. Hartzler (1816-89), David Morrell (1828-1905), J. S. Hartzler (1857-1953), Andrew Yontz (1864-1938), Raymond Hartzler (1893-), C. Norman Kraus (1924-), and Ellis Croyle (1930-). The first meetinghouse was a frame building erected south of Topeka in 1856, replaced by a larger brick structure in 1879. The congregation reached a peak of 225 members in the early 1920's. In 1924 after several years of growing dissatisfaction, about half of the congregation, which then numbered 150, withdrew from the Indiana-Michigan Conference and later merged with a small congregation in Topeka, Ind., belonging to the Central Conference, now called the Topeka Mennonite Church (GCM).

The group who remained with the conference erected a frame building with a seating capacity of 300, at the south edge of town, which was dedicated in May 1925 and is still in use. The membership in 1955 was 189, largely rural. The original families came almost exclusively from the Amish settlement in Fairfield Co., Ohio. C.N.K.

Maple Hill Conservative Amish Mennonnite Church, Middlefield, Ohio: see **Maple View**.

Maple Ridge United Mennonite Church (GCM), Pitt Meadows, B.C., was organized on Nov. 18, 1945, by Mennonites who had come from the prairie provinces since 1934. On Jan. 1, 1948, the membership was 25. Since there has been no increase from the outside, and the members are dependent on occasional employment in the peat and lumber industries, the church has grown little, and the church life has never been completely organized. It is served by preachers from other congregations, principally by A. I. Loewen, Abbotsford, who receives partial support from the Canadian Conference. Regular services in German are held on Sunday morning in a rented hall. No official membership was reported in 1954. C.G.T.

Maple River Mennonite Church (MC), one mile west of Brutus, and 14 miles northeast of Petoskey, Mich., was organized in 1883, when the meetinghouse was built by settlers who had come from Waterloo Co., Ont., in 1879 (Abraham Detwiler and Jonas Brubacher families). Abraham Detwiler and Jonathan Gehman were the first preachers. The Wisler Old Order Mennonite schism occurred here in 1886 and seriously handicapped the congregation, since both ministers withdrew with the Wisler group (which has since died out). Christian Detwiler, who was ordained after the schism, served until his death in 1917. The congregation, a member of the Indiana-Michigan Mennonite Conference, was revived by the action of the conference mission board, which located Clyde X. Kauffman as a minister here in 1921; the congregation was reorganized that year. In 1955 the membership was 64, with Kauffman still serving as pastor, assisted by Earl Hartman. C.X.K.

Maple View Amish Mennonite Church, north of Wellesley, Waterloo Co., Ont., was organized in 1859 with John Jantzi (1806-81) as bishop by members of the Steinman (q.v.) congregation in Wilmot Township who had moved a few miles northward into Wellesley Township, and was long called the Wellesley congregation. It is a member of the Ontario A.M. Conference. Meetings were at first held in the homes until a meetinghouse was erected which was to be used only as a funeral chapel. When the house began to be used for regular worship services (1886) a group opposed to this withdrew to continue as the Wellesley Old Order Amish. They were joined by a group which withdrew the same year and for the same reason from the near-by Mornington (Poole) A.M. congregation. In 1954 the Old Order group still had three districts, with a total of 260 baptized members. In 1912 again a conservative faction broke away from the Wellesley A.M. group to organize a separate congregation, called the

Lichti group after its leader, Bishop Jacob Lichti. This group built a meetinghouse a half mile east of the Wellesley A.M. church. It continues to use German exclusively, sings from the *Ausbund,* and has no Sunday school. Thus it is in a sense "Old Order," although it has no fellowship with the Wellesley "House Amish" Old Order group. In 1954 it had 200 members, and was called the Cedar Grove A.M. congregation.

The Poole (Mornington) A.M. (q.v.) church was an outgrowth of the Wellesley A.M. settlement. It was formally organized in 1874 although it did not build a meetinghouse until 1886. The meetinghouse was the occasion of an Old Order split paralleling that at Wellesley in the same year, called the Mornington Old Order Amish group. In 1904 a second schism occurred in the Poole A.M. congregation, led by Bishop Nicholas Nafziger, which built a meetinghouse in that year, but continues to use the German language and the *Ausbund* and has no Sunday school. It parallels the Lichti congregation and in 1954 had 175 members. It is locally called the Nafziger church, although its official name is Mornington. Mornington and Cedar Grove are reckoned with the Beachy Amish (q.v.) group. In 1928 a new frame church was erected, and the name Maple View was adopted to replace the name Wellesley.

Bishops who served the congregation before the use of the meetinghouse were John Jantzi, Christian Gascho, Christian Wagler, and Christian B. Zehr. Samuel L. Schultz (1883-) has served as bishop since 1941. In 1954 Samuel V. Leis, Chris S. Streicher, and Allen Y. Bender were serving as ministers. An outpost was operated at Crosshill. The total membership at the two places was 457. The congregation has been slow in adopting the English language for its services and long retained the *Ausbund* as its hymnal.

Thus in 1954 there were six congregations on three distinct levels, with a total of 1,092 members, the outgrowth of the original Wellesley congregation of 1859. J.C.F.

Maple View Conservative Mennonite Church, formerly called Maple Hill, was organized near Middlefield, Ohio, in 1937, under the direction of the Maple Grove C.A.M. Church. The congregation, with a membership (1956) of 107, worships in a basement church. The bishop of the Maple Grove congregation, Roman Miller, serves here. The preachers are Noah D. Miller, Eli E. Hostetler, and Mahlon Miller. S.C.

Marbach, Johann (1521-81), a German Lutheran theologian, studied at the University of Wittenberg, was called to Strasbourg in 1545, made professor of theology and president of the church convention in 1553, and died there on March 17, 1581. He was a zealous Lutheran and was often engaged in dispute with Johann Sturm, with Zanchi, the rector of the University, as well as with the Reformed clergy of the city.

Marbach made it his particular task to fight the Schwenckfelders and the Anabaptists. Against the former he preached seven successive sermons in

1556; the latter he tried to convert through church inspections. According to his statement, five councilmen met to deal with the Anabaptists pointed out by the inspectors. These councilmen, known as the *Wiedertäuferherren* (Anabaptist Committee), were chosen annually. Usually one or two preachers met with them. "Marbach generally came alone. Sometimes he had with him something the sectarians had written, in order to refute their doctrine. The sectarian was then given a definite period to repent; at its termination he was summoned; if he did not recant, he was banished from the city; if he returned, he was imprisoned" (Horning, 16; Hulshof, 232).

Marbach was present at the trial of the Anabaptists Veit Heilgenstein of Saarbrücken and Johannes Novesianus; because they persisted in their error they were expelled from the city. The same fate met Johannes Schlaf of Neuss (Records of the council, I and II, 1556).

In 1556 Marbach was invited by Palatine Elector Otto Heinrich to head a church inspection in his domain. It was reported that in the Neustadt Amt there were many Anabaptists and Schwenckfelders throughout the mountains, who met in woods and remote places. In Edenkoben the inspecting group converted an Anabaptist, and in Kreuznach two. In Dirmstein they disputed in vain with two Anabaptists, in Heppenheim with one who had gone to Moravia and had returned with a commission to the local brethren. At Stromberg six Anabaptists were in prison; they declared that they had left the church only because they did not believe that the immoral and ignorant local preachers possessed the Spirit of God.

In August 1557 Marbach conducted the disputation with the Anabaptists at Pfeddersheim (*q.v.*). He also took part in the colloquium at Worms (Sept. 11 to Oct. 7, 1557), and signed the document which the Protestant theologians issued after this debate, titled *Prozess, wie es soll gehalten werden mit den Wiedertäufern durch etliche Gelehrten, so zu Worms versammelt gewesen, gestellt* (Hege, 93 ff.).

The official opinion which he formulated for Landgrave William of Hesse on Sept. 1, 1569, concerning the unbaptized children of the Anabaptists, states that it is obligatory upon the state to baptize such children forcibly, even against the wishes of the parents. The marginal notes made by the landgrave on this document, however, repudiate the use of force in matters of faith (Hochhuth, 213-20).

In 1557 Marbach was instrumental in banishing three Anabaptists, Niklaus Fuchs, Wendel Haman, and the wife of Martin Spanner, when they refused to accept the Lutheran faith. Again in 1558 three Anabaptists were brought before the Anabaptist Committee and expelled. Church inspections revealed the presence of Anabaptists at four localities in the country. At "St. Oswald" Marbach learned that the Anabaptists held monthly meetings on the Murhof or in the forest of Eckbolsheim or on Lichtenberg, "numbering 50, sometimes 200, indeed, a year ago 600." The inspection of 1579 found David Zoller at Barr, Andreas Maurer at Heiligenstein, and two others at Wasslenheim (Horning, 22).

In spite of all his efforts Marbach did not succeed in eradicating Anabaptism from Strasbourg and its vicinity. His suggestion to conduct a house to house inspection in the city was rejected by the city council. Until the middle of the 19th century there was a Mennonite congregation in Strasbourg (see Alsace). NEFF.

C. Schmidt, *Der Anteil der Strassburger an der Reformation in der Churpfalz* (Strasbourg, 1856); W. Horning, *Johannes Marbach* (Strasbourg, 1887); A. Hulshof, *Geschiedenis van de Doopsgezinden te Straatsburg van 1525 tot 1557* (Amsterdam, 1905); Chr. Hege, *Die Täufer in der Kurpfalz* (Frankfurt, 1908); K. W. H. Hochhuth, "Mitteilungen aus der Protestantischen Secten-Gesch. in der Hessischen Kirche," in *Ztscht für die historische Theologie*, 1859, 213-20; *ML* III, 24 f.

Marburg (pop. 24,000), a city in Hesse-Nassau, Germany, was a center of the Anabaptist movement in Hesse (*q.v.*) and the neighboring Thuringia (*q.v.*) in the Reformation period. Melchior Rinck (*q.v.*) was cross-examined here by Balthasar Raidt, the pastor of Hersfeld, and the theological professors of the University of Marburg. On this occasion he wrote his confession of faith on five points. In the Marburg Colloquy (1529) between Zwingli and Luther Campanus (*q.v.*) took part.

In 1536 four Hessian Anabaptist leaders, including Hermann Bastian, who probably stemmed from Marburg, were imprisoned in Marburg, and were kept in light confinement alternately here and at Wolkersdorf. Philip of Hesse (*q.v.*) requested an official opinion of various university cities. The theological faculty of the University of Marburg also sent one; it has, however, been lost. Marburg seems to have rendered a mild judgment; for a year previous Gerhard Noviomagus (*q.v.*) had expressed to Philip his opposition to severe penalties against the Anabaptists. This was also the position of Adam Krafft (*q.v.*), who had been a professor at the university and a pastor at Marburg since 1528. The prisoners were repeatedly examined. A written confession of faith was found on one such occasion with the title, *Verantwortung und Widerlegung der Artikel, so jetzund im Land zu Hessen über die armen Davider, die man Wiedertäufer nennet, ausgangen sind.* Finally Martin Bucer (*q.v.*) was called, who debated with the prisoners from Oct. 30 to Nov. 1, 1538, and succeeded in converting them.

Nevertheless there were remnants of Anabaptist groups in Hesse and vicinity for a long time after. The General Synod held in 1571 adopted a resolution with the following import: Since the Anabaptists now and again come secretly and dare to mislead the common people with their seductive teachings from the right way of salvation to destruction, the superintendents shall diligently watch for them and their meetings and conventicles, also lead them and oppose them with teaching and admonition from God's Word as much as possible. The prince ought to renew his mandates threatening all converts to Anabaptism with severe penalties, expelling those from the country, who refuse to recant.

The Synod of Marburg in 1573 recommended that the property of Anabaptists to which they fell heir after banishment be confiscated to prevent the return of such Anabaptists to poison others.

In 1575 the pastor of Alsfeld reported to the Marburg Synod that one of his parishioners had been infected with Anabaptism for fifty years and could not be persuaded to change his mind. Two Anabaptists, Martin Richter and Hans Kuchenbecker, had drawn the attention of the authorities, while the others were living quietly. Kuchenbecker had been examined at Marburg in 1577, and made a courageous confession. He was given two months to change his mind, at the end of which he was to be expelled if he persisted in his error.

On Oct. 7, 1578, the pastor Tielmann Noll was summoned before the Marburg Synod to answer charges of Anabaptist leanings. His reply clearly shows that he had received genuine inspiration from his association with the Anabaptists. He then had to pass an examination on all the articles of the Confession of Augsburg, and for a year withdraw from all social activity, or forfeit his position. After this the Anabaptists did not come to public attention, but their quiet life remained an influence for a long time to come. (See **Hesse** for bibliography; *ML* III, 34 f.)   NEFF.

Marcelis Goverts Gasthuis is a home for the aged at Leeuwarden (*q.v.*), Dutch province of Friesland, founded for the benefit of the poor members of the Waterlander congregation in 1669 by Marcelis Goverts (d. 1669). Goverts, married to Mayke Markus (d. 1664), was a member of the Leeuwarden city council and its city architect. For this reason there is some doubt whether he was a Mennonite, since at this time the Mennonites did not hold magisterial offices; but Goverts may have been an exception. The Gasthuis, located on the Stadsgracht (now Oostergrachtswal), was completely remodeled in 1766, the Leeuwarden congregation having received a large legacy from Dirk Zeper for this purpose. In 1877 a new home with the same name was built on the Noordsingel. (*Leeuwarder Gemeenteblad*, Dec. 1933.)   vDZ.

Marck Jettyezoon, a Dutch martyr belonging to the revolutionary wing, was arrested during the recapture of the Oldeklooster (*q.v.*), Dutch province of Friesland, in 1535 and beheaded at Leeuwarden on April 10, 1535. (K. Vos, *Menno Simons,* Leiden, 1914, 228.)   vDZ.

Marcus Cornelisz, a bagmaker of Westkapelle, a village on the island of Walcheren (Holland), was beheaded on April 30, 1535, at Middelburg, capital of the Dutch province of Zeeland, because he refused to "make an offering at the burial of his children, as God has not commanded it. The dead have no help or ease that can be given by those living under the sun. One must confess not to priests but to God; thus the preachers have taught him, and there is no purgatory." Marcus Cornelisz had attended an Anabaptist meeting at Middelburg shortly before Christmas of 1534, where Damas Jacobsz (*q.v.*) of Leiden urged his listeners to march to Amsterdam and other towns to take these towns by force, but Marcus did not agree with such ideas and had left the meeting. He had been arrested before Jan. 14, 1535, and was tortured on March 8. During the trial he recanted. He was 25 years of age. (*DB* 1908, 8; Mellink, *Wederdopers,* 320, 322; *ML* I, 371.)   NEFF, vDZ.

Marcus de Ledersnijder, an Anabaptist martyr, was seized at Kortrijk (Courtrai) (*q.v.*) in Flanders, Belgium. In spite of torture he refused to return to the Catholic faith, and was therefore burned at the stake at Kortrijk on Dec. 12, 1559 (van Braght has erroneously 1558). He was a weaver and his official name was Marcus (Marcx) van de Gheinste. His property was confiscated. (*Mart. Mir.* D 201, E 583; Verheyden, *Courtrai-Bruxelles,* 34, No. 9; *ML* II, 626; III, 35.)   HEGE, vDZ.

Marcus de Smit (in *Offer* and van Braght's *Martyrs' Mirror* called *Marcus,* the brother of Hans de Smit; in the official records *Marcus* (Martin) *de Smet*), an Anabaptist martyr, burned at the stake on the Vrijdagsmarkt of Gent, Belgium, on Aug. 7, 1559, at 7:00 in the morning, with five other martyrs; some others arrested with them had suffered martyrdom shortly before. A letter by Hans de Vette (*q.v.*) states that this group of 12 members had been arrested at Gent on Pentecost of 1559. They are commemorated in two hymns: "Ick moet een liet beginnen" (I must begin a hymn), found in *Nieu Liedenboeck* of 1562 and *Lietboecxken van den Offer des Heeren* of 1563 (No. 14), and "Een eeuwighe vruecht die niet en vergaet" (An eternal joy, which does not pass away), found in *Veelderhande Liedekens* of 1569. (*Offer,* 348, 556 ff.; *Mart. Mir.* D 246, E 620; Verheyden, *Gent,* 25, No. 64.)   vDZ.

Marcus(z), Pieter, was a preacher and elder of the High German Mennonite congregation meeting at the Barrevoetersteeg at Haarlem, Holland, and later of the united Flemish-Frisian-High German congregation (Vlaemschen Blok) on Klein Heiligland at Haarlem. He was a bitter opponent of Galenus Abrahamsz (*q.v.*) and of Collegiant principles. As a representative of the Haarlem congregation at the Leiden Flemish conference of June 1660, he was one of the four men appointed to draw up a common confession out of the four Dutch confessions (*Olyftack* 1626, Jan Cents confession 1630, Dordrecht confession 1632, and Concept of Cologne), which, however, never came into being. Pieter Marcus was also one of the delegates sent by this conference to Amsterdam to depose Abrahamsz and Spruyt from their offices, without result however. Soon thereupon the "Lammerenkrijgh" (*q.v.,* War of the Lambs) broke out, which in 1664 divided the Flemish Mennonites into Lamists (*q.v.*) and Zonists (*q.v.*). Pieter Marcus sided with the Zonists, and in 1671, when the Flemish congregation at Haarlem was also divided, he and Isaac Snep (*q.v.*) were in the conservative wing.

Concerning the life of Pieter Marcus no data were available. He died before 1685.   vDZ.

DB 1863, 132, 137; Blaupot t. C., *Holland* I, 345; H. W. Meihuizen, *Galenus Abrahamsz* (Haarlem, 1954) 72, 74.

Margaret of Austria (Margaret of Savoy) (1480-1530), a daughter of Emperor Maximilian, was a stadholder of the Netherlands, both Belgium and Holland, from 1507 until her death. Although Anabaptism did not rise in these countries before 1530, an Evangelical anti-Catholic movement, usually called Sacramentism (*q.v.*), arose in the last years of her government. Since it was also her task to suppress heresy, she occasionally concerned herself with heretics. On May 25, 1527, she wrote a letter to the Court of Holland at The Hague concerning the martyr Wendelmoet Claesdochter (*q.v.*), who is listed in *Offer des Heeren* (*Inv. Arch. Amst.* I, No. 1 b; *Offer,* 422-29).   vDZ.

Margaret (1522-86) of Parma, the natural daughter of Emperor Charles V, regent of the Netherlands 1559-67, governing in the name of her half brother Philip II (*q.v.*) of Spain. Following the policy of her predecessor, Mary of Hungary, she vigorously opposed the rise of heresy, though less consistently than Philip. In general her conduct of the government lacked independence and was influenced by all sorts of moods and opinions. At first she was under the staunchly Catholic influence of Cardinal Granvelle, and absolutely refused to lighten the persecution of heretics. After his departure she expressed the opinion that it was enough to punish those who caused insurrection, held secret meetings, or possessed bad books. She asked the king to pardon the Anabaptists imprisoned at Utrecht, Middelburg, and other places, if they would recant. When the king refused to spare their lives she ordered their execution in December 1565, at the same time expressing her opinion that such measures were harmful. On Aug. 20, 1565, she wrote a letter to Count John de Ligne, Duke of Aremberg, stadholder of Friesland, urging him to keep a watchful eye on the Anabaptists and other sects. In December 1567, when Alva came, she left the Netherlands protesting against the harsh measures which he was instructed to execute against the "heretics." (*ML* III, 35 f.)   NEFF.

Margaretha, wife of the peasant Hans of Schlüchtern (Schlüechta) in the Palatinate, Germany, one of the 14 Anabaptists who were cross-examined on Sept. 16, 1535, in the castle at Passau, where they lay in prison. She states that she had been baptized upon confession of her faith ten(?) years before by Jörg of Ingersheim (see **Leserlin**), and that she came from Moravia, and wished to return to the Oberland. Like her husband, she could not be moved from her faith. (*ML* III, 35.)   W.W.

Margarethe of Heilbronn, a widow, a prisoner in the castle at Passau, Bavaria, in 1535. She confessed that she had been baptized five years previously by a preacher named Hans, who had since died. In spite of chains she remained true to her faith. (*ML* III, 35.)   W.W.

Margenau, located on the Kurushan River, a tributary of the Molotschna River, was a village of the Molotschna Mennonite settlement, Gnadenfeld volost, Berdyansk district, Ukraine, founded in 1819. The village consisted of some 300 inhabitants and was primarily agricultural. During the famine of 1932-33, more than 50 persons died. Under the Soviets many individuals were exiled. When the German army approached in 1941, the Margenau Mennonite population was sent to Asiatic Russia.

Only a few remained during the German occupation and have since reached America. (*ML* III, 36.)
                                                C.K.

Margenau - Alexanderwohl - Landskrone Mennonite Church was composed of Mennonites living in the villages listed in the name, Molotschna settlement, Ukraine. The Margenau church was established in 1832, in which year a church building was erected in the village of Margenau. Originally Margenau belonged to the Flemish group of the Ohrloff-Petershagen-Halbstadt church (*q.v.*). In 1842-74 the church was known as the Margenau-Alexanderwohl Mennonite Church. Until 1890 the Alexanderkrone Mennonite Church had been a part of the congregation. After the emigration of the Alexanderwohl Mennonite Church to Kansas in 1874 the reorganized church in Russia with that name became a part of the Margenau church. In 1910, when the Landskrone group built a church, it seems to have become an independent congregation. After the Revolution, however, it was again an integral part of the Margenau church. In 1905 the Alexanderwohl group consisted of 355 members and 325 children and the Margenau church had 1,382 members and 1,492 children. (It is not clear whether these statistics include Landskrone.)

The first elder was Heinrich Wiens (1842-47), who was removed from his office when he opposed the reform efforts of Johann Cornies. For 14 years the congregation was cared for by Heinrich Töws, the elder of the Pordenau Mennonite Church. He was succeeded by Bernhard Peters (1861-87), Heinrich Koop (1887-1901), Peter Friesen (1901-7), Gerhard Plett (1907-28), and Heinrich T. Janz (1928-32). The last elder had to leave the congregation, because of the high taxes which neither he nor the congregation could pay. The congregational life gradually disintegrated because of the antireligious attitude of the Soviet government. One of the last and most impressive services conducted was the ordination of Heinrich T. Janz as elder conducted by his retiring predecessor, Gerhard Plett, who had baptized 1,543 members during his 20 years of service. The ordination took place at the church at Landskrone, on May 13, 1928.   C.K.

Friesen, *Brüderschaft,* 705; *Unser Blatt* III, 201; H. Dirks, *Statistik,* 62-63; A. A. Töws, *Mennonitische Märtyrer* I (N. Clearbrook, 1954) 116 ff.; *ML* III, 36.

Margenau-Schönsee: see Margenau-Alexanderwohl-Landskrone Mennonite Church.

Margokerto, a former Mennonite mission station on the island of Java (*q.v.*), Indonesia, formerly Dutch East Indies, operated by the Dutch Mennonite Mission Association, since 1940 an independent congregation. Missions started here in 1880. The membership in 1953 was 132, not including the 229 children. The pastor is R. Nitihardjo. (Reports of the Dutch Mennonite Mission Association.)   vDZ.

Margoredjo, the first missionary colony of the Mennonite mission on Java, Indonesia, former Dutch East Indies, is situated on the north side of Mt. Muria, ten miles from Taju (see map in article Java). The founder of this colony was Pieter Anton Jansz (*q.v.*), the son of the first missionary in Java,

Pieter Jansz, who had worked for many years without visible results in Japara. His son therefore tried another method, namely, evangelization by means of cultivating the land. He had recognized that the religious life of the Javanese was closely interwoven with their economic life, and that it is almost impossible for a Christian to remain true in a Mohammedan community. In 1880 he therefore sent a request to the colonial government to have a virgin forest given to his care. On Aug. 26, 1881, he received an area of 400 acres, on which he erected Margoredjo. The mission school at Japara, which his father had taken over from missionary Schuurmann, was now transferred to Margoredjo. He also built a teachers' seminary here in 1903 to train native teachers. All the native teachers in the Mennonite concession received their training here. After 30 years the seminary was closed for lack of funds.

From 1888 to 1901 Johann Fast worked with P.A. Jansz. In 1895 he built a church here, which was dedicated on Nov. 7, 1897, and a second missionary residence. In 1893 missionary Johann Hübert came to Margoredjo and took charge of the church at Kedungpendjalin (q.v.). In 1899 Johann Klaassen (q.v.) took charge of the medical work in connection with evangelism. The congregation grew in the faith. Attendance was good. The first missionary doctor was Dr. Bervoets, who operated the hospital with two nurses, H. Goosen and S. Riechert. In 1915 he took charge of the central hospital located at Kelet. From 1905 to 1937 N. Thiessen was in charge of the mother church at Margoredjo, also doing evangelistic work in the subsidiary congregations of Tegalamba, Tawangredjo, Kembang, Dukuhseti, Banjutawa, Taju, Puntjel, Bumiardjo, Udjungwatu, and Bandngardjo.

Since 1928 the Margoredjo church has been independent. Its first native preacher was Rubin. Since 1931 S. Harsesudirdjo has been the elder of the congregation, while Hardjosuwito (since 1939), Armujadi, and Martohadi (both since 1941) are preachers. In 1937 it had a membership of 1,830 souls; in 1953 the membership numbered 970 baptized members and 1,144 children.

During the Japanese occupation 1942-46 the congregation had to endure many hardships. The beautiful church of Margoredjo was destroyed by a band of nationalistic Mohammedans. After 1946 a period of new growth began.   D.A., J.M.

Records of the Dutch Mennonite Mission Association; *Uit Verleden en Heden der Doopsgezinde Zending* (n.p., 1947, 26-28); *ML* III, 35.

Margriet, the wife of Jan Inghels of Brugge, Belgium, was (re)baptized there in 1537. In the next year she was arrested and persuaded by the inquisitor to recant. Notwithstanding the fact that she penitently returned to the Catholic Church she was sentenced on Aug. 17, 1538, to be buried alive. Margriet was the first victim of Anabaptist persecution at Brugge. (Verheyden, *Brugge*, 31, No. 4.)
vDZ.

Margriet Dregge, widow of Hendrik Bosbas, an Anabaptist martyr, was sentenced to death on March 27, 1536, at Antwerp, Belgium, because of Anabap-

tism. She was put into a sack and thrown into the Scheldt River. Her small property was confiscated. (*Antw. Arch.-Blad* VII, 392, 426; XIV, 14 f., No. 152.)
vDZ.

Margriet Jan Herkensdochter, an Anabaptist martyr, drowned at Utrecht, Netherlands, on June 11, 1539. Particulars about this martyr were not available except that she was the wife of Steffen van Halteren of Holthuizen in the Bishopric of Münster, Westphalia.
vDZ.

Berigten van het Hist. Genootschap Utrecht IV, 2 (1851) 139; Mellink, *Wederdopers*, 237.

Margriete van den Berghe, an Anabaptist martyr: see **Grietgen van Lier**.

Margriete van Halle, an Anabaptist martyr: see **Grietgen Bonaventuers.**

Margriete (Margriet), Jeroons Huysvrouwe, an Anabaptist martyr, executed at Antwerp, Belgium, on July 6, 1557, with Claerken Boucket. They were put into a sack and drowned. Margriete, whose official name was Marguerite Venneau, was the wife of Jeronimus van der Capellen (q.v.), who had suffered martyrdom at Antwerp on May 22, 1557. The name of Margriete, who died valiantly, is found in hymn No. 16 of the *Lietboecxken van den Offer des Heeren*, "Aenhoort Godt, hemelsche Vader" (Hear, O God, heavenly Father).
vDZ.

Offer, 553 note, 565; *Mart. Mir.* D 185, E 569; *Antw. Arch.-Blad* VIII, 434, 438, 469; XIV, 22 f., No. 249; Wolkan, *Lieder*, 63, 71.

Margriete Willems uyt Hitland, an Anabaptist martyr, sentenced at Amsterdam, Holland, on July 10, 1535, to be hanged and strangled, which was a rather unusual way of executing women. Margriete, who was the widow of Willem de Propheet (Willem de Cuyper, q.v.), had been (re)baptized by Jan Volkertsz (q.v.) "four or five years ago," i.e., about 1531; Jan Volkertsz had also performed her marriage. Margriete was one of the Anabaptists who had sailed from Amsterdam in March 1534 en route to Münster (q.v.), but were arrested at Bergklooster (q.v.). She then was released, but soon after arrested again because of Anabaptist activity, also being charged of having contact with the Amsterdam Anabaptist bishop and leader Jacob van Campen (q.v.). It is not clear whether she recanted or not. (Grosheide, *Verhooren*, 108 f.; Mellink, *Wederdopers*, 104, 147, 191, 346.)
vDZ.

Margriette Wynants, an Anabaptist martyr: see **Grietje van Brussel**.

Maria van Beckum: see **Beckum.**

Maria (1505-88), Queen of Hungary, daughter of Philip I, wife of King Louis, who fell in the battle of Mohacs in 1526, was regent of the Netherlands 1530-55, governing in the name of her brother Charles V. It was during her reign that the Anabaptist movement arose in the Netherlands and its severe persecution was instituted. She is described as a very capable woman, who was at first not hostile to the Reformation. At the death of her husband she received a letter of condolence from Luther.

Melanchthon was personally acquainted with her. In 1539 Pope Paul III accused her of "Lutheranism." Nevertheless she always complied with the wishes of her brother throughout her official life. A number of persecution orders were issued, and inquisitors searched the country. The Anabaptists especially suffered relentless persecution; the order of 1535 referred primarily to them. When the Dutch court, inclined to lenience, asked the regent for instructions, she ordered the death of all the victims. (*DB* 1906, 21-23, 29; *ML* III, 36.)   vDZ.

Maria of Montjoie (Monschau, *q.v.,* in the Eifel, Germany, near the Belgian border), an Anabaptist martyr, who was drowned in 1552 after an imprisonment lasting nearly two years. She valiantly resisted all pleas and threats to give up her faith. On the way to the place of execution she sang cheerfully. She said, "I have been the bride of a man, but today I hope to be the bride of Christ, and to inherit His kingdom with Him." At the water's edge they held her two hours, hoping to persuade her to forsake the truth. She said, "I adhere to my God; proceed with what you have come here for." She died courageously with the words, "O heavenly Father, into Thy hands I commend my spirit." Her death is described in a song, "Ach fröhlich will ich singen," found in the *Schön Gesangbüchlein,* Trier copy, No. 96; *Ausbund,* No. 25; Wackernagel, *Kirchenlied* V, 1082 f.   NEFF, E.C.

Mart. Mir. D 131, E 525; Wolkan, *Lieder,* 100-2, 136; E. Bax, *Het Protestantisme in het Bisdom Luik* II (The Hague, 1941) 422-24; Ernst Crous, "Auf Mennos Spuren am Niederrhein," *Der Mennonit* IX (1956) 10 f.; *ML* III, 36.

Maria Janssen, an Anabaptist martyr: see **Maeyken Janssens.**

Mariawohl, a village in the Molotschna Mennonite settlement, South Russia, with about 250 Mennonite inhabitants before World War I. An important battle was fought here in 1920.   A.KE.

Marie Baernt Gerytsdochter, a native of Achtersloot near IJsselstein, Dutch province of Utrecht, who had been (re)baptized in the spring of 1534 by Gerrit Ghysen of Benschop in his house at Benschop. She was a daughter of Brechte Lambrechtsdochter and married to Gheryt Kievit of Benschop, who was put to death at Amsterdam in 1540 because of revolutionary activities (he had apparently robbed some Catholic churches). Marie also belonged to the revolutionary wing of Anabaptism, being a follower of Jan van Batenburg (*q.v.*) and Appelman (*q.v.*), to whom she was married after the death of her first husband. She was apprehended in May 1544 and executed at The Hague on June 26, 1545, by drowning. She probably repented and returned to the Catholic Church, because she was buried in consecrated earth. Marie Baernt Gerytsdochter is one of the most striking examples of revolutionary Anabaptism, which had nothing to do with real and peaceful Anabaptism.   vDZ.

Inv. Arch. Amst. I, Nos. 328, 744 f.; Grosheide, *Bijdrage,* 146 f.; Mellink, *Wederdopers,* 232, 240, 411.

Marie Kerckhoffs, an Anabaptist martyr, burned at the stake on July 27, 1573, on the Houtmarkt at Maastricht, Dutch province of Limburg. Marie was a native of Maastricht and lived there; she was about 30 years of age and the mother of four children. She had been (re)baptized in a house at Maastricht by Henrick Kroch (see **Krufft**) from Germany together with some others, whose names she refused to tell. Even in severe torture she gave no further information. Marie was typical of the loyal Mennonite martyrs; she refused to be comforted by Catholic priests, saying that she "desired to live and die in her faith"; and that sins could only be forgiven by God, but not by priests; for this reason she did not attach importance to the Catholic sacrament of confession. She also held a low opinion of the Mass. Quietly and faithfully she spoke about her faith, and steadfastly suffered martyrdom.   vDZ.

W. Bax, *Het Protestantisme in het Bisdom Luik* II (The Hague, 1941) 312 f., 602-4.

Marie (Marijken) **'s Keysers,** a daughter of Joos van Deynse, and a sister of the martyr Olyverynken 's Keisers (*q.v.*), had received baptism upon her faith at Gent, Belgium, in 1568 or 1569. She was arrested and died in prison at Gent, on May 10, 1573. (Verheyden, *Gent,* 62, No. 220.)   vDZ.

Marie von der Kuhlen, an Anabaptist who was arrested in 1559 and tried at Waldfeucht, district of Millen in the duchy of Jülich, Germany. She had been (re)baptized six years before at Lichterwald in Jülich by Elder Lemken (*q.v.*), together with about 20 persons, whose names she did not know, all from the Dutch Maas district (now Dutch province of Limburg). It is not known whether Marie died as a martyr or not.   vDZ.

W. Bax, *Het Protestantisme in het Bisdom Luik* I (The Hague, 1937) 302.

Marie Sioucke huysvrouwe, a Dutch martyr belonging to the revolutionary wing of Anabaptism, was arrested on April 7, 1535, when the Oldeklooster (*q.v.*) was reconquered. She was drowned at Leeuwarden on April 14, 1535. (K. Vos, *Menno Simons,* Leiden, 1914, 228.)   vDZ.

Marie Vlamincx (Vlemincx) (in *Offer* and *Martyrs' Mirror* called *Mariken*), an Anabaptist martyr, strangled and burned at the stake on Jan. 31, 1551, at Lier in Brabant, Belgium, together with Gielis van Aerde, Tanneken van Roosbroecke, and Godevaert Mertens. The *Offer* and the *Martyrs' Mirror* give 1550 as year of execution without exact date; the exact date is found in *Antw. Arch.-Blad.* Marie was a woman of 75; she was born in St-Truyen, Belgium. Neither in the hymn "Alsmen screef duyst vijfhondert en daertoe noch vijftich jaer," found in a number of Dutch hymnals including (No. 17) the *Lietboecxken van den Offer des Heeren,* nor in the account given by van Braght are there many particulars. Marie frankly confessed her faith. When she was asked whether she desired to confess her sins to a (Catholic) priest before she died, she answered that she repented the fact that she had formerly confessed her sins to mortal ears.   vDZ.

Offer, 568-77; *Mart. Mir.* D 96 f., E 494; *Antw. Arch.-Blad* VII, 393; XIV, 18 f., No. 199; Wackernagel, *Lieder,* 126; Wolkan, *Lieder,* 63, 78; *ML* III, 73.

Marienburg, a city (1939 pop. 27,318) on the Nogat River in West Prussia. The castle, built in 1274, was the capital of the Teutonic Knights, falling to the Poles in 1460. In the second half of the 17th century many foreigners, including Mennonites, were admitted to the castle grounds and allowed to pursue their trades there. Their competition with the citizens caused the latter to send a complaint to the king, and after decades of strife the city took the castle in lease, and the Mennonites, who had hitherto not been granted citizenship, were now made citizens. On Sept. 13, 1772, Marienburg came again into the possession of the Prussians. It had a population of 4,575 at that time.

Beginning in the latter years of the 17th century the Mennonites held services on the castle grounds, and later in Sandhof near Marienburg in private homes. In 1906 the Heubuden (*q.v.*) congregation built a meetinghouse in Marienburg; services were held here every Sunday and church holiday, but there was no organized congregation. In 1940 there were 350 Mennonites in Marienburg. The group was dissolved when the Russians came in the spring of 1945 and the Mennonite population was evacuated westward. The meetinghouse was converted into a cinema. A.D.

E. Dormann and H. Eckerdt, *Geschichte des Kreises Marienburg* (1862, 1868); W. Hunsberger, "The Danzig Mennonite Church Buildings Today," *Menn. Life* IV (July 1949) 10; *ML* III, 36.

Marienburger Werder, a level lowland along the Baltic Sea at the mouth of the Vistula River, consisting of the Gross-Werder (large marsh) between the Vistula and the Nogat, and the Klein-Werder between the Nogat and Lake Drausen. With the Danzig Werder to the west of the Vistula and the lowlands lying north of the Vistula at Danzig and Elbing they constitute the Vistula-Nogat delta. About 160 sq. miles of cultivated land lie from 3 to 7 feet below sea level. The Marienburg Werder was occupied by the Teutonic Order in 1242 and the Danzig Werder in 1309. In the second half of the 13th century several villages were settled in the Gross-Werder by German settlers. Throughout the 14th century dikes were built on both sides of the Vistula and Nogat and most of the Werder was settled. In 1456 the Danzig Werder came into the possession of the city of Danzig, and in 1466 the Marienburg Werders passed into the possession of the Poles.

In 1520-30 the Reformation made its appearance in the Werders. Many of the peasants and dike workers accepted Lutheranism. The Lutherans as well as the Mennonites were benefited by the Confederation of Warsaw adopted in 1585 by the Prussian estates, promising mutual toleration. But by 1608 the bishop of Culm gave orders to the Landtag not to tolerate the Mennonites. Likewise the bishop of Ermland ordered in 1648 that religious liberty should be granted only to the Lutherans and should not include the Mennonites.

In 1642 the chamberlain Willibald von Haxenberg (*q.v.*) succeeded in extorting 80,000 florins from the Mennonites, giving the landed estates an occasion to rise to their defense. When the Mennonites appealed to King Ladislaus IV they received from him the *Privilegium* of Dec. 22, 1642 (Mannhardt, p. LX). In spite of recurrent hostility on the part of the Landtag at Marienburg and the parliament at Warsaw the Mennonites were able to maintain themselves in the lowlands, where good use could be made of their industry and skill.

From 1328 on, there are reports of broken dikes causing the Werders to be flooded and ruined by the Vistula and the Nogat. In 1540 and 1543 the Vistula broke through its dike and flooded the Danzig Werder. For many years most of the lower Werder remained a desolate area largely covered with water. Then came the Dutch, who offered to restore the lost territory at their own expense. On Nov. 28, 1547, the Danzig city council granted the village and estate of Reichenberg to Philippus Edzema, and granted him permission to settle it with people of his nationality (Dutch). In the same year the Dutch were granted Scharfenberg and Landau, in 1550 Wesslinken, in 1552 Schmerblock, in 1556 Breitfelde, in 1601 Schönrohr, as well as Hochzeit and Neunhuben. These villages, covering over 10,000 acres, were known as the Dutch villages. They were granted many liberties by the Danzig city council, which were maintained until 1857 in spite of the objections of the other villages.

These Dutch (Mennonite largely) immigrants attained significant success in a short time; the first five villages, which at first paid 90 marks a year, were soon paying 768 marks. Both in the drainage of the marshes and the improvement of the soil their work was of lasting importance and influence. The consequent export of grain made rapid increases. Whereas at the close of the 15th century 22,000 tons of grain were shipped via Danzig from Poland and Danzig, by 1575 Polish Prussia alone exported 100,000 tons. Their influence on cattle raising was also important, for they introduced the superior Dutch breeds of cattle and horses.

In 1582 the Mennonites made an appeal to the government to be relieved of the fee charged them for not complying with the demands of the state church regarding communion, church attendance, and infant baptism, stating that they had freely and openly admitted their faith 30 years before when they entered the country, and nothing had been said of the requirement of this crushing fee.

On March 15, 1526, the Vistula broke through its dike near Schöneberg, and flooded the lower areas of the Gross-Werder for many years, compelling the inhabitants to emigrate. In 1550 the Polish king leased the Tiegenhof area with 20 villages to Simon Loysen (*q.v.*) and his brothers, who then built a new center of management on the left bank of the Tiege. In 1562 they invited Mennonites from Holland to settle in this area, which was largely covered with water and overgrown with reeds. The Mennonites built dams on the Haff, Lake Drausen, and lower on the Nogat, Vistula, and the Tiege, and set up windmills to make the land arable. In 1578 Hans Loysen leased these restored lands to the Mennonites. About 1581 Ernst Weiher took this land from Loysen in payment of a debt; he signed a new contract with the Mennonites, which his widow renewed in 1601 for a period of 40 years (according to H. Donner). The Mennonites were very successful. Everywhere there were now grassy meadows, orchards, and gardens (Hartwich). The market town founded soon after 1600 by Melchior Weiher beside the castle was called Weihershof, and later Tiegenhof.

About 1565 the estates of the Teutonic Knights, which had been acquired by the Polish crown, Heubuden, Leske, Klein Montau, Thörichthof, Markushof, etc., were leased out to Mennonites. The low places in the Bärwalde region were also settled with Mennonites. In 1565 the council of Elbing parceled out the 14 sq. miles of the Ellerwald, which had been a communal pasture, and the citizens rented them to Dutch Mennonites, who began the systematic drainage and cultivation of this land. (See Farming . . . in West Prussia.)

In the 1530's many Dutch Sacramentists and Anabaptists immigrated to the lowland to the right of the Nogat, to Polish Prussia and the Danzig region. Some Mennonites also came from the duchy of Prussia, where Dutch Sacramentists had been settling since 1528. On the former Teutonic Knight estates 11 villages were settled, including Wickerau and Markushof. They built the dam on the west side of Lake Drausen, drained this lowland, and by 1631 established 15 villages here, including Thiensdorf and Augustwalde, by 1676 five more villages. Fifteen of these were probably Dutch settlements. After 1680 the river islands in the Vistula near Danzig and in the Nogat, which could be drained after the dikes had been built, were also reclaimed, an area of 110 sq. miles in 550 years, known as "Kampen," and inhabited for the most part by Mennonites.

The draining of these lands below sea level not only created new farm land, but also increased production on the higher lands by lowering the water table. Although the Dutch had the lowest, least valuable land, they improved the soil so consistently that their villages in a short time not only equaled but surpassed the more elevated villages of the Teutonic Order in the number of cattle and productivity of the soil. This settlement of Flemish and Frisian Mennonites in the Vistula-Nogat delta is the cradle of Mennonitism in Russia and of a large block of that in America.

Exact dates cannot be given for many of the Dutch settlements in the delta, for there was no formal settlement. The land was leased out by the owners to the Mennonites. Not until the law of March 2, 1850, was passed did the Mennonites receive title to the land.

The settlements of the period of the Teutonic Knights were made in the form of closed villages. Homes were separate from barns and stables; the dwelling houses frequently had the characteristic Vorlaube, and the land was divided into parcels. The settlers of the 16th century (Dutch) built isolated farms surrounded by their land, or in even rows along a dike so that the farm buildings faced the land. In the lower villages dirt embankments had to be thrown up around the houses to prevent spring floods. Dwelling houses and farm buildings were joined under one roof, sometimes forming a right angle or even a rectangle. Roofs were thatched with straw or reed.

In the southern part of the Gross-Werder in and around Marienburg the Heubuden Mennonite church has been in existence since the middle of the 16th century. In the Elbing region of the Gross-Werder in Tiegenhof and in Bärwalde, the Flemish group was organized, while the Frisians living here united in 1585 to form the Orlofferfelde (q.v.) congregation. In 1735 the Flemish group was divided into four parts because of the wide area it covered: Tiegenhagen, Rosenort (Elbing), Ladekopp (Orloff), and Fürstenwerder (Bärwalde). Each division had its own preachers and deacons; one elder served all. In the Klein-Werder the Thiensdorf congregation was formed.

On Sept. 13, 1772, Marienburg passed to Prussia, and in 1793 the Danzig Werder also. The Elbing region had been controlled by Prussia since 1702. In 1788 began the great migration of the Mennonites to South Russia, and in 1851 to eastern Russia. In 1874-92 many Mennonites emigrated from Russia, also some from Prussia, to the United States and Canada.

In 1937 there were 4,100 Mennonites in the Gross-Werder, 1,550 in the Klein-Werder, and 300 in the Danzig Werder, a total of 5,950 members. The Werder was lost to the Mennonites in 1945, when it was occupied by the Russians and all the Mennonites were evacuated.   A.D.

H. Bertram, Danziger Deichverband 1407-1907, Die Eindeichung und Besiedlung des Weichseldeltas (1926); W. L. Baume and O. Kloeppel, Das Weichsel-Nogat-Delta (1924); M. Toeppen, Beiträge zur Geschichte des Weichseldeltas (1894); B. Schmidt, Bau- und Kunstdenkmäler des Kreises Marienburg (1919); C. Parey, Der Marienburger Kreis (1864); E. Dormann and H. Eckerdt, Geschichte des Kreises Marienburg (1862 und 1868); Felicia Szper, Nederlandsche Nederzettingen in West-Pruisen (Enkhuizen, 1913); Br. Schumacher, Niederländische Ansiedlungen (Königsberg, 1902); H. Donner, notes of 1735-1805; W. Mannhardt, Die Wehrfreit der Altpreussischen Mennoniten (Marienburg, 1863); Horst Quiring, "Die Auswanderung der Mennoniten aus Preussen," in Gesch.-Bl., 1954; H. S. Bender, "Von Danzig bis Elbing," loc. cit.; Herbert Wiebe, Das Siedlungswerk niederländischer Mennoniten im Weichseltal zwischen Fordon und Weissenberg bis zum Ausgang des 18. Jahrhunderts (Marburg a.d. Lahn, 1952); Inv. Arch. Amst. I, Nos. 1070, 1124-26, 1552-63, 1570-73, 1576, 1675, 1677, 1680, 1688, 1691-96, 1703-12, 1739-45; II, Nos. 2626, 2646, 2650 f.; II, 2, Nos. 722, 734-37, 741 f., 746, 752, 755, 798, 801, 804-8; ML III, 36-39.

Marienhafe (Marienhove), a hamlet in East Friesland, Germany, where Leenaert Bouwens (q.v.) in 1563-65 baptized 11 persons. Since there was never a Mennonite congregation at Marienhafe, it may be assumed that the newly baptized joined either the Emderland or the Norden congregation.   vDZ.

Mariental Mennonite Brethren Church, a subsidiary of the Rückenau (q.v.) M.B. Church of South Russia, was established as a schism from the Alexandertal congregation. In 1887 Heinrich Ewert (preacher of the Mennonite Church), Johann Penner, and Jakob Hain joined the Mennonite Brethren following a visit to Rückenau. Gerhard Claassen (a teacher) joined them, as well as some other members; these organized a small congregation with a church in Mariental. They were then joined in 1896 by Johann Wiebe, the elder of the Mennonite Church, who became the elder of the small congregation. In

1900 Peter Köhn of Waldheim (a graduate of St. Chrischona, Switzerland) was called to preach for them; he soon realized that this group could not exist as a Mennonite Brethren congregation, and aided in reorganizing it as an Alliance (q.v.) congregation (Allianzgemeinde), so that members could be received without rebaptism. Köhn, who was held in high esteem by all groups, also found opportunity to preach in the Mennonite church. In 1907 Köhn returned to his native town because the small congregation was unable to support him. Then Jakob Töws was ordained elder (he had also previously been a Mennonite preacher) and served until he was banished to Siberia in 1925.   B.H.

Mariental, the name of two villages in Russia. The older was established in 1820 in the Molotschna Mennonite settlement in South Russia and from 1870 belonged to the Gnadenfeld district. The second village was founded in 1863 in the Alexandertal settlement in the province of Samara. In 1887 the Mennonite Brethren built a church here. In 1905 the congregation numbered 98 souls; in 1913 the membership was 250 souls. They suffered severely during the Revolution. (ML III, 39.)   NEFF.

Marientaubstummenschule (Mary School for the Deaf), at Tiege, Molotschna, South Russia, was organized in 1881 and named after Czarina Maria on the occasion of the 25th anniversary of the reign of Alexander II, who granted the patent for the school under date of Dec. 21, 1881. It did not actually get started until 1885, and did not have its own building until 1890, having been conducted in a house in Blumenort owned by Gerhard Klassen, a great friend and supporter of the school. A Protestant Armenian, A. G. Ambartsumov, trained in Switzerland, was largely responsible for the idea of the school and was the first teacher 1885-91. The school was established by the Halbstadt district civil government (later joined by the Gnadenfeld district), with the moral support of the churches, and the two representatives of the two districts on the board of directors (a total of nine directors) always had to include one elder or preacher. The school in its full development had a nine-year course equal to the regular elementary school curriculum with five teachers and 40 pupils. It was supported by freewill offerings coming from all Mennonite groups in Russia, and had a small endowment fund. The Mennonite General Conference, though not directly responsible, gave it warm support. The school was a great success. P. M. Friesen said of it, "This first charitable institution of the Mennonites of Russia is a precious jewel (kostbarer Schmuck) and deserves all love and zealous support." The school was finally closed by the Soviet government.†   H.S.B.

Friesen, Brüderschaft, 655-57; A. Görz, "Kurzgefasster Bericht über die Marienschule für Taubstumme in Blumenort in Südrussland," in H. G. Mannhardt's Jahrbuch der Altevangelischen Taufgesinnten oder Mennoniten-Gemeinden (Danzig, 1888); ML III, 39.

Marienwerder (Polish, Kwidzyn), a town (1939 pop. 20,484), East Prussia, Germany (Polish since 1945), founded by the Teutonic Knights in 1233. In 1720 the Mennonites began to appear in the city as quietly naturalized citizens, whereas there had been scattered Mennonites in the Marienwerder Upper Lowland since 1650, and in the Lower Lowland in a closed group, which was later known as the Tragheimerweide congregation (q.v.), since 1550. In 1937 there were 78 Mennonites living in Marienwerder, including 18 unbaptized children. Services were held every fourth week in the Protestant church. In 1945, in the final stages of World War II, most of the Mennonite families were evacuated to West Germany or Denmark. (ML III, 39.) E.Tg.

Marietta (Ohio) CPS Camp No. 8 was opened in June 1941 and was closed in April 1943. It was operated as a co-operative camp by the Brethren and Mennonites until May 1942, when the latter became the sole operating agency. The camp was located seven miles southeast of Marietta on the crest of a hill overlooking the Ohio River. It was the first Forest Service camp operated by the MCC, the assignment consisting primarily of work in the forest nursery.   M.G.

M. Gingerich, Service for Peace (Akron, Pa., 1949) 126.

Marietta Mennonite Mission (MC), located at Essex and Porter Streets, Marietta, Pa., was founded in 1928 by the district mission board of the Lancaster Mennonite Conference. In 1951 the entire membership (40) with the minister, John Hiestand, withdrew from the Lancaster Conference to form the Congregational Mennonite Church (q.v.), which has remained unaffiliated. The deacon alone remained in the conference. No formal membership was reported in 1956.   M.G.

Marijn Amare, an Anabaptist martyr: see **Marijn Euwout.**

Marijn (Martijne) **Euwout,** an Anabaptist martyr, burned at the stake on Dec. 10, 1561, at Brugge, Belgium. In van Braght's Martyrs' Mirror this martyr is erroneously called Marijn Amare. She was born at Middelburg, Dutch province of Zeeland. Living at Brugge, she was arrested there with a large number of members on Nov. 10, 1561, when a meeting of the Brugge Mennonite congregation was surprised outside the town. Marijn and her comartyrs are celebrated in a hymn, "Genade ende vrede moet Godvresende zijn" (Mercy and peace should be to the God-fearing), found in Veelderhande Liedekens of 1569 and other Dutch hymnals and reproduced by Wackernagel. In this hymn she is called Martijne without a family name. The Bibliographie lists Marijn Amare as identical with Martijntgen Aelmeers (q.v.), but this is an error. vDZ.

Mart. Mir. D 288, E 655; Verheyden, Brugge, 48, No. 32; Bibliographie II No. 16; Wackernagel, Lieder, 130.

Marijntgen (Marijtgen) **van Male** (or Martynckin Maelbouts, Malebosch), an Anabaptist martyr, beheaded on Dec. 12, 1564, at Gent, Belgium, with her sister Pierijntgen. They were natives of Thielt in Flanders and daughters of a Zegher. Other particulars are lacking. Van Braght's Martyrs' Mirror names this martyr twice: first as Marijntgen van Male, and then as Martijntgen Maelbouts. In neither case does he give the exact date of execution. This martyr is listed among the martyrs of Gent in a hymn found in the *Lietboecxken van den Offer des Heeren* of 1578. The account on this martyr found in *ML* III is incorrect. (*Offer*, 652; *Mart. Mir.* D 301, 306; E 666, 670; Verheyden, *Gent*, 30 f., No. 103; *ML* III, 44.)   vDZ.

Marijtgen (Marritgen), wife of Huyge Jacobsz Kraen (*q.v.*), an Anabaptist drowned on April 25, 1534, at the Hague, Holland. She was a native of Hazerswoude, Dutch province of South Holland. The account given by van Braght's *Martyrs' Mirror*, stating that she was drowned at Haarlem in 1532, is not correct. Recent research has proved that both Marijtgen and her husband Huyge were among the revolutionary Münsterites (*q.v.*) who sailed in March 1534 en route to Münster; this fact seems to have been unknown to van Braght.   vDZ.

   Mart. Mir. D 34, E 441; *Inv. Arch. Amst.* I, No. 745; Mellink, *Wederdopers*, 190.

Mariken, an Anabaptist martyr: see **Maria Vlamincx** and **Maeyken Goossens**.

Mariken (Marijtgen, Maritgen Adriaens), an Anabaptist martyr, was sentenced on Aug. 21, 1552, at Leiden, Dutch province of South Holland, to be buried alive. When she was led to the place of execution she prayed, "Lord, strengthen us, who suffer for Thy Word, which few are willing to do. I am not worthy to suffer for Thy name; but, Lord, Thou shalt make me worthy." Mariken and three other martyrs, sentenced to death on the same day, are celebrated in the hymn "Eylaes ick mach wel suchten" (Alas, I must make complaint), written by the martyr Adriaen Cornelisz (*q.v.*); this hymn is found (No. 18) in *Lietboecxken van den Offer des Heeren* and also in *Nieu Liedenboeck* of 1562. In this hymn Mariken is called a young woman. Van Braght's *Martyrs' Mirror* erroneously gives 1550 as the year of her death. The martyr Mariken named in hymn No. 6 of the *Lietboecxken van den Offer des Heeren* is either identical with this martyr or with Mariken Jansdochter (*q.v.*). (*Offer*, 526, note 1, 578 ff.; *Mart. Mir.* D 97, E 495; Wolkan, *Lieder*, 61.)   vDZ.

Mariken (Maeyken) **Fransse**, in the official records called Mariken Filiers (Filgiers), born at Gorinchem, Dutch province of South Holland, an Anabaptist martyr, burned at the stake at Antwerp, Belgium, on June 28, 1559, because she "obstinately persists in the doctrines of the Anabaptists." The accounts of *Offer des Heeren* and van Braght's *Martyrs' Mirror* are incomplete. Mariken Fransse is commemorated in the hymn "Aenhoort Godt, hemelsche Vader" (Hear, O God, heavenly Father), No. 16 of the *Lietboecxken van den Offer des Heeren*, which was also inserted in the *Nieu Liedenboeck* of 1562.   vDZ.

   Offer, 566; *Mart. Mir.* D 244, E 618; *Antw. Arch.-Blad* IX, 2, 8; XIV, 26 f., No. 293; *ML* III, 39.

Mariken (Marrijtgen) **Jansdochter**, an Anabaptist martyr, sentenced to death on Aug. 21, 1552, at Leiden, Dutch province of South Holland, to be burned at the stake if she persisted in error and to be buried alive if she recanted. She did not forsake her faith and in consequence she was burned; when she was standing on the execution place, she said to the bystanders, "There is no other way to salvation," and she died with the words of Stephen (Acts 7:59), "Lord Jesus, receive my spirit." Mariken Jansdochter, together with a few other martyrs put to death at Leiden in 1552, is celebrated in a hymn composed by Adriaen Cornelisz (*q.v.*), beginning "Eylaes ick mach wel suchten" (Alas, I must make complaint), found both in the *Lietboecxken van den Offer des Heeren* (No. 18) and *Nieu Liedenboeck* of 1562. Perhaps the martyr, who is also called Mariken and is named in hymn No. 6 of the *Lietboecxken van den Offer des Heeren*, is identical with Mariken Jansdochter. (*Offer*, 526, note 1, 578 ff.; *Mart. Mir.* D 132, E 526.)   vDZ.

Mariken van Meenen (Maeyken Eghels), an Anabaptist martyr, drowned at the Steen castle at Antwerp, Belgium, on Sept. 5, 1562, with several other martyrs. Mariken, who was a native of Haerlebeke near Kortrijk, Flanders, is commemorated in the hymn "Lieve broeders, ick groet u met sanghen" (Dear brethren, I greet you with songs), found in the *Nieu Liedenboeck* of 1562 and *Tweede Liedenboeck* of 1583 and reproduced by Wackernagel. The account found in van Braght's *Martyrs' Mirror* on Mariken and her fellow martyrs is rather insignificant, and erroneously gives as the date of execution of a number of martyrs Aug. 15, 1561. (*Mart. Mir.* D 288, E 655; *Antw. Arch.-Blad* IX, 141, 149; XIV, 32 f., No. 364; Wackernagel, *Lieder*, 140.)   vDZ.

Mariken Vrancken (Vrencken), an Anabaptist martyr, who was drowned at Stockheim "int Lant van Ludich" (Liege in Belgium?) together with her husband Thysken. The year of their execution is unknown, but it must have happened before 1547, in which year Metken (*q.v.*), Mariken's sister-in-law, gave the information concerning Thysken's and Mariken's death during her trial in August 1547 at Valkenburg, Dutch province of Limburg. Particulars about Mariken Vrancken and Thysken are unknown.   vDZ.

   W. Bax, *Het Protestantisme in het Bisdom Luik* I (The Hague, 1937) 326, 399.

Marinus van Dale, an Anabaptist martyr, drowned on Oct. 31, 1563, in the Steen castle at Antwerp, Belgium, because he had been rebaptized and "pertinaciously persisted in the doctrines of the Anabaptists." His property, some furniture and a few tools, was confiscated and publicly sold on June 27, 1562. Hence Marinus must have been imprisoned before this date. (*Antw. Arch.-Blad* IX, 142, 150, 162; XIV, 32 f., No. 368.)   vDZ.

Marion (Junction), S.D., is a town (pop. 775, about one third Mennonites) in Turner County, in the southeastern part of the state. It was laid out in August 1879 and named after the daughter of one of the officials of the Milwaukee Railroad Co. It is on the eastern edge of a large Mennonite settlement and consequently serves as an important Mennonite trading center. The Tieszen Home for the Aged is located here. It also has two chiropractic clinics operated by the grandsons of Derk Tieszen, who came from Russia in 1874 and became well known as a "bone-setter." J.D.U.

Marion County, Kan., is located north of the Santa Fe Railroad between Emporia and Hutchinson, north of Harvey County and east of McPherson County. It has a land area of 957 square miles and a population of 16,307 (1953). The first white settlers in the county located on Doyle Creek near the present town of Florence in 1858. In 1859 the population was 74. The Santa Fe trail ran through the northeast corner of Marion County and crossed to the southwest into McPherson County. Railroads crossing the county are the Atchison, Topeka, and Santa Fe; and the Chicago, Rock Island, and Pacific. The primary occupation is agriculture. Some of the most significant towns are Marion (county seat), Florence, Peabody, and Hillsboro.

Marion County has a large Mennonite population. Towns with a predominantly Mennonite population are Hillsboro, Lehigh, and Goessel. The Mennonites are located primarily in the southwestern part of the county. The first Mennonites to come to Marion County were M. W. Keim and his friends from Johnstown, Pa., who bought 5,000 acres of land from Case and Billings during the winter of 1869-70. The next Mennonite settlement in the county was established by Peter and Jacob Funk in 1873, who had come from Russia via Sommerfield, Ill., and purchased land from the Santa Fe through the agent A. E. Touzalin. They established the Brudertal settlement (see **Brudertal** Mennonite Church). The next group to settle were the Krimmer Mennonite Brethren under the leadership of Jacob A. Wiebe, who settled west of Marion (Center), in the village of Gnadenau (*q.v.*) in 1874. Mennonites from Poland established the Johannestal Mennonite Church (*q.v.*) north of Hillsboro and the Friedenstal Mennonite Church (*q.v.*) near Tampa. The Alexanderwohl Mennonites from Russia settled in seven villages in the southwest corner of Marion County in 1874. In the center of the settlement the town of Goessel (*q.v.*) is now located. This group has spread into neighboring Harvey and McPherson counties. In addition to these groups, the Mennonite Brethren gradually concentrated in the Hillsboro area. They maintain the Mennonite Brethren Publishing House (*q.v.*) and Tabor College (*q.v.*) in Hillsboro.

The General Conference Mennonite churches in Marion County are as follows: First of Burns (*q.v.*), Alexanderwohl (*q.v.*), Goessel (*q.v.*), Tabor (*q.v.*), Brudertal (*q.v.*), First of Hillsboro (*q.v.*), Johannestal (*q.v.*), Lehigh (*q.v.*), and Friedenstal (*q.v.*) at Tampa. The Mennonite Brethren have the following churches: Ebenfeld (*q.v.*), Hillsboro (*q.v.*), Tampa (*q.v.*), Gnadenau-Lehigh (*q.v.*), and Steinreich (*q.v.*) near Florence. The Krimmer Mennonite Brethren have the Springfield church (*q.v.*). The Gnadenau mother church has joined the Mennonite Brethren. The M.C. group has the Catlin church (*q.v.*) near Peabody. (See also **Kansas;** *ML* II, 39 f.) C.K.

Marion County, Mo., is located in the eastern part of the state about 50 miles south of the Iowa state line and on the Mississippi River. About 100 Mennonites are located in the eastern and central parts of the county, two families in adjoining Rolls County. The first Mennonite settled in Marion County in the late 1880's or early 1890's, coming here from Lancaster Co., Pa. There are two Mennonite (MC) churches in Marion County: Pea Ridge, 12 miles west of Palmyra, and the Hannibal Mission Church, 1530 Lyon St., Hannibal. The Palmyra Mennonite (MC) Church was closed in 1955. The former members are now in one of the two remaining congregations. The total membership (1956) is 108. J.F.Kr.

Marion County (Ohio) Mennonite Church (MC), now extinct, was founded by five Cullom, Ill., families who moved to the neighborhood of Morral in 1918-19. One member was Eli J. Christophel, a deacon. High land values and internal dissension prevented a normal congregational development. The group organized a Sunday school in 1920 and visiting ministers conducted services until 1923, when Levi L. Hartzler of West Liberty was appointed minister. He served until his death the next year. In 1923 one of the original settlers returned to Illinois. Between that date and 1927 the entire group moved away, some to Texas and some to West Liberty, Ohio. J.S.U.

Marion (S.D.) Evangelical Mennonite Brethren Church, located in Turner County, was formerly known as the Bruderthaler Church and also as "Wall's" Church. The congregation was organized with 11 members in 1893. The first church, erected in 1901, was replaced by the present structure in 1922. The membership in 1957 was 141. Ministers who have served the church are Benjamin Becker, Henry C. Unruh, D. P. Schultz, A. T. Duerksen, J. J. Gerbrandt, John R. Doerksen, C. A. Classen, and H. P. Fast. S.J.S.

Marion (Kan.) Mennonite Brethren Church, organized in 1884 by Elder Jacob Ehrlich as an affiliate of the Ebenfeld M.B. Church, was located one and one-half miles northwest of Marion, Kan. Ehrlich was succeeded by Johan J. Berg as leader. Its baptized membership remained small. As a result of some strong external influences the church decided to leave the Mennonite Brethren Conference, and affiliated with the German Baptists in 1889. A.E.J.

Marion Mennonite Church (MC), located five miles west of Howe, Lagrange Co., Ind., a member of the Indiana-Michigan Mennonite Conference, began as a mission outpost of the Shore congregation, near Shipshewana, Ind. On Dec. 10, 1944, the Marion Sunday school was organized under the direction of the Indiana-Michigan District Mission Board, with 18 charter members under the leadership of Willard Sommers. In 1950 the group was organized as an independent congregation, and on Nov. 12, 1950, Paul W. Haarer was ordained as minister to assist Sommers. The membership in 1955 was 78. The meetinghouse, built in 1903 by the Methodist Church and sold by them to the Mennonites, is a frame structure with a seating capacity of approximately 130. P.W.H.

Marion Mennonite Church (MC) is located one mile north of Marion and five miles south of Chambersburg, Franklin Co., Pa. Among the family names associated with the early history of the congregation were Hege, Bender, Burkholder, Shank, Whitmore, Over, Gingrich, Garman, Kriner, Gsell, Snively, Stauffer, and Lesher. The first meetinghouse was built of brick at Brown's Mill, eight miles south of Chambersburg. In 1867 this church was removed to the present site, and was replaced in 1898 by the present larger brick church. For the members who were left in Peters and St. Thomas townships when the church was moved away, a church was built one mile southwest of Williamson in 1869, both churches having been served by the same ministers ever since, although steps have been taken to organize the Williamson group into a separate congregation.

The following ministers have served the church (with dates of ordination): Jacob Hege 1832, Benjamin Lesher 1850, Jacob W. Hege 1892, George S. Ernst 1898, W. W. Hege 1907, J. Irvin Lehman 1922, and Norman H. Martin 1937. J. Irvin Lehman, one of the present ministers, is a great-great-grandson of the first minister.

In 1896 a Sunday school was started, and in 1912 young people's Bible meetings. The first evangelistic meetings were held in 1904, conducted by Abram Metzler. Among the most active leaders of the church was W. W. Hege, who promulgated young people's meetings, teacher-training classes, mission study classes, and Bible conferences. The membership of the congregation in 1954 was 100 but the approximate membership of the Marion, Williamson, Pleasant View, and Pond Bank congregations, the last three formerly outposts of the Marion church, was 321.   J.E.M.

Marital Avoidance, a question in the practice of the ban (q.v.), which has played an important and sad role in the history of the Anabaptist-Mennonite brotherhood, especially in Holland. As early as the conference of Emden in 1547 this question was raised, whether in the case of married couples, when one spouse has been placed under the ban by the church, all association between them must be avoided, a course that would closely resemble divorce. Adam Pastor and Frans de Kuiper answered the question in the negative, but the other elders present agreed with Menno Simons that marital avoidance was the proper method, but that instead of making rigid regulations, each case should be independently decided.

From now on the Mennonites were divided into two opposing camps in this matter. One party wanted to limit avoidance between spouses to spiritual matters (i.e., church affairs), and permit marital association on the same basis as before the banning. The stricter party, on the other hand, demanded complete separation from the person banned, which was to be observed also by married couples.

In 1550 Menno Simons replied affirmatively to an inquiry of the Groningen congregation in his appendix, "Answer to Several Questions" (Opera 1681, 474): "Whether married couples shall avoid one another on account of the ban," because the ban was a

regulation adopted by the brotherhood, to which all members were bound without exception. But Menno cautioned against ruthless application of the regulation. The application should not burden the conscience of the persons concerned. Also the Wismar Resolutions of 1554 (Point 3) required marital avoidance, but added that no violence should be done the conscience in the matter. The predominant tone was still one of moderation.

But this spirit soon changed. Leenaert Bouwens (q.v.), the most radical promoter of the ban, came to the fore. In 1556 he pronounced the ban on Swaentje Rutgers, who refused to consent to the avoidance of her husband on the ground that she did not want to forsake him in his spiritual need, but wanted rather to support him as much as possible. Menno Simons tried to mediate. He wrote to Emden in November 1556 when he was asked for advice, disapproving the excommunication of Swaentje Rutgers, pointing out the position of the Wismar Resolutions, and urging moderation and kindness. But in vain; nor did oral negotiations ease the situation. At the conference in Harlingen (1557) the influence of Leenaert Bouwens won. After first resisting, Menno finally consented to the severe interpretation. He is reported to have said, "I agree in everything; I accept your marital avoidance."

At a meeting in 1557 in Wüstenfelde Menno also sought to win Zylis and Lemke, the South German representatives, to favor marital avoidance. Zylis most vigorously opposed it. To him marital avoidance seemed an abomination, according to Matt. 19:5-6. Lemke, however, who remained with Menno for some time, adopted his position and offered to win his brethren in South Germany for it. But this did not happen, for Lemke became a pronounced opponent of marital avoidance. At the large conference held at Strasbourg in 1557 it was definitely repudiated. "It is still the sincere wish of those gathered here," they wrote to Menno Simons, "to the Dutch brethren, that they should not advise that a man and wife should separate on account of the ban, for it would result in more damage and offense than glory to God and the winning of souls, especially since the command of marriage is weightier than that of marital avoidance." Dirk Philips attacked the resolutions of Strasbourg in his booklet, Lieflijcke Vermaninghe of 1558 (BRN X, 249-65).

Menno Simons replied to this letter on June 11, 1558, with A Thorough Instruction and Account of Excommunication, in which he holds to his requirement of marital avoidance: "The heavenly marriage between Christ and our souls must be maintained firmly and unbroken, and . . . we may therefore not yield or deviate in the slightest to father or mother or husband or wife in any disobedience to His Word, for God our Lord will, shall, and must alone be the God of our conscience and the only Lord of our souls and not our father or mother, husband or wife."

This writing evoked a storm of disappointment among the South Germans. Zylis and Lemke replied with warmth, and Menno Simons could not refrain from replying to their reproaches in an angry tone. It is his last writing: A Thorough Reply to

Zylis and Lemke's Unmerited Malicious Calumniation (Jan. 28, 1559). In it he broke off fraternal relations with the South German brethren. In the same year Dirk Philips, Leenaert Bouwens, and other Dutch elders went to South Germany and banned their brethren who disagreed with them. Menno suffered from this strife. He is reported to have said shortly before his death, "How sorry I am to have consented to marital avoidance!"

After Menno's death Leenaert Bouwens and Dirk Philips with their followers carried the question of the ban and marital avoidance to the extreme. It is said to have occurred more than once that members of the severe party came into a house at night to take away from a banned husband a wife who was still questioning whether she should leave him or stay with him. There was no thought of yielding: "And although the banned husband pleaded and requested with tears, with his poor innocent children, with great pathetic and pitiful cries and weeping, that the unbanned mother might be permitted to stay with her poor little children, this did no good and they would not be moved to pity by such a sad situation." Many men could not discover for a long time, and some all their lives, what happened to their wives (Buruma, 42).

When the division between the Flemish and Frisian Mennonites occurred (1566-67), it sometimes happened that the husband adhered to the Frisians, while the wife belonged to the Flemish, with the result that married couples divided their money and children, went their separate ways and never reunited.

Several years later a division occurred among the Frisians on the matter of marital avoidance. Hoyte Renix, Lubbert Gerrits, Jan Heyndrixz, and Pieter Willemsz opposed marital avoidance. Lubbert Gerrits put his opinion into writing in his *Short, Simple Explanations.* Marital avoidance, he said, had been handed down by Leenaert Bouwens and Dirk Philips, but "if we read the Scriptures from Genesis to Revelation we find no case of its application. We will no longer do violence to the Scriptures and strive against God and God's Word."

When Lubbert was thereupon banned, he founded the party of Young Frisians. The strict party of Frisians also underwent a division on the matter of marital avoidance. The Jan Jacobsgezinden founded a party of their own in order to carry out their extreme interpretation of marital avoidance.

It was inevitable that this extreme interpretation of avoidance in marriage would lead to all sorts of disorder and offense. The author of *Vriendelijcke Aenspraeck aen alle Doopsghesinde over het Stuck ofte Puynct der Echt-mijdinghe* (1613) lamented: "How many families have been destroyed by marital avoidance! How many men and women have been disgraced! How many have lost their livelihood and their daily bread because the husband or wife had been punished and was unable to be at one with the congregation." "I must weep and with sad heart write this. But the Lord knows that I am telling the truth."

Hence it is not surprising that on several occasions the government intervened with legal regulations. The States of Friesland on April 8, 1597, strictly forbade the exercise of the ban which would lead to a complete separation and bring in its train other avoidance of civil and domestic life and living.

The quarrels over the question of marital avoidance resulted in a number of Dutch Mennonites, especially of the strictest branches, leaving the Mennonite Church in the 17th century and joining the Reformed Church. After 1700 marital avoidance was no longer practiced. The practice had been most strictly maintained by the Janjacobsz group (*q.v.*) even after all other branches had dropped it. The Waterlanders never practiced it, and the Flemish only rarely.

The Frankenthal Disputation (*q.v.*) of 1571 included a topic (No. 8) on the subject, "Whether Ban or Unbelief Separates a Marriage." The South German Anabaptists took a clear position contrary to the Dutch Mennonites, answering "No." The confession known as the Concept of Cologne (1591) dealt with this topic also.

In the Hutterite literature there is an interesting hint regarding a possible Hutterite practice of marital avoidance in the renowned *Church Regulations* (*Gemeinde-Ordnung*) of Andreas Ehrenpreis (*q.v.*) of 1640. Here Item III reads as follows: "It also happened that several excommunicated and shunned men lie with their wives in their beds. This [the discipline of marital avoidance] has been too little watched and heeded" (Beck, *Geschichts-Bücher*, 464). We may assume that most likely the principle had never been strictly observed among the Hutterites, and in later times was given up altogether. The ban, it was felt, cannot actually break the bonds of marital relations.

The Old Order Amish of North America still practice marital avoidance, although the strictness of the practice varies with the local traditions and the severity of the bishop. Marital avoidance was not one of the issues, however, that caused the original Amish division of 1693-97 (contrary to Neff, article **Ban**), although the general question of avoidance of banned persons was the major cause of the schism.   NEFF, H.S.B.

Y. Buruma, *Het huwelijk der Doopsgezinden in de zestiende eeuw* (1911); Kühler, *Geschiedenis* I, *passim;* ML I, 526-28.

Maritgen, the wife of Hans de Vette: see **Miertgen.**

Maritgen (Mariken), an Anabaptist martyr: see **Marie Vlamincx.**

Maritgen (Adriaens), an Anabaptist martyr: see **Mariken.**

Maritgen Davidsdr., an Anabaptist martyr of Leiden, Dutch province of South Holland, who was drowned with two companions at Alkmaar on June 7 or 17, 1539. (*DB* 1909, 8, 22 f.; *ML* I, 397.)
                                                  NEFF.

Maritgen Jacobsdochter, wife of Willem Heynricsz, was arrested on May 28, 1539, at Haarlem, Holland, and died about Sept. 22 of this year, when she was trying to escape from the St. Jans gate and crashed on the street. She was probably a follower of David Joris (*q.v.*).   vnZ.

Bijdragen en Mededelingen Hist. Genootschap Utrecht XLI (Amsterdam, 1920) 200 f., 208, 212-14, 218; Mellink, *Wederdopers,* 184 f.

Maritgen Jansdochter, an Anabaptist martyr: see **Mariken Jansdochter.**

Maritgen Thonisdochter, of Amsterdam, an Anabaptist martyr, a follower of David Joris (*q.v.*), was arrested on May 29 in the house of Lambert Duppijns (*q.v.*) at Haarlem, Dutch province of North Holland. After severe torture she was drowned there on June 3, 1539.   vdZ.

Bijdragen en Mededelingen Hist. Genootschap Utrecht XLI (Amsterdam, 1920) 201, 208, 210; Mellink, *Wederdopers,* 184.

Maritgen van Waestene: see **Miertgen.**

Maritgen Willem van Damsdochter, the wife of Jan van Halteren of Haarlem, was arrested there on May 24, 1573, because of rebaptism. On September 17 of the same year she died in the St. Jans tower after she had given birth to a child. The expression found in the records, that "she died as a Christian," seems to indicate that she forsook her Mennonite faith.
                    vdZ.

Bijdragen en Mededeelingen van het Historisch Genootschap Utrecht (Amsterdam, 1920) 201, 208, 216.

Maritgen Ysbrandsdochter, an Anabaptist martyr. She was the wife of Jan van Leyden (*q.v.*), and lived at Leiden, Dutch province of South Holland, where she kept the inn "Three Herrings." Here she was (re)baptized in November 1533 by Jan Matthysz of Haarlem (*q.v.*). In March 1534 she was one of the Anabaptists who sailed from Amsterdam en route to Münster, Westphalia, but being arrested at Bergklooster (*q.v.*) she was pardoned, apparently having recanted. Back in Leiden, however, she continued to gather revolutionary Anabaptists in her house, while her husband reigned in Münster as "King of Zion." In another house, also belonging to Maritgen, the Anabaptists also used to meet; here a plan was made to attack the city of Leiden (and perhaps also Amsterdam), but this project being betrayed, Maritgen was arrested on Jan. 23, 1535, and on Feb. 11, or shortly after, put to death at Leiden by burning at the stake. (*N.N.B.Wb.* V, 1163; Mellink, *Wederdopers,* 188, 195, 201.)   vdZ.

Mariupol (Mariopol) Mennonite Brethren Church. Mariupol is a city on the Sea of Azov in the Russian province of Ekaterinoslav, Ukraine. Northwest of Mariupol was the Bergthal Mennonite settlement, which was sold in 1874 when the Mennonites moved to Canada. This settlement became a part of the larger Catholic and Lutheran settlement known as the Planerkolonie (*q.v.*), which established daughter settlements west and east in the Don River Basin. One of the villages west of the river was Neuhoffnung, where Eduard Wüst (*q.v.*) was the minister of a separatist movement. Through his evangelistic work Protestants and Catholics were converted.

Around 1866 baptism by immersion was introduced at Mariupol. Among those baptized were J. Fitz, Schröder, Preiss, and Liedtke, who made contact in the villages near the Don River with Heinrich Bartel, Regehr, and Abr. Cornelssen of the Mennonite Brethren. Others who were working here were Johann and Karl Foth, W. Berchthold, Leppke, and Wölk. The number of Mennonite Brethren increased.

In the 1880's many of the Mennonite Brethren emigrated to North America. Those of Lutheran and Catholic background who remained in Russia encountered difficulties in registering as Mennonite Brethren with the Russian government. The Mariupol Mennonite Brethren group, which was then primarily of non-Mennonite background, joined the Baptist Union in 1887 as the Belachvetch Church in the Mariupol district and as the Liebental Church in the Don area. Some of these Baptists came to America and joined the Ebenfeld Mennonite Brethren of Kansas and Wittenberg, S.D. In 1886 the Mariupol Mennonite Brethren Church in Russia had a membership of 300 and a total population of 538. C.K.

Friesen, *Brüderschaft,* 427; J. F. Harms, *Geschichte der Mennoniten Brüdergemeinde* (Hillsboro, 1924) 67; J. A. Malinowsky, *Die Planerkolonien am Asowschen Meere* (Stuttgart, 1928).

Mariupol Mennonite Settlement: see **Planerkolonie.**

Marius (Mayer), **Augustin** (1485-1543), a Catholic theologian, dean of the theological school of the University of Vienna, Austria, and in the same year cathedral preacher in Regensburg, Bavaria, Germany, which was the time when Balthasar Hubmaier (*q.v.*) resigned his pastorate there. During this period Hans Denk was also in Regensburg and had some contact with Marius (preface to *Eyngelegte schrifft,* p. 1, reprinted by E. Dürr and Paul Roth in *Aktensammlung,* 584 ff.). Marius was probably instrumental in procuring for Denk a position in the local "Stift"; Denk resigned this position when he turned to Protestant doctrine (Staehelin, 428).

On Feb. 25, 1525, Marius received a call to Freising as suffragan, but remained in Regensburg over a year longer while he raised the sum he had to pay Rome for this position. In Freising he successfully attacked "false doctrine and heresy" (according to Gropp, his first biographer). In 1526 he was called to Basel to take the position of the suffragan, who had joined the Reformed Church, "in order to help to keep the sinking Catholic religion upright" (Reininger, 117).

Like Oecolampadius and his colleague Thomas Geyerfalk, Marius and his colleague Leonard Rebhan of St. Peter were commissioned to refute the teachings of the imprisoned Anabaptist leader "Karlin N." probably Karl Brennwald (*q.v.*), in a disputation. Oecolampadius wanted Denk also to take part in the disputation. In the entire history of the Anabaptists this is one of the few attempts to combine Catholic and Protestant forces in an effort to combat Anabaptist teaching.

Four articles were to be discussed: infant baptism, government, the oath, and discipleship (*Nachfolge*). The theses were drawn up by Karlin and presented to Oecolampadius and Marius shortly before the end of June 1527, as follows:

(1) Infant baptism is an abomination before God and idolatry. (2) The government is instituted by God; but if the government acts contrary to the

command of Christ, it is not Christian, and obedience to it is not obligatory. (3) The swearing of oaths is forbidden; it is not permissible for anyone to swear. For what is more than Yea and Nay is of the evil one; therefore one must not swear at all, not for any reason. (4) In short, he who teaches and acts contrary to Christ is a deceiver.

Before the disputation Marius declared to the council that he could not engage in debate with Karlin in the presence of Oecolampadius, since the latter was a *Freitäufer;* it was known that he had permitted postponing the baptism of children until their third year (Staehelin, *Briefe* II, 93, note 8). Another factor may have been the decree of the pope prohibiting disputation with heretics (Anshelm, 361). Marius requested and received permission to present his refutation in writing. He later published the address he delivered before the council with his official opinion.

The disputation was not held, but Karlin explained his four theses orally to the council. The Protestant and Catholic theologians were to present their arguments within four days.

The statement made by Bullinger and later by Hottinger (*Helvetische Kirchen-Geschichte* III, 387), that Oecolampadius disputed with the Swiss Brethren on these questions in St. Martin's church on June 10, 1527, is an error (Staehelin, *Briefe,* 78).

A few days after the theologians had handed in their opinions, the council issued a mandate against the Anabaptists (July 6, 1527), ordering compulsory baptism of infants, prohibiting adult baptism and religious meetings in the forests, and setting severe penalties on lodging Anabaptist preachers (Staehelin, *Das Buch,* No. 49). The opinions of the theologians appeared in print, Oecolampadius' on Aug. 15, 1527 (see Basel), and Marius' three years later.

The instigation to publish Marius' refutation was made by Johann Faber (*q.v.*), Hubmaier's opponent and Vicar General of Constance; he was later made court chaplain and confessor to Duke Ferdinand, and in 1529 provost at Ofen. On his journey to the Reichstag at Speyer in 1529 he visited Marius, who had moved back to Freising. The book by Marius appeared there in 1530 with the title, *Eyngelegte schrifft so uff anmutung eins Ersamen Raths zu Basel wider Carlin N. widerteufer D. Augustinus Marius Thompredicant und Wichbischoff überantwortet hat;* it has 44 pages (copies may be found in the state library of München, Exeg. 1179, city library of Frankfurt, Misc. var. 678, No. 1, and city library of Augsburg, Th. H. Marius 1530). Marius based his reply on the statements presented to the council by Karlin, taking them verbatim from the court records. It maintains a remarkably conciliatory tone (Blanke, *Corpus Reformatorum* XCIII 122). He comments that Karlin, a "poor, deceived Anabaptist," has not correctly understood the Holy Scripture, on which he bases his doctrine, recognizing the dead letter but not the spirit, and admonishes Karlin to "lay aside his errors and to desist from his erroneous interpretation of the doctrine of Christ."

Marius sent his reply to Johann Faber on March 31, 1529, asking him to present it to Cardinal Matthias Lang (*q.v.*) of Salzburg and to Bishop Con-

rad von Thüngen of Würzberg, whom he was to meet at the Reichstag in Speyer (Staehelin, *Briefe,* 300). The latter two are known to have been very severe in their opposition to the Anabaptists; in both Würzburg (*q.v.*) and Salzburg (*q.v.*) Anabaptists had been put to death for their faith. This booklet apparently drew the primate's attention to Marius, for on April 24, 1529, Bishop Conrad of Thüngen recommended Marius to the Würzburg chapter as cathedral preacher, offering a considerable sum from his own purse toward Marius' salary (Birkner, 87). Marius was well informed on the teachings of the individual reformers, and for this reason the bishops were glad to have his service (Birkner, 110).

In May 1529 Marius entered his position as cathedral preacher, and in 1536 he was appointed suffragan of Würzburg. At the Reichstag in Augsburg in 1530 he was one of the Catholic theologians who drew up the refutation to the Confession of Augsburg.   HEGE.

J. Birkner, *Augustin Marius* (Munich, 1930); R. Reiniger, *Die Weihbischöfe von Würzburg (Archiv des Historischen Vereins von Unterfranken und Aschaffenburg* XVIII, Würzburg, 1865); E. Staehelin, *Das Buch der Basler Reformation* (Basel, 1929); idem, *Briefe und Akten zum Leben Oecolampads* II (Leipzig, 1934); Dürr and Roth, *Aktensammlung zur Gesch. der Basler Ref.* II (1933); Val. Anshelm, *Berner Chronik* VI (Bern, 1833); Fritz Blanke, *Corpus Reformatorum* XCIII; *ML* III, 40 f.

Marken-Binnen, a hamlet in the Dutch province of North Holland, where from early times Anabaptists were found. They soon formed a congregation of the Waterlander branch, but being rather conservative it in 1674 joined the Zonist (*q.v.*) conference. Its membership was always very small. With the neighboring congregations of Krommeniedijk, Uitgeest, and Knollendam it formed the union of "the four congregations," in which, however, each of them had a great measure of independence. From about 1675 Marken-Binnen had no preachers of its own, but was served by those of Uitgeest and of Knollendam. In 1678 it contributed 28 guilders to the needs of the Swiss Brethren in the Palatinate and in 1726, 33 guilders for the Lithuanian Mennonites. After the congregation of Uitgeest had died out about 1750, Marken-Binnen was served by Knollendam until Marken-Binnen itself was dissolved. The *Naamlijst* of 1815 stated that this had happened, but it seems that the seven remaining members of Marken-Binnen did not unite with the congregation of Knollendam until 1828. Then in 1829 the old meetinghouse of Marken-Binnen was sold.   vDZ.

Inv. Arch. Amst. I, Nos. 892, 1164, 1180; II, 2, Nos. 227 f., 242; *Naamlijst* 1815, 107; *DJ* 1837, 4; *DB* 1907, 37, 45, 46 ff., 72-76; 1918, 50; *ML* III, 41.

Markham, in York Co., Ont., is a town (pop. 3,000) approximately 20 miles northeast of Toronto. Mennonites have lived in this area since 1803. Some of them reside in town but most live north and east of town. Seven Mennonite churches with 323 members are located in this area. Four are members of the Ontario Mennonite Conference (MC), namely, Widemans, Cedar Grove, Almira, and Hagerman's with a membership of 218. Three are Wisler or Old Order Mennonite, namely, Almira, Reesor, and Altona, with 105 members. In addition, the United

Missionary Church has two congregations with 264 members in the area of Markham and Gormley, and the Brethren in Christ (Tunkers) have (1957) 162 members in the Markham district, in two congregations, Vaughn and Heise Hill. (*ML* III, 41.)

P.H.Gr.

Markham (Alberta) United Missionary Church had 37 members in 1953, with M. L. Baker as pastor.

Markirch (French, Sainte-Marie-aux-Mines), an Alsatian town in the Leber Valley (Dep. Haut-Rhin), near the junction of three departments, Haut-Rhin, Bas-Rhin, and Vosges. There were Anabaptists in the Markirch Valley in the early years of the movement, as is indicated in a complaint made by the mining association to Count Egenolph III on May 29, 1561. It is directed against the "Anabaptists, Schwenckfelders, and divisions of these: Bilgerer (from Pilgram Marpeck?), Gabrielites, Sattlerites, and the like." This would indicate that the first Anabaptists here came from Strasbourg. They were quite numerous and lived on remote farms as well as near the town. They were possessed of a strong missionary zeal; the document mentioned above complains that "they creep into the houses everywhere, teach and preach without a calling, surround the common people with their subtleties." It points out the danger to which they expose the country by opposing military service.

But the count was not to be moved to expel them, not even when the chancellery at Ensisheim on July 5, 1562, ordered him in rather rude terms finally to take serious steps to get rid of Anabaptists, Sattlerites, and the like. This period of calm lasted until the Thirty Years' War. In the terror of 1635-36, the population was nearly wiped out by hostile attacks, hunger, and plagues. The survivors moved to quieter regions, so that the country lay desolate. Traces of these refugees are found in the Münster Valley and in Strasbourg. The records of the church convention of Dec. 9, 1640, mention a Jakob Mangold, an "Anabaptist Schwenckfelder, who has recently come from Markirch, where this sect has long had its synagogue." Does this mean that the Anabaptists in Markirch had built a church? Other records state that they met in a forest between Markirch and Schlettstadt. Tradition confirms this; the spot is still known.

By 1643 there were again Anabaptists in Markirch, this time Swiss Brethren refugees from Switzerland. Parson Jean le Bachelles reported that 12 families had settled there, who had elders come from Switzerland to serve them for communion, baptism, and weddings. Toward the end of the century the Swiss also brought with them their divisions. Jakob Ammann (*q.v.*) went to Markirch in person to put his way through. A meeting for the purpose of reaching an agreement with the followers of Hans Reist (*q.v.*) was held at Markirch on Nov. 9, 1697; here Ammann also wrote the letter to his opponents in Switzerland in 1700, confessing that he had grievously erred. He also worked vigorously to acquire for his brethren the privilege of exemption from military service and the oath.

These privileges and the prosperity soon achieved by the Brethren aroused the envy of the people.

Complaints reached the court at Paris. In 1712 Louis XIV ordered the expulsion of all Anabaptists from Alsace. Count Christian II of Birkenfeld, who had married the last heiress of Rappoltstein, was an officer and a favorite of the king; hence he was compelled to execute the king's orders, however reluctant he might be. He gave the exiles certificates showing that they had lived honorably, been industrious, lived in peace and harmony with their neighbors, and had been forced to emigrate solely on account of their religion. Thus 500-600 persons emigrated from Markirch to Montbéliard and Lorraine, which were not under French dominion at that time.

Very soon the disastrous consequences of this withdrawal became apparent. Many fields lay waste and the count's revenues declined. An appeal was made by several noblemen of Alsace to permit a limited number of Mennonites to settle in the valley, which was granted. Because the number was limited, most of their children had to leave the country when they were grown. Nevertheless the congregation remained rather large. Jacob Goldschmidt was its elder for a long period, until about 1804. In 1789, at the election and ordination of an elder by the elders of Montbéliard, Colmar, and Salm, a total of 128 votes was reported. During the 19th century there was a steady decline. Many joined the Reformed and Lutheran groups, largely because they had to emigrate from the community. Emigration also took place to the interior of France, where many were lost to Catholicism, and also the emigration to America depleted the congregation.

Meetings were held in the homes of the members. In the present century few remained; they met in the Weiler Valley. In 1938 they met in Chatenois (Kestenholz). The congregation was served by outside ministers. It has now completely died out. The nearest living Mennonite congregation is Le Hang (*q.v.*).

P.So.

D. L. Gratz, *Bernese Anabaptists* (Goshen, 1954) 38, 46, 85, 87 f.; *ML* III, 41 f.

Markstay Mennonite Mission (MC), located near Sudbury, northern Ontario, was opened in 1936 by Walter McDowell and Arthur Gingrich under the Ontario Mennonite Mission Board, the first impulse to it having been given by Linford Hackman. The work had periods of progress and decline, but never developed into a strong congregation. In 1954 the total membership was 7, although by 1948 over 75 had professed conversion and 22 had been baptized as members. At various times outposts have been established and summer Bible schools and Sunday schools conducted at such places as Mountville, Whitefish, Nairn, and Virginiatown near Kirkland Lake. (*ML* III, 42.)

A.Gi.

Markushof, a village (pop. 650) in the Klein-Werder of Marienburg, formerly West Prussia, Germany, was settled by Dutch colonists in the early 17th century or even earlier, probably mostly by Mennonites. They suffered severely from many hardships; repeatedly Markushof was flooded by the Vistula River (very severely on April 21, 1681, and in 1737). In these calamities they were financially supported by the Dutch Mennonite Committee of Foreign Needs. In May 1724 a number of Mennonites expelled from Lithuania (*q.v.*) temporarily settled near Markushof, among whom was Elder David Penner. On Jan. 31, 1744, a conference of several West Prussian congregations was held at Markushof to face the new situation when the King of Prussia had granted freedom of religion to the Mennonites. The Mennonites living at Markushof belonged to the Frisian congregation of Thiensdorf (*q.v.*), but in 1791-1890 Markushof was the seat of an independent congregation.

In 1790, after 12 years of strife, about 400 persons, with four preachers and five deacons, withdrew from the Thiensdorf congregation, which had a membership of 2,000 (including children). The smaller group and the congregations of Orlofferfelde and Danzig wanted to continue to permit mixed marriages between members of the Frisian and Flemish groups, which had been allowed in the Frisian churches until 1772, and to accept the children of these marriages as well as others who wished to join by baptism. The larger part of the Thiensdorf congregation and four other Frisian congregations rejected this position. On April 21, 1791, the papers of the division were signed. The smaller group then built a church in Markushof, in which Elder Heinrich Donner of Orlofferfelde preached the first sermon on Christmas Day. In 1792 Johann Sperling, the first elder of the congregation, was ordained by Donner.

The membership remained at about 450, including children. The baptized membership in 1852 was 288, and in 1887, 292. The elder of the Markushof congregation then was Heinrich Wiehler (from 1860) and the preachers were Cornelius Wiehler, Hermann Pauls, and Franz Wiehler. Differences began to disappear and some co-operation became possible. In 1865 Thiensdorf built a new church. Elder Siebert of Markushof invited Thiensdorf to use his church during the building. The preachers of the two groups then preached on alternate Sundays, and in the autumn communion was observed on two Sundays served by both elders together.

On March 25, 1888, the Nogat River broke through its dam near Jonasdorf, and seriously damaged the Markushof church. Then the Mennonites of Holland, Hamburg-Altona, and Danzig raised a considerable sum to be given for a new church on condition that the Thiensdorf and Markushof groups merge and build a church at Preussisch-Rosengart instead of Markushof, which is near Thiensdorf. On March 4, 1890, the united group adopted the name Thiensdorf-Markushof. The old church was repaired to the extent that services could be held in it until the dedication of the church in Preussisch-Rosengart on June 14, 1894. A.D., vDZ.

Felicia Szper, *Nederlandsche Nederzettingen in West-Pruisen gedurende den Poolschen tijd* (Enkhuizen, 1913) 121, 125, 171 note 3; *Inv. Arch. Amst.* I, Nos. 1571-79, 1649, 1666, 1679, 1683, 1688, 1696; II, Nos. 2626, 2635, 2650; II, 2, Nos. 735, 808, 856 f.; Mannhardt, *Jahrbuch* 1883, 17, 19; 1888, 12; *ML* III, 43.

Marlboro (N.J.) was the location of CPS Unit No. 63, established at the New Jersey State Hospital in 1942. Unit 63, Mennonite administered, was the first CPS unit to be placed in a New Jersey state institution. An 82-page history and report of the unit published by the CPS men is entitled *p. r. n.* The MCC conducted a psychiatry and Christian service school at this hospital in February 1945. The unit was closed in 1946. M.G.

M. Gingerich, *Service for Peace* (Akron, Pa., 1949) 221-22, 313-14.

Marlette (Mich.) United Missionary Church had 13 members in 1954. B. H. Surbrook was its pastor.

Marne Brotherhood, a name given to one of several congregations which formed a certain union found in the northeast part of the Dutch province of Groningen, commonly called "De Marne." In this region (according to G. E. Frerichs, *DB* 1906, 44 f.) Menno Simons may have found shelter after he had left the Roman Catholic Church in 1536. About 1640 Jan Luies (*q.v.*) is said to have been the elder of the Marne Brotherhood; soon afterward this congregation was divided into five congregations, Houwerzijl, Ulrum, Leens, Kloosterburen, and Vliedorp, all belonging to the Groningen Old Flemish branch. In 1816 the remnants of these congregations were united into one congregation, viz., Mensingeweer (*q.v.*). Repeatedly, but very severely in 1717, the Marne region was struck by floods. vDZ.

Inv. Arch. Amst. II, 1977 f.; *Tegenwoordige Staat der Vereenigde Nederlanden* XXI (Amsterdam, 1793) 310-18; *Groningsche Volksalmanak* 1918, 1-21; 1921, 6-13.

Marnix, Philips van: see **Aldegonde.**

Maronier, Jan Hendrik, b. 1827 at Rotterdam, d. 1920, a Remonstrant preacher successively at Zevenaar, Leiden, Utrecht, and Rotterdam, wrote an excellent biography of the Remonstrant Jacobus Arminius (*q.v.*), *Jakob Arminius* (Amsterdam, 1905), and *Geschiedenis van het Protestantisme . . . 1648-1789* (Leiden, 1907), besides a number of smaller works including some opposing the Roman Catholic Church, and of particular interest, *Het inwendig Woord* (Amsterdam, 1890), which treats Hans Denk and the Mennonites of Holland. "Menno Simons did not know the doctrine of the inner word (*q.v.*), nor did Dirk Philips." Hans de Ries acknowledges in addition to the Scriptures "another unwritten Word of God." With the exception of Nittert Obbesz there is no trace of opposition to the doctrine of the inner word, states Maronier (page 221). (*ML* III, 43.) vDZ.

Marpeck (Marbeck), **Pilgram** (d. 1556), author and leader of the South German Anabaptists 1530-56. I. *Introduction.* Concerning the life and work of this man, the most important of the German Anabaptists in the middle of the 16th century, little was known until very recently. This is understandable, for the great *Geschicht-Buch* of the Hutterian Brethren did not record his name, nor do the abundant hymns of the Anabaptists name him, although more recent investigation has revealed numerous contacts between Marpeck's circle and the Hutterites in Moravia. Indeed Marpeck's great work, the *Verantwortung,* his reply to Schwenckfeld's *Judicium,* which in turn was a reply to Marpeck's *Buch der Bundesbezeugung,* or *Vermahnung,* was first found and noted by them, and as was proved very recently, they even used Marpeck's book as the basis for decision in debatable questions. What a pity it is that this work in the ensuing time was to sink away into oblivion, so much the more so since it is precisely this work that has called to attention the existence of a third great Anabaptist book of the same period, the knowledge of which had likewise vanished from the later Anabaptists. The book referred to is the *Testamentserläuterung,* which is one of the most important of the works preceding Marpeck's great work and was probably written under his leadership and supervision by a close circle of fellow believers.

As a result of recent research the Anabaptist world of today is the recipient of three Anabaptist books that have been hitherto almost unknown; first the *Bundesbezeugung,* which will be briefly referred to in this article as the "Baptism booklet" of 1542; second the *Testamentserläuterung* (Testament Explanation); and third the *Verantwortung (Answer)* to Schwenckfeld's *Judicium* (Critique) concerning the baptism booklet. We become acquainted with these men who collaborated with Marpeck in his work, and who after its completion subjected it to a critical survey, after which it was released for general use ("to each and all who will have it"). These men were Pilgram Marpeck, Leopold Scharnschlager, the leader of the Swiss Brethren in the Grisons, Sigmund Bosch, Martin Blaichner, Valentin Werner, Antoni Müller, and Hans Jacob, several of whom are also known as the authors of hymns.

II. *Marpeck's Origin and Education.* Pilgram Marpeck was a native of Tirol, Austria. This could be gathered from his language and way of writing even if there were no record in the Tirol court records. His family lived in prosperity at Rattenberg on the Inn in the 15th and the beginning of the 16th centuries. Records in the government archives show that Jakob Marpeck, who is mentioned under the date of Nov. 23, 1489, as a judge at Rattenberg, was a member of this family. Likewise under Aug. 10, 1494, a Heinrich Marpeck is named as judge at the same place, who served until 1502. He was in the city council, in 1511 was the mayor, and in 1514 was still in the council. The family coat-of-arms shows a bird on a sphere.

Pilgram Marpeck attended the Latin school in Rattenberg. Thus he received a "scholarly education," which can be discerned in his writings, which contain not only numerous Latin words but also a Latinized sentence construction. He united with the miners' brotherhood of Rattenberg as one of the last to do so, as is shown by an old notation of Feb. 26, 1520, which also records that he was married by that time. This disproves the assumption by Gerber that he had been a cleric. The Tirolese authorities would not have given him the office of mining judge, to which he was called on April 20, 1525, if he had been a renegade monk or cleric. Two years previously, on Feb. 24, 1523, he had been a member of the Rattenberg outer council and after June 11, 1525, also a member of the inner council.

In the 1520's Marpeck had the reputation of being a competent mechanic or engineer in the mines of the lower Inn Valley. His annual salary as mine judge amounted to 65 pounds, and he received an additional 3 pounds for court dress. As a private contractor in the mining business he delivered ore from Schneeberg and Gossensass to Kitzbühel in 1520. When he received the office of mine judge, he loaned to the state treasury the sum of 1,000 guilders, which were put to his credit. This indicates that he was in good financial circumstances. He owned two houses, which were assessed for a tax of 3 florins for the "Turkish Tax," as was also his daughter's property. The Gilg (Egidius) Marpeck who on this occasion was taxed 2 florins and according to Josef Beck was also an Anabaptist was doubtless a close relative.

His good financial status put Pilgram into a position to undertake the education of three orphan children and to make journeys to South Germany.

When Marpeck became an Anabaptist is not clear, but on Jan. 28, 1528, he was removed from his position as mine judge; the reason was certainly that he refused to "investigate" (aid in catching) Anabaptists as requested by the authorities in Innsbruck. The Anabaptist preacher Leonhard Schiemer had been executed in Rattenberg as a martyr two weeks earlier, and Hans Schlaffer likewise on February 4 of that year. It seems most probable that Marpeck was influenced by these missionaries, although he had probably previously attended some Anabaptist meetings conducted by a certain Paul in near-by Kitzbühel and in the Münichau Castle, whose owner, Helena von Freiburg, favored the movement (Marpeck later had connections with her). This could have been in November and December of 1527, since a report of such meetings was given to the authorities in Salzburg on December 9 of that year. But although there is no evidence as to Marpeck's baptism, he must have been an Anabaptist at least in conviction when he fled from Rattenberg soon after his dismissal from his office, which he turned over to his successor on February 3, for his property was confiscated. But it is possible that he was not baptized until he was in Augsburg.

Marpeck's sacrifice of his position must certainly be connected with his ideas about the office of judge. He himself reported concerning his religious experiences thus (paraphrased): "Educated in the papacy by God-fearing parents, he turned from this and became a proclaimer of the Wittenberg Gospel. But when he found that in the places where God's Word was preached in Lutheran terms a carnal freedom was felt, it disinclined him somewhat, so that he could not find rest with the Lutherans. At that time he accepted baptism as a testimony of his faith, in this looking only upon God's Word and command."

It is known that this was in general the course of Anabaptist development in Tirol. When Marpeck became suspected of being an Anabaptist who could not be tolerated in the country, he found it advisable to leave his home, leaving behind all his possessions. In 1529 he received his inheritance. His property, in accord with the mandate of April 1, 1528, which stipulated that the possessions of people of other creeds who "had left and become fugitive," must be confiscated into the state treasury, was inventoried and the order given to the authorities at Rattenberg to confiscate all of Marpeck's property; it was in the first place to be used for the education of the three orphans. But this was not done; for soon afterward it was transferred to Christoph Philip von Liechtenstein, the manager of the castle and the bailiff of Rattenberg, who valued it at 400 guilders, whereas it had been valued by other persons at 3,500 guilders.

III. *Marpeck's Residence in Strasbourg. Connection with the Lutheran and Reformed Churches.* Johannes Walch, who was deacon in Nürtingen in 1578 and was later removed from his office on account of inclinations to Anabaptism, reported that Marpeck first went to Augsburg after his expulsion. In May 1528 he arrived at Strasbourg (*q.v.*); very soon he became the leader of the Anabaptists there. Here there was a strong church movement. Men of various religious parties collected here (though not all at one time), including Kaspar Schwenckfeld, who later became Marpeck's opponent, Melchior Hofmann, Sebastian Franck, whose *Paradoxa* were popular, Johannes Bünderlin of Linz, once a leader of the Anabaptists of that place, Jakob Kautz, Wilhelm Reublin, Jakob Wiedemann of Memmingen, personalities who had a good reputation in Anabaptist circles. They held their meetings in the home of the notary Fridolin Meiger and in the houses of Lukas Hobelmacher and Klaus Bruch. Foreign and native Anabaptists assembled here, of whom the former group was supported by the common treasury. Marpeck had first settled in Steintal, where he worked for a salary in the city forest, about 25 miles southwest of Strasbourg, just south of Schirmeck. He lived here with his wife, and in his house Anabaptist meetings were held.

In 1530 (1528?) he moved into the city; here he had numerous friends, patrons, and followers who honored him like a god (*numinis instar*). An excellent intellect, blameless Christian conduct, acquaintance with the Scriptures, an earnest character who did not regard temporal possessions, he in the beginning became a ward of Capito, Bucer, Zell, and Blaurer. The Strasbourg clergy were full of his praise and lauded his intellectual gifts. His courageous zeal was proved in many situations. The total citizenry of Strasbourg profited from his presence; for he built for the city the extraordinarily complex water system and wood floating flumes in the valleys of the Ehn and Brerisch (Steintal) in Alsace, and of the Kinzig and Murg in Baden, whereby Strasbourg, which was poor in wood, had access to the wealth of the Black Forest.

To be sure, public opinion soon changed. Marpeck was inconvenient to the clergy. He contradicted them and boldly expressed his opinions. Then they accused him of having led many good hearts into error by his violence, of being unfit for the office of Christian preaching and for the management of a church for the sanctity of which he was working, indeed of being unusable, a stiff-necked heretic, who like all sectarians was lacking in love, to which the Holy Scriptures admonish so urgently. On Aug. 17, 1531, Bucer wrote to Blaurer that this Pilgram was intent on his own pleasure and his own supposed knowledge; otherwise he and his wife were of unblamable conduct.

Known to the government as an obstinate heretic, namely, as an opponent of infant baptism (which he called a sacrifice to Moloch, a robbery of souls and murder) and then as a man who, according to reports, was misleading the good citizens and to whom well-meant arguments meant nothing, Marpeck was imprisoned. Capito's intercession, and probably still more the fact that he was needed for the city's water works engineering, restored to him his freedom, without his having given the required oaths to renounce Anabaptist company and doctrine.

At the beginning of December 1531 Marpeck requested of the council permission for a public debate with the clergy, but he was granted only a colloquium before the assembled council and the "committee of twenty-one," the public being excluded. The date set was Dec. 9, 1531. In 23 articles Marpeck presented his doctrine, corresponding to the two booklets which he had previously published, but which were suppressed by the council on the suggestion of the censors. Bucer was his opponent. Marpeck defended adult baptism vigorously. Only he who received it (he argued) might be a member of the kingdom of God; among the Catholics on the one side, and the Bucer following on the other, more dissension and envy were felt than divine zeal. He accused Bucer and his followers, "that they did not preach freely under the Cross of Christ but under the protection of the princes and cities." One should therefore not be surprised that the Word of God was bearing no fruit; even at that day there was no Christian order in Strasbourg.

Bucer replied with more loquacity than thoroughness and was repeatedly criticized by Marpeck, especially when he admitted that he had called upon the government for support and when he compared circumcision with baptism (Zwingli's "symbol of initiation"). The decision of the council was that it had perceived from the charge of the clergy that Pilgram was mistaken in this matter and therefore commanded that if he persisted in his opinion and was planning to overthrow infant baptism, which the council did not consider unchristian, and to set up a separate church, this must not be permitted; in this case he must leave this city and region not to return unless he abjured his error; in the contrary case he would be dealt with in a manner that one would rather escape. The document bears the date of Dec. 18, 1531.

Two days later Marpeck notified the council that he would leave the region. But if, impelled by the Spirit of God, he should be led thither again he would endure what God would send him. Since he would not be able to sell his little household in a short time he asked for a period of grace of three or four weeks, then requested the payment of the credit that he still had with the council for the wood floating from Einbach (Black Forest). He was then granted a period of four weeks to prepare for his departure, but at the same time it was made clear to him that the council was displeased by his saying "that infant baptism is not proved with divine Scripture." Therefore Pilgram left, but not without having asked the people of Strasbourg to reflect on the things of God, in order that the city might be preserved in the future from the shedding of blood in matters of faith, that it might therefore end the persecution of these pitiable people who had no place of refuge. He finally gave the council a copy of Bucer's talk at the disputation and his reply, in order that they could see that it was not his, but God's will that was bidding him leave. The city informed Countess Elisabeth of Fürstenberg on Dec. 18, 1531, that they had dismissed Pilgram Marpeck, her overseer in the forestry at Einbach, "on account of obstinate insistence on his erroneous opinion," and had put in his place two men skilled in trade and in forestry. To be sure, they were also suspected as Anabaptists, but since they kept their convictions to themselves and did not disturb anyone with them, she might tolerate the two.

A third disputation with Marpeck was held before a special commission of the Council on Jan. 18, 1532, but the verdict remained unchanged: Marpeck had to go. Thus Marpeck left Strasbourg in January 1532. Bucer and Blaurer expressed themselves with very frank satisfaction over this fact. Blaurer wrote to Bucer on Jan. 24, "Your report concerning Marpeck will be dear and useful to all our people, but still more your earnest reply to his nonsense. Share it with us. An evil of this kind usually sticks obstinately with people who have once been spotted by it, but superstition knows how to deceive simple people by a pious bearing." On Feb. 2 Bucer replied to Blaurer's words with flattery. Not all of Blaurer's friends were happy with Marpeck's withdrawal. His own sister Margarete had taken a deep interest in him and Bucer was now zealously engaged in changing her opinion.

It might have been expected that Marpeck, like so many of his Tirol countrymen, would go to Moravia. Perhaps, however, the unfavorable reports that he had received from there a year earlier kept him away. In the Moravian Anabaptist group there had been violent dissension in the winter of 1530, which threatened its very existence and resulted in a division into two wings. It was Wilhelm Reublin (q.v.) who allegedly rebelled against the elders "on account of offensive misconduct of the ministers (Diener)," and left Austerlitz with his following, going to Auspitz. On Jan. 26 he wrote a long report about this to Marpeck. Apparently there were older connections between the two. Reublin spoke of the love which he had always had for Pilgram, and mentioned a writing by his brother-in-law Kaspar Schueler which he had sent to Pilgram. These statements by Reublin must always be compared with the corresponding statements of the Hutterite Geschicht-Buch, to get at the real truth. Reublin did not leave a good memory in Moravian Anabaptist circles. Whether his reports affected Marpeck or not, the Geschicht-Buch does not show any incidents that imply any later connections with Marpeck.

Until recently the whereabouts of Marpeck from the time he left Strasbourg in 1532 until his controversy with Schwenckfeld in 1542-44 was unknown. The discovery of the Kunstbuch codex (see below) containing numerous letters of Marpeck and his circle has cast considerable light on his movements. He apparently traveled widely. In 1534 he was back in Strasbourg but had to flee again. On Dec. 4, 1540, he wrote a letter from near Ilanz in the Grisons

(Switzerland) to the "dear ones" near Strasbourg in the Kinzig and Leber valleys. In 1541 he probably made a trip to Moravia to visit the Hutterites. On Aug. 15, 1544, he wrote a letter from Chur in the Grisons to the churches in Württemberg. Most likely he spent at least 1540-44 in the Grisons, and possibly some of the time 1532-40. In late 1544 he moved permanently to Augsburg. Kiwiet and Fast believe that the Vermahnung (1542) and the first part of the Verantwortung (1542-44) were written in the Grisons.

IV. Marpeck and Schwenckfeld. Schwenkfeld's Attitude to the Anabaptists. Marpeck's connections with the Silesian nobleman Caspar Schwenckfeld von Ossig extend back to the time when both lived in Strasbourg. Schwenckfeld expressed himself very differently at different times concerning the life and teaching of the Anabaptists. His views are found in the excellent book by Ecke. Only the most important ought to be stated here. In the 1550's Schwenckfeld wrote, "What horrible errors I have heard from the Anabaptists when I was among them I would rather tell you by mouth than in writing" (Ecke, 203). He named the leaders and told only evil things about them; i.e., about Ludwig Hätzer, Balthasar Hubmaier, and others whom he knew personally. But the intimate contact which he himself had in Strasbourg and probably also later with Marpeck, whose frank Anabaptist opinions he knew, proves that he thought differently about Anabaptism and the Anabaptists at that time and therefore took them under his protection.

Something of the earlier friendly relationship between the two is echoed in the open letter which Marpeck wrote Jan. 1, 1544, to Schwenckfeld (Verantwortung, 55). Mindful of the old friendship he vigorously expressed his displeasure concerning the present unexpectedly hostile attitude of Schwenckfeld toward him. He wrote, "I would not have thought it of you that you would behind my back send letters into the world against me, and without asking or informing me would make charges against me, since you in the earlier days dealt with me so much in matters of faith. You are now doing it too since the first letter I sent you from Ulm. Now you have composed a whole book against me and selected in particular 38 articles 'how I shall hold them concerning Christ,' and sent them out everywhere so that I must defend myself about them toward many who know my teaching."

Marpeck complained further that Schwenckfeld had associated with Valentin Ickelsamer (q.v.) and that the two had worked against him. Ickelsamer is known not only as a religious polemicist but especially also as one of the oldest German grammarians. Entangled in the quarrel between Carlstadt and Luther he later adhered to Schwenckfeld, and in 1542, when Schwenckfeld's polemics with Marpeck were beginning, he published a letter which Schwenckfeld had sent to him during a severe illness: His (Schwenckfeld's) prayer had saved his life. It is necessary to consider this grammarian here because Marpeck speaks of him in his large book. As far as Schwenckfeld is concerned his procedure against Marpeck was so much the more spiteful because Marpeck had in earlier days supported him.

Marpeck wrote that he was not aware that in all his life he had ever done an evil deed to Schwenckfeld, much rather he had wished and done him all kinds of good.

Concerning the origin of Schwenckfeld's hostility to Marpeck there is information in an Olmütz (Olomuce) manuscript (Sign. III 19), which refers to a letter that Marpeck wrote to Helene Streicher in Ulm and which greatly excited Schwenckfeld. It reveals, as do also allusions found in Marpeck's *Verantwortung,* that Schwenckfeld had expressed a negative opinion of the Anabaptists in Anabaptist circles (Schwenckfeld's propaganda against the Anabaptists is also seen from his 54th *Rede* in Marpeck's *Verantwortung,* 171-73). Thus it is learned that the zealous Anabaptist Magdalena Marschalk von Pappenheim was "tempted with unfathomable things" by "false prophets," with writings that contained untruths and slander of the Anabaptists and especially of one of their brethren. It is probably safe to assume that Marpeck is meant. Helene Streicher, Schwenckfeld's friend, expressed herself similarly. She sent to Marpeck a writing that contained a number of charges which had been made by their opponents against the Anabaptists, charging that the Anabaptists held to externalities instead of holding to the spirit of Christ's teaching, "whether it be baptism or whatever it may be." Under such circumstances the Anabaptist brotherhood proceeded to place into the hands of its members a confession of faith which gives the testimony of their doctrine in 25 large sections, the *Vermahnung.*

V. *Marpeck's Vermahnung* (called the *Bundesbezeugung* or baptism booklet of 1542). In 1542 a book of 200 pages appeared, which in accord with the custom of the time bore the somewhat long-winded title: *Vermannung; auch gantz klarer gründtlicher un(d) unwidersprechlicher bericht zu warer Christlicher . . . puntssvereynigung allen waren glaubigen frummen und gutthertzigen menschen zu hilff und trost mit grund heyliger schrifft durch bewerung warer Tauff und Abendmals Christi sampt mitlauffung und erklärung irer gegensachen und Argumenten wider alle vermeynte Christliche Pündtnus so sich bissher un(d) noch under dem nammen Christi zutragend.* Neither the author nor the place of its publication is named. The document is signed by "the believing (*christgläubig*) comrades of the covenant of the tribulation that is in Christ." In Marpeck's *Verantwortung,* the last of the three Anabaptist writings which are closely interrelated, this writing is also called the "booklet of the sign (*Bezeugung*) of the covenant" or briefly the Baptism booklet, probably mostly because most of it deals with the problem of baptism.

In our day this book has been a bibliographical rarity, for only two copies were known, one in the British Museum and the other in the Württemberg state library in Stuttgart. Christian Hege performed a valuable service when he published it in the book commemorating the fourth centennial of the founding of the Mennonites (1925), since this booklet by Marpeck for reasons stressed in the introduction to the edition of Marpeck's larger work, the *Verantwortung,* was the first one for a long time in which the South German Anabaptists defended

their teaching in print. That it was also of great significance for its content is clear from the sharp condemnation it was given by its opponents. Even though the author's name is not stated in the book, the contemporaries had no doubt about who it was. Caspar Schwenckfeld thought there were two authors; one was undoubtedly Pilgram Marpeck, who was probably assisted by Leopold Scharnschlager.

The modern publisher of the *Taufbüchlein* has described its contents and importance with the following words (paraphrased): "The *Vermahnung* is an exposition and a suggestion for the congregations on the right use of baptism and communion. It, however, rejects all supersensory (*übersinnliche*) meaning, but it makes the highest demands of its members in respect to their position of faith and their moral conduct. With baptism Marpeck demands a penitent frame of mind, a believing submission to God through Christ, obedience to the will of God. Communion is simply a memorial meal and is held 'for the renewal, strengthening and comfort of the soul, and for nothing else.' The members are to examine themselves earnestly to see whether they stand in the right love toward friend and foe and whether their love for Christ is strong enough that they would be able to give up their lives for Him. Partaking of the Lord's Supper with open sinners is unworthy, if they have not been rebuked with a brotherly rebuke, since otherwise the innocent partakes of the sin of the guilty. The Anabaptists always kept referring to his concept of a pure church, when an attempt was made by the state church to compel them to transfer their membership. Their objections often had the consequence that the Protestant clergy decided to introduce 'church discipline' " (*Gedenkschrift,* 182).

Marpeck's argumentation, Hege adds, is evidence of a thorough knowledge of the Bible and a keen thought process, and is in many cases supported by excellent figures of speech. The language of the book is gentle, and contrasts strongly with the harsh tone found in the works of most of the reformers. The impression it made in its own circles must have been so much the more significant, since even an opponent like Schwenckfeld, though against his will, is compelled here and there to give it recognition. Although the problem of baptism is treated with particular detail, the chapter on infant baptism and the treatment of original sin should also be pointed out. He expounds his views as follows: After Peter (page 215) had admonished the people they grew anxious in heart and asked, What shall we do? Be converted, he replied, be sorry for your sins and let each one be baptized in the name of Jesus Christ for the forgiveness of his sin, and thus you shall receive the gifts of the Holy Ghost. Because the children who cannot talk are still unknowing and cannot be converted and have also not yet been perverted by their own carnal reason, they cannot receive any forgiveness of their sins in baptism, because they do not have any knowledge or guilt concerning their sins, either before God or in themselves. Therefore the baptism of infants is a mere work of mockery before God.

VI. *Schwenckfeld's Judicium Concerning the Baptism Booklet of 1542 and Marpeck's Reply.* About

Schwenckfeld's attempt to win favor for his own teaching in Marpeck's circles there is information in this reply which Pilgram Marpeck addressed to Helene Streicher, Schwenckfeld's friend, and hitherto probably also Marpeck's friend, which is now printed as a supplement to the first part of Marpeck's *Verantwortung* to Schwenckfeld's *Judicium* (pp. 179-88).

Helene Streicher, entirely taken in by Schwenckfeld's teaching, wrote to Marpeck, "Since Christ's word and teaching are spirit and life, one must rise to it and must not make earthly elements, baptism or anything else, a condition for salvation." Marpeck referred her to the Scripture, that no Christian may refuse a demand of the Lord. Since Christ has commanded baptism the believer must hold himself to the command. We need "the physical elements" according to the Word and command of Christ, without denying the inward working of the Spirit. The true believer knows only of one baptism, namely, the baptism of the Lord, of the washing away of sins in the blood of Christ, i.e., through spirit, water, and blood, "which serve as one." "Of course where spirit and life do not follow in this physical use of the elements, the elements probably will remain only mere elements"; here Paul's statement in I Cor. 3 applies, "Neither he who waters nor he who plants is anything, but he who gives the growth. The external should not be separated from the inward, as it is imagined today."

These words are a rejection of Schwenckfeld's doctrine as shared by Helene Streicher, and thus also of other opinions of Schwenckfeld's, suggesting that the Anabaptists had no true knowledge of Christ. In conclusion Marpeck wrote to her, "Please accept this my writing out of a sincere intention; I could not leave my opinion unrevealed to you. You told me that you could not be of our opinion. Know that I cannot accept yours either." This letter, said Walpurga Marschalk von Pappenheim, was sent by her Aunt Magdalena to Mrs. Streicher in Ulm. When it reached Schwenckfeld, Walpurga wrote, he became heated and wrote against "Brother Pilgram and Miss Magdalena." In the *Judicium* is found what moved him. It is probably to be expected that Schwenckfeld would not leave Marpeck's booklet on baptism without a critical faultfinding, but it was not to be expected that this would turn out to be so bitter and hate-filled as is the case. First it must be said, that the *Judicium* also makes an attempt to distinguish between the Anabaptists (concerning whom many good things are granted) and their leaders.

The *Judicium* attack on the baptism booklet has been passed down in two forms. First in the Wolfenbüttel manuscript (V, 33), "Uiber das new Büchlein der Taufbrüder im 1542 Jare ausgangen Judicium," and second in those extracts with which Marpeck preceded his 100 answers (Schwenckfeld's *Reden*).

In Marpeck's circles the *Judicium* was very disturbing, for Schwenckfeld's opinions were clearly revealed. This can also be gathered from Schwenckfeld's instruction to see to it that the *Judicium* would not fall into other hands than those of the Anabaptists, "so that it may be of benefit to them and that

they can accordingly correct their errors; for I hope that many finally will come to the truth and become better acquainted with Christ, the reigning king of heaven."

The propaganda of this document did not remain concealed from the Anabaptists; it induced them to issue an immediate reply, the writing of which was also taken in hand at once and of which at first only the first part, finished by Jan. 1, 1544, was given to the public. In it only the first of the seven points charged against them by Schwenckfeld is treated. Therefore Marpeck also apologized at the end of the first part, "that they had allowed this one part without the completion of the other to be issued; this happened on account of the haste, so that our fellow members and other goodhearted people will not be overtaken by such false erroneous spirits and be prejudiced or taken unawares, and if one of them might already be entangled he could loose himself from the entanglement." The second part would then produce what was still lacking. For each of the 100 *Reden* by Schwenckfeld there is a reply by Marpeck, of which replies 54 come in the first part, which is 206 manuscript pages in length, about one fourth of the entire book.

Marpeck preceded his work with an open letter to Schwenckfeld which contains really bitter comments about people who play themselves up as removers of splinters without seeing the beams in their own eyes. He wished for Schwenckfeld a knowledge of himself, without which any other knowledge is vain. After the dealing they had with him and the warnings sent to him they had not expected such a proceeding against them, and now he had even forged together 39 articles, "as I allegedly had them from Christ, so that I must apologize to all who know my confession of faith. It is this that compels me to reply."

And now Marpeck proceeds with the individual points. First he defends himself against the charge of incompetence, that the composers of the baptism booklet were much too presumptuous, that they considered all who did not agree with their baptism as not being Christians. We say, that those who are not baptized according to the order of the Lord we do not have to judge or condemn. As they are outside they do not concern us. Every true believer, however, must obey the commands of the Lord, even in detail. We confess the baptism of Christ as a baptism of a rebirth and the washing away of sins. It issues from the teaching, "No baptism without preceding teaching, without the accompanying Gospel and faith."

With the 17th *Rede* Schwenckfeld begins the condemnation of the baptism booklet, which he finds fault with in almost all its parts. The whole contrast in the concept of the problem of baptism Marpeck crystallized in his prayer in his reply in the 34th *Rede* of Schwenckfeld: "O Lord, see how this generation attempts to destroy your own baptism. . . . You command baptism and so it is reasonable to keep it for the sake of your command as well as for the sake of the one for whom it is commanded. With their reason, which you have condemned, they separate your water bath into parts, the water from the word, in order to do away with your command under the pretext of not permitting the external water to be made a requirement for salvation. Even if we did not understand why you have commanded baptism we would obey for the very reason that you have commanded it, just as Peter once did when he let you wash his feet." The 46th *Rede* contains the texts where all the Bible citations are assembled which speak against Schwenckfeld. There is sharp antithesis between the demands of the Gospel and what Schwenckfeld does. When Schwenckfeld speaks of baptism he separates indivisible baptism into parts, accuses it of being a water baptism thought up by man, and accuses us of calling the element that is water the narrow gate to the kingdom of heaven, whereas we mean the whole inward and outward work of the only baptism, to which all matters ordained of the Lord belong and wherein they have their origin through true faith.

VII. *The Second Part of the Verantwortung and the Testamentserläuterung.* Before the contents of the second part of the *Verantwortung* are considered it should be once more stated that the first part was worked out hastily and that therefore some details had to be supplemented and especially a stronger apparatus of Biblical proof citations for single points had to be assembled. So it happens that the second part of the *Verantwortung* in its entire presentation bears a different face than the first. Not only does it go more deeply into individual points and treat anew what Marpeck had already said, but it also has a much greater amount of proof material from the Holy Scriptures.

In the study of the two parts with regard to their sources it must be obvious that in the second part when it deals with Bible citations, they often refer to the *Testamentserläuterung,* where one may find many more citations on a matter than his presentation contains, whereas in a similar case in the first part not a single reference is made to this source, not even where one should have unquestionably expected it. For this no other explanation can be found, but that in the years 1542-44 when they were just working on a refutation of Schwenckfeld's accusations this book "called the *Testamentserläuterung"* was not available and was not to be finished until the conclusion of the first part, and indeed was prepared for the purpose of creating a broader area of defense. From the citations which are made in the second part of the *Verantwortung* the existence of the book could be ascertained. It is in fact still extant in two libraries, in Zürich and in Berlin. Its full title is *Testamenterleutterung. Erleuterung durch ausszug aus Heiliger Biblischer schrifft. tail und gegentail sampt ains tails angehangen beireden zu dienst und fürderung ains klaren urtails von wegen underschaid Alts und News Testaments unnd ire beder Sündtvergebung, Opffer, Erlösung, Gerechtigkait, Gnad, Glauben, Gaist, Folck unnd anderm, so grundtlich lautter und nutzlich nie ersehen genant Testamenterleutterung.* No place and year of publication are given. It is an octavo volume with over 800 pages of text, and a further 11 pages with title, preface, and index. Kiwiet has now shown that it was finished in May 1550 (dissertation, p. 77).

The foreword announces the purpose of the book: Since there are widely divergent views on the question of the distinction between the Old and New Testaments, between the Mosaic assembly and the new church, some saying that the sufferings of Christ are retroactive into the Old Testament and also had already delivered a forgiving of sins to eternal life in the Old Testament as it is now in the New (which agrees with Schwenckfeld's preaching), but others (like Marpeck and his circle) deny this and say that this (reconciliation to salvation, redemption, comfort, etc.) is found in the Old Testament only figuratively, but not in essence; neither is the spirit of divine promise for eternal life there, but all this was only promised. The Fathers, i.e., the believers in the old covenant hoped to receive all this only through the Incarnation of Christ, His suffering, His death, and His resurrection; therefore the *Testamentserläuterung* presents the total material from the pure text of the Holy Scripture, in order that each one who hungers for the truth may form a judgment for himself. What reason would there have been, say those on one side, for Christ after His death to have had to descend to hell and proclaim the Gospel there among the dead and the spirits, if "the [Old Testament] Fathers" had already had possession of forgiveness to eternal life?

Thus the foreword presents further motives which we find again collectively in the *Verantwortung.* All the citations concerning forgiveness of sins, reconciliation, redemption, salvation, comfort, etc., are presented from the Bible and indeed first from the old and then from the new covenant, wherein now a hungry man "may refresh himself as in a garden of roses or on a flowery meadow in the splendor of colour." And here the foreword goes on to say, the period before Christ's Incarnation is designated with the word "yesterday" and those of the new covenant with "today." The foreword then explains the word "Wesen" and "wesentlich" (essence and essential); to the Anabaptists these words mean that "yesterday" prefigured, but the "today" accomplished, things for eternal life which were not present "yesterday" but were to be expected only in the future, as Paul says in Col. 2: "These things are a shadow of that which was to come, but the 'Wesen' is Christ."

Finally there are in the foreword explanations as to possible understandings of certain individual verses: "And it is to be noticed where 'yesterday' and 'today' 'Wesen' is promised. One should pay attention to the words which are 'today' and which cannot be figures and thus refer to 'yesterday's' time. There are also promises for 'tomorrow,' that is, for Christ's return from heaven. Consider these places in the Old Testament which speak of future affairs as of the present as if they had already happened, which were of course still to be fulfilled." The author promises himself great benefit from the book, because here matters of revelation are explained with clear judgment and understanding of the Scripture.

The name of the author of the *Testamentserläuterung* is not given: We discover that several persons took part in composing it. They conceal its authorship, because many people ask more about the author than about the truth and consider further whether he is of high [Schwenckfeld] or low [Anabaptist] rank, or they ask what faith he is, and accordingly buy the books. The author therefore has referred the reader only to the Word of God and left his own name unstated partly also for this reason that he did not "collect" the book without co-operation.

The very fact of the unusually frequent citation [92 citations by name] of the *Testamentserläuterung* by Marpeck when it was a matter of proving something, leads to the conclusion that the book originated in Anabaptist circles. The citation never occurs in a polemic intention, but always in agreement. For example when *Red und Antwort* 73 says: "Our testimony is this, also especially in the book called the *Testamentserläuterung* . . ." or in *Red und Antwort* 79: "We have a great collection of right clear Scripture against it; for this one may merely read in the *Testamentserläuterung* . . . ." In *Red und Antwort* 81: "More is proved in the *Testamentserläuterung;* in that same book one should also read all the articles concerning 'today's' 'Wesen.' " Briefly stated: the assemblage of Bible citations corresponds exactly with the trend of the *Verantwortung.* The *Testamentserläuterung,* like it, always refers to it as a source book for proving and strengthening a fact, as a work that stands immediately after the Bible and which one cites as one wants to draw more Bible verses, as if one wanted to say, "There our proofs are found." Finally the numerous citations of the *Testamentserläuterung* agree verbatim with the *Verantwortung.* They formed an essential preparatory work for the second part of the *Verantwortung.*

In the light of the above it is clear that the second part of the *Verantwortung* was written after May 1550. Kiwiet's careful study has shown that it had two authors, having been begun by Marpeck (d. 1556) and finished by Scharnschlager, the date of finishing being March 1558. The transition from Marpeck to Scharnschlager is clearly evident in the difference in style and structure, as well as in the fact that Marpeck cites various sources, while Scharnschlager cites only Schwenckfeld. The Scharnschlager section occupies pp. 409-578 in the printed *Verantwortung;* it was without doubt written after Marpeck's death in 1556. The second part of the *Verantwortung* was delayed in circulation among the brethren (it was never printed, only copied) because of the necessity (following the unity achieved among the Anabaptists at the Strasbourg conference of 1555) of securing the approval of the brethren "in all lands" so that it might stand as their common testimony. A copy, for instance, was sent to Moravia. Kiwiet holds (p. 79 f.) that it was not released for general circulation until 1571.

VIII. *Schwenckfeld's Judicium Concerning the Second Part of the Taufbüchlein and Marpeck's Reply.* Pilgram Marpeck had sent the first part of his *Verantwortung,* which he had just finished, to Schwenckfeld (*Verantwortung,* 50); "but," says a notice in the Zürich manuscript, "concerning it he, Schwenckfeld, never gave an answer. And so he has died." The date "1571" is struck out. But in his *Judicium* Schwenckfeld had after all shown the way that Marpeck must go. We now wish, says Schwenckfeld (*Verantwortung,* 129), to look at the other points also and see what they write about original sin and especially about the Word of God, the church, communion, and sonship to God, also about the faith and spirit of the patriarchs and prophets, and we want to give our best judgment to them about these points.

Concerning original sin, says Schwenckfeld, they do not hold, as the church teaches in agreement with the Holy Scriptures, that "it is a corruption of human nature since Adam's fall in which all men are conceived and born, but rather that sin has its origin and inheritance in the knowledge and the understanding of the good; but that the inheritance becomes effective only when they can distinguish between good and evil, which Schwenckfeld calls an old Pelagian error long since refuted by the church. Marpeck rejects this view on the basis of the Bible and the example of Christ: original sin becomes effective only in the understanding of good and evil which became a part of human nature in Adam and Eve only after they had eaten of the fruit of the tree of the knowledge of good and evil contrary to the prohibition of God. In this sense all men inherited it, but neither original sin nor real sin are reckoned so by God until the knowledge of good and evil is present, so that man out of his fleshly nature forsakes the good and does the evil." One should let the children live upon the promise of Christ until one can teach them and they can believe, confess, and desire it. The Lord did not give in vain the sayings of Christ that we should become like children. Accordingly, says Marpeck, the Moravian congregation included the following declaration in the 16 articles which they adopted several years back, namely, that children before the age of reason have no sin except the inherited tendency to sin, which does not affect the salvation until it breaks out in actual sin. Therefore baptism is not ordained for them.

Schwenckfeld denies that men become children of God by faith and consequent baptism. But, answers Marpeck, if that is so then Paul (Gal. 3) would be condemned, who attributes the sonship of God to faith and baptism, as also the Lord Himself says, "He who believes and is baptized will be saved." But who will be saved if not the children of God? If Schwenckfeld gives consideration to what sonship means, we have long ago considered it. We call him a child of God who believes the Gospel from his heart and experiences the working of the Holy Spirit so that he desires baptism. And if Schwenckfeld says that the Anabaptists had no conception of the Word of God, we answer that we stand on I Peter 1 and on the Saviour who has Himself and through His apostles proclaimed the Gospel word. He who hears these words and believes them he will be born as a child of God, and such words will become spirit and live in him by faith and by the Holy Spirit.

In the 71st section Schwenckfeld laments, without going into detail, "that no Christian can be a magistrate or worldly ruler, nor can assume authority over cities or countries or people since such authority belongs to earthly rulers and not to true Christians." In answer Marpeck first gives the correct statement of the Anabaptists as follows: that since the kingdom of Christ is not of this world no true Christian dare have authority over cities, countries, and people (as earthly rulers), nor exercise defense or use force, since this belongs to the earthly and temporal rulers and can only lead to results such as happened in the Peasants' War. Our understanding is that true Christians have no commandment in the Gospel to exercise any power such as that of the worldly arm in the kingdom of this world. We should like to know, says Marpeck, "on what basis in the Evangelical Scriptures and the Christian conscience he would advise a true Christian to frivolously enter into such worldly government or office, and whether, after he is not such, he should conduct the affairs of this world according to God's commandment without abuse, and how long his conscience would keep him in such governmental office if he would not desire to suffer damage to his soul." Marpeck's teaching clearly is not directed in any way against the worldly authority, as the opponents of the Anabaptists claimed.

In the matter of the church, as discussed in this connection, there is no fundamental exposition of the concept of the church but rather a fixing of the foundation on which it stands, and this is not Peter, as Schwenckfeld accuses the Anabaptists of saying, but the Lord Himself who produced in Peter his confession.

A favorite topic of Schwenckfeld is his teaching concerning the men of the old covenant, the patriarchs and prophets, who he claims were already Christians. He says that the Anabaptists are guilty of a serious error in that they will not admit that the fathers, patriarchs, and prophets are Christians, children of God, and friends of God, like us. Against this teaching of Schwenckfeld Marpeck teaches, in harmony with the statements and references in the *Testamentserläuterung,* that the fathers who believed the promises of God died in hope of the incarnation of Christ and went to Hades, received there from the Lord grace, comfort, salvation, peace, and redemption, and were reconciled (Eph. 4:11 and I Peter 3:4). The faith of the fathers included the future incarnation of Christ, but they were not because of this Christians.

Schwenckfeld introduces the discussions of the communion with the statement that here, as in the matter of baptism, one must ask whether the Anabaptists have the right understanding of it and the right practice. He denies both. Marpeck takes up the debatable interpretation of the words of institution of the communion which is given by Luther, Zwingli, and others and says, we have written about this in our testimonies so clear and without any fog or darkness that all of those who are taught of the Spirit agree with us. If, however, Schwenckfeld writes that our communion service is based upon works not its use of bread and wine, like water and baptism, and a commitment to obedience, we answer: Christ gave His disciples bread to eat and wine to drink and would not command them to dispute about it. Our understanding of the Lord's words is that everything depends upon the interworking, making alive, and making pious by the Holy Spirit. What the pious believers produce by their faith is God's work. Bread and wine and water are and remain material elements and are not

a part of the essence, but are only commanded to be used and so it can not be shown (as we are accused) that we make the creature into God and God into a creature. We confess that the Lord gives food and drink to the soul and the inner man by His holy flesh and blood, and that the nourishment of our spirit and our soul must be only spiritual. Bread and wine cannot be food and drink for the soul, but are used as a memorial for proclaiming the death of Christ and as a thanksgiving to Him. How can Schwenckfeld accuse us of not knowing anything about the spiritual food? We will not obscure the secret of a communion but rather reveal it, but without the hair-splittings of this *Judicium.*

Schwenckfeld's own writings refute his attitudes. For this purpose the *Verantwortung* gives extensive extracts from Schwenckfeld's writings in five chapters, dealing with the following subjects: "von der leiblichen Stell," of the knowledge of Christ, of the worship of Christ, of the communication of Christ, of the word and creaturehood of Christ, of a clear report, after such extracts from Schwenckfeld's book against Bucer had already been given as an appendix to the 89th *Red und Antwort.*

The question which receives the most thorough discussion is the incarnation of Christ. While Schwenckfeld presents Jesus primarily as the Saviour in His glorification, Marpeck emphasizes the *Ecce homo.* The suffering Redeemer had died for mankind, but he emphasizes that the two aspects are not to be separated. If one should separate the humanity of Christ from His deity, all comfort and hope for humankind would be gone, "since He is to be our faithful Mediator, High Priest, and merciful Advocate." "And so they say that the humanity (flesh) of Christ, which is now in and with the Word of God, is our refuge, yea of all sinners. Without this no man could be saved or come to the eternal God."

In the latter portions of the *Verantwortung* Marpeck treats again the doctrine of the communion and the essence of the church and gives an overview of everything, not without once more touching upon the basis of Schwenckfeld's bitter attempt, who does not want to be considered to be Anabaptist, since he sees how such people are slandered, persecuted, and crucified. But for this very reason his teaching is not from God nor from His Word and he therefore cannot be a servant of God.

Herewith the polemic between the two men comes to an end, of whom the one presents Christ chiefly in His glory, the other crowned with thorns, smitten and hanging on the cross as the Saviour of mankind, of the poor and the oppressed. Marpeck apparently did not expect a reply to his book, although he calls out to Schwenckfeld, "Just write the world full of books against us." This Schwenckfeld did not do. He had difficulty, indeed, to meet the arguments of the Anabaptists, who had anchored themselves in the words of the Bible by the use of *Testamentserläuterung.* In Schwenckfeld's extensive correspondence Marpeck's name appears only rarely, and then only in such fashion as to indicate clearly his bitterness against this Anabaptist leader.

IX. *Effects of the Verantwortung.* The most recent studies of Marpeck's book have shown that it was not given to the public without the testing of the elders of the entire church. Only after the approval by the elders, whose names have been preserved through the attentiveness of a noble lady, Walpurga von Pappenheim, could believers secure copies. Because of the size of the book probably not many were able to take advantage of the privilege. But the larger congregations, even beyond South Germany, very likely possessed it. And when uncertainty or difference of opinion about some point of doctrine arose among the members of the church, the *Verantwortung* was called upon for the decision on which one could take his position. A proof of this is found in the Olmütz manuscript, which also contains the text of the *Verantwortung*. Two brethren of the church in 1571 disagreed concerning the question "about the Holy Scriptures and the dead letter through which spirit and life come." On this occasion a number of Anabaptists were called in and given an explanation of the matter from the pen of the former (by then dead) co-worker of Marpeck, Leupold Scharnschlager. The document was the "Unterscheid," in which the following appears: "Dear Brethren, I think you have noticed in the 4th chapter of the 96th *Antwort* of the book of the *Verantwortung* against Schwenckfeld's *Judicium*, how this passage is used against Schwenckfeld. It is my opinion that the word 'letter,' as it is used in Romans and in II Corinthians, refers to the Old Testament, and not to the New, which contains the spirit which is able to make alive and the grace through faith. For this reason it behooves us not to give the name 'dead letter' to the Holy Scriptures of the New Testament, since such Scripture, which calls itself the Holy Scripture which speaks, according to II Peter 1, of the holy man of God and of the holy Gospel, is written and inspired by the Spirit of God. The Holy Scripture itself is the spoken word of God, and for this reason I would not call it a dead letter, but would call it the Holy Scriptures, as it calls itself." Now if we look in the 4th chapter of the 96th *Antwort* (concerning the Word of God) we find the following: "That the invisible spiritual content, meaning understanding and sense of the Holy Scriptures and of the outwardly preached word . . . is the word to which the Holy Scripture gives honor and power as God's natural almighty word, which is spirit and life, yea God Himself."

X. *Marpeck's Later Years and Death.* From 1544 until 1556 Marpeck's name appears on the tax books and the building records of the city of Augsburg in Bavarian Swabia. There he secured employment as an engineer. His first assignment was the improvement of the city water system, the aqueducts. He built waterways for the floating of rafts of wood (*Pilgerholz*). From 1546 until his death his salary as a city employee (*Stadtwerckmeister*) was 150 florins per year. From as early as 1545 Marpeck's activities as an Anabaptist elder were a matter of annoyance to the city authorities, and he was sent a number of warnings to desist therefrom. But somehow he managed to retain his position until his death in 1556. Known warnings to Marpeck, either from the mayor of Augsburg or the Council, are dated July 16, 1545, May 6, 1550, Sept. 26, 1553, and Sept. 25, 1554. Marpeck was paid quarterly on the Ember days. The first three payments for 1556 are

entered in the *Baumeisterbuch* in a normal manner, but under the payment date of Dec. 16, 1556, for Marpeck is the notation, "Is dead."

LOSERTH, J.C.W.

XI. *Marpeck and His Group in the Light of the Newly Discovered Kunstbuch Codex.* An entirely new light is thrown on Marpeck's role in the history of Anabaptism by the discovery in July 1955 in the Bürgerbibliothek in Bern, Switzerland, of a large manuscript codex of 370 pages, copied for the most part by Jörg Maler, who finished it on Sept. 4, 1561, and gave it the title *Kunstbuch*. It contains 42 documents originally written between 1527 and 1555 (only seven written before 1540, and all of these in 1527 except one early 1528 and one in 1530). All but two of the 37 documents of 1540-55 were written either by Marpeck (16) or Leopold Scharnschlager (6) or members of the Marpeck circle. A complete analysis of the contents of the documents was given by Heinold Fast in *ARG*, the abstract of which is herewith presented in full as a quotation:

"The earliest writings of the collection do not belong to the Marbeck circle, but they seem to have had an influence on it. Some of them are known from other sources and published by Lydia Müller in her *Glaubenszeugnisse oberdeutscher Taufgesinnter* (Leipzig, 1938). The authors are Hans Hut, Lienhart Schiemer, Hans Schlaffer, and others. Their theological thinking centered around the discipleship under the cross which led them to martyrdom. Fast derives the main themes of this piety from Thomas Müntzer, though he is aware that it was not the war-waging Müntzer who found his followers among the Anabaptists, and that his spiritualism and eschatology were strongly moderated by them. It is probable that Marbeck was converted to Anabaptism by the impression made by the martyrdom of Schiemer and Schlaffer in the vicinity of his home town in the Tyrol. Fast raises the question how far this may indicate an influence of their theology on Marbeck. The presence of a letter by Hans Has suggests an influence also by Lutheran ideas. And a tract by Christian Entfelder, a pupil of Hans Denk, leads to the question of Marbeck's dependence on mystical thinking. The paper does not intend to give definite answers to these questions. After it has sketched the theological thinking of Marbeck in part four, it repeats it in detail in part five. The stress lies on part three and its survey of Marbeck's activities in striving for the unity of the different Anabaptist groups.

"The survey follows the places to which Marbeck paid his visits or wrote his letters: Strassburg and its surroundings, the Grisons, Württemberg, Appenzell, St. Gall, Moravia, and Augsburg. Everywhere the Anabaptists had been split into parties shunning and fighting one another. The Marbeck circle seems to have been a separated group, too. It is not always clear when the separation began and how long it existed. But in the forties it is most definitely to be seen in Appenzell as well as in Moravia. In Appenzell the Marbeck group opposed the so-called Swiss Brethren, in Moravia the Hutterites. The questions at stake were the ban and community of goods. Marbeck advocated a less rigorous attitude with respect to both. In his view the radicalism of the

Swiss Brethren in Appenzell and of the Hutterites did not agree with the freedom of the gospel. It was also the cause for the splitting of the Anabaptist movement. Marbeck consistently fought for a re-union of the separated groups. His success was limited to winning smaller circles for his own party. Among them was Jörg of Augsburg, called Maler, the later transcriber of the codex. The Anabaptist synods at Strassburg 1554/55 seem to have shown better results in uniting the movement. They also must have grown out of the endeavors of Marbeck. The new material does not refer to these events, but the author points to other publications (Kiwiet) which make the relationship probable."

Kiwiet's study has led him to the conclusion that Marbeck and his followers constituted a distinct group among the German Anabaptists, differing from the Swiss Brethren. On the other hand, they also differed clearly from the Spiritualists. Kiwiet claims an origin for the Marpeck group independent of the Swiss Brethren with Hans Denk as their founder. He also claims that Denk was not a Spiritualist and thus rehabilitates Denk as a full Anabaptist. His conception of the Marpeck group and of Marpeck's role in Anabaptist history can best be given in his own words (from an unpublished paper scheduled to appear in MQR for October 1957):

"Until recently the only possible distinction between Anabaptists seemed to be the radical and the moderate type of an Anabaptist. With such a division Denck was usually grouped among the radicals, while Marbeck was put together with the Swiss Brethren among the moderates. These categories prevented a clear insight into Anabaptist history. Another questionable point was the eschatological and spiritual (in distinction from spiritualistic) tendencies among many Anabaptist groups. Mennonite scholars had no explanation for these tendencies as they clearly were not present among the Swiss Brethren. Because of these just mentioned tendencies some church historians still persisted in claiming a dependence of the Anabaptists on Thomas Müntzer. A study of Marbeck and Hans Denck gives the explanation of the other type of Anabaptist, which also originated free of Müntzer, although it shared with him the eschatological and spiritual interest which was common to many theologians in South Germany.

"Within the field of Anabaptist history it is very interesting to notice the origin and development of these two main movements within Anabaptism, one having the Scriptures as its principle, the other having love and obedience as its center. Both discovered the free church from a different angle, one from Bible study and the other from theological considerations. These two types of Anabaptists provide a Scriptural as well as a theological foundation for the free church principles.

"Within the ecumenical discussion about the meaning of the church Marbeck provides very valuable material. He not only gives an exposition of a free church theology, but he also has related his teaching to that of the Catholics, the Lutherans, and the Spiritualistic circles. In all three of these areas the discussion is still very relevant; the discussion with Rome, the discussion about the value and fu-

ture of the state churches, and the problem of ever rising free circles who incline to give up all historic church forms. As far as I know, Marbeck is the only one in church history who has presented us a thorough free church theology."

Another significant recent discovery is that by Frank Wray (first published in ARG, 1956), who has shown that much of the Vermahnung is in fact a translation (from the Low German) and revision of a significant part of Bernhard Rothmann's Bekenntnisse van beyden Sacramenten, Doepe unde Nachtmaele der predicanten tho Munster (Nov. 8, 1533). That this pre-Münsterite writing could be used and accepted by the Marpeck group proves on the one hand that the pre-Münsterite Anabaptists in Westphalia were good Anabaptists, and also that there was some literary exchange between the Middle German and South German groups. H.S.B.

Johann Adam, Evangelische Kirchengeschichte . . . Strassburg (Strasbourg, 1922); Johann Wilh. Baum, Capito und Butzer (Elberfeld, 1860); Beck, Geschichts-Bücher; Gustav Bossert, Jr., "Nebenkirchliche Bewegung," Blätter für württembergische Kirchengeschichte (Stuttgart, 1930) 1-41; C. A. Cornelius, Gesch. des Münsterischen Aufruhrs II (Leipzig, 1860); Ernst Correll, "Anabaptism in the Tyrol," MQR I (October 1927); Karl Ecke, Schwenckfeld, Luther und . . . apostol. Ref. (Berlin, 1911); H. Eels, Martin Bucer (New Haven, 1931); Robert Friedmann, "Täufergemeinschaften in Mähren," Archiv für Ref.-Gesch., 1931; Samuel Geiser, Die Taufgesinnten-Gemeinden (Karlsruhe, 1931); Camille Gerbert, Gesch. der Strassburger Sectenbewegung, 1524-35 (Strasbourg, 1889); A. Hulshoff, Geschiedenis der Doopsgezinden te Straatsburg (Amsterdam, 1905); E. E. S. Johnson, Corpus Schwenckfeldianorum VIII (Leipzig, 1927); Ludwig Keller, "Marbeck," ADB XX (Leipzig, 1884); L. Keller, Monatsheft der Comenius-Gesellschaft V (1896) 311-13; Walther Köhler, in RGG III; J. ten Doornkaat Koolman, "Graubünden," ML II; J. Loserth, "Wiedertäufer in Tirol," Ztscht . . . für Tirol u. Vorarlberg (Innsbruck, 1895) 279-88; idem "Marbeck," ML III; idem, "Studien zu Pilgram Marbeck," Gedenkschrift (Ludwigshafen, 1925) 134-78; idem, "Pilgram Marbeck, sein Leben u. sein Werk," Quellen u. Forschungen . . . (Vienna, 1929) 1-60; A. H. Newman, History of Antipedobaptism (Philadelphia, 1897) 189-249; Horst Quiring, "The Anthropology of Pilgram Marbeck," MQR IX (1935) 155-64; T. W. Röhrich, "Strassburgische Wiedertäufer," Ztscht für die histor. Theologie (Gotha, 1860); Friedrich Roth, Augsburgs Reformationsgesch. III (Munich, 1907); Chr. Aug. Salig, Vollst. Hist. der Augspurgischen Confession III (Halle, 1735); Traugott Schiess, "Ilanzer Schulmeister," Bündnerisches Monatsblatt (Chur, 1916) 73-89; Paul von Stetten, Gesch. der . . . Stadt Augsburg I (Frankfurt and Leipzig, 1743); J. C. Wenger, "The Life and Work of Pilgram Marpeck," MQR XII (1938) 137-66; idem, "Pilgram Marpeck's Confession of Faith," MQR XII (1938) 167-202; idem, "The Theology of Pilgram Marpeck," MQR XII (1938) 205-56; idem, "A Letter from Wilhelm Reublin to Pilgram Marpeck, 1531," MQR XXIII (1949) 67-75; idem, "Pilgram Marpeck's Summary of His Confession of Faith," MHB IX, 3; W. Wiswedel, "Die Testamentserläuterung," Blätter f. württemberg. Kirchengeschichte XLI (1937) 64-76.

Original copies of Marpeck's Taufbüchlein, the Vermanung of 1542, are in the British Museum, the Budapest University Library, and the Stuttgart State Library. This book was reprinted in the Gedenkschrift, 1925. Original copies of Marpeck's Testamentserläuterung are in the Zentralbibliothek of Zürich, and in the Preussische Staatsbibliothek, Berlin (now Marburg). This work has never been republished. Manuscript copies of the Verantwortung, the reply to Schwenckfeld, are in the Zürich Stadtbibliothek, in the Bayerische Staatsbibliothek at Munich, and in the Studienbibliothek of Olmütz, Czechoslovakia. Loserth transcribed and published the Verantwortung in Quellen u. Forschungen zur Geschichte der oberdeutschen Taufgesinnten im 16. Jahrhundert. Pilgram Marbecks Antwort *auf Kaspar Schwenckfelds Beurteilung des Buches der Bundesbezeugung von 1542* (Vienna and Leipzig, 1929); Heinold Fast, "Pilgram Marbeck und das oberdeutsche Täufertum. Ein neuer Handschriftenfund," *Archiv für Reformationsgeschichte* XLVII (1956) 212-42; Jan J. Kiwiet, "Pilgram Marbeck, sein Kreis und seine Theologie" (unpublished doctoral dissertation, University of Zürich, 1955); Frank Wray, "The Vermanung of 1542 and Rothmann's Bekenntnisse," *Archiv für Reformationsgeschichte* XLVII (1956) 243 ff.; Lydia Müller, *Glaubensbekenntnisse oberdeutscher Taufgesinnter* (Leipzig, 1938; ML III, 25-34.

Marquardt, Hans, of Wissenhorn, an Anabaptist leader, was a chaplain in Constanz, Germany, about one year, then for three years Protestant preacher in the canton of Bern, Switzerland, joined the Swiss Brethren, and became an effective leader. He was very likely for a while in Memmingen (*q.v.*) and Moravia (*q.v.*). In the summer of 1532 he went to St. Gall, where his sermons had a large following. Here he was captured. After an arrest of eight days he was granted a disputation which lasted three days. With no small skill he defended his views against the mayor Joachim Vadian (*q.v.*) and the Reformed preachers, Dominicus Zili, Christoph Schappelar, and Jakob Riner. What he said concerning the oath, infant baptism, and the government is not without significance. He was expelled from the city, and all trace of him is lost. NEFF.

E. Götzinger, *Joachim von Watt (Vadian): Deutsche historische Schriften* III (St. Gall, 1879) 455 ff.; ML III, 43.

Marquette (Man.) Mennonite Brethren Church was organized on July 15, 1934, as a branch of the North End M.B. Church of Winnipeg. The church is a member of the Manitoba Provincial and the Canadian District Conferences. In 1954 the baptized membership was 22, with Isaak Penner as leader, and John Klassen assistant.   H.NE.

Marri Tiene, an Anabaptist martyr, who is not named in van Braght's *Martyrs' Mirror*. She is named in acrostic in the song, *Met menschlijcke tongen niet.* (Wolkan, *Lieder,* 80.)   NEFF.

Marriage, the most intimate form of fellowship between man and woman, with the family (*q.v.*) the most ancient human institution, took various forms in the ancient world, was transformed and made sacred in Christianity as unbreakable monogamy. Marriage was taken by Paul (Eph. 5) as a symbol of Christ's union with the church, and was to be only in the Lord. The relation between husband and wife was to be one of profound Christian love and mutual service, grounded in the relation of each to Christ. It was to be kept absolutely pure. Jesus taught that the indissoluble union of one man with one woman was an original part of God's creation, and could be broken only by adultery (Matt. 9). The equality of man and woman in the church and in the Christian faith as taught by Paul (Col. 3) had a powerful elevating effect upon the status of woman in marriage and in society. Nevertheless the patriarchal type of marriage and family life continued to be dominant among Christians in the Middle Ages and on into modern times. The developing ascetic ideal of monasticism, by which celibacy was elevated

above marriage as holier and preferable, interfered with the full realization of the Christian ideal in marriage. In the Middle Ages also the church developed the sacramental concept of marriage, which contributed to the absolute control of marriage by the church, with prohibited degrees of consanguinity.

The Reformers, while doing away with monasticism and celibacy, also abolished the sacramental concept of marriage. Luther especially pointed to its secular elements. Various ends were to be served. Households were considered fiscal units in the political structure of society. Marriage was a worldly business, so that Christians might even marry unbelievers (Luther, *Vom Eelichen Leben,* 1522). Anabaptist sentiments were truly in contrast to external interpretations of this sort. In Anabaptist tradition the marriage bond has always been valued as a mystical association and form of piety. This view and Anabaptist-Mennonite insistence on the community-bound order and service of the marriage union in Christian fellowship contributed in its way to the opposition against ecclesiastical controls. Their objection applied to Roman Catholic canon law as it did to later Protestant state church interference.

The Anabaptist emphasis upon personal choice and responsibility in matters of religion on the one hand, and upon strict obedience to the teachings of Christ and the New Testament on the other, strengthened measurably the moral character of marriage. By its consecrated view of life Anabaptism obliterated the sacramental marriage concept. It placed obedience to Christ in the first place, with three significant consequences: (1) because of the separation of the true (Anabaptist) church from the world and all other Christian groups, marriage was restricted to members of the group alone; (2) in case a marriage partner did not follow the spouse in joining the Anabaptists, some felt it would be right and necessary to separate from or even divorce the unbelieving partner, since otherwise there would be an "unequal yoke with unbelievers" (although this was by no means universal); and (3) the Anabaptist missioner felt obliged to leave his family to go on missionary tours if sent by the church. All of these attitudes and practices were subject to severe criticism by opponents in the state churches.

More severe, but unwarranted criticism was directed against the Anabaptists with the frequent charge (Zwingli the first) that they practiced communism of wives, or at least were guilty of gross immorality. These charges were pure inference from the purported Anabaptist teaching of community of goods and arose before Münster (1534-35), and even before the Hutterite communities were established (1528-35).

The Münsterites (1534-35), however, introduced polygamy; but, except for the "King," Jan van Leyden, they were not guilty of the gross immorality which the vivid imagination of their contemporaries and later writers often attributed to them. The Münsterite regulations about marriage were clear and severe. According to the "Twenty-one Münsterite Articles," marriage with unbelievers (i.e., non-Münsterites) was strictly forbidden. Believers were to have a "new marriage," which of course opened the door to separation from "unbelieving spouses." Strict marital fidelity was required. Adultery, also seduction and rape, were punishable by death. Detmer has shown that the introduction of polygamy, although based on the example of the patriarchs and kings of the Old Testament, was due to Jan van Leyden's own personal decision, and that he had to break the opposition of the better elements and the preachers by long days of disputation. It was not a real part of even radical Münsterism. The apocalyptic mood in Münster, which recognized Jan van Leyden as a prophet, gave him great authority. He himself began the polygamy. He prophesied that the people of God must multiply, and enforced the rule that all men and women of proper age must marry and reproduce. The decline of the number of men in Münster made it easy (and necessary if the rule of all marrying was to be obeyed) for polygamy to be practiced.

Another dark case of a different sort which was wrongly exploited by Justus Menius (*q.v.*) was that of the "Blood Friends" (Blutsfreunde aus der Wiedertaufe) of Northwest Thuringia and near-by Hesse of 1550, which occurred in the latter days of Anabaptism in Thuringia. Led by Ludwig von Tüngeda this small group renounced the regular Anabaptist basic doctrines of baptism and the Lord's Supper, and declared that the true sacrament consists in the fleshly mingling of the brethren and sisters who are united with Christ, which they called "Christerie." Wappler (*Thüringia*) has shown that it is completely false to consider these apostates as a party of Anabaptists, since they had openly repudiated the main Anabaptist teachings. The Thuringian and Hessian Anabaptists, as Wappler and others have shown, maintained high standards of marriage ethics.

Marriage Among the Mennonites; The Marriage Problem in the "Separated" Organized Congregation; Forms of Courtship. It would be incorrect to call Menno Simons the most outspoken "ethical prophet" of Anabaptism merely because (1) in the stately series of his writings the most conspicuous place is occupied by his rejection of the lumping together of the peaceful Anabaptists with the warlike apocalyptic Anabaptists of Münster, and (2) Menno at the same time teaches the absolute principle of the suffering church. Much rather does his ethical significance lie in the fact that it was under his essential influence that the first congregational organizations arose. It was he who began to order the widely scattered groups according to a unified direction in a world of persecution. The strongly pietistic spirit that sets in with him is no longer borne and upheld by the mighty idealism such as that of the High German Anabaptists. Historically Menno's writings are an honest attempt to prove the innocence of those oppressed by suspicion, and so he is concerned in presenting the true concept of those first Mennonites about marriage: how they base it entirely on the New Testament. "Every age has its own liberty and usages. Concerning marriage we are directed by the Lord Himself, not to the liberty and usage of the fathers . . . but to the beginning of creation, to Adam and Eve. . . . So we too teach, use, and consent to no other marriage, . . . namely one man and

one woman. . . . They are one flesh and they shall not part from this and from one another . . . except for adultery. . . ." "Concerning the shameful vice that we are said to have our wives in common . . . the God-fearing would rather die ten deaths than do such a thing." Menno's contemporaries, such as Adam Pastor, wrote in the same vein.

But it was not this polemic that became historically significant for the Anabaptist position on marriage. Separation from the world, which was still stressed, even if no longer in the first fullness of conviction, took on a certain new stamp. No longer does immoderate enthusiasm stream into the congregations—it was in general broken under the armed resistance of the intolerant public powers. The separation of the congregations from the world in those places where in a sense their existence was assured, meant certainly a selection of those most purified in the Anabaptist concept of Christianity. Very soon this development into which original Anabaptism had been pushed from without and within, was bound also to determine the question of the marriage of members of the congregation.

Martyrdom, then as later, created and inspired a conjugal fellowship of consecration unto suffering and death. Here and there, however, groups of Mennonites could establish themselves in refugee settlements or otherwise shielded settlements. Under such less disturbed auspices marriage and its prerequisites were given a more elaborate interpretation and specific directions. As a possible gateway into the religious community marriage was now placed under conditions designed to preserve permanently the purity and resolute "separation from the world" of the congregations. Adam Pastor expresses himself (I Cor. 7:39) very precisely in this sense: that one is not to enter into a marriage with persons who are not of the Lord's house (i.e., outside the brotherhood): "That one take for marriage not a renegade partner who is without God but a believing partner who adheres to God." Dirk Philips stresses the importance of this marriage of the mind. He sets the congregation as the judge of one of the most essential problems which was to disturb the future of Anabaptism-Mennonitism for a long time to come. The ground to control the matter decisively grew out of the congregation's right of discipline. It lay in the hands of the "Diener" (elders and lay preachers), who were economically relatively independent of the congregation. This position, energetically defended by Menno, elevated the rules about marriage set by the congregation to a considerable height, guaranteed for the very reason that church discipline had been by that time made a basic regulation.

Under the penalty of the ban, marriage was to be concluded in the presence of the congregation and by its commissioned ministers. They examined the couple to be married, obligating them to the most important articles concerning marriage. Wedded thus "within" the congregation, marriage would undoubtedly be concluded "in the Lord." The fact that they had been married "before God and His holy church" was often enthusiastically affirmed in the confessions of Anabaptist martyr couples. "Outside marriage," i.e., marriage with an "unbelieving person in the world," is a later development fraught with much conflict.

Dirk Philips' last writing and one of considerable influence (*Van die Echt der Christenen,* 1569), deals with the marriage of Christians on a Scriptural basis. In general the Mosaic law (Deut. 7:3 ff.) is also cited by him, in order to confirm marriage with believers as an absolute goal. This regulation was applied with heroic and inexorable Anabaptist moral severity. When it was violated, reconciliation of the offender with the congregation was granted only when the unbelieving partner was "recognized," i.e., was received by baptism into the brotherhood. If this did not happen, the partner who wanted to be reconciled had to "desist from" the unbelieving partner. The Flemish branch (including Dirk Philips) took a position similar to that of the Frisians. They "do not accept those who were married outside the brotherhood however long and sincerely they lament, seek, write, ask, and beseech, but all their life long have to remain separated from their brotherhood, or the unbelieving one with whom one is married must become believing or die." The Waterlander branch did not share this stern concept, having accepted the Wismar resolutions (1554) with their freer spirit: "The persons who marry outside the congregation shall be excluded and avoided until they show an upright and Christian life before God and the brethren; then after a period of trial they shall be received again."

It is conspicuous that "mixed marriage" was always considered as a conflict from within, as a threat to purity, but not as a threat to the existence of the brotherhood. Such a fear did not seem to exist; at least it was not expressed. The concept, spread particularly by the fanatical David Joris, that the marriage of true believers would finally bring forth the kingdom of God, had apparently found a convinced following in the very circles of Menno. Wherever it arose there was, however, no thought at all of the dangers mentioned above. In general, the following contradictory views of marriage can be observed among the Dutch Anabaptists:

(1) One position was the absolute marriage law of the severe Frisian type, oriented according to the Old Testament, in which marriage was allowed only among church members. Not until later did the custom develop of acceptance into fellowship only after they have been rebaptized. At first the expulsion of offending members was relentlessly carried out and this law applied even and precisely against members of less strict congregations.

(2) A second position was a moderated marriage law oriented according to the New Testament, definitive in the sense of the resolutions of Wismar and Strasbourg (1555 f.), represented especially in the Waterlander branch, by which persons marrying outside the brotherhood were again received after giving evidence of "upright Christian life before God and the brethren," and were excluded only until such evidence was produced.

The Concept of Cologne, a document of unification of some (Young) Frisians and High Germans of 1591, to be sure, still breathes the old severity of concept, but also speaks against a ruthless solution and thus approaches the New Testament marriage

law: "We confess also out of the Holy Scriptures of the Old and New Testament that no freedom is left to a believer to marry anyone except one who has become with them through faith a member of the body of Christ and a brother or sister.... Transgressors . . . are worthy of punishment before the congregation and one shall have no brotherly unity with them [to be excluded from communion], unless one feels a worthy fruit of penitence and repentance; they are to be admonished to observe faithfully their marriage vow, neither to leave their spouse nor to conclude a second marriage."

The Dordrecht Confession of 1632 breathes the spirit of the Old Testament law as it does in other points where it represents a violently dominating reaction toward all previous efforts of unification on the basis of milder premises. It says: "Like as the Fathers had to marry among their brotherhood or race, so also believers of the New Testament are permitted no other freedom than to marry among the elect race and spiritual brotherhood of Christ, namely those who are already united with the brotherhood as one heart and one soul, have received one baptism and stand in one brotherhood, faith, teaching, and life, before they are united through marriage." Such unions were then called "marriage in the Lord."

In the Amish congregations in America, among the Mennonites in Switzerland and France, and among the Mennonite Brethren in Russia this last concept has prevailed in part to this day. In the negotiations for unification between the Amish and Mennonites in the Palatinate in 1873 a basic stipulation was made that marriage between members of these congregations shall not be opposed by either group. The West Prussian rural congregations practiced the marriage law oriented by the Old Testament until the end of their existence. Thus Article IX of the confession of faith of the Mennonites of Prussia of 1895 says: "When a member marries outside our branch this act is considered a voluntary separation out of our brotherhood. The position of the Gemeindeverband (*q.v.*) is more moderate. In the case of mixed marriages in the congregations composing it, if the promise to raise the children as Mennonites is not given, the Mennonite partner is considered as excluded from the congregation."

For a considerable part of the Mennonites the confession of Cornelis Ris of 1766 is valid; it became definitive for the Mennonite congregations in Russia, for some urban congregations of North Germany, as well as for the Mennonite congregations of the Palatinate and Hesse. The spirit of its marriage law, completely oriented according to the New Testament (Article XXXI), is as follows: God also controls human marriages "but in such a way that human freedom is not annulled thereby, be it that He institutes it graciously according to His kindness, or be it that He legally permits it in disfavor and for punishment." Marriage is therefore to be "an affair in which man is permitted to proceed in his freedom in so far as God's holy requirements do not limit it; as this is clearly shown in the prohibition of marriage with unbelieving persons. . . ." Further examples are cited from the

Scriptures. Incidents of divine displeasure are pointed out, where the evil and the dangers of carnal marriages in which one follows only the impulses of nature are presented. "Therefore it is exceedingly important that whoever wants to enter the state of matrimony shall examine himself well and not decide before he is convinced in faith and with a good conscience that in this decision he is pleasing the Lord Christ. Those who marry thus can with reason hope that it is taking place in the Lord. . . ." If a marriage is thus begun, "the man who is the head of the wife, . . . shall be a worthy image of Jesus Christ in his relationship toward his church . . . the wife will become blessed through bearing of children, her seed will be blessed, and all things will serve them for the best. But to be happy herein we consider it necessary in so far as it is at all possible, to remain in one's own religious brotherhood, in order to avoid the many unpleasant consequences that usually arise out of differing education, manner of living, and points of view in the teaching of children and other things, which is often discovered too late. . . ." For young people it is proper and useful to ask advice of parents, besides God and close relatives, and to obey them, "but all in the fear of the Lord."

In more recent times there were other reasons than purely religious strivings for preventing marriages outside the brotherhood. In West Prussia release from military duty for Mennonites was limited to those who, for example, could prove that they had for several generations occupied land without military duty. Anyone who married outside the brotherhood lost his Mennonite right to release from military duty. On the other hand the Prussian state also prevented the increase in the number of Mennonites by prohibiting transfer of membership from other groups to the Mennonites. The congregations maintained themselves at a definite limited number. With the repeal of the privilege of release from military duty the greatest part of the congregations of West Prussia were quite ready to permit marriage with members of other Christian creeds. On the other hand it is known that Swiss Anabaptists in the principality of Montbéliard about 1710 married Calvinists in order to be able to stay in the country. To what extent the regulation of the authorities that change in creed be affirmed by an oath was effective (for the Anabaptists who had only apparently become Calvinistic) is unknown.

Two closely related motives determined the nature and manner of courtship by withdrawing the right of the individual to choose his marriage partner and transferring it to the elders or other ministers of the congregation; for the guarantee of a marriage of faith on the one hand, and for the preservation of the moral purity of the congregation on the other hand. "Youths and maidens shall not go about together too freely," says the introductory sentence of the second article of a resolution of a conference of Frisian congregations which had to be announced annually between 1639 and 1716. Another motivation also effective as a pattern was the formal adoption of customs out of the holy Scriptures as was inherent in Anabaptist Biblicism. This was most pronounced among the former Swiss

Anabaptists in the Vosges area of France. Their courtship was accomplished in a most complete analogy with Genesis 24. In the place of the servant who went out for Abraham to win a wife for his son, the deacon ("the Steckelmann") mounted a horse for his mission even if the bride's house was the very next one. Then the traditional customs were repeated, such as presenting a drink, gifts, etc. And the result of the commission was indicated by the attitude expressed by the bride. This drastic usage of Biblical imitation has never been found in any other group than in this remote one in the Vosges region.

In all the Anabaptist-Mennonite groups of whatever religious and ethical shading, there was at least the custom that preachers or elders functioned as commissioned wooers. He who did not accept this arrangement was subject to church discipline. This custom was practiced most severely in those places where mixed marriage was opposed with the sharpness of the Old Testament law. Carel van Gent reports from the Flemish congregations that about 1600 among them the arrangement of weddings was diligently and dictatorially exercised by the ministers. In the Flemish and Frisian congregations at Danzig the stipulations seem to have been less sharp; there the courtship was not exclusively the affair of the leaders. In 1765 it was announced to the brotherhood that the ancient, praiseworthy habit of using two men to make the proposal of marriage, who after a week or two of time granted the prospective bride for reflection returned for the decision, had fallen into decline. The practice that some bridegrooms proposed for themselves, and others even became engaged without the knowledge of their parents, was punishable. (See **Umbitter**.)

The decision concerning the so-called "obstacles to marriage" was in the hands of the church or secular authorities, but it was not only conditions of a religious kind which were also decided in the congregations. Thus there was almost everywhere a prohibition of marriage of cousins. There was no lack of efforts to renew this prohibition. The great conference at Groningen in 1683, which argued for two days concerning granting an exception, is well known. Almost half of the over 100 preachers out of 29 congregations had "with concern" voted in its favor. The decision was then left to the congregation concerned. Also the Ibersheim (Palatinate) conference of 1805 had the question of the marriage of cousins on its agenda, but came to no conclusion. At that time the prohibition had already been frequently disregarded.

Relations between the fiances generally were kept under the severity of church discipline. In harmony with the Mosaic laws offenses against chastity were to be punished as adultery.

The equating of the engagement vow with the marriage vow had already very early given rise to difference of opinion, especially between Adam Pastor and Dirk Philips. The latter was more lenient, saying, "Not the mere vow alone binds the marriage, because things may lie concealed which cause the marriage vow to be ineffective." He recognized the need that there be an inclination and attitude of the heart, but "they shall not be married earlier than is favored by the Lord and His church." That the brotherhood would recognize only a marriage concluded before it and through it was already a strictly executed demand of the Swiss Anabaptists. The solemn modesty of Mennonite marriage customs is pictured in travel accounts out of various Mennonite areas. Another common phenomenon of the Mennonite congregations was early marriage. It is interesting to note, for example, that the enlargement of the area of the city of Crefeld in 1738 was caused in part by this fact. A new building plan was recommended to the king on account of the prospective increase in the number of households, most of whom at that time were Mennonite.

The Anabaptist-Mennonite Attitude on the Indissolubility of Marriage; Divorce; "Marital Avoidance" as a Problem of Church Discipline.

The command of Jesus (Matt. 5:32) which names adultery as the only possible ground for divorce becomes a point of judgment repeated in all the Mennonite creeds. The Wismar resolutions give the unfaithful one the right to return to the spouse upon repentance and reform. In the case of "premeditated" (*mutwillig*) adultery, the innocent party might marry again after consultation with the congregation.

An increasingly serious question was whether unbelief entering into the marriage did, after all, part the marriage. The booklet, *Concerning Divorce* ("Von der Ehescheydung auss den worten Christi . . ."), attached to the Confession of Schleitheim (1527) says nothing more than that divorce may be based singly and alone on adultery. But it was precisely unbelief that had a decisive effect on a wide circle of South German Anabaptists.

Considering the well-organized and politically isolated communities of the Hutterian Brethren, it seems inevitable that the unbelief of a marriage partner must be recognized as a reason for divorce. About 1550 this was considered as justified, especially in consideration of the need for training children in the "true faith." Now it is very evident that this severity had its source in the threat to the communistic system (*Gemeinschaft*) imposed by an unbelieving partner. For unbelief means certainly a criticism of this "Gemeinschaft," which was indeed the very heart of the faith of the Hutterites. Divorce was allowed, then, for protection and for resistance. "The believing partner is not obliged by conscience to cling to a renegade from the faith and from the community. If he nevertheless associates with such an one he becomes unclean and ceases to be in the brotherhood." The later compromise also has meaning in this sense: that a living together of believing and unbelieving marriage partners is permitted "only outside and near the brotherhood." In the case of danger to the believer in such a case the shepherds and guardians of the "Lambs of Christ" could then point him back to the brotherhood.

It was inevitable that there where the preservation of the pure "community of the saints" (*Gemeinschaft der Heiligen*) was striven for with full earnestness, church discipline also began to shape marriage fellowship. But then there could be no more serious consequences of inward and outward division

than those phenomena which attended the conflict concerning theory and practice of "marital avoidance" (*Ehemeidung*). It meant nothing less than that the faithful spouse had to avoid all communication with a marriage partner who had been punished by the brotherhood. The question of being received back again was to be decided by the brotherhood. At times the wedding was repeated. Furthermore children were to be taken away from parents who had both been excluded. Marital avoidance had an effect so much the more ruthless since that punishment of expulsion could be simply the consequence of any offense that had been vainly warned against repeatedly. This kind of divorce for the reason of unbelief was a phenomenon peculiar to Hutterites. The regulation regarding marital avoidance had no connection with it. A reference in the *Gemeindeordnungen* of 1640 (Ehrenpreis) which were to reform certain lacks, shows that the regulation was finally evaded in practice.

Among the Dutch Mennonites the conflicts about marital avoidance were most violent in the middle of the 16th century. At the Emden conference of 1547 Adam Pastor and François (Frans) de Kuiper rejected the application of marital avoidance, whereas Menno Simons wanted to see it applied (though not as a severe general rule). "See to it that in this matter you do not try to bring any one farther than he is taught in his heart by God: In his conscience is able . . . to bear and to feel." This is in agreement with Point 3 of the Wismar resolutions. But Menno Simons was not able to put his milder point of view across. Leenaert Bouwens, who actually expelled a woman who wanted to stand by her expelled husband at least spiritually, defeated him and also Dirk Philips.

The High German circles resisted as early as the Anabaptist conference at Strasbourg in 1557: "It is still the sincere wish of the Brethren assembled that they would like to advise that man and wife should separate for reason of the ban, for then more damage and sin would follow than praise to God and the winning of souls." Menno, who had yielded to the influence of Bouwens, based his reply on the heavenly marriages between Christianity and our souls which are to be maintained unbroken. Therefore neither father nor mother, neither husband nor wife, may yield to any disobedience against his word even in the least. God alone should be the master of our conscience, and not our father or mother or husband or wife. Zylis and Lemke, the delegates of the "High Germans," opposed him in person and in writing, basing their argument on the word of the Lord (Matt. 19:5, 6) repudiating marital avoidance as an abomination. In Menno's reply to Zylis and Lemke he complained about this. The break between the High German and Low German Anabaptists was accomplished. Menno is said in his last days to have deeply lamented this fact. The High Germans remained steadfast in their rejection of the effectiveness of church discipline on marriage. In the Frankenthal disputation of 1571 the Mennonites answered the questions whether the ban and unbelief separates a marriage: "We believe that nothing may part a marriage but adultery. But if the unbelieving one for the sake of the believing one wants to part, as Paul says in I Cor. 7, I let them part. But we believe that the cause for the parting shall not lie in the Christian."

Buruma reports the consequences which the harsh position of Bouwens and his associates produced after Menno's death in Holland. Those who favored banning entered at night the homes of those who had been banned and took the marriage partner away from the screaming children. "Many a man could not for a long time, others throughout their lives, find out what happened to their wives." Then the divisions began. Among the Frisians Lubbert Gerrits represented the opinion, which was soon to become dangerous to him, that the Scriptures from Genesis to Revelation contain no confirmation of marital avoidance. Then when he was banned, the party of the Young Frisians formed itself about him, who "no longer wanted to fight against the Word of God." In the older Frisian party the Jan Jacobs group was formed in order to maintain the most severe position in marital avoidance.

In the last decade of the 16th century gradually a general moderation set in. The Concept of Cologne (1591) rejected marital avoidance. The economic consequences of the practice of marital avoidance were lamented in an anonymous document of 1612, the *Vriendlijcke Aenspraeck:* "How many households have been ruined by marital avoidance! How many lost their sustenance . . . because the husband or the wife was penalized and could not go along with the congregation to communion!"

The state soon set itself in opposition to such damage to family life. In 1597 the States of Friesland prohibited the execution of the ban which usually entailed complete divorce, and other avoidances in civic and domestic relationships.

It has not been sufficiently investigated whether the division of the Swiss and Alsatian Mennonites into Amish and Reist branches was caused in part because of the requirement of marital avoidance, but thus far no evidence has been found to that effect. At any rate that division (1693-97) revolved around separation according to I Cor. 5:11. Jakob Ammann thought that the "true Christian order was lost to some extent" in this point in the Swiss churches. Footwashing and avoidance were, at least until 1800, special practices of the Amish, who took them along to America. Among the Old Order Amish in America to this day marital avoidance is practiced, though it is relaxed in the milder groups.

Marital avoidance among Mennonites is one of the most peculiar events in the history of Christianity. It meant really a temporary separation, although the defenders of the use of avoidance specifically repudiated this argument. In addition to religious doubts concerning marital avoidance, the danger of adulterous acts was warned against which might break the marriage completely. In general, no definite influence of marital avoidance upon the development of the laws of divorce can be proved.

The Anabaptist-Mennonite Marriage and the Legal Demands of "State and Church." Typically Political-Legal-Religious Conflicts and Their Solution. Only in the occasional struggle in behalf of nonresistance, is there a record comparable with the matter of marriage in the history of religious

intolerance of Anabaptist Mennonitism in faith and matters of conscience. Out of the abundance of the facts, to date little investigated, only several typical phenomena regarding intolerance by the state regarding marriage will be presented.

In Zürich, the original Anabaptist area, all means were tried to subdue Anabaptist obstinacy. As early as 1526 an Anabaptist "register" was introduced for people who refused to have their children baptized. A regulation soon followed according to which only those marriages solemnized in the church were to be valid. When the Anabaptists did not concern themselves about this, the government declared the children of marriages not thus solemnized in church as illegitimate and deprived them of their rights of inheritance. This regulation was valid for a long time. Even in 1614 one of the Anabaptist leaders (Hans Landis) was sentenced to death partly on this basis, because he resisted the government by a marriage independent of the government. Bergmann shows that the Anabaptists, through their "solemnizing of marriage," brought about an extensive reform. Until the Zwinglian reformation and after it, marriage was considered legally valid merely by the spouses living together. But then the great morals mandate of 1530 (which was to remove the cause for Anabaptist criticism) ordered a "going to church" before marital association.

Concerning the canton of Bern, Ernst Müller reported similar developments. Even in 1661 when the Anabaptists were called to account for their refusal to have their marriages solemnized in the church they answered, "This isn't necessary." The fact that the authorities regarded their marriages as a concubinage and withdrew the inheritance rights of the children did not trouble them. As late as 1810 the council of Bern invalidated a marriage performed by a Mennonite preacher. The legal rights of domicile, relationship, and inheritance have recently again been made dependent on the proclamation and solemnizing of the marriage by the local state church pastor.

The unconcern with which the Swiss exiles, e.g., in the Palatinate, "allowed themselves to be married in their small conventicles," evoked angry attention on the part of the Reformed Church Council of Heidelberg. One of the first court documents (1655) regarding Mennonites protests that "one very recently dragged a woman into his house under the pretense that she was his wife, although nobody knew where and how they were married." Then the Church Council expected that the Elector would soon prevent such offensive evils. But reports increased, stating that the Anabaptists, in disregard of the mayor and the pastor, without previous proclamation, and contrary to the law of the country, performed marriages. In 1662 an electoral mandate was issued requiring that those who had let themselves be married without a proclamation were to be fined three guilders, and future cases 18 guilders. Soon afterwards this penalty was reduced to 12 guilders, i.e., factually a fee was set at this sum. Somewhat more light on the marriage laws affecting the Palatine Mennonites in the early 18th century is found in connection with the negotiations in the case of several (very few) transfers to the "tolerated religions." "Mixed marriages" did not occur, i.e., "before errors were renounced" no Anabaptist person was permitted to be married to a member of one of the tolerated religions. The result was that among the Mennonites it had actually become a custom to persuade the clerk of the court (Oberamt) to produce proclamation certificates on the basis of which they could perform their own marriages. At least there are no official records of obligations on the part of the pastor, although there were protests against the infringement by "Oberamt" proceedings. A generally valid Palatine regulation for Mennonite marriage affairs seems not to have existed. In general here, too, the ecclesiastical power interest retreated behind the financial interest of the state. Also the distribution of the Mennonites over many areas, each with differing laws of marriage, put them into a varying legal situation though nevertheless into a favorable one. The Mennonites were treated uniformly only in matters of separation such as the Reformed marriage law at Heidelberg. But a strict Mennonite church discipline, and the effort to handle legal problems as much as possible within the brotherhood, prevented such cases from occurring.

In the Margraviate of Baden-Durlach the Anabaptists emigrating from Bern (after 1710) found more tolerant conditions than in the Palatinate. In 1729 it was decided that marriages were to be announced to the Oberamt which was to conclude the marriage contract after an examination; this was to be done in writing in the presence of a state church pastor. The pastor thereby was merely to say: "God bless your marriage, and be mindful of your duty," and to abstain from all ceremony and prayer. Under like conditions the Anabaptists were free to be married in a church in any case by a Protestant clergyman. But they seem not to have taken advantage of this privilege.

A "most submissive petition" presented by the Mennonite congregation of Hochberg in 1747 shows graphically how even these mild regulations did not fit the Mennonite religious customs. The fact that they were to be asked officially whether they were thinking of marrying one another "contradicted their regulations, which are ordered only according to Divine Scriptures." "He who was seeking a wife would name to the elders of the congregation the person in whom he had confidence. These should then act as fathers who advise their children. If no serious objections arose it was then decided when the persons in question must make their declaration before the whole congregation. Thereupon after the weal and the woe of the married estate is presented to them from the Word of God they are asked if they are minded to marry one another." If a free "yes" should follow on both sides, then a minister would immediately perform the wedding ceremony in the name of God. Up to this moment the two could still leave one another, "although in such a case the withdrawing party is not without censure of the congregation in order thereby to prevent all libertinism." Against this custom received from their fathers the official decree was in absolute contradiction. "We must previously lead our newly betrothed persons into the chancellory and there

have their finished betrothal reported officially before it has actually happened; since a real betrothal on their own authority without reference to the congregation is not free to them, they may not even call it a betrothal." A matter so sacred should be handled only before God; therefore the helpmeet would be sought for them by the congregational leaders. The presenters of the petition added that in their brotherhood no vagabond and unknown people would be married, but only such as were incorporated into their meeting. In this manner all disorder would be prevented. The repeated Mennonite proposal that "immediately after the marriage some of the leaders of our brotherhood obediently announce themselves to the electoral Oberamt and answer all questions concerning the newly married orally or in writing," was "once and for all" rejected by the authorities. Nevertheless within the jurisdiction of Baden-Durlach certain valuable rights of custom were granted to the petitioners. The marriage regulation prescribed to them was applied in only a few localities. Usually an official marriage certificate was drawn up for a small fee, and the time and place of the wedding announced to the clerk. A part of the Mennonites of Baden thus actually enjoyed the right of "civil marriage," more than a century before its general introduction within the German Empire. In marriage affairs the Protestant marriage laws were valid for all the Mennonites of Baden, to be sure. But in the first decade of the 19th century a ducal decree accorded the Mennonites equality and fully released them from any connection with the established church. In so far as at first the marriage registers were kept for the Mennonites by the pastors, the latter performed this duty as state officials and not as church officials. Soon thereafter Mennonite church officials were allowed to keep the records of births and deaths of their members. In the cases of marriage they had to testify to the secular authority the age of the betrothed persons. The betrothed had to appear within the courthouse, and upon a fee received official consent to let themselves be married in their own manner. It is noteworthy that in 1804 in the neighboring (Austrian) Breisgau "six Anabaptist fathers" were denied equal status with their brethren by the government of Baden. Soon the Peace of Pressburg transferred Austrian Breisgau into Baden. The Mennonites in the territories of the Palatinate, etc., owe the benefits of freedom and tolerance principally to the French Revolution of 1789. (See **Emancipation**.)

In Prussia the entanglement of the Mennonites in obligations to pay church fees was solved much more slowly. The edict of 1789 concerning the future establishment of the "Mennonite concerns" ordered taxes which were paid, in part at least, until the revolution of 1918. Until the Civil Marriage Laws of 1875 were established it remained the legal duty of the state church pastor to keep marriage records, as for instance in Danzig. The Crefeld Mennonites owe their release in 1738 from state church taxes and the right to proclaim marriages themselves, to the mercantile interests of the Prussian king, especially his friendship for the von der Leyen industrialists. In Neuwied the Mennonites did not object to the proclamation of their marriages in the Reformed Church, nor was any obstacle put in the way of the performance of Mennonite weddings.

In the Netherlands, noted for its tolerance, the Mennonites had for a long time little freedom in this respect. The Reformed state church held the sole right of performing valid marriages. To the extent that Mennonite congregations claimed the right to perform legal marriages independently, they were compelled to conform to the state law. Only in a few cities such as Dordrecht, Leiden, Haarlem, and Vlissingen, did the respect for the Mennonites socially gradually give them independence. The first to receive the right for their own fully valid marriages were the Frisian congregations. In Groningen and Overijssel as late as 1601 the right of inheritance was denied to all couples married outside the Reformed Church. Meanwhile, however, the right of performing marriage ceremonies was gradually granted to other creeds. A necessary condition was notification to the magistrate. On Sunday at the city hall the couples of the religions "that were only tolerated" were to present themselves—Catholics, Mennonites, Jews, etc. There a legal marriage consent was then given with the words of the sheriff: "God bless your marriage, don't forget the poor." The strict groups of the Mennonites had the congregational ceremony precede the civil ceremony. Sections of the more liberal groups recognized the official civil marriage of its members without a proclamation or ceremony of their own.

A comparative study of the laws which concerned the legitimacy of Anabaptist and Mennonite marriages up till the time of the recognition of civil marriages could proceed in a unified way in the following manner. First, one would test the legal status in comparison with the degree of freedom of conscience, i.e., the extent to which freedom of conscience had become a positive legal right. Of necessity, in this connection, the actual relationship between the church and the state would need to be clarified. It is by no means the case that the so-called separation of church and state, which on the whole did determine the relationship between the state and the Mennonite congregations, guaranteed freedom of conscience. Thus for example in Prussia the Mennonites were invited for economic reasons, and were "tolerated" in a sort of "law of separation," often, however, under strong objections by the church. Corresponding to these on the side of the state were the efforts for the preservation of the greatest extent of religious unity possible. The relatively tolerant Prussian General Law of 1794 still contains the obligation for the members of merely tolerated religious societies to have their marriages recorded by the privileged churches. A degree of consideration is given the Mennonites in that they were assigned to churches most closely related to them (Lutheran or Reformed). The incorporation of official records of the marriages of the adherents of non-state church groups in the records of the state churches is the main point; the fees charged were another element. Freedom of conscience and religion, as far as it concerned marriage law (marriage obstacles, laws of divorce),

found a guarantee in the general laws of Prussia to this extent that the adherents of all creeds were considered equal. In the Palatinate and Baden-Durlach a customary right of Mennonite marriages is to be noted, the grounds of which have not yet been clarified, which recognizes no interference by the state church. The ecclesiastical marriage laws, however, remained unaltered. The attainment of full recognition and equalization by the Mennonites was slow in progress. The law of the German empire of Feb. 6, 1875, recognized the purely civil nature of the registration of marriages, and thus eliminated any control by or favor to the state church.

In 1653 the English Anabaptist "Independents" achieved the same principle. The tolerated continental Mennonites strove for religious independence and responsibility, while subjecting themselves to the regulations of the dominant church concerning the laws of marriage. In the 1870's when there was a struggle in Germany concerning an obligatory civil marriage some of their leaders, especially the West Prussian Mennonites, had some doubts about the introduction of civil marriage laws. The fear of a depreciation of marriage which seemed to be increasing was countered by the favorable experience of the Palatine Mennonites who were subject to the civil marriage regulations of the code of Napoleon. Soon, however, the West Prussian Mennonite congregations decided to consider members as excommunicated who were married only according to civil law. For some time, in consideration of changed circumstances, the Mennonite congregations there were advised to use the marriage formula of the Protestant church synods.

Fundamentally the Anabaptist-Mennonite view of marriage reflects and represents the concern for the voluntary "community of the saints." In this perspective marriage is seen as its germ cell. It is cared for and cultivated as a religious "Gesinnungsehe," a community of the spirit. Marriage and the family are submitted to rules of conduct arising from the New Testament and are also dedicated to the principles of the Sermon on the Mount. The example of persecuted and martyred couples and families has, from the beginning of Anabaptist-Mennonite history, testified to their religio-ethical traditions, discipleship, and discipline. Issues of various kinds sprang from contacts and conflicts with the "world." Insistence on a community-bound Christian fellowship in marriage and family caused strong congregational measures for protection and preservation, including orders of separation (marital avoidance).

The Anabaptist-Mennonite marriage concept, positions, and conflicts in relation to it, the customs and folklore of many cultural backgrounds constitute other (external) aspects of study and evaluation.

Marriage and family life within the full scope of the Anabaptist-Mennonite movement still awaits its historian. Archival and other documentary records, numerous monographic including biographic inquiries are now put at the disposal of researchers into expanded or new fields as at no other moment in historiography. Important criteria testing the essence of pertinent principles have been provided in H. S. Bender's classic *Anabaptist Vision*. Here then are the prerequisites needed to overhaul, to construct, and to reconstruct an edifice of world-wide Anabaptism's contribution in the history of Christian culture.

As these remarks are to stress that which is genuinely meaningful in the concept, status, and custom of marriage in Anabaptism, reference is also made to Robert Friedmann's signal work on the Hutterian brotherhood. He has assembled and studied nearly all the essential sources. The article Ehe (*ML* I) in some little measure gave attention to the central role of the Hutterites. Friedmann's separate treatment of the views and practices of their Haushaben society is a deeply appreciated substitution for my endeavors in the early 1920's. Finally, it should be said that the above article deals chiefly with the European continent. The original study touched on the English Anabaptist influence on religious and secular developments. Irvin Horst's discussion of the Anabaptists in England (*ME* II) has opened the way for a thorough exploration of the Anglo-Saxon significance of the view of marriage, the family, and laws pertaining to the status of women.

Mennonites in North America. The European Mennonite immigrants to America brought with them their well-established marriage ideals and practices. But since the restrictions and regulations imposed by the state churches in Europe upon the "sects" were not imposed in the new free world of Pennsylvania and the other states of the United States and the provinces of Canada into which the later immigrants came and to which internal migration took place, there was a noticeable evolution in regard to marriage. While the prohibition of outside marriage was long maintained, it has now disappeared among most Mennonites of all branches; it is still maintained in all the most conservative groups, and even in such a progressive group as the Bergthal Mennonite Church in Manitoba. In practice most marriages are within the group, but where more outside marriages take place, weakening influences upon essential Mennonite doctrines and practices have been observed. Courtship customs have likewise changed to free selection of partners through a period of relatively free and unchaperoned courtship.

High standards of marriage fidelity and lifelong monogamy are maintained, with divorce almost unknown and separation rare. Marriage laws vary from state to state, and also in the Canadian provinces, but the European custom in some countries of having a civil and a religious ceremony is unknown. Everywhere a religious ceremony performed by a clergyman is permitted, and in fact a civil marriage is almost unknown among Mennonites. In earlier days, in certain regions, such as the province of Ontario, Mennonite ministers seldom secured the right to perform marriage ceremonies, so that Mennonites frequently went to authorized clergymen of other faiths for the ceremony. In Ontario also the publishing of the banns (advance announcement in the church of the intent to marry) was long required. This custom was long prevalent in the 18th and 19th centuries among both Mennonites and Amish in the eastern states, and is still followed by the Old Order Amish. Prohibition of marriage between cousins has at times been the subject of church regulations in various Mennonite groups. Among the Old Order Amish the rule is still maintained that only bishops may perform a marriage ceremony. This has been true among other groups as well, but in modern times it is common to permit ministers without the full bishop or elder authority to perform the marriage ceremony. (See **Divorce; Family; Marriage, Hutterite Practices; Marital Avoidance; Mixed Marriage; Weddings.**) E.H.C., H.S.B.

Y. Buruma, *Het huwelijk der Doopsgezinden in de zestiende eeuw* (Amsterdam, 1911); Ernst Troeltsch, *The Social Teaching of the Christian Churches* (N.Y., 1936); Marianne Weber, *Ehefrau und Mutter in der Rechtsentwicklung* (Tübingen, 1907); A. Hegler, *Geist und Schrift bei Sebastian Franck* (Freiburg, 1892); Müller, *Berner Täufer;* H. Detmer, *Bilder aus den religiösen und sozialen Unruhen in Münster während des 16. Jahrhunderts:* III, "Uber die Auffassung von der Ehe und die Durchführung der Vielweiberei in Münster während der Täuferherrschaft" (Munster, 1904); Wappler, *Thüringen;* Adam Pastor, *Unterscheit tuschen rechte leer unde valsche ler* (1552), reprinted in *BRN* V, especially chapter 12, against "Veelheit der Wynen"; S. F. Rues, *Tegenwoordige Staet der Doopsgezinden of Mennoniten in de vereenigde Nederlanden* (Amsterdam, 1745); A. Michiels, *Les Anabaptistes des Vosges* (Paris, 1860); C. Bergmann, *Die Täuferbewegung im Kanton Zürich bis 1660* (Leipzig, 1916); H. G. Mannhardt, *Die Danziger Mennonitengemeinde* (Danzig, 1919); G. E. Lenski, "Marriage in the Lutheran Church, A Historical Investigation" (unpublished doctoral dissertation at the American University, 1936), contains material on the Anabaptists; H. W. Schraepler, "Die rechtliche Behandlung der Täufer in Württemberg, Hessen, Baden, Kurpfalz und der deutschen Schweiz in den Jahren 1525 bis 1618" (unpublished doctoral dissertation at Tübingen University, 1956) contains a section entitled, "Die Auffassung der Täufer von der Ehe und die sich daraus ergebenden Probleme"; Hans Hillerbrand, "Die täuferische Auffassung von dem Staat" (doctoral dissertation at Erlangen University, 1957) contains a chapter on the Anabaptist attitude in marriage.

Marriage, Hutterite Practices. In general the Hutterites had an ascetic outlook on life; in fact were it not for their acceptance of marriage their way of life could best be characterized as "monastic." Marriage, however, was to them a part of their principle of absolute obedience to the commandments of God. As God once had ordered His chosen people to multiply and be fruitful, all His children are to accept this "ordinance" of procreation and act accordingly. "God, however," wrote Ulrich Stadler in 1536, "will wink at our marital work . . . on behalf of the children and will not reckon it upon those who act in fear and discipline." Naturally, emotional engagements of any kind in things connected with marriage were completely ruled out. Courtship and romance simply did not exist among the old Hutterites, and even among the Brethren of today are more or less frowned upon, although the general practice in selecting of the spouse was changed substantially about one hundred years ago. In former days the wife was called by the husband only "marital sister" (*eheliche Schwester*).

Peter Riedemann (*q.v.*), in his *Rechenschaft unseres Glaubens* of 1540, has a special chapter "Concerning Marriage," in which he expressly declares that the two partners must not come together through their own action and choice but in accordance with the will of God. "One should not ask his flesh but the elders that God might show through them what He has appointed for him. This then one should take with gratitude as a gift from God . . ." (100). One case is known, in 1541, where a young man had asked a girl to marry him without previously consulting the elders of the church. This was considered such a break with the rules of the church that this marriage was never realized (Riedemann, 25th epistle).

The practice of choosing a spouse was indeed peculiar with the Brethren and extremely impersonal. Two reports of this practice have been given by outside observers. In 1578 Stefan Gerlach, a professor at the University of Tübingen, came to Moravia to visit his sisters, who had joined the brotherhood some years previously. He now wrote in his *Konstantinopolische Reisebeschreibung* what he saw and heard. "On a certain Sunday of the year the elders call all young people together and place the boys on one side and the girls on the other side such that they face each other. Two or three boys are then suggested to each girl, one of whom she has to accept. Of course they are not really compelled, but on the other hand there is not much chance to act against the counsel of the elders" (Bossert, 1107). According to Christoph Erhard (*q.v.*) (p. 12) such matching took place only once a year and was done exclusively by the elders.

In 1612 the Polish nobleman Andreas Rey de Naglovitz visited the colonies in Moravia and wrote about them to a friend in France in a letter in Latin, in which he also described the Hutterite marriage practices, only he reversed the procedure; namely, each young man was given a choice of three girls (whom he had possibly never seen before) and he had to accept one of them as the will of God, "whether young or or old, poor or rich" (as Riedemann had written in his *Rechenschaft*). Should, however, one of the two absolutely refuse such a partner, then he or she had to wait for another six months. Apparently by 1612 this practice was performed twice a year (Hruby, 129).

The wedding itself was performed apparently right after this matching meeting so as to exclude any period of courtship. (Today among the Brethren such a period lasts as a rule hardly more than four days, say from Thursday to Sunday, when the wedding takes place.) At the wedding meal the bridegroom used to sit with the men, and the bride with the women, and it was only after the meal that the couple was led to their assigned room (*Stube* or *Oertel*) in one of the big community houses (see **Bruderhof**).

During the 17th century these practices began to decline as in general the common life deteriorated. There had been some opposition to the former strict method of matching, and the young people asked to be told before the meeting with whom they were to be mated. Thereupon Andreas Ehrenpreis (*q.v.*), the outstanding bishop of the brotherhood in Slovakia, assembled all the elders in Sobotiste in 1634, and gave them a *Gemeindeordnung* concerning matching, a sort of renewed regulation of this important brotherhood function. He first referred to Abraham who had sent his servants to Mesopotamia to get a wife for his son Isaac, and so forth. As in all other areas of life so also in this area of

selecting a spouse all self-will should be subdued. Whatever is done in the brotherhood should be done in accordance with the will of God (*Klein-Geschichtsbuch*, 214-18).

The Hutterites continued such strict practices, in part at least, until far into the 19th century. (As for an unpleasant disagreement in this matter which led to a three-year period of shunning, see *Klein-Geschichtsbuch*, 284.) But during their stay in South Russia things were radically changed, strangely enough, not by a decision of the elders but apparently by a fiat of the great sponsor of the Hutterites in the Molotschna district, Johann Cornies (*q.v.*), the Mennonite trustee of the government. This change must have happened around 1845. D. H. Epp in his book on Johann Cornies (1909) reports in detail the event which eventually led to changes of great consequences. A young girl was about to be compelled to marry a man whom she did not want in any case. She then fled from her confinement and ran straight to Cornies begging him for help. Cornies quickly realized the precarious situation and at once put the girl on some distant farm and at the same time prevailed upon the Hutterian Brethren to abandon altogether the former practice (Epp, *Johann Cornies*, 146-52). Apparently the brotherhood accepted this advice (as the practice had been most unpopular anyway by that time), and ever since young people may decide for themselves whom they want to marry. To be sure, much strictness remains, and the elders and parents have to approve any such choice before one can speak of engagement. Only a few days after their approval the wedding will take place. There is no room for courtship within the brotherhood, just as there is no room for divorce. But as a rule these marriages are very successful and the two partners share their life in mutual respect and love. Today the couple receives not only one room but usually a small house or a few rooms in a bigger house in anticipation of a growing family.   R.F.

Zieglschmid, *Klein-Geschichtsbuch*; F. Hruby, *Die Wiedertäufer in Mähren* (Leipzig, 1935); *TA Württemberg*; D. H. Epp, *Johann Cornies* (Ekaterinoslav and Berdyansk, 1909); Peter Rideman, *An Account of Our Religion, Doctrine, and Faith* (London, 1950); Chr. Erhard, *Historia . . . der Münsterischen Wiedertäufer* (Munich, 1580).

Marritgen Jans: see **Marytge(n) Jan de Gortersdochter.**

Marritgen Nadminx, an Anabaptist martyr from Alkmaar, Dutch province of North Holland, who was drowned at Amsterdam on May 21, 1535, with eight other Anabaptist women. According to van Braght's *Martyrs' Mirror* these martyrs were thrown into the water at night, with heavy stones around their necks. The statement (*DB* 1909, 20) that Marritgen left Alkmaar on Jan. 21, 1536, and was executed on May 25, 1536, with 25 comartyrs is incorrect. The official records show that the date of execution given by van Braght is correct. Only the name is written inaccurately; it should be Marritgen Nannincxdochter. She had been (re)baptized just outside the town of Leiden, Holland, in the spring of 1534 by Adriaen Leertouwer (Adriaen Lourisz, *q.v.*). The trial records make clear that she had nothing to do with revolutionary Anabaptism; she was very aggressive against the Catholic Church.

vDZ.

Mart. Mir. D 413, E 764; Grosheide, *Verhooren*, 67, 70; Mellink, *Wederdopers*, 145, 172, 189; *ML* III, 197.

Marschalck (Zoller), **Haug** (1489-1535), a personality long shrouded in obscurity, a writer of popular literature, of considerable influence in the early days of the Reformation through his broadsides. He was a soldier, serving first in the imperial army, entering the service of the city of Augsburg, Germany, as a soldier in 1508; in 1519 he was in the expedition against Ulrich of Württemberg, took part in the Peasants' War in 1525, and marched against the Turks in 1529. He died in 1535 in Augsburg.

Marschalck adopted the new Protestant doctrine with enthusiasm and defended it with his broadsides. But when he realized that it did not produce the expected fruit he turned away in disappointment. In his booklet *Spiegel der Blinden* this is clearly expressed. "We have not yet received full vision, although the light is breaking through everywhere. . . . The Wittenberg preachers are on the right road; too bad that so few take heed to their words, and still fewer take their admonitions to heart. . . . We should seek Christ alone, trust in Him alone, and call upon Him alone without any mediator. And we should love our brethren and do good. Even the teachers and preachers of the new doctrine walk before the mirror of the blind in consequence of their lack of constancy; they are probably worried about the decrease of the breadbasket. . . ."

These are ideas with which the Augsburg Anabaptists occupied themselves. It is possible that he was acquainted with Eitelhans Langenmantel. In his booklet *Der Blindenführer* he presents views that coincide with those of Hans Denk. But there is no evidence that he joined the Anabaptist circle.

NEFF.

K. Schottenloher, *Philipp Ulhart* (Munich, 1921) 37 f.; Otto Clemen, "Haug Marschalck, genannt Zoller, von Augsburg," in *Beiträge zur Bayrischen Kirchengesch.* IV; F. W. Roth, "Wer war Haug Marschalck, genannt Zoller von Augsburg?" in *loc. cit.* VI; *ML* III, 43 f.

Marshallville Reformed Mennonite Church, located at Marshallville, Wayne Co., Ohio, had 22 members in 1948. The first members moved here about 1820, but no meetinghouse was built until 1860. J.L.K.

Marten Goudsmid (Merten Goltsmeth; official name, *Martin Berchmans*) of Maastricht, Dutch province of Limburg, belonged as early as 1528 to a group of opponents of the Roman Catholic Church, apparently Sacramentists (*q.v.*); later he joined the Anabaptists; in 1533 he used to receive Anabaptists in his house and read the Scriptures to them. Then his traces are lost. He probably left the Anabaptists soon after. vDZ.

DB 1917, 119 (No. 105) 188; W. Bax, *Het Protestantisme in het Bisdom Luik* I (The Hague, 1937) 75, 77, 81 f., 102, 217.

Marten Jansen, an Anabaptist martyr: see **Maerten Jansz Corendrager.**

Marten of Vilgraten: see **Marthin of Vilgraten.**

Martens, a Dutch Mennonite family, of whom there are still a number of descendants. Marten Martens of Sexbierum, a blacksmith at Leeuwarden, Dutch province of Friesland, living there from about 1720, was married to Jitske Hendriks, a daughter of Hendrik Klazes, Mennonite preacher at Leeuwarden. Of their 12 children, the youngest, Sibrant Martens (1741-1816), educated in the Collegiant (*q.v.*) orphanage "D'Oranjeappel" at Amsterdam, became a Mennonite minister. He served the congregations of Hijum, Friesland, 1776-83, Noordeind van Graft en Rijp 1783-84, and 1784-1816 Friedrichstadt on the Eider, then belonging to Denmark, now Germany. He was married to Elsje Woudbeek. Of their three sons, Marten Martens (d. 1852), after training at the Amsterdam Mennonite Seminary, was minister of the congregation of Holwerd, Friesland, 1798-1849. He wrote *Feestrede of Dankbare uitboezeming op het eerste Eeuwgetijde der Kweekschool . . .* (Groningen, 1836), a rhymed sermon held at Holwerd. A number of letters which he wrote to his father while he was a student and soon after, and which contain important information on this period of Dutch history and on the seminary, are now in the possession of the author of this article. Marten Martens was married to Amelia Johanna Brouwer, a daughter of Petrus Brouwer, Reformed minister of Blija near Holward. (This Petrus Brouwer was of Mennonite descent; one of his ancestors was Minne or Menno Brouwer, who was about 1640 a Mennonite preacher in Kollumerland, Friesland, and who, according to a family tradition, was a grandson of Menno Simons, his mother being a daughter of Menno Simons.) It is not clear whether Hero Martens of Hijum, who in the early 18th century was a preacher of the Mennonite St-Annakerk-Biltzijl congregation, belonged to this family. Whether E. M. Martens-Dupuy (Amsterdam, 1841-1931), who was a warm promoter of missions and friend of the Gemeetedagbeweging (*q.v.*), belonged to this family is uncertain.

There have been a number of Dutch preachers bearing this name, who are known not to have been related to this Martens family: Reinier Martens, *ca.* 1610 at Molkwerum, Cornelius Martens, elder of the Groningen Old Flemish congregation at Bierum *ca.* 1625-d.85, Berend Martens, elder of the Ukowallists (*q.v.*) in the province of Groningen from 1653.

A widespread Martens (Martensz, Martensen, Martin, Mertens) family, probably not related to these families, but undoubtedly of Dutch descent, was found in West Prussia (Thiensdorf, Orlofferfelde, Rosenort, Elbing, Tiegenhagen, Ladekopp, Fürstenwerder, Heubuden, Danzig, and Königsberg) and later also in Russia and America. In 1930 Heinrich Martens, from Russia, was the leader of the Mennonite emigration to Brazil (*q.v.*). Simon Martensz (d. *ca.* 1612) was a Mennonite elder at Danzig. vDZ.

Martens family papers; Reimer, *Familiennamen*, 113; *DJ* 1850, 45 f.; *DB* 1874, 70; 1879, 3, 9, 10, 13, 87, 92, 111; 1895, 107, 115; 1919, 125, 139-41; 1917, 61; *Inv. Arch. Amst.* II, 1942, 2026, 2925.

Martens (Martenss, Martensen, Martin, Martins, Mertins, Mertens), a Prussian Mennonite family name, which is recorded as early as 1619. The early Dutch form "Marten" is the equivalent of the German and English Martin, as a given name. The added "s" was attached to indicate that the bearer was a son of "Marten." The name occurred in the congregations at Danzig, Thiensdorf, Orloff, Rosenort, Elbing, Tiegenhagen, Ladekopp, Fürstenwerder, Heubuden, and Königsberg. From Prussia the name was transplanted to Russia. B. H. Unruh lists many with this name in the Chortitza and Molotschna settlements. Abraham Martens (*q.v.*), Johann Martens (*q.v.*), Johann Johann Martens (*q.v.*), Jacob Martens (*q.v.*), and K. K. Martens (*q.v.*) were outstanding leaders in Russia.

From Russia the name was transplanted to North and South America. J. G. Rempel lists Abram A. Martens and Wilhelm G. Martens as ministers (GCM) in Canada. J. H. Lohrenz lists Franz W. Martens (*q.v.*), Henry A. Martens, and Jacob J. Martens as outstanding M.B. leaders. Heinrich Martins was a leader of the first Witmarsum settlement of the Mennonites in Brazil, later living at Blumenau.   C.K.

J. G. Rempel, *50 Jahre Konferenzbestrebungen, 1902-1952;* Reimer, *Familiennamen* 113; J. H. Lohrenz, *The Mennonite Brethren Church* (Hillsboro, 1950) 310 ff.; B. H. Unruh, *Die niederländisch-niederdeutschen Hintergründe . . .* (Karlsruhe, 1955).

Martens, Abraham, was ordained in 1893 as the leading minister in the Lugovsk (*q.v.*) Mennonite Brethren Church of Neu-Samara.   B.H.

Martens, Franz (1869-1942), a Mennonite elder, was born in Hutterthal near Melitopol, South Russia. He was a public school teacher for 17 years, and chairman of the district (*volost*) school board for 17 years. He was elected minister of the Nikolaifeld (*q.v.*) Mennonite Church in 1894 and elder in 1902. His attempts to reform the traditional church practice in regard to baptism, communion, and church discipline led to his resignation from the Nikolaifeld church and the founding of the Orloff Evangelical Mennonite Church in 1907, of which he was elder until 1924, when he left for Canada. He died in Kitchener, Ont., Jan. 21, 1942.   G.L.

Friesen, *Brüderschaft,* 724-27; G. Lohrenz, *Sagradowka* (Rosthern, 1947) 73-76.

Martens, Jacob (1870-1920), an elder of the Memrik (*q.v.*) Mennonite Church, was born at Tiegenhagen, Molotschna Mennonite settlement in South Russia, in 1870. He attended the Halbstadt Zentralschule, became a member of the Ohrloff-Halbstadt Mennonite Church, and married Katharina Janzen in 1891. For a while he resided at Ohrloff, Zagradovka settlement. In 1900 he moved to the Don Basin and in 1905 purchased a farm in the village of Kalinovo of the Memrik settlement. He was elected chorister (*Vorsänger*) and in 1910 elected and ordained minister. After the death of Elder P. Janzen, Jacob Martens became the elder of the Memrik Mennonite Church in 1919. In February 1920 he died of typhoid fever. He was an outstanding farmer, minister, and promoter of education.   C.K.

H. Goerz, *Memrik* (Rosthern, 1954).

Martens, Johann (b. June 7, 1875), of the Chortitza Mennonite settlement, Ukraine, where he attended

the Zentralschule and the normal school. For thirteen years he taught the elementary school, and was also the Oberschulze. During the Revolution he was ordained as a minister and in 1924 became the elder of the Schönwiese Mennonite Church, Alexandrovsk. In 1929 he had to leave his home and in 1930 he and his wife with two children were exiled to Bogoslov, near Sverdlovsk in the Ural Mountains. In 1936 they were permitted to return to the Ukraine, but in 1938 Martens was arrested and imprisoned in Zaporozhe, and then exiled to northern Russia. No further word has been received from or about him.   C.K.

A. A. Töws, *Mennonitische Märtyrer* I (North Clearbrook, 1949) 97.

Martens, Johann Johann (1885-1935), was the son of Johann Martens, a minister of Olgafeld, Fürstenland Mennonite settlement, near Melitopol, Ukraine. He was chosen minister and then elder of the Fürstenland Mennonite Church. In 1926 he emigrated to Canada, where he served as minister and elder of the Mennonite churches at Eyebrow and Fitzmaurice, Sask. He died May 5, 1935.   C.K.

A. A. Töws, *Mennonitische Märtyrer* II (North Clearbrook, 1954) 456.

Martens, Kornelius K. (1880- ?), Russian Mennonite Brethren teacher and elder, was born Nov. 15, 1880, in Wernersdorf, Molotschna, South Russia, the oldest of the five children of Kornelius Johann Martens and Helena Wolf Martens. After his father's death his mother married David Huebert of Margenau, who had four sons. To this second marriage eight children were born. On July 3, 1903, K. K. Martens married Sarah Friesen, a daughter of Julius Friesen of Waldheim, Molotschna. They had eight children. Of these Kornelius and Sarah were teachers, Tusnelda a physician, and Elfriede a nurse. After the death of his first wife, Martens married (July 6, 1934) Anna Klassen, a daughter of David Klassen of Ekaterinoslav. Martens received his education in the Zentralschule in Gnadenfeld, the Normal School in Halbstadt, and the University of St. Petersburg, besides much private study. He was a member of the Mennonite Brethren Church. In 1914 he was ordained for the ministry and later he became the elder (bishop) and leader of the M.B. Church of Sparrau.

After completing his course at Halbstadt Martens taught a village school in Siberia for three years. In 1903-12 he taught school at Ignatyevo; he founded a Zentralschule in Nikolayevka. Following that he continued his education in St. Petersburg (1912-14). In 1914-22 he served as teacher and rector (principal) of the Gnadenfeld Zentralschule. During the time of his residence in Gnadenfeld he was also inspector of the schools of the volost of Gnadenfeld. For two years he was the "Oberschulze" of the volost. In 1922 he was forced to resign from his teaching and rectorship, because he refused to join the Communist organization. He then moved to Grossweide, where he began farming. While he resided there, he became a member of the Church Commission (*KfK*), having been elected at the General Conference (*Bundeskonferenz*) in Moscow in 1925. He was elected as editor, treasurer, and secretary of the Mennonite paper *Unser Blatt (q.v.)*, which was published in Melitopol. For this paper he wrote a number of valuable articles. His other writings could not be published, because the printing of Christian books was prohibited at that time. Only a few of his poems, such as "Die letzte Nacht im Vaterhause" and "Die alte Weide," have found their way into some of the American papers. Martens also had an active part in the work of the printing association "Raduga" of Halbstadt. In the cause of nonresistance he was one of the official representatives of the Mennonites.

In 1930 Martens and his family were forced to leave their home in Grossweide and to seek refuge in various villages. Two years later he was asked to teach German and Latin at the University of Stalino, Donbass. On Aug. 6, 1937, he was arrested and after one year he was sentenced to a ten-year exile in Siberia. Shortly before the arrest he said, "Soon my turn will come and my whole crime is that I have faithfully served my Lord and Saviour." Since 1938 no information has been received from or about him. His three daughters, Sarah, Tusnelda, and Elfriede. believe that he has died. G.D.H.

Martha Baerts, an Anabaptist martyr, was secretly beheaded on Nov. 20, 1560, in the Gravensteen castle at Gent, Belgium, with Soetken van den Houtte and Lynken Pieters. Martha was a native of Oudenaerde in Flanders. Van Braght's *Martyrs' Mirror* gives her name simply as Martha, and erroneously gives Nov. 27 as the date of her death. (*Mart. Mir.* D 277, E 646; Verheyden, *Gent,* 27, No. 76; *ML* III, 44.) vDZ.

Mart(h)in (Marten) of Vilgraten in Tirol, Austria, an Anabaptist martyr, who was beheaded with Caspar Schuester (*q.v.*) of Schöneck in 1538 at Michelberg in the Puster Valley. Van Braght's *Martyrs' Mirror* gives the place of execution as Ries near Brixen in the Flucht Valley and names both men twice, viz., for 1528 and 1538. Both martyrs wrote several songs. The only known one was "Merckt auf und nemt zu Hertzen, Wie Gott will suchen heim," No. 33 in the *Ausbund,* also found in the *Lieder der Hutterischen Brüder,* p. 87, together with "Erzürn dich nicht, o frommer Christ," by Kaspar Schuester. NEFF.

Beck, *Geschichts-Bücher,* 135; Wolkan, *Lieder,* 142, 171; Zieglschmid, *Chronik,* 187; *Mart. Mir.* D 19, 43, E 429, 449; *Die Lieder der Hutterischen Brüder* (Scottdale, 1914); *ML* III, 44.

Marti, Jakob, was an elder of the Swiss Brethren, who together with the elders Peter Ramseier and Peter Oberli made a trip to the congregations of Swiss descent in the Palatinate in 1742, visiting the congregations of Freudenberg, Weierhof, Rauhof, and Schafbusch-Niederrödern. They tried to bridge over some differences among the Palatine Mennonites, which had been caused by the spirit and obstinate attitude of Elder Abraham Zeisset. But they did not apparently succeed, for in 1766 Marti again stayed in the Palatinate, this time together with Ramseier and Niklaus Knör. But peace was not restored until Oct. 14, 1782, at a conference on Himmelhäuserhof. Marti was not present at this conference, having probably died before. Delbert Gratz lists him not as an elder but as a deacon. He was a native of Sumiswald in the Emmental and lived at Büderichgraben. vDZ.

Müller, *Berner Täufer,* 212 f.; Delbert L. Gratz, *Bernese Anabaptists* (Scottdale, 1953) 80.

Martijn Pietersz, beheaded at Rotterdam, Holland, on Dec. 22, 1534, had attended Anabaptist meetings at The Hague, and had also planned to go to Münster, Westphalia, in March 1534, but did not actually go. He had been (re)baptized in April 1534; thereupon he visited Haarlem, Flanders, and the Dutch province of Zeeland; he also repeatedly stayed in Amsterdam. He was arrested in December 1534 at Rotterdam and put to death, not for Anabaptism, but for pocket-picking. There would be no reason for naming him here except for the fact that his confession gives very valuable material concerning the spread of Anabaptism in the Netherlands in 1534. (Mellink, *Wederdopers,* 208, 223 f.; *DB* 1905, 171.) vDZ.

Martijne (Martijntje) **Amare:** see **Martijntgen** (van) **Aelmeers.**

Martijnken (Martijntgen) **Meere,** an Anabaptist martyr, burned at the stake on Aug. 9, 1573, at the Vrijdagsmarkt at Gent, Belgium, with two other women. Martijnken, the sister of the martyr Calleken Meere (*q.v.*), was a native of Wyncle in Flanders and unmarried. These three women were gagged to prevent them from speaking to the crowd gathered around the execution place. This fact or something else displeased the bystanders, and they nearly created a riot. Soldiers then began to clear the market place. (Verheyden, *Gent,* 64 f., No. 229.) vDZ.

Martijntgen (van) **Aelmeers,** an Anabaptist martyr, known under different names: Martijne Amare, Martijntgen (van) Aelmeers, Martincke Aelmaers. She was a young unmarried woman, who was executed with six others at Hondschoote (*q.v.*) in Flanders, Belgium. Particulars of the execution are lacking, but it probably occurred on April 20, 1563. This martyr is listed twice by van Braght's *Martyrs' Mirror:* (*a*) D 297, E 655, where she is called Martijntgen Aelmeers; and (*b*) D 298, E 655, where her name is Martijne (Martijntgen) Amare. *Bibliographie* II, No. 16, wrongly identifies her with Marijn Amare (Marijn Euwouts), but this martyr died at Brugge in 1561. Martijntgen Aelmeers was the sister of the martyr Nicasen van Aelmeers (*q.v.*). Until recently no particulars were known, the date of the execution usually being assumed to have been April 20, 1563. The records published in the *Jaarboek* show that her name was Martijnken Alcmaers, and that she was a daughter of Loys Alcmaers. She was a native of Steenwercke in Flanders, and the execution took place on March 23, 1562. vDZ.

Jaarboek van het Central Bureau vor Genealogie VIII (The Hague, 1954) 78, 83; *Bibliographie* II, No. 16.

Martijntgen Maelbouts: see **Marijntgen** (Marijtgen) **van Male.**

Martin, a family of Swiss descent widely represented in the Mennonite Church (MC). The progenitor of many of these Martins was David Martin, who arrived in Pennsylvania in 1727 and settled in what is now the Weaverland area of Lancaster County. Many of his descendants still live in that area, while others have moved farther west in Pennsylvania, and to other states, as well as to Ontario. More than a score of Martins served in the ministry of the Lancaster Mennonite Conference in the first two centuries of the life of the family in Pennsylvania. Martins worthy of note in the Lancaster area are Henry Martin, a bishop at Weaverland from 1809 until his death in 1825; Jonas Martin who became a bishop in 1881 at Weaverland and who led a schism from the conference in 1893, the so-called Martinites (Old Order Mennonites); Abraham L. Martin, of the Pequea district of the Lancaster Conference, ordained bishop in 1921 and active for many years; Elmer G. Martin (1894-), bishop at Mellinger's since 1946; C. Z. Martin (1893-), minister since 1923 at Columbia. In 1954 there were 16 ministers in the Lancaster Conference bearing the name Martin, and only 14 in the rest of the Mennonite Church (MC), viz., Ohio, Ontario, Virginia, Maryland. A. D. Martin (1878-1913) was a Mennonite preacher at Scottdale, Pa., and for a number of years was in charge of the Mennonite Book and Tract Society work, as well as serving as secretary-treasurer of the Mennonite Publishing House.

The Old Order (Wisler) Mennonite schism in Waterloo Co., Ont. (1889), was led by Bishop Abraham Martin (1834-1902), ordained bishop in 1867, who served at the Martin meetinghouse. Many, probably most, of the ministers in the Waterloo Old Order group have been Martins. In 1954 two of the three bishops of the group were Martins, and four of the remaining nine preachers.

The leading historian of the family was Isaac W. Martin (1861-1954), but his genealogical studies are at this writing not yet published.   J.C.W.

Martin Box Chapel, a Mennonite Brethren mission in the Ozarks, located near Marshall, Ark., had its beginning with the extension work of the Southern District Conference together with daily vacation Bible school work of Tabor College. In the summer of 1946 a corps of workers, under the direction of Mr. and Mrs. David Richert, were sent into this field, and the work was well received in the various communities. In the spring of 1947, Mr. and Mrs. Richert were requested to take over the work on a full-time basis. The pastor (1957) is Ed Hinz.
          A.W.E.

Martin Old Order Mennonites. Aaron Martin, born Aug. 30, 1918, in Lancaster Co., Pa., joined with the Jacob Stauffer group in eastern Snyder Co., Pa., but in 1945 led one of the two-way schisms in that congregation. Martin was ordained to the ministry after this schism, June 4, 1945, and four weeks later bishop. In 1950 the group had 28 members and used the meetinghouse a few miles west of the Susquehanna Trail. Further divisions, a total of four in seven years, have reduced the group to small fractions each

with a bishop, minister, and deacon, all using the same meetinghouse at different times.   I.D.L.

Martin Old Order Mennonite Church, located three miles north of Waterloo, Ont., was organized *ca.* 1824. Its meetinghouse, built in 1848, was long the center of the large Mennonite settlement in Woolwich Township, north of Waterloo Township. It was named "Martin's" probably because the site of four acres was on the farm of pioneer Peter Martin and had been reserved by Henry Martin in 1824 for the purpose of a meetinghouse and burial grounds, even though the land was not actually purchased (by the "Mennonite Society of British North America" according to the deed) until 1848, when the meetinghouse was erected. The meetinghouse was long the only one north of Waterloo and served all the Mennonites in Woolwich Township.

In 1889 the Old Order schism created a serious break in the Ontario Mennonite body. The bishop at Martin's at that time, Abraham Martin, led most of his congregation in his refusal to accept the newer methods of church work (Sunday school, etc.) which had been accepted by most of the Ontario Mennonite congregations, and made Martin's the strongest unit in the Ontario Old Order group (which included smaller groups at Selkirk-Rainham and Markham). In 1925 a schism in the entire Ontario Old Order group resulted in an almost half-and-half division at Martin's. The new progressive group, which permitted automobiles and telephones, joined with a similar group at Markham to form the Waterloo-Markham Conference. In 1955 this group had at Martin's 150 members with Amsey M. Martin serving as bishop, and Urias Martin as preacher. The more conservative group had some 200 members, with Addison Gingerich as bishop and Daniel B. Martin as minister. The two groups use the meetinghouse on alternate Sundays. The meetinghouse is an excellent example of the older style of architecture and interior arrangement and furniture. In 1900 it was enlarged to 42 x 64 ft.
          J.C.F.

Martin von Neck, an Anabaptist martyr: see **Nauk, Martin.**

Martin du Petitz (Petis), an Anabaptist martyr, burned at the stake on Oct. 21 or 22, 1551, at Antwerp, Belgium, with Peter Bruynen (*q.v.*) and three others. Martin was a native of Kortrijk (Courtrai) in Flanders and a chairmaker by trade. He was sentenced to death because he "had been rebaptized and persisted in his heresy." Van Braght's *Martyrs' Mirror* mentions him as "another brother," not giving his name.   vDZ.

Offer, 177, note 1; *Antw. Arch.-Blad* VIII, 405, 415, 417; XIV, 18 f., No. 206; *DB* 1864, 99; *Mart. Mir.* D 128, E 498.

Martin (Maerten) **van der Stra(e)ten,** an Anabaptist martyr, born about 1534 at Kortrijk (Courtrai) in Flanders, was burned at the stake at Gent, Belgium, on Dec. 4, 1572; his wife Beliken de Jaghere (*q.v.*) also died as a martyr at Gent, on March 17, 1573. Martin had received baptism on his faith at Middelburg, Dutch province of Zeeland. By trade he was a maker of felt hats. Van Braght's *Martyrs' Mirror* contains six of his letters. Three of them Martin wrote to his wife, who was his fellow prisoner, comforting her and admonishing her with the words of Scripture and the Apocrypha to have patience and endurance in her suffering. The fourth letter was written to Anna Servaes, the fifth to Servaes Jansz. In the sixth he wrote words of admonition and comfort to Adam v. L. and his wife. These letters all contain exhortations and admonitions to keep the faith; personal information in them is scarce. Incidentally the information is given that Martin and Beliken had married three years before; the marriage had been performed in the congregation. In the letters Martin also sent greetings in the name of Adriaen, Hansken, Margriet, Lou, and Dingentgen, all imprisoned with them. The identity of Adriaen, Hansken, Margriet, and Dingentgen is easily established; they were Adriaen Rogiers, Hansken van Oudenaerde, Grietgen van Sluys, and Dingentgen van Hondschoote. Lou could not be identified. (*Mart. Mir.* D 623, 631-40, E 954-60; Verheyden, *Gent,* 59, No. 205; *ML* III, 44.) vDZ.

Martin Taelman, an Anabaptist martyr, of whom little is known. He was an old man, born at St.-Maria-Horebeke in Flanders, and living in Brugge, where he worked as a ropewalker. He was burned at the stake on March 25, 1572, at Gent, Belgium. (Verheyden, *Gent,* 58, No. 203.) vDZ.

Martin, Thoni, an Anabaptist martyr, a native of Grönenbach, Bavaria, Germany, which belonged to Kempten. Because of his faith he was led to his death on Oct. 23, 1593, at the advanced age of 80 years. He was accompanied by a Catholic clergyman to the site of execution, which was set up before the court of the abbey. While the clergyman was urging the steadfast Martin to recant, the church prince angrily opened his window and shouted to the executioner to lay the head of the obstinate heretic at his feet. W.W.

Haggenmüller, *Geschichte der Stadt und der gefürsteten Grafschaft Kempten* II (1847) 107 f.; Wiswedel, *Bilder* II, 58; *ML* III, 44.

Martin (Maerten) **van de Walle,** an Anabaptist martyr, burned at the stake on Oct. 15, 1558, at Brugge, Belgium, with three other men. Martin was a silkweaver, a native of Gent, and 33 years of age. He had been (re)baptized in 1551 at Antwerp by Gillis van Aken (*q.v.*); later he lived at Gent, and from 1557 at Brugge. Meetings of the congregation were sometimes held in his home, attended by members from the city and from the country. Martin apparently was a widower; he left two children. The martyr Jan van de Walle was his brother. (*Mart. Mir.* D 202, E 569; Verheyden, *Brugge,* 46, No. 28.) vDZ.

Martindale (Pa.) Mennonite Church (MC), a member of the Lancaster Conference, formerly called Fairview, had a meetinghouse on the northeast corner of the town square by 1854. In 1848 the widow of Christian Zimmerman gave a tract for burial purposes west of the town, which became the location of a new meetinghouse in 1886. The Old Order Mennonite schism of 1893 in this area resulted in two branches, both using the meetinghouse, and after 1926 three used this commodious stone house, since the O.O.M. group had a schism. The meetinghouse still has the singing table and a table on the floor for a pulpit. After the 1893 division the Mennonite (MC) congregation was very small, and was cared for by the ministers of the Weaverland congregation. This small group became the especial care of I. B. Good and the membership grew. In 1948-49 a 60 x 86 ft. brick meetinghouse was built northwest of the town, the O.O.M. groups retaining the old house. In 1954 the membership was 266 with John D. Burkholder and Alvin Martin as ministers. I.D.L.

Martindale Old Order Mennonite Church, Lancaster Co., Pa. After the Martinite (Wisler) division of 1893 the new group continued to worship in the stone meetinghouse built in 1886 by the Mennonites of the Lancaster Conference (MC), of which they were then a part; in fact, there were very few left in the parent body in this congregation. The one Zimmerman cemetery, located south of the church, continues to be used by them. The Lancaster Conference and the O.O.M. both used the same meetinghouse, and after the division of 1926 into the Groffdale and Weaverland conferences, all three groups used it. By 1949, with the Lancaster Conference membership built up (279 in 1956), they built a new church to the north, leaving the old building for the two conferences.

The two groups continued to grow under their own ministers. The Groffdale Conference, earlier under Joseph Wenger as bishop, now Aaron Z. Sensenig as bishop, and Harry H. Martin as minister, is a part of the Weaverland circuit with George G. Horst also as minister. The membership is about 275. The Weaverland Conference with 160 members is in charge of Joseph O. Weaver, bishop, and John B. Weaver, minister. Martindale and Weaverland are in a circuit too. I.D.L.

Martindale (Groffdale) Old Order Mennonite Conference is the result of a schism in 1926 in the Weaverland O.O.M. Conference, which had broken from the Weaverland Mennonite Church (*q.v.*) in 1893. The 1954 membership was reported to be 1200 in round numbers, meeting in meetinghouses, with Aaron Z. Sensenig as bishop. They still share the use of the Weaverland O.O.M. meetinghouse. They represent the most conservative O.O.M. group in Lancaster County and separated from the Weaverland group on the issue of the use of automobiles, which they reject. They use German almost exclusively in preaching, have no Sunday schools, and reject most modern conveniences. I.D.L.

Martine (Martijntken) **Dhanins,** a daughter of Joost (Jan) van Sleidingen, a member of the congregation of Gent, Belgium, died there in August 1573, while in prison because of her faith. Her sister Janneken, arrested with her, suffered martyrdom at Gent on Aug. 17, 1573. (Verheyden, *Gent,* 64, No. 228.) vDZ.

Martin's Mennonite Church (MC), with its present meetinghouse in east central Wayne Co., Ohio, about three miles southeast of Orrville, was founded by Lancaster County Mennonites in 1834. William Westheffer and Henry Martin were the first ministers. The congregation erected a log meetinghouse in 1835. Being rather conservative, the congregation did not organize a Sunday school until 1880. The congregation of 197 (1955) members, with Stanford Mumaw as pastor, is a member of the Ohio and Eastern Mennonite Conference. Earlier the Pleasant View (q.v.) and Martin's congregations were counted in a sense as one congregation with alternating services in the two meetinghouses but a joint ministry. In 1930 the connection severed and each became a fully independent congregation. The Wisler schism of 1873 cost heavily in membership at both Martin's and Pleasant View, the County Line-Chestnut Ridge (q.v.) O.O.M. congregation having been formed from this schism. J.S.U.

Martin's Creek Mennonite (MC) Church, located two miles north of Berlin, Holmes Co., Ohio, a member of the Ohio and Eastern Conference, was organized in 1860 by former members of the Old Order Amish in this community, the first settlers having come in 1824. The first meetinghouse, 25 x 48 ft., was erected in 1875, its second in 1906, when the membership was about 200, which was remodeled in 1955 to seat 550. The first bishop was Fred Hege, who was followed by Jonathan Zook, Fred Mast, and Joseph Mast. After a period of nonresident bishops, D. D. Miller, who is now (1956) serving, was installed as bishop-pastor. He is assisted by Warren Miller. The membership in 1955 was 357. The congregations at Berlin (1939) and Millersburg (1956) have been organized out of Martin's Creek. In addition the Flat Ridge Mission Church, 10 miles south of Newcomerstown, is sponsored by the Martin's Creek congregation. H.S.B.

Martins, Heinrich H., Elder of the Busau Mennonite Church, Crimea, Russia, b. February 1860 at Brodske, Prussia, d. Oct. 17, 1905, at Montanai, Crimea. He was baptized in 1880, married Anna Friedrichsen in 1886, was elected minister in 1893 and elder in 1901. Of his twelve children four preceded him in death. He was a very effective minister during his brief term of service. C.K.

H. Dirks, "Nekrolog des Aeltesten der Busauer Gemeinde Heinrich Martins," *Menn. Jahrbuch,* 1905/6, 84; "Die Geschichte der Busauer Mennonitengemeinde," *Unser Blatt,* May 1927, 236 ff.

Martinsburg Mennonite Church (MC), a member of Allegheny Mennonite Conference, located on the southern outskirts of Martinsburg in the Morrison's Cove area, Blair Co., Pa., dates back to 1790 when Mennonites migrated to this area from eastern counties and Virginia. The original settlers included families with the names of Rhodes, Kauffman, Snyder, Shank, Newcomer, Stoner, and Bassler. In the early days, a log building was used for worship and school purposes. In 1853 a new frame church was erected about one mile east of the present building. This was used until 1916, when a brick building was erected on the outskirts of Martinsburg. Because the congregation was scattered another meetinghouse was built about three miles south of

Martinsburg in 1900, known as the Pleasant Grove Church. Church and Sunday-school services were alternated between these two places until 1945, when Pleasant Grove was abandoned. This congregation established a mission station at Ore Hill in 1902, and took an active part in the opening of Altoona Mission. The congregation at Roaring Spring, about five miles west of Martinsburg, where a meetinghouse had been erected in 1898, was at first a part of the Martinsburg congregation. In 1912 it seceded to join the General Conference Mennonite Church.

The earliest ministerial help for these people came from Huntingdon County. The first resident minister and bishop was apparently Frederick Rhodes, who was ordained about 1840. A prominent leader was Abram Metzler (1862-1924, ord. bishop 1906). In 1956 the bishop is D. I. Stonerook and the pastor Clyde Fulmer, with a membership of 86. Ministers ordained at this place now serving elsewhere include Henry B. Ramer (1901), Duchess, Alberta; Isaac Metzler (1913), bishop at Accident, Md.; Clayton F. Derstine (1914), bishop at Kitchener, Ont.; and A. J. Metzler (1924), bishop at Scottdale, Pa. E.C.B.

Ammon Kaufman, "Martinsburg Mennonite Church," *Southwestern Pennsylvania Conference News,* March-April 1948.

Martinshof, a large farm near Bad Rappenau in the district of Sinsheim in Baden, Germany, which was acquired by Mennonites in the middle of the 18th century. A Mennonite congregation was organized here, closely associated with Bockschaft. The two were served by the same preachers. According to an entry in the Protestant church books at Treschklingen, one of the first weddings of this congregation was performed at the Martinshof on April 24, 1768 (Jakob Krehbühl and Katharina Plötscher). This congregation was served in the last decades of the 18th century by Elder Abraham Zeisset (q.v.) of Hasselbach; preachers of the Martinshof congregation then were Hans Kaufmann and Hans Bechtel. In 1862 the farm changed ownership and the buildings were removed. The site is now in a bare field. The Mennonites here then met in Bad Rappenau (q.v.). HEGE.

K. Noll, *Geschichte von Rappenau* (Rappenau, 1907) 172 f.; Dutch *Naamlijst; Menn. Gesch.-Bl.* 1936, 23; *ML* III, 44.

Martyr Books, The martyr's death suffered by thousands of Protestants made the deepest impression on their world. Relatives, friends, acquaintances, and fellow believers regarded them with unbounded grateful esteem. The letters they wrote in prison, their confessions of faith, their letters of farewell, the poems they composed, went from hand to hand and were read with enthusiasm. Descriptions and songs which described their steadfast faith in the grip of torture and death found enormous sale. Soon the desire arose to collect these testimonies into one book, in order to preserve them for posterity.

Thus the first book of martyrs came into being in 1552 with the title, *Historien der Heyligen auserwöllten Gottes Zeugen, Bekennern und Märtyrern, so in angehender ersten Kirchen Altes und Neues Testament, zu jeder zeyt gewesen sind,* written by Ludwig Rabus (*q.v.*) of Memmingen. Among others it contains descriptions of the death of Hendrik of Zutphen (Dec. 11, 1524), Willem of Zwolle (Oct. 29, 1529), and Leonhard Kaiser (Aug. 16, 1527); a second edition was printed in 1571-72.

In 1554 the first edition of J. Crespin's (*q.v.*) noted book, *Le livre des martyrs depuis Jean Huss jusqu'en 1554,* came out and went through many revised editions. The translations and excerpts made by Christoph Raab, published in 1582 and 1591 at Herborn, and by Paulus Crocius, *Grosses Märtyrerbuch und Kirchenhistorien,* published at Bremen in 1607, 1617, 1682, and 1722, also deserve notice. (Concerning John Fox's *Book of Martyrs* of 1559, see **John Fox.**)

On March 18, 1559, Adriaen van Haemstede (*q.v.*) finished his book at Antwerp titled: *De Gheschiedenisse ende den doodt der vromer Martelaren die om het ghetuyghenisse des Euangeliums haer bloedt ghestort hebben, van den tyden Christi af, tot den Jare M.D. LIX toe, byeen vergadert op het kortste, Door Adrianum Corn. Haemstedium,* a book which was of influence on the martyrology of the Dutch Mennonites, and also contains a few accounts of Mennonite martyrs.

Another (non-Mennonite) martyrbook deserving mention is the *Groot Christen-Martelaersboeck Ghenoechsaem vervattende een kerckelycke Historie van den Opgangh, Voorgangh en Ondergangh der vervolgingen,* etc., by Abraham Philippus Mellin, preacher at Anthonypolder (Dordrecht, 1619). It is refuted by *De ontledinge van dry verscheyden niew ghereformeerde Wederdoopers door Arnoudt van Gelouwe* (Antwerp, 1656).

The first Anabaptist-Mennonite martyr book is the important Dutch collection, *Het Offer des Heeren* (*q.v.*), which was published in 1562 with the title, *Dit Boec wort genoemt Het offer des Heeren, om het inhout van sommighe opgheofferde kinderen Godts: De welcke voortgebracht hebben wt den goeden schat haers harten Belijdingen, Sendbrieven ende Testamenten, dewelcke sy metten monde beleden, ende metten bloede bezegelt hebben, Tot troost ende versterckinghe der Slachtschaepkens Christi, die totter doot Geschict zijn, Tot lof, prijs ende eere desgeens diet al in allen vermach, wiens macht duert van eewicheyt tot eewicheyt, Amen.* By 1599 it had gone through 11 editions (n.p., printed either at Emden or Amsterdam). In all editions a collection of songs was added (first edition, 1563), which has the title, *Een Lietboecxken, tracterende van den Offer des Heeren, int welcke oude ende nieuwe Liedekens wt verscheyden Copien vergadert zijn, om by het Offerboeck ghevoecht te worden, want het van eender materyen roert als van verraden, vanghen ende dooden, aengaende der Slachtschaepkens Christi, die de stemme haers Herders Jesu Christi getrouwelyck gehoorsaem zijn gheweest totter doodt toe. . . .* This first edition contains 25 songs, the first of which treats the sufferings of Christ and the others the death of the Anabaptist martyrs during 1526-61. It is the oldest hymnal of the Dutch Mennonites, and was much used in church services along with three other hymnals, *Veelderhande Liedekens, Nieu Liedeboeck,* and *Tweede Liedenboeck.* The complete *Offer* (with *Lietboecxken*) was reprinted

in the edition of 1570 with a valuable scholarly introduction and notes, edited by S. Cramer in *BRN* II (The Hague, 1904). Both before and after the publication of the *Offer des Heeren* a number of small booklets were published containing letters, accounts of trials and executions, and hymns of martyrs. The first of the Anabaptist martyrbooks is the small booklet giving an account of the martyrdom of Michael Sattler and his associates at Rottenburg (Württemberg) under the title *Ayn newes wunderbarliches geschicht von Michael Sattler zu Rottenburg am Neckar sampt andern 9 mannen seiner lere und glauben halben verbrannt und 10 wyaber ertrenkt,* 1527 (copy in the Wolfenbüttel Library). Another account of the Michael Sattler martyrdom appeared about the same time as an appendix to the *Brüderliche Vereinigung* of 1527. These booklets were published not later than 1533. Dutch revised editions appeared in 1560 and 1565, and the story was included in *Het Offer* and by this route got into the *Groot Martelaarsboek* (Big Martyr book) and following martyr books. The "Testament" (letter of farewell) and a hymn written by Anneken Jans (*q.v.*), put to death at Rotterdam in 1539, were published in the very year of her death. A rhymed account of the suffering and death of the ladies of Beckum (*q.v.*), put to death at Delden in 1544, was published in Low German by 1545 and soon after in Dutch. A somewhat larger collection of Anabaptist martyr material concerning Thomas von Imbroich (d. 1558) and Soetken van den Houtte appeared about 1565 and concerning Reytse Aysesz about 1577. The Mennonite Library at Amsterdam has a volume of 1577 (repr. 1584) containing letters of Jacob de Keersmaecker, Hendrick Alewijnsz, Joost Verkindert, Thys Joriaensz, and Herman Timmerman, another volume of Jan Woutersz (1579), one of Christiaen Rycen or de Rycke (1588), and one of Joos de Tollenaer (1599).

Further collections of martyr stories, made especially by Jacques Outerman (*q.v.*) and Joost Govertsz (*q.v.*), led to the first genuine Mennonite book of martyrs, published in 1615 at Haarlem by Hans de Ries (*q.v.*) and the Waterlander Mennonites. The printer was Jakob Pouwels Houwaert and the publisher Daniel Keyser at Haarlem. Its title was *Historie der martelaren ofte waerachtighe getuygen Jesu Christi die d'evangelische waerheyt in veelderley tormenten betuygt ende met haer bloed bevesticht hebben sint het Jaer 1524 tot desen tyt toe waerby oock gevoecht syn haer bekentenissen, disputatien ende schriften uytdruckende haerl. levende hope crachtich gelove ende brandende liefde tot Godt ende syne heylige waerheyt.* The preface states that the book lays no claim to exhaustiveness, and that further stories were still to be collected for later publication.

The Old Frisians, led by their elder Pieter Janszoon Twisck and Syvaert Pietersz, had the work reprinted at Hoorn in 1617. This edition is exactly like the Haarlem edition, except that the foreword is different, and a confession of faith with 33 articles has been added, also 41 additional martyr stories, with 21 listed in an appendix. Ten stories were omitted, as well as a disputation of Herman van Vlekwijk because of its Arian content. The title of this edition reads *Historie der warachtighe getuygen Jesu Christi . . . sint het Jaer 1524 tot desen tijt toe.*

Thus the Old Frisians had produced a work that they called the great book of sacrifice. But they completely overlooked the fact that the Haarlem book contained accounts of some martyrs who held false views of the humanity of Christ. In order to correct these errors they printed a new edition in 1626 at Hoorn omitting the questionable passages. The martyr stories listed in the appendix of the first edition were inserted in chronological order and seven more added, two of them in an appendix. Otherwise this edition is like the 1617 edition. This edition has a somewhat modified title, *Historie van de Vrome getuygen Jesu Christi . . . .*

In reply to the charges which the third edition raised against the editors of the first, Alenson (*q.v.*) published his *Tegen-Bericht,* defending Hans de Ries and his co-workers. This led to the fourth edition of the book, which was published in 1631 at Haarlem by the press of Hans Passchiers van Wesbusch with the title, *Martelaers-Spiegel der werelose Christenen t'zedert anno 1524.* Not including the foreword and introduction, which cover 56 pages, and the table of contents, which contains 6, the book has 864 pages. In many of the copies a page was inserted with the title, *Onnoselheydts peyl van't Munsters onheyl,* a repudiation of any relationship with the Anabaptists of Münster, and in some copies an appendix was bound in, containing the confessions of faith by Hans de Ries and Lubbert Gerritsz in forty articles. De Hoop Scheffer thinks that Hans de Ries supervised this edition and adopted the additions in the Hoorn editions of 1617 and 1626. Several martyr stories of the 1617 edition taken from the chronicles of Curtius were omitted here, and persons mistreated but not killed are given separate treatment. Only four new accounts are added; there is also a short note on several martyrs previously mentioned.

The foreword of the 1631 edition is a masterpiece of style. It recounts the heroic steadfastness of the martyrs in the face of pain and death, praises their oral and written statements, and finally refutes the arguments of their judges in justifying the death sentence. The first Reformation martyrs treated in the book are Hans Koch and Leonhard Meister in 1524; the last Anabaptist martyr is Hans Landis, 1614.

The last and most significant martyrbook of the Dutch Mennonites is the *Martyrs' Mirror* by Tieleman Jansz van Braght (*q.v.*): *Het Bloedigh Tooneel der Doops-gesinde en Weereloose Christenen, die om het getuygenisse Jesu hunnen Zaligmaker geleden hebben en gedoodt zijn, van Christi tijdt af, tot dese onse laetste tijden toe, verzameld uit verscheidene geloofweerdige Chronieken, gedenkschriften en getuigenissen.* It was published at Dordrecht in 1660; the second and last Dutch edition, which was published in Amsterdam in 1685, was illustrated with over 100 etchings by Jan Luiken (*q.v.*). In this edition the words "of Martelaarspiegel" were added after the word "tooneel" in the title. The foreword of the first edition says that the author had originally intended to reprint the *Groote Offerboeck* of 1631, with the addition of only a few recently discovered martyr accounts. Actually it

turned out to be an entirely different book. Part I contains the history of the Christian martyrs from the time of Christ to 1600, arranged by centuries, each century being concluded with a history of baptism. The confessions of faith are valuable: of 1627 (23-27), of 1630 (27-32), of 1632 (32-37), and the one consisting of 33 articles (385-432). The second part deals with Mennonite martyr history. (For information about later editions see **Martyrs' Mirror.**)

Güldene Aepffel in Silbern Schalen (European editions without place in 1702 and 1742, American edition at Ephrata in 1745, 519 pp.), though not an abridgment of the *Martyrs' Mirror,* contains martyr stories, testimonials, letters, and confessions of the martyrs Michael Sattler, Thomas von Imbroich, and Susanna van Houte. Isaak van Dühren's *Geschichte der Märtyrer oder kurze historische Nachricht von den Verfolgungen der Mennonisten* (Königsberg 1787, reprints Königsberg 1788, Stuttgart 1863, and Winnipeg 1939), 169 pp., contains three parts, the first of which (*Verfolgungen . . . von den Catholiken*) reported on 102 Dutch martyrs and is taken from van Braght's *Martyrs' Mirror.* The other two parts (*Verfolgungen . . . von den Lutheranern* and *Verfolgungen . . . von den Reformirten*) are based on various sources, including Mathesius, Gottfried Arnold, Gerber, Crespin (see van **Dühren**).

The 1831 (Philadelphia, Pa.) German edition of John Fox's Martyr Book (*Allgemeine Geschichte des Christlichen Marterthums*), which includes in the title the following: "Vermehrt mit vielen wichtigen Nachrichten über die späteren Verfolgungen der wehrlosen Taufgesinnten und Anderen, in Deutschland," includes "Verfolgungen der Mennoniten," pp. 787-934, a condensation of the full text of the van Braght book.

The importance of the books of martyrs must not be underestimated. They have been instrumental in stirring and keeping the interest of Mennonite churches and have at various times won warm friends for the presentation of Mennonite history.

A careful bibliographical report of all editions of *Het Offer* and the other Dutch Mennonite martyrbooks was published in *Bibliographie des Martyrologes Protestants Néerlandais* (The Hague, 1890).   NEFF.

Martyr Hymns: see **Song Writing.**

Martyrdom, Theology of. In 1933 the German church historian Ethelbert Stauffer (of Palatinate Mennonite parentage) published a study in the *Zeitschrift für Kirchengeschichte* (III, 1933, 545-98), entitled "Täufertum und Märtyrertheologie" (English translation under the title, "The Anabaptist Theology of Martyrdom" in *MQR* XIX, 1945, 179-214), which soon became a minor classic in the ongoing discussion of interpreting the essence of Anabaptism and its implied "theology." Stauffer's thesis is briefly as follows: In the period of post-canonical Judaism (since about 175 B.C.) a new viewpoint impressed itself on the then flourishing apocryphal literature: the idea that suffering and martyrdom for one's faith are the very meaning of the happenings of history, for a double reason: (a) they represent a causal necessity in the great fight between the divine and the satanic order. The great Adversary does not allow a pure realization of God's plan, at least not in this present aeon or world period. (b) Such suffering, however, serves at the same time a very great purpose: it ushers in the new aeon. Death becomes victory, martyrdom is an expiating sacrifice, and Satan will be overcome only by such nonresistant suffering. That was the teaching of Dan. 3 (the three men in the furnace) and of the Second and Third Book of the Maccabees (e.g., the story of the mother and her seven sons). In short, the apocalyptic, pre-Christian literature offers this double justification of martyrdom: causally it is inescapable, and teleologically ("what for") it is absolutely meaningful.

The New Testament continued this apocalyptic trend even further; the Cross becoming the very center not only of salvation but also the vindication of all martyrdom for conscience' sake. In fact the idea of *Nachfolge* or discipleship (*q.v.*) would almost be without meaning if it were not connected with such earthly tribulations. The believer's conflict with the "world" is the surest indication that the disciple is true to the master, testifying for another reality and preparing for the coming of the kingdom. Two figures of speech soon became generally accepted: the disciple must become a "soldier" [occasionally also called a "knight"] of Christ who "fights the good fight" to the bitter end, and secondly, baptism is called death just as death is a sort of baptism by blood. This remarkable "theology of history" may be found with many writers of the first centuries after Christ (sometimes called the period of the "Church under the Cross"), and received its final formulation in the famous *Church History* of Eusebius (*q.v.*), a favorite later on with the Anabaptists.

Stauffer now claims that this "theology of martyrdom" (which he occasionally also calls appropriately the "apocalypse of martyrdom") is the "hidden sanctuary or crypt of Anabaptist Christianity" (*MQR*, 205). It is the very core of Anabaptist thought, its "theology of history," and the final directive toward the narrow path of renouncing the world and accepting conflicts and death, if need be. The true Christian must suffer in this world, but in so doing he is preparing for the kingdom of God which might come at any time (i.e., when the number of martyrs is full). The "suffering church" is the true church of God throughout all history. In documenting his thesis, Stauffer could refer to an outstanding array of original source material: Conrad Grebel's famous letter to Thomas Müntzer of 1524, Balthasar Hubmaier's *Taufbüchlein* of 1525, with its motto "Die Wahrheit is untödtlich," Menno Simons' tract *Of the Cross of Christ* (of 1556), the Hutterite *Chronicle* with its long list of martyrs and its special register of all these witnesses to truth, and finally the numerous martyrs' books (*q.v.*), ending with van Braght's *Martyrs' Mirror* of 1660. The *Ausbund* and the Hutterite *Lieder,* as well as the numerous Dutch Mennonite hymnals, likewise contain ample material in this regard; in fact all evangelical Anabaptists are one in this basic outlook, theology, vision, or whatever

this position might be called. A summary of the main ideas of Stauffer's essay follows.

(1) "The path of martyrdom of the people of God through history." The 45th hymn of the *Ausbund* (by Hans Büchel) has the characteristic title: "A new hymn in which a disciple laments because he met tribulations for the sake of God's Word; but the Lord answers kindly by telling him how He has fared in this world." This hymn very well reflects the mood and outlook of a typical Anabaptist believer. He is supposed to have "the patience and faith of the saints" (Rev. 13:10; see **Gelassenheit**), understanding that he is one in an endless tradition of fighters for God who thus challenge the prince of this world, and reach victory only through the Cross. Menno Simons' great tract *Of the Cross* explains this necessity in so many words: expect the Cross and be glad, for suffering (for the sake of Truth) is the sign of election. Letters and hymns produced on the eve of execution abundantly show this generally accepted attitude and faith, for which God is more real and concrete than anything else on this earth.

The Cross is the measure and the center of all Anabaptist "theology of martyrdom." No escape into a religion of either pure inwardness (like Pietism, *q.v.*) or of pure spiritualism (like the Spiritual Reformers, *q.v.*, or later the Quakers, *q.v.*) appears possible from this point of view. "The Anabaptist apocalypse of martyrdom is the testimony of a theological realism to which God is more real than anything called world" (*MQR*, 204). In the great controversy between Pilgram Marpeck and Caspar Schwenckfeld, for instance (to Stauffer apparently not yet known), the distinction is well formulated: while Schwenckfeld seeks the "halo of glory," Marpeck knows that the disciple will find nothing but a "crown of thorns" (Marpeck, *Verantwortung,* 160).

(2) "The apocalyptic interpretation of persecution." The new world epoch or aeon, the kingdom of God, which began with Jesus Christ, stands altogether under the sign of the Cross. However, Christ's disciples possess also the great promise of the "Holy Remnant" (as the prophets of old called it); they will inherit the kingdom and will see how those who once persecuted them now will find their bitter reward, namely, closed doors to the new and shining realm. The martyr stands in the center of a battle of two aeons (see, e.g., the *Ausbund,* 78th hymn); life is nothing but "the warfare of the Cross" (Menno Simons), which must be carried out to its very end. The blood of the martyrs is the seed of the coming aeon, martyrdom is actually victory over the victor. And this triumph was foretold long ago in Rev. 1:7, "They shall see whom they have pierced."

At this place a word of caution might be appropriate. Although the basic theology of the Anabaptists seems to have centered around this idea of the two aeons (the "City of God" vs. the "City of the Devil"), it would yet be erroneous to assume that the Anabaptists were radical believers in apocalypses, such as adventists or millennialists. Nothing is further from their thought. They almost never speculated about "the end" (with perhaps the exception of Melchior Hofmann, *q.v.,* and to some extent Hans Hut, *q.v.*). At all times they were more concerned with the narrow path to be walked on than with the goal to be expected. Of course, this path receives its meaning and justification from this particular "theology of history." In a sense they felt that their walking the narrow path and their obedience to God's commandments realized already in the here and now some aspects of the coming aeon. That becomes especially clear in Stauffer's third section of his study,

(3) "Baptism, Confession and Defenselessness." Anneken of Rotterdam's moving "Testament to her infant son" (1539, *Mart. Mir.* D 48-50, E 453 f.) serves as a fine illustration that the life and death of an Anabaptist receives its deeper meaning alone through this "theology of martyrdom." Baptism is the sealing unto suffering and death. Conrad Grebel said the same in his letter to Thomas Müntzer. Occasionally martyrdom is called "the dubbing of the retainer of Christ." It is always understood as the *Bundessiegel,* the seal of the covenant of God with His people.

Confessions with Anabaptists are something basically different from the formulated creedal systems (called Confessions of Faith) of the established churches. For the Anabaptists they are rather testimonies in the old sense of being statements of the "confessors of faith," that is, expressions of their concrete and substantial faith. "I shall testify with my blood," said a martyr in the early days, "what I have taught and confessed with my mouth."

Defenselessness, nonresistance, and "Gelassenheit" are then the natural consequences of such a martyr attitude. Compare Menno Simons' pertinent passages in his tract *Of the Cross* (*Works,* p. 184 f.). The disciples of Christ are sent out like sheep among wolves (Grebel), and must accept their fate with true yieldedness to the will of God. It is taken for granted that no Anabaptist can ever wield a sword. Naturally, he will be obedient to the authorities of this world as long as no conflict arises with his own conscience. Beyond that he is bound to deny such obedience since he is bound to a higher authority. Actually, he is already living in a world of a different dimension, and therefore stands under its laws rather than under those of this world.

Critical Evaluation. When Stauffer's article was published in 1945, the editor of the *Mennonite Quarterly Review,* Harold S. Bender, wrote a lengthy editorial (178) in which he claimed that in a certain sense this "theology of martyrdom" is no "theology" at all. This set of ideas certainly moves the disciple to his fight, but it does not tell concretely what he is fighting for. "We must look elsewhere for a statement of the positive contents of the faith for which the Anabaptist bleeds and dies." Thus Stauffer's study gives us the background or mood of the Anabaptist movement rather than its very theme. If genuine Anabaptist theology is to be recovered, our search has to go on until a proper formulation of the positive contents is found. H. S. Bender's own suggestion of a "theology of discipleship," to be sure, may find a somewhat similar criticism, namely, that discipleship, likewise, is not really a "theology" in the proper sense of the term. But

it seems that in the background of both discipleship and martyrdom there may easily be found a common denominator which gives meaning and content to both. And that is the dualistic idea of the "two realms" (or cities): that of God and that of the prince of this world. Tentatively one could call this idea the "theology of the kingdom" (*q.v.*). It is true that the Anabaptists rather seldom developed this theme; yet it is still their basic outlook. Only upon such an idea of two different dimensions of the world (or of human existence) will the idea of martyrdom assume meaning, answering the eternal question, "Why is it that the just (or the saint) must suffer at all times?" The Christian answer will always have an eschatological if not a downright apocalyptic aspect. It is the philosophy of history of the Christian, or (from another angle) his dynamic theology of salvation.

In general, it may be said that the idea of the suffering church (or the church under the Cross) is a part of the very core of the Anabaptist genius, without which the entire problem of evangelical Anabaptism cannot be understood nor can it be properly demarcated against related Christian movements such as Pietism and Spiritualism. (See also **Concerning a True Soldier of Christ; Eusebius; Gelassenheit.**) R.F.

E. Stauffer, "The Anabaptist Theology of Martyrdom," *MQR* XIX (1945) 179-214; H. W. Meihuizen has published a number of important studies on the theology of the martyrs as found in the *Offer des Heeren:* "De Geloofswereld onzer Martelaren, voor zover die af te lezen valt uit het Offer des Heeren," in *Algemeen Doopsgezind Weekblad* V (1951) Nos. 35-50; see also Kühler, *Geschiedenis* I, 247-69; A. Orley Swartzentruber, "The Piety and Theology of the Anabaptist Martyrs in van Braght's *Martyrs' Mirror,*" *MQR* XXVIII (1954) 5-26, 128-42.

Martyrs, derived from the Greek *martys* (witness), are blood witnesses; i.e., persons who, clinging to their convictions, suffered the blood penalty. Usage has limited the word in general to apply only to those who suffered a violent death for their convictions. Socrates was, for instance, a pre-Christian martyr.

The Christian martyrs are blood witnesses, who suffered violent deaths for the sake of their Christian faith. This concept of martyrdom presupposes that the penalty was not applied for insurrection or any other crime, but was based on the victim's religious faith. There are martyrs in this sense only where religious persecution reigns. This was the case in the early centuries after Christ until Constantine's recognition of Christianity. The first Christian martyrs were the victims of Jewish persecution (Stephen, Acts 7, and James, Acts 12). An incomparably larger number found death at the hands of the pagan government of the Roman Empire.

1. *Christian Martyrs in the Christian State.* When the Catholic Church, with the aid of the government, developed into a strong organization, martyrdom did not cease, as one might suppose. Instead, the large church, having won recognition, now applied the very methods of suppression which it had formerly suffered, to all extra-ecclesiastical groups that refused to recognize its creed, its power politics, and its lax moral standards. There were

therefore martyrs at once among the heretics (*q.v.*), or those who in general opposed the prevailing church doctrine. The first victim of this kind was Priscillian together with six others in 385, who were publicly executed at Trier. The Donatists (*q.v.*), against whom Augustine counseled violent measures, had many martyrs. To a much larger extent this was true of the Waldenses (*q.v.*) and Albigenses (*q.v.*), especially after the Inquisition was instituted as a permanent ecclesiastical court, operated with state aid, which caused a terrifying number to lose their lives far into the Reformation, including also Lutheran and Reformed "heretics."

The real martyr church of the Reformation period and long after was the Anabaptist. The development of this movement in the first centuries after its inception cannot be separated from this fact. There was no religious movement that was so radically suppressed at that time as the Anabaptist movement. Catholic and Protestant government and clergy with few exceptions attempted to exterminate it by the same methods.

2. *Executions in Catholic Countries.* In the Catholic countries the Inquisition was in full authority. It was expressly recognized by the temporal government, which offered its arm to carry out its verdicts. Numerous state regulations threatened every Anabaptist with death. Members of the two large Reformation parties were also threatened with severe punishment, but the full severity of the law was not always applied. "In Bavaria and in Austria and also in the domain of the Swabian League not only their supposed connection with Lutheranism, but also adult baptism *per se* and the assumption that they were the originators of the Peasants' War and born revolutionaries brought the most cruel punishment upon them. Whereas in Austria the death penalty was not always carried out against the Lutherans in consideration of the nobility, there was no such deterrent against ruthless measures for Anabaptists, such as imprisonment, torture, beheading, drowning, hanging, and burning, usually without a proper trial" (K. Müller, II, 1, p. 332). Precisely in these Catholic lands the Anabaptists were often more numerous than the Lutherans or Reformed. The latter frequently were afraid to promote their doctrine without state protection, whereas the Anabaptists, who were almost nowhere tolerated, spread rapidly everywhere as a movement whose center of gravity lay in the laity.

3. *Blood Witnesses Under Protestant Government.* It is a conspicuous fact that there were Anabaptist martyrs also in Protestant countries. One would have expected that there would be no room for the persecution of dissenters in places where protest against Roman tyranny was so strong. But the Anabaptists were even here by no means tolerated. They were therefore the only martyrs in these regions. There were, to be sure, voices raised to oppose this kind of suppression of religious convictions and to warn of the danger inherent in it. Luther was at first of this opinion. Other reformers also wanted God's Word to be the sole judge in religious matters. But when this method did not accomplish their aim they took another course (see **Punishment**). In the Netherlands, after Roman Catholicism had been largely replaced by Calvinism, no Mennonite was put to death. In the Southern Netherlands (now Belgium) executions ceased at the end of the 16th century, because Mennonitism had been nearly extirpated.

4. *Reasons for the Persecution.* What were the real reasons for this course of action against the Anabaptists? The sentence passed on Anneken Heyndricks (*q.v.*) in Amsterdam in 1571 may show us what the "capital crimes" were. A verbatim excerpt from the criminal records of the city, which is given by van Braght (*Mart. Mir.* D 538, E 874), follows:

"Whereas Anneken Hendrik's daughter, alias Anna de Vlaster, formerly citizeness of this city, at present a prisoner here, unmindful of her soul's salvation and the obedience which she owed to our mother the holy church and his royal majesty, as her natural lord and prince, rejecting the ordinances of the holy church, has neither been to confession, nor to the holy, worthy sacrament for six or seven years since, (but has dared) to go into the assembly of the reprobated sect of the Mennonists, or Anabaptists, and has also held conventicles or meetings at her house; and has further, about three years ago, forsaking and renouncing the baptism received in her infancy from the holy church, been rebaptized, and then received the breaking of bread according to the manner of the Mennonist sect, and was married to her present husband in Mennonist manner, at night, in a country house; and though she, the prisoner, has, by my lords of the court, as well as by divers ecclesiastical persons, been urged and repeatedly admonished to leave the aforementioned reprobated sect, and she nevertheless refuses to do it, persisting in her obstinacy and stubbornness, so that she, the prisoner, according to what has been mentioned, has committed crime against divine and human majesty, as by said sect disturbing the common peace and welfare of the land, according to the import of the decrees of his majesty, existing in regard to this; which misdemeanors, for an example unto others, ought not to go unpunished; therefore, my lords of the court, having heard the demand of my lord the bailiff, seen the confession of the prisoner, and having had regard to her obstinacy and stubbornness, have condemned her, and condemn her by these presents, to be, according to the decrees of his royal majesty, executed with fire, and declare all her property confiscated for the benefit of his majesty aforesaid. Done in court on the 10th of November, in the year 1571, in the presence of the judges, by the advice of all the burgomasters, in my knowledge, as secretary, and as was subscribed: W. Pietersz."

This sentence is typical of many. It contains a long series of charges raised against the Mennonites: neglect of public church attendance and confession, communion, participation in Mennonite services, adult baptism and communion "in the Mennonite manner," marriage within the brotherhood, and stubborn resistance toward conversion attempts.

All of this deals with purely religious matters. But adhering to this faith made one suspect politically and was labeled as disobedience not only to the church, but also to the state. This shows how closely hand in hand the state worked with the church. In its cross-examinations the state used the clergy, who frequently engaged in lively dispute with the Mennonites. But in order to induce the state to take aggressive action, great stress was put on the political danger and on the religious obligation to take action against that sort of "blasphemy."

This verdict is also of legal interest, in that it illustrates how the violation of the regulations and mandates against the Mennonites could at all times be the incontestable basis for severe action against them. The fact that the injustice was of earlier date, that is, before the passing of these mandates, which bound the conscience and which in every instance overstepped the boundaries of state authority, was consistently ignored.

In very many instances punishment was made easier by applying all sorts of slander and false generalizations without examination. There was no hesitation in attributing the grossest excesses to these people, who actually insisted very earnestly on moral conduct. The events in Münster, with which the quiet Anabaptists had nothing in common, were applied without distinction to all Mennonites. The few aberrations, which accompany any movement, were considered characteristic of the entire movement. The chronicle of the Hutterian Brethren (Wolkan, 187) contains this passage on the subject:

"On all sides many slanders and evil words were given out about them, and obvious lies, as that they had goat feet and ox hooves and that if they gave people a drink from a small bottle, the people would have to act as they did. The lie was also circulated that they had their wives in common, that everything was in confusion. Likewise that they kidnaped children and ate them, they were accused of stealing people and of breaking up marriages, because frequently one party of the marriage left the unbelieving party who would not follow, and go to the brotherhood. Yea, they were called Anabaptists, garden brethren, deceivers, sectarians, revolutionaries, fanatics, and the most terrible things."

Special efforts were made to dispose of the leaders, in the hope that the movement could thus be smothered. Most of these died a violent death, as Felix Manz, Michael Sattler, Balthasar Hubmaier, Hans Hut, George Blaurock, Eitelhans Langenmantel, and others. But owing to the priesthood of the believer, which they held and practiced, the loss of their leaders was not sufficient to stop the movement. To be sure, the absence of their influence may have contributed to the rise of radical elements here and there, who were guilty of excesses which a thoughtful leadership would have prevented (Münster).

5. *Modes of Execution.* The methods of execution offer a picture of inhuman cruelty. The intention was that they should have a deterrent effect on the populace. Torture was often applied, principally to extort from the victims information about their brethren, where they stayed and where they met, or to force them to recant. The Hutterian chronicle has a graphic description of these methods (Wolkan, 184):

"Some were racked until the sun could have shone through them, so that some were torn and died, some were burned to ashes under the name of heretic, some roasted on pillars, some torn with glowing tongs, some locked into houses and all burned together, some hanged to trees, but some executed with the sword, killed and cut to pieces. Many were gagged or had their tongues tied so that they should be unable to speak or defend themselves, and were thus led to death. . . . Like lambs they were led to the slaughter in droves and murdered according to Satan's kind and nature. . . ."

In the execution of the Anabaptists and Mennonites medieval methods of capital punishment were maintained. The following practices were used to put the victims to death; in most cases burning at the stake both for men and women; sometimes the victims were not burned alive but were first strangled; in the Netherlands occasionally a little sack of gunpowder was placed around the martyr's neck to shorten the death struggle. When a "heretic" recanted, he nevertheless was put to death; in these cases men were usually beheaded and women drowned. But martyrs who remained loyal were sometimes also beheaded or drowned. It was the instruction both of Charles V and Philip II, that male heretics were to be decapitated and females drowned, but often men were drowned and women beheaded. Sometimes the victims were executed by being hanged. In a few cases also women martyrs were buried alive. It is not clear whether these awful practices were regulated after a certain method. Apparently the mood of the judges was decisive as to the method of execution.

The executions took place publicly; but in the course of time there were a large number of secret executions, because the crowds gathered around the execution places often showed sympathy with the victims and not seldom revolted against the executioner, the officers, and the Catholic priests, who were always present. Secret executions were numerous at Antwerp and Gent, Belgium.

6. *The Number of the Anabaptist Martyrs.* The number cannot be determined with any certainty. Documentary evidence has been preserved only in part, some of it probably intentionally destroyed. In the "Anabaptist hunts" in the territory of the Swabian League and in the Netherlands as well as in other regions where regular trials were dispensed with, there was most likely no record of even the names or number of victims. Nevertheless an attempt has been made to determine the number from oral and written sources. For the Netherlands, Samuel Cramer has conservatively set the number at 1,500 (*DB* 1902, 150 ff.). He based this figure on the fairly complete records of Antwerp and Gent, estimating the number in the other provinces on this basis, which should yield a sufficiently reliable result. W. J. Kühler also surmised that the number of martyrs was at least 1,500 (*Geschiedenis* I, 270); N. van der Zijpp (*Geschiedenis,* 77) is of the opinion that the number of martyrs in Belgium and in the Netherlands should be estimated as at least 2,500, on the basis of his studies on Mennonite martyrdom in the Netherlands. The best collection

of data on the fate and testimonies of the martyrs is found in the *Martyrs' Mirror* (*q.v.*) by Tieleman J. van Braght, who lists about 800 Anabaptist martyrs by name. A larger number is given in summary form, because data and names were lacking. This ENCYCLOPEDIA gives brief articles on all known martyrs.

For South Germany the list in the Hutterite *Geschicht-Buch* is of particular importance. According to the list given in Beck (*q.v.*, pp. 278 ff.) the number of martyrs up to the year 1581 was 2,169. But the numbers given for the individual districts do not agree with this figure, totaling only 1,396. It is not clear how this difference is to be explained. (For Tirol the list of 1581 gives the number as 338, whereas a government declaration of Nov. 11, 1539, set the number of Anabaptists executed at over 600. —Hege.) Wolkan presents a list that deviates in some instances from the above, and gives a total of 1,580 martyrs by 1542. Beck has on page 310 an additional list that was found on Julius Lober (*q.v.*) in 1531, listing 390 martyrs.

None of these lists can claim to be exhaustive; in Beck all the executions recorded in the court records in Switzerland, and in Wolkan some of them, are lacking, nor can they offer absolute reliability, since they are sometimes based on oral information, as in the case of the 350 in Alzey (see **Palatinate**) and the 600 who were said by Sebastian Franck to have been executed at Ensisheim (*q.v.*). Nevertheless the total must not be underestimated, and would probably exceed rather than fall below 4,000.

The first Anabaptist execution was not perpetrated in 1527 (Felix Manz, *q.v.*), as has hitherto been asserted, but in 1525 when Eberli Bolt (*q.v.*) died at the stake in Schwyz. Bolt was an Anabaptist, but was executed in a Catholic canton for being a Protestant.

7. Steadfastness and Courage of the Anabaptists. Steadfast and willing to endure the supreme sacrifice, most of the martyrs went to their death with cheerful countenance and with a prayer on their lips. Men and women, occasionally children, were unwavering in their loyalty to their faith. Naturally they did not push themselves into martyrdom. But they did not purchase their freedom by denying their convictions, which were based on God's Word, when they were in the hands of their persecutors. Neither skilled argument, nor severity, nor kindness confused them. "Many were promised great gifts and wealth if they would recant, or splendid benefices, or power and office. Others were asked to say only a little word as desired of them, and they would be released. But they would not accept dishonorable release. Some were told merely to utter an oath, indeed only a small oath, to gain their release. . . . With many they dealt strangely, . . . day and night with great cunning and slyness, also with many sweet and smooth words by monks and priests, . . . with much false doctrine and testimony, with much threatening . . . and slander, also with lies and terrible reviling, but this did not cause them dismay" (Wolkan, 185 f.). There were, however, a considerable number of recantations.

8. What Was the Source of Their Strength? Full of admiration, indeed frequently full of consternation, the people and sometimes the executioners witnessed the steadfastness and the courage of the martyrs. Whence came the strength to endure all this? This question is raised in many writings of the Reformation period, and its answer was not always easy. Luther, who had once thought quite differently concerning the Inquisition and the execution of John Huss, saw in their joy a delusion of hell; likewise did Faber of Heilbronn (see the significant quotation in the article **Faber**). Justus Menius (*q.v.*), the passionate opponent of the Anabaptists, could hardly conceal his amazement at the courage of several Anabaptists, nevertheless he explained it as impudence and foolhardiness. "For it can very easily happen that such a desperate, hard-hearted man in his damnable unbelief is as stiff and defiant, indeed much stiffer and more defiant than a holy, pious Christian in his true faith. . . ."—"The whole world has of course seen with what brash frivolity the poor people died, who were executed . . . at Rheinhardsbrunn" (see **Kolb, Andreas**) (*Der ander Teil,* 314).

The Anabaptists had a different idea of the source of their strength. "They could freely say with the holy apostle Paul: Who can separate us from the love of Christ? Shall tribulation, or distress, or persecution, or famine, or nakedness, or peril, or sword? Rom. 8:35. But they found and showed it to be true that according to the testimony of the apostle, neither death, nor life, nor things present, nor things to come, shall be able to separate us from the love of God, which is in Christ Jesus. Through this love they overcame all things and performed glorious deeds beyond the power of man" (*Mart. Mir.* D 542, E 356).

The martyrs had the unshakable certainty of being on the right road, which God had unequivocally shown them in the Holy Scriptures. Their knowledge of the Bible, revealed in their trials and other oral and written expressions, is amazing. During their persecution they had learned that this life cannot be the final fulfillment. Hence they saw even in a martyr's death the transition to a fuller and richer life. "Their holy spirit regarded the things that happen in the world as a shadow, assured of better things. Thus they were taught by God not to know anything, nor to seek anything but the eternal heavenly possession alone" (Beck, XXI).

Furthermore the martyrs lived in the conviction that true followers of Christ must necessarily draw upon themselves the hatred of the world. As they took all the sayings and demands of the Bible seriously, so also did they regard the experiences of Jesus and the apostles in the world, which they foretold for all true Christians. All expressions of principle concerning martyrdom refer to Christ's suffering and death as Lord and example to the church. Martyrdom was for them the inevitable consequence of witnessing to the truth. Nowhere is this so clearly expressed as in Menno Simons' booklet to his oppressed brethren, *Of the Cross of Christ.* Since the truth evokes hatred and persecution, therefore these are evidence of walking in the truth. Thus the temptations of martyrdom serve to make the victims so much the surer and firmer in their conviction. The assurance that even in suffering they were in communion with Christ gave them joy and called forth thanks for being counted worthy of suffering death for His sake.

But in spite of all their courage and steadfastness the martyrs were free of fanaticism. Of the letters printed in the *Martyrs' Mirror* many are written to wife, children, or relatives. They do not treat the natural bonds of marriage and family with contempt. They commend their dear ones to the loving care of the brotherhood, and mention how difficult it is to leave them alone. This feeling comes to graphic expression in a letter written by Hendrik Verstralen (*Mart. Mir.* D 542, E 877): "The only and eternal God . . . keep you, my dearest wife and sister in the Lord, my flesh, my bone, the dearest among all creatures on earth. For this I have confessed more than once before the lords, if the whole world were mine, I would give it, if I could keep my wife and children with a good conscience; but for the Lord's sake I must now contrary to nature forsake everything—the spirit must overcome the flesh. O my Janneken, my lamb, how hard it is for me to part from you and the children! Oh, how deep you are buried in my heart; which is now a great conflict for me; may the Lord help me to gain the victory, so that the crown of life may be prepared for me with all the elect saints of God, who have forsaken everything for the Lord's sake."

The petition for strength to endure, found in this letter and repeated in many others, is a sign of the sobriety of the martyrs, as is also their prayer for forgiveness of sins. They did not share in the error that a martyr's death would in itself assure God's grace or be of special merit. The wish for martyrdom therefore was far from their minds. They did not consider it treason to the cause to avoid the catchpolls as long as possible. Menno himself by no means walked carelessly into the arms of those who had set a price upon his head.

Because they were fully aware of the seriousness of death for Christ's sake they did not hesitate to urge upon their judges the responsibility for their wicked conduct. Like the voice of an Old Testament prophet sounds the cry of Hans Blietel (*Blüetl, q.v.*): "Repent, reform, and desist from your unrighteous, wicked, and vicious life; for if you do not do this, the eternal God will visit you for your sins, and He shall require the innocent blood at your hands, and punish you for it" (*Mart. Mir.* D 72, E 473 f.).

The frequency of martyrdom in their time and the prophecies concerning it in the Bible convinced them that the end time was approaching. Persecution of the truth in itself they regarded as evidence that the power of Antichrist was at work, and so it is not surprising to find that they viewed their persecutors as representatives of Antichrist, an idea that Luther expresses frequently in relation to the papacy.

9. The Effects of Martyrdom. The consequences of the martyrdom of the Anabaptists are of enormous significance. First of all this is true for the movement itself. The blood of the martyrs was the seed of the Anabaptist congregations. "Persecution contributed greatly to the spread of Anabaptism. The believers, driven from city to city, everywhere laid the foundation for new beginnings. Everywhere the simple manner of proclamation, the touching cohesion of the members among themselves, the earnest and strict life of the adherents, the thousands of joyous and simple martyrdoms, the wonderful poetry that grew out of the bloody persecution and constant danger of death, and the feeling that this condition was the seal of true Christianity, were extremely effective" (K. Müller, 333). In precisely those places where the movement was met with the greatest tolerance, as in the realm of Philip of Hesse, it was soon extinct.

Martyrdom gave Anabaptist literature its strongest incentives, especially in hymnology (*q.v.*). (See **Het Offer, Lietboecxken, Ausbund.**)

Toward the outside martyrdom was the most effective propaganda for the new movement. The man of the common people, with his natural sensibilities, was not blinded by the artificial attempts of the judges to justify their conduct.

One of the last formal executions was that of Hans Landis (*q.v.*) on Sept. 20, 1614, at Zürich. Nevertheless many other Mennonites died in the following years as a result of bad treatment in prison. These must be included at least indirectly among the martyrs. The last martyr in the Netherlands died in 1574, and the last in Belgium in 1597.

Growing scruples against the death penalty for heretics, the obvious ineffectiveness of the severe measures, frequently also political necessity, led to the abandonment of the death penalty. At that point Mennonite history ceases to be martyr history. Toleration and complete religious freedom were by no means achieved, at least not in many countries. Once more under the Communist rule in Russia hundreds of Mennonites are estimated to have perished. It was, of course, not persecution for their Mennonitism, but punishment for being Christian is usually given a political veneer. But "God knows how many lost their lives in Russia, according to the verdict of the Soviet merely as reactionaries. But their rejection of much that a government separated from God asked of these alleged reactionaries stemmed from their inner relationship to God" (Kroeker). (See the article **Martyrdom, Theology of.**) P.S.

K. Müller, *Kirchengeschichte* II (Tübingen, 1911, II, 2, 1919); Wolkan, *Geschicht-Buch;* Zieglschmid, *Chronik;* Beck, *Geschichts-Bücher;* J. Kroeker, *Das Bekenntnis der russischen Märtyrerkirche* (Berlin, 1936); *Mart. Mir. passim; Der ander Teil der Bücher D. Martin Luthers* (Wittenberg, 1551); A. Orley Swartzentruber, "The Piety and Theology of the Anabaptist Martyrs in van Braght's *Martyrs' Mirror,*" *MQR* XXVIII (1954) 5-26, 128-42; I. M. J. Hoog, *De Martelaren der Hervorming in Nederland* (Schiedam, 1885); Kühler, *Geschiedenis* I, 245-77; N. van der Zijpp, *Geschiedenis der Doopsgezinden in Nederland* (Arnhem, 1952) 59-77; *ML* III, 44-49.

Martyrs (Russia). The suffering of the Mennonites behind the Iron Curtain (1917-) has been called "martyrdom." A. A. Töws collected materials on this subject and published them under the title *Mennonitische Martyrer der jüngsten Vergangenheit und der Gegenwart* (2 vv., 1949 and 1954). Certainly never since the days of the 16th-century persecution of the Anabaptists have their descendants suffered so severely as they have under modern Communism since its establishment in 1917. Hundreds have been executed and many thousands have perished in prisons, slave labor camps, and concentration camps (*q.v.*). Although much has been done to gather the accounts of the suffering, the death, and the witness of this most recent "martyrdom" among Mennonites, no systematic study exists along these lines. Considerable material has been collected in addition to the two volumes by Töws. The Canadian Mennonite periodicals contain much information, as do also the numerous books which have been published by Mennonites and non-Mennonites dealing with this question. Much more should be done to obtain all possible information from those who have escaped the death of "martyrdom" and are now living in Western Europe, Canada, or South America. Most important for a systematic study of this question would be an investigation of the accounts by survivors in Russia, to obtain information about the number that perished, details about their suffering and death, and the testimony and results of their death.

One of the basic questions arising in the investigation of the martyrdom of Mennonites or any other religious group behind the Iron Curtain is the degree to which their suffering has been due to their faith in God. Did they originally not, above all, suffer because they belonged to a certain social and economic group, regardless of their religious affiliation or convictions? Many of the Mennonites who died during the early days of the Revolution were well-to-do individuals of the bourgeoisie, the prosperous class, which according to the Marxist theory had to be liquidated in order to usher in the classless society of a social utopia. Though these revolutionary Marxists were as a rule also antireligious, they were in most cases annihilating an enemy on a political and economic battlefield. That these sufferings were borne with the courage and the testimony of a Christian in many cases is a fact and is to the credit of those who had enjoyed days of prosperity and now with Job experienced the presence of the Lord in a more real sense while they were led through the valley of death.

The real antireligious persecution came later with the liquidation of the "kulaks" in 1929 ff. Lenin relaxed the original plans of socializing the country overnight. After his death Stalin proceeded with collectivization and the liquidation of the kulaks (i.e., those who would possibly be opposed to the collectivization, etc.). Many thousands of Mennonites were sent to concentration and slave labor camps in 1933-38. Some were executed. Among these kulaks were many ministers and other sincere Christians. Simultaneously the organized church life of the communities was checked by taxing ministers and church buildings so heavily that services had to be discontinued. Again many ministers and faithful church members were imprisoned and exiled. Also many of the Mennonite teachers, who were accustomed to express their Christian convictions daily in their classroom work, were deprived of their position or exiled. The teachers as a class suffered possibly just as much as the ministers. In fact, since in many instances they combined these two professions, many a teacher was dismissed because he was also a minister. No one will ever be able to measure the cup of suffering endured for the sake of their faith by these two professions, which were hit hardest during the trying years. But again we cannot simply label all the sufferings they endured as 100 per cent religious martyrdom. Former economic status, social and cultural affiliations, and at times their German background were probably counted against them as much as their deeply rooted Christian convictions.

Some of these who were well-known leaders and confessors and are known to have died as a result of the suffering inflicted upon them during these trying years are D. J. Classen, H. H. Dirks, A. A. Dück, B. B. Dyck, H. H. Ediger, S. S. Ediger, H. H. Funk, A. A. Klassen, Johann Martens, K. K. Martens, J. A. Rempel, J. J. Wiebe, etc. Biographies of these and others are included in the ENCYCLOPEDIA.

C.K.

Bethel College Historical Library, Displaced Persons File; *Der Bote* 1923- ; *Die Mennonitische Rundschau,* 1923- . A. A. Töws, *Mennonitische Märtyrer* I (Winnipeg, 1949), II (North Clearbrook, 1954); D. Dalin and B. Nicolaevsky, *Forced Labor in Soviet Russia* (New Haven, 1947).

Martyrs, Anonymous. There were a number of Anabaptist-Mennonite martyrs whose names have not been preserved, and about whose fate, testimony, and sufferings nothing is known. Van Braght's *Martyrs' Mirror* occasionally mentions large numbers of anonymous martyrs. Delbert Gratz (*Bernese Anabaptists*) mentions eight martyrs whose names are not known, executed at Bern, Switzerland, in 1530-32. Concerning a few of these pious anonymous persons there is some information.

A man from Vueren (Veurne, Furnes in Belgium?) was executed there and died loyally for his faith. This happened (according to the Dutch martyrbook of 1615) in 1553. He was commemorated in the hymn, "In bitterheyt der sielen, claghe ick dit jammer groot" (In bitterness of soul I lament this great distress). This song, No. 11 of the *Lietboecxken van den Offer des Heeren,* was very popular among the Dutch Mennonites and was sung until the 18th century. It has been included in a number of Dutch hymnals, including *Veelderhande Liedekens* of 1569 and also Stapel's *Lusthof der Zielen* (*q.v.*), until the last (7th) edition of 1743. (*Offer,* 547-50; Wackernagel, *Lieder,* 139; Wolkan, *Lieder,* 62, 78.)

Verheyden mentions some anonymous martyrs at Gent, Belgium. On Aug. 27, 1568, a man was burned at the stake outside the Muyde-poorte. Another martyr, a native of Merendree, was burned on Feb. 6, 1569, in the territory of Gent St-Pieters, and two others on Aug. 2, 1569, on the Vrijdagsmarkt. A woman was also burned at the stake on Oct. 3, 1569. (Verheyden, *Gent,* 48, No. 153; 51, No. 169; 53, Nos. 175-76; 55, No. 181.)

Génard reports on the following anonymous martyrs at Antwerp, Belgium: a Mennonite man, burned at the stake on Oct. 12, 1569, because "he persisted in his false creed" (*Antw. Arch.-Blad* XII, 420; XIV, 70 f., No. 787); another Mennonite man, burned at the stake on the market place on Sept. 10, 1571, while "persisting in his false opinions" (*ibid.* XIII, 77; XIV, 86 f., No. 971); an unknown woman, burned at the stake on May 18, 1573, on the market place of Antwerp, because of her Mennonite opinions (*ibid.* XIII, 111; XIV, 90 f., No. 1020). Willem Bax mentions two women who were executed at Gangelt, near Millen, in 1556 and a man who was drowned in the neighboring Waldfeucht about 1558. vDZ.

Delbert Gratz, *Bernese Anabaptists* (Scottdale, 1954) 20 ff., Nos. 5, 6, 9, 26, 27, 30, 31, 33; W. Bax, *Het Protestantisme in het bisdom Luik* . . . II (The Hague, 1941) 364 f.

Martyrs' Mirror. In 1660 a stately volume of 1290 pages appeared, entitled *Het Bloedig Tooneel Der Doops-gesinde, En Weereloose Christenen. Die/om het getuygenisse Jesu hares Salighmaeckers/geleden hebben/en gedoodt zijn/van Christi tijdt af/tot dese onse laetste tijden toe. Mitsgaders, Een beschrijvinge der H. Doops, ende andere stucken van den Godsdienst, door alle de selve geoeffent. Begrepen in Twee Boecken. Zijnde een vergrootinge van den voorgaenden Martelaers-Spiegel, uyt vele geloofweerdige Chronijcken/Memorien/Getuygenissen/etc. Door T. J. V. B. Gedruckt tot Dordrecht, by Jacob Braat, Voor Jacobus Savry, woonende in 't Kasteel van Gendt. In 't Jaer 1660.* The author was Tieleman Jansz van Braght (*q.v.*), the elder of the Flemish Mennonite congregation at Dordrecht. The preface of the book is signed "Dordrecht July 23, 1659." The Introduction contains in succession (1) a note of the printers to the readers; (2) a note of van Braght to his "dear friends and companions in Jesus Christ, our Saviour"; (3) a general address to the readers; (4) a short summary of the book; (5) a treatise, "The true church of God and its Origin, Expansion and Immovable Stability Through all Centuries"—in this section are found the three major confessions of the Dutch Mennonites; viz., the *Olyftacxken* (*q.v.*) of 1627, that of Jan Cents (*q.v.*) of 1630, and the Dordrecht Confession (*q.v.*) of 1632; (6) a treatise concerning the ungodly and false church; (7) a laudatory poem by Cornelis van Braght, entitled "Martyrs' Crown for Jesus Christ the Saviour and those Nonresistant Crossbearers who Follow in His Train."

Van Braght's martyr book, usually called in Dutch the *Martelaersspiegel,* i.e., *Martyrs' Mirror* (this word actually appears first in the second edition, 1685) is divided into two parts. Part I, containing 450 pages, followed by an index, deals with Christian martyrdom from the time of Christ to 1500, although in its last chapter (pp. 397-408) a number of later martyrs are found, who like Christian Gasteyger and Thomas van Imbroek (*q.v.*), whose confession is inserted here, suffered because of their rejection of infant baptism. Part I concludes with a "confession of faith according to the Holy Word of God" in 33 articles. Part II (840 pp.) contains (1) Preface, (2) Introduction, and (3) three laudatory poems, followed by an index and the accounts of the Anabaptist and Mennonite martyrs, beginning with Hans Koch and Leonhard Meyster (these two men were, however, not Anabaptists). In this part van Braght deals with 803 named martyrs, 613 of whom

were executed in the Netherlands and Belgium, and 190 in other European countries. Besides these a large number of anonymous martyrs are mentioned.

At the outset van Braght, as he writes in the Introduction, only intended to re-edit the Dutch martyr book of 1631, amplified by some new material, but gradually it became clear to him that the work should be entirely rewritten. Van Braght's sources were: first the existing Dutch martyr books, in particular the *Martelaersspiegel* of 1631. But the number of martyrs was increased by the studies he made in other works of church history, and by information he secured from archives, e.g., those of the cities of Dordrecht and Amsterdam. He also received valuable information from Switzerland and Germany. Hence he was able not only to verify and to add to previous information and to insert a large number of official documents with authentic court sentences, but also to give accounts of many martyrs hitherto unknown.

Of course, the masterly work of van Braght is neither complete nor without error. He did not do scholarly work in the method of modern historiography, and too often he uncritically inserted accounts without checking them. There are mistakes, both in the names of the martyrs and in the dates of their execution. Some martyrs are named twice. The question has arisen whether van Braght may have falsified history. This accusation was made by Christian Schotanus in *Van de Gronden der Mennisterij* (Leeuwarden, 1671), while Hermann Haupt called the *Martyrs' Mirror* a prejudiced book, composed mostly from impure sources (*DB* 1899, 72; *ML* III, 53). W. Wilde, a Dutch Roman Catholic, attacked van Braght in two papers published in *Studiën* (1877, 1-88; 1894, 270-332) and in *Zonderlinge Critiek* (Amsterdam, 1900). (See *DB* 1899, 70-72; 1900, 192-210.) Also Karel Vos (*DB* 1917, 161, 170-74) and recently A. F. Mellink (*Wederdopers,* 419 and *passim*) accused van Braght of partiality. But Samuel Cramer proved (*DB* 1899, 65-164; 1900, 184-210) that van Braght, though sometimes too unsuspecting and naive, and a few times careless, may in general be called reliable. Those who criticized van Braght and accused him of omitting a large number of Anabaptists who were executed, forget that van Braght only wanted to list such martyrs as gave testimony to a Biblical faith and held the strict nonresistant principles. For this reason he excluded all those Anabaptists put to death because of their religious convictions who had contacts with or were influenced by the Münsterite or other revolutionary principles, though occasionally a few Münsterites were inserted in the *Martyrs' Mirror,* of whose real opinions van Braght was not aware. The fact that van Braght, a champion of Trinitarianism and averse to all kind of Unitarianism, did not do justice to a martyr like Herman van Vlekwijk (*q.v.*) is a shortcoming in his work, which is, however, excusable not only on the basis of his personal convictions, but also by the fact that the martyr book of 1626 had likewise omitted a few sentences from the accounts of some anti-Trinitarian martyrs. The same explicable imperfection may be noted concerning the doctrine of the Incarnation. In summary it may be said that van Braght's *Martyrs' Mirror* is a reliable, trustworthy book, as has been stated not only by Cramer, but also by other outstanding historians like Ludwig Keller, Chr. Sepp, J. G. de Hoop Scheffer, F. van der Haeghen, Adolf Fluri, L. Knappert, and W. J. Kühler.

The second edition of van Braght's *Martyrs' Mirror* was published in 1685 at Amsterdam by Hieronymus Sweerts, Jan ten Hoorn, Jan Bouman, and Daniel van den Dalen. This second edition was not edited by van Braght, who died in 1664, but by an anonymous unknown editor. The title of the second edition was slightly modified, reading *Het Bloedig Toneel of Martelaers Spiegel der Doopsgezinde of Weereloose Christenen,* etc. The text does not differ from that of the first edition, except for small additions. Only a few documents were added in Part II, and a summary account at the end of this part, concerning the persecutions in Switzerland in 1671. This new edition is noteworthy for its 103 illustrations (49 in Part I, 54 in Part II), the beautiful etchings of Jan Luiken (*q.v.*).

The first German edition of van Braght's book was translated and published in 1748-49 in the cloister at Ephrata, Pa., in an edition of 1,300 copies, 1,512 pages. The prior of the cloister, the learned Peter Miller of Alsenborn near Kaiserslautern, was the translator; in addition 14 other cloister brethren were also engaged in this work: 8 in the print shop and 6 in the paper mill. The title was as follows: *Der blutige Schau-Platz oder Märtyrer-Spiegel der Taufs Gesinnten oder Wehrlosen Christen, die um des Zeugnuss Jesu ihres Seligmachers willen gelitten haben, und seynd getödtet worden, von Christi Zeit an bis auf das Jahr 1660. Vormals aus unterschiedlichen glaubwürdigen Chronicken, Nachrichten und Zeugnüssen gesammlet und in Holländischer Sprach heraus gegeben von T. J. V. Braght. Nun aber sorgfältigst ins Hochteutsche übersetzt und zum erstenmal ans Licht gebracht.* This edition adds a list of Swiss Brethren martyrs executed in Bern 1529-71, copied from the *Tower-book* by Hans Lorsch in 1667 and preserved by Christian Kropff. It appears in all later English and German editions. In connection with the last martyr listed, Hans Haslibacher, of 1571, a portion (stanza 21 to the end) of the "Haslibacher Lied" was reprinted from the *Ausbund.*

The Ephrata edition was published by the Franconia Conference Mennonites (MC) with the definite purpose of strengthening the nonresistant faith of the church in the face of the rising threat of war. In 1745 the leaders of the church wrote to Amsterdam, requesting help in translating and publishing van Braght's great work. "As the flames of war appear to mount higher, no man can tell whether the cross and persecution of the defenseless Christians will not soon come, and it is therefore of importance to prepare ourselves for such circumstances with patience and resignation, and to use all available means that can encourage steadfastness and strengthen faith. Our whole community has manifested a unanimous desire for a German translation of the *Bloody Theater of Tieleman Jansz van Braght,* especially since in this community there is a very great number of newcomers, for which we consider it to be of greatest importance that they should become acquainted with the trustworthy witnesses who have walked in the way of truth, and sacrificed their lives for it."

In 1780 a reprint of this edition of the *Martyrs' Mirror* was made in Pirmasens (Palatinate). To the Ephrata title was added the following: *Nachwärts von der Brüderschaft zu Ephrata in Pensylvanien ins Deutsche gebracht und daselbst gedruckt worden, Anno 1748. Nunmehro von der vereinigten Brüderschaft in Europa nach obiger Uebersetzung und Druck aufs neue zum Druck befördert.* A peculiarity of this edition is the anonymity of most of the copies, whereas some have on their title page this statement: "Nunmehro von etlichen der Brüderschaft nach obiger Uebersetzung und Druck aufs neue zum Druck befördert. Pirmasens, Gedruckt bey Johann Friedrich Seelig, Hochfürstl. Hof- und Canzley-Buchdrucker 1780." These "several of the brethren" were no doubt Amish Mennonites who lived in the vicinity of Pirmasens. According to a letter written to Peter Weber (*q.v.*) on Sept. 16, 1778, in Kindenheim, most of the work of putting out this edition was done by Elder Hans Naffziger of Essingen. This edition included the etchings by Jan Luiken; 1,000 copies were printed.

The book was very widely used in the Palatinate, especially by the Amish. It served in many instances as a devotional book. This was also true of the Mennonites in Switzerland and Alsace-Lorraine (Michiels, *Anabaptistes*). In the German language the book came out in the following American editions: Lancaster 1814; Philadelphia 1849 (Shem Zook); Elkhart 1870; Scottdale 1916; and Berne 1950. English editions appeared in Lampeter Square, Pa., 1837 (J. D. Rupp, translator); London, England, 1853 (Hanserd Knollys Society); Elkhart 1886 (J. F. Sohm, translator); Scottdale 1938 and 1950.

J. B.(out) edited an abridgment of van Braght's 1685 edition under the title, *'T merg van de Historien der Martelaren,* published at Haarlem in 1699 (reprints at Amsterdam 1722, 1736, 1769). Another abridgment (120 pp.), translated by Peter Miller (Theophilus), was published at Ephrata, Pa., in 1745 under the title *Das Andenken einiger heiligen Märtyrer,* apparently as a foretaste of the edition of the full volume which followed in 1748. L. D. G. Knipscheer published in 1953 at Amsterdam a small collection entitled *Verhalen uit de Doopsgezinde Geschiedenis.*

The 105 etchings which the noted artist Jan Luiken supplied to the 1685 edition of the *Martyrs' Mirror* were published as a collection in the book *Théatre des Martyrs* (n.p., n.d.) and reprinted in *Schouwtooneel der Martelaren* (Amsterdam, 1738). They were used in the Pirmasens German edition of 1780. The original copper plates were in the possession of a Dr. Schmidt in Munich in 1924, where they were examined by H. S. Bender.

vDZ., H.S.B.

Hans Alenson, *Tegen-Bericht op de Voor-reden vant Groote Martelaer Boeck, BRN* VII (The Hague, 1910) 139-266; *DJ* II (1840) 102 f.; Chr. Sepp, *Geschiedkundige Nasporingen* II (Leiden, 1875) 9-136; A. Brons, *Entwickelung und Schicksale der altevangelischen Taufgesinnten oder Mennoniten* (Emden, 1912) 219-25; *Pirmasenser Geschichtsblätter* XI, No. 1; A. Michiels, *Les Anabaptistes des Vosges* (Paris, 1860); A. Fluri, *Beiträge zur Geschichte der Bernischen Täufer* (Bern, 1912); J. G. de Hoop Scheffer, "Onze Martelaarsboeken," *DB* 1870, 45-90;

S. Cramer, "De geloofwaardigkeit van van Braght," *DB* 1899, 65-164; *idem*, "Nog eens de geloofwaardigkeit van van Braght," *DB* 1900, 184-211; S. W. Pennypacker, *A Noteworthy Book* (Philadelphia, 1881); L. A. Miller, *Konkordanz zu dem Märtyrer-Spiegel* (Arthur, 1918); F. Pijper, *Martelaarsboeken* (The Hague, 1924); Gerald C. Studer, "A History of the *Martyrs' Mirror*," *MQR* XXII (1948) 163-79; *Inv. Arch. Amst.* I, No. 2287; *ML* III, 49-53.

Martyrs' Synod

Martyrs' Synod. In Augsburg (*q.v.*), Bavaria, Germany, a center of the Anabaptists in the 16th century, the leading figures of the movement met on Aug. 20, 1527, in a conference that was of great significance in the history of the brotherhood. Because a large number of the delegates died a short time afterward as martyrs, this meeting has been called the Martyrs' Synod.

Previous to this meeting there was only one general statement issued by the movement as a whole, namely, at a meeting on Feb. 24, 1527, at Schleitheim (*q.v.*), in the canton of Schaffhausen in Switzerland, where representatives of the Brethren agreed on a statement of doctrine and practice regarding the points in which they were at variance with Zwingli's state church. It laid the foundation for bridging over the differences between the Swiss and South German groups. Whereas the Schleitheim decisions were written down and later published, the Augsburg synod left no written statements. But there are several documents written by Anabaptist leaders of that time, which throw some light on the nature of the meeting and its religious position, such as Jakob Dachser, Hans Denk, Oswald Glait, Balthasar Hubmaier, Eitelhans Langenmantel, and Sigmund Salminger.

From the scant information from other sources it is clear that a definite program had been arranged and carried out. Those present expressed a firm determination to proclaim the doctrines and ethical principles they had accepted as right, and not to be deterred from it by persecution and danger of death.

More than 60 representatives came from South Germany, Switzerland, and Austria. Hans Denk (*q.v.*) was most likely present. The others present whose names are known were Hans Beck (*q.v.*) of Basel, also called Beckenknecht; Eucharius Binder (*q.v.*) of Koburg; Burghard Braun (*q.v.*), also called Burkhart of Ofen; Jakob Dachser (*q.v.*), a former Catholic priest of Ingolstadt; Leonhard Dorfbrunner (*q.v.*), formerly a Teutonic Knight of Nürnberg; Jakob Gross (*q.v.*) of Waldshut; Hans Gulden of Biberach in Franconia; Lukas Haffner of Augsburg; Siegmund Hofer; Hans Hut (*q.v.*) of Haina in Franconia; Jakob Kautz (*q.v.*), formerly a Lutheran preacher in Worms; Hans Kiessling (*q.v.*) of Friedberg near Augsburg; Gregor Maler (*q.v.*) of Chur; Eitelhans Langenmantel (*q.v.*) of Augsburg; Hans Leupold (*q.v.*) of Augsburg; Joachim März (*q.v.*) of Franconia; Marx Mayer (*q.v.*) of Alterlangen near Nürnberg; Hans Mittermaier (*q.v.*) of Ingolstadt; Georg Nespitzer (*q.v.*) of Lauingen, also called Jörg of Passau; Leonhardt von Prukh (*q.v.*); Sigmund Salminger (*q.v.*), a former Franciscan monk of Munich; Peter Scheppach, an artist of Augsburg; Leopold Schiemer (*q.v.*), a former Franciscan monk of Judenburg; Hans Schlaffer (*q.v.*), a former priest of Upper Austria; Leonhard Spörle (*q.v.*); Ulrich Trechsel (*q.v.*); Thomas Waldhausen (*q.v.*), a former Catholic priest of Grein, hence also called Thomas of Grein; Jakob Widemann (*q.v.*) of Memmingen; Andreas Widholz (*q.v.*), a guild master, in whose house services were held (Keller, *Apostel*, 218; Keller, *Staupitz*, 325 f.; Keller, *Reformation*, 426-28; Nicoladoni, 107; Neuser, 27).

Some of the important leaders were not present: Hubmaier was in Moravia; Pilgram Marpeck was still at Rattenberg on the Inn; Georg Blaurock was wandering in the mountains of Switzerland; Felix Manz had been martyred by drowning on Jan. 5, 1527, in Zürich, and Michael Sattler at the stake on May 21, 1527, in Rottenburg on the Neckar; Conrad Grebel had died of the plague in Maienfeld, Grisons, in the summer of 1526.

The conference appointed missionaries, who went out in all directions in two's and three's to all the countries where their fellow believers lived, to teach, comfort and strengthen them, or to build new brotherhoods. Their speech was so impressive that frequently a few hours sufficed to establish a new congregation (Cornelius, II, 49). Of their converts they demanded an upright life; when a brother sinned, he was to be admonished, and if he was in need he should be aided by the brethren; anyone who was unwilling to do this should not request baptism (Wiswedel, II, 50). Their opponents were surprised by the rapid spread of the movement. Unable to understand it, they asserted of some of the preachers that they carried little flasks of a magic potion, which they passed around through the audience to put a spell upon them (see **Hans Hut**; also Wiswedel, II, 178).

Hans Denk, Gregor Maler, and Hans Beck were sent to Basel and Zürich (Röhrich, 33); Ulrich Trechsel and Peter Scheppach to Worms and the Palatinate (Röhrich, 33); Hans Mittermaier, Leonhard Schiemer, and Leonhard Dorfbrunner (Nicoladoni, 107) to Upper Austria; Georg Nespitzer to Franconia (Keller, *Reformation*, 429); Eucharius Binder and Joachim März to Salzburg; and Leonhard Pruckh and Leonhard Spörle to Bavaria. None of these evangelists were able to work long; some were apparently seized in the rising wave of persecution before they reached their assigned field.

As soon as the Augsburg authorities learned of the synod, they took steps toward wiping out the movement. Urban Rhegius, the head of the local Protestant clergy, on Sept. 6, 1527, published a booklet, *Wider den neuen Tauforden*, with an addition, *Notwendige Warnung an alle Christ-gläubigen durch die Diener des Evangeliums in Augsburg*. Already on Aug. 24, 1527, the city council had made arrests and applied torture (Keller, *Reformation*, 428), and used the extorted statements to warn other governments of these messengers; on Sept. 16 they sent a message of this kind to Ulm (Roth, *Reformationsgeschichte* I, 264), and on Sept. 20 to Strasbourg (Röhrich, 32) and Nürnberg (Schornbaum, 39).

By this measure the suppression of Anabaptism in German-speaking regions was given a new impetus; political charges went hand in hand with attacks on their doctrine. Even before the meeting of the synod

35

a number of polemics had been issued against them; Zwingli, Oecolampadius, Bucer, Johannes Eck, Johann Landtsperger, Konrad Schmid, and Johannes Bader had written such booklets. In 1527, following the synod, and in 1528, other polemics were published by Wenzeslaus Linck, Andreas Althamer, Johann Faber, Ortolf Fuchsberger, Thomas Venatorius, and again Urban Rhegius. Melanchthon now also took up the fight against the Anabaptists.

At the same time a new general persecution was inaugurated by the temporal authorities. In the last quarter of 1527 and the first half of 1528 not a month passed without a decree or mandate having been issued (see **Mandates**). The most cruel was the decision of the Swabian League passed at Augsburg on Feb. 22, 1528, authorizing a band of four hundred armed horsemen to hunt the Anabaptists and bring them to headquarters. All who would not recant were burned at the stake without trial, those who did recant were beheaded; women were executed by drowning (Kühn, 1016 and Schornbaum, 117). Two weeks after this decree was passed Joachim Helm, a citizen of Augsburg, wrote: "It is such a misery, that the whole city of Augsburg is saddened. They are daily beheading some, at times four or six, and at times ten persons" (*Archiv für Ref.-Gesch.,* 1916, 154).

The first martyrs among the participants at the synod were Joachim März and Eucharius Binder, both of whom died at the stake in Salzburg on Oct. 27, 1527. Leonhard Spörle was executed on Nov. 12, 1527, at an undesignated place. Hans Hut was suffocated by a fire in his cell at Augsburg, Dec. 6, 1527. Leonhard Dorfbrunner was burned at the stake at Passau in January 1528. Leonhard Schiemer was beheaded on Jan. 14, 1528, at Rattenberg on the Inn, and his corpse burned. Hans Schlaffer was beheaded on Feb. 4, 1528, at Schwaz in Tirol, Eitelhans Langenmantel on March 11, 1528, at Weissenhorn near Ulm, one of the four headquarters of the Swabian League. Thomas Waldhausen was burned on April 10, 1528, at Brno in Moravia; Hans Leupold was beheaded on April 25, 1528, at Augsburg. Hans Mittermaier was executed in 1529 at Linz, and Jakob Widemann in 1535 at Vienna.

Other participants in the synod were victims of the strains of persecution. Hans Denk died of the Plague at Basel in November 1527. Several preachers languished in prison in Augsburg, until, broken in body and soul, they recanted in order to gain their release, as was the case with Jakob Dachser, Sigmund Salminger, and Jakob Gross.

Two other participants in the synod, who were seized several years later in Franconia, recanted in the face of death and were released under oath not to return to the region after making a public confession in church. George Nespitzer renounced his faith in Brandenburg on Aug. 21, 1530. Marx Mayer was arrested at Creglingen near Ansbach in June 1530, and was sentenced to death in accord with a decision of Margrave George (Schornbaum, 189). But the mayor and the council of Ansbach made a protest on Aug. 13, claiming that the decision of the margrave was not valid in this case, since the prisoner could not be charged with sedition (Schornbaum, 191). Mayer recanted and

was released. But he then joined the Puschenhamer (*q.v.*) group, misguided followers of Hans Schmied, who based his doctrines on dreams. Against them the margrave had issued a mandate on June 20, 1531 (Schornbaum, 270 f.). Marx Mayer was beheaded on July 6, 1531, as an adherent of this group, whose teachings were not at all like those of the Anabaptists (see the sentence in Schornbaum, 327-29).

It is worth noticing that in spite of the cruel persecution, no Anabaptist took recourse to violent resistance, nor was there evidence of a planned attack against the government in all the cross-examinations even on the rack. The prophecies concerning the punishment of the persecutors, which Hans Hut at first proclaimed, and which were interpreted as revolt against the temporal government, he soon abandoned (Schornbaum, 188). Nor were they construed as criminal by the authorities when they learned that they were repeated only in the circle of intimate friends (Schornbaum, 191.)

Although several delegates fell from their faith under the severe pressure of persecution, nevertheless the other participants in the synod were faithful shepherds of the congregations entrusted to them. Some of the writings of these martyrs are still unpublished, and are found in various archives: Hans Hut (*Vom Geheimnis der Taufe*), Eitelhans Langenmantel (*Vom Nachtmahl des Herrn*), Hans Schlaffer, (Beck, 64; excerpts in Beck, 651-53 and Wiswedel, II, 191-201), Thomas Waldhausen (Beck, 66 and Keller, *Reformation,* 434), and Leopold Schiemer (Beck, 62; excerpts in Wiswedel, II, 174-86).

Some scholars have doubted that the meeting known as the Martyrs' Synod ever took place, and J. J. Kiwiet goes so far as to call it a fiction of Ludwig Keller. Walter Fellman (*Hans Denck Schriften,* 17 f.) gives probably the best analysis of what actually happened, based on the latest research. Several meetings were held, the chief one on Aug. 24, 1527, in the house of Mathias Finder, a butcher. It was at this meeting that the missioners were delegated. One meeting had been held two or three days before this at the house of Gall Fischer, a weaver, one of the deacons of the Augsburg Anabaptist congregation. In these two meetings both Denk and Hut were present, with about 60 others. A third meeting was held in the house of Konrad Huber, also a deacon of the Augsburg congregation, where Hut was present, but Denk absent. Hut calls this latter meeting a "council." Although none of the sessions was a synod in the formal sense that a body of delegates deliberated and adopted binding resolutions, yet there was a consideration of certain points at issue and at least a sort of agreement, in addition to the appointment of missioners. In this sense the term conference would be justifiable.

Fellman holds that the conference consisted largely of representatives from the areas where Hut had been preaching, i.e., mostly south and east of Augsburg. Denk was not the presiding officer, as Keller supposed. The major theological point at issue was Hut's chiliastic teaching. He had, among other things, prophesied the second coming of Christ to take place in the spring of 1528. The conference decided, with Hut's agreement, to drop certain of the concrete details of the Hut prophecy, but approved the central idea of the return in 1528. Fellman holds that the urge to send out missioners was based on the concept of the near return of Christ and the urgency of strengthening the congregations and inaugurating a vigorous evangelistic campaign before the end. At least some of the decisions of the conference are reported in the "Epistle of Hans Hut," sent with some of the missioners, which has been published by Lydia Müller (*Glaubenszeugnisse*, 12). HEGE, H.S.B.

Beck, *Geschichts-Bücher*; C. A. Cornelius, *Geschichte des Münsterischen Aufruhrs* II (Leipzig, 1860); Chr. Hege, *Pilgram Marbecks Vermahnung*, reprint from *Gedenkschrift zum 400-jährigen Jubiläum der Mennoniten* (1925) 178-282; L. Keller, *Ein Apostel der Wiedertäufer* (Leipzig, 1882); *idem, Reformation; idem, Johann von Staupitz u. die Anfänge der Reformation* (Leipzig, 1888); Joh. Kühn, *Deutsche Reichstagsakten unter Kaiser Karl V.* VII (1935); J. Loserth, "Studien zu Pilgram Marbeck," in *Gedenkschrift zum 400-jährigen Jubiläum der Mennoniten* (1925) 134-78; *idem, Quellen und Forschungen zur Geschichte der oberdeutschen Taufgesinnten im 16. Jahrhundert* (Leipzig, 1929); W. Neuser, *Hans Hut* (Berlin, 1913); A. Nicoladoni, *Johannes Bünderlin von Linz* . . . (Berlin, 1893); T. W. Röhrich, "Zur Gesch. der strassburgischen Wiedertäufer" in *Ztscht für die hist. Theol.*, 1860; Fr. Roth, *Augsburgs Reformationsgeschichte* II (Munich, 1904); *TA Bayern* I; Wiswedel, *Bilder* II; Walter Fellmann, *Hans Denck, Schriften*, Part II, *Religiöse Schriften* (Gütersloh, 1956); J. J. Kiwiet, "Hans Denk and His Teaching" (B.D. dissertation, Baptist Theological Seminary, Rüschlikon, Zürich, 1954); Lydia Müller, *Glaubenszeugnisse oberdeutscher Taufgesinnter* (Leipzig, 1938); *ML* III, 53-56.

Mary, name of many Dutch martyrs, spelled in different ways: Maeyken, Maria, Marie, Marijtgen, Mariken, Maritgen, Marritgen, Marytgen, and Mayken.

Mary Joris, an Anabaptist martyr, who, "removed from her husband and children," was sentenced to death with Joriaen Simons (*q.v.*) and Clement Dirks (*q.v.*), and languished in chains in Haarlem, Holland. Since she was pregnant the execution was postponed until she should be delivered; but she died in prison before it happened (1557). Joriaen, Clement, and Mary are celebrated in a hymn, "Hoort toe ghy Christen scharen" (Hear, ye multitudes of Christians), inserted in *Nieu Liedenboeck* of 1562 (re-edited by Wackernagel), while Mary's name is also found in the hymn "Hoort vrienden al hier in dit aertsche dal" (Hear all ye friends in this earthly dale), hymn No. 20 of the *Lietboecxken van den Offer des Heeren*. According to the *Bibliographie* this martyr was probably the wife of the bookseller Dionys, who was also arrested but escaped from prison, and her name was Mary (Maritgen) Servaes. This surmise is based on S. Ampzing's history of Haarlem; but this book is not very reliable.
NEFF, vDZ.

Offer, 257, note 1, 590; *Mart. Mir.* D 178, E 563, 565; Wackernagel, *Lieder*, 133; Wolkan, *Lieder*, 79; *Doopsgez. Lectuur* 1856, 339; S. Ampzing, *Beschryvinge . . . der Stad Haerlem* (Haarlem, 1628) 449; *Bibliographie* II, 717, No. 397; *ML* II, 435.

Mary-Martha Home, located at 437 Mountain Avenue in Winnipeg, Man., was established in 1925 and is an outgrowth of the Winnipeg city mission of the Mennonite Brethren Northern District Conference. Since 1948 it has, however, been supervised by the Manitoba Provincial Conference of the M.B. Church. At first rooms were rented, but in 1933 a house was purchased providing a home for Mennonite girls working in the city. Anna J. Thiessen was matron of the home 1925-47. Other workers who have assisted are Sarah Warkentin (Mrs. J. Voth), Elizabeth Unruh (Mrs. I. Friesen), Lena Isaak (Mrs. G. Sawatzky), and Tina Friesen. A. B. Peters has for 12 years conducted the preaching services in the home. The purpose of the home is to give spiritual aid to the girls, assist them in finding employment, and to provide for them a home while in the city. Since 1925, 2,200 girls coming from various Mennonite churches have been placed and helped. At present (1949) there are 12 in the home and 117 are on the list who are working in the factories or homes of the city, but are connected with this home. The Dorcas Circle, organized in 1929, arranges for the girls to do handwork for mission or relief and for visiting the sick. Martha Thiessen has been matron since 1947. G.D.H.

Mary Martha Girls' Home (GCM), located in the city of Vancouver, B.C., was founded in 1935 by the General Conference Mennonite Church to gather for spiritual guidance and care the large number of Mennonite girls working in this city. This service is rendered by the pastor of the Mennonite (GCM) Church. An experienced girl serves as matron of the Home. At the beginning, approximately 45 girls made use of the Home but this number soon increased considerably. Then for a period the number decreased greatly until it rose during the new immigration, which started toward the end of the 1940's. On Thursday the Home is full of life, because then the girls working in the private homes have their weekly half-day off. They enjoy social as well as spiritual fellowship, as the pastor then leads in an hour of Bible study, which is always well attended. Sunday is observed in a similar manner, but then the girls share in the worship with other Mennonites in the near-by church (located at 659 East 52nd Avenue). This Home has proved a great blessing for the girls, as well as for the churches as a whole. (See also **Bethel Girls' Home** in Vancouver.) The first superintendent of the Home was J. H. Janzen, 1935-37, with his wife as matron. In 1937-46 J. B. Wiens, the pastor of the Vancouver G.C.M. church, was superintendent, with his wife as matron. In 1945 Tina Lehn became the matron, with the J. B. Wienses as spiritual advisers. J.B.W.

Mary Oth, an Anabaptist martyr, a widow, from Rees in the territory of Cleve, Germany, was drowned on June 11, 1539, at Utrecht, Netherlands, together with nine other women. Particulars are lacking. She may have been a follower of David Joris (*q.v.*). vDZ.

Berigten Historisch Genootschap Utrecht IV, 2 (1851) 139; Mellink, *Wederdopers*, 237.

Maryboro Mennonite Church (MC), now extinct, in Maryboro Twp., Wellington Co., Ont., lying adjacent to Waterloo County on the northwest. Several Mennonite families moved here after the middle of the 19th century. By 1872 the Mennonite Conference

(MC) of Ontario supplied a minister every eight weeks; meetings were held in the home of Jacob Good. Families attending were Dan Geiger, Andrew Thaler, William Beisel, Solomon Sitler, Jacob Shantz, David Eby, Isaac Cressman, Michael Schantz, Isaac Clemmer, Menno Heckendorn, John Heckendorn, and Weavers. By 1891 communion was served annually with appointments at four-week intervals. Ministerial help supplied for neighboring Wallace also served here. Cheaper land attracted the settlers, but interest declined as new congregations arose. By 1903 regularity of appointments ceased as several members returned to Waterloo County.   J.C.F.

Maryboro United Missionary Church was located five miles west of Moorefield, Ont. In September 1949 the Ontario Conference decided to move the church building to the town of Palmerston, Ont. At that time the membership was 14 with H. R. Priddle serving as pastor.   H.R.P.

Maryken (Mariken), an Anabaptist martyr, who (*Mart. Mir.* D 664, E 983) was executed with Hans van Munstdorp and three other martyrs at Antwerp, Belgium, in 1573, is apparently identical with Maeyken Wens (*q.v.*).   vDZ.

Maryland, a state (pop. 2,343,000), one of the original colonies, lies on the southern border of Pennsylvania, extending for almost four fifths of the length of Pennsylvania. The total of almost 2,000 baptized Mennonites in the state belong to the Mennonite Church (MC), including one Conservative Mennonite congregation, except for a small Old Order Amish congregation in St. Mary's County and one in Garrett County, with a total of 171 members. The two old original Mennonite communities in Maryland (Washington County and Garrett County) lie immediately south of the Pennsylvania border and are extensions of the Mennonite communities on the Pennsylvania side.

(1) Washington County, Md., bordering Franklin County, Pa., first received Mennonite settlers of Lancaster County, Pa., background shortly before the Revolutionary War, the oldest congregation (Miller) near Leitersburg, the second (Clear Spring) near Clear Spring in 1810, and the third (Stouffer) near Edgemont in 1820. From these have grown two later congregations (Paradise, 1897; Maugansville Home, 1923) and three mission stations (Pinesburg, 1923; Flintsone, 1925, just across the border in Allegany County, and Pondsville, 1954). These nine congregations, with a total of 831 members, constitute about one half of the Washington County, Md., and Franklin County, Pa., Conference (organized in 1790), which is closely related to the Lancaster Conference and is very conservative in customs, practices, and activities. It has one institution, the Mennonite Old People's Home at Maugansville, Md., founded in 1923. The Brook Lane Farm Mental Hospital, operated by the MCC, is located near Hagerstown, but is not under the conference. In the same county is one congregation, Black Oak Bethel near Hancock, founded in 1953, which belongs to the Ohio and Eastern Conference.

(2) The second original settlement was made in Garrett County as an integral part of the Amish settlement in southern Somerset County, Pa. The Maryland side center of the settlement is Grantsville, which began in a small way about 1770. This area is in the valley of the Casselman River and so has long been called the Casselman Valley district. The original settlement here was Old Order Amish, founded quite early, and largely built up by immigrants from Hesse and Waldeck in 1830-60. Since numerous Amish families from here moved westward to Holmes County, Ohio, and Johnson County, Iowa, before 1860, the community never grew large. Furthermore it ultimately became almost totally Conservative Amish (*q.v.*) or Beachy Amish (*q.v.*), with the exception of those who joined the Mennonite (MC) congregation called Springs, whose meetinghouse is located just two miles across the border in Pennsylvania, and which has been built up largely from transfers from the several Amish groups in the community. This congregation in turn began to establish Mennonite (MC) outposts in Maryland, which by 1900 had resulted in the organization of three congregations, Casselman (first meetinghouse 1889), Oak Grove (first meetinghouse 1900), and Glade near Accident (first meetinghouse 1908). The Conservative meetinghouses at Maple Glen and Cherry Glade were built in 1881. About 60 miles southwest of Grantsville an Old Order Amish settlement was started about 1850 near Gortner, not far from Oakland. By 1898 a Mennonite (MC) congregation had been established here, called Gortner. The last new settlement, formed from the Springs congregation, was that which resulted in the Pinto congregation (1927), about 15 miles south of Cumberland. From Pinto a mission church was established in Cumberland in 1952. Seven other Mennonite (MC) mission points were established in the area around the older churches in northern Garrett County 1935-55. All of these Mennonite congregations and missions in Garrett County and Allegany County belong to the Allegheny Conference (MC). A total of twelve congregations and missions had 417 baptized members here. The Conservative congregation had 230 members, although part of the membership lived across the line in Pennsylvania. A children's home conducted by this congregation and the Conservative Conference for many years was closed in 1950.

In Eastern Maryland in the past 30 years nine mission stations have been established by the Lancaster Conference with a total membership of 178, one at Cottage City (1927), Maryland, at the eastern edge of Washington and one in Baltimore (1952). On the eastern shore of Maryland are two congregations of the Ohio and Eastern Conference, Holly Grove near Westover in Somerset County (1919), and Snow Hill (1953) in Worcester County near the Atlantic Coast, the two having a total membership of 109. A Beachy Amish congregation has recently been established near Chestertown across the Chesapeake from Baltimore, with 30 members. An Old Order Amish settlement was established in St. Mary's County near the James River in 1950. Mennonite and Amish membership in Maryland is distributed as follows: Washington County-Franklin County

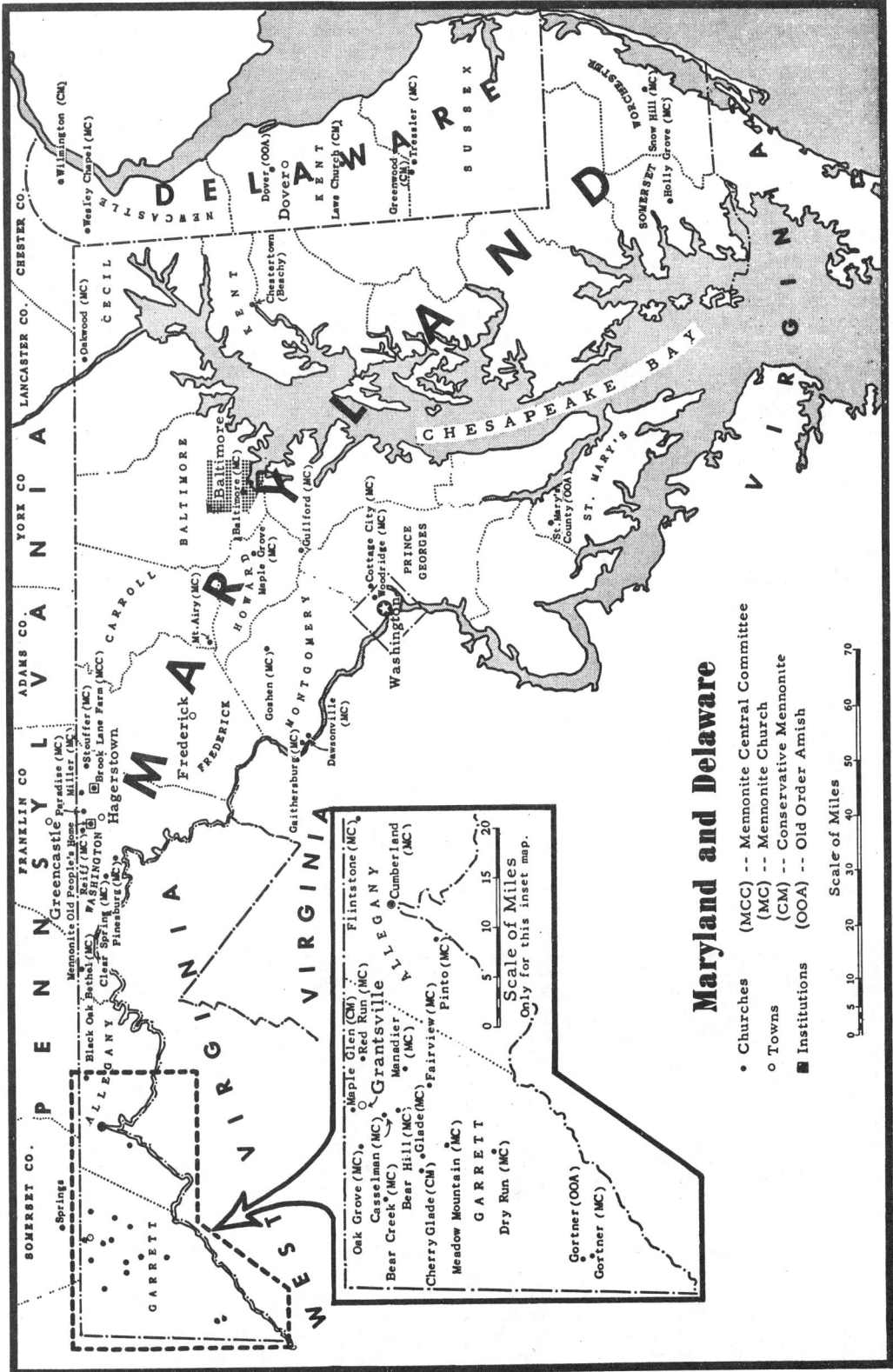

Maryland and Delaware

- Churches   (MCC) -- Mennonite Central Committee
- Towns   (MC) -- Mennonite Church
- Institutions   (CM) -- Conservative Mennonite
              (OOA) -- Old Order Amish

Scale of Miles

0   10   20   30   40   50   60   70

Conference 9 congregations with 831 members, Allegheny Conference 12 with 417, Lancaster Conference 9 with 178, Ohio and Eastern Conference 3 with 159, Conservative Conference one with 230, Beachy Amish one with 30, and Old Order Amish 2 with 71, a total of 37 congregations or missions with 1,916 members.   H.S.B.

Marytge(n) Jan de Gortersdochter (Maritgen Jans), the mother of the Anabaptist leader David Joris (*q.v.*), was arrested at Delft, Dutch province of South Holland, in January 1539 (not 1538 as stated in G. Brandt, *Historie der Reformatie* I, 134). She recanted ("abjuring her rebaptism") and was after some trials beheaded at Delft, shortly before Feb. 26, 1539. (*DB* 1917, 160 ff.; Mellink, *Wederdopers,* 215 f.)   vDZ.

Marytgen Davidsdochter from Leiden, Holland, an Anabaptist martyr, was drowned on June 7, 1539, at Alkmaar, Dutch province of North Holland, with three other martyrs, because she had been (re)baptized. Mellink is of opinion that she was a follower of David Joris (*q.v.*). (*Inv. Arch. Amst.* I, No. 748; *DB* 1909, 8, 22; Mellink, *Wederdopers,* 173, 204.)   vDZ.

Marytje Simons, of Gouda, Dutch province of South Holland, an Anabaptist martyr, was sentenced to death on July 3, 1542, by the Court of Holland and burned at the stake at The Hague that very day or the following, because "she had been rebaptized and calumniated the Holy Catholic Church." (*Inv. Arch. Amst.* I, Nos. 247, 747.)   vDZ.

März (Mertz), **Joachim,** an Anabaptist martyr, a native of Bamberg, Germany, was won to Anabaptist doctrine by Hans Hut (*q.v.*) and baptized by him in a village near Koburg in the summer of 1526 together with Eucharius Binder (*q.v.*). Like Hans Hut he was an Anabaptist missionary, at first in the region of Königsberg in Franconia and the valleys of the tributaries of the Main. In the statements made by the prisoners he was usually named with Hans Hut, and seems to have accompanied him on his journeys. Early in 1527 he was in the region of Bamberg (Wappler, 239), Nürnberg, and Augsburg (Wappler, 245), and later in Passau. From here he went to the Martyrs' Synod in Augsburg with Hans Hut, Eucharius Binder, and Georg Nespitzer (Roth, 232), and there was commissioned to evangelize in the region of Salzburg (Roth, 232 and 234). But their work was of short duration. They were imprisoned in Salzburg with Binder, and burned at the stake on Oct. 25, 1527.   Hege.

A. Nicoladoni, *Johannes Bünderlin von Linz und die Oberösterreichischen Täufergemeinden in den Jahren 1525-1531* (Berlin, 1893); Fr. Roth, *Augsburgs Reformationsgeschichte* I (München, 1901); Wappler, *Thüringen; ML* III, 57.

Maskowitz (Moskowitz, Moskowice; Czech, *Mackovice*), a village near Znaim in southern Moravia, annexed to the Frischau parish. The owner of Frischau, Peter Certorejsky of Certorej, called the Anabaptists into his territory, to settle in four desolate villages. In Frischau they built their first Bruderhof in 1531; this was soon followed by another

at Maskowitz. It had a more difficult lot than most of the Hutterite settlements. Some of its leaders are known. Hans Schlegl died here on Feb. 21, 1587; Walser Hasenfelder on Aug. 9, 1590; Paul Iltzmüller on Feb. 15, 1591, and Leonhard Reuss on Nov. 20, 1591; all of them were preachers.

The quarrel between the son of their patron and the Frischau Hutterite settlement in 1597 soon involved the Maskowitz Brethren as well. The baron, knowing the Brethren to be in his power, did not adhere to the promises made by his father both orally and in writing, and imposed an intolerable amount of robot work on them, so that they were unable to keep up their own work in the Bruderhof and in the fields. Besides this, he roughly mistreated them, knocking out the teeth of one of them. He also confiscated their horses for military service. When the Brethren made gestures of leaving, he promised to improve their conditions, but never kept his promise; indeed, in a period of 21 weeks they had only two days free of robot work. The Brethren finally gathered their possessions to leave; Certorejsky took from them all their goods, causing them a loss of 5,000 florins, and drove them from the Frischau Bruderhof, not sparing the sick or aged. The Maskowitz Bruderhof remained, and in 1598 the baron, aware of the damage he had done himself, recalled the exiled Frischau settlers.

In the war with Bocskay (*q.v.*) a regiment was raised in the region of Znaim; in 1605 Maskowitz suffered 18 weeks of great expense and trouble in consequence. In the following year troops passing through inflicted all sorts of violence on them, and took away their horses. In the spring of 1609 three companies of Hungarian troops lodged in the Maskowitz Bruderhof for two days and nights, followed by two more companies, causing much trouble and consuming great amounts of goods.

The chronicles of the Hutterites record that in the spring of 1608 Berka instigated an attempt to convert them by force. Two companies of horsemen surrounded the Bruderhof for two hours awaiting word from Brno; they withdrew in haste when word reached them of Berka's defeat there. In 1611 new troops were raised, again injuring Maskowitz as well as other Bruderhofs. Nevertheless Christian Steiner, having served as preacher for over 30 years, died in peace on Nov. 5 of that year.

In the Moravian rebellion at the beginning of the Thirty Years' War the Maskowitz household suffered indescribable hardship. On July 22, 1619, it was plundered by Dampierre's troops; "By Oct. 15 it had been attacked 30 times and robbed of anything that could be found; in addition to much other movable property, much grain, flour, several barrels of wine, four horses, twelve oxen, and an entire herd of hogs; they also seized two brethren, tortured them, cut off the ear of one, in order to extort information about money and other things." A list of martyrs states that in 1619 Peter Klein, an old man, was cut down and Konrad Spör was shot down. The next year brought more oppression. On March 24 imperial troops fell upon Maskowitz at three in the morning, plundered everything, drove away the cattle and stock, and finally set fire to the house. Scarcely had the house been rebuilt, when new troops came. Most of the Maskowitz brethren did not await them, but in the second half of December 1621 fled into the region of Pausram, Austerlitz, and Nikolsburg; a part of them returned and met misfortune; on Jan. 6, 1622, imperial troops of Walloons, French, Spaniards, Neapolitans, Kroats, and a Fugger band from Swabia broke in. They stripped the inmates of their clothing, and drove them, some of them stark naked, out into the wintry cold. Several Brethren were senselessly tortured to make them reveal their hidden money. "With the sisters that they seized they dealt horribly." The Fugger band was guilty of the worst behavior in these days. Finally a French commander restored order to the extent that the brethren could again venture out to cook and bake. The soldiers took all their horses. On April 22 another band attacked them. The horsemen of Löbl, who had received heavy contributions from the brotherhoods at Kromau and Eibenschitz, now plundered Maskowitz, hauling away 18 loads of goods. In an attempt to come by the reputed wealth of the brethren, a vain attempt was made to lure the Maskowitz elder, Michel Kocher, to Nikolsburg.

After the issuance of the mandate of Sept. 28, 1622, Cardinal Franz von Dietrichstein (*q.v.*) personally directed the expulsion of the Hutterites from Maskowitz. They had to leave "with empty hands," leaving all their cattle, grain, and larger pieces of equipment. They managed to take away secretly very little, with some help from the soldiers. Most of the people of the two Bruderhofs of Maskowitz and Olekowitz, led by the preachers Michel Kocher, Thoman Wilhelm, and Albrecht Grob, "in very bad weather" moved to their brethren in Transylvania (*q.v.*). (Beck, *Geschichts-Bücher;* Wolkan, *Geschicht-Buch;* Zieglschmid, *Chronik; ML* III, 57 f.)

P.DE.

Masontown Mennonite Church (MC), located one mile east of Masontown, Fayette Co., Pa., a member of the Allegheny Conference, is perhaps the oldest organized Mennonite congregation west of the Allegheny Mountains. Mennonites settled in the region about Masontown around 1790. Jacob Newcomer was the first minister of this group. Peter Longeneker, formerly of Berks Co., Pa., was the first resident bishop. This congregation was under the supervision of the Lancaster Co., Pa., bishops some time before the Southwestern Pennsylvania (now Allegheny) Conference was organized in 1876. J. N. Durr (*q.v.*), who was largely responsible for the organization of the conference, was ordained to the ministry here at the early age of 18 in 1872 and to the office of bishop at the age of 20. Nicholas Johnson, the third bishop, is given the credit for conducting the first Sunday school in the Mennonite Church (MC) in the United States. This service was held on the upper floor of a springhouse on his farm in 1842. The present brick meetinghouse, the third one built, was erected in 1871, with a seating capacity of 200. The first was a log church, a half mile north of the present site, which was also used for school purposes. The second meetinghouse was a frame building about one mile east. The membership in 1956 was 138, with Paul M. Roth as pastor.

Other ministers who served this congregation were Walter Campbell, A. J. Metzler (present bishop), Lloy A. Kniss, Elmer D. Hess, J. A. Brilhart, Ed. Miller, S. F. Coffman, Christian Deffenbaugh, David Johnson, and Joseph Bixler.

P.M.R.

Masonville (Pa.) Mennonite Church (MC), Manor Twp., Lancaster Co., Pa., is one of the older Lancaster Conference congregations. A meetinghouse was built here in 1760, long known as Bachman's because it was built on land donated by Christian Baughman. In 1893 a new brick meetinghouse was erected on near-by land and the name changed to Masonville. Christian Kauffman (1765-1840) was one of the first bishops in the immediate area. The congregation was a part of the Manor circuit. In 1954 Christian K. Lehman was bishop with Benjamin Miller as preacher. The membership was 162. Slackwater, formerly an outpost of Masonville, is now an independent congregation with 26 members and Frank K. Garman as pastor.

I.D.L.

Mast (Mest, Maust, Moist), an Amish Mennonite family, was planted first in Berks-Lancaster counties, Pa., during the colonial period by immigration from Switzerland or the Palatinate, Germany, and by the first quarter of the 19th century six lines were established, with a large offspring at the present time. Three of these lines are quite numerous in Mennonite circles throughout the United States. Jacob Mast (arrived in 1737), Jacob Mast (arrived in 1750), and Abraham Mast with two brothers, Jacob and Christian, arrived here in America after the colonial period, which had closed in 1776, when it was no longer required for all male persons above 15 years of age to be marched from the ship to the courthouse to sign their allegiance to the King of Great Britain.

Among the outstanding representatives of the family have been the following: bishops (MC) Jacob Mast (1738-1808), John P. Mast (1826-88), Frederick Mast (1856-1932), John S. Mast (1861-1951), Emanuel A. Mast (1856-1932), Isaac S. Mast (1874-1955), Daniel E. Mast (*q.v.,* 1848-1930, OOA). Russel Mast is a pastor (GCM) at Freeman, S.D., John L. Mast (MC) a minister at Belleville, Pa., and Aaron Mast (MC) a bishop of the Belleville congregation. Fifteen others, mostly Old Order Amish, were serving as bishops and ministers in 1954. Among those using the spelling Maust were bishop Sherman (Upland, Cal., M.C.) and preacher Earl J. (C.A.M.) of Pigeon, Mich.

C.Z.M.

C. Z. Mast, *A Brief History of Bishop Jacob Mast and Other Mast Pioneers, and a Complete Genealogical Family Register* (Elverson, Pa., 1911); Henry J. Otto, *Decendants of Jacob D. Mast from the Year 1832 to 1952* (Nappanee, 1952); Moses C. Mast, *Mast History of Eli D. Mast and Rebecca (Miller) Mast and Their Descendants* (Cadwell, Ill., 1952).

Mast, Andrew J., was born in Holmes Co., Ohio, June 10, 1873. Because of his father's early death he was reared in the home of his uncle, Andrew Mast, who was an Amish minister. About 1894 he went to Arthur, Ill., and then to Gibson, Miss., where a small Amish colony was just being started. There he was married on Oct. 26, 1896; on Oct. 24, 1897, he was ordained to the ministry and on

June 4, 1899, bishop of the colony. Five years later he with his family moved to Arthur, Ill., where he served as bishop until his death on March 17, 1949. He was an outstanding and very influential Old Order Amish leader.   L.A.M.

Mast, Daniel E., an Old Order Amish leader, was born in Holmes Co., Ohio, on Oct. 16, 1848, and died at his home near Hutchinson, Kan., on Sept. 29, 1930. He was baptized into the Old Order Amish Church in Holmes County in 1867. In November 1870 he was married to Catherine Miller, who died 16 years later. A few months later, in April 1886, a widower with eight children, he moved to the vicinity of Hutchinson. In October 1888 he married as his second wife Elizabeth Stutzman, who died in a little over five years. As his third wife he married Elizabeth Kauffman of Oregon, who died 25 years later. He then married Barbara Helmuth, who preceded him in death by six months. He was the father of 16 children.

Mast was ordained deacon in 1891 and minister in 1914. In his early married life he tried to arouse an interest in the Amish churches in Holmes County to start Sunday schools, but sentiment was too strong against them. Later in Kansas he took an active interest in the Sunday school as long as health permitted. He was very influential in his church as deacon and minister.

During the time of his ministry he visited nearly all the Old Order Amish churches in North America, his main themes being "Salvation Through Christ," and the "New Birth Through the Holy Spirit." Nearly all his conversations in visiting were spiritual, often getting a spiritual conversation started before the team was fully unhitched. When the *Herold der Wahrheit* (q.v.) was started in 1912 he took an active interest in writing and took advantage of the opportunity to spread out among the churches his deep knowledge of the Word of God; he had written many articles ahead at the time of his death. Most of his writings are printed in a 784-page book, *Anweisung zur Seligkeit* (Baltic, Ohio, n.d., ca. 1930). A selection was printed in English in *Lessons in the Sermon on the Mount* (Weatherford, Okla., 1953).   L.A.M.

Mast, Jacob (1738-1808), was born in Switzerland. He migrated to America an orphan boy in company with his four sisters and younger brother John. All were in the care of their uncle Johannes Mast and landed in Philadelphia, Pa., on Nov. 3, 1750. Their first abode in the new world was in the vicinity of Hamburg, Berks Co., Pa., where the Amish had founded their first organized congregation in America by 1749. In that year Bishop Jacob Hertzler arrived from Switzerland and became their first leader. During 1754-64, "the years of bloodshed" in Berks County, when the Indians returned to reclaim the land, the Masts were driven from their home in 1760, and found refuge at the headwaters of the Conestoga, where Jacob Mast in 1764 took out a warrant for land comprising 170 acres for 325 pounds, situated in Caernarvon Twp., Berks Co., Pa.

Jacob Mast was married at the age of 25 to Magdalene Holly, who had accompanied him on his voyage to America. To this union were born 12 children, all of whom married and had offspring. In 1786 he succeeded Jacob Hertzler as bishop, the second Amish bishop in America and the first ordained here. He was one of the charter members of the present Conestoga Mennonite (MC) Church near Morgantown, which became the first permanent Amish Mennonite church in America. His manuscripts indicate a fair education for the times. The record of his public sale of personal property shows that he owned a goodly number of books.

As bishop, Mast presided over the following congregations in Berks County: Northkill, Maiden Creek, Tulpehocken, and Conestoga; in Chester County, one congregation Goshen, where a meetinghouse had been built near Malvern; the earliest in Lancaster County was in the vicinity of Compassville, and White Horse; these were also under his oversight. He died in 1808 and was buried on his farm.   C.Z.M.

C. Z. Mast, *A Brief History of Bishop Jacob Mast and Other Mast Pioneers, and a Complete Genealogical Family Register* (Elverson, Pa., 1911).

Mast, John P. (1826-88), was born near Elverson, Pa., and was a lifelong resident of Caernarvon Twp., Berks Co., Pa. He was a great-grandson of Bishop Jacob Mast (q.v.) and was himself an able and faithful leader in the same district where his great-grandfather had served for 22 years. As a preacher he was practical and eloquent. He drew his lessons from everyday life and had a wide acquaintance in Amish Mennonite circles in both the United States and Canada. He was married to Anna Zook, but had no children. He was ordained to the ministry in his thirties by a unanimous vote from his congregation. He died June 11, 1888. His name was for many years a household word throughout his community.   C.Z.M.

Mast, John S. (1861-1951), a leader in the Amish Mennonite (MC) church in Lancaster-Berks Co., Pa., b. Nov. 30, 1861, in Caernarvon Twp., Berks Co., Pa., d. Jan. 3, 1951, on his home farm. He was a son of John M. Mast and Rebecca Stoltzfus. His early years were spent on his father's farm and in the community. At the age of 17 he attended Miss Bertolet's private school in Morgantown. He was married in 1885 to Christiana Zook. To this union three children were born, two of whom died in infancy. Christian Z. Mast, the historian of the Conestoga Valley, was a surviving son. On May 6, 1894, Mast was ordained to the ministry. He rendered over fifty years of active service in the pulpit and was an active participant in the work of the Ohio-Eastern A.M. Joint Conference. In the early 1900's he began a wide ministry as a speaker in Bible conferences. He was elected to the office of bishop by vote of his congregation and ordained in 1908. The following churches were in his charge: Conestoga at Morgantown, Pa., Millwood and Maple Grove at Gap and Atglen, Pa.; Long Green, Md.; Westover, Md.; and Mattawana, Pa. His ability to speak in both German and English took him as an evangelist into different parts of the United States and Canada.   C.Z.M.

Mastenbroek, Fenna (1787-1826), of Sneek, a daughter of Pieter Mastenbroek and Janneke ten Cate, was the Mennonite author of many books and articles in periodicals, now all forgotten, which in the 19th century were very popular. She wrote particularly for women; among her books are *Lectuur voor vrouwen* (2 vols., Groningen, 1815-16), *Zedelijke verhalen uit den Bijbel, voor vrouwen en meisjes* (2 vols., Sneek, 1822), and *De kunst om gelukkig te worden. Een geschenk voor jeugdigen* (The Hague, 1826).

A Mennonite Mastenbroek family, not related to that of Sneek, is found in Ouddorp. (Blaupot t. C., *Friesland,* 239; *N.N.B.Wb.* III, 825 f., *DB* 1890, 116.)
vDZ.

Masuria (Mazuria, Mazury, Masuren), now Olsztyn, Poland, a lake area in the southeastern part of the former German province of East Prussia, one of the territories early settled by Anabaptist refugees from Holland. The little extant information indicates that they settled primarily in the vicinity of Johannisburg about 1535, but were soon compelled to leave their homes there. HEGE.

G. Sommerfeld, "Die Beziehungen Georgs des Frommen, Markgrafen von Ansbach, zu seinem Bruder, Herzog Albrecht I. von Preussen," in *Ztscht für Kirchengesch.,* 1911, 105; *ML* III, 58.

Matheeux Maurisz (Mattheeuw Marinissen), an Anabaptist martyr, burned at the stake on March 13, 1572, at Middelburg, Dutch province of Zeeland. (*DB* 1908, 17, erroneously gives 1569 as the year of execution.) Matheeux and his wife Magdalene Jansdochter lived at Middelburg, outside the Langevyle gate of the city. Matheeux, 43 or 44 years of age, had been (re)baptized about 1559. Both he and his wife, who suffered martyrdom on the same day, are said "to belong to the sect of the Mennonites." vDZ.

W. te Water, *Kort Verhaal der Reformatie van Zeeland* (Middelburg, 1766) 148; *ML* III, 61.

Mathesius, Johannes (1504-65), a Lutheran theologian, pastor of the miners at Joachimsthal in northern Bohemia from 1545 until his death. He was one of the most zealous literary opponents of Anabaptism in the second half of the 16th century. Approximately 1500 of his sermons have been handed down in manuscript, among them 17 sermons on Luther's life. These sermons were delivered in 1562-64, and represent one of the first biographies of Luther. However, because of the intermittent nature of his connections with Luther, not all of the material on the reformer was derived from personal experience as was formerly generally assumed, or from his notes on Luther's table talks (*Tischreden,* delivered in the summer and fall of 1540). Rather he adapted to his records numerous transcripts from other manuscripts and "changed not only the text but also the content of Luther's speeches; indeed on occasion he even perverted them to a contrary meaning" (Volz, 148).

In these sermons on Luther he also enlarged in a derogatory way on the Anabaptists, whose suffering he had observed in 1526-27 as private tutor at the Odelzhausen castle between Augsburg and Dachau on the Glon River in Bavaria, and also in 1528-29 with Zacharia Weixner, a pastor in Bruck on the Amper. He labeled their doctrine as "Turkish and devilish madness" and their ministers as "apostles of the devil. It is as if the devil has stirred up an ungodly and seditious rabble." These characterizations indicate his manner of fighting. He did not bother to gather evidence for his defamations. In addition he charged the most prominent Anabaptist leaders, Balthasar Hubmaier and Hans Denk, with teaching revolt and horrible unchastity. Other preachers he accused of monkish hypocrisy and witchcraft, through which they deluded the common man, as he had seen in numerous examples on the Lech and on the Glon. There the rabble allowed themselves to be rebaptized and "drowned in droves." He gives the knowledge and abilities of the Anabaptists no mean testimonial, when he says, "The bishops and their scholars, and those who hold to Antichrist, were much too weak and unlearned to refute the Anabaptists with definite Scripture and show the people the right way."

On the historiography (*q.v.*) of the Anabaptists Mathesius exerted a malicious influence through his false assertions, since his writings on Luther were widely circulated. His representation was copied uncritically by later historians (see **Anabaptisticum**) and for centuries greatly injured the reputation of the Mennonites. Not until recent research was developed could his unfounded accusations be refuted. HEGE.

G. Loesche, *Johannes Mathesius, Ausgewählte Werke* III; *Luthers Leben in Predigten* (2d ed., Prague, 1906); H. Volz, *Die Lutherpredigten des Johannes Mathesius* (Leipzig, 1930); *ML* III, 58 f.

Matheus Sauvaige, an Anabaptist martyr, was burned at the stake on March 3, 1535, at the market place of Antwerp, Belgium. He was a gunsmith, born at Loreynen (?). Other particulars are lacking. (*Antw. Arch.-Blad* VII, 318; XIV, 12 f., No. 135.)
vDZ.

Mathijs Baseliers, an Anabaptist martyr, burned at the stake with three others on May 20, 1573, at Antwerp, Belgium, because he had been (re)baptized, had attended forbidden meetings (of the Mennonites) and had held such meetings in his house. (*Antw. Arch.-Blad* XIII, 113, 115, 176; XIV, 90 f., No. 1024.)
vDZ.

Mathis (Mathies, Matthiesen, Mattis, Matis), a Mennonite family of Dutch descent, found in West Prussia, Germany. In the Danzig-Neugarten congregation (Frisian) the name is found from 1680. They were especially found in the Heubuden (*q.v.*) congregation. Jakob Mathis was a preacher of the Heubuden Old Flemish congregation 1745-62 and Peter Mathies 1757-65. In 1796 and following years some of them moved from West Prussia to Russia.
vDZ.

Reimer, *Familiennamen; Naamlijst;* B. H. Unruh, *Die niederländisch-niederdeutschen Hintergründe der mennonitischen Ostwanderungen* (Karlsruhe, 1955) *passim,* see Index.

Mathisz (Matthysz), **Hughe:** see **Mattheissen, Hugo.**

Mathys van Castele, an unknown Anabaptist martyr, who was beheaded at Antwerp, Belgium, in

1535 (exact date unknown). (*Antw. Arch.-Blad* VII, 367; XIV, 14 f., No. 146.)   vDZ.

Matrei, a village in Tirol, Austria, between Innsbruck and the Brenner Pass, where the Anabaptist movement found many adherents in the 16th century. Many of them emigrated to Moravia. In 1544 two persons who knew the plan of an Anabaptist family to migrate but did not reveal it were fined 50 florins. Others were called to account for sheltering and feeding Anabaptists. A considerable emigration to Moravia took place in 1560 (see **Hans Mändl**).   HEGE.

G. Loesche, *Archivalische Beiträge zur Gesch. des Täufertums und des Protestantismus in Tirol* (Vienna, 1926) 30; *ML* III, 59.

Mats, a Mennonite family found in Westzaan and Zaandam, Dutch province of North Holland. Arian Cornelisz Volger (1) of Akersloot in North Holland, who died in 1609, is said to have belonged to the Catholic Church; while he was still a young man, he went to Alkmaar to buy a vest, and came back with a Bible; soon after, he joined the Mennonites. His son Jan Ariansz Volger (2) settled at Westzaan and changed his family name to Mats (the reason is not known). Aerjan Jansz Mats (3), the son of (2), became a preacher of the Frisian Mennonite congregation of Westzaan and Zaandam until 1667. His son Klaes Aerjansz Mats (4), d. 1694, was a preacher of the "Oude Huys" (Frisian) congregation of Westzaandam and Westzaan 1681-*ca.* 94. Other members of this family were deacons of the Mennonite congregations of Zaandam and Westzaan until the 20th century.

Most members of this family were wood dealers and shipowners. In the early 18th century they moved from Westzaan to Zaandam and greatly contributed to the prosperity of this town. Gradually the Mats family, which by marriage was related to many well-known families of Zaandam and the Zaanstreek (Zaan district) like Schoen, Duyvis, van Gelder, Ouwejan, Rogge, Corver, and van de Stadt, came to great wealth. So for example Jacob Dirksz Mats (about 1716-53), a grandson of Klaes Aerjansz (4), equipped a fleet of seven sailing vessels ("Groenland-vaarders") for whaling near Greenland. vDZ.

S. Lootsma, *Het Nieuwe Huys* (Zaandam, 1937) 189-200; J. M. van Gelder, *Stamboek der familie van Gelder* (Amsterdam, 1899) 193 ff.

Matschidl, Michael (*Kleinmichel*), a Hutterite chosen as deacon in 1539, and as preacher in 1542, was captured at Ortenburg in Carinthia, Austria, with his wife Lisel and Hans Gurtzham (*q.v.*). After a cross-examination, in which they acquitted themselves with credit, they were taken to Vienna. Here they were put into a prison with Hans Staudacher (*q.v.*), to the great joy of both. After Staudacher's execution, concerning which Matschidl wrote a letter on Dec. 5, 1546, in Moravia, he and Gurtzham remained in prison three years. Then a fire broke out, and the prisoners were freed. Matschidl and his wife reached Moravia uninjured, and he died there in 1553 at Altenmarkt. He wrote several epistles, which are preserved in Pressburg. NEFF.

Mart. Mir. D 73, E 474; **Beck,** *Geschichts-Bücher,* 167 f.; Wolkan, *Geschicht-Buch,* 205 f., 259; Zieglschmid, *Chronik,* 267 f.; *ML* III, 59.

Matschilder, Michiel: see **Matschidl, Michael.**

Matsqui (B.C.) Mennonite Brethren Church, a member of the Canadian Conference since 1945, when it was organized with 71 charter members who had settled at Matsqui. The leader and minister was A. D. Rempel. A building was remodeled into a church; in 1947-49 the congregation met in the basement of a new church. Together with three neighbor congregations it maintains a Bible school and a private high school. The disastrous flood of May 1948 covered the homes of the members and also caused the death of one church member, Cornelius Isaaks. In 1954 the membership was 185, with G. A. Konrad and Johann F. Klassen as ministers in charge.   G.A.K.

Mattawana Mennonite Church (MC), near Mattawana, Pa., a member of the Ohio and Eastern Conference, was formerly called the River Church. Amish families, Hooleys and Yoders, from Lancaster and Berks counties, Pa., settled along the Juniata River near Lewistown as early as 1793. When the congregation was organized is not known, but in 1818 the ministers were Christ King and Christ Yoder, and Daniel Stutzman was deacon. In 1840-68 there were no resident ministers, the church being served by ministers from Kishacoquillas Valley. Outstanding personalities in the history of this church were Michael Yoder (1831-1923), ordained to the ministry in 1868 and bishop in 1885, and Shem Zook (*q.v.,* 1798-1880), an author, publisher, and educator. The first meetinghouse was built in 1871, at which time the congregation affiliated itself with the Eastern Amish Mennonite Conference. The congregation has remained small. Other resident ministers were John S. Yoder, John E. Kauffman (bishop), Samuel K. Yoder, Harry E. Kauffman, and Milo M. Yoder. In 1954 the membership was 127, under the ministry of Samuel Kauffman bishop, and Ross Metzler and M. M. Yoder ministers.   J.A.H.

Mattheissen (Matheisen, Mathysen, Mathisz), **Hugo,** a Dutchman, who in 1562 leased from the city of Danzig, West Prussia (then Poland), a large tract of swampland in the Danzig Nehrung to reclaim and cultivate it. Probably he was a "locator," i.e., he leased the land to rent it out to immigrants, who usually were Dutch Mennonites. His name (Hugo Matthias) is found in a letter of 1569 written to the city of Danzig by King Sigismund of Poland. About 1550 he was a preacher of the Danzig Anabaptist congregation. This was stated by Jan van Sol (*q.v.*) in his confession before the judges of Brussels in 1550. He related that Hughe Matthyszoon had formerly been a weaver at The Hague, Holland, and had preached at Amsterdam and 's Hertogenbosch, and that he had been a copperplate engraver and during his first years in Prussia a peddler.   vDZ.

F. Szper, *Nederl. Nederzettingen in West-Pruisen* (Enkhuizen, 1913) 45 f., 50, 236 f.; *DB* 1917, 135; Horst

Penner, *Ansiedlung mennonitischer Niederländer im Weichselmündungsgebiet* (Weierhof, 1940) 5; *MQR* XXIII (October 1949) 235; *Gesch.-Bl.* VII (1950) 22.

Mattheus Bernaerts (Mattheus or Matthijs van Linken), an Anabaptist martyr, was burned at the stake at Gent, Belgium, on Dec. 4, 1572, with three other martyrs. Mattheus was 40 years of age and a native of Meenen in Flanders. He had been baptized by Elder Leenaert Bouwens and was "a minister of the church of God, in the Word of the Holy Gospel, and also in the deaconship to provide for poor needy members of Christ" at Gent. Mattheus and his three companions died faithful. He left a will to his three small children, in which he makes a beautiful, Biblical confession of his faith, and admonishes them to abstain from the evil works of the world and to lead an honorable godly life. "O my dear children," he concludes, "neglect not to thank your Lord and God before eating and drinking; and when you lie down to sleep and when you arise, upon your knees, with folded hands, entreat Him for His grace." He added two short prayers, one to be used before and the other after meals; these are excellent models. (*Mart. Mir.* D 619-23, E 947-51; Verheyden, *Gent*, 59, No. 207; *ML* I, 196.) NEFF, VDZ.

Mattheus Jacobszoon: see Jacobsz, Mattheus.

Mattheus Keuse (Kuese), an Anabaptist martyr, b. at Roesselare, Flanders, a tailor 31 years of age. In 1567 he left the town of Gent in Belgium because of fear of persecution, since his child had not been baptized. After a stay in the Netherlands, leaving his family behind at Dordrecht, he returned to Flanders, but on his way to Gent he was apprehended at Brugge. Here, remaining loyal to his Lord, he was burned at the stake on Aug. 7, 1573 (not 1574 as is stated in *Mart. Mir.*). (*Mart. Mir.* D 676, E 992; Verheyden, *Brugge*, 62, No. 69.) VDZ.

Mattheus Pottebacker (Mattheus de Smidt or Smet), an Anabaptist martyr, beheaded with two other martyrs on Nov. 9 (or 4), 1559, in the Steen castle at Antwerp, Belgium. Mattheus had been (re)baptized by Gillis van Aken (*q.v.*). His name is found in the hymn "Aenhoort Godt, hemelsche Vader" (Hear, O God, heavenly Father), found in the Dutch hymnals *Nieu Liedenboeck* of 1562 and *Lietboecxken van den Offer des Heeren* (No. 16) of 1563. VDZ.

Offer, 567; *Mart. Mir.* D 262, E 633; *Antw. Arch.-Blad* IX, 5, 10; XIV, 26 f., No. 302; Wolkan, *Lieder*, 63, 72; *ML* III, 385.

Mattheus de Smidt, an Anabaptist martyr: see Mattheus Pottebacker.

Mattheus de Vik (Mattheeuws de Vick, de Vicht, de Vecht), an Anabaptist martyr, arrested with Christiaen Langedul, Cornelis Claesz, and Hans Symonsz on Sunday morning, Aug, 10, 1567, at Antwerp, Belgium, while attending a meeting. After imprisonment and torture they were sentenced to death at Antwerp on Sept. 13, 1567. At the place of execution they addressed the bystanders and Mattheus said: "Citizens, that we suffer here, is for the truth, and because we live according to the

Word of God." Thereupon his words were drowned out by the roll of soldiers' drums, and the victims bound together two by two, after having been strangled by the executioner, were burned in their little huts of straw, thus giving a striking testimony of their faith. VDZ.

Mart. Mir. D 345, E 704; *Antw. Arch.-Blad* IX, 460, 462; X, 66; XIV, 46 f., No. 524.

Mattheus Wens was a Mennonite of Antwerp, Belgium, a mason by trade and a deacon of the congregation. His wife Maeyken Wèns (*q.v.*) was apprehended and put to death at Antwerp on Oct. 6, 1573. While she was in prison Mattheus wrote her a letter, and Maeyken wrote her reply on the back of the same sheet and returned the letter. This letter, a unique martyrs' document and the only extant autographic letter of a martyr, is now in the Amsterdam Mennonite Archives. Maeyken's letter is found in van Braght's *Martyrs' Mirror*; that of her husband was published by S. Cramer in *DB* 1904, 119 f. VDZ.

Matthias (1557-1619), Emperor of the Holy Roman Empire, the son of the only Hapsburg leaning toward Protestantism, Maximilian II, educated as a Catholic and devoted to the church. In 1593 he was appointed governor of Austria by his brother Rudolf II. In this capacity he requested his councilors on July 5, 1600, to work out an opinion on how to expel the Anabaptists who managed mills, estates, and dairy farms in the country. The answer given on July 17 pointed out how seriously "food was taken from the Christian population" by the competition. They noted that "they had often advised how to rid the land of this kind of sectarian people and offensive intentional enemy of the Christian religion," and recommended absolute eradication (copies of these documents are in the national archives in Vienna). Thereupon Matthias induced Rudolf to issue the mandate of March 23, 1601, for Lower and Upper Austria. He argued that his brother had reported to him that in both regions there were Anabaptists who were injuring native industry by illegally engaging in crafts; besides, it was not known what they did with the money thus acquired. He therefore gave orders to expel all Anabaptists immediately, making use of the police if necessary. Landowners who continued to employ Anabaptists should be fined 500 ducats (copy in the *Patentsammlung des Haus-, Hof- und Staatsarchivs* in Vienna).

When Matthias, at the request of Rudolf, supported the Counter Reformation in Hungary, the rebellion headed by Bocskay (*q.v.*) broke out, which caused severe damage to the Hutterite Bruderhofs situated in Slovakia, especially those in Lewär, as well as several in Moravian territory, where the troops were mustered (see **Maskowitz**). The treaty of peace concluded between Bocskay and Matthias on June 23, 1606, put an end to these oppressions.

The quarrel between the Hapsburg brothers soon involved the Moravian Hutterites in renewed suffering. In order to assume the government assigned to him by the archdukes and to depose his brother, who was sinking into insanity, Matthias drew up an army, which was joined by Hungarian troops, and he frequently quartered them on the Hutterian Bruderhofs. Also the troops acquired in Moravia liked to lodge in the Bruderhofs. The treaty of June 24, 1608, ceded to Matthias the government of Hungary, Austria, and Moravia; on Nov. 16 the Pressburg Reichstag elected him king of Hungary. In the following year Matthias again turned his attention to the Anabaptists, who had been taken back by the barons of Lower Austria. He asked the authorities to report on what had previously been done about them and especially what had been done to those coming from Germany (copy in the national archives for Lower Austria in Vienna).

The Passau attack on Bohemia was followed by the mustering of new troops in Moravia, causing the Bruderhofs of Maskowitz, Stiegnitz, Olekowitz, and Niembschitz considerable hardship. Matthias marched to Bohemia, from which archduke Leopold had to retreat with his Passau troops, and was crowned as king of Bohemia on May 23. On June 13, 1612, Rudolf died, and Matthias was elected as emperor at Frankfurt.

The Moravian diet decided on Aug. 15, 1612, to assess each of the Hutterite Bruderhofs 100 florins (*Pamatkenbuch* in the Moravian national archives in Brno). Matthias had been represented at this diet by his younger brother Maximilian, who had a clock made by the Priebitz Bruderhof, which was famed for its clocks. In September 1613 Johann Dionysius von Zierotin, the negotiator, informed the archduke that his clock was finished, and would cost 170 florins, because the Brethren had made an identical clock for Cardinal Dietrichstein for that price. (Copy in the Zierotin archives in Blauda.)

It is reported that the emperor ordered the Dominican prior Stallhofer to expel the Hutterites from Zierotitz and Gaiwitz, and that this was done (from a manuscript in the Moravian archives in Brno). Beyond this incident the Brethren had peace during the remainder of Matthias' reign. In Slovakia they even rebuilt their Bruderhofs in Sobotiste and Protzka. On Aug. 18, 1618, the diet at Brno in the presence of archduke Ferdinand decided to assess the Moravian Bruderhofs a war tax of 50 florins in addition to the current 100 florins. Not long after, Matthias died, and the destruction of the Moravian Hutterite settlements set in.   P.DE.

A. Gundely, *Rudolf II. und seine Zeit* (1862-65); F. Krones, *Handbuch der Geschichte Oesterreichs* . . . (1878 f.); Beck, *Geschichts-Bücher*; Wolkan, *Geschicht-Buch*; Zieglschmid, *Chronik*; M. Uhlirz, *Handbuch der Geschichte Oesterreichs* (1927-30); ML III, 59 f.

Matthias van Balck (Matthias Belkensis): see **Matthijs van Balk.**

Matthias Servaes von Ottenheim (Kottenem, Kottenheim), an Anabaptist martyr, was born in 1536 in the district of Mayen, near Coblence, Germany. He was a linen weaver. His wife, Aeltgen (Adelheid) van Tongeren (in the bishopric of Liége), apparently did not understand German, for in one of his letters Matthias asked for a Dutch New Testament for her. Servaes was baptized at Andernach, Germany, and lived for a time at Brohl. His simple manner won him the respect and affection of his fellow believers. He was ordained a preacher of the Anabaptists by Zelis from the Eifel, an itinerant Anabaptist preacher, who courageously cared for his brotherhood in the time of persecution. He was distinguished by his natural eloquence and noble character. Preaching and baptizing he traveled with Heinrich von Krufft, a Jülich Anabaptist, through the regions of the lower Rhine. "Heinrich Krufft and Servaes are the chief preachers who are accustomed to teach their people and baptize around Gladbach, Dülken, Süchteln and the vicinity in many villages. He could not tell where Krufft lived, for Krufft does not stay long at a place. Meetings were held between Gladbach and Viersen in a stone quarry," we read in the confession of Thies von Dülken.

In 1565 Servaes was in Cologne to minister to the sorely tried church there. In the midst of severest persecution the Cologne Anabaptists had continued their meetings. But one evening their place of meeting was betrayed and all attending were captured. There were about 56 persons, Servaes among them. They were taken to the Bayen tower, where their names were recorded. When they were asked who their preacher was Martin Servaes freely acknowledged his calling. The trial was directed chiefly against him. With deceit and cunning, with beseeching and threatening they beset him; to learn the names of other Anabaptist preachers they placed him on the rack; with the severest torture they sought to learn who had ordained him and to obtain information which would lead to the detection of others. But "I pressed my lips together, yielded myself to God, suffered patiently and thought of the Word of the Lord: Greater love hath no man than this, that he lay down his life for his friends," he writes in noble humility and simple heroism. During his imprisonment he engaged in several discussions with Cassander (*q.v.*), an important Catholic scholar. His faithfulness to his convictions deeply impressed Cassander as well as others who disputed with him. Eberhard, the Bishop's chaplain, is said to have kindly commended him to the Lord, he writes in a letter. "And if we were where the duke wishes, we would be free." The judges became more lenient and kindly in feeling. "The affair would probably be all right," they observed, "if it would not finally end in revolution." Thus the quiet meetings of the Anabaptists were considered seditious and illegal. Their steadfast devotion to their faith was in the eyes of the authorities an obstinate adherence to heresy which merited death. This is expressed in an old tower chronicle of Cologne, which records of Servaes, "Anno 1565, on Saturday, the thirtieth or last day of June, Mattheis Servays of Cottenheim, preacher and baptizer, by vocation a linen weaver, Hermann von Daverkhausen, and Jost Böterknap, a tapestry weaver of Brussels, all three Anabaptists, because of their obstinacy and also because they held secret meetings at night contrary to law . . . , and because they have repeatedly administered baptism contrary to imperial mandates, further because they stubbornly persist in their heretical faith and rebaptism, will not desist from their error nor listen to pious admonitions, have been delivered from the Cunibert tower to the duke and the bailiff according to custom." A great crowd is said to have assembled at the site of the execution. The hymn written to commemorate his death describes the crowd and the pity felt by some that he should die for such a deed. Servaes had pardoned his enemies, and suffered martyrdom happy for the privilege of giving his life for the glory of God.

The nobility of his character is seen in the letters he wrote in prison to his family, his brethren, and the members of his church. Concerning this epistle Goebel says, "They are true pearls of Christian life and on a par with the most beautiful testimonies of Protestant martyrs. Where do we find in them, breathing as they do the peace of God, and the spirit of conciliation, any seditious, traitorous ideas that threaten temporal authority? Besides practical admonitions to his fellow elders Servaes writes a happy confession of his Biblical faith. Patiently he bears his bonds to the glory of the heavenly Father. Yea, he is willing to endure even greater suffering, not to secure his place in heaven, but to the greater honor of God. It is not fanaticism, which probably also makes superhuman endurance possible, that speaks from his open letters, but the peace of a heart that hopes soon to enter into the heavenly home."

His death is sung in the hymn, "Hinweg ist mir genommen," that names Heinrich von Krufft in acrostics; it is No. 1095 f. in Wackernagel, *Kirchenlied* V, and No. 24 in the *Ausbund*. Another hymn, beginning with the words, "Mit Angst und Not ruf ich dich an," and spelling the name of Servaes in acrostics, was written by him (Wackernagel, No. 665, and *Ausbund*, No. 41). Van Braght's *Martyrs' Mirror* contains 10 letters by Servaes, all written in prison and addressed as follows: one to H. K. (i.e., Heinrich Krufft); one to his brother; one to I. N.; one to the congregation of Cologne; one to his mother, his brother Johann, his brother-in-law Leonhard, and his two sisters; one to his wife, who was also in prison; one to I. N. and his brethren; one to his wife Aeltgen; one to F. V. H.; and one to Maria West.   O.H.

Rembert, *Wiedertäufer;* Wolkan, *Lieder,* 49, 91, 100; M. Goebel, *Gesch. des christlichen Lebens in der rheinisch - westphälisch - evangelischen Kirche* I (Coblenz, 1849) 217; Wackernagel, *Kirchenlied; Mart. Mir.* D 327-43, E 688-703; *BRN* VII, see Index; *DB* 1868, 45-48; E. Crous, "The Mennonites in Germany Since the Thirty Years' War," *MQR* XXV (October 1951) 237; *Der Mennonit* IX, No. 1 (January 1956) 11; Leonhard Ennen, *Geschichte der Stadt Köln* IV (Cologne and Neuss, 1875) 816-20; *ML* I, 338 f.

Matthijs van Balk (Matthias van Balck, Matthias Belkensis, or Maes de Schoenmaker), probably a native of Balk, Dutch province of Friesland, was a leader in the revolutionary wing of Anabaptism. After the fall of Oldeklooster (*q.v.*) in March 1534 he fled from Friesland to Ommelanden, Dutch province of Groningen, where he met with other revolutionary leaders like Jan van Batenburg (*q.v.*), whom he won over to his group. About his activity during the Münster (*q.v.*) period nothing is known. In the summer of 1536 he was among the Anabaptist leaders who met at Bocholt (Boekholt), Westphalia, where he defended the Münsterite principles of force and polygamy against Jan Matthijsz van Middelburg and Jan Smeitgen van Tricht. He is said then to have been of an advanced age. Here his trace is lost.   vDZ.

K. Vos, *Menno Simons* (Leiden, 1914) 41; *DB* 1917, 120 (No. 119), 138; 1919, 193; Kühler, *Geschiedenis* I, 201; Mellink, *Wederdopers, passim,* see Index.

Matthijs (Matthijsz, Matthysen), **Hans,** was from about 1580 an elder of the High German Mennonite group at Haarlem, Holland, who later joined the Waterlander congregation. It seems that he was present at the disputation (*q.v.*) held at Leeuwarden in 1596 between the Reformed minister Ruardus Acronius (*q.v.*) and the Mennonite Elder Pieter van Ceulen (*q.v.*); for in a letter dated Leeuwarden, Dec. 14, 1596, and addressed to the noted Waterlander Elder Hans de Ries (*q.v.*), then at Emden, Germany, he wrote about this dispute, of which he expected little result. In 1608 he played a somewhat unclear role in a quarrel caused in the United Waterlander-High German congregation of Haarlem by the controversies of Leenaerdt Clock (*q.v.*) and Denijs van Hulle. Concerning his person and activity there is little information. A letter found in the Amsterdam archives (II, 2, No. 656) seems to indicate that he was living at Leeuwarden in 1612, an elder of the local congregation. In 1613 he published *Brief om overghelevert te worden aen de leraren der Vlaemscher Mennoniten . . .* (Haarlem, 1613). In the same year he was one of the delegates at the Waterlander conference held at Workum, Friesland, to consider disciplinary measures against Rippert Eenkes (*q.v.*). If the name Hans Martens, found in a report of 1618 (*Inv. Arch. Amst.* II, 2, 662), refers—as is probable—to Hans Matthijs, he was still living in 1618 and active in solving the matter of Rippert Eenkes.   vDZ.

Inv. Arch. Amst. I, Nos. 476, 493, 527; II, Nos. 1358, 1362 f.; II, 2, No. 656; *DB* 1864, 41, 51, 53 f.; 1897, 112; 1903, 59 f., 64.

Matthijs van Lind, an Anabaptist martyr: see **Tijs (Thijs) van Lind.**

Mat(t)ijs Olbrantsz: see **Thijs Olbrants.**

Matthysz, Hughe: see **Mattheissen, Hugo.**

Mauer: see **Meckesheim.**

Maugansville, Md., population 700, is an unincorporated village in the northern part of Washington County, three miles northwest of Hagerstown. Mennonites (MC) live in and around the village. The Reiff (*q.v.*) Mennonite Church is located two miles to the northwest, while the Paradise Mennonite Church (*q.v.*) and the Miller Mennonite Church are situated east of the village, the latter church two miles from Leitersburg. These three churches had a combined membership of 564 in 1954. The Mennonite Old People's Home (*q.v.*) is located near Maugansville.   M.K.H.

Mauhadih Mennonite Mission Station (GCM), India, was opened on Jan. 11, 1911, by P. J. Wiens. The address is Mauhadih, via Champa, M.P., India.

Mauhadih is located about 25 miles south of Champa, which lies on the Bengal-Nagpur railroad line, 400 miles west of Calcutta. The first small house of worship was built of sun-dried brick in 1911. This was replaced by a spacious, burnt-brick church in 1920. The congregation was organized in 1915 or 1916. The Indian pastor of the church in 1949 was Samson Walters. There are 159 baptized members and 134 unbaptized children. During 1918-38 the boys' orphanage and middle school were located in Mauhadih. In 1937 there was a devastating flood. Fearing a recurrence of this, the school was moved to Jagdeespur, about 30 miles south. In 1954 the Mauhadih mission station was moved to a new location on higher ground, about two miles northeast of the old site. Here in New Mauhadih there is a primary school with over 100 children. There is also a dispensary under the supervision of the medical staff of the Champa Christian Hospital. New Mauhadih is chiefly an evangelistic station seeking to bring the Gospel to the approximately 355 villages in that area.   A.E.I.

Maulbronn, a city and district of Württemberg, Germany, where the Anabaptist movement found many adherents in the 16th century. Its spread was facilitated by the forests on the border between Württemberg and the Electoral Palatinate. Only one martyr is known in the region; in 1529 Georg Baumann of Bauschlott was put to death, because after recanting he had rejoined the Anabaptists (Beck, 32 and Wolkan, 59). Most of the Anabaptists escaped persecution by emigrating to Moravia to join the Hutterian brotherhoods, who carried on an active evangelization around Maulbronn well into the 17th century. Frequent searching parties for the Anabaptists failed to disclose them.

A Hutterite preacher, Matthias Binder (*q.v.*), who was visiting his mother in Frickenhausen, was imprisoned in Maulbronn on April 15, 1573, and was kept here for a long time. The prison of the Cistercian monastery at Maulbronn was apparently a favorite of the authorities, for there were prisoners here from all parts of the country. On June 2, 1573, orders came from Stuttgart to the abbot to fasten Binder by a chain or otherwise in the cell that had been occupied in 1567-69 by Blasius Greiner (*q.v.*) and others, and to put them on small rations (Bossert, 371). The abbot tried unsuccessfully to win Binder for the church or at least to extract from him a promise to stay out of Württemberg (Bossert, 374-76; Wolkan, 383). He was then taken to the prison of Hohenwittlingen (*q.v.*). From prison in Maulbronn he wrote two letters to the brotherhood in Moravia which were published by Bossert (369-71, and 373-74).

While Binder lay in prison in Maulbronn, the Hutterites sent other missionaries to Maulbronn, whose sermons were heard by large audiences, especially in the Bretten forest. Orders were accordingly issued to the foresters on July 21, 1574, from Stuttgart, to keep a sharp lookout for these meetings, especially for the leaders, and to turn them over to the authorities; a reward was promised for capture, and punishment for carelessness or for aiding them to escape (Bossert, 418).

During those years the migration to Moravia from Maulbronn became rather extensive. To thwart it the authorities directed the abbot and the bailiff of Maulbronn not to grant permission for the sale of property, unless the seller could prove that the place to which he was going had nothing to do with the Anabaptists. If the people mentioned their poverty and the prospect of better nutrition, they should be advised against going to Moravia and promised that they would not be allowed to starve in Maulbronn (Bossert, 417). In spite of these measures the emigration to Moravia continued; sometimes the refugees left all their property behind (Bossert, 422 and 499); nor could the forest meetings be prevented. In July 1596 attendance at an Anabaptist service was punished by a day in prison and a small fine (Bossert, 687), and in 1607 with three days in prison; whoever sheltered a preacher had to atone with eight days in prison and a fine of ten guilders (Bossert, 793).

The scope of the emigration to Moravia can be estimated from the fact that by 1613 Anabaptist property to the value of 25,593 florins had been confiscated; i.e., nearly half of the amount confiscated by the order of 1571 in the duchy of Württemberg. This amount is evidence that the Anabaptists valued their faith above their possessions. HEGE.

Beck, *Geschichts-Bücher;* Bossert, *TA Württemberg;* Wolkan, *Geschicht-Buch;* Zieglschmid, *Chronik; ML* **III,** 61.

Maurer, Hans, an Anabaptist martyr, from Flass, a village in Tirol, Austria, Bozen district, was taken to Gufidaun (*q.v.*) with six other brethren, including Christian Alseider and Valtin Gsäl (*q.v.*) and executed there in October 1533. In prison they wrote several letters to their brethren, two of which have been preserved.   NEFF.

Beck, *Geschichts-Bücher,* 108 f.; Wolkan, *Geschicht-Buch,* 75; Zieglschmid, *Chronik;* Loserth, *Anabaptismus,* 510; H. Amman, *Die Wiedertäufer in Michelsberg* (Programm, Brixen, 1896); *Mart. Mir.* D 33, E 444, where the date is erroneously given as 1536; *ML* **III,** 61.

Maurer, Wendel, an Anabaptist martyr, executed in 1581 at Bretten, Germany. (Beck, *Geschichts-Bücher,* 279; *ML* **III,** 61.)

Maurice (Moritz) (1521-53), Duke and Elector of Saxony, Germany, the son of Henry the Pious (*q.v.*), who introduced the Reformation in Albertine Saxony, succeeded his father to the duchy in 1541, attained to the electorship after the Schmalkaldian War, in which he fought on the emperor's side in spite of his sympathetic interest in the reformers, then deserted the emperor, compelled the signing of the treaty of Passau of 1552, and died in 1553 of a wound received in the victorious battle of Sievershausen, "a man of cool political calculation and full of religious indifference."

When Maurice assumed the government in 1541 at the age of 20 years, there were in the duchy some isolated Anabaptists, in spite of the bloody persecution under his predecessor, the strictly Catholic Duke George (*q.v.*). At the end of July 1543 two women and a man were seized in Beyernaumburg, a village east of Sangerhausen, where Anabaptists had been imprisoned earlier, and were ordered by the duke to be cross-examined by the preachers of

Beyernaumburg, Kaltenborn, and Nienstedt. Further information concerning them is unfortunately missing. In Mühlhausen in Thuringia (q.v.), which was jointly ruled by Maurice and the landgrave of Hesse, he ordered the violent extermination of Anabaptists in 1545, but was unable to overcome the tolerant attitude of Philip of Hesse, his father-in-law. And so the Anabaptist leader Christoph von der Eichen was permitted to leave the country with his wife and child, though his return to Mühlhausen was forbidden on penalty of death. On the whole, there were hardly any heresy trials under Maurice; matters of faith played a subordinate role in his politics. The final eradication of the Anabaptist movement in Saxony was reserved for his less gifted brother and successor, the strictly Lutheran August.   G.H.

P. Wappler, *Die Stellung Kursachsens und des Landgrafen Philipp von Hessen zur Täuferbewegung* (Münster, 1910); *idem, Die Täuferbewegung in Thüringen von 1526-1584* (Jena, 1913); *ML* III, 167 f.

Maurice of Orange (1567-1625), the son of William and his second wife Anna of Saxony, was born Nov. 14, 1567, d. in 1625. After the death of his father in 1584 Maurice succeeded him as stadholder of a large part of the Netherlands. He continued the struggle with Spain with vigor, displaying more talent as a general than as a statesman. In his later years he was a fanatical Calvinist, though probably from political rather than religious considerations, and as such he persecuted the Remonstrants (q.v.). Toward the Mennonites he was tolerant. When the magistrate of Middelburg (q.v.) oppressed the Mennonites living in that city, and Maillaert de Poorter and Joost Leonisse (Joos Loysen) in the name of the Mennonites appealed to the prince, he wrote a letter dated March 4, 1593, ordering the Middelburg authorities to leave to the Mennonites all the liberties his father had granted them. As Duke of Mörs and Lord of Crefeld, he also protected the Mennonites of this area in 1622 against his bailiff Sterckenburg, who wanted to execute the Mennonites of Crefeld for holding meetings.   vDZ.

G. Brandt, *Historie der Reformatie* I (2nd ed. Amsterdam, 1677) 780 f., where the letter of 1593 is found in full; Blaupot t. C., *Holland* I, 214; *DB* 1908, 40; *DJ* 1930, 136, note 1; *Der Mennonit* IX, No. 7 (July 1956) 107; *ML* III, 167.

Maurik, van, a Dutch Mennonite family found at Utrecht, Amsterdam, Haarlem, and Rotterdam. A number of its members served as deacons and at least three of them were Mennonite ministers. Aert Thonisz van Maurik was appointed preacher in the Flemish congregation of Utrecht in 1653 (*DB* 1874, 81). He was the ancestor of many generations of Mennonites. His son (or his cousin?) Willem van Maurik (q.v.) was a physician and a minister at Utrecht and Amsterdam. Matthys van Maurik (d. 1737) of Utrecht prepared the translation of two books by Herman Schijn (q.v.). The first was published in 1727 at Amsterdam and Utrecht, *Geschiedenis der Protestantsche Christenen, in't Vereenigd Nederland genaamd Mennoniten,* a translation of Schijn's *Historia Christianorum, qui in Belgio Foederatione inter Protestantes Mennonitae appellantur* of 1723. The second was published in 1738, after his

death, at Amsterdam, *Uitvoeriger Verhandeling of Vervolg van de Geschiedenis der Mennonieten,* a translation of Schijn's *Historia Mennonitarum plenior deductio* of 1729. This Matthys van Maurik was a deacon of the Utrecht congregation in 1721-24, 1728-32, and 1736-37. His son Willem van Maurik Matth.zn of Utrecht, after studying at the Amsterdam Lamist seminary, was a preacher of the Vlaemsche Blok congregation at Haarlem 1738-*ca.*60.

vDZ.

Maurik (Maurick, Mourik), **Willem** (Wilhem) **van,** b. *ca.* 1625 at Utrecht, d. 1710 at Amsterdam, was a physician and a Mennonite minister. On Feb. 21, 1658, he was chosen as preacher of the Utrecht Flemish congregation. Being rather progressive and of Collegiant (q.v.) inclination, he was soon involved in trouble with the conservative part of the congregation, particularly with his co-preacher Robbert Jansz van Hoog(h)veldt (q.v.), who was very conservative. Van Hoogveldt severely censured van Maurik's officiating in the Waterlander congregation of Rotterdam, and accused him of heresy. Then van Maurik, acting with three co-preachers, Arent van Heuven, Johann Andriesz van Aken, and Goris van Aldendorp, who were in sympathy with van Maurik, published a confession of faith, *Een Belydenisse aengaende de voornaemste Leer-stucken* (Utrecht, 1659). Though this confession was couched in orthodox terms, its moderation, laying more stress upon Christian practice than upon Christian doctrine, displeased the conservative leaders of the congregation; van Hoogveldt wrote his *Korte doch nodighe Waerschouwinghe* (n.p., 1659), and the conservatives felt obliged to present a number of questions to van Maurik and his three colleagues. They at first refused to answer, but finally reluctantly gave a reply. This seems to have satisfied the conservatives; at least in January 1660 peace was restored. But the quarrel arose anew. Apparently at the instigation of van Hoogveldt the city government presented twelve questions, which had been drawn up by the Reformed minister Cornelis Gentman (q.v.; see also **Geuzenvragen**), to van Maurik. Van Maurik did not reply and the city governors dropped the matter. But now the conservatives, charging van Maurik and his three colleagues with Collegiant sympathies and heresy, arranged a meeting in which the leaders from the outside (*buitenmannen*) were invited to make a decision. The meeting was held at Utrecht July 29-Aug. 11, 1661. Among the buitenmannen, all of whom were conservative leaders, were T. J. van Braght from Dordrecht, Bastiaan van Weenigem and Jean Boenes from Rotterdam, and Isaac Snep from Haarlem. On Aug. 10 they suspended van Maurik, van Aldendorp, van Heuven, and Andriesz from their office. Deep dissension arose in the congregation because many members were in sympathy with the suspended preachers. Finally in July 1664 van Maurik with his following withdrew from the main body and began to hold separate meetings. The root of the conflict was the question whether the Flemish church was the true and only Christian church on earth. Van Hoogveldt and the conservatives affirmed this question, van Maurik and his followers denied it. The division lasted until 1675, when the two groups reunited. In 1673 van Maurik had moved to Amsterdam. Here he was at once appointed preacher of the Lam and Toren congregation (united Flemish and Waterlander church) and worked in harmony with Galenus Abrahamsz (*q.v.*), with whom he was so congenial. On April 19, 1706, he stood at the deathbed of Galenus. On May 16, 1706, he commemorated his colleague in a funeral sermon, which was published: *Lykreden. Op Galenus Abrahamsz* (Amsterdam, n.d.). He also published some posthumous works of Galenus. Besides this and the *Belydenisse* mentioned before, van Maurik published *Wydt-loopiger Verhael van de beklaeglycke onlusten . . . teghen R. van Hoochvelt* (Utrecht, 1662) and *Verantwoording tegen het Placcaet van de stad Bern*. In Amsterdam, as a member of the Committee for Foreign Needs, van Maurik was also active in behalf of the oppressed Swiss Mennonites.   vDZ.

DB 1916, 150-93; *Inv. Arch. Amst.* I, No. 1254b; H. W. Meihuizen, *Galenus Abrahamsz* (Haarlem, 1954); *passim*, see Index.

Maurissus van Dale, an Anabapist martyr, b. 1518 or 1519 at Bellem near Gent, Belgium, a sheriff of Gent, joined the Mennonite congregation at Gent. In the records he is called a "bishop of the Mennonites." Further particulars about him were not available. On June 25, 1573, he was burned at the stake outside the Peterselle gate of Gent. Adriaen van Haemstede (*q.v.*) erroneously listed him in his martyrbook as a Reformed martyr. (Verheyden, *Gent*, 63, No. 223; *idem*, "Mennisme in Vlaanderen," Ms.)   vDZ.

Mauthausen in Upper Austria, an important station for the Anabaptists going from Tirol to Moravia. A decree issued by Ferdinand in Vienna on March 18, 1534, to the council of Mauthausen contains strict orders not to permit the Anabaptists to pass either by land or on the Danube, but to drive them away at once. Wolfgang Brandhuber (*q.v.*) preached at Mauthausen about 1527-29 and may have established a congregation here.   LOSERTH.

Mauthausen, Marktarchiv 9; G. Loesche in *Jahrbuch der Gesellschaft f. d. Gesch. des Prot. in Oesterreich* XL f., 179; *ML* III, 61 f.

Mauve, Anton (Anthony), b. Sept. 18, 1858, at Zaandam, Dutch province of North Holland, baptized at Haarlem in November 1858, d. Feb. 5, 1888, at Arnhem, one of the best (if not the best) landscape painters in the Hague School, in which the finest traditions of the Old Dutch painting were brought to a new and fuller fruition under the influence of the impressionistic views of nature that had already produced in French art in the Barbizon School an era of rich and worthy revival. Mauve, as well as his equally gifted contemporary, P. J. C. Gabriel, kept himself rather aloof from the Romanticism characteristic of the Naturalism of the Hague School. His work is distinguished by its disciplined yet delicate portrayal, in the cool, luminous, yet tender and clear tone of his oils and water colors. The beauty of "het Gooi" and particularly that of the Laren landscape was in a sense discovered by Mauve.

It is probable that Mauve influenced Vincent van Gogh, who was a cousin of his wife (Colmjon, 45).

Many of Mauve's paintings are found in the Mesdag Museum; the reason for this is probably the fact that Mauve and H. W. Mesdag were close friends. The Rijksmuseum of Amsterdam also has a large collection. Mauve paintings are numerous in many European and even some American museums.

Anton Mauve was the son of a Mennonite pastor, Willem Carel Mauve (1803-69), who served the congregations at Enschedé 1830-36, Zaandam-Oost 1836-39, and Haarlem 1839-63; he was the author of a small catechism on Biblical history (Haarlem, 1846). He came into the Mennonite brotherhood from the Reformed Church.   H.F.W.J., C.K.

Archives of the Zaandam-Oost Mennonite Church; E. Pekema, *Iets over de Doopsgezinde gemeente te Enschedé;* G. Heeringa, *Uit het verleden der Doopsgezinden in Twenthe* (1934); Germen Colmjon, *The Hague School* (Rijswijk, 1951) 41; E. B. Greenshields, *Landscape Painting and Modern Dutch Artists* (New York, 1906) 155; Frank Rutter, "A Consideration of the Work of Anton Mauve," *Studio* XLII (1908) 3-16; H. P. Baard, "Anton Mauve," *Palet Serie* (1947); *ML* III, 62.

Maximilian I (Maximilian Joseph) (1756-1825), first king of Bavaria, Germany. When he assumed government in Bavaria (*q.v.*) as Elector Maximilian IV Joseph of Zweibrücken on Feb. 16, 1799, he brought about a radical change in the treatment of the Mennonites in the Palatinate. His Jesuit-educated predecessor, Charles (Karl, *q.v.*) Theodore, had passed several suppressive measures, which Maximilian, king since 1805, felt to be unjust, and which he removed in his reforms. By decreasing the Catholic influence on affairs of state, he removed the legal restrictions on the Mennonites and put them on a civil plane with other citizens. On April 17, 1801, the right of redemption (*jus retractus, q.v.;* also *Gem.-Kal.* 1912, 120-34) was liquidated. In addition, on Oct. 20, 1811, they were permitted free exercise of their faith, churches without bells, and the regulation of the oath in accord with their wishes.

After the Palatinate was ceded to France, Maximilian Joseph was interested in settling Mennonites on farms in South Germany. A number of German princes sought them out as master farmers (Correll, 130-33). An attempt was to be made to open the Donaumoos (*q.v.*), northwest of Munich, for agriculture, leading to the founding of Maxweiler (*q.v.,* named after the king) by eight Mennonite families from the Palatinate. The Mennonites also acquired a number of suppressed monasteries (1803) in Upper Bavaria and Franconia, which Catholic peasants, partly because of superstitious reasons, were reluctant to accept (*Gem.-Kal.* 1912, 91, and Correll, 134). Thus the first emigration of Mennonites from the Palatinate and from Alsace took place to southern Bavaria. A large number of the Maxweiler families went to America about the middle of the 19th century, but after 1880 new settlements of Mennonites from Baden and Württemberg were made in southern Bavaria.   HEGE.

E. Correll, *Das schweizerische Täufermennonitentum* (Tübingen, 1925); *ML* III, 63.

Maxmill Hutterite Bruderhof near Scotland, Hutchinson Co., S.D., founded in 1900. Joseph Wipf, who had been chosen preacher in the Bon Homme Bruderhof in 1891, moved with 17 families to Maxmill and settled the colony there. Wipf was born in Russia, and died in 1917. Samuel Hofer was chosen preacher in 1911. In 1918 the Bruderhof sold its property and settled the Maxwell Bruderhof near Pigeon Lake, Man. In 1947 the New Elm Springs Bruderhof bought this site and rebuilt it.   D.D.

Maxweiler, a village in the Neuburg district of Bavaria, Germany, on the Danube, a former Mennonite settlement which helped to open the Donaumoos (*q.v.*) for agriculture. Maximilian Joseph (*q.v.*), who was acquainted with Mennonite agricultural skills in the Palatinate, granted the Palatine Mennonites who had settled in Donaumoos 270 acres of wooded land per family, where they were to do pioneer work. The number of families in the settlement rose from 8 to 25 in 50 years, 12 of whom lived in Maxweiler, which they established, and 13 in the surrounding villages.

Immediately after they arrived they organized a congregation in the hunting lodge assigned to them while their houses were in building, and chose two preachers from their midst, Daniel and Heinrich Müller, who were ordained by elder Heinrich Zeiset of Willenbach, near Heilbronn. At first they assembled in the home of preacher Müller, and later in the church they built in Maxweiler in 1832, which contained several rooms for school purposes. They taught their own children or had them taught by a member of the settlement. In 1848 the government provided a teacher for them; they were to raise one fourth of his salary. At their request religious instruction was left to them.

In spite of all their efforts, which were recognized with great praise by the authorities, the struggle for existence was very difficult in the settlement because of the low productivity of the soil. Therefore beginning in 1852 the young men were attracted to America, where there were better prospects and where they would be exempt from military service, to which the second generation of settlers was subject (Correll, 83). They were soon followed by other members of their families. Between 1852 and 1855 most of them emigrated to Lee County in Iowa (*q.v.*), and joined the Mennonites who had recently come from the Palatinate and from nearby Eichstock (*q.v.*) in the congregation of Donnellson (*q.v.*) and West Point, where the former preachers at Eichstock, David Ruth and Jacob Krehbiel, were located (Rupp, 10), with whom they had been acquainted in Germany. The rest of the Maxweiler Mennonites settled in Summerfield, Ill. All left the settlement on the Donaumoos.

The two Iowa churches formed a union in 1859. They thereby laid the foundation for the General Conference Mennonite Church, which was constituted in Wadsworth, Ohio, in 1861, with the addition of six other congregations, including Summerfield.

The church at Maxweiler has since the emigration of the Mennonites served the village as a school. The Mennonite farms passed into the hands of Protestant peasants.   HEGE.

Ernst Correll, "Die Mennoniten im Donaumoos," in *Gem.-Kal.* 1922, 80-91; H. P. Krehbiel, *The History of the General Conference of the Mennonite Church of North America* (Canton, 1898); Jakob Rupp, *Entstehung*

und Auflösung der Gemeinde zu Maxweiler bei Neuburg an der Donau (Moundridge, 1924); Cornelius Krahn, "Zur Auswanderung der Mennoniten von Maxweiler und Eichstock," *Gesch.-Bl.*, December 1938, 81; "Haus- und Handbuch für die Familie David Ruth zu Eichstock, 1852," and "Stammbuch der evangelischen Mennonitengemeinde in Westpoint, Lee County, Iowa . . . 1864" (the last two in BeCHL); *ML* III, 63 f.

Maxwell Hutterite Bruderhof in Manitoba. In 1918 many of the Hutterian Brethren in the United States went to Canada because of Canada's more liberal provisions for conscientious objectors to war. The Bruderhof at Maxwell, S.D., consisting of 29 families and their preacher Samuel Hofer, made a settlement near Headingly, Man. Samuel Hofer was chosen minister on Jan. 15, 1911, and confirmed on March 17, 1918, in South Dakota. Other preachers are Jörg Waldner, chosen Aug. 4, 1929, confirmed Dec. 16, 1934, Jörg Wipf, chosen Jan. 31, 1937, and Joseph Hofer, chosen 1919 and confirmed March 18, 1928. In 1947 the Bruderhof had 78 inhabitants, of whom 28 were baptized members.   D.D.

May City (Alberta) United Missionary Church, organized in 1907, had 33 members in 1953, with Lloyd Torgerson as pastor.   M.G.

Mayak Bible School, located in Davlekanovo village, Ufa, Russia, the last of the three Bible schools established by the Mennonites of Russia after World War II, was founded in September 1923 by Karl Friedrichsen (*q.v.*), a Mennonite preacher, who had served as a Bible teacher in the Davlekanovo Zentralschule in 1913-22. He was the director, and apparently the sole teacher of the school throughout its history. The government permit for the school was issued July 27, 1923, and withdrawn in November 1926. Friedrichsen appointed a school council of four local ministers, including the two local elders (Mennonite and Mennonite Brethren) to assist him. Financial support came from widely scattered sources, including small contributions from the Emergency Relief Commission at Newton, Kan., and from "Licht dem Osten" at Wernigerode, Germany. The school sessions were held in the Davlekanovo Mennonite Church. The course was a three-year curriculum leading to a diploma, the school year Sept. 15-May 1.

Enrollment in the school never was more than seven at one time (1924-25), five in the last full year, with a total of 13 different persons, all men, in the entire first three years, of whom three graduated in April 1926. The enrollment of the final school year is not known. Of the 13 students, nine were M.B., one Mennonite, two Freie Gemeinde, and one Baptist. They came from Siberia (6), Turkestan (5), Alt-Samara (1), and Ufa (1). A picture of the teacher and five students enrolled in April 1926 appeared in *Unser Blatt* for June 1926 (I, 203).

The school was definitely a ministerial training school, one of three started in 1923. The other two, Tchongrav in the Crimea and Orenburg, had to close before April 1926. Similar shorter preachers' courses planned for Slavgorod and Orenburg in 1926 were not permitted by the government. A general Mennonite Bible School planned by the *KfK* (*q.v.*), for Melitopol, which was to begin in the fall of 1927, for which permission had been orally promised on Oct. 20, 1926, by the government but never granted in writing, had to be given up.   H.S.B.

K. Friedrichsen, "Die Majak-Bibelschule," with financial report, *Unser Blatt* I (1926) 138 f.; idem, "Schluss-akt der Majak-Bibelschule in Davlekanovo," *Unser Blatt* I (1927) 220-22; idem, "Die Allgemeine Mennonitische Bibelschule," *Unser Blatt* I (1926) 280-84; *Der Bote* II, No. 27, 6.

Maycken (Martine) 's Heeren, an Anabaptist martyr, b. at Belle (Bailleul), Flanders, and living at Brugge, Belgium, a widow, was apprehended at Brugge in February 1568 with 13 other Mennonites, of whom only four, including Maycken, remained steadfast. Maycken was burned at the stake at Brugge between April 13 and July 28, 1568. (Verheyden, *Brugge,* 54, No. 52.)   vDZ.

Mayer, Mar(c)x, an early Anabaptist leader from Alterlangen near Nürnberg in Germany, about whose Anabaptist activity not much is known. In August 1527 he was with many other leaders at the Martyrs' Synod (*q.v.*) at Augsburg. In June 1530 he was arrested at Creglingen near Ansbach, Germany, but he recanted and was released. Soon afterward he joined the sect of the Puschenhamers and was beheaded on July 6, 1531. (*TA Bayern* I, 189, 191, 327-29.)   vDZ.

Mayes County (Okla.) Old Order Amish Settlement is located southwest of Choteau, Okla. Among the first Amish families who came there (1910) were Rudy Yoder and M. K. Yoder from Custer Co., Okla., Eli Mast from Ford Co., Kan., David Plank from Reno Co., Kan., R. B. Detweiler from Geauga Co., Ohio, and Eli Miller from Tuscarawas Co., Ohio. The first bishop of the group was M. J. Troyer, and L. M. Yoder was the first minister. There has always been only one district. In 1956 the membership was 64.   N.Y.

Mayken (i.e., Maria, Mary), the name of a number of martyrs: see **Maeyken.**

Mayrl, Hans, an Anabaptist leader, was seized early in 1530 in or near Petersburg in the Tirol, Austria, together with his wife. On April 26 of that year the judge was reprimanded for being too lenient with the prisoners. The judges had received orders to act "not in accord with their conscience, but in accord with the imperial mandate." The orders were further to apply the rack. Two councilors from Innsbruck and two from Hall should be called to the trial; the Anabaptist preacher should be executed, and others pardoned according to their deserts. If Hans Maryl should recant, he might be "pardoned to beheading" and be buried in consecrated earth. Very likely the sentence was carried out.   W.W.

G. Loesche, *Archivalische Beiträge zur Geschichte des Täufertums und des Protestantismus in Tirol* (1926) 33 f.; *ML* III, 64.

Mayton Mennonite Church (MC), now extinct, located near Mayton, Alberta, had its origin with the arrival of the first settlers on March 11, 1901, from northwestern Iowa. Amos S. Bauman, a minister, came with his family in the spring of 1903. S. F.

Coffman organized the Mayton congregation. On July 27, 1903, A. S. Bauman was ordained bishop by lot, and on Aug. 3, 1903, Noah Gerber was ordained to the office of deacon. John K. Lehman was ordained minister in 1906. In the meantime Bishop Bauman had left the church, to join the Mennonite Brethren in Christ Church. In 1915 Lehman with his family moved to Oregon because of his wife's ailing health. In 1918 they, however, returned, but moved to Tofield, Alberta. At about the same time most of the rest of the congregation also moved to Tofield, where they were amalgamated in the Salem (*q.v.*) congregation. A few members continued to live at Mayton, but held their membership with the West Zion church, near Carstairs, Alberta.   E.S.

Meade Bible Academy, located 12 miles southeast of Meade, Kan., operated by the two Mennonite churches in the community (E.M.B. and Emmanuel), was established in 1945 as a 2-year high school and in 1948 became a full 4-year accredited school. It was originally the outgrowth of the Meade Bible School started in 1936 in the E.M.B. church basement, which in turn was preceded by a German Bible School conducted 1927-30 by missionary G. T. Thiessen. The academy in 1955 had an enrollment of 71, a staff of six, a modern fireproof administration building erected in 1955, two frame classroom buildings, and a large teacherage.   J.L.E.

Meade County, Kan., is located in the semiarid area of southwestern Kansas along the Oklahoma border. It was not until the late 19th and early 20th centuries that this part of Kansas was transformed from prairie grazing land into tilled agricultural units. Mennonites from Jansen, Neb. (Kleine Gemeinde), and Inman, Kan., were among the early settlers. The first two Mennonite families were those of Peter F. Rempel and Jacob B. Friesen, both from Nebraska, who settled on homesteaded land approximately ten miles south of Meade (pop. 1500) in 1906. Today there are two Mennonite congregations in Meade County with a combined membership of 400. One congregation belongs to the Evangelical Mennonite Brethren Conference (*q.v.*) and the other, the Emmanuel Mennonite Church (*q.v.*), is at present unaffiliated but was formerly a part of the Kleine Gemeinde (*q.v.*). The family names of Bartel, Ediger, Friesen, Isaac, Loewen, Rempel, Reimer, and Wiens predominate.   J.W.F.

Meade Evangelical Mennonite Brethren Church, located eight miles south and four miles east of Meade, Kan., a member of the Evangelical Mennonite Brethren Conference of the United States and Canada, was organized on June 10, 1910, with 14 members, by Elder Henry E. Fast of Mountain Lake, Minn. The first church, built in 1920, has twice been replaced by larger buildings. In 1930 the Nebo congregation united with the Meade congregation. The present membership is 244. The following ministers have served the church: A. M. Doerksen (ordained 1914), Peter F. Friesen, G. T. Thiessen, H. R. Harms, D. J. Ediger, J. E. Wiens, B. A. Wiens, Orlando Wiebe, John N. Wall, H. P.

Wiebe, Alvin D. Kleinsasser, and Arnold Wall, who is now the pastor. The Meade Bible Academy (q.v.) is a co-operative project supported jointly by the E.M.B. Church and the Emmanuel Mennonite Church (q.v.). H.St.

Meade (Kan.) Kleine Gemeinde Mennonite Church was transplanted from Jansen, Neb. (q.v.), in 1906-8. The influences of more evangelistic Mennonite groups, the adjustment to the American environment as a whole, and the determination of the leader to maintain the status quo caused the disintegration of the church. The *Diener-Konferenz* in 1937, attended by Canadian Kleine Gemeinde ministers, could not settle the problems. The attendance at the two churches dwindled to a mere handful. Separate meetings were initiated in one of the church buildings by some dissatisfied members, which brought about the organization of a new church. H. R. Harms of the Evangelical Mennonite Brethren Church was asked to serve this group, which was officially organized as an unaffiliated Emmanuel Mennonite Church (q.v.) in 1944. The services and activities of the Kleine Gemeinde ceased, although its elders still lived in the community. Most of the members that had not joined the local Evangelical Mennonite Brethren Church joined the Emmanuel Mennonite Church. C.K.

Daniel J. Classen, "Meade—A Changing Community," *Menn. Life* VI (1951) 14 ff.

Meadow Mennonite Church (GCM) in Mingo, 12 miles southeast of Colby, Thomas Co., Kan., a member of the Western District Conference, was organized Sept. 19, 1937, with charter members under the leadership of John H. Epp, who later also served the church as the first resident pastor. The first building was a frame structure with a seating capacity of 90. The present building, a brick structure with a seating capacity of 200, was dedicated Nov. 30, 1952. In 1954 the membership was 82, mostly rural, with J. W. Bergen as pastor. Other ministers who have served are Wm. C. Voth and Walter H. Regier. W.H.R.

Meadow Valley Old Order Mennonite Church, Weaverland Conference, is located in Ephrata Twp., Lancaster Co., Pa. Its meetinghouse was built in 1916. Joseph E. Hostetter is the bishop, Henry W. Martin and Luke N. Good the ministers, and Martin L. Zimmerman deacon. The membership (1955) is 255. I.D.L.

Meadows (Ill.) Mennonite Church (GCM), on U.S. Highway 24 midway between Chenoa and Gridley, a member of the Central District Conference, was organized in 1891, when a white frame building was constructed three quarters of a mile north of Meadows. In 1908 it was moved to its present location in Meadows and remodeled. It was again remodeled, enlarged, and rededicated Sept. 6, 1953, with a seating capacity of 300. The membership in 1954 was 248, mostly rural; the minister was L. E. Troyer. Past ministers (all deceased): Andrew Vercler, Joseph Kinsinger, Aaron Roszhart, George Gundy. L.E.T.

Meadows Mennonite Home, Meadows, McLean Co., Ill., until 1951 called Mennonite Old People's Home, was legally organized as a non-profit corporation on June 6, 1919, by representatives from the Central and Defenseless Mennonite conferences and is supported by these conferences. The main building was erected in 1922, and a west wing added in 1951. On Jan. 6, 1944, the Constitution and Bylaws were revised, and again Feb. 6, 1954, when the name of the institution changed to "Meadows Mennonite Home." Superintendents and matrons who have served the Home are Mr. and Mrs. J. H. Klassen, 2 years, Mr. and Mrs. G. I. Gundy, 22 years, and Mr. and Mrs. Frank R. Mitchell, since 1947. F.R.M.

W. B. Weaver, *History of the Central Conference Mennonite Church* (Danvers, Ill., 1926).

Meadville Mennonite Mission was located on the southern plateau of the Welsh Mountain, three miles north of White Horse, Lancaster Co., Pa. John L. Musser, then superintendent of the Welsh Mountain Samaritan Home, conducted a summer Bible school in the schoolhouse with success. Thereafter, on July 28, 1954, the ministers of the Hershey district opened Sunday school and services in the same building. The schoolhouse was used until the spring of 1951, when a frame structure 32 x 46 ft. was erected a short distance east of the schoolhouse. In 1955 Galen Hostetter was serving as pastor, with a membership of 41. I.D.L.

Mechanic Grove Mennonite Church (MC), a member of the Lancaster Conference, is located near a small rural town by this name, four miles south of Quarryville, Lancaster Co., Pa. When members began to move into this formerly Scotch-Irish area services were desired. In 1877 Amos Herr preached in the village. The 20 members in the fall of 1881 built a frame structure 46 x 35 ft., which served the congregation until 1949, when it was extensively remodeled and enlarged. In 1954 Abram D. Metzler and J. Harold Breneman were serving as ministers, with a membership of 149. In 1920 a schism occurred, led by John W. Swarr, a preacher who led the group into the General Conference Mennonite Church. This group, called the Calvary Mennonite Church, had 57 members in 1954. I.D.L.

Mechanicsburg, Pa., in the beautiful Cumberland Valley is a quiet town of 6,786, seven miles southwest of Harrisburg. The Union House cornerstone was laid June 12, 1798, with Christian Newcomer, a United Brethren bishop, present. It was a house "wherein Christian preachers of all denominations are to enjoy the privilege of preaching." How many decades Mennonites (MC) used this house is not definitely known, but it was only in the early 1950's that they ceased to do so. I.D.L.

Mechel, von, an old publishing house in Basel, Switzerland, which was apparently the only printing office willing to publish whatever the Swiss Mennonites of the late 17th and 18th centuries wanted published. It is well known that this period around the turn of the 17th century was one of harsh persecution by Swiss authorities (mainly in Bern), a time when large-scale emigration to Alsace and the Palatinate took place. And yet, a number of books, tracts, hymns, and prayers were published, to be sure without any indication as to place, year, and author, which soon became standard devotional material of the Brethren. Careful study of all evidence makes it certain that it was this Mechel publishing house where Mennonites found a willing support, not only at the time of the establishment of the firm in 1685, but all through the following centuries, the last publication known from this house being the *Ausbund* of 1838.

The history of the Mechel house has never been fully studied. The founder of the firm was Johann Conrad von Mechel (1642-1715), who after having been an itinerant journeyman in his trade all over Europe, married in 1681 a daughter of the well-known Basel printer family of J. J. Decker, and opened his own shop in 1685. Since the Deckers had bought the still older Basel printing office of Henricpetri (16th and 17th century), it is not surprising to find woodcuts and colophons of the Henricpetri era on Mechel productions. The elder Johann Conrad was succeeded by his son of the same name (called Hans Conrad, 1681-1734). After the latter's death the firm was continued by his widow Anna Maria, nee Christ, and her twin sons Johann Conrad and Johann Jakob (born 1730), the "Gebrüder Mechel." The last name of interest to us is Jakob Heinrich von Mechel, active 1830-40.

Paul Wernle calls this firm "the pietistic publishing house of Basel" (Wernle, 602). Among other books it published the *Basel Gesangbuch* of 1743 and later editions, and another Reformed *Gesangbüchlein* of 1726 and later editions. Most remarkable is also the publication of a *Totentanz* with 41 woodcuts from 1576, eight editions between 1715 and 1842. (The woodcutter was the well-known Basel artist Gregor Sickinger, the rhymes to the plates come from a certain Fröhlich, both around 1576.)

No one has ever noticed the close ties between this press and the Swiss Mennonites which, however, are quite apparent. An advertising list at the end of the 1822 Mechel edition of the Dordrecht Confession of Faith contains nine Swiss Mennonite books and ten other books much in demand by the Brethren. The Mennonite books are as follows: *Ausbund*, 1809 (earlier editions seem to have come from the same place); *Ernsthafte Christenpflicht*, 1796; *Güldene Aepffel*, 1742 (and also 1702); Schabalie, *Die Wandelnde Seele*, 1811 (and before 1770); *Kleines Handbüchlein*, etc., 1801; *Glaubensbekenntnis*, 1822 (and earlier 1742); D. Philips, *Enchiridion*, 1822; *Ein Sendbrief* (about 1720); and G. Roosen, *Unschuld und Gegenbericht*, 1753. It is most likely that *Das Gebätt* by Hans Reist (around 1700) was also printed here, as well as earlier editions of the *Ausbund* (1695 or 99). A *Namenbüchlein* (see A-B-C-Books) of 1740 was much in use by the Mennonites. Also popular were other Mechel publications such as the *Geistliches Lustgärtlein*, 1815; Joh. Arndt's *Paradiesgärtlein*, 1737; *Abschied der zwölf Patriarchen*, 1744; *Sieben Busspsalme*, etc., 1751; and Thomas à Kempis (in Teersteegen's translation), 1752 (Friedmann, 98). It is remarkable that in 1822 books more than a century old were still advertised to Swiss Mennonite readers.

A special feature of this publishing firm was its hymn prints. It not only printed official (Reformed) hymnals but also the *Ausbund*. The 1809 and 1838 editions bear the firm's name, but there is evidence that already around 1695-99 one or two *Ausbund* editions must have been produced by this press, and most likely one or several 18th-century printings as well (Friedmann, 170 f.). Besides this most important Mennonite hymnal a number of Anabaptist hymn-pamphlets and pamphlet collections were printed here, recognizable by their characteristic colophons and inscriptions on the title page. One *Ausbund* appeared bound or printed with (same size, same type) *Fünf schöne neue geistliche Lieder*, 1695 (among them also the Thessalonica hymn), in 1696 followed by the *Neuaufgerichtetes geistliches Liederbüchlein* (Neff, MQR IV, 1930, 208), and in 1699 by 20 *neue geistliche Lieder*, with an appendix *Drey Geistliche Lieder* (Wolkan, *Lieder*, 157 ff.). The same *Drey Geistliche Lieder*, 1699, are also found in the rare volume which contains the oldest (1564) edition of the *Ausbund*. Here they are bound together under one cover. In 1708 another collection of hymns "gedruckt zu Basel" appeared (Neff), and so on. Their Mechel origin is fairly certain. Most remarkable is one volume (at Goshen College Library) containing not less than 96 such hymn pamphlets (with 310 hymns) covering the period from 1709 to 1803 or even later, all of the same size. Among them are found the *Haslibacher Lied* (q.v.), the *Reist-Lied*, "Es ist eine wunderschöne Gab," even one hymn from the oldest *Ausbund* edition, "Wach auf, wach auf," which may be as old as 1540.

There can be no doubt that all these books and pamphlets come from the same press. Two of these books show the same colophon, a circle of 13 death's heads with the circumscription: pope/emperor/king/prince/count/baron/noble/commoner/peasant/rich/poor/old/young. In the center stands the verse from Jesus Sirach, "Mensch du musst sterben" (Eccl. 14:18; see Friedmann, 157 f., and plate III). This emblem is contained in *Güldene Aepffel* (1702, 1742) and the *Sendbrief* (1720), both still advertised in 1822. Likewise the inscription "Gedruckt im Jahr da wahre Buss von Nöten war" appears more than once on the title page (Neff and Friedmann, pl. III); since these books are advertised by Mechel in 1822, one may safely assume their origin at this press.

Many of these books and pamphlets bear on their title page woodcuts, some of the early 16th century (once the Henricpetri colophon is used), all of which indicates a fairly uniform publishing policy. This policy is all the more remarkable since it does not conform to the leading style of the period (baroque) but rather uses and re-uses Renaissance or even pre-Renaissance cuts, apparently inherited from the Henricpetri office. Only the death's heads circle is contemporary (around 1700) but it fits very well with the spirit of the reprint of the old Basel *Totentanz* (originating as far back as 1451) in 1715. A characteristic specimen of the Mechel prints is the *Namenbüchlein* of 1740 (Bey Johann Conrad von Mechel sel. Wittib) with a woodcut (a family praying before meal), decidedly of early 16th-century origin (Friedmann, plate V; original at Goshen College Library).

With the *Ausbund* edition of 1838, the connection between the Swiss Mennonite and Amish groups (in Alsace and the Palatinate) and the Mechel publishing house seem to have come to an end. Much gratitude is due to Mechel, for without its readiness to print all these books the literary history of the Swiss Mennonites would have been much poorer. R.F.

Historisch-Biographisches Lexikon der Schweiz; Paul Wernle, *Geschichte des Schweizerischen Protestantismus im 18. Jahrhundert* I: *Vernünftige Orthodoxie und Pietismus* (Tübingen, 1923); R. Friedmann, *Mennonite Piety Through the Centuries* (Goshen, 1949; here the relationship between Mennonites and the Mechels is studied for the first time); personal information from the Univ. Library of Basel and the Oeffentliche Basler Denkmalpflege; Chr. Neff, "A Hymn of the Swiss Brethren," *MQR* IV (1930) 208 ff.

Mechelen (Malines), a town in Belgium (pop. 1950, 61,380), which in 1507-30 was the seat of the regent Margaret of Austria (*q.v.*). Though Anabaptist activity was not very strong here, there must have been some Anabaptists at Mechelen, for in September 1539 a number of them were put to death here (number and names unknown). In 1554-56 Elder Leenaert Bouwens baptized five persons at Mechelen. (*Inv. Arch. Amst.* I, No. 215.) vdZ.

Mechtelt Melis, an Anabaptist martyr of Antwerp, Belgium, drowned there in a sack on Sept. 23, 1552. She was born at The Hague, Holland, and was married to Adriaen Wouterssone, who was executed on the same day as his wife by burning at the stake. (*Antw. Arch.-Blad* VIII, 420, 422, 424; XIV, 20 f., No. 219.) vdZ.

Meckesheim, a village (pop. 2,246) in the Heidelberg district of Baden, Germany, mostly Protestant, was formerly the seat of a Mennonite church, the first of whose members immigrated from Switzerland after the Thirty Years' War. A list of 1731 enumerates the heads of the 16 families (Müller, *Berner Täufer,* 210). The Dutch *Naamlijst* of 1766 lists this congregation as Honingerhof and Meckesheim, with Hans Bechtel as preacher from 1732 and elder from 1743; the preachers were Georg Bechtel, David Kaufmann, and Michael Bachmann. The *Naamlijst* of 1775, where the congregation is called Mauer and Meckesheim, lists Hans Bechtel as still the elder, and Michael Bechtel, Jakob Hursch (obviously Hirsch), and Johannes Neff as preachers, all appointed in 1772. The *Naamlijst* of 1780 lists Mauer as an independent congregation, with Jakob Hursch as elder from 1778; the Meckesheim congregation then had Johannes Neff (from 1772), Michael Bechtel (from 1774), and Christian Sander (later called Sauter) as preachers (from 1776). In the *Naamlijst* of 1786 Mauer and Meckesheim were united again, with Abraham Mayer as preacher from 1781 and as elder from 1784, and Michael Bechtel, Christian Sauter, and Jakob Müller (from 1783) as preachers. Finally in the *Naamlijst* of 1793 the congregation is called Meckesheim, Schatthausen, and Baiertal, with the same ministers as in 1786 and in addition Heinrich Landis, from 1790. A list

of preachers of 1787 reveals that services were held alternately in Mauer and Schatthausen (*Menn. Geschicts.-Bl.,* 1936, 25), later also in Beiertal; in 1840, however, an independent congregation was organized here. The Meckesheim congregation was weakened by emigration. Mannhardt (*Jahrbuch* 1888) mentions a baptized membership of 25 in 1887, with Heinrich Mosemann serving as elder (preacher 1856, elder 1870) and Heinrich Bechtel (from 1875) serving both as preacher and deacon. Services then were held each Sunday in a rented room. In 1896 it transferred its headquarters to Mönchzell (*q.v.*) and in 1916 it united with Sinsheim (*q.v.*) after an existence of about two hundred years. (*ML* III, 65.) Hege, vdZ.

Meckville Mennonite Church (MC), a member of the Lancaster Conference, began as a mission station in the Meckville area, Bethel Twp., Berks Co., Pa. After some disappointing experiences in joint work with the Church of the Brethren, and then in a purchased schoolhouse which burned to the ground, the mission board in 1932 built a brick building, 36 x 50 ft., near one of these schools. In 1954 Aaron M. Shank and Cletus Doutrich were serving as ministers with a membership of 65. I.D.L.

Medals: see **Commemorative Medals.**

Medaryville (Ind.) CPS Camp No. 28, about five miles north of Medaryville, was opened in the Jasper-Pulaski Game Preserve when the Bluffton, Ind., Camp No. 13 was moved to this location in early April 1942. It was a Mennonite administered camp, and was the site of a handicraft institute in September 1944 and a conscription institute in March 1945. The men worked in a tree seedling nursery and on a game farm and participated in emergency farm work. The *Peace Sentinel* was published by the camp from July 1942 to March 1946. The camp was closed in April 1946. M.G.

M. Gingerich, *Service for Peace* (Akron, Pa., 1949) 126-28.

Medemblik, a town (1947 pop. 4,930) in the Dutch Province of North Holland, where there has been a Mennonite congregation since very early times. Leenaert Bouwens (*q.v.*) baptized a total of 63 persons here in 1563-65. From the close of the 16th century the attitude of the government was remarkably tolerant in permitting the Mennonites to perform their own marriages, merely notifying the authorities of the union. But otherwise the magistrates were less tolerant: in 1628 Hans Alenson (*q.v.*), preaching here, was imprisoned for some time on the instigation of the Reformed ministers and then banished from the town. The small congregation (in 1675, 50 baptized members) belonged to the Waterlander branch. There was also a Frisian congregation, which was still smaller and in 1730 united with the former. On several occasions (e.g., 1727, 1733, 1736) the congregation contributed liberally to the needs of the Prussian and Lithuanian Mennonites. In 1826 the combined membership was only 16; by 1847 the number had risen to 31, in 1901 to 53, and in 1938 to 73; since then somewhat less (42 in 1957). Until 1883 the congregation had its own preacher. After having none for six years, it joined the neighboring Enkhuizen for services. But in 1901 it again acquired a preacher of its own (Th. H. van Vens 1901-5, F. J. de Holl 1905-13, J. M. Erkelens 1913-19). In 1919 it united with the congregation of Twisk (*q.v.*).   vDZ.

Inv. Arch. Amst. II, 2, Nos. 261-71; Blaupot t. C., *Holland* I, II, *passim*, see Index; *DB* 1889, 134; *ML* III, 65.

Medemblicker Nieu Liedtboeck, a Dutch hymnbook, printed at Wormerveer 1646, of which there is apparently no copy left. (*DJ* 1837, 65.)   vDZ.

Medendorp, a Mennonite family, which seems to have stemmed from De Meeden (*q.v.*), a village in the Dutch province of Groningen, where Alle Pieters (1595-1641), one of its ancestors, was a Mennonite preacher. In the 17th and 18th centuries the Medendorps belonged to the Old Flemish branch. They were found particularly in the city of Groningen, where Alle Pieters Medendorp (1705-56) became a preacher of the Old Flemish congregation, serving from 1733 until his death. He was an active trustee of the Dutch Mennonite Committee for Foreign Needs, and as secretary of the Groningen Old Flemish Conference he corresponded with Prussian Mennonites. His son Christoffer Medendorp (1733-1818), a merchant, moved from Groningen to Leer, East Friesland, Germany.

There is also a Reformed branch of the Medendorp family, to which belonged Lambert Medendorp, born at Appingedam, Dutch province of Groningen, d. 1690, Reformed minister (1678-90) at Larrelt, Leer, and Emden in East Friesland. (*Inv. Arch. Amst.* I, Nos. 1097, 1636. 1664.)   vDZ.

Medford (Okla.) Mennonite Brethren Church, now extinct, located three miles north of Medford, was organized on Nov. 12, 1899, through the initiative of J. F. Harms and daughter Tina, David Harms, Sam Hodel, John J. Wiens, and Mrs. Susanne Wiens. The first meetinghouse was an old schoolhouse moved to its new location in October 1901 and dedicated on Jan. 25, 1903. The congregation was dissolved on Sept. 20, 1909, because most of the members had moved away.   P.C.H.

Medford Mennonite Church (GCM), located two miles north and two east of Medford, Grant Co., Okla., a member of the Western District Conference, was organized in February 1897 with 13 charter members and H. J. Gaede as first minister. The first building was erected in 1909, the present one dedicated in 1954. The membership in 1954 was 98. Other ministers who have served are John Lichti, Albert G. Schmidt, Ernest Bergen, and Henry D. Penner, the present pastor.   H.D.P.

Medicine. Many of the early Swiss Brethren of Reformation times were well educated, and a list of the Brethren in 1526 mentions a doctor and his wife as being among the group. After the persecution the Brethren largely became peasants in more isolated districts with little opportunity for economic advancement or formal schooling. Lack of reference to medical affairs in their writings leads one to

suppose that they had little acquaintance with professional medicine. They were acquainted with the violent deaths accorded to martyrs. As farmers they were acquainted with the cause-and-effect relationships of exposure, violence, nutrition, and disease. It is known from family lists that the birth and death rates were high. Midwifery was practiced among them and booklets on this art ascribed to Aristotle and Albertus Magnus were used. As economic and educational opportunities increased during the 19th century the medical history of the Mennonites is similar to that of the European people of their class and location. A significant contribution to medical advance came through the work of Dr. Peter Dettweiler (*q.v.,* d. 1904), of Alsatian Mennonite parentage, but resident in Bavaria, who discovered that the cure of tuberculosis is not dependent on specific locations and thus became the father of the sanatorium movement.

The Hutterites of the 16th century developed medical practice far in advance of their day. They may have had personal contact with Paracelsus. Their surgeons and bathers (barbers) attended the nobility, conducted famous baths in Moravia, and recognized the contagious nature of certain diseases; the Brethren followed sanitary practices and applied principles of child training consonant with modern concepts of mental hygiene. The excellent work of the physician-surgeons played a large part in developing friendly relations between them and the nobility. Their profession was respected and at least one of the bathers, Sebastian Dietrich, became the general overseer of the entire brotherhood. Dabbling in alchemy, on the other hand, was considered highly improper. The contact of the Hutterite surgeons with the nobility tended to cause dissatisfaction with the simplicity of life practiced by the brotherhood. Frequently they drifted away from their brothers. The death, near the end of the 18th century, of the one remaining physician and his apprentice within a week was taken to be a providential sign that they should get along without professional medical care. The Hutterite chronicles record wave after wave of pestilence decimating the settlements. Unlike their neighbors who fled in panic to the forests leaving the sick to die in utter helplessness, the Hutterites nursed their victims of the plague and gave orderly burial to their dead.

In 1874-77 the Hutterites emigrated to South Dakota and later to Canada. Here they give their children only elementary school education and have not produced any physicians. However, they avail themselves of the medical facilities of near-by towns. At the middle of the 20th century their birth rate was 45.19 per thousand population and their death rate a mere 4.4, making them one of the most rapidly growing population groups on record. Their colonies have recently been intensively studied because of a reported low incidence of mental illness. (See further **Medicine Among the Hutterites.**)

The Dutch Mennonites were less isolated and economically and socially more favored than their Swiss brethren. One of their unique institutions, that of the deaconesses, had far-reaching results in the medical world. Theodore Fliedner, a pastor of Kaiserswerth, Germany, received some inspiration for founding his famous institution while visiting among the Mennonites in Holland, although the Dutch deaconesses do not deserve the whole credit. The Mennonite deaconesses of Holland were not nurses but rather women ordained to the office of overseer of the poor and needy. They were important in staffing the projects pioneered by the Dutch Mennonite minister Jan Nieuwenhuizen (q.v.). These projects included an old ladies' home, orphanages, and a home for feeble-minded children. These deaconesses also furnished the inspiration for an order of Mennonite deaconess nurses in Russia and the United States. (See further **Medicine Among the Dutch Mennonites.**)

The immigrants from North Germany to Russia (1789-1820) took with them their medical customs and practices. Babies were delivered by midwives. One practitioner recorded the 13,000 deliveries at which she assisted. These women received no particular stipend but were exempt from paying taxes. The mortality rate was high. In the Chortitza settlement, of the 6,874 children born between 1880 and 1922, 2,008 died in infancy and childhood, a rate of nearly 30 per cent. Trained physicians were scarce and only one was reported among the 60 villages of the Molotschna settlement in 1880.

The sense of brotherhood led the Russian Mennonite settlers to provide for the aged and infirm. From early days the feeble-minded, the deaf, and the epileptic inherited twice the amount the healthy siblings received. Such funds were placed in trusteeship and came to have a stabilizing influence in the economy of the community as well as providing for institutional care. By about the end of the 19th century the settlements had old people's homes, orphanages, a school for the deaf, and a hospital for those with nervous diseases including epileptics. To staff these institutions a school for deaconess nurses was opened at Neuhalbstadt in 1909. The doctors were generally Mennonites who had taken training either in German or Russian universities.

While these institutions were the product of united community action, the first Russian Mennonite hospital was the result of a private venture of faith. Franz Wall, a Mennonite minister, inspired by the noble example of George Müller of Bristol, England, converted his home at Muntau, Molotschna, into a hospital in 1880.

The Mennonites in Russia were interested in helping others in need. One thousand rubles were collected and given to aid wounded soldiers during the Napoleonic invasion. During the Crimean War 5,000 sick and wounded soldiers were transported and cared for in the settlements. As a result of exposure to the diseases of the soldiers, especially dysentery and typhus, a number of the Mennonites died. At the time of the Boxer Rebellion in China 5,000 rubles were sent to the Red Cross to be used for the sick and wounded. In the Russo-Japanese War, in addition to Red Cross support, a group of twenty Mennonite young men volunteered to aid sick and wounded soldiers. Of these, a number died, including a Mennonite doctor. In World War I thousands of Russian Mennonite men served on hospital trains and in special hospitals. Mennonite doctors had responsible positions in these

services. This medical service was civilian and staffed by volunteers, who had the legal right to serve in the forestry service. The Zemstwo Union was a civilian organization. (See also **Medicine Among the Mennonites in Russia.**)

The Mennonites of America were earlier suspicious of the ways of the world in education and science. Hence unscientific means for obtaining cures were often used. Among them was a system of incantations known as "powwowing" (q.v.) or "Braucherei." The formulae used were supposed to have some magic qualities, and were not true prayers as some supposed. References to the Virgin, saints, archangels, and the use of Latin words point to a Catholic origin, possibly pre-Reformation and peasant. Powwowing is frowned upon officially, but is still practiced in a few culturally retarded communities. People in such areas lack scientific standards of evaluation and tend to patronize irregular practitioners, maintain a belief in magnetism and other devices, and place reliance on herbs, home remedies, and advertised nostrums. However, since virtually all childbed deliveries now take place in hospitals, and immunization of children is routine, modern medical practices are being fully accepted.

In some Mennonite groups "anointing" (q.v.), based on James 5, has been practiced sporadically. Occasionally, in most recent times, individuals have been influenced by the "divine healing" movement, and a few have attempted to practice it. However, vigorous counteraction in teaching and discipline has prevented any significant spread of the aberration.

In Mennonitism throughout the world missionary work and the rise of hospitals and charitable work was a 19th-century development, sometimes influenced by Pietism, sometimes the natural result of a strong tradition of the ministry of Christian love to the needy, which found expression in service to non-Mennonites after the spirit of isolationism began to break down. The value of medical work became very clear on the missionary field, and the first missionary effort by the Dutch Mennonites in Java and Sumatra soon developed a medical emphasis. With some modification that pattern is typical of Mennonite medical missions, whether in India, pre-Communist China, Ethiopia, Tanganyika, the Belgian Congo, or Puerto Rico. It consists of a hospital center staffed by a medical missionary and missionary nurses, assisted by native workers who assume more responsibility as they receive training. In time a school of nursing develops, and native assistants or even doctors are added to the staff. In addition to the central hospital there are a series of outstations in charge of a missionary nurse or visited on schedule by the missionary doctor. In Asia and Africa a leprosarium is generally added. Missions in South America do not include hospital work, because of the governments' policy of excluding foreign doctors.

The first Mennonite hospitals in North America were established in the communities of the Russian immigrants about 1900 and later. The General Conference Mennonites developed nursing schools under the direction of a deaconess order. The Mennonites (MC) did not develop community hospitals so early.

The first of their hospitals was an outgrowth of a tuberculosis sanatorium established (1907) as an act of mercy in a non-Mennonite community. It is owned by their board of missions. Recently this board has begun operating a number of community hospitals whose constituency is not primarily Mennonite. The two nursing schools of the group are under the general Board of Education and one of the schools is of the collegiate type. It is estimated that there are now about 1,000 Mennonite nurses in North America. Among them are a number of male nurses.

In earlier days it was unusual to see a Mennonite physician. Family histories reveal that the physicians who came from Mennonite homes often did not remain members of the church. A study in 1947 revealed that one third of the doctors from such homes were no longer Mennonites. Most of these transferred membership after starting practice and attributed the change to a "broadening" viewpoint, or learning to appreciate other religious views and becoming less dogmatic. Fully half of these physicians did not practice in Mennonite communities, explaining that these lacked cultural or educational opportunities, or that some Mennonites were unscientific, patronized quacks, and were generally unappreciative of a physician's services. A Mennonite Medical Association (q.v.) was founded to help in correcting this difficulty.

World War II had a great effect on Mennonite medical affairs. The reservoir of doctors, nurses, and medical auxiliaries was tapped by the MCC to carry on the medical phase of its relief work throughout the world. Fifteen hundred men drafted to Civilian Public Service worked in mental hospitals as aids, and about 170 women volunteered to do similar work. Other young people worked in general hospitals, veterans' hospitals, in public health and sanitation, hookworm and typhus control, or in health education. Others were used as "guinea pigs" in scientific investigations on typhus, pneumonia, infectious hepatitis, nutrition or metabolism experiments. Similar experience was continued after the war in the "I-W" and voluntary services programs.

One of the results of this experience has been an increased interest in mental health. The MCC has established three mental hospitals since 1945, and a fourth is under consideration. Another mental hospital is sponsored by the Lancaster Conference (MC) and yet another in Ontario is sponsored by the M.B. group. These institutions represent pioneer experiments in the value of personal service religiously oriented, combined with a restful rural atmosphere.

Sickness insurance is a relatively new phenomenon on the American scene. The brotherhood has always had an alms fund in the care of the deacon, and the community often turned out en masse to do the season's farm work of the sick or injured member. It is interesting to note that there existed a Beneficial Society in the Franconia (MC) district as early as 1888 and that they paid sickness benefits. In 1902 the Menno-Friendly Beneficial Association was formed at the First Mennonite Church (GCM) in Philadelphia for the purpose of giving relief "to

members who shall be confined to their homes by reason of sickness or disability or accident." Local efforts are illustrated by the Health Society of Yarrow, B.C., organized in 1935. This group contracted for medical care by a Mennonite doctor for $12.00 per year for each member's family. A similar plan was sponsored by the Health Society of Coaldale, Alberta. A more extensive movement took place in the Mennonite Church (MC). As a result of official conference action Mennonite Aid, Inc., was authorized in 1949 to set up a plan for payment of hospital and surgical benefits. At the beginning of 1955 it had over 5,000 members. In Europe Mennonites normally take advantage of the state medical insurance plans, such as the German and Swiss *Krankenkasse*. The Mennonites of Mexico and South America have had special medical problems. Since the Mexican group migrated seeking isolation, it is not surprising that they are not aware that their health and sanitary practices are poor and their medical care inadequate, being limited largely to the ministrations of the bone-doctors (*Knochenärzte*), midwives, and such patent medicines as may be purchased at the village stores. Knowledge of nutrition is meager. Milk is sold for cash rather than consumed by the family. Sanitary installations are scarce. Immunization is not practiced and the childhood diseases, especially enteritis, take a heavy toll. Villages may be 40 to 50 miles from a doctor and almost as far from a telephone. The MCC relief services offered in various ways to assist in raising the health standards, but difficulty with government regulations and the attitudes of the settlers made it necessary to abandon the clinics. In 1954 plans were under way to have the MCC administer a local hospital in Cuauhtemoc.

The Brazilian immigrant group of 1930 included trained nurses and others who had some elemental knowledge of medicine, but no doctor. Medical services had to be obtained at a hospital 40 miles distant until Dr. Peter Dyck from Russia and his wife, a trained nurse, arrived to establish a hospital in Witmarsum. This medical work was supported financially by the Dutch Mennonites. The colonists had their own dental clinic. When the Witmarsum colony was abandoned this hospital passed out of Mennonite hands.

In many ways the most difficult health problems were presented by Paraguay. The settlers included those from Canada in search of isolation, Russian refugees stranded in Europe but refused admittance to Canada often because of trachoma or tuberculosis, and refugees from Siberia long stranded in Harbin, China. When the Canadian group arrived in 1928 about one tenth died on the way into the Chaco from dysentery and typhus. The Paraguayan government offered free immunizations against typhoid, but only a few immigrants took advantage of this. The Harbin group, too, was decimated by an epidemic of scarlet fever. Medical care was inadequate. Practical nurses and midwives did what they could. Because of poor roads and great distances the Paraguayan doctors were almost inaccessible. The MCC sent Dr. John R. Schmidt, and later his wife, a trained nurse, to bring medical aid. Dr. Schmidt found that 75 per cent had trachoma and about

50 per cent had hookworm. Rickets and tuberculosis of the bone were common. Hookworm control was initiated and trachoma was treated with the sulfa drugs. An adequate hospital was built to supersede the old clay-floored dispensary. A small mental hospital was erected. A North American surgeon, a dentist, and an eye specialist spent terms of various lengths giving their specialized services. A school of nursing was set up, and colonists were trained in pharmacy, anesthesia, and other auxiliaries. Promising young men were sent to Asuncion or abroad to learn medicine and young women to learn nursing. Thus a most difficult problem gave way to relentless will backed up by the world-wide resources of the Mennonite brotherhood. Several European non-Mennonite doctors have been employed by the Paraguayan settlements, particularly Fernheim. In 1954 the first Mennonite doctor, a son of Fernheim but trained in the United States, began practice in the Friesland colony.

It is typical that a leprosarium was to be established in gratitude to Paraguay for offering a new home and a new outlook on life, to be jointly operated by the MCC and the Mennonite settlements with considerable financial assistance by the American Mission to Lepers. Instead of the leprosarium as originally planned, however, a series of clinics was set up, where ambulatory treatment is emphasized. (See **Lepers, Paraguay Mission to.**)

H.C.A.

Frank C. Peters, "Noncombatant Service Then and Now," *Menn. Life* X (January 1955) 31-35.

Medicine Among the Dutch Mennonites. Among the Dutch Mennonite ministers of the 17th and 18th centuries there is a striking number of medical doctors. One of the first leaders of the Dutch Anabaptists, Obbe Philips, had been a barber-surgeon, and even before the end of the 16th century some Dutch Mennonites attended the universities to obtain medical training. Among the first was Jan Willemsz (1583-1660), who obtained his doctor's degree about 1610. During the 17th and especially the 18th centuries there were many Mennonite physicians in Holland. Their unusually large number had two principal causes: first, the wealth the Dutch Mennonites had attained by this time enabled them to devote time and money to scholarly pursuits, and at the same time made them eager to partake in university "higher life"; second, they nonetheless still held to the old Mennonite view that talents should be made subservient to the welfare of one's fellow men; in brief, the ethical responsibility of faith caused them to choose medicine rather than, for example, law. Some of them were called to high positions; Govert Bidloo (1649-1713) became professor of anatomy at the University of Leiden and chief physician to stadholder King William III; his nephew Nicolaas Bidloo (b. 1670) became the personal physician of Czar Peter the Great of Russia, and founder of the medical school at Moscow; and Matthias S. van Geuns (1735-1817) was a professor in the medical faculties of the universities of Harderwijk and Utrecht. A large number of the Mennonites who had studied medicine before the Seminary was founded were both physicians and preach-

ers. Particularly after about 1650 the congregations apparently demanded well-trained preachers, and yet wished to maintain the principle of the unsalaried ministry, and since university training seemed a guarantee of adequacy to the task of leading a Mennonite congregation, they often called physicians as preachers and elders. A few of the outstanding doctor-preachers were Jan Willemsz at De Rijp, Joannes de Backer at Amsterdam, Anthoni Jacobsz Roscius at Hoorn, Jacob Cornelis van Dalen at Amsterdam, Galenus Abrahamsz at Amsterdam, Jacob Ostens at Rotterdam, Antonius van Dale at Haarlem, Petrus Teckop at Leiden, Klaas Toornburg at De Rijp, Christoffel Tirion at Utrecht, Herman Schijn at Amsterdam, Willem Bosch at Haarlem, Gerardus de Wind at Middelburg, Abraham van Loon at Gouda, Maarten Harp at Den Ilp, Frederik Toger at Leiden, Jacobus van Zanten at Haarlem, Jan van Beekhoven de Wind at Haarlem, Johannes Nettis at Alkmaar, Petrus Belkmeer at Enschedé, Pieter Schagen at Westzaan. After the founding of the Amsterdam Mennonite Theological Seminary in 1735, the physician preachers gradually disappeared. The last was Pieter Schagen.

The Mennonites of Amsterdam have organized the Mennonite Public Health Association, which is actually a nursing service for all classes of people. Subscribers are entitled to six weeks of nursing service per year.

vDZ.

Medicine Among the Hutterites. As the article **Medicine** has already demonstrated, there was a distinct difference between the medical experiences among 16th-century Anabaptists in general and the unique practices of the Hutterites. Their settled and well-developed community life in Moravia and Slovakia almost necessitated attention to medical care and hygiene, and thus led to developments which singled them out among all the rest of the nonurban population of early modern times. Since the situation has been given careful historical study, a fairly correct picture can be offered in the following.

(a) Hygiene. The Brethren were among the earliest to conduct what today would best be called boarding schools. Accordingly, much attention was directed to have these schools (from nursery age to about 14 years of age) on their Bruderhofs well controlled and supervised. Peter Walpot (*q.v.*) issued his famous school discipline in 1568, in which almost modern principles of hygiene were set forth to be strictly obeyed. The Brethren were sensibly aware of contagion; thus particular care was directed to an early discovery of children's diseases, whereupon such children were separated, their clothing and linen as well as their food being kept completely from that of the rest. There were sicknesses like scurvy, eczema, even syphilis, and attention was needed to prevent epidemics. The enemies accused them of negligence and claimed a high child mortality (see **Handbüchlein** and **Fischer, Chr. A.**), but the Brethren defended themselves effectively, and actually could point to their numerous strict regulations for such group living.

(b) Bathing and Bathhouses. The 16th century in general experienced a decline in bathing. Bathing for cleanliness was deemed by the Hutterites

not necessary more than once in four weeks. But for health's sake bathing found quite elaborate attention among the Brethren. To quote the archfoe of the Hutterites, Christoph A. Fischer, who involuntarily had to admit the fame of these Hutterite bathhouses: "Every Saturday their baths are packed full of Christians [i.e., Catholics]. And not alone the common people but also noble persons come running to them if they ever need treatment, as if Anabaptists were the only ones who possessed this art in the entire region" (Fischer, *54 Erhebliche Ursachen* 1607, "32. Ursach," p. 85). These bathhouses were administered by professional "Bader" (caretakers of the baths), who also functioned as barber-surgeons and generally replaced physicians, as these latter were a rather rare profession in the 16th century. These Bader must have been quite numerous among the Hutterites of the later 16th century, again a proof that the Anabaptist way had great attraction for all walks of life.

(c) Bader-Ordnungen. Although generally highly respected the Bader nevertheless had to conform to the general pattern of communal life of the Hutterites. Apparently this posed a real problem for these rather independent people who quickly gained also a clientele outside the brotherhood. Thus it is not surprising that strict regulations, called "Bader-Ordnungen," were issued from time to time, particularly during the 17th century when a certain decline in discipline set in. The earliest regulation is no longer extant, but we hear of such documents of 1592, 1633, 1635, 1637, 1654, and 1657 (with the exception of the first named they all come from the period of Bishop Andreas Ehrenpreis, *q.v.* The Bader-Ordnung of 1654 was published in an English translation, *MQR* 1953, 125-27). They insisted on cleanliness, asked the barber-surgeons to continue in the study of pharmacy and other medical knowledge, regulated the practice of blood-cupping, and so on. Special emphasis is laid upon the proper behavior of these important brethren: there should be no arrogance among them and no overbearing, in spite of the fact that they enjoyed certain privileges which differentiated them from the rest on the Bruderhof (e.g., horseback riding).

When traveling from Bruderhof to Bruderhof, these barber-surgeons often carried along a whole wagonload of extracts, pills, electuaries, ointments, etc. Needless to say, the Bader were also much in demand outside the Hutterite communities, which made their exceptional position even more difficult. They received payment for their services, and these sums, too, presented a temptation. As the rest of the brotherhood were largely rural in character, the adjustment of these men posed a permanent problem.

(d) Personnel. The Hutterite *Chronicle* mentions at least three doctors or physicians among the Brethren: Georg Zobel (d. 1603) of Nikolsburg, who was called twice to the Imperial Court of Rudolph II at Prague (the first time, 1581, he stayed six months and is said to have cured the emperor; the second time, 1599, he was supposed to help to stop an epidemic in Prague); Balthasar Gollar (d. 1619), likewise of Nikolsburg, the personal physician of Cardinal Dietrichstein (*q.v.*), who otherwise fought

Anabaptism by all means at his disposal. In 1608-9 Goller was also the personal physician of the Imperial Ambassador, Count Herberstein, on his trip to Constantinople. At the outbreak of the Thirty Years' War Goller was slain in Nikolsburg and his pharmacy was destroyed. The third was Conrad Blössy, a former citizen of Zürich, Switzerland, who in 1612 went back to that city and rendered great assistance in fighting an epidemic there.

The number of barber-surgeons mentioned in the sources is quite considerable. One, Sebastian Dietrich (*q.v.*) of Markgröningen in Württemberg, even became head bishop or Vorsteher of the entire brotherhood (1611-19). (For more names of such barbers see Friedmann, 130-35.)

(e) Training and Education. Very little is known about the training of the physicians. Most likely they got their training before joining the brotherhood, although the profession of barber-surgeon could also be learned at certain Bruderhofs, e.g., in Nikolsburg, or at the places of their bathhouses. It is also known that Paracelsus, the most famous physician of his century, lived in Moravia 1537-38 on an estate where Hutterites also were admitted. But no sources about possible contacts have become known. It is, however, highly revealing that the Hutterian Brethren of today have preserved two very old medical books. The one, of 1575, was bought by Andreas Ehrenpreis in Sobotiste, Slovakia, in 1638 from a Hungarian book peddler. It is a manuscript book of 230 leaves octavo, entitled *Antidotarium, Composita oder Recepta der Schaden- und Wundarzney,* etc., by Lienhard Gargasser, 1575. The other, called *Arzney Handbüchl, vieler Krankheiten Zustände Causam et Curam,* etc., is also handwritten, copied by the Hutterite barber-surgeon Johannes Spengler in 1635 while practicing his art at the mineral bath of Trenchin-Teplic, Slovakia. It comprises 470 octavo leaves, containing mostly prescriptions of remedies and good counsel as to how to cure ailments. The name of Paracelsus is mentioned in it at many places; unfortunately the original from which this book was carefully copied is no longer known. Both books are now in the possession of the Hutterites in Western Canada.

(f) Later Period. The tradition of having doctors or barber-surgeons around on the Bruderhofs was never abandoned. The *Klein-Geschichtsbuch* (380-81), for instance, expressly mentions for the year 1780 (when the brotherhood had settled in the Ukraine) that the Brethren wished to have again a trained doctor with them, and accordingly dispatched the young and able brother Christian Wurz to study with the French house physician of Count Romanzov, the protector of the Brethren. At first Christian kept rigidly and faithfully to his Hutterite background, but after a while he got "to love the world," even put on a wig, and soon became fully secularized. He later went to Moscow. The chronicle states sadly, "In a few years three members left our faith; they were among the most skilled and learned ones."

Again in 1792, the same chronicle reports the death of a barber-surgeon. "Thus the brotherhood had no one any more who would understand blood-cupping and other medical practices. This fact became a real concern to the brethren" (*Klein-Geschichtsbuch*, 388). In 1814 again the death of another brother-medicus Zacharias Wipf is reported. He had served his brotherhood for 16 years both in the pharmacy and in the art of medicine (*Klein-Geschichtsbuch*, 423).

(*g*) *In America* naturally the need for doctors has been more easily met than at any time before. Nevertheless the Brethren continued to have their own "bonesetters" (chiropractors), experts in medicinal herbs, and, of course, experienced midwives. Joseph Eaton reports that some of these bonesetters and masseurs are so much in demand that the Brethren set up a special office for one of them. It seems that they are not especially trained in their art but practice it rather out of a certain natural gift and intuition (Eaton, 164, 170). All Bruderhofs have plenty of house remedies for all emergencies. As to psychic disturbances, the friendly atmosphere of the community and the opportunity of talking confidentially to the preacher work strongly toward a high level of mental health.   R.F.

J. Loserth, *Communismus*, chapter "Die Arzneikunst und Bäder der Wiedertäufer," 275 ff.; John L. Sommer, "Hutterite Medicine and Physicians in Moravia in the 16th Century and After," *MQR* XX (1953) 111-27 (with an English translation of a Bader-Ordnung); R. Friedmann, "Hutterite Physicians and Barber-Surgeons," *ibid.*, 128-36; J. W. Eaton and R. J. Weil, *Culture and Mental Disorder, A Comparative Study of the Hutterites* (Glencoe, Ill., 1955); Zieglschmid, *Klein-Geschichtsbuch*.

Medicine Among the Mennonites in Russia. The use of medicine among the early Mennonites of Russia, as in Prussia, was similar to that of any rural area. In the early pioneer days of the Ukraine there was little opportunity for the settlers to avail themselves of the help of medical doctors, drugs, and hospitalization. The traditional bonesetters (*Knochenärzte*) and midwives functioned. Some of the bonesetters (similar to chiropractors) and midwives had through innate gifts, years of experience, and the knowledge conveyed from generation to generation achieved a wide reputation. The ministers or the teachers were often also advisers in health matters. Health rules, recipes, and the practice of the Knochenarzt were transplanted from Russia to the Great Plains of America, where they have been preserved in some forms to this day, particularly in Mexico and South America. Even the popular contemporary chiropractors in Mennonite communities can no doubt be linked to this tradition, e.g., the Tieszen clinic at Marion, S.D. Schmiedehaus relates that the Mennonites of Mexico still use such medicines as *Schlagwasser, Wunderöl, Kaiseröl, Alpenkräuter, Grossmutters Abführtee*, and Dr. Bell's horse medicine.

With the increase of the Russian population in the Ukraine, the government helped provide medical aid to the people. As the Mennonites advanced culturally and economically, they also became interested in better medical care. The Russian zemstvo (rural administration) made some provision for trained physicians around 1850. The primary purpose was to prevent the spread of epidemics. Only at a few places were hospitals erected. One of the first doctors to practice in Chortitza was Karnitzky. A Bernhard Schellenberg became the first "Feld-scher," a trained assistant to the physician. Among the first midwives who had received some training was Charlotte Voroshevskaya. She was succeeded by Margarete Wieler and later Susie Penner.

The first Mennonite doctor in Russia very likely was Jacob Esau, who was educated at the University of Kiev and became the physician of the Chortitza settlement around 1880. Considerable improvement was made during this period. A small hospital was erected, and two or three assistants (*Feldscher*) assisted Esau. An apothecary was located next to his office. Medicine, examination, and treatment were free. In addition to this arrangement, the Mennonite factories of Chortitza also employed doctors, among whom were Voth, Hausknecht, Knieast, Ebius, Glückman, Meder, and Heinrichs. Judging by the names, only the first two and last were Mennonites. The factory owners also established a hospital of their own next to that of the zemstvo. One of the most successful doctors with one of the longest terms of service was Theodor Hottmann, who practiced medicine in connection with the zemstvo hospital 1902-37. Hottmann was joined by Dr. David A. Hamm.

In 1908 a new zemstvo hospital was erected between the villages of Rosenthal and Chortitza. The services of the zemstvo hospital were available to all Chortitza Mennonite villages and four neighboring Russian villages. The hospital and doctors were supported by the Chortitza volost (district). For the services given to the Russian village, the provincial zemstvo furnished medicine and instruments as well as two medical assistants and nurses.

During World War I the Chortitza Mennonites maintained a 75 to 100 bed Red Cross emergency hospital in addition to the regular hospital. Many of the Mennonites served in this unit.

Less information is available about the medical care among Mennonites of other settlements in Russia, even in the Molotschna settlement. In most of the other more recent and smaller settlements, the Mennonites availed themselves of the medical facilities of their neighboring Russian communities. The Molotschna settlement apparently did not have the zemstvo facilities. Franz Wall established a hospital at Muntau (see **Muntau Hospital**) in 1880. During the last phase of its existence, this hospital prospered under Dr. Erich Tavonius, who served 1900-27. Other small Mennonite hospitals existed at Waldheim and Ohrloff in the Molotschna settlement as well as in the Neu-Samara settlement. Bethania (*q.v.*), near Chortitza, was a mental hospital. On the island of Chortitza a hospital for tubercular patients was established and a sanitarium called Alexandrabad.   C.K.

D. A. Hamm, "Das Gesundheitswesen in Chortitza," *Menn. Life* X (April 1955) 84 f.; Maria Hottmann, "Dr. Theodor Hottmann," *Mennonitisches Jahrbuch 1953* (Newton, 1953) 39-48; "Doktor Erich Tavonius," *Unser Blatt* II (1927) 307-9; Walter Schmiedehaus, "Mennonite Life in Mexico," *Menn. Life* II (April 1947) 29-38; C. W. Wiebe, "Health Conditions Among the Mennonites of Mexico," *Menn. Life* II (April 1947) 43 f.

Medina County, Ohio, originally a part of Western Reserve of Connecticut, was organized in 1818. It is the home of three Mennonite congregations with a total of 425 baptized members: Wadsworth (GCM) with 254 members, Lower (OOM) with 40 members, and Bethel (MC) with 131, in the southeastern part of the county, all derived from original Mennonite settlers from Bucks Co., Pa., in 1829, soon joined by others from Maryland, from Lancaster and Lehigh counties, Pa., and from Canada. The first Mennonite school of higher education (GCM) was located in Wadsworth in 1867-78.

J.S.U.

Medway Reformed Mennonite Church, located at Medway, Clark Co., Ohio, had eight members in 1948. The meetinghouse was built in 1872, but sold before 1948; the privilege of worship is, however, retained.

J.L.K.

Meeden, a village in the Dutch province of Groningen, where there was a Mennonite congregation belonging to the Groningen Old Flemish and closely connected with that of Beerta (*q.v.*) in the early 17th century. It was always small, reaching its highest point in 1773 with a baptized membership of 100, but then rapidly decreasing. Since the end of the 18th century it has been merged with Midwolda (*q.v.*). Originally meetings were held in a private home. In the 18th century a plain meetinghouse was erected, and a new one was built in 1871. This was used until a new church of the united congregation of Midwolda, De Meeden, and Beerta (now called Winschoten), was built at Winschoten in 1931.

vDZ.

Blaupot t. C., *Groningen* I, *passim*, see Index; *DB* 1872, 192; 1879, 4; *ML* III, 65.

Meenen (Menin), a town in West Flanders, Belgium, center of Anabaptist-Mennonite activity in the 16th century. There was a congregation from at least 1545. Leenaert Bouwens (*q.v.*) baptized 26 persons here in 1554-56 and in 1577-61 another 21 (or perhaps 46). About this time Joris Wippe (*q.v.*) (he was not a burgomaster of Meenen, as has been supposed), who was executed at Dordrecht, Holland, in 1558, was a member of the congregation, as was also Leenaert Plovier (*q.v.*), a cloth merchant, executed at Antwerp in 1558. Pieter van der Meersch (*q.v.*) was a preacher of the Meenen congregation until 1564; Jacob de Keersgieter (de Rore) (*q.v.*) baptized here about 1566. Since baptism was still performed at Meenen in 1578, it is probable that the congregation existed at least until this time. The Meenen congregation was often struck by severe persecution, particularly in 1561 and 1569, while in 1567 during a raid a number of Mennonites escaped; their property, however, was confiscated. Eight Mennonites arrested here were executed at Kortrijk (*q.v.*) in 1569: Absolon de Zanger and Willem van Haverbeke in 1561, and Pieter den Ouden, Fransoois de Timmerman, Jan van Raes, Jan Wattier, Wouter Denijs, and Kalleken, the wife of Anpleunis van den Berge. A number of Anabaptists of Meenen suffered martyrdom in other Belgian towns, particularly at Gent and Antwerp. This indicates that there must have been a rather strong Anabaptist-Mennonite movement at Meenen. In 1578 (or 79) the martyr Michiel Buyse (*q.v.*) was baptized at Meenen.

About 1581 the remaining members of the congregation fled to the Netherlands. Some of them, e.g., the Apostool (*q.v.*) and the van der Meersch (*q.v.*) families, emigrated to Haarlem, Holland, where they founded important weaving mills and linen bleacheries.

vDZ.

A. L. E. Verheyden, "Mennisme in Vlaanderen," ms.; *idem,* Gent, 68, note 1; Kühler, *Geschiedenis* 1, 439.

Meer (Mehr), **Jan ter** (1594-1672), was a Mennonite elder at Gladbach, Germany (see **München-Gladbach**). Of his life and activity not much is known; he was an elder from 1628 or earlier. After 1652 when the Mennonites were forced to leave Gladbach, ter Meer apparently moved to Crefeld (*q.v.*) with many members of the Gladbach congregation, while others moved to Nijmegen (*q.v.*) in the Netherlands. In 1656 ter Meer, then living at Crefeld, ordained Jan Godtschalks van Elten, who had moved from Gladbach to Nijmegen in 1654, as a preacher and deacon of the Nijmegen congregation. The Jan ter Mehr who in 1677 wrote a letter to the Mennonites at Nijmegen in the name of the Crefeld congregation cannot be the same person. Possibly he is a son of the former. (*Der Mennonit* IX, No. 8, Aug. 1956, 123; *DB* 1874, 15 f., 22.)

vDZ.

Meer, Theodorus van der, a Dutch Reformed minister, was the author of a pamphlet against Galenus Abrahamsz (*q.v.*), entitled *Het gekraay van een Sociniaense Haan onder Doopsgesinde Veederen* (Amsterdam, 1663), in which Galenus is accused of teaching Socinian (*q.v.*) doctrines.

vDZ.

H. W. Meihuizen, *Galenus Abrahamsz* (Arnhem, 1954) 84.

Meerlanders: see Merlanders.

Meersch, van der (sometimes Vermeersch), a family originally found in Flanders and at Antwerp, both Reformed and Mennonite. Pieter van der Meersch, b. at Meenen (*q.v.*), married to Maria van der Molen, who was probably a sister of the noted Flemish Elder Jacob Pietersz van der Meulen (*q.v.*), was a preacher of the Mennonite congregation at Meenen (*q.v.*). In 1564 he fled to Haarlem, Holland. His son, also Pieter van der Meersch, b. 1560 at Meenen, died before 1608 at Haarlem, a grain dealer, married to Maeyken Boutens, was a preacher of the Haarlem Flemish congregation, as was his grandson Arent van der Meersch, b. 1601 at Haarlem, d. 1667 at Amsterdam. Like his father Arent was a grain dealer. He was married to Sara de Veer of Amsterdam, and some of this family served as deacons at Amsterdam. Abraham van der Meersch, probably belonging to the same family, studied at the Mennonite Theological Seminary at Amsterdam and in 1733-48 served as a Mennonite preacher in Dordrecht. Another Abraham van der Meersch (b. 1643 at Amsterdam, d. 1728 at 's Graveland), a son of Arent, was a wealthy linen merchant in Amsterdam, and a deacon of the Lamist (*q.v.*) Mennonite congregation in 1681-86 and again in 1691-96. In this capacity he tried to found a theological seminary, but found little sympathy for this idea among his co-deacons. In 1721, at the age of 71 years, he wrote an autobiographical sketch, the original manuscript of which is still found in the Amsterdam

Mennonite archives. It gives important information not only concerning his business and his family, but also on several pages expounds his views concerning the Mennonite doctrines of the non-swearing of oaths, believers' baptism, and nonresistance, with which he wholeheartedly agreed. In Amsterdam most of the van der Meersch family belonged to the Lamist church, but a few of them were Zonists (q.v.). A branch of this family lived at Rotterdam. Here Pieter van der Meersch was a deacon of the Old Flemish Mennonites, and Elisabeth van der Meersch was married to Michiel Comans (q.v.). In the 16th century a van der Meersch family was found at Hoorn, of which Israel Jacobsz van der Meersch, the author of *Gewyde Poezie,* a volume of devotional poems, was a member. Israel Jacobsz, however, left the Mennonite church in 1605 and joined the Reformed. Pieter van der Meersch, of Amsterdam, published in 1713-44 a number of devotional books translated from the English. In the 18th century most members of the van der Meersch family left the Mennonite church. Abraham van der Meersch (1720-92) was a noted Remonstrant (q.v.) preacher. He was a grandson of the linen merchant Abraham van der Meersch mentioned above, who wrote his autobiography for this grandson.

A branch of probably the same van der Meersch family is found in Prussia from about 1668, at first at Danzig. Cornelius van der Meersch was about 1750 a (Mennonite) distiller of brandy and merchant of lace at Königsberg in East Prussia. It is possible that the Vermeersch family at Harlingen, Friesland, one of whom was Gillis Vermeersch (q.v., d. 1721), originally belonged to the same branch.

It could not be decided whether the martyrs Joris van der Meersch (q.v.) executed at Gent, Belgium, in 1570, and Hans Vermeersch executed at Waestene, Flanders, in 1559 were members of the same family.

vDZ.

Ned. Patriciaat II (1911) 330-33; Mennonite archives of Haarlem and Amsterdam; *Inv. Arch. Amst.* I, No. 772; *Gesch.-Bl.* VII (1956) 22, 27, No. 62.

Meeting Calendar: see **Calendar of Appointments.**

Meetinghouses. The following series of articles treats by countries the places of meeting for worship used by the Anabaptists-Mennonites through the centuries, the names given to such places, the dates of the first meetinghouses, and any items of particular interest relating to the functions of meetinghouses. See the article **Architecture** for a treatment of the architectural aspects including style. The countries are treated in the following order: *A.* Netherlands; *B.* Switzerland; *C.* South Germany; *D.* Northwest and Northeast Germany; *E.* Russia; *F.* North America.

A. Netherlands. During the period of persecution the Anabaptist-Mennonites had no regular place to hold their meetings. They met, as the martyr Claes de Praet (q.v.) says (*Offer,* 246), "there where Christ and His apostles held their meetings, in the woods, in the fields, on the seashore, and sometimes in homes." In larger towns such as Amsterdam meetings were held in private homes from the beginning. For the sake of safety meeting places were constantly changed and messengers (*weetdoeners*) visited the members to announce the place and the hour of the next meeting.

From about 1575, when persecution had ceased, the Mennonites gradually began to hold their meetings at fixed places, although as late as 1654, for example at Nijmegen (q.v.), the magistrates did not allow Mennonite meetings to be held at regular places; at Deventer no meetinghouses could be built until 1688. About 1600 the smaller congregations usually met in the home of a member, who placed a room at the disposal of the congregation. Larger congregations at this time or even earlier probably rented or bought houses or warehouses, which were then in simple style adapted for use as meetinghouses. Of these first meetinghouses nothing is known and of most congregations it cannot be exactly stated when they acquired a meetinghouse. It is very questionable whether the Mennonites of Amsterdam had a meetinghouse as early as 1578, as is suggested by Brandt, but the Waterlanders as well as the Frisians and the Flemish had meetinghouses here before 1600. More exact dates are available concerning Rotterdam. Here the Old Flemish Mennonites possessed a house in which they held meetings as early as 1580, whereas the Frisian congregation obtained a meetinghouse in 1593, and the Flemish congregation bought a house in 1609, which was remodeled for meetings. The present Mennonite church at Amsterdam has its origin in an old meetinghouse which had been used since 1608. Utrecht acquired a meetinghouse about 1610, the Waterlanders at Leiden in 1613, the Middelburg congregation in 1616. The two former meetinghouses of Harlingen, Friesland, no doubt dated from before 1600; the former meetinghouse of the Haarlem Flemish congregation, called "d'Oly-block," is also of about 1600. During the 17th century many meetinghouses were built in the province of Friesland, but it is possible that at least some of these were rebuilt from meetinghouses originally built some decades before. Balk built a meetinghouse in 1629, the Leeuwarden Waterlander congregation in 1631, Hindeloopen 1653, Sneek 1654, Grouw 1659, Warns and Joure both 1664, Akkrum *ca.* 1667, Irnsum 1684, Surhuisterveen 1685, Holwerd 1692, and Drachten 1693.

By 1700 all the congregations had meetinghouses except the conservative Janjacobsz group (q.v.), which was opposed to special meetinghouses. Many small congregations of the Groningen Old Flemish branch also had no meetinghouses, but continued to meet in the homes of the members as late as the end of the 18th century. At present a few newly founded congregations and circles (*kringen*) do not yet have meetinghouses, but use rented rooms or halls. The Breda (q.v.) congregation holds its meetings in the Lutheran church.

Nearly all the Dutch Mennonite churches now have one or more rooms for catechetical classes, Sunday schools, ladies' circles, and other church activities. Sometimes the sexton's quarters are a part of the church building, and in a number of congregations, particularly in the country, the parsonage is next to the church, and in a few attached to the church.

Since the 18th century Dutch Mennonite meeting-houses have been called churches (*Doopsgezinde kerk*). The earlier word *vermaning* (literally admonition," or place where the people are stimulated to faith and Christian life), formerly very common, especially in the province of Friesland, is now obsolete.   vDZ.

B. Switzerland. The first Mennonite meetinghouse built in Switzerland is that of the present Holee Street congregation in Basel, which was then known as the Basel-Binningen Church. Most of its members live in adjoining Alsace, and the congregation belongs to the Alsatian Mennonite Conference. The church was built in 1847 at 141 Holee Street, and was completely rebuilt in a modern style in 1932 at the same location. The Emmental (*q.v.*) congregation, with its seat at Langnau, built a meetinghouse at Kehr, in the outskirts of Langnau in 1888, and renovated and enlarged it in 1947. In 1899 the Emmental congregation built chapels at Bomatt on the Emme, and at Aebnit, near Bowil, west of Bomatt. The Bomatt church was renovated in 1955.

In 1893 the Kleintal congregation built a church at Moron, which was renovated in 1943. In 1894 the Chaux de Fonds congregation built one at Les Bulles, renovated in 1944. The Sonnenberg (*q.v.*) congregation bought some of the buildings of an inn on Fürstenberg (Mont Tramelan), and converted a dance hall into a spacious meeting place; it was considerably enlarged in 1947. The Jeangis-boden (Sonnenberg) congregation acquired its church in 1900; this meetinghouse has been the site of the meetings of the Swiss Mennonite Conference. It was renovated in 1950.

Near the Swiss border in Alsace the Grosslützel (Grand Lucelle) congregation (formerly Delsberg-tal) converted a tavern into a church. In 1956 this meetinghouse, which was severely damaged by military occupation in World War II, was renovated. The Schänzli congregation in Basel acquired a chapel on the street from Basel to Muttenz in 1891. A new church was built there in 1903 and renovated in 1954. The spacious Chaux d'Abel meetinghouse on the Jura plateau, which was built in 1905, belongs to the YMCA, of which a number of Mennonites are members.

For the purpose of maintaining a German school the Kleintal congregation in 1921 built a school at Perceux, above the cave called the "Goat Chapel," in which, according to tradition, the Mennonites met for worship in times of persecution. The congregation also built a school on the heights of Mont-bautier in 1923, in which the Mennonites meet for worship. Les Mottes, north of Tramelan, is the third meeting place of the Sonnenberg congregation. In 1928 a spacious room for meetings was built into a home. Also in Tramelan a room in a Mennonite home was rented for this purpose in 1941 and renovated in 1955. The most modern Mennonite meetinghouse in Switzerland was built at Courgenay in 1938 by the Pruntrut (Porrentruy) congregation. In 1956 a room was privately built into a new home at Reconvilier and placed at the disposal of the Mennonites.

The word "church" is not used by the Mennonites of Switzerland for their meeting places, but rather the word "chapel." Before these meetinghouses were built, the Swiss Mennonites met in rotation in barns, usually in the forenoons. A meal of nutritious peasoup was then served the members, many of whom had come on foot from a considerable distance.   S.G.

C. South Germany. From the time of the Reformation to about the middle of the 17th century the Anabaptists and sometimes the Mennonites had to meet secretly for their worship services. During the severest persecutions they at times met in forests (e.g., at Immelshausen until as late as 1654) or on remote farms (e.g., betweeen Kriegsheim, *q.v.*, and Pfeddersheim in 1608), often at night.

With the concession of Charles Ludwig, Elector of the Palatinate, granted in 1664, they were permitted, in villages where four or five families were living, to hold meetings of not more than 20 persons. For this the living room of a home was sufficient. Services were regularly held in rotation among the members.

Very likely, especially in the larger congregations, the need was felt by the first quarter of the 18th century of having a large room of their own for regular use, equipped in the simplest manner possible. Here it is not yet a matter of a building, but merely of parts of residences or other farm buildings which could be remodeled and furnished for the purpose. There are, of course, no records of dates, etc., from this period; nevertheless certain conclusions can be drawn on the basis of evidence in the congregations at Ibersheim, Kriegsheim, Friedelsheim, Weierhof, etc. The hall furnished in 1756 in Erpolzheim, which is still in use, may serve as an example from this period. In some instances the owners of the estates put rooms at the disposal of the Mennonite renters.

Toward the end of the 18th century meetinghouses were built in many places. They had to be built off the street and in the style of a farmhouse, in order not to be noticeable from the outside. Such buildings arose in 1770 at Weierhof, 1777 at Sembach, 1779 at Eppstein and Friedelsheim, 1783 in Heppenheim a.d. Wiese. Of these, Eppstein probably, in spite of frequent remodeling, has best preserved the type of Mennonite churches of that period (low room, rectangular windows, low pulpit), whereas the only other church remaining from that period which is still in use, namely, the Sembach, has been more radically altered.

In the early 19th century, when all legal restrictions were removed from the Mennonites in the Palatinate and Hesse, churches were built in the simple style of the Reformed churches of the vicinity. Churches of this kind were built in Altleiningen in 1811 (abandoned in 1956 because of a dilapidated condition), Monsheim 1820, Uffhofen 1829-30, Kühbörncheshof 1832, Friedelsheim 1836, Weierhof 1837, Deutschhof 1842, Ernstweiler 1843, etc. Of the few Amish congregations of South Germany only Ixheim built a church, erected in 1847, which was still in use until 1937. In other cases private rooms or rented halls were used. The Branchweilerhof congregation has for a long time been using the old arched, former Hospitalkirche. The Friedelsheim congregation (*q.v.*) in 1807 acquired by legal contract the right to the use of the Protestant church (until 1902).

In Baden, Württemberg, and Bavaria, where the congregations were subject to a great deal of change, since many of the members were renters on large estates, few meetinghouses were built. The churches in Baiertal and Streichenberg (Baden), built after 1800, were sold in the past century. Likewise the meetinghouse in Bildhausen near Schweinfurt, and the building intended for both church and school at Maxweiler. Also the attractive little church at Giebelstadt, built in 1867, had to be given up in 1953, because it was too far from Würzburg, the Mennonite center. The only churches left in this area were the one belonging to the Hasselbach congregation, built in 1846, and the one at Eichstock, built in 1856. In 1945, however, the Heilbronn congregation acquired the former MCC "neighborhood home," and in the same year the Ingolstadt congregation built a suitable room for the purpose. Everywhere else private rooms or space belonging to other churches is used.

In Frankfurt a congregational home was acquired in 1955, in which the MCC also has working quarters; in Kaiserslautern, on the other hand, the congregation is the guest of the MCC in the building erected by the MCC. Modern meetinghouses with additional rooms were built at Backnang in 1955 and in Enkenbach in 1956. They will no doubt point the way for further new meetinghouses, since the old style of building with only the one room which is used for regular worship services is no longer adequate for the manifold needs of congregations. For instance, in 1948 a hall was built at Sembach for worship services as well as youth activities.

As to terminology, the word "church" was not used east of the Rhine before about 1800, but is freely used now. The meetinghouse at Weierhof is, however, called a "Lehr." Elder Schmutz of Baden in an article in the *Mennonitische Blätter* in 1856 called these churches "meetinghouse, congregational house, or house of God." But later the word "Kirche" (church) was also adopted here and there. In the case of rented halls the word "Saal" is used.

P.S.

Paul Schowalter, "Mennonite Churches in South Germany," *Menn. Life* VII (January 1952) 14; *idem*, "Der Kirchenbau in den Mennonitengemeinden von Pfalz-Hessen," *Gem.-Kal.*, 1953, 36-43.

D. Northwest and Northeast Germany. It is known that the congregations in East Friesland had meetinghouses at least as early as 1600, although they were long required to worship "in private." The earliest known date for a meetinghouse in Emden, Leer, Norden, or Neustadt-Goedens is 1649 for the Ukowallist group in Emden. Emmerich built a meetinghouse about 1676. Crefeld built in 1693; Neuwied not until 1768, Emden in 1769. In Friedrichstadt the Alte Münze, owned by the deacon, was in use before 1652 when it was purchased by the congregation. In Hamburg-Altona the first meetinghouse was in the rear part of a private house purchased about 1619 (public services were not permitted until 1622). The first "real" meetinghouse (as B. C. Roosen calls it) was built in 1675.

The degrees of toleration granted to Mennonites in East and West Prussia, Danzig, and the lower Vistula region in Poland varied greatly; as a consequence the first meetinghouses were erected at widely differing times. The first meetinghouse built for that purpose was probably the one of 1586 at Muntau in the Culm-Graudenz area, rebuilt in 1898, which is in a sense the oldest Mennonite meetinghouse anywhere in the world. Its fate since 1945 is unknown. The meetinghouse of the Schönsee congregation near Culm, built in 1618, is the oldest Mennonite meetinghouse still standing in its original form. It was converted to a private dwelling *ca.* 1948. The Elbing-Ellerwald congregation built its first meetinghouse in 1590. In Danzig the Mennonites were not allowed to build meetinghouses until well into the 17th century, and then they were not to appear like public buildings but private dwellings. The Frisian congregation built first, *ca.* 1638, the Flemish congregation *ca.* 1648. The country churches were not allowed to build until a century or more later—Thiensdorf 1728, Orlofferfelde 1751, Rosenort 1754, and in 1768 four meetinghouses with permission of the Bishop of Culm—Fürstenwerder, Heubuden, Ladekopp, and Tiegenhagen. Obernessau near Thorn was built in 1778. Before the meetinghouses were built the congregations worshiped in various private homes of members. H.S.B.

The early meetinghouses of the Mennonites along the Vistula River in Danzig, Prussia, and Poland were simple structures resembling the homes or schools of that day. Some resemblance to the early Mennonite meetinghouses in the Netherlands can be detected. The smaller meetinghouses were usually one-story buildings like Schönsee (see *ME* I, "Illustrations," p. 8). Later two-story buildings were erected where needed to accommodate the growing membership. As a rule, the second story consisted of a balcony similar to the structures in the Netherlands. The main floor was for women and the balcony for men, as in the present Singel Church of Amsterdam. The pulpit was located on the long side with an elevated bench for the ministers and deacons. From the outside the meetinghouse could hardly be recognized as a place of worship. The old churches at Ellerwald, Fürstenwerder, and Heubuden were of this type (*ME* I, "Illustrations," p. 8). Usually the meetinghouse was a frame building, extremely plain, located in an open field.

The Thiensdorf church, erected in 1728, is thought to have been the first meetinghouse in Prussia. This indicates worship services had previously been held in private homes or public buildings such as schools. Later the meetinghouses were constructed of brick and resembled the surrounding non-Mennonite churches, sometimes having a steeple or a cross. Typical of this change in architecture were the churches of Rosengart and Elbing (*ME* I, "Illustrations," p. 8). Arched windows became common.

C.K.

E. Russia. The Mennonite meetinghouses of Poland and Russia were patterned after the early structures in Prussia. A typical structure was the Chortitza church, and for the Mennonite Brethren, the meetinghouse at Einlage (*ME* I, "Illustrations," p. 10). Gradually a new style of meetinghouses evolved. Brick buildings replaced the former frame structure. An adjustment to the Russian environment became noticeable. Heavy brick fences as a rule surrounded the churches. The most extreme adjustment to the Russian environment was found in the Einlage church. The early meetinghouse in Russia closely resembled the school building found in every village. The pattern of the meetinghouse in Russia and Prussia was transplanted to the Great Plains of North America. Some of the churches built after this pattern were the First Mennonite Church of Beatrice, Neb.; the Hoffnungsau Mennonite Church near Buhler, Kan.; the Kleine Gemeinde Church near Meade, Kan.; and the numerous meetinghouses of the early Mennonites in Manitoba and Saskatchewan as well as Mexico and Paraguay. (See also **Architecture,** where literature is listed.)   C.K.

F. North America. The Swiss and South German Mennonite immigrants who came to America before the Revolutionary War had never worshiped in meetinghouses in their homelands, nor had the Lower Rhine and Crefeld immigrants of 1683-95 (the first Crefeld meetinghouse was built in 1695); only the few families from the Hamburg-Altona congregation had had one (the Altona meetinghouse was built in 1675). But with all restrictions removed in free America Mennonites of all kinds except the Amish built meetinghouses apparently as soon as the size of the congregation required it and economic conditions permitted. Meanwhile meetings were held in homes, which were sometimes built with a large room especially built to accommodate church services. An illustration is the Christian Herr house near Lancaster, built in 1719 with such a room, the oldest Mennonite building used for worship still standing in America.

The Amish immigrants, however, elevated the practice of holding meetings in homes into a principle. To this day the Old Order Amish basically forbid the building of meetinghouses for worship purposes. The only Amish meetinghouse built in America before 1830 was the one called Chester Valley, near Malvern, Chester Co., Pa., built in 1795. The congregation here, however, died out within a generation after this. The next Amish meetinghouse was the Beech church near Louisville, Ohio, about 1830, followed by the Clinton Frame church near Goshen, Ind., in 1848. The Rock Creek church, near Danvers, Ill., was built in 1853 and the neighboring Partridge (Metamora) church in 1854. Congregations in Ohio which were leaving the "Old Order" Amish began to build meetinghouses, such as Walnut Grove (West Liberty) in 1857, Oak Grove, near Smithville, and Walnut Creek, both in 1862, Central at Archbold and Martens Creek near Millersburg in 1869. The Ontario Amish churches did not begin to build meetinghouses until the 1880's. Sometimes the building of a meetinghouse became the definite sign or cause of a break between the progressive and old order elements.

American Mennonites never in principle opposed meetinghouses. The first one built was in Germantown, Pa., in 1708. The second Germantown meetinghouse, of 1770, is the oldest American Mennonite meetinghouse still used for regular services. The only other meetinghouse built before 1800 and still standing at the original location was built at Landisville, west of Lancaster, Pa., in 1740 as a residence, but was used as a meetinghouse long before 1790; it is now used as a dwelling for the sexton. The Byerland meetinghouse, also in Lancaster County, built about 1755, is still standing but has been moved several miles away. In order of erection the oldest meetinghouses in the original settlements in Eastern Pennsylvania were Skippack 1725, Towamencin 1728(?), Hereford 1732, Swamp 1735, Salford 1738(?), and Deep Run 1746, all in the Franconia Conference. Dates of the earliest meetinghouses in the Lancaster district are not known before the first one at Abbeyville, built in 1747 or earlier, and New Danville, built in 1755. Apparently the first Lancaster Mennonites waited a generation before building meetinghouses. Most of their early meetinghouses were built after 1750; by 1800 the Lancaster Conference had at least 27 known meetinghouses. The earliest known meetinghouses in other areas, with dates of erection, were: *Western Pennsylvania*—Scottdale (Pennsville) 1800, Blough 1837, Masontown 1840; *Ontario*—Vineland 1810, Kitchener 1813, Markham 1817; *Ohio*—Fairfield County, two meetinghouses about 1810-15, Rowland in Canton 1823, North Lima 1824(?), followed by Midway almost at the sametime, Sonnenberg 1834, Bluffton (GCM) 1840; *Virginia*—Mill Creek near Luray in Page County (a union church) 1800, six erected 1823-28, viz., Trissels 1823, Pike 1825, Brennemans 1826, Weavers 1827, Hildebrand and Springdale; *Maryland*—Housers, Beaver Creek 1763, Strasburg (in Franklin County, Pa.) 1812, Millers 1835; *Indiana*—Clinton Brick 1845, Yellow Creek 1849, Holdeman 1851, Berne (GCM) 1852; *Illinois*—Union near Washington 1858, Sterling 1859, Summerfield (GCM) 1858.

The immigrants from Russia 1874-80 had had meetinghouses in their homeland and proceeded to erect them in their new homes very soon after arrival. The first meetinghouses of the General Conference Mennonite Church were immigration houses (Alexanderwohl, Hoffnungsau, etc.) and schoolhouses; the first Krimmer Mennonite Brethren meetinghouse was Gnadenau near Hillsboro, Kan., built in 1876; the first Mennonite Brethren meetinghouse was Ebenfeld near Hillsboro, built in 1876.

The first meetinghouses in Pennsylvania were simple, plain, and functional, designed only for an assembly for worship, but often serving a double use as schoolhouses, or with schoolhouses or even sexton's quarters attached. This style was generally followed by the later congregations. Later, when Sunday schools and other activities were introduced, basements were added to accommodate the children's classes, and more recently educational wings or sections with classrooms and other facilities have been built. For the most part this has been the pattern of the meetinghouse type and development throughout American Mennonite history, except that some of the groups from Russia brought with them a different type of meetinghouse design.

The descendants of the Swiss-South German Mennonites and the Amish from Alsace, Bavaria, and

Hesse universally called their buildings meeting-houses (*Versammlungshaus*), or "Gmeehaus" (*Gemeindehaus*) in Pennsylvania Dutch, until recent decades, when the term "church" has partially superseded it. (See also **Architecture.**) H.S.B.

Megander, Kaspar: see **Grossmann, Kaspar.**

Mehoude (originally Meaude), a former Dutch Mennonite family. stemming from French Flanders and because of persecutions emigrating to Dutch Zeeland-Flanders, where its members belonged to the Mennonite congregations of Cadzand and Aardenburg, later also of Vlissingen. In the early 18th century this family joined the Reformed Church.
vdZ.

Mehrning, Jakob, of Holstein, Germany, author of the book *S. Baptismi Historia: Das ist/Heilige Tauff-Historia/In welcher Die Wahrheit der Ersten-Ein-vnd Eygentlichen Tauffordnung Jesu Christi, Aus heiliger Schrift deutlich widerholt/darzu aus vielen Alten vnd Newen/Kirchenhistorien/durch alle Hundert Jährige Zeiten/von Anfang der Tauff bisshieher/bezeuget/Vnd wie solche fast nach allen Hauptstücken/offt verändert/vnd in schändliche Missbräuch verkehret sey worden . . . . Anfänglich durch den hochgelehrten H. Johan. Montanum kurtz/vnd mit blossen Allegaten in Niderlandischer Sprach beschrieben/Nach dessen Todt aber aus seinen hinderlassenen Schrifften/vnd andern Autoren vollkomlich vermehret/vnd in die Hochdeutsche Sprach übersetzet/Durch Jacob Mehrning aus Holstein/der Göttlichen Wahrheit Studiosum* (Dortmund, 1646 and 1647). The book, containing XVII plus 1128 pages, is a complete original revision of the booklet by Joh. Montanus and at the same time its translation from Dutch to German. Its purpose was to promote baptism by immersion practiced by the Dompelaers, but it grew into a veritable historical arsenal on the "baptism ordinance of Christ," though with what critical right is another question. Under point five of the foreword the Mennonites are expressly taken to task, "since some of them understand little of this mystery." Nothing is known concerning the author's personal life. No doubt he is partly responsible for the confusion caused by the Dompelaers in the Hamburg-Altona church. The assumption by "many" that the *Tauff-Historia* is not Mehrning's work, but that of Chr. Raselius, is seen to be untenable when the two are compared.
O.S.

Jöcher, *Gelehrtenlexikon;* Moller, *Cimbria Literata;* B. C. Roosen, *Gesch. der Mennoniten-Gemeinde zu Hamburg und Altona* (Hamburg, 1886); *ML* III, 65.

Meihuizen, a widely branched Dutch Mennonite family. On account of persecution a number of Swiss Mennonite families moved to Holland at the beginning of the 18th century. Among them were Samuel Peter and his wife Barbara Fr(e)y (*q.v.*) and five children from Gontenschwil (at that time in the canton of Bern, now in Aargau). In 1711 they are said to have belonged to the Reformed Church, but "having a great desire to the religion of the Swiss Brethren." When they left Switzerland in the fall of 1714 Samuel Peter was not yet a Mennonite, although his wife had apparently united with

them; but in the Netherlands both Barbara and Samuel Peter were Mennonites from the beginning. They settled in Kalkwijk near Hoogezand in the province of Groningen, where they continued to farm as they had done in Switzerland. They adopted the name Meihuizen after a village Maihusen in the Catholic canton of Lucerne, from which an ancestor had fled to Protestant Gontenschwil in 1532. Samuel Peter and Barbara Frey, the former of whom died in 1758 at the age of nearly 87, and the latter in the following year at the age of 86, are the progenitors of this numerous family. A descendant of this family is Hendrik Wiebes Meihuizen, b. at Arnhem on Aug. 29, 1906, married to Minke Wartena, b. 1910, a Mennonite pastor, serving at Wieringen 1933-36, Veendam-Pekela 1936-38, and from 1938 at The Hague. Since September 1955 he has been the chief editor of the *Algemeen Doopsgezind Weekblad.* He is the author of a number of publications, including *Doopsgezinde Kenmerken en Eigenaardigheden* (Amsterdam, 1948, 2nd ed. 1948); *Galenus Abrahamsz* (Haarlem, 1954); *Een Dader des Woords, in memoriam Ds Albert Keuter* (Amsterdam, n.d.-1946); *De Doopsgezinde Broederschap* (The Hague, n.d.-1955); some sermons; a number of historical studies, particularly "De Geloofswereld onzer martelaren," in *Algemeen Doopsgezind Weekblad* V (1951); "Spiritualistic Tendencies and Movements Among the Dutch Mennonites of the Sixteenth and Seventeenth Centuries," *MQR* XXVII (October 1953); "De Verwachting van de wederkomende Christus en het rijk Gods bij de oude Doopsgezinden," in *Stemmen uit de Doopsgezinde broederschap* III (1954, No. 2); "Het geloof in de Heilige Geest onder de oudste Nederlandse Doopsgezinden," in *Stemmen* III (1954) No. 5.

The family tree, provided with an excellent introduction on the Swiss Mennonites in Holland, was drawn up by the minister Jacob Dirks Huizinga.
vdZ.

J. D. Huizinga, *Stamboek of Geslachtregister der Nakomelingen van Samuel Peter (Meihuizen) en Barbara Fry* (Groningen, 1890); the genealogical part of this book was reprinted with additions in 1922 (n.d.) and 1946 (n.d.); *DJ* 1928, 114-26; *ML* III, 65 f.

Meindert van Emden: see **Meynardt van Emden** (van Delft).

Meister (Meyster), **Leonhard,** an Anabaptist (?) martyr executed with Hans Koch (*q.v.*) at Augsburg, Bavaria, Germany, in 1524 for his faith (according to Mehrning probably a Waldensian). He was the author of the oldest song in the *Ausbund,* "Ach Gott Vater im höchsten Thron." NEFF.

J. Mehrning, *S. Baptismi Historia* (Dortmund, 1646 and 1647); Wolkan, *Lieder,* 8 and 140; *Mart. Mir.* D 1 f., E 413 f.; *ML* III, 66.

Meiszrod, Barbara, an Anabaptist martyr, baptized by Heinz Kraut (*q.v.*), made her house a center for the meetings of the Anabaptists in Mühlhausen in Thuringia. A meeting of this kind was surprised in October 1537, the participants arrested, tried on the rack on Oct. 11, and ten of them drowned, including Barbara, in the Unstrut between Mühlhausen and Ammern. (Wappler, *Thüringen; ML* III, 66.)

Melanchthon, Philip (1497-1560), the German reformer, friend and co-worker of Martin Luther, the son of an armorer, George Schwarzerdt, whose wife was a niece of Johann Reuchlin. After his father's death he attended Latin school and at the age of 12 entered the University of Heidelberg, followed by the University of Tübingen in 1512, earning the M.A. degree there in 1514, which gave him the right to lecture. In 1518 Reuchlin recommended him as professor of Greek at the University of Wittenberg; on Aug. 29 he delivered his inaugural address, which made a deep impression on Luther. A fast friendship was soon formed between them, with a lasting effect on the course of the Reformation. They complemented each other well. Luther, the religious genius and creative spirit, Melanchthon, the man of the pen, the keen scholar, who clothed Luther's ideas in scholarly form. Their friendship went through some difficult trials. Melanchthon was again and again offended by his friend's violent manner, severe judgment, and rough treatment of opponents; and Luther suffered under Melanchthon's timidity, hesitation, scruples, and fear. Melanchthon's last years were saddened by dogmatic strife brought on by his undecisive character, until death gently released him from the "rage of the theologians."

Melanchthon, generally a mild theologian, dealt with extraordinary harshness and increasing roughness with the Anabaptists. He had not the least understanding for them. He saw in them only "irreligious fanatics and murderous revolutionaries, enemies of temporal government, however peaceful they may seem" (a letter to Myconius, February 1530), "a fiendish sect, which must not be tolerated" (a letter to Myconius, Oct. 31, 1531). Therein lies deep tragedy, for in his ideas he was much closer to them than was Luther. He held to freedom of the will, and sponsored the separation of religious and moral civil life (opinion to Philip of Hesse in 1524), favored the reinstatement of the ban (church inspector's protocol), recognized in the immorality of the populace the damage done by the doctrine of justification, which was being used as a convenient bed of ease. He had temporary doubts concerning the validity of infant baptism.

In mid-December 1527 the "Zwickau prophets," Nikolaus Storch, Thomas Drechsel, and Marcus Stübner, came to Wittenberg. They made a tremendous impression on Melanchthon. He wrote about them to Spalatin. Their "divine inspiration" he recognized as fanaticism, but to their objections to infant baptism he could find no answer until a letter from Luther (Jan. 13, 1522) freed him from his doubts. It is reasonable to assume that his later severity against the Anabaptists stemmed from his inability to come to terms decisively and effectively with the arguments of the Prophets. It is significant that his basic characterizations of Anabaptism, developed in later years, did not depart substantially from his analysis of the Prophets.

In 1522 Melanchthon became acquainted with Thomas Müntzer, who is said to have disputed with Melanchthon and Bugenhagen (*q.v.*). From Alstedt Müntzer wrote at Easter in 1524 a letter to Melanchthon, in which he accused the Wittenbergers of neglecting the inner revelation, too much consideration of the weak, and servility to the princes. Further contacts between them have not been proved. He probably did not write the *Historie von Thomas Münzer,* which was long the principal source on Müntzer's activities in the Peasants' War (Brandt, 223).

At first Melanchthon took a tolerant attitude toward the Anabaptists and the Zwickau prophets, whom he identified with the former. In the letter to Frederick mentioned above he rejected the application of violent measures. Their "conventicle nature should not be stopped with violence, but with Scripture and judicio spiritualium hominum." But he soon changed his position; his attitude became increasingly harsh. Already in his *Unterricht der Visitatoren* of 1528 he placed every deviation from Lutheran doctrine under the punitive arm of temporal government as sedition. The mandate issued on Jan. 17, 1528, by the Elector of Saxony, who was somewhat influenced in this instance by Melanchthon, threatened all who did not follow Lutheranism with loss of life and property.

In July 1527 Melanchthon was commissioned by the Elector to conduct an inspection (visitation) of the churches in Thuringia. Among his companions were Friedrich Myconius (*q.v.*) and Justus Menius (*q.v.*). On this tour of inspection he encountered at least the teachings of those whom he called Anabaptists, if not the Anabaptists in person (letter to Camerarius Oct. 23, 1527). He appended to his "Visitation Articles" a brief instruction to pastors on methods of effectively refuting Anabaptist arguments against infant baptism. His first major work against the Anabaptists, the *Adversus anabaptistas Philippi Melanchthonis iudicium,* is an elaboration of this basic argument. It was finished by Jan. 23, 1528, and printed in April 1528. A German translation by Justus Jonas, *Underricht Philip Melanchthon Wider die Lere der Wiederteuffer,* appeared in October of the same year.

It was dedicated to Friedrich Pistorius, the abbot of a monastery in Nürnberg. It deals with the sacraments, their number, and particularly with baptism, the baptism of John and the apostles, and infant baptism. He attempted to refute the "frightful, abominable, diabolical doctrine and error of the Anabaptists" and defended infant baptism on the grounds that it was the New Testament parallel to circumcision in the Old Testament.

Hardly two years later he expressed himself definitely in favor of the death penalty for Anabaptists in the letter to Friedrich Myconius of February 1530: "At first when I began to become acquainted with Storch and his following, to whom the whole family of Anabaptists owes its existence, I was possessed by a foolish tolerance. Others were also of the opinion that heretics are not to be destroyed with the sword. At that time Duke Frederick was violently angry with Storch, and if he had not been protected by us, the mad and thoroughly bad man would have been executed. Now I regret this lenience not a little. What disturbances, what heresies did he not stir up afterward? For you must think thus: As an armed race is said to have come forth from the teeth of a dragon, so have all these sects of Anabaptists and Zwinglians come forth from him. . . .

All the Anabaptists, even if they are blameless in all other respects, reject some part or other of their civic duties. Though the matter in and for itself may be insignificant, yet at this time and in so many crises it is extremely dangerous. . . . Therefore it is my opinion concerning those who hold beliefs that are, to be sure, not seditious, but still obviously blasphemous, that the government is under obligation to kill them" (Wappler, *Kursachsen,* 13 f.).

On Jan. 18, 1530, six Anabaptists were executed at Reinhardsbrunn in Saxony (see **Kolb, Andreas**). This execution evoked great excitement. Elector John now requested an opinion of the Wittenberg theologians. It was composed by Melanchthon and handed in at the end of October 1531 under the title, *Gutachten an den Kurfürsten Johann von Sachsen.* Following a lengthy introduction it said:

"In the matter of punishments distinctions must be made. For there are three kinds of Anabaptists: First the instigators and those who have made a second beginning; secondly followers and misled ones, who openly hold seditious beliefs, for instance, that it is unfitting to hold government office, that Christians must share their goods among each other, that a Christian should not swear an oath, not even to the government, that the churches should be reformed and the ungodly destroyed, that it is wrong to pay interest, and similar articles; in the third place there are many who erred because of lack of understanding, but could be persuaded to recant.

"The first class is to be killed with the sword, because they persisted contrary to the electoral mandate in holding meetings; for they have thereby shown themselves disobedient to the government. But the second class who hold obviously seditious articles of faith and persisted in them in spite of warning and instruction, should as revolutionaries also be put to death. . . . Finally those of the third class, who have erred because of ignorance, should be shown mercy after they have been instructed and have recanted their error, after they have made public confession and have been warned not to repeat the error. But if they do not desist from their error—'for many of them are possessed by the devil' —they should be expelled from the country, provided that no seditious beliefs or malicious intentions are found in them, or be punished by some other mild penalty" (Wappler, *Kursachsen,* 26 f.).

At the end of 1532 Luther and Melanchthon warned the council of Münster (Westphalia) and Bernhardt Rothmann of the Zwinglians and fanatics. (See **Germany**.)

Three years later Melanchthon wrote his booklet, *Etliche propositiones wider die lehr der Widerteuffer* (erroneously dated 1528). It is a reply to Rothmann's *Restitution,* and the second edition of the same year bears the title, *Wider das gotteslästerliche und schändliche Buch, so zu Münster im Druck neulich ist ausgegangen.* In it he refutes the teaching of the Anabaptists of Münster concerning the violent erection of the kingdom of God, since the kingdom of Christ is spiritual, and concerning community of goods and polygamy. It is incomprehensible that he failed to distinguish between the peaceful and the revolutionary Anabaptists. "And it does no good," he writes, "to say that they are not all

thus. But on the contrary, because the devil has torn them away from the true doctrine, as one devil is about as impious as another, and they are all together striving every moment against the kingdom of God and temporal order and rule, therefore one Anabaptist is like another, and the fact that they do not all make so much noise and innovation is due merely to lack of opportunity." In point 24 he calls the doctrine that "Christ did not take His flesh from the flesh of Mary, a terrible, abominable blasphemy. In it one can see that they conceal other poison and blasphemy concerning Christ."

From Melanchthon a different verdict might have been expected concerning the Anabaptists. He had far better opportunity to become acquainted with them. On Dec. 1, 1535, he took part in a long cross-examination of Anabaptists imprisoned in Jena. It lasted several days. Melanchthon and his colleagues used all their ingenuity and great learning to convince the prisoners of their error. Results were meager. In a report to the Elector of Saxony (*Bericht an den Kurfürsten Johann von Sachsen*) on Jan. 19, 1536, he wrote "Against the obstinate it is necessary to apply serious punishment. And even some may not be malicious in other respects, nevertheless we must resist the shameful sect, in which there is so much horrible and shameful error" (Wappler, *Thüringen,* 149). Several days later, the Anabaptists in Jena, who remained true to their faith, were executed.

In the letter to the elector cited above, Melanchthon urged the publication of an official writing which would reveal what "coarse, seditious, shameful, and harmful articles the Anabaptists hold." He was commissioned to write it. On April 10, 1536, a new mandate against the Anabaptists was issued for Saxony, using the executed Anabaptists as a warning to others. The following are the main articles of their faith, as he states them, by means of which they deceived the simple folk in body and soul: (1) Christians should not and can not be in an office of government, which take the sword; (2) Christians should have no other government over them than the preachers of the Gospel; (3) Christians are forbidden to swear an oath, and to swear is sin; (4) Christians are obliged to give their possessions to the common good, and shall have no property; (5) If one partner in a marriage is a true believer and the other is not, then the believer may leave the unbeliever and court another, merely on account of his faith; (6) That infant baptism is wrong; (7) Infants have no sin; "original sin," so-called, is not in fact sin; (8) That alone is sin which man of his own free will commits.

In addition Melanchthon wrote a booklet that was by electoral command to be given to every pastor in the electorate with the obligation to read it from the pulpit every third Sunday. Its title was *Verlegung etlicher unchristlicher Artikel, welche die Wiederteuffer fürgeben.* This booklet of instruction appeared in two editions in 1536. It contains very sharp language for the gentle reformer. He called Anabaptism a "horrible devilish sect." He maintained that the government was obliged "to resist and punish such shameful, murderous doctrine, since it teaches only revolt, theft and murder, besides immorality and adultery"; events at Münster proved this, he held. He called them Manichaeans and expressed the hope that like them, they would not increase or remain long. The Anabaptist sect, he said, was simply a diabolical deception, which must be punished with force and wiped out.—What the Anabaptist thought of this booklet is shown by the statement of a prisoner, that there was not a true word in it (Wappler, *Inquisition*, 78).

In May 1536 Philip of Hesse also requested an opinion of the Wittenberg theologians, for advice in dealing with the Anabaptists imprisoned in his realm. The opinion was delivered on June 5, 1536 (see **Punishment**). It was composed by Melanchthon and signed by Luther, Bugenhagen, and Cruciger. The title was *Das Weltliche Oberkeitt den Widertaufferen mit leiblicher straff zu weren schuldig sey*. (One edition of the pamphlet bore the subtitle: *Melanchthonis Iudicium: Ob christliche Fürsten schuldig sind, der Wiedertäufer unchristlicher Sekte mit leiblicher Strafe und mit dem Schwert zu wehren*.) This booklet states most definitely that Anabaptists are to be punished with the sword.

Also in a letter to Henry VIII of England, Sept. 25, 1538, Melanchthon sponsors the severest punishment for the Anabaptists. In his opinion of Feb. 5, 1539, concerning religious conditions in the duchy of Jülich, he cautions that "there is much vermin of Anabaptists there" (Rembert, *Wiedertäufer*, 267).

The Anabaptist question occupied Melanchthon once more at the disputation of Worms in 1557 in the summarizing statement which he drew up, called *Prozess, wie es soll gehalten werden mit den Wiedertäufern*. His attitude had not grown more lenient. As seditionists and blasphemers, he said, they should be killed with the sword, according to Leviticus 24. Two years later, in 1559, when the question was asked: Does a pious government do wrong in killing Anabaptists who cling to their terrible errors? he replied with lengthy argument: If they are obstinate and stubbornly persist in their error, they may be killed as revolutionaries. In this final declaration of Melanchthon against the Anabaptists (entitled *Ob fromme Obrigkeiten unrecht tun, wenn sie an schrecklichen Irrtümern festhalten-de Wiedertäufer töten*) he contends that on the basis of natural law the Anabaptists should be killed. (*C.R.* IX, 1002-4.)

One can only lament this verdict of Melanchthon's, which has been fraught with such dire consequences in church history. Two hundred years were to pass before religious toleration was given its due.   NEFF.

Corpus Reformatorum I, III, IV, IX; J. v. Döllinger, *Die Reformation* I; G. Ellinger, *Philipp Melanchthon. Ein Lebensbild* (Berlin, 1902); H. Engelland, *Melanchthon, Glauben und Handeln* (München, 1931); W. Gussmann, *Quellen und Forschungen zur Geschichte des Augsburger Bekenntnisses* (Leipzig, 1911); Fr. Nippold, *Was gibt den heutigen Universitäten das Recht und die Pflicht zu Melanchthon-Feiern* (Bern, 1897); N. Paulus, *Protestantismus und Toleranz im 16. Jhdt.* (1911); C. Schmidt, *Philipp Melanchthon* (Eberfeld, 1861); G. Ellinger, *Philipp Melanchthon* (Berlin, 1902); J. W. Richard, *Philipp Melanchthon* (N.Y., 1907); P. Wappler, *Inquisition und Ketzerprozesse in Zwickau zur Reformationszeit im Zusammenhang der Entwicklung der Ansichten Luthers u. Melanchthons* (Leipzig, 1908); idem, *Die Stellung Kursachsens und des Landgrafen Philipp von Hessen zur Täuferbewegung* (Münster, 1910); idem, *Die Täuferbewegung in Thüringen* (Jena, 1913); J. S. Oyer, "The Writings of Melanchthon Against the Anabaptists," *MQR* XXVI (1952) 259-79; W. W. Wiswedel and R. Friedmann, "The Anabaptists Answer Melanchthon," *MQR* XXIX (1955) 212-31; O. Clemen, *Melanchthons Briefwechsel, Supplementa Melanchthoniana* (Leipzig, 1926); Robert Stupperich," Melanchthon und die Täufer," *Kerugma und Dogma* III (1957) 150-170; *ML* III, 66-69.

Melander, Dionysius (1486-1561), appointed with Bernhard Algesheimer by the city council of Frankfurt (*q.v.*), Germany, as the first Protestant preachers, under the pressure of the uprising of the citizens on April 20, 1526. For a decade the two preachers were very successful and influential, since they had the guilds on their side. "What the preachers ordered was done," writes Scheffers Kreinchen in a contemporary chronicle (Dechent, 125). This was demonstrated in the first of a long series of requests presented to the city council concerning the Anabaptists. When Anabaptists began to preach outside the city walls in 1528, the two pastors demanded that the council suppress them; the council complied with the edict of March 24, 1528, which forbade giving them shelter or lodging. This position was still in force in 1704, for when some Mennonite refugees from Switzerland wanted to settle in the city in that year, they were refused, "after they had in a discussion clearly expressed their doctrine" (Dechent, 114).

A presumptuous attitude on Melander's part led to the hostility of wide circles toward him, especially of the colleagues who had for years supported him but now accused him of moral lapses. In February 1535 he requested his release. The council consented, giving him through Wolfgang Capito (*q.v.*) a testimonial of honorable life and conduct (Dechent, 144). After Easter Melander left Frankfurt and entered the service of Philip of Hesse, who had heard him preach at the Marburg disputation, and now appointed him court preacher.

In this new position Melander again came into contact with the Anabaptists. Characteristic of his attitude at this time is his opinion on measures passed by the government council on Aug. 7, 1536, when he said that the populace must be urged to reform its conduct; offenses must be punished, "in order that the Anabaptists may not take from us an excuse for setting up a new church" (see **Hesse**). He incidentally gives the Anabaptists a good testimonial in stressing that they, the preachers, must clean their own house in order to deprive the Anabaptists of a pretext for leaving the established church. The government really made an effort "through positive work to remove the foundation from the accusations of the Anabaptists and to remove existing offenses by suitable measures. Clearly and plainly Bucer expressed this in a letter written to Philip in Wittenberg on Nov. 17, 1538" (Diehl, 5). This positive work was to be accomplished through the church discipline of Ziegenhain published in 1539, which Melander helped to draw up (Thudichum, 595), and in connection with this, also a result of dealings with the Anabaptists, the Order of Confirmation which led to the introduction of confirmation (*q.v.*) in all Protestant countries.

There is no record of any further efforts made by Melander to suppress the Anabaptists. He died on July 10, 1561, in Kassel at the age of 75 years.

HEGE.

H. Dechent, *Kirchengeschichte von Frankfurt am Main seit der Reformation* I (Leipzig and Frankfurt, 1913); W. Diehl, *Zur Geschichte der Konfirmation* (Giessen, 1897); K. W. H. Hochhuth, "Mittheilungen aus der protestantischen Secten-Geschichte in der hessischen Kirche," in *Ztscht für die hist. Theol.* XXVIII (1858); Fr. Thudichum, *Die deutsche Reformation 1517-1577* II (Leipzig, 1909); *ML* III, 69.

Melchior, an Anabaptist martyr, who was executed at Schwäbisch-Gmünd (*q.v.*), Germany, together with Wolfgang Esslinger (*q.v.*) and five other brethren in 1531. (*Mart. Mir.* D 32, E 439 f.; *ML* III, 65.)

Melchior von Salzburg, a knight, an Anabaptist martyr, who baptized and preached in Augsburg, Germany, in 1527. He was burned at the stake at Passau in 1528.

HEGE.

Fr. Roth, *Augsburgs Ref.-Gesch.* I, 2nd ed. (Munich, 1901) 252; *idem, Zur Gesch. der Wiedertäufer in Oberschwaben* III (Augsburg, 1901) 80 and 99; *ML* III, 69.

Melchiorites, the followers of Melchior Hofmann (*q.v.*) after his conversion to Anabaptism in 1530 in Strasbourg (*q.v.*), Alsace. Among them baptism was performed as a sign that the adult convert was forsaking the world, the flesh, and the devil, and entering into a covenant with God. Members called themselves "Bundesgenossen" or (Dutch) "Bondgenoten" (*q.v.*) (Covenanters). Hofmann transplanted the movement to northwest Germany and the Netherlands. There were also some Melchiorites in England (*q.v.*). Hofmann's chiliasm and allegorical interpretation of the Bible, particularly the book of Revelation, as well as the prevalent social, political, and religious conditions, were the factors that determined the chiliastic, revolutionary form adopted by the movement after Hofmann's imprisonment in Strasbourg. Basing their view on Revelation they considered it their obligation to set up the kingdom of God and destroy the ungodly. A group of Melchiorites attacked the Oldeklooster (*q.v.*) monastery near Bolsward, Friesland. Jan van Geelen (*q.v.*) stormed the Amsterdam city hall on May 10, 1535. With the fall of Münster (*q.v.*) on June 25 of that year, the radical form of the movement soon lost most of its followers. With Jan van Batenburg, the group of Melchiorites known as "Covenanters of the Sword" disappeared, although there was occasional revolutionary Anabaptist activity until 1544.

But the spirit of the original Bundesgenossen in Strasbourg was not extinct. Such Melchiorites could now be called "Covenanters under the Cross." They had always protested against the radical form of the movement, as early as 1533 when it first appeared. Among them were men like Jan Volkertsz Trypmaker, Jacob van Campen, and Obbe and Dirk Philips. After the catastrophe of Münster it was the special merit of Menno Simons (*q.v.*) that the peaceful Melchiorites were gathered together and were able to withstand the severe persecution. The earlier names were now replaced by such designations as Obbites, Dirkites, Mennists, and finally Doopsgezinden. It appears that small groups of Melchior-

ites persisted in Middle Germany as late as 1560 and after.

C.K.

A. Hulshoff, *Geschiedenis van de Doopsgez. te Straatsburg van 1525 tot 1557* (Amsterdam, 1905); W. I. Leendertz, *Melchior Hofmann* (Haarlem, 1883); Kühler, *Geschiedenis* I; K. Vos, "Kleine bijdragen over de Doopersche beweging in Nederland tot het optreden van Menno Simons," *DB* 1917; *DB* 1919, 198 *et passim;* Mellink, *Wederdopers, passim;* F. O. zur Linden, *Melchior Hofmann* (Haarlem, 1885) *ML* III, 69 f.

Melis Jansz, an Anabaptist martyr, beheaded at Leeuwarden, Dutch province of Friesland, on Feb. 11, 1539, because he had been (re)baptized and held "heretical opinions concerning the sacrament and the Catholic doctrines."

vDZ.

J. Reitsma, *Honderd jaren uit de Geschiedenis der Hervorming . . . in Friesland* (Leeuwarden, 1876) 63.

Melitopol, a city (pop. 75,000) in South Russia on the Molotschna in the province of Taurida. As a trade center Melitopol was important to the villages in the volosts of Halbstadt, Prischib, and Eichenfeld. In 1914 among other German Protestant groups there was a small Mennonite congregation there with a church of its own. Some of the members lost their lives in the Machno (*q.v.*) reign of terror during the spring of 1919.

The Mennonite church in Melitopol is of particular historical interest, since it was the scene of the last meeting of the general conference (*Bundeskonferenz*) of the Russian Mennonites (*q.v.*). The church had been closed for some time because the congregation had not registered promptly in the winter of 1923-24, and was unable to raise the necessary funds. It was opened on Aug. 9, 1925, when outside funds were donated, and was used every Sunday.

At the Ukrainian Mennonite general conference of Oct. 5-9, 1926, there were present 83 delegates and 14 visitors, representing 22,380 members. The meeting was watched over by two government officials (Kotelnikov and Schön). The discussions were determined by the pressures and difficulties of the time; ways and means were sought to alleviate them in the spirit of unity and love. Their desire was, as P. Penner (Lichtfelde) said in the conference address, to promote the kingdom of God, to the exclusion of any selfish interests.

This striving found expression in the reports given by representatives of the several districts on work done in the 20 months following the general conference held in Moscow in January 1925. Efforts had been made to elevate the inner life of the church and to resist the destructive spirit of the age. Everywhere church services were well attended.

A resolution passed on these reports states as a confession of faith, "that everywhere in the churches even in the most difficult circumstances an effort is being made to grow as a church of Christ on protective Biblical principles in the generally upset circumstances of life. One of the first requirements toward this end must be mutual loving understanding and the peaceable, fraternal co-operation between the various branches; the reports show us that in all the congregations there is an awakening to the recognition of this need and the efforts in this direction are being made. This is grace and true mercy from

God, which watches over the churches, and only in the strength of this grace can we approach our goal. . . . In surveying our widely scattered Mennonite brotherhood we are filled with the conviction that there is resident in our people a capital of religious strength, inner warmth and tenderness, and that our peculiar Mennonite confession presents a rich mine of healthy folkstrength and our Biblical church organization offers a fruitful field for developing the same."

The addresses and talks on the seriousness of the situation were in harmony with the above. The difficult tasks of church work, particularly pastoral care, are in the foreground. The proposals made here had as their object the elevation of the religious and moral life of the brotherhood. Consideration was given to the long recognized need for a Bible school, for expanded evangelization, for unity among the children of God, and expansion of work for the youth. The missionary spirit, which had to a large extent grown lax, was to be revived.

Regarding youth work the government representative reminded the conference that the instruction of children under eighteen was prohibited. The conference planned to work toward procuring government permission to give this instruction. But this was not achieved, nor was the Bible school set up. Already during the conference sessions there were indications of suppression. H. Reimer, the pastor of Rückenau, was sentenced to a month of hard labor for issuing birth certificates, and his congregation was dissolved. At the conference the government representative also raised objections to letting *Unser Blatt* circulate outside the Ukraine and recommended that they obtain government permission for this, as they had done for their foreign subscribers.

The discussions of the delegates revealed that the congregations had been losing capable leaders by the emigration of many preachers. In 1926 there were only 46,829 Mennonites, including children, in the Ukraine; of these, 9,000 baptized members met in 23 churches in the Molotschna. (*Unser Blatt* I, 28; II, 46-53, 58-59, 85-88, 113-16, 120-21, 151-55; *ML* III, 70 f.)   HEGE.

Melk, a town (pop. 3,175) of Lower Austria, situated in the upper entry to the Wachau, with a famous old Benedictine abbey. According to the Passau court records in the archives at Munich, Hans Hut (*q.v.*) introduced the Anabaptist movement here, when he stopped briefly in the spring of 1527 on his return from Vienna. When he went on to Styria, he took with him two highly respected citizens whom he had won, Eibmann and Simon Fleischhacker. In 1528 Jörg Krautschlögel (*q.v.*), a leader in Melk who had recently been in Krems (*q.v.*), was in Melk. A Passau court record describes him as "a fat person, a small beard, and was tolltaker on the bridge at Vienna, a leader of the deceiving sect of the Anabaptists, lived especially in Melk and wherever he could mix in, in order to spread the heresies." The authorities of Lower Austria, urged on by Ferdinand, took energetic action in Melk, reporting to the king on March 4, 1528, that in Melk several Anabaptists had been questioned. These were imprisoned and Wolfgang

Künigl (*q.v.*) was appointed to prosecute them. The outcome of the trial was that Krautschlögel and two other Anabaptists were beheaded in October and their bodies burned. These are the three victims mentioned but not named in the martyr list. People traveling from Tirol to Moravia used to end the river trip at Krems or Stein rather than at Melk.

P.DE.

A. Nicoladoni, *Johannes Bünderlin von Linz und die oberösterreichischen Täufergemeinden in den Jahren 1525-1531* (Berlin, 1893); J. Loserth, "Wiedertaufe in Niederösterreich," in *Bl. des Vereins für Landeskunde von Niederösterreich* XXXIII (Vienna, 1899); Beck, *Geschichts-Bücher*; Wolkan, *Geschicht-Buch*; Zieglschmid, *Chronik; ML* III, 71.

Melles, Jacob: see Rengers.

Mellin (Mellinus, Melling), **Abraham Philippus** (dates of birth and death unknown), was in the early 17th century a Reformed pastor at St. Anthonispolder, Dutch province of South Holland. He published the *Eerste deel van het Groot Rechtgevoelende Christen Martelaers-Boeck* . . . (Dordrecht, 1619). This martyr book deals only with the Christian martyrs until 1520; Mellin's intention to continue his work and list also the martyrs of the Reformation period was not carried out. Mellin's book, which shows evidence of thorough scholarship, was used by T. J. van Braght for his *Martyrs' Mirror*. In 1656 it was severely criticized by the Catholic Arnout van Gelouwe (*q.v.*).   vDZ.

B. Glasius, *Godgeleerd Nederland* II ('s Hertogenbosch, 1853) 492 f.; Gerald C. Studer, "A History of the Martyrs' Mirror," *MQR* XXXII (1948) 163-79, particularly 169; *Bibliographie* II, 435-40.

Mellinger, John H. (Dec. 7, 1858-May 13, 1952), an outstanding lay leader and the father of the missionary movement among Lancaster Conference Mennonites (MC), was born in Paradise Twp., Lancaster Co., Pa., the son of Jacob Mellinger, of the Benedict Mellinger line, and Elizabeth Hershey, of the Andrew Hershey and Peter Eby lines. He was married on Nov. 16, 1882, to Barbara K. Denlinger. They started farming north of Vintage in 1883, and the same year were baptized by Benjamin Herr at the Hershey meetinghouse. Here they farmed until 1895 when they purchased a smaller farm on Lincoln Highway East, retiring in 1912. In 1924, after his wife's death, Mellinger went to his son Jacob. His last days were spent in the Amos Mellinger home (a granddaughter). Of the six sons and one daughter, Jacob, John, Enos, and Jesse survived.

Sunday schools, approved by Conference in 1871, did not come into his district until 1887 when John was asked to be the superintendent at Paradise. Here he contributed missionary spark which sent John M. Kreider to Missouri, Abram Metzler to Martinsburg, A. Hershey Leaman and Mary Denlinger to Chicago (the first M.C. home mission), and J. A. Ressler (the first M.C. foreign missionary) to India. On Sept. 15, 1894, the Mission Advocates (*q.v.*) were organized in his home. With the organization of the Lancaster Sunday School Mission (*q.v.*) 16 months later, which he headed, quarterly mission meetings were held in the Paradise-Kinzer district. Whenever any rural or city missions were started, regardless of the distance, he was personally interested. When the larger succeeding organization, the Eastern Mennonite Board of Missions and Charities (q.v.), was organized in 1914 he was chosen president, serving until October 1934; thus he was chairman of the mission movement here over 38 years.

Although he passed through the lot for the ministry three times, his work was elsewhere. He and M. S. Steiner wrote the constitution for the forerunner of the Mennonite Board of Missions and Charities (q.v.). He aided in the organization of the Franconia Mennonite Mission Board (q.v.). He helped to locate the Falfurrias (Tex.), and the Tampa-Ybor City (Fla.) mission fields. He turned the adverse tide in a Philadelphia Quaker meeting in 1919 (?) that caused the Quakers with Mennonite support to feed the German children following World War I (Quaker Child Feeding). He helped to organize the Mennonite Central Committee in 1920 and served as a member on it until his retirement in 1934. He was promoter of the Old People's Home and the Associated Sewing Circles, chairman of the board of the Millersville Mennonite Children's Home for 20 years from the beginning. He was the moving spirit in 1922 and 1924, when $65,000 were successfully loaned to the Russian Mennonite immigrants in Manitoba, Saskatchewan, and elsewhere in Canada.

Mellinger's greatest contribution was in his outstanding leadership in the field of missions. Though a layman, he exercised extraordinary influence in the Lancaster Conference over a long period of time. Its extensive current program of foreign and home mission owes very much to him. I.D.L.

Mellinger, Martin (1763-1842), a prominent deacon for 52 years in the Mellinger Mennonite Church (q.v.) just east of Lancaster, Pa., named after him. His correspondence with his cousin Peter Weber (q.v.) of Kindenheim, Palatinate, Germany, published in the MQR V (1931) 42-64, contains much valuable historical information. H.S.B.

Mellinger meetinghouse was a union meetinghouse built by the Lutherans, Reformed, Mennonites (MC), and Dunkards in 1861 three quarters of a mile southwest of Schoeneck in northern Lancaster Co., Pa. The Shirk home east of town was the first Mennonite meeting place in this area. The ministers of the Indiantown Mennonite Church (q.v.) held services here once a month until 1921, and in 1942 relinquished all rights to the building. The services became more frequent in the Hammer Creek-Indiantown district and in 1926 led to the revival of the Cocalico meetinghouse. I.D.L.

Mellinger Mennonite Church (MC), located one mile east of Lancaster, Pa., on the Lincoln Highway, is one of the strongest and largest congregations of the Lancaster Mennonite Conference. With Jacob and Felix Landis, Martin Bare, Jacob Kreider, Joseph and Dorous Buckwalter, and others, Mennonite immigrants from the Palatinate, able to buy land from the London Company by 1722, the fertile acres soon became a prosperous Mennonite community. The settlers first worshiped in private homes. But at least by 1767 had a meetinghouse,

called Lampiter. A schoolhouse adjoining was added later. Martin Bare as minister signed the Dordrecht Confession at the 1725 conference in Germantown. Benjamin Landis was his early co-worker as preacher followed by Jacob Hartman, Bishop Tobias Kreider, and John Stauffer in the 18th century. Martin Mellinger (1763-1842), an immigrant from the Palatinate, was a prominent deacon. When a new meetinghouse, now a sexton's house, was built in 1855, it was named in his honor. A new meetinghouse was built on the present site in 1884, with extensive remodeling in 1894. The present large brick meetinghouse replaced it in 1914. This has always been one of the two largest congregations in the Lancaster Conference, and has remained largely rural, although located only three miles from the center of Lancaster. In recent years the city is rapidly moving to engulf the congregation and its building. Among the prominent ministers of more recent times have been John and Tobias Kreider, David Buckwalter, Adam Ranck, John L. and Sanford B. Landis. In 1956 the membership was 600, with Elmer G. Martin as bishop, and David L. Landis and Harry S. Lefever as preachers. I.D.L.

Memelniederung (Lowland of the Memel River) the name given in 1928-41 by the *Gemeinde-Kalender* to the Mennonite congregation in East Prussia near Tilsit, formerly known as the Lithuanian congregation (Litthauer Gemeinde), except in two issues, 1926 and 1927, when it was listed as Adlig Pokraken. At the earliest appearance of the congregation in the Dutch *Naamlijst* it already bore the name "the congregation in Lithuania." (See **Lithuania**.) H.S.B.

Memmingen, a city (pop. 25,250) in Bavaria, Germany, located on the Aach, 35 miles southeast of Augsburg, to which the Anabaptist movement came in the 16th century. The cities of Ulm, Biberach, Isny, Memmingen, Lindau, and Constance met in Memmingen Feb. 26-March 1, 1531, to discuss the Anabaptist situation. Their agreement is known as the Resolutions of Memmingen (q.v.).

In 1527 a flood of Anabaptists passed from Switzerland to the north and northeast, touching Memmingen, and winning some of its citizens. In January 1528, in the absence of the city preacher Christoph Schappeler, Simprecht Schenk of Wertingen advised the city authorities to expel them rather than to "punish them painfully." Thereupon the council forbade the lodging or sheltering of Anabaptists in its realm. In December of the same year the city council resolved to send all Anabaptists to the preachers, whether native or foreign; those who would not recant should be banished from the city. In case of banishment an eight-day period of grace was given, in hope that the penitent would return to the church. Nevertheless imprisonment was also used, as was reported to Mindelheim in May 1528, in order to instruct them in the Scripture, and if that failed, to detain them. A different case was that of a guild master, who as a member of the council had helped to pass the regulation prohibiting Anabaptists in the city. To the complaint of the city authorities that he nevertheless offered shelter to such persons, he replied that it was brotherly to give shelter to the poor exiles, and that it was better to obey God than man. It is to be assumed that he complied with the order to "put an end to it in eight days."

In 1529 after the second diet of Speyer with its sharp mandate against the Anabaptists, little Memmingen and its sister Protestant cities, led by the Protestant clergy, defied the imperial edict by adhering to its lenient Anabaptist policy. In October 1529 several men and women were instructed in the presence of the council; when there were no results, they were told to "spend their money elsewhere." Others who sympathized with them were punished "with words," and ordered "not to have meetings." Adherents should not baptize, but "we do not forbid other discussion of God's Word."

Through 1530 there was not much stir, but by the end of March 1531 it was decided to call to account those who did not attend church services in order to discover the Anabaptists. A month later one of the preachers proposed that they close the city gates on Sunday and put the citizenry under oath not to shelter Anabaptists. In the process the surprising discovery was made that one or another refused to give the oath "for conscience' sake." Hans Binder "could not be convinced by Scripture that he was in error and would not desist." The banishment was carried out; "they were to leave within a day's time and not return." Early in January 1532 some Anabaptist suspects were cited before the mayor; he ordered them to attend the church services, one of the sermons being on baptism. These measures were apparently successful. Not until 1535 were the Anabaptists mentioned again. In adjacent Woringen, which was under the jurisdiction of Memmingen, there were some who were interested in Anabaptism. It seems there were only women in the group. The council decided in case of arrivals from the outside (there had previously been some additions from Kaufbeuren, q.v.) to send two preachers and two church wardens to talk with them "at some suitable place, but not before the people." Then there was silence.

The moderate measures of the authorities were sufficient to control the movement. On only two other occasions are they mentioned. In 1574 a forest worker from near-by Eisenberg was tried on a charge of having joined them. His description of the people is of interest not only for church history, but also for cultural history: "They guard themselves against all sins and direct their lives in accord with God's commands, they do violence to no man, they leave the matter with God, they do not swear, they do not drink, they are chaste, and their life is to be to the praise and honor of God, and they have a fine brotherly love among each other; furthermore they are patient in cross and suffering and thank God without ceasing." In 1710 occurs the last Anabaptist trace: a Swiss woman came to the city via Ulm, and herself requested the pastor's instruction (Anna Margarete Cramer).   R.Do.

Fr. Dobel, *Memmingen im Reformationszeitalter, Das Reformationswerk zu Memmingen unter dem Drucke des Schwäbischen Bundes 1525-1529* (Memmingen, 1877); R. Dollinger, "Die Freie Stadt Memmingen und das Wieder-

täuferedikt Karls V.," in *Zeitwende* V, No. 11; *ML* III, 72 f.

Memmingen, Resolutions of (*Memminger Beschlüsse*). Early in 1531 some of the imperial cities of Swabia, Germany, of Zwinglian creed formulated agreements on matters concerning the Reformation, which also dealt with the treatment of Anabaptists. They were closely connected with the resolutions of the 1530 diet of Augsburg, the religious aspects of which failed to satisfy some of the Protestants, whereupon the evangelical estates on Dec. 31, 1530, formed the League of Schmalkald, in order to bring about clarification on the most important questions and to give each other mutual support in case of infringement of their rights. Unity in the punishment of the Anabaptists was another of their objectives.

The cities of Upper Germany, fearing subjection to the Confession of Augsburg, sought to come to an understanding on several points, including the checking of the Anabaptist movement. Representatives of Ulm, Memmingen, Biberach, Isny, Lindau, and Constance met in Memmingen Feb. 26-March 1, 1531, to discuss these points. Reutlingen was not represented on account of an epidemic of the plague, but presented a written opinion drawn up by its preachers. The city council of Ulm appointed its mayor Bernhard Besserer and Konrad Sam to draw up a draft of the points under consideration. In point of both statesmanship and theology the principles they formulated show understanding for the ideas and demands of the Anabaptists. On many a disputed point they sided with the Anabaptists.

The decisions drawn up by Ambrosius Blaurer (*q.v.*) and unanimously accepted, declare that in baptism and communion all additions and deviations from the ordinances as instituted by Christ must no longer be countenanced; the use of oil, salt, and exorcism of devils were named as such additions. Nor should infant baptism be compulsory, "in order that the accusations of the Anabaptists might be somewhat moderated and their mouths closed." They were to see that "we observe infant baptism freely and without compulsion, and in accord with the requirement of love grant this custom or omit it." The weak should, however, be permitted to perform an emergency baptism in case the life of the child is in danger, although for the child "there is no danger toward God, if it should happen to die without outward baptism." The effort of the city representatives to meet the reproach of the Anabaptists that not enough attention was paid in Protestant cities to moral living, is shown in the decisions concerning the punishment of the laity and the clergy.

The decisions concerning the punishment of the Anabaptists show that the Swabian cities were not in accord with the course taken against them in the empire and did not approve of severe penalties in matters of faith. They said:

"On account of the Anabaptists we wish very sincerely that they be treated as tolerantly as possible, so that our Gospel be not blamed or impugned on their account. For we have hitherto seen very clearly that the much too severe and tyrannical treatment exercised toward them in some places contributes much more toward spreading them than toward checking their error, because many of them, some out of stubbornness of spirit and some out of pious, simple steadfastness, endured all dangers, even death itself, and suffered with such patience that not only were their adherents strengthened, but also many of ours were moved to regard their cause as good and just.

"Thus it is contrary to the right of Christian government to force faith upon the world with the sword and other violent compulsion and uproot evil therein, which should be resisted alone through the mighty Word of God, and the person erring in faith shall not be suddenly knocked down, but should be tolerated in all Christian love as a harmless person." If he refuses to render the oath and military service, and does not yield after instruction from God's Word, he should be banished from the city. An outsider, who "teaches his error to others, should be kept out of the city." A citizen in a similar case should first be fined, then imprisoned, and if he still persists in his error, banished from the city. However, anyone who "under the pretense of Anabaptism incites other disturbances and revolt," shall be punished in accord with the imperial mandate as a sectarian and revolutionary. Anyone permitting himself to be baptized should be banished. Anyone who has been baptized and has been called to account for it, shall go to the preacher for instruction. Every citizen shall be under oath to report all Anabaptists of whom he knows to the authorities.

The delegates assumed that they could not be reproached in this position by God or either temporal or religious authorities. The decisions state that there were in the cities many God-fearing persons, who thought the government was discriminating against them in not tolerating them, while it tolerated others who with their teaching, life, and seditious acts disgraced the name of Christian. Therefore the cities would punish Catholics in the same manner if "in order to teach others they stir up disturbance or revolution."

The decisions of Memmingen did not adapt themselves to the imperial mandates of 1528 and 1529 nor to the imperial law of 1529 on the punishment of the Anabaptists. They furnish an interesting insight into the attitude of Upper Germany, especially in the territory of the persecuting Swabian League (q.v.). They have thus far received little attention in the pertinent literature.   HEGE.

K. Th. Keim, *Schwäbische Reformationsgeschichte bis zum Augsburger Reichstag* (Tübingen, 1855); Th. Pressel, *Ambrosius Blaurer* (Elberfeld, 1861); Fr. Thudichum, *Die deutsche Reformation* II (Leipzig, 1909); *ML* III, 73 f.

Memorial Mennonite Church (GCM), located at Altoona, Pa., was begun as Bethany Mission in 1913 by the Eastern District under the General Conference Board of Missions. The workers' home was erected in 1918. Jacob Snyder Board of Roaring Spring, Pa., became active director. Elizabeth Voth and Martha Franz served as workers until 1924. The permanent church building was erected in 1920 and dedicated as Memorial Mennonite Church, on Feb. 27, 1921. During George M. Bergen's service 1921-24, the congregation was organized with 48 members.

Early in 1925 Louis H. Glass, a railroad-engineer and evangelist, became the leader. Mrs. Edith Stiffler and daughter resided in the workers' home and helped with the work. Their ten-year period of service brought the congregation to its highest point with 95 members. Ill health caused Glass to resign in December 1936 and Mrs. Stiffler closed her service at the same time. Grover Klink served only 18 months as leader and was succeeded by Emerson F. Slotterback, who served till 1942. Much unemployment and a shifting population "on the hill" made work very difficult and the membership slowly decreased. There was no dependable lay leadership. Delbert E. Welty came and sought to rally the forces, but to no avail. The Board closed the field on Aug. 24, 1945. The Salvation Army bought the buildings and is carrying on the work.   A.J.N.

Memrik and Kalinovo Mennonite Church, located in the Memrik (q.v.) settlement, Bachmut district, province of Ekaterinoslav, Ukraine, was organized in the early days of the settlement, which had been founded in 1885 by settlers from the Molotschna settlement. The first ministers, elected on Aug. 27, 1885, were Jacob Wiens, Peter Janzen, and Abram Warkentin, all ordained by J. Töws. The congregation first met in private homes and in schools, then purchased one of the mansions of the noblemen in the village of Memrik and rebuilt it as a church. In 1887, when the congregation was visited by Kornelius Dirks, Johann Schartner, and Abram Görz from the Molotschna, the following additional ministers were elected: Johann Dück, Jacob Berg, Dietrich Peters, and Franz Janzen.

On June 28, 1887, in the presence of Elder Abram Görz, Peter Janzen was ordained as elder. In 1898 the congregation built a church 120 x 50 ft. In 1899 Jacob Pankratz, Jacob Penner, and Peter Dyck were ordained ministers, and in 1910 Jacob Martens, Peter Schellenberg, and Bernhard Harder likewise. The congregation observed footwashing in connection with the Lord's Supper. When Elder P. Janzen died of typhoid fever in 1918 Jacob Martens succeeded him, but died of the same disease in February 1920. He was succeeded temporarily by Franz Enns who had come to Memrik from the Terek settlement. In 1922 Jacob Pätkau (q.v.), a teacher and minister, was ordained elder. Under him Bible conferences and song festivals became popular. Pätkau was a member of the K.f.K. and coeditor of *Unser Blatt* (q.v.).

The Memrik church was soon nationalized and religious instruction for youth under 18 years of age was forbidden by the state. The taxes for the ministers and the church building increased constantly. After Elder Pätkau left (1929) under pressure the other ministers were also soon silenced. The church building was closed. By 1935 most of the ministers had been exiled. For a time the Mennonites and the Mennonite Brethren worshiped together at Kotlyarevka. The Kalinovo church was used as a reading room, granary, and children's home. During the German occupation (1941-44) it was used as a barracks.

In 1905 the Memrik Mennonite Church had a total membership of 2,215 including 1,183 unbaptized children. The contribution for benevolences

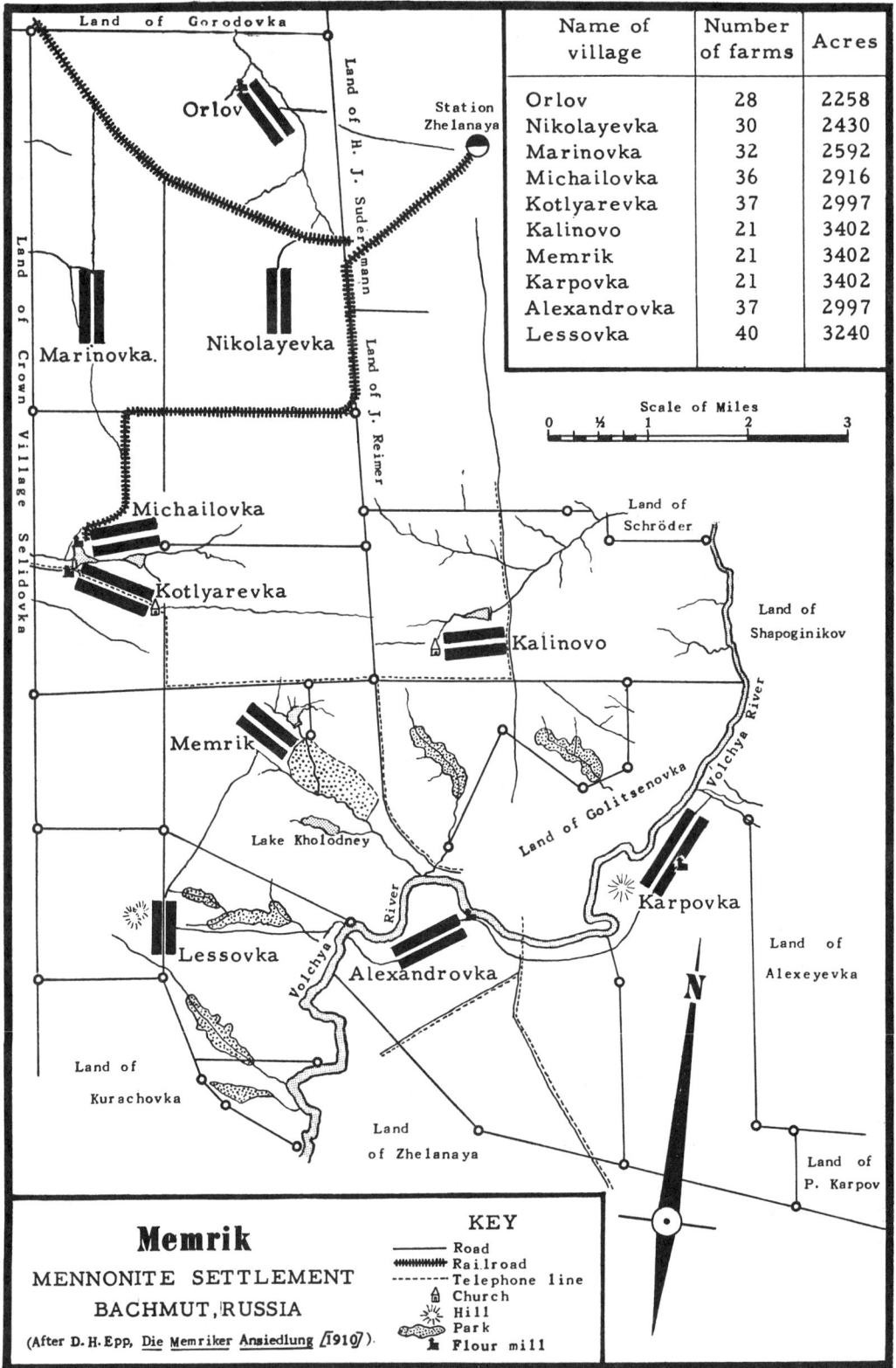

Name of village	Number of farms	Acres
Orlov	28	2258
Nikolayevka	30	2430
Marinovka	32	2592
Michailovka	36	2916
Kotlyarevka	37	2997
Kalinovo	21	3402
Memrik	21	3402
Karpovka	21	3402
Alexandrovka	37	2997
Lessovka	40	3240

Memrik

MENNONITE SETTLEMENT

BACHMUT, RUSSIA

(After D. H. Epp, Die Memriker Ansiedlung [1910])

KEY

Road
Railroad
Telephone line
Church
Hill
Park
Flour mill

was 1,649 rubles. In 1910 the total population was 470 families with 3,019 persons. C.K.

D. H. Epp, *Die Memriker Ansiedlung* (Berdyansk, 1910); H. Dirks, *Statistik (1905)*; H. Goerz, *Memrik* (Rosthern, Sask., 1954); *ML* III, 74.

Memrik Mennonite Settlement, Bachmut district, Ekaterinoslav province, Russia, was founded in 1885 on the Volshya River, a tributary of the Samara, which in turn flows into the Dnepr. The settlement was located in the Don basin near the Catherine railroad, which connected it with the Sea of Azov. The next larger city was Yuzovka (now Stalino) some 20 miles away.

The settlers came from the Halbstadt and the Gnadenfeld districts of the Molotschna settlement. A total of 32,400 acres of land were purchased from the noblemen Kotlyarevsky and Karpov in 1884 for the price of 600,000 rubles. A total of 221 families with 1,367 persons settled in ten villages on this land. In three of the villages each of the 21 farmers owned 162 acres, while in the remaining seven villages, consisting of a total of 40 farms, each owned 81 acres. The latter were called "half farms." The names of the villages, later Russianized, were Alexanderhof (Alexandrovka, *q.v.*), Bahndorf (Orlov), Ebental (Nikolayevka), Karpovka, Kotlyarevka, Marienort (Kalinovo), Memrik, Michaelsheim (Michailovka), Nordheim (Marinovka), and Waldeck (Lessovka).

The necessary qualifications of a settler were that "the head of the landless family conduct a quiet and moral life, be industrious and in possession of a wagon, plow, harrow, two horses, two cows, and the necessary means to establish a home." The land was mostly unbroken prairie. Although the quality of the land was excellent the settlers underwent the usual difficulties of pioneering. All settlers were expected to repay the loan and interest within 15 years to the Molotschna settlement, which sponsored the settlement. Originally Memrik was under the administration of the Molotschna settlement. Because the distance was over a hundred miles, Memrik tried to establish its own district or volost (*q.v.*) administration but failed. In 1888, contrary to the wishes of the settlers, it was incorporated in the neighboring Russian Golitzynov. The group was represented in this office by a settlement leader. The following served in this capacity: Heinrich Martins, Daniel Abrahams, Peter Dirks, Johann Köhn, and Julius Dörksen. In 1921 the settlement had its own volost office and administration for a short time. The settlement also had its own fire insurance agency, organized in 1901; Hermann Janzen, Jr., was its administrator for many years.

During the 1890's some Molotschna Mennonites purchased and settled on a part of a large estate some 12 miles from the Memrik settlement, which they named Ossokino. In the center of the settlement they built their school, which also served on Sunday for worship. The settlers belonged to the Memrik-Kalinovo Mennonite Church. During and after the Revolution this settlement suffered severely and disintegrated. In 1888 Molotschna Mennonites established the village of Alexandropol (30 farms), some 18 miles northeast of Memrik, near

the station Ocheretino. The village prospered and had its own school and church buildings. Most of the settlers belonged to the Mennonite Brethren Church (see **Alexandropol** Mennonite Brethren Church). The settlers were in close contact with the Memrik settlement.

The Memrik settlement had to solve many economic problems in its early life. Grasshoppers, gophers, and other plagues caused great damage. The prices of the products were low. Originally the farmers followed the rotation cycle of wheat, feed, and summer fallow. They sowed mostly summer wheat, which was replaced by winter wheat around 1905. The "German Red" cattle became significant. Later Holsteins were introduced. Markets for agricultural products were found in Yuzovka (Stalino), Mariupol, Berdyansk, etc.

Industry and commerce developed rapidly, particularly the milling industry. Steam mills were located in Bahndorf, Alexanderhof, Kotlyarevka, Karpovka, and near the station Zhelanaya (Heinrichs and Andres). One of the manufacturers of agricultural machinery was Julius Legin at Waldeck (started in 1895), who before World War I produced annually about 1,000 reapers, 600 plows, 300 fanning mills, etc., with an annual turnover of 150,-000 rubles. Among the business people were H. Hamm of Zhelanaya and David Warkentin of Kalinovo. At times efforts were made to establish coal mines on the land owned by the Mennonites, but this never developed into large industry.

During the first years of the Memrik settlement elementary education was given in homes. Soon schools were erected in each of the villages. By 1910 most of the villages had modern larger school buildings made of brick, and residences for the teachers, both being modeled after the pattern established by the Molotschna Mennonites. Outstanding teachers were Peter Schellenberg, Jacob Koop, Jacob H. Janzen, Cornelius Unruh, and H. Goerz.

In addition to the elementary schools (six grades) there was also at Kotlyarevo a secondary school (*Zentralschule*) started in 1918 with D. P. Wiens and H. Goerz as teachers, which had to be closed after a few years. Another secondary school, established at Ebental in 1920, was gradually taken over by the state. Attendance became obligatory in 1930. As a rule the director was a non-Mennonite. Gradually all Mennonite teachers were forced to give up their positions or adjust to the Communist philosophy of education.

In 1914 the estimated property of the settlement (population of some 3,500) amounted to 11,145,000 rubles. During World War I some 240 young men were drafted into forestry and medical service. During the Revolution in 1918 Machno (*q.v.*) and his bands inflicted great suffering on the settlement, murdering many inhabitants, and taking or destroying much property. During the struggle between the Soviet and White armies the Memrik settlement again suffered severely. Drought and starvation were severe. At last in 1922 some help came from America (MCC). Conditions improved somewhat during the NEP period under the Soviets. Only some 30 families emigrated to Canada in 1923-27. Very few managed to escape from Russia via Moscow in 1929.

In 1930 a great number of the farmers (kulaks) were sent to Siberia. During 1937-38 some 240 men were exiled, none of whom returned nor was any information ever obtained about them. The remaining population was organized into three collective farms under the following names: Thälmann, Petrovky, and Karl Marx. The headquarters of these collectives were located in the former Mennonite Brethren church of Kotlyarevo.

During the outbreak of the German-Russian War in 1941 some young men were drafted. In September 1941 all men between 16 and 65 were sent to Asiatic Russia. On Oct. 5 the remaining population received orders to appear at the station Zhelanaya, and from here they were also transported eastward. It is likely that they were sent to Kazakhstan in Siberia. When the German army reached Memrik there were only a few Mennonites left in the villages; Russian population had been moved into the villages. What happened to the villages in 1943 when the German army withdrew from Memrik is not known. The few Mennonites they had found in Memrik were taken to Germany. Thus only a few of the Memrik Mennonites reached America after World War II.   C.K.

D. H. Epp, *Die Memriker Ansiedlung* (Berdyansk, 1910); H. Goerz, *Memrik* (Rosthern, Sask., 1954); *ML* III, 74 f.

Menalda, a Dutch Mennonite family, usually merchants, in the province of Friesland (Bolsward, Harlingen, later also Groningen and Leeuwarden). There are a number of Mennonite preachers of this name: Jan Menalda (1726-1801), of Harlingen, who studied at the University of Utrecht and the Amsterdam Mennonite Seminary, and served at Huizen 1751-64, Leeuwarden 1764-71, and Rotterdam 1771-1801. His son Eke Menalda (1759-1831), educated at the Amsterdam Mennonite Seminary, served at Middelburg 1784-1831. Thomas Menalda (1736-94) of Bolsward studied at the University of Franeker and the Amsterdam Seminary and served at Makkum 1761-71 and Zwolle 1771-94. His son Simon Menalda (1763-1822), after studying at the Franeker University and the Amsterdam Seminary, was a pastor of the Bolsward congregation 1789-1813. Rein Sickes Menalda (b. *ca.* 1660), the grandfather of Jan Menalda, in 1700 conducted an important trade to the Baltic Sea ports. In 1721 he became burgomaster of Harlingen, one of the earliest instances of a Mennonite in government office.

To this family also belonged Cornelis Benjamin Menalda (1862-1950), of Leeuwarden, registrar of the Provincial States of Friesland, and for many years a trustee of the F.D.S. (Conference of Friesland) and the A.D.S. (General Dutch Mennonite Conference), and his daughter Wilhelmina Jacoba Menalda (1891-1946), who was the secretary of the Elspeetsche Vereeniging (*q.v.*) and also participated in the compilation of the new Dutch Mennonite hymnal, the *Doopsgezinde Bundel* (*q.v.*).   vDZ.

Menaldum (Menaem), a village in the Dutch province of Friesland, where Leenaert Bouwens (*q.v.*) baptized 7 persons in 1563-65 and 81 in 1568-82. In the 17th century it was the seat of a Mennonite congregation, belonging to the Jan Jacobsz group (*q.v.*). About 1623 the district governor made trouble for the Mennonites here because they did not want to have their marriages performed by the magistrate. A Sierck Annes was even punished by having his furniture confiscated. Later on the congregation is called Old Flemish. The small congregation, of which there is no further information, united with the Jan Jacobsz congregation at neighboring Franeker (*q.v.*) shortly after 1743.   vDZ.

J. Loosjes, "Jan Jacobsz en de Jan-Jacobsgezinden" in *Ned. Archief voor Kerkgeschiedenis* XI (1914) 234 f.

Mendon (Mich.) United Missionary Church was founded in 1950. In 1956 the pastor was Elmer Miller. The congregation is a member of the Indiana Conference.

Meneest or **Meneese,** a name by which 19th-century Mennonites (MC) were sometimes known in the areas in which they lived in eastern Pennsylvania, Ohio, and possibly elsewhere. Theodore Bean, historian of Montgomery County, Pa., states that the Mennonites call themselves "Meneest." This is evidently a corruption of the Dutch and German *Mennist* (*q.v.*).   J.C.W.

T. W. Bean, *History of Montgomery County* (Philadelphia, 1884) 369.

Menius, Justus (Jodocus Menig) (1499-1558), a Protestant theologian, entered the University of Erfurt, Germany, joined the circle of Humanists around his uncle Mutianus Rufus and Crotus Rubianus, went to the University of Wittenberg on Melanchthon's advice, became vicar in Mühlberg near Gotha in 1523, pastor in Erfurt in 1525, and superintendent of Eisenach 1529-57. In 1541-44 he served as temporary pastor in Mühlhausen, Thuringia, went to Gotha in 1546 and there succeeded his friend Fr. Myconius (*q.v.*) as superintendent of Gotha, without, however, giving up his position in Eisenach. Menius was a zealous promoter of the Reformation, taking an active part in the program of church inspection. In the last years of his life he participated actively in the theological disputes of the time. He became involved in a violent conflict with Amsdorf, whose thesis of the harm in good works he contested, defending the necessity of good works as evidence of the new life. This caused him to retire from his offices to the pastorate of the Thomaskirche in Leipzig, where he remained until his death, Aug. 11, 1558.

Menius had extended contacts with the Anabaptists. In his official position he came upon them again and again, and especially tried to refute them in several writings. In 1528, when the Anabaptist leader Melchior Rink (*q.v.*) was an itinerant preacher in Thuringia, Menius joined the bailiff of the Wartburg in writing a report to the elector of Saxony, warning him of Rink's activity. On Jan. 18, 1530, six Anabaptists were put to death in the district of Hausbreitenbach at Reinhardsbrunn, creating a great excitement, particularly since no seditious doctrines could be proved against them. Myconius expressed his misgivings in a letter to Melanchthon, who did not, however, share them. In order to silence criticism and to justify the position of the government, Menius wrote his booklet (1530), *Der widerteuffer lere und geheimnis, aus heiliger Schrift widerlegt;* Myconius was to have written it with Menius, but this plan was not carried out. In token of his agreement with its content Luther provided it with a foreword, which shows not a particle of understanding for the Anabaptist position. The lengthy and tedious book was dedicated to Philip, Landgrave of Hesse, in order to move him, who was always inclined to be lenient in matters of faith, to more aggressive action. Menius shows some familiarity with the teachings of his opponents if one disregards the vociferous and fanatical manner in which he calls them hypocrites and servants of the devil. The following paragraph is characteristic of his understanding of the Anabaptist concerns:

"The rabble rousers lodge only with the poor and their greeting is: The peace of God be with you. They preach that they belong only to the poor, to whom God has sent them out, and wherever they go they pretend special piety with peculiar prayers and read the Gospel to the poor people. But what they teach is only good works, such as that one must help his neighbor with gifts and loans and that goods should be held in common, one should injure no one, but conduct oneself friendly and brotherly among each other, none should rule over another, but all should be brethren and sisters alike."

Menius gives a list of "Erroneous doctrines of the Anabaptists," which he then refutes, though of course in a frequently tortuous and petty manner. The articles of faith that he names are as follows: (1) The Word of God shall be preached to none but those who are in the Anabaptist order and are sealed with the sign of the covenant. (2) Faith in Jesus Christ alone, without our good works and suffering, makes one neither pious nor blessed before God. (3) Infant baptism is against God and a sin, neither useful nor necessary for children; therefore only the adults and aged should be baptized. (4) The bread and wine of communion are not the real body and blood of our Lord Jesus Christ. (5) Jesus is not the actual and true Son of God. (6) All the damned and ungodly and even the devil himself will finally be saved.

In addition he reproaches them with regard to their attitude to the external rules of life and especially to the government, such as the oath, property, marriage, divorce, etc. Upon Luther's advice Menius at the end of the book makes the charge against the Anabaptists that their preachers do not have the proper call, and preach in corners instead of the open, although he would of course be the first to urge the government to interfere in such a case of open preaching. The above "erroneous articles" show that he must have received them at least in part from individual Anabaptist leaders; the sixth is strongly reminiscent of Denk. The first article is a self-contradiction, since the Word of God was to precede baptism, hence could not possibly be limited to baptized persons.

But the Anabaptists did not disappear, but on the contrary became more numerous in the district of Hausbreitenbach. Menius was almost always one of the commissars whose duty it was to notify the authorities of suspects and to cross-examine those arrested. Again and again he urges the authorities to take decisive steps.

At the close of 1538 the elector had two Anabaptists put to death, Hans Köhler (*q.v.*) and Hans Scheffer, not for sedition but for "blasphemy." Some of the people objected to this verdict and contested the right of the government to execute anyone for his belief. Menius was again compelled to resort to his pen to justify the elector's course of action, and wrote *Wie ein jeglicher Christ gegen allerley Lere, gut und böse nach Gottes befehl sich gebürlich halten sol,* in which he tries to present the rights and duties of the clergy and the temporal authorities toward the Word of God. To the clergy he grants only spiritual weapons in the struggle against heresy, but to the temporal authorities he makes it a duty to punish severely any teachers of false doctrine as "open blasphemers and murderers of souls," who endanger the peace and security of the subjects in a high degree. The tone of this book is even sharper than that of the previous one, and the threat of punishment by the government much more obvious.

However, the desired results were still not materializing. When Menius came to Mühlhausen as pastor in 1541 he found there an Anabaptist center. The city council hesitated to proceed against them. Therefore Menius directed a new book against it in 1544 titled *Von dem Geist der Widerteuffer.* Luther again contributed a foreword, full of praise for this irrefutable book by Menius, "so that if a cow had understanding, she would have to say it was the truth and could not be otherwise." The tone of the book is as usual quite intolerant, borne by a fanatical hatred. In content it is largely identical with the first book. The questions concerning the Scripture, faith and works, baptism, original sin, communion, family, marriage, government, etc., are discussed in thesis and antithesis. Again, and at great length the Anabaptist call to preach is contested and the charge of corner preaching repeated. The repeated statement that the Anabaptists were not being punished because of their faith is peculiar. He says, for instance, "And no one may think or say that he is punished for the sake of his faith. For if some one had a peculiar faith, he could not offend any one nor could he be judged for it or punished. But because this sect not only believes erroneously for itself, but blasphemes the true faith, God's Word, the sacraments, and God Himself and in their outward life pervert all the divine order, . . . therefore they are no longer to be judged according to their false hypocritical gestures, but rather according to their evident works."

A noteworthy discussion concerns the charge made by the Anabaptists that the clergy lived ungodly lives and that their teaching had little effect on their hearers. "A distinction must be made between a person with his life, conduct, and works, and his office and teaching, and where the office and teaching are right and pure, but the person blameworthy, follow the office and teaching and let the person with his works go." Is it any wonder that the Anabaptists, who always regarded doctrine and life as a unit, opposed such a position?

But this is not all of Menius' literary opposition to the Anabaptists. In 1551 he wrote a booklet entitled *Wider die Blutsfreunde aus der Widertauffer.* "Blutsfreunde" (Blood Friends) was the name of a degenerate wing of Anabaptists, which had little in common with the quiet branch. They advocated a libertinistic ideal of freedom, which led them to excesses of a flagrant character under the assumption that Christ had died for all sins. It is not strange that Menius attacks them with sharp words. But this booklet brought the quiet Anabaptists also into bad repute. From this time on little is heard of further contact between Menius and the Anabaptists.

Menius was one of the bitterest literary and personal enemies of Anabaptism on the Lutheran side during the period of the Reformation. With strong prejudice, frequently against his better knowledge, he interpreted as the work of the devil the fruit he could not fail to see. Hence his opposition is by no means free of the fanaticism with which all heresy was to be eradicated in favor of Lutheran pure doctrine. By his books Menius for a long time determined the character of writing about the Anabaptist movement in Middle Germany.   P.S.

G. L. Schmidt, *Justus Menius* (2 vv., 1867); P. Wappler, *Die Stellung Kursachsens und des Landgrafen Philipp von Hessen zur Täuferbewegung* (Münster, 1910); *idem, Thüringen;* the writings of Justus Menius of 1530, 1538, and 1544 in *Der ander Teil der Bücher D. Martin Luthers* (Wittenberg, 1551); *ML* III, 75-77; original prints of the 1530 and 1544 titles in GCL.

Mennist (*Menist*, and in the 18th century erroneously *Benist*), a Dutch and German term for "Mennonite." The earliest known appearance of the term was in a mandate of Countess Anna of East Friesland in 1545, where it was used to distinguish the followers of Menno from the Davidjorists and the Batenburgers. It was frequently used in the Netherlands as well as in government decrees of other countries, such as the Palatinate. In North Germany the term "Mennonisten" was long current. But since the 19th century only the designation "Mennoniten" has been preserved in German-language regions. (*ML* III, 77.)   HEGE.

A letter written by King John of Poland in 1660 calls the Dutch Mennonite immigrants "Minnists." Hans Alenson in his *Tegen-Bericht* (*BRN* VII, 242) says that the Frisians in 1626 were the first to use the name Mennist or Mennoniet. Though the term Menist is still commonly used in Friesland, the Dutch Mennonites at present are generally called Doopsgezind (*q.v.*).

In the Dutch and Frisian languages there are a number of expressions and sayings dealing with Mennonites; for example, the name "Mennistenhemel" (heaven) given to an area on the Vecht River in the province of Utrecht, where wealthy Mennonites built their stately country homes in the 18th century. A "Menniste hemel" is also found at Ureterp, Friesland. A number of these names and sayings were collected by D. M. van der Woude and published: "De Mennisten over de tong" (*DJ* 1941, 39-48) and "Menniste Namen" (*DJ* 1942, 44-50).

Also frequently mentioned are "Mennisten leugen" (lies) and "Menniste streken" (tricks), meaning distorted truths or half-truths. These expressions probably originated in a 16th-century story about Menno Simons: Menno was once traveling in a coach which was stopped by police looking for him. When they asked whether Menno Simons was in the coach, Menno is said to have asked the passengers, "Is Menno Simons in here?" and replied to the officers, "They say he is not here." The same story is told of Hans Busschaert (*q.v.*). (See J. G. de Hoop Scheffer, "Mennisten-streken," *DB* 1868, 23-48.)

A familiar expression in Dutch literature is "Menniste Zusje" (girl), meaning a young woman dressed in the modest Mennonite way and apparently an example of virtue, but doing things on the sly. C. N. Wybrands in 1913 published an important study on this material, entitled *Het Menniste Zusje.* Menniste Zusje is also the common Dutch name for the flower of the *saxifraga nutans.* (See **Mennonite.**)
                vDZ.

Menniste-Bouwers-Federatie is a Dutch Mennonite association for Mennonite youth (12-18 years), founded at Amsterdam in March 27, 1948. The purpose of the association is to get the children of Mennonites together in special meetings, where they are entertained by various activities, such as sports (also camping) and games. The association is divided into a number of districts and local groups, which are found in 20 congregations. The total membership in 1956 numbered about 1,000.   vDZ.

Menniste-buurt, a hamlet in the Dutch province of North Holland. In the *Naamlijst* of 1780 the Oude-Zijpe (*q.v.*) congregation is called that "aen de Menniste-buurt in de Zuidzijpe of Oudezijp bij Petten."   vDZ.

Menniste Zusje: see Mennist.

Menno Bible Institute (GCM), located near Didsbury between Edmonton and Calgary, Alberta, was founded in 1937 by the Mennonite Conference of Alberta, which still owns three acres of land, the school, two dormitories with accommodations for 80 students, and two teacherages. The enrollment rose from 8 in 1937 to 52 in 1941 with two instructors. In 1941-51 three teachers taught 45-55 students a year. Since then the enrollment has declined. In 1956, the 20th year, 27 students registered for the five-month term. During the last two years four teachers have taught. The Didsbury church was the place for instruction the first 10 years. Now a fine school is used. M.B.I. is an active member of the Evangelical Teacher Training Association.   W.P.

Menno Chapel Mennonite Church (MC), better known as the New Stark (Ohio) Mennonite Church, and often called simply Chapel, a member of the Ohio Mennonite Conference, was not organized until 1876 but some of the members had moved in from Stark Co., Ohio, as early as 1839. Children and grandchildren of Bishop John Thut of Bluffton made up the majority of the congregation, never very large. Menno Chapel was built a mile west of New Stark in 1878. John Blosser (*q.v.*) was bishop for many years. He was followed by his brother Noah, who took his congregation into the General Conference of Mennonites of North America when it disagreed with the discipline of the Ohio and

Eastern A.M. Joint Conference about 1924. After his death ministers connected with the Witmarsum Theological Seminary (*q.v.*) at Bluffton, Ohio, served the congregation. Later the members joined with the few remaining members of the New Stark Presbyterian Church to form the New Stark Community Church. J.S.U.

Menno Colony, located in the Chaco district of Paraguay, was the first Mennonite settlement to be founded in the country, its first settlers arriving at the colony site in April 1928, from Manitoba and Saskatchewan. After the passing of the Canadian School Act of 1915, which was to enforce the use of the English language for all instruction in schools, and because of the Canadian war effort during those years, of which the Mennonites also felt the effects, there developed among their settlements along the Red River and in Saskatchewan a desire to find a new homeland for themselves and their children. On Feb. 11, 1921, six delegates from the Red River settlements went to Paraguay to investigate settlement possibilities and returned with a very favorable report, contrary to that given by the delegation of five Saskatchewan Mennonites who had made the same trip in 1920. Through the help of a New York banker, Samuel McRoberts, the Paraguayan government was approached with a request for granting of certain privileges which the Mennonites demanded. The Paraguayan government reacted very favorably and on July 26, 1921, passed Law #514, giving them all the requested privileges and freedoms. The Mennonites today refer to this law as the "Privilegium." However, economic conditions in Canada delayed Mennonite emigration until 1926, when McRoberts formed the Inter-Continental Company in Winnipeg to buy their land in Canada, and the Corporacion Paraguaya in Paraguay to sell them lands there in return. Their first Chaco land purchase consisted of 137,920 acres, lying about 500 ft. above sea-level.

The first group of 51 families (309 persons) left Altona, Man., on Nov. 23, 1926, followed by other groups, totaling 279 families, in all approximately 1,765 persons, by 1930. Upon arrival the first group in Paraguay was welcomed by President Eligio Ayala on Dec. 29, 1926, in Asuncion, and then continued its journey to Puerto Casado. There the immigrants discovered that the Corporacion Paraguaya had not surveyed the land they had bought while still in Canada, and the group had to wait until April 1928 to take possession of their land. Many became discouraged and 355 returned to Canada, while 147 died of a typhoid epidemic and the difficult climate. It was undoubtedly the most difficult period any Mennonites in Paraguay have ever experienced. The 1937 population was 1,722 in 309 families. The January 1950 population of the colony was 3,370 in 52 villages with 560 families. The July 1955 population was 4,006 with a land area of 800,-000 acres owned by Menno and its daughter colony, about six times the original area.

The eastern border of the colony is located 110 miles due west of Puerto Casado. The distance from Puerto Casado to Sommerfeld, the capital of Menno Colony, is 155 miles. The first villages to be established shortly after their arrival in 1928, with an average of more than the intended 16 families each, were Bergtal, Laubenheim, Waldheim, Gnadenfeld, Weidenfeld, Reinland, Bergfeld, Osterwick, Blumengart, Schöntal, Halbstadt, Strassberg, Chortitz, and Silberfeld (abandoned in 1934). In 1950 Menno Colony had 43 villages in the old colony and an additional 6 villages in the new daughter colony located approximately 70 miles south of the colony. In 1955 the total number of villages was 60. As in other Chaco Mennonite settlements the chief cash crops are cotton, sorgo, peanuts, and for home consumption such crops as beans, watermelons, mandioca, and other vegetables. The colony has many orange, lemon, and grapefruit orchards. The houses are usually built of adobe brick and frequently in two-story style as formerly in Canada.

All the immigrants came to Paraguay in one of the three church groups—Chortitz Church under the leadership of Martin C. Friesen; Sommerfelder Church under Heinrich Unruh, and the Bergtal Church under Aron Zacharias. The first two groups together numbered 1,535 souls and the latter only 227. Later the Sommerfelder, Chortitz, and a part of the Bergtal group merged into the Chortitz Church, the latter group, however, retaining its administrative independence. After the death of Zacharias the rest of the Bergtal people joined the united group. The colony has one church building at Osterwick, the village of Elder Friesen, the schools serving as meetinghouses in the other villages. While still in Canada these church groups elected a committee to discharge all business in connection with emigration and resettlement, which consisted of the following: Martin C. Friesen and Abram A. Braun (East Reserve), Heinrich Unruh and Abram J. Friesen (West Reserve), Peter Peters and Peter J. Dyck (Sask.). In 1928 in Paraguay this committee was changed to include Jakob Braun, Johann Derksen, Isaak K. Fehr, Bernhard Penner, Kornelius Wiebe, and Jakob Neufeld. Today the committee, called the Chortitzer-Komitee, is made up of one representative from every three leguas of land, totaling nine members. The secretary is elected out of the committee members by themselves, and the administrator (*Vorsteher*) is elected out of the committee members by the colony. The secretary and administrator are salaried. This committee is entirely responsible for all colony affairs of whatever form, except church matters, which are handled by the leading ministers. Disputes are settled by the ministers and elders. Its 1951 administrator was Jakob B. Reimer. Previously Jakob Braun had filled this post for many years. There is also the traditional "Waisenamt" (office to care for widows and orphans, and the inheritance of property) brought along from Russia via Manitoba.

Instruction in the schools is carried on by self-educated laymen, and there are usually four classes in each school; namely, *Fibler,* beginners; *Katechismer,* Katechism class; *Testamentler,* the older students studying the New Testament; *Bibler,* the Bible study and graduating class. The average school attendance is for five years. In 1947 the colony built its own 30-bed hospital, and since 1949 has had its own doctor, either German or Paraguayan, as may be available. All surgical work is done in Filadelfia, Colony Fernheim, in return for which Menno Colony shares the expenses of that hospital. The colony has also its own co-operative store that handles all buying and selling, and a small industrial establishment, including a sawmill and cotton gin, operated by the co-operative.

Because Menno was the first colony to be established in the Chaco its settlers suffered untold hardships and reverses. It is creditable indeed that, coming from a more abundant life in Canada, more of them did not become discouraged. In contrast to subsequent Mennonite immigrants to Paraguay from Russia, few people of Menno Colony have a desire to emigrate to Canada. Although the colony has a difficult financial struggle most of its people are happy and satisfied. In 1955, however a group of some 50 conservative families, dissatisfied with the change gradually coming into Menno's life under the leadership of the more progressive elder and Chortitzer Komitee, decided to migrate to the Santa Cruz region of Bolivia, where a few families from Fernheim had settled a few years earlier. C.J.D.

Walter Quiring, "The Canadian Mennonite Immigration to the Paraguayan Chaco 1926-27," *MQR* VIII (1934) 32-42; *idem, Russlanddeutsche suchen eine Heimat, Die deutsche Einwanderung in den paraguayischen Chaco* (Karlsruhe, 1938); *idem, Deutsche erschliessen den Chaco* (Karlsruhe, 1936); Ministerio de Economia, *Las Colonias Mennoniticas en el Chaco Paraguayo* (Asuncion, 1934); Schmieder and Wilhelmy, *Deutsche Ackerbausiedlungen im südamerikanischen Grasland, Pampa und Gran Chaco* (Leipzig, 1938); Friedrich Kliewer, *Die deutsche Volksgruppe in Paraguay, eine siedlungsgeschichtliche, volkskundliche und volkspolitische Untersuchung* (Hamburg, 1941); Annemarie Krause, *Mennonite Settlement in the Paraguayan Chaco* (Chicago, 1952); J. W. Fretz, *Pilgrims in Paraguay* (Scottdale, 1953); *ML* III, 90-93.

Menno Colony Co-operative, Chaco, Paraguay, was founded in 1936 as a mutual aid organization, hence pays no dividends as most co-operatives do. It advances necessary short-term consumer credit, and uses its profits for the enlargement of facilities, and a smaller part to support the hospital and other welfare activities. The co-operative is under the general direction and control of the Chortitzer-Komitee, which is the general incorporated or registered organization of the Menno Colony and which has general responsibility for the economic aspects of Menno Colony life. H.S.B.

Menno Linden, a very old splendid linden tree which stands before a small house near Fresenburg, between Hamburg and Lübeck in North Germany, which is now a poorhouse. According to tradition this house was occupied by Menno's printer, and the tree was planted by Menno himself, hence the name. This story, though it is quite improbable, shows how tenaciously Menno's memory has attached itself to the locality where he spent the last years of his life. On Sept. 6, 1922, a brief gilded inscription was put on the tree. In 1954 the Menno Stone was moved from its location in the adjacent field to the Menno Linden. NEFF.

Menn. Bl., 1902, with picture; H. van der Smissen, *Mennostein und Mennolinde zu Fresenburg* (Hamburg, 1922); *ML* III, 95.

Menno Mennonite Church (GCM), located 20 miles west of Ritzville, and 19 miles northwest of Lind in Adams Co., eastern Washington, a member of the Pacific District Conference, was organized in 1879 near Freeman, S.D., with J. R. Schrag and Joseph Kaufman as elected ministers. In 1888 Schrag and a number of families moved west to Polk Co., near Dallas, Ore. In 1891 they settled near Eugene, Ore., and in 1900 the entire congregation moved by covered wagon to their present location, where they pioneered on homestead land. The first church, built in 1908, was replaced by a modern structure in 1950. A new parsonage was completed in 1952. The membership of the congregation in 1954 was 164, mostly rural, and living within a radius of 20 miles of the church. Other ministers who have served this church are John Waltner, D. D. King, D. B. Hess, M. J. Galle, E. J. Miller, Willard Wiebe, Paul Boschman (assistant), and Lester E. Janzen.
W.W.W.

H. D. Burkholder, *The Story of Our Conferences and Churches* (n.p., 1951).

Menno Mennonite Church, Menno Colony, Chaco, Paraguay, the church of the Manitoba Mennonites who founded Menno Colony in 1927. In 1956 it had 1,359 baptized members. Martin C. Friesen, the single elder, who has served as elder from the beginning, is assisted by twenty-one preachers and six deacons. In 1953 (according to Fretz) there was only one meetinghouse in the colony located in the village of Osterwick, the residence of the elder. The village schools serve as the regular meeting places for worship, but general assemblies are held in the Osterwick church.

The original immigrants, coming largely from the West Reserve in Manitoba, were largely Sommerfelders (*q.v.*), and since they brought their elder (Friesen) with them, they constituted the dominant element in church life. The Chortitzer Church group, composed largely of people from the East Reserve in Manitoba, which actually differed little from the Sommerfelders, also brought their leader, Heinrich Unruh, with them, but they were smaller and later merged with the Sommerfelders. The Bergthaler Church, a very small group, led by Aron Zacharias, has practically lost its identity. The Menno Church, in contrast to the Old Colony group in Mexico, is moving progressively forward and strengthening its religious life and outlook. H.S.B.

J. Winfield Fretz, *Pilgrims in Paraguay* (Scottdale, 1953).

Menno Monument, in Witmarsum, Dutch province of Friesland, was erected on the site where the meetinghouse of the Witmarsum Mennonites once stood. Tradition says that the house of Herman and Gerrit Jansz stood here, where Menno first preached after leaving the Roman Catholic Church in 1536, and often stayed, and where he was probably married. These traditions are, however, rather improbable. The monument, a large stone obelisk about 10 feet high, was dedicated on Sept. 11, 1879. On the front it has the words, "In memory of Menno Simons, b. at Witmarsum in 1496. Heb. 12:7"; on the left side: "According to tradition Menno preached to his first followers here"; on the right side (facing the village two miles distant): "For three centuries the Mennonites of Witmarsum assembled at this place"; on the back: "I Cor. 3:11. 1536." The petition of the Dutch Mennonites for contributions to support the project was not universally complied with. Christian Schmutz of Rappenau (Baden) and others rejected the idea of such a monument. The stiffest resistance was encountered in America, where an article in the periodical *Zur Heimath* called it idolatry and a defamation of Menno Simons. On July 3, 1936, in connection with the close of the Mennonite World Conference, a wreath was placed at the foot of the monument in a solemn ceremony. (*DB* 1880, 164; *Menn. Bl.*, 1878, 22, 55 ff.; 1879, 63; 1880, 37; 1907, 81; *ML* III, 94 f.) Neff.

Menno Simons (*ca.* 1496-1561) was the outstanding Anabaptist leader of the Low Countries during the 16th century. His followers became known as Mennonites (*Mennisten*). He was not, however, as is popularly assumed, the founder of the movement in the Netherlands. He became its leader after it had been in existence in that area for a number of years. His significance lies in the fact that he assumed the responsibilities of leadership at the crucial moment of the movement when it was in danger of losing its original identity under the influence of chiliastic and revolutionary leaders who succeeded in winning large followings. He maintained original peaceful Biblical Anabaptist concepts and won many who had been in danger of being swallowed up by the Münsterites (*q.v.*).

Menno was born in 1496 (exact date unknown) in the little village of Witmarsum, Dutch province of Friesland. Little is known about his youth and parental home. His parents, who lived in Witmarsum, were very probably dairy farmers. His father's first name was Simon, hence the son's name Menno Simons(zoon). Since Menno did not enter the priesthood until the age of 28, it can be assumed that he made the decision for this career not so early in life. He may have received his training in a monastery of Friesland or in a neighboring province. Menno knew Latin, and Greek was not entirely foreign to him. During his study he acquainted himself with some of the Latin Church Fathers. He did not read the Bible as such before his second year as a priest. Naturally he knew large sections of it, e.g., through the Roman missal.

Hardenberg used Menno Simons as an example of men who had "stupid teachers" and who without "learning and sound judgment ran away from monasteries." He also states that he met Menno as a rural priest. Hardenberg received his training at the Aduard Monastery near Groningen (1527-30) at the time when Menno was serving as a priest in Friesland. What occasion brought the two together? Was Menno also a graduate of Aduard? In that case Hardenberg did not speak very respectfully of his alma mater. In any event not too much significance can be attached to his statement regarding Menno's training since he was jealous of Menno's success and not inclined to give an objective evaluation. He says of Menno that he "took the Bible into his hands

without formal training causing such great damage among Frisians, Belgians, the Dutch, . . . Saxons, . . . all of Germany, France, Britain, and all surrounding countries that posterity will not be able to shed sufficient tears because of it" (Spiegel, 117).

In 1524 at the age of 28, Menno was ordained priest at Utrecht. His first parish was Pingjum near Witmarsum, where he served as a vicar, with two colleagues. Judged by his reminiscences he was not deeply convinced of the sacredness of his duties, for he states that he joined his fellow priests in "playing cards, drinking. . . ." But during the first year he was suddenly frightened. While he was administering the Mass he began to doubt whether the bread and the wine were actually being changed into the flesh and blood of Christ. First he considered these thoughts the whisperings of Satan; but he was unable to free himself through sighings, prayers, and confessings." We conclude, therefore, that Menno Simons was not entirely free of influences from a movement which had become quite strong at that time in the Netherlands and whose adherents were known as Sacramentists.

The Sacramentists denied the actual presence of Christ in the Lord's Supper, i.e., Transubstantiation. This thought was first advocated publicly by Cornelis Hoen (*q.v.*). The Sacramentists (*q.v.*) were promoters of a reform movement in the Low Countries advocating the removal of abuses in the Catholic Church and a return to a Biblical Christianity, although they were not specifically "Lutheran" or "Reformed." This Sacramentist movement became the seedbed for the message proclaimed by Melchior Hofmann (*q.v.*) and his evangelists when they penetrated the Low Countries from Emden in 1530. Hoen's views regarding the Lord's Supper were published in Switzerland by Zwingli at the very time that Menno was entertaining doubts.

After Menno had been tormented for about two years by his doubts he finally turned to the Bible and searched it for help on his particular problem. "I did not get very far in it before I saw that we had been deceived," is Menno's summary of the result of his search. In the Scriptures he found certainty regarding the Lord's Supper. He found that the Sacramentist view, which interprets the meaning of the Lord's Supper as being symbolic, was the Biblical one. Now he was torn between two authorities: the Bible and the church. Thus far he had avoided the use of the Bible, for he saw that the Bible had taken Luther, Zwingli, and others out of the Catholic Church; now he was on the same path. Which of the two authorities would win? He wanted to be loyal to both. In the meantime Menno found help by reading certain writings of Luther, who taught him that the Scriptures should have the first place. Luther also taught him that if violations of the tradition of the Catholic Church have a Biblical basis they can not lead to eternal death. He may have read Luther's *Von der Menschenlehre zu meiden* . . . (Krahn, 43). Gradually the Scriptures became the authority for Menno, and the source of his sermons. Soon Menno became known as an "evangelical preacher," yet he complains that in those days "the world loved him and he the world."

Thus Menno, influenced by the Sacramentists and Luther, began to place the Scriptures above the authority of the church.

Melchior Hofmann, a lay preacher and follower of Luther, had traveled on long journeys as far as Baltic regions. In Strasbourg he came into contact with the Anabaptists and was baptized there in 1530, apparently not by the Swiss Brethren or by the group represented by Pilgram Marpeck. During the same year he introduced believers' baptism in Emden, East Friesland (q.v.), where he found the soil well prepared by the Sacramentist movement. As the symbolic meaning of the Lord's Supper had become the center around which its followers gathered, so now believers' or adult baptism became the point around which many Sacramentists and sympathizers of the Reformation gathered. Jan Volkerts Trypmaker (q.v.), a follower of Hofmann, who had been baptized by him, baptized Sicke Freerks Snijder in Emden. The latter then went to Leeuwarden, the capital of the Dutch province of Friesland, where he soon died a martyr's death, being executed because of his "re-baptism." Menno, who lived near Leeuwarden, heard about this event. "It sounded strange to me," says he, "to hear of a second baptism." This made a deep impression on him, although the idea as such was probably not entirely new to him (Krahn, 24). The thought of believers' baptism was now constantly in his mind. He "searched the Scriptures diligently and considered the question seriously but could find nothing about infant baptism." He also consulted his colleague, the Church Fathers, Luther, Bucer, and Bullinger. In their writings he found various reasons given for infant baptism, in which "each one followed only his own mind." He saw himself deceived by all on the question of baptism. The Scriptures, in which he found no definite reference to infant baptism, convinced him that believers' baptism was the true Christian practice. By 1531 he was thoroughly convinced that believers' baptism was Scriptural.

This, however, did not yet cause Menno's withdrawal from the Catholic Church. Instead he accepted a call to become the pastor of his home church at Witmarsum, where he remained until he joined the Anabaptists in 1536. This step may in part be explained by the course which the Anabaptist movement was taking at this time. Hofmann had placed great emphasis on prophetic visions and the Second Coming of the Lord, but under the pressure of persecution he ordered a cessation of baptism for two years (1531-33). After he had been imprisoned in Strasbourg in May 1533 the Anabaptist movement of the Low Countries came under the influence of persons who exploited the chiliastic aspect of the Hofmannite teaching, and threw off Hofmann's restriction on baptizing. Jan Matthijs (q.v.), Jan van Leyden (q.v.), and others like them became prominent leaders. Aided by the results of the severe persecution they transformed a part of the peaceful Biblical Anabaptist movement into a militant Old Testament "Israel," each citizen of which was expected to help Christ usher in the millennium, which Hofmann had prophesied would start in Strasbourg, and which they variously prophesied to come at Münster, Amsterdam, and other places. Particularly the attempt to establish a "New Jerusalem" at Münster (q.v.) in 1534-35 affected the course and future of Anabaptism. Menno Simons, although convinced that the Catholic Church was in need of a reformation, also realized that the Melchiorite movement, which had started well with a reformation program, had now accepted some very unchristian principles and practices. Publicly from the pulpit, and privately, he denounced its evils. As early as 1532 some people in the vicinity of Witmarsum had been baptized. Menno even had some discussions with leaders of the Münsterite movement early in 1534. It is possible that among the men with whom he debated was Jan van Geelen (q.v.), who organized an armed defense at the Olde-Klooster (q.v.) near Bolsward. On April 7, 1535, this group was defeated; among those who lost their lives were Peter Simons (q.v.), who may have been Menno's brother, as well as some members of his congregation. This was a turning point in Menno's life. On July 25, 1535, the "New Jerusalem" at Münster came to a tragic end. Few escaped and the leaders were tortured to death.

All this made a great impression on Menno and brought his inner life to a crisis and final decision. Had he not received some valuable insight through the Anabaptist movement in its earlier and peaceful days? Did he not know that among the Anabaptists were many with a sincere desire to live a consecrated Christian life? What had he done to prevent this tragic development through which so many were misled, although it was said that he "could silence these persons beautifully"? He now states, "The blood of these people, although misled, fell so hot upon my heart that I could not stand it, nor find rest in my soul. . . . I saw that these zealous children, although in error, willingly gave their lives . . . for their doctrine and their faith. And I was one of those who had disclosed to some of them the abominations of the papal system. But I continued in my comfortable life and acknowledged abominations simply in order that I might enjoy physical comfort and escape the Cross of Christ.

"Pondering these things my conscience tormented me so that I could no longer endure it. . . . If I continue this way and do not live agreeably to the Word of the Lord . . . , if I through bodily fear do not lay bare the foundations of truth, nor use all my powers to direct the wandering flock who would gladly do their duty if they knew it, to the true pastures of Christ—Oh, how shall their shed blood, shed in the midst of transgression, rise against me at the judgment of the Almighty and pronounce sentence against my poor, miserable soul!"

Menno continues his account by stating that his "heart trembled within" him and that he "prayed to God with sighs and tears that He would give" him, "a sorrowing sinner, the gift of His grace" and create within him "a clean heart and graciously through the merits of the crimson blood of Christ forgive" his "unclean walk . . ." and bestow upon him "wisdom, Spirit, courage . . . so that" he might "preach His exalted adorable name and holy Word in purity, and make known His truth to His glory."

Thus the gradual acceptance of the evangelical truth and the willingness to take upon him the "cross of Christ" came to Menno in the crucial days of the disastrous end and defeat of the radical Melchiorites at Bolsward and Münster. He was challenged and found the courage to become the shepherd of the flock without a leader. For some nine months after the defeat at Bolsward in April 1535, he preached "the word of true repentance" more openly from his pulpit, "pointing the people to the narrow path, reproving all sin and wickedness, adultery, and false worship," but he also presented "the true worship, . . . baptism and the Lord's Supper, according to the doctrine of Christ," to the extent that he had at that time received from God insight and grace (*Complete Writings,* 670 f.).

This Menno did, not only in preaching from his pulpit and in personal contact with the people, but also through a writing which was to be the first of many. Jan van Leyden, who had assumed the blasphemous role of a "Second David" of the "New Jerusalem" at Münster, was the reason for this writing entitled *The Blasphemy of Jan van Leyden.* The pamphlet, which was not printed until 1627, was written after the defeat at Bolsward but before the defeat of Münster, with the intention of publication. But Münster collapsed, and Menno left the Roman church; hence the urgency and possibility of having it published diminished (*Complete Writings,* 33).

After nine months of the more dedicated and open presentation of his views, Menno's position must have become known. This endangered his life, and so he quietly renounced all "worldly reputation, name and fame," infant baptism, easy life, and "willingly submitted to stress and poverty under the heavy cross of Christ." He left his home community and parish, likely by night, to start an "underground" life. According to available information this was most likely in January 1536 (Krahn, 35). For a year he probably found shelter in the province of Groningen, at times crossing the border into East Friesland. He "sought out the pious" and found "some who were zealous and maintained the truth." He dealt with the erring and "reclaimed them from the snares of damnation and gained them to Christ." Thus we find Menno continuing his labors as a voluntary underground evangelist. In addition to this work he was also studying the Word of God and writing pamphlets to strengthen and guide those in need of spiritual help and to win those in danger of losing their evangelical faith. Some of his writings he probably had started in Witmarsum, such as "The Spiritual Resurrection" (*Van de Geestlijke Verrijsenisse,* published *ca.* 1536) which was soon followed by "The New Birth" (*De nieuwe Creatuere, ca.* 1537) and "The Meditations on the Twenty-Fifth Psalm" (*Christelycke leringhen op den 25. Psalm, ca.* 1538). One of the most important writings was the *Foundation-Book* (*q.v.*) (*Dat Fundament des Christelycken leers,* published 1539-40). The contents of these writings reveal that Menno had found the foundation and salvation in Jesus Christ and that he was challenging his readers to accept Christ and become His disciples.

While Menno was seeking out the pious and studying and writing in seclusion, he soon became known among the Anabaptists as a capable and devoted leader. One day "some six, seven, or eight persons" came to him who were of "one heart and one soul" with him, "beyond reproach as far as man can judge in doctrine and life, separated from the world after the witness of Scriptures and under the cross, men who sincerely abhorred not only the sect of Münster but the cursed abomination of all other worldly sects." They prayerfully requested Menno in the name of "those pious souls who were of the same mind and spirit" that he should make "the great sufferings and need of the poor oppressed souls" his concern, since their hunger was so very great and the faithful stewards so few. They urged him to use the talents which he had received from God in His vineyard (*Complete Writings,* 671).

When this request to become an elder or bishop of the scattered Anabaptists came to Menno he was again greatly troubled. He realized that his talents were limited, that on one hand he was weak by nature and timid by spirit, and that on the other hand the wickedness and tyranny of the world was great; yet he saw a great hunger and need among the God-fearing, pious souls who "erred as do harmless sheep which have no shepherd." The delegation and Menno agreed to pray about this matter for a season. When they came again Menno surrendered his "soul and body to the Lord . . . and commenced in due time . . . to teach and to baptize, to till the vineyard of the Lord, . . . to build up His holy city and temple and to repair the tumbledown walls" (*Complete Writings,* 672).

This marks the call and the assuming of the office of an elder by Menno Simons. When his baptism took place is not known. It is possible that this occurred while he was still at Witmarsum during the time that he was publicly preaching "the true baptism and the Lord's Supper." But it is more likely that he was not baptized upon confession of his faith until he left Witmarsum. A Catholic priest preaching believers' baptism publicly and also receiving a second baptism could not remain unnoticed by the authorities even in a little village like Witmarsum. This consideration makes us inclined to believe that he was baptized soon after his withdrawal from the Catholic Church in January 1536.

Much effort has been made to determine where Menno Simons lived after he left the Catholic Church early in 1536 (see Frerichs, 1 ff.; Vos, 64 ff.; Krahn, 32 ff.). Menno himself wrote in 1544 that he "could not find in all the countries a cabin or hut in which my poor wife and our little children could be put up in safety for a year or even half a year" (*Complete Writings,* 424). This was his fate from 1536 until 1554. During the first years Menno probably spent most of his time in the Dutch province of Groningen. However, he could hardly stay anywhere for any length of time. Tjaard Renicx of Kimswerd in the province of Friesland was executed at Leeuwarden in January 1539 because he had sheltered Menno. Syouck Haeyes confessed in 1542 that he had heard a sermon by Menno outside Leeuwarden. An official document of Leeuwarden of May 19, 1541, states that Menno, one of the principal leaders, made it a practice to come to the province of Friesland once or twice a year, winning many followers.

On Dec. 7, 1542, one hundred guilders were offered by the authorities of Leeuwarden for the apprehension of Menno, who appeared by night at different places to preach and baptize. This indicates that Menno returned to his native province of Friesland at times in all secrecy but only for a short time. Menno found no permanent home during this time in any of the Dutch provinces.

Soon after his renunciation of Catholicism in 1536 Menno was also in the German province of East Friesland, where Ulrich von Dornum (*q.v.*) of Oldersum (*q.v.*) sheltered religious refugees, and according to tradition he found shelter here under Dornum's protection. However, Menno's statement must not be forgotten, that he and his family never found a place where they could live unmolested "for a year or even half a year." When and where Menno married his wife Geertruydt (*q.v.*) is not definitely known. In 1544 he spoke of their "little children." Peter Jansz confessed on June 14, 1540, that Menno had baptized him at Oldersum "about four years ago" (Vos, 243). This shows that Menno traveled early and extensively after his withdrawal. It will be shown later that he soon became well known in East Friesland. However, it is doubtful that he ever met Ulrich von Dornum or was a guest in his home during Dornum's lifetime, since the latter died early in the spring of 1536 (Ohling, 49). If this did occur, Menno had to proceed directly from Witmarsum to Oldersum. Ulrich was a staunch promoter of the Reformation, a friend of Carlstadt and Sebastian Franck, an admirer of Hans Denk, and a sympathizer with the Anabaptists. Two of his daughters married Anabaptists; one of them in 1551 married Christoffer van Ewsum (*q.v.*), who sheltered Menno in Groningen and whom Alba called a "principal Mennist" (Ohling, 24).

East Friesland (*q.v.*), where Melchior Hofmann had baptized some 300 persons in the city of Emden (*q.v.*), became a refuge for the Sacramentists of the Low Countries and other persecuted minorities. Even Carlstadt (*q.v.*) found shelter on the estate of Ulrich von Dornum. Menno, as has been said, also found his way to East Friesland soon after his withdrawal from Witmarsum. At this time John a Lasco (*q.v.*) was the superintendent of the East Friesland churches under the ruler, Countess Anna of Oldenburg.

In January 1544 Menno had a theological discussion with a Lasco. The objective of this discussion was to win Menno and his followers to the Reformed Church. That Menno was called upon to represent the Mennonites makes it clear that he was known in East Friesland as their spokesman. Anna, personally a tolerant ruler, was compelled by the emperor to do something about the numerous religious groups found in her domain. She consented to expel those which a Lasco would designate as "heretical." The latter's first objective was to win those who were spiritually closest to his own views. The discussion was held on Jan. 28-31, 1544, when the articles pertaining to the Incarnation, baptism, original sin, justification, and the call of ministers were discussed. Although the two men did not agree concerning all articles, Menno and his followers were dismissed by a Lasco in a friendly manner. Menno had promised to present a written confession regarding the Incarnation, and he now wrote "in a secluded place" under the title, *A Brief and Clear Confession and Scriptural Declaration Concerning the Incarnation. . . .* A Lasco had it printed in 1544 without Menno's knowledge or consent and used it against him. The following decree of Countess Anna in 1545 announces that the followers of David Joris (*q.v.*) and Batenburg (*q.v.*) should be "corrected on their neck" (executed) if they would not leave the country. The "Mennisten," however, were to be examined by the superintendent, and if they did not surrender were to leave the country. The term "Mennisten" designating followers of Menno appeared for the first time in any official document in the 1545 decree. This again, as well as the fact that Menno left East Friesland before this announcement was published, indicates that he was well known in this area as an Anabaptist leader (Krahn, 59 ff.).

In May 1544 Menno went to the Lower Rhine region, to the area of Cologne and Bonn. A Lasco wrote to Hardenberg on July 26, 1544, that Menno was in the bishopric of Cologne, where he was "misleading" many. This area had long been a fertile ground for the evangelical and Sacramentist movement. Menno was also successful there, and associated with the Anabaptist leaders Zyllis and Lemke. Matthias Servaes (*q.v.*), who died a martyr's death here, refused at any cost to "renounce" the principles for which Menno Simons stood. This indicates the degree of success of Menno's work in this area.

Menno's activities here coincide with the last years of the bishopric of Archbishop Hermann von Wied of Cologne, who had to give up his position in 1546 because he was promoting an evangelical reformation in the Catholic Church. Hardenberg, an active reformer of this area, influenced by a Lasco, interfered with Menno's activities. Menno was also in all probability active at the following places in the Maas River region: Vischersweert, Illekhoven, and Roermond. Several martyrs of this area testified that they had heard sermons by Menno in 1545. Under the rigid Catholic rule of the successor of Hermann von Wied in 1546, Menno had to leave this district. He now proceeded to the province of Schleswig-Holstein.

In the fall of 1546 Menno attended a discussion at a country place near Lübeck with the followers of David Joris, led by the latter's son-in-law Nicolaas Meyndertsz van Blesdijk (*q.v.*). Joris himself had left Emden for Basel early in 1544. David Joris (*q.v.*), an extreme left-wing Anabaptist of the Low Countries, who had been ordained elder by Obbe Philips in 1535, before Menno, had never been in full harmony with the peaceful Anabaptist representatives such as Dirk and Obbe Philips or Menno Simons. He placed too much emphasis on personal visions and "revelations" without checking them against the Scriptures. Menno and his followers opposed all revolutionary and mystical fanaticism. In addition to their spiritualistic conception of the Scriptures, Menno opposed the Jorists for considering it unnecessary to baptize or to organize churches during the time of persecution. Menno was supported in this discussion by the elders Dirk Philips, Leenaert Bouwens, Gillis van Aken, and Adam Pastor, and the group excommunicated Joris.

Another question arose when it became apparent

that Adam Pastor (*q.v.*), a former priest, who had been ordained *ca.* 1542 as an Anabaptist elder by Menno and Dirk, turned heretical in his Christological views. At a conference at Emden in 1547 no agreement could be reached. Meetings at Goch (1547), the Lower Rhine, and Lübeck (1552) followed. Since no agreement could be reached, Pastor was excommunicated at once. Pastor apparently deviated from the others on a number of other questions also, such as church discipline and relationship to government. He was more liberal than the group. His views regarding Christ differ considerably from those of Menno. Whereas Menno emphasized the deity of Christ, Pastor emphasized His humanity. Pastor believed that Jesus became the Saviour because God endowed Him and ordained Him for this task; but in essence He was not divine or equal with God. Menno on the other hand also deviated somewhat from the accepted orthodox creed, which sets forth the divine and the human nature as equally present in Christ, in stressing His divinity above His humanity. His peculiar conception of the Incarnation (*q.v.*) of Christ he had adopted from Melchior Hofmann. It became for him an essential part of his concept of the church. Christ in the Incarnation passed through Mary's womb like a ray of sunshine through a glass of water without taking on any of her "sinful flesh." Only thus, he claimed, could the Saviour be perfect, and only because of this can the work of His salvation, the church of Jesus Christ, be perfected.

Menno's traveling schedule indicates that he spent some time during the years after 1546 at Lübeck, Emden, the Lower Rhine, Leeuwarden, Danzig, etc. He still had no permanent home, although it is likely that his family did not accompany him on these trips of a shorter duration. In April 1549 Menno stayed overnight at the home of Klaas Jans, who was executed on this account at Leeuwarden on June 1. During the same summer he spent some weeks with the "Elected and Children of God in the Country of Prussia," as becomes apparent from a letter which he addressed to these believers on Oct. 7, 1549. This indicates not only that the Anabaptists of the Low Countries had spread as far as Danzig, but also that Menno's guidance, counsel, and authority were needed to iron out some difficulties which had risen. His co-worker Dirk Philips became the first elder of the Danzig Mennonite Church. It is possible that Menno's visit to the Anabaptists in Danzig and Prussia was not limited to this one occasion, although definite information is lacking.

In search of a field of labor and a refuge Menno had moved from the Low Countries to the province of East Friesland and was now on his way to Mecklenburg. He no doubt resided for some time in the Hanseatic city of Wismar. He was here during the winter of 1553-54 when a group from a Lasco's church arrived by boat from London as a refugee congregation. Since the Lutheran city of Wismar did not welcome this Reformed group, the Mennonites went out over the frozen ice of the harbor to the boat to meet them and to provide them with help and aid. This led to a religious discussion. On Feb. 6, 1554, the a Lasco group met with Menno and

his followers, having invited Martin Micron of Emden to serve as their man. The Incarnation was again among the topics discussed. The discussion ended in hostility, with the Mennonites accusing the Reformed of publishing a list of the Mennonites located in Wismar which had speeded up their expulsion from the city. An exchange of writings between Menno and Martin Micron (*q.v.*) resulted from this discussion.

Before this occurred Menno and certain other elders met in Wismar for a conference, at which they agreed on certain rules of church practice and discipline known as the Wismar Articles (1554). These articles deal primarily with the relationship between partners in a mixed marriage, i.e., believer and unbeliever, the matter of appealing to a court, and nonresistance. During this time Menno also wrote and published his book against the accusations of Gellius Faber (*q.v.*), entitled *Een Klare beantwoordinge . . . (Reply to Gellius Faber)* which was published in the Anabaptist print shop at Lübeck in 1554. In this, the longest book that Menno produced, can be found the account of his "Conversion" or the "Renunciation of the Church of Rome," which he presented in order to defend the calling of the Anabaptist ministers.

On Nov. 11, 1554, the city council of Wismar decreed that all Anabaptists were to leave the city. Menno had already left during the summer and gone to Lübeck. He and his followers proceeded together to the town of Oldesloe in the province of Holstein. In the vicinity of this town Bartholomeus von Ahlefeldt had since 1543 been gathering oppressed Anabaptists on one of his large estates, called Wüstenfelde (desert field). Here at last Menno found shelter and protection. His printer began to print his books, and Menno took the opportunity to revise his early editions and write several new books. Although von Ahlefeldt was often challenged to expel the Mennonites he remained their protector, having learned to appreciate them when he was in Holland.

The Mennonites aimed at nothing less than the establishment of a true Christian and apostolic church. With Paul they were determined to present to Christ His bride without spot and wrinkle and to keep themselves pure and clean as far as the world around them was concerned and also to keep the world out of the church. They were doing this through church discipline, using the ban and avoidance. Questions regarding the application of church discipline led to controversies. Menno had meetings with his fellow workers in Emden, Franeker, and Harlingen. Dirk Philips and Leenaert Bouwens favored a rigid application of church discipline. Others were lenient. Menno mediated between the two extremes. Menno made his last trip to his home province, Friesland, in 1557 to settle a dispute over this question. But in vain. This matter was to occupy the minds and hearts of the Dutch Mennonites for at least another century. After his return he wrote to a friend, "If the omnipotent God had not preserved me last year as well as now, I would already have gone mad. For there is nothing upon earth which my heart loves more than it does the church, and yet I must live to see this sad affliction upon her" (*Complete Writings,* 1055). Certain reports indicate that Menno was won over by the more rigid church disciplinarians toward the end of his life.

Through Zyllis and Lemke, Menno's friends and co-workers of the Lower Rhine area, the question of church discipline was presented at a large conference of South German Anabaptists which met at Strasbourg in 1557. Some 50 representatives of congregations in various South German countries, such as Moravia, Switzerland, and Alsace, were present. The assembled elders sent an appeal to Menno and his co-workers not to go to extremes in the matter of ban and avoidance, through which even family life was disrupted. Menno and Dirk Philips responded in writing, defending the more rigid position. Menno now emphasized that the heavenly marriage between Christ and the soul is more important than the relationship of man and wife in the earthly marriage. This controversy saddened the last days of his life.

During his last years Menno was crippled. The earliest portraits show him with crutches. His wife preceded him in death, although it is not known when she died. The children included at least two daughters and a son Jan. The son probably also preceded the father in death. One of the daughters gave some information about Menno to the historian Pieter Jans Twisck. According to all available information Menno died at Wüstenfelde on Jan. 31, 1561, 25 years after his withdrawal from the Catholic Church. He was buried in his own garden. The Thirty Years' War destroyed the estate on which the Anabaptists had settled, so that the exact location of the grave is no longer known. In 1906 a simple stone was erected at the approximate place, which was popularly known as the "Menno field." Not far from it the Menno Linden, supposedly planted by Menno himself, and the Menno House, in which his books were supposedly printed, still stand.

Menno Simons was a Biblicist in the truest and best meaning of the word. He turned away from tradition and became Bible-centered in all his beliefs and practices. Once he had turned to the Bible, he took it for the Word of God and made it the cornerstone of all his work. His writings are filled with Bible quotations. His approach to the Bible differs from that of the other reformers. It is above all Christ-centered. Every book and every little pamphlet he wrote have on the front page the motto, "For other foundation can no man lay than that is laid, which is Jesus Christ" (I Cor. 3:11). Christ-centeredness marks his theology and the practices he derived from the Bible. Discipleship *(Nachfolge)* or a fruitful Christian life were very strongly emphasized. But this emphasis on true Christian living does not take place in a vacuum or as a matter merely between the individual and his God, but rather within the congregation, the church of Christ. Menno's faith is therefore not only Christ-centered but also church-centered: his chief concern was the achievement of the true church of Jesus Christ or the body of Christ. Again and again he refers to I Cor. 12:13, 25-27, and Col. 1:18-24. The prerequisites for church membership according to Menno are regeneration and willingness to bear the cross of Christ.

These two are inseparable. Discipline was as natural in the church of Menno Simons as any normal function of the healthy body.

Behind these views lie first of all Menno's personal experience in the Catholic Church, and the experience which he had with the Reformers and Münsterites. With Luther he rejected the Catholic Church, which did not preach justification by faith, but he also had to reject the Lutheran Church because of its one-sided emphasis on "faith alone." On the other hand he could not accept the radical movement which attempted to usher in the kingdom of God by force. Instead he developed a theology of martyrdom, of suffering for God.

Menno's significance lies in the fact that he prevented the collapse of the northern wing of the Anabaptist movement in the days of its greatest trial and built it up on the right Biblical foundation. He did this as its leader, speaker, and defender, through his preaching as he journeyed from place to place, and through his simple and searching writings. Particularly the *Foundation-Book* did much to restore the original Anabaptist concepts and principles, which were in grave danger of being lost. His writings were effective not so much because of their superior and logical qualities as a theological system, but because behind them stood a man formed according to the Scriptures who sincerely and honestly wanted to give all for the Christian church and the glory of God. Through Menno's courageous and devoted life a distinctive witness in the Reformation movement, representing a Christian brotherhood and a Christian way of life, was preserved, which have meanwhile become quite generally recognized as an integral part of Protestantism and include such basic principles as separation of church and state, freedom of conscience, voluntary church membership, democratic church government, holy living, and the Christian peace witness in a world of strife.

The questions pertaining to the linguistic peculiarities, the editions and printers of Menno's writings have found some interest among scholars; and a considerable amount of investigation has been made. G. E. Frerichs wrote a detailed article on "Menno's taal" (Menno's Language) (*DB* 1905). He concluded that Menno's first writings were linguistically colored by the language of the place in which he was living, and which he (Frerichs) thought to find in the province of Groningen, called "Ommelanden." Karel Vos calls the writings and the linguistic coloring of this period (1537-41) an *Oosters gekleurd* dialect, meaning with "an eastern coloring." The term *Oosters* (eastern) is, however, relative. "Eastern" is viewed from the standpoint of the province of Holland, which was the leading one in the economy and the culture of the Netherlands for a long time, and whose language became the standard. A slight deviation from its language under the influence of linguistic peculiarities of the regions east and northeast of the province of Holland is designated as an *Oosters gekleurd* dialect. Such peculiarities in the writings of Menno Simons, which are characteristic of the province of Groningen, are designated by Vos as *Oosters gekleurd.*

Later, when Menno Simons was living in East

Friesland and Holstein, his language was necessarily adapted to the language of this country since he was printing primarily for the people of that territory. Vos refers to the language in which Menno wrote and printed his books in East Friesland and the Hanseatic cities as the Oosters language (not only an *Oosters gekleurd* dialect). Menno even revised his earlier Dutch writings and had them reprinted at Lübeck, Oldesloe, and Wüstenfelde in the Oosters language. The later writings printed first in Oosters were translated into the Dutch for use in the Netherlands proper. The question of the linguistic peculiarities in the various editions and writings of Menno Simons deserves a more thorough investigation and would be one of the most significant tasks in preparing a scholarly edition of Menno's writings. The following is merely a brief outline of Menno's printers and printing facilities as far as they can be determined at this time.

It is very difficult to determine where and when Menno's early writings were printed and who the printers were. Jan Claesz (*q.v.*) was beheaded Jan. 19, 1544, because he had 600 copies of Menno Simons' books printed at Antwerp. He sold 200 of them in the province of Holland and sent the rest to Friesland. These books must have been some of Menno's earliest writings. A little information is found in the copy of the *Foundation-Book* (1539-40) in the British Museum, which has an entry by Johan Enschede of Haarlem pertaining to the type used in the book. Nijhoff-Kronenberg (*Ned. Bibliographie* I, p. 540) states that this book and Menno's *Voele goede leringhen op den 25. Psalm* (*ca.* 1537) and *Een corte vermaninghe . . . van de wedergeboorte* (*ca.* 1537) were both printed in the same print shop. It should be possible to discover more details about the print shop by the type that was used (see also Vos, 296). It is likely that others of Menno's books were published in East Friesland during the time he was living there. To what an extent, if at all, Nicolaes Biestkens (*q.v.*) of Emden, who printed for the Mennonites, printed Menno's writings, should be investigated. Probably no writings of Menno appeared between 1542 and 1551. After 1551 Menno and the Anabaptists had a printer at Lübeck. When the underground print shop here was discovered, the authoritites found ten tons of books. The printer then moved from Lübeck to Oldesloe, and in 1554 to Wüstenfelde, where he continued to function as Menno's printer. At this time an Oosters edition of the *Foundation-Book* appeared with a certain "B. L." as printer. All of Menno's writings, both new and revised editions, appeared now in Wüstenfelde in rapid succession. Von Ahlefeldt protected Menno and his printer, B. L., whose full name is not yet known, against all attacks. In 1558 a Dutch edition of the *Foundation-Book* appeared, probably in Wüstenfelde (BRN VII, 253). The printer must have continued his work even after Menno's death in 1561. In 1562 another Dutch edition of the *Foundation-Book* appeared. In 1616 an unchanged Dutch reprint of the 1539-40 edition was published.

The writings of Menno Simons have been published more often than the writings of any other Anabaptist leaders. The *Foundation-Book* was trans-lated into German in 1575. The first large collection appeared in Dutch as *Sommarie* (1600-1) which was followed by the *Opera ofte Groot Sommarie* (1646) and the *Opera Omnia Theologica* (1681). In America the first complete edition of Menno Simons appeared in 1871 in English and in 1876 in German. In 1956 a new enlarged English edition, the first practically complete edition in any language, was published. An urgent task in Mennonite research would be to prepare a scholarly edition of Menno's writings, in which the various early and later editions and translations would be fully taken into consideration, similar to the edition of Dirk Philips' writings published in Volume X of the *BRN*.

Turning to the research pertaining to the life, work, and beliefs of Menno it must be said that no other Anabaptist leader has been the subject of as many biographies as Menno. All major aspects of his life, times, and activities, have been investigated, primarily by Dutch, but also by some German scholars. Much of the biographical information was published in the *Doopsgezinde Bijdragen* (1861-1919). A. M. Cramer wrote the first significant biography (1837). J. G. de Hoop Scheffer, Christiaan Sepp, and G. E. Frerichs published much biographical information in *Doopsgezinde Bijdragen*. The first most complete scholarly biography of Menno was produced by Karel Vos (1914) based on extensive archival research. W. J. Kühler published his findings along these lines in his history of the Dutch Mennonites during the 16th century (1932). In the German language early biographies appeared, written by C. Harder (1846) and B. C. Roosen (1848). A recent German biography, with a theological interpretation of the views of Menno and his followers, was written by Cornelius Krahn (1936). In America John Horsch presented the only full-length English biography (1916).

The Amsterdam Mennonite Library has an authentic letter written by Menno Simons himself; it is undated and is addressed (after 1554) to a widow. This letter is the only extant manuscript in Menno's handwriting. It was printed, with somewhat modified spelling, in *Opera Omnia*, page 336.†

None of the portraits of Menno, circulating since the early 17th century, can be considered historically true. The most acceptable one is the engraving made about 1608 by Christoffel van Sichem (*q.v.*). Recently the Dutch artist Arend Hendriks made a beautiful etching of Menno.   C.K.

Sources: Menno Simons, *Opera Omnia Theologica* (Amsterdam, 1681); *idem, Die vollständigen Werke* (Elkhart, 1876); *idem, Die vollständigen Werke* (Baltic, Ohio, 1926); Menno Simons, *The Complete Works* (Elkhart, 1871); Menno Simons, *The Complete Writings* (Scottdale, 1956); Hans Alenson, "Tegen-Bericht op de voor-Reden vant groote Martelaer Boeck," 1630, *BRN* VII (The Hague, 1910); I. H. V. P. N., *Het beginsel en voortganck der geschillen, scheuringen, en verdeeltheden onder de . . . Doopsgesinden;* E. F. Goverts, "Archivstücke aus dem Reichsarchiv Hansborg," *Ztscht d. Zentralstelle für Niedersächsische Familiengeschichte* (Hamburg, 1923) No. 5; Obbe Philips, "Bekentenisse . . ." (Amsterdam, 1584) *BRN* VII; *Inv. Arch.*

Amst. I, Nos. 241 f., 257-60, 323, 343, 356, 367, 417, 463, 617, 619 f., 631, 640.

Biographies: J. Horsch, *Menno Simons, His Life, Labors and Teachings* (Scottdale, 1916); H. S. Bender and J. Horsch, *Menno Simons' Life and Writings* (Scottdale, 1936); C. H. Smith, *Menno Simons, An Apostle of the Nonresistant Life* (Berne, ca. 1936); C. Krahn, *Menno Simons* (Karlsruhe, 1936); idem, "The Conversion of Menno Simons: A Quadricentennial Tribute," *MQR* IX f. (1935-36); A. M. Cramer, *Het leven en de verrichtingen van Menno Simons* (Amsterdam, 1837); C. Harder, *Das Leben Menno Symons* (Königsberg, 1846); F. Bastian, *Essai sur la vie et les écrits de Menno Simons* (Strasbourg, 1857); J. G. de Hoop Scheffer, "Eenige opmerkingen en mededeelingen betr. Menno Simons," *DB* 1864, 1865, 1872, 1881, 1889, 1890, 1892, 1894; F. C. Fleischer, *Menno Simons (1492-1559)* (Amsterdam, 1892); S. Cramer, "Menno Simons," in *HRE;* idem, "Menno's Leven," in *DB* 1904; K. Vos, *Menno Simons* (Leiden, 1914); Kühler, *Geschiedenis* I; Rob Limburg, "Menno Simons, de Herder der verstrooide Kudde," in *Cultuurdragers in bewogen dagen* (The Hague, n.d.-1941) 112-53.

Other Literature: G. J. Boekenoogen, "De portretten van Menno Simons," *DB* 1916; G. E. Frerichs, "Menno's taal," *DB* 1906; idem, "Menno's verblijf in de eerste jaren na zijn uitgang," *DB* 1906; B. C. Roosen, *Menno Simons, den evang. Mennoniten-Gemeinden geschildert* (Leipzig, 1848); Sibold S. Smeding, "The Portraits of Menno Simons," *Menn. Life* III (July 1948); H. van der Smissen, *Mennostein und Mennolinde zu Fresenburg* (n.p., n.d.); G. Ohling, *Ulrich von Dornum . . .* (Aurich, 1955); Mellink, *Wederdopers;* B. H. Unruh, *Die niederländisch-niederdeutschen Hintergründe der mennonitischen Ostwanderungen* (Karlsruhe, 1955); Friedrich Brune, *Der Kampf um eine evangelische Kirche im Münsterland 1520-1802* (Witten, 1953); S. Hoekstra, *Beginselen en Leer der Oude Doopsgezinden, vergeleken met die van de overige Protestanten* (Amsterdam, 1863); J. H. Wessel, *De leerstellige strijd tusschen Nederlandsche Gereformeerden en Doopsgezinden in de zestiende eeuw* (Assen, 1945); N. van der Zijpp, *Geschiedenis der Doopsgezinden in Nederland* (Arnhem, 1952); J. P. Müller, *Die Mennoniten in Ostfriesland* (Emden, 1887); idem, "Die Mennoniten in Ostfriesland," *Jahrbuch . . . Emden* IV (1881) 58-74, and V (1882) 46-79; C. A. Cornelius, *Der Anteil Ostfrieslands an der Reformation bis zum Jahr 1535* (Münster, 1852); E. Kochs, "Die Anfänge der ostfr. Reformation," *Jahrb. der Ges. für bild. Kunst und vaterl. Altertümer zu Emden* XIX (1916-18) 109-273; XX (1920) 1-125; H. Dalton, *Johannes a Lasco* (Utrecht, 1885); R. Dollinger, *Geschichte der Mennoniten in Schleswig-Holstein, Hamburg und Lübeck* (Neumünster, 1930); Julian Heins, *Menno Simonis. Ein dramatisches Gedicht* (Danzig, 1844); *Catalogus Amst.* 1919; *DJ* 1936, 40-69; K. Vos, "Menno Simons in Groningen," in *Groningsche Volksalmanak* 1919, 139-46; E. Crous, "Auf Mennos Spuren am Niederrhein," *Der Mennonit* VIII (1955), Nos. 10-12, and IX, Nos. 1-2; N. van der Zijpp, *Menno Simonsz* (Amsterdam, 1950); *ML* III, 177-90.

Menno Simons Kerkje, a former meetinghouse in Witmarsum, Dutch province of Friesland, where Menno was supposed to have preached his first sermons after leaving the Catholic Church in 1536. It stood here for 50 years, about two miles from the village. In 1878 it was torn down because it was too small and old, and the Menno monument (*q.v.*) was erected on its site. The Mennonites of Witmarsum built a new and spacious church in the village. H. Thepass made engravings of both the interior and the exterior of the Menno Church, which were edited by M. Stoffels at Zaandam. (*DB* 1880, 164; *Menn. Bl.,* 1902, 49, shows a picture of the old church; *ML* III, 95.)

Menno Simons Lectureship, endowed by the John P. Kaufman family, is a function of Bethel College, North Newton, Kan., which came into being in 1953, when Roland H. Bainton delivered the Menno Simons Lectures on March 8-10 on "Sixteenth Century Anabaptism." The raising of funds and the organizational setup were started in 1947. The lectureship is devoted to the promotion of research in Anabaptist and Mennonite history, thought, life, and culture, and the implications and relationship of these to the whole of society. The results of this research are presented to the public through annual lectures which are, if feasible, published in book form. The speakers are chosen by a committee composed of the president of Bethel College, one representative of the John P. Kaufman family, and one faculty member. In 1957 this committee was composed of Ed. G. Kaufman, D. C. Wedel, and Cornelius Krahn. Some of the lectures have been published in the quarterly magazine, *Mennonite Life,* and some are to appear in book form. The following are the lecturers and topics 1953-56: Roland H. Bainton—"Sixteenth Century Anabaptism," March 8-10, 1953; Wilhelm Pauck—"The Reformers and the Anabaptists," Jan. 24-27, 1954; Franklin H. Littell—"The Free Church," Oct. 31-Nov. 3, 1954; Robert Kreider—"Anabaptism Speaks to Our Day," Nov. 6-8, 1955; and Martin Niemöller—"Relevance of Christian Nonresistance in Our Present World Situation," Nov. 11-14, 1956.   C.K.

Menno Simons Mennonite Church (GCM), now extinct, located in Butterfield, Watonwan Co., Minn., a member of the Northern District Conference, was organized in 1887 by Mennonites of Swiss origin coming from the Lemberg area of Austria 1880-83. Their leader was Daniel Brubacher. The group was small—exact figures are not available, and in 1915, when their minister and elder Heinrich Kintzi, who succeeded Brubacher, resigned, the congregation merged with the Salem Mennonite Church in Butterfield. Disharmony between the two groups in the Salem congregation soon set in and in 1921 a breach occurred. The Swiss members severed their connection with Salem church, reorganized, and in 1922 erected a new building in Butterfield, known as the Mennonite Church of Butterfield (*q.v.*).   J.J.F.

Menno Stone, the monument to Menno Simons erected on the supposed location of the house where Menno Simons is supposed to have spent the last years of his life, was erected by the Mennonite congregation of Hamburg in 1902 near the village of Fresenburg, about half way between Hamburg and Lübeck in North Germany. It is a simple shaft of granite bearing a bronze plate with a supposed picture of Menno Simons. It was dedicated on Aug. 26, 1906. Sometime after World War II, the bronze plate was stolen from the monument. With the aid of students of the University of Kiel, who wanted to express gratitude for the MCC student feeding program there in 1948 ff., the Hamburg congregation moved the monument the short distance from the field where it stood to the road near the Menno Linden (*q.v.*).   Neff, H.S.B.

H. van der Smissen, *Mennostein und Mennolinde zu Fresenburg* (Hamburg, 1922); *ML* III, 112.

Menno Township, Mifflin Co., Pa., was named after Menno Simons by action of the court in 1837 because of the large number of Mennonite settlers in that vicinity. The township is 6½ miles long, extends from the summit of Jack's Mountain to the summit of Stone Mountain, and is bordered by Huntingdon County on the west and Union Township on the east. See **Mifflin County.**   J.A.H.

Menno-Berg, the name of a wavelike elevation near Oldesloe, Schleswig-Holstein, Germany. Here was located Wüstenfelde (*q.v.*), the village where Menno Simons lived the last years of his life; it was completely destroyed in the Thirty Years' War. The Menno Stone (*q.v., monument*) placed here to mark the site was moved to the Menno Linden after World War II. (*Menn. Bl.,* 1900, 5; *ML* III, 93.)
          Neff.

Menno-Blatt, a 4-page (9 x 11½ in.) Mennonite periodical in the German language, issued monthly for the Fernheim settlement of Paraguay since 1930; its editor and publisher until 1955 was Nikolai Siemens. He was succeeded in 1956 by Peter Klassen. The first issue was December 1930, preceded by a 2-page *Flugblatt* in October 1930. The small hand press, which was a gift of the MCC, was first set up in Lichtfelde (*q.v.*) in the home of the typesetter Peter Rahn, and later in the home of the editor in Friedensruh, until it was placed in its permanent quarters in Filadelfia. Originally a 4-page supplement, *Kämpfende Jugend,* was added, but later discontinued. The economic distress caused by drought and grasshoppers in 1935-37 compelled them to discontinue the youth supplement. In content the *Menno-Blatt* serves all the Mennonites in the Chaco as an informative journal to keep them in contact with each other and with their friends and brethren in Europe and North America. This paper is perhaps unique in the history of Mennonite colonization, in that it appeared in the first year of a new settlement in a primitive country and continued its publication even in the crises of pioneering. In 1955 it was taken over by Fernheim Colony and made an official publication. (*ML* III, 94.)   F.K.

Mennofonds, a fund established by the Algemeene Doopsgezinde Sociëteit on Jan. 5, 1920, for the purpose of borrowing money from congregations and individuals at a low interest rate and investing it at a higher rate to obtain means for raising the salaries of the ministers. This plan, though the planned amount of one and a half million guilders was not reached, has been very successful. Klaas Dekker Jzn, a deacon of Zaandam, had suggested the plan. The treasurers of the A.D.S. have taken charge of the fund. In 1947 the total borrowed amount was redeemed.   vDZ.

De Zondagsbode, Dec. 19, 1920; *DJ* 1921, 50-56; *Verslag* (report) of the A.D.S., 1946-47, p. 18.

Menno-Friendly Benefit Association, a mutual burial aid association, was organized about 1908 in the First Mennonite Church (GCM) of Philadelphia to serve General Conference Mennonites in the Philadelphia area. Its assessment rate in 1953 was 50¢ per month. It aids members in times of disability and death.   H.S.B.

Mennonisten-Lexikon. The theological journal, *Altes und Neues aus dem Schatz theologischer Wissenschaften* (Wittenberg, 1701 ff.), an important journal of the 18th century, which changed its name a number of times, published in 1730 under the title *Fortgesetzte Sammlung von alten und neuen theologischen Sachen* a lengthy article, "Kleines Mennonisten-Lexikon oder Nachricht von denen Lehrern der Mennonisten." The article is a listing of the Mennonite authors and a description of their works. The compilation begins with Apostool (*q.v.*) and ends with Wybrandt (*q.v.*). First on the list are the writers of devotional literature, as catechisms, sermons, and Bible studies. Most of these works and authors had been previously discussed in Hermann Schijn's Mennonite history, which is almost in every case cited as source. Since the discussions contain no critical notes, they are of no particular value today except to show that in Lutheran circles at that time Mennonite literature merited a review in such publications.

Since in that period the Dutch Mennonites, in their position of security, were the most active writers, they are naturally considered first in this lexicon. A few errors, probably due to faulty proofreading, do not disturb too seriously, as when 1339 is given as the date of the origin of the Mennonites in Friesland, or 1661 as the date of Menno's death. In general the lexicon is well informed. The biographical notes contain several items of interest. A Dutch Mennonite linguist by the name of Anton Dahlem is mentioned, who was for a time a Mennonite preacher. Connections with Danzig are revealed by the booklet written against the Socinians by Petrus Johann Twiskerus, *Disputationes de Deitate Christi contra Montanum Socinianum,* which was printed in Danzig in 1650.

This lexicon was supplemented by occasional references to contemporary Mennonite publications. In 1704, under the title *Unschuldige Nachrichten,* appeared a short article, "Nachricht vom neuen Zustand der Mennoniten." It is mostly a report on the followers of Galenus Abrahamsz de Haan, with whom many Socinians allied themselves. It also tells of the persecution of the Mennonites of Jülich-Palatine lands, "which soon subsided through the intercession of the lord of Dyckfeld, who induced the glorious King William of Great Britain to come to their defense."

In further reviews the attitude of the publishers

is unmistakably revealed. Concerning the *Korte Historie der Mennoniten* by Herman Schijn they cautiously mention that he protests against the designation *Wiedertäufer* and denies connections with the Münsterites and Müntzerites. That the publishers are not of Schijn's opinion is clearly revealed in their evaluation of the Latin edition of his book (1723): "There is so little history in this book that it should be called *Apologia* instead of *Historia*." Also in the discussion of K. van Huysen's historical treatises the protest against the alleged derivation from Münster, which was taught by every history of theology, was not taken seriously (1716). On the other hand, in the *Fortgesetzte Sammlung* (1720) the publishers very joyfully discuss J. Chr. Jehring's (*q.v.*) history of the divisions and disputes among the Mennonites and repeat Jehring's verdict: "Because of these dissensions the foundation of the Mennonites is a poor one, built up on lies."

It is evident that the publishers of the first Mennonite Lexicon, in spite of their good historical information, were enmeshed in the spirit of intolerance prevalent in the 16th century. (*ML* III, 95.)

H.Q.

Mennonit, Der, a 16-page 9 x 12 in. illustrated Mennonite monthly journal, was established by the Mennonite Central Committee in 1948, to serve first of all the Mennonite refugees from Russia, the Danzig area, and Poland, who were scattered widely over Germany (and Denmark), South America, and Canada, but also to serve all German-speaking Mennonites, especially in Europe. It was to serve as a bond of union and fellowship across international boundaries and also to stimulate the spiritual life of the churches, to strengthen the sense of the historic Mennonite heritage and to promote its modern revival and application, and to promote interest, conviction, and activity in the fields of missions, evangelism, Christian education, and Christian service.

The first editors were H. S. Bender, C. F. Klassen, and Peter Dyck, all MCC workers stationed in Europe, assisted by other MCC workers and by a widely representative editorial council from all Mennonite countries around the world. The managing editors have been H. S. Bender 1948-51, Peter J. Dyck 1951-52, C. F. Klassen with Cornelius Wall 1952-54, and Gerhard Hein 1954- . Beginning with January 1957 the *Mennonit* was taken over from the MCC by a publication commission composed of representatives of the German-speaking European conferences (German Vereinigung, *q.v.*, Swiss Conference, Alsatian Conference) and the MCC. At first issued as a bimonthly, the journal became a monthly with the issue of July 1950.

H.S.B.

Mennonite, the name now given to the churches which descend from the Anabaptists from the Reformation period, except those in the Netherlands, who since 1796 have been officially registered as *Doopsgezinden* (*q.v.*), and the Hutterian Brethren (*q.v.*). For a time the German name *Taufgesinnte* (*q.v.*), or *Altevangelisch Wehrlose Taufgesinnte* (*q.v.*) was used by certain North German and the Swiss Mennonites, who still officially carry this name though it does not appear in common usage either

by the Swiss Mennonites themselves or by others in referring to them. In France, even in modern times the name *Anabaptistes* has had some currency as a designation for French Mennonites but is now discarded, and *Täufer* has had some popular currency in Switzerland and Alsace. "Mennonite" is the only name that has ever been used in Russia and in North and South America.

The term "Mennonite" has gone through three forms historically in the Dutch language—Men(n)ist, Mennonist, and Mennonite(e), the last two also in the German and English.

In America the form "Mennist" has been generally used only in the colloquial form "Menischt" in the Pennsylvania Dutch or "Meneest" (*q.v.*); however, C. Henry Smith reports a letter of 1643 by the French Jesuit traveler, Father Jaques, referring to "Anabaptists, here called Menists" in the Manhattan Island, N.Y., settlement. Smith also reports a later document of 1657 which refers to "Mennonists" at Gravesend, Long Island. The 1712 and 1727 English editions of the Dordrecht Confession use the term "Mennonist." The petition of 1775 to the Colonial Assembly of Pennsylvania regarding exemption from military service refers to the church as the "Society of Menonists," and Morgan Edwards, in his *Materials Towards a History of the American Baptists* (1770), calls them Mennonists. A study of the book titles in Bender's *Two Centuries of American Mennonite Literature . . . 1727-1928,* shows the first use of "Mennonite" in titles to have been in 1813, 1835, and 1837. After 1837 Mennonist practically disappears except in the *Lancaster Calendar of Mennonist Meetings* of 1854 and following years. The two first American Mennonite hymnals, *Unpartheyisches Gesangbuch* and *Kleine geistliche Harfe* reprinted the title page relatively unchanged in later editions, carrying the term "Mennonist" along, the former book even in the 1941 edition. The General Conference Mennonites (Oberholtzer group in Pennsylvania) used Mennonite from their beginning in 1847-48. Jacob Stauffer's *Eine Chronik oder Geschicht-Buechlein* of 1859 still used Mennonist.

In Holland the term "Men(n)ist" was used roughly for the first century of Mennonite history, although it occurred as late as 1670 in a Dutch edition of a book by Stephen Crisp. The first use of the term in a public document was in an edict of 1545 by Countess Anna of East Friesland, issued at Emden, in which she distinguished the followers of Menno Simons from those of David Joris and Jan van Batenburg. In his reply to Gellius Faber (1554) Menno Simons objected to the designations Mennists, Obbenites, or Dirkites, saying "We are not thus divided." The form "Mennonite" appeared in Holland as early as 1643 in a book title by Gerrit van Vryburgh, but it did not displace Mennist until near the end of the 17th century. The variant spellings Mennonyt, Mennonijt, and Mennoniet also appeared at times. *Mennonist* appeared in the latter part of the 17th century along with *Mennonit*. A book of 1686 called *Lantaerne* spoke of "Mennonistendom." Mennist (Mennonist, Mennonit) became a party name in Holland about the turn of the 16th to the 17th century. The strict wing of the Flemish and Frisians claimed it, while the Waterlanders and

High Germans adopted the name "Doopsgezinde" (*q.v.*), which ultimately became the general designation when all the parties reunited about the end of the 18th century. Some, like Rippert Eenkes, the preacher of the congregation at Workum, objected (1607) to the name Mennonite, "because we do not call ourselves for Menno, but for Christ." After the division of the Lamists and Zonists in 1664, the latter preferred the name "Mennonite," while the former rejected it, using "Doopsgezinde" instead.

The usage in Germany followed that of Holland, except that Mennonit finally won out over against Taufgesinnte. Mennonist was used for a time during the 18th century. Roosen's *Christliches Gemüthsgespräch* (Hamburg, 1702) used it, as did the 1742 edition of *Güldene Aepfel* (South Germany or Basel) and von Dühren's *Geschichte der Märtyrer* (Königsberg, 1787). The Elbing Waldeck Catechism of 1778-97 and its later editions of 1833 and 1837 also used it. But "Mennonit" was in use in the German translations of Deknatel and others at the middle of the 18th century; and Rues, *Aufrichtige Nachrichten* (1743), used "Mennoniten." There is no trace of "Mennonist" after 1800 except in traditional titles reprinted.

It is a historical anomaly that the South German Mennonites, who were excommunicated by Menno Simons and who never were under his influence personally, preferred to use his name in their group identification, whereas the Dutch, who were Menno's immediate followers, finally rejected it. "Mennonite" was of course a useful protective name, referring to a well-known peaceful leader and group, and served to displace the opprobrious name Anabaptist or Wiedertäufer which suffered from its connection with the Münsterites.

Question has at times been raised as to who among the modern descendant groups or conferences is properly entitled to use the name "Mennonite" without a modifying prefix for its denominational designation. Certainly the national groups in Germany, France, and Switzerland have a historical right to the unadorned name. In Russia the original and continuing main body, from which all other groups separated (M.B., K.M.B., Kleine Gemeinde), continued with historical justice to use the simple name "*Mennonite*," and descendants of the group in North America are properly called Mennonite, although they have chosen for their denominational name General Conference Mennonite Church. (The Swiss and South German elements in the General Conference Church can also rightly claim the simple name "Mennonite.") In North America the original and continuing body, from which all other schismatic groups before 1874 separated (Funkite, Reformed Mennonite, Church of God in Christ, Stauffer Mennonite, Defenceless, Central Conference) before the arrival of the Russian Mennonites, with the same historic propriety uses the name Mennonite Church. In any case, the use of the unadorned name by any particular group in Europe or America does not and cannot mean that such a group is the only legitimate "Mennonite" church. All groups which bear the name Mennonite, simply or with a prefix, and thus claim to be in the line of historic descent of the Mennonite

faith are equally "Mennonite"; their legitimate claim to the title might much better be tested by their adherence to the original Anabaptist-Mennonite faith. Some modern groups of Mennonite or partial Mennonite background have deliberately decided to drop the name Mennonite in favor of another (e.g., United Missionary Church, formerly Mennonite Brethren in Christ until 1953, apparently holding that the former name was a handicap in evangelism and missionary outreach). H.S.B.

(S. Muller), "De oorsprong en beteekenis der benamingen van Mennoniten en Doopsgezinden," *DJ* 1837, 39-50; Pieter Leendertz, "De Naam Doopschgezinden," *DB* 1861, 33-50; *Gbl.* 1886, 90; Ottius, *Annales Anabaptistici* (Basel, 1680) 117, 119; Chr. Hege, *Ein Rückblick auf 400 Jahre mennonitischer Geschichte* (Karlsruhe, 1935) 15, 28 f., 47 f.; *ML* III, 102.

Mennonite, The, a 16-page, 8 x 11 in. weekly, is the official English language organ of the General Conference Mennonite Church. Authorized in October 1885 by a resolution of the Eastern District, the paper was first conceived by N. B. Grubb (*q.v.*), a Philadelphia pastor who felt the need of an English paper for city pastoral work, and A. B. Shelly, who desired something for the younger generation that did not read German. Until 1902 it was published in Quakertown, Pa., by the Eastern District Conference, although the General Conference adopted it as its official English language paper in 1893.

N. B. Grubb, pastor of the First Mennonite Church of Philadelphia, was the first editor of this paper, which was published monthly during its Eastern District tenure. After Grubb's resignation in 1892 A. S. Shelly edited it until 1902 while at the same time serving as pastor of the Hereford Mennonite Church of Bally, Pa.

When the General Conference assumed publication of the paper in 1902, the printing was done in Berne, Ind., while H. G. Allebach, who was living in Pennsylvania, edited it until 1905. I. A. Sommer served as editor 1905-11, followed by C. H. A. van der Smissen 1912-14. Silas M. Grubb, a son of the first editor and an associate editor for five years, held this position for 21 years, 1915-36, the paper's longest editorship. He was followed by J. R. Thierstein 1937-41, Reynold Weinbrenner 1941-48, Jacob J. Enz 1948-49, and J. N. Smucker 1950- .

Beginning with Thierstein's editorship the paper was edited and printed in Kansas, the Bethel College Press, now the Mennonite Press, in North Newton, doing the printing. The printing continues to be done in Kansas, although since 1950 the paper has been edited from the editor's home, which is now in Goshen, Ind.

The Christian Exponent was absorbed by *The Mennonite* in 1929 and was maintained as a department until June 1930. In 1931 the *Missions Quarterly,* published by the Board of Foreign Missions, was also absorbed. During the depression years of 1934-35 the paper was published jointly as a biweekly with the *Christian Evangel,* the official organ of the Central Conference of Mennonites, William B. Weaver sharing the editorship with S. M. Grubb.

Since the beginning the paper has carried as its motto, "Other foundation can no man lay than that is laid, which is Jesus Christ." This motto from I

Cor. 3:11 is to remind readers that the church's foundation is Christ, on which Menno Simons built. The paper is devoted to the interest of the Mennonite church, and the cause of Christ in general. Its basic content consists of devotional articles, general articles of information and inspiration, news of General Conference activities, including missions and relief work, and news of General Conference congregations and schools.

In 1923 the Conference asked that a page be devoted to the interests of young people. This has continued as an important feature until the present. Editors of this section have been C. E. Krehbiel 1923-26, Austin R. Keiser 1927-29, 1930-35, Amelia Mueller 1935-36, Bernhard Bargen 1936-39, Reynold Weinbrenner 1939-45, Esko Loewen 1945-53, Leola Schultz 1953-54, Lois Duerksen 1954-55, Maynard Shelly 1955-56, Robert Schrag 1956- .

In 1948 a number of associate editors were appointed who were to serve as contributors and also as an editorial board. Meeting regularly with the editor they plan editorial policy, help to determine and define issues, and suggest ways of improving the paper.

In 1951, *The Mennonite* and *Der Bote,* the official German publication of the General Conference, began to circulate under the Every Home Plan, which allows each General Conference congregation to request a copy of either paper for each family. In return for this service congregations are encouraged to make a yearly contribution of $1.00 per subscription, though the subscription price for others is $2.50. The deficit incurred is assumed by the Boards of the General Conference Mennonite Church. The paper has a circulation of 15,000.   J.N.S., M.SH.

Mennonite Aid Association of the Indiana-Michigan (MC) Conference District was organized in 1911, as a mutual fire and storm insurance society. In 1953 it had 2,608 members with $22,222,000 of property covered.   H.S.B.

Mennonite Aid Plan (German, *Unterstützungsplan*), a Mennonite mutual fire and storm property insurance association, was organized by authorization of the Indiana Mennonite (MC) Conference at its meeting of Oct. 13, 1882. The following statement in the *Herald of Truth* for Nov. 1, 1882 (p. 330), gives an authentic account of the nature and purpose of the organization: "The subject of aiding each other in case of loss by fire among the brotherhood was presented and discussed. The plan of collecting by general contributions seems of late years not to accomplish the desired results, and a necessity exists for a more systematic plan, by which, according to the admonition of the apostle, each brother may give according as the Lord has prospered him. An arrangement of this kind will also obviate the necessity of brethren identifying themselves with the general insurance companies, to which many of the brethren are opposed.

"It was suggested, in order to give this question a definite form, that an arrangement or system of collection similar to that which has now been maintained already some twenty years by the brotherhood in Canada, be entered into.

"This plan has worked well and given very good satisfaction and has now been accepted by all the churches. The plan is briefly as follows: Each church or meeting district appoints a valuator (or a committee as may be determined on) whose duty it is to get the valuation of the property of every brother or sister who may desire to enter into this plan, and make a record of the same in a book provided for the purpose. A copy of this valuation list shall be furnished by each district valuator or committee to a central man, or general secretary, who shall be chosen by the district valuators. In case of fire, the district valuator shall ascertain the amount of the loss and report the same to the central man, who levies the proportionate assessment, and each church being notified of the amount to be raised, makes the collections and sends them to the central man, who pays it over to the party sustaining the loss, and takes a receipt for it.

"The above is simply a brief sketch of the plan. In its practical workings some changes and modifications may be needful, as the committees or valuators appointed may deem most practical. But the above will give an idea of it so that every one may judge of its feasibility.

"The conference accepted the plan and gave permission to the brotherhood to enter into such an agreement."

The Aid Plan was, however, not a conference-controlled organization, but a voluntary association of property owners; membership was not restricted to the Indiana Conference, and the third report includes "districts" in Michigan, Ohio, Illinois, Missouri, and at Mountain Lake, Minn. Gradually the service of the organization spread into other states and in 1912 the headquarters office was moved to Freeman, S.D., where it has remained ever since, with the name slightly changed to "Mennonite Aid Plan of South Dakota." This was the first all-Mennonite organization. In 1911 the Indiana-Michigan (MC) Conference organized its own Mennonite Aid Association, since when only a few from the Indiana area have continued in the Aid Plan. In 1953 the Aid Plan was serving 4,000 members in 17 states, chiefly in North and South Dakota, Nebraska, Minnesota, Montana, and the remaining prairie and Rocky Mountain states, with a few in Iowa, Pennsylvania, California, and Washington, with a total property evaluation of $40,000,000. The assessment rate was 1 mill. D. J. Mendel and his son D. S. Mendel of Freeman, S.D., have been long-time secretaries of the organization. Rules and Regulations have been printed at irregular intervals, last in 1951. Minutes of the annual meeting of the association have been printed every year since 1882.   H.S.B.

Mennonite Aid Plan, West Liberty, Ohio, was organized April 1, 1896, as a mutual fire and storm insurance association to serve the Mennonites (MC) of the Logan and Champaign County settlement. In 1953 it had 205 members with a property coverage of $2,323,000.   H.S.B.

Mennonite Aid Plan of the Pacific Coast, a material aid fire and storm insurance association serving Mennonites of all branches in California, Idaho, Oregon, and Washington, was organized in 1922 at Reedley, Cal., its present head office. In 1953 it had 2,500 members with a property coverage of $18,000,000.

H.S.B.

Mennonite Aid Societies, Association of (*AMAS*), was organized in July 1956 as a representative organization for counsel, promotion, education, and fellowship, for all Mennonite and Brethren in Christ mutual aid societies of North America, of which 26 have already joined. All member societies have one vote each, and elect a board of seven directors, which was initially composed of the following: Harold L. Swartzendruber (Goshen) chairman, J. Winfield Fretz (North Newton) vice-chairman, Howard Raid (Bluffton) secretary-treasurer, S. S. Wenger (Lancaster), Jacob Wedel (Moundridge), and William T. Snyder (Akron) representing the MCC. The association meets annually in March.

H.S.B.

Mennonite Aid Society of Mountain Lake, Minn., a mutual burial aid society, was organized May 24, 1897, to serve Mennonites everywhere including missionaries in foreign countries. In 1953 it had 4,139 members, with an annual assessment rate of $12 per member.

H.S.B.

Mennonite Aid Society of South Dakota, a mutual aid fire and storm insurance association, was organized in March 1922 in Turner Co., S.D., its office now being in Freeman, to serve all branches of Mennonites. In 1953 it served 241 members, chiefly General Conference Mennonites, with $2,000,000 of property covered.

H.S.B.

Mennonite Aid Union of Kansas, an unincorporated mutual assessment association, was organized in 1906. Most of the founders were former members of the Mennonite Aid Plan of Freeman, S.D., who felt it would be more economical to organize a society for local Mennonites than to have one whose members were widely scattered. As of 1955 the society had a membership of 2,107 covering 2,464 risks for a total evaluation of $16,435,887.50. Up to 1956, the society did not insure business properties in towns and cities. Only Mennonites in good standing are admitted. This excludes members who belong to secret societies or who have been expelled from church on account of unchristian living. The headquarters as of 1956 are at North Newton, Kan.

J.W.F.

Mennonite Aid Union (Ont.), the oldest Mennonite mutual fire and storm property insurance organization, was organized on April 9, 1866, by authorization of the Ontario Mennonite Conference given in September 1864. Its original constitution declared that it was an effort to return to apostolic conditions, and every brother was urged to give his portion willingly in love to cover losses. At first serving only members of the Mennonite Church (MC), in 1919 it made members of the Brethren in Christ Church eligible for participation. It serves the Ontario and Alberta-Saskatchewan areas. In 1953 it had 2,442 members, covering property valued at $25,000,000.

H.S.B.

L. J. Burkholder, *A Brief History of the Mennonites in Ontario* (n.p., 1935).

Mennonite Benefit Association, New Hamburg, Ont., was organized in 1948 to serve Mennonites of all branches, primarily in Ontario, but also elsewhere in Canada, with aid to cover losses due to hospitalization, surgery, disability, and burial. In 1953 it had 750 members, with an annual assessment of $25 per member.

H.S.B.

Mennonite Bible Academy, Beatrice, Neb. A keen interest in education among the early Mennonites who came to Beatrice was first expressed by classes taught in private homes. In 1881 the first classes were taught by Helene Hamm, and later Mrs. William Penner. After Johannes K. Penner, an able minister and teacher, arrived in Beatrice in 1888, classes grew too large for his home. Recognizing the need for additional room and for instruction in the English language, the congregation built a two-room schoolhouse near "Onkel Lehrer" Penner's home three and one-half miles west of Beatrice, and one-half mile east of the First Mennonite Church, and hired an additional instructor. This school provided half-day instruction alternating between German and English. In later years the school was changed into a two-year course offering a fully accredited ninth grade plus Bible and other church-related subjects. Since students came only from the two local Mennonite churches, the attendance was small. In 1948 the accredited high-school subjects were dropped and a one-year course in Bible and other church-related subjects was offered. The school was closed for one year in 1950. When it later became clear that Nebraska state law prevented young people from being taken out of school for a year before continuing their high-school studies, the school was not reopened. The two-room, two-story frame building was dismantled in 1954 and the lumber sold at auction. Investigations were made of the possibilities of opening a parochial elementary grade school. Problems of transportation, cost, and possible attitude of non-Mennonite neighbors if children were taken out of the small country schools, and the difficulty of competing with superior facilities of the Beatrice public schools were factors to be considered before a parochial elementary grade school could be established. Public school consolidation was also a factor to be taken into consideration.

J.T.F.

Mennonite Bible Mission (GCM), located at 4221 South Rockwell St., Chicago: see **Grace** Mennonite Church.

Mennonite Biblical Seminary, a graduate school for the training of ministers, missionaries, and other church workers, is a school of the General Conference Mennonite Church administered directly by a Board of Trustees, nine in number, elected by and responsible to the General Conference. Additional members of the Board in an advisory capacity represent the three colleges of the General Conference and the alumni of the Seminary. The present Mennonite Biblical Seminary is a continuation of former seminaries, particularly the Mennonite Seminary which operated as a department of Bluffton College 1915-21 and the Witmarsum Theological Seminary into which the former was reorganized in 1921. This latter institution operated independently of the College until 1931 when it was provisionally discontinued. The board, however, continued to meet regularly and to plan for reopening of the institution. This was accomplished in two steps; first, the reorganization of the old board into a new board elected by the General Conference and the turning over of all assets of the former board and institution, and secondly, the opening of a seminary in September 1945 at a new location in Chicago under the name of Mennonite Biblical Seminary.

The Seminary as reopened was conducted in affiliation with Bethany Biblical Seminary, an institution of the Church of the Brethren, which confers the degree. Under the affiliated program Mennonite Biblical Seminary provides a number of faculty members who join the Bethany staff in teaching combined classes of students of both schools. The first president was Abraham Warkentin, who served from 1945 until his death in 1947. S. F. Pannabecker functioned as dean beginning in 1946 and continued as president after the death of Warkentin until 1957, also teaching in the fields of missions and church history. Other full-time faculty members during the first ten-year period were Don. E. Smucker in the field of Christian social ethics, Jacob J. Enz in Old Testament, and Marvin J. Dirks in music. All of these were serving in 1954-55. A number of others have assisted part time or for short periods. Besides the teaching faculty the staff has included a librarian and a director of public relations as well as a business manager and a matron, the latter two serving on a part-time basis. The number of Mennonite students in the affiliated program has varied from 15 the first year to as high as 45, with an average of 35.

While participating in the joint work of the affiliated program Mennonite Biblical Seminary has its own faculty and student organizations and its own physical plant located in the 4600 block on Woodlawn Avenue on the south side of Chicago. Here are provided student rooms and apartments, faculty apartments, business office, quarters for guests, library, and auditorium. Mennonite interests of the institution are centered at this location. Two projects incidental to Seminary activity became significant for the church. One was the provision for housing young Mennonites in the city studying in other institutions and tying them in with the Seminary fellowship. The second was the organization of the Woodlawn Mennonite Church, the congregation of which was based largely on Seminary residents but reached out into an active Christian effort in the local community. A third activity, stimulated in part by the Seminary but actually independent of it, was the mission center established by the General Conference in the same block as that occupied by the Seminary.

At this time of writing Mennonite Biblical Seminary is completing its first decade in the Chicago location. During this period about $250,000 has been invested in property for Seminary use. The number of students who have attended totals 162 with 72 graduates as follows: Master of Theology 2,

Bachelor of Divinity 53, Master of Religious Education 17. All degrees have been given by Bethany Biblical Seminary.

The most recent movement is one for an inter-Mennonite co-operative program in ministerial education, in which the Mennonite Biblical Seminary and the Goshen College Biblical Seminary, with any other interested Mennonite seminaries or groups will participate in a project called the Associated Mennonite Biblical Seminaries. This calls for the relocation of the campus of M.B.S. at the south edge of Elkhart, Ind., and the erection of a new plant there ready for occupancy by September 1958, as well as reorganization of the academic program.   S.F.P.

Mennonite Board of Charitable Homes (and Missions) was organized at Marshallville, Ohio, in 1899, and merged with the Mennonite Evangelizing and Benevolent Board (*q.v.*) in 1906 to become the Mennonite Board of Missions and Charities (*q.v.*). The phrase "and Missions" was added to the name in 1903. This Mennonite (MC) board was organized as the result of a mistake, not in competition with the Evangelizing and Benevolent Board. It was mistakenly assumed that an organization to hold property in Ohio would need to be incorporated in Ohio, and the desire to take over the Orphans' Home founded at Orrville, Ohio, in 1896, and to establish the Old People's Home at Marshallville, Ohio, in 1899, was the occasion for the organization and incorporation. The first president was M. S. Steiner of Columbus Grove, Ohio, and one of the five directors was A. B. Kolb, president of the M.E.B. Board. The officers of the new board almost throughout its history were M. S. Steiner president, C. Z. Yoder vice-president, D. C. Amstutz secretary, and A. Burkholder treasurer. M. S. Steiner, an aggressive man of vision, was the leader. The *Mennonite Yearbook and Directory* was begun in 1905 by this board. In 1905 the Eastern Mission Committee was appointed "to oversee and manage any institutions in the Eastern States that may come under the supervision of the Board." The committee was J. H. Mellinger, S. S. Krabill, and S. H. Musselman, all of Lancaster County, Pa., and later leaders in the formation of the Eastern Mennonite Board of Missions and Charities in 1914. In the merger of 1906, M. S. Steiner became the president of the new board.   H.S.B.

Levi Hartzler, *A Brief History of Mennonite Missions* (Elkhart, 1955).

Mennonite Board of Education was founded in 1905 as the official educational corporation of the Mennonite Church (MC). Its first task was to receive from the Elkhart Institute Association all its assets including Goshen College (*q.v.*), and to operate Goshen College. In 1909, at the request of Mennonites in Kansas, it established Hesston College (*q.v.*), and has continued to operate both schools to date. In 1949 it took over the La Junta Mennonite School of Nursing (*q.v.*), which it operated until its closing in 1958. In 1950 it created the General Educational Council as an autonomous body to represent the interests of the total educational program of the church, including locally operated elementary and secondary schools and colleges as well as the schools under the Board.

The Board holds full title to all properties and assets of the schools under it, and administers all endowment and annuity funds. Earlier the Board had operated its two colleges through the Local Board for each school. In 1942 the administrative structure was changed, the local boards were discontinued, and the Executive Committee of the Board assumed direct operational control working through the presidents of the schools.

The membership of the Board from the beginning was constitutionally provided by election by the district conferences and the Mennonite General Conference, ex officio members being the presidents and business managers of the schools under the Board. Later two representatives elected by each Alumni Association were added, and several members-at-large elected by the Board. In 1957 the total membership of the Board was 39, with a term of appointment of four years. A number of men have rendered long-term and outstanding service in the work of the Board: Presidents, John Blosser 1902-17, D. A. Yoder 1929-48, and Nelson Kauffman 1948- ; others were D. D. Miller, member of the Board 1906-41, and vice-president or secretary 1906-20; J. S. Hartzler, member 1906-18, secretary or treasurer 1910-16; S. F. Coffman, member 1906-39, secretary 1929-39; Aaron Loucks, member 1906-28, vice-president 1913-18; O. O. Miller, member 1920- , financial agent and on executive committee 1925-56; J. B. Smith, member 1917-22, 1930-47, vice-president 1933-45; H. R. Schertz, member 1923-49, president 1924-29, vice-president 1929-31, treasurer 1933-44; C. F. Yake, member 1935-53, secretary 1939-49; S. C. Yoder, member 1916-40, president 1918-24.   H.S.B.

Mennonite Board (Council) **of Education** (*Schulrat*), Russia, came into being in the Molotschna Mennonite settlement after the Agricultural Association (*q.v.*), which had been established through J. Cornies (*q.v.*), had lost its leadership in matters pertaining to education. The Molotschna Mennonite Schulrat, approved by the Fürsorgekomitee (*q.v.*) at Odessa in 1869, consisted of four, later six, members, of whom at least one was a minister. The members were nominated by the Mennonite communities (the minister by the church). The Fürsorgekomitee approved the candidates. The Chortitza Board of Education (Zentralschulrat) was also established in 1869. Similar organizations functioned in some of the larger daughter settlements.

The Schulrat inspected schools, conducted two teachers' conferences annually, examined teaching candidates, and had general supervision of education. At the teachers' conferences curricula, methods, textbooks, etc., were discussed. Lectures and teaching demonstrations were given. Minutes were kept at all meetings and the attendance was obligatory. The 60 schools of the Molotschna settlement were divided into some ten districts in each of which local teachers' conferences were held. Here local problems were presented and discussed in greater detail.

In 1871 the Fürsorgekomitee was discontinued and the Schulrat was placed under the Russian State Department of Education. Through this transfer gradually great difficulties arose, which became significant factors in causing the great emigration of 1874. Such men as Isaak Peters and Dietrich Gaeddert, leaders of the emigration movement, were also members of the Board.

Outstanding members of the Molotschna Schulrat were Philip Wiebe, A. Voth 1869-83, J. Klatt, and P. H. Heese 1884-96. Many improvements were made during this time, especially on the level of elementary education. The Bible, generally used as a reader in elementary schools, was replaced by a German reader and a Bible history. Books on church history and a German grammar were produced. All books were written by Mennonite authors and were approved by the government. Secondary schools for girls were introduced (*Mädchenschule*) and teachers' training courses (*Lehrerseminar*) were added to some of the Zentralschulen mainly through the efforts of the Board. Many educators received medals of distinction and other honors from the State Department of Education.

From 1869 to 1905 the Chortitza Schulrat was mostly in the hands of two excellent educators, Heinrich Epp (*q.v.*) and A. A. Neufeld (*q.v.*). The church elder of the Chortitza settlement was always a member of the Board, as was also the director of the Chortitza Zentralschule.

The Schulrat in general played a very significant role in raising the educational level among the Mennonites of Russia, particularly in view of the fact that it confronted almost insurmountable difficulties from the Russian government. The State Department of Education sometimes refused to appoint candidates and sought to be responsible for the inspection of the schools. Gradually the Schulrat consisted mostly of ministers who had permission to supervise and inspect religious and German instruction in the Mennonite schools. Under these conditions its influence and significance decreased, but the Mennonite Teachers' Association (*q.v.*) had meanwhile taken over its major functions.   C.K.

D. P. Enns, "Mennonite Education in Russia," *Menn. Life* VI (July 1951) 28 ff.; idem, "Die mennonitischen Schulen in Russland," *Menn. Jahrbuch,* 1950 (Newton) 7 ff.; Peter Braun, "Eduction System of the Mennonite Colonies in South Russia," *MQR* III (July 1929) 175 ff.; Friesen, *Brüderschaft,* 645 ff.; L. Froese, *Das pädagogische Kultursystem der mennonitischen Siedlungsgruppe in Russland* (thesis at the University of Göttingen, privately mimeographed, 1949) 89 ff.

Mennonite Board of Guardians, an immigration aid committee of American Mennonites formed on Dec. 2, 1873, at Summerfield, Ill., to aid the Mennonites emigrating from Russia to the United States. It was created by the merger of two earlier committees, the aid committee appointed on Oct. 9, 1873, by the Indiana-Michigan Mennonite (MC) Conference and composed of John F. Funk (*q.v.*), Isaac Kilmer, and Bernhard Warkentin (*q.v.*), and a similar committee appointed on Nov. 17, 1873, by the Western District Conference (GCM), composed of Christian Krehbiel (*q.v.*), Daniel Baer, and Bernhard Warkentin (*q.v.*). The new Board of Guardians was composed of Christian Krehbiel president, David Goerz secretary, John F. Funk treasurer, Bernhard Warkentin agent, and Kilmer and Baer as members. It announced its purposes to be to negotiate with the railroads to secure the most favorable terms, to speed up the collection of gifts and loans from all the peace churches, and to solicit the co-operation of all the conferences. Funk seems to have been a moving spirit in the organization; he had already in the November number of his paper, the *Herald of Truth,* issued a stirring appeal for immediate action to help the immigrants on the part of all Mennonites, "whether old or new Mennonites, Reformed Mennonites, Evangelical Mennonites, Swiss Mennonites, Amish Mennonites, or by whatsoever other peculiar name they may be known." The Board contacted the prospective emigrants in Russia with direct offers of aid in the form of gifts and loans, and gave them counsel as to procedures in reaching America. It unfolded a vigorous and extensive program of aid, negotiated with railroads and steamship companies, and became in effect the director and guardian of the emigration as a whole. Its field of work naturally remained the United States, but it co-operated closely with a similar committee in Ontario led by Jacob Y. Shantz (*q.v.*), as well as with the Mennonite Executive Aid Committee of Eastern Pennsylvania Mennonites, organized in April 1874 with which it had hoped to arrange a merger, but failed. It had a reliable Mennonite merchant in Hamburg, Germany, Heinrich Schuett, as its agent in that important port. Considerable sums of money were raised for the immigrants, both as contributions and loans, especially to help the many poor in some of the immigrant groups, although the original intent of the Board had been only to aid in the passage money. By 1875 the Board was deeply involved in aiding in actual colonization, working in Kansas through the Kansas Central Relief Committee, organized in April 1875, of which Bernhard Warkentin was secretary. After this committee was dissolved on May 16, 1876, the Board handled its colonization aid directly with the colonists.

The chief work of the Board of Guardians was accomplished by the end of 1875; but minor activity continued for another six or seven years. The loans of the Board were serviced for many years. Records are incomplete but documents are extant of as late as 1886, signed by David Goerz, secretary, and John F. Funk, treasurer, showing that loan repayments were still being collected. The total official receipts of the Board amounted to $40,484.16, of which $23,595.49 was used to provide passage for the destitute. The officers and members of the Board apparently remained unchanged throughout its history; at least Funk and Goerz still carried their office until 1886. No record is known of its formal dissolution. Some of the account books of the Board, as kept by its treasurer, John F. Funk, are in the Mennonite Church Archives at Goshen College. The records of David Goerz, the secretary, were destroyed in the burning of the office of the Western Publishing Company at Halstead, Kan., in 1876.

H.S.B.

Kempes Schnell, "John F. Funk, 1839-1930, and the Mennonite Migration of 1873-1875," *MQR* XXIV (1950) 199-229; C. Henry Smith, *The Coming of the Russian Mennonites* (Berne, 1927).

Mennonite Board of Missions and Charities, Elkhart, Ind., is the general mission board of the Mennonite Church (MC), consisting of elected directors representing all district conferences eligible for affiliation with the Mennonite General Conference, two representatives each of the Mennonite Publication Board and the Mennonite Board of Education, four members elected by the General Conference, eight members at large, and officers and administrative secretaries members ex-officio. The Board meets annually in June in some major Mennonite community to review and act on the missions, relief and service, and institutional program for which it is responsible. The stated purposes of the organization are (1) to systematize and extend evangelistic work; (2) to establish and support home and foreign missions, (3) to care and provide for orphans, the aged, the needy, and the afflicted; (4) to carry on relief and service work; and (5) to receive and manage all properties and funds for the above purposes.

The MBMC stems from the Mennonite Evangelizing Committee, Elkhart, organized by the local Mennonite church in 1882 to collect and disburse funds for the purpose of defraying the expenses of ministers traveling to visit scattered members and churches. In 1892 the name was changed to the Mennonite Evangelizing Board of America (*q.v.*) with membership from other district conferences and in 1896 to the Mennonite Evangelizing and Benevolent Board to include charitable work in its functions. In 1899 the Mennonite Board of Charitable Homes was organized and incorporated in Wayne Co., Ohio, to operate a children's home and an old people's home. Four years later that name was changed to the Mennonite Board of Charitable Homes and Missions. A merger of these two boards was effected in 1906 and the present name of Mennonite Board of Missions and Charities selected.

Leaders responsible for the early developments of the Mennonite Evangelizing Committee included J. F. Funk, J. S. Coffman, C. K. Hostetler, A. B. Kolb, and Joseph Summers. G. L. Bender served the Mennonite Evangelizing Board of America and the Mennonite Evangelizing and Benevolent Board as both secretary and treasurer and then became the first treasurer of the Mennonite Board of Missions and Charities in 1906, serving in that capacity until 1921. Leaders who served the Mennonite Board of Charitable Homes and Missions and continued as leaders of the Mennonite Board of Missions and Charities included M. S. Steiner, president 1906-11; C. Z. Yoder, vice-president 1906-11, president 1911-20; and D. S. Yoder, fifth member on the Executive Committee 1906-18. Since 1920 four men have served as president: D. D. Miller 1920-36, J. N. Kaufman 1936-44, S. C. Yoder 1944-49, and John H. Mosemann 1949- . Three men have served as secretary of the Board since 1906: J. S. Shoemaker 1906-21, S. C. Yoder 1921-44, and J. D. Graber 1944- . Vice-presidents of the Board since 1911 included D. D. Miller 1911-16, D. G. Lapp 1916-27, Levi Mumaw 1927-35, Edwin J. Yoder 1935-48, J. B. Martin 1948- . The following treasurers have served since 1921: V. E. Reiff 1921-34, D. D. Miller 1934-39, E. C. Bender 1939-51, and H. Ernest Bennett 1951- . S. E. Allgyer was a member of the Missions Committee of the Board 1914-37, serving much of that time as field worker. Another person constantly associated with the committees of the MBMC for the first three decades was Daniel Kauffman. In 1948 the secretaryship for Relief and Service was established. Those serving in this secretaryship include Levi C. Hartzler 1949-53 and Boyd Nelson 1953- . A secretaryship for publicity and church relations was established in 1953 with Levi C. Hartzler appointed to serve. In 1955 Nelson E. Kauffman was appointed to serve as the first secretary for home missions and evangelism, on a part-time basis, and Henry Weaver, Jr., as first secretary for radio evangelism. A secretaryship for personnel was established in 1956 and Dorsa J. Mishler appointed first secretary.

Foreign Missions. The Mennonite Evangelizing and Benevolent Board began mission work in India in 1899. Further development of the foreign mission program under the MBMC follows: Central Argentina 1917; Bihar, India, 1940; Chaco, Argentina, 1943; Puerto Rico 1945; China 1948-51; Japan 1949; Belgium 1950; Sicily 1950 (administered by the Virginia Mennonite Board of Missions and Charities); Alaska 1952; England 1952; France 1953; Israel 1953; Uruguay 1954; Brazil 1954; and Cuba 1954 (administered by the Franconia Mennonite Board of Missions and Charities); Ghana, W. Africa, 1956; and Jamaica 1956 (administered by the Virginia Mennonite Board of Missions and Charities). In July 1952 the American Mennonite Mission in India was amalgamated with the India Mennonite Church to form the Mennonite Church in India, an indigenous organization served by the missionaries and funds sent from American churches through MBMC. The trend toward the indigenous church continues on most of the mission fields under the Board.

Home Missions. The MBMC encourages local congregations and district conferences to develop home missions. The Board does operate home missions when requested by local congregations or district boards and/or when the project can develop best as a church-wide mission. City missions under the MBMC with date of founding include the following: Mennonite Home Mission, Chicago, 1893; Ft. Wayne, Ind., 1903-53; Canton, Ohio, 1904; Kansas City, Kan., 1905-46; Toronto, Ont., 1907; Lima, Ohio, 1910; Peoria, Ill., 1919; Detroit, Mich., 1926; Spanish Church, Chicago, 1932; Mathis, Tex., 1936; La Junta, Col. (Spanish), 1940; Denver, Col., 1941-54; Bethel Church, Chicago, 1944; Kansas City, Mo., 1946; Ninth St., Saginaw, Mich., 1950; Cleveland, Ohio, 1951; East Side, Saginaw, 1954; Hope Rescue Mission, South Bend, Ind., 1954; Mennonite House of Friendship, Bronx, N.Y., 1956; St. Louis, Mo., 1956; Corpus Christi, Tex. (Spanish), 1956; and Defiance, Ohio (Spanish), 1957. Rural missions under the MBMC include Culp, Ark., 1935; Camp Rehoboth, St. Anne, Ill., 1953; Black Mt. Mission, Ganado, Ariz., 1954.

Charitable Institutions. In keeping with its purposes, the MBMC has continued and enlarged the institutional program begun by the Mennonite Board of Charitable Homes and Missions: West Liberty (Ohio) Orphans' Home 1896; Rittman (Ohio) Old People's Home 1901. In 1917 another children's home was established in Kansas City, Kan., and in

1950 the Mennonite Youth Village, White Pigeon, Mich., a summer camp program, was launched. Three more homes for the aged—Eureka, Ill., 1922, Froh Bros. Homestead, Sturgis, Mich., 1952, Sunset Home, Geneva, Neb., 1955—and a home for retired church workers, Rockome, Arcola, Ill., 1952, have been added to the institutions serving the aged. In 1907 a sanitarium for tuberculosis patients was established near La Junta, Col. (closed 1956); and the La Junta city hospital was taken over in 1919 forming the Mennonite Hospital and Sanitarium. Since 1915 the La Junta Mennonite School of Nursing has been affiliated with the Mennonite Hospital and Sanitarium. Recently the MBMC has contracted to operate four community hospitals: Lebanon, Ore., 1950; Greensburg, Kan., 1950; Rocky Ford, Col., 1954; Glenwood Springs, Col., 1955.

Relief and Service. Since 1926 when the Mennonite Relief Commission for War Sufferers (*q.v.*), founded in 1917, dissolved to become the Mennonite Relief Committee of the General Mission Board, the relief and service program has been administered through that committee. Foreign relief work, refugee aid, and mental health work are carried on through the Mennonite Central Committee, all-Mennonite relief agency. In 1944 MRC organized a voluntary service program. In 1948 a secretary for relief and service was appointed by the MBMC to serve as secretary of MRC. Since 1952 the permanent draft program has greatly increased the work of MRSC (the name of the committee was changed in the 1953 revised MBMC constitution) in the areas of service to conscientious objectors and in the voluntary service program. Six full-time administrators and four secretaries comprise the MRSC office staff.

Radio Evangelism. The Board at its 1953 annual meeting set up an administrative committee for radio evangelism and entered into an agreement with Mennonite Crusaders, Inc., Harrisonburg, Va., to make *The Mennonite Hour,* established in 1951, the official Mennonite (MC) broadcast. In 1955 a secretary for radio evangelism was appointed to serve as executive secretary for the radio evangelism committee. A building was purchased in Harrisonburg by the MBMC and dedicated as the radio headquarters on Jan. 11, 1956. Also in 1956, Mennonite Crusaders, Inc., dissolved and Mennonite Broadcasts, Inc., is responsible for the following broadcasts: *The Mennonite Hour* (English), *Luz y Verdad* (Spanish), *Menonaito Awa* (Japanese), and the Navaho Bible Hour; it also has an affiliate relationship with *Heart to Heart,* a women's broadcast. Programs in French, German, and Hindi are now in the planning stages. In addition radio Bible correspondence courses are being administered in English, Spanish, and Japanese.

Finances. Total contributions the first year (1882) to the Mennonite Evangelizing Committee reached $27.36. Contributions in 1892 totaled $959.31. The 1897 treasurer's report shows designated contributions for foreign missions for the first time: $153.05. Contributions during the first year of the MBMC, 1906-7, totaled $42,564.69. By 1930 annual contributions had reached $175,598.40 but dropped back to $128,672.87 in 1940. Due to the foreign relief and

CPS programs during World War II annual contributions reached $914,102.55 in 1946. They dropped back to $561,838.41 in 1950, but have been increasing gradually since. The 1954-55 figure reached $1,011,006.54. Property and cash assets of the MBMC as of March 31, 1955, were $1,950,000. L.C.H.

Mennonite Book and Tract Society

Mennonite Book and Tract Society (1889-1908) was founded in May 1889, near Orrville, Ohio, by a number of Mennonites "to awaken a greater interest for good literature and supply the same." The first formal business meeting was held on Oct. 10, 1892, and the last on Nov. 11, 1907. The Society published ten books and one catalog, at least thirty-three tracts, possibly many more, and Sunday-school materials: *Beams of Light* (1906-8), *Book and Tract Messenger* (*q.v.*), and primary (1906-) and advanced (1907-) lesson helps. The first president was J. S. Coffman, followed by J. S. Lehman, John Blosser, and D. H. Bender. Other officers were: vice-president, David Burkholder, Aaron Loucks; tract editor, J. S. Coffman, A. D. Wenger; secretary, M. S. Steiner. The official place of business of the Society was the address of the treasurer: G. L. Bender, Elkhart, Ind., 1889-98; J. A. Ressler, Scottdale, Pa., 1898-1902; John W. Weaver, Spring Grove, Pa., 1902-5 and A. D. Martin, Scottdale, 1905-8, when the Society's business was merged with the work of the Mennonite Publishing House. J.A.H.

J. A. Hostetler, "History of the Mennonite Book and Tract Society," MQR XXXI (1957), p. 105.

Mennonite Book Concern

Mennonite Book Concern, Berne, Ind., had its beginning in 1882, when Joel Welty opened a bookstore, with his brother Dan Welty assisting him in the store. The two brothers secured S. F. Sprunger (*q.v.*), then commonly known in Berne as "der Sam," to make the selection of books. Two years later Sprunger became a partner in the firm, and the store went under the name of Welty and Sprunger. In 1884, when the General Conference convened in Berne, the bookstore became a church institution and has remained as such. Welty and Sprunger became the publishing agents for what later became known as the Mennonite Book Concern.

Revenue from this store was the major source of subsidy for General Conference periodicals and Sunday-school literature until 1929. Its manager also served as business manager for G.C.M. publications until 1939. Managers following Welty have been J. F. Lehman 1895-1929, Ferdinand J. Wiens 1930-36, Fred von Guten 1937-51, and Howard Culp 1951- . E.S., M.Sh.

Eva P. Sprunger, *A History of the Mennonite Church in Adams County, Indiana* (Berne, 1938) 205; H. P. Krehbiel, *The History of the General Conference Mennonite Church of North America* I and II (St. Louis, 1898, and Newton, 1938).

Mennonite Bookstore

Mennonite Bookstore, Rosthern, Sask., was established in 1947 by the General Conference Mennonite Board of Publication to serve as its Canadian retail outlet. Managers of the store have been John R. Dyck 1947-54, Henry A. Wiens 1954-55, and David D. Reimer 1955- . M.Sh.

Mennonite Boys League

Mennonite Boys League, an organization for boys 9 to 14 years old of the General Conference Mennonite Church, came into existence through appointment in 1954 of a Boys Work Committee by Mennonite Men (*q.v.*), the Conference Laymen's organization. The members of this committee were Erwin C. Goering, Clinton Kaufman, and Menno Schrag. The League began to function in August 1955 when the first unit of some 25 boys was established in the First Mennonite Church of Newton, Kan. Other units soon followed in Pennsylvania and Indiana—with manifest interest throughout the conference. The purpose of the League is "to carry out an intensive program of wholesome activities geared to the interest of young boys; to lead boys into a saving relationship with Christ; to foster consistent Christian living, and instill the Mennonite faith as founded on the Word of God." M.Sh.

Mennonite Brethren Bible College

Mennonite Brethren Bible College, at 77 Kelvin Street, Winnipeg, Man., is a theological institution of the Canadian Conference of the Mennonite Brethren Church. It seeks to provide an adequate preparation for young men and women who desire to serve as ministers, teachers, missionaries, choir leaders, and workers in other fields of Christian service. The educational program of the College has been determined in part by present-day educational standards, in part by the great variety of interests and needs of the young people of the church, and in part by the demands of a constantly expanding missionary and educational program of the Conference. The College has been authorized by the Board of Education to offer the following courses: (1) The Theological Degree Course (Th.B.), designed for those who wish to major in theology and practical work as ministers of the Gospel, which covers five years. (2) The Religious Education Course (B.R.E.), offered to meet the needs of those who seek preparation in the fields of Christian education, missionary service, and local church leadership, which covers four years. (3) The General Bible Course, designed especially for students who cannot secure adequate College training. (4) The Sacred Music Course, an intensive course of instruction offered to meet the advanced music standards of the present day. It seeks to prepare the students for the ministry of music in churches, schools, and communities. (5) "Liberal Arts" courses are offered in psychology, philosophy, history, English, and German.

The Mennonite Brethren Bible College was founded in response to a longfelt need within the denomination. Official expression of this need was given by the late J. A. Toews, in his report on Christian Education presented to the Canadian Conference in July 1939 at Coaldale, Alberta. Although the challenge presented by Toews found a favorable response among the Brethren, no definite steps were undertaken until 1943, when a recommendation was accepted by the Conference to found a Bible College in Canada, to be controlled and financed by the Conference, and that such a College be centrally located. The Educational Board, which was elected by the Conference, took immediate steps to open the school in Winnipeg in the fall of 1944. A. H. Unruh was elected by the Conference as the first president of the College. To relieve Unruh of administrative responsibilities, the Conference extended a call to J. B. Toews of Buhler, Kan., in the summer of 1945, to assume the responsibility as president of the College. Both Unruh and Toews deserve much credit for establishing the school on a sound academic and spiritual basis. Ben Horch has built up the music department of the school and his unique contributions in the field of church music have been greatly appreciated by the whole constituency. In 1948, when Toews accepted a call to the pastorate of the Mennonite Brethren Church of Reedley, Cal., H. H. Janzen became president of the College. Under President Janzen's able administration, the College has enjoyed steady progress. In October 1950 the College was accredited in the College Division by the Accrediting Association of Bible Institutes and Bible Colleges (U.S.A.). A change in the administration was necessitated by H. H. Janzen's resignation from the presidency in the summer of 1956 in order to accept a mission appointment in Europe. He was succeeded on Sept. 1, 1956, by J. A. Toews.

The growth of the College necessitated the erection and acquisition of new buildings. Bethany Hall, a spacious, two-story frame building, was purchased at the same time as the administration building (1944). It is used as a music hall at present (1955). Ebenezer Hall, a new structure 67 x 54 ft., with basement and two stories, was built in 1946 and serves as dormitory for married couples and for women students. McIntosh Hall and Carmen Hall were purchased in 1950 and 1951 as dormitories for the men students. A modern library building (L-shaped, 125 ft. frontage, 90 ft. north side) containing an auditorium, two classrooms, seven music rooms, and four spacious offices was completed in the summer of 1956.

After a brief history of ten years the positive and constructive influence of the College may be noticed in all parts of the far-flung Canadian constituency. To date (1955) 860 students have enrolled for longer or shorter terms of study. Among these have been foreign students from the United States, South America, Germany, Holland, Switzerland, and Japan. Of the 146 graduates (1954) a large number are engaged in teaching in public schools, Bible Schools, and Christian high schools. Others serve as pastors, home mission workers, etc., and a goodly number have gone forth to the foreign mission fields (24 by 1955). Through annual courses for ministers, for Sunday-school superintendents and teachers as well as through Bible and missionary conferences, the College has served as a unifying factor in the life of the Conference.

The Voice, official publication of the Mennonite Brethren Bible College, is published bimonthly in the interest of sound Christian teaching. Denominational principles and practices are given special emphasis.

The doctrinal position of the College is frankly conservative, holding to those distinctive principles for which evangelical Mennonites have always stood. Although its doors are open to Christian young men and women of other evangelical denominations, the College is a Mennonite institution whose primary concern it is to serve the needs of the Mennonite Brethren churches and the larger Mennonite brotherhood.   Jo.A.T.

Mennonite Brethren Church. The Mennonite Brethren Church, which constitutes an integral part of the general body of Mennonites, had its beginning among the Mennonite settlements of southern Russia in 1860. Here it established itself in its doctrinal position, experienced its early growth and spread, and made some definite contribution toward Mennonite life and history. In the migration of Mennonites from Russia to North America 1874-80, there were also members of the Mennonite Brethren Church and so the church was in part transplanted to America. Here it has experienced its largest expansion and growth, and made its chief contribution toward the sum total of Mennonite life and activity. As a fruit of its foreign mission effort the Mennonite Brethren Church has become established in India, China, Belgian Congo, Africa, where through the converts that have been won, indigenous M.B. churches have sprung up. Through Mennonite immigrations from Europe into Paraguay and Brazil since 1930 the M.B. Church has also been transplanted to this continent, and through foreign mission effort converts from among the Indian tribes in Paraguay and from the nationals in Colombia have been won, resulting in the beginning of indigenous churches in these two countries. A fair historical presentation of the M.B. Church therefore calls for a treatment of (I) the M.B. Church in Russia; (II) the M.B. Church in North America; and (III) the M.B. Church in Other Countries.

I. *The Mennonite Brethren Church in Russia.*

1. *The Religious Awakening Which Led to the Beginning of the Mennonite Brethren Church.* A settlement of Mennonites, mostly of Dutch origin, migrated from Prussia into South Russia in 1788, and settled at Chortitza, province of Ekaterinoslav. In 1803 a still larger group migrated and established the Molotschna settlement, in the province of Taurida, further south. These colonists struggled with poverty, epidemics, and other hardships during their pioneer years, but ultimately succeeded in making their settlements some of the most prosperous in the Czar's domain. They enjoyed a limited amount of self-government, exemption from military service, and freedom of religion. As there was a lack of ministers and of strong religious leaders from the beginning, the spiritual life in these settlements was low during the first half century. In culture and education there was retrogression, and the schools prior to 1850 were of an inferior quality.

Beginning with 1845 a religious awakening spread over the settlements. For this there were several contributing factors. In 1835 a new group of settlers had come from Prussia, Brenkenhoffswalde, and founded the village of Gnadenfeld, Molotschna. They had formerly come in touch with the Moravian Brethren and had received inspiration and stimulus from them. This group exerted some influence on their surroundings and were later the

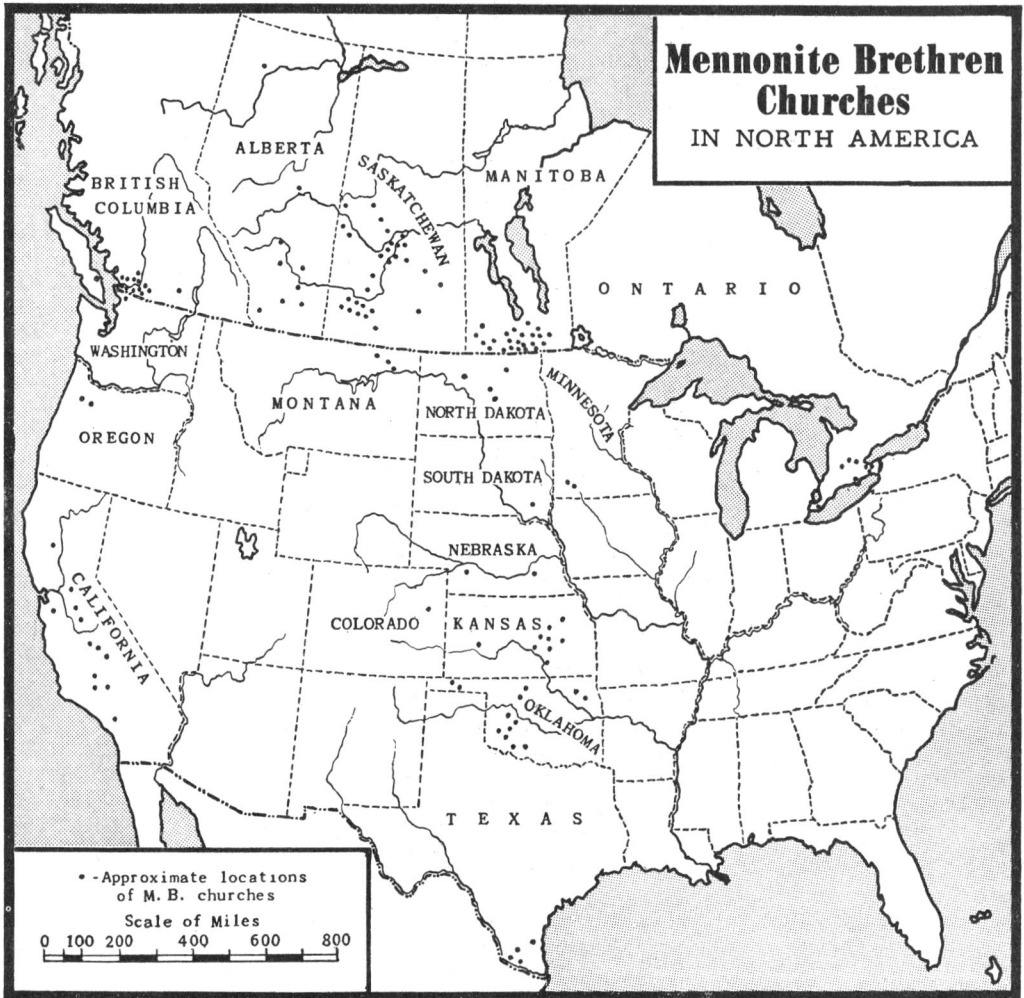

Mennonite Brethren Churches IN NORTH AMERICA

• - Approximate locations
of M. B. churches
Scale of Miles
0 100 200   400   600   800

center of new religious life. Another factor in the spiritual awakening had its origin in a settlement of Lutheran Pietists, who had located at Neu-Hoffnung, south of the Molotschna settlement. This church called Edward Wüst from Germany to come and be their pastor, and he served them from 1845 until his death in 1859. Wüst was a powerful personality and a very effective speaker, a man of deep emotions and of strong religious convictions. His message was definitely evangelical, stressing repentance, conversion, and a life consistent with the Christian faith.

Wüst's work had a remarkable influence on his own congregation as well as on the neighboring Mennonites, whom he occasionally also served as guest speaker. Many of them attended the annual mission festivals which Wüst instituted, and some also his regular church services. The result was that Wüst gained an entrance into the Mennonite settlements. In various places groups began to meet for prayer and for the study of the Bible. Those participating in such gatherings called themselves "Brethren." This revived religious life was not gen-

erally understood in the settlement and was at times suppressed rather than nurtured. Among those taking an opposing attitude were ministers and even church elders. Some unsound manifestations accompanied the movement in its early stages and this may partly account for the antagonistic position many took. The movement itself was, however, the most remarkable religious awakening and the most influential revival of spiritual life in the history of the Mennonites in Russia.

2. The Beginning of the Mennonite Brethren Church. As the groups of Brethren increased and became more united, they raised objections to certain practices and inconsistencies of conduct on the part of members of the church and insisted on church discipline. Since this was not carried out as they believed that it should be done, they requested that communion service be administered to them separately. This the church elders declined to do. Thereupon a group of the Brethren met in December 1859 and held a communion service among themselves. This event soon became known and

caused a great turmoil in the church. Some of the Brethren were called before the church and were asked to apologize and to promise that they would refrain from this in the future. They, however, did not concede to this, but rather justified their action and claimed Scriptural ground for the step they had taken. Thereupon six members of the Gnadenfeld church were asked to withdraw from the congregation.

On Jan. 6, 1860, a number of the Brethren met in the village of Elisabeththal, Molotschna, and took steps to form a separate church. They drew up a written statement addressed to the elders of the church, in which they declared themselves an independent church and stated their reasons for taking this step. They also stated their intention to remain within the Mennonite brotherhood of the settlement. This document was signed by 18 men. This event is regarded as the beginning of the Mennonite Brethren Church, and the 18 men as constituting the first congregation. Abraham Cornelsen, Johann Claassen, and Heinrich Hübert appear to have been the leading men. Upon receiving this document the elders of the church met and forbade this organization and ordered that no separate religious meetings should be held by the Brethren. They also referred this matter to the local Mennonite council of the settlement. This council forbade the holding of any religious meetings of a private or secret nature.

Several years of acute trials for the Brethren and of strained relationships between them and the existing Mennonite Church followed. The young M.B. Church, however, grew and was able to continue. Through the prolonged efforts of Johann Claassen, in which he applied to the higher government officials in St. Petersburg, the M.B. Church at last received recognition and legal status in the Mennonite settlements. Meanwhile groups of Brethren in the older Chortitza settlement had likewise organized themselves into a church and joined in fellowship with those in the Molotschna settlement. These Brethren in Chortitza for some time met with persecution and passed through a period of severe testings.

In its position the early M.B. Church strongly stressed repentance from sin, conversion as a personal experience of faith in Christ, a life of prayer, and a conduct consistent with the teachings of the Bible. In general the M.B. Church continued to adhere to the teachings of Menno Simons, renouncing military service, abstaining from taking oath, and adhering to a simple way of life. The immersion form of baptism upon a personal confession of faith in Jesus Christ was early instituted and required for church membership. Church discipline for improper conduct of members was practiced. The ministry was elected from among the membership. On May 30, 1860, the M.B. Church assembled and elected Heinrich Hübert as elder and Jacob Becker as minister.

3. *Growth and Activity of the Church.* In spite of difficulties within and opposition from without, the M.B. Church continued to grow and to spread. The years 1865-72 marked a period of peace, of prosperity, and of rapid growth. The Molotschna congregation, with its center at Rückenau, was fortunate in securing a number of able and devout leaders. Among these were Jacob Jantz, Christian Schmidt, Johan Fast, and Abraham Schellenberg, and a little later David Dürksen and David Schellenberg. The Chortitza congregation, centered in the large village of Einlage, increased even more rapidly, and for a number of years was the largest M.B. congregation. Its early elders and leading men were Abraham Unger and Aaron Lepp. In 1873 Elder Heinrich Hübert moved to the new Kuban settlement, east of the Black Sea, where land had been procured for a settlement of the Mennonite Brethren. Here also a congregation developed. The M.B. Church also spread to the new settlements of Friedensfeld and Tiege-Zagradovka, to the settlements east of the Don River and at Mariupol, and still further east to the Volga River.

The several M.B. churches convened for their first general conference (*Bundeskonferenz*) May 14-16, 1872. The congregations from Chortitza, Molotschna, and Kuban participated. At this time the total communicant membership numbered 600. Since then a conference was held annually, until the revolution following World War I brought about conditions which made its continuation impossible. The conference was the means by which the M.B. Church remained united as one body, by which it maintained and expressed its position, and by which it directed and promoted its common activities.

A Confession of Faith was drawn up in 1873, adopted by the conference and printed in 1876. This Confession of Faith was thoroughly revised in 1900 and then adopted by the conference as well as by the separate churches. It was published at Halbstadt in 1902. Later the M.B. Church in North America adopted this Confession of Faith as its statement of belief and conduct and in 1917 had it translated into English and published.

The emigration to America in 1874-80 drew considerably from the membership of the M.B. Church, including some of its leading ministers. After this period the church again increased, and in 1885, when it celebrated its 25th anniversary, the M.B. Church in Russia had a total membership of 1,800, and 7 congregations with meetinghouse and 10 other places of worship. The ministry consisted of 4 elders and 35 other ministers.

A period of industrial and economic expansion and growth among the Mennonites of Russia marked the three decades following 1885, which was accompanied by a rapid advance in education and in cultural life. Village schools were greatly improved. Higher institutions of learning, known as "Zentralschulen," were established at various centers. The Mennonite Brethren Church did not establish its own schools or other institutions, but cooperated in this with the existing Mennonite body, thus contributing its share and reaping of the benefits.

The M.B. Church zealously undertook home mission work from the very beginning and continued this as long as possible. With the organization of the church into a conference, the conference directed and promoted this work. A number of effective evangelists and itinerating ministers (*Reiseprediger*) have done very useful work for the church. In 1890 the M.B. Church began a foreign mission among the Telugus of the Hyderabad State, South India, by sending the Abraham Friesens to this field as their first missionaries. In its foreign mission effort the M.B. Church co-operated with the American Baptist Foreign Mission Society and affiliated itself with this body. A total of 18 M.B. missionaries were sent from Russia to this field. The three mission stations, Nalgonda, Sooriapet, and Jangaon, were built by them, and the work in this responsive field proved to be very successful. The records, closing the year 1910, show a total of 3,000 baptized church members in the indigenous church. When World War I broke out in 1914 and the M.B. Church in Russia found it impossible to continue the mission, the American Baptist Mission took it over completely and has continued since.

In publication efforts the M.B. Church found its expression in the periodical *Friedensstimme,* which was published by Abraham Kroeker 1903-20, and which can be regarded as the official organ of the church.

When the M.B. Church celebrated its 50th anniversary in 1910, it had spread still further east to include congregations in Orenburg, Russian Turkestan, and Omsk, Siberia; it had advanced southward, where congregations had begun in the Crimean peninsula; it had extended to the west, where congregations had been established in Poland. The total membership at this time was 6,000. With the coming of World War I and the revolution with its period of chaos and the famine that followed, calamities and untold sufferings became the fate of the Mennonite Brethren as well as of other Mennonites in Russia. The change to an atheistic and communistic government made it difficult for evangelical churches to maintain themselves. From 1923 to 1929 many of the Mennonite Brethren migrated to Canada; others later found a new home in South America. We can hardly speak of a functioning M.B. Church in Russia since 1929.

II. *The Mennonite Brethren Church in North America.*

1. *The Settlement of the Mennonite Brethren in North America.* When the government of Russia instituted universal military service in 1870, the Mennonites, who had thus far enjoyed complete exemption from such service, were in danger of losing their privileges. The government had decreed that Mennonite settlers should be under obligation to render such service beginning with 1880. Though this order was later modified so that Mennonite young men could substitute work in the forestry department instead, many decided to emigrate to America. In 1874 this emigration to the New World set in, and in the decade which followed many Mennonites left Russia to establish their home in the United States, settling mainly in Kansas, Nebraska, Minnesota, and Dakota. No M.B. members settled in Canada at this time. They were not able to form closed settlements in America, as they had done in Russia, but they were fortunate in pro-

curing vast stretches of fertile farm land in the Middle West, where they established themselves in large settlements. Through industry and thrift they managed to found their homes and at the same time took care of their spiritual needs. Worship services were at first held in homes and in schoolhouses, and as soon as possible they erected church buildings.

Among these immigrants were about 200 M.B. families, though most of these were not in the first groups which came. Several families settled in Harvey and Reno counties, Kan., in 1874, and others came into this community later. This group established the Ebenezer congregation, east of Buhler, the first M.B. congregation in America. A large congregation, the Ebenfeld M.B. Church, began in Marion Co., Kan., in 1875. Similar congregations had their beginning in Kansas at this time in Goessel and Lehigh, and a little later in Hillsboro and Marion. The one at Marion joined the German Baptists in 1895.

A congregation known as the Henderson M.B. Church began in York and Hamilton counties, Neb., in 1876. This grew rapidly and was for some time one of the largest M.B. churches in America. Several smaller congregations began in Nebraska, one in Boone County, which continued only a few years, and one at Jansen, which has recently discontinued. Of the Mennonite Brethren coming from the Volga settlement in Russia, congregations were established at Eldorado, Sutton, Hastings, and Culbertson, Neb. Of these only the one at Culbertson has continued to the present.

Among the Mennonites settling in Cottonwood Co., Minn., 1875-76, were several members of the M.B. Church. These began their own services and started a congregation. Through baptism of new converts and the coming of later immigrants a church of more than 100 members grew up in a few years. This church was for many years one of the largest in the M.B. constituency. It was long centered in the rural community at Bingham Lake, but has ultimately developed into the two congregations, Mountain Lake and Carson.

An M.B. congregation began in Turner Co., S.D., in 1876, which is today known as the Dolton or Silver Lake M.B. Church. Several other groups of M.B. members settled in other parts of South Dakota and began services, but these have not materialized into permanent congregations.

2. *The Establishment of the Mennonite Brethren Church.* In the establishment of the Mennonite Brethren Church the local congregation fulfilled a very important spiritual function. As a rule the members came from homes marked by simplicity, piety, and religious fervor, where daily worship in the family was kept up. Church services were therefore usually also well attended. The Sunday morning church service in early years consisted of hearty congregational singing, a short prayer service led by a lay brother, and two sermons by ministers. The Sunday school, which was instituted almost immediately, was for many years conducted on Sunday afternoon. Christian young people's societies began in the larger congregations in 1898. These societies have proved to be of immense value in occupying

the young people and keeping them attached to the church. Church choirs began at the same time, and worship in song occupied an important place in services. The use of musical instruments in church began some time later.

The M.B. Church has held to the plurality of ministers until recently and in many places still does. In early years the presiding minister of a larger congregation held the position of elder (now discontinued) and was assisted by other ministers and by deacons. Ministers as well as deacons were elected from the ranks of the congregation by ballot and after they had proved themselves worthy of their office, were ordained. The ministry was not professional in the sense that it was trained in an institution or employed by the church for full-time service with a stipulated salary. These men usually made their living by farming, and only where need arose did the church give them some support. Their ministry, however, gave evidence of deep consecration to God, and their messages showed that they had attained a thorough knowledge of the Scriptures through constant study. They manifested a grave concern for the spiritual welfare of the individual members, and pastoral house to house visitation was much practiced by this type of ministry. In recent years many of the larger congregations have, however, selected and employed a full-time minister with a stipulated salary.

The M.B. Church in America apparently lacked strong leadership in the five years prior to 1879. In the following years, a number of outstanding men either came with later immigrating groups or emerged from the existing congregations. Among those who have had a leading part in establishing the church and who left their impress on it were Abraham Schellenberg, Cornelius Wedel, Johann Fath, and David Dyck in Kansas, J. J. Regier in Nebraska, Heinrich Voth in Minnesota, and Heinrich Adrian in South Dakota. These men stood out as the leadership of the church and of its activities for many years.

On Oct. 8-20, 1879, representative delegates from M.B. churches in Kansas, Nebraska, Minnesota, and South Dakota met at Henderson, Neb., and organized a conference. The purpose for organizing was to build up the churches in their spiritual life, to give united expression to the position the church holds on various points, and to work unitedly in the various church activities. Such a general conference was held annually 1879-1909, and since then triennially. These conferences have been a very important factor in the upbuilding of the M.B. Church and in the furtherance of its various activities.

3. *The Growth and Spread of the Mennonite Brethren Church.* To show the growth and spread of the M.B. Church during its 75 years of history in North America, the time may conveniently be divided into three periods of equal length. In 1874-99 the church had not only established itself in the localities already mentioned but it also spread into new areas. Through effective home mission work on the part of the conference, a congregation materialized near Winkler, Man., in 1888. This was the first one in Canada and it grew into one of the largest in the conference. Through new settlements of Mennonite

Brethren coming from the United States, several small congregations began in the region west of Rosthern, Sask., about 1895. In this area the churches of Dalmeny, Hepburn, Bruderfeld, Waldheim, Laird, Neu-Hoffnung, Aberdeen, and Borden developed. There were at this time also the beginnings of churches in North Dakota (McClusky, Munich, Harvey, and Sawyer), Colorado (Joes and Denver), Texas (Premont, Los Ebanos, and missions Grulla and Chihuahua), and Oregon (Dallas and Salem). The most noted expansion was, however, in Oklahoma, where the government opened vast tracts of land for homesteads, and many young farmers from M.B. churches in Kansas and Nebraska settled on these lands. Churches sprang up at Corn, Gotebo, Okeene, Süd-Hoffnungsfeld near Isabella, Nord-Hoffnungsfeld near Fairview, North Enid, and Medford.

Statistics for this period are meager. The earliest ones published appeared in *Zionsbote* for 1888 (No. 2) and are quoted by P. M. Friesen (in *Brüderschaft*). These give the following figures: churches and places of worship 18, total church membership 1,266, elders 7, ordained ministers and deacons 29, unordained ministers and deacons 23. Toward the close of the 19th century the membership of the M.B. Church in America was probably a little over 2,000.

During the period 1899-1924 the church continued to increase steadily in numbers and to spread into further new areas. A Mennonite settlement in Southern Saskatchewan, centered at Herbert, led to the formation of a cluster of congregations, among which the larger ones were Herbert, Main Centre, Bethania, Green Farm, Elim, and Woodrow. Through new settlements in Montana, M.B. congregations began at Lustre, Volt, Larslan, and Chinook. In Michigan two small congregations began, which later discontinued. Churches also began at Paxton, Neb., at Hooker and Boyd in western Oklahoma, and at Collinsville and Inola in eastern Oklahoma. Several further congregations also began in California, among which the principal ones are Reedley, Orland, Lodi, Shafter, Rosedale, Bakersfield, Los Angeles, and Escondido. The total membership of the M.B. Church in 1924 stood at 8,422.

The period 1924-49 shows a very rapid growth of the M.B. Church in Canada. This increase was mainly due to the immigration of many Mennonites from Russia, 1923-30. Among them a fair percentage were Mennonite Brethren. These either joined existing M.B. congregations or formed new ones where they settled. At present the M.B. Church is well represented with congregations in the provinces of Ontario, Manitoba, Saskatchewan, Alberta, and British Columbia, and in each of these provinces they are organized into provincial conferences. Through this influx from Russia the church not only gained in numbers, but also received some strong leaders, able ministers, and well-qualified teachers, who have contributed much toward the spiritual welfare and the educational advance of the church. Leading congregations in Canada are in Winnipeg, Kitchener, Vineland, Coaldale, Abbotsford, Sardis.

In the United States the M.B. Church shows a steady growth during this time, but not a noted spread into further new territory. Here its constituency is composed of three district conferences: the Central District Conference comprising the congregations in Minnesota, North Dakota, South Dakota, Nebraska, and Montana; the Southern District Conference comprising those of Kansas, Oklahoma, Texas, and Colorado; and the Pacific District Conference comprising those of California, Oregon, and Washington.

The total membership of the M.B. Church, according to the statistics compiled by A. A. Schroeter, as of Jan. 1, 1948, was 19,169. Of these, 9,500 represent 59 local churches in the United States, and 9,579 the 83 congregations in Canada. In 1954 the the total was 24,136, with 11,930 in the United States in 65 congregations, and 12,206 in Canada in 81 congregations.

4. *The Doctrinal Position and Organization of the Mennonite Brethren Church.* The Mennonite Brethren Church has from the beginning held to the verbal and plenary inspiration of the Holy Scriptures, and it expects its members to conform to teachings of Scripture in faith and in conduct. The Confession of Faith as adopted in 1902 is intended to give a brief summarized statement of faith as understood to be the teaching of the Scriptures. The M.B. Church holds to the teachings and practices generally held by Mennonites. Participation in military service is forbidden. Conversion, in which the individual repents from sin and in faith accepts Jesus Christ as his personal Saviour, is regarded as essential for salvation and for membership in the church. The immersion form of baptism is required and no other form permitted. The Holy Communion service is observed and the washing of saints' feet is practiced. In the congregations of the United States an almost complete change has come from the use of the German language in worship services to that of the English, while in Canada German is mostly held to.

The General M.B. Conference has remained the channel through which the church as a whole maintained its organization, defined its position on doctrine and practice, and conducted its activities. In 1900 the Conference drew up a charter in order to incorporate itself under the state law of Kansas. In 1908 it framed a constitution to regulate its activities. This constitution was thoroughly revised in 1936 and was enlarged to cover the newer department of conference activities. According to the provisions in this constitution, the spiritual welfare of the church is supervised by the Committee of Reference and Counsel; its property and funds are taken care of by the Board of Trustees; the various phases of activity, such as foreign missions, city missions, publication, education, relief, Sunday school, and youth interests, are directed by the respective boards elected by the conference for this purpose. The General M.B. Conference has been meeting once every three years since 1909, when it elects its officers and boards and provides for the continuation of its work. The three district conferences in the United States and the Canadian conference convene annually and they confine themselves mainly to their home mission program, to care for the churches in their respective areas, and to matters of local interest. In addition there are provincial conferences in Canada which meet annually.

5. *The Activities of the Mennonite Brethren Church.* The M.B. Church has from its very beginning had a warm heart for missions and has to the present regarded these as its most important form of activity. The constituency has usually been liberal in its contributions for this purpose, many young people have consecrated themselves for this service.

Home missions, until 1909 conducted by the General M.B. Conference and since then by the district conferences, have been basic in the activity of the church. This work consisted in arranging and holding prolonged evangelistic meetings in the congregations and in neglected communities. Such meetings often resulted in revivals and conversions and largely account for the rapid increase of the church. Extension work among Russians in North Dakota, Saskatchewan, and later also in other parts of Canada, resulted in the formation of several Russian M.B. congregations. Work among Mexicans in Oklahoma and in Texas has resulted in conversions among these people and in the beginning of congregations. A number of other new churches and mission projects have been started, an indication that home mission work is expanding.

A city mission under the direction of the General M.B. Conference has been conducted at Minneapolis, Minn., since 1910. In 1948 the City Mission Board also began a mission among the Jews in Winnipeg, Man. A number of city missions are carried on by the several district conferences.

The M.B. Church in North America has from its early years felt a special urge to do foreign mission work. In 1884 it began to send financial support to missions with which it was acquainted and continued this for 14 years. A Foreign Missions Committee was appointed by the Conference in 1889 which was instructed to find a mission field among the North American Indians and to look for suitable workers. This plan was carried out in 1894 when a mission to the Comanche Indian tribe in southern Oklahoma was begun. A mission to the Telugus of the Hyderabad State in Southern India was established in 1899 and the Conference has since taken over mission fields in Southern China, Western China, Belgian Congo, Africa, and in Paraguay, Brazil, and Colombia, South America. In all 137 missionaries have been sent forth and supported by the M.B. Conference. Besides these many have gone out and worked in other missions. The Foreign Missions financial statement for the fiscal year ending Oct. 1, 1948, shows the total receipts to be $256,602.22; the disbursements for the same period are $255,952.91.

The M.B. Church began its publication activities in 1884, when the conference elected a committee of three to arrange for the editing and printing of a church paper. This resulted in the founding of the *Zionsbote* (*q.v.*) in 1885 with J. F. Harms as editor. At first this periodical appeared quarterly, since 1886 monthly, and since 1899 weekly. It is still the M.B. church organ and is printed mainly in the German language. J. F. Harms began an M.B. Publishing

House at Medford, Okla., in 1898. The press was moved to McPherson, Kan., in 1907 where the church established a publishing house under the management of A. L. Schellenberg, who also became editor of the *Zionsbote* at that time. In 1912 the conference transferred its publishing interests to Hillsboro, Kan., where it erected a publishing house in 1913. P. H. Berg served as business manager 1929-48. The *Christian Leader* (*q.v.*) was published in English as a monthly paper 1936-48 and since then twice a month. In Canada the *Mennonitische Rundschau* (*q.v.*) serves as an unofficial church organ for Canada. The *Konferenz-Jugendblatt* (1945-) serves as the official youth organ for Canada. The *Mennonite Observer* (1955-) is the Canadian English paper.

The M.B. Church early realized the need of establishing its own school to provide Biblical instruction as well as general education for her young people. This sentiment was expressed at the conference in 1883. In 1884 J. F. Harms began a private school at Canada, Kan., which provided elementary instruction in German, English, and Bible. A school association (*Schulverein*) took over this school in 1886 and continued it at Lehigh, Kan., two years longer. A similar school was begun at Buhler, Kan., a little later with J. F. Duerksen as teacher. The M.B. Conference undertook its first project in education at McPherson in 1899, when by arrangement with the faculty and board of trustees of McPherson College it began a German Department School in the college building. This school was under the direction of J. F. Duerksen and continued until 1904. From the students of these early schools came a number of outstanding leaders, evangelists, ministers, missionaries, educators, and other workers of the M.B. Church, such as M. M. Just, J. H. Pankratz, D. F. Bergthold, F. J. Wiens, H. W. Lohrenz, H. S. Voth, and others.

In the winter of 1907-8 a school association was organized among members of the M.B. Church and members of the K.M.B. Church. This association established Tabor College at Hillsboro as a Christian college to meet the educational needs of the two churches. The school began its first term of instruction in the fall of 1908 with H. W. Lohrenz, P. C. Hiebert, and P. P. Rempel as teaching staff. These were soon joined by D. E. Harder and H. F. Toews. Tabor College continued under the direction of the association until 1933, when it was taken over by the M.B. General Conference, which has since operated the institution through its Board of Education. The college has provided training for many useful workers of the church.

Though the educational interests of the M.B. Church have largely centered in Tabor College since 1908, other institutions have likewise contributed toward the education and training of many of her young people. Among those in the United States are Corn Bible School and Academy, Corn, Okla.; Immanuel Bible School and Academy, Reedley, Cal.; Pacific Bible Institute, Fresno, Cal. In Canada M.B. churches established Bible schools at Herbert, Sask., Winkler, Man., Hepburn, Sask., and Coaldale, Alberta. In 1948 there were nine Bible schools and five church high schools serving the constituency of the Canadian M.B. Church. In 1944 the Canadian M.B. Conference established M.B. Bible College, Winnipeg, Man., for training ministers, evangelists, Bible school teachers, and missionaries. In 1955 the Mennonite Brethren Biblical Seminary was established by the Board of Education at Fresno, Cal., as the official seminary of the church. Meanwhile the Pacific Bible Institute, founded in 1943 as a two-year institute, had grown into a four-year Bible College.

The M.B. Church has carried out an extensive program of relief work for many years, under the direction of its Board of Relief and General Welfare. In its foreign relief effort and in rehabilitation this Board is affiliated with the MCC, and P. C. Hiebert served as chairman 1920-57.

During World War II many young men of the M.B. Church were drafted for service. Of these a large number agreed to do only Civilian Public Service. The M.B. Church, in collaboration with other Mennonite bodies, participated in caring for their spiritual nurture and meeting their needs in camp.

III. *The Mennonite Brethren Church in Other Lands.*

I. *India.* The Mennonite Brethren Church has been transplanted to India through foreign mission effort. The M.B. Church in Russia sent its first missionary, Abraham Friesen, to India in 1890 and a mission was begun among the Telugus in the southeastern part of the Hyderabad State. Since this work was affiliated with the American Baptist Telugu Mission, the resultant indigenous church was Baptist and with the discontinuance of the M.B. Mission from Russia, when World War I broke out in 1914, the whole work was taken over by the Baptist Mission.

The American M.B. Church sent its first missionary, N. N. Hiebert, to India in 1899 and a mission was begun among the Telugus in the southern part of the Hyderabad State, west of the field worked by the Brethren from Russia. In this field, which has from time to time been enlarged so that it now covers an area of 10,000 square miles having a population of 1,500,000, the work has greatly prospered. The conference has, since the beginning of the mission, sent 46 missionaries to this field and has eight main mission stations, where it operates the work. Evangelism has been strongly emphasized in the mission and has occupied the major part of the missionaries' time and effort. An indigenous church has sprung up, known as the "Andhra Mennonite Brethren Church," which now totals over 12,000 communicant members. This church holds to the doctrinal principles of the American M.B. Church and is similar in organization and church polity. The membership of the whole constituency is composed of 57 local churches. In each of the eight station-fields these churches are organized into a "field association." All the churches of the whole mission area are organized into a convention, which corresponds to the M.B. Conference in the homeland. This convention bears the name "Andhra Mennonite Brethren Convention," and holds its meetings annually.

2. *China.* The M.B. Church entered China through its missionaries. Several members of the M.B. Church labored as missionaries in the Mennonite

Mission in Shantung and Honan province, China. This mission was of an inter-Mennonite constituency and the resultant indigenous church was consequently also of a similar type. In 1911 F. J. Wiens opened an M.B. mission among the Hakkas at Shanghang, Fukien Province, South China. As this work continued to prosper, the M.B. Conference took over the mission in 1919 and sent additional missionaries to this field. Though the work could be carried on only with much interruption, due to revolution in the land on account of which all the missionaries had to leave the field in 1929, a promising indigenous church came into existence, which at one time numbered over 500 members. In 1949 one missionary family was still working in this field and there was still an indigenous church which showed signs of growth. In 1945 the M.B. Conference took steps to establish a mission in the provinces Kansu and Shensi, West China. Missionaries were sent to this area and work was begun. An indigenous M.B. Church from Chinese converts was established. All missionaries were forced out of China by the Communist government by 1952.

3. *Belgian Congo, Africa.* In 1924 A. A. Janzen began a mission among the Negro tribes in the southwestern part of the Belgian Congo, locating the station at Kafumba, Kwango District. H. G. Bartsch began a mission at Bololo, Dengese Province, about 400 miles northeast of Kafumba, in 1933. Both of these missions began independently of the M.B. Conference. In 1943 the General M.B. Conference took over the responsibility of the two missions in Africa and sent additional missionaries to the field. The station at Bololo was shifted to Djongo Sanga, a more suitable location, and in 1949 this field was given over to a neighboring mission. In the Kwango District the work has expanded and three mission stations have been established. Besides aggressive evangelism, schools are conducted, hospital work is carried on, and the printing of Christian literature in the vernacular is done. An indigenous church from the African converts is organized, which numbers over 2,000 communicant members.

4. *Paraguay, South America.* Displaced Russian Mennonites emigrated to Paraguay by way of Germany, Poland, and China in 1930-32 and founded the colonies Fernheim and Friesland in the Chaco of Paraguay. Among these were members of the Mennonite Brethren Church who organized themselves as congregations and established places of worship at six centers. These have a total church membership of over 800. With the further immigration beginning 1947 the colonies Volendam and Neuland were established. Among these were likewise some Mennonite Brethren, who organized themselves into congregations. These number about 500 members.

In 1935 the Mennonites of Paraguay organized among themselves a Mission Society and began a mission to the Lengua tribe of Indians, who lived in their vicinity. Since the colonists struggled with poverty in their pioneer days, they appealed to Mennonites in other lands for the support of this mission. Contributions for this purpose soon came from the M.B. Church in North America, and in 1937 mission workers from there arrived and joined in the work.

The North American M.B. Conference was approached and asked to take over the responsibility and supervision of the mission. This was done in 1946, and since then missionaries have come partly from North America and partly from Paraguay. The financial support comes mainly through the Board of Foreign Missions of the North American M.B. Church. Some of the Lengua Indians have professed faith in Christ and have been baptized. An indigenous church is in its beginning stages.

5. *Brazil, South America.* In 1930-32 displaced Mennonites from Russia made two settlements in southern Brazil, one near Curitiba, Parana State, and the other in the Krauel, St. Catharina State. Among these were members of the M.B. Church, who united themselves into local churches. These numbered 450 members in 1948. The M.B. churches in Brazil united into a conference in 1948. The same year this conference was admitted into the General M.B. Conference of North America as a district conference. In 1945 the North American M.B. Church took steps to begin a mission in Curitiba, Brazil, and accepted and sent there the first missionaries. This mission has materialized into an orphanage and school and is in part supported by the churches in Brazil. The Krauel Colony dissolved 1949-52, and a new colony was established at Bage, Rio Grande du Sul, almost entirely of M.B. members.

6. *Colombia, South America.* The North American M.B. Church began a mission in the northern part of Colombia in 1945. The field touches the Atlantic in the North and the Pacific in the southwest. Its western part is largely an elevated tableland, while the eastern part, known as the Chaco, is a vast lowland plain. The mission has established three stations and work is being done partly among the regular Colombian nationals, partly among the Negroes of the Chaco, and recently work has also begun among the Indian tribes. Several converts have received baptism and an indigenous church has begun. J.H.L.

Friesen, *Brüderschaft;* P. Regier *Kurzgefasste Geschichte der Mennoniten Brüder-Gemeinde* (Berne, 1901); J. F. Harms, *Geschichte der Mennoniten Brüdergemeinde 1860-1924* (Hillsboro, n.d., ca. 1924); *Glaubensbekenntnis der Vereinigten Taufgesinnten Mennonitischen Brüdergemeinde in Russland* (Halbstadt, 1902); Year Books of the General Conference of the Mennonite Brethren Church in North America; J. H. Lohrenz, *The Mennonite Brethren Church* (Hillsboro, 1950); H. J. Wiens, *The Mennonite Brethren Churches of North America, An Illustrated Survey* (Hillsboro, 1954); G. W. Peters, *The Growth of Foreign Missions in the Mennonite Brethren Church* (Hillsboro, 1952); Mrs. H. T. Esau, *First Sixty Years of Mennonite Brethren Missions* (Hillsboro, 1954); ML III, 102-6; A. H. Unruh, *Die Geschichte der Mennoniten-Brüdergemeinde 1860-1954* (Winnipeg, 1954).

Mennonite Brethren Collegiate Institute, a church high school, was established in September 1945 in Winnipeg, Man., in a few rooms in the building of the M.B. Bible College. In 1947 it erected its own building. Up to 1956 the school had a total enrollment of 1,042 students, of whom 226 had been graduated. In 1955-56, 163 students were enrolled. In 1955-56 grades seven and eight were added. The principals have been Henry Wall, Gerhard Lehrenz, William Neufeld, A. K. Dürksen, and Victor Adrian. H.S.B.

Mennonite Brethren Home for the Aged, Inc., located in Reedley, Cal., founded in 1942, is operated and owned by the Pacific District Conference and managed by a committee, of which H. R. Martens has been the chairman since its origin. The present capacity (1954) is 48 and the personnel consists of 16. A. R. and Kathryn Jost are the house parents. (*Yearbook of the Pacific District Conference of the M.B. Ch. of N.A., 1942-54.*)   C.K.

Mennonite Brethren in Christ Church was the name from 1883 to 1947 of a religious denomination which since the latter date has been called the United Missionary Church (*q.v.*). It was formed on Dec. 29, 1883, by the union of two bodies, the Evangelical United Mennonite (*q.v.*), and a Brethren in Christ group in Ohio, known as the Swankites, who had separated from their mother body in 1828. The Evangelical United Mennonites in turn had been formed in 1879 by a union of the Evangelical Mennonites (*q.v.*) of Pennsylvania (formed in 1857 from the Oberholtzer group (later General Conference Mennonites) and the United Mennonites (*q.v.*). The latter group had been formed in 1875 from two groups in Ontario—the Reformed Mennonites (organized in 1874) and the New Mennonites, a scattered group which had its origin about 1860. Daniel Brenneman, who had been expelled from the Indiana Conference of the Mennonite Church (MC) in 1874, had joined the Reformed group with his followers. It was this Ontario-Indiana-Ohio group which formed the backbone of the M.B.C. from the beginning and continued to form the heart and majority of the United Missionary Church. The outstanding early leaders of the M.B.C. were Elder Daniel Brenneman (1834-1919) and Elder Solomon Eby (1834-1930), Waterloo Co., Ont., who however left the group to join the Pentecostal movement in 1912.

The organized work of the M.B.C. really got under way about 1879-80. Brenneman established the conference organ, the *Gospel Banner*, in 1878. The earliest foreign missionary, Eusebius Hershey, went out to Liberia in 1890, with private support to be sure, but organized foreign mission work was in operation long before the United Missionary Society was established in 1920. The first camp meeting, an institution which has been a powerful spiritual influence in the group, was held at Fetter's Grove, west of Goshen, Ind., in 1880. The Reading Course for Ministers was first adopted in 1882. The first home mission was established in Grand Rapids, Mich., in 1880.

In 1883 when the M.B.C. Church was formed, the three district conferences had the following statistics: Ontario, 43 appointments (congregations and mission points) with 909 members; Pennsylvania, 14 appointments with 286 members; Indiana-Ohio-Michigan, 22 appointments with 452 members, a total of 79 appointments with 1,647 members. In 1947, when the new name (United Missionary Church) was adopted and before the schism of the Pennsylvania conference, the total membership was 13,313, with congregations in Michigan, Iowa, Nebraska, Washington, and Alberta, in addition to the original locations.

The Mennonite Brethren in Christ Church represented in its beginning a breaking forth of new life in the Mennonite brotherhood, with emphasis upon evangelism and aggressive work, conversion and Christian experience with a warm, rather emotional piety, and a stronger supervisory organization. Actually it was the invasion of a Methodistic type of piety and sanctification or holiness emphasis (entire sanctification, second work of grace) with a Methodistic church organization with district superintendents and well-organized conferences. All this was in strong contrast to the slower moving, more stolid type of piety and less organized church polity of the Mennonite Church (MC), from which the Ontario and Indiana groups had come. The sense of distance between the new and the old groups has therefore been great, and no fraternization or rapprochement has ever taken place. In fact, although the traditional Mennonite distinctive principles and practices were taken over by the new group and long maintained, such as nonresistance and nonconformity, and feetwashing, these points have gradually received less emphasis, and the decision in 1947 to change the name to drop the name "Mennonite" is an index of a substantial move away from the historic Mennonite anchorage. The name Mennonite was finally felt to be a handicap because of its associations. Daniel Brenneman, however, before he died in 1919, is reported to have stated that if he had known that the old church would change so much and so rapidly into a more progressive pattern, he would never have left it.

Since the doctrines, practices, and church polity of the M.B.C. Church are carried forward in the United Missionary Church, its lineal continuing body, a report on these points will be given in the article on the latter body.   H.S.B.

J. A. Huffman, *History of the Mennonite Brethren in Christ Church* (New Carlisle, Ohio, n.d., 1920); *The Test of Time,* Indiana Conference 75th Anniversary booklet; *Doctrines and Discipline of the Mennonite Brethren in Christ,* editions of 1883, 1888, 1897, 1910, and 1916, et seq.; *ML* III, 96.

Mennonite Brethren in Christ Church *of Pennsylvania* is the body which continued the denominational name after the General Conference of the M.B.C. on Nov. 3, 1947, changed its name to United Missionary Church (*q.v.*). The group, formerly the Pennsylvania Conference of the M.B.C., has had a continuing organized existence since 1857, when it separated from the Oberholtzer (GCM) group and called itself the Evangelical Mennonites (*q.v.*). Although the 1947 M.B.C. General Conference voted a paragraph of the name-changing resolution which says, "One Annual Conference, the Pennsylvania, did not concur in the necessity for the present change in the church name, and was voted full and unqualified relationship to the General Conference of the body, while it continues to use the name Mennonite Brethren in Christ," the separation was in fact complete and the Pennsylvania Conference no longer sends delegates or exercises any fraternal relations to the General Conference of the U.M.C. Thus one of the component parts of the U.M.C. body, which had merged with the United Mennonite Church (at a special conference on Nov. 6, 1879, at

Upper Milford, Pa., when it had nine congregations with 175 members) to form the Evangelical United Mennonites, withdrew after 68 years of collaboration and reverted to independent status. The basic causes for the separation in 1947 were differences in polity and administration, but there was apparently also a doctrinal difference. The Pennsylvania Conference had gradually accepted a degree of Calvinist theology, particularly the doctrine of eternal security, whereas the rest of the U.M.C. continued on its original Arminian basis, with the emphasis on the "second work of grace." However, for some years the fellowship had become increasingly less close, with practically no interchange of ministers. The Pennsylvania Conference had long had its own independent foreign and home mission boards and Bible school.

At the time of the separation in 1947 the Pennsylvania Conference had 38 congregations (officially called "appointments"), each with a responsible pastor, organized into two districts with district superintendent, the Allentown and Bethlehem districts, with 2,340 and 2,177 baptized members respectively, in addition to work in six appointments under the Home Mission Society and 22 missionaries, with 88 additional members, for a total of 4,605 members. In 1955 the Conference had 4,635 members. All of the congregations are in Eastern Pennsylvania except three in New Jersey (Jersey City, Newark, and Staten Island), which have a total of 337 members.

The Conference has an extensive series of subsidiary organizations: Board of Foreign Missions (which supports M.B.C. missionaries under other boards but operates no foreign work itself), the Board of Home Missions and the Home Missionary Society, the Board of Publications and Printing, the Board of Education, which has operated the Berean Bible School in Allentown, Pa., since 1950, the Beneficiary Society, the Home and Farm at Center Valley, Pa., the Laymen's Benevolent Society, the Ministers' Retirement Fund, the Menno Youth General Committee, and several annual Camp Meetings, Sunday School Conventions, and an annual Ministerial Convention.

The conference is thoroughly organized, is aggressively evangelistic, fundamentalistic, and premillennial in doctrinal emphasis, and emphasizes a warm type of piety. It recognizes the nonresistant position, but not many of its young men take the CO position and there is no conference discipline on this point. It maintains the practice of footwashing and baptism by immersion.

The Conference has never had its own periodical organ, but beginning with March 7, 1953, it has had a four-page weekly news supplement to the *Gospel Herald* published by the Union Gospel Press at Cleveland, Ohio. The Conference has long had a friendly relation to this publishing house and its periodical, the publishing house having been founded by a leading minister of the Conference, W. B. Musselman. The Conference long used its Sunday-school helps. The Conference publishes a yearbook of approximately 120 pages with comprehensive reports.

Candidates for the ministry in the Conference must serve a probationary period of three years un-

der license, must pass a three-year reading course, and serve one year successfully as pastor before being ordained. In 1953 the Conference was supporting 35 foreign missionaries, with receipts of $52,361.25.   H.S.B.

Mennonite Brethren in Christ Publication Society. The Mennonite Brethren in Christ Church as a conference owned a printing establishment from 1879 on, previously owned by the United Mennonite Conference. The first office and shop were at Goshen, Ind. It published the English and German editions of the *Gospel Banner,* and was administered by a managing committee. The 1879 conference elected a publishing committee of six, three each from Ontario and Indiana. In 1879 a bookstore was added, which operated under the firm name of United Evangelical Mennonite Publication Society. In 1885 the name was changed to M.B.C. Publication Society to correspond with the change in conference name, and the conference printing plant was moved to Kitchener (then Berlin), Ont. Since the name of the Publication Society apparently never appeared on the masthead of the conference organ, the *Gospel Banner,* as publisher it must not have carried any responsibility for the paper as publisher, although the conference raised funds to support the rather precarious enterprise. Private persons or Gospel printing companies were contracted by the conference as publishers; H. S. Hallman of Kitchener filled this role for most of the twenty years 1888-1908. The statements regarding the publisher of the *Gospel Banner* in H. S. Bender's *Two Centuries of American Mennonite Literature* (1929, pp. 128 f.) are erroneous.

The name of the Publication Society appeared as publisher on the title pages of the conference disciplines published in 1880 (Goshen), in 1888 (Berlin), and in 1897 (Berlin), and also of the conference hymnal (*A Choice Collection,* Goshen) in 1881.   H.S.B.

Mennonite Brethren Publishing House, the official publishing house of the Conference of the Mennonite Brethren Church of North America, had its inception in 1904 in Medford, Okla. Before this time the *Zionsbote,* the official organ of the Mennonite Brethren Conference, had been issued since 1884 with J. F. Harms as editor. Printing of this periodical had been done in Elkhart, Ind., in Canada, Kan., McPherson, Kan., and Medford, Okla., Editor Harms having resided at the latter three places.

At the 1903 conference the decision was reached to purchase a conference printing plant in Hillsboro. The churches were to raise the money for this purchase within 30 days. Sentiment in the churches, however, showed that they would rather establish a new conference publishing house; consequently J. F. Harms purchased machinery and a suitable building in Medford, where he resided at the time. Thus the Mennonite Brethren Publishing House was begun. Here the *Zionsbote, Lektionsblaetter,* and *Golos,* a periodical in the Russian language, and other publications were produced. In 1906, since Harms was unable to continue as editor and manager of the new publishing house, the conference decided to move the business to McPherson. This was done and A. L. Schellenberg became the new editor and manager.

Early in 1913 a printing establishment was purchased in Hillsboro, Kan., and the entire business was moved here. Through this purchase the *Vorwaerts,* a weekly paper, was acquired. In 1939 this became the *Hillsboro Journal* and in 1953 it was amalgamated with another local paper. In 1915 a large building was constructed to house the printing and publishing plant, and modern equipment was installed. In 1922 a complete bookstore was added. A major addition to the building was completed in 1950. Other additions and equipment have been added from time to time.

A. L. Schellenberg continued to serve as editor and manager 1907-27, with the exception of 1919-22. P. H. Berg was manager in 1930-48 and editor 1951-53. Others who have served in leading positions for shorter periods of time are J. D. Fast, A. J. Voth, and J. J. Gerbrandt. Orlando Harms has served as editor and manager since 1954.

Since 1936 English Sunday-school quarterlies and the *Christian Leader,* an English Conference periodical, have been produced in addition to the above-named German publications. In addition to these, many books, pamphlets, and much job work has been produced throughout the years. In 1953 and 1954 two editions of the *Mennonite Brethren Church Hymnal,* the first official songbook of the denomination, were produced.

The Mennonite Brethren Publishing House is the property of the Conference of the Mennonite Brethren Church of North America and is controlled by the Publication Board, part of which is elected at each triennial general conference. The size of this board has varied through the years but at present it consists of seven members who represent the various districts of the Conference.   O.HA.

Mennonite Broadcasts, Inc., a subsidiary operating agency of the Mennonite Board of Missions and Charities (MC) and controlled by it, was established in 1956 as successor to Mennonite Crusaders, Inc. (*q.v.*). Headquarters and studio are located at 1111 North Main Street, Harrisonburg, Va., where a full-time staff of seven to ten persons is at work. The officers in 1957 were Lewis Strite chairman, Daniel Suter vice-chairman, Richard Weaver secretary, Harley Rhodes treasurer, all of Harrisonburg. The mission board controls the agency by recommending and approving members of the board of directors. Broadcasts in 1956 were *The Mennonite Hour, Luz y Verdad* (Spanish, originating in Puerto Rico), *Menonaito Awa* (Japanese, originating in Japan), and Navaho Bible Hour (Arizona). The Heart to Heart program, a women's broadcast originating in Harrisonburg, is affiliated, though financed and administered independently. A European broadcast in several languages is to begin in 1957 (French, Italian, and possibly German and Russian). The mission board purchased the headquarters building in 1956. Mennonite Broadcasts is financed through voluntary contributions, largely received from the radio audience. It does not receive mission funds.

An extensive publishing program is also carried on, including the periodical publications, *Mennonite Broadcasts Informer* and *Prayer Calendar,* and booklets containing collections of radio sermons, as well as study booklets for the Bible correspondence which it conducts in English, Spanish, and Japanese.

In 1957 Mennonite Broadcasts was broadcasting over seventy stations in the United States and foreign countries. Of this number, fifty-six were in the United States, two in Canada; others were in Ceylon, Costa Rica, Ecuador, Jamaica, Liberia, Tangier, Panama, Philippines, Puerto Rico, and Viet-Nam.
      H.S.B.

Mennonite Brotherhood Aid Association of Bluffton, Ohio, was established in 1949 to serve General Conference Mennonites in the Bluffton-Pandora area with financial assistance (loans) on a mutual basis in establishing a modest home, getting an education, or getting a start in farming, business, or a profession. In 1954 it had 151 members with about $6,000 out on loan at $3\frac{1}{2}$ per cent interest.   H.S.B.

Mennonite Central Committee, the joint relief and service agency of nearly all North American Mennonites, was composed in 1957 of representatives of the following seventeen distinct Mennonite bodies or agencies (with years of adherence); viz., Mennonite (MC) 1920, General Conference Mennonite 1920, Mennonite Brethren 1920, Lancaster Conference (MC) 1920, Krimmer Mennonite Brethren 1920, Evangelical Mennonite (Defenceless) 1930, Church of God in Christ, Mennonite 1940, Brethren in Christ 1940, Conservative (Amish) Mennonite 1941, Old Order Amish Mennonite 1942, Evangelical Mennonite Brethren 1944, Nonresistant Relief Organization of Ontario 1944, Conference of Historic Peace Churches (Ontario) 1944, Mennonite Central Relief Committee of Western Canada 1944, Canadian Mennonite Relief Committee of Manitoba 1944, Canadian Mennonite Board of Colonization 1944, Beachy Amish Mennonite 1956. Since conferences are entitled to one representative for each 25,000 members or fraction thereof, the first two groups have two representatives each, and since there are two members-at-large, the total MCC membership in 1957 was 20. In addition there were three associate members, United Missionary Church (Indiana Conference) since 1930, the Missionary Church Association since 1940, and the Emmanuel Mennonite Church at Meade, Kan., since 1952. At the beginning, in 1920, two additional groups were represented, the Central Conference (merged in 1947 with the GCM group) and the Pacific Branch of the Relief Committee for the Suffering Mennonites of Russia (discontinued about 1925). The MCC was incorporated at Lancaster, Pa., on Aug. 27, 1937; before this it had no constitution or bylaws, operating solely on the basis of the authorizing resolution of July 27, 1920, which date may be considered as its date of origin at Elkhart.

The committee, which meets annually, operates through an executive committee elected by its annual meeting, at first composed of the three officers, enlarged in 1930 to four, in 1944 to five, in 1948 to six, which meets as frequently as necessary, averaging six meetings per year. The direct administration of all MCC work is through an executive secretary, who was Levi Mumaw at Scottdale, 1920-35, and then Orie O. Miller at Akron, near Lancaster, Pa., 1935-57. Since 1935 the executive headquarters has been at Akron, where the MCC in 1957 owned six office and residential buildings and employed an average staff of fifty. In addition the following regional offices were maintained with a total staff of ten: Waterloo, Ont., Newton, Kan., Reedley, Cal., each with a clothing and food center, besides the clothing and food center at Ephrata, Pa. Foreign centers, with owned or leased buildings, were maintained at Sao Paulo, Brazil; Montevideo, Uruguay (owned); Asuncion, Paraguay (owned); Kaiserslautern, Germany (owned); Frankfurt, Germany; Amsterdam, Holland; and Basel, Switzerland. The Ailsa Craig (Ontario) Boys Home was also owned property (since 1955). Three mental hospitals were owned and operated through an incorporated agency (Mennonite Mental Health Services): Brook Lane Farm near Hagerstown, Md., Kings View Homes at Reedley, and Prairie View Mental Hospital at Newton. The MCC also still owned considerable holdings (some 200,000 acres) near the Mennonite settlements in the Paraguayan Chaco through its purchase of Corporacion Paraguaya (q.v.) in 1937. The total net dollar assets of the MCC in 1957 were $1,900,000. Long-time office members and staff workers of the MCC have been P. C. Hiebert, chairman 1920-54, chairman emeritus 1954- ; O. O. Miller, member 1921- , executive secretary 1935-57; Levi Mumaw, executive secretary 1920-35; M. H. Kratz, vice-chairman 1920-39; H. S. Bender, assistant secretary 1930- ; H. A. Fast, vice-chairman 1943- ; C. F. Klassen, executive committee member 1944-54; J. J. Thiessen, executive committee member 1948- ; Allen Yoder, executive committee member 1920-30, 1934-44; D. M. Hofer, member 1920-44; John H. Mellinger, member 1920-36; H. F. Garber, member 1936-56; J. B. Martin, member 1944- ; J. N. Byler, director of relief 1945- ; William T. Snyder, director of Mennonite Aid 1945- , executive committee member 1954- ; J. Harold Sherk, executive secretary of the Peace Section 1949- ; Delmar Stahly, director of Mental Health Services 1949- .

In 1957 the MCC had worker teams in Holland, Germany, France, Austria, Switzerland, Greece, Jordan, Indonesia, India and Nepal, South Viet-Nam, Korea, Japan, Argentina, Paraguay, Uruguay, and Brazil. The Latin America projects were all in connection with the Mennonite refugee settlements made there in 1930 and since. Discontinued fields of service were England, Egypt, Italy, Hungary, Poland, Denmark, China, Formosa, Philippines, Puerto Rico, and Mexico.

Two departments of MCC service are organized as sections with membership bodies: the Peace Section (1947), successor to the Mennonite Central Peace Committee (1939), of which H. S. Bender has been the continuous chairman, and the Mennonite Aid Section (1943), of which J. W. Fretz has been the continuous chairman. Other important departments are Mennonite Mental Health Services, Inc. (1946 first form of organization), of which H. A. Fast was chairman to 1957; the Voluntary Service Office (1946) and the I-W Services Office (1952). The latter two were merged into one de-

partment in 1955. The Mennonite Resettlement Finance, Inc., a holding agency for certain Paraguay financing, was in existence 1948-55. Menno Travel Service, Inc., was set up as a subsidiary travel agency in 1947. It maintains a main office at Akron, subsidiary offices at Goshen, Newton, and in Europe at Amsterdam.

The MCC was originally created in July 1920 to operate a joint Mennonite famine relief program in Russia, requested by the several Mennonite relief committees of North America at that time engaged in sending aid to Mennonites in Russia. The Mennonite *Studienkommission* of four delegates from Russia, who were at that time visiting the United States and Canada, had strongly urged such a united organization. Upon completion of the active program in Russia (1920-25) the Committee intended to disband but did not formally do so. It was reactivated by the emergency of 1929-30 when the call came to aid several thousand Mennonite refugees who had come out of Russia into Germany October to November 1929. Its second task therefore was the resettlement of many of these refugees in Paraguay in 1930, since when it has continuously aided the colonies there, especially the Fernheim, Neuland, and Volendam colonies, which it originally sponsored. The third field of service was War Sufferers Relief during and following World War II, beginning in Poland in September 1939. The total program finally included work in twelve western and central European countries, including Egypt. This program was chiefly the distribution of food and clothing, and included community services and peace testimony. At the peak of the work (summer of 1947) 317 workers were simultaneously in service in Europe. The program in Jordan for Arab refugees was begun in 1950. The work in the Far East, with programs in eight countries, was begun with war emergency relief services in Bengal, India (creation of the inter-Mission organization Mennonite Relief Committee in India, MRCI), and entrance into China in 1945. Puerto Rico work began in 1943 in connection with CPS.

In all areas where Mennonite churches were located, especially in Europe, the MCC work led to close and fruitful interaction between North American and local Mennonites. Out of this interaction came among other things a monthly publication, *Der Mennonit,* published by the MCC at Basel in 1948-56 and later at Frankfurt (continued by a European Board), the European Mennonite Bible School at Basel (est. 1950) under an international Mennonite board, Mennonite Voluntary Service in Europe (1950) under a European Mennonite committee, the International Mennonite Peace Committee (1947), and the Christian Education Materials Project (CEMO) at Basel (1952).

The war emergency relief needs in Europe have almost disappeared (1957), so that the continuing MCC program in Europe is greatly reduced though still continuing in certain special services and in contact with European Mennonites. The relief program in the Far East (Korea, Indonesia, and South Viet-Nam in particular) was also reduced, but not so greatly as in Europe.

In the course of its relief effort the MCC became

a member of the following inter-group relief organizations sponsored by the United States State Department: American Council of Voluntary Agencies (1944), Council of Relief Agencies Licensed for Operation in Germany (Cralog, 1946), Licensed Agency for Relief in Asia (LARA, 1947), and Co-operative for American Remittances to Europe (CARE, 1945).

The fourth major field of MCC service was the operation of Civilian Public Service (*q.v.*) assumed in 1941. At this time the MCC also became a member of the National Service Board for Religious Objectors (NSBRO). The fifth field of service was the resettlement of Russian and Danzig Mennonite refugees after World War II, the former in Paraguay (4,849 persons in 1947-52) and the latter in Uruguay (1,184 persons 1948-52). Voluntary Service for young Mennonite in North America was begun in 1945 as the sixth field of service. The seventh field was that of Mental Health Service, begun in 1949 with the establishment of the mental hospital Brook Lane Farm at Leitersburg, Md. The eighth program was one of aid to the Old Colony Mennonites in Mexico (1950-56). The ninth and last new field was the I-W Service Program begun in 1952 with the renewal of the United States draft of conscientious objectors in that year, which had been suspended 1947-52.

In the course of its various activities the MCC has issued numerous publications—periodicals, books, and pamphlets. Some of the periodicals have been the monthly *MCC Services Bulletin* (1945-), the monthly *I-W Mirror* 1953-), and various area relief newsletters such as monthly *European Relief Notes* 1945-), the monthly *Der Mennonit* (1948-56), and the biweekly *Unser Blatt* (1947-50) at Gronau, Germany. Books issued have been: P. C. Hiebert and Orie O. Miller, *Feeding the Hungry. Russia Famine 1919-25* (1929); Melvin Gingerich, *Service for Peace, A History of Mennonite Civilian Public Service* (1949); Emily Brunk, *Espelkamp* (1951); John D. Unruh, *In the Name of Christ, A History of the Mennonite Central Committee and Its Service 1920-1951* (1953); J. Winfield Fretz, *Pilgrims in Paraguay, The Story of Mennonite Colonization in South America* (1953); *Proceedings of the Fourth Mennonite World Conference August 3-10, 1948* (1949).

The pamphlets and booklets issued have included a group of titles published by the Peace Section, another group by the Mennonite Aid Section, and the CPS "Core Course Booklets," and some individual titles. PEACE SECTION: Edward Yoder, *Must Christians Fight* (1943, German translation, *Sollen Christen sich an der Kriegsführung beteiligen,* 1949); *Peace Section Handbook with Draft Manual* (1942, later called *Manual of Draft Information*); Edward Yoder, *Compromise with War* (1944); Edward Yoder and Don. E. Smucker, *The Christian and Conscription* (1945); Howard Charles, *Before You Decide* (1948); Melvin Gingerich, *What of Noncombatant Service* (1949). MENNONITE AID SECTION: J. W. Fretz, *Mennonite Colonization* (1944); J. W. Fretz, *Mennonite Colonization in Mexico* (1945); J. W. Fretz, *Christian Mutual Aid* (1947); CORE COURSE BOOKLETS: *Mennonites and Their Heritage.*

A Series of Six Studies Designed for Use in Civilian Service Camps (1942) as follows—No. 1, H. S. Bender, *Mennonite Origin in Europe;* No. 2, C. Henry Smith, *Mennonites in America;* No. 3, Edward Yoder, *Our Mennonite Heritage;* No. 4, Ed. G. Kaufman, *Our Mission as a Church of Christ;* No. 5, G. F. Hershberger, *Christian Relationships to State and Community;* No. 6, P. C. Hiebert, *Life and Service in the Kingdom of God.* OTHER TITLES: *Twenty-five Years, the Story of the MCC 1920-1945;* M. C. Lehman, *The History and Principles of Mennonite Relief Work* (1945); Esko Loewen, Editor, *Mennonite Community Sourcebook* (1946); Irvin B. Horst, *A Ministry of Goodwill, An Account of Mennonite Relief Work Following World War II* (1950). The official MCC handbook appeared first in 1943 and 1945 as *Handbook of Information on the Mennonite Central Committee,* then under the title *Handbook of the Mennonite Central Committee* in editions of 1950 and 1954.

The size of MCC operations at the heights of its program may be indicated in part by a summary of the income during the five years Dec. 1, 1947, to Nov. 30, 1952: total income $9,239,601.73; War Sufferers Relief cash $2,008,276.24; War Sufferers Material Aid $5,242,153.33; Mennonite Aid $1,472,-636.39; Mental Health $207,588.92; Voluntary Service $136,303.29; Peace Section $79,305.24.

The following statements taken from the MCC *Handbook* (pp. 7-8, and 27-29) and prepared by Irvin Horst upon the basis of statements adopted at various times by the MCC and constituent bodies indicate the foundation of faith and commitment upon which the work of the MCC has been established and continued.

"In a very real sense the MCC is an organization which spontaneously grew out of the desire of the Mennonite brotherhood to feed the hungry, clothe the naked, and to testify by loving service to the Gospel of peace and love. This desire to respond with a witness of Christian peace and love grew in vision and compulsion as various emergencies were faced both within and without the brotherhood. Relief and peace services were an integral part of the Mennonite witness and way of life in the world. Where the various Mennonite and Brethren in Christ bodies retained their faith and ideals they were moved to remain firm in the position of nonresistance and to be energetic in showing mercy and love toward enemies as well as toward all mankind. To implement these compulsions they desired an organization to provide a channel for sharing their gifts and services 'In the Name of Christ.'"

"The experiences of relief and peace work during the past thirty-six years have indicated the wisdom of organizing a common agency to meet common emergencies and tasks, particularly when such emergencies were greater than any one group could have well performed alone. Through a common witness the various groups were able to speak as one voice against war and militarism; through a common representation the various bodies were able to reach and assist, as in no other way, the Mennonites in Russia, Holland, France, Germany, Switzerland, Brazil, Paraguay, Uruguay. What little the Mennonites of North America with their slender resources have been able to do for a suffering world was multiplied in effectiveness by co-operative administration of these resources, whether it was in Russia, France, India, China, or any of the other countries in which relief and peace services were expended.

"The Mennonite position regarding relief and service is a part of the particular Christian faith and way of life which has its background and origin in the Anabaptist movement of Reformation times. This movement, as others before and after, under the providence of God was a fresh and vital discovery of the living truth and spirit of the New Testament. The experience was so compellingly real that it sought an uncompromising fufillment of the Gospel in life; it was so powerful that it survived the most obliterating persecution, to persist down to our own times. This heritage, in so far as it still lives in the Mennonite bodies of North America, motivates and guides the service program of the Mennonite Central Committee. Its principles, if accepted and put into practice, become for us in our own time, we believe, a unique experience of fellowship with Christ in loving discipleship and service to others.

"*A. The Central Position and Authority of Christ and the Bible.* While recognizing the hand of God in history and the voice of the Holy Spirit in the experiences of the church and individual Christians, we accept the Bible, particularly the New Testament, as the final authority for faith and action. Relief and service have validity for us only as the motivation, spirit, and methods of work are in keeping with the Bible. We advocate voluntary and sacrificial service because it is enjoined by Christ and the apostles. We have confidence in the Bible as a guide to a realistic understanding of the place and work of the Christian in the world. While recognizing the tools of human training and learning, we believe the Bible is a reference to eternal truth which transcends all indefiniteness and obscurity of human thinking. 'If you seek God with all your heart and would not be deceived, do not depend upon men and the doctrine of men, however old, holy and excellent they may be esteemed, for one theologian is against the other, both in ancient and modern times; but build upon Christ and His Word alone, upon the sure teaching and practice of His holy apostles . . .' (Menno Simons).

"*B. The Christian Life as Discipleship.* The Christian life is a transformed life, separated from sin and the world and consecrated to good works in imitation of Christ. 'And he that taketh not his cross, and followeth after me, is not worthy of me. He that findeth his life shall lose it; and he that loseth his life for my sake shall find it' (Matth. 10:38, 39). The inner experience will result in outward expression. Christians not only hear but are also 'doers of the word.' Christian discipleship signifies the total devotion of one's life and possessions to kingdom service. We believe that discipleship includes the welfare of the brotherhood, but more especially an unlimited response and continual outreach to the needs of all mankind, both spiritual and material. 'Even as the Son of man came not to be ministered unto, but to minister, and to give his life a ransom for many' (Matth. 20:28). As disciples of Christ we desire to be more conscious of His leading than the number of persons helped, the total tons of clothing distributed, and whether or not our services are recognized and commended by the world. We are convinced that God leads us forth into the needs of the world at all times with all our resources, but at the same time we know that evil will continue in the world and that we dare not be frustrated or relinquish our services when at times it seems to triumph.

"*C. Relief and Service, A Christian Witness.* As a part of the life and outreach of the Christian brotherhood, relief and service can be a testimony to the redemptive and reconciling power of the Gospel. Because of this conviction, we are concerned about the Christian faith and character of worker personnel. We are equally concerned that the spirit and methods of service and distribution be Christian, that is, that they are spiritual, sympathetic, merciful, without discrimination and without prejudice. This concern also causes us to use Christian insignia and to speak frequently of the motto, 'In the Name of Christ.' In contrast to some other types of relief, we believe it is important that our own workers be present on the field and represented at distributions. Mennonite relief seeks to be humanitarian plus a Christian witness. Mennonite relief, however, is not mission work in the sense of organized, direct evangelistic appeal to man's spiritual need, but rather in the sense that all of the Christian's life and action is a witness to the Gospel. 'Let your light so shine before men, that they may see your good works, and glorify your Father which is in heaven' (Matth. 5:16).

"*D. The Emphasis on Christian Love and Nonresistance.* In common with various other Christian groups, Mennonites share the conviction that Christian love and nonresistance are applicable to all human relationships. This conviction finds its basis in the teaching and example of Christ and the apostles (Matth. 5:38-48; Rom. 12:17-21). Hate and violence, whether on the personal or national level, are the antithesis of Christ and the Gospel Relief and service are ways of affirming our good faith in the doctrine of nonresistance in that they provide positive, creative expression of peace and good will. Relief and service are not only a witness to the way of Christian love but they can become a method of overcoming evil, of reconciling an enemy. 'Therefore if thine enemy hunger, feed him; if he thirst, give him drink; for in so doing thou shalt heap coals of fire on his head. Be not overcome of evil, but overcome evil with good' (Rom. 12:20, 21). Real nonresistance, however, is far more than an intellectual concept or even a doctrinal belief to be proved by Scriptural texts; it is part of a way of life which spontaneously reflects the presence of the indwelling Christ. On the relief field and in service projects love and nonresistance often lead to a special concern for despised minorities, neglected persons, prisoners, political outcasts. 'Inasmuch as ye have done it unto one of the least of these my brethren, ye have done it unto me' (Matth. 25:40).

"*E. The Christian Brotherhood and Mutual Aid.* The Mennonite concept of the church is that of a true brotherhood, a community of believers, as contrasted to that of an organization or institution. In the Christian brotherhood no degrees of position exist and there is mutual concern and responsibility for the spiritual and material welfare of each member. The community of believers is necessary to sustain the spiritual life and strength of the believers, to nurture the oncoming generation, to teach new disciples, and to give a corporate witness. We recognize that the brotherhood in itself has no validity except as an instrument of God toward these ends. We believe that we have a primary responsibility, when necessary, to bring relief and service to the brotherhood. 'Bear ye one another's burdens, and so fulfill the law of Christ . . . . As we have therefore opportunity, let us do good unto all men, especially unto them who are of the household of faith (Gal. 6:2, 10).'"   H.S.B.

J. D. Unruh, *In the Name of Christ, A History of the Mennonite Central Committee and Its Service 1920-1951* (Akron, 1952); *ML* III, 97-99.

Mennonite Central Committee Aid Section. The Mennonite Aid Section was established by the Mennonite Central Committee on March 17, 1944, upon recommendation of the Rehabilitation Study Committee, appointed by the MCC in 1943 to study the rehabilitation needs of CPS men who faced World War II demobilization. The demobilization needs were largely met by the individual conferences, but the Aid Section functioned to co-ordinate the various assistance plans. The largest work of the Aid Section came with the movement of the Mennonite refugees from Europe to the Western Hemisphere after World War II. The Aid Section is composed of representatives appointed by the various Mennonite groups. The Sectional meetings are advisory to the MCC on matters coming under the Aid Section purview, for the most part in the following areas: (1) To assist Mennonite refugees to countries of their choice where they may settle and earn a livelihood; countries of destination for this assistance have been Canada, Paraguay, Uruguay, and Argentina. (2) To assist in economic and community development after arrival in the country of resettlement. (3) Operation of a vocational trainee program which provides opportunity for foreign young men and women to live in American Mennonite homes for one year while receiving practical training in their field of interest. (4) To assist the Council of Mennonite and Affiliated Colleges in the processing of students from areas abroad where MCC relief workers are stationed.   W.T.S.

Mennonite Central Relief Committee of Western Canada. With the outbreak of World War II in 1939, the Mennonites of Western Canada began the organization of provincial relief committees. In January 1940 meetings were held in Altona, Man., Coaldale, Alberta, and Yarrow, B.C. These meetings appointed provincial committees, each of which delegated two representatives to a meeting on March 15, 1940, in Winnipeg, Man., which in turn formed a central executive committee known as the Mennonite Central Relief Committee. Officers from the beginning have been continuously B. B. Janz, chairman, J. J. Thiessen vice-chairman, C. A. DeFehr

treasurer. Up to about 1954 all the committee funds were sent to the Mennonite Central Committee. Since then most of the contributions have been sent directly to committee-supported projects in Paraguay. The committee appoints a regular member to the MCC.   H.S.B.

Mennonite Charité (GCM), a private charitable corporation, was organized and incorporated in 1908 by the First Mennonite Church of Halstead, Garden Township Mennonite Church, First Mennonite Church of Christian, and some citizens of Kansas to maintain charitable institutions such as a Christian hospital, a home for the aged, and orphanages, and to employ physicians and nurses. The place of business was Halstead and some of the first directors of the organization were Christian Krehbiel, Arthur E. Hertzler, John C. Goering, and C. E. Krehbiel. The Charité reported regularly to the Western District Conference. Primary purpose of the organization was to help the Halstead Hospital in its financial crises. In 1931 the Mennonite Charité was dissolved and its funds, consisting of $6,000, were turned over to the church building fund of the Western District Conference (GCM). At that time P. P. Wedel functioned as president and C. E. Krehbiel as secretary.   C.K.

Charter and By-laws of Mennonite Charité (Halstead, 1908); *Minutes of the Mennonite Charité* 1909-1931. Original and printed minutes in the BeCL.

Mennonite Children's Home, 1620 S. 37th St., Kansas City, Kan., was established in 1917 in response to the many requests for child care that came to the workers in the Mennonite Gospel Mission (*q.v.*) here. J. D. Mininger, the mission superintendent, was one of the initiators of this venture in child welfare. The Home is owned and operated by the Mennonite Board of Missions and Charities, Elkhart, Ind., which delegates the actual administration to the local Board of Directors.

The Home is licensed by the state of Kansas to care for 46 children. The building was planned and arranged to care for these children in five groups: six preschool children, ten younger schoolboys, ten older schoolboys, ten younger schoolgirls, and ten older schoolgirls. The children range in age from two to twelve years. The Home is also licensed to place children in foster and adoptive homes. Over 1200 children have either been placed in homes or been given temporary care in the Children's Home since 1917. The present (1956) superintendent is Glen Yoder.   G.Y.

Mennonite (MC) Children's Home, located on the east edge of Millersville, Pa., was opened on March 22, 1911, with Levi and Lydia Sauder in charge. In the first year 56 children were accepted. The beautiful 62 x 50 ft. brick building and a similar building near by for the steward and nurses were built on the farm of Abram B. Eshleman, Millersville-Rohrerstown deacon. The chairman of its Board of Directors has included John H. Mellinger, 20 years; Simon H. Heistand, 20 years; and John M. Hertzler at present (1955). Levi Sauder (1878-1940) was superintendent until his death. Gideon Eberly followed in 1941-51, John M. Hertzler five months, Isaac L. Frederick two years, and Chester Steffy

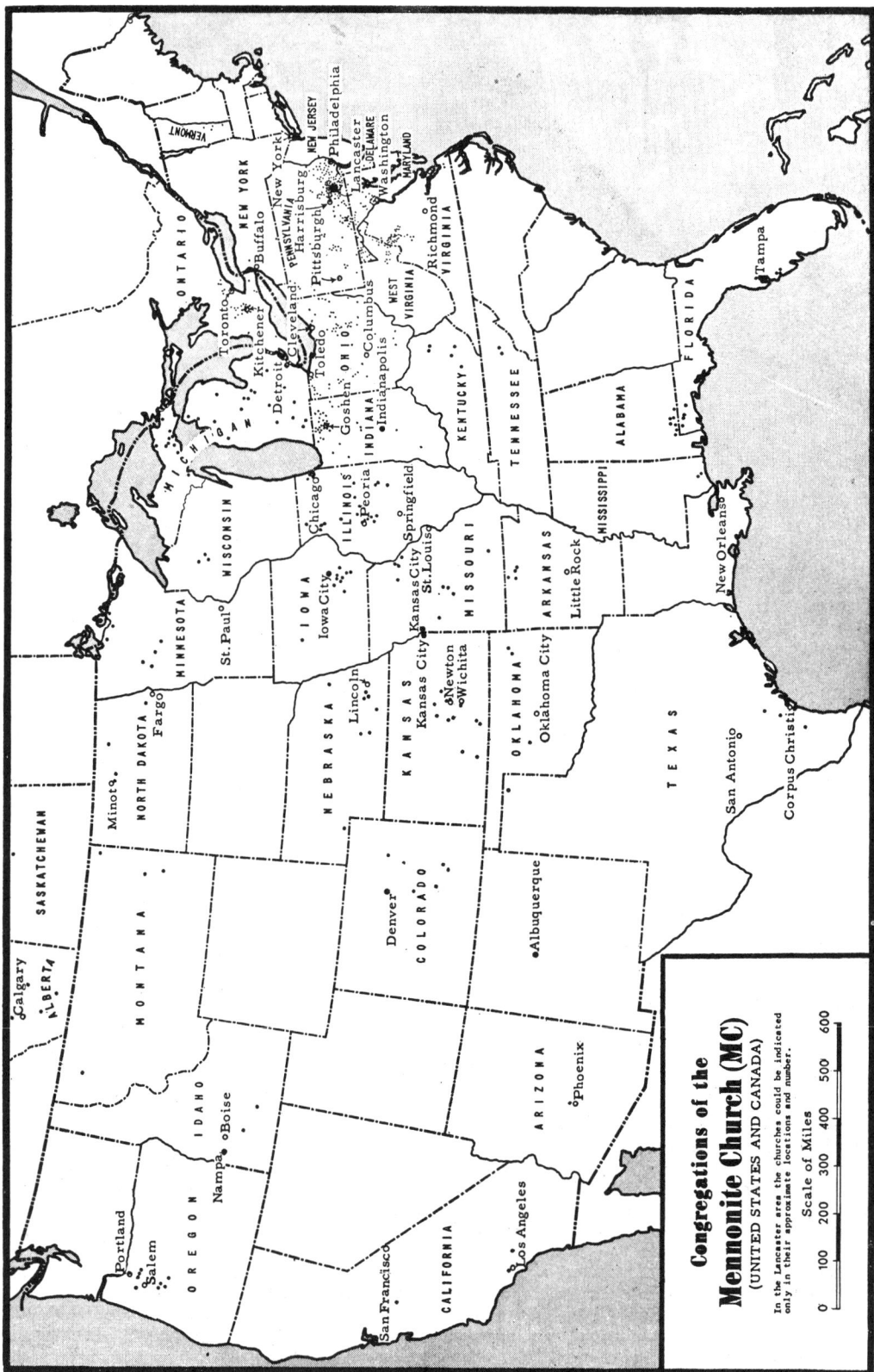

Congregations of the Mennonite Church (MC)
(UNITED STATES AND CANADA)

In the Lancaster area the churches could be indicated only in their approximate locations and number.

Scale of Miles

0   100   200   300   400   500   600

since Dec. 27, 1953. The superintendent also has charge of the orchard-truck farm. The Christian day school was opened for the children of the Home in 1940 and is operated by the Home. To date 1,220 children have entered the Home. The number of children "in ward" (1955) is nineteen.

I.D.L.

Mennonite Church, sometimes familiarly called the "old" Mennonite Church in contradistinction to certain schismatic "new" Mennonite groups formed from it, such as the Reformed Mennonites (*q.v.,* founded in 1812 in Lancaster County, Pa.), the Eastern District of the General Conference Mennonite Church (*q.v.,* founded in 1847 in the Franconia area in Bucks and Montgomery counties, Pa.), and the Indiana and Ontario districts of the United Missionary Church (*q.v.,* formerly called Mennonite Brethren in Christ, *q.v.,* founded in 1875). It is the oldest (1683 ff.) and largest (77,369 baptized members in 1956) Mennonite body in North America. The total membership in 1956 was 81,472, distributed by countries as follows: United States 70,513, Canada 6,856, foreign mission areas 4,103 (India 1,613, East Africa 1,212, Japan 86, Argentina 655, Puerto Rico 335, Sicily 73, Belgium 28, Ghana 26, Honduras 28, Cuba 13, Jamaica 30). In 1956 it was composed of 20 district conferences—three in Canada, fifteen in the United States including Puerto Rico, and three abroad formed from missions, viz., India, Japan, and Argentina, besides two dependent mission conferences, viz., East Africa and Bihar in India. The conferences with date of organization and membership in 1956 are as follows in chronological order: Franconia 1725, 5,404; Lancaster 1775, 15, 046; Washington County, Md., and Franklin County, Pa. 1790, 1,673; Ontario 1820, 3,895; Virginia 1835, 4,621; Ohio and Eastern 1840, 11,269; Indiana and Michigan 1853, 8,649; Illinois 1872, 3,293; Allegheny 1876, 2,590; Iowa and Nebraska 1876, 4,336; South Central 1876, 3,407; Alberta and Saskatchewan 1904, 797; Pacific Coast 1906, 2,186; Conservative Mennonite 1910, 5,585; North Central 1920, 766; Ontario Amish Mennonite 1918 (1924), 2,450; South Pacific 1948, 436; Puerto Rico 1955, 339; India 1912, 1,501; Argentina 1923, 655. (For further information about the district conferences, see the pertinent articles.)

The Mennonite General Conference (*q.v.*), which was organized in 1898 and meets biennially, is an advisory body of considerable importance, but the authority of the church resides in the district conferences, not all of which are officially represented in the General Conference sessions. In 1957 the following conferences participated in the general work and fellowship of the church, but without official delegates in the General Conference: Conservative, Franconia, Lancaster, Ontario Amish, and Washington-Franklin. All of these but the last, however, had official representatives in the General Council of the General Conference. The Mennonite Church thus existed prior to its General Conference and exists apart from it today. The mark of "belonging" to the general body of the church is intercommunion and pulpit fellowship.

The Mennonite Church historically has two ecclesiastical backgrounds, but only one ethnic. Ethnically the body of the membership is Swiss-South German in origin, except for the small number of families from the Lower Rhine area and Hamburg-Altona who settled in Germantown in 1683-1707. Only scattered individual families of Dutch, Prussian, or Russian background are to be found in its membership today, and no entire congregations of such persons, or of Lower Rhine background. Only one congregation today is exclusively of Swiss background, viz., Kidron, Ohio. The one Dutch congregation at New Paris, Ind., founded in 1853, has died out.

Ecclesiastically the group has two constituent backgrounds, viz., Mennonite and Amish Mennonite. The following conferences are exclusively (with minor exceptions) Mennonite: Franconia, Lancaster, Virginia, Washington-Franklin, and Ontario. Exclusively Amish are the Conservative and Ontario Amish Mennonite conferences. The rest are of mixed background, resulting largely from mergers in 1916-25. The sense of Amish background has practically vanished in all but the Conservative and Ontario Amish conferences. The differences have largely disappeared, although locally some echoes of earlier differing traditions still remain. The European geographic backgrounds of the Mennonite and Amish elements, however, were rather distinct. The Mennonite element all came originally from the Palatinate in 1707-56 or Switzerland 1710-56, whereas the Amish came either from Switzerland and the Palatinate (a small number) in 1730-56 or from Alsace-Lorraine, Zweibrücken, Bavaria, and Hesse-Cassel 1815-60, with stragglers down to 1900. The relative proportion of Mennonite and Amish background elements in the sixteen North American conferences is about 70 per cent to 30 per cent. Omitting the two entirely Amish conferences, the ratio of the rest of the church is 75 to 25, with some 22,000 members of Amish background.

The only Mennonite (i.e., non-Amish) settlements made directly from Europe (except the Swiss settlement in Wayne County, Ohio, 1817-30) were those in the Franconia and Lancaster districts; all other Mennonite settlements or congregations further west are derivative from these. Most Amish settlements were founded directly from Europe, but all Amish settlements west of Ohio except Illinois are derivative.

Organizationally the work of the Mennonite Church at large is carried on by three major church-wide boards—the Mennonite Board of Missions and Charities (organized in final form in 1906), which carries on foreign and home missions, charitable homes, and relief and service work, the Mennonite Board of Education (organized in 1905), which operates Goshen and Hesston colleges, the La Junta School of Nursing, and the Mennonite Publication Board (organized in 1908), which works through the Mennonite Publishing House. All these boards are autonomous and self-perpetuating, but are anchored basically in the district conferences by a membership elected directly by them. All the district conferences also have their own mission boards, largely for home missions; the Lancaster, Franconia, and Virginia conference boards, however, also have foreign missions, the former operating an extensive program in Africa. Some of the district conferences also operate institutions such as schools (e.g., Indiana-Michigan has Bethany Christian High School, Ontario has Rockway School, Virginia has Eastern Mennonite College), or homes for the aged (e.g., Ontario has Fairview), and sponsor mutual aid organizations. In most district conferences the mission boards publish periodicals promoting the work of the conference in missions, evangelism, and service. On the other hand, the General Conference, although it does not operate any institutions either directly or indirectly, does carry on a certain amount of promotional and advisory activity and certain administrative assignments through its standing committees such as the Commission for Christian Education, Peace Problems Committee, Ministerial Committee, Music Committee, etc. In matters of finance there is no church-wide budget, except a budget for the specific general conference activities. Funds for the church-wide boards, district boards, and local institutions are secured by offerings or solicitation, locally or generally as the case may be.

In church polity the Mennonite Church uses traditionally elements of several types of polity, but basically it has a synodal polity with the district conferences having general authority over the congregations. Reserved to the congregations are all local matters, including selection of ministers and ownership of church buildings. Matters of doctrine and practice, including discipline, are the prerogative of the district conferences, which have the power to discipline ministers and congregations. The traditional triple congregational ministry of bishop, preacher, and deacon still prevails in most district conferences, although there is a significant trend away from the office of bishop. For example, two district conferences, South Central, and Ohio and Eastern, have recently suspended bishop ordinations, and are using the idea of district superintendent in some form. In the other conferences, bishop districts (dioceses) of from two to ten congregations or mission stations are the rule, although in areas with Amish background the general pattern is a bishop in each major congregation. In the Lancaster Conference the bishops as a body constitute a sort of upper house in the conference, and are called a "bishop board," which exercises considerable power. In the other conferences all ordained men have equal voice in conference work, regardless of office. The office of deacon is declining in some areas.

The Mennonite Church has suffered a number of schisms. Interestingly, none was due to a major issue in doctrine, all being due primarily to differences over progressive and conservative attitudes in church work or strictness in discipline, or to miscellaneous and personal difficulties. These schisms are all described under the pertinent articles: Funkites in Franconia 1778, Reformed Mennonite or Herrites in Lancaster 1812, Stauffer in Lancaster 1845, Eastern District General Conference Mennonite or Oberholtzer division in Franconia 1847, Church of God in Christ or Holdeman in Ohio 1859 (actually not a true schism), Defenseless or Egly among the Amish of Indiana, Illinois, and

Ohio in 1864, Old Order Mennonite or Wisler in Indiana and Ohio in 1871-72 (Ontario similarly in 1889, Lancaster in 1893, Virginia in 1903), Central Illinois or Stucky Amish in 1871 (organized first in 1898), Mennonite Brethren in Christ or Brenneman division in Indiana and Ontario about 1875. Progressive groups also broke off in several places in 1924-30 (Indiana, Ontario, Ohio, Pennsylvania) which never organized a conference but transferred gradually to the General Conference Mennonites.

In contrast to these schisms the reunion of the largest section of the Amish body with the main body of the Mennonite Church, beginning with the adherence of Amish conferences to the Mennonite General Conference in 1898 ff. and to the general church-wide boards in 1892 ff., should be noted as a major achievement in Mennonite unity in North America, exceeding in size of membership involved the total of all the schisms listed above.

The history of the Mennonite Church falls readily into four major periods: Colonial 1683-1783; Westward Migration 1783-1860; Strain and Stress (overlapping) 1840-90; Great Awakening 1890-1910; Consolidation and Forward Movement 1910-57.

Colonial Period, 1683-1783. Although advance contingents came early, such as the first Lower Rhine urban immigrants, who began to arrive at Germantown in 1683 and formed a congregation apparently as early as 1690 with William Rittenhouse as preacher, and also a few from the Palatinate in 1707 and Switzerland (1710 to Lancaster), the main body of rural immigrants (about 4,000-5,000) came from the Palatinate in 1717-56, splitting about equally between the Franconia district twenty to fifty miles north of Philadelphia and the Lancaster district fifty to eighty miles west of Philadelphia. The small number of Colonial Amish settled approximately at the junction of Lancaster, Chester, and Berks counties in 1738-56. The two Mennonite settlements remained distinct, without organic union, as did the smaller Amish group. However, delegates from the two Mennonite settlements met conjointly as early as 1725, probably in Germantown, to adopt the Dutch Dordrecht Confession of Faith of 1632 as their own and arrange for its publication in English (1727). Since the Amish in Europe had already adopted this Confession, Dordrecht became and has remained the accepted confession of the Mennonite Church of North America. In the colonial period the major Mennonite books published in America (Germantown or Ephrata) were the hymnal *Ausbund* (q.v., 1742), the martyr book (*Güldene Aepfel* (1745), the *Martyrs' Mirror* (1748), the devotional Bible history *Die wandelnde Seele* (1768), the catechism *Christliches Gemüthsgespräch* (1769), the prayerbook *Ernsthafte Christenpflicht* (1770), and two books by a native author, *Spiegel der Taufe* (1744) and *Eine Restitution* (1763) by Bishop Heinrich Funck of Franconia.

In the colonial century the Pennsylvania Mennonites established their solid communities, successfully transferring their traditional faith and practice from Europe and retaining the German language. But they were subject to considerable pietistic influence, largely through literature, and suffered some loss from the Wesleyan revivalistic influence in the latter part of the period and on into the 19th century. A Lancaster bishop, Martin Boehm (*q.v.,* excommunicated about 1777), was a cofounder of the United Brethren Church and led a considerable body of Mennonites, including several ministers (e.g., Christian Newcomer, *q.v.*), into the new group which he formed with Philip Otterbein, which was in process of crystallization from 1767 on (notable meeting in Isaac Long's barn in that year). About the same time (1770) began the small rather pietistic movement called the River Brethren (Brethren in Christ, *q.v.*), led by Jacob Engel (*q.v.*), a Mennonite layman in western Lancaster County, although the real emergence of the group did not take place until 1785 with the first baptisms by Engel. A considerable part of the new group was composed of former Mennonites. The Mennonites have been described by some writers as having had a part in the Great Awakening of 1744 ff., but this has not been proved. Culturally they were an integral part of the large Pennsylvania German block of Eastern Pennsylvania.

The French and Indian Wars (1756-53) and the Revolutionary War (1776-83) created considerable difficulty for the nonresistant Mennonites, who successfully maintained their position of complete nonparticipation in war. In this they were helped by the Quakers, who controlled the provincial government of Pennsylvania to 1756 and who had great influence even after that. The first schism, the one led by Bishop Christian Funk of Franconia (1778), occurred over the question of paying the war tax and in general supporting the American revolutionary side against England, although military service was not involved.

Westward Migration, 1783-1860. The end of the fighting, and the creation of more stable conditions made possible the great American westward migration across the Alleghenies into the vast central plain of Western Pennsylvania, Ohio, Indiana, Illinois, and Iowa, as well as into Ontario. The shortage of available land in the East furnished considerable pressure. Many Mennonites joined the migration, some going northwest into Ontario, some straight west to western Pennsylvania (Somerset and Westmoreland counties, etc.) and on into Eastern Ohio, and some south through the Cumberland Valley from Harrisburg into Maryland, and on down into the Shenandoah Valley in Virginia. By 1840-50 derivative settlements (families from Virginia, Eastern Ohio, and Ontario) were being established in western Ohio and northern Indiana, with small and scattered settlements soon after in Illinois. The few Mennonite settlements in Missouri and Kansas were made mostly after 1870. The movement reached Colorado, North Dakota, and Oregon, as well as Alberta and Saskatchewan (from Ontario and Nebraska chiefly) about the turn of the 20th century or soon thereafter. California received only scattered settlers, with the first organized congregation in 1921. Michigan received its Mennonites mostly after 1900 (a few 1865-1900, chiefly from Ontario). The total Mennonite (non-Amish) population west of Indiana and west of Ontario in Canada has never been large, and in 1956 was less than 6,000 baptized members.

The Amish also shared in the westward migration, although many of the Amish settlements were made directly from Europe as follows: Waterloo County, Ont., Somerset County, Pa. (partly from Hesse, partly from Lancaster County), Stark and Fulton counties and part of Wayne County, Ohio, central Illinois, and part of Wayland, Iowa. These were mostly Alsatian Amish settlements made in 1825-60. Derivative settlements from Lancaster County were made in Mifflin County, Pa., and Fairfield County, Ohio, West Liberty, Ohio, Topeka, Ind., Cass County, Mo., Hubbard, Ore., and partly Wayne County, Ohio, all made from ultimately Lancaster County Amish stock. Holmes County, Ohio, Elkhart and Lagrange counties, Ind., and Johnson County, Iowa, were made largely of Hessian Amish stock from Somerset County, Pa. Leo, Ind., Wayland, Iowa, most Nebraska settlements, Pigeon, Mich., Fairview, Ore., and Tofield, Alberta, were derivative, settled largely by Amish families from Ohio, Ontario, or Illinois, ultimately from Alsace. Characteristic names enable a fairly accurate tracing of derivation. The Amish (Mennonite) settlements west of Indiana are nearly twice the size of the Mennonite, almost 10,000 in membership.

The total membership of all district conferences west of Indiana and Ontario in 1956 was 15,811. West of the Mississippi in the U.S.A. it was about 11,400.

The 19th-century westward migration was completely rural, largely based on free or very cheap government homestead land. (Numerous attempted smaller settlements vanished for various reasons.) All carried with them substantially the traditional faith and practice of the mother communities. Gradually, however, the freer life of the frontier resulted in a less conservative and more flexible type of church life and attitude, and prevented the development of the somewhat radical conservative trend or purely static condition which characterized sections of the East until recent decades. Most of the newer methods of church work and activities which came into the Mennonite Church in the 20th century developed in the newer midwestern settlements in Ohio and Indiana.

Strain and Stress, 1840-90. The limits of this period overlap somewhat the previous one because of the nature of the historical developments. It can be characterized as one of strain and stress, because it was in the fifty years of this period that all the major schisms among both the Mennonite and Amish wings occurred. Outside influences, especially from the Alleghenies westward and in Ontario, but also in Eastern Pennsylvania and Virginia, put great pressure upon the tradition-bound Mennonite communities. Chief among these influences were the Sunday school and revivalism, the Methodist (English) and United Brethren and Evangelical (German) evangelists and camp meetings, a pietistic type of literature, etc., all of which had weighty influence, and resulted in the loss of many members to the more aggressive denominations. Many Mennonite leaders, pressed by conservative laymen, were inclined to resist most innovations, and often those who wanted progress had great difficulty in making their influence felt, or tended to become seriously dissatisfied. The struggle over the German language and the transition to English added to the strain and stress.

At times it seemed that the main body might be so weakened by the struggle and the defections right and left that it would completely disintegrate, as some communities actually did. But the outstanding leadership of several able and devoted men of vision in the Midwest, in particular Bishop John M. Brenneman (1817-95) of Allen County, Ohio, and John F. Funk, publisher (1835-1930), and J. S. Coffman (1848-99), evangelist, both of Elkhart, Ind., did much to turn the tide, both in progress and in unity. The outside influences did in some respects have a wholesome influence.

The Great Awakening, 1890-1914. The work of Brenneman, Funk (1864 on), and Coffman (1879 on), assisted and supplemented by others, soon began to bear fruit. Sunday schools were accepted and did their good work in Bible teaching and lay activity from 1863 on (first Sunday schools at Masontown, Pa., and Kitchener, Ont., about 1840). The spirit of evangelism and revival was spread by J. S. Coffman's widespread itinerant work, followed by others who imitated him such as J. S. Shoemaker, Daniel Kauffman, D. D. Miller, S. G. Shetler, Noah Stauffer, and A. D. Wenger. New life was awakened, and thousands of young people were gathered in who otherwise would have been lost to the Mennonite Church. The spirit of missions arose (first home mission, Chicago 1893; first foreign mission, India 1899), church schools were established (Elkhart and Goshen 1894-1903, Ontario Bible School 1907, Hesston 1909), Sunday-school conferences were held (1891 the first in Indiana), young people's meetings began to spring up (first in Elkhart, Ind., and Smithville, Ohio, about 1893). It was a remarkable awakening to new spirit and life internally, and to a new sense of mission and outreach to the world. The church was transformed, first in the Midwest and Ontario, then in the East as well. Finally the General Conference was launched in 1898 and the three great church-wide boards established in 1905, 1906, and 1908.

Consolidation and Forward Movement, 1914-57. A splendid fruit of the new spiritual life and activity was the growing sense of unity and the need for closer co-operation among the scattered congregations, settlements, and conferences, which manifested slightly varying traditions, and at times varying degrees of progress. The consolidation of the results of the Great Awakening and the unifying of the church were manifested in various ways, e.g., in the growing strength of the General Conference which at first was supported by less than half of the church, in the formation of the three boards with their church-wide representation and operation, particularly in the earlier period the mission board at Elkhart, and in the growing influence of the central church publishing house at Scottdale, with the church organ, the *Gospel Herald,* and its vigorous editor, Daniel Kauffman. It was manifested also in the formal merger of the Amish and Mennonite conferences in 1916-25. The growth and wider influence of the church schools at Goshen and Hesston, joined by Eastern Mennonite College in 1917, was also both a token and a force in the consolidation and unification. In spite of serious tensions in the twenties and thirties over the degree of change

permissible in the traditional expression of nonconformity to the world (with the Midwest changing more rapidly and substantially than the East) the church on the whole moved vigorously forward on all fronts and maintained its unity. The delayed awakening in the East (Lancaster and Franconia) has been largely compensated in the last two decades.

World Wars I and II had significant effects upon the church. On the one hand the severe testing of its nonresistant position, through the military draft and related war measures such as the sale of war bonds and war industry, brought a significant rallying of strength and clarification of position. While certain weaknesses were revealed, basically the church took a united and strong stand and contributed much to the clarification and unification of the nonresistant position of the entire North American Mennonite brotherhood. On the other hand, the experiences of Civilian Public Service, with the great foreign relief effort after World War II, and the development of voluntary service, has greatly stimulated and challenged the church and its youth. Another result was the growing discovery and appreciation of other branches of the Mennonite brotherhood.

Outside currents of influence were not without their effect on the church also in this period. Modernism had scant influence, but the Fundamentalist-Modernist controversy in America had its echoes within the church, which although it succeeded in keeping out of the outright Fundamentalist movement, because of strong sympathies for the general anti-modernist position was definitely influenced by it. One fruit of this influence was the adoption of a statement of doctrinal position by the General Conference in 1921, called *A Statement of Christian Fundamentals,* the only original general doctrinal statement ever adopted by the church. It was in this period too (1910-40) that millennialism made considerable inroads with the result that a substantial number of both ministers and lay members followed this type of prophetic interpretation. Dispensationalism, however, has been rejected. There has apparently been a decline in interest in millennialism in the past decade.

The growth of confidence in education and its value for the cause of the church has been marked in the past quarter of a century. In higher education two full four-year colleges and one junior college have had an extraordinary growth in attendance (1956-57 over 1,000 college students) and plant and resources. In secondary education nine four-year high schools have been established across the continent since 1942 in addition to the two at E.M.C. and Hesston, with a total enrollment of over 1,500 in 1956-57. In elementary education a remarkable development has taken place since 1939 when the first Mennonite Christian day school was established in Eastern Pennsylvania (preceded by two Amish schools in Delaware of 1925 and 1938 and an Amish school of 1938 in Pennsylvania). In 1956-57 there were 88 such schools in operation, 20 of them Amish. Pennsylvania alone had 45 elementary schools, most of them in the Lancaster area. Almost every congregation throughout the church also had a summer Bible school of two weeks' duration.

The changing concept of the minister's work has also led to the demand in various quarters for a better trained ministry, and along with this the preference for the one-pastor system with full or partial support. In Ontario, Ohio, Indiana, Kansas, and Illinois this change has come rapidly in the past decade. To serve this demand the Mennonite Board of Education established at Goshen College the Biblical Seminary (beginning in 1933, separate organization in 1944), which since 1947 has offered a full graduate course, and has graduated about 200 persons from all curriculums. E.M.C. has also added an advanced Bible training program. However, the majority of congregations are still served by ministers without full support and only a small amount of special training.

The publication work of the church has also shown a significant expansion in the past generation. Whereas John F. Funk's Mennonite Publishing Company in Elkhart (organized 1875, although his publishing work had begun in Chicago in 1864) published chiefly the church paper *Herald of Truth* and the large historical volumes such as *Menno Simons Works* and the *Martyrs' Mirror,* and hymnbooks, it had little original production by Mennonite writers to issue. Funk's influence was exercised chiefly through the *Herald* and Sunday-school helps. He was also handicapped by a bilingual constituency. With the shift to English in 1890-1910, the establishment of the Mennonite Book and Tract Society (*q.v.,* 1892-1908), and the Gospel Witness Company (*q.v.,* 1905-8), followed by the general church agency, the Mennonite Publishing House (*q.v.,* est. 1908 at Scottdale), and the emergence of two capable writers, Daniel Kauffman (*q.v.*) and John Horsch (*q.v.*), the literary output expanded in quantity and improved in quality. The periodical literature and the Sunday-school helps became increasingly influential. By 1930 a younger generation of writers, many of them associated with the three colleges of the church, but particularly Goshen College and Biblical Seminary, emerged, and the past fifteen years have witnessed the flowering of a historical, theological, and practical literature outstanding in American Mennonite history. The Conrad Grebel Lectureship (see **Lectureships**), established in 1952, has contributed measurably to this.

The rise and growth of the missionary and philanthropic interest in the church in the past 50 years has been a notable development, greatly intensified in the last decade. Foreign mission fields were entered as follows: India 1899, Argentina 1917, East Africa 1934, Bihar (India) 1940, Argentine Chaco 1943, Puerto Rico 1945, Ethiopia 1948, Japan 1949, Sicily 1949, Honduras 1950, Belgium 1950, Luxembourg 1951, England 1952, Somalia 1953, France 1953, Israel 1953, Alaska 1954, Brazil 1954, Uruguay 1954, Cuba 1954, Jamaica 1955, Viet-Nam 1957. The remarkable growth in home missions in the past twenty years has brought the number of mission outposts operated either by congregations alone or by mission boards to over 300, scattered over many states outside of original Mennonite territory, including Vermont, New York, North Carolina, Kentucky, Tennessee, Alabama, Florida, Georgia, Texas, Minnesota, northern Michigan, northern Ontario, north-

ern Alberta. New types of mission activity have developed such as Negro missions (25 in number), Jewish missions, missions among the Mexicans. Radio broadcasting with a basically evangelistic purpose has developed into a major thrust, with the Mennonite Hour, established in 1952, since 1955 operating under the Mennonite Board of Missions and Charities, with over 70 stations, and a Spanish broadcast with 10 stations, to which additional foreign language broadcasts in Italian, French, German, and Russian are to be added. A European studio was established in Basel, Switzerland, in 1957.

A remarkable growth in charitable institutions is also to be noted. The church now maintains five children's homes and eighteen homes for the aged, owns two hospitals in North America, and operates four more as well as one mental hospital. It has been a strong supporter of the Mennonite Central Committee from its beginning in 1920, and carries on in addition a large voluntary service program of both summer short-term and year-round units in numerous states and provinces. Much of this is administered by the Mennonite Relief and Service Committee (*q.v.*) under the general mission board, but the Lancaster Conference mission board also operates a vigorous program of voluntary service.

Organized mutual aid (*q.v.*) has also developed in a large way, particularly since 1910. District organizations for mutual aid in property losses have become almost universal. The first such was in Ontario, beginning in 1867. The Mennonite Aid Plan (*q.v.*), organized in Indiana in 1882, served a larger area. In 1945 a church-wide organization, Mennonite Mutual Aid, Inc. (*q.v.*), was set up under the General Conference to provide hospitalization and surgical aid, also burial aid; automobile accident aid was later added. Today the concept of organized aid of various types is generally accepted. The strong position against commercial life insurance in all forms originally taken still generally holds, although in recent years some modified forms of insurance with investment features are coming into use.

The church has in general maintained a strong position in regard to nonconformity to the world, holding that the full Christian life will of necessity express itself in nonconformity to the world in life and conduct. Its ideals include simplicity in life and costume, rejecting attendance at the theater including motion pictures, the wearing of jewelry, the swearing of oaths, lodge membership, divorce, smoking and drinking, participation in politics and office-holding, membership in labor unions, participation in war or carnal strife of any kind, and advocating simplicity in worship without the use of musical instruments. There is universal observance of the ordinance of footwashing, the prayer veil for women, and close communion. In the application of this principle of nonconformity and simplicity the church in general has maintained a conservative position, with real church discipline, seeking to avoid the evils of legalism and formalism on the one hand and worldliness on the other, though not always successfully. While weaknesses have manifested themselves frequently at various times and places, in general the church has maintained its principles and ideals. Among the means used to this end in recent years have been pronouncements by the General Conference on various major questions of practical Christian living, including the following: Peace, War, and Military Service (1937), Industrial Relations (1941), a Declaration of Christian Faith and Commitment (Nonresistance) first by an all-Mennonite study conference at Winona Lake (1950), Race Relations (1955), and Christian Separation and Nonconformity as a Whole (1955). The declarations of position and commitment, while not having the force of confessions of faith, nevertheless carry great weight and influence.

Among the outstanding leaders of the Mennonite Church through the 275 years of its career in America the following might be noted: *Franconia District*: Jacob Gottschalk (1666-1763?) of Germantown and Skippack, first bishop in America; Heinrich Funck (d. 1760), bishop and writer at Franconia; Christopher Dock (d. 1771), noted schoolmaster on the Skippack; Abraham Godschalk (1791-1838), minister at Doylestown; Josiah Clemmer (1827-1905), bishop at Franconia; and Andrew Mack (1836-1917), bishop at Bally; *Lancaster*: Hans Herr (1639-1725), first bishop in the Lancaster area; Christian Burkholder (1746-1809), writer and bishop at Groffdale; Peter Eby (1765-1843), bishop at Pequea; Christian Herr (1780-1853), bishop at Pequea; Amos Herr (1816-97), preacher at Willow Street; Jacob N. Brubacher (1839-1913), bishop at Mount Joy; Noah Mack (1861-1948), bishop at New Holland; and John H. Mellinger (1858-1952), lay leader and long-time president of the Lancaster mission board; John S. Mast (1861-1951), Amish bishop at Morgantown; *Virginia*: Peter Burkholder (1783-1846), bishop and writer in Rockingham County; Samuel Coffman (1822-94) and L. J. Heatwole (1852-1932), also bishops there; George R. Brunk (1871-1938), bishop and writer at Denbigh; *Ontario*: Benjamin Eby (1785-1863), bishop and writer at Kitchener; David Sherk (1801-82), minister and writer at Preston; S. F. Coffman (1872-1954), bishop and writer at Vineland; Oscar Burkholder (1886-1956), bishop at Breslau; *Western Pennsylvania*: Abram Metzler (1862-1924), bishop at Martinsburg; Daniel Kauffman (1865-1944), J. A. Ressler (1867-1936), and Aaron Loucks (1864-1945), all bishops at Scottdale, Kauffman and Ressler being also writers and editors; N. E. Miller (1880-1930), bishop at Springs; S. G. Shetler (1871-1942), bishop at Johnstown (Holsopple); *Ohio*: John M. Brenneman (1816-95), bishop at Elida; John K. Yoder (1824-1906), bishop at Smithville; M. S. Steiner (1866-1911), minister at Columbus Grove and early missions leader; David Plank (1833-1912), bishop at West Liberty; John Blosser (1855-1921), bishop at Rawson and early educational leader; C. Z. Yoder (1845-1939), minister at Smithville and early missions leader; E. L. Frey (1856-1942), bishop at Wauseon; J. B. Smith (1870-1951), minister and writer at Elida and educator; S. E. Allgyer (1859-1953), bishop at West Liberty and evangelist and missions leader; *Indiana*: John F. Funk (1835-1930), bishop, writer, and publisher at Elkhart; John S. Coffman (1845-99), evangelist at Elkhart; D. J. Johns (1850-1942), bishop at Goshen; J. S. Hartzler (1857-1953), minister and educator at

Elkhart and Goshen; D. D. Miller (1864-1955), bishop, evangelist, and educational and missions leader at Middlebury; *Illinois*: J. S. Shoemaker (1853-1936), bishop at Freeport and early publications and mission leader; Samuel Gerber (1863-1929), bishop at Tremont; C. A. Hartzler (1876-1947), bishop at Tiskilwa; H. R. Schertz (1886-1954), bishop at Metamora; *Iowa*: Sebastian Gerig (1838-1924), bishop at Wayland; Abner Yoder (1879-1942), bishop at Parnell; *Nebraska*: D. G. Lapp (1857-1951), bishop at Roseland; *Kansas*: T. M. Erb (1865-1929), bishop at Hesston; D. H. Bender (1866-1945), bishop at Hesston and educator; Noah Oyer (1891-1931), minister and educator at Hesston (and Goshen, Ind.); Foreign Missions: *India*: M. C. Lapp (1871-1923) and George J. Lapp (1879-1951), bishops; *Argentina*: T. K. Hershey (1879-1956), bishop. (See the pertinent biographical articles for all of these men.)   H.S.B.

C. Henry Smith, *The Mennonites of America* (Goshen, 1909); *idem, The Mennonite Immigration to Pennsylvania in the Eighteenth Century* (Norristown, 1929); *idem, The Story of the Mennonites* (Berne, 1941); J. S. Hartzler and Daniel Kauffman, *Mennonite Church History* (Scottdale, 1905); Daniel Kauffman, *The Conservative Viewpoint* (Scottdale, 1918); *idem, Doctrines of the Bible* (Scottdale, 1928); *idem, Fifty Years in the Mennonite Church 1890-1940* (Scottdale, 1941); *idem, Mennonite Cyclopedic Dictionary* (Scottdale, 1937); H. S. Bender, *Two Centuries of American Mennonite Literature, A Bibliography of Mennonitica Americana 1727-1928* (Goshen, 1929); *idem, Mennonite Sunday School Centennial 1840-1940* (Scottdale, 1940); *idem,* "The Founding of the Mennonite Church in America at Germantown 1683-1708," *MQR* VII (1933) 227-50; J. C. Wenger, *History of the Mennonites of the Franconia Conference* (Telford, Pa., 1937); *idem, The Doctrines of the Mennonites* (Scottdale, 1943); *idem, Historical and Biblical Position of the Mennonite Church on Attire* (Scottdale, 1944); *idem, Separated Unto God: A Plea for Christian Simplicity of Life and for a Scriptural Nonconformity to the World* (Scottdale, 1951); *idem, Introduction to Theology* (Scottdale, 1954); G. F. Hershberger, *War, Peace, and Nonresistance* (Scottdale, 1944, rev. ed. 1953); *idem, The Mennonite Church in the Second World War* (Scottdale, 1951); J. S. Hartzler, *Mennonites in the World War* (Scottdale, 1921); John Umble, *Mennonite Pioneers, Biographical Sketches of Some of the Leading Men and Women in the Mennonite Church Who Have Served in the Institutions of the Church in the Home Land* (Elkhart, 1940); *idem, Ohio Mennonite Sunday Schools* (Goshen, 1941); *idem, Goshen College 1894-1954* (Goshen, 1955); *idem,* "Extinct Mennonite Churches in Ohio," *MQR* XVIII-XIX (1944-45) 36-38, 89-116, 186-92, 225-50, 41-58, 215-37, and XX (1946) 5-52; *idem,* "Seventy Years of Progress in Sunday School Work Among the Mennonites of the Middle West," *MQR* VIII (1934) 166-79; Roy H. Umble, "Mennonite Preaching 1864-1944," doctoral dissertation at Northwestern University 1949; John F. Funk, *Mennonite Church and Her Accusers* (Elkhart, 1878); "Fifty Mennonite Leaders," the title of two series of biographical sketches which appeared in the *Gospel Herald,* Jan. 10—Dec. 19, 1929; Jan. 18, 1934—Jan. 3, 1935; John Horsch, "Alt-Mennoniten," *ML* I, 43-46; Ed. G. Kauffman, *The Development of the Missionary and Philanthropic Interest Among the Mennonites of North America* (Berne, 1931); M. S. Steiner, *John S. Coffman, Mennonite Evangelist* (Spring Grove, Pa., n.d.—1903); Alice Gingerich, *Life and Times of Daniel Kauffman* (Scottdale, 1954). For further bibliography, see the articles on the several district conferences, and on specific doctrines, ordinances, and practices. See also the published proceedings of the Mennonite General Conference (*q.v.*) and the district conferences.

Mennonite Church Buildings, Inc., a nonprofit corporation formed in 1956 as a subsidiary of Mennonite Mutual Aid (*q.v.*), a standing committee of the Mennonite (MC) General Conference (*q.v.*), to take over the assets of Mennonite Educational Buildings, Inc. (*q.v.*), and to continue its program of aiding in the financing of college buildings with the enlargement of scope to include all types of church buildings, such as meetinghouses and buildings for missions and publishing purposes. The initial officers were Abram Hallman (Akron, Pa.) president, H. Ernest Bennett (Elkhart) vice-president, Harold L. Swartzendruber (Goshen) secretary-treasurer. Additional members of the board of directors were Melvin Lauver (Akron, Pa.), Joseph Buzzard (Scottdale), William Yoder (Columbiana, Ohio), and Howard Mellinger (Sterling, Ill.).

H.S.B.

Mennonite Church Extension Society (*Eine Mennonitische Kirchenerweiterungs-Gesellschaft*) of the Western District Conference (GCM) was incorporated on Nov. 17, 1904, by Christian Krehbiel, Joseph Schrag, Jakob Isaak, J. W. Penner, H. Banman, Peter Goertz, David Goerz, J. J. Krehbiel, and C. F. Claassen. Christian Krehbiel was the president, David Goerz secretary, and C. F. Claassen treasurer. The purpose of the society was the promotion of public worship through the establishment or furnishing of churches at places where the Western District Conference did mission work, or where a local congregation was being organized and needed help to acquire a meetinghouse. As soon as newly established congregations became independent and self-supporting these churches became their property. The society collected funds and raised membership dues which enabled it to build churches. Membership dues were $5.00. Little information is available of the actual activities of the Extension Society and of the time when its work came to a close. C.K.

The above information is contained in a twelve-page pamphlet entitled *Eine Mennonitische Kirchenerweiterungs-Gesellschaft.*

Mennonite Collegiate Institute was founded at Gretna, Man., in 1889 by a group of progressive Mennonite pioneers who had settled in the West Reserve in 1875. Its purpose was to train teachers for the Mennonite elementary schools which were then operated as private schools and after 1890 partly as public schools. From the very start the M.C.I., a private school, was supported by voluntary contributions and student fees. Until 1908 classes were held in a small building. In 1908 a three-story structure with two classrooms and room for about 20 boarding students was built. In 1912 the plant was enlarged to about three times its former size.

After World War I the Mennonite constituency which supported the M.C.I. and received the benefits of the school was greatly expanded by immigration of Mennonites from Russia (see **Manitoba**). Therefore in 1944 a building fund was started for the construction of a new building to take care of the growing student body, quadrupled in size. The new building, a modern plant with five classrooms, two large and well-equipped laboratories, and a chapel, was completed in 1946 at a total cost of some $60,000. Since the school had offered boarding facilities for boys only, four private residences were

bought and converted into girls' boarding houses. In 1948 the old school building was converted into a boys' residence and infirmary. In 1952 a large auditorium capable of seating 1800-2000 was built. In 1955 a new dormitory was erected to accommodate 150 students.

Since 1916 the M.C.I. has taught the full general course for grades 9 to 12. It is not an accredited collegiate but prefers to have its students write the Departmental Examinations at the end of June. The State Department of Education fully recognizes the work of the M.C.I. In addition to the prescribed subjects, stress is placed on the German language and Mennonite heritage. In the last eight years of its operation seven Isbister scholarship winners have been graduated from the school, and fourteen Manitoba scholarship winners. The school had 179 students in 1955-56. The first principal was H. H. Ewert, who was succeeded by G. H. Peters. The staff now consists of P. J. Schäfer, Principal, and six teachers. (†*ME* I) (*ML* III, 99.)   P.J.S.

Mennonite Colonization Board, headquarters at Newton, Kan., was organized in the spring of 1924 to give financial aid to the movement of Mennonite immigrants from Russia to Canada. The board was constituted at a meeting held at the Alexanderwohl Mennonite Church north of Newton, where by popular election at the meeting seventeen members were elected representing six Mennonite branches (MC, GCM, MB, KMB, EMC, CGC) from Pennsylvania to Kansas, nine from the latter state. The first officers were D. E. Harder, president, D. H. Bender, vice-president, J. G. Regier, secretary-treasurer, all from Harvey County, Kan., with J. G. Wiens and O. O. Miller as additional members of the executive committee. Later J. M. Sudermann became president and executive secretary, P. C. Hiebert, secretary, and H. E. Suderman, treasurer. These men, with O. O. Miller and John Lichti, constituted the executive committee to the close of active operations in 1926. In 1947 the MCB was dissolved and its assets turned over to the MCC.

The MCB had two active projects. The one was financial aid to immigrants to Canada. By Aug. 1, 1925, $15,000 had been raised and sent to Canada, $12,000 as loans to be repaid. The second project, colonization of Russian Mennonites in Mexico, arose because of the inability of some of the prospective Russian emigrants to pass the Canadian health requirements. The Board failed in its attempt to secure admission of these people to the United States, and then turned to Mexico because of the favorable attitude of the Mexican government as well as the earlier (1922) actual establishment of an Old Colony Mennonite settlement from Manitoba in the state of Chihuahua. When the possibility of settlement in Mexico was reported to the Mennonites in Russia there was immediate response and a considerable movement to Mexico set in at once via Tampico and Vera Cruz. The first two groups of six families, a total of fifteen, arrived on July 1, 1924, and settled on a tract of their own choosing near Rosario, state of Chihuahua. By October about 200 persons had arrived. By the end of 1924 approximately $14,000 in cash and supplies had been contributed to this settlement by the Board from donations received in the United States. The Rosario settlement, suffering serious reverses due to climate, also due to the divisive effects of the founding of a second (San Juan) colony near Irapuato about 550 miles south of Rosario, finally disintegrated and by the end of 1925 almost all had gone on to Canada. The Irapuato settlement was organized by several private individuals in the G.C.M. church in Kansas, who solicited individuals to leave the Rosario settlement and finally diverted 24 families from Rosario to Irapuato. In spite of additional aid which the MCB finally gave in an attempt to aid and save the Irapuato colony, it too disintegrated, the settlers moving to Canada. A third settlement was attempted at Las Animas near Irapuato by a private individual, A. A. Rempel, himself an immigrant from Russia to the United States a few years earlier, chiefly for his own relatives. A total of 18 families were received by Rempel in November 1924, but by the end of January 1925 they left to go to Rosario (10 families) and Irapuato or Canada. A fourth settlement was attempted at El Trebol, Durango, about 500 miles south of Rosario, by 24 families from Russia arriving in late 1925. This colony also disintegrated, most going to Canada, although a few families still live here. Most of the Russian Mennonites who remained in Mexico (some 35 persons) finally located at Cuauhtemoc (*q.v.*), a town adjacent to the Old Colony settlement in Chihuahua. This group was organized into a G.C.M. congregation in 1938. The total number of immigrant families (1957) from Russia to Mexico was 124, with about 600 persons. The last group of eight families arrived in December 1925. The MBC aided all of the four settlements, although its only own project was Rosario. The total funds received by the Board were: for Canada, loan $11,050, donations $3,096, total $14,146; for Mexico, loan $10,105, donations $22,800, total $32,905 plus two cars of supplies and one car of milk cows.

The failure of the MCB colonization effort in Mexico 1924-25 can be attributed to the following causes: (1) lack of sufficient aid funds to carry the settlements through to self-support; (2) lack of sufficient rainfall in the areas chosen, at least without expensive irrigation; (3) fear of the degrading influence of the Mexican population; (4) no opportunity to earn money by hiring out during the pioneer years as in Canada and the United States because of the low wage scale; (5) the changed attitude of the new Mexican president Calles (succeeding the tolerant Obregon), who in early 1925 issued a decree to the effect that "in the future not more than ten families of foreigners shall be permitted to colonize any particular farming locality."

When the MCB was liquidated in 1947 it had succeeded largely through the help of C. F. Klassen (*q.v.*) in collecting most of the loans advanced to the settlers in Canada and Mexico and had been able to discharge all its financial obligations. The remaining assets were contributed to the MCC relief fund.   J.M.S.

S. C. Yoder, *For Conscience Sake* (Goshen, 1940) 154-59; files of J. M. Suderman and H. P. Krehbiel (BeCL); *ML* III, 99 f.

Mennonite Commission *for Christian Education* (MC) was organized in 1937 by action of General Conference. It was an enlargement and reorganization of the General Sunday School Committee (1915-37) and a merger of other General Conference committees active in Christian education, viz., Young People's Bible Meeting Committee (1909-37), and Young People's Problems Committee (1921-37). The Commission was charged with the responsibility to co-ordinate, promote, and supervise the Christian education agencies operating in the local congregations, not including the church schools under the direction of the Mennonite Board of Education.

The Commission is composed of 12 members. At first six were elected by General Conference, one each by the Mennonite Board of Missions and Charities, Mennonite Publication Board, and the Mennonite Board of Education, and three by the Commission itself. In 1941 General Conference adopted a revised constitution by which ten members are elected by General Conference and two by the Commission itself.

The Commission meets semiannually. In these meetings the Commission works as a cabinet, each of the officers and divisional secretaries for the various phases of education giving his report. The Field Secretary is the executive officer of the Commission, and with each divisional secretary forms a committee of two to implement recommendations from the Commission and to plan a program of promotion in each area of interest. The scope of Commission work is seen in the present (1957) list of divisional secretaries: (1) Sunday schools, (2) summer Bible schools, (3) weekday Bible schools, (4) church camps, (5) Christian service training, (6) missionary education, (7) church music, (8) junior activities, (9) young people's activities, (10) adult activities, (11) home interests, (12) audio-visual aids, (13) Sunday evening services. Each secretary is to study his respective field, to carry on a program of promotion in co-operation with field secretary, to co-operate in the planning of curriculum materials, and to collect pertinent statistics.

During 1941-56 the Commission published annually the *Handbook for Christian Workers*. It has also published many pieces of promotional literature.

The Commission has co-ordinated the teaching efforts of the Church, and has contributed to improved teaching efficiency. The Commission has led the church in facing educational problems, such as child evangelism; it has taken the lead, through its Curriculum Committee, in planning needed curriculum materials. It has sponsored Sunday-school conventions and workshops, and has brought the attention of the church to special teaching emphases through its annual teaching themes, such as "Christian Training for Every Member" (1943), "Christian Nonresistance" (1953), "Every Member Evangelism" (1954), "Christian Nonconformity" (1955), and "Knowing and Using the Bible" (1956). The Curriculum Committee is at the heart of the educational program. It is responsible both to the Commission and the Mennonite Publication Board (*q.v.*). Its work in stating objectives and outlining curriculum materials for summer Bible school and Sunday-school use is worthy of note.

The first officers of the Commission were as follows: A. J. Metzler, chairman; O. O. Miller, vice-chairman; Paul Erb, secretary-treasurer; fourth member, Jesse B. Martin; and I. W. Royer, fifth member. J. R. Mumaw was first field secretary. In 1957 the officers are Richard Detweiler, chairman; Noah Good, vice-chairman; J. J. Hostetler, secretary-treasurer, and Paul M. Lederach, field secretary. Fourth and fifth members are no longer elected. Paul Mininger was long chairman of the Curriculum Committee.   P.M.L.

Mennonite Community, The, a 36-page periodical published by the Mennonite Community Association (*q.v.*) at Scottdale, Pa., January 1947 to October 1949; at first a bimonthly, in January 1948 it became a monthly. In November 1949 responsibility for its publication was assumed by the Mennonite Publishing House. Stressing the social implications of the Gospel, the journal conceived of the Christian community as church-centered and was concerned that its economic, social, educational, and cultural life should be a true expression of the Gospel to which the church adheres. Emphasis was placed on social ethics, stewardship, brotherhood, Christian education, and health practices. In January 1954 the *Mennonite Community* and the *Christian Monitor* (*q.v.*) were discontinued and replaced by a new periodical, *Christian Living* (*q.v.*), combining the interests of both, and described as "A Magazine for Home and Community." The editor of the *Mennonite Community* was Grant Stoltzfus to August 1952, after which an editorial committee with Ralph Hernley as chairman had charge of the journal.
        G.F.H.

Mennonite Community Association (MC) was organized in 1946, its stated purpose being "to support and strengthen the Christian community as expressed in Mennonite teachings and practices; to stimulate community interests—religious, social, cultural, economic—among the Mennonite people; to publicize the Mennonite way of life through the medium of publications and any other means deemed advisable by the Association."

The major undertaking of the Association was the founding of the *Mennonite Community* (*q.v.*) magazine which it published from January 1947 to October 1949. Beginning in November 1949 and continuing to December 1953 the magazine was published by the Mennonite Publishing House. Beginning in January 1954 the *Mennonite Community* and the *Christian Monitor* were discontinued and a new periodical, *Christian Living* (*1 Magazine for Home and Community*), took their place. The Mennonite Community Association maintains a close relationship to the new periodical, two of its officers serving as consulting editors of *Christian Living*.

In 1950 the Association, in co-operation with the John C. Winston Company, published the *Mennonite Community Cookbook,* a compilation of 1,400 favorite family recipes collected by Mary Emma Showalter from Mennonite communities in the United States and Canada. Since 1949 the Association has co-operated with the Committee on Economic and Social Relations of the Mennonite Church

(MC) in sponsoring an annual Conference on Christian Community Relations. The Association also supports the work of the Mennonite Research Foundation (*q.v.*), and since 1953 has awarded several scholarships annually to advanced students who show promise in the area of Christian community leadership.   G.F.H.

Mennonite Community Church (GCM), located in Fresno, Cal., and previously known as the General Conference Fellowship of Fresno, was organized on Nov. 21, 1954, and affiliated with the Pacific District Conference in 1955. Ground-breaking services for a new church, with a seating capacity of 180, took place in August 1955. The building was dedicated in April 1956. The minister (1957) is Peter J. Ediger; there are 57 members.   P.J.E.

Mennonite Country Church (GCM), located near Monroe, Snohomish Co., Wash., a member of the Pacific Conference, was organized on June 14, 1944. The first settlers arrived in 1911, coming from Oklahoma and Pretty Prairie, Kan. The church, a cement block building with seating capacity of 150, was dedicated in February 1946. In 1956 the membership was 52, with Donald Emmert as pastor.
        D.R.E.

Mennonite Crusaders, Inc., organized in June 1951 and incorporated in Virginia June 16, 1952, was an organization of interested Virginia Mennonites created to operate *The Mennonite Hour* (*q.v.*). In 1956 it changed its name to Mennonite Broadcasts, Inc. (*q.v.*). In June 1953 it entered into an agreement with the Mennonite Board of Missions and Charities to operate and promote a Mennonite broadcasting program co-operatively and thus it became an officially endorsed and supervised agency. Headquarters were at Harrisonburg, Va., where it maintained its studio. The officers were Lewis Strite president, Richard Weaver vice-president, Harley Rhodes secretary-treasurer, Norman Derstine program director, B. Charles Hostetter radio pastor. Besides its periodical publications, *Mennonite Hour Informer* and *Mennonite Hour Prayer Guide,* it began in 1952 a series of publications consisting of collected sermons of the radio pastor. It also operated a Bible correspondence course. Mennonite Crusaders was financed by voluntary contributions, largely from the radio audience. In June 1955 it was broadcasting over 32 stations in the United States, in addition to two in Canada, Radio Ceylon on four beams, Quito, Ecuador, Manila in the Philippines, with eight programs, two in Puerto Rico, and one in the Virgin Islands.   H.S.B.

Mennonite Cultural Problems Conference. General cultural developments by the latter 1930's had made a number of American Mennonite leaders conscious of the need for periodic discussion of common problems on an inter-Mennonite basis. Acting on this awareness, Harold S. Bender, Guy F. Hershberger, Melvin Gingerich, and J. Winfield Fretz took the initiative in organizing a program for a one-day discussion of some of the common problems confronting Mennonites. It was called a Conference on Mennonite Sociology and was held on Dec. 31, 1941, in the YMCA Hotel in Chicago, 47 of the 53 invited guests being present. It was unanimously agreed that further conferences should be held. A committee drew up a two-day program for a conference to be held on Aug. 7-8, 1942. There were 119 registered guests at the first session of what came to be known as the Conference on Mennonite Cultural Problems.

The first six sessions were held annually, but from 1949 on it was decided to meet every two years, usually on Mennonite and Brethren in Christ college campuses on a rotating basis. Although this conference had a spontaneous origin by a group of interested individuals, it was decided at the first meeting to place the responsibility for future conferences in the hands of a more permanently organized group. The group chosen was the Council of Mennonite and Affiliated Colleges, which is a loosely organized association of college administrators. This Council appoints the program committee for the Cultural Conference sessions and assumes financial responsibility for the publication of the conference proceedings, which have appeared regularly.

The significance of the Cultural Conference sessions is becoming more apparent as the results of its first ten sessions can be appraised. It provides the occasion for a periodic meeting of Mennonite and affiliated college faculty members to discuss common cultural problems. It stimulates intellectual inquiry and academic research in areas and on problems that universities and non-Mennonite colleges would normally not touch. It provides a method for regularly collecting and publishing research data, which in turn become valuable documentary material for further reference and study.   J.W.F.

Mennonite Cyclopedic Dictionary, *A Compendium of the Doctrines, History, Activities, Literature and Environments of the Mennonite Church* (Scottdale, 1937), a condensed reference manual of 445 pages, with mostly short articles, was not only edited but also largely written by Daniel Kauffman (*q.v.*). The subject matter is limited largely to the Mennonite Church (MC). It includes, besides a large number of biographies and brief sketches of congregations and institutions, thumbnail genealogical reports on 382 Mennonite families.   H.S.B.

Mennonite Deaconess Home and Hospital was founded in Beatrice, Neb., as the result of a jubilee celebration on Jan. 27, 1905, which commemorated the founding of the Mennonite church in the Beatrice community and the 25th anniversary of the ministry of Gerhard Penner and Peter Reimer. A block of ground in the city of Beatrice was donated to the Mennonite church as a site for the proposed hospital. The church elected a group of 12 men to serve as a board for the building and operation of the hospital. Building operations began in 1910 and on July 16, 1911, the hospital was dedicated. The work of the hospital is conducted by a small group of deaconesses.

A nurses' training school was conducted by the hospital for a number of years, which was later reorganized on a two-year basis and for a number of years trained practical nurses. The hospital has

sought to serve the church as means of expressing Christian love and concern for our fellow men through care of the sick, and has been a means of interpreting Mennonite principles to the community.

The hospital is now engaged in a building program which will result in a new hospital building of 50 beds. The existing building will then be used for chronically ill and convalescent patients.

In 1956 the administrator was Edmund P. Zehr; the superintendent of nursing was Martha Thimm, with a staff of five deaconesses.   E.Z.

Mennonite Disaster Service, an organized program for a service by Mennonite laymen in the United States and Canada to aid the victims of natural disasters such as floods, tornadoes, storms, earthquakes, and fire by cleanup and reconstruction work, largely in damaged homes. Such work supplements the familiar Red Cross operations which primarily provide emergency food and medical supplies, clothing, and shelter in addition to direct financial aid. MDS operates typically by assembling groups of men who at their own expense and with their own tools proceed to the disaster area and work at their own expense for a period of several days or weeks doing what they can to make damaged homes livable again.

The idea of MDS arose after World War II. The first organization was made at Hesston, Kan., in 1950 in the local Mennonite Church (MC); it was made inter-Mennonite in 1951. The second organization was formed in Northern Indiana and Western Ohio, where in 1953 a group was formed to work in the tornado area at Flint, Mich. As the idea spread, other local MDS organizations were formed, usually inter-Mennonite in character. The need for larger co-ordination and counsel led to a request by several conferences for co-ordination on a national basis. On May 15, 1954, the Executive Committee of the MCC created by appointment the Disaster Service Co-ordinating Committee. This committee also has the responsibility of liaisonship with the United States Government, particularly in matters relating to Civil Defense, and the American Red Cross. In 1956 it was composed of representatives of the following Mennonite Conferences: M.C., G.C.M., E.M.C., C.M., the Brethren in Christ, and the MCC headquarters office. Provision is also made for Canadian representation. It meets annually with representatives of the local or regional disaster organizations. Most of the local units also meet annually. The program is decentralized, with local units springing into action as needed, and without centralized administration. In 1957 the organized regional Mennonite Disaster Service units in active existence were as follows: Arizona-California, British Columbia, Idaho, Illinois, Indiana-Michigan, Iowa-Missouri, Kansas, Manitoba, Minnesota, Nebraska, New York State, Eastern Ohio, Western Ohio, Oklahoma, Western Pennsylvania, Lancaster County, Pa., Eastern Pennsylvania, and South Dakota.   W.T.S.

Mennonite Educational Buildings, Inc., a nonprofit corporation organized in 1950 to take over the assets of Mennonite Educational Finance, Inc. (*q.v.*) and continue its program of financing Mennonite

(MC) college building erection on a long-term loan basis. Its officers were Edwin Yoder president, and C. L. Graber secretary-treasurer. In 1957 it transferred its assets to Mennonite Church Buildings, Inc., (*q.v.*) and was dissolved.   H.S.B.

Mennonite Educational Finance, Inc., was organized in 1928 to secure funds on a loan basis from the constituency of Goshen College to supply long-term loans to the college to finance the erection or remodeling of college buildings. It financed Coffman Hall, the remodeling of Kulp Hall, and the erection of three college cabins. It also financed a building for Hesston College. Officers throughout were Edwin Yoder (Topeka, Ind.) chairman, and C. L. Graber (Goshen) secretary-treasurer. In 1950 it transferred its assets to Mennonite Educational Buildings, Inc. (*q.v.*) and was dissolved.   H.S.B.

Mennonite Educational Institute (M.E.I.), at Clearbrook, formerly Abbotsford, B.C., the first Mennonite high school in British Columbia, was founded in 1944. The need for Mennonite high schools in British Columbia became more and more obvious as the Mennonite population increased. A small group of Mennonite Brethren parents in the Abbotsford district decided to begin such a school, and classes were announced (grades 9, 10, and 11) for the fall of 1944, when 43 enrolled, together with a smaller group of Bible students, using the Bible School building. F. C. Thiessen was the first principal, with I. J. Dyck and H. H. Nikkel as teachers. Six local Mennonite Brethren churches (South Abbotsford, Abbotsford, Arnold, Clearbrook, Matsqui, and East Aldergrove) and one General Conference Mennonite Church (Abbotsford United Mennonite) officially supported the school, but the 403 pupils (1955-56) came from 20 different congregations. A commodious new building located just north of the Clearbrook M.B. Church was dedicated at Christmas of 1946, when the student body numbered 164. In 1954 a Junior High School with four classrooms, a library, and a gymnasium were added; two additional classrooms were added in 1956.

The curriculum includes all the courses of the public schools for grades 7-13, as well as classes in music, Bible, Mennonite history, and German. The staff in 1955-56 consisted of 14 teachers, with I. J. Dyck as principal. The graduates numbered 38 in the year 1953, 47 in 1954, 38 in 1955, 35 in 1956, and 56 in 1957. Of the 260 graduates in 1946-55, 140 are engaged in teaching, 27 in business, 21 in nursing. The *Students' Call,* a monthly paper edited by the students, and the annual, *Evergreen,* cover all school activities. In scholastic endeavors, students of the M.E.I. have monopolized the scholarships offered locally. The school has two excellent choirs and a good sports program. A readily noticed Christian spirit pervades the school life, and is given opportunities for expression in the morning devotions, prayer meetings, and the testimony meeting at the end of each week. This is the largest of all Mennonite high schools, with an enrollment of about 450. I. J. Dyck has been principal since 1945.

C.F.K.

"Mennonite Educational Institute," *Konferenz-Jugendblatt,* September-October 1955, 11, 13; *Evergreen* (School Annual) for 1954 contains a history of the school.

Mennonite Educational Institute, Altona, Man. By 1905 it was felt that the building of the Mennonite Collegiate Institute (*q.v.*) at Gretna should be remodeled or replaced by a new building. Some felt that the new building, if any, should be constructed at Altona, which would offer a more convenient site. In an open meeting in May 1905, a majority vote was cast for the Gretna site. Those favoring Altona thereupon raised money for a new school, and somewhat later the Gretna supporters also raised money for a new building. By 1908 the two schools were built and in operation. The Gretna school was incorporated as the Mennonite Collegiate Institute (M.C.I.) and the Altona school as the Mennonite Educational Institute (M.E.I.).

The M.E.I. was built on the present site of the Agricultural Hall and Fair Grounds of Altona. In January 1926 the building was burned to the ground and has not been rebuilt. The object of the school was to train Mennonite teachers for the schools in the Manitoba Mennonite settlements. The principals of the school have been J. J. Balzer, G. G. Neufeld, J. S. Schultz, and Gerhard Friesen.   H.H.H.

Mennonite Evangelizing Board of America, the first mission board of the Mennonite Church (MC), was organized at the Salem Church south of Elkhart, Ind., on Jan. 20, 1892, as the successor to the Evangelizing Committee which had been organized Oct. 13, 1882. The constitution reads: "The object of this organization shall be to collect means and maintain a treasury for the purpose of carrying on a general missionary work." The money was to be used to send men wherever needed, "but especially among scattered members of the church, and churches not supplied at all or unsufficiently supplied with laborers." Whereas the Evangelizing Committee had been composed solely of local men in Elkhart County, the new board was to be general, with representatives invited from all the Mennonite and Amish conferences in sympathy with the work. Headquarters, however, were to continue at Elkhart. To begin with, fourteen members were "elected" from Indiana, Ohio, Illinois, Missouri, Kansas, and Nebraska. The officers were F. W. Brunk president, Herman Yoder vice-president, A. B. Kolb secretary, Josiah Sommers treasurer, all laymen, and all from the Elkhart and Goshen area. In 1894 G. L. Bender was elected treasurer, to begin his long career of treasurer and chief executive officer of the central mission organization of the church. At the annual meeting held on Oct. 7, 1896, the name of the board was changed to Mennonite Evangelizing and Benevolent Board, to indicate a merger with the Benevolent Organization of Mennonites, which had been incorporated in Indiana on April 23, 1894, "to support, maintain, and carry on Home and Foreign Missions, Hospitals, Orphans' Homes, Training Schools for the Education of Nurses, Deaconesses and Bible Students," also with headquarters at Elkhart, and considerable overlapping of membership. The new Mennonite Evangelizing and Benevolent Board was now incorporated.

The first act of the new board was to "accept" the Chicago Home Mission, which had been started as an independent work in 1893. This launched the board on a direct mission career. Its first foreign mission project was the establishment of a mission in India, J. A. Ressler and W. B. Page and his wife going out in 1899. The mission was located in Dhamtari.

The Home and Foreign Relief Commission (*q.v.*), which was organized in 1897, a committee under the Mennonite Evangelizing and Benevolent Board, withdrew from the parent organization and organized itself independently on Nov. 22, 1897. It continued in existence as a companion organization to the Board until 1906-7, when the latter became the Mennonite Board of Missions and Charities. Its chief work was to send relief to India in 1897-98 and support famine orphans in India in the years immediately following.

The final stage of organization of the Mennonite Evangelizing and Benevolent Board was the merger with the Mennonite Board of Charitable Homes and Missions (*q.v.*) at a joint meeting of the two boards at Rittman, Ohio, on May 22, 1906. Thus at last the general mission and charitable organizations of the church were unified and a strong and broad base created for the expanding work of the Mennonite Church in these fields. Officers of the Evangelizing and Benevolent Board in 1896-1906 were A. B. Kolb president to 1905, J. K. Hartzler, Daniel Shenk, A. R. Zook successive vice-presidents, the latter 1900-5, C. K. Hostetler secretary to 1905, except for the first year when G. L. Bender served, G. L. Bender treasurer throughout except for the first year when C. K. Hostetler was treasurer. In 1925, in preparation for the merger, the following officers were chosen: J. S. Shoemaker president, D. S. Yoder vice-president, I. R. Detweiler secretary, G. L. Bender treasurer. The minutes of the Board to and including 1897 were reprinted in the *Gospel Herald* for March 11, 18, and 25, 1952 (254-57, 278-80, 302).　　H.S.B.

Levi Hartzler, *A Brief History of Mennonite Missions* (Elkhart, 1955).

Mennonite Evangelizing Committee, the first organization for evangelistic and mission work in the Mennonite Church (MC), was organized on Dec. 28, 1882, at Elkhart, Ind., by members of the Elkhart congregation acting as private persons. The pastor, J. F. Funk, was the leading spirit in promoting it, and the chairman for several years. The report of the organizing meeting states that it was decided to form a "local permanent organization consisting of a managing committee of three, plus a secretary and treasurer." The first election placed J. F. Funk, Martin Wenger, and Henry Brenneman on the managing committee and Joseph Summers and J. J. Hostetler as treasurer and secretary. The Committee actually was an unofficial organization formed to carry out the decision of the Indiana Conference of Oct. 13, 1882, "that means should be collected for the purpose of defraying the expenses incurred in traveling to visit scattered members and churches." A meeting of the Committee on March 15, 1883, decided to enlarge its purpose to include fund-raising, "also to preach the Gospel where our church and

doctrines are not known." It decided to activate the conference request to hold quarterly offerings. It also decided that it should work under the Elkhart congregation. At the first annual meeting J. F. Funk and J. S. Coffman were elected president and secretary respectively, Coffman serving a number of years. The members of the managing committee for several years were Martin Wenger, Noah Hoover, and Henry Brenneman. Later A. B. Kolb was a leading member. Although the Committee was local, it held most of its meetings as public sessions in the Mennonite meetinghouses south of Elkhart, and did much to promote interest in evangelism through its programs. The last meeting was held on Jan. 20, 1892, when the Committee was transformed into the Mennonite Evangelizing Board (*q.v.*). The work of the Committee was usually small (e.g., 1887, $118.61), although in 1890 it reached a peak of $718.97. The minutes of the Committee were printed entire in the *Gospel Herald* for March 4, 1952, pp. 230-33.　　H.S.B.

Mennonite General Conference is the over-all representative body of the Mennonite Church (MC), formally organized in 1898. Since the locus of authority in the Mennonite Church is the district conference, and the general boards and institutions of the church are independent and self-perpetuating, the General Conference has remained from the beginning advisory and consultant in relation to the district conferences and general boards. In fact four district conferences of the church (Franconia, Lancaster, Washington Co., Md. and Franklin Co., Pa., and Ontario Amish) have never formally joined the General Conference, although they participate in varying degrees in General Conference work and all but the third work in the General Council of General Conference. They are fully a part of the Mennonite Church nevertheless. In spite of its lack of authority the pronouncements of the General Conference in matters of faith and life carry great weight, and the work of the committees which it has created and directs has had and still has great value and influence for the church at large.

In 1957 the committees of the General Conference were the following: Executive Committee, General Council, Commission for Christian Education, Peace Problems Committee, Committee on Economic and Social Relations, General Problems Committee, Ministerial Committee, Mennonite Mutual Aid, Committee on Worship (projected for creation at 1957 session).

The General Council, established in 1951, which acts as the interim representative body for the General Conference, is composed of the officers of the G.C., a representative from each G.C. committee, each district conference and each church-wide general board, with a total membership in 1957 of 35. It has become an important body, meeting three or four times between the biennial sessions of General Conference. It recommends the General Conference biennial budget, approves the biennial conference program, counsels the General Conference committees at their request, and acts in emergencies for the General Conference. It does not have administrative responsibility for General Conference committees;

they are directly responsible to the General Conference. Since 1953 the conference has had an executive secretary. The first incumbent is Paul Erb, still serving.

The delegate body of General Conference was formerly constituted of all the ordained bishops of the church, delegates elected by conference, and one representative from each General Conference committee. In 1955 the basis of representation was changed so that now the delegate body consists of all members of the General Council and delegates elected from the district conferences at the rates of one delegate to 200 members, but bishops from non-electing conferences are recognized as delegates ex officio. The number of delegates in attendance in recent sessions averages 125-150, with a total audience varying from 1,500 to 6,000.

The sessions of General Conference are held biennially in the odd years, usually entertained by the larger Mennonite communities. They combine business sessions for the delegates with general and inspirational addresses.

A preliminary session was held in 1897 at Elida, Ohio, the first regular session at Wakarusa, Ind., in 1898.

The proceedings of the conference have been regularly printed, and since 1925 include the full text of all reports and the text of most or all of the programmed sermons and addresses.   H.S.B.

H. S. Bender, "The Function and Authority of General Conference, A Review of Past History," *Gospel Herald* XXXVII (1944) 289 f., 306, 316 f.; *Proceedings of the Mennonite General Conference, Including Discussions Leading to Its Origination* (1890-1919) (Scottdale, 1921).

Mennonite Girls' Center (MC), located at 412 E. Lincoln Ave., Goshen, Ind., was founded for the purpose of providing a Christian home for Mennonite girls who are working in Goshen. This 16-room building was purchased in May 1947 and dedicated on Dec. 1, 1947, with 16 roomers. The Indiana-Michigan Mennonite Mission Board and the Women's Missionary Auxiliary sponsor the work of the Center and appoint a committee of four members for a term of two years, which effects its own organization and appoints a fifth member who serves as executive vice-chairman and manager. This committee also secures the matron in charge of the Center. The Center has served more than 165 girls from 12 different states and various denominations, providing Christian fellowship, conveniences, various activities, and social contacts.   A.Br.

Mennonite Girls' Home (Reading, Pa.). Because many girls from outside this immediate area were working as domestics in Reading, and a few were attending night school or taking nurses' training in the city hospital, the Girls' Home was opened at 704 N. 12th Street in 1935, to serve as a home for those who roomed away from their place of employment and as a congregating center for the others on hours off duty. These benefits, with a licensed placement agency, made this a real home for such girls. Margaret Horst was for many years matron of the Home. As a home and girls' center only it has continued over the years, with Elsie Gehman as chairman of the management. It is sponsored by the

Eastern Board of Missions and Charities, and has been a real asset to Mennonite missions in the city. In 1937 alone, 63 girls had contact with the Home, and in two years 150 girls from thirteen states and numerous conferences used its facilities.   I.D.L.

Mennonite Girls' Home (Saskatoon, Sask.). With the immigration of Mennonites from Russia to Canada in 1923-30, many girls worked in Saskatoon to aid their parents, who had lost their possessions during the Revolution in Russia, in establishing new homes and in repaying the transportation debt to the Canadian Pacific Railway Company. The Home Mission Board (GCM) was interested in the spiritual welfare of the girls in the city and on the recommendation of David Toews of Rosthern established the Girls' Home (dedicated on Jan. 29, 1931), with the following aims: (*a*) to provide the girls with a home as a substitute for their parental home; (*b*) to find suitable employment for the girls and, where necessary, to protect them from exploitation; (*c*) to give them the necessary spiritual guidance. J. J. Thiessen and Mrs. Thiessen were in charge of the home from the beginning until its closing in 1956.

On Thursday afternoon and evening, when the girls were off duty, they gathered in the Girls' Home for relaxation, recreation, and fellowship. Whenever possible the girls attended the church services in the First Mennonite Church of Saskatoon. During their association with the Mennonite Girls' Home and the church many of the girls were received into the church by baptism.

The largest attendance was registered in the depression years. During World War II many girls went home to the parental farms to replace their brothers who were drafted. At the close of the war and the following years, with the coming of the Mennonite refugees to Canada, the number of Mennonite girls working in the city again increased. Since the establishment of the home over 500 girls of various denominations have availed themselves of the services of the Mennonite Girls' Home in Saskatoon. The twenty-fifth anniversary of the home was celebrated on Jan. 29, 1956.   J.J.Th.

Mennonite Gospel Center (MC), 1238 Washington Ave., Kansas City, Mo., was one of the two descendants of the Mennonite Gospel Mission (*q.v.*) of Kansas City, Kan., the other being the Morris Gospel Hall, R. 2, Kansas City, Kan. The Center was organized in 1946. Edward Yoder was superintendent from the beginning of both locations until he withdrew from the Mennonite Church to start an independent work in 1951, when the membership was 41. Morris Gospel Hall was destroyed by the great Kansas City flood about that time, and F. B. Raber took charge of the Gospel Center. In 1956 John T. Kreider was in charge, with a membership of 39.   H.S.B.

Mennonite Gospel Mission, Ft. Wayne, Ind.: see **Fort Wayne** First Mennonite Church.

Mennonite Gospel Mission (MC), Kansas City, Kan., was opened in 1905 at 200 S. 7th Street, under the direction of a local mission board appointed by the Missouri-Iowa and the Kansas-Nebraska district conferences; later the work was taken over by the Mennonite Board of Missions and Charities. In February 1946 the Mission was discontinued and the Argentine Mennonite Church (q.v.) was organized as its direct successor, acquiring 130 of the 176 members of the Mission.

The following served as superintendents in the order named: J. F. Brunk, J. D. Charles, C. A. Hartzler, J. D. Mininger, Wm. Smith, and Edward Yoder. Many persons have contributed years of service as mission workers, assisting the superintendent and matron. J. D. Mininger (q.v.) was the long-time superintendent and outstanding leader. The original building at 200 S. 7th Street was sold and a church was built at 3701 Metropolitan Ave., Kansas City, Kan., and dedicated Feb. 25, 1925. Additional places of worship were located at Morris, Kan., and at 1238 Washington Ave., Kansas City, Mo. When the Argentine Mennonite Church was organized these two places were continued as missions under the joint name of Twin City Missions (q.v.), the Washington Avenue place being called the Mennonite Gospel Center (q.v.).   R.P.H.

Mennonite Gospel Mission, Norristown, Pa.: see Norristown First Mennonite Church.

Mennonite Gospel Mission, a project of the Pigeon River Conservative Mennonite Church, is located near Vassar, Mich. Work was begun here by Emanuel Swartzendruber in 1939. In 1945 Orie Kauffman took charge of the mission, moving into the community in 1948. In 1950 a new church was dedicated. The membership in 1956 is 15; Elam Bender is pastor in charge of the mission.   Or.K.

Mennonite Gospel Mission Church, Peoria, Ill., was opened in 1914 by the Home Mission Committee of the Central Conference (GCM). Jacob Sommer, who was assisting at the Mennonite Gospel Mission in Chicago, was called to open this new work in Peoria. The first service was held in a rented store building at 920 North Adams St., with 37 in attendance; in 1916 the present building was erected at 1001 North Adams St. At present (1956) there is a church membership of 148, which affords a strong working group for constant need of mission work in a city such as Peoria, and the minister is Samuel Ummel, with Melvin Norquist as assistant.   S.U.

Mennonite Hilfs-Plan (Aid Plan) of Moundridge, Kan., a mutual fire and storm insurance association, was organized Jan. 13, 1900, to serve all branches of Mennonites in the prairie states, chiefly Kansas. In 1953 it served 3,000 members with $20,000,000.

Mennonite Historical Association (Society) *of North America* was founded at the General Conference Mennonite Church sessions at Bluffton, Ohio, Sept. 2, 1911, by individuals interested in collecting and preserving historical material pertaining to the Mennonites. Those present at this first meeting were N. B. Grubb, H. P. Krehbiel, Eddison Mosiman, C. H. Regier, J. R. Toews, Gerhard Penner, C. H. A. van der Smissen, S. M. Grubb, H. D. Penner, N. W. Bahnmann, H. A. Bachmann, S. K. Mosiman, J. H. Langenwalter, J. S. Krehbiel, A. J. Krehbiel, G. Wiebe, H. H. Ewert, G. A. Haury, J. W. Kliewer,

John H. von Steen, Hermann Wiebe, and D. C. Welty. A second meeting was held on September 5, at which time N. B. Grubb was elected president; S. K. Mosiman, vice-president; H. P. Krehbiel, secretary; G. A. Haury, treasurer. Twenty-two charter members joined the newly founded organization, each one paying one dollar membership dues.

The next meeting of the Association took place in connection with the General Conference Mennonite Church sessions at Meno, Okla., at which time S. M. Grubb presented a paper, "The Importance of Collecting Historical Material of Our Denomination." H. R. Voth was elected president; S. K. Mosiman, vice-president; H. P. Krehbiel, secretary; and G. A. Haury, treasurer. The executive committee was given authority to make changes in organization in line with the needs and to ask the Conference to set aside at the next session a whole evening for the Mennonite Historical Association. During the General Conference sessions in Reedley, Cal., in 1917 the Association presented its first report. From then on the reports were printed with the Conference minutes. A constitution had been printed in German and in English. The dues were now one dollar for five years, and ten dollars for a lifetime. Membership was 117. H. R. Voth, who had done most in collecting materials, was chairman at this time. The classification of some 6,400 items was under way. G. A. Haury was also actively engaged in collecting materials. Some of the material was kept in the vault of the Herald Publishing Company and some at Bethel College, both at Newton, Kan. Periodicals, books, photographs, manuscripts were being collected, filed, and catalogued "during the late hours of the night" in the home of the chairman, H. R. Voth. At the Freeman Conference sessions in 1923, the officers H. R. Voth, H. P. Krehbiel, and G. A. Haury reported that 2,110 items of the 10,240 objects collected had been catalogued. The pressing question as to where to place and make available the collected material was answered when Bethel College offered space in the newly erected Science Hall.

The reports of the Association for 1925 indicate that plans were under way to establish a Mennonite Memorial Museum on the Bethel College campus to house the collection. The reports of 1926 and 1929 also emphasized this need. When the report of 1933 was given, the chairman, H. R. Voth, had passed away and the work came to a near standstill. The executive committee of the Association, consisting of P. H. Richert, P. H. Unruh, A. J. Dyck, and H. P. Krehbiel, stated that "the extensive collection of the historical material continues to be stored rent-free in a fireproof vault owned by H. P. Krehbiel." The latter was the chief promoter of the Association at this time. In 1938 he proposed the erection of a Mennonite Historical Institute. C. E. Krehbiel also became active in the Association at this time. However, meanwhile the Mennonite historical libraries (q.v.) at Bethel College, under the able direction of A. Warkentin, and at Bluffton College, under the senior historian C. Henry Smith, had become the chief centers of collection and preservation of Mennonite materials within the General Conference Mennonite Church.

The special Historical Committee, which gave its first report at the Conference sessions in 1941, was now appointed by the Executive Committee of the General Conference, consisting of J. R. Thierstein, H. P. Krehbiel, A. Warkentin, and H. A. Fast. This interim committee worked in close harmony with the Bethel College Historical Library. The bulk of the material remained in the H. P. Krehbiel vault but material received at this time was placed in the Bethel College Historical Library with a college or conference label. The Conference made $25.00 available monthly for the cataloguing of such materials. The members appointed to this special committee at the 1941 Conference were A. Warkentin, H. A. Dyck, P. A. Penner, E. E. Leisy, and C. Henry Smith. In 1947 a permanent Historical Committee (q.v.) of the General Conference Mennonite Church was appointed, with A. Warkentin as chairman, Cornelius Krahn as secretary, and C. Henry Smith, A. J. Dyck, E. E. Leisy, and Paul R. Shelly as members, which took over the responsibility of the old Mennonite Historical Association, and the latter was dissolved. The collection of the Association located in the H. P. Krehbiel vault at Newton was transferred to the Bethel College Historical Library, some of which was later transferred to the Mennonite Biblical Seminary Library, Chicago, and other Mennonite libraries.

The Mennonite Historical Association was the first organization among the Mennonites of North America to pioneer in the preservation of valuable Mennonite documents. C. H. Wedel (q.v.), who died when this organization was coming into being, had laid the foundation, and inspired the younger generation to preserve records of the heritage which would have otherwise been lost. A list of the materials collected by the Association is to be found in the Bethel College Historical Library.   C.K.

Minute Book of the Mennonite Historical Society (Association), 1911-31, kept by H. P. Krehbiel, contains constitution, minutes, membership lists, and articles received (BeCL); reports of the Mennonite Historical Association in *Minutes and Reports of General Conference Mennonite Church*, 1917, 1920, 1923, 1926, etc.

Mennonite Historical Bulletin is published by the Historical Committee of the Mennonite General Conference (MC). The first issue appeared in April 1940 and for two years it remained a four-page semi-annual publication. Since 1942 four issues a year have been published, two of which have been eight-page since 1952. It features biographies, local church history, family history, book reviews, and other articles of a semipopular nature. The *Bulletin* has maintained the same format, 8½ by 11 in. Editors have been John C. Wenger, Edward Yoder, Grant Stoltzfus, Melvin Gingerich, and John A. Hostetler, who is the present editor (1956).   M.G.

Mennonite Historical Library of Bethel College (or Bethel College Historical Library), North Newton, Kan., had its beginning at the turn of the century, when C. H. Wedel (q.v.), the first president of Bethel College, engaged in Mennonite research, taught Mennonite history, collected materials, and published books along these lines. The C. H. Wedel Collection and the acquisitions for the college library

in his days are evidence of this. Historical books and artifacts were kept in the Bethel College Museum located in the Science Hall. Various faculty members were in charge of this growing collection, which also contained Mennonitica. In 1932-33 the Museum was reorganized by a committee headed by Abraham Warkentin. The Museum proper was now transferred to Alumni Hall, and the Mennonite books and documents of the Museum, together with those from the college library, became the nucleus of the present Bethel College Historical Library. The cataloging of books was begun on March 30, 1937, by Mrs. P. S. Goertz, who continued this work for a number of years and devised a cataloging system for Mennonite libraries based on the Dewey Decimal Classification system. By Jan. 1, 1940, 1,130 books had been cataloged. Warkentin served as director of the library from the reorganization until 1944, when Cornelius Krahn succeeded him. In 1933-53 the Historical Library was housed in the basement of the Science Hall, in which a vault had been established. During the summer of 1953 the Historical Library was moved to its present location, the basement floor of the new college library building. Some of the rooms have been furnished by friends of the library in memory of their relatives. John and Linda Warkentin furnished the director's room in memory of Abraham Warkentin; Mrs. Elva Leisy furnished the office in memory of her father, H. P. Krehbiel; Cornelius J. and Aaron J. Claassen established the Cornelius Jansen Collection and furnished the vault, etc.

The new rooms were planned to house the following major divisions of the Mennonite Historical Library: books, periodicals, archives, photographs, charts, microfilms, slides, works of art, special collections, and *Mennonite Life*, (q.v.).

(1) In the book division it is aimed to collect books and pamphlets dealing with any phase of Anabaptist-Mennonite history. The number of cataloged books in 1955 was over 10,000, exclusive of reference books, periodicals, annual publications, etc. The 16th- and 17th-century items are kept in the vault of the library.

(2) In the periodical division all official Mennonite papers, some Mennonite community papers, conference reports, school publications, church bulletins and yearbooks are kept on display for a year, then bound. Some 200 current periodicals are received.

(3) The archives contain church records, diaries, special collections—some of which are special memorial units, such as the Rodolphe Petter Collection, A. A. Friesen Collection, J. H. Janzen Collection, and Cornelius Jansen Collection (see **Archives**). A large special fireproof vault houses this material.

(4) Several thousand photographs and slides dealing with various phases of the Mennonites covering a period of centuries are being cataloged. Over 2,000 cuts used in *Mennonite Life* have been cataloged and filed. Slides on Mennonites and church history are made available for classes, lectures in churches, etc.

(5) Microfilms are kept in a special room with a microfilm reader. The collection contained over 100,000 exposures in 1955, owned by the college and the General Conference Historical Committee. Many

documents pertaining to the Mennonites of America have been microfilmed, but the greater portion consists of European Anabaptist sources. Most important among them are the Archives of the Mennonite Church of Amsterdam, the largest collection of this kind, which has been completely microfilmed.

(6) The Mennonite Art Collection contains original etchings and paintings by Rembrandt, J. Ruisdael, the Mesdags, D. Wohlgemuth, and many contemporary Mennonite artists. In addition to this there are many etchings of Mennonite leaders, etc.

(7) Several hundred different Bible translations and editions, some going back to the 16th century, have been collected. The library has a nearly complete collection of the Mennonite songbooks used in Prussia, Russia, and America.

An increasing number of graduate and undergraduate students as well as interested laymen avail themselves of the research opportunities, for which three special study-rooms are available. Numerous dissertations and theses have been written on the basis of the facilities offered by the library. The Historical Library is constantly in use in the production of *Mennonite Life,* the MENNONITE ENCYCLOPEDIA, and other publications.

The Historical Library collects books, documents, etc., from the churches and homes of its constituency and purchases rare Mennonitica through funds made available through the college, special donations from individuals, and the allowances of the G.C. Board of Education and Publication. Although it is the aim to collect everything pertaining to the Mennonites everywhere, the library is probably most complete in the areas dealing with the Mennonites of Holland, Prussia, Russia, Poland, and the Prairie States and Provinces. It is the only library of its kind west of the Mississippi River.

Since 1947 the director has been ably assisted by John F. Schmidt, who is particularly in charge of the archives, periodicals, photographs, microfilms, and slides.   C.K.

Peter J. Wedel, *The Story of Bethel College* (North Newton, 1954) 489 ff.; John F. Schmidt, "The Story of a Library," *Menn. Life* IX (April 1954) 68 ff.

Mennonite Historical Library of Bluffton College is a collection of books, periodicals, microfilm, pictures, vertical file material, etc., by and about Mennonites, concerning their history, doctrine, and culture. It is especially designed to serve the Mennonite constituency of Bluffton College, viz., the Eastern, Central, and Middle District conferences of the General Conference Mennonite Church, but is open to anyone who desires to use its materials.

The collecting of materials for the Mennonite Historical Library was begun by C. Henry Smith (d. 1948). About 1928 Edna Hanley, then librarian of Bluffton College, began to arrange the material as a separate collection. Especially significant in the growth of the library was the accession of the Grubb Collection of Mennonite History, the lifetime collection of Mennonite materials by father and son, Nathaniel B. Grubb and Silas M. Grubb of Philadelphia, Pa., and the C. H. Smith Collection of Mennonite History donated by C. Henry Smith in 1943.

The entire collection contains approximately 4,000 books, files of about 250 Mennonite periodicals, about 6,000 frames of microfilm and other materials as maps, clippings, etc. The Library is particularly strong in materials on Swiss, South German, and Eastern American Mennonite materials and also Mennonite family histories.   D.L.G.

Mennonite Historical Library of Goshen College, Goshen, Ind., a research collection of books, pamphlets, periodicals, microfilms, photocopies, manuscripts, maps, pictures, museum items, and other materials relating to Anabaptist and Mennonite history. The collection was begun by action of the Alumni Association of Goshen College in 1906 at the suggestion of C. Henry Smith. Collection of materials began in earnest in 1924, when H. S. Bender and Ernst H. Correll came to the faculty. Since that time the collection has grown steadily through the gifts of books and other materials received from many individuals and agencies, and through purchases with funds allocated from the budget of the Goshen College Library or provided by the Mennonite Historical Society, an organization of Goshen College faculty and students.

From time to time the holdings have been augmented by the accession of large groups of materials representing the personal collections of individuals. Notable among these have been the books and papers of John F. Funk (1835-1930), Elkhart, Ind., publisher and leader in the Mennonite Church; S. D. Guengerich (1836-1929), Wellman, Iowa, publisher, schoolteacher, and lay leader among the Amish Mennonites (Old Order); W. J. Kühler, professor of church history in the theological faculty of the University of Amsterdam and the Mennonite Seminary there, and librarian of the Library of the United Mennonite Church (*Bibliotheek der Vereenigde Doopsgezinde Gemeente*) in Amsterdam; and Christian Hege (1869-1943), Frankfurt, Germany, one of the coeditors of the *Mennonitisches Lexikon.* The most outstanding of these collections, however, is the library collected by John Horsch (1867-1941), Scottdale, Pa., the first American Mennonite to devote major time to research in Anabaptist history. This collection, which has been kept separate as a memorial to Horsch, is particularly rich in German and Swiss Reformation history and is of value to those who are studying the Reformation movement in these countries, as well as to the student of Anabaptist and Mennonite history.

At present (April 1957) the collection contains more than 13,000 books, pamphlets, and bound periodicals. The microfilm collection includes approximately 150 items. Among the books and microfilms are 150 items with an imprint date of 1600 or earlier, many of which cannot be found elsewhere in the United States. There are more than 22 vertical file drawers of pamphlets, folders, photocopies, maps, photographs, etchings, engravings, seminars, term papers, manuscripts, and other materials of varying importance. Additional manuscript materials, numbering in the thousands and belonging to the Mennonite Historical Library, are deposited in the Archives of the Mennonite Church (*q.v.*).

As the property of Goshen College, the **Mennonite** Historical Library is administered as part of the Goshen College Library. Since 1949 Nelson Springer has been in charge of it. It was housed in the basement of the Memorial Library Building at Goshen College, occupying one large room, which served as reading room and stacks. Adjacent rooms housed the Archives of the Mennonite Church. The close proximity of these two collections was of mutual benefit to their administration and use. In late 1958 the library and archives were transferred to the new building of the Goshen College Biblical Seminary.

While the users of the Mennonite Historical Library have included many persons from many places, the faculty and students of Goshen College use its resources constantly. The fine quality of scholarship which has characterized the *Mennonite Quarterly Review,* published by the Mennonite Historical Society of Goshen College since 1927, would have been impossible without the resources of the collection. While H. S. Bender has been more active than any other individual in the building of the collection, he has also drawn most heavily on its resources for his research and editorial work and for his course in Mennonite History in the Goshen College Biblical Seminary. Other men on the Goshen College faculty who have done outstanding research in Mennonite history, doctrine, and life have included Ernst H. Correll, Robert Friedmann, Melvin Gingerich, G. F. Hershberger, John Umble, John C. Wenger, Edward Yoder, and S. C. Yoder. The location of the central editorial office of the MENNONITE ENCYCLOPEDIA in an adjoining room has enabled the editorial staff to draw constantly on the resources of the collection. N.P.S.

R. Friedmann, "The Mennonite Historical Library of Goshen College," in *The American-German Review* IX, No. 2 (December 1942) 12-14; N. P. Springer, "The Mennonite Historical Library at Goshen College," and "The Holdings of the Mennonite Historical Library," *MQR* XXV (1951) 296-306, 307-19.

Mennonite Historical Library of the Mennonite Biblical Seminary in Chicago, Ill., was begun by Abraham Warkentin, the first president of the institution, who was intensely interested in the matter and had previously served as collector for the Historical Committee of the General Conference. Coming to the Seminary in 1945 he brought much historical material and continued gathering. The largest quantity of material in the beginning came from the collection of the Mennonite Historical Association made by such men as H. R. Voth and H. P. Krehbiel, which had been gathered at Newton, Kan., and stored in the H. P. Krehbiel vault. This provided sets of early church periodicals as well as books and pamphlets of interest. Noteworthy items were also contributed from duplicate items in the Bethel College Historical Library. Duplicate files at Bluffton College provided a large supply of church periodicals. Continued additions to the library are financed from certain memorial funds and a grant of $200 given annually since 1952 by the General Conference Historical Committee for the acquiring of research material in the field of Mennonite literature.

The Historical Library is located in a fireproof vault on Seminary property with convenient arrangements for access and study. The accessions at the present time (1955) number 1,560 volumes and include valuable historical books from Holland and Germany, as well as several hundred volumes of bound Mennonite periodicals in English, German, and Dutch. S.F.P.

Mennonite Historical Series, sponsored by the Historical Committee (*q.v.*) under the General Conference Board of Education and Publication, was started in 1949 when *From the Steppes to the Prairies* appeared. The Committee members at that time were S. F. Pannabecker, chairman; Cornelius Krahn, secretary; J. Herbert Fretz, J. H. Janzen, E. E. Leisy, and J. D. Unruh. The second publication was Leland and Marvin Harder's *Plockhoy from Zurikzee. The Study of a Dutch Reformer in Puritan England and Colonial America* (1952). The third was the study by Gustav E. Reimer and Gustave R. Gaeddert, *Exiled by the Czar. Cornelius Jansen and the Great Mennonite Migration, 1874* (1956). Hans Fischer's *Jakob Hutter* is in print (1956). The Historical Committee selects, edits, and publishes the books of this series through the means of budget allowances and other sources, and the Mennonite Publication Office, Newton, Kan., markets the books. As a rule the books consist of original studies in the field of Anabaptist-Mennonite history and thought. C.K.

Mennonite Historical Society (of Goshen College) was founded in October 1924, after an earlier organization by the same name founded on the Goshen College campus in 1921 by John J. Fisher and others had discontinued. The membership of the Society, which has varied from 50 to 125, is limited to the faculty and students of Goshen College and occasional persons from the immediate community. The Society has regularly held three or four meetings during the school year, at which scholarly and popular addresses are given. It has given strong support to the Mennonite Historical Library at Goshen College, having contributed over $8,000 for this purpose. It has been the publisher of the *Mennonite Quarterly Review* since its founding in 1927, and has been the publisher (since 1953 editor only) of the scholarly monograph series known as "Studies in Anabaptist and Mennonite History," in which eight volumes have been published since 1929. Subsidies have been granted to others. The officers in 1957 were H. S. Bender president (since the beginning in 1924), G. F. Hershberger vice-president (1925-32, 1935-), J. C. Wenger secretary (1947- , following Silas Hertzler 1927-41 and John Umble 1941-47), J. Howard Kauffman treasurer, and S. C. Yoder as a member of the executive committee (1943-). Ernst Correll was an active member of the organization 1924-29, having been a cofounder. The Society is governed by a board of fifteen directors, twelve of whom are faculty members and three students. In addition to the officers listed above the following have been long-time directors and are still serving: W. H. Smith since 1930, Nelson Springer since 1938, Carl Kreider since 1945, and Melvin Gingerich since 1947. H.S.B.

Mennonite Historical Society of Iowa was organized Sept. 7, 1948, at Wellman, Iowa, with Thomas Miller as president. Its purpose is to promote the local history of the Mennonites and Amish Mennonites in Iowa, particularly in the local settlements around Kalona, Wellman, and Wayland, including preservation of historical records and materials. It holds occasional public meetings, usually annually. Elmer G. Swartzendruber, local historian, was the prime mover in organizing the society.   H.S.B.

Mennonite Home (MC), a home for the aged in Lancaster, Pa. Through the vision of the Sunday School Mission, the foresight of Abram B. Eshleman of Millersville, and the gift of a site by John L. Landis, the Mennonite Home, 1520 Harrisburg Pike, Lancaster, Pa., was opened on April 1, 1905. Jacob H. Mellinger (1866-1934) was the first steward. John L. Landis (1834-1911) donated two adjoining farms, which made it possible for the Home to operate on a self-supporting basis ever since. Abram K. Diener (1842-1911) was the second steward 1906-8, followed by Jacob Benner (1851-1917) until 1911. Tobias E. Moyer (1863-1933) served until his death, followed by John N. Wissler until 1937. Phares N. Frank (1881-1944) served until his death, followed by Jacob Thomas for 16 months and Jacob D. Mellinger since 1946. The board of trustees, headed by Bishop Jacob T. Harnish, is composed mostly of deacons. Many additions have been made to the building, so that the present residential capacity is 135, of whom 123 are aged guests.   I.D.L.

Mennonite Home for the Aged, Albany, Ore., was established in 1946, and is operated by a local board of five men under the Pacific Coast Conference (MC). In 1956 it had 57 guests; the superintendent and matron were Mr. and Mrs. Joel D. Roth.
                                                    H.S.B.

Mennonite Home for the Aged, Eureka, Ill., is operated by the Mennonite Board of Missions and Charities (MC). Authorized in 1921, the Home was dedicated July 23, 1922. It is located on a hill north of the city, and accommodates 47 persons, including the workers. Five acres of the 18-acre tract are used for the buildings, garden, and orchard. In 1946 the institution became a licensed nursing home. J. D. Smith served as superintendent of the Home from its beginning until his retirement in 1947, when Clayton Sutter was appointed to the office. Earl Greaser became superintendent of the home in 1956.
                                                    M.G.

C. F. Derstine, "The Mennonite Home for the Aged," *Christian Monitor,* January 1923.

Mennonite Home for the Aged (GCM), located at Frederick, Pa., had its beginning when N. B. Grubb (*q.v.*) purchased the former Frederick Institute on Feb. 11, 1896. It was a three-story brick building erected in 1857, with three acres of land. On March 24, 1896, the Eastern District Conference (GCM) purchased this property from Grubb. The Mennonite Home for the Aged was dedicated and officially opened on Sept. 1, 1896. The buildings consist of the main building, a south wing added in

1928, the three-story Stetler property located across the street and occupied by members of the staff, 22 acres of adjoining land purchased later, and the administrator's residence erected in 1954. A $400,000 building program was instituted in 1957 to add 39 rooms, a chapel, and an elevator.

In 1956 there were 31 guests and a staff of 10. The Home is controlled by a board of managers of nine members elected by the Eastern District Conference. In 1956 they were Freeman H. Swartz, chairman; Vernon F. Detweiler, secretary; Harry M. Detwiler, financial secretary and (now also) treasurer; William H. Mohr, vice-chairman; Eugene S. Oberholtzer, Stanley Stauffer, Lester Shaffer, Willis A. Moyer, and Stanley Fretz. Mr. and Mrs. Wilmer S. Shelly were the administrators.   W.S.S.

Mennonite Home Mission (MC), a congregation located at 1907 South Union Avenue, Chicago, Ill., a member of the Illinois Conference, was started as a mission station in 1893 by Dr. S. D. Ebersole, Dr. W. B. Page, M. S. Steiner, and J. S. Coffman, assisted by Mennonite medical students and other Mennonites living in Chicago. It had its beginning in a four-story building at 639 West 18th Street. From there it moved to its present location. There have been 17 different nationalities represented in the church and 20 in the Sunday school. In the (1956) membership of 123, about 50 per cent were of non-Mennonite background. The ministers in charge of the church in 1956 were Laurence M. Horst and James Christophel (licensed minister). One of the outstanding events in the history of the congregation was a combined missionary meeting, dedication service, and twenty-fifth anniversary celebration, which lasted four days in January 1919. The outstanding superintendent in the history of the mission was A. Hershey Leaman (1878-1950), who served the mission as pastor 1905-20.   E.Le.

Emma Oyer, *What God Hath Wrought* (Elkhart, Ind., 1949).

Mennonite Homes: see **Refugee Camps.**

Mennonite Hospital, located at Bloomington, Ill., came into being through a growing concern on the part of Mennonite leaders in the Central and Evangelical (then Defenseless) Conference churches in Central Illinois, that provision be made by and in behalf of the Church, for the carrying out of Christ's command to "heal the sick." They were encouraged and aided by Bloomington physicians, particularly Dr. E. P. Sloan, nationally known surgeon, who served for many years as chief of the medical staff. The Mennonite Sanitarium Association (*q.v.*) was organized on Jan. 23, 1919, its membership consisting of delegates from the constituent churches. (The name was subsequently changed to Mennonite Hospital Association, *q.v.*) A board of five directors was chosen, consisting of Emanuel Troyer, who served as president until his death in 1942, Benjamin Rupp, John Kinsinger, Allen Miller, and J. H. King. The board was subsequently enlarged to nine members, three being elected each year by the Association at its annual meeting in January.

A property was purchased on North Main Street

in Bloomington, and the first patients entered on May 1, 1919. While plans were afoot for the construction of a new building, it was learned that the Kelso Sanitarium at 807 North Main Street was available and by action of the Association it was purchased at a cost of $75,000, the purchase being made by five men making themselves personally responsible for the amount, for which fact many of them paid heavily in later years. In 1931-32 the present main building was added to the single fireproof structure in the Kelso plant. After weathering the depression, the institution grew rapidly in favor and patronage, and the southern east wing of 45 rooms was added in 1941-42. In 1944-45 the Troyer Memorial Nurses' Home with a capacity of 80 was built; and in 1956 the northern east wing was completed, giving the hospital a total capacity of 130 beds.

Benjamin Rupp was the first superintendent of the hospital, serving in that capacity until 1927, at which time N. O. Hoover became administrator and held that position for more than 29 years. The present administrator is Theodor F. Kaap, Jr. The hospital also operates the Mennonite Hospital Training School for Nurses (q.v.) with a usual complement of 65 girls in training.

In 1956 the institution served a total of 7,357 at an operating cost of $719,384.91. Births numbered 901. Total assets of the institution are listed by the auditor as $1,147,261.99, with a net worth of $772,-354.19. Not more than 4 per cent of its patients come from its constituent churches. The hospital seeks to render a service in behalf of the church and in the spirit of Christ, and the testimony of many who are served by it attests to the fact that it is serving that purpose.   R.L.H.

Mennonite Hospital and Sanitarium, La Junta, Col., is a general hospital with a separate building for the treatment of tuberculosis, operated by the Mennonite (MC) Board of Missions and Charities, Elkhart, Ind. The purpose of the hospital is to provide medical, surgical, and nursing treatment for the sick and to provide for nursing education; the sanitarium is limited to patients with tuberculosis. The ultimate purpose is to carry a witness for Christ by ministering to both body and soul.

Since tuberculosis patients were generally sent to an arid climate for treatment in those early days, many found their way to the west, and Mennonites from eastern sections of the Mennonite Church (MC), principally Virginia and Ohio, settling in Colorado found themselves confronted with the problem of caring for these sick people. At first some of them were taken care of in homes, but the need of an institution for their care was evident. Individuals such as D. S. Brunk, D. S. Weaver, and J. F. Brunk of the La Junta-Holbrook settlement then conceived the idea of organizing a sanitarium. Steps were immediately taken to organize a stock company for this purpose, and some certificates of stock were sold. The proposed plan was then presented to the Kansas-Nebraska Mennonite Conference meeting in Hubbard, Ore., in 1905, which passed a resolution approving the project. However, the association idea was soon dropped, and the proj-

ect was taken over by the Mission Board. A fund of $10,000 from the Mrs. Snavely Estate in Ohio was used for the proposed sanitarium. It was built on a hill overlooking the Arkansas Valley, about 5 miles west of La Junta, and dedicated Oct. 28, 1908, with accommodations for 38 patients.

Very early in the development it was felt that the service should be adapted also to take care of general medical and surgical cases, and an appeal was made to the Mission Board to build a new hospital. The Board then leased a building located in the city and owned by the La Junta City Hospital Association, a 25-bed institution built with very limited resources. This equipment was turned over without cost to the Board, and on Jan. 1, 1920, four nurses from the Sanitarium, Lydia Heatwole, Ada Burkhart (Ziegler), Ruth Erb (Ebersole), and Gladys Grove, began to operate the institution for the care of general medical, surgical, and obstetrical cases. At the General Conference session of 1921 final approval was given to the Mission Board to proceed in building a hospital. The original sanitarium was then sold and the sale price applied to the new building, which was built in La Junta in 1927 and dedicated on Easter Day of 1928. In 1946 a new wing was built to this hospital. In 1949 a new nurses' home was built for students in the La Junta Mennonite School of Nursing, which was established in 1915. The general hospital is a 108-bed institution, with 18 bassinets. During the last 10 years (1944-54) the average number of patients admitted annually was 2,994; the average number of babies born annually was 724.

The tuberculosis wing of this new institution had been operated as a tuberculosis sanitarium since it was built in 1928, but the reduction of the incidence of tuberculosis led to such a reduction of patient census that the state, which had been paying for all patients, directed the closing of the sanitarium on March 1, 1955. This marks the end of a 46-year period of experience in ministering to those afflicted with this disease. Many are helped physically, some were helped spiritually, and many nurses were trained to care for the sick. From the beginning, Christian services were held in which patients were invited to participate. In late years, a chaplaincy program has been organized and executed in the institution. From the La Junta nursing school movement has developed the present Goshen College Collegiate School of Nursing.   A.H.E.

Mennonite Hospital School of Nursing. The Mennonite Hospital (q.v.), Bloomington, Ill., organized in 1919, included in its organizing statement provision for a school of nursing, which was established at the very beginning, the first class graduating in 1922.

The hospital and the School of Nursing are under the control of the board of trustees as one institution. Responsibility for the formulation of the curriculum in its relationship to the State Department of Registration and Education and to co-ordinate the factors which go into the education of Christian nurses falls to the School of Nursing Advisory Committee, composed of the Director of Nursing Service and Education, Educational Director, President of the Board of Trustees, hospital administrator, a member of the Alumni Association, a member of the faculty of the Illinois State Normal University, and a lay member of the Mennonite constituency.

The course requires 1,374 hours of formal classroom work during the three-year period. Applied nursing experience is gained in the hospital itself. College credit is received for work done at Illinois State Normal University, and there is opportunity for co-ordination with Bluffton College, Bluffton, Ohio, to receive a Bachelor's degree in Nursing.

The School of Nursing has graduated 439 nurses, many of whom have entered some form of full-time Christian service. Graduates are now serving in Liberia, British West Africa, Belgian Congo, and Nepal, in addition to the United States.

N.O.H., T.F.K.

Mennonite Hospitals and Homes, Association of, founded in 1952, serves as a fellowship for counseling and inspiration, composed of representatives of most of the North American institutions included under the title. It meets annually in connection with the annual meeting of the American Hospital Association. The officers in 1956 were H. J. Andres (Newton) president, H. Ernest Bennett (Elkhart) executive secretary.   H.S.B.

Mennonite Hour, The, the official broadcast of the Mennonite Church (MC) through the Mennonite Board of Missions and Charities (*q.v.*), was formally begun in June 1951, under a private organization of Mennonite men, largely at Harrisonburg, Va., who formed the Mennonite Crusaders (*q.v.*) to take over the half-hour Sunday broadcast of a male quartet from Eastern Mennonite College called "Crusaders for Christ," which had begun in March 1951 over the local Harisonburg station WSVA. In January 1952, B. Charles Hostetter became the radio pastor, a position he still held in 1957. In June 1953 the Crusaders entered into an agreement with the MBMC, whereby the planning and promoting of the broadcast became a co-operative venture under an administrative committee of the Board called "Radio Evangelism Committee." The Crusaders, who had been incorporated in Virginia June 1952, continued to operate and finance the broadcast, however, and did so until 1956, when its name was changed to Mennonite Broadcasts, Inc. (*q.v.*). The *Mennonite Hour* is a half-hour program, basically of worship and preaching. The radio pastor delivers a ten-minute sermon, and music is provided as a cappella singing by the Mennonite Hour Chorus, composed largely of community people and students of Eastern Mennonite College. The program director is Norman Derstine, a local Mennonite minister; music director, Earl Maust of the E.M.C. faculty. The international English version is called "The Way to Life." In early 1957 the Mennonite Hour was broadcast over seventy stations in the United States and foreign countries. Of this number, 56 were in the United States, two in Canada, plus broadcasts in Ceylon, Costa Rica, Ecuador, Jamaica, Liberia, Tangier, Panama, Philippines, Puerto Rico, and Viet-Nam. The weekly listening audience was estimated in 1957 at five million. The program is self-sustaining, supported largely by voluntary contributions from the listening audience. The *Mennonite Hour Informer* has been published monthly since 1952, and the *Mennonite Hour Prayer Guide* monthly since 1953.   H.S.B.

Mennonite Indemnity, Inc., a reinsurance corporation serving all Mennonite Aid societies desiring to participate, incorporated in Pennsylvania in 1957. Sixteen societies were the initial participants. A board of twelve directors is elected by the stockholders. The first officers were S. S. Wenger (Lancaster) president, Elvin Souder (Souderton) vice-president, Wayne W. Martin (Goodville, Pa.) secretary-treasurer; the capital was $150,000. The MCC nominates the board of directors and exercises a paternal influence.   H.S.B.

Mennonite Land Settlement Association was formed by a group of Mennonites (GCM) interested in organizing an inter-Mennonite settlement of landless people, particularly young married couples living in Ontario and western Canada. The Association was organized in 1953 to assist in buying livestock, machinery, and if possible, suitable farm lands. Any member of any branch of Mennonites in Canada was eligible to join the association. While not an official agency of the church, the Mennonite Land Settlement Association was organized with the express purpose of strengthening the church, by establishing new Christian communities.

Because of high costs of land and farm machinery, it was found impossible to raise the necessary capital to launch an effective settlement program. The ease of getting city jobs at high wages by farm young men further complicated the aid program. Because the Association has been unable to achieve its purposes, it is now inactive.   J.W.F.

Mennonite Land Settlement Board was organized in July 1924 to take over from the Canadian Mennonite Board of Colonization the work of land settlement. It had nine members, three each from the CMBC, the Central Mennonite Immigration Committee, and the Canadian Pacific Railway. Its work was financed by the Canada Colonization Association, a subsidiary of the C.P.R. In 1929 the Board was discontinued and its work taken over by the Canadian Colonization Association (see **Canadian Mennonite Board of Colonization**). The original executive committee was David Toews, chairman, T. O. F. Herzer, and A. A. Friesen.   J.G.

Mennonite Life, a 48-page illustrated quarterly magazine, published by Bethel College, North Newton, Kan., "in the interest of the best in the religious, social, and economic phases of Mennonite culture." The magazine, begun in January 1946, presents Mennonite principles, doctrines, culture, and history in a popular and illustrated form based on thorough research, to readers in all Mennonite groups and branches the world over. A large staff of co-workers contributes articles from all parts of the world where Mennonites reside, and the resources of the Bethel College Historical Library are constantly used to illustrate and check contributions. During the first ten years of publication over 3,000 ilustrations appeared on its pages, most of which had never before appeared in print and were rather unique. Many works of Mennonite artists, poets, and writers of fiction have been published. Annually in April all books and articles dealing with Anabaptist-Mennonites published during the preceding year are listed under the title "Mennonite Bibliography." The same issue publishes reports on "Mennonite Research in Progress" in the field of Mennonite beliefs, history, culture, etc. The issue of January 1956 contains an exhaustive index of authors, titles, and topics for the first ten years (1946-55). The circulation of the magazine has been between 2,000 and 3,000, but an edition of 4,000 is printed. The issue during the first year (1946) was semiannual.

Mennonite Life is published by Bethel College under the auspices of an executive board. The chief responsibility of the editorial work rests with the editor, Cornelius Krahn (1946), and John F. Schmidt, assistant editor (1947). Among the associate editors and contributors the most active have been J. W. Fretz, Melvin Gingerich, Erland Waltner, M. S. Harder, and Andrew Shelly. The subscription price is $3.00 per year. C.K.

Mennonite Medical Association, an organization formed in 1944 for Mennonite (MC) physicians and Mennonite medical students. Its officers (1956) are president, Galen Miller, Elkhart, Ind.; secretary-treasurer, Charles Neff, Street, Md.; vice-president, Meryl Grasse, Calico Rock, Ark. Samuel J. Bucher, Harman, W. Va., is the editor of the *Mennonite Medical Messenger,* a quarterly which publishes news items from the various members of the Association. There are 105 members in the Association. The Association has an adoption program whereby physicians and students in the states "adopt" those physicians who are serving in relief or missionary work in order to develop a closer link with those who are serving in foreign lands. S.J.B.

Mennonite Men or **Men's Brotherhood** is an organization within the General Conference Mennonite Church with divisions in district conferences and local congregations. The first organization of this type within the Conference originated in 1918 in the Zion Mennonite Church at Souderton, Pa., after Maxwell H. Kratz of Philadelphia had challenged the men at the Eastern District Conference during the preceding year to greater activity within the local congregations and the Conference. The "Mennonite Men" of the Eastern District Conference has met annually since 1918. They raised money for the Mennonite immigrants from Russia to Canada to help them pay for their transportation and had an active part in developing the Eastern Conference camp, Men-O-Lan (*q.v.*).

In 1945 at the General Conference Mennonite Church sessions at Bethel College steps were taken to organize "Mennonite Men" on a General Conference scale. Ever since the "Mennonite Men" of the General Conference reports about its work at all triennial Conference sessions.

At the Northern District Conference sessions in 1950 held at Mountain Lake, Minn., the Northern District "Mennonite Men" was organized. As a rule they meet in conjunction with the district conference sessions. One of the outstanding projects of this district was the purchase of a bulldozer which arrived at Fernheim Colony, Paraguay, in 1952. The brotherhood raised $18,468.94 for this purpose.

The Western District "Mennonite Men" was organized in September 1950. They have assisted youth fellowship in the development of Camp Mennoscah (*q.v.*), in purchasing a linotype for the Mennonites in Brazil, and numerous other projects. They have published *The Spotlight* since 1950.

At present the General Conference "Mennonite Men" is trying to organize additional districts. One of the projects is to assist the Mennonites of Paraguay in road construction. Another project is in the field of boys' work and youth activities. Officers in 1957 were John O. Schrag president, Menno Schrag vice-president, and Carl M. Lehman secretary. C.K.

"Mennonite Men at Work," *Menn. Life* IX (October 1954) 167-71; *Reports and Official Minutes of the General Conference Mennonite Church, 1947, 1950, 1953, 1956.*

Mennonite Mental Health Services, Incorporated, an agency holding title to mental hospitals established by the Mennonite Central Committee, and responsible for policy guidance and technical consultation in the operation of those hospitals. It was incorporated on Dec. 12, 1952, as a successor to a Mental Health Services Committee which as the Homes for Mentally Ill Planning and Advisory Committee formed by MCC on Jan. 3, 1947, had planned the three-hospital program. Initial members, all of whom were directors of the corporation, were George Classen, Titus Books, Dr. Paul M. Nase, and Henry Martens, in additon to officers H. A. Fast president, E. C. Bender vice-president, Delmar Stahly secretary, and Orie Miller treasurer. At its annual meeting on Dec. 27, 1956, the MCC approved a reorganization of its mental health program and called for a change of function and make-up of MMHS during the ensuing year. At a meeting of the new members on April 6, 1957, officers elected were Dr. H. Clair Amstutz chairman, Robert Kreider secretary, Orie Miller treasurer. Other members at that time were Dr. Otto Klassen, Dr. Norman Loux, H. A. Fast, and Frank Peters. Although the stated purpose of MMHS changed little, the reorganization effected during 1957 was significant and involved the establishment of responsible local boards for the operation of each mental hospital, administrative responsibility having theretofore rested directly with the Executive Committee of the MCC. A more specific policy code was established by MMHS, with a full-time staff member responsible for representing the concerns of the Corporation in co-ordinating the various hospital programs and in serving Mental Health interests of Mennonite churches in liaisonship with professional, voluntary, and governmental organizations within the field. The corporation maintains an office in connection with the Mennonite Central Committee at Akron, Pa. See **Brook Lane Farm, Prairie View Hospital,** and **Kings View Homes.**) D.S.

Mennonite Migration Aid Society was founded after World War I to aid Mennonites from Russia in their attempt to settle in North America. The business office was in Newton, Kan., and the Executive Board consisted of H. P. Krehbiel, president, C. E. Krehbiel, secretary, and J. G. Regier. Other members were P. H. Unruh, Gerhard Regier, and P. H. Richert. According to the files of the president of this organization the primary purpose seems to have been to settle a group of Mennonites from Russia in Mexico at San Juan, Irapuato, and Gto. The Society dealt with Mennonite immigrants from Russia, the government of Mexico, land agents of Mexico, the Dutch Immigration Bureau, of Rotterdam, and the Mennonite congregations who supported the project. The settlement in Mexico was unsuccessful. The activities of the Society and the settlement have not been fully investigated.   C.K.

Mennonite Mission Board (MC) *of Ontario.* The Mennonite Conference of Ontario, seeing the need for urban evangelization within the conference area, organized the City Mission Board in 1907 when the Toronto Mission began, and four years later the Mennonite Board of Finance. In 1914 the conference, to build up isolated and declining congregations in the conference district, appointed a committee of five to provide for rural mission work in Ontario. A constitution was prepared and at the 1915 session the Mennonite Board of Rural Missions was established. After some years it seemed advisable to unify the various mission interests in Ontario; accordingly, on Sept. 11, 1929, the former organizations were dissolved and the Mennonite Mission Board of Ontario was fully organized in their place. In 1953 changes were made in the constitution to provide for a missions council. Until 1952, when a conference charter was inaugurated, this mission board was also the charatered body of the conference for the holding of properties.   J.C.F.

Mennonite Mission Church (MC), 1530 Lyon Street, Hannibal, Mo., formerly known as the Mennonite Gospel Mission, 2313 Market Street, is a member of the South Central Conference, with a membership in 1956 of 77. Mennonite services were first conducted in Hannibal by members of the Palmyra Mennonite Church in 1927. Nelson E. Kauffman was appointed the first superintendent by the Missouri-Kansas District Mission Board in 1934, and the congregation was organized in August 1934. A church was built at 1530 Lyon Street in 1936. Young men have been given missionary apprenticeship experience there since 1939. Nelson E. Kauffman served as the minister from August 1934, and bishop from September 1940, with Harold Kreider as minister. In 1956 Kauffman moved to Elkhart, Ind., and Kreider became pastor of the congregation.   N.E.K.

Mennonite Missionary Messenger, an illustrated 4-page monthly, published by the Home and Foreign Relief Commission (MC), Elkhart, Ind., devoted to mission interests, "especially to the care and support of orphans," appeared first in April 1901 as a supplement to the *Herald of Truth;* it ran only a few months. A. C. Kolb was editor.   N.P.S.

Mennonite Mutual Aid, Inc., was incorporated in 1945 as an Indiana nonprofit corporation sponsored

by the Mennonite General Conference (MC) to provide a means within the church for its members to carry out the historic Mennonite practice of sharing financial burdens and providing loan aid to those in need of assistance. The first project was assisting in the rehabilitation of returning Civilian Public Service men. At present loan aid is given to any member, provided satisfactory local credit is not available and the applicant merits assistance. Financial counsel and vocational placement services are provided. A plan for sharing expenses of hospitalization, surgical and burial aid is carried on by a subsidiary Pennsylvania nonprofit corporation called Mennonite Aid, Inc. (*q.v.*). Another subsidiary Pennsylvania nonprofit corporation called Mennonite Automobile Aid, Inc. (*q.v.*), has been organized to share costs of automobile collision and comprehensive expenses. Another Indiana nonprofit corporation, the Mennonite Foundation (*q.v.*), is recognized by the Treasury Department of the United States as a depository for tax exempt funds, therefore bequests, legacies, or gifts of property to the Mennonite Foundation are deductible as provided by law. Orie O. Miller has continued as president of Mennonite Mutual Aid from its beginning. C. L. Graber has been secretary-treasurer from its beginning to 1954 and continues as its treasurer. Original Board appointees, made by Mennonite General Conference, and still active members are Guy F. Hershberger and H. A. Diener. Also Simon Gingerich and John H. Alger were original appointees but recently retired from active participation. Later appointees now serving are E. C. Bender, vice-president; Harry Wenger, John D. Burkholder, J. Robert Kreider, H. Ralph Hernley, Abram P. Hallman, and Harold L. Swartzendruber, secretary.
          H.L.S.

Mennonite Mutual Aid Association, Kalona, Iowa, a mutual fire and storm insurance organization, organized originally in 1913 as the Mennonite Aid Plan of Iowa, was reorganized and incorporated in 1948 under its present name, in Washington County. It has permission to do business in this county and any other adjoining it. In 1957, with a property coverage of $14,000,000, it had over 800 members. Membership in the association is open to "persons of the Mennonite or Amish faith who are in good standing in their church."   L.G.G.

L. G. Guengerich, "The Mennonite Aid Plan of Iowa," *MHB,* December 1946.

Mennonite Mutual Aid Society of Bluffton, Ohio, a mutual fire and storm insurance association, was organized June 5, 1866, to serve the Swiss Mennonites of Allen, Putnam, and Hancock counties, Ohio, but no longer restricts its membership to Mennonites. It was incorporated April 10, 1907. In 1953 it had 852 policy holders with a property coverage of $7,500,000.   H.S.B.

Mennonite Mutual *Fire Insurance Association* of Intercourse, Pa., was organized Aug. 17, 1893, to serve all branches of Mennonites and Amish in Pennsylvania. In 1953 it served 8,116 members with a property coverage of about $38,000,000.
          H.S.B.

Mennonite Mutual *Insurance Association of Ohio,* a mutual fire and storm insurance association, with office at Orrville, Ohio, was organized in 1897 to serve all branches of Mennonites. In 1953 it had 5,550 members with over $55,000,000 property coverage. H.S.B.

Mennonite Mutual Insurance Company of Kansas. When the Mennonites migrated from Prussia to Kansas in the latter 19th century, they brought with them the system of mutual insurance. (See **Tiegenhöfer Privat Brandordnung;** also **Insurance.**) The minutes of the earliest organization of the Newton Mutual Fire Insurance Company were destroyed by fire, but is is certain that the association was in operation in 1879 and for at least a brief time previously. An early experience of the fire association was the fire at Halstead, Kan., the headquarters of the association, which destroyed the Mennonite Book Concern, one of the company's risks. In 1880 the company was incorporated and chartered as the Mennonite Mutual Fire Insurance Company of Kansas.

Outstanding among the organizers and founders of this association were David Goerz, Bernhard Warkentin, William Ewert, H. Richert, and B. Buhler. The headquarters of the association today are at Newton, Kan.

At first this insurance company accepted only Mennonites as members, but in time began to include others. In 1937 the name of the organization was changed to Midland Mutual Insurance Company (*q.v.*); it is a commercial mutual and is no longer a strictly Mennonite company. J.W.F.

Mennonite Observer, a 12-page, 10¼ x 12½ in. weekly companion to the *Mennonitische Rundschau,* has been published by the Christian Press at Winnipeg, Man., beginning on Sept. 21, 1955, with Leslie Stobbe as editor. The first six numbers had only eight pages. H.S.B.

Mennonite Old People's Home (MC), Maugansville, Md., was opened Jan. 1, 1924, with Ben Stauffer as superintendent, who served until 1938. He was followed by Laban Eshleman 1938-44, S. L. Horst 1944-47, Henry Hostetter 1947-53, Samuel J. Diller 1953-. The average number of guests is 20. It serves the Washington Co., Md., and Franklin Co., Pa., Conference district. S.J.D.

Mennonite Old People's Home (MC), located near Rittman, Ohio, is a charitable institution built in 1901 on a 155-acre farm given by D. C. Amstutz to the Mennonite Board of Missions and Charities for such a home. Board members were Christian P. Steiner, Menno S. Steiner, David S. Yoder, Lewis J. Lehman, and Abram Metzler. The first building, having a capacity of 34 inmates, burned to the ground in 1919, but through the untiring efforts of S. E. Allgyer, the present home, with a capacity of 41 inmates, was dedicated on Jan. 1, 1939. Since that time, under the care and direction of Aaron J. Peachey and wife, who are still (1956) serving as superintendent and matron, approximately 280 different persons, from at least eight states and seventeen different denominations, have been cared for.

The present members of the board are Melvin Hartzler, chairman; Herman Brenner, Lloyd Sommer, and Melvin Rohrer. A.J.P.

Mennonite Orphan and Childrens Aid Society was organized in Halstead, Kan., in 1893 for the purpose of caring for orphans and other needy children either by keeping them at an orphan home or placing them with Christian families. This organization was started in order to give opportunity to a wider circle to share in the Christian service to homeless children which was started when the Leisy Orphan Aid Society (*q.v.*) was incorporated in 1884. The organization held annual meetings and printed its activity reports. Annual memberships were available for $5.00 and life memberships for $100.00. A total of 426 membership certificates were issued. Later the Mennonite Orphan and Childrens Aid Society merged with the Leisy Orphan Aid Society. C.K.

Mennonite Orphan and Childrens Aid Society of Halstead Kansas. Reports 1894-1911.

Mennonite Pioneer Mission, an agency of the Bergthaler Mennonite Church of Manitoba, began mission work in Chihuahua, Mexico, in 1944. Because of visa and other difficulties, the work had to be abandoned in 1948. In the same year work was begun among Indians and other settlers in the Lake Winnipeg area of Manitoba. Mr. and Mrs. J. M. Unrau were the first missionaries. To these have been added Mr. and Mrs. Edwine Brandt, partial support; Mr. and Mrs. Henry Neufeld, Helen Willms, Mary Janzen, Mr. and Mrs. Larry Klippenstein, and Mr. and Mrs. Otto Hamm, besides associate workers in the public schools of the area. Mr. and Mrs. Peter Falk are supported under the Congo Inland Mission and Anne Penner under the General Conference board in India. The 1956 budget was $24,500.

The mission board members are elected by the several congregations. The following are in the present (1955) executive committee: George Groening, chairman; Bernie Leoppky, vice-chairman; H. J. Gerbrandt, secretary; J. N. Braun, treasurer. Plans are now under way to amalgamate this work with that of the Canadian Conference of Mennonites (GCM) in 1957.

The mission has been publishing a bimonthly bilingual, six-page periodical, which is sent to all members of the church. H.J.G.

Mennonite Press is a joint venture of the Board of Education and Publication of the General Conference Mennonite Church and Bethel College (*q.v.*) of Newton, Kan. It came into official existence July 1, 1949, after a two-year period of negotiations, its purpose, as expressed in the charter, being "to merge their respective printing interests in a jointly operated Press." It is controlled by a separate board consisting of five members, two of whom are selected by each of the two parties to the venture for indeterminate tenure and a fifth being elected by these four. The first chairman of the Board was H. J. Andres. The Mennonite Press is responsible to the Conference through the Conference Board of Education and Publication, and to the Bethel College through its board representatives. It is located at

2513 North Main St., North Newton. Official reports showed net assets of $20,827.37 at the close of 1949, and $52,135.50 on June 30, 1954. It began with five full-time employees in 1949; in 1954 there were nine. The Press does general letterpress and offset-process printing, as well as extensive mailing operations for various church bodies. The first manager was Bernhard Bargen. Dan Epp is the present (1957) manager.   B.B.

Mennonite Publication Board (MC) was organized in 1908, and chartered in the State of Indiana. For ten years previous to this, conviction had been developing in the Mennonite Church (MC) that the denomination should own its publications. The Kansas-Nebraska Conference so expressed itself in 1898. By November 1907, when the Mennonite General Conference met at Kokomo, Ind., nine conferences had appointed representatives on a proposed church-wide publishing organization. General Conference approved the plan and appointed three representatives. The Board was organized at Goshen, Ind., on Jan. 8, 1908, and elected the following officers: J. S. Shoemaker, president; Jonathan Kurtz, vice-president; S. H. Miller, secretary; Abram Metzler, treasurer. Shoemaker had served as chairman of the organizing committee, and was president until 1933. Succeeding presidents have been D. D. Troyer, M. H. Shantz, Simon Gingerich, John C. Wenger, and E. C. Bender.

The Board purchased the assets of the Gospel Witness (*q.v.*) Company and the Mennonite Book and Tract Society (*q.v.*) of Scottdale, Pa. It also purchased the church periodicals published by the Mennonite Publishing Company (*q.v.*) at Elkhart, Ind. Publishing headquarters were established at Scottdale as the Mennonite Publishing House (*q.v.*). The *Gospel Herald* (*q.v.*) was established as the official organ of the church and began publication, with other periodicals, in April 1908.

This Board now has a membership of more than thirty, including representatives from all district conferences, from the Mennonite General Conference, and members at large. It meets annually to hear reports, elect officers, and consider needs and policies. Between meetings its business is conducted by the Executive Committee. The Board produces and distributes books, periodicals, tracts, and educational materials. Its net worth as of Dec. 31, 1956, was $1,019,223.72. It owns the publishing headquarters at Scottdale and retail outlets at Scottdale, Lancaster, New Holland, and Souderton, Pa.; Goshen, Ind.; Kitchener and London, Ont.; and Bloomington, Ill. The general management of the affairs of the board is in the hands of a Publishing Agent, who is appointed by the Board. The Board is autonomous in its operation, but reports to the biennial sessions of the Mennonite General Conference. Officers following the 1957 election were: E. C. Bender, president; Clarence Lutz, vice-president; Harold Zehr, secretary; C. L. Graber, financial agent; John C. Wenger, fifth member of Executive Committee. A. J. Metzler is the Publishing Agent. Annual reports have been published every year since the beginning (1908) in the *Gospel Herald*.   P.E.

Mennonite Publishing Company, Elkhart Ind., the successor to the firm of John F. Funk and Brother, was chartered in 1875 and completed its chartered life of fifty years, although it sold its periodical publications (*Herald of Truth* and *Mennonitische Rundschau*) in 1908 to the Mennonite Publication Board (*q.v.*) which had just created the Mennonite Publishing House (*q.v.*) as the publishing agency for the Mennonite Church (MC). The Mennonite Publishing Company was a stock company, whose stock was widely held in the eastern Pennsylvania section of the Mennonite Church. Due largely to a bank failure and a fire it was forced to bankruptcy in 1903 with heavy loss to its stockholders. Its president throughout its history and business manager until about 1900, was John F. Funk (*q.v.*, 1835-1930), an outstanding leader in the Mennonite Church (MC). The Mennonite Publishing Company did an outstanding service in its book and periodical publications both in German and English, serving not only the Mennonites and Amish Mennonites but also a large block of the Russian Mennonite immigrants, particularly in Manitoba. For the latter group it published the *Mennonitische Rundschau* (*q.v.*) and hymnals, catechisms, and confessions of faith.

Due to Funk's deep historical interest the Mennonite Publishing Company and its predecessor, John F. Funk and Brother, published two notable large historical works, Menno Simons' *Complete Works* (English 1871, German 1876), and the *Martyrs' Mirror* (German 1870, English 1886). Funk became the major publisher for the Mennonite Church (MC), publishing its hymnals, catechisms, confessions, yearbooks, Sunday-school literature, etc. Through his press as well as his personality Funk wielded immeasurable influence upon the cause and molded the course of its history in the second half of the 19th century, working for unity and progress. It was a tragedy that in his later years he lost much of the confidence of the church he once had, so that from about 1900 on his publishing work decreased in size and influence.

During the years 1880-1900, the Mennonite Publishing Company became the center of a group of younger progressive men, who found in its activities almost the only available outlet for their desire to serve in the church and who made significant contributions to the new day in the church. Among these were A. B. Kolb, A. C. Kolb, F. W. Brunk, J. S. Coffman, G. L. Bender, and John Horsch.   H.S.B.

Mennonite Publishing House (MC), Scottdale, Pa., is the headquarters and chief place of business of the Mennonite Publication Board (*q.v.*). It is a church-owned nonprofit institution. Proceeds above expenses and additional capital for expansion go into subsidies for literature and other forms of church work. It dates from 1908, when the Mennonite Publication Board was chartered and made Scottdale its place of business. Three years previously the Gospel Witness Company had been organized and had begun the publication and sale of religious literature. Jacob S. Loucks, Aaron Loucks, and A. D. Martin had an important part in these first steps in the development of a church-owned publishing house. The assets of the Gospel Witness Company were purchased by the Mennonite Publication Board, and the two privately owned buildings which had been used by the Gospel Witness Company were rented until purchased in 1914. Expanding business made it necessary to build a new four-story building in 1921-22. Again in 1948-49 a three-story annex was added to this building. Together with the growth in floor space there has been commensurate addition of machinery and equipment and an increase in personnel. The number of employees in 1957 was about 175.

Aaron Loucks was the General Manager of the Publishing House from its beginning in 1908 until 1935, when A. J. Metzler became his successor (since called Publishing Agent). Others who had a large part in developing this business were Daniel Kauffman, M. K. Smoker, J. A. Ressler, Levi Mumaw, Henry Hernley, George Cutrell, C. B. Shoemaker, C. F. Yake, and J. L. Horst.

The Mennonite Publishing House is engaged in printing, publishing, and bookselling. It publishes periodicals (*Gospel Herald, Christian Living, Youth's Christian Companion, Words of Cheer, Beams of Light, Christian Ministry, Christian School, El Heraldo,* and *The Way*), tracts, books, and educational materials (*Herald Uniform Sunday School Series, Herald Summer Bible School Series*). It prints most of its own published materials and does much work for district conferences, institutions, and other organizations of the Mennonite Church (MC), although most of the district conference organs are not published by it. It sells by mail order and through eight retail stores (Scottdale, Lancaster, New Holland, and Souderton, Pa.; Kitchener and London, Ont.; Goshen, Ind.; and Bloomington, Ill.). Sales in 1956 totaled $1,289,646.86. The net worth of the Publishing House as of Dec. 31, 1956, was $1,019,223.72.

The Mennonite Publishing House is organized into five divisions: editorial, production, sales, finance, and personnel. The head of the institution is the Publishing Agent, who has an Assistant Agent. Heading the divisions, respectively, are the executive editor, the production manager, the sales manager, the treasurer, and the personnel director. Annual reports of the House have been published regularly in the church organ, the *Gospel Herald,* from the beginning in 1908, and an annual catalog has appeared every year since that time.   P.E.

Mennonite Quarterly Review, a quarterly scholarly journal of 80 pages published by the Mennonite Historical Society, Goshen College, Goshen, Ind., first issue dated January 1927. It was preceded by the *Goshen College Record Review Supplement* (3 numbers in 1926). It is devoted largely to learned articles on Anabaptist and Mennonite history and theology, but also to current Mennonite issues and affairs, with sections on bibliographical and research notes and book reviews. It is the only journal of its kind, and its files are a rich treasury of historical materials. The editor from the beginning has been H. S. Bender. The circulation in 1956 was about 600.   H.S.B.

Mennonite Relief and Service Committee. In 1926, after more than eight years of service, the Mennonite Relief Commission for War Sufferers (*q.v.*) came to an end as a separate organization and its functions were assumed by a committee of the Mennonite Board of Missions and Charities (*q.v.*) of Elkhart, Ind. The new committee was known as the Mennonite Relief Committee, later renamed the Mennonite Relief and Service Committee. The Mennonite Relief Committee (MRC) and the Mennonite Relief and Service Committee (MRSC) have maintained a policy of supporting the work of the Mennonite Central Committee (MCC), and in addition of maintaining relief and service projects under their own administration.

During 1937-40 the MRC administered a relief program in Spain. Six workers were sent to the field and a total of $57,000 was contributed to the work by the Mennonite churches, besides a small amount of support by the Mennonites of the Netherlands. In addition, the MRC workers distributed large quantities of food contributed through the International Commission for the Assistance of Child Refugees to Spain.

From the beginning of the relief projects associated with World War II the MRC served the Mennonite Church (MC) constituency in supporting the MCC program with funds and personnel. During 1937-48 a total of 572 Mennonite relief workers were in the field, of whom 282 (49 per cent) were from the MRC constituency. In September 1945 the MRC opened a relief work under its own administration in Ethiopia. After the Eastern Mennonite Board of Missions and Charities (*q.v.*) established its mission in Ethiopia in 1949 the relief project in that country was taken over by the EMBMC. In 1944 an MRC unit of relief workers was working in India under general MCC administration and in 1946 a unit was working under similar arrangements in China. In 1946-48 an MRC unit was operated in Belgium, and 1947-49 one was operating in Poland. On Jan. 1, 1950, the MRC took over from the MCC administration of the La Plata, Puerto Rico, project and has administered it continuously since that date.

One of the wartime functions of the MRC was the raising of funds for the support of the Mennonite Church (MC) share of the Civilian Public Service (*q.v.*) program. During much of the time the quota for this service was fifty cents per member per month, which amount the MRC collected and paid to the MCC. Beginning March 1944 the MRC also administered for its constituency a CPS dependency support fund which continued for three years. During this period allowances of more than $130,000 were paid to CPS dependents. This does not include dependents from the Lancaster, Franconia, Virginia, Washington County, Md., and Franklin County, Pa., conferences, nor from the congregations of Fulton County, Ohio, which administered their own CPS dependency programs.

The MRC also administered a fund to provide tuition grants-in-aid for ex-CPS men studying in Mennonite colleges. This fund consisted of the surplus remaining in the CPS and the CPS dependency funds at the close of CPS, in addition to continued contributions from the churches as needed. During

1946-50 a total of 240 students at Goshen, Hesston, and Eastern Mennonite Colleges received grants-in-aid in payment up to a maximum of 27 months each. Total grants received by these men amounted to nearly $80,000, of which nearly $66,000 was paid by the MRC.

In 1943 the Mennonite Board of Missions and Charities authorized the administration of a voluntary service (q.v.) program by the MRC. The first such service unit was of eight weeks' duration in the summer of 1944, with an enrollment of five workers, including the leader. In the four successive summers of 1945-48, the number of units with the number of workers was as follows: three with 15 workers, seven with 30 workers, 13 with 56 workers, and 16 units with 77 workers. In 1948 L. C. Hartzler was appointed the first full-time secretary of the committee with the title Secretary for Relief and Service. From this time the voluntary service program of the MRC experienced a steady growth, with long-term units in addition to the short-term summer units. In 1953 the MRC was renamed the Mennonite Relief and Service Committee. In 1953 Boyd Nelson succeeded Hartzler as Secretary for Relief and Service.

When the Selective Service System resumed the conscription of conscientious objectors in 1952 the MRSC established a I-W counseling service with responsibility for all I-W (see volume I, 697) men in the MRSC constituency. Beginning with age 16 a register is kept of all prospective I-W men. These men receive regular mailings of literature giving information regarding the services of the church to conscripted men. Financial support of I-W men in Pax (q.v.) and voluntary service units is the responsibility of the MRSC. A number of I-W centers and units are also administered under the direction of the I-W counseling service of the MRSC.

During the fiscal year 1956-57 the MRSC consisted of six appointed members, and the three chief officers of the Mennonite Board of Missions and Charities ex officio. The administrative staff consisted of Boyd Nelson, secretary for Relief and Service; Ray Horst, director of Voluntary Service; and Victor Esch, I-W Services counselor. During 1956-57 thirteen I-W units were under MRSC direction. The MRSC reported 27 short-term service units for the summer of 1956 with an enrollment of 22 men and 63 women. On Dec. 1, 1956, 25 long-term voluntary service units were in operation under MRSC administration with an enrollment of 167 persons, many of them being I-W men.   G.F.H.

Mennonite Relief Commission for War Sufferers was organized in December 1917 with headquarters at Elkhart, Ind., its stated purpose being "to solicit, receive, hold and dispense or distribute funds or supplies for the relief of war sufferers." From the beginning of World War I the periodicals of the Mennonite Church (MC) stressed relief for war sufferers as an essential part of the Gospel message for nonresistant Christians. Following the entrance of the United States into the war, funds for this purpose began to flow into the treasury of the Mennonite Board of Missions and Charities (q.v.). The MRCWS was then organized for the effective ad-

ministration of a work which had begun in a more or less spontaneous manner.

The Commission was made up of one representative each from the district mission boards of the Mennonite Church (MC) plus three members appointed by the Mennonite Board of Missions and Charities. It was organized with Aaron Loucks president, E. G. Reist vice-president, Levi Mumaw secretary, and G. L. Bender treasurer. Since the treasurer was also the treasurer of the Mennonite Board of Missions and Charities, and the vice-president an officer of the Eastern Mennonite Board of Missions and Charities (q.v.), the relief program of the Mennonite Church was thus closely associated with its mission program.

In January 1918 the MRCWS took action to support the work of reconstruction in France under the administration of the American Friends Service Committee, and also the work of the American Committee for Armenian and Syrian Relief, later known as the Near East Relief. This action was followed by regular monthly contributions to these two organizations. The MRCWS also organized among the women's sewing circles of its constituent congregations a program of sewing and knitting for the support of the relief work. The Eastern Mennonite Board of Missions and Charities co-ordinated its relief efforts with those of the MRCWS as did also the Nonresistant Relief Organization (q.v.), organized in 1917 by the Mennonite and Brethren in Christ congregations of Ontario.

By April 30, 1919, the receipts of the relief agencies of the church under the leadership of the MRCWS had amounted to more than $463,000. A report of the secretary-treasurer of the Mennonite Central Committee (q.v.), summarizing all Mennonite relief activities for the decade 1917-27, shows total contributions of approximately $2,500,000 for this period, of which amount approximately one half was contributed through the MRCWS and the agencies closely associated with it. The report shows a total of $339,000 contributed to the Near East Relief and $291,000 to the French reconstruction program. Of these two amounts all but $45,000 was contributed through the MRCWS and its affiliates. Most of the remainder of the contributions of the MRCWS were for relief work in Austria, Germany, and Eastern Europe, and (after the organization of the MCC in July 1920) for the support of Russian relief.

More than 50 Mennonites gave terms of personal service to the French reconstruction work. Some thirty served in the Near East Relief. These with others who served in Eastern Europe and in Russia make a total of nearly 100 men and women who served in foreign relief work under the auspices or sponsorship of the MRCWS.

Soon after its organization efforts were made to open foreign work to be administered directly by the MRCWS. As early as 1918 inquiry was made into the possibility of opening such work in Serbia or in Russia. When the first Mennonite contingent sailed for the Near East in January 1919, it was accompanied by William A. Derstine and Aaron Loucks, the president of the MRCWS, who explored the possibilities of an independent work in that region. When this proposal was found inadvisable the Mennonite workers entered service directly under the administration of the Near East Relief.

In the summer of 1920 the MRCWS co-operated with the relief agencies of other Mennonite groups in organizing the Mennonite Central Committee as a central Mennonite relief agency which then became responsible for the relief program in Russia. In May 1926 the MRCWS came to an end as an independent organization, when its work was taken over by the Mennonite Relief Committee, later known as the Mennonite Relief and Service Committee of the Mennonite Board of Missions and Charities.   G.F.H.

Mennonite Relief Committee: see Mennonite Relief and Service Committee

Mennonite Relief Committee of India was organized in 1942 at the suggestion of the Mennonite Central Committee primarily to serve refugees whose coming to India from neighboring war-stricken countries was anticipated. The first meeting of representatives from the five Mennonite and related missions in India was held at Champa, C.P., on April 9, 1942, at which time plans for a relief program were considered and an organization effected. It was agreed that members should be elected to MRCI by the respective missions on the basis of one representative for every 15 missionaries or fraction thereof. This representation is as follows: M.C. (Dhamtari) two, M.B. (Hyderabad) two, B.C. (Saharsa) one, G.C.M. (Champa) two, and M.B.C. (Ragandih) one. The membership of eight has been maintained except in 1945-51, when the MCC had a director in India (along with other MCC workers) who also served on the MRCI. While war refugee needs were less than anticipated, MRCI had occasion to render aid to some such persons. The main relief projects, however, have been carried on in Bengal following the tidal wave disaster of 1943, in refugee camps of North India and Pakistan following the partition of the country in 1947, and in local communities of the several mission areas in times of crop failure.

The MRCI marked the first attempt at any organic relationship between the four Mennonite bodies and the Brethren in Christ working in India. This organization has emphasized a peace testimony along with its relief program and has aided in bringing together the historic peace churches found in India for conferences on peace. Two such conferences have been held in India since 1952 with members of the Brethren in Christ, Church of the Brethren, Friends, and Mennonite churches participating.   S.M.K.

Mennonite Religious School at Winnipeg, Man., operating in 1932-46, was located in the Schoenwiese Mennonite Church and supported by the following churches: Schoenwiese, Schoenfeld, Lichtenau, Springstein, and Elim Mennonite church. The subjects of instruction were introduction to the Scriptures, the Christian faith, church history, the Mennonite heritage, church hymnology, and the German language. The teachers were the local ministers: J. H. Enns, J. J. Schulz, D. Loewen, and P. Dirks. The school offered a four-year course. It was fol-

lowed by the Bible School at Altona and the Canadian Mennonite Bible College at Winnipeg.
                                             J.H.E.

Mennonite Research Fellowship was organized in 1945 at Bluffton, Ohio, to meet the desire of a number of Mennonite college faculty members to promote scholarship in the fields directly related to the Mennonite church, its history, faith, and life. It had 13 charter members. Membership is by invitation to scholars who are communicant members of some Mennonite congregation and who have a demonstrated capacity and achievement in research. Candidates for membership must have a minimum of publications directly related to Mennonites and the quality of writing must be at least on a Master's Degree level. The organization consists of a president, vice-president, and secretary-treasurer, who serve as the Executive Committee. The meetings are arranged for on an annual or biannual basis as circumstances may dictate.   J.W.F.

Mennonite Research Foundation, a semiautonomous organization, chartered by the Mennonite (MC) Board of Education (*q.v.*) with office at Goshen, Ind., was founded in February 1947 to serve the research needs of the Mennonite Church (MC) by carrying on or aiding research and publication in such fields as Mennonite history, theology, sociology, education, evangelism, and current activities and problems. It is controlled by a board of seven directors appointed by the Executive Committee of the Mennonite Board of Education including representatives from the three major boards of the Mennonite Church (MC), education, publication, and missions, and its three colleges, Goshen, E.M.C., and Hesston. Officers from the beginning have been Paul Erb, chairman, H. S. Bender, secretary, A. J. Metzler, treasurer. Melvin Gingerich has been director of research from the beginning, with G. F. Hershberger serving as acting director 1955-57. The budget is supplied by contributions from the boards and a group of private supporters known as Mennonite Research Associates, plus fees charged for services rendered.   H.S.B.

Mennonite Resettlement Finance, Inc., was incorporated as a nonprofit organization on Dec. 16,, 1946, to function as the trustee of funds received from the Mennonite Central Committee and others for the purpose of aiding and assisting in the migration, location, resettlement, and rehabilitation of Mennonite refugees and other individuals or groups served by the MCC. The members, constituting the Board of Directors and numbering not less than five and not more than eight, were appointed by the MCC for terms of one year. The officers—chairman, vice-chairman, secretary, and treasurer—were elected by the MRF Board members.

From the beginning of its function as a trustee, the economic problems of the settlement in South America, particularly in Paraguay, became a major concern of the MRF. Responsibility for receiving and administering additional loan funds was lodged in the MRF, as well as the trusteeship for receiving repayment on loans and for reinvestment. From time to time adjustments were made on the debts of immigrants.

On Dec. 30, 1954, the MRF was dissolved by action of the MCC annual meeting, and its functions and assets were transferred to the parent organization, the MCC. The directors at the time of liquidation were E. C. Bender, C. A. DeFehr, C. L. Graber, Abe M. Hallman, Raymond Schlichting, Elvin R. Souder, and William T. Snyder.   W.T.S.

Mennonite School of Nursing, Beatrice, Neb., was founded at the Mennonite Deaconess Home and Hospital at Beatrice in 1911 shortly after the hospital was opened, and continued until 1929. The course of study was three years and included courses which led to high-school graduation and upon graduation from the School of Nursing eligibility for registration. Special courses in Bible, ethics, and the deaconess work were given. The school gave training to 27 girls; of these a number became ordained deaconesses and have devoted their lives to the care of the sick. The school was under the leadership of Sister Marie Wedel, Sister Elise Hirschler, Sister Sarah Rempel, Sister Magdalene Wiebe, and Herman Wiebe. In 1941-47 a two-year course in practical community nursing was offered under the leadership of Mrs. Ursula Penner Frantz.
          E.P.Z.

Mennonite Settlers Aid Society, an organization incorporated in 1927 with headquarters at Newton, Kan. Its purpose was to assist General Conference Mennonites who were looking for farm land to settle in solid Mennonite communities. The Society reserved large tracts of land for periods of time in which General Conference Mennonites could ask for membership and buy land. The Society did not finance settlers nor did it buy the land directly. It merely negotiated for large blocks of land with agencies such as railroads and lumber companies. One of the first aids of the Society was to reserve 50,000 acres of cutover timberland in northeastern Washington through the Great Northern Railway.

Three settlements were attempted—one each at Elk, Deer Park, and Newport, Wash. None of these settlements flourished, although there is still a small Mennonite community at Newport, with a baptized membership (1955) of 54. This land was not suitable for general farming purposes. The Aid Society eventually disintegrated because it never enjoyed strong support. A number of the families attracted were Mennonite refugees who had come from Russia to the United States after World War I. The original founders and directors of the Settlers Aid Society were H. P. Krehbiel president, P. H. Unruh vice-president, A. J. Dyck secretary, and P. P. Buller and D. D. Unruh.   J.W.F.

Mennonite Song Festival Society (GCM) became a permanent organization June 8, 1930, at a business meeting held in connection with a Sängerfest (song festival) at the Alexanderwohl Mennonite Church near Goessel, Kan. The officers for this new society were John W. Unruh, president; Carl Krehbiel, vice-president; Isaac Balzer, secretary; and Weldon Rupp, treasurer. Other leaders in carrying on the work of

this annual spring song festival for more than a quarter century include Walter H. Hohmann, G. F. Friesen, and the late Paul G. Baumgartner. This festival has become the largest Mennonite gathering of its kind in Kansas and probably in the United States.

Sängerfests were held in the communities of Newton, Moundridge, Goessel, and Buhler in the early 1920's, to which music organizations of the surrounding churches were invited. In accord with the newly adopted constitution this Sängerfest was now held at the various churches upon invitation, and all Kansas, Oklahoma, and Nebraska churches were invited to participate. The host church erected a large tent on the church grounds and by having the choirs sing in the church and tent alternately, a large listening audience of several thousand was accommodated quite adequately. Within a few years, however, the local churches were unable to accommodate such vast crowds, and in 1934 it was agreed to have the festival at Bethel College. Permanent bleachers were erected on the slopes of Kidron Creek and the festival was held out-of-doors. In the case of inclement weather the festival was held at Lindley Hall at Newton. Upon completion of the Bethel College Memorial Hall in 1942, Joliffe Auditorium became the meeting place for this festival. The constitution as revised in 1947 stipulates that "Memorial Hall is to be considered the home of the song festival unless it becomes necessary to meet elsewhere."

Approximately 30 churches from the Western District Conference participate in this annual festival. The idea of having a massed choir make up a part of the program has continued at every festival. This choir has sung such oratorios as the *Holy City, Elijah,* and practically all of the *Messiah.* At other times as many as 12 anthems, carefully selected by the officers, have made up an evening's program. German and English chorales and Gospel hymns are sung by the massed choir as well as by the entire audience. To complete the afternoon and evening programs mixed choirs and men's choruses, ladies' choirs, young people's choirs, ensembles, and in later years children's choirs have sung at the festival. Between 500 and 800 singers participate annually.

The Mennonite Song Festival Society endeavors to fulfill its stated purpose: "To glorify the name of God in song; to create opportunities for fellowship between the different Mennonite churches; to stimulate interest in church choir work; to constantly strive to improve the quality of the singing of choirs and congregations."   E.N.

Mennonite Spanish Church (MC), 1014 South Blue Island Ave., Chicago, Ill., on the near west side of the city, was organized under the Mennonite Board of Missions and Charities in 1934 with 14 charter members. The main services are bilingual, Spanish and English. The membership in 1956 was 64. Pastors who have served the church are David Castillo (4 years), Lester Hershey (5 years), D. Parke Lantz (one year), Elvin V. Snyder (one year), John Litwiller (2 years), and Mario Snyder (3 years). It serves the Latin-American community of Chicago.
          D.Be.

Mennonite Teachers' Association *(Lehrerverein)*, an organization established in the Chortitza, Molotschna, and other Mennonite settlements of Russia after the Russo-Japanese War (1905-6). Until then associations of this nature had been forbidden in Russia. A new educational organization was particularly urgent because the Mennonite Board (Council) of Education (*Schulrat, q.v.*) was losing its significance because of constant difficulties with regulations of the Russian Department of Education. The Mennonite Teachers' Association took over some of the functions of the Board, such as arranging for teachers' conferences where problems pertinent to education were discussed, such as methods, curricula, textbooks, and visual aids. Gradually the achievements and qualifications of the new organization were recognized by the constituency. Although there were some difficulties in working harmoniously with the Board there was co-operation among them. Major difficulties arose when a reactionary policy of the government set in. When World War I broke out the Association was forbidden because of its German background. After the March Revolution in 1917 the Association was revived and accomplished some significant tasks. Gradually it was discontinued because all teachers were expected to join the professional organizations of the Soviets.

The Mennonite Teachers' Association and its local branches in the various Mennonite settlements played a very significant role in improving standards of education through the means of a professional exchange of thoughts and experiences, and fellowship and mutual encouragement.   C.K.

D. P. Enns, "Mennonite Education in Russia," *Menn. Life* VI (July 1951) 28 ff.; Peter Braun, "The Education System of the Mennonite Colonies in South Russia," *MQR* III (July 1929) 179 ff.; Leonhard Froese, *Das pädagogische Kultursystem der mennonitischen Siedlungsgruppe in Russland* (thesis at the University of Göttingen, privately mimeographed, 1949) 96.

Mennonite Teachers' Association (or **Conference**) **of Kansas** (*Mennonitischer Lehrerverein*) was founded in 1886 for the purpose of promoting Christian education among the Mennonites who had recently come from Russia, Prussia, and Poland. It was a continuation of a similar organization in Russia. H. H. Ewert of Halstead, Kan., called a first meeting of teachers in the spring of 1886, and a second meeting during the summer, at which a constitution was adopted, which was slightly revised and reprinted in 1910 and 1925. The Mennonite Teachers' Association grew out of the Kansas Conference of Mennonites (*q.v.*), which became the Western District Conference (GCM) and had originally concerned itself chiefly with matters of education. The Association met twice annually, during the Christmas and summer vacations. Local or district meetings of the Association were held at various places. These meetings took place in the school of the local teacher, where one of the teachers presented a demonstration lesson which was later criticized and used for discussion. A public program followed. The Mennonite Teachers' Association organized and sponsored the German Teachers' Institute (*q.v.*), which had its first session Aug. 6, 1894.

During World War I, when the feeling against the use of German was strong, the Association experienced a setback from which it never recovered. In 1924 the Association published the *Lehrplan für Ferien-Bibel-Schulen* (Lesson Plan for Vacation Bible Schools) prepared by a special committee. The *Bethel College Monthly* (Jan. 15, 1927) reports the 65th meeting, which was held on Dec. 28, 1926, at Newton. During the Christmas vacation of 1932 the 71st meeting was held (*Mennonite Weekly Review*, Jan. 11, 1933). The last meeting was held in 1941 at the First Mennonite Church of Newton. The interest in the organization had apparently disappeared.

In Nebraska the Mennonite teachers founded a Mennonite Teachers' Association in 1898, which included the teachers of Jefferson, Gage, Cumming, Hamilton, and York counties. The first meeting was held in Jansen. The activities were similar to those in Kansas, but the organization was discontinued at an earlier date. It is probable that similar organizations existed in Dakota and Minnesota.

The contributions made to Mennonite education by the Association during the difficult pioneer conditions have never been fully investigated and evaluated. A very valuable source for this purpose would be the questionnaires filled out by the 31 existing Mennonite schools in Kansas in 1892-93 (in BeCL), which give much information pertaining to schools, teachers, textbooks, etc.

H. H. Ewert (*q.v.*) organized a number of activities along the line of the Teachers' Association among the Mennonites of Manitoba. Before the turn of the century he introduced local monthly teachers' conferences in the various school districts under his supervision. The program was very much the same as in Kansas. During World War I these conferences were discontinued, and after the war attempts to revive them were not very successful. In 1900 Ewert created a German Teachers' Conference (*Lehrerkonferenz*) for Southern Manitoba, which met annually, alternating between Gretna and Winkler. Later Altona and Plum Coulee were added. The conferences usually lasted two days. First they were conducted in German and after World War I in English. In 1929 the Mennonite teachers who had come from Russia organized another (German) Teachers' Conference in Manitoba, which has its regular meetings. In 1948 it was decided at a teachers' conference to publish the *Mennonitische Lehrerzeitung* (later *Mennonitische Welt*), which appeared 1948-52.   C.K.

H. P. Peters, *History and Development of Education Among the Mennonites of Kansas* (Hillsboro, 1925) 78 ff. (contains translated constitution); *Statuten für den Mennonitischen Lehrerverein von Kansas* (1886, 1910, 1925); P. J. Schaeffer, *Heinrich H. Ewert . . .* (n.p., 1945) 76-86; Theodore Schmidt, "The Mennonites of Nebraska" (thesis, University of Nebraska, 1933) 45 ff.

Mennonite Teachers' Institute: see German Teachers' Institute.

Mennonite Theological Seminary: see Amsterdam Mennonite Theological Seminary.

Mennonite Union Aid is an organization serving the members of the Church of God in Christ, Mennonite, throughout North America in times of disaster caused by lightning, fire, and storm. The office is located at Montezuma, Kan. The organization began to operate on Oct. 1, 1943, and was adopted by the General Conference in November 1946. It functions under the direction of an Executive Board, a Board of Directors, and 41 local committees representing 41 districts in the United States and Canada. Mortgage certificates are recognized by loan companies. In April 1957 the assessed valuation was over $14,000,000, with 1,765 members.   A.U.

Mennonite Voluntary Service, European organization: see **Mennonitischer Freiwilligendienst.**

Mennonite Weekly Review, published at Newton, Kan., by the Herald Publishing Co., appeared in its first introductory issue of Aug. 9, 1923, as a supplement of *Der Herold.* Its purpose was set forth in an editorial by H. P. Krehbiel, president of the Herald Publishing Co.: "When the Herald Publishing Co. was organized in 1920 the principal purpose was to create an institution through which literature in the German language would continue to be prepared, published, and circulated in behalf of our Mennonite people. But it was also recognized that in the central West the English language was rapidly coming into prominence among the incoming generation. . . . A year ago . . . it was decided to proceed to the establishment of an English Mennonite periodical suitable particularly to the needs of the Middle West."

Regular and independent publication as a 4-page, 6-column paper was begun Sept. 18, 1923. Gradually it became a 6- and 8-page paper, with space devoted to family, church and community events, articles on current issues, school reports, and a summary of news around the world. After mostly local circulation for ten years, the *Mennonite Weekly Review* later assumed the character of "A Mennonite Family Paper—Published in the Interest of Mennonites Everywhere," with readership extending into most branches of Mennonites throughout North America. Special columnists and contributors serving over a period of years include Peter Brown, J. W. Fretz, Melvin Gingerich, Cornelius Krahn, John P. Suderman, Andrew R. Shelly, and Ida M. Yoder. The 12-page tabloid format was adopted in 1951. Editors have been A. J. Krehbiel 1923-25, H. P. Krehbiel 1926-35, Menno Schrag 1935- . Assistant editors have been Abe Epp 1925-26, Menno Schrag 1927-28 and 1931-35, Ferdinand Wiens 1928-30, J. Richard Blosser, associate editor, 1946- .   M.S.

Mennonite Welfare Board (MC) of Ontario was organized in 1939 by the Ontario Conference as a board under which the Poor and Charity Funds administered by various committees were brought under the administration of the deacon body of the conference. Its purpose is to see that the welfare needs are met equally among the churches. Each deacon presents the needs of both laymen and ministers for his congregation. A levy of 15-30 cents has been sufficient as dues per member. The Board meets in September and in March. Special needs may be cared for by the Executive Committee between regular meetings. The Board contributes funds for needy Mennonites in the Braeside Home

for the Aged in Preston. Considerable income is derived from endowment sources. Since 1948 the child welfare work in Ontario has been under this organization. The deacons are encouraged to co-operate in presenting the needs of all members with serious reverses caused by illness and other misfortune. In 1954, 18 cases were helped with a sum amounting nearly to $3,200.   J.C.F.

Mennonite Women's Missionary Association (GCM): see **Women's Missionary Association.**

Mennonite Women's Missionary Society, the first women's organization in the Mennonite Church (MC), was organized in 1918 as the result of the initiative of Clara Eby Steiner of Columbus Grove, Ohio, the widow of M. S. Steiner, an early General Mission Board president. She served as the general secretary from the beginning until her retirement because of ill health in 1926. Because of misunderstandings between the organization and the officers of the Mennonite Board of Missions and Charities, the organization was in effect forced to dissolve in 1927, when the Board appointed a General Sewing Circle Committee to co-ordinate the work of the local sewing circles in their sewing for missions and relief. The MWMS did a good work in co-ordinating the work of the local sewing circles and stimulating missionary interest and giving on the part of the local sewing circles of the Mennonite Church. It operated through local and state branches, of which there were 20 in 1920. Since in certain sections the sewing circles worked under conference or district mission board organizations, and since there was little co-ordination across state and conference lines the pioneer work of the MWMS was not easy. The treasurer throughout its history was Ruth A. Yoder of Bellefontaine, Ohio. Presidents changed a number of times, the first being Mary Burkhard of Goshen, Ind. The organ of the Society was the *Monthly Letter.*   H.S.B.

Mennonite World Conference has held the following sessions: (1) Basel, Switzerland, June 13-16, 1925; (2) Danzig, Free City of Danzig, Aug. 31-Sept. 3, 1930; (3) Amsterdam, Elspeet, and Witmarsum, Netherlands, June 29-July 3, 1936; (4) Goshen, Ind., and North Newton, Kan., Aug. 3-10, 1948; (5) Basel and Zürich, Switzerland, Aug. 10-15, 1952; (6) Karlsruhe, Germany, Aug. 10-16, 1957. The proceedings of the first five conferences have been published as follows: (1) *Bericht über die 400jährige Jubiläumsfeier der Mennoniten oder Taufgesinnten* (Karlsruhe, n.d.-1925?) pp. 183; (2) *Mennonitische Welt-Hilfs-Konferenz* (Karlsruhe, n.d.-1930?) pp. 192; (3) *Der Allgemeine Kongress der Mennoniten* (Karlsruhe, n.d.-1936?) pp. 183; (4) *Proceedings of the Fourth Mennonite World Conference* (Akron, 1950) pp. 341; (5) *Die Gemeinde Christi und Ihr Auftrag. Vorträge und Verhandlungen der Fünften Mennonitischen Weltkonferenz* (Karlsruhe, 1953) pp. 410. Editor of the first three was Christian Neff (*q.v.*), of the fourth H. S. Bender and P. C. Hiebert, of the fifth Paul Schowalter and H. S. Bender.

The father of the Mennonite World Conference, and its recognized leader for the first three sessions, though he was never officially elected its chairman, was Christian Neff, pastor of the Weierhof, Germany, Mennonite congregation and president of the Conference of South German Mennonites. The South German Conference issued the call for the first session at his proposal. He issued the call personally for the two following conferences. The first conference was based upon the idea of the 400th anniversary of the founding of Anabaptism in Switzerland in 1525, the second upon the need for co-operative effort to meet the urgent need for aid to Mennonite refugees from Russia then being settled in Paraguay, Brazil, and Canada, the third upon the 400th anniversary of Menno Simons' conversion from Roman Catholicism in 1536. The several relief agencies (MCC, Dutch, German) joined in sponsoring the Danzig meeting. The Dutch A.D.S. was the chief sponsor of the third conference. The programs of these three sessions were naturally oriented around the three distinct occasions listed above, and the promotion of the idea of a world conference was made easier (some Mennonites were hesitant and many rather indifferent) by the nature of the three occasions.

Attendance at the first conference was small, with only one delegate from North America, H. J. Krehbiel, the president of the General Conference Mennonite Church, and only a few from Holland, France, and Germany. In spite of the historical setting the first conference devoted a major session to the question, "How can we improve the spiritual life of our congregations?" The chief speakers were W. J. Kühler and T. O. Hylkema from Holland, Jacob Kroeker, Michael Horsch, and Christian Schnebele from Germany, and David Geiser from Switzerland. The moderators were Samuel Nussbaumer and Fritz Goldschmidt from Basel.

The program of the second or Danzig conference was devoted exclusively to the history of past Mennonite relief efforts (addresses by Christian Neff and W. J. Kühler), current relief operations (H. S. Bender from the United States, S. H. N. Gorter from Holland, Christian Neff and Michael Horsch from Germany). C. F. Klassen, David Toews, B. H. Unruh, H. S. Bender, and S. H. N. Gorter spoke on the conditions of the Mennonites in Russia since 1917, the flight from Russia, and the emigration to South America and Canada. Two moderators were elected, P. B. Westerdijk of the Netherlands, and David Toews of Canada. The attendance from beyond the local area was small, with only three from Canada, and three from the United States. A general resolution was adopted by the conference summarizing the work of the sessions, accompanied by an appeal to the Mennonite brotherhood everywhere to support the relief. work being carried on in behalf of the Russian Mennonite refugees and emigrants.

The program of the third conference at Amsterdam in 1936 was strongly historical and descriptive. N. van der Zijpp gave the major commemorative address, "Menno Simons' Significance for the Mennonite Brotherhood." Historical-descriptive addresses were given on Holland (J. Yntema), Germany (Christian Neff), Switzerland (Samuel Geiser), Russia (B. H. Unruh), United States (H. S. Bender), Canada (David Toews), Mennonite settlements

in South America (B. H. Unruh) and in Paraguay (Fritz Kliewer), on missions (C. Nijdam and O. O. Miller), on relief·work and colonization (S. H. N. Gorter, P. C. Hiebert, and David Toews), on Mennonites and Culture (C. Henry Smith and Frits Kuiper), on Mennonites and Youth (P. R. Schroeder and Erich Göttner). The conference closed with a commemorative ceremony at Witmarsum, having spent the first two days in Amsterdam with services in the Singel Church, and the last two days in Elspeet at the Brotherhood House grounds. An appeal was made by the conference for a world-wide collection on behalf of the debts of the Russian Mennonite immigrants in Canada, and an international Mennonite relief office was created at Karlsruhe, Germany (by the several Mennonite relief agencies, not by the world conference), with B. H. Unruh as director, to be supported by the relief agencies in Europe and North America. The latter attempt failed after a year or so, and the response to the collection appeal was not as large as hoped for. The chairman of the A.D.S. was chosen as moderator of the conference, with Christian Neff as honorary moderator; assistant moderators were Emil Händiges (Germany), C. F. Klassen (Canada), and P. R. Schroeder (United States). The attendance was much larger than in the previous conferences, with a large number from Germany, a few from France and Switzerland, and about fifteen from North America (six from Canada). An important side meeting on nonresistance was held at Fredeshiem near Steenwijk, Netherlands, immediately following the conference close, attended by some twenty persons, mostly from Holland and North America, at which an International Mennonite Peace Committee was created and a message sent to all Mennonites on behalf of the peace position.

The coming of World War II made the calling of the fourth world conference in 1940 in the United States, as planned, impossible; and the traditional world conference leader, Christian Neff, died in 1946. The MCC then assumed the leadership and called the conference to meet in the United States in August 1948, serving the large attendance by holding sessions at two centers, Goshen, Ind., and North Newton, Kan., with similar two-and-a-half-day programs at each place. The program was planned by the Committee of Guidance and Counsel representing the leading North American conferences, together with the chairman and vice-chairman of the MCC, the latter two men also being designated as moderator (P. C. Hiebert) and assistant moderator (H. A. Fast) of the conference sessions. The very full program was devoted to the following major topics, each being given a session with an average of three speakers: Relief, Nonconformity to the World, Faith and Life, Missions, Young People's Work, A Young People's Program, the Peace Testimony, Colonization, Institutions and Mennonite Life, and Christian Education. The conference sermon was by P. C. Hiebert. The developments among Mennonites during World War II and after (1936-48) were thoroughly reported by Emil Händiges (West Prussia), Dirk Cattepoel (Germany), H. W. Meihuizen (Holland), and Samuel Geiser (Switzerland and France), and similar reports were given on the new refugee settlements in Paraguay and Brazil. Some 45 major addresses were delivered in addition to shorter testimonies. The attendance was very large, although only a few came from overseas: Netherlands 8, Germany 6, France 3, Switzerland 2, Paraguay 2, Brazil 2, India 3, China 1, a total from overseas of 27. The MCC aided in the travel expenses of most of the official delegates from Europe. No official resolutions or appeals were issued by the conference, except one making provision for a fifth conference through authorization of a Preparatory Commission to be constituted by representatives from Mennonite conferences throughout the world who might choose to participate.

In the 1952 conference held on the grounds of the St. Chrischona Seminary near Basel, Switzerland, the program development and attendance reached a new level. The general theme of the program, "The Church of Christ and Her Commission," was developed largely around several sub-themes such as (1) the nature of the church; (2) the concept of the church held by the Anabaptist forefathers and its realization in history and the present in Holland, Central Europe, and America; (3) the work of the church and its expression in missions and evangelization; (4) the church and the world; (5) the Mennonite Church and the rest of Christendom; (6) the church and her youth. There was a review of current world Mennonitism in six descriptive addresses, with a summary address on the total situation of world Mennonitism. Samuel Gerber of Les Reussilles, Switzerland, preached the conference sermon. Two new features marked this conference, the use of discussion groups following the major addresses, and the setting up of side meetings for women, youth, missions, scholars, publishers, and editors, peace testimony, nurses, and voluntary service. One day was spent in an historical celebration in Zürich, at which addresses were given by the president of the Zürich Cantonal Reformed Church, Oskar Farner, and Fritz Blanke of the Zürich theological faculty, in the Grossmünster Church, and a memorial tablet was dedicated to Conrad Grebel and Felix Manz. The officers of the Preparatory Commission were elected as officers of the conference (H. S. Bender, chairman, Hans Nussbaumer, vice-chairman, Ulrich Hege, C. F. Klassen, H. W. Meihuizen, the five constituting the executive committee). A noteworthy feature of this conference also was the adoption of a conference message to the world Mennonite brotherhood. The attendance was very large, averaging 600 in the day sessions. The 218 delegates were distributed as follows: Europe 104, North America 111, Indonesia two, Paraguay one.

The sixth world conference, by action of the Basel conference, is to be held at Karlsruhe, Germany, Aug. 10-16, 1957. The conference theme will be "The Gospel of Jesus Christ in the World." The Preparatory Commission is in full charge of the program, and works through a local committee on arrangements. For the Basel and Karlsruhe conferences simultaneous translation equipment (IBM) has made possible translation of all addresses and business in three languages (English, German,

French), but the official language has been German. A trilingual conference hymnal has been published.

From a meeting oriented primarily to historical occasions, with a limited attendance and certain uncertainties and hesitancies, the world conference has developed into a large-scale session with significant addresses and discussions on major doctrinal and practical themes of current interest and concern to Mennonites as a whole, and with an increasing warmth of fellowship and practical value. The conference is basically an inspirational and discussion conference, with no jurisdiction whatsoever over its constituent groups, but responsive to their wishes. It has demonstrated a growing value and won increasing acceptance, and its regular five-year sessions can contribute much to the strengthening of worldwide Mennonitism and the effective discharge of its spiritual tasks.   H.S.B.

Mennonite Writers Fellowship, established in 1951 by the editorial staff of the Mennonite Publishing House to promote better religious writing, holds annual meetings and writers' workshop at Laurelville Mennonite Camp near Scottdale, Pa., and issues a quarterly multilithed release, the *Christian Writer.* In 1956 it had 227 members, with officers as follows: John A. Hostetler chairman, Helen Trumbo vice-chairman, Elizabeth Showalter secretary-treasurer.
                                                 H.S.B.

Mennonite Yearbook and Directory (MC) was first published in 1905 by the Mennonite Board of Charitable Homes and Missions, at Scottdale, Pa. Issued as an annual publication, it contained articles, ministerial directories, statistical data, and names of institutional personnel. In 1905-13 it also contained the Almanac. The 1906 issue was published by its founder, and the 1907-8 issues were published by the Mennonite Board of Missions and Charities. The publication was not issued in 1909-12, but appeared again in 1913 with the Mennonite Publishing House, Scottdale, as its publisher. During these four years (1909-12) some information and statistical data appeared in the *Family Almanac (q.v.).* Except for one issue dated 1914-15, the *Mennonite Yearbook and Directory* has been published annually by the Mennonite Publishing House. It contains articles and biographical sketches of general church interest, church organizations and institutions including domestic and foreign missions, with names of their personnel. The Conference Directory for the Mennonite Church (MC) gives names and addresses of congregations by conference districts with the membership and ministry for each congregation. Conference directories are also given for the Conservative Mennonites, Old Order Amish Mennonites, Old Order (Wisler) Mennonites, and affiliated congregations. The Ministerial Directory includes lists of names and addresses of ordained men for Mennonite bodies throughout the world. The issues of 1905-7 inclusive were edited by a compiling committee of three. Those who served on this committee were Aaron Loucks 1905-7, M. S. Steiner 1905-7, J. S. Shoemaker 1905-6, D. H. Bender 1907. No names appear in the 1908 issue. The 1913 issue was edited by J. A. Ressler, Daniel Kauffman, and H. F. Reist. Beginning with the 1914 issue the editors were J. A. Ressler 1914-24, John L. Horst 1925-42, Ellrose D. Zook 1943- . The 1956 issue contained 136 pages and had a circulation of 8,600. The size has remained at 6 x 9 in., and except for typographical changes in format it is similar to the first issue. It has become in a sense a world Mennonite directory, with lists of Mennonite ministers and total church membership for all Mennonite groups.   E.D.Z.

Mennonite (MC) **Youth Fellowship** (generally called "MYF") is a general church-wide organization for the stimulation and guidance of young people in Christian life and service. MYF was organized at Eureka, Ill., in 1948, after extensive study by the Commission and approval by the General Conference. It serves the youth organizations in the Mennonite (MC) congregations. In January 1955 there were 121 member units. There is an annual meeting, usually held in connection with other church-wide meetings. The general organization promotes youth work concepts, participates in the production of program materials, and prepares promotional literature. There is a general council, consisting of the president, vice-president, secretary, treasurer, secretaries in the areas of faith, fellowship, and service, representatives of the *Youth's Christian Companion* staff and the Mission Board, and the sponsor. The sponsor is the Secretary of Young People's Activities of the Commission for Christian Education, to which MYF is generally responsible. Officers are elected by the delegates at the annual meeting. Area secretaries are appointed by these officers and the sponsor. An executive office is maintained at Scottdale, Pa.

The local units of MYF are not uniform in organization of functioning, nor do all carry the MYF name, but they are expected to function in supplying young people's needs in accordance with local conditions and standards. The general organization furnishes to the local units only such guidance as they wish or can use. In some districts, particularly in the Middle West, there are also district MYF organizations, conference-wide or state-wide. P.E.

Mennonite (GCM) **Youth Organization** *of Saskatchewan* was initiated with the help of Olin Krehbiel of Berne, Ind., largely as the result of the influence of the General Conference sessions held at Saskatoon in 1938. In June 1941 the first youth retreat was held, and in the same year a youth conference at Laird. Here a constitution was adopted connecting the organization with the Young People's Union of the General Conference; but this was changed July 1949 to connect it with the Canadian Conference. In 1942 the daily vacation Bible schools were started and still enjoy a great popularity. The executive Committee of the Mennonite Youth Organization of Saskatchewan at first consisted of five members, but in 1946 it was enlarged to nine members.

Most of the interests of this organization have centered on the Rosthern Youth Farm, since the activities and projects are mostly on this farm. Here the first and largest projects were started. In 1941

and 1942 the first retreats were held at the Rosthern Dominion Experimental Farm. In the winter of 1943-44 the experimental farm was bought from the government for $20,000, consisting of 640 acres and buildings that the government built for about $60,000. In 1944 the Invalid Home was opened and now (1954) has about 80 patients in two houses. In 1945 the Elim Gospel Beach in South Saskatchewan was bought and in 1947 paid in full. In 1946 the first children's home was built and in 1953 the Crippled Children's Home was opened. Combined, these homes are able to take about 20 children. In 1951 the Invalid Home in Herbert was started, which now has about 20 patients. This farm also organizes workshops for youth, the first one in 1952. The farm supplies the town of Rosthern with pasteurized milk. Besides this the farm supports missionaries in foreign and domestic fields. The main endeavor comes from the Youth Organization, particularly H. W. Friesen and J. C. Schmidt. J.G.R.

Mennonite Youth Service (MC) is an 8-page quarterly published by the Lancaster Mennonite Conference. In order to increase Christian testimony and to provide suitable activities for Christian development, especially among the young people, the Lancaster Mennonite Conference encouraged the organizing and conducting of Christian worker groups in the local congregations. As early as 1939 groups were organizing for Christian service, such as distributing tracts and other Gospel literature, making scrapbooks, advertising the Gospel in trolley cars and buses, and visiting shut-ins. At the fall session of Conference in 1946 a resolution was passed to prepare a folder to give suggestions and guidance concerning objectives, opportunities, methods of organization, and safeguards in the organizing and conducting of the Christian worker groups. This folder was distributed among the congregations in the conference area. The years which followed saw a rapid increase in the organizing of these worker groups. At the spring session of Conference in 1950 a committee was selected to give guidance to the Christian worker groups within the conference. About a year later this committee, known as the Youth Christian Service Activities Committee, planned for the publication of a monthly paper for the promotion and guidance of Christian service activities by the worker groups.

The first issue of *Mennonite Youth Service* was published in July 1951, with a circulation of approximately 3,000 copies. It was printed monthly thereafter, with one exception, until October 1954, when it became an 8-page paper and was printed quarterly. It contained reports of the various activities of the worker groups, testimonies by young people of blessings received, also articles giving encouragement and helpful suggestions. News notes and poems also added interest to its pages. It is intended that this little paper shall aid in enlisting the interest and support of the several thousand young people of the Lancaster Mennonite Conference and surrounding areas to the great task of witnessing to the saving power of Christ through Christian service.

H.H.W.

Mennonitentag. In the constitution of the German Mennonite *Vereinigung* (*q.v.*) adopted in 1934, provision is made for an annual "Mennonite Day" "to reflect on the Gospel and the Mennonite confession of faith as the foundation of our church life in the past and present." The first Mennonite Day was held on Ascension Day, May 30, 1935, in Altona. Since then the plan has been to hold the meetings annually in rotation in various parts of Germany. Further Mennonitentags were held: Gronau and Emden 1936, Berlin 1937, Regensburg and Munich 1938, Crefeld 1939. Later attempts to revive these meetings have been fruitless. (*ML* III, 106.)

NEFF.

Mennonites of America, The, by C. Henry Smith, the first and thus far only comprehensive work on American Mennonite history, was published by the author at Goshen, Ind., in 1909, printed by the Mennonite Publishing House at Scottdale, Pa., 484 pp. illustrated. It was Smith's Ph.D. dissertation at the University of Chicago, and chapters I-IV were published in the same year as a booklet of 147 pages to fulfill the doctoral requirements. Its content was ultimately absorbed in revised form into the author's *Story of the Mennonites* (Berne, 1941). Smith also wrote a booklet of 71 pages, *Mennonites in America* (Akron, 1942), as one of the CPS Core Course booklets called *Mennonites and Their Heritage,* published by the MCC.

H.S.B.

Mennonitische Auslese, a German-language periodical edited and published by Arnold Dyck, Steinbach, Man., of which only one issue appeared in 1951. It was intended to be a Mennonite "digest" and to appear biannually. On its 85 pages the editor presents articles from Mennonite papers, e.g., *Der Bote* and *Mennonitische Rundschau.* The 25 illustrated articles deal with the Mennonites the world over including numerous biographical sketches. Lack of subscriptions compelled the publisher to give up his plan. The *Mennonitische Auslese* may be considered a continuation of the *Mennonitische Volkswarte* (*q.v.*) and *Warte-Jahrbuch* (*q.v.*).

C.K.

Mennonitische Blätter, the oldest periodical of the German Mennonites (not published since 1941), was founded on Jan. 1, 1854, by Preacher Jakob Mannhardt (*q.v.*) of Danzig. Determinedly and faithfully following the motto of Menno Simons (I Cor. 3:11) he considered it "as the beautiful goal of our work to bring about a closer community among our congregations, to awaken or revive the consciousness that we belong together and of our brotherhood on a basis of faith and work and so to lead to deeper bonds of union, and help to cultivate and promote the kingdom of God and its concerns everywhere in our churches." In nine points he drew up the program of work for the paper. Above all else it was to present historical information, then articles on the faith and organization of the brotherhood, excerpts from the writings of our Reformers, contemporary events in the churches, articles of a devotional nature, on home and foreign missions, religious news, hymns (of the martyrs), and notices of various

kinds. Assisted by a staff of co-workers, including B. C. Roosen of Hamburg-Altona, Heinrich Neufeldt, of Ibersheim, Johannes Risser of Sembach, and Johannes Molenaar of Monsheim, he successfully carried out his program. Under his leadership the *Mennonitische Blätter* became a mine of historical research and a reflection of the intellectual and spiritual life of the German Mennonites of the time. In 1874 old age compelled him to retire from its direction.

Mannhardt was followed by Hinrich van der Smissen (*q.v.*), who had been called as pastor of the Ibersheim congregation the year before. For fifty years (1874-1924) he conducted the paper with skill. During the first five years he was supported by his older cousin Johannes van der Smissen, pastor of the Sembach congregation. As the interest of the churches was stirred by the historical research of Ludwig Keller (*q.v.*), the periodical became the vehicle of publication of many articles in the field of Mennonite history.

In 1888 H. G. Mannhardt (*q.v.*) became an associate editor and the paper was published twice a month. After six months, when H. G. Mannhardt resigned, the paper ended its bimonthly appearance. The volumes 1887-89 printed sermons by preachers of various congregations; volumes 1890-91 offered interesting and entertaining supplements. Both of these innovations were experimental. During World War I the paper was able to continue its work. The postwar period was more difficult. The volume of 1924 appeared in double numbers. In September 1925 it ceased publication until 1927.

Then the *Vereinigung* (*q.v.*, a German Mennonite conference) intervened. At its request Pastor Emil Händiges assumed the editorship of the revived paper on Jan. 1, 1927, with the voluntary assistance of H. G. Mannhardt and Christian Neff of Weierhof. When the former died (July 1927), Pastor Erich Götner stepped into his place. Thus the paper was able to fulfill a great and important mission in reviving, strengthening, and uniting the German Mennonites (*Menn. Bl.,* 1929, 1 ff.). In 1939 the issue numbered 1,450 copies. The last issue was dated March 1941, when it was forced to cease publication by order of the German government. (*ML* III, 107.)

NEFF.

Mennonitische Druckverein, Der (Mennonite Printing Association), the first Mennonite publishing organization in America. Soon after the founding of the Eastern District Conference on Oct. 28, 1847, John H. Oberholtzer (*q.v.*), who had taken the leadership in the new conference, decided to publish a periodical which would promote and unify the church. It was also his hope that the old breach might be healed through such a paper. Accordingly with a certain heroism he purchased a hand printing press with his much-needed money and set it up in his locksmith shop near Milford Square, Bucks Co., Pa. His first publication was *Verhandlungen des Hohen Rathes der Mennoniten Gemeinschaft* (*gedruckt bey Johann H. Oberholtzer,* n.p., n.d.), a broadside, published in 1848. This would suggest that he set up his print shop at once after the division. He wrote, edited, set type, printed, and mailed out his first paper, *Der religiöse Botschafter,* a biweekly, on June 9, 1852, the first successful Mennonite periodical in America. It required tremendous efforts to continue this work together with his busy ministry. Sometimes he worked all night in the shop without sleep to get the copies out. Perhaps, more than will ever be known, this paper helped to form the bond of fellowship among scattered groups of Mennonites hungering for new life in the church, which led to the General Conference Mennonite Church in 1860.

Oberholtzer continued his printing until 1856, when, on account of financial difficulties, a group of local Mennonites formed a stock company under the name "Der Mennonitische Druckverein" and took over the press. The constitution of this organization was printed by Oberholtzer under the date of May 31, 1856. Oberholtzer continued to edit the paper until 1867, although the name was changed on July 30, 1856, to *Das Christliche Volksblatt.* A young man, John G. Stauffer, then established the press in the village of Milford Square. Stauffer entered the business in November 1856 and after six months' apprenticeship assumed the management and acted as compositor, printer, foreman, and in part as bookkeeper and assistant editor. The chief business of the Druckverein was the publication of the *Volksblatt,* but some book and job printing was also done.

For many years Stauffer and his younger brother, Daniel G. Stauffer, continued as printers in Milford Square, publishing a number of religious periodicals for Mennonites and other groups, The present *Quakertown Free Press,* in the near-by town of Quakertown, is an outgrowth of this printing venture.

The Druckverein erected a brick building in Milford Square as a printing house. The annual meeting of the stockholders on Dec. 1, 1866, decided to transfer its publication work to the newly established school (Mennonitische Bildungsanstalt) at Wadsworth, Ohio, provided that certain conditions could be met, giving as one of the chief reasons the expectation that the professors and students would participate in the publication. This plan failed to materialize, however, and the publication continued at Milford Square. The name of the paper was changed to *Der Mennonitische Friedensbote* beginning in January 1867, when it also became a monthly instead of semimonthly. The publication was placed under a Publication Committee, but the printing was henceforth taken over by J. G. Stauffer as a private venture, who apparently at this point purchased the printing establishment from the Druckverein. The Druckverein continued to be the publisher of the *Friedensbote* until the end of 1871. At that point the Eastern District Conference took over the publication with J. G. Stauffer continuing as printer. The conference, at its meeting in October 1871, accepted the proposal of the Druckverein to take over the *Friedensbote* and appointed a Publication Board of five members to handle the journal and any other publications desired by the conference.

Following is a list of the known imprints of Oberholtzer and the Druckverein: *A. Oberholtzer imprints:* (1) *Verhandlungen des Hohen Rathes der Mennoniten Gemeinschaft* (broadside in 1848, reprinted as broadside in 1849); (2) *Religiöser Botschafter* (1852-56, then *Das Christliche Volksblatt* 1856-66); (3) J. H. Oberholtzer, *Aufschluss der Verfolgungen gegen Daniel Hoch* (1853, pp. 168); Part II, Samuel B. Bauman, *Eine Erleiterung an Benjamin Eby* (1855, pp. 108); (4); *idem, Lieder für die Tauf-Kinder* (broadside, 1854?); (5) Gottfried Arnold, *Geistliche Erfahrungs-Lehre* (1854, pp. 504); (6) *Constitution des Mennonitischen Druck-Vereins* (1856). B. *Druckverein imprints:* (1) C. N. Hall, *Komm zu Jesu* (1857, pp. 96); (2) *Das unparteiische biblische Fragenbuch* (1859, pp. 121); (3) J. H. Oberholtzer, *Der wahre Character von J. H. Oberholtzer* (1860, pp. 115); (4) *Gemeinde-Ordnung . . . Summerfield* (1861, pp. 36); (5) A. Hunzinger, *Das Religions-, Kirchen-, und Schulwesen der Mennoniten oder Taufgesinnten* (1862, pp. 162); (6) *Katechismus* (1863, pp. 105).

H.S.B.

H. P. Krehbiel, *History of the General Conference* (n.p., 1898) 364 ff.; "Life of J. H. Oberholtzer," *The Mennonite,* March 1895, 44; A. J. Fretz, *Stauffer-Stover Family History* (1899) 264; J. B. Battle, *History of Bucks County, Pennsylvania* (Philadelphia, 1887) 1067 f.

Mennonitische Flüchtlingsfürsorge (Mennonite Refugee Care). The arrival of many Mennonite refugees to Germany from Russia after World War I, their number constantly increasing as revolutionary bands violated the villages of the Ukraine, called for organized assistance in alleviating their distress, in which all the Mennonite congregations in Germany were to take part. In South German circles it was discussed several times. In April 1920 a meeting was held at Heilbronn with representatives chosen by the Mennonites of Russia to explore possibilities for settlement (see **Emergency Relief**). The South German Conference then sent its traveling evangelist, Abram Warkentin, himself a former Russian Mennonite, to investigate conditions in the refugee camps in North Germany. He visited about 70 families in August and September 1920 and found them in a desperate situation, many of them in rags and undernourished (*Menn. Bl.,* 1920, 77-78). A number of the refugees had already been taken in by Mennonite families.

Now an organized and centralized program of support was inaugurated on Nov. 22, 1920, when the Flüchtlingsfürsorge was organized in Ludwigshafen with its seat at Heilbronn. Its purpose is "to assist with pastoral and material aid the German refugees from Russia, especially the brethren in the faith, who have been sorely tried in soul, spirit, and body in consequence of war and anarchy." An attempt was made to find the Mennonite families and support them with money, clothing, and food. An effort was made to give permanent aid by finding employment for them in industry and on farms. A considerable number of families settled in Gronau in Westphalia and worked in the textile mills of the van Deldens. Others were settled on state lands east of Lübeck in Lockwisch and Westerbeck near Schönberg in Mecklenburg-Strelitz in the winter of

1920 and summer of 1921; this was made possible by loans from the German Mennonite congregations. But the settlers soon emigrated to America with the exception of one family. The loans were fully paid back; some of the funds were donated to the conference of the South German Mennonites for benevolent purposes.

Other refugees were given work and lodging for their families in the Lechfeld (q.v.) camp, a former army drill ground which was given for agricultural purposes to the Mennonite Fürsorgekomitee, the Mennonite relief organization called "Christenpflicht" (q.v.), and the union of German Baptists. This farm yielded about 50,000 marks in 1923 for charitable purposes. The refugees who could not be used in farming were given other work such as basket making or the manufacture of work clothing. At the same time a camp was kept in Lechfeld for Mennonite refugees whose admission to Canada was postponed for reasons of health. The German government consented to this arrangement after the Heilbronn committee had given a guarantee that it would take care of all expenses and assume political responsibility for the inmates.

To meet the increasing scope of its work the committee changed its name on May 9, 1922, to "Deutsche Mennonitenhilfe" (German Mennonite Aid) and transferred its seat to Oberursel near Frankfurt. Most of the refugees were able to emigrate to Canada with the support of the Canadian Mennonite Board of Colonization.

At this time calls were coming from Russia for German literature, especially for Bible and school books. The German Mennonite Aid was able to send the Mennonites in the Ukraine 12,000 textbooks and 4,000 Bibles. This committee also supported the publishers of the *Mennonitisches Lexikon* in ordering for Russia one hundred copies of the first volume, which offer was gratefully accepted by the Russian Mennonite churches. Before World War I, however, only the first two installments could be sent to the 900 subscribers in Russia; after that no further shipments to Russia were possible.

The committee was dissolved on Dec. 16, 1926. The work of the Mennonitische Flüchtlingsfürsorge and the Deutsche Mennonitenhilfe was done during the period of inflation of German currency, enormously increasing the difficulty of the task. But thanks to the co-operation of the Mennonites in countries with stable currency, it was possible to render the Mennonite refugees from Russia genuine assistance throughout the period to relieve their great need.   HEGE.

Deutsche Mennonitenhilfe, ihre Entstehung und Arbeitsgebiete (Oberursel, 1924); Chr. Neff, *Bericht über die Mennonitische Welthilfskonferenz vom 31. August bis 3. September 1930 in Danzig*, 67-68; ML III, 107 f.

Mennonitische Friedensbote, Der, a continuation of *Das Christliche Volksblatt* (q.v.) under a new name from 1867 to 1881, when it was merged with *Zur Heimath* to form *Der Bundesbote* (first issue January 1882). It was an eight-page semimonthly, 10 x 12 in., published by the Eastern District Conference (GCM) at Milford Square, Pa. The editor was A. B. Shelly.   H.S.B.

Mennonitische Geschichtsblätter, published by the Mennonite Historical Society (*Mennonitischer Geschichtsverein, q.v.*) of Germany, is an annual publication in the field of Mennonite history. It was edited in 1936-40 by Christian Hege and appeared annually, each issue consisting of 64-100 pages. It suspended publication 1941-48, but was revived in 1949, with Horst Quiring as the editor, assisted by Ernst Crous and Paul Schowalter. · The issues of 1949-55 consisted of 48-80 pages each. The content of the magazine has remained the same throughout the years of its publication. Questions pertaining to the Mennonites and Anabaptists, particularly in Germany, are discussed. Numerous historical articles, short biographies, bibliographies, and book reviews have appeared. The magazine is the only European publication completely devoted to Mennonite history. (*ML* III, 110.)   C.K.

Mennonitische Heime, e.V. (Mennonite Homes, Inc.) was organized on June 17, 1949, at the Thomashof, Germany, and registered Oct. 12, 1949, at Neustadt a.d.W., Palatinate, under the name *Mennonitisches Altersheim e.V.*, to operate homes for the aged on the basis of the Mennonite faith. Seven years later, on June 24, 1956, its purpose was changed to a general charitable service to old people, youth, and children, and its name changed to the present form. Its field of service is West Germany, where it now (1957) operates three homes for the aged with 215 guests, practically all Mennonite refugees from West Prussia, Poland, and Russia. The homes are "Marienburg" at Leutesdorf on the Rhine, near Neuwied; "Friedenshort" at Enkenbach, Palatinate, near Kaiserslautern; and "Abendfrieden" at Pinneberg, near Hamburg in the North. All three homes are in rented buildings. The inmates receive a daily support from the state, mostly based on their claims to reparations as refugees. In addition the MCC contributes relief food, and many inmates work in the homes and in attached acreage in food production. The homes are thus self-supporting.

The organization operates through an executive committee, a council, and a members' annual meeting. In 1957 the association had some 1,000 members, who were expected to contribute a remuneration of one-half Mark monthly toward overhead expense. The Executive Committee in 1957 was composed of Fritz Hege president, Richard Hertzler executive secretary, Otto Regier, Gertrud Schowalter, and Gottfried Horsch. The homes have achieved great significance in German Mennonite life. In addition to the spiritual work in the homes through visiting ministers from all Germany, other indirect and unplanned benefits include stimulation to greater giving by the members, larger inter-area Mennonite contact, and to scattered needy individuals, capital loans from the association's surplus, for building of homes for refugees, etc.   R.HE.

Mennonitische Hilfskasse (Mennonite Aid Fund), a fund of the Mennonites of the Palatinate and Hesse, Germany, with its seat in Monsheim, which was incorporated on June 30, 1905. According to its constitution it has the following aims: (1) support of the needy in the Mennonite congregations of the Conference in special cases; (2) care of the widows and children of its preachers, as well as of preachers no longer able to serve; (3) support of individual congregations under special conditions, such as the building or major repairs of church buildings. On Dec. 6, 1912, four paragraphs were added to the constitution to provide a pension fund for ministers.

The new tax laws necessitated some changes in the constitution. In 1933-34, when the organization was put on a purely church basis, aim (1) was dropped. In 1947 another change was made in order to insure the character of an "organization for the public welfare." On the basis of a decision of Jan. 30, 1951, the executive expenses of the Palatine-Hessian Conference are borne by the Aid Fund.

On June 13, 1882, the Fund was originally organized as the "Mennonitische Central-Hilfskasse" at the instigation of Hinrich van der Smissen, pastor of the Ibersheim Mennonite Church. Several congregations of North Germany—Emden, Hamburg-Altona, and Leer—participated in the project.

When the *Vereinigung* (Conference of Mennonite Churches in Germany) organized in 1886, the North German churches withdrew from the Fund. The funds in the treasury, 2,677 Marks, were given to the Palatine-Hessian Conference, and the name of the Fund shortened to "Mennonitische Hilfskasse" on Dec. 13, 1886. Participation by all the congregations of the conference was attained in 1891, when a resolution was passed at the conference meeting in Sembach on May 21 to give more general and faithful support to the Fund. At this time the congregations at Ernstweiler, Kühbörncheshof, and Neudorferhof joined the project; Eppstein, Friesenheim, and Uffhofen continued their annual contributions. Ibersheim had joined in 1888. Hamburg-Altona contributed until 1915.

The development of the Fund was promoted by Jakob Ellenberger, pastor at Friedelsheim, who served as its chairman for many years. In 1900 Thomas Löwenberg, the minister of Ibersheim, succeeded him. In 1907 Löwenberg called for a contribution to celebrate the twenty-fifth anniversary of the Fund; over 7,000 Marks were contributed. A far greater sum, over 32,000 Marks, was collected in 1916 to operate the provision for the pensioning of preachers. On Dec. 31, 1918, there were nearly 100,000 Marks in the treasury.

The Fund was wiped out by the inflation of German currency in 1922-23, which left less than 1,800 Marks at the end of 1924. It had to be built up anew; only by sacrificial giving could the work progress. By Dec. 12, 1939, the treasury had accumulated RM 49,099, and on July 20, 1948, the date of the second currency reform, RM 65,498.21. Since this second devaluation it has been impossible to raise any considerable sum. In 1926 the annual assessment was raised to 250 Marks; by 1933 it was reduced to 200, and by 1935 to 150 Marks. In 1937 both the chairman, Rudolf Stauffer of Ibersheim, and the treasurer, David Galle, Weierhof, resigned. Fritz Stauffer of Kaiserslautern was chosen chairman, and Heinrich Rink of Kaiserslautern treasurer.

In 1957 Christian Galle of Weierhof was chairman, and Heinrich Rink was still treasurer.

Extraordinary services were rendered by the Fund during World War I and also in the very difficult postwar period, with the support of the American Mennonites. In 1957 the fund held 17,000 Marks and supported three retired ministers; since the income of the fund was not sufficient, the congregations added about 2,000 Marks by pro rata contributions. A substantial part of the capital is loaned to the Mennonitische Siedlungshilfe (*q.v.*; Mennonite Settlement Aid). *ML* III, 108 f.) C.G.

Mennonitische Jugendwarte, a periodical published 1920-39 by the Youth Commission of the Conference of the South German Mennonites (*q.v.*). The Youth Commission was created in 1919; at its first session, Feb. 27, 1920, at Weierhof, it considered its first obligation to be the publication of a quarterly, "whose contents consider the interests of youth and should therefore perform the function of advising, teaching, and stimulating young people."

Emil Händiges, minister of the Ibersheim Mennonite Church, was appointed editor. Since the duties of the editor as traveling evangelist had taken him into many homes, the periodical was gratefully received in all the homes of the conference. The subscription list, extending as far as West Prussia, numbered 1,000 in its early period. The great topics of faith and a Christian world view, questions of youth, suggestions on good literature, and also articles on Mennonite history were published by the paper. The youth movement, which was at that time developing spontaneously, was reflected in the reports: Youth Days were held now and again, youth groups were organized left of the Rhine, and leaders chosen. In March 1924 Händiges resigned. The editorship was temporarily assigned to a committee, which functioned until Feb. 28, 1927, when Walter Fellmann, pastor of the Monsheim Mennonite Church, became editor. After 1929 it appeared in six issues (later only four) annually with 750 subscribers. The last issue was August 1939, but it continued two years as a bimonthly supplement to the *Gemeindeblatt*. (*ML* III, 109.) W.F.

Mennonitische Lehranstalt, Gretna, Man.; see **Mennonite Collegiate Institute.**

Mennonitische Lehrerzeitung, a 16-page quarterly edited by Victor Peters, Horndean, Man., first issue July 1948. With the July 1950 number it changed its title to *Mennonitische Welt* (*q.v.*) and became a monthly. As the title indicated, its purpose was to serve Mennonite teachers in Canada, especially those still speaking German, with educational, literary, and cultural material, definitely oriented within Mennonitism, but also concerned to promote the maintenance of the German language among Canadian Mennonites beside the English. H.S.B.

Mennonitische Rundschau, Die, the oldest Mennonite periodical published continuously under one name, first issue June 5, 1880, the direct successor to the *Nebraska Ansiedler* (*q.v.*, first issue June 1878), was established by the Mennonite Publishing Co. (John F. Funk) to serve the newly established

Russian Mennonite communities in the prairie states and Manitoba. It appeared as a 4-page semimonthly, 10 x 15½ in., until the end of 1882, and has continued as a weekly ever since. A semimonthly edition was published from 1883 on "for readers in Europe and Asia," apparently to keep the Mennonites in Russia in contact with American Mennonites. The edition was still being published in 1889, when the publisher described it as in "format somewhat smaller, but it contains all the Mennonite news which appears in the weekly edition in addition to other reading matter out of the latter." The subscription price was given as 50 cents, 3 marks, or 1 ruble. Since January 1899 was the first time that the subscription price for the weekly edition was given in terms of German and Russian money, it is probable that the "European edition" continued until then.

The *Rundschau* was the paper of the Russian Mennonites for decades, and still carries something of this general character, although on Oct. 24, 1945, it came into the ownership of a company composed of men from the M.B. Church who have made it more of an M.B. organ, though it is not yet conference-owned. The rise of other periodicals for the Russian Mennonites, such as the *Bote* of Rosthern, Sask. (since 1924), has naturally divided the field. Editors of the *Rundschau* have been as follows: John F. Harms 1880-85; 1886-96 no one was officially listed as editor, J. F. Funk himself presumably carrying the responsibility; D. F. Jantzen 1896-98; G. G. Wiens 1899-Aug. 26, 1903; M. B. Fast Jan. 27, 1904-Oct. 12, 1910; C. B. Wiens Oct. 19, 1910-June 9, 1920; William Winsinger June 16, 1920-Oct. 10, 1923; Hermann H. Neufeld Oct. 17, 1923-Oct. 17, 1945; H. F. Klassen Nov. 14, 1945- . Publishers and places of publication have been: Mennonite Publishing Co., Elkhart, Ind., to July 8, 1908; Mennonite Publishing House, Scottdale, Pa., to Oct. 17, 1923; Hermann Neufeld through the *Rundschau* Publishing House, Winnipeg, Man., to Oct. 24, 1945, in which the Mennonite Publishing House retained a substantial financial interest for a number of years, but which was legally owned by H. H. Neufeld, which changed its name to Christian Press, Ltd., on March 27, 1940, but was sold to a stock company Oct. 24, 1945, which has continued to publish the *Rundschau* under the same firm name. Changes in size and format of the *Rundschau* have been frequent: 4 pp. to the end of 1898, with format 1884-Sept. 1890 of 13 x 13 in., Oct. 1890-98 of 14½ x 21½ in.; 8 pp. 1899-Nov. 6, 1901, same format; 16 pp. Nov. 6, 1901, with change to 10½ x 14 in. format until Sept. 2, 1908, when it was changed to 9½ x 12 and probably 20 pp. (definitely known as 20 pp. beginning January 1909), and continuing in this size and format to Oct. 17, 1923, when it became 16 pp., and on June 9, 1926, changed in format to 10½ x 13½. In 1942-50 it was 8 pp. with three changes in format, 1942—12½ x 17 in., 1947 —13 x 19 in., 1950—13½ x 20 in. In 1951 it again became 16 pp., with format 11¾ x 15¼ in. From Nov. 1901, the *Herold der Wahrheit* was combined with it until the latter's discontinuance Sept. 2, 1908. The *Christlicher Jugendfreund,* published 1878-1951, became a department of the *Rundschau*

in June 1951. The circulation of the *Rundschau* in 1957 is 7,400.

An English companion to the *Rundschau* called *Mennonite Observer* is being published by the Christian Press as a 12-page weekly beginning Sept. 21, 1955.   H.S.B.

Mennonitische Siedlungshilfe e.V. (Mennonite Settlement Aid, Inc.), was founded on July 24, 1953, at Ludwigshafen on the Rhine, Germany, and registered there as a charitable organization on Sept. 18, 1953, with the purpose of promoting the construction of dwellings, meetinghouses, and rural settlements for Mennonite refugees and other needy persons, also the gathering of scattered Mennonites into community settlements and counseling and aiding them in economic, cultural, and religious matters. It furnishes financial aid through loans with funds secured primarily from the American Mennonites through the MCC. It also serves as an advisory council for the MCC Pax units working at home-building in Germany. It played a major role in the creation of the Mennonite settlements at Backnang near Stuttgart, Bechterdissen near Bielefeld, Enkenbach near Kaiserslautern, and Wedel near Hamburg. Its work in this field of home building continues.

Through the help of the MSH hundreds of Mennonite refugees from Danzig and West Prussia have been gathered together again into communities and congregations, and have again found a home, spiritual fellowship, and a solid base for living. R.He.

Mennonitische Studentenhilfe (Mennonite Student Aid). During the period of inflation of German currency, 1922-23, an association was formed in Munich, South Germany, with this name, whose objective was to lighten the economic need of Mennonite students and to offer them a home in which they would have inexpensive living and opportunity for Christian association. In January 1922 the association secured a four-story house between the Institute of Technology and the University of Munich, in which Mennonites and non-Mennonites could live. When living quarters were put under state control in 1926 the association could no longer function. It was nevertheless possible to assist several Mennonite students with loans of several thousand Marks, making it easier for them to attend the university. (*ML* III, 109.)   HEGE.

Mennonitische Vierteljahrschrift, an attempted quarterly review edited by John Horsch, of which only one number appeared, in October 1900, with 16 pages, 7 x 10 in., published at Berne, Ind. H.S.B.

Mennonitische Volkswarte (since 1937 *Mennonitische Warte*), an illustrated monthly magazine of 32-40 pages, was published and edited for four years (1934-38) by Arnold Dyck at East Kildonan, Man. The magazine made a unique contribution in making full use of Mennonite art, photography, fiction, poetry, etc., for the first time in American Mennonite history, in presenting the various aspects of culture of Mennonites of German background. Many of its contributors, like the editor himself, were writers, artists, and teachers. The magazine placed more emphasis on the cultural aspect than the specifically religious, which is taken care of in the traditional Mennonite publications. The magazine built up a storehouse of information during its brief existence and influenced and inspired *Mennonite Life* (*q.v.*). Lack of support and sufficient circulation made it necessary for the publisher, who sacrificed heavily, to discontinue its publication. The *Warte-Jahrbuch* (*q.v.*) followed the same pattern, but likewise did not survive. (*ML* III, 109.) C.K.

Mennonitische Warte: see Mennonitische Volkswarte.

Mennonitische Welt, a 24-page, 8 x 10½ in. monthly, which was the successor to *Mennonitische Lehrerzeitung* (continuous volume numbering), and which appeared from July 1950 to December 1952. With the issue of January 1951 the publisher was indicated as Canadian Mennonite Publishers, Ltd., Winnipeg, Man. (changed in May 1951 to Mennonite Publishers of Canada, Ltd., also Winnipeg). The editor was Victor Peters of Horndean, Man., until May 1951, when Walter Quiring and Victor Peters appear as joint editors, Peters dropping out with the April 1952 number. The last number published was dated December 1952. The journal combined literary and cultural interests with religious and historical, maintaining the Mennonite faith, life, and work as its focus, but not competing with the regular church organs. It announced a policy of serving German-speaking Mennonites everywhere and solicited contributions internationally. H.S.B.

Mennonitischer Freiwilligendienst (Mennonite Voluntary Service), usually known as MFD, is an international European Mennonite organization whose purpose is to give young people, on a Christian and Mennonite basis, opportunity to render aid to needy persons or communities in the name of Christ and thereby to give a testimony of their desire to serve sacrificially in the cause of peace and construction. The organization was composed in 1957 of the following official conference representatives: Germany—Richard Hertzler, France—Jean Jacques Hirschy, Netherlands—Lenie de Groot, Switzerland—Samuel Gerber, MCC in Europe—Milton Harder. MFD arose out of the voluntary service work of the MCC in Europe in building houses after World War II, which in 1948-51 operated an average of four short-term summer work camps annually in a total of seven different countries with a total of 1,537 participants. In 1950 the MCC created a council for the summer work out of representatives appointed by the conferences, which then became an independent organization, the MFD. The MFD also joined AIG (Arbeitskreis Internationaler Gemeinschaftsdienste) and UNESCO.

The work of MFD is carried on through an executive secretary who was Lamarr Kopp in 1954-57, an American Mennonite loaned by the MCC, with headquarters at Kaiserslautern since 1956. Finances for the organization are provided by appropriations from the participating conferences. Direct support of the summer work camps is given by the MCC through relief food shipments and by appropriations from the German government through its Bundesjugendplan (Federal Youth Plan). Although the camp leaders are Mennonites, most of the participants are non-Mennonites. In 1956 one third of the 256 participants were Mennonites, the rest being from 24 denominations and 15 countries. In recent years the following have been among the work projects: clean-up work (1) in the Swiss Alps following an avalanche catastrophe and (2) in Holland following the coastal flood disaster; construction of homes for refugees in Germany, construction of children's homes in France, and reconstruction of a damaged Protestant high school in Austria.

The significance of MFD for the Mennonite brotherhood lies first of all in the fellowship of Mennonite youth from various countries, then further in the opportunity for contact with Christian youth from other countries and circumstances, but also in the privilege of putting into practice the command of Christ to love one's neighbor as himself, and to give an example to others of this spirit. R.He.

Mennonitischer Geschichtsverein (Mennonite Historical Society). Research in Mennonite history, begun in the middle of the 19th century by German historians, has revealed the bias with which the origin and growth of the Anabaptist-Mennonite brotherhood has been treated in most works of history. This revelation stirred up a desire in Mennonite circles for further information on their own history.

The constitution of the Vereinigung (*q.v.;* i.e., Conference of German Mennonite Churches) provided for the publication of historical material; its support indeed made the publication of several historical works possible. At a meeting of this conference on June 20, 1932, in Altona (*q.v.*), the task of promoting the publication of historical materials was put in the hands of a committee organized for that purpose, and in April 1933 the Mennonitischer Geschichtsverein was founded. The executive committee of four members was composed of Christian Neff of Weierhof, Ernst Crous of Berlin, Christian Hege of Frankfurt, and Hendrik van Delden of Gronau. Five other members of the society were chosen to work with the executive committee: A. Driedger of Heubuden, Erich Göttner of Danzig, Fritz Kliewer of Berlin, B. H. Unruh of Karlsruhe, Walther Köhler, an outstanding Reformation scholar of the University of Heidelberg. The society has its seat at Weierhof. The general meeting of the society was in the beginning regularly held in connection with the Mennonite Day (*Mennonitentag*).

The constitution defines the work of the society as collecting documents and copies of material on Mennonite history, publishing source material and articles on this history, collecting and distributing works on Mennonite history, supporting the publication of works on the subject, and the promotion of family history. The annual fee is a minimum of two marks. By 1939 the society had 280 members.

Since 1936 (suspended 1941-48) the society has published the biannual *Mennonitische Geschichtsblätter* (*q.v.*) with 60-100 pages, which the members receive free of charge. The periodical presents matter on various events in the changing history of the

Mennonites. For more exhaustive treatments provision is made in a special series of pamphlets, the *Schriftenreihe* (Historical Series). The first issue of this series appeared in 1938 with the title, *Beiträge zur Geschichte der Mennoniten, Festgabe für D. Christian Neff zum 70. Geburtstag.* (*ML* III, 110.)

HEGE.

Before the German collapse in 1945, five issues of the *Geschichtsblätter* were published (1936-40), and three numbers of the Historical Series (*Schriftenreihe*) (1938-41) appeared. The first volume of this series is mentioned above. The second was *Beiträge zur Geschichte rheinischer Mennoniten, Festgabe zum 5. Mennonitentag* (1939). The third contained Horst Penner's *Ansiedlung Mennonitischer Niederländer im Weichselmündungsgebiet von der Mitte des 16. Jahrhunderts bis zum Beginn der preussischen Zeit,* and Gustav E. Reimer's *Die Familiennamen der westpreussischen Mennoniten* (1940). Reimer's active solicitation resulted in a membership of over 800.

After the political collapse and the death of Hege (1943) and Neff (1946) the work was resumed in 1947 by a general meeting at Thomashof. Membership reached 856, but after the currency reform (1948) receded to about 600. In 1948 the general meeting was held at Gronau in Westphalia; here the Göttingen Mennonite Research Center (*Mennonitische Forschungsstelle Göttingen*) was established; in 1952 a new constitution was adopted; in 1953 legal rights acquired. In 1949-56 eight issues of the *Geschichtsblätter* appeared (Nos. 6-13), and in 1954 the fourth number of the Historical Series, viz., Paul Peachey's *Die soziale Herkunft der Schweizer Täufer in der Reformationszeit.* In 1955 the general meeting held at Göttingen elected the following executive officers: Ernst Crous, Horst Quiring, Paul Schowalter, Gerhard Hein, and Gerrit van Delden. An assisting council was also elected: Harold S. Bender, Abraham Fast, Samuel Geiser, Fritz Hege, Kurt Kauenhoven, Cornelius Krahn, Gustav E. Reimer, Walther Risler, Otto Schowalter, Erich Schultz, B. H. Unruh, and N. van der Zijpp.

E.C.

Mennonitischer Kirchenkonvent: see **Molotschnaer Kirchenkonvent,** and **Chortitzer Kirchenkonvent.**

Mennonitischer Lehrerverein: see **Mennonite Teachers' Association.**

Mennonitischer Verein *Deutsche Muttersprache* (Mennonite Association for the German Mother Language) was founded in Winnipeg, Man., in 1952, to aid Mennonite families of German background in preserving their German language and culture by encouraging the use of High German in their homes and churches, by organizing German classes, by offering a German correspondence course, encouraging the establishment of German libraries, etc. The officers of the organization are elected at the annual meeting usually held in the fall. Minimum membership dues are $1.00. Some of the leading ministers and educators are actively participating in the cause. In 1955 it had a membership of 1,500.

C.K.

Mennonitischer Zentralausschuss (Mennonite Central Committee) was established in 1950 at Frankfurt, Germany, to serve as a liaison between the Mennonite Central Committee (of the United States and Canada) and the German Mennonite churches. The latter are represented on the committee by one representative delegated by each of the three German Mennonite conferences as follows: Vereinigung (*q.v.*), Verband (*q.v.*), and Elders' Committee of the Conference of (former) West and East Prussian Mennonite Churches. The European director of the MCC usually serves as chairman. The members in 1957 were Cornelius Wall, Ulrich Hege, Abraham Braun, and Otto Wiebe. Meetings are held as needed to review the MCC program in Germany and its relations to the German Mennonite brotherhood and its work.

H.S.B.

Mennonitisches Gemeindeblatt (until 1918 with the added phrase "for Austria"), the official organ of the Mennonite brotherhood of Kiernica-Lemberg in Poland, was founded in 1913 as a 4-page 10 x 13 in. monthly paper, published in Lemberg (*q.v.*). Its purpose was to inform the scattered Mennonites of Galicia concerning events in the brotherhood and to preserve their love and loyalty to the church and to the entire Mennonite brotherhood. The contents of the paper were chiefly composed of news of their own congregations, preaching services, changes of address, reports on meetings and their organization. In addition it contained religious meditations and articles from the field of Mennonite history and literature.

The first editor was Arnold Bachmann (d. 1920). At the outbreak of World War I in August 1914 the paper had to suspend publication for several years, resuming publication in December 1917 with Heinrich Pauls as editor. In 1920 Leopold Gesell took it over. It appeared irregularly until 1928, when Alfred Bachmann became editor and published it quarterly. In 1932 Arnold Bachmann became editor. He served until 1939, when the paper ceased publication, the Mennonites in that year having been resettled in the Warthegau. The last number extant is Volume XXV (1939) No. 2. The paper was read for the most part by members of the group whose organ it was, but it also had a number of subscribers among the Mennonites in other countries. (*ML* III, 110.)

A.BA.

Mennonitisches Jahrbuch, a Russian Mennonite annual reviewing current Mennonite activities in the area of missions, charitable institutions, schools, and general church life, edited 1904-11 by Heinrich Dirks (*q.v.*), elder of the Gnadenfeld Mennonite Church (Molotschna settlement) and former missionary, then in 1913-14 by D. H. Epp, under the authority of the Allgemeine Bundeskonferenz (Conference of Mennonites in Russia). Epp greatly enlarged and enriched it with numerous historical articles on Mennonite congregations, institutions, etc., in Russia together with the annual minutes of the conference sessions. The 1914 (10th) issue (for the year 1913) had 226 pages. This was the nearest approach to a scholarly or historical journal published by the Mennonites in Russia. The prohibition of German publications brought its career to an end. (*ML* III, 111 f.)   H.S.B.

Mennonitisches Jahrbuch is a 48-page yearbook edited by Cornelius Krahn and published by the General Conference Mennonite Publication Office in cooperation with the G.C.M. Board of Missions since 1948, when it replaced the *Bundesbote-Kalender* (*q.v.*). The *Jahrbuch* aims to present illustrated articles of interest to its Mennonite readers in Canada, South America, and Germany. Many of the articles deal with the problems of Mennonite refugees, resettlement, relief, and progress and developments in the religious, educational, and economic aspects of Mennonite life in general and in the above areas in particular.   C.K.

Mennonitisches Lexikon. One of the great enterprises of Mennonite historical scholarship is the *Mennonitisches Lexikon,* an encyclopedia of the Anabaptist-Mennonite movement from its beginning in 1525 to the present day, covering all countries to which the movement has spread. An invaluable mine of information, thorough, authentic, comprehensive, it is an indispensable tool for students of Anabaptist-Mennonite history and a landmark in Mennonite historiography. Christian Neff (1863-1946) of Weierhof in the Palatinate, Germany, and Christian Hege (1869-1943) of Frankfurt, Germany, the founders and coeditors of the *Lexikon* until their death, and writers of a majority of the articles, served also as publishers. The two men formed a well-balanced team, with Hege the managing editor, carrying on together with devotion and sacrifice for over thirty years, until death called them both from their unfinished task. As they worked, what had been originally planned in 1913 as a two-volume work to be completed in ten years, grew into a three-volume work, each volume containing fifteen installments of 48 pages each, of which two volumes and six additional installments (a total of 36) had appeared by September 1942, extending into "Ob."

During the thirty years of their endeavor, the courage and faith of the editors of the *Lexikon* were put to severe tests and disappointments. With but slender resources of their own, and compelled to pay for many of the contributed articles in accord with European custom, they had to depend heavily on advance subscriptions and on donations from churches and interested groups and individuals. The Dutch Mennonites, who had the wealth and might have aided the enterprise strongly, failed to do so. The Russian Mennonite churches, which were among the heaviest original supporters, were early eliminated as a result of World War I, which broke out less than fifteen months after the first installment appeared in May 1913. The German currency inflation of 1922-23 was a heavy blow. If it had not been for direct financial assistance from friends in the United States and Canada at that time, promoted largely by H. P. Krehbiel and H. H. Ewert of the General Conference Mennonite Church, the enterprise would have failed financially. When Hege lost his private income in 1934 (except for a

small pension) as financial writer on a Frankfurt newspaper, the German Mennonites, primarily through the organization known as "Mennonitisches Hilfswerk Christenpflicht," led by Michael Horsch, came to the rescue with a regular, though slender, monthly stipend to enable Hege to continue his editorial work unhindered for the remaining years of his life.

World War II was the final catastrophe. Both men sacrificed practically all their personal resources to keep the *Lexikon* going, and upon their decease no resources were available to continue the unfinished project. Many of the original contributors had died in the course of the 35 years since 1913, and a number of the promising younger German Mennonite scholars fell on the battlefields. The end of the war left the German Mennonites in a seriously weakened state, financially and otherwise. A great work seemed destined to remain incomplete, although approximately 75 per cent of the remaining articles from "O" to "Z" as planned by the original editors, had been assembled in wholly or partially complete manuscript form, and a considerable body of notes intended for the supplementary volume of revisions and additions had also been gathered, all of which fortunately survived the devastation of war, since Hege had retired from Frankfurt to the relative security of Eichstätt in central Bavaria, and Neff remained in the rather remote village of Weierhof in the Palatinate. Eberhard Teufel of Stuttgart-Fellbach became the custodian of Hege's materials after his death, including the remaining manuscripts and supplementary notes.

At this stage, in 1945-46, soon after the close of the war, the American Mennonite scholars and publishers interested in the publication of the MENNONITE ENCYCLOPEDIA drew up plans which included sufficient financial and moral support to make possible the completion of the *Lexikon* in a reasonable time, provided German Mennonite scholars would resume the leadership in the project laid down by Hege and Neff. The MENNONITE ENCYCLOPEDIA organization offered to furnish the paper for printing and whatever financial subsidy was needed, in return for translation rights in the English language, giving the *Lexikon* in turn translation rights for the ENCYCLOPEDIA. Fortunately H. S. Bender, as the representative of the ENCYCLOPEDIA, was able to negotiate such an agreement in September 1946 in Germany with Christian Neff and with the surviving heir of the late Christian Hege, his daughter Adele Hege of Eichstätt, Bavaria. Bender, one of the coeditors of the MENNONITE ENCYCLOPEDIA, was designated by Neff to be coeditor of the *Lexikon* in place of Hege. Upon the death of Neff in December 1946, Ernst Crous, a German Mennonite scholar, formerly librarian in the Prussian State Library in Berlin, now living in retirement in Göttingen, Germany, was designated to be the successor of Neff as the other coeditor.

Since the new editors were unable to finance the enterprise themselves and therefore could not serve as publishers as their predecessors had done, they secured the agreement of the two Mennonite church conferences in Germany to take over this function. This was done through the creation of a "Lexikon

Committee" composed of six men, viz., the two editors, plus one official representative of each conference, Abram Braun of Ibersheim for the Vereinigung der Deutschen Mennoniten-Gemeinden, and Fritz Hege of Reutlingen for the Badisch-Württembergisch-Bayerischer Gemeindeverband, and two co-opted members, namely Gerrit van Delden of Gronau as treasurer, and Heinrich Schneider of Karlsruhe as printer. The two conferences guaranteed to underwrite one half of the possible deficit (Vereinigung two sixths and Verband one sixth), while the MENNONITE ENCYCLOPEDIA assumed the other half. The Lexikon Committee became the official manager of the enterprise and publisher, but with no functions in the field of editorial control. To aid them in the editorial work the editors secured the assistance of a board of associate editors composed of the following scholars: for Germany, Emil Händiges of Monsheim, B. H. Unruh of Karlsruhe, Horst Quiring of Stuttgart, Otto Schowalter of Hamburg, Gerhard Hein of Sembach, and Eberhard Teufel of Stuttgart; for Switzerland, Samuel Geiser of Brügg bei Biel; for Holland, N. van der Zijpp.

Ernst Crous has carried the main burden of the editorial work, with H. S. Bender as assistant and counselor. After an interruption of slightly more than eight years publication was resumed in January 1951 with installment No. 37; No. 41 appeared in the summer of 1957, reaching the letter "R." The new printer is the Mennonite firm of Heinrich Schneider in Karlsruhe. The size of the edition was formerly some 3,500, but since 1951 has been less.

The coverage of the *Lexikon* has been strong in strictly historical articles, particularly in Anabaptism and European Mennonitism, less strong in the field of American Mennonitism and in the areas of missions and education, and the social, economic, and cultural aspects of Anabaptist-Mennonite history and life.　　　　　　　　　　　　　　　H.S.B.

Mennonursing, since 1947 called *The Christian Nurse,* an 8-page 6 x 9 in. journal, the official organ of the Mennonite (MC) Nurses' Association, printed at Scottdale, Pa., was founded in March 1945 as a quarterly and changed to a bimonthly in 1949. The first editor was Verna Zimmerman, followed by Elizabeth Erb 1945-46, Orpah Mosemann 1946-51, Mabel Brunk 1951-52, Clara Headrick 1952-54, Ruth Lederach 1954-56, and Margaret Brubacher Ashley 1956- .　　　　　　　　　　　　　　　M.Sw.

Mennoscah, Camp, located on the Ninnescah River one and a half mile southwest of Murdock, Kan., with a camp site of 160 acres, was acquired in 1948 as the General Conference Western District Young People's recreation grounds. The camp was opened in 1949. By 1954, six cabins had been built in addition to the dining hall and kitchen. The camp is in use throughout the summer, primarily by young people but also by other groups such as Mennonite Men (*q.v.*). The first managers and caretakers were Mr. and Mrs. A. Theodore Mueller.　　　　C.K.

Loris Habegger, "Realizing a Dream," *Menn. Life* IX (January 1954) 16-18.

Menno-Stiftung (Menno Endowment). Heinrich Neufeld (*q.v.*), the pastor of the Ibersheim (*q.v.*), Palatinate, Germany, Mennonite congregation, published in commemoration of the third centennial of the death of Menno an appeal to all the Mennonite churches in the Old World and the New to create a general fund for the support of the widows of Mennonite ministers and a large endowment for Mennonite. students of theology (*Menn. Bl.,* 1859, 23). Carl J. van der Smissen, pastor of the Friedrichstadt congregation, took up the idea and named it *Menno-Stiftung.* He envisioned a comprehensive world-wide federation of Mennonites. The proposal was warmly welcomed by Johannes Risser (*q.v.*) and Johannes Molenaar (*q.v.*), with the amendment that a fund be established in each congregation for church expenses and needs under this name. Christian Schmutz (*q.v.*) of Rappenau, however, rejected the idea. Only the Friedelsheim congregation has a "Menno-Stift," which has served the congregation well. (*ML III,* 112.)　　　　　　　　　NEFF.

Mennoville Mennonite Church (GCM), near El Reno, Canadian Co., Okla., now extinct, was established about 1891 as the first Mennonite church of Oklahoma. In 1893 the congregation built a small frame church, which is located southwest of the Darlington Mennonite mission station. For a while it was a fair-sized congregation, but most of the members moved away. The last service in the church was held in 1952. The original church building, the oldest in Oklahoma, is now in custody of the Western District Historical Committee.
　　　　　　　　　　　　　　　　　　C.K.

Marvin Kroeker, "Mennonites in the Oklahoma 'Run.'" *Menn. Life* X (July 1955) 114; files of the Western District Historical Committee.

Meno (Okla.) is a small town about 16 miles west of Enid in Major Co., Okla., in a wheat-growing area. Most of the 175 inhabitants are Mennonites of Polish and Russian Mennonite descent, and members of the New Hopedale Mennonite Church (GCM). The Oklahoma Bible Academy (*q.v.*) is located here. "Meno" is a corruption of "Menno" (after Menno Simons). The town has a grain elevator with a capacity of 190,000 bu. and can easily handle 300,000 bu. per year. It handles also flour, feed, coal, fertilizer, and other commodities. It also has a good bank which has deposits of $707,354.93 and the depositors are guaranteed up to $10,000.
　　　　　　　　　　　　　　　　　　H.U.S.

Men-O-Lan, Quakertown, Pa., is the camp site of the Eastern District Conference (GCM), located one mile east of Finland, Milford Twp., Bucks Co. Development started in 1938 with twenty-three acres of woodland donated by J. Walter Landis, which was increased to ninety-two acres in 1954. The first camp program was held in July 1941. Equipment, buildings, and land were evaluated at $74,410 in 1956. Developments include three workers' cabins, seven cabins, auditorium, dining hall-kitchen, washrooms, nature trails, artificial lake, two wells, caretaker's apartment, and the Landis Memorial Chapel. Weekly Sunday-school services are held in the chapel. Program planning is the responsibility of the Retreat Committee. The camp is administered by a Board of Managers of nine members elected by the Eastern District Conference.   M.SH.

J. E. Fretz, "Retreat Camp Grounds Men-O-Lan," *Menn. Life* II (July 1947) 6 f.; *Report of the Eastern District Conference,* 1938, 1956.

Menonit, Der, a drama by Ernst von Wildenbruch (1845-1909), a superpatriotic German author, written in 1877. It has for its setting the Mennonites of East Prussia during the Wars of Liberation from Napoleon (1806-13), and as its theme a young Mennonite's conflict between patriotic duty and conscience, loosely based on an actual incident in which a young Mennonite who had served in the army was refused membership in his congregation. The drama, poor in literary quality, shows not the least understanding of the position of the Mennonites, portraying them as self-centered and stupid egoists. The play reached the Mannheim stage in 1882. Mennonite reaction was prompt. Articles were published in a number of Mennonite journals, written by Mennonites such as H. van der Smissen and H. G. Mannhardt, and a letter by Wildenbruch written in reply to the protest by the consistory of the Danzig Mennonite Church was published in the *Mennonitische Blätter.* (See **Literature**.)   E.H.B.

Berthold Litzmann, ed., *Ernst von Wildenbruch, Gesammelte Werke* VII (Berlin, 1912) 135-233; "Der Menonit," *MQR* XVIII (January 1944) 22-35; H. van der Smissen, "Die Mennoniten auf der Bühne," *Menn. Bl.,* XXIX (November 1882) 86 f.; H. G. Mannhardt, "Die Mennoniten in der dramatischen Literatur," *Jahrbuch* 1883, 23-73; idem, "Der Bischof Eylert und die Mennoniten," *Menn. Bl.,* XXXI (March 1884) 17-20; "Noch einmal der *Menonit,* Correspondenz zwischen dem Vorstand der Gemeinde zu Danzig und Ernst von Wildenbruch," *Menn. Bl.,* XXXV (1888) 61 f., 74 f., 97 ff., 110 f., 119; "Amerikanische Urtheile über Wildenbruchs *Menonit,*" *Menn. Bl.,* XXXVIII (1891) 142.

Mensingeweer, a village in the Dutch province of Groningen, in the former Marne (*q.v.*) region. In 1607 Jan Cornelissen is called the "bishop and preacher of the Mennonites at Mensingeweer." There was, however, no congregation here. The Mennonite congregations in this region greatly decreased both in number of congregations and in membership in the 17th century. On Nov. 11, 1816, Houwerzijl (or Vliedorp), Ulrum, den Hoorn, Rasquert, and Obergum merged. A centrally located church was built at Mensingeweer, dedicated on April 4, 1819, and soon also a parsonage. An organ was acquired in 1899. The baptized membership numbered 21 at the time of the merger; 75 in 1861; 95 in 1900; 75 in 1956. The first minister was S. K. de Waard, serving here 1821-26, followed by J. Leendertz 1832-37, I. de Stoppelaar Blijdenstein 1838-39, W. Bruin 1840-44, D. S. Huizinga 1846-47, H. ten Cate Hoedemaker 1849-50, H. A. van Gelder 1851-53, J. P. Müller 1854-57, A. Vis 1861-63, J. A. Oosterbaan 1863-66, G. Vrijer Azn. 1868-73, A. Sipkema 1874-81, F. J. de Holl after a long vacancy 1897-1900, T. J. van der Ploeg 1901-3, E. Pekema 1904-7, C. C. de Maar 1907-10, F. H. Pasma 1913-16, P. Vis 1917-20; after another period of vacancy it was served by the pastor of Noorbroek 1924-45, and the pastor of Uithuizen 1946-50; since 1954 J. Lange has been the pastor of the Mensingeweer congrega-

tion. Recently a new parsonage was acquired at Eenrum. There is a ladies' circle.   vDZ.

S. E. Wieling, *Inwijding van de Nieuwe Kerk der Doopsgez. Gemeente Mensingeweer* (Groningen, 1819); P. Vis, "Gedenkrede" (Ms. 1919); *DJ* 1850, 59 f.; *ML* III, 115.

Mental Hospitals, Mennonite. The earliest beginnings of Mennonite interest in the care of the mentally ill are hidden in obscurity. We know, however, that the first Mennonite mental institution, and the only one established in Europe, was "Bethania" (*q.v.*), founded in 1910 by the Allgemeine Bundeskonferenz (*q.v.*) of the Mennonites of Russia, and located near Alt-Kronsweide in the Chorititza district. Motivated by a spirit of Christian compassion and of mutual aid and modeled after the Bethel institution near Bielefeld, Germany, Bethania built up a truly honorable record of service. But the disruptions of World War I, the following Communist revolution, and finally the flooding of this area by the large Dnieprostroy dam brought this great Mennonite venture to a close in 1927. Mennonite patients were given preference in the Bethania program, but as a matter of fact it cared for many non-Mennonite Russian and Jewish patients. Its treatment program followed the most enlightened practices of the time. It admitted as patients the mentally ill, both acute and chronic, epileptics, and the mentally retarded.

In the United States and Canada the pioneering years reveal little interest in an institution for the mentally ill. But as Mennonite communities stabilized and the interest in missions and education increased and the conference organization and program of service became more effective, there emerged an increasing concern for the mentally ill. This interest asserted itself in hospital circles and in sessions of conference. However, considerations of cost, the lack of leadership trained in this service, and especially the lack of a great inner compulsion caused hesitation and checked all positive action.

The only exception to this was an indirect continuation of Bethania, the Bethesda Mental Hospital (*q.v.*), of the Mennonite Brethren Church of Ontario, at Vineland, Ont. It was begun in 1932 by Mr. and Mrs. Henry Wiebe, who had formerly worked in Bethania and came to Canada in 1924. They took the first patient into their home near Stratford, Ont., in 1932, then purchased a farm near Vineland in 1937 where they began their work in the full sense of a private institution. In 1947 it was taken over by the Ontario District M.B. Conference.

World War II in an unexpected manner focused Mennonite attention on the tragic plight of the mentally ill and made them sensitively conscious of this field of human neglect. Some 1,500 young Mennonite conscientious objectors in the United States who were drafted into the Civilian Public Service program sought service in mental hospitals in order to relieve the critical shortage of attendants in these institutions. Seeing the need and seeking to meet it "in the name of Christ," they caught a vision of a great service of Christian love the Mennonite church could and should render.

When this concern was presented to the MCC annual meeting on Dec. 27, 1944, it received a sympathetic hearing but it was thought best to refer this matter to the MCC "constituent groups for whatever expression they may have to give." The General Conference Mennonite Church, convening for its triennial conference session in North Newton, Kan., in June 1945, was the first to take action. It urged the Board of Christian Service "to co-operate with the MCC" in establishing a mental institution and to proceed independently if the MCC failed to act. Other conferences in due course took similar favorable action.

This strong resolution was presented to the MCC Executive Committee at its next session only four days later. Greatly heartened by this initial response the Executive Committee appointed a Study Committee ". . . to ascertain the extent of mental illness and mental deficiency among our people, and thus the need for church-administered institutional care; second, to survey the types of institutional care which can best be provided; and, third, to present the informational bases upon which decisions can be made as to whether there should be a joint conference effort in this institutional program."

The extensive study which brought together the results (1) of a questionnaire mailed to 1,070 Mennonite ministers, (2) of investigations of various types of mental institutions, and (3) of interviews with heads of mental health departments of state and federal governments, gave a survey not only of the extent of mental illness in the MCC constituency, but also of the probable cost of a mental hospital program and the available resources of personnel. It was a sobering and yet challenging report.

Plans matured slowly but events pressed for decision. A master plan was adopted by the MCC annual meeting on Jan. 3, 1947. This plan, now realized, envisioned the establishment of three small mental institutions strategically located in the east, the west, and in the central area. Brook Lane Farm (q.v.) near Leitersburg, Md., with a capacity of 23 patients, was dedicated in November 1949; Kings View Homes (q.v.) near Reedley, Cal., with a capacity of 31 patients, was opened in March 1951; and Prairie View Hospital (q.v.) near Newton, Kan., with a capacity of 40 patients, was dedicated March 14, 1954. Various improvements and enlargements have since been made in all three institutions. Plans are now being drawn for a fourth institution in the North central states area, with a probable location in Indiana.

The emphasis in these institutions has been on treatment rather than on custodial care, but a limited number of chronic patients have been admitted. Psychiatrists had to be recruited from non-Mennonite ranks but great care was used to secure a staff sympathetic to Mennonite Christian concerns in this undertaking. Voluntary service personnel used as attendants and staff workers wherever possible likewise had to measure up to certain standards of character, motivation, and quality of service. Mennonite patients are to receive preference but to date considerably more than half of those admitted have been non-Mennonites.

The management of the MCC mental health institutions has been placed under an incorporated board called Mennonite Mental Health Services (q.v.).

The Lancaster Mennonite (MC) Conference also established a mental hospital, Philhaven (q.v.), near Lebanon, Pa., as an outgrowth of the experiences of CO's in World War II. Established in 1952 and since enlarged, it is now the largest Mennonite mental hospital, caring for both chronic and acute cases.

A small mental hospital was established in Filadelfia in Fernheim Colony, Paraguay, which to the present has been only a home for custodial care. Plans are now being made, with the help of MCC, to replace it with a modern type of mental health facility. (*Menn. Life* IX (July 1954), Mental Health Issue.)   H.A.F.

Mente Jan Heynendochter (Clementia Heymen), wife of the Anabaptist martyr Bartholomeus van den Berge (q.v.) of Dieteren, now Dutch province of Limburg, was arrested with her husband on the charge of Anabaptism. Whereas Bartholomeus remained steadfast, Mente recanted. She did not, however, save her life thereby; on Feb. 1, 1535, she was drowned in the Maas River at Maastricht, Dutch province of Limburg. Her confession during the trial reveals some facts concerning the Anabaptists: the water with which she had been baptized was taken from a pump; Leenaert van Ysenbroeck (q.v.), who had baptized her in Dieteren, pronounced the baptismal formula according to Matt. 28:19; the Anabaptists did not observe holidays, for "one day is as good as the other." vDZ.

W. Bax, *Het Protestantisme in het bisdom Luik* I (The Hague, 1937) 114; Mellink, *Wederdopers,* 306.

Meppel, a city in the Dutch province of Drente, where there has been a Mennonite church since 1880. On Jan. 11, 1880, the congregation dedicated a church, for which Tj. Kielstra (q.v.) of Zwartsluis preached the dedicatory sermon. An organ was installed in 1897. Kielstra served the two congregations at Meppel and Zwartsluis (q.v.) until 1886, and was followed by H. Koekebakker, who also had charge of both churches. Since 1893 the Meppel congregation has had its own preacher. B. P. Plantinga served until 1897 (during his term a congregation was organized at Assen (q.v.), which the Meppel minister looked after), A. Binnerts Szn 1897-1902, W. J. Kühler 1902-5, and Th. H. van Veen 1905-40. In 1942-46 the Meppel congregation was served by the pastor of Steenwijk. In 1946-49 W. J. Fleischer served at Meppel, H. R. Keuring 1950-52, and L. Laurense 1953- . The union with Assen lasted until 1916. In the next year this congregation secured a pastor of its own. In 1918-40 the Meppel ministers also had pastoral charge of Zwartsluis, and since 1950 again of Assen. In 1896 the membership was 78; in 1939 it was 90, and in 1956, 145. A new parsonage was acquired in 1946. There is a women's circle, a Sunday school for children, and youth groups for ages 12-16. (*Inv. Arch. Amst.* II, 2, No. 272; *DB* 1880, 166 f.; *ML* III, 115 f.) vDZ.

Mepsche, de, a noble family of governors in the Dutch province of Groningen. Whereas most of them, and particularly Johan de Mepsche, in the 16th century were ardent Catholics and devoted

servants of the Spanish regime of the Duke of
Alba (*q.v.*), which was persecuting the Anabaptists
and Mennonites, a cousin, also named Johan de Mepsche, of Den Ham, joined the Mennonites about
1580, and leaving his country, his property, and his
social rank for his faith he fled to Danzig, Prussia.
He is said to have died of the plague at Danzig
in 1588. The hypothesis that he may have been
the ancestor of the Mennonite Hamm family in
Prussia is probably tenable. (*DB* 1906, 35, 44; *Gesch.-
Bl.* VIII, 1951, 33.)   vɒZ.

Meran (Italian, *Merano*), a city (pop. 22,000) in
the Adige Valley, Austria (now Italian), until the
beginning of the 15th century the capital of the
Tirol and an important center on the trade route
between Germany and Italy over the Jaufen pass
through the Passei Valley. In the upper Adige (*q.v.*)
Valley, the Vintschgau, Anabaptists were found in
1527. Cardinal Matthäus Lang (*q.v.*) of Salzburg
notified the authorities of Meran and the villages
in the Vintschgau of their presence. Upon the proclamation of Ferdinand's mandate of Feb. 24, 1528,
offering pardon to all Anabaptists who would voluntarily report to the authorities, recant, and ask for
mercy, a few appeared. In Meran several Anabaptists were brought before the magistrate, but the
records do not indicate the outcome of the trial.
In May 1529 Georg Blaurock preached here as
he passed through the town on his way to the Eisack
Valley to take charge of the congregation there,
which had been orphaned by the execution of its
preacher Michael Kürschner (*q.v.*). His visit did
not lead to the establishing of a congregation in
Meran. (Loserth, *Anabaptismus*, 463 f., 485; *ML*
III, 116.)   HEGE.

Mercer County, Pa., bordering Ohio, has two Amish
(one now Mennonite) settlements. The Old Order
Amish settlement northwest of Jackson Center,
consisting of 109 baptized members in 1956, began
in 1942 when Jacob J. Byler with his four brothers
and families moved there from Atlantic, in Craw-
ford County. Other families left Atlantic for the
Jackson Center settlement because of the munitions
plant established two miles from Atlantic. Eli K.
Byler of Geauga Co., Ohio, served as their first
bishop. In 1956 the bishop was Henry M. Miller.
For an account of the Mennonites (MC) near Had-
ley in the same county, see **Maple Grove** Mennonite
Church.   J.A.H.

Mercken, an Anabaptist martyr, burned at the stake
on Nov. 23, 1566, at Gangelt in the duchy of Jülich,
Germany, just across the Dutch border. At least one
other woman died with her; an old chronicle indicates that a number of Anabaptists were executed
here at the same time. Mercken was (re)baptized
about 1550 by Theunis van Hastenrath (*q.v.*) at
Langenrade in the district of Born, now Dutch
province of Limburg. After her baptism she is said
to have moved to Lübeck, Germany, with Palmen
(i.e., Peter Palmen) and Heilcken (the wife of
Jacob, of Heel).   vɒZ.

W. Bax, *Het Protestantisme in het bisdom Luik* I
(The Hague, 1937) 406; II (The Hague, 1941) 364 f.;
DB 1909, 121, 126.

Mercy Hospital, Inc., Moundridge, Kan., is a nonprofit institution of the Church of God in Christ,
Mennonite. The conviction that the total work of
the Church of Christ includes caring for the sick
was shared by many of its members. A large house
was purchased and remodeled into a 15-bed hospital
equipped with modern facilities for major surgery
and obstetrics and dedicated Oct. 15, 1944, and
officially opened four days later. In 1953 a new
brick fireproof addition was added, which included
a clinic, emergency room, six patient rooms, an
operating room, a dining room and kitchen, an
office, and a waiting room, all modern and air-
conditioned.
The staff consists of a resident doctor, administrator, board of directors consisting of three executive
board members and four regular board members.
The personnel including two to three registered
nurses numbers sixteen.
The nurses' home is located across the street from
the hospital. The first budget (1944) was $20,000;
the present (1956) assets total $104,771.88. The
hospital board is responsible to the over-all board,
which in turn is responsible to the C.G.C. General
Conference.   P.G.H.

Mergriet Horstmans, an Anabaptist martyr, drowned
at Utrecht, Netherlands, on June 11, 1539. She was
the widow of Anthonis van Aldenberch, from the
Bishopric of Münster, Westphalia. No further information about her was available, except that she
had been (re)baptized. (*Berigten Hist. Genootschap
Utrecht*, IV, 1851, p. 139.)   vɒZ.

Meridian Church of God in Christ Mennonite
Church, located two miles east and two north of
Hesston, McPherson Co., Kan., was organized by
David S. Holdeman soon after he moved to this
area from Indiana in 1873. Religious services were
at first held in his home and later in the district
schoolhouse. He was a benefactor of the community
in various ways. In 1874, when many Mennonites
immigrated from Russia to Kansas, he was chosen
as treasurer of the Kansas Relief Committee.
His sons John A. and Daniel B. were ordained to
the ministry in 1882. A church was built in 1907
and enlarged in 1921 to a seating capacity of 300.
It was replaced in 1953 by a new church, capacity
450. Nine ministers and four deacons have been ordained by the congregation, of whom the following
are serving in 1957: Frank H. Wenger, Harry D.
Wenger, Paul D. Wenger, and Milferd Wenger,
ministers, and A. L. Yost, Orville E. Wiggers, and
G. H. Dyck as deacons. The background of its members is largely Pennsylvania-German. The ministry
is unsalaried. Religious services consist of Sunday
morning and evening worship services, midweek Bible study, and Sunday school. The Sunday school
was organized in 1909. Footwashing with close communion is practiced. The membership in 1957 was
194.   A.L.Y.

Merlanders (or Meerlanders, i.e., Moravians) are
said to have founded a small congregation near
Aachen, Germany. They were "standing by themselves" and practiced communism, calling themselves the "Dutch congregation." Apparently this

account concerns a congregation of Hutterites (*q.v.*) at Aachen, which was founded there by Hans Raiffer (*q.v.*) in 1557. A note concerning these "Merlanders" is found in Nicolai's insertions in the Dutch edition of Bullinger's *Der Widertöufferen Ursprung.* Nicolai calls them also "Apostolic Anabaptists." In 1612 Elder Jan Gerritsz (*q.v.*) of Danzig identified the Merlanders as Hutterites. (*BRN* VII, 461, 467; *Inv. Arch. Amst.* II, No. 2926.)   vDZ.

Mersch, van der, a Dutch Mennonite family of Flemish descent. Lieven van der Mersch (b. about 1545 at Lendelede, West Flanders, d. about 1580 at Haarlem, Holland) fled to Vlissingen in the Netherlands about 1575; then he lived at Dordrecht for some time and thereupon settled at Haarlem, where he joined the Mennonites. It is not clear whether he belonged to the Mennonites before he left Flanders. Johannes van der Mersch, lord of Zuidland and Velgersdijk (Haarlem, 1679-Amsterdam, 1775), married to Petronella van Oosterwijk, was a descendant. He was a wealthy merchant at Amsterdam, a shipowner and one of the principal wholesale dealers of the Dutch East Indies trade. A few members of this family served as deacons of the Mennonite church. Jan van der Mersch (*q.v.*), a weaver, a native of Kortrijk, Belgium, who died there as a martyr in 1569, probably did not belong to this family. Since the name van der Meersch (*q.v.*) is often incorrectly written van der Mersch, it is sometimes not clear whether a person whose name is spelled van der Meersch really belongs to this family or to the van der Mersch family. (*Ned. Patriciaat* VIII, 1917, 298-302.)   vDZ.

Merten Perboom, an Anabaptist, baptized about Christmas time by Leenaert van Ysenbroeck (*q.v.*) in the Palmenhuys near Born, in the duchy of Jülich, now Dutch province of Limburg, upon his arrest and trial at Maastricht, Limburg, on Jan. 29, 1535, recanted and was beheaded at the Vrijthof square of Maastricht on Feb. 1, 1535. His confession is remarkable for its information about early Anabaptism: Merten was baptized after Leenaert had read from a book (a New Testament?). Anabaptists did not believe in purgatory. They believed that if one party of a married couple had not been rebaptized they were living in adultery. For this reason Merten had forced his wife to be baptized against her will. He also gave some information about a plan of the Anabaptists to meet in Ysenbroeck and to march to Amsterdam. This shows that early Anabaptism in this region was largely infected with revolutionary ideas.   vDZ.

W. Bax, *Het Protestantisme in het bisdom Luik I* (The Hague, 1937) 73, 114 f.

Mertz, Joachim: see **März.**

Mertz, Melchior, of Mentzingen, the unknown author of an Anabaptist hymn: "Wacht auff ir frommen Christen Vnd greiffets dapffer an." (Wolkan, *Lieder,* 242; *ML* III, 116.)

Mesdag (Mesdach, Mesdagh, Mestach, Van Mesdag), an old name of frequent occurrence in Flanders, which was also borne by many Mennonites. A Mennonite martyr of this name was Jacob (Jaques)

Mesdag (*q.v.*), a miller and weaver of Poelkapelle, who was arrested for his faith at Kortrijk (Courtrai) in Belgium, on March 1, 1566, put into heavy chains, and after 20 months of bitterest imprisonment, was burned at the stake together with three Mennonites in front of the courthouse on Nov. 8, 1567. In prison he wrote a long, deeply moving letter of farewell, full of sincere, immovable faith, to his "dear and greatly beloved chosen sister Susanneken," on Sept. 9, 1567 (*Mart. Mir.* D 358-366, E 715-21). This Susanna Mesdag, later living in Haarlem, Holland, was a member of the Flemish Mennonite congregation and died there about 1603.

In the course of the 16th and 17th centuries a number of Reformed and Mennonite emigrants from Flanders bearing a variant of this name are encountered in the Dutch and Frisian cities, as in Middelburg, Leiden, Haarlem, Alkmaar, Bolsward, and Harlingen; in the 17th century a portrait painter Salomon Mesdach (Reformed; d. 1644) lived in Middelburg, whose self-portrait is in the national museum in Amsterdam.

Concerning the early Mennonites of this family: About 1580 Vincent Mesdag, a miller near Kortrijk in Flanders, fled to Haarlem; his son Gillis Mesdag, a weaver, later a cloth merchant, moved to Leiden, where he played some part as a member of the Vincent de Hondt (*q.v.*) congregation. About 1600 another Pieter Mesdag (1537-1604) and another Gillis Mesdag, both flax merchants, moved from Flanders to Harlingen. Jaques Mesdag, a nephew of the martyr Jaques Mesdag, a thread twister, left Dixmuide, Flanders, and settled at Alkmaar. One of the descendants of this thriving Mesdag family in Holland, which has produced many respected merchants, industrialists, bankers, physicians, and pharmacists, was the attorney Taco Gillisz Mesdag, who lived in Bolsward 1752-1814; one of his daughters was the grandmother of the famous painter Sir Laurens Alma Tadema (1836-1912), who lived in London after 1870. The descendants of Taco Mesdag settled mostly in the province and city of Groningen. Of this Groningen family mention should be made of the following:

Hendrik Willem Mesdag, b. Feb. 23, 1831, at Groningen, baptized Oct. 20, 1850, d. July 10, 1915, at The Hague, a gifted painter of marine scenes, belonging to the Hague School, founder of an important collection of modern painting, in which especially the impressionistic art of Holland and France (the schools of Barbizon and The Hague) are represented in well-selected pictures; in 1903 the collection was given as a gift to the nation. He was not only very wealthy, but also a strong, leading, and farsighted personality, who promoted the essential interests of art and artists with a generous hand and clear judgment. Also as the energetic president of the artist club "Pulchri Studio" in The Hague he performed meritorious service for many years. For a long time before he devoted himself to art (1866) he had been in his father's bank; then for two years he studied under the Dutch landscape painter Willem Roelofs in Brussels (on the advice of his cousin, L. Alma Tadema, who lived there until 1870, and who also belonged to a Mennonite family) and settled in The Hague in 1868. In addition to marine pictures he painted a large panorama of Scheveningen. In Groningen a street and a public square were named for him, and in The Hague a street.

Taco Mesdag, a brother of the above, b. Sept. 21, 1829, at Groningen, baptized Oct. 20, 1850, d. Aug. 4, 1902, at first a banker and grain dealer at Groningen, then moving to Scheveningen, near The Hague; he was a landscape painter of mediocre talent. One of his pictures adorns the church council room of the Mennonite church in Groningen.

Sientje Mesdag, nee van Houten, b. Dec. 23, 1834, baptized March 28, 1852, d. March 20, 1909, wife of H. W. Mesdag and sister of the statesman, minister, and philosopher Samuel van Houten (q.v.), painted landscapes and still life, the latter showing more talent.

Geesje (Gesina) Mesdag, née van Calcar, b. at Hoogezand on July 21, 1850, d. at Scheveningen April 12, 1936, the wife of Taco Mesdag and painter of landscapes and interiors. To this family also belonged Willem Mesdag, b. Rotterdam 1896, Mennonite pastor at West-Zaan-Zuid 1924-29, Zijldijk 1929-34, Sneek 1934-46, and Zeist 1946- .

H.F.W.J., vDZ.

G. Mesdag, Jr., *Het Geslacht Mesdag* (Groningen, 1896); G. van Mesdag, *Het Geslacht Mesdag* (n.p., 1943-46); *Jierboekje fan it Genealogysk Wurkforbân* (Ljouwert, 1955) 67 f.; *DB* 1901, 211; *ML* III, 116 f.

Meshovius, Arnold (1591-1667), professor at the University of Cologne, wrote a book in 1617 about the Anabaptists: *Historia Anabaptistica, Libri septem.* He was an orthodox Catholic and the intention of the book is to "frighten Catholics away from the pestilence of these disgusting people," and "confirm them in the faith, in the doctrine, and in the practices of the Catholic Church more and more." A glance at his sources—Ambrosius Blaurer, Bullinger, Cochläus, Oecolampadius, Luther, Zwingli, Melanchthon, etc.—shows that this is a piece of propaganda. Anabaptists are revolutionaries; he discusses Carlstadt, Thomas Müntzer, Hutten, the Münsterites, and ends with the year 1536. He has nothing to say about the peaceful Anabaptists. The book was given recognition by the Catholic Church and was probably the basis for suspicions against the Mennonites in Polish Prussia. The author announced the planned continuation of his book to cover the period 1536-1618, likewise in seven books. Apparently he did not get this done. (*ML* III, 117.)   H.Q.

Messchaert (Messchert), an old Dutch Mennonite family, whose progenitor Dirk Messchaert (b. 1555) came from Meenen, West Flanders, Belgium, and settled in Haarlem, Holland, in 1580. Later the family was distributed in Rotterdam and Hoorn and several villages in North Holland. In Rotterdam, more than 20 members of this family have served as deacons since 1658. They belonged to the Waterlander congregation. Dirk Jans Messchaert, who had been chosen as deacon with some other members, opposed the church board about 1665 because of their complacent attitude to the Collegiants (q.v.). In Hoorn the Messchaert family belonged to the strict conservative Mennonites. In the 18th century some of them were in sympathy with the pietistic

views of the Moravian Brethren (Herrnhuter). Dirk Messchaert of Hoorn, married to Janneken Beets, in 1736 joined this group and sent their son Peter to the Moravian school at Herrnhut. Nicolaas Messchaert of Hoorn in 1771 received a visit from the Count von Zinzendorf (q.v.). To this family also belonged Nicolaes Messchaert, b. July 19, 1774, at Hoorn, died of the plague July 13, 1833, at Utrecht, who had not studied at a university or the Amsterdam Seminary, but was trained by P. van Dokkumburg (q.v.), pastor of Koog-Zaandijk; he was pastor of the Mennonite church at Noordzijpe (Oude Sluis) 1794, Blokzijl 1796, Grouw 1800, and Rotterdam 1802-33, and was also a writer and school inspector. In the library of the Amsterdam Mennonite Church some of his sermons are found. He published *De zegen van den openbaren Godsdienst* (Rotterdam, 1825) a sermon preached at Rotterdam on the occasion of the fiftieth anniversary of the church; a sermon preached at Rotterdam May 6, 1827, commemorating his 25 years as a minister in Rotterdam entitled *De Aanmoediging en het Loon van den Getrouwen Evangeliedienaar* (Rotterdam, 1827); *Leerredenen ter verklaring van het Evangelie van Johannes* (Delft, 1825-31); and *Onderzoek naar den inhoud en het wezen des Christendoms* (Rotterdam, 1835).

Willem Messchert, b. March 3, 1790, at Rotterdam, d. there Feb. 14, 1844, was a brewer, later a bookdealer, also writer and poet of mediocre talent. He joined the *Réveil* (q.v.), a revival movement in Holland, about 1825, and leaving the Mennonite Church he joined the Reformed Church in 1829.

Johannes Martinus Messchaert, b. Aug. 22, 1857, at Hoorn, baptized there in 1876, was a concert singer, professor at the conservatory in Amsterdam (1881-1905), the conservatory at Frankfurt (from 1905), the University of Berlin (from 1911), and at the conservatory of Zürich (from 1920). He was a high-minded, gifted, and distinguished artist, who made incomparable achievements in the field of the oratorio as well as the song in all the capitals and music centers of Europe and earned great fame. In Hoorn a monument was erected to him on May 24, 1930; a street had already been named for him both in Hoorn and Amsterdam. His portrait by Jan Veth is in the museum at Amsterdam. In 1885 he married Johanna Jacoba Alma, of an old Mennonite family in Friesland. He died at Zürich, Switzerland, on Sept. 10, 1922.   H.F.W.J., vDZ.

Blaupot t. C., *Holland* I, 63; II, 99, 143 f.; *Ned. Patriciaat* XVI (1926) 212-36; *N.N.B.Wb.* II, 907; *Inv. Arch. Amst.* II, 2, Nos. 400-12; *DJ* 1840, 111; *DB* 1864, 120; 1895, 122-25; 1901, 21; 1911, 70; *Catalogus Amst.*, 294, 313, 319; J. H. Letzer, *Muzikaal Nederland 1850-1910;* P. Frank, *Kurzgefasstes Tonkünsterlexikon* (1926); W. Lütjeharms, *Het philadelphisch-oecumenisch streven der Hernhutters, . . .* (Zeist, 1935) 56, 78; *ML* III, 117.

Messenger of Truth is the official organ of the Church of God in Christ, Mennonite. It began as a monthly 4-page supplement, 8 x 11 in., to the *Botschafter der Wahrheit* in January 1903. John D. Dueck was acting editor for three years. On Feb. 18, 1906, F. C. Fricke was chosen editor, which office he filled for 36 years. Reuben J. Koehn became the editor Jan. 1, 1943. During the 54 years of its existence the *Messenger of Truth* has been printed in Hillsboro, Kan., Ithaca, Mich., Scottdale, Pa., and Newton, Kan. It is printed at present (1957), by Herald Publishing Co. of Newton, as a biweekly of 12 pages, 8 x 11 in. The circulation is a little over 3,000.   P.G.H.

Messiah College, located at Grantham, Pa., was founded in Harrisburg, Pa., by the Brethren in Christ Church in 1909, primarily in response to a need for trained workers in foreign mission work. This foreign mission program, which had been started on a small scale in the 19th century, had grown to such an extent that the need for missionaries with a broad educational foundation was apparent. The church responded to this need by launching the institution under the name Messiah Bible School and Missionary Training Home. In 1911 the school was moved from Harrisburg to Grantham, eleven miles south, with a more suitable environment and a less limited site. At the time, in addition to religious and Christian service education, it provided courses in secular fields including education for public school teachers. In 1920 junior college courses were added, and in 1921 the first class to complete a junior college program of study in the state of Pennsylvania was graduated from Messiah Bible School.

The growth of the institution and the expansion of the program made desirable a change in name. Consequently on May 12, 1924, the school was rechartered as Messiah Bible College. Pennsylvania State University accredited the junior college division in 1928. On May 6, 1946, the Pennsylvania State Council of Education officially approved the institution as a junior college.

The growth of the College has been steady and continuous. Upon recommendation of a study committee surveying higher educational needs in the Brethren in Christ Church, the general conference of 1948 requested the college to provide more adequately for the education of ministers, missionaries, and Christian workers by providing a five-year theological course on the collegiate level leading to the Th.B. degree. To meet this demand the educational program was expanded and the financial standing of the institution strengthened. The court approved amendments to the charter on Jan. 15, 1951, changing the name to Messiah College and granting legal authority to confer degrees. The Pennsylvania State Council of Education approved Messiah College as a degree-granting institution on Feb. 12, 1951.

The College is governed by a board of fourteen trustees appointed by and subject to the General Conference of the Brethren in Christ Church.

The Messiah College campus consists of 72 acres located on the eastern edge of the town of Grantham. Its educational plant consists of five buildings as follows: the administration building, a large four-story brick structure erected in 1911, containing offices, classrooms, chapel, library, and rooms for seventy men students; Hill View, remodeled in 1946 from a private residence, housing the music department; Science Hall, a two-story building erected in 1914; the auditorium-gymnasium, with an auditorium seating 1,000, erected in 1935; and Musser

Industrial Arts Building, a two-story building erected in 1940. Four additional buildings are used for housing: the women's dormitory, a four-story building with rooms for eighty women students, erected in 1948; the apartment hall, providing six family-unit apartments, erected in 1952; the president's home; and Lawn Annex, a combined apartment and dormitory building. A new library is in process of construction. When it is finished, Messiah College's investment in buildings, grounds, and equipment will exceed $700,000.

In 1956-57 Messiah College had a teaching faculty of 23 and a full-time enrollment of 111. Seventy per cent of the enrollment is from Pennsylvania, but twelve states and several foreign countries contribute students. Three fourths of the students are members of the Brethren in Christ Church, as are four fifths of the faculty. The school publishes the bimonthly *Messiah College Bulletin* and a student annual called *The Clarion.*

Presidents of the school from the beginning have been S. R. Smith, 1910-16; C. N. Hostetter, Sr., 1917-22; Enos H. Hess, 1922-34; C. N. Hostetter, Jr., 1934- .   H.S.B.

Metamora (Ill.) Mennonite Church (MC), originally known as the Partridge Creek or Springbay Church, was organized in 1833 by Christian Engel in the home of his son John Engel one mile west of Metamora. Christian Engel, the first Amish bishop in America west of Ohio, served as bishop of this congregation until his death in 1838. The Partridge congregation at one time had 13 ordained ministers, four of whom were bishops. Services were held in the homes until 1854, when the Partridge brick church was built, which served until 1889, when a frame building was erected one mile east of Metamora. For many years services were held every other Sunday, alternating with the Roanoke Church.

The Metamora and Roanoke congregations together purchased an abandoned Baptist church building seven miles north of Eureka in 1905, rebuilt it, and called it the Harmony Church. When the Roanoke congregation built its own meetinghouse it left the Harmony work in charge of the Metamora congregation. Services were held regularly each alternate Sunday in the Metamora church. On intervening Sundays the congregation divided between the Union church near Washington, Ill., and the Harmony church. In 1929 the Harmony and Union churches were closed. The Harmony building was moved to Pleasant Hill, near Morton, and is being used by the congregation there as a house of worship. The membership of the Metamora congregation in 1955 was 388, with Roy Bucher as pastor and Howard J. Zehr as bishop. The congregation is a member of the Illinois Conference. H. R. Schertz (1886-1954) served as minister in 1917-54, bishop 1941-54, and outstanding leader of the Metamora Mennonite Church, with the exception of a period of about three years (1920-23), when he served as superintendent of the Chicago Home Mission. (*ML* III, 117.)   H.R.S., H.S.B.

Metken, an Anabaptist martyr, wife of Jacob Vrencken, born at Roosteren, Montfort district, in the duchy of Gelre, now province of Limburg, was baptized in 1535 by Jan Smeitgen van Tricht (*q.v.*) in the home of Herman van den Berge (*q.v.*), heard Menno Simons preach in 1545 in Visschersweert (*q.v.*), where she lived, was imprisoned at Valkenburg (Dutch province of Limburg) on Aug. 22, 1547, and soon afterward, remaining steadfast, suffered a martyr's death; her two sisters and her brother had been executed earlier. She was the mother of five children and 35 years of age. Her husband, also a Mennonite, had left Visschersweert five or six days before she was arrested. Her confession gives interesting information about the Mennonite faith and Mennonite practices and doctrines. Metken's daughter Mariken of about 12 years, was also examined. She reported that she had often seen her mother reading a little booklet, "which she called the New Testament." Mariken, though she had never been in a church, knew the Lord's Prayer and the Apostles' Creed in the Dutch language. Her parents had also taught her a prayer (to be spoken before the meals), which she then recited. This is indeed a fine example of true Christian education.

NEFF, vDZ.

Inv. Arch. Amst. I, No. 343; *DB* 1864, 147 ff.; 1890, 56, 60; W. Bax, *Het Protestantisme in het Bisdom Luik* I (The Hague, 1937) 325-27, 398-401; *ML* III, 118.

Metselaer, Gommer de, an Anabaptist martyr: see **Gom(m)er de Metser.**

Metselaer, Jacob de, an Anabaptist martyr: see **Jacob Daneels.**

Metselaer, Jelis de, an Anabaptist martyr: see **Gillis van Havre.**

Metselaer, Peter, an Anabaptist martyr: see **Peter Witses.**

Metzler, a Lancaster Mennonite family. Yost Metzler, who came to Philadelphia on Sept. 9, 1738, and his son Valentine, aged 12, settled in Lancaster Co., Pa., the father dying early. Valentine (Feb. 14, 1726-July 24, 1783) was married on Nov. 19, 1749, to Anna Nissley (Nov. 3, 1727-March 29, 1793). He lived on the site east of the present Stehli Silk Mill, Lancaster. He was ordained in the 1760's as minister and in 1778 as bishop. His children included (1) Maria, wife of Bishop Jacob Hostetter, (2) Abraham, who lived at Metzler Meetinghouse, W. Earl Twp., Lancaster County, (3) John, (4) Henry of Strasburg, a preacher, (5) Ann, wife of Christian Hess, a preacher in the Hershey (Hess) congregation in the Pequea, (6) Christian, an active church worker of Roseville, (7) Martin of Warwick, and (8) Elizabeth Fry of Landisville. At least by 1831 descendants of Abraham were living in Beaver Twp., Columbiana Co., Ohio, where the Metzler congregation was founded in neighboring Mahoning County. From here Noah Metzler went to Yellow Creek, Elkhart Co., Ind., where he became a preacher. Other descendants of Abraham in Pennsylvania were Bishop Abram of Martinsburg and his sons, Isaac Metzler of Glade, Md., and Abram J. Metzler of Scottdale, Pa. Abram Metzler (*q.v.*), superintendent of the West Liberty Children's Home, was also a descendant. I.D.L.

Metzler, Abram (1854-1918) a native of Mahoning Co., Ohio, was a progressive worker in the Mennonite Church (MC), being especially interested in Sunday-school work and in the young people's Bible meetings. In November 1899 he was chosen as superintendent of the Mennonite Orphans' Home at Smithville, Ohio. A few months later the home was removed to West Liberty, Ohio, and he accompanied the children to the new location. It was he who succeeded in establishing the children's home at West Liberty financially and in every other way. He wrote articles and poems for the *Herald of Truth,* and juvenile stories for the *Beams of Light* and the *Words of Cheer.* He resigned in 1917 because of a breakdown in health, and died Oct. 27, 1918, during the influenza epidemic. J.C.W.

John Umble, *Mennonite Pioneers* (Elkhart, 1940) 21-38.

Metzler Mennonite Church (MC) in West Earl Twp., Lancaster Co., Pa., a member of the Lancaster Conference, was named for Jacob Metzler, who on May 6, 1927, donated 60 perches of land to the trustees of the congregation. This was the home district of Bishop Christian Burkholder (1746-1809). Earlier the members had worshiped in private homes or at Groffdale, which was always a part of the circuit. Jacob Weber and Jacob Stauffer, two of the ministers here, led the schism which resulted in the Stauffer Mennonites (Pike meetinghouse) in 1845. The Metzler meetinghouse was enlarged in 1864. A new one 40 x 62 ft. was built in 1897 and renovated and enlarged in 1952. In 1956 the congregation numbered 235, with Eli G. Sauder, John S. Martin, Amos H. Sauder, and Paul S. Wenger as preachers. I.D.L.

Meulen, Jacob ter, b. Oct. 3, 1884, at The Hague, Holland, a Dutch Mennonite, married to Wilhelmina Bosboom, studied history and was librarian of the Peace Palace at The Hague 1924-52. He is particularly known for his publications on the Dutch Pacifist Hugo de Groot (Grotius), collaborating with P. J. J. Diermanse in publishing *Bibliographie des écrits imprimés de Hugo Grotius* (The Hague, 1950). He was one of the first Dutch pacifists and an active member of the Mennonite Peace Association (Arbeidsgroep, *q.v.,* tegen de Krijgsdienst). Jacob ter Meulen is the son of François Pieter ter Meulen (1843-1927), who after studying Latin and Greek lived at The Hague and became a painter; he was an active president of the painters' association Pulchri Studio.

Hendrik ter Meulen (1841-73) was an uncle of Jacob ter Meulen. He studied at the Amsterdam Mennonite Seminary and served as pastor at Hoorn on the island of Texel 1865-68 and at Rottevalle-Witveen 1868-73. In the *Doopsgezinde Bijdragen* he published a paper, "Iets over de Gezangen bij de Doopsgezinden." vDZ.

Meulen, van der (van der Muelen, van der Molen, Vermeulen), is a common family name in Flanders and the Netherlands, both Mennonite and non-Mennonite. There were two martyrs by this name: Pieter van der Meulen (*q.v.*) and Tanneken van der Meulen (*q.v.*), both of Gent. Jacob Pietersz van der Meulen (*q.v.*) was a noted elder of the Old Flemish Mennonites at Haarlem, Holland. Quirijn van der Meulen (*q.v.*) (Krijn Vermeulen) was an elder at Danzig, Prussia; Jacob van der Meulen (*q.v.*) a preacher at Leiden, Holland. In Leiden too there were in the 17th-18th centuries a number of deacons by this name. In recent times Karst Sybrand van der Meulen (b. 1838 at Sneek, d. 1927 at Amersfoort), educated at the Amsterdam Theological Seminary, served as pastor at Terschelling 1863-65 and Nieuwe Niedorp 1865-1904; in 1904 he retired. His son Sipke Inne van der Meulen (b. 1889 at Nieuwe Niedorp) studied at the university and the seminary at Amsterdam and was a minister of Terschelling 1913-16, Balk 1916-22, Ytens 1922-29, Akkrum 1929-43, and Heerenveen 1943-54. In 1954 he retired.   vDZ.

Meulen, Jacob Pietersz van der (also Vermeulen, van der Muelen, van der Mullen, van der Moelen, van der Molen) (d. after 1631), was an elder of the Old Flemish (Huiskopers) Mennonite congregation of Haarlem, Holland. About 1590 he and Hans de Wever (Hans Busschaert, *q.v.*) banned the "Bekommerden" (*q.v.*) and their leader Quirijn van der Meulen (*q.v.*) of Danzig, and also Paulus Bussemaker (*q.v.*) of Danzig and his group called "Heylsamen" (*q.v.*). But in 1598 he was banned himself by Hans de Wever, because he refused to exclude a member of his congregation for bankruptcy. Then Jacob Pietersz and his followers, called Vermeulensvolk or Bankroetiers, formed a congregation of their own. Yet he was the man who, perhaps having become wise by experience, sought to restore peace; in 1600 when Hans de Ries (*q.v.*), the Waterlander elder, wrote a letter to him to make peace, he eagerly took up the idea. After the negotiations had been carried on for some time by letter, a conference was held at Haarlem on June 29, 1605, between de Ries and his followers and Jacob Pietersz and his adherents. Here the different views of both groups concerning intermarriage, marital avoidance, ban, rebaptism of members of other churches who wished to join the group were discussed. Apparently the Waterlanders could not agree with the rather conservative principles of the Vermeulensvolk; at any rate the negotiations were broken off. A second meeting of Jacob Pietersz and de Ries in October 1606 likewise failed to heal the breach between the two groups.

Concerning the private life of Jacob Pietersz there is little information. He was probably born in Flanders and died at a very advanced age. He was probably a businessman, because he is said to have once stayed for a long time at Vilna, Lithuania, on business. Kühler is of the opinion that he was "one of the cleverest and most versatile of the educated Mennonites" of this period. With a sympathy rarely found at that time, he spoke about the poor Indians of America, who were victims of the covetousness and fanaticism of the Spaniards.

Jacob Pietersz, believing that the rise of Catholicism in the Netherlands about 1600 represented a danger, wrote a remarkable book on the Apostolic Succession. The title reads: *Successio Apostolica, Dat is, Naecominghe oft de Naetredinghe der Apo-*

stelen . . . (Alkmaar, 1600). In this book he defends the thesis that true apostolic succession is not guaranteed by an unbroken line of consecrated clergymen (as taught in the Catholic Church) who are warranted to administer the holy offices of the church, but that the "apostolic successors" are those who follow Christ and obey His commandments; they are not committed to any succession of place or person, but only to the succession of the evangelical confession. The Christian church is apostolic, not on the basis of the succession of its ministers, but on the basis of its spiritual relationship with the church of the apostles, and the true Christian is not the one who belongs to a church in which there is a continuous chain of ministers from the days of old, but the one who knows the voice of the Good Shepherd and who bears witness of the forgiveness of sins. Whoever thus believes is a member of the church, and the church is found wherever such believers have united. All the rest are the synagogue of Satan.

Van der Meulen's *Successio Apostolica* was countered by two Catholic authors: the Jesuit Fransciscus Costerus wrote *Toetsteen van de versierde apostolische successie eens wederdoopers Jacob Pietersen van der Molen* (Antwerp, 1603) and V. P. (probably Simon Walraven, *q.v.*) published *Successio Anabaptistica, Dat is Babel der Wederdopers, eensdeels in Duytsland, maer principael in Nederlandt,* . . . (Cologne, 1603, reprint Cologne, 1612, reedition in *BRN* VII by S. Cramer with introduction, The Hague, 1910).

Besides his *Successio Apostolica* Jacob Pietersz van der Meulen published a number of books: *Een gantsch Claer Grondighe bewijsinghe ende Onderrechtinghe van der Doope* (1581, reprint Haarlem, 1627); *Verantwoordinge eender Requeste* (1597); *Defensio, wt de Heylighe Godlijcke Schrifture, dat strijdende Menschelijcke Vernuft, opinie ende schadelijcke dwalinghe wech neemt,* . . . (Alkmaar, 1599); *Ondersoeckinge der Pausgesinde Leere* (1600); *Declaratio, oft Openbare vertooninghe* . . . *teghen sekere gedichte Calumnien,* . . . (Alkmaar, 1600); *Collatio: S. Scripture, Dat is, Verghelijckinge der H. schrifturen in verscheyden geloofs-saken,* . . . (Dordrecht, 1602, reprint with appendix, Dordrecht, 1602); *Vertoogh aen de Succesoors des Jesuijts D. Francisci Costeri,* . . . (Alkmaar, 1604); *Dialogus, Dat is een t'samensprekinghe tusschen verscheyden persoonen,* . . . (Dordrecht, 1602); *Ontschuldinghe oft Nootelicke verantwoordinghe tegen Lasterlijcke Schriften* (1603); *Christelijcke Onderrichtinghe, oft een clare Onderwijsinghe, met grondighe Belijdenisse der voorneemste Poincten der heylsamer Leere,* . . . (Alkmaar, 1609); *Historia Ecclesiastica. Een Kercken Historie,* . . . (Haarlem, 1614), with an appendix to this work entitled *Historia der Kerckenhandel* . . . (Haarlem, 1614), in which *Kerckenhandel* he also gives an account of two disputations he held with Catholics at Haarlem in 1614, the first on Jan. 14, the second shortly after. He published further: *Apocalypsis, ofte de Openbaringhe Joannis* (Haarlem, 1614); *Proeve van de Kerckelijcke Regeeringhe, ofte Ordinatien der Ghemeynten Christi* (Haarlem, 1621); *Evangelische Expositien* (Haarlem, 1623); *Veilighe Wech ofte Raet om hem in't bannen ofte veroordelen niet te vergrijpen* (Amsterdam, 1631). His book *Verclaringe uyt de Godtlycke Schriftuere, Hoe haer de Gemeente Christi moet bewysen neflens die Broeders die (na datse haer in de Gemeenschap der Geloovigen hebben begeven) wederom vervollen zijn,* published after his death in 1645, apparently is the reprint of an older writing from the time of his quarrels with the *Bekommerden* or the *Heylsamen* (about 1590).   vdZ.

Inv. Arch. Amst. I, Nos. 495-98, 500, 507, 510-14, 516, 518; M. Schagen, *Naamlijst der Doopsgezinde schrijveren* (Amsterdam, 1745) 67 f.; *Catalogus Amst.,* 193, 194, 195, 197, 212, 213; *BRN* VII, 8 f. 64 f., 69 f., 74 f., 79, 82, 87; *DB* 1876, 35; 1910, 31; Kühler, *Geschiedenis* II, 2, 126-30; *ML* III, 118.

Meulen, Jacobus van der (d. 1693), apparently a physician, was the preacher and later the elder of the Waterlander congregation at Leiden, Holland. On May 5, 1670, he was appointed preacher, but on Sept. 16 of that year he was suspended because he had preached publicly at Rijnsburg (*q.v.*), the Collegiant center. On Dec. 16, 1675, he was readmitted to the pulpit and on July 24, 1679, he was called to the eldership in the congregation, serving until his death on Oct. 22, 1693. At his instigation catechetical instruction was started in 1682. A number of his relatives were deacons of the Waterlander and from 1701 in the United Leiden congregation.   vdZ.

Inv. Arch. Amst. I, Nos. 805, 840; L. G. le Poole, *Bijdragen tot de kennis van het kerkelijk leven onder de Doopsgezinden te Leiden* (Leiden, 1905) 64, 71-73, 79 and *passim.*

Meulen, Quiryn van der (Crijn, Krijn, Cryn Vermeulen), was the elder of the Danzig congregation following Dirk Philips (*q.v.*) in the last decades of the 16th century. His letters that were preserved in the records of the Heubuden (*q.v.*) church were signed by his Flemish name Cryn Vermoolen. In the disputes on the ban which divided the Dutch Mennonites into two camps he was on the side of the merciful use of the ban. (H. G. Mannhardt's judgment, p. 45, concerning Cryn's severe rule in the church is based on error.) This generosity led to tensions within the Danzig congregation and beyond in the West Prussian churches, who on the basis of a correspondence with the leaders of the Flemish wing in Holland placed the milder Frisians under the ban. In 1580 Cryn still had the confidence of all the Mennonites of West Prussia. He was one of several delegates sent by the West Prussian churches to the conference of elders in Haarlem and Emden. He was saddened by what he heard about the strife between the Frisians and Flemish. "I confess that in Haarlem I showed my feeling, which was inclined to peace, though in my worry I received no help." He requested that men be sent to Danzig to teach the brethren that which he himself could not understand, and declared that if he was proved to be in error he was willing to be dismissed from his eldership. When these men came to Danzig, he expressed himself freely on his concern upon their request that he do so.—The name "Bekommerden" (*q.v.*, i.e., Concerned Ones) for the lenient wing of the Frisians is derived from their concern or worry about the severe application of the ban.

Van der Meulen's frankness aroused offense in Danzig. He was accused of having destroyed the peace of the congregation. On the advice of the Haarlem church representatives of the three Frisian congregations of Montau, Elbing, and Olde Tooren (Thorn), a total of 35 brethren met and confronted Cryn and his friend Hans van Schwindern with their charge of guilt, and presented to them a confession they had worked out in advance. It contained six charges: (1) Cryn and Hans had criticized the elders in the west and had thereby created disturbance in the brotherhood. (2) In spite of the wishes of the West Prussians that they attend a conference of elders in Holland they had not complied, but had rather burdened the Danzig church with "weaknesses and liberties." (3) Cryn had promised in Haarlem that he would remain quiet, but did not do so. (4) Cryn and Hans had censured the deceased Dirk Philips (for his strict conception of the ban) against the will of the congregation. (5) Cryn and all those who thought as he did did not rebaptize those who joined the brotherhood from some other branch, and did not apply the strict ban. (6) In addition to this charge, there was his "peculiar understanding" of the truth.

Cryn defended himself in a letter. The tone and content of this letter show his superiority. The charges had no justification, and as to his view of the ban, he maintained, "We would prefer to have matters go according to Christ's teaching and take their course after fraternal discussion." His personality and the strength of his conviction caused many of his opponents to waver. The confession of guilt was probably read to the 35 delegates of the three churches in Danzig in the home of Harmen Borgerlinck (Sept. 25, 1586), but they did not yet dare to pass judgment on Cryn and his supporters. But when they arrived in Holland and there received sanction the committee met once more in Danzig early in 1588; however, the representatives from Elbing and Thorn left at once. And so Hilchen Smit (Schmidt), the elder of the Montau congregation, with his delegates and 55 brethren from the Danzig congregation, was obliged to carry out the expulsion of Cryn and Hans van Schwindern. The act was direful. The cleavage between the Frisians and the Flemish, which was bridged over by Cryn and men like him, now became open. As early as March a protest was made to the leaders by the Elbing congregation, disapproving the hard course taken by the Montau group. They begged for patience and long-suffering toward Cryn.

Cryn continued to live in Danzig as an ordinary member of the congregation. Alenson's *Tegenbericht* (*BRN* VII, 190) reports that in a colloquy with Wolff Uohll, who had come to Danzig from Moravia with Jan Gerrits, Cryn upheld Menno's view of the Incarnation. He applied his energy to writing. The Amsterdam Mennonite Library and the Danzig Church Library each have a copy of a beautiful Schottland Bible which he had printed at his own expense. The foreword contains the statement, "Men vindse te koop bij Krijn Vermeulen de jonghe, Cramer, woonende opte lege zydt van Schotlandt bij Danswick 1598" (To be bought of Krijn Vermeulen, Jr., merchant, living on the lower side of Schottland at Danzig, 1598). (Mannhardt, *op. cit.*)

Krijn van Vermeulen is not to be confused with the Danzig Mennonite alchemist Krijn van Mollem (*q.v.*).   H.Q.

Succssio Anabaptistica and Alenson's *Tegenbericht, BRN* VII, 65 and 190; H. G. Mannhardt, *Die Danziger Mennonitengemeinde* (Danzig, 1919); *ML* III, 118 f.

Meurs, van, a Dutch Mennonite family, found in the 17th and 18th centuries at Rotterdam, where its members originally belonged to the Flemish congregation. Aelbert (Albregt) van Meurs (son of Huybrecht van Meurs), b. *ca.* 1640 at Rotterdam, d. there March 9, 1712, was banned from the Flemish congregation in 1669 because he had attended services and taken communion with the Waterlanders. He then joined the Waterlander congregation, becoming a deacon in 1673 and a preacher in 1675. Until 1700 he served in the Waterlander congregation and after their merger with the Flemish, he served this united congregation.

His son Aelbert van Meurs de Jonge was a deacon of the Rotterdam congregation 1711-15. In 1718 he and Jan Suderman protested the appointment of David van Heyst, of Amsterdam (see Jan Suderman and Aelbert van Meurs, *Protest, gedaen tegen de maniere van't beroepen van den Heere D. van Heist . . . nevens eene korte verantwoordinge van hun gedragh diesaengaande.* Rotterdam, 1718), as preacher. They were opposed by M. van Oudenaerden and Adriaen van Alkmaer of Rotterdam and Herman Schijn and H. van Dam of Amsterdam. vDZ.

K. Vos, *Geschiedenis der Doopsgezinde Gemeente te Rotterdam* (1907, repr.) 24, 25, 26, 27, 44, 47.

Meurthe et Moselle, a departement in northeastern France, in the former province of Lorraine, composed of parts of the two departements Meurthe and Moselle, after the rest had been ceded to Germany in 1871. Two Mennonite churches in this area, Repaix and Lunéville-Dieuze, were thereby divided into two groups, but continued to have their meetings on both sides of the new border, the former until it was dissolved and the latter until World War I.

The Mennonites of Meurthe et Moselle are descendants of refugees from Switzerland who settled in Alsace and were driven out by Louis XIV. In the east-central part of Lorraine, later the departement of Meurthe, they formed the "Welschland" congregation, and in the northeastern part, later called the departement of Moselle, the German-Lorraine (Deutsch-Lothringen) congregation. The former congregation extended farther and farther westward. Families from Salm and Le Hang in southeastern Lorraine were added, thus forming congregations throughout the southern part of Meurthe et Moselle. Living scattered among the French-speaking Catholic population had a disintegrating effect, so that some of these congregations could not maintain themselves. In 1939 *Christ Seul* (*q.v.*), the official church organ, was sent free of charge as a means of evangelization to all known Mennonite addresses in this area, a total of 155. Many of these families had no connections with an organized congregation. In 1939 three small congregations were

still in existence: Baccarat, many of whose members lived in the adjoining departement of Vosges, Lunéville-Repaix, and Toul, which also extended into the departement of Meuse. In 1955 the membership, including children, of these three congregations was 220. (*ML* III, 119.)   P.So.

Meuse (German, *Maas*), a departement in northern France, formed from the former province of Lorraine. Many Mennonites settled there after the beginning of the 19th century. They came from the east from various parts of Lorraine. As long as the German language was in use they called themselves the "Welschland" congregation; in 1880 an elder signed his name as Peter Kennel, "elder from the Welschland congregation." When French predominated the name became "Assemblée de la Meuse." For a long time its seat was the town of Vaucouleurs. An old list, probably from the first half of the 19th century, names 27 meeting places in the region around Vaucouleurs extending north beyond St. Mihiel. Meetings were held in the homes of the more prosperous members. As the urge to go west continued, an independent congregation was organized in the departement of Haute-Marne. On account of the great distance the Mennonites around St. Mihiel also organized, but this group disappeared after the death of their elder André Greabill about 1870. A division occurred in 1885, strife among the elders led to the organization of the Toul congregation. All of this, in addition to emigration to America, weakened the congregation. The great distances between members also had a paralyzing effect on the spiritual life. The center of the church in 1939 was the town of Ligny-en Barrois, 10 miles southeast of Bar-le-Duc, the captial of the departement. Only ten places of meeting were left, scattered from Vaucouleurs to Revigny, west of Bar-le-Duc and north as far as Clermont-on-Argonne. In 1954 the membership, including children, was 90, with Emile Muller as preacher. (*ML* III, 119 f.)

P.So.

Meuslin, Wolfgang: see **Musculus.**

Mexican *Mennonite* (MC) *Mission Work.* The Mennonite Church (MC) began mission work in Argentina in 1917. Growing interest in Spanish-speaking people resulted in the appointment of D. H. Bender and S. E. Allgyer by the Mennonite Board of Missions and Charities to investigate mission needs among Mexicans from Brownsville, Tex., all along the Mexican border to California. This investigation was carried out in February and March 1920. Recommendation to open mission work in Phoenix, Ariz., was brought to the annual meeting of the Board in May 1920. Fifteen years later, in 1935, another committee was appointed to make a similar investigation. T. K. Hershey and William Detweiler served on this committee and made an extensive investigative tour along the border. As a result T. K. Hershey spent the winter of 1936-37 with a trailer preaching and distributing literature among Mexicans along the Texas border. In May 1937, Amsa Kauffman took over the responsibility for the work. Small groups of believers were established in several

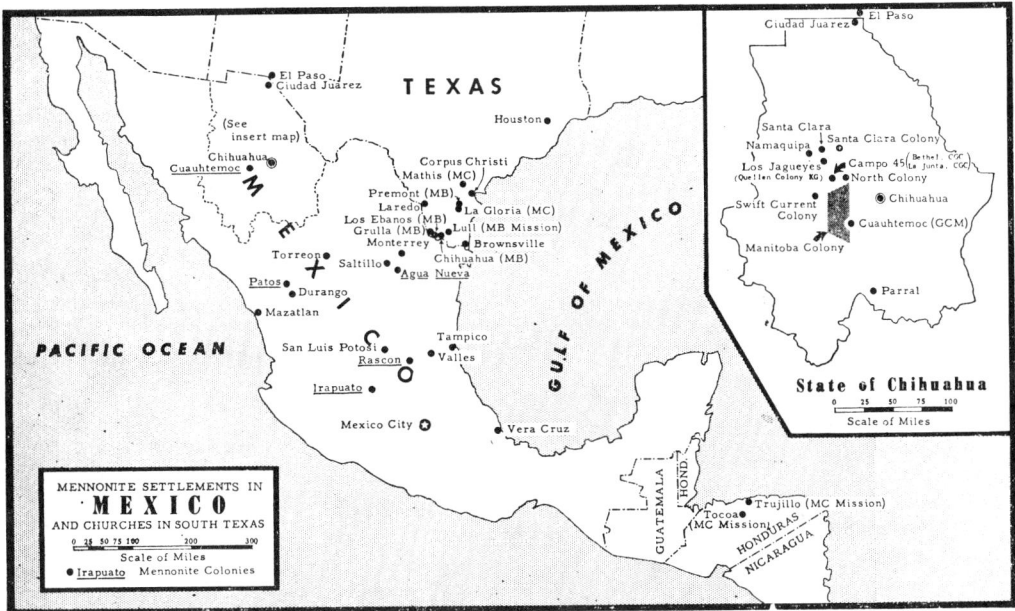

MENNONITE SETTLEMENTS IN
MEXICO
AND CHURCHES IN SOUTH TEXAS
0 25 50 75 100   200   300
Scale of Miles
● Irapuato   Mennonite Colonies

State of Chihuahua
0   25   50   75   100
Scale of Miles

towns, but finally the center of the program was located at the town of Mathis.

Other workers followed Kauffman after his call to serve as pastor in Indiana, some attempting to support themselves as they sought to witness in a voluntary capacity. The program was greatly strengthened by the setting up of a Voluntary Service unit at Mathis in 1952, activities of which included housing construction, kindergarten, maternity home, crafts, and other community service. A small church was built in 1949, and a new and larger one was begun in the winter of 1954. J. Weldon Martin has been the pastor since 1951.

In addition to this Mexican program in Texas there are Spanish language churches for Mexicans in La Junta, Col., Chicago, Ill., and Archbold, Ohio. The work in La Junta was organized in 1923; David Castillo has been pastor since 1940. The membership in 1955 was 44, with an average attendance of approximately 56; a weekly radio program is conducted over the local station. The Mexican work in Chicago was opened in 1932 by J. W. Shank, missionary on furlough from Argentina. Mario Snyder has been pastor since 1953; the membership in 1955 was 53, and the average Sunday-school attendance 107. The work at Archbold, Ohio, has largely been the fruit of the labors of William S. Florry. He began Sunday school and services among the migrant Mexicans of his community in 1940 and now the Mexican congregation worships in a building of its own. The baptized membership is only three, but the attendance much larger. In 1956 and early 1957 work was opened among Spanish-speaking people in Corpus Christi, Tex., with Don Brenneman as pastor; Los Angeles, Cal., with Bernard Kroeker as pastor; Defiance, Ohio, with Victor M. Ovando as pastor.

J.D.G.

Mexico is a federal republic of North America, though it belongs geographically partly to Central America. It extends southward from the United States to Guatemala and British Honduras. The Rio Grande River is its northern boundary line. The Sierra Madre mountain ranges extend in the north-south direction shaped like a huge wishbone with two forks reaching north from Mexico City. Between the ranges lie a number of valleys and plateaus of differing altitudes. The country has great diversity of climate because of its location in both temperate and tropical zones and its varied altitudes. Annual rainfall varies from three inches in northern Lower California to 82 inches in the tropics. The country as a whole suffers from a lack of natural water supply. Large areas of Mexico are unproductive. In 1940 only 7.6 per cent of the land area was under cultivation. Of the unproductive land 80 per cent is known as "seasonal" land in that it will produce crops only during the rainy season, which in most parts of the country is from May or June to September. Only about 6.5 per cent of the land does not require irrigation. Much of the farming is done on plateaus at altitudes of 5,000 feet or over. The drop in altitude along the mountains is so sudden that streams tend to flood quickly during rainy seasons and to revert to dry gullies in the winter. Few streams of any length are found on the level plateaus and for this reason in many areas the possibilities for extensive irrigation projects are limited.

Politically Mexico has had a stormy history. Being a Spanish colony, it was for years exploited under the imperialistic colonial system. It has had its national heroes who struggled valiantly to emancipate the country and bring political freedom to its people. The United States governmental organization has been generally the model after which Mexico has patterned. The government, both national and local, is less stable and democracy less mature than is the case in the United States and Canada. Nevertheless, noticeable progress has been made in the second quarter of the 20th century, in that revolutions have been fewer and orderly elections have become more commonplace.

The significance of Mexico for Mennonites is in the settlement of over 16,000 Mennonites there. In 1922-27 several thousand Mennonites from the Old Colony and the Sommerfelder Mennonites in Manitoba (and some from Saskatchewan) emigrated to Mexico. These groups represent the most conservative elements of the Mennonites who had come from Russia to Canada in the 1870's. They left Canada out of protest to the secularization processes, the chief of which was the Canadianization to which they were being subjected in the public schools. The Mennonites were opposed to the requirement to conduct their schools in the English language, which they considered an abrogation of a privilege granted them originally when they immigrated. Rather than surrender what to them seemed freedom of education, they decided to emigrate.

A delegation of six men investigated colonization possibilities in a number of South American countries, but nowhere but in Mexico were they able to secure the desired privileges. Alvaro Obregon, the president of Mexico at that time, by presidential decree granted them the privileges they sought, such as freedom from military service, freedom from the swearing of oaths, freedom to conduct their religious life and observe their church regulations without molestation or restrictions, freedom to establish and conduct their own schools and select their own teachers without hindrance from the Mexican government, and freedom to dispose of property or establish any economic system which they might voluntarily adopt. The largest Mennonite settlement in 1950 was located in the state of Chihuahua, consisting of over 12,000 Mennonites, more than 90 per cent of whom are Old Colony Mennonites. About 6 per cent are Sommerfelders, a slightly less conservative branch. There are also a few Church of God in Christ and General Conference Mennonites. A small settlement of Old Order Mennonites and Old Order Amish from Pennsylvania established in the state of San Luis Potosi in 1944 failed. Some 3,000 (1950) Old Colony Mennonites are located in the state of Durango, 500 miles south of the Chihuahua settlement. A new settlement of Swift Current, Sask., Old Colony Mennonites and a Kleine Gemeinde (q.v.) group of Manitoba originated in 1948 on the Los Jagueyes ranch northwest of the Cuauhtemoc settlement. The total Mennonite population of Mexico in 1950 was about 16,000. Almost without exception the Mennonites in Mexico are engaged in agriculture. Their pattern of settlement is according to agricultural villages very similar to the pattern brought from Russia by way of Canada. New land has always been bought in large blocks and redistributed to the purchasers in family-sized farms. The chief crops produced are oats, some corn, beans, and dairy products. A generally diversified type of farming is most common. Mennonites have contributed much to the production of such commodities as but-

ter, cheese, beef, pork, oats, and beans for the commercial market. Fruits and vegetables are grown only in limited quantities on irrigated lands. The few Old Colony Mennonites that engage in business and industry in towns are not considered members in "good standing." Few of them have shops and stores in the rural villages. The Mennonites engaged in industry and business are members of the G.C.M. group. The Church of God in Christ Mennonites have a flourishing mission station in rural Mexico in the central region of the Old Colony settlement.

The future of the Mennonites in Mexico seems somewhat uncertain. Some think of Mexico as a somewhat temporary stopping place on a pilgrimage to a yet unknown land, others as a permanent place of settlement. The entire Mennonite settlement in Mexico presents an interesting experiment in the contact of two different cultures. Mexico has a Latin culture, which includes the Spanish language, the Roman Catholic religion, and many moral standards and customs alien to those of the Mennonites, who are a Germanic Protestant group with generally higher standards. The influence of the Latin culture is felt by the Mennonites, and outsiders can notice many adaptations that the Mennonites have made to it. The Mennonites, though a minority group, have made a significant impact on the Mexicans, especially in agricultural methods, and have introduced modern farming machinery and highly superior types of livestock. Slowly Mexican neighbors have been imitating these examples. The process of cultural interaction is continuing. The privileges which the Mexican government granted the Mennonites have been scrupulously upheld up to this time. The severe drought of 1951-54 placed a very heavy strain on the economic welfare of the settlements. Several hundred returned poverty-stricken to Canada in 1954-55.

Since 1947 the Mennonite Central Committee has carried on a program of social welfare and relief, largely for the Mennonites, with headquarters in Cuauhtemoc. Hospital service, primarily in Cuauhtemoc, has been a major part of the program. In the drought period considerable direct relief was given, particularly in seed wheat. (See also **Old Colony Mennonites.**)   J.W.F.

J. W. Fretz, *Mennonite Colonization in Mexico, an Introduction* (Akron, 1945); W. Schmiedehaus, *Ein feste Burg ist unser Gott. Der Wanderweg eines christlichen Siedlungsvolkes* (Cuauhtemoc, 1948); W. Quiring, *Im Schweisse deines Angesichts, Ein mennonitisches Bilderbuch: Paraguay, Brasilien, Argentinien, Uruguay und Mexiko. Mennonite Life* published the following articles on Mexico: Vol. II (April 1947) contains the articles: J. W. Fretz, "Mennonites in Mexico"; A. D. Stoesz, "Agriculture Among the Mennonites in Mexico"; C. Wiebe, "Health Conditions Among the Mennonites in Mexico"; P. C. Hiebert and W. T. Snyder, "Are the Doors of Mexico Open to Mennonite Immigrants?" W. Schmiedehaus, "Mennonite Life in Mexico"; Vol. IV (October 1949): W. Schmiedehaus, "New Mennonite Settlements in Mexico"; P. J. B. Reimer, "From Russia to Mexico—The Story of the Kleine Gemeinde"; Vol. VII (January 1952): Charles Burkhart, "Music of the Old Colony Mennonites [in Mexico]"; ML III, 120-23.

Meyer, a common family name, found also among the Mennonites. As early as 1526-32 a number of Anabaptists in the Swiss cantons of Zürich, Schaffhausen, Bern, and Lucerne had this name. Among them was Hans Meyer (Pfistermeyer, *q.v.*), an active preacher. Later there were Anabaptists in the canton of Aarau, most of whom emigrated to Alsace and the Palatinate in the 17th and 18th centuries, and from there to America. Several members of this family served as preachers at Immelhausen in Baden, Germany, in the 18th century. One Meyer family emigrated from Switzerland to the Netherlands in the early 18th century. Dutch ministers with the name Meyer, but not related to the above family, are Joost Jurriaensz Meyer, a preacher of the Old Frisian (Arke Noach) congregation at Amsterdam 1709-d.49, and J. A. A. Meijer (b. 1913), pastor at Ternaard 1940-46 and Zutphen 1946- . (See also **Moyer.**)   vDZ.

Paul Peachey, *Die soziale Herkunft der Schweizer Täufer in der Reformationszeit* (Karlsruhe, 1954) 113, Nos. 91-94; 117, Nos. 188 f.; 121, No. 259; 133 f., Nos. 536-50; Delbert Gratz, *Bernese Anabaptists* (Scottdale, 1953) 47, 89; *Naamlijst,* issues of 1766-93.

Meyer, Christian (1842-1916), a German archivist, son of a forester, began his career in the national archives in Munich and in 1871 was appointed city archivist for Augsburg, Germany. He published numerous works on the history of Bavaria, especially of Augsburg, Prussia, and the Hohenzollerns. Among his early historical works was a study, *Anfänge des Wiedertäufertums in Augsburg,* published in the periodical he edited, the *Zeitschrift des Historischen Vereins für Schwaben und Neuburg* I (1874) 207-53, in which he gave information on the Anabaptist leaders in Augsburg (Hans Denk, Hans Hut, Jakob Gross, and Siegmund Salminger) and published 22 documents from the city archives of 1526-27. The publication of archives on the Anabaptist congregation in Augsburg was continued by Friedrich Roth in the same periodical, Vols. XXVII and XXVIII. Another of Meyer's noteworthy contributions to the study of Anabaptist history from a chronicle of Augsburg in the Bavarian State Library was published under the title, "Zur Geschichte der Wiedertäufer in Oberschwaben" (*Ztscht für Kirchengesch.* XVII, 1896, 248-58). (*ML* III, 123.)
                                                   HEGE.

Meyer (Meyger, Meiger), **Fridolin,** a notary in Strasbourg, Alsace, united with the Anabaptists there in 1528. He was baptized by Jakob Kautz (*q.v.*). His home became the occasional meeting place of the members, and he was one of their preachers. Meyer seems to have had earlier connection with persons who later became Anabaptists or were akin to them in spirit. In 1523 he had, for instance, published a booklet by Otto Brunfels (*q.v.*), *Von der Zucht und underweysung der Kinder, Ein Leer und vermanung* (Röhrich, 36). On Dec. 15, 1528, he was cross-examined by Bucer and Capito on baptism. No records of the interrogation have survived, but bound into excerpts from the cross-examination is a four-page manuscript leaflet on the oath that is said to be from Meyer's hand (Röhrich, 36). Meyer was released from prison upon promise not to return to the city, but was seized again at a meeting of the Anabaptists at which Hans Bünderlin (*q.v.*) and Wilhelm Reublin (*q.v.*) were also present (Cornelius, 275). In a hearing on March 16, 1529, Meyer

denied the intention of the Anabaptists to hold all things in common. He was pardoned, but unless he would desist from his belief he was to leave the city (Cornelius, 273).   HEGE.

J. Adam, *Evangelische Kirchengeschichte der Stadt Strassburg* (1922); C. A. Cornelius, *Geschichte des Münsterischen Aufruhrs* II (Leipzig, 1860); T. W. Röhrich, "Zur Geschichte der strassburger Wiedertäufer," in *Ztscht für die historische Theologie,* 1860; *ML* III, 123.

Meyer, Hans: see **Pfistermeyer, Hans.**

Meyer, Sebastian (1465-1545), a Reformed theologian, of Neuburg on the Rhine, Germany, a former Franciscan, who had occasionally worked in Strasbourg, Alsace. At the very beginning of the Reformation he was inspired by the evangelical spirit. He came to Bern, Switzerland, and was the first to preach Reformation doctrine. In 1523 he participated in the colloquy of Zürich. But Catholic power prevailed and he was expelled from Bern in 1524. He went to Basel, left the Franciscan order, married and then went to Augsburg, where he preached for a long time. After the Reformation was accomplished in Bern he returned to fill the gap caused by the death of Berchtold Haller (*q.v.*) and Franz Kolb (*q.v.*).

For the Anabaptist movement Meyer was of importance in that he represented the Reformed Church in the disputation at Bern (*q.v.*) March 11-17, 1538. He sought to establish the nature of the true church on the basis of Ephesians 4, and made serious charges against the Anabaptists, accusing them of having forsaken the true Christian church and as self-chosen prophets having set up a synagogue of Satan; but they had not succeeded; the Reformers had opened entire cities and countries to the Gospel. In strict contrast to this position was that of the Swiss Brethren. Their conception of the church could not be one of church politics. They replied to Meyer that Christianity was not a matter of an external confession by entire cities and kingdoms, but an inward personal life. Sebastian Meyer participated actively in the campaign to wipe out the Anabaptists. To what extent he was responsible for the violent measures passed against them cannot be determined.   S.G.

Manuscript record of the Anabaptist Disputation of 1538 in U.P. 80, state archives of Bern; E. Marti, *Menschenrat und Gottestat. Geschichte der Berner Reformation* (Karlsruhe, 1931); S. Geiser, *Die Taufgesinnten-Gemeinden* (Karlsruhe, 1931); *ML* III, 123 f.

Meyere, Boudewijn de (d. 1651), a colleague of Jacques van Maldegem (*q.v.*), left the Catholic Church to join the Anabaptists, was ordained preacher in 1633, and elder in 1638; he served until his death in 1681. De Meyere at first lived just outside Aardenburg, probably being a farmer. He was apparently a wealthy man, for in 1654 he made a liberal contribution for the building of a new meetinghouse in Aardenburg. During his ministry the Aardenburg congregation had many difficulties with the Reformed city governors; in 1643 they prevented the members living outside the town, including de Meyere, from entering the town to attend the church services. Then a petition signed by de Meyere was sent to the States-General at The Hague, with the result that the city magistrates were required to give all members free access to the church. In 1654 there were difficulties concerning the erection of the new meetinghouse. In the spring of 1649 de Meyere had a debate with the Catholic Arnout van Gelouwe (*q.v.*), who with two other Catholics attended a Mennonite service at Aardenburg conducted by de Meyere. At the close of the service van Gelouwe accused de Meyere of errors in dogma. They disputed for some time in the meetinghouse, and in the afternoon in de Meyere's home, which was then in the hamlet of Eede, two miles from Aardenburg.

For nearly a century members of the de Meyere family were devoted members of the Aardenburg Mennonite congregation. Jan de Meyere, probably Boudewijn's brother, was a deacon; Boudewijn's daughter Susanna was married to the preacher Ghysel Hebberecht (*q.v.*). (*DB* 1876, 81, 112; 1877, 1-42 *passim; ML* III, 65.)   vDZ.

Meyli (Meili), **Hans,** an old man, a Swiss Brethren preacher, of the canton of Zürich, Switzerland, was imprisoned in 1637 with his sons Hans and Martin for about three years.   vDZ.

Ein wahrhaftiger Bericht von den Brüdern im Schweizerland, 11; S. Geiser, *Die Taufgesinnten-Gemeinden* (Karlsruhe, 1931) 383; *Mart. Mir.* D 812, E **1111.**

Meylin, Barbara and **Elizabeth,** apparently the wives of Hans and Martin Meili, were imprisoned in 1639 at the Oetenbach prison in Zürich, Switzerland. They, however, managed to escape. (*Mart. Mir.* D 813, E 1112.)

Meyn (Mein, Mayn, Main), a Dutch Mennonite family found at Zaandam, North Holland, where some members of this family were preachers: Cornelis Gerritsz Meyn, serving 1663-81; Gerrit Pietersse Meyn, serving from 1693; Cornelis Gerritsz Meyn 1727-75, and perhaps Gerrit Cornelisz Meyn, all of the Frisian congregation. A number of the Meyn family also were deacons. Some members of this family belonged to the Flemish congregation of Zaandam, and after 1687 to the United Flemish and Waterlander congregation of West-Zaandam (Nieuwe Huys); of these mention should be made of Meyndert Arendsze Meyn (d. March 4, 1704), who in 1673 organized a support action among the Mennonites of the Zaan district in behalf of the Dutch army, then at war with England and France. This action, launched in gratitude for the exemption of the Dutch Mennonites from military service, brought in a sum of about 30,000 guilders besides a large quantity of clothing for the common cause. This Meyndert A. Meyn was a merchant; in 1695 he was appointed as one of the directors of the Dutch Whaling Company.   vDZ.

S. Lootsma, *Het Nieuwe Huys* (Zaandam, 1937) 18, 26, 29, 31, 102 f., 189-97; *DB* 1873, 170-74.

Meynardt (Meynart, Meyndert) **van Delft:** see **Meynart van Emden.**

Meynart van Emden (or van Delft), a Dutch Anabaptist elder and leader of the revolutionary Münsterite (*q.v.*) wing, who was extremely active in various parts of the Netherlands. In November 1533

he was one of the 12 "apostles" sent out by Jan Matthijsz (*q.v.*) of Haarlem. He baptized at Amsterdam, The Hague, Brielle, and other places. The martyrs Anneken Jans of Brielle, Jan Everts of Middelburg, and Cornelis Cornelisz Kelder of The Hague were among those baptized by Meynart. He was still living in 1548; about his further life and his death nothing is known. By trade he was a weaver.   vDZ.

Inv. Arch. Amst. I, Nos. 203, 205; Grosheide, *Verhooren,* 23, 181-84, idem, *Bijdrage,* 95, 97; *DB* 1917, 98, 105 f.; Mellink, *Wederdopers, passim; Groningsche Volksalmanak 1909,* 72.

Meynert, Hermansz (Harmenszoon), an Anabaptist martyr, a sawer of wood from Balk in Friesland, Netherlands, who was burned at the stake with five brethren in Amsterdam on Aug. 6 or 8, 1552; he had been baptized by Gillis van Aken (*q.v.*). Further particulars are lacking. (*Mart. Mir.* D 142 f., E 535; *ML* III, 124.)   vDZ.

Miami Amish Mennonite Church, unaffiliated, located in the southern part of Miami Co., Ind., and serving the Amish Mennonite community of Miami and Howard counties, was organized in 1939 with 18 members. At first, services were held in homes but in June 1946 a brick school was converted into a church. In 1956 the membership was 49. Levi Sommers was the first minister of the congregation. On April 18, 1948, Ezra Miller and Enos Miller were ordained to the office of minister and a year later Ezra Miller was ordained bishop. In 1956 they were still serving.   E.MI.

Miami County, Ind., organized as a county in 1834, was named for the Miami Indians. What is now Howard and Miami counties was part of the Miami Indian Reservation which was created in 1826. The Indians who did not wish to come under civil law were obligated to migrate to Kansas by 1845. Beginning in 1848 Amish settlers from Ohio began to locate in the Howard-Miami (*q.v.*) area. The first congregation organized was what would now be called Old Order Amish, though it was not until 1854 that the division between the Old Order Amish and the less strict Amish Mennonites occurred in the Howard-Miami area. The latter built their first house of worship (MC) in 1871 along the Howard County line, in Section 31 of Harrison Township, Miami Co. The membership of this congregation in 1956 was 378. The Old Order Amish have a congregation in Miami County with 32 members, and the Beachy Amish one with 49 members. J.C.W.

Glenn L. Troyer, *et al., Mennonite Church History of Howard and Miami Counties* (Scottdale, ca. 1917).

Miami Hutterite Bruderhof, located near New Dayton, Alberta, was founded in 1923. George Waldner, who was chosen to the ministry in 1906, left the Milford Bruderhof to found this Bruderhof. P. Hofer was chosen as minister in 1927. In 1957 the Bruderhof had a population of 120, with 17 families and 43 members.   D.D.

Michael Matschilder, an Anabaptist martyr: see **Matschidl, Michael.**

Michael Sattler: see **Sattler, Michael.**

Michaelsburg Mennonite Church of the Fürstenland Mennonite Settlement, Ukraine, was a subsidiary of the Fürstenland Mennonite Church (*q.v.*), which in turn was a daughter of the Chortitza Mennonite Church. The school building of Michaelsburg served as a place of worship. In 1905 there was a total population of 255, of whom 97 were baptized members. (Dirks, *Statistik,* 1905, 60.) C.K.

Michailov, Peter, pseudonym of Peter the Great while he lived for several months in 1697 in Zaandam, Dutch province of North Holland, and Amsterdam as a worker in order to learn shipbuilding on the dock of the East India Company, where he came in contact with the local Mennonites. (*Menn. Bl.,* 1911, 45; *ML* III, 124.) HEGE.

Michalin Mennonite community and church was located near Machnovka in the province of Volhynia, Polish Russia. The community was settled in the later years of the 18th century by families from the Graudenz area of the Vistula River but the congregation seems not to have organized until 1811, when David Siebrandt was elected minister. He was called to be elder in 1816, and was succeeded in 1852 by Johann Schröder. In 1874-78 the entire group emigrated to Kansas, where in the following year the congregation became the Gnadenberg Mennonite Church (*q.v.*). J.F.S.

Michelians (German, *Michelianer*), a Pietistic group within the state church in Württemberg, Germany, which derives from Johann Michael Hahn (*q.v.*). In contrast with Old Pietism, which accepted the creed of the church, the Michelians deviated further from church doctrine. The writings of Hahn are even more influenced by Theosophy than those of Oetinger, going back to Jakob Boehme. Ascetic traits point back to medieval Mysticism (e.g., the high regard for celibacy). Old Pietism used expressions adopted from church catechisms and hymns; Hahn has a different kind of language.

The core of the piety of the Michelians is sanctification (*q.v.*). This doctrine was developed by Hahn in his struggles with other streams of Pietism in Swabia. Old Pietism earnestly cultivated the feeling of human sinfulness, to such an extent that a countercurrent arose in the followers of M. Christian Gottlob Pregizer (d. 1824), which advocated joy for the forgiveness of sins by looking at Jesus and the finished sacrificial work of redemption. In opposition to these divergent ideas on justification by faith, the Michelians stressed righteous living; justification is not merely something that happened long ago outside the believer, but a process taking place within him (in contrast to the Pregizians). Whereas the Pregizians ascribe sinlessness to the Christian, the Michelians believe that it is possible for a Christian to sin. Whereas the Old Pietists continued to look at the old life, the Michelians stressed rest and joy in redemption.

The Michelians describe the second birth as an inward process that progresses by degrees, "whereby Christ, through the medium of the working of His Spirit on the mind of the believer, must accomplish and suffer within each one personally what He once historically accomplished and suffered, . . . in order to prepare him for pure sonship and blessed perfection." They stress progress in sanctification through "undismayed watchfulness of a penitent heart." This end is furthered by the brotherhood, in which the like-minded "reveal to each other the state of their spirit and impart counsel and admonition, comfort, and encouragement."

The doctrines of creation and redemption taught by Hahn, related to those of Oetinger, and Boehme, do not insist on the external forms of existing church ordinance, but stress the "free agreement of such as do not stand under the law, because Christ is in them as spirit and impulse, truth and life." The insistence upon the inner life as well as the teaching on sanctification reveal significant points of contact with Anabaptism.

The slight emphasis upon organizational matters made it possible for the Michelians to remain within the state church, follow its creed, honor its public services and sacraments, recognize the office of preaching, and thus to respect the entire institution of the state church as a legal religious educative agency. A conspicuous trait is their effort to live in peace with all other creeds.

The first spread of the Hahn brotherhoods took place in Württemberg, in the regions of Cannstatt, Böblingen, and Herrenberg, principally through the personal work of the founder. These circles treasure, besides the Scripture, the works of F. Christian Oetinger and Ph. M. Hahn, but also those of Gerhard Tersteegen, the mystic poet of the Reformed Church.

About 1870 the Michelians adopted a new constitution. It embraced at that time 26 circles with 100 localities; the southernmost was in the Baar, the northernmost the cities of Frankfurt, Mannheim, Speyer, etc. In each district two conferences are held annually. Supervision and leadership are in the hands of a committee of six older brethren. In 1939 the number of adherents was estimated at 15,000. The center is the Stuttgart circle with its seat in Stuttgart.

Michael Hahn was a prolific writer. After his death in 1819 all his works were published, comprising 15 volumes. The headship of the entire brotherhood was entrusted to Anton Egeler in Nebringen; he served in this capacity until his death in 1850. He was succeeded by the schoolmaster Kolb of Dagersheim. In addition to the conferences arrangements were made for meetings of the brethren. Kolb published *Ordnung für Reisebrüder* (Directive for Traveling Brethren) on their visits to the congregations. He appointed 24 unmarried brethren and 24 substitutes for the 12 districts to visit the individual brotherhoods.

Since the Gemeinschaftsbewegung (*q.v.*) in Württemberg has taken on a new life (e.g., Liebenzell mission), trying actively to carry out its historic mission (evangelization, etc.), the Michael Hahn brotherhood plays an important role beside Old Pietism in Swabian Pietism and beyond its borders.

In the middle of the 19th century the Michelians also found their way into the Mennonite churches of Baden. In the Mennonite congregation of Dühren - Ursenbacherhof (*q.v.*) the Elder Heinrich Kaufmann received a young girl of a Protestant family into the church without rebaptism as an adult, and the council of elders of the conference of Württemberg and Baden in consequence deposed him from office in 1858. His members in large part remained loyal to him and under his leadership organized a separate congregation, which was joined by the Heimbronnerhof (*q.v.*) congregation, and in 1900 by Bretten. The division was complete.

The two small congregations do not rebaptize persons coming into the brotherhood from the state church, but recognize infant baptism. From the beginning they conducted Sunday afternoon Bible study, in which members of the other churches participated, whereas only their own members attended the Sunday morning services.

The Michelian custom of two brethren preaching at each service, based on the sending out of Christ's disciples two by two, was also adopted by these two churches; furthermore, they remain seated while preaching. The connection with the Michelians was personal, not official. The preachers of these two Mennonite churches took part in the conferences of the Michelian group, and the latter participated in the Sunday afternoon services of the Mennonites.

Connections between the two groups were maintained alive by the later elders and preachers, especially Heinrich Musselmann of the Ursenbacherhof and Heinrich Kaufmann in Dühren (d. 1920). Later the contacts became rare.   W.F.

D. Haug, *Die Sekte der Michelianer nach ihrer Lehre und ihrem Verhältnis zu anderen pietistischen Partheien in Württemberg* (Stuttgart, 1839); *Die Hahnische Gemeinschaft, ihre Entstehung und seitherige Entwicklung* (Stuttgart, 1877); C. Grüneisen, "Abriss einer Geschichte der religiösen Gemeinschaften in Württemberg," in *Ztscht für die historische Theologie,* 1841; ML III, 124-26.

Michelsburg (not Michelsberg, as is often found in Loserth and Wolkan), a castle in Tirol, Austria, near St. Lorenzen in the Puster Valley, about 3 miles from Bruneck, in a district of the same name, which, though small, played a significant part in the Anabaptist movement.

As early as 1527 we hear of confiscations of the property of Anabaptists who fled the country. In December 1527 the warden of Michelsburg received orders from the Brixen authorities, who held the castle in lease, to be on the lookout for Anabaptists coming from the region of Venice, since there were some among them "who preach Anabaptism in corners." A year later the judge of Michelsburg searched for Anabaptists, who apparently escaped. The Brixen authorities ordered them pursued, and on April 27, 1529, the Michelsburg warden, Balthasar Gerhard, managed to arrest five Anabaptists, including the leader in the district, Gregor Weber of Pflaurenz, preacher and trusted friend of Jakob Hutter (*q.v.*). Soon afterward eight additional brethren and sisters fell into his hands, whom he delivered to Brixen for trial. Thus an exchange of correspondence took place between the authorities in Innsbruck and the authorities of Brixen. Innsbruck considered it an infringement on its rights for Brixen to try these important cases, but finally granted that in case of emergency it would be permissible. Later dispute arose concerning the property confiscated from Anabaptists in Brixen territory, which Innsbruck thought should be turned over to the national coffers. Brixen usually had to yield.

The cross-examination of the Anabaptists arrested at Michelsburg revealed that there were numerous other Anabaptists there. Some of them escaped, but Kaspar Mayrpaulle, Wilhelm Sambsfeuer, Marx in der Au, a Rader woman and three other women fell into the hands of the authorities. Weber, Mayrpaulle, and the Rader woman were burned at the stake on June 17, and Sambsfeuer beheaded. A great crowd watched the execution, including two brothers of Weber; the widow of an earlier martyr took the occasion to become an Anabaptist and have herself arrested. The others were kept for months in a vile dungeon full of vermin waiting to hear from Innsbruck whether they should be taken there for trial, Innsbruck having said Brixen should pass sentence on its own Anabaptists. The prisoners were taken back to Michelsburg and released upon promise to leave the district.

In December again two men and four women of the Anabaptists were arrested. The warden Gerhard wished to deal leniently with them, but was reprimanded by Brixen, blamed for the spread of the Anabaptist movement, and ordered to spare neither money nor effort to wipe them out. Thereupon Gerhard arrested so many that the new prison in the Michelsburg overflowed, and some had to be sent to Bruneck for trial, though the sentence had to be passed in Michelsburg. After several had been executed, some declared themselves willing to return to the church; they were required to recant from the pulpit on three successive Sundays, and promise not to leave the district for three years and never to leave Tirol. Some were also apparently converted by the pastor of St. Lorenz, among them a sister of Jakob Hutter. But other Anabaptist missionaries and preachers continued to appear. To gain control of the situation Gerhard assessed each person who gave them lodging a fine of 50 florins. Innsbruck, however, objected to his taking the money for himself, and reduced the fine by half.

The struggle with the Anabaptists was taken up with new vigor when Christoph Ochs became the judge of Michelsburg in 1531. He received the highest praise from the local as well as the Innsbruck authorities, and was frequently called to give reports or advice on the situation. He made special efforts to seize backsliders, and dealt most severely with them. Two of these, Georg Schräffl of Rungen and his servant, were executed in the summer of 1531, and other "simple-minded folk" were released after they recanted. In January 1532 Gerhard was reprimanded for negligence; this led to the arrest and probable execution in February of Michel Ebner and his servant.

The records give a graphic account of the activities of Jakob Hutter, Hans Amon (*q.v.*), and Georg Fasser (*q.v.*) at this time in the region. A surprise visit by Ochs and his henchmen to Huber's home at Getzenburg on the evening of Feb. 21 found only children in the house, but food cooked for many people. Likewise a few days later, of 40 persons assembled for "the breaking of bread," only seven were seized, the rest, including Hutter, escaping. In June Innsbruck demanded more strenuous efforts, for it was learned from the confession of Friedrich Brandenburger, who had meanwhile been executed, that Hutter was staying near by with a peasant "called Pirker in the castle of Michelsburg," and had held meetings. In addition, migrations to Moravia were increasing.

Then Ochs began to use spies, one of whom succeeded in gaining the confidence of the Brethren so completely that they took him to a meeting at Getzenberg and even offered to baptize him. But before he was able to notify Ochs, most of them had fled, only five falling into his hands. One of these, Ottilie Luckner, was released on the ground of many petitions sent in for her; but she at once returned to the Brethren and was again arrested by Ochs with four others. Of these at least one, Andreas Zimmerman, was put to death, and perhaps others also. The court records again give a clear picture of the fearless work of the missionaries from Moravia. While the above were still on trial, Ochs surprised six Anabaptists in a gorge and seized three of them. It was reported that they met in droves at Getzenberg. One of their preachers, Jorg Fasser, preached to groups of as many as thirty. During October Ochs often lay in wait on the Kniepasshof next to the forest, where Hans Amon had spent a day in hiding with 20 brethren and sisters and even held a meeting. But again Ochs arrived an hour too late! Nevertheless he succeeded in seizing four brethren, one of whom, Christoph Schuhknecht, was the son of Andreas Zimmermann, who had been executed shortly before. He and two of his companions and Valentin Luckner, who had been arrested before, were beheaded after Oct. 20, 1532.

All of these measures were unavailing, though one of Och's spies was a pretended Anabaptist. In December 1533 Brixen reported to Innsbruck that the entire district was full of Anabaptists. The people, instead of obeying the edicts against sheltering them, assisted them and their missionaries. Even the warden of Neuhaus was protecting them. But when Gerhard and Ochs arrived to make arrests, the Anabaptists, who had been freely going in and out of Neuhaus, had fled. Very few were added to the four brethren in the dungeon of Michelsburg in February 1534.

Michelsburg is not again mentioned in the court records until 1536, the year of the great persecution. Ochs arrested the daughter Anna of the judge of Schöneck, who was the wife of a prominent citizen. He held her under arrest in his home because of her station, then on government orders, "that there be no murmuring among the people," put her into the castle. At her trial she was at first steadfast, but then on her father's plea recanted. She was pardoned at her own request and because of feminine "silliness."

A Moravian missionary, Kasper Huber, seized in early 1537, stated that Offerus Griesinger (q.v.) was considered the leader of the Anabaptists of Tirol and established many contacts between the Tirol and Moravia. In the same year Hans Grünfelder (q.v.) died, who had formerly gathered and cared for the Anabaptists in Michelsburg. The government notified Gerhard that there were many Ana-

baptists in the Puster Valley. In spite of increased watchfulness Offerus came to the Puster Valley in June 1538 to gather a group for Moravia. When Ochs discovered this, he had all the bridges and passes guarded while his men searched the countryside. Offerus escaped, but Martin of Villgraten (q.v.) and Kaspar Schuster were caught and beheaded in Michelsburg.

In 1538 Bernhard, Cardinal of Trient, ordered the pastor of St. Lorenzen to devote all his energy to the eradication of the sectarians. Just at this time an exciting incident occurred in Michelsburg. Agnes von Waldhofen, a widow belonging to an old noble family, took all her cash and jewels and her little daughter to join the Brethren in Moravia. In spite of all precaution by local and higher authorities to prevent her leaving the country she apparently made her way successfully to Moravia. But in the region of Lüsen (q.v.) Ochs arrested the wife of the Anabaptist leader Lienhard with two others. The government put an increased number of men at the disposal of Ochs to reach the most outlying parts of the district. The records of Ambras of 1540 tell of three Anabaptists of the Puster Valley who were condemned to serve on the galleys, but recanted and were pardoned.

The greater the pressure of persecution, the greater became the wish of the steadfast brethren to emigrate to Moravia. In April 1544 orders were given by Brixen to guard the roads and bridges, especially at night, in order to prevent the entry of missionaries. The orders were not too strictly obeyed, for in September a group of Michelsburg citizens was arrested in Bavaria en route to Moravia. In 1548 some left from Mühlbach, in 1553 from Bruneck. Four years later a transport from this region fell into arrest at the end of their journey on the Danube. But the movement continued in Michelsburg. In 1561 Gregor Prunner confessed that he had "gone about in the forest" and gathered his brethren.

In 1582 a mandate of Bishop Johann Thomas again complains about the increase of the Anabaptists in the Puster Valley. In August 1591 it became the scene of an execution. Georg Wenger, "one of the most active of the Anabaptists," had been seized in St. Lorenzen and tried after 30 days' imprisonment. The authorities were determined to find out who had sheltered him. But he refused to give any information, saying that he would not betray even an enemy, much less a friend. On Aug. 27, he was delivered to Michelsburg. Here he was racked so badly that the wounds were visible for 13 weeks. After two weeks he was lodged in a vermin-infested cell in Brixen. He had to keep his head covered to protect it from the scorpions. But he defied all force as well as the attempts of the clergy to convert him. He was executed at St. Lorenzen on Aug. 5, 1592.

The list of martyrs of the Hutterian chronicles records a total of 48 executions in the Puster Valley, half of them at Michelsburg.

Still the communications between Michelsburg and Moravia did not cease. In 1602, on the basis of statements made by a brother seized on his return to Moravia, a search was made in the valley for those who had lodged him, and in 1604 several persons were arrested on suspicion of being Anabaptists. P.DE.

F. A. Sinnacher, *Beiträge zur Gesch. der bisch. Kirche in Säben und Brixen* VII (Brixen, 1830); J. v. Kripp, *Ein Beitrag zur Gesch. der Wiedertäufer in Tirol* (*Programm*, Innsbruck, 1847); Beck, *Geschichts-Bücher;* J. Loserth, *Anabaptismus;* H. Ammann, *Die Wiedertäufer in Michelsburg und deren Urgichten* (*Programm*, Brixen, 1896); Wolkan, *Geschicht-Buch; Chronik;* G. Loesche, *Tirolensia, Täufertum und Protestantismus* (Leipzig, 1926); *ML* III, 126-29.

Michelsdorf and **Urszulin**, two villages, a mile apart, located approximately thirty miles northeast of the Polish town of Lublin, were the center of a Swiss-Volhynian Amish Mennonite congregation *ca.* 1795-1837. The Mennonites who settled in Urszulin and Michelsdorf came from Montbéliard, France, leaving there in 1791 and proceeding eastward upon the invitation of the Polish Prince Adam Czartoryski. Known members of the party were Moses Gering, Johann Graber, Johann Lichti, Peter Kaufman (wife Elisabeth Graber), Anna Roth, Christ Graber (wife Marie), and Christen Stucky (wife Marie). There may have been others in the party, possibly including someone with the name of Flückinger.

Although the group may have proceeded directly to Urszulin, there is some evidence that they spent a few years in the Russian province of Podolia, possibly near Adampol. Sometime before 1800 and maybe as early as 1795, they located in Urszulin, and soon also in Michelsdorf. Joseph Mündlein, of the Galician Mennonite settlements, joined the group soon after their arrival and is known to have been its elder in 1802. The group was reinforced in 1797 by a few Swiss Amish Mennonite families who had unsuccessfully attempted to join the Hutterite colony at Vishenka on the Desna River in the northern Ukraine. Never fully satisfied with the productivity of the land, the larger part of the Urszulin-Michelsdorf settlement moved to the village of Poutschy (Eduardsdorf) in Volhynia about 1815. The remaining members left in 1837 for Horodyszcze, Volhynia.

The Urszulin-Michelsdorf congregation was Amish, and adhered to the Amish Discipline of 1779. In addition to Mündlein (d. 1810) church officials were Christian Graber, Christian Stucky, Johannes Flickinger, and Johan Graber. Names introduced into the Swiss-Volhynian churchbooks for the first time included Voran, Wolbert, Senner, Schwartz, Sutter, and Mauer. M.H.S.

Martin H. Schrag, "European History of the Swiss-Volhynian Mennonite Ancestors of Mennonites now Living in Communities in Kansas and South Dakota" (unpublished Master's dissertation, 1956).

Michiel Beernaerts, an Anabaptist martyr, burned at the stake on June 18, 1559, at Antwerp, Belgium, identical with the martyr called Jelis Bernaerts (*q.v.*) in van Braght's *Martyrs' Mirror* and Gielis Bernaerts in *Offer.*

Michiel van Bruyssel, an Anabaptist martyr: see **Michiel Willems.**

Michiel Buyse (Buesse, Buerse), an Anabaptist martyr, was captured in Gent, Belgium, on Jan. 13,

1589, with Joos de Tollenaere and Josyntgen Swynts (Sijntgen Wens). "After much temptation and torment in which they constantly remained steadfast" they were condemned to die as heretics. On April 13 they were secretly hanged on a pillar in the Gravensteen castle at Gent. Then the executioner hung the corpses of the men on the gallows outside, while Sijntgen was buried beneath it. Michiel was 40 years of age, and married. By trade he was a weaver. In 1578 or 1579 he had been (re)baptized at Meenen. (*Mart. Mir.* D 764, E 1069; Verheyden, *Gent,* 68, No. 247; *ML* I, 313.) O.H.

Michiel de Cleercq, an Anabaptist martyr: see **Michiel the Widower.**

Michiel Egbertszoon, an Anabaptist, who was put to death at Amsterdam on May 14, 1535, in a cruel manner. He was one of the revolutionary Münsterites and had participated in the assault on the Amsterdam town hall on May 10-11, 1535. He was a weaver. (Grosheide, *Verhooren,* 63 f.; Mellink, *Wederdopers,* 143, 145, 164.) vDZ.

Michiel Geldoff, an Anabaptist, a barber-surgeon of Maastricht, Dutch province of Limburg. He was (re)baptized by Jan Smeitgen (*q.v.*) in an attic shortly before Christmas of 1534, was arrested on Jan. 28, 1535, with a large number of members of the Maastricht congregation, and after trial, forsaking his faith, was beheaded at Maastricht on Feb. 6, 1535. His confession is very remarkable: he accused the Catholic priests of immoral conduct; the Catholic religion he considered an invention of popes and bishops; one could be a member of the church only after conversion; he held chiliastic views concerning the kingdom of God. vDZ.

W. Bax, *Het Protestantisme in het bisdom Luik* I (The Hague, 1937) 120, **374.**

Michiel (Gerritsz), an Anabaptist martyr, burned at the stake at Breda, Dutch province of North Brabant, in August 1571 (not 1572 as is stated in *Martyrs' Mirror*). Michiel was an uncle of Cornelis de Gyselaer (*q.v.*), arrested with Michiel and executed some time before him, and was married to the widow of the martyr Valerius de Schoolmeester (*q.v.*). He refused to take an oath and during his trial and torture gave some information on his life. He had been baptized six years previously at Middelburg by Joachim de Suyckerbacker (Joachim Vermeeren, *q.v.*); he had later lived at Zierikzee and at the time of his arrest he was living at Princenhage near Breda. He possessed three books, a New Testament printed by Nicolaes Biestkens (*q.v.*), a copy of the *Offer des Heeren*, and a volume of letters by the martyr Jacob de Keersmaeckere (Jacob de Rore, *q.v.*). Michiel was apprehended with some others on Aug. 5, 1571, when a Mennonite meeting in Klundert (*q.v.*) was surprised by the officials. He remained steadfast and willingly suffered martyrdom. (*Mart. Mir.* D 603-5, E 929; *DB* 1912, 36, 42; *ML* III, 124.) vDZ.

Michiel van Houcke, a Mennonite martyr, burned at the stake at Gent, Belgium, on March 2, 1560, together with four others. Michiel was a native of Nevele, Flanders, and only 23 years of age. (Verheyden, *Gent, 26,* No. 70.)   vᴅZ.

Michiel Jans(en) was a preacher and leader of the Flemish party in the Mennonite congregation at Harlingen, Friesland, in 1566, when the Frisian-Flemish schism arose. He attacked Ebbe Pieters (*q.v.*), then the leader of the Frisian party in the congregation. Being an old man, he apparently died soon after December 1566. (*DB* 1893, 20 f., 34, 40.)
                                                    vᴅZ.

Michiel Jans(s)en, a writer of hymns, two of which, composed in 1531 and 1532, are found in the *Geestelijck Liedt-Boecxken* of David Joris (*q.v.*). (Wolkan, *Lieder,* 59; *ML* II, 391.)   vᴅZ.

Michiel Jansz(oon), a native of Oosterhout in Brabant, Netherlands, who (according to the confession of Jan van Sol at Brussels in 1550) moved from the Netherlands to Danzig, West Prussia, Germany. Here he and Thonis Barbier were "buyldrager," i.e., deacons for the care of the poor of the congregation. Shortly before 1550 he died at Elbing. He is not identical with the two foregoing Michiel Jansens. (*DB* 1917, 137.)   vᴅZ.

Michiel de Leertouwer, an Anabaptist martyr: see **Jelis Bernaerts.**

Michiel Matschilder, an Anabaptist martyr: see **Matschidl, Michael.**

Michiel N., an Anabaptist martyr, found in the 1578b edition of the *Offer des Heeren* (*Offer,* 15, 624 f.), who was executed at Gent, Belgium, in 1592, is identical with Michiel de Cleercq (Michiel the Widower, *q.v.*).   vᴅZ.

Michiel Pietersz, of Hoorn, Holland, an Anabaptist martyr, executed by beheading at Delft, Dutch province of South Holland, on Jan. 7, 1539, with 10 others. Michiel apparently was a follower of David Joris (*q.v.*). (*Inv. Arch. Amst.* I, No. 749; *DB* 1899, 158-60; 1917, 160-67.)   vᴅZ.

Michiel Ratgheers, an Anabaptist martyr, burned at the stake at Sluis, Dutch Zeeland Flanders, on March 15, 1563. Michiel, who was born in Aardenburg near Sluis, and who was a basketmaker by trade, had stayed for some time at Brugge, Belgium, where he was arrested because of Anabaptism. He recanted and was released, but later he continued to speak slightingly of the Roman Catholic sacraments, particularly the practice of infant baptism.
                                                    vᴅZ.

H. Q. Janssen, *De Kerkhervorming te Brugge* (Rotterdam, 1856) I, 11; II, 243 f., where the sentence pronounced on Michiel is found.

Michiel Seyn (Syen), an Anabaptist martyr, drowned on June 26, 1562, at the Steen castle at Antwerp, Belgium, because he had been rebaptized (by Gillis van Aken, *q.v.*) and "persisted in his rebaptism." Michiel was born at Dermonde (Dendermonde?) in Flanders and was a chair-bottomer by trade. A Mennonite family with the name Seijen (*q.v.*) or Seyen was found in Amsterdam and other

Dutch towns in the 17th and 18th centuries. (*Antw. Arch.-Bl.* IX, 137, 141; XIV, 32 f., No. 358.) vᴅZ.

Michiel Stevens of Oosterhout, a potter, an Anabaptist martyr, was beheaded at Vught near Hertogenbosch, Dutch province of North Brabant, on Sept. 9, 1538, with Jan Block of Gent and Adriaen of The Hague, both weavers. In the sentence Michiel is called "boersdreger," i.e., purse bearer; he was therefore probably a deacon who had charge of aid to poor members. (*Mart. Mir.* D 42, E 447; *DB* 1917, 189.)   vᴅZ.

Michiel Verhaghe, a Mennonite preacher or elder, active in Flanders about 1566, of whom there are no further particulars. (Verheyden, "Mennisme in Vlaanderen" Ms.)   vᴅZ.

Michiel van Waelhem, an Anabaptist martyr, sentenced by the court of Holland in The Hague (?) "to die by the sword," because he was one of the Anabaptists who had sailed for Münster and were arrested at Bergklooster (*q.v.*). (*Inv. Arch. Amst.* I, No. 745.)   vᴅZ.

Michiel the Widower (Michiel de Cleercq), an Anabaptist martyr, was seized at Gent, Flanders, Belgium, in July 1592 with Bartholomeus Panten and a sister Kalleken N. (*q.v.*). After a trial on the rack, in which they courageously confessed their faith, the men were hanged in the Gravensteen castle; Kalleken was released. The sparse information by van Braght's *Martyrs' Mirror* is considerably supplemented by the data from the official records published by Verheyden. Michiel the Widower's official name was Michiel de Cleercq. He was born about 1552 at St. Antelinks, near Aalst in Belgium. By trade he was a weaver. H. Q. Janssen (*Kerkhervorming in Vlaanderen* I, 377) lists him among the Calvinists. This is wrong. Initially he joined the Calvinists. He then lived at Sluis, Dutch Zeeland Flanders. He wanted to become a Reformed clergyman but was disqualified by the classis of Brugge (1579). From about 1581 Michiel lived at Gent, joining the Mennonite congregation in 1588. From now on, both in his firm conviction and his fearless activity, he was a strong pillar in the struggling congregation at the time when it was sorely tried by the loss of its leaders by persecution. Michiel de Cleercq and Bartholomeus Panten were the last Mennonite martyrs to die at Gent. The date of their execution was Sept. 15, 1592. (*Mart. Mir.* D 779, E 1082; Verheyden, *Gent,* 70 f., No. 250; *ML* III, 124.)   Nᴇғғ, vᴅZ.

Michiel Willems (van Braght, *Martyrs' Mirror:* Michiel van Bruyssel, i.e., Brussels in Belgium), an Anabaptist martyr, a silk weaver, who was arrested at Gent, Belgium, with his wife Barberken (Barbele Pieters, *q.v.*) in 1576 (not 1573 as stated in the *Martyrs' Mirror*). They were put to death "after manifold temptations and trials of their faith, ... not for any evil deed, but only for the obedience of the truth of Jesus Christ." Michiel was burned on July 19, 1576, at the Vrijdagsmarkt and Barberken beheaded in the Gravensteen castle. (*Mart. Mir.*

D 643, E 965; Verheyden, *Gent*, 67, No. 242; *ML* III, 124.)   NEFF, vDZ.

Michiel Zeepzieder: see **Seifensieder, Michael.**

Michielken (van) Huls(t), an Anabaptist martyr, burned at the stake at Antwerp, Belgium, on Oct. 19, 1571. She was a native of Bocholt in the territory of Cleve, Germany, and had been (re)baptized about 1553 by Leenaert Bouwens (*q.v.*) in a wood near Antwerp. Further information was not available. (*Antw. Arch.-Blad* XIII, 78 f., 162; XIV, 86 f., No. 974.)   vDZ.

Michiel(l), a bookseller of Leiden, Dutch province of South Holland, an Anabaptist martyr, (re)baptized on Nov. 25, 1534, in the home of Jacob van Wijnssen at Deventer by Hendrik Kistemaecker, was beheaded at Kempen (*q.v.*) in Overijssel on Feb. 15, 1535, with two brethren and a sister of his faith. He rejected the Catholic doctrines of the Mass and shared the views of Melchior Hofmann concerning the Incarnation. (*DB* 1875, 59, 62 f.; *ML* III, 129.)
vDZ.

Michiels, Alfred (1813-92), a French literary historian, who achieved fame in the second half of the 19th century by his important works on the history of art in Flanders, on the relations of France with Alsace-Lorraine, on the Franco-Prussian War, etc. He was born in Paris in 1813, the son of a Flemish mother and French father, studied law in Strasbourg, made a foot tour through Germany, journeyed to England and Belgium, and finally settled as a librarian in Paris.

On his travels Michiels became acquainted with the Mennonites in the Vosges, and dedicated to them a book with the title, *Les Anabaptistes des Vosges* (Paris, 1860) which went through several editions. It is a charming account, written from the point of view of a Catholic Frenchman, of a segment of Mennonite life in the Vosges. As a metropolite Michiels feels himself transported into a legendary world, when he finds on the plateau of the Salm a group who, "hostile to luxury, exciting pleasures, vanity, and ambition, lead a peaceful, happy life." Conversation with their elders and preachers reveals that they are well informed on their history: they treasure the old Anabaptist writings; excerpts from Menno Simons, the *Martyrs' Mirror*, and the Dordrecht Confession are "alive in them in every respect." This loyalty to tradition goes so far that they pattern their customs entirely on Biblical examples. Not without some inward merriment Michiels tells his Parisian friends about the marriage customs of the group. When a young man wished to marry he went to the deacon, who performed the suit like Eliezer of the Old Testament and had the nickname "Steckelmann" (*q.v.*). He swung himself upon his horse, rode to the girl's home, and asked her for a drink of water from a well. If she granted the request the Steckelmann entered the house and asked for the hand of the daughter for the young man.

If these and similar customs seemed peculiar and incomprehensible to the author and to the modern reader, the positive aspects of Mennonite separation

from the world so impressed him that he presents them as exemplary for community life: their simplicity, their wholesome, solid way of life, especially their mutual aid in cases of adversity. One who suffered misfortune through no fault of his own experienced the substantial help of the brotherhood. Only if it was apparent that he was incompetent, he and his wife had to work in subordinate positions, but their children were well provided for by the brotherhood. "Honneur donc aux Anabaptistes!" (*ML* III, 129.)   H.Q.

Michielsz, Simon, a Dutch Mennonite elder: see **Simon Michielsz.**

Michigan was admitted to the Union in 1837; it has an area of 58,216 square miles and a population of over five and a quarter million. In it live approximately 5,500 Mennonites, many of them recent converts in the Mennonite Church (MC) or the United Missionary Church (UMC). By the close of the Civil War (1865) Mennonites (MC) were living in three counties of Michigan: (1) Barker Street (*q.v.*) had been established in St. Joseph County in 1863 and lasted a little over sixty years before it disintegrated; it never had more than 64 members. (2) Branch County was the seat of the Pleasant Hill congregation established in 1865, the home church of the well-known Bishop C. D. Beery (1815-78). Pleasant Hill was rather weak by the time of the Brenneman division of 1874, and eventually the Mennonite Brethren in Christ (now UMC) took up the work at Pleasant Hill and have built it up to a membership (1955) of 104. (3) Kent County contained two congregations, Caledonia (*q.v.*) established in 1864, which remained rather weak numerically until its dissolution a half century later; and Bowne (*q.v.*) established in 1865 and having in 1955 a membership of 104. Resident bishops of the Bowne congregation were John P. Speicher (1833-94), ordained preacher in 1867 and bishop in 1869; Bishop Jacob P. Miller (1850-1927), who moved from White Cloud to Bowne in July 1911 and lived there until March 1916; and T. E. Schrock, ordained preacher at Bowne in 1931 and bishop in 1936. Before 1879 these were the only counties in Michigan which contained established Mennonite congregations, although individual families were located in various other counties, who were often visited by traveling preachers such as John M. Brenneman of Ohio, and John F. Funk and Daniel Brenneman of Elkhart County, Ind. In 1880 a preacher Cornelius Unruh with a small flock of 25 members was living in Okemos, Ingham Co., Mich., and another small group at Hammond in Kent County was hoping to build a meetinghouse. In 1880 a settlement was begun in Antrim County at Mancelona. Some Mennonites (MC) were also living in Mecosta County at a place called Wheatland. About the same time a number of Ontario Mennonite families settled in Tuscola County, but within a few decades most of them moved away. One of the last residents was Daniel Lehman, preacher of Fairgrove, Tuscola County, who died about 1922.

Between 1879 and 1899 three permanent settlements were made in Emmet, Huron, and Newaygo

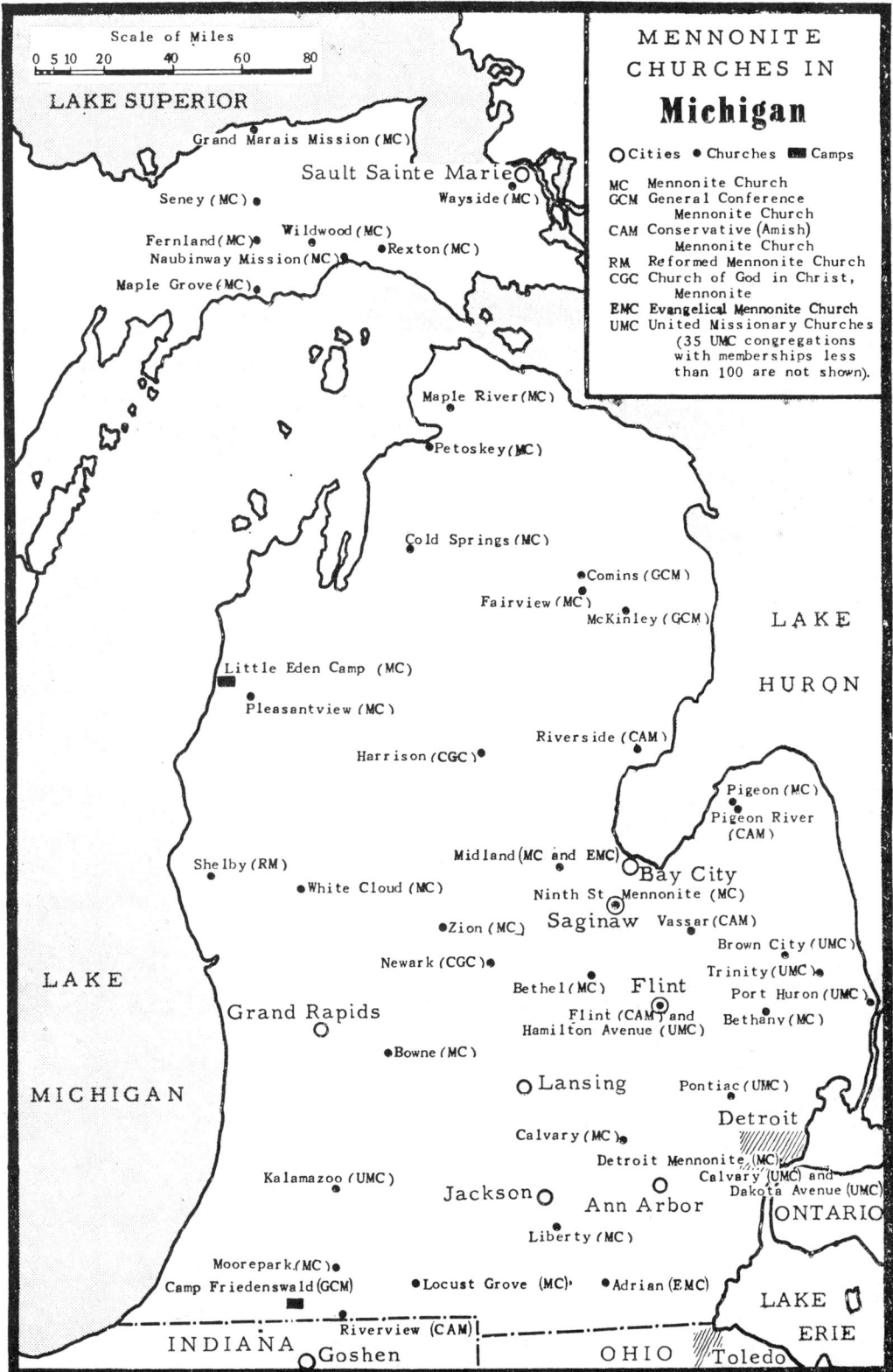

MENNONITE CHURCHES IN **Michigan**

◯ Cities ● Churches ◼ Camps

MC   Mennonite Church
GCM General Conference Mennonite Church
CAM Conservative (Amish) Mennonite Church
RM   Reformed Mennonite Church
CGC Church of God in Christ, Mennonite
EMC Evangelical Mennonite Church
UMC United Missionary Churches (35 UMC congregations with memberships less than 100 are not shown).

Scale of Miles
0 5 10 20 40 60 80

LAKE SUPERIOR

Grand Marais Mission (MC)
Sault Sainte Marie
Seney (MC)
Wayside (MC)
Fernland (MC)   Wildwood (MC)
Naubinway Mission (MC)   Rexton (MC)
Maple Grove (MC)

Maple River (MC)

Petoskey (MC)

Cold Springs (MC)

Comins (GCM)
Fairview (MC)
McKinley (GCM)

LAKE HURON

Little Eden Camp (MC)
Pleasantview (MC)

Riverside (CAM)

Harrison (CGC)

Pigeon (MC)
Pigeon River (CAM)

Shelby (RM)
White Cloud (MC)

Midland (MC and EMC)
Bay City
Ninth St. Mennonite (MC)
Zion (MC)
Saginaw   Vassar (CAM)

Newark (CGC)
Bethel (MC)   Flint
Brown City (UMC)
Trinity (UMC)
Port Huron (UMC)
Flint (CAM) and Hamilton Avenue (UMC)
Bethany (MC)

Grand Rapids

Bowne (MC)

MICHIGAN

LAKE MICHIGAN

Lansing
Pontiac (UMC)
Detroit
Calvary (MC)
Detroit Mennonite (MC)
Kalamazoo (UMC)
Jackson
Ann Arbor
Calvary (UMC) and Dakota Avenue (UMC)
ONTARIO
Liberty (MC)

Moorepark (MC)
Camp Friedenswald (GCM)
Locust Grove (MC)
Adrian (EMC)
LAKE ERIE

Riverview (CAM)

INDIANA   Goshen   OHIO   Toledo

counties. The Maple River congregation near Brutus in Emmet County was established in 1879 and led by Abraham W. Detweiler (1828-1912), who was originally of Ontario, but had left the Caledonia congregation to start a colony in Emmet County. Because of Detweiler's leadership the congregation itself was often called Detweiler's (*q.v.*). About 1886 there was a division in the congregation parallel to the Wisler schism (*q.v.*) in Indiana of 1871, and Detweiler went with the conservatives (Wisler's Old Order Mennonites). This Wisler congregation, although its establishment greatly weakened the other portion of the congregation, was destined to live for only half a century. In 1921 a number of these Wisler families returned to the congregation which was a part of the Indiana-Michigan Conference (MC). After the division of 1886 Bishop Henry Shaum of Indiana went to Maple River and ordained 1887 Christian Detweiler (1845-1917) to the ministry, but the congregation grew progressively weaker. In 1912 seven members communed, and in 1919 three. The District Mission Board (MC) then arranged for the ordination of Clyde X. Kauffman of Indiana, and in 1921 he located in the Brutus area and attempted to revive the congregation. In a few years he had over 50 members, but later the membership dropped back to 25. In 1952 Earl Hartman of the Olive Church in Indiana was ordained to serve at Maple River; he moved to Brutus in 1954, and in 1955 was made pastor of the congregation, which in that year numbered 64.

In 1894 the Berne (now Pigeon) congregation (MC) was organized in Huron County, Mich. Mennonite families began to move into the area about 1888, and the first services were held in a private home in 1890. The first meetinghouse was built in 1897. That same year Peter Ropp (1864-1944) was ordained preacher; he served at Pigeon until 1923 when he moved to Imlay City (where he was ordained bishop in 1926). Pigeon was in the Ontario Conference until 1916 when it became affiliated with Indiana-Michigan (MC). Later pastors were S. J. Miller and Donald E. King, who was ordained bishop in 1957. The present membership is 98.

The original settlers in Newaygo County came largely from the Shore congregation (MC) in Indiana; they located near White Cloud in 1897-99. The group started a Sunday school the first year, and in 1899 Bishop P. Y. Lehman (1836-1925) of Indiana organized the congregation. In 1900 John F. Funk (*q.v.*) ordained Jacob P. Miller (1850-1927) as preacher, and in 1901 P. Y. Lehman ordained Miller as bishop. (Ten years later, in July 1911, Miller moved to Bowne, Kent Co., Mich.) The long-time pastor of the White Cloud congregation (formerly called Union) was T. U. Nelson (1870-1950), who was ordained in 1909. The present pastor is Edward D. Jones, who has been a preacher since 1935, and the membership (1955) is 75. The meetinghouse was partly destroyed by fire Dec. 25, 1956.

In 1900-20 five additional Mennonite congregations (MC) were established in Michigan by colonization. Largest of all the Mennonite congregations of Michigan (MC) is Fairview (*q.v.*) with its 401 members in 1955. Amish Mennonite settlers from Indiana began to locate in Oscoda County in 1900.

In 1903 Eli A. Bontrager (1861-1956), preacher of the West Market Street (Nappanee) congregation, moved to Fairview, and the next year Bishop D. J. Johns (*q.v.*) of Goshen, Ind., organized the Fairview congregation with 35 charter members. In 1906 Menno Esch was ordained as a preacher, and in 1909 as bishop. In 1952 Esch ordained Harvey Handrich as bishop. Sentiment against the nonresistance of the Fairview Mennonites during World War I led to the burning of the meetinghouse of 1904 during the night of April 4, 1918, but a new church was immediately erected in its place, and was ready for use, first in the basement only, by January 1919.

Mennonite settlers began moving into Manistee County in 1903, and the next year Bishop E. A. Mast (1856-1932) of the Howard-Miami congregation in Indiana, from which the settlers had come, organized a congregation which was named Pleasantview. The first meetings were held in a log cabin, but in 1906 the church erected a new meetinghouse. Among the pastors who served the congregation were Joseph S. Horner (1864-1945) 1903-11, and Claude C. Culp (1893-1953) 1919-53. The present (1956) pastor is Warren C. Shaum, and the membership is 29.

Mennonite settlers from the Emma congregation (MC) in Indiana began to locate in Midland County in 1910, and three years later the District Mission Board placed William Haarer there as a licensed pastor. He remained three years. In 1916-38 Eli A. Bontrager (1861-1956) was a minister at the Midland Church. In 1926 his son Floyd was ordained preacher, and in 1934 bishop. The congregation purchased an old lodge hall and moved it onto their church lot in 1917 for use as a meetinghouse. In 1928 the congregation built a new meetinghouse. The present (1955) pastor is Clarence R. Yoder, and the membership is 134.

Mennonite families began to locate at Imlay City in Lapeer County in 1917. Some came from the Pigeon congregation in Huron County, others from other places including Ontario. One of the settlers was Peter Ropp (1864-1944), a preacher formerly of the Pigeon congregation. The Imlay City congregation was organized in 1918. In 1926 Ropp was ordained bishop. Paul A. Wittrig, the present pastor, was ordained in 1938. The membership in 1955 was 35.

The last Mennonite Church (MC) to be established in Michigan by direct colonization was the Bethel congregation near Ashley in Gratiot County. The settlers came from the large Amish Mennonite churches in Illinois beginning in 1918. Sunday school was organized in 1920, and church services were inaugurated later that same year by Bishop George H. Summer (1871-1937), who had been ordained preacher by the Waldo congregation in Illinois in 1906 and bishop there two years later. Summer located at Ashley in 1920. The meetinghouse was built in 1922. Daniel S. Oyer (1882-1954) served as deacon of the congregation 1923-42, when he was ordained bishop, serving 1942-d.54. The present (1955) pastor is John M. Landis, and the membership is 134.

The remaining churches and mission stations of

the Mennonites (MC) in Michigan have all been established since 1937 with the exception of Detroit (1926). In 1937-52 eleven mission stations were established in the Upper Peninsula of Michigan; these stations now have a total of 190 members (1955). Ten other stations and congregational outposts were established in Lower Michigan in 1941-55 with a membership of a little over 400 counting Detroit (which was established in 1926). The largest of these is Locust Grove in St. Joseph County with 192 members, an outpost of the Shore congregation in Lagrange County, Ind. The total membership (MC) of the ten Michigan independent congregations (not under another congregation or a mission board), those with full status in Conference, is 1,272, and the remaining 17 outposts and mission stations have 444 members, a total for the state of 1,716 Mennonite (MC) members. Only six congregations have a membership of approximately one hundred or above.

The General Conference Mennonites are represented by one congregation and one mission station in Michigan, Comins and McKinley. The congregation at Comins in Oscoda County resulted from the energy and vision of F. F. Stutesman, formerly of the Mennonite Church (MC), who started a Sunday school in Comins after a Methodist Sunday school had died. Stutesman's Sunday school was a union or nondenominational effort, but was apparently attended by a number of Mennonite families which were living in the area and which had been worshiping with the Methodists. Stutesman became sufficiently concerned to see a Mennonite church started that he came to Middlebury in 1924 to interview Emanuel Troyer, the field secretary of the Central Conference Mennonites (since 1945 merged with the General Conference Mennonites). Troyer held a series of meetings at Comins the fall of 1924, and the next summer Troyer and Allen Yoder organized the Mennonites of the area into a congregation. In the late summer of 1925 the Comins Mennonite Church was accepted as a member of the Central Conference of Mennonites. That same year the Comins congregation built its first church building. In 1927 H. E. Nunemaker accepted the pastorate. By 1927 the membership was 26. In 1955 the pulpit was supplied by Howard Johnson of Fairview, and the membership had risen to 173. The McKinley Mission (GCM), southeast of Fairview in Oscoda County, was established in 1951 and the membership in 1955 was three.

The Old Order Amish began to settle in Oscoda County, Mich., in 1900. They came from Geauga County, Ohio, and other locations. But the Amish seem not to have been permanently successful in Oscoda County. By 1955 the membership had dwindled to 20, and the remaining members no longer had any ordained men to care for them. Since 1925 the Amish have established a colony in St. Joseph County in southern Michigan, around Centerville. Here they have three districts with a total of 146 members (1955). There are also some Amish families in the Stoll District at Jerome, Hillsdale Co., Mich.

Historically the Evangelical Mennonites were not represented in Michigan but they now have two small congregations, Adrian and Midland. The First Mennonite Church (EMC) of Adrian (q.v.) in Lenawee County (north of Wauseon, Ohio) was organized in 1949; in 1954 it had a membership of 34. The Midland congregation in Midland County is even younger, having been founded in 1953. In 1955 it had a membership of 28.

The Reformed Mennonites (q.v.) are represented in Michigan by only one congregation, the Shelby Mennonite Church in Oceana County. It was established in the years immediately following the Civil War, a little before 1870. It has not prospered. The 1955 membership is approximately 50. The ministers are Omar Near and Lawrence Zimmerman. About 1900 a second Reformed Mennonite congregation was established at Rochester in Oakland County near Detroit, but it died in the 1930's.

When John Holdeman (q.v.), founder of the Church of God in Christ, Mennonite, wrote his English *History of the Church of God* (1876), he reported that his group had spread to "Canada, Michigan, Iowa, Missouri, Kansas, Virginia, and Maryland, and is still increasing more and more" (p. 241). Eighty years later, however, the CGC group was represented in Michigan by only two congregations, Newark in Gratiot County, and Harrison in Clare County. Newark was established as a congregation in 1890 and has prospered; the membership stands at 285 in 1955. Meetinghouses were built in 1903 and 1920, and the latter enlarged in 1947 and again in 1953. The Harrison (q.v.) congregation in Clare County was established in 1912, and has a membership of 59.

The Old Order or Wisler Mennonites no longer have any members in Michigan. As was noted above, the Maple River or Detweiler congregation (q.v.) near Brutus in Emmet County divided about 1886. Even prior to the division at Brutus, however, Jacob Wisler had ordained Jonathan Gehman to the ministry. A later preacher was Henry Brenneman. The bishop, Daniel G. Brubaker, originally of Ontario—he settled at Brutus before his marriage and later brought a bride from Ontario—was still living in 1957, an aged man of about 90. (His home is now at Elverson, Pa.) The two groups, M.C. and O.O.M., alternated in the use of the meetinghouse. For a number of decades the Wisler congregation was the stronger of the two, the number of attendants about 1920 often being in the neighborhood of 80 or 90. But in 1921 some of the Wisler families began to unite with the M.C. congregation and others moved to various communities. About 1936, fifty years after its founding, the Wisler services ceased at Brutus. In another decade or so the last member had died.

The group with the largest number of members in Michigan is the United Missionary Church, formerly M.B.C., although as their historian J. A. Huffman writes, they have "but little Mennonite stock." The first mission stations were started in Huron and Lapeer counties in the "thumb" of Michigan in 1880. The first meetinghouses were built in 1884. In rapid succession a series of missions was founded: Grand Rapids (1897), Caro (1900), St. Clair (1903), Bad Axe (1903), Port Huron (1903), Flint (1904), Pontiac (1908), etc. Some stations have died out, but the general movement has been definitely forward. The Michigan Conference was organized in 1920 and includes twenty congregations with 1,110 members. The chain of eighteen congregations across southern Michigan belongs to the Indiana Conference (UMC) and embraces a total of 1,004 members. The following five U.M.C. congregations in Michigan have over 100 members: Brown City in Sanilac County, 132; Port Huron in St. Clair County, 165; Calvary in Detroit, 111; Dakota Avenue in Detroit, 264; and Pleasant Hill in Branch County (originally MC), 104.

The Conservative Mennonites (CAM) are represented in Michigan by three well-established congregations with a total of 602 members (1955): Pigeon River in Huron County, which began about 1902 and now has 270 members (1955); the Riverside congregation at Au Gres in Arenac County, founded about 1911 and now having 100 members; and the Riverview congregation in St. Joseph County near White Pigeon, established as an extension of the C.A.M. settlement in the vicinity of Middlebury, Ind., with a membership of 174. The mission in Flint was founded in 1929, and now has 39 members; the mission in Vassar (1938) had 15 members in 1955; and the Mount Morris mission north of Flint (Genesee County) has four members; it was established in 1951. The Fairhaven mission at Sebewaing (southwest Pigeon, Huron Co.), founded in 1938, and the National City mission, Iosco County, have as yet no resident membership. The oldest and chief congregation, Pigeon River, was host to the first session of the Conservative A.M. Conference (q.v.) in 1910. Emanuel Swartzendruber (1893-), its present bishop, ordained preacher in 1934, and bishop in 1944, has oversight of all the Conservative congregations and missions in Michigan except Riverview, where Orie Kauffman is in charge.

The Missionary Church Association was founded in 1898 as a schism from the Defenseless Mennonite Church, now Evangelical Mennonite Church (q.v.). That very year an M.C.A. congregation was founded in Elkton, Mich. In 1918-47 the following nine mission stations and/or congregations were established: Eastlawn in Detroit (1918), East Detroit (1923), Roseville, northeast of Detroit (1929), Royal Oak, north of Detroit (1937), Flint (1940), East Lansing (1940), Jackson (1945), Sturgis (1945), and Loomis (1947). By 1954 there were 14 M.C.A. congregations in Michigan including Augusta, northeast of Kalamazoo (1954), Bad Axe in Huron County, east of Pigeon (1952-53), Battle Creek in Calhoun County (1953), Clare in Clare County some fifty miles northwest of Saginaw, and Wayne, a few miles southwest of Detroit (1952-53). There are also (1954) two unorganized M.C.A. congregations or mission stations in Michigan; viz., Midland, and Mt. Clemens, northeast of Detroit. When the Missionary Church Association began to appoint district superintendents in 1909, Michigan was one of nine districts given a superintendent. The three states, Michigan, Ohio, and Pennsylvania, now constitute (1954) the Eastern District, a territory with the following organized congregations: Michigan, 14; Ohio, 11; and Pennsylvania, 3. These 28 churches, plus Michigan's two unorganized churches, have a total membership of 1,432.

One other related denomination is represented in Michigan, the Brethren in Christ (q.v.), a group founded by Jacob Engel (q.v.) about the close of the Revolutionary War. This body is represented in Michigan by seven small congregations founded since 1880, most of the meetinghouses having been built in 1915-35. The membership of these churches totaled 153 in 1954. These congregations have all been under the care of Bishop E. J. Swalm of Duntroon, Ont., since 1954 because of the advanced age of the previous leader, Henry Schneider of Merrill, Mich., who now has the status of bishop emeritus.

The successful colonies of Mennonites in Michigan have not been numerous. The state has rather proved to be the "mission field" for the various groups of Mennonites in Indiana. Four bodies, M.C. (1,716 members), U.M.C. (2,114 members), C.G.C. (344 members), and C.A.M. (602 members), constitute over 85 per cent of all the Mennonites in the state. Indeed, two of these, the M.C. and the U.M.C., together comprise about 70 per cent of the total.

J.C.W.

A. W. Climenhaga, *History of the Brethren in Christ Church* (Nappanee, 1942); John Holdeman, *A History of the Church of God* (Newton, 1876 and 1938); J. A. Huffman, *History of the Mennonite Brethren in Christ Church* (New Carlisle, 1920); W. H. Lugibihl and J. F. Gerig, *The Missionary Church Association* (Berne, 1950); W. B. Weaver, *History of the Central Conference Mennonite Church* (Danvers, 1926); *ML* III, 129 f.

Michigan Conference *of the United Missionary Church* was organized in 1896 as a mission conference under the Ontario Conference, later becoming an independent conference. The earliest congregations in the district had been formed as the result of the work of a young Canadian convert, Peter Cober, and Daniel Brenneman. Other early workers were Samuel Shirk, D. U. Lambert, and J. Schlichter. The first presiding elder was E. O. Anthony. In 1954 the conference had 43 congregations and mission stations, with a total membership of 2,049, of which 16 congregations with 964 members were in the South District, 24 congregations with 1,038 members were in the North District, and 3 unorganized churches had 47 members; most of the churches are small, the following 5 having more than 100 members each: Detroit (Dakota Ave.) 243, Port Huron 177, Brown City 126, Yale Trinity 123, Pontiac 106.

H.S.B.

Michigan Mennonite Mutual Auto Aid, a mutual insurance association for members of the Mennonite (MC) and Conservative Mennonite churches in Michigan, covering damage to automobiles in accidents, organized at Fairview, Mich., in 1939, with 150 members in 1953.

H.S.B.

Micronius, Martinus (*Marten de Cleyne*) (*ca.* 1522-59), a Reformed theologian of the Reformation period, studied at the University of Basel under Bullinger (q.v.), who influenced him deeply. In 1550 he became pastor of the Dutch congregation in London, which was under the leadership of John á Lasco (q.v.). When it became difficult for him to stay here under Queen Mary, he and his group in 1553 sought a new home in Denmark, in Wismar, Lübeck, and Hamburg. He was rejected everywhere by the strict Lutherans. After a short stay in Emden he became pastor in Norden in 1554, and died there on Sept. 12, 1559.

In Wismar Micronius met Menno Simons. The Mennonites living here received the refugees with sympathy and willingness to help them. Soon they were engaged in religious disputations, in which Hermes Backereel wished to represent the refugees in debating with Menno Simons, who had been living here in concealment. After the first meeting Micronius was called from Emden. In the discussion of disputed points on Feb. 6, 1554, Micronius expressed his surprise that Menno's concept of the Incarnation was not among these topics. Then it was discussed for eleven hours, after which they ate a meal together. On Feb. 15 the discussion on the Incarnation was continued in the home of a Mennonite. This time the debate became so heated that Micronius and his party were finally driven out. Their relations with the refugees had an unhappy result for the Mennonites. Micronius reported that Menno was living in Wismar and that the government was tolerating Anabaptists. This ungrateful recompense for the fraternal care they had given the refugees upon their arrival worried Menno deeply. It also made it necessary for Menno to leave Wismar; he took up residence in Fresenburg in 1554.

Micronius as well as Menno published an exact report on the course of the two debates. On June 18, 1556, appeared Micronius' booklet, *Een waeraechtigh verhaal der t'zammensprekinghe tusschen Menno Simons en Martinus Mikron van der Menschwerdinghe Jesu Christi*, to which Menno replied with *Een gants duytlick en bescheyden antwoort* . . . Oct. 15, and *Een seer hertgrontlijck Sentbrief aen M. Micron* . . . of Sept. 16, 1556 (Menno Simons, *Opera*, 1681, 543-618). The discussion was closed with Micronius' *Een apologie of verandtwoordinghe* . . . in 1558. A first edition of each of Micronius' works is found in the Amsterdam Mennonite Library. C.K.

J. H. Gerretsen, *Micronius, zijn leven, zijn geschriften, zijn geestesrichting* (Nijmegen, 1895); S. Cramer, article in *Theol. Tijdschrift*, 1896, 304 ff.; F. Pijper, in *BRN* I, 421 ff.; *HRE; RGG;* K. Vos, *Menno Simons* (Leiden, 1914); J. Horsch, *Menno Simons* (Scottdale, 1916); C. Krahn, *Menno Simons* (Karlsruhe, 1936); *ML* III, 130 f.

Middelburg, capital of the Dutch province of Zeeland (pop. 21,500), has since very early times been the seat of an Anabaptist congregation with a rich history. Already in 1532 the magistrate had learned that there were Anabaptists in the city. He searched for a "Melchiorite" Jan Matthijsz Blauwaert (Jan the Goldsmith, not to be confused with Jan Matthijsz of Haarlem, of Münsterite notoriety) and four others because they were sowing the Melchiorite seed among the simple populace. Between 1535 and 1571 at least 18 Anabaptists were put to death here. Jan Everts (*q.v.*) was beheaded on April 19, 1535, and in the same year Marcus Cornelisz (*q.v.*) and Cop Heyne (*q.v.*); the latter had been a Münsterite, but was converted at Amsterdam. Of Münsterite ideas there is no further trace among the Anabaptists of Middelburg. Marcus Cornelisz declared that neither he nor the others had anything to do with them. The people were obviously on the side of the martyrs. Gillis Matthijsz (*q.v.*), a surgeon, was executed in the prison one night in 1564, for fear of the populace. Other martyrs executed at Middelburg were Maeyken Daniels, Jan Hendricksz, Andries van Laerbeke, all in 1559, Dirck Jansz in 1561, Willeboort Cornelisz in 1564, Hendrick Alewijnsz, Mattheeux Maurisz, Magdaleena Jansdochter, Hans Marijnsz, Gerrit Duynherder, Bastiaen Corsz, Maeyken Jans, Aelken Jans, all in 1569, and Anneken Jans van Woerden in 1571. Other Anabaptists who were martyred at other places are known to have been citizens of Middelburg or the vicinity. These are indications that Middelburg was an important Anabaptist-Mennonite center. The existence of a large congregation here explains why Leenaert Bouwens baptized only 13 converts here (in 1557-61). The martyr Valerius de Schoolmeester (*q.v.*) was active here in 1563-64 and 1566.

The bloody persecutions ceased when the city passed into the power of William of Orange in 1574. At once the Calvinist preachers, though they were in the minority, began to molest the Anabaptists. In 1576 the government gave them a hearing and made it obligatory for the Anabaptists to swear the oath. Without it they could not be citizens or carry on a trade or craft. When William visited the city in 1577 the Anabaptists presented a petition to him. In his reply of Jan. 26, 1577, William promised them release from this obligation. On this occasion the words were used which have become of great significance to the Dutch Mennonites because they marked the beginning of religious freedom for them: "His Excellency commanding and charging the magistrates of Middelborgh and all others whom this may concern, not further to oppress the petitioners contrary to their conscience, with regard to the oath and otherwise."

But the magistrate did not follow this regulation and in April 1578 again demanded the oath, closing the shops of 40 merchants (evidence of their prosperity). In addition the magistrate demanded that the Mennonites serve as armed guards. Thereupon they sent another petition to the prince. In reply he wrote to both the governor of Zeeland and the councilors of Middelburg (June 23, 1578), with emphatic instructions to give the magistrate of Middelburg express orders to leave the petitioners in peace; they were to keep their domicile beside the other citizens, carry on their business as well as they could, and were not to be in any way molested or disturbed. But the magistrate paid no attention; another letter from William was needed (July 26, 1578): "And therefore we order and demand expressly of you to cease to molest the aforesaid persons, who are Mennonites, or to prevent them from carrying on trade and crafts."

New disturbances soon followed. An attempt was made to disturb and prevent their services (June 1580) and to compel them to take their armed guard duty. The Mennonites were willing to pay taxes, serve as guards to prevent and aid in case of accident or fire, and even dig trenches, but refused to bear arms. At first William of Orange, to whom the Mennonites had addressed a letter (signed by Arendt Pietersz, Jan van Son, Matthys Hermansz, and Aert Conincx, apparently preachers or deacons of the congregation), was unable to do anything for the oppressed Mennonites, but in 1582 he again intervened on their behalf. After another letter had been sent by the Mennonites he decided on Jan. 29, 1582, that all Mennonite men should pay a special tax. Since this was very high, a new ruling was passed in 1588, whereby the brotherhood paid the fee of 1,200 florins annually. This amount was reduced to 800 in 1626, 600 in 1659, 420 in 1681, 350 in 1708, and was dropped in 1795. After the death of William of Orange (1584) the magistrate of Middelburg apparently continued to thwart the Mennonites, for on March 4, 1593, William's son and successor, Stadholder Maurice of Orange, in reply to a letter written by Maillaerd de Poorter and Joost Leonisse in the name of the Middelburg Mennonite congregation, admonished the magistrate of Middelburg not to interfere with the privileges granted the Mennonites by his father. It was always the Reformed Church which set the magistrates against the Mennonites. In 1578 Hans de Ries (*q.v.*), visiting Middelburg, was imprisoned here for about a month and banished from the territory.

After 1550 the membership increased rapidly, especially after the arrival of the foreigners, mostly Mennonite merchants from Belgium. In 1580 some Anabaptists arrived from England. In 1574 the male membership was about 90, in 1581 about 130. In the 17th century it continued to grow. Many immigrants from Flanders joined the Mennonites in Middelburg. Elder Bastiaen Willems baptized 42 persons here in 1632-33. Numerous complaints were made by the pastor of the Reformed Church concerning these transfers, which were not limited to foreigners. In 1656 these complaints were still heard. Hermann Faukelius (*q.v.*), the zealous pastor of Middelburg, appeared several times in the Mennonite church services in 1620 and in July 1621, read a paper to the congregation, which was published under the title, *Babel, dat is de Verwerringhe der Wederdoperen*. In 1660 the synod called the attention of the government to the "great and dangerous errors" which tended to creep in especially among the Mennonites; this is a reference to Socinianism. The 12 articles ("Geuze vragen," *q.v.*) set up for this purpose were presented to the Mennonite preachers for signature. Joost Isenbaert complied; Adriaen van Eeghem (*q.v.*) and his cousin Thomas refused to do so and were forbidden for some time to preach.

The Middelburg congregation, which belonged to the Flemish wing, at first was rather conservative. In 1632 their representatives, Elder Bastiaen Willemsen and Preacher Jan Winckelmans, signed the Dordrecht confession. But through the influence of its excellent elder Adriaan van Eeghem it grew more progressive; in the schism between Galenus Abrahamsz and Samuel Apostool, called the "Lammerenkrijgh" (*q.v.*), it took a moderate position, as did most of the Zeeland congregations. When Samuel Apostool (*q.v.*), the leader of the conservative wing, visited Middelburg in 1665 to persuade the congregation to join the stricter Zonist group and to co-operate in the *Verbond van Eenigheydt* (*q.v.*), although Joost Isenbaert signed, the congregation led

by Adriaan van Eeghem would not involve itself in the quarrel.

Besides the Flemish congregation there was also in Middelburg a congregation of the (Groningen) Old Flemish or Ukowallists (*q.v.*). This group apparently is identical with a congregation mentioned in 1576-78, called "Voetwasschers" (Footwashers). Of this group Gerrit Gerrits was a preacher in 1663, while in 1681 Claes Pieters and Winink Alberts attended a conference of the Groningen Old Flemish. In 1663 the elders of this wing, Derk Sierts (Huizinga) and Luirt Luirts (Huizinga), visited Middelburg on their great preaching journey. This Old Flemish congregation had died out or merged with the main Middelburg congregation before 1710.

After the restless history of the 16th and 17th centuries the life of the congregation developed more quietly. The calm was broken in December 1732 when 12 Mennonite families from Dannenberg in Prussia settled on the island of Walcheren in the vicinity of Middelburg. In the following years several of their brethren, who had found a temporary home near Wageningen (*q.v.*), also moved to Walcheren. The Committee for Foreign Needs assisted in buying farms for these people. But the new settlers did not feel at home here, and one after the other they returned to Prussia. Since the sale of these homes did not bring enough to cover the original cost, to say nothing of additional expenses incurred in making the settlement, Middelburg suffered a considerable financial loss through this episode.

Old Mennonite families formerly of Middelburg are de Clerq, van Da(e)le, Dobbelaer(e), Dyserinck, van Eeghen (Eeghem), Fa(c)k, Goudeseboys, d'Hoye, van Houcke (Hoecke), van de Steenkiste, Strubbe, Ta(c)k, de Wind, Winckelmans (Winkelman); most of these families have died out, a few in the course of time joined the Reformed Church, and many others left Middelburg during the 17th and 18th centuries, moving elsewhere, particularly to Haarlem and Amsterdam.

The congregation of Middelburg, whose baptized membership was about 270 in 1600, decreased rapidly in the 18th century. Figures about the 18th century were not available, but in 1847 the baptized membership had decreased to 92. After that there was some increase: 102 in 1861, 187 in 1900, 209 in 1911, but 132 in 1939, and 107 in 1957. The congregation formerly was rather well-to-do. The small congregation contributed liberally to the needs of the Mennonites in Poland and Prussia: in 1727, 255 florins; in 1733, 727 florins; in 1736, 530 florins. Among the ministers who have served here there are a number of outstanding men. Bastiaen Willemsen, named above, died in 1636 or 1637. Adriaan van Eeghem served here in 1655-1709. In 1705-52 Gerardus de Wind, a physician, was its preacher. Johannes Nettis, also a physician, 1729-73, Gerrit Boothamer 1751-90, Abraham Wynands 1773-78, Sjoerd Ysbrandi 1778-83. Eke Menalda served 1784-1831, Sicco Rekker 1790-1832, Alle M. Cramer 1832-71, K. R. Pekelharing 1849-84, Tj. Kielstra 1885-1901, P. Sybolts 1901-6, P. H. Veen 1907-19, Jacob Koekebakker 1919-40, Miss A. H. A. Bakker since 1940. In 1808 an agreement was reached with the neighboring Vlissingen (*q.v.*) congregation to have the Middelburg preachers serve both congregations. This union lasted until 1898. In 1920 a similar agreement was made with Goes (*q.v.*); this union (1955) still exists.

Originally the congregation may have met for its services in the homes of its members; in 1629 Pieter van de Vegte bought a building in the Hoogstraat, which was adapted as a meetinghouse. It was used until June 18, 1889; a new church in the Lange Noordstraat was dedicated on July 7, 1889. The old church is now used by the Salvation Army. The congregation of Middelburg always took good care of its poor members. They not only supplied them with money, food, clothing, and fuel (usually peat), but in the economically difficult period of the French occupation in August 1807, moved a number of poor Mennonite children to the province of Drenthe to work in textile mills. In 1838 Pastor A. M. Cramer (*q.v.*) initiated a project to create work for the unemployed (not only Mennonites) during the winter months. Until the 19th century the congregation possessed a "Fund for the prevention of poverty," directed by four "comissaries" and the pastor of the congregation. There is a ladies' circle and a West Hill Sunday school for children.   vDZ.

The Middelburg Archives contain a manuscript by G. Boothamer, "Geschiedenis van de Doopsgezinde Gemeente te Middelburg uit de boeken en geschriften ter kerkekamer berustende tot den tegenwoordigen jare 1773"; this ms. contains very valuable information; *Inv. Arch. Amst.* I, 424-34, 439, 441 f., 452, 580, 887, 1072, 1168, 1195-2085; II, Nos. 1645-67, 2094-2108; II 2, Nos. 273-95, 503, 518, 571, 608; *DJ* 1837, 24; 1850, 42; 1930, 115-41; *DB* 1863, 113 f.; 1875, 36 f., 99; 1877, 5; 1879, 7, 93 f.; 1883, 88, 114, 106; 1890, 142; 1900, 28; 1905, 118, 157 ff.; 1906, 111 ff.; 120, 122-24; 1908, 1-64; 1912, 113 note 2; K. R. Pekelharing, "Geschiedenis der Hervorming in Zeeland," in *Archief Zeeuwsch Genootschap* VI (1866); Blaupot t. C., *Holland* I and II, *passim;* C. P. van Eeghen, *Adriaan van Eeghem* (Amsterdam, 1896); Kühler, *Geschiedenis* I and II, *passim;* Mellink, *Wederdopers,* 317-19; *Catalogus Amst.,* 150 f., 294; *Algemeen Doopsgezind Weekblad* XI, No. 47 (Feb. 23, 1957); *ML* III, 131 f.

Middelharnis, a village on Overflakkee, an island in the Dutch province of South Holland, was once the seat of a Flemish Mennonite church, which dated back to the early days. Elias Jansz van Wijlvliet, Coenraet Jansz van Wijlvliet, and Coenraet Philipsz Block of Middelharnis were present at the Flemish meeting in June 1660 at Leiden. Later on the congregation belonged to the Zonsche (*q.v.*) Sociëteit. The congregation was always small in membership. It had declined to 12 male members by 1747. The congregation was always very poor and for nearly a century Rotterdam contributed to the minister's salary. Also the congregations of Amsterdam and Haarlem supported it, particularly when the church needed repairs in 1779. In 1805 the church was sold (it still exists as a warehouse), and the congregation ceased to exist. Its last preachers were Pieter Beets until 1753, Jacob van Loon 1755-57, Jan Nieuwenhuyzen 1758-63, T. G. van Grouw 1764-70, Abr. Tersier 1771-1805. In the 18th century it was united with Sommelsdijk (*q.v.*), where there was also a church. On Dec. 7, 1540, Paulus Harrouts (*q.v.*) of Middelharnis was burned at the stake at Zierikzee.

In 1617 the Mennonite elder François de Knuyt. (*q.v.*) of Zierikzee held a public dispute at Middelharnis with the Reformed pastor Abr. Stamperius on infant baptism.

Inv. Arch. Amst. I, Nos. 1164, 1180; II, Nos. 2109-41; *DB* 1864, 121; 1880, 50; 1908, 106-14; *ML* III, 132.

Middelhoven, a Dutch Mennonite family at Zaandam, province of North Holland. Most of them belonged to the Waterlander congregation of Zaandam, and after the merging of Waterlander and Flemish congregations (1687) to this united church. But in the Frisian congregation there were also members of the Middelhoven family. From the 18th century they were mostly lumber dealers. Jacob Dirks Middelhoven was a preacher of the Waterlander congregation *ca.* 1680-91. In this year he asked to be discharged from his preaching office, because his trade—he was a confectioner or pastry cook—demanded all his time. He was somewhat liberal in his views, and (from 1697) ardently participated in the Collegiant (*q.v.*) meetings at Rijnsburg. He published a funeral sermon on Pieter Pietersz of Koog aan de Zaan (*Lyckrede ofte Aenmercking des Doods* . . . , Amsterdam, 1680). This Jacob Middelhoven seems to have moved to near-by Krommenie (*q.v.*) shortly after 1691; his son Jacob was a deacon there in 1729. Many members of the Middelhoven family until recent times served as deacons of the West-Zaandam congregation, one of whom was Willem Jacobsz Middelhoven, who died in 1888, having served for nearly 55 years.   vDZ.

S. Lootsma, *Het Nieuwe Huys* (Zaandam, 1937) 31, 44, 70, 76, 114 f., 169; *Catalogus Amst.,* 250; *DJ* 1926, 139-41.

Middelie, a village in the Dutch province of North Holland, south of Hoorn, the center of Anabaptist activity from the earliest times (Walraven Herberts of Middelie was executed at Utrecht in 1535) and soon the seat of a Mennonite congregation, of which, however, little is known. Leenaert Bouwens baptized 25 persons here in 1563-65. Soon afterward the congregation joined the Frisian branch, and in the 17th century the Frisian conference of North Holland. At an early time the congregation of neighboring Axwijk (*q.v.*) had united with Middelie. The congregation contributed in 1733 and 1736 to the needs of the Prussian Mennonites. It seems to have had a hymnal of its own (see **Middelier Lied-Boeck**), replaced in 1854 by the *Groote Bundel* (*q.v.*), which was in turn replaced in 1946 by the *Doopsgezinde Bundel.* Until 1892 it was served by untrained preachers, among whom in the 18th century were some members of the Hartog (*q.v.*) family. The last untrained preachers were Hendrik Bakker, serving 1809-38, and H. W. van der Ploeg, serving 1839-92, who was examined and appointed preacher candidate by the Conference of Friesland (Friesche Doopsgezinde Sociëteit). He was followed by A. van der Goot, serving 1892-1930. After the departure of van der Goot the pulpit became vacant, but in 1936 an agreement was made with the congregation of Den Ilp (*q.v.*) to have its pastor also serve at Middelie. This lasted until 1953, when the Middelie-Axwijk congregation united with Edam-Monnikendam. The old meetinghouse was remodeled in 1860 and 1907; it acquired an organ in 1865.

The baptized membership, numbering 140 in 1726, 119 in 1788, and again 140 in 1847, was 187 in 1901, 184 in 1939, and 109 in 1957.   vDZ.

Inv. Arch. Amst. I, Nos. 102, 412, 1131, 1179; II, 2, No. 140; Blaupot t. C., *Holland* I and II, *passim; DJ* 1850, 21; *DB* 1887, 130 f.; 1900, 116; *De Zondagsbode* XXIV (1910-11) No. 47; *ML* III, 132.

Middelier Lied-Boeck, a Dutch Mennonite hymnal, printed at Haarlem 1651. It was used by the congregation of Middelie (*q.v.*) until 1854. This hymnal contains 131 hymns without notes, all composed by J. H. Pos.   vDZ.

Middelstum, a village in the Dutch province of Groningen. Close to Middelstum was the castle of the Ewsum family, to which half of the land of Groningen belonged, and which was favorable to the Anabaptists. Christoffer van Ewsum (*q.v.*) was undoubtedly one of them. The Middelstum congregation belonged to the Groningen Old Flemish branch; in 1710 it numbered about 50 members, in 1767, 20. In 1783 a merger was effected of the Middelstum, Westeremden, and Huizinge congregations. A new church was built in Huizinge (*q.v.*) in 1815. The membership was 36 at the time. In 1863 the church in Huizinge was sold and a new church with a parsonage was built in Middelstum, where the congregation has had an almshouse from early times (sold in 1890). Until 1865 the congregation was usually called Huizinge and Westeremden, now always Middelstum. The baptized membership was 68 in 1861, 74 in 1900, 37 in 1957. Since the church and parsonage have been established at Middelstum it has been served by J. Hoekstra 1856-74, J. F. Bakker 1875-77, C. Leendertz 1878-1908. In 1911-26 the congregation was served by Karel Vos (*q.v.*), the noted historian, who wrote numerous articles for the *Mennonitisches Lexikon.* Since his death the pastorate has been vacant. Services were conducted by J. M. Vis of Noordbroek 1928-45; in 1946 an agreement was reached with Leermens-Loppersum to have its pastor also serve at Middelstum.

Old Mennonite families found in and around Middelstum are van der Molen, Gaaikema, Doornbosch, Wiersema, Noordhoff, and particularly Huizinga (*q.v.*). Many members of the Huizinga family have served the Middelstum congregation as lay preachers.

Middelstum is important in Mennonite history because of a meeting held here on Sept. 18-22, 1628, to consider the offer of reconciliation made by the Frisians to the Flemish. The irreconcilable attitude of the Flemish Elder Jan Luies (*q.v.*) prevented the adoption of the agreement, and caused the rise of the Groningen Old Flemish branch.   vDZ.

Inv. Arch. Amst. I, No. 558 V; Blaupot t. C., *Groningen* I and II, *passim; DJ* 1840, 43, 52; *DB* 1864, 169; 1879, 5, 86; *N.N.B.Wb.* III, 797 f.; K. Vos, "Doopsgezinde familien onder Middelstum," in *Groningsche Volksalmanak* 1921, 95-115; *ML* III, 133.

Middle District Conference of the General Conference Mennonite Church comprises 20 churches with a membership of 5,237, located in Ohio, Indiana, Illinois, Iowa, and Missouri. This district conference had its beginning in 1868, when four churches of Lee Co., Iowa, and the church at Summerfield, Ill., organized to carry on home missionary work. Other Mennonite churches were invited to this first meeting, but only the above five churches responded. A conference was organized and the name "Western District Conference" was adopted. Its purpose was to promote home mission work and a spiritual ministry among scattered Mennonite families in the "north and west." Christian Krehbiel, a minister in the church at Summerfield, Ill., was the leader in this movement. By 1888, 30 churches, including a number of churches in Kansas, had affiliated with this district. The churches in Kansas, because of the close proximity to each other, had organized a local conference. When the Western District Conference met in 1888 in its twenty-first session, it was decided to divide the area into two districts. The western churches, which then were chiefly the churches of Kansas, organized and adopted the name "Western District Conference." The churches of Ohio, Indiana, Illinois, and Iowa then reorganized and chose as their name "Middle District Conference." In 1888 the Middle District was composed of six congregations: Berne, Ind.; Dalton, Ohio; Summerfield, Ill.; Donnelson, Iowa; West Point, Iowa; and Franklin, Iowa. In the course of the years other Mennonite churches within the area came into the district conference.

The Middle District Conference, in its constitution, states that it seeks to unite the Mennonite churches within its area in fellowship and in evangelization and service. The major home mission project of the district is the Lima (Ohio) Mission Church (now First Mennonite Church of Lima). There is also active interest in the home mission efforts carried on in Chicago, Ill. The standing committees of the district are the Home Mission Committee, Education Committee, Young People's Committee, Women's Work Committee, and Peace Committee. The district actively supports Bluffton College and elects members to its board of trustees. The district shares in sponsoring the program of summer camps at Camp Friedenswald. Mennonite Biblical Seminary in Chicago receives the support of the churches of the district. The four churches near Bluffton took the initiative in promoting plans for a home for elderly people and were joined by other churches. The home was dedicated and opened in 1955.

The first session of General Conference was held in 1860 in a church (Lee Co., Iowa) of this district. In fact much of the interest which led to the organization of the General Conference had its origin in the Middle District. Daniel Krehbiel and Christian Showalter, both from the churches of Lee County, urged and supported the union movement which led to the organization of the General Conference. Then, too, it was within the Middle District that the first Mennonite school in America for training ministers and Christian workers was established. This school was opened in 1868 at Wadsworth, Ohio, and served as the forerunner of Witmarsum Theological Seminary located at Bluffton.

In view of the fact that the churches of the Middle District and the churches formerly of the Central

Conference of Mennonites (but now G.C.M.) are located in the same general area it was proposed by the Middle District that the two districts merge and be known as the Central District. This proposal was favorably received by both district conferences. The merger was completed at the joint session of the two conferences held at Normal, Ill., April 25-27, 1957. The newly organized conference is known as the Central District of the General Conference Mennonite Church.   A.E.K.

H. P. Krehbiel, *History of the Mennonite General Conference* I (n.p., 1898).

Middle East Relief *and Refugee Administration* (MERRA) was organized to deal with the various problems created by the large-scale evacuation of refugees from Poland, Greece, and Dodecanese to the south early in 1941. These refugees were placed in camps in countries to the east of the Mediterranean and Egypt. MERRA was a fusion of the Repatriation Office with the Relief Section of the Minister of State Office, both British. The impact of the refugee movement by the British Military necessitated a single organization to move refugees and administer the camps where these people were temporarily housed. The exact date of MERRA's organization is not known because fire destroyed the records. One document has given July 1, 1942, as the official date of organization.

MERRA was active in administering refugee camps for a period of three years. During this brief period the Mennonite Central Committee, Inc., Akron, Pa., assigned a total of 15 of its foreign relief workers to refugee camps at El Shat and Tolumbat, both in Egypt. In May 1944 MERRA was absorbed by UNRRA (United Nations Relief and Rehabilitation Administration), a United Nations civilian organization of world-wide scope. At this time MERRA became the Balkan Mission, an administrative section of UNRRA. MCC was not a part of MERRA.   J.N.B.

Middlebury, Ind., a town (1950 pop. 839) in Middlebury Twp., Elkhart Co., Ind. For many years there have been many Amish and Mennonites in the vicinity of this village. As early as 1868 the Brenneman brothers, Daniel of Indiana and Henry of Ohio, preached to a "large, attentive, and very orderly audience." But no effort was made to locate a Mennonite church in the town before 1902, when a Sunday school was conducted in private homes. In 1904 the Middlebury Mennonite Church (MC) was organized with 32 charter members as a sort of outpost of the Forks congregation. In 1911 the first meetinghouse was built, a brick structure. In 1923 the congregation, along with a number of others in Indiana, suffered a schism on questions of discipline and conference authority. At this time about 100 members withdrew and became an independent congregation called Warren Street Mennonite Church, which later joined the Central Conference. In 1956 the two congregations had a total of 462 members of whom 62 were in the Warren Street congregation. A large number of Old Order Amish and Conservative Mennonites live in the territory surrounding Middlebury, which is their shopping center.   J.C.W.

Middlebury (Ind.) Mennonite Church (MC). As early as 1868 the Brenneman brothers, Daniel of Indiana and Henry of Ohio, preached to a "large, attentive, and very orderly audience" in Middlebury. But no effort was made to locate a Mennonite meetinghouse in the village before 1902. In that year the Mennonites conducted a Sunday school in private homes. On May 10, 1903, the Sunday school was more formally organized and preaching services were begun in Prescott Hall, with D. D. Miller of the Forks Amish Mennonite Church preaching the first sermon. In 1904 the Middlebury congregation was organized with 32 charter members as a sort of outpost of the Forks congregation. A. J. Hostetler, who had been ordained deacon at Forks in 1896 and preacher in 1898, became the first pastor of the congregation, and D. J. Johns served as bishop. Simon S. Yoder, who had been ordained deacon in the Forks congregation in 1903, joined Middlebury a few years later, and in 1907 was ordained preacher. In 1911 the first meetinghouse was built, a brick structure, on Lawrence Street, enlarged in 1950-51. In 1923 the congregation, along with several others in Indiana, divided over the issue of how strict the discipline of the church ought to be, and how much direction conference ought to give its constituent congregations. In this division Hostetler remained with the Indiana-Michigan Conference (MC), together with 110 members, while Yoder and about 100 members withdrew and soon joined the Central Conference as the Warren Street congregation. Hostetler's group continued to grow, and by 1956 had a membership of 400. Wilbur Yoder has been pastor since 1936. In 1941 Simon S. Yoder was received back into the fellowship of the Indiana-Michigan Conference (MC) following his return to the Middlebury (Lawrence Street) congregation. Paul M. Miller was chosen bishop by the congregation in 1956.   J.C.W.

Middlesex Reformed Mennonite Church, located near Carlisle, Cumberland Co., Pa., had 17 members in 1948. The meetinghouse was built in 1870.
                J.L.K.

Middleton, Humphrey, an English Anabaptist martyr, was executed during the reign of Mary, the Catholic queen of England, in London in July 1555. (*ME* II, 217.)

Midland, Mich., Old Order Amish community, now about extinct, was established 14 miles north of Midland in 1909 by settlers from Elkhart and Lagrange counties in Indiana. It never prospered, the only resident bishop having been Peter Yoder, who served in this office 1925-28. The last family moved away in 1930.   D.J.T.

Midland (Mich.) Mennonite Church (MC) was organized in June 1913, the first families having arrived from Emma, Ind., in 1910 (Jacob Emmert) and 1912 (A. D. Miller). The first meetinghouse was a remodeled log dwelling in 1916, located five miles north of Midland. The second, a former Grange hall 3½ miles southwest of the city, was used in 1917-28; then a new meetinghouse of cinder block was built on the same site. The first resident minister was E. A. Bontrager 1916-39 (following

Will Haarer, who served as unordained leader 1913-16). F. F. Bontrager (ordained 1926) has served as bishop-pastor since 1934, but Clarence Yoder (ordained 1936) is now (1956) serving as pastor, assisted by Erie Kindy, since Bontrager has charge of the mission outpost at Clare, 30 miles northwest of Midland. In 1956 the membership was 134.   H.S.B.

Midland Mutual Fire Insurance: see Mennonite Mutual Fire Insurance Association.

Midsland, on the Dutch island of Terschelling (q.v.), was in the 16th century the seat of a Mennonite congregation, whose meetinghouse was renovated in 1690, but which soon after, at any rate before 1731, died out or joined the main congregation of West-Terschelling. (DB 1861, 87, 92.)   vDZ.

Midway Mennonite Church (MC), located near Columbiana, Mahoning Co., Ohio, is a member of the Ohio and Eastern Mennonite Conference. The first meetinghouse was built about 1825 on land deeded to the church by Jacob Oberholtzer, who was the first Mennonite minister in Ohio, having arrived here in 1806. A new brick church was constructed in 1869 to replace the older building. An addition was constructed in 1899. The building has been remodeled twice since that time. For many years the members and the ministers were a part of the circuit of the three churches—Midway, North Lima, and Leetonia, rather than assigned to a specific church. The bishops who served since about 1866 were Joseph Bixler, John Burkholder, and Albert J. Steiner. In 1956 Paul Yoder was bishop-pastor, and Ernest Martin minister, with a membership of 164. It was called Oberholtzer's until 1898.   P.R.Y.

Midwolda, a village in the Dutch province of Groningen. The Mennonite congregation here was in existence by the 17th century, but was then usually called Woldampt. Concerning its history there is little information; in 1637 it was mentioned as the Midwolda congregation. In the 17th century it belonged to the Old Flemish branch. Amme Hikke(n)s (q.v.) was its elder at this time. During the 18th century the name Widwolda is not found in the Naamlijst, since the Mennonites of Midwolda were united with the Beerta (q.v.) and Meeden (q.v.) congregations; but from 1793 the congregation is listed as Midwolda-Beerta-Meeden, and in 1794 a parsonage was built at Midwolda. Until 1793 the preachers had always been chosen from the members of the congregation; in that year Huizinga was called in from the outside; the first preacher who received training at the Amsterdam Mennonite Seminary was Taco Kuiper, serving here in 1804-7. He was followed by S. E. Wieling 1808-22, J. F. Boersema 1827-66, J. Oosterbaan 1866-72, J. F. Bakker 1873-75, A. H. ten Cate 1877-83; after a vacancy of ten years a call was accepted by Joh. A. Wartena, who however did not live at Midwolda, but at Winschoten (q.v.). Concerning the membership there are no figures for the 17th and 18th centuries; in 1834 the baptized membership of the Midwolda-Beerta-Meeden congregation numbered 65, 100 in 1861, 119 in 1897.

About the middle of the 19th century the congregation became liberal in its theology. In May 1869 the question was discussed whether persons should be admitted to the church without baptism, i.e., only on confession of faith; and in 1871 it was decided that baptism was not obligatory for membership. In 1893 the church in Midwolda was sold, and the pastor moved to Winschoten (q.v.), which now became the center of the united congregation; services were to be held alternately in Beerta, Midwolda, de Meeden, and Winschoten. In Midwolda a hall has been rented for the purpose, but Beerta and de Meeden had churches. In Winschoten the preaching service was at first held in the Lutheran church. On Oct. 11, 1931, a new Mennonite church was dedicated there. Since about 1920 no services have been held at Midwolda; only seven members were living there then. The congregation now carries the name Winschoten. For ministers and membership, see **Winschoten.**   vDZ.

DB 1879, 5; 1870, 178; 1872, 192; 1887, 148; 1894, 168; Blaupot t. C., *Groningen* I, 93, 214, 238; *ML* III, 133.

Mierdemann (Mierdman), **Steven,** a book printer, who had a publishing business at Antwerp, Belgium, in 1543-45, and in England in 1551-53. In 1554 he fled to Emden, East Friesland, Germany. Here he published in 1556 "the first genuinely Lutheran Bible in the Low German tongue," called *Den Bibel in Duyts.* The text for this Dutch Bible had been prepared by Jan Gheylliaert, also an emigrant from Flanders. The historical books of the Old Testament followed the text of the Dutch Bible printed at Antwerp by Jacob van Liesveldt (q.v.). For the other books of the Old Testament and of the New Testament they took the German Zürich Froschauer (q.v.) Bible (first ed. 1548, repr. 1549, 1556). The Mierdemann-Gheylliaert Bibles were also in use among the Mennonites in the Netherlands and northern Germany; Menno Simons may also have used this edition. After 1560, when a new Bible in the Dutch language was published at Emden by the Mennonite printer Nicolaes Biestkens (q.v.) van Diest, the Mierdemann Bible probably soon was discarded. Among the Dutch Reformed the Mierdemann Bible was replaced by the Calvinist Dutch edition edited by Jan N. Utenhove and Godfried van Winghen and published by Gillis van der Erven at Emden. The assertion of Samuel Muller (DJ 1837, 56) that there was a Mierdemann edition of 1528 at Emden, is a mistake.   vDZ.

DB 1890, 62-64; K. Vos, *Menno Simons* (Leiden, 1914) 259 f.; I. le Long, *Boekzaal der Nederduytsche Bybels* (Amsterdam, 1732); *Nederlandse Bijbels en hun uitgevers 1477-1952* (Amsterdam, n.d., 1952).

Mierevelt (Miereveldt), **Michiel Janszn van** (1567-1641), a noted Dutch portraitist, lived all his life in Delft (q.v.) and painted many pictures of the princes and princesses of the house of Orange-Nassau, also of Elector Frederick (q.v.) V of the Palatinate, the dethroned king of Bohemia. Many of the pictures painted by his pupils in his studio were signed by him; this practice had a depreciating effect on his reputation as well as on the value of his paintings. The portrait of Lubbert Gerritsz (q.v.), a Mennonite preacher, which is in the national museum at Amsterdam, is the product of a pupil (Cat. 1907, No.

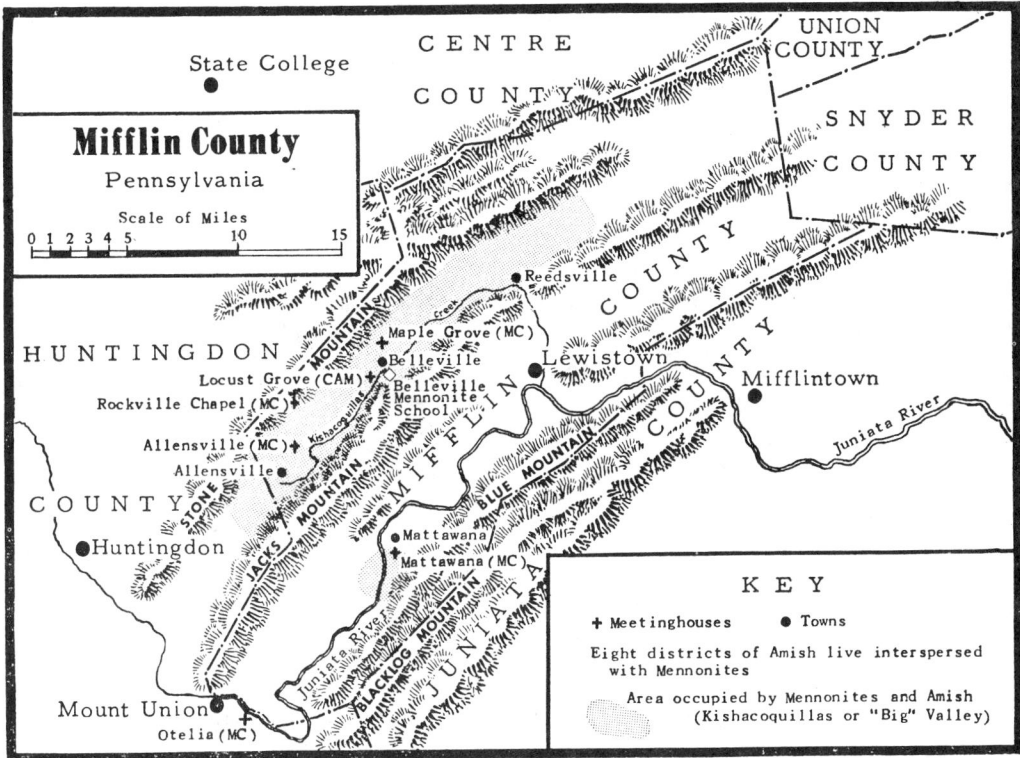

Mifflin County
Pennsylvania
Scale of Miles
0 1 2 3 4 5   10   15

KEY
+ Meetinghouses   ● Towns
Eight districts of Amish live interspersed
with Mennonites
Area occupied by Mennonites and Amish
(Kishacoquillas or "Big" Valley)

1606). But the best made by him in person are of great artistic value. After unremitting work he left a fortune at his death and a respected school of portraitists, of whom Paulus Moreelse and Jan van Ravesteyn were the most outstanding. His son-in-law, the excellent copper etcher Willem Jacobszn Delff, made some excellent reproductions of van Mierevelt's works.

In foreign countries Mierevelt also enjoyed great fame. The court of England invited him to come to London; he was, however, unable to go because of the epidemic of the plague prevalent in the city. Duke Albertus of Austria, Stadholder of the southern Netherlands where the Anabaptists had been so terribly persecuted, called him to Brussels, and he was granted the very unusual privilege of practicing his "Mennonite religion" undisturbed, as the historian Joachim van Sandrart reports. The poet Joachim Oudaen (q.v.), who was closely associated with Mennonites and Collegiants, composed his epitaph. Of his contacts with the Mennonites nothing is known but the fact that he was a member of the Mennonite Church. About 1600 there was at Delft a Flemish, a Frisian, and possibly a Waterlander Mennonite congregation. His father, Jan Michielsen Mierevelt (1528-92), a silver smith and copperplate engraver at Delft, is also said to have been a Mennonite.   H.F.W.J., vDZ.

J. van Sandrart, *Academie der Bau-, Bild- und Malerey-Künste 1675-83* (*Academia nobilissimae artis pictoriae*), later edition of three folio volumes under the title *Teutsche Academie* (ed. J. J. Volkmann, 1768-75); A. Houbraken, *Groote Schouburgh der Nederlandsche Konstschilders* (3 vv., 1718-19); Van der Aa, *Biogr. Wb.* VIII (Haarlem, 1869); *ML* III, 133.

Miertgen (Maritgen, Mynken Sduucs), an Anabaptist martyr, born at Komen (Commines) in Flanders, the wife of Hans de Vette. In July 1559 a number of members of the Mennonite congregation of Gent, Belgium, were arrested. Most of them were put to death on July 5 and Aug. 7, 1559, among them Hans de Vette on July 5. Two women, Tanneken Gressy (Tanneken Godtbetert) and Miertgen, who were pregnant when they were arrested, had their execution postponed until they had given birth to their children; and then the execution for some reason or other was again postponed until June 27, 1560, when they were secretly beheaded in the Gent Gravensteen castle and immediately buried. Miertgen, who with the other martyrs of this group is commemorated in the hymn "Ick moet een liet beginnen" (I must begin a song), No. 14 of the *Lietboecxken van den Offer des Heeren,* faithfully suffered imprisonment and martyrdom. She is said to have spoken from the window of her prison to the passers-by and to have thrown letters into the street. Van Braght (*Martyrs' Mirror*), who calls this martyr Maritgen van Waestene (Warneton in Flanders), where Hans and Miertgen probably had lived before they moved to Gent, gives 1559 as the year of execution. (*Offer,* 348, 559; *Mart. Mir.* D 246, 249; E 620; Verheyden, *Gent,* 26, No. 74.)   vDZ.

Mifflin County in central Pennsylvania, organized in 1789, contains large settlements of Amish and Mennonites. The beautiful Kishacoquillas Valley, enclosed by Stone and Jacks Mountains, and extending about 30 miles across the central part of the county, is host to the Mennonite and Amish inhabitants of the county. There are five Mennonite meetinghouses in the county. The first settlers known were Michael Yotter (Yoder), whose name occurred on the assessment roll of Union Township in 1791, and Christian Zook, who warranted land in 1792. That Amish Mennonites were in the county as early as 1760 (S. W. Peachey) cannot be substantiated. Family names of early Amish settlers who came to Mifflin County from Lancaster, Berks, Chester, and Union counties were Yoder, Zook, Byler, Hooley, Hartzler, Peachey (Bitsche), Renno, and Kauffman. The first Amish minister was probably "Long" Christian Zook, the first bishop Hans Beiler (*q.v.*). In 1850 there were three Amish church districts with a membership of 290. In 1900 the total membership in Mifflin County was 863: Belleville 155 and Allensville 110 in the Eastern A.M. Conference; Peachey (3 districts) 250, Old School (2 districts) 159, Locust Grove 110, and Mattawana 79 across the mountain and in the Eastern A.M. Conference.

The present Mennonites in Mifflin County all stem from the early Amish settlers. The settlement has gradually gained in membership in its 160 years of history, even though at various times some of its families have moved westward to Ohio, Indiana, Iowa, Missouri, Nebraska, and North Dakota. Since 1849 there have been various schisms in the Amish group so that there are now eight differing Amish and Mennonite branches or conferences in the county, totaling 1,796 members. Farming is the chief occupation, with special emphasis on dairying. The three villages in the heart of the settlement in Kishacoquillas Valley are Allensville, Belleville, and Reedsville.

Shem Zook (*q.v.*), Samuel Yoder, and J. K. Hartzler were outstanding Amish Mennonite leaders of the county. The four Mennonite churches belong to the M.C. branch. Of these, only Maple Grove (Belleville) is a member of the Allegheny Conference; the others belong to the Ohio and Eastern Conference. Locust Grove (CM) members conduct mission points at Woodland and Crenshaw. Following is a summary of Amish and Mennonite membership in the county in 1956:

Name of Church	Origin	Building Erected	Founder or Organizer	Membership
Mennonite (814)				
Mattawana	1793	1871	Sol Yoder	125
Maple Grove (Belleville)	1863	1868	Solomon Byler	281
Allensville	1863	1869	Solomon Byler	361
Rockville	1934	1941	Eli K. Zook	56
Conservative (402))				
Locust Grove	1898	1899	Abraham D. Zook	402
Old Order Amish (580)				
Old School Byler	1792		Hans Byler	40
Renno (3 dist.)	1863		Abraham Peachey	205
Nebraska (Yoder)	1880		Yost H. Yoder	70
Speicher (Beachy)	1911		John B. Zook	205
Nebraska (Zook)	1945		Christ. Y. Zook	60

J.A.H.

S. W. Peachey, *Amish of Kishacoquillas Valley, Mifflin Co., Pa.* (Scottdale, 1930); J. W. Yoder, *Rosanna of the Amish* (Huntingdon, 1940); idem, *Rosanna's Boys* (Huntingdon, 1948); the Yoder books portray Amish life and customs of the Mifflin County area; J. K. Hartzler, "Fifty Years with the Amish Mennonite Churches of Pennsylvania," *Herald of Truth* (June 1, 1902); J. A. Hostetler, "Life and Times of Samuel Yoder," *MQR* XXII (October 1948); *idem,* "The Amish Family" (MA thesis, Penn State, 1951).

Migrant Work. In the United States thousands of families annually follow the harvest season work from Texas to Michigan, Florida to New York, and up the coast in California. Since 1940 Protestant groups have generally co-ordinated their religious, educational, and health concerns for migrants through the Home Missions Council of North America (later the Division of Home Missions of the National Council of Churches of America).

Full-time Mennonite migrant workers were sponsored by California General Conference Mennonites at Shafter as early as 1941. That same year a Mennonite Women's United Service Committee of the Defenseless, General, and Central conferences was organized with migrant work as a major service objective.

The Mennonite Central Committee in co-operation with the Home Missions Council pioneered in placing a team of six to ten voluntary service workers to do a more thorough job in a given area. The first such summer unit was in operation in Utica, N.Y., in 1949, and shortly thereafter a year-round unit at Coalinga, Cal. A children's nursery, evenings of recreation, visual education, a traveling library service, visiting nurse, vacation Bible school, Sunday schools, and a wide range of counseling and visitation constitute such a total unit approach. It is an effort to provide the help and influence of a Christian church community to an unstable, migrating community of Christians and non-Christians. Though not aimed specifically toward becoming a continuing mission church, its fruition has been just that. By 1956 the Brethren in Christ had taken over the Coalinga work as a mission project.

Of the individual Mennonite groups the Lancaster Conference (MC) has developed one of the most extensive ongoing ministries to the migrants. Their year-round migrant service, much like the MCC's, began in 1951 with a unit of five workers at Redland, Fla. A year later a similar group was located in the Everglades of Florida at Immokalee. In both camps the Mennonites have regular chapel services in buildings provided by the government-built camp or the local migrant committtee of the near-by city. In 1951 a Gospel Quartet spent several months with Negro migrants in Potter County, Pa. This has developed into a continuing program with child care as the core of the work. Spanish migrant work in their own neighborhood was begun in Lancaster County in 1950. Of particular significance is an annual fellowship meal and meeting sponsored by local Mennonite churches which reaches 1,000 Puerto Rican migrants at one time.

Other similar missions to migrants include that of the Mennonite Church (MC) with the Indians in New Mexico, in Maryland, and other states. The G.C. Mennonites have developed a mission church at Eloy, Ariz., for poor whites and Spanish and Negro migrants.   E.ED.

Migrations of Mennonites. Mennonites and their history are characterized by severe persecution and subsequent migrations. The Mennonites of Swiss background migrated primarily to South Germany,

France, and Pennsylvania; most of the Mennonites east of the Mississippi River are of this background. Smaller groups of Swiss Mennonites also went to Holland, Polish Russia, and Prussia.

During the 16th century the Mennonites of the Low Countries went primarily eastward to Danzig and Polish Russia, and only during the second half of the past century did their descendants begin to come to America, with the exception of the first Dutch-German Mennonite families who settled in Germantown, Pa. Those coming during the last century settled mostly in the prairie states and provinces, and are thus located west of the Mississippi River. All Mennonites that have migrated to South America are of this background.

Dutch - North German Mennonite Migrations. When Anabaptism established itself in the Low Countries under most adverse conditions, migration to other countries was often the only chance for survival. The Anabaptists from Flanders went to the northern provinces of the Low Countries. On the other hand, German East Friesland became the haven of religious refugees from the Low Countries as a whole. Menno Simons, Dirk Philips, Leenaert Bouwens, David Joris, and many other early leaders and their followers found shelter there. Another German province which soon became a haven of Anabaptist refugees was Schleswig-Holstein. Wüstenfelde near Oldesloe became a Mennonite settlement with Menno Simons as leader. Soon Altona and Friedrichstadt attracted refugees.

As early as 1530 Anabaptists found their way to the Vistula Delta and the migration to this area continued for a long time. Menno Simons and Dirk Philips were instrumental in establishing congregations here. From here the Mennonites moved along the Vistula River even into Poland after the triangle between Danzig, Elbing, and Marienburg had been occupied. Until the middle of the 18th century the surplus population was absorbed in new settlements along the Vistula. Thus far all migration had been on a scale involving small groups. From now on organized large-scale migration of Mennonites of Dutch background became common.

When Catherine the Great issued her Manifesto in 1763 inviting farmers from Western countries to settle in the Ukraine, the Mennonites of Prussia and Danzig were soon attracted, because they were continually encountering restrictions in their economic and religious life. Later the matter of exemption from military service became important. The approximate number that emigrated to Russia in 1787-1870 was 1,907 families, with a total of some 8,000 persons. This constituted a true mass migration of Mennonites in comparison with previous movements. Of this number about 400 families settled at Chortitza (*q.v.*), some 1,049 at Molotschna (*q.v.*), some 438 at Samara (*q.v.*), and 20 families were reported to have gone to Vilna.

While the migration eastward was still in progress the Mennonites of Russia and Prussia were again studying the map to find a place where they would find complete exemption from military service, which they were in danger of losing in Prussia and Russia. In 1873-84 some 18,000 Mennonites left Russia to settle in the United States and Canada.

Although the Chortitza settlement (Old Colony) was much smaller than the Molotschna settlement, it furnished almost half of the emigrants. Only a small number of the Samara Mennonites, the newest settlement, left. The chief reasons for this mass migration were unwillingness to accept a compulsory alternative service program and the objection to a Russianization program inaugurated by the Russian government. Only a small number of Prussian Mennonites joined this movement, whereas all of the Swiss Volhynian Mennonites of Polish Russia joined, half of the Swiss Galician Mennonites came to America, and many of the Low German Mennonites of Poland came to the United States as congregations (Karolswalde, Michalin, etc.).

An even larger migration of Mennonites from Russia occurred after World War I, when in 1922-30 some 25,000 Mennonites went to Canada (21,000), Mexico, Brazil, and Paraguay. The reasons for this mass migration were the threat of a complete disintegration of the religious, cultural, and economic way of life of the Mennonites. A much larger number would have escaped if the "Red gate" had not rather suddenly closed. During the German occupation of the Ukraine in 1941-43 some 35,000 were evacuated by the German army to be settled in the Vistula area where they had come from some 150 years ago. Because of the outcome of the war nearly two thirds of them were forcibly repatriated by the Russian army in 1945-46, while some 12,000 found their way to Canada and South America.

In Russia itself great migrations have taken place. Between 1850 and 1914 many new settlements originated in the Ukraine, Crimea, north of the Caucasian Mountains, along the Volga River, Siberia, Central Asia, etc. After the Revolution mass exiles and concentrations in slave labor camps contributed to the dispersion of Mennonites. Large numbers were sent to northern European Russia and to Asiatic Russia. Again during the invasion of the Ukraine by the Germans in 1941 many Mennonite settlements were dissolved, the total population having been sent to Asiatic Russia by the Soviet government. This happened to the settlements east of the Dnieper River with the exception of those which the invading German army was not expected to reach. The exact location of the majority of the Mennonite population and its centers since this mass migration has not yet been fully determined. Kazakhstan, east of the Ural Mountains, is known as a new center of the Mennonite population.

All the Mennonites of Prussia and Poland fled in 1945 when the Russian army approached. Some were interned for some time in Denmark, while the others escaped to West Germany, where many of them have established new homes. A large number of the Danzig and Prussian and some of the Galician Mennonites migrated to Uruguay and Canada in 1948-52.

Migrations have also taken place among the Mennonites of America. After World War I many Old Colony Mennonites moved from Manitoba and Saskatchewan to Mexico and some Sommerfelder Mennonites moved to the Chaco of Paraguay. In general, the Mennonite population trend in Canada and the United States has been from the east to the west and from the country to the city. A considerable number of Russian Mennonites from Paraguay have come to Canada. There have also been some migrations within the boundaries of Brazil. Witmarsum was dissolved and New Witmarsum and Bage were established.   C.K.

C. Henry Smith, *The Story of the Mennonites* (Newton, 1950); *idem*, *The Coming of the Russian Mennonites* (Berne, 1927); *Mennonite Life Maps and Charts* (North Newton, 1953); Horst Quiring, "Die Auswanderung der Mennoniten aus Preussen 1788-1870," *Menn. Life* VI (April 1951); S. C. Yoder, *For Conscience Sake* (Goshen, 1940); Ernst Müller, *Berner Täufer*; B. H. Unruh, *Die niederländisch-niederdeutschen Hintergründe der mennonitischen Ostwanderungen im 16., 18. und 19. Jahrhundert* (Karlsruhe, 1955).

Swiss-South German Migrations. The first migrations from Switzerland or South Germany were of Anabaptists fleeing persecution to a haven of refuge with Hutterites in Moravia, throughout the 16th century. This was not on a mass scale but included a considerable number of families, sometimes blocks or a whole congregation. Hutterite missioners invited the harried brethren to come, promising toleration and the security of a large group fellowship. The numbers leaving sometimes were so large, or other resources taken along so great, that the civil authorities took steps to stop the movement, both by counter-persuasion and by penalties, including confiscation of property and imprisonment, both of those departing and the missioners. To go to Moravia meant of course for the Swiss Brethren not only a migration but a conversion to Hutterianism.

The next migration, also caused by persecution, which became very severe in Switzerland in the 17th century, was from the cantons of Bern and Zürich down the Rhine to Alsace and the Palatinate on both sides of the Rhine, as well as certain adjoining territories such as Durlach or Zweibrücken. Since the earlier Anabaptists in these territories were almost completely wiped out by 1600-30, all the later Mennonite settlements in these areas were made by emigrants from Switzerland. The heaviest movement was in 1650-90. Some Bernese Anabaptists migrated to the Jura region of the Bishopric of Basel early in the 18th century, and about 1711 some emigrated to Holland. In 1714 the Anabaptists were ordered expelled from Alsace, and many left to found the community in Montbéliard, at that time ruled by Württemberg. From 1700 on there was an almost constant internal migration of families from Alsace westward into interior France, northward down the Rhine into Hesse, into Wittgenstein, and finally into Waldeck, where it reached its limit. Mennonite farmers were seeking land to rent and tolerable living conditions and freedom of worship. Mennonites from the Palatinate moved eastward in South Germany into Württemberg, Franconia, and Bavaria from about 1800 on. Others went from Alsace and the Palatinate to Galicia about 1784-85, and some of them later to Volhynia. Shortage of land forced some migration of Swiss Mennonites into Alsace in the late 19th and early 20th centuries.

But the greatest migration of the Swiss-South German Mennonites, both from Switzerland direct and from France, Germany, and Galicia-Volhynia,

was to North America. This migration was of the greatest significance for the future of the Mennonite movement. Beginning in 1683, one hundred years before the emigration from West Prussia to Russia begun in 1788, it lasted much longer (200 years) and ultimately moved more people. It was, of course, a part of the great Atlantic migration from western Europe to America, in which the Mennonites played a small role, although they have the honor of founding the first permanent German settlement in America at Germantown. This total migration falls into six successive waves: (1) Lower Rhine to Germantown, 1683-1705, 100 persons; (2) Palatinate and Switzerland to Eastern Pennsylvania (Franconia and Lancaster districts), 1707-56, 3,000-5,000 persons, mostly Mennonite, possibly 300 Amish; (3) Alsatian, Bavarian, and Hessian Amish to Ohio, Ontario, Indiana, Illinois, 1815-80, possibly 3,000 persons; (4) Swiss Mennonites to Ohio and Indiana, 1830-60, possibly 500 persons; (5) Palatine Mennonites to Ohio, Indiana, Illinois, possibly 300 persons; stragglers of the last three groups continued to come after the Civil War (1861-65) until toward the end of the 19th century; (6) Galician and Volhynian Mennonites to Kansas and South Dakota, 1875-80, about 400 persons. A total of possibly 8,000 persons crossed the Atlantic in the two centuries. Almost all of the first three waves found fellowship together in what is known as the Mennonite Church (MC). Including some Amish who never joined (remaining Old Order) and the schismatic groups, Oberholtzer (GCM), Holdeman (CGC, a minority part only), Reformed Mennonites, Evangelical (Defenseless) Mennonites, and Central Conference (GCM), the total Mennonite membership in the United States and Canada in 1956 of the descendants of these 8,000 immigrants of 1683 to 1883 number approximately 120,000 or three fifths of the total Mennonite membership. Since only 10,000 of this number are in Canada, the 110,000 in the United States (not counting the United Missionary Church) is over two thirds or about 70 per cent of the total number of Mennonites in the United States. A small Dutch group from Balk came to New Paris, Ind., in 1853.

This group of immigrants has been widely distributed by internal migration. A considerable movement to Southern Ontario from Eastern Pennsylvania took place in 1785-1840, accompanied by a southward movement to Maryland and Virginia. A movement westward (also from Virginia) across the Alleghenies into Western Pennsylvania and Ohio and finally from Ohio and Ontario to Indiana and Northern Illinois took place in 1800-60. All this was Mennonite. An Amish movement westward from Eastern (and Western) Pennsylvania into Ohio, Indiana, and Iowa (some to central Illinois) took place in 1800-60. Some Amish from Illinois and Ontario reached Iowa and Nebraska in 1845-80. Mennonites from Pennsylvania and Virginia reached Missouri and Kansas in 1865-90, and some went into North Dakota, Oregon, and Alberta in 1890-1920. Some Amish reached Oregon from Ohio and Missouri, also Iowa and Nebraska in 1880-1910. A small movement of Mennonites from Ontario reached Saskatchewan and Alberta in

1907-20. All these westward movements were part and parcel of the general internal westward migration in both the United States and Canada. Whereas the migrations across the Atlantic had as a major motive the search for religious toleration and freedom from military service, with economic betterment, the internal migrations were solely motivated by the search for cheaper land and economic betterment.

The Dutch Mennonites rendered significant financial aid to the harried Swiss and Palatine Mennonites in their migration to Pennsylvania in the first half of the 18th century. It is doubtful if many could have succeeded in the move without this help, since most of the Swiss were penniless exiles, and the Palatines had suffered heavily from the French invasions and the heavy exactions and economic restrictions of the successive Palatine rulers. H.S.B.

The internal German migrations are well surveyed in the article "Germany" by Ernst Crous (*ME* II, 491-93), those of the Bernese in Europe and in the 19th century to Ohio and Indiana by Delbert Gratz, *Bernese Anabaptists and Their American Descendants* (Goshen, 1953) 57-78 and 128-40. C. Henry Smith's *The Mennonite Immigration to Pennsylvania in the 18th Century* (Norristown, 1929) covers the early story thoroughly. His *Story of the Mennonites* (Berne, 1941) is almost the only source for the 19th century.

Mijleman, Franciscus (1610-67), a Jesuit who was active in the Dutch province of Groningen in 1639-67, and who gave some information about Anabaptism in this area in his booklet *Ommelands Eere*. In his book *Vast ende klaer bewijs hoe dat Christus Jesus . . . in sijn H. Mensch-wordinge heeft uyt sijns H. Moeders, en Maegts Maria suyver Lichaem aengenomen onse Nature* (Antwerp, 1661), he also attacked the doctrine of the Incarnation (*q.v.*) as taught by Menno Simons. (*DB* 1906, 41-43; *N.N.B.Wb.* III, 900.) vDZ.

Mildam, a hamlet in the Dutch province of Friesland, near Heerenveen, the seat of a Mennonite congregation belonging to the Groningen Old Flemish branch (the *Naamlijst* of 1731 erroneously calls it Frisian). In 1648 it had a small meetinghouse. The preachers listed are Jacob Poppes (1648), Frank Wybes (1681), Jan Rykels (1683), Jan Jans Heide (1696-1764), serving 1725-64, Klaas Eites, *ca.*1722-46, Dirk Gerrits 1747-d.70. The membership numbered about 50 in 1710, 62 in 1733, 39 in 1754. About 1765 the congregation of Mildam merged with that of neighboring Knijpe (*q.v.*), hence it is then called Mildam and Knijpe or Knijpe and Mildam. It died out about 1800. (Blaupot t. C., *Groningen* I, 128; *DJ* 1840, 43; *DB* 1879, 3, 90; 1890, 94.) vDZ.

Milder, Johannes (*ca.*1628-88), a Hutterite leader, born in the brotherhood in Hungary, a tailor by vocation, was chosen preacher on March 4, 1660, in Sobotiste (*q.v.*) and ordained on March 13, 1661. He experienced all the vicissitudes of the Thirty Years' War as they affected this settlement of the Hutterian Brethren with their many tribulations, quartering of troops, and oppression. Sobotiste was the Bruderhof from which a delegation was sent to Holland in 1665 to ask aid, which they received.

Milder, in co-operation with the leader Johannes Rieger and his colleague Benjamin Poley, was outstanding in his fearless opposition to the efforts of Georg Szelepesenyi, the archbishop of Gran, royal chancellor and regent of Hungary, to catholicize the Brethren. On March 11, 1574, the three were summoned to Pressburg where about three hundred Lutheran and Calvinist preachers and teachers were assembled, who were subsequently expelled, imprisoned, and some of them sentenced to serve as galley slaves. The three Brethren were ordered by the agents of the Counter Reformation either to become Catholic or to leave the country. For days they were urged with promises and threats, at least to permit their children to be baptized. They replied that this was impossible, and said that they wished nothing but to serve and to make their living without harming anyone. The noblemen present gave them the best testimonial, finding only the one fault that they were not Catholics.

When Milder, Rieger, and Poley were about to go home, the archbishop had three halberdiers take them by force to the cathedral on Palm Sunday, when he held the High Mass. But the splendor of the cult did not make the desired impression on the three Brethren standing amid the worshipers; hence the archbishop had them brought to his castle in the train following his carriage and then dismissed them with orders to make their final decision within two weeks.

Upon their return to Sobotiste the three Brethren reported their experience to the brotherhood and received their approbation. In April they reported to the archbishop's committee that they intended to remain steadfast. But the expected expulsion did not follow; it is said that the bishop of Wiener Neustadt intervened. While Sobotiste was left in peace, there was no cessation of attempts to convert the Brethren in Trentschin. On March 3, 1676, the three Brethren were again summoned to Pressburg and confronted with the same promises and threats as in the previous year and then dismissed. Some of the landlords also took advantage of the situation and oppressed them. Then followed the quartering of troops in the period of the Turkish war, especially 1686-87, as well as internal difficulties, such as the abandonment of communal living in Velke Levary (*q.v.*).

In the summer of 1687 the leader Johannes Rieger died. The preachers of the Bruderhofs in Sobotiste, Levary, Trentschin, Dechtitz, Schatmannsdorf, and St. Johannes on Aug. 20 unanimously chose Milder as leader of the brotherhood. After less than 33 weeks in this office he died on March 28, 1688, at the age of sixty. (Beck, *Geschichts-Bücher;* Wolkan, *Geschicht-Buch;* Zieglschmid, *Chronik;* ML III, 133 f.) P.De.

Milford, Neb., is a town (pop. 900) in the southeastern end of Seward County, which is in the southeastern part of the state. The three Mennonite (MC) churches in the community, Milford, East Fairview, West Fairview, have a total of 796 members. Approximately 650 Mennonites live within shopping distance of the town. The main settlement is west of town, but there are Mennonites living all around it. Approximately 18 per cent (75 families) of the Mennonites live in town; about one third of the businesses are owned and operated by Mennonites.

Mennonites have been living in this area since 1873. Near the town is the Rest Home for the Aged, privately operated by a Mennonite family. (*ML* III, 134.)   L.O.S.

Milford Defenseless Mennonite Church, now extinct, located in Seward Co., Neb., had its beginning in the late 1890's, when settlers came from Groveland and Flanagan, Ill. In 1891 they built a church. C. R. Egle from the Flanagan area was chosen the first minister. After a number of years Joseph Rediger from Groveland succeeded him, serving as pastor for a number of years. Silas Miller also served the church. For a time Rediger apparently preached in German and Miller in English. At the beginning there were about 40 members and at the most 100. Some of the members came from the Amish church near by.

In 1915 a revival took place in which many were converted. Shortly thereafter there was some difference of opinion as to doctrine and the church was dismissed from the conference. The building was then sold to the group, who later sold it for salvage. About four or five, however, remained with the Defenseless Mennonite Conference. Others became affiliated with the Mennonite Brethren in Christ.
E.E.Z.

Milford Mennonite Church (MC), located in Milford, Seward Co., Neb., a member of the Iowa-Nebraska Mennonite District Conference, was organized on Nov. 19, 1925, with 81 charter members, under the leadership of L. O. Schlegel, bishop, and William Schlegel, minister, as a schism from the East Fairview Mennonite Church (*q.v.*). After a period of attempted affiliation with the General Conference Mennonite Church the congregation returned and was received as a member of the Iowa-Nebraska Conference (MC) on Aug. 8, 1938. The first meetinghouse, a frame structure, was erected in 1926, modernized and enlarged to a seating capacity of 400 in 1953. The 1956 membership was 205 with L. O. Schlegel as bishop and W. A. Eicher and Milton Troyer as ministers. On June 3, 1956, Milton Troyer was ordained bishop and L. O. Schlegel resigned from active service.   L.O.S.

Milford (Buck Ranch) Hutterite Bruderhof, founded in 1918 near Raymond, Alberta, by the members of the Bruderhof in Milford, S.D., and their preachers Johann Kleinsasser and Jerg Waldner; they sold the holdings in South Dakota and bought the Big Ben site. In 1947 the Milford Bruderhof numbered 125 souls, with 60 baptized members.   D.D.

Milford Square, Bucks Co., Pa., was the location of the press of John H. Oberholtzer, founder in 1847 of what is known as the Eastern District Conference (GCM) in southeastern Pennsylvania. On June 9, 1852, he issued here the first number of a new church periodical entitled *Religiöser Botschafter* (*q.v.*). To bear the burden of publication there was organized in 1856 the Mennonite Printing Union (in German, Mennonitischer Druck-Verein, *q.v.*) to take over the Oberholtzer printery, which was later sold to J. G. Stauffer. In 1856 the name of the paper was changed to *Das Christliche Volksblatt*,

and in 1867 to *Mennonitischer Friedensbote*. From Milford Square were also issued a number of books, booklets, catechisms, constitutions, conference reports, periodicals, etc., beginning in 1855 with Gottfried Arnold's *Geistliche Erfahrungslehre*. When the 1860 sessions of the General Conference Mennonite Church were held it was proposed to create a mission board, with one treasury to be maintained at Franklin Center, Lee Co., Iowa, the other at Milford Square, Bucks Co., Pa., but the plan seems not to have been adopted. The Mennonite (GCM) publisher J. G. Stauffer (*q.v.*) also issued periodicals such as the *Himmelsmanna* (1876-), *Reformer & Agriculturist* (1876-) for a number of years at Milford Square before removing to Quakertown, Pa., in 1880. Stauffer published also B. C. Roosen's *Menno Symons den Mennoniten Gemeinden geschildert* at Milford Square in 1874. And Peter High Stauffer issued an eight-page periodical from Milford Square entitled *Our Home Friend*. For years the name Milford Square stood for the publication interests of the General Conference Mennonite Church, especially in the East. (*ML* III, 134 f.)   J.C.W.

Military Service in Europe. The ancient Mennonite principle of nonresistance has often led to conflicts with the state, until in the course of the 19th century, partly under compulsion and partly from conviction, the principle was abandoned almost completely in Europe. This change was at the same time the result of the change in the form of warfare. Formerly war was the business of mercenary troops; now it is the affair of the entire nation. Hence the Mennonites of Europe in their adjustment to the society surrounding them reached the point where they sacrificed their nonresistance.

The Swiss Mennonites with some difficulty preserved their full nonresistance for a long time. The regulation of Sept. 3, 1815, granted them the privilege of hiring substitutes for their service in the army. When their nonresistance was denied them in 1874, they secured the privilege of noncombatant service in the army, which they have used in most cases.

In the Netherlands the "fine Mennonites" (*Fijne Mennisten*) strictly maintained the principle of nonresistance, while the "coarse Mennonites" (*Grove Mennisten*) in the late 17th and 18th centuries considered a war of self-defense justified, but nevertheless forbade their members to become soldiers. By considerable (more or less) voluntary gifts of money they induced the government to continue to grant them freedom from military service (union of Utrecht, 1579). During the wars with England in 1606 and 1672 they paid about 500,000 florins. During the siege of Kampen, Groningen, Deventer, etc., they fulfilled their civic duty by fighting fires under a constant rain of bullets. But in the arming of the civilians in North Holland and Friesland in 1785 some Mennonites hastened voluntarily to bear arms, and even though this step was frowned upon by the brotherhood, and some Mennonites were actually expelled from membership for serving on a warship in 1793, and others were not admitted to baptism, nevertheless nonresistance was no longer a required article of faith. In 1796 a law was passed which abrogated the old privilege given to the Mennonites by Prince William I of Orange, but which still made it possible to avoid military service by sending a substitute. In 1810 Napoleon invaded the "Batavian Republic" and compelled the Mennonites to bear arms. But it was not until the war with Belgium (1830) that the practice of nonresistance was generally abandoned, though not by all. At the end of the 19th century the tenet of nonresistance was abandoned and in its stead the obligation to "Christian meekness" was adopted. The system of employing substitutes was abolished by a law of 1898; from that time on, military service was compulsory for all, including the Mennonites, who accepted it without much objection. After World War I the principle of nonresistance was revived in certain small circles and the "Arbeidsgroep (*q.v.*) tegen de Krijgsdienst" was organized, followed by the "Vredesgroep" (*q.v.*) after World War II. (See **Conscientious Objectors.**)

The Mennonites of France were permitted by a decision passed in the French Revolution to perform their military service in building fortifications and roads or in transportation or to purchase their release. Thus until the reign of Napoleon III they were free of the obligation to render full military service.

The Mennonites of Galicia were given a promise of freedom from military service in 1789, which was rescinded by Austria at the close of the 19th century.

Most consistent in their refusal of military service were the Hutterian Brethren (*q.v.*). They even refused to perform services indirectly supporting war. In Russia the substitution of forestry for military service did not satisfy them, and they (with many Mennonites) emigrated to America.

In South and West Germany the Mennonites enjoyed the privilege of voluntary freedom from military service until 1806. As late as 1803 the Ibersheim conference passed the resolution that "bearing arms is contrary to the teaching of Christ and of our faith." But Napoleon paid no attention to creeds when he conscripted all the young men of the age of 21 in the territory of the federation of the Rhine. To hire a substitute for 2,000 florins was possible only for the wealthy. Thus the law of Jan. 7, 1805, in Bavaria, Dec. 17, 1820, in Hesse, and Aug. 22, 1818, in Baden, meant the end of nonresistance in those countries, although the provision was made for the hiring of a substitute.

The Mennonites of East Friesland lost their freedom from military service under the reign of the Hannoverian kings. On the basis of the more liberal position of the Rhenish Mennonites, Hermann von Beckerath, a member of the Crefeld congregation and minister of state in 1848, declared in the Parliament of Frankfurt that the Mennonites were willing to perform armed service. Immediately a protest was made by the Mennonites of West Prussia (Heubuden, Sept. 14, 1848), stating that for most of their members it was still a matter of deepest conviction not to bear arms. (The document is printed in complete form in Mannhardt, 192.)

The Mennonites of West Prussia fought longest to preserve nonresistance. Under the Polish government they could employ a substitute; only the Danzig Mennonites had to serve in guard and fire-fighting duty in 1733-34, and were then released upon payment of 5,000 florins, later reduced to 2,000. Serious difficulties arose when West Prussia was incorporated into militarized Prussia. In 1723 the recruiting agents of Frederick William forced some young Mennonites living in Lithuania to enter the army for a short time. Under the tolerant reign of Frederick the Great, however, they were granted freedom from military service "forever." In return for the privilege they had to pay 5,000 Thalers annually to the cadet school in Culm after 1773. In the Wars of Liberation they collected voluntary sums of 10,000 and 30,000 Thalers; nevertheless they had to suffer much annoyance, especially on the part of minor officials. A graphic picture of these struggles is given by Elder Heinrich Donner (*q.v.*) (*Gem.-Kal.* 1932). They maintained the principle of nonresistance and expelled several young Mennonites from membership for performing military service.

When universal military conscription was introduced in Prussia, an order of cabinet of March 3, 1868, gave them the privilege of serving in the noncombatant functions of the armed forces. This provision became valid for the entire German army in 1871. Only in Bavaria and Württemberg was military service forced upon the Mennonites. But in the Franco-Prussian War some of the Mennonites voluntarily took up arms, and in World War I only a few Mennonites took advantage of the order of the cabinet. One report states that about one third of the West Prussian Mennonites took noncombatant service in World War I. In World War II the German Mennonites as such no longer asked for noncombatant service.

Since 1918 (until 1945) there was among the German Mennonites no thought of refusing military service. All the Mennonites without exception accepted the call to military training in 1933. For later developments see below.

The Mennonites of Russia were released from military service in 1800 "for all time." In gratitude many young Mennonites served in the hospital units during the Crimean War; several lost their lives. When military service became compulsory in 1874, lengthy negotiations with General Todtleben led to the enactment of a law permitting the Mennonites to perform their service to the state in forestry service. In World War I many voluntarily accepted service in the medical corps, which was at that time still under the Red Cross and not a part of the army. Under the treaty of Brest-Litovsk of 1917, the Germans occupied the Ukraine for a time. When they were preparing their withdrawal self-defense military units (*Selbstschutz*) were organized in the German settlements, particularly in the Mennonite settlements of Chortitza and Molotschna. After the withdrawal the Mennonite Selbstschutz (*q.v.*) did a small amount of fighting with the Machno guerrillas but were speedily overcome. After the re-establishment of the Russian army under the Soviet government the Mennonites were granted the privilege of noncombatant service until about 1933-35. (See **Nonresistance** for North America.) H.S.B.

A. Brons, *Ursprung und Schicksale der . . . Mennoniten* (Emden, 1912); W. Mannhardt, *Die Wehrfreiheit der Altpreussischen Mennoniten* (Danzig, 1863); N. van der Zijpp, *De vroegere Doopsgezinden en de Krijgsdienst* (Wolvega, 1930); E. Händiges, *Die Lehre der Mennoniten* (Kaiserslautern, 1921); Chr. Neff, "Die Wehrlosigkeit der Mennoniten und der Weltkrieg," in *Die Eiche,* April 1924; John Horsch, *Die biblische Lehre von der Wehrlosigkeit* (Scottdale, 1920); J. S. Hartzler, *Mennonites in the World War* (Scottdale, 1921); Friesen, *Brüderschaft; ML* III, 135 f.

Mill Creek Union Church is located in the village of Hamburg two miles west of Luray, Page Co., Va. This old weatherboarded log church, still standing, was built around 1800. The land was given by Joseph Mauck, a Mennonite, and the church built on it was to be open to all orthodox denominations. Mennonite preachers in Rockingham County held infrequent services here for a rapidly declining membership in Page County during the 19th century. For a number of years Mennonites and other interested parties have held an annual *Harmonia Sacra* Singing in this ancient church.　H.A.B.

Mill Run Mennonite (MC) Mission, located in a suburb of Altoona, Pa., with a population of a few hundred, is an outgrowth of the Altoona mission work and is located about three miles north of the Home Mission at 2504 Fourth Avenue. The Southwestern Pennsylvania (now Allegheny) Mission Board authorized the opening of the work in November 1927; a plot of ground was purchased for a building site, and a chapel was built, dedicated in 1928. A mission home was erected in 1933, and in 1937 a school adjacent to the chapel was purchased to provide more space. The former chapel was converted into a residence. At first the work was carried on under the supervision of the Altoona Mission, but it now has its own workers and organization under the direction of the Allegheny Mennonite Mission Board. In 1956 the membership was 30, with Sidney Martin as pastor.　J.L.H.

Joseph Nissley, in *Mennonite Yearbook and Directory,* 1929; John L. Horst and Ammon Kaufman, *Seventy-fifth Anniversary Observance of Southwestern Pennsylvania Conference* (1951).

Mill Stream, The, is a 32-page periodical issued 10 times a year by Lancaster Mennonite School, Lancaster, Pa., since 1942, edited by a student staff. It carries school news, articles by students and teachers of the school, poems and essays from English classes, and solicited contributions by persons not in school.　N.G.

Millbach: see **Royer** Mennonite Church.

Millbach (Pa.) Mennonite Mission (MC) was operated by the Ephrata, Pa., Mennonite Church in 1945-47 in a former Baptist church located about one mile north of Kleinfeltersville in Lebanon Co., Pa., primarily for Lancaster County Mennonite families moving northward for cheaper land. In 1947 the Millbach work was moved to the Tulpehocken Brethren church building between Myerstown and Richland.　I.D.L.

Millen, a village now in the Dutch province of Limburg, in the 16th century belonging to the duchy of Jülich, Germany. In the 1530's it was a center of Anabaptist activity. Later there were also Mennonites here. Theunis van Hastenrath (*q.v.*) baptized in Millen about 1550. About 1550 one group of seven Anabaptists and then one of eleven were beheaded in the territories of Millen and neighboring Born (*q.v.*). In 1591 the Concept (*q.v.*) of Cologne was signed by Diderich Verwer for the Millen congregations ("vanwegen aller Gemeynten in 't Lant van Millen").　vDZ.

Rembert, *Wiedertäufer,* see Index; W. Bax, *Het Protestantisme in het bisdom Luik* I (The Hague, 1937) *passim;* II (The Hague, 1941) 365; *Mart. Mir.* D 98, E 496.

Millennialism: see **Chiliasm.**

Miller, an American family name of Swiss origin. (For the European history of the family, see **Müller.**) It is the most common family name in the Mennonite Church (MC) and in the Old Order Amish and Conservative and related Amish groups, but it is completely missing from the lists of ordained men in all other Mennonite groups in North America, except three in the General Conference Mennonite Church; it is not found in any group in Canada. In 1956, of the O.O.A. ordained men, 131 bore the name Miller, 63 in Ohio and 37 in Indiana. In the other Amish groups 28 more ordained men were Millers. In the Mennonite Church (MC) there were 93 ordained men bearing this name, six of these in Indiana and eleven in Pennsylvania. Miller is distinctly a midwestern Amish name; very few families of Millers descend from the early Mennonites in colonial Pennsylvania, although Jacob Miller was one of the first (1710) Mennonite settlers to arrive in Lancaster County from Switzerland. Among the church leaders of the past with this name should be mentioned the Mennonite bishops Moses B. Miller (1819-1902), bishop in the Johnstown (Pa.) district from 1848; Noah E. Miller (1880-1930), bishop at Springs, Pa., from 1921; D. D. Miller (1864-1955), bishop near Middlebury, Ind., from 1906. Jonas B. Miller (1870-1952) was an influential Conservative minister at Grantsville, Md., from 1897. Moses J. Miller (1811-97) was an influential Old Order Amish bishop in Holmes County, Ohio, from 1847. Among the currently active workers in the Mennonite Church are O. O. Miller of Akron, Pa., long executive secretary of the MCC, and Ernest E. Miller of Goshen, Ind., missionary to India and president of Goshen College 1940-54, both sons of the above D. D. Miller, Paul M. Miller, bishop and professor in the Goshen College Biblical Seminary, D. D. Miller, bishop at Berlin, Ohio, Ira E. Miller, minister and dean of Eastern Mennonite College at Harrisonburg, Va., Paul R. Miller, bishop at Walnut Creek, Ohio, Ivan J. Miller, Conservative bishop at Grantsville, Md. (Eight Miller genealogies, mostly of Amish families, are listed in the article **Genealogies,** *ME* II, 461.)　H.S.B.

Miller, D. D. (1864-1955), a Mennonite (MC) bishop and leader, was born in Lagrange County, Ind., on Dec. 10, 1864, a son of Daniel P. and Anna (Hershberger) Miller. He prepared himself for teaching school, and followed the profession for twenty years. On May 26, 1889, he married Nettie Hostetler. They had thirteen children, of whom eleven grew to maturity: Orie O., Ernest E., Truman T., Ida, Clara, Wilbur W., Kathryn, Bertha, Alice, Samuel S., and Mabel. All became schoolteachers for longer or shorter periods. Orie O. Miller (b. 1892) became executive secretary of the Mennonite Central Committee, Ernest E. Miller (b. 1893) president of Goshen College, and Samuel S. Miller (b. 1908) a bishop in the Indiana-Michigan Conference (MC). As a young man D. D. Miller went west to Cass County, Mo.; while there he united with the Amish Mennonite Church. After some time he returned to Indiana and became a member of the Forks A.M. Church in his home community. There in 1890 he was chosen as deacon, one year later as preacher, and in 1906 as bishop, D. J. Johns performing all three ordinations. About a year after his ordination he voluntarily adopted the "plain coat" so that his ministry would be more effective among the Mennonites (MC), although his Amish Mennonite church did not require it. He traveled far and wide in the Amish Mennonite and Mennonite brotherhoods, served as an evangelist and a Bible Conference instructor times without number, and exerted a strong influence everywhere he went. His sermons were well prepared, his voice was strong and clear, his thought processes clear and direct. As a disciplinarian he was somewhat strict, yet not a legalist. He wrote considerably for the *Gospel Herald,* the organ of the Mennonite Church (MC), and contributed several sections to the large *Bible Doctrine* book of 1914. He was active in his local conference, first the Indiana-Michigan Amish Mennonite Conference, and then in the Indiana-Michigan Mennonite Conference (MC) after the merger of 1916. He was the first moderator of the united conference, and frequently thereafter. He was active in the Mennonite General Conference (MC), on the Mennonite Board of Education (MC), and especially on the Mennonite Board of Missions and Charities (MC), of which he served as president 1920-35, and as treasurer 1939-40. He continued to serve a large bishop district in the churches of Indiana until his health collapsed in his eightieth year, early in 1944. Burial was in the Forest Grove Cemetery, southeast of Middlebury.   J.C.W.

Miller, Jonas B. (1870-1952), Amish Mennonite minister and leader, was born at Grantsville, Md., on Dec. 10, 1870, the oldest of the three sons and three daughters of Bishop Joel J. and Savilla (Beachy) Miller. He was the sixth generation of the Miller family, Amish pioneers, who settled in the Casselman River region in 1793. He was married to Barbara Swartzentruber on Oct. 5, 1893. They raised a family of four sons and seven daughters on their small farm near Grantsville, among them Bishop Ivan J.

Miller was an avid reader and lover of books, and an able student, public speaker, and writer. He was a member of the Amish Mennonite Church and ordained to the ministry by his father on May 30, 1897, serving over 52 years. He was one of the original members of the Conservative Amish Mennonite Conference and one of its early influential leaders. He served as English editor of *Herold der Wahrheit* 1917-49, **when** he was succeeded by his

son Evan. In his preaching and writing he was a staunch advocate of conservatism in faith and practice. He died Sept. 20, 1952, at Grantsville and is buried in the Maple Glen cemetery.   I.J.M.

Miller, Moses J. (1811-97), an Amish bishop and leader, was the second Amish child and the third white child born in Holmes Co., Ohio. His parents, with three other families, all young people, moved from Somerset Co., Pa., to the western wilderness in Walnut Township, arriving on May 6, 1810. Indian raids drove them back to Somerset County during the War of 1812, but in 1815 they returned to Holmes County. In 1834 Moses married Katherine Dunn, an Irish girl. They became the parents of ten children, of whom only three outlived their father. He was ordained minister in the Amish Church in 1835 and bishop in 1847. He was one of 14 bishops and ministers in the Holmes-Tuscarawas congregations to attend the first Amish ministers' meeting held in Wayne Co., Ohio, in June 1862. Three Moses Millers were present at that conference: Moses J. (*Gross* or Big Mose) Miller of Walnut Creek; Moses H. Miller of Winesburg; and Moses Miller of Shanesville. One of the latter was known as *"Klein* (Small) Mose" and was so designated in the conference report. There was also another Moses B. Miller from Johnstown, Pa. The subject of this sketch, "Big Mose," took an active part in the conference discussions and took a broad-minded, conciliatory attitude in current issues. He strongly advocated leniency in enforcing the ban between man and wife, favored allowing nonmembers in the counsel meeting when Christian duties were under consideration, and urged tolerance on the mode of baptism, "in the house" or "in a running stream." Moses J. Miller did not attend the general Amish ministers' meeting again until it met in Wayne County in 1865. Nineteen Holmes-Tuscarawas bishops, ministers, and deacons attended. Since the report does not include the statements of individual ministers his reactions cannot be stated with certainty. Tradition records that he cast his lot with the old order during the period when meetinghouses were built and other "new things" introduced. He attended no more of the Amish conferences, not even the one held in the vicinity of Walnut Creek, Holmes Co., Ohio, in 1869. By this time Abraham Mast and a few other Holmes County ministers had become regular attendants and led one of the five Amish congregations into the progressive Amish Mennonite group. Tradition records that Moses J. Miller was a wise counselor and able leader, keeping his people in the old paths.   J.S.U.

Miller, Noah E. (1880-1930), a Mennonite (MC) pastor, evangelist, and Bible teacher, was born Jan. 13, 1880, the son of Elias M. and Catherine J. Miller. He was an active member of the Southwestern Pennsylvania (now Allegheny) Mennonite (MC) Conference and lived his entire life in the vicinity of Springs, Somerset Co., Pa. He was married to Hannah, daughter of Bishop J. N. Durr, Martinsburg, Pa., June 6, 1907, to which union were born three sons and three daughters. He was ordained to the ministry in the Springs congregation (MC) May 11, 1912, and as bishop Oct. 5, 1912. He was known and widely used throughout the church. At different times he served as secretary and moderator of Southwestern Pennsylvania Conference and president of the Southwestern Pennsylvania Mission Board. He was an instructor for the winter Bible school at Eastern Mennonite School for about ten years and was serving in this capacity at the time of his death. At various times he served on the Young People's Bible Meeting Committee and the Young People's Problems Committee of Mennonite General Conference. He was secretary of the Mennonite General Conference at the time of his death, March 18, 1930.

J.L.H.

Miller, Peter, prior of the monastery of the followers of John Beissel in Ephrata (q.v.), Lancaster Co., Pa., stemmed from Alsenborn near Kaiserslautern, Germany, studied theology at the University of Heidelberg, and in the first half of the 18th century emigrated to the United States, settling in Ephrata. Here he translated van Braght's great martyrbook, the *Martyrs' Mirror* (q.v.), from Dutch into German, thereby fulfilling a wish of the Mennonites of America, who had in October 1745 asked their brethren in Amsterdam to find a reliable translator to print a German edition for them. Over two years later, on Feb. 10, 1748, the Amsterdam Mennonites replied that it was impossible to comply with the American request on account of the difficulty of finding a translator and the high costs of such a project (Brons, 219).

Meanwhile the Mennonites of Pennsylvania had approached the brothers in the monastery on the subject of publishing a German edition of the *Martyrs' Mirror* in Ephrata, since they had a printing shop with two hand presses—the second-oldest German printery in America. One of these presses has been preserved in the Franklin Institute in Pennsylvania. From this shop other books had appeared for the Mennonites (Bender, p. 2): *Güldene Aepffel in Silbern Schalen* (q.v., see also **Beissel**) and *Die ernsthafte Christenpflicht* (q.v.). They are among the oldest German books printed in America. Since there was no further demand for printing the press was not used for some years.

An entry in the diary of a Moravian Brethren missionary dated March 20, 1748, states that while he was in Ephrata visiting the monastery the Mennonites were just concluding a contract for the translation and printing of the *Martyrs' Mirror* (*Frankfurter Bücherfreund* V, Nos. 3 and 4; *Menn. Bl.,* 1908, 20). Now this important work of the Dutch Mennonites was to be made accessible to German readers. The printing was begun in 1748; it continued through three years, frequently delayed by a paper shortage, which the brothers manufactured themselves. For this printery with its primitive equipment this great work was a very meritorious achievement.

With his translation Peter Miller rendered the Mennonites of Germany and America a most important service. The *Martyrs' Mirror* is also of importance in the history of American literature, since it was the largest book printed in America before its independence. It is a folio volume of 1,512 pages. The translation was checked, as the conclusion of the book states, by Henry Funck (q.v.) and Diel-

mann Kolb (q.v.), the ministers of the Mennonite congregations of Franconia (q.v.) and Salford (q.v.). Five editions of the German *Martyrs' Mirror* have followed, all of them reprints of the original German translation by Peter Miller.

The printing of the German *Martyrs' Mirror* is also significant to the economic history of America. It was the occasion for the casting of type in America. Previously all type used in Ephrata had been obtained from Christopher Sauer in Germantown, the first printer of German books in the American colonies, who had it sent from Frankfurt, Germany. The brothers of the monastery made contact with Benjamin Franklin, who also owned a print shop, who furnished them matrices from which they made their own fonts, as stated in the conclusion of a religious book printed in the monastery (Gustav Mauri).

HEGE.

Bender, *Two Centuries;* A. Brons, *Ursprung, Entwickelung, und Schicksale der . . . Mennoniten* (Emden, 1912); G. Mauri, "Der Buchdrucker Christoph Sauer in Germantown," in *Gutenberg-Jahrbuch* 1934, 229; J. C. Wenger, *History of the Mennonites of the Franconia Conference* (Telford, 1937); ML III, 136 f.

Miller Amish Mennonite Church at West Liberty, Ohio, now extinct, existed from 1883 to about 1902. It was made up of progressive members of the Warye-Plank faction of the Oak Grove (q.v.) and Walnut Grove (q.v.) congregations. The introduction of English and four-part singing, the change of Sunday school to the forenoon (leaving the afternoon open for visiting), and English sermons by visiting ministers from Indiana, who organized the congregation under the Indiana Amish Mennonite Conference, attracted many young people to their services. Locally the group was known as the "Miller people" because Bishop Eli Miller of the Clinton Frame Mennonite Church in Elkhart Co., Ind., organized the congregation and ordained Samuel Detweiler as their minister. Weak ministerial leadership and a Church of God camp meeting caused a decline in the membership. Most of the small remaining membership united with the Bethel Mennonite Church (q.v.) in West Liberty. A few families returned to the Oak Grove and Walnut Grove congregations during the late 1890's.

J.S.U.

Miller Mennonite Church (MC), now extinct, located in the western outskirts of Clarence, N.Y., was built by the Strickler family on Ulrich Strickler's farm. Ulrich's brother-in-law, a Miller, was to preach there. John Strickler, a son of pioneer Ulrich Strickler, was also a preacher here. This point likely represents the independent action of some Mennonites of Erie Co., N.Y., after the middle of the 19th century, when disturbances were affecting several congregations of the Mennonite Conference (MC) of Ontario, of which these east of the Niagara River were to be a part. About 1825 the Miller church, already in disuse, was converted into a residence. Its structure of stone is still substantial a century later (see **Strickler's** Mennonite Church). J.C.F.

L. J. Burkholder, *A Brief History of the Mennonites in Ontario* (Toronto, 1935) 55.

Miller Mennonite Church (MC), located near Leitersburg, Md., was established before 1800. After services had been held in private homes for many years, a stone meetinghouse was built by Martin Bachtel (their minister) upon his farm near Fiddlersburg, which served until 1835, when a stone church was built on the present site, donated by Jacob Miller, which was surrounded by many families of the Miller name. The present brick church was built in 1926. The bishop in 1835 was Peter Eshleman, ordained in 1828. Ministers who have served the congregation were Christian Strite, ordained 1850; Jacob Oberholtzer, 1863; Adam Baer, 1876; his son Henry H. Baer, 1883; J. C. Miller, 1893; D. M. Strite, 1901; John D. Risser, 1920. M. K. Horst was serving as bishop in 1954. Sunday school has been conducted there since 1893. The 1956 membership was 183, with Daniel M. Strite and Samuel L. Martin as ministers.　　　J.D.R.

Miller Mennonite Church (MC), located in Miller, Hand Co., S.D., a member of the Iowa-Nebraska Conference, was organized in 1928 with 17 charter members under the leadership of Bishop Lee O. Schlegel. The first pastor was Wm. Schlegel, who served until 1932. Paul J. Glanzer, the present (1956) minister, began to serve in 1950. Services were held in a schoolhouse until 1947, and in a Seventh-Day Adventist church until 1954, when a new frame church was built. The membership in 1956 was 23.　　　P.J.G.

Miller Mennonite Church (MC), now extinct, was located on the North Fork in Union Magisterial District, Pendleton Co., W. Va., two miles below (north) the mouth of the Seneca. Samuel and Sara Miller gave the land here for a church which was to be used by "all orthodox denominations." This was the first church built in West Virginia under the auspices of the Mennonites of the Middle District of the Virginia Conference. The Brethren Church became active in the area and the Mennonites lost out. There was more promising work elsewhere in the West Virginia field for the Mennonites. The church was moved to Roaring Creek in 1913.　　　H.A.B.

Millerovo, a town in the Don area of Russia, where in the beginning of the 20th century some Mennonite industrialists, businessmen, and farmers settled. A few large mills and factories employed several hundred workers. In 1926 there were 231 Mennonites living in Millerovo and vicinity. Since the early days Millerovo had a Mennonite Brethren church. Wilhelm Dyck (q.v.) was chosen leader of the group in 1910. In the yearbook of 1913 J. J. Nickel was listed as deacon. In 1927 J. Pätkau, the minister of the church, reported on a harvest festival which was conducted in the M.B. church in Millerovo at which a collection was raised for home missions. There was also a small group at Millerovo belonging to the Mennonite Church. A.J.K., C.K.

Friesen, *Brüderschaft*, 464; *Unser Blatt* III (1927) 75; *Der praktische Landwirt*, 1925, No. 5, p. 2; *ML* III, 137 f.

Millerovo Mennonite Brethren Church, located in the town of Millerovo, in the Don region of Russia, was rather isolated from other Mennonite settlements, being at least about 400 miles from the closest Mennonite community. The first settlers, David J. Klassen, Wilhelm J. Friesen, who was a teacher, Johann Nick l, and J. Siemens, three of whom were business partners, and Wilhelm Isaac Dyck, a businessman and minister, came to Millerovo in the spring of 1903, seeking better business opportunities for a flour mill. This group immediately selected a place for a church, built a frame structure with a seating capacity of 40-50, and then organized an independent M.B. Church under the leadership of Wilhelm I. Dyck. The membership did not exceed 140, and consisted mainly of business people and laborers. They conducted all of their services in the High German language. W. I. Dyck was assisted in the work of the church by the ministry of David Johann Klassen, Johann Penner, and Abram Rempel. Rempel also succeeded W. I. Dyck as the leader of the church 1919-23. By 1924 most of the members, on account of hardship because of the Revolution, emigrated to Canada, and the church ceased to exist.　　　I.J.T.

Miller's (John Miller's) Mennonite (MC) meetinghouse, the former name of the present River Corner (q.v.) meetinghouse in Conestoga Twp., Lancaster, Co., Pa.　　　I.D.L.

Millersville, a town (pop. 2,551) in Lancaster Co., Pa., located two miles southwest of Lancaster, was started in 1764 by lottery by John Miller, a Lancaster blacksmith, who purchased of Michael Mayer on May 8, 1749 (surveyed to his father in 1737), 217 acres and more land until he had 460 acres. It was called Millersburg until about 1800, then Millerstown until 1855, when it assumed its present name. Michael Cryder and Peter Kegy were among the first residents. Abraham Herr, George, John, and Bernard Mann, John Correl, John and Michael Shank, Jacob Frantz, Christian Musselman, Andrew Kauffman, Martin Funk, and Peter Eshleman were some of the early Mennonite settlers in that vicinity. In 1854 the normal school, which today is the Millersville State Teachers College, had its beginning in the town. The Millersville Mennonite Church (MC), with a meetinghouse in town, has 375 members, and the entire surrounding area has many Mennonite families. The Mennonite Children's Home has been located here since 1911. (*ML* III, 138.)　　　I.D.L.

Millersville Mennonite (MC) Church in the town of Millersville, two miles southwest of Lancaster, Pa., dates back to 1757, when a log meetinghouse was built to serve the Abraham Herr, John Correl, Michael Shenk, Peter Eshleman, Jacob Frantz, and Andrew Kauffman families. Benjamin Hershey, living one mile west of Lancaster, was the first bishop. Among the leading ministers who have served here were Andrew Kauffman, John Shenk, Benjamin Hertzler, Christian S. Herr, and more recently Daniel Lehman and Daniel Gish. Among the sons of the congregation serving elsewhere have been John D. Charles, Chester and Daniel Lehman, and Clyde Shenk. The old church was replaced in 1851 by a new brick building, which in turn was replaced in 1897 by the present church, with renovations in 1927. Jacob G. Hess, Landis Shertzer, and J. Herbert Fisher were the ministers in 1955 with a membership of 375. The Millersville Mennonite

Children's Home (*q.v.*) is near by. The ministers share a circuit with the ministers of the Rohrerstown congregation.   I.D.L.

Milltown, or Cedar Spring Mills, in Lower Allen Twp., Cumberland Co., Pa., a few minutes' walk from the Susquehanna River, was a Mennonite (MC) preaching point (Lancaster Conference) as late as 1884. Little is known about this place. Caspar and Adam Weber built a mill at this place in the late 1780's hence the name "Milltown."   I.D.L.

Milltown Hutterite Bruderhof, founded in 1918, one fourth of a mile south of Bernard Siding, Man., was the first Hutterite settlement in Manitoba, the members coming from South Dakota, where they had experienced persecution during World War I. Joseph Kleinsasser, who was born in Russia Nov. 10, 1869, and came to South Dakota with his parents in 1874, was chosen minister on March 12, 1901, and confirmed Dec. 2, 1902, by the Milltown (S.D.) Bruderhof. On Feb. 11, 1934, he was chosen elder for the entire Schmied (*q.v.*) group in Canada and South Dakota, and served in this office 13 years; he died April 16, 1947, having been a preacher 46 years. Michael D. Waldner was chosen to the ministry on Jan. 31, 1943. In 1947 the population of the Bruderhof was 95, of whom 28 were baptized members.
D.D.

Millwood Mennonite Church (MC), located two miles northeast of Gap, Lancaster Co., Pa., since 1945 a member of the Lancaster Conference, was formed in 1877 with 22 families consisting of 124 members from the Old Order Amish community in this district, under the leadership of Gideon Stoltzfus, who had been ordained a minister in 1868 by the Old Order Amish, and was ordained bishop in 1888, serving in this office until his death in 1913.

The congregation met in members' homes every two weeks until 1882, when the first meetinghouse was built (frame 36 x 50 ft.), which served the congregation until 1937, when the present brick structure was erected. John A. Kennel, ordained bishop in 1926, assisted by LeRoy S. Stoltzfus, ordained bishop in 1949, were serving as bishops in 1955. Ministers and deacons that have formerly served were Samuel Lantz, John M. Stoltzfus, Daniel Stoltzfus, Amos B. Stoltzfus, M. S. Stoltzfus, Frank Stoltzfus, George B. Stoltzfus, John P. Kennel, Aaron Mast, and Isaac G. Kennel. Since 1929 the congregation has established the following mission outposts which together with the home congregation constituted the Millwood district membership of 431 in 1954: Coatesville (1929), Parkesburg (1938), Homeville (1945), Newlinville (1949), and Kennett Square (1951). In 1954 the Millwood congregation proper had 222 members, with Reuben G. Stoltzfus as preacher in addition to the two bishops.

In 1909 the Millwood congregation built a second meetinghouse, known as Maple Grove, but continued to function as one congregation. In 1945 a division occurred, the more conservative one-third minority withdrawing under Bishop John Kennel's leadership to join the Lancaster Conference (the only congregation of Amish background in the conference) and taking the Millwood meetinghouse. The more progressive two-thirds majority (1954 membership 458) continued the congregation's membership in the Ohio and Eastern A.M. Conference, taking Maple Grove (*q.v.*) meetinghouse. (*ML* III, 138.)
L.S.S.

Miloradovka Mennonite Brethren Church was located 65 miles west of the city of Dnepropetrovsk, earlier known as Ekaterinoslav, in South Russia, in the midst of rolling prairies and fertile valleys. Gerhard Pries, Bernhard Rempel, Daniel Löwen, Gerhard Dyck, Jakob Unger, Johann Funk, Peter Driediger, and Johann Penner were among the first settlers who arrived in 1889, a group of young farmers who were unable to acquire farms in the older settlements because of the scarcity of land. The church was organized in 1895, and built its first meetinghouse of brick with a seating capacity of 250 about 1908. Most of its members were farmers and used the Plattdeutsch in their homes and the High German in their worship services. The membership reached a peak of 110, with the following ministers serving this congregation: Abraham Wall (leader), Johann Funk, Gerhard Dyck, Johann Funk, Jr., Isaac Funk, David Dück, and Jakob Bergen. Peter Rempel was one of their outstanding choir directors.

This congregation experienced two great revivals, one in 1911 and another in 1921, through Baptist influences. A mass funeral became necessary in 1918 when a minister of the church and six young men of the village were murdered by bandits. In 1929 severe persecution began. The last known membership is given as 25, but the church disintegrated completely in the fall of 1933, when the last leaders left and the believers were subjected to severe persecution. David Dyck, a former minister of this congregation, is living in Grassy Lake, Alberta. J.J.T.

Milotitz, a region in southeastern Moravia, which included the villages of Svatoboric and Wäzenobitz (Slavic, *Vacenovice*), containing Hutterite Bruderhofs. During the Hungarian Wars and in the period of rebellion at the beginning of the Thirty Years' War they were severely damaged. The Bruderhof Wäzenobitz was burned down in June 1665 by attacking Hungarians; four brethren met a violent death. A band of Turk and Tatar marauders seized the Milotitz castle in July, and inflicted much loss on the Hutterites living near by.

In 1615 the treatment which the Wäzenobitz Bruderhof received from Albrecht Wenzel Eusebius von Waldstein, lord of Milotitz, was especially rough. He imposed such heavy labor upon them that both they and their horses were seriously injured, and refused to pay them for the goods they made for him. When he finally began to repay them in produce, he required the Brethren to pay several hundred florins for it, thus doubly injuring them. When they complained and declared their inability to pay he had their housekeeper arrested in his castle until some neighboring noblemen interceded for them. Unable to endure the treatment any longer, the preachers withdrew to Schädowitz and the entire colony prepared to vacate. Then Waldstein finally yielded and promised to pay his debts and take a more friendly attitude; so the Brethren promised in return to stay. The case of Waldstein shows that besides the numerous Moravian nobles who appreciated the Hutterian Brethren and were kindly disposed to them, there were occasionally some who wished to enrich themselves forcibly at their expense.

P.DE.

Beck, *Geschichts-Bücher;* Wolkan, *Geschicht-Buch;* Zieglschmid, *Chronik; ML* III, 138.

Mils, a village near Hall (*q.v.*), one of the earliest centers of Anabaptism in Tirol, Austria. In August 1529 in a forest near Mils 20 persons were seized in a worship service and taken to Hall on the Inn. On Sept. 14 they were put into solitary confinement to prevent their encouraging each other. They received instruction in Catholic doctrine from Christoph Landtsperger, and most of them recanted. Two women, Anna Malerin (*q.v.*) and Ursula Ochsentreiberin (*q.v.*), remaining constant to their faith, suffered a martyr's death. (*ML* III, 138.)   HEGE.

Miners Village Mennonite (MC) Mission was opened in 1931 in the woods on the edge of the ore-mining village with this name in Lebanon Co., Pa. The present mission building is leased from the Bethlehem Steel Co. The membership in 1956 was 40, with Noah S. Boll as pastor. Two women workers at the mission live in the building.   I.D.L.

Mininger, Hiram J. (1870-1953), a Church of God in Christ Mennonite preacher, the son of John and Susanna (Johnson) Mininger, was born on Jan. 8, 1870, in Hatfield, Montgomery Co., Pa. He grew up on the farm and attended the district school until the sixth grade and one summer of German Sunday school conducted by the Franconia Mennonite Church. He married Katie Bechtel, whose parents were also Mennonites, in September 1889. Nine sons and seven daughters were born to this union. He wrote: "At the time when we were married very few of the Mennonite youth joined the church before marrying. Soon after marriage we informed the local pastor, Bishop Josiah Clemmer, that we wished to change our way of living and would like to join the church, upon which it was openly announced and a class of 12 couples received instructions every other Sunday for several months on changing our lives and how to live when affiliated with the church, and were baptized." Mininger was a truth-seeker and gave much time to reading the Bible and to prayer. He became deeply interested in church history. He soon felt a need for a new birth, which he obtained when he earnestly sought the Lord and His ways through much prayer and fasting. When the door to a fuller fellowship in the Mennonite church seemed to close, he, his wife, and a few others joined the Church of God in Christ Mennonites, when John Holdeman and Tobias Unruh held meetings in Pennsylvania in March 1898. A few years later they moved to Ithaca, Mich., where Mininger was ordained to the ministry in March 1904. After serving the Newark congregation at Ithaca as associate minister for many years, he took charge of the congregation at Wauseon, Ohio. He preached with great fervor and emphasis the whole truth as he believed it. He was a pioneer in the evangelistic field, devoting much time and effort to conducting revival meetings.   P.G.H.

Mininger, Jacob D. (1879-1941), a Mennonite (MC) leader, mission worker, and evangelist, was born near Sellersville, Bucks Co., Pa., on June 9, 1879, the third son of Joseph M. and Eliza Detweiler Mininger. As a youth he united with the Mennonite Church and early had convictions for mission work.

On July 27, 1904, he was married to Hettie B. Kulp of Danboro, Pa. One daughter and two sons were born to them: Ruth (Mrs. M. T. Brackbill), a teacher at Eastern Mennonite College, Harrisonburg, Va.; Paul E., a bishop, and president of Goshen College, Goshen, Ind.; and Edward P., a physician at Elkhart, Ind.

J. D. Mininger spent four and a half years (1904-9) as superintendent of the Mennonite Old People's Home, Marshallville, Ohio, and three years in Holbrook, Col., where he was ordained to the ministry on October 5, 1911. Then in April 1912 he was appointed superintendent of the Mennonite Gospel Mission, Kansas City, Kan., where he served until his death, almost 29 years later. The outreach of the mission was greatly extended during those years, as he discovered varied ways of ministering to the spiritually needy.

Mininger was used church-wide as an evangelist and conference speaker, a frequent theme of his messages being the victorious Christian life. He wrote and edited many tracts, which he called Victory Leaflets. *Exalting Christ in the City* is a mission study text which he wrote as a veteran missionary. He rendered unusual service as counselor and pastor to the conscientious objectors imprisoned in the U.S. Military Disciplinary Barracks at Ft. Leavenworth in World War I and after. Through the years he was a member of various committees and boards of the church. At the time of his death he was a member-at-large of the Mennonite Board of Missions and Charities and a member of the executive committee of the Mennonite Board of Education. He died Jan. 4, 1941, and was buried at Maple Hill Cemetery, Kansas City, Kan.   R.M.B.

Minister of Music is an office which has only recently entered the Mennonite churches of America, and is still unknown in Europe and elsewhere, although in some of the larger Protestant denominations it has been the practice for some time to make a professionally trained person responsible for the music program of a congregation. With the traditional Mennonite interest in music and with the growing multiple responsibilities of the pastor of a congregation, whose first responsibility it is to preach the Gospel, and to counsel and visit the members of the church, it has become desirable to make one person responsible for the musical work of the congregation. At times this office also includes the leadership of the young people's activities. As a rule such an individual has had some theological as well as musical training. Congregations (only GCM) which at present (1957) employ full- or part-time ministers of music are Bethel Mennonite Church, Mountain Lake, Minn.; Bethel College Mennonite Church, North Newton, Kan.; Bethesda Mennonite Church, Henderson, Neb.; First Mennonite Church, Berne, Ind.; First Mennonite Church, Newton, Kan.; First

Mennonite Church, Reedley, Cal. In some churches which have had such an office it is at the moment vacant; others are planning to create it.   **C.K.**

Ministerial Retirement Benefit Plan of the United Missionary Church, a recent development, begun in 1940. In the earlier history of the church ministers were only partially supported and were expected to provide a portion of their own living. The Retirement Plan came as a consequence of a supported ministry, giving full time to ministerial work. It was inaugurated as a result of an agreement that pastors would pay a small percentage of their salaries into the fund, and that the church which they serve would also pay into the fund a certain amount annually. Each congregation is expected to pay into the Retirement Fund 50¢ per member annually, and the pastor is expected to pay one per cent of his salary up to $1200 per annum, and 2 per cent of the portion over that amount. The maximum benefit paid to any retired minister is $35 per month and to widows of deceased ministers a maximum of $100 per year. In 1948 a Death Benefit Insurance was incorporated into the Retirement Fund, with a maximum death benefit of $1000.   **J.A.Hu.**

Ministers' Bible Week, an annual institution, usually held on a college campus for the ministers and interested laymen and students of the community, for which occasion special speakers or Bible expositors are invited. The first Bible Week in connection with Bethel College (q.v.) took place in 1915 after the initiative had been taken at the Western District Conference session in October 1914. This Bible Week was originally held in connection with a course for ministers and Sunday-school workers. In 1952-53 J. E. Hartzler endowed a lectureship in connection with the Bible Week, which is known as the Hartzler Bible Lectureship. A similar Bible Week is being held at Tabor, Freeman, and Bluffton colleges. The Canadian Mennonite Bible College and the Mennonite Brethren Bible College of Winnipeg as well as the Gretna Collegiate Institute and Rosthern Junior College and the many other academies and Bible schools have been conducting a Bible Week for their students and constituency. Spiritual and intellectual guidance and stimulation have been given. (See also **Ministers' Week.**) C.K.

Ministers' Manuals, handbooks or service manuals for ministers, usually containing forms and instructions for administration of the ordinances of baptism, communion, and footwashing, and for ordination, reception, discipline, and dismissal or transfer of members, order of service in worship, and other items of service to ministers in the performance of the duties of their office. Sometimes prayers for various occasions are included. Among German-speaking European and American Mennonites such manuals have been given various names: *Formularbuch* (Palatinate), *Leitfaden* (Baden), *Handbuch für Prediger* (Russia and North America).

The history of ministers' manuals among Anabaptist-Mennonites begins with Balthasar Hubmaier's two pamphlets of 1527, *Eine Form zu taufen* and *Eine Form des Nachtmahls Christi*. The Hutterian Brethren also had manuscripts prescribing the ritual for the ordinances; Peter Riedemann's

Rechenschaft of 1545 contains a "Taufordnung." Beck's *Geschichts-Bücher* (pp. 648-50) reprints from the original codices several forms: "Des Tauffens weis, oder wie man tauffen soll" (1561); "Vom Abentmal Christi" (1529-56); "Form des Nachtmals Christi" (1561); "Vom Bann oder Ausschluss und Wiederaufnehmen" (1529-65).

The oldest known printed manual is probably the one found as an appendix to the second edition of a book by Jan Gerritsz van Emden (Amsterdam, 1650), *Drie Evangelische Predicatien, . . . daar in zeer leerelyk aangeweezen, en verklaard word hunne maniere van Doop, en Avondmal, de Reden, en Woorden, die zy gebruiken in deeze Heilige Handelinge, en Godsdienst. . . . Hier achter volgen Eenige stichtelyke Gebeden, en Meditatien, dewlke mede ter Zee gebruikt kunnen worden.* Schijn-Maatschoen (*Geschiedenis* III, 58-75) reprints most of the manual material. This manual was translated into German by Elder Jakob Siebert of the Thiensdorf congregation in West Prussia and printed there in 1800 under the title *Drei geistreiche Predigten . . . .* It was used by the Rudnerweide and Kronsweide congregations in Russia (reported by Friesen, *Brüderschaft,* 82). It contained a manual or order of worship consisting of three sermons, articles of faith, information regarding baptism, the Lord's Supper, Christian doctrines, the election and installation of deacons, ministers, and elders, the marriage ceremony, excommunication, reception of repentant members, footwashing, etc. Elder Franz Goerz (q.v.) of the Rudnerweide Mennonite Church in Russia still used this manual.

It is likely that this manual was in use in many congregations in handwritten form. The Bethel College Historical Library has an old copy of this "Formularbuch" formerly in use by the Michalin Mennonite Church (q.v.), Poland, which has a preface by Johann Siebert (q.v.) in which he states that this book was translated from the Dutch by his father, Jakob Siebert, and that the sermons dated back to the days of Menno Simons. Gerardus Maatschoen (*Geschiedenis* III, 58-75) assumes that Hans de Ries (q.v.), the noted Waterlander preacher, was the author of these sermons. The Michalin copy consists of a sermon preceding the articles of faith, the articles of faith; a sermon preceding the baptismal sermon, the baptismal sermon; the sermon preceding the Lord's Supper, the sermon at the Lord's Supper; about the election of ministers, deacons, and elders; about excommunication, the acceptance of excommunicated members, and a marriage ceremony.

J. C. Jehring, in his *Gründliche Historie* (Jena, 1720, pp. 264-74), published a *Formular so bei Einsetzung und Ordination der Lehrer und Aeltesten unter den Mennoniten gebräuchlich ist. Aufgesetzet von Abraham Dircks, gewesenem Lehrer und Aeltesten der Taufgesinneten Gemeine zu Amsterdam,* which he took from Part III of a Dutch hymnal of the Flemish at Altona (*De CL. Psalmen,* Hamburg, 1685; first ed., Amsterdam, 1652), titled *Het deerde Deel, vervattende de Belydenisse des Gheloofs met de voornaemste zeden, wetten, kerkelycke Ordre en discipline in de Christelycke Gemeynte.* Dircks, he says, lived *ca.* 1626.

An interesting report on the forms for baptism and communion used in the Old Flemish (Jan-Jacobsgezinden, q.v.) Church on the island of Ameland, Holland, written by the Old Flemish preacher C. P. Sorgdrager apparently in the late 18th century, is described in *Mennonitische Blätter* for 1913 (p. 75), in the article "Kirchliche Gebräuche bei den alten Flamingern auf der holländischen Insel Ameland um 1800." This manuscript was, however, not printed as a ministers' manual. Sorgdrager did publish *Vragen aan de Dopelingen met derselver antwoorden*.

The only regular ministers' manual published in modern times for the Dutch Mennonites is *Kanselboek: ten dienste van de Doopsgezinde Gemeenter in hederland* (62 pp.) published in 1948.

The first manual printed in Switzerland or Germany was Valentin Dahlem's *Allgemeines und vollständiges Formularbuch für die Gottesdienstliche Handlungen in denen Taufgesinnten, Evangelisch Mennoniten-Gemeinden* (Neuwied, 1807). It was printed for the congregations of the Palatinate at the request of the Ibersheim conference of 1803. The first 145 pages contain the manual of forms, the second section (146-293) a collection of prayers for the minister's use, the third section (299-336) the ministers' manual of the congregations in Baden and Württemberg in the Neckar regions, prepared by the ministers of this group east of the Rhine and printed at their request in the Dahlem book.

In 1852 the Palatine churches replaced the 1807 manual with one prepared by Johannes Molenaar, *Allgemeines Formularbuch* (Monsheim, 1852) of 279 pages, but without the "Neckar" appendix. The "Neckar" congregations published their own manual in 1876 under the title *Leitfaden zum Gebrauch bei gottesdienstlichen Handlungen zunächst für die Aeltesten und Prediger der gesammt-Mennoniten Gemeine in Baden,* prepared by Ulrich Hege and printed at Sinsheim in 1921 (154 pp.). The *Handbuch zum Gebrauch bei gottesdienstlichen Handlungen zunächst für die Aeltesten und Prediger der Mennoniten-Gemeinden in Nordamerika* (Berne, Ind., 1893, pp. 124), published by the General Conference Mennonite Church, and often reprinted, was based on manuals of the Palatinate and Baden.

For whom the Mennonite Publishing Company at Elkhart, Ind., printed the following small 47-page booklet about 1875 is not known: *Ein Verlobungs-, Copulirungs- und Strafannehmungsbuch. Nebst schönen, geistreichen Sprüchen. Von dem ehrsamen Lehrer Oheim Heinrich Schmidt, wohnhaft und Mitnachbar in Antonowka, bei der Kreisstadt Kanjew, Volhynisches Gouvernement im Kaiserthum Russland.* It is not strictly a service manual but contains sermons to be used at the occasions of betrothal, marriage, and restoration of disciplined persons. Schmidt is identified as having been ordained on April 7, 1861, at Antonowka by Elder Tobias Unruh. The first and apparently only manual published for the Mennonite Brethren Church was Heinrich A. Neufeld's *Handbüchlein für Prediger und Gemeindeglieder* (Winnipeg, n.d.-1927, 24 pp.).

The Mennonite Church (MC) since 1890 has used the *Confession of Faith and Ministers Manual*, edited by John S. Coffman and John F. Funk and published at Elkhart. Besides the manual proper it contains the Dordrecht Confession, Shorter Catechism, and forms for use at funeral services. The eighth edition appeared at Scottdale in 1925. In 1944 this was combined with other materials under the title *Mennonite Church Polity* and published by authorization of the Mennonite General Conference.

The Old Order Amish ministers' manuals have been handed down largely in manuscript form. The oldest known manual is that prepared by Bishop Johannes Naffziger of Essingen, Palatinate, Germany, at the request of the Amish congregations in Holland and sent to them in a letter dated March 16, 1781. (Several manuscript copies of this manual are in the GCL.) It was printed at Elkhart in 1916 as a 31-page pamphlet under the title, *Ein Alter Brief,* and reprinted at Kutztown, Pa., in 1926. Another independently composed manual was written by Joseph Unzicker, apparently in Europe in the early 19th century. (Several manuscript copies of this manual also are in GCL.) John Umble has edited the Unzicker manual in the article, "An Amish Minister's Manual," *MQR* XV (1941) 95-117, and described all the manuscript manuals in GCL in "Manuscript Amish Ministers' Manuals in the Goshen College Library," *MQR* XV (1941) 243-53. L. A. Miller assembled material from several manuscript manuals and added his own revision and comments to produce the first printed Old Order Amish ministers' manual. Its title is: *Handbuch für Prediger. Zum Gebrauch für gottesdienstliche Handlungen so wie den Diakonen, Diener zum Buch und Bischöfen ihr Beruf anbefohlen wird und wie verschiedene Lehren oder Predigten ordentlich und ehrerbietig ausgeführt werden die Zuhörer zu Jesu leiten wiedergeboren und selig werden* (Arthur, Ill., n.d.-1950).

Goshen College Library also has a manuscript Mennonite (not Amish) manual used in Virginia, entitled *Ordnung und Gemeinde Regel, von Daniel Good, Aelt. der Gemeinde in Rockingham County, Virginia.* Bishop A. G. Clemmer (d. 1939) is reported to have used a manuscript ministers' manual of his own. H.S.B.

Ministers' Meetings or Conferences.

A. Mennonite Church (MC). Ministers' meetings as distinct from the official annual or semiannual conferences are widely held in the Mennonite Church, usually semiannually. In their earliest occurrence, as for instance in Ontario, they were meetings of all the ordained men in a local area or even one bishop district. In each of the three districts in Ontario, Waterloo, York, and "Twenty" (Vineland), semiannual ministerial meetings (called *Kleine Zusammenkunft*) were held from the beginning, at least as early as 1830 and probably earlier, and have continued to the present. They may even have preceded the annual conference (called *Grosse Zusammenkunft*). Earlier they preceded the traditional spring baptismal and communion services, and no doubt gave attention to matters relating to these services, including discipline. More recently the ministerial meetings have been largely inspirational and educational meetings for the consideration of matters relating to the improvement of ministerial service, including however also expository studies and theological and practical topics.

In the Franconia Conference it has been a longstanding tradition that the bishop calls a meeting of the ministers and deacons of his bishop district to fix communion and baptismal dates and to consider matters of discipline or "housekeeping" which may need attention. This meeting was called the *Kleiner Rath* in contrast to the annual conference, which was called *Grosser Rath*. These meetings were essentially different from the later ministers' meetings for inspiration and instruction.

In the Indiana-Michigan Conference four ministerial meetings are held in addition to the annual conference, two in northern Indiana meeting semiannually (one east of Goshen, and one west), and two annual meetings, one for Michigan, and one for the entire ministerial body, usually meeting in December. The last meeting is of recent origin, starting in 1945. The northern Indiana meetings are much older, dating from about 1890, but the one for Michigan began only in 1919.

All of these meetings are similar in character, being on an inspirational and practical nature to help the ministers in their work, but not transacting any business.

In Ohio the ministerial meetings are of more recent origin. The northeastern Ohio meetings date to about 1913, the Wayne County meetings to about 1945; the western Ohio meetings began in 1955. In other states and conference districts ministers' meetings are of more recent origin. Sometimes they are called Ministers Fellowship (Illinois) or Ministers Retreat (Allegheny). The date of origin of the ministers' meetings in other conference districts is as follows: Virginia 1912, Lancaster 1933, Missouri-Kansas 1936, Pacific Coast 1936, Franconia 1938, Allegheny 1938, Illinois 1943, Alberta-Saskatchewan 1945 (combining with Christian Workers' Meeting), North Central 1946, Allegheny Retreat 1954.

H.S.B.

B. General Conference Mennonite Church. The practice of holding a ministers' conference as distinct from the annual official general or district conference in the General Conference Mennonite Church goes back to 1886, when the Eastern District conference sessions authorized the holding of such a gathering "to discuss subjects and topics relative to the labor and success of the ministers of our church." Such a ministers' conference was announced in the *Mennonite* to be held on June 14, 1886, at the West Swamp Church in Pennsylvania. Bad weather on this date made a postponement to Aug. 2 necessary. However, the six ministers who appeared on June 14 devoted some attention, under the chairmanship of A. M. Fretz, to "The Duty of the Pastor at the Sick Bed." At the Aug. 2 session the ministers discussed the choice of sermon texts, the preparation of sermons, avoiding duplication in funeral sermons, and the minister's duty to youth. N. B. Grubb presided at this session.

From the Eastern District the idea of ministers' meetings apparently spread rapidly to other sections, for by the fall of 1891 the *Christlicher Bundesbote* carried announcements and reports of such conferences held in the Middle District and also the West-

ern District conferences. The idea was also promoted in the organizational session of the Northern District Conference at Mountain Lake, Minn., in that same year. In the ministers' conference held at Newton, Kan., on Sept. 21, 1891, chaired by Christian Krehbiel, some of the topics discussed were the Mennonite attitude toward life and health insurance, the dismissal of ministers, the slandering of ministers, and the question of admitting to church membership such who do not agree with the church on the practice of footwashing, abstinence from tobacco, and prohibition of alcoholic drinks.

The practice of holding ministers' conferences has spread to and continues in all districts of the General Conference but the frequency of meeting and the program patterns vary from district to district. In the Eastern District Conference the ministers' conference has become the "Quarterly Conference" which includes also congregational officers and other church leaders. (See also **Ministers' Retreats.**) E.W.

Ministers, Hutterite, *Special Honors Accorded to.* One of the features that have impressed visitors to Hutterite Bruderhofs ever since the very beginning and which occasionally also caused internal problems is the treatment allotted to their ministers (*Diener des Wortes, q.v.,* i.e., elders or bishops). While in general a puritanical way of life and a democratic sharing of all goods prevailed, ministers as a rule were given somewhat better quarters and better food wherever possible. This was naturally resented by some strict members of the group and it likewise aroused surprise, perhaps even criticism, by foreign observers.

The *Chronicle* of the Hutterites is quite frank in this regard, reporting as early as 1540 an internal conflict on this count. A certain Herman Schmid (of the more radical wing of the brotherhood) openly censured the practice "that the brotherhood treats their ministers with special food and drink" (Zieglschmid, 211). An ensuing meeting (without the ministers) readily reaffirmed that it is according to divine Scripture that those who serve the group spiritually as shepherds should receive "double honors" in things temporal. Schmid, however, was disavowed and excommunicated. He went to Hesse, where Peter Riedemann (*q.v.*) at that time was imprisoned, and asked Riedemann for his intercession.

Riedemann now (1540) wrote a lengthy epistle to the brotherhood in Moravia, "Concerning the Office of the Ministers and What is Due Them" (*Der Diener Amt und Gebühren halben*), now in the *Chronicle* (Zieglschmid, 212-23), in which he discussed the issue in general along the lines approved by the brotherhood. He wrote it "impartially," inasmuch as he could not know whether or not he might ever profit from such an "opinion." This great letter then became a real cornerstone of Hutterite practice for all the future and thus created a tradition within the brotherhood, which is still alive today. The gist of this rather elaborate document is the reference to I Tim. 5:17, "Let the elders that rule well be counted worthy of double honour, especially they who labour in the word and doctrine." As it is the Word of God, the brotherhood should by all means conform to it.

This principle was repeated in 1556, when Hänsel Schmidt or Raiffer explained the practice of the brotherhood to Swiss Brethren around Kreuznach in a seven-point statement. Point 4 deals again with what should be allotted to ministers in all things temporal (Zieglschmid, 363). The "double honor" principle is expressly mentioned. Again in 1652 this seven-point statement is reproduced by Andreas Ehrenpreis (*q.v.*) in his great *Sendbrief,* one of the few Hutterite documents ever printed. The brotherhood has accepted this practice as a matter of course ever since 1540.

Visitors and guests, however, did not approve this policy. We hear, for example, of Polish Brethren (Anti-Trinitarians: see **Polish Church**) who lived on a Bruderhof for a whole year (1569/70) to learn how to run a community farm, and who now strongly criticized this usage; in fact, they called the Brethren for this reason outright "hypocrites." Likewise later visitors had a similar impression, and of course all the local antagonists, e.g., Catholic clergymen such as Erhard and Christof A. Fischer (*q.v.*). Indeed this practice has to the present day aroused surprise, amazement, and sometimes resentment. It seems incongruous in the face of the uttermost strictness and Puritanism among the Brethren in general, that the food and living conditions of ministers and elders are distinctly better and more ample. Today, as an expression of honor, the ministers do not eat with the other brethren and sisters in the common dining hall but separately in their own rooms.

With the Society of Brothers a similar practice was the rule, but it has been abandoned in recent years, although certain privileges are still granted the ministers. (Zieglschmid, *Chronik;* Wolkan, *Geschicht-Buch.*) R.F.

Ministers' Retreats (GCM). The idea of a retreat for ministers and other Christian workers was first given official approval at the General Conference sessions held at North Newton. Kan., in 1945. The first retreat of this kind was held at Spirit Lake, Iowa, in the summer of 1946. Designed to promote spiritual fellowship and understanding, to serve as a workshop to discuss pertinent problems, and to provide opportunity for relaxation and recreation, the policy has been to hold such retreats annually except when some other conflicting gathering make this inadvisable. While the responsibility for planning the retreat was at first in the hands of the Board of Education, since the constitutional reorganization in 1950 this responsibility rests with the Committee on the Ministry functioning under the Board of Missions. E.W.

Ministers' Week, the name in the Mennonite Church (MC) for a special series of addresses and discussions provided for ministers in service by the colleges and Bible schools of the church, originally offered for a school week, but later often reduced to three to five days, although still called a "week," and usually scheduled at the end of the six weeks' Winter Bible School. Topics of practical value to the working minister are offered, including Bible exposition, homiletics and pastoral work, doctrine, church program and problems, and Christian education. The first known Ministers' Week was offered by Hess-

ton College in 1925. Johnstown (Pa.) Bible School followed in 1926, Goshen College in 1927, Ontario Bible School and Eastern Mennonite College in 1928, Canton (Ohio) Bible School and others later. Hesston and Johnstown were later transferred to conference sponsorship. Attendance has usually included most of the active ordained men of the region served. In recent years attendance has declined, and in a few cases the ministers' week has been discontinued, or replaced as at Goshen by the School for Ministers lasting three weeks. For shorter meetings of one or two days see **Ministers' Meeting.**

Similar programs for ministers have been provided at the colleges of other Mennonite groups such as Bethel, Bluffton, Canadian Mennonite Bible College for the General Conference Mennonite Church, M.B. Bible College for the Mennonite Brethren in Canada. (See **Ministers' Bible Week.**) H.S.B.

Ministry (Netherlands). In the early period of Anabaptism in the Netherlands there are found a number of names and functions of ministers: bishop, elder (*oudste*), baptizer (*doper*), preacher, deacon, purse bearer (*buydeldrager;* in charge of financial matters), servant (*dienaer*), and servant of the poor (*armendienaer*). In those times of persecution and insecurity, when the congregations had not yet been fully organized, there was no sharp distinction between the various offices. Not yet strictly observed was the difference between elders, whose task it was to baptize, to administer the communion, to perform marriages, to ordain elders, preachers, and deacons, and to ban, and on the other hand preachers, who were only to preach or to read the Scriptures in the meetings, and there are a number of instances where a deacon preached and even performed baptism. Though we are informed only about a few cases, we may assume that as a rule elders, preachers and deacons were ordained by laying on of hands. This did not imply a doctrine of apostolic succession (*q.v.*). The word "Bishop" is rarely found; it was apparently too suggestive of Catholicism. About 1545 the differences between the offices became clearer, and elders, preachers, and deacons were usually well distinguished. Preachers then used to be chosen from the deacons, while the elders were chosen from the preachers. In the times of Menno Simons there were only a few elders, traveling about, who formed a kind of council of elders, meeting from time to time (Goch 1547, Lübeck 1552, Wismar 1554) to discuss and to decide upon the matters of the church, also to discuss and resolve the question whether new elders should be ordained. But by the close of the 16th century most local congregations had obtained their own elder. He was chosen by the preachers and deacons (*dienaerschap*) of the local congregation and ordained by an elder from abroad. Thus it is found in the confessions. In the Concept of Cologne (*q.v.*) 1591 the "bishop or *leeraer*" is to be chosen by the congregation and after being examined is to be ordained by elders with the laying on of hands. Ordination of deacons is not mentioned here. In the Flemish Olijftacxken (*q.v.*) confession, 1626, preachers, elders and deacons are named, together being the shepherds of the church, who after fasting and prayer are to be examined concerning their faith and their moral conduct and thereupon to be ordained by laying on of hands. The Jan Cents confession of 1630 (High German-Frisian), Article X, mentions the following officers in the church: prophets, shepherds, preachers (this means elders; the word "Oudste" is not found in this confession), "hulpers" (i.e., assistants, who were the preachers), and governors. They are to be appointed by the congregation after fasting and prayer. Laying on of hands is not mentioned, but obviously assumed. The Dordrecht confession (*q.v.*) of 1632 (Flemish), Article IX, deals with the ministry only in general terms. The distinction between bishops, or elders, and preachers (*leeraers*) is not quite clear. Laying on of hands is emphatically demanded. Both the "Diaken-Dienaren," who were to care for the poor, and the deaconesses, who were to look after the poor, the sick, and the afflicted, are mentioned among the ministry. It is expressly stated that the congregation which appoints the minister shall choose as deacons men who, if necessary, can also preach. The practice, no doubt, generally agreed with these resolutions. Laying on of hands for ordaining deacons in all these groups had disappeared by 1650, in some branches even long before.

After the Dutch Mennonites had been divided into numerous branches by their deplorable schisms, practices in the various groups differed.

Waterlander (*q.v.*) practices are revealed by the resolutions of the Emden meeting in 1568 and the Amsterdam meeting of 1581. In the Emden resolutions a difference is made between a "leeraer" (i.e., elder) and a "vermaner" (admonisher), who was chosen to "the service of admonishing," i.e., preaching. The deacons, if they were able to do so, were also authorized to preach. In the resolution of Amsterdam in 1581 the "leeraer in den vollen dienst" (minister in full service) is spoken of and during this meeting Jacob Jansz (Schedemaker, *q.v.*), who until then had been a "vermaner" (preacher), was "asked, admonished, and ordered" to accept the full office of the eldership (*leerampt*). Upon his assent he was ordained with the laying on of hands. The expression "leeraer in den vollen dienst" was the common title of the elder among the Waterlanders; the word "Oudste," though it is found in Articles XXVI and XXVII of the Waterlander confession by Hans de Ries and Lubbert Gerritsz (1610), was unusual among the Waterlanders. About 1610 the distinction between the offices of elder and preacher was no longer strictly observed in this group, and soon after the preachers usually also performed baptism and administered communion, which in other Mennonite branches was reserved to elders as their special assignment and prerogative. As a typical remnant of the old difference between the functions of elder and preacher we note the retention of the phrase "asked, admonished, and ordered" to accept "the full service of the *leerampt*," but practically the difference between "leeraer in den vollen dienst" (elder) and "leeraer" soon disappeared. Another remnant of the old distinction is seen in the practice, commonly found among the Waterlanders until the 18th century, of inviting a minister from another congregation for the purpose of performing baptism and administering the communion, though

the "leeraer" of the congregation was fully qualified to do this himself.

The extreme conservative groups in the Netherlands, e.g., the Janjacobs-gezinden (*q.v.*), Groningen and Danzig Old Flemish, and Old Frisians, until the end of the 18th century maintained the distinction in function and responsibility between elders and preachers. These groups maintained the traditions from the times of Menno Simons, e.g., that of traveling elders. Among the Old Frisians of North Holland these men were called "landsdienaren." The Groningen Old Flemish called them "oudsten," or "opzieners," but in the last decades of the 18th century even the name "commissaris" is found. There is much information on the manner of choosing elders in this group: when they wanted to appoint an elder, a number of preachers who were candidates for the eldership visited all the congregations; the one who gathered most votes was then chosen. This system lasted until the end of the 18th century. From about 1750 among this group only the elders, not the preachers, were ordained by laying on of hands.

Among the Flemish and the Frisians, and after 1665 among the Lamists and Zonists, the distinctions between elder and preacher also gradually fell into discard (Galenus Abrahamsz was never ordained as elder), though there are during the 18th century many examples of appointing and ordaining preachers to special eldership, both among the Lamists and Zonists. During the 18th century in a few congregations (Leiden, Rotterdam, Amsterdam bij 't Lam, Bovenknijpe) there were "ouderlingen." They were chosen from the deacons and had to supervise the finances of the congregation.

Deacons were chosen from the male membership. Until about 1685 deacons were usually chosen by the meeting of the brethren (*Broedervertoeving*), but from this time on in a number of congregations, especially those of larger cities like Amsterdam, Haarlem, Leiden, Rotterdam, gradually the practice was introduced of having the church board (preachers and deacons) appoint the new members of the board, who in the 18th century were often chosen for life. The rural churches rarely accepted this practice of co-optation, which lasted in Rotterdam, for example, until 1924.

As long as the congregation had lay preachers (*leekepreekers*) who did not receive a salary, or at most a small remuneration for the loss of their earnings from private business (*liefdepredikers*), each congregation had two or more, up to as many as seven preachers. When a preacher had been chosen he was subjected to a thorough examination. In the stricter groups like the Old Flemish this was an examination on the confession. He then became a minister on probation (*proefdienaar*). This they formerly called "in de proeve staan." The preachers from about 1550 until about 1700 like the deacons were usually chosen out of the congregation by the male members of the congregation, but from the 18th century on in a number of congregations preachers were appointed by the church boards. About 1700 and occasionally even some three decades before, as the desire and ability of the local candidates diminished, and the congregations, particularly those of the larger cities, grew more and more demanding, preachers were often called in from abroad, who were then given a salary. At the same time, in 1680, Galenus Abrahamsz at Amsterdam started to train young men for the ministry, which training was continued in 1735 by the Amsterdam (Lamist) Theological Seminary, founded in this year, whereas the Amsterdam Zonist congregation began a ministers' training course some years later. Besides this, a number of ministers, like Pieter van Dokkumburg (*q.v.*) at Koog aan de Zaan and Pieter Beets (*q.v.*) at Zaandam, took up the training of ministers, who after their training were examined by a church board or by the trustees of the Conference in Friesland (Friesche Doopsgezinde Sociëteit) and appointed ministerial candidate (*proponent*). During the entire 17th century and even before, the congregations liked to have a physician as their preacher, the university training giving some warranty for scholarly education (see **Medicine among the Mennonites**). Thus a number of congregations in the 18th century obtained well-trained ministers; but in the country churches the untrained and unsalaried ministers far outnumbered the others until about 1825.

From the 19th century on, the Dutch Mennonite congregations have been governed by a church board (*Kerkeraad, Kerkbestuur*), consisting of a number of male members (since 1900 also in many congregations female members), which with a few exceptions are now chosen by all the members of the congregation. The pastor usually is a member of the church board, often its secretary. In most congregations the trustees are called deacons. In some congregations there are still special deacons (deaconesses) for the care of the poor. The members of the church board (deacons) have no particular spiritual office, since preaching, baptizing, performing marriages, giving catechetical instruction, etc., is left to the pastor(s). Occasionally a deacon preaches. The congregations are wholly autonomous, both material and spiritual matters being discussed and resolved by the local church board. Most congregations now have only one pastor; a number of small congregations have united to be served by the same pastor. Only a few large congregations are served by two or more (two each in Leeuwarden, Groningen, Utrecht, Texel, Zaandam, Rotterdam; The Hague three, Haarlem four, Amsterdam six). The pastor is usually called "dominee"; the old "leeraar" has gradually become rare. Since 1911 there have also been women in the ministry (in 1957, 25 out of a total of 109 pastors). The great majority of pastors now have been trained at a university and the Amsterdam Seminary, but in 1957 there are still ten pastors who have had no university or seminary training.

Since the distinction between elders and preachers is now unknown in the Netherlands, the pastor is both elder and preacher. Pastors mostly take up their office simply by being introduced by an older pastor (usually a relative or a friend) and by delivering an installation sermon. Laying on of hands, which had been rarely practiced for more than a century and a half, now sometimes takes place. Pastorship is generally a full-time job; only a few pastors have some side employment. This makes high demands upon the Dutch brotherhood. Most salaries are provided by the local congregations; but many congregations which are unable to pay an adequate salary receive a subsidy from the A.D.S. (in 1956 some 75,000 guilders paid to 64 congregations). For the insurance of the pastors in cases of illness or old age there are a number of pension funds.

Nearly all the pastors have joined the A.N.D.P.V. (*q.v.*) (General Dutch Mennonite Pastors' Association), founded in 1927; a number of them are members of the (interconfessional) union of Dutch pastors, an association for the material interests of ministers. vDZ.

Kühler, *Geschiedenis* I, 292, 300 f., 369, 400, 434; idem, III, 2-4, 7-21; S. F. Rues *Tegenwoordige Staet der Doopsgezinden* (Amsterdam, 1745) 40, 54 f., 67, 99 f., 110-16, 121, 148-50; *Inv. Arch. Amst.* II, Nos. 283, 668, 676, 686; *DJ* 1840, 33-52; N. van der Zijpp, *Geschiedenis der Doopsgezinden in Nederland* (Arnhem, 1952) 55 f., 126-29, 182-84, 222; H. W. Meihuizen, *Galenus Abrahamsz* (Haarlem, 1954) 32, 131 f.; *DJ* 1837, 86-125, 1840, 33-52; *BRN* VII, 528 f.; Blaupot t. C., *Groningen* I, 130-39; *DB* 1877, 67-72, 76, 80-82, 84; 1878, 30 f.; 1879, 9; 1889, 28-30; 1906, 149-51; 1910, 191; J. Willemsz, *Grondigh Ondersoeck oft Klaer Betoogh* (De Rijp, 1652); *Oud Gebruyck van de Vryheit van Spreecken in de Gemeente der Doopsgesinden* (1665); W. K. Loopes, *Ontlediging der Christel. Kercken-Order ende des zelfs Ampten* (Amsterdam, 1684, repr. 1699) 14 and *passim*.

Ministry (German, *Diener am Wort, Lehrer*, Dutch, *dienaar, leraar*) *of Mennonites of Prusso-Russian Background*. Among the Mennonites of Danzig, Prussia, Poland, and Russia Dutch traditions pertaining to the ministry were retained over many generations and even transplanted to the prairie states and provinces of North America and South America in a somewhat modified form. The Danzig church record, beginning with the activities of Peter Classen in 1667, gives a list of ministers from the days of Dirk Philips to the 19th century, and a list of the elders (*oudsten*) and preachers (*dienaar int' woort*) from 1598 to 1805, together with interesting information on the election of elders, ministers, and deacons. The congregation always had one elder and from two to five ministers and a number of deacons. At times the elder had a coelder. A number of candidates were nominated at a congregational meeting, and the one receiving the largest number of votes was considered elected. On Aug. 17, 1800, the election procedure differed considerably from the previous method, in that the church council nominated candidates, from whom the congregation elected the one they wished to have serve as minister. The candidate with the highest number of votes had 41, the next had 30, and the third had 20. The one with 41 votes was considered elected.

In later days it frequently occurred that candidates elected were not willing to accept the responsibilities of the ministry. On the other hand, the candidate who was elected was on "probation" for some time before he was ordained. There was always a possibility that he would remain a candidate and never be ordained. The following entry in the Danzig church record on Feb. 1, 1801, is characteristic: "In the country church where Jacob Bartsch resigned from his ministerial duties and Gerhard Fast was deprived of his ministerial duties, there was an election of a deacon and minister. First two deacons were· chosen. Gerhard Dyk with 25 votes, Klaas Reimer with 24 votes. Of these two deacons one was elected minister. Klaas Reimer was elected with 21 votes. Both men accepted the office. May the Lord strengthen them." (Klaas Reimer founded the Kleine Gemeinde in Russia.) On Feb. 10, 1805, the congregation elected two ministers, both of whom refused to accept the call. In the early 19th century it became extremely difficult to find members of the congregation willing to serve as lay ministers (Mannhardt). This led to the calling of theologically trained salaried ministers. Jacob van der Smissen, the first such minister, began serving the Danzig Mennonite Church on July 9, 1826. Elbing followed this practice. This changed the traditional Mennonite pattern of a multiple lay ministry. The theologically trained and salaried minister served as elder and pastor of the congregation, assisted by the deacons. The lay ministers were "retired"· and died out. In the rural Prussian and Polish churches, with the exception of Lemberg, Galicia, the old system prevailed until World War II, at which time the Mennonites of this territory were dispersed.

With the change in the function of the minister came also changes in preaching. Originally the minister delivered the sermon seated on a somewhat elevated chair without a pulpit (Mannhardt, 106). On both sides of the preacher sat the co-ministers. The sermon was delivered without notes in the Dutch language. During the second half of the 18th century the Dutch was changed to German. The first German sermon in the Flemish Mennonite Church of Danzig was preached by Gerhard Wiebe of Elbing on Sept. 19, 1762. "Since the congregation was not used to this he did not find general approval." With this gradual shift from Dutch to German it became common for a minister to stand while preaching and to follow an outline. This necessitated the introduction of a pulpit. Hans von Steen complained that "the beautiful simplicity is disappearing more and more from Menno's church." The change was probably brought about by developments in the Mennonite churches of the Netherlands, where the practice of writing out sermons and delivering them verbatim no doubt originated. Numerous sermons from the beginning and middle of the 18th century have been preserved in the Bethel College Historical Library coming from Prussian, Old Colony, and Kleine Gemeinde ministers. Some were written by the Dutch minister Pieter Pietersz, and (according to entries on the cover) were delivered in various congregations and at times also repeated in the same congregation. This practice prevailed in Russia until men like Bernhard Harder (q.v.) began to preach without notes. Among the conservative groups, such as the Old Colony Mennonites, the old practice has been retained to this day.

The Mennonites of Russia retained the multiple unsalaried lay ministry until the end of the 19th century. With the improvement of educational facilities and the raising of the educational standard within the congregation it became necessary to deviate from this old practice, just as had been the case in Danzig and in Holland. In Holland in the early days the congregation frequently elected the ministers from the ranks of practicing physicians. In Russia the teaching profession was considered most suitable for the ministry. Before World War I the Mennonites of Russia had some 32 elders in the Mennonite Church and 15 in the Mennonite Brethren Church, with a total of 500 ministers. Of this total about one third were or had been teachers with a secondary school training. Two thirds had only an elementary education. Twenty-five of these ministers had received theological training in some place following the pattern of the urban Mennonite churches of Germany and the Netherlands. They encountered difficulties with the government in establishing a seminary. The outbreak of World War I and the consequent Revolution prevented the Mennonites of Russia from building their own theological seminary.

On April 8, 1910, the Halbstadt Church meeting regarding the establishment of a church fund for the theological training of ministers stated that it would be impossible in the future to follow the old practice pertaining to the ministry, and that without intending to break with the practice of electing and maintaining a lay ministry, the time had come when the minister deserved remuneration. The ministerial candidate should also have an opportunity to obtain theological training in short-range Bible courses as well as in theological seminaries; for this purpose a budget of 2,060 rubles was to be created, and the money raised by a special method (Friesen, 760). Numerous attempts were made to create a theological seminary in connection with the secondary Mennonite schools in Russia or by establishing Bible schools (q.v.). Not all of the plans could be realized. However, the Bible courses offered for ministers in larger congregations were of great significance.

Some of the older congregations with cultural centers and secondary schools had quite a high ratio of ministers with a secondary and theological education. Statistics of the Chortitza Mennonite Church of 1928 reveal that of the total of 18 ministers and 10 deacons of the church and its subsidiaries, 10 had a secondary education including religious training and one had theological training. A similar situation was recorded regarding the Nikolaipol Mennonite Church and the Kronsweide Mennonite Church (*Unser Blatt* III, April 1928, p. 176; May 1928, p. 193).

In the prairie states and provinces of North America the Mennonites of Prussian, Polish, and Russian background continued the practices to which they had been accustomed in the old country. Gradually an adjustment to the environment and to new needs took place. This change was first effected in the United States. One of the reasons which speeded up the shift from the unsalaried multiple lay ministry to a single theologically trained and paid minister was the change from the German to the English language in worship services. As in Russia, Prussia, and Holland the rise of the educational level of the laity also caused the downfall of the old system here. In the United States in the congregations of the General Conference Mennonite Church, the Mennonite Brethren Church, and the Evangelical Mennonite Brethren Church the change is nearly complete. A minister is hardly ever elected from the members of the congregation to serve for a lifetime without special preparation and remuneration. As a rule he continues his training beyond college at a seminary or Bible school. After he has received a call from the congregation he enters into a contract with the congregation for one or a number of years. The old division of duties whereby the minister preaches only and the elder (*q.v.*) is responsible for administering baptism and the Lord's Supper has been discontinued. The present pastor takes care of all ministerial and elder duties, although much of the work of administration may be done by the church council of the congregation or the board of deacons.

The former Prusso-Russian pattern has been retained most fully among the Mennonites in Canada, Mexico, Brazil, Uruguay, and Paraguay, with Canada showing greater changes than the other countries. With the rapid changes from German to English it will most probably follow the usual pattern of the United States. Most of the Canadian congregations in the G.C.M., M.B., and other groups still have one elder or leader and a number of ministers, up to five or even ten. However, there is a tendency toward a salaried one-minister system. The Russo-Canadian Mennonites have thus far drawn heavily upon the teachers from Russia. They are now producing their own ministers. Young men are being prepared in the two Canadian Mennonite Bible colleges of Winnipeg; many of them go on to other Mennonite colleges and seminaries.

A recent study reveals that in the United States there is a constant turnover in the ministry. The practice of electing a lifetime minister from the membership of the congregation is past. Most of the G.C.M. congregations have had from two to five ministers within the last 25 years, indicating that the tenure is from five to twelve years. It is likely that the situation is similar among the M.B., E.M.B., and K.M.B. groups. The larger congregations apparently have a slightly higher rate of change in the ministry than the smaller congregations.

All ministers of the General Conference Mennonite congregations of the United States are partially or fully supported, whereas in Canada 50 per cent are self-supporting. In the United States 69 per cent are fully supported, and 28 per cent partially supported. Almost all G.C.M. ministers in the United States serving congregations of more than 150 are fully supported. In most of the larger congregations the salary of a minister is equal to that of a faculty member in a Mennonite college. In some of the large congregations an assistant minister or a minister of music is employed. The Mennonite Brethren situation is very similar to that of the G.C.M., except in Canada, where there are as yet few fully trained and salaried ministers. The old ministerial pattern is best preserved in C.G.C. congregations, which are mostly of Polish background.

A unique incident is related by H. B. Schmidt, which may have represented a general practice among the Mennonites of Prussia and Poland. When the brethren of the Friedenstal Church (Tampa, Kan.) visited him to ask him to become their minister they gave him a farewell kiss (which had originally been a general practice but was then restricted to this occasion).

The trend toward a supported ministry began in the Eastern District Conference before World War I and spread westward to the Western District Conference, and is now nearly completed. The process was a little slower in the Northern District.

Fifty per cent of the Canadian General Conference churches have from two to four ministers, the other 50 per cent having only one. Most of the elders serve more than one congregation. About half of the congregations have called their ministers from within the congregation in the last ten years.

In some of the congregations it is a practice to license a ministerial candidate to preach before he is ordained. This is in keeping with the old tradition in the Danzig Mennonite Church. It is also in keeping with the Anabaptist emphasis that the minister and his family are expected to be the best representatives of a consecrated disciplined congregation. A high ethical standard is still emphasized more than eloquence and education.   C.K.

Harold W. Buller, "The Problem of Pastoral Responsibility in the General Conference Mennonite Church in Its American Environment" (dissertation, Princeton, 1952); P. M. Friesen, "Der geistliche Charakter der Gemeinde und der Predigerschaft," *Brüderschaft*, 730-66; M. Shelly, "Practices and Trends in Mennonite Congregations," *Proceedings of the Study Conference on the Believers' Church* (Newton, 1955) 27 ff.; P. K. Regier and I. I. Friesen, "Values and Problems of the Lay and the Supported Ministry," *ibid.*, 197 ff.; H. G. Mannhardt, *Die Danziger Mennonitengemeinde* (Danzig, 1919); Cornelius Krahn, "The Office of an Elder in Anabaptist Mennonite History," *MQR* XXX (April 1956) 120 ff.; "Danzig Mennonite Church Record" (BeCL); K. Friedrichsen, "Die Allgemeine Mennonitische Bibelschule," *Unser Blatt* I, 280; II, 101.

Ministry in Switzerland, South Germany, France, and North American Groups of This General Background. Very early in Swiss-South German Anabaptist history the congregations adopted a form of leadership which gave considerable responsibility to the bishop-elder in each congregation. The Schleitheim Confession of February 1527 calls this office the "Hirtenamt" or pastoral office. How early the threefold ministry of bishop-elder, preacher, and deacon developed is not clear, but by the time of the Strasbourg Discipline of 1565 it was well established. It has been maintained to modern times in all the Swiss, French, and South German congregations, as well as North American, except in the Palatinate, where the single pastor system with trained and salaried pastors was introduced soon after the beginning of the 19th century (first case, Ibersheim in 1813). The plural ministry has been maintained in all those congregations in Europe which did not adopt the system of the trained single pastor. Here usually there is also a plural eldership, the larger congregations having as many as four or five elders; in Alsace the practice has commonly been to have only one elder, with several preachers. In the Badisch-Württembergisch-Bayrischer Gemeindeverband, all the ordained men of all the congregations of the conference constitute a conjoint ministry, the elders being actually ordained for the entire conference, though with local congregational connections. In the Palatinate the office of deacon has virtually disappeared.

In North America the early Pennsylvania settlements of Swiss and Palatine immigrants continued the ministerial pattern of their homelands as did the Alsatian Amish immigrants of the 19th century settling farther west. One notable change took place in the Mennonite congregations, however, namely, the development of a district or diocesan bishop with charge over a number of congregations. This pattern probably was a result of the establishment of daughter congregations from an original base congregation whose bishop retained pastoral charge at all the meeting places of the total congregation. The ministers also in such cases served in rotation in a circuit. Amish congregations retained more rigidly the pattern of one bishop for each congregation. Among the Old Order Amish to this day a congregation is not considered fully organized until it has its own bishop, who is usually chosen very promptly after the formation of a new "district." In all North American groups with a plural ministry, ministers are chosen exclusively out of the congregation and serve for life unless "silenced" for heresy or misconduct. The lot (*q.v.*) has been commonly used in the choice of candidates for ordination, and is still widely used.

The practice of a single pastor ministry, with training and full or part salary, has been slow in coming in the Mennonite Church (MC), but since World War II has been rapidly increasing except in the four eastern conferences—Franconia, Lancaster, Franklin-Washington, and Virginia—and in the western conferences of Iowa-Nebraska, North Central, and Pacific Coast. A recent study shows that now about 40 per cent of M.C. ministers are ordained without the lot. Some 60 congregations, mostly in the Middle West, now have single pastors with salary. This is almost wholly the case in Illinois and Ontario, and largely so in Ohio and Indiana. The office of deacon usually retreats in significance or is dropped in these cases. Ministers are still chosen or called by the congregations for life or an indefinite term, although in a few cases recently a three- or five-year term has been specified. The practice of licensing ministers for a probationary period a year at a time has been coming in rapidly in the past ten years.

A significant trend of the past ten years has been the reconsideration of the office of bishop. The bishop district system having been largely broken down west of the Allegheny Mountains because of the growing adoption of the practice of having a bishop in each congregation, the office of bishop has lost much of its former prestige. Two conferences (the South Central and the Ohio and Eastern) have suspended the ordination of bishops and are experimenting with a system of district superintendents. The Ohio and Eastern Conference has adopted the practice of only one ordination, with assignments to various types of ministerial duty—deacon, pastor, and supervising bishop. Thus the ministerial system has come into flux, with the outcome not yet clear. The district superintendent plan is in effect the reintroduction of the district or diocesan bishop concept with limited tenure and supervisory functions rather than pastoral.

The Hutterian Brethren developed a ministerial system in which each local Bruderhof (congregation) had at least one preacher (*Diener der Worts*) and one deacon (*Diener der Notdurft*), while the whole brotherhood had one bishop-superintendent (*Vorsteher*). (See also **Bishop, Elder, Deacon.**)

H.S.B.

Mennonite Church Polity. A Statement of Practices in Church Government (Scottdale, 1944); Paul Peachey, "Anabaptism and Church Organization," *MQR* XXX (1956) 213-28; *Report of the Study Conference on Church Organization and Administration* (Scottdale, 1955); H. S Bender, "The Historical Background of Our Present Ministerial Offices," *Gospel Herald* XLII (Oct. 25, 1949) 1051 and 1061.

Ministry, Call to the. A distinction is properly made between two aspects of the call to the ministry: a direct and inner call (*vocatio immediata* or *interna*), which comes from God, and an indirect or outward call (*vocatio mediata* or *externa*), given through a human agency, the church. The two must work together. This is the prerequisite for a blessed, fruitful discharge of the duties of the minister's office, and the preliminary requirement for a healthy church life. The one-sided emphasis of the former as a rule leads to disorderly, undisciplined conditions, and the exclusion of all participation by the church is often a principal cause of disintegration of church life.

It is the teaching of the Bible and apostolic practice that the call proceeds from God and takes place through the church. The church chooses those called by God and ordains them to service. Acts 1:21-26 says, "Wherefore of these men which have companied with us all the time that the Lord Jesus went in and out among us, beginning from the baptism of John, unto that same day that he was taken up from us, must one be ordained to be a witness with us of his resurrection. And they appointed two, Joseph called Barsabas, who was surnamed Justus, and Matthias. And they prayed, and said, Thou, Lord, which knowest the hearts of all men, shew whether of these two thou hast chosen, that he may take part of this ministry and apostleship, from which Judas by transgression fell, that he might go to his own place. And they gave forth their lots; and the lot fell upon Matthias; and he was numbered with the eleven apostles."

When it became necessary to fill the office of deacon, with which also the proclamation of the Word was connected, the Twelve did not simply impose a man selected by their power upon the church, but they called the church together (Acts 6:2-6) and said, ". . . Brethren, look ye out among you seven men of honest report, full of the Holy Ghost and wisdom, whom we may appoint over this business. . . . And they chose Stephen . . . whom they set before the apostles: and when they had prayed, they laid their hands on them."

Other passages of Scripture agree with these. The elders at Ephesus are reminded by Paul of their divine calling and admonished (Acts 20:28), "Take heed therefore unto yourselves, and to all the flock, over the which the Holy Ghost hath made you overseers, to feed the church of God, which he hath purchased with his own blood." In Eph. 4:11 the apostle writes, "And he [Christ] gave some, apostles; and some, prophets; and some, evangelists; and some, pastors and teachers." Compare this with I

Cor. 12:28: "And God hath set some in the church, first apostles, secondarily prophets, thirdly teachers . . . ." We hear thus that Christ gives, God determines ("hath set") and calls individuals as bearers of spiritual office, and the church takes them, so to say, from the hand of God and of Christ and ordains them to service.

The outward call to the office, if it is to have meaning in the kingdom of God, must be based on the inner call. In II Cor. 3:5 and 6 Paul writes, "Not that we are sufficient of ourselves to think any thing as of ourselves; but our sufficiency is of God; who also hath made us able ministers of the new testament; not of the letter, but of the spirit: for the letter killeth, but the spirit giveth life." And in I Cor. 2:12 and 13 he especially emphasizes, "Now we have received, not the spirit of the world, but the spirit which is of God; that we might know the things that are freely given to us of God. Which things also we speak, not in the words which man's wisdom teacheth, but which the Holy Ghost teacheth; comparing spiritual things with spiritual." Only he who is in possession of the Holy Ghost is called by God to any spiritual office in the Christian church. He has personal life-connection with Christ, from which strength flows to him to plant the seeds which grow into eternal life.

The teaching and practice of the apostolic church is based on the idea of the priesthood of all believers (q.v.). In the post-apostolic period this fundamental Christian principle was adhered to. Justin and Irenaeus testify with joy that the church of Christ is the priestly race of promise, and Tertullian asserts that because all Christians are priests, they also have the right to administer the ordinances. Also Origen and Augustine emphasize the priesthood of all believers. And yet this principle had long since been abandoned in practice. The example of Old Testament priesthood was more and more imitated in the Christian (Catholic) church. The calling of church officials became solely the affair of the church authorities, which set up exact directions for it. In these specifications there are echoes of the idea of the priesthood of believers. Thus the demand is repeatedly made that appointments to church offices should not be made without consulting the congregation. But it was never done. At the Roman Catholic Council of Trent in 1545-63 (*Sessio XXII* c. 4) all participation by the laity in the calling and appointment to spiritual office was eliminated.

The Reformation restored validity to the concept of the priesthood of all believers. Now the question of the call to the ministry in the Christian church became current again. How beautifully Luther expresses it in his booklet, *An den christlichen Adel deutscher Nation:* "For all Christians are truly of the 'spiritual estate,' and there is among them no difference at all but that of office. . . . If a little group of pious Christian laymen were taken captive and set down in a wilderness, and had among them no priest consecrated by a bishop, and if there in the wilderness they were to agree in choosing one of themselves, married or unmarried, and were to charge him with the office of baptizing, saying mass, absolving and preaching, such a man would be as truly a priest as though all bishops and popes had

consecrated him" (*Works of Martin Luther,* II, Philadelphia, 1915, 67). And in a *Kirchenpostille* Luther preaches: "Hence every Christian has the power which the pope, bishops, priests and monks have in this case to retain or to remit sins. . . . All of us indeed have this power; but let no one presume to exercise it openly, unless he is chosen by the church to do so."

Here Luther represents the absolutely correct Protestant conviction that all worthy and responsible members have the right to exercise the functions of spiritual office, but that for the sake of order only the person to whom the office has been entrusted by the church may do so. Luther afterwards modified his conception of the priesthood of believers because of the attitude of the Zwickau prophets and Thomas Müntzer. He placed increasing emphasis on the preaching office and put the greatest stress on the orderly call to the office, limiting the participation of the congregation and giving the state increasing rights and duties.

In the third chapter of his exposition of several chapters of Exodus (1524-26) Luther distinguishes two types of call: The first comes only from God, without the use of an intermediate means; but this call must have outward signs and evidence. The other call, which comes through men, needs no sign. Those who say, "We are called of God," must prove that God and men have called them. In his exposition of Psalm 82 he argues as follows: "It does them [the Anabaptists] no good to assert that all Christians are priests. It is true that all Christians are priests, but not all are pastors; for over and above being a Christian and a priest, he must also have an office and an assigned parish." Hence, "unless they [the "corner preachers"] furnish good evidence and proof of their calling and commission from God to this work in a definite parish, they should not be recognized or listened to, even if they were like angels or Gabriel himself. For God wants nothing done by one's own choice or worship, but all on command and call, especially the office of preaching, as Peter says in II Pet. 1," etc. Therefore "Let everyone consider: If he wants to preach or teach, let him prove the call and command that drives and compels him or be still. If he refuses, then let the government commend such fellows to the proper master, whose name is Master Hans" (i.e., the hangman).

Luther goes still further in his booklet *Von den Schleichern und Winkelpredigern* (1532). He actually warns against the restoration of apostolic custom: "People are too wild and forward." Just as it is not permitted to push oneself uncalled into the (civil) council, much less should it be allowed that "in a spiritual council, that is, the office of preacher, a foreign intruder should push his way in or a layman should venture to preach uncalled in his church. It shall be and remain the charge of the prophets (the pastors)." To them and not to the members he grants the right of protest against an erring preacher and thus no doubt also the right of calling the preacher.

In the Lutheran Church the conception of a twofold call, immediate and indirect, was retained. But the former is not understood as the call that comes through the Holy Spirit as the prophets and apostles experienced it, but merely as the inner conviction of the capability of performing the functions of the office of preacher, knowing that one has the required gifts and the knowledge, especially the gift of teaching ability and eloquence, and that one agrees with the faith of the church and has the urge and the joy to serve according to the intentions of the church. The latter or indirect and outward call consists either in the congregational choice or in the church governing body's selection of a candidate for the administration of any spiritual office. Fundamentally the participation of the church is required. The sentence, "The call is the concern of the entire congregation," occurs again and again in the rules and doctrines of the church; therefore the members must in some way be heard. But actually their participation is extremely slight. The call remains solely the concern and the task of the church authorities with the co-operation of the state. The conditions of the call are as follows: (1) an unspotted reputation; (2) the proper age; (3) adequate health and absence of disturbing bodily defects; (4) adequate education, required since 1552. As a rule, two examinations are required; one (*pro licentia concionandi*) to acquire the permission to preach and to be a candidate for the ministry, the other (*pro ministerio*) for admission to a spiritual office; three examinations are given in Old Prussia, Saxony, and several Thuringian states; (5) since 1533 a statement has been required of the candidate, confessing as his own the faith that he is to proclaim; (6) the gratuitousness of the giving of the office, so that all simony is excluded.

The same practice is, on the whole, found in the Reformed Church. According to Calvin's *Institutes* (IV, c III, 17) the call must be made with the consent and approval of the congregation; other pastors must have charge of the election. Accordingly, in accord with the Geneva Rules, the pastors elect, and the laymen declare their assent. The Helvetian Confession of 1556 (*Confessio Helvetica Posterior*) makes the following assertion regarding the call: God gives the church preachers, who are to be regarded as the successors of the apostles, even of the prophets, by equipping believing men with the gifts necessary to leadership in the church; but only those are to be considered servants of the church, who have been chosen and regularly ordained by the church. "The call and the choice are made by the church or by those whom the church has appointed for the purpose." In the Reformed Church, too, as a rule the call to the office is issued by the church authorities; the individual congregation has only the right of suggestion or of limited choice.

More faithfully than these Anabaptism has preserved the principle of the congregational call to the ministry and has given the priesthood of believers its full place. The call is the business of the individual congregation and is given to a mature member of the congregation by a vote of the congregation. The oldest confession (*q.v.*) of the Anabaptists states it thus (*Mart. Mir.* D (I), 433 f., E 395; translated from the German Pirmasens edition of 1780): "Therefore shall the believers who lack preachers, after they have sought the face of God

in ardent prayers (Acts 6:6), turn their eyes to a God-fearing (Acts 16:2; I Tim. 3:7) brother who keeps his body in subjection (I Cor. 9:27), and in whom the fruit of the Holy Spirit (Gal. 5:22) is evident. He, when he has been chosen through the votes of the members (II Cor. 8:19), shall be examined by the elder and overseer of the congregation (I Tim. 3:10), whether he agrees with the congregation in all matters, according to the rule of God's Word, so that he may be capable of instructing others in the way of truth which he himself understands and knows (Matt. 15:14; Isa. 9:15). And he, if he is found capable (Tit. 1:8), shall arise in the name of the Lord to proclaim the will of God to the people. If it is evident that God has entrusted him with the preaching of the Gospel (Gal. 2:7), namely, that he rightly divides the Word (II Tim. 2:16) and with it brings forth fruit (Isa. 55:11; Col. 1:6), then the church, if it is in need of it, and if after the examination he is found to be of one mind with the congregation, can elect him by a regular vote (II Cor. 8:19) as elder and preacher in full office; the elders (I Tim. 1:14; II Tim. 1:16; Acts 13:3) confirm it by the laying on of hands and permit him to work and labor in the Lord's vineyard (I Cor. 3:9), and also administer Christian baptism and the Lord's Supper with all that pertains to it."

The regulations in other Mennonite confessions, though shorter, have the same provisions. This is still the doctrine and practice of the Mennonite churches everywhere; i.e., that the call of the ministry is the exclusive right of the individual congregation. It is carried out by means of the vote, to which all mature members, in most churches including women, are eligible. A prerequisite of the congregational call is the divine call, which consists, not in receiving special revelations, but in the inner urge to preach given by God and in the possession of the necessary qualifications. Formal training, which at times and in many places was rejected as unscriptural, is coming more and more to be viewed as essential. In Holland, in the city churches of Germany, and in the country churches of the Palatinate it has become a requirement. The country churches of West Prussia, the Verband (*q.v.*), as well as the churches of Russia and America still reject this as an absolute requirement.

Before 1795 some of the Mennonite congregations in the Netherlands were required to ask the consent of government in order to call a minister, or the called ministers were obliged to get approval in order to be allowed to accept the invitation. Usually the congregation did not comply with this law and called ministers without notifying the government. In 1745 at Almelo (*q.v.*) and in 1765 at Enkhuizen (*q.v.*) difficulties arose because the church board neglected to ask for the required approval. In both cases the government conceded.

In former times Mennonite congregations frequently asked the Lamist congregation at Amsterdam for consent to call ministers. Among others, this happened in the case of Den Burg in 1713 and 1714, Cadzand in 1758, Grouw in 1799 (when notified that the minister they intended to call did not belong to the Lamist Sociëteit), and Ameland in

1807. Consent was asked because Amsterdam gave subsidies to these congregations. After the A.D.S. (Dutch General Conference) was established in 1811, the congregations which received subsidies from the A.D.S. were required to have the approval of this organization for the calling of the ministers they chose.

The opponents of 16th-century Anabaptism made vigorous attacks on the right of the Anabaptist preacher to preach; i.e., they challenged his call. This topic was one of the church questions discussed in practically all the disputations held by state church authorities with the Anabaptists. The great Bern debate (*Berner Gespräch*) of 1538 is a striking example of this. The whole concept of corner preacher (*Winkelprediger*) as applied to the Anabaptists also expresses this. The Anabaptist answer was usually simply, "God has called us." But they did also commonly recognize the call by the congregation as soon as an ordered congregational life was set up. (See the Schleitheim Confession, 1527, article V.) (*ML* I, 198-200.)

The call to the ministry in the Mennonite churches of Europe (with the exception of the Netherlands) and of America has commonly been of two types: (1) by direct vote of the members of the congregation, or (2) by a nominating vote of members of the congregation followed by the casting of the lot (*q.v.*) if more than one candidate receives votes. Most of the groups in Europe and America use only a vote without the lot, and have done so throughout most of their history. In earlier times the minister, who was a lay-minister without special training or salary, was always chosen from the midst of the congregation. The employment of trained and salaried ministers usually means a call to someone from outside the congregation. In South Germany, France, and Switzerland the lot was used at certain times and places, and the 18th and 19th century immigrants from these areas to America brought the lot with them. It was consequently used regularly until recently in the Mennonite Church (MC), and all branches of the Amish. The Old Order Amish still use this method exclusively, but in the Mennonite Church it is being rapidly replaced by a direct vote or call from the outside. The lot ceased to be used in Europe by the end of the 19th century, with certain small exceptions. In the Palatinate the calling of trained ministers from the outside began in the first quarter of the 19th century.

A theological examination of candidates for ordination by the executive committee of a conference or by a special committee designated for this purpose, with or without a written questionnaire, has been introduced into about half of the conferences of the Mennonite Church (MC).

The early practice in the Mennonite (MC) and Amish churches in America was to expect every male member to be available for a call to the ministry, and refusal of a call was considered a very serious matter and at times subject to discipline. Some baptismal vows included a commitment to accept a call to the ministry if one should be received. Occasionally inability or unwillingness to preach after ordination resulted in a complete non-

functioning in the ministerial office. This was tolerated more readily than was refusal to accept ordination. The call to the ministerial office as expressed through the vote of the congregation and the lot was considered a divine call which could not be refused, whether one had an inner call or not. In more recent times it has been common to ask the candidate voted for whether he has an inner call from God. One who professes no such call is commonly excused from the lot. However, by many the vote and the lot are still considered sufficient evidence of a divine call.

The call to the ministry for service in special appointments under mission boards in foreign or home fields of service, or in institutions, does not usually require action by the congregation from which the candidate comes.

In the M.B.C.-U.M. Church a candidate for the ministry may offer himself for service but must receive an endorsement by vote of his home congregation before he can be used in an appointment to the pastoral ministry elsewhere. A period of probation, usually three years under licensure, must precede full ordination.

The practice of licensing, whereby a candidate for ministerial service may be authorized to serve in a preaching or pastoral appointment, either in full charge or as an assistant to an ordained minister, is coming into many district conferences of the Mennonite Church (MC). In this case the call is extended by the bishop in charge, often without any vote by the congregation from which the candidate comes, but frequently with a vote by the congregation where he is to serve. In the case of a mission station, no vote is taken. Licensure is usually for a year at a time only. (See **Berufung**, *ML* I, 198-200.)

NEFF, H.S.B., vDZ.

Minnesota, one of the United States of America, is bounded on the north by Canada, east by Lake Superior and Wisconsin, south by Iowa, and west by the Dakotas. Its area is 84,068 square miles. The chief towns are Minneapolis and the adjoining capital St. Paul. The state is known as the land of 10,000 lakes and attracts many vacationists. Its climate is healthful. The winters are cold but invigorating. Mining and lumbering are among its industries, but the state is noted largely for its prosperous agriculture.

The first Mennonite settlers in Minnesota came in 1873 from the Crimea, Russia, into the village of Mountain Lake, in the southern part of the state, which was hardly more than a railway station then. Other groups, all of Dutch-Prussian-Russian background, came in succeeding years; by 1880 some 350 families had come to this Cottonwood County village, which became the center of a large Mennonite community. Some of these families made their homes in the village and set up places of business, but most took up neighboring farm lands. A few families chose more outlying districts but later came back. Leaders in the early years were the four pioneer elders, Aaron Wall, Heinrich Voth, Gerhard Neufeld, and Heinrich Regier. Other personalities of note were Jacob Balzer, I. I. Bargen, and John

Rempel, who were instrumental in organizing school and church life.

A smaller contingent of Mennonites came to Butterfield, in Watonwan County, the county east of Cottonwood, in 1880-83. This group, of Galician (Swiss) origin, came from the Lemberg (*q.v.*) area in Austria. A few families of this group located in outlying districts, but only temporarily. Most of these people live in or near Butterfield. The Butterfield and Mountain Lake area is really one community. Through the years a number of families have drifted away to western states, and some to the cities, but many have come back. The majority of the Mennonites in this locality are prosperous farmers, but a goodly number have set up flourishing business establishments. Some have gone into professions, such as medicine, nursing, teaching, and the ministry.

A small group of Mennonites has been living at Warroad, a town of about 1,500, in Roseau County in northwestern Minnesota, since 1934. Most of this group came originally from the Mountain Lake and Butterfield area. They had left Minnesota in 1916 and settled near Lostwood, in northwestern North Dakota, but because of continued crop failures moved to Warroad. Their number was increased by some families from Alsen and Munich, N.D., and others coming direct from the Mountain Lake and Butterfield community. They are all of Dutch-Prussian-Russian background. A congregation (GCM) was organized in 1939 and a country church was built. Its membership (1954) is 86.

The first Mennonite church in the Mountain Lake community, now called Gospel Mennonite Church, was organized in 1876, and was open to all who wished to affiliate with it. In 1888 a split occurred, due to the introduction of Sunday school. A small group in the congregation led by Aaron Wall (*q.v.*) severed its connection and reorganized as a separate congregation, which later was instrumental in forming the Evangelical Mennonite Brethren Conference (*q.v.*). The original church became a member of the General Conference and the Northern District Conference. A third branch of Mennonites represented in the community are the Mennonite Brethren. The first M.B. church was organized in 1877. The following data indicate the constituency of these conferences in Minnesota in 1954; G.C.M. with a membership of 1,822 in 7 churches, including the church at Warroad; M.B. with 452 members in 2 churches; and the E.M.B. with 255 members in one congregation.

The last migration of Mennonites into Minnesota was that of the Mennonite (MC) Church. One group came from Cullom, Ill., to settle in 1894-97 at Alpha, in Jackson County, on the Iowa border some 20 miles straight south of Mountain Lake. This congregation had 77 members in 1954. The next congregation of this branch was Lake Region at Detroit Lakes, 180 miles northwest of Minneapolis, founded in 1926, most of the members coming from Nebraska. In 1954 it had 87 members. A series of seven mission churches have been established by this branch in the past ten years in northern Minnesota (Cass Lake 26 members, Ogema 51, Queeton 15, Leader 26, Loman 20, Menahga 26, International

Falls 50). The total membership in these missions was 214. Thus the total membership of the Mennonite Church (MC) in Minnesota in 1954 was 378.

The total membership of all branches of Mennonites in Minnesota in 1954 was 2,907.　J.J.F.

Jubiläumsfeier zum Andenken an das 50-jährige Bestehen der Mennonitenansiedlung von Mountain Lake, Minnesota 1875-1925 (n.p., n.d.); F. S. Schultz, *A History of the Settlement of German Mennonites from Russia at Mountain Lake, Minnesota* (Minneapolis, 1938); G. S. Rempel, *A Historical Sketch of the Churches of the Evangelical Mennonite Brethren* (Rosthern, 1939); *ML* III, 139.

Miropol: see **Friedensfeld** and **Novo-Kovno.**

Mishawaka (Ind.) United Missionary Church (MBC), founded in 1903, had a membership of 52 in 1953, with Lloyd Murphy as pastor.　J.H.H.

Missel, Hans, an Anabaptist martyr, still a young man, was betrayed and arrested at Langenschemmern in the Biberach district of Württemberg, Germany, and was taken to Warthausen and beheaded on Dec. 13, 1571. He went to his death with joy. The executioner testified of him, "This man is better than all of us together." His suffering is described in the song, "Merkt auf, ihr gelibten Brüder mein," found in *Lieder der Hutterischen Brüder* and in Liliencron's anthology.　NEFF.

Mart. Mir. D 561, E 893 f.; Wolkan, *Geschicht-Buch,* 359-61; Zieglschmid, *Chronik,* 466 ff.; *Die Lieder der Hutterischen Brüder* (Scottdale, 1914) 693-97; R. Liliencron, *Zur Liederdichtung der Wiedertäufer* (Munich, 1875) 49-51; *ML* III, 140.

Mission Advocates, the first missionary organization in the Lancaster Mennonite (MC) Conference, originated at a meeting in the home of John H. Mellinger, Harristown, Pa., on Sept. 15, 1894. It was a layman's movement with C. M. Brackbill, John H. Mellinger, Abram Metzler, Jr., J. A. Ressler, and others as a nucleus, an outgrowth of Bible Studies through the district. At the second meeting they contributed $7.75 to encourage the new Chicago Mission. After 16 months, to comply with Bishop Board wishes they organized the Mennonite Sunday School Mission, and missions began to appear. Here was the seedbed for the Eastern Board of Missions and Charities, which is now touching four continents.　I.D.L.

Mission Association, *Dutch Mennonite:* **Doopsgezinde Zendings Vereeniging:** see **Dutch Mennonite Missions Association.**

Mission Board of the E.M.B. Church, known as the *Commission on Missions of the Evangelical Mennonite Brethren,* was organized in 1889, originally consisting of only three members. At the present time, according to the recently revised constitution, nine members serve on this board. Three members are elected each year and the term of office is three years.

The Commission functions as a co-operating Board, processing and recommending a missionary candidate to the societies with which the Evangelical Mennonite Brethren is affiliated: Congo Inland Mission, Far Eastern Gospel Crusade, and Gospel Missionary Union. It also recognizes and keeps in touch with all E.M.B. missionaries going out under any nonaffiliated mission societies. The annual budget is nearly $100,000. The number of missionaries served by the Commission is 70, located in Japan, India, Africa, and South America.

The officers at present are O. H. Wiebe, chairman; H. H. Dick, Executive Secretary; H. P. Nickel; B. B. Janz; Arthur Fast; Reuben Warkentin; Max Eisenbraun; A. P. Toews; and H. P. Wiens.

O.H.W.

Mission Home for the Aged, located in Hillsboro, Kan., one block north of the Salem Hospital and Salem Home for the Aged, is operated by the same board as the Salem Home. It was opened in 1920 as the Bethesda Sanitarium under the direction of Dr. and Mrs. J. V. Wiebe. After Dr. Wiebe's death it continued as the Mission Home for the Aged under the supervision of Miss Marie Schmidt and others until taken over by the Salem Home for the Aged Board, which is made up of representatives of the several Mennonite churches in Hillsboro and community. Each Home has its own matron and nurses. In 1957 the occupants of the Mission Home were transferred to the remodeled former Salem Hospital and Home and the activities of the Mission Home as a separate institution terminated. The enlarged institution now operates under the name Home for the Aged, Inc.   D.V.W.

Mission Mennonite Belge (MMB) was set up in 1955 as the legal holding corporation for the mission work of the Mennonite (MC) Board of Missions and Charities in Belgium. It is a subsidiary to the European Mission Council described in the article **Mission Mennonite Française.**   H.S.B.

Mission Mennonite Church (GCM), a rural congregation near Mission City, B.C., organized in 1940 by settlers from the Canadian prairies, now called United Mennonite Church. The first settlers were Johann Dueck, Peter Enns, David Lietz, and Peter Penner, who came in 1934-37. In 1940 a meetinghouse seating 180 was built. The members are largely engaged in dairying, poultry raising, and berry culture. In 1954 the membership was 116, with Peter J. Froese as pastor.   C.G.T.

Mission Mennonite Française (MMF), legal holding corporation in France for the mission work of the Mennonite (MC) Board of Missions and Charities, organized Sept. 19, 1954, in co-operation with the French Mennonites. The original officers were Pierre Widmer chairman, René Kennel secretary, Max Schowalter treasurer. MMF is a subsidiary to the European Mission Council of the MBMC, which was created by the MBMC Sept. 1, 1953, to plan and make recommendations for its mission work among the French-speaking peoples of Europe, particularly France and Belgium. In 1956 the members of EMC were David Shank chairman, Pierre Widmer executive secretary, Orley Swartzentruber, Jules Lambotte, René Kennel, Max Schowalter, Robert Witmer, and John H. Yoder. The MMF fields of service in 1957 were the work carried on by the Orley Swartzentrubers in Paris, and the PAX unit at Orleansville, Algiers.   H.S.B.

Mission News is a bimonthly paper published by the Franconia Mennonite Board of Missions and Charities (MC). It was first published in March 1937 as a four-page paper. Later it developed into an eight-page paper. At present (1955) it is a 16-page paper, approximately 8 x 10 in. in size. It is printed at the Mennonite Publishing House at Scottdale, Pa., with an edition of 2,100. The purpose of this paper was given by President Isaiah G. Ruth in the first issue as follows: "The object of the undertaking is to inform our people as to the work which is carried on by the Board and the mission stations under its supervision." The editors were 1937-39 Claude Shisler and Jacob M. Moyer; 1940-55 J. Silas Graybill and Elmer B. Kolb.   J.S.G.

Mission News Bulletin, published biweekly by the Mennonite Board of Missions and Charities, Elkhart, Ind., was first issued on Jan. 21, 1925, and continued through Dec. 22, 1947. Since that time the mission and financial information contained in the *News Bulletin* has appeared in the *Gospel Herald* under "Mission News" and "Your Treasurer Reports." The *News Bulletin* began as a one-page 8½ x 11 inch release and continued as such until June 6, 1928, Vol. 4, No. 11, when the format was changed to a one-page 8½ x 14 inch mimeographed sheet and continued in that form until discontinuance. It was distributed free to a selected list of ministerial and lay leaders in the Mennonite Church (MC). Since April 1953 the Mennonite Board of Missions and Charities has published a multigraphed monthly *Mission-Service Newsletter* which supplements material appearing in the *Gospel Herald*.   L.C.H.

Mission Quarterly; German edition, *Missions Quartalblatt,* was a 16-page, 6 x 9 in., quarterly published by the Home and Foreign Mission boards of the General Conference Mennonite Church from September 1924 to February 1931. The German issues were published in March, June, September, and December, while the English edition was published in February, May, August, and November. Most of the content was duplicated in the two languages. Since the purpose of the periodical was to acquaint church members with mission fields and missionaries and to promote the missions cause, its contents consisted mainly of reports and letters from missionaries, information from the mission boards, and editorials emphasizing missions. The home missions editor was A. S. Shelly of Germantown, Pa., until February 1928, when J. M. Regier of Pandora, Ohio, succeeded him. P. H. Richert of Goessel, Kan., edited the foreign missions section. It was sent free of charge to all families in General Conference churches.   J.F.S.

Mission Worker, The, "A monthly periodical published in the interest of mission work by the Mennonite (MC) Home Mission" in Chicago, A. H. Leaman editor, was published from December 1906 to November 1908 as an 8-page (from January 1908 16-page) 6½ x 9½ in. monthly. Beginning with May 1908 it was published by the Mennonite Publishing House at Scottdale, Pa., and from June 1908 John Thut was editor. It was discontinued with the establishment of the *Christian Monitor* in January 1909.   H.S.B.

Missionary Banner, an illustrated 16-page monthly, published first in 1938 at New Carlisle, Ohio, then at Winona Lake, Ind., and Pandora and Springfield, Ohio, and now at Elkhart, Ind., by the United Missionary Society, the missionary organization of the United Missionary Church. R. P. Ditmer served as editor of the first 14 volumes, 1938-52; Roy P. Adams, 1952-53, and Richard S. Reilly, 1954- .
                                                                    N.P.S.

Missionary Church Association, founded on Aug. 29, 1898, at Berne, Ind., has been deeply influenced by Mennonite character and tradition, since a number of the founders came out of the Defenseless Mennonite Church (now the Evangelical Mennonite Church). Several of the early leaders in the Missionary Church Association, including J. E. Ramseyer, William Egle, Joseph Egly, David Roth, and Henry Roth, were ministers in the Defenseless Mennonite Church originally. A. E. Funk of Eastern Pennsylvania, a minister in the General Conference Mennonite Church and a close associate of A. B. Simpson in the Christian and Missionary Alliance, was elected the first president of the M.C.A. in 1898. B. P. Lugibihl of the C. and M.A., and D. Y. Schultz were also strongly influential leaders in the beginning of the M.C.A. J. A. Sprunger, a General Conference Mennonite minister, also wielded an influence, but did not associate with the M.C.A. at its founding. A number of people followed the early Mennonite leaders in establishing the first Missionary churches in Berne and Grabill, Ind., Archbold, Ohio, Groveland, Ill., and Elkton, Mich. In addition to the Mennonite sources, the C. and M.A., through its early German Branch and the influences of its strong missionary and Bible conferences, played a major role in the formation of the new church.

Bethany Home and Bible Institute (the antecedent of the Fort Wayne Bible College) was established by the B. P. Lugibihls in 1895 in Bluffton, Ohio. J. E. Ramseyer, D. Y. Schultz, J. A. Sprunger, and others were engaged to assist in the Bible Institute at Bluffton. J. E. Ramseyer was principal for the first two years (1895-97), followed by D. Y. Schultz (1897-1900). The Bible Institute was closed in 1901 after six years of ministry. In 1904, after wide investigation for a new and more advantageous site, the school was reopened as the Fort Wayne Bible Training School in Fort Wayne, Ind. The school is now known as the Fort Wayne Bible College with a strong and varied program of training. It is owned and controlled by the Missionary Church Association although operated under a broad interdenominational policy. S. A. Witmer has been president for twelve years beginning in 1945.

J. E. Ramseyer was the president of the M.C.A. for 44 years (1900-44), and during that long period was its great and highly respected leader. He was also the president of the Fort Wayne Bible College 1912-d.44. Other founders of Fort Wayne Bible College were D. Y. Schultz, B. P. Lugibihl, William Egle, David Roth, and Henry Roth.

From 1900 to 1907 most of the churches founded had some Mennonite background. These included Pandora, Ohio, in 1900; Elbing, Kan., in 1902; Swanton, Ohio, in 1904; Archbold, Ohio, Pettisville, Ohio, and the First Church, Fort Wayne, Ind., in 1905; and Woodburn, Ind., in 1907. After 1908 the church grew largely through other influences and sources which have weakened the Mennonite character of the church.

The particular issues which led to the expulsion of the early leaders from the Defenseless Mennonite Church were the baptism with the Holy Spirit as a crisis experience following regeneration, certain truths related to eschatology, immersion as the only mode of baptism, and divine healing. J. E. Ramseyer brought the conflict in the church to a crisis by being rebaptized by immersion in August 1896. Others followed his example in baptism, and these with others became the nucleus of the new church.

In 1904 the official organ of the M.C.A., *The Missionary Worker,* was established with D. Y. Schultz as its first editor 1904-11. It has continued as a bimonthly denominational periodical. The German organ, *Botschafter des Heils in Christo,* was founded earlier but was approved by the General Conference of the M.C.A. in 1903 as an official organ of the church. William Egle served as its editor until 1927 with the exception of 1919-22, when H. C. Thiessen was the editor. The paper was discontinued in 1927.

The strong distinctives of the M.C.A. have been its emphasis upon the deeper life and upon foreign missions. Separation from the world, nonresistance with some modification, and the ordinances of baptism and the Lord's Supper are taught and practiced. Footwashing, once quite widely practiced, has practically died out.

The M.C.A. in 1957 had 113 local churches with approximately 7,000 members. There are 95 ordained pastors and 25 licensed ministers serving in churches. The churches are distributed as follows: Indiana 16, Ohio 24, Michigan 17, Illinois 9, Pennsylvania 3, Maryland 1, Tennessee 3, Arkansas 2, Missouri 1, Kansas 6, Nebraska 2, Colorado 1, Oregon 2, California 18, Arizona 3, Hawaii 4.

Foreign missionary work is carried on in sixteen countries around the world with a staff of 100 missionaries including 10 in the Hawaiian Islands. The M.C.A. operates its own fields in Sierra Leone, Africa; Ecuador, S.A.; Jamaica, Dominican Republic; Haiti, and the Hawaiian Islands. It has cooperated closely with other boards, particularly the Christian and Missionary Alliance, in sending and supporting missionaries in other countries.

The M.C.A. has had close relations for many years with the Evangelical Mennonites, the United Missionary Church, and the Christian and Missionary Alliance. Off and on there have been special efforts at merger between the M.C.A. and the first two. Negotiations are in progress at the present time with the U.M.C. The M.C.A. has been a member of the National Association of Evangelicals and its foreign department of the Evangelical Foreign Missions Association since their inception.

The M.C.A. headquarters is located at 3901 South Wayne Avenue, Fort Wayne, Ind., in a memorial building to J. E. Ramseyer, dedicated in 1950. J. A. Ringenberg succeeded J. E. Ramseyer as president in 1944, and Jared F. Gerig was elected to that office in 1952.   J.F.GE.

Walter H. Lugibihl and Jared F. Gerig, *The Missionary Church Association, Historical Account of Its Origin and Development* (Berne, 1950); Mrs. J. E. Ramseyer, *J. E. Ramseyer, Yet Speaking* (Berne).

Missionary Guide, an illustrated 16-page (sometimes 12, sometimes 18) bimonthly, published by the Illinois Mennonite Mission Board, "for the promotion of the interests of the Illinois Mennonite Conference and her subsidiaries." The editors have been J. N. Kaufman and C. Warren Long, 1944; Raymond M. Yoder, 1945-48; and Harold Zehr, 1948 to the present.   N.P.S.

Missionary Meetings, which serve the purpose of awakening and reviving a missionary spirit, are held regularly in the Mennonite churches in America, South Germany, West Prussia, and Switzerland. In 1830 a meeting of this kind was held in Heubuden (Danzig). Since 1817 the West Prussian Mennonites had been supporting Protestant missionaries with regular contributions and private gifts (*Menn. Bl.,* 1856, 55). When the Dutch Mennonite Mission Association (*q.v.*) was organized in 1847, the interest of German Mennonite friends of missions was soon turned to it. In the annual missionary meetings of the West Prussian churches this fact found lively expression in sermons and addresses. These meetings were well attended (*Menn. Bl.,* 1877, 66) and continued down into recent times.

The Mennonites of Russia also gathered for missionary meetings from an early period. On Oct. 4, 1857, "our this year's missionary meeting was held at Berdyansk" (*Menn. Bl.,* 1858, 18). Thus they became important in the life of the church.

Somewhat later missionary meetings were organized in South Germany. The initial impulse came from America. At the meeting of the General Conference Mennonite Church at Wadsworth in December 1876, it was proposed that annual missionary conferences be held to support the newly established foreign mission. The plan was carried out. Today such meetings are very frequent in the Mennonite churches of America. Some are quarterly (e.g., West Liberty, Ohio, M.C.), some semiannual, some annual. Some have been carried on for several decades.

In Switzerland the first known missionary meeting was held in the Emmental on March 9, 1890. Two years later the congregation of Giebelstadt-Würzburg followed its example and held such a meeting annually on a Catholic holiday. The farewell service for the outgoing missionaries, P. Löwen and his wife, and Peter Nachtigall with his wife, in 1911 in Würzburg became an inspirational celebration. Thereupon it was decided at the following meeting of the preachers of the conference of Baden and Hesse to hold a mission meeting annually. The first took place in Monsheim on May 1, 1913. Since then it has been held alternately in Monsheim and Kaiserslautern. The Gemeindeverband of Baden, Bavaria, and Württemberg has been conducting such meetings in Heilbronn since 1915. A similar meeting was held annually on the Deutschhof near Bergzabern until World War II.

Great blessing results from these meetings; they not only benefit foreign missions, but also serve to strengthen and revive the home churches. (See also **Angas, William Henry;** *ML* III, 142.)   NEFF.

Missionary Messenger, The, the official organ of the Eastern Mennonite Board of Missions and Charities of the Lancaster Mennonite Conference (MC), began as a 4-page quarterly in April 1924, became a 12-page 7¾ x 10¾ in. monthly in May 1925, a 16-page since December 1930 with an occasional 16-page supplement in recent years. Orie O. Miller was the first editor; his successors with time of beginning have been: J. P. Sauder, March 1932; Menno E. Miller, May 1935; Howard Charles, May 1941; Mahlon Hess, October 1941; Irvin B. Horst, July 1946; J. Lester Brubaker, February 1947; Paul N. Kraybill, May 1951. It touches all phases of missions, relief, and service, and some general church life. The subscription list of 4,900 reaches the entire conference, serving especially well by "keeping all the issues before all of our people all the time."   I.D.L.

Missionary News and Notes, the organ of the Women's Missionary Association of the General Conference Mennonite Church, 722 Main St., Newton, Kan. Its primary purpose is to propagate missionary interest among women of the Conference constituency and solicit their participation in the support of all Conference missionary endeavors. It was first published in 1926 as a monthly (except July and August) four-page leaflet with variable format. It is now (1957) published as a 16-page monthly, size 7 x 10 in., printed by the Herald Book and Printing Company of Newton. Its highest circulation, 6,650, was reached in 1947; the current circulation is 6,274. The editors have been Mrs. P. R. Schroeder 1926-29; Mrs. R. A. Goerz 1929-45; Mrs. H. J. Andres 1945-48; Mrs. A. D. Klassen 1949-56 (partial); and Mrs. Ira Sprunger 1956- . A German edition appeared in 1929-45. The German editors were Mrs. F. H. Klassen 1937-39 and Mrs. Gerhard Friesen 1939-45. At first the German edition was mimeographed and published separately but in April 1936 the separate issues were combined in one publication. *Missionary News and Notes* is now published entirely in English.   J.S.A.

Missionary Sewing Circle Letter, the monthly organ of the women's missionary and sewing circle work of the Mennonite Church (MC), at first 4 pages, 5 x 7 in., later usually 8 pages, called *M.S.C. Monthly* beginning in August 1944. It was published by the General Sewing Circle Committee of the Mennonite Board of Missions and Charities, a committee appointed by the Board, until March 1948, when a new name was given to the committee, Women's Missionary Sewing Circle Organization of the Mennonite Board of Missions and Charities. In January 1952 the format was enlarged to 6 x 9 in., still 8 pages, and has remained so to date. In October 1954 the title was changed to *Women's Missionary and Service Monthly* to correspond to the change of the organizational name to Women's Missionary and Service Auxiliary of the Mennonite Board of Missions and Charities.   H.S.B.

Missions, Board of: see **Board of Missions** (GCM).

Missions, Board of Foreign, of the Mennonite Brethren Church of North America: see **Board of Foreign Missions.**

Mission-Service Newsletter, a 6-page, 8½ x 11 in., monthly multilithed publicity release, published by the Mennonite (MC) Board of Missions and Charities, first number April 1953, mailed free to all ordained men and church workers of the Mennonite Church (MC). The editor from the beginning has been Levi C. Hartzler. It is the successor to the *Mission News Bulletin* (*q.v.*), published 1925-47.   H.S.B.

Missions, Foreign Mennonite. Modern Protestant mission work finds its stimulus and origin in the 18th-century Pietist movement and the evangelical awakening which followed it. Certain special characteristics mark this flowering of the missionary movement in the "Great Century," such as the multitude of zealous missionaries, the stress upon individual conversion, the dependence for financial support upon a voluntary supporting society, and the development of an understanding on the mission field that the new movement had the status of a minority in an antagonistic world. In the main these characteristics represent a new emphasis and new direction in mission purpose and method and could come into being only in the wake of a broad spiritual awakening. The lack of a deep spiritual revival as an immediate aspect of the Reformation is one of the main factors in explaining the lag of Protestant interest in the cause of missions. In other words, when the medieval idea of the state church with state support and state control and enforced membership was taken over by the classical reformers and introduced into the new Protestant movement and with Protestant princes uninterested, unwilling, or unable, the cause of Protestant missions could only wait for a new stimulus to individual responsibility and voluntary participation. The territorial church concept of the Reformers inhibited outreach beyond the national borders.

Early Anabaptist Missions (1525-1600), though conducted against the opposition of both Protestant and Catholic authorities and eventually suppressed, represent an attempt to introduce an apostolic sense of mission 200 years before the Protestant church as a whole was ready. A strong evangelical strain ran in the early Reformation leaders and was picked up by the Swiss Brethren and the Dutch Mennonites, both of whom represented the moderate, spiritual phase of the "Left Wing Reformation." In them was developed to a higher degree the logical Reformation emphasis on individual conversion, apostolic call to witness, and voluntary church fellowship. Early Anabaptist missions, thus, were a precursor to the modern missionary movement. They grew out of a deep sense of responsibility for evangelism and the spontaneous testimony of warm hearts to a faith that could only be transmitted by voluntary witness and appropriation. This spontaneous expansion through evangelism (*q.v.*) is evident from the earliest Anabaptist congregation at Zollikon in 1525 (Blanke, *Brüder in Christo*) to the last roving missionaries of the Moravian Hutterites about 1650. It accounts for the rapid expansion in Switzerland, where 38 congregations are reported organized in the canton of Zürich alone in the two years 1525-27 and a similar number in the canton of Bern. It appears in the Martyrs' Synod (*q.v.*) held in Augsburg in 1527, where in addition to ironing out doctrinal misunderstandings missionaries were assigned to the various fields of labor in central Europe. It appears again in the North in the rapid expansion of Anabaptism in the Low Countries, though here one must distinguish between the politico-eschatological Münsterites and the deeply religious Dutch Mennonites. It is seen pre-eminently in the Hutterites, whose missioners (*q.v.*) were part of an organized program to preach the Gospel and gather the Lord's people to the Moravian colonies which, in the later 16th century, were prospering. The evangelists were driven by zeal or persecution into ever widening circles where the indistinct national boundaries of the day made little difference. In this process, although they sailed no boundless seas to "Greenland's icy mountains" or "India's coral strand," they encountered the problems of modern missions and displayed the qualities of character and the methods of that movement.

F. H. Littell ("Anabaptist Theology of Missions") points out specific ways in which the early Anabaptist missions foreshadowed the modern movement: (1) they rejected the parish pattern and coercion for Pauline methods of persuasion and faith in which the proper order was first, preach, secondly, believe, and lastly, baptize; (2) they interpreted the Great Commission's "Go ye therefore" as applying to all believers at all times; (3) the lay believer became the carrying power of the movement; and (4) they had a supreme confidence in the power of God so that the suffering of the martyr church was its authentication and believed that in this very process "the Master was gathering His people from the far corners of the earth and that in His own good time God would give them the kingdom" (Stauffer, "Anabaptist Theology of Martyrdom").

Loss and Recovery of Evangelistic-Missionary Zeal. The very success of the evangelical Anabaptist movement stimulated opposition to it in a day when torture and death were accepted means of suppression. Persecution in various ways and to varying degrees became current wherever the Anabaptists went. The earlier effect was to spread the movement and to increase the challenge to faithfulness; the Hutterite Chronicle, the early South German and Swiss *Ausbund,* and the Dutch *Het Offer des Heeren* and *Martyrs' Mirror* glory in accounts of faithfulness unto death and in conversions by such vivid testimony. The later effects were not so favorable; trained leaders were lost and replaced by equally devoted but perhaps less qualified men; eventually missionary zeal was lost and replaced by an inner aspiration for piety and faithfulness to a more traditional type of religious life. The period of Mennonite exclusiveness had arrived. Although severe persecution ceased, irritating discriminations by the authorities continued, and the typical Mennonite became the "Quiet in the Land," emphasizing the virtues of simplicity, honesty, and adherence to the faith of the fathers, but without imagination or judgment as to opportunities or responsibilities of the higher faith in Christ. The 16th-century Anabaptists had been "in the world but not of the world"; the 18th-century Mennonite was neither "in the world" nor "of the world." This explains the continuing lack of evangelistic zeal for a long period after persecution and discrimination had passed.

The recovery of evangelistic-missionary zeal was a complicated process in which not only the challenge of a new viewpoint toward religious opportunities was necessary but also a reinterpretation of secular social responsibilities. It was the complication of balancing one of these against another that made Mennonite adjustments to the new movements of the 19th century so difficult. By approximately the early 19th century the Dutch and North German Mennonites were giving up much of the traditional Mennonite way of life. Nonresistance and nonconformity gradually vanished here and elsewhere. Liberal theology also made its inroads in Holland and North Germany. But Pietism also exerted its influence in Holland, Hamburg, West Prussia, South Germany, and Switzerland. In Russia and America conservative-traditional Mennonitism was maintained, but warmer pietistic and evangelical currents of influence opened the door to missions by the end of the 19th century. It was in the nexus of this social and religious adjustment that evangelism and missions returned to the Mennonites, receiving at first only a hesitant welcome. The process occupied the greater part of the 19th century and in Europe involved stimulating contacts with Baptists and Lutheran Pietists. In America it came largely through the German Evangelical arm of the Methodist awakening, or through the Moody type of revivalistic evangelism. The contacts were many and complex and it was not simply outside pressure that won Mennonites to renewed evangelistic and missionary zeal, but also the dawning consciousness that this was an essential aspect of Anabaptist-Mennonite faith.

Missionary Interest among European Mennonites was first aroused through efforts of the English Baptists to secure support for their Serampore (India) work. William Henry Angas (*q.v.*), an English Baptist preacher, was instrumental in organizing, in 1821, in Holland the Aid Society to support this work, which was predominantly Mennonite in membership. In 1824 Angas toured the Continent, paying attention to Mennonite congregations in Prussia, Poland, Bavaria, Switzerland, and France, and making a deep impression on them. As a result of his visit in the Palatinate a special conference in 1824 authorized a missionary box in every church and a mission offering once a month for support of the Baptist work. Shortly afterward, in 1830, there was held the first mission festival in West Prussia in the Heubuden church. Contributions raised were sent to the Berlin Mission. The growing sentiment for missions brought about in 1847 the reorganization of the Dutch Aid Society for the support of Baptist Missions into a Dutch Mennonite Missionary Association (*q.v.*). Prominent in this reorganization was Samuel Muller (*q.v.*), who had been president of the previous organization and carried over in the same capacity in the new society. Muller, deeply spiritual, formerly minister of the Amsterdam congregation and professor in the Seminary, was one of the most influential Mennonite leaders of the period. As were most early missionary societies, this was a private organization seeking voluntary support from all who were interested; though there was some Mennonite opposition as an innovation, it came to draw popular support, though it never won the entire brotherhood. The Palatinate and Prussian congregations now directed their contributions to the new Mennonite society, as did those of North Germany, Bavaria, and Russia, as well as a few congregations in America.

The first volunteer for foreign service was Pieter Jansz (*q.v.*), a teacher from Delft, Holland, who was sent out in 1851 to the Netherlands overseas possessions in Java (*q.v.*), locating at Japara. He was followed by H. C. Klinkert (*q.v.*) in 1856, Thomas Doyer (*q.v.*) in 1857, and R. D. Schuurman (*q.v.*) in 1863. Another mission field was opened in Sumatra in 1871 but staffed by the Russian Mennonites, Heinrich Dirks (*q.v.*) being the first missionary.

The rise of missionary interest among the Mennonites in Russia presents a vivid case of the influence of Pietist and Awakening forces on staid Mennonites. The Mennonite colonies in Russia were laid down roughly in three strata. The first colonists (1788-98), forming the Chortitza settlement, came originally from the financially poorer class of West Prussian Mennonites, consequently with less training and breadth of vision. The settlement was marked by early quarrels and slow progress and at the middle of the 19th century was still closed to innovations. The second group (1803-8), forming the Molotschna settlement, were from a more well-to-do background, with broader training and more initiative. They progressed more rapidly and took the lead in educational and religious moves. The third was a group of later arrivals (1819-40) from scattered settlements up the Vistula River, where they had had more prolonged contacts with other Protestants and particularly intimate relations with the Herrnhuters (*q.v.*). They formed the congregations of Rudnerweide, Alexanderwohl, Gnadenfeld (*q.v.*), and Waldheim (*q.v.*) and were scattered within the Molotschna settlement where they became focal points of new ideas. Rudnerweide, a Frisian congregation, immediately showed progressive tendencies by associating and uniting with a Flemish congregation. Then, with Alexanderwohl and Ohrloff, another progressive congregation, it joined in organizing a Molotschna branch of the Bible Society in St. Petersburg, and in supporting the Moravian missionary work as early as 1827. Under the first elder, Franz Görz, there were found at Rudnerweide mission study hours and a warm, evangelical type of sermon not common elsewhere.

Gnadenfeld, whose pastor Wilhelm Lange (*q.v.*) had formerly been Lutheran, had intimate Moravian contacts in Prussia at Brenkenhoffswalde (*q.v.*), where the congregation is said to have received many blessings, such as "a clear knowledge of the Scriptures, living Christianity, and understanding and love for missions and schools." This background made Gnadenfeld open to the ministrations of the near-by Lutheran Pietist minister Eduard

Wüst (*q.v.*), who further cultivated the pietistic-evangelistic emphasis. Here in 1860 was one of the main centers of the Mennonite Brethren as they emerged with their revival activities. In spite of some controversy Gnadenfeld presented a relatively undisturbed picture of developing spiritual life with stimulating effect on other congregations through evangelical, educational, and missionary activities. It was from this same Gnadenfeld that the first Russian Mennonite missionary volunteer came. Heinrich Dirks offered himself to the Dutch society and in 1867 was sent out to Sumatra. His service on the field and later service at home promoted the cause of missions among the Mennonites of Russia and Europe.

The Russian Mennonites organized no mission society of their own, but additional missionaries were like Dirks sent out under the Dutch society, and in fact the main support of the society came from Russia. The Mennonite Brethren made Baptist connections and sent a student to the German Baptist Seminary at Hamburg. When their first missionary, Abraham Friesen, was ready in 1889, he was sent out under the American Baptist Mission Union to South India, where he started a work for the Mennonite Brethren at Nalgonda, Hyderabad. Following him were A. J. Hiebert in 1898 and Heinrich Unruh in 1899. This was carried on at first in co-operation with the Baptists but later absorbed by the American Mennonite Brethren mission established in this area in 1900.

North American Mission Interest. As among European Mennonites, the mission interest of the Mennonites in North America arose contemporaneously with and in relation to the Evangelical awakening but was hindered by the social environment where secular innovations were pressed along with new forms of religious work. Thus opposition to political enticements, secular schools, and city occupations developed a reaction which tended to oppose all innovations including Sunday schools, midweek prayer meetings, evangelism and missions. Mennonites responded with varying degrees of opposition or approval to the new methods and activities, in accord with their background, contacts, and development. All of the Mennonite immigrants to America settled in what were at first closed communities with linguistic and religious distinctions which discouraged outside influences.

1. *General Conference Mennonite Church.* The first serious struggle over new methods of work came in connection with the John H. Oberholtzer (*q.v.*) schism of 1847 in the Franconia Conference (MC) in which 16 congregations, in whole or in part, comprising about one fourth of the members of the Franconia Conference, separated from the main body and organized the East Pennsylvania Conference of the Mennonite Church, later to be the G.C.M. Eastern District Conference (*q.v.*). Among the innovations soon introduced under Oberholtzer and the new conference were Sunday-school work, publication of literature, and ministerial training. Missions also were envisaged, for in a letter to European Mennonites in 1858 Oberholtzer inquired about how the Dutch Mission Society operated (*Menn. Bl.,* December 1858, 63). Contacts were

soon made with the South German Mennonite immigrants who had recently settled in Iowa and were already sending back contributions to the Dutch work (*Menn. Bl.,* September 1857, 50). Certain Canadian churches associated with Daniel Hoch (*q.v.*) joined with Ohio churches in a conference in May 1855, and recognized "the high duty to support missions for heathen" (*Rel. Botschafter,* June 25, 1855, 125). This surge of missionary interest in many quarters was part of the growing sentiment which brought about the organization in 1860 of the General Conference of the Mennonite Church of North America (now General Conference Mennonite Church, *q.v.*). In the union conference both home and foreign missions were commended to the churches and three treasuries were set up for the receipt of funds. Plans were made also for continuing and enlarging Oberholtzer's publications and for setting up an educational institution to train ministers and missionaries. To further these ends Daniel Hege (*q.v.*) was set aside as an itinerant minister to visit all Mennonite congregations explaining the new move and the opportunities for new work, and to solicit funds for the proposed institution. The building for the new school, located at Wadsworth, Ohio, was completed and dedicated in 1866 and Carl Justus van der Smissen (*q.v.*), pastor of the Friedrichstadt Church in Schleswig-Holstein, was secured as principal. The influence of the Wadsworth institute, though it lasted but ten years, and the influence of the van der Smissen family in the cause of missions cannot be overestimated. Deeply spiritual, in contact with the Dutch movement and the Java mission, van der Smissen impressed students and through them congregations. Perhaps most important is that from the first graduating class in 1871 came the one, Samuel S. Haury (*q.v.*), who was to become the first missionary sent out by the General Conference. As a missionary candidate, he made it necessary for the General Conference to organize a board which became in time the Foreign Mission Board (*q.v.*) of the General Conference. Various possible fields were investigated, Java under the Dutch society and Alaska; but finally in 1880 Haury was located among the American Indians in Oklahoma. This was the beginning of General Conference work among the American Indians which came to include the Arapahoe, Hopi, and Cheyenne in Oklahoma, Arizona, and Montana. The Hopi work was started by H. R. Voth (*q.v.*), who in addition to evangelistic work made notable contributions to Hopi anthropology by collections of Hopi artifacts now in the Chicago Museum of Natural History. The outstanding name in the Cheyenne mission was that of Rodolphe Petter (*q.v.*), who came from Switzerland in 1890 to join the Indian mission and become the foremost linguist in the Cheyenne language. His dictionary, grammar, Bible translations, and other publications are monumental works. The first mission field on foreign soil to be opened by the General Conference was that in India, started in 1900, in response to famine needs; the second was that in China begun as an independent venture in 1909 by H. J. Brown but taken over by the General Conference in 1914; more recently work was begun in Colombia (1945), in Japan (1950), and in Taiwan

(Formosa) (1954). In addition to the several factors mentioned above which contributed to the development of missionary interest among the General Conference Mennonites must be mentioned the coming of the Russian Mennonite immigration toward the end of the 19th century. Ten thousand settled in the prairie states and another eight thousand in Manitoba. Their conscious Mennonite heritage, their emerging interest in missions, their experience in education and co-operative enterprises, and their resources in personnel and finances stimulated all church activities but none more than missions.

Mennonite Brethren in Christ. The Evangelical movement under Jacob Albright in the early 19th century among the Germans in Pennsylvania came close home to the Mennonite congregations there, and among the thousands who thronged this movement were many Mennonites. Some joined the Evangelical church; some attempted to remain in their own church. William Gehman (*q.v.*), a minister in the Upper Milford congregation associated with Oberholtzer's group, under Evangelical influence started holding prayer meetings. Criticism developed against this new spiritual exercise and the emotional religion with which it was associated. As a result, in 1858 Gehman and others were stricken from the list of ministers. With like-minded members they then organized the Evangelical Mennonites, who in turn made contact with groups in Indiana, Ontario, and Ohio of similar experience and by a series of unions formed in 1883 the Mennonite Brethren in Christ (*q.v.*). Because of their background in the revival movement they immediately adopted its type of program and entered aggressive work. Home missions and particularly city missions were prosecuted with zeal, and an increasing proportion of their membership came from people of non-Mennonite origin. It was from this group that the first American Mennonite missionary to a foreign land appeared. Eusebius Hershey (*q.v.*), for forty years an inveterate traveling home missionary, announced in 1883 that the church would have a foreign missionary before long. In 1890 he left his family at home and without board appointment or assurance of support sailed for Africa. Aged 67 and not physically strong, he succumbed to the African climate after six months of work through an interpreter. His greatest contribution was the legacy of inspiration of a completely devoted life. Two others from this group left in the 90's for foreign service—William Shantz (1895) and C. F. Snyder (1897), both to China where they worked under the Christian and Missionary Alliance. The first work directly sponsored by the M.B.C. church was opened in Nigeria, Africa, by A. W. Banfield in 1901 and taken over by the church in 1905. This was well supplied with workers and has been a successful effort. Other fields in which this Mennonite branch has labored are Armenia (1898-1920), India (1928), and Colombia (1942), with also many individual workers supported by the church but working under other boards.

3. *Mennonite Church* (MC). Among the mass of remaining Mennonites, often referred to as the "Old" Mennonites, who were located largely east of the Mississippi River and in Ontario, evangelism and missions were slower in entering. John C. Wenger has characterized the group in recent times as (1) conservative in faith, (2) strict in discipline, and (3) active in missions, publication, education, and mutual aid. The activity came in part from the stimulus of prolonged contacts with outside influences such as Sunday schools and evangelism. The influences were mediated by men like John F. Funk (*q.v.*) and J. S. Coffman (*q.v.*). The former, a Pennsylvania teacher and later businessman in Chicago where he had contacts with Moody, relocated his printing business in Elkhart in 1867 and became the center of a movement for publication, education, and missions. The latter, a Virginia minister, became the pioneer evangelist and almost singlehandedly introduced "protracted" meetings in the church during the 1880's. Both worked together for promoting education for service in the Elkhart Institute (1894), which later became Goshen College (1903), as well as stimulating the organizing of the Mennonite General Conference in the late 90's. They had an uncommon ability to retain the confidence of conservatives while introducing progressive ideas. Mission interest, both home and foreign, entered and became fruitful in the closing years of the century through organization of the Mennonite Evangelizing Committee (1882) and the Mennonite Benevolent and Evangelizing Board (1892), which in 1905 became the Mennonite Board of Missions and Charities. The first city mission was opened in Chicago in 1893 and the first foreign work in India in 1899. The India work was a response to famine conditions which were vividly reported by George Lambert (*q.v.*), who had just returned from a world tour appalled by the suffering. He was sent out to accompany a shipload of food, and the first missionaries, J. A. Ressler and Dr. and Mrs. W. B. Page, followed shortly. Beginning with orphanage, education, and evangelistic work, the India work has developed into a strong indigenous church work. Other fields entered have been Argentina 1917, Tanganyika in East Africa 1934, Bihar in India 1940, Chaco in Argentina 1943, Puerto Rico 1945, Ethiopia 1948, Japan 1949, Sicily 1949, Belgium 1950, Honduras 1950, Luxembourg 1951, Alaska 1952, England 1952, Israel 1953, France 1953, Somalia 1953, Cuba 1954, Brazil 1954, Uruguay 1954, Jamaica 1955, Viet-Nam 1957, Ghana 1957. In this group several district conferences have entered into foreign and home mission work in addition to the main older board, these being Lancaster (Eastern Mennonite Board of Missions and Charities in 1917), Virginia (1949), Conservative (1951), and Franconia (1954). An independent mission was begun in the Amazon region of Brazil in 1955.

4. *Mennonite Brethren Church.* The Mennonite Brethren with their Russian origin and evangelical beginnings were better prepared for aggressive work when they came to America in 1874. From Russia Abraham Friesen (MB) went to India under the American Baptist Mission Union in 1889 and thus a pattern of Baptist co-operation had been set up. The mission emphasis is indicated by the incorporation of the Mennonite Brethren in 1900 under the name "American Brethren Mission Union," later revised to "Conference of the Mennonite Brethren

Church of North America." The first American missionaries to join the Mennonite Brethren work in India were Mr. and Mrs. N. N. Hiebert and Elizabeth Neufeld, who arrived in the Telugu (Hyderabad) field in 1899. Additional missionaries were sent out and a strong evangelistic program carried on which spread to several major stations in the Hyderabad area. The next field entered by the Mennonite Brethren was China where individual missionaries joined the work of the China Mennonite Mission Society (q.v.) in Shantung, and where in 1911 F. J. Wiens opened the work in Fukien among the Hakkas. M.B. work began in the Belgian Congo on a private basis in 1912, coming under the official board in 1923. The mission in Paraguay to the Indians called "Light to the Indians," begun by the colonists in 1932, was turned over to the M.B. mission board in 1946. Additional M.B. foreign mission fields are Curitiba in Brazil (1946), Colombia (1945), and Japan (1950). They also have a work among the American Indians.

5. *Other American Mennonite Groups.* By 1900 most Mennonites were convinced of the validity of mission work and it was only a matter of time and opportunity before the remaining groups began to express interest. The Krimmer Mennonite Brethren, who merged with the Mennonite Brethren in 1957, have had a remarkably high missionary interest, although as a very small group they never had a mission board of their own. Mr. and Mrs. H. C. Barthel, K.M.B. members, started a mission in the Shantung province of China in 1901, which led to the formation of an inter-Mennonite China Mennonite Mission Society in 1912 to operate this work. The Evangelical Mennonite Brethren became one of the chief supporters of this mission. In 1921 two K.M.B. missionaries started a work in Inner Mongolia. Individual workers are supported in other fields by the K.M.B. Conference. The K.M.B. conference mission work is carried forward by three committees, the Foreign Missions Committee, the Home Missions Committee, and the City Missions Committee. The E.M.B. conference operates its mission program through the Commission on Missions, and through the Congo Inland Mission Board, on which it has three members. It operates no direct foreign work of its own but supports conference-recognized workers in several fields under other denominational boards. The Church of God in Christ Mennonites have recently begun mission work in Mexico, and among the Navaho Indians and the Mexicans in the Southwest of the United States, under their General Mission Board.

The Central Conference of Mennonites (q.v.) and the Evangelical Mennonite Church (q.v.) (then Defenseless Mennonites) joined in opening work in Africa which developed into the Congo Inland Mission (q.v.) organized in 1911, which is now a large co-operative work in which the G.C.M. church is also associated. A few of the smaller groups, such as Evangelical Mennonites (Kleine Gemeinde), Church of God in Christ Mennonites, and Conservative Mennonites, have only recently been drawn into mission work, while the most conservative groups still hold aloof, such as Reformed Mennonites, Old Colony, Hutterites, and Old Order

Amish. In 1956 an Old Order Amish mission committee started work among the Indians in far Northwest Ontario.

The total foreign missionaries in service under the major American Mennonite mission boards in all fields as of July 1, 1957 (including those on furlough and under appointment, but not short-term service workers), with the total membership by groups, was as follows: *General Conference Mennonite Church*: missionaries 127, members 25,295; *Mennonite Church* (MC): missionaries 266, members 4,103; *Mennonite Brethren Church*: missionaries 196, members 30,904; *Congo Inland Mission*: missionaries 93, of which 44 are duplicates of the GCM figure, members 16,000 (all in GCM figures); missionaries 638, members 50,302. The total annual contributions of the American Mennonites to foreign missions now runs over $1,000,000. The following table lists the numbers of foreign missionaries by boards and countries, not including short-term service workers (I-W, etc.).

Country	M.C.	M.B.	G.C.M.	Total
Alaska	5			5
Algeria	2			2
Argentina	22			22
Austria		5		5
Belgium		23	9	32
Brazil	8	5		13
Colombia	2			2
Congo, Africa		68	44	*161
Cuba	6			6
Ecuador		5		5
England	6			6
Ethiopia	33			33
France	4			4
Germany		5		5
Ghana	4			4
Honduras	13			13
India	32	42	45	119
Israel	4			4
Jamaica	4			4
Japan	18	12	18	48
Luxembourg	12			12
Mexico		11		11
Paraguay		20		20
Puerto Rico	28			28
Somalia, Africa	8			8
Taiwan (Formosa)			11	11
Tanganyika, Africa	41			41
Uruguay	10			10
Viet-Nam	4			4
Total	266	196	127	638
American Indians		9	27	36

* The total figure includes other Mennonite bodies.

In 1940 the Dutch Mennonite mission field in Java was turned over to the Malay Mennonite Church, which had become independent in that year. The Dutch board then in 1950 took over from the Dutch Reformed Church a mission field in the territory of northwest New Guinea, which has about 60 congregations and mission stations. The Russian Mennonites had developed a mission among the semi-primitive people (Ostyaks) of north-central Siberia after World War I about 300 miles north of Tomsk (see **Ob Mission**). It was in operation as late as 1928.

The development of the missionary enterprise among the Mennonites of North America since 1900 has been noteworthy in size and significant in influence upon the brotherhood as a whole. It has meant a great enlargement of vision, a stimulus to outreach in various other areas of work, an intensification of spiritual commitment, a growth in stewardship, and emphasis upon the majors in the Christian faith and life.

For additional treatments on aspects of missions and evangelism among Mennonites, see the following articles: **Evangelism, City Missions, Missionary Meetings, Negro Missions, Rural Missions,** the various conference mission boards, the various foreign fields, such as China, India, Japan, etc., the various major stations in the mission fields, biographies of outstanding missionary leaders, etc., also in the supplement in Vol. IV the articles **Home Missions** and **Jewish Missions.** The Dutch Mennonite Mission Association has published annual reports since 1848, and the Mennonite Board of Missions and Charities since 1915. **S.F.P.**

Ed. G. Kaufman, *The Development of the Missionary and Philanthropic Interest Among the Mennonites of North America* (Berne, 1951); Ira D. Landis, *The Missionary Movement Among Lancaster Conference Mennonites* (Scottdale, 1938); E. R. Storms, *What God Hath Wrought* (a history of M.B.C.-U.M.C. missions) (Springfield, 1948); G. W. Peters, *The Growth of Foreign Missions in the Mennonite Brethren Church* (Hillsboro, 1952); Mrs. H. T. Esau, *The First Sixty Years of Mennonite Brethren Missions* (Hillsboro, 1954); F. H. Littell, "The Anabaptist Theology of Missions," *MQR* XXI (1947) 5-17; Ethelbert Stauffer, "The Anabaptist Theology of Martyrdom," *MQR* XIX (1945) 179-214; *ML* I, 54 f.; II, 274 f.; III, 141 f.

Missions Quartalblatt: see **Mission Quarterly.**

Mississippi, population 2,170,194, the twentieth state admitted to the Union (1817), has one Mennonite (MC) congregation, Gulfhaven, located about five miles north of Gulfport in the far south of the state, founded in 1922, with 62 members in 1956, and a mission (MC) in Gulfport founded in 1947, with 22 members in 1956. Both belong to the South Central Conference. A CPS project under the MCC, Camp Landon, near Gulfport, has since 1945 been serving the Negro community. In January 1957 it was taken over by the General Conference Mennonite Church. **H.S.B.**

Mississippi was considered by the Old Colony Mennonites (*q.v.*) for settlement in 1920 when they had difficulties in Manitoba and Saskatchewan. After the delegation had returned from South America in 1919, another delegation was sent to Alabama and Mississippi. After a visit by a land agent named Peters from Mississippi a delegation from Canada investigated the land and conditions offered in Mississippi in 1920. Although there was some question as to whether the "freedoms" promised by Peters would actually be granted, it was decided on June 1, 1920, that a delegation make a down payment of $250,000 on the land; at the border, however, the delegation with the money was stopped and sent back by the United States officials. Evidently patriotic organizations like the American Legion prevented the immigration of nonresistant Mennonites into Mississippi. The chronicler David Harder wrote, "Since we could not find out why the border was closed to us, we are compelled to accept it as a guidance of God, who wanted to spare us unforeseen hardships. Very likely the offer of freedom

was the hoax of a land speculator." Thus the Old Colony Mennonites chose Mexico instead of Mississippi. **C.K.**

Missive, *van de Sociëteit der Doopsgezinde gemeenten in Vriesland en Groningen, geschreeven aan de Doopsgezinde Christenen, welke zich uit Dantzig in Pruissen hebben nedergezet in de Staaten van Haare Majesteit Catharina de Groote, Keizerin aller Russen* (Leeuwarden, n.d.-1788) (Missive of the Conference of Mennonite Congregations in Friesland and Groningen, Written to the Mennonite Christians from Danzig, Prussia, Who Have Settled in the States of Her Majesty Catherine the Great, empress of all Russians) is an official letter, signed by the trustees of the Mennonite Conference of Friesland (FDS), Netherlands, drawn up at the special request of Jakob (von) Trapp(e) (*q.v.*), the Russian director of settlements, at this time visiting the Netherlands and contacting the Dutch Mennonites. Alarmed by the information given by Trappe that the new settlers in Russia were torn by doctrinal differences, the Mennonite Conference of Friesland, which held a special meeting to discuss the question, resolved to send a letter to the settlers. This letter, drawn up by pastor Heere Oosterbaan (*q.v.*), and dated July 31, 1788, is a warm plea for moderation. It urged the Mennonites in Russia to avoid banning members who as Flemish married members of the Frisian branch and to live in peace and harmony. The letter, written in German, was printed in Dutch; it was reprinted in full by Blaupot ten Cate in *Geschiedenis der Doopsgezinden in Friesland* (Leeuwarden, 1837) 354-63. **vDZ.**

Missoula (Mont.) CPS Camp No. 103 was a Forest Service camp under the administration of the MCC but with the men chosen from other agencies in addition to those from the MCC. The men were trained as "smoke jumpers," learning how to parachute to the sites of forest fires. Over 200 men were members of the camp between its opening and closing dates May 1943—January 1946. A 48-page book entitled *Smoke Jumpers,* produced by the men of the camp, gives pictures of the unit's work as well as a description of its activities. **M.G.**

M. Gingerich, *Service for Peace* (Akron, Pa., 1949) 139-47.

Missouri, pop. 3,945,653, admitted to the Union in 1821 as the 24th state, has had Mennonites within its borders since 1860, when the first ones (Amish Mennonites) located on the western border of the state, below Kansas City in Cass County (near Garden City). In 1868 they organized the Sycamore Grove (MC) congregation, which in 1956 had 224 members. The next settlement was made in 1866-68 in the Morgan County-Moniteau County area near Versailles and Fortuna. First to come were Swiss Mennonites from Berne, Ind., and Polk County, Iowa, followed by others from Rockingham County, Va. In 1871 the settlement peaceably divided into two congregations, Mount Zion (MC) and Bethel (GCM), with 54 and 131 members respectively in 1956.

The third location to be settled was in northeastern Missouri, northwest of Hannibal in Shelby Coun-

Mennonite Church (MC)	
Name of Church	Address
1. Mt. Pisgah	Cherry Box
2. Pea Ridge	Palmyra
3. Palmyra (extinct)	Palmyra
4. Mennonite Mission Church	Hannibal
5. Mennonite Gospel Center	Kansas City
6. Sycamore Grove	Garden City
7. Mt. Zion	Versailles
8. Providence	Versailles
9. Lick Creek	Edwards
10. Berea	Birch Tree
10a. Walker	Walker
General Conference Mennonite	
11. Bethel	Fortuna
Old Order Amish Mennonite	
12. Bowling Green, North	Curryville
13. Bowling Green, South	Curryville
14. Green Ridge	Green Ridge
15. Jamesport	Jamesport
Church of God in Christ Mennonite	
16. Emmanuel (Bethany)	Rich Hill

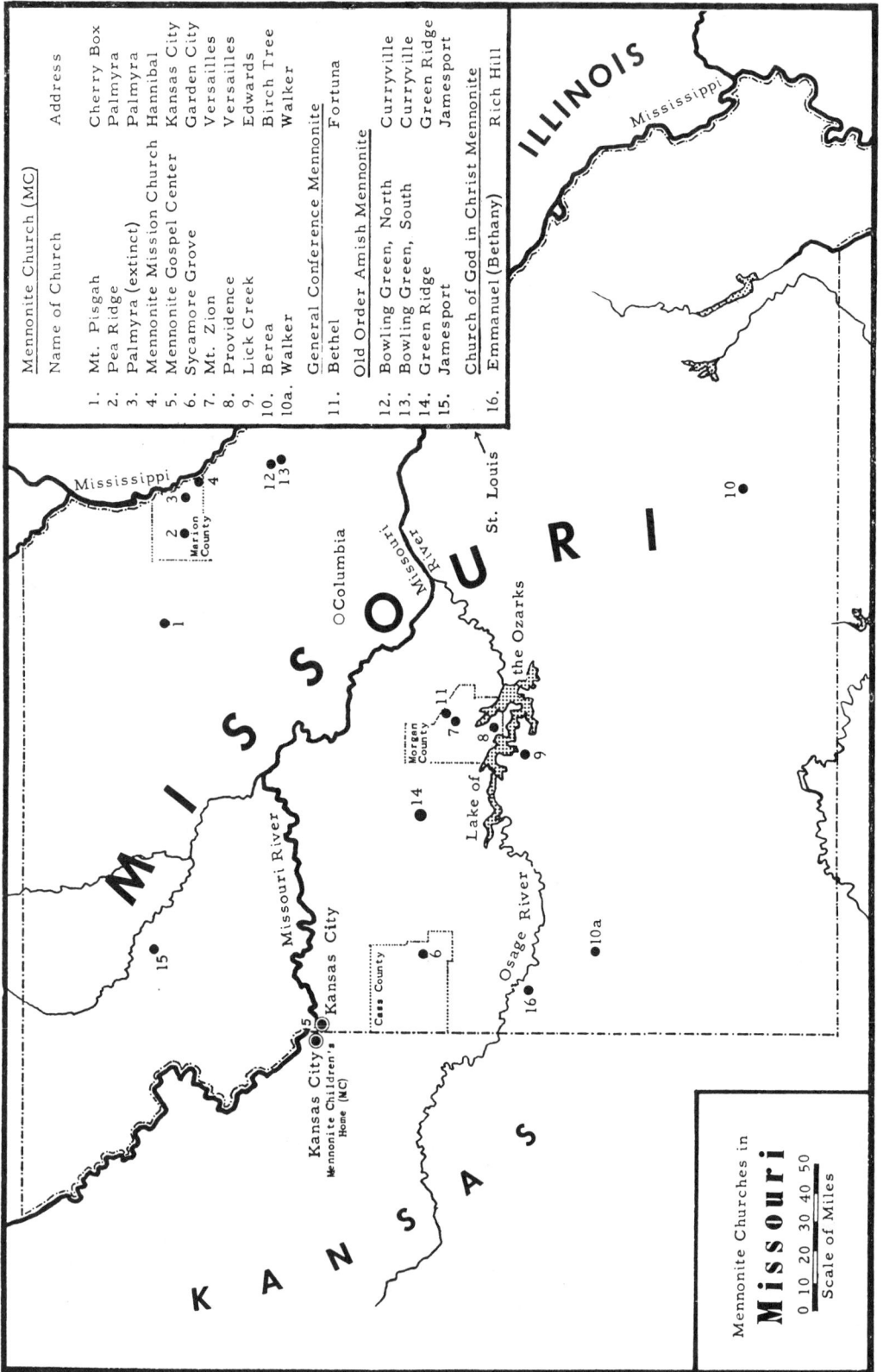

Mennonite Churches in
Missouri

0 10 20 30 40 50
Scale of Miles

ty and later in Marion County. The Mount Pisgah (MC) congregation, formerly called Cherry Box, was founded in 1868 by settlers chiefly from Sterling, Ill.; in 1956 it had 48 members. A daughter congregation, Berea (MC), was settled in 1895-99 in the far south in Shannon County. In 1956 it had 25 members. A third small congregation in the Marion County area, Palmyra, founded by settlers from Lancaster County, Pa., in 1884, was dissolved in 1955, part joining the Pea Ridge congregation, which had been started about 1909 as a mission from Palmyra and in 1956 had 28 members.

In addition to the original settlements missions have been established at various places by the Mennonite Church (MC). The first was in Kansas City (Mennonite Gospel Center), dating from 1947, with 29 members. The larger Argentine church (MC) with 109 members, is on the Kansas side of the city. At Hannibal the Mission Church, now with 76 members, was started in 1934. The three additional missions in central Missouri still in existence (at Edwards, Warsaw, and Walker, started in 1939, 1949, and 1954) have a total of only about 30 members. The total membership of the Mennonite Church (MC) in Missouri in 1956 was 514.

The remaining Mennonites in Missouri consist of four Old Order Amish districts, with a total of 131 members, located in three widely scattered areas of the state (see map) and are of more recent origin. The Emmanuel Church of God in Christ congregation at Rich Hill along the Osage River, near the western border of the state, was organized in 1923; it had 93 members in 1956. The total Mennonite and Amish membership in the state in 1956 was 869. There are no Mennonite institutions in the state. **H.S.B.**

Missouri-Iowa Mennonite Conference (MC) was organized in 1873 (first meeting at the Bethel Church, Moniteau County, Mo., on Oct. 24, 1873) as the Mennonite Conference of Missouri, Iowa, and eastern Kansas, later extended to include the few Mennonite (MC) congregations west of Illinois in Louisiana, Texas, Minnesota, and North Dakota. When the merger and reorganization of the Mennonite and Amish Mennonite conferences west of Indiana took place in 1920-21, this conference was dissolved, and its congregations redistributed among the Missouri-Kansas (later South Central, *q.v.*), Iowa-Nebraska (*q.v.*), and Dakota-Montana (later North Central, *q.v.*) conferences. In 1920 the Missouri-Iowa Conference included the following 17 congregations, with a membership of 723: *Missouri* 434—Mount Zion at Versailles 89, Bethel at Garden City 110, Proctor 14, Palmyra 24, Pea Ridge 40, Mount Pisgah at Cherry Box 42, White Hall at Oronogo 65, Jasper 16, Oakland 17, Berea at Birch Tree 49, and five missions: *Iowa* 57—Liberty at South English 50, Coal Creek at What Cheer 7; *Minnesota*—Alpha 42; *North Dakota* 89—Fairview at Surrey 43, Spring Valley at Baden 46; *Montana* 24—Bloomfield 20, Coalridge 4; *Texas*—Tuleta 49; *Louisiana*—Lake Charles 15, Allemands 13. Among the outstanding leaders of the conference were D. D. Kauffman (d. 1896) of Versailles, J. M. Kreider (d. 1946) of Palmyra, J. R. Shank of Carver, J. D.

Mininger (d. 1941) of Kansas City, and Andrew Shenk (d. 1937) of Oronogo, Mo.

The conference had a district mission board for home mission work, organized in 1898, and a Sunday school conference, organized before 1905. **H.S.B.**

Missouri-Kansas Mennonite (MC) Conference, formed in 1921, changed its name in 1946 to South Central Mennonite Conference (*q.v.*).

Mitarbeiter, Der, a monthly German periodical founded in 1906 in the interests of the Canadian Mennonite Conference and 'Gretna Collegiate Institute, where it was edited and published. H. H. Ewert served as editor throughout its publication. David Toews and N. W. Bahnmann served temporarily as assistant editors. In 1913 the paper had 500 readers, 230 in Manitoba and 225 in Saskatchewan. Special collections were raised to subsidize the paper.

During World War I the publication of the paper was suspended for about two years. In 1925 at the Canadian Mennonite Conference it was decided to discontinue the publication of the paper. However, H. H. Ewert continued it privately by founding a publishing company and raising the funds necessary to subsidize it. In December 1934, just before his death, the paper was discontinued. The paper had a definite influence among the Mennonites of Canada in promoting and maintaining high religious and educational standards. Major credit goes to H. H. Ewert (*q.v.*). **C.K.**

Paul J. Schaefer, *Heinrich H. Ewert* (Gretna, 1945) 108; "Zum Abschied," *Der Mitarbeiter,* December 1934; *ML* III, 143.

Mithelfer, a short-lived, monthly religious magazine of 32 pages, size 6 x 9 in., published from March 1926 to April 1927 with Abram Kroeker and N. N. Hiebert of Mountain Lake, Minn., as editors and owners. It was printed and mailed by the M.B. Publishing House, Hillsboro, Kan. The content of the magazine included sermon outlines, doctrinal articles, Sunday-school material, Christian dialogues, poems, editorials, and information on the current religious outlook. The first issue of some eleven hundred copies was mailed as a sample to Mennonite leaders and laymen. The actual subscription list varied between 400 and 500, and therefore the magazine proved financially impossible. **A.E.J.**

Mittermaier, Hans, an Anabaptist martyr, a native of Ingolstadt, Bavaria, Germany, therefore called Hans (Hänslein) of Ingolstadt. He was baptized by Hans Hut (*q.v.*) about 1527. It is possible that he became a leader soon after his joining the brotherhood, for he was one of the participants in the Martyrs' Synod (*q.v.*) at Augsburg at the end of August 1527. He was sent with Leonhard Dorfbrunner (*q.v.*) as a missionary to Upper Austria. Dorfbrunner did not reach the field assigned him, for he was captured in Passau and died there at the stake in January 1528. Mittermaier went on to Linz (*q.v.*), and there served the "brotherhood in the land of the Ems" with Wolfgang Brandhuber (*q.v.*) after the complete destruction of the Anabaptist congregation in the town of Steyr. But his work was of short duration. In 1529 the two men with 75 members were seized in Linz, and put to death together, some by beheading and the others by burning.

In the accounts given by the Hutterite chronicle and the *Martyrs' Mirror* (D 24, E 433) Hans Ni(e)-dermai(e)r is named as the preacher of the group, but according to the court records of Linz which were sent to the council of Augsburg, he is probably identical with Mittermaier.   HEGE.

Fr. Roth, *Augsburgs Reformations-Geschichte* (Munich, 1901) 232, 262; Wolkan, *Geschicht-Buch*, 47; Zieglschmid, *Chronik*, 65; Beck, *Geschichts-Bücher*, 88; *ML* III, 143.

Mittersill, a castle in the Austrian province of Salzburg. This medieval castle has a twofold significance in Anabaptist history. (1) It was here that the Hutterite brother Veith Grünberger (*q.v.*) was imprisoned while on a mission trip in 1569. The *Chronicle* says that he was brought to the "Schloss gen Mitterschl (Nidersol)," where he lay for five weeks before being moved to Salzburg (where he lay seven years before regaining his freedom). The dungeon where he was kept still exists; it is a foul, dark place far down without light or any provision whatsoever for human existence. A tiny opening near the ceiling served as the only connection with the outside world. (2) About 1900, Mittersill castle was modernized by a nobleman who happened to be also an outstanding book connoisseur. This nobleman (Baron Grundherr) in 1919 bought the entire collection of Hutterite codices of the library of the cathedral chapter of Bratislava (*q.v.*) in Slovakia, a total of 25 unique and invaluable handwritten books in excellent condition. The canons of Bratislava needed money and the Baron wanted to adorn his castle. Around 1928 the place changed hands, and the depression in the early 1930's forced the sale of the entire castle. The manuscript collection was bought by a secondhand book dealer in 1936, and was later sold by him to the City Archives and Library of Bratislava. At present (1956) this library owns a total of 29 such codices, four of them of different derivation. A description of the Mittersill collection may be found in the printed Catalog of the Cathedral Library of Bratislava by N. Knauz, made in 1870.   R.F.

R. Friedmann, "Of Hutterite Books," *Menn. Life* VII (April 1952) 81 f. (illustrated); H. S. Bender, "Rediscovery of the Schloss Mittersill Hutterite Codices," *MQR* XXX (January 1956) 77; N. Knauz, *A Poszonyi Kaptalannak Keziratai* (Esztergom, 1870) 324 pp.; Zieglschmid, *Klein-Geschichtsbuch,* 483 f.

Mixed Marriage. Marriage of Mennonites with non-Mennonites was formerly more or less strictly forbidden. In the early period of Anabaptist history there was no thought of such marriage. That was the time of gathering the brotherhood and fortifying it against the pressure and persecution from the outside. The sacredness of marriage was a religious and moral obligation that was taken for granted. With righteous indignation they repudiated the charge of community of wives, which was raised again and again. Their high moral sense in the matter of marriage is obvious in the confessions of the early martyrs.

Not until the brotherhood was well established was there any proscription of mixed marriage. In Menno Simons there is no mention of it. But Dirk Philips (*q.v.*) speaks of it. Before him Adam Pastor (*q.v.*) had already concluded from the words of I Cor. 7:39, "only in the Lord," that matrimony should be concluded only with members of the brotherhood. The *Brüderliche Vereinigung* of Schleitheim states that one should take in marriage only a member of the "believing people."

Dirk Philips goes still further. In his booklet *Concerning the Marriage of Christians (Van die Echt der Christenen)* he says, "This we indeed confess, that marriage consists first of all in this, that the hearts of both persons are thus inclined, but that they do not marry unless it is pleasing to the Lord and to the brotherhood." By this measure an attempt was made to keep the church pure. By exercising an influence on the choice of a marriage partner the brotherhood could prevent the marriage of a brother or sister with someone in another branch. Not only was marriage with a member of another creed forbidden, but marriage with a member of another Mennonite wing as well.

Dirk Philips was the exponent of the strictest party. "Deut. 7:3 clearly shows how great a sin and danger to souls there is in a union between a believer and a heathen or unbeliever; for here through Moses God Himself says quite expressly that the unbelievers, the heathen daughters, will mislead the believers who have once known and accepted the truth and are inscribed in the number of the saints, so that they will be turned away from the living God to idols. A believer dare not accept any marriage other than the first one, which God instituted in Eden and was later renewed and confirmed, that is, with one man and one woman, two believers, whom God Himself joins. This is a true marriage, and from this each one who fears God can understand how unreasonable, how wrong, yea, how utterly ungodly it is to dare to act contrary to the pure, good, and holy command of the Lord. . . ." This strict concept of marriage was shared by the Mennonites in South Germany and especially of Alsace-Lorraine. The *Abred* (Agreement) of Strasbourg of 1568 says expressly that those who believe in the Lord shall not marry an unbeliever (Müller, 51; *Gem.-Kal.* 1906, 136). The *Ordnungsbrief* (conference decisions) for the Alsatian congregations, agreed upon at Steinselz on April 28, 1752, says in point two, "When a brother or a sister unites himself with or marries a worldly person, but with sorrow and penitence desires to be received, the request shall not be denied, but with the stipulation and on the condition that he bring with him his wife whom he has married contrary to God and His Word; if this could not happen, he must leave her, but provide for her physical needs and separate himself for the sake of the kingdom of heaven and earnestly beseech God that she may be converted and recognize the truth."

Article 8 of the Essingen *Ordnungsbrief,* of Nov. 22, 1779, says that "marriage shall take place with the foreknowledge and consent of the preachers and elders and when feasible of the parents, in the Lord and not with the world" (*Gesch.-Bl.*, 1938, 53).

In all the Mennonite confessions of faith the religious and moral significance of marriage is stressed beside its divine origin, together with the requirement of agreement of faith. The *Olyftacxken* of 1627 says that a brother or sister may marry if he will, but only in the Lord. But God has never ordained that a believer should unite with an unbeliever, but that the Lord is angry with such and has declared that they are flesh, who refuse to let His Spirit govern their lives; therefore we discipline all who follow their carnal desire herein like other carnal sinners. The *Concept of Cologne* of 1591 strictly forbids mixed marriage, saying that the Scripture leaves no liberty to marry anyone except one who has become a member of the body of Christ through faith. No brotherly communion should be held with those who transgress, unless one feels their genuine penitence; they should then be admonished to keep the marriage vow faithfully, and neither to leave the mate nor to incur another marriage (Hege, 151). Also the confession of 1630 (Jan Cents) agrees that "only in the Lord" means that a believer does not have the liberty to unite himself in marriage with an unbeliever. The *Dordrecht Confession* of 1632, article 12, deals with marriage; "in the Lord" means that marriage may be entered into only with one in the spiritual family of God, who are united first with the church as one heart and one soul, have received one baptism and stand in one faith, doctrine, and life.

This position is still held by the Amish branch of the Mennonite brotherhood in America, as formerly in Switzerland and France. The Mennonite Church (MC) and related groups maintained this rule until into the 20th century.

A more liberal position was taken by Cornelis Ris in his confession of 1766: In order to be happy in marriage we consider it necessary wherever possible to stay within the brotherhood, in order to prevent impurity and many unpleasant consequences which often arise between persons with a different upbringing and manner of life in the training of the children and in other matters. It is therefore not only proper but also beneficial to take the advice of parents and relatives. But only in the fear of the Lord.

This is the standpoint of the Dutch and North German congregations, as well as of the Mennonites of Baden and Hesse. The prohibition of mixed marriage does not exist there. One who marries outside the brotherhood remains a member as before and loses none of the rights of membership.

In the West Prussian country congregations marriage outside the church automatically excluded one from the church. Article IX of *Glaubensbekenntnis der Mennoniten in Preussen* of 1895, "On Christian Marriage," says, "When a member marries outside the brotherhood, the act is regarded as a voluntary parting from the brotherhood."

The Russian Mennonites of all branches and their descendants in North America maintained the prohibition of mixed marriages. The most conservative Russian Mennonite groups in Canada, such as the Old Colony group (but also the Bergthaler), still maintain this rule and apply it to intermarriage with other Mennonite groups. (See also **Marriage** and **Divorce**.) NEFF.

A. Hunzinger, *Das Religions-, Kirchen- und Schulwesen der Mennoniten oder Taufgesinnten* (Speyer, 1830); Chr. Hege, *Die Täufer in der Kurpfalz* (Karlsruhe, 1908); *ML III*, 139 f.

Mizpah United Missionary Church, located 5½ miles southeast of Cass City, Sanilac Co., Mich., was organized Nov. 15, 1895, with a membership of nine. In 1957 L. W. Sherrard was serving as pastor, with a membership of 47. J.KI.

Möckmühl, a town (pop. 2,000) in Württemberg, Germany, at the confluence of the Seckach River with the Jagst. Since 1914 there has been a Mennonite congregation here, which had its seat formerly in Rossach (*q.v.*) near Schöntal (Württemberg); it was joined by members of the Lobenbach congregation when this congregation merged with the one in Heilbronn (*q.v.*). The Möckmühl congregation meets every two weeks in a rented hall and in 1955 had 23 members with 2 children living in six villages. It is a member of the Verband (*q.v.*), the conference of Baden, Württemberg, and Bavaria. (*ML III*, 143.) HEGE.

Moded, Herman (also called Herman Strijcker) (1530-1603), a Dutch Reformed divine. His career was very changeful. He became Reformed about 1558 and was made court chaplain and professor at the University of Copenhagen, Denmark; later he preached in Flanders; after 1567 he was preacher of the Dutch refugee church at Norwich, England. In 1572 he organized the Reformed congregation in Zierikzee, Dutch province of Zeeland. From 1580-88 he was the preacher of the Reformed congregation in Utrecht. After 1595 he lived in Middelburg (Zeeland). One of the books he published dealt with the Mennonites; it was originally written by Pieter Pauwels in Norwich; Moded corrected and enlarged it and published it with the title *Grondich bericht, Van de eerste beghinselen der Wederdoopsche Seckten ende wat veelderley verscheyden tacken, een yder met zyn aert ende dryven, daer wt gesproten zyn* (Middelburg, 1603). Robbert Robbertsz (*q.v.*) replied to it with *Een cleyn briefken, tegen Harmen Modeth, Predicant* (Middelburg, 1603). (*N.N.B.Wb.* III, 862 ff.; *ML III*, 143.) VDZ.

Modern Devotion (Latin, *Devotio Moderna;* Dutch, *Moderne Devotie*), a medieval revival in the Netherlands in the Roman Catholic Church of which Geert (de) Groote (Deventer, 1340-84) was the soul and animator. The movement resulted in the organization of the Brethren (*q.v.*) of the Common Life (Broeders des gemeenen levens) and finally also in the Windesheim monastic order, to which a number of monasteries and nunneries both in the Netherlands and Germany belonged. Though the Modern Devotion remained thoroughly Catholic—there are no traces either of deviation from Catholic doctrines or of fundamental criticism of the Catholic hierarchical system—yet this movement criticizing the immoral conduct of the clergy, particularly by the stress it laid upon Biblical piety—in pre-Reformation times the Bible was a nearly unknown book even among the clergy—created a type of new devoutness, *devotia moderna,* which proved to be very wholesome and of great blessing, preparing the soil for the Biblicism of Sacramentalism and Anabaptism. There are, however, no direct connections between the Modern Devotion of the 14th century and the Sacramentist-Anabaptist movement in the early 16th century. W. J. Kühler overaccentuates the influence of the Modern Devotion on Anabaptism; N. van der Zijpp holds the opinion that it had no direct influence on the rise of Anabaptism in the Netherlands.   vdZ.

W. Moll, *Kerkgeschiedenis van Nederland voor de Hervorming* II, 2 (Arnhem, 1867) 164-78; Kühler, *Geschiedenis* I, 24-32; L. Knappert, *Het Ontstaan en de Vestiging van het Protestantisme in de Nederlanden* (Utrecht, 1924) 33-52; R. R. Post, *De Moderne Devotie* (Amsterdam, 1940); A. Hyma, *The Brethren of the Common Life* (New York, 1951); N. van der Zijpp, *Geschiedenis der Doopsgezinden in Nederland* (Arnhem, 1952) 28.

Mödling, a town (pop. 48,000) in Lower Austria, situated at the edge of the Vienna Woods. In 1536 the Hutterian Brethren sent Georg Fasser (*q.v.*) and Leonhard Lanzenstiel (*q.v.*) as missionaries to Tirol. On April 25 they started out, but were seized two days later at Neudorf in Lower Austria "a half mile of field road" from Mödling and placed in stocks. On the next day the Mödling judge transferred them to the local prison and asked why they had been arrested. They replied, "For the sake of the divine truth and righteousness." On the way to Mödling and in the prison, which they shared with criminals, they zealously confessed their faith and defied all attempts to convert them; nor did they change their view after nearly a year of imprisonment. In prison Lanzenstiel and Fasser wrote six letters to the brotherhood in Moravia (found in a codex, division 5 of the University Library of Budapest), to which Hans Amon replied with four (found at the same place). In order to conceal the place of origin they were given peculiar place headings: "From the village where Oswald keeps house and Martl cooks," i.e., Tischlawitz; or "From the town where the kitchen is in the cellar and Walser keeps house," i.e., Gostal (Kostel). Released "by a special miracle," Fasser and Lanzenstiel hastened to Moravia, where they were received by the Brethren in the border village of Drasenhofen. Fasser died the death of a martyr in Pögstall, having been sent out again in 1537. The martyr list names four executions in Mödling, concerning which no details are known.   P.DE.

Beck, *Geschichts-Bücher;* Wolkan, *Geschicht-Buch;* Zieglschmid, *Chronik;* ML III, 143 f.

Moencopi Mennonite Mission (GCM) is located about two and one-half miles east of Tuba City, Ariz., which is a government post for the Western District of the Navaho Reservation, approximately 75 miles north of Flagstaff. Mission work was begun at Moencopi in about 1905. Among the missionaries then on the field were J. R. Duerksen, J. B. Fry, and Mary Schirmer. J. B. Fry was given charge of Moencopi mission work. The work is being carried on under the direction of the Home Missions section of the Board of Missions.

The present workers (1956) are Mr. and Mrs.

Henry A. Kliewer, members of the Immanuel Mennonite Church of Downey. A church council consisting of all adult members was organized Oct. 18, 1955. It is hoped that soon a more complete organization will be formed. The work carried on at present consists of regular Sunday school and morning worship services, Sunday evening services, midweek children's classes, and adult Bible class. During the winter months special sewing classes are held for the women. Plans are being worked out for men and older boys. Visitation is a very important phase of the work. The present (1956) membership includes three Hopis, two Navahos, one Acoma, one Eskimo, and one Cherokee.   H.A.K.

Moerbeek, van, a former Dutch Mennonite family found at Dordrecht, Haarlem, and Amsterdam. Adam Abrahamsz van Moerbeek (b. about 1720 at Cleve, Germany) served a few years as preacher of the Hoorn congregation on the island of Texel and 1749-d.93 at Dordrecht; he was also a noted philologist. His son Jacobus van Moerbeek studied at the Amsterdam Seminary 1778-86 and served the congregations of Wieringen 1787-92 and Huizen 1792-c. 1825. Abraham van Moerbeek, of Haarlem, studied at the Theological Seminary at Amsterdam and became a ministerial candidate in 1777. Thereupon he studied medicine at the Leiden University, obtaining his M.D. degree in 1782. Returning to Amsterdam, he served for about one year as an assistant preacher, then he resigned, devoting himself to his medical practice, but continued his service to the church by his appointment by the board as doctor of the poor.   vdZ.

Naamlijst; Inv. Arch. Amst. II, Nos. 1701-7, 1712; *N.N.B.Wb.* IX, 687; *DJ* 1850, 85, note 1; *DB* 1868, 97.

Moeriaan, a former Dutch Mennonite family, found in Alkmaar and particularly in the Zaan district of the province of North Holland. Simon Poulusz Moeriaan (d. 1757), an oil miller, was a deacon of the Frisian congregation at Wormerveer. The best-known member of this family was Dirk Symonsz Moeriaan (1654-April 20, 1728) of Zaandijk. He was a merchant, owner of an oil mill, shipowner, also owner of whaling vessels, and apparently a wealthy man. Besides all these businesses he still found time to devote to the Mennonite church. In 1679 he became a preacher, and later an elder of the Waterlander congregation of Koog aan de Zaan, serving for nearly 49 years until death, at first in the Waterlander, and after its merging (1690) with the Flemish in the united congregation of Koog-Zaandijk. Dirk Symonsz' influence extended beyond his home congregation into the Waterlander Conference. Being rather conservative, it was due to his influence that his congregation and also a number of other Waterlander churches in North Holland joined the Zonist (*q.v.*) conference. In 1722 he and Maarten Mol (*q.v.*) tried to bring about a complete union between the Zonists and the Lamists, but failed to achieve it. Dirk Symonsz was often invited to preach and baptize in other congregations. In 1699 he ordained Jan de Lanoy as an elder of the congregation at Hamburg. He had been trained for the ministry by E. A. van Dooregeest (*q.v.*). His colleague Abr. Verduin commemorated his death in a funeral sermon, *Heil in de Dood* (published at Haarlem, n.d.). vDZ.

Kühler, *Geschiedenis* III, 8; *Inv. Arch. Amst.* I, Nos. 909, 918, 925; II, Nos. 1429 f.; *DB* 1898, 88 f.; B. C. Roosen, *Geschichte der Menn.-Gemeinde Hamburg* I (Hamburg, 1886) 49, 61; II (1887) 10; S. Lootsma, *Het Nieuwe Huys* (Zaandam, 1937) 64; (J. de Lange CJzn) *Beknopte Gesch. der Doopsgez. gemeente te Alkmaar* (n.p., n.d.-1927) 30, 91, 97, 162.

Mohadi, M.P., India, is a village 28 miles (or 40 miles by motorable road) east-northeast of Dhamtari, a station of the American Mennonite (MC) Mission. Four acres of land for mission premises were purchased by the Mission in 1920. The mission bungalow and Christian workers' and servants' quarters were finished by 1922. R. R. Smucker and family became resident at Mohadi in 1923, and with Indian Christian workers carried on evangelistic work among the villages of the district. A small medical dispensary also was opened by the missionaries.

Mohadi was regarded as purely an evangelistic station with the missionaries free for village and home visitation work and touring. The district is large, including Bindra-Nawagarh Zamindari (a small Indian state) and a large area of villages extending west to the Dhamtari-Mohadi border and east for many miles to the border of the American Evangelical Mission territory. A church was organized with a membership of about 50 and an Indian deacon. The pastoral work was performed by the missionaries whether resident or nonresident. In 1954 the membership was 33. (*ML* III, 144.) G.J.L.

Moibanus, Ambrosius (1494-1554), a Lutheran divine, who is considered as the coreformer of Silesia, Germany, with Johann Hess. In his efforts to promote Luther's teachings on every hand, the Anabaptists, who had been there since 1526, and the Schwenckfelders were in his way. Both had many adherents among the nobility and in the country. Balthasar Hubmaier (*q.v.*) even dedicated his book (1527) *Das ander Biechlein von der Freywilligkeit des Menschens* to Frederick II, Duke of Liegnitz.

Ten years later Moibanus wrote a book which he also dedicated to the duke and which attacked the Anabaptists and the Schwenckfelders. It appeared in 1537 with the title *Das herrliche Mandat Jesu Christi vnseres Herrn vnd Heilandes. Gehet hin jnn die gantze welt vnd prediget das Evangelium . . . Marci XVI. Denen zu einem vnterricht, so das Predigampt vnd die Sakrament Christi für vnnötig zur Seelen heil achten wollen, gehandelt* (copy in Wolfenbüttel). The book reproaches the ruler for tolerating the two brotherhoods. The consequence of the book was a heightened persecution of the Anabaptists in Liegnitz, Brieg, and Wohlau, and their emigration to the gravure of Glatz. Now Moibanus set about to persuade Baron Johannes von Bernstein in Helfenstein not to tolerate the two groups. In this attempt he was supported by Melanchthon, who in 1541 dedicated to the baron a booklet printed in Breslau on the duty of princes. HEGE.

D. Erdmann, *Luther und seine Beziehungen zu Schlesien, insbesondere zu Breslau* (*Schriften des Vereins für Ref.-Gesch.*) 1887; P. Konrad, *Dr. Ambrosius Moibanus* (*Schriften des Vereins für Ref.-Gesch.*) 1891; *ML* III, 144.

Mol, a former Dutch Mennonite family, many of whose members served the church as deacons and preachers. An important branch of this family lived at Jisp (*q.v.*), province of North Holland. In the Waterlander congregation of Jisp (or Wormer-Jisp) Maarten Jansz Mol and Jacob Jansz Mol were preachers about 1675. Jan Maartensz Mol of Jisp, who died before 1697, apparently a son of Maarten Jansz Mol and preacher of the same congregation, was the author of a much-used catechetical booklet, *Kort Onderwys des Christelyken Geloofs* (Amsterdam, 1697, repr. 1698, 1710, 1723, 1740). His son Maarten Jansz Mol, of Jisp, was an elder of the Wormer-Jisp congregation, serving from about 1700 until at least 1731. He must have been a wealthy man, as most members of this Jisp branch were. He was the owner of an oil mill, at the same time participating in whaling; in 1701-31 he sent 41 whaling boats to Greenland and 1732-33 two vessels to Davis Street. Pieter Pietersz Mol, living about the same time at Jisp, and likely related to the former, became a deacon of the church in 1695 and was probably the author of *Nutte Zamenspraak tusschen een Geestelyke en een Wereldling* (Amsterdam, 1741). This Pieter Mol was also an important owner of whaling boats. In 1700-8 he sent 34 vessels to the whaling grounds near Greenland, and in 1709-19 together with his son Jan Mol 47. The members of this Jisp Mol family were rather conservative in their religious opinions, and though they were members of the Waterlander congregation they were much in sympathy with the Zonist (*q.v.*) principles.

There are, besides the Jisp branch of this Mol family, a number of Mennonite preachers bearing the same family name, of whom it could not be decided, whether and in what way they were related with the Jisp family.

Jan Pietersz Mol served at Alkmaar about 1720; Jan Pietersz Mol (the same person?) was preacher of the congregation of Almelo 1731-41. In 1740 he was invited to Danzig, West Prussia, to reconcile the quarreling parties in the Danzig Flemish congregation and to restore peace. Mol, however, did not go (*Inv. Arch. Amst.* II, No. 2656). Other preachers of this name were Willem Mol, serving at Winterswijk 1739-45 and Zuid-Zijpe 1745-48 (?), whose father Nicolaas Mol also seems to have been a Mennonite preacher or elder. Cornelis (Jacobsz) Mol, a native of Wormer, was in 1743 an assistant preacher at Krommenie; Pieter Mol served the congregation of Enkhuizen 1787-89 and Hoorn 1789-d.1804. Hendrik Jansz Mol, from about 1735 until about 1762 a preacher of the Old Flemish congregation at Blokzijl, was not related to the former.

These preachers were all lay preachers, not having received a special training for the ministry. vDZ.

Naamlijst, passim; Kühler, *Geschiedenis* III, 8; *Inv. Arch. Amst.* I, Nos. 918, 925; II, No. 1429; *DB* 1898, 88; Marten Schagen, *Naamlijst der Doopsgezinde schrijveren* (Amsterdam, 1745) 68, 69; information from J. Aten at Wormerveer (descendant of Maarten Jansz Mol.)

Mol, de, Mennonites from Antwerp, Belgium, later found in Hamburg, Germany. Pieter de Mol fled from Antwerp with his sister Pereira de Mol and her husband François Noë before 1600. In 1621 a Jan de Mol was chosen as a deacon of the Old Flemish congregation on Achterburgwal at Amsterdam.

vdZ.

B. C. Roosen, *Geschichte der Menn.-Gemeinde Hamburg,* (Hamburg, 1886) 10 f.; *Inv. Arch. Amst.* II, 2, No. 5.

Molalla Mennonite Church (MC), now extinct, located at Molalla, Ore., a member of the Pacific Coast Conference, was organized with 40 members in 1935, when Joe Yoder was ordained as minister for the congregation, largely out of a number of Swedish converts who had been members of the Hopewell Mennonite Church. At first a hall at an unsatisfactory location near the rodeo stadium was used, but in 1937 a meetinghouse was built on Third Street. When the Sweet Home congregation was organized in 1939 about half of the Molalla membership united with this group. From that time on the membership declined seriously. When Yoder left for Arizona in 1945 J. S. Roth was made minister in charge. In 1951 the work was closed. (*ML* III, 144.) H.S.B.

Molanus, Jacobus Gualterus (Jacob Wouter Molenaar), and four other Reformed ministers on the Dutch island of Texel in 1649 had Claas Arentsz, the Mennonite elder of Nieuwe-Zijpe, arrested, because during a baptismal service on Texel he had spoken disparagingly of infant baptism. Arentsz had to dispute with Molanus and his colleagues. The dispute was broken off, but after a few weeks continued. Then Arentsz was assisted by three Mennonite preachers of Amsterdam, one of whom was Galenus Abrahamsz. After these disputations Molanus published *Christen-Kinder-doops-Waerheijdt, voorafgegaan door een: Corte sommarische ende oprecht verhaal van de handelinghe ende 't samensprekinghe der Gereformeerden Praedicanten in' eylandt Texel met Claas Arentz, Menniste Bisschop uit de Nieuwe Zijp met meer andere Bisschoppen ende vermaanders* . . . (1650). An unknown author calling himself J.G.L.V.C.W.M.D. (apparently the initials of a motto) answered with *Christelycke Antwoort op het Boeck J. Molani, ghenaamt Christen - Kinder - doops - Waerheydt* (Amsterdam, 1650). Neither the book by Molanus nor the reply is at present extant.

vdZ.

Blaupot t. C., *Holland* I, 195-97; H. W. Meihuizen, *Galenus Abrahamsz* (Haarlem, 1954) 39 f., 200, note 27.

Molenaar family. Hessel Ockes (d. 1720), a Mennonite at Workum, Dutch province of Friesland, had a son Hylke Hessels (1703-75), married to Anke Wopkes Knoop of Bolsward. Hylke inherited a "molen" (sawmill) from his father; hence his family name became Molenaar. His son Claes Hylkes Molenaar inherited the mill in 1774. Another son was Wopko (Wopke) Hylkes Molenaar (*q.v.*), minister at Crefeld and ancestor of the Crefeld branch of the family. A son of his was Isaak Molenaar I (*q.v.*), also minister at Crefeld, and a grandson Johannes Molenaar (*q.v.*), minister at Monsheim. Isaak Molenaar I had a son Isaak (II), and Isaak (II) had a son Isaak (III). They were all Mennonite preachers. A grandson of Johannes was **Heinrich Molenaar**

(*q.v.*). Two brothers of Isaak Molenaar I, Nicolaus (1778-1840) and Jacob (1788-1816), in 1812 founded the oldest bank at Crefeld. The only son of Nicolaus, Gustav Wilhelm (1811-64), followed his father in the bank. Most prominent of his 13 children were Alfred (1841-1922), Emil (1851-1929), and Willy (*q.v.,* 1852-1921), the latter being the founder of the Berlin Mennonite Church. Alfred was also a banker and held honorary positions in the civil administration of Crefeld. W.Ri., vdZ.

Die "Heimat" (Crefeld) IV (1925) 189-96; *Rheinisch-Westfälische Bank in Krefeld, früher Deutsche Bank 1901-1951; DB* 1903, 110.

Molenaar, Heinrich (1870-), a grandson of Johannes Molenaar (*q.v.*), was born at Zweibrücken, Germany, June 16, 1870, planned to follow in the footsteps of his Mennonite ancestors, but finally decided to study modern languages in preparation for teaching. His first and—as he was fond of saying—favorite position was at the Weierhof (*q.v.*) school under Ernst Göbel, whom he regarded with respect. He also taught at schools in Kaiserslautern, Weissenburg in Baden, Nürnberg, Bayreuth, Darmstadt, Neustadt a.d.Weinstrasse, and Munich. Besides his duties as a teacher he was actively and sacrificially engaged in the solution of social and philosophical problems. To develop life physically as well as spiritually and mentally in accord with the laws of God was a special interest of the teacher Molenaar.

He was therefore widely known as an opponent of vaccination and the use of tobacco. He gave many public addresses, wrote articles for periodical literature and pamphlets to promote his views. Some of these were his lectures on Comte's Positivism: *Die Religion der Menschheit,* and *Positive Weltanschauung.* He created a universal language, and founded the Franco-German league in which he worked long before World War I to improve understanding between the two countries. In the fields of music and poetry Molenaar's warmth found varied expression and form. The sonnet was the form he used most successfully. Two volumes of verse were *Kriegsgedichte* (Bayreuth, 1914), and *Geharnischte und friedliche Sonette* (Frankfurt, 1931).

Heinrich Molenaar was by nature a fighter. Even where one can not agree with him his friends recognize that in his blood lay something of the inheritance from the old Anabaptist forebears, which was devoted to building up society in a narrower or wider circle. (*ML* III, 144.) G.Go.

Molenaar, Isaak, I (1776-1834), a Mennonite minister, was born on Sept. 3, 1776, at Crefeld, Germany, the son of Wopko Molenaar (*q.v.*), studied at the Mennonite Seminary in Amsterdam (1794-99) and at the University of Jena, where he met Schiller in the home of Johann Jakob Griesbach, a professor of theology. Schiller mentions him with honor in his letters to Wilhelm von Humboldt, suggesting Molenaar for the position of tutor to the Humboldt sons.

Molenaar completed his studies at Amsterdam. In 1804 he was called as preacher to Zutphen, in 1806 to Groningen, in 1808 to Zaandam-West, in

1814 to Leiden, where he was on friendly terms with his old friend of student days, now Professor Siegenbeek (*q.v.*), and the professors van Voorst, van der Palm, Kemper, Borger, and Willem Bilderdijk, a conservative who lectured in history and who mentioned Molenaar's intellect and scholarship with praise. The sermon he preached at Leiden on Oct. 3, 1814, to commemorate the relief of Leiden was published: *Kerkelijke Aanspraak ter viering van Leiden's ontzet* (n.p., n.d.).

In 1818 Molenaar was called to Crefeld. He preached his first sermon there on Oct. 18 and continued his fruitful work for 16 years, until his death on April 19, 1834. A volume of his sermons was published in 1836 with a biographical foreword by Professor Sack of the University of Bonn (see **Crefeld**). A collection of his sermons, entitled *Leerredenen* (Amsterdam, 1836), was published in the Dutch language by van der Palm, Siegenbeek, and Muller.

An interesting estimate of Molenaar's character is given by Princess Wilhelmine of Prussia: "In Cleve I had the pleasure of meeting the Mennonite preacher Molenaar, whom I had learned to love long ago through a splendid sermon which dear old Pastor Reuss gave me on the words 'Maria-Rabbuni.' Unfortunately he is very sickly, but all love, gentleness, and humility—and so simple!" Of interest is also his correspondence with Willem de Clerq (*q.v.*), published in the *Mennonitische Blätter* (1916, 74, and 1918, 4 and 12).

In an article, "Izaäk Molenaar aan Willem de Clercq" (*DB* 1911, 63-92), C. B. Hylkema calls him one of the forerunners and fathers of the Dutch *Réveil* (1830-50). As a Pietist he occupied a very unusual position among the Dutch Mennonites, shared by few—Willem Messchert (*q.v.*) of Rotterdam, Jan ter Borg (*q.v.*) of Amsterdam, and Doyer of Texel—where the Mennonite preachers in general had adopted a rationalistic Christianity. In this respect certainly he was a unique personality for his time. NEFF.

W. Bauer, "Prinzess Wilhelmine von Preussen," 246, taken from *Menn. Bl.* 1911, 37; *N.N.B.Wb.* IV, 998; *DJ* 1837, 36; *DB* 1901, 4; 1911, 62 ff.; S. Lootsma, *Het Nieuwe Huys* (Zaandam, 1937) 161, 164-66; *ML* III, 145 f.

Molenaar, Isaak, II (1813-91), a Dutch Mennonite minister, son of Isaak Molenaar I, was born at Crefeld, Germany, in 1813, died at Zwolle, Jan. 12, 1891. After studying at the Amsterdam Mennonite Seminary, he served the congregation of Irnsum, Dutch province of Friesland, 1837-78. His advice to divide the united congregation of Irnsum-Poppingewier into two separate congregations was published at Irnsum in 1870 (*Aan de leden der Doopsgezinde Gemeente*). (*ML* III, 146.) vDZ.

Molenaar, Isaak, III (1848-1935), a Dutch Mennonite minister, a son of Isaak Molenaar II, was born at Irnsum, Dutch province of Friesland, on Dec. 7, 1848, studied at the Amsterdam Mennonite Seminary 1868-73; served as preacher in Berlikum 1872-75; in Almelo 1875-77; in West Zaandam 1877-1914; retired on June 21, 1914, and died on Oct. 12, 1935. After his resignation a collection of his sermons,

entitled *Preeken* (Amsterdam, 1915), was published by the church board of Zaandam. In 1897 he published a study on S. Hoekstra Bzn, entitled *Professor Hoekstra* (Haarlem, 1897); he also wrote the articles "Hoekstra" and "Opzoomer" in the *Realenzyklopaedie für protestantische Theologie und Kirche*, third edition. D. Attema wrote a sketch of his life and work in the *Zondagsbode*, Oct. 20, 1935. (*ML* III, 146.) NEFF.

Molenaar, Johannes (1810-68), a German Mennonite minister, was born at Zaandam in Holland, Oct. 27, 1810, spent his youth in Crefeld, Germany, where his father Isaak Molenaar I (*q.v.*) served the Mennonite congregation as pastor, attended the Gymnasium in Kreuznach, studied theology at the University of Bonn, married Alwine Beindorff, a highly educated woman, poet and composer, in 1836 became preacher of the Mennonite congregation at Monsheim (*q.v.*) and made his influence felt far beyond the confines of his parish.

With his fellow ministers Jakob Ellenberger (*q.v.*) of Friedelsheim and Johann Risser (*q.v.*) of Sembach he was in close fraternal sympathy. Together they compiled a ministers' manual (*q.v.*) in 1852 and a hymnal (*q.v.*) in 1854, which latter was principally his work. He drew Albert Knapp (*q.v.*) of Stuttgart into collaboration. He also worked out a catechism (*q.v.*) in 1841, which he published in a new edition in 1854 and which in shortened form is still in use in the congregations of the Palatinate and Hesse.

In addition Johannes Molenaar published a collection of sermons, for every Sunday and church holiday, with the title *Evangelische Stimmen* (1884), and also *Andenken an die beiden heiligen Tage der Taufe und der ersten Abendmahlsfeier*. He also translated some of the popular writings of his brother-in-law J. de Liefde (*q.v.*) from the Dutch: *Des Christen Einnahme und Ausgabe*, for the benefit of the rescue home at Hassloch in the Palatinate, *Der Sträfling*, and other stories.

Molenaar was active in the founding of the rescue home at Rockenhausen in the Palatinate. He was well acquainted with a number of Protestant ministers, as Ohly, Helferich, and Mallet. W. H. Riehl (*q.v.*), author and professor of cultural history, was a frequent guest in his home, and gave him this tribute: "Among the educated preachers of the Mennonites there are, by the way, men before whose scholarship and education the light of many a Catholic and Protestant divine may be as dim as a street light in Westrich." He was also a personal friend of Hermann von Beckerath (*q.v.*) and Heinrich von Gagern, minister of state.

Johannes Molenaar was an enthusiastic sponsor of the Evangelical Alliance (*q.v.*), and took part in their meetings in Berlin (1857) and Geneva (1861). He was also a loyal co-worker on the *Mennonitische Blätter* (*q.v.*). His description of a trip in Switzerland is particularly interesting (*Menn. Bl.*, 1861 and 1862).

Molenaar's work at Monsheim was not without its difficulties. In 1838 a part of the congregation, dissatisfied with his preaching, left Monsheim and joined the Ibersheim congregation. In his family life he endured great sorrow. His wife was afflicted with a long nervous illness until her death in 1865. His strength was broken. He had to have an assistant. Three years later, on Oct. 19, 1868, he died. Upon his death Christian Böhmer, a Protestant minister, wrote a warm poem, and a member of his congregation also wrote a poem, *Denkmal der Liebe* (*Monument of Love*). (*Menn. Bl.*, 1870, 14.)

NEFF.

J. Ellenberger, *Bilder aus dem Pilgerleben* II (n.p., 1783); *DB* 1868, 1-5; W. H. Riehl, *Die Pfälzer, Ein rheinisches Volksbild* (Stuttgart, 1858) 375; *Allgemeine lutherische Kirchenzeitung*, No. 166, Oct. 30, 1839; *ML* III, 145; *DB* 1868, 1, 3 f., 5; 1886, 16.

Molenaar, Willy (1852-1921), a lay leader of the Berlin Mennonite Church, was born on Nov. 18, 1852. He was a descendant of the Crefeld branch of the family; his father was a grandson of Wopko Molenaar (*q.v.*), a nephew of Isaak Molenaar (*q.v.*) of Crefeld, and a cousin of Johannes Molenaar (*q.v.*). Like his grandfather Nikolaus and his father Gustav, Wilhelm was a banker, in partnership with his brother Rudolf, in the Molenaar banking firm. In 1900 he was made director of the Augusta Insurance Company, but had to retire after a few years because of a hearing difficulty. In 1883 he married Maria von Beckerath, a Mennonite of Crefeld. In his parental home he had learned to love music and the arts; he was a collector of paintings (sale on Nov. 13, 1906) and helped to found the German Art Association in Berlin. He took an active part in the political, economic, and artistic life of his time. But he was also devotedly interested in the Mennonite brotherhood, sparing no pains or money to promote it. He was a member of the first curatorium of the Vereinigung (*q.v.*), which he had helped to organize. Until 1907, when he was forced to withdraw on account of eye trouble, he was chairman of the Berlin congregation, and remained an honorary chairman until his death, on Dec. 29, 1921. Many an article (*Menn. Bl.*, 1911-16) shows his interest in following Bernhard Brons as a link between the intellectual life of the time and his brotherhood. The medal struck for the twenty-fifth anniversary of the founding of the Berlin congregation upon his suggestion bore the inscription, "Gott die Ehre, frei die Lehre."

E.C.

E. Harder, *Festschrift zur Feier des 25-jährigen Bestehens der Berliner Mennonitengemeinde* (Berlin, 1912); *Menn. Bl.*, *passim*; *ML*, III, 146.

Molenaar, Wopke (Wopco, Wopko) (1739-94), a German Mennonite preacher, was born Sept. 30, 1739, at Workum, Dutch province of Friesland, the son of Hylke Hessels, owner of a large sawmill. He studied at the Lamist (*q.v.*) seminary in Amsterdam, served at Franeker 1767-70, and in 1770 became the first theologically educated preacher of the Mennonite congregation in Crefeld. An endowment from the von der Leyen family (1766) enabled the Crefeld congregation to request the seminary to send a trained preacher. Molenaar and Sino van Abbema came. Van Abbema served in Crefeld 1771-88. The funeral address given by Molenaar at the burial of the last lay preacher, Wynand Peter Wynandsz (1777), indicates that the transition from the lay to a salaried ministry was not easy for either the congregation or the minister. Especially the spiritualistic circles appear to have remained aloof, probably in view of the "enlightened" position of the new preachers. That Molenaar was rationalistic is proved by his membership in the "enlightened" circle of Engelbert von Bruck. Wopke Molenaar was married to Hester Tirion, of Crefeld. He was the progenitor of the Molenaar family in Crefeld. He died on April 27, 1794.

D.C.

K. Rembert, "Zur Geschichte der Crefelder Familie Molenaar," *Heimat* IV, 189 ff.; *Beiträge zur Geschichte rheinischer Mennoniten* (*Schriftenreihe des Mennonitischen Geschichtsvereins*, No. 2, 1939); *Inv. Arch. Amst.* II, 2350; *ML* III, 146 f.

Molkwerum, a small village of scarcely 200 inhabitants in the southwest corner of the Dutch province of Friesland, was once the seat of a very large Mennonite congregation, of whose history not much is known. The congregation dates from the middle of the 16th century or even before. Leenaert Bouwens (*q.v.*) baptized 39 persons here in 1551-54, 19 or 21 in 1557-61, and 36 in 1563-65, a total of 94 or 96 within 14 years. Soon the congregation must have increased greatly. One can hardly imagine that in this picturesque little hamlet at the beginning of the 17th century there were more than 1,000 Mennonites in three or four congregations, the largest of them being Waterlander (formerly Young Frisian) with 407 baptized members about 1600. In 1650, when the membership comprised 174 men and 233 women, it was decided to build a new church, commonly called the Groote Vermaning. This was a period of prosperity derived from shipping (it must have been in this period when 70 Molkwerum ships lay at the dock in Riga on the Baltic at one time). The Mennonites at this time made large contributions to Mennonites in other countries. In 1672, though trade was weakened by war, an offering of 259 guilders was raised for Swiss Mennonites. The war with England during this period seriously hampered the Mennonite shipping industry. Their preachers had to keep reminding the members that the weapons of their warfare were not carnal but spiritual; one shipper who had armed his boat was expelled from membership. The Waterlander congregation was served by lay preachers until 1808; among them was Harmen Reynskes (*q.v.*), serving here 1690-94, later preacher of the Amsterdam Zonist congregation, whose progressive ideas, considered Socinian (*q.v.*) by the conservative members, nearly caused a schism in the Molkwerum congregation.

At the beginning of the 18th century Molkwerum suffered the decline in trade affecting all the shipping towns on the Zuiderzee. The Mennonite congregations of Molkwerum also decreased rapidly. In 1695, when both the Groote Vermaning and the Kleine Vermaning joined the F.D.S. (Conference of Friesland), their membership numbered 167 and 97 baptized members. The union of the large group (Waterlander) with the smaller one (Flemish, commonly called Kleine Vermaning) in 1732 did little good; the combined congregation then numbered scarcely 200 members. All sorts of other factors contributed to the decline; a division in 1755-67, and in the 18th century a conflict between a more liberal preacher and a conservative one, difficulty with the Reformed clergy, and finally trouble with the authorities (in 1705 the congregation had to surrender to the Reformed congregation a considerable legacy, which had been left to the Mennonites). In 1838 there were only 20 members left.

Until 1797 the congregation was served by lay preachers chosen from the members. The last of these preachers was Nanne Jans, who served 1755-d.97. After Cornelis Gerbens van Grouw, a lay preacher called in from outside the congregation who served here 1796-1806, the Molkwerum congregation in 1808 joined the neighboring one of Hindeloopen (q.v.) in supporting a (trained) pastor; in 1873 Molkwerum joined the congregation of Stavoren (q.v.) for the same purpose. The membership, which had risen to 55 in 1910, in 1939 was 29. Wijtse S. van der Zijpp was treasurer 1867-1909. In 1921 a new church was built. On May 16, 1948, when there were only 12 members left, they decided to merge with the congregation of Warns (q.v.), only two miles from Molkwerum. Thereupon the small meetinghouse was sold.   vDZ.

Inv. Arch. Amst. II, 2, No. 295; Blaupot t. C., *Friesland, passim; Naamlijst* 1808, 77; *DB* 1874, 86 f., 142; 1895, 105-16; 1900, 228; 1903, 81, 91; *De Zondagsbode* XXIV (1910-11) No. 3; *ML* III, 147.

Mollem (Mullem), **van**, a former Dutch Mennonite family, of Flemish origin, stemming from Mollem near Gent, Belgium, or Molhem near Brussels, during 17th-18th centuries members of the Flemish congregation at Amsterdam, where some of them were deacons. As early as 1573 a Dierck Mullem (or van Mollem) is found at Rotterdam, where he was a book printer (*Rotterdamsch Jaarboekje*, 1931). In 1582 he published the hymnal by Hans de Ries. He was probably an emigrant from Flanders and a Mennonite. Mathijs van Mollem (d. Oct. 24, 1689) was a preacher of the Flemish congregation at Rotterdam *ca.* 1655-86. To this family also belonged Jacob van Mollem (b. 1623), a merchant of Amsterdam, who in 1681 founded a silk factory at Utrecht, which was managed by him and later his son David van Mollem (1670-1746). Their luxurious country seat "Zijdebalen" near Utrecht, built in 1693 and in 1719 enlarged with splendid parks adorned with a large number of beautiful statues, had a wide reputation (see *N.N.B.Wb.* III, 876, and S. Müller Fzn, "Zijdebalen" in *Bouwkunst* 1912, repr.). Both Jacob van Mollem, married to Maria Sijdervelt, and David, married to Jacoba van Oosterwijck, were faithful Mennonites.

It could not be ascertained whether Corijn (Krijn) van Mollem (who is confused with Krijn or Quirin Vermeulen in *ML* III, 119), a Mennonite of Flemish descent living in Danzig, West Prussia, who in August 1612 perished during his attempt to make gold (*Inv. Arch. Amst.* II, Nos. 2925, 2927, 2935) was related to the above van Mollems.   vDZ.

Möller, A. von (Angelica von Lagerström) (d. 1879), author of popular and juvenile German literature 1846-61, taught foreign languages in Danzig, 1850-52 in Königsberg, then having been expelled from the city as a member of a free church was housekeeper in the home of Gottfried Kinkel in London, returned to Königsberg in 1864, where she died on Nov. 20, 1879. In 1851 she published a popular book titled *Die Mennoniten*. The story is centered around Danzig during and after the siege of 1813 and has as its theme the young man concerning whom Bishop Eylert (q.v.) wrote, and who was the hero of Wildenbruch's *Menonit*. On the whole the treatment differs from Wildenbruch's and the attitude toward the Mennonites is much friendlier.

    E.C.

S. Pataky, *Lexikon deutscher Frauen der Feder* (Berlin, 1898, under both names); J. N. Weisfert, *Biographisch-litterarisches Lexikon für . . . Königsberg und Ostpreussen* (Königsberg, 1898); *ML* III, 147.

Möller (Müller), **Georg**, an Anabaptist martyr from Schönau near Zwickau, Germany, joined the Anabaptists after hearing sermons by Georg Köhler (q.v.) in Riestedt near Sangerhausen and by Heinz Kraut (q.v.) in March 1535. He was baptized by Heinz Kraut on July 10 with his brother Jobst Möller (q.v.) in the home of Georg Knoblauch behind the cathedral in Halberstadt (q.v.). He began at once to preach repentance (Jacobs, 469) in the vicinity of Riestedt. He was seized with Georg Köhler on the morning of Sept. 2, 1535, and taken to the prison in Sangerhausen, where an Anabaptist woman, Petronella, was detained. Two days later Köhler and Möller were subjected singly to a lengthy cross-examination by the Catholic authorities. The bailiff Philipp Reibitzsch reported at once to George, Duke of Saxony (q.v.), with the comment that he was greatly surprised by their free confession of their faith and the frank answers to the questions asked them; the presence of the executioner had not intimidated them (*Thüringen*, 130 and 392).

The answers, published by Eduard Jacobs from the court records (pp. 496-508), give important information on the history of the Anabaptist movement in Central Germany. Georg Köhler, in answer to the question how he had come to join the Anabaptists, said that he had first been admonished by Georg Knoblauch—whose wife Greta Knoblauch (q.v.) had been executed in April 1534 at Sangerhausen, and with whom he had been baptized six months later by Heinz Kraut—to turn to God, be obedient to Him, repent, and deny the world, pride, and drunkenness. Georg Möller had also been deeply influenced by Knoblauch, whose house in Halberstadt was long an Anabaptist center.

As in other countries, the Anabaptists in Saxony were suspected of seditious intentions. Köhler declared that they had made no conspiracy against the government, that God had ordained government, and killing was forbidden in the Ten Commandments (Jacobs, 504). And Möller said in reply to the question as to the whereabouts of his brethren that God's followers were all beloved of Him and were ready to endure all persecution for God's sake (Jacobs, 472).

The Anabaptists put great stress on clean moral living, as is shown by their statements on marriage. Among them marriage was not begun with excessive eating, drinking, and pride, as is the usage in the world. "By their simple and moral conduct," writes Jacobs, "they stand high above the unrefined generation of their day, in many cases sunken in gluttony and drunkenness. . . . It is indeed no trifling matter that our friends of God could say that they tolerated no adulterer, gambler, or glutton, nor any with an undisciplined or evil life and conduct in their brotherhood; they were not permitted to speak ill or laugh in derision at anyone" (Jacobs, 485 and 529).

The questioning on doctrinal points covered infant baptism, original sin, confession of faith, communion, confessional, and forgiveness of sin. Baptism they regarded as the covenant of a good conscience with God, which an infant cannot enter into. Infants are not tainted by original sin or any other kind of sin. God has instilled a clean spirit into them. It is therefore not possible that they could be in the power of the devil whom the parson must drive out. God has not granted the devil so much power over a child that has done no wrong. Concerning communion both repeated what they had been taught by Heinz Kraut, who later became a martyr in Jena, "that God is a living God and a spirit, over whom no man has any power." Therefore, declared Köhler, he did not believe that in the form of the bread the body of God was concealed or was pure flesh and blood. Möller answered that he did not believe that God would permit Himself to be transformed into bread by a priest or a sinful man. In reply to the question of what benefit communion was to them Möller replied that it was of no special benefit; he thought that as the grain of wheat must suffer much before it becomes bread, so also a disciple of Jesus must suffer much before he becomes a real Christian (Jacobs, 508). Communion they regarded as a meal of the covenant which obligated them to faithful discipleship. That included being willing to give up home, property, wife, and child, indeed even life (Jacobs, 475, 500, 503, and '507). Asked about the confessional and absolution Köhler said that he placed no value on the forgiveness of sin as the church taught it. Nobody was able to forgive sin except those sins which his neighbor had committed against him. The forgiving of sins pertained to God alone. To that end He did not need a man, but required a penitent heart.

The records state that Köhler had answered freely without the use of the rack and had in conclusion declared that he would adhere to his opinion, come what might. Likewise Möller said he would adhere to his confession of faith, hoping that God would strengthen and illumine him in doing so. Albrecht, Cardinal of Mainz, on Sept. 24, 1535, advised Duke George to have them beheaded and also to put Petronella to death unless she recanted, as soon as the consent of the council of Quedlinburg and the official of Sachsenberg arrived, since Petronella had been baptized in his district by schoolmaster Alexander, who had already been martyred, "that such an unchristian undertaking be seriously punished and eradicated" (*Thüringen*, 130).

The arrest of these two men led to further executions, also under Lutheran authority, since they named their brethren when asked to do so. John, the young Duke of Saxony, had in the absence of his father sent the records of the trials to Cardinal Albrecht, administrator of Halberstadt, with the request to seize the Anabaptists named by the prisoners and try them, "that we may see behind their intrigues" (Jacobs, 519). The Anabaptists who remained steadfast were drowned by order of the cardinal at Gröningen near Halberstadt (Jacobs, 536).   HEGE.

Eduard Jacobs, "Die Wiedertäufer am Harz," in *Ztscht des Harz-Vereins für Gesch. und Altertumskunde* XXXII (1899) 422-536; P. Wappler, *Inquisition und Ketzerprozesse in Zwickau zur Ref.-Zeit* (Leipzig, 1908); *idem, Thüringen; ML* III, 147 f.

Möller (Müller), **Heinrich,** an Anabaptist martyr from Schönau near Zwickau, Germany. With his brothers Georg (*q.v.*) and Jobst (*q.v.*) he joined the brotherhood in the spring of 1535. He was married to Anna Wedekind, the daughter of the martyr Greta Knoblauch (*q.v.*) from her first marriage; Anna had been baptized by Heinz Kraut (*q.v.*) in November 1534 in her stepfather's home with her sister Ursula and her brother Hans (Jacobs, 440) seven months after her mother's execution. After his marriage Heinrich Möller moved to Eisleben.

On Nov. 20, 1535, an Anabaptist meeting at Hans Peissker's (*q.v.*) mill at Kleineutersdorf in Saxon territory was surprised and 16, including Heinrich and Anna, were taken and cross-examined. The report to the ducal council at Weimar said that Heinrich Möller placed no value on "our sacrament" (*Thüringen*, 398). With his father-in-law Heinrich was then taken to Neustadt on the Orla, where Lutheran clergymen endeavored to convert them (*Thüringen*, 140 and 151), as was reported to John Frederick, Elector of Saxony (*q.v.*), "to move them to desist from their seditious and unchristian articles and conduct" (*Thüringen*, 414). Since the content of the articles of examination was not sent to the elector, he sent the minister of Neustadt and other scholars to re-examine the prisoners and to write up the statements and confessions of each separately and present them to him (*Thüringen*, 415).

The prisoners were then subjected to further questioning concerning their faith by scholars in the presence of the council of Neustadt and the bailiff of Arnshaugk. Their statements were sent to the professors of the University of Wittenberg (who had gone to Jena to escape the plague) who were to send their opinion with the records to the elector (*Thüringen*, 422). There are no records of Heinrich's statements. Since he was not amenable to the teaching of the divines he was beheaded at Neustadt (Wappler, *Inquisition*, 112). His father-in-law and his wife recanted and were released with the penalty of church penance (*Thüringen*, 422).   HEGE.

Eduard Jacobs, "Die Wiedertäufer am Harz," in *Ztscht des Harz-Vereins für Gesch. und Altertumskunde* XXXII (1899); P. Wappler, *Inquisition und Ketzerprozesse in Zwickau zur Reformationszeit*, 1908; *idem, Thüringen; ML* III, 148 f.

Möller (Müller), **Jobst,** an Anabaptist martyr from Schönau near Zwickau, Germany, was baptized with his brother Georg Möller (*q.v.*) in the home of Georg Knobloch (*q.v.,* also Knoblauch) at Halberstadt on July 10, 1535, by Heinz Kraut (*q.v.*). Three weeks later Möller married Ursula Wedekind, a daughter of the martyr Greta Knobloch (*q.v.*) from her first marriage. Ursula's first husband had been executed in 1534 in Frankenhausen. (*Thüringen,* 127.) The marriage was of short duration. On Nov. 20, 1535, Jobst and Ursula were taking part in a meeting of Anabaptists in the home of the miller Hans Peissker (*q.v.*) at Kleineutersdorf near Orlamünde in Saxony (*q.v.*), which was disbanded by Peter Wolfram, bailiff of the Leuchtenburg. As the catchpolls closed in on them the little group began to sing the Luther hymn, "Nun bitten wir den Heiligen Geist," and cried to God to help them to be firm. Sixteen persons were taken to the Leuchtenburg, including Jobst Möller and his wife, Hans Peissker, Heinz Kraut, Heinrich Möller (*q.v.*) and his wife, and Georg Knobloch. On the way to prison they sang religious songs and called to the curious onlookers in the villages they passed through to repent. In the Leuchtenburg they were at once cross-examined. When asked what they thought of the sacrament (communion) all the prisoners said they did not agree with the Lutheran doctrine.

Since the prison was not large enough for 16, and a guard of 12 men would have been required, the men were divided between Jena, Kahla, Neustadt on the Orla, and the Arnshaugk castle, while the women remained at the Leuchtenburg. Jobst Möller, Heinz Kraut, and Lorenz (Hilarius) Petsch were taken to Jena (*q.v.*). Here they were questioned on Dec. 1 and 6 in the presence of the mayor and several members of the city council by Philip Melanchthon (*q.v.*), Kaspar Cruciger (*q.v.*), and the city pastor Anton Musa (*q.v.*) concerning their doctrinal position, including the Trinity, communion, forgiveness of sin, and baptism, as well as on civil matters such as community of goods, government, oath, and marriage. They said they had had no connections with the Münsterites, and could therefore say anything, either good or bad, about them.

Lorenz Petsch, who stemmed from Emseloh near Sangerhausen, and, as Melanchthon reported, had lived in villages where the Gospel was not preached and had consequently received no instruction, was separated from the rest. He had not yet been baptized and was from the beginning of the examination inclined to recant; he escaped from prison the day before the others were put to death.

The statements made by Jobst Möller, Heinz Kraut, and Hans Peissker have been published from the court records in *Corpus Reformatorum* II. Though the brief summary does not always correctly interpret the meaning, it nevertheless affords an insight into the principal doctrines of the Anabaptists in Saxony.

Concerning the doctrine of the Trinity they said, according to the text of the court record: "God the Father must be seen in omnipotence, the Son in righteousness, and the Spirit in kindness. Likewise they confess the eternal Deity of Christ together with the humanity He assumed, in which He suffered; they say nothing wrong about the two natures in Christ; but they say they are not educated and cannot talk much on these high articles." On the question as to how they had received pardon for their sin, the record gives their reply, "They must sincerely ask for forgiveness and must thereafter walk in righteousness, believe and trust God's Word,

do the will of the Father, and the sins would be forgiven. In short, one must practice truth and righteousness." "Concerning the sacrament of baptism they say, infant baptism is not commanded, and all children are saved, whether of Christians, heathen, or Turks. God is not such a God that He would damn an infant on account of a little water; for all His creatures are good. And they deny original sin in children, for they have not willed to sin, but only when man is grown and sins voluntarily does original sin become valid. . . . The children are of the kingdom of heaven . . . and even if they sin it does not harm them, for they do not yet know what is good or what is bad" (*Corp. Ref.* II, 995, 999, and 1000).

Melanchthon at once reported to John, Elector of Saxony (*q.v.*), the results of the examination, but does not quite do justice to their statements on civil matters. The brief summary of these statements gives the impression that Heinz Kraut and his companions rejected all government and taught that "Christians should have no government at all except the preachers" (*Corp. Ref.,* 1004), and "a Christian can not be a ruler, who punishes with the sword," while according to the court record Heinz Kraut declared that "if the government deprived him of his faith he must not obey it. For he had only one Lord, God alone. He left his former government because it had interfered with his conscience. But he recognized government that rewards the good and punishes the wicked, and gives it whatever it requires. But neither he nor his brethren could assume the responsibility of government. To preach the Gospel no government permission is needed, but only the consent of his brethren and those who accept the Word" (*Corp. Ref.* II, 1000 f.). The statements of the prisoners on property rights are quoted in Melanchthon's report as a rejection of all personal possession and the requirement of complete community of goods (*op. cit.,* 1004), whereas the court records show that they had no common possessions. "But a Christian must part from his possessions and his lands which he does not need for himself and his family" (*op. cit.,* 998). On marriage it was their belief that no marriage could exist if the partners were not of the same faith, but the dissolution of the marriage should be postponed for a time until the erring partner has had an opportunity to place himself under God's Word, which should be a matter of prayer to God (*op. cit.,* 1001).

Since the prisoners showed no inclination to give up their faith, the elector on Jan. 9, 1536, ordered that the records be presented to the doctors of law then in the city of Jena for their official opinion on the method of punishment, "in order that this seductive sect be eradicated" (*Thüringen,* 404).

The cross-examination of the prisoners at Kahla and Leuchtenburg was reported to John of Saxony by Melanchthon on Jan. 19, 1536, together with suggestions on punishment. Concerning the wavering father of a family he wrote, "With this one I beg you not to hasten punishment. For I hope that when his master Heinz Kraut, who lies in Jena, and a few other stubborn ones are executed, he will let himself be instructed. On the obstinate ones it is necessary to inflict serious punishment. And even though some may not be otherwise untractable, nevertheless this harmful sect must be resisted, in which there are so many terrible, dangerous errors. But with the poor obstinate women I think it is not necessary to hurry, but first deal earnestly with their husbands." John wrote a letter on Jan. 23 concurring with Melanchthon's opinion (*Corp. Ref.* III, 16 f.).

The jurists of Jena wished to have the prisoners questioned further on a few points before giving their opinion, first in kindness, and then if they made no statements, on the rack. This was done on Jan. 26, 1536. The instruments of torture produced no statements beyond what they had already said. On the next day they were condemned to death and beheaded.

The death sentence gives as the reasons for inflicting this penalty that the prisoners had allowed themselves to be baptized a second time, contributed to the spread of their ungodly, seditious doctrine, and held meetings at Kleineutersdorf. They had also, in spite of the application of much zeal and Christian teaching, not yielded their erroneous faith, but always said they would persist in it. Of Heinz Kraut it was said that he had participated in the revolt of Frankenhausen (*Thüringen*, 409-14).

The women held in the Leuchtenburg, the wives of Jobst and Heinrich Möller, were naturally crushed by the news of the execution, as Melanchthon hoped. On Jan. 13 they had still resisted his attempts to convert them, and were described by Melanchthon as stubborn (*Corp. Ref.* III, 21). But now the widows were incapable of further resistance and yielded to pressure. They were joined by Ursula Meurer, a girl of 16 years. On March 3, 1536, the elector ordered that the women should make a public recantation in the church at Kahla (*Thüringen*, 423).

The execution of the three Möller brothers illustrates how the families of religious minorities in both Catholic and Protestant countries were torn apart, merely because they refused to join the state church. It is also evidence of the impression made on pious natures by steadfastness and suffering of believing Christians. The courage of Greta Knobloch, the mother-in-law of Jobst and Heinrich Möller, "was most highly praised by the populace, so that much annoyance to the preachers resulted from it and they were compelled to preach against it openly from the pulpits several times" (*Thüringen*, 109).

The martyrdom of the Möller brothers and their companions brought new converts to the Anabaptist movement. Hans Hamster, a young man of 33 and a brother-in-law of the Möller brothers, who had not yet been baptized, was now heart and soul in the cause (*Inquisition*, 100). He gave up his previous position because the lord of the place would not tolerate Anabaptists and moved away, but was seized in August 1538 on Saxon territory and was put through four cross-examinations. Each time he refused to make the required recantation, and finally said that he would willingly suffer and die for his faith. John sent his confession to the court in Wittenberg on Sept. 25. The court apparently hesitated to pronounce a verdict, for John sent a

reproof on Oct. 14. It is not definitely known that Hamster shared the fate of his brothers-in-law, for the pertinent Zwickau records have disappeared (*Inquisition*, 114-17).

While these trials were in progress in Jena, Melanchthon planned to have a public warning against the Anabaptists issued. On Jan. 19, 1536, he wrote John in connection with his report on the answers of the prisoners, "Perhaps it would be advisable for your Excellency to have a public writing issued, which would show what coarse, seditious, and dangerous articles the Anabaptists have, wherefore such earnest measures must be taken against them" (*Corp. Ref.* III, 17). The elector agreed with the proposal and assigned the composition to Melanchthon, asking him to send it to him and his brother for approval (*Thüringen*, 407). Then in February Melanchthon drew up a guide for pastors, with the title, *Des Herrn Philipp Melanchthons Widerlegung auf etliche aufruhrische Artikel so die Wiederteufer treiben und verteidigen*, which presents the teachings of the Anabaptists, in somewhat distorted form, and refutes them. At the end he says, "We also command that in all places the pastors and preachers shall give the people a thorough and clear report of these and other erroneous articles" (*Corp. Ref.* III, 28-34).

Since the execution of these persons who had been seized at an evening service of worship at Kleineutersdorf within the homeland of the Reformation caused great excitement, Melanchthon felt it necessary to defend the severe sentence pronounced against them in another booklet. It was published in Wittenberg in 1536 (without date) and had the title, *Verlegung etlicher unchristlicher Artikel; welche die Widerteuffer furgeben* (38 pp.). In the preface Melanchthon says that on account of these articles, which all Anabaptists hold in common, several had recently been punished in these lands. With the exception of infant baptism the pamphlet deals not so much with questions of dogma as with questions of civil right, as the Anabaptist position on government, property, and divorce, imputing motives to them that are in many instances incompatible with the earnest character of the Anabaptists of Saxony. At the close he writes, "The Anabaptists have in addition more errors on both sacraments and their practice, and on other articles, of which others have already written before, and which cannot all be discussed here for lack of time." A second edition of this pamphlet appeared in Zwickau in 1536 without naming Melanchthon as the author.

Melanchthon's report to John on the statements of the martyrs executed in Jena found an echo in the mandate of April 10, 1536, in a warning reference to the executions, "that everyone may know how to guard himself against such blasphemous and seditious sects and that kind of seditious punishment."

In view of the fact that princes, theologians, and jurists were occupied for months with the religious confessions made by the condemned prisoners, it is appropriate to inquire what Anabaptist wing the Saxon group adhered to. Melanchthon noted in his pamphlets that "the Anabaptists are not alike." The jurists of Jena wanted to know definitely whether sedition could be charged against Jobst Möller,

Heinz Kraut, and Hans Peissker, before giving their official opinion. The question was therefore to be asked the prisoners, whether they had any connections with the Münsterites; the answer was negative in both examinations, even with the application of torture. Melanchthon was also well aware that this was not the case; for he added to his account the statement that among the Münsterites more and worse errors were found.

That these Anabaptists had not the remotest idea of revolt is clear from their statement that only such persons were admitted to membership as would pledge themselves to commit no civil crime, but would obey God's command. Heinz Kraut demanded sincere penitence and devotion to God before he baptized anyone. Georg Köhler said on Sept. 4, 1535, as recorded in the official report of the trial at Sangerhausen, "When one wishes to be baptized he comes to the baptizer and says kneeling: Dear Brother, I desire the bond of a good conscience with God and request baptism. The baptizer then says, And do you believe that Christ is the only begotten Son of God and is eternal, will you submit yourself entirely to Him alone, be obedient to Him as to a God and Lord, and if necessary die for His sake? If the answer is yes, the brother appointed to the task performs the sacred act, repeating first the baptism of John word for word. Then he wets his finger three times in the water, draws three crosses on the head and brow of the candidate, and says, I baptize you in the name of the Father, Son, and Holy Ghost. He then earnestly admonishes the brother to follow the covenant, be obedient to God, avoid sin, and yet always consider himself a sinner in the sight of God" (Jacobs, 470).

This serious conception of discipleship coincides with the doctrine and thought of the High German Anabaptists, whose representatives met on Aug. 20, 1527, in the Martyrs' Synod at Augsburg. That there were contacts between the Saxon and Upper German Anabaptists is known, for the Synod sent Hans Mittermaier, of Ingolstadt, as a missionary to Saxony in 1527.   Hege.

Corpus Reformatorum II and III; E. Jacobs, "Die Wiedertäufer am Harz," in *Ztscht des Harzvereins für Geschichte und Altertumskunde* XXXII (1899); Chr. Thomas, *Philipp Melanchthon, Verzeichnis von den Wiedertäuffern, so in Jena gefangen gesessen und Anno 1536 enthauptet worden. Melanchthonis Articul wieder die Wiedertäuffer, die damals zu Weimar, Leuchtenburg und Jena gefangen gesessen, auch damit die meisten zu rechte gebracht 1536* (Halle, 1693); P. Wappler, *Inquisition und Ketzerprozesse in Zwickau zur Ref.-Zeit* (Leipzig, 1908); idem, *Thüringen; ML* III, 149-52.

Möllinger, a well-known name among the Mennonites of the Palatinate, Germany, whose progenitor, Ulrich Möllinger, immigrated from the canton of Bern, Switzerland, in the middle of the 17th century, and settled on the "Mainzer Hofgut" in Guntersblum near Oppenheim, and then on the Kirschgartshäuserhof near Mannheim. The dates of his birth and death are not known.

His son Jakob Möllinger (b. about 1660) was hereditary lessee of one fourth of the Hemshof. Johannes Möllinger, a grandson of Jakob, was ordained preacher and elder of the Friesenheim congregation (see *Namenlistbüchlein* 1805, 43).

Better known than Jakob and his descendants was his younger brother Vincenz and his family. Vincenz Möllinger (b. Nov. 22, 1668, d. Dec. 1748) settled in Dühren near Sinsheim a. Elsenz, where he married Veronica Magelin (1664-1753). In 1710 he settled with his family on the Nonnenhof near Bobenheim, in 1714 in Eppstein near Frankenthal, and in 1718 in Mutterstadt. When he died at the age of 80 he left his widow, four married sons, and three married daughters, whom the parents had reared "with great love and care." Some of the four sons became famed beyond the Mennonite circles.

Mellingers are found in America in Lancaster County, Pa., in Columbiana and Mahoning counties, Ohio, and at Sterling, Ill. (*ML* III, 152.)   G.H.

Möllinger, David (1709-86), an outstanding German Mennonite farmer, "the father of agriculture in the Palatinate," was born Jan. 24, 1709, at Dühren near Sinsheim, Baden. He married Maria Kindig of the Immelhäuserhof (*q.v.*) on Feb. 8, 1732. In farming he was a pioneer. At first he lived in Mutterstadt in the Palatinate, where his father Vincenz was farming, and in 1732 moved to near-by Cronau, where he increased his small patrimony (500 florins) "through trade and crafts." In 1744 he bought land near Monsheim.

Möllinger's success at extensive farming was widely acclaimed. He distilled liquor, brewed beer, made vinegar, fattened cattle, and cultivated the land. He was the first to manufacture liquor from potatoes. A by-product of his distillery was some valuable cattle feed. To feed his cattle he also raised certain kinds of clover. In 1769 he lost much of his hay through a flood of the Rhine. Then he transferred his meadows to the higher lands and planted grain on the lower. He purchased part of a neighboring wooded hill, planted the bare top of the hill in clover and scattered limestone over it, which he ground in a mill driven by horsepower, and raised an amazingly good crop. A complete revolution in the system of crop rotation followed. Instead of letting every field lie fallow each alternate year, the soil was improved by the use of clover, his stand of cattle was trebled, the fertility of the soil increased, and the prosperity of the farmer improved. "All of this the Palatinate owes a single man, a Mennonite" (Schwerz). He died at Monsheim (*q.v.*) on May 3, 1786.

The monthly periodical of the historical society of Frankenthal (*Frankenthaler Altertumsverein*) of June 1904 published a guest book of his family containing more than 350 entries, some of them very important persons, a glowing tribute of the high esteem he enjoyed.   Neff.

Ernst Correll, *Das Schweizerische Täufermennonitentum* (Tübingen, 1925) 122-26 contains an excellent description of Möllinger's "model farming"; J. N. Schwerz, *Der Ackerbau der Pfälzer* (Berlin, 1816); Ernst Crous, "The Mennonites in Germany Since the Thirty Years' War," *MQR* XXV (October 1951) 235-62; "Aus dem Stammbuch der Familie Möllinger," *Gem.-Kal.*, 1933, 116-25; *ML* III, 152 f.

Möllinger, Jakob (1695-1763), a famous Mennonite clockmaker, was born Dec. 4, 1695, at Dühren, Germany, oldest son of Vincenz Möllinger, d. Jan. 17,

1763, at Neustadt on the Haardt, Palatinate, Germany. His shop is said to have been one of the most important in all Germany. It produced the "Altpörtl-Uhr" in Speyer and the handsome clock in the Dreifaltigkeitskirche in Worms (the latter is now in a museum at Worms; see *Wormser Zeitung*, No. 552). A census list of Mennonites of 1743 indicated that he had six sons, one of whom was court clockmaker to the Count of Wartenberg.

Ernst Crous, "The Mennonites of Germany Since the Thirty Years' War," *MQR* XXV (October 1951) 235-62; "Graf und Uhrmacher," *Gem.-Kal.*, 1932, 125 ff. (taken from *Pfälzische Geschichts-Blätter*, 1905); *ML* III, 153.

Möllinger, Johann Albert, a German Mennonite farmer, b. Sept. 16, 1823, at Pfeddersheim, Hesse, d. April 30, 1906, was a member of the Nationalverein, an association which as early as the 1860's promoted the unification of Germany under Prussia, from 1862 to 1906 a member of the Second Chamber of the Hessian parliament, and for 18 years president of the Department of Agriculture of Hesse (*Menn. Bl.*, 1906, 53). His wife Angelica died Nov. 4, 1939, at the age of one hundred years. (*ML* III, 153.)
NEFF.

Möllinger, Joseph, b. Nov. 7, 1715, at Eppstein, Palatinate, Germany, d. April 27, 1772, at Frankenthal, was like his brother Jakob (*q.v.*) a clockmaker at Neustadt on the Haardt. He was called to Zweibrücken as clockmaker and minter of money to the Duke. Besides his professional skill he was known for his benevolence. (*ML* III, 153).

Möllinger, Martin (1698-1774), a German Mennonite elder, was born at Dühren, Baden, Germany, on Nov. 12, 1698. For 20 years (1753-73) he served as preacher and elder of the Mennonite congregation at Mannheim (*q.v.*), after he had farmed for three years at Mutterstadt and 25 years at Monsheim. He died at Mannheim, Jan. 17, 1774.

Through Martin Möllinger, at the instigation of the Danzig Elder Hans van Steen (*q.v.*), the correspondence between the West Prussian and South German Mennonites was begun (*Gem.-Kal.*, 1935, 112 ff.). The letters and poems of David Möllinger were read with pleasure by the West Prussian Mennonites. A song of 40 stanzas and the letters were copied by Hans van Steen and placed in the archives of the Danzig Church. The *Familiennachrichten des Martin Möllinger zu Mannheim vom 1. Februar 1766* (published in *Gem.-Kal.*, 1940) contains a brief biography in addition to data on his ancestors and brothers and sisters. (*ML* III, 153).   G.H.

Mölln: see **Refugee Camps.**

Molotschna Mennonite Settlement, located in the province of Taurida, Russia, on the Molochnaya River, was the second and largest Mennonite settlement of Russia (*q.v.*). Chortitza (*q.v.*), founded in 1789, was the oldest and next in size. Chortitza was established by Mennonites of Danzig and Prussia who had followed the invitation of Catherine the Great issued through her representative George von Trappe. The basis for this invitation was the fact that the Russian government needed good farmers in the Ukraine on land just acquired through a war with Turkey. Land along the Vistula River in Prussia had become scarce and the Mennonite families were large; hence the Mennonites, who were by tradition farmers, were forced to seek other occupations, not all of which were open to Mennonites. Among the first settlers establishing the Chortitza settlement were many artisans and laborers who longed to have their own farms. In 1787 Frederick William II of Prussia issued an order of cabinet which forbade the Mennonites to enlarge their landholdings. The "Mennonite Edict" followed in 1789 with further restrictions. Frederick William III further increased restrictions when he issued a declaration supplementary to the Mennonite Edict in 1801. All Mennonite efforts to have the edict changed were in vain. It became apparent that these restrictions were aimed to undermine the Mennonite principle of nonresistance. Mennonites who gave it up could purchase all the land they wanted.

Beginning. In spite of the reports of hardships experienced by the Chortitza settlers a new movement to the steppes of the Ukraine began in 1803. Elder Cornelius Warkentin of Rosenort, who had been in Russia in 1798, was in correspondence with Kontenius (*q.v.*) and found out that there was land available for several thousand families on the Molochnaya east of the Dnepr. This was the major topic of discussion at the West Prussian Mennonite ministers' conference on Aug. 10, 1803. Of particular significance was the special *Privilegium* which Czar Paul I had given the Mennonites in 1800. The first Molotschna group arrived at Chortitza in the fall of 1803 and continued its trip in the spring. Other groups followed, making a total of 365 families during 1803-6. The immigrants were on the average much more prosperous than those who had gone to Chortitza.

Various things hindered the emigration movement. The German authorities kept 10 per cent of the property of those leaving the country. For a while passports were refused. Also the Napoleonic wars stopped the emigration for a time. In 1819-20 again 254 families went to the Molotschna. More groups followed. In 1835 the migration to the Molotschna came to a close, with a total of 1,200 families (Unruh, 231) and an estimated population of 6,000. The land complex of the settlement consisted of 120,000 dessiatines (324,000 acres) located east of the Molochnaya River along its tributaries the Tokmak, Begemthsokrak, Kurushan, and Yushanlee, about 100 miles southeast of the Chortitza settlement. To the west resided non-Mennonite German settlers, to the north and east Ukrainians, and to the south nomadic tribes. Around 1870 the Molotschna settlement consisted of the following villages, besides many large estates located within the boundary of the settlement.

The Villages of the Molotschna Settlement in 1860 (Based on Isaac, *Molotschnaer Mennoniten*, 72-73)

These are the names of the 60 Molotschna villages and hamlets with years when founded, number of "full farms" (175 acres), "half size farms," and individuals (landless) who had only a house and possibly a few acres of land (1860), and total acreage of each village.

Molotschna
MENNONITE SETTLEMENT, RUSSIA (1914)

Scale of Miles

0 1 2 3 4 5 6 7 8 9 10 15 20

to Zarekonstantigovka

Tchernigovka

Tokmak

Begim Tchokrak

Kaytulak

Klippenfeld

Felsenthal

Factory location

Hamberg

Tiemerzdorf

Liebenau

Schönsee

Fürstenau

Ladekopp

Prischib

Hoffenthal

Alt-Nassau

Münteau

Weinau

Durlach

Bogdanovka

German, Lutheran, and Catholic Colonies

to Federovka

Ingul

Tokmak

Halbstadt (Molochansk)

Neuhalbstadt

Peterhagen

Waldheim

Hierschau

Landskrone

Friedendorf

Gnadenheim

Alexanderwohl

Fürstenwerder

Tiegerweide

Kuruschan

Old People's Home

Rosenort

Tiegenhagen

Fischau

Lindenau

Schönau

Lichtenau

Blumstein

Münsterberg

Ohrloff

Tiege

Blumenort

Molochnaya

Dove River

Waltschia

Altonau

Yushanlee

Conteniusfeld

Sparrau

Grossweide

Kurudu-ushan

Gnadenthal

Margenau

Nicolaidorf

Rückenau

Mariawohl-

Paulsheim

Gnadenfeld

Kleefeld

Lichtfelde

Neukirch

Prangenau

Friedensruh

Alexanderkrone

Steinfeld

Elisabetthal

Alexanderthal

Steinbach

Schardau

Pordenau

Marienthal

Rudnerweide

Neigenka

Franzthal

Pastwa

Tschanlee

Yushanlee

Juschanlee

Apa

to Zarekonstantigovka

Neu-Hoffnung

Neu-Stuttgart

Heidelberg

Gnadenfeld

Halbstadt

Melitopol

Zarevoderovka

AZOV

Village	Founded	Full Farms	Half Farms	Landless	Acreage
Halbstadt	1804	21	—	28	5192
Neu-Halbstadt	"	—	—	39	2259
Muntau	"	17	8	38	5327
Schönau	"	19	4	24	4722
Fischau	"	16	12	23	4854
Lindenau	"	19	4	29	4938
Lichtenau	"	18	6	26	4808
Blumstein	"	20	2	51	5888
Münsterberg	"	22	—	24	4997
Altona	"	21	2	31	5200
Ladekopp	1805	20	—	29	4762
Schönsee	"	19	2	26	4633
Petershagen	"	17	6	19	4330
Tiegenhagen	"	19	4	24	4822
Ohrloff	"	21	—	26	4908
Tiege	"	20	—	23	4503
Blumenort	"	19	2	23	4503
Rosenort	"	19	2	27	4776
Fürstenau	1806	20	2	37	5283
Rückenau	1811	14	12	34	4978
Margenau	1819	19	10	31	5551
Lichtfelde	"	16	8	27	4876
Neukirch	"	17	6	26	4633
Alexandertal	1820	15	12	26	4808
Schardau	"	16	8	28	4719
Pordenau	"	19	2	27	4676
Mariental	"	17	6	36	5065
Rudnerweide	"	28	10	46	7778
Grossweide	"	21	6	31	5551
Franztal	"	10	28	25	5251
Pastwa	"	17	2	23	5292
Fürstenwerder	1821	18	4	33	4752
Alexanderwohl	"	25	10	26	6691
Gnadenheim	"	22	4	29	6388
Tiegerweide	1822	22	4	32	5465
Liebenau	1823	20	—	22	5594
Elisabethtal	"	22	6	29	4460
Wernersdorf	1824	29	2	45	5640
Friedensdorf	"	27	6	26	7209
Prangenau	"	16	8	33	6388
Sparrau	1838	32	16	37	4936
Konteniusfeld	1832	25	10	33	8618
Gnadenfeld	1835	34	12	38	6691
Waldheim	1836	34	12	56	8862
Landskrone	1839	36	8	34	9439
Hierschau	1848	30	—	30	8489
Nikolaidorf	1851	22	—	8	6561
Paulsheim	1852	25	2	10	4207
Kleefeld	1854	37	6	38	4995
Alexanderkrone	1857	40	—	25	8662
Mariawohl	"	21	—	4	8100
Friedensruh	"	28	4	24	3858
Steinfeld	"	29	2	6	6302
Gnadental	1862	30	—	9	5524
Hamberg	1863	25	2	5	4779
Klippenfeld	"	27	—	14	5343
Fabrikerwiese	"	3	—	10	959
Felsental	1820	—	—	—	—
Yushanlee	1811	—	—	—	—
Steinbach	1812	—	—	—	—

Economic Life. Recently published information shows that the Mennonites who came to the Molotschna had been more prosperous in West Prussia on the average than the Chortitza settlers, and included a number of experienced and aggressive farmers. Also they could profit from the experiences of the Chortitza settlers, and the soil was good. Johann Cornies (*q.v.*) and the Agricultural Association (*q.v.*) headed by him did much to overcome the pioneer difficulties. Cornies successfully demonstrated on his estate which crops were most suitable for the steppes and introduced and constantly improved cattle, sheep, horses, etc. He introduced summer fallow and suitable grains for the steppes. His introduction of fruit trees and an afforestation program were of great consequences far beyond the Mennonite settlement. Through the support of the Guardians' Committee (*q.v.*) of the government his experience and experiments bore fruit even among the nomadic tribes of the neighborhood and the Russian population.

Alexander Petzholdt, who visited the Molotschna Mennonites in 1855, gives a very good description of the agricultural life at that time. Their machinery was comparatively primitive; they were raising mainly sheep, cattle, horses, silk, and grains, including summer wheat, rye, barley, and oats. He found that the Mennonites had planted 7½ million fruit and shade trees (Petzholdt, 180). Industry was in its early stages, with a number of mills, silk factories, carpenter and smith shops, brick factories, oil presses, breweries, etc. The products were much in demand among the population outside Molotschna. Some 500 non-Mennonites found employment among the Mennonites at that time (p. 187).

Around 1850 great changes took place in the life of the Molotschna Mennonites. With the increase of the population, the improvement of agricultural machinery, and the introduction of the hard winter wheat, a more intensive farming came about. Winter wheat became the chief crop and as a result factories of agricultural machinery and a milling industry developed. In addition many branches of business were introduced. Favorable soil and climatic conditions, the industry of the majority of the farmers, and farsighted leadership made the Molotschna settlement a garden spot of the Ukraine and one of the most successful Mennonite settlements of Russia (see also **Agriculture, Business**). However, the settlement also had to solve a growing problem usually referred to as the landless (*q.v.*) question. The table "Villages of the Molotschna Settlement" gives a vivid picture of the land distribution. By 1860 the great majority of the population was landless. The number of families had increased rapidly, and parceling out a normal-sized farm (175 acres) was prohibited. The surplus population usually obtained some land to build little cottages at the end of the village and eked out a meager living as laborers or artisans. Unfortunately the landowners resisted all attempts to provide the landless with better opportunities to secure land or the right to vote. Since only the owners of farms had the right to vote, the landless were denied this right. Finally in 1866 the landless population had persuaded the Russian government to distribute the community surplus and reserve land, which had been rented out mostly to the well-to-do farmers. Each family thus received 16 dessiatines (some 40 acres) of land and with it the right to vote. By 1869 the land had been distributed among 1,563 families.

This was, however, only a partial and temporary solution of a continuously increasing problem. Gradually a colonization system was developed by which the surplus population was given the opportunity to establish their own homes on new settlements called daughter colonies or settlements. The administration of the mother settlement created funds for the purchase of new lands, and supervised the purchase, the financing, and the distribution of the land. Most of the daughter settlements originated on this basis, although some smaller settlements were started through private initiative. The following are the names of the most important settlements or the areas in which they were located; many scattered villages and estates are not mentioned. It is worthy of note that the Chortitza settlement had established daughter settlements much earlier, the first in 1836 at Bergthal. But the Molotschna established more settlements than Chortitza in 1862-1901.

Molotschna Daughter Settlements

Name	Province	Year Established	Number of Villages	Acreage
Crimea	Taurida	1862 ff.	25	108,000
Kuban	Kuban district	1863	2	17,550
Brazol (Schönfeld)	Ekaterinoslav	1868	4	150,000
Zagradovka	Kherson	1871	16	56,130
Auli Ata	Turkestan	1880	4	9,450
Memrik	Ekaterinoslav	1885	10	32,400
Neu-Samara	Samara	1890	12	59,400
Davlekanovo	Ufa	1894	scattered	—
Orenburg	Orenburg	1894	8	29,700
Suvorovka	Stavropol	1894	4	10,800
Olgino	Olgino	1895	2	11,920
Terek	Caucasus	1901	15	76,960

In addition to this, Molotschna Mennonites purchased in their neighborhood and in various other provinces smaller and larger estates. Also they established places of business and industries. The largest and best-known estates were those of Johann Cornies at Yushanlee and Tashchenak; Brodsky near Melitopol, Crimea; and Apanlee.

In the large Mennonite settlements in Siberia many villages were established by Molotschna settlers. They had over 100 villages with an acreage of over one million.

According to the estimates for forestry service taxation, the property of the Molotschna settlement before World War I (1914) amounted to 51,600,000 rubles ($25,800,000), which was no doubt a low estimate.

The Mennonites of the Molotschna settlement, like most of the other Mennonites of Russia, lived in villages (*q.v.*), which were administered by a *Schulze* (mayor). The total settlement had an administration under the leadership of an *Oberschulze* located at Halbstadt (*q.v.*). In 1870 the settlement was divided into two administrative units (volost), Halbstadt and Gnadenfeld. Halbstadt included 31 villages and two estates, while Gnadenfeld had 26 villages and one estate (see map). In addition to these two, Ohrloff was also significant as a cultural center. The local administration (*obshestvo*) was subject to the district administration (*okrug*), which in turn was subject to the Guardians' Committee (*q.v.*).

The men who served as Oberschulze at Halbstadt, Molotschna, were Klaas Wiens 1804-6, Johann Klassen 1806-8 and 1812-14, Gerhard Reimer 1809-11, Peter Töws 1815-20, Johann Klassen (Ohrloff) 1824-26, Johann Klassen (Tiegerweide) 1827-32, Johann Regier 1833-41, Abraham Töws 1842-47, David Friesen 1848-64, Franz Dück 1865-66, Abraham Driedger 1867, Kornelius Töws 1868-72, Abraham Wiebe 1873-78, Peter Dück 1879-81, Klaas Enns 1882-84, Johann Enns 1885-88, Peter Neufeld 1889-98, Franz Nickel 1899-1906, Dietrich Dyck 1906-10. When Gnadenfeld became an independent volost the following served as Oberschulze: Wilhelm Ewert 1870, Franz Penner 1871, Peter Ewert 1872-75 and 1877-78, Gerhard Fast 1876, David Unruh 1878-87, and Gerhard Dörksen 1887.

Molotschna had a mutual fire insurance agency and a *Waisenamt* (*q.v.*), which took care of the orphans of the settlement and regulated inheritance.

Cultural and Religious Life. In the early days cultural and religious life was on a higher level in the Molotschna than in Chortitza. This was probably due mostly to the fact that the Molotschna Mennonites had stayed in their home country (West Prussia) longer, had there undergone more influences in education and had more vital religious experiences because of contacts with Pietistic groups, and were of a generally higher economic status. However, as settlers they had to overcome the same hardships and problems of pioneering as the Chortitza people. In the realm of education (*q.v.*) they had the advantage of having Johann Cornies (*q.v.*) as an outstanding pioneer. Teachers like T. Voth, H. Heese (*q.v.*), and H. Franz paved the way to higher goals. In addition to an improved elementary educational system a secondary educational system followed gradually with its Zentralschulen, Mädchenschulen, as well as teacher training and business schools (see **Education Among the Mennonites of Russia**). The Molotschna Mennonites were also ahead of the other Mennonite settlements in Russia as well as in America in the realm of hospital (*q.v.*) and deaconess (*q.v.*) work.

The Mennonites of the Molotschna settlement were mostly of the Flemish (*q.v.*) branch. Only the village of Rudnerweide was of the Frisian (*q.v.*) branch. In 1805 the first 18 villages were organized into one congregation, the Ohrloff-Petershagen-Halbstadt Mennonite Church (*q.v.*), with Jakob Enns as elder. Klaas Reimer (*q.v.*) separated from this group in 1814 and founded the Kleine Gemeinde (*q.v.*). Another separation occurred in 1823 which resulted in the organization of the Lichtenau-Petershagen Church (*q.v.*). Later this congregation was subdivided into the Margenau-Schönsee (*q.v.*), Pordenau (*q.v.*), and Alexanderkrone (*q.v.*) congregations. In addition to these the following congregations were organized among the settlers that came later: Rudnerweide in 1820 (*q.v.*), consisting of the Frisian Mennonites alone, Alexanderwohl in 1820 (*q.v.*), Gnadenfeld in 1834 (*q.v.*), and Waldheim in 1836 (*q.v.*), which were all of the same Old Flemish or Groningen Flemish background. The latter two represented a conservatism which had been softened and awakened through Moravian and Pietistic influences. In addition to these congregations there existed independent congregations in most of the daughter settlements of the Molotschna.

Gnadenfeld became the center of an active religious life, promoting better education and missions. Heinrich Dirks (*q.v.*) of Gnadenfeld was the first Mennonite missionary from outside Holland. It was in these circles that the Pietist Eduard Wüst (*q.v.*) found response and caused a revival. This revival was welcomed and promoted by men like Bernhard Harder (*q.v.*), but also caused a break resulting in the founding of the Mennonite Brethren Church (*q.v.*) in 1860. However, the difference between these two groups was never as great in the Molotschna as in Chortitza. Men like P. M. Friesen tried to combine the best characteristics and traditions of both, founding the "Allianz" group or Evangelical Mennonite Brethren (*q.v.*) in 1905. The Mennonite Brethren as well as the Friends of Jerusalem (*q.v.*) established settlements on the Kuban (*q.v.*) River in the Caucasus. In 1880 Hermann Peters (*q.v.*) led a group of Molotschna Mennonites to Central Asia (*q.v.*), where they found like-minded chiliasts in the followers of Klaas Epp (*q.v.*). As a whole the Molotschna Mennonites maintained a balanced and active program of Christianity that aimed to manifest itself in all areas of life.

When the Mennonites of Russia in the 1870's had to accept state service, the Mennonites of the Molotschna led in the negotiations with the government and also in the emigration to America. The Molotschna Mennonites went mostly to the United States, while the Chortitza Mennonites and their daughter settlements preferred Canada. Of the total of some 18,000, half must have come from the Molotschna. The now available passenger lists have not yet been investigated as to where the immigrants came from. Those that stayed accepted forestry service (*q.v.*) and later also hospital work.

In 1905 the Molotschna settlement had the following congregations (the figures in parentheses indicate the year of founding and the total membership including children): Halbstadt (1895; 1174), Lichtenau (1823; 3338), Petershagen (?; 722), Schön-

feld and branches (1868 ff.; 763), Blumenfeld (1872; 135), Rosenhof (1870; 419), Ohrloff (1804; 980), Herzenberg (1881; 80), Alexanderkrone (1890; 1305), Neukirch (1863; 890), Alexanderwohl (1820; 680), Schönsee (1830; 1425), Gnadenfeld (and branches) (1834 ff.; 1151), Pordenau (1842; 1771), Rudnerweide (1820; 2548), Margenau (1832; 2876), Waldheim (1836; 219). The Mennonite Brethren were organized as the Rückenau Mennonite Brethren Church, with a number of branches (1860; 1977).

In 1926 the total membership (including children) of the combined Mennonite congregations in the Molotschna was 15,036, of the Mennonite Brethren 2,501, and the Evangelical Mennonite Brethren 810, a total of 17,347. Another source says there were 20,706 Mennonites in the Molotschna settlement in 1922. Taking into consideration the natural increase it may be concluded that some 4,000 must have emigrated to America in 1922-26.

After World War I. World War I had the same effect on the Molotschna settlement as on the other settlements in Russia. The suffering inflicted by the Bolshevik Revolution, the bandits of Machno (*q.v.*), the civil war, drought, and starvation was gradually overcome, partly through American Mennonite relief (*q.v.*). According to a report entitled "American Mennonite Relief Scheme" there was a population of 20,706 in the Molotschna in 1922, of whom 11,134 received relief food. The Association of Citizens of Dutch Origin (*Verband Bürger holländischer Herkunft, q.v.*) did much to prevent great disaster, and to help to restore the economic, cultural, and religious life. The NEP (*q.v.*) period made this restoration possible. Soon, however, the great Mennonite emigration to Canada set in (1921), which was discontinued by 1927. Again in 1929 a small number succeeded in leaving Russia for Canada. How many of the 25,000 emigrants from Russia who went to North America after World War I came from the Molotschna has never been established.

In 1930 the collectivization and the deportation of "kulaks" to the slave labor camps (*q.v.*) began. Most of the churches were closed and ministers exiled. The meetinghouses were turned into club houses, nurseries, schools, granaries, etc. All schools became state schools with a Communistic curriculum and philosophy of life. The Mennonite teachers either had to adjust themselves or be exiled.

In 1937-38 in the Molotschna, just as in the other Mennonite settlements, many hundreds of men were taken by night and exiled. Little is known about their fate. Numerous exclusively Russian villages were established among the Mennonite villages of the Molotschna settlement. When the war between Germany and Russia broke out in 1941 many of the Mennonite men and women had to dig trenches west of the Dnepr River. Some were taken prisoners of war there by the German army. During the early days of the German attack the Soviets sent all Mennonite men over 16 years of age eastward. When the German army approached the total remaining population was ordered to meet at the stations of Halbstadt, Stulnevo, Tokmak, Lichtenau, and Feodorovka on Oct. 1, 1941. Those that came to Lichtenau and Feodorovka were loaded on freight trains and sent east. Those who came to the depots of Halbstadt, Tokmak, and Stulnevo waited for five days, when the German army overran the territory, so that none of these were sent eastward. As a result of this evacuation and deportation in the Molotschna some 20 of the Mennonite villages had no Mennonite population left when the German army approached in 1941. They were Altonau, Münsterberg, Blumenstein, Lichtenau, Lindenau, Ohrloff, Tiege, Blumenort, Rosenort, Kleefeld, Alexanderkrone, Lichtfelde, Neukirch, Friedensruh, Prangenau, Steinfeld, Elisabethtal, Schardau, Pastwa, and Grossweide. In some other villages the population had shrunk to half its normal size. Since the war information has been received from many of those evacuated; seemingly most of them were settled in Kazakhstan, Siberia. Here their life was at first extremely hard. Many perished and many members of families have not yet been able to locate each other to reunite. During the most recent years conditions seem to have improved. Even worship services have been arranged for, at places.

During the German occupation of the Molotschna the Mennonites who had remained in the area began to revive their former way of living in the realm of agriculture, religious life, and education. Gradually the Mennonites began to farm privately; ministers were elected, churches reopened, and religious instruction and baptismal services were held. All this was of short duration. In the fall of 1943, when the German army withdrew, the total remaining Molotschna Mennonite population also went westward by wagons to be settled in the Warthegau, their old ancestral home along the Vistula River in western Poland. When the Red army invaded Germany in 1945, the newly resettled Mennonites fled westward with the local population. At the end of the war some of the refugees found themselves in the Russian zone of Germany. Most of them were forcibly repatriated. Even some of those who had escaped into the British, American, and French zones were seized and returned to Russia. It is estimated that some 35,000 Mennonites had been evacuated from Russia to Germany in 1943, but only some 12,000 of them found their way to Canada and South America; the rest were sent back to Russia. We can assume that of these 12,000 emigrants not more than half were from the Molotschna settlement. With the help of American Mennonite relief agencies they found new homes in South America and Canada. Little is known about the present fate of the 60 villages and hamlets which constituted the Molotschna settlement, one of the most prosperous undertakings in Mennonite history, except that their former Mennonite inhabitants have been scattered over Siberia, Central Asia, Canada, and South America. Recent correspondence received from Russia indicates that some Mennonite families either stayed in the Molotschna villages or returned after World War II. If the report regarding the village of Liebenau is typical, there must be a number of Mennonite families residing in the Molotschna villages today. An eyewitness reported in 1957 that of the 53 original prewar buildings of Liebenau, only 8 still stand. Among the 15 families living

in the village, there were some Mennonites, some of whom had intermarried with Russians. Liebenau and the neighboring Russian village of Ostriekovka together formed a collective farm. (*Menn. Rundschau,* July 10, 1957, p. 2.) Similar reports have come from other places in the Molotschna settlement.

There are also indications of worship services attended by Mennonites in the Molotschna region; whether Baptist - sponsored or Mennonite is not known. Now that there is greater freedom of movement in Russia, people from Northern and Eastern Russia return to visit their home community in the Molotschna. Whether nostalgia and newly won freedom will make it possible for greater numbers to return and to concentrate in some areas or villages remains to be seen. (See also **Russia, Ukraine,** and articles under churches and institutions referred in this article.)   C.K.

Friesen, *Brüderschaft;* F. Isaac, *Die Molotschnaer Mennoniten* (Halbstadt, 1908); H. Görz, *Die Molotschnaer Ansiedlung* (Steinbach, Man., 1951); B. H. Unruh, *Die niederländisch-niederdeutschen Hintergründe der mennonitischen Ostwanderungen* (Karlsruhe, 1955); A. Klaus, *Unsere Kolonien* (Odessa, 1887); C. E. Bondar, *Sekta Mennonitov v Rossii* (Petrograd, 1916); Adolf Ehrt, *Das Mennonitentum in Russland von seiner Einwanderung bis zur Gegenwart* (Berlin, 1932); D. G. Rempel, "The Menn. Colonies in New Russia . . . 1789-1914" (unpublished doctoral dissertation at Stanford University, California, 1933); C. Krahn, ed., *From the Steppes to the Prairies* (Newton, 1949); D. H. Epp, *Johann Cornies* (Ekaterinoslav and Berdyansk, 1909, and reprint Steinbach, Man., 1946); J. Quiring, *Die Mundart von Chortitza in Süd-Russland* (Munich, 1928); Gerhard Fast, "The Mennonites under Stalin and Hitler," *Menn. Life* II (April 1947) 18 ff.; A. Petzholdt, *Reise im Westlichen und südlichen europäischen Russland im Jahre 1855* (Leipzig, 1864); J. Neufeld, "Die Flucht, 1943-46," *Menn. Life* VI (January 1951) 8 ff.; Horst Quiring, "Die Auswanderung der Mennoniten aus Preussen 1788-1870," *Menn. Life* VI (April 1951) 37 ff.; H. Dirks, *Statistik* (Gnadenfeld, 1906); "Statistik . . . ," *Unser Blatt* II (1926) 51; "Aus vergilbten Papieren," *Unser Blatt* I (1926) 171 f.; D. H. Epp, "Historische Uebersicht über den Zustand der Mennonitengemeinden an der Molotschna vom Jahre 1836," *Unser Blatt* III (1928) 110-12, 138-43; Hermann Epp, "From the Vistula to the Dnieper," *Menn. Life* VI (October 1951) 14 ff.; H. Dirks, *Mennonitisches Jahrbuch* (1903-13); *Die Mennoniten-Gemeinden in Russland . . . 1914 bis 1920* (Heilbronn, 1921); *ML* III, 154-58.

Molotschna Agricultural Association was organized at Halbstadt in the Molotschna Mennonite settlement, Ukraine, in 1912. During the first year a membership of 90 was reached. A subdivision of the association was a society concerned with the improvement of the breeds of horses and cattle at Molotschna. The promoter of the association was Johann Wiebe of Ohrloff, a nephew of Johann Cornies. Little is known about the scope of its activities. (Dirks, *Jahrbuch, 1911-12,* 164.)   C.K.

Molotschna Fire Insurance, Molotschna Mennonite settlement, South Russia, was organized in the early days of the settlement on principles established earlier among the Mennonites of Prussia. Each village had a fire warden (*Brandschulze*), and each district (*volost*) a fire marshal (*Brandältester*). A special commission inspected the houses to see whether they were built and maintained in line with the instructions of the fire insurance organization. Every village had and maintained a fire engine located in a special building in the center of the village next to the school.   C.K.

H. Goerz, *Die Molotschnaer Ansiedlung* (Steinbach, 1951) 184.

Molotschna Home for the Aged, located on the Kurushan River in the Molotschna Mennonite settlement, South Russia, was started on 90 acres of community land owned by the Halbstadt *volost* (district) in 1903 as a centennial monument to the founding of the Molotschna settlement. The land was donated, and the capital for the building of a 40,000 ruble structure was raised through assessment. The large modern brick building opened in 1906 was equipped to house 50 guests, but was to be enlarged to accommodate 100. The charges for the guests per person were 10 rubles per month. The cost of maintenance for 50 guests amounted to 6,000 rubles per year. The home was managed by a committee of which Elder A. Görz was the chairman in 1910. Among those who served as house parents were Mr. and Mrs. J. Epp and F. Willms.   C.K.

P. M. Friesen, *Brüderschaft,* 661; H. Goerz, *Die Molotschnaer Ansiedlung* (Steinbach, 1951) 150; Dirks, *Jahrbuch, 1911-12,* 113.

Molotschnaer Evangelische *Mennonitenbrüderschaft* was organized at Yushanlee, Molotschna, Russia, on May 16, 1905, the protocol of the founding being signed by Isaak Ediger, Peter Schmidt, H. Günter (as elders), A. Nachtigal (minister), N. Ediger, P. Enns, C. Klaassen, J. Boschmann, P. Stobbe, P. Ediger, J. Dick, J. Boldt, J. Enns, Jakob Dick, H. Harder (members). In 1905 the congregation had a council of elders (*Aeltestenrat*), with Isaak Ediger as leading minister; in 1910 the elder was H. Günter.

The reason for founding a new congregation by accepting and soliciting members from other congregations was given as follows: (1) "That members of a church of God must believe with all their heart in Jesus Christ . . ." and (2) "There was a desire for fellowship with all children of God who are concerned with walking uprightly before God. . . ." Some of the members of the Mennonite Brethren Church were voted into the council of elders: Jakob Reimer, Peter Unruh, and Jakob Kröker.

The background and cause for the founding of this congregation was the influence and work of men like Fr. Wil. Bädeker (*q.v.*) and Ströter, who emphasized unity of believers, the body of Christ or the congregation, the second coming of Christ, etc. A warm evangelism prevailed in the group and it was an aim to have fellowship with children of God outside their own group on broader scale than was customary among the Mennonites of Russia. Baptism by immersion was practiced, but sprinkling and pouring were also recognized. (For additional details concerning the background see **Evangelische Mennoniten-Gemeinden.**) The congregation had a place of worship in the village of Lichtfelde.

Under the Soviets the new congregation disintegrated. Many of its members were exiled and others emigrated to Canada and South America. In Canada they organized into similar congregations which later joined the Mennonite Brethren Church; in

Brazil they organized and joined the General Conference Mennonite Church, while in Paraguay they still exist as the Evangelische Mennoniten-Gemeinde.   C.K.

Friesen, *Brüderschaft,* 722-24; H. Dirks, *Statistik . . .* (1905) 59, 69.

Molotschnaer Mennoniten-Kirchenkonvent (a conference of ministers and elders) was organized by the ministers and elders of the churches of the Molotschna Mennonite settlement around 1850, although (according to Isaac) it was probably loosely functioning under different names before this date. Many of the documents published by Isaac even before 1850 bear such titles as "Vorstand" or "geistlicher Lehrdienst." Sometimes the term "Kirchenkonvent" is used to refer to the ministers of a single congregation. Gradually the name "Molotschnaer Mennoniten-Kirchenkonvent" came into use to include the elders and ministers of all congregations of the Molotschna settlement. The Kirchenkonvent met regularly to discuss significant questions pertaining to the spiritual life and well-being of the individual churches and the total brotherhood. Resolutions passed at the meeting were presented to the individual congregations for approval.

At the time of the revival caused by evangelists like Eduard Wüst (*q.v.*), with the result that several new Mennonite branches were founded, the Kirchenkonvent dealt with the problems arising from this movement. When the General Conference (*Allgemeine Bundeskonferenz, q.v.*) was founded in 1910, this body took care of most of the problems, particularly the executive committee of this Conference, known as the *Kommission für Kirchenangelegenheiten (q.v.)* or *KjK.*   C.K.

H. Görz, *Die Molotschnaer Ansiedlung* (Steinbach, 1950); F. Isaac, *Die Molotschnaer Mennoniten* (Halbstadt, 1908).

Molotschnaer Mennonitischer Schulrat (Molotschna Mennonite School Board) was created in 1869 to supervise and promote the educational program of the Halbstadt and Gnadenfeld districts of the Molotschna settlement, Ukraine, South Russia. The seal of the organization was in Russian ("Petchat Molotchanskago Mennonitskago Utchilishchnago Soveta"). This organization took over the responsibilities and functions of the Agricultural Association (*q.v.*) in the realm of education. The first chairman of the organization was Philipp Wiebe. Other members were Peter Schmidt, Andreas Voth, Franz Dyck, and Peter Isaak. Representatives of the ministry during the first years were Isaac Peters of Pordenau, Dietrich Gaeddert of Alexanderwohl. Later significant members were Aron Rempel, Gustav Rempel, Daniel Unger, Abr. Görz, Heinrich Ediger, Gerhard Klassen, Heinrich Franz, H. A. Neufeld, Heinrich J. Janzen, Heinrich Jantz, Peter A. Ediger, Heinrich Unruh, J. K. Klett, P. H. Heese, David Nickel, Peter Unruh, Jacob Esau, Johann Dürksen, Benjamin Ratzlaff, and David Claassen.

Branches of the Molotschna Schulrat were formed in the Crimea, Brazol, Zagradovka, etc. The periods of the Schulrat activities can be divided as follows: (1) Under Andreas Voth the foundations were laid. He created a fund of 2,000 rubles to help young men prepare for the teaching profession, and received from the government the silver medal "For Zeal." Before he retired all the schools in the Molotschna settlement had adopted a uniform curriculum and had introduced the Russian language as a subject. He promoted teachers' conferences (*Lehrerkonferenzen*) and the introduction of Mädchenschulen (secondary schools for girls), a parallel to the Zentralschulen (secondary schools for boys). (2) The second period followed under P. H. Heese and J. K. Klett (1884-96), both of whom deserve much credit for the continued interest in the improvement of the elementary and secondary education among the Mennonites of the Molotschna settlement and in Russia in general. (3) The third period of the Molotschna Mennonite Schulrat is marked by a decline (1896-1914). During this period of Russian nationalism when the Mennonite educational system was subjected to the Department of Education, the activities of the Schulrat were paralyzed. Other organizations took its place. (See **Mennonite Teachers' Conference**, Russia.)   C.K.

Friesen, *Brüderschaft*, 645; D. P. Enns, "Die mennonitischen Schulen in Russland," *Mennonitisches Jahrbuch* (Newton, 1950); Peter Braun, "The Educational System of the Mennonite Colonies in South Russia," *MQR* III (1929) 169-82.

Momber, a widely ramified family, which is found in the records of the Danzig Mennonite Church as far back as 1650, and which lived for the most part in Danzig until the end of the 19th century. The progenitor of the family, Anthony de Momper (b. 1580 in Amsterdam, d. about 1610 in Danzig), emigrated from the Netherlands to Danzig on account of religious oppression, and changed the name to Momber.

The Dutch ancestors of Anthony Momber can be traced back to 1440 in Brugge, Belgium. Jean de Momper I and his son Jean de Momper II (1485-1540), noted landscape painters in Brugge, were Catholic. The next son, Jodocus (Joos) de Momper I, alias van Lyons (b. 1516 in Brugge, d. 1580 in Antwerp), also a painter, became a Calvinist. His son Bartholomäus I (b. 1535, famed painter, publisher, art dealer, and guildmaster in Amsterdam) was the father of Jodocus (Joos) de Momper II (1564-1635), who is still known for his landscapes in various European galleries, and who was a painter, etcher, and guildmaster in Antwerp, a friend of van Dyck and probably also of Rembrandt. Van Dyck and de Momper painted each other's portraits.

Another son of Jodocus I, Hendrik de Momper (Momboir, b. 1540 in Amsterdam), was the father of the emigrant Anthony de Momper mentioned above. Anthony as well as his brothers Hendrick and Hans, who stayed in Amsterdam, became Mennonites. Another Anthony Momber was a member and probably a deacon of the Flemish congregation of Amsterdam in 1629 (*Inv. Arch. Amst.* II, 2, No. 571). Anthony's descendants in Danzig were craftsmen. Many served in various offices in the Mennonite congregation in Danzig. Abraham Momber, the oldest representative listed in the church records of Danzig (Oct. 3, 1650-May 20, 1712), was chosen deacon by the Flemish congregation in Danzig in 1694, and preacher in 1703. His wife Maria de Veer (1661-1742) was appointed as deaconess of the congregation in 1720. Anton Momber (1670-1735) was widely known as the founder of the first coffeehouse in Danzig (about 1700), in which German and foreign newspapers were read and which was comparable to the London coffeehouse. At the home of Jacob Momber (1704-72), a merchant, the elders of the congregation held a meeting to discuss arrangements for the care of the poor and a place for religious services during the bombardment of Danzig in 1734.

His son Hans Momber I (1742-1815), a deacon and preacher in the Flemish congregation, was according to the church chronicles, "gifted with rich talents and skilled in speaking and writing." For several years he collaborated with Peter Thiessen and Jakob de Veer in compiling the first German hymnal for the Danzig church, translating some hymns from the Dutch and writing others himself. Some of his hymns are still to be found in the Danzig hymnal. He had a special gift for composing hymns for special occasions, some of which have been preserved. He was a leader in the merger of the Flemish and Frisian branches of the brotherhood in 1808.

His cousin Berend Momber (March 15, 1755-April 25, 1840), a merchant, was the first Mennonite to acquire citizenship when Danzig was incorporated in Prussia. The Danzig state library contained his extensive manuscript of the history of his family during the siege. His wife Cäcilie lost her life in the bombardment of the city in 1813.

August Momber (March 9, 1807-Dec. 16, 1882) established the linen business that grew from small beginnings into one of Danzig's leading industries. In 1869 he became a member of the church council. He took an active part in the change in the position of the congregation on nonresistance, mixed marriages, and the admission of members of related groups. He cheerfully sacrificed for the common good, and enjoyed the esteem of all.

When he lost his sight in 1880 his son Julius Momber (Dec. 25, 1839-Dec. 5, 1900) succeeded him on the church council. He and his brother Otto (Jan. 30, 1847-May 5, 1929) carried on the paternal business.

Julius was from 1876 an active member of the church council and promoter of the Vereinigung (*q.v.*; Conference of German Mennonite Churches). In the political life of his city he filled several posts of honor, and was also a patron of the arts.

The oldest son of August Momber, Albert Momber (July 26, 1837-June 6, 1909), was a teacher in the Danzig Gymnasium and in 1901 took the place of his deceased brother Julius on the church council. He was a highly honored figure in the public life of the city. The name was still common in the congregation at the time of its dispersal in 1945. Some members of this family were found in Königsberg (*q.v.*), East Prussia, while Hermann Momber was a "possementierer" (lacemaker, or merchant) and a distiller of brandy about 1735. Others were found in Berlin.   W.M.

H. G. Mannhardt, *Die Danziger Mennonitengemeinde* (Danzig, 1919); *Menn. Bl.; ADB* XXII, 158-60; family archives; *Gesch.-Bl.* VIII (1956) 22, 27 f.; *ML* III, 158 f.

Mömpelgard: see **Montbéliard**.

Momper, Jodocus de, a painter: see **Momber.**

Monatsblätter *aus Bethel College,* later *Monatsblätter,* successor to *School and College Journal,* was the 16-page, 6½ x 9, monthly periodical published by the board of directors of Bethel College January 1903-June 1918, when it was succeeded by the *Bethel College Monthly,* an all-English publication. From January 1903 to December 1909 it was a separate publication issued in a parallel series with the *Bethel College Monthly.* From January 1909 to June 1918 it was published in combination with the *Bethel College Monthly,* appearing ten times a year during this period. Its purpose was to promote the denominational and religious interests of Mennonites through the publication of articles of Biblical, historical, and general cultural interest. Its aim was to gain friends for higher education among Mennonites. David Goerz, its editor 1903-8, wrote extensively on deaconess work and his travels to India and Russia. Other editors were P. H. Richert, P. J. Wedel, Emil R. Riesen, J. H. Langenwalter, J. F. Balzer, and H. H. Wiebe. J.F.S.

Mönchshof, an estate near Schweinfurt, Bavaria, Germany, which was farmed by Mennonites until the end of the 19th century, who together with those at Bildhausen (*q.v.*) formed a Mennonite congregation (*Menn. Bl.,* 1856, 80), which has been merged with the Trappstadt (*q.v.*) congregation since the 1880's. (*ML* III, 160.) NEFF.

Monchy, de, a Dutch family of French Protestant descent, which about 1650 moved to the Netherlands as military officers, settling at Gouda. Many members of this family, from about 1740 living at Rotterdam, Holland, were Mennonites. The first de Monchys in Rotterdam were brewers and distillers; after about 1800 they were mostly engaged in trading, banking, and the directorate of the Holland-America Line. Two of them were noted physicians of Rotterdam. S. J. R. de Monchy (b. 1880 at Rotterdam), also a Mennonite, was burgomaster of Arnhem 1921-34 and of The Hague 1934-50. Marius Jacobus de Monchy, b. 1909 at Rotterdam, a musician and composer, is an organist in the Rotterdam Mennonite Church. The following members of this family served in the Rotterdam Mennonite church council: Engel Pieter de Monchy I (1793-1883), a merchant, later president of the Nederlandsche Handel-Maatschappij (Dutch Trading Co.), a member of the First Chamber of the States-General, who also was a trustee of the A.D.S. (Dutch Mennonite General Conference); then Michiel Marinus de Monchy (1820-98), a merchant, thereupon president of the Rotterdam Bank, Salomon Jean René de Monchy (1824-1917), director of a trading company, Engel Pieter de Monchy II (1836-1919), a broker, all three sons of Engel Pieter de Monchy I, Salomon Jean René de Monchy II (1863-1930), a merchant, and Henri Gérard Jean de Monchy (1882-), son of Engel Pieter de Monchy II, director of a trading company. vDZ.

Ned. Patriciaat XXV (1935) 142-62; *N.N.B.Wb.* I, 1342-45; IV, 1006 f.

Mönchzell, a village in the Heidelberg district of Baden, Germany, pop. (1933) 582, railway station Meckesheim on the Elsenz, was from 1896 to 1916 the seat of a Mennonite congregation. Previously Meckesheim (*q.v.*) had been the center; in 1916 the congregation merged with the Sinsheim (*q.v.*) congregation. Services were held every two weeks on the Mönchzell estate. There were approximately 36 members. The family names were Bechtel, Fellmann, Mosemann, and Binkele. (*ML* III, 160.) W.F.

Mongolia, a highland on the continent of Asia, which now belongs to Russia. In Inner Mongolia, the smaller southern division of the country, the Krimmer Mennonite Brethren of America opened a mission in the city of Chotzeshan, about 250 miles north of Peking, with several subsidiary stations. Buildings were erected for evangelization, school, and hospital. The inhabitants of the city and the district showed a wish for the Gospel and participated actively in the services. The establishment of the Communist regime in China in 1950 put an end to the mission. (*ML* III, 160). HEGE.

Monnikendam (Monnickendam), a town (1947 population 2,762, with 169 Mennonites) in the Dutch province of North Holland, from the beginning of the Reformation a center of Protestant activity. On Nov. 20, 1527, Wendelmoet Claes (*q.v.*) of Monnikendam was burned at the stake in The Hague. Though this martyr is listed in *Offer des Heeren* and the later Dutch martyrbooks including van Braght's *Martyrs' Mirror,* she was not an Anabaptist in the strict sense but a "Sacramentist" (*q.v.*), a group which helped to prepare the soil upon which Anabaptism could flourish.

In Monnikendam there were soon many Anabaptists. In 1534 the Catholic priest of Monnikendam reported that probably two thirds of the city was "contaminated with the Anabaptist doctrine." In 1535 the persecution in North Holland began, with its center in Monnikendam. Many Anabaptists hid in the reeds or fled to Amsterdam. Therefore the number of Anabaptist victims who were natives of Monnikendam is not very high. At Monnikendam Arent Jacobsz was executed in 1539 with his wife and son. Among the Anabaptists of Monnikendam revolutionary Münsterite influence was very strong, and many of them were in the boats which crossed the Zuiderzee in March 1534 en route to Münster. When the persecution subsided there was a large group of peaceful Anabaptists in the city. Leenaert Bouwens (*q.v.*) baptized 62 persons here in 1563-65 and later another six persons. Pieter Willems Bogaert (*q.v.*), who was a preacher (*ca.* 1565) and elder (1588) of the Frisian congregation at Monnikendam, presented to William of Orange the considerable sum the Dutch Mennonites had raised to help in the liberation of Holland from the Spanish yoke. Concerning the history of the Mennonites of Monnikendam there is little information. Besides the Frisian congregation there was a Waterlander congregation, with which the Frisian seems to have merged soon after 1600.

In 1675 the Monnikendam congregation, then numbering 150 members, requested admission to the Lamist Sociëteit. Some four decades earlier it had joined the Rijper (Waterlander) Sociëteit. In all the collections organized by the Dutch Committee of Foreign Needs, several times in 1672-1736 in behalf of the persecuted Mennonites in Switzerland, the Palatinate, Jülich, Prussia, and Lithuania, the congregation of Monnikendam contributed liberally, though their number was rather small and decreased with the decline in the population of the town whose business of shipping to the Baltic Sea was severely injured by the wars in which Holland was involved at that time.

In 1771-1806 Jan Nieuwenhuyzen (q.v.), founder of the "Maatschappij tot nut van 't Algemeen" (q.v.), served the Monnikendam congregation as preacher. He was followed by Govert Jans van Rijswijk 1806-8, Reitze de Vries 1809-14, and 1817-58, Jacob Julius 1860-62, J. van der Ploeg 1863-83, S. J. Dekker 1884-91, J. N. Wiersma 1894-96, E. M. ten Cate 1896-1904, E. Pekema 1907-9, F. F. Milatz 1910-18, and P. H. Veen 1919-33. After a vacancy of nearly two years in the pulpit the congregation made an agreement in February 1935 with the neighboring Edam (q.v.) congregation, and has since been served by the Edam pastor.

Concerning membership no figures were available for the 19th century. In 1847 the baptized membership numbered 60; it was 85 in 1897, 74 in 1955. There is a ladies' circle. The present church dates from the 19th century; it has a copper lectern from the 17th century, no doubt from a former meetinghouse. vdZ.

Inv. Arch. Amst. I, Nos. 20, 31, 75, 80, 94, 98-100, 110, 113, 116 f., 137, 445, 708, 860, 1164, 1180; II, Nos. 2142 f.; II, 2, No. 296; Blaupot t. C., *Holland* I, 24, 44, 332, 355; II, 204, 232; Kühler, *Geschiedenis* I, 87, 173-75, 340, 349; Mellink, *Wederdopers*, 158-64 and *passim*; *ML* III, 160.

Monnikendam, Keizer van, an Anabaptist martyr: see **Arent Jacobssen.**

Monroe County (Miss.) Amish settlement, now extinct. A small colony of Old Order Amish moved to western Monroe Co. and eastern Chickasaw Co., Miss., from Newton Co., Ind., in the winter of 1895-96. The address of the settlement was Gibson and Aberdeen. The first to acquire land in Monroe County were John T. Yoder and Eli E. Miller, when they purchased two plantations with 3,300 acres. The settlement at its largest consisted of about 25 families. By 1904 all of the Amish settlers had sold their land and moved back north. About 1937-38 a few families again bought homes near Aberdeen, and in 1949 about 8-10 families were living in Monroe County, but no congregation developed. J.A.H.

Monroe First Mennonite Church (GCM), located in Monroe, Snohomish Co., Wash., a member of the Pacific District Conference, was organized on April 22, 1918, with 33 charter members, with the help of P. R. Aeschliman. The first settlers came from Oklahoma and Kansas in 1911. The congregation purchased the present church site in 1922. The hall, completely remodeled in 1946, seats 250. The membership in 1956 was 86, with George W. Kopper as pastor. G.W.K.

Monschau (Mondschau, Monjoie, Monjou, Montjoie), a town in the Eifel (q.v.) Mountains in the district of Aachen, Germany, the birthplace of the martyr Maria van Montjoie (q.v.), executed there in 1552. It is not very likely that Maria's death was an isolated instance, but about Anabaptism-Mennonitism in Monschau there is not much information. Elder Theunis van Hastenrath visited Monschau about 1550, but did not preach or baptize in the town. Ottius published a letter of 1557 which states that there were in the Eifel area more than 50 congregations, most of them with a large membership, of Moravian Hutterites (see **Merlanders**). Later there was a Mennonite congregation in or near Monschau. On Jan. 24, 1711, Jan Helgers, preacher of Burtscheid near Aachen, wrote a letter to Abr. Jacob Fries at Amsterdam, informing Fries, the treasurer of the Dutch Committee of Foreign Needs, that the Mennonites of Monschau had been expelled from hearth and home and were now planning to settle in the Dutch province of South Holland; Jan Pluys, their preacher, had already moved there, and they hoped to earn their living by farming. vdZ.

J. H. Ottius, *Annales Anabaptistica* (Basel, 1672) 130; *Inv. Arch. Amst.* I, No. 1305; *DB* 1909, 123; *Der Mennonit* IX (1956) No. 1, p. 10; No. 7, p. 108; Walter Scheibler, *Geschichte der Evangelischen Gemeinde Monschau 1520-1939* (Aachen, 1939) 15-33, "Die Wiedertäufer im Monschauer Land."

Monsheim, a village near Worms, Rhenish Hesse, Germany, since 1820 the seat of a Mennonite congregation. Previously the center had been Kriegsheim (q.v.). At the time of the engagement of the first trained minister, Leonhard Weydmann 1819-36, a new church was built at Monsheim and a parsonage was bought near by. Official records show that the Amsterdam Mennonite Church contributed 600 gilders for this church and parsonage; the proceeds from the sale of the old church in Kriegsheim were also applied to this purchase. The land for the site was apparently donated by the Möllinger family in Monsheim. Much of the work of the building was done by the members according to a fixed schedule and assessment. A workman lost his life in the erection of the building.

In 1836-68 the preacher of the Monsheim congregation was Johannes Molenaar (q.v.), who is known for his formulary, catechism, and hymnal, as well as other literary works. In 1838 several families who were dissatisfied with his work joined another congregation.

In 1859, when the last lay preacher of the neighboring Obersülzen (q.v.) congregation died, that congregation joined with Monsheim for preaching services, though keeping its own organization in all other respects. In 1866 Obersülzen built a church of its own. In that year the congregation at Oberflörsheim (q.v.), which had for some years been served by Molenaar, merged with Monsheim. In 1867 Adolf Ellenberger succeeded Molenaar as pastor at Monsheim, and served until 1889.

Until 1872 the Monsheim congregational singing was led by choristers (*Vorsänger*). "Anyone who has ever had the opportunity to hear such singing will never have a moment's doubt as to its artistic or edificatory value," says one of the old church documents. In 1872 the Monsheim church acquired an organ. In 1881 a new church constitution was adopted, which had been drawn up in 1869 and circulated among the members. It stipulated that the preacher should as a rule have formal training, and the council should have at least six members. Baptism was to be administered in the late summer and communion observed four times annually.

In 1886 the congregation joined the Vereinigung (Conference of German Mennonite Churches), represented in Berlin by Christian Finger, who was also chosen treasurer of the council. In 1886 a fund was established for the congregation. His successor was his son Hermann, who served on the council 1907-29. On Sept. 5, 1889, the congregation was incorporated through the efforts of Jakob Finger (q.v.), the brother of Christian Finger, minister of state. In the fall of 1889 the old parsonage was sold and a new one bought. In 1892 the church was remodeled. The preachers of the congregation in more recent times were Philipp Kieferndorf 1889-94, Gerhard Haake 1896-99, Johannes Hirschler 1899-1926, Walter Fellmann 1927-45, Emil Händiges 1945-54, and Alexander Prieur 1954- . The constitution stipulates that at least 30 services are to be held in Monsheim each year, and 20 in the subsidiary congregation in Obersülzen. In 1895 the Monsheim congregation had about 300 members; in 1939 only about 200, who lived in many neighboring villages. The membership in 1955 was 286, including 74 refugees from the East.　　　　W.F.

Ernst Correll, *Das schweizerische Täufermennonitentum* (Tübingen, 1925); *ML* III, 160 f.

Mont des Oiseaux (German, *Vogelsberg*), the location of a Mennonite children's home in Northern Alsace located within a few rods of the German border near the village of Weiler some three miles from Wissembourg, commonly called the Weiler Children's Home. In the summer of 1945 the Mennonite Central Committee, with the help of several French relief organizations, opened the Weiler Children's Home under the direction of Mme. Roger Georges, for the purpose of giving good food and care to approximately forty undernourished or temporarily homeless war-suffering children between the ages of two and six years. As soon as conditions permitted, the MCC sent food, clothing, and American personnel to the home. The home is surrounded by a beautiful forest which provides unusual opportunity for educational and recreational activities.

In the spring of 1947 Mme. Georges was replaced by an American representative, Mary Byler. During the years that followed, a state-recognized kindergarten was opened, summer Bible camps were organized for children between the ages of 7 and 14, and the main building was enlarged and equipped with modern conveniences. More significant than these physical changes, however, were the changes in the nature and purpose of the work. With time, the need for war relief naturally decreased and the home, trying always to help where the need seemed the greatest, found itself caring for children from divorced or separated parents, illegitimate children, or children whose parents were ill. Increased attention was given to the mission opportunities these homes and children presented.

In 1951 the "Association Fraternelle Mennonite," an official organization of the French Mennonite churches, purchased the children's home property for 6,000,000 French francs (approximately $17,142) plus a 25 per cent sales tax. Then followed a five-year period of transition as MCC help decreased and French participation increased. By the fall of 1956 the home was operating independent of MCC help (except for continued shipments of food and clothing) and under the direction of Regina Nussbaumer, Basel, Switzerland. It is probable that within the near future the home will prepare to receive mentally retarded children in order to meet what appears to be the most urgent present-day need and also in order to receive increased governmental financial support.　　　　M.B.C.

Mont Tramelan, a Mennonite school situated in a French-speaking area of the Bernese Jura, Switzerland. The language of instruction is German. The enrollment is some thirty; the teacher is P. Pulver. This school, like those at La Chaux d'Abel, Montbautier, and Moron, is subsidized by the state, while those of Jeangisboden, La Paturatte, and Le Perceux are financed privately.　　　　vDZ.

Montana was admitted to the Union in 1889. In 1955 the total Mennonite membership in the state was over 800. Soon after 1900 Mennonites began to arrive as individuals and as family groups. The first congregation established was Mountain View (MC), founded in 1903 near Creston not far from Kalispell in the far northwest corner by Amish Mennonite settlers from Oregon. In 1955 it had 98 members. Old Order Amish families settled in Dawson County in 1903, and General Conference Mennonites in 1906.

The Old Order Amish lost several members through migration; the rest joined the Red Top Mennonite (MC) Church near Bloomfield, Dawson Co., which was organized in 1917. A church was built by this group in 1936 and enlarged in 1952. The membership of the church in 1955 was 59. Some members of the Red Top Mennonite Church moved to the near-by city of Glendive and organized the Little White Chapel congregation in 1948. It acquired a church in 1949, which was remodeled in 1952. The membership in 1955 was 39. Another small Mennonite (MC) group was reported at Coalridge, Sheridan Co., with 10 members in 1955, organized as a congregation in 1916.

General Conference Mennonites who settled in Dawson County in 1906 organized the Bethlehem Mennonite Church (q.v.) at Bloomfield in 1910. The first meetinghouse was built in 1912 and was enlarged several times. Membership of this group was 155 in 1955. Several families of this group settled in Glendive, building their own house of worship in 1948. In 1950 it became an independent congregation, with a membership of 60 in 1955.

General Conference Mennonites and Mennonite Brethren settled along the Missouri River at Frazer and Wolf Point and north as far as Lustre and Larslan in eastern Valley County during the early years of World War I (1915-16). The Northern District (GCM) sent workers to the Lustre-Bethel area from 1917 on. In 1924 the groups at Lustre and Volt organized as the Bethel Mennonite Church (q.v.). This congregation numbered 84 members in 1955. The Bethel Mennonite Church (q.v.) at Wolf Point is first reported in 1935. In 1955 this congregation totaled 83 members.

The Mennonite Brethren organized a church at Lustre (q.v.) in 1917, erecting a church building in 1923. A group at Volt also organized in 1917 but has been affiliated with the Lustre group. The total Lustre M.B. congregation numbered 133 in 1952. The group at Larslan (q.v.) was organized in 1945, and in 1952 reported a membership of 37. Small groups of Mennonite Brethren existed for brief periods at Chinook, Whitefish, Hydro, and Poplar.

The Evangelical Mennonite Brethren were also represented in the original settlement of the community about Lustre (q.v.). This group was organized in 1917, building its first meetinghouse the same year, and a new church ten years later. In 1954 its total membership was 103.

All of the Mennonite churches in Montana are located in the far northeast corner of the state, except the congregation at Creston in the far northwest corner.

All Mennonite groups in Montana passed through a particularly painful crisis during World War I. The use of German was prohibited in the church services and the minister at the Bethlehem Mennonite at Bloomfield was abducted and held prisoner under threat of being lynched. (See *Menn. Life*, October 1952.)

One institution is being sponsored in Montana on an inter-Mennonite basis, viz., Lustre Bible Academy.

The G.C.M. Church established extensive mission work among the Cheyenne Indians on the Tongue River Reservation in Southwestern Montana. This was begun in 1904 by Mr. and Mrs. G. A. Linscheid, followed by others, including Mr. and Mrs. Rodolphe Petter in 1916. Churches have been maintained at Busby (q.v.), Lame Deer (q.v.), and Birney (q.v.) with a total membership of 283 in 1950.

In 1952 there were 11 Hutterite Bruderhofs in Montana, with a total population of 919. The four Dariusleut (q.v.) Bruderhofs, settled in 1935 and 1945-47, were located near Lewistown, the seven Lehrerleut Bruderhofs, all settled in 1945-50 mostly between Choteau and Valier, with one almost at the Alberta border near Sweetgrass, and south of Augusta. By 1955 an additional Lehrerleut Bruderhof was settled near Cut Bank, almost at the Alberta border. (See article **Hutterian Brethren**, with maps.) J.F.S.

John H. Lohrenz, *The Mennonite Brethren Church* (Hillsboro, 1950); G. S. Rempel, *A Historical Sketch of the Churches of the Evangelical Mennonite Brethren* (Rosthern, 1939); *Menn. Life* IX (July 1954) and VII (October 1952); *Minutes and Reports*, Northern District Conference (GCM); "Missions, Home and Foreign, of the General Conference Mennonite Church" (Mennonite Biblical Seminary, Chicago, 1953); Chris A. Buller, "Fifty Years in Dawson County, Montana," *Menn. Life* IX (July 1954); Rufus M. Franz, "It Happened in Montana," *Menn. Life* VII (October 1952).

Montanus, Herman, a Reformed "alumnus" in Leiden, later a Remonstrant (q.v.) preacher, and finally, attracted by Socinianism, he joined in the criticism of the traditional doctrines of the church. In 1647 he wrote a booklet on the inadequacy of infant baptism, with the title *Nietigheydt van de Kinder-doop, noyt voor desen soo overvloedelyk ende klaerlyk uyt kerckelycke historien, Oudvaderen, en voornamelyck uyt de H. Schrift bewesen* (Amsterdam, 1647, 1648, 1700, 1702, 1848). On the basis of the sources he proves that infant baptism is unscriptural, and that in spite of Tertullian's protest Augustine established the ceremony as a general church custom in the fourth century. He attributes the gradual replacement of adult baptism by infant baptism to Augustine's doctrine of original sin, which counts newborn infants as sinful. Montanus names all those who through the centuries protested against infant baptism, and shows (at least apparently) that in certain localities of Italy adult baptism was practiced throughout the Middle Ages. The Mennonites are mentioned only once in a marginal note. Does this indicate that Montanus was interested primarily in the criticism of the church, and only secondarily in faith? Or did he assume that Mennonite practice was known? He names (p. 91) Pacimontanus, i.e., Hubmaier (q.v.), who died at the stake in Vienna, and who opposed Luther's teaching. On the whole the book still deserves to be read as a compilation of material opposing infant baptism, aside from the considerable material on the subject which had already been written by the Mennonites. (*ML* III, 162). H.Q.

Montanus, Johannes Fabricius: see **Fabricius Johannes.**

Montau, a Mennonite congregation in former West Prussia, near Neuenburg (Schwetz district). According to documents preserved in Danzig this settlement had existed since 1568, for on Feb. 2, 1568, a number of Dutch Mennonites had moved in from the Danzig Werder—Thomas and Peter Jansen, Leonhard von Rho (garbled; probably Leenaert van Rhoon), Bernhard von Baygen (Berent van Bargen), Andreas (Andries) Unrau, and their companions and relatives—and concluded a rental contract with Hans Dulzky of Roggenhausen; it included the villages of Montau and Sanskau, an area of 50 hooves. The further settlement of the Schwetz-Neuenburg lowlands apparently radiated from here. The documents also indicate the Dutch origin of the settlers. Other evidence of this origin is seen in the architecture and in the Dutch Bibles preserved in some of these homes. Dutch was the language used in preaching until the 18th century. Later, when the Mennonites spread over the entire lowland, a subsidiary church was built at Obergruppe in 1776.

In course of the 16th and 17th centuries there were several additional immigrations from Holland. The Montau group was the first to settle near the left bank of the Vistula River, and gradually spread out over a wide area; as early as 1598 a number of Mennonites from Montau settled near Sanskau to begin the cultivation of this area. Others settled at Gruppe, Deutsch-Westphalen, Gross-Lubin, Neunhuben, Dragass, all in the neighborhood of Montau. In the late 18th century some of its members moved to Brenkenhoffswalde and to Deutsch-Kazun. The area of Montau was in the 17th and 18th centuries struck by various calamities. About 1620 the Mennonites had some difficulty with the governors, but in 1623 obtained freedom from military service and quartering. About 1657 during the Swedish-Polish war Mennonite property was severely damaged by the passing armies; the floods of the Vistula repeatedly damaged the fields and the houses, particularly in 1677, when a number of farms were destroyed and many people and cattle perished, and many fields were ruined by the sand washed over them. A few years later they suffered a total crop failure. In 1727 the passing armies (Polish, Saxon, Swedish, Russian) plundered the farms to such an extent that they had to sell some of their land to pay their taxes. After 1772, when this area was occupied by Prussia, conditions were somewhat improved; but during the Napoleonic wars (1806-15) the congregation again suffered severely. In many of their tribulations the Montau Mennonites were financially supported by the Dutch Mennonites.

In the 16-18th centuries the Montau congregation belonged to the Frisian Mennonite branch. At a conference held in Montau in 1586 delegates from Danzig, Elbing, the "Kleine Marienburger Werder," Montau, and Thorn resolved to side with the Frisian party in the Netherlands. The first elder was very probably Hilchen Schmidt (Hylke Smit), who was commissioned by the Haarlem congregation in 1588 to depose Quiryn van der Meulen (q.v.) from the office of elder in Danzig.

The date of the building of the first church is not certain. But records show that there was one in 1568. This was a frame building with thatched roof. By 1859 it had become so badly ruined by several floods of the Vistula that it had to be practically rebuilt. The congregation later had two large churches, one in Montau with a small tower and a clock, which was built in 1898, Sister (a deaconess) Marie Schröder having willed a large amount to the congregation for this purpose. It had two stained glass windows. The other church was in Gruppe (q.v.), without a tower, built in 1865. The congregation had no cemetery. Concerning the membership there are no exact figures before 1789. In the 16th and 17th centuries the congregation must have been rather small, apparently not more than 100 baptized members, but during the 18th century there was a rapid increase. In 1789 the membership (including children), numbered 847; 829 in 1845, 536 in 1917, 375 in 1941 (300 baptized members and 75 children).

Montau was served by the following elders after about 1661: Hans Baltzer (1628-1706), from ca. 1661 until 1702; David Schroeder served probably 1702-6. He was followed by David Block (1663-1756), preacher from 1714, elder 1738-56; Frans Gerts (d. 1757), preacher 1725, elder 1756-57; Abraham Schroeder (1718-81), preacher 1754, elder 1758-81; Steffen Kerber (1732-1800), preacher 1767, elder 1781-1800; Peter Kerber (1759-1814), preacher 1795, elder 1801-14; Peter Kerber, Jr. (1782-1821), preacher 1801, elder 1814-18; Hans Goerz (1792-1829), preacher 1814, elder 1821-29; Peter Foth (1793-1850), preacher 1826, elder 1830-50; Isaac Kopper (1809-56), preacher 1831, elder 1850-56; Peter Bartel (1813-

79), preacher 1840, elder 1856-79; Gerhard Kopper (1840-1928), preacher 1871, elder 1881-1925; Wilhelm Tyart (1868-1932), preacher 1897 in Gruppe, elder Montau-Gruppe 1926-32; Bernhard Kopper, preacher 1924, elder 1934-45.

For centuries the congregation held to the old doctrines and practices, including nonresistance. The North German law issued on Nov. 9, 1867, threatening to deprive the Mennonites of their old privilege of freedom of military service also confused the congregation in Montau. After much correspondence and several audiences at Berlin, the church council accepted a new church constitution drawn up by Elder Peter Bartel, which permitted members to accept noncombatant service, as offered by the Order of Cabinet of March 3, 1868, but threatened to excommunicate those choosing military service; this was, however, never carried out. The question of military service caused the Obergruppe congregation to split off from the Montau church in 1869; the new group refused to tolerate soldiers as members, whereas the Montau congregation did not exclude such members. In 1920 the breach was healed, and the combined brotherhood was then called the Montau-Gruppe congregation.

Church records were kept since the 17th century. The important documents were preserved in the Danzig archives. In the village of Gruppe the congregation had an almshouse.

A large endowment for ministers' salaries vanished during the inflation of 1923. The members were mostly farmers, though there were also tradesmen and craftsmen among them. In 1939 the congregation had about 400 members, who lived in the neighboring villages and the cities of Graudenz and Neuenburg. Between 1918 and 1939, while the area belonged to Poland, some German members of the congregation were expelled to Germany; other emigrations also took place. Though there were some transfers from other denominations, the membership declined by about one hundred. In 1945 the congregation was dissolved by mass flight westward like all the other Prussian congregations.

G.K., vDZ.

L. Stobbe, *Montau-Gruppe. Ein Gedenkblatt an die Besiedlung der Schwetz - Neuenburger Niederlassung* (Montau, 1918); H. Wiebe, *Das Siedlungswerk niederländischer Mennoniten im Weichseltal* (Marburg a. d. Lahn, 1952) 18 ff., 47, 73 ff.; Felicia Szper, *Nederl. Nederzettingen in West-Pruisen gedurende den Poolschen tijd* (Enkhuizen, 1913) 139 f., 203, 206; *Inv. Arch. Amst.* I, Nos. 1564, 1609, 1647 f., 1652, 1667 f.; II, 2626, 2651; *ML* III, 162 f.

Montauerweide, in the Marienburg Marsh near the Vistula, West Prussia, was in 1730 rented in long-lease to a number of Dutch farmers; soon the majority of the inhabitants were Mennonites, belonging to the congregation of Zwanzigerweide, later Tragheimerweide (q.v.). Among the names are Unrau (6), Stobbe (3), Penner (2), Sibert (2), Schultz (2), Harder, Claass, Tgart, Ewert, Harm, Pauls, Jantz, Nickel, Ediger, Frantz, Bartel, Woelms, Block Baltzer.

vDZ.

Felicia Szper, *Ned. Nederzettingen in West-Pruisen* (Enkhuizen, 1913) 122 f.; H. Wiebe, *Das Siedlungswerk niederländischer Mennoniten im Weichseltal* (Marburg a. d. Lahn, 1952) 40, 84 f.

Montbautier, a Mennonite school in the Bernese Jura, Switzerland; the teacher is A. Amstutz, and the enrollment about thirty. Although it is located in a French-speaking area, the teaching medium of this school is German. It is subsidized by the government. vdZ.

Montbéliard (Mömpelgard), a town (pop. 13,600) in eastern France, close to the Swiss border, 12 miles south of Belfort, is located in a densely settled industrial region. It was once the capital of the gravure of Montbéliard, which was a possession of Württemberg from 1397 to 1796.

The first Mennonites came to Montbéliard as refugees from Bern, Switzerland, in the early 18th century. They had connections with other Mennonites who had fled to the bishopric of Basel in the Swiss Jura and to the gravure of Neuchatel. Others came from the Rappoltstein area which was especially hard hit by the order of Louis XIV expelling the Mennonites from Alsace in 1712. Many Mennonites, especially from the Markirch (Ste-Marie-aux-Mines) (Leber) Valley, went to Montbéliard, and a rather strong congregation was organized in this region. The Mennonites settled exclusively on the estates of Duke Leopold-Eberhard, who had dispossessed many of his subjects and found these foreigners very welcome, the more so when they soon proved themselves to be honest and competent farmers. Their presence was naturally resented by the populace, but they were protected by the counts, although the counts made it clear to the Mennonites that they were merely tolerated and refused to give them any written contracts. The Mennonites were permitted to have their own cemetery, which is still in use, and to organize a school, and they were released from the oath. But they were refused permission to build a church. They began a church record in 1750, the first church record among the Swiss Mennonites. Among the Mennonite family names found in the region of Montbéliard in 1759 were Roth, Frey, Schmucker, Mosimann, Meyer, Krähenbühl, Kohler, Baumgartner, Eicher, Schuhmacher, Oberli, Kauffman, Hostetler, Gerber, and Wählti. From 1765 Hans Rich was for a long time the elder of this Amish congregation.

In 1790 there was a wave of emigration to Poland, the reason for which is no longer clear, when several groups from Montbéliard and some from the Upper Alsatian congregations emigrated to Poland. The old church book, which dates back to 1750, says of the migration: "So Samuel Stoll (preacher) and Christian Känel (elder) with their companions and travelers went away together on Sept. 22, 1790, from Montbéliard to Poland in the Palantinä Värsowie. Hans Schindtler led them as far as Ulm, so they arrived in Ulm on Oct. 4; then they traveled on the Danube to Vienna and arrived on Oct. 24, 1790. May God the Father lead them further." A list compiled in 1793 contains 36 family names with a total of 50 persons (including children) who comprised the congregation.

The French Revolution, which united Montbéliard with France, brought much unrest into the congregation. All citizens had to swear an oath and be enrolled in the National Guard. The Mennonites protested. The central government granted their request and peace was restored in the congregation. Nor were they drafted in the Napoleonic wars. The idea of sending delegates to the emperor with a petition in 1809 originated in Montbéliard.

Up to this time the Mennonites had been renters. But gradually they began to acquire property. This is probably the reason why there was no movement to the interior as was the case in the Lorraine congregations. The German language could also be maintained much longer here. There was repeated influx from Alsace and Switzerland. On the other hand the congregation lost many members to other churches through marriage, and many emigrated to America.

Services were held in private homes in and around Montbéliard, as far as the adjacent portions of the Jura, where many Swiss families had settled. When the congregation built a church in 1833 the mountain families formed a congregation of their own, known as the Seigne congregation (*Sennergemeinde*). This congregation, which had at first a rather large membership, gradually died out, the families moving into the vicinity of Montbéliard and Porrentruy (Pruntrut) in Switzerland.

The Montbéliard congregation also survived a critical period. The determined holding to the German language, which only a few understood, conflict between leading personalities, and lack of contact with other Mennonites had a baneful effect. But conditions soon changed. Ministers from Switzerland visited the congregation. The French language was adopted for singing and preaching. Conference activity increased, and signs of a new life became apparent.

The Montbéliard congregation suffered least during World War I, since it was not in a zone of combat. Also many of its members were citizens of Switzerland and were consequently not drafted. Religious services could continue regularly. After the war a new increase came from Alsace with increased life, so that the old "du Canal" church, in use from 1832, became too small. A new church was built at la Prarie and dedicated in 1930, with a seating capacity of 400. Services are held here every Sunday, besides Sunday school, prayer meetings, Bible study, hymn sings, and evangelistic meetings. The membership, numbering 250 in 1795, 150 in 1887, was 300 in 1956, including unbaptized children. P.So.

Church records; Delbert L. Gratz, *Bernese Anabaptists* (Scottdale, 1953) 85, 87-89; Mannhardt, *Jahrbuch* 1888, 42; *ML* III, 163 f.

Monterey Mennonite Church (MC), located on Route 1, Bird-in-Hand, at the little village of Monterey in Upper Leacock Twp., Lancaster Co., Pa., is a member of the Ohio and Eastern Conference. The first meetings of the congregation were held the first Sunday of October 1946. The membership is largely urban. Glenn Esh was ordained by the congregation and serves as its minister; O. N. Johns is the bishop. The membership in 1956 was 200. G.Es.

Montevideo (pop. *ca.* 750,000), the capital of Uruguay, has had some Mennonite inhabitants ever since the first European Mennonite immigrants, largely refugees from the Danzig area with a few from the Lemberg area of Poland and a few from Russia, arrived in October 1948. In 1956 there were approximately 200 of these immigrants living in the city. A congregation, the Montevideo Mennonite Church which meets at Vilardebo 964, has been organized in the city; it had 220 members in 1956 and belongs to the Uruguay Mennonite Conference (affiliated with the General Conference Mennonite Church in North America). There is also a Mennonite Brethren congregation of 79 members, which meets at Calle Pedro Berro 1114, called the El Ombu congregation, since many of its members live in the El Ombu colony. There is also an M.B. Bible School in the city. The Mennonite Church (MC) of North America established a mission in the city in 1954 with four workers. The MCC has had a center in the city since 1948, and now owns the house at Vilardebo 964. The Mennonite Biblical Seminary, a bilingual (Spanish and German) training school, operated by a board composed of representatives from all the Mennonite groups in South America who desire to co-operate and supported by the mission boards of the M.C. and the G.C.M. churches in North America, was established in 1956. It also is located at Vilardebo 964.   H.S.B.

Montezuma Church of God in Christ Mennonite Church is located near Montezuma, Gray Co., Kan. The first members arrived in 1912. In this group there was Peter A. Friesen, the first resident minister, who served the congregation until 1918. Before 1915 the worship services were conducted in homes and in a small frame meetinghouse, which was later enlarged, and in 1946 replaced by a new brick structure with a seating capacity of 900. The German language, formerly used in the services, has now been replaced by the English. The members are of Dutch-Russian Mennonite descent and the Low German dialect is still spoken in many homes. The Sunday school was organized in 1935. Three sewing circles are functioning. Several members of the congregation are actively engaged in missionary work. The local burial plan organized in 1940 is operating successfully. Bethel Home (q.v.) for the aged was built in 1950. The membership in 1957 was 386, with Daniel J. Koehn as minister in charge. The congregation survived the dust storms and extreme drought of the 1930's.   A.Un.

Montfoort, Pieter van, a Catholic priest, was a negotiator of the Court of Brussels (Governess Maria of Hungary) with the Anabaptist kingdom of Münster in 1534-35. Jan van Geelen (q.v.), who acted as the ambassador of Münster, visited van Montfoort at Amsterdam and Brussels and, while preparing Anabaptist revolts in the Netherlands, received from van Montfoort a safe-conduct. After van Geelen's death during the attack on the Amsterdam town hall on May 10, 1535, the negotiations were broken off, and van Montfoort, having incurred the wrath of the hoodwinked authorities by his gullibility, was sentenced to death, but pardoned in March 1537.   vdZ.

Inv. Arch. Amst. I, Nos. 127, 153; *DB* 1899, 1-20; Grosheide, *Verhooren*, 20 f.; Mellink, *Wederdopers, passim,* see Index.

Montgelas, Maximilian Joseph (1759-1838), a statesman of Bavaria, Germany, was appointed state and conference minister on Feb. 21, 1799, by Elector Maximilian Joseph (q.v.). His influence was determinant in the change in the political system of Bavaria. It is due to his progressive views that the Mennonites were granted full citizenship upon their request in 1801 and that the right of redemption (see **Jus Retractus**) passed against them on April 29, 1726, was annulled on Aug. 17, 1801. HEGE.

E. Correll, *Das schweizerische Täufermennonitentum* (Tübingen, 1925); *ML* III, 164.

Montgomery County, Pa., a heavily populated county in southeastern Pennsylvania in which the Mennonites first settled in 1702 at Skippack, an outpost of the Germantown congregation (q.v.). Gradually the Skippack settlement expanded, and new settlements were made at Towamencin, Salford, Worcester, Providence, Franconia, and Plains, all by 1740. The large Souderton congregation was established in 1879, and since 1930 a large number of mission stations, bringing the total baptized membership (1955) of the Franconia Conference (MC) congregations and mission stations in Montgomery County to about 2,900. The Oberholtzer division of 1847 resulted in the formation of several new permanent congregations (GCM) in the county: Schwenksville (1847), Souderton (1887), and Lansdale (1928), with a combined membership in 1955 of over 1,200. The Mennonite Brethren in Christ have only a few congregations in the county: Royersford, Graterford, Harleysville, and Hatfield, with a total membership of 307 in 1956. The Brethren in Christ have three congregations: Graterford, Souderton, and Stowe, with 175 members in the three churches. Montgomery County was the scene of the Funkite (q.v.) schism of 1778. The Franconia Conference Mennonites have a large home for the aged at Souderton, the Eastern Mennonite Home, built in 1916, and enlarged in 1921. The Eastern District Conference (GCM) has a Home for the Aged at Frederick, established in 1896. The Christopher Dock Mennonite (High) School (MC) was established near Lansdale in 1954. The two most valuable Mennonite historical items in the county are the alms books of the Skippack and Franconia congregations, kept by the deacons since 1738 and 1767 respectively. Montgomery County was the home of the colonial Mennonite writer, Bishop Henrich Funck (q.v.), of the famous schoolmaster Christopher Dock (q.v.), and of the Hunsickers, father and son, who founded Freeland Seminary (now Ursinus College) at Collegeville, in 1848. It should also be mentioned that of the congregations of the Franconia Conference only in Skippack was footwashing observed as a church rite before the 20th century. Both the Skippack congregation of the Franconia Conference, and the (independent) Lower Skippack congregation (q.v.), still observe the ceremony. From the Skippack congregation the practice gradually spread, mostly since 1900, to the other congregations of the conference. The name "Franconia Conference" derives from the Franconia Meetinghouse in Franconia Township, which has long been the chief place of meeting of the ministerial body in conference sessions.   J.C.W.

Montgomery Female Institute was a private girls' school organized at Collegeville, Montgomery Co., Pa., about 1851 by a Mennonite bishop (previously in succession MC and GCM), who had become an independent, Abraham Hunsicker (1793-1872), and two other persons, J. W. Sunderland and Luannie Sunderland. In their announcement the founders expressed this position: "We believe the female mind endowed with powers and capabilities quite equal to those of the other sex. . . . We have a twofold object in view,—first, to provide correct and thorough instruction in the ordinary branches of learning . . . ; second, to afford. . . a more extensive course in the sciences and liberal arts. . . ." The institution was incorporated in 1853. Sunderland served as president. The name was soon changed to Pennsylvania Female College. The last class of graduates completed their work in 1875. The total number of graduates from 1853 through 1875 amounted to over 100. After 1875 the school ceased to exist.   J.C.W.

Theodore W. Bean, *History of Montgomery County* (Philadelphia, 1884) 419 f.

Monthly Letter of the Mennonite Women's Missionary Society (*q.v.*) was the first publication of the Women's Missionary organization of the Mennonite Church (MC). It began as an annual letter in 1919 (first issue March 1), became a quarterly in 1920, and a monthly in 1921. It was a single sheet broadside, 8½ x 10 in., until Vol. IV (1922) when it became a 4-page folder, continuing as such to the end of 1927. It was edited by the general secretary of the organization who was Clara Eby Steiner (Mrs. M. S. Steiner) from the beginning until her retirement in 1926. The society was disbanded at the end of 1927 and the paper discontinued with the November-December 1927 issue (complete file in GCL). It was succeeded by the *Missionary Sewing Circle Letter* (*q.v.*), published by the General Sewing Circle Committee of the Mennonite Board of Missions and Charities, which began publication July 1930.
H.S.B.

Montreux, France: see **Münsterrol.**

Monument Mennonite Mission (MC), the first mission of the Mission Advocates of Lancaster Co., Pa., located in a Union meetinghouse on Linville Hill, Lancaster County, was opened on Sept. 21, 1895. It continued intermittently until 1926. The neighboring congregations of Mt. Pleasant and Kinzer very definitely and variously benefited from the work. Isaac E. Hershey and Emanuel E. Keneagy were the first superintendents. The closing of the nickel mines near by in the first decade of this century affected the attendance.   I.D.L.

Moody, Dwight Lyman (1837-99), the leading evangelist of American Protestantism in the 19th century (beginning in 1870), whose work was of immeasurable influence upon American religious life. He was also the founder of the Northfield School at Northfield, Mass. (1879, 1881), and of Moody Bible Institute at Chicago, Ill. (1886), the finances for which came from the enormous profits of the songbooks which he and Sankey published (*Gospel Hymns,* etc., over $1,250,000 in royalties).

Moody's revivalistic work indirectly influenced the Mennonites of North America, particularly the more English-speaking Mennonite Church (MC). The Moody Bible Institute has had considerable influence on Mennonites through the attendance of Mennonite students from about 1895 on, through its publication, the Moody Monthly, and through its radio programs (WMBI) and the summer Bible conferences which it has sponsored throughout the country.

A major source of Moody's influence on the Mennonite Church (MC) was through John F. Funk (*q.v.*). Funk became acquainted with Moody in 1861 when they were fellow teachers at the Milwaukee Depot Mission Sunday School. They were close friends for several years. Funk regarded highly his association with Moody, and records in his unpublished memoirs that he owed to Moody the vision of better things in the Mennonite Church, including Sunday schools, young people's meetings, and evangelism. He described to a friend Moody's influence by saying that Moody was so full of religious enthusiasm that one could not help being moved or drawn by him into a blessed religious experience. Without doubt, a significant contribution to the Great Awakening in the Mennonite Church (MC) in 1875-1900 was Moody's indirect influence in various ways, especially through Funk.
H.S.B.

Richard Day, *Bush Aglow; the Life Story of D. L. Moody* (Philadelphia, 1936); W. R. Moody, *D. L. Moody* (New York, 1900, 1930).

Mooi-Land, a Dutch Mennonite home for the aged at Doorwerth, near Arnhem, province of Gelderland. It was opened on June 13, 1936, and enlarged in 1952.   vdZ.

Moravia, in the 16th century often called "the promised land" of the Anabaptists. During the Middle Ages it was a margravure and part of the Kingdom of Bohemia. As such it experienced also the rise and spread of Hussitism in the 15th century. When this pre-Protestant movement settled down to become a quiet sectarian church, several names appeared for it, such as Bohemian Brethren (*q.v.*) and Picards (a nickname erroneously derived from Beghards). Under this last name the movement was widely spread also in Moravia during the 16th century, to be sure among the Czech-speaking population only and with practically no contact with the German-speaking people of that land.

In 1526 the last king of Bohemia (and incidentally also king of Hungary) fell in a battle against the Turks, and Archduke Ferdinand of Hapsburg (*q.v.*), his brother-in-law and later emperor, became king of Bohemia and of (a small part of) Hungary. Being a staunch Catholic he naturally tried to make Bohemia and Moravia thoroughly Catholic, an endeavor in which, however, all the Hapsburgs failed up to 1620. The provincial estates (*Landstände*) were exceedingly jealous of their local autonomy and resented all aggressive interference from the government in Vienna, Austria. They elected (and the Hapsburgs approved) a governor (*Landeshauptmann*) from their midst as head of the provincial (thoroughly feudal) government and also as their spokesman in Vienna at the Hapsburg court. On the other hand King Ferdinand was never certain whether his orders to this governor were actually carried out or not; thus he often sent his orders instead to the Bishop of Olmütz (Olomouc), the ecclesiastical ruler of Moravia. Moravia had three "royal" cities: Olmütz, Brno, and Znaim (Znojmo); provincial diets (*Landtage*) were held alternately in these three cities, with proceedings in the Czech language (for details see **Olmütz**). Until 1636 Olmütz was the capital of Moravia; after that year Brno became the capital. There were many smaller cities, too, such as Nikolsburg or Austerlitz, but they had the character of large manorial estates rather than of cities in the modern sense. Here the lords could act more or less as they pleased.

It was these lords (some of them Protestants) who practiced such a degree of religious toleration that this country rightly stands out in the 16th century as a unique area of refuge for those fleeing religious persecution. Perhaps only Poland could compete with it to any extent; the rest of Europe knew nothing but persecution of those who did not conform. Franticek Hruby discusses at great length the roots of this liberal attitude. He is certain that it was by no means derived from economic motives only (sectarians being usually good and reliable workers); perhaps the Hussite-Picard tradition of more than half a century had something to do with it, and likewise the old feudal pride in independence. In short, not only Anabaptists of all shades but many other left-wing groups of the age of the Reformation found a welcome refuge in Moravia for shorter or longer periods. As far as the records go, there was only one execution for reasons of nonconformity in Moravia, namely, the burning at the stake of the Anabaptist brother Thoman Waldhauser in Brno in 1528 (*Geschicht-Buch,* 45 f.). But at that time Brno had a city government and was rather cool to manorial or feudal tradition.

Perhaps the earliest report on sectarian activities is found in a printed book of 1526 by Oswald Glaidt (*q.v.*), which records a religious debate in Austerlitz in March 1526, sponsored by a nobleman John Dubchansky, who wanted to achieve a sort of unification of all non-Catholics (Utraquists, Lutherans, and independent groups, one of them called Habrovans). Oswald Glaidt, the recorder, was at that time not yet an Anabaptist. A few weeks after this debate, Balthasar Hubmaier (*q.v.*), since May 1525 an Anabaptist preacher, arrived in Nikolsburg (*q.v.*) upon the express invitation of the nobleman Johann von Liechtenstein (*q.v.*), lord of Nikolsburg and himself a sympathizer with Hubmaier's views. Most likely Liechtenstein was later baptized by his illustrious guest. From that time on Anabaptism found a foothold in Moravia. Glaidt also went to Nikolsburg, as did Hans Hut, Ambrosius Spittelmaier, Jacob Wiedemann, and many more. Soon Anabaptism experienced its first split: Hubmaier and Spittelmaier defended the use of the sword (*Schwertler*), while Hut, Glaidt, and Wiedemann opposed it, hence were derisively called *Stäbler* (staff-bearers; see **Hutterian Brethren**). As persecutions intensified elsewhere, a stream of refugees now poured into Moravia, coming from Tirol and other

Hapsburg areas, as well as from South Germany, Bavaria, Württemberg, etc. In the 1530's three main groups are observed: Hutterian Brothern (destined to survive all the vicissitudes of history), Gabrielites (*q.v.*), who first left for Silesia but around 1545 joined the Hutterites, and Philippites (*q.v.*), some of whom likewise joined the first-named group, while others returned to Germany, when for a few years even Moravia attempted to expel its Anabaptists. Besides these three main groups there were also "Swiss" Brethren, i.e., Anabaptists who did not practice community of goods. Whether they were actually Swiss is not known, but it is certain that small groups of them existed as late as 1591 and even 1618 (Beck, *Geschichts-Bücher,* 152, note). There were also the Pilgramites, apparently the followers of Pilgram Marpeck (*q.v.*). Leopold Scharnschlager (*q.v.*) was for a while their leader (in the 1530's). But the number of independent groups other than Anabaptists was far greater. Several published lists and other reports show that at certain places, such as Austerlitz, there existed at least 13 or 14 sectarian (non-Catholic) groups. The earliest list, of 1556 (Krebs, 511), enumerates 20 such sects. De Wind published several such lists (of 1567 and later) which name, besides Picards, Lutherans, and Calvinists, various Anabaptist groups (one called Austerlitzer Brüder), then "Arians, Samosatenes, and Sabbatarians" (apparently all three names for the anti-Trinitarian Socinians, all of whom were immigrant Italians), then Adamites and similar marginal groups, practically all of them (except the Socinians) German-speaking people now living in Czech surroundings. De Wind also names some of the more outstanding manorial lords who made the opportunities for these groups available. Besides the lord of Nikolsburg (Liechtenstein), there was the lord of Austerlitz, Ulrich von Kaunitz, who was perhaps the most broad-minded of all (Austerlitz was said to have been at times a real "Babel"), then Johann von Lipa, lord of Kromau and Schäkovitz (incidentally the man who also offered a safe refuge in 1537 to Paracelsus, the famous physician of that day), Heinrich von Lomnitz, lord of Jamnitz, who is said to have ransomed Anabaptist brethren from the dungeon of Passau (*MQR* 1955, 61), and, strangely enough, also the Abbess of Maria-Saal near Brno, the mistress of Auspitz (*q.v.*), another well-known center of Anabaptism. Apparently she needed reliable tillers of the soil and skilled craftsmen more than anything else. Later the lords of Selovitz, the Zierotin (Zerotin, *q.v.*) family, became outstanding as protectors of the Hutterian Brethren and broad-minded lords. Three of these Zierotins, Friedrich (d. 1598), Karl, and Ladislaus Velen (1619-21), were also governors of Moravia and exerted a beneficent influence regarding the life of the Anabaptists in Moravia.

Only twice did it happen that King Ferdinand had his way and the lords had to yield; viz., 1535-36 and 1547-51. These were hard times for the Anabaptists (and most likely also for the other left-wing groups). In 1535 Ferdinand came for the first time personally to a provincial diet, and prevailed upon the reluctant lords to expel all "heretics." It was then that the Philippites left Moravia for good (except a few remnants; see **Pulgram**), and that Jakob Hutter addressed his famous letter to the governor Johan Kuna von Kunstadt, to be sure without success. The Brethren had no choice and began wandering hither and thither. Fortunately, the stern measures did not last for very long, and in 1537 new Bruderhofs could be established again on various estates (see **Schäkovitz**). In 1546 Ferdinand came again to Moravia. Things looked favorable for the Hapsburgs; the Turks had been defeated (at least for the moment) and Ferdinand's brother, Emperor Charles V, held the Protestants in check in the Schmalkaldian War. Now the danger for the Brethren was even more serious than a decade earlier. They began new settlements in near-by Slovakia (*q.v.*), then belonging to the Kingdom of Hungary, where the Hapsburgs had not yet gained much influence. But even here the situation became somewhat critical in 1548-53 (see **Holitsch**). Thus the brotherhoods shuttled back and forth between Moravia, Lower Austria, and Slovakia. Nowhere did they find a place of rest. It may have been in these dark years that they began to dig out the underground tunnels found all over that area and called in Czech *Lochy* (*q.v.*), i.e., *Löcher,* meaning holes. They are pathetic witnesses of persecution. The Hutterites, however, tried again to write to the governor (Wenzel von Ludanitz) in 1545, with small success, as could have been anticipated. (Beck, 169-73.)

But the political scene changed again; the Turks threatened again from Hungary, and Charles V was defeated by the Schmalkaldians. Thus around 1551-52 peace came for the Brethren, making it possible for them to develop permanent settlements (Bruderhofs). From 1551 until about 1600 the peace was but very little disturbed. The Hutterian Brethren called this period the "Golden Era." Their number multiplied now by leaps and bounds, mainly because of newcomers from many countries (Germany, Switzerland, Austria, etc.); their activities were so successful that the jealousy of the surrounding population was aroused. Jesuits arrived in Nikolsburg in the 1570's, but neither they nor other priests (Erhard, *q.v.,* Fischer, *q.v.*) could do much harm to the brotherhood which was so powerfully protected by the nobles.

The Hutterites were, however, not the only Anabaptists in Moravia, although they are the only ones of whom there is a continuous record. It is known that until the end of the 16th century Swiss Brethren also lived in Moravia (though in small numbers) and Pilgramites, the Marpeck group. As for the Swiss Brethren (besides what Beck had to say; see above) a remarkable event is known through a Dutch booklet, *Het Brilleken* of 1630 (*Mart. Mir.* D I, 400 f., E 365-67), which tells of the visit of "Greek Brethren" from Thessalonica to these Brethren in Moravia around 1550, and also of the flight of one of these Swiss Brethren (who later tells this story) around 1620. As for the Pilgramites one of their most precious possessions, Marpeck's *Verantwortung* (1542), was copied in Moravia (now preserved in the library of Olmütz). This manuscript contains a letter of 1571 by a certain Wernhard Riepl of Klein-Teschau, Moravia,

concerning certain theological arguments among these brethren, referring back to a tract by Leopold Scharnschlager (Loserth, *Quellen,* 35). This is apparently the latest reference available for the existence of the Marpeck group in Moravia and elsewhere.

One of the "'administrative" centers of the Hutterites between 1565 and 1620 was the Bruderhof at Neumühl, ten miles east of Nikolsburg, which became the residence of four successive head bishops or *Vorsteher,* viz., Walpot, Kräl, Braidl, and Dietrich (for details see **Neumühl**). It was here that the large chronicle was written, where all the outgoing and incoming correspondence was handled and filed away, where some of the famous codices (*Epistel-* and *Artikel-Büchlein*) were written, and where important community regulations (*Gemeindeordnungen, q.v.*) were formulated. It was also here that Polish anti-Trinitarian visitors were entertained. All practical and doctrinal decisions of the second half of the 16th century seem to have originated at this place.

Unfortunate conditions brought this flowering to a bitter end. A Turkish-Hungarian war brought the invasion of undisciplined hordes, who inflicted severe tribulations upon the brotherhood: murder, rape, torture, arson, carrying away of women and children, war in its worst aspect, coming upon people who were nonresistant and therefore helpless in the face of such dangers (see **Böger**). Three hymns in the Hutterite hymnal tell of those terrible years (the "Botschkai Lieder," *Lieder d. Hutt. Brüder,* 804-12). The detailed story is also told in all their chronicles. In addition to all this tribulation came intensified demands from the Emperor Rudolph II (residing in Prague) for money (actually war loans), which the Brethren emphatically refused to give, thus provoking renewed threats (correspondence in the *Geschicht-Buch,* 443-46 and 477-80). And then the Catholic Counter Reformation (*q.v.*) came into full swing in the formerly liberal margraviate of Moravia (see **Dietrichstein**, Cardinal Franz von, the new lord of Nikolsburg). The number of Bruderhofs declined but they still were strong spiritually and in organization.

Then once again it appeared that good fortune would make it possible for the brethren to continue their work, internally by building up their brotherhood, externally by sending out missioners to the farthest corners of the German-speaking territories (such as East Prussia; see **Elbing**). When in the Bohemian Rebellion of 1618-19 the Hapsburgs lost their old kingdom, and Frederick, the prince-elector of the Palatinate, became the ruler (later called "the Winter-King," 1619-20), things looked somewhat hopeful again. Frederick himself was a Calvinist, but for the moment he was definitely graciously inclined toward all sectarians. When he came to visit Moravia he also stopped at some Hutterite colonies (such as Kromau), where he was given presents and promised his royal protection (Hruby). This did not last longer than one winter, however. In 1620 Frederick lost the battle at the White Mountain (near Prague) and had to flee; with it the fate of the Protestants (and Anabaptists) in the Hapsburg lands was sealed. Emperor Ferdinand II, supported by Cardinal Franz von Dietrichstein, now insisted upon total expulsion of all non-Catholics. No lord could any longer protect the Hutterian Brethren, who thus suffered both from the unrestrained military hordes (e.g., Dampierre's cavalry), and the ruthless orders of the authorities. The severity of this suffering through war can still be felt in reading the moving three "Pribitz hymns" of 1620-22 (*Lieder d. Hutt. Brüder,* 821-38; see also **Pribitz**). Lives were lost and goods destroyed or confiscated. And then one Vorsteher, Hirzel (*q.v.*), betrayed a number of hiding places of their savings, thus leaving the Brethren nearly penniless.

After 1622 no Anabaptist could remain in Moravia any longer. A few lords tried still to employ some single individuals on their estates, but as the Thirty Years' War progressed also these had to be sent away. Slovakia promised at least for a while a safe refuge (see **Slovakia**). As for the non-Hutterites, there is no knowledge at all concerning their fate.

And yet the crafts of the Brethren even after that tragic war continued to attract the interest of Moravian nobles. As Hruby proved, the famous Habaner ceramics (*q.v.*) were found throughout the 17th century in the inventories of Moravian castles and manor houses. The same is true regarding the Hutterite cutlery (knives) and their beautifully worked clocks, to be found on many a tower. But otherwise Moravia like Bohemia had been thoroughly reconverted to Catholicism. The old feudal independence faded away and the great period of Moravian history was over.

In 1918 Moravia became part of the Czechoslovakian Republic. At that time it still had more than 600,000 Germans among its 2.7 million population. When, in 1937, two Hutterite Brothers from America visited the country they reported that remnants of their old settlements were still extant and that even some vague recollections lingered on here and there. Today, all Germans have been expelled from Czechoslovakia, and the country has become completely Slavic.   R.F.

Loserth, *Communismus;* Fr. Hruby, *Die Mährischen Wiedertäufer* (Leipzig, 1935, with new Czech source material); P. Dedic, *Die religiösen und kirchlichen Verhältnisse in Mähren im 16. Jahrhundert* (1922, dissertation in manuscript at the University of Vienna, Evangelical-Theological Faculty); H. De Wind, "A Sixteenth Century Description of Religious Sects in Austerlitz, Moravia," *MQR* XXIX (1955) 44-53; for older works see Friedmann's bibliography in *Archiv für Ref. Gesch.* XXVI (1929) 176-78; *ML* II, 711-17.

Moravian Church (or Moravian Brethren), the name in America and England of the church known in Europe as *Unitas Fratrum, Brüder-Unität,* or *Herrnhuter (Gemeinde).* Its history is divided into two distinct parts, viz., the "old" (1457) and the "new" (1722 or 1736) *Brüder-Unität.* Whereas the former group was nearly exclusively made up of members of Czech nationality (both in Bohemia and Moravia), the new *Brüder-Unität* has been predominantly German. Its spiritual and organizational center was and still is Herrnhut in Saxony; its guiding spirit was the inspired and "pietistic" leader Ludwig Count von Zinzendorf (*q.v.*). This new, re-established church, in many ways similar to the German Lutheran state church and yet independent

of it as well as of any state, now became very aggressive, evangelizing and doing extensive mission work. Soon it spread to West and East, that is, to England and America on the one side and to Russia on the other.

Since the article **Bohemian Brethren** (*q.v.*) discusses the historical background, and the article **Moravians in the Netherlands** (*q.v.*) the particular development of this group during the 18th and 19th centuries, the present article will restrict itself to contacts between Moravians and Anabaptism.

As far as the "old" church (in Czech called *Jednota Bratrska*) is concerned, its contacts with Anabaptists in Moravia (none in Bohemia) are minor, apparently primarily because of language barriers. The Anabaptists never worked among non-German groups and, on the other hand, the Moravians not among non-Czech people. Moravia (*q.v.*) in the 16th century was a most tolerant country; thus both groups could live peacefully side by side without too many visible contacts. In 1534 the Bohemian Brethren abolished their practice of adult baptism, retaining only a form of "confirmation" with their adolescents, thus adding another reason for mutual distance. Early in the 17th century the last bishop of the Bohemian Brethren, John Amos Comenius (Komensky), more than once expressed his admiration for the Hutterian Brethren and his sympathy for their suffering while being expelled from Moravia. He called their constitution "perfect as with no other society in the world" (*Fragen über die Unität,* 1633), and again in 1661, "I have known these simple Brethren from my youth on, and I know that they always held to their faith."

In the 18th century, however, when a new church arose in Herrnhut burning with missionary zeal, contacts with Anabaptists became almost inevitable, even though the two groups represent rather different spirits of Christian witnessing. J. T. Müller in his excellent study of 1910 (see bibliography) collected all available evidence concerning these contacts, a condensation of which may also be found in Friedmann's book, *Mennonite Piety* (51-54). Since contacts with Dutch Mennonites are dealt with in another article, and of contacts with Mennonites in Germany and Switzerland nothing essential has become known, this article is concerned exclusively with contacts with Hutterites, both in Slovakia and in Russia.

The first document of significance is a letter of Count Zinzendorf of 1727, handed to a Slovakian Hutterite brother visiting Herrnhut. In this letter the basically different orientation becomes quite apparent: "To follow the ordinances of the perfect church [most likely he meant the practice of community of goods] . . . is not our primary concern. . . . Each one should ground himself in Jesus Christ and thus receive regeneration from above. It is on this that we base all brotherhood. . . . We believe in an invisible church of Jesus in the spirit."

A second letter by Zinzendorf (1731) to the brethren in Slovakia deals with the Lord's Supper and its meaning. Again the difference between the new spirit of Pietism (*q.v.*) and that of old-type Anabaptism becomes obvious. "The coming together (at least twelve times a year), the testing, eating, drinking, believing, possessing [of sacramental grace], feeling, enjoying—this is what I must testify out of a sincere love." Most likely the Hutterian Brethren in Slovakia had little understanding for this kind of "subjectivism" and emotionalism. Their Lord's Supper (*q.v.*), celebrated usually twice a year, meant something very different to them. They were rather ignorant of the new trend of "enjoying one's own salvation"; to them the Supper meant simply commitment to the path of discipleship and strengthening of the spirit of genuine community and brotherhood.

In 1782 a Hutterite brother Jakob Walter (*q.v.*) of Sobotiste in Slovakia, on his way to his brethren in the Ukraine, passed through Herrnhut and there received help and support; likewise some later emigrants from Slovakia. Apparently the Moravians considered them as some remnants of the older *Unitas Fratrum*.

Quite remarkable is the contact of the Hutterite Brethren with Moravians in Russia, the Hutterites living in Radichev (*q.v.*) in the Ukraine, the Moravians in Sarepta on the Volga River, some 700 miles to the East. This contact covers the period of 1797 to 1811; the main actors were Johannes Waldner (*q.v.*), the Vorsteher at Radichev, and Johann Wiegand (or Wygand), pastor of the Brüdergemeinde in the Volga district. In 1802 the latter visited the Hutterite Bruderhof and thereupon reported in detail of his experiences (Zieglschmid, *Klein-Geschichtsbuch*, 413-18). He assured the reader that "not only the Moravians but also the Hutterites consider as the sole foundation of all righteousness and salvation the merit of Jesus Christ" (Zieglschmid, 415). But immediately afterwards he lamented the formalistic rigidity of the Hutterites, who had not changed since the 16th century, and he likewise deplored their lack of a missionary spirit. The two groups exchanged writings, and in one of his letters Johannes Waldner highly praised Spangenberg's *Idea Fidei Fratrum* (one of the basic texts of the Moravians). But the gulf between the two groups remained unbridged, mainly due to the Moravians' insistence on infant baptism. In 1803 Wiegand asked Herrnhut for some relief work among the Hutterites, and added that such help might also promote further rapprochement and in the long run perhaps even complete fusion. When Wiegand died in 1808 Waldner sent a letter of sympathy to his successor, full of personal warmth and appreciation even though he could not avoid saying, "There are a number of points between us which separate us. . . . But we want to bear with each other in the love of Jesus since we are one in the great work of redemption and reconciliation through the blood of Jesus" (Friedmann, 54).

The archives of the Herrnhut center still have the gifts received from Johannes Waldner, namely, one booklet containing catechetical instructions and the form for the ceremony of (adult) baptism (50 pages), two sermons to be preached at Easter time on the occasion of the Lord's Supper (*Abendmahlsrede*) of 1644 (140 pages), one sermon for Christmas concerning the deity of Christ, written at Kesselsdorf (*q.v.*), Slovakia, in 1657, and a hymn describing the exodus of the Carinthians in 1756

and the new beginning in Transylvania until 1760, 50 stanzas in 19 pages (perhaps composed by Matthias Hofer). The archives hold also the entire correspondence mentioned above, including letters by Waldner to Wiegand's successor Friedrich Gregor.   R.F.

J. T. Müller, "Die Berührung der alten und neuen Brüderunität mit den Täufern," in *Ztschr für Brüdergeschichte*, 1910; idem, *Geschichte der Böhmischen Brüder*, 3 vv., 1922-31 (v. I: 1400-1528; v. II: 1528-1576; v. III: 1548-1793 [Polnische Unität] and 1575-1780 [Bömisch-Mährische Unität]); R. Friedmann, *Mennonite Piety Through the Centuries* (Goshen, 1949); Zieglschmid, *Klein-Geschichtsbuch;* J. Loserth, "Deutsch-Böhmische Wiedertäufer, ein Beitrag zur Geschichte der Reformation in Böhmen," in *Mitteilungen des Vereins für die Geschichte der Deutschen in Böhmen*, 1892; for Comenius see M. Spinka, *John Amos Comenius, That Incomparable Moravian* (Chicago, 1943); Beck, *Geschichts-Bücher*, 169-73; ML I, 279-85.

Moravians in the Netherlands. In the Netherlands the Moravian Brethren or "Brüdergemeine" are usually called Her(r)nhutters after their center Herrnhut in Silesia, Germany. In the Netherlands they established a center at 's-Heerendijk near IJsselstein in 1736, moving to Zeist in 1746, both in the province of Utrecht. They still occupy the estate at Zeist. These Hernhutters opened a mission in the Dutch colony of Surinam as early as 1735. Though sometimes vehemently attacked and made suspect by the Reformed Church, a number of Reformed ministers and others protected and assisted them. They also found much contact with Mennonites. Among their first Mennonite friends were Jacob Schellinger of Amsterdam, who loaned money for the purchase of 's-Heerendijk in 1736, and Joannes Deknatel (*q.v.*), the noted pastor of the Amsterdam Lamist congregation, who was on very friendly terms with Count von Zinzendorf, the general leader of the Brethren movement. The revivalism and evangelism of the Brethren, promoted and supported especially by Deknatel, took root among the Mennonites. Places of extensive Moravian influence among the Mennonites about 1740-50 were Amsterdam, Haarlem, Hoorn, Groningen, Blokzijl, Norden, Akkrum, Oldeboorn, and Terhorne. A number of Mennonites, though not many, definitely joined the movement, including Jacob and Cornelis Schellinger of Amsterdam, Jan Broeks and Sybern Claases of Terhorne, Gerrit Synes and others of Akkrum, Volkert de Graaf, the minister of Blokzijl. Jan van Calker of Kampen joined the Brethren in 1741; in 1743 he sold his property and moved to Herrnhut, but soon returned to the Netherlands, settling at Sappemeer. Other Mennonites, like Deknatel, Dirk Messchaert of Hoorn and his wife Janneken Beets, Joost Daams, the preacher of Haarlem, Maria Voorhelm, the wife of J. H. Schneevogt of Haarlem, also joined the Moravians, but later left them. Many Mennonites participated in Moravian communion services, usually held in the homes of the members or adherents.

In a few towns congregations were founded, which received a large proportion of their members from the Mennonites, e.g., Akkrum, where a (small) Hernhutter congregation was in existence *ca.*1746-97. After Deknatel had become somewhat estranged from Zinzendorf (in 1748) and no longer supported the movement, the interest of the Mennonites in the Moravian Brethren decreased. VDZ.

W. Lütjeharms, *Het philadelphisch-eucumenisch streven der Hernhutters in de Nederlanden in de achttiende eeuw* (Zeist, 1935) *passim; Inv. Arch. Amst.* II, No. 1454.

Mörchingen: see Morhange.

Morden, Man., a town (pop. 1,862) located 6 miles west of Winkler and 60 miles southwest of Winnipeg, is the seat of the Mennonite Brethren Old People's Home, an M.B. congregation with 176 members, and a local unit of the Bergtal Mennonite (GCM) Church. (*ML* III, 167.) H.S.B.

Morden (Man.) Mennonite Brethren Church, a member of the Northern District Conference, was organized Jan. 12, 1930, with 32 members, under the leadership of D. D. Toews. John Andres served as its first pastor. He was followed by John F. Braun and F. H. Friesen, the present (1955) minister. The membership in 1955 was 176, half of whom live in the country. The congregation at first rented Alexander Hall, and in 1935 purchased a brick building which it used for its meetings for some time. In 1946 a new church, which has a seating capacity of 400, was erected in the town of Morden. D.J.R.

Morgan and **Moniteau Counties,** Mo., are located in the central part of the state along the Missouri Pacific Railroad. The Mennonites settled in Piolet Grove Twp., Moniteau Co., and Moreau Twp., Morgan Co. This settlement has two Mennonite churches. Mt. Zion Mennonite (MC) Church (in Morgan County) has a membership of 54 (1955). The Bethel Mennonite (GCM) Church (in Moniteau County) has 141 members (1955).

In October 1865 Christian Luginbühl, P. P. Lehman, Sr., and Ulrich Welty, of the Sonnenberg settlement in Wayne Co., Ohio, made a trip through Missouri and Iowa to find land for a settlement. Christian Luginbühl bought a farm 8 miles south of Tipton, Mo. In April 1866 he, together with four other men, moved with their families from Wayne County to this new settlement. In the following decade more came from Wayne County. Most of the Polk Co., Iowa, Swiss Mennonite settlement moved here in 1867-68. Numerous families came from Rockingham Co., Va., and various other Mennonite (MC) settlements in Ohio, Pennsylvania, and Michigan. In 1871 the church divided peacefully into the two present congregations. D.L.G.

Jesse H. Loganbill, *Souvenir Album of the Fiftieth Anniversary of the Founding of the Bethel Mennonite Church in Morgan and Moniteau Counties near Fortuna, Missouri* (Berne, 1917); Peter P. Hilty, *Seventy-fifth Anniversary of the Bethel Mennonite Church* (California, Mo., 1942); D. L. Gratz, *Bernese Anabaptists* (Scottdale, 1953).

Morgantown, Pa., is a village of 365 inhabitants on the headwaters of Conestoga Creek in Berks County. Amish Mennonites and Mennonites (MC) live in and around the town. It is near the center of the oldest permanent Amish settlement in America, they having arrived there approximately 200 years ago. Three Mennonite churches are located in the adjacent area—Conestoga (*q.v.*), Oley (*q.v.*), and Rock (*q.v.*), as well as the Conestoga Christian Day School. Farming is the chief occupation of the community, although many local businesses are Mennonite owned. The area was originally settled by Welsh in the 18th century. The village has also a Methodist and an Episcopal church. The Pennsylvania Turnpike goes by the town. There are mining developments near by. G.M.S.

Morhange (German, *Mörchingen*), a town (pop. 1,914) in Lorraine (*q.v.*), France, 25 miles southeast of Metz, was the seat of a small Mennonite congregation, which was founded about 1720 by Alsatian Mennonites of Swiss Amish descent after the Mennonites had been expelled from Alsace (*q.v.*) in 1712 by decree of Louis XIV. The Morhange congregation was never very large and was further weakened by emigration to America in the early 19th century. Nevertheless it built a small meetinghouse in 1856 near the town and a cemetery on the Hinsingen estate near Gros-Tenquin, the home of elder Joseph Hirschy. About 1893 they were joined by the families of the Dieuze (*q.v.*) congregation who lived on the German side of Lorraine, while those living on the French side joined the Nancy (*q.v.*) congregation. Nevertheless the membership showed a steady decline, chiefly because the families were small. Early in World War I bloody battles were fought near Morhange; when peace came there was no minister left. Services were, however, begun again, conducted in French by visiting ministers. In 1940 the membership (children included) numbered 35. Charles Baechler (d. 1952) was ordained minister in 1939, but there was no elder in the congregation after World War I, the congregation being served by elders from Toul, Sarrebourg, and Montbéliard. Meetings ceased at the beginning of World War II (1939). During the war the chapel was damaged and has not been repaired. The remaining members joined either Diesen or Pont-a-Mousson, a branch of Toul. P.So., J.H.Y.

Morija Deaconess Home, located at Neu-Halbstadt, South Russia, was the first and only Mennonite deaconess home to be established in Russia, opened on Dec. 3, 1909. A 3-year course offered theoretical as well as practical instruction to Mennonite girls, who offered to dedicate their lives as Christian nurses in Mennonite charitable institutions. The deaconess home also served as a mother house, keeping and caring for the nurses in sickness and old age. The institution was organized as a private charitable organization, all Mennonite churches participating, the initiators being Franz Wall, head of the Muntau Hospital, Peter Schmidt, a rich landowner, and Dr. E. Tavonius, the father of Dr. Erica Tavonius at Fernheim, Paraguay. The home accepted up to 40 nursing students every year. After the Revolution first the religious aspect of the school was changed and in 1927 the last Mennonite head nurse was removed and the deaconess home turned into a medical institute under a Communist leader. (*Menn. Rundschau,* 1929, No. 34; *ML* III, 167.) J.A.K.

Morning Star Bible School, since 1949 called the Coaldale Bible School, a school of the M.B. congregations in Alberta, particularly the Coaldale congregation, was founded in 1929. In 1934 the first separate building was erected, the Coaldale M.B. Church having served as meeting place until that time, and in 1949 the present commodious building was erected. In the first 25 years of its existence, over 800 students attended. Among the earlier teachers were A. J. Schierling, J. A. Toews, Sr., J. H. Quiring, D. Ewert, and J. A. Toews, Jr. In 1956 A. P. Regier was serving as principal with a total faculty of three. The school has since 1931 offered a three-year course in Bible and Teachers Training. The peak enrollment was 101 in 1948-49.   H.S.B.

Morning View Mennonite (MC) Mission Church, six miles west of Linville, Va., belonging to the Virginia Conference, started about 1924 as a Sunday school that had formerly been a union school. Later the work was carried on in a vacant building near by until it became too small to accommodate the congregation. In 1928 a frame church was built. This church was remodeled and enlarged in 1956. Sunday school is held each Sunday, and preaching twice each month. The membership in 1955 was 42, with Ernest G. Gehman and Clayton Showalter in charge. (*ML* III, 168.)   T.S.

Mornington Old Order Amish settlement, located in Mornington Twp., Perth Co., Ont. When about 1890 a meetinghouse was built north of Poole, a group led by Christian L. Kuepfer and Andrew Kuepfer as ministers and Solomon Kuepfer deacon, continued to worship in homes as had been done from the original organization in 1874. For a few years Old Order Amish bishops from Ohio served communion. In 1891 Samuel Miller and David Miller of Holmes Co., Ohio, helped the Old Order Amish in Mornington to organize a congregation. Christian L. Kuepfer became bishop in 1891, and Solomon Kuepfer was ordained minister in 1911. No Sunday schools were conducted and the German language was used. Ministers have been John J. Kuepfer (1865-1945), ordained minister 1897 and bishop 1913; Jonathan Kuepfer, minister 1916; Henry S. Albrecht, minister 1924 and bishop 1934; and Daniel Steckley, minister 1931.

The congregation held services every two weeks alternating with the Wellesley Old Order group, using the *Ausbund*. The membership of 135 comprised some 40 families, and services were held at about 30 homes.

About 1945 dissatisfaction led to cleavage in this group. Samuel Steckley was ordained bishop to assist the senior bishop, Henry Albrecht, with the majority of the young people under this leadership. In 1954 this Mornington Old Order Amish district stands divided as follows: Samuel Steckley, ordained minister in 1945 and bishop in 1946, Joseph Z. Kuepfer and Daniel Steckley ministers, Menno J. Kuepfer deacon, as the leadership for 26 families with a membership of 40. The total number of worshipers is 116, with 5 adherents. Services are held in 30 different homes.

Under the leadership of Solomon S. Kuepfer bishop, Jonathan Kuepfer, Simon Kuepfer, and Gideon Streicher ministers, Christian W. Kuepfer deacon, there are 20 families with a membership of 80 and a total of 162 worshipers and 8 adherents. They have worship in 21 homes. (*ML* III, 168.)   J.C.F.

Moron, a small village on an elevation with the same name in the Bernese Jura, Switzerland. The beautifully situated village at an elevation of 3,300 ft., lies three fifths of a mile east of the highway from Biel to Pruntrut (Porrentruy). Moron, attractively surrounded by meadows and fir forests, is the center of the Kleintal (*q.v.*) Mennonite congregation. The inhabitants are almost exclusively Mennonite. Most of them are the descendants of refugees from the Emmental in the 18th century. The Mennonite census list (*Verzeichnis aller Wiedertäuffer nach Namen, Zunamen, Heimat, Wohnort in jedem Oberamt aufgenommen: Kontrollbücher* I and II in the state archives in Bern) of 1823 enumerates a number of families who settled in Moron and the vicinity. The narrower circle of the Kleintal congregation with its seat in Moron, including the communes of Souboz, Sornetan, Monible, Chatelat, and Saicourt, showed a Mennonite membership of 147 persons, and that of the Münster (Moutier) district 469 persons. About 1850 Peter Studer of Malleray and David Nussbaumer of La Cote Souboz were preachers. Meetings were held in the farmhouses. Toward the end of the 19th century the desire and the need arose for a suitable building. In 1892 the chapel on Moron was built under the leadership of Christian Gerber, and dedicated in November.

In the midst of the French-speaking region the Mennonites in the Jura have always made an effort to preserve the German language, considering it a necessary condition for their existence. To this end the new chapel of Moron was to serve, by having on its ground floor a German school, where Gottlieb Loosli (*q.v.*), the elder of the congregation, taught for many fruitful years, especially through the addition of a Sunday school and baptismal instruction.

In 1904 the revival movement in the Jura also seized the Moron congregation, and in the revival meetings held by evangelist Fritz Schüpbach from the Emmental many awoke to new life. Even though the movement was considered extreme in certain circles, it left a trail of blessing in its wake. The girls' society formed in the interest of home missions has continued its service to the present.

In the history of the development of the Moron congregation Loosli's work played an essential part in the organization of choruses, song services, annual celebrations, and revival meetings. The regular meetings are held the first and third Sunday afternoon of every month.

Loosli's death in 1931 was a serious loss for Moron; a second blow was struck in the passing of Elder Hans Geiser on Aug. 28, 1938. (For a more extended account of the history of the Moron congregation, see **Kleintal**; *ML* III, 168 f.)   S.G.

Morozovo (Neu-Hochfeld), a village in South Russia, founded in 1872 in the province of Ekaterinoslav (*q.v.*), volost Nikolaipol (formerly Nikolaifeld), by Mennonites from the Chortitza settlement (*q.v.*). The village owned 5,270 acres of land. In 1913 the population was 350, mostly Mennonites. (*ML* III, 169.)

Morris, Man., a town (pop. 1,193) 40 miles south of Winnipeg on the (now) Morris River, which runs through the Mennonite settlement into the Red

River. Morris is located in a predominantly Mennonite locality. An estimated 200 Mennonites live in town. There are two Mennonite churches in town with a small membership, without full-time pastors, the United Mennonite Church (GCM) and a Bergtaler Mennonite Church.

About six to eight miles northwest of Morris, on the banks of the Morris River, the villages Rosenhof and Rosenort were founded in the fall of 1874 by the Evangelical Mennonite Church (Kleine Gemeinde). Just before World War I these villages broke up and the settlers nearly all moved on their farms. In 1882 about one fourth of the congregation organized into a part of the Church of God in Christ Mennonites (Holdeman). In 1955 the Evangelical Mennonite Church numbers over 1,000 souls with 500 baptized members who worship in a large church built in 1949, about eight miles from Morris. The Holdeman Church numbers about 500, with approximately 250 baptized members, who worship in a church built in 1950, located 2½ miles from the other church. The social relationship between the two churches is good. In 1950 both the town and the rural municipality suffered severely from a major flood. The whole population had to be evacuated to neighboring Mennonite settlements like Lowe Farm and Steinbach, and for seven weeks from the beginning of May to the middle of June the entire area was covered with from one to eight feet of water. The main occupation is grain farming. (*ML* III, 169.)   P.J.B.R.

Morris Gospel Hall (MC) was a preaching outpost of the Kansas City, Kan., Mennonite Gospel Mission. In 1946 it had 22 members. It had its beginning in 1931 as an extension Sunday school of the Mennonite Gospel Mission. In 1946 it became an organized congregation of the South Central Conference with 16 charter members. It was administered in 1946-51 as part of the Twin City Missions, which had a total of 38 members in that year. The work was discontinued in 1951, when the building was destroyed in the great flood. Edward Yoder was the superintendent throughout.   Ed.Y.

Morrison Mennonite Church (MC), also known as the Mennonite Brick Church, located about four miles northwest of Morrison, in Whiteside Co., Ill., belonging to the Illinois Conference, was organized in 1868. The meetinghouse was dedicated on Jan. 1, 1873. The membership in 1956 was 16, with Aaron D. Nice as pastor.   A.D.N.

Mortier, Jean (Jan) **de,** was an elder of the Waterlander congregation at Leiden, Holland. He was one of the group of Waterlander, High German, and Frisian leaders who on March 16, 1614, sent a letter to the Mennonites of Bergischland and South Germany to promote peace with them. De Mortier signs this letter "Jan de Mortier, bishop of the church of Walloons at Leyden"; hence it is known that the Waterlander congregation in which he served was composed of French-speaking Walloons, apparently immigrants from southern Belgium. (*Inv. Arch. Amst.* I, No. 544.)   vdZ.

Morton, Ill., a town (pop. 2,241) in Tazewell County, ten miles southeast of Peoria. Mennonite pioneers

came to the county in 1830. In 1941 the Pleasant Grove and Goodfield congregations (MC) united and erected a church building in Morton, where approximately half of the 193 members now reside. Rural members live within a six-mile radius mainly south and west. Evangelical Mennonites, earlier known as Defenseless Mennonites, are located five miles southwest, and the Pleasant Hill (MC) congregation five miles west. There are approximately 500 Mennonites within a six-mile radius. The Apostolic Christian Church (*q.v.*) has one of its larger congregations in Morton. The town is noted for its small industries, which include two potteries, two manufacturers of grain elevators, a fence factory, and a washing-machine factory. Mennonites are employed locally and in large industries in Peoria. A number of Mennonites operate their own businesses.   L.A.B.

Morton Mennonite Church (MC), in the city of Morton, Tazewell Co., Ill., a member of the Illinois Conference, is a merger of two older rural congregations, Pleasant Grove, near Tremont, Ill., whose meetinghouse was erected in 1879, and Goodfield, near Goodfield, Ill., whose building was erected in 1883. The church was dedicated on May 4, 1941. In 1957 the congregation had 200 members with Kenneth G. Good as bishop.   R.D.R.

Morveldinck (Mordelvinck, Maerlincx), **Rolef** and **Jan,** brothers who were put to death at Deventer, Dutch province of Overijssel, on May 18, 1542. With some relatives and adherents they lived at Emlichem and, calling themselves "de vrome Kinderen van Emlichem," they plundered the farms. They were Anabaptists only in name, followers of Jan van Batenburg; in the sentence they are called "adherents of the Crechting group and Davidjorists." (*Inv. Arch. Amst.* I, No. 246; *DB* 1917, 141, 177; 1919, 18.   vdZ.

Mos (Moser), **Wolfgang von,** an Anabaptist martyr, a native of Mos in the Adige Valley of Tirol, Austria, was arrested in 1529 with seven or eight other Anabaptists, at Vill in the Adige. Each was separately examined. Wolfgang confessed that he had been taught and baptized by Michael Kürschner (*q.v.*), who had died a martyr's death on June 2, 1529. The eight or nine brethren and sisters were executed on Nov. 16, 1529. Wolfgang Moser was one of the two companions of Jörg vom Hause Jakob (George Blaurock?) when Jörg was imprisoned at Basel, Switzerland, in February 1529. Moser was expelled from Basel, but returned in March with his wife Küngolde. He was again expelled from the city upon *Urfehde* (*q.v.*), which his wife, however, refused to render. He returned to the Adige and there lost his life.   E.H.B.

Mart. Mir. D 27, E 435; Zieglschmid, *Chronik,* 74 f.; Paul Peachey, *Die soziale Herkunft der Schweizer Täufer in der Reformationszeit* (Karlsruhe, 1954) 47, 121, No. 262; Paul Burckhardt, *Die Basler Täufer* (Basel, 1898) 48 f.

Mosa Mennonite Church (MC), located in Mosa Township, about 40 miles west of London, Ont. Early families were Brubacher, Moyer, Snyder, Bergey, Woolner, King, McKay, Saylor, Devitt, and Cressman, who had come from Waterloo County and from the Niagara frontier. In 1875 Henry Mc-Kay was called to the ministry here and served until 1902. In 1877 Abram B. Brubacher was ordained minister. By 1883 he inclined to the conservative group and moved to eastern Ohio. In 1907 Nathaniel Bergey was ordained minister. In 1905 under I. R. Shantz of Alberta the membership was strengthened. Over the years services have been held in Cashmere Schoolhouse, S.S. No. 5, Mosa, Austen School, Presbyterian church in Bothwell, in Clachan Hall. By 1934 the membership was reduced to eleven. In recent years it has been revived and the new Bethel Church built. See also **Clachan, Aldboro, Austen, Bothwell.** (*ML* III, 169.) J.C.F.

Mosbach, a town and formerly a district of the Palatinate (now Baden), Germany, which included in addition to the Mosbach district also the present Sinsheim district. Shortly after the Thirty Years' War Swiss Mennonites settled in the desolate and depopulated region, arriving in complete poverty and finding employment on the estates of the nobles. As laborers they were welcome, but the exercise of their religion was made difficult. They at first had to meet secretly in the woods for their service, until they were permitted to meet in groups of not more than twenty. In 1652 several families came to Neckarelz in the Mosbach district. Some of them moved away. The census of 1925 listed 41 Mennonites living in the Mosbach district. (*ML* III, 169.)
HEGE.

Moscorovius, Hieronymus, was an elder of the Polish Brethren (Socinians, *q.v.*) in Rakov, Poland, who in 1612 together with Valentinus Smalcius (*q.v.*), a preacher of this group, wrote a letter to the (Frisian) Mennonite congregation of Danzig, Prussia, in which they asked to arrange a union between the Mennonites and the Polish Brethren. Other letters followed, insisting on the union. There were— so they said—differences between both groups: the Polish Brethren did not strictly reject the swearing of oaths, but there were many principles on which they agreed: both the Brethren and the Mennonites were opposed to infant baptism and bearing arms; both meant to be a church of believers, using the ban; both laid much stress on Christian morals. Moscorovius repeatedly insisted on holding a meeting to discuss the problem. This meeting, however, was never held, because the Mennonites did not wish to unite with the Brethren. The leaders of the Danzig Mennonite congregations wrote a number of letters to Dutch Mennonite leaders, Hans de Ries (*q.v.*) and Reinier Wybrands, asking their advice and their coming in person if necessary. This, however, did not happen. In 1628 the Polish Brethren were suppressed by order of the Polish government. (*Inv. Arch. Amst.* I, No. 664; II, Nos. 2925-39.)
vDZ.

Moscow (Russian, *Moskva*), founded in 1295, capital of Soviet Russia, population 4,137,018 (1949), has played a significant role in the history of the Mennonites of Russia. Occasionally young men attended the University of Moscow. During World War I, when Mennonite young men served in hospital units under the All-Russian Union of Zemstvos for Relief of Sick and Wounded Soldiers and other or-ganizations, Moscow was the headquarters of these activities. After the Revolution some young men remained in Moscow and others were attracted to study or work in the capital, among them C. F. Klassen (*q.v.*). The American Mennonite Relief (*q.v.*) operated in Moscow under the direction of A. J. Miller. The Mennonites of Russia maintained an office of the Allrussischer Mennonitischer Landwirtschaftlicher Verein (*q.v.*) in Moscow, with Peter Froese as president, which also published *Der Praktische Landwirt* (1925-26.) The office address was Taganskaya Ulitsa. This organization also served as Mennonite center (*Menobshestvo*) in Moscow advising and helping many of the Mennonite immigrants to Canada. In 1928 all activities had to be discontinued. Most of the 25,000 Mennonites who left Russia 1923-30 went through Moscow, particularly during the last phase of their migration. In 1929 thousands of Mennonites who planned to leave Russia were stranded in Moscow for many weeks until they were given permission to leave or were forcibly returned home or exiled. During the first years after the Revolution the Mennonites of Russia, under the leadership of Peter F. Froese, took part in the work of the United Council of Religious Bodies in advising the conscientious objectors to war. In 1925 the Allgemeine Bundeskonferenz (*q.v.*) of Mennonites of Russia convened in Moscow. A complete investigation as to the number of Mennonites who have resided in Moscow has not been made. At present there are very few there. Moscow is the headquarters for the All-Union Council of Evangelical Christian Baptists, with whom Mennonites of Russia and America have contact. C.K.

Mosellanus, Franciscus, a Reformed theologian, one of the most influential clergymen during the rule of the Calvinist Elector Frederick III (*q.v.*) of the Palatinate, Germany. He was the deacon of the Heiliggeistkirche in Heidelberg 1568-70, and inspector of the Bacharach district 1570-73. He was appointed to represent the national church at the Frankenthal disputation (*q.v.*), but he did not actually take part in the debate (May 28-June 19, 1571) with the Anabaptists. (*ML* III, 169.) HEGE.

Mosemann, John Heer (1877-1938), a Mennonite (MC) bishop and leader, was born in Lancaster, Pa., on Dec. 1, 1877, the fifth of the eleven children of Philip and Elizabeth Heer Mosemann, who immigrated from near Trappstadt, Bavaria, Germany, in 1854-55. On Dec. 22, 1901, he married Lillie Swarr Forry. Their six children are Paul, Martha, Esther (Mrs. John R. Mumaw), John, Rhoda (Mrs. J. Clarence Denlinger), and Daniel. His formal education was limited to a short course at the Millersville Normal School 1898-99.

Mosemann became a member of the church in 1895 and was ordained a minister in the Chestnut St. (Lancaster) congregation in 1904, where he served until his death in 1938, being ordained bishop in 1926. He was active in the early missionary and Bible conferences of the Eastern Pennsylvania conferences, and participated in the organization of the Rockland Street Mission in Lancaster, and in founding the later outposts of the East Chestnut Street Mennonite Church.

In the Lancaster Conference Mosemann was active in numerous capacities, serving as secretary of the Conference 1931-37. He was a member on the Publishing Committee of the Mennonite Publication Board 1924-31, was coeditor of *The Way* 1917-38, and wrote numerous tracts and articles. He was a promoter of Christian education, and served as instructor in the winter Bible school at Eastern Mennonite School. Throughout his ministry he supported his family by means of retail marketing and the manufacture of peanutbutter. His death came Aug. 28, 1938, in Lancaster, with burial in the Millersville Mennonite Church Cemetery.   J.H.M.

Moser, a Mennonite family, numerous among the Mennonites in Switzerland, both in the Emmental and the Bernese Jura. From Switzerland many of them because of oppression or hardships moved to Germany (Palatinate) and Alsace. From Courtelary, France, a Moser family emigrated to America in 1754. Others, mostly from Alsace, also settled in the United States in the early 19th century. In the Palatinate the Mosers never were numerous. The Dutch *Naamlijst* names Peter Mos(s)er as an elder of the Bockschaft congregation in 1757, and Christian Moser (d. 1789 or 90) as a preacher (before 1769) and from 1782 an elder of the Rheingrafenstein congregation near Kreuznach. In America there are many Mosers. Abraham J. Moser published a paper, "Aus dem Leben der Schweizer Mennoniten" in *Christlicher Bundesbote* of Aug. 1, 1885. Nicolaus Moser (*q.v.*) and John Moser (*q.v.*) belonged to this family, but not Wolfgang Moser (*q.v.*). The name Musser is in all probability a variant of Moser.   vDZ.

Moser, John (1826-1908), a General Conference Mennonite elder and leader, was born Aug. 2, 1826, in Wayne Co., Ohio, the oldest son and fourth child of Jakob and Barbara Wahli Moser, who had immigrated among the early settlers to the Sonnenberg Swiss settlement in Ohio in 1821 from Am Stalden, Jura, Switzerland. John married Anna Lehman on Jan. 15, 1852. They moved to Riley Twp., Putnam Co., Ohio, near Bluffton, the following spring, where their ten children were born. He joined the Sonnenberg church on April 10, 1846, and was chosen minister of the Putnam County congregation on Oct. 9, 1853. On Jan. 24, 1864, he was chosen bishop of this congregation, which office he carried out with zeal and fidelity during a period when many changes were introduced into the congregation. During his pastorate of over 50 years he baptized nearly 1,000 persons, married over 200 couples, and, besides his regular sermons nearly every Sunday, officiated at several hundred funerals. He took great interest in the church organizations, such as Sunday schools, young people's societies, missions and evangelistic endeavors, all of which were begun during his ministry. He participated in the ministers' meetings of the Swiss congregations. During his ministry the Swiss congregations of Allen and Putnam counties joined the General Conference Mennonite Church.

A farmer by occupation, he learned the gunsmith's trade and supplied the settlement with rifles of high quality.

Moser compiled the letters of the Amish schism and had them published in 1876 as an answer to the strict avoidance practiced by the Reformed Mennonites and defended in the writings of Daniel Musser. He died July 10, 1908, and was buried in the cemetery of the St. John's Mennonite Church.

D.L.G.

Mennonite Yearbook and Almanac (1909) 22-24 with picture; P. B. Amstutz, *Geschichtliche Ereignisse der Mennoniten Ansiedlung in Allen und Putnam County, Ohio* (n.p., 1925) 124-26 with picture; Johannes Moser, *Eine Verantwortung gegen Daniel Musser's Meidungs-Erklärung* . . . (Lancaster, 1876); *ML* III, 170.

Moser, Nikolaus, an elder of the Swiss Mennonites in Friedersmatt near Bowil, Switzerland, who tried in vain to prevent the break between the Amish (*q.v.*) and the Reist (*q.v.*) groups. In 1709 he wrote a letter to the Mennonites in Holland on behalf of his oppressed brethren describing their desperate plight and expressing his earnest desire that they be reunited. He is said to have died in prison. NEFF.

Inv. Arch. Amst. I, No. 1255 a; Müller, *Berner Täufer*, 255; S. Geiser, *Die Taufgesinnten-Gemeinden* (Karlsruhe, 1931) 417, 426; *ML* III, 170.

Moser, Wolfgang: see **Mos, Wolfgang von.**

Mosheim, Johann Lorenz von (1694-1755), a noted German Protestant theologian, professor of theology in Helmstädt and chancellor of the University of Göttingen. In his meritorious church history, *Institutiones historiae ecclesiasticae recentiores* (Helmstädt, 1741), he treats the Mennonites extensively and indeed much more moderately and correctly than other historiographers of that time. He admits that he read the book by Herman Schijn (*q.v.*), *Historia Christianorum,* but does not agree that they should not be called *Wiedertäufer.* He accuses them of maliciously and cleverly concealing their issue, a charge which Gerardus Maatschoen (*q.v.*) vigorously and skillfully refutes. In his writings, *Versuch einer unparteiischen Ketzergeschichte* (Helmstädt, 1746) and *Anderweitiger Versuch einer vollständigen und unparteiischen Ketzergeschichte* (Helmstädt, 1748), he does not mention the Mennonites. The former book does not go beyond the Middle Ages (Waldenses); the latter deals mainly with Michel Servetus.   NEFF.

Schijn-Maatschoen, *Geschiedenis* II, 54 ff.; *DB* 1882, 54; *ML* III, 170.

Mosiman, Samuel K. (1867-1940), a prominent educator in the General Conference Mennonite Church, president of Bluffton College for 25 years, was born near Middleton, Ohio, Dec. 17, 1867, the second of the fourteen children of Christian and Anna Kinsinger Mosiman. His education included one year at the National Normal Institute at Lebanon, Ohio, and further work at Wittenberg Academy and Wittemberg College, Springfield, Ohio, where he received his B.A. in 1897, and M.A. in 1905. McCormick Theological Seminary, Chicago, conferred the B.D. degree upon him in 1905, and Halle University, Germany, the Ph.D. degree for studies in Hebrew, Aramaic, Syriac, and Arabic in 1907. Honorary degrees conferred were Litt.D. from Wittenberg College in 1930 and LL.D. from Bluffton College in 1939.

His first wife (1902), Amelia Krehbiel, died in 1905. In 1909 he married Emilie Hamm. There were no children. In 1897-1903 he served as superintendent of the Mennonite Indian Mission school at Cantonment, Okla. The year after returning from Europe he was professor of Greek and philosophy at National Normal Institute. The following year (1909) he started his career at Bluffton College, which then was Central Mennonite College.

For the year 1908-9 Mosiman served as one of three members on an administration committee of the college. The next year he was elected president, in which capacity he served faithfully and efficiently until 1935. Central Mennonite College, maintained by the Middle District (GCM), became Bluffton College in 1913, directed by a board of fifteen members representing five branches of Mennonites. The first B.A. degrees were conferred on the class of 1915. During his administration five substantial new buildings were erected, the campus enlarged, the curriculum and faculty greatly expanded, for a period even including a theological seminary.

In addition, especially as a minister of the Gospel, he was active in the First Mennonite Church of Bluffton, of which he was a member, served as secretary and president of the Middle District Conference, vice-president of the General Conference, member of the Federal Council of Churches, chairman of the Association of Ohio College Presidents and Deans, and on numerous boards and committees.

While serving as a missionary to the American Indians Mosiman edited for a short time a periodical, *The Cheyenne and Arapaho Sword*, in the interest of the Mennonite mission at Cantonment (1900-1). While at the seminary he submitted a thesis, "The Existence of Maccabean Psalms in the Psalter," for the purpose of obtaining the Nettie F. McCormick Fellowship in Hebrew for 1904-5. His doctoral dissertation, "Eine Zusammenstellung und Vergleichung der Parralleltexte der Chronik und der älteren Bücher des Alten Testaments," is a recognized piece of research. He also contributed to the *International Standard Bible Encyclopedia*.

J.S.Sc.

Mosimann (Mosiman, Mosemann, Moseman), a Swiss Mennonite family. Between Signau and Lauperswil in the Emmental in the canton of Bern, Switzerland, there is a hill called Moosegg, meaning Moss Ridge, where the first traces of the Mosimann family appear. The first appearance of the family in the records as Anabaptists is in 1633, when Madlena and Elsbeth Mosemann were taken before the Bernese authorities for belonging to this forbidden sect. From that time until 1670 the Bernese records report nine similar cases against members of the Mosimann family. This is one of the few families that had members who remained in the Emmental region during the times of severe persecution; it is still found in the congregation. Until 1952 Fritz Mosimann was an elder in the Langnau congregation. Others moved to Alsace and Montbéliard in the first years of the 18th century. Fritz Mosimann of the Pfastatt-Mulhouse congregation (1954) was a popular painter of Alsatian landscapes.

From Alsace (and Switzerland) several families came to America and others moved to Germany. Several Mosimann families established their homes in America during the 19th century, locating in Lancaster Co., Pa., Butler Co., Ohio, and central Illinois. Among the outstanding Mosimann personalities have been Jakob Mosemann (1795-1876), who emigrated from the Trappstadt congregation, Germany, settling near Bowmansville, Lancaster County. He was ordained preacher (1822) and bishop (1825) in Germany and continued as bishop in the Lancaster Conference, where he was an outstanding preacher and teacher. His grandson John H. Mosemann (*q.v.*, 1877-1938) was also an outstanding bishop (preacher 1904, bishop 1926) in the Lancaster Conference. The latter's son John H. Mosemann was in 1956 a professor in the Goshen College Biblical Seminary and bishop of the Goshen College congregation. Another grandson of Jakob was David H. Mosemann, long a minister in the East Chestnut St. (MC) congregation in Lancaster. Samuel K. Mosiman (*q.v.*, 1867-1940) was president of Bluffton College in 1908-35, and a leader in the General Conference Mennonite Church. Michael Mosimann, born *ca.* 1820 in Lorraine, came to the United States in 1831, became a leading bishop in central Illinois, later joining the Defenseless Mennonite Church.

D.L.G.

Mottencop: see **Stupmann, Wilhelm.**

Moultrie County, Ill.: see **Douglas-Moultrie Counties.**

Moultrie, a village in western Columbiana County, Ohio, near which there was a small settlement of Mennonites (MC) which organized the Georgetown Mennonite Church (now extinct) about 1840. In 1850 Jacob Newcomer donated one-half acre of ground on which the meetinghouse now stands. Henry Newcomer and Henry Walters served as ministers. The church never had Sunday school. The last services were held in 1885.

W.D.S.

Moundridge, a town (1950 pop. 942) in McPherson Co., Kan. The first Mennonite settlers to come to this area were South German Mennonites who came to Kansas in 1874 via Illinois and Iowa. They founded Christian (*q.v.*) near Moundridge, which was later given up. However, the Mennonites of Moundridge and its community are primarily of Swiss-Volhynian background, who came to Kansas in 1874. Moundridge has a number of stores, a milling company, a co-operative creamery organized in 1932, Co-op Elevator Association organized in 1944, Farmers Co-op organized in 1936, Co-op Federal Credit Union organized in 1947, the Citizen's State Bank, and other businesses. In the early days it had a preparatory school, which is now replaced by a modern high school. The *Moundridge Journal* has been published since 1886. The Mercy Hospital (*q.v.*), operated by the Church of God in Christ, Mennonite, is located at Moundridge.

Moundridge has two General Conference churches — the First Mennonite Church of Christian and the West Zion Mennonite Church (*q.v.*). In its immediate community the following churches are located: Hoffnungsfeld (see **Hopefield**) Mennonite

Church, Eden Mennonite Church (*q.v.*), Garden Township Mennonite Church (*q.v.*), Emmanuel Mennonite Church (*q.v.*) and the Lone Tree (*q.v.*) and Meridian (*q.v.*) Church of God in Christ, Mennonite congregations. The latter three are not of Swiss-Volhynian but Polish-German background.

C.K.

I. G. Neufeld, "Jacob Stucky—Pioneer of Two Continents," *Menn. Life* IV (January 1949) 46; *The Seventy-Fifth Anniversary Services of the Swiss Mennonites, Sept. 5, 1949* (n.d.); P. P. Wedel, *Kurze Geschichte der aus Wolhynien, Russland nach Kansas ausgewanderten Schweizer-Mennoniten;* L. L. Spalding, "What We Found in Moundridge," *Menn. Life* VII (July 1952) 131; ML III, 170.

Moundridge Preparatory School was founded in Moundridge, Kan., in 1909, sponsored by the Mennonite School Association (*Mennonitischer Schulverein*), which consisted of representatives of the West Zion Mennonite Church, the Eden Mennonite Church, the First Mennonite Church of Christian, and the Garden Township Mennonite Church, all of the General Conference branch. The booklet *Mennonitischer Schulverein* (Moundridge, 1909) contained information about the board of directors (J. C. Goering, chairman, S. S. Baumgartner, secretary), the constitution, the purpose of the school, curriculum, and rules. Among the teachers were P. P. Wedel and Helena Isaac. The school was closed in 1918. (*Jahresheft des Mennonitischen Schulvereins,* 1910 ff.)

C.K.

Mount Airy Mennonite Church (MC), formerly a mission outpost of the Maple Grove (*q.v.*) church, near Ellicott City, Md., is now an independent congregation, with a membership of 18, and Irvin S. Martin as pastor.

I.D.L.

Mount Bethel (Pa.) Mennonite (MC) Church. Mennonites living in northeastern Northampton County, Pa., in the latter part of the 18th century built a meetinghouse on the land of Jacob Kappes of Upper Mount Bethel Township. In 1822 the Mennonites of the area built another meetinghouse near what became later the intersection of Broadway and South Fourth Street in Bangor, Pa. The settlement seems not to have thrived, although the following Mennonite names were represented in the area in 1754: Gross, Culp, Tyson, Moyer, Swartz, Funk, Hess, Fry, Snyder, Martin, Weaver, Bender, Bower, Bowman, Grub, and Nice. Jacob Moyer (1791-1859) of the Swamp district of the Franconia Conference used to go to Northampton County to administer communion to the members there. And John Geil (1778-1866), a preacher of the Lexington congregation of the Franconia Conference, used to preach in Northampton County. The members who were left in the area in 1847 cast their lot with John H. Oberholtzer's new conference, which ordained David Henning (1806-81) to serve as preacher. But shortly after Henning's ordination he united with William Gehman's Evangelical Mennonites. In 1878 Henning and a woman named Elizabeth Warch as "survivors of the said Mennonite Society" conveyed the church property to the Lutherans, and the Mennonite congregations expired. In 1935 the old residents in Northampton County spoke of the former Men-

nonites with high regard, calling them "Old Meneese" (corruption for Mennist, an old German name for Mennonite).

J.C.W.

J. C. Wenger, *History of the Mennonites of the Franconia Conference* (Telford, Pa., 1937) 232-37.

Mount Calvary Mennonite Church (MC), located near Westward Ho, Alberta. The first settlers were the Mervin R. Stanton, John C. Harder, and Earl Buschert families, arriving in 1936. Sunday school was held in the Westward Ho school until 1945 as a mission of the West Zion Mennonite Church near Carstairs. On July 8, 1945, the congregation organized and dedicated its new church. Abraham Reist was given pastoral charge of the congregation by the Alberta-Saskatchewan Mennonite Conference in 1948, having served the congregation for some time before this. The membership was 30 in 1955.

E.S.

Mount Carmel Mennonite Brethren in Christ Church, near Mt. Carmel, Pa., had 95 members in 1955, with Herbert W. Hartman as pastor.

Mount Clinton Mennonite Church (MC), located one-half mile west of Mount Clinton, Rockingham Co., Va., belongs to the Central Bishop District. Services were held in schoolhouses before the Civil War for Burkholder, Layman, Myers, and Showalter families who had settled in the Muddy Creek "basin." The Weavers, Drivers, Brunks, Heltzels, Heatwoles, and Pences followed after the war. The first meetinghouse was dedicated on Jan. 3, 1875, under the local leadership of Jacob and Joseph N. Driver. The old frame church was replaced by a brick structure on the opposite (north) side of the highway in 1916. This church is one of the four home churches of the Middle District of the Virginia Conference. Today few Mennonites live in this area. It must depend to some extent on Mennonite families who do not live near here. Sem S. Weaver was a resident minister for many years. The membership in 1956 was 109, with C. K. Lehman as pastor.

H.A.B.

Mount Hermon Mennonite (MC) Church at Bergton, Hardy Co., W. Va., under the Virginia Conference. In the early years occasional meetings were held at the Moyer school by ministers on their way to more distant points in West Virginia. About the turn of the century services were held more regularly. Later services were held at the Capon Run schoolhouse in Virginia, two miles south. In 1937 a meetinghouse was built between the two schools, a short distance north of the Virginia and West Virginia line. The membership in 1956 was 65, with Linden M. Wenger as pastor, and Rowland Shank as assistant pastor.

T.S.

Mount Hermon Mennonite Church (MC), also known as Mutton Hollow Church, located in the Blue Ridge Mountains between Lydia and Geer, Green Co., Va., is a mission church under the Virginia Conference. The congregation was organized in 1938 and services were first held in a Brethren church. In April 1947 a new stone building was dedicated. The membership in 1957 was 20, with Warren A. Kratz as minister.

D.R.H.

Mount Joy, Pa., a town (pop. 3,600) located in a fertile and prosperous farming area on the Lancaster-Harrisburg Pike, 13 miles west of Lancaster, was settled in 1735 by Scotch-Irish immigrants from Mountjoy, Donegal, Ireland. The Heistands and Nissleys, Mennonites, had settled there by 1750. Swiss Mennonites claimed the lands back from the highway, but gradually also obtained those over the highway from the Scotch-Irish. By the twentieth century the Swiss had also come into town. A large Mennonite congregation (MC), called Mount Joy, with 394 members, worships in the town, and numerous other congregations surround it.   I.D.L.

Mount Joy Mennonite Church (MC), located in Mt. Joy, Lancaster Co., Pa., was organized in 1908 when the present brick meetinghouse, 54 x 88 ft., was built in the southwestern part of the town. It remained a part of the Kraybill circuit until 1949. The membership in 1955 was 381, with Henry E. Lutz as bishop and Henry F. Garber, Amos L. Hess, and Henry W. Frank as ministers.   I.D.L.

Mount Joy United Missionary Church, Markham, York Co., Ont., was organized in 1876. In 1957 the membership was 129 with Herbert Shantz serving as pastor.   S.S.S.

Mount Olivet Mennonite Church (GCM), located at 2nd and Ohio Streets in Huron, S.D., was organized on July 17, 1945, under the Evangelization Board of the Northern District Conference (GCM) with 17 charter members. On May 12, 1946, this congregation joined the General Conference. In 1956 the church had a membership of 85, and was building a new church and parsonage. Four ministers have served the church in the following order: Jacob A. Friesen, Alfred Regier, B. J. Nickel, and Vernon Buller.   V.H.B.

Mount Pisgah Mennonite Church (MC), located about five miles northwest of Leonard, Shelby Co., Mo., and sometimes known as the Cherry Box congregation, was organized probably about 1868, with perhaps 20 charter members. Benjamin Lapp was the first minister and Christian Lapp the first deacon. In 1870 Benjamin F. Hershey, from the Science Ridge congregation, Sterling, Ill., moved into this community and is thought to have been the first bishop of the congregation. The first church was built probably in 1872 about one and one-half miles south of Cherry Box. It was replaced by the present church, located a quarter mile south of Cherry Box, in 1899; this church was remodeled in 1956. The congregation has never been large; the membership in 1956 was 48. Other bishops who have served the congregation were David Kauffman, Daniel Kauffman, J. M. Kreider, Nelson Kauffman, and Daniel Kauffman, the present bishop. Other ministers who have served are John Brubaker, Wallace Kauffman, L. J. Johnston, George Bissey, John M. Yoder, and Daniel Kauffman (ordained bishop in 1952).
      J.M.Y.

Mount Pleasant, Iowa, is the county seat (pop. 4,610) of Henry County (*q.v.*), in the southeastern part of the state. In 1874-76 Prussian Mennonite immigrants, who later settled in Kansas and Nebraska, lived in this city temporarily through the influence of Cornelius Jansen (*q.v.*), who resided in Mount Pleasant in 1874-76. During World War II, from February 1943 to September 1946, Civilian Public Service Unit No. 86, under MCC administration, was located at the Mount Pleasant State Hospital. Conscientious objectors were again employed at the hospital in a Mennonite I-W unit under the new Selective Service program following World War II.   M.G.

M. Gingerich, "Mennonites in Mount Pleasant," *The Palimpsest* (Iowa City) December 1942; M. Gingerich, *Service for Peace* (Akron, Pa., 1949) 229-31.

Mount Pleasant Christian Day School, Fentress, Va., founded by the Mount Pleasant Mennonite (MC) Church, opened in the fall of 1941 with one teacher and seven grades. Since then the eighth grade and first and second years of high school have been added. For a few years the school was conducted in a reconditioned store building, but now has permanent quarters in a new building. The work is financed by the Mount Pleasant Mennonite Church, for the most part by freewill offerings taken in the regular morning church sessions twice a month, and operated by a board of trustees chosen by the congregation.

The teachers of the school have all been Mennonites and the children for the most part have come from the Mennonite homes of the community. It is the purpose of the school to give the children a Christian education under a wholesome environment. The school is open to all, regardless of ability to support it, and to date with only a few exceptions all the children of the immediate church community have attended here.   A.D.W.

Mount Pleasant Mennonite Church (MC), formerly called Blanchard, located six miles southeast of Continental, Putnam Co., Ohio, was founded soon after 1830 by the Myers and Shank families from Leiters Ford, Md. The first meetinghouse, built before 1840 near the site of the present building, which was erected in 1918, was displaced in 1866 by one located about four miles farther east. The congregation has always been small, and had no resident minister 1886-1906. A. J. Steiner was ordained for this place in 1906, but was called to North Lima, Ohio, in 1908. For various reasons the pastoral supply was quite irregular until 1950 when Norman O. Smith, the present (1956) pastor, took charge. The membership, which was 40 in 1912, was 47 in 1956.
      H.S.B.

John Umble, *Ohio Mennonite Sunday Schools* (Goshen, 1941).

Mount Pleasant Mennonite Church (MC), located near Paradise in the northern tip of Bart Twp., Lancaster Co., Pa., was begun as a mission in 1898 in a former United Brethren meetinghouse by the Lancaster Sunday School Mission under the leadership of B. F. Book and Christian M. Neff. A congregation emerged, which in 1956 numbered 78 with Amos W. Weaver and C. Marvin Eshleman as ministers and G. Parke Book as bishop. A Christian day school for the community adjoins the meetinghouse.
      I.D.L.

Mount Pleasant Mennonite Church (MC), located in Norfolk Co., Va., is a member of the Virginia Conference. The first settlers came into this area in 1900 and were organized into a congregation on Sept. 17, 1905, by Anthony Heatwole, bishop from Waynesboro, Va., with 16 charter members; J. D. Wert was ordained as pastor. Other ministers who have served the congregation were A. D. Wenger, S. H. Brunk, Amos D. Wenger, and Clayton D. Bergey, who is currently serving the congregation of 174 members (1956). The first meetinghouse was built in 1910 and enlarged in 1952. (*ML* III, 170.)   A.D.W.

Mount Pleasant Mennonite Church (MC), now extinct, was located two miles west of Mount Sidney in the North River District, Augusta Co., Va. The church was built in 1870. The congregation probably reached its height in the 1890's. Appointments were filled by Southern and Middle District ministers. The Mennonites moved farther south or left the state. Services discontinued here about 1940. The meetinghouse was sold in 1954. Isaac Grove (1820-99) and Jacob Harshbarger (1855-1906) were the early local ministers.   H.A.B.

Mount Pleasant United Missionary Church, located 1½ miles north of Zephyr, Ont., was organized in 1889. In 1957 it had a membership of 24, with Edward N. Chester as pastor.   E.N.C.

Mount Vernon Mennonite Church (MC) was begun by the Strasburg congregation as an outpost located in a frame meetinghouse close to the Octoraro Creek in Chester Co., Pa. On June 24, 1948, J. Lloyd Kreider was ordained pastor. The meetinghouse was greatly enlarged and the grounds renovated in 1956. The membership in 1956 was 39.   I.D.L.

Mount Vernon Mennonite Church (MC), located along the Brown's Gap Road, at the foot of the Blue Ridge Mountains, one mile east of Port Republic, Rockingham Co., Va. Services were begun here in an abandoned church building, 20 x 60 ft., in January 1954. The present membership is 26, of whom 17 are natives of this rural community now populated mostly by descendants of English settlers. The congregation is part of the Middle District of the Virginia Conference. Three weekly worship services and other activities for the various age groups are under the direction of the pastor, Hubert R. Pellman, and four non-native married couples.   H.R.Pe.

Mount View Mennonite Church (MC), located near High River, south of Calgary, Alberta. Elias W. Bricker of Ontario was the pioneer settler in this district, coming with the first home-seekers' excursion sponsored by the Canadian Pacific Railway in 1889. Around 1900-1 other Mennonite families arrived. On April 30, 1901, a meeting was held in Bricker's home, in charge of S. F. Coffman, and a congregation was organized with 11 charter members. Early services were held in the Maple Leaf schoolhouse. In 1902 a church 28 x 42 ft. was built, enlarged in 1939. The membership in 1955 was 19; there was no resident pastor. The following

ordained men have served the congregation: Norman B. Stauffer, Isaac Miller, A. H. Wambold, Menno Gingrich, Owen O. Hershberger, Howard O. Stauffer, and Harold Boettger.   E.S.

Mount View United Missionary Church, Mt. View Twp., Whatcom Co., Wash., was organized in 1902. Two years later a meetinghouse was erected with a seating capacity of 200. Since 1917 the congregation has conducted an annual camp meeting at Mount View. In 1949 Arcie Grout was the pastor, with 12 members.   A.Gr.

Mount Zion Mennonite Church (MC), in Morgan Co., Mo., six miles northeast of Versailles, belongs to the South Central Conference District. It was organized in 1868. In 1871 the congregation was divided on doctrinal questions, particularly on the ordinance of footwashing. One group formed the Bethel Mennonite Church (GCM) of Fortuna, Mo., in Moniteau County; the other was known as the Mount Zion Mennonite Church. The first services were held in a schoolhouse. In 1876 the first church building was erected, replaced in 1905 by the present building. Mount Zion was for some years the church home of Daniel Kauffman, for many years editor of the *Gospel Herald*. In 1956 the membership was 54, with Leroy Gingerich as pastor.   L.G.

Mount Zion United Missionary Church, located five miles east of Queensville, Ont., was organized in 1889. In 1957 it had 17 members with Edward N. Chester as pastor.   H.W.Ha.

Mountain Home schoolhouse is the site of an extinct Mennonite (MC) rural mission church under the Virginia Conference, on the Virginia-West Virginia line four miles west of Criders, Va. About 1885 Mennonite ministers were invited to conduct services at this as well as other schoolhouses in this community. Preaching services were held here once a month until 1955. Here the minister stood in West Virginia and preached to his congregation in Virginia. The pastor in recent years was Ray Emsweiler.   T.S.

Mountain Lake, Minn., a village of about 2,000 located in the southwestern part of the state in Cottonwood County. In 1873, when the first Mennonites came to this area, it was a little village; by 1880 about 295 Mennonite families had settled in the Mountain Lake community. At the turn of the century the population of the village was 595. Most of these Mennonites came from the Molotschna settlement in Russia. However, a number of Manitoba Mennonite families joined the settlement, who were of Chortitza background. Most of the inhabitants of Mountain Lake at the present time are Mennonites. They also predominate in the surrounding farming area.

In the early days the Mennonites of Mountain Lake had progressive leadership in the realm of education. I. I. Bargen started the Mountain Lake Preparatory School (*q.v.*) in 1886. This school still exists, although its purpose and name have changed, as the Mountain Lake Bible School. There are three Mennonite groups represented in the **Mountain Lake** community. The General Conference has a membership of 1,394 (1956) in three congregations—Bethel Mennonite Church (*q.v.*), First Mennonite Church (*q.v.*), and Gospel Mennonite Church (*q.v.*). Three additional G.C.M. churches are located in the communities of Butterfield (*q.v.*) and Delft (*q.v.*). The Mennonite Brethren have 452 (1956) members in two churches, Mountain Lake and Carson. The Evangelical Mennonite Brethren Church of Mountain Lake consists of 255 members. Of these nine churches four are located within the city limits—three G.C.M. and one M.B.

Mountain Lake has a hospital (see **Bethel Deaconess Hospital**), nurses' home, Basinger Clinic, Mennonite Aid Society (*q.v.*), and the Eventide Home. The hospital and the old people's home have served the community over many decades. The present building of the hospital was opened for service in 1921 and the Eventide Home in 1950. The *Mountain Lake Observer*, published locally since 1894, has at times been in Mennonite hands.

Great changes have taken place in the community. The High German language has been replaced by English. Low German is still spoken among people over 25 years of age. Sixty-three per cent go to Mennonite colleges. Only 35 per cent of the young men were conscientious objectors during World War II. In only 19 of the 34 marriages in 1950, were both partners Mennonites.

When Saskatchewan invited settlers in its pioneer days, 157 families from Mountain Lake accepted the invitation. Many other families and young people have gone to other states and to the cities. On the other hand, non-Mennonites have moved into the city. J.J.F., C.K.

Seventy-five years in Minnesota, 1874-1949. Mennonite Churches in Mountain Lake Community (n.p. n.d.); *Jubilaeumsfeier, Mountain Lake, Minnesota, 1875-1925* (n.p., n.d.); *Brosamen aus Erfahrungen der Mennoniten in und um Mountain Lake, Minnesota* (n.p., n.d.,); Calvin Redekop, "A Changing Mountain Lake," *Menn. Life* XI (April 1956); F. P. Schultz, *A History of the Settlement of German Mennonites from Russia at Mountain Lake, Minnesota* (Author, 1938); ML III, 171 f.

Mountain Lake Bible School, formerly known as the Mountain Lake Preparatory School (*Deutsche Vorbereitungs-Schule*), Mountain Lake, Minn., was started by I. I. Bargen (*q.v.*) in 1886, who had organized a School Association (*Schulverein*) of 30 members for this purpose. After two years this organization was dissolved and I. I. Bargen resigned, but J. J. Balzer continued the school. Through his efforts a new School Association was organized in 1896.

The 1905-6 catalog makes provision for two classes of the lower level and four classes of upper level instruction in addition to some elementary school classes. The curriculum indicates that Balzer, who was a graduate of the Gnadenfeld Zentralschule, Russia, patterned his school after the one he was graduated from. In 1901 a commodious building was erected. The enrollment in 1901-2 was 83, 1902-3 was 106, 1903-4 was 116. More than half the students were adults.

In 1912 the Schulverein was dissolved and the control of the school was assumed jointly by five different Mennonite churches in the Mountain Lake community, who administered it until 1936, when another reorganization took place. Since that time the school has been known as the Mountain Lake Bible School (*q.v.*) and offers in its Bible department a Bible course of two years and six months for adults, and in its parochial department (in which the term consists of nine month) the regular state-required subjects of the first six grades and some courses in Bible and German. In addition to this the Bible School maintains a kindergarten. Among the outstanding teachers have been J. J. Balzer (1886-1914) and Cornelius Wall (1936-1946). In 1954 the school had an enrollment of 105 and five teachers. C.K.

Catalogs of Mountain Lake Deutsche Vorbereitungs-Schule and the Mountain Lake Bible School; J. E. Hartzler, *Education Among the Mennonites of America* (Danvers, Ill., 1925) 116 ff.; M. S. Harder, "The Origin, Philosophy, and Development of Education Among the Mennonites" (University of Southern California, dissertation, 1949) 244 ff.; ML III, 172.

Mountain Lake (Minn.) Evangelical Mennonite Brethren Church originated when Elder Aaron Wall and the ministers Johann Becker, Heinrich Fast, Sr., Peter Schultz, Heinrich E. Fast, and deacon Cornelius Friesen together with a group of fifteen families who had withdrawn from the first and larger of the two pioneer Mennonite churches of Mountain Lake began to meet in the homes for fellowship. This group organized as a church in January 1889 as the Bruderthaler Mennoniten-Gemeinde and built a meetinghouse. In the community it was later commonly known as the "Valley Church" because of the location of the church building about a mile north of the village of Mountain Lake, Midway Twp., Cottonwood County. The name was later changed to "Evangelical Mennonite Brethren Church" to accord with the name of the conference to which it belongs and which it helped bring into being and organized in October 1889. The conference was originally known as the "Defenseless Mennonite Brethren of North America."

The first meetinghouse was dedicated June 16, 1889. In 1892 another church was built and the first edifice used as a dining hall, and for a short time (1893-96) as a Bible school. This first building was razed in 1944.

From the very beginning the church stressed Christian education and instituted a Bible school in 1893 known as the Bruderthaler Gemeindeschule. In 1896 a three-story Bible school was built near the church, in which an elementary Bible school was held until 1925. Thereafter for several summers daily vacation Bible school was conducted here. This building was razed in 1947 and the material used for building a modern parsonage in Mountain Lake.

At least 35 members coming from this church have served in various conferences and denominations as missionaries, pastors, or Bible teachers; and a number of its younger members are now in training for Christian service. Other pastors of this church have been D. A. Regier, John N. Wall, H. P. Wiebe, Wm. M. Loewen, and H. A. Brandt. The baptized membership in 1957 was 273. D.A.R.

G. S. Rempel, *A Historical Sketch of the Churches of the Evangelical Mennonite Brethren* (Rosthern, 1939).

Mountain Lake (Minn.) **First** Mennonite Church (GCM), organized in 1878, until about 1938 called the Mennonite Church of Mountain Lake, had no conference affiliation until 1917, when it joined both the Northern District Conference and the General Conference. The first elder, Gerhard Neufeld, arrived in 1878 from South Russia, whence all members in the early years came. The most common names are Neufeld, Harder, Derksen, Dick, Falk, Friesen. About half of the members are farmers. The first meetinghouse was built in 1882. The second meetinghouse, also a wooden structure, was erected in 1911 with a seating capacity of about 350. It was replaced by a modern brick building with a seating capacity of 710, dedicated in August 1956. In 1947 a brick parsonage was built. As late as 1936 the language of worship was German. In 1937 English was introduced and gradually gained ground, so that at present it is all English, with the exception of a single German Sunday-school class. In 1947-55 L. R. Amstutz was the pastor. He is the first minister called from outside the congregation. The Sunday school was organized about the middle nineties. The first C.E. Society was started in 1906. At present there is also a Junior C.E. Society and a Youth Fellowship organization. There are three mission societies, a men's chorus, and a mixed choir.

Outstanding individuals in the history of the church have been Elder Gerhard Neufeld 1878-1910; Jacob Stoesz, elder 1910-18; I. J. Dick, assistant pastor 1914-20, elder 1920-47; D. D. Harder, minister 1892-1940; I. I. Bargen, who taught in the Sunday school for about 50 years. The membership in 1956 was 423. L. R. Amstutz was succeeded as pastor in 1955 by Willard W. Wiebe. I.J.D.

Mountain Lake (Minn.) Mennonite Brethren Church is an outgrowth of the Carson Mennonite Brethren Church. Since members living in and south of Mountain Lake could not attend the Carson church regularly because of the distance, another meetinghouse was built about five miles south of Mountain Lake. Elder Voth served as pastor of both churches until 1918, when he moved to Canada. In 1901 the building was moved to its present location in Mountain Lake. In 1913 a new church building was constructed, which was enlarged in 1948. N. N. Hiebert served as pastor in 1918-29, succeeded by H. E. Wiens, Dan E. Friesen, and John G. Baerg, the present (1956) pastor. The Mountain Lake and Carson churches conjointly convene at quarterly meetings, alternating the place of meeting. An annual mission festival is jointly observed on July 4, when, as a result of a sale arranged by women's missionary societies, large sums are collected for the work of missions. The congregation has missionaries serving in Africa, Japan, Colombia, Brazil, and other foreign fields. The membership in 1955 was 276. J.A.W.

Mountain Lake Preparatory School: see Mountain Lake Bible School.

Mountain Mennonite Church (MC), now extinct, was located in Clinton Twp., Lincoln Co., Ont., in the settlement known as the "Twenty," some 20 miles west of the Niagara River south of Lake Ontario. It and the Moyer church below the escarpment were practically one congregation using two places of worship at the peak of strength. One staff of ministers served both every Sunday in the late 80's. As the families on the mountain either moved away or failed to gather the young people into the church the attendance waned. The church was sold in 1915. From that time Moyer church was the one place of worship. J.C.F.

L. J. Burkholder, *Brief History of Mennonites in Ontario* (Toronto, 1935) 61.

Mountain Top Schoolhouse, five miles west of Bergton, Va., near the top of Shenandoah Mountain, is the meeting place of a rural mission (MC) church of 16 members. Pastoral care is given by the Northern District of the Virginia Conference. T.S.

Mountain View Amish Mennonite Church, located 1½ miles northwest of Salisbury, Somerset Co., Pa., was built in 1953, as an outpost of the Beachy (*q.v.*) congregation, which conducts public worship services here every Sunday, preaching services and Sunday school being held on alternate Sundays. E.N.H.

Mountain View Bible College, Didsbury, Alberta, was founded in 1926 by the Mennonite Brethren in Christ (UMC). The school had an enrollment of 35 in 1956-57 and offered work leading to degrees in music, theology, and sacred literature. A fifth year of work leading to the Th.B. degree has been added. An administration building, a music studio, a library and classroom buildings in addition to dormitories comprise the plant. The Conference Tabernacle is also located on the campus. Two of the eight faculty members in 1956 held master's degrees and four had bachelor's degrees. Gl.E.

Mountain View Church of God in Christ Mennonite Church, located north of Bonners Ferry, Boundary Co., Idaho, was organized in 1936. The meetinghouse, built in 1943, was made of lumber from the local woods. The church had 92 members in 1955, with Ernest Dirks and Eddie Justus as ministers in charge. The ministry is unsalaried. The members are of Mennonite and Norwegian descent. H.Hol.

Mountain View Mennonite Church (MC), located 10 miles east of Kalispell and 2½ miles northeast of Creston, Mont., originated in 1903, when Jacob Roth, bishop in the Amish Mennonite Church, moved to Creston from Oregon. Other early settlers were John Eicher, Lee Neuschwander, Peter and Samuel Sutter, Ed Ruckdashel, Joseph Murer, Andrew Bachman, and Peter Eyman. Norman Leroy Kauffman came in the spring of 1911.

In the spring of 1904 a Sunday school was organized. Preaching services in the German language were held every two weeks. Four different buildings were used for these services before the church was built in 1913. During these years this congregation was a part of the Western Amish Mennonite Conference, but in 1916 it joined the Pacific Coast Mennonite Conference and in 1923 became a member of the Alberta-Saskatchewan Conference. In 1955 the membership was 98. The following ministers have served the congregation: Jacob Roth, D. D. Kauffman, Joseph Whitaker, Christ Snyder, John W. Oesch, John G. Hochstetler, who is the present (1955) bishop, and D. D. Brenneman, the present minister.   J.G.H.

S. G. Shetler, *Church History of the Pacific Coast Mennonite Conference District* (Scottdale, 1931).

Mountain View Mennonite Church (MC) is to be built in west-central North Carolina, seven miles south of Hickory. Clayton Gotshall and family of the Franconia Conference in Pennsylvania, while doing some follow-up work, located a former Mennonite family here. Work was begun among the local people. Services are being held in a dwelling house. Truman Brunk of the Southeastern District of the Virginia Conference has bishop oversight of this work.   H.A.B.

Mountain View Mennonite Church (MC), the first mission church of the Southern District of the Virginia Conference, is located on the Back Creek, near Lyndhurst, in the Blue Ridge Mountains, in the South River District of Augusta County. The church was built in 1900 and rebuilt in 1953. The early sponsors were Anthony P. Heatwole, Erasmus Shank, and Martin Brunk. Two local ministers, B. Frank Hatter and Silas Brydge, were ordained in the 1940's. In 1957 the membership was 59, with B. Frank Hatter as pastor.   H.A.B.

Mountain View (Alberta) United Missionary Church had 24 members in 1953, with Amsey Frey as pastor.

Mountville Mennonite Church (MC), located in the town of Mountville (pop. 1,000) in Lancaster Co., Pa., three miles from the Susquehanna River, is the third meetinghouse for the Manor District, built in 1898, a substantial brick church 50 x 74 ft. In 1955 Elmer F. Kennel was pastor, with 102 members. (*ML* III, 172.)   I.D.L.

Moyer (Moyers, Mayer, Meyer, Meyers, Myers), a large family, some branches of which have many Mennonite members. The various Swiss immigrants to colonial America who bore the name Meyer were not all related to each other. The *Moyer Family Genealogy* of 1896, a huge volume of over 700 pages, treats various immigrants, some of whom were Mennonites, others not. Among the Mennonite immigrants may be mentioned Christian Meyer (d. *ca.*1751) of Switzerland, who was in Pennsylvania by 1719, settling on the Indian Creek in Lower Salford Twp., Montgomery Co. One of his sons, Christian Meyer, (*ca.*1705-87) was a deacon in the Franconia district of the Franconia Conference (MC), and another son, Jacob Meyer (1730-78), was a preacher at Perkasie (now called Blooming Glen). Immigrant Hans Meyer (d. *ca.*1748) came to Pennsylvania by about 1720 and located in what is now Upper Salford Twp., Montgomery Co. (then Skippack Twp., Philadelphia Co.). A third Mennonite Meyer immigrant was a preacher Peter Meyer, born in Switzerland about 1723, who emigrated to America about 1741 with his mother, three brothers, and a sister. He located in Springfield Township, Bucks Co. In 1773 he was ordained preacher in the Swamp district of the Franconia Conference. His brother

Jacob (1721-90) Meyer settled in Saucon Township, now Lehigh County. He was ordained a preacher in the Swamp district in 1752 and bishop in 1763. Jacob's son Samuel Meyer (d. 1832) was also a preacher at Saucon. The variant form Moyer is found widely in the Franconia Conference to this day, and is also common in Ontario to which some members of the family removed. Especially worthy of mention in Ontario was Dilman Moyer (1807-73) of the Twenty congregation at Vineland, now called the Moyer Mennonite Church, ordained bishop in 1850. Daniel Moyer (1812-64), a preacher of the Yellow Creek district in Indiana (MC), was ordained about 1850 and lived near Jamestown where he served the Shaum (now Olive) congregation until his death in a railway accident. Arthur Moyer (1890-1924), of Lehigh County, Pa., served as superintendent of the Welsh Mountain Industrial Mission (MC), New Holland, Pa., until he was shot and killed by a thief in 1924. At the present time in the Franconia Conference among the ordained Moyers are the following: Jacob Moyer, bishop, and Elmer Moyer, preacher at Souderton, and Wilson Moyer, preacher at Blooming Glen. Among the Moyers who were preachers in the General Conference Mennonite Church were Samuel Moyer (1812-91), two of his sons, Manasseh Moyer (1845-1903) and Jacob Moyer (1842-1909); Manasseh's son John F. Moyer (1885-1955) was on the staff of Bethel College, and S. T. Moyer (1893-) is a missionary in India. Elmer Moyer (1889-) served as secretary of the Ontario Conference of the Mennonite Brethren in Christ Church 1917-33.

In Europe the name Meyer was apparently never prominent in Mennonite circles; Delbert L. Gratz lists Meyer as an Aargau family which left Switzerland because of the severe persecution in the 18th century. The name appeared in a list of Anabaptists in Montbéliard, Württemberg (now in France) in 1759. A Meyer family from Alsace located in Wayne County, Ohio, in 1872, several of whose present-day descendants are in active church work; Elmer Meyer has been deacon at Pleasant Hill, Ohio, since 1936; J. C. Meyer has been professor of history at Western Reserve University, Cleveland, Ohio, since 1923. Willard Moyer is a preacher in the Conservative Mennonite Church at Pigeon, Mich. The Hutterian Chronicle records the selection of a preacher named Hannss Meyer in 1632 and his ordination three years later. (See also **Meyer.**)   J.C.W.

A. J. Fretz, *A Genealogical Record of the Descendants of Christian and Hans Meyer* (Harleysville, 1896); *idem, Genealogy of the Moyer Family* (Milton, 1909); E. R. Mueller, *Moyer Family History* (Halstead, 1948).

Moyer, Manasses S. (1845-1903), a leader in the General Conference Mennonite Church in its formative years, was born in Springfield Twp., Bucks Co., Pa., on Sept. 25, 1845, the son of Samuel and Elizabeth Shelly Moyer. After teaching in schools in Pennsylvania he attended the Mennonite school at Wadsworth, Ohio. Then he taught English at this school in 1871-75. He also taught at Sonnenberg, Wayne Co., Ohio; Bluffton, Ohio; and Lee Co., Iowa. He was married to Anna M. Eyman in Iowa on April 19, 1874. Five children grew to adulthood.

Most of his active life Moyer served in the ministry. He was ordained in 1873 and served as assistant to Ephraim Hunsberger, the pastor at Wadsworth. In 1878 he was called to the Bethel Mennonite Church, in Moniteau Co., Mo., and was ordained elder in 1879. In 1901 he accepted a call from the newly formed Mennonite church at Deer Creek, Okla., serving until his death. He was active in the work of the General Conference, serving on the Home Mission Committee for a number of years. He also was a member of the Foreign Mission Board 1899-1903. He died on Dec. 3, 1903.

Three character traits stand out in the accounts of Moyer's life. He was a tactful leader. In some of the internal difficulties in the Mennonite school at Wadsworth he was recognized as a leader of even temperament and wisdom. He had a conservative disposition, which was noticed at board sessions. He was a man of action when he arrived at a decision.

P.R.S.

Mennonite Year Book and Almanac (Quakertown, Pa., 1905); H. P. Krehbiel, *The History of the General Conference of the Mennonites of North America* (n.p., 1898).

Moyer (Mooyer), **Pieter Jansz,** a Dutch Mennonite elder, serving in the Flemish congregations of Amsterdam 1624-42 and Leiden 1642 until his death (before 1661). Moyer, who was one of the four authors of the Flemish confession called the *Olyftack* (1626), also participated in the Middelstum (*q.v.*) Flemish conference of 1628. In 1649 he was at Hamburg with Isaac Jansz Snep, T. T. van Sittert, and Tobias Govertsz to settle the quarrel in the congregation concerning baptism by immersion or sprinkling. On this occasion he also visited the burial place of Menno Simons. The following two writings by Moyer have been preserved: *Wederleg van Conradi Vietoris Bewijs-redenen voor der Martinisten Kinderdoop* (Haarlem, 1632) and *Volgher op Conradi Vietoris Voorlooper* (Haarlem, 1632). In these books Moyer shows himself as a sharp opponent of infant baptism, but at the same time somewhat more progressive than most Flemish leaders were.

vDZ.

H. W. Meihuizen, *Galenus Abrahamsz* (Haarlem, 1954) *passim; Inv. Arch. Amst.* I, Nos. 558 V, 566; II, 1238, 1240 b, 1242, 1855, 1859; Schijn-Maatschoen, *Geschiedenis* III, 243; *DB* 1881, 38; Blaupot t. C., *Holland* II, 221 f.

Moyer Mennonite Church (MC), at Vineland, Ont., now known as the First Mennonite Church of Vineland, was organized in 1801, by settlers from Bucks Co., Pa. Six families came in 1786, 8 families came in 1799, and by the close of 1800 there were some 60 persons in this part of Ontario. At the time of organization, an estimated 100 persons constituted the congregation. With the permission of the Franconia Conference (*q.v.*) Valentine Kratz was ordained minister in 1801 and John Fretz deacon. A log schoolhouse was used at first for the services. In 1810 a site was provided on the farm of Jacob Moyer for the first meetinghouse and cemetery. Samuel Moyer was the first schoolteacher. Jacob (d. 1833) Moyer became minister in 1802, bishop in 1807. Shortly before his death the stone wall bounding the present cemetery was built.

The Moyer congregation reached its greatest strength by 1850. Other bishops who served "The Twenty," as it was called, were Jacob Gross, ordained in 1834, and Dilman Moyer, ordained in 1850. Other ministers were Jacob Moyer, Jr., Abraham Moyer, Daniel Hoch, Abram K. Hunsberger, Daniel Honsberger, John F. Rittenhouse, and Abraham Rittenhouse. The congregation experienced an unusual amount of difficulty through misunderstandings and schisms. First Bishop Jacob Gross withdrew to the Evangelical Association about 1849, with a considerable following. Daniel Hoch (*q.v.*) left in 1849 and he and his followers used the church east of the Pond at Jordan. For a time he co-operated with the John H. Oberholtzer (*q.v.*) group in eastern Pennsylvania, then later with the Mennonite Brethren in Christ. The M.B.C. movement of 1874-75 took several members. Again, the division of 1889 separated several families of the Old Order Mennonites, who worshiped in a frame building at the west side of the cemetery grounds. Sunday school was conducted in the late 1840's, with lessons from the New Testament, for the preservation of the German language. The ministry of more recent date consisted of S. F. Coffman (*q.v.*), who was ordained in Chicago in 1895, came to Vineland shortly thereafter, and was ordained bishop in 1903. He was followed by Wayne North as minister, ordained in 1955. The membership now (1955) numbers 74. (*ML* III, 172 f.)   J.C.F.

Muara Sipongi, a former mission station of the Dutch Mennonites on Sumatra (*q.v.*), opened by the missionary Nikolas Wiebe on Sept. 26, 1890, three hours distant from Pakanten (*q.v.*). The region, which is inhabited by the Ulus, "a poor, deeply deteriorated, apathetic, insensitive, and sleepy people," suffered a terrible earthquake in 1892. With a wide participation by the native population the church was dedicated in October 1895. In 1901 Wiebe was followed by Johann Thiessen, who made Muara Sipongi a main station beside Pakanten. In 1911-27 Peter Nachtigal worked there with untiring faithfulness. In 1927 the station was turned over to the supervision of a German missionary society and is served by native workers. (*ML* III, 173.)   NEFF.

Mugango Mennonite Church (MC), located 17 miles south of Musoma, Tanganyika, Africa, is in the Jita and Ruri tribes. The Africa Inland Mission began work among these tribes and turned it over to Elam Stauffer of the East Africa Mennonite Mission on Oct. 1, 1936. The first baptismal and communion services were held at Butata, Majita, on Aug. 13, 1936; four were baptized and 25 received into fellowship from the former mission. On March 14, 1937, two were baptized at Mugango and three received into fellowship. Since all the work of the Majita field is under the supervision of the Muango station, the full beginning of the church there was the result of these two services. The total of this beginning was 34 members. The membership in 1956 was 270. W. Ray Wenger arrived at Mugango on April 10, 1938, and had pastoral oversight of the work until his death June 9, 1945. He was ordained bishop at Mugango on April 24, 1941, for the South Mara area of Musoma District. Elam Stauffer has present pastoral oversight of the Mugango-Majita churches. (*ML* III, 173.)   E.W.S.

Mühldorf, a town on the Inn in Upper Bavaria, Germany, in which, according to a Hutterite chronicle, five brethren were executed for their faith. (Beck, *Geschichts-Bücher,* 277; Zieglschmid, *Chronik,* 233; *ML* III, 173.)

Mühlhausen in Thuringia, Germany, situated on the Unstrut (pop. 36,755), until 1802 a free imperial city, during the Peasants' War the seat and site of execution of Thomas Müntzer (*q.v.*), later a temporary center of the Anabaptist movement in northern Thuringia.

Anabaptism found its way into Thuringia about 1527 apparently from Franconia, where Hans Hut (*q.v.*) was working. The first head of the Thuringian Anabaptists was Hans Römer, a furrier of Eisenach. After him his disciple Ludwig Spon of Ershausen became "the soul of the movement" in this area. The preacher Alexander, who also baptized in this region, was seized and beheaded in Frankenhausen in 1533, "one of the noblest characters of Anabaptism."

Early in May of that year seven Anabaptists including Ludwig Spon were imprisoned in Mühlhausen and Treffurt after they had been warned to give up their conventicles in the neighboring villages. They declared that they would rather die than recant or betray their brethren. They would probably have been executed if Philip of Hesse, who had jurisdiction over the region with the dukes of Saxony, had not objected. The seven prisoners were instructed for a while by Balthasar Raidt (*q.v.*), the pastor at Hersfeld, and released after half a year.

Almost at once the Mühlhausen Anabaptists began to propagandize for their cause in the wider vicinity of the city. They had good success in the village of Neunleiningen, ten miles east. A number of men and women were imprisoned and tried in September 1534. Alerted to the presence of Anabaptists in Mühlhausen by the statements of the prisoners, persecution began anew in the city. A citizen of Mühlhausen, Klaus Scharf, on the rack betrayed the names of his brethren; they were arrested, but soon released when the city council was convinced of their innocence. Klaus Scharf was also given his freedom, but again held Anabaptist meetings in his house.

A center for the Anabaptists in the city was for a time the home of Barbara Meissrod (*q.v.*), who had been baptized in the fall of 1534 by Heinz Kraut (*q.v.*). In early 1535 Peter Reusse (*q.v.*) baptized several women of Mühlhausen. Meetings were also held in the neighboring Gunzelhof, where as many as 20 gathered at one time and where the preacher Mattes baptized. Anabaptists of the city also met in the forests.

The growth of the movement in Mühlhausen stirred up the wrath of the authorities again in 1537; Barbara Meissrod and several others who had met in her home were arrested and examined on the rack. Other arrests followed. George, Duke of Saxony (*q.v.*), who as patron of the city was at once informed of the affair, ordered the immediate execution of the Anabaptists by drowning. On Nov. 8, 1537, ten were put to death; they were thrown into the Unstrut and their bodies buried on the river bank. Among these were Barbara Meissrod, Jakob Storger, and Klaus Scharf. They went to their death singing "Nun bitten wir den Heiligen Geist." On the way to their execution they are said to have called out to the spectators words derogatory to infant baptism and the Mass, and a call to repentance. A few days later two other Anabaptists were put to death at the same place. Four were driven from the city.

This procedure of terror apparently wiped out the Anabaptist movement in Mühlhausen. But after the death of George in 1539, when the Reformation was introduced into the city, the Anabaptists also became active again, especially since Sebastian Thiel, the pastor of Niederrode near Mühlhausen, was not unfriendly to the movement. Thiel was, to be sure, punished for his attitude at the instigation of Justus Menius (*q.v.*), who had been put in charge of the reform of the church in 1542, but the Anabaptist movement nevertheless revived to the sorrow of the Eisenach Superintendent, who spared no effort in speaking and writing to eradicate the movement during his two years of office. The preachers were required to preach against them from the pulpit and pray for their conversion. He wrote a new polemic, *Von dem Geist der Widerteuffer,* which he dedicated to the city council on April 3, 1544.

This booklet had the desired effect. Several citizens and peasants were ordered arrested and cross-examined by the preachers. Those who refused to recant were imprisoned; among these was Ludwig Spon, who was once more at the head of the brotherhood. A year later six brethren were examined, among whom was Christoph von der Eichen (*q.v.*), who was repeatedly imprisoned and escaped death only through Philip's intervention. He was banished from Mühlhausen with his family, but kept reappearing in the city and the vicinity, obviously a leader, whereas Ludwig Spon disappeared from the records.

Until the 1570's a small remnant seems to have maintained itself under the leadership of Christoph von der Eichen, who caused the authorities of Mühlhausen much concern. The complaints of the pastors were unceasing. In 1564 the governments involved made it mandatory to take serious steps to wipe them out. In September 16 Anabaptists were summoned to a cross-examination, of whom 12, including Christoph von der Eichen, appeared. They were examined at length and strictly admonished to desist from their "horrible error," but in vain. Christoph von der Eichen was questioned a number of times and was finally executed as an "arch-Anabaptist" at Langensalza in the early 1570's. The same fate befell the last Anabaptist of whom there is record in Mühlhausen, Hans Dohn of Lauterbach, who stayed with his brother in the vicinity, and whose doctrine was of a strange dualistic and anti-Trinitarian nature.

After the middle of the 16th century there was beside the Anabaptist movement a libertinistic group, the "Blood Friends," whom Justus Menius in his book, *Von den Blutsfreunden aus dem Widertauff* (Erfurt, 1551), associates with the Anabaptists; but the cross-examinations of the arrested "Blood

Friends" revealed that they would have no part in adult baptism and attacked the teachings of the Anabaptists (Wappler, *Thüringen,* 190, 193, 205). Several "Blood Friends" were arrested in Mühlhausen in 1551, one of whom probably died at the stake, and others were banished from the city. This group caused the Anabaptist reputation irreparable damage in northern Thuringia.   G.H.

P. Wappler, *Die Stellung Kursachsens und des Landgrafen Philipp von Hessen zur Täuferbewegung* (Münster, 1910); *idem, Thüringen; ML* III, 173-75.

Muhr, Hans (d. 1528), an Anabaptist martyr, was arrested in the summer of 1527 in Styria, Upper Austria, with a number of brethren, among them Leonhard Alexberger, Hans Penzenauer, Sigmund Peutler, Matth. Pürschinger, and Hans Schützenecker. They were asked to recant, but they insisted that they would adhere to the doctrine they had received from Hans Hut (*q.v.*) until they were shown something better from the Word of God. This statement impressed the authorities of Styria where there was a lack of theologians. The council believed, according to its report to Vienna, that they had listened to the preaching of Hans Hut out of love to the Word of God rather than any malicious intent. King Ferdinand (*q.v.*) commanded on Sept. 10, 1527, to begin criminal proceedings against the prisoners, but to pardon those who would recant and accept church penance (*q.v.*) and pay the cost of the trial.

The trial was conducted by Wolfgang Künigl (*q.v.*) before 35 judges and spectators. The accused were given an opportunity to defend themselves in writing. They declared that it had never entered their minds to act contrary to the imperial laws, brotherly love, and Christian order, as was asserted in the public charge; on the contrary they gave the emperor what was the emperor's and were subject to all human law for the Lord's sake. In their meetings they instructed each other from the Word of God, but not with the idea of doing anything wrong or instigating revolt. Their doctrine was not an innovation, but the teaching of Christ. The baptism they taught they would maintain to the end. Concerning the sacrament of the altar they read nothing in the Bible, but they valued communion as Christ instituted it very highly. They did not believe that the body of Christ was in the form of bread; for Christ said in Matthew 24 and Mark 14, that if anyone said to them, lo Christ is here or Christ is there, they should not believe it.

Künigl was not satisfied with their promise to stop holding secret meetings if they did not also forsake their doctrine. He said he was not obliged to enter into a debate with them on their view of the Scriptures; imperial and clerical law forbade the laity to dispute matters of faith.

The judges were not unimpressed with the statements of the Anabaptists; their verdicts complied only in part with the mandates requiring the death penalty for those who refused to recant. The delegate from Linz, Michael Widmer, said it was difficult for a layman inexperienced in divine and temporal law to make a decision in such a case. But he would obediently subdue his conscience and his reason and sentence them to two additional months

of instruction by learned Christians; if they then would not recant, they should be forever banished from the hereditary crown lands; eight delegates from Styria decided that if they did not respond to efforts to convert them, they should be branded on the forehead and expelled; two delegates from Gmunden and Vöcklabruck thought they should also be blinded. The verdict was finally reached that they should be kept in prison until they returned to the right and Christian faith.

Ferdinand, however, declared that this verdict was inadequate and ordered that the six prisoners be burned at the stake if they refused to recant. On the rack they again refused to recant, and confessed that before they had been summoned they had taken communion together and mutually encouraged each other to remain true to their faith. They were executed on March 30, 1528.   HEGE.

J. Jäkel, *Zur Geschichte der Wiedertäufer in Oberösterreich* (1889) 32-35; A. Nicoladoni, *Johannes Bünderlin von Linz* (Berlin, 1893) 74-84; *ML* III, 175.

Muiden, a town in Holland on the IJsselmeer west of Amsterdam, where in 1569 two Anabaptist martyrs, Thijs Joriaensz (*q.v.*) and Jan Claesz (*q.v.*), were burned at the stake. The latter, a "young fellow of about twenty-five years," lived in the neighboring town of Weesp and moved to Muiden with Thijs Joriaensz to attend religious services. They were arrested and imprisoned in the castle near Muiden. Six months later they were taken to The Hague, and after another six months returned to Muiden, where they were put to death together. Elder Leenaert Bouwens (*q.v.*) had baptized 18 persons here in 1563-65 and another five about 1568. This presupposes the existence of a congregation at Muiden, which is corroborated by the fact that Thijs Joriaensz went to Muiden "to serve the congregation of God with the Word." Very little is known about this congregation. It was still in existence in 1681, apparently united with that of Weesp (*q.v.*), which was served by the ministers of the Amsterdam Lamist congregation. The membership was only 12 in 1675, and presumably died out soon after.   NEFF., vDZ.

Mart. Mir. D 480, E 828; *Inv. Arch. Amst.* I, No. 789; II, 2, No. 2343; *DB* 1872, 61; 1918, 50; *ML* III, 175.

Mukedi station of the Congo Inland Mission in Africa was founded in 1922. This was the first station located in the Leopoldville province of Belgian Congo, and the second major expansion of the work among the Bampandi tribes. It is approximately 75 miles northwest of Nyanga and separated from the rest of the stations by the wide and treacherous Loange river. A large medical work is carried on with both general and maternity hospitals for Congolese. The mission medical station also serves a large number of European and American personnel of government, business, and missions located in the area. There is also a three-year teacher training school for Congolese preparing to teach in village or regional schools and a two-year Bible school open to graduates of elementary grades. Both these schools accept students from other C.I.M. stations and other missions in the language area.

Data for 1955: 12 missionaries, 9 native church

leaders, 127 teachers in Christian day schools, 1,193 baptized members, 1,138 professed Christians awaiting baptism, average daily attendance of 3,570 at all mission day schools of Mukedi and district, 180 communities where the Word is preached regularly, 21 Congolese medical helpers, 1,402 hospitalized patients, 13,223 new cases treated, 564 surgical operations performed.				H.A.Dr.

Mulberry (Fla.) was a Mennonite-administered unit under the Brethren-directed CPS Camp No. 27, located approximately 30 miles east of Tampa. The unit engaged in a hookworm eradication program. The unit was opened in September 1943 but in April 1946 it was moved to Bartow, Fla. The Mulberry camp was one of a number selected by the MCC for relief training program, which lasted from November 1943 to May 1946.				M.G.

M. Gingerich, *Service for Peace* (Akron, Pa., 1949) 252-56.

Mulder, a common Dutch family name, both Mennonite and non-Mennonite, the Dutch word *mulder* meaning miller. There have been a number of Mennonite ministers by this name, among whom were Claes Mulder, a mason, who was a (lay) preacher at den Burg on the island of Texel until 1710, and at Rotterdam 1710-25, and Abraham Mulder (b. 1893), who at first was an archivist and then became a Mennonite (lay) pastor and served at Aardenburg 1932-41, Giethoorn 1941-46, and Dordrecht 1946. He published some papers on Mennonite history; e.g., "De oudste bewaard gebleven brieven van onze Middelburgse gemeente," "Voordopers Doperdom," and "Menno Simons' Uitgang uit het Pausdom," all published in *Doopsgezind Jaarboekje,* 1930, 1934, and 1936. He also wrote *Uit Verleden en Heden van de Doopsgezinde Zending* (n.p., 1947), a booklet to commemorate the centennial of the Dutch Mennonite Mission Association.				vdZ.

Of special interest is the Mennonite Mulder family found in the "peat colonies" district in the Dutch province of Groningen. Its ancestor (1) Hindrik Wichersz moved from Giethoorn (*q.v.*) to Veendam (*q.v.*) to break up the peat moors (the peat being used as fuel), as did the two following generations, being at the same time landowners and farmers. From about 1750 the members of this family are also engaged in business. Most of them then lived at Sappemeer (*q.v.*). Since about 1860 many of them have been in the professions as engineers, bankers, teachers, and lawyers, spreading all over the Netherlands, and even migrating to South Africa. This Mulder family is related by marriage to other Mennonite families such as Calkema, Van der Goot, Meihuizen, Romkes, Ubbens, and Verveld.

Two grandsons of (1) Hindrik Wichersz were Mennonite preachers at Sappemeer; viz., (2) Hendrik Jacobsz, a farmer, serving the Waterlander congregation 1700-33, and his brother (3) Harm Jacobsz, a tanner, serving the same congregation 1730-72 and the united Waterlander and Groningen Old Flemish congregation 1772-80. The eldest son of (3) Harm Jacobsz, (4) Jacob Harms, was the first to take the family name of Mulder. He had a textile shop at Hoogezand. His brother (5) Heike Harms Mulder, an oil miller, was a preacher of the Sappemeer congregation 1786-d.1833, with which both the Old and New Swiss (*q.v.*) Mennonite congregations of Sappemeer had merged. He was the last unsalaried minister of this congregation. Great-grandsons of his were (6) Edsge Marten Mulder (1844-1922), who after studying at the Mennonite Theological Seminary served the congregation of Wormer-Jisp 1869-71, and then resigned to study medicine, afterwards being a physician at Graneker, and his brother (7) Marten Edsge Mulder (1847-1928), professor of ophthalmology at the University of Groningen. A great-grandson of (4) Jacob Harms Mulder was (8) Alje Mulder (b. 1846 at Groningen, d. 1919 at Groningen), who after studying at the Mennonite Theological Seminary served as pastor at Wormer-Jisp 1873-74, Zijldijk 1874-88, and Leermens-Loppersum 1888-1905, retiring in 1905.

A number of members of the Mulder family in the 19th century left the Mennonite Church, joining the Reformed and the "Gereformeerde" (Calvinist-Reformed) churches.				G.N.S.

J. Huizinga, *Stamboek van Fiepke Foppes en Diever Olferts* (Groningen, 1887); idem, *Stamboek . . . van Samuel Peter en Barbara Fry* (Groningen, 1890); E. de Waard et al., *De Waarden en het Geslacht de Waard* (n.p., n.d.–Groningen, 1937); *Naamlijst;* family papers.

Mulhouse, France: see **Pfastatt.**

Mulier (des Mulier, Mullier), a French-speaking Mennonite family, to which belonged Jan de Mulier, who in 1614 was a preacher of the Walloon (French-speaking) Waterlander congregation at Leiden, Holland. Bartholomeus Mulier, from Waarschoot, East Flanders, Belgium, settled as a farmer about 1626 at De Biezen near Aardenburg, Dutch Zeeland Flanders. Pierson des Muliers (*q.v.*) was probably also a member of this family. In 1547 is found an Anna Muliers in Amsterdam, who was imprisoned because of sympathy with the Anabaptists, but escaped from prison.				vdZ.

Le Poole, *Leiden,* 61, 53, 83; *DB* 1876, 107; 1889, 95; *Inv. Arch. Amst.* I, Nos. 341 f.

Muliers, Pierson (Piersom) **de(s),** a Mennonite at Brugge, Belgium, warned by a member of the council of Brugge, fled with his wife Claudine le Vettre (*q.v.*) to Meenen (*q.v.*). There he was betrayed by a neighbor. Again he escaped through a warning by a councilman; but his wife, because she would not abandon her infant son, was seized in 1567 by the inquisitor Titelman (*q.v.*) and burned at the stake in Ieper (*q.v.*) the following year. She is said to have been a beautiful woman, who sang well. Their betrayer had to flee from the city. Pierson's account books were saved by the councilman who rescued him. After leaving Belgium, Pierson de Muliers lived at Hoorn, Holland, and then moved to Leiden (before 1589). He married again, first Peronne Hennebo (d. 1589 at Leiden), then Isabeau de la Motte, and died in 1591. The children of his first marriage were baptized illegally by the parson: Pieter (d. 1568), Nicolaas, Jan (b. 1567), and Margriete, who died at Calais, France, at the age of sixteen. Peronne's children, Maria and Martha, were born at Hoorn: Martha married the preacher Dirk Volkerts Velius (*q.v.*), the chronicler of Hoorn;

their son was Pieter Velius. Isabeau was the mother of Margriete des Muliers, who lived at Gouda. Claudine's son was Nicolaas Mulerius, who obtained his M.D. degree at the University of Leiden in 1589 and soon after left the Mennonite Church to join the Reformed. (*Mart. Mir.* D 384, E 737; *DB* 1875, 28-31; *ML* III, 175 f.) K.V.

Mullem, van: see **Mollem, van.**

Müller (Dutch and French, *Muller;* English, *Miller, q.v.*), a common Mennonite family, of Swiss origin, which means that the early bearers of the name were employed in or owners of a mill. There are a large number of Anabaptist-Mennonite Müllers, who are obviously not all descendants of a common ancestor. Among the earliest Anabaptists there were in 1525-33 a number of Müllers in different parts of Switzerland (Peachey, p. 113, No. 96; 118, Nos. 191-95; 121, No. 263; 134, Nos. 561-65). Among these 16th-century Anabaptist Müllers in Switzerland the following are named: Elsi Müller, of Basel, Hans Müller (*q.v.*), of Medicon (Geiser, 155, 148), and Heinrich Müller, of Meisterschwanden, emigrated from Switzerland to Moravia (*ib.,* 163). Hans Müller (*q.v.*), of Grüningen, was imprisoned for his faith at Zürich in 1635-38 (378, 385). Van Braght's *Martyrs' Mirror* (D 813, 820, E 1111 f.) names Catharina Müllerin and Ottilla Müllerin and Ulrich Müller. Just Müller (Jobst Möller, *q.v.*) died as a martyr at Jena, Germany, in 1536 (Geiser, 242). (See also **Möller, Georg,** and **Möller, Heinrich.**)

In the 17th century the Müllers were found in Aargau and in the Thun region of Switzerland (Gratz, 47, 48). During the 17th and early 18th centuries many of them left Switzerland because of persecution. Some of them settled in South Alsace; others were in the congregations of Les Bulles and Montbéliard (Gratz, 38, 87). Hans Müller, of Magenheim in Alsace, as early as 1660 signed the German translation of the Dordrecht Confession approved in this year at Ohnenheim. Other members of the Müller family emigrated to the Palatinate, Germany. In 1671 Hans Müller, then 80 years old, and Michael Müller (b. 1640) settled in the Palatinate (*Inv. Arch. Amst.* I, No. 1248; Müller, 203). A number of Müllers have served as preachers in Mennonite congregations in Alsace and in the Palatinate. The Dutch *Naamlijst* of 1766-1802 names seven of them. In 1936 there were 69 Müllers in 14 Mennonite congregations in Germany—23 in West Prussia, 13 in Northeast Germany, and 33 in South Germany; they were most numerous in Tiegenhagen (ten), Neudorferhof (nine), and Regensburg (nine).

Shortly before 1740 some of the Müller family emigrated from Switzerland to the United States. They were Amish. Other Müllers moved from Alsace to America in the 1740's. Abraham Müller was a preacher of the Conestoga Township congregation in 1793. Joseph Müller, a Hutterite preacher from Moravia, visited *ca.* 1780 the Mennonite congregations in West Prussia (*ME* II, 84). Of the Hutterite congregation at Lewar (*q.v.*), then Austria, now Rumania, Heinrich Müller was an elder from 1742. At Einsiedel, Galicia, Jacob Müller was an elder from 1786 and Johann Müller from 1799.

In the 17th century a Swiss Müller family settled in the Palatinate, Germany. Christian Müller, b. at Gerolsheim and married to Barbara Stauffer, lived at Wallertheim, Palatinate, as did their son Heinrich Müller (1715-95), a farmer, who was a preacher (ordained 1771) of the congregation. Johannes Müller, son of Heinrich, continued the Wallertheim branch of this family, whereas another son, Christian Müller (1752-94), moved to Crefeld. He was a tailor and was married to Elisabeth Schmidt. One of his sons was Samuel Muller (*q.v.*), who became a Dutch Mennonite minister and professor, and who spelled his name, as all his descendants did, without the umlaut. Another son of Christian Müller of Crefeld was Johannes Müller (1786-1853), who moved to Amsterdam and founded a bookstore annex to a publishing house. Dr. Johann Peter Müller (*q.v.*) was a son of this Johannes Müller.

The Muller Dutch Mennonite family is descended from Samuel Muller. Some of his children were Christiaan Muller (1813-96), the Mennonite pastor of Koog-Zaandijk (1838-68), Elisabeth Muller (1815-85), married to Pastor A. M. Cramer (*q.v.*), Frederik Muller (1817-81), the founder of a well-known bookstore and print shop at Amsterdam (his daughter Henriette was married to Pastor A. K. Kuiper, *q.v.,*), Hendrik Muller (1819-98), a merchant at Rotterdam, a member of the Provincial States of South Holland and the First Chamber of the States-General (1881-98), Pieter Nicolaas Muller (1821-1908), a banker and literary man, and Femina Geertruida Henriette Muller (1826-1909), founder of the union of kindergartens at Amsterdam. Among Samuel Muller's grandsons were Pieter Lodewijk Muller (1842-1904), professor of history at the universities of Groningen and Leiden, Samuel Muller Fzn (1848-1922), state archivist and historian at Utrecht, Jacob Wybrand Muller (1858-1945), professor at the universities of Utrecht and Leiden, Samuel Muller Hz (1852-1915), a noted historian; Hendrik Pieter Nicolaas Muller (1859-1941) was an ambassador of the Netherlands at Bucharest and Prague; and Samuel Cramer (*q.v.*) and Gerrit Kalff, professor of Dutch literature at the University of Leiden. Of these, Cramer was a Mennonite pastor, while others have served as deacons. Frederik Muller wrote a study on the present Amsterdam Mennonite Singel Church (*DB* 1863). vDZ.

J. W. Muller, *Das Geschlecht Müller aus Gerolsheim* (Amsterdam, 1950-51); *Ned. Patriciaat* XIX (1930-) 152-62; *Winkler Prins Encyclopedie* (6th ed., 1952) 61-64.

Müller, Anthoni, an elder in the High German Anabaptist brotherhood, who co-operated in composing the significant writings of 1544-46 known as Pilgram Marpeck's (*q.v.*) *Verantwortung* and the *Testamentserläuterung.* These two comprehensive works were only recently made available for examination, and with Marpeck's *Vermahnung* are very important source materials on the doctrine of the Anabaptists in the time of their origin. Nothing else is known about Anthoni Müller's life and work. HEGE.

J. Loserth, *Quellen und Forschungen zur Geschichte der oberdeutschen Taufgesinnten im 16. Jahrhundert* (Vienna, 1929); *ML* III, 176.

Müller, Ernst (1849-1927), a Reformed clergyman and historian, was born in Bern, Switzerland, on May 10, 1849, the son of the apothecary Christian Müller. His youth was spent in Bern. He studied theology in the universities of Bern, Jena, Tübingen, and Leipzig. In 1873 he entered the service of the Reformed Church in the canton of Bern. His first pastorate was Reichenbach in the Bernese Oberland, where he preached 1874-84. In the latter year he took a similar position at Langnau in the Emmental (*q.v.*), serving there until his death on March 26, 1927. He was an enthusiastic promoter of many charitable undertakings.

In the Emmental he came in contact with the Mennonites and became acquainted with their manner of life and their principles. He was deeply interested in the Anabaptist movement and took great pains to study its history from the original sources. His great book, *Geschichte der bernischen Täufer,* which was published at Frauenfeld in 1895, deserves all respect. The foreword states correctly, "The justification for the existence of this book lies in the fact that this part of Swiss church and cultural history has never been presented, and is intended to fill a gap not only here, but also in the history of the great spiritual movement of the Reformation, which is customarily known as Anabaptism." Again in the introduction, "Above all it will be of interest to the Mennonites to have a presentation of their history, for this brotherhood is a church of martyrs, the justification of whose existence and whose strength lie in its history. The willingness to sacrifice and the devotion to ideals revealed by those who suffered for their faith deserves to be snatched from oblivion as a monument to the character of our people."

In recognition of his work the University of Jena in 1904 conferred upon him an honorary doctor's degree. (*ML* III, 176.) S.G.

Müller, Gallus, an outstanding opponent of the Anabaptists in Tirol, Austria, in the 1530's and 1540's, was one of the few who tried to counter the Anabaptist movement by peaceable means rather than by bloodshed and influenced the pertinent measures of the government in this direction. All that is known of his life and career is the material found in connection with the records of Anabaptist persecution.

Gallus Müller was born at Fürstenberg, studied theology, and was said to have accepted a pastorate in 1522. In 1526, when he was pastor at Tübingen and professor at the university, he was one of the theologians chosen by Ferdinand, who was then the ruler of Württemberg, to attend the religious colloquy held on May 21, 1526, at Baden in Aargau, Switzerland. There he became acquainted with Eck (*q.v.*) and Johann Faber (*q.v.*). When the exiled Duke Ulrich returned to Württemberg and adopted a Protestant program for the University of Heidelberg, there was no longer room for Müller. He then was appointed court preacher for the government of Upper Austria in Innsbruck, and assumed the position in May 1535. Ferdinand agreed to his appointment because he was aware that other rulers sought him, and because he needed a learned

clergyman for ecclesiastical negotiations. His sermons were very popular and were attended by great crowds. His first difficult assignment was to convert Jakob Hutter (*q.v.*), who had just been brought to prison. Müller no doubt did all that lay in his power, but against a man who had made up his mind to adhere to his faith and if necessary seal it with his blood, even more eloquent speakers than Müller would have failed.

In March 1537 the pastorate of Ingolstadt was offered Gallus Müller, but he preferred to remain in Innsbruck. He now took pains to convert the Anabaptists captured at Imst and in Petersberg, especially Sebastian Hubmaier (alias Glaser, *q.v.*), Hans Grünfelder (*q.v.*) of Lüsen, both of whom were executed, and the Hellriegel family. He was successful only with Oswald Hellriegel and N. Knaufel.

Meanwhile Matthias, Cardinal and Archbishop of Salzburg, called a meeting of the provincial synod in Salzburg. Ferdinand appointed Müller as one of the representatives, with detailed instructions on his policies. The records show that he was really in earnest about removing the offensive practices of the clergy and in the church. By meeting these just complaints on the part of the populace, by teaching, and by raising the moral standards he did more to eliminate the growth of Separatism than by the bloodiest persecution.

Persecutions were of course not lacking. In April 1538 Lienhard Lochmeier (*q.v.*), an Anabaptist leader, was brought in, and Müller working with the suffragan of Brixen persuaded him to make a public recantation; but when they also requested that he try to convert some of his brethren, he accepted the plea of his fellow prisoner Offerus Griesinger (*q.v.*) to repent and reject the pardon offered him. There were voices that blamed this backsliding on Müller's overzealousness. The law took its course with Lochmeier. Müller was equally unsuccessful with Ursula Hellriegel (*q.v.*) and Georg Liebich (*q.v.*), who was imprisoned in the Vellenburg. But he succeeded with two backsliding Anabaptists in June 1539.

Like Faber in Vienna, Müller was the official adviser of the government in Innsbruck, and very conscientious in formulating and in executing the mandates passed against the Anabaptists. It was he who drew up the mandate of Nov. 28, 1539, in which the Anabaptists are called not only sacramentists, iconoclasts, and falsifiers of the Scripture, but also revolutionaries, "who think of revolt by day and night, and taking away with them their earthly goods they commit themselves to improper and unheard-of communion and brotherhood." As a measure of combating them the mandate ordered cutting off their food supply; and in those places where they were not vigorously pursued soldiers should be quartered until the heresy was wiped out. This mandate was sent out on Dec. 16, with orders to have it affixed to the church doors and read to the people on the following Sunday and holiday, and once a month thereafter.

Müller was now appointed by Ferdinand to the vacant parish of Tirol-Meran, but declined on the ground that he was too old for the position. Not a popular figure with the local priests, he became a hated one, when in August 1546 he was assigned to the task of rooting out concubinage among the clergy. The authorities, temporal and ecclesiastical, were ordered to support him in the reform. The synod which met in Brixen a week later made celibacy mandatory for the clergy; Müller was one of the leaders responsible for calling this meeting.

In June 1540 Müller was honored by accompanying the Bishop of Trent to the religious colloquy which was held in Hagenau. In the next year, when Ferdinand was enraged by the offensive conduct of the clergy, he ordered a pastoral inspection; again Gallus Müller was one of the two men appointed by the bishop to make this inspection in the Inn Valley in 1542.

In 1543 the pastorate of Tirol-Meran again fell vacant, and this time Müller accepted it. In consideration of his services in "the conversion of Anabaptists," his church tax was sharply reduced. This concession was a step in raising the clerical standards; for "the growth of the sects not only in Tirol, but also in the entire Roman Empire is caused by the great dearth of priests, so that even on excellent benefices it was impossible to place skilled and learned priests."

In Meran (q.v.) Gallus Müller had to cope not only with Anabaptists, but also with Lutherans. The latter had such a large following among the people, including the nobility and the mayor, that they were able to call a preacher of their own in 1544 to preach in their homes. Though Müller tried to correct the matter, he was reproached by the government with harboring the "vagrant" priests. Müller replied in self-defense that the Lutheran preacher had so large a following among the most respected classes, that he had been threatened with physical violence, that a mob of women had treated him very roughly; he therefore asked for protection and satisfaction. The preacher was then banished, the mayor deposed from office, and the women who had led the mob put into prison on bread and water; peace was thus temporarily established. Müller, for reasons of age and health, decided to resign from his benefice at Meran and retire to Tirol. The resignation was accepted, but Müller had to remain until a competent successor could be found. Meanwhile the authorities were ordered to see that he received adequate protection and honor, and to punish any who offended him.

A few weeks before, Charles V had written from Gent requesting Müller's participation in a disputation to be held at Innsbruck between the Catholics and the Protestants; there is no information on his work in that colloquy nor of his death.   Loserth.

Loserth, *Anabaptismus; idem, Zwei biographische Skizzen aus der Zeit der Wiedertäufer in Tirol;* papers of Beck published in *Ztscht des Ferdinandeums für Tirol und Voralberg,* third series, 277-302; *ML* III, 176-78.

Müller (Möller), **Hans,** an Anabaptist martyr from Königsberg (q.v.) in Franconia, Germany, was seized in 1530 and drowned at Frankenhausen in Thuringia. (Wappler, *Thüringen,* 92 f.; *ML* III, 179.)

Müller, Hans, an Anabaptist of Medikon. Grüningen district of the canton of Zürich, Switzerland, was arrested in 1529 because of his Anabaptist views. When he was ordered to attend church he replied that he would confer with his brethren; the city council also met with weighty matters were to be discussed, and they should follow the Golden Rule and let him do likewise. A letter he wrote in prison to the council reveals his knowledge of the Bible, when he explains that his conscience should not be forced, faith being a free gift of God. In another letter he asks for patience with him, for "faith cannot be picked up like a stone." The magistrate Berger said of him that he was otherwise a "fine, upright fellow." (*ML* III, 178.)   Neff.

Müller, Hans, a member of the Swiss Brethren community in the Grüningen district of the canton of Zürich, Switzerland, was arrested in 1635 as an obstinate Anabaptist; he was held for 20 weeks "under much cross, strife, and temptation" and was then released for a month to consult with his brethren whether they would join the state church. He was then again seized and imprisoned, and released on the condition that if he could not join the church, he should at least be obedient to the government in other respects. In 1639 he is said to have been seized again, but to have escaped. His wife was therefore taken in his stead and the order proclaimed in the Reformed churches that no one should give him food or drink. He accepted the offer of safe-conduct and presented himself to the authorities, whereupon they imprisoned him for 60 weeks, 16 of them in chains. He escaped on Good Friday. His wife too, who had been hard pressed, escaped. Their property was confiscated. From it the government drew an annual rental of 1,000 guilders (*Mart. Mir.* D 811, E 1109). The fugitives evidently settled at Gerolsheim and Wallertheim in the Palatinate, Germany. Some of their descendants moved to Crefeld and to Holland, and achieved wealth and distinction. (*ML* III, 178 f.)   Neff.

Müller, Hans (Hans von Utikon), was imprisoned in the monastery prison in Zürich, Switzerland, in 1639. When he became seriously ill, "some of his companions" helped him escape. But he died soon afterward of the consequences of his imprisonment. (*Mart. Mir.* D 814, E 1113.)   vDZ.

Müller, Heinrich, of Meisterschwanden, an Anabaptist martyr, also known as Heinrich Sumer, organized an emigration of Swiss Mennonites to Moravia, was chosen preacher there in 1581, was seized in Zurzach, Switzerland, in 1582 with Jakob Mändl (q.v.), taken to the town of Baden, and crossexamined there in the courthouse in the presence of a large crowd of spectators. All attempts to convert them having failed, they were sentenced to die by drowning. On the way to the site of execution "they spoke cheerfully to the crowd admonishing them to repent and be converted from their sinful life to God. They sang together joyfully . . . lifting their voices in lovely melody and praise to God. They sang so harmoniously that the multitude . . . marveled." Mändl was drowned first; another effort was made to convert Müller, but he rejected it and died. Three songs were written upon their death. Neff.

Beck, *Geschichts-Bücher*, 281; Wolkan, **Geschicht-Buch,** 408-10; Zieglschmid, *Chronik; Die Lieder der Hutterischen Brüder* (Scottdale, 1914) 752-56; Wolkan, *Lieder,* 234 f.; *Mart. Mir.* D 749, E 1057; J. Heiz, *Die Täufer im Aargau* (Aargau, 1902) 41, 79; *ML* III, 179.

Müller, Jakob (1753-1827), born at Ibersheim, South Germany, was the first elder of the Mennonite Church at Einsiedel, Galicia, and an outstanding pioneer leader of that settlement. A number of his letters written to relatives in the Palatinate, which were printed by Bachmann, contain valuable information about the early Mennonite settlement in Galicia. He died Sept. 11, 1827, having served the congregation for 43 years.   C.K.

P. Bachmann, *Mennoniten in Kleinpolen 1784-1934* (Lemberg, 1934) 134-43.

Müller, Jakob, b. 1834 in Ehrenfeld, d. 1914 at Rohatyn, Galicia, formerly Austria, now Poland, was an elder (ordained 1883) of the congregations at Lipovce and Podusilna. For a time he lived on the estate "Tura" at Lipovce, which he sold in 1892 to rent an estate near Davidov. Peter Bachmann then succeeded him as elder.   C.K.

Peter Bachmann, *Mennoniten in Kleinpolen 1784-1934* (Lemberg, 1934) 280, 288.

Müller, Johann (1773-1835), became elder of the Einsiedel Mennonite church, Galicia, on Sept. 11, 1827, after the death of the first elder, Jakob Müller. His correspondence with relatives in the Palatinate and with Elder Johann Donner was published by Peter Bachmann. In 1830 Johann Müller and six others bought a part of the estate Zavidovice and established the daughter settlement Neuhof (*q.v.*), where he died Aug. 22, 1835.   C.K.

Peter Bachmann, *Mennoniten in Kleinpolen 1784-1934* (Lemberg, 1934) 203-11.

Müller, Johann, b. 1802 at Einsiedel, Galicia, d. there on March 2, 1857, was the father of the estate dealer (*Güterhändler*) Peter Müller. He was elected elder 1839. He maintained a lively correspondence with the Mennonites in South Germany and Prussia and visited the latter. In 1849 he bought a part of the estate Horozanna near Falkenstein and there with others established a new settlement.   C.K.

Peter Bachmann, *Mennoniten in Kleinpolen 1784-1934* (Lemberg, 1934) 218-30.

Müller, Johann, b. 1823 at Navarya, Galicia, formerly Austria, d. 1888 in Blyszcsyvody, married Magdalene Kintzi, was ordained minister in 1846 and elder June 19, 1864, at Neuhof. He co-operated with his brother, the real estate dealer (*Güterhändler*) Peter Müller, in establishing the Ehrenfeld settlement in 1864, of which he was elder. In 1865 he established a school fund for Mennonite students and in 1871 he published the *Glaubensbekenntnis für Taufgesinnte der galizischen Mennonitengemeinden.*   C.K.

Peter Bachmann, *Mennoniten in Kleinpolen 1784-1934* (Lemberg, 1934) 250 f.

Müller, Johann Peter (1829-1907), a Dutch Mennonite minister, was born at Amsterdam on Sept. 24, 1829. He studied theology at the Mennonite Seminary in Amsterdam, served the congregations of Mensingeweer 1854-57, Rotterdam 1857-61, retired

for reasons of health in 1861, then served at Zwartsluis 1867-72, and Emden 1872-1904; then he retired. In 1869 he received the title of Doctor of Theology at the University of Leiden. He is the author of the books, *Geschiedenis der ontwikkeling van het christologisch dogma in de Grieksche Kerk* (his doctoral dissertation) and *Die Mennoniten in Ostfriesland vom 16. zum 18. Jahrhundert,* a work which was unfortunately not completed. The first part was published at Emden in 1887; the second part without place or date of publication. Müller also published *Drei Predigten* (Emden, n.d.-1890). He was influential in the formation of the Vereinigung (*q.v.;* Conference of German Mennonite Churches) after an attempt to form such a union at Friedelsheim in 1874 had failed. Johann Peter Müller was married to M. Th. Rutgers of Baflo, Groningen; his son Paulus Müller (1863-1924) was director of a publishing house at Amsterdam. Johann Peter Müller died March 25, 1907. (*ML* III, 179.) NEFF., vDZ.

Müller, Johannes (1598-1672), a Lutheran preacher and theologian, wrote while he was in Hamburg, Germany, the book *Anabaptismus. Das ist: Wiedertauffer Irthumb, wie dieselbige in der Mennisten Glaubens Bekändtnis zu Hoorn gedrucket, an den Tag gegeben, vnd zu verführung einfältiger Christen ausgestrewet werden* (Hamburg, 1645; second ed. Hamburg, 1668; third ed. Lübeck-Leipzig, 1695). The immediate occasion for writing this book was the transfer of a member of the state church to the Mennonites. The book deals with the 33 articles of the confession of faith drawn up by the Old Frisian leaders P. J. Twisck (*q.v.*) and Sywaert Pietersz and found in the preface of the *Groot Offerboek* (i.e., *Historie der Warachtighe getuygen Jesu Christi . . . ,* Hoorn, 1617). A separate edition of this confession was edited and published in Hoorn 1620, and is also found in van Braght's *Martyrs' Mirror* (D I 409-50, E 373-490). From the 33 articles Müller extracts 26 errors. Though his theological equipment is obviously superior, the book is not an adequate refutation, but a polemic, which though correct on a few points (such as original sin) does not understand the Biblicistic concern of the Mennonites. The effects of this refutation are not known. O.S.

B. C. Roosen, "Kurze Zusammenfassung der Gesch. der Hamburg-Altonaer Menn.-Gem.," in *Ztscht für Hamburgische Gesch.* III (1848) 78-108; *ML* III, 179.

Müller, Johannes, a master in the guild of goldsmiths in Ulm, Württemberg, Germany, influential in the treatment of religious questions in the second decade of the Reformation. He was a member of the rather large Anabaptist congregation in Ulm. In 1528 he became a voting member of the city council (Keim, 120 and 265). The scant records indicate that he tried to establish Anabaptist principles. When the council discussed the 18 articles of the Ulm church order (chiefly the work of Martin Bucer, *q.v.*) in May 1531 he proposed leaving the matter of baptism open (*op. cit.,* 225). Even though his suggestions did not carry, it is nevertheless worthy of note that in the following month the council invited the clergy of the city and district to the city hall (*Rathaus*) to express their view on the 18 articles, so that none should have occasion to complain of compulsion (Thudichum, 640). He appears to have been influential in the attitude toward the Anabaptists in other imperial cities of upper Swabia. He also had some contacts with Oecolampadius (*q.v.*), whose position on infant baptism was more liberal and who maintained connections with Bucer; the two sent their greetings to him through Ambrosius Blaurer (*q.v.*) and Konrad Sam (Schiess I, 251) on July 1, 1531. It is not impossible that he had a voice in determining the attitude of tolerance toward the Anabaptists in the decisions of Memmingen (*q.v.*), the idea of which was conceived in Ulm.   HEGE.

K. Th. Keim, *Die Reformation der Reichsstadt Ulm* (Stuttgart, 1851); T. Schiess, *Briefwechsel der Brüder Ambrosius und Thomas Blaurer* I (1908); Fr. Thudichum, *Die deutsche Reformation* II (Leipzig, 1909); *ML* III, 179 f.

Müller, Karl (1852-1940), a German Lutheran church historian, professor of history at the universities of Berlin, Halle, Giessen, Breslau, and (1903-22) Tübingen. In addition to the studies he made in various fields of ancient and medieval church history, his most significant work is his *Kirchengeschichte* (Mohr, Tübingen), a comprehensive history of the church, which, however, he was unable to finish. Written in a good literary style, the book not only gives facts, but presents them in their interrelationship and interprets their development. Volume II (Part I published in 1902 and Part II 1919) offers a rather extended discussion of the Anabaptists, with a clear distinction between the revolutionary and peaceful branches of the movement. The concerns of the Anabaptist movement, which he considers the third large Reformation group beside the Lutheran and the Swiss wings, find a sympathetic evaluation; e.g., "It was significant enough that in the midst of the dissolution of all relationships there was here a brotherhood which placed holiness of living above all else and at the same time gained a footing among the lower classes, filling them with an independent religiosity" (p. 330).

Of Müller's many writings several are of indirect interest to the Mennonites for their treatment of certain problems: *Kirche, Gemeinde und Obrigkeit nach Luther* (1910); *Luther und Karlstadt* (1907); *Die Waldenser und ihre einzelnen Gruppen bis zum Anfang des 14. Jahrhunderts* (1886).

Müller was on the board of directors of the Association for Reformation History (*Verein für Reformationsgeschichte*), and was responsible for the publication of "Quellen zur Geschichte der Wiedertäufer." (*RGG* IV, 263 f.; *ML* III, 180.)   P.S.

Müller, Peter, b. 1825 in Einsiedel, Galicia, d. 1873 in Podusilna, known as a "Güterhändler" (real estate dealer), played an unusually important role in the economic life of the Mennonites of Galicia. His grandfather Johann Müller (1773-1835) and his father Johann Müller (1803-57) were elders, of the Einsiedel congregation. Thus far the Mennonites had spread by purchasing smaller estates for daughter colonies. Peter Müller changed the course of the economic development completely. In 1862-72 he purchased six large estates (Viszenka, Blyszczyvody, Troscianiec, Dobrovlany, Lipovce, and Podusilna) and urged Mennonites to sell their small farms and

borrow money to buy portions of the estates. Thus through the activities of Peter Müller the crowded settlements were gradually abandoned and the Mennonites settled on scattered estates.

As a result the old settlement of Einsiedel disintegrated in the 1870's. Peter Müller even went to the Palatinate to invite Mennonites to come to Galicia. A number of families and individuals came. Also in the preservation of archival material Peter Müller rendered valuable service to the Mennonites of Galicia. He copied 24 of the early letters, which Peter Bachmann used in his book, *Mennoniten in Kleinpolen* (p. 168). The era of Peter Müller marked the turning point in the history of the Mennonites of Galicia, bringing prosperity, cultural adjustment, and a widening outlook. On the other hand, now that the Mennonites were scattered over a large area and their former isolation was broken they were in serious danger of being submerged in a general process of secularization and disintegration.
                                                            C.K.

Peter Bachmann, *Mennoniten in Kleinpolen 1784-1934* (Lemberg, 1934) 168.

Muller, Samuel (1785-1875), a Dutch Mennonite theologian, was born in Crefeld, Germany, on Jan. 18, 1785. He was a son of Christian Müller and Elisabeth Schmidt. His mother died when Samuel was only six years old, his father when he was nine. In Crefeld he spent a "youth without joy," went to Amsterdam in 1801 to study theology at the Mennonite Seminary under Gerrit Hesselink (*q.v.*) and ancient languages at the Athenaeum under van Lennep. The regular services of the Amsterdam Mennonites did not satisfy him. "His heart had needs which could not be filled by the offerings of the preachers" (Sepp). He was appointed ministerial candidate and served at Zutphen.

Samuel Muller preached his first sermon on Dec. 6, 1806, at Zutphen; in 1809 he went to Zaandam-Oostzijde, and in 1814 he was called to Amsterdam. His work here was fraught with blessing. Although he stood on a basis of evangelical supernaturalism, he considered the orthodox pietism of his colleague Jan ter Borg (*q.v.*) such a threat to the brotherhood, that he felt compelled to raise his voice in warning. (See Muller's letter to the church council, *DB* 1897, 27 f.) Ter Borg resigned.

Meanwhile Muller in 1827 succeeded Rinse Koopmans as professor (*q.v.*) at the seminary. At his request Wopko Cnoop Koopmans (*q.v.*), Rinse's son, was given the other Mennonite professorship. On Oct. 7, 1828, he delivered an inaugural address in Latin, *Oratio de muneris sancti ratione recte aestimanda* (*Concerning the Virtue of Reason in Sacred Matters*) (Amsterdam, 1829). Muller lectured in dogmatics, pastoral theology, and Mennonite history. In the field of history he was a pioneer. He not only wrote articles on the subject himself, but succeeded in interesting a number of his students in the history of the church. He began to systematize the comprehensive library in Amsterdam, finding many a valuable document in the process. In 1854 he published the first catalog of the Library. He was editor of the *Naamlijst* (*q.v.*) of 1829 and published in 1837, 1840, and 1850 a *Jaarboekje voor de Doopsgezinde Gemeenten in de*

Nederlanden, commonly called Muller's *Jaarboekje.* Of the edition of 1837 he was the sole author. Here, after a list of congregations and ministers, there are four studies in Mennonite history, on the names "Mennonites" and "Doopsgezinden," on Dutch Mennonite editions of the Bible, on the relation between the Mennonites and the Dutch government, and on the lay ministry among the Mennonites; he wrote on the importance of Dutch Mennonite history and on some poems of Vondel (*q.v.*) (published in *DJ* 1840), and an excellent paper on the history of theological training among the Dutch Mennonites (*DJ* 1850). His greatest strength, however, lay not in the field of history, but in pastoral theology, especially homiletics.

Until 1836 Muller remained a preacher of the Mennonite congregation in Amsterdam. When he resigned he published a collection of sermons, *Leerredenen.* From now on he could devote himself entirely to the education of future ministers, and he did this with great devotion. It was his aim to raise the Mennonite brotherhood and its preachers to the same level of learning as that of the other churches: he succeeded, as he reports in the *DJ* 1850, 188.

In addition to his work as an educator Muller found time to serve in other capacities. He was for many years on the directing board of the Association for the Common Welfare (*Maatschappij, q.v., tot nut van't algemeen*), the Dutch Bible society, and the Teyler (*q.v.*) Theological Society. He lent a strong hand in the founding of the A.D.S. (Dutch General Conference) in 1811, and gave the festival address at the celebration of the fiftieth anniversary of the society; he was active in organizing the Dutch Mennonite Mission Society (*q.v.*) in 1847 and for many years served as its chairman.

Muller wrote relatively little, for he felt himself called to work within the Mennonite brotherhood rather than the outside world. He wrote a number of historical articles in *DJ* and *DB;* a number of articles for other magazines, some criticisms, three biographical sketches for the Society for Dutch Literature, a volume of sermons, also *Feestrede ter viering van het 50 jarig bestaan der A.D.S.* in 1861, and *De Geschiedenis van het ontstaan en de Vestiging der A.D.S.* (n.p., Amsterdam, 1861). Twice the University of Leiden conferred an honorary doctor's degree upon him, in philosophy in 1827, and theology in 1836.

In 1844 Muller sharply criticized J. H. Halbertsma (*q.v.*) who attributed the decay of the Dutch Mennonites to their "obsolete orthodoxy" (see Muller's *Beoordeeling van eenige Kerkredenen van J. H. Halbertsma,* Amsterdam, 1844), and when shortly after 1850 Professor Jan van Gilse (*q.v.*) introduced liberal theology into the Amsterdam Mennonite Seminary and about 1870 Liberalism had penetrated into most of the Dutch congregations, Muller was earnestly grieved and occasionally sounded a warning note.

In 1856 Muller resigned from his chair at the seminary. He was of more than ordinary importance, wielding a wide influence upon the brotherhood and helping individual congregations in need. His was a powerful, positive personality with a determined will. This virtue, practiced to excess, led

to a sharpness of utterance and a hardness that estranged many from him, including some of his students. His aspiration was always rather in the direction of high attainment than of winning personal approval. Nevertheless he was always able to distinguish between a cause and the personalities involved, as is shown by his friendship for ter Borg, even after the latter had begun to entertain views that seemed ruinous to Muller; and likewise when Jan de Liefde (*q.v.*), under the influence of the pietistic "Réveil" (revivalism), in 1845 left the church and severely criticized the spiritual conditions of the Dutch Mennonite brotherhood. A stenciled copy of Muller's diary is found in the Amsterdam Mennonite library.

On April 15, 1812, Muller married Femina Geertruida Mabé, a widow from Haarlem. She died in 1870, leaving eight children. Muller's descendants include a number of important scholars. vDZ.

Chr. Sepp, *Levensschets van Dr. Samuel Muller* (Leiden, 1876); idem, *Proeve eener Pragmatische Gesch. der Theologie in Nederland* (Amsterdam, 1868) *passim; DJ* 1910, 21-34 (with portrait); N. van der Zijpp, *Gesch. der Doopsgezinden in Nederland* (Arnhem, 1952) *passim;* Walther Risler, "Samuel Muller, ein Krefelder als Professor am Mennonitischen Prediger-Seminar in Amsterdam" in *Die Heimat* XXVII, 1956, Nos. 1-2 and 3-4; *DB* 1867, 4; 1884, 49; 1885, 55 f., 92-95; 1888, 128; 1897, 11-70 *passim;* 1898, 20, 129; 1901, 9, 17-23, 144 f., 149, 162; *ML* III, 180 f.

Müller, Ulrich, an Anabaptist martyr, a preacher in the gravure of Kyburg of Switzerland, was seized on Aug. 31, 1640, taken to Zürich, and imprisoned in the monastery tower until he died after 35 weeks in chains. (*Mart. Mir.* D 820, E 1119; *ML* III, 181.)

Müllerin, Catharina, an aged woman, was arrested at Zürich, Switzerland, in 1639; after enduring many hardships she was finally released. (*Mart. Mir.* D 813, E 1111.) vDZ.

Müllerin, Ottila, was imprisoned in 1639 at Zürich, Switzerland, with Barbara and Elisabeth Meylin and Barbara Kolbin. Notwithstanding severe examination they all remained steadfast. After some time they succeeded in escaping from prison. Ottila Müllerin apparently was the wife of Hans Müller (*q.v.*). (*Mart. Mir.* D 813, E 1112.) vDZ.

Mullingar Mennonite Brethren Church of north Saskatchewan, located 5 miles south of Mullingar or 110 miles northwest of Saskatoon, was organized in 1928 under the leadership of M. K. Unrau, with a membership of 23. That same year logs were gathered for the erection of a church building. The pioneering conditions were rugged. Approximately 95 individuals have been members of the church. Most of these have moved away. In 1954, when the membership had dwindled to eight, the group became an affiliate of the Glenbush (*q.v.*) M.B. Church and the building was sold. B. J. Derksen was the last pastor of the Mullingar congregation. J.H.E.

Müllner (Müller), Ulrich (d. 1531), an Anabaptist martyr from Klausen (*q.v.*) in Tirol, Austria. He was arrested with his wife by the church authorities of Brixen at Christmas 1527, because the Anabaptists had held meetings in his house. He was apparently not yet a member of the brotherhood. Georg, Bishop of Brixen, reported the results of the trial to the Innsbruck government on the next day, and asked what punishment should be meted out. The government officials replied that the bishop should inquire of the learned men in his district and pass their opinion on to the government. At the same time the Innsbruck authorities sent the bishop copies of all the mandates that had been printed, with the request that he publish them in Brixen (Loserth, I, 567).

In the meantime the Müllner joined the Anabaptists. In 1531 he was arrested again. He freely admitted belonging to the group, and was therefore executed in October 1531. His steadfastness made a deep impression on the people and was recounted decades later by eyewitnesses (Loserth, I, 500; II, 196). Müllner was the father of minor children, who were deprived of their father's property. Three years later their guardian appealed for its return to them (Loserth, I, 540). (Loserth, *Anabaptismus; ML* III, 181 f.)   HEGE.

Mülner, Johannes, an Anabaptist martyr, was burned at the stake on Jan. 30, 1528, at Bamberg, Germany.

P. Wappler, *Die Stellung Kursachsens und des Landgrafen Philipp von Hessen zur Täuferbewegung* (Münster, 1910) 450; *ML* III, 182.

Mumaw, Henry A. (1850-1908), an influential Mennonite (MC) layman, physician, and early educational leader in the Mennonite Church (MC), was born near Winesburg, Holmes Co., Ohio, Jan. 27, 1850, the son of George Mumaw and Catharine Brenneman, second of eight children. On June 27, 1872, he married Malinda Blosser; they had three children. He graduated from the Smithville (Ohio) High School, attended Alliance College, Alliance, Ohio, and taught in the public elementary school near his home for a time, also in certain business schools at Wooster and Wadsworth, Ohio. He moved to Elkhart about 1878 and was for a time employed in the shop of the Mennonite Publishing Company. In February 1886, he was graduated from the Hahnemann Medical College in Chicago and practiced as a homeopathic physician in Nappanee and Elkhart, Ind., also for a time at Orrville, Ohio. He died on April 1, 1908, at Elkhart.

Mumaw's interest in publication led him to found the *Words of Cheer,* a Sunday-school paper for children, which he published for two years, 1876-78, at Orrville, then sold to the Mennonite Publishing Company at Elkhart. It is still published under the same name at Scottdale, Pa. His interest in education led him to establish several business schools, most of them of short duration: Elkhart and English Training School (later called Elkhart Normal School) in 1882-85; Elkhart Institute of Science, Industry, and Art in 1894, from which he withdrew in 1898 to found Elkhart Normal and Business College in the same year. The latter has continued in operation to date as the Elkhart Business College. The Elkhart Institute (*q.v.*) was taken over in 1895 by the Elkhart Institute Association and made a church school, which was moved to Goshen in 1903 to become Goshen College. Mumaw was the first president of the Elkhart Institute Association, and

his son-in-law Aaron C. Kolb (d. 1935, married to his daughter Phebe, who lives in Kitchener, Ont.) the first secretary.   H.S.B.

Mumaw, Levi (1879-1935), the second of nine children of Amos and Catherine (Shaum) Mumaw, was born near Winesburg, Holmes Co., Ohio, Nov. 6, 1879. When he was a child the family moved to Elkhart Co., Ind., and after 16 years returned to Ohio, settling in Wayne County. He was married June 9, 1903, to Fannie Shoemaker (d. 1921). In 1923 he was married to Alice Hershey, Manheim, Pa., who survived him. No children survived.

In 1910 Mumaw was called to Scottdale to serve as treasurer of the Mennonite Publishing House. In a few years the work of secretary was combined with that of treasurer and he continued to serve as secretary-treasurer of the Publishing House until his death. It was in this period of 25 years of devoted service to the publishing interests of the Mennonite Church that he made his greatest contribution.

Other important offices were given to Mumaw. He was chosen secretary of the Mennonite Relief Commission when it was organized in 1917. When the various Mennonite groups organized the Mennonite Central Committee in 1920 he was elected executive secretary-treasurer, which office he held until his death in 1935. When the Mennonite Relief Committee (under the Mennonite Board of Missions and Charities) replaced the Mennonite Relief Commission in 1926, by action of both the Mission Board and Mennonite General Conference, he was elected secretary and continued to serve in that capacity until his death. He was vice-president of the Mennonite Board of Missions and Charities 1927-35. By virtue of the offices which he held in these bodies he served on the executive committees of the Mennonite Publication Board and the Mennonite Board of Missions and Charities.

Mumaw was song leader in the local congregation for many years, and was often called to serve in this capacity in church-wide meetings. When the *Church Hymnal,* published first in 1927, was in preparation he took care of all business matters relating to its compilation, and read the proof for both words and music. He died at Scottdale on June 4, 1935.   J.L.H.

John Umble, *Mennonite Pioneers* (Elkhart, 1940) 137-51.

Mummasburg, Pa., five miles northwest of Gettysburg, was laid out as a town in 1820, and the Mennonite meetinghouse built by 1823 from community funds. The first preachers were Bishop Abraham Roth, David Reiff, and George Throne, followed by Christian and Daniel Shank with Martin Whisler. Earlier they worshiped in a building where Flohr's Schoolhouse between New Salem and Cashtown now stands. There a cemetery holds some of the early settlers. In spite of a schism in 1927, when the Fairfield General Conference Mennonite Church was formed, and another in the forties, when the Bethel Mennonite Church, now in the Ohio and Eastern Mennonite Conference (MC), was formed, the congregation in 1956 numbered 54 members. Amos W. Myer and Roy M. Geigley are the ministers assisting Bishop Richard Danner.   I.D.L.

München-Gladbach, a city (1950 pop. 122,388) in Rhineland, Germany (formerly often only Gladbach, now Mönchen-Gladbach). In the 16th and 17th centuries there were many Anabaptists in the city, and particularly in the country around it. The first information about them concerns the execution of Vit (*q.v.*) tho Pilgrams, who is recognized in the cross-examination as an Anabaptist, in the district records as a Lutheran, and in the *Martyrs' Mirror* as a "High German brother." He was seized in the winter of 1532 but was released upon the petition of friends and relatives. In 1537 he was again seized, put on the rack after a lengthy imprisonment in Grevenbroich, and after another trial with torture in Gladbach, in which he persisted in his faith as fully as in the first trial he was burned at the stake on May 26 in Gladbach with a sack of powder around his neck. The region around Gladbach was full of Anabaptists. In Odenkirchen (*q.v.*) the pastor and chaplain were Anabaptists; Adam Pastor (*q.v.*) lived there for a time and Theunis van Hastenrath had baptized there. In 1554 Grevenbroich horse guards appeared in Hardt "on account of Anabaptists." From the records of the second church inspection of Jülich in 1550 (the first one of 1533 did not include Gladbach) it is seen that there were numerous "innovators" in the Gladbach region, for the authorities were ordered to present a list of Anabaptists, Sacramentists, etc., to the secretary.

Theunis van Hastenrath confessed that he had baptized four persons in Gladbach broich and in Hoeven; of these four Paetzgen Bruwers is still named as one of the unchurched in the inspection of 1560. This inspection says concerning Gerhard von Schechtelhausen, that he could not comprehend that the true body and blood of Christ were actually in the sacrament; but he accepted it with the word in spirit and in faith. The stadholder of Gladbach was ordered to be on the look-out for suspicious books and booksellers. The government and the church tried with all measures to stop the movement. They brought the noted clergyman Matthys von Aachen, who stayed in Gladbach a week, preached against the Anabaptists, and disputed with them. It is worthy of note that the people of Gladbach in the church inspection of 1560 asserted that they knew of no Anabaptists or rebaptized persons. They had recognized that the quiet industrious people who were for the most part native Gladbach people, had nothing to do with fanaticism of the Münsterite Anabaptists. Nevertheless the persecutions continued.

Theisz Rueden from Dülken, who was imprisoned on July 26, 1565, in Cologne with other Anabaptists, said that in the previous year he had been baptized between Gladbach and Viersen by Heinrich Krufft (*q.v.*) and Matthias Servaes (*q.v.*), the leaders who had been preaching and baptizing in the region of Gladbach. The only other preacher he knew was "das Lämpgen," who however had been deposed from his office. This was Lambert Kramer (or Lemken, *q.v.*), who was important for the history of the Gladbach congregation and who stood with Zillis in the question of the ban and avoidance in marriage against the inexorable position of Menno

Simons. He is expressly called "a High German preacher," and represented the moderate point of view of the High Germans. Matthias Servaes, who was also imprisoned in Cologne in 1665, favored unity and did not approve of excessively severe discipline, and in this spirit he admonished his Brethren in his correspondence from the prison.

In the same year the pastors of Jülich and Düren were dealing with the Anabaptists in the Gladbach district. They were to try to turn these erring ones from their error through the mercy of the Almighty. They and their preachers should be granted safe-conduct in writing.

In 1653 the Gladbach Anabaptists stated that they had been living there for more than one hundred years and had been the first to begin the trade of weaving and had propagated it. It is a question how in spite of all the decrees, of all the persecution and suppression, they were able to stay so long at one place. The answer is given in a letter to the duke by the abbott Hecken in 1574: in the city and parish there were 150 Anabaptist families who "for their promotion (*Fortpflanzung*) had their preference above all others with the (ducal) officials." The magistrate (*Vogt*) Johann Gryn was holding his hand over them but the church did not relent in its persecution. In 1575 Daem auf der Scheuten was expelled from the country. His estates were inventoried and his three children were compulsorily baptized. Johannes Vits was ordered with other Anabaptists to appear before the theologians. The abbey did not permit any non-Catholic renters to lease its estates and did not allow the Anabaptists to have any Catholic servants. The *Kirchenvroge* (der Sent) in its first question deals with the Anabaptists. But the congregation continued and in 1591 sent Toenis Comes as its representative to the Anabaptist conference at Cologne. In 1599 they were again banished from Gladbach and their estates confiscated. Most of them found a refuge in Rheydt, where the official hunted them up. As their chief minister and leader Claes in Sittard is named. This is Claas Wolters, "the preacher" who in the list of Gladbach Anabaptists of 1622 is named as the first of those living in the parish. His full name was Claas Wolters Kops (*q.v.*) of Aldenhoven. It was said he was born in 1559, the son of Wolter Kops in Hoen and Bilken ter Meer, and it is supposed that the father was pastor Wolter N., who is named in 1540 at Odenkirchen as being suspect of Anabaptism, and who preached in Hüls and Crefeld about 1550. Claas Wolters in 1611 in Haarlem, Holland, induced Leenaerdt Clock to leave the "Bevredigde Broederschap" (*q.v.*). Abraham Rietmacher of Aachen made this charge against Claas: It was an offense among the Anabaptists that some carried on a great mercantile business and even admitted *Diener am Wort* into their businesses in order to collect much money and property. This statement is aimed at the "High German preacher," who is designated as Claas Wolters. According to the list of 1622 he was carrying on a great mercantile business with yarn and linen cloth and had much capital and also a great estate. In the list 151 families and individuals are listed, most of them weavers and merchants. Two were elders in the congregation. Some had come to the congregation from Cologne. The edicts became sharper. In 1639 a number, mostly those without financial means, emigrated to Nijmegen and became citizens there. Soon the fate of those who had remained in Gladbach was also to be decided. They had to leave their home. A list drawn up by them in 1654 names 142 families and individuals with their wives, the number of children, vocation, property, and servants. In the signature of this list they describe themselves as "those who have themselves baptized upon their confessed faith." This is still the name by which Gladbach Anabaptists called themselves; they had never called themselves "Taufgesinnte" or indeed "Mennonites"; for as High Germans these terms did not describe them.

The fact that they had in 1639 purchased from the Count Palatine the right to remain in residence in Gladbach was of no benefit to them in 1642. They had to seek a new home. Many remained in the neighborhood to await developments. Others settled in Crefeld, Nijmegen, and Goch. Later they are found in Wickrath and Rheydt, until they also had to leave these places and then settled in Crefeld. A list of 1669 names 65 persons who had not availed themselves of the privilege of selling their possessions. Not until well in the following century had all Mennonite property passed into other hands. Some individual Anabaptists tried in vain to return to Gladbach. One single one, Johann Floh, succeeded in 1667 by giving the promise that he would introduce Dutch bleaching for the especial benefit and profit of business. He was even allowed to enlarge his possession at Lüpertz in Harterbroich, but in 1694, in the final expulsion from the Jülich district, he had to leave Gladbach permanently. But even in 1743 his grandson Jacob Preyer still owned the house and the bleaching establishment there.

The ducal officials lamented the expulsion. Their income had declined so sharply that the magistrate (*Vogt*) at Gladbach proposed in 1705, "that the expelled Anabaptist be again soon admitted in the country for the sake of business." But in vain. The congregation of the High German Mennonites in Gladbach had come to an end in 1654.   W.N.

Rembert, *Wiedertäufer;* Brasse, *Urkundenbuch und Geschichte der Stadt und Abtei Gladbach;* Redlich, *Jülich-Bergische Kirchenpolitik* II, 7; Növer, *Die alte Handweberei,* p. 74; *Mitteilungen der Westdeutschen Gesellschaft für Familienkunde* (1935) p. 311; Risler, "Das München-Gladbacher Mennonitenverzeichnis," in *Beiträge z. Gesch. rhein, Menn.,* 1939, 94-130; Bax, *Het Protestantisme in het bisdom Luik en vooral te Maastricht* (The Hague, 1937); P. C. C. Guyot, *Bijdragen tot de Geschiedenis der Doopsgezinden te Nijmegen* (Nijmegen, 1845) 44, 59, 60-62; *Inv. Arch. Amst.* I, No. 536; *DB* 1874, 6 ff., 68 ff.; *ML* II, 116.

Munich (*München*), capital of Bavaria (*q.v.*), Germany, pop. (1950) 831,017, in which there were Anabaptists for a time during the 16th century; like the Lutherans they were violently persecuted and subdued within a few years. Even before Emperor Charles V issued his mandate against the Anabaptists the dukes William IV and Louis issued one on Nov. 15, 1527, "one of the strictest edicts ever passed in religious matters" (Winter, 16). As in other cities, most of their followers were craftsmen, some of whom became martyrs. As early as 1527 a small congregation was formed which met quietly in the

suburbs. As soon as these meetings became known severe persecution set in. Until their trial those who were seized were thrown into the dungeon of the Falkenturm, a tower from which no one ever emerged without severe (capital) punishment; "some had their limbs cut off, some were beheaded, some were cast into the Isar and drowned, and some were burned alive at the stake" (Winter, 35).

One of the first martyrs burned at Munich was Georg Wagner (*q.v.*) of Emmering. He was executed on Feb. 8, 1527, on the square of the Frauenkirche. His steadfastness made a deep impression and was described in a broadside of the day. It was repeatedly printed; it appeared in the *Jahrbuch für die evangelisch-lutherische Landeskirche Bayerns* (1906) and in the *Rheinisch-Westfälischen Gustav-Adolf-Blatt* of Feb. 1, 1909, from a copy in the central library of Zürich.

This execution did not have the effect expected by the church and the government. After Wagner's execution Leonhard Dorfbrunner, a Teutonic Knight from Nürnberg (*q.v.*), preached for a short time in Munich and baptized four persons there in the fall of 1527, Christof Schufler and his wife, and Georg Schachner (Nicoladoni, 206). The latter was chosen as head of the group, and had been a leader in the Augsburg brotherhood, helping to introduce a systematic care of the poor (Roth, 11 and 86).

After the decree of the dukes was issued, persecution increased in Munich. Three weeks later Martin Pasensner of Jesenwang was made inquisitor to seek the Anabaptists out (Winter, 30 and 177). In a short time he seized Augustin of Perwanger of Günzlhofen (*q.v.*) at Fürstenfeld-Bruck and his brother Christoph, who were beheaded on Jan. 7, 1528, together with a miller (Beck, 24). On Jan. 28 of that year six men were burned alive in a hut and the wives of two of them with a widow Baumgartner drowned and then burned (Jörg, 744 and Sender, 188). One of them, Hans Feyerer (*q.v.*), was a preacher (Beck, 24). In the same year another Anabaptist preacher, Oswald Binder (*q.v.*), and Buntzer, the head of the congregation, concerning whom nothing more is known, were beheaded at Munich (Roth, 84). Oswald may be identical with Oswald Schäffler, of whom the Hutterian chronicles say that he was a preacher and was beheaded in Munich in 1528 (Beck, 29).

But the number of Anabaptist martyrs in Munich is not limited to these 15 persons. A list compiled by the Hutterian Brethren in 1581 names only eight, and a supplementary list three more (Beck, 277 and 310). A contemporary chronicler, Clemens Sender, in his *Chronik der Stadt Augsburg,* which extends to the year 1536, gives the number of martyrs as 32, commenting that the three women among them "were much more stubborn than the men" (Sender, 189). The last martyr to die in Munich was Christian Gasteiger (*q.v.*), who was captured at Ingolstadt on May 30, 1586, and beheaded on Sept. 13, at Munich.

The period of Enlightenment finally brought about a change in the treatment of religious minorities. Under Maximilian I Joseph (*q.v.*) an effort was made to settle Mennonites from Lorraine and the Palatinate in south Bavaria; several families settled near Munich and organized a congregation, meeting in the farm homes. After 1880 Mennonites from Baden also took farms in the neighborhood. The two groups united in 1892, and employed a preacher (Emmanuel Landes) with Regensburg and Eichstock (*q.v.*). In 1939 the congregation had 130 members and 40 children, and in 1956 it had 185 baptized members and 32 children. Most of them are farmers, and live in 18 villages. Services are held in a hall in Munich. The congregation belongs to the Vereinigung (*q.v.*).   HEGE.

Beck, *Geschichts-Bücher;* Zieglschmid, *Chronik;* Chr. Hege, "Die Ansiedlung badischer Mennoniten in Südbayern," *Menn. Bl.*, 1905, 68 f., 75 f.; J. E. Jörg, *Deutschland in der Revolutionsperiode von 1522-1526* (Freiburg, 1851); A. Nicoladoni, *Johannes Bünderlin von Linz* (Berlin, 1893); Fr. Roth, "Zur Gesch. der Wiedertäufer in Oberschwaben," in *Ztscht les hist. Vereins für Schwaben und Neuburg* XXVIII (1901); Cl. Sender, *Chronik der Stadt Augsburg* (1894); V. A. Winter, *Gesch. der baierischen Wiedertäufer im 16. Jahrhundert* (Munich, 1809); Wiswedel, *Bilder* II; *ML* III, 182 ff.

Munich (or **Rosehill**) Mennonite Brethren Church is located eight miles east of Munich, Cavalier Co., N.D., and is a member of the M.B. Central District Conference. It was organized Dec. 27, 1897, under the leadership of Johann Enns, who served the congregation as minister 15 years. At that time the church had approximately 60 members. A church building was erected in 1898 and remodeled in 1927. Ministers who served this congregation were John Guenther for 32 years, B. B. Fadenrecht, contemporary with him for 18 years, David Hooge 1942-47, G. W. Schroeder 1948-54, and Arthur Harder 1955-57. The membership in 1956 was 62. David Hooge, G. W. Schroeder, Arthur Harder, and Leroy Schroeder were also teaching in the Community Bible Academy.   A.A.D.

Münichau, Helene von: see **Freyberg, Helene von.**

Munsels, Leonhard: see **Leenhart Munsels.**

Münster, a village southeast of Colmar, Alsace, formerly the seat of a Mennonite congregation, now extinct.

Münster, a Mennonite family of Hamburg, Germany. Its ancestor, Hans Münster (1588-1626), was probably a farmer in the Wilster Marsch, Holstein, Germany. His son Elias Jansen Münster moved to Glückstadt (*q.v.*), from where his son Jan Elias Münster (d. 1716) moved first to Hamburg, then to Altona, where he was a merchant and deacon of the Mennonite church, as were his sons and grandsons Herman, Jan Elias, Peter, and Peter Münster, Jr. Most of them took part in whaling and equipped whaling vessels, as had Jan Elias in 1681-1714. Whether Cornelis Jan Munster (d. 1717), a cloth merchant, who in 1676 moved from Bommel, Dutch island of Overflakkee, to Rotterdam and here in 1679 became a preacher of the Flemish congregation and 1688-91 served as elder, was a member of the same family, is doubtful.   vDZ.

B. C. Roosen, *Gesch. der Menn. Gemeinde Hamburg* I and II (Hamburg, 1886-87), *passim;* Wanda Oesau, *Hamburg's Grönlandsfahrt* (Glückstadt, 1955) 131 f.; *DB* 1908, 115.

Münster Anabaptists (usually called "Münsterites"). Münster, capital (1955 pop. 150,000) of Westphalia, Germany, has a university, has been a bishop's see since the 8th century, and became a member of the Hanseatic League during the 13th century. The buildings in the center of the city revealed its bloom during the Middle Ages until World War II, when 90 per cent of them were destroyed. Most famous among its churches are the cathedral (1225), St. Ludger (1200), St. Martin (14th century), and the Gothic St. Lambert (14th century). The population of Münster is predominantly Catholic.

Reformation of Münster. In 1532-35 Münster became a center of radical Anabaptism, in which many persecuted religious and social reformers found refuge. Peculiar economic, social, and religious conditions in the city brought this about. The city was ruled by a city council and the bishop, who had his own court. The fact that Münster was a member of the Hanseatic League speeded up the participation of the guilds of the city in public affairs. At the time of the Reformation, the guilds participated in the government, leaving the common people in the background. When Luther's reformation spread, his ideas were brought into the city by merchants. The cathedral school of Münster spread Humanism. Early religious reformers were Johann Glandorp and Adolf Clarenbach (*q.v.*). By 1524 the religious reform movement was assuming definite forms. The peasant revolt of 1525 stirred the masses of Münster, who began to demand improvements in economic, social, and religious conditions. Criticism was directed against some monasteries which were creating strong competition for the weaving industry. By 1527 Bernhard Knipperdolling (*q.v.*) had become the leader of the masses.

In 1531 the religious unrest of the city received stimulation and guidance from Bernhard Rothmann, a former priest who had visited Wittenberg and Strasbourg, and was in touch with the reformers of these centers. He preached the Lutheran message. When the authorities wanted to stop him, he was protected by the powerful guilds of the city. During the same year he published a confession of faith which reveals no fanatic influences. This gave direction to the masses. On Feb. 18, 1532, the Lambert church was taken over by his followers. By Aug. 10 of that year all the churches except the cathedral were occupied by evangelical ministers: Brixius of Norden, Henric Rol (*q.v.*), Gottfried Stralen, P. Wertheim, and G. Nienhoven. The guilds and the common people were taking over and the council and bishops were losing out. Rol and Dionysius Vinne (*q.v.*), representatives of the Wassenberg (*q.v.*) reform movement who had arrived at the end of 1532, furthered the religious activities of the city. Early in 1533 Heinrich Staprade (*q.v.*) and Johann Klopreis (*q.v.*), also Wassenberg reformers, arrived. The reform movement of Münster gradually divided into two major camps: the conservative Lutheran group and the democratic Sacramentarian wing which was ready to accept Anabaptist ideas.

Anabaptism in Münster. Melchior Hofmann (*q.v.*), who had spread Anabaptist beliefs and practices in East Friesland and the Netherlands since 1531, also secured followers in Münster. Thus far there had been severe criticism of Catholic and some Lutheran practices, but with the preaching and practice of believers' baptism the representatives of the radical reform movement of Münster introduced a new motto and symbol. On Aug. 7 and 8, 1533, a religious discussion was held between the Wassenberg representatives adhering to Anabaptist ideas and Catholic and Lutheran ministers. Those favoring Anabaptist innovations were ordered by the city council to have their children baptized. Rothmann was removed from his office. On Nov. 8, 1533, his *Bekentnisse van beyden Sakramenten Doepe vnde Nachtmaele . . .* was published. In addition to his name, it bore the signatures of Rol, Klopreis, Vinne, Staprade, and Stralen, dated Oct. 22, 1533. Concerning baptism this confession says it "is dipping into water, which the candidate desires and receives as a true sign that he has died to sin, been buried with Christ, and arises in a new life, henceforth to walk not in the lusts of the flesh, but obediently according to the will of God" (Keller, 131). This booklet prepared the way for the practice of baptism upon confession of faith.

On Jan. 5, 1534, Bartholomeus Boeckbinder and Willem de Cuyper, representatives of Jan Matthys (*q.v.*) of Haarlem, who had been baptized by Melchior Hofmann, appeared in Münster. They baptized Rothmann, Klopreis, Vinne, Rol, Stralen, and Staprade. Now Jan van Leyden (*q.v.*) and Gerrit Boekbinder appeared in Münster. Gradually peaceful Anabaptism grew into a caricature. Rothmann wrote *Eyne Restitution . . .* , which appeared October 1534, in which he urged a restitution of the apostolic church. On Feb. 9, 1534, the city hall was seized, and on Feb. 23 Bernhard Knipperdolling became mayor of Münster. On Feb. 27 all those who refused to be baptized were expelled from the city. Johann Lenning and Theodor Fabricius, who had been sent to Münster by Philip of Hesse to restore the evangelical order, had to leave without accomplishing their task. Münster became the refuge of all persecuted, desperate people and the "New Jerusalem" of radical Anabaptism. Evangelists spread the news that the Lord had chosen Münster to establish His kingdom on earth. Particularly many of the sorely oppressed Dutch Anabaptists, who were suffering severely under Catholic authorities, considered this a God-sent message. Many sailed from Amsterdam and other cities across the Zuiderzee en route to the "New Jerusalem." Most of them were arrested and returned to their homes, or imprisoned, many being put to death. Others were prevented by the magistrate from leaving their home communities. Nevertheless, large numbers succeeded in reaching Münster.

Meanwhile, Bishop Franz of Waldeck, the ruler of the territory, had begun the siege of the city. Already before this event the original Anabaptist principle of nonresistance had been weakened through the fanatical view that the "children of Jacob" would be actively engaged in helping God punish and annihilate the "children of Esau," at the time of the establishment of the kingdom of God. On April 4, 1534, Jan Matthys, a fanatical representative of this view, was suddenly seized by a foolhardy inspiration to go outside the city walls

with a few followers to disperse the besieging army, as in the days of Israel. He fell in this attempt. Jan van Leyden took his place in the city, cleverly exploiting the situation. He appointed 12 elders and gave them authority in the city. Early in 1534 he published a tract entitled *Bekentones des globens und lebens der gemein Criste zu Monster* (Confession of Faith and Life of the Church of Christ at Münster), which was sent to Philip of Hesse. In December 1534 Rothmann published an appeal to take up arms in revenge and in defense of the church of Christ at Münster (*Eyn gantz troestlick bericht van der Wrake unde straffe des Babilonischen gruwels . . .*). A unique episode in the drama of Münster was Hille Feicken who sacrificed herself in an attempt to kill the bishop as Judith had beheaded Holofernes in Israel. She was captured and put to death.

In addition to armed resistance, two new characteristics were soon promoted by Jan van Leyden. One of them, not entirely unknown in Anabaptist history, was the principle of community of goods. Marxian writers like K. Kautsky (*Vorläufer des neueren Sozialismus,* 3rd ed., Berlin, 1947), and scholars like Hans van Schubert have investigated and presented the basis and the purpose of this institution of community of goods. Schubert (*Der Kommunismus der Wiedertäufer in Münster und seine Quellen,* Heidelberg, 1919) attempted to trace the idea of the community of goods back to early Christian writers and Plato. One has the feeling that it is hard to establish an unbroken line of this principle from Plato to the Münsterites. The Bible-reading Anabaptists, interested in the restitution of the early Christian church, found enough information and inspiration in the Jerusalem church, in which community of goods was practiced. In their attempt to establish a "New Jerusalem" they simply imitated the pattern before them.

More complicated is the reason for introducing polygamy. Jan van Leyden introduced it against the judgment of some of the more serious ministers such as Rothmann, Rol, and Klopreis. It probably was originally an impulse of the "king of the new Zion." On the other hand, in the "New Jerusalem," the capital of the "New Israel" in which the children of light were fighting the children of darkness, according to the pattern of Israel in the Old Testament, "King David" could with the same justification introduce this Old Testament practice. In addition to this, it served at the same time as a social welfare practice since the number of men continued to decrease during the siege of the city. One of Jan van Leyden's wives was "Queen" Divara, the widow of Jan Matthys; another wife was the daughter of Bernhard Knipperdolling.

The New Testament beliefs of the Anabaptist movement of Swiss background were transplanted to Strasbourg, where the Lutheran lay evangelist Melchior Hofmann became superficially acquainted with them. In Münster they were transformed through the fanaticism of Jan Matthys and Jan van Leyden into a carnal Old Testament-oriented earthly "kingdom of God." Not much of the early vision, spirit, and essence of Anabaptism were retained. Naturally it is hard to distribute a proper balance of the blame for this development. The ruthless persecution which Anabaptists underwent in the Low Countries could produce only fanaticism among people without true leadership, seeing no way out.

Jan van Leyden found some opposition. Rol and some others who did not agree with Jan van Leyden had left Münster in the spring of 1534. A revolt led by Heinrich Mollenhecke was brutally suppressed. On Aug. 31, 1534, a second powerful attack of the besiegers was repulsed after which Jan van Leyden was proclaimed "king of the New Zion" by Johann Dusentschuer (Jer. 23:2-6; Ezek. 37:21). Jan had a throne erected at the market square where he held court. Anybody who opposed the dictator was crushed. One of Jan van Leyden's ambassadors was Jan van Geelen (q.v.), who traveled through the Netherlands recruiting followers for the "New Jerusalem" at Münster, distributing Rothmann's latest book, *Van der Wrake* (Concerning Revenge), and trying to create "Zions" in the Netherlands at Amsterdam (q.v.) and Bolsward (q.v.). Jan van Leyden sent out 27 apostles, including Vinne, Klopreis, Stralen, and Slachtscaep, most of whom were put to death. The expected help from the Netherlands could not reach Münster, although individuals succeeded in getting into the city. Jan van Leyden with a small male population managed to keep the enemy outside the walls. The aged and ill were sent outside the city in order to preserve the meager supplies. Finally on June 25, 1535, the bishop's army gained entrance through betrayal from within. Heinrich Gresbeck led a group through a gate into the city. Jan van Leyden, Bernhard Knipperdolling, and Bernhard Krechting were cruelly tortured, displayed in various parts of the country, and put to death on Jan. 23, 1536. Their corpses were hung on the tower of St. Lambert's church. The cages are still hanging on the same tower. Most of the male population were put to death; only a few, e.g., Hinrich Krechting (q.v.) managed to escape. Rothmann evidently also escaped, although no trace of him was ever found.

After 1535. Scholars do not agree what the future religious affiliation of Münster would have been if the Anabaptist catastrophe had not occurred. The Catholic writer Tücking states that without the will of the bishop the Reformation would not have succeeded in Münster nor any other place. Ludwig Keller, on the other hand, states that if it had not been for the Anabaptists, the city of Münster would have remained evangelical like some of the neighboring cities. Brune says that it is a tragedy that Hermann von Wied, Duke of Cleve, and Franz von Waldeck, who later favored the Reformation, prevented it at this time. Although it is true that Protestantism was suppressed in the city of Münster and other places of Westphalia during the Catholic Counter Reformation, it is nevertheless likely that the result would not have been very different if the Münster tragedy had never occurred. Wherever possible, the Catholic Church took advantage of any situation to gain lost ground and to fortify its position. The Münster incident was used by the Catholics to defeat not only Anabaptism, but also Protestantism in general, while the reformers used the Münsterite label for all Anabaptists, including the peaceful wing. Even modern Protestant scholarship has not fully overcome the effects of this prejudice.

Protestantism, and with it Anabaptism, indeed experienced a setback in Münster and the surrounding territory, from which it never fully recuperated. It is, however, wrong to assume that Anabaptism immediately died out in the province of Westphalia after 1535. As in some other places Anabaptism continued in Westphalia for many decades. Numerous smaller and larger congregations existed. Among them were Dortmund, Osnabrück, Soest, Minden, Coesfeld, and Lemgo. Gradually they disappeared. Since they could exist only as an underground movement, information concerning these congregations is scarce. In a recent study, *Der Kampf um eine evangelische Kirche im Münsterland,* Friedrich Brune has presented the history of the struggle of the Protestant church in and around Münster. This book also contains valuable information pertaining to the courageous small Anabaptist groups. In his report regarding the Catholic attempts to exterminate Protestantism during the Counter Reformation, he relates that in 1612 Bishop Ferdinand was particularly interested in converting the numerous Anabaptists. Brune states that at this time Anabaptists were by no means a dangerous revolutionary or fanatical sect. The people called them "Tibben" (q.v.), while they themselves addressed each other simply as brethren, Christians, or church of Christ. They were pious, industrious, and reliable citizens and highly honored by their neighbors. They were found in the following cities in 1612: Warendorf, Freckenhorst, Harsewinkel, Beelen, Bocholt, Ahaus, Ottestein, Wessum, Wüllen, and Vreden. Even one of the Catholic priests of Warendorf was an Anabaptist sympathizer. Severe measures of the Counter Reformation necessitated the emigration of these Anabaptists to Gronau (q.v.), Emden (q.v.), Hamm (q.v.), Emmerich (q.v.), Winterswijk (q.v.), or Zutphen (q.v.). (Brune, 55, 122.)

Brune believes that many who had been attracted by the Münsterite movement did not really share the radical views promoted by the leaders, and returned to a sane evangelical Biblical Christianity, and that it is an error to mention only the sobering effect of catastrophe on misled radical Anabaptists, since many of the Anabaptists of Westphalia had nothing to do with this radicalism. Many of those called Anabaptists should be classified as evangelical Christians because "it is a fact that on the whole gradually in the time of sobering and quietness some of the Anabaptists joined the Evangelicals, above all in later times the Reformed Church" (p. 56). (For a detailed treatment of this question, see the article **Westphalia,** the places listed above, and **Münsterites in the Netherlands.**)

Münster in the Press. No other topic of the Reformation and particularly the Anabaptists has received as much attention throughout the centuries as the Anabaptists of Münster. Opponents of the movement in the Catholic and Protestant churches, scholars and journalists in all groups, fiction writers and artists, have through four centuries found this subject a fertile field. Even today novels and dramas dealing with some phase of the Münsterite movement appear almost annually.

During the beginning of the Anabaptist movement of Münster, Bernhard Rothmann and his coworkers published a number of writings as mentioned above. Correspondence between representatives of the Münsterite movement and the chief Reformers, such as Melanchthon and Martin Luther, has been published (Bahlmann, 122). Immediately after the collapse of Münster numerous reports were published under the usual name *Newe Zeittung,* in which the tragedy of Münster was described. Bahlmann lists at least 20 of these pamphlets in his bibliography for 1535 (p. 142). Among the early reporters on the Münster tragedy was Urbanus Rhegius, who wrote *De Restitutione regne Israelitici . . .* (1536), which was reprinted and also translated into German (Bahlmann, 155). He had previously written *Widderlegung der Münsterischen . . .* (Wittenberg, 1535). Very popular was *Warhafftige historie, wie das Evangelium zu Münster angefangen, vnd darnach durch die Widderteuffer verstöret . . .* by Henricus Dorpius, which was published in 1536 and reprinted in the same year with a preface by Bugenhagen at Strasbourg. It was again published and edited by Friedrich Merschmann at Magdeburg in 1847. C. A. Cornelius claimed that Fabricius actually wrote the book or furnished the main source of information. Even though presented from a biased point of view this source is very valuable because of its early date. The Amsterdam Mennonite Library has a Dutch translation of it in manuscript form (see **Corvinus**).

Another early writer was Antonius Corvinus (*q.v.*), who wrote *Acta: Handlungen . . .* (1536) and *De miserabili Monasteriensium Anabaptistarum obsidione . . .* (1536). (The tract of 1536 entitled *Waarachtige Historie . . .* mentioned in *ME* I, 720, was not written by Corvinus but by Dorpius. See above.) Konrad von Heresbach (*q.v.*) of Cleve reported his observations to Erasmus in two letters, which were used to produce a tract entitled *Konradi Heresbachii J. C. Historia Anabaptistica . . .* which went through a number of editions (see **Heresbach**). Justus Menius (*q.v.*) wrote *Von dem Geist der Widerteuffer,* with a preface by Luther (1544).

Lambertus Hortensius (*q.v.*) wrote *Tumultuum Anabaptistarum . . .* (Basel, 1548), of which numerous editions and translations appeared, particularly Dutch. Hortensius presents a detailed though somewhat biased account of the events in Münster. Most of the editions are illustrated.

J. Sleidanus (*q.v.*) wrote *De statu religionis . . .* (1555), which appeared in numerous Latin editions and in German translation. Heinrich Bullinger (*q.v.*) wrote among other things *Der Widertöufferen ursprung . . .* (Zürich, 1560). G. Nicolai translated the book and added to it what he deemed necessary for readers of the Low Countries. It was published at Emden in 1569. (*BRN* VII, 667.)

Hermann Hamelmann (*q.v.*), a Lutheran minister of Oldenburg, wrote *Historiae renati evangelii . . .* around 1570, in which he relates important information and data although presented in a somewhat biased manner. The book was first published at Lemgo in 1711. In 1913 Kl. Löffler published Hamelmann's *Reformationsgeschichte Westfalens* (Latin). Hermann von Kerssenbroick (*q.v.*), who

attended the cathedral school in Münster at the time when the Anabaptist movement started, later wrote two books: *Anabaptistici furoris Monasterium . . .* (which was copied by hand. In 1730 and 1750 inadequate editions appeared, in 1771, 1900, and 1929 German editions were published) and *Belli Monasteriensis contra Anabaptistica . . .* (Cologne, 1545).

The only actual witness living in Münster during the Anabaptist reign who survived to write an account of it was Heinrich Gresbeck (*q.v.*), who caused the downfall of the kingdom by showing the bishop's army how to enter the city. His *Bericht von der Wiedertaufe in Münster* was published by C. A. Cornelius in *Die Geschichtsquellen des Bistums Münster* II (Münster, 1853). B. N. Krohn published *Geschichte der fanatischen und enthusiastischen Wiedertäufer . . .* (Leipzig, 1858) and compiled over 50 volumes of material which was destroyed in Hamburg during World War II. J. H. Ottius treated the Münsterites in *Annales anabaptistici . . .* (Basel, 1672).

Since 1800 scholars have paid considerable attention to the Anabaptists of Münster. Among those who have made substantial contributions in this field of investigation during the 19th century we name H. Jochmus, J. Hast, H. A. Erhard, H. F. Jacobson, D. Harting, J. C. Fässer, K. Ziegler, K. Hase, M. Goebel, H. Kampschulte, K. Rembert, H. Detmer (for titles of their contributions, see Bahlmann, "Die Wiedertäufer zu Münster. Eine bibliographische Zusammenstellung," pp. 167-70, *Ztscht f. v. Gesch. u. Alterthumskunde,* Münster, 1893).

The most important contributors in this field of research, who introduced a more objective method of investigation during the past centuries, were C. A. Cornelius, Ludwig Keller, and Joseph Niesert. These men not only freed the account of the usual preconceived denominational notions about the Anabaptists, but they also made available most of the sources on the subject. Niesert published *Beiträge zu einem Münsterischen Urkundenbuche* I (Münster, 1823) and *Münsterische Urkundensammlung* I (Coesfeld, 1836). Cornelius published *Berichte der Augenzeugen über das Münsterische Wiedertäuferreich* (Münster, 1853) and *Die niederländischen Wiedertäufer während der Belagerung Münsters 1534 bis 1535* (Munich, 1869). Keller published some sources in his *Geschichte der Wiedertäufer . . .* (Münster, 1880) and *Die Gegenreformation in Westfalen und dem Niederrhein* (3 vv., Leipzig, 1881-95).

Especially Cornelius and Keller were instrumental in introducing an objective scholarly method of research not only on the Münster Anabaptists but on Anabaptists in general. Among the writings of Cornelius, the following should be mentioned: *Geschichte des Münsterischen Aufruhrs . . .* (Leipzig, 1855) and *Historische Arbeiten vornehmlich zur Reformationszeit* (1899). Keller wrote the book already referred to, *Geschichte der Wiedertäufer . . .* (Münster, 1880); *Zur Geschichte der Wiedertäufer nach dem Untergang des Münsterschen Königreichs* (1882); *Die Wiederherstellung der katholischen Kirche nach den Wiedertäuferunruhen in Münster 1535-37* (1882). Other scholars who made valuable contributions during the past century were Johann Döllinger in his *Die Reformation . . .* (3 vv., 1848);

Leopold Ranke, *Deutsche Geschichte im Zeitalter der Reformation* (3 vv.); Paul Bahlmann, *Beiträge zur Geschichte der Kirchenvisitation im Bistum Münster 1571-73;* W. E. Schwarz, *Die Akten der Visitation des Bistums Münster . . . (1571-73)* (Münster, 1913).

During the 20th century some outstanding contributions have been made in the realm of further investigation by Friedrich Brune in *Der Kampf um eine evangelische Kirche im Münsterland, 1520-1802* (Witten, 1953) which presents valuable information on the Anabaptists in Westphalia after 1535. The book has an up-to-date bibliography on the Protestant movement within Westphalia. Heinrich Detmer made numerous contributions regarding Rothmann, etc. Klemens Löffler wrote *Die Wiedertäufer zu Münster 1534-35* (Jena, 1923), which constitutes an eyewitness account based on Kerssenbroik, Dorpius, and Gresbeck. Hugo Rothert published *Westfälische Geschichte* (Vol. II, 1950) and *Der Kampf um Münster 1531-35* (1925), which discusses the Anabaptists. Hans von Schubert investigated the basis of the Münsterite communism in *Der Kommunismus der Wiedertäufer in Münster und seine Quellen* (Heidelberg, 1919). Ernst Reichel wrote *Die Vorstellungen der Münsterischen Wiedertäufer über ihr Verhältnis zur Welt und zu ihren Mitmenschen* (Tübingen, 1919). H. Rothert's *Das Tausendjährige Reich der Wiedertäufer zu Münster, 1534-55* (Münster, 1948) was published the second time.

Melchior Hofmann, the initiator of North German and Dutch Anabaptism, has received considerable attention during the last decades. The most recent study was made by Peter Kawerau on *Melchior Hofmann als religiöser Denker* (Haarlem, 1954). As the title indicates, it is an attempt to reconstruct the theological content and the basic religious concern of the writings of Hofmann. Writers who previously dealt specifically with Hofmann were A. Hulshof, *Geschiedenis van de Doopsgezinden te Straatsburg* (Amsterdam, 1905); W. I. Leendertz, *Melchior Hofmann* (Haarlem, 1883); F. P. zur Linden, *Melchior Hofmann, ein Prophet der Wiedertäufer* (Haarlem, 1885). In addition to these writings, all major books on Dutch Anabaptism deal with Melchior Hofmann. The writings of Hofmann were published in *Bibliotheca Reformatoria Neerlandica* V (Hague, 1903). Rothmann's *Restitution* was published in *Flugschriften aus der Reformation* VII (Halle, 1888), and his *Bekenntnisse van beyden Sacramenten* and *Van erdesscher unnde tytliker gewalt* were published with introduction by Detmer and Krumbholtz, in *Zwei Schriften des Münsterschen Wiedertäufers Bernhard Rothmann* (Dortmund, 1904). Detmer wrote *Johann von Leiden . . .* (2 vv., Münster, 1903-4).

The relationship between the Münsterites and the peaceful Anabaptists has always been a controversial subject from the time of the writings of Menno Simons against Jan van Leyden to the present. Many have written about it. The opponents of the Anabaptists emphasized the similarities between the fanatical Münsterites and the Biblical Anabaptists, while the Mennonite writers denied or minimized the relationship between the two. Kautzky and others have claimed that Anabaptism was a revolutionary movement and not a religious reformation. E. B. Bax in *Rise and Fall of the Anabaptists* (London, 1903) concludes that the Anabaptists were "the forerunners of Modern Socialism, and, as such, let us spare them a passing tribute of recognition!" Gabriel d'Aubarede wrote in a similar vein in *La Revolution des Saints* (1946).

In 1917 Karel Vos (*q.v.*) published an article on this subject in *Doopsgezinde Bijdragen,* to which W. J. Kühler responded in the same yearbook in 1919. They continued their controversy in *De Gids* of 1920 and 1921. Kühler presented his final views in his book, *Geschiedenis der Nederlandsche Doopsgezinden in de zestiende eeuw* (Haarlem, 1932). He maintained that the Biblicist type of Anabaptism, with the exception of the practice of adult baptism, had existed in the Netherlands before Melchior Hofmann's coming in 1531, that the Münsterite development was a deviation from the Anabaptist Biblical line, and that Menno Simons and others continued to promote true Anabaptism. Vos claimed with Kautzky that Anabaptism was primarily revolutionary; after the tragedy of Münster it became a "peaceful" movement. John Horsch entered this discussion when he wrote "Is Dr. Kühler's Conception of Early Dutch Anabaptism Historically Sound?" (*MQR* VII, 1933, 48-64, 97-126). The most recent publication on the Münster Anabaptists is that by A. F. Mellink (*q.v.*), *De Wederdopers in de Noordelijke Nederlanden* (Groningen, 1954). The author follows the Kautzky-Marxian line, considering the whole problem as an economic struggle of the desperate masses who used a religious vocabulary to state their needs.

One of the urgent and significant tasks in Anabaptist research is to investigate the following questions objectively. To what extent does Münster Anabaptism contain original Anabaptist views? Which of the ideas and practices of the fanatical Anabaptists were caused by local conditions in Münster and the Netherlands? It is one-sided to present the Münster struggle purely as an attempt of the lower classes to improve their economic status. On the other hand, it is also one-sided to dissociate the Münsterite radicals from all Anabaptist ties. Münster Anabaptism is unthinkable without the social and economic developments of the city as well as the preaching of Luther's message by Rothmann and others. Only on this soil could the Lutheran lay evangelist Melchior Hofmann and the fanatical Jan van Leyden plant their seed successfully. This does not give the Catholic Church of Münster any reason to wash its hands in innocence regarding the tragedy of Münster. These conditions, including those created by the church, were a part of the background for the tragedy.

A recent striking discovery has been made which shows that Pilgram Marpeck's *Vermanung* of 1542 is largely a revision of Rothmann's *Bekenntnisse van beyden Sacramenten* of 1533 (Frank Wray, "The *Vermanung* of 1542 and Rothmann's *Bekenntnisse,*" *Archiv für Ref.-Geschichte* XLVII, 1956, 243-51).

Münster in Fiction, Drama, and Art. In the realm of literature and art the Münster Anabaptists have proved very attractive. Before World War I three dissertations were written on the topic of the Münsterite Anabaptists in German literature. Hermann Bitter wrote *Der monsterschen ketter bichtbok* (Münster, 1908); Wilhelm Rauch wrote *Johann von Leiden, der König von Sion, in der deutschen Dichtung* (Leipzig, 1912); and Hugo Hermsen, *Die Wiedertäufer zu Münster in der deutschen Dichtung* (Stuttgart, 1913). Hermsen lists six publications in this area by contemporaries and 21 novels and dramas from 1777 to 1904. August E. Scribe wrote the opera *Le Prophéte* with music by Meyerbeer (Paris, 1849), which was translated into German.

Some of the most significant novels and dramas along these lines during this century are the following: Bernhard Kellermann, *Die Wiedertäufer von Münster* (drama) (Berlin, 1925); F. Reck-Malleczewen, *Bockelson* (Berlin, 1937); H. Specht, *Heil'ge Feuer* (Nordhorn); H. S. Rehm, *Das tausendjährige Reich* (Rothenfelde, 1925); Ludwig Wegmann, *König im Käfig* (Münster, 1935); F. Dürrenmatt, *Es steht geschrieben* (drama) (Basel, 1945); H. Müller-Einigen, *Die Menschen sind alle gleich* (Bern, 1946); F. Th. Czokor, *Der Schlüssel zum Abgrund* (Hamburg, 1955); H. Paulus, *Die tönernen Füsse* (Bonn, 1953); Ypk fan der Fear, *De breugeman komt* (Drachten, 1953); B. Stroman, *Obbe Philipsz* (Hilversum, 1935); G. Hoogewerff, *De Zwaardgeesten* (The Hague); M. Jacobse, *De drie kooien* (poems) (Kampen, 1947).

In the realm of art the Münsterite incident has also been popular. The most significant contemporary artist to deal with the subject was Aldegrever, who produced paintings and etchings of the most significant leaders. His works have been reproduced by Geisberg in *Die Münsterischen Wiedertäufer und Aldegrever* (Strasbourg, 1907). George Tumbült in *Die Wiedertäufer* (Leipzig, 1899) deals at great length with the objects of art pertaining to the Münsterite Anabaptists. H. Schmitz in his book *Münster* (Leipzig, 1911) also devotes a chapter to the Münster Anabaptists in art. The catalog of an Anabaptist exhibition of 1935 in commemoration of the 400th anniversary contains much information about art and other items pertaining to Münsterite Anabaptists. The title is *Die Wiedertäufer. Katalog der Ausstellung des Landesmuseums der Provinz Westfalen in Münster i.W. in der Galenschen Kurie, August-November 1935* (illus.). The most significant modern artist dealing with the subject is Joseph Sattler, whose 30 etchings pertaining to the Münster Anabaptist kingdom are reproduced in *Die Wiedertäufer* (Berlin, 1895). Ida C. Ströver, "Die Wiedertäufer in Münster," in *Westfälische Kunsthefte* IV (1933) contains 35 drawings. Some of the emergency bank notes (*Notgeld*) circulated in the city of Münster during the inflation of 1922-23 depict Jan van Leyden and the history of the Münsterites.

A question which needs investigation is the course of Anabaptism in Westphalia after 1535. Brune has given a good account of what happened to the Protestant movement and indicated the way regarding the Anabaptists. Keller has also done some work regarding the Anabaptists. The archives of Westphalia, particularly the records of the Church inspections of the Counter Reformation, partly published, contain much information. Local archives of places where Anabaptists lived also furnish information. Much of the source material has been made available by Niesert, Keller, Cornelius, and the annual publication, *Zeitschrift für vaterländische Geschichte und Alterthumskunde; Die Geschichtsquellen des Bistums Münster*. The most important archives are the Staatsarchiv Münster and Bischöfliches Diözesanarchiv of Münster. The most comprehensive bibliography of the Münster Anabaptsts can be found in Bahlmann, "Die Wiedertäufer zu Münster" (*Zeitschrift f. v. Gesch. u. Alterthumskunde* LI, Münster, 1893); Klemens Löffler, "Zur Bibliographie der münsterischen Wiedertäufer" (*Zentralblatt f. Bibliothekswesen* XXIV, 1907); F. Brune, *Der Kampf um eine evangelische Kirche im Münsterland, 1520-1802* (Witten, 1953) 181-87; K. Hase, *Das Reich der Wiedertäufer*, 2nd ed. (Leipzig, 1860), 146-74; K. W. Bouterwek, "Zur Literatur u. Geschichte der Wiedertäufer . . . ," *Ztscht d. Berg. Geschichtsvereins* I (1863); *Realencyklopädie f. prot. Theologie u. Kirche* XIII, 539. Hans Schiedung, *Beiträge zur Publizistik und Bibliographie über die Münsterischen Wiedertäufer* (dissertation, Münster 1934) does not deal with bibliography. Most of the books mentioned in this article are found in BeCL, GCL, and AML. (*ML* III, 185 f.)   C.K.

Münster Anabaptists in the Netherlands. Not only in the city of Münster but also outside the city Jan van Leyden had a large number of adherents, particularly in Holland. They had been won over to the revolutionary principles by the propaganda of Münster, e.g., by Rothmann's *Van der Wraecke*. Besides this, conditions in Holland in 1534 promoted this course: growing persecution, economic conditions such as unemployment and famine in many cities, and finally the declining kingdom. Most of the Dutch Anabaptists were disciples of Melchior Hofmann and eagerly shared his chiliastic views, and when the expected kingdom of God failed to come on earth, this fact, added to the other adversities, psychologically prepared the soil for the luxuriant germination of the seeds of sedition and insurrection sown by the Münster emissaries like Jan van Geelen (*q.v.*). Many of the Dutch Anabaptists abandoned their peaceful principles and the Biblical faith. Revolts and assaults took place (March 1535) at Oldeklooster (*q.v.*) near Bolsward, Friesland, and on the town hall of Amsterdam (May 10-11, 1535). The Anabaptists had apparently planned attacks on Leiden, Woerden, The Hague, Oudewater, and other towns; Benschop, IJsselstein, and Poeldijk were important centers of revolutionary activity, and a number of the Amsterdam Anabaptists also held the Münsterite views. After the fall of Münster, June 1535, most of these revolutionary Anabaptists returned to peace, as for example Jan Matthijs van Middelburg (*q.v.*) and Jan Smeitgen (*q.v.*); but others desperately persisted in their rebellious ideas. Of this group after the death of Jan van Geelen, Johan van Batenburg became the leader; hence they were often called Batenburgers. Even after his death (Vilvoorde 1538) the revolutionary Anabaptists did not yet die out. Until 1544 their adherents were active in the Netherlands. Hundreds of them were put to death.

Karel Vos (*q.v.*) and following him A. F. Mellink (*q.v.*) are of the opinion that until *ca.* 1544 the Dutch Anabaptists were nearly all of the revolutionary type, a gathering of the poor, unemployed, illiterates, in short "the dregs of the population" (Vos in *De Gids,* 435, 436, 441 f., 448; Mellink, 419), and that with a few exceptions the Dutch martyrs between 1531 and 1540 were revolutionaries (Vos, *DB* 1917, 169 ff.). Vos and Mellink also consider the Dutch Mennonites in general, even Menno Simons, to have sprung up from the Münsterites (Vos, *Menno Simons,* 36-42). Vos accused de Hoop Scheffer and Kühler of falsifying history for reasons of "Mennonite prudery," by refusing to accept the descent of Mennonitism from Münsterism (Vos, in *De Gids,* 434). And Mellink (*Wederdopers,* 367, 419) even exceeds Vos by claiming that all history as written by Mennonites is falsification, from van Braght to Kühler.

This theory has been well refuted by Kühler and others. It should be pointed out that a number of outstanding leaders of the Dutch Anabaptists, such as Jacob van Campen, Jan Paeuw, and Paulus van Drunen, definitely rejected Münsterite doctrines, that among the Anabaptists in Belgium (Antwerp, Gent, Brugge) there are few traces of sympathy with Münster, and that both Menno Simons and Dirk Philips wholeheartedly repudiated Münsterism. Already in his *Foundation Book* of 1539, Menno sharply criticized in unambiguous terms such Münsterite doctrines as the "sword" and polygamy.

After the Münster episode the rulers and governors of many countries in Western Europe found a strong motivation for the persecution of the Anabaptists. Though they mostly were well aware of the fact that there were peaceful as well as revolutionary Anabaptists, neither ecclesiastical nor temporal authority attempted to make a distinction between them—hence the increase of persecution in Holland, where thousands were put to death. In Germany the events of Münster were also made a pretext for severe suppression of the Anabaptist-Mennonites.

Catholic, Lutheran, and especially Dutch Reformed (Calvinist) historians dealing with Anabaptist-Mennonite history never tire of telling the story of Münster, and in spite of better information by open-minded and neutral historians like Gottfried Arnold (*q.v.*) historians have continued to recent times to assert that as the Swiss-German Mennonites are the spiritual descendants of Thomas Müntzer (*q.v.*), the Dutch Mennonites are the children of Münster (see **Historiography**). Guy de Brez (*q.v.*), one of the first opponents of the Mennonites in writing, warned the governments against them. Now, he says, they are peaceful and law-abiding, sweet lambs, but they may soon be wolves, rebellious again, as they have formerly been. This insinuation, copied and expanded by a large number of Calvinist authors, who until the 18th century felt themselves obliged to caution against "Mennonite boldnesses," has frequently been the cause of annoying and even harsh measures by the magistrates against the Mennonites. For this reason Galenus Abrahamsz (*q.v.*) and Herman Schijn (*q.v.*) published their writings, energetically denying the Münsterite descent of the Mennonites and refuting their Calvinist opponents.

Thus Münster and Münsterism in many ways caused incalculable harm to the cause of the loyal Anabaptism and Mennonitism, which, as Neff says (*ML* III, 186), "were able to maintain themselves to the present only by their endurance and faithful adherence to Biblical concepts."   vDZ.

K. Vos, *Menno Simons* (Leiden, 1914); *idem,* "Kleine Bijdragen over de Doopersche beweging in Nederland tot het optreden van Menno Simons," in *DB* 1917, 74-202; *idem,* "Revolutionnaire Hervorming," in *De Gids* IV (1920) 433-50; A. F. Mellink, *Wederdopers;* J. G. de Hoop Scheffer, *Geschiedenis der Kerkhervorming in Nederland . . . tot 1531* (Amsterdam, 1873) 611 ff.; W. J. Kühler, "Het Nederlandsche Anabaptisme en de revolutionaire woelingen der zestiende eeuw," in *DB* 1919, 124-212; *idem,* "Het Anabaptisme in Nederland" in *De Gids* I (1921) 250-78; N. van der Zijpp, "Menno en Munster," in *Stemmen uit de Doopsgez. Broederschap* II (1953) 6-20; Galenus Abrahamsz, *Verdediging der Christenen, die Doopsgezinde genaamd worden* (Amsterdam, 1699); H. Schijn, *Geschiedenis dier Christenen, die . . . Mennoniten genaamd worden* (Amsterdam, 1743); John Horsch, "Menno Simons' Attitude Toward the Anabaptists of Münster," *MQR* X (January 1936) 55-72; *ML* III, 185 f.

Münsterberg (Montagne de Moutier), in the Emmental (*q.v.*) in the Bernese Jura, Switzerland, where a small congregation was formed by refugee Mennonites from the Emmental (*q.v.*) in the early years of the 18th century. Some may have come somewhat earlier. As early as 1595 the prince-bishop Jakob Christof demanded of the provost in Münster that the filth of the damned sect of the Anabaptists in the Holy Roman Empire be removed. Upon the insistence of several Jura communities the prince-bishop in 1731 ordered the expulsion of the Mennonites, but withdrew his mandate when the landowners appealed in behalf of the quiet, orderly mountain dwellers. Nevertheless the toleration was arbitrary, they were not permitted to buy land, and they must remain in the mountains. Thus the congregation of the Münsterberg was able to organize and develop unmolested. Peter Ramseier (b. 1706) was chosen as preacher in 1730, and elder in 1732. Ramseier must have been an important preacher in the brotherhood, for he was called to peace conferences in the Palatinate with other brethren four times—in 1762, 1766, 1770, and 1782, in an attempt to heal a schism among the Palatinate brethren.

Early in the 19th century the Münsterberg congregation reached a period of considerable prosperity. With members living on isolated farms in the adjacent communities of Perfitte, Eschert, Grandval, Roche, and Courrendlin the congregation numbered 258 souls. The elder and preacher at that time were respectively Peter Sprunger and Peter Habegger. Traces of blessing were also left by the Mennonite schoolteacher Johann Baumgartner, who implanted the Word of God into the hearts of the children. The deacon was Peter Lehmann, whose son Peter Lehman (*q.v.*) became preacher in 1848.

On account of difficult economic conditions many Mennonites on the Münsterberg decided to emigrate to America. In March 1852 a company of about one hundred left Münster and settled in the virgin forests of Indiana. From the dense oak forests the pioneers built log houses and valuable farms, and built the thriving town of Berne (*q.v.*), Ind., named after their homeland.

In 1874 when freedom from military services was no longer granted in Switzerland, another considerable group emigrated from the Münsterberg congregation to America; the Münsterberg congregation shrank in size. The above Peter S. Lehmann was one of the leaders in this emigration, and died in 1899 as the elder of the Berne Mennonite congregation.

In the 20th century, when the Münsterberg congregation faced dissolution through repeated emigrations, the few remaining families united with the Kleintal (q.v.) congregation.

In 1939 there were only three families left in the Münsterberg part of the Kleintal congregation. In the hospitable home of the blind aged Christian Habegger (Combe de Roche) monthly meetings were held every summer, at which one of the ministers of the Kleintal congregation preached. S.G.

Chronik der Familie Lehmann; S. Geiser, *Die Taufgesinnten-Gemeinden* (Karlsruhe, 1931); N. G. Frankhauser, "Emmentalische Täuferansiedlung in Amerika," in *Alpenhornkalender* 1934; D. L. Gratz, *Bernese Anabaptists* (Scottdale, 1953); *ML* III, 184.

Münsterberg, the name of two villages in the Mennonite settlements in Russia. The first was founded in the southwest of the Molotschna (q.v.) settlement in South Russia in 1804 by Mennonites from West Prussia and named for a village in the old home country. It was one of the nine oldest Mennonite villages of the Molotschna settlement and embraced 4,592 acres of land. Some of the land was salty. The land on the elevations was fertile. The lower lands with their fields and orchards suffered from floods. The families that arrived later usually settled on the higher land. In 1913 the village had two motor-driven mills, a tile factory, and four large shops. It had about 400 Mennonite inhabitants in 70 families. During and after the Revolution the village suffered under Communism. Many inhabitants were sent into exile and some have come to America.

A second village with this name was founded by Molotschna Mennonites in the Zagradovka settlement in 1874 in the province of Kherson. It contained 3,200 acres and had a population (1913) of about 250. In October 1919 the village was attacked by bandits, and most of the inhabitants lost their lives. Neither of the two villages is occupied by Mennonies today. HEGE.

G. Lohrenz, *Sagradowka* (Rosthern, 1947); *ML* III, 184, f.

Münstermaifeld, near Coblenz in Germany, where in the 17th century a number of Amish families settled, whose descendants were still found there in the 19th century. (*DB* 1885, 12.) vDZ.

Münsterrol (French, *Montreux*), a former (Amish) Mennonite congregation in France, some five miles from Belfort (q.v.). The congregation was founded about 1750 by immigrants from the Swiss Jura. Their first ministers were Klaus Engel of Münsterrol, Peter Klopfenstein of Bourogne, and Michael Müller of Chavanatte. The Münsterrol congregation is not found in the *Naamlijst.* vDZ.

Delbert Gratz, *Bernese Anabaptists and Their American Descendants* (Scottdale, 1953) 93.

Muntau, a village in the northwest of the Molotschna Mennonite settlement (q.v.) in South Russia. It was one of the oldest settlements of Mennonites emigrating from West Prussia, Germany, to the province of Taurida. In June 1804, 21 of the 162 families who went to Russia in 1803 and spent the winter in the Chortitza settlement (q.v.) settled here. The beginnings on the grass-covered steppes were extremely difficult for these settlers. They could not build their homes until 1805-6. The village owned 4,870 acres of land. In 1913 the population was about 400, mostly Mennonites. The land, with an 18-inch layer of fertile topsoil, was well suited to the raising of grain. In 1830 a forest was planted, which was kept in prime condition and was very beautiful. The industries of the village included a mill and a starch factory. In 1852 the village built its own school. An endowment given by Franz Wall in 1889 made possible the erection of a hospital, which was enlarged in 1911 and offered the best of service to the people in the vicinity. In 1913 there were three doctors and eight nurses on duty. In that year there were 643 patients with 9,523 days of nursing care. (*ML* III, 186 f.) HEGE.

Muntau Hospital, located in the Molotschna Mennonite settlement, Ukraine, was established as a private enterprise in 1880 (or 1889?) by Franz Wall. After the death of the founder in 1906, his son Franz Wall, Jr., continued the work, assisted by his sister Elisabeth, a nurse. Before World War I it was enlarged to a 60-bed capacity. Franz Wall was exiled after the Revolution, and his sister came to Canada. The leading doctor was Erich Tavonius, who served the hospital as physician 1900-27. In 1909 Morija (q.v.), a deaconess institution closely connected with the Muntau Hospital, was established to train nurses. In 1913 Dr. Tavonius headed the hospital, assisted by Dr. Seiler as oculist and Dr. Büttner. After the Revolution the hospital was nationalized. (Dirks, *Jahrbuch 1913*, 179; *Unser Blatt* II, 1927, 307.) C.K.

Munter, Jan, b. 1570, d. about 1620, and his wife Sara van Tongerloo, b. 1578, d. after 1639, members of the Waterlander congregation at Amsterdam. As owner of the former bakery of the East India Company, he placed this building at the disposal of a group of English Brownists (q.v.) in 1608, who under the leadership of John Smyth (q.v.) had separated from the main body. In 1615 this group, then led by Thomas Pigott (q.v.)—Smyth had died in 1612—merged with the Mennonite Waterlander congregation. The English, using their own language in the meetings, continued to hold services in the "Jan Munter's bakhuis" until 1639, the year of Pigott's death. vDZ.

J. G. de Hoop Scheffer and W. E. Griffis, *History of the Free Churchmen* (Ithaca, N.Y., n.d.-1922) 143-46, 166-68.

Muntzenheim, a village near Colmar, Upper Alsace, France, formerly the seat of a Mennonite congregation, now extinct, the remaining members having joined the Colmar (q.v.) congregation. At Muntzenheim a preachers' conference was held in 1896, which was the beginning of new conference activity in Alsace. vDZ.

Müntzer, Thomas (1488/9-1525), was perhaps the most controversial figure of the period of the German Reformation, a man who has been called at various times the "beginner of the great Anabaptist movement," the forerunner of modern socialism, the beginner of the mystical-spiritualistic movement in Germany, a religious socialist, the leader in the Peasants' War 1525, and other such designations, none of which really fit this versatile man who during the decisive last five years of his life (1520-25) changed his position almost from year to year. Karl Holl's assertion that most of the catchwords or slogans of the German Reformation during its formative period were made current by this fiery and restless mind is acceptable. Noble and deep thoughts mingle in his writings with rather coarse and rude expressions, not to say offensive passages; genuine spirituality alternates with fanciful inspirationism. At the end, in spite of his position as a priest and preacher, one may legitimately ask: Was he still a Christian?

The literature about Müntzer is extensive but not too enlightening, providing for each author an occasion for personal interpretation of an ambiguous personality, thereby using categories often wanting in precision. Praise and blame, love and hatred speak from these writings, but no author seems to be able to be fully neutral and detached. But since Müntzer has quite persistently been called the "originator of the great Anabaptist movement" it is desirable that a careful and objective study be made of his relation to Anabaptism.

Thomas Müntzer was born in Stollberg in the Harz Mountains ca. 1488-89. He received a good academic education which familiarized him with the Bible and the mystics, and with Plato and St. Augustine and the classic Christian writers, which were required in higher education at that time. He had a brilliant and dynamic mind. In 1513 he became a Catholic priest, was soon promoted as provost (Propst) of a monastery, and in 1519 he became father-confessor of a nunnery. It was about that time he also became acquainted with Martin Luther. In 1520 he was a priest in Zwickau (Saxony), where he met Nicolaus Storch, the inspirationist and "'prophet'" who proclaimed that the Bible is secondary to the direct revelation of God to His chosen servants. Müntzer felt akin to this viewpoint and began to develop his own doctrine of the "spirit." Soon unrest and disturbances set in (they were to follow this man from now on wherever he chanced to preach) and he had to flee the city in April 1521.

Next Müntzer was in Prague (until February 1522), where he drew up the "Prague Manifesto" in four different versions, two in German, one in Czech, and one in Latin. This Manifesto was the real program for his further life. He wanted to start a "new church," the church of the spirit. He called it the "spirit of the fear of God." The German and Czech versions of the Manifesto appealed to the plain people (*Am Volk zweifle ich nicht*); the Latin version, much milder, addressed itself to the scholars, the humanistically educated readers. The Manifesto is a visionary document, but like all of Müntzer's later writings is confused and without clear-cut orientation. Certainly its program was not Scriptural in any concrete sense. Müntzer had little success in Bohemia, the old land of John Hus, and as he left it he began a period of restless wandering. He passed through Wittenberg during Luther's absence at the Wartburg and lodged in the home of Carlstadt, who was sympathetic to some of his ideas but unwilling to go all the way with him.

From Easter of 1523 until August 1524 Müntzer was a priest or preacher (things were still fluid in these years) in Allstedt, a small town in the Harz area, in the neighborhood of rich ore mines which produced a restless class of miners (*Bergknappen*), always eager to promote social changes. His sermons were attended allegedly by 2,000 hearers even though Allstedt had hardly more than a few hundred population. In Allstedt he now wrote a number of liturgical tracts concerning (infant) baptism and the German Mass. These liturgical writings are a clear indication that his reforms were a deviation from Catholicism in degree only, not in substance. He did not propose the establishment of a completely new church. He distributed the sacraments in both elements (instead of the one of the Catholic practice) and read the Mass in German interspersed by German hymns instead of using the Latin—that is all. As for baptism the records are contradictory; some say that every two months he baptized all the infants, others that he postponed baptism until the children were six or seven years of age. He never in his life baptized adults.

In Allstedt he married, like Luther, a former nun, and reared children. This fact seems to indicate his break with the old church, but one cannot claim that the new church in Allstedt was Protestant or Lutheran in any specific sense. The Reformation was still in its formative years. For the time being he had not yet broken with Luther; in fact, he sent him a rather conciliatory letter on July 9, 1523. In this same year he also wrote a letter to his brethren in Stollberg. Of all his writings this letter breathes a spirit nearest to the evangelical spirit of the later Anabaptists. It is the only document of this kind and has been carefully analyzed by Annemarie Lohmann. Unfortunately, he soon pursued other directions: in the winter of 1523-24 he founded the Allstedt League, a strange conspiratorial society which was to carry out the Prague program, if necessary even with violence. Here Müntzer lost altogether his sense of reality and embarked on a road of romantic fanaticism. Luther recognized this correctly when he called Müntzer a *Schwärmer* (fanatic). The new church should be radical; "ungodly people" should not be allowed to exist. Soon a nearby Catholic chapel went up in flames.

The two princes of Saxony, Duke John and Prince Elector Frederick the Wise, were embarrassed by Müntzer and did not know what to do, being themselves in favor of the Lutheran reforms. Therefore as they passed through Allstaedt they invited Müntzer to preach for them and explain his theology. On July 13, 1524, he preached in the castle in the presence of the princes his famous "Sermon on Daniel." In it he claimed that the authorities were given the sword to eradicate the ungodly, but insisted that if they did not do their duty the sword would be taken away from them (Dan. 7) and given to the people; "for the ungodly have no right to live except as the elect grant it to them." Obviously the princes were now even more confused than before and asked Luther for advice. No persecution was considered for the moment, as Luther still advised lenience. But unrest in Allstaedt prompted Müntzer to flee at night over the city walls. On Aug. 15, 1524, he arrived in Mühlhausen, Thuringia, and soon became a preacher in a church here. This city was to become his real misfortune, for here he met another preacher, Heinrich Pfeiffer, who might be called a real social-revolutionary comparable to John Ball of the English Peasants' War of 1381. Soon the Mühlhausen city council was overthrown and things looked almost like events ten years later in Münster. But after two months, early in October 1524, Müntzer had to flee again. This time he turned south, stopping in Nürnberg, where he may have met Hans Denk, the rector of the School at St. Sebald's. Müntzer's fiery mysticism might have impressed this sensitive man, but his stay was too short to produce any major influence upon him. In Nürnberg Müntzer also had (later, most likely) two new tracts printed: the *Hochverursachte Schutzrede* (a vitriolic pamphlet in which he called Luther *das geistlose, sanftlebende Fleisch zu Wittenberg*) which attacked the Protestant doctrine of original sin, and the *Ausgetrückte Emplössung des falschen Glaubens,* of which more is to be said later.

November and December 1524 Müntzer spent in the South, in Griessen in the Klettgau (Swabia) near Schaffhausen, and in Basel, Switzerland, where he was the guest of Oecolampadius and Hugwald. Not much is known about these eight weeks of restless wandering, but it may be assumed that they merely increased his "prophetic" fancies. Bullinger's claim that he met and converted Hubmaier on this trip is without any foundation and is rather unlikely, even though Griessen is only 15 miles distant from Waldshut, where Hubmaier was living.

In February 1525 Müntzer was back in Mühlhausen, to which city Heinrich Pfeiffer had returned by the end of December 1524. At this point Müntzer placed upon the rebellious peasants his last hope and chance of carrying out his apocalyptic program. Between February and May of this year he may rightly be called the preacher of the peasants, encouraging them mainly during the last three weeks to violent action—expecting at any moment the great crisis of mankind. On May 15 the tragic battle at Frankenhausen was fought (or rather not fought by the confused and discouraged peasants), followed by the senseless massacre which ended the Peasants' War in Thuringia. Müntzer, who tried to hide, was caught, imprisoned, and soon tortured to make him yield a full confession of all his misdeeds. He recanted, accepted the Mass according to Catholic rites, and wrote a farewell letter to his followers in Mühlhausen which is a complete turnabout from his former position. On May 27, 1525, he was beheaded. His symbol and heraldic sign had always been " a red cross and a naked sword."

The biographical sketch has indicated that Müntzer could not possibly have been the "beginner and originator of the great Anabaptist movement" (as in our day Böhmer and Holl have claimed). In view, however, of the persistency of this claim further discussion is needed. We may distinguish here between the factual and pragmatic evidence on the one hand, and on the other, the possible influences from the viewpoint of a history of ideas where evidence is usually of a more indirect nature.

Factual evidence for Müntzer's connection with the Anabaptists is almost completely lacking. Harold S. Bender has proved this with great thoroughness. The legend of such causal influences started with Bullinger in his *Der Widertoufferen Ursprung* (Zürich, 1560), where he claims that Müntzer was the beginner of Anabaptism "down there in Saxony." That was written 35 years after Müntzer's death and naturally without any documentation. Bullinger also says that Hubmaier was "completely confused by Müntzer" (*er sey durch ihn ganz verkehrt worden*), again without any proof. The fact is that Bullinger in none of his earlier books ever mentioned such a theory, and it must be assumed that he more or less invented it later. Bender conjectures that he did so for the purpose of freeing the Zürich Reformed Church from any "reproach" that Anabaptism had its origin in Zürich—which it actually had.

Unfortunately, Bullinger's invention was an appealing theory and has been repeated many times since, in part perhaps because the Müntzer story is so much better known than the story of the early Anabaptists. Neither Holl nor Böhmer seems to have been very familiar with the origins of the Anabaptists (e.g., Conrad Grebel); hence they were inclined to follow the pattern which was first set by Martin Luther, namely, to lump together all nonconformists, "left-wing" groups and individuals, as fanatics (*Schwärmer*), without much discrimination of categories. Since the tragic events of Münster (1534-35) provided evidence that violence could also develop in connection with some forms of Anabaptism (though not with the evangelical type) there was little hesitation to give Bullinger full credence.

What are the facts? Müntzer himself never baptized adults; in fact he somewhat minimized the significance of baptism in general. "Neither Mary, the mother of God, nor the disciples of Christ had been baptized with water." True baptism takes place only through the Holy Spirit. To be sure, he also says, "As they made babes into Christians, Christians became children," but nowhere does he follow up this idea, and for all practical purposes continued to baptize children, either as infants or as six- and seven-year-olds. In 1524 he published a new baptismal liturgy, *Von der Tauff wie man die heldt* (dealing with infant baptism of course). Annemarie Lohmann, who carefully analyzed the issue, says that adult baptism was definitely contrary to Müntzer's basic ideas. Nevertheless, she too speculates that it was perhaps "Müntzer's interpretation of the cross as a sort of baptism" which might have influenced people who were then seeking "an external symbol for the inner baptism of the cross." . . . "All this is, of course, but a conjecture and lacks any proof. . . ." It is not very clear how this connection is to be understood.

Now as to concrete contacts. First of all, the very

first act of adult baptism took place in Zürich in January 1525, when contacts with Müntzer were out of the question. His sojourn in the Klettgau in December 1524 did not produce any known contact with the Conrad Grebel circle in Zürich. Moreover the long letter by Grebel to Müntzer of Sept. 5, 1524, shows that Grebel and his friends were familiar with Müntzer's two earlier tracts, *Von dem getichten Glauben,* and *Protestation odder Empbietung* (both written in Allstedt, 1524). Both these tracts were still rather moderate in tone, the former dealing in the main with the idea of the "cross," the other criticizing infant baptism. Grebel now wrote that he was glad to find in these tracts some familiar ideas and he welcomed Müntzer as a brother in the spirit. But then he reproached Müntzer on two points: one, his emphasis upon church liturgy (*Deutsche Messe*), and two, because of certain rumors that Müntzer was advocating the "sword." This the Grebel friends emphatically opposed and therefore warned the unknown "brother" not to continue in this way. Müntzer never received this letter, and the Grebel circle had no further knowledge about Müntzer's activities. Thus nothing can be deduced from this letter, except that no real contact existed and that Zürich went ahead with their new brotherhood of regenerated Christians independently of anything outside their circle. One indirect contact between Müntzer and the Grebel group was the visit of a brother of Hans Huiuf (one of the Grebel group in Zürich), who came from Halle to Zürich and had known Müntzer.

The same holds true with regard to Müntzer's supposed influence on Hubmaier (who was baptized by Reublin at Easter of 1525), Bullinger's claim notwithstanding.

Three additional possible contacts must be investigated: Hans Denk, Hans Hut, and Melchior Rinck. Müntzer's contact with Denk in Nürnberg, if it took place at all (Fellmann denies it), was very brief and superficial; moreover it had nothing to do with Denk's later turn to Anabaptism, and can therefore be dismissed. The situation with regard to Hans Hut, however, is different. He must be called a former friend of Müntzer who supposedly spent a few days in Hut's home in Bibra. Hut then received a manuscript from Müntzer, the *Ausgetrückte Emplössung des falschen Glaubens* (1524), and was asked to manage its publication. (Hut as a book peddler might have been better acquainted with printers willing to risk such a publication.) Hut thereupon approached the journeymen of the Nürnberg printer Hans Hergott, who in the absence of the master actually printed the pamphlet clandestinely. When the councilmen of Nürnberg heard of it, the journeymen and Hut were imprisoned and the book edition was destroyed. (Only one or two copies survived.) In his court trial in 1527 Hut openly admitted this act. Was he then a Müntzerite? To some extent, yes, mainly with regard to Müntzer's apocalyptic expectations that the end of this world-aeon had drawn near and that the new era was about to come at any moment, indicated by wars and rumors of war. Müntzer's apocalypticism seems to have appealed to Hut's frame of mind, but not his doctrine of the sword. At the battle of

Frankenhausen Hut was present; whether as an itinerant book peddler or as a curious onlooker is hard to say. He had no part whatever in the events and soon left. A year later, in the spring of 1526, in Augsburg, he was baptized by Hans Denk and became truly a "new man."

It might be argued that in spite of his conversion, Hut nevertheless promoted certain Müntzerite ideas throughout his itinerant activities as an Anabaptist missionary up to his early death in 1527.

What about this argument with its crucial bearing on the question of Müntzer's relation to later Anabaptism? True enough, Hut preached "the cross," that is, the suffering church, and in this message sounded somewhat like a Müntzerite. But an analysis reveals that it is only the key word "cross" which is the same as with Müntzer; its meaning, however, is very different with Hut, as will be shown presently. The same holds true with regard to Hut's "spiritualism," i.e., the idea that the Word of God can be interpreted rightly only by those who are filled by a spirit akin to that of the Holy Scriptures. No word of direct inspiration or of dreams can be found in all of Hut's teaching, as far as is known. Again, the key word "spirit" is the same, but the content is different. If Hut was a "spiritualist," he was a Biblical one, as were Michael Sattler and all the early Anabaptists, but he really was not a spiritualist at all. Müntzer, on the other hand, was an inspirationist (like David Joris a decade or so later), and understood the idea of the "spirit" much more subjectively than any Anabaptist. To him the "inward scripture" outbade the "Holy Scripture." Lydia Müller thinks that this was also the position of at least some leading Anabaptists but cannot prove it. Anabaptists at no time minimized the unconditional Biblical faith.

Finally, it is known that Hut passionately opposed the "sword." In Nikolsburg in 1526 he debated this issue with Hubmaier, who defended the use of the sword under certain conditions. When Hut saw the impasse he left Nikolsburg, continuing his Anabaptist mission of cross and love. Incidentally, Müntzer, his former friend, had very little to say concerning this Christian love; Lohmann expressly states that "the idea of love drops inadvertently into the background," all the more when Müntzer preached the needed eradication of the ungodly. Thus Hut cannot be a useful witness for Bullinger's theory and its late defenders, even though some common key words actually appear in both camps. It is their meaning which matters, not the terms as such.

There remains one last contact with later Anabaptism: Melchior Rinck. This contact is a real one. Rinck was openly a Müntzerite, and in fact he even boasted that God had spared him at Frankenhausen that he might carry out Müntzer's plans more successfully and bring them to a happy end. He apparently owed to Müntzer his first spiritual awakening and was grateful for that, but perhaps understood only part of Müntzer's message. Rinck's own later writings do not continue Müntzer's fancies concerning dreams and the violent overthrow of the ungodly. After becoming an Anabaptist in May 1527 at Worms as a result of his contact with Hans

Denk and Jakob Kautz, he became one of the most effective leaders of early Anabaptism in Thuringia, until he too experienced the very cross of all true confessors in martyrdom sometime after 1545, having been in prison since 1531. In no way may he be called a "beginner" of Anabaptism or even one of its leading figures. And after becoming an Anabaptist he shows no trace whatever of Müntzer's ideas. He could not have been a channel of transmission of these ideas into Anabaptism.

But what about indirect influences on later Anabaptism by Müntzer's writings? A brief review of some of the major points of possible contact and similarity in the realm of ideas between Müntzer and the Anabaptists, in other words, continuities of Müntzer's ideas, reveals the following facts.

Cross. To Müntzer the cross meant two things: outwardly human suffering through sickness, poverty, and the hostility of people; and inwardly *Anfechtung,* i.e., doubt, error, and unbelief. A "cross" of such a kind is utterly foreign to the Anabaptists, who become "disciples of Christ" only through rebirth and determination to follow the commandments of Christ. On the other hand, suffering for the sake of truth, the idea of a "church under the cross" (Grebel) never occurred to Müntzer, who had no revealed truth in the first place to be witnessed to and no church either. Thus even though the term "cross" appears frequently in Müntzer's writings—sometimes also called "the bitter Christ" (vs. the "sweet Christ" of Luther)—it means something different. When he vaguely indicates that whoever experiences the cross experiences inner spiritual baptism, that idea is not in itself to be equated with the Anabaptist doctrine of the cross.

Spirit. To a certain extent all early Anabaptists had a good share of spiritualism in their understanding of the Holy Scriptures; but the latter remained the rock foundation upon which they built their faith. No fanatical dreaming can ever be found among them, and Lydia Müller's claim that the appreciation of the Scriptural Word drops into the background with the Anabaptists just as with Müntzer is simply a misstatement, since she confounds the occasional Anabaptist term "inner word" with Müntzer's inspirationism.

Gelassenheit, i.e., yielding to the will of God and not following one's own imaginations, was a frequent term in Müntzer's earlier writings when he was still under the influence of the German mystics, and also a central idea with the Anabaptists. Müntzer had learned a great deal from these German mystics, through whose writings he apparently grew spiritually in the earlier period of his life. But soon he gave it up; it was "basically against his very nature," which nature was unrest, passion, activity, and challenge. A man who wanted to kill all the ungodly could have little Gelassenheit, even though he might preach it as an ideal.

Adult baptism. Concerning this little needs to be added. Müntzer was not interested in it (as so many radical spiritualists were not), and would hardly have understood its new meaning with the Anabaptists as a sealing of the inner rebirth, making men determined to walk the narrow path of discipleship.

Lord's Supper. Remembering his liturgical tracts (*Deutsche Messe*) it becomes evident that to Müntzer the celebration lacked completely the Anabaptist meaning of a symbol of sharing, akin to the "lovefeast" idea. Lohmann expressly states that Müntzer's tracts were extremely "conservative" in character, i.e., nearer to a modified Catholicism than to Lutheranism or any radical idea. For that reason he continued to the end to speak of the "Mass" and not of the Lord's Supper.

Church. This is perhaps the most difficult item of all, and has never been fully studied. Most authors think that here at least are to be found similarities with Anabaptism. The Anabaptist idea is that of a voluntary free church of genuine believers as opposed to the ecclesiastical institution of both Catholicism and Lutheranism (state church, people's church). A careful analysis, however, will destroy even this most persistent argument. To be sure, in the Prague Manifesto of 1521 Müntzer passingly said that in Bohemia the "new church" would arise. It was to be the church of the new aeon, the church without the ungodly, an apocalyptic vision, no concrete reality. This is theory. But what was Müntzer's practice? First, he remained to the very end of his life a priest-preacher both in Allstedt and in Mühlhausen city churches, and hence never actually opposed an institution of that kind (either Catholic or Lutheran in nature). Second, his Allstedt League was anything but an Anabaptist brotherhood; it was rather a secret society to promote the imminently expected kingdom of God by means of wiping out, if need be by the sword, all (Catholic) superstition— a chapel was burned down—and all ungodliness. Of a restitution of the primitive church in the Anabaptist sense there is no trace whatever, since Müntzer completely lacked the idea or vision of discipleship and obedience to the Word of God.

It is true that at times Müntzer also taught that the true reign of Christ could come only by genuine "kenosis," that is, emptying oneself of all worldly desires and humbling oneself to the will of God. But then he contradicted himself by claiming (at another place) that those who were prepared to the "fear of God" were now entitled to reign and rule, for they alone knew the will of God. Obviously no doctrine of the church could follow from such a confused theology. Since he continued as a state church preacher, it cannot be claimed that the "believers' church" originated with Müntzer.

Eschatology. This may be omitted here, since it is but marginal with the Anabaptists. Hans Hut, to be sure, was much attracted by it, but when it came to preaching the new birth and discipleship he voluntarily restrained himself and kept his apocalyptic ideas silent. With Müntzer it was the exact opposite. Only by these ideas about the change of the world did he find an inner justification for all his violent and revolutionary actions.

The writings of Hans Denk have recently been carefully studied by the editor of the new 1956 edition of Denk, Walter Fellmann, for evidence of possible literary influence of Müntzer's writings on Denk. Surprisingly Fellmann found twenty-four passages in Denk which echo Müntzer's terms or phrases, and concludes that "the literary dependence on Müntzer's mysticism is noticeable." J. J. Kiwiet thinks that this may be explainable through a possible common source of both, i.e., the writings of the German mystics, particularly *Theologia deutsch*, rather than a borrowing by Denk from Müntzer. Grete Mecenseffy ("Die Herkunft des oberösterreichischen Täufertums") believes that Hans Hut's mystical ideas had their origin in Müntzer's writings. Granting both Fellmann's and Mecenseffy's point, it remains only to say that the mystical ideas were not the essence of Anabaptism and that no evidence has been brought forward which would contradict any of the points made above.

In summary we may agree with Annemarie Lohmann that the years 1524-25 appallingly show how this erstwhile mystically minded man, who knew so much about suffering and human tragedy, became more and more shallow (*Verflachung*). Since all his six major tracts and sermons date from 1524, it is after all this Müntzer whom we have to consider first, not the man of the Prague Manifesto (1521), confused and equivocal though this document also appears. This weakening of Müntzer's former spiritual position is a tragedy in itself, the result not of any "kenosis" but of a self-centered and romantic fanaticism.

That Müntzer represented a tremendous spiritual power for his time, being a passionate awakener, is true enough. That he was a "beginner of Anabaptism" in any sense whatever is, however, just as incorrect as the opposite claim which sees in him a forerunner of modern socialism. Since his writings are contradictory, such attitudes might be read into them; but any such interpretation does not do justice to his true nature.

But what was Müntzer then, after all? Were it not for his activism, Müntzer might be placed beside David Joris, the inspirationist. This activism, however, with all its hazy orientation toward a goal to be achieved by the sword, brings him into the neighborhood of the "kingdom of Münster" of 1534-35. Müntzer had little essential in common with evangelical Anabaptism, which arose when he was about to pass from the scene, and which became victorious simply by being a "church under the cross."

R.F.

Karl Holl, "Luther und die Schwärmer" in his *Gesammelte Aufsätze* (2nd and 3rd ed., Tübingen, 1923) 420-46; Heinrich Böhmer, "Thomas Müntzer und das jüngste Deutschland," in his *Gesammelte Aufsätze* (Gotha, 1922) 187-222; H. Böhmer and P. Kirn, *Thomas Müntzers Briefwechsel* (Leipzig, 1931, containing also the four versions of the *Prague Manifesto*); Otto Clemen, "Das Prager Manifest Thomas Müntzers," *Arch. f. Ref.-Gesch.* (1933) 73-81; Joachim Zimmerman, *Thomas Münzer, ein deutsches Schicksal* (Berlin, 1925); Annemarie Lohmann, *Zur geistigen Entwicklung Thomas Müntzers* (Leipzig, 1931), the best work of all; Otto H. Brandt, *Thomas Müntzer, Sein Leben und seine Schriften* (Jena, 1933), an excellent edition of Müntzer's tracts in modernized German together with other source material; Carl Hinrichs, *Thomas Müntzer, Politische Schriften mit Kommentar* (Halle, 1950), contains Müntzer's last three and most important writings; idem, *Luther und Müntzer* (Berlin, 1952); H. S. Bender, *Conrad Grebel* (Goshen, 1950) 198 f. and *passim*; idem, "The Zwickau Prophets, Thomas Müntzer and the Anabaptists," *MQR XXVII* (1953) 3-16 (basic); Wiswedel, *Bilder I*; idem, "War Thomas Müntzer wirklich der Urheber der grossen Taufbewegung?" in *Mühlhauser Geschichtsblätter XXX* (1929) 268-73; idem, "Inner and Outer Word," *MQR XXVI* (1952) 171-93; K. Schulz, "Thomas Müntzers liturgische Bestrebungen," *Ztscht f. Kirchengesch. XLVII*

(1928); Paul Wappler, *Die Täuferbewegung in Thüringen* (Jena, 1913); W. Metzger, "Müntzeriana," *Thüringisch-Sächsische Ztscht f. Gesch. u. Kunst XVI* (1927); Grete Mecenseffy, "Die Herkunft des oberösterreichischen Täufertums," in *Archiv für Ref.-Gesch. XLVII* (1956) 252-8; George H. Williams, ed., *Spiritual and Anabaptist Writers* (Library of Christian Classics XXIV, Philadelphia, 1957), reprints Müntzer's "Sermon Before the Princes" in English, with an introduction, pp. 47-70, also Grebel's letter to Müntzer with an introduction, pp. 71-85; Walter Fellman, *Hans Denk Schriften*, Part 2: *Religiöse Schriften* (Gütersloh, 1956); Robert Friedmann, "Thomas Müntzer's Relation to Anabaptism," *MQR XXXI* (1957) 75-87.

The Böhmer school produced the following monographs, in all of which Heinrich Böhmer's thesis concerning Müntzer as the beginner of the Anabaptist movement is discussed and conditionally respected: K. Ecke, *Schwenckfeld, Luther und der Gedanke einer apostolischen Reformation* (Berlin, 1911); H. Neusser, *Hans Huth* (Berlin, 1913); C. Sachsse, *Balthasar Hubmaier als Theologe* (Berlin, 1914); L. Müller, *Der Kommunismus der mährischen Wiedertäufer* (Leipzig, 1928); Annemarie Lohmann, *Zur geistigen Entwicklung* (Leipzig, 1931).

A considerable number of socialist-Marxist studies in Müntzer have appeared since Engels' work on the great Peasants' War. The latest book is by a Soviet-Russian scholar, M. M. Smirin, *Die Volksreformation des Thomas Müntzer und der grosse Bauernkrieg* (Berlin, 1952; 675 pages), in which the author distinguishes between the "Reformation of the Princes" (Luther) and the "Reformation of the working people" (Müntzer); A. Meusel, *Thomas Müntzer und seine Zeit* (Berlin, 1952) repeats the same idea; see also K. Kleinschmid, *Thomas Münzer* (1952). Of similar character are the earlier volumes: P. Friedländer, *Thomas Münzer (Redner der Revolution VI*, Berlin, 1926), and L. G. Walter, *Thomas Munzer 1489-1525 et Les Luttes Sociales à L'Epoque de la Reforme* (Paris, 1927); and to a lesser extent Michael Freund, *Thomas Müntzer. Revolution als Glaube, Eine Auswahl aus den Schriften Thomas Müntzers und Martin Luthers zur religiösen Revolution und zum deutschen Bauernkreig* (Deutsche Schriften V, Potsdam, 1936); ML III, 187-91.

Muravyevka, a village in the Mennonite settlement of Alt-Samara or Alexandertal (*q.v.*) in the province of Samara, about 80 miles north of the city of Samara, was founded in 1863 by Mennonites from West Prussia, when the Russian government granted permission for 100 additional families to immigrate. In 1913 the village had 59 Mennonite inhabitants and maintained a German school. (ML III, 191.)

HEGE.

Muria is the name of the conference of the Mennonite congregations around Mount Muria on the island of Java (*q.v.*), Indonesia. In 1940 the congregations in this territory, which resulted from the work of the Dutch Mennonite Mission Association in this area in 1851-1940, became independent, and a number of them formed a kind of conference. The Muria conference started with 10 congregations with a membership of about 2,000; now (1955) it consists of 30 congregations with nearly 4,000 members.

VDZ.

Muristalden *Teachers' Seminary*, a teacher-training school in the canton of Bern, Switzerland, founded by Pietists within the Reformed Church in 1854. The founder was Pastor Friedrich Gerber. Its founding occurred in a politically restless time, when political liberalism was accompanied by religious liberalism. Its purpose was to train teachers in a thoroughly Christian spirit. Tuition fees cover about one third of the cost, the rest being raised by voluntary contributions. Annually about 20 young men are graduated. The young Mennonites of Bern who plan to teach usually attend Muristalden. One of the teachers at this school was Dr. Adolf Fluri, who was the author of the valuable *Beiträge zur Geschichte der bernischen Täufer* (Bern, 1912). A.-T.

Gedenkschrift zum 50-jährigen Bestand des Evangelischen Seminars auf dem Muristalden, Bern 1854-1905; Hugendubel, Lebensbild von Pfarrer Friedrich Gerber (Basel, 1908); Hadorn, "Gesch. des Pietismus der Schweiz" (Ms.); ML I, 615 f.

Murphy Hutterite Bruderhof near Glenwood, Alberta, founded in 1927 by members of the East Cardston Bruderhof. Joseph Hofer was chosen as their preacher in 1927. In 1947 the Bruderhof numbered 58, with 20 baptized members.   D.D.

Murton, John, an English refugee, belonged to a congregation of Independents in Amsterdam in the early 17th century. At first this church had some interest in the Mennonites, but after John Smyth (*q.v.*) with a number of adherents left the Independents, planning a union with the Waterlander Mennonites (effected in 1615), Thomas Helwys (*q.v.*), then the leader of the Independent group, turned more and more to Calvinism. In 1611 the Independents returned to England; about 1614 Helwys died and Murton became the leader of the group in London (occasionally called an Anabaptist congregation). Murton was an inspiring leader and during his leadership, which lasted until after 1645, the Independent congregation, which met at Newgate in London, flourished, though persecution by the state church and internal controversy continued to weaken it. Murton protested against the persecutions in an address to the King of England pleading for freedom of religion: "A most humble supplication of many of the king Majestys loyal subjects . . . who are persecuted only for differing in religion." Still more than his predecessor Helwys, Murton was in sympathy with the doctrines of Calvinism. In 1620 he published *A description of what God hath predestinated concerning man.* Not all the members agreed with this Calvinism; this was apparently the reason why shortly after 1620 Elias Tookey (*q.v.*) and 15 others were expelled. They held the Anabaptist views of free will and believers' baptism, and in 1624-26 contacted the Dutch Mennonites for a union, which, however, was not effected.

Of Murton's personal life not much is known. Neither the year nor place of his birth or death are available. On Aug. 23, 1608, he was married at Amsterdam to Jane Hodgkin. The marriage certificate says that he was born about 1583 and had lived at Gainsborough, England, before he came to Amsterdam. During his stay in Amsterdam he was a furrier. He is said to have been a zealous and capable man.   vDZ.

Inv. Arch. Amst. II, Nos. 1351, 1367; J. G. de Hoop Scheffer and W. E. Griffis, History of the Free Churchmen (Ithaca, n.d.—1922) 148, 153, 178 f., 190, No. 53.

Musa, Antonius (*ca.* 1490-1547), a Lutheran clergyman, city pastor in Jena, Germany, beginning 1524, was one of the inspectors chosen in Saxony after the passing of the mandate of Jan. 17, 1528, against the

"Anabaptists, Sacramentalists, and fanaticism." He was also assigned the task of cross-examining a number of Anabaptist prisoners and of persuading them to rejoin the church. On Dec. 1 and 6, 1535, he questioned Heinz Kraut (*q.v.*), Jobst Möller (*q.v.*), and Hans Peissker at Jena in the presence of several members of the city council and Philip Melanchthon (*q.v.*) and Kaspar Cruciger (*q.v.*). The three were executed on Jan. 26, 1536, at Jena. On Jan. 13, 1536, Musa together with Melanchthon and Cruciger worked on the conversion of four imprisoned women on the Lüchtenburg near Kahla, and on the next day with Melanchthon three men imprisoned in Kahla. Several weeks of work were required to achieve this end, whereupon the prisoners were released in February and March.

Among those who recanted were Anna and Ursula Möller, whom Melanchthon had described to the Elector of Saxony as being particularly obstinate (*Corp. Ref. III, 21*). Their resistance melted when they were informed that their husbands had been beheaded, since they refused to enter the Lutheran Church. Those who yielded to such compulsion were released without punishment, even when seditious intentions were evident, as Musa thought was the case with the Anabaptists who had been freed (letter of Musa to Stephen Roth, city clerk of Zwickau in *Corp. Ref.* III, 12-14).

The resistance of the Anabaptists to adopting the Lutheran creed is understandable in the light of conditions in many parishes. Thus after his church inspection Musa wrote to Stephen Roth that there were very few educated men who preached Christ; some ranted against the Papists, others against the secular government; but very few taught what repentance, faith, and love are (Clemen, 74). On Oct. 3, 1534, he wrote to Roth that those who were everywhere reckoned as preachers of the Gospel did not preach Christ (Clemen, 77), and on May 22, 1537, he wrote that the preachers were abusing the pulpit to rant against the papacy; meanwhile the dear congregation snored, correctly feeling that it was no concern of theirs (Clemen, 67).

After the Anabaptist executions in Jena, which stirred up much excitement, Musa was no longer comfortable there. On Feb. 22, 1536, he wrote to Roth that he was about to resign his position on account of the intrigues of some ungodly persons (Clemen, 67). He would have liked to go to Zwickau if there had been a vacancy for him. In 1538 he was made superintendent at Rochlitz. He died in 1547.   HEGE.

O. Clemen, Beiträge zur Ref.-Gesch. aus Büchern und Handschriften der Zwickauer Ratsschulbibliothek I (Berlin, 1900); Corpus Reformatorum II and III (1835 and 1836); Wappler, Thüringen; ML III, 191 f.

Musculus (Meusslin), **Wolfgang** (1497-1563), a clergyman who in 1512 entered a Benedictine monastery at Lixheim, Alsace, left it in 1527 and became a Protestant. For a time he served as deacon at the minster in Strasbourg. In 1531 he was called to the church of the Holy Cross in Augsburg (*q.v.*), Germany. Here he attacked the Anabaptists in speaking and writing, but was of a more lenient nature than his colleague Urban Rhegius (*q.v.*), who had left Augsburg on Aug. 26, 1530. The peak of the

Anabaptist movement in the city was already past. The leaders of the brotherhood had been in prison for three and one-half years. Soon after his arrival Musculus and his colleague Bonifacius Wolfhart began his attempts to convert them. Jakob Daschser (*q.v.*), who had been in prison since Aug. 28, 1527, and had written 40 hymns there (Kamp, 27), recanted on May 16, 1531; Jakob Gross (*q.v.*) after over three years in prison did the same on June 22. Other members of the Augsburg Anabaptist group were imprisoned in the meantime and released upon recantation. Some were expelled from the city, and threatened with beheading if they returned (Roth, II, 407).

The discussions of the city preachers with the Anabaptist prisoners led Musculus to write a pamphlet on the oath in order to make it clear to the populace that swearing is not forbidden; many citizens were refusing to give the required oath before the court. In 1530, on the occasion of the meeting of the Reichstag, when the oath was required of all citizens, some of them preferred to be put out of the city (Roth, II, 408). The booklet was published on July 28, 1533, in Augsburg with the title, *Ain frydsams vnnd Christlichs Gesprech ains Euangelischen auff ainer, vnd ains Widerteuffers, auff der andern seyten, so sy des Aydschwurs halben thund*, and contains 34 pages. It is written in the form of a dialogue, in which a Protestant named Friedenreich tries to persuade an Anabaptist named Adolf that swearing is not forbidden. It is the oldest polemic against the Anabaptists on the subject of the oath, though the Confession of Augsburg (*q.v.*) had three years previously taken a position in Article 16, which says, "Here the Anabaptists are damned" because they teach that to render "the required oath is not Christian." Martin Micronius (*q.v.*) in 1555 published a Dutch translation of Musculus' booklet with the title *Een claere, ende Scriftelicke onderrichtinghe van den Eedt, wat hy sy: ende hoe dat hy gebruijct ende misbruijct can werden Waer toeghedaen is een clein anhancksel, den seluen handel angaende, Door Marten Mikroen.*

Musculus also refuted the doctrines of the Anabaptists in his commentaries on the Gospels (Roth, III, 247). After the Augsburg Interim in 1548 Musculus had to leave the city and fled to Bern, where he was employed as professor of theology.   HEGE.

F. Grimme, "Wolfgang Musculus," in *Jahrb. der Gesellschaft für lothringer Geschichte und Altertumskunde* V, 2 (1893) 1-20; A. Kamp, *Die Psalmendichtung des Jakob Dachser* (Greifswald, 1931); Fr. Roth, *Augsburger Reformationsgesichte* (1904 and 1907); ML III, 192.

Music, Church. Music, vocal and instrumental, was a regular part of Old Testament temple worship. The early Christians used vocal, but not instrumental, music in their worship. Christ and His disciples in the upper room before the betrayal "sang an hymn." The Apostle Paul (Eph. 5:19; Col. 3:16) urged his churches to sing "psalms, hymns, and spiritual songs," and James advised a "merry" Christian to "sing psalms" (Jas. 5:13). John the Revelator pictures the victorious Christians singing the song of Moses and the Lamb in the future glory. Paul and Silas sang praises in prison (Acts 16:25), as many persecuted Christians and martyrs have done since.

The early Christian congregational singing, one-part in character, was gradually supplanted by liturgical singing (promoted greatly by Ambrose, Bishop of Milan, 333-97, and still more by Pope Gregory the Great, 598-604), which became the exclusive function of the clergy, assisted by special male choirs, who sang only in Latin in the West. The organ was introduced into church music in the West by Charlemagne (*ca.* 800). In the Middle Ages only the small groups outside the church such as the Albigenses and Waldenses continued congregational singing, in the vernacular, and also used singing in their evangelistic efforts. Because of the effective use of singing by the "heretical" groups, alert Roman Catholic leaders like Berthold of Regensburg (d. 1272) urged the use of singing in the vernacular by the church because "the heretics were leading people astray" by "composing songs and teaching them to the children in the streets."

But it was the Lutheran Reformation which first restored congregational singing in the vernacular, though with the retention of the organ. Luther's first published order of service (*Deutsche Messe*, 1526) provided for two or three hymns to be sung by the congregation. Luther himself composed some songs and wrote some hymns. Lutheranism, however, as did Anglicanism, retained the liturgical type of worship service.

It was the Reformed phase of the Reformation which did away with the liturgy altogether and made congregational singing the people's part in the worship service. At first, however, Zwingli, though a lover of music, banished both singing and the organ from the church service, basing his position on Amos 5:23. It was not until 1598 that singing was reintroduced into the worship in Zürich.

Although Conrad Grebel himself, in line with Zwingli, also opposed all music including singing in worship, the early Anabaptists made much use of singing almost from the beginning, and many Anabaptists wrote hymns, over 130 Anabaptist hymn writers being known. One section of the *Ausbund* consists of hymns which were "composed and sung at Passau in the castle (prison) by the Swiss Brethren," as the title states. Without doubt hymns were a factor in Anabaptist evangelism, both sung and read. Christian Neff says (*ML* II, 86), "A flood of religious songs poured over the young brotherhood like a vivifying and refreshing stream. The songs became the strongest attractive force for the brotherhood. They sang themselves into the hearts of many, clothed in popular tunes. They were mostly martyr songs, which breathed an atmosphere of readiness to die and a touching depth of faith. And those that did not report on martyr steadfastness admonished the listener to a devout faith, which was to prove itself in love. Sanctification and its demonstration in life and death is their glorious content." By the middle of the 16th century five printed Anabaptist hymnals had appeared, in addition to numerous song leaflets and handwritten materials (the Hutterite hymnal was not published until 1914, although hymn codices have been preserved from as early as 1570).

Congregational singing has thus been a regular part of Anabaptist-Mennonite worship from the beginning. In Europe it has largely remained one-part singing in Holland, but by the second half of the 19th century was developing into four-part singing, especially by congregational choral groups, in South Germany, France, Switzerland, and somewhat later in Russia and North America.

The use of the reed organ and pipe organ in worship was introduced into the Dutch Mennonite churches in the fourth quarter of the 18th century (first case in Utrecht in 1765), but not until considerably later elsewhere. It was little used in Russia at any time, and is still not permitted in the more conservative groups in North America including, for instance, the Mennonite Church (MC). It came into general use in the other American groups about the turn of the 20th century. About one third of North American Mennonites now use the organ or piano in worship.

Choirs (q.v.) are not used at all in regular worship anywhere in Europe, and in North America only in those groups which use an instrument in worship, and even then not uniformly. Choirs are, however, often used for special occasions in South Germany, France, Switzerland, and now again Russia, as well as in South America and most North American groups including the M.C., but not in the strictly conservative groups. Before the use of an instrument, and now in groups not using it, the congregational singing has been and is led by a song leader called a chorister (q.v.) or Vorsänger.

The church music of the Mennonites is completely nonliturgical. Since Mennonites have produced almost no composers of church music of their own, although in Anabaptist times they produced many of their own hymns, they have used the tunes (q.v.) of other Protestant churches. They have thus also been influenced by their environment and affinities in the type of church music used. Pietism, Methodism, and revivalism have all had their influence. This influence has been particularly noticeable in the past two generations in South Germany, France, Switzerland, Russia, and America; Holland and North Germany have remained largely untouched. This has resulted in the displacement of much of the older, slower music of the chorale type by a faster and lighter type commonly known as the "gospel song." Recently a wholesome return toward the solider type of music is noticeable, while retaining the best of the gospel songs.

Conscious effort has been made in certain North American groups to maintain and improve the quality of congregational singing as well as the quality of music used. "Singing classes" or "singing schools" were widely used in the Mennonite Church (MC) for this purpose, both to teach the rudiments of music and improve hymn interpretation. Chorister training conferences and church music institutes have also been held in this group. A standing committee of the Mennonite General Conference, the Music Committee created in 1909, has sponsored these and other measures, as well as having responsibility for editing hymnals for the church. Among the outstanding leaders of church music in the Mennonite (MC) Church have been C. H. Brunk (1845-1921), J. D. Brunk (1872-1926), S. F. Coffman (1872-1954), J. W. Yoder (1872-1956), and Walter

E. Yoder (1889-　). All of these men have also composed some music for hymns which are included in the hymnals of the church.

The church music of the Old Order Amish is unique among Mennonite groups by virtue of their four century-long traditional and continued use of both hymns and tunes. The sole hymnal used in the regular public worship is still the ancient Swiss Brethren hymnal, the Ausbund (first ed. 1564), probably the oldest Christian hymnal in continuous use. This hymnal, though indicating the tunes to be used with the hymns, has never printed any notes, and no tune-book has ever been published. The tunes have been handed down from the beginning by memory; many of them have been identified as coming directly from 16th-century religious and folk-tunes. J. W. Yoder transcribed some of the Amish tunes and published them with the words in Amische Lieder (1942). Recordings have also been made of a number of the tunes, which have been deposited in the Library of Congress and Goshen College Library. Rote perpetuation of the 16th-century tunes has naturally resulted in considerable "distortion."

The Old Colony Mennonites in Manitoba, Mexico, and Paraguay have had a similar experience in their church music as the Amish, except that their tunes go back only about half the length of time. They are still using as their hymnal essentially the Geistreiches Gesangbuch of their Russian-Prussian ancestors, first published as a noteless hymnal in 1767 at Königsberg. The tunes indicated in the hymnal have been handed down by rote, and hence have also been subject to distortion, although for a short time the Franz Choralbuch of 1860 was used in Russia by a part of the later "Old Colony" immigrants to Canada. Both Old Order Amish and Old Colony Mennonites, as well as the Hutterites, still sing in what is called the "old" or "slow" style. (See also Chorister, Choir, Hymnology, and Tunes.)

H.S.B.

Charles Burkhart, "Church Music of the Old Order Amish and Old Colony Mennonites," MQR XXVII (1953) 34-54; Rosella Duerksen, "Anabaptist Hymnody of the Sixteenth Century. A Study of Its Marked Individuality Coupled with a Dependence upon Secular and Sacred Music Style and Form" (unpublished dissertation, Union Theological Seminary, N.Y., 1956); ML II, 85 f.

Music, Church, in the Netherlands. During the persecution hymn singing in Anabaptist-Mennonite meetings was practiced as circumstances permitted it. After persecution ended hymn singing was regularly practiced. The singing was led by a "voorzanger" (precentor); musical instruments including organs were not tolerated as being too worldly. Not until 1765 was a pipe organ placed in a Dutch Mennonite meetinghouse. This first organ was built in the church of Utrecht. Other congregations soon followed: Haarlem (Klein Heiligland) in 1771, Leiden 1774, Rotterdam 1775, Amsterdam (Lamist church) 1777, Zaandam (Nieuwe Huys) 1784, Amsterdam (Zonist church) 1786. Though there was here and there some resistance against organs, yet the introduction nowhere led to discord.

During the 19th century nearly all congregations acquired organs, mostly pipe organs, sometimes a simple harmonium. By 1905 only seven congregations in the Netherlands had no organ; this was not because they were opposed to organs but because the money was lacking. Now (1955) all Mennonite churches are provided with organs.

Musical instruments, other than organs, are not used in Dutch Mennonite churches. Congregational singing is always in unison. Sometimes, particularly on special days like on Christmas or the installation of a new pastor, there is choir singing. Choir singing as a regular part of the order of service, as practiced among some American Mennonite branches, is unknown in the Netherlands.

In the 16th and early 17th centuries it was the common practice to sing two hymns at the meeting, one at the beginning and one at the close. During the 17th century the custom gradually developed to sing three times during a meeting. This practice was obviously borrowed from the Calvinist liturgy. Now singing three times and occasionally once or twice more is usual in Dutch Mennonite services.

The first Dutch Mennonite hymnbooks used in the 17th century, such as *Veelderhande Liedekens* (*q.v.*) of 1560 and following reprints, *Een Nieu Liedenboeck* (*q.v.*) of 1562, *Lietboecxken van den Offer des Heeren* (*q.v.*) (at the same time the hymns found in the *Offer* itself) of 1563 and following editions, *Het Tweede Liedeboeck* (*q.v.*) of 1583, *Veelderhande Schriftuerlycke Nieuwe Liedekens* by Leenaerdt Clock, of 1597, and *Sommige andachtige ende leerachtige Gheestelicke Liedekens* (*q.v.*) of 1597, are without notes, as are most 17th-century hymnals, such as the *Kleyn* and the *Groot Hoorns Liedtboeck* (*q.v.*), the *Rijper Lietboecxken* (*q.v.*), Stapel's *Lusthof der Zielen* (*q.v.*), and many others, and also some 18th-century hymnals like Alle Derks' *Lusthof des Gemoeds* (*q.v.*). As late as 1814 a reprint of the *Kleyn Hoorns Lietboeck* appeared without notes. In all these hymnals a melody (or often two) is suggested at the top of each hymn to which the hymn can be sung. These tunes, obviously all familiar to the congregations, were derived from both spiritual and secular songs. Often it was the tune of a psalm. A large number of the old secular songs with their melodies are found in Florimont van Duyse, *Het Oude Nederlandsche Lied,* 3 vv. (1907). The first Dutch hymnbook to break with the tradition of having no notes was the *Lietboeck* by Hans de Ries of 1582, in which the entire section containing psalms has notes, while in the following sections only a few hymns have notes, the others having only the indication of a tune. The 18th- and 19th-century hymnals, being usually collections of hymns borrowed from other hymnals, mostly non-Mennonite, took over the melodies from these hymnbooks together with the texts.

Later hymnals used by the Mennonites, such as *Protestantenbond-bundel* (*q.v.*), *Leidsche Bundel* (*q.v.*), and the *Doopsgezinde Bundel* (*q.v.*, 1944), contain a list which shows the source of each hymn and melody as well as the composer. Only the *Doopsgezinde Bundel* indicates Mennonite composers, including in its supplement seven melodies composed by Jacob Bijster (b. 1902), the organist of the Haarlem Mennonite congregation.

There are no Dutch Mennonite composers, either of secular or of church music. Pastor W. H. toe Water composed the music of the Elspeet Broederschapshuis song, while Pastor L. Bonga wrote both the words and the music of the hymn of the Friese Doopsgezinde Jongerenbond (*q.v.*).   vDZ.

N. van der Zijpp, *Geschiedenis der Doopsgezinden in Nederland* (Arnhem, 1952) 108, 110 f., 112-14, 242 note 14; *DB* 1863, 19 f., 1904, 244; D. F. Scheurleer, *De Souterliedekens* (1894); F. C. Wieder, *De Schriftuurlijke Liedekens* (The Hague, 1900); Wolkan, *Lieder*; J. A. N. Knuttel, *Het geestelijk lied in de Nederlanden voor de Kerkhervorming* (1906).

Music, Church, in Prussia, Poland, Russia, and Descendant Communities in North America. The articles **Hymnology** of the Mennonites of West and East Prussia, Danzig, and Russia, **Choirs** in Prussia and Russia, **Chorister,** and **Choral-books** have treated extensively various aspects of Mennonite church music in this area. The Mennonites of Dutch-Prussian background did not differ greatly in their attitude toward music from the Swiss Brethren, or from the Reformed Church, which used music in worship only to a limited degree. Mennonites, being non-liturgical in their worship, placed more emphasis on the preaching of the Word of God. In fact, there are some claims that the early Prussian Mennonites did not sing during their worship services (*ME* II, 875). If this was the case, it was likely because they were compelled to worship God quietly in order not to attract attention. The singing was as a rule in unison and restricted to congregational singing without instrumental accompaniment. The early hymnbooks had no notes, but indicated for each hymn a melody, which was transmitted by rote from generation to generation. The hymn tunes were either brought from Holland or borrowed from the Lutherans. The singing was slow, very much as it is found today among the Old Colony Mennonites of Mexico or the Amish and Hutterites. Only after Mennonite spiritual life had been influenced by the pietistic revival movement in Prussia and Russia through German Pietism and the English Baptists, was the traditional singing transformed by faster singing and new melodies. A significant development along these lines was the introduction of written and (later) printed choral-books through which four-part singing and modified faster melodies were introduced. These were first used in the schools, later by village and community choirs, but only gradually and with opposition in congregational singing. The great promoter of improved singing in Russia in school, home, and congregation was Heinrich Franz (*q.v.*), who published the *Choralbuch* (*q.v.*) in 1860. After this came the lighter gospel songs of T. Köbner (*Glaubensstimme*) and E. Gebhardt (*Heimatklänge,* etc.), which were introduced by the Mennonite Brethren, who had adopted them through their Baptist contacts. The Mennonites of Russia used ciphers instead of notes in their melody books.

Even though the congregations gradually accepted a more modern form of music, four-part singing was introduced only with difficulty in some places. Some groups consistently refused the faster and modified melodies, clinging to the old-fashioned slow tunes. This form of singing was transplanted by the Mennonites of the Old Colony in Russia to Canada in the 1870's and from there by the Old Colony Mennonites to Mexico in the 1920's.

Already in Russia congregational singing and the renditions by choirs reached high levels. After the Revolution song festivals and choir schools were among the few church activities left to them. *Unser Blatt* reported about them regularly in 1925-27, when this publication ceased and the choirs had to discontinue their work. (By 1956 the choirs were reported singing again.) The Mennonites of this tradition in North and South America, regardless of conference affiliation, continue these practices on even a larger scale. As a rule congregations have no regular orchestras, but congregational as well as choir singing is almost always accompanied by an organ or piano. All these activities can also be found in G.C.M. or related congregations and communities of Pennsylvania-German or Swiss background.

High schools of Mennonite communities usually rank high in their performances. The musical organizations of communities like Berne, Ind., Kansas, South Dakota, and Manitoba are strong; their programs and the annual rendition of *The Messiah, The Seven Last Words,* and *The Creation* by Bethel College, Bluffton College, Tabor College, and Freeman College are attended by thousands of people. Some congregational choirs have become noted for the quality of their performances; this can also be said of the college choirs and other musical organizations which travel regularly to give programs in the constituency. The Mennonite Singers of Bethel College made two trips to Europe where they sang in Mennonite and non-Mennonite communities.

The music festivals of Manitoba under the direction of K. H. Neufeld and Neil Unruh, the Mennonite Symphony Orchestra of Winnipeg under the direction of Ben Horch, and the Bornoff School of Music in Winnipeg under the direction of John Konrad, have done much to maintain traditions brought from Russia and to improve the standard of musical performance. F. C. Thiessen and K. H. Neufeld did much to improve church music in the M.B. Church in Canada, and H. C. Richert likewise in the same group in the United States.

Similar activities in vocal and instrumental music can be found in the solid Mennonite communities of the other provinces of Canada and the United States. The colleges have done much to improve and foster good quality of music through their educational programs. At the time when the Mennonites changed from the German to the English language there was a general decline in quality of music, since the traditional German hymn was replaced by the lighter gospel song. In this process the Mennonite colleges have made a very significant contribution in keeping alive the tradition of singing hymns and singing them well. The effects of this are noticeable in the congregational singing of the constituency and in the newer hymnbooks which have been published during the last years (see **Hymnology**). Walter H. Hohmann, Lester Hostetler, and also other leaders have done much to improve the standards of music. Graduates of Mennonite schools are also teaching or directing choirs in non-Mennonite communities. (See also **Minister of Music.**)

The contributions of the Mennonites as composers of hymn tunes are not as significant as their accomplishments in musical performances. Few, if any, of their works have found a general acceptance beyond their own circle. Of the 558 hymn tunes of the *Christian Hymnal* of the Church of God in Christ Mennonites, twenty-two are of Mennonite origin, an unusually large number of hymns of Mennonite origin in a Mennonite hymnal. Among the composers of tunes of the Great Plains, Walter H. Hohmann and Herbert C. Richert have probably been most productive. The latter published *Young People's Sacred Songs,* for which he wrote all the hymn tunes. In addition to this the *Mennonite Brethren Church Hymnal* contains eight of his hymn tunes. Among Hohmann's compositions and arrangements are *Immortality* (North Newton, 1945), *Bless Thou the Lord* (Chicago, 1948), *Jesus Put Forth His Hand* (Chicago, 1949), and *Hymns and Chorales for Men's Voices* (Newton, 1955). No doubt other Mennonite musicians have composed music for hymns, published or unpublished. C.K.

Musical Instruments have only comparatively recently been introduced into Mennonite churches as an aid in worship. The first instrument was the pipe organ, installed in the Mennonite church of Hamburg-Altona, Germany, in 1764, and in the Mennonite church at Utrecht, Netherlands, in 1765. Other Dutch Mennonite churches followed in rapid succession. The Prussian Mennonites introduced their first organ in the Neugarten church in 1778; the Danzig church installed one in 1806, after which others followed. The introduction of the organ made the old chorister (*q.v.*) or Vorsänger system obsolete. Gradually this honored office disappeared, although in some churches the organ and Vorsänger competed for some time. The Danzig Mennonite Church introduced a written Choral Buch in 1806 specifically for the organist. It contains 111 different chorale titles, of which 86 are Bach harmonizations.

The introduction of musical instruments in the Mennonite churches of Russia occurred considerably later. Here it was primarily the reed organ which was used in churches. Only a few of the Mennonite and Mennonite Brethren churches introduced this instrument (Gnadenfeld) before World War I. The guitar was also used, particularly at youth meetings in Mennonite Brethren circles in connection with the lighter Gospel songs. An extreme wing of the M.B. used in its early stage various musical instruments such as barrel organs, drums, flutes, and violins, most of which were soon discarded (A. H. Unruh, 113).

Among the more conservative Mennonites of Russia and also among those who later settled in Canada and Mexico the use of musical instruments in worship services was not tolerated. The Old Colony Mennonites still forbid instruments entirely. In the early days of the Reformation the more radical reformers, e.g., Zwingli, Calvin, and the Anabaptists, discarded the use of musical instruments. This became a tradition perpetuated for centuries. It was taken for granted that the musical instrument was to be used only for worldly entertainment; the introduction of musical instruments in the church would mean the opening of the gates of the church to secular and sinful influences. Today in the General Conference Mennonite Church, the Mennonite Brethren, the Evangelical Mennonite Brethren, the Krimmer Mennonite Brethren, the Evangelical Mennonite Brethren, the Evangelical Mennonites, and the Mennonite Brethren in Christ, the use of the musical instruments has been accepted for worship services. The Brethren in Christ General Conference in 1955 authorized the use of musical instruments by congregations desiring them. Those churches who can afford the cost and have a sense of appreciation install pipe organs. If not, they may have an electronic organ, a reed organ, or a piano. The latter is used particularly in churches where the lighter Gospel songs are preferred above the chorales and hymns.

The first pipe organ installed in an American Mennonite church was at West Swamp, Pa., in 1874. By 1890 most of the Eastern District Conference (GCM) churches were using either a pipe or reed organ. The Berne (Ind.) Mennonite Church installed a reed organ in 1890 and a pipe organ in 1914. Eva Sprunger's centennial history of the Berne church (*First Hundred Years*) says, "Instrumental music was considered sinful and was not allowed. . . . It was not until 1901 that opposition was sufficiently overcome to pass a resolution permitting the use . . . in the Sunday School." The Western District (GCM) passed a resolution in 1881 leaving the decision regarding the use of musical instruments in worship to the individual congregations.

All schools of the General Conference and most other groups use musical instruments. The first musical instrument was an organ used at the Wadsworth (Ohio) school, which had been brought from Europe by C. J. van der Smissen, whose grandmother Hillegonda J. Deknatel, had received it from her father, Johannes Deknatel, of Amsterdam. Later this organ was used at Bethel College, where it is now a part of the Kauffman Museum collection.

Reed organs were introduced into the Swiss, French, and South German churches east of the Rhine about the turn of the 19th century. Pipe organs are, however, to this day not in use.

The Mennonite Church (MC), and the more conservative groups of Swiss-South German background, such as the various Amish groups and the Old Order Mennonites, have maintained a form of worship in which the instrument has no place. The prohibition of instruments is based in part on a long-standing tradition, but is also based on the desire to maintain strong congregational singing and the fear that the use of instruments will harmfully affect this. In some areas of the Mennonite Church for a time, and always among the more conservative groups, the use of musical instruments has been forbidden even in the home. Some conferences, such as the Virginia Conference (MC), made it a conference regulation for a time that ordained ministers should not have instruments. George R. Brunk, Sr., was a vigorous opponent of musical instruments and largely responsible for the introduction of this spirit into the Virginia Conference. From the beginning instruments have not been allowed in the buildings of the Eastern Mennonite College, nor are they used in the music department there. The same rule applied at

Hesston College from the beginning until about 1950. No such policy has been applied at Goshen College. **C.K.**

Music Issue, *Menn. Life* III (April 1948); A. H. Unruh, *Die Geschichte der Mennonitenbrüdergemeinde* (Winnipeg, 1954); N. van der Zijpp, *Geschiedenis der Doopsgezinden in Nederland* (Arnhem, 1952) 108, 242 note 14.

Musselman (Musselmann, Moselmann), a Mennonite family name, probably Swiss in origin, found in both Europe and America. Mennonite Musselmanns are still found in Germany, viz., in Baden, Bavaria, and Württemberg, and formerly also in the Palatinate. Worthy of mention is Elder Johannes Musselmann (1881-1955) of the Heilbronn (*q.v.*) congregation in Württemberg, who was ordained preacher in 1924 and elder in 1937. Jacob Musselman emigrated from Europe (according to tradition, from Germany) in 1743 and settled in Bucks County, Pa. He bought land which included the first Swamp (MC) meetinghouse (near the present West Swamp General Conference Mennonite Church), but for which no deed had been granted. His son Michael Musselman was ordained preacher in the Swamp district before 1773. Michael's son Samuel Musselman (1764-1842) became a bishop (MC) in the Swamp district. The name Musselman is also found in Lancaster County, Pa. One of the members of the Lancaster County Musselman family was the promising John S. Musselman (1881-1913), superintendent of the Welsh Mountain Industrial Mission and a volunteer for the India Mission field, who died of typhoid fever before leaving home. Prominent fruit canners of Adams County, Pa., were C. H. Musselman and Ivan Z. Musselman. Samuel H. Musselman (1855-1929), father of Ivan Z. Musselman, was a prominent lay leader in the Lancaster County Mennonite (MC), treasurer of the district mission board, and fellow commissioner with S. C. Yoder in the visit to the South American mission field, 1919-20. About 1803 Peter Musselman removed from Pennsylvania to Ontario, where he served as a Mennonite (MC) preacher. The last minister in the Mennonite Church in Jo Daviess County, Ill., in the 19th century was Michael Musselman, a member of the Bavarian settlement which was made in the county about 1840. Perhaps the most prominent General Conference Mennonite preacher with this name was Samuel M. Musselman (1875-1938) of Bucks County, Pa., who served pastorates in Pennsylvania, Ohio, Iowa, and Kansas. Three representatives of the family served prominently in the ministry of the Mennonite Brethren in Christ Church, Pennsylvania Conference: Harvey B. Musselman, ordained 1893; his son, B. Bryan Musselman, ordained 1916; and William B. Musselman, ordained 1886. **J.C.W.**

Musselman, Harvey B. (1868-1956), an outstanding leader of the Mennonite Brethren in Christ Church in Pennsylvania, was born in Lehigh Co., Pa. He entered the ministry in 1890 and was ordained in 1893 by the Pennsylvania Mennonite Brethren in Christ Conference. He was married to Annie M. Bans in 1888, to which union were born three children. He held pastorates at Royersford, Spring City, Lehighton, Weissport, Bethlehem, and Mt. Carmel, Pa.; served as presiding elder for 18 years; and was president of the Orphanage and Home Board, the Foreign Mission Board, and the Executive Board of the M.B.C. Conference.   J.A.Hu.

Musselman, Samuel H. (1855-1929), an outstanding lay leader in mission and Sunday-school work in the Lancaster (MC) Conference, was born on the Musselman homestead near New Holland, Pa., on Oct. 24, 1855, the son of Christian Musselman and Catherine High. In Nov. 22, 1877, he married Anna Zimmerman. They were baptized at Weaverland in 1878. In 1893 he (with I. W. Martin) organized the first Weaverland Sunday school and served as superintendent for 25 years. As chairman of the Welsh Mountain Board, he saw his dreams materialize in an industrial mission (1898) and the Red Well evangelistic work. For years he was an active worker on the Weaverland Missions Committee in their enlarging program into Chester County. He saw this committee amalgamated with the Eastern Board of Missions and Charities. He was active in the Lancaster Sunday School Mission and served on the Executive Committee of the Mission Board. In the fall of 1919 he with S. C. Yoder made an inspection trip to the Argentine in prospecting for a mission program there. He was a mover for the Oreville Old People's Home and served on this Board from 1903 for many years. He died Nov. 26, 1929.   I.D.L.

Musselman, William Brunner (1860-1938), a prominent leader of the M.B.C. Church in Pennsylvania, was born in Lehigh Co., Pa., the son of Jonas and Lucy Musselman. He began to preach in 1883 and in 1886 was ordained by the Pennsylvania Mennonite Brethren in Christ Conference. In 1879 he was married to Mary A. Oberholtzer. To them were born 10 children, 5 boys and 5 girls. He held pastorates at Reading, Bethlehem, and Allentown, Pa., and served as presiding elder, member of the executive board of the general conference, and president of the Gospel Worker Society. He was a member of all of the general conferences from 1888 to 1916.   J.A.Hu.

Mussen, Beene Gerrits (d. in 1783 at an advanced age), was in 1727-83 an elder of the congregation of Giethoorn-Noord (*q.v.*), Dutch province of Overijssel. This was a Danzig Old Flemish congregation, and during Mussen's eldership still had contacts with the Flemish congregation at Danzig, West Prussia. Mussen guided his congregation according to conservative, strict principles. In 1768 he banned Berend Thijssen Rijkmans, who, being more progressive than his elder, had attended the meetings of the Giethoorn-Zuid congregation. A number of members sided with the banned brother. By the intervention of the provincial government of Overijssel and mediation of the Mennonite congregations of Haarlem and Amsterdam the quarrel was reconciled, but some years later the majority of the members of Giethoorn-Noord left the congregation to found a new, less conservative congregation at Zuidveen (*q.v.*) in 1774.

Mussen (according to tradition) did not write his own sermons, but read sermons written by the Amsterdam Danzig Old Flemish Elder Peter van Dijk,

which sermons had been given to Mussen by van Dijk's heirs. Mussen taught from the catechism by Pieter Boudewijns (*q.v.*). (*DB* 1878, 14-26; *Naamlijst, passim.*)   vDZ.

Mutual Aid. The Anabaptists strove to reproduce as nearly as possible the life of the early Christian Church and to imitate the life of Christ. The Mennonites, being direct descendants of the Anabaptists, have tried to do the same. In doing this they have insisted on the right of the individual to interpret the Scriptures for himself without the aid of priest, but by the illumination of the Holy Spirit. This emphasis on individual freedom under the guidance of the Holy Spirit manifested itself in daily life in not being bound by law but living by the Spirit. It is this freedom from legalism and a dependence upon individual conscience in the grace of God that enabled them to live out their convictions despite all opposition and persecution. It is these principles that gave them the vision and confidence to try to establish a "Kingdom of Heaven" on earth in their own communities. It was not an attempt to build a kingdom on a universal scale. It was simply a kingdom of voluntary believers, adding others who wished to join their group. It was in such an atmosphere of freedom and Christian brotherliness that mutual aid could flourish. Mutual aid had its roots intertwined with the very roots of Mennonite religious principles.

Another distinctive principle of the Mennonites was the belief in the complete separation of the church from the state and from dependence upon it for any kind of support. In applying this principle they manifested a willingness to provide the necessities of life for all within their group. Positively, they believed in the possibility of a way of life based on mutual love and respect for fellow believers, so that an organization of Christians could be established on a community basis where love and brotherhood could be expressed in daily life, since a true follower of Christ would so conduct himself as to place the welfare of others before his own. This was Jesus' own teaching, although history reveals that not all His professed followers have accomplished His ideal or even aimed at it.

Another Mennonite principle has been an emphasis on the simple life, applied in matters of clothing, food, furnishings, and in all outward appearance. With this simplicity were stressed industry and thrift. Frugality and industry generally produce prosperity, at least in a material sense. It was so with the Mennonites; but they aimed at a reasonable prosperity for the group rather than for only a few within the group. The concept of a brotherhood church leveled all class distinction, and brought condemnation upon anyone who tried to exploit another. Likewise, emphasis on simplicity tended to counteract any feeling of sophistication and superiority. With few outward possessions to display individuality, the tendency to covet was reduced to a minimum. With a minimum of jealousy, selfishness, and sophistication, there is possible a maximum of mutual aid and brotherly helpfulness.

One evidence of the high regard of the Mennonites for each other's welfare was their opposition to claiming interest on loans. They refused to accept interest themselves and paid it unwillingly to others. Money, they believed, should be lent for the benefit of the borrower rather than the lender. Proper fraternal relations forbade the exploitation of the needs of a brother; besides, the practice was contrary to the teachings of Scripture: "You must not exact interest on loan to a fellow-countryman of yours, interest on money, food, or anything else that might be exacted as interest" (Deut. 23:19). Again they read in the sacred Word that the Christian "does not put out his money on interest, nor take a bribe against the innocent" (Psalm 15:5).

These principles of the earlier Mennonites and the Anabaptists are based on the literal interpretation of the Sermon on the Mount. An attempt to live out these teachings and imitate the Apostolic community can scarcely help but result in mutual aid, if not semi-communism. Christian brotherhood and mutual aid are inseparable. A second source of mutual aid practices may be found in the cultural patterns of the medieval and Reformation periods, where certain forms of mutual aid were expressed in the village communities. The Mennonites have, throughout their history, lived in rather compact communities and when they migrated they did so in groups rather than by individual families. This in itself is an evidence of the loyalty to, and dependence upon, one another.

The evidence of the practice of mutual aid among Anabaptists is clear and cumulative. From the beginning in Zürich they insisted on the obligation of a brother to help his brethren in need. This emphasis lies behind the repeated and continued charge of their opponents that they advocated and practiced communism, which was, however, not true. Hans Leopold, a Swiss Brethren martyr of 1528, said of the brethren, "If they know of any one who is in need, whether or not he is a member of their church, they believe it their duty out of love to God to render help and aid." Heinrich Seiler, a martyr of 1535, said, "I do not believe that it is wrong that a Christian own property of his own, but yet he is nothing more than a steward." Heinrich Bullinger, the bitter enemy of the Brethren, wrote in 1560, "They teach that every Christian is under duty before God from motives of love to use, if need be, all his possessions to supply the necessities of life to any of the brethren who are in need." A Strasburg Protestant who had visited a Swiss Brethren baptismal service near that city in 1557 reported that a question addressed to all candidates for baptism was "whether, if necessity required it, they would devote all their possessions to the service of the brotherhood and would not fail any member that is in need, if they were able to render aid." (All quotations from the *Anabaptist Vision*.)

Russia. Two examples of mutual aid in an extreme form in Mennonite history are the Hutterites (*q.v.*) with their practice of Christian communism (from 1528 on) and the short-lived Plockhoy (*q.v.*) co-operative colony on the Delaware in colonial America (1662 ff.). A third, more normal example is the large number of mutual aid practices of the Mennonites in Russia (1788-1917).

The following will present a representative picture of mutual aid in a typical Mennonite community in Russia as it existed in the 19th century. The Mennonites grouped themselves into small farm villages of 20 to 30 families each, each family having 65 dessiatines (175 acres) of land. The land was divided into strips so distributed that all would share the good and the bad land wherever there was difference in its fertility. Each village had a common pasture and each family had several acres for gardening immediately adjoining the house. In the Volga region the title to the land rested in the village; in South Russia it rested in the head of the family. C. Henry Smith gives a good brief description of some mutual aid activities in one village community: "While these colonies were not communistic in their organization, yet the villages frequently undertook municipal enterprises for the common good. Some villages had a common granary stored with grain for the lean years and for the benefit of the poor. Occasionally also they held tracts of land for later distribution as the population grew. In 1820 the communal sheep flock of the Old Colony (Chortitza) consisted of 1,000 merinos, and the annual income from the communal ferry across the Dnieper was two to three thousand rubles. The communal distillery also netted a substantial profit for the common treasury that year" (*Coming*, 34).

During the early days in Russia the villages had no banks for their money, since in a rural community of the 18th century money played only a very small part in the life of a people. What little cash people had was kept at home. One of the older immigrants who remembers life in those Russian villages remarked that it was much easier to help someone else when the money was kept within constant reach. In later years, banks of mutual credit were established, which accepted deposits from any person and transacted all legal commerical business, lending money not only for agricultural purposes but for promotion of manufacturing and trade. But these banks were based on membership, and money was lent to members only. The *Waisenamt*, however, established before the mutual credit bank, was most characteristic of the village community and its mutual aid practices. It was in fact a trust organization formed to assist minors who were orphaned, and to administer their inheritance funds. The money could be invested, saved, or distributed according to the best interests of the parties concerned. Evidence that the *Waisenamt* satisfactorily served a need is the fact that it is still in existence in a number of Mennonite communities of Russian background, especially in Canada and Paraguay.

Another interesting illustration of mutual aid among the Russian Mennonite villages was the practice of assisting a widow at the death of her husband. Immediately after her husband's death the widow would name "two good men" to take charge of her affairs. This was not compulsory, but it was generally done. The widow usually chose the closest friends of her husband, who considered it both an honor and a religious duty to serve in such a capacity. All service was rendered free even if it took many days with teams of horses to perform the necessary work. Problems with regard to children, finances, or even remarriage were all first discussed by the widow and her advisers before action was taken. This was an effective way of helping a member who had sustained misfortune; it offered an opportunity for the friends of the deceased to show their appreciation for his friendship, and at the same time was a way of relieving the widow of undue worry and the fear of exploitation. Moreover, there were no lawyers' fees to be extracted from whatever financial balance the husband may have left. It was an expression of mutual aid of the simplest yet most genuine sort.

To improve their economic condition and the quality of their livestock, the Russian Mennonites practiced mutual ownership of stock to a limited degree. A high-grade stallion, bull, ram, or other male animal might be purchased by the community and thus made available to each farmer to improve his herd. During the winter months, when these animals could not be fed in the common pasture, they were taken from one farmer to another for several weeks at a time, thus distributing the cost of feeding and care. The reputation of the Mennonites for raising high-grade stock spread far and wide and in this way representatives from Jewish, Russian, and other German communities came to the Mennonites for advice on how to improve their own herds as well as to buy stock from them.

A further evidence of the way mutual aid pervaded the spirit of the Russian Mennonites was the community land fund for the purchase of new lands for the oncoming generation. When a new area was opened up for settlement any Mennonite married couple having no other farming land was entitled to one farm and a lot in the new settlement. Parents from both sides usually supplied the young couple with means sufficient to equip the new farm. If they were unable to do so, the couple was given a start at the expense of the community through a common fund, repayable or not repayable, as in each case was considered most advisable. In this way young people were helped to begin life on their own, and at the same time given a sense of status in the community. As the land in the new communities was paid for by the settlers, the money was put into a revolving fund for the future purchase of another settlement. In this way generation after generation could be provided for. Following this method, the Mennonites expanded within the course of a century from a poor immigrant group of 8,000 to a flourishing population of 45,000 (by 1914, 100,000), generally prosperous farmers and landowners.

Another instance of mutual aid among the Russian Mennonites was the fire insurance plan (*Brandordnung*) which had been brought along from West Prussia in the late 18th century. Each member had his property valued as he saw fit. No premiums were paid. The officers in the associations held their offices without pay as honorary positions. After a loss by fire or storm, each member contributed pro rata according to the value of his own property. The aim of this plan was to levy the assessment in proportion to the ability to pay. The clearing of the debris and the hauling of brick and stone and other building material for reconstruction was then done jointly by the whole village free of

charge. Likewise the heavy work, such as setting up the frame of the building, was done free of charge. The insurance money paid out in cash to the loser was actually only for building material. This is an excellent example of mutual sharing of the loss from an unavoidable hardship.

One of the universal practices of the Mennonites has always been to provide for their own aged and poor. In Russia this was done in an admirable way, admirable in the sense that it did not tend to degrade the recipients to the point of being outcasts or of losing complete self-respect. The poor were given an opportunity to contribute something of value in return for the charity they received. It was the practice for each village to have a common fireproof storehouse at one end of the village to which each farmer contributed in times of prosperity to provide against lean years, perhaps a sack of wheat, a sack of rye, and a half sack of barley. This not only served as a source of supply for the dependent poor, but also as an emergency source for any member of the community who might suffer a crop failure.

The freedom which Catherine the Great and her successors granted the Mennonites to develop their culture in the way they thought best resulted in the turning of vast treeless steppes in Southern Russia into productive farm lands and prosperous villages. Given this complete independence, the Mennonites developed their thriving economy built entirely around and on the idea of mutual aid. Mutual aid was practiced not only in the economic, social, and political aspects of life, but pervaded almost every activity. The ideals and principles of working together for the common welfare of all became the accepted way of doing things. To carry on activities on a selfish, extremely individualistic basis without thought of the effect on others would have been considered a gross sin, causing one to be avoided by his fellow men. This would have been the severest punishment for anyone in a small village where fellowship and companionship were the very basis of happiness. It is likewise a significant fact that this extensive practice of mutual aid was not discontinued when prosperity came. The tendency was rather to increase the mutual services. The practices of mutual aid can thus not be said to be desirable or practical only in times of grave necessity or in times of struggle for existence.

America. Because the Mennonites in America are scattered widely from Pennsylvania to California, and from Ontario to British Columbia, and because of the differences or divisions within the Mennonites themselves, it is impossible to speak of American Mennonites as one group. The illustrations that will be used in this part of the study are, however, as representative of the various groups of Mennonites as possible who in general have common basic beliefs and attitudes regardless of minor differences in policy and practice. But some mutual aid practices seem to be universally characteristic of Mennonites. One of these is the practice of providing for their own poor and orphans. It is very unusual for Mennonites to send their dependent members to county or state institutions. If the particular local church conference does not have an institution for the purpose of caring for its aged and poor, provision is often made in private homes of friends or of relatives. At least 38 homes for the aged and 7 children's homes are maintained by the American Mennonites. A second mutual aid practice which is common to many Mennonite communities is that of providing hospital care. At least 14 hospitals are owned in whole or in part by Mennonites. Often these hospitals and old people's homes are located in the same locality, thus making it convenient to provide medical care for the aged and also making it easier to manage the two institutions under one head. The fact that Mennonites are concerned with such matters as care for their own sick and for their economically underprivileged reveals the depth of feeling and the sense of mutual responsibility that they have for each other. It is likewise an evidence that the Mennonites assume the care for and welfare of their own dependents as part of their Christian duty.

A third type of mutual aid among Mennonites is fire and storm insurance societies. It seems significant that the mutual aid organizations are especially strong wherever losses from causes beyond the control of man are suffered, such as sharing responsibility for losses due to fire, storm, accident, sickness, and death. Such a mutual insurance plan is undoubtedly the oldest form of organized mutual aid among the Mennonites. The earliest records available show that mutual insurance was practiced by some Mennonites in Europe in the beginning of the 17th century, and had its origin among the Mennonites in Germany in 1623, when a group then living in West Prussia organized the *Tiegenhöfer Privat Brandordnung*. This association was still in operation with its office at Tiegenhof up to the time of the Russian invasion in 1945, which wiped out the Mennonite communities there. Practically every American Mennonite region has its own fire insurance society based on the principle of mutual aid. These societies are very old in America, some dating back at least a hundred years. Very often they existed for years in unorganized forms without written constitutions whereby to govern themselves, and many of them did not keep records of proceedings of business conducted.

Mutual aid developments of more recent years include the burial aid society, the hospital and medical aid society, the automobile accident insurance plan, and the loan aid plan. A complete list of all known North American Mennonite Mutual Aid organizations operating in 1956 follows, 69 in total.

Mennonite Mutual Aid Organizations in the United States and Canada, 1956
I. *Property Insurance Societies - 36*

Name	Address	Year Organized	Membership
Alberta Menn. Mutual Aid Society	Coaldale, Alberta		450
Amish Aid Ins. Plan of Ohio Districts	Millersburg, Ohio	1937	5,000
Amish Aid Plan of Ind. and Mich.	Shipshewana, Ind.	1934	3,316
Amish Aid Plan of Kan., Okla. & Oregon	Partridge, Kan.	1890	560
Amish Aid Society of Eastern Pa.	Ronks, Pa.	before 1850	1,500
Amish Menn. Aid Society of Iowa	Kalona, Ia.	1885	160
Amish Menn. Storm and Fire Aid Union	Wellesley, Ont.	*ca.*1858	1,096
Amish Mutual Fire Ins. Ass'n	Parkesburg, Pa.	1922	850
Brotherhood Mutual Ins. Co.	Fort Wayne, Ind.	1917	10,000
Brotherly Aid Plan	Lancaster, Pa.	1950	950
Canada and States Menn. Ins. Ass'n	Mt. Lake, Minn.	1874	4,000
Canadian Menn. Mutual Ins.	Altona, Man.	1923	500
Fire and Storm Aid Plan of the Ref. Menn. Church	Lancaster, Pa.	1923	900
Franconia Menn. Aid Plan for Mutual Fire Ins.	Lansdale, Pa.	1936	1,000
Ill. O.O. Amish Mutual Aid Plan	Arthur, Ill.		820
Man. Menn. Mutual Ins. Co.	Steinbach, Man.	1874	2,800
Menn. Aid Ass'n	Topeka, Ind.	1911	2,608
Menn. Aid Plan	West Liberty, Ohio	1896	205
Menn. Aid Plan of the Pacific Coast	Reedley, Cal.	1922	2,500
Menn. Aid Plan of S.D.	Freeman, S.D.	1882	4,000
Menn. Aid Society of S.D.	Marion, S.D.	1922	241
Menn. Aid Union	Baden, Ont.	1864	2,442
Menn. Aid Union of Kan.	North Newton, Kan.	1906	2,050
Menn. Hilfs-Plan	Moundridge, Kan.	1900	3,000
Menn. Mutual Aid Ass'n	Kalona, Ia.	1913	600
Menn. Mutual Aid Society	Bluffton, Ohio	1866	852
Menn. Mutual Fire Aid Plan	Hagerstown, Md.	1924	475
Menn. Mutual Fire Ins. Ass'n	Intercourse, Pa.	1893	8,116
Menn. Mutual Fire Ins. Co. of Sask. Ltd.	Waldheim, Sask.	1917	
Menn. Mutual Hail Ins. Co. for W. Can.	Hepburn, Sask.	1916	3,145
Menn. Mutual Ins. Ass'n of Ohio	Orrville, Ohio	1897	5,550
Menn. Union Aid	Montezuma, Kan.	1942	1,410
Prairie Menn. Mutual Fire Ins. Co.	Herbert, Sask.	inc.1941	600
Red River Mutual Fire Ins. Co.	Altona, Man.	1874	5,500

Name	Address	Year Organized	Membership
Virginia Menn. Property Aid Plan	Harrisonburg, Va.	1911	1,286
Wash. Co. Menn. Mutual Ass'n	Wayland, Ia.	1950	130
*Menn. Indemnity, Inc.	Goodville, Pa.	1956	

*A reinsurance organization of Mennonite Insurance Societies

II. *Automobile Aid Insurance - 7*

Name	Address	Year Organized	Membership
Brotherly Aid Liability Plan for the Lancaster Menn. Conf.	Leola, Pa.	1955	484
Goodville Mutual Casualty Co.	Goodville, Pa.	1926	18,000
Menn. Automobile Aid, Inc.	Goshen, Ind	1954	(1957) 1,686
Michigan Menn. Mutual Auto Aid	Fairview, Mich.	1939	150
Mutual Auto Aid of the Menn. of Wash. Co., Md.	Hagerstown, Md.	1945	264
Pigeon River Menn. Mutual Auto Aid	Owendale, Mich.	1950	75
Virginia Menn. Automobile Aid Plan	Harrisonburg, Va.	1933	761

III. *Burial Aid Societies - 14*

Name	Address	Year Organized	Membership
Alberta Menn. Relief Society	Coaldale, Alberta		450
Beerdigungs-Verein zu Leamington, Ont.	Leamington, Ont.	1935	
Menno-Friendly Beneficial Assoc.	Philadelphia, Pa.	1908	
Menn. Aid, Inc.	Goshen, Ind.	1949	1,276
Menn. Aid Society	Mt. Lake, Minn.	1897	4,139
Menn. Burial Aid Soc.	Altona, Man.	1910	
Menn. Mutual Burial Aid	Halbstadt, Man.	1940	276
Pacific Menn. Aid Soc.	Reedley, Cal.	1941	650
Menn. Mutual Supporting Soc. of Arnaud-St. Elizabeth	St. Elizabeth, Man.	1934	680
Mutual Burial Fund	Montezuma, Kan.	1940	274
Mutual Support Society	Starbuck, Man.	1926	855
Niagara Mutual Funeral Soc.	Niagara-on-the-Lake, Ont.	1934	2,146
Vineland Beerdigungs-Kasse	Vineland, Ont.	1934	2,450
West Abbotsford and Clearbrook Menn. Church Funeral Aid	Abbotsford, B.C.	1952	263

IV. *Medical, Surgical, and Hospital Aid Plans - 6*

Name	Address	Year Organized	Membership
Bethesda Menn. Health Society	Yarrow, B.C.	1935	
Coaldale Menn. Health Society	Coaldale, Alberta	1943	
Menn. Aid, Inc.	Goshen, Ind.	1949	(1957) 18,655
Menn. Health Society	Coaldale, Alberta	1931	300
Menn. Hospital Soc. Concordia	Winnipeg, Man.	1928	1,663
Menn. Mutual Aid of Ont.	St. Catharines, Ont.	1944	2,550

V. *Loan Aid Organizations - 6*

Name	Address	Year Organized	Membership
Christian Service Foundation	Ft. Wayne, Ind.	1949	
Crosstown Credit Union Society Ltd.	Winnipeg, Man.	1944	1,336
G.C. Menn. Mutual Service & Aid Assoc.	Newton, Kan.	1945	
Menn. Brotherhood Aid Assoc.	Bluffton, Ohio	1949	151
Menn. Mutual Aid, Inc.	Goshen, Ind.	1945	
Western Canada Menn. Land Settlement Ass'n	Plum Coulee, Man.	1954	450

The spirit of mutual aid has also been vigorously expressed in migration and colonization aid, sometimes on a large scale. The Dutch Mennonites made substantial cash contributions to Swiss and Palatinate Mennonites migrating to Pennsylvania in 1710-50, in addition to direct relief contributions. The attempted (though failing) settlement of Lithuanian Mennonites in Holland, and the successful settlement of some Swiss Mennonites in Holland, both in the early 18th century, were also financed by the Dutch. The migration of the Russian Mennonites to Canada and the United States 1874-80 was strongly aided by cash and loan contributions raised by the existing American Mennonite groups through regional "aid committees." Similar aid was given to the large group of immigrants from Russia to Canada in 1922-25 and the smaller groups of 1930-31 and 1947-50. The colonization of the major Russian Mennonite settlements in Paraguay (1930, 1947-50) and the Danzig Mennonites in Uruguay (1948-51) was possible only because of the large amounts of financial aid, including loans for land purchase, made by North American Mennonites through the Mennonite Central Committee. The Mennonite Economic Development Associates (MEDA), a group of American businessmen, is supplying substantial amounts of finance capital to aid small-scale industrialization in the colonies. Many young conscientious objectors from the Mennonite congregations in the United States (PAX boys, *q.v.*) have contributed substantially in labor to the building of homes for Mennonite refugees in Germany (1952 ff.), to which considerable cash amounts were also furnished by contributed funds from America. During and after World War II the major Mennonite bodies in the United States raised considerable sums of money to aid their men in CPS service by financing their maintenance while at work on government-assigned projects, by supplementing their meager wages in certain cases, by supporting dependent wives and children, and by furnishing rehabilitation loans after discharge.

The co-operative barn-raisings among the Old Order Amish are also worthy of note as examples of mutual aid, along with the practice of co-operative planting and harvesting of crops for sick or disabled farmers, a practice which is found in other Mennonite groups as well.

In the South American Mennonite colonies established in Paraguay and Brazil since 1926 and 1930, the spirit of mutual aid has also expressed itself in an organized way in the founding of co-operatives.

Thus it is evident that the ancient and original spirit of mutual brotherhood aid has not only survived among the Mennonites of North and South America, but has experienced a substantial revival and more extensive and intensive application.

Among modern European Mennonites there has been and is almost no organized expression of the spirit of mutual aid which was present in the earlier centuries in largely unorganized form, except in the Danzig-West Prussian area as noted above. (See **Community; Community of Goods; Insurance; and Life Insurance.**) J.W.F., H.S.B.

J. Winfield Fretz, "Mutual Aid Among the Mennonites," *MQR* XIII (1939) 28-58, 187-209; *idem*, "Mennonite Mutual Aid, A Contribution to the Development of Christian Communtiy" (Ph.D. Thesis, University of Chicago, 1941); *idem, Christian Mutual Aid, A Handbook of Brotherhood Economics* (Akron, 1947); *idem, Mennonite Colonization, Lessons from the Past for the Future* (Akron, 1944); *idem, Pilgrims in Paraguay* (Scottdale, 1953); H. S. Bender, *The Anabaptist Vision* (Goshen, 1944, reprint from *MQR* XVIII, 1944, 67-88); C. Henry Smith, *The Coming of the Russian Mennonites* (Berne, 1927); C. Krahn, J. W. Fretz, and R. S. Kreider, "Altruism in Mennonite Life," in Sorokin's *Forms and Techniques of Altruistic and Spiritual Growth* (Boston, 1954); "A Directory of Mennonite Insurance and Mutual Aid Organizations" (Mennonite Research Foundation, Goshen, 1956).

Mutual Aid Board. The General Conference Mennonites created the Mutual Aid Board at its 1945 general sessions for the immediate purpose of aiding the rehabilitation of young men who had served as conscientious objectors during World War II, since these young men had served without pay and without the discharge bonuses that were given to the men in the military service. The function of the board was to assemble funds on a gift or a loan basis from individuals or conference organizations. These were to be loaned to G.C.M. young men at a low rate of interest. The purpose for which loans were made varied, but among the most common were assistance to young couples in setting up housekeeping, buying livestock and equipment to start farming or to

establish a business, completing a college or university education, and purchasing or remodeling modest homes. In 1950 the General Conference reorganized and created the Board of Christian Service which absorbed the Board of Mutual Aid and thereafter made it the committee on Mutual Aid. Thus after 1950 the Board of Mutual Aid no longer officially existed but its work has been expanded. In 1957 it was incorporated. Its services are no longer confined to young men in the service of their country, but provides assistance to all members in need of vocational and economic help to the extent that means are available and deemed necessary by the Mutual Aid Committee. J.W.F.

Mutual Auto Aid *of the Mennonites of Washington Co., Md.,* established at Hagerstown, Md., Dec. 26, 1945, serving 264 members (1953) of the Mennonite Church (MC). H.S.B.

Mutual Burial Fund, organized in January 1940, serves six Church of God in Christ Mennonite congregations: Montezuma, Copeland, Greensburg, Scott City, and Cimarron in Western Kansas, and Crowley, Col. The Fund has a membership of about 800, in 377 families. This plan takes care of all the funeral expenses, including the casket, embalming, undertaker fees, and grave digging. The caskets are made by a brother at an average cost of $90.00. The average complete service of a funeral is $325.00. The members save at least 50 per cent on their funeral expenses.

The expenses for making the caskets as well as those of the funeral directors are taken from the church treasuries. This plan makes it possible for all members to have a more uniform burial, the poor being well provided for. A.Un.

Mutual Support Society of Starbuck, Man., was founded in 1926 by Peter J. Dyck, Elder Johann Klassen, Gerhard Braun, Franz Klassen, and Jacob Rempel, under the name "Starbucker Beerdigungskasse," as a burial aid society, chiefly for the new immigrants from Russia in 1922-25. In 1955 the membership was 855 including children. The burial aid, which was originally $30 per adult and $20 for children under 12, was $250 per adult and $150 for children in 1955. The annual membership fee is $2.00 for adults ($3.00 for one above 40 years of age) and $1.00 for children. H.S.B.

J. H. Rempel, "Etwas über die 'Starbucker Beerdigungskasse," *Menn. Rundschau* LXXIX (1956) 11.

Muys, Douwe Douwensz, usually called only Douwe Douwensz, was a Dutch Mennonite preacher of the Waterlander congregation of Hindeloopen, Friesland. Being rather progressive, he disagreed with some conservative elements of the Waterlander group, and was thereupon attacked by Cornelius van Huyzen (*q.v.*) of Emden. Muys replied with *Den gesuiverden Toetsteen, of Aanmerkingen op't boek van K. v. Huizen, genaamt Toetsteen van de leere der Doopsgesinde* (Workum, 1714). The years of his serving are unknown. He had died before 1731. (Schijn-Maatschoen, *Geschiedenis* II, 626, 627 note.) vDZ.

Myconius (Mecum), **Friedrich** (1490-1546), a reformer in Thuringia, Germany, pastor in the small town of Buchholz in Saxony, and finally pastor and superintendent in Gotha. Here he carried out a thorough reformation of church and school. He took part in the church and school inspections of 1527 and 1533 and in many theological meetings and discussions. After the death of Duke George he introduced the Reformation in Leipzig and Annaberg.

In these positions Myconius came into frequent contact with the Anabaptists. After the execution of six Anabaptists at Reinhardsbrunn (*q.v.*) he had some qualms against such violent measures, but was set at rest by Melanchthon (*q.v.*), to whom he had turned for counsel. He planned to write a booklet against the Anabaptists with Menius (*q.v.*), but the latter wrote it alone. After his death in 1546 Menius became his successor as superintendent of Gotha.   P.S.

"Myconius" in *RGG* and *HRE;* Paul Wappler, *Die Stellung Kursachsens und des Landgrafen Philipp von Hessen zur Täuferbewegung* (Münster, 1910); *idem, Thüringen; ML* III, 192.

Myconius (Geisshüsler), **Oswald** (1488-1552), a Reformed theologian, born at Lucerne, Switzerland, studied philology at the universities of Bern and Basel, became a Humanistic professor in Basel and Lucerne, then Zürich (1516 f.), where he promoted Zwingli's call to the ministry of the city. In 1520 he turned his attention to the study of the Scriptures. Zwingli had in him an assistant for his Bible study groups well-versed in languages and in the Bible. Myconius as a layman was commissioned by the city council to hold these studies in the Fraumünster Church. His thorough but popular exposition soon attracted large audiences from all ranks. Thus even though he was not a preacher he was an effective promoter of the Reformation.

It is to be assumed that some future Anabaptist leaders also participated in these meetings, for Myconius was acquainted with some of them. Conrad Grebel (*q.v.*) was in the party in 1518, when Myconius, with Vadian (*q.v.*) and Johann Zimmermann (Xylotectus), made the first scientific ascent of Mt. Pilatus, which had been shrouded in superstition (Hagenbach, 348). Grebel later left Myconius. With Zwingli, Leo Jud, and Kasper Megander (*q.v.*), Myconius took part in the disputations with the Swiss Brethren, including that of Jan. 17, 1525, which led to the founding of the broherhood in Zürich (Blanke, 37-40). Myconius also participated in the debate with Balthasar Hubmaier (*q.v.*) on Dec. 21, 1525 (Hagenbach, 333). He reported that they had taken part in "nine friendly discussions and serious disputations" with the Anabaptists (Blanke, 45).

When the battle of Kappel (Oct. 11, 1531) claimed the lives of Zwingli and Oecolampadius' assistant, who had also been the pastor of the church of St. Alban in Basel, Myconius succeeded into his position; and upon the death of Oecolampadius in August 1532 he as Zwingli's friend was made the antistes of the Basel church. He also held the chair of New Testament at the university. Myconius now became a prominent opponent of the Swiss Brethren,

though after 1531 the death penalty was no longer inflicted upon an Anabaptist in Basel. With Heinrich Bullinger (*q.v.*), who had just published his first book against the Anabaptists, *Von dem unverschämten Frevel,* and who became the antistes of the Zürich church after Zwingli's death, Myconius carried on a lively correspondence.

In the synod of Basel (*q.v.*) of May 1533 Myconius expressed his distaste for the carelessness of the dress of the Swiss Brethren; though the clergy was now wearing civil garb, he did not wish it to be everyday clothing, lest something equally ordinary be expected of the sermon (Hagenbach, 347). In contrast to the Swiss Brethren, who required ethical conduct and faith as condition of membership in their brotherhood, Myconius advocated government intervention to preserve moral conduct and faith by means of strict laws; these laws were, however, constantly broken, so that even the sharpest measures against gluttony, intoxication, and profanity were ineffective. "Lack of respect for the services ordained by the state church, disregard of the Word and the sacrament were made criminal offenses and as such were severely prosecuted" (Hagenbach, 348).

Nevertheless Myconius left a little freedom of action to the Swiss Brethren at first, as is seen in his letter to Wolfgang Capito (*q.v.*) dated June 26, 1533, admitting that there were in Basel no sects that denied the deity of Christ or the regulation of civil uprightness among men (Cornelius, 264). But he was soon attacking in speech and in writing the Swiss Brethren doctrines that differed from those of the Reformed Church.

In his first church regulation, the *Basler Konfession* of Jan. 21, 1534, he took a position against Swiss Brethren doctrine. This creed had been outlined by Oecolampadius, but written by Myconius. Like the Augsburg Confession this creed also contained a section on "errors of the Anabaptists," which calls them mobsters and designates their teaching as malicious opinions when they say "that one should not baptize infants (which we baptize according to the custom of the apostles and the early church and because baptism takes the place of circumcision), and that one may under no circumstances swear an oath, and that Christians may not be a part of the government, together with all the others that are opposed to the sound, pure doctrine of Jesus Christ, and that we not only do not accept, but also reject as an abomination and blasphemy" (Hagenbach, 469 f.). The creed was presented to the guilds and sworn to by the members. For over three centuries it remained the official creed of the church in Basel. Until 1789 all citizens, and until 1780 all clergymen in Basel were bound by this creed (*Theologischer Jahresbericht,* 1911, 654). This same creed was also adopted in Mühlhausen in Alsace, and was known as the *Mühlhauser Konfession* (Hagenbach, 353).

Ten days after the release of the creed Myconius issued a pastoral letter, which presents a sad picture of the rudeness of the age and an accusation against the conduct of the Catholic clergy, with the entirely unfounded assertion that "Papists and Anabaptists make common cause, one group believing that by killing one's enemy they are doing a work pleasing to God, and the other group would have liked to destroy the Word and the uprightness of the Gospel; for when it came to battle, the Anabaptists turned their backs before they had seen the foe, and the others, having perceived the serious impression of the enemy, likewise sought their safety in flight. Neither party marched out to face the enemy, but only to look after itself" (Hagenbach, 409). Myconius completely ignored the fact that the Anabaptists were nowhere tolerated by the Catholics, and that they defended their teaching with the Word itself.

In his later years, racked by physical pain, he confessed to Bullinger in 1547 in a penitent mood that he too had been lacking in a true trust in God. "Our own sins stand in our way. When we clergymen urge repentance we are admitted nowhere, and we ourselves are occasionally guilty of serious missteps. Love has grown cold in all, even in those who commend love to others. All, learned and ignorant, great and small, are blinded by the prevalent ungodliness. We do not love God and are attached only to the world. Therefore the Gospel preached for many years has borne no greater fruit. Our passions, not the Word of God, govern us, who ought to lead others" (Hagenbach, 367).

Myconius died on Oct. 14, 1552, at Basel, almost at the same time as his colleague Johann Gast (*q.v.*), who had been deacon of the church of St. Martins since 1529 and in 1544 wrote a violent polemic against the Anabaptists.

Conrad Grebel and Oswald Myconius were intimate friends for some ten years prior to Grebel's break with the Zwinglian Reformation. Nine letters of Grebel to Myconius have been preserved covering the period from Jan. 30, 1519, to Nov. 4, 1521, all of which have been published in the original Latin and in English translation by Edward Yoder in the *Mennonite Quarterly Review* (1928).   HEGE.

Fritz Blanke, reprint of Zwingli's *In Catabaptistarum strophas elenchus* (*Corpus Ref.* XCIII, Leipzig, 1936); C. A. Cornelius, *Gesch. des Münsterischen Aufruhrs* II (Leipzig, 1860); K. R. Hagenbach, *Johann Oekolampad und Oswald Myconius, die Reformatoren Basels* (Elberfeld, 1859); Edward Yoder, "Nine Letters of Conrad Grebel [to Myconius]," *MQR* II (1928) 229-59; *ML* III, 193 f.

N

Naaktlopers. On Feb. 10-11, 1535, a number of Anabaptists had a meeting in the Zoutsteeg at Amsterdam, Netherlands. Suddenly Henrick Henricxz Snyder, who was looked upon as a prophet, removed
his clothing, threw it into the fire, and ordered
those present to do the same. Infected by the mania
of their leader they all obeyed and thereupon followed him, marching naked along the streets and
crying, "Woe, woe, the wrath of God [is coming]
over this city." They had no revolutionary intentions, because they had all thrown away their weapons. Soon the seven men and five women were apprehended. The women were executed on May 15,
the men on Feb. 25, 1535, all by beheading.   vDZ.

An account of this incident is found in C. A. Cornelius, *Die Niederländischen Wiedertäufer während der
Belagerung Münsters* (Leipzig, 1869) 19 ff., and L. Hortensius, *Het Boeck van den Oproeren der Weder-doo-
peren* (Enkhuizen, 1660) 104 ff.; *Inv. Arch. Amst.* I, Nos.
68, 94 f., 193; Grosheide, *Verhooren*, 57 f.; *DB* 1917,
155 f.; Kühler, *Geschiedenis* I, 176 f.; Mellink, *Wederdopers*, 122-24.

Naaldeman, Heinrich: see Hendrik Naeldeman.

Naamlijst *der Doopsgezinde schrijveren en schriften
van 1539 tot aan 1745* is an anonymous bibliography
of 136 pages, published at Amsterdam in 1745. The
author of this valuable book is Marten Schagen
(*q.v.*). The Amsterdam Mennonite Library has a
copy of this book with a number of handwritten
annotations, probably by Schagen himself.   vDZ.

Naamlijst *der tegenwoordig in dienst zijnde predikanten der Mennoniten in de Vereenigde Nederlanden* is a register of names, reporting the Dutch
Mennonite congregations with their elders and
preachers and the years when they began to serve.
From 1743 on, the congregations in Prussia were
also included, and from 1765 on also those of South
Germany and France, while occasionally some information was given about the Mennonite congregations of Switzerland and America. Beginning in
1782 some information was added concerning the
congregations, called *Kerknieuws*. Though sometimes a little inaccurate, the *Naamlijst* is a valuable
contribution to our knowledge of both the congregations and their ministers. A letter written on Aug.
30, 1764, by Jacob Hirschel (Hirschler, elder at
Gerolsheim) to the editor in Amsterdam (*Inv. Arch.
Amst.* II, 2, No. 690) shows that the composers
tried to obtain firsthand information. Under somewhat varying titles the following editions are still
extant: 1731, 1743, 1755, 1757, 1759-76, 1787-94, 1796,
1798, 1800, 1802, 1804, 1806, 1808, 1810, 1815 (edited
by A. H. van Gelder), and 1829 (by Samuel Muller),
all published at Amsterdam and mostly together
with a register of Remonstrant (*q.v.*) congregations
in the Netherlands and their ministers. There was
also a German edition of the *Naamlijst* 1759 and of
1802 (see **Namensverzeichnis**). The *Naamlijst* was
followed by the *Doopsgezind Jaarboekje* (*q.v.*), first
published in 1837.

Of the *Naamlijst van de Leeraren bij de Doopsgezinden in Vriesland, Groningerland en de Vijf
Eilanden* there is only one issue (Leeuwarden, 1779),
composed by F. van der Ploeg (*q.v.*) who was at
that time the Mennonite minister at Dokkum. (*ML*
III, 198.)   vDZ.

Naarden-Bussum, a Dutch Mennonite congregation:
see **Bussum**.

Nabels, Eduard, was a physician and an elder of
the United Waterlander and High German congregation at Rotterdam, Holland, serving from before
1620 until after 1647. He served in a stirring period
of the Rotterdam congregation, in which there was
a quarrel between the Waterlander group and the
former High Germans, which led to the departure
of most High Germans in 1636. They took vigorous
action against Nabels for laxity in maintaining the
practice of banning and in the matter of mixed
marriages, as well as for unorthodoxy in the doctrine
of the Incarnation. Nabels was also active outside
his Rotterdam congregation: in 1629 he secured a
privilege of exemption from the office of sheriff for
the Waterlander Mennonites in Holland. In 1626 he
sided with Nittert Obbesz (*q.v.*), who was then
involved in a quarrel with the Amsterdam Waterlander preachers and Hans de Ries.   vDZ.

K. Vos, *Geschiedenis der Doopsgez. Gemeente te Rot-
terdam* (repr. 1907) 22, 43; *Inv. Arch. Amst.* I, No. 447;
II, No. 2196; II, 2, No. 332-67, *passim*; *DB* 1906, 140-44;
Kühler, *Geschiedenis* II, 174.

Nachrichten aus der Heidenwelt, an 8-page, 7 x 10
in. missionary paper published monthly from January 1877 to December 1881 by the General Conference Mennonite Church in co-operation with Western Publication Co., Halstead, Kan., edited by C. J.
van der Smissen, with a children's section edited by
Christian Schowalter. The paper was discontinued
when the *Christlicher Bundesbote* (*q.v.*) was started
in January 1882, and resumed in January 1885 as a
4-page 9 x 12½ in. paper published at Berne, Ind.
The last issue appeared in December 1887. Its purpose was to give information concerning G.C.M.
Indian mission work. (*ML* III, 196.)   C.K.

Nachrichten, Unschuldige, the first German theological journal, founded at Leipzig, Germany, in
1701 by Valentin Ernst Löscher. Löscher was succeeded as editor by Michael Heinrich Reinhard,
Löscher again, Johann Erhard Kapp, and Johann
Rudolf Kiesling. Its name was changed a number
of times; in 1701 it was called *Altes und Neues aus
dem Schatz theologischer Wissenschaften;* 1702-19
*Unschuldige Nachrichten von alten und neuen theo-
logischen Sachen;* 1720-50 *Fortgesetzte Sammlung
von alten und neuen theologischen Sachen;* 1751-61
*Neue Beiträge von alten und neuen theologischen
Sachen.* It expired in 1761.

It was supplemented for the first 50 years by the
Theologische Annales (1715-54), in five volumes,
each for a period of ten years, the first volume of

which went through a second edition, and 1735-42 by *Frühaufgelesene Früchte der theologischen Sammlung von Alten und Neuen.* Excerpts from the first 40 volumes were published by Johann Christian Ammon (*Kernhafter Auszug* . . . 1745-52) and Benedikt Born or rather Benjamin Bieler (*Neueröffnete Schatzkammer* . . . 1746-47). "Every month or at shorter intervals a periodical went out into the world, filled with discussions on old and new books, quotations from unprinted sources, articles on questions of scholarship, refutations, church news, and the like. . . . There is in existence no clearer mirror of the thought process of Lutheran orthodoxy in the first half of the 18th century than this paper, which is also an excellent collection of source material for church history" (Blanckmeister, 20). A complete index in five volumes for the years 1701-50 and individual indexes for the following years reveal a frequent mention of the Anabaptists, the Mennonites, and the writings by and about them.

E.C.

F. Blanckmeister, *Der Prophet von Kursachsen Valentin Ernst Löscher und seine Zeit* (Dresden, 1920) 19-21, 167-75; *ML* III, 196.

Nachtigal (Nachtegaal), a Prussian Mennonite family name which probably originated in the Netherlands and may be related to the Nagtegaal family of Ameland. It was found in a number of Prussian families from the early 18th century, particularly at Jeziorka, Schönsee, and Montau. Among the Mennonites expelled from Dannenberg (*q.v.*) in Lithuania (*q.v.*) in 1732 there was a Jonas Nachtigal who settled in the Netherlands with the aid of the Dutch Committee of Foreign Needs and farmed at Serooskerke on the island of Walcheren (*q.v.*) in the province of Zeeland. In 1739 he returned to West Prussia with the larger part of this group.

In the early 19th century some Nachtigals emigrated from West Prussia to Russia. Among them was David Nachtigal, of the Montau area, who settled in Rudnerweide on the Molotschna. Outstanding members of this family were Abraham Nachtigal (*q.v.*) and the missionary Peter Nachtigal (*q.v.*), who served in Sumatra. vDZ.

Reimer, *Familiennanmen*, 114; B. H. Unruh, *Die niederlandisch-niederdeutschen Hintergründe der mennonitischen Ostwanderungen* (n.p., n.d.-1955) 368; *Inv. Arch. Amst.* I, Nos. 1922 f. and 2183-99 *passim.*

Nachtigal, Abraham (1876-1950), a leading Mennonite Brethren minister, was born May 11, 1876, in Franzthal, South Russia, the son of Peter Nachtigal. He studied with Kornelius Unruh (*q.v.*) in Orloff, and supplemented his education by much reading. In Russia he was a member of the Allianz-Gemeinde (*q.v.*) in Lichtfelde and for 19 years its leading minister. He taught school a few years, and later served as manager of a Mennonite forestry (*q.v.*) service camp. As a gifted evangelist and youth worker he served both in Russia and Canada as an itinerant minister. In his home church he was valued as minister, Bible school teacher, and youth worker. Besides numerous articles in the church papers he published two booklets, *Unter dem Kreuz* and *Gesegnete Spaziergänge eines Vaters mit seinem Vierzehnjährigen* (Yarrow, 1947).

Nachtigal was married three times. His first wife was Mariechen Warkentin; this union was blessed with eight children. After her death he married Frida Noeg, with whom he had five children. Anna Dick became his third wife. The family came to Canada in 1924. After a year's stay in Ontario they lived in Arnaud, Man., for eleven years, where he was the leading minister of the M.B. Church. In 1935 the family moved to Yarrow, B.C., where Abraham Nachtigal died after a lengthy illness on Feb. 6, 1950. He was interred in the Yarrow cemetery.

J.A.Ha.

Nachtigal, Peter (1881-1928), a Mennonite missionary, was born at Gnadenfeld in South Russia on May 13, 1881, received his training at the Johanneum at Barmen and in Rotterdam, was sent out by the Dutch Mennonite Missionary Society on Oct. 17, 1911. He took charge of the station at Pakantan in Sumatra (*q.v.*), serving with unusual success until his premature death on Jan. 5, 1928. His post was not filled after his death. His widow is living on the Lautenbacherhof, Württemberg, Germany.

NEFF.

De Zondagsbode XLII (1927-28) No. 11, p. 48; *Brieven* 1928, II; *80ste Jaarverslag* (annual report of 1927 of the Dutch Missionary Association) 15-18; *ML* III, 196.

Nadler (Ritter), **Hans**, an Anabaptist preacher of Erlangen, whose trade was selling needles to shoemakers and tailors. He was baptized with his wife by Hans Hut (*q.v.*) in 1527, henceforth preaching wherever he went. He escaped imprisonment by flight to Moravia. In Nikolsburg he took part in a great Anabaptist meeting, at which 72 persons were baptized.

Nadler returned to Erlangen, was arrested there on Jan. 17, 1529, and cross-examined. In reply to the question why he was so bold as to keep returning to Erlangen he said God had given him the grace to return to his wife and children; he had never baptized, was not ordained to do so; his parents had indeed told him that he had been baptized, but he personally knew nothing of it; for he had been a child and had no understanding and knew nothing about faith; therefore he had himself baptized upon his faith. Concerning communion he said he did not believe that the body of Christ is in the bread, but one receives it in spirit. Concerning possessions he said that if they were used as Christ commanded, they could serve toward salvation. He would not act contrary to the government, for it is ordained of God. Concerning nonresistance he said, it is not the business of a Christian to fight. There were among them brethren who wanted all the brethren to lay down their arms, and he did so; but it was not a law of the brotherhood. He vigorously denied that they were instigating revolt; they should mutually show only love and faithfulness, offend no one, but do good to all. On Feb. 13, 1529, he was tried again, this time with torture. He remained true to his faith. Upon his request he was permitted to sell his property and move to Moravia with his wife and three children. Nothing more is known about him. NEFF.

C. A. Cornelius, *Geschichte des Münsterischen Aufruhrs* II (Leipzig, 1860) 281; *TA Bayern* I, 131-41; Wiswedel, *Bilder* II, 40-44; *ML* III, 196.

Naeldeman, leader of the "Franekeraars": see **Hendrik (de) Naeldeman.**

Naeldemansvolk were the followers of Hendrik Naeldeman (*q.v.*) at Franeker, Friesland. Here in 1556 a group of moderate Dutch Mennonites, who opposed the practice of strict marital avoidance (*q.v.*), disagreed with Menno Simons, Dirk Philips, Leenaert Bouwens, and other conservative leaders. They were also called "de nieuwe gemeente" (new congregation) or Franekeraars (Franickers). Soon they joined or merged with the Waterlanders (*q.v.*). At other places also mention is made of the "Hendrik-Naeldemansvolk," for example at Vlissingen (*q.v.*), where Cornelis de Compasmaker was said to be their leader. (*BRN* VII, 460, 464 f.; *DB* 1894, 36, 39.)
VDZ.

Naeldenverkooper, Evert, an Anabaptist martyr: see **Evert Hendricks.**

Naenken (Naentgen, Adrienne) **Bornaige,** an Anabaptist martyr. Because of her Anabaptist conviction she had fled from Lier, Brabant, to Gent, Flanders, Belgium, where she soon was arrested and burned at the stake on April 11, 1551, with four other Anabaptists, all of Lier. On the way to the site of execution Naenken said, "This is the day for which I have so greatly longed." In the *Offer des Heeren* she is called simply Naenken. These martyrs from Lier are commemorated in the hymn, "Doemen vijftienhondert schreve, daertoe een en vijftich jaer," found in the *Lietboecxken van den Offer des Heeren.*
NEFF, VDZ.
Offer, 517-21; *Mart. Mir.* D 106, E 503; Verheyden, *Gent,* 13, No. 23; Wolkan, *Lieder,* 61; *ML* III, 195.

Naentgen (Naenken) **Leerverkoop(st)er,** an Anabaptist martyr, listed by van Braght (*Mart. Mir.* D 244, E 618), who after trial on the rack was drowned with two sisters in a washtub at Antwerp on March 17 or 19, 1559. She is identical with Adriana Lambrechts (*q.v.*). Her name is found in the hymn, "Aenhoort Godt, hemelsche Vader" (Hear, O God, heavenly Father), No. 16 in the *Lietboecxken van den Offer des Heeren.* (*Offer,* 566; *ML* II, 626.)
VDZ.

Nafziger (Nafzger, Naffziger, Nafzinger, Naffzer, Naftziger, Nofziger, Noffsinger, Nofsker, Naftiger), a Mennonite name of Swiss origin, found in the 18th century in the Palatinate, where Johannes Nafziger (*q.v.*) was an elder of the Essingen congregation until about 1790, and in Alsace, where Christian Nafziger was an elder of the Froensberg congregation from 1765 until after 1810, while Christian Nafziger, Jr., was an elder of the Stroeter congregation from about 1765 until after 1810. In Hesse (*q.v.*) Hans Nafziger was a preacher in the district of Nassau-Weilburg 1786-*ca.*1815, and Peter Nafziger about the end of the 18th century on the Kammerhof in the duchy of Hesse-Darmstadt. A branch of the Nafzigers settled in Luxembourg early in the 19th century and furnished several preachers there, the last being Elder Christian Nafziger. Another branch settled in Bavaria about the same time, from which Christian Nafziger (*q.v.*) emigrated to Canada in 1826 to found the Amish Mennonite settlement in Wilmot Township, Waterloo County. Peter Nafziger (1789-1885) moved from here to Butler County, Ohio, in 1831, where he became a prominent bishop. John Naffziger (1802-56) immigrated from Lorraine in 1837 to the Metamora settlement in Woodford County, Ill., where he served as a bishop. Nafzigers have been numerous in the central Illinois Amish Mennonite settlement (especially Hopedale and Metamora), the Fulton County, Ohio, settlement, and in Butler County, Ohio.
H.S.B.
Ernst Correll, "The Value of Family History for Mennonite History, with Illustrations from Nafziger Family Material," *MQR* II (1928) 66-79, 151-54, 198-205; *Naamlijst.*

Nafziger, Christian (1776-1836), a pioneer German Mennonite immigrant to Canada, stemmed from the Palatinate and settled for a time near Munich, Germany. He led the emigration of the Amish Mennonites to Canada, leaving in late 1821 to find a place of settlement in the New World. In January 1822 he landed in New Orleans and covered the 1,000 miles to Lancaster County on foot. The Lancaster Mennonites pointed out to him the settlement possibilities in Canada, where Pennsylvania Mennonites had already settled in 1796-1800 and after. In Waterloo County, Ont., he found a Mennonite settlement which impressed him favorably. In the summer of 1822 he made contact with the governor of Upper Canada, who put at his disposal for settlement a large tract of land west of Waterloo in Wilmot Township. Each family could acquire 150 acres, and in addition, free of charge, another 50 acres.

On his return trip to Germany Nafziger stopped in London to have the agreement with Governor Maitland ratified by George IV. In the next year the first Amish Mennonite families from Germany settled in Wilmot Township, including such names as Bechler, Brennemann, Gingerich, Burky, Goldschmidt, Kropf, and Moser. Nafziger himself did not emigrate to Canada until 1826, when some other Amish Mennonites of Bavaria came with him. In this group there were two ordained men, Bishop Peter Nafziger (1789-1885), who led the new congregation until 1831 and then moved to Butler County, Ohio, and Christian Steinmann (1792-1865). Christian Nafziger can be considered the pioneer of the many German emigrants to Canada in the following years. He died on May 5, 1836. HEGE.
L. J. Burkholder, *A Brief History of the Mennonites in Ontario* (Toronto, 1935); Heinz Lehmann, *Das Deutschtum in Ostkanada* (Stuttgart, 1931); *ML* III, 197.

Nafziger, Johannes (b. *ca.* 1706), an elder of the Amish congregation in Essingen near Landau in the Palatinate, Germany, supposedly spent his youth on the Mechtersheimerhof near Germersheim. The records in the archives in Karlsruhe mention him for the first time in 1738. He later moved to Essingen and leased an estate from the Baron of Dalsberg. He married Barbara Holly. In 1731 he was chosen preacher and then elder. He must have been a leader in the brotherhood. In 1765 he journeyed to the Netherlands with two other brethren, where some Swiss Amish had founded congregations. There were all kinds of disorder and strife to be regulated. They remained nine weeks to install new preachers and to make the observance of communion possible. These congregations needed help several times. In 1770 we find Johannes Nafziger again one of the delegates. Later a written directive for the regulation of congregational life was requested. On March 26, 1781, Nafziger complied with a long letter, in which he described the ceremonies of baptism, marriage, choice and ordination of preachers and deacons as he practiced them. This letter appears to have become a sort of ministers' manual for the Amish congregations in South Germany, for several copies made at a later time have been preserved in the Goshen College Library.

Nafziger was active in the publication of the *Martyrs' Mirror* (*q.v.*) in 1780 in Pirmasens. On Sept. 16, 1778, he wrote a letter to Peter Weber of Kindenheim which reports the details of the contract with the printer and the copper plates he obtained from Amsterdam for the illustrations. "We hope it will by the grace of God be a beautiful book," he says at the close of the letter, which gives evidence of his business acumen.

The closing years of Nafziger's life were clouded by a most noteworthy instance of intolerance on the part of the Catholic Church. He was the elder who baptized the two girls mentioned in the article **Punishment.** The girls were to be punished by death, and he with a fine of 500 florins and exile. Nothing further is known about the execution of the sentence, nor of the date or place of Nafziger's death.

P.S.

Chr. Neff, "Eine Bekehrungsgeschichte," *Gem.-Kal.*, 1906, 54-78; Ernst Correll, "The Value of Family History for Mennonite History: Illustrated from **Nafziger** Family History Material of the Eighteenth Century," *MQR* II (1928) Nos. 1, 2, and 3; "An Amish Church Discipline of 1781," *op. cit.* (1930) No. 2; *ML* III, 197 f.

Nafziger Old Order Amish Church, located in Mornington Twp., Perth Co., Ont. About 1903 some differences arose in the Mornington Old Order Amish Church at Poole, which resulted in some of the ministers and some of the lay members withdrawing under the leadership of Bishop Nicholas Nafziger (ordained 1896, d. 1944). In 1904 the group supporting Nafziger built a meetinghouse west of the corner at Poole. Services are held every Sunday in the German language with singing from the *Ausbund*. This congregation is not connected with any conference. They have no Sunday schools and no evening meetings. The membership in 1954 was 154, and the congregation consisted of 56 families and 234 worshipers. The first ministers besides Nafziger were Peter Spenler and John Albrecht. John Gerber (ord. 1909, d. 1929), from West Branch, Mich., joined this group in 1924. Samuel Nafziger, son of Bishop Nicholas, was ordained minister in 1933. Moses Nafziger, nephew of Nicholas, was ordained minister in 1933 and bishop in 1940. Valentine Gerber (d. 1928), ordained minister in Holt Co., Neb., was in his later life connected with this congregation. The present leadership consists of Moses Nafziger, bishop; Samuel Nafziger and Joseph Steckley, ministers; and Jonas Jantzi, deacon. An account of the Amish Mennonites in Canada

was given in the John Baer German *Almanac* in 1903.

J.C.F.

Nagar Kurnool, a Mennonite Brethren Mission station in India located near the large village Nagar Kurnool, 80 miles south of Hyderabad, Andhra Pradesh (formerly Hyderabad State). Sanction for possession of the site and permission to erect the buildings was procured by D. F. Bergthold in 1907. The buildings constructed include a missionary's dwelling house, a church and school building, hostels for school children, a hospital, and living quarters for indigenous workers.

Resident missionaries at this station have been Mr. and Mrs. D. F. Bergthold, Mr. and Mrs. F. A. Janzen, Mr. and Mrs. J. H. Lohrenz, Mr. and Mrs. J. N. C. Hiebert, Dr. Katharina L. Schellenberg, Catherine Reimer, Mr. and Mrs. J. J. Kasper, and Mary Doerksen. The missionaries in 1951 were Mildred Enns and Rosella Toews.

The work at the station includes the regular worship services and other activities of the church; a school, which for some time was a middle school, but in recent years only a primary school; and a hospital. For some time the mission press and publication activities were centered here. In 1923-29 the Bible School of the Mission was located at Nagar Kurnool. The station field, comprising an area of 1400 square miles and having 200,000 inhabitants, has been a responsive field for evangelism. At present the indigenous church numbers over 1,000 members. (*ML* III, 198.)

J.H.L.

Nagtegaal, a Mennonite family found since at least the 18th century on the Dutch island of Ameland (*q.v.*), where the descendants are still serving as deacons. The Nachtigal family found in Russia and America and formerly in Prussia may be related to this Dutch family.

vDZ.

Nairn Amish Mennonite Church, located 3 miles south of Ailsa Craig, and about 20 miles northeast of London, Middlesex Co., Ont., a member of the Ontario A.M. Conference, was organized in 1949 with 20 members under the leadership of Wilfred Schlegel. In 1947 the congregation bought a well-built Presbyterian church, seating capacity 350. In 1955 the membership was 63, with Wilfred Schlegel still serving as pastor.

W.Sc.

Nalgonda, a Baptist mission station in India, 60 miles from Hyderabad, was founded in 1890 by a Mennonite from Russia named Abraham Friesen (*q.v.*), who had been a student in the Baptist seminary in Hamburg, Germany, on behalf of the Baptist Missionary Union of Boston. For a considerable time it was maintained by the Mennonite Brethren in Russia. In 1897, when Friesen left on a furlough trip to Russia, the congregation among the Telegus numbered 700 members. Other Mennonite Brethren of Russia volunteered to serve as missionaries in this work of evangelization with Friesen. In 1898 Abraham Hübert came to the field, followed in 1899 by Heinrich Unruh, and in 1904 by Cornelius Unruh and Johann Wiens. About 1912 J. A. Penner went to India; in 1940 he was still in Mahbubnagar. An agreement was reached by which the Mennonite

Brethren of Russia would be responsible for the total expenses of evangelization, and the Baptist Union for the expenses of youth work and the care of the sick.

The development of the Nalgonda Mission encouraged the Mennonite Brethren in America to open a mission station in India. As early as 1884 they had offered the Baptist mission a sum of money for the education of a native preacher. Since they had raised a larger sum than necessary for this purpose, they organized a Missions Committee in 1885 to take care of these surplus funds. As the missionary opportunities expanded, it was decided at a conference meeting in Reno County, Kan., to establish an independent mission in the same general area of Nalgonda in India, which was founded with the arrival of the first missionaries Oct. 27, 1899.

HEGE.

J. F. Harms, *Geschichte der Mennoniten-Brüdergemeinde* (Hillsboro, 1924); A. H. Unruh, *Die Geschichte der Mennoniten-Brüdergemeinde 1860-1954* (Winnipeg, 1954); G. W. Peters, *The Growth of Foreign Missions in the Mennonite Brethren Church* (Hillsboro, 1952); *ML* III, 198.

Namaka Mennonite Brethren Church, located three miles south of Namaka, Alberta, formerly a member of the Evangelical Mennonite Brethren Conference, but since 1942 a member of the Canadian M.B. District Conference, was organized in 1927 with 30 members. The church was built in 1932. The presiding minister of this church 1927-47 was A. A. Toews. Other ministers were A. P. Willms, G. Dirks, A. G. Martens, Heinrich Klassen, and C. Penner. The presiding minister in 1955 was Gerhard Dirks, and the membership was 34.   A.A.T.

Namenbüchlein: see A-B-C Books.

Namensverzeichnis *der sämtlichen remonstrantischen Gemeinden in und ausserhalb der Batavischen Republik. Veränderte Ausgabe vom Jahre 1802* (Danzig) is the German edition of the Dutch *Naamlijst* (*q.v.*) of 1802. A corrected edition with the same title appeared in 1805. In spite of imperfections this book has value even today. The appendix has a brief biography of Menno Simons. It closes with an index of places.

In 1823 an entirely new list was published in Danzig, *Namensverzeichnis der Aeltesten und Lehrer der mennonitischen Gemeinen in Süd-, Ost-, Westpreussen, Lithauen und Polen, nebst derjenigen in Russland und in den neu angesiedelten Kolonien* (1823 Danzig), reprinted in 1835 with a changed title, by Agathon Wernich in Elbing. The preface states, "This edition contains, in accord with the decision adopted at Marienburg on Sept. 18, 1834, the names of the congregations found in East and West Prussia, Lithuania, Poland, and in the German settlements of the Russian Empire; and the names of the elders, preachers, and deacons, with the towns or districts where they reside, in order that this book may if necessary be used as an address book." It is a very valuable list.

A new edition of this list was issued in 1843; the fourth edition followed in 1857 in Danzig with the altered title, *Namensverzeichniss der in Deutsch-land, Ost- und Westpreussen, Galizien, Polen und Russland befindlichen Mennoniten-Gemeinden sowie ihrer Aeltesten, Lehrer und Vorsteher* (1857, Danzig). It contains a preface signed by J. Mannhardt (*q.v.*) in the name of the elders and preachers of the West Prussian congregations, which expresses regret for the incompleteness of the list; the congregations in Alsace and Crefeld had not sent the requested information. Hence blank spaces were left in the book for the insertion of entries. This register contains the names of the elders, preachers, and deacons of Prussia, Hesse, Bavaria, Baden, Galicia, Poland, and Russia. A fifth edition appeared in 1881.

The *Jahrbuch der altevangelischen taufgesinnten Mennoniten-Gemeinden* (*q.v.*) of 1883 and 1888, published by H. G. Mannhardt, does not contain a register of congregations in West Prussia nor those in Switzerland, France, and Poland. A list of preachers and congregations in Holland is contained in the *Jaarboekje* (*q.v.*). The *Mennonitischer Gemeinde-Kalender* (1892-   ) publishes a list of ministers in Germany, Switzerland, and France. A list of preachers and congregations in Russia appeared in 1905 with the title, *Statistik der Mennonitengemeinden in Russland* (Appendix to the *Mennonitisches Jahrbuch* 1904-5). The *Mennonite Yearbook and Directory* (*q.v.*) publishes an annual list of all the Mennonite ministers in North America, including Europe and South America in recent years. The *Meeting Calendar of All the Mennonite Churches in Eastern Pennsylvania,* appearing annually since at least 1880, contains a complete directory of all ordained men in the three easternmost conferences of the Mennonite Church (MC). All individual denominational or conference yearbooks contain a directory of ministers and congregations. (*ML* III, 198 f.)   NEFF.

Names *Given to the Anabaptists-Mennonites in the Netherlands.* Besides the names used by the Dutch Mennonites themselves like Doopsgezinden (*q.v.*) and Mennisten (*q.v.;* also Menisten, Benisten), Mennoniten, Mennonieten, there were from the very beginning of Anabaptism in the Netherlands a large number of group names. The first Anabaptists called themselves Bondgenooten or Vrienden. By their opponents, both Catholic and Reformed even as late as the 17th century, they were usually called Wederdopers. After the various schisms there were the names Waterlanders, Vlamingen (Flemish), Oude Vlamingen, Groninger Oude Vlamingen, Dantziger Oude Vlamingen, Vriezen (Friezen), Oude or Harde Vriezen, Jonge or Zachte Vriezen, Hoogduitsers (High German Mennonites) or Overlanders, in the 17th century Lamisten and Zonisten, Grove and Fijne Mennisten. Often the names of the different branches or local groups were derived from a leading person: Melchiorieten (from Melchior Hofmann), Davidjoristen (after David Joris), Adamieten (after Adam Pastor), Obbiten (after Obbe Philipsz), Batenburgers (after Jan van Batenburg), Dirckisten (after Dirk Philipsz; the variant Dreckisten is an unkind corruption of the name Dirckisten), Naeldemansvolk (group), Thomas Bintgensvolk, Jacob Keestvolk, Jan Jacobszvolk, or Janjacobsgezinden, Pieter Jeltjesvolk, Vermeulensvolk (after

Jacob Pieters van der Meulen), Robbert Robbertsz-volk, Jan Evertsvolk, Twisken (after Pieter Jansz Twisck), Uckowallisten (after Uko Walles), Gale-nisten (after Galenus Abrahamsz), Apostoolsen (after Samuel Apostool), Foppe-Onesvolk, Lausoms-gemeente, Jan Schellingwousvolk.

Stilstaanders, Zierikzeeërs, and Neutralisten are the names given to the Mennonites who refused to take sides in the Flemish-Frisian conflict in 1566. Huiskopers and Contra-Huiskopers are denomina-tional designations given to some Flemish groups. Bekommerden and Heylsamen are found in Fries-land and Danzig. Bevredigden and Afgedeelden are two groups of Mennonites in North Holland in the early 17th century. Meerlanders are Hutterites; Wevers mean the followers of Hans Busschaert de Wever; Franickers or Franekers were Waterlanders, as was also the Nieuwe Gemeente (*BRN* VII, 460, 464 f.); Blaauwe Schuur-Menisten are the Water-landers at Harlingen and Nes, Ameland; Voetwas-sers were found in the province of Zeeland, Kome-jannen, being a branch of the Waterlanders, in North Holland; the meaning of the denominations Hamersch (*DB* 1897, 103, note) and Russchers (*DB* 1877, 34) is unknown. For Tibben, a denomination found in Groningen and Overijssel, see the article. The names Kleyn Hoopken and Allerkleinste Hoop-ken are names assumed by a few conservative sep-arate congregations who did not want to have any connections with other congregations.

Formerly there circulated also a number of nick-names or contemptuous terms, given to the Men-nonites by the non-Mennonite population, or by op-posing Mennonite branches. The following are known: Swermers (Schwärmer, fanatics) or Rot-geesten (mobsters) (*BRN* VII, 238), Winkelpredi-kers (corner preachers), Dreckwagen (garbage cart), the name given by Leenaert Bouwens to the mod-erate Waterlanders; Bankroetiers, Borstentasters, Clerckschen (Clarichen), Sandtdooperen (*BRN* VII, 461, called thus after the tumultuous occurrences at 't Zandt), Maliapen (*DB* 1872, 32), Nieuwe Jeru-zalemmers (after Münster, the new Jerusalem), Tib-ben, Eyckenplancken (*DB* 1897, 79), Reinen (clean ones), Stroopslikkers (syrup-lickers), Koekvreters (cake eaters), Sloddermenisten (*BRN* VII, 20, grub-by Mennonites, meaning uncertain), Vuile Goten (*DB* 1877, 34, dirty gutters; this expression probably was derived from the old doctrine of Incarnation as taught by Melchior Hofmann and Menno Simons, that Christ had passed through Maria as water through a pipe), Olieblokken (*DB* 1877, 34, obvious-ly after the meetinghouse Den Vlaemschen Oly-Block at Haarlem).

A. Montanus, *Kerkelijke Historie van Nederland* (1671), p. 197, enumerates the following names of the Dutch Mennonites: Mennisten, Huttieten, Hoog-duitschen, Zwitserschen, Apostolischen, Separatis-ten, Oude en Jonge Friesen, Vlamingen, Voetwas-schers, Borstentasters (or Borstenslagers), Haken-en-Oogen, Zwaardgeesten, Stilzwijgenden, Neutra-listen, Huiskoopers, Contra-Huiskoopers, Franekers, Gooischen, Zuiveren, Libertisten, Hoterschen, Au-gustianen, Waterlanders, de Drekwagen, Leonard-Klokschen, Claes-Woltersensvolk, Harde and Slappe Friezen, Collegianten, Hollanders or Pieter-Jansvolk,

Afvallige Vlamingen, Groningers or Jan-Lucasvolk, Jacob Pieters Vermolensvolk, Vincent de Hondts-volk, Hendrik Dirks Apeldoornsvolk, Robbert Ro-bertszvolk, Bevende Broeders. This list obviously is very uncritical; not all "collegianten" were Men-nonites, and "Bevende Broeders" apparently were Quakers and not Mennonites.   vDZ.

Names, Mennonite, of Persons and Places. Quite frequently one hears the remark, "That is a Men-nonite name," or "That is not a Mennonite name." This indicates that there are specific names con-sidered to be "Mennonite." This is one of the char-acteristics of Mennonites of various countries and areas. They have perpetuated not only certain fam-ily names and given names, but also names of settle-ments, villages, institutions, etc. Many names of European origin have been transplanted to North and South America.

Family Names. Because of their withdrawal from the world, enforced by persecution and their princi-ple of nonconformity, Mennonites have in certain countries perpetuated their faith and traditions with-in the group into which very few "outsiders" found entrance. At times conversion to the Mennonite faith and intermarriage with outsiders were almost completely absent for generations. This was true among the Swiss, German, and Dutch Mennonites in the past and is true today among the Swiss, French, South German, Russian, and American Men-nonites almost to the same degree, although inter-marriage is more common in our day than it was heretofore. Among the Mennonites of the Nether-lands and North Germany this isolation has been given up long ago. Scarcely any Mennonite family names of the 16th century are found among the Mennonites of the Netherlands today. One reason is that during the 16th and early 17th centuries there were hardly any family names in existence in Hol-land in general. Instead, in addition to the given name a person retained his father's given name. Thus "Menno" added to his name "Simonsz" which meant that he was Simons' son. Menno's son in turn would add "Mennosz" to his given name. Not until the second quarter of the 17th century were family names handed down from generation to generation. In many cases the father's given name became the family name. Thus Peter Claasz became Peter Claas-sen; Jakob Friesz became Jakob Friesen; Abraham Dirksz became Abraham Dirksen, etc. Of these original Dutch Mennonite family names, which really were "petrified" given names, very few have survived in the Netherlands. This is mostly due to the fact that the Dutch Mennonites gave up the principle of isolation and nonconformity nearly 200 years ago. In the process of adjustment, intermar-riage with non-Mennonites was so frequent and common that few of the original "Mennonite" names survived within the Mennonite fold. Also in modern times many "liberal" elements have transferred from the Dutch Reformed Church to the Mennonite Church bringing new family names into the broth-erhood. The same is true in such German congrega-tions as Crefeld and Emden.

However, among the Mennonites of Prussia, Dan-zig, and Poland and their descendants in Russia and

America, the 16th- and particularly the 17th-century Mennonite names have survived in large numbers. It is true that many new names were added in Prussia and Danzig which by now are also considered full-fledged "Mennonite" names. Many of the names ending in "ski" or "sky" are definitely of Polish origin (Sawatsky, Tillitzki, Schepansky, Koslowsky, etc.). In some instances the original name may have been changed by accepting the Polish ending. On the other hand, some of the older names died out and cannot be found either in Europe or America. A study made by Franz Crous reports a very interesting study on the frequency of the most common Mennonite family names among the Mennonites of Germany. He reports for East Germany 454 names in 15 congregations in the following order of frequency of baptized bearers of the name down to 100: Penner 469, Wiebe 388, Wiens 363, Dyck 281, Claassen 263, Klaassen 190, Pauls 190, Harder 188, Bartel 185, Janzen 180, Janz 178, Froese 170, Reimer 165, Franz 156, Neufeld 154, Enss 144, Thiessen 133, Friesen 121, Wiehler 120, Fieguth 112, Ewert 110, Fast 108, Regier 107, Driedger 105, Albrecht 104. In Northwest Germany he found 660 names in 9 congregations, of whom only 19 had more than 10 bearers, the first ten being: von Beckerath 45, van Delden 32, Fast 24, Brons 23, Penner 21, Claassen 21, Fieguth 20, Stroink 20, van der Smissen 17, Kruse 15. South Germany had 478 names in 40 congregations; following were the leading names in order of frequency: Schmutz 154, Hege 149, Krehbiel 121, Fellmann 119, Horsch 108, Stauffer 107, Schowalter 98, Landes 98, Eymann 87, Lichti 86, Hertzler 79, Musselmann 70, Dettweiler 69, Hirschler 68, Weber 67, Galle 60, Lehman 55, Bachmann 54, Guth 54, Blickensdorfer 53, Beutler 52, Funk 52.

From Prussia, Poland, and Russia these names were transplanted starting in 1874 to the Great Plains of North America and again after each of the world wars to North America as well as South America. The Swiss-South German names were in a similar way transplanted from Switzerland, France, South Germany, Volhynia, and Galicia to Pennsylvania, Ohio, Indiana, and other states during the many waves of migrations beginning in the 18th century. A statistical study of the frequency of the American Mennonite names has not been made. C. Henry Smith in *The Story of the Mennonites* lists names peculiar to certain settlements in America. The genealogies (*q.v.*) and family histories (*q.v.*) are a source information regarding family names. The more frequent Mennonite family names have all been treated in the MENNONITE ENCYCLOPEDIA.

The total of different traditional family names among the Mennonites of Europe, exclusive of Holland and the newer families in Emden and Crefeld, has been determined to be about 600. Of these, 167 names of Swiss-South German origin, and 105 names of West Prussian and Northwest German origin are treated in this ENCYCLOPEDIA, in addition to most of the 15 Hutterite family names. The article **Amish** (*ME* I, 97) lists 100 Amish family names.

Given Names. Besides the patronymic system of names, the given names were primarily names taken from the Bible like those of the Puritans and other religious groups. Among the Russian Mennonites

there were certain cycles and traditions according to which the same names would be repeated in the family. The oldest son would be named after the father or grandfather, and the oldest daughter after the mother or grandmother. The succeeding children would be named after uncles and aunts. The Alexanderwohl Mennonite Church record, started in Germany during the 17th century and continued in Russia and Kansas, is an interesting source of information on this practice. During 1695-1799 (Prussia), 921 given names were checked. This list contained only 40 different names, all the others being repeated. Heading the list of male members in frequency was Peter (90), followed by Jakob (74). Among the female names, Ancke (Anna) ranked highest (107) with Marike (Maria) following (79). The names still had a Dutch ending, indicating the cultural and linguistic adherence to their background. In 1860-75 (Russia), among the 1,328 Alexanderwohl names checked there were only 54 different given names, which indicates the unbroken tradition of repeating the same names in the family. The names had become Germanized. Peter still ranked highest (118), followed by Heinrich (116) and Jakob (98). Maria (143) was now more frequent than Anna (101), after which Helena (95) followed. After the Alexanderwohl congregation had moved to Kansas in 1874 great adjustments were made to the new environment. How rapidly they were made is indicated by the change in given names. In 1919-25, 175 names were checked, of which 109 were different. Entirely new German and English names had been added, very few of which are repeated. A complete adjustment was made by the time World War II ended. Of the 168 names checked of the children born 1945-53 there appear 122 different names, most of which are typically American names rather than Bible names. Hardly any are repeated more than two or three times and most of them appear only once. Most popular was "Clifford." At the end of the alphabet was "Zyleene."

Although no other American Mennonite church has a record of over 200 years it can safely be assumed that the changes which have taken place in given names are very much the same. The Alexanderwohl Mennonite Church has always been one of the more conservative Mennonite congregations. It can be assumed that some others have made this adjustment much more rapidly. On the other hand, such groups as the Amish, the Hutterites, and the Old Colony Mennonites still perpetuate the tradition of giving their children only the Biblical names commonly in use in their circle. In South America Spanish influences are beginning to be noticeable in the choice of given names, while in Russia it had already become a practice in some circles before World War I to add Russian endings to the given names. Since World Wars I and II Russian names have become very frequent. Another Russian practice accepted by the Mennonites of Russia was the adding of the father's given name to the bearer's given name somewhat similar to the original Dutch practice. P. M. Friesen would be called Peter Martinovitch Friesen, Martin being the given name of his father.

Settlement and Village Names. The Mennonite

settlement (colony) names, particularly in Russia, were frequently the name of the river on which they were located (Chortitza, Molotchna, Kuban, etc.), or the owner from whom the settlement had been bought (Ignatyevo), the province in which they were located (Orenburg, Samara), or the name of the Russian town or village next to which they were located (Arkadak, etc.). In North and South America the selection of a name for a settlement was somewhat different. In Manitoba the name for the largest two settlements was derived from the fact that the government "reserved" the land for the Mennonites to the east and west of the Red River, and therefore the names "East Reserve" and "West Reserve" originated. In Saskatchewan the two large Mennonite settlements received their name from the nearest large places at which the Mennonites settled, "Hague settlement" and "Swift Current settlement." These in turn were transplanted by the migrants to Mexico next to the "Manitoba" settlers of Mexico. In the United States there are few Mennonite settlements consisting of a larger group of villages in existence since the immigrants settled on individual farms. The Alexanderwohl (*q.v.*) settlement with a number of villages was an exception. In Mexico, Paraguay, Uruguay, and Brazil the Mennonites have perpetuated the tradition of establishing themselves in a compact settlement. The major settlements of Paraguay are Menno (*q.v.*), Fernheim (*q.v.*), Friesland (*q.v.*), Volendam (*q.v.*), and Neuland (*q.v.*). In Brazil the name "Witmarsum" and in Paraguay "Friesland" indicate that the settlers wished to emphasize their Dutch background.

The Mennonites of Prusso-Russian background have been most loyal in perpetuating village names from Prussia to Russia and to the Great Plains of North America and Mexico and South America. Some of the names have been repeated in many of the settlements established by them. A complete study of this will appear under the article **Village Names.** C.K.

Reimer, *Familiennamen*; Franz Crous, "Mennonitenfamilien in Zahlen," *Gesch.-Bl.*, August 1940; Herbert Wiebe, "Mennonitische Familiennamen in den Weichselniederungen von Graudenz bis Thorn," *Gesch.-Bl.*, August 1939; Mel Voth, "Given Name Changes in the Alexanderwohl Community" (a research paper, BeCL, 1954).

Nampa, a city (pop. 17,500) located in Canyon Co., Idaho, in the southwestern part of the state, about 30 miles from the Oregon line. The average rainfall is only approximately 11 inches, but irrigation provides moisture for growing crops. About 140 Mennonites (MC) live in this area, 60 per cent of whom are farmers. David Garber was the first Mennonite to arrive here, coming in February 1899. Others soon followed and in the same year the Nampa Mennonite Church (*q.v.*) was organized by George R. Brunk, Sr. The present membership is made up of families from practically every state where Mennonites are found, with a few added from the community. The congregation operates two mission Sunday schools. A congregation of General Conference Mennonites lives around Caldwell, eight miles northwest of Nampa. The Nampa Mennonite Christian Day School is owned and controlled by the local Mennonite church (MC). The average enrollment is about 60, with a corps of three teachers. E.S.G.

Nampa Mennonite Children's Home. In the fall of 1939 the city welfare representative asked the Mennonite Church (MC) of Nampa to provide a home for a family of five girls. A member of the congregation agreed to furnish living quarters if the congregation would help support the project. This they agreed to do. This group of five children formed the nucleus from which the children's home grew, until at one time there were 19 children. In the winter of 1947 the Pacific Coast Conference Mission Board assumed responsibility for the home. It was discontinued in 1950. R.E.G.

Nancy, capital (pop. 121,000) of the former province of Lorraine, a city in the department of Meurthe-et-Moselle (*q.v.*), in northeastern France. In the second half of the 18th century some Mennonites located in the vicinity of the city. The Mennonites had been expelled from Alsace by Louis XIV in 1712; many of them turned to Lorraine, which was at that time not a part of France. Several families had also settled on farms in the bishopric of Metz, and lived there unmolested, since they were considered **Swiss.**

In 1766, when Lorraine became French, Louis XV inquired about the Mennonites. Since the reports were favorable, they were left in peace until the Revolution brought freedom of religion to all.

The families lived widely scattered on isolated farms and mills; they met as a congregation in the homes of the more prosperous members. As is often the case with small groups, they were subject to disintegrating influences and the congregation declined steadily. The union of part of the congregation with Lunéville-Dieuze (*q.v.*) in 1893 did not stem the decline. In World War I the congregation was in the zone of battle. Meetings were disrupted. The elders of the congregation died during or right after the war; the congregation was unable to organize again. Although there are still several families in the city and the vicinity, there have been no services there since the war. The MCC operated a children's home at Nancy in 1945-50. (*ML* III, 199.) P.So.

Nanlo, a county in southern Hopei province, China, with an area of 350 square miles and population estimated at 221,000. Mission work was begun in 1920 by the General Conference Mennonite Board of Missions. A primary school and an organized church established at Nanlo City, as well as ten or twelve regular preaching places in the country, were cared for by an evangelist, a schoolteacher, and a Bible woman, with the help of missionaries and itinerant workers. Mission buildings were occupied by the Japanese military forces in 1938 and the work badly disrupted and forced to discontinue in 1942, though the Chinese church continued active. S.F.P.

Napajedl (Napayerle, Napeürl), a market town (pop. 4,700) on the March River in Moravia, in the 16th century in the possession of the barons of Zierotin. The Hutterite chronicles state that "Sir Paul" in 1545 "gave the Hutterian Brethren two houses to try for a year." But conditions were not favorable, and they moved away at the end of the year.

P.DE.

Beck, *Geschichts-Bücher*, 164; Wolkan, *Geschicht-Buch*, 201; Zieglschmid, *Chronik*, 258; *ML* III, 199.

Napier Mennonite Church (GCM), located three miles east of Schellsburg, Pa., a member of the Eastern District Conference, was organized June 22, 1913, with Herman Snyder as the first pastor. The church originated as a home mission project and became a self-supporting church in May 1955. The membership in 1956 was 86. Leon Detweiler served as pastor for a number of years. Other pastors were Jacob Snyder, Stephen Yoder, Adam Wolfe, Jacob Yoder, Andrew R. Shelly, Willard Claassen, George Gregor, Walter M. Wolfe. Donald Janis was serving as interim pastor in 1956.

P.R.S.

Napoleon I, Emperor of France 1804-15, rescinded the exemption of the Mennonites from military service in the lands under his dominion. He generally, though not always, permitted them to employ substitutes, but since it was very expensive to hire one very few could do it.

The Mennonites of the Palatinate and Rhenish Hesse tried in vain to maintain their principle of nonresistance. At the momentous conferences in Ibersheim (*q.v.*) in 1803 and 1805 this was expressly stated. The latter conference passed a resolution to observe a day of fasting, penitence, and prayer. Möllinger (*q.v.*), pastor of the Ruchheim (Palatinate) congregation, was sent to Paris to appeal to Napoleon in person, but he was not given audience. The Mennonites had to render military service.

On June 19, 1808, a conference of the elders and preachers of the Mennonites of Alsace-Lorraine meeting on the Bildhäuserhof near Schlettstadt decided to send two brethren to Paris on a similar mission (see **Donnersberg** and **Alsace**). They presented an interesting document requesting the privilege of serving in the transportation corps. If the statement of Elder Augsburger of the Salm congregation is correct, this petition was granted (see **France**).

In 1810, when the Netherlands were incorporated into the French empire, Napoleon interfered with the Dutch churches. They were compelled to subscribe to state loans, which caused the loss of large sums, since the loans soon became valueless. In consequence, most congregations were unable to pay the salaries of their ministers. An indirect result of this financial deterioration was the founding of the Algemeene Doopsgezinde Sociëteit (*q.v.*) in 1811, since the congregation of Amsterdam was no longer able to support the Seminary. A futile attempt was made by Napoleon to unite all the Protestant churches of the Netherlands, including the Mennonites, into one single Protestant church.

Another project, viz., to organize the Mennonite congregations into one body, which was to contact the government by six "corresponding congregations," i.e., Amsterdam, Haarlem, Harlingen, Leeuwarden, Groningen, and Zwolle, was only committed to paper, but never really came into being (see **Naamlijst** 1815, 58-61; *Biogr. Wb.* III, 783).

The Mennonite congregations were compelled to ask Napoleon's consent whenever they called a new minister, and in 1812, when Rinse Koopmans (*q.v.*) was chosen professor of the Amsterdam Seminary, his appointment had to be approved by Napoleon, but since the approval failed to come, he could not officially take up his office until June 8, 1814. The order that each minister had to have his sermon approved before it was preached was generally disregarded.

The order that Mennonites serve in the French armies was also usually evaded, though a number of young Mennonites were seized and compelled to go to Paris as imperial guards, and even to serve in the Grand Army on its march into Russia in 1812. A number of young Mennonites in the Palatinate were drafted into Napoleon's army and also served on the march into Russia in 1812.

NEFF, vDZ.

W. Mannhardt, *Die Wehrfreiheit der Altpreussischen Mennoniten* (Danzig, 1863); *Naamlijst* 1815, 58, 59, 62, 64, 69 f.; *Biogr. Wb.* III, 783; *DB* 1872, 126; 1912, 112; *ML* III, 199 f.

Nappanee, a town (pop. 3,800) in the southwestern part of Elkhart Co., Ind., in a very fertile section of farming land. A collection center of the Brethren Service Relief and the E.V. Publishing House, the headquarters of the Brethren in Christ Church, are located here. Of the 13 churches within the city, three are Mennonite, namely, North Main St. (MC), First Mennonite (GCM), and United Missionary. The first Mennonites to settle in Locke and Union townships in which Nappanee is located came about 1857-60. There are also two churches of the Conservative Mennonites and nine districts of Old Order Amish in the territory surrounding Nappanee.

H.F.N.

Nappanee First Mennonite Church (GCM), located in Nappanee, Ind., first known as the Amish Mennonite Church and later as the West Market Street Mennonite Church, is a member of the Middle District Conference. Before 1923 the congregation was a member of the Mennonite Church (MC). The congregation was organized in 1875 after groups of settlers had met for worship in homes and schoolhouses since 1853. The first meetinghouse was erected in 1878, rebuilt in 1910, and remodeled in 1926 and 1955, a frame structure with a seating capacity of about 250. In 1955 the membership was 164, with Earl L. Salzman as pastor.

J.J.EN.

Nappanee (Ind.) United Missionary Church was organized April 3, 1897, under the leadership of Daniel Brenneman. In 1957 the congregation had 74 members, with L. L. Rassi serving as pastor.

R.McB.

Nassau, until 1866 an independent duchy of Germany, area 1,830 sq. mi., later a part of Hesse. As at the close of the Thirty Years' War Mennonites fleeing from Switzerland had been welcomed to rebuild the devastated land of the Palatinate (*q.v.*), so one hundred years later they were invited by Nassau to leave the Palatinate and settle in Nassau to raise the productivity of the few fertile sections. The Palatine Mennonites had been conspicuously successful in raising the agricultural level by means of new methods of farming and the use of fertilizers (Correll, 110, 115, 120 f.).

In 1710 the Duchess of Nassau still refused to receive Mennonite refugees from Switzerland, claiming that she was well provided with farmers (Müller, 289). But later regents welcomed farmers who understood the newer methods of agriculture and cattle raising. The Dutch *Naamlijst* of the years 1766-1802 names Bäntz Jungerich (Güngerich) as the elder of the Swiss Mennonites in Nassau-Siegen; the issue of 1793 names Peter Schanz as the elder of the congregation in Nassau-Weilburg. The great famine of 1770-72 became the occasion of the invitation given Palatine Mennonites to settle in Nassau. In the late 1770's several families from the region of Heidelberg and Mannheim rented estates in the vicinity of Wiesbaden and Usingen, where there was much wasteland. A leader among these Mennonites was Valentin Dahlem (*q.v.*), to whom Baron von Kruse, the head of the government, gave his estate near Wiesbaden in hereditary lease. After the increase in size of the country in 1803 and 1806 the Mennonites were assigned to the task of teaching the peasants. Very soon the ministers of state reported that the Mennonites were a good example to the people, that the cultivation of clover was improving the soil, that more land could be put under profitable cultivation, and that the cattle industry was thriving (*Menn. Bl.,* 1895, 19).

The Mennonites in southern Nassau organized a congregation in 1790 with its seat in Wiesbaden. Valentin Dahlem was chosen preacher, who lived at first at Mosbach and later on the Koppensteinerhof near Wiesbaden. In 1830 the congregation was composed of fourteen families. Dahlem's influence extended beyond his immediate congregation. He is the author of the first formulary of the South German Mennonites, which was used in the congregations of the Palatinate and Hesse until 1852 and of Baden until 1876.

While the Wiesbaden congregation was coming into being, an Amish settlement was made in the northern and eastern parts of the country. Their members lived scattered over eight districts: Braubach, Dillenburg, Eltville, Idstein, Montabaur, Rennerod, Runkel, and St. Goarshausen. They held their services in the various homes of the members. About 1830 this congregation had a membership of 130 souls in 17 families (*Menn. Bl.,* 1896, 36). The family names represented there were Bender, Ehrismann, Hochstätter, Nafziger, Quetsch, Schanz, Schlabach, Spring, Stähly, and Unzicker (*Menn. Bl.,* 1896, 15 and 22). On May 21, 1867, the Amish preachers and elders in Hesse, the Palatinate, Rhenish Prussia, and Nassau met on the Offental estate to change their church regulations. They decided to let each member decide what position he would take on footwashing, nonresistance, and mixed marriages (*Menn. Bl.,* 1867, 38-40). A part of this congregation emigrated to America, and the others lived so widely scattered that the congregation was dissolved. In 1881 its membership had declined to twenty-five. (See also **Hesse-Nassau.**)　　　　Hege.

Ernst Correll, *Das schweizerische Täufermennonitentum* (Tübingen, 1923); Müller, *Berner Täufer*; C. Spielmann, "Die Mennoniten und ihre Bedeutung für die

Kultur in Nassau," in *Annalen des Vereins für nassauische Altertumskunde und Geschichtsforschung* XXVI (1894), reprinted in *Menn. Bl.,* 1895, 19-21, 27-29, 36 f.; W. Wittgen, "Die Mennoniten in Nassau, ihre Bedeutung für die Landwirtschaft," in "Die Landwirtschaft" *Blätter für Landwirtschaft, Weinbau und Genossenschaftswesen* (Wiesbaden, 1917) No. 17; J. Mannhardt, *Verzeichnis* (1881); *ML* III, 200 f.

Natalyevskaya, a volost in the Alexandrovsk district, Ekaterinoslav province, Ukraine, which had three Mennonite villages: Andreasfeld (Andrepol), Neuschönwiese (Dmitrovka), and Eugenfeld (Yakovlevo).

National Association of Evangelicals (N.A.E.), founded in 1944 as a conservative counterpart to the National Council of the Churches of Christ in America, representing some 3,000,000 American Christians belonging largely to the smaller, strictly orthodox evangelical denominations in the United States, the moderate wing of the Fundamentalist movement. From the beginning the Mennonite Brethren, the Evangelical Mennonites, and the Brethren in Christ have been denominational members. The N.A.E. has a series of subsidiary and affiliated organizations, to which its denominational members may or may not belong, as they individually decide.　　　　H.S.B.

J. D. Murch, *Co-operation without Compromise, a History of the National Association of Evangelicals* (Grand Rapids, 1956).

National Mental Health Foundation, Inc., established in May 1946, represented a layman's movement toward an improved, representative, and democratic mental health program, especially through stimulating research and providing information regarding the causes and prevention of mental afflictions and the needs and care of the mentally ill. The Mennonite Central Committee joined with the American Friends Service Committee and the Brethren Service Commission in helping to finance its operations. Orie O. Miller served on its Board of Directors until it dissolved, and various Mennonites filled key staff positions. On Sept. 13, 1950, it was merged with the National Committee for Mental Hygiene and the American Psychiatric Foundation into the National Association for Mental Health. It owed its origin largely to the stimulus provided by CPS men of Mennonite, Brethren, and Quaker connection, who had worked in mental hospitals and as a consequence got a vision of the need for a better type of care for the mentally ill.　　　　W.T.S.

National Service Board for Religious Objectors (NSBRO), a voluntary association of religious organizations, which acted and is still acting as spokesman for the churches and conscientious objectors to the Selective Service System in matters regarding the administration of the draft of conscientious objectors, was created on Nov. 26, 1940, as a merger of the short-lived National Council for Religious Objectors with the Civilian Service Board. The NCRO had been established on Oct. 11, 1940, by joint action of the Mennonite Central Committee, the American Friends Service Committee, and the Brethren Service Committee. The NSBRO Board of Directors was composed of seven members, representative of the above three groups and the Fellowship of Reconciliation, the Commission on World Peace of the Methodist Church, the Disciples of Christ, and—from 1942—Walter van Kirk of the Department of International Justice and Goodwill of the Federal Council of Churches of Christ in America. The Fellowship of Reconciliation in 1944 withdrew its membership to become only a consultative member, and in 1946 the Friends ceased to be active, ultimately withdrawing their membership. From 1946 on, the NSBRO was largely in the control of the Mennonites and Brethren. To enable other interested groups to share in the work of the NSBRO the Consultative Council was created by the Board of Directors on April 16, 1941. Ultimately 39 groups, largely denominational bodies, joined this council.

The function of the NSBRO was to serve as the liaison between the churches and other groups having conscientious objectors to military service among their members. Although it did not administer any Civilian Public Service (q.v.) projects or camps, it performed a very valuable service. It was not the sole channel to the National Selective Service office for those groups who administered CPS, since they could and did on occasion deal directly with Selective Service, but it nevertheless carried most of the liaison work. For this purpose it was organized into the following sections: Camp Section, Complaint Section, and Assignment Section. The Camp Section worked in connection with the selection of sites for CPS camps; the Complaint Section helped men who were not properly classified or were denied their claim to conscientious objector status; the Assignment Section was the channel for transmitting the assignment to the proper CPS camp for the CO's who were being drafted.

The NSBRO official publication is the *Reporter,* first issued as a monthly magazine in July 1942, then as a semimonthly from November 1942 to February 1946, and thereafter irregularly, usually as a 4-page journal 8½ x 11½ inches. Other mimeographed publications were the *Camp Directors' Bulletin,* which had reached issue No. 180 by June 1946, and the directors' *General Letter* to all CPS men, which was issued 164 times between December 1942 and August 1946. There were also numerous other bulletins and memoranda.

The first officers of the NSBRO Board of Directors were M. R. Zigler, chairman; Orie O. Miller, vice-chairman; Paul J. Furnas, treasurer; and Paul Comly French, executive secretary and director. French served until 1946.. During most of this time J. N. Weaver, a Mennonite, was in charge of the Assignment Section. Additional members of the Board in the early days were Arthur L. Swift, Jr., Charles F. Boss, Jr., Walter W. van Kirk, and James A. Crain. With the transfer of M. R. Zigler to Geneva, Switzerland, in 1952, Orie O. Miller became the chairman and Harold Row, of the Brethren, vice-chairman. Ora M. Huston served for a time as executive director after Paul C. French's withdrawal in 1946. He was succeeded by A. Stauffer Curry, and he in turn by Leroy Doty, all of the Brethren. The headquarters of the NSBRO has always been in Washington, D.C.

The work of the NSBRO was much reduced after the discontinuance of the CPS camp system, but the resumption of the draft of CO's in 1950 made its continuance very desirable. It continues to play a vital role as the liaison with the National Selective Service headquarters in Washington.

The budget of the NSBRO was supplied by regular appropriations from the three Historic Peace Church service agencies, by contributions from members of the Consultative Council, and by general contributions solicited by the NSBRO office, which for some years had the valued service of Leroy Dakin for this purpose.   H.S.B.

Melvin Gingerich, *Service for Peace* (Akron, 1949); *Conscientious Objection,* 2 vv. (Selective Service System, 1950).

Naubinway (Mich.) Mennonite Church (MC), located at the northern tip of Lake Michigan in the Upper Peninsula, is sponsored by the Indiana-Michigan District Mission Board. Work was begun there in 1943 by Clarence Troyer from a neighboring mission station. In 1946 Ora C. Wyse and family came from Midland, Mich., to carry on the work. Already some are in mission work in other fields and two are preparing for medical work. In 1947 an old Presbyterian church was bought, remodeled, and repaired with the help of a service unit and others. The membership in 1956 was 12, with O. C. Wyse as pastor.   O.C.W.

Nauk, Martin (Marthin von Nockh, also Martin von Neck), of Deutschnofen in southern Tirol, Austria, an Anabaptist martyr, one of the Anabaptist leaders of Neumarkt (q.v.) in the Adige Valley. In November 1529 the authorities seized Wolfgang Stroel (Strölen) and his wife and Nauk's wife; Nauk escaped. This was reported to Ferdinand, who replied with two decrees, Nov. 27 and Dec. 9, 1529, that Stroel and his wife were to be taken to the criminal court, which would be held by the judge of Kaltern. Nauk's wife was to be spared until the birth of her child. Since the cross-examination of the Stroels revealed that they had been baptized by Michael Kneusser (Kürsner?), search should be made for him as the "principal" and also for the fugitive leaders Wolfgang of Moos and Martin Nauk of Deutschnofen. Nauk must have fallen into the hands of his pursuers in January 1530, for the Innsbruck authorities ordered that Martin Nauk and Benedikt Gamper (Campner, the former priest?) of Breitenberg should be examined further on some specified articles of faith. The report of the questioning stated that the two men were leaders and were said to have misled many people. They died as martyrs in Neumarkt.   P.De.

Zieglschmid, *Chronik,* 74 f.; *Mart. Mir.* D does not list Nauk, E 435 f.; *ML* III, 201.

Naumenko Mennonite Brethren Church, a subsidiary of the Einlage M.B. Church (q.v.), in the Naumenko (Petrovka) Mennonite settlement, province of Kharkov, South Russia, was founded in 1889 by emigrants from the Molotschna and Chortitza settlements who had settled on private land at Petrovka, Vassilyevka, Elenovka, and Barvenkovo. Gerhard Siemens of Neplyuevo was the leading minister. Later the ministers Abraham Pätkau and Johann

Schellenberg of Yazykovo also served here. In 1905 the settlement had a population of 700 Mennonites, most of whom were members of this church.

At first the Naumenko M.B. Church seemed to flourish, especially economically, but soon suffered a serious reverse. Wilhelm Dyck, who later moved to Canada, David Klassen, Abram Martens, and Jacob Thiessen served the church until 1910. At this time Abr. Unruh of the Orloff Zentralschule and Jacob Froese, both living at Barvenkovo, also ministering to the church after 1910, extended their ministry to the Russian people and were as a result arrested and imprisoned, but were released in about one month. The M.B. Conference that was to be held at Naumenko at this time was forbidden by Russian authorities, and when the permission finally came from St. Petersburg it was too late.

Nothing definite seems to be known about this church after World War II and little about its fate during and after the Revolution. Some members left the settlement during the great westward move in World War II. (Friesen, *Brüderschaft*, 450; *ML* III, 201.) P.H.B.

Naville, van de (van den Navyle, Naevijle, van den Avyle, Aville), a Mennonite family of French Flemish descent, in the 17th and 18th centuries found in the Dutch congregations of Aardenburg (*DB* 1877, 11; Jan van den Navyle was a deacon here 1657-79), Cadzand, Vlissingen, and Middelburg. Most of them were farmers. This family is apparently not related to the French Flemish de Neufville (*q.v.*) family. vDZ.

F. K. van Lennep, *Verzameling van Oorkonden betrekking hebbend op het geschlacht Van Eeghen in Nederland* (Amsterdam, 1918) see Index.

Nazarene is the name of a Christian denomination founded about 1840 in Hungary, whose adherents also called themselves "Disciples of Christ" and "Believers in Christ." The origin of the name Nazarenes can no longer be ascertained. Although the first men of the group were John Denkel and John Kropatchek, who were converted and baptized by Fröhlich in Zürich in the summer of 1839, Louis Hencsey can be considered as the real founder of this religious movement. He was baptized May 8, 1840, at Hauptwyl, canton of Thurgau, Switzerland. What he received here by way of religious life he proclaimed with fiery zeal in his native Hungary, and soon won numerous adherents. When he died in 1844 his brother and other gifted men like Joseph Bela and Stephan Kalmar continued his work. Kalmar founded the most influential Nazarene congregation in Pacser. The Nazarene group is identical with the Apostolic Christian Church (*q.v.*). It has no connection with the Church of the Nazarene in the United States.

The Nazarene doctrine is simple. The Bible is their only and absolute norm of religious knowledge. The reading of the Scriptures is considered an unquestioned duty; fulfilling its commands is the way of salvation. The principal command is to bear the cross for Christ's sake, and to practice self-denial and love. Absolute nonresistance, patient bearing of all insults, rejection of military service and the oath, and abstention from cursing, are among their principles. They baptize by immersion after the age of 18 years. The offices of the church consist of bishops, who draw no salary but depend entirely on voluntary offerings, evangelists, presbyters, teachers, singers, managers whose duty is to take care of the material aspects of church life, secretaries, and deacons who have charge of the care of the poor. On all of these points they are very close to the Mennonites. Direct contacts can, however, not be shown.

In 1848-78 the Nazarenes suffered severe persecution in Hungary. Since 1895 they have been tolerated in principle, although they were never granted exemption from military service and their young men were constantly sent to prison. Strife within the brotherhood led to its decline. In 1935 they numbered about 25,000 members. Their chief location was formerly near Szegedin in South Hungary, but they were also found in Transylvania, Austria, Jugoslavia, and Rumania. A few came to the United States locating in Ohio. Bela himself came to America in 1850. Information concerning their status in 1956 was not available. NEFF, H.S.B.

G. Schwalm, in *Jahrbücher für protestantische Theologie* (1890); *DB* 1891, 67; 1904, 160 ff.; *Menn. Bl.*, 1903, 55, where interesting letters are mentioned; Hermann Ruegger, Sr., *Apostolic Christian Church History* I (Chicago, 1949), which is the English edition of his *Die Evangelisch Taufgesinnten* (Zürich, 1948); *Nazarenes in Jugoslavia* (Syracuse, 1928), which is the English edition of a booklet prepared by C. Stäubli of Pfäffikon-Zürich in March 1928, telling of the persecution of the Nazarenes in Jugoslavia in 1924-28 because of their refusal to accept military service; *ML* III, 201.

Nebraska, admitted to the Union as the 37th state in 1867. "Nebraska" is the Otoe Indian name for the Platte River, and means "flat water." It was first used by the French explorer Bourgmont in 1714. It was applied to the Platte watershed by John C. Freemont in 1841, and later to the state. It is near the center of the Great Plains region of North America, the eastern border formed by the Missouri River. Its dominant surface characteristic is its undulating prairie. The mean altitude is approximately 2,500 feet above sea level. The population of the state was 1,371,000 in 1952; its area is 77,227 sq. miles. It is predominantly a rural state; it has only 36 towns with more than 2,500. The chief natural resource is the rich soil of the loess region, a triangular area of approximately 42,000 square miles extending over the southeastern half of the state. The climate is characterized by rather light rainfall, low humidity, severe winters, hot summers, frequent changes in the weather, and considerable variation in rainfall and temperature from year to year. The average annual rainfall varies from 34 inches in the southeast to 16 inches in the west. Omaha (pop. 251,117) is Nebraska's principal trading center, with livestock market receipts from more than twenty states. Other important trading centers are Lincoln (state capital, pop. 100,000), Grand Island, Hastings, Scottsbluff, North Platte, Norfolk, Fremont, and Beatrice.

The first Mennonites to settle in Nebraska were a group of three Amish Mennonite families (MC) who came from the East and settled west of Milford in April 1873. In August 1874, 28 immigrant families from Russia under the leadership of Peter

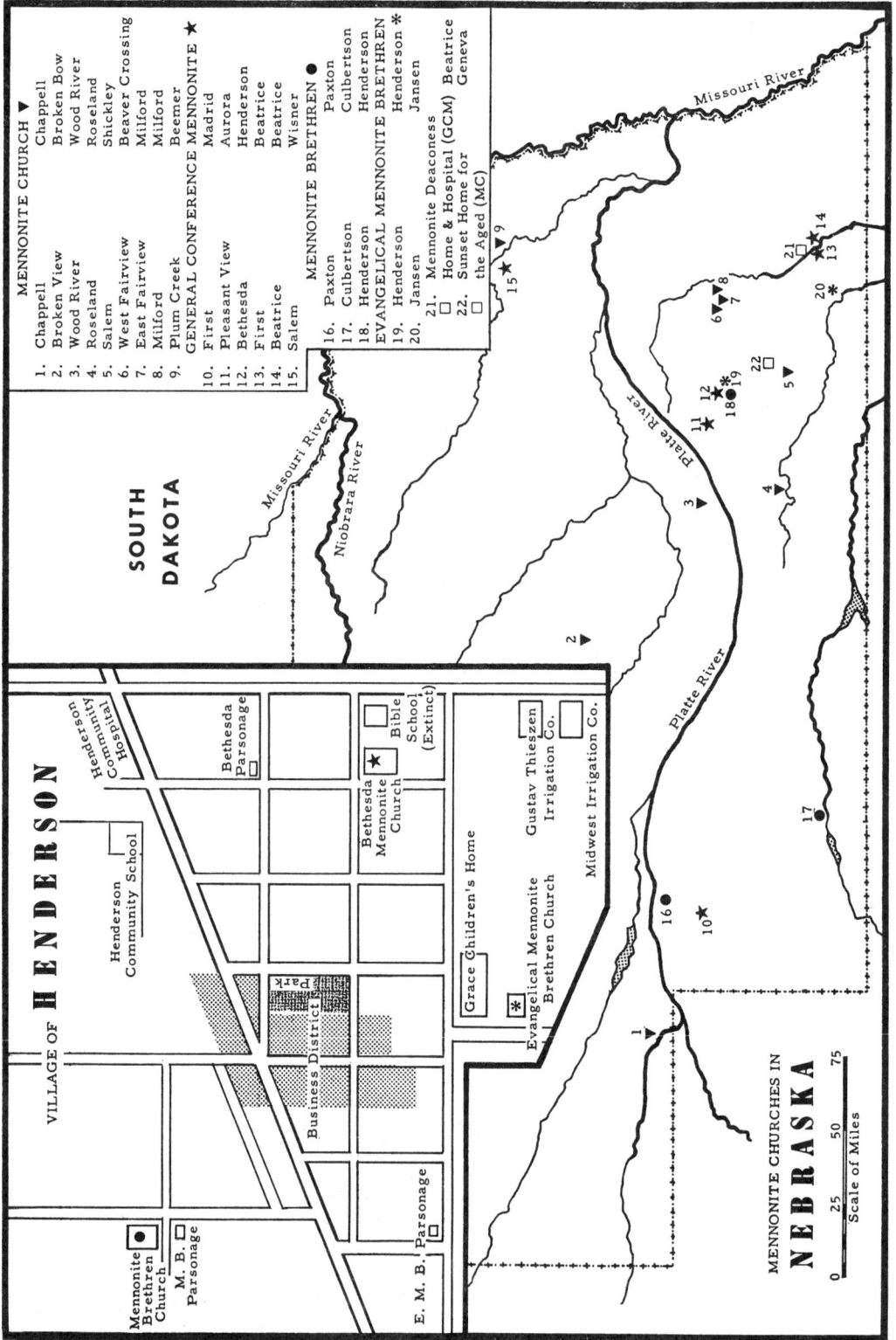

MENNONITE CHURCH ▼

1. Chappell — Chappell
2. Broken View — Broken Bow
3. Wood River — Wood River
4. Roseland — Roseland
5. Salem — Shickley
6. West Fairview — Beaver Crossing
7. East Fairview — Milford
8. Milford — Milford
9. Plum Creek — Beemer

GENERAL CONFERENCE MENNONITE ★

10. First — Madrid
11. Pleasant View — Aurora
12. Bethesda — Henderson
13. First — Beatrice
14. Beatrice — Beatrice
15. Salem — Wisner

MENNONITE BRETHREN ●

16. Paxton — Paxton
17. Culbertson — Culbertson
18. Henderson — Henderson

EVANGELICAL MENNONITE BRETHREN ✳

19. Henderson — Henderson ✳
20. Jansen — Jansen

21. Mennonite Deaconess □
    Home & Hospital (GCM) — Beatrice
22. Sunset Home for □
    the Aged (MC) — Geneva

SOUTH DAKOTA

Missouri River

Niobrara River

Platte River

Missouri River

VILLAGE OF **HENDERSON**

Henderson Community Hospital

Henderson Community School

Bethesda Parsonage □

Bethesda Mennonite Church ★

Bible School (Extinct) □

Park

Business District

Grace Children's Home □

Evangelical Mennonite Brethren Church ✳

Gustav Thieszen Irrigation Co.

Midwest Irrigation Co.

Mennonite Brethren Church ●

M. B. Parsonage □

E. M. B. Parsonage □

MENNONITE CHURCHES IN
NEBRASKA

Scale of Miles
0   25   50   75

Jansen arrived in Beatrice and in September, under the leadership of Elder Jacob Buller, another group of Russians arrived in Lincoln. From this group 37 families (206 persons) settled in York and Hamilton counties near Henderson. From these three early settlements the largest Mennonite settlements of the state, Milford, Beatrice, and Henderson, have developed. With the exception of the Mennonite Brethren in Christ and Grace Bible Institute, the other present Mennonite congregations over the state have been a part of the expansion programs of these three original settlements.

The United Missionary Church congregations in Nebraska resulted from an evangelistic movement occurring around the turn of the century. Seven congregations have been established, all of which are small or have become extinct. The Grace Bible Institute (*q.v.*) of Omaha was organized in 1943 and serves as an inter-Mennonite school.

The Kleine Gemeinde of Jansen (*q.v.*), founded by 36 families from Russia, became extinct with the removal of the group to Meade, Kan., in 1906-8.

The Mennonite congregations in Nebraska (in 1954 numbering 25 with 3,832 members) with their conference affiliation, location, and membership numbers in 1954 are as follows: E.M.B.—Ebenezer at Henderson (96), EMB Church at Jansen (70), total 166; G.C.M. Northern District Conference—Bethesda at Henderson (1,014), First at Madrid (44), Salem at Wisner (14); G.C.M. Central District Conference—Pleasant View at Aurora (180); G.C.M. Western District Conference—Beatrice at Beatrice (180), First (originally called Wehrlose Mennoniten-Gemeinde) at Beatrice (333), Kilpatrick at Beatrice (extinct); total G.C.M., 1,765; M.C.—Plum Creek at Beemer (137), West Fairview at Beaver Crossing (156), East Fairview at Milford (444), Chappell (63), Wood River (102), Salem at Shickley (257), Roseland (17), Broken View at Broken Bow (42), Milford (196), total M.C., 1,414; M.B.—Culbertson (14), Henderson (274), Paxton (74), total M.B., 362; U.M.C.—Bloomington (extinct), Cambridge (extinct), Franklin (15), Lewellen (30), Milford (30), Weeping Water (50), total U.M.C., 125.

Other Mennonite institutions in the state are (1) Abbott Mennonite Mission (MC), established at Abbott in 1951, sponsored by Wood River Mennonite (MC) Church; (2) Grace Bible Institute (*q.v.*), Omaha; (3) Grace Children's Home, Henderson, sponsored by the E.M.B. Church; (4) Mennonite Hospital at Beatrice, sponsored by the G.C.M. churches of Beatrice; and (5) Sunset Home for the Aged at Geneva, established in 1951, sponsored by the M.C. congregations of eastern Nebraska.

D.P.M.

Theodore Schmidt, *The Mennonites of Nebraska* (Lincoln, 1933); Gustav E. Reimer and G. R. Gaeddert, *Exiled by the Czar. Cornelius Jansen and the Great Mennonite Migration, 1874* (Newton, 1956); W. C. Andreas, "Highlights and Sidelights of the Mennonites in Beatrice," *Menn. Life* I (July 1946) 21; J. J. Friesen, "Remaking a Community, Henderson, Nebraska," *Menn. Life* V (October 1950) 10; Jacob T. Friesen, "A Rural Church—Beatrice, Nebraska," *Menn. Life* VIII (April 1953) 80; D. Paul Miller, "The Story of Jansen, Nebraska," *Menn. Life* IX (October 1954) 173; idem, "The Story of the Jansen Churches," *Menn. Life* X (January 1955) 38; ML III, 201 f.

Nebraska Ansiedler, a four-page monthly, published at Lincoln, Neb., 1878-88, but printed at Elkhart, Ind., as a supplement to the *Herald of Truth* of Elkhart, Ind., particularly in the interests of the Russian Mennonite settlers in Nebraska, but also for circulation among the Mennonite immigrants from Russia to other states. With the stated purpose of giving a Christian interpretation to news, it contained articles on crops, animal husbandry, school affairs, domestic and foreign news, market prices, and other features. It began in June 1878, and ran until April 1880. It was replaced by the *Mennonitische Rundschau*. N.P.S.

Nebraska Conference of the United Missionary Church was organized in 1896 as the third conference of the church. It at first included all the territory west of Indiana, but the Pacific (Washington) Conference was organized from this conference in 1906. In 1955 the conference had 774 baptized members, with 16 ordained ministers and 8 probationers in 20 congregations, and one district superintendent, for an area roughly 2,500 by 900 miles. Congregations were located as follows by states: Nebraska seven, Iowa four, South Dakota three, California two, Kansas one, Colorado one, and Oklahoma one. H.S.B.

Neck, Martin von, an Anabaptist martyr: see **Nauck, Martin.**

Neckties. In reference to changes in the conventions of clothing Mennonites in general have been characterized by two tendencies: (1) resistance to cultural change, even to the point of adding a religious sanction to what was at one time a new form of clothing or a new convention of daily life; (2) the adoption in the long run of what has become generally accepted in society and is no longer regarded as in any sense a new fashion or style. This is illustrated by the history of the necktie in the Mennonite (MC) Church. In the 19th century when the old-style colonial cravat was displaced by more modern forms of the necktie, the Mennonites often clung to the bow tie as more conservative, as being less of a conformity to a worldly style than the four-in-hand or long tie. The tie, however, was universally worn by the Mennonites in the East. About 1890, as a result of the influence of some non-Mennonites in Kansas who advocated a certain type of "holiness," sentiment arose in certain parts of the Mennonite Church (MC) against the wearing of any form of necktie. The editor of the unofficial church organ of the group, John F. Funk, objected vigorously to the new view in the *Herald of Truth* (1891, p. 231), but it had considerable influence in the midwest nevertheless. In one of the largest conferences (Indiana-Michigan, MC) a prohibition of the necktie for ordained men was introduced in the 1920's. In the East, especially in the Lancaster Conference (MC), the tie has never been fully banished, even for ordained men. In the East the bow tie is to some extent the "approved" form of the tie in so far as ties are approved at all, and it is worn by some of the members. In the Amish Mennonite congregations founded in the first half of the 19th century from Alsace-Lorraine, the general practice was for the men to wear the standard lapel sack coat, but no neckties or white stiff collars, the shirt with attached soft collar being used instead. In the final synthesis of the "plain" attire for Mennonite (MC) ministers, which came in the first quarter of the 20th century, the costume became the "plain" or collarless coat with no necktie but a stiff white collar. In many cases in the second quarter of the 20th century the plain or clerical vest was added to this ministerial costume. Recently some preachers are adopting a costume which includes the clerical vest with stiff white collar, but a lapel coat instead of the "plain" or clerical coat. The final product appears much like the standard clerical attire worn by certain Lutheran, Anglican. and Catholic clergymen. Another trend is the dropping of any clerical garb altogether, which results in the wearing of the standard American male costume in the mid-20th century, which is lapel coat, shirt with soft attached collar, with or without necktie.

Many lay Mennonites are not recognizable by the kind of tie they wear, however, and the widespread practice is to wear a four-in-hand tie. In congregations with an Amish Mennonite background many of the older men wear no tie at all, but among the young men of the Old Order Amish in Lancaster County a small black bow tie is commonly worn as a part of the Sunday attire. As to color, among the conservative-minded black is preferred in any kind of tie.   J.C.W.

Nederduytsche Concordantie ofte Harmonie is a Dutch Bible concordance compiled by an unknown Mennonite author, published at Haarlem in 1645. In this remarkable work a large number of "all most instructive and important statements of the Scriptures" are "gathered and placed in alphabetic order."   vDZ.

M. Schagen, *Naamlijst der Doopsgezinde schrijveren* (Amsterdam, 1745) 24.

Nederlandsche Geloofsbelijdenis, official confession of the Dutch Reformed Church, was drawn up about 1561 by Guy de Brez (*q.v.*), following the confession of the French Calvinists, which had been approved by the Synod of Paris in 1559 and presented to Henry II, king of France. On the night of Nov. 1-2, 1561, a copy of the printed confession was thrown into the garden of the regent Margaret of Parma (*q.v.*) at Brussels to inform her about the doctrines of the Dutch Calvinists. This confession was approved by the Synod of Armentières in 1563. The approval given by the Dutch General Reformed Synod at Dordrecht in 1619 made it the official confession of the Reformed Church in the Netherlands.

In this confession de Brez tried to prove that the Calvinists were very different from the Anabaptists or Mennonites. Two articles of the confession deal with the Anabaptists (*Wederdoopers*): Article 34, concerning baptism, states: "We [the Calvinists] reject the error of the Anabaptists . . . who reject the baptism of the children of believers"; Article 36, dealing with the office of the magistrates, concludes, "For this reason [i.e., because the public authorities are of God] we reject the Anabaptists and all other revolutionary people, and in general

all those who reject the authorities and magistracy, who wish to overthrow the administration of justice and to introduce community of property, who throw into disorder modesty, which God has established among men."

Though it is clear that this judgment on the Anabaptists-Mennonites is untrue, the confession has never been changed or corrected, still being generally accepted by the Reformed Church.   vDZ.

Nederlandse Protestantenbond (Dutch Protestant Union), an association of liberal Christians founded in 1870, in which Mennonites, Lutherans, Reformed, and other Christians co-operate for the promotion of liberal Christianity. The Protestantenbond now has about 20,000 members and 108 local chapters. The chapters, spread all over the Netherlands, function as a kind of Christian community, often with a church and a pastor of their own. These churches are found particularly in towns where there is no Mennonite or Remonstrant congregation and where the Reformed Church is fundamentalist. Originally some leaders of the Protestantenbond hoped for a total union of all Dutch liberal Christians into one single church, but this has proved to be an unrealizable ideal, since the Remonstrants, Reformed, and Mennonites all wished to maintain their own organizations. Mennonites have from the beginning warmly supported the Bond. Among the founders was the Mennonite pastor Gerrit ten Cate (*q.v.*) of Drachten. Many Mennonites, particularly in the Diaspora, are members, and a number of Mennonite pastors also serve in Protestantenbond churches for preaching and catechetical instruction.

In 1882 the Protestantenbond edited a hymnal (5th ed. 1910), in 1919 followed by an appendix. This *Protestantenbond-bundel* was also used in many Mennonite congregations. The first of these to introduce it were Texel in 1885, Middelburg in 1889 and Deventer in 1890. In 1940 it was in use in 80 Mennonite congregations. In 1944 the Protestantenbond together with the Remonstrants and Mennonites published a new hymnal. This hymnbook, augmented with a supplement, is now used in all Mennonite congregations (see **Doopsgezinde Bundel**).   vDZ.

Neef, Barbara, an Anabaptist martyr, died in the canton of Zürich, Switzerland, in 1643 after the birth of a child, in consequence of imprisonment in chains. (*Mart. Mir.* E 1121.)

Neel, Mypeis, an Anabaptist martyr of Rotterdam, Holland, was executed at The Hague on June 8, 1535. Particulars are lacking.   vDZ.

K. Vos, *Geschiedenis van de Doopsgezinde gemeente Rotterdam* (1907, reprint) 6.

Neelken, an Anabaptist martyr, No. 49 in the hymn "Aenhoort Godt, hemelsche Vader" (Hear, O God, heavenly Father), which is hymn No. 16 of the *Lietboecxken van den Offer des Heeren.* In this hymn Neelken is called a "dochter" (daughter), which usually means an unmarried woman. She was executed at Antwerp, Belgium, in 1559. Van Braght (*Mart. Mir.* D 244, E 618) states that she suffered martyrdom with Betgen and Mariken

Fransse. It is not clear which martyr is meant here. Génard believes that she is identical with Neelken Jacobs (q.v.), the wife of Adriaen Pan, executed on June 28, 1559. But in this case the word "dochter" would be rather strange.   vdZ.

Neelken, the wife of Adriaen Pan, an Anabaptist martyr: see **Neelken Jacobs.**

Neelken, the wife of Paulus van Druynen (q.v.), an Anabaptist martyr, was burned at the stake on Sept. 11, 1538, at Vught, Dutch province of North Brabant (DB 1917, 189). Van Braght (Mart. Mir. D 42, E 448) mentions her only incidentally.
                                                                  vdZ.

Neelken (Cornelia) **Clercx,** the wife of Henrick de Timmerman, an Anabaptist martyr, executed on March 16, 1535, at Antwerp, Belgium, by being tied into a sack and drowned. She was charged with the crime of having been rebaptized. (Antw. Arch.-Blad VII, 319, 367; XIV, 14 f., No. 140.)   vdZ.

Neelken Jacobs (Cornelia van Rommerswael), an Anabaptist martyr, drowned on June 28, 1559, at Antwerp, Belgium, after giving birth to a child. Neelken was married to Adriaen Pan (q.v.), who suffered martyrdom in Antwerp on June 18, 1559. They had formerly lived at Nijvele (Nivelles) in Flanders, but moved to Antwerp, where they were arrested. Their furniture was confiscated and publicly sold while they were in prison, even before they were sentenced. Neelken, who like her husband died steadfast, is commemorated in the hymn on Adriaen Pan, "Duysternis gaet van henen, wanneer dat licht coemt aen" (Darkness passes away when the light appears), found in Offer des Heeren. In Offer and following Dutch martyrs' books, including van Braght's Martyrs' Mirror, this martyr is called simply Neelken (Neeltgen).   vdZ.

Offer, 342, note, 346 f.; Mart. Mir. D 244, E 618; Bibliographie II, No. 573; Antw. Arch.-Blad. IX, 3, 9, 16, XIV, 26 f., No. 295; ML III, 204.

Neelken (Nelleken) **Jaspers,** an Anabaptist martyr, erroneously considered Reformed, a girl 17 or 18 years of age, was burned at the stake at Antwerp, Belgium, on June 27, 1570 (not 1571, as in Mart. Mir.), after giving a valiant testimony to her faith. The death sentence states that she was rebaptized and was "persistent in her heresy." Her father Jasper Hermansz (q.v.) and her mother Maeyken Janssens (q.v.) had both been executed as martyrs at Antwerp in 1569, Jasper on June 22, and Maeyken on Nov. 22. While in prison Neelken wrote a letter, dated Dec. 12, 1569, which reveals her firm faith and joy in suffering. She said that she wanted to follow the example of her parents and two youths who had been executed, though they had not yet been baptized. She is commemorated in a hymn composed by an anonymous 16th-century author, entitled "Aen Neelken Jaspers" (n.p., n.d.).
                                                      NEFF, vdZ.

Mart. Mir. D 407, E 762; DB 1899, 91, 108, 121, 139; Antw. Arch.-Blad XIII, 2, 61; XIV, 76 f., No. 853; Catalogus Amst., 100; ML II, 394.

Neeltgen, an Anabaptist martyr, a woman of 75 years, was burned at the stake on Jan. 24, 1570, at Maastricht, Dutch province of Limburg, together with her daughter Trijntgen. They had been arrested on Nov. 24, 1569, and were severely tortured. Neeltgen and Trijntgen belonged to the small Mennonite congregation of Maastricht, of which Arent van Essen (q.v.) and his wife Ursel (Ursula) had suffered martyrdom on Jan. 10, 1570. When Ursel was led to the execution place, Neeltgen had loudly called from the window of the prison, so that all the people gathered to observe the execution could hear: "Dear sister, contend manfully, for the crown of life is prepared for you." Neeltgen herself died also steadfast. The martyrdom of Neeltgen and Trijntgen, and of Arent van Essen and his wife is commemorated in the songs "Anhördt fründe Ersame," "Nun hört jhr Freundt ehrsamen," and "O Mensch, bedenck die kurtze Zeit," found in the old German hymnal, Ein schon gesangbüchlein, of about 1570.
                                                                  vdZ.

Mart. Mir. D 502, E 844; W. Bax, Het Protestantisme in het bisdom Luik II (The Hague, 1941) 306-10; Wolkan, Lieder, 92, 101, 136; Ausbund, 28; ML III, 204.

Neeltje Jans, an Anabaptist martyr, drowned at Leiden, Holland, on Nov. 13, 1554. In the sentence she is said to have associated with heretics, obviously Anabaptist groups; she did not believe in the Catholic doctrine of the Mass, and would have been (re)baptized if there had been an opportunity. Neeltje was sentenced to be burned at the stake if she should persist in her heresy. From the fact that she was drowned it may be inferred that she recanted.   vdZ.

I. M. J. Hoog, "Onze Martelaren," in Kerkhistorisch Archief III (1898) 442 f.

Neff (Neef, Nef, Näff), a Mennonite family name found in Switzerland, South Germany, and North America. The name is of Swiss origin, occurring as early as 1529 (or 1533) in St. Gall, when the citizen Othmar Nef (called Bublerin) was named as an Anabaptist. The Martyrs' Mirror names Barbara Neff (Neef) (q.v.) in the canton of Zürich. The family probably emigrated to the Palatinate at the end of the 17th century, where in 1685 Hans Neff was living at Gundersheim and Heinrich Neff in Ibersheim. Other Mennonites in the Palatinate with this name were Johannes Neff at Mechtersheimerhof in 1738, Oswald Neff at Erbesbüdesheim in 1743, David Neff at Kleinkarlbach, and Michael and Johannes Neff at Kriegsheim, who came from Kleinkarlbach in 1768. The family was no longer named in Erbesbüdesheim after 1768. A Jacob Neff (1676-1743), the son of Oswald, settled in Dürkheim. His grandson Jakob Neff married a daughter of Peter Weber (q.v.) of Hardenburg and emigrated to America, as did in 1840 Johannes Neff (son of Abraham Neff) (1783-1855), married to Magdalena Krehbiel, and many other members of the Neff family in the 18th and 19th centuries. Jakob Neff was listed as a preacher in Conestoga Township in Pennsylvania in 1790.

The best known of the Neff families was the one located at Assenheim, which is very likely related to the above Neffs. The progenitor, Johann Peter Neff,

was born at Erpolzheim in 1717 (the son of Nikolaus Neff?) and came to Assenheim in 1747 through
his marriage with Veronica Resch. He served as
minister of the Erpolzheim congregation 1755-69,
and of the Ruchheim congregation 1769-90 (*Naamlijst*). Johann's son Johannes (1748-1829) was the
founder of the Neff line in Baden, which settled
at Hoffenheim near Sinsheim and from there spread
to Württemberg and Bavaria. He was ordained in
the Mauer-Meckesheim congregation in 1772. Dr.
Hermann Neff (1891-1950), who practiced medicine
in Grünheim, Saxony, was a member of this family.
He published a number of articles in Mennonite
periodicals on ethical and historical problems concerning medicine. Peter, the second son of the progenitor Johannes (1750-1813), a preacher of the
Ruchheim-Assenheim congregation from 1777 and
an elder 1786-*ca.* 96, continued the line in the Palatinate. As elder of the Assenheim congregation he
signed the Ibersheim Resolutions (*q.v.*). A Jakob
Neff was an elder of the Erpolzheim congregation in
1790. Of greatest importance for the Mennonite
brotherhood was Peter's great-grandson Christian
Neff (*q.v.*, 1863-1946), pastor of the Weierhof congregation 1887-1945.

The name Neff is also found in the records of
the Mennonite congregation at Danzig, Prussia, as
early as 1693, but it is an open question whether
this Neff family (the name is also written Newe
or Neue) is related to the Swiss-South German Neff
family.   P.S., vDZ.

Mart. Mir. E. 1121; Paul Peachey, *Die soziale Herkunft der Schweizer Täufer* (Karlsruhe, 1954) 113, No.
101; *Naamlijst* 1776, 52; 1775, 46; 1780, 45; 1793, 46,
56; Fritz Braun, "Nineteenth Century Emigrants from
. . . Friedelsheim," *MQR* XXX (April 1956) 146; Elizabeth Neff, *A Chronicle Regarding Rudolf and Jacob
Näf . . . and Their Descendants* (Cincinnati, 1886); Reimer, *Familiennamen*, 114.

Neff, Christian (1863-1946), an outstanding leader
of the Mennonites of Germany, long-time (1887-
1939 and 1940-43) pastor of the Weierhof, Palatinate,
Mennonite Church, and scholar and Mennonite historian, was born Feb. 18, 1863, on the Hemshof
near Ludwigshafen, one of the six children of Peter
and Barbara Schowalter Neff. He was married on
Dec. 28, 1889, to Babette Lydia Krehbiel of the
Weierhof. One son and three daughters survive the
parents. He attended the elementary school in Ludwigshafen, then the Weierhof school 1874-75, the
Latin School in Ludwigshafen 1875-79, and the
Gymnasium at that place 1879-83. He studied theology at the universities of Erlangen, Berlin, Tübingen, and in the fourth year Erlangen again, being
influenced more particularly by Professors Zahn and
Frank at Erlangen, and Kaftan and Treitschke in
Berlin. He was also influenced strongly by Prof.
Tobias Beck.

On Dec. 11, 1887, Neff was ordained to the ministry in the Weierhof congregation, serving there as
the beloved pastor for almost 55 years, and for much
of this time also as a teacher in the Weierhof school
where he taught religion for many years, but also
for some years German and history. He soon became a widely influential Mennonite leader not only
in South Germany but also in the entire country and

beyond. He was the outstanding leader of the Conference of the South German Mennonites (*q.v.*) organized in 1887, of which he was for 40 years (1903-
43) the chairman. He likewise was for many years
an active leader in the Vereinigung der Mennoniten
im Deutschen Reich (*q.v.*), from 1905 a member of
its board of directors. He was also the initiator and
leader of the Mennonite World Conference (*q.v.*),
and planner of its sessions of 1925 (Basel, Switzerland), 1930 (Danzig, Germany), and 1936 (Amsterdam, Netherlands). From 1892 he was the secretary
of the Palatinate-Hesse Mennonite Ministers' Conference; soon elected its chairman, he served in this
office for decades. He was an active supporter of
foreign missions and from 1913 on was for many
years a member of the Dutch Mennonite Mission
Board. He was the initiator of the Youth Commission of the South German Conference (1919) and
frequent contributor to its monthly journal, the
Mennonitische Jugendwarte (1920-39).

As an able writer, editor, and historian, Christian
Neff was almost constantly in literary production
throughout his active career. He was a member of
the editorial board of the *Christlicher Gemeinde-
kalender* (*q.v.*) from the beginning (1892) and in
virtually every year of its issue contributed major
articles, often of outstanding historical research and
literary quality. He was an associate editor of the
Mennonitische Blätter from 1891 to its end in 1941.
An extraordinary contribution was his numerous
articles in the *Mennonitisches Lexikon,* of which he
was coeditor and publisher, with Christian Hege
(*q.v.*), from 1913 until his death. He was the editor
of the excellent hymnal of the South German Mennonites, *Gesangbuch der Mennoniten* (Ludwigshafen, 1910), and author of three pamphlets in the
series *Schriften der Konferenz der Süddeutschen
Mennoniten;* namely, (1) *Was sind Mennoniten?*
(1913); (2) *Die Mennoniten keine Wiedertäufer*
(1914); (3) *Die Mennoniten keine Baptisten noch
Methodisten* (1914). He was the editor of the reports
of the Mennonite World Conferences of 1925, 1930,
and 1936, and of the book *Gedenkschrift zum 400-
jährigen Jubiläum der Mennoniten* (Ludwigshafen,
1925), for which he wrote a substantial article on
Conrad Grebel. He edited the *Mennonitisches Adress-
buch* (Karlsruhe, 1936). In 1925 he was given the
honorary degree of Doctor of Theology by the University of Zürich, Switzerland, in connection with
the first Mennonite World Conference. In 1913 he
spent several weeks on a visit to the North American Mennonite churches, attending the first All-
Mennonite Convention. A complete bibliography of
his writings is found in *Beiträge zur Geschichte der
Mennoniten* (Weierhof, 1938) 89-96, with a supplement in *Mennonitische Geschichtsblätter* VI (April
1949) 11-13. He died Dec. 30, 1946, and was buried
in the Weierhof Mennonite cemetery.   H.S.B.

Paul Schowalter, "Zum Gedenken an Christian Neff,"
Gesch.-Bl., VI (April 1949) 2-11; *idem,* "Christian Neff,
Ein Lebensbild,"* in *Gem.-Kal.* 1951, 17-39; Cornelius
Krahn, "Christian Neff (1863-1946)," *The Mennonite*
LXII (Jan. 14, 1947) 6 f.

Negri, Francesco (1500-64), of Bassano, Italy, humanist and reformer, by some erroneously called
an Anabaptist because of his temporary support of

the position of Camillo Renato (*q.v.*) on the sacraments at Chiavenna in the 1540's, entered a Benedictine cloister at Padua in 1521. Influenced by Lutheran writings, he fled the monastery in 1525, and in 1529 was in Strasbourg, where he attended the lectures of Capito and Bucer. He visited Venice, Padua, and Brescia in 1530, then returned to Strasbourg. In 1531 when he requested that he be permitted to work for the Reformation in the Italian-speaking parts of Switzerland, Capito recommended him to Zwingli as an able and learned man. He went to Tirano (then under the jurisdiction of the Rhaetian Leagues) as a teacher in 1531, and in 1538 moved to Chiavenna where he taught classical languages. He helped found the evangelical community there, and was on good terms with Bullinger and other Swiss leaders. During this time he wrote a *Catechism* and in 1546 published his *Tragedia del libero arbitrio* in which he bitterly attacked the Catholic Church. Although placed on the Index in 1548, this work was widely read by Italians and went into several later editions. Negri helped many Italian fugitives from the Roman Inquisition to make fresh starts in the Leagues. In 1547 when Camillo Renato became involved in a dispute with Agostino Mainardi, pastor of the church at Chiavenna, Negri sided with the former on the interpretation of the origin of the sacraments (although personalities were also in question) and thereby received the epithet "Anabaptist," which was likewise applied incorrectly to Renato. However, Negri accepted the verdict of a special synod which supported Mainardi's position and in the second edition of the *Libero arbitrio* (1550) included an orthodox confession which contained a specific disavowal of Anabaptism. He had no objection to infant baptism in principle (he had his child baptized in 1548, although there was some difficulty over the precise form to be used). The radical evangelical leader in north Italy, Pietro Manelfi (*q.v.*), reported Negri's presence at the council in Venice in September 1550 where Christological questions were discussed, but there is no other evidence for this. In 1550 Negri published the narratives of the martyrdom of some Italians and in the ensuing years was in contact with the ex-bishop Pierpaolo Vergerio who was wrongly accused of Anabaptism by some contemporaries. By 1556 Negri had settled once again in Tirano but he continued to maintain close contacts with Chiavenna, and in fact undertook a tutoring assignment there in 1560. He visited Poland in 1562 or 1563 and died of the plague at Cracow in 1564.

DeWind.

Bullingers Korrespondenz mit den Graubündnern, ed. T. Schiess, XXIII-XXV of *Quellen zur Schweizer Geschichte* (Basel, 1904-6); F. C. Church, *The Italian Reformers, 1534-1564* (New York, 1932); G. Zonta, "Francesco Negri l'eretico e la sua tragedia 'Il Libero Arbitrio,'" *Giornale storico della letteratura italiana* LXVII (1916) 265-324; *ML* III, 203.

Negro Missions. The first mission among the Negroes in America was begun in 1898 by the Lancaster Mennonites (MC) when they established the Welsh Mountain Industrial Mission for Negroes living in the wooded area at the junction of Lancaster, Chester, and Berks counties called the Welsh Mountain. Noah Mack (*q.v.*) was the superintendent of the mission until 1910. The first convert was baptized in 1917, but a permanent congregation was not established until later. In 1924 the industrial phase of the work was discontinued, but the work has continued as a purely mission program. In 1899 the Krimmer Mennonite Brethren evangelistic mission was opened at Elk Park, N.C., which has been continued to the present. A small number of converts have been organized into several congregations with six Negro ministers. The work has always been in charge of one or more white K.M.B. couples. H. V. Wiebe was the first worker (1899-1907), assisted by J. M. Tschetter (1902-12). P. H. Siemens spent over 25 years (from 1925 on) as an outstanding worker there. In 1955 there was an attendance of 180 at the Sunday morning services.

Negro missions have had extensive development only in the Mennonite Church (MC), which now has at least 27 missions or congregations. In 1933 the Lancaster Colored Mission was established in Lancaster city. Additional missions among colored people have been established by the Lancaster Conference as follows (with date of establishment), all in Pennsylvania unless otherwise indicated: Philadelphia in 1935; Reading 1938; Andrew's Bridge 1938; Mt. Vernon in Oxford 1946; Newlinville near Coatesville 1946; Harrisburg 1951; Steelton 1952; Lincoln University 1954; York 1954; New York City, Harlem, 1954; Edgemont near Harrisburg 1955; West Chester 1955; Tampa, Fla., 1952; and Freemanville, Ala., 1956. These missions were opened to minister to the spiritual needs of a predominantly Negro population; a number of them are conducted on an interracial basis with membership of both races.

Additional missions have been established in other conference districts as follows: Harrisonburg, Va., 1935; Bethel in Chicago, Ill., 1945; Youngstown, Ohio, 1947; Gladstone in Cleveland, Ohio, 1948; Ninth Street in Saginaw, Mich., 1949; Buckeye near Phoenix, Ariz., 1951; Newport News, Va., 1952; St. Anne at Rehoboth, Ill., 1953; East Side in Saginaw, Mich., 1955; Madisonville, La., 1955; Fort Wayne, Ind., 1955. At least five additional Negro missions have been established in various places, which are no longer operated at least as Mennonite (MC) missions, among them Los Angeles, Cal., 1940, and Rocky Ridge near Souderton, Pa., 1931. The Rocky Ridge Mennonite (MC) Church has continued as an interracial church with a few Negroes among its 89 members in 1956. From this congregation came the first Negro minister in the Mennonite Church, James Lark, who was ordained at Chicago in 1946, and made bishop there in 1954 (discontinued his bishop office in 1956). He is at present the only ordained Negro minister in the Mennonite Church (MC); although there is an elected deacon at the Ninth Street Church in Saginaw. The four rapidly growing young churches at Saginaw, Cleveland, Chicago, and Youngstown have co-operated as a group in various ways with considerable sharing of ideas.

In 1951 there were 385 Negro members in 29 different predominantly Negro Mennonite (MC) congregations. In 1957 the number was more than 500. The first record of Negro members in the

Mennonite Church (MC) was in 1896 when Bishop Jacob N. Brubacher baptized a few colored people in Juniata County, Pa., as the result of the revival movement in this area inaugurated by J. S. Coffman, M. S. Steiner, and A. D. Wenger. There is an earlier, as yet unverified, report of Negro members in the small Lancaster Conference congregation at Marietta, Pa., about 1800.

No regular missions among the Negroes have been established by any other Mennonite group in North America. However, the General Conference Board of Missions (GCM) on Jan. 1, 1957, took over Camp Landon at Gulfport, Miss., as a Voluntary Service community project, which had been established in 1946 as a CPS project and administered by the MCC until 1957. It works exclusively among Negroes.   H.S.B.

Robert Stoltzfus, "Mennonite Mission Work Among the American Negro" (1953) and Vern L. Miller, "Negro Evangelism" (1951, seminar papers in GCL); Leroy Bechler, "Facts, Considerations, and Membership of Negroes in the Mennonite (MC) Church, 1955" (unpublished paper).

Neiss (Neuss), **Andreas von,** an Anabaptist martyr: see **Andreas von Neiss.**

NEK (*Natuur en kunst;* English, Nature and Art), a Dutch Mennonite student association, which was formed out of the student association E.T.E.B.O.N. (*q.v.*) at Amsterdam on Nov. 17, 1838, by A. Winkler Prins (*q.v.*) together with D. Harting, P. Leendertz Wzn, H. C. C. Dronrijp Uges, and J. G. de Hoop Scheffer, and continued until Aug. 8, 1849, having held about 100 meetings during this time. It admitted 17 members only, and had as its main purpose the writing of humorous or satirical verse. The members came from the universities of Amsterdam, Leiden, and Utrecht, among them the later noted authors J. J. L. ten Kate and J. Kerbert, also H. Kretzer and A. Winkler Prins. The literary periodical *Braga* was founded by members of the group (first number Dec. 1, 1842), but had only a short life in spite of its high quality.   K.V.

A. Winkler Prins, *Feestavonden van de Studentenvereeniging NEK;* H. A. Lunshof, *Leven zonder demon* (Amsterdam, 1950) 50-63; *ML* III, 203.

Nelleken, an Anabaptist martyr: see **Neelken Jaspers.**

Nellis, Johannes, apparently from the Lower Rhine, Germany, author of an Anabaptist hymn that bears his name in acrostic form: "Ich weiss eine Jungfrau reine." (Wolkan, *Lieder,* 100; *ML* III, 204.)

Nembsche (Nemtschan, Niemtscha; Czech, *Nemcany*), a village near Austerlitz (*q.v.*). Under John, Baron of Kaunitz (*q.v.*), the Hutterian Brethren settled there in 1560. Not much is known of this Bruderhof. In 1570 the poet Christoph Hueter or Schiffmann died there. At Easter of 1600 the Bruderhof was abandoned by the Brethren "on account of the many taxes and burdens of the military men which they could not carry." (Beck, *Geschichts-Bücher;* Wolkan, *Geschicht-Buch;* Zieglschmid, *Chronik;* ML III, 252.)   P.DE.

Nem(b)schitz (Niemtschitz; Czech, *Nemcice*), the name of eleven villages in different parts of Moravia,

three of which are mentioned in the Hutterian chronicles:

(1) Gross-Niemtschitz, on the left bank of the Schwarza between Nikolsburg (*q.v.*) and Nusslau (*q.v.*). To this place the "Stäbler" (*q.v.*) came from Nikolsburg in 1529. From here they sent four messengers to the barons of Kaunitz at Austerlitz (*q.v.*) with a petition for admission, which was granted them. The trial of the miller Nikolaus Geyersbühler (*q.v.*) shows that there were Anabaptists there at a later period. "Although he could neither read nor write and was not a leader or preacher, he was sent by the brotherhood to his old home to bring Anabaptists to Moravia." He was beheaded at Innsbruck in 1566/7.

(2) Klein-Niemtschitz in the domain of Panowitz, in which Anabaptists had settled at Gurdau (*q.v.*), Rackvitz, and Seitz, had a Hutterite Bruderhof, date of founding unknown, which was abandoned in 1559; the chronicles say that the Brethren were driven out and moved to Pellerditz (*q.v.*); they opened a Bruderhof in that year under the Baron of Wickow.

(3) Klein-Nembschitz near Pralitz (in the chronicles usually called "Nembschitz bei Präles"; see **Klein-Nembschitz**), on the road from Brno to Znaim in the Kaunitz domain on the left bank of the Iglawa, noted for its fruit and vineyards. Baron Siegmund von Zastrizel gave the Brethren a Bruderhof here in 1562 with several gardens and a mill. This Bruderhof prospered and soon became one of the most important in the country. In 1564 three men were confirmed in the ministry: Klaus Braidl (*q.v.*), a shoemaker, later head of the entire brotherhood, Valentin Hörl, and Hans Langenbach; and Leonhard Dax (*q.v.*), who was well known on account of his long imprisonment in Alzey, was chosen to the ministry. Here Leonhard Lanzenstiel (*q.v.*), the head of the entire Moravian brotherhood, died in 1565.

An important institution of this Bruderhof (3) was Peter Walpot's school. Here he published on Nov. 15, 1568, his famous address to the teachers which shows evidence of pedagogical skill. To the "sisters in the cotton rooms" Paul Glock (*q.v.*) addressed his eighth letter written in prison in Württemberg in 1569. The skill of the craftsmen of the Bruderhof is proved by the order given in 1569 by the wealthy nobleman Albrecht von Boskowitz and Tchernahora for a fountain and water conduit to be connected with the city water system in the guilding of his new town house, at the price of sixty florins and five measures of wheat (copy of the letter in the private archives of the Prince of Liechtenstein in Vienna.) In 1606 Niemtschitz suffered severe arbitrary violence at the hands of armies on route to Hungary. Great offense was caused among the Brethren in 1610, when the bishop Georg Riedel had to be deposed because he neglected the duties of his office for experiments in alchemy.

This settlement was especially hard pressed in the Moravian uprising. After the inhuman treatment of the Pribitz Brethren at the hands of the Polish troops of the imperial army, the Brethren fled with their neighbors to Pausram. The terrible distress of the Brethren, who were subjected to all sorts of mistreatment, is related in the *Geschicht-Buch*. On Dec. 28, 1620, soldiers broke into the abandoned house and plundered it completely, "and burned the best buildings. What the soldiery did not find in the earth, the baron of Kaunitz, who should have protected the Brethren, had his men dig up and take away, so that they lost everything at once."

On Jan. 3, 1621, two men who had ventured back to the ravaged house were cut down by soldiers. Nevertheless the Brethren began again in March to live there and to build; then soldiers came again and robbed them, and raped two sisters. Again the Brethren began anew, and then some troops of the Brno garrison broke in on July 15, "plundered everything and took away thirty-five loads of booty, grain and all that they found."

After the suppression of the rebellion Niemtschitz fell to Cardinal Dietrichstein (*q.v.*), who had this Bruderhof as well as those in Nikolsburg (*q.v.*) and Tracht (*q.v.*) completely plundered even before the general expulsion of the Anabaptists. P.DE.

Beck, *Geschichts-Bücher;* Zieglschmid, *Chronik;* Loserth, *Communismus;* Wolkan, *Geschicht-Buch; ML* III, 252 f.

Nen, a Mennonite family at Zaandam, Holland, of which a number of members have served the Mennonite congregation. Jacob Jansz Nen, a lumber merchant, was in the early 18th century a reader in the West Zaandam Nieuwe Huys congregation, while his son Klaas Jacobsz Nen (1701-55) was a preacher of this congregation from 1726 and an elder from 1730 until his death. His colleague Adriaen Loosjes preached his funeral sermon, *De gezegende Naagedachtenis des Rechtvaardigen,* published in 1755 at West Zaandam. Neeltje Jans Nen (d. 1796 at Zaandam) was a deaconess of the same congregation and contributed to the church its silver communion service. vDZ.

S. Lootsma, *Het Nieuwe Huys* (Zaandam, 1937) 57 f., 67, 80, 109, 186.

Nepluyevka (Nepluyevo), a Mennonite settlement located in the province of Ekaterinoslav, Ukraine, Russia, established in 1870, consisted of two villages, Steinau (Starozavodskaya), and Blumenfeld (Kisslitchevatoye), consisting of 10,800 acres. The land was owned by the nobleman Nepluyev and the settlers came from the Chortitza Mennonite settlement. The villages were located 10 miles from the city of Nikolaipol on the Dnieper River. (*ML* III, 204.) C.K.

Nepluyevka (Nepluyevo, Nikopol) Mennonite Brethren Church, about 8 miles from the city of Nikopol in the volost of Tchortomlek, Ekaterinoslav province, Russia, was first known as the Steinau Mennonite Brethren Church; the Russian name was adopted about 1897 by order of the Russian government. Peter Wiebe, Isaac Töws, Peter Löwen, Jacob Siemens, and Jacob Friesen were among the first settlers who came from the Chortitza settlement to this fertile area in 1870, and settled in two villages, Steinau and Blumenfeld. They organized the congregation about 1885, and in 1907 built their first

meetinghouse of brick, with a seating capacity of over 500. The membership, which did not exceed 100, consisted mostly of farmers who used High German in their services, but Low German in the homes. The church functioned under the elder of the Einlage M.B. Church, Aron Lepp, and later was led by Heinrich Friesen, Isaak Töws, Gerhard Siemens, and Peter Wiebe, with Johann Löwen as the choir director. This church experienced a great revival in the winter of 1906-7, and also in the winter of 1911-12. In 1907 Heinrich Friesen, one of their leading men, began extension work among the Russians in the surrounding villages, and thus a Russian evangelical church came into being, which bought the M.B. church building in 1918 and used the material to build two churches for themselves. Much of the land under cultivation was only rented to the Mennonites and this weakened the stability of the settlement. A number had already moved away before World War I; and afer the Revolution of 1918, especially during the severe Bolshevist persecution, the membership scattered, some moving to Siberia, others to Steinfeld, Friedensfeld, and other places, and the church ceased to exist about 1932. (*ML* III, 204.) J.J.T.

Nepluyevka (Nepluyevo) Mennonite Church formed a unit with the neighboring Borozenko Mennonite Church (*q.v.*). In 1906 the two villages of the Nepluyevka settlement had a membership of 106, while together with Borozenko they had a membership of 442 and a total population of 1,036. Ministers who served the Borozenko-Nepluyevka Mennonite Church were Isaak Ens (ordained 1889), Cornelius Penner (1889), Peter Friesen (1893), Jacob Block (1895), Johann Funk (1900), Franz Penner (1900), Abr. Olfert (1902), Martin Hamm (1902), Heinrich Klassen (1902), Heinrich Sawatzky (1906). Worship services were conducted in various schools. There is no later information available. (Dirks, *Statistik,* 1905, 7, 61; Friesen, *Brüderschaft,* 701.) C.K.

Nerdaenus: see **Antonides, Henricus.**

Nes in East Friesland, Germany. In 1551-56 Leenaert Bouwens baptized five or eight persons here, who may have joined the Emderland (*q.v.*) congregation. vDZ.

Nes, one of the three Mennonite churches on Ameland (*q.v.*), a Dutch island in the North Sea; it is smaller than the Hollum (*q.v.*) congregation and larger than Ballum (*q.v.*), the other congregations on the island. Leenaert Bouwens (*q.v.*), who visited Ameland eight times, baptized only three in Nes, and those on his first journey, between 1551 and 1554. The Nes congregation belonged to a more lenient wing than the other two, and was therefore less interested in the stern Bouwens. In the division of 1557 between the stricter Flemish and Frisians on one hand and the more lenient Waterlanders on the other, the Nes congregation sided with the Waterlanders. In the 18th century this Waterlander congregation belonged to the Humsterland Sociëteit (see **Groninger Doopsgezinde Sociëteit**). In 1599

Jan Jacobs (*q.v.*) of Harlingen, who favored a stricter application of the ban, won some adherents at Nes, most of whom belonged to the Flemish group, but now turned to the Jan Jacobs faction. For some unknown reason another division occurred in Nes probably about the middle of the 17th century, which led to the founding of the Foppe Ones or Laus Ooms (*q.v.*) congregation. In 1804 the Foppe Ones and Jan Jacobsz congregations united. In 1854 a union was formed with the Waterlanders, the resulting congregation being called the Ameland Mennonite Church. It included the Mennonites of Hollum and Ballum and was served by two preachers, one of whom had to live in Nes. In 1883 the Ameland congregation was divided into two independent congregations, viz., Hollum-Ballum and Nes. From that time until 1930 Nes had its own preacher, G. E. Frerichs, serving from 1878 in the Ameland congregation, and 1883-84 only in Nes. Then the pulpit was vacant until it was filled by J. B. du Bury 1895-1902, Menno Huizinga, Jr., 1902-8, W. Leendertz 1909-22, Miss M. T. Gerritsma 1923-26, and J. A. P. Bijl 1926-30. After a vacancy of three years Nes united with Hollum and Ballum for ministerial services. Nes had a membership of 84 in 1898, 40 in 1956. The church used is still the "Blue Barn" of the Waterlander group. An organ was installed in 1896.   J.W.S.

K. S. Gorter, "Uit de vroegere geschiedenis der Doopsgezinde gemeenten op Ameland," in *DB* 1889, 1-50; 1890, 1-30; 1897, 250; *ML* III, 204.

Nespitzer (Nospitzer), **Georg**, a citizen of Passau, Bavaria, Germany, therefore also called Jörg of Passau, b. at Stadtlauringen near Schweinfurt, a weaver by trade, was baptized at Easter 1527 by Hans Hut (*q.v.*) and became like him a successful Anabaptist preacher. After he became acquainted with the large Anabaptist congregation at Nikolsburg (*q.v.*), he stayed briefly in Strasbourg, and then went to Augsburg (*q.v.*), where he participated in the Martyrs' Synod (*q.v.*) and was sent out as a missionary to Franconia. Upon the suggestion of Hans Hut and Hans Denk (*q.v.*) he was made leader of the Augsburg congregation. Under his brief but active leadership in the spring of 1528 the congregation, some of whose first leaders were languishing in prison, increased in strength. His work also took him out to the surrounding communities; he held services at Göggingen near St. Radegundis, in Wellenburg near St. Severin, in the valleys of the Lech and Wertach, and baptized a number of new members, most of whom were soon seized and imprisoned or expelled from the city.

Nespitzer again and again urged his hearers to repent. Great distress would come upon the Brethren, "which would begin at Easter." When news of executions came, he comforted the brotherhood. "Now you see that persecution is setting in against the house of God. Be of good cheer. Indeed, the Lord will not tarry long, He will come to our aid." After the time of tribulation the time of the establishment of the kingdom would begin.

The poverty that overtook the refugee Brethren in Augsburg Nespitzer sought to ease by appointing deacons; these were Georg Schachner of Munich,

Augustin Bader (*q.v.*), and two who later died as martyrs, Hans Leupold (*q.v.*) and Bernhard Zurgkendorfer of Göppingen.

Persecution at other places became more severe. Nespitzer's brother-in-law Eucharius Binder (*q.v.*) was surprised at a meeting with 36 Brethren in Salzburg on Oct. 27, 1527, and was burned to death with them in the building. At the Easter service in Augsburg in 1528, which was led by Nespitzer and Hans Leupold, the city council had all those participating arrested (43 men and 45 women). Leupold was beheaded on April 25, 1528, and Nespitzer and the others from outside the city were expelled; he preached for a time in Franconia and then went to Strasbourg in 1529, where he was seized. In the face of the persecution before him he rendered the required recantation and lived in seclusion in Leutershausen near Ansbach (Wappler, 36), leading a God-fearing life, as the mayor and council of the city reported (*TA*, 196). When it was discovered that he had once belonged to the Anabaptists he was arrested but released upon public confession in the church and an oath of loyalty (*TA*, 197).

Two epistles from Nespitzer's hand have been preserved (*TA*, 168 f., and Wappler, 306 f.), in which he urged an earnest, penitent life.   HEGE.

Fr. Roth, *Augsburger Reformationsgeschichte* (2d ed., 1904); *idem*, "Zur Geschichte der Wiedertäufer in Oberschwaben," *Ztscht des Hist. Vereins für Schwaben und Neuburg*, 1901, 8; *TA Bayern* I; Wappler, *Thüringen*; Wiswedel, *Bilder* II, 48-51; *ML* III, 204 f.

Nesselbach Mennonite Church, a congregation in northern Württemberg, near Crailsheim, Germany, belonging to the Verband (*q.v.*). It was founded about 1890. It has always been small in size, having 20 baptized members in 1956. Its present elderpastor is Jakob Glück. Services are held on the first Sunday of each month in rotation in Nesselbach, Klumpenhof, and Erkenbrechtshausen.   H.S.B.

Nestler, Hermann (b. 1879), teacher at the Gymnasium in Regensburg, Bavaria, Germany, and superintendent of education in Passau, author of the meritorious book, *Die Täuferbewegung in Regensburg; Ein Ausschnitt aus der Regensburger Reformationsgeschichte* (Regensburg, 1926). This book relates in detail the rise of the Anabaptist movement in Regensburg (*q.v.*) and its suppression. The numerous court records of Anabaptist trials (82 in number) in the Regensburg city archives are especially valuable; they are given verbatim. (*ML* III, 205.)   NEFF.

Netherlands. The term Netherlands is here used as it existed geographically and politically in 1957, i.e., without Belgium (*q.v.*), but including Limburg (*q.v.*), which in the 16th century belonged to Jülich (*q.v.*), and also including IJssel Lake and other coastal inlets. This area, covering 15,765 square miles in 1950, had a population of 9,625,499.

In the history and life of the Netherlands the Anabaptist-Mennonites have occupied an important place, in the first place by their numbers. Originally they comprised a large segment of the population of the provinces of North Holland, Friesland, and Groningen. In Friesland it has been estimated that

Mennonite congregations in the

NETHERLANDS

- Congregations
- ★ Brotherhood Houses
- □ Children's Homes
- ○ Larger towns
- † Old People's Homes

(See also maps of Provinces of Friesland, Groningen, and North Holland.)

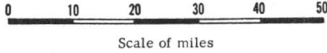

0   10   20   30   40   50

Scale of miles

1   Giekerk
2   Veenwouden
3   Zwaagwesteinde
4   Warga
5   Poppingawier
6   Terhorne
7   Akkrum
8   Oldeboorn
9   Tjalleberd
10 Woudsend

11 Koog†Zaandyk
12 Wormer-Jisp
13 Middelie
14 Westzaan
15 Purmerend
16 Den Ilp
17 Landsmeer
18 Monnikendam
19 Knollendam
20 Krommenie
21 De Rijp

NORTH SEA

IJSSEL LAKE

NORTH HOLLAND

FRIESLAND

GRONINGEN

DRENTE

OVERIJSSEL

GELDERLAND

UTRECHT

SOUTH HOLLAND

ZEELAND

NORTH BRABANT

LIMBURG

GERMANY

BELGIUM

Rhine

JUIST
BORKUM
ROTTUM
SCHIERMONNIKOOG
AMELAND
Hollum   Nes
Ballum
TERSCHELLING
Terschelling
VLIELAND
TEXEL
Emden

Uithuizen
Ternaard   Mensingeweer   Bijldijk
Holwerd   Middelstum
Blija   Dantumawoude   Oldehove   Loppersum
Oude Biltzijl   Leermens
StAnnaparochie   Kollum   Noordhorn
Berlikum   Grijpskerk   Den horn   Groningen †
Franeker †Leeuwarden   (Pieterszijl)   Noordbroek
Witveen   Surhuisterveen   Roden   Sappemeer   Winschoten
Harlingen   Baard   Rottevalle   Veendam   Oude Pekela
Pingjum-Witmarsum   Ylens   Grouw   Drachten   Nieuwe Pekela
Oosterend   Makkum   Sneek   Irnsum   Ureterp   Assen   Stadskanaal
Waal   Bolsward   Lippenhuizen
Den Burg   Workum   IJlst   Joure   Gorredijk   Bovenknijpe
Den Horn   Hindeloopen   Koudum   Heerenveen   Wolvega
Den Helder   Stavoren   Warns   Fredeshiem   Emmen
Hypolitushoef   Balk   Steenwijk   Samen Een   Hoogeveen
Zijpe   N.   Medemblik   Giethoorn   Kraggehuis
s.   Twisk   Blokzijl   Meppel
Barsingerhorn   Nieuwe Niedorp   Enkhuizen   Zwartsluis
Schoorl ★   Noordoostpolder   ALMELO
Broek op Langendijk   Hoorn   Kampen   Zwolle   Borne
Alkmaar   N.Einde v. Graft   Hengelo
Heilo   Graftdijk   Enschede   Gronau
Castricum   Graft   Beemster
Wormerveer   21 12   13   Edam   Zutphen   Colmschale
Beverwijk   14 19 16   Deventer
IJmuiden   17   18   Elspeet   Apeldoorn   Winterswijk
Haarlem   Zaandam   Nieuwendam   Doetinchem (Kr.)
Hoofddorp   AMSTERDAM   Arnhem
Aalsmeer   (Seminary)   Naarden-Bussum   Doorwerth
Hilversum   Baarn   Wageningen
Leiden †   Amersfoort
THE HAGUE   Bilthoven ★   †Schaerweyde
Voorburg-Rijswijk   Utrecht   Zelst ★ †Heerewegen
Gouda   Oud-Wulven   UTRECHT   Tiel
Delft   Gorkum   Nijmegen
ROTTERDAM
Ouddorp   Dordrecht
'sHertogenbos
Vught
Breda   Eindhoven   Krefeld
Middelburg   Goes
Vlissingen
Aardenburg   Antwerp
Cologne
Brussels   Heerlen
Maastricht   Aachen
Liége

they composed one fourth of the entire population. But their importance lay also in their participation in the culture of the Netherlands. Many of Holland's most famous poets and painters, e.g., Carel van Mander, Joost van den Vondel, van der Goes, Lambert Jacobsz, Ruysdael, Jacob and Adriaen Backer, van Mierevelt, father and son van Hoogstraten, were Mennonites. Distinguished scholars in all areas of knowledge, businessmen of note, and top bankers were produced by the Mennonites. After 1795 there were also Mennonites in high official positions. Some of these were cabinet ministers, one of whom was C. Lely, who laid the plans for the reclamation of the Zuiderzee, and others were governors of the Dutch East Indies or mayors of the large cities, as Amsterdam, The Hague, and Haarlem.

But there is still another reason for the importance of the Mennonites in the Netherlands. Whereas in other parts of Europe they were either completely wiped out or after severe persecution reduced to a small percentage of the population, in the Netherlands the Anabaptists, after the first half century of persecution, were permitted to develop in comparative peace and live in accord with their type of faith, their undogmatic Christianity, which was true to the Gospel but without binding formulations and was especially strong in its practical aspects.

I. THE RISE OF ANABAPTISM (1530-56)

1. *The Early Leaders of Anabaptism.* It was slightly later than in Switzerland, Germany, Tirol, and Moravia, that Anabaptism appeared in the Netherlands. In 1530 Jan Volkertsz Trypmaker (*q.v.*) brought baptism upon confession of faith from Emden to the Netherlands. He had there come in contact with Melchior Hofmann (*q.v.*), a chiliast and Anabaptist Reformer, who had shortly before united with the Anabaptists in Strasbourg. In Friesland as well as in Amsterdam Trypmaker's sermons enjoyed a large following, while elsewhere, as in South Limburg, baptism upon confession of faith found entry into a small circle of friends of the Reformation. The movement spread with great speed; for at that early date there was already evident a growing spirit "of unecclesiastical independence and Biblical renewal of life, which can be best characterized as the Anabaptist spirit" (Kühler).

The fruits could mature here so quickly because the soil was ready for the movement. Even before 1530 there were in the Netherlands many friends of the Reformation, which had developed especially from the circles of the Devotio Moderna and their acquaintance with the Bible. It was in these circles that the preaching of Trypmaker and others was to crystallize baptism upon confession of faith as an external symbol into an Anabaptist church or brotherhood. Many of these congregations must have reached a large membership within a few months. Men like Obbe Philips (*q.v.*), who was the leader of a large congregation at Leeuwarden (*q.v.*) in Friesland, and Jacob van Campen (*q.v.*), who died as a martyr at Amsterdam in 1535, were a strong support. An eager expectation of the imminent kingdom of God prevailed. Hofmann's visits in the Netherlands (1531, 1532) and his writings had further strengthened these expectations. Those who

were converted were baptized (the ceremony was simply the expression of the personal connection with God), and then patiently awaited the coming of the kingdom, living true to the evangelical demands of nonvengeance, nonswearing of oaths, uprightness, and love of one's neighbor.

2. *Persecutions.* The imperial government at Brussels, and Charles V (*q.v.*) most of all, viewed the increasing decline of Catholicism and the growth of the Anabaptist movement with deep disfavor. Various proclamations were issued, beginning in 1521, against the spread of the Reformation. The proclamation of June 10, 1535, opposed the Anabaptists exclusively. It was of extreme severity and announced that anyone who refused to recant, who had rebaptized others, or who claimed to be a prophet, apostle, or bishop, would be sentenced to death by fire; any who were rebaptized but recanted, or who harbored Anabaptists, would be sentenced to death by beheading, or in case of women, by drowning. This threat was repeated through provincial and local authorities. The Frisian Stadholder in 1534 commanded by means of proclamations that "the damned sect of the Anabaptists" be exterminated. Thus the government insisted on severe persecution; nevertheless the authorities of the cities and provinces were reluctant to obey, and sabotaged the supreme commands, often because they were benevolently disposed to the Anabaptists as if they themselves had been members of the group.

But in the long run the Anabaptists met with severity, especially in the imperial crown lands, the provinces of Holland, Zeeland, and in the southern Netherlands. (During this time the emperor acquired all the provinces of the Netherlands: Friesland in 1524, Utrecht 1527, Overijssel 1528, Groningen 1536, Drenthe 1537, Gelderland 1543.) In the recently acquired areas the persecution was in general less severe; Groningen had only one Anabaptist martyr.

The severity reached its height, even the lesser authorities now co-operating, when the Münster episode of violence occurred and Jan van Leyden, who obtained the upper hand in the government of the "new Zion" in 1534, began to make himself felt in the Netherlands. On the whole, it may be said that the Dutch Anabaptists turned away from these horrors. A meeting of thirty-two Anabaptist leaders held at Spaarndam, near Haarlem, at the end of 1534 or early in 1535, for the most part repudiated all violence. Obbe Philips had broken completely with the violent element by 1534. But many Anabaptists, incited by interminable persecution, weary of passively waiting for the kingdom of God, lent an ear to the commands of the sly seducer to come to Münster, or fell into the trap of his criminal emissary Jan van Geelen (*q.v.*). Then when there were riots even in the Netherlands, i.e., the seizure of the Oldeklooster (*q.v.*) by a troop of revolutionary Anabaptists (March 30, 1535) and the attack on the city hall of Amsterdam (May 10, 1535), and other acts of violence here and there, the mania of persecution knew no bounds. Revolutionary and peaceful Anabaptists were lumped together into one class, although the authorities knew very well that there was a great difference between them, and that the latter had no other desire than to avoid all violence and in faithfulness to the Gospel to await the coming of the Lord. Men and women fared like Jan Pauw (*q.v.*), who said his heart did not testify to him to defend himself with a knife (beheaded March 6, 1535).

On June 25, 1535, Münster fell; Jan van Leyden's wicked role as king was finished, his unholy influence on the movement in the Netherlands ended. But for several years the revolutionary followers of Jan van Batenburg (*q.v.*) made the country unsafe and brought ill fame upon the peaceable Anabaptists, who would have nothing to do with him.

The persecutions continued to claim many martyrs. It has never been possible to determine their exact number. Kühler's estimate of about 1,500 is too low; 2,500 is probably more nearly correct. In the northern Netherlands Reytse Aysesz (*q.v.*) was the last to lay down his life for his faith. He was executed at Leeuwarden on April 23, 1574. In the South the last martyr was executed at Brussels in 1597. (See **Anneken vanden Hove**.)

3. *Organization of the Congregations.* At places Anabaptism was completely rooted out; e.g., at Maastricht and in the entire province of Limburg; elsewhere the movement persisted, and in these congregations a firm organization and church discipline arose concerning preaching, baptism, and the Lord's Supper. Of great importance was the fearlessness of the elders, who in almost complete disregard of danger—they were, of course, most sought after by the police—traveled about the country to preach and to serve with baptism and communion. Obbe Philips had been baptized by Bartel (Bartholomëus) Boeckbinder (*q.v.*). In 1534-36, the period of great difficulty, he had powerfully opposed all violence and ordained both his brother Dirk Philips (*q.v.*) and Menno Simons (*q.v.*) as elders. Although he grew discontented and withdrew from the brotherhood as early as 1540, his work must be remembered with gratitude. Other men took his place, especially Menno Simons, who had left the Catholic priesthood in January 1536, and after a period of quiet study of the Bible began in 1539, both by word of mouth and in writing, his task as the leader of the Dutch Anabaptists. In December 1542 a price was set on his head, in consequence of which he had to live outside the country. He stayed successively in East Friesland, the Rhineland, Wismar, and in his last years at Wüstenfelde, near Oldesloe. Dirk Philips also lived outside the Netherlands, at Danzig. But both of these elders made frequent journeys for longer or shorter periods to the Netherlands, and in addition strengthened the believers through writing. Menno died in 1561, Dirk in 1568. Other elders continued their work. The most influential of these was Leenaert Bouwens (*q.v.*), elder from 1553, who with great zeal promoted the spread and strengthening of the brotherhood, and whose baptismal lists still bear witness of his indefatigable work; he baptized over 10,000 persons in 1551-82.

Thus the brotherhood seemed to be facing a promising and great future; the severe persecution did not prevent its spread; the Münsterite danger was past. David Joris (*q.v.*), ordained as elder by Obbe

Philips in 1535, but motivated by ambition rather than love for the Gospel, arrived at the doctrine that it is possible to conform to the world. He was opposed by Menno (1539 ff.) by means of the principles of the Gospel and finally sought refuge in Basel (1544), but continued contacts with his followers in the Netherlands.

4. *Differences Within the Congregations.* Even though dangers from without had subsided, quarrels arose within the very circle of the brotherhood. In 1547 Adam Pastor (*q.v.*), an elder, was excommunicated on account of deviating views on the Trinity. On this occasion Dirk Philips and Menno Simons assumed the authority to ban, which properly belonged to the brotherhood. This was a basic alteration that became more and more incisive: Is the first authority the individual or the congregation? Finally the great conflict in Menno's life came, which had its basis in this question. Here a disparity of views among the Anabaptists became evident, which had actually existed from the very beginning and is still noticeable among the Dutch Mennonites. Whereas some experienced faith as a personal and inner relationship with God, considered baptism as a personal union between their conscience and God, knew nothing of dominant position either of the congregation or of the elders, wanted to make only a lenient use of the ban, and were disinclined to any formulating of the faith because they feared that the word of man might acquire more respect and power than the Word of God (in general the Spiritualist position), others held fast to the concept of the visible church as a church without spot or wrinkle, in which every individual subjected himself to the common brotherhood, recognized and desired the authority of the elders who would govern the congregation and apply the ban strictly against the unworthy and unbelieving, and demanded a firm system of doctrine expressed in a confession of faith, which to be sure never acquired complete authority as in other churches but was nevertheless of great authority and a means of separating the worthy from the unworthy. The latter party was in the majority.

II. THE PERIOD 1557-1664

5. *Ban and Avoidance.* In 1556 the strife flared up. Menno, who had at first taken a very moderate course in the application of the ban, now adopted a stricter course in compliance with the wishes of Dirk Philips and especially of Leenaert Bouwens. The section of the brotherhood that opposed them, the moderate wing, withdrew and were called Franekeraars (*q.v.*) or Scheedemakers (after their elder Jacob Jansz Scheedemaker, *q.v.*), but were most generally called Waterlanders (*q.v.*) because they had a large following in Waterland of North Holland. Fortunately the strife did not reach the point of banning one another, but the cleavage that had been revealed was not easy to bridge over.

6. *Separation from the German Congregations.* Division also arose between the Dutch and the German elders. Besides Menno's strict views of the ban (*q.v.*), his doctrine of the Incarnation (*q.v.*) of Christ was the cause of a division which was completed at a large conference of German Anabaptists

at Strasbourg in 1557. This was the beginning of the divisions in the brotherhood, which was still suffering persecution, one such division following upon the other, so that an opponent could speak with a measure of correctness of a "Babel of Anabaptists."

7. *Rise of the Waterlanders.* The Waterlanders quietly built up their brotherhood, in which there was no place for dominating elders; they soon achieved a regulated, organized congregational life and an arrangement for mutual assistance in preaching. Excellent men served their congregations: Hans de Ries (*q.v.*), Cornelis Anslo (*q.v.*), Anthony Roscius (*q.v.*), etc. Most of the Waterlander congregations were in the province of North Holland, but they had some congregations in other areas, some as far away as Belgium. They were the more progressive of the Anabaptists, but not liberal in the 19th-century sense of Modernism. They held to a strictly Biblical concept of preaching and faith, and among them was found a deep mystical conception of Christ. They were liberal in the sense that they were less conservative than the other wings, less firmly bound to tradition in clothing and church government. They were also peaceable toward the Frisians (*q.v.*) and Flemish (*q.v.*) as well as to the Remonstrants (*q.v.*), Collegiants (*q.v.*), and even the Catholics. Strange to say, it was these liberal Waterlanders who formulated the first confession of faith (1577), which was, however, by no means to be a binding rule of faith. The liberality in the lines drawn in this confession is significant. They recognized as true members of the church of Jesus Christ all men on earth who had achieved a renewal of the inner man through the power of God through faith. These Waterlanders called themselves Doopsgezinden, not Mennonites. They did not want to be named after a man.

8. *Division Between Frisians and Flemish.* Ten years after the first division a second one arose among the Dutch Mennonites (1567). Again Franeker was the scene of the conflict. Here as elsewhere a number of Flemish had settled to escape severe oppression in Flanders. The difference in their manner of life, customs, and habits led to conflicts between them and the Frisians. A number of minor personal differences of opinion and increasing opposition between the two most powerful elders, Dirk Philips and Leenaert Bouwens, the former on the side of the Flemish and the latter on the side of the Frisians, were factors in the impasse reached when Jan Willemsz (*q.v.*) and Lubbert Gerritsz (*q.v.*), who had been called as outside mediators (*buitenmannen, q.v.*) to settle the dispute, could not achieve more than a compromise. No lasting results were achieved, and the rupture broke open again. The Frisians and the Flemish banned each other in 1567. Later attempts at reconciliation such as the Peace of Humsterland (*q.v.*) of 1574 were a complete failure.

But this was not the end of divisions. Twenty years later there was a third flare-up in Franeker. Among the Flemish were Thomas Byntgens and his followers (*Huiskopers*), opposed to Jacob Keest (*Contra-Huiskopers*). At the bottom of this dispute

about the purchase of a house lay a deeper conflict between the more conservative and the more moderate elements. Attempts to preserve unity failed, and soon the Flemish were divided into two camps. Not only in Franeker, but everywhere, even among the Mennonites who were not of Flemish origin, there were the Huiskopers (*q.v.*), usually called Old Flemish, and Contra-Huiskopers (*q.v.*), usually called Flemish or "Soft" Flemish.

The Old Flemish, the more conservative, banned from their midst the Vermeulensvolk (*q.v.*) or Bankrottiers (*q.v.*) in 1593, and soon afterward the Borstentasters (*q.v.*), who, however, soon returned or dissolved. Here and there small groups split off from the Old Flemish, but these also soon reunited with the larger group or died out.

In 1628 and the following years the Groningen Old Flemish divided from the (Soft) Flemish (in 1637 there was another division among the Groningen Old Flemish) on the grounds that the latter permitted mixed marriages and were lax in their application of the ban and avoidance. The Groningen Old Flemish were extremely conservative in clothing and home furnishings. They long practiced footwashing. Most of their following was in the province of Groningen and they were a closely knit brotherhood. Men like Jan Luies (*q.v.*) and Uko Walles (*q.v.,* who was banished by the government on account of his peculiar views on Judas, and upon his return banished again in 1644) had great influence among them. The Danzig Old Flemish (*q.v.*) were just as conservative as the Groningen Old Flemish, but differed from them in the practice of footwashing in that only elders and visitors from a distance took part.

Nor did the Frisians avoid divisions. In 1598 in Friesland Jan Jacobsz (*q.v.*) of Harlingen and Pieter Jeltjes (*q.v.*) of Kollum were involved in a dispute. Jan Jacobsz, who was very strict, had acquired a considerable following, and the Jan-Jacobsgezinden soon had a number of congregations in Friesland as well as elsewhere, e.g., at Hoorn and Amsterdam. Their last congregation, on Ameland, united with the other local congregations in 1855.

9. *Attempts to Unify.* The continuing separations were certainly not favorable to the welfare of the brotherhood. Some, who believed that the church of God could not exist where there were so many divisions, turned their backs to the brotherhood. Others, of all parties except the extreme Old Flemish and Old Frisians, insisted upon reunion. As early as 1591 most of Young Frisians and High Germans united. Before the merger an agreement was drawn up known as the Concept of Cologne (*q.v.*). Soon, especially upon the insistence of Hans de Ries, many Waterlanders joined the union, which became known as the Satisfied Brotherhood (see **Bevredigde Broederschap**). A new spirit arose among the Mennonites. To be sure a request of the Satisfied in 1603 to the Frisians and Flemish to merge had no success; on the contrary, about 1613 a large number of Young Frisians and High Germans separated from the Satisfied Brotherhood (see **Afgedeelden**) under the leadership of Leenaerdt Clock (*q.v.*); but the wish for unity had after all made itself felt.

About 1610 the Frisian and Flemish congregations in Harlingen united. Also in 1626 four preachers of the Flemish congregation in Amsterdam sent their confession, the Olijftacxken (Olive Branch), as an overture of peace to "the dear brethren, ministers, and elders of the congregations in Groningen, Friesland, Overijssel, Utrecht, Haarlem, and Zeeland." In 1630 an agreement was actually reached between the Flemish on one side and the United Frisians and High Germans on the other. The United Frisians and High Germans had also drawn up a confession for this purpose, named after Jan Cents. This beginning of an agreement led in 1639 to a complete unification of the two branches. The *Olijftacxken* was also very successful. In 1632 most of the Old Flemish united with the Flemish, on the basis of the Confession of Adriaen Cornelis (*q.v.*), also called the Dordrecht Confession because the conference had been held at Dordrecht. There were still remaining apart the group of the Old Frisians and several congregations of the Old Flemish; likewise the Groningen and Danzig Old Flemish pursued their former course; the others had now found their way to each other.

Only the Waterlanders were still standing to one side, for no fault of their own. Although their great leader Hans de Ries died in 1638 his spirit remained among them, which constantly worked in the direction of unification. In 1626 the Flemish had not offered their *Olive Branch* to the Waterlanders, perhaps because the differences were too great. There were indeed deep differences between them. The Flemish were more dogmatic and the Waterlanders not at all so; their confessions stressed faith much more than theology. The Waterlanders, who wanted to be bound only to the Holy Scriptures, viewed with concern the authoritarian position of the *Olijftacxken*. In addition there were differences in church regulations. The Waterlanders observed communion seated around a table, the Flemish while at their seats. Nevertheless the Waterlanders in their conference of 1647 decided to offer Christian peace to the others. The Flemish reply, which was not given until 1649, was negative: if the Waterlanders really wanted peace they would have to begin to adapt themselves in life and teaching to the other Mennonites. Thus the general unification remained a pious wish.

10. *Lamists and Zonists.* Soon a new division was to rock the brotherhood. It occurred in the same church, bij 't Lam, at Amsterdam where on April 26, 1639, the reunification of the Frisian and Flemish was so joyfully celebrated, and where two of the preachers in 1664 were Galenus Abrahamsz de Haan (*q.v.*) and Samuel Apostool (*q v.*). The latter was a man of the old type in whom there was still something of the idea that the Mennonite Church was the only true church, and who devoted all his preaching activity to the strengthening of this idea and insisted on a fixed confession. Galenus, on the other hand, in consequence of his association with the Collegiants and his leading role in peace meetings, was more liberal and warned against attaching too much value to the visible church. Both had a following. After much conflict mockingly called the "Lammerenkrijgh" (War of the Lambs)

a schism occurred in 1664. Apostool with 500 members moved into a new meetinghouse, called "de Zon" (the Sun); Galenus with his following stayed "bij 't Lam." And so the more liberal Lamists stood opposed to the more conservative Zonists. This opposition was not confined to Amsterdam; the schism reached all of the Netherlands. And even if the quarrel had lost the violence of the former days, nevertheless any opportunity to achieve unity was destroyed for two centuries. The old partisan designations "Frisian" and "Flemish" disappeared in this new quarrel. Several remnants of the Old Frisians or Old Flemish remained by themselves, but gradually either united with the Zonists or disappeared. But most of the Waterlanders soon united with the Lamists, in Amsterdam already in 1668, and in many places soon afterward. From now on two types of Mennonites were referred to, viz., the Fijne (Fine) Mennisten (Groningen and Danzig Old Flemish, Janjacobsgezinden, etc.) and the Groove (Coarse) Mennisten (Lamists, Zonists, and Waterlanders). Thus the period of 1557-1664 was a time of division, approach, and new division.

11. *Attempts by the State Church to Suppress the Mennonites in Spite of General Toleration.* Many changes took place in the mutual relationships between church and state and also in the internal organization of the Dutch Mennonite church. At the beginning of this period bloody persecution still dominated. This ended with the coming of the Eighty Years' War (the war of liberation from Spain 1568-1648) and the rise of Calvinism in the Netherlands. To be sure there were among the Calvinists some who wished to continue the previous proceedings against the Anabaptists; but William of Orange (*q.v.*), who was becoming a more and more powerful leader in the revolt against Spain, emphatically opposed them; he wanted toleration. When the Mennonites at Middelburg had difficulties with the authorities established by the Calvinistic preachers, he defended them and secured for them release from the oath and military service. The Union of Utrecht (1579) designated that no one was to be persecuted for his faith. But the Reformed, as the followers of Calvin's doctrine called themselves in the Netherlands, and especially their preachers, tried with all the means at their disposal to interfere with the liberty of the Mennonites to confess their faith freely. In the first place came a long series of violent polemics against the Mennonites, to which the Mennonites replied in writing. But also the synods, especially the provincial ones, sometimes demanded severe measures against the Anabaptists, for which however they usually found no hearing. Looking through their fingers the magistrates tolerated the Anabaptists and saw to it that Calvinistic intolerance would not oppress "our best citizens." On several occasions the building of a Mennonite church was temporarily prevented, as at Franeker in 1611, at Haarlem in 1626, and at Leeuwarden in 1631. The frequent interference of the Reformed preachers in the worship services of the Mennonites was odious, but their attempts to convert the Mennonites failed. Several times the Mennonites had religious disputations with the Reformed clergy, such as the debate by Peter van Coelen with Ruardus Acronius at Leeuwarden in

1596. But these debates were soon abandoned, since the authorities regarded them with disfavor and a number of times forbade them.

Difficulties with the government on the oath and military duty occurred repeatedly, even after the intervention of Prince William in Middelburg, whereas Prince Maurice followed his father's attitude. But these differences did not lead to oppression. The Anabaptists generally obtained the rights of citizenship, substituting a vow "by manly truth" for the oath.

The release from the bearing of arms was obtained by paying a fee or a poll tax and fulfilling their obligation to the government in special services, such as providing food, extinguishing fires, and digging trenches. There was also some difficulty with regard to marriage. Mennonite marriages were usually concluded before the secular authorities, after the bans had been published three times in a Reformed service. Here and there rules were passed excluding Mennonite children from inheritance, but very likely these severe rulings were only laxly enforced.

Gradually the attitude of the government to the Anabaptists changed. This change has been recorded in two resolutions: in 1583 the "Closer Union" of Utrecht states that the Reformed religion is to be maintained and perfected in the United provinces, "without permitting public instruction . . . for several other religions in the presently united provinces." On the basis of this regulation the Reformed preachers considered it their right to annoy the Mennonites and to prejudice the government against them. The regulation passed in 1651 even designated that "the sects and religious parties" which were excluded from the public protection and are merely tolerated were to hold their services in all quietness, and only in the places where they had previously held their meetings. Both of these resolutions were occasionally seized upon by the Reformed Church to annoy the Mennonite congregations, as happened at Sneek in 1601, but on the whole the Mennonites were able to live and worship relatively undisturbed.

Now the motive of the Reformed in interfering was a different one: the charge that many heresies were being taught among the Mennonites, such as "the horrible error of Socinus" (*q.v.*). Actually the Mennonites, never having been theologians, were not always immune to the Socinian opposition to the doctrine of the Trinity, the Satisfaction of the Atonement, and other questions.

12. *Participation in the Civil Life of the State.* Although the attitude of the government toward the Mennonites had changed (however, the stain of Münster still clung to them in the eyes of the state), the attitude of the Mennonites to the state also underwent a profound change. Good friends of the fatherland, thankful for the ground upon which they lived and for the protection they received —this they had always wanted to be, even when their principles forbade active participation in the conflict with national enemies. Already in 1574 a large sum of money was presented to Prince William in his military camp at Roermond in the name of the Mennonites. In 1666 and again in 1672 the Mennonites raised large loans which made it possible for the state to carry on its war with four foes.

In Friesland in 1666, 50,000 guilders was raised, in 1672 again 400,000 guilders, and in 1673 again a significant sum was raised. This assistance more than anything else added to the appreciation for the Mennonites by the state and the public.

Much earlier than this the Mennonites of the Netherlands had been aware of a task in this world. When their expectation of the coming kingdom was not fulfilled, their attention gradually shifted more to this world. An appreciation of the national community, the state, culture, and art, arose, first among the Waterlanders. By 1581 the Waterlanders permitted their members to hold government offices, and after that time many of this branch held such offices. They did not shut their congregations off from the world; Joost van den Vondel (*q.v.*), a poet and dramatist, felt himself at home among them and served the Amsterdam Waterlander congregation as deacon. Hans de Ries (*q.v.*) was a friend of the humanist Dirk Volkertsz Coornhert (*q.v.*), whom Kühler called the Sebastian Franck of the Netherlands, and was strongly influenced by him. But the fact that a Carel van Mander (*q.v.*) could be a member of the Old Flemish group (1602) shows that a change was in progress here too. The fact that among the Mennonites, with the exception of the extreme groups, there was strong sympathy for the Remonstrants, who were likewise under persecution by the Reformed Church, speaks for itself. This sympathy was mutual; the Remonstrants at first used Hans de Ries' confession of faith. On the other hand, when the Remonstrants at Rotterdam proposed a union with the Waterlander Mennonites, objections arose. The Flemish now also began to be more open to the world and seemed to be receptive to Socinianism (*q.v.*), for which their Elder Jacques Outerman had to answer to the authorities in 1626. Finally during this time the Flemish as well as the Waterlanders took part in the Collegiant (*q.v.*) movement; their free-speaking meetings were frequently held in Mennonite meetinghouses.

13. *The First Historical Writings.* However great the changes had been, the bonds with the past remained. This is shown by the interest in the martyrs. In the very earliest time testimonies and songs about the martyrs were loyally gathered and by 1599 had been published at least eleven times (first in 1562) in the *Offer des Heeren.* In 1615 Hans de Ries published a new *Historie der Martelaren (History of the Martyrs)*, which appeared in a second edition in 1631 under the title *Martelaers-Spiegel (Martyrs' Mirror)*, the first use of this title in Mennonite literature. The Old Frisians, who considered themselves the true spiritual descendants of Menno Simons and were unable to accept such a work by the Waterlanders whom they did not regard as true Mennonites, published a new edition of this work in 1617 under the title *Historie der Warachtige Getuygen (History of the Genuine Witnesses)*, with some additions, but without the important foreword by Hans de Ries, substituting for it a confession of faith. It also enjoyed a second edition in 1626 under the title *Historie van de Vrome Getuygen (History of the Pious Witnesses)*, in which the "unorthodoxies" in the martyr book of 1617, which they had thoughtlessly accepted from the book of 1615, were

now corrected. Then T. J. van Braght, preacher of the Dordrecht congregation, published in 1660 his *Het Bloedig Tooneel der Doops-gesinde en Weerlose Christenen* (*The Bloody Theater of the Mennonite and Nonresistant Christians*), which was reprinted in 1685 with Jan Luyken's etchings under the somewhat modified title *Het Bloedig Tooneel of Martelaers Spiegel* (*The Bloody Theater or Martyrs' Mirror*).

III. THE PERIOD OF DECLINE 1665-1810

14. *Differences Between the Lamists and the Zonists.* Very soon after the division between the Lamists and the Zonists occurred, attempts were made to heal the breach (1672, 1684, 1685, 1691), but in vain. To be sure, the other small schismatic groups merged again into the larger streams, but the two main streams, Lamists and Zonists, remained separate throughout the 18th century, with opposite courses. The Lamists, often called the "Coarse," paid little attention to doctrinal confessions, were rather free in their attitude toward tradition, and had much association with the Collegiants and the Remonstrants. Even though some nuances were evident, they were mostly Spiritualists (*q.v.*) advocating an individual concept of faith, with the congregation occupying a secondary place. The Zonists, on the other hand, preferred to call themselves Mennists or Mennonites, as if they were still on the platform of Menno Simons. They had a very high regard for the authority of the congregation, held fast to the ban even though perhaps more in name than in actuality, and laid great stress on the extant confessions of faith; even not rarely leaning toward confessionalism. In 1665 they published *De Algemeene Belijdenissen* (*q.v.*, General Confessions; i.e., Concept of Cologne, Outerman's Confession, Olyftack, Jan Cents' Confession, and Dordrecht Confession). Shortly after this a somewhat surprising trend to confessionalism is found among the Waterlanders; some of them forsook their spiritualism, and now stressed the confession of Hans de Ries, and many of their congregations, particularly in the province of North Holland, joined the Zonist Conference. Again about 1750 there was among the Dutch Mennonites an unusual interest in confessions. The Danzig Old Flemish produced one in 1743, the Groningen Old Flemish Conference (Sociëteit) one in 1755. Neither group had ever before drawn up a confession. The Zonist Conference in 1766 approved a confession drawn up for them by Cornelis Ris (*q.v.*). This confession, however, never came into general use among the Dutch Mennonites. Many of the Zonists, except for adult baptism, felt themselves more closely related to the Reformed Church than with their brethren in the Lamist camp. In the final period of the 18th century not only did many of them transfer their membership to the Reformed Church, but in 1766 the preachers Cornelis Ris and Jan Beets (*q.v.*) at Hoorn actually promoted the idea of a union with the Reformed.

15. *Readiness to Help the Needy.* However different, even hostile, some of the Dutch Mennonites of this time were to one another, in one matter they always co-operated harmoniously, namely, when aid was asked for oppressed or suffering brethren. How frequently this aid was asked! In 1696 they helped their brethren in the Palatinate. The sum of 20,000 guilders was raised to support the refugees who came to Crefeld and Groningen. In 1711 one hundred Swiss families came to the Netherlands, followed by others in 1713, for whom land and homes had to be procured. For this purpose the sum of 30,000 guilders was raised in 1711, and another large sum in 1713. Likewise in 1713 they helped the Mennonites in Prussia and Poland. For this work a permanent committee was established, the Committee for Foreign Needs (see **Fonds voor Buitenlandsche Nooden**) which had a definite fund after 1725. In 1732 they were able to provide shelter for more than 100 persons who had come from the Danzig area to the island of Walcheren and to Wageningen. Until 1790 occasional collections were raised for the Mennonites of Poland and Lithuania, who suffered from floods and other calamities. The Committee was dissolved in 1804; but occasionally relief was still given, as in 1886 for the Mennonites in the Marienburg Werder in Prussia, who had suffered severe losses by floods, and especially after 1920 for the Russian Mennonites. Not only were those of the "household of faith," the Mennonites in various countries, financially supported by the Dutch Mennonites, but also others; e.g., Waldensians, the Salzburg refugees, Polish Unitarians, and also many Reformed.

16. *Forming Conferences.* Schisms and strife had caused many to leave the brotherhood. There was reason for concern for the future. Discipline grew visibly lax. In 1700 the United Flemish and Waterlander congregation at Rotterdam invited all Christians to communion, with no question as to whether they had been baptized as adults. Small congregations were no longer entirely self-supporting and threatened to die out. Mutual assistance was necessary. Out of this need various conferences (*Sociëteit*) arose. Among the stricter Mennonites these conferences at first served to provide supervision of the teaching doctrine and discipline.

The Waterlanders seem to have been the first to recognize the need of common consultations. As early as 1568 their delegates met, meeting again in 1581, 1618, and 1647. Also the Groningen Old Flemish (25 congregations in Groningen, 10 in Friesland, 4 in Holland, and 5 in East Friesland) had apparently met regularly in the first half of the 17th century. This developed into the Groningen Old Flemish Sociëteit. Although in the later period this conference no longer met regularly and many congregations outside the province dropped their membership in it, it existed until 1815. Beside this first sociëteit there was a second in the province of Groningen. the Humsterland Sociëteit, which originally embraced 10 congregations in Groningen and Friesland. It existed until 1825.

In North Holland the Frisian congregations had in all probability also united into a conference in the first half of the 17th century. This Frisian Sociëteit met regularly until 1818, but dissolved in 1841 into the Rijper Sociëteit. This latter (Waterlander) Sociëteit had been meeting since about 1640. A noticeable characteristic of this conference was the fact that whereas all the other conferences consisted of preachers and deacons, the Rijper Sociëteit held two meetings, one for the preachers and one for the deacons. The former was discontinued in the late 18th century; at present the deacons meet regularly in De Rijp.

In 1675 the delegates of the Lamist congregations of South Holland met (the Amsterdam and Haarlem congregations also belonged to this conference). This conference also gave the initiative for the founding of the Sociëteit of Friesland, which united a large number of Mennonite congregations in this province and until 1791 also included three congregations in the province of Groningen. The Sociëteit of Friesland met for the first time in 1695. It is still in existence, all the 47 congregations in the province of Friesland being members.

In addition a Zonist Sociëteit arose in 1674. The first objective of this conference was the application of the confession of faith. In 1674 it issued the *Grondsteen van vreede en verdraegsaemheyt tot opbouwinge van den tempel Christi onder de Doopsgezinde* (Foundation Stone of Peace and Tolerance for the Building of the Temple of Christ among the Mennonites). Some Waterlander congregations joined it. An attempted union with the Frisian Sociëteit in North Holland failed in 1723. Nor did a planned merger with the Groningen Old Flemish Sociëteit in 1766 succeed. The Zonist Sociëteit met until 1796 when the Amsterdam congregation dropped its membership. These conferences not only benefited the congregations by preventing their disintegration, using the means of mutual support, but they also brought together like-minded groups.

There were many changes in church life in the 18th century. The office of elder, as the one who alone could administer baptism and communion, gradually fell into decline. It was maintained longest among the Groningen Old Flemish (until 1749). Everywhere else local ministers also administered baptism and communion; their burdens were thereby increased. In many instances these brethren, chosen from the congregation, of whose piety there was no question but whose education was slight, did not feel equal to the task. There are reports that they were less competent than the Reformed and Remonstrant preachers and that therefore many members left the Mennonite congregations. In addition, the love for the office of preaching was decreasing, so that congregations that had formerly had four to six preachers now had none. A desire arose for more educated preachers. An early solution to the problem was to choose for the ministry men who had studied medicine and therefore had some scholarly training. Examples of such physician-preachers were Anthony Roscius, who died in 1616 at an early age; Jan Willemsz in De Rijp (b. 1587); Galenus Abrahamsz de Haan, who assumed the ministerial service in the Lamist congregation in Amsterdam (d. 1706); the Zonist preacher and historian Herman Schijn (d. 1727); and Gerardus Maatschoen (d. 1751). But the congregations wanted more. Especially in the conference of South Holland the question of theologically trained preachers arose a number of times. Galenus Abrahamsz offered to acquire special training, and the Lam en Toren congregation at Amsterdam paid the expenses. So Galenus

began his activity in 1680, serving until 1703. The church board was unable to find a successor for him when he retired. Oncoming preachers now had to study under Remonstrant professors in order to follow the lectures at the Remonstrant seminary, which had existed at Amsterdam since 1639. But when this practice issued in Remonstrant graduates being called to Mennonite congregations, while there was a dearth of preachers among the Remonstrants and furthermore when difficulty arose between the Mennonites and the Remonstrants on the question of baptism, the Amsterdam Mennonite congregation decided to establish its own seminary. Attempts to interest the entire brotherhood in this project failed. The co-operation of other congregations was very slight, and the Zonists had doubts and objections. In 1735 Tjerk Nieuwenhuis (*q.v.*) became a professor of the seminary; he was succeeded by Heere Oosterbaan (*q.v.*) and Gerrit Hesselink (*q.v.*). The seminary soon thrived.

The Zonists also took steps to this end. Their conference in 1733 appointed their Amsterdam preacher Petrus Smidt as professor. Many oncoming preachers, however, continued to receive their training from other preachers, who made it one of their tasks to lead young people into the office of the ministry.

Still, all of these measures were not sufficient to halt the steady decline in membership. Whereas in the 17th century the small conservative groups sometimes disappeared unnoticed, now the main groups also declined in number, as the membership in almost all of the congregations decreased. In Haarlem the number of baptized Mennonites decreased from about 3,000 in 1708 to 488 in 1834; in Hoorn, where in 1695 there were about 450 Mennonites, the number decreased to 212 in 1747 and 119 in 1845. Vlissingen dropped from 230 members in 1660 to 99 in 1757 and 22 in 1834. In Friesland, where there had been some 20,000 members in 1666, the number fell below 13,000 in 1796; one third of the members had been lost since 1739. It was still worse in South Holland. Of the 27 congregations in existence there at the end of the 18th century only three remained—Leiden, Ouddorp, and Rotterdam. Whereas the number of Mennonites in the Netherlands in 1700 was still estimated at 160,000 souls, in 1808 there were only 26,953. From 1700 to 1800 exactly 100 Dutch Mennonite congregations disappeared. In 1837 there were only 15,326 baptized Mennonites in Holland.

What were the reasons for this decline? The general decline in interest that eventuated in indifference is striking. But specific causes of various kinds can also be given. The Mennonite congregations around the Zuiderzee, e.g., Hoorn, Makkum, Hindelopen, Molkwerum, were the victims of the economic decay of these towns when the thriving Baltic trade disappeared. Many Mennonites were no longer satisfied with the occasionally very simple sermons of the lay preachers, and sought edification with the Remonstrants and the Reformed. Others—and their number was not small—went over to the established church in order to procure for themselves and their descendants the right to accept honorable government positions. Increasing wealth and luxury, about which Galenus Abrahamsz had already complained, also led to indifference on the part of many. Some who were unhappy in the separation of church life from the general life of the country went to the free-speaking meetings of the Rijnsburger Collegiants; but these also declined from the middle of the 18th century. Led by the new spirit of the Enlightenment, and influenced by the current literature, Mennonites of this type finally turned their backs on the brotherhood altogether.

Finally, the Reformed clergy was still watchful against heresy, even though not with the same violence as in former times, attacking especially Socinianism, which they thought they saw—and sometimes not mistakenly—in the Mennonites. Real Socinianism, however, passed over into a wider liberalism. In 1722 a doctrinal formula was drawn up for Mennonite preachers in Friesland to sign, which was to determine their orthodoxy. All but one refused to comply, not primarily because they were sympathetic to liberalism, but because they considered the signing of such a formula as un-Mennonite. For the time being the matter remained quiescent, but finally the Reformed clergy managed to have the capable preacher Johannes Stinstra (q.v.) at Harlingen deposed from his office by the government of Friesland on the grounds of heresy, and required to remain inactive until 1757.

But aside from these and a few other instances, the Dutch government was benevolent in its attitude. As early as 1671 bequests could be made for the Mennonite poor in Amsterdam. In Friesland—here and in the province of Zeeland the Mennonites had most to suffer from the hostility of the Reformed clergy—a bequest to the Molkwerum congregation was still forbidden in 1705, and in Witmarsum until 1753. Even though full legal equality was not attained until 1796, in many respects the magistrate came to the defense of the Mennonites. Thus it was gradually found satisfactory to have Mennonite marriages solemnized before their own congregations, provided the government were notified beforehand or within a definite period afterward. Since the time of the Batavian Republic (1796) civil marriages have been obligatory for all persons in the Netherlands including Mennonites.

17. *Relaxation of Church Regulations*. The ancient landmarks of the brotherhood gradually fell into decay. Mixed marriages (with someone outside the brotherhood), which had in the previous period been the occasion for much strife, were, to be sure, still forbidden by the "Fine" Mennonites, but for the most part nothing happened if a Mennonite married a non-Mennonite. Also the ban, at least the "great ban," in which the church member was excommunicated from the congregation, hardly ever was used after the mid-18th century. But the small ban, which meant exclusion from communion until correction of the error, was still applied, e.g., when young men sailed on armed boats. About 1765 a woman was refused communion at Terhorne because she was wearing a gold cap. In 1701 (records of the Frisian Sociëteit in North Holland) there was some complaint that decline was taking place in the attitude on mixed marriage, the ban, footwashing, and the furnishing of or sailing on boats with arms.

Especially in the principle against bearing arms was there laxity of application. The doctrine was defended in books, and now and then the ban was pronounced against an offender (in Texel as late as 1793), and the Zonist Sociëteit called the bearing of arms "a deviation from the Mennonite principles," but the doctrine was less and less regarded. After 1784 many Mennonites, especially in North Holland, enrolled in the militia, although this practice was by no means generally approved. In 1799, when the old Mennonite privilege of release from the bearing of arms was canceled, there was no general movement of protest. Only a few congregations complained. Upon a petition of the congregations of Haarlem and Rotterdam made to Louis Napoleon in 1806 this privilege was restored, but when the Netherlands was incorporated into France in 1810 it was again abrogated. The issue did not become acute until the introduction of compulsory military service in 1898.

Although the Waterlanders had early broken through the separation of the church from the world, in which the Lamists soon followed, in the 18th century the conservatives tried passionately to keep the church away from the world, but without success. They too had to surrender to the spirit of the time. It is noteworthy that the Zonist hymnal of Amsterdam of 1796 had more of a rationalistic spirit than the hymnal published by the Lamist congregation in 1792. The conservatives were turning about-face; the "liberals" remained true to their genius; the liberals had very early seen the untenability of isolation. Indeed, as noted above, by 1700 the Rotterdam congregation decided to invite all Christians to communion, without requiring adult baptism; the visible church had ceased to be considered a reflection of the kingdom of God. It is characteristic that in 1700 and a few times later some were baptized in the Waterlander congregation at Grouw and other congregations, and "were not received into our brotherhood, but were baptized into the general Christian church." In this, Collegiant influences are clearly discernible. The extent of friendly relations between the Mennonites and the Collegiants here and there is indicated by the fact that in 1715 the two groups in Groningen used the same meeting-house, Mennonite services being held in the morning and Collegiant services in the afternoon. The Mennonite church council of Zwolle went still further, deciding in 1808 that henceforth baptism as an infant would be accepted as valid in the case of members of the Reformed Church who wished to transfer to the Mennonite congregation. This extreme position also prevailed at other places. In the early 18th century Remonstrant ministers preached at Mennonite services, e.g., in the Waterlander congregation at Leeuwarden. Nevertheless the Mennonites valued their independence; for in 1796 when the Remonstrants circulated among all the ministers of the Protestant churches in the Netherlands a proposal that all unite with them into a single Christian brotherhood all the Mennonite congregations except Dokkum (q.v.) rejected the idea; in Dokkum this union was formed in 1798.

18. *Prayer and Singing*. Within the congregational life there were also many changes. Silent prayer

was gradually replaced by audible prayer, the Waterlanders and Lamists having completed the change by 1661. In 1770 silent prayer was still practiced in a number of congregations. Audible prayer was introduced in the Ameland congregations in 1789; the last congregation to hold fast to silent prayer was Aalsmeer, which gave it up in 1867.

In many congregations the singing was now accompanied by an organ. The first organ in a Dutch Mennonite church was installed in the Utrecht Church in 1765; it was followed by Haarlem in 1771, Rotterdam in 1775, Amsterdam bij 't Lam in 1777, and by Zaandam Nieuwe Huis in 1784.

The hymnal also underwent changes (see **Hymnology**). There had been singing in the Anabaptist-Mennonite churches from very early times, usually Biblical hymns and martyr hymns. Later, numerous collections of hymns were made: Hans de Ries's hymnal of 1582, the various Hoorn hymnals (issued as late as 1732 for the Groningen Old Flemish and the Balk—*q.v.*—congregation in 1814), Alle Derk's *Lusthof des gemoeds* with its supplement the *Achterhofje,* which were used here and there until the 19th century. In addition, some non-Mennonite hymnals were used; e.g., D. R. Camphuizen's *Stichtelijcke Rijmen* (Devotional Poems) or the much-used *Lusthof der Zielen* (Pleasure Garden of the Soul) by the Remonstrant notary Claes Stapel of Hoorn. The Psalms in various versions were also sung. Besides the mediocre versification of the Psalms by the Reformed minister Petrus Dathenus (*q.v.*), a new translation was introduced in the Lamist church in Amsterdam in 1684, which was replaced in 1770 by the versification by the poetic society Laus Deo, Salus populo (*q.v.*), which had been used by the Zonist congregation since 1762. Since 1713 Haarlem had had its own version of the Psalms, which was also used in other congregations. Later also the new Reformed version of 1773 was introduced here and there; and the evangelical Reformed hymns of 1807 and also its supplementary volume were used in many congregations.

Between 1792 and 1811 at least four new hymnals were produced, consisting for the most part of hymns taken from the previous books, viz., 1792 the *Kleine Bundel* (Lamist Amsterdam), 1796 the *Groote Bundel* (Zonist Amsterdam), 1805 the *Old Haarlem Bundel,* 1811 the *Uitgezochte Liederen* (Leiden and Zaandam-West). These collections were used in other congregations besides the ones they were published for. (See **Hymnology**.)

19. *Church Architecture.* In this period, in which the Mennonites became prosperous, not to say wealthy, new churches were built, even though the government did not permit building in the open. Besides the characteristic frame churches which were built in North Holland and of which a number of beautiful specimens are still standing, e.g., in Krommenie, West-Zaan Zuid, and Zaandam, there were also "barn" churches, like those still standing at Zijldijk and Nes in Ameland. But also larger churches were built in the 18th century, like the splendid church at Rotterdam, which was destroyed on May 13, 1940, during World War II. (See **Architecture**.)

20. *Benevolent Institutions.* The economic well-being of the Dutch Mennonites was expressed not only in church architecture and equipment, but also in the provisions made for the care of the aged and orphans. By 1630 Gerrit Franken van Hoogmade established the Bethlehem hofje (old people's home) at Leiden, and bequeathed it to the Waterlander congregation. In 1634 Elisabeth van Blenckvliet, the widow of Jaques van Damme, contributed an orphanage to the Flemish congregation of Den Blok in Haarlem. About the same time some other hofjes were established at Amsterdam and Haarlem. The Waterlander congregation of Leuwarden acquired its Marcelis Goverts Gasthuis in 1669. In the course of the 17th and 18th centuries many congregations, even small ones, acquired hospitals and orphanages, sometimes given by individuals, sometimes built by the congregations. The Flemish congregation at Leiden in 1660 established the Hoeksteen hospital, and the United Flemish and Waterlander congregation at Zaandam built an orphanage. (See **Homes for the Aged** and **Orphanages**.) Also the care of the widows of ministers was taken in hand. In 1794 the Rijper Sociëteit established a fund for this purpose, and in 1804 the Frisian Sociëteit followed suit and others also followed later (see **Pensioen Fonds**).

But their benevolence was not limited to members of the Dutch Mennonite congregations. The contributions raised for fellow believers in other countries as well as for non-Mennonites, e.g., for the oppressed French Reformed under Louis XIV, have already been mentioned. The contribution of the Dutch Mennonites for the common national welfare has not been slight: the association for the rescue of shipwrecked persons, the fund for the widows of shipwrecked sailors, the seminar for navigation, the Maatschappij tot Nut van't Algemeen (*q.v.*) founded by Jan Nieuwenhuizen (*q.v.*), all were established principally on Mennonite initiative.

Among the many who might be named with honor for their contribution to the common welfare or to scholarship, an outstanding benefactor was Pieter Teyler van der Hulst (*q.v.*) of Haarlem, who at his death in 1778 bequeathed his property for the establishment of the Teyler Foundation (*q.v.*), which supports an excellent museum and has done much for the promotion of scholarship in Holland, especially theology.

21. *Confessional Equality.* The political changes in the Netherlands in the last fifteen years of the 18th century were extensive. The whole nation was divided into two parties, the Orangist (Monarchist) party and the Patriot party which was strongly influenced by ideas coming from France. Most of the Mennonites joined the Patriots (*q.v.*). Even though they did not forget the privileges and the protection which they had always enjoyed at the hands of the House of Orange, they were still only a tolerated sect in comparison with the Reformed Church, and whereas the Reformed clergy and the regents, their natural opponents, were fiery Orangists, it was to be expected that the Mennonites, who as individualists warmly accepted the new French ideas which fitted so well their religious ideal and their true position, should feel quite at home among those who stood for "liberty, equality, and brotherhood."

Actually the republic did away with the hated position of inferiority and brought them the desired equality with the Reformed Church. In the National Assembly of May 23, 1796, a resolution was unanimously adopted, "that since religion is now separated from the state there shall no longer be a preferred religion in the free Netherlands."

22. *Founding of the General Mennonite Conference* (A.D.S., i.e., *Algemeene Doopsgezinde Sociëteit, q.v.*). The difficult times which followed did not pass without affecting the life of the brotherhood. One result was the reuniting in 1801 of the two Amsterdam congregations, the Lamist and the Zonist. The general impoverishment of the people also affected the congregations. For instance, through a reduction of the fixed income of pensioners and other causes, the annual income of the Amsterdam congregation was reduced by 34,000 florins. It became impossible for the congregation to maintain the Seminary without outside help. And so in 1811 it finally became possible to accomplish what had been impossible in 1735, namely, the establishment of a general conference (A.D.S.). Almost all the Dutch congregations joined the new conference. The A.D.S. now took on the care of the Seminary and thus continued the work which the Amsterdam congregation had for three quarters of a century carried on alone for the welfare of the whole brotherhood and which had already become such a great blessing to the church. Furthermore the A.D.S. took upon itself the task of financial assistance for the salaries of ministers in the weak congregations. So in 1811 a new era dawned for the Mennonites in the Netherlands.

IV. THE MODERN PERIOD 1811-1957

23. *The Amsterdam Mennonite Seminary.* In the first years of the new era little was accomplished in the new direction. The Mennonite congregations also had to bear their share of the troubles of the French Empire, viz., the large reduction in financial income, and the loss of freedom. The year 1815 brought liberation. Now the new age could begin, which brought about the equalization of the Mennonites with all other denominations, which so many had longed for in the 18th century.

During this period practically all the congregations came to the place where they secured preachers who had received scholarly training in the Seminary, but there have always been laymen here and there who carried on the work of preaching without training. Only one congregation, that of the Old Frisians at Balk, refused to join the A.D.S.

The Seminary carried on a work of real blessing. Professor Hesseling died in 1811; Rinse Koopmans (*q.v.*) was his successor, although he could not begin his work until 1814. After his death two professors were chosen, and since then there have regularly been two. These have been Samuel Muller (*q.v.*) 1826-56, W. Cnoop Koopmans (*q.v.*) 1826-49, J. van Gilse (*q.v.*) 1849-60, S. Hoekstra Bzn (*q.v.*) 1857-92, and J. G. de Hoop Scheffer (*q.v.*) 1860-90. Hoekstra and de Hoop Scheffer were from 1877 also professors at the University of Amsterdam, which was opened in that year. In that year the instruction in the Seminary was reduced in amount, and the students were sent to the university to take their exam-

inations. The later professors were all university professors also: Samuel Cramer (*q.v.*) 1890-1912, I. J. le Cosquino de Bussy (*q.v.*) 1892-1916, W. J. Kühler (*q.v.*) 1912-46, J. G. Appeldoorn 1916-33, W. Leendertz 1946-56, and J. A. Oosterbaan 1956- . Since the death of de Bussy there has been only one professor besides one or two lecturers.

Two of the professors in the Seminary require special mention. The first was Samuel Muller (*q.v.*), who was responsible for raising the Seminary to a high level and whose ideal it was to give the Mennonite preachers a scholarly education on a level with that of the older denominations. He brought a new spirit into the brotherhood and gave the impulse to an intensive study of Mennonite history. The second was Sytse Hoekstra (*q.v.*), who found (or created) a type of modernism (liberalism) which suited the Dutch Mennonites, and of whom Muller testified that he was "probably the keenest thinker which Holland produced in the 19th century in this field." Mennonite history was taught at the seminary by Muller, de Hoop Scheffer, Cramer, Kühler, and since 1946 by N. van der Zijpp. W. F. Golterman has since 1946 been lecturer in practical theology.

24. *Theological Alignments.* Following 1815 there was at first no spiritual revival in the brotherhood. A moderate supernaturalism was in general dominant, which gave due recognition to the Biblical events of salvation, but gave them a strong moralistic interpretation. Men liked to speak about the teachings of the good Jesus. A Christianity of virtue and enlightenment was preached. According to a tract of this time, the intention was to protect from decay the Mennonite body and its concern for a rational knowledge of God, for the general welfare, and for the consideration of virtue and piety. There was as much opposition to the Neology of the time which rejected everything, as there was toward a cheap sort of fanaticism. It was not until 1830 that a fresher spirit appeared; now there was a growing piety; Muller's influence was making itself felt; again preaching had Biblical theology for its content. But in opposition to this other persons arose, such as the Deventer minister J. H. Halbertsma (*q.v.*), who advocated a liberal rationalism. But the opposite extreme also affected the brotherhood; the Dutch revival movement known as the *Réveil* (*q.v.*) found supporters among the Mennonites. Never has a pietistic element been completely missing in the Dutch brotherhood. Among the supporters of the Réveil were Isaac Molenaar (*q.v.*), who was a minister in Leiden until 1818 and thereafter in Crefeld; Jan ter Borg (*q.v.*), who served in Amsterdam until 1828; Willem de Clercq (*q.v.*), who, like Willem Messchert (*q.v.*), left the brotherhood. Others were Jan de Liefde (*q.v.*), Johannes Molenaar's brother-in-law, who was a preacher in Zutphen until 1846, and Assuerus Doyer (*q.v.*), pastor at Zwolle. P. van der Goot (*q.v.*), preacher at Rotterdam and 1851-75 at Amsterdam, was a warm supporter of the Réveil in its later stages. Throughout the 19th century a noticeable pietistic tendency persisted in the Dutch brotherhood and likewise a more theological trend which rallied around Samuel Muller, especially in his later years.

At first, when the modernistic theology arose in the Dutch universities after 1842, the Mennonites were quite cool toward it, holding fast to supernaturalism. However, "under van Gilse the modernistic tendency approached the Seminary, and under Hoekstra and Scheffer in 1857 and 1860 it made its entry" (Cramer). This disturbed many. They wanted to hold fast to the Biblical, historical Christian note in the life of faith. D. S. Gorter (*q.v.*), a minister in several village congregations, who was known for his *Doopsgezinde Lectuur* (*q.v.*), wrote in 1856, "But this I know, I do not want to be either liberal or orthodox . . . but only Biblical." Pastor Sybrandy of Haarlem, who also feared a dangerous development, made a proposal in the meeting of the A.D.S. in 1866 that each candidate for ordination should be required to deliver an exposition of the Scripturalness of adult baptism, but the proposal was lost, with eleven of the seventeen votes against it. By no means all of those who voted against it were modernistic; among them there were certainly some who were moved by the fear of an un-Mennonite formalism.

By about 1871 modernism had won a general victory throughout the congregations, but there were still congregations and preachers, such as the ministers Taco Kuiper (*q.v.*) at Amsterdam and Jan Hartog (*q.v.*) of Utrecht, who rejected it. The change to modernism in the congregations had not produced many difficulties. Only in the Groningen congregation was there tension when, in 1867, the ministers J. W. Straatman (*q.v.*) and C. Corver (*q.v.*) proposed (1) that baptism be made optional, (2) to gradually do away with the communion service, (3) to permit the preachers to omit hymns, prayer, and Scripture from the service, and (4) to give them the privilege of choosing freely the content of their sermons on the major Christian holidays. When their proposals were rejected both pastors resigned. As a result of radical liberalism baptism was abolished in the Midwolda congregation; for a number of years no communion services were held in the Winterswijk (*q.v.*) and Franeker (*q.v.*) congregations.

The great majority of the Mennonites were modernistic, but because of Hoekstra's influence they did not usually belong to the radical left wing. Here and there were also quite a number who stood on the "right" as more evangelical. In Amsterdam there was an "Association for the Maintenance of God's Word in the Mennonite Congregations," which had a preacher of its own in 1892-1912 in the person of C. P. van Eeghen, Jr. (*q.v.*). The "leftists" and "rightists" both were able to find a place in the body of the brotherhood, and both bore with one another in a brotherly way. They not seldom even learned to appreciate each other.

25. *The Activities in the District Conferences and Groups.* It has been noted that at the beginning of this period the Mennonites were suffering heavy losses in membership. About 1830 the trend was halted. By 1855 a growth was reported, and although in the following years a number of Mennonites joined a schismatic Reformed group (known as the *Doleerenden,* i.e., "Troubled Ones") especially in the countryside in Groningen and Friesland, a growth in membership continued which was largely due to transfers from the Reformed Church of those who could not stand the increasingly (since 1875) confessional character of that church. Hence the period of 1880 to 1900 is characterized by growth.

Much credit is due to the A.D.S. for the manner in which it helped the brotherhood, both in the training of preachers and in strong financial support of the weak congregations. Various other organizations also made their contributions. The Mennonite conference in Friesland (Friesche Doopsgezinde Sociëteit) was still active. In 1826 a new conference (Sociëteit) was organized in Groningen, which also included the congregations of East Friesland in Germany. In North Holland the old Rijper Sociëteit continued its good work on behalf of the congregations. In 1840 the congregations in Overijssel, Gelderland, and Utrecht formed an association, which was joined in 1858 by the congregations in South Holland and Zeeland, and which in 1885 called itself the Zwolsche Vereniging.

In the 19th century a number of district organizations, called Rings, were established for the purpose of helping to maintain a good supply of preaching, particularly when a pulpit was vacant or the preacher ill. Each Ring served about 10-15 congregations. The oldest is Ring Akkrum (1837), followed by Ring Bolsward (1840), Ring North Holland with two chapters (1844), Ring Dantumawoude (1850), Ring Twenthe (1856), Ring Arnhem (1856), Ring Zwolle (18.....), Ring South Holland-Zeeland (18.....), and finally in the 20th century, split off from Ring Arnhem, Ring Utrecht-het Gooi (1947). The Groningen Sociëteit also acts as a Ring.

In 1861 the Haarlem Vereniging of Mennonite congregations was founded, which among other things furnished certifications and looked after scattered members living outside the regular congregations. From 1896 on visiting preachers were provided to minister to Mennonites living where there were no congregations. The Haarlem Association continued until 1925.

In 1794 the congregations in North Holland and in 1804 those in Friesland established a Fonds (foundation) for the support of the widows of Mennonite preachers, and in 1810 a similar fund, the Zwolsche Fonds, was established, which merged with the older North Holland Foundation in 1897. In 1835 the Groningen Sociëteit had also established a foundation for widows. At the same time foundations were established to pay pensions to retired and invalid ministers, such as the Zaansche Fonds (1848; see **Algemeen Emeritaatsfonds**), the Friesche Emeritaatsfonds, and the Groningen Fonds (1917). In 1929 the A.D.S. established a foundation for the increase of pensions. In 1865 the Foundation for the Increase of Salaries was established, and in 1917 the Menno Foundation was established for the same purpose, while in 1912 the Dienstjaren Fonds (*q.v.*) accomplished the same purpose by granting supplementary payments to preachers who had served ten years or more and had low salaries. The A.D.S. established a general Pensioenfonds in 1946.

26. *New Congregations.* Since 1811, 30 new congregations have arisen, some of them at places where there had been a Mennonite congregation in earlier

times. The 25 are Mensingeweer 1816, Tjalleberd 1817, Beverwijk ca. 1825, Stadskanaal 1848, Pekela 1852, Arnhem 1852, Wolvega 1861, Koudum 1867, St. Anna-Parochie 1871, Huizen-Hilversum 1878, Meppel 1879, The Hague 1881, Apeldoorn 1896, Assen (as Kring or circle 1896, as a congregation 1898), Breda 1896, Dordrecht 1896, Wageningen 1896, Zwaagwesteinde (Kring 1904, congregation 1942), Amersfoort (Kring 1905, congregation 1923), IJmuiden 1909, Bussum (Kring 1909, congregation 1915), Baarn (Kring 1909, congregation 1921), Delft (Kring 1918, congregation 1923), South Limburg (Kring 1924, congregation 1931), Eindhoven (Kring 1929, congregation 1936), Zeist (Kring 1929, congregation 1931), Haarlemmermeer 1950, North East Polder 1953, Roden 1954, Emmen 1957, Buitenpost 1957.

There are now (1957) in the Netherlands 136 congregations, of which, however, a considerable number have joined with other neighboring congregations in a pastoral circuit with one common pastor. In addition there are 24 circles (Kring). The total baptized membership is 38,446. Detailed statistics of membership appear at the end of the article. In January 1957, 16 congregations had no pastors, but there were a total of 109 pastors serving in congregations, besides three in general work. Of the 112 preachers 25 were women. In most of the congregations new meetinghouses and parsonages have been built since 1811. Four meetinghouses, completely destroyed during World War II, i.e., at Rotterdam, Wageningen, Vlissingen, and Nijmegen, have been rebuilt by the support of the Noodfonds, a fund established by the A.D.S., to which congregations and private persons have liberally contributed, in addition to state aid.

Since 1811 only two Mennonite congregations have become extinct, the small one at Appelsga (q.v.), which was founded at the beginning of the 19th century, and Maastricht (q.v.). The property of the Maastricht congregation, which became extinct in 1815, was taken over by the state. The Dordrecht congregation also died out and lost its capital, but a new congregation arose in 1879. In 1853 most of the Old Frisian congregation at Balk, which had stood quite alone in maintaining its old customs and insisting on the wearing of outmoded clothing, emigrated to North America, settling near Goshen, Ind. A chief reason for the emigration was that it was no longer possible to secure exemption of the young men from military service.

A number of congregations which were located side by side in the same town merged during this period; e.g., Joure in 1816, IJlst 1817, Grouw 1827, Sneek 1838, Ameland 1855, Aalsmeer 1866, Oldeboorn 1886, Wormerveer 1899, Westzaan 1930, and Zaandam 1949. The Swiss congregations at Kampen (1822) and at Groningen (1824) also joined older Dutch congregations.

27. *Congregational Life*. The inner life of the brotherhood has also experienced changes. In the 1870's much attention was given to the question of baptism, and a number of articles on the subject appeared in the *Doopsgezinde Bijdragen*. As has been noted above, members of other denominations who had been baptized as infants could be admitted

into the church at Zwolle and elsewhere in 1808 without baptism upon confession of faith. Although this was not universally approved it came to be a permanent practice in the brotherhood. In a meeting of the Ring South Holland-Zeeland in 1864 the general opinion was that such candidates should be rebaptized. But in 1871 the Midwolda congregation in Groningen decided that one could become a church member without being baptized. The congregation at Vlissingen actually voted to accept transfer members without baptism, action which stirred up trouble. In 1879 a conference was held in Amsterdam under the leadership of Jacobus Craandijk, pastor of Rotterdam, to discuss this matter. Here Jeronimo de Vries, pastor at Haarlem, proposed that baptism be made optional, and added that he had no objection to its complete elimination. On the opposite side were the Amsterdam leaders (Pastor T. Kuiper, H. S. van Eeghen, F. Muller, and others), who insisted that there must be adult baptism on confession of faith: "It is Christ's command." No agreement was reached.

In many congregations it became a custom to accept members of other creeds without adult baptism, which is now the general practice. Personal choice as to baptism or no baptism in admission to the church, as had been practiced at Midwolda, did not appeal to the churches, even though now and then an individual was admitted without baptism.

The Lord's Supper, although especially in Friesland it still enjoys a warm participation which is shown in faithful attendance, is no longer the heart of the congregational life as it formerly was, although in recent times a change to a higher evaluation has been noticeable. In Winterswijk, after it had not been observed for several years, the Lord's Supper has been observed again since 1910. In Franeker it was abandoned in 1915, but observed again regularly since 1934. The Lord's Supper is usually observed once a year; in some congregations the members are seated around the table, in others they remain at their places while the pastor(s) and deacons hand them the bread and wine. In Amsterdam both methods are used.

Now congregational singing in all the congregations is accompanied by an organ. About 1910 the last congregation decided to install one. After 1811 the content of the songbooks also changed somewhat. Amsterdam introduced *Christelijke Gezangen* (2 volumes) in 1848, in 1849 Rotterdam adopted the Remonstrant hymnal in a revised form. In 1851 Haarlem adopted a new hymnal, *Christelijke Kerkgezangen*. Amsterdam introduced its two new hymnals, *Christelijke Liederen,* in 1870. All these hymnals were also adopted in other places. In 1882 the Dutch Protestant Union compiled a hymnal, in 1920 a continuation of this hymnal appeared, which was also adopted in many Mennonite churches, first in Texel (1885). Haarlem received new hymnals once more in 1895 in two books, of which the first was a selection of Mennonite hymns, and the second the Protestant Lutheran one with some changes. In 1897 the ministers J. Sepp and H. Boetje issued the *Leidsche Bundel* (q.v.), which was widely used. In 1900 it was followed by a selection from the Psalms. Thus there were still in the congregations ten or more different hymnbooks in use. This diversity in hymnals remained until after World War II, when the new *Doopsgezinde Bundel* was introduced, which is now used in all but one or two congregations.

In 1911 at Bovenknijpe Miss Anna Zernike, the first woman preacher in the brotherhood, delivered her initial sermon (see **Zernike, Anna**); the meeting of the A.D.S. of 1905 had made this possible. Women also were made members of the church councils, the first ones shortly after 1900. Now nearly all the congregations have women on their church boards.

Since the beginning of the 20th century the usual worship service has no longer been the sole form of congregational life. Lectures and "devotional hours" are held. In addition Sunday schools and youth work, choirs, and sewing societies were founded everywhere, and later sisters' associations and occasionally also brothers' associations, while also youth associations are found nearly everywhere.

The relationship to the state has remained as it was regulated in 1796. The church is separated from the state. There is no longer any privilege granted to members of a particular church. By means of this equalization it became possible for Mennonites to occupy a relatively high percentage of state offices, even the highest. When the law of 1815 and again that of 1817 offered the Mennonites the use of some funds as state contributions for the pastors' pay for many congregations and a children's supplementary grant for the preachers, at first a few could not make up their mind to accept them. An important sum was actually raised for this support to prevent the acceptance of state funds, but gradually the doubt disappeared, and now the supplementary "Rijkstraktement" and "Kindergelden" are generally accepted. By the law of Sept. 10, 1853, each congregation is a church unit and has the legal rights of a person. When the government wants to reach the Mennonites as a whole it addresses itself to the A.D.S. In 1898 once more the old Mennonite privilege of release from military service was discussed. In that year a law was passed making it a personal obligation to serve, which did away with the hiring of a substitute which had been valid since 1799. This older regulation, according to which any one who had to become a soldier could employ a substitute, was often made use of by the Mennonites. No opposition to this new ruling came from the church. But there were difficulties. This was shown in World War I. Finally the law of alternative service was formulated (1925) in favor of the Mennonites and other antimilitary groups, giving those who had conscientious scruples the opportunity of service in a number of nonmilitary state tasks.

The work of the Mennonite Missionary Association (*q.v.*), which was founded in 1847, has been of great importance. Above all, thanks to the activity of P. van der Goot (*q.v.*), this mission work was also supported since 1855 by Mennonite congregations in Germany and Russia. In the Netherlands there was on the whole no great love for the mission work; in later years this noticeably changed;

especially since the funds no more flowed in from foreign countries many Dutch Mennonites felt the support of the mission to be their obligation. The annual meeting of the A.D.S. (General Dutch Mennonite conference) of 1957 resolved that missions are henceforth not to be promoted by a special mission association; they are to be the concern of the whole Dutch Mennonite brotherhood.

The Mennonites of the Netherlands have felt themselves more drawn to works of mercy than of missions. Especially in the first half of the 19th century many devoted their strength and time to the Association for the General Welfare (Maatschappij tot Nut van 't Algemeen), especially for the improvement of the school system and popular education, as well as the system of savings banks. The Amsterdam Mennonite Church established its own savings bank in 1844. The Mennonite congregations of Amsterdam, Haarlem, and several others, have their own system of care for their sick. Haarlem has a Mennonite school; Amsterdam and a number of other congregations conduct their own social service. In 1912 an association was formed for the care of neglected Mennonite children, but this was of short duration. The Mennonites preferably worked in the general organizations such as the Groene Kruis (*q.v.,* Green Cross), an association instituted by the Mennonite minister F. C. Fleischer (*q.v.*), or in "Tot Steun" (*q.v.*), an association for the care of neglected children and also for the care of the sick and the fight against tuberculosis.

Many congregations have for a long time had their orphanages and old people's homes. Recently three such homes for the aged were founded for more general use: Spaar en Hout at Haarlem (1930), Mooiland at Heelsum near Arnhem (1936), and Avondzon at Velp near Arnhem (1939). Others were founded after World War II. The Groningen congregation has since 1929 had a rest home.

The Hollandsch Doopsgezind Emigranten Bureau (*q.v.,* Mennonite Emigrant Committee), which supported Mennonites in their emigration from Russia and gave good support to the new Mennonite settlement in Brazil, began functioning in 1924. In 1938 the Commissie voor Buitenlandsche Noden (Commission for Foreign Needs, *q.v.*) awakened to new activity. In 1939 the Doopsgezinde Hulpfunds (Mennonite Relief Bureau) was established to aid Mennonites and others (Jews expelled from Germany).

In many respects the Mennonites have gone their own way, but there has always been some co-operation with others, especially with the liberal part of the people. There was opportunity for common work in the field of social service, but also in more spiritual fields. Together with the liberal Reformed, the Remonstrants, and the Evangelical Lutherans, the Protestant Union was established in 1870. In 1923 the Central Commission of Liberal Protestantism came into being, from which among other things the liberal Christian radio originated. The A.D.S. is a member of this Central Commission, but only as a representative of a majority of the Mennonite congregations, not of all. Several Mennonites are members of this Commission.

In 1917 the Gemeentedag-Beweging (*q.v.,* Movement for Church Conferences), now called Gemeenschap voor Doopsgezind Broederschapswerk (*q.v.*), was organized for the purpose of strengthening the general, provincial, and personal religious life, and the congregational life of the Mennonites in the Netherlands. This movement, in which at first especially the more orthodox Mennonites felt at home, has been a blessing to many, and by creative initiative has refreshed spiritual life. The first Gemeentedag was held Aug. 2-4, 1917, at Utrecht. In 1918 Gemeentedagen were held at Utrecht, Wormerveer, and Heerenveen, in 1919 at eight places. The Algemeen Gemeentedag has been held regularly at Elspeet since 1928. Here in 1925, at first on a small scale, later more extensively, a conference site was created which has become the center of the movement, sometimes also called the Elspeetse Vereniging (Elspeet Association).

The "work groups" and the commissions within the Elspeetse Vereniging have developed into great significance. Among these groups were the Arbeidsgroep van Doopsgezinden tegen de Krijgsdienst (*q.v.,* Work Group of Mennonites Against Military Service), which worked for a revival of the old principle of nonresistance, the Commission for Mennonite Catechism Camps, and above all the Commission for Mennonite Crisis Work (for unemployed).

The youth work has grown greatly. The beginning was a meeting for young members held at Lunteren in 1922, which soon developed into an annual Youth Conference held customarily in Elspeet. One fruit of this was the Doopsgezinde Jongeren-Bond (*q.v.*) or DJB (Mennonite Youth League). Out of a similar youth conference held in Friesland in 1922 developed in 1924 the Friesche Doopsgezinde Jongeren-Bond (*q.v.*) or FDJB, which remained in close association with the general Youth League. In 1941 this general Youth League, which included youth of 18-35 years of age, had 70 circles with a total of approximately 1,000 members. These circles had regular meetings locally, and in addition sent delegates to the provincial and general youth meetings. It should be noted in contrast to the plan in other Mennonite groups that the youth work in Holland is not a work for the benefit of youth, managed from above, but its leadership and work are actually in the hands of the young people.

The Gemeentedag-Beweging also sought and found new contacts with foreign Mennonites and other related groups. Foreign delegates have repeatedly taken part in the Elspeet meetings, and Dutch delegates and youth groups have attended meetings in foreign countries. Contacts were also made with the Quakers in England. In 1925 a brotherhood house was built at Elspeet, in 1929 a second called Fredeshiem (*q.v.*) near Steenwijk, and in 1932 a third was built at Schoorl (*q.v.*). These houses have a double purpose; they are not only to serve as convenient places to hold conferences, but also as retreat places for vacationers and those in need of relaxation. At Giethoorn (*q.v.*) there are two youth camp houses, Kraggehuis and Samen-Een. In 1937 the Amsterdam and Utrecht congregations jointly purchased the brotherhood house at Bilthoven (*q.v.*).

In 1923 the A.D.S. was reorganized in such a way as to become a general representative body of the Mennonite congregations in the Netherlands. Various kinds of work are now done by the A.D.S. which were formerly done by other organizations. For instance the ministry to the Mennonites in the diaspora was taken over by the A.D.S. New forms of work were also inaugurated, and since then the weekly journal, the *Zondagsbode,* has become its official organ. In 1940 an organic association was established between the A.D.S. on the one hand and the Elspeetsche Vereniging, the Mennonite Youth League, and other organizations on the other. In 1927 the General Mennonite Preachers' Association (ANDPV) was founded, which meets twice yearly.

The Dutch Mennonite press is quite extensive. In addition to the *Zondagsbode,* established in 1887, other journals have appeared, such as the *Brieven* (*q.v.*), published since 1918 by the Elspeetsche Vereniging (since 1925 as a monthly), and *De Hoeksteen,* published by the Youth League. Since about 1910 gradually some fifty circles and congregations have begun to publish a monthly periodical. Beginning in 1731 the directory (*Naamlijst*) of Mennonite ministers was published, though irregularly, which later was continued in a sense as *Mullers Jaarboekje* (1837, 1840, 1850), *Gorters Doopsgezinde Lectuur* (1854, 1856, 1858), the *Doopsgezinde Bijdragen,* and the *Doopsgezinde Jaarboekje.* The last has appeared annually since 1901, The *Bijdragen* were published 1860 to 1919 (not published in 1866, 1871, 1913-15). They are a treasure house of historical materials. The Amsterdam congregational library has a large collection of historical works which are of great value to the church as a whole and support the work of the Mennonite Theological Seminary.

27. *During and After World War II.* On May 10-14, 1940, the Netherlands were overrun by the German armies. On May 14, the Dutch government capitulated and the war in a strict sense came to an end, but the following German occupation, in the southern Dutch provinces lasting until September 1944 and in the northern until April-May 1945, often was for the Dutch population as grievous and unbearable as the war, not only because of the constant air raids, both by the Germans and also by the English and Americans, but also because of the harsh measures of the German occupation officials, who according to the godless and inhuman principles of Nazism did all they could to smother democratic as well as religious life. Particularly the Jews were mercilessly persecuted; only a small percentage of them survived the occupation; the others were murdered or transported to Germany to die a cruel death in the extermination camps.

The German occupation forces at first left the Christian churches rather undisturbed, but particularly from the fall of 1943, though church services in general remained unmolested and free, church life was much hindered by the occupation regime, and little by little all congregational activity except church services was made impossible. It was the apparent intention of the occupation to replace in every sector of life the Cross of the Redeemer by Hitler's heathen cross (*Hakenkreuz*). The press was censored, and religious periodicals, including the Mennonite ones, were nearly all discontinued from 1943 on. All Mennonite congregational publications, and also *Brieven* (*q.v.*) and *De Hoeksteen* (*q.v.*) were suppressed. The *Doopsgezind Jaarboekje* for 1943 (published in November 1942) was the last to be published. The *Zondagsbode* (*q.v.*) had earlier already been forbidden by the Germans (last issue: June 21, 1942). Not only was the press eliminated; church conferences were prohibited and the lectures at the Amsterdam Theological Seminary were forbidden, although for some time they were conducted secretly in private homes. Charity by the churches was restricted, by the order of the Reichskommissar in Holland that all property of the deacon's offices was to be placed at the disposal of the Nazi government, which order was followed by no Dutch church (the order was later rescinded).

In the course of time secret organizations were founded everywhere to fight the occupying enemies and to frustrate their noxious measures, both those destroying material welfare and those wrecking religious values; in this underground movement also many Mennonites, including a number of pastors, were active. Some of them, whose activities were found out, were executed or died in prisons and concentration camps. Among these modern martyrs were two Mennonite ministers, A. Keuter (*q.v.*) and A. de Croix (*q.v.*).

During the occupation period the A.D.S. co-operated with the other Dutch churches in drawing up messages to be read from the pulpits in which strong protests were made against the intolerable orders and practices of the Nazis, as for example the persecution of the Jews. Repeatedly delegates were sent to the High Commissioner to point out the will of the churches not to tolerate the Nazi assault on Christian faith and morals.

The Arbeidsgroep van Doopsgezinden tegen de Krijgsdienst (*q.v.*, i.e., Mennonite Work Group Against Military Service), doomed to inactivity and silence, together with the Dutch Quakers, found a Christian task in taking starving children to the country from the large cities like Amsterdam. Others organized an exodus of children from the heavily bombed city of Rotterdam to the northern provinces of Friesland and Groningen, where life was comparatively safe and food less scarce.

After liberation from the Germans in 1945 national and church life had to be reorganized. Gradually the wounds of the war and occupation were healed. In the Mennonite brotherhood, through the leadership of the A.D.S., a relief fund (*Noodfonds*) was founded for the rebuilding of destroyed and damaged churches. Besides the meetinghouses which had been completely destroyed, such as Rotterdam, Wageningen, Vlissingen, and Nijmegen, some others (Aardenburg, Goes, Zutphen, IJmuiden, Arnhem, and the parsonages of Hengelo and Hollum on the island of Ameland) had been damaged. The brotherhood houses of Elspeet and Schoorl also sustained considerable damage. All have now been restored; the new church of Vlissingen was dedicated on Feb. 20, 1949, Wageningen April 29, 1951, Rotterdam Dec. 21, 1951, and Nijmegen May 25, 1952.

Immediately after the war was over, in the southern provinces as early as the fall of 1944, representatives of the American MCC came to the Netherlands with their extensive relief program "in the Name of Christ," distributing food and clothing. They gave highly appreciated help to the pillaged and famishing Dutch people both Mennonites and non-Mennonites. It was then that Dutch Mennonites thankfully became aware of their coreligionists across the ocean. These incidental contacts, strengthened particularly after the MCC had moved to its center at Koningslaan 58 in Amsterdam, where contacts could be more regular and thorough, have been—as it seems to the writer—stimulating and fruitful both for the Dutch and the American Mennonites. In this process light was thrown not only on the differences, which are large, but also on the common background and the unity of their Christian endeavors. At present the Dutch A.D.S., the Dutch Peace Group (*Vredesgroep*), and the MCC are co-operating in the management of the Mennonite conference and peace center at Heerewegen.

As a result of events, continuing the trend of its reorganization in 1923, the A.D.S. after the war became more influential in local church life, though each congregation retained in principle its autonomy as before. In 1949 the constitution of the A.D.S. was significantly amended: since then representation is no longer based on the financial contributions made to the A.D.S. by the congregations, but on the membership of the congregations. Besides the regular representation, delegates of the Mission Association, the Peace Group, and certain other associations are now admitted to the meetings of the A.D.S. as advisory members. Since 1946 the A.D.S. has had a full-time secretary (now R. de Zeeuw). In 1946 by creating a general Pension Fund (Pensioenfonds) the A.D.S. took over the responsibility for the pensions of retired ministers and widows; in 1955 the Dienstjarenfonds (*q.v.*) was taken over, and in 1956 a strong financial action was launched to raise the salaries of the ministers.

After the war (1948) a new foundation was established, called the Stichting voor Bizondere Noden (for special needs), which attempts to cope with the financial and material needs, both in the several sectors of the Mennonite brotherhood and beyond it. Each year at Pentecost an offering is taken in all Mennonite churches of Holland to enable this foundation to carry out its tasks, among which have been relief work in Vienna (together with the Peace-Group), the sending of Red Cross packages to the Mennonite congregations in East Friesland (Germany), aid to Mennonite refugees in Western Germany, relief action after the Dutch flood of Feb. 1, 1953, which had severely afflicted large areas of the South Holland and Zeeland islands, and founding the Van de Water House (*q.v.*) at Schoorl in 1951, where a number of DP's from East Europe found shelter. The foundation is still sending clothes and food to Berlin, and operating the Mennonite children's home at Houten (*q.v.*).

After the war the Work Group Against Military Service was changed into the Vredesgroep (Peace group); it started with renewed devotion and new activities. Only a small number of members have joined this group (600 out of 38,000 Mennonites), but about 40 per cent of the active pastors have done so.

The Youth associations of the Dutch Mennonites, Jongerenbond (*q.v.*), Elfregi (*q.v.*), and Menniste Bouwers (*q.v.*), were co-ordinated in the Doopsgezinde Jeugdraad (*q.v., Mennonite Youth Council*), since 1957 called the Doopsgezinde Jeugd Centrale. The several women's circles were organized into the Landelijke Federatie van Doopsgezinde Zusterkringen General Federation of Mennonite Women's Circles), 3,000 members, holding yearly delegate meetings in the Brotherhood house at Elspeet.

The Gemeentedagbeweging, also called the Elspeetse Vereniging, received a new name: Gemeenschap voor Doopsgezind Broederschapswerk (*q.v., Fellowship for Mennonite Brotherhood Work*) and resumed its activities. It now holds regularly an annual conference of members of Mennonite congregational boards at Elspeet.

The Dutch Mennonite Mission Association (*q.v.*) had much difficulty in resuming its work after the war. During the war contacts with the missionaries and the mission fields in Java became impossible; moreover because of the Japanese invasion in the Dutch East Indies (during which inflamed Mohammedans seriously damaged churches and hospitals, and some of the missionaries lost their lives), and finally after the declaration of independence of the Republic of Indonesia in December 1948, the fields were closed for Dutch missionaries. Fortunately the mission churches had organized as independent Mennonite congregations in 1940. Now only two Dutch Mennonite missionaries, viz., Jan Matthijssen and R. Kuitse, are in Java, the former as a general worker and the latter as an instructor in the school for the training of native ministers at Malang. In 1952 a new mission field was opened on Dutch New Guinea (*q.v.*).

The Dutch brotherhood introduced a new hymnal in 1945 called *Doopsgezinde Bundel,* which was to replace several older hymnals, and which now is used in all the congregations except one or two.

Great changes took place in the Dutch Mennonite press. The former *Zondagsbode* did not reappear; in 1945-46 a temporary periodical, *De Noodbrug,* was published by the A.D.S., and since October 1946 the *Algemeen Doopsgezind Weekblad* (*q.v.*), a weekly, has been the official paper of the A.D.S. The *Doopsgezind Jaarboekje* too made its reappearance for the first time after the war in 1949. The *Brieven* (*q.v.*) were resumed in 1946, but have been discontinued. As compensation for the dicontinuance of *Brieuen,* a monthly supplement, called *Fundamenten en Bouwstenen* (Foundations and Buildingstones) has been added to the *Algemeen Doopsgezind Weekblad* since 1956. *De Hoeksteen* (*q.v.*), edited by the Youth League, has been continued, and some new periodicals are being published by the Mennonite Youth Council. The Peace Group continues to publish its printed letter (*Brief*).

In 1954 a group of eleven young Mennonite ministers organized an Ecclesiologische Werkgroep (Ecclesiological Work Group) and published *Doopsgezind Belijden Nu.* In this booklet they criticize the Dutch Mennonite brotherhood for its liberal and individualistic views and its lack of a concept of objective truth. They stress the importance of a confession of faith, and offer a specimen of such a confession. This confession has not had much of an echo among the Dutch Mennonites, who, notwithstanding the fact that faith was deepened by the experiences of the war, with a turning away from too much moralism to more evangelical ideas, still do not in general place a high value on strict definitions in an objective creed, and who, even at present, are mostly individuals and spiritualists and are still predominantly liberal. However, there is a noticeable increase in ministers who hold an evangelical position as compared to prewar times.

New congregations founded after World War II are Haarlemmermeer in 1950, Noord-Oost-Polder (an area reclaimed from the former Zuiderzee) in 1953, Roden in 1954, and Emmen and Buitenpost in 1957. Moreover a large number of Mennonite circles (Kring) have been organized. New meetinghouses, apart from those destroyed during the war and since rebuilt, were built at Heerlen for the congregation of South Limburg (dedicated in November 1939) and at Zutphen (dedicated on Dec. 9, 1949). In 1940 new churches were dedicated at Gorredijk (on April 7, just before the outbreak of the war) and Hilversum (on Oct. 27, 1940, a few months after the war had broken out). After the war five new meetinghouses were erected: in Roden (1955), in the north section of Haarlem (1955), De Koog on the island of Texel (1955), in the west section of Amsterdam, formerly called Slootermeer (1956), in Warga (1956), and Buitenpost (1957). The latter two were erected by international Mennonite Voluntary Service units. A new home for the aged was opened at Heemstede near Haarlem in 1956. There are plans for more such homes. A new Brotherhood House was founded at Paterswolde near Groningen in 1956.

The Dutch Mennonites, though eager to preserve their own type of undogmatic Christendom and their own pattern of church life, co-operate with the ecumenical movement and take part in its activities. They are represented in the Dutch Ecumenical Council, and sent official delegates to the world assemblies at Amsterdam (1948) and Evanston (1954).   vDZ.

N. van der Zijpp, *Geschiedenis der Doopsgezinden in Nederland* (Arnhem, 1952); W. J. Kühler, *Geschiedenis* I, II, and III; S. Blaupot ten Cate, *Friesland; idem, Groningen* I and II; *idem, Holland* I and II; Anna Brons, *Ursprung, Entwickelung und Schicksale der . . . Mennoniten* (3rd ed., Amsterdam, 1912); Mellink, *Wederdopers;* Schijn-Maatschoen, *Geschiedenis* I, II, and III (Amsterdam, 1743-45); S. F. Rues, *Tegenwoordige Staet* (Amsterdam, 1745); I.H.V.P.N., *Beginsel em Voortganck der Geschillen* (Amsterdam, 1658; reprinted in BRN VII, 489-564); H. Bullinger and G. Nicolai, *Teghens de Wederdopers* (reprinted in BRN VII, 267-487); V. P. *Successio Anabaptistica* (reprinted in BRN VII, 1-87); J. H. Ottius, *Annales Anabaptistici* (Basel, 1672); S. Cramer, "Mennoniten" in *HRE* (1903) 594-616; C. Henry Smith, *The Story of the Mennonites* (Newton, 1950); P. van der Meulen, "Dutch Mennonites Unite During Crisis," *Menn. Life* III (July 1948); Pieter Langendijk, "Simplicity Laments Corrupted Manners," *op. cit.,* X (July 1955); H. W. Meihuizen, "Basic Beliefs of the Dutch Mennonites," *op. cit.,* XI (October 1956); Henk van Bilderbeek, "A Confession for Our Day," *op. cit.,* XI (October 1956); ML III, 225-41.

Membership Statistics

(The statistics are taken from three sources; the first column from S. Blaupot ten Cate, the second from the *Doopsgezinde Bijdragen* for 1900, the third and fourth columns from the *Doopsgezind Jaarboekje* of 1940 and 1957; the figures indicate the baptized membership in the 138 congregations.)

Province of Friesland

	1837	1900	1940	1956
Akkrum	321	424	256	181
Ameland (the "Fine")	270	300	211	
Ameland (the "Coarse")	50			
Ballum				41
Hollum				105
Nes				40
St. Anna-Parochie	----	57	127	129
Appelsga	----	7	----	----
Baard	86	94	70	54
Balk	35	83	90	85
Berlikum	12	56	86	142
Bolsward	157	235	171	125
Bovenknijpe	123	178	119	94
Dantumawoude	207	278	270	244
Drachten and Ureterp	183	220	227	214
Franeker	95	128	183	120
Gorredijk and Lippenhuizen	118	166	156	150
Grouw	275	419	310	205
Hallum	20	56	152	155
Harlingen	272	556	404	367
Heerenveen	144	235	224	209
Hindeloopen	57	48	57	48
Holwerd and Blija	165	260	100	92
IJlst	135	101	86	81
Irnsum	60	154	108	96
Joure	200	360	277	240
Koudum	----	39	31	28
Leeuwarden	270	1,000	1,250	1,011
Makkum	90	89	57	48
Molkwerum	20	42	26	----
Noordoostpolder				60
Oldeboorn (Oude Huis)	142			
Oldeboorn (Nieuwe Huis)	146	493	274	182
Oudebildtzijl	34	98	161	140
Poppingawier	27	91	52	45
Rottevalle and Witveen	72	101	124	145
Sneek	310	434	427	465
Staveren	25	89	59	56
Surhuisterveen	68	80	100	131
Terhorne	119	138	87	83
Ternaard	----	69	89	113
Tjalleberd	104	92	121	100
Veenwouden	36	136	173	200
Warga	159	180	86	80
Warns	108	149	105	101
Witmarsum and Pingjum	50	80	71	50
Wolvega	----	92	85	107
Workum	74	97	108	89
Woudsend	34	50	41	31
Ytens (formerly Kromwal)	65	122	90	95
Zwaagwesteinde	3	----	85	100
Total	**4,941**	**8,176**	**7,386**	**6,672**

Province of North Holland

	1841	1900	1940	1956
Aalsmeer (Uitweg)	64			
Aalsmeer (Zijdweg)	105	654	721	648
Aalsmeer (Nieuwe vermaning)	120			
Alkmaar	116	440	867	656
Amsterdam	1,641			
Nieuwendam	23	5,010	7,781	5,500
Baarn	----	----	139	160
Barsingerhorn	240	435	284	210
Beemster	166	267	206	180
Beverwijk	15	141	467	467
Broek op Langendijk	26	100	177	116
Burg, Waal, and Oosterend op Texel	400	695	670	572
Bussum	----	----	305	429

	1841	1900	1940	1956
Edam	26	80	139	104
Enkhuizen	43	86	115	89
Graft, Noordeinde (1836)	50	70	60	45
Oost Graftdijk	50	38		
West Graftdijk	24	40	67	65
Haarlem	593	2,250	4,608	3,458
Haarlemmermeer	----	----	----	150
Helder and Huisduinen	132	349	170	233
Hoorn	121	142	190	115
Den Hoorn op Texel	45	42	43	----
Hilversum—Huizen	----	291	600	780
Den Ilp—Landsmeer	47	72	119	80
Knollendam	60	130	85	35
Koog-Zaandijk	499	531	488	390
Krommenie	116	180	215	170
Medemblik	31	37	66	39
Middelie-Axwijk	135	185	163	109
Monnikendam	33	103	76	75
Nieuwe and Oude Niedorp	32	161	141	109
Pumerend	84	246	185	180
De Rijp	160	184	90	68
Terschelling	132	140	170	144
Twisk-Abbekerk	127	156	128	72
Westzaan-Noord	83	146	144	
Westzaan-Zuid	105	116	81	170
Wieringen	140	275	403	330
Wormer and Jisp	58	96	121	80
Wormerveer Noord	78			
Wormerveer Zuid	167	460	458	369
IJmuiden	----	----	170	225
Zaandam Oost	268	503	454	
Zaandam West	483	753	763	1,014
Noord Zijpe	100	76	108	40
Zuid Zijpe	88	81		46
Total	**7,026**	**15,761**	**22,237**	**17,722**

Province of Groningen

	1840	1900	1940	1956
Groningen	370	1,017	1,142	1,163
Den Horn	100	67	85	44
Leermens-Loppersum	48	98	98	92
Mensingeweer	48	100	80	75
Middelstum	65	74	36	37
Midwolda c.a. (now Winschoten)	65	120	129	104
Noordbroek and Nieuw Scheemda	85	82	45	28
Noordhorn	60	89	69	70
Oude and Nieuwe Pekela	----	40	42	52
Pieterzijl (now Grijpskerk)	48	87	82	49
Sappemeer	350	494	265	270
Stadskanaal	----	106	73	85
Uithuizen	30	98	89	95
Veendam	160	240	160	127
Zijldijk	65	83	68	69
Total	**1,494**	**2,795**	**2,463**	**2,360**

Province of Drente

	1840	1900	1940	1956
Assen	----	45	71	86
Meppel	----	89	90	145
Emmen	----	----	30	43
Roden	----	----	----	39
Total	**----**	**134**	**191**	**313**

Province of Overijssel

	1840	1900	1940	1956
Almelo	73	125	162	192
Blokzijl	150	151	70	75
Borne	30	64	60	60
Deventer	80	255	427	325
Enschedé	65	180	560	625
Giethoorn Noord	60			
Giethoorn Zuid	314	490	436	389
Hengelo	85	154	429	353
Kampen	97	172	150	127
Steenwijk (formerly Zuidveen)	135	190	185	167
Zwartsluis	40	31	21	21
Zwolle	85	219	203	240
Total	**1,214**	**2,031**	**2,703**	**2,574**

Province of Gelderland

	1847	1900	1940	1956
Apeldoorn	....	82	410	325
Arnhem	....	390	912	840
Nijmegen	28	244	325	135
Wageningen	....	65	146	240
Winterswijk	13	45	76	140
Zutphen	63	117	92	150
Total	**104**	**943**	**1,961**	**1,830**

Province of Utrecht

	1847	1900	1940	1956
Amersfoort	....	....	242	275
Utrecht	100	553	1,030	752
Zeist	....	....	333	313
Total	**100**	**553**	**1,605**	**1,340**

Province of South Holland

	1847	1900	1940	1956
Delft	....	....	116	134
Dordrecht	....	65	131	150
's Gravenhage	....	(1898)860	3,020	2,926
Leiden	43	460	429	500
Ouddorp	35	9	21	31
Rotterdam	195	(1898)500	1,252	989
Total	**273**	**1,894**	**4,969**	**4,730**

Province of Zeeland

	1847	1900	1940	1956
Aardenburg	50	71	100	100
Goes	14	51	37	50
Middelburg	92	194	138	107
Vlissingen	18	60	172	180
Total	**174**	**376**	**447**	**437**

Province of North Brabant

	1847	1900	1940	1956
Breda	....	41	61	103
Eindhoven	....	....	110	205
Total	**....**	**41**	**171**	**308**

Province of Limburg

	1847	1900	1940	1955
Zuid Limburg	....	....	101	160
Total	**....**	**....**	**101**	**160**

Summary by Provinces

	1840	1900	1940	1956
Friesland	4,941	8,176	7,386	6,672
Groningen	1,494	2,795	2,463	2,360
Drente	....	134	191	313
Overijssel	1,214	2,031	2,703	2,574
Gelderland	104	943	1,961	1,830
Utrecht	100	553	1,605	1,340
North Holland	7,026	15,761	22,237	17,722
South Holland	273	1,894	4,969	4,730
Zeeland	174	376	447	437
North Brabant	....	41	171	308
Limburg	....	....	101	160
Total		**15,326**	**32,704**	**44,234**	**38,446**

Total Mennonites According to the National Census (including children)

	Dec. 31 1859	Dec. 31 1899	Dec. 31 1930	May 31 1947
Friesland	5,762	14,943	12,371	13,442
Groningen	4,743	4,550	3,797	4,275
Drente	286	641	655	923
Overijssel	2,877	3,460	3,561	3,940
Gelderland	465	1,701	2,695	3,403
Utrecht	340	1,088	2,199	2,912
North Holland	15,713	26,508	28,124	28,492
South Holland	963	3,883	7,284	8,237
Zeeland	335	645	634	642
North Brabant	55	275	452	758
Limburg	14	92	240	396
Total	**41,813**	**57,786**	**62,012**	**67,420**

Netherlands States-General, the highest legislative and executive power in the Netherlands in the 16th-18th centuries, repeatedly acted in behalf of the oppressed and persecuted Mennonites abroad.

On Feb. 19, 1660, the States-General addressed the magistrates of Zürich, Switzerland, to demand for the Mennonites in this canton free departure with their property. At the same date a letter was sent to the magistrates of Bern, Switzerland, with an urgent request to release the arrested Mennonites. In 1687 the States-General sent Adolf de Vreede, a Dutch Mennonite, as an ambassador to Bern, to inquire into the conditions of the Mennonites, many of whom were then imprisoned in Bern. On March 24, 1695, the States sent a message to John William, Palatine Elector, in behalf of the oppressed Mennonites in this territory, asking compensation for the property confiscated from the Mennonites, and on June 24 of that year passed a resolution to intervene with John William in behalf of the Mennonites in the duchy of Jülich, Germany.

On March 10, 1710, a letter was sent to the government of Bern, interceding for the persecuted Bernese Anabaptists. Upon a petition by the Dutch Mennonites, the States resolved to instruct Louis Runckel (q.v.), their delegate in Switzerland, at Schaffhausen, to compile a complete list of the Mennonites then in prison for their faith, and to be concerned for the interests of the Swiss Mennonites. The expenses of this work by Runckel were defrayed by the States. Again and again the secretary of the States corresponded with Runckel, and the Mennonite archives of Amsterdam contain a large number of copies of letters by Runckel on the situation of the Bernese Anabaptists. When the government of Bern finally decided to deport a number of Mennonites to America, these were released by order of the States when the boats on which they were transported down the Rhine arrived at Nijmegen (q.v.) in the Netherlands. Again on Jan. 22, 1715, the States interceded by letter with the Bernese magistrates in favor of the Mennonites, still oppressed.

In 1732 the Dutch Mennonites drew the attention of the States-General to the situation of the East Prussian (Lithuanian) Mennonites, who were persecuted by Frederick William II of Prussia. On April 22, 1732, the States contacted Reinier van Reede tot Ginckel, their ambassador in Berlin, instructing him to present to the king a request which emphatically demanded that the privilege of religious freedom for the Mennonites be maintained and persecution cease. An extended correspondence between Ginckel and the Dutch States during the years 1732-38 shows what was done and how seriously the States were concerned with the interests of the East Prussian Mennonites.

Finally on Dec. 23, 1749, a resolution was passed in the States to intervene with the king of Poland in behalf of the Mennonites in West Prussia, especially of those in Danzig, who were in serious difficulty with the Polish officials. On this matter there are also many letters in the Amsterdam Mennonite archives showing how C. van Gemert, representative of the Dutch States at Danzig, and C. Calkoen, their ambassador at Dresden, defended the interests of the Mennonites in this area. vDZ.

Inv. Arch. Amst. I, Nos. 1746-1865; *Mart. Mir.* D 832-36, E 1131 ff.; Müller, *Berner Täufer*, 167, 184, 185-87, 193 f., 259-70, 280, 283.

Nette Lipkes (Lupkes, Lypkens) (d. 1567), a Dutch Anabaptist preacher at the time of Menno Simons. The two met in 1557 at Dokkum, Friesland, where Nette apparently was a preacher, and went together via Franeker to Harlingen, where the discussion on the ban took place. Afterwards, about 1562, Nette seems to have been an elder in 't Oversticht, Dutch province of Overijssel. In 1566, when the strife between the Frisians and Flemish (*q.v.*) broke out, he was one of the elders called in to mediate. Finally he sided with the Flemish group. He died at Dokkum in 1567. vdZ.

Menno Simons, *Opera Omnia* (1681) 486b, 487a; *Writings*, 1010; *BRN* VII, 63, 258 f.; *DB* 1893, 12-76, *passim*; 1894, 39.

Nettes, Johannes, b. 1707 at Alkmaar, d. 1777 at Leiden, was a physician at Middelburg, Dutch province of Zeeland, and an elder of the local Mennonite congregation 1729-72. In 1742 he obtained his medical degree at the University of Leiden. He was renowned as an oculist and eye surgeon, operated on the eye of a princess of Orange. In 1742 he retired from the ministry, moved to Leiden, and devoted himself to the practice of medicine. vdZ.

F. Nagtglas, *Levensberichten von Zeeuwen* II (Middelburg, 1893) 268; *DB* 1868, 92.

Netzebruch, former Polish territory, acquired by Prussia in 1772, whereas the lower Netze had come into Prussian hands earlier. Netzebruch is now Polish again (since 1945). Large areas of this region between the Vistula and the Warthe were marshy, others wooded. As early as 1738 Mennonite families from Poland had tried to make this land arable, but were interrupted by the first Silesian War. When oppression at the hands of a landlord in the region of Schwetz became more and more marked, three Mennonites from the village of Jeziorka on the Tuchel Heath made a successful personal appeal to Frederick the Great to have this region admitted into eastern Ostmark; they also received permission for 32 Mennonite families to settle in this desolate region, which they turned into fertile land for grain and meadow by industry and perseverance. A *Privilegium* of Feb. 7, 1765, granted them free exercise of their religion, recognition of their word in place of the oath, freedom from military service for themselves and their posterity, and the erection of their own schools. For their buildings they were permitted to use the necessary wood free of charge. Each family received at least 40 "Magdeburg Morgen" of land, and several families received more.

In May and June 1765, 35 families with 194 persons came to Driesen, a town on the eastern border of Prussia and founded the settlements between Driesen and Friedeberg: Brenkenhoffswalde, Franzthal, and Neu-Dessau. The Mennonites in Neu-Dessau soon moved into the other two villages; by 1787 there were 266 Mennonites living in Brenkenhoffswalde and Franzthal. Of all the settlers, according to one report, "the Mennonites proved themselves most industrious and most useful." And the Department of Foreign Affairs declared them to be "excellent, useful citizens of the state, even though they do not bear arms."

In a few years all the land in the Netzebruch had been bought up and settled, so that there were no possibilities for Mennonite sons to settle there. In 1785 a Mennonite family emigrated to Vishenka in Little Russia, and joined the congregation organized on the estate of Count Romanzov. Several other families were about to follow, but the Department of Foreign Affairs decided that the Mennonites should be kept in the country and ordered that they should be permitted to buy land in other parts of the Netzebruch (*Menn. Bl.,* 1928, 91).

The Brenkenhoffswalde congregation met in the homes of the members until the available rooms were too small. The government then gave them a building site for a church free of charge, and the funds for the building were donated by the Dutch Mennonites; on Nov. 8, 1778, the congregation met for the first time in their own church. In 1787 Franzthal also acquired a small church, funds having been raised among the Mennonites of Hamburg and Holland by the preachers Jan de Jager (*q.v.*) and Johannes Deknatel (*q.v.*).

In the period of the Enlightenment at the beginning of the 19th century many groups hostile to the government were formed, and in consequence all meetings of private groups were prohibited, including the Mennonites. The only exception made to this ruling concerned meetings held under the auspices of the Bohemian Brethren (*Herrnhuter*). The Mennonites at once formed connections with the Brethren and continued to meet unmolested. This fraternal association between the two brotherhoods, furthered by the Brethren traveling evangelists, Gottlieb Jahr and Niederschuh, had a stimulating effect on the Mennonites and led to a number of beneficial practices in the Brenkenhoffswalde congregation, such as the consecration of infants (*q.v.*), which was not yet observed by the West Prussian Mennonites, mission work, and the employment of their own teachers in their schools.

At the end of 1831 the church board of the Brenkenhoffswalde congregation was informed by the government that all privileges were to be withdrawn. The Mennonites were given their choice between accepting full military service, paying 5 per cent more in taxes, or emigrating. A petition to Frederick William III brought this reply: "My dear children, no matter how much I would like to help you, I am unable to do so." Thereupon they decided to emigrate to Russia. Since Nicholas I had prohibited such immigration, the Mennonites sent him a petition in the summer of 1832 for permission for 40 families to join their brethren in the Molotschna settlement (*q.v.*); the petition was not granted until the fall of 1833. Meanwhile some families had moved to other places. In July 1834, 28 Mennonite families and 10 Lutheran families who had now become Mennonites (Johann Lange and his son-in-law Johann Preuss, Gottfried Rabe, Johann Rabsch, Hermann Lenzmann, Johann Glöckler, Michael Kant, Christian Dosso, Christian Herfort, Gottlieb Strauss), besides two unmarried Lutherans (Karl Brüsso and Karl Klatt), emigrated to the Molotschna, arriving on Oct. 8, 1834, and remained for the winter in the villages of Alexanderwohl, Friedensdorf, Rudnerweide, Grossweide, Pastva, and Steinbach. In the following spring the immigrants built the village of Gnadenfeld (*q.v.*), which later became the center for the eastern Molotschna settlement (*Jahrbuch* 1909, 107), and had much influence on the rise of the Mennonite Brethren. (See **Brenkenhoffswalde.**) HEGE.

"Aus der Gnadenfelder Gemeindechronik," in Heinrich Dirks' *Mennonitisches Jahrbuch* (Berdyansk, 1909) 33-46; (1910) 106-16; A. Hänseler, "Mennoniten im Netzebruch," in *Brandenburg. Ztscht für Heimatkunde und Heimatpflege* IV (Eberswalde, 1926) 205 ff. (reprinted in *Menn. Bl.*, 1928, 90-92); B. H. Unruh, "Die Mennoniten in der Neumark," *Gem.-Kal.* 1941, 58-76; Herbert Wiebe, *Das Siedlungswerk niederländischer Mennoniten* (Marburg, 1952) 45 f.; *ML* III, 206 f.

Neuanlage, a Mennonite village name found in the West and East reserves of Manitoba; Hague, Sask.; Jansen, Neb.; twice in the Cuauhtemoc Old Colony Mennonite settlements, and Durango, Mexico; and in the Menno and other Chaco colonies of Paraguay. (*ML* III, 207.) C.K.

Neubergthal Rudnerweide Mennonite Church, having some 150 members in and around the village of Neubergthal, five miles southeast of Altona, Man., is one of the ten congregations of the Rudnerweide (*q.v.*) Mennonite Church, all of which are organized as sections of a single congregation, rotating ministers every Sunday. H.H.H.

Neuburg on the Danube, the former capital of the duchy of Pfalz-Neuburg, in which Anabaptist teachings were spread very early. Otto Heinrich, Count Palatine, on Jan. 28, 1528, issued an order against the "new Christians." According to the chronicles of the Hutterian Brethren three Anabaptists were executed for their faith in Neuburg in the 16th century, among them the successful preacher Andreas (*q.v.*) of Neiss. Southwest of Neuburg the Maxweiler (*q.v.*) Mennonite settlement was made in 1802; its inhabitants emigrated to America about the middle of the 19th century. HEGE.

K. Schottenloher, *Pfalzgraf Ottheinrich und das Buch* (Münster, 1927) 83; Wolkan, *Lieder; idem, Geschicht-Buch,* 182; Zieglschmid, *Chronik,* 233; *ML* III, 207.

Neuchâtel (German, *Neuenburg*), a canton in northwestern Switzerland, area 305 sq. miles, consists of the former districts of Valagin and Neuchâtel. Neuchâtel was open to the influence of the Reformation at an early date. Under the protection of Bern, with which Neuchâtel had been associated since 1406, William Farel (*q.v.*) brought the Reformation to the canton about 1530. It was a decisive victory for the Reformation that the princes and nobility all adopted the Protestant faith. It became the policy to tolerate only Protestantism, especially when Neuchâtel came under the rule of Frederick William I (*q.v.*) of Prussia in 1707 (until 1848).

Closely allied to the Swiss Confederation by old treaties and common interests, Neuchâtel was admitted into the Confederation in 1814 as the twenty-first canton. A revolution freed it from Prussian domination in 1848, when the republic was declared. Since then freedom of religion and conscience has

been assured and compulsory civil marriage introduced, and the registration of births made independent of the baptismal record.

The Anabaptist movement never reached the significance in Neuchâtel that it had in the cantons of Zürich and Bern, in part because of the difference in language, but it was for the Swiss Brethren a place of refuge when persecution reached its height in Bern. The date of the first immigration can no longer be ascertained, but by the middle of the 17th century many had escaped to the mountains of the canton. A few families wandered into the Val de Ruz and into the region of La Chaux de Fonds and Le Locle.

As in the Jura, the Anabaptists became pioneers in agriculture and cattle raising in Neuchâtel. Their success soon stirred up the envy of the native population; the competition led to an economic struggle against them. Ernst Müller wrote, "We find in the Neuchâtel Jura exactly the same social and political movement of the populace against the immigrants with their economic superiority as in the Bernese Jura."

The early 18th century brought a new influx of Mennonites, but also a renewed opposition to them. The complaints of the populace produced an order that the Mennonites then in the canton should be tolerated, but no others should be admitted.

The mayor of Valagin is indeed said to have registered the complaint in Bern that church unity in the canton was threatened by the settlement of Mennonites, since a law of 1707 stipulated that the Protestant faith should be the only one tolerated. Negotiations between the government of Bern and Frederick William (*q.v.*) of Prussia resulted in the order on April 21, 1734, "that these Mennonites, Pietists, and Anabaptists shall be tolerated in view of the testimonial given them by the council that these people live as good citizens." Thereupon the Bernese government wrote to the governor on Dec. 21, 1734, and to the Prussian council in Neuchâtel, that Valagin complained about the settlement of sectarians on its territory, and besought the governor to take the necessary steps to "get rid of these encumbering people." The king replied that the Mennonites were to be tolerated, both because of the good repute of their conduct and because it was wrong to persecute for their religion persons who live as good citizens. After further negotiations the king wrote, "Any spirit of persecution is obnoxious to me and I cannot understand why one wants to drive these poor people out of the country, since they do no harm to anyone and do nothing that could jeopardize the welfare of the state. They seem to me to be deserving of sympathy and it would always be more worth while to draw them to you with kindness and Christian love with a good example, than to deprive them of the refuge they have sought with you. It is therefore my wish that they be tolerated until I find it advisable and necessary to order otherwise." Finally the mayor of Valagin had to admit that there was no good reason for disturbing the Mennonites, and that they rather deserved gratitude for their industry and their general character.

But the noble intentions of the great king were

not nobly accepted. Agitation against the Mennonites continued. The people of Valagin assembled, ostensibly to preserve their old rights and liberties, and the mayors of the villages and the council of Bern challenged the king. Thereupon the king replied on June 4, 1735, that those sectarians who had settled in Neuchâtel and Valagin since 1724 should be sent out in 1736, but very few families were hit by this arrangement.

In spite of all difficulties the Mennonites were able to maintain themselves in Neuchâtel, though in some instances they changed their location. They came on Sunday from great distances to the spacious room of some farmer for mutual edification. For a long time the central point for such meetings was the hamlet Bressels near Locle (see **Locle-Bressels**). In 1894 a suitable church was built under the direction of Elder Henri Ummel in Les Bulles near Chaux de Fonds, in which the Mennonites of the canton meet, with about 150 members. From the 18th century on, the Mennonites of Neuchâtel adhered to the Amish wing.   S.G.

Fallet-Scheurer, "Geschichtsbilder aus dem Bauernleben des 17. und 18. Jahrhunderts," in *Schweizer Bauer,* 1929; Müller, *Berner Täufer;* S. Geiser, *Die Taufgesinnten-Gemeinden* (Karlsruhe, 1931); D. L. Gratz, *Bernese Anabaptists* (Scottdale, 1953); *ML* III, 208 f.

Neu-Chortitza (Novo-Chortitza), one of the major villages of the Baratov Mennonite settlement (*q.v.*) in the province of Ekaterinoslav, Ukraine, Russia, established in 1872. Neu-Chortitza and Gnadenthal comprised 10,000 acres of land and had a population of 550 in 1914. In 1874 the villages Grünfeld, Steinfeld, and Hochfeld were added, which formed the Schlachtin Mennonite settlement (*q.v.*). The church serving these settlements was the Neu-Chortitza Mennonite Church (*q.v.*).

During the Revolution and under Stalin's regime the settlements suffered very severely. Many of the inhabitants were sent into exile. During the German occupation (1941-43) the former life was somewhat revived. Some 600 inhabitants of the Neu-Chortitza village alone left for Germany in October 1943, of whom approximately 550 were forcibly returned to Russia after the collapse of Germany. Thus relatively only a few of the settlers reached Canada and South America. (*ML* III, 207.)   C.K.

Neuer Haus- und Landwirtschaftskalender (Odessa, 1913) 50, 75; *ML* III, 207, 278.

Neu-Chortitza (Novo-Chortitza) Mennonite Church was organized in 1872 in the Baratov Mennonite settlement (*q.v.*), as a subsidiary of the Chortitza Mennonite Church (*q.v.*). When the Schlachtin settlement was established in the neighborhood in 1874, its villages also became a part of the Neu-Chortitza Mennonite Church. In 1905 the membership was 1,045, with a total population of 2,569. Jacob Päthkau served as the elder of the congregation in 1910-18. He was succeeded as elder by J. A. Rempel 1920-29, who was the last elder of the congregation. Other ministers, with dates of ordination, were Peter Klassen (ordained 1890), Jacob Epp (1852), Gerhard Dyck (1856), Gerhard Ens I (1860), Anton Sudermann (1870), Gerhard Ens II (1870), Dietrich Epp (1872), Cornelius Rempel

(1879), Jacob Klassen (1900), Abr. Penner (1880), Heinrich Dyck (1884), Klaas Wiebe (1884), Aaron Warkentin (1890), Peter Penner (1890), Jacob Bärg (1892), Abraham Kröger (1897), Dietrich Görzen (1898), Wilhelm Sawatzky (1905). The congregation had places of worship at Neu-Chortitza and Grünfeld. During the Revolution and under Stalin the congregation suffered severely. In 1923, 500 persons from this congregation emigrated to Canada.

Elder J. A. Rempel was very active in his congregation and also in representing the Mennonites to the government. He served many congregations all over Russia. In 1925 he was delegated to attend the first Mennonite World Conference at Basel. In 1929 he was sent into exile, where he perished in 1941. Peter Funk, a co-minister, was also exiled in 1930. Worship services were discontinued. During the German occupation (1941-43), religious life was revived. The leading minister then was Jacob Friesen, who later emigrated to Drake, Sask. The church records of the congregation (according to a niece of Elder Jacob Päthkau) were burned under the Soviet government. The majority of the members of the Neu-Chortitza Mennonite Church were taken to Germany with the retreating German army in 1943. However, only a fraction of them reached Canada and South America, the majority having been sent back by the Russian army.   C.K.

H. Dirks, *Statistik* (1905) 6, 61; A. A. Töws, *Mennonitische Märtyrer* I (Abbotsford, 1949) 34-46.

Neu-Dessau: see Netzebruch.

Neudorf (Czech, *Nová Ves Ostrozská,* also Waltersdorf), a village near Lundenburg in Moravia, in the former domain of the Zierotin family. Under the protection of the wealthy John of Zierotin the Hutterian Brethren opened a Bruderhof here in 1570. In 1605 the Bruderhof, located on the border, suffered severely in the Hungarian war; imperial troops plundered the Bruderhof and killed four Brethren, including the householder Jakob Köppel, and led three away captive. In December 1620 most of the inmates fled before the inhuman cruelties of the imperial troops to Sobotiste in Hungary; many succumbed to illness and the rigors of the journey on the way. On Jan. 23, 1621, troops burned down the house in Neudorf with all the property and goods in it. That was the end of the settlement. (Beck, *Geschichts-Bücher;* Wolkan, *Geschicht-Buch;* Zieglschmid, *Chronik;* *ML* III, 207.)   P.DE.

Neudorferhof, an estate farmed by five Mennonite families near Obermoschel in the Palatinate, which has since 1816 been the seat of a Mennonite congregation. Its members live scattered through a number of villages. Formerly the Mennonites on these farms belonged to the Rheingrafenstein (*q.v.*) congregation, and held their services in the hall of the castle and on the Dimrotherhof. Since 1816 services are held only on the Neudorferhof. For five years the members met in a living room and 1821-86 in a room in the house of the leader Johann Zerger, which was furnished for the purpose. In 1885 the congregation built a meetinghouse of its own, and dedicated it in 1886 (*Gbl.,* 1886, 55 f.).

After the death of the first preacher, Abraham

Hertzler of the Antoniushof (1817), the congregation was served by Jakob Galle (*q.v.*), preacher of the Uffhofen congregation. On Nov. 7, 1819, Johannes Weber of the Neudorferhof was ordained to the ministry. In 1841 Jakob Schowalter of the Bangerterhof took his place. In 1862 the vote fell on two brothers, Jakob Weber and Johann Weber.

In 1878 the congregation joined with Ernstweiler (*q.v.*) and Kühbörncheshof (*q.v.*) to employ the first salaried preacher, Samuel Blickensdörfer of the Kohlhof. In 1879 he accepted the pulpit in Sembach, leaving the one in Neudorferhof vacant. Then in 1880 Abraham Hirschler took the position, and gave it his untiring devotion for 50 years. He lived in Kaiserslautern. In 1930 he retired. In 1931 Abraham Harder of Thiergart, West Prussia, was installed as preacher in Ernstweiler. Four years later (1935) he moved to Paraguay. Hugo Scheffler, previously the pastor of the congregation in Sembach, took his place in 1935; Scheffler emigrated to America and was succeeded by Gerhard Hein, who is still (1957) serving. The affiliated congregations took the name Kaiserslautern (*q.v.*).

On July 16, 1890, the congregation was incorporated. Baptismal services are held every other year in the fall. Communion is observed four times a year. In 1941 the congregation had 110 baptized members, and 96 in 1956. In 1951 the congregation detached itself from Kaiserslautern and joined the Sembach congregation.

In 1923 the inhabitants of the estate organized a co-operative with a specific division of labor, the individual holdings of each family, however, remaining intact. The work in the fields and in the vineyards is done in common. The cattle are housed in commonly owned barns. The proceeds of the entire establishment flow into a common treasury, from which the needs of all the families are met. At the end of the year the net gain is divided according to the individual holdings. NEFF.

Frankfurter Illustrierte Zeitung, No. 5, Feb. 9, 1933, p. 117, with photographs; *ML* III, 207 f.

Neue amerikanische Calender, Der, a 32-44 page almanac, published in the German language by Johan Räber, an Amish layman at Baltic, Ohio, from 1930 to the present. In addition to usual features of almanacs, it contains the "Schriften und Lieder" used in Old Order Amish church services, inspirational articles and poems, articles on church history, and a list of Amish ministers arranged according to bishop districts within states. Since 1951 the *Calender* has also carried lists of ministers among the Old Colony Mennonites in Mexico and the Hutterian Brethren in Canada and the United States. (GCL has a complete file.) N.P.S.

Neue Zeytung *von den Wiedertaufern und ihrer Sekt*. This is the title of a pamphlet published in 1528 against the Anabaptists. The appendix contains thirteen articles added by Urban Rhegius, "which they consider true," which he refuted item by item in his booklet *Nothwendige Warnung*. Ranke considered these thirteen points the actual teaching of the Salzburg Anabaptists, and made several citations from them; he thereby does this group of Anabap-

tists grave injustice, for this is a polemic against the Anabaptists, and the excerpts from it which are known lead to the conclusion that the Anabaptists were not capable of much good. Nevertheless we learn a few things which may approximate historical truth. With all necessary reservations, the following may be stated:

In the pamphlet Eitelhans Langenmantel (*q.v.*) is named; he is known to have been one of Denk's disciples. It is said that he denied predestination, for God cannot be made responsible for sin. A native inborn way of doing good is really possible, and there are sinless human beings. Christ accepted as an exemplary teacher, but not as the fulfillment of the law or as the Son of God. The denial of the Sonship of Christ, which was first preached by Haetzer, is now also to be found among the simple Anabaptists in Salzburg and with Langenmantel. Christ they believed to be only a prophet, who by word and example brought the natural moral law closer to human consciousness and strengthened the desire of the heart for God.

We shall not examine how nearly these statements correspond with fact, although many certainly are not true. It is certain that the influence of Denk is shown here, even though in a somewhat exaggerated and distorted form. He was by no means an isolated thinker. He had his circle of followers, and as is shown in the polemic of Rhegius, even congregations that were attached to him. H.Q.

U. Heberle, "Johannes Denk und die Ausbreitung seiner Lehre," *Theologische Studien und Kritiken* (1855); Leopold Ranke, *Deutsche Geschichte im Zeitalter der Ref.* III, 407 ff.; *ML* III, 210.

Neuenburg: see **Neuchâtel.**

Neuenburg (Malashovka), a Mennonite village name of the Chortitza settlement, Ukraine, transplanted to West Reserve of Manitoba, and Cuauhtemoc, Mexico.

Neuendorf (Neudorf), a village name found in the Chortitza settlement, Ukraine; East and West reserves of Manitoba; Swift Current, Sask.; Cuauhtemoc and Durango, Mexico; and Neuland, Paraguay. C.K.

Neuendorf Mennonite Church was a subsidiary of the Chortitza Mennonite Church (*q.v.*) in the Ukraine. In 1905 the total population was 1,620, of whom 732 were baptized members. Neuendorf had a meetinghouse, but was otherwise an integral part of the mother church. (Dirks, *Statistik*, 1905, 60.) C.K.

Neuenschwander (Niswander, Neiswander, Nicewander, Neuschwanger, Neuen, Nisewander, Newswanger), meaning a man from Neuenschwand, near Langnau, canton of Bern, Switzerland. The word Neuenschwand means a place where the forest was recently cleared. The first person of this family known to have been an Anabaptist was Uli Neuenschwander from Eggiwil, who appeared at the Bern disputation March 11-18, 1538. In 1551 Mathis Neuenschwander fled from his Emmental home because of his Anabaptist faith. Peter Neuenschwander and family left their home in Langnau in 1729 and settled at Cortébert in the Jura. A son Michael lived on the Münsterberg. The latter's son Michael moved to the Normanvillars settlement in France and in 1823 migrated to Wayne Co., Ohio, becoming one of the first settlers in the Chippewa settlement. In 1833 the family moved to Putnam Co., Ohio, to become the first Mennonite settlers there. A son, John B. Neuenschwander, founded the Mennonite settlement in Polk Co., Iowa, by settling there in 1849. This family moved to Moniteau Co., Mo., in 1868, becoming one of the pioneer families in that settlement. Peter M. Neuenschwander (*q.v.*) was a bishop at Berne, Ind. The Dutch *Naamlijst* of 1802 lists Ulrich Neuenschwander as an elder of the congregation at Boliou (?) in the county of Limousin, France, ordained in 1782.

Another family that some claim were originally Neuenschwanders are the Newschwangers who first appear in Lancaster Co., Pa., in the 18th century. Of this family Emmanual Newschwanger (1758-1846) ministered to the Diller (MC) congregation near Newville, Pa., for many years. In Virginia, Abraham Nisewander (1774-1846) served a number of years in the Rockingham County Mennonite ministry. In later generations the name became common in the Church of the Brethren. Other families of this name have been located in Ontario, Kansas, and Oregon.

A Neuschwander family emigrated to Oregon from Switzerland in the 1880's settling eventually near Silverton.   D.L.G.

Daniel Kauffman, *Mennonite Cyclopedic Dictionary* (Scottdale, 1937) 264; D. L. Gratz, *Bernese Anabaptists* (Scottdale, 1953) *passim.*

Neuenschwander Mennonite Church (now extinct) was located at Berne, Ind. Peter M. Neuenschwander (1854-1946) was ordained to the ministry at the age of 17 at Moron in the Bernese Jura. In 1876 he came with his parents and other families to America, settling near Berne, and became an assistant minister in the church there. In 1879, when a large meetinghouse was built, he and several other families withdrew from this church and formed a congregation which was allied throughout its existence with the loosely organized Conference of Swiss Congregations. The reason for Neuenschwander's withdrawal from the larger church was the liberal practice of the other ministers in dress and church policy. In 1883 Peter M. Neuenschwander was ordained a bishop of the Neuenschwander Church by Bishop Christian Sommer of the Sonnenberg Mennonite Church. The group met in a small church located about one-half mile west of Berne, and for many years resisted modern innovations such as automobiles and electricity. The aged bishop preached every other Sunday to his small flock until 1944. The group was served occasionally by ministers from Sonnenberg until about 1950, when the remaining few members joined other Mennonite churches in the vicinity.
                                                      D.L.G.

Eva F. Sprunger, *The First Hundred Years* (Berne, 1938) 222-23; D. L. Gratz, *Bernese Anabaptists* (Scottdale, 1953) 155.

Neues Buchstabir- und Lesebuch, *Besonders bearbeitet und eingerichtet zum Gebrauch Deutscher*

Schulen. Enthaltend das ABC, und vielerley Buchstabir- und Leseuebungen, compiled by Benjamin Eby (*q.v.*), was published by Heinrich Wilhelm Peterson at Berlin (now Kitchener), Ont., in 1839. A second edition, entitled *A B C-Buchstabir- und Lesebuch,* was printed by Heinrich Eby at Berlin in 1842, "for the use of German schools in Canada." This small booklet of 144 pages became very popular. It was reprinted again in 1847 at Berlin, and by J. F. Funk at Elkhart, Ind., 1869, 1871, 1882, 1896, 1909. It was used in German schools in the churches in Canada, and in Sunday schools for the teaching of German. It contains the alphabet, 81 exercises in orthography, the words graded from one to six syllables, a dictionary, rules of syntax, a list of the Old Testament books including the Apocrypha, some Bible history, a short history of printing, the Ten Commandments, the Apostles' Creed, the Lord's Prayer, some sample letters, wise sayings, the multiplication tables, and two addresses to children.

                                                      S.F.C.

Neu-Falkenstein in Galicia (*q.v.*), a village, formerly Austrian, now Polish, about 20 miles from Lemberg, where a number of Mennonite families from the Palatinate, Germany, settled in 1784-85. They formed a small congregation which held its first communion service on Christmas Day of 1785. Neu-Falkenstein was the center of the Mennonites in Galicia until about 1800, when Einsiedel (*q.v.*) became the center. (*DB* 1865, 101 ff.) Neu-Falkenstein is probably identical with Falkenstein (*q.v.*).   vDZ.

Neuf-Brisach (German, *Neubreisach*), a village (pop. 1,400) in département Haut-Rhin, Alsace, situated 10 miles east of Colmar (*q.v.*), on the bank of the Rhine, opposite the German town of Breisach, is the seat of a Mennonite congregation, which in 1950 numbered 65 baptized members and 43 children. The congregation was formed by a group of members of the Colmar congregation which at first met at Wolfganzen. Benjamin Peterschmitt, an elder at Colmar from 1891, was their first elder, serving until 1932. The present elder is Jean Peterschmitt, of Rheinfelderhof (*q.v.*), where most members of the congregation, nearly all of whom are farmers, are living, and where the school of the congregation is located. In 1924 the congregation acquired a house just outside Neuf-Brisach, called "Bethel," which has been equipped as a meetinghouse.   vDZ.

P. Sommer, "Assemblée de Neuf-Brisach," in *Christ Seul* (October 1932) 6 f.

Neufeld (Neufeldt, Nifeld, Nyfelt, Neuenfeld, Nieufelt, Newfield), a Mennonite family name, appeared for the first time in the Danzig Mennonite church records in 1694. Reimer lists the origin as referring to land reclaimed from the sea. The name was common among the Mennonite congregations of Danzig, Prussia, and Russia, from where it spread to the United States, Canada, and South America. The *Universal Biography* lists two teachers of philosophy at Danzig, George H. Neufeld (d. 1673) and Konrad N. Neufeld (d. 1656), both sons of George N. Neufeld. C. Henry Smith refers to a study of Mennonite names in Prussia made in 1912, which lists 161 Neufelds.

Among the Mennonites of Russia the name Neufeld was very common. A. A. Neufeld (*q.v.*) was an outstanding educator. Peter Neufeld (*q.v.*) was elder of the Chortitza Mennonite Church. Isaak Neufeld of Waldheim, Molotschna, was a manufacturer of agricultural machinery. David P. Neufeld, son of Peter Neufeld, minister of the Ohrloff Mennonite Church, was an educator. Gerhard J. Neufeld was a physician at Davlekanovo, Ufa. Wilhelm P. Neufeld was minister of the Schönsee Mennonite Church and perished in exile. Heinrich D. Neufeld, founder of the secondary school at Ohrloff, Zagradovka, was murdered by the Machno bandits. Cornelius G. Neufeld, educator, died in Shafter, Cal.

The name is found quite frequently in central Kansas, where Mennonites from Russia settled in 1874 ff. Of 330 members of the Bethel Mennonite Church of Inman, Kan., 61 are Neufelds. The name appears more frequently than any other in the Inman telephone directory, 29 times in all. But the name is found at other places also. In the General Conference *Handbook of Information* of 1954 there are fifteen ministers by that name listed for Canada and six in the United States. In the *Civilian Public Service Directory* the name occurs twelve times, nine from Kansas, two from California, and one from Oklahoma. G. B. Neufeld is a missionary in the Congo, and Jacob H. Neufeld a missionary in the Chaco, Paraguay.

Who's Who Among the Mennonites (1943) lists the following: Harry Neufeld, missionary, Los Ebanos, Texas; Herman H. Neufeld, former editor and publisher of *Mennonitische Rundschau;* N. J. Neufeld, physician, Winnipeg; Peter T. Neufeld, pastor of Bethel Mennonite Church, Inman, Kan. Peter T. Neufeld's grandfather, Peter Neufeld, came to Kansas in 1875, whose grandfather, Hermann Neufeld, had immigrated to Russia from Prussia in 1803. In addition, Cornelius K. Neufeld, a musician, should be mentioned. J. G. Rempel lists the following General Conference ministers of Canada: A. Neufeld, New Westminster, B.C.; A. J. Neufeld, Lena, Man.; B. G. Neufeld, Manitou, Man.; Gerhard Neufeld, Oliver, B.C.; H. H. Neufeld, Abbotsford, B.C.; J. G. Neufeld, Didsbury, Alta.; J. H. Neufeld, Gem, Alta.; Johann Neufeld, Tofield, Alta.; Abram G. Neufeld, Whitewater, Man.; Cornelius G. Neufeld (elder); David P. Neufeld; Gerhard G. Neufeld (elder). P.T.N., C.K.

A. A. Töws, *Mennonitische Märtyrer* I and II (N. Clearbrook, 1949 and 1954); J. G. Rempel, *Fünfzig Jahre Konferenzbestrebungen, 1902-1952* I and II.

Neufeld, Abraham A. (1862-1909), a Mennonite teacher in a secondary school in South Russia, was born March 15, 1862, at Fürstenau in the Molotschna Mennonite settlement, the child of simple Mennonite farmers. His industry and gifts moved his father to send him to the Zentralschule in Ohrloff, where he completed the three-year course in two years. Then he entered the Realschule in Berdyansk, and refusing the scholarship offered him in favor of needier students, he supported himself by giving private lessons and later, when he was married, by journalistic work. In 1883 he took a philological course at the University of Odessa. During all his school years he showed an unusual capacity for and love of work. He was not satisfied merely to follow the lectures of the professors, but was inspired to independent study. After three years at Odessa he attended the University of Berlin for two years, where one of his professors was Theodor Mommsen, and then returned to Russia.

Now Abraham Neufeld's public work began. He devoted all his energy to Mennonite education. For a few years he served as a secondary school teacher in Berdyansk and Bachmut, and from 1890 for 15 years as principal of the Chortitza Zentralschule. His influence on the Chortitza school constituency was profound. The church conference and the teachers' association entrusted to him the supervision of the elementary and secondary school system. The higher school authorities also held him in high esteem. To provide educational facilities for his children Neufeld moved to Berdyansk and founded there a secondary school with the rights of a government school. At the same time he was considerate of the rights of other Mennonite sons, and tried to build for them a school characterized by honor and thoroughness. After a short period of successful work he died at Berdyansk on Jan. 9, 1909. Neufeld had many offers of high positions outside the Mennonite constituency but he remained faithful to his people. Neufeld's lecture, *Die Chortitza Centralschule 1842-1892,* given at the time of the 50th anniversary, was published by H. Ediger (Berdyansk, 1893). A.B.

H. Goerz, "A. A. Neufeld, Erinnerungen," *Menn. Warte* II (1944) 49-55 (interesting and informative personal reminiscences concerning Neufeld); Friesen, *Brüderschaft;* H. Epp, *Menn. Jahrbuch* 1909, 128-31; *ML* III, 210 f.

Neufeld, Heinrich August (1826-1900), a Mennonite preacher, born at Danzig, Oct. 30, 1826. He was educated at the universities of Halle and Leipzig, Germany, lived a while in Danzig, working on the new hymnal, was ordained by Jakob Mannhardt on April 17, 1856, as pastor of the Ibersheim (*q.v.*) Mennonite church, serving there until 1869, and at Friedrichstadt (*q.v.*) 1869-99. In 1899 he retired and moved to Danzig to live with his sister, and died there on Oct. 19, 1900. His sermons, which he had published in various Mennonite collections of sermons, as well as his numerous devotional articles in the *Mennonitische Blätter,* bear eloquent witness of his childlike faith and depth of spirit (*Menn. Bl.,* 1894, 14).

Worthy of note is Neufeld's appeal to all the Mennonite congregations in the Old World and the New (*Menn. Bl.,* 1859, 23; 1860, 34), to raise an endowment in commemoration of the third centennial of the death of Menno Simons. He also wrote articles in appreciation of his colleagues Johann Risser, Jakob Ellenberger I, Johannes van der Smissen, and Jakob Mannhardt in the *Mennonitische Blätter.* (*ML* III, 211.) NEFF.

Neufeld, Hermann Abram (1860-1931), an itinerating minister and elder of the Mennonite Brethren Church, was born at Yarkivka, Ekaterinoslav province, South Russia, June 24, 1860, the seventh of the twelve children of Abraham and Helena Unrau

55

Neufeld. On Feb. 6, 1883, he married Katharina Klassen and established his home at Sergeyevka, Taurida province, South Russia, working in an iron foundry for a living. They had thirteen children. In 1892-1923 they lived at Nikolayevka, Ekaterinoslav province.

In 1884 Neufeld joined the M.B. Church. The following year he began to preach in his local church and in 1886 was ordained to the ministry. In 1890 he began a very active service as an itinerating minister (*Reiseprediger*) in the M.B. Conference, which lasted twenty-five years. During this time he conducted many meetings in all the M.B. churches of Russia, visiting Turkestan twice and Siberia four times. He also made two trips to Germany, where he took part in Bible conferences. In 1905 he was ordained elder and became one of the outstanding leaders of the M.B. Conference in Russia, and served on various important boards and committees.

In 1923 Neufeld emigrated with his family to Canada, establishing his home at Winkler, Man. Here, too, he immediately became active in the ministry, his particular service being that of Bible expositor in the Canadian M.B. churches. He also wrote many valuable articles for periodicals in Russia as well as in Canada. He wrote and published a booklet entitled *Handbuch für Prediger*. He died at Winkler, on Sept. 28, 1931, and was buried in the local M.B. cemetery. H. H. Neufeld, a former editor of the *Mennonitische Rundschau*, and K. G. Neufeld, a musician, are sons of Hermann A. Neufeld.

J.H.L.

Friesen, *Brüderschaft;* Dirks, *Statistik,* 1905; J. H. Lohrenz, *The Mennonite Brethren Church* (Hillsboro, 1950).

Neufeld, Peter J. (1823-1909), an educator and printer of the Mennonites of Russia, was born at Ladekopp, Molotschna, on Dec. 23, 1823. From the age of eleven or twelve to eighteen he attended the Zentralschule of Halbstadt, after which he succeeded his teacher, Johann Voth. In 1843 he succeeded Heinrich Franz in the Gnadenfeld school. In 1841 Neufeld was baptized. In 1847 he married Laura Lange, the daughter of the Elder Wilhelm Lange of Gnadenfeld. He was greatly influenced by the spiritual and cultural life of the Gnadenfeld community. In 1851 Neufeld resigned his position at Gnadenfeld and spent six years as a teacher in Odessa to perfect himself in the Russian language and to obtain a Russian teacher's certificate. In 1857 he became the teacher of the Steinbach school sponsored by Peter Schmidt. After nine years of teaching he studied photography in Kharkov. In 1866 he returned to Halbstadt, gave private instruction, and functioned as a photographer until 1870, when he returned to Steinbach for one year of teaching. In 1871-74 and 1878-86 he taught at the Halbstadt Zentralschule and in 1876-77 at the Gnadenfeld Zentralschule. In 1886 Neufeld retired from teaching and established a print shop in Halbstadt, which he sold in 1897 to H. J. Braun and Company, which later became the Raduga (*q.v.*) Publishing Company. His wife died in 1900. They had thirteen children. His son Wilhelm P. Neufeld was educated in Germany, and was a minister and teacher in the Gnadenfeld and Halb-

stadt Zentralschulen. Peter J. Neufeld died at Halbstadt on Nov. 22, 1909.

C.K.

H. Dirks, "Peter Neufeld," *Menn. Jahrbuch*, 1910 (Berdyansk, 1911) 78-91; Friesen, *Brüderschaft,* 597-99; *ML* III, 211.

Neufeld, Peter P. (1875-1927), a Mennonite teacher and elder, was born Dec. 4, 1875 (1876), at Nepluyevka, Ukraine. He attended the Chortitza Zentralschule 1892-96. After passing the teacher's examination at Alexandrovsk, he became teacher in the Rosental village school. In 1898 Neufeld married Helena Krahn. One daughter was born to them who now resides in Winnipeg. His wife died as a refugee, fleeing from Russia to Germany during World War II.

After teaching seven years at Rosental, Neufeld taught seven years at Schönwiese. In 1914 he was called to teach German at the Chortitza Mädchenschule (*q.v.*). During the Russian Revolution he taught for two years in the Chortitza elementary school. On June 26, 1921, he observed his twenty-fifth anniversary as a teacher. On Nov. 2, 1914, Neufeld was ordained as minister. On April 17 (18), 1922, he was ordained elder of the Chortitza Mennonite Church, after which he devoted his full time to his work in the church. Neufeld attended the last Bundeskonferenz at Moscow in 1925, at which time he was elected a member of the KfK (*q.v.*). He was an unusually successful teacher, and an effective preacher and elder, who had acquired a very good education. He died at Chortitza on Jan. 21, 1927. (*Unser Blatt* II, 1927, 214, 245, 279.)

C.K.

Neufville, de, an old French family. Robert de Neufville became a Protestant and left his native country, lived in Antwerp in 1545, and in England from 1550 on. During the reign of Mary, when the Protestants were no longer safe in England, a large number of Reformed found refuge in Holland; but another group, led by John á Lasco (*q.v.*), of which Robert de Neufville was a member, vainly sought admission to Copenhagen, Lübeck, Wismar, and Hamburg. In 1554 this company came to Emden and in 1555 to Frankfurt, where Robert de Neufville became elder of the French church in 1573, and where the family became resident and acquired wealth.

One of Robert's 19 children was Daniel de Neufville (b. 1554 at Emden), who went to Holland in 1600, and settled first in Haarlem and then in Amsterdam, where he founded the great mercantile house of the family. At Haarlem he was married to Maeyken Koppens (Coppens) of the Flemish Mennonite congregation. It is not certain, though it is probable, that Daniel became a Mennonite; his many descendants were Mennonites. Most of them lived at Amsterdam, where they were members of the Flemish congregation and after the schism of 1664, of the Lamist congregation. By marriage they were related to a large number of Amsterdam Mennonite patrician families such as van Halmael, Block, van Beeck, Rutgers, van Gelder, Verhamme, de Wolff, van Lennep, Blaupot, de Clerck, Bierens; a small branch of this family lived at Haarlem in the 17th and 18th centuries.

The de Neufville family became very wealthy. Its first members in Holland were engaged in the textile trade, particularly silk. But in the early 18th century most of them were also bankers. Daniel de Neufville (Amsterdam 1643-78) founded a bank at Amsterdam, which in the 18th century developed into one of the largest banking houses of western Europe. In 1763, when political circumstances caused its bankruptcy, more than 40 banks in Holland, Hamburg, and Berlin were also bankrupt. Other banking houses owned and carried on by members of this family in the 18th century were the world-known banking company of M. and J. de Neufville in London and that of Jean de Neufville at Amsterdam, with whom the newly independent United States·of America in 1778 negotiated for a considerable loan. This loan was however, never made and both Jean de Neufville and his son Leendert emigrated to Pennsylvania in 1785, where they lived in rather poor circumstances (*N.N.B.Wb.* VIII, 1211). The de Neufville family were loyal Mennonites. Many of its members served as deacons in Amsterdam and Haarlem.

To this family also belonged Christina Leonora de Neufville (1713-81), a daughter of Leendert de Neufville (1677-1755), of Amsterdam, and Aleyda Oosterling (1683-1730), for her time a learned woman, deeply interested in philosophical, theological, and ethical questions. She cannot be called a poet, although she wrote her moralizing *Bespiegelingen, voorgestelt in dichtkundige brieven* (1741) in verse form. She was a member of the Mennonite congregation in Amsterdam, and made a generous contribution for the organ installed in the Lamist Singel church (*DB* 1863, 24).

Of somewhat greater significance, though not outstanding, are Margaretha Jacoba de Neufville (1775-1856), a daughter of David Matheus van Gelder de Neufville (1751-1814) and Elisabeth Barnaart (1747-94). The father and the entire family were members of the Mennonite Church in Amsterdam, but nevertheless he was also a city councillor, bailiff, and (during the Napoleonic domination of the Netherlands) assistant mayor of Amsterdam. His daughter was crippled, and remained unmarried, preferring to live in seclusion on her parents' country estate near Haarlem, reading and writing. Her best work, *De kleine Pligten* (2 vv., 1824), is a sequel to the novel by Elisabeth Wolff and A. Deken, and in moralizing letters depicts domestic and social life in Amsterdam in the French period. Besides several translations of stories, including some for children, she wrote two novels, *De Schildknaap* (1829) and *Elisabeth Basmooth* (2 vv., 1836). The first of these is important because it is the first attempt in modern Dutch literature to write a historical novel.   H.F.W.J., vDZ.

A. C. de Neufville, *Histoire généalogique de la maison de Neufville* (Amsterdam, 1869); Heinrich von Nathusius-Neinstedt and Alfred von Neufville. *Beiträge zur Geschichte des Hauses Neufville* (Frankfurt, 1897); *Nederl. Patriciaat* VI (1915) 275-78; *N.N.B.Wb.* III, 910; *Jaarboek Amstelodamum* XXXIX (1942) 53 ff.; P. A. A. Boeser, *Leven en Werken van Margaretha Jacoba de Neufville* (Leiden, 1889); G. Kalff, *Geschiedenis der Nederlandsche Letterkunde* VII (Groningen, 1910) 132 f.; *ML* III, 211 f.

Neu-Halbstadt, a village in the northwest of the Molotschna (*q.v.*) Mennonite settlement in South Russia, at the eastern end of the Halbstadt (*q.v.*) district, was founded in 1843 by Johann Cornies (*q.v.*), and admitted only craftsmen at that time. It covered 550 acres of land, whereas the village of Halbstadt, founded in 1804, owned 5,500 acres. Both villages prospered. Shortly before World War I "splendid buildings arose, especially in Neu-Halbstadt, built by retired farm owners and village residents, which would be an ornament to any city" (Blank, 106).

Thus Neu-Halbstadt developed into the intellectual and economic center of the Mennonite villages of the Molotschna territory. Here the volost management had its seat, which was responsible for fire protection and the orphanage; here were several educational institutions and industrial establishments. The oldest school is the Zentralschule in Halbstadt, founded in 1835, which transferred its headquarters to Neu-Halbstadt and added a two-year normal course, where Mennonite teachers received their training. The course was later enlarged and in 1914 the school was attended by 150 students. A small private experiment in Neu-Halbstadt resulted in the Girls' School in Halbstadt, the oldest secondary school for girls among the Russian Mennonites. It developed into a Gymnasium for girls. Also the deaconess house Morija (*q.v.*) was founded here in 1909, which gave the deaconesses their training and cared for them in their old age.

Two industrial concerns that should be mentioned were the Franz and Schröder farm machinery manufacturing company and the Raduga (*q.v.*) Publishing Company.   A.B.

E. Blank, "Die Halbstädter Wolost," in *Haus- und Landwirtschafts-Kalender für deutsche Ansiedler im südlichen Russland* XLIII (Odessa, 1910) 104; *Menn. Jahrbuch,* No. 10 (Berdyansk, 1914) 91; *ML* III, 212.

Neuhof, once a Mennonite village near Lemberg in Galicia (*q.v.*). Led by Elder Johann Müller of Einsiedel several Mennonites bought about 540 acres of land in 1830, about eight miles west of Grodek, and founded on it the village of Neuhof with six Mennonite families. Jakob Müller, one of the first settlers, was chosen preacher there in 1839. In 1862 a church was built, which also contained a schoolroom. The number of Mennonite families had in the meantime increased to twelve. Then the Mennonites sold their land in Neuhof and moved to larger farms. In 1933 only four farms were still owned by Mennonites; on three others some aged Mennonites were receiving their living.

Maintaining the church and school life became increasingly difficult as Neuhof declined, especially since Roman Catholic Poles and Greek Catholic Ruthenians settled in Neuhof. But the Mennonites successfully preserved their German school and culture. In 1938 the group numbered fourteen. In 1939, when German troops marched into Neuhof, the inhabitants decided suddenly to emigrate. With a neighboring congregation they were settled in Greifenort near Buk in Warthegau.   H.Pa.

Peter Bachmann, *Mennoniten in Kleinpolen 1784-1934* (Lemberg, 1934) 208-20; *Menn. Bl.,* 1940; *ML* III, 212.

Neuhof, a village near Wertheim in Baden, Germany, was the seat of a Mennonite congregation in

1908-*ca.* 44. The membership was very small, never exceeding twenty. Heinrich Fellmann was the preacher from the beginning and the elder from 1924 until the end. (*Gem.-Kal.* 1941, 151.)

vDZ.

Neuhoffnung (*Nadezhdino*), a common Mennonite village name which was found in the following settlements: Alexandertal, Samara, Russia; West Reserve, Man.; Cuauhtemoc and Durango, Mexico; and Menno, Chaco, and Sommerfeld, Villarrica, Paraguay.

C.K.

Neuhorst, a common Mennonite village name which was found in the following settlements: Chortitza, Ukraine, Russia; West and East Reserves, Man.; Hague, Sask.; Cuauhtemoc and Durango, Mexico; and Neuland, Paraguay.

C.K.

Neu-Hutterthal Mennonite Church: see **New Huttertal** Mennonite Church.

Neukirch, a village in the south of the Molotschna Mennonite settlement (*q.v.*) in South Russia, which was settled in 1820 by 21 Mennonite families from Marienburg, Elbing, and Tiegenhof in (former) West Prussia, Germany. By 1910 there were 168 Mennonite families with 526 persons living on 52 farms in the village, which embraced 4,400 acres of land. A church was built in the village in 1865. (See **Neukirch** Mennonite Church.)   HEGE.

Neuer Haus- und Landwirtschafts-Kalender für deutsche Ansiedler im südlichen Russland, 1911, 111-12; Mannhardt, *Jahrbuch* 1888, 68; *ML III,* 212.

Neukirch Mennonite Church in the Molotschna (*q.v.*) Mennonite settlement, South Russia, was organized in 1863. A church building was erected in 1865. Heinrich Harder was the first leader of the congregation. Originally the church was associated with the Orloff Mennonite Church (*q.v.*) and was under the spiritual guidance of Elder Abraham Görz. When and to what extent this congregation became independent is not quite definite. In 1905, in addition to the two leading ministers, the congregation was served by Cornelius Fast, Abraham Harder, Jacob Thiessen, Gerhard Epp, Jacob Wiens, and Abraham Dück. At that time the congregation had a membership of 402 and a total population of 890. Little is known about the later development of the congregation.   C.K.

Dirks, *Statistik,* 1905, 16, 62; Friesen, *Brüderschaft,* 703 f.; *Neuer Haus- und Landwirtschafts-Kalender* (1911) 111.

Neu-Kronsweide: see **Kronsweide.**

Neuland Agricultural Co-operative (*Cooperativa Agricola de Neuland*), located in Colony Neuland of the Paraguayan Chaco, was officially organized on June 1, 1949, but had been functioning since August 1947 as a branch office of the Fernheim Co-operative. Its membership is 596 and it is based upon Paraguayan law No. 13,635 of 1942. Founded upon the advice of the colony and MCC leaders, its objectives were to facilitate adequate distribution of funds made available by the MCC; to handle all buying of colony necessities and all sale of produce; and to establish small industries which would meet the needs of the immigrants. Its only capital during the first year was maintenance and loan funds made available by MCC. Its shares are currently valued at 25 guaranies payable in cash upon purchase. The turnover of the first seven months in 1949 (June-December) was 381,458 guaranies, and profits are used to expand the co-operative facilities or are paid to the members in the form of shares. The president of the co-operative is responsible to the colony administration (*Amt*) in all matters and acts as the financial arm of the colony. A shortage of capital, lack of proper markets and transportation facilities, and the instability of the Paraguayan currency have been the chief difficulties for the colony. Nevertheless, the co-operative has done much to help the immigrants over the first difficult years of pioneering and guarded them against exploitation by outsiders.

C.J.D.

Neuland Colony, located in the Paraguayan Chaco, was organized on June 4, 1947, under the leadership of Peter Derksen, by 299 Mennonites who had fled from Russia during World War II to Germany and Poland. There the MCC made contact with them and was instrumental in arranging for their emigration to Paraguay in 1947-48. They arrived at station Fred Engen on March 1, 1947, and were the advance group of the many transports that were to follow later. A second group of 150 came a week later, the others all being delayed in Asuncion and Buenos Aires because of the Paraguayan Revolution which was raging in full force at that time. With communications to Asuncion broken, these two groups waited three months for the rest of their party and for MCC representatives, then finally decided to begin settlement on their own and accordingly left Fernheim and Menno Colony, which had given them temporary shelter, and established the first seven Neuland villages: Neu-Halbstadt, Neuendorf, Einlage, Lichtenau, Heimstätte, Rosental, and Alt-Chortitza. The first months on the new land were especially trying because all heavy baggage of the immigrants had been held up in Buenos Aires by the revolution, leaving the settlers without tools or equipment of any kind. Much credit is due the Fernheim and Menno settlements for their liberal help to the new immigrants in those days, through lending or giving tools, building houses and wells for them, and in general helping them over the first difficult period. Fernheim built two wells in every village and a house for every widow. In September those delayed in Buenos Aires by the revolution joined the rest in the Chaco and were received largely by the Menno Colony, which assumed the same responsibilities as Fernheim had earlier. In April 1948 the transport *Stuart Heinzelmann* brought an additional 803 immigrants, in July 1948 the *Charlton Monarch* brought 667, and in November 1948 an additional 133 of the second *Volendam* transport came to Neuland. Twenty-eight family members came in July 1950 to join their families, making a total colony population of 2,314 in August 1950, or 641 family units, of which 253 families were without a father or husband. The names of the additional villages established are Kronsfeld, Schönhorst, Sandhorst, Neu-Chortitza, Altenau, Grossweide, Gronau,

Neuhorst, Steinfeld, Schöntal, Nikolaifeld, Neuhof, Waldhof, Waldrode, and Tiege.

The average annual birth rate in 1947-50 was 53.7, and the average number of deaths 11.3. Total landholdings are 276,670 acres (110,625 hectares), of which a large percentage is typical Chaco jungle growth. This land was purchased by and still is the property of MCC. By Jan. 1, 1950, 6,340 acres (2,536 ha.) had been placed under cultivation. In addition the colonists had by that time built 473 houses, 174 wells, and had acquired 515 horses, 740 draft oxen, 1,209 cows, 1,619 cattle, and 278 wagons. The difficulties of pioneering are accentuated by the absence of many family heads, by severe insect plagues as grasshoppers, ants, and cotton worms, by poor transportation facilities and long distances from markets, and by an inadequate well-water supply. However, the settlers are largely courageous and reasonably optimistic. Churches have been organized, schools built, and industry established to saw lumber and manufacture furniture, an oil press for extraction of edible oils, a stone-burr mill, and other essential services. A 20-bed hospital is in operation. All colony affairs and administration are the responsibility of a five-man committee elected by all colony members for a three-year term. The chairman (1950) of this committee—now Peter Dürksen—is the colony administrator (*Oberschultze*).

P.Du.

Neuland Mennonite Brethren Church: see **Gnadental M.B. Church**.

Neuland Mennonite Church (GCM), located in Neuland Colony in the Paraguayan Chaco, was organized on Nov. 12, 1947, under the leadership of Hans Rempel of Einlage, Neuland. Its members are largely of the immigrant groups from Russia that came to Paraguay via Germany through the help of the MCC in 1947-48. It has been a member of the General Conference Mennonite Church since August 1950, and consisted of 670 members in 1956. Worship services were held regularly every Sunday morning in the village schools, but a meetinghouse has been erected in Neu-Halbstadt. Sunday school, youth programs, Bible study, prayer meetings, and other church activities are being sponsored. The church has several choirs. For congregational singing the *Gesangbuch der Mennoniten* is used. Communion services are held several times each year depending on the desire of the members. Its leader (1954) is still Hans Rempel, assisted by 20 ministers and deacons, many of whom have been recently elected. Five ministers receive financial support from the G.C.M. churches in North America. H.Re.

Neumair, Hans, a confectioner, an Anabaptist martyr, who was executed with Leonhard Haslinger (*q.v.*) and a number of others at Wels, Austria, on June 8, 1528.

A. Nicoladoni, *Johannes Bünderlin von Linz* (Berlin, 1893) 187; Beck, *Geschichts-Bücher*, 280; ML III, 213.

Neumann, Caspar (1648-1715), a Catholic divine, son of a tax collector of Breslau, Germany. He studied theology at the University of Jena, became court chaplain in Altenburg and professor of theology in

two Gymnasiums in Breslau. As a convinced Catholic he wrote several books on the Bible, the Catholic Church, and also a compendium of religions in his *Trutina Religionum*. In it he discussed all the religions he knew, including the branches of the Christian faith. A special chapter, "Pantheon Fanaticum," treats the Anabaptists. The sources he cited show that he wrote in the customary vein of church polemics.

Neumann put the Mennonites into a group with Müntzer and Münster. Nevertheless he attributed gentler teachings to them, remarking that it was difficult to learn their teaching. He was apparently not acquainted with a Mennonite confession of faith. In an alphabetical list of famous Anabaptists he named Blaurock, Rink, Manz, and Menno, and also Jan Matthys and Müntzer. As an expression of his age the book is of interest, but it offers nothing new to Anabaptist literature. H.Q.

C. Neumann, *Trutina Religionum quae hodie sunt, ubi singularum Aetas Fontes Dogmata* (Leipzig, 1731); ML III, 213.

Neumannovka (Neumanufka) and Kutuzovka (Kotozufka), two villages in eastern Volhynia, Russia, located 25 miles northwest of Zhitomir, were the seat of a Swiss-Volhynian Mennonite congregation 1861 to 1874. The group moved from Eduardsdorf (Poutchy) in western Volhynia, 14 miles west of Dubno, to Kutuzovka in 1861 because of new land made available by the abolition of serfdom by Czar Alexander II. Initially the group settled not only in Kutuzovka but also in the neighboring village of Neumannovka, three miles farther northeast. A church was erected between the two villages and the entire Mennonite settlement was called Kutuzovka. The land was owned by the Mennonites and considerable economic progress was made in the short time they lived there. Surplus products were sold in Zhitomir and Kiev. The church was served by Elder Jacob Stucky and ministers Jakob D. Goering and Johann Goering. The names of Dirks and Ortman were added to the church here. The village of Lindenthal was located between Kutuzovka and Zhitomir and was populated by West Prussian Mennonites. Virtually the entire Kutuzovka settlement emigrated to the United States in 1874. Seventy-three families under the leadership of Elder Stucky left Kutuzovka on Aug. 6, 1874, most of these settling in McPherson County, Kan. They organized the Hoffnungsfeld (*q.v.*) Mennonite Church near Moundridge. The Eden Mennonite Church (*q.v.*) was later formed by members of the Hoffnungsfeld church. M.H.S.

P. P. Wedel, *Kurze Geschichte der aus Wolhynien, Russland, nach Kansas ausgewanderten Schweizer-Mennoniten* (n.p., 1929); P. R. Kaufman, *Unser Volk und seine Geschichte* (n.p., n.d.—ca. 1931); Martin H. Schrag, "European History of the Swiss-Volhynian Mennonite Ancestors of Mennonites Now Living in Communities in Kansas and South Dakota" (unpublished master's dissertation, 1956).

Neumark, an area of West Prussia: see **Netzebruch**.

Neumarkt, a market town in the Adige Valley, Tirol, Austria (now belonging to Italy), formerly in the domain of Enn and Caldif. Here the Anabaptist movement found early entry, for the records show that property of fugitive Anabaptists was confiscated as early as 1527. In May 1528 two citizens of Neumarkt were called to Bozen to sit in on the trial of the imprisoned Anabaptists. In the early summer of 1529 Georg Blaurock (q.v.) apparently came as far as Neumarkt in his work in southern Tirol; for from this time on the movement spread rapidly. In September the authorities became aware of the situation, and in November the Innsbruck government ordered energetic preventive measures.

After the imprisonment of Georg Blaurock and Hans Langecker (q.v.) in August 1529 their work was carried on by Benedikt Gamper of Gamperhof near Leifers. He was especially hunted by the authorities, for he had been a people's priest in Bruneck. He preached and baptized in the vicinity of Neumarkt, in the villages of Vill and Tramin. On Nov. 16, 1529, four brethren and three sisters were seized in Vill and taken to the Vill castle. The judge, Jörg Tschander, was given directions by the Innsbruck government to have competent and pious priests convert them, and to report the names of those who recanted and deliver the obstinate ones to the criminal court. They were to be thoroughly interrogated concerning their preachers and leaders in the region. If the prisoners gave the names of persons in other districts, the pertinent authorities should be notified. Tschander was physically unable to conduct the trial, and was replaced by Hans Plattner of Salurn. On Dec. 3, 1529, the jury was called, and the judge was warned to carry out the mandates strictly.

The supervisor of the parish of Enn and Caldif was accused on December 3 of permitting Anabaptists to go about in his territory. He reported that of the eight prisoners only one had repented. The government ordered that the others be executed. This was done on Dec. 22. Very soon the leaders Martin Nauk (q.v.) and Benedikt Gamper were captured, and put to death as martyrs. Thus it is clear that the nine executions listed in the Hutterian chronicles in Neumarkt all occurred at the turn of the year 1529-30.

On June 11, 1531, the government warned all the neighboring authorities that 40 Anabaptists were reported to have built a hut in Brantental, in the jurisdiction of Deutschnofen. The judges of these regions, including Neumarkt, should co-operate in catching them. A hunt, very secretly carried out, resulted in the seizure of four men and three women, in Kaltern, Karneid, and Bozen. On June 27 Innsbruck ordered that all backsliders, leaders, and impenitent ones should be executed. The "principal" had, however, escaped. The others were executed on or before July 19. On August 1 Innsbruck reported that the escaped prisoner and the leader were living in a mountain hut in the district of Bozen, and two weeks later added that they were in a cave near Leifers.

A tabulation of property confiscated from Anabaptists of 1532 states that in the region of Enn and Caldif many Anabaptists had been executed and many had fled.

Although Neumarkt is hardly mentioned after this, it can be assumed that the Anabaptist movement was indeed suppressed, as in the rest of the

country, but by no means extirpated. On Aug. 20, 1539, Innsbruck again ordered the authorities in the Adige to seize an active Anabaptist preacher. The trouble was, as the Innsbruck authorities reported to the king, that the parishes were filled with ignorant priests. Among the populace the Anabaptists found many friends. On Nov. 12, 1560, the government ordered that vigorous steps be taken against those who aided them. And in November 1592 the secondary authorities were accused of negligence in the matter.   P.DE.

Beck, Geschichts-Bücher; Loserth, Anabaptismus; Wolkan, Geschicht-Buch; Zieglschmid, Chronik; Loesche, Tirolensia; ML III, 213 f.

Neumeister, Erdmann (1671-1756), a Lutheran clergyman at the church of St. Jakob in Hamburg, Germany, a noted author of church hymns and violent opponent of Mennonites and Pietists, author of a booklet against Jakob Denner (q.v.): Anmerckungen über Jacob Denners Postille, betitult Einfältige und christliche Betrachtungen über die Jährlichen und Heiligen Evangelia . . . nebst treumeynender Warnung für derselben (Hamburg, 1731). Two of his hymns have been adopted into the South German Mennonite hymnal: "Jesus nimmt die Sünder an" and "Jesu grosser Wunderstern."

His polemic against Denner is one of the worst of the writings of the 18th century. He disposes of his opponent with a tone of superiority; he denies Denner, a dyer without scholarly training, any right to preach and teach the Word of God. In 73 paragraphs he refutes the supposed errors in Denner's book, setting up the Lutheran Church as the true church and treating the Mennonites and Calvinists as ruinous sects. In all of Denner's words he scents self-contradiction, which he triumphantly exposes by manipulating the words. The entire presentation reveals his annoyance at the great audiences Denner's sermons attracted. He expressly warns his readers and his own congregation for the sake of their souls not to attend Denner's meetings, on the basis of II Pet. 3:16, 17. (Menn. Bl., 1880, 71; 1881, 23, 29, and 37; ML III, 214.)   NEFF.

Neumühl, Moravia, in the 16th century a large mill on the Eisgrub estate belonging to the Liechtenstein family, located on the left bank of the Thaya River; it is today a village with a population of 400 with a new mill, which is on the same site as the above. Here in Tracht the Hutterian Brethren built a Bruderhof in 1558. The settlement around this mill became one of the most important Anabaptist settlements of Moravia, the residence of the "bishop" and leader of the entire brotherhood.

On Jan. 25, 1570, the delegates of the Polish antiTrinitarians (q.v.) arrived at Neumühl to confer with the Brethren on the subject of unification with them, whose leader was Peter Walpot (q.v.), whereupon a correspondence followed, but which did not lead to a union. After Walpot's death on Feb. 5, 1578, Hänsel Kräl (q.v.) of Kitzbühel was chosen as leader of the entire brotherhood. He died here on Nov. 14, 1583, at the age of 63. Again the ordained men of the brotherhood met at Neumühl and chose as bishop Klaus Braidl (q.v.) of Hesse, who had been a Hutterite preacher for 20 years.

On May 14, 1590, Klaus Braidl called all the elders of all the Bruderhofs together at Neumühl for an important conference. The refusal of the Brethren to pay war taxes, which had in recent years led to the confiscation of cattle and produce, was used as an accusation against them with the charge that they enjoyed the benefits of the land, but would do nothing for its welfare. Since in 1585-87 in the general increase in the Moravian population there was also an increase in the number of craftsmen who were in competition with the Hutterite craftsmen, there was also increased agitation against the Brethren. Therefore the elders addressed a petition to Frederick of Zierotin, rejecting the charges, but insisted upon their belief that for conscience' sake they could not contribute anything for purposes of war; the general taxes they were willing to pay. They also requested permission, in view of their large population, to purchase more grain, also permission to brew beer as formerly. In conclusion they suggested a tax on their houses which had kitchens; this tax of 12 florins was imposed upon them by the Landtag. The amount of beer they brewed in Neumühl is shown in an account of Eisgrub: in 1593 they brewed no less than 217 barrels of beer, which they sold at a gain of 225 florins.

Klaus Braidl may be considered the originator of most of the later craftsmen's regulations. Concerning these there are occasional references in the chronicles; e.g., that of Jan. 8, 1591, passed at a meeting of all the leaders and managers assembled at Neumühl, where "the points were discussed, what the shoemakers, the cutters, menders, and buyers should not permit."

The Turkish war brought troublous times in 1595; confiscations injured the Bruderhofs, including that of Neumühl, where a certain brother Heinrich was shot to death through the open door. In 1596, however, Neumühl became the scene of violence, introducing a chain of similar events and hardships. On August 26 about six o'clock in the evening, a mob of about 30 men attacked the Neumühl Bruderhof to gain possession of the wealth the Brethren were reported to have stored here. The bandits mistreated the inhabitants and ruined furniture, without finding the treasure. After two hours of plundering they left with 16 horses. They were seized in the neighborhood of Vösendorf and Vienna, where they confessed. The horses were returned to the Brethren through the mediation of Zierotin.

On Sept. 20, 1596, the imperial commissaries reported an empty treasury; thereupon the treasurers suggested obtaining a loan from the "wealthy" Hutterites. A committee of three officials was appointed to negotiate with the Brethren for a loan of several thousand florins. On October 25 Klaus Braidl was summoned to the castle of Selowitz with six elders; the discussion was continued through six days. With the exception of Zierotin, the commissioners were unfavorable to the Brethren and tried by all possible means to extort the money from them, using the threat that if the Brethren were unwilling to do the emperor this favor, they could not count on his protection in future attacks. After the elders had repeatedly asserted that these reputed treasures were nonexistent, the committee demanded a written

statement, which was sent to Prague with a letter from Zierotin, assuring the treasurer that he had previously tried in vain to obtain a loan from the Brethren; for with their large number of children, sick and aged persons, and the heavy taxes, their expenses were very heavy; there could therefore be no great capital in reserve. In 1597, while the Neumühl Brethren were greatly occupied with the offensive conduct of Hans Zuckenhammer (q.v.) and in addition had to suffer the quartering of four squadrons of horsemen for five days, the government continued its efforts to obtain the loan. On the suggestion that the reason for the Hutterite refusal of the loan was the fear that the money would be used for war purposes, a letter was written by Prague on Feb. 4, 1597, requesting 10,000 Talers for the repayment of an urgent debt, and accusing the Brethren of a lack of good will. A year later a certain Jew of Nikolsburg, Pisker Löw, claimed to have a letter from the emperor demanding the loan of 10,000 florins. The Brethren, suspecting that this request was not genuine, refused to pay the sum; Pisker was finally ordered to apologize to the Brethren. Zierotin had meanwhile died. It was thereupon decided to have the Landtag meeting on Jan. 2, 1601, impose upon the Hutterian Brethren a poll tax, "under the pretext that this tax would be used nowhere but for the payment of internal taxes." Meanwhile the Bruderhof suffered further depredations through the quartering of military troops, who took away much material and many horses. In July 1600 it was the cavalry of Count Thurn; in the autumn of 1601 the cavalry of a certain Hodicky stayed three weeks; in 1602 the infantry of Schönberger stayed five weeks; finally the Thurn Cavalry came again.

At the court it was decided that since the Brethren were suffering so much confiscation of cattle, horses, and other goods in lieu of the war taxes which they refused to pay, this would be a favorable time to renew the request for a loan. The letter on the subject called attention to the great sacrifices all classes in Moravia had made in the defense of the country, while the Jews and the Anabaptists, who had more provisions than anyone else in Moravia, had hitherto paid very little. On July 28, 1604, an imperial order was sent to the provincial governor, Karl von Liechtenstein, calling for both groups to deliver either a large loan or wagons and horses for the artillery with the necessary drivers. The negotiations with the Brethren, which included an official delegation to Neumühl on August 26, were futile, since Braidl could show how impoverished the brotherhood was. In the course of the negotiations the governor secured a list of all the Bruderhofs: there were at that time 37, with an average of 200 adults each (with children this might mean a total populace of at least 15,000). The governor advised the imperial office that little could be expected from new tax levies, since the brotherhood was so poor that many members were forsaking the brotherhood and there were few new converts. So the attempt was dropped.

On April 1, 1610, three major buildings at Neumühl were accidentally burned. The war in the fall of 1619 brought new and severe losses to Neumühl, when 12,800 Moravian troops and 10,000 Hungarian troops lay two months in the vicinity. The constant plundering practically ruined the Bruderhof. In December 1620 the entire population of Neumühl fled to Göding and Wesseli in view of the imminent danger of attack, returning sometime later. In 1621 the brotherhood was twice put under heavy pressure to deliver war loans, wagons, and men for military service, which they steadfastly refused. The third attempt in May-July, which included charges of treason and threats of complete extermination of the brotherhood and delivering of the women and children into serfdom, resulted in the betrayal by several weak brethren (the bishop and several other leaders had been in prison for several months) of most of the hidden money of the brotherhood, which was in turn followed by the excommunication of the bishop (Hirzel) and several other leaders. Cardinal Dietrichstein (*q.v.*) reported on June 29, 1622, that he was (on request) preparing an edict calling for the expulsion of the entire brotherhood from Moravia, which soon followed. Neumühl, however, was apparently the last of the Bruderhofs to be expelled. It was still in existence in November 1623, but must have been lost soon thereafter.   P.DE.

Beck, *Geschichts-Bücher;* Loserth, *Communismus;* Wolkan, *Geschicht-Buch;* Zieglschmid, *Chronik;* Fr. Hruby, *Die Wiedertäufer in Mähren* (Leipzig, 1935); M. Witzany, *Die Markgrafschaft Mähren und die Marktgemeinde Eisgrub;* P. Dedic, *Die religiösen und kirchlichen Verhältnisse in Mähren* (1922); A. Riep, *Der Markt Tracht* (Brno, 1930); *ML* III, 214-18.

Neuneich, an Amish Mennonite congregation in the Sundgau in southern Alsace on the Swiss border, named after a farm by this name near Ligsdorf in the Glaserberg area (now reverted to forest) a few miles from Lucelle (Lützel), about 12 miles from Basel. The congregation was in existence in 1779 when its elder, Peter Kaufmann, represented it at the Amish conference at Essingen (*q.v.*), Palatinate. It is probable that the later congregations of Lucelle (*q.v.*) and Basel-Binningen (*q.v.*), now called Holée, formed at the end of the 18th century, are descendants of this congregation, and that Birkenhof (*q.v.*) is the direct descendant. Pierre Sommer believes that the Neuneich area, which lies in the remote northern part of the Jura Mountain chain, where the summits reach 2,000-2,500 ft., was a place of refuge for Anabaptists in the mid-16th century, but there is no documentary evidence for this. Where the families of this area came from is also not known, possibly in part from the Jura area further south and east, possibly from the Markirch, Alsace, area whence the Mennonites were expelled in 1710. It is also possible that they came from the Montbéliard area after 1740, when the Mennonites were again tolerated in French territory about the time when the Florimont (Normanvillars) settlement was made. Two Peter Kaufmanns living in the latter area in 1791 (Gratz, 91) may have been relatives of the Peter Kaufmann, elder of Neuneich in 1779, who died at Hirtzbach in 1797. Since the Amish of these areas moved frequently as necessary to find farms to rent, and since they had no meetinghouses in the 18th century, it is difficult to determine congregational identities or boundaries.

Neuneich was, however, for a time a main meeting place of the Amish families in this general area.
                                                                    H.S.B.

Pierre Sommer, "Assemblée de Birkenhof (Neuneich)," *Christ Seul,* February 1933, 4 f., and "Assemblée de Bâle (Holée)" April 1933, 4-6; Delbert Gratz, "Normanvillars," in *Bernese Anabaptists* (Scottdale, 1953) 89-95.

Neunhuben, a village in the Polish district of Schwetz, west of the Vistula River, was in 1659 ff. settled by Dutch colonists who may have been Mennonites. In the course of time they all left this area on account of repeated floods. Then in 1745 the village was bought by a number of Mennonite farmers from the neighboring villages of Montau (*q.v.*), Schönsee (*q.v.*), and others. In the land leases of Neunhuben the following Mennonite names are found: Kopper, Rosenfeldt, Goerz, Klieuwer, Bartel, and Geddert. The Mennonites of Neunhuben belonged to the Montau congregation.   vDZ.

H. Wiebe, *Das Siedlungswerk der niederländischen Mennoniten im Weichseltal* (Marburg a.d.Lahn, 1952) 25 f., 59 note 23, 100-4; *ML* III, 219.

Neunhuben, a congregation southeast of Danzig, originated in 1659 (*Menn. Gesch.-Bl.,* 1940, 4) and united with the Mennonite congregation in Danzig, but acquired a degree of independence in 1791. In 1826, when the city congregation in Danzig employed a salaried preacher, the rural congregation of Neunhuben joined the Fürstenwerder (*q.v.*) congregation as a subsidiary and built a small church at Quadendorf (*q.v.*) in 1845, where the members met twice a month. At the close of the 19th century 30 families belonged to this congregation; then it began to decline through emigration. In 1941 it had a membership of 67, including children, living in four villages. With Fürstenwerder it belonged to the Conference of the East and West Prussian Mennonite Congregations (*q.v.*). It ceased to exist with the extinction of West Prussian Mennonitism in 1945 as a result of the Russian invasion. (*ML* III, 219.)   HEGE.

Neu-Osterwiek, a branch congregation of the Chortitza (*q.v.*) Mennonite Church in the Ukraine, South Russia; one of the meetinghouses of the Chortitza congregation was located here.

Neurecht, a village in Mexico in the northeast of the settlement made by Mennonites of Canada in Chihuahua in 1922.

Neureinland, a village in Mexico in the south of the settlement made by Mennonites of Canada in Chihuahua in 1922.

Neu-Samara (*Pleshanovo*), a Mennonite settlement in the northern part of the fertile province of Samara, Russia, located about 125 miles east of the city by the same name. It was founded in 1890 as a daughter settlement of Molotschna (*q.v.*) and embraced 59,400 acres of land. In 1926 it numbered 3,071 Mennonite and 66 non-Mennonite inhabitants, who lived in thirteen villages and five single farms. The settlement suffered severely before and during World War II. (*ML* III, 219; see also **Pleshanovo.**)

Neu-Schönwiese (Russian, *Dmitrovka*), a Mennonite settlement near Alexandrovka in South Russia. In the church organization it was a subsidiary of the Schönwiese Mennonite Church, and was founded in 1868. The land, 3,788 acres, was bought of Russian estate owners, and was of such quality that the settlement soon achieved prosperity. But here too the civil war of 1918 had a devastating effect. On Nov. 15, 1918, the inhabitants fled to Schönwiese, but returned in 1919; they suffered the loss of all their property. (*ML* III, 219.)   D.H.E.

Neuss, a town on the Rhine, formerly belonging to the bishop and elector of Cologne, Germany. A letter written by Hans Busschaert (*q.v.*) in 1570 (found in *Antw. Arch.-Bl.* XII, 26 f.) indicates that a Mennonite congregation existed at Neuss, of which there is, however, no further information. Andreas of Neuss (see **Andreas von Neiss**) was a Hutterite elder who baptized at Paurbach in Moravia about 1535. (Wolkan, *Lieder,* 29 f.)
A Mennonite family by the name of Neuss (or Neiss), the ancestors of the American Nice (*q.v.*) family, is found in the 17th century in the German Rhineland, particularly at Crefeld.   vDZ.

Neustadt, a village in Mexico, in the southern part of the Chihuahua settlement made by Canadian Mennonites in 1922.

Neustadt a.d.W. (*an der Weinstrasse,* earlier *an der Haardt*), an old city (pop. 26,674) in the Palatinate, Germany, the center of the Palatine wine industry, 16 miles southwest of Ludwigshafen (*q.v.*). There is evidence of an Anabaptist congregation here in the 16th century, but little specific information. An elder of this area, named Farwendel (*q.v.*), joined the Hutterites in Moravia in 1565. The Hutterite Chronicle (*Chronik,* 415) calls him "ein alter diener oder leerer der Schweizer Brüder Gemain bei der Newstat an der Haart," and tells how he was in prison at Oggersheim near Worms when he decided to go to Moravia. The Branchweilerhof (*q.v.*), which lies about one mile east of the city, has been a Mennonite settlement and congregation since 1683. The Mennonite Central Committee maintained here its relief headquarters for the French Zone of Germany (December 1946 to the fall of 1950) and for a time for all Germany. It carried on a relief food and clothing program here, and beginning in 1948 a special religious program for children by Elizabeth Wiebe. When the MCC left, Miss Wiebe continued her work, and ultimately a general evangelistic program was started in 1957, leading toward establishment of a Mennonite Brethren congregation. On Oct. 15, 1949, an MCC children's home was established at Bad Dürkheim about 10 miles north of Neustadt.   H.S.B.

Neustadt-Goedens, a town in East Friesland, Germany, 5 miles southeast of Jever and 20 miles east of Aurich, once the seat of a Mennonite congregation. This is the place of origin of the Dutch van Geuns (*q.v.*) family, which has been Mennonite since the time of the Reformation, and whose progenitor Steven Jansz van Geuns (Goedens) came to Groningen about 1720. Another well-known family

of Neustadt-Goedens was the Cremer (Kremer, Cramer, Kramer) family, many of whom were deacons and preachers in the local congregation. Neustadt-Goedens was the home of Hinrich Krechting (*q.v.*), who escaped from Münster in 1535.
In Goedens Leenaert Bouwens (*q.v.*) baptized 20 persons in 1551-65; hence a congregation came into being here soon after 1550. They were at once given protection by the van Freydag family, from whom they received favors in subsequent periods as well. In the 17th century the congregation belonged to the Old Flemish Mennonite branch, and until 1790 remained a member of the Groningen Sociëteit. Its Golden Age it experienced in the 17th century concurrently with the city, which at that time had a considerable linen industry and trade with Oldenburg. The highest membership, 67, was reached in 1736. In 1710 it was about 60, 56 in 1754, and 66 in 1767. Preachers who served here were Lubbert Alberts (1626-91), Albert Tobias Cramer 1679-92, Jan Jacobs 1693-1726, Pieter Alberts Zwart 1728-50, Lubbert Jansz Cremer 1738-87, Hinrich Pieters Swart (Zwart) 1756-d.75, Jan van Kalker 1782-88, Jan W. van Douwen 1789-98, and Taco Kuiper 1799-1804. In 1741 Pieter Zwart received from the counts van Freydag permission to build a church. In the 19th century the decline began. In 1804-36 the congregation had no preacher; in 1820 it had 20 members, in 1840 only 11. In 1836-42 Jakob van der Smissen, the retired preacher of Friedrichstadt and Danzig, came to fill the pulpit for several years. In 1895 there was only one member left, who lived in Wilhelmshaven.   vDZ.
Inv. Arch. Amst. II, Nos. 2800-10; *Naamlijst* 1810, 83; *DJ* 1837, 35; 1840, 45 and list facing page 52; *DB* 1879, 8; 1885, 6; 1895, 184; 1898, 222 f.; 1906, 192; Blaupot t. C., *Groningen* I and II, see Index; *ML* III, 219.

Neutäufer, a name sometimes given in Switzerland and South Germany to the Apostolic Christian Church (*q.v.*) called properly "Gemeinschaft Evangelisch Taufgesinnter" or "Fröhlichianer." The Neutäufer are a rather widely disseminated denomination in Switzerland. Since some of its adherents were originally Mennonites they were called "Neutäufer" to distinguish them from the older "Alttäufer." The group owes its origin to Samuel Heinrich Fröhlich (*q.v.*), born in Brugg in the Swiss canton of Aargau July 4, 1803, who stemmed from an old French Huguenot family with the name De Joyeux. When the family fled from France in the period of persecution it settled in German-speaking Switzerland and changed its name to Fröhlich. Samuel Fröhlich studied theology at the universities of Zürich and Basel, but was not in sympathy with the spirit of rationalism found in the universities at that time. After severe inner struggles, in October 1825, "finally a view of faith on Jesus Christ, the Crucified" came to him which brought him "rest and peace and light and created room in me for a new creation." He served as a pastor of the Reformed Church at Leutwil in the canton of Aargau for a short time. Since he taught a rebirth through repentance and faith, and baptism upon confession of faith, he was opposed by the church consistory. On Oct. 22, 1830, he was hastily summoned and told that he had been eliminated from the list of Aargau clergy, and that he was strictly forbidden to perform any church function such as preaching and baptizing.

Fröhlich then had himself baptized in Geneva by Pastor Bost, who had likewise been expelled from the church. From now on he preached the Gospel in private meetings, began to baptize, and "to help to gather the children of God." In August 1832 he made connections with Christian Gerber near Langnau (*q.v.*), the leader (Vorsteher) of the Emmental Mennonite congregation. When it developed that there was some agreement in the matter of baptism Fröhlich himself traveled to Langnau and visited Gerber (1763-1849), who was at that time nearly seventy years old. At a meeting of all the ministers and deacons Fröhlich presented his beliefs. Gerber and several others, like Christian Baumgartner, a Mennonite preacher living in Labach near Langnau, agreed with him. Fröhlich's "earnest pure teaching of the Gospel, which aroused the sleepy," soon found entry, especially since Gerber and Baumgartner complained about the lethargy and laxity of the preachers. Thus Fröhlich found favorable soil in Langnau and from now on held regular meetings here, which were well attended. The court record reports that "at a public meeting he gave the admonition like a preacher and in the evening often taught, so that the old simple doctrines now seem to some as foolishness." He won several members of the Langnau Mennonite congregation, who now began to separate from the others. They demanded that communion be held almost every Sunday according to Acts 2:46, hoping thereby to lead the congregation back to the apostolic position. These innovations attracted many. By Sept. 2, 1832, Fröhlich's audience was estimated at 400-500 persons. Fröhlich was therefore summoned before the government and banished. He then went to East Switzerland.

This move, however, caused severe divisions in the Mennonite congregations in the Emmental. In spite of negotiations, unity could not be achieved and discord increased. Gerber and Baumgartner began at Christmas time 1834 to observe communion separately with several of their companions. This matter then came before the brotherhood in the Jura. In January 1835 four preachers, David Baumgartner, Hans Zingg, Jakob Nussbaumer, and Ulrich Lehmann, came to Langnau to settle the trouble, but accomplished little. The elders and ministers of the Langnau congregation continued to hope for improvement, but the meetings remained separate. In East Switzerland and in the vicinity of his home in Aargau many Mennonites grouped themselves around Fröhlich. The movement spread also in the cantons of St. Gall, Appenzell, Thurgau, and Zürich. In the Emmental the division became even greater when Fröhlich sent to the Emmental George Steiger from Toggenburg, one of his followers, a young man of 21 years. Steiger declared that the adherents of the old order were all spiritually dead as long as they were not baptized by immersion. Just as Jakob Ammann had done in his time (1694-97) Steiger insisted that the Langnau church discipline was too lax. He succeeded in drawing about 64 persons out of the Mennonite congregations and a similar number from the Reformed Church in Langnau and

uniting them into a separate congregation by rebaptism. But they first had to confess that they had until then been children of the devil. This baptism by Steiger destroyed all hope of healing the schism in the Mennonite congregation. The Swiss conference meeting in March 1835 decided to expel Gerber and Baumgartner with their following from the Mennonite brotherhood; this was done on the first Sunday of May by the elders of the Jura churches. Thus complete separation had come. Fröhlich's followers were now called "Fröhlichianer" or "Neutäufer."

Soon after the division Ulrich Steiner (*q.v.*) was installed as elder of the Langnau Mennonite Church. In his booklet *Angenehme Stunden in Zion* he describes how seriously he was grieved by this course of events, which caused him severe trials until God gave him light. The light of the rising sun with its golden glow seemed to him a symbol of the old church, since through all the storms of persecutions it had shone as a bright light. As a symbol of the new brotherhood he believed he saw the light of the full moon as a reflection of the former.

In February 1836 Fröhlich made an attempt to make contact with the Reformation Committee of the Baptist Association in London, with the view of bringing about a unification of his group with the Baptists. He also negotiated with Johann Gerhard Oncken (*q.v.*) in 1846 for the purpose of union. All these attempts failed; Fröhlich was alone with the congregations which had originated through him and which called themselves "Taufgesinnte Gemeinschaft." On Oct. 30, 1836, Fröhlich again visited Langnau, staying at Bäregg for several days until the police began to pursue him. In 1844 Fröhlich was finally expelled from Switzerland and found refuge in Strasbourg with a Johann Diebold. Here too he tried to find his way to the Mennonite congregations, but the Mennonites explained to him that only those ministers who were ordained for the proclamation of the Word by the laying on of hands of their elders were admitted as preachers. Since the "Alttäufer seemed to regard the letter more than the Spirit" no agreement was reached. From Strasbourg Fröhlich tried to serve his congregations by means of pastoral letters, some of which are still extant. In late July 1852 he once more visited the Langnau congregation, holding a meeting in a barn. Again on his last trip in Switzerland in 1856 he passed through Langnau. He died on Jan. 15, 1857.

In the canton of Bern the Neutäufer have considerable congregations, not only in the Emmental but also in other parts. In Bern they built an old people's home called the Mattenhof in 1903. In 1908 a part of the congregation under Elder Fritz Zehnder separated and built a meetinghouse of its own in Bärau near Langnau.

On the whole the Neutäufer are rather hostile to the state church, for which reason there were serious difficulties with the clergy of the church in the first decades of their existence. A clergyman of Bern whose name is not given published a pamphlet in 1864 with the title *Gemeinfassliche Belehrung über die Sekte der Neutäufer und ihre Lehre,* "to preserve the members of the Evangelical Reformed State Church from error and seduction."

For the nurture of the Neutäufer congregations in Alsace, Strasbourg, and elsewhere, Fröhlich on Jan. 1, 1847, ordained G. Martin Mangold in addition to Johann Diebold. Mangold is credited with the publication in 1853 of the *Zionsharfe,* the Neutäufer hymnal, using songs out of the former *Harmonika.* But this cannot be true, since the first edition is dated 1844. But he is the author of the book *Blicke in die Vergangenheit, Gegenwart und Zukunft, oder Enthüllungen wichtiger prophetischer Weissagungen und Anmerkungen über die Offenbarung Jesu Christi an seinen Knecht Johannes* (Zürich, 1862). Mangold here presents himself as a prophet illuminated by God, who has the task of explaining the Revelation of John. At the very beginning he calls infant baptism the basic error, which has set the whole ecclesiastical building on a false foundation. The rejection of infant baptism is, to be sure, understandable, but what follows is particularly striking, and is actually nothing more than unwholesome presumption. The fallen star of Rev. 8:10-11, he says was the Church Father Augustine, who must be regarded as the "destroyer of divine fundamental truth." The Reformation and the whole Protestant church he saw as the second beast out of the abyss, which like the first beast, the papacy, killed the two witnesses of God, the Law and the Gospel, and is therefore called the false prophet. The beast with seven heads was, in his interpretation, the combination of traditional church doctrine with the seven sacraments, through which the body of the orthodox world church is held together. The new church constitution of the Reformation had "like the Lamb in the church of God only two sacraments." Both branches (Lutheran and Reformed) he interprets as the two horns of the beast which have extended their might over lands and kingdoms. At the end Mangold also discusses the Mennonites and Baptists, "who to be sure, at first stood in the truth but gradually fell into externalities," which had lost "the divine anointment and the power," and had turned into a "saltless salt."

After Fröhlich's death Mangold emigrated to America and established several congregations there, which spread to the states of New York, Illinois, and Ohio. (See **Apostolic Christian Church.**) In Austria, where there are a few Neutäufer, and in Hungary, Jugoslavia, and Rumania, where there are more, they are called Nazarenes (*q.v.*). During World War I many of them had to undergo long imprisonment in Hungary because they refused military service. On the whole the Neutäufer are rather narrow, rejecting communion with other believers, even those who maintain the same principles, and holding strictly to tradition.   S.G.

Die Umtriebe der Neutäufer (Bern, 1841); *Die Sekte der Neutäufer* (Bern, 1864); S. Geiser, *Die Taufgesinnten-Gemeinden* (Karlsruhe, 1931); G. Martin Mangold, *Blicke in die Vergangenheit, Gegenwart und Zukunft* (Zürich, 1862); Herrmann Ruegger, *Aufzeichnungen über Entstehung und Bekenntnis der Gemeinschaft Evangelisch-Taufgesinnter* (Zürich, 1948); English translation, *Apostolic Christian Church History* I (Chicago, 1949); Delbert L. Gratz, *Bernese Anabaptists* (Scottdale, 1953).

Neutralists. After the Frisian-Flemish schism of 1567, by which the stricter Mennonites in the Netherlands were divided into two branches, a few con-gregations did not wish to side with either group. In Zierikzee (*q.v.*) they were called "Stilstaanders" (*q.v.*), elsewhere "Neutralists." (The name is found in A. Montanus, *Kerkelijke Historie van Nederland,* 197.) The Neutralists were numerous in the district of Baarderadeel in Friesland, where the name was used as late as the 18th century. (*ML* III, 219.)
vDZ.

Neuwerk Hutterite "Bruderhof" near Fulda, Germany: see **Rhönbruderhof.**

Neuwied, a town (pop. 20,670) in the former Prussian Rhine Province of Germany, since 1945 in Rhineland-Palatinate, seven miles northwest of Coblenz. In 1574 the Anabaptists were expelled from the gravure of Wied (Fahr and Irlich). An influx of Mennonites and the organization of a congregation was not possible until Count Frederick of Wied founded Neuwied as a residential town in 1652, and offered freedom of worship to all creeds. The Mennonites who came to Neuwied at that time stemmed from Jülich and Monschau, the Palatinate, and Switzerland. They were peasants and craftsmen (weavers and clockmakers). After they had been living here in peace for about twenty years the counts tried in 1678 to compel them to attend the Reformed Church now and then; when they refused to comply they were given a guarantee of religious liberty on Dec. 16, 1680, "in consideration of their persistent plea and their quiet life and conduct." This document names the families of Linschet, Krey, Rupp, and Sintzenich. In 1694 a number of oppressed Mennonites from the Palatinate settled near Neuwied. In 1710 the Count of Neuwied was disposed to grant citizenship to the Mennonite refugees from Switzerland. In 1767 a number of Mennonites from Württemberg settled at Neuwied.

After Count Frederick's death some difficulties arose on the questions of reception into the guilds and guard duty; but on the whole the Mennonites of Neuwied could live according to their beliefs. Indeed, the count even encouraged the building up of the congregation. Lorentz Friedenreich (*q.v.*), the elder of the congregation, wrote in 1769 that they were not only given protection and toleration like all other churches, but were encouraged to invite more Mennonites to come from the Palatinate; they would have invited more if economic conditions had permitted. But for weavers and peasants these were not too favorable; hence the membership remained small, never exceeding eighty.

Until 1768 services were held in homes as required by the government. In 1768 Count Alexander ordered the Mennonites to erect a suitable church near the castle grounds. With generous assistance from their brethren in Holland a small church could be built, with an adjoining residence for the needy, and on Nov. 6, 1768, the church was dedicated in the presence of the count's family. In 1826 an organ was put into the church, and in 1861, as a gift from the count, a small tower with a bell.

The intellectual life and manner of living were no different here from other Mennonite communities of the time. Simplicity, tolerance, and quietness were characteristic of them. When Lavater, together with Basedow and Goethe, visited the Neuwied congregation on July 19, 1774, he noted in his diary, "Visited the Mennonites Friedenreich and Kintzing, splendid faces full of simplicity and honesty, and around them—many boys and daughters and mothers' faces equally noble, innocent, affectionate, went into their church without tower or bell, spoke of their services, looked into their orthodox catechism —Basedow asked whether they would receive one who did not believe in the Trinity—received the reply—not to communion—looked over their artistic clocks—microscopes." In the 18th century the following ministers served at Neuwied: Thielmann Rupp *ca.* 1760, Lorentz Friedenreich, elder 1758-*ca.* 95; Jakob Jutzy (?), elder 1758-*ca.* 98; Heinrich Friedenreich 1788, Peter Weber 1793. In the 17th century the following served the congregation: Heinrich Rupp (d. 1637), a *Vorsteher,* in whose home the meetings were held for a time; Tillmann Rupp (d. 1649), a *Vorsteher* for 26 years, and his son Leonhard (d. 1683) for 18 years.

Concerning their legal status Fischer wrote in 1777: "The Mennonite brotherhood has its own distinctive organization, which differs from the three tolerated churches; it has no particular organization, but rather stresses quietness and inner piety, where no superior gives orders, but all regulations depend on the consent of all members. Thus a church inspection would not be of practical use, because they are allowed freedom of religion, and the rulers of the land have so little prescribed their doctrine or even sanctioned it, that one is not concerned with their doctrine but only considers whether their toleration is harmful to the state."

In the 19th century a deep change took place in the life of the congregation. Economic conditions induced many to emigrate to America. Furthermore, several families died out, and others joined the Reformed Church. (In 1817 there were including the children 76 members; in 1850, 40; in 1900, 88; in 1940 hardly 25.) The old spirit was dying. There was no one who would take charge of the preaching. And so it was decided to employ a salaried minister. With financial support from Holland and a fund raised by the members, trained preachers served the congregation in 1829-1909. Of these preachers, Karl Harder (*q.v.*) was outstanding; he preached at Neuwied 1858-69 and was given honorable mention by the royal poet Carmen Sylva in her autobiography, *Mein Penatenwinkel.* In 1867 the Neuwied congregation joined the A.D.S. (Dutch General Conference). Pastor Harder was followed by August Billau 1871-92, Adolf Siebert 1893-98, and Gerhard Haake 1898-1910. After this the ministers of the Crefeld Mennonite Church took over the pastoral care of the congregation, with regular preaching appointments.

After World War II a number of Mennonite refugees from West Prussia settled in the neighborhood of Neuwied. With the help of the MCC the congregation was built up. In 1948 Gerhard Fast became preacher, and in 1952 Otto Wiebe, formerly of Marienburg, West Prussia, elder. The baptized membership numbered about 360 in 1956.

An MCC unit of Pax men (Mennonite CO's from the United States doing their two years of I-W service in Europe) built a series of 14 one-family houses and 8 two-family houses in Torney near Niederbiber a few miles from Neuwied in 1950-54. A chapel was built in Niederbiber in 1955, and certain services are now held here. One of the houses was occupied for almost a year by a group of Pax men who had set up a cement block factory and made blocks (bimsblocks) for the houses they were building in Espelkamp (*q.v.*).

The traveler going from Andernach to Laach Lake is acquainted with the Mennonite farms and small Mennonite cemetery near Eich. They are the remains of a small Swiss ("Schwitzer") congregation, but which, reduced in number, later reunited with Neuwied.

A small Mennonite Brethren congregation was established in Neuwied about 1950, which acquired a meetinghouse in 1956, and had about 15 members.   D.C., H.S.B.

D. Cattepoel, "Die Neuwieder Mennoniten-Gemeinde," in *Beiträge zur Geschichte rheinischer Mennoniten* (1939) 144-53; E. Crous, "Lavater, Basedow und Goethe bei den Mennoniten in Neuwied," in *Menn. Bl.,* 1930, 107 f.; Christian Neff, "Peter Weber, ein mennonitischer Pietist," *Gem.-Kal.* 1930, 61-102; *Der Mennonit* VI (February 1953); *Inv. Arch. Amst.* I, Nos. 1146, 1257, 1259, 1431 f., 1543; II, 2811-17; *DB* 1868, 172; 1885, 10 f.; B. C. Roosen, *Geschichte der Mennoniten-Gemeinde zu Hamburg-Altona* II (Hamburg, 1887) 58; *ML* III, 219-21.

Neuwied (Germany) Mennonite Brethren Church was founded in 1951 by refugees from Russia and Poland. Most of these have now emigrated to Canada, but the congregation has been continued as a mission under the leadership of J. W. Vogt, supported by the M.B. Foreign Mission Board. In 1956 the congregation had acquired a meetinghouse and had 60 members, with J. W. Vogt as pastor. Only 9 of the original 25 members are still members, the rest having emigrated to Canada. H.S.B.

New Amish, a name sometimes given to the Apostolic Christian Church (*q.v.*) in the United States because several of its major congregations (e.g., Morton, Ill., and Croghan, N.Y.) were located in Amish Mennonite communities and won a considerable number of adherents from them. (See **Neutäufer.**)

New Bremen (N.Y.) **First** Mennonite Church (MC) was established on Nov. 11, 1941, with 76 charter members, most of whom had been members of the Amish Mennonite Church of Croghan, N.Y. The congregation is not affiliated with any Mennonite conference. D. A. Yoder, Goshen, Ind.; S. C. Yoder, Goshen, Ind.; and Simon Gingerich, Wayland, Ia., have served as bishops of the congregation. J. Lawrence Burkholder, Goshen, Ind., was the first pastor (1942-44). The 1955 membership was 190; Gordon Schrag was the pastor 1945-56. A new meetinghouse was built one mile north of town. B.F.Z.

New Carlisle (Ohio) United Missionary Church was organized in 1898. In 1954 the congregation had 140 members with R. P. Ditmer serving as pastor.   A.TA.

New Conestoga Mennonite Church (OOM) is located on the east bank of the Conestoga River, two miles west of the village of St. Jacobs, Ont. In 1894 land was purchased and a frame building erected to serve the Old Order (Wisler) Mennonites of this vicinity, known as the South Woolwich community. The ministers have been Daniel M. Brubacher, Ezra L. Martin, Tobias Martin, Israel Weber, and Irvin W. Shantz. The membership has been small.

J.C.F.

New Danville Mennonite Church (MC), in Lancaster Co., Pa., a member of the Lancaster Conference, was built on land of Bishop Hans Burkholder and Melchior Brenneman, pioneers of 1717. The cemetery is still there. In the overflow from the Lampeter-Strasburg settlement of 1710 many of the new arrivals in 1717 came into this area. The first meetinghouse, built in 1755 in this stump land, was called Stumptown. It was replaced in 1855 and 1878 by stone churches, and therefore became known as the Stone Church. The new one of brick built in 1907 gradually took on the present name of the near-by town. This was the home district of Bishop Martin Boehm, organizer of the United Brethren Church. The membership in 1956 was 260, with David N. Thomas as bishop and James H. Hess as the minister. A three-room Christian day school near by is sponsored by the district. I.D.L.

New Danville Reformed Mennonite Church is located five miles south of Lancaster, Pa. The meetinghouse was built in 1837, and was known as the Stumptown church. It was organized under the leadership of Bishop Abram Snavely, one of the first ministers in that district. This frame building has been used ever since, with a small addition about 60 years ago. Other ministers who served the congregation were John Kohr, Sr., Elias H. Hershey, John Kohr, Jr., Henry Fisher, Levi Weaver, and Christian Howry. The ministers of this group are not assigned to one particular meetinghouse, but alternate in the churches in the county. Likewise the members attend the meetings wherever they are; it is therefore hard to give exact membership figures. The present alternating ministers are Jacob L. Kreider, J. Henry Fisher, Clyde Weaver, Ray Eshleman, Willis Weaver, and Earl M. Basinger. The total Reformed Mennonite membership in Lancaster County was about 300 in 1948. J.L.K.

New Elm Springs Hutterite Bruderhof, near Magrath, Alberta, was founded in 1918 by the New Elm Spring Bruderhof near Ethan, S.D., who sold all their land and bought the New Elm site. Their preachers are Johann P. Entz, chosen here in 1923, and Jakob J. Waldner, chosen a few years later. In 1947 the Bruderhof numbered 107, with 40 baptized members. D.D.

New Elm Springs Hutterite Bruderhof at Valier, Mont., was founded in 1947 by several families and preacher Jakob Waldner of the New Elm Springs Bruderhof in Alberta. In 1947 the Bruderhof numbered 85, with 40 baptized members. D.D.

New Elm Springs Hutterite Bruderhof, near Ethan, S.D., was founded in 1911. In 1918 the Brethren sold the property and founded the New Elm Springs Bruderhof near Magrath, Alberta. In 1936 the Maxwell Bruderhof near Pigeon Lake, Man.,

bought this site and settled on it. Their preacher Joseph Hofer was chosen to the ministry in 1919 by the Maxwell colony in Manitoba. In 1939 Samuel Wollman was also chosen. In 1947 the Bruderhof numbered 146, with 56 baptized members. D.D.

New Guinea. The western part of this island, administered by the Dutch government, is populated by a hundred Papua tribes, most of whom are ancestor worshipers. In 1855 some Dutch Reformed missionaries started mission work in New Guinea, which was, however, not very successful until 1907. Since 1907 complete clans have been converted and batpized, and a number of Christian congregations have been established. The method of conducting missions has been that of a comprehensive approach, proclaiming the Gospel, establishing schools and hospitals, and social work.

In 1950 the region of Inanwatan (*q.v.*) was transferred to the Dutch Mennonite Mission Association (*q.v.*). R. E. H. Marcus was sent to this field in 1950, and P. Messie in 1953, as well as a number of teachers, physicians, and nurses. P. Messie returned to Holland in 1956. The center of the Dutch Mennonite activity at present is no longer Inanwatan but Teminabuan.

In 1956 the churches of New Guinea constituted the autonomous Evangelical Christian Church, governed by one general and several regional synods composed of native ministers, with the Dutch missionaries as advisers. In this Evangelical Church Mennonites co-operate with the Reformed, but are free to preach the Gospel in Mennonite manner and to administer adult baptism. The design of the foundation of this Evangelical Church is to renovate the old Papuan society into a Christian community from which pagan traditions and the practice of magic and ancestor worship are eliminated.

W.F.G.

New Hamburg, Ont., a town (pop. *ca.* 2,000) situated in Waterloo County, 12 miles west of Kitchener. It is a trading center for the Wilmot Township Mennonites of the Baden, Biehn, Geiger, and Shantz Mennonite (MC) congregations, and for the Amish Mennonites of the Steinman and East Zorra congregations. A small Reformed Mennonite church stands close to the town on the bank of the Nith River. The chief industries are textiles and brass working.

J.C.F.

New Hamburg Mennonite Brethren Church, a former congregation located in New Hamburg, Waterloo Co., Ont., a member of the Canadian M.B. Conference, was organized Nov. 20, 1932, under the leadership of Peter Goertzen. The membership in 1948 was 17, most of whom lived in town. The congregation met with the members of the United Mennonite Church in a rented hall. The ministers who served the church were D. Derksen, P. Goertzen, A. Block, and P. Friesen. The group, already small, suffered greatly when some of its members moved to areas where they could enjoy the fellowship of larger churches. On June 10, 1950, it chose to join the M.B. Church of Kitchener as an affiliate. While I. T. Ewert supplied the pulpit, G. Wiebe served as their local leader, with David Dick succeeding him. The pulpit supply became difficult, and so the group dissolved and its members joined the M.B. Church of Kitchener on Sept. 29, 1952.

J.J.T.

New Holland, a town (pop. 3,000) located 13 miles northeast of Lancaster, Pa., on Highway 23. With Hans Groff settling to the northwest, the Weaver brothers and David Martin to the east, the Rancks to the southeast, and Dorus Eby to the southwest, this area was left for John Diffenderfer, the 1728 immigrant. David Martin brought him, his family, and all his worldly possessions from the port of entry to this area. With the aid of Swiss Mennonite neighbors he soon had a shelter and a cow. His son Michael laid out the town in 1760, on 268 acres patented to him, first called Säue-Schwamm (Hog Wallow) for very apparent reasons, later Earltown after Hans Groff, then New Design until the 1760's. Then New Holland was adopted, honoring the country that so graciously made possible the journey of many to this country. The town became a trading center for the Mennonites on the fertile acres around. The silk mill, the concrete works, and more recently the overshadowing New Holland Machine Company, are industries here. A Mennonite (MC) meetinghouse is also found in the town.

I.D.L.

M. G. Weaver, *A History of New Holland, Pennsylvania . . . 1728-1928* (New Holland, 1928).

New Holland Mennonite Church (MC), located in eastern Lancaster Co., Pa., was organized for a number of retired farmers and near-by farmers from the Weaverland, Groffdale, and Hershey congregations. In 1910-22 services were held in the Methodist church, with Noah H. Mack as minister. In 1922 the present large meetinghouse was built in the town. Noah Sauder was the first local minister, ordained Dec. 20, 1923. Six ordinations have been held here to date. Mahlon Witmer as bishop, and Noah N. Sauder and James H. Martin as ministers serve a congregation of 258 members (1956).

I.D.L.

New Hopedale Mennonite Church (GCM), located at the northeast corner of Meno, Major Co., Okla., a member of the Western District, was organized June 13, 1895, in the basement of the Benjamin P. Jantz home with 25 charter members. Johann Ratzlaff was called to be their elder and pastor. In 1914 Ratzlaff retired for reasons of health and was followed by J. B. Epp, who served for five years, and was replaced by J. J. Ratzlaff. The following ministers assisted at the two meetinghouses: J. J. Ratzlaff, David H. Schmidt, Tobias P. Wedel, Tobias P. Unruh, Karl Schartner, Heinrich T. Neufeld, and Albert J. Unruh. Mr. and Mrs. Harold Ratzlaff are missionaries in India from New Hopedale. A group that had worshiped separately from the beginning later organized a congregation called West New Hopedale, taking over 50 members from New Hopedale.

H. U. Schmidt was pastor 1921-48; the pulpit was supplied until 1955 by various temporary ministers. In 1955 Arnold A. Epp was regularly appointed to this church and served several months. Ben J. Nickel then served until June 1957. A new meetinghouse has recently been built. The membership in 1956 was 308.

H.U.S.

New Huttertal Mennonite Church (GCM), located near Bridgewater, S.D., a member of the Northern District Conference but not of the General Conference, was organized in Russia and transplanted to America in 1874. It is of Hutterite background. Paul Tschetter served as its first leader in America. Previous to 1888, when the first meetinghouse was constructed, services were held in homes and schools. The meetinghouse was remodeled in 1952. The 1956 membership was 150, largely rural. Other ministers who have served this congregation are Joseph Wipf, John D. Hofer, David J. Wipf, Paul J. Tschetter, Jacob I. Walter, Albert Ewert, and Abe M. Wiebe.

J.D.U.

New Jersey State Hospital CPS Unit No. 63, located at Marlboro, had a maximum of 103 men. It was approved by Selective Service in November 1942 and closed in December 1946. Most of the men served as attendants to the mental patients in the institution. The Unit published an 82-page history and report of its work under the title *p. r. n.* (See **Marlboro.**)

M.G.

Melvin Gingerich, *Service for Peace* (Akron, Pa., 1949) 221 f.

New Market (Iowa) United Missionary Church was organized in 1893. In 1948 the congregation had 50 members, with J. B. Starkey serving as pastor.

J.B.ST.

New Mennonites, a colloquial name given locally to several schismatic groups separating from older established Mennonite bodies, both by the older group and the general public. Its counterpart designation, "Old Mennonite" (*q.v.*), has likewise been used to designate the original group from which the new had broken off. Three instances of this usage have occurred: (1) the Reformed Mennonites (*q.v.*), who separated from the Lancaster (MC) Conference in Eastern Pennsylvania in 1812; (2) the Oberholtzer (*q.v.*) group (Eastern District Conference, GCM), which broke off from the Franconia Conference (MC) in Eastern Pennsylvania in 1847-48; (3) the Mennonite Brethren in Christ (*q.v.*, now United Missionary Church), who broke off from the Mennonite Church (MC) in Indiana and Ontario in 1874-75. While the term "New Mennonite" was earlier fairly common in Pennsylvania, Indiana, and Ontario, it has gradually almost died out.

The term "New Maneest" has sometimes been used to refer to the Apostolic Christian (*q.v.*) Church in Illinois, New York, and Ohio, but the more common term in these districts has been "New Amish," although the Apostolic group has had no connection with the Amish either in Europe or America and was not a schismatic group in North America. In Switzerland the Apostolic group has commonly been called "Neutäufer," a term which historically has some justification since about half of the original group in 1832 was drawn from the Emmental

(Switzerland) Mennonite (*Täufer*) congregation. (See also **Nieuwe Zwitsers**; *ML* III, 214.) H.S.B.

New Mexico, admitted to the union in 1912 as the 47th state, population 681,187. There is in the state one Mennonite (MC) congregation, located at Albuquerque, founded in 1950, having 13 members in 1956; it is a member of the South Pacific Conference. H.S.B.

New Miami Hutterite Bruderhof, near Conrad, Mont., was founded in 1947 by several families and preacher Johann Wipf of the Miami Bruderhof at New Dayton, Alberta. The Bruderhof has a population of 108, with 45 baptized members. D.D.

New Milford Hutterite Bruderhof, near Augusta, Mont., was founded in 1946 by several families and preacher Joseph Kleinsasser from the Bruderhof in Milford, Alberta. In 1947 it had a population of 108, with 45 baptized members. D.D.

New Pittsburg Church of God in Christ Mennonite Church, now extinct, located in Chester Twp., Wayne Co., Ohio, was organized in 1859 with John Holdeman as minister and a membership of 20. During the first 19 years services were conducted in homes of the members. In 1878 a modest meetinghouse was built. This congregation became extinct in 1883, when nearly all its members moved to Missouri or other congregations. P.G.H.

New Providence Mennonite Church (MC), located in a small town of that name in Lancaster County, Pa. By 1766 it had a log meetinghouse for the Groff, Eshleman, Herr, Funk, Brubaker, and Gochenauer families who had settled there. Johannes Bowman served them early as preacher. The Strasburg ministers helped them at first. In 1882 they built the Mechanic Grove meetinghouse for their southern constituency. Jacob T. Harnish as bishop, Abram D. Metzler and A. Clyde Hostetter as ministers served this congregation of 137 members in 1956. I.D.L.

New Raymer (Col.) was the address of a permanent side camp under the administration of the Fort Collins (*q.v.*) Civilian Public Service Camp No. 33 during World War II. It was known as Buckingham Side Camp, and was located on an abandoned farm site in an arid region about 70 miles east of Fort Collins. The campers, under Mennonite direction, built fences, reseeded grasslands, drilled wells, and built stock water tanks. M.G.

Melvin Gingerich, *Service for Peace* (Akron, Pa., 1949) 122, 158, *et passim*.

New Rosebud Hutterite Bruderhof near Crossfield, Alberta, was founded in 1939 by several families from the Beiseker Bruderhof with their preacher, who was chosen in Beiseker in 1933. In 1944 Darius Tschetter was chosen minister. In 1947 this Bruderhof numbered 70, with 28 baptized members. D.D.

New Rosedale Hutterite Bruderhof was founded in 1944, 15 miles southwest of **Portage La Prairie,** Man., by Andreas Hofer and eleven families from

the Rosedale Bruderhof near Elie, Man. In 1947 the population of the colony was 87, of whom 32 were baptized members. D.D.

New Springvale Hutterite Bruderhof near Beiseker, Alberta, was founded in 1935 by several families from the Springvale commune near Rocky Ford, Alberta, with their preacher Jakob Wurz, chosen to the ministry in 1913. Franz A. Wollmann was chosen preacher here. In 1947 the colony numbered 165, with 70 baptized members. D.D.

New Stark Mennonite Church is the more commonly used name for Menno Chapel (*q.v.*), erected west of New Stark, Ohio, in 1878, and abandoned several years ago. J.S.U.

New York (State). As early as 1643 Mennonites are known to have been living on Manhattan Island, now New York City. A French Jesuit traveler, Father Jaques, in a letter of 1643 from Manhattan mentions "Anabaptists here called Menists" as one of the religious groups found on the island. Mennonites were reported in another document of 1657 at Gravesend on Long Island. The term Anabaptist appears frequently in early colonial New York records. However, no record of an organized congregation from this early time has been found, and no permanent settlement was made by them.

The only Mennonites to settle in the state of New York were settlers from Eastern Pennsylvania, largely from Lancaster County, who located in Niagara County (Falls Church) in 1810 ff. and in Erie County (Clarence Center or Good's Church) in 1824 ff. The former congregation was very small and soon died out. The latter was more substantial but had practically died out by the beginning of the 20th century. Several families of Krehbiels from the Palatinate located at Clarence Center in 1831 ff., and a small fraction of this congregation followed a Krehbiel preacher in 1875 into the General Conference Mennonite fellowship, but the group was small and ultimately died out. The Clarence Center congregation was revived by new arrivals beginning in 1920 and is now a flourishing congregation with 187 members. A Conservative Amish Mennonite congregation was started in the same community at Alden about the same time and now has 188 members. An Old Order Amish settlement was founded recently at Conewango Valley, N.Y., which now has two congregations with a total of 113 members, with a small neighboring congregation near Sinclairville. An independent Conservative congregation existed at Clarence 1921-48.

In 1833 ff. a large Conservative Amish Mennonite settlement was established near Croghan and Lowville in Lewis County, in the northeastern part of the state, by immigrants direct from Alsace and Lorraine, increased by settlers coming from the Amish community west of Kitchener (see **Ontario**), Ont. In 1955 this settlement had three congregations with a total of 631 members, one of which was at Woodville, some 50 miles nearer the St. Lawrence River. In 1941 a group withdrew from the Conservative church to form the New Bremen Mennonite Church, an independent congregation which in 1955

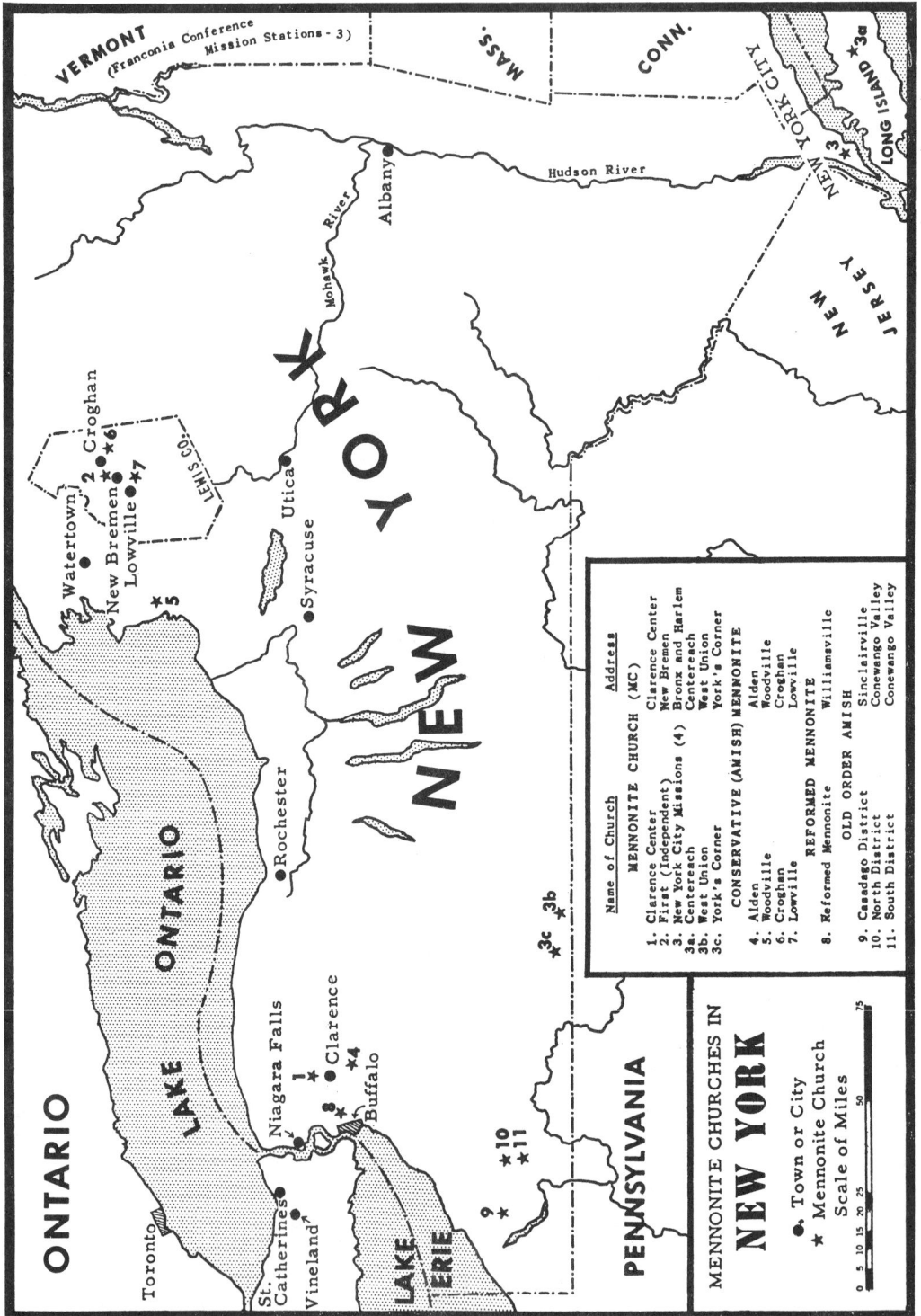

MENNONITE CHURCHES IN
NEW YORK

●. Town or City
★ Mennonite Church
Scale of Miles

0 5 10 15 20 25   50   75

Name of Church	Address
MENNONITE CHURCH (MC)	
1. Clarence Center	Clarence Center
2. First (Independent)	New Bremen
3. New York City Missions (4)	Bronx and Harlem
3a. Centereach	Centereach
3b. West Union	West Union
3c. York's Corner	York's Corner
CONSERVATIVE (AMISH) MENNONITE	
4. Alden	Alden
5. Woodville	Woodville
6. Croghan	Croghan
7. Lowville	Lowville
REFORMED MENNONITE	
8. Reformed Mennonite	Williamsville
OLD ORDER AMISH	
9. Casadego District	Sinclairville
10. North District	Conewango Valley
11. South District	Conewango Valley

VERMONT (Franconia Conference Mission Stations-3)

MASS.   CONN.

NEW YORK CITY

LONG ISLAND   ★3a

★3

Hudson River

Albany●

Mohawk River

NEW JERSEY

Croghan
2 ★6
Watertown●
New Bremen●
Lowville●★7

LEWIS CO.

●Utica

NEW YORK

●Syracuse

★5

ONTARIO

LAKE ONTARIO

●Rochester

Toronto●

St. Catherines●
Vineland●

Niagara Falls
1 ★
8 ★●Clarence ★4
Buffalo

LAKE ERIE

9 ★

10 ★
11 ★

3c ★ 3b ★

PENNSYLVANIA

had 194 members. A large block of the Conservative members withdrew in 1849 to form an Apostolic Christian congregation.

Thus the total of Mennonites and Old Order Amish in the state in 1955 was 1,119, distributed as follows: Conservative Mennonite 819, Mennonite (MC) 187, Old Order Amish 113. A Reformed Mennonite congregation was established at Williamsville, N.Y., near Clarence, about 1834, which had 34 members in 1948. The Mennonite Brethren in Christ have a congregation of 48 members on Staten Island, a borough of New York City, and a mission in Binghamton on the south-central border of the state.

New York City and Long Island have become a locus of mission work for the Lancaster and Franconia Mennonite (MC) conferences in recent years. The Lancaster Conference has four stations, with a total of 52 members, three in the Bronx (1949, 1951, and 1954), and one colored mission in Harlem (1954). The Franconia Conference has a work at Centereach, Long Island, with 10 members, started in 1953. The House of Friendship, a mission to Jews, was established as an outpost of the Maple Grove congregation (Ohio and Eastern Conference) near Atglen in Lancaster County, Pa., in 1956. Further mission stations have been established in the western part of the state as follows: by the Lancaster Conference at York's Corners in Allegany County in 1952, and at West Union in Steuben County in 1954, by the Conservative Mennonites at Williamsville in 1936, and by the Clarence Center Mennonite Church (MC) at Arcade in Allegany County in 1956. H.S.B.

New York, a village in the Ignatyevka Mennonite settlement in the province of Ekaterinoslav, in South Russia. The Chortitza settlement bought an estate here in 1888 for its landless members and founded six villages in the following year. Of these villages New York, with a population (1913) of 926, and Nikolayevka became the centers of the settlement. Each of the two villages had a Zentralschule, a Mennonite Brethren meetinghouse, and a Mennonite meetinghouse. With its subsidiaries Borissovo and Grigoryevka (*q.v.*) and with the forestry service unit at Azov, the New York Mennonite congregation had a membership of (in 1905) 2,275. For the M.B. congregation in this settlement see **Nikolayevka** Mennonite Brethren Church. (*ML* III, 223.) C.K.

New York Hutterite Bruderhof (Dariusleut), located near Maybutt, Alberta, was founded in 1924; the population in 1950 was 110, with Jacob Hofer as head minister. (*ME* II, 15.) D.D.

New York Mädchenschule (secondary school for girls) was established in the Bachmut Mennonite settlement (*q.v.*), South Russia, in 1907 after the New York Zentralschule had been established. The next year a second class was added. The sponsor of the school was J. J. Thiessen of Ekaterinoslav (*q.v.*). The leading teacher was Viktoria Klein. Other teachers were Miss L. P. Ediger, Miss H. A. Leonhard, Miss A. D. Rempel, Johann Bärg, and Dietrich Dyck. A supporting Mädchenschul-Verein aided the school. In 1913-14 there were 40 members in the

fourth class. Little is known about the later development of the school. (Dirks, *Jahrbuch 1913,* 107.) C.K.

New York Mennonite Church, Bachmut (*q.v.;* Ignatyevka) Mennonite settlement, Ukraine, Russia, was established in 1892 by settlers who had come from the Chortitza settlement. The first elder was Abraham Unrau, who was assisted by the ministers Isaak Hildebrand, Johann Nickel, Jakob Lehn, Franz Bückert I and II, and Jakob Wiebe I and II. In 1905 the congregation had a total membership of 1,834, with 606 baptized members. The Grigoryevka (*q.v.*) and the Borissovo (*q.v.*) Mennonite churches were branches of the New York Mennonite Church. The Azov Forestry Service Camp (*q.v.*) received its spiritual guidance from this congregation. The total membership of the New York church and the two branches, including the camp, was 2,275 in 1905. Little is known about the fate of the congregation since World War II. C.K.

Friesen, *Brüderschaft,* 701; Dirks, *Statistik,* 34, 64; *ML* III, 223.

New York Zentralschule was established in the Bachmut Mennonite settlement (*q.v.*), South Russia, in 1905. In 1910 the school consisted of four classes with five teachers. It was supported by the local Mennonite population. C.K.

Newark Church of God in Christ Mennonite Church, located two miles west and four miles south of Ithaca, Mich., originated in the 1880's when the Brown, Diller, Peters, Eicher, Gable, and other families settled here and held services in their homes. Jacob Litwiller, F. C. Fricke, and Peter Litwiller of an adjoining congregation were ordained to the ministry in the early 1890's. F. C. Fricke served as elder for many years. In 1902 a church was built, replaced by a larger church in 1920, which was remodeled and enlarged in 1947 and again in 1954. The membership in 1957 was 265. Nine other ministers and five deacons have been ordained in the history of the church; Glenn Litwiller was the presiding minister in 1957. The ministry is unsalaried. C.M.

Newark (N.J.) Mennonite Brethren in Christ Church was organized Dec. 21, 1941. In 1956 the congregation had 46 members with LeRoy S. Heller serving as pastor. R.H.G.

Newaygo County (Mich.) Amish settlement, now extinct. A group of Old Order Amish began to settle about seven miles north of White Cloud, Mich., on the banks of Diamond Loch Lake in 1895, including Manasses D. Schmucker and Samuel Yoder, who purchased an old sawmill and produced lumber from which many of the dwellings of the oncoming settlers were built. Other early Amish settlers were Daniel Miller, a minister from Lagrange Co., Ind., Dave Yoder of Elkhart Co., Ind., John Fry and Samuel Miller from Ohio. Newcomers purchased land northeast of White Cloud. Names characteristic of the settlement were Kauffman, Hochstetler, Stutzman, Troyer, Chupp, and Schrock. Gradually all the ministers and many others left.

A number of Amish families joined the Union Mennonite Church at White Cloud.   T.U.N.

Newcomer, Christian (1744-1830), one of the founders of the United Brethren in Christ, was born of Mennonite parents in Lancaster County, Pa., the son of Wolfgang Newcomer. He was married to Elizabeth Baer in 1770. Baptized a Mennonite at about the age of 17, he felt a call to the ministry and withdrew from the Mennonite Church when he was living in Washington County, Md., about 1777, to associate himself with Philip Otterbein, a Reformed minister, who was active as a revival preacher. Martin Boehm (q.v.), a former Mennonite bishop in the Lancaster Mennonite Conference, was with Otterbein a co-founder of the United Brethren Church, which was fully organized and named in 1800. Otterbein and Boehm were the first two bishops elected, Newcomer the third, elected in 1813 and serving in that office until his death. His valuable diary, *The Life and Journal of the Rev'd Christian Newcomer,* published in 1834, gives information about his early years as a Mennonite.
                                         H.S.B.

Newkirk Mennonite Church (MC), now extinct, located in farming community in Kay County, Okla., about 25 miles southeast of Arkansas City, Kan. Mennonite settlers coming to this locality from Sterling, Ill., were the David Ebersole, Dan Ebersole, John Frey, Abe Frey, and Dan·Frey families. In 1907 Christian Reiff and his family came from Newton, Kan., to serve this congregation as minister. The membership at the time of organization was 13, and increased to 22. Because of drought the families gradually moved away; by 1911 the congregation was discontinued.   V.E.R.

Newman, Albert Henry (1852-1933), an American church historian, is the most important of the few Baptist scholars who have made a contribution to the history of Anabaptism in the Reformation time. Besides Newman there were only Henry S. Burrage (q.v.), H. C. Vedder, and William J. McGlothlin (q.v.). Besides these and the Mennonites there are no other American historians who have made any significant contribution to Anabaptist historiography.

Newman was born in Edgefield Co., S.C., on Aug. 25, 1852, the son of John Blackston and Harriet Whitaker Newman. After graduating from the Mercer University in Macon, Ga., in 1871, he acquired his theological education at the Baptist Rochester Theological Seminary at Rochester, N.Y., receiving his degree in 1875. Having chosen Semitic languages as his field of teaching he studied for one year at Southern Baptist Theological Seminary and in January 1877 was asked to succeed Whittemore as professor of church history at this seminary. In 1881 he joined the group which at that time founded McMaster University in Toronto, Ont., at which place he taught for 20 years as professor of church history. In 1901 he was called to the new Southwestern Baptist Theological Seminary in connection with Baylor University in Waco, Tex. In 1921 he was given the lectureship in church history in a newly founded theological school of Mercer University.

Here in January 1927 he celebrated the 50th anniversary of his professorship of church history.

Of Newman's writings the best known is the book published at Philadelphia in 1897, *A History of Antipedobaptism from the Rise of Pedobaptism to A.D. 1609.* Other publications were *The Baptist Churches in the United States* (2 vv., 1894) and *A Manual of Church History* (2 vv., 1899 and 1903); "The Reformation from a Baptist Point of View," in the *Baptist Theological Quarterly,* 1880; "The Significance of the Anabaptist Movement in the History of the Christian Church," in *Review Supplement to the Goshen College Record,* January 1926; *Adam Pastor, Antitrinitarian Antipaedobaptist* (a reprint from *Papers of the American Society of Church History, Second Series* V, 1914).

In the first of his books Newman gives a short survey of the struggle against infant baptism in the old church and a history of the struggle of the Middle Ages carried on by the Petrobrusians, Arnoldists, Waldenses, Taborites, and Bohemian Brethren and describes the Anabaptist movement from its beginning in Zürich, Switzerland, with Grebel, Manz, and Hubmaier in Austria, Moravia, and Bohemia, and finally with Melchior Hofmann down the Rhine. The kingdom of Münster he sees in its true light as an aberration, not as a result of the movement. After a chapter on Menno Simons in the northern group of the Mennonites he turns his attention to the Anabaptists in Italy and Poland. Finally in three chapters the history of the Anabaptist movement in England and the rise of the Baptist Church in 1609 is described.

The presentation is characterized by thoroughness, impartiality, and a benevolent understanding. Newman is the first historian writing in the English language who assigned to the Anabaptist movement its proper position, free of doctrinaire distortion. It is not saying too much to assert that Newman's work is the only satisfactory and complete scholarly history of the Anabaptist movement in the English language, unless Smithson's briefer discussion should be named. Of great value is the extensive bibliography at the end of the volume, which gives 400 titles of nothing but Anabaptist sources.   H.S.B.

Frederick Eby, *Newman, The Church Historian* (Nashville, 1946); *Monatshefte der Comenius-Gesellschaft,* 1897, 342-43; *ML* III, 221 f.

Newport News, Va., a city (pop. 55,000) in the southeastern part of the state, has a large port on Hampton Roads as well as large shipyards. From this port many loads of cattle and horses were sent abroad by UNRRA (q.v.). Many of the Mennonite young men who served as attendants on UNRRA ships in 1946 and later, generally spent a number of days in the city before embarking. Two Mennonite (MC) churches are located in the city. Calvary Mennonite Church on Wickham Avenue, with a membership of 12, is a church for Negroes. The other is Huntington Avenue Mennonite Church (q.v.), with a membership of 50. Twelve miles north of Newport News is the Providence Mennonite Church (q.v.), located near Oyster Point, with a membership of 35. Fourteen miles northwest of the city is Denbigh and the nearby Warwick River Mennonite (MC) Church (q.v.), which has

300 members. All of these congregations belong to the Virginia Conference except Providence, which belongs to the Ohio and Eastern Conference.

E.W.C.

Newport News (Va.) Mennonite Mission (MC): see **Huntington Avenue** Mennonite Church.

Newton, the county seat (1956 pop. 13,603) of Harvey County (*q.v.*), Kan., is located southeast of the state's geographical center, about 23 miles north of Wichita on the Santa Fe Railroad. The area within an approximate 50-mile radius around the city contains the largest Mennonite concentration west of the Mississippi River, with many churches of the General Conference Mennonite Church, the Mennonite Church (MC), the Church of God in Christ Mennonites, and some Mennonite Brethren. In Newton are the General Conference Mennonite Headquarters and Publication Office, First Mennonite Church of Newton (GCM, *q.v.*), Bethel Deaconess Hospital and Home for Aged (GCM, *q.v.*), and Mennonite Central Committee regional office. North Newton (*q.v.*), incorporated as a separate municipality about one-half mile north of the city proper and almost entirely populated by Mennonites, is the seat of Bethel College (*q.v.*), Bethel College Mennonite Church (*q.v.*), the Mennonite Press (*q.v.*, all GCM), and the MCC Relief Clothing Center. Prairie View Hospital (*q.v.*), an MCC mental hospital, is one and one-half miles east of Newton. In 1956 a third Mennonite church, the Newton Mennonite Fellowship (*q.v.*), was founded.

Founded as the Atchison, Topeka and Santa Fe Railroad built its tracks westward to the town site in July 1871, the town was named after Newton, Mass., the home of many Santa Fe stockholders. Completion of the railroad to Newton made it the northern end of the Chisholm Trail, over which Texas cattle ranchers drove great herds of Texas longhorns to Kansas railroads for shipment to eastern markets. Intercepting the bulk of the cattle trade, previously controlled by the Kansas Pacific R.R. (now Union Pacific) at Abilene some 60 miles to the north, Newton was the principal eastward shipping point for Texas cattle. The town's turbulent cowboy era, from August 1871 to January 1873, ended as the rails advanced south and west and the cattle trade transferred to other points.

In 1874 and the years immediately following, Mennonites bought large blocks of land from the Santa Fe, settling east, north, and west of Newton, in Harvey and the adjoining counties of Butler, Marion, McPherson, and Reno. Newton thus became the business and trading center of the Mennonites living within a radius of some 25 miles. Large purchases of tools and machinery were made by Mennonites whose financial resources were sometimes limited to promises.

In 1877 a few Mennonite families from South Russia, coming to Newton via Summerfield, Ill., settled just east of the town. These were followed by more Mennonite immigrants from West Prussia and Russia who bought land in the same area. First worship services were held in their homes two and one-half miles east of Newton at "Goldschar." In

September 1878 they organized themselves as a congregation, later called First Mennonite Church of Newton. The congregation began to worship at the present church site on East First Street after completion of a frame building there in 1881.

Among the pioneer Mennonite businessmen of Newton was Bernhard Warkentin (*q.v.*), who built Harvey County's first flour mill at Halstead (*q.v.*) in 1873 and organized the Newton Milling and Elevator Co. about 1886. His mills were some of the first to be equipped for milling the hard Red Turkey wheat, which he helped to introduce to Kansas farmers on a large scale. The extensive milling industry in Newton is largely a monument to his pioneer efforts in that field. Other Mennonite names associated with the milling industry were Rudolph Goerz, son of David Goerz and founder and president of Goerz Flour Mills Co., now American Flours Inc., and Peter M. Claassen, founder and operator of the Claassen Flour Mills.

Mennonites were instrumental in founding and developing some of the city's early financial institutions. Cornelius F. Claassen founded a finance company (now Regier Loan and Abstract Co.) in 1888 and sold the business to J. G. Regier in 1904. When the Kansas State Bank was incorporated in 1902 with Bernhard Warkentin as president, C. F. Claassen became vice-president, then president in 1908. Herman E. Suderman came to the Midland National Bank (founded 1893) as vice-president in 1902, becoming president in 1919. Mennonite Mutual Fire Insurance Company (*q.v.*), now Midland Mutual Fire Insurance Co., was incorporated by Mennonites of central Kansas in 1880, and in 1893 was moved from Halstead to offices in Newton. First directors were David Goerz, Herman Suderman, Peter Harms, John Siemens, and Jacob W. Regier.

Mennonite publication work began in Newton in 1897 with *Das Kansas Volksblatt,* published by William J. Krehbiel and David Goerz. The *Volksblatt* was sold to the Kansan Printing Co. in 1899 and subsequently in 1900 to the Western Book and Printing Co., founded that year by H. P. Krehbiel. The name of the paper was changed to *Post- und Volksblatt* in 1903 and to *Der Herold* (*q.v.*) in 1909, this name being retained until publication ended in 1941. The company name also changed to Herold Book and Publishing Co. in 1909, and in 1920 to the present name, Herald Publishing Co. (*q.v.*). In 1923 the company began publication of *Mennonite Weekly Review* (*q.v.*), its present main concern. Other periodicals published in Newton as of 1956 were *The Mennonite* (*q.v.*) and *Mennonite Life* (*q.v.*).

Newton has numerous Mennonite business proprietors and tradespeople who play a large part in community life. The city has a large Mennonite population which has always been on the increase.

R.M.S.

W. E. Connelley, *A Standard History of Kansas and Kansans* (New York, 1918) 2292; L. L. Waters, *Steel Rails to Santa Fe* (Lawrence, 1950) 146; R. W. P. Muse, "History of Harvey County—1871-1881," in *Atlas of Harvey County, Kansas—1882* (Philadelphia, 1882); J. E. Entz, "First Mennonite Church—Newton (1878-1953)," *Menn. Life* VIII (October 1953) 153-55; *The Newton Kansan,* Fiftieth Anniversary Number, LI (Aug. 22, 1922); *ML* III, 222 f.

Newton Bible Church had its beginning when on April 4, 1955, the following request with 28 signatures came to the board of deacons of the First Mennonite Church of Newton: "Having felt a definite need for an interdenominational church in Newton, . . . we the undersigned now would like to ask for our church letters so that we might unite as the Newton Bible Church. . . ." This request was granted. The newly organized church worships on Old Main Street and has Lawrence Friesen as pastor (1957).   A.Ep.

Newton (Kan.) **First** Mennonite Church (GCM) had its beginnings in 1877, when a few Mennonite families immigrating from West Prussia settled east of Newton. Among them were Herman Sudermann, Sr., Herman Sudermann, Jr., and William Quiring. In 1878 with the coming of Peter Claassen, a minister from Prussia, the church secured its charter and joined the Western District Conference (GCM). Services were held in a rented Baptist church until their new building was dedicated in 1881 on East First Street. In 1897 and 1902 the church was enlarged, and in 1932 replaced by a new brick church seating 700.

Its first Sunday school was organized in 1881, its first choir in 1888 or 1889, Christian Endeavor in 1898, Junior Endeavor in 1920, Mission Sewing Society in 1887, and Mission Study Circle in 1933. From this church have come thirteen ministers, eighteen missionaries, and five deaconesses. Ministers who have served the congregation include Peter Claassen, B. Regier, Sr., Abr. Suderman, Jacob Toews, J. R. Toews, B. Regier, J. E. Entz, Abram Warkentin, and D. J. Unruh. The present membership (1956) is 811, served by Arnold Epp as pastor. In 1955 a group withdrew to form the Newton Bible Church (*q.v.*).   J.E.E.

Newton Mennonite Fellowship is the beginning of a third Mennonite congregation in the city of Newton, Kan., which is being formed to minister to the growing Mennonite population in Newton. On Sept. 17, 1956, the board of deacons of the First Mennonite Church, which took the lead in forming the new congregation, met in joint session with the board of deacons of the Bethel College Mennonite Church, when action was taken to invite the Western District Home Missions Committee to assist in guiding further developments. The Home Missions Committee called a meeting of the pastors and church board members of all the Western District Conference churches located within an approximate radius of 30 to 35 miles of Newton. During this meeting, at which 23 congregations were represented, the following motion was adopted: "Moved that the Home Mission Committee take necessary steps toward the establishment and organization of a third Mennonite church in Newton, Kansas." A survey revealed interest and a fertile field for another Mennonite church. After several meetings with interested individuals, the first public worship service was called for the evening of Feb. 24, 1957, which took place in the Sister Frieda Memorial Chapel. Since that time regular weekly worship services take place in the chapel for which a Planning Committee is responsible (1957).   A.Ep.

Newton-Jasper County (Ind.) Old Order Amish settlement was begun about 1872, when several Amish families from Ohio settled near Rensselaer in Jasper County but soon moved some 15 miles west into Newton County near the small town of Mount Ayr. Others joined them from near Goshen, Ind. Until 1914 this group constituted one congregation, but in that year another group of Amish from Daviess County, Ind., settled about 15 miles further east in Jasper County, near the small town of Parr, creating a second congregation. In 1914-23 the two groups were served by one ministerial body, with services alternating. At the peak the number of families was about sixty.

About 1910 a large group, possibly half, left for Mississippi to found a new colony on cheap land, but the experiment was a failure. Meanwhile the group left behind gradually dwindled, and when in 1947 their last bishop left, only 10 families remained, which in 1957 had declined to three families without a minister. The four successive bishops of the Newton-Jasper settlement were David Hochstetler, his son Wallie Hochstettler, David Miller, and Albert Anderson. About one third of the present Burr Oak Mennonite (MC) congregation (53 members) descends from the Old Order Amish group.   H.J.St.

Newton Siding Mennonite Brethren Church, located in the Municipality of Portage la Prairie, Man., a member of the Manitoba Provincial and the Canadian District M.B. conferences, was organized on Nov. 25, 1928. Its new church building burned down in 1940 after being used for only 10 months. The basement was used for the services until 1946, when the superstructure was rebuilt. The 1954 baptized membership was 139. A. A. Loewen was the leading minister, and D. A. Dyck assistant. H.Ne.

Newtown Community Chapel (MC) of Sarasota, Fla., is a mission outpost among the Negroes of Sarasota. Bible classes followed by Sunday school were conducted for a period of about eight months in this community by the Tuttle Avenue Mennonite Church. In the winter of 1952-53 a block building was constructed to seat 200. Since then an addition for Sunday-school classes has been built. Workers were supplied by the home congregation. In the fall of 1953 Michael Shenk, of Denbigh, Va., was called to serve as pastor. He was replaced in 1956 by Mervin Sherk, of Lebanon, Pa. The attendance averages 75 (1956). There are twelve baptized members and several more under instruction. The program is making progress among the colored people and has overcome many barriers. Newtown Community Chapel is under the Virginia Conference.   M.S.A.

Niagara Falls Mennonite settlement was located near the village of Sanborn about 12 miles east of Niagara Falls, N.Y. The first families to locate here were Hans Witmer in 1810 and his brother Abraham Witmer in 1811, who came from Lancaster County, Pa. David Habecker (1791-1889), the first and only resident minister in this church, came with his family to this settlement from Pennsylvania in 1832 and was ordained to the ministry two years later. The meetinghouse was erected on the Habecker farm soon after 1830. The Ontario Calendar of Appointments lists no meetings at this place in 1854, but in 1862 it lists them every two weeks, alternating with Clarence. The membership was never large.

After Habecker had become unable to minister because of age and Jacob Krehbiel had left the Mennonite Church (MC), the latter had charge of the remaining members at the Falls. The congregation was represented in the triennial meetings of the General Conference (GCM) 1884 to 1908, at which time only five members were listed. The meetinghouse, located on the Shank farm, fell into disuse and was torn down.   J.C.F.

D. K. Cassel, *History of the Mennonites* (Philadelphia, 1888) 170.

Niagara Mennonite Brethren Church: see **Virgil.**

Niagara United Mennonite Church (GCM), located in Niagara-on-the-Lake, Ont., had its beginning in 1934, when Mennonite settlers came to the Niagara district as fruit farmers. In the fall of 1937 they built a church two miles from Niagara-on-the-Lake. On Feb. 1, 1938, at a meeting in the new church under the leadership of Peter Kroeker, the Niagara United Mennonite Church was organized. Because of the rapid growth in membership it became necessary to build a larger church in 1949. In 1956 the membership of the congregation was 540. Most of the members are fruit farmers. Since 1947 J. A. Dyck has been the minister in charge of this congregation.   J.A.D.

Nicasen (van) Aelmeers (Nicasius Aelmare), an Anabaptist martyr burned at the stake at Brugge on Dec. 10, 1561, the brother of Martijntgen van Aelmeers (*q.v.*), was named twice by van Braght (*Mart. Mir.* D 297, E 663, where the date of execution is given as 1562; and D 288, E 655, where the correct date is given, but his name is given as Nikasen Amare). Verheyden (*Brugge,* 49) lists him (No. 35) as Nicasius Aelmaere, born at Steenwercke in Flanders. On Nov. 10, 1561, a meeting of the Brugge congregation held just outside the city was surprised by the police and a number of the members were seized, bound two by two, and taken to the prison. They remained steadfast and on Dec. 10 four other martyrs died with Nicasen: Marijn Eewouts, Andries de Molenaar, Adriaen Brael, and Lucas Hendricx; they were followed on the next day by Jan Christiaens, Maeyken Frans, Jelis Outerman, Anthonis Keute, Francijntgen, the wife of Andries de Molenaar (Meulenaer), Hans (Hansken) Lisz (*q.v.*) and Hansken Parmentier (*q.v.*) (*ML* I, 49; III, 254.)

vDZ.

Nice (Nyce, Neiss, Neuss), a Mennonite family name found widely in Montgomery County, Pa., most of the descendants, if not all, springing from two brothers, Jan and Hans Neuss of Crefeld, Germany, who arrived in Germantown (*q.v.*) about 1684 and 1702 respectively. Jan was ordained Mennonite deacon at Germantown in 1690, and Hans preacher in 1702. Hans soon left the Mennonite Church, moving to Montgomery County in 1720,

and died in 1736. Among the prominent representatives of this name may be mentioned Henry Nice (1804-83), ordained preacher in the Franconia congregation (MC) of Montgomery County in 1839; and Bishop Henry Nice (1822-92), born in Montgomery County, who served in Sterling, Ill., for most of his ministry. Henry Nice had four ordained (MC) sons: Bishop John Nice of Morrison, Ill.; Philip Nice, a preacher in Illinois, and Jonas Nice, a preacher in Nebraska, Louisiana, and Virginia; and Henry Nice, a deacon. Howard G. Nice (b. 1899) has served as a minister in the Eastern District and Western District conferences of the General Conference Mennonite Church.   J.C.W.

Nice, Henry (1822-1902), a prominent bishop in the Illinois Mennonite (MC) Conference, was born in Montgomery County, Pa., on April 17, 1822. He married Levina Tyson in 1842. One of their eight children was Bishop John Nice of Morrison, Ill. Henry Nice lived near Wadsworth, Ohio, in 185?-65, where he was ordained to the ministry in the General Conference Mennonite Church in 1853. In 1865 he moved to Sterling, Ill., where he was ordained bishop in the Science Ridge (MC) congregation in 1868. In the same year he moved to Morrison, serving there as bishop and pastor until his death in 1902. He was one of the organizers of the Illinois Mennonite Conference in 1872 and its outstanding early leader.   H.S.B.

Nicholas I, Emperor of Russia 1825-55, was benevolent to the Mennonites. In 1835 he gave the immigrant Prussian Mennonites under Wilhelm Lange (*q.v.*) permission to settle 40 families from Brenkenhoffswalde (*q.v.*), although he had previously forbidden any new immigration, and on Dec. 31, 1854, he gave an interesting document of praise to the Molotschna Mennonites for their part in the Crimean War in gifts of money and the care of the wounded and sick. To Johann Cornies (*q.v.*), the great promoter of agriculture, he showed appreciation. He was therefore held in high esteem by the Mennonites of Russia. (Friesen, *Brüderschaft,* 80, 488; *ML* III, 255.)   NEFF.

Nickel (Nikkel, Neckel), a Prussian Mennonite family name which was first recorded in the Danzig Mennonite church in 1669. It also appeared in Thiensdorf, Orlofferfelde, Tragheimerweide, Montau-Gruppe, and Schönsee. Heinrich Nickel and Gabriel Frantz, who was the preacher of the Waterlander (Frisian) congregation of Schönsee (*q.v.*) in the Culm Lowland in 1732-33 had some troubles with the Catholic bishop of Culm, who threatened to expel the Mennonites from the Schönsee territory. Finally a permit to stay was obtained from the bishop upon payment of 10,000 guilders, which amount, besides several hundred guilders as tips for the officials, was procured by the Dutch Mennonite Committee of Foreign Needs at Amsterdam. The Dutch *Naamlijst* names the following ministers of this family: Peter Nickel, *ca.* 1740-d.59, a preacher of the Waterlander congregation at Schönsee; Jacob Nickel 1755-*ca.*65 and Geert (Gerit) Nickel 1782-*ca.*95, preachers in the Stuhmsche Lowland

(Schweingrube, *q.v.*). Hans Nickel served at Nieschewski near Thorn about 1750-85, and Abraham Nikkel (1739-1823) was preacher 1766 and elder 1779-1823 of the Nieschewken church. Franz Nickel was a preacher at Deutsch-Kazun (*q.v.*) 1780-*ca*.1800. Members of this family emigrated from Prussia and Danzig to Russia, and from there to the United States, Paraguay, and Uruguay. Abraham Nickel (*q.v.*) of Jamerau played a significant role in Prussia. Gerhard Nikkel (*q.v.*) of Russia was a Mennonite missionary in Java (*q.v.*). In Canada Jacob D. Nickel (b. 1898), an elder and evangelist in Rosemary, Alberta; Johann J. Nickel, an elder from Arkadak, Russia, now of Herbert, Sask.; and Valentine E. Nickel, the minister of the Swift Current (Sask.) Mennonite Church, should be mentioned. In the United States Peter E. Nickel, the former minister of the Hillsboro Mennonite Brethren Church, and P. E. Nikkel of Merced, Cal., are listed in *Who's Who Among the Mennonites*. J. W. Nickel of Canada has served a number of churches (GCM) in Canada and the United States and among the Mennonites of Paraguay. Arnold Nickel of Mountain Lake, Minn., served the Bethesda Mennonite Church, Henderson, Neb., and is now (1957) pastor of Eden Mennonite Church. Helen Nickel, of Mountain Lake, was a missionary in India (GCM). David Nickel was an elder of the Rudnerweide Mennonite Church from 1891 to 1924. He was succeeded by his son Abraham Nickel.

C.K., vDZ.

Reimer *Familiennamen*, 114; J. G. Rempel, *Fünfzig Jahre Konferenzbestrebungen 1902-1952* (Steinbach, 1952); B. H. Unruh, *Die niederländisch-niederdeutschen Hintergründe der mennonitischen Ostwanderungen* (n.p., n.d., Karlsruhe, 1955) *passim; Unser Blatt*, 1927, 302; *Inv. Arch. Amst.* I, Nos. 1088, 1597, 1600 f., 1604 f., 1611, 1614.

Nickel, Abraham (1743-1820), a Mennonite deacon of Jamerau (*q.v.*) in (former) West Prussia, Germany, was born June 4, 1743, and died Feb. 23, 1820. He was a deacon in the Waterlander (Frisian) congregation at Schönsee in the Culm Lowlands (Niederung) from 1766, and elder from 1779. He is known for his audience with the Prussian king, Fredrick William III, and his consort in Graudenz in 1806, when he represented the Mennonites in presenting a contribution of 30,000 Talers, while his wife presented to the queen a basket of fresh butter. The queen, deeply moved by the loyal and simple manner of the donors, gave the woman the shawl she was wearing with the words, "In memory of this moment." In commemoration of this incident a monument of black granite in the form of a rounded obelisk was erected in the churchyard of the Schönsee Mennonite Church, with an account of the incident inscribed on it. (*Menn. Bl.*, 1892, 146; 1907, 18-20; 1911, 50-53 and 68 f.; *ML* III, 223.)

NEFF.

Nickel, Abraham D. (1887-1935), an elder of the Mennonites of Russia, was born Oct. 29, 1887, in Steinfeld, a village in the Gnadenfeld district of Taurida, South Russia, the fifth child of David D. Nickel and Margaretha Dück of Grossweide. His father was the teacher of the village school in Steinfeld, and was later the elder of the Rudnerweide Mennonite Church. He was educated in the Zentral-

schule in Gnadenfeld, and the teacher-training courses at Halbstadt (*q.v.*), and in his eighteenth year became a teacher, an office he held for fourteen years. On May 22, 1906, he was baptized by his father upon the confession of his faith. In 1912 he married Katherina Käthler of Ebenfeld in South Russia. They had seven children. During World War I he was drafted to serve the state as bookkeeper of a medical corps.

In 1922 Nickel was chosen by his congregation to the ministry and in 1927 to the eldership, and was ordained by his father, whom he succeeded. In 1924 he moved to Grossweide, the neighbor village to Rudnerweide, where the church was located, and from here he served the congregation as its last elder. In 1934 the church was closed and taken over as a clubhouse by the Soviet government. Then all religious services were forbidden and he in consequence had to leave his church work in January 1935. Since that time the Rudnerweide congregation has ceased to exist. The shepherd was overpowered and the flock scattered.

In 1923 Nickel became ill with inflammatory rheumatism, which crippled both feet. At first he was able to move about with crutches, but later he had to be carried to church in a chair. In this way he served his church until the end. Deprived of all rights and means of subsistence by the Soviet government, he and his family suffered severe hunger. In 1935 he escaped to the Caucasus with the aid of some friends and found a place of refuge in the village of Sablya near Dolinovka. There he developed an intestinal cancer and died on June 3, 1935.

J.D.N.

Nickel, David D. (1853-1940), a Mennonite teacher and elder of Russia, was born in Rudnerweide, a village in the Gnadenfeld district of the Molotschna settlement in South Russia, on Aug. 30, 1853, the eighth child of David A. Nickel and Helena Janzen. His father had come to Russia as a child from the Stuhm area of West Prussia in 1819. His parents and all his brothers and sisters emigrated to Mountain Lake, Minn., in 1878; David remained in Russia. He was baptized on June 5, 1872. On June 19, 1875, he married Margareta Dück of Pordenau. Ten children grew to maturity. Three of their sons became elders and another a minister in the Mennonite Church. One son, three daughters, and three sons-in-law were exiled by the Soviets; some died there and some are missing.

David D. Nickel was trained as a teacher and worked at this vocation for eighteen years in Orechov, Neu-Halbstadt, and Steinfeld in the Molotschna settlement. In 1881 he was chosen as preacher and in 1891 as elder of the Rudnerweide Mennonite Church. In 1891 he moved to Grossweide. In 1927 he retired from his duties as elder, but continued to work for the kingdom of God as his strength permitted. In these 46 years of service for the church he also worked outside its borders. In 1896 he and Elder H. Unruh of Muntau were given an audience with the newly crowned Czar Nicholas II and as symbols of true submission presented him with bread and salt. In 1898, 1899, and 1900 he visited and served the Mennonite settlements of Samara in Orenburg; in 1902 those in Terek and

Suvorovka; in 1909-11 in Siberia the settlements at Omsk, Pavlodar, and Barnaul; in 1913 those in the Caucasus. He also served for many years on the Molotschna Mennonite school board.

In 1931 under pressure from the government he was compelled to leave his house and property at night and flee. In Chortitza in the home of his youngest married daughter he spent the rest of his life in wretched outward circumstances. The general destruction of the congregations and churches grieved him deeply. His mind and body, however, kept their vigor until he was struck by a cerebral hemorrhage. Ten days later, on Aug. 31, 1940, he died, and was buried in Chortitza. A deacon of the Mennonite Brethren congregation, Wiens, conducted the simple graveside service. J.D.N.

Nikkel (Nickel), **Gerhard** (1862-1932), a Russian Mennonite missionary in Sumatra, was born at Gnadenfeld in the Molotschna Mennonite settlement, South Russia, on Dec. 6, 1862. He received a secondary education and was a teacher for a number of years. He attended the Missionshaus at Barmen, Germany, for about six years. After some study in Holland he married Anna C. Kuipers of Haarlem, and went to Sumatra in 1888 under the Dutch Mennonite Mission Society. He worked in the mission station of Pakantan (*q.v.*). After the death of his wife he returned to Russia with his six children in 1900. At first he served as evangelist and later as minister and manager of the Razien Forestry Camp near Voznesensk. After this he returned to Gnadenfeld, bought a farm, and was elected elder of the church. Under the Soviets he was exiled to the Don Basin area in the Bachmut region, where he died in 1932. C.K.

A. A. Toews, *Mennonitische Märtyrer* I (Clearbrook, 1949) 281; *ML* III, 254.

Nickel Mines Mennonite Church (MC), located in a former mining community in Paradise Twp., Lancaster Co., Pa. The ministers of the Paradise District of Lancaster Conference bought and repaired an abandoned Episcopal meetinghouse, and services were started on Sept. 29, 1935. In 1952 Paul C. Mast (now at Lansing, N.C.) was ordained as local pastor. The missionaries Edgar Denlinger and Irene Stauffer were from this congregation. The membership in 1956 was 40, with C. Marvin Eshleman as pastor. I.D.L.

Nicknames of the Mennonites: see **Names** given to the Anabaptists-Mennonites in the Netherlands.

Niclaes, Hendrik (Heinrich) (1502-80), founder of the Familists (*q.v.*) or the "House of Love," also called Nicolaites, was a native of Münster, Westphalia, Germany, had visions as a boy, entered a Latin school at the age of nine, but three years later worked in his father's business until he married and took over a business of his own. At the age of twenty-seven he was arrested on a suspicion of Lutheran beliefs, and then moved to Amsterdam. Here he was arrested on a suspicion of being a "Münsterite." After his release he stayed nine years longer in Amsterdam. At the age of thirty-nine while he was living in Emden, East Friesland, where he owned a thriving business, he had prophetic visions and gathered a following. In his fifty-ninth year he was again imprisoned and tried on the rack. He escaped to Kampen, Dutch province of Overijssel, and from there to London and Cologne. He was a prolific writer. Nippold names fifty-one titles from his pen, which deal with a mystical pantheism. The disloyalty of some friends embittered the last years of his life. With David Joris (*q.v.*) he carried on a brief literary dispute. Other Anabaptist connections cannot be claimed, as some older histories erroneously assert. In Holland he had few adherents. Only in Dordrecht was there a group of followers until about 1614. Among his most influential followers was Christoffel Plantijn (1520-89), noted printer at Antwerp. NEFF.

F. Nippold, "Heinrich Niclaes und das Haus der Liebe," in *Ztscht für die historische Theologie* III and IV (1862); *BRN* VII, *passim*, see Index; J. Lindeboom, *Stiefkinderen van het Christendom* (The Hague, 1929) 201-9; Kühler, *Geschiedenis* I, 387-94; *ML* III, 224.

Nicodemus, Gospel of (*Acts of Pilate*), is an apocryphal Gospel which contains a supposedly official report of the procurator concerning Jesus. Both Justin Martyr (*ca.* 150) and Tertullian refer to a report supposedly made by Pilate to Emperor Tiberius. In these references and in the Gospel of Nicodemus is seen the tendency to use Pilate as a witness to the history of the death and resurrection of Christ. This Gospel in the first sixteen chapters contains an elaborate account of the trial, crucifixion, and burial of Jesus. Part II, which has thirteen chapters of varying length, is an elaboration of the sentence, "He descended into hell," from the Apostles' Creed. This book cannot be older than the fourth century, although the central idea, the delivery of the righteous Fathers (Patriarchs) from Hades, is exceedingly ancient and was common in the second century (James, 95). Quasten states, "During the Middle Ages, the influence of the Acts (of Pilate) in the field of literature and art was tremendous" (118).

During Reformation times a German translation was published by Philip Ulhart in Augsburg in 1525. Schottenloher conjectures that Viet Bild translated it, and that he also was the author of a book which appeared in the same year which set out to prove the descent of Christ into hell and to convince those who were in doubt about this article in the creed (*Philip Ulhart,* 120).

The *descensus ad inferos* idea occurs in Pilgram Marpeck's *Verantwortung* (317), and has a crucial significance for him, for it is through Christ's death, resurrection and ascension that the believers of the Old Covenant were forgiven and put on a par with those of the New. In this way Marpeck was able to vouchsafe salvation to the patriarchs and yet retain a basic distinction between the Old and New Covenants. The descent into Hades was an issue between Marpeck and Schwenckfeld, as well as between the former and Bucer. For Schwenckfeld the descent must be interpreted spiritually, which meant it should be removed from the realm of history (*Corpus Schwenckfeldianorum* V, 421). Marpeck's view of the descent into hell is Biblically derived and maintains the same simplicity and lack of detail found in the New Testament. He insists on it for theological reasons, and the closest affinities to the Gospel of Nicodemus occur in his confession (*MQR* XII, 1938, 176, 180), and it is at this point that Bucer strongly criticizes Marpeck's interpretation of Ephesians 4:8 and I Peter 3:19 (compare the report of this in the *Strassburger Täuferakten* (unpublished) under Nos. 55, 56, and 75 of the report on Marpeck's views by Bucer). If he had read the Gospel of Nicodemus he does not quote it as Scripture, not even in the same way as he uses the Testament of the Twelve Patriarchs.

In more recent times the book has found some popularity among Mennonites. The two Ephrata editions of 1748 and 1764 were read and one nineteenth century edition of Philadelphia was used among the Mennonites. According to Friedmann, a Canadian Mennonite proposed its translation into English in 1941 in order that it might be accessible to a generation not able to read German. The preface to that work begins: "Everybody who has read this book must admit that it is very close to the truth, and it rightly can be said that Nicodemus is its author since it is drawn up with such beautiful and true details" (Friedmann, 222). As in the second century, so among the Mennonites this type of literature was used as Sunday afternoon reading and was a major source of entertainment. W.KL.

M. R. James *The Apocryphal New Testament* (Oxford, 1954); Johannes Quasten, *Patrology* I (Westminster, Md., 1950) 115-18; Robert Friedmann, *Mennonite Piety Through the Centuries* (Goshen, 1949); K. Schottenloher, *Philip Ulhart* (Munich and Freising, 1921).

Nicodemus Letterknecht van Wtgheest, pseudonym of Jan Theunisz (*q.v.*), under which he published a manuscript by Nittert Obbesz (*q.v.*) and gave it the title *Raegh-besem* (Amsterdam, 1625). vDZ.

Nicolaas Geyers, an Anabaptist martyr: see **Geyersbühler.**

Nicolaes de Penty, an Anabaptist martyr, born at Douai, France, and secretly drowned in the Steen castle prison at Antwerp, Belgium, on April 4, 1562, because he "persisted in his rebaptism." His furniture, clothing, and tools were confiscated and publicly sold on Jan. 30, 1562; this indicates that he was then already in prison. Further particulars are lacking, and his trade is not mentioned. He must have been an artisan. (*Antw. Arch.-Bl.* IX, 131, 140, 161; XIV, 30 f., No. 352.) vDZ.

Nicolaes de Stevele, an Anabaptist martyr of Armentières, France, executed on Oct. 7, 1575, at Antwerp, Belgium, because of rebaptism, is identical with Claes of Armentières (*q.v.*). vDZ.

Nicolai, Antonius (Anthonys Claesz), of Wasenaar, was a Reformed minister of Workum, Leeuwarden, and Stiens in Friesland, Netherlands. He retired in 1599. Nicolai was an opponent of the Mennonites; in 1583 he wrote a book, *De magistratu of van den Overheyt,* which was repeatedly discussed in the Reformed synods of Friesland. (*DB* 1911, 42.) vDZ.

Nicolai, Friedrich Christoph (1733-1811), a friend of Lessing, a literary critic and bookdealer of Berlin, in 1781 published the following tract: *Geistlicher Diskurs und Betrachtung, was für eine Gottseligkeit*

und Art der Liebe erfordert wird by Dr. Gratianus Amandus de Stellis. This is a reprint of a booklet published in 1618 in Appenheim; it contains two tracts, one of which is a revision of Hans Denk's (*q.v.*) *Von der wahren Liebe* (1527) and the other Christian Entfelder's (*q.v.*) *Von wahrer Gottseligkeit* (1530). (*Comeniushefte* 1901, 194; *ML* III, 224.) NEFF.

Nicolai, Gerhard, became a Reformed clergyman of Norden, East Friesland, Germany, in 1567 and died soon after. He published a Dutch translation of Bullinger's (*q.v.*) book, *Der Widertöufferen ursprung* (Zürich, 1560), to which he added a number of articles that he thought might be of interest to his Dutch readers. These insertions, though often incorrect and always unkind, are important to the understanding of Mennonite history. They were published by Samuel Cramer with an introduction (*BRN* VII, 267-487). Nicolai's book was published in Emden in 1569 by Johann Malet, who in his foreword dedicated it to Amalia, Countess of Neuenahr, wife of Elector Palatine Frederick III. The title is *Teghens de Wederdoopers, ses boecken Henrici Bullingeri, nu eerst vvt de Latijnsche Tale in Nederduytsch overgestelt, door Gerardum Nicolaj, in zijnen leven Kerckendienaer tot Norden in Oostvrieslandt. Die daer by ghevoecht heeft de Wederlegginghe der leeringen van Menno Symons, Dierick Philips, Adam Pastor, Hendrick Niclaes, ende meer andere.* vDZ.

B. Becker, "Nicolai's inlassching over de Franckisten," in *Ned. Archief voor Kerkgeschiedenis* XVIII (1925) 286 ff.; *ML* III, 224.

Nicolai, Idzardus (Idzerd Klases), b. at Franeker ca. 1560, d. 1611, a Reformed minister at Tjummarum in Friesland ca. 1590-92, Franeker 1592-99, Hallum 1599-1603, and Minnertsga 1603-11, wrote an extensive book against the Mennonites under the title *Grontlicke onderwijsinghe teghen allerleye dwalinghen der Wederdooperen deses tijts in de Nederlanden* (Franeker-Amsterdam, 1609, two vv., 800 pages). An abbreviated version was printed in Franeker with the title, *Leere der Waerheyt, van eenighe Leerstvcken die door de Drijvers der nieuwicheden berispt ende ghelastert worden.* (*N.N.B.Wb.* V, 371; *ML* III, 224.) vDZ.

Nicolai, Melchior (1578-1659), a rather quarrelsome Württemberg theologian of the Lutheran orthodox wing, and a staunch fighter against Anabaptism in his home country. In 1604 he was made deacon in Waiblingen, and in 1608 minister in Stetten in the Rems Valley, in Württemberg. At both places he had many contacts with local Anabaptists and fought aggressively against their further spread. In 1619 he became professor at the University of Tübingen. In 1627 he was general superintendent and member of the consistory of the state church of Württemberg, the highest office possible. Later he became provost (*Probst*) of the Stiftskirche in Stuttgart.

The trend of the time and his own bent of mind made him a polemical writer. "Against all calumniators and heretics," writes his biographer F. Wagner in 1685, "against Papists and Calvinists and Anabaptists he defended the true **religion**" [i.e., Lutheranism]. He was known for his battle against the Jesuits in Dillingen. The book of greatest interest to us is his *Gründliche, mit Gottes Wort und der Antiquität bevestigte Widerlegung eines wiedertäufferischen Büchleins handelnd* I. *Von der Kindertauff,* II. *Von dem heiligen Abendmahl,* III. *Von der Gemeinschaft der Güter,* IV. *Von dem Ampt der Obrigkeit,* V. *Von dem Eydschwur* . . . *(Stuttgart, bey Johann Weyrich Rösslin, 1659)* (286 pages quarto).

Nicolai's book is the most elaborate answer of Lutheranism to one of the basic doctrinal documents of the Hutterites, namely, the *Article Book* (*q.v.*), which was originally drawn up in 1547, much enlarged in 1577, and condensed again in the time of the Vorsteher Andreas Ehrenpreis (*q.v.*) around 1648-55. This book in its present extant form contains five articles, but strangely enough all known manuscripts have as Number Five an article "Concerning Divorce," while an article "Concerning the Oath" (as Nicolai claims) has thus far not been found among the extant manuscripts. In this regard Nicolai's book is of some value for research in Anabaptist doctrinal writings. It is surprising that Nicolai should battle Hutterites (who had long since ceased mission work in his country) and not the Swiss Brethren (remnants of whom were still around). The latter, however, had no doctrinal writings as comprehensive as the "big" book of Hutterite origin. It is not known whether Nicolai used the Ehrenpreis condensation (as Bossert claims) or the original "Article book" (comprising some 250 leaves) as is suggested by a reference in the book to the Anabaptists in Markt Gröningen (see **Dietrich, Sebastian**).

Nicolai is not very familiar with the Anabaptists, referring time and again to Thomas Müntzer and Jan van Leyden as his main witnesses, never to the evangelical Brethren whom he should have known better from personal contacts in the Rems Valley. However, what arouses this churchman is the Anabaptist principle of nonconformity and separation from the world. Their critique of the authorities (*Obrigkeit*) seems to provoke him above all, and as he has no pertinent argument from a theological standpoint he indulges in slanderous conjectures: if these brethren should gain power in the state they would certainly behave like the Münsterites and would use brute force (*loc. cit.,* 251 ff.). It is obvious that an argument like this was much out of date in 1659, a century and a quarter after the unfortunate Münster episode, and proves only the propagandistic intentions of this book.

That Nicolai devotes much space to a defense of infant baptism and the demonstration of the Anabaptist error on this point is understandable from his position as orthodox state churchman. There is hardly any new argument in the material he has to present.   R.F.

R. Friedmann, "Eine dogmatische Hauptschrift der Hutterischen Täufergemeinschaften," *Archiv für Ref.-Gesch.* XXIX (1932) 1-8; F. Fritz, "Die Württembergischen Pfarrer im dreissigjährigen Krieg," *Blätter für Württembergische Kirchengeschichte* (1926) 55 f.; see also *ibid.* (1928) 64; G. Bossert, Jr., "Aus der nebenkirchlichen religiösen Bewegung der Reformationszeit in Württemberg," *Blätter für Württembg. Kirchen-Geschichte* (1929) 39; ML III, 224 f.

Nicolaites, followers of Hendrik Niclaes (*q.v.*): see **Familists.**

Nicolschütz: see **Nikoltschitz.**

Niebuhr, Hermann Abramovitch (1830-1906) a Mennonite industrialist in Russia, was born July 24, 1830, in the village of Kronstal of the Chortitza Mennonite settlement in South Russia. His grandparents had immigrated from West Prussia in 1789 and were as poor as all the rest of the Mennonite settlers at that time. Hermann Niebuhr was the oldest of 14 brothers and sisters. His parents were well-to-do, owning two full farms, each of 175 acres, and two windmills. When he was only eight years old he was taught by his father the milling process with a windmill; but this type of milling did not satisfy the alert boy, and so at the age of 19 years he left his father's business to become a miller on a treadmill. He remained here in service for four years and then with his father's help bought a treadmill of his own in Chortitza. This date is considered the date of the founding of what became the great firm of H. A. Niebuhr and Company. In 1853-72 Niebuhr owned alternately wind- and treadmills, or sometimes both at the same time. Not until 1872 did he build a large steam-driven mill, and in 1882 the second one. In 1879 his only son Jacob entered the father's business. Hermann Niebuhr died at Chortitza Aug. 20, 1906.

When Hermann Niebuhr died he left 10 windmills and motor-driven mills, of which the largest, in the city of Alexandrovsk, ground 7,000 pood (*ca.* 125 tons) of wheat and the smallest 1,000 pood (18 tons) daily. After Niebuhr's death the milling business of eleven mills passed to the heirs as a corporation and continued to work with great success. Thirteen years after the death of the founder in the autumn of 1919, when the entire business became nationalized, the heirs owned besides this milling business (valued at 5 million rubles and the largest in all Russia) about 46,000 acres of land, on which there were eight farms and six additional mills of various sizes; they also owned a banking house which during World War II was enlarged into the Chortitzaer Kommerzbank with a capital of 5 million rubles, a stone quarry with 451 acres of land near the station of Yanzezo, which contained valuable granite (also with a capital of 5 million rubles), and a sanatorium "Alexanderbad" near Kitchkas on the Dnieper with 432 acres of land which was furnished with a capital of 1 million rubles. The sanatorium, with three Berlin physicians at the head, was modernly equipped and could take care of 250 patients. During World War I the income of the Kommerzbank and of the stone quarry was withheld by the czarist government in consequence of the general hatred against the Germans. In 1919 the entire work was nationalized. (*ML* III, 225.)   D.H.E.

Niebuhr, Jakob G. (1847-1913), a Russian Mennonite industrialist, born Oct. 20, 1847, at Kronstal, Chortitza, South Russia, who built up and owned the J. G. Niebuhr factory at Olgafeld, Fürstenland settlement, and New York, Bachmut, which employed 350 people and had an annual production of 450,000 rubles. This industry was one of the largest among the Mennonites of Russia.

Jakob G. Niebuhr lost his father, Jakob Niebuhr, early. After two years of school he worked for his uncle Abraham Niebuhr of Chortitza, who had a small mill. For a while he worked for the pioneer industrialist A. J. Koop of Chortitza, serving as foreman for eleven years. In 1881 he started his own factory at Olgafeld, Fürstenland settlement, manufacturing parts for fanning mills. Soon he produced plows, among them the "Bugger" plow, very common among the Mennonites of Russia. Before World War I, he produced 4,500 of these plows annually. In 1898 Niebuhr started another factory at New York. He made inventions in the realm of improving reapers and drills. Of the latter he produced 4,500 annually. He also manufactured numerous other machines, including those for the growing milling industry (see **Agriculture** among the Mennonites of Russia).

During the later years his sons, Jakob J., Peter J., and Gerhard J. Niebuhr, were his assistants. Annually they produced 20,000 larger agricultural machines. In addition to three factories, they owned two mills, one at Olgafeld and the other at Yelenovka. In 1912 their property was estimated at 1,500,000 gold rubles. Because of the anti-German feeling during World War I, the business declined rapidly, and was sold for a token price on Oct. 15, 1915. In 1929 Gerhard Niebuhr escaped via China and went to Paraguay. Peter Niebuhr, who served under the Soviets as engineer of the Niebuhr factory, was exiled in 1933 and died. Jakob J. Niebuhr escaped to Canada in 1942.   C.K.

Jakob J. Niebuhr, "Jakob G. Niebuhr Fabriken," *Menn. Life* X (January 1955) 25-30.

Niederausmass and **Oberausmass**, two villages in West Prussia, Germany (Polish before 1772 and after 1919), belonging to the territory of the city of Culm (*q.v.*), were largely inhabited by Dutch families who settled there shortly after 1600. Most of them may have been Mennonites: Niederausmass was a Mennonite village belonging to the Schönsee (*q.v.*) congregation and had a Mennonite school.
vDZ.

H. Wiebe, *Das Siedlungswerk niederländischer Mennoniten im Weichseltal* (Marburg a.d.Lahn, 1952) 13, 33, 97; *Menn. Life* X (April 1955) 76, 78.

Nieder-Chortitza (Russian, *Nizhnaya-Chortitza*), a village of the Chortitza Mennonite settlement, province of Ekaterinoslav, Russia, volost Marianovka, founded in 1803 by Mennonites coming from the Danzig region. In 1912 the village had 5,192 acres of land and a population of 742. During World War I the Mennonite population consisted of 185 families or 835 persons. The 175 farms consisted of 6,712 acres.

During the Russian Revolution and the early Soviet regime the Mennonites of this village suffered severely. In 1919 twenty-one persons were murdered, during the famine of 1921-22, twenty-four died of starvation, and during 1933-34 thirty-five perished. During 1929-41 eighty-three persons were exiled. Before the Germans arrived to occupy the Ukraine in 1941, 289 persons were evacuated, of

whom only 13 returned. This indicates that almost half of the population either perished or was exiled or evacuated under the Soviets. When the German army returned to Germany, the remaining population was taken along; some were repatriated by the Russian army from Poland and East Germany, and the remainder reached Canada and South America after World War II.   C.K.

K. Stumpp, *Bericht über das Gebiet Chortitza* (Berlin, 1943); *Neuer Haus- und Landwirtschafts-Kalender* (Odessa, 1913) 49 and 74; *ML* III, 264.

Niederflörsheim, a village near Monsheim, Rhenish Hesse, Germany, where a number of Swiss Mennonites settled at the close of the Thirty Years' War. In a decision of Feb. 16, 1652, the church council in Heidelberg issued a warning to the Palatine government regarding the Mennonites, since "it is known what a dangerous and stubborn sect they are." The list of Mennonites of 1664 (in the state archives in Karlsruhe) named three Mennonite families, which had grown to five by 1680; among them are the names of Christian Borckholder, Christian Clementz, and Julius Schmidt. In 1685 Osthofen issued an exact list, in which only three families were named: Johann Clemens, a decrepit old man with his wife, who was supported by his son-in-law; Christian Borckholder, the son-in-law mentioned above, with a wife and child, a farmer; and Peter Clemens, sixty-four years old, unmarried, supports himself from his vineyard; they are neighborly and give no one cause to complain. Later a Christoffel married into the community. In 1773 twelve Mennonites were counted in the village. At present there are five Mennonites living in Niederflörsheim; they belong to the Monsheim congregation. (*ML* III, 225.)
NEFF.

Niedermaier, Hans: see **Mittermaier.**

Niederrödern, a village in Alsace, seven miles east of Wissembourg, was one of the oldest meeting places for the present Mennonite Deutschhof-Geisberg (*q.v.*) congregation. The castle there, belonging to the Deutschhof estate, was leased by Baron Hatzel to Christian Gingerich, a Mennonite, on April 22, 1711, according to the records in Strasbourg. The church records (1724) of Niederrödern show that the estate was "given in lease to the Anabaptists Jakob Bassler and Hans Krayenbühl [Krehbiel]." Another tradition says that Krehbiel occupied the farm in 1716, coming from the Pfrimmerhof near Sippersfeld in the Palatinate. In 1755 he took on his son-in-law Christian Lehmann (from the Geisberg or the Zweibrücken congregation) as a partner. He is the progenitor of the Lehmann (*q.v.*) family living on the Kaplaneihof and Deutschhof. After Hatzel's death (1762) the estate fell to the Elector Palatine and then to Prince Maximilian of the Palatinate and Zweibrücken, who later became the king of Bavaria. But in the course of the French Revolution it was confiscated and in 1794 sold to the two sons of Lehmann and the widow of Daniel Hirschler on very favorable terms. After these families died out, David Schmitt of the Deutschhof (1870) and then his nephew Friedrich Schmitt of the Haftelhof came into the possession of the castle estate.

The Mennonites who had settled in other places near by met for worship in rotation at Schafbusch, Geisberg, and the Haftelhof, and for a long time in the Niederrödern castle. In 1875 a neat little meetinghouse was built, for which the community and the state put 2,000 franks at their disposal. It was dedicated on June 6. In the following decades it was used less and less, and by 1942 was used only once a year.

Hans Krehbiel is named as the first preacher of the Deutschhof-Geisberg congregation. The Dutch *Naamlijst,* which calls the congregation Schaafbusch and Rödern, names the following ministers: Daniel Hirschler, elder 1736-*ca.*70; Jakob Lehmann, preacher *ca.*1740-*ca.*86; Johannes Grebeil (Krehbiel), preacher before 1775; Ulrich Schowalter, preacher 1771-*ca.*80; Elias Thätweiler (Dettweiler), preacher from 1775, elder 1778 until after 1802; Johannes Müller, preacher 1780 until after 1802; Heinrich Schmidt, preacher 1790 until after 1802; Christian Heinrich Hirschler (from 1827) and Friedrich Schmitt (from 1921) lived at Niederrödern.

In 1792 a register of births, marriages, and deaths was begun, apparently by order of the authorities, in duplicate. It extended only to 1798, however. The church record of the Deutschhof congregation, opened in 1855, and dated back as far as memory could recall contains data about the Mennonites in Niederrödern. P.S.

Naamlijst 1766-1802; Menn. Bl., 1855, 41; 1875, 63; *Gbl.,* 1875, 53; "Dettweiler Family History" (ms); *ML* III, 251.

Niedorp (formerly commonly called Nierop), two Dutch villages, Nieuwe Niedorp and Oude Niedorp, in the province of North Holland (*q.v.*). Soon after 1530 the Anabaptists were numerous here. On March 6, 1535, the attorney-general of the Court of Holland, Reinier Brunt (*q.v.*), made a raid on Nieuwe Niedorp and arrested eight Anabaptists; he had them executed in Monnikendam (*q.v.*), where he had set up his headquarters. Several days later he seized three more, and had them hanged on the spot; the house of Jan Walichs, where they had worshiped, was torn down; and in June 1535 others were apprehended. Still others escaped, for example, Jan Gijsbrecht, who in 1542 fled from Niedorp to Emden, East Friesland.

Afterward a Mennonite congregation developed in each village, though probably neither was large. The Oude Niedorp group belonged to the Frisian branch and was a member of the Frisian Sociëteit in North Holland. The group in Nieuwe Niedorp called itself the United Waterlander and Flemish congregation, and later belonged to the Zonist Sociëteit.

The two Mennonite congregations united in 1803 under the name Oude en Nieuwe Niedorp. In 1857, both church buildings being in a state of collapse, it was decided to build a new one in Nieuwe Niedorp. It was dedicated Oct. 25, 1857, by Inne Thyssen Taconis. The old church of Oude Niedorp was demolished in 1860. The 1857 meetinghouse of Nieuwe Niedorp was replaced by a new one in 1879. The baptized membership was 32 in 1847, 64 in 1861, 164 in 1900, and 109 in 1957. During most of the 18th century the pulpits of both Oude and Nieuwe Niedorp were vacant. In 1813-31 Johannes Michiels Bakker served here, and in 1841-65 Inne Thyssen Taconis, the last untrained preacher; he had been appointed as ministerial candidate by the Conference of Friesland. Taconis was followed by K. S. van der Meulen 1865-1904, D. Haars 1905-35, Miss T. Rothfusz 1942-46, and Mrs. E. Franken-Liefrinck 1949- . From August 1940 until March 1941 P. J. Smidts, pastor of Den Helder, who was forced to leave this town because of the war, lived in Nieuwe Niedorp, taking care of the congregation. There·is a Sunday school for children, and a ladies' circle. vDZ.

Inv. Arch. Amst. I, Nos. 99, 101, 131, 137, 226, 240, 249, 896; II, Nos. 2144 f.; Kühler, *Geschiedenis* I, 174; Blaupot t. C., *Holland* I and II, see Index; *Naamlijst* 1810, 69; *DB* 1861, 162 f.; 1860, 165; 1909, 15, 22; *ML* III, 251.

Niehove, a village in the Dutch province of Groningen, where Leenaert Bouwens in 1568-82 baptized 25 persons. A separate congregation of Niehove is not known. The Mennonites baptized by Bouwens may have joined the Humsterland (*q.v.*) congregation. At Gaaikemaweer, a hamlet near Niehove, meetings were held in the 16th and 17th centuries. vDZ.

S. K. de Waard, *Aanteekeningen uit de Geschiedenis der Doopsgez. in't Westerkwartier* (Groningen, 1901) 9.

Nieland, where Leenaert Bouwens (*q.v.*) baptized some eight persons in 1551-56, is a hamlet in the Dutch province of Groningen. Whether it was Wester- or Oosternieland could not be ascertained. (See also **Nieuwland.**) vDZ.

Niellius, Carolus (Charles de Nielles), a Reformed preacher in Antwerp in 1560, and at Wesel 1569-98, and then in the Reformed congregations at Frankfurt and Hanau (to which congregation he dedicated his *Consolation de la conscience troublée*). He translated the confession of faith written by Obbe Philips (*q.v.*) into French and published it with a treatise on Jan Willems of Roermond (*q.v.*). The book has the title *Recognoissance d'Obbe Philippe, par laquelle luy et ceux qui ont enseigné et enseignent entre les anabaptistes . . . n'ont nulle vocation légitime. Avec un Discours des faicts exécrables du nouveau roy des Anabaptistes Jan Wilhems et de ses complices, executez à Cleves, Wesel et autres lieux, l'an 1550* (Leiden, 1595). vDZ.

N.N.B.Wb. I, 1372; *BRN* VII, 101 f.; Kühler, *Geschiedenis* I, 209; *ML* III, 251 f.

Niembschitz: see **Nembschitz.**

Nierop, Derk Pietersz van: see **Pieters, Dirk.**

Nierop, Dirk Rembrandtsz van: see **Rembrandtsz, Dirk.**

Nieschewski, a village near Thorn (Torun), Poland, the seat of a Mennonite congregation from the early 17th century until 1945, usually known as the Obernessau (*q.v.*) congregation. It may have been founded by Dutch colonists, since family names here were all pure Dutch. About the time of its

founding there is no exact information, because all
land leases have been lost.   vDZ.

Niesert, J., was the author of the important work,
Münsterische Urkunden-sammlung (2 vv., Coesfeld,
1826-27).

Nieu Geestelijck Liet-boeck, *ghenaemt den Bloem-
pot,* a Dutch Mennonite hymnbook: see **Volkertsz,
Jan.**

Nieu Geestelyck Liedboecxken, *getoghen uyt den
Ouden en Nieuwen Testament,* a Dutch Mennonite
hymnbook compiled by Claes Ganglofs (*q.v.*), which
consisted of eleven hymns without notes. There are
four editions: 1593, 1606, 1615, and 1633, all at Groningen.   vDZ.

Nieu Gheestelijck Liedtboecxken, Een, a Dutch
Mennonite hymnal: see **Soetken Gerrits.**

Nieu Kleyn Trompetjen, Een (*inhoudende al nieuwe Gheestelijcke Liedekens, die noyt voor desen in
druck gheweest en zijn*), is a small collection of
Dutch Mennonite hymns, of which L. P. is the author. It contains 55 hymns without notes on 219
pages. Only one edition is known, published at
Kampen in 1611.   vDZ.

Nieu Liedenboeck, Een, *van alle nieuwe ghedichte
Liedekens, die noyt in druck en zijn gheweest, ghe-
maect wt den Ouden ende Nieuwen Testament, nv
eerst by den anderen vergadert, ende nieus in Druck
ghebracht* (n.p., 1562) was one of the first hymnals
of the Dutch Mennonites. It contains 257 songs in
alphabetical order without notes. It was appparently
printed by Nicolaes Biestkens (*q.v.*). Only one copy,
found in the Amsterdam Mennonite Library, has
been preserved. It was called the new hymnal, because there had been an earlier (first) hymnal, entitled *Veelderhande Liedekens* (*q.v.*), which had
also been published by Nicolaes Biestkens, and of
which there were two editions, both lost, in 1560
and 1562. A second (enlarged) edition of this *Nieu
Liedenboeck* appeared in 1583, with the title *Het
Tweede Liedeboeck* (*q.v.*). Many hymns of the
Nieu Liedenboeck were included in the 1569 edition
of *Veelderhande Liedekens* and in a large number
of 17th-century hymnals.   vDZ.

F. C. Wieder, *De schriftuurlijke Liedekens* (The
Hague, 1900) 149 f.

**Nieu Medemblicker Liet-boeck, met schriftuerlike
liedekens,** mentioned by Blaupot ten Cate (*Holland* II, 213), is the same Dutch Mennonite hymnal
as *Medemblikker* (*q.v.*) *Nieu Liedtboeck.*   vDZ.

Nieu Sangh-boec, Een (A New Songbook), *inhoudende eenighe Psalmen, Lof-sanghen ende Geestelijcke Liedekens seer stichtelijcken om te singhen
voor ende nae de Predicatie.* This Dutch Mennonite
hymnal was printed in 1628 at Dokkum (all copies
apparently lost). A third edition of *Een Nieuw
Sangh-boeck* appeared at Dokkum in 1650 in one
volume containing two parts of 210 and 550 pages
in a small size. This edition, of which a copy is
found in the Amsterdam Mennonite Library, contains (*a*) 22 Psalms in the rhymed version of Dathe-

nus (*q.v.*); (*b*) Part I of the hymns being a collection of 41 *Geestelijcke Liedekens* (spiritual hymns);
(*c*) Part II of the hymns with a separate title page
and a new pagination, entitled *Sommighe Nieuwe
Schriftuerlijcke Liedekens,* containing 107 hymns obviously mostly taken from other hymnals; fourteen
of these hymns are signed with the device "Hier
nae beter" (Later better) and the letters J. S. (Jan
Sents). After hymn No. 30 there is found an address "Tot den Leser" (to the reader); probably the
following 77 hymns had not been included in the
first and second editions of this hymnal. The whole,
both psalms and hymns, is without notes.
   There is a reprint, published at Leeuwarden in
1679, with the title *Een Nieuw Sangh-boeck, ofte
anders genaemt, Jan Sents Liedtboeck.* This reprint
is quite similar to the 1650 edition, except for a few
accidental alterations. It is also without notes. The
preface to this 1679 edition states that this hymnbook
was used in the congregations of Friesland. vDZ.

Nieu Schriftuerlijck Liedtboecxken, Een, a Dutch
Mennonite hymnal: see **Alckmaer, J. C. van.**

Nieukerck, Joost Willemsz, b. 1587 at Nijkerk,
Dutch province of Gelderland, d. 1645 at Amsterdam, was a wealthy grain dealer at Amsterdam,
who became bankrupt in 1627. Because he was
known as a strictly honest man the Amsterdam city
government exempted him from the usual bail.
Nieukerck was a member of the Amsterdam Waterlander congregation, and a deacon until he resigned
because of his bankruptcy. He was married to Sara
van den Vondel, a sister of the poet Joost van den
Vondel (*q.v.*). His sister Adriaantje Willems was
married to the Amsterdam Waterlander preacher
Pieter Andriesz Hesseling (*q.v.*). His other sister,
Hester Willems, was married to the deacon Reyer
Claesz Anslo, a brother of the Elder Cornelis Claesz
Anslo (*q.v.*). (*N.N.B.Wb.* VIII, 1219-21.)   vDZ.

Nieuw Geestelijck Kruyt-Hof, Het, is a Dutch Mennonite hymnal, the second part of the hymnbook
Syons Wijn-bergh (*q.v.*).   vDZ.

**Nieuw Sangh-boeck, ofte anders genaemt, Jan Sents
   Liedt-boeck,** a Dutch Mennonite hymnal: see
   Nieu Sangh-boec.

Nieuw-Brongerga: see **Knijpe.**

Nieuwe Gemeente (New Congregation), a name
given to the Mennonites at Franeker, Friesland,
whose leaders were Joriaen Heynsz and Hendrik
Naeldeman (*q.v.*). (*BRN* VII, 460, 464 f.)   vDZ.

Nieuwe Niedorp: see **Niedorp.**

Nieuwe Pekela: see **Pekela.**

Nieuwe Zijpe: see **Barsingerhorn** and **Wieringerwaard.**

Nieuwe Zwitsers: see **Swiss Mennonites in the Netherlands.**

Nieuwendam, once an independent village northeast
of Amsterdam, now incorporated into the city. A
Mennonite church was built in the village in 1843

with the support of Mennonites living here, and especially of the Cleyndert family. It was dedicated on July 9, by Jan Boeke, minister of the Amsterdam congregation. Its care was the responsibility of the Cleyndert family for decades. The church is now property of the Amsterdam congregation.

In 1842 the membership of the Nieuwendam congregation was 23, 52 in 1918, 35 in 1940, and 450 in 1955. It was originally served by preachers of Amsterdam, Haarlem, De Zaanstreek, and the students of the Mennonite seminary, then by the Amsterdam preachers and by the Ring of North Holland, now by the Amsterdam pastors. Miss C. W. Brugman served here 1947-55 and W. Veen since 1955; the latter is at the same time the pastor of Den Ilp-Landsmeer (*q.v.*). The church now serves Mennonites who live in the suburb of North Amsterdam.   vDZ.

Inv. Arch. Amst. II, Nos. 256-64; II, 2, Nos. 297; Blaupot t. C., *Holland* II, 200 f.; *DJ* 1954, 53; *ML* III, 253.

Nieuwenhuis, a common Dutch family name, which also occurs among the Mennonites. There are at least four Mennonite branches, apparently unrelated.

(1) Nieuwenhuis (Nienhaus, Nyenhuis) family found at Enschedé and Winterswijk. The origin of this family probably was Neuenhaus (Nienhuis) in the gravure of Bentheim, Germany, not far from the Dutch border. From the early 17th century the name is found in the town of Steinfurt (Burgsteinfurt, *q.v.*), not far from Neuenhaus. Here members of the Nieuwenhuis family were still found in the 18th century. In the meantime some of them had moved to Enschedé in the Dutch province of Overijssel. They are found here from the early 18th century, and perhaps already in the 17th century, usually being engaged in textile business and manufacturing; some of them were deacons of the church. By marriage the Nieuwenhuis family in Enschedé was related to other well-known Mennonite families, such as Hoedemaker, Naber, Stenvers, van Lochum, Warnaers, and ter Mors. In the 19th century this Enschedé branch died out. In the Mennonite congregation of Winterswijk, Dutch province of Gelderland, there were in the 18th century also a number of Nieuwenhuises. They had moved in from Enschedé.

(2) Nieuwenhuis family of Amsterdam. This family, found here in the 16th-18th centuries, seems to have moved in from Steinfurt and probably belonged to the same branch as the Enschedé-Winterswijk family. In the 18th century they spelled their names in different ways: Nieuwenhuis, Nieuwenhuys, Nieuwenhuizen, Nieuwenhuysen. A relationship of the Amsterdam Zonist deacon Maarten Nieuwenhuizen, and Maarten Nieuwenhuizen of Haarlem, father of pastor Jan Nieuwenhuizen (*q.v.*), with them could not be ascertained.

(3) Nieuwenhuis family of Harlingen, Friesland. The first of this family we find here is Feddrik Tjerks about 1740, who was married to Geertje Everts Oosterbaan, and father of Tjerk Nieuwenhuis (*q.v.*), the first professor of the Amsterdam Mennonite seminary. With the latter this family died out in the male line.

(4) Nieuwenhuis family of Westzaan, province of North Holland. Willem Nieuwenhuis, b. *ca.* 1760 at Westzaan, d. 1806 at Groningen, was trained for the ministry by H. van Gelder and P. Beets, both preachers of Zaandam, and examined and appointed ministerial candidate by the church board of West Zaandam. He served as pastor at Norden, East Friesland, 1796-98 and at Groningen (Pelsterstraat congregation) 1798-1806.

Benjamin Nieuwenhuis (Nieuwenhuizen), of Westzaan, b. there about 1712, d. 1780 at Kampen, was a Mennonite minister at Kampen 1737-80; his grandson Benjamin Nieuwenhuis, b. *ca.* 1810 at Kampen, d. Feb. 7, 1847, at Medemblik, was educated at the Amsterdam Mennonite seminary and served the congregation of Medemblik 1835-47.
                                                            vDZ.

Nieuwenhuis, Tjerk, a Mennonite theologian, b. Nov. 5, 1708, at Harlingen, the son of Feddrik Tjerks and Geertje Everts Oosterbaan, d. Aug. 9, 1759, at Amsterdam, married Eva van Maurik, was the first professor at the seminary founded by the Lam en Toren Mennonite congregation in Amsterdam. Having specialized in philology and philosophy at the University of Franeker, he went to Amsterdam in 1731 to attend the lectures of Professor Cattenburgh at the Remonstrant seminary. During an illness of Professor Clericus he was asked to lecture on logic.

The Mennonite church council saw in Nieuwenhuis the man they needed to fill the position of professor at the seminary. Nieuwenhuis accepted and completed his doctorate at Franeker. Then he made a journey to England and France to meet men of learning and visit libraries, and on Nov. 28, 1735, he assumed his duties and delivered his first lecture on the subject, "The Benefits of Philosophy and the Excellence of Revealed Religion." This address and all his lectures were given in Latin. He lectured on both theology and philosophy. His position is revealed by the title of his initial address, namely, that philosophy—he means especially that of John Locke—is of great importance but is inadequate compared with revealed religion, viz., Christianity. Nieuwenhuis left no writings. Pastor K. de Vries of Amsterdam published a funeral sermon in his honor, *Lijkrede over het afsterven van T. Nieuwenhuis* (Amsterdam, 1759).   vDZ.

Inv. Arch. Amst. II, Nos. 2481, 2483; *DJ* 1850, 99-111; Chr. Sepp, *Johannes Stinstra en zijn tijd* I and II (Amsterdam, 1865 and 1866) *passim,* see Indexes; *DB* 1918, 74-77, 81-84; *ML* III, 253.

Nieuwenhuizen (Nieuwenhuyzen), a Dutch Mennonite family found in Amsterdam and Haarlem. Maerten Nieuwenhuyzen was from 1729 a preacher of the Flemish and Frisian Kruisstraat congregation at Haarlem, and after 1747, when this congregation merged with the Flemish Klein-Heiligland congregation, until 1760 of the United congregation. His son was Jan Nieuwenhuyzen (*q.v.*). In Amsterdam a Maerten Nieuwenhuizen was a deacon of the Zonist congregation in 1791.   vDZ.

Nieuwenhuizen (Nieuwenhuyzen), **Jan,** a Mennonite preacher, b. Sept. 4, 1724, at Haarlem, d. Feb.

24, 1806, at Monnikendam, the son of Maarten Nieuwenhuyzen, was trained to be a bookseller, then studied theology and became a minister, serving at Middelharnis 1758-63, Aardenburg 1763-71, and Monnikendam 1771-1806. He left a number of sermons and a treatise *Over de voortreffelijkheid der wijsheid.*

Nieuwenhuizen is known as the founder of the *Maatschappij tot Nut van 't Algemeen* (*q.v.*). This society, which he founded on Oct. 16, 1784, had its seat in Edam until 1787 and in Amsterdam since then; it is based on Christian kindness and was planned and intended to promote the welfare of the public.

For a long time Nieuwenhuizen had been concerned with the sad state of the populace; he reflected on what measures might help the people out of their moral decline and improve their material lot. He came to the conclusion that earnest leadership and better instruction was the first essential. "In order to achieve what I considered necessary for my fatherland, nothing seemed more necessary than to form a society of true and upright friends of mankind, who would be willing to support my efforts through their co-operation and modest contribution." He talked his idea over with his son Martinus (*q.v.*) and found it favorably received by others, especially by his Mennonite colleague J. A. J. Hoekstra at Edam and the Lutheran pastor J. C. Loggers.

The society, usually known as "Het Nut," covers a wide scope. Although in some local sections the educational work degenerated into a sort of entertaining play (this happened in the early 19th century), the society has been of benefit, especially in creating libraries, savings banks, nursery schools, and vocational schools. There were in 1955 more than 300 local units, with about 40,000 members; their 2602 libraries contain over 250,000 books; there are 133 savings banks, 90 nursery schools, and more than 100 other schools and courses. Thus the work of Jan Nieuwenhuizen has borne rich fruit.

Jan Nieuwenhuizen was married to Gezina (Geesje) Wynalda (1722-87) of Haarlem. A collection of her poems, entitled *Verzaameling van Zeede- en Stichtelijke Haarlemmerhout en Tuin Gezangen,* was published at Haarlem in 1756 by her husband, who was still a bookseller at Haarlem.   vDZ.

Naamlijst 1806, 70 f.; N. C. Wertz, *Jan Nieuwenhuizen* (address delivered at the general meeting of the Het Nut on Aug. 13, 1806); *N.N.B.Wb.* II, 993; *DB* 1884, 45; 1887, 126; 1889, 115 f.; *DJ* 1907, 21-31 with portrait); *ML* III, 253 f.

Nieuwenhuizen, Martinus (Maarten), the son of Jan Nieuwenhuizen, b. Dec. 9, 1759, at Middelharnis, d. March 6, 1793, at Haarlem. He studied medicine at the University of Franeker and settled in Edam as a physician. He supported his father in organizing the *Maatschappij tot Nut van 't Algemeen,* serving as its secretary until his death. When the office of the society was transferred to Amsterdam in 1787, he moved with it. In 1791 he was appointed to the committee of the Mennonite Zonist congregation at Amsterdam to publish a new hymnal, the *Groote Bundel* (*q.v.*, 1796). Nieuwenhuizen offered to write some hymns himself, and

received offers of hymns from noted poets. The *Doopsgezinde Bijdragen* (1890, 74) has a poem from his pen on Menno Simons, written for the portrait by L. Garreau (1788). G. Brender à Brandis and M. C. van Hall delivered funeral orations for him, which appeared in print in 1793. (*N.N.B.Wb.* II, 993 f.; *ML* III, 254.)   vDZ.

Nieuwezijl (Niezijl) is a village in the Dutch province of Groningen, where Leenaert Bouwens (*q.v.*) in 1551-54 baptized five persons, and where a Mennonite congregation later came into being, which joined the Friesche Sociëteit (Conference of Friesland) in 1695 (membership then only 11), but soon after that date merged with the Pieterzijl (*q.v.*) Mennonite congregation. (*DB* 1895, 4 f., 20; *ML* III, 254.)   vDZ.

Nieuwland, an area north of Leeuwarden, Dutch province of Friesland, where Leenaert Bouwens (*q.v.*) in 1563-65 baptized 12 persons and in 1568-82 another 94. This considerable number indicates the existence of a Mennonite congregation, of which, however, nothing is known. Perhaps the converts joined the congregation of Leeuwarden, which for reasons of safety may have held its meetings outside the city. In 1594 a Mennonite meeting held on the Nieuwland in the home of Johannes Gaukes and led by Peter van Coelen (*q.v.*) was disturbed by the Reformed minister Ruardus Acronius. The elders of the Jan-Jacobsz group in 1604-31 baptized 53 persons in Nieuwland. (Blaupot t. C., *Friesland,* 131.)   vDZ.

Nieuwpoort, a town in the Dutch province of South Holland, where Leenaert Bouwens (*q.v.*) baptized 12 persons in 1563-65. Of a Mennonite congregation at Nieuwpoort nothing is known. These converts may have constituted the original core of the Mennonite congregation in the neighboring town of Vianen (*q.v.*).   vDZ.

Nieuwpoort, West Flanders, Belgium, was in 1534-35 the seat of an Anabaptist congregation, mostly consisting of Anabaptists from Holland, who often stayed here some time before crossing the channel to England.   vDZ.

A. L. E. Verheyden, "Le protestantisme à Nieuport," in *Bulletin . . . d'Histoire de Belgique* LXVI (Brussels, 1951) 2.

Nieuw-Scheemda, during the 16th-18th centuries usually called Scheemder-hamrik, is a hamlet in the Dutch province of Groningen and formerly seat of a Mennonite congregation. Of the origin and history of this congregation not much is known. S. Blaupot ten Cate's assumption that the congregation of Scheemder-hamrik is identical with the Klei(n) Oldampt (*q.v.*) congregation is questionable. In 1650 Peter Jansen was a preacher of the Scheemderhamrik congregation, which belonged to the Groningen Old Flemish branch and at this time had no meetinghouse, meetings being held in Dirk Jans's home. From the early 18th century the congregation of Scheemder-hamrik, whose membership probably never surpassed twenty, was always united with the congregation of neighboring Noordbroek (*q.v.,* later mostly called Noordbroek and Nieuw-Scheemda). It was apparently not until the early 19th century that a meetinghouse was built at Nieuw-Scheemda, which was remodeled in 1840 and used until 1919. In 1921 it was sold, after its organ had been transported and installed in the Noordbroek church. (*DJ* 1840, 46; 1850, 57; *DB* 1879, 6, 9, 89; Blaupot t. C., *Groningen* I, 92, 213; *ML* III, 265.)

vDZ.

Nieuwvaart: see Klundert.

Nieuwvliet "in 't lant van Cadsant" is a hamlet in Dutch Zeeland-Flanders, where a Mennonite congregation existed from the 16th to the 18th century. The congregation, which was composed of refugees from Belgian Flanders in 1614 and the following years and which was always small, had a preacher of its own only a part of the time, but had a church. After 1771 this meetinghouse was apparently no longer used. In the lists of Mennonite congregations it is mentioned for the last time in 1775. On July 10, 1779, the members joined the neighboring congregation of Aardenburg (*q.v.*). The Nieuwvliet congregation is often called Cadzand (*q.v.*) or Groede (*q.v.*).

vDZ.

Inv. Arch. Amst. I, No. 1166; *DB* 1879, 20; 1883, 112; 1884, 45, 108, 113 f.; a history of the congregation, *DB* 1889, 90-116; *ML* III, 254.

Nijdam (Nydam), a widely ramified family of farmers, still found in the Dutch province of Friesland and elsewhere in the Netherlands, whose ancestor, as far as is known, was Willem Willems Nydam (about 1550-1635), living at Nydamstra Estate (state farmhouse) near Irnsum. He belonged to the Reformed Church, as did the first generations of his descendants; but since the 18th century there have been a number of Mennonite Nijdam families, particularly near Akkrum and Grouw. Cornelis Nijdam (*q.v.*) was a descendant of Willem Willems Nydam. (W. Tsj. Vleer, *Het Nijdamstra-boek*, n.p., 1956.)

vDZ.

Nijdam, Cornelis, b. April 24, 1884, at Leeuwarden, d. July 12, 1946, at Amsterdam, a Dutch Mennonite minister, studied theology at the universities of Groningen and Amsterdam and at the Amsterdam Mennonite Seminary, and served as pastor in the following congregations: Noordeind van Graft 1909-12, Veenwouden 1912-26, Borne 1926-30, Amsterdam 1930-33, and Zeist 1933-46. By his kindness, his simplicity, his untiring work, and particularly by his strong evangelical faith Nijdam was a great blessing to the Dutch brotherhood. Influenced by the pietistic theology of Friedrich Schleiermacher, and inspired by contacts with English Quakers, a Biblical faith and practical Christianity were firmly linked in him throughout his life. Nijdam was always a warm friend and a promoter of missions. In 1915 he became a member of the executive board of the Dutch Missions Association, in 1923 its secretary, and served as its chairman from 1934 until his death; in 1926-30 he was also the editor of *Onze Zending,* a monthly dedicated to the interests of the Mission Association. Nijdam was one of the first members and leaders of the "Vereeniging voor Gemeente-

dagen," now "Vereniging voor Doopsgezind Broederschapswerk" (*q.v.*), founded in 1917. He wholeheartedly welcomed the spiritual renewal of the Dutch brotherhood for which this association was striving. In 1924-27 he was treasurer of this association, and 1927-34 its president. In 1922 in collaboration with P. Vis (*q.v.*) and W. H. toe Water (*q.v.*), he instigated the founding of the "Friese Doopsgezinde Jongeren Bond" (*q.v.*) (Youth Association of Friesland). From the beginning (1924) he was on the committee for the Elspeet Mennonite Brotherhood Home, serving as secretary of this committee 1925-32 and its president 1932-46.

In September 1945 Nijdam was appointed president of the A.D.S. (*q.v.*; Dutch General Mennonite Conference), of which he had been for many years a trustee. He entered his presidency with great plans, but his premature death prevented him from carrying out his intentions. One of his projects, a general Mennonite weekly, which was to be read by all the Dutch Mennonites, was realized after his death. *De Noodbrug* (*q.v.*), a temporary periodical published by the A.D.S., was edited by Nijdam and S. H. N. Gorter (*q.v.*).

Nijdam published a large number of articles in *De Zondagsbode* and *Brieven;* he also contributed to the *Doopsgezind Jaarboekje*. Besides this he published some sermons and separately *Het Nieuwe Huis* (Bergum, 1916), *De Doopsgezinde Zending* (Wolvega, n.d.), and *Een Winter in de Oase, brieven uit Biskra* (Haarlem, 1934). Nijdam was married to Anna A. Vogelsang, Th.D.

vDZ.

De Noodbrug, September 1946; *DJ* 1949, 36 f.; C. Nijdam, "Spiritual Reconstruction," *Menn. Life* II (January 1947) 31-33; H. Craandyk, "In Memoriam—Cornelis Nijdam," *op. cit.,* 33 f.

Nijmegen (German, Nimwegen), a city in the Dutch province of Gelderland with (1951) a population of 112,800 (231 Mennonites). The first mention of Anabaptists in this city occurs in 1539; on April 19 of this year three unnamed Anabaptist men were burned at the stake here, and shortly after two women were drowned in the Waal River. Two other victims of persecution in this city are known: in 1557 (van Bragt gives the year as 1556) Gerrit Hazenpoet was burned at the stake, and in 1569 (van Bragt 1572) Jan (Johan) Block (*q.v.*) met the same fate. But the city government did not always take such strong action against the Anabaptists; as early as 1565 Jan van den Berg was expelled from the city with his whole family because he refused to have his children baptized.

The next mention of Anabaptists is made in 1639. The city, which had become predominantly Reformed, suffered a terrible epidemic of the plague in 1635-37, losing about half of its inhabitants. It therefore considered bringing weavers in from other places for its linen weaving industry. During this time many Reformed came here from the duchy of Jülich (*q.v.*), Germany, where they were oppressed because of their religious faith. Mennonites came too; in 1639 a Mennonite acquired the rights of citizenship, and two others in 1640. Instead of giving the customary oath they were received upon their vow of truthfulness ("by mannen-waerheyd"). In

1642 and the following years more Mennonite weavers came to Nijmegen from Jülich, who practiced their craft, becoming citizens in the same way. The number of Mennonites there in 1652 was considerable. The complaint of the Reformed to the government that the Mennonites were meeting regularly for services indicates that there was an organized congregation. In 1654-57 new refugees came, strengthening the congregation, which Guyot estimates at 180 souls. The Mennonites of Nijmegen belonged to the United Flemish, Frisians, and High Germans and used this name although there were never any divisions there. After the Lamist-Zonist (*q.v.*) schism the Nijmegen congregation held to the conservative Zonist views. In 1664 Willem Kops, Jan Welsinck, and Pieter Willemsz signed the *Verbondt van Eenigheydt* (*q.v.*) in the name of the Nijmegen congregation.

A man of importance who did much to promote the financial status of the brotherhood was the deacon Jan Godschalks van Elten (*q.v.;* d. 1700), who came from München-Gladbach, Jülich, and obtained citizenship in 1655. In 1665 the council of the Reformed Church protested that the Mennonites had a fixed place of meeting; thereupon they were forced again to meet in the homes of the members. In 1706 they bought a house which they remodeled as a church. In 1728 they found another place in the Remonstrant church on the Arminiaansche Plaats, which was now sold to the Mennonites.

In the 18th century the membership suffered a sharp decline. In 1655 the membership including children was estimated at 180, the number of baptized members in 1783 was 99, in 1798, 39, and in 1847 only 28. The French occupation brought a time of trial and difficulty. In 1794 the church was used as a stable. But by 1802 it was again in use as a church. After 1860 the membership increased rapidly. The 28 members of 1847 grew to 240 by 1900. In 1940 the membership stood at about 200, in 1955 at 135. The congregation of Nijmegen seems to have had as its first regular (lay) preacher and elder Thomas Ameldonck, who came from Goch (*q.v.*) and served at Nijmegen 1672-89. After his decease the congregation was for some time served by elders from the outside, but in 1690 two preachers had been appointed, i.e., Jan Ameldonck Leeuw, the son of elder Thomas Ameldonck, and Laurens Hendriks. They were followed by Hendrik Laurens (son of Laurens Hendriks) and Pieter Hendriks (Pieter de Eger, or van Egen), who were both appointed elders in 1724. Laurens Hendriks served until 1759, in which year he retired; Pieter van Egen served until his death in 1770. They were followed by Cornelis Bruyn, serving 1773-82, J. H. Floh, who was their first minister trained at the Amsterdam Seminary, 1782-83, Evert Akkeringa 1784-99, Herman I. van Hinte 1799, Abraham de Vries 1800-1, Pieter Hollenberg 1801-5, Sybren Sybrandi 1805-7, Coenraad Bavink 1807-10, Anthonie Doyer 1811-18, Cornelis S. van Geuns 1819-22, Abraham Doyer 1825-28, Jan Boeke 1828-30, Klaas Sybrandi 1830-34, J. ten Cate Fennema 1835-60, J. Attema 1861-81, P. Feenstra Jr. 1881-91, B. Haga 1891-1917, Y. S. Buruma 1917-50, H. C. Valeton 1950—.

During World War II the church was destroyed in September 1944; a new church was dedicated on May 25, 1952. There is a Sunday school for children and a ladies' circle. The city is now predominantly (79 per cent) Catholic.

In 1710 a number of Mennonites from Switzerland, who were to be deported to the English colonies in America, were set free by the Dutch authorities at Nijmegen on April 9, when their ship, sailing down the Rhine, passed Nijmegen. They were cordially received by the Mennonites of Nijmegen.

vDZ.

P. C. G. Guyot, *Bijdragen tot de geschiedenis der Doopsgezinden te Nijmegen* (1845); B. Haga, *De Doopsgezinde Martelaren te Nijmegen (Geschriften t. b. v. de Doopsgezinde in de verstrooiing)* (Amsterdam, n.d.); *Inv. Arch. Amst.* I, Nos. 1261, 1772; II, Nos. 2154-74; *DB* 1874, 1-33; 1875, 67-92; *DJ* 1953, 38-40; *Algemeen Doopsgezind Weekblad* XI (1955 f.) Nos. 36 and 40.

Nijpkerke: see **Nukerke.**

Niklas, Nikolaus, an Anabaptist martyr: see **Claes Claesz.**

Nikolaidorf, a village in the Molotschna (*q.v.*) settlement, South Russia, on the south bank of the Apanlee River, was founded in 1852 by Mennonites from West Prussia. In 1914 it had 319 inhabitants and 4,100 acres of land.

Another village with this name was founded by Mennonite immigrants in Barnaul (*q.v.*), province of Tomsk (Siberia), in 1909. The village belonged to the Orloff Mennonite Church and had a school which gave instruction in both Russian and German. (*ML* III, 254.) Hege.

Nikolaifeld (Nikolaipol), a common Mennonite village name in Russia named after Czar Nicholas. The name appeared in the following Mennonite settlements: Zagradovka, Borissovo, Yazekovo, and Don Ukraine; Aulie-Ata, Central Asia; Suvorovka, Caucasus; Barnaul and Omsk, Siberia; and Neuland, Paraguay. (*ML* III, 254.) C.K.

Nikolaifeld (Nikolaipol) was a village in which the administration (*volost*) of the Yazekovo Mennonite settlement (*q.v.*), near Chortitza, Russia, was located. The village was established in 1869 and had 4,300 acres of land in 1918, and under the Soviet regime as a collective farm 2,650 acres. In 1914 the population was 221; in 1941 it was 610. Thirteen persons were murdered in 1919, three starved to death in 1933-34, and 113 were exiled during 1929-41. During the German occupation of the Ukraine in 1941-43 the economic and cultural life was somewhat revived. When the Germans withdrew the population was evacuated to Germany, whence probably half of it was returned to Russia by the Russian army, and the other half found its way to America. C.K.

K. Stumpp, *Bericht über das Gebiet Chortitza* (Berlin, 1943); *ML* III, 255.

Nikolaifeld (Nikolaipol) Mennonite Church was located in the Yazekovo Mennonite settlement (*q.v.*) of Ukraine, 15 miles north of Chortitza in South Russia. The congregation was established in 1869. Originally it was a subsidiary of the Chortitza Mennonite Church (*q.v.*). Early ministers were Peter

Penner (ordained 1865), Isaak Klassen (1871), Anton Löwen (1871, leading minister), Martin Dyck (1876), Heinrich Rempel (1876), Heinrich Siemens (1880), Heinrich Löwen (1885), Jacob Siemens (1888), Cornelius Lehn (1888), Aaron Klassen (1905), Klaas Quiring (1908), Peter Schulz (1908).

The church was located in the village of Nikolaifeld (Nikolaipol). In 1905 the total population of the church was 1,046, of whom some 240 were members. The church contributions during that year amounted to 1,345 rubles. In 1928 the total population was 1,009, with 472 members. In these 25 years the congregation had indeed grown, but the surplus population had gone to daughter settlements and particularly to Canada. Of the total population, 58 had a Zentralschule education, 10 a normal training, 4 a secondary training, and 2 university training. Heinrich D. Epp (*q.v.*), a teacher of the local Zentralschule and minister of the church, was ordained elder in 1920. At that time the church became independent. He was assisted by five ministers and three deacons, most of whom had a secondary education and had been teaching. On Nov. 12, 1926, the congregation observed the fortieth anniversary of the ministry of Heinrich D. Epp, for which occasion the elders Isaak Dyck, Johann Martens, Peter Neufeld, and others came. In 1935 the church was confiscated and Heinrich D. Epp left the community.

During the war the members of the church were scattered. At the time of the German occupation of the Ukraine (1941-43) the congregation had meetinghouses in the villages of Nikolaifeld, Adelsheim, and Hochfeld. Each village had a choir. Information about the religious life and the hardships of the congregations under the Soviets is not available. (See also **Yazekovo** Mennonite settlement, and the respective villages.) Some of the members have meanwhile found their way to Canada and South America. (See **Nikolaipol.**) C.K.

H. Dirks, *Statistik*, 1905, 61; Friesen, *Brüderschaft*, 70; *Unser Blatt* II (April 1927) 206; K. Stumpp, *Bericht über das Gebiet Chortitza* (Berlin, 1943); *ML* III, 254.

Nikolaifeld Mennonite Church was the congregation in the Suvorovka Mennonite settlement, province of Stavropol, Caucasus, with its meetinghouse in the village of Nikolaifeld. The settlement was established in 1894 and consisted of two villages; the congregation was organized in 1901. Cornelius Harder (*q.v.*) was the first leading minister, assisted by Jacob Enns and Jacob Janzen. In 1905 the total membership of the church was 405, with 173 baptized members. Little is known about the later development of the congregation. (Friesen, *Brüderschaft*, 717; Dirks, *Statistik*, 1905, 40, 65.) C.K.

Nikolaifeld Mennonite Church, located in the Zagradovka settlement, province of Kherson, South Russia. The Zagradovka settlement was established 1872-79, comprising seventeen villages. The settlers had come from various places. In this heterogeneous mass there was not a single minister. The first election of ministers was held Oct. 22, 1872. Three men were elected to preach; next year a few more were added. On June 2, 1874, the congregation was organized as the Tiege Mennonite Church, and

Wilhelm Voth was elected and ordained elder of the congregation. Services at first were held in schools and large sheds, but in 1888 construction of a large church in the village of Nikolaifeld began. The first service in the new church was held May 5, 1891, after which the congregation was renamed the Nikolaifeld Mennonite Church.

Among the first ministers were capable men, some of whom had belonged to the Gnadenfeld "brother" circle; most of them had been affected by the wave of reformation that had swept through the Mennonite villages of Russia during the 1860's and which is to be identified with such names as Eduard Wüst and Bernhard Harder. The Nikolaifeld ministers preached the necessity of rebirth and sanctification of life; they did not read their sermons as was customary at that time but spoke extemporaneously. Bible conferences, prayer meetings, visitation of members in their homes, mission circles, etc., were introduced.

Elders of this church were Wilhelm Voth 1874-95, Gerhard Warkentin 1895-1902, Franz Martens 1902-7, Johann Voth 1908-21, Franz Wiens 1921-24, Heinrich Voth 1925- . Martens, Wiens, and H. Voth were teachers by profession.

In 1907 Martens and most of the ministers left the church and organized the Orloff Evangelical Mennonite Church. The reason for this action was their desire to establish a "pure" church. Admissibility to baptism and communion, as well as church discipline in general, were the problems.

Martens was followed by Johann Voth, the son of the Elder Wilhelm Voth. Voth resigned in 1921. His successor, Franz Wiens, resigned and joined the Evangelical Church. Heinrich Voth, no relative of the above-named Voths, now was elected and ordained as elder; he was young, energetic, and capable. He was sent into exile in 1931 and the church building converted into a granary by the Soviets. All ministers either were sent into exile or else killed. Under ruthless Soviet pressure all organized religious life had ceased to exist.

In 1922 the congregation had 1,241 members. In the course of time subsidiary congregations were established (1) near the station Zuvorovskaya in the Caucasus, (2), Pissarev, (3) Trubetzkoy, and (4) Durilino. Missionaries from the congregation in foreign fields were Johann Wiebe, German East Africa; Peter J. Wiens, Champa, India; Suse Richert, Java; Helena Goossen, Java. G.L.

Friesen, *Brüderschaft*, 462-64, 709-11, 724-27; G. Lohrenz, *Sagradowka* (Rosthern, 1947) 64-79.

Nikolaipol, the name of numerous Mennonite villages in Russia. In the province of Ekaterinoslav Mennonites from the Chortitza and Kronsweide established the Nikolaipol settlement in 1869-72 with eight villages, one of them also called Nikolaipol, originally Nikolaifeld, with 5,130 acres of land. In 1912 it had a population of 314 and was the seat of a Mennonite congregation, which built a church between Nikolaipol and Franzfeld in 1888. To this congregation belonged the Mennonites of the following villages: Eichenfeld (Dubovka, *q.v.*), Neu-Hochfeld (Morozovo, *q.v.*), where in 1905 a congregation of the "Evangelical Mennonite Brethren" was also organized, Adelsheim (Dolinovka, *q.v.*), Franzfeld (Varvarovka), Reinfeld (Tchistopol), Paulsheim (Pavlovka), and Petersdorf (Nadeschovka). Dubovka, the village destroyed during the Revolution, most of whose male population was killed on Oct. 26, 1919, was also a part of this congregation, which had a membership of 500. The Mennonite Brethren had a subsidiary congregation and chapel in Nikolaipol, whose members also lived in the above eight villages. Before World War I the settlement was very prosperous, and many of the settlers were able to replace their simple homes with stately residences. All the villages had schools from the beginning. In the village of Nikolaipol a large Zentralschule was built in 1906, with an enrollment of about 100. It was later changed into an agricultural school and taken over by the government.

In 1892 another village called Nikolaipol was founded in the province of Ekaterinoslav, Santurinovskaya district, Bachmut area, Borissovo (*q.v.*) settlement (daughter settlement of Chortitza), with 204 inhabitants in 1912.

A congregation with this name was founded in 1881 in Asia, in the region of Sir-Darya, at the foot of the Thian-schan Mountain (on the Talash River) in Turkestan by Mennonites from the Am Trakt settlement (*q.v.*), whose members lived in five villages. The congregation built a hospital near Tashkent in the village of Nikolaipol in 1908 for the care of sick Kirghiz.

One of the villages in the Slavgorod settlement (formerly Barnaul, *q.v.*), province of Omsk, was called Nikolaipol.   HEGE.

Dirks, *Statistik*, 1905; D. H. Epp, *Die Memriker Ansiedlung* (Berdyansk, 1910); W. Quiring, *Die Mundart von Chortitza in Süd-Russland* (1928) 31 f.; *Neuer Haus- und Landwirtschafts-Kalender*, 1913, 32, 50, 52, 70; *Menn. Jahrbuch*, 1908, 87; *ML* III, 255.

Nikolaipol Mennonite Brethren Church, located at Nikolaipol, Aulie-Ata (*q.v.*), 150 miles northeast of Tashkent (*q.v.*) in Central Asia, started as an independent Mennonite Brethren congregation among the followers of Abram Peters (*q.v.*), and Claas Epp (*q.v.*), who had come from the Molotschna and Trakt settlements looking for a refuge to escape military service and to meet Christ at His second coming. This Mennonite Brethren church was freer in the form of baptism, admitting members who were not immersed. The organization of the church took place in 1887 (Dirks, 1889), with Heinrich Kröker as its first elder. In 1905 Heinrich Kröker was elder, assisted by the ministers Jakob Janzen, Jakob Mantler, Johann Klassen, Aron Dyck, and Franz Braun. The congregation at that time numbered 377, with 173 baptized members. The history of this church is not quite clear. Johannes Janzen gives the information that the M.B. church underwent a reorganization challenged by the work of the more vital Evangelical Mennonite Church. The Nikolaipol M.B. Church maintained a special status within the Mennonite Brethren Conference of Russia although fellowship was maintained (Friesen, 482). From all information available, this congregation must have been more or less independent. Little is known about the later development and the

present status of this congregation, although it can be assumed that it is still in existence.   C.K.

J. Janzen, "The Mennonite Colony in Turkestan," *MQR* IV (1930) 282-89; Friesen, *Brüderschaft*; H. Dirks, *Statistik* (1905) 58, 69; *Unser Blatt* (October 1925) 10.

Nikolaital (Novo-Sofievka), a village in the Novo-Sofievka district of Ekaterinoslav, South Russia, founded in 1865, one of seven villages constituting the Mennonite settlement of Borozenko (*q.v.*). In 1913 it had 96 inhabitants with 2,676 acres of land.

W. Quiring, *Die Mundart von Chortitza in Süd-Russland* (Munich, 1928) 31; *ML* III, 255.

Nikolayev Mennonite Church in the Orenburg Mennonite settlement, Russia, first consisted of Mennonites from the Molotschna settlement who settled in the province of Orenburg (Chkalov) in 1895. The church was founded in 1897 under the leadership of Johann Bärgmann, who was assisted by Peter Dück, David Littke, Henrich Janzen, and Abraham Bärgmann. In 1905 the total population of the church was 1,238, with 494 baptized members. The first church building was located in the village of Stepanovka. In 1913-14 the old church was torn down and a large new church of brick was erected. In 1906 a second church was built of brick in the village of Chernozernoye. The elder Johann Bärgmann also lived in this village. In addition to the early ministers mentioned above, Jacob Wolff was ordained in 1906 and Heinrich Brucks in 1911. The Mennonites maintained for a time a Bible school, called "Pniel."

After the Revolution, the congregation suffered severely. The ministers had to give up their work. Many members of the church emigrated to Canada and others were exiled. The lowest economic and spiritual status of the settlement was reached during World War II. This settlement was evidently spared the fate of many of the others of having its population completely removed. Recent reports indicate that the religious life of the settlement has been revived. (See **Orenburg** Mennonite Settlement.)   C.K.

Peter Dyck, *Orenburg am Ural* (Clearbrook, 1951); Dirks, *Statistik* (1905) 33, 64; Friesen, *Brüderschaft*, 717; Cornelius Krahn, "Revival Sweeps Mennonite Settlement in Russia," *Menn. Weekly Review*, Jan. 31, 1957, p. 11.

Nikolayevka, the name of a number of Mennonite settlements in Russia and Siberia, most of which were given German names at their founding.

Two settlements with this name were made in the province of Ekaterinoslav (*q.v.*). One was that of 1884 in the Santvinovka district, which in 1913 had 289 inhabitants and 6,525 acres of land. Another was made in 1885 (originally called Ebental) in the Memrik settlement, a daughter colony of the Molotschna settlement, Golitsinovka district, Bachmut area, with 209 inhabitants and 2,592 acres of land. The settlers had great difficulties to overcome, but in two years a school was opened, and in the next year a schoolhouse was built. In 1889 a third village was given this name, one of seven villages in the Ignatyevka settlement, a daughter settlement of Chortitza, in the Zhelezyanskaya district of the Bachmut area.

In the Terek (*q.v.*) settlement in the Caucasus, a daughter of the Molotschna settlement at the mouth of the Sula River, where it flows into the Caspian Sea, was given this name in 1901. Also a village in the Orenburg-Dyeyvka (*q.v.*) settlement was so named, a daughter settlement of Chortitza, Uranskaya area of the province of Orenburg, which was founded in 1894-1901 and contained 15 villages.

The name occurs likewise in a number of Mennonite settlements made in Siberia. One of these was in the province of Omsk, ten miles from the town of Slavgorod in the Slavgorod settlement (formerly Barnaul, *q.v.*) which consisted of 58 villages with (1925) a population of 13,173. Another was 45 miles west of Slavgorod in the Tchaiatchi settlement.   HEGE.

Dirks, *Statistik* (1905); D. H. Epp, *Die Memriker Ansiedlung* (Berdyansk, 1910); W. Quiring, *Die Mundart von Chortitza in Süd-Russland* (Munich, 1928); *ML* III, 255.

Nikolayevka Mennonite Brethren Church, located in the Bachmut Mennonite settlement (New York), province of Ekaterinoslav, South Russia, was founded in 1889 by Mennonites coming from the Chortitza settlement. The congregation was at first affiliated with the Einlage M.B. Church under the leadership of Gerhard Regehr. It became independent in 1905, when Hermann A. Neufeld (*q.v.*) was ordained elder. Other ministers who served the congregation were Cornelius Grunau, who later emigrated to the United States, Abraham Pätkau, Paul Wiebe, Johann Schellenberg, Johann Siemens, Peter Wiebe, David Block, Wilhelm Klassen, Peter Janzen, Peter Krause, Johann Fröse, Johann Klassen, Peter Siemens. In 1905 the total population of the congregation was 501 and the number of baptized members was 146. For a while the Mennonites and the Mennonite Brethren worshiped at the same place on alternate Sundays. In 1923 Hermann A. Neufeld emigrated to Canada and a number of other members followed. Little is known of the congregation after this date. So far as is known, the congregation survived the troubles of the 1920's and 30's but its fate was sealed during World War II.   P.H.B., C.K.

Dirks, *Statistik*, 1905; Friesen, *Brüderschaft*, 476; A. H. Unruh, *Die Geschichte der Mennoniten-Brüdergemeinde* (Winnipeg, 1954) 201.

Nikolsburg, a city and domain in the former Brno area of the margravure of Moravia, belonged since the middle of the 13th century to the Lower Austrian branch of the old noble family of Liechtenstein. In 1566 the domain fell to Emperor Maximilian II, who in 1575 ceded a part of it to the Baron Adam von Dietrichstein.

In the third decade of the 16th century Nikolsburg became noted as the center of Moravian Anabaptism. Indeed, throughout the entire 16th century Moravia was considered the promised land of religious tolerance. Here lived, besides the Catholics and the Utraquists, Bohemian Brethren who had fled from persecution in Bohemia to Moravia, and in general all those of any creed who were persecuted in any other country.

Already in 1524 the Protestants had established a congregation at Nikolsburg under the protection of Leonhard of Liechtenstein (*q.v.*). Their preacher was Hans Spittelmaier, assisted by Oswald Glaidt, (*q.v.*). At the beginning of July 1526 Balthasar Hubmaier arrived from Augsburg. Contemporary reports indicate that he had an extraordinary following throughout Nikolsburg; something like 12,000 Anabaptists are reported to have gradually found their way into the city and the vicinity. To them this Moravian spot became a sort of "Emmaus."

Anabaptists streamed together here from South Germany and from Austria. All the records of their trials at courts to which the Anabaptists at Schwaz in Tirol, in Augsburg, and in other places, were subjected in 1528-29, give the information that most of them either had been baptized in Nikolsburg or perhaps lived there for some time. Some of them were Hubmaier's friends. Some of the noted names were Hans Hut (*q.v.*) who found ten leaders (*Vorsteher*) already serving the Anabaptists in Nikolsburg; also Hans Nadler (*q.v.*), Georg Nespitzer (*q.v.*), and the better known Leonhard Schiemer (*q.v.*), who was the first Anabaptist bishop in Upper Austria. Another was Hans Schlaffer (*q.v.*), "who had previously been a Roman priest." In his statement Schlaffer said that in Nikolsburg baptisms were performed in the following manner: "First there was a sermon for the congregation. Then they baptized whoever came and desired it. Not everyone was questioned apart, nor an account demanded of him. Therefore our dear Hans Hut differed with Dr. Balthasar and the great division arose between him and the Brethren." In Nikolsburg there was probably also the Anabaptist preacher Thomas Waldhauser (*q.v.*). This was stated by Jacob Wiedemann and Philipp Jäger.

In Nikolsburg Hubmaier did a great deal of writing supported by the publisher Simprecht Sorg, called Froschauer. Here he wrote his well-known tracts, most of which he dedicated to the heads of the Moravian people, e.g., the Lords Leonhard and Hans von Liechtenstein, the magistrate Johann von Pernstein, the chief chamberlain Arkleb von Boskowitz, and Johann Dubcansky von Zedenin and Habrowan, in order to win their favor for Anabaptism. Here in Nikolsburg, however, Hubmaier found opponents among the Anabaptists themselves, such as Hans Hut, with whom he debated twice, once in Bergen and once in Nikolsburg. At the first of these debates the question considered was "whether one should use the sword or whether one should pay taxes for war or not." According to the position one took on these questions he belonged to the Schwertler (*q.v.*) or to the Stäbler (*q.v.*). In the second disputation, as Hans Nadler of Erlangen stated in 1529, seven subjects were debated: baptism, the sacrament of the Lord's Supper, God's judgment, God's verdict, the end of the world, the new kingdom, and the coming of Christ. This disputation at Nikolsburg created considerable excitement beyond Moravia, as can be seen from the wide distribution of the so-called Nikolsburg Articles (*q.v.*), the refutation of which became a serious matter for the opponents of the Anabaptists, and which were placed on the Index in Rome.

While Hubmaier was developing his extensive work in Nikolsburg the Austrian government was eagerly trying to arrest him. But his death as a martyr in May 1528 did not stop the progress of Anabaptism; not only did the government fail to get it under control, but it even spread to a much wider extent. It was injured by divisions more than by persecutions; these divisions finally led to the separation of the followers of Wiedemann and Jäger, the Stäbler, from their brethren, the Schwertler; the Stäbler moved to Austerlitz, which now became a chief center of Anabaptism in Moravia.

The Anabaptists who remained in Nikolsburg were later usually called collectively Swiss Brethren. They occupied several villages in the vicinity of Nikolsburg and shared on the whole the changing fate of their other brethren in Moravia, who, to be sure, after Jakob Hutter (q.v.) became their leader, soon surpassed their former brethren in numbers and in ability. The Nikolsburg Anabaptists furthermore, upon the death of Leonhard of Liechtenstein, lost the protection which he had given them. Besides in Nikolsburg, they were found in Pollau (q.v.), Bergen, Wisternitz, Voitelsbrunn, Tasswitz, Urban, some in Znaim (q.v.), and Eibenschitz (q.v.), and in the mountain city Jamnitz, where Oswald Glaidt was their leader for a considerable period of time until his martyrdom in 1545. LOSERTH.

How many believers reached Nikolsburg at Hubmaier's time is seen from the confession of Hans Nadler (q.v.) of 1529, when he said that when he was staying in Nikolsburg for about 14 days in 1527 he himself watched how "they publicly baptized in the churches about 72 persons on one day." The parting of Leonhard von Liechtenstein from the Stäbler, who were driven out in 1528, was not unfriendly. He accompanied them to Unterwisternitz, gave them drinks, and freed them from the tax; from there they went on to Austerlitz.

Between the Schwertler who had remained in the Nikolsburger domain or settled in the villages of Bergen, Klentnitz, Pollau, Tracht, Voitelsbrunn, and Wisternitz, and the Hutterian Brethren there was no fellowship. To the government at Vienna, however, all Anabaptists were equally thorns in the flesh. The government gave instructions to the representatives traveling to the Landtag of Moravia on Jan. 2, 1540, that they should persuade the estates nowhere to tolerate the Anabaptists, who were reputedly spreading widely in the Nikolsburg domain and other places. The estates rejected this idea on January 4 to the extent that they declared that they did not openly tolerate the Anabaptist brotherhood but could not forbid the individual lords to keep their Anabaptist subjects, because otherwise whole strips of land would have become desolate and the lords would then furthermore no longer be in a position to furnish the money for important public undertakings, such as aid against the Turks, etc.

From 1543 on gradually the influx of the Swiss Brethren, in this case the former followers of Hubmaier, into the Hutterian brotherhood began; Hans Klopfer of Pollau and his group were the first of these. In the persecution of 1550 Mayden Mountain near Pollau offered them a refuge where they "had in many places pits and holes, in which they maintained themselves for a time, also in the clefts of the rocks and in the hollows and in the high mountains." Especially severe was the persecution of those who had fled to Pulgram; they were relentlessly driven out and plundered.

In 1556, when the Hutterian Brethren began to live in Nikolsburg, numerous Anabaptists from the neighboring area in Lower Austria, especially from Laa and Falkenstein, found their way to this place. The establishment of the Bruderhof (which is still standing) was followed in the next years by Bruderhofs in Bergen and Voitelsbrunn, which the Anabaptists developed, by making use of a healing spring there, into a noted and widely patronized bathing resort. In 1569 they suffered severely in the entire country, when during the famine in Nikolsburg a loaf of bread cost 45 Kreuzer.

A new section of Hutterite history in the Nikolsburg domain is introduced by the ceding of the domain to Adam von Dietrichstein (q.v.). He had called in the Jesuit Cardaneus for the conversion of the Lutherans in his domain in 1579. Adam experienced a certain embarrassment from the zealous Jesuit in that he had wanted the Anabaptists to be an exception in the work of conversion on account of their usefulness. Adam stated this in a letter he wrote from Prague on May 24, 1579, to Cardaneus in which he excused his (in the eyes of a zealous missionary) serious negligence in respect to the Anabaptists with the explanation: "Not everything can be done at the moment as one would like to see it." That in spite of this request Cardaneus (according to the Geschicht-Buch) did not avoid conflicts with the Anabaptists, resulted first from the fact that they refused to give him the required greeting. In January 1580 Cardaneus even announced the conversion of several Anabaptists, and in 1582 again the conversion of several Anabaptist women in Unterwisternitz; but on the whole there were only some individual conversions.

The new priest of Nikolsburg, Christoph Erhard (q.v.), wrote to the Jesuit Possevinus on June 17, 1584, that the oppression of Lutheranism had to be sure been successful, but for the complete and enduring conversion of the domain of Nikolsburg also the Hutterites would have to be made Catholic without an exception. A hindrance to the complete conversion was of course the undisciplined conduct of many a Catholic priest, newly established in the parishes of the domain, concerning which also Erhard, who had been made dean, soon complained. Also an evil and calumnious pamphlet was circulated in Nikolsburg in 1587, which appeared anonymously against the Hutterites, but failed to accomplish its purpose. Nor can it be said that the pamphlets of two renegade Hutterites, namely, that of Hans Jedelshauser (q.v.) and the one of Johann Eysvogel (q.v.) in Cologne had any more effect. The former charged the Hutterites with envy, quarrelsomeness, and ill will, and charged the Vorsteher of the entire brotherhood, Klaus Braidl (q.v.), as well as the noted physician Jörg Zobel (q.v.) with moral misdemeanors. The latter, when he left the Austerlitz brotherhood, had his song of calumniation printed in 1586. Zobel, the great physician of the brotherhood, who mostly lived in Nikolsburg, had even been called to the imperial court at Prague and been able to heal Rudolf II. Even the abbot of the nearby monastery Klosterbruck, who requested the help of the emperor in his quarrel with the Hutterites (in a private audience), did not allow this to move him to cease addressing Jörg Zobel as "dear friend" and to invite him to a visit, and even to have him called for in a carriage. In 1599 Zobel was called to Emperor Rudolf in Prague a second time, "because of the infection which reigned at that time violently in Bohemia, in the good hope and confidence that he would be able to give counsel for the illness in the emperor's fortress."

The influx to Moravia, especially into the Nikolsburg domain, continued especially in these years. On May 28, 1587, Rudolf Stumpf reported from Zurich to Theodor Beza (q.v.) that now especially many Anabaptists were moving from the canton of Zürich to Moravia, and Erhard estimated the influx out of the "German and Oberland" regions in this year alone at 1,600 persons.

In 1589 there was complaint about a heavy tax imposed by the estates. Adam von Dietrichstein had died on Feb. 5, 1590, and had passed on the inheritance to his three sons, Maximilian, Sigismund (who in spite of his extreme youth became the underchamberlain in 1597), and Franz, who at the age of 29 was made cardinal by Pope Clemens VIII and afterwards, under pressure, became bishop of Olmütz.

On May 12, 1592, Thoman Haan (q.v.), of Nikolsburg, died a martyr's death as a true confessor at Freiburg, Bavaria.

Although in consideration of his clerical office he should not have admitted the heretics, Cardinal Franz von Dietrichstein (q.v.) was much more tolerant when he, coming from Rome, assumed the rulership of Nikolsburg in 1599. To be sure, economic reasons determined his position, for he recognized the great advantage accruing to him from this Anabaptist settlement and he knew how to enrich himself, as he demonstrated later as governor of Moravia.

A really hostile attitude of the cardinal did not appear until the Moravian "rebellion" in 1619, in the course of which he, having been sent to Vienna for negotiations, decided with the emperor against the estates who had commissioned him, whereas the Anabaptists, who were most barbarously treated by the imperial troops in southern Moravia, naturally sided with the estates protecting them. In the Nikolsburg domain, however, a difficulty for the Brethren arose from the fact that their baron was opposed to the protectors of the Hutterian Brethren in the country. And since he furthermore was the highest dignitary of the Roman Church, which was considered as idolatry by the Hutterites, their attitude in Nikolsburg was self-evident.

The cardinal, having heard that the Brethren of his domain sided with the rebels, ordered his magistrate to consider their expulsion. The magistrate Johann von Denée, in a letter of August 7, reported the situation to his master, especially of the conduct of the imperial troops against the Brethren in the domain. He reported that the miller Christoph had been killed, and the wounded Duke of Saxony, to whom Denée had offered a room in the castle, had preferred to commit himself to the care of the Hutterite physicians. On August 17 the cardinal wrote to his officer Brus that in case the Hutterites of Nikolsburg, who were guilty of treason, refused to send to him as their lord secret messages, Brus would be permitted to punish them physically himself. On September 5 the official was compelled to report to the bishop that his famous Hutterite doctor Kolert had been killed without any reason by one of the gentlemen quartered in the castle. Dietrichstein, who from Vienna had a view over the whole situation, which was changing day by day, on September 14 again permitted his official Brus to deal with the Brethren as he thought best. Two days later the Czech secretary in Nikolsburg announced the mandates sent from Vienna and complained about the defiant attitude of the Hutterite householder. On September 25 followed the announcement from Nikolsburg to Vienna that several Anabaptist subjects were yielding service to the enemy.

On October 19 the Nikolsburg Bruderhof was "severely plundered, also the sick robbed." Denée on November 13 announced to the cardinal that he had confiscated and taken away from the Bruderhof all the flour and the drugs and that he had expelled the Brethren completely out of the estate and he had let them take along only the simplest kind of equipment. The cardinal's answer from Vienna on November 17 was reproachful; the Anabaptists should not have been allowed to take along any possessions at all.

Meanwhile Puchheim had begun the siege of Nikolsburg, which, after the arrival of reinforcements from Olmütz (Olomouc) including field pieces from Olmütz, was to lead finally to the conquest of the city and even of the castle in the middle of January 1620. Of course both had to be yielded soon again to the imperial troops and so came back into the cardinal's possession. In Nikolsburg the Vorsteher of the entire brotherhood, Rudolf Hirzl, and two brethren lay imprisoned from June 2, 1621, until the cardinal had by treachery gained from him the betrayal of the treasure of the brotherhood in Neumühl (q.v.). The cardinal had been made governor and now fulfilled his threat, that when he returned to Moravia he would not tolerate the Brethren in the country. He sent his officials with soldiers to the Bruderhofs in Nikolsburg, Tracht, and the newly won Niemtschitz, "had all the rooms, chambers, attics, and grain and flour storage places, also the attics and rooms where the people lived, sealed shut so that no one could go to his place any more, and soldiers guarded the houses." After this the imperial orders were read to the assembled Hutterites, denying them protection even in Hungary and Transylvania, and offering them conversion to Catholicism as the only way to save their lives and possessions. Two hundred and thirty persons declared themselves willing to do this, "mostly careless and indifferent people, who had previously been a burden and difficulty to the brotherhood." Most of the Brethren, however, were steadfast. Jakob Braitensteiner, the manager of the Tracht Bruderhof, answered the cardinal "to his face in the presence of many people of the world," that he would not trust his salvation to a faith whose followers "had burned down their houses, cut down their men, and raped their women and daughters." With the cardinal and his followers people of that kind were "good Christians, even if they acted worse than the Turks. But the good, God-fearing people who nourish themselves with the faithful works of their hands and do no man an injury must leave the country."

Most of the Brethren were expelled; they were not allowed to take much with them, especially no tools. "The elders appealed to the cardinal, pointed out the great economic services of the Brethren to the country and the injustice that was being done to them if they took away from them their cattle, their possessions, their tools, their property, without compensation. It was all in vain." Wherever they looked for help in their oppression, they were referred to their enemy, the cardinal, as the only one who had any power.

When the elders once more presented a humble written supplication and asked for pity for their poor brotherhood, the prince of the church replied to them with laughter and mocking words: "You have brought to me only a written supplication from your elders. But I will give you a printed reply," and sent to them the mandate of expulsion which was issued at Brno on Sept. 28, 1622, which was applied so harshly that even the petition they presented to the emperor asking for shelter for the winter or a refuge for their aged sick and weak was rejected.

From almost all the 24 Bruderhofs of the country the Brethren had to leave in October "with empty hands" (see *ML* II, 715). Nikolsburg had been destroyed before that date; the Brethren from Nikolsburg were then lodging in Schächnitz in Hungary. The patents of April 13, 1623, and of March 1624, in the latter of which the cardinal ordered that the few scattered Brethren who had again been received by a few of the barons, be cut down after two weeks without a trial or hung to the nearest tree, drove most of this scattered people out of the country. The very last Hutterites who had been anxiously and secretly employed by their patrons were finally expelled from Moravia by the mandates of 1628 and 1650, where, however, for a long time not only the buildings but also the beautiful majolica ware of the Brethren served to remind the inhabitants of them.   P.DE.

J. Loserth, *Doktor Balthasar Hubmaier und die Anfänge der Wiedertäufer in Mähren* (Brno, 1893); *idem, Anabaptismus; idem, Communismus;* Lemker, *Nachricht von der Unterdrückung der evangelisch-lutherischen Lehre auf der Herrschaft Nikolsburg* (Lemgo, 1748); Adauctus Voigt, *Leben Franz Fürsten u. Kardinals von Dietrichstein von* Fulgentius Schwab (Leipzig, 1792); Falke, *Gesch. des fürstlichen Hauses Dietrichstein* II; Christoph Erhard, *Gründliche kurtz verfaste Historia* (Munich, 1589); F. Kl. Schenner, "Quellen zur Gesch. Znaims im Ref.-Zeitalter," in *Ztscht des deutschen Vereins für die Geschichte Mährens und Schlesiens* VII f. (1903 f.); P. Dedic, "Die kirchlichen und religiösen Verhältnisse in Mähren im Ref.-Jahrhundert" (Dissertation, University of Vienna, 1922); Wolkan, *Geschicht-Buch;* Zieglschmid, *Chronik;* Beck, *Geschichts-Bücher;* Fr. Hruby, *New Additions to the History of the Moravian Anabaptists* (Czech language) (Prague, 1929); *ML* III, 256-60.

Nikolsburg, Articles of. The articles of faith drawn up under this title by enemies of the Anabaptists have had disastrous consequences for the Anabaptists. In the trials of the Brethren in the imperial cities in South Germany they played a considerable role. They have been published by Nicoladoni, Cornelius, Jörg, and Schornbaum in the following form:

(1) The Gospel shall not be preached openly in the churches, but only into the ears and secretly in the houses; (2) Christ was born in original sin; (3) Mary is not the mother of God, but only the mother of Christ; (4) Christ is not God, but a prophet, to whom the Word of God was entrusted; (5) Christ has not made "satisfaction" for the sin of the whole world; (6) Among Christians there shall be neither violence nor government; (7) The Last Judgment is due in two years; (8) The angels were conceived with Christ and assumed flesh with Christ.

But the Articles of Nikolsburg were distributed not only in this version. In the state archives of Nürnberg in the *Ansbacher Religionsakten* there is an undated document that has been printed by Jörg and Cornelius, which also contains eight articles which are expressly called Articles of Nikolsburg. In the archives of the church of St. Thomas in Strasbourg these articles are found with "several additions by Hut" and with the title, "Articles which Anabaptists in Augsburg have confessed, and learned by careful questioning of the tweny-five still imprisoned there" (Cornelius, II, 281). And finally they are found in the Chronicle of Clemens Sender. Later works then cite Sender.

Until a few decades ago historians accepted these articles without question as the work of the Anabaptists themselves. Indeed, this seemed the more probable because the Martyrs' Synod (q.v.), in which Denk and Hut probably participated, was held in Augsburg on Aug. 20, 1527. Cornelius (q.v.) was the first historiographer of recent times to oppose this idea. He thought, as did Loserth (q.v.) and Sachsse (q.v.), that Hubmaier must be rejected as the author. Loserth assumes that the articles were not formulated until the cross-examination of Hut and his brethren in the summer and fall of 1527, in which Urban Rhegius made use of Hut's own booklet and the information from Nikolsburg. That such doctrinal statements were discussed in Nikolsburg is today considered out of the question. Wilhelm Neuser, who discusses these articles at length in his book on Hans Hut (1913), believes that these statements supposedly confessed by Hut were in their essence discussed at Nikolsburg; but this assumption must be rejected.

Again the articles were thoroughly discussed by Erich Meissner in his doctoral dissertation, *Die Rechtsprechung über die Wiedertäufer und die antitäuferische Publizistik* (University of Göttingen, 1921). Although the author does not yet arrive at a generally satisfactory solution of this problem, we are convinced on the basis of some sources that were unknown to Meissner, that the articles did not originate with the Anabaptists, but were falsely attributed to them by their enemies.

The earliest dated version of these articles is in the state archives in Augsburg. They were discussed in detail in Hut's trial. Hut is said to have confessed to them, as the court record of Nov. 4, 1527, reports. And so it has hitherto been assumed that they reached the public through Anabaptist hands. But Meissner proves that the articles were known to the Augsburg city council before the opening of the inquisitory proceedings against Hut. For there is in the archives of Augsburg another document, not yet published, a questionnaire drawn up for the first trial of Hut on Sept. 16, 1527. Even the very thorough and scholarly Friedrich Roth seems to have overlooked it. This manuscript is undated and is written in an almost illegible hand. It consists of 84 questions that were used for the first day of Hut's trial on September 16. Among them the articles of Nikolsburg are clearly recognizable. But Hut answered these questions definitely and briefly in the negative. And now that Hut's life and work have been made known and the Hutterite *Geschicht-Buch* is available, it can be positively asserted that Hut did not teach at least the two articles of Nikolsburg, that Christ is not God, and that He did not make satisfactory atonement for the sins of man. For two hymns composed by Hut, the "Communion Hymn" and the second one composed by him as "a prisoner of Christ," very clearly state his belief that Christ is God, and that through His death on the cross we have obtained salvation from the Father.

Concerning his attitude toward government, note Nadler's statement on Feb. 13, 1529, "Neither Hans Hut nor the pastor at Eltersdorf (Wolfgang Vogel), nor any other brother has said anything about revolt and the like," which corresponds with Hut's reply to this question before the court. The *Geschicht-Buch* confirms this idea: "This is the Hans Hut, who at Nikolsburg could not agree with Balthasar Hubmaier in the matter of the sword" (p. 47). Certainly the Hutterite chronicles would not have said of Hut that he died as a true servant of Jesus Christ if he had harbored such radical ideas as the articles of Nikolsburg attribute to him.

When Hubmaier, especially in his *Rechenschaft,* repeatedly attacked Hut sharply and charged him with deceptive and revolutionary teaching, he was certainly not thinking of the statements in the articles of Nikolsburg, but of Hut's rejection of the "sword" and of "war taxes."

That the Anabaptist preachers in Nikolsburg discussed the eight articles is impossible. According to the *Geschicht-Buch* the questions under discussion concerned "whether one should use the sword or not, and whether one should pay taxes for war." But at the same time it is indicated that other "doctrines" were also discussed. This is confirmed by the Anabaptist Hans Nadler of Erlangen, who said they also talked about "seven other decisions," namely baptism, communion, the judgment, the end of the world, the new kingdom in Revelation, and the coming of Christ (Cornelius, 281). But the chief topics of discussion were the sword and the payment of war taxes.

The discussion at Nikolsburg did not concern the Nikolsburg articles, but the "seven decisions,"

as Nadler confirms. But these originated with Hut, as he himself said in his epistle. Ambrosius Spittel-mayer (*q.v.*) also names these "seven decisions" in his cross-examination (*TA,* 49 f.); likewise Julius Lober (*q.v.*). Meissner's surmise is probably correct: "The problem of the Nikolsburg disputation with which the authorship of the Nikolsburg articles is inextricably connected by the report of Hut's trial of November 4, seems to be especially complicated by a persistent confusion. The seven decisions play a part here."

But how did the city council of Augsburg come to connect the Nikolsburg articles, all of which are included in the Augsburg questionnaire, with the Nikolsburg disputation? Meissner suggests, probably correctly, that there was a sort of preliminary sketch, not yet published, upon which the questionnaire was based. On the basis of this sketch Hut was to be questioned about his connections with Hubmaier. That there was only a sketch is clear from the fact that the court record of November 4 contains nearly fifty questions, and the sketch only four: (1) The council believes that many articles have been set up by Hut for the disputation at Nikolsburg; Hut shall show what these articles are; (2) What else he did there; (3) When he stayed there and when he left; (4) In any case the council wants to know what the Anabaptist secrets are and what their articles are.

The admission of the council in point four is worthy of notice. They had in their possession the "Augsburg Interrogatorium," but they saw in it not the "Anabaptist secrets and articles," but merely an interrogatorium. In order to learn something definite about the Nikolsburg disputation they again referred to the questionnaire, which contains a long list of heretical doctrinal statements. Indeed, Hut replied briefly to it in his cross-examination of September 16, and so they hoped certainly to learn more about it.

From the above sketch of the questions for the trial of November 4 it may be safely concluded that the Augsburg council did not take the "Nikolsburg articles" from a dependable Anabaptist source, for the statement that the council wanted especially to learn the Anabaptist secret and articles would be odd if they had been for "two months in possession of fourteen doctrinal statements of dogmatic theological and revolutionary content, whose origin lay in guaranteed Anabaptist circles" (Meissner).

Since there is no Anabaptist source as a preliminary basis we must look through the literature to see whether the Augsburg city council could not have received its information there, and in this review the work of Urban Rhegius, the violent opponent of the Augsburg Anabaptists, comes first to mind. This theologian was one of the skilled polemicists of the time. His argumentation is often artificial and casuistic, but in the capacity to exploit the statements of his opponents in his favor he achieves amazing results (Meissner). This capability of casting scanty material that contains little that shows guilt, into a devastating charge, Rhegius reveals in his first book against the Anabaptists, *Wider den neuen tauforden, notwendige Warnung an alle Christgläubigen durch die Diener des Evangelii zu*

Augsburg am 6. Tag September anno 1527. Loserth and Meissner also say that it is highly probable that Rhegius influenced the formulation of the articles.

So much at least is certain today, that it is no longer right to seek an Anabaptist origin for the Nikolsburg articles, and equally wrong to claim that they represent Anabaptist doctrines as they were set up for discussion in the disputation of Nikolsburg.   W.W.

A. Nicoladoni, *Johannes Bünderlin von Linz und die oberösterreichischen Täufergemeinden* (Berlin, 1893); C. A. Cornelius, *Gesch. des Münsterischen Aufruhrs* II (Leipzig, 1860); J. E. Jörg, *Deutschland in der Revolutionsperiode von 1522-1526* (Breisach, 1851); *TA Bayern* II; Wappler, *Thüringen;* Wiswedel, *Bilder* I; idem, "Die Nikolsburger Artikel," in *Ztscht für bayrische Kirchengeschichte*, 1938, 34-36; *ML* III, 260-62.

Nikoltschitz (Nickelschitz; Czech, *Nicolcice*), a village in the Zierotin domains in Moravia. Under the protection of Frederick of Zierotin, whom the Brethren called "our Fritz," they founded a Bruderhof here in 1570.

In 1602 this Bruderhof suffered considerably at the hands of the soldiers quartered in the region. On April 6, 1605, six horsemen broke in, stabbed one brother, shot another through the arm. At Christmas the Brethren were attacked while hauling grain to Olmütz, and one of them wantonly killed. In the following years troops on the way to and from Hungary fell upon the Nikoltschitz Bruderhof and others in the neighborhood, requisitioned much, and took away horses. At the beginning of the Thirty Years' War Nikoltschitz endured great suffering. On Sept. 18 and 21, 1619, Dämmerschitz and Nikoltschitz were plundered by Dampierre's army; doors, windows, and chests were broken, and many things taken. On October 18 "poor Nikoltschitz" was plundered for the third time, this time by Hungarian troops. Scarcely had they rebuilt and repaired this damage, when imperial troops broke into the Bruderhof on Jan. 28, 1621, and took leather, salt, lard, wool, and copper kettles. "Thereafter they continued to plunder until nothing was left." All the cattle were driven away from Nikoltschitz. The lists of the 24 Bruderhofs abandoned by compulsion in October 1622 found in the Breslau codex, the codex of Braitmichel in Gran, and codex Dreller in Sobotiste, include Nikoltschitz; this is correct. Most of the manuscripts erroneously name Nikolsburg (*q.v.*) in its place, but Nikolsburg was destroyed before this date. (Beck, *Geschichts-Bücher;* Zieglschmid, *Chronik;* Wolkan, *Geschicht-Buch; ML* III, 262 f.)   P.De.

Niles United Missionary Church, located just outside the city limits of Niles, Mich., is a member of the Indiana Conference. The meetinghouse was built in 1951. Ministers were Joseph Kimbel in 1951, Russel Miller 1951-53, Delmer Horn 1953-55, and Lloyd Murphy 1955- . The membership in 1956 was 20.   D.J.H.

Nimrich, Hemes, an Anabaptist preacher, was taken with several brethren to the gallows at Wittgenstein, Germany, in 1605, severely lashed, and then driven from the city with whips. Nothing more is known of him at present. (*Mart. Mir.* D 803, E 1103; *ML* III, 263.)

Ninth Street Mennonite Church (MC), Saginaw, Mich., was begun in 1950 as a mission for the colored people of the city and is still operated under the Mennonite Board of Missions and Charities, with partial support from the Board, though organized as a congregation. In 1956 the membership was 58, with LeRoy Bechler as pastor.   H.S.B.

Nippold, Friedrich (1838-1918), a German Protestant theologian, professor of church history in a number of universities: Heidelberg 1867-71, Bern 1871-84, and Jena 1884-1907, then lived in retirement in Oberursel. He was one of the founders of the Protestant League. In his youth he had become well acquainted with the Mennonites on both sides of the Dutch border. Until his death he was appreciative of and friendly toward the Mennonites. While he was teaching at the University of Jena he gave friendly assistance in the organization of the Vereinigung (*q.v.*) (a Mennonite conference in Germany), and participated in the examination of the first Mennonite theological students. In his writings he warmly defended the Mennonites. Among his articles and books were: *Berner Beiträge zur Geschichte der Schweizerischen Reformationskirchen* (1884); a new edition of Hagenbach's *Kirchengeschichte* (1885-87); *Handbuch der neuesten Kirchengeschichte* (1880-1906); various articles in the *Protestantische Jahr-Bücher* (especially 1887). Special mention must be made of his important monograph, "David Joris von Delft. Sein Leben, seine Lehre und seine Sekte," in *Zeitschrift für die historische Theologie*, 1863, 3-166, and 1864, 483-673.

Nippold was one of the first historians to take a position contrary to traditional biased historiography against the Mennonites. As early as 1861 he published in the *Allgemeine kirchliche Zeitschrift* (618-28) a treatise, "Die niederländischen Taufgesinnten," in which he demonstrated that the prevailing principle of the brotherhood in the Reformation period as well as later was not the rejection of infant baptism, but the establishment of the kingdom of God on earth, and that in the Netherlands they were "one of the most important ecclesiastical phenomena on Protestant soil." Even though external changes have come about in the process of development, nevertheless "the contrast of the simple Biblical standpoint with symbolic Christianity remains."

In another article in the *Protestantisches Monatsblatt* (December 1865) Nippold discussed the "Anabaptist Tendencies in Their Significance for Understanding the Period of the Reformation," and in his greatest work, *Handbuch der neuesten Kirchengeschichte* (third edition, Vol. I, 1889, p. IX f.), in which he traces a parallel between the various churches back to the Reformation, he presents a thorough correction of the customary manner of presenting church history, by showing that the basis is found in the central point of the Gospel, in a sketch of the kingdom of God. "But this very Gospel is buried under all sorts of dogmatic repainting." The need of a thorough correction of the traditional presentation of church history is very clear, and is being more strongly voiced by professional historians year by year, says Nippold. (*ML* III, 263 f.)

                                               HEGE, NEFF.

Nissley (Nisley, Nissli, Nüssli), a family name found among the Mennonites of the Lancaster Conference (MC) in eastern Pennsylvania and elsewhere, and among the Old Order Amish in the states of the midwest to which they have migrated: Indiana, Illinois, Iowa, and Kansas. The progenitor of the family was named Jakob Nissley from the Swiss Emmenthal, who died in Lancaster County in 1752. The spelling of his family name seems to have been uncertain. According to tradition it may have been Nutt or Nolt; but more likely it was Nuss or Nüssli. In any case his descendants are almost uniformly known by the name Nissley. Among them may be mentioned three bishops in the Lancaster Conference: Samuel Nissley (1761-1838), who was ordained as preacher in 1790 in the district west and north of Lancaster, and as bishop before 1800; Christian Nissley (1777-1831), who became a preacher in the Mount Joy area in 1812, and bishop in 1820; and Peter R. Nissley (1864-1921), who was ordained as a preacher in the Kraybill congregation in 1904, and bishop in 1911. There were numerous other Nissleys in the ministry in the Lancaster Conference. One of the best known of them was Joseph M. Nissley of Mount Joy, Pa., who served for many years as superintendent of the Altoona (Pa.) Mission, beginning in 1919. The Amish Nissleys may have a different progenitor from the above Jakob. In 1955 there were three Old Order Amish bishops named Nissley, one being Ira Nissley of Kalona, Iowa.   J.C.W.

Nitsche, Richard, author of *Geschichte der Wiedertäufer in der Schweiz zur Reformationszeit,* 107 pages (Einsiedeln and New York 1885), written from the Catholic point of view.

Nitschmann, David (1696-1772), chief bishop of the Moravian Brethren, who was consecrated on March 13, 1735, in Berlin, Germany, in the home of the court chaplain Daniel Ernst Jablonski, undertook many trips to America in the service of the Brethren. In this way he came to Amsterdam, where he became the friend of Johannes Deknatel (*q.v.*), the pietistic Mennonite preacher. In 1738, while he and Count Zinzendorf were staying in the Rönneburg Castle near Büdingen, Hesse, he wrote a letter to Deknatel dated June 19, 1738. He also wrote a second letter to Deknatel from Pennsylvania, dated Jan. 3, 1741. (*Menn. Bl.,* 1858, 32; *ML* III, 264.)
NEFF.

Nittert Obbesz: see **Obbes, Nittert.**

Nivenius, Johannes (Johan van Nieuveen), rector of the Old School in Amsterdam, wrote an account of the Anabaptist attack on Amsterdam in 1535 in Latin verse. It appeared in 1552 under the title *Tumultus Anabaptistarum in noblissimo totius Hollandiae emporio Amsteldamensi, nuper exorti descriptio.* C. G. Plemp (*q.v.*) published a Dutch translation in 1631 and also an enlarged and revised Latin edition in Antwerp, 1632. (*ML* III, 264.)   vDZ.

Niverville (Man.) **Chortitz** Mennonite Church is a subsidiary of the Chortitz Mennonite Church (*q.v.*), which originated in the early days of the settlement of the Mennonites on the East Reserve of Manitoba. The present elder of the total church, P. S. Wiebe, lives in the village of Chortitz. Originally a group worshiped a few miles from Niverville in the Reinland schoolhouse. After World War I a church was built in Niverville, which has recently been replaced by a new building with a seating capacity of 250-300 and a full basement. The church has a young people's program and Sunday-school activities. The local minister is P. F. Wiebe.
C.K.

Niverville (Man.) Mennonite Brethren Church, a member of the Manitoba Provincial and the Canadian District conferences, was organized on Oct. 8, 1933, with 69 members. In 1937 a new church building was erected. Three ministers and one deacon have been ordained. The baptized membership in 1955 was 140, with William W. Dyck as the leading minister.   H.NE.

Niverville (Man.) Mennonite Church (GCM) originated after World War I, when Mennonites from Russia settled in and around Niverville. In 1955 the congregation had 139 baptized members, with Jacob J. Klassen as leading minister and Wilhelm Buhler as deacon. The meetinghouse is located in the town of Niverville.   C.K.

Nizhnaya-Chortitza: see **Nieder-Chortitza.**

Noah's Ark, a former Mennonite meetinghouse in Amsterdam: see **Arke Noachs.**

Noë, a Mennonite family of Belgian Brabant, which lived in Antwerp. François Noë and Pereira de Mol were married there and about 1568 fled to Hamburg from Alba's (*q.v.*) catchpolls. François, the oldest of their children, became a rather wealthy man in Hamburg. Closely connected with the name of his son François Noë II is the first blossoming of the village of Altona and also the formation of a Mennonite congregation in Altona (*q.v.*). For it was François Noë II to whom Count Ernst von Schauenburg translated into action his proclamation of freedom to practice the crafts. The count assigned to Noë a place near Altona where he could build houses and settle people of all faiths, without the guilds being permitted to object. Under Ernst's successor the boundaries were more sharply defined. By thinking of his brethren in inviting settlers, Noë laid the foundation of the Altona congregation; for freedom of religion went hand-in-hand with freedom of crafts. Services were, of course, held in private. At the same time Noë had become a wealthy landowner, building nine houses in three years, many more than any other "privileged" person.

Little is known of Noë's business. He delivered to the count a sort of plush. The craftsmen he had brought in did not work for him, but only paid him rent, which in Hamburg was more expensive than in Altona. Nor is much known of his life. He died before 1636, for in that year his name in the record is followed by "deceased." None of his descendants showed his skill. They were soon lost to the Mennonite brotherhood.

Joost Noë, also a Mennonite, perhaps a relative

of François, who later fled from Antwerp to Franeker in Friesland, was a friend of the martyr Lenaert Plovier (*Mart. Mir.,* where he is erroneously called Nose, D 270, E 641). Other members of the Noë family, of which there are still some Mennonite descendants, are found in the 17th century at Danzig, in West Prussia (Kordt Noweh von Hamburg was a member of the Danzig congregation in 1681), Leeuwarden, and Amsterdam.   O.S., vdZ.

Bolton, *Historische Kirchennachrichten von Altona* I (1790); R. Ehrenberg, "**Gewerbefreiheit und Zunftzwang** in Ottensen und Altona **1543-1640**," in *Altona unter Schauenburgischer Herrschaft* (1892); R. Dollinger, *Gesch. der Menn. in Schleswig-Holstein, Hamburg und Lübeck* (Neumünster, 1930); B. C. Roosen, *Gesch. der Mennoniten-Gemeinde zu Hamburg und Altona* I (Hamburg, 1886) 10 f., 25, 29, 32 f., 36, 44; G. A. Wumkes *Stads- en Dorpskroniek van Friesland* II (Leeuwarden, 1934) 86, 313, 554; *ML* III, 264 f.

Noëlle Mazille, an Anabaptist martyr, the wife of Antoine Rogne (Anthonie de Rocke, *q.v.*), was drowned in a tub at Antwerp in the night of Aug. 20, 1558, because she refused to recant. Her name is found in the hymn "Aenhoort Godt, hemelsche Vader" (Hear, O God, heavenly Father), No. 16 of the *Lietboecxken van den Offer des Heeren.* vdZ.

Offer, 565; *Mart. Mir.* D 202, E 583; *Antw. Arch.-Blad* VIII, 447, 464; XIV, 24 f., No. 260; *DB* 1899, 109; Wolkan, *Lieder,* 63, 72; *ML* III, 64.

Nogaies, a nomadic, very warlike branch of the Tartars, who lived on the steppes of South Russia when the Mennonites founded the Molotschna (*q.v.*) settlement there, and who resented their coming, for they occupied a number of Nogai meadows. The Nogaies in revenge became guilty of theft, and on one occasion murdered four Mennonite men. The government then interfered and compelled the Nogaies to abandon their nomadic life. They later became friends with the Mennonites. In 1860 the tribe emigrated to Turkey. (*ML* III, 265.)   A.B.

Nolan Mennonite Brethren Church, now extinct, located in northeastern Michigan, had its beginning in 1907 when a number of M.B. families settled on land cleared of timber. Abraham Richert of Corn, Okla., organized the church and H. F. Janzen became its leader. Because of economic difficulties the settlers left and the church discontinued in 1919.
                                                            H.E.W.

Nold, Jacob (1765-1834), the first Mennonite (MC) bishop in Ohio, was born in Milford Twp., Bucks Co., Pa., of parents who came from the Palatinate, Germany, in 1754. He was ordained to the ministry March 30, 1794, and served the Swamp congregation, where he was later ordained a bishop. In 1813 he and Abraham Wismer conducted a tour of preaching appointments in Lancaster County. In the same year he and a few others came to Ohio evidently looking for a location. Four years later, in 1817, he moved to Ohio with his family, locating in Columbiana County just east of Leetonia. He was extremely active and energetic and is said to have been instrumental in effecting the organization of several congregations in Medina, Stark, and Wayne counties, serving these congregations as bishop, going from one to the other on foot or on horseback. Foot-

washing was optional in the Columbiana-Mahoning congregation in the early years, many being opposed to it. In order to have fellowship with the Wayne-Stark County Mennonites who favored it, Nold introduced footwashing in his home congregations as the result of great effort. This counsel with the Wayne-Stark group in time grew into the Ohio Mennonite Conference. Bishop Nold had a son Jacob Nold (1798-1864), who was the first Mennonite deacon in the Leetonia area, and who had a third edition of Christopher Dock's (*q.v.*) *Schulordnung* published at Columbiana, Ohio, in 1861.   W.D.S.

Nonconformity. *General.* Nonconformity has been and still largely is a major doctrine in the faith and life of the Anabaptist-Mennonite brotherhood. It is anchored directly to the Scripture passage (Romans 12:1, 2) in which Paul says: "I beseech you therefore, brethren, by the mercies of God, that ye present your bodies a living sacrifice, holy, acceptable unto God, which is your reasonable service. And be not conformed to this world: but be ye transformed by the renewing of your mind, that ye may prove what is that good, and acceptable, and perfect, will of God." Other Scripture passages are also used, such as (I John 1:15, 16) "Love not the world, neither the things that are in the world. If any man love the world, the love of the Father is not in him. For all that is in the world, the lust of the flesh, and the lust of the eyes, and the pride of life, is not of the Father, but is of the world"; and (I Peter 2:11) "Dearly beloved, I beseech you as strangers and pilgrims, abstain from fleshly lusts, which war against the soul." The German has no exactly corresponding term for nonconformity, although the phrase "Nichtgleichstellung mit der Welt" and its counterpart "Weltförmigkeit" have often been used. "Weltlichkeit" corresponds to the English term "worldliness."

The concept of nonconformity is not unique to Anabaptists or Mennonites, but it has found an unusually intense and detailed application among them, particularly in earlier groups and at certain times in their history, such as 16th-17th century Holland, and 19th-20th century North America, especially among the more conservative bodies. In the course of Christian history all earnest Christian groups who have taken the concept of discipleship seriously and have sought to apply Christian ethical principles vigorously to their everyday life, have had to come to grips with the problem of the relation of the Christian to the world, to society, and to culture. This has been true in the early church, in the monastic solution to the problem of worldliness in the medieval church, in the medieval sects such as the Waldenses, in the Anabaptists of the Reformation period, in the various pietistic movements including the Moravians, and the Wesleyan movement and its modern descendants, etc. The practical answers have not always been the same, but the general principle of nonconformity to the spirit, ideals, and culture of the non-Christian world or a seriously diluted Christian culture, sometimes called sub-Christian, and an attempt to mold life after the image of Christ, has been the same.

The content of the concept of nonconformity as

held by Mennonites has been compounded out of a complex of ideas and factors. One of these is the clear Biblical teaching on holiness and purity of life, on obedience to the teaching of Christ and "following after Him," and on taking up the cross, particularly the cross of suffering. The positive and negative aspects, nonconformity to the world and conformity to God's holy nature and will, are commonly teamed together, but at times the negative idea has become dominant, probably in part because of the easy availability of the negative word, and the lack of a corresponding positive word, the nearest being "holiness." However, Mennonites have seldom used the word "holiness" and are reluctant to do so in modern times because of its association with certain types of "holiness" doctrine and piety current in America. Another idea in the complex is that of being "pilgrims and strangers" on the earth, with "no abiding city here" but with a "citizenship in heaven." This involves the relativization of human society and culture and emphasis upon the transcendent value of relationship to God and of the future life with Him in a world to come, and easily turns into an other-worldly emphasis of either indifference to or rejection of many cultural values and expressions. Another idea is that of asceticism, the deliberate denial of certain material and human values for the good of the spiritual life or as an expression of anti-worldliness. Even just the emphasis on high Christian ethical ideals of purity, love, and righteousness, with which contemporary non-Christian or "nominal" Christian ethical ideas and practices stand in contrast, logically merges into a concept of nonconformity, derived from other ideas. Then there is the concept of a people of God, separate from other people and from the world. This is a major idea in the Old Testament, and carries over into the New Testament concept of the kingdom of God and the Church of Christ. (John 10: "I am the good shepherd, and know my sheep." "My sheep hear my voice." Luke 12: "Fear not, little flock; for it is your Father's good pleasure to give you the kingdom." John 17: "I pray not that thou shouldest take them out of the world, but that thou shouldest keep them from the evil. They are not of the world, even as I am not of the world." II Cor. 6: "Be ye not unequally yoked together with unbelievers." "Wherefore come out from among them, and be ye separate." "I will be their God, and they shall be my people." I Peter 2: "But ye are a chosen generation, a royal priesthood, an holy nation, a peculiar people." "But are now the people of God." Gal. 6: "The Israel of God.")

The persecution and oppression of the Anabaptists and Mennonites by the state and church authorities not only of the Reformation period, but of the following centuries until the 19th century, added intensity and urgency to the idea of nonconformity, but did not create it. Mennonites were not considered citizens in most areas until late in the 18th century and beyond, or were at least treated as a special class of citizens or inhabitants, and given special privileges of exemption from military service and the oath, which set them apart from the ordinary citizen of the country. The often intense and bitter opposition of the state church clergy to all

dissenters, whom they called "sects," intensified this feeling of separateness. And the fact that in most areas the church and state were coextensive contributed to an identification by the Mennonites, sometimes too radically, of the state church structure with the world per se. Both state and church shared in the persecution and both tolerated unholy and worldly living, hence the idea of a separation from both merged imperceptibly into the idea of nonconformity. The rise of pietistic influence upon the Mennonites, first in Hamburg and then in the Palatinate in the 18th century, and soon also in West Prussia in certain sections, and the strong influence of the Gemeinschaft movement (*q.v.*) in South Germany, Alsace, and Switzerland in the late 19th and 20th centuries contributed further to the general idea of nonconformity. However, the very familiarity of Mennonitism with Pietism and the Gemeinschaft movement also contributed to the breakdown and ultimate disappearance of the uniquely Mennonite emphasis on nonresistance, nonparticipation in state affairs, and general withdrawal from public life. Mennonite conformity in these areas now became more a general all-Christian emphasis upon a warm piety and personal holiness. In this process the conscious Mennonite tradition itself was de-emphasized and often discredited and even broken off completely, even to the point of abandoning the name Mennonite because of its connection of nonconformity.

The propagation and maintenance of the idea and practice of nonconformity among Mennonites has been carried largely by three forces—tradition, indoctrination, and discipline. In the close-knit self-conscious congregation or settlement group, with strong solidarity, deeply rooted tradition, and distinct separation from the surrounding culture, it has usually been taken for granted with little written regulation or deliberate group decision. In times of struggle with the forces of accommodation and strong environmental influence, usually more weight has been put upon deliberate teaching and specific regulations adopted by conferences or ministerial leadership. The device of church schools to support nonconformity has also been consciously introduced. All of these methods have operated with varying success and the emphasis has shifted from one type of action to another as deemed necessary.

The problems related to the practice of nonconformity have caused much trouble in Mennonite history and have been major factors in schisms, particularly in Holland and the United States. It is notable that practically never has any significant Mennonite schism occurred over doctrinal questions. It was more often questions of discipline, particularly in relation to nonconformity, that led to breaks in personal and group relations. The Dutch schisms from 1560 to 1700 practically all involved major or minor aspects of nonconformity. In America the labels "progressive" and "conservative" as applied to different orientations in Mennonite groups usually refer to attitudes on nonconformity or separation from the world, although they also at times refer to methods of church work and forms of worship.

The close interrelation of nonconformity and nonresistance should also be noted. History reveals that the maintenance or loss of one involves the other, and that as groups weaken on nonconformity they tend to weaken on nonresistance. While this is not absolutely true and need not be so, it has occurred often enough to give considerable ground for a generalization. The reason is probably not to be found in the logical connection of the two ideas, but rather in the fact that both positions are not popular in Christendom and can only be maintained by vigorous effort and readiness to oppose main elements in Western culture.

The following discussion will deal with the ideal and practice of nonconformity among the Mennonites under the following subdivisions: (1) Netherlands; (2) Europe, aside from the Netherlands; (3) The Mennonite Church (MC), and related groups in North America; (4) the General Conference Mennonite Church in North America; and (5) Other groups in North and South America.

H.S.B.

C. J. Cadoux, *The Early Church and the World* (New York, 1925); G. J. Heering, *The Fall of Christianity* (New York, 1943); H. R. Niebuhr, *Christ and Culture* (New York, 1951); George R. Brunk, *Ready Scriptural Reasons* (Scottdale, 1926); Daniel Kauffman, *Doctrines of the Bible* (Scottdale, 1928); Richard R. Caemmerer, *The Church in the World* (St. Louis, 1949); H. R. Niebuhr, W. Pauck, and F. P. Miller, *The Church Against the World* (New York, 1935); J. C. Wenger, *Separated unto God; a Plea for Christian Simplicity of Life and for a Scriptural Nonconformity to the World* (Scottdale, 1951); C. Henry Smith, "Mennonites and Culture," *MQR* XII (1938) 71-84; *Proceedings of the Fourth Mennonite World Conference* (Akron, 1950), containing the following papers: "The Divine Imperative of Nonconformity to the World" by Frank and Harry Wenger; "The History of Nonconformity Among Mennonites" by Donovan Smucker; "The Purpose and Power of Nonformity" by Pierre Widmer; and "The Limitations of Nonconformity" by Paul Mininger.

(1) *Netherlands.* Nonconformity as a practice of difference in dress and of difference in style of living as compared with other Christians and non-Christians is at the present time not found among the Dutch Mennonites. They dress like other people, partake in the cultural life and the common amusements like theater and cinema, and have no objection to smoking or drinking alcoholic beverages; they do not reject voting and by far the majority assume the obligation of serving in the army. In all these matters the church does not give any regulations or prohibitions, leaving to each member individually the decision on his private attitude to life.

This free responsibility of the Dutch Mennonites is largely due to the fact that they, at least since the early 17th century, have not lived in separated and closed groups like the Mennonites of some other countries, but have lived in towns and from early times have been engaged in businesses of various kinds, closely associated with other Christians. Besides this, the fact that they esteemed the government and the country where they were permitted to live quietly may have largely contributed to the loss of nonconformity in the sense of antithesis to the pattern of life of other Christians. In a higher sense the Dutch Mennonite always has been aware of a difference between the "world" and the "kingdom of God," and being convinced in his heart that

the "world" is always to be appraised lower than the kingdom of God, he has the responsibility of faith to decide in each case where he is to draw the line between "world" and the kingdom. Thus he has to practice what may be called ethical nonconformity.

For the early Anabaptists and Mennonites in Holland these matters were quite different. They were a plain people, living in a period of persecution; and led by their eschatological views they expected the destruction of this world and the coming of the new aeon in the near future, which drew a sharp line between the church and the world, and between Christian life and worldly life. Though they did not make any special regulations or prohibitions before the resolutions of Wismar in 1554 (found in *BRN* VII, 52-54, and K. Vos, *Menno Simons,* 123-27, and *Writings,* 1041 f.), their attitude toward the world involved a special style of life, and even after the eschatological belief was dropped, they observed a plain style of living, including plain dress, houses, furniture, and food, though they never practiced asceticism, for example never prohibiting the use of beer, then the common beverage. Many from abroad, who visited and studied the Dutch Mennonites, like Benthem (1698) and Rues (1741), were struck by their "humility in dressing" and their "simplicity of life."

But after the congregations became established and organized, a difference appeared between those who wanted to maintain strictly the old plainness, and those who regarded these matters as insignificant and did not want to make any regulations.

One of the sources of the Flemish-Frisian schism in 1566-67 was the feeling of the Mennonites of Friesland that those from Flanders were dressed too worldly. The Flemish immigrants on their part accused the Frisians of paying too much attention to their houses and furniture. In the preface to the martyr's book of 1615 Hans de Ries states that the simplicity of the Mennonites had been changed into pomp and show; possessions having increased while the souls became impoverished, their clothing had become magnificent, but "the inward adornment" had been lost. From then on, the lamentations about luxury and worldliness are numerous. One illustration is Jacob Cornelisz van Dalen (*q.v.*), a preacher in the Waterlander congregation at Amsterdam, who in 1652 published a collection of sermons along this line under the title *Onciersel en cieraet van de godsalige vrouwen* (Disfigurement and Adornment of the Godly Women), in which he attacked the inclination to ostentation both in dress and furniture and the custom of pompous weddings, "in which the Mennonites follow outright those who serve the world." Galenus Abrahamsz (*q.v.*) of Amsterdam in his sermons often urged the congregation to soberness of clothing and house appointments and repeatedly warned against superabundance in food and drinks. Peter Langendijk (*q.v.*) in his poem *De Zwitsersche Eenvoudigheid* (Swiss Simplicity, lamenting the depraved morals of many Dutch Mennonites) of 1713 exaggerates somewhat, but nevertheless it is true, as was also observed by some Prussian immigrants settling in Holland in 1734 (*Inv. Arch. Amst.* I, No. 2041), that many

Dutch Mennonites did not differ much from other people as to the style of their living.

Sometimes regulations were drawn up concerning the matter of nonconformity. The Waterlanders in their delegates' meeting at Amsterdam 1647 renewed the resolutions of 1581 to urge the preachers to warn against the loss of nonconformity in matters of dress, meals, homes, and trade (*DB* 1877, 62-93), and the Frisian Conference of North Holland drew up twelve articles in 1639, enlarged in 1697, which deal with nonconformity in various matters (Blaupot t. C., *Holland* II, 223-28). These resolutions, however, did not prohibit, but merely gave advice. The Groningen Old Flemish group passed a resolution in their conference at Loppersum in 1659 (Blaupot ten Cate, *Friesland*, 307 f.), making a number of restrictions and forbidding certain things; these regulations were strictly maintained for about a century, and many were banned for breaking the precepts and inclining to unseemly luxury in dress and furnishings. The extremely conservative groups of Danzig Old Flemish and Jan-Jacobsgezinden, all together called "Fijne Mennisten," may have had regulations of the same kind, watching that the members did not trespass even in small matters like the style of haircutting.

Of such regulations nothing is found either among the Lamists of the 17th and 18th centuries, or among the Zonists. In the matter of refusing to accept office in the government the Zonists were stricter than the Lamists, though some Mennonites of both groups, particularly in the country, served as sheriffs, bailiffs, and in other functions even in the 17th century. In general there was no objection against business and trade, though Mennonites are said to have objected to the reprehensible practices as often found in business. Mennonite merchants and bankers had a reputation of great fairness and honesty. Yet some Mennonites objected to business, particularly for preachers. Binnert Tjallings of Grouw, when he was appointed preacher in 1781, retired from business because it seemed improper to him to be a preacher of the Gospel and at the same time to be involved in worldly matters of business. Klaas Rinses Koopmans had also taken this step when he became a preacher of the Leeuwarden congregation in 1772. "Outside marriage" (marriage with non-members of the church) originally was not allowed, as is stated in the Waterlander resolutions of 1568 and held by the Groningen Old Flemish until the 18th century, but among the Waterlanders, "outside marriage" was found as early as about 1620, and a few decades after also in the Lamist and Zonist congregations. Originally the Mennonites, when they had a difference with other members of the congregation, did not take the matter to a secular court. It cannot be stated how long this aversion to litigation lasted among the Dutch Mennonites (in 1613, Mennonites of Amsterdam did not ask the decision of the court), but apparently it soon disappeared, for as early as 1620 there are cases of Mennonites settling their disputes before the secular courts. A privilege granted by Prince William I of Orange in 1577 exempted the Dutch Mennonites from rendering an oath. This privilege is still in force and strictly observed by the Dutch Mennonites.

From the beginning until the end of the 17th century the Mennonites in the Netherlands did not take up military service; during the 18th century this doctrine gradually fell into decline, though there were a number of cases even in the last decades of the 18th century to show that on this point nonconformity had not yet been entirely lost. In the Napoleonic period (about 1810) some Mennonites were forced to serve in the army, but it was not until 1830 (Dutch war with Belgium) that Mennonites became volunteer soldiers. Though until 1898 there was no compulsory military service in the Netherlands, those who had objections having the opportunity of hiring a substitute, from about 1860 on there has been a rather high percentage of Mennonites in the army, especially in the higher ranks.

Surveying the matter of nonconformity as a whole, the Dutch Mennonites, though originally "separate," now do not differ from other Dutchmen.   vDZ.

H. W. Meihuizen, "Die Gemeinde in der Welt, aber nicht von der Welt," in *Die Gemeinde und ihr Auftrag* (Karlsruhe, 1953) 210-18; N. van der Zijpp, *Geschiedenis der Doopsgezinden in Nederland* (Arnhem, 1952) 133-56; C. N. Wijbrands, *Het Menniste Zusje* (repr. 1913); S. Hoekstra, *Leer der Oude Doopsgezinden* (Amsterdam, 1863); Yearbook *Amstelodamum* XXV (1928) 71; Irvin Horst, "Simplicity Laments Corrupted Manners," *Menn. Life* X (July 1955) 129.

(2) *Europe, aside from the Netherlands.* The Mennonites of Switzerland, South Germany, and France, believing strongly in the spiritual principle of nonconformity, have sought to apply it practically in nonconformity in life and separation from the world. The first three centuries of their history with its severe persecution added to their strong distrust of the "world." In these centuries when they were rejected by society in general, often oppressed and restricted in their manner of life, occupation, and even place of residence by official decrees, and subject to exile, the problem of nonconformity to the world was not a difficult one. They rejected the holding of civil office and all participation in government, as well as all litigation and swearing of oaths. They clung tenaciously to the Biblical doctrine of peace and nonresistance, and therefore rejected all participation in war and military service. They accepted the stigma associated with not practicing infant baptism which was, in the lands where they dwelt, a universally observed rite. They strictly opposed marriage with persons outside the brotherhood. They maintained a general simplicity in costume, home furnishings, and manner of life, although no specific or uniform costume was developed except that the Amish (after 1697) required the beard for men, and the wearing of hooks and eyes instead of buttons by all. Since these Mennonites and Amish were always strongly rural and very conservative in general, there was little direct contact with society and its changing culture, and little tendency to "worldly" fashions and practices. European rural society was itself conservative and slow in changing, and "fashions" as such were considered to be the prerogative of the urban and upper classes, not permitted to peasants and rural people. Thus a good, consistent general position on nonconformity was maintained until into the 19th century.

The 19th century witnessed a gradual transformation of the relationship of these groups to the society and culture round about them. As the old restrictions imposed by law fell away and modern culture began to penetrate the relatively isolated rural Mennonite groups, the Mennonites began to participate in the general culture and gradually lost their sense of distinctiveness and with it the desire to be different from the surrounding culture. This occurred most rapidly in the North German urban Mennonitism (Hamburg, Emden, Crefeld, Danzig), then in the Palatinate, and last of all in the rest of South Germany, Alsace-Lorraine, and Switzerland. The threat to nonresistance and nonconformity under the Napoleonic regime led to the calling of two special conferences of the Palatine congregations at Ibersheim in 1803 and 1805, where resolutions were passed reaffirming the historic Mennonite position on these two principles, with specific prohibition of military service and office holding. But this did not prevent the gradual loss of both positions. By the beginning of the 20th century the distinctive Mennonite position on nonconformity had disappeared practically everywhere, and office holding and military service were tolerated, even though not universally accepted. No distinctive practices in costume were maintained except the resistance to the cutting of women's hair in the second quarter of the 20th century. The prayer veiling gradually disappeared. Only the nonswearing of oaths remained as a remnant of distinctiveness everywhere. In Switzerland resistance to noncombatant military service has remained relatively strong, though not universal, down to the present day. In general in France and Switzerland, also in the Verband (q.v.) in South Germany, a certain spirit of simplicity and opposition to the crasser forms of worldliness has persisted, such as card playing, dancing, theater attendance, and the use of cosmetics. For Germany as a whole the verdict of Ernst Crous (article **Germany**, *ME* II, 490) may well stand, "Thus the world overcame nonconformity"; but this is not quite true for the Verband congregations in the South, where both the ideal and practice of nonconformity are still held to a certain extent.

However, this loss of outward nonconformity did not come without a struggle in some areas. Evidence of this is to be found in the content of the *Gemeindeblatt der Mennoniten,* founded in 1870 as the organ of the Verband. From its beginning there was in its columns a vigorous effort to maintain the sense of separation and holiness which had for centuries characterized the Mennonites. Ulrich Hege of Reihen, the first editor, wrote many articles on church discipline, on opposing marriages outside the church, etc. He published various excerpts from Anabaptist writings, including Menno Simons and the *Martyr's Mirror,* on such topics as baptism and communion. A sample article on the subject of nonconformity was (July 1887) "Gleichförmigkeit mit der Welt," in which the writer points out that Christians are forbidden to love the world, and the Apostle Paul calls for not being conformed to the world; but that there are, alas, many lukewarm Christians in contemporary Christendom. The writer admits, of course, that there are no detailed appli-

cations of the principle in Scripture, but finds that the general principle is quite clear. Since Christians cannot be conformed to the world, he argues, there is no other possible view for a believer to take than that of nonconformity; God's Word demands it, and Scripture must be obeyed.

In the West Prussian Mennonite rural group around Danzig and Elbing, and along the lower Vistula and the Vistula delta, the development was very similar to that in the South German, French, and Swiss Mennonites, with the exception that some dancing and patronage of local inns (*Wirtshäuser*) was tolerated in the 20th century.

In the urban Mennonite congregations in Germany, such as Emden, Crefeld, Hamburg-Altona, Danzig, Elbing, and Königsberg, the accommodation to the world, the acceptance of office holding and military service, and the dropping of any outward expression of nonconformity to the world came much earlier, and paralleled more nearly the history in Holland, with which there were close connections. This was due probably as much to the greater wealth of the families as to the influence of the urban environment.

In Russia the ideal and practice of nonconformity was made both more easy and more difficult by the pattern of settlement in the closed colonies, founded from 1789 on, and the grant of cultural autonomy to Mennonites by the Russian state, including special recognition of the Mennonite principle of nonresistance. The level of ethical and cultural life of the Mennonites was on the whole so much higher than the surrounding Russian culture and morals that there was little pull away from Mennonitism toward accommodation to the surrounding world. The principle of nonresistance was never exposed to real danger by any acculturation process, and when the government threatened to withdraw exemption from military service the threat of emigration caused a restoration of the privilege. Since the Mennonites who came to Russia from West Prussia had no particular form of costume or similar outward regulations, although in general simplicity of dress and manner of life, sobriety of deportment, and high standards of business dealings prevailed, costume never became a serious issue in Russia, particularly since the rural Mennonite settlements were far removed from the influences of urban culture and fashion. However, the prevalent complete separation from the Russian society made a practical identification of Mennonite Church and Mennonite community almost inevitable, and the retention of unbaptized persons and of spiritually indifferent baptized persons in the general complex of Mennonitism tended to obscure clear-cut ethical and behavior lines and to confuse thinking on the church and the world. The reaction of the Kleine Gemeinde (1812) in the Molotschna, and the Mennonite Brethren movement (1860) in the Molotschna and Chortitza settlements, was by the clear testimony of its leaders directed largely against the dilution of spiritual and ethical standards and performance in the Mennonite settlements and the encroachment of "worldliness," with which, in their mind, the established church leadership seemed either unable or unwilling to cope. Hence these two groups, as well as all the other schismatic groups in Russia (K.M.B., Peters group, etc.), taught and disciplined vigorously on matters of nonconformity and worldliness, and succeeded in promoting a relative elevation of general patterns of living both in their own groups and in the general Mennonite society. They were strong against the moral looseness which had developed in the toleration of drinking in the inns, for instance, and related undesirable practices. However, although these new Mennonite groups emphasized general strictness of discipline and simplicity of dress and manners, they did not develop uniform costume patterns. The Kleine Gemeinde, however, was inclined to a considerable degree of legalism and formalism along with its spiritual strength (Friesen, *Brüderschaft*).

The attitude toward alcohol and tobacco among Mennonites in general deserves a special note. It is only in the late 19th and the early 20th century that prohibition of drinking and smoking (see **Alcohol** and **Tobacco**) became a fixed part of Mennonite nonconformity either in Europe or America. Where it has done so, it has come in from outside influences, such as the temperance movement. It is interesting to note that in the most radically culturally nonconformed American group, the Old Order Amish, there is still no general prohibition of drinking and smoking. The same has been true of smoking in the conservative nonconformed groups in Eastern Pennsylvania, including the Franconia and Lancaster conferences, where dress nonconformity has been strictly maintained, but where smoking has only recently been disappearing. H.S.B.

Ernst Crous, "Mennonites in Germany Since the Thirty Years' War," *MQR* XXV (1951) 235-62; *idem*, "Wie die Mennoniten in die deutsche Volksgemeinschaft hineinwuchsen," *Gesch.-Bl.* 1939, 13-24.

(3) *Mennonite Church (MC) and Related Groups in North America.* American Mennonites in the 20th century are divided into several distinct groups, some of which differ rather sharply from other groups in the matter of nonconformity. The stricter groups, such as the Old Order Amish, Old Order Mennonites, and Old Colony, almost identify certain items of 18th- or 19th-century culture with the will of God, while the culturally more liberal groups have but little sense of difference from the world and its culture except on nonresistance, the rejection of the oath, and secret societies. A middle position is taken by the largest group of American Mennonites, the Mennonite Church (MC). A typical member of this body would, ideally at least, hold that nonconformity applies to every area of life. In business it means the avoidance of the "unequal yoke" with unbelievers, i.e., not entering into business partnership with non-Christians, maintenance of strict standards of honesty and integrity, a willingness to remain content with a smaller business in order to have much time and energy left for the life and service of the church, and the rejection of litigation to collect debts. In relation to the state he would not hold any office which would violate the principle of nonresistance, such as an executive, legislative, or judicial position, or serving as sheriff, constable, etc., and for some it means not even voting for any political office, although serving on a local school board might be al-

lowed. As to costume, the fashions of the world are rejected (although the general conventions of contemporary culture are followed), no jewelry is worn, and in certain large parts of the church at least a considerable portion of the members still maintain a "plain" garb which differs from the common dress, more particularly for women, but also for men, especially at church services. The mustache is avoided because it originally had a military association. The Old Order Amish and the Church of God in Christ Mennonites require the beard. The oath is rejected absolutely, and instead a simple affirmation is used for legal documents and in court. In general demeanor one seeks to be restrained and quiet, rather than loud, talkative, or boastful. In recreation various activities are forbidden, such as card playing, theater attendance, commercial motion pictures, pool-playing and dancing. Membership in secret societies is rejected because of the oath, hierarchical titles, religious relativism, and the secrecy practiced. Marriages with "outsiders," i.e., non-Christians or non-Mennonites is almost unknown; it was formerly forbidden completely though now more often than not tolerated, except in the most conservative groups. Meetinghouses are simple and functional, and in no case carry steeples or bells. Musical instruments are not used in worship. Women members wear a veil on their heads during worship in obedience to I Corinthians 11. Both a highly liturgical service and a noisy type of religious enthusiasm are rejected for a more sober and quiet form of piety and worship. In economics there is a strong emphasis on mutual and brotherly aid and stewardship rather than on individualism which puts an undue emphasis on self-seeking and wealth-seeking, although materialism is a constant temptation. In earlier times even taking interest from a brother was not permitted; in the 20th century this has been reduced to limiting the rate of interest to what is considered reasonable. There are, however, still Mennonites who do not charge interest on money loaned to a needy person.

The standard of nonconformity upheld by the church has been high, but the level of performance has sometimes sagged. Sometimes also what was intended to be only a consistent Biblical emphasis on nonconformity has tended to become the freezing of neutral social conventions of the past which are without any direct moral or spiritual significance or value in life or witness. Nonconformity has also at times been confused with a rejection of modern inventions, or identified with a rejection of the fine arts or the maintenance of the German language. This has been particularly true with the Old Order Amish, Old Order Mennonites, and Old Colony Mennonites, who have variously rejected the automobile, telephone, electricity, carpets, curtains, pictures, etc., and maintained certain German dialects, such as Pennsylvania German and Plattdeutsch.

Some groups and sections have identified ruralism with nonconformity, forbidding living in town or working in industry or business, and restricting occupations to farming and farm-related work. This has often meant a retreat into a pattern of rural sociological group life and withdrawal, with a consequent denial of evangelistic responsibility or witness, and even complacency about the group's spiritual life. Again, nonconformity patterns have sometimes been advocated on the grounds of "distinctiveness," that is, using outward marks of separation as devices to aid in the maintenance of spiritual nonconformity and to resist the process of acculturation, and to help ward off temptation to ungodliness. There has been some confusion between the concepts of nonconformity and separation, and between principles and applications. There has been a confused identification of "worldliness" with mere variation in cultural convention from age to age and place to place. There has also been considerable difference as to the degree of severity of discipline to be used to maintain nonconformity. Some have confused nonconformity with uniformity, or have felt that uniformity—e.g., in costume—is necessary to maintain nonconformity. Problems have also arisen when foreign mission work has been undertaken in lands with their own cultural conventions which are quite different from those of North America or the North American mother churches. Confused attempts have been made to impose the particular external nonconformity practices—e.g., in costume—of the sending group upon the newer indigenous churches, with attendant tensions and problems.

The struggle to maintain true Scriptural nonconformity continues to be a major problem for the Mennonite Church (MC). With the acceleration of cultural change in American life and the pervasiveness of modern American urban cultural influences through almost universal advertising, periodical reading, radio, and television, even the most withdrawn groups are subjected to pressures to surrender principles, not to speak of the more open groups. Universal compulsory education up to and including high school with the accompanying generally lower ethical standards often constitutes a severe test. Consequently increasingly recourse is being taken to church high schools and elementary schools, some sixty of the latter and ten of the former having been established in recent years. Attempts have been made to forbid radio and television in the homes, often largely because of the concern to keep out influences militating against standards of nonconformity.

As the former barriers to intercourse with the larger society and general culture fall, such as language, rural remoteness, or costume, the more open groups discover it increasingly difficult to maintain a clear and strong position on nonconformity. The moving line of demarcation between the church and the world is increasingly hard to define; sincere and honest people differ on where to establish it. The result is a certain amount of internal tension, which at times has resulted in local schisms and some estrangement between areas and groups or between the generations. The problem of unity becomes intensified, and the threat of undue diversion from more urgent spiritual tasks to struggles over the definition of the nonconformity frontier and the details of application becomes very real. Considerable numbers of members in certain areas become alienated by the atmosphere of what seems to them legalism and formalism and arbitrary action of church leaders and leave the church. On the other hand, bishops and pastors, alarmed by trends which they find difficult to comprehend or halt and fearful for the loss of real nonconformity and spiritual decline, are tempted to reach for increasingly repressive and authoritarian measures to meet the need. That in the face of all this the Mennonite Church (MC) has maintained unity and solidarity together with substantial spiritual and practical nonconformity and an increasingly strong evangelistic and mission outreach as well as a large general service program, and also largely retained its youth, is an indication of the vitality both of the spiritual heritage and the spiritual forces at present at work in the group.

The tensions within the Old Order Amish group in recent years over the degree of nonconformity and separation from the world, as well as over other questions, have become so serious as to result in repeated local schisms and the formation of new groups, such as the Beachy Amish. There has also been a constant and significant loss of members to the Conservative Mennonite Church and the Mennonite Church (MC). (See also **Dress**.)

J.C.W., H.S.B.

Biblical and Practical Nonconformity (published by the Bible School Board of the Lancaster Conference, Lancaster, 1950); *Declaration of Commitment in Respect to Christian Separation and Nonconformity to the World* (A statement of position adopted by the Mennonite General Conference, MC, Scottdale, 1955); General Problems Committee, *A Book of Standards* (Scottdale, 1940); *Bible Teaching on Nonconformity* (Scottdale, 1940); David Sherk, *Nonconformity to the World* (Elkhart, 1882); J. C. Wenger, *Historical and Biblical Position of the Mennonite Church on Attire* (Scottdale, 1944); *Proceedings of the Fourth Mennonite World Conference* (Akron, 1948) contains the following papers: Frank and Harry Wenger, "The Divine Imperative of Nonconformity"; Don. E. Smucker, "The History of Nonconformity Among the Mennonites"; Pierre Widmer, "The Purpose and Power of Nonconformity"; Paul Mininger, "The Limitations of Nonconformity."

(4) *The General Conference Mennonite Church,* organized in 1860, though now composed of groups with different cultural and ethnic backgrounds, had its original nucleus in a Pennsylvania-German group of Mennonites who seceded in 1847 from the Franconia Conference of the Mennonite Church (MC) in Eastern Pennsylvania. The secession was in large part a reaction against an overemphasis on literalistic adherence to nonconformity as expressed in traditional forms of dress and personal and social conduct. The new conference assumed that the changes it advocated could be made without sacrifice of the New Testament principle of separation from the world. It argued that adherence to traditional church regulations was not necessarily practicing the principle of apostolic nonconformity to the world; nor that departure from these traditions was necessarily violating Christian principles of separation from the world as taught in Rom. 12:1, 2. In brief, it claimed that many of the old forms were outmoded and actually hindered the most effective kind of Christian witnessing.

The coming of the large number of Mennonite immigrants from Switzerland in the middle of the 19th century to Ohio and Indiana, and toward the end of that same century of immigrants from Russia, Prussia, and Poland to Kansas, Nebraska, South Dakota, and Minnesota, strengthened the General

Conference membership, giving new life, more spiritual strength and vigor, and more advance in the major concerns of the Conference such as the development of Sunday schools, higher education, missions, trained ministers, congregational church government, and a greater degree of individual freedom of choice in such matters as dress and social conduct.

In principle the General Conference Mennonites have always stressed nonconformity to the world. In practice, however, there has been wide variation in interpreting this principle. Since the Conference, in the United States at least, has no centralized ruling system, and since each congregation is its own authority in matters of faith and conduct, and because of a heterogeneous background, time has tended to accent rather than minimize differences in observance of separation from the world. In many instances local congregations leave matters, except in extreme cases, almost totally up to the individual believer.

In the most recent revised General Conference constitution, the part dealing with "The Basic Faith" says with regard to the separated life: " . . . membership in oath-bound secret societies, military organizations, or other groups which tend to compromise the loyalty of the Christian to the Lord and to his church is contrary to such apostolic admonitions: 'Be not unequally yoked with unbelievers' (II Cor. 6:14-15), and that the Church should be 'holy and without blemish' (Eph. 5:27)." In addition to these and several other references the "Statement of Doctrine" of the Cornelis Ris *Articles of Faith* is approved as authoritative conference practice.

The fact that there is no uniform pattern of nonconformity in General Conference Mennonite churches does not imply that there is no effort on the part of individual congregations to exercise control over members in an effort to secure genuinely devout forms of behavior. Most congregations have exercised discipline on members whose conduct deviated too far from defined norms. The areas in which discipline has been most frequently exercised are in matters of military service, secret societies, and moral matters such as fornication, adultery, and remarriage of divorced individuals. Such practices as the use of tobacco and alcoholic beverages are generally discouraged but are not forbidden. Matters relating to attendance at theaters, motion pictures, and professional sports, or the use of radios, television, and other modern conveniences are handled variously from congregation to congregation. In few, if any, congregations is a member suspended or expelled for purchasing these items or engaging in any of these activities.

There is general recognition of the need for stronger emphasis on the separated life for modern Christians within the General Conference Mennonite congregations. This was evidenced by the calling of a special conference on "The Believers' Church" in 1955, and by the appointment of the Study Committee for matters pertaining to church discipline. Efforts are being made to solicit full general approval toward developing a consecrated type of Christian living and establishing a "pure" church. Close cooperation with other Mennonite bodies in fields of peace, voluntary service, relief, education, hospital service, and mutual aid has greatly strengthened the concerns for Christian nonconformity in the General Conference.   J.W.F.

(5) *Other Groups in North and South America.* The strictest and most intense application of nonconformity in North and South America, aside from the Old Order Amish, has been practiced by the Old Colony Mennonites in Manitoba, Mexico, and Paraguay. This has included not only nonresistance affairs, and rejection of many modern inventions, and nonparticipation in civic and governmental but also rigid maintenance of the German (and Low German) language, certain regulations in costume, and strong traditions regarding house building, home furnishings, village layout, etc. In all this they have become stricter and more nonconformed than they had been in Russia and at first in Manitoba. As in the case of the Amish some more progressive elements (e.g., the Rudnerweide group) have broken away from the strict traditions of the Old Colony and are accommodating themselves increasingly to the surrounding culture. The Hutterites in North America have also been very strict in nonconformity.

The Church of God in Christ Mennonite and the Kleine Gemeinde have maintained a relatively strict application of nonconformity, though without much distinctive costume. The latter group, now called Evangelical Mennonites, are increasingly open to change and are beginning to accommodate themselves culturally.

The M.B., K.M.B., E.M.B., and Evangelical Mennonites, while maintaining ideally a strong position on nonconformity, have modified their practical application of nonconformity in recent decades. None of these groups, except the K.M.B., has ever had distinctive costume requirements, but all have emphasized simplicity, nonparticipation in worldly amusements, and an unworldly spirit. They have in general accommodated themselves more readily to cultural change than the more conservative groups. The K.M.B. group in its earlier days in Kansas had certain strict costume regulations (see **Krimmer Mennonite Brethren**). On the whole this group of conferences has maintained a generally stricter position on drinking, smoking, worldly amusements, and the use of cosmetics than the more liberal Mennonites of North America; but in general in outward expression of nonconformity, in business practices, in nonresistance, and litigation there has been less difference.   H.S.B.

Nonnenberg, Gotthard von: see Gotthard of Nonnenberg.

Nonresistance is the term which in Anabaptist-Mennonite history has come to denote the faith and life of those who believe that the will of God requires the renunciation of warfare and other compulsive means for the furtherance of personal or social ends. The term itself is derived from the words of Jesus, "Do not resist one who is evil" (Matt. 5:39). The term pacifism (*q.v.*) is likewise derived from the words of Jesus, "Blessed are the peacemakers" (Matt. 5:9); hence true Christian pacifism may be thought of as synonymous with Christian nonresistance. Certain forms of pacifism or nonviolence (q.v.), however, being based more upon humanitarian, philosophical, or political considerations than upon New Testament ethics, are not to be confused with nonresistance as here defined. Nonresistance was held by Anabaptists universally from the beginning, except for the revolutionary fringe in Münster and related elements (1534-40), and for the short-lived Hubmaier group in Moravia (1526-28). It was characteristic of all Mennonite groups in Europe until into the 19th century, and has been universally held by all American Mennonites until the present day. In Russia it was held by all groups until World War II.

Christian nonresistance is more than conscientious objection (q.v.) and more than refusal to engage in military service (q.v.) or to participate in war (q.v.). The doctrine of nonresistance is founded on the way of love and the cross as portrayed in the New Testament. Jesus Christ, "when he was reviled, did not revile in return, when he suffered he did not threaten," and in doing so gave His disciples an example that they should follow in His steps, having died that men should live unto righteousness in this present world. As God through Christ reconciled men unto Himself He in turn gave unto them the ministry of reconciliation, God making His appeal of love through the Christian disciple who does not repay evil for evil, who does not avenge himself, who loves his enemies and prays for those who persecute him. This is the way of love and the cross as lived by Christ, which culminated in His death on the cross of Calvary. The doctrine of nonresistance holds that the Christian disciple must enter into this same experience with Christ, being crucified with Him, following His steps, forgiving even as He forgave. During World War I a Mennonite minister counseling his brethren as to their manner of life for that time said: "We cannot take the place of Christ in the work of redemption, but we can take our place as His followers and share in the love which prompted Him to lay down His life for His enemies." (This and the quotations on the following page are taken from the author's *War, Peace, and Nonresistance*.)

The doctrine of nonresistance has implications for every phase of the Christian's life, first of all in personal relations. The Christian brotherhood is a community of forgiven sinners whose attitude toward one another is that of unbounded forgiveness, unto "seventy times seven." Its members do not seek the highest position; they live in humble subjection one to another out of reverence for Christ who in washing the disciples' feet is their great example in humble, loving service. In the wider social relationships the emphasis is on doing justice, loving mercy, and walking humbly before one's God. Doing that which is just to others takes precedence over seeking justice for one's self or for one's group. Instead of going to law for the settlement of differences the Christian would rather suffer himself to be defrauded. In economic relationships the Christian community does not think in terms of buyer and seller or of management and labor, each seeking his own good; it thinks of itself as a brotherhood whose

members are laborers together with God, in honor preferring one another.

This way of love and nonresistance characterized the Anabaptists from the beginning. Walter Rauschenbusch says, "Their communities were prophetic. . . . They stood against war, against capital punishment, against slavery, and against coercion in matters of religion before others thought of it." Sixteenth-century Catholic opponents said they found among them "no lying, deception, swearing, strife, harsh language . . . , but . . . humility, patience, uprightness, meekness, honesty, temperance, and straightforwardness. . . . They call each other brethren and sisters, . . . they use no weapons of defense. . . . They do not go to law before judicial courts."

Menno Simons said: "The regenerated do not go to war, nor engage in strife. They are the children of peace who have beaten their swords into plowshares and their spears into pruninghooks, and know of no war. . . . Since we are to be conformed to the image of Christ, how can we then fight our enemies with the sword? . . . Spears and swords of iron we leave to those who, alas, consider human blood and swine's blood of well-nigh equal value." Conrad Grebel, the first leader of the Swiss Brethren, said: "True, believing Christians are as sheep in the midst of wolves. . . . They . . . must reach the fatherland of eternal rest, not by overcoming bodily enemies with the sword, but by overcoming spiritual foes. They neither use the worldly sword nor engage in war, since among them taking human life has ceased entirely, for we are no longer under the old covenant."

The Anabaptists recognized the state (q.v.) as ordained of God for the maintenance of order by means of the sword in the sub-Christian society of this world. They did not believe, however, that the disciple of Christ was called to perform this coercive function. The (Swiss Brethren) Schleitheim Confession of Faith, adopted in 1527, says: "The sword is ordained of God outside the perfection of Christ." The (Dutch Mennonite) Dordrecht Confession of 1632 says: "We believe and confess that the Lord Jesus has forbidden His disciples and followers all revenge and resistance, and has thereby commanded them not to 'return evil for evil, nor railing for railing'; but to 'put the sword into the sheath.' . . . Also, if necessity should require it, to flee, for the Lord's sake, from one city or country to another, and suffer the 'spoiling of our goods,' rather than give occasion of offense to anyone; and if we are struck on our 'right cheek, rather to turn the other also,' than revenge ourselves, or return the blow. . . . And we are, besides this, also to pray for our enemies, comfort and feed them, when they are hungry or thirsty, and thus by well doing convince them and overcome the evil with good."

The old Anabaptist hymnal, the *Ausbund* (q.v.), the *Offer des Heeren,* with the *Lietboecxken* of 1562, the oldest documents about the Dutch martyrs, and T. J. van Braght's *Martyrs' Mirror* (q.v.), first published in 1660, are filled with accounts of the Anabaptists who suffered for their nonresistant faith. In the 18th century the Mennonites of Pennsylvania published new editions of these works with the avowed purpose of encouraging steadfastness and strengthening the faith of the brethren, "as the flames of war appear to mount higher." Since "no man can tell whether the cross and persecution of the defenseless Christians will not soon come, . . . it is therefore of importance to prepare ourselves for such circumstances with patience and resignation, and to use all possible means that can encourage steadfastness and strengthen faith."

In 1775 during the American Revolution, following an appeal by the Pennsylvania Assembly to assist the country and its people in such manner as is consistent with their nonresistant faith, the Pennsylvania Mennonites and Dunkers in a joint petition thanked the Assembly for its advice and its liberality in granting freedom of conscience. The petition said the Mennonites and Dunkers were ready at all times to help those in need and distress, "it being our principle to feed the hungry and to give the thirsty drink; we have dedicated ourselves to serve all men in everything that can be helpful to the preservation of men's lives, but we find no freedom in giving, or doing, or assisting in anything by which men's lives are destroyed or hurt." On various occasions in the following 175 years similar sentiments were addressed to the American and Canadian governments by the American Mennonites, as in 1915, 1917, 1919, and other times.

In 1937 the Mennonite Church (MC) at its biennial conference adopted a statement of position on *Peace, War, and Military Service,* saying: "We are constrained as followers of Christ to abstain from all forms of military service and . . . support of war," from service in civil organizations allied with the military, from "the financing of war operations . . . through voluntary contributions," from participation in the manufacture of munitions and from making financial profit out of war. This statement also expressed a willingness "at all times to aid in the relief of those who are in need, distress or suffering, regardless of the danger in which we may be placed in bringing such relief, or of the cost which may be involved in the same. If our country becomes involved in war, we shall endeavor to continue to live a quiet and peaceable life in all godliness and honesty; avoiding joining in the wartime hysteria of hatred, revenge, and retaliation; manifest a meek and submissive spirit, being obedient unto the laws and regulations of the government in all things, except in such cases where obedience to the government would cause us to violate the teachings of Scriptures so that we could not maintain a clear conscience before God."

Four years later the same group issued a declaration of the principle of nonresistance as applied to industrial relations: "We believe that industrial strife, unfair and unjust practices by employers or employees, and every economic and social condition and practice which makes for suffering or ill will among men is altogether contrary to the teaching and spirit of Christ and the Gospel."

In 1941 the General Conference Mennonite Church (GCM) at its triennial meeting adopted a similar statement on nonresistance in which it said: "We believe that war is altogether contrary to the teaching and spirit of Christ and the Gospel; that therefore war is sin, as is all manner of carnal strife;

that it is wrong in spirit and method as well as in purpose, and destructive in its results. Therefore, if we profess the principle of peace and nevertheless engage in warfare and strife, we as Christians become guilty of sin and fall under the condemnation of Christ the righteous judge." (*Minutes and Reports of the 29th Session of the General Conference of the Mennonite Church of N.A.,* 1941, p. 164.)

As a positive expression of nonresistance in the form of Christian love and service, and as an alternative to military service, the G.C.M. statement says: "We . . . express our willingness . . . at all times to aid in the relief of those who are in need, distress or suffering, regardless of the danger in which we may be placed in bringing such relief, or of the cost which may be involved in the same. We are also willing to render such services as housing, road making, farming, forestry, hospitalization, and recreational work during time of war. Wherever we render such service it shall always be our purpose to spread the Gospel of Christ by word as well as deed."

In 1954 the Mennonite Brethren Church at its General Conference session also adopted a statement in which it said: "The Mennonite Brethren Church believes in nonresistance because: (1) Nonresistance is a Biblical principle clearly exemplified by Jesus Christ. (2) The Church as the body of Christ is a fellowship of the redeemed, therefore: The members are a separated people. John 17:16. They accept Christ as their pattern. I John 2:6. Their lives are controlled by redemptive love. Rom. 5:5. Since the responsibility of the Church is to represent Christ, its Head, and to evangelize the world, participation in any form of war becomes impossible for its members. (3) The practice of the redeemed in Christ demands that every phase of their life in all relationships, such as personal, social, national, and international, be governed by the supreme law of love, and is not limited to an abstinence from military service. It is a general attitude of the Christian as he seeks the redemption of his fellow men. (4) Human life is sacred unto God, and a Christian has no right to destroy life. (5) War is evil, brutal, and inhuman. It glorifies might, greed, and selfishness. The nature of war remains incompatible with the new nature of a regenerated Christian." (*Year Book of the 46th General Conference of the M.B. Church,* 1954, p. 121.)

In Europe, following a long period of persecution for their nonresistant faith, the Mennonites experienced first a period of toleration and then in course of time a gradual loss of the principle for which the fathers had died. In Holland the latter tendency was first manifested as early as the late 17th century. This tendency in the first instance may have been caused in part by the influence of Calvinism, which was very great from the 17th century on, not only on the more liberal Lamists (who, for example, took over the Calvinist liturgy, pulpit, and organ), but also on the stricter Zonists, and in part by the worldliness and economic prosperity. Although a number of Dutch Mennonites performed military service during the Napoleonic wars (1796-1815) most of the leaders of the church were opposed to voluntary service in the army as late as

1850. At that time it was still possible to secure exemption from service by hiring a substitute. When the new law requiring military service was passed by the Dutch parliament in 1898, however, without any exceptions or special privileges for Mennonites, even the leaders of the church failed to offer any objections. By the first quarter of the 20th century individual Dutch Mennonites were holding important political positions, a Mennonite deacon even serving as Minister of the Navy, and during the time of World War I there was only one known conscientious objector among the Mennonites called up for military service in Holland. By this time the Dutch Mennonites as a whole were persuaded that the nonresistant position was no longer valid, although as late as 1890 such an important leader as Tjepke Kielstra took his stand firmly for New Testament nonresistance.

In Switzerland the Mennonites suffered persecution for nearly three centuries, and were not granted complete religious toleration until 1815. Most of those who had not been put to death were driven out, eventually finding homes in Alsace, in the Palatinate, and many in America. As a result of the persecutions the few Mennonites who remained in Switzerland developed a spirit of self-depreciation and when that country adopted universal conscription in the mid-19th century those who did not emigrate to escape conscription accepted noncombatant service, which was their privilege, although by the mid-20th century about 15 per cent took full service. Officially, however, the Swiss Conference maintained the nonresistant position.

Following the Napoleonic wars, conscription for military service became the universal practice on the continent of Europe. In Germany as elsewhere when this occurred those Mennonites who took their nonresistance most seriously migrated to new homes where their faith and their way of life would be respected. In the 1780's the Mennonites of West Prussia were required to give financial support to the military academy at Culm. They also suffered other forms of oppression, such as restrictions in land ownership. As a result of this situation large numbers of the Mennonites moved to Russia in 1788-1820, where they were exempt from military service.

No doubt the Mennonites of West Prussia who migrated to Russia were those who took their nonresistance most seriously. Nevertheless, those who remained in West Prussia and the Vistula delta did not give up their position without a struggle. During the Napoleonic wars, for example, when one of the members of the Elbing congregation volunteered for service and fought at Waterloo, he was excommunicated. Following the enactment of the Prussian universal military training law in 1814 the Mennonites appealed for exemption, which was granted, but only on condition that they pay a heavy tax in addition to that paid for the support of the military academy. In the Revolution of 1848, when the Frankfurt Assembly drew up a constitution for the proposed new German confederation, a non-Mennonite delegate from Danzig suggested a provision for the exemption of Mennonites from military service. Astonishing as it may seem, however, a Mennonite delegate from Crefeld, in northwestern Germany, opposed the suggestion, with the result that it was turned down. Since the proposed German confederation did not materialize, the new constitution never went into effect. From what happened at the Assembly, however, it is clear that the influence of the Mennonites of the Lower Rhine, who were rapidly losing their nonresistance, made it more difficult for their brethren of northeastern Germany to maintain their faith.

In the 17th century large numbers of persecuted Mennonites had also moved from Switzerland into the Palatinate and other parts of southern Germany. They continued to suffer many hardships here, however, both from persecution and from the wars at the end of the century. As a result, many of these South German Mennonites moved to America in the first half of the 18th century. As the pressure of militarism increased and opportunities for migration opened up, some Mennonites of all parts of Germany continued to migrate to America and to Russia during the late 18th and the 19th centuries.

The end of full nonresistance among the Prussian and all of the North German Mennonites came following the founding of the North German Confederation in 1867. In that year a new universal military service law was enacted, with no exemption for Mennonites. After the law was passed the Mennonites appealed to Berlin, but the only concession they received was the cabinet order of March 3, 1868, permitting noncombatant military service for those who had scruples against regular service. After the cabinet order was issued many of those Mennonites who were genuinely nonresistant migrated to Russia and America. Those who remained at first accepted noncombatant military service. This was especially true of the North German Mennonites after the cabinet order of 1868. It soon became clear, however, that there was little difference in principle between noncombatant and regular service. As a result, the Mennonites of Germany gradually gave up all objection to army service, and in World War I most Mennonites in the army were in the regular service. Only a few chose the noncombatant service provided for by the law, although about one third of those in West Prussia did so. Thus, for more than a century the process of adaptation went on until it culminated in the almost complete abandonment of the nonresistant faith by the Mennonites of Germany.

Before the opening of World War II (1934) in fact, the *Vereinigung der Mennonitengemeinden im Deutschen Reich,* the official conference which included the churches of northern Germany and the Palatinate, had taken official action openly disavowing the nonresistant position by stating that the privilege of exemption from full military service would no longer be claimed. The Mennonites of Germany as a whole had become convinced that the old Mennonite position was no longer valid, and that they owed it to their country to assume the full burden of citizenship like their fellow citizens. The older status of exemption had been based upon the conception of the Mennonites being a special class of citizens, with limited rights and exceptional privileges. Ernst Crous has shown

(*MQR* XXV, 241-44) that the process of accommodation by which the German Mennonites changed their convictions on nonresistance seemed right and good to them and was not viewed as compromise, although viewed historically it appears as such.

In France the story is much the same as elsewhere in Europe. After 1870 the French military laws made no provision whatever for conscientious objectors, and military service came to be generally accepted by the Mennonites in that country. From 1870 to 1914 Alsace, being annexed to Germany, was subject to German military law.

When the Mennonites migrated from Prussia and elsewhere in western Europe to Russia during the latter part of the 18th century the principle of nonresistance was one of the factors responsible for the move. When they came to Russia they, like all other German immigrants, were guaranteed complete exemption from military service. This policy of exemption was continued according to promise until 1870. In that year, however, the Russian government issued a ukase abolishing all special privileges to non-Russian settlers in South Russia, including exemption from military service effective in 1880.

The imperial edict caused great concern among the Mennonites, and from the beginning some of them considered the situation serious enough to warrant emigration. Numerous official delegations were sent to St. Petersburg in 1871-73 with appeals to the government to withdraw its order regarding military service. As these efforts proved fruitless, however, an emigration to America, which began in a small way in 1873, actually assumed mass proportions in the following year. In 1873 the total population of the Mennonites in Russia was 45,000, and before the migration movement was concluded one third of this number had gone to the prairie regions of the United States and Canada.

The Russian government now became alarmed, realizing too late that it had not taken Mennonite nonresistance seriously enough. Determined to hold as many of them as possible the Czar sent General von Todtleben to the colonies in April 1874. After acquainting himself with the faith and the convictions of the Mennonites he offered them civilian service of an entirely nonmilitary character as an alternative to military service. The result was the alternative forestry service (*q.v.*) program for conscientious objectors (*q.v.*) operated by the Mennonites under the Russian government from 1880 through World War I and financed by them. By the time of World War I the annual enrollment in this service was about 1,000 men. During the war itself about 12,000 Mennonites were engaged in government service, about 6,000 in the forestry and another 6,000 in the Mennonite hospital and medical corps. Practically no Mennonites entered the army.

The coming of the Russian revolution in 1917 following three years of war proved to be a very severe test for the nonresistant faith of the Russian Mennonites. In 1918 some Mennonites in the Ukraine organized a Self-Defense Corps (*q.v.*) (*Selbstschutz*) at the suggestion and with the help of officers of the German army of occupation. There was some actual fighting between armed Mennonites and groups of Russian bandits. This serious lapse no doubt increased the difficulties experienced by Russian Mennonites who were sincerely and genuinely nonresistant, and who were the great majority.

Some form of alternative service was granted by the Soviet government upon individual application quite regularly down to 1927, on the basis of the Lenin decree of 1919 (which has never been repealed). Thereafter it became increasingly difficult, although cases are known to have been granted as late as 1935. In some cases also the CO's are reported to have been shot, and in other cases the alternative service amounted to forced labor in concentration camps. Many of the Mennonite men who were brought out of Russia in 1943 by the German army of occupation were drafted into the German army.

From the time of the first Mennonite immigration to America in the late 17th century to the present time, concern for the principle of nonresistance has always been a major cause for the emigration of Mennonites from Europe. This was especially true after the introduction of universal military service in Europe by Napoleon early in the 19th century. The coming of the Swiss Mennonites and the Alsatian Amish to Ohio, Indiana, Illinois, and Iowa in the mid-19th century are cases in point. Further illustrations would be Mennonite groups coming from Prussia to Kansas and Nebraska as well as other Mennonites and Amish groups from Germany to Pennsylvania, Ohio, Illinois, and Iowa. By far the largest migration before World War I was that from Russia in the 1870's, and this was brought about almost entirely by the Russian threat to the nonresistant way of life of the Mennonites. These successive waves of immigration accordingly strengthened the American Mennonite devotion to the principle of nonresistance.

Although there have always been individuals who did not follow the teachings of the church, the American Mennonites during the wars from the 18th to the 20th centuries have maintained a fairly consistent testimony against military service. The nonresistant faith of the Pennsylvania Mennonites was not only stated in their declaration to the Pennsylvania Assembly in 1775; it was also demonstrated by the assistance and relief which they brought to the war sufferers of that time. There were also numerous cases of Mennonites on the American frontier in colonial times who suffered in various ways, some of them even being murdered at the hands of hostile Indians, such as in Page County, Va., and Berks County, Pa. In all of these trials there is no case on record of any Mennonite using force against the enemy. In 1789 Benjamin Rush said: "Perhaps those German sects of Christians among us who refuse to bear arms for the purpose of shedding human blood, may be preserved by divine providence as the center of a circle, which shall gradually embrace all nations of the earth in a perpetual treaty of friendship and peace."

The period before the Civil War (1860-65) was one of spiritual decline among the American Mennonites. For a long time no peace literature had been produced and in many cases the young men were not prepared to meet the test of war and conscription when it came, and a considerable number of them accepted military service.

This failure became the occasion for a revival of teaching on nonresistance and a cause for a great awakening in the Mennonite Church. In June 1863 appeared two little booklets on nonresistance, "the first trickles of a stream of literature that has flowed into the church in growing volume since." One was entitled, *Warfare, Its Evils, Our Duty,* and was written by John F. Funk, the young minister who was to found the *Herald of Truth* in Chicago the following year. The other, entitled *Christianity and War,* was written by John M. Brenneman, Mennonite minister of Elida, Ohio. The *Herald of Truth,* which began publication in January 1864, promoted the cause of nonresistance from the very beginning. In an editorial in the January 1865 issue of the *Herald,* Funk discussed various alternatives to military service and evaluated them as to their consistency with the nonresistant faith. He presented a convincing case against the hiring of substitutes. "It is now generally admitted to be wrong," he says, "and there is probably scarcely a single one who professes to hold to the doctrine of nonresistance, that would be willing to send a man to do that which he himself . . . considers altogether against the gospel of Jesus Christ."

While the testimony of the church leadership was clear on the question of hiring substitutes, there is evidence of confused thinking on the matter of the commutation fee, service to sick and wounded soldiers, and noncombatant service in the army which some accepted, both in the North and in the South. The church at that time showed a weakness in not being able to grapple adequately, on the basis of its own principles, with the issues at hand. The considerate attitude of the government, however, especially in the North, in recognizing the scruples of nonresistant people when they were effectively presented, makes it seem certain that if the Mennonites had been sufficiently advanced in their thinking to conceive and promote a comprehensive program of civilian alternative service in harmony with their principles, it would have been granted them. As it was, however, such a program was not developed until the time of World War II.

During the Civil War the Mennonites of Virginia, located within the Confederacy, were very hard pressed. Much of their property was destroyed. Some of them suffered imprisonment. Some remained in hiding in the mountains for months at a time. Others managed to escape to the North where some of them remained permanently. The vigorous leadership of Bishop Samuel Coffman, who stood courageously for the nonresistant faith at the risk of his own life, enabled the Mennonite Church in Virginia to maintain a fairly consistent nonresistant record, considering the seriousness of the military situation and the period in the history of the church when these events occurred.

The great awakening in the Mennonite Church (MC) which followed the Civil War, and the spiritual developments of the next half century, prepared the Mennonites of America to meet the problems of World War I with greater effectiveness than they did those of the Civil War. When the war came a firm position was taken against noncombatant as well as combatant military service, and the wartime experience was such as to clarify effectively the issues here at stake and to gain the recognition of the government for the principle of nonresistance as well as its co-operation in an effort to find acceptable alternatives for military service. Relief and reconstruction work abroad in the last year of the war and immediately following (1917-19), the farm furlough, and proposals near the end of the war for the assignment of conscientious objectors to projects of land reclamation and agricultural and educational service helped to set the pattern for later Civilian Public Service and comprehensive relief and voluntary service programs, both home and foreign, developed during and following World War II, which functioned both as an alternative to military service and as a positive service and witness for peace in the modern world.

These gains were made, however, only because the men in the army camps and in the home communities were willing to pay for them with the necessary price, often in the form of genuine suffering. The experience of the men in the camps was often not a happy one. C. Henry Smith says they "were frequently roughly handled. . . . In all the camps they were subject to ridicule. . . . Some . . . were brutally handled in the guardhouse; they were bayoneted, beaten, and tortured by various kinds of the water cure; eighteen men one night were aroused from their sleep and held under cold showers until one became hysterical. . . . Men were forced to stand at attention, sometimes with outstretched arms for hours and days at a time . . . exposed to the inclemencies of the weather as well as to the jeers and taunts of their fellows until they could stand no longer, . . . occasionally tortured by mock trials, in which the victim was left under the impression to the very last that unless he submitted to the regulations the penalty would be death. Every conceivable device—ridicule, torture, offer of promotion, and other tempting inducements were resorted to in order to get them to give up their convictions; but with only few exceptions the religious objectors refused to compromise with their consciences." (*Story of the Mennonites,* 794 ff.)

In World War I the total number of objectors in the United States who were court-martialed and sentenced was 503. Of these, 360 were religious objectors; and of the latter, 138 were Mennonites. Prison sentences ranged all the way from one year or less to life. Life sentences were given to 142 men, and 17 men were even sentenced to death. Sentences from five to thirty years were very common. None of these severe sentences were fully served. Within a few months after the close of the war most of the prisoners had been given their freedom by Presidential pardon.

The darkest chapter in the entire story of the treatment received by the conscientious objectors in World War I is that of the four Hutterian Brethren—Joseph, Michael, and David Hofer, and Jacob Wipf. After spending two months in the guardhouse in a military camp these four men were court-martialed and sentenced to twenty years' imprisonment. They were taken to Alcatraz federal prison in California, where they suffered very cruel treatment, from which Joseph and Michael Hofer died.

The brotherhood in the home community was also tested. In some communities Mennonites were most severely criticized, and even abused. In Kansas and Illinois and in other places a number of meetinghouses were painted yellow. In at least two cases meetinghouses were burned to the ground. In Kansas several men were tarred and feathered because of their nonresistant objection to the purchase of bonds. One minister in Ohio was dragged from his home at night, and his hair was clipped from his head. In South Dakota a mob, with the connivance of a local bond committee, actually robbed the Hutterian community of livestock worth $40,000. This, with other abuses, was responsible for driving the Hutterites out of the state into Canada. No doubt this is the worst example, but it would be possible to enumerate cases of mistreatment and mob violence by the score.

One of the effects of World War I was to arouse all of the peace churches to the need for an aggressive program of peace teaching and peace action. The various Mennonite groups appointed official peace committees who were responsible for carrying on this program. The Brethren and Friends groups did likewise. Following the war, the amount of peace literature produced by all of these groups was greater than ever before in their history. Peace conferences sponsored by the peace groups, both individually and co-operatively, were a common thing during this period. The most important of the co-operatively sponsored meetings was that held at Newton, Kan., in 1935, at which time the name "Historic Peace Churches" was first used. This meeting created an unofficial Continuation Committee (the Mennonite member appointed by the MCC) whose duty it was to plan for future conferences and to guide the co-operative efforts of the Historic Peace Churches. Among these co-operative efforts was the bringing of a testimony for the Christian way of peace to the official bodies of other Christian denominations. In 1937 representatives of the Historic Peace Churches called on President Franklin D. Roosevelt, each of the three groups (Mennonites, Friends, and Brethren) presenting a letter stating its views on war and peace, and refusal to bear arms. A similar delegation visited the President again on Jan. 10, 1940, with concrete proposals for alternative service in case universal military training and service should be adopted.

In 1939 various Mennonite groups, realizing the need for a united position, organized the Mennonite Central Peace Committee, which then drafted a proposed plan of action in case of war; this plan received official approval on Sept. 30, 1939. The other Historic Peace Churches also gave official approval to this plan of action. As a result of these efforts the provision for conscientious objectors in the Selective Training and Service Act of 1940 was more generous and satisfactory than that of the draft law of 1917. Under the new law all persons "who, by reason of religious training and belief," were conscientiously opposed to all forms of military service, should, if conscripted for service, "be assigned to work of national importance under civilian direction." The implementation of this law resulted in the CPS system of World War II and the revised civilian work program inaugurated in 1952 (as described in *ME* I, page 698).

The experiences of World War II had a profound effect for both the Mennonite conscientious objectors and their churches. For four years the principle of nonresistance and its applications were put under a strenuous test, in both the United States and Canada. Civilian Public Service (*q.v.*) in the United States with over 4,000 Mennonite CO's in service for several years, and the vast effort of administration and financial support for it required of the associated Mennonite bodies (the entire Mennonite brotherhood of North America was united in its stand and co-operated in CPS), was a tremendous experience for all, whose great and lasting effects are still being measured. Much thorough thinking on the basic principle of nonresistance went on throughout the period, with a resultant clarification and deepening of understanding and .commitment. Some of the side effects on the churches will be reported later on in this article, but it should be said here that by the end of the war the nonresistance position of the Mennonites in North America was solidified as never before. The Canadian Mennonite experience with Alternative Service (*q.v.*) had a similar significance. The ripest expression of this fuller understanding and conviction found its precipitate in a powerful and moving declaration of nonresistant faith as set forth in "A Declaration of Christian Faith and Commitment" adopted at a "Study Conference on Nonresistance held by Representatives of the Mennonite and Brethren in Christ Churches of North America held at Winona Lake, Indiana, November 9-12, 1950." A further and more elaborate and theological statement, incorporating much of the Winona Lake statement but twice as long, was adopted by the Mennonite Church (MC) as its position at its General Conference, Aug. 23, 1951, entitled "A Declaration of Christian Faith and Commitment with Respect to War, Peace, and Nonresistance." Both statements are to be found in *Twenty-Seventh Mennonite General Conference,* Scottdale, 1951, pp. 41-50.)

The experience of both of the world wars served to stimulate and expand the Mennonite relief and service programs as forms of a positive world-wide witness for peace. The reconstruction work in France, followed by the Near East Relief and the Russian famine relief, were supported by the Mennonites both with funds and personnel. The latter project led to the formation in 1920 of the Mennonite Central Committee, which has become the great relief and service organization of North American Mennonitism, and which has also carried the banner of a united Mennonite nonresistance testimony. The total amount contributed by the American Mennonites and distributed through its own organizations for the relief of war sufferers in Europe and the Near East during the period of World War I and immediately afterwards is estimated at about $2,500,000. The Mennonites of Holland also contributed several hundred thousand dollars for the work in Russia. During the Spanish Civil War (1937), the American Mennonites (MC) carried on a relief work in that country, contributing about $57,000.

This record of work in migration, relief (*q.v.*), voluntary service (*q.v.*), and civilian service (*q.v.*) of North American Mennonites as an alternative to military service from 1940 on constitutes a 20th-century Mennonite peace testimony which is world-wide in its scope. The story of the Mennonite migrations for conscience' sake has attracted wide attention, and their relief and humanitarian service projects have touched many countries on every continent on the globe, except Australia. Their record as conscientious objectors in the United States and Canada is likewise well known.

This world-wide witness was bound to have a profound effect upon the Mennonites themselves. It gave them a new vision of their own faith and life, and of the Anabaptist contribution to theology, and brought a deepened conviction that the Christian Gospel and the message of love and nonresistance which according to the New Testament is an integral part of it were sorely needed in their world. Those Mennonites who had formerly given up their nonresistant faith were challenged to espouse it once more, which some of them did. Even as early as 1915 a spirit of renewal was beginning to stir among the Mennonites of the Netherlands, which by 1950 had done much to turn the church in the direction of its original evangelical and nonresistant principles. This spirit was first symbolized by Jan Gleijsteen, the one and only Dutch Mennonite who took his stand as a conscientious objector when called up for military service during World War I. Gleijsteen served a term in prison for taking this stand. At the same time some young ministers, T. O. Hylkema, J. E. van Brakel, and J. M. Leendertz, through a study of the Bible and church history, began to find their way to the early and historic position of the Dutch Mennonite church on nonresistance and related Biblical principles. In this they were helped to some extent by their contacts with the English Quakers at Woodbrooke. In 1917 Hylkema and his associates organized the Gemeentedag movement, the aim of which was to bring the church to a more thoroughly Biblical faith. Included in its emphasis was nonresistance. During the 1920's and 1930's there gradually developed among the Dutch Mennonites a vigorous body of opinion opposing military service and militarism. In 1922 this led to the formation of a Committee against Military Service (*Arbeidsgroep, q.v.*) with over 300 members, which some fifteen years later prepared a *Mennonite Peace Manifesto*, appealing to its members "to witness vigorously to our peace testimony in our congregations everywhere," and calling "all Mennonites throughout the world to fulfill the task entrusted to us by the history of our Mennonite forefathers, in the propagation of the Gospel of peace." This *Manifesto*, signed by representatives of Mennonites in various countries at the organization of an International Mennonite Peace Committee in the summer of 1936 following the third Mennonite World Conference, was widely circulated among the Mennonites of the world.

By adopting pertinent legislation in 1926 the Dutch government liberalized its military laws so as again to give some recognition to conscientious objectors. Following the war a program of alternative service was inaugurated, with service camps for conscientious objectors similar to those in the United States. The program included service in mental hospitals and other similar assignments. In 1952 several hundred Dutch conscientious objectors were engaged in this service, about thirty of them being Mennonites. In 1952 also two Dutch Mennonites whose CO position was not recognized by the government were serving prison sentences.

Following the war the organized peace work of the Dutch Mennonites also underwent some change. The earlier Committee against Military Service became the Mennonite Peace Group (*Doopsgezinde Vredesgroep, q.v.*). This change of name symbolized a changing emphasis in the group's peace teaching and peace work. If the earlier emphasis was largely one of antimilitarism, the later emphasis was increasingly that of Biblical nonresistance, so that by 1950 the Biblical position was dominant in the Dutch Mennonite peace movement. The fact that by 1953 the Peace Group had a membership of nearly 700 members, among whom were 32 per cent of the Dutch Mennonite ministers, is evidence enough that Dutch Mennonitism had made much progress in the recovery of its earlier faith.

The principles of the Peace Group are set forth in the following declaration, adopted at its founding on Sept. 2, 1946. "The Mennonite Peace Group, in obedience to Jesus Christ our Lord, and moved by His love, seeks in a world torn by sin to give a witness for the peace spirit and a purely spiritual arming which seeks to overcome the evil by the good. It knows that it can achieve this only as its members, in union with Christ, in prayer and consecration, allow their weakness to be renewed by His strength. It seeks to reach this goal by: (1) striving for a personal life witness by its members (acceptance of Christ's command to love, even the enemies, as their obligation) in Biblical nonresistance; readiness to sacrifice the selfish ego, whatever heavy sacrifices of time and money the Lord may require; (2) strengthening in our churches the attitude of caring for one another in the spirit of mutual responsibility and intercession; (3) lending spiritual and material support to those who come into difficulties because of their Christian peace testimony (in particular, help to those who in obedience to Christ feel called to refuse military service; co-operating in establishing in our country an alternative service of life like the Civilian Public Service in America); (4) co-operating in relief work." (*Doopsgezinde Vredesgroep Brief*, December 1949, "Verklaring.")

The International Mennonite Peace Committee mentioned above was organized following the third Mennonite World Conference in Holland in the summer of 1936. Participating in the formation of the new organization were members of the Dutch Mennonite Committee against Military Service and representatives of several peace committees from North America. Harold S. Bender of the United States was chosen chairman of the committee, and

Jacob ter Meulen of the Netherlands secretary-treasurer. The achievements of the new organization, however, were very modest. Moreover, with the coming of World War II the connections between America and Holland were broken, so that the International Mennonite Peace Committee became inactive. In the summer of 1949, however, an international Mennonite peace conference in Holland provided the occasion for its revival. In its reorganized form Harold S. Bender again became chairman, and Carl F. Brüsewitz of Holland was chosen secretary. It has continued in a modest program of activity to the present. In Holland the Peace Group, with the help of American Mennonites, established a peace center at Heerewegen near Zeist.

The most significant feature of the 1949 conference, however, was the presence of representatives of the German, French, and Swiss Mennonites, as well as those of Holland and America. Representatives from each of these countries were also named officials of the new organization. The new organization held a second international Mennonite peace conference at Heilbronn, Germany, in the summer of 1950, and a third conference in France in 1951. In 1952 it held a meeting in connection with the Fifth Mennonite World Conference in Basel. Several similar meetings have been held since then.

The participation of the German, French, and Swiss Mennonites in this movement was of much significance, indicating a growing interest in nonresistance. However, even in 1957 it was uncertain whether or not this interest would grow into a movement as significant as that of the Dutch Peace Group. The leaders of the movement in these countries were only a few, and their following was not large. And yet there were signs that the movement had genuine life. In Germany a peace conference for German Mennonites was held in 1949. In both 1949 and 1950 the question of nonresistance was discussed at official conferences of the German Mennonites. The constitution of the new West German Republic provided that no one should be compelled against his conscience to perform military service. When the question of remilitarization arose, the German parliament took steps to enact legislation to implement this constitutional provision, and the German churches were given the opportunity of stating their position on conscientious objection. In 1950 the German Mennonite conferences officially went on record as supporting the position of the conscientious objector. This did not necessarily mean that the great body of German Mennonites had come to accept nonresistance in faith and practice once more. It did mean, however, that those who took that position would have the support of the church. Moreover, the editor of the official South German Mennonite periodical, the *Gemeindeblatt,* was personally committed to nonresistance; and in the middle of the century the pages of this periodical were carrying articles on nonresistance by influential members of the church.

Inductions into the new German army were scheduled to begin in 1957. In the meantime a German Mennonite Peace Committee had been organized, which in turn was represented on the Central Agency for Conscientious Objectors organized by the various peace groups for handling objector affairs with the German government similar to the operations of the National Service Board for Religious Objectors (*q.v.*) in the United States. Under the German conscription system men registering as conscientious objectors were to be examined by twelve regional committees and if their claims were recognized were to be assigned to civilian service under the Labor Ministry of the federal government. Government-operated camps were to provide projects in land reclamation, disaster service, health services, and construction of welfare and charitable institutions. Private agencies were also to be licensed for giving alternative service employment to objectors. At the time of this writing it was impossible to know the extent to which the German Mennonites would take their position as conscientious objectors under the provisions of the new law.

By 1948 the editor of the French Mennonite periodical, *Christ Seul,* was also committed to nonresistance, and his journal likewise promoted the cause. He was also an influential evangelist and youth leader whose sincere peace convictions showed signs of bearing fruit. He, along with several other French Mennonites, had notified the government that although they had previously served in the army they could not do so again. Youth meetings were discussing nonresistance, and even an all-day conference of the French Mennonite ministers in the summer of 1950 was devoted to a consideration of the ancient nonresistant testimony of the church, an event without precedent within the memory of those present. This meeting revealed an interest in testifying to the French government against its intolerant attitude toward the conscientious objector, which later was done. Present at the French ministerial conference were also representatives of the Swiss Mennonites, including the president of their conference, indicating a serious interest in nonresistance on their part. That in the mid-20th century a new interest in nonresistance had been aroused in the European Mennonite churches there could be no doubt.

In all of this the European Mennonite peace leaders were working closely with the American Mennonites. In the summer of 1949 three representatives of the peace section of the MCC, Harold S. Bender, Erland Waltner, and C. J. Rempel, spent several months in Europe on a preaching mission, holding conferences and doing what they could to encourage their brethren in the recovery of their nonresistant witness. During the year 1949-50 Guy F. Hershberger served in a similar way, his work including a study of the general pacifist movement in Europe. In the summer of 1951 Bender and Waltner engaged in a second preaching mission and, in addition to their labors among the Mennonites, participated in conferences with peace leaders in the German evangelical churches. Similar missions were sent to the Mennonite colonies in South America about the same time.

This outward reach of the Mennonite peace witness into the general Christian peace movement was manifesting itself in a number of ways. The Dutch Mennonite Peace Group was making its influence felt upon Dutch Christianity in general. Since 1949 the Dutch Peace Group and American Mennonites had been holding occasional conferences with representatives of the Friends and the Church of the Brethren in Europe, and a European Historic Peace Church Continuation Committee was organized in that year, with the British Friends, the European representatives of the Brethren Service Committee, and MCC workers (plus later representatives of the Dutch Peace Group) participating. A conference of these groups in 1950 took steps toward the presentation of the concerns and convictions of the Historic Peace Churches to the World Council of Churches before the time of its world conference in 1953. This presentation was made in the form of a booklet *Peace Is the Will of God* (Amsterdam, 1953). Since then the European Mennonite peace witness and work has continued under the leadership of the International Mennonite Peace Committee assisted by American MCC workers John H. Yoder, Albert Meyer, Ernst Harder, Milton Harder, Paul Bender, and others. In the summer of 1957 a number of peace conferences were held in meetings associated with the sixth Mennonite World Conference. At the same time the Mennonites of the Latin-American countries were also growing increasingly conscious of their responsibility to strengthen the witness of peace among themselves, and to make that witness felt beyond their own circles through the publication of peace literature and by other means. This was true both of the Mennonite colonists who had recently settled there as immigrants, and of the Mennonite missions in those parts. The same was also true of Mennonite missions in Africa, India, and in other parts of the world. During 1955-57 Melvin Gingerich gave a two-year term of service under the Peace Section of the MCC bringing the peace witness to the people of Japan, working with Japanese Christians and peace workers in that country. In September 1957 he was succeeded by Paul Peachey in this ministry. Thus at the middle of the 20th century there was a growing conviction among Mennonites that nonresistance was an integral part of the Gospel of Christ. And the Mennonite peace witness was growing ever more world-wide in its scope.

Another effect of the growing interest in the Christian peace testimony was a deepened concern among Mennonites for the wider social implications of the Gospel and of the principle of nonresistance in particular. "A Declaration of Christian Faith and Commitment," adopted by a study conference called by the Peace Section of the MCC at Winona Lake, Ind., in 1950, says: "We . . . have the responsibility to bring to the total social order . . . the utmost of which we are capable in Christian love and service. . . . For this reason the social order, including our own segment of it, must be constantly brought under the judgment of Christ. . . . We must practice an increasingly sharper Christian control of our economic, social, and cultural practices among ourselves and toward others, to make certain that love truly operates to work no ill to our neighbor, either short-range or long-range. Knowing how much the selfishness, pride, and greed of individuals, groups, and nations, which economic systems often encourage, help to cause carnal strife and

warfare, we must see to it that we do not contribute thereto, whether for the goals of direct military operation or to anything which destroys property or causes hurt or loss of human life."

In 1951 a conference at Laurelville Mennonite Camp, sponsored by the Committee on Industrial Relations of the Mennonite Church (MC), adopted "A Statement of Concerns" which said: "We are further concerned that the church should acquire a better understanding of the principles of social justice contained in the Gospel of Christ, and urge our preachers and teachers to study and to set forth the social obligations expressed and implied in the teachings of the Old Testament prophets, of our Lord, and of all the apostles. We are deeply concerned that the social conscience of all our people may be aroused and sharpened, so that we may sense more and more the implications of Christian love and brotherhood in the complex details of modern life. We believe that our Christian testimony to the world about us can be effective only as we confess unsocial conduct to be sin and cleanse our lives of its defilement."

"A Declaration of Christian Faith and Commitment with Respect to Peace, War, and Nonresistance," adopted by the Mennonite Church (MC) in 1951, repeated the admonition of the Winona Lake statement to "practice a sharper Christian control of our economic, social, and cultural practices," and added that "Christian love must hold primacy in all our economic and labor relations, that we cannot participate in activities, organizations, investments, or systems which use the methods of force and violence, compromise Christian ethics, or do not permit the full exercise of Christian love and brotherhood, and that we seek in our own practices to work out this love and brotherhood in concrete applications."

In 1955 the Committee on Economic and Social Relations sponsored a study conference on Christian race relations which drafted a statement which later that same year was officially adopted by the Mennonite Church (MC). This statement, "The Way of Christian Love in Race Relations," condemned racial prejudice and discrimination as a sin, as "a violation of the basic moral law which requires a redemptive attitude of love and reconciliation toward all men," and as "a major cause of present-day international conflict and war" in which a nonresistant people can have no part.

The growth of the Mennonite peace witness also seems to have been accompanied by deepened convictions and a more complete commitment to the principle of nonresistance by the rank and file of the Mennonite brotherhood in America, as reflected in the percentage of conscripted men who chose alternative service. In World War II 46.2 per cent of all conscripted Mennonites and 59.2 per cent of conscripted members of the Mennonite Church (MC) chose alternative service under the CPS system. Under the alternative service work program reinstituted in 1952, however, the figure for the Mennonite Church (MC) had been raised to 88 per cent and that for Mennonites as a whole had been raised proportionately, although precise figures were not available in every case.   G.F.H.

Nonresistance in Germany. The 19th century witnessed a general decline in nonresistance among the German Mennonites. In South Germany for some time payment instead of personal service was allowed. Those with strong nonresistant convictions emigrated to America (1830-60). After 1871 payment was no more possible. In West and East Prussia in the last quarter of the 18th century the Mennonites were required to give financial support to the military academy at Culm and had to face restrictions in gaining more land. Consequently large numbers emigrated to Russia. When the Prussian universal military training law was passed in 1814 the Mennonites were granted exemption, but still had to pay a fee in place of personal service. After the revolution of 1848 (equal rights, equal obligations!), when a new universal military law with no exemptions for the Mennonites became imminent and in 1867 became reality, the Mennonites again and again appealed to Berlin. Their appeals to the parliament, which now had to decide the question, were futile; but the king as commander-in-chief of the army succeeded at least (1868) in granting them a cabinet order permitting noncombatant military services for those who had scruples against full service. As a result of this legislation Mennonites with strong nonresistant convictions again emigrated to Russia (from 1853) and later to America (from 1874). Among those who remained the question of following the cabinet order or accepting full service remained in dispute, but more and more the full service was accepted, especially in World War I (about one third to one half of all males of the Mennonite congregations had to enter the army; about 10 per cent of them killed in action). So in 1933, when again universal military conscription was at hand, the Vereinigung (*q.v.;* Union of Mennonite Churches in Germany) resolved not to ask for more exemption from the law; its constitution of June 11, 1934, published in 1936, explained this development; and indeed there were no Mennonite conscientious objectors in World War II. (See **Germany**.) E.C.

Peter Froese, *Liebreiche Erinnerung von der Wehrlosigkeit* (1850); W. Mannhardt, *Die Wehrfreiheit der Altpreussischen Mennoniten* (Marienburg, 1863); John Horsch, *Die biblische Lehre von der Wehrlosigkeit* (Scottdale, 1920); Wilbur J. Bender, *Nonresistance in Colonial Pennsylvania* (Scottdale, 1934); G. F. Hershberger, *Nonresistance and the State, the Pennsylvania Quaker Experiment in Politics 1682-1756* (Scottdale, 1936); C. H. Smith, *Christian Peace: Four Hundred Years of Mennonite Peace Principles and Practice* (n.p., 1938); E. J. Swalm, *Nonresistance under Test* (Nappanee, 1838); John Horsch, *The Principle of Nonresistance as Held by the Mennonite Church* (Scottdale, 1927); S. C. Yoder, *For Conscience Sake* (Goshen, 1940); G. F. Hershberger, *Christian Relationships to State and Country* (Akron, 1942); Jacob Sudermann, "The Origin of Mennonite State Service in Russia 1870-1880," *MQR* XVII (1943) 23-46; Edward Yoder, *Compromise with War* (Akron, 1943); Edward Yoder, *Must Christians Fight* (Akron, 1943); G. F. Hershberger, *War, Peace, and Nonresistance* (first ed., Scottdale, 1944, third rev. ed., Scottdale, 1953); Edward Yoder and Don. E. Smucker, *The Christian and Conscription* (Akron, 1945); Melvin Gingerich, *Service for Peace: A History of Mennonite Civilian Public Service* (Akron, 1949); *idem, What of Noncombatant Service* (Akron, 1949); G. F. Hershberger, *The Mennonite Church in the Second World War* (Scottdale, 1951); Ernst Crous, "The Mennonites in Germany Since the Thirty Years'

War" (section on nonresistance), *MQR* XXV (1951) 241-44; S. A. Yoder, *Middle-East Sojourn* (Scottdale, 1951); John D. Unruh, *In the Name of Christ: A History of the Mennonite Central Committee and Its Services, 1920-1951* (Scottdale, 1952); Don. E. Smucker, "The Theological Basis of Christian Pacifism," *MQR* XXVII (1953) 63-86; John A. Toews, *True Nonresistance Through Christ* (Winnipeg, 1955); *Peace Is the Will of God* (Amsterdam, 1953); H. P. Krehbiel, *War—Peace—Amity* (Newton, 1937); *Erfahrungen der Mennoniten in Canada während des zweiten Weltkrieges—1939-1945* (Steinbach, 1948); Edward Krehbiel, *Nationalism, War and Society* (New York, 1916); Krahn, Fretz, Kreider, "Altruism in Mennonite Life," in Pitirim A. Sorokin's *Forms and Techniques of Altruistic and Spiritual Growth* (Boston, 1954); Cornelius Krahn, "Public Service in Russia," *The Mennonite* LVIII (June 8, June 22, August 31, and September 21, 1943); Gustav Reimer and G. Gaeddert, *Exiled by the Czar* (Newton, 1956); C. Henry Smith, *The Story of the Mennonites* (Newton, 1950); Peace Study Conferences, Moundridge 1953, Winona 1950, etc.; *Inv. Arch. Amst.* I, Nos. 428 f., 431, 433, 436 f., 441, 453 f., 570-84, 887, 1471, 1559, 1638, 1736, 2359, 2471; II,. Nos. 2994, 3290 f., 3293-3319; II, 2, Nos. 37, 211-15, 309-12, 330; *DB* 1864, 113, 115 f.; 1867, 103; 1873, 144; 1877, 17 *et passim;* 1878, 29; 1879, 27 *et passim;* 1880, 53, 56-60; 1881, 1-32, 87; 1882, 91-94; 1883, 35; 1884, 33; 1887, 120; 1891, 20; 1898, 123-49; 1903, 94; 1904, 45, 53 f.; 1905, 23 f.; 1907, 128-33, 157, 160; 1908, 36-47, 114; 1909, 154 f.; 1910, 9, 22; 1919, 39-41, 63-67; J. Dyserinck, "De weerloosheid volgens de Doopsgezinden," *De Gids* I (1890) 104-61 and 303-42; *De Zondagsbode,* Jan. 10, 1915; K. Vos, *De Weerloosheid volgens de Doopsgezinden* (Geschr, t.b.v. de Doopsgezinden in de Verstrooiing, No. 52, Amsterdam, 1924); J. M. Leendertz, *Een Doopsgezind getuigenis tegen militair geweld* (Wolvega, n.d.-1924); *Evangelie en Krijgsdienst* (1929); N. van der Zijpp, *De vroegere Doopsgezinden en de Krijgsdienst* (Wolvega, 1930); H. Bremer, *De basis van ons weerloos Christendom* (n.p., n.d.-1952); T. O. Hylkema, *Wat de Bijbel zegt: Dienende weerlose liefde? ... Of niet?* (n.p., 1953); J. M. Leendertz and T. O. Hylkema, *Nieuw Leven in een Oude Broederschap* (n.p., 1956); E. Crous, article "Germany," *ME* II, 495-97.

Nonresistant Relief Organization (NRRO), a fundraising organization created in 1917 by the several Mennonite and Brethren in Christ bodies in Ontario. A preliminary meeting of ten persons representing four groups of nonresistant churches was held in the Wideman Mennonite Church (MC) near Markham, Ont., on Nov. 17, 1917, to consider the status of nonresistants under the Canadian Military Service Act of 1917, and to devise a practical expression of appreciation to the government for past exemptions from military service. L. J. Burkholder of Markham was chairman of the meeting and David W. Heise of Gormley, Ont., was secretary. The permanent organization was effected in Kitchener, Ont., on Jan. 16, 1918, by representatives of the following bodies: Ontario Conference (MC), Markham district (OOM), North Waterloo district (OOM), United Missionary Church (MBC at that time), Brethren in Christ (Tunker), Amish Mennonite, United Mennonite (GCM), Mennonite Brethren, and Stirling Avenue (GCM, at that time independent). Each group is entitled to three representatives. A fund of $70,000 was contributed and presented to the government in appreciation for exemption privileges, and at government request was distributed to various relief organizations for war sufferers in Europe. Contacts were maintained with the government in the interpretation and application of the Military Service Act as it affected members of the churches, to maintain exemption privileges. The organization was active in raising funds for China famine relief in 1920, Russian famine relief 1921, support of Russian immigrants to Canada 1923, Spanish relief 1937, drought relief in the Canadian Northwest 1937-38, evacuees' relief in England 1939, European relief through the MCC 1939, co-operation with Western Canada relief organizations, support of relief homes in England 1941, food and clothing shipments for MCC relief from 1946 on. The organization, for the sake of better service, was co-ordinated with the Conference of Historic Peace Churches in 1946, but functions as an organization as before. Since 1944 it has regularly appointed a member on the MCC. It now works through the regional office at Waterloo.

S.F.C.

Nonviolence is a term used to characterize the strategy of coercion without the use of physical force, for the furtherance of social ends, such as that used by the Indian leader, Gandhi, as well as by certain types of western pacifism. While illustrations of so-called nonviolence can be cited which approach the spirit of New Testament nonresistance, the latter is not to be equated with the Gandhian type of nonviolence, which is aggressively coercive in its strategy as well as non-Christian in its basic philosophy.

The chief source of Gandhi's philosophy was the Hindu idea of suffering as a means of appeasing the gods. As the Hindu endures self-inflicted suffering in order to wrest from heaven some good for himself, so the nonviolent coercionist may employ the hunger strike, the picket line, non-co-operation, and similar strategies to compel his social or political opponent to do him good. Gandhi's followers even threw themselves before the wheels of British military vehicles, risking their lives in an effort through embarrassment and frustration to thwart the imperial power and thus compel it to do that which the coercionist desired.

While such a strategy is preferable to violence and bloodshed it is in reality a form of warfare rather than the New Testament way of peace. Nonviolent coercion is a strategy for compelling the other party to do one good, to do that which is just. New Testament nonresistance is not a strategy. It is the way of love and the cross, not seeking suffering for the achievement of some social end, but rather following Christ in sacrificial service for the good of the other party, whether this good is reciprocated or not.

In nonviolent coercion the primary aim is to obtain the good for oneself or one's cause, although there may be love for the one against whom the coercion is directed. The greater the love, however, and the nearer the way of the cross is approached, the more will be the aim to appeal to the other party and win him to the way of love, rather than to embarrass him and to compel him, and thus the nearer will be the approach to New Testament nonresistance.

The nonviolent protest of the Negro minister Martin Luther King and his followers against discrimination in transportation facilities in Montgomery, Ala., in 1956-57, inasmuch as it was a strategy of simply declining the use of the buses, without aggressive acts of embarrassment or attempts to restrain others from using the buses, and inasmuch as great emphasis was placed on prayer and on love for those who engaged in unjust discrimination, would seem to be more a strategy of appeal and less one of compulsion, and thus would seem more nearly to approach New Testament nonresistance than is the case of most forms of nonviolence.   G.F.H.

R. B. Gregg, *The Power of Non-Violence* (Philadelphia, 1934); K. Shridharani, *War Without Violence* (New York, 1939); Guy F. Hershberger, *War, Peace, and Nonresistance* (Scottdale, 1944, rev. ed. 1953).

Noodbrug, De (Emergency Bridge), a Dutch Mennonite periodical, edited by S. H. N. Gorter and C. Nijdam, which was published by the A.D.S. (Dutch General Mennonite Conference) after the end of World War II, to replace *De Zondagsbode* (*q.v.*), which had been forbidden during the war by the German Nazi regime then occupying the Netherlands. The first issue of *De Noodbrug* appeared in June 1945, the last (12th) number in September 1946, when it was succeeded by the *Algemeen Doopsgezind Weekblad* (*q.v.*).   vDZ.

Nooddruft, Louwerens, an Anabaptist martyr: see **Laurens Janssen.**

Noodfonds vanwege de A.D.S. is a fund established in 1944 by the A.D.S. (Dutch Mennonite General Conference) to raise money for the rebuilding of Mennonite churches in the Netherlands which were destroyed during World War II. More than 600,000 guilders were raised by congregations and individuals, making it possible to rebuild the four churches of Vlissingen, Wageningen, Rotterdam, and Nijmegen, and to aid a few other congregations in repairing meetinghouses and parsonages damaged in the war.   vDZ.

Noomen (Noome, Nome, Nomen), a Dutch Mennonite family, found in the Zaan region and particularly at Zaandam, North Holland, where many members of this family have been deacons. Klaas Noome, a farmer and weaver, was a Mennonite preacher at Zaandam as early as 1543. In this year he was arrested because he read the Bible, but escaped en route to Haarlem. Krelis Jansse Noome was a preacher of the Frisian congregation (Oude Huys) at Zaandam 1651-69. Pieter Noome is said to have preached a remarkable sermon before Czar Peter I of Russia, then staying at Zaandam (about 1700). A lateral branch of this family is the van Lijnen Noomen family.   vDZ.

S. Lootsma, *Het Nieuwe Huys* (Zaandam, 1937) 11, 80, 85, 94, 189, 191, 194.

Noordbroek and the adjacent **Nieuw-Scheemda** (*q.v.*) are villages in the Dutch province of Groningen (*q.v.*), the seat of a Mennonite congregation. Its origin is still unknown. It is however known that there were at first two congregations, one of them in Noordbroek, the other, as Blaupot ten Cate supposes, called Nieuw-Scheemda or Scheemder-hamrik, another name for the place "Klein-Oldambt," which name is found on the list of preachers and in the records of the Groningen Sociëteit (Conference) of the Old Flemish until 1743. Both congregations belonged to this Sociëteit. Noordbroek was also the home of the noted Elder Uko Walles (q.v.), who was banned in 1637. Both congregations suffered grievously in the "Martini" flood, which put a part of the province of Groningen under water in 1686. In Klein-Oldambt four men and eight women, and twenty-seven children perished, besides many cattle; in Noordbroek the damage was limited to cattle. In 1717 another flood caused a great deal of damage, drowning many cattle. In 1738 there were still two independent congregations, which apparently united about 1740. In 1811 a new church was built in Noordbroek, and in 1840 one in Scheemda, and also a parsonage in Noordbroek. The church in Nieuw-Scheemda was used until 1919. The membership, which stood at 93 in 1733, had sunk to 50 by 1795; in 1840 it had risen to 85, in 1900, 82, and in 1957 decreased to 28. The first minister whose name has come down to us was Albert Feyes (d. 1650), elder; others were Claes Jansen, Hendrik Sybes, Jacob Alberts, preachers in the 17th century, and the preacher Albert Hendriks (d. 1760) serving from 1722, Peter Harms (d. 1768) from 1733, Albert Jans (d. 1770) from 1738, Jan Peters (d. 1760) from 1751, Harm Roelofs (d. 1791) from 1753, Otto Willems 1764-88, Jacob Harkes 1776-96, Hendrik Bavink 1786-89, and Pieter Harmens de Vries 1790-96. Isaack ten Kate (d. 1839), who served here in 1796-1836, was the last untrained preacher of the congregations, the first preacher educated at the Amsterdam Seminary being Jacob Bodisco, who served at Noordbroek and Nieuw-Scheemda 1840-49. He was followed by H. ten Cate Hoedemaker 1850-52, F. J. Klaasesz 1853-58, J. ten Bruggencate 1859-71, P. E. Lugt 1872-74, B. ten Bruggencate 1874-1900, Iz. Hulshoff 1901-3, J. H. van Giessen 1904-6, and J. M. Vis 1907-45. After Vis's resignation the pastor of Sappemeer was charged with the preaching and catechetical service in Noordbroek. vdZ.

Inv. Arch. Amst. II, Nos. 2146-49; Blaupot t. C., *Groningen* I, *passim*, see Index; *DJ* 1840, 52; 1850, 57; *DB* 1879, 5, 7 f.; *ML* III, 265.

Noordeind van Graft en Rijp, a Dutch Mennonite congregation: see **Graft.**

Noordholland, Vriesche (Friesche) Doopsgezinde Sociëteit in, was a conference of Mennonite congregations of the (Old) Frisian branch in the Dutch province of North Holland. It was founded about 1628 to assist in maintaining the old Mennonite principles and practices. In 1639 twelve articles were drawn up, in 1697 somewhat altered and augmented, which summarized these principles. Until 1729 these articles were regularly read at the sessions of the Conference, always being "adopted without comment." After 1729 the reading was omitted.

Another purpose of the Conference was to organize the preaching, baptism, and communion services in the member congregations. For this purpose conference elders (called *Landsdienaren*), usually two, visited the congregations. After about 1730 three "commissarissen voor den predikdienst"

organized the services in congregations where there was no minister. The third, and from about 1730 the most important, business of the Conference was to give financial support to weak congregations.

The Conference was presumably established by the Old Frisian congregation at Hoorn and particularly its Elder Pieter Jansz Twisck (q.v.). The following 19 congregations were members: Amsterdam Frisian congregation (when this congregation merged in 1752 with the Zonist congregation the latter became a member), Aalsmeer aan de Uiterweg, Hoorn, Medemblik, Alkmaar (Ridderstraat congregation), Edam, Zaandam-West (Oude Huys), Westzaan op 't Zuid, Wormerveer op 't Zuid, Oosthuizen (later called Beemster), Middelie and Axwijk, Venhuizen, Twisk and Abbekerk, Lange- and Koedijk, Oude Niedorp, Barsingerhorn and Kolhorn, Huisduinen and Den Helder, Burg and Waal on the island of Texel, Hippolytushoef and 't Stroe on the island of Wieringen. Purmerend was a member in the 17th century and again after 1793. Amsterdam withdrew in 1802.

Until 1798 meetings were held annually, at first on various dates, and after about 1740 on the second Wednesday of June. After 1798 the meetings were held only every two years. Originally they met at different places, then for a long period at Edam, 1709-19 in Alkmaar, and 1719-1804 in rotation at Hoorn, Alkmaar, Amsterdam, Zaandam, and Wormerveer, and 1806-18 in Alkmaar. Since 1818 no meetings have been held. In 1841 the Conference merged with the Rijper Sociëteit (q.v.). vdZ.

Blaupot t. C., *Holland* II, 70-81, and 223-28 (containing the twelve articles); *DB* 1872, 53 f.; *DJ* 1935, 34-45; 1940, 59 f.

Noordhollandsche Ring van Doopsgezinde Gemeenten (North Holland Circle of Mennonite Congregations) is an organization founded in 1844 to arrange for regular services in congregations without a minister, the preachers of the other congregations of the group serving these congregations in rotation. (*DJ* 1850, 35 f.; *Inv. Arch. Amst.* I, Nos. 945-51.) vdZ.

Noordhollandsche Weduwenfonds (Fund for the Relief of Widows of Mennonite Pastors in the Dutch Province of North Holland): see **Fonds tot Ondersteuning.**

Noordhorn, a village in the Dutch province of Groningen (q.v.), where there is a Mennonite congregation. Not much is known about the origin of this congregation; it was apparently founded in an early period. Leenaert Bouwens (q.v.) baptized 29 or 32 persons here in 1551-82. In 1621 Mattheus Janssen of Noordhorn, who was appointed as a delegate of the Landdag (legislature) of the province of Groningen, was not admitted to its sessions because he was a Mennonite. The Noordhorn congregation was formerly called Humsterland (q.v.) and also Oldehove and Ter Horne, where the old church stood. This old church, which was difficult of access and in need of repairs, was replaced in 1838 by a new one more centrally located in the village of Noordhorn, where a parsonage was also built. Since that time it has been known as the Noordhorn congregation. For a long time, 1818-71, Gerrit Bakker was the preacher here, who took an active part in the organization of the Groningen Sociëteit (Conference) and was its first secretary. During this time the membership rose from 40 to 90. In 1872 a new parsonage was built. In 1877 Noordhorn was one of the few congregations which did not require adult baptism in receiving a member of another creed; it was also one of the first Dutch Mennonite congregations to allow women to vote. The baptized membership was 85 in 1861, 89 in 1900, but only 70 in 1957. During the last half century the following pastors served here: A. de Jong 1898-1910, R. D. Boersma 1912-22, Miss F. Tieks Koening 1936-42, J. H. Rawie 1942-46, and S. S. Smeding 1946- . Since 1946 the pastor of Noordhorn has also been the pastor of the Grijpskerk (q.v.) congregation. To the Noordhorn congregation also belongs the Mennonite Kring (circle) of Oldehove (q.v.). The congregation has a ladies' circle, a youth group, and activities of youth workers (age 12-15).   vdZ.

Inv. Arch. Amst. II, Nos. 2150-53; Blaupot t. C., *Groningen* I, 52, 86, 206, 238; II, 40; *DJ* 1837, 34 f.; 1840, 27 f., 1850, 60; *DB* 1861, 152; 1877, 148; 1906, 46; *ML* III, 265.

Noord-Oost-Polder (Northeast Polder), an area of 128,520 acres reclaimed from the Zuiderzee, Netherlands, in 1940, now consisting of fertile arable land. On Jan. 23, 1948, the Mennonites living here formed a Kring (circle), which in 1953 became an independent congregation. Services are held biweekly in a rented hall at Emmeloord. H. H. Gaaikema, the pastor of the Harlingen congregation, has charge of this congregation. The baptized membership in 1955 was 41, and 60 in 1957.   vdZ.

Noor(t)dijk, Pieter, b. *ca.* 1660 at Amsterdam, d. on Nov. 20, 1708, at Amsterdam, a Dutch Mennonite minister, trained for the ministry by Galenus Abrahamsz (q.v.), was a preacher of the Utrecht congregation in 1685-1704, and of the Lamist congregation in Amsterdam in 1704-8. In January 1699 he was invited to replace Galenus Abrahamsz as the preacher of the Amsterdam Lamist congregation and as a professor of its seminary, but he declined and Galenus retained his position. Again after the death of Galenus (1706) Noortdijk was invited to become a professor of the seminary, but he again refused.   vdZ.

H. B. Berghuys, *Geschiedenis der Doopsgez. Gemeente te Utrecht* (n.p., n.d., Utrecht, 1926) 41, 43-45; H. W. Meihuizen, *Galenus Abrahamsz* (Haarlem, 1954) 169 f., 181, 187, 192; *DB* 1918, 53, 67.

Norden, a town (pop. 16,800) in East Friesland (q.v.), Germany, in the (formerly Prussian) district of Aurich. It has been the seat of a Mennonite congregation since the second half of the 16th century. The publications of J. P. Müller and Jan ten Doornkaat Koolman give much information on the history of the Norden congregation, which once occupied a leading place among the Mennonites.

Since Anna (q.v.), regent of East Friesland in 1528-40, offered protection to all victims of religious persecution, Mennonite refugees from Holland settled in the town of Emden (q.v.) about 1530; Menno Simons also came about 1542 and preached there

until 1545. Leenaert Bouwens (q.v.) visited Norden three or four times in 1563-65, baptizing 15 persons, and about 1575 two more. In that time, or even earlier, congregations were formed in Emden, Aurich, Leer, and Norden, which were not seriously disturbed until the Thirty Years' War and which were given many a concession by the government.

Under Enno III (q.v.), 1599-1625, when the center of Mennonitism in East Friesland moved from Emden to Norden, the Lutheran clergy began to use their influence upon the authorities to have the Mennonite worship services suppressed, who were accustomed to gather "when the church bells rang and Christian sermons were delivered and thus drew many simple Christians to themselves." The count was persuaded to announce a mandate on Nov. 21, 1612, against the open preaching of Mennonite doctrine. After many years of effort on the part of the Mennonites the count consented to permit the 400 Mennonites living in the principality the free exercise of their religion for ten years in return for a fee of 12,000 Talers; but the services were not permitted to be held publicly.

During the Thirty Years' War, when deep misery passed over the country, the attitude toward the Mennonites underwent a change. Enno's son Rudolf Christian (1625-28) issued a letter of protection on May 26, 1626, for which an annual payment of six Talers was to be made by each Mennonite family.

By the end of the war there were sixty Mennonite families in Norden, who were divided into two branches after the beginning of the 17th century— the moderate Waterlanders (q.v.), and the rigidly traditional Groningen Old Flemish (q.v.). The division was due less to matters of faith than to differences of opinion, especially in matters of dress. After the coming of Uko Walles (q.v.), a peasant with an unusual gift of oratory who belonged to the stricter branch of the Old Flemish and had a great following in Norden after 1633, the clergy of Norden again raised complaint and demanded the expulsion of Uko, but were not successful; instead, Ulrich II gave the Old Flemish a special letter of protection on Nov. 26, 1635.

Because the Mennonites refused to give up the letter of protection when Christine Charlotte assumed the government as princess in 1665, she issued a mandate on June 20, 1666, forbidding them to hold worship services, and threatening expulsion from the country in case of transgression; but the mandate was not enforced. On the contrary, on Dec. 7, 1666, the Old Flemish received their letter of protection upon payment of 400 Talers, and the Waterlanders upon payment of 800 Talers; these were renewed on Dec. 19, 1690, by Prince Christian Eberhard, 1690-1708, in return for a large sum of money.

A petition made by the Mennonites to Prince George Albrecht on Jan. 22, 1709, for permission to admit persons of other churches into the Mennonite brotherhood was refused with the comment that they could hope for such a privilege only if they gave him a gift of 3,000 Talers. In this negotiation the government official explained in defense of the Mennonites that they were much less wealthy than formerly, for the richest had joined the Lutherans, other wealthy ones had died, and the Mennonites were heavily burdened with large families; but on the other hand, they made themselves of use everywhere and were of benefit to the country. On April 10, 1709, the Old Flemish, and on April 16 the Waterlanders, received their letters of protection upon payment of the stipulated sum.

From 1723 on, the center of the brotherhood in East Friesland was gradually transferred from Norden to Leer (q.v.). The Old Flemish congregations of Emden and Norden in the 17th century seem to have been served by the same minister. In 1715 the two congregations separated, and henceforth each had its own minister.

The last prince of East Friesland, Carl Edzard, 1734-44, was friendly toward the Mennonites. The letter of protection of May 30, 1738, shows understanding of both wings. In 1739 the Mennonites were ordered to keep a record of births. Marriages could be performed by the Mennonite preachers, but had to be registered with the pastor of the established church. On Oct. 14, 1739, the Mennonites were ordered to keep church records. After the death of Carl Edzard, East Friesland passed to Prussia on Aug. 19, 1744. For a new letter of protection the Mennonites in Norden and Leer were required to pay 1800 Talers. King Frederick William also gave them a letter in return for a payment of 900 Talers.

The Waterlanders in Norden had a church and a parsonage, as well as an almshouse on the west side of the square. The Old Flemish met for worship in a leased house. When they were notified that the lease could not be renewed, they reached an agreement with the Waterlanders to use their church when the home congregation was not using it. On April 13, 1780, the Old Flemish congregation, which had a membership of 56 besides 49 children, united with the Waterlanders, so that there was in Norden, as there had been for some time in Emden and Leer, a single united congregation, which adopted a constitution on June 29, 1793. Ministers of the Old Flemish congregation in 1715 were Cornelis Eppes and Claes Folkerts. Gerrit Hilbrantsz served until about 1740, Heert Cornelisz (d. 1761) 1721-ca.55, Job Abrahamsz 1732-d.67, Jan Warners 1733-ca.54, Rijke Jansz 1755-ca.68, Harmen Allertsz (Alless) Kremer 1755-ca.68. All these ministers had been chosen out of the congregation. The following three ministers, though still untrained, were called in: Nolle Abeles Venema, serving 1768-75, Hendrik J. Blaauw 1775-76, and Daniel Rieken (Ricken), a Swiss Mennonite, 1777-d.79. Concerning the Waterlander congregation the list is not complete: preachers in 1690 were Jan Oom Hendricks (Jan Hendriks Bakker), Jannes Abrams, and Pieter van Geuns. Pieter van Geuns served this congregation from before 1690 until 1740, and Marcus Arisz 1741-85.

The Lutheran clergy continued to interfere in the internal affairs of the Mennonites in Norden and to secure financial advantages for themselves. On May 19, 1795, they presented a long letter of complaint to Frederick William II (q.v.) of Prussia, chiefly on the ground that the Mennonites were having their own preachers deliver their funeral sermons, instead of calling in a Lutheran clergyman and paying him

a louis d'or. On Aug. 5, 1795, the king's decision rejected all the points in the Lutheran complaint.

The Mennonites were now seriously planning to replace their old church, which looked more like a barn than a church, with a more suitable edifice. A house was bought, remodeled, furnished with an organ. Services were conducted in Dutch until 1885. Until then the Amsterdam Mennonite hymnal was also used; after 1885 the hymnbook of the Reformed Church in East Friesland was adopted.

In 1802 the Lutherans attempted to require contributions from Mennonites for repair of Lutheran churches. The Mennonites refused, saying that they did not use the Lutheran churches and that they had built their own without Lutheran assistance. The Lutherans replied that the Mennonites had after all used Lutheran services, such as visits to the sick, funeral sermons, etc., and had used the Lutheran church bell for their funerals. Again the Lutheran demands were rejected. In 1826 there was again some difficulty when the Mennonites and Reformed were required to contribute toward the Lutheran almshouse, although they were supporting their own poor. This problem was solved by giving Mennonites and Reformed permission to make use of the Lutheran almshouses.

When the new constitution for Hannover was to be drafted, the Mennonites of Norden presented a petition for equal recognition with other denominations (June 1831). It was refused. But in 1848, in view of the political movements in Germany, which among other things granted equal status to all creeds, a law was passed making civil rights independent of church affiliation.

The membership of the Norden congregation has steadily declined. In the Waterlander congregation 208 took communion in 1698; 116 in 1737. The membership of the Old Flemish church in 1715 numbered about 70 baptized members, 51 in 1733, 56 in 1769 after it had merged with the small congregation of Krummhörn (q.v.), a few years previously. At the merger the baptized membership of the united congregation was 140; in 1890, 104 and 92 children; in 1940 this number had decreased to 68 and 12 children; in 1955 the number was 125. After the merger the united congregation at first was served by the preacher of the former Waterlander congregation, Marcus Arisz, who served until 1785. Other ministers serving here were Hendrik Bavink 1781-86, Arend van Gelder 1785-95, Dirk Huizinga 1802-9, Jan van Hulst 1809-44, Johannes Pol 1847-84, L. Hesta 1884-89, and C. A. Leendertz 1889-1931. In 1934 Abraham Fast, pastor of Emden, took upon himself the charge to serve also in Norden. In 1957 he was succeeded by his son Heinold Fast.

Formerly there were many contacts between the congregations of Norden, both the Old Flemish and the Waterlander, and Holland. In 1681 Galenus Abrahamsz, the minister of the Amsterdam Lamist congregation, was called to Norden to settle a quarrel in the Waterlander congregation. In the following years this congregation was several times financially supported by Amsterdam for the salary of its preachers. In 1686 and again in 1718 both congregations, having been struck in previous years by severe floods, received aid from the Dutch congregations. Johannes Deknatel (*q.v.*), the pietistic minister of Amsterdam, was a native of Norden. It was Deknatel who trained the Norden preacher Marcus Arisz for the ministry. Both Arisz (1719-85), a native from Amsterdam, and his wife Catharina Leeuw of Haarlem, were influenced by Deknatel and friends of the Moravian Brethren, which caused some conflicts in the Norden congregation.

Among the outstanding Mennonite families of Norden are Cremer (Antje Cremer ten Doornkaat, married to Isaak Brons, was born in Norden), Brouwer (Brouer), ten Doornkaat, and Stroman. (See **East Friesland.**)   HEGE, vDZ.

Jan ten Doornkaat Koolman, *Kurze Mitteilungen aus der Gesch. der . . . Norder Gemeinde . . .* (Norden, 1903); *idem, Mitteilungen aus der Gesch. der Mennoniten-Gemeinde zu Norden im 19. Jahrhundert* (Norden, 1904); L. Hesta, "De laatste bladzijde van de Gesch. der Out-Vlaamsche gem. te Norden," *DB* 1895, 75-100; J. P. Müller, *Die Mennoniten in Ostfriesland . . .* (Amsterdam, 1887); *Inv. Arch. Amst.* I, Nos. 1095, 1147; II, Nos. 1872, 2814-48; *DJ* 1840, 45 f., 57; 1850, 63; *DB* 1862, 152; 1863, 102; 1875, 54; 1879, 8; Blaupot t. C., *Groningen* I, 226 f.; *Zondagsbode* XVII (1903-4) Nos. 29-36; *ML* III, 270-72.

Nordheim (Marinovka), a village in the Memrik settlement (*q.v.*) in the province of Ekaterinoslav, Russia, which was settled in 1885 by 32 landless and poor Mennonites from the Molotschna and Chortitza settlements. At first the inhabitants had hardly enough to shelter them from the cold and rain; but in a few years they became prosperous through industrious cultivation of a basically good soil. In 1887 the village built a school. In 1912 it had a population of 203.   HEGE.

D. H. Epp, *Die Memriker Ansiedlung* (Berdyansk, 1910) 89-91; *Neuer Haus- und Landwirtschafts-Kalender* (Odessa, 1913) 51; *ML* III, 272.

Nordheim Mennonite Church (GCM) of Dundurn, Sask., about 30 miles south of Saskatoon, was one of the first churches to be organized after the immigration of Russian Mennonites in 1923, being organized in 1925 by Elder Johann J. Klassen, an immigrant from Russia. This congregation has four meeting places (churches): one in the village of Dundurn; the Pleasant Point Church, 9½ miles northeast of Dundurn; the Hanley Church, 10 miles west of Hanley; and the fourth, 11 miles east of Elbow, Sask. This meetinghouse is owned jointly by the Mennonite Brethren and the General Conference Mennonites. The congregation belongs to the Conference of Mennonites in Canada. It had 285 baptized members in 1956, with G. J. Warkentin as minister in charge.   G.J.W.

Nordheim Mennonite Church (GCM), located near Winnipegosis in the rural municipality of Mossy River, 6½ miles northwest of Fork River, Man., a member of the General Conference of Mennonites of Canada, was organized in 1933 with 38 members, under the leadership of Gerhard Goertzen. In 1956 the membership was 114, mostly rural. The meetinghouse, a log structure with a seating capacity of 400, was built in 1935. Other ministers who have served the congregation are Jakob Martens, Abram Bergen, and C. C. Janzen.   C.C.J.

Nordhorn, an industrial town in Germany near the Dutch border, where there are a number of Mennonites, mostly engaged in textile industries, e.g., the Stroink family. About 1880 services were occasionally held in a private house, but the plan to found a congregation was never carried out. The Mennonites of Nordhorn have joined the Gronau (*q.v.*) congregation.   vDZ.

Nördlingen, a town (pop. 13,000) in Bavaria, Germany, situated on the Eger, formerly a free imperial city, in which the Anabaptist movement occasionally found a following. Soon after the origin of the Swiss Brethren in Zürich, a congregation of former Catholics was formed in Nördlingen, which left it to the parents to decide whether they would baptize their infants after birth or have them consecrated by the laying on of hands (*q.v.*) in the presence of the congregation (Roosen, p. 76 and 86), baptism on confession of faith to follow later.

Little is known about this group. Ambrosius Spittelmeier (*q.v.*), who was seized in Erlangen and executed on Feb. 6, 1528, had planned a visit to the Nördlingen congregation. In 1531 the city authorities succeeded in capturing two foreign Anabaptists, Melchior Gram of Geisslingen and Stephan Baltzer of Weil. They were banished from the city for refusing to swear a required oath. On March 30, 1534, the magistrate issued an order to expel all Anabaptists. Later on the Anabaptists who did not join the state church emigrated to Württemberg and Moravia.   HEGE.

H. Clauss, "Wiedertäufer in der ehemaligen Reichsstadt Nördlingen," in *Jahrbuch des Historischen Vereins für Nördlingen und Umgebung* (1933) 144-48; B. C. Roosen, "Pieter Beets über die Einsegnung der neugeborenen Kinder," in *Menn. Bl.*, 1900, 76 and 86; *ML* III, 275.

Norfolk County is located in southeast Virginia. In the eastern part of the county, about 12 miles from Norfolk and 2 miles from Fentress, a Mennonite settlement of approximately 225 persons was located in 1957. A few families were living across the county line east in Princess Anne County. To the west in the same county was the Portsmouth settlement of approximately 90 persons. The Portsmouth area church is known as Deep Creek and the Fentress church is named Mount Pleasant. Both have Christian day schools. The first Mennonites arrived in the county in 1899 and the first church was dedicated in May 1910. Several Conservative Amish Mennonite families were living in the county. They were affiliated with the larger settlement near Kempsville, Princess Anne County.   L.H.W.

Norma Mennonite Mission (MC), located at Norma, near Vineland, N.J., was opened in a Jewish refugee community by the Mission Board of the Lancaster Conference. The meetinghouse is a church, 24 x 40 ft., that had been closed. It was dedicated as a mission in January 1957. Amos Horst is the bishop in charge (1957).   D.S.K.

Normal, Ill., a twin city (pop. 12,000) with Bloomington on its south, in McLean County, is the site of Illinois State Normal University. Mennonites living in and around the city are almost all of the

Central District Conference (GCM). The First Mennonite Church of Normal with 230 members, is located within the city, at University and Church Streets. Approximately 400 Mennonites live within the trading area of Normal.　　　　R.L.H.

Normal First Mennonite Church (GCM), Normal, Ill., was organized in March 1912, with 35 charter members, as the result of the interest and efforts of Peter Schantz, Sr., minister of the East White Oak Mennonite Church, not far from Normal, in providing opportunity for fellowship and worship for Mennonites who then lived in Bloomington and Normal. Services were held in rented quarters until a church was built at the present location, Church and University Streets. This frame structure was remodeled in 1951. The church had a membership of 230 in 1957, with H. N. Harder as pastor.　　　　R.L.H.

Normanvillars, a Mennonite settlement on the border of the Sundgau (southern Alsace) and the Territory of Belfort, in a forest area called by that name, some 10-15 miles northeast of Montbéliard, southeast of Belfort, and north of Delle in Switzerland. The settlement was established in 1747-80 by Mennonite families coming from the Swiss Jura to the south and a few Amish families coming from the Montbéliard area to the southwest. By 1791, according to a military census, 23 of the 97 families in the commune of Florimont were Mennonite. By the end of the 18th century the rather extended settlement was divided into two organized congregations, both meeting in homes, the one to the north called La Maie (later Belfort, q.v.), the one in the south called Florimont (q.v.). The first meetinghouse at Normanvillars, the Chapelle des Fermes, was erected in 1849 after many members had emigrated. The beginning of emigration to America was in 1819. A number of families settled in Putnam County, Ohio, others in western Waterloo County, Ont. For a detailed account of the Normanvillars settlement see D. Gratz, *Bernese Anabaptists and their American Descendants* (Scottdale, 1950) 89-95 *et passim.*　　　　H.S.B.

Norris Square Mennonite (MC) Church (formerly Mennonite Home Mission), located in Philadelphia, Pa., began as a mission Sunday school in the spring of 1899, with Joseph Bechtel, a building contractor, as superintendent. It was sponsored by the "Lancaster County Sunday School Mission" (now the Eastern Mennonite Board of Missions and Charities), who sent Amanda Musselman and Mary Denlinger as full-time city missionaries. The Lancaster and Franconia conferences alternated in supplying preachers for Sunday services until 1922, when J. Paul Graybill was stationed as pastor-superintendent (now bishop of the congregation). Originally at 1930 East York St., the work is now located at 2147-51 North Howard St. and belongs to the Lancaster Conference. The present name was adopted in 1938, an important year in the organization of the congregation, when a deacon, Joseph Bromley, Sr., was chosen from within the congregation. In 1946 Jacob Frederick was chosen minister in a simi-

lar way, to assist the pastor-superintendent, Clarence Y. Fretz. Teaching the Bible has been a prominent feature of the work from the first; large-scale literature distribution for the last twenty-five years; and open-air evangelism for the last five years. The summer Bible school movement in eastern Mennonite (MC) churches had its beginning here in 1927, and the weekday Bible school movement in 1931. During the depression of 1932 eighteen hundred families were helped. In 1956 the total baptized membership was 33, with Jacob Frederick as pastor. C.Y.F.

Alta Mae Erb, *Studies in Mennonite City Missions* (Scottdale, 1937) 38-44; Clarence Y. Fretz, "Mennonitism in Philadelphia," *Christian Monitor,* June-July, 1945 (Scottdale) 133, 134, 165, 166; Ira D. Landis, *The Missionary Movement Among Lancaster Conference Mennonites* (Scottdale, 1938) 41-47; John C. Wenger, *History of the Mennonites of the Franconia Conference* (Telford, 1937) 333.

Norristown First Mennonite (MC) Church in Norristown, Pa., a member of the Franconia Conference, was founded in 1919 as the Mennonite Gospel Mission, the first mission station in the Franconia Conference. Meetings were held first in a residence purchased at 21 W. Marshall St. In 1924 a one-story brick auditorium annex was erected. In 1949 a Jewish synagogue adjacent to the residence was purchased and renovated and is since then the meetinghouse. In the same year the congregation became self-sustaining. In 1956 there were 71 members.

At the beginning the work was in charge of resident superintendents, among whom were Elmer Moyer (1919-20), Allen Freed (1920-21), Willis K. Lederach (1921-28), William G. Detweiler (1928-31), Llewellyn Groff (1931-34), William Hoffman (1934-35), and Paul Mininger (1935-36), although the pulpit was supplied by visiting ministers until 1936. On Nov. 10 of that year Markley H. Clemmer was ordained for Norristown as the first resident pastor; he is still serving. Harold K. Weaver was ordained deacon in 1941. J. C. Clemens served as visiting pastor in 1929-31, succeeded by several others. Paul M. Lederach was ordained as an associate pastor in 1944. He served until 1950. On Nov. 10, 1956, Paul M. Hackman was ordained to assist in the work. The church at Norristown pioneered in young people's Bible meeting and summer Bible school work in the Franconia Mennonite Conference. It has been largely responsible for the establishment of two other missions—Bridgeport, Pa. (opened in 1946), and Conshohocken, Pa. (opened in 1948). P.M.L.

Norristown (Pa.) State Hospital was the location of Civilian Public Service Unit No. 66, from December 1942 to October 1946. Over 160 men served in this unit, which was under Mennonite administration. The average was 100 men for much of the period. Although the men served primarily as attendants in the mental hospital, after a period of time they were being used in nearly all of the activities of the institution. *Files* is a 48-page yearbook published by the men in the unit. Norristown has continued to be a center for work for men in I-W service.　　　　M.G.

Melvin Gingerich, *Service for Peace* (Akron, Pa., 1949) 222-23.

North Abbotsford Mennonite Brethren Church, located at Abbotsford, B.C., a member of the Canadian District M.B. Conference, was organized on Dec. 27, 1935, with 24 members. George Rempel was elected leader of the group. Other leaders have been George Doerksen, C. C. Peters, and J. J. Doerksen; assistant ministers have been George Rempel, D. P. Esau, C. C. Peters, G. P. Warkentin, J. J. Doerksen, J. P. Wiebe, A. A. Toews, A. H. Wieler, and G. Giesbrecht. The church has two choirs and an extensive program of Christian activity for the young people. The 1954 membership was 287, with H. H. Nikkel as pastor, assisted by J. F. Redekop.

J.J.D.

North America. The first Mennonites in North America were Dutch "Menists" reported to be in Manhattan (now New York City) and Gravesend, Long Island, near New York City, as early as 1644. Nothing is known of them except these reports, and no permanent settlement was made. Plockhoy's ill-starred colony on the Delaware, south of Chester, Pa. (1663-65), was scarcely Mennonite. Permanent Mennonite settlement began in 1683 (really not until 1685) at Germantown, near Philadelphia, Pa., with a small group from the Lower Rhine and Hamburg (*ca.* 100 families 1683-1705). The major immigration began in 1707-10 from the Palatinate and Switzerland into the territory north and west of Philadelphia, Pa., continuing until about 1756, when it was relatively stopped by the French and Indian War (1756-63), and was not resumed in force until after the close of the Napoleonic Wars in 1815. By that time Eastern Pennsylvania was filled, and the new groups located west of the Alleghenies and on west to central Illinois or to Ontario. The major element in the migration of 1815-60 was of Amish from Alsace, Bavaria, and Hesse, although also a considerable body of Swiss came in this period to Ohio and Indiana. While the German and Swiss immigration slowed to a trickle after this, a very large migration from Russia brought another ethnic group to North America in 1874-80, followed by a later, still larger movement from Russia in 1922-25, a small one 1930-39, and a larger one again in 1947-50. A minor movement of this ethnic element came from South America (chiefly Paraguay) to North America in 1950-57. (For a fuller account, see **Migrations.**)

Until 1824 all Mennonite immigrants from Europe to America settled only in the United States. Internal migration from Eastern Pennsylvania to Ontario (*q.v.*) in 1785-1840 established a substantial Mennonite base there. This furnished the attraction for all later substantial Mennonite movements to Canada. First were the Amish from Alsace-Lorraine and Bavaria in 1824 - 50, located adjacent to the Pennsylvania Mennonites west of Kitchener. The very large migration from Russia to Manitoba in 1874-80 was made possible largely by the leadership of Jacob Y. Shantz (*q.v.*), a Mennonite of Kitchener, and the financial aid of the Ontario Mennonites. The large later movements from Russia to Canada (almost all the Russian immigrants of 1922-25 and later came to Canada) were made possible largely by the aid of Russian Mennonites already in Mani-

toba and Saskatchewan. The freer immigration policy of the Canadian government, in contrast to the restrictive policy of the United States, together with the greater availability of land for settlement in Canada, of course played a major role in the diversion of the 20th-century immigration to Canada. Since 1880 almost no Mennonites have immigrated to the United States, whereas the majority of the Canadian Mennonites are descendants of immigrants who arrived after 1920. This fact, coupled with the conservatism of the Manitoba Mennonites in general has resulted in retention of the German language among the Canadian Mennonites (with the exception of Ontario), in contrast to the United States where the use of German was effectively ended by World War I.

The third country of North America to have Mennonite settlements, Mexico, received them first in 1922 from Manitoba. Except for a very few who came from Russia in 1922-25, all Mennonites in Mexico came from Manitoba and Saskatchewan. All of them are of Russian origin, and all have maintained the German language, including the Kleine Gemeinde group, which came from Manitoba in 1947-49. The only substantial Mennonite emigration from North America has been that of the Old Colony Mennonites from Manitoba and Saskatchewan in 1926-30 (later groups 1945-48) who went to Paraguay.

Internal migration has scattered the Mennonites of North America westward from Pennsylvania, the east-central states, and the midwestern and prairie states and provinces to the Pacific Coast in both the United States and Canada.

In 1956 North America had 215,000 baptized Mennonites, with a total population of some 300,-000. The baptized members are distributed as follows by groups and countries.

Body	U.S.	Canada	Total
Mennonite (MC)	70,513	6,586	77,369
Gen. Conference	35,764	14,005	49,769
Menn. Brethren	11,095	12,967	24,062
Old Order Amish	16,794	260	17,054
Old Order Menn.	3,887	1,915	5,802
Ch. of God in Christ	4,161	1,439	5,600
M.B.C. (Pa.)	4,635	....	4,635
Sommerfelder	....	3,785	3,785
Beachy Amish	2,677	....	2,677
E.M.B.	1,564	936	2,500
E.M. (Kleingemeinde)	25	1,900	1,925
Old Colony	....	2,155	2,155
Evan. Menn.	2,210	....	2,210
Rudnerweide	....	1,824	1,824
Chortitz	....	1,408	1,408
K.M.B.	1,527	176	1,703
Reformed	662	218	880
Stauffer	357	....	357
Weaver	60	....	60
Total	155,931	49,844	205,775
Hutterites	2,900	7,560	9,460

(Taken from *Mennonite Yearbook and Directory* 1957, Scottdale, Pa.)

The above table indicates that North American Mennonitism at the mid-20th century is not unified in one common fellowship. It is true that all, except the Old Colony group in Manitoba and Mexico and the Old Order Mennonites in the United States and Canada, co-operate organizationally in the Mennonite Central Committee in relief work, peace work, and service projects. But denominationally they remain distinct. The present groups are, however, by no means all the result of divisions, at least in North America. The Old Order Amish division and the M.B. and K.M.B. divisions were imported from Europe and have been maintained in North America. The latter two groups have just merged (1957), and a large block of the O.O.A. has gradually merged with the M.C. branch. Of the groups formed by division in North America (see pertinent denominational articles) the Central Conference has merged with the G.C.M. branch (1950), and the E.M. and E.M.B. groups work together in a joint conference (1952), and the Conservative (Amish) Mennonites have practically joined the M.C. The spirit of co-operation and mutual recognition is growing among the various major and minor groups, but no further organic union is in prospect for some time to come.

The history of North American Mennonitism cannot well be viewed as a whole, not only because of the lack of organic union, but also in part because of difference in time of arrival of the successive waves of immigrants, and in part because of the relative isolation geographically and culturally of the various groups from one another. The national boundary between Canada and the United States has had little significance. However, a more detailed account of the general and spiritual history of the North American Mennonites will be found under the articles **Canada** and **United States**, so divided for convenience only. H.S.B.

H. S. Bender, "The Mennonites of the United States and Canada," *MQR* XI (1937) 50-75; C. Henry Smith, *The Mennonites of America* (Goshen, 1909); idem, *The Story of the Mennonites* (Berne, 1941).

North Brabant, a Dutch province south of the Maas, population (1947) 1,180,133. There was a slight Anabaptist-Mennonite activity in this province during the 16th century. Anabaptists there were found at 's Hertogenbosch, Breda, Vught, and a few other places, but only in small numbers. In 1571 a small Mennonite congregation at Klundert (*q.v.*) in the west part of this province was exterminated by persecution. In the 17th century a Mennonite congregation existed, called "Brabandt, Breda en Oosterhout, united with Geertruydenberg." This congregation, belonging to the Flemish branch and regularly supported by the Flemish congregation of Rotterdam, died out shortly after 1670. Now the province of North Brabant is predominantly Catholic (90 per cent of the population in 1947). There are now (1957) only two Mennonite congregations, Breda (*q.v.*) with 91 members and Eindhoven (*q.v.*) with 205. There is a Mennonite Kring (circle) at 's Hertogenbosch-Vught, at Bergen op Zoom and at Tilburg. In 1909 there were about 331 Mennonites in North Brabant, in 1930, 452, and in 1947, 758. (*DB* 1912, 30-44; *ML* III, 269.) vDZ.

North Carolina, a state in southeastern United States on the Atlantic Coast immediately south of Virginia, population slightly over 4,000,000. Until 1955 no Mennonite congregations had ever been established in the state, except the Negro congregations established through the Krimmer Mennonite Brethren mission work in the far western part of the state

near Elk Park since 1899. There are six preachers and eleven deacons in these congregations, with an attendance of about 180 at the Sunday morning services. This group is, however, not directly a part of the K.M.B. conference. In 1955 the Virginia Mennonite Conference established a mission in Hickory, 45 miles northwest of Charlotte, in the west-central part of the state, which in 1956 had 22 members.

Traces of resident Mennonites in North Carolina might be seen in the following facts. In 1778 the Colonial Assembly of North Carolina adopted a resolution stating "that all Quakers, Moravians, Dunkards and Mennonists . . . shall be admitted to the rights of citizens." Again in 1779 a resolution was adopted that the same categories of persons be exempted from the draft. There are other references to "Mennonists," all noted in *Records of the Moravians in North Carolina* III (Raleigh, N.C., 1926). Further the *Herald of Truth* for May 1866 reports a conversation with a soldier who knew of a Mennonite congregation in the state. J. F. Funk reported that J. S. Coffman was once sent to visit the supposed Mennonite congregation in North Carolina about 1880. According to Funk's oral report to the writer in 1926, Coffman found the group very much disorganized and not recognizable as Mennonites. H.S.B.

H. S. Bender, "Mennonites in North Carolina," *MQR* I (July 1927) 69-71.

North Central Conference of the Mennonite Church (MC) was a part of the Missouri-Iowa Conference until the merger in 1920 of all Mennonite (MC) and Amish conferences west of Indiana. It was then organized as the Dakota-Montana Conference in 1921. In 1945, because of its enlarged borders, the name was changed to the North Central Mennonite Conference. This was the smallest of the conferences organized at the time of the merger, and each of the other conferences (four) agreed to send a delegate to the annual conference held the second Thursday in June. In 1946 the Illinois Conference District requested that they be permitted to discontinue sending a delegate because they felt this conference could carry on without their help. The other conferences are still sending delegates, who are greatly appreciated. I. S. Mast served as the only bishop until 1926, when Eli G. Hochstetler was ordained. The district includes congregations in eastern Montana, North Dakota, Minnesota, and Wisconsin, having a total membership in 1956 of 766 in 10 congregations and 12 mission outposts, with 4 bishops, 20 ministers, and 4 deacons. The district annually sponsors a winter Bible school and a fall mission meeting. Since 1945 an annual ministers' conference has been held. F.E.K.

North Clinton Mennonite Church (MC), located one-half mile northwest of Wauseon, Ohio, was organized as a separate congregation under the Ohio and Eastern Mennonite Conference in late 1957 as an extension of the West Clinton congregation, with E. B. Frey as bishop and Olen B. Nofziger as minister in charge. A 40 x 80 brick meetinghouse was erected in 1956, with a seating capacity of 300. The initial membership was about 150. H.S.B.

North Dakota. Mennonites first began to move into this state in the late 1890's. The first group of 10 Swiss Mennonite (GCM) families came from Freeman, S.D., in 1898, and settled in the Starkweather area in Mansey and Cavalier counties. In this same period Low German Mennonites (GCM) also moved in from the Mountain Lake, Minn., and Henderson, Neb., communities. The fact that land was available at reasonable prices seems to have been the special attraction. Land agents of the Great Northern Railroad Company were especially anxious for settlers to come. The first Old Order Amish came in 1894.

The first congregation of the Mennonite Church (MC) was established in 1903 at Minot (Surrey), when a group settlement was made by Amish Mennonites from the vicinity of Belleville, Pa. A second congregation was organized at Kenmare in 1905, which died out about 1939. Later congregations were organized at Wolford in 1916 and at Casselton in 1929.

Settlements were later made in a number of counties in the state, viz., McHenry, Billings, Burleigh, Wells, McLean, Rolette, Sheridan, Pierce, Walsh, Ward, Mountrail, and perhaps others. The settlements in Cavalier County near Alsen, Munich, and Langdon have always been the strongest. In this vicinity there are three General Conference Mennonite churches, one Mennonite Brethren, and one Church of God in Christ Mennonite church. In 1939 several of the churches in this area co-operatively established a Bible school at Munich. For many years the school operated only during the five winter months. One full-time teacher was engaged, usually assisted by several of the local ministers. The peak enrollment (35) was reached in 1941. In 1951 this Bible school became Bethany Bible Academy with G. W. Schroeder as superintendent. In 1954 the Academy had two instructors and 13 students.

While agriculture has remained the predominant vocation through the years, some of the Mennonites have ventured into business, especially in the Alsen and Munich area. Statistically, there are 1,000-1,100 Mennonites in the state, besides the 75 members of the one Hutterian Brethren colony in the state, distributed as follows: G.C.M. 313, M.B. 493, M.C. 218, C.G.C. 36. These congregations are as follows: Bethel (GCM) at Dresden, 40 members; Zion (GCM) at Arena, 31; Salem (GCM) at Munich, 166; Swiss (GCM) at Alsen, 76; Rosehill (MB) at Munich, 70; Harvey (MB), 206; McClusky (MB), 25; Sawyer (MB), 98; Kief (MB), 44; Lakeview (MC) at Wolford, 109; Red River Valley (MC) at Casselton, 45; Fairview (MC) at Minot, 55; Rockway Gospel Chapel at East Minot (MC), 9; North Unity (CGC) at Wales, 28; Grafton (CGC), 8; Old Order Amish at Wolford, 8; Forest River Farm, Hutterian Brethren, at Inkster, 75.   J.D.U.

North Dakota Amish. Of the sixteen states which now contain established Old Order Amish communities, North Dakota was one of the last to receive the Amish. An interest in colonization to North Dakota began to manifest itself among the Amish in Indiana in 1893, and in Mifflin County, Pa.,

about 1896. A delegation of Amishmen from Elkhart County, Ind., consisting of Reuben L. Bontreger, Eli J. Bontreger, R. A. Yoder, J. A. Miller, and D. D. Kauffman, visited North Dakota in 1893. They were favorably impressed with the vast area of level country, recommended the Turtle Mountain district in Rolette County for prospective settlers. In the spring of 1894 four families from Indiana moved to North Dakota—R. A. Yoder, John D. Bontreger, Joni Hershberger, and M. H. Hochstedler, besides an unmarried John A. Yoder. These families settled near Rolla in Rolette County, but later moved to the Island Lake region near Mylo and Wolford.

In 1895 a mass movement of immigrants to North Dakota began, including many members of the Church of the Brethren as well as Amish, from several counties in Indiana and from Ohio and Kansas. Two special trains consisting of about ten coaches and some thirty cars carried the immigrants and their movables. Eli J. Bontreger, who was ordained a minister in 1894, and R. L. Bontreger left Indiana and with their families moved to North Dakota in 1895.

Several families in Mifflin County, Pa., became interested in the Dakotas about 1900. Jonas Renno, who owned and operated the Renno Mill near Belleville, moved there in 1898. Aaron Yoder, who married Renno's daughter, established his home there in 1901. In January 1903 D. D. Miller learned of a considerable group of Mennonites and Amishmen who were contemplating moving from Mifflin County to North Dakota. At Miller's suggestion the Belleville and Allensville, Pa., congregations (MC) met jointly on March 1, 1903, and ordained I. S. Mast to serve as minister for the new congregation about to move to Dakota. This group boarded the train at Reedsville, Pa., on March 30, 1903, and arrived at Surrey, N.D., on April 2. Some of the Nebraska families who moved to North Dakota were David Yoder, Solomon Yoder, and Isaac Kauffman.

For the next eight years families continued to come to Rolette and Pierce counties. Most of them filed claims on government land. The Amish settlement in North Dakota probably reached its peak in 1903, when there were about fifty families in the settlement, and two church districts.

Now (1956) Amish life in North Dakota is almost extinct. In 1903 families began to leave. In 1909 many families left for Colorado and elsewhere. The reasons for the disintegration of this apparently promising Amish community were in part severe winters, in part the limited medical and community service, and in part inability to adjust to the new environment. Many of the remaining members joined the Lakeview Mennonite congregation, organized in 1916, which is largely composed of members of Amish descent.

Eli J. Bontreger served as bishop of the North Dakota Amish church 1895-1910. He was succeeded by Jacob Graber and A. R. Gingerich. Bontreger continued to assist the Amish congregation, visiting the church twice a year until 1936, when Mahlon L. Yoder was ordained bishop. The Amish church in North Dakota now has only three members, and Mahlon L. Yoder is the present minister and bishop.

There was also at one time a small Old Order Amish settlement at Kenmare, N.D., also one at Bloomfield, Mont.   F.E.K.

North Dallas Mennonite Brethren Church, sometimes called the Salt Creek Church, located northwest of Dallas, Polk Co., Ore., a member of the Pacific District Conference, was organized in 1904 with 24 charter members. Ministers were Jacob Toews, Abraham Buhler, P. C. Hiebert, H. S. Voth, John Enns, Dietrich Bartel, and H. F. Klaassen. In 1917 a group began to assemble also in Dallas, which organized in 1919 and received the North Dallas congregation into its membership on Jan. 7, 1923, as an integral part of the new Dallas (*q.v.*) congregation.   G.H.J.

North Danvers Mennonite Church (GCM), located three miles northeast of Danvers, McLean Co., Ill., a member of the Central District Conference, was organized in 1871 with a ministry composed of Bishop Joseph Stuckey, John Strubhar, John Stahly, Christian Imhoff, Joseph Stalter, Michael Miller, and Jacob Miller, who represented the three orders of the Amish ministry—bishops, ministers, and deacons. The new church building was erected in 1872, remodeled in 1917. The membership in 1956 was 265, mostly rural. Other ministers have been Joash Stutzman, Peter Schantz, Joseph Clark, Joseph King, John Kohler, and Hugo J. Mierau. William B. Weaver was a long-time pastor, 1923-52. H.J.M.

North Easthope Reformed Mennonite Church is located in Perth Co., Ont., 12 miles northeast of Stratford. The land for the original building was purchased in 1871 under the leadership of ministers Christian Zimmerman of Perth County, and John Honderich of Waterloo County. In 1882 the building was moved and enlarged. In 1902 the building was again moved and with an addition. Other ministers who served the congregation were Joseph Wilhelm of Perth County, and Frederick Weicker of Waterloo County. Since the ministers of this group are not assigned to one particular meetinghouse, but rotate in serving the three churches, one in Perth County and two in Waterloo County, the membership worshiping at one church cannot be determined. The present ministers (1955) are Harvey Gamp, Abram Honderich, and Aaron Yost, all of Waterloo County. The membership of the three groups is small.   H.Ga.

North End Mennonite Church (MC), Steven Street, Lancaster, Pa., was started at Dillerville in 1934. When the grounds were needed for the expanding Armstrong Linoleum Company, the building was salvaged and used in a larger brick building at the present site. Earl M. Wert, who is still serving (1957), was ordained for this mission group on Feb. 24, 1946. The membership is 38.   I.D.L.

North Enid Mennonite Brethren Church, also known as the Enid Country M.B. Church, is located three miles north of Enid in Garfield County, Okla. It is one of two Mennonite Brethren congregations in the area, the other being the City M.B. Church located in Enid.

Shortly after the opening of the Cherokee Strip in north-central Oklahoma, 1893, Mennonites began to settle in this area. Mennonite Brethren from Hamilton County, Neb., some of whom had come to America in the 1874 immigration from Russia, were among the original thirty charter members who organized as a congregation April 5, 1897. Klaas Penner was elected as their first leader in 1895; Peter Regier became the first ordained minister (1897 ff.) to serve this congregation as a pastor. In the years that followed others came from Nebraska as well as Kansas and the Dakotas.

The first meetinghouse was built and dedicated in 1898; this was replaced by a larger building (40 x 60 feet) in 1911, which is still used for worship. Two smaller buildings are used for Sunday-school classrooms. A parsonage in Enid was purchased in 1954. For several decades after 1921 the church operated a Bible school.

Though most of the early members were farmers, now about half of the members live in Enid. In its sixty years of existence more than 400 have been baptized and received into its membership; its present membership (1957) is 212.

The following ministers have served this congregation: Peter Regier, John Bese, John D. Hiebert, Gerhard Voth, P. P. Regier, Cornelius Grunau, G. A. Wiens, D. J. Dick, J. K. Siemens, A. A. Smith, P. C. Grunau, R. C. Seibel, and Clarence Hiebert, the present pastor.   C.H.

P. C. Grunau, "North Enid Mennonite Brethren Church," *Menn. Life* IX (October 1954).

North Fork (Cal.) Civilian Public Service Camp No. 5 was located 50 miles northeast of Fresno and one-half mile northwest of North Fork at an altitude of 2,600 feet, near the base of the Sierra Nevadas. Opened in May 1942, it remained in operation until March 1946. It occupied the site of an abandoned Civilian Conservation Corps camp, and its work was chiefly fire prevention and fire fighting under the direction of the United States Forest Service. During the life of the camp 4,689 man-days were spent in fighting forest fires and 14,232 days in fire suppression.   M.G.

Melvin Gingerich, *Service for Peace* (Akron, Pa., 1949) 138-39.

North Georgetown Mennonite Church (MC), now extinct, 10 miles southwest of Salem, Ohio, near the village of New Alexandria, Columbiana County, was organized about 1840. In 1858 a small frame building was erected on land donated by Jacob Newcomer. Christian Holdeman (1788-1846), the father of the John Holdeman who founded the Church of God in Christ, Mennonite, settled nearby in Knox Township, Columbiana Co., in 1825, moving to Wayne County in 1844. Henry Newcomer and Henry Walters were ministers. In 1879 the membership of this group was reported as about 15 members. The church never had a Sunday school; the last service was held in 1885.   W.D.S.

North Goshen Mennonite Church (MC), located on Eighth Street in Goshen, Ind., a member of the Indiana-Michigan Conference, is an outgrowth of Sunday-school work begun by the Goshen College

Province of
NORTH HOLLAND
Netherlands

Places of Mennonite
congregations underlined

* extinct congregations

** Children's Homes

† Old People's Homes

Canal

Railroad

larger towns ✪

Province border

Waterland area

Scale of Miles

0   5   10   15   20   25

WADDEN

TEXEL

Oosterend

Waal

Den Burg

Den Hoorn

SEA

Dike

Den Helder

Huisduinen   Hippolytushoef

Zijpe   Wieringerwerf

                          Middenmeer

Kolhorn*

Schagen   Barsingerhorn   Medemblik

                              Twisk

Schoorl   Abbekerk   Enkhuizen
Brotherhood House   Nieuwe Niedorp
                          Oude Niedorp   Grootebroek*
              Broek op Langendijk
Koedijk*   Venhuizen*
                                        Hoorn
                  Alkmaar   Schellinkhout*
Marken-Binnen   Groot-Schermer*   Oosthuizen
  Akersloot*
Krommeniedijk*   Beemster
  Uitgeest*   Graft   DeRijp   IJSSEL
            W♦O-Graftdijk
Krommenie   Knollendam   Middelie
                              Axwijk
        Wormerveer   Jisp   Edam
Beverwijk   Westzaan   Wormer   Purmerend
        Koog-Zaandijk †   Monnikendam
IJmuiden   Velsen   Den Ilp
                    Zaan-   Landsmeer
SEA   dam   Ransdorp*   LAKE
                    Nieuwendam
Haarlem ** AMSTERDAM   Durgerdam*
  †6   †3
    Hoofddorp   Muiden*

                        Weesp*   Huizen*
    Aalsmeer   Bussum
                                    UTRECHT
            Uithoorn*   Hilversum
                                    Baarn
SOUTH HOLLAND
        Leiden   UTRECHT
                    Utrecht 10 mi.S↓ Zeist (Heerewegen)
                            ↓12 mi. S.E.

NORTH

YPCA as early as 1915. In 1936 an abandoned Baptist church near Wayland, Iowa, was hauled to Goshen, rebuilt, and dedicated in May 1937. This building has since been enlarged twice. Paul Mininger was pastor of the congregation when it became independent from the Goshen College Mennonite Church in 1942. The membership in 1957 was 328, with Paul Mininger serving as bishop, and Russell Krabill as bishop-pastor. John C. Wenger also served the congregation as deacon and minister prior to 1951. R.Kr.

North Holland (*Noordholland*), a province of the Netherlands between the North Sea and IJssel Lake (formerly Zuiderzee), area 1,016.4 sq. miles, population (1947) 774,273, with 28,492 Mennonites. In the Reformation period the area was smaller; but much land has been reclaimed since 1564, including Beemster Lake under the direction of J. A. Leeghwater (*q.v.*) 1610-14, Purmer 1622, Wormer 1626, Schermer 1632-35, and Haarlem Lake 1848-52. Since the 16th century many a fertile polder has been created; in 1597 Zijpe, 1610 Wieringerwaard, 1847 Anna Paulovnapolder, 1932 Wieringermeerpolder. Many Mennonites settled on these new lands as farmers. The province of North Holland in its present form dates from 1813. Formerly the boundary was formed by the IJ, and during the 17th and 18th centuries the southern part with the cities of Amsterdam and Haarlem belonged to South Holland rather than North Holland. In the following account the present status is understood.

The earliest traces of Anabaptists in North Holland are found about 1530; in that year Jan Volkertsz Trypmaker (*q.v.*) founded the congregation in Amsterdam; Melchior Hofmann (*q.v.*) baptized probably 50 persons here in 1531; and Anabaptists are also found in other places. Especially in 1533-34 the number increased rapidly. In Amsterdam 100 baptisms were performed on some days. In Monnikendam (*q.v.*) two thirds of the population were "contaminated," and in Westzaan about 200 persons were baptized in the winter of 1533-34.

Now the government began its violent measures of suppression and put many to death. Nevertheless the movement grew in strength. In this province, where the Anabaptists were more numerous than in any other Dutch province, the spirit of Münster (*q.v.*) was evident, but not dominant. To be sure, about 3,000 persons crossed the Zuiderzee on the way to Münster on March 24, 1534, following the call of Jan van Leyden, but these people were not revolutionaries. They were seized at the Bergklooster (*q.v.*) in Overijssel. Among them were many wealthy persons. The Anabaptist preachers above all rejected violence, as is seen in a ministerial conference held in Spaarndam near Haarlem in late 1534 or early 1535. The small following of Münster in North Holland is seen in the fact that Jan van Geelen (*q.v.*), the emissary from Münster, in his attempt to storm the Amsterdam city hall (May 10, 1535), actually had only elements from other places at his disposal, and also from the fact that the procurator of the Court of Holland needed only a small number of soldiers for his ruthless persecution. The Anabaptist movement was not eradicated

by his raids in 1534 nor by the severe edict of June 10, 1535, which was aimed principally at the Anabaptists.

The Anabaptists remained numerous in North Holland and began to organize congregations. Menno Simons also was influential here. Jan Claesz (*q.v.*) of Alkmaar, who had some of Menno's books printed in Antwerp, and had distributed 600 copies of them, was executed for this deed in 1544. In 1556 Menno again visited North Holland. The elder Leenaert Bouwens (*q.v.*) baptized many here. When the outstanding elders, Menno, Bouwens, and Dirk Philips, adopted a stricter application of the ban, many congregations of North Holland were unable to follow their lead and adhered to the more lenient application. These were then known as the Waterlanders (*q.v.*) because they lived in the area called Waterland (between the IJ River and Hoorn); they were always the most influential and largest Mennonite branch in the province. They differed from the other groups by their individual piety, not considering their own group to be the only true church; they were also less negative to the world and to culture. But the other groups were also found in the province; especially in Haarlem and Amsterdam there were important congregations of the Flemish (*q.v.*) branch. A considerable number of Frisians were found particularly at Hoorn and Alkmaar.

In North Holland many difficulties remained even after the Spanish had been expelled (about 1580) and the government was in Reformed hands, though there were not so many difficulties as in the other provinces.

Concerning the oath (*q.v.*), the States-General decided that the Mennonites were to be excused from it in favor of a simple assertion. Regarding marriage it was decided in 1580 that Mennonites must report their marriages to the magistrate or the Reformed pastor. In 1606 marriage within one's own congregation was approved, provided the government was informed of the event. This regulation became the general practice but many difficulties arose in this connection. On the whole the Mennonites were excused from bearing arms, while on their part the Mennonites did all they could to support the government in other ways. Donations of money were repeatedly made. In 1673 the rural churches of North Holland alone raised 30,000 guilders besides clothing and bedding. The strict practice of nonresistance was abandoned. Especially among the Waterlanders it was repeatedly charged in the first half of the 17th century that their merchant ships were furnished with guns to protect them against pirates. Among the stricter branches, however, the principle was held throughout the century and well into the next, though it may have been more theory than practice.

In the early days there was opposition to holding government office, but by 1581 a change was becoming evident among the Waterlanders; in a conference held in that year it was decided that holding minor offices was permissible, provided there was no bloodshed connected with them. In the communities where the Mennonites were in the majority, when they were elected to the offices of bailiff or even mayor, they were permitted to withdraw from the office upon payment of a fine, which was, however, seldom paid. Nevertheless many Waterlanders held important administrative offices in the first half of the 17th century. Until the 18th century the Frisians retained their aversion toward holding government office.

The Mennonites were not recognized by the government; they were merely tolerated. This was the theory; the practice was different. Although there were occasional difficulties regarding marriage, inheritance, and the building of churches, the government protected these citizens, who were of such benefit to the welfare of the country. Thus the magistrate of Amsterdam took their part when the British government refused to give them money due them on the ground that they would not swear to their rights of possession. Again the Amsterdam government in 1642 took steps to aid the oppressed Mennonites in Switzerland. It was also the lenient attitude of the government that prevented the Reformed from undertaking suppressive steps. When the Reformed pastor in 1597 wanted to hold a public debate with Lubbert Gerritsz (q.v.), the government forbade it. But when it was a question of Socinianism, the government sometimes interfered. In 1626 Jacques Outerman (q.v.), preacher at Haarlem, and in 1663 Galenus Abrahamsz de Haan had to answer for their teachings at court. The testimony of both was accepted. No wonder that the Dutch Mennonites rejoiced in this privilege; Hans Vlamingh, a Mennonite merchant of Amsterdam, wrote to a friend in Switzerland in 1659, that the Mennonites there were permitted to meet freely, sometimes 2,000 at one time and place, that in Amsterdam and elsewhere they had orphanages and almshouses, free of taxation, that they could perform their ordinances free of molestation; the government accepted their word instead of the oath; they were citizens like anybody else, but exempt from war and military service, for which they paid a certain tax.

The Mennonites were important in the cultural life of North Holland. Famous poets and painters in the Golden Age were Mennonites or of Mennonite descent or were associated with Mennonites. Many were engaged in commerce, thus contributing greatly to the economic prosperity of Amsterdam and Haarlem. The Zaan River region, now an important industrial district, owes its prosperity largely to its Mennonite merchants and manufacturers. Also in shipping and deep sea fishing the Mennonites played a significant part.

The consequence of this was a great prosperity and increasing luxury; the dangers therein were pointed out on many an occasion. Galenus Abrahamsz de Haan complains about the decline of the brotherhood. The complaint was certainly not unfounded. Not only in luxurious living did the changing spirit of the Mennonites express itself. The Mennonites no longer stood outside a world that they considered entirely evil; spiritually, too, contacts had been established with others. There was frequent connection with the Collegiants (q.v.); yet there was also a large proportion of Mennonites who did not favor this connection, and this differ-ence caused strife in many a congregation, Waterlander as well as Flemish.

Another indication of the change in spirit was the fact that in many places the branches began to unite in the 18th century. It is therefore so much the more lamentable that a new division took place in 1664 at Amsterdam between the Lamists (q.v.) and the Zonists (q.v.), which split the congregation into two camps.

The 18th century was a time of decay; many congregations declined rapidly in numbers, especially those around the Zuiderzee, which bloomed in the Baltic trade and nearly perished in its decline. Edam dropped from 80 to 12 members in the 18th century; in Hoorn, where there were four congregations, the total membership dropped from 450 to less than 100. But other congregations also showed a decrease; Amsterdam from more than 2,300 (about 1700) to 1,385 in 1832, Haarlem from 3,000 in 1708 to 485 in 1834.

Twenty small congregations in North Holland died out. Some were combined with others. Many had no preacher in the first half of the 18th century. The various conferences (Sociëteit) performed a good work: the Waterlander or Rijper Sociëteit (q.v.), which must have been organized in the first half of the 17th century, though there is no record of it before 1694; the Frisian Sociëteit of North Holland, which was in existence in 1639 and merged with the Rijper Sociëteit in 1844; the Zonist Sociëteit, which met from 1674 to 1796, and the South Holland or Lamist Sociëteit, which initiated the founding of the Mennonite seminary in Amsterdam, but soon disappeared from the scene. These conferences preserved many a congregation from extinction by looking after the preaching needs.

The organizing of the Algemeene Doopsgezinde Sociëteit (q.v.) was also of great significance in North Holland. All the congregations could gradually be provided with educated preachers, and many received financial support. In the 19th century no congregations died out. Still the membership decreased here and there, and rarely did the membership keep pace with the increase in the population. Only in Amsterdam and Haarlem did the rate of increase exceed the rate of increase in the population. In the Gooi district a new congregation was organized at Bussum in 1915; in Hilversum the old Huizen congregation was revived. Also in IJmuiden, a rapidly rising town on the locks of the North Sea canal, there has been a Mennonite congregation since 1909. The Haarlemmermeer congregation dates from 1950; and in the Wieringermeer, reclaimed from the former Zuiderzee, there is now also a congregation. According to the official Dutch census the number of Mennonites (including children) in the province of North Holland was 15,713 in 1849, 26,508 in 1900, and 28,492 in 1947. The baptized membership numbered 5,052 in 1771, 7,800 in 1847, 11,332 in 1900, and 17,722 in 1957. (For a view of the membership of the present congregations in Holland, see the table in the article **Netherlands**.) (*ML* III, 272-75.)   vɒZ.

North Kildonan, Man., a municipality (township) with an area of nine sq. miles, which is a northeastern suburb of Winnipeg, lying immediately adjacent to the city. Mennonites began to settle in this area in 1928 when it was purely rural, and have since built up a rather compact settlement of some 1,500 persons, practically all located in a single ward, which has a total population of about 2,300. Meanwhile the area has become largely urban, and the Mennonites are all workers in the urban area of Winnipeg and its suburbs. Practically all these Mennonites are of the newer immigration from Russia in 1922-25, 1930-31, and 1947-51. There are two Mennonite churches in the district, one Mennonite Brethren with about 500 members, and one General Conference Mennonite with 340 members. This is a unique urban Mennonite settlement, and is still rapidly growing. A.J.Dɪ.

North Kildonan Mennonite Brethren Church in North Kildonan, a suburb of Winnipeg, Man., a member of the Manitoba Provincial and the Canadian M.B. District conferences, was organized in 1929 by poor Mennonite immigrants from Russia. Immediately they began the erection of a church, which was thrice enlarged by 1937. The last enlargement in 1941 brought the size of the main auditorium to 40 x 62 ft. with a full basement. The baptized membership in 1956 was *ca.* 500, with W. Falk as the leading minister. H.Nᴇ.

North Kildonan Mennonite (GCM) Church, located in North Kildonan, Man., a suburb of Winnipeg, is a member of the Canadian Conference. It was formerly a subgroup of the Schoenwiese Mennonite Church (*q.v.*) of Manitoba. The first Schoenwiese families located here in 1929. The first meetinghouse, erected in 1935, was replaced in 1951 by the present meetinghouse on Pentland Ave. In 1956 the membership was 340, with Victor Schroeder as pastor. J.H.Eɴ.

North Lima Mennonite Church (MC), formerly known as Metzler's, located one-half mile south of North Lima, Mahoning Co., Ohio, is a member of the Ohio and Eastern Conference. The Mennonite community in Mahoning and Columbiana counties began in 1806 or earlier, one of the oldest Mennonite settlements in Ohio. Jacob Oberholser was living there by that year and was the first preacher, organizing soon after arrival the first congregation at what is now called Midway. In 1817 Jacob Nold, a bishop from Bucks County, arrived and located near Leetonia, where a meetinghouse was erected in 1819. The settlement near North Lima was begun in 1821. The first meetinghouse at the present site (Metzler's Church) is thought to have been built about 1824 by a group of families either related to the Metzlers or bearing the name; David Metzler, a deacon, who had come from Lancaster County about 1821, donated the land. Until 1948 the North Lima, Midway, and Leetonia congregations functioned largely as one organization, rotating services (except Leetonia after *ca.* 1915), the membership being served in a circuit by the total ministry. A. J. Steiner, ordained bishop in 1910, was the last circuit bishop, retiring about 1950, when his son David C. Steiner was ordained (1952) as bishop

for North Lima alone. The present (1956) membership is 116. In 1872 a division occurred in the district, the Old Order or Wisler group withdrawing to form the Pleasant View congregation, which used the three meetinghouses jointly with the regular Mennonite congregation until 1898, when it built its own meetinghouse. J.A.S.

James A. Steiner, "Mahoning and Columbiana County Mennonite Churches," in *Ohio Evangel* X (September-October 1956) 2-4.

North Main Street Mennonite Church (MC), located in Nappanee, Elkhart Co., Ind., is a member of the Indiana-Michigan Conference. The early Mennonite families began to settle in Locke and Union townships in Elkhart County about 1853-63. Services were held in a near-by schoolhouse every four weeks. About 1878 a small building was purchased in Nappanee. A Sunday school was organized, which apparently created new interest. On May 15, 1880, David Burkholder was ordained minister, which sets the date when the congregation was organized. In 1893 a new brick building was built by the 43 members of the conregation. Preaching services were now held every two weeks. The first evangelistic meetings were held by J. S. Coffman (*q.v.*) in 1894. The membership in 1906 was 117. The meetinghouse was enlarged in 1912, 1921, and 1952. It now has a seating capacity of 450.

In 1923, when a division occurred in the church, Ezra Mullet (then pastor) withdrew with a group to the West Market Street Mennonite Church (MC). Members of the West Market Street Church who desired to stay with the conservative group adhering to the conference transferred their membership to the North Main Street congregation. The West Market Street congregation later united with the General Conference Mennonite Church. D. D. Troyer was responsible for the worship services until Homer F. North was ordained as minister on Aug. 1, 1926. North was ordained bishop in 1954.

Bishops who have served in the congregation are David Burkholder, Jacob Christophel, Ray F. Yoder, and Homer F. North; ministers were Frank Hartman, Noah Metzler, Ezra Mullet, and D. D. Troyer. In the fall of 1952 the church sponsored the opening of a mission Sunday school in Osceola, just west of Elkhart, and Maurice Long was ordained in 1954 as minister for the work in Osceola. In 1955 the membership was 372, with Homer F. North as pastor. H.F.N.

North Mennonite settlement, Mexico: see **Ojo de lad Yegua** Mennonite settlement.

North Newton, a village (pop. about 400) in Kansas, was incorporated as a town in 1935 under a mayor-council form of government in order to provide for utilities (streets, sewers, etc.) on the Bethel College (*q.v.*) campus and the development of postal services for the college community. The village had grown around the Bethel College campus, established in 1893, and is located immediately north of Newton (*q.v.*). It includes the Bethel College campus, the residential sections, a business area, the MCC relief center, and the Bethel College Mennonite

Church (*q.v.*). Mayors of North Newton have been J. E. Regier, Paul Baumgartner, Jacob H. Lingenfelder, and John F. Schmidt. J.F.S.

North Salem Amish Mennonite Church, erected 1885, now extinct, was located about 14 miles southwest of Huntsville, Ohio. Among the first settlers about 1874 were the following families: Bishop Jonas Yoder of Lagrange Co., Ind.; Joseph Hartzler, Gideon Zook, and David Hartzler, a preacher, from Noble Co., Ind.; several families from Tennessee, and a little later the I. K. Stoltzfus, E. B. Stoltzfus, and David Stoltzfus (a preacher) families from Hartford, Kan. In the late 1890's the families began moving to the West Liberty, Ohio, community about 20 miles south. Services were discontinued entirely in 1906, the meetinghouse sold, and even the bodies in the cemetery removed to cemeteries near **West Liberty.** J.S.U.

North Star (*Nordstern*) Mennonite Church (GCM) at Drake, Sask., was organized on Feb. 6, 1906, under the leadership of John Gerbrandt with 20 charter members, who had immigrated to Canada the year previously from the Johannesthal and Bruderthal churches in Kansas and Alva, Okla. Gerbrandt had been elder of the Johannesthal congregation and was elected to the same office in his new charge. In 1906 H. H. Bartel, also of the Johannesthal congregation, became assistant minister. During the first two years services were held in the Gerbrandt home. In 1907 a church building was erected four miles west of the village of Drake and in 1928 another in the village. In 1956 a new and larger church was built in the village of Drake and the separate services in the old churches were discontinued. In that year the membership was 270. Paul Schroeder was serving as elder and Edwin S. Bartel and J. J. Friesen were assistant ministers. J.G.

North Unity Church of God in Christ Mennonite Church, located west of Langdon, Cavalier Co., N.D., began with the coming of Jacob Toews in 1888, at which time the services were conducted in the homes. A Sunday school was organized in 1923. The present church building was purchased in 1926. In 1921 Peter Toews was ordained and has since been the residing minister; until that time the church was served by adjoining congregations. The membership, of Dutch and Norwegian descent, was 31 in 1956. P.T.

North Woolwich Old Order Mennonite Church, located north of the village of Floradale, Woolwich Twp., Waterloo Co., Ontario, was known as the "Hembling appointment" 1857-75. The services were probably first held in a log school, then in a little church purchased from the Evangelical Association about 1868 and moved northward in 1872. In 1900 the site was enlarged and a new brick structure erected. In 1928 this building was lengthened and grounds acquired to provide cemetery space. The ministers in this congregation were Abraham W. Detweiler, Joseph Gingerich, and John B. Bowman. In 1955 the minister was Osias Gingerich (1917-   ), ordained 1943; the membership was under 200.

This meetinghouse is used also by the Waterloo-Markham Old Order Mennonite group under Bishop Amsey Martin (b. 1899), ordained as minister in 1940 and as bishop in 1941. This membership is approximately 100. The total O.O.M. membership in Ontario in 1954 was 1,071. J.C.F.

Northampton County, Pa., with Easton, its county seat, the seventh county established in Pennsylvania, in 1752, was an Indian purchase, based "on a (1737) walk," which led to the war with the Indians in 1755. It is situated in the east central part of the state, between the Kittatinny and South Mountains, and is watered by both the Lehigh and Delaware rivers. The Scotch-Irish were here by 1732, followed by more Scotch-Irish, Moravians, Mennonites, and other Germans. This was the land of David Brainerd, missionary to the Delawares, and the scenic Delaware Water Gap.

The Mennonite farmers were chiefly in Allen, Lower Mount Bethel, Washington, and Saucon townships. At Hellertown a union schoolhouse was built probably in the middle of the 18th century and a second in 1802, deeded to Samuel Kauffman for "the Menoists" and Samuel Rothrock "for the Baptice Societice." This was burned down and rebuilt in 1854 and again in 1891. Mennonite names are common in the adjoining cemetery.

In Allen Township at Siegfried's Bridge on the Lehigh River a half acre of ground was purchased by Jacob Baer, Jacob Heston, John Ziegler, and Samuel Landis, and with John Ziegler and Samuel Funk as a committee, a school-meetinghouse 26 x 30 ft. was built on it in 1802, for the purpose of leading the children "from the home to the school, the school to the church, and from the church to Heaven." In the first half century the membership varied between 60 and 100. The ministers included Valentine Young, Samuel Musselman, Christian Bliem, John Bechtel, William Gehman, John Oberholtzer, Christian Clemmer, David Henning (1806-81), William Shelly, Henry Diehl, Jonas Musselman, and Samuel Moyer. In 1860-80 the membership dwindled and services were held every four weeks by Samuel Landis, Lewis Taylor, and Jonas Y. Shultz. The cemetery contains the Mennonite names of Bliem, Bechtel, Coppes, Funk, Gerhard, Geisinger, Heistand, Baer, Landis, Latshaw, Scherrer, Seiple, Swartz, Young, and Ziegler. In August 1884 efforts were made to repair the building and improve the burying grounds. By 1908 the building was sold to the school board, but apparently never used as a school.

Siegfried's meetinghouse was built in the borough of Northampton, with Jacob Showalter, Sr., as leader. By 1771 Joseph, John, and Jacob Showalter, Jr., with Peter Bassler moved to Lancaster County, that they might live with coreligionists. With a congregation in 1798 in Mount Bethel Township, a union log house was built in Bangor in 1806 and one of brick in 1822. In 1849 in Lower Mount Bethel Township another was built. Northeast of Bangor, near Richmond, was the Rothrock meetinghouse, torn down in 1916. Although six Mennonite churches once stood in Northampton County with a numerous Mennonite pioneer group, their descendants moved away or left the Mennonite (MC) Church. The only services of this group now held in the county are the two missions started at Bethlehem and Easton since 1951 by the Franconia Mennonites, and at Bender in 1955 by Lancaster Mennonites of the Weaverland congregation.

Northampton County has always been a stronghold, however, of the Mennonite Brethren in Christ Church of Pennsylvania. Its second largest congregation in Pennsylvania is Bethlehem with 376 members, founded in 1887. Other congregations are Easton with 162 (20 members in 1911) members, Nazareth with 58, Northampton with 38, and Walnutport with 53. Their total in the county is 647 baptized members. **I.D.L.**

W. H. Egle, *The Commonwealth of Pennsylvania;* D. K. Cassel, *Mennonite History* (Philadelphia, 1888); J. C. Wenger, *History of the Mennonites of the Franconia Conference* (Telford, 1937).

Northern District is one of the three districts of the Virginia Mennonite Conference (MC). The entire church in the Shenandoah Valley was originally under one leadership. Around 1840 the territory was divided into three districts. What was north of the highway leading from West Gay Street, Harrisonburg, Va., through Park View to Mt. Clinton, Va., to a point about one and one-half miles west of the Eastern Mennonite College, then with the Hopkins Mill road to Singers Glen, Va., then by an imaginary line somewhat north by west indefinitely, was known as the Lower District (because the valley drains in that direction). By conference action the name was changed in 1942 to its present form.

Among the early family names in this vicinity were Funk, Brunk, Trissel, Showalter, Shank, Rhodes (then Roth), Brenneman, Good, Acker, Geil, Driver, Huber (now Hoover), Wenger, Heatwole, and Kauffman (now Coffman), who settled here in 1773-90 and perhaps still later. Early dates are difficult to verify because of the burning of county records during the Civil War.

The original and oldest congregation in the district is Trissels (1822), with 125 members, followed by Zion (1885) with 138, Lindale (1895) with 183, and Bethel (1915) with 108. Seven additional organized congregations with 466 members and eleven rural missions with 219 members, a total of 675, have been established in the mountains immediately to the west, mostly in West Virginia, the oldest of these outposts going back to 1868, the newest established in 1955. The total baptized membership in the district in 1956 was 1,229, about one fourth of the total Virginia Conference membership.

Originally there was only one bishop in charge of the district. Lewis Shank (d. 1942), bishop in charge in 1901-38, was followed by J. L. Stauffer (ord. 1938), who has been assisted since 1945 by Bishop Timothy Showalter and since 1954 by Bishop J. Ward Shank. **T.S.**

Northern District Conference of the General Conference Mennonite Church comprises 31 congregations located in Montana, North and South Dakota, Minnesota, and Nebraska. The first impetus to organize the handful of congregations in these states into a conference was given by J. B. Baer, the traveling home missionary for the General Conference, who persuaded Elder Gerhard Neufeld of the First Mennonite Church of Mountain Lake, Minn., to allow a "trial conference" to be held in his church on Oct. 12-13, 1891. Representatives came from at least eight of the churches in the northern area along with guests from other district conferences. Discussion at the conference centered on mission and publication work. Baer served as chairman of the conference while Christian Schowalter, of the Donnelson, Iowa, church, served as secretary. Although a second conference was held the following year, it was not until the third conference session held in South Dakota in 1894, that a committee of three was appointed to draw up a constitution. The ministers J. J. Balzer, Jacob Hege, and Christian Mueller, who were appointed to this committee, presented a document for adoption at the conference held at Mountain Lake in 1895.

The first constitution was, of course, in German. It was translated into English some years later and revised in 1951. In form and scope of organization the Northern District follows the pattern of the General Conference. It believes "in the congregational form of church government, whereby the local church retains maximum freedom of self-determination. It is a deliberative body carrying powers of recommendation but not of legislation." In matters of faith and practice the Northern District Conference has accepted the Statement of Doctrine adopted by the General Conference in 1941. The constitution established the following purpose of the conference: "To unite into one conference all Mennonite congregations not already in another district conference and who desire to affiliate themselves with this conference, in the states of North and South Dakota, Nebraska, Minnesota, and Montana. To promote the growth and expansion of the kingdom of God: (*a*) by establishing one another through mutual instruction and admonition from the Word of God; (*b*) by the exercise of Christian fellowship among the churches; (*c*) by co-operation with the work undertaken by the various boards of the General Conference Mennonite Church." Through the years there has been a strong mission emphasis in the Conference. The pioneer General Conference missionaries to India and China came from this district: the P. A. Penners to India, the H. J. Browns and Aganetha Fast to China.

While the Conference has sponsored no schools, congregations in various communities have done so. The congregations in the Mountain Lake, Minn., area established Mountain Lake Bible School; in the Freeman, S.D., area the congregations founded Freeman Academy—later Freeman Junior College; in the Munich, N.D., and Lustre, Mont., areas Bible schools were also established. This was also true at Henderson, Neb., although the Bible school there has become extinct.

The first statistical report (1908) listed 14 congregations with a membership of 1,467; two of these were in Nebraska, three in North Dakota, four in Minnesota, and five in South Dakota. The 1956 Conference Report listed a total of 32 congregations with a combined membership of 6,150 members. Contributions made by these congregations totaled

$583,044. The congregations also reported 85 young men in I-W service (q.v.), 28 in noncombatant military service, and 53 in active military service.

J.D.U.

Northern District Conference of the Mennonite Brethren Church, organized in 1910, was the former name of the present Canadian Conference of the M.B. Church (q.v.).

Northern Light, authorized as a quarterly publication in 1942 by the Young People's Organization of the Northern District Conference of the General Conference Mennonite Church. Hermie Preheim, Marion, S.D., served as the first editor of the paper. Publication was discontinued in 1950.   J.D.U.

Northern Minnesota Mission of the Mennonite Brethren Central District Conference. This mission was begun in 1926 by John H. Wiens, who under the Northern Gospel Mission Union, took over a mission at Mildred, Minn. From there the mission established preaching centers connected with Sunday schools and daily vacation Bible schools. A number of young people have attended Bible schools and have gone out as missionaries to various mission fields at home and abroad. For 30 years this mission has continued with the same workers still on the field.

Another mission center has been opened among the Chippewa Indians at Ponemah on the Red Lakes Indian Reservation. This work had a hard beginning since these Indians were isolated from the white people and resented the white man's religion. Art Unrau and his wife together with Sarah H. Balzer and Marie Peters started Bible classes with the Indian boys and girls at the school. At present (1956) Sam Fast and his wife are in charge of this station. Another mission station was opened at Ericksburg near International Falls, in charge of Tina Ediger and a co-worker.

The conference together with the various Mennonite churches at and around Mountain Lake, Minn., and various mission friends have supported this mission work.   H.E.W.

Norwich, capital of the county of Norfolk, England, was in the 16th century an Anabaptist center. There was here a small Anabaptist. congregation probably founded by immigrants from Holland, of Flanders, who had left their countries by 1536 because of persecution. For the same reason some Mennonites from Flanders settled at Norwich about 1567. These Anabaptist-Mennonites apparently had a great influence on the population of Norwich, most of which was opposed to the Anglican state church, censuring its moral laxity, its lack of church discipline, the arrogance of its clergy, and the domination by the state in church affairs. This Separatist-Puritan movement in Norwich, with its ideal of the church as a body of believers, free of the state and its interference, was often called Anabaptist by Anglican churchmen and government officers, but this terminology is, strictly speaking, not correct, because these Puritans did not embrace the principle of believers' baptism on confession of faith with rejection of infant baptism. Yet there was some affinity with

Anabaptism, especially concerning the free church idea as formulated by Robert Browne (q.v.) in 1582: "The Church planted or gathered is a company or number of Christians or believers, which, by a voluntary covenant made with their God, are under the government of God and Christ and keep His laws in one holy communion."

The following of these "Anabaptists" must have been considerable. In 1571 half of the population of Norwich, including some 3,000 immigrants from Holland and Flanders, are said to have shared the views of the Anabaptists. In 1580 Robert Browne and his friend Robert Harrison were active in Norwich, but in the fall of 1581 Browne and Harrison had to leave England and moved to the Netherlands, first to Middelburg in the province of Zeeland, then to Amsterdam. A number of Puritans accompanied them, and others followed later. Some of them came into contact with the Dutch Waterlander Mennonites at Amsterdam (see **John Smyth**) and finally joined them in 1615, but most of them in the course of time returned to England. Norwich always remained a strong center of congregationalism, opposed to the hierarchy of the English state church.

VDZ.

J. G. de Hoop Scheffer and W. E. Griffis, *History of the Free Churchmen* (Ithaca, n.d., 1922) 7 f., 10; H. E. Dosker, *The Dutch Anabaptists* (Philadelphia, 1921) 293 f.; *ML* III, 276.

Nospitzer, Georg: see **Nespitzer, Georg.**

Noviomagus (Geldenhauer) (1482-1542), a professor of theology at the University of Marburg, Germany, was at first a monk and also reader and secretary to Charles V, became a Protestant in 1526, lived for a time in Strasbourg, where he became acquainted with the Anabaptists. After the publication of the imperial mandate of Jan. 4, 1528, he wrote a booklet in Latin, which was translated into German in the same year with the title, *Ein sentbrief an Kayser Carol des namens den Fünften, Alzeyt merer des Reichs . . . Gerardi Noviomagi, In welcher wird gehandlet, Ob man ein ketzer mit recht möge peinlich und leyblich strafen oder nicht. Auss dem Latein verteutscht* (Nürnberg, 1528, 12 pages).

In the spring of 1529 he published another Latin booklet, which was also translated into German, with the title, *Des Desiderius Erasmus von Rotterdam Anmerkungen zu den päpstlichen und kaiserlichen Gesetzen über die Häretiker. Einige Briefe des Gerhard Noviomagus über die evangelische Sache und die Strafen der Häretiker an Kaiser Karl V., an die auf dem Reichstag zu Speyer versammelten Fürsten, an Karl, Herzog von Geldern, an Philipp, den Fürsten von Hessen.* A second German translation followed on March 1, 1530, probably printed in Augsburg, by Hieronymus Gebweyler in Hagenau. In the introduction Noviomagus repeated the statements of Erasmus (q.v.) in his book against the Spanish monks, published in the previous year, which annoyed Erasmus, since it would probably lead to the conclusion that he was the author and had attacked the mandate of Charles V of Jan. 4, 1528, which was to be presented to the Diet of Speyer for ratification. To clear himself of this suspicion Erasmus wrote a counter pamphlet with the title *Briefe gegen gewisse Leute, die sich falscherweise rühmen, Evangelische zu sein* (Freiburg, November 1529), declaring that although he had warned against exaggerated severity, he had not denied the right of the government to kill heretics if it was necessary to secure public tranquillity.

In 1532 Noviomagus entered the service of Hesse. He was made professor of history and in 1534 professor of theology at the University of Marburg. Here he had to deal with the Anabaptist question a number of times, and expressed his lenient attitude, especially in official opinions and at cross-examinations, in opposition to the prevalent views of theologians and jurists. In a letter to Philip of Hesse in 1535 he designated tolerance and gentleness as the most effective means of winning the Anabaptists to the Protestants. Philip heeded this counsel. In an order of early 1536 the officials were directed to have the Anabaptists instructed by the clergy; if they persisted in their belief they should be exiled, but they could keep their property. In early August Noviomagus and pastor Dietrich Fabritius began the indoctrination of the Anabaptists imprisoned in Wolkersdorf—Johannes Schnabel, Peter Lose, and Leonhard Fälber; but their efforts were in vain (see **Hesse**). HEGE.

L. Prinsen, *Gerardus Geldenhauer Noviomagus, Bijdrage tot de kennis van zijn Leven en Werken* (The Hague, 1898); Fr. Thudichum, *Die deutsche Reformation* II (Leipzig, 1909); *TA Hesse; ML* III, 278.

Novo-Chortitza: see Neu-Chortitza.

Novo-Kovno, a village in the province of Ekaterinoslav, volost Nikolayevka. Since 1888 there had been in the village a branch congregation of the Friedensfeld (Miropol) Mennonite Brethren Church, consisting in 1905 of 11 members and 36 adherents. (Dirks, *Statistik*, 67; *ML* III, 278.) C.K.

Novo-Moskovsk, an area in the Alexandrovsk area of the province of Ekaterinoslav, Russia, where Mennonites from West Prussia settled in 1799 and founded the village of Kronsgarten, which served as a model for the native Russian villages around them in the plan of the farms and also in the tilling of the soil. "Externally these [Novo-Moskovsk] Russian villages (like Yodgornoye) are like the Mennonite villages. The same plan of buildings and arrangement of the farm, the gardens before the homes, trees along the streets, orchards, fences along the street, made of red tile and carefully laid drainage tile."

K. Lindemann, *Von den deutschen Kolonisten in Russland* (Stuttgart, 1924) 59; *ML* III, 278.

Novo-Nikolayevka, one of two villages comprising the Mennonite Trubetskoye settlement in the province of Kherson, Kazatskaya district, South Russia, founded in 1904.

W. Quiring, *Die Mundart von Chortitza in Süd-Russland* (Munich, 1928) 34; *ML* III, 278.

Novo-Podolsk, a Mennonite village in the Russian province of Ekaterinoslav, volost Kamenskaya.

Novo-Podolsk Mennonite Brethren Church, located in Kherson province of South Russia in the village of Krivoy, had its beginning about 1895 when the

Russian government tried to settle several communities with a mixed population, consisting of one third Mennonites, one third Russians, and one third Jews, in the hope that the Mennonites would teach the others how to be prosperous farmers. These ethnic groups refused, however, to integrate, and the Mennonites organized the Mennonite Brethren Church under the leadership of Franz Peters, who was succeeded by Franz Wieler, assisted by Peter Unger and Gehard Wieler. Most of the first settlers, of whom Peter Unger, Franz Wieler, and Peter Krause are known by name, came to this plains area from the Old Colony near Chortitza to escape population pressure at home. The membership is not known to have exceeded 75. In 1932 most of the ministers and able-bodied men were banished by the Soviet Government, and the congregation disintegrated under the pressure of severe persecution. J.J.T.

Novopokrovsk, a volost in the province of Ekaterinoslav, Russia, in which the Mennonite villages of Elisabeththal and Gerhardsthal were founded in 1860 and 1861, each with about 2,700 acres of land and (in 1926) 126 inhabitants.

Neuer Haus- und Landwirtschafts-Kalender (Odessa, 1913) 50; *ML* III, 278.

Novosibirsk, formerly Novonikolaevsk, one of the chief cities of Novosibirsk Region, Siberia, Soviet Russia, was founded in 1896. The city is located on the Ob River and the Trans-Siberian railroad, 390 miles east of Omsk and has a population of about 500,000. It is connected by railroad with Barnaul, Semipalatinsk, and Central Asia. The city is sometimes referred to as the "Chicago of Siberia," specializing in the manufacture of agricultural machinery, trade of farm products, and timber. It is also an agricultural and educational center. During World War II entire industrial plants were removed bodily from European Russia to Novosibirsk.

Although Mennonites settled south and east of Novosibirsk at the turn of the century, they hardly reached this territory and city at that time. Under the Soviets, however, many Mennonites were exiled to this region. From correspondence published in *Der Bote* and the *Mennonitische Rundschau*, it has become apparent that numerous Mennonites are today located in the city of Novosibirsk and the surrounding regions. Some of the Mennonites work in factories and in the hospital. Now that they are free to move about, some of those from the surrounding areas are moving into the city. According to information, some of the Mennonites came originally from Chortitza, the Molotschna, and other settlements of the Ukraine. Some Mennonites are located in the city of Berdsk, south of the city of Novosibirsk.

Peter Bergmann, born in 1934, Schönsee, Molotschna, sent a picture of himself and his wife which is clear evidence that they are living under satisfactory conditions. Jakob Esau, also formerly from the Molotschna, sent a picture to relatives of eleven young men, five of whom are listed as ministers. He himself writes that after having spent seven years in the "school of Daniel," meaning in a concentration camp, he has now started to preach the Gospel. He is grateful for the Bible which he received. Evidently these young men are all active in the city of Novosibirsk, possibly in the Baptist church. Whether the Mennonites are conducting worship services on their own is not clear.   C.K.

Webster's Geographical Dictionary (Springfield, 1955); *Der Bote*, March 2, 1955, p. 8; Sept. 28, 1955, p. 8; Nov. 23, 1955, p. 7, 12; April 4, 1956, p. 7; April 25, 1956, p. 7; *Mennonitische Rundschau*, July 19, 1950, p. 3; March 10, 1954, p. 4; Oct. 20, 1954, p. 6; Oct. 12, 1955, p. 6; March 7, 1956, p. 3; March 21, 1956, p. 8; May 2, 1956, p. 11; June 20, 1956, p. 14, 15; Oct. 17, 1956, p. 3; Jan. 30, 1957, p. 5.

Novoslobodka (formerly Rosengart), a village in the Chortitza Mennonite settlement in the province of Ekaterinoslav, Russia, founded in 1824, had in 1912, 238 inhabitants, who belonged to the Chortitza Mennonite Church.

Neuer Haus- und Landwirtschafts-Kalender (Odessa, 1913) 47 and 74; *ML* III, 278.

Novo-Sofievka (formerly *Nikolaithal*), a volost (*q.v.*) in the province of Ekaterinoslav in the Mennonite Borozenko settlement (*q.v.*), a daughter of the Chortitza settlement, founded in 1865, with the following seven villages: Novo-Sofievka, Felsenbach (Mariapol), Blumenfeld, Steinau, Hamburg, Neubergthal, and Hoffnungsort. Novo-Sofievka had 2,675 acres of land and (1912) 96 inhabitants.
                                                      HEGE.

W. Quiring, *Die Mundart von Chortitza in Süd-Russland* (Munich, 1928) 49; *ML* III, 278 f.

Novo-Stepnoye, one of four villages comprising the Mennonite settlement of Samoylovka near Bachmetyevka in the province of Kharkov, a daughter colony of the Molotschna settlement, founded in 1888.

W. Quiring, *Die Mundart von Chortitza in Süd-Russland* (Munich, 1928) 35; *ML* III, 279.

Novo-Zhitomir, a Mennonite village in the Russian province of Kherson, volost Krivoi-Rog, Ukraine.

Nuevo Leon Mennonite settlement, located approximately 500 miles southeast of the Manitoba Mennonite settlement near Cuauhtemoc, Chihuahua, Mexico, was started in 1944 by 38 families, but was soon discontinued because of lack of water and other unfavorable conditions.   C.K.

Nukerke (Nieukerke, in Anabaptist literature mostly called Nijpkerke or Nipkerke), a village (pop. *ca.* 2,400) in the Belgian province of East Flanders, where Leenaert Bouwens (*q.v.*) baptized 20, or perhaps even 43 persons in 1551-61. Even before Bouwens visited Nijpkerke, there was a Mennonite congregation here, which together with a number of other congregations in Flanders wrote a letter to the ministers at Antwerp (see **Kortrijk, Adriaen van**). Jan de Swarte (*q.v.*), executed in 1563 at Rijssel, France, was a preacher of the congregation at Nijpkerke. Nothing is known of the congregation after this execution. It died out probably soon after because the members moved elsewhere for fear of persecution. Nukerke is still a center of the weaving industry; in the 16th century most of its inhabitants were weavers.   vDZ.

Nunkirchen, Thieleman von, an Anabaptist martyr: who was executed at Blankenberg in the Duchy of Julich in 1552 by the sword, with three fellow martyrs, William van Bierk, Christophel uyt de Geistens, and Christiaen uyt den Eukeraat. (*Mart. Mir.* D 148, E 526).

Nürnberg, a former free city (pop. in 1950, 360,017) located in Middle Franconia, Bavaria, Germany. In the Reformation period the city played an important role. It was the center of intellectual life. Great scholars like Willibald Pirkheimer (*q.v.*), great painters like Albrecht Dürer (*q.v.*), and great poets like Hans Sachs lived and worked here. The Reformation found early entry into the city, with the preachers Andreas Osiander (*q.v.*) and Lazarus Spengler (*q.v.*) as its most important representatives. The imperial diet met here twice, in 1522 and 1524. The most important historical event to take place here was the Peace of Nürnberg of 1532.

Signs of Anabaptism appeared here very early. It is possible that Diepold of Thon, near Nürnberg, a peasant who was holding religious meetings in February 1524 in the neighborhood of Nürnberg with a large attendance, which were forbidden him, and Gallus, a journeyman weaver of Nördlingen, who fared similarly on May 6, 1524, were forerunners of the new movement. For it is known that at the beginning of the Reformation there were Waldensians in and around Nürnberg.

Meanwhile Hans Denk (*q.v.*) had come to Nürnberg in the fall of 1523. After serving for a year as rector of the school of St. Sebald, he became involved in a theological dispute with Osiander, and was expelled from the city on Jan. 20, 1525. Here in Nürnberg he met Ludwig Haetzer (*q.v.*), Hans Hut (*q.v.*), and Hans Schlaffer (*q.v.*). Hans Hut was working for a book binder named Valantin, and lived in Denk's house at various times. Later, in 1526, after he had been baptized as an Anabaptist at Augsburg by Denk, Hut won Wolfgang Vogel (*q.v.*), the pastor at Eltersdorf near Nürnberg, for Anabaptism. The city council of Nürnberg ordered Vogel's execution on March 26, 1527, as a seditious person, because he "sought to form an association for the elimination of all the ungodly and establish a new kingdom of Christ, where only equality is to reign."

In 1526 Prince Casimir of Brandenburg issued a proclamation to his subjects in Nürnberg warning them of the "adherents of the malicious company, who held nothing at all of the original baptism of infants, nor of the sacrament of the altar, and supposed that in a short time Christ would return and begin a temporal reign, and that the sword of righteousness (as they called it) would be placed in their hands to destroy and kill all authority and those that did not accept their rebaptism and were not related to their fellowship, also that there is no eternal punishment in sight for the damned and the devil will be saved, together with other improprieties."

The council was also zealous in warning against the Anabaptists. On March 21, 1527, it wrote in a letter to the city of Strasbourg in reply to a question about the Nürnberg church constitution, that in all the towns and villages of the area Christian evangelical preachers had been installed, who had previously been tried and examined as to their possible contamination with Anabaptism, for the Anabaptists believed that Christ was only a man, that He was begotten in sin, that He had not done satisfaction for the sins of mankind, that no Christian could be a ruler, that God will return in person to the earth to establish a physical reign in which all government will be destroyed, and all things should be held in common. No Anabaptist was to be tolerated in the city, because the sect is especially inclined to sedition. In addition, the council forbade the printing, sale, or possession of the booklets of these teachers of false doctrine. In a similar vein the council had three days previously written to the city of Regensburg, mentioning Hans Hut and giving an exact description of him, and on March 26 likewise to the Elector of Brandenburg.

The Nürnberg council was constantly on the alert to counter Anabaptism. On Sept. 11, 1527, it sent George Grün to Erlangen to attend the examination of the imprisoned Ambrosius Spittelmaier (*q.v.*). On the next day it sent a letter to the city of Ansbach asking for information about Spittelmaier, so that Nürnberg would be able to help in exterminating this "ungodly and misleading faction," and enclosed thirty-five questions which Spittelmaier answered in his examination on Sept. 20, 1527.

On Sept. 23, 1527, another letter was sent to Ansbach, with the intention of "exterminating the poisonous new sect of the Anabaptists with zeal." The letter continued that there would be no purpose in sending to Ansbach the court records of the Anabaptists in prison in Nürnberg, since they were poor peasants who had themselves not baptized but were misled. From Augsburg they had received news that Hans Hut, the leader of the Anabaptists, had been imprisoned, and that they should examine Spittelmaier, who said he was an emissary of Hut, on the enclosed questions. Again on Dec. 21, 1527, Nürnberg wrote a letter to Ulm containing the same unfounded accusations against the Anabaptists as those written to Strasbourg and Regensburg.

At the same time the council had a work published with the title *Grundtliche vntterrichtung eins erbarn Rats der Statt Nürnberg Welcher gestalt jre Pfarrher vn Prediger in den Stetten vn auff dem Land das volck wider etliche verfürische lere der Widertauffer in jren predigen auss heyliger Götlicher schrifft zum getreulichsten ermanen vnnd unterrichten sollen.* It contains 42 pages. The author is unknown. It obviously stems from Lutheran circles in Nürnberg, for it contains strictly Lutheran teaching. It was published in 1528 or later, for Hans Hut's death in Augsburg is mentioned in it. The introduction to the book reproduced the current accusations against the Anabaptists, charging them with fomenting revolt and sedition. "The evil, devilish poison must be counteracted with state measures and also especially with instruction on the basis of the Word of God." This is followed by a profusely verbose instruction on baptism, based largely on the Old Testament.

Then comes a presentation of Anabaptist teaching in twelve points. Point 8: "They say no preacher shall stay in one place but travel about as the apostles did." Point 11: "But some say there is no devil but sin and evil desire and inclination of man." Then these twelve points are refuted, again largely on the basis of the Old Testament. The argument is often picayune and anything but convincing. This booklet shows not an iota of understanding of the Anabaptists, but apparently contributed considerably to the struggle against them.

On Jan. 25, 1528, the council of Nürnberg requested of the council of Regensburg the names of the Anabaptists living there or being held in their prison. Upon inquiry by Dr. Hiltner, the legal adviser of the city of Regensburg in 1530, as to the measures to be adopted in the case of Anabaptists, Nürnberg gave a circumstantial reply describing the procedure within its jurisdiction.

When the captains of the Swabian League received the command in February 1528 to put to death without trial all who were suspected of Anabaptism, the council of Nürnberg protested and proposed milder measures, probably for fear that innocent persons might become victims of these severe measures. Nonetheless it is significant that Nürnberg never again sponsored the death penalty for Anabaptism after the case of Vogel.

In May 1528 six Anabaptists were in the Nürnberg prison. They were visited by Dr. Wenzeslaus Linck (*q.v.*) and the pastor of St. Clara's Church, who instructed them in Lutheran doctrine. Several Anabaptist expellees from Augsburg who had come to Nürnberg were conducted out of the city on May 16, 1528, by two city soldiers and were compelled to swear that they would never enter the city again.

In July 1528 the city council demanded advice from its lawyers and theologians on the proper punishment of Anabaptists. The jurists met on July 8; three favored the death penalty and three opposed it. Of the theologians, Dominicus Sleupner and Wenzeslaus Linck voted against the death penalty, and Osiander for it. Cartheuser made the decision the duty of the council. This official opinion was given twice. Then on July 14, 1528, the Nürnberg city council issued an edict: "All who recant their error of Anabaptism shall be accepted in mercy; those who persist in it shall be expelled beyond a distance of ten miles from the city."

In January 1529 twenty persons of both sexes were arrested in the country because they had been rebaptized. Thereupon the council, on Jan. 25, 1529, for the third time asked the official opinion of the jurists and the theologians. The reply was to the effect that "since this error was on the increase, punishment should reasonably follow. In addition it might be advisable to issue another mandate ordering that anyone who was rebaptized should have his eyes put out." The twenty arrested Anabaptists not only adhered to their baptism, but also believed that the sacrament did not contain the actual body and blood of Christ; the council then had them given instruction. Those who were converted were left in peace; those who persisted were expelled, contrary to the advice of the clergy and lawyers who wanted more severe penalties; the Anabaptists had to give an oath that they would not again come near the city.

On April 29, 1531, the Nürnberg scholars rendered another official opinion. This time the theologians took a lenient and generous position, and only some of the jurists favored the death penalty. A noteworthy event was the result of the consultation of May 30, 1531, concerning the "dreamers of Windsheim," also called "Puschenhamer." "It is difficult to proceed against them; one does not know whether they may simply have been misled. In this case, if the man in question were in Nürnberg's jurisdiction, he would be expelled from the city. They, however, would leave the decision to the prince." The opinion of the jurists and theologians in the case of the Anabaptists of Baiersdorf (Uttenreuth) issued on June 3, 1531, had a different tone, "It is above all necessary, useful, and fruitful, first of all to institute a church constitution in the margravure." These *Schwärmer* shall be overcome by the Word of God, taught and indoctrinated. But they must not be released without punishment because, as the example of Müntzer has shown, they are intent upon the destruction of the government. They must therefore not be permitted to gain the upper hand. The originator, Hans Schmid, shall be burned at the stake, the others killed with the sword. But those who are amenable to teaching shall be branded. Above all, the prince is to issue a severe edict.

In April 1535, when it was learned that some were holding a "synagogue" behind St. Jacob's Church, the council had them arrested. The Anabaptists from Carinthia, who were staying at the inn "To the White Rooster" at St. Lorenz, were ordered to leave the city at once. The innkeeper was warned against admitting such guests and ordered to notify the authorities at once if any arrived.

Peter Riedemann (*q.v.*) was imprisoned in Nürnberg for four years and ten weeks (1532 - July 19, 1537) in the tower called "Lug ins Land." Osiander and other theologians tried in vain to convert him. In 1536 the council had a whole Bible brought to him with Melanchthon's booklet on baptism, but in vain.

In the cross-examination of Jan. 30, 1539, Jakob Hölin of Schorndorf named a Konrad Hefner of Nürnberg as leader of the Anabaptists; nothing else is known about him. During Mosheim's residence in Nürnberg two Anabaptists appeared there on Oct. 9, 1539; they had been imprisoned at Passau and released. The Nürnberg city council had some clergymen examine them on their doctrine, and when they were convinced that these men had repudiated Anabaptist doctrine they were released with the warning not to spread Anabaptist teachings.

In March 1541 the Anabaptists in Nürnberg ventured to come into the light. The council, informed of this matter, had them all arrested. The tailor Lorenz Holzmann, whom three theologians tried to convert, persisted in his Anabaptist ideas and refused to recant. Thereupon the council made him pay the trial fee, swear not to return within a radius of ten miles of the city, and ordered him expelled. On April 19 he was to be led from the city, so that he would not mislead his wife and other people or persuade them to such error. When this sentence was read to Holzmann he asked for the council's permission to appear with his wife before Master Vetter, the preacher of St. Sebald, to discuss the matter with him. This permission was granted, and Vetter succeeded in converting him from his error. Holzmann was then pardoned, but penalized by having to stand on two Sundays before the church with his wife. Heinrich Meilendorfer, another Anabaptist, was punished with four weeks in prison; his wife, who had led him into this error, was forged to a "bench and irons" for four weeks. Others were treated more leniently. Thus Anabaptism was suppressed in Nürnberg. But traces continued to appear for a long time to come.

Since 1948 there has been a small Mennonite congregation at Nürnberg, numbering 25 baptized members in 1956. It has no meetinghouse and is served by ministers from the outside. NEFF.

Beiträge zur bayrischen Kirchengeschichte X (1913) 57 ff.; *Hist. Ver.-Blatt für Schwaben und Neuburg* (1874); Joh. Heberle, "Johann Denk und die Ausbreitung seiner Lehre," in *Theologische Studien und Kritiken* (1855) 817-90; Hermann Nestler, *Die Wiedertäuferbewegung in Regensburg* (Regensburg, 1926); Friedrich Roth, *Die Einführung der Reformation in Nürnberg* (Würzburg, 1885); *TA Brandenburg;* Franz von Soden, *Beiträge zur Geschichte der Reformation und der Sitten jener Zeit mit besonderem Hinblick auf Christoph Scheurl* II (Nürnberg, 1885); Wiswedel, *Bilder* II; Austin Patterson Evans, *An Episode in the Struggle for Religious Freedom, The Sectaries of Nuremberg 1524-1528* (New York, 1924); *Grundtliche untterrichtung, eins erbarn Rats der Statt Nürnberg, Welcher gestalt, jre Pfarrher vn Prediger in den Stetten un auff dem Land, das volck, wider etliche verfürische lere der Widertauffer, in jren predigen ausz heyligerr Gotlicher schrifft, zum getreulichste ermannen vnnd vnterrichten sollen* (Nürnberg, 1527-28); *ML* III, 279-81.

Nursing Education. Until recently the training of nurses has been the function of general hospitals who have organized schools of nursing under their direction, using their own clinical facilities in so far as they are adequate, and sending their nursing students away to larger hospitals for specialized clinical experience (called affiliation). Now more collegiate schools of nursing are being established, which are operated by colleges or universities in affiliation either with their own hospitals or independent hospitals.

The first formal training of nurses was that established by Pastor Fliedner at Kaiserswerth, Germany, in 1836. Florence Nightingale's school established in 1860 at St. Thomas Hospital in London was the first significant nurses' training course in an English-speaking country. The first similar school in the United States was established at Roxbury, Mass., near Boston, in 1872. By the turn of the century the original typical one-year training was being extended to three years, and high-school graduation was beginning to be required for entrance.

The first American Mennonite schools of nursing were established in the 20th century in the midst of the rising standards of nursing education. The first was the Bethel Deaconess Hospital (*q.v.*) School of Nursing (GCM) at Newton, Kan., established in 1908 soon after the hospital was opened. This school has trained and still trains both deaconess and non-deaconess nurses, the number of deaconesses having greatly declined in recent years. It originated in connection with Bethel College and is affiliated with the General Conference Mennonite Church.

The second school was the Mennonite School of Nursing at Beatrice, Neb., established in 1911 and continued to 1929 as a small 3-year school operated by the Mennonite Deaconess Home and Hospital. In 1941-47 a two-year course in practical nursing was offered.

The third school was the La Junta (Col.) Mennonite (MC) Hospital and Sanitarium School of Nursing, established in 1915 and operated by the hospital under the Mennonite Board of Missions and Charities until 1949, when it was placed under the Mennonite Board of Education as an independent school. Though it was a quality school of high standards it was forced to discontinue through decline in the patient census at the hospital with which it was affiliated. The last class was to be graduated in 1958. A course in practical nursing was instituted by the hospital in 1957.

The Salem Home and Hospital, founded by the K.M.B. Church at Hillsboro, Kan., in 1918, began a training school for nurses and deaconesses but it was never fully developed and was later discontinued.

The Mennonite Hospital at Bloomington, Ill., an institution supported by the members of the Central Conference of Mennonites and the Evangelical Mennonites in Illinois, which was established in 1920 by taking over the existing Kelso Sanitarium with its school of nursing, has had a school of nursing from its beginning in 1920.

The Mennonite Hospital at Mountain Lake, Minn., also had a training program for a time.

In Russia a three-year training school for nurses was established in 1909 by the Deaconess Home Morija in Neu-Halbstadt, Molotschna. It was a private undertaking, was built primarily with the funds furnished by Peter Schmidt of Steinbach, and was supported by voluntary contributions. It was opened Dec. 3, 1909, but was practically destroyed in 1918 when it was plundered by bandits.

A training school for nurses was established in Filadelfia, Fernheim Colony, Paraguay, in 1945, in connection with the colony hospital, by Mrs. John Schmidt, wife of Dr. John Schmidt. It was operated for only a short time, and offered what was in effect a course in practical nursing.

The Mennonite Church (MC) in India has a school of nursing attached to the Dhamtari Christian Hospital at Dhamtari, M.P., established in July 1951, with a three-year course.   H.S.B.

Nussbaumer (Nussbaum), a Swiss Mennonite family name, first recorded as an Anabaptist family in Ichertswil, Lüterkofen district, in the Bucheggberg region of the canton of Solothurn, Switzerland. Most of the Mennonite Nussbaumers are descended from this family. Others have come from various villages in the Emmental, especially Gross Höchstetten. The Emmental family may have been the forerunners of the family in the Bucheggberg. As early as the mid-16th century Anabaptist members of this family were living near Péry in the Jura.

Barbli Nussbaum of Allmendingen had to pay a fine of 100 pounds in 1563 because she was an Anabaptist. The records speak of several members of the family who had difficulties with the authorities in the early part of the 18th century for the same reason.

Members of the Nussbaumer family moved to Basel and Alsace, where they have furnished a number of ministers for the Mennonite churches. An outstanding leader of the Swiss Mennonite Conference for many years was Samuel Nussbaumer (*q.v.*, 1866-1944), Basel. His son, Hans Nussbaumer, a prominent elder in the Alsatian Mennonite churches, has served as secretary of the Alsatian Conference for many years.

The first party of the 19th century, consisting of four Swiss Anabaptist families, who left their Jura homes in 1817 for America, included Hans Nussbaum, who settled in Wayne Co., Ohio. Later this family moved to Ashland Co., Ohio, where Hans served the Mennonite Church as a minister.

Various immigrants of this family settled in each of the 19th-century Swiss Mennonite settlements: Sonnenberg, Wayne Co., Ohio; Allen-Putnam Co., Ohio; and Berne, Ind., where some have become leaders in the church.   D.L.G.

D. L. Gratz, *Bernese Anabaptists* (Scottdale, 1953) 129-30.

Nussbaumer, Samuel (1866-1944), outstanding elder and leader of the Swiss Mennonites, was born July 5, 1866, as fifth child of Daniel and Marianne Gerber Nussbaumer at Wittwald near Eptingen in the canton of Baselland, Switzerland. The family moved to a farm in the Bernese Jura in 1889 located near Montfaucon. He was baptized in the Sonnenberg congregation in 1889, and here ordained as a preacher shortly thereafter and in *ca.* 1900 as elder. He attended the St. Chrischona Bible School 1890-91. In February 1897 he married Elise Scheidegger. Among the six children who grew to maturity is Elder Hans Nussbaumer of Schweighof, Altkirch, Alsace. In 1904 the family moved to Les Fontaines near Tramelan, and in 1911 near Basel, where they occupied the farm called Sternenhof at Dornach and where he became the elder of the Schänzli Mennonite congregation at Basel. He served many years (*ca.* 25) as president of the Swiss Mennonite Conference, and was widely known, respected, and loved as a preacher, pastor, Bible teacher, and leader. He was an also an outstanding farmer, and for a number of years member of the cantonal legislature as a representative of the Evangelical People's Party. (*Zum Andenken an Samuel Nussbaumer, ca.* 1944.)   H.S.B.

Nusslau (Nussla, Nuslau; Czech, *Nosislava*), a market town in Moravia between Selowitz (*q.v.*) and Nikoltschitz (*q.v.*), belonging to the lands of the Zierotin family. As in Nikoltschitz, the Brethren began to settle here in 1570 and contributed a substantial fee to the owners of the land.

According to the chronicles the Brethren in Selowitz also moved to Nusslau, probably because they wanted to cultivate vineyards and hop farms here under the favor of the lords. The fate of this

Bruderhof is closely connected with that of Nikolt-schitz. In July 1600, much of their goods was consumed by the compulsory quartering of troops, in 1601 by the quartering of 5,000 foot soldiers in the neighborhood. Five years later the Hohenlohe and Münsterberg armies plundered the Bruderhof.

The "good time" was over with the death of Frederick of Zierotin. His successors were too much concerned with their own advantage; this created tensions. In 1615 the Brethren thought very seriously of emigrating, "because with inadequate food, with much robot labor, also all sorts of gifts and fees, they were hard pressed and also with the lords there were always strife and unpleasantness, so that one could not trust himself to endure it." The school and tannery were already located at another place. But in the end the baron promised them better food and treatment, and they decided to stay.

In the rebellion the Hutterite Bruderhofs suffered great misfortune. On Jan. 5, 1621, imperial troops plundered Nusslau and "laid it in ashes." An aged sister died in it. On March 30 Polish auxiliaries struck down the superintendent of the Nusslau mill and an apprentice. In September 1622 the expulsion of the Brethren from Moravia led to the complete abandonment of the Bruderhof.   P.DE.

Beck, *Geschichts-Bücher;* Wolkan, *Geschicht-Buch;* Zieglschmid, *Chronik; ML* III, 282.

Nut, Het: see **Maatschappij tot Nut van't Algemeen.**

Nyabasi (Tanganyika) Mennonite Church (MC), located 46 miles east of Shirati, is in the Kuria tribe. Work in this tribe was begun by Clinton Ferster on Jan. 1, 1940. Doctor Noah Mack joined them in June of the same year. The beginning of the church dates from Nov. 17, 1940, when two were received into church fellowship and the first communion service was held. Noah Mack had pastoral oversight of the church until Simeon Hurst arrived June 13, 1941, who has had charge since that time. The present (1956) membership stands at 24.   E.W.S.

Nycolson, John: see **Lambert.**

Illustrations

Contents

I. Martyr Scenes
1. Maria and Ursula van Beckum, Deventer, 1544; 2. Dirk Willemsz Rescuing His Captor, 1569

II. Martyr Scenes
1. Johan Knel, 1550; 2. Jaques d'Auchy, Leeuwarden, 1559.

III. Martyr Scenes

1. A Camouflaged Church Service, Holland; 2. Unknown Martyr, Holland.

IV. Mandates
1. *Mandate of King Ferdinand of Austria, 1528; 2. Mandate of the City of Regensburg, 1539.*

6

V. Mandates

1. *Mandate against Menno Simons, 1542;* 2. *Mandate of the City of Bern,* 1597.

VI. Manuscripts

1. A Menno Simons Letter, *ca.*1549. 2. Maeyken Wens' Letter, Holland, **1573.**

VII. Manuscripts

1. Johann Reimer, School Motto, Blumenort, Russia, 1832; 2. A Christopher Dock School Motto of *ca.*1750.

VIII. Manuscripts

1. A Deep Run, Pa., School Motto of 1783; 2. A Songbook Title Page, Deep Run, Pa., School, 1828.

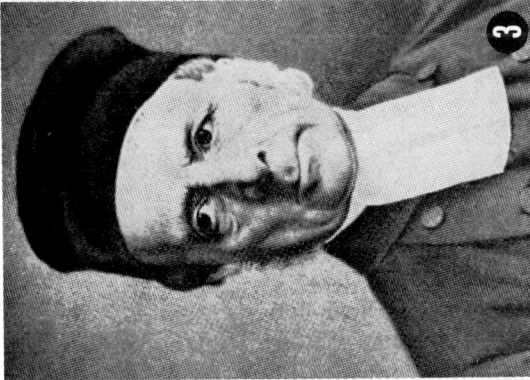

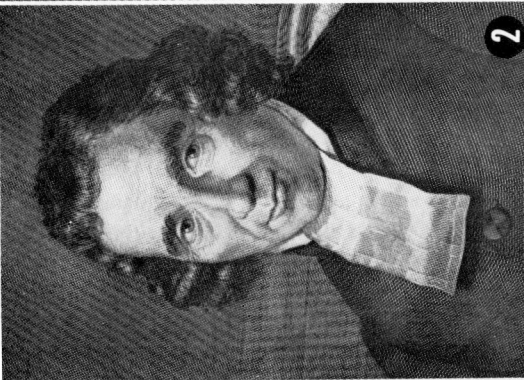

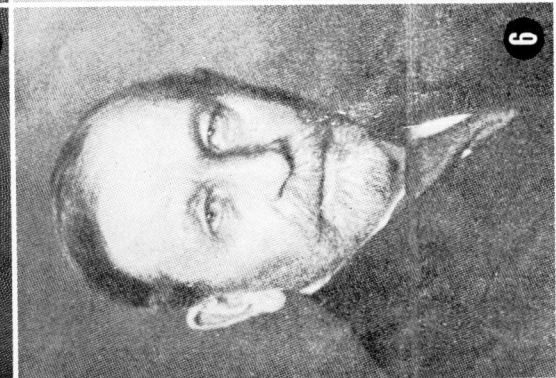

IX. Portraits

1. Samuel Muller (1785-1875), Amsterdam, Neth.; 2. Jan Nieuwenhuizen (1724-1806), Haarlem, Neth.; 3. Jakob Mannhardt (1801-85), Danzig, Ger.; 4. Cornelis Nijdam (1884-1946), Amsterdam, Neth.; 5. Jakob Kroeker (1872-1948), Wernigerode, Ger.; 6. Hermann Gottlieb Mannhardt (1855-1927), Danzig, Ger.; 7. David Möllinger (1709-68), Monsheim, Ger.; 8. Samuel Nussbaumer (1866-1944), Basel-Dornach, Sw.

11

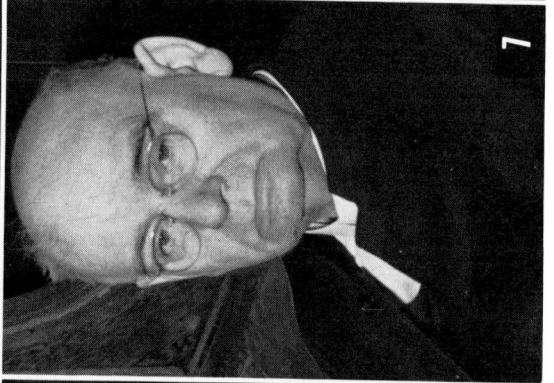

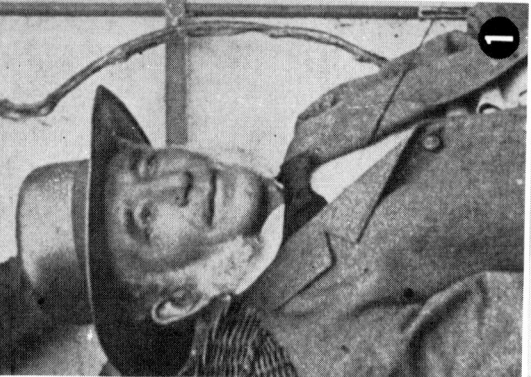

X. Portraits

1. Cornelius Jansen (GCM) (1822-94), Beatrice, Neb.; 2. Samuel K. Mosiman (GCM) (1867-1940), Bluffton, Ohio; 3. Jacob H. Janzen (GCM) (1878-1950), Waterloo, Ont.; 4. Pieter Jansz (1820-1904), Kaju-Apu, Java; 5. Henry W. Lohrenz (MB) (1878-1945), Hillsboro, Kan.; 6. Daniel J. Johns (MC) (1850-1942), Goshen Ind.; 7. Daniel Kauffman (MC) (1865-1944), Scottdale, Pa.; 8. Daniel D. Miller (MC) (1864-1955), Middlebury, Ind.

Der Hutterischen
Widertäuffer Tauben-
kobel: In welchem all ihr Wüst/ Mist/ Kott
vnnd Vnflat/ das ist/ ihr falsche/ stinckende/ vnflättige
vnd abscheuliche Lehrn/ was sie nemblich von Gott/ von Christo/ von
den H. Sacramenten vnd andern Artickeln deß Christlichen Glaubens halten/
werden erzählet/ alle kürtzlich vnd treulich auß ihren eygnen Büchern/
so wol getruckten als geschribnen/mit Anzeygung deß Orths/
wo ein jedtliche zufinden/verfasset.

Auch deß grossen Taubers deß Jacob Hutters Leben/
von welchem sich die Widertäuffer Hutterisch nen-
nen/angehenckt:

Durch CHRISTOPHORVM ANDREAM Fischer D.
Pfarrherrn zu Velsperg.

Mit Röm: Kays: Mayest: Freyheit.
Getruckt zu Ingolstatt/ in der Ederischen Truckerey/
Durch Andream Angermeyr.

ANNO M D C VII.

Testamenterleü-
terung.

Erleütterung durch außzug
auß Heiliger Biblischer sch:ifft/ tail vnd
gegentail/sampt ainstails angehangen beireden/
zü dienst vnnd fürderung ains klaren vrtails/von
wegen vnderschaid Alts vnd News Testaments/
vnnd jre beder Sündtuergebung/ Opffer/
Erlösung/Gerechtigkait /Gnad/Glauben/Gaist /
folck vnnd anderm /so grundtlich/ lautter
vnd nutzlich nie ersehen/ genant
Testamentereütterung.

*
* *

Liß in der Vorred gar dahinden / wirstu
beschaid vmb des Büchmachers
nammen finden.

XI. A. Portraits
1. Cornelius Franz Klassen (MB) (1894-1954), Abbotsford, B.C., and Frankfurt, Ger.; 2. Christian Neff (1863-1946), Weierhof, Ger.

XI. B. Book Title Pages
3. An Anti-Hutterite Work by C. A. Fischer, *Taubenkobel*, 1607. 4. Pilgram Marpeck's *Explanation of the Testaments*, 1550.

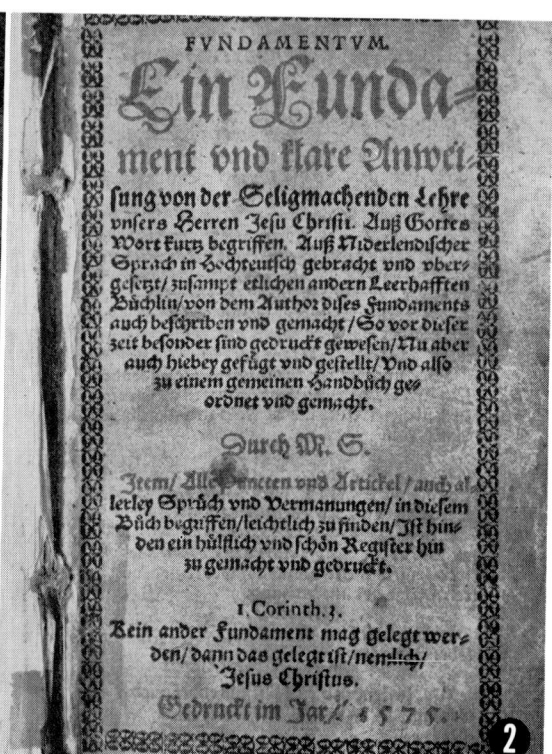

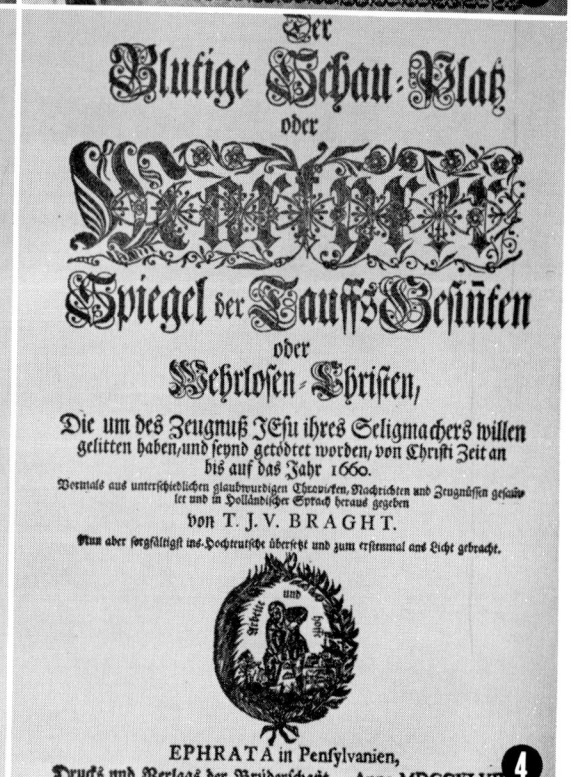

XII. Book Title Pages

1. Menno Simons' *Foundation Book*, first Dutch edition, 1539; 2. Menno Simons' *Foundation Book*, first German edition, 1575; 3. *Martyrs' Mirror*, first Dutch edition, 1660; 4. *Martyrs' Mirror*, first American edition in German, 1748.

Index of Illustrations

Asterisk (*) indicates a portrait; *italics,* a book

Explanation of Illustrations

The illustrations in the MENNONITE ENCYCLOPEDIA appear as pictorial supplements at the end of each of the four volumes. They are grouped according to the topics they illustrate. For instance, pictures of Mennonite colleges are grouped under the heading "Colleges," and appear in Volume 1, since this volume includes the letter "C." In the case of portraits, however, pictures are presented only for those persons for whom articles appear within the volume. An alphabetical index indicates the location of the pictures by pages in the supplement. In the text of the volume itself, the symbol (†) at the end of the article indicates that an illustration for the article appears in the pictorial supplement of that volume. The choice of illustrations has been limited by availability.

The co-operation of the many individuals and institutions who have secured or contributed pictures is here gratefully acknowledged, even though individual recognition is not given. The larger number of illustrations have been drawn from two chief sources: the Bethel College Historical Library, North Newton, Kan. (Cornelius Krahn, director) and the Goshen College Mennonite Historical Library, Goshen, Ind. (Nelson Springer, curator). In addition the Archives of the Mennonite Church at Goshen College (Melvin Gingerich, custodian), the Library of the United Mennonite Church at Amsterdam, Netherlands (N. van der Zijpp, director), and the Library of the Mennonite Research Center at Göttingen, Germany (Ernst Crous, director), deserve recognition for their contributions. The following periodicals kindly granted us the use of pictures which they had published: *Mennonite Life,* North Newton, Kan., and *Der Mennonit,* Frankfurt a.M., Germany.

The principle of selection of pictures has varied according to the type of matter to be illustrated. Thus, only a few typical dwellings were chosen, in cases where the dwelling represents a distinct type. But in the case of meetinghouses and institutions, age, historic importance, style, and regional and denominational representation, have all played a part in the decision, along with the availability of good photographs. Under "Art" only works of genuine merit, and artists of established reputation, have been chosen. For title-pages chiefly first editions, where available, of titles of historic significance have been used.

The Martyr Scenes presented on Plates I, II, and III are taken from the Dutch edition of the *Martyrs' Mirror* of 1685, and are reproductions of the Jan Luyken etchings. The mandates on Plates IV and V are reproduced from the originals in the Goshen College Library, as are the book title pages on Plate XI:3 and Plate XII:2, 3, and 4. The manuscript letters on Plate VI are reproduced from Bethel College photographs of the originals in the Amsterdam Mennonite Library. The mottoes on Plates VII and VIII are specimens of the illuminated manuscripts discussed in the article under that title. The first specimen is reproduced from the original in the Bethel College Library; the third and fourth specimens are from originals in the Goshen College Library; the second specimen is from the Henry Borneman Collection, reproduced from Borneman's book, *Pennsylvania German Illuminated Manuscripts* (Norristown, 1937), and is printed by permission of the publishers, the Pennsylvania German Society.